For Reference
DISCARD
Not to be taken from this room

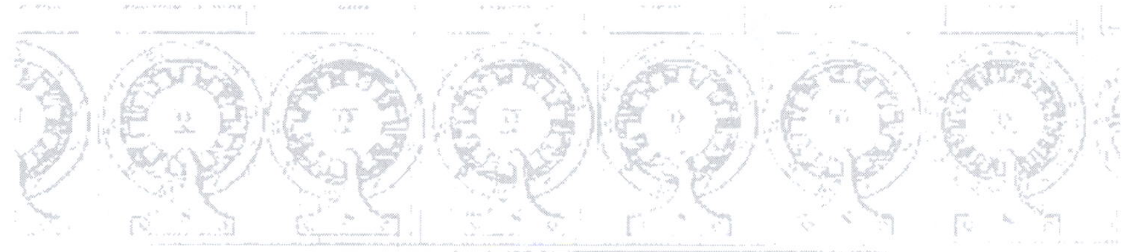

2nd edition

ENCYCLOPEDIA OF PHILOSOPHY

APPENDIX: ADDITIONAL ARTICLES
THEMATIC OUTLINE
BIBLIOGRAPHIES
INDEX

2nd edition

ENCYCLOPEDIA OF PHILOSOPHY

DONALD M. BORCHERT
Editor in Chief

MACMILLAN REFERENCE USA
An imprint of Thomson Gale, a part of The Thomson Corporation

Detroit • New York • San Francisco • San Diego • New Haven, Conn. • Waterville, Maine • London • Munich

Encyclopedia of Philosophy, Second Edition

Donald M. Borchert, Editor in Chief

For more information, contact
Macmillan Reference USA
An imprint of Thomson Gale
27500 Drake Rd.
Farmington Hills, MI 48331-3535
Or you can visit our internet site at
http://www.gale.com

LIBRARY OF CONGRESS CATALOGING-IN-PUBLICATION DATA

Encyclopedia of philosophy / Donald M. Borchert, editor in chief.—2nd ed.
p. cm.
Includes bibliographical references and index.
ISBN 0-02-865780-2 (set hardcover : alk. paper)—
ISBN 0-02-865781-0 (vol 1)—ISBN 0-02-865782-9 (vol 2)—
ISBN 0-02-865783-7 (vol 3)—ISBN 0-02-865784-5 (vol 4)—
ISBN 0-02-865785-3 (vol 5)—ISBN 0-02-865786-1 (vol 6)—
ISBN 0-02-865787-X (vol 7)—ISBN 0-02-865788-8 (vol 8)—
ISBN 0-02-865789-6 (vol 9)—ISBN 0-02-866098-6 (vol 10)
1. Philosophy–Encyclopedias. I. Borchert, Donald M., 1934-

B51.E53 2005
103–dc22

2005018573

This title is also available as an e-book.
ISBN 0-02-866072-2
Contact your Thomson Gale representative for ordering information.

Printed in the United States of America
10 9 8 7 6 5 4 3 2

contents

volume 1
PREFACE TO 2ND EDITION
INTRODUCTION TO 1ST EDITION
LIST OF CONTRIBUTORS
LIST OF ARTICLES

ENCYCLOPEDIA OF PHILOSOPHY
2nd edition

Abbagnano–Byzantine Philosophy

volume 2
Cabanis–Destutt de Tracy

volume 3
Determinables–Fuzzy Logic

volume 4
Gadamer–Just War Theory

volume 5
Kabbalah–Marxist Philosophy

volume 6
Masaryk–Nussbaum

volume 7
Oakeshott–Presupposition

volume 8
Price–Sextus Empiricus

volume 9
Shaftesbury–Zubiri

volume 10
APPENDIX: ADDITIONAL ARTICLES
THEMATIC OUTLINE
BIBLIOGRAPHIES
INDEX

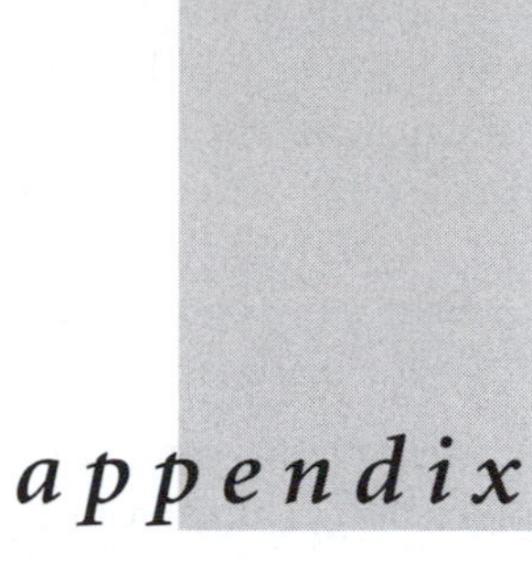

appendix

ALBERT THE GREAT

(before 1200–1280)

According to the near-contemporary testimony of Tolomeo of Lucca (*Historia Ecclesiastica* [1317], 22.19) and confirmed by other, later sources, Albert the Great (Albertus Magnus) was more than 80 years old when he died on November 15, 1280, establishing the turn of the thirteenth century as the *terminus ante quem* of his birth. He was born in the town of Lauingen in Schwaben in the diocese of Augsburg, at the time a part of Bavaria, the son of a knight in the service of the counts of Bollestadt. He was already a student in the *studium litterarum* at Padua when, in 1223, Jordan of Saxony came in search of recruits to the Dominican Order among the young men in residence at the new university. Albert received the habit from Jordan sometime around Easter of 1223 and was sent to Cologne for his novitiate. By 1228 he had become a lecturer (*lector*), and he served in that office in Dominican communities at Heldesheim, Freiberg, Regensburg, and Strassburg. In 1243 or 1244 he was sent to Paris by John of Wildeshausen, where he became a master of theology in 1245 and lectured on Peter Lombard's *Sententiarum* (Sentences).

In the fall of 1245 Thomas Aquinas was sent to Paris, also at the direction of John of Wildeshausen, and in 1248 he and probably other Dominicans accompanied Albert to Cologne, where Albert was to establish the first *studium generale* (or liberal-arts college) in Germany. He served as Provincial of Teutonia from 1254 to 1257, during which time he was summoned before the papal curia to defend the Dominican Order against the attacks of William of Saint-Amour. He was well received by the curia, and his lectures and debating were found to be extraordinary. In January of 1260 Pope Alexander IV appointed him bishop of Regensburg, but he served less than two years before submitting his resignation, after instituting many reforms in his diocese. Although retired, he was directed by Pope Urban IV, in 1263, to preach to the Germans a crusade to the Holy Land, and this he did, until Urban's death in 1264.

It is said that after the death of Thomas Aquinas, Albert traveled to Paris one last time to defend the views of his former student, but this story, related at the canonization proceedings for Aquinas in 1319, is not fully consistent with other known facts about Albert's final years and, indeed, appears to interpret the events in Paris in 1277 in a manner that places far too much importance on the connection, if any, between Aquinas and the doctrines that were being formally condemned. The complete absence of any official correspondence after August 18, 1279, in the face of a full and active participation in the life of the Church and his order right up until that date, has suggested to some that Albert's memory, and perhaps other aspects of his mental life, had begun to fail him at that time, but there is no good reason to suppose, as some have done, that this decline began as early as 1277. Whether he was already in decline or not, he and his Dominican brothers were apparently not unprepared when death finally took him away on November 15, 1280.

WRITINGS

Albert was committed to the preservation and propagation of the philosophical ideas of antiquity, in particular the philosophy of Aristotle, which he saw himself as introducing to the Latin west. Like Aristotle, he produced a body of philosophical work that spanned the discipline in both breadth and depth. As in the case of Aristotle, some of the works attributed to Albert in his corpus are not actually from his hand, and other works known to have been written by him have yet to be found. Little is known with any certainty about the chronology of the corpus, but there are good reasons for thinking that the bulk of his philosophical writings, in particular, his Aristotelian paraphrases, were completed between the years 1250 and 1270.

His corpus can be divided into three main categories: philosophy (nine treatises in logic, five in metaphysics, and three in ethics), theology (thirty treatises), and what we would call natural science but what throughout the medieval period was known as natural philosophy (twenty-two treatises). His method in most of his writings is the paraphrastic style employed by Avicenna (ibn Sīnā), as opposed to the line-by-line commentary characteristic of the works of Averroes (ibn Rushd), and his logical works in particular are deeply influenced by the work not only of Avicenna but also of al-Fārābī and Robert Kilwardby. Although Aristotle's scientific writings had been condemned in 1210 by Innocent III and the University of Paris established a commission to purge the Aristotelian corpus of heretical ideas in 1231, Albert encountered no difficulty in making use of Aristotelian ideas when he began to work on his *Summa de creaturis* (Treatise on creatures), before 1246, and his commentary on the *Sententiarum* of Peter Lombard, completed in 1249. It was probably not until the condemnation of 1277 that Aristotelianism as such encountered any serious resistance at the universities.

PHILOSOPHY

Part of what was at issue in the condemnation of 1277 was the relation between philosophy and theology, which the so-called Latin Averroists argued were separate disciplines corresponding to entirely distinct objects of knowledge, and hence governing different sorts of truths. The truths of theology were grounded in divine revelation and prophecy, while those of philosophy were grounded in human reason, and the mendicant orders were concerned to keep the two disciplines separate, on the grounds that philosophy, an inherently skeptical discipline, might intrude itself into theology in an unwarranted way, calling into question conclusions drawn in a domain in which it had no authority. In this context, Albert's insistence on the importance of knowing and understanding the philosophy of the ancient Greeks is striking and serves to illustrate his intellectual integrity.

Albert's approach to ancient philosophy has been criticized by late-twentieth-century historians of philosophy as an unrealistic syncretism of Aristotelianism and Neoplatonism. The complaint is that the two systems are philosophically and philologically incompatible, and any attempt to reconcile them is not only doomed to failure but is also methodologically misguided. It is worth noting, however, that this view is itself grounded in historical research based upon certain a priori assumptions about the relation between Plato's philosophical system and Aristotle's. Albert's Neoplatonism was essentially the Neoplatonism of the Greek commentators on Aristotle, which was itself an attempt to syncretize Plato and Aristotle, and it is fair to say that in antiquity the disparities between the two systems were not viewed as they have been by modern commentators. In fact, Albert, in offering a Neoplatonic harmonization of the two systems, is simply following the example, not only of his Arabic sources, but of a tradition that extends back to the Hellenistic period. The view that the systems are beyond harmonizing is of rather recent vintage and is subject to modification.

METAPHYSICS

Albert's metaphysics focused primarily on a theory of causation that can be traced to such sources as Aristotle, Avicenna, Pseudo-Dionysius, and the *Liber de causis* (*The Book of Causes*). He adapted the Neoplatonic notion of emanation of form, but in his system the causation is by attraction rather than by pure emanation from the One. He preferred attraction to pure emanation because he identified the One with the Good, and the Good, by its very nature, is diffusive of itself and of being (*diffusivum sui et esse*), that is, it causes other things to be by means of a kind of "calling to resemblance." (Albert here treats the word for good, "bonum," as cognate with the verb "boare" [to call]. This appeal to homespun etymology was also common in antiquity, particularly in Plato but also in Aristotle.) By virtue of this "calling to resemblance," the Good is not merely the first mover, as Aristotle's unmoved mover is, but is also the first producer, that is, the Creator—a role for the First Cause that is not found in Aristotle's *Metaphysics* (bk. ?), but rather is drawn from the *Liber de causis*, which Albert regarded as Aristotelian in provenance.

LOGIC

Albert's logical works consist, for the most part, of paraphrases of the treatises of the Organon (from Gr. "organōn," instrument, tool), so-called in the medieval period because logic was viewed not as a part of philosophy but rather as an implement that is necessary for the advancement of philosophy. The Organon consisted of

Aristotle's *Categories*, *De interpretatione* (On interpretation), *Topics* (including the *De sophisticis elenchis* [On sophistical refutations]), *Prior Analytics*, and *Posterior Analytics*. Yet Albert moved beyond Aristotle in a number of areas, most notably in his treatment of universals, which was grounded on the notion of form found in Plato and Aristotle. Aristotle had objected to the separability of the Platonic form and argued that forms are immanent in particulars. Drawing again upon Aristotle's Greek commentators, Albert argued that the universal must be analyzed into three *modi essendi*, or modes of being. Although a universal is a metaphysical unity, it may be considered under three aspects: as an entity in its own right, really existing separately from a particular, as in the mind of God (*ante rem*); as an entity that informs a particular, causing it to be the thing it is (*in re*); or as an entity in human thought (*post rem*). The distinction between the universal *in re* and the universal *post rem* is grounded in the Aristotelian notion of abstraction, which is discussed in more detail below under the heading of "Natural Science." Although Albert achieves here another notable syncretism, it is worth noting that he does not treat universals as substantial forms, as Plato and Aristotle both do.

NATURAL SCIENCE

Albert's interest in the natural world was driven by his belief that all knowledge is interconnected, and he pursued scientific questions with such intensity that critics, such as Henry of Ghent (*De scriptoribus ecclesiasticis* 2.10) suggested that he neglected theology and philosophy. Of particular interest with regard to his scientific writings is his attitude toward the distinction between rationalism and empiricism, a distinction that had been of great interest in antiquity but that had faded during the early medieval period as a consequence of both the ascendancy of rationalism under the influence of Neoplatonism and the decline in scientific investigations during periods of social and political upheaval. Working against the grain of the prevailing rationalism, Albert's attitude towards work in the natural sciences was decidedly empiricist: *experimentum solum certificat in talibus* ("Experience alone gives certainty in such matters" (*De vegetabilibus et plantis*, VI, 2.1). Although "experimentum" (here translated "experience") is reminiscent of our word "experiment," the modern concept of scientific experiment, in which a hypothesis is tested against observational data for confirmation or falsification, was unknown at this time.

For Albert, as for his contemporary Roger Bacon, the other great experimentalist of the thirteenth century, scientific "experiment" consisted in the gathering of observational data only, not the comparative analysis of data against hypotheses with controlled variables (The Latin word "experimentum" is cognate with the Greek word "empeiria" [experience], from which we get the English word "empiricism.") As in Aristotle's treatises on nature, observational data served only to illustrate or confirm a priori hypotheses, never as a means of hypothesis formation. But Albert is not a strict Aristotelian in this matter. For natural philosophers in the Aristotelian tradition, such as Aquinas, experience must be understood in terms of an inductive process leading from sense perception of particulars to the formation of general concepts in the soul, as described in Aristotle's *Metaphysics* (A.1) and *Posterior Analytics* (B.19).

In this account, the specific features of particulars are the proper objects of sense perception, but memory functions to gather together the perceptual information from similar particulars into what Aristotle calls an *empeiria* (experience) of the natural kind involved, and the rational faculty called *nous* in Greek (variously translated into English as either intellect or understanding) abstracts from *empeiria* an intelligible object, which then resides in *nous* and is a likeness (*homoiōma*) of the immanent form present in the particulars. Since these intelligible objects are different in kind from the perceptual objects that are the proper objects of the perceptual faculties, Aristotle is properly regarded not as an empiricist but as a rationalist. Nonetheless, experience clearly plays an essential role in the acquisition of knowledge of universals.

For Albert, although scientific knowledge is of the universal, the mechanism by which the universal comes to reside in the soul is by the "calling to resemblance" of the emanation of the intelligences. Intelligences illuminate the human rational faculty in accord with the doctrine of causation by attraction, and universal concepts form in the soul not because of the capacity of human intellect to abstract them but because the First Cause uses the intellect in its causal process. In Albert's and Bacon's reliance on experience, though different in kind from later notions of experience, we see the beginnings of the movement that would, by the time of the Renaissance, establish empiricism as the dominant scientific attitude, an attitude that, in time, would drive a wedge between natural philosophy and first philosophy and separate the natural sciences from philosophy.

See also al-Fārābī; Aristotelianism; Aristotle; Avicenna; Bacon, Roger; Liber de Causis; Neoplatonism; Peter Lombard; Pseudo-Dionysius; Thomas Aquinas, St.

Bibliography

WORKS BY ALBERT

Alberti Magni opera omnia, edited by the Institutum Alberti Magni Coloniense. Münster, Germany: Monasterium Westfalorum, 1951–.

Alberti Magni opera omnia. 21 vols., edited by Petri Jammy. Lyon, France: 1651.

Alberti Magni opera omnia. 38 vols., edited by Auguste Borgnet and E. Borgnet. Paris: L. Vivès, 1890–1899.

WORKS ON ALBERT

Bianchi, Luca. *Il vescovo e i filosofi: La condanna pariginia del 1277 e l'evoluzione dell'aristotelismo scolastico*. Bergamo, Italy: 1990.

Craemer-Ruegenberg, Ingrid. *Albertus Magnus*. Munich, Germany: Beck, 1980.

D'Ancona Costa, Cristina. *Recherches sur le "Liber de causis."* Paris: J. Vrin, 1995.

Hoenen, Maarten, and Alain de Libera. *Albertus Magnus und der Albertismus: Deutsche philosophische Kultur des Mittelalters*. Leiden, Germany: Brill, 1995.

Kovach, Francis J., and Robert W. Shahan, eds. *Albert the Great: Commemorative Essays*. Norman: University of Oklahoma Press, 1980.

Libera, Alain de. *Albert le Grand et la Philosophie*. Paris: J. Vrin, 1990.

Pegis, Anton. "St. Albert the Great and the Problem of Soul as Substance." In his *St. Thomas and the Problem of the Soul in the Thirteenth Century*, chap. 3. Toronto: St. Michael's College, 1934.

Weisheipl, James, ed. *Albertus Magnus and the Sciences: Commemorative Essays, 1980*. Toronto: Pontifical Institute of Mediaeval Studies, 1980.

Zimmermann, Albert. *Albert der Große: Seine Zeit, sein Werk, seine Wirkung*. Berlin: de Gruyter, 1981.

Scott Carson (2005)

COUNTERFACTUALS

A conditional is a sentence, statement, proposition, or thought of the form

If A then C

"A" is called the *antecedent* of the conditional and "C" the *consequent*. Philosophers have traditionally divided conditionals into two main groups, *indicative*, which can be symbolized as [A→C], and subjunctive ([A□→C]). The so-called *counterfactual* conditionals that have been the subject of so much discussion in analytic philosophy are subjunctive conditionals of the form

If it were to be the case that X then it would be the case that Y (if X were to happen, then Y would happen)

and

If it had been the case that X, then it would have been the case that Y (if X had happened, then Y would have happened)

Subjunctive conditionals of the form "If she be gone, he is in despair" are not at issue.

It is because the antecedents of such subjunctive conditionals usually state something that is not in fact the case or "contrary-to-fact," or is at least assumed not to be the case by the thinker or utterer of the conditional, that they have come to be known as *counterfactuals*.

It is not clear that there is any interesting difference between present and future tense indicative and subjunctive conditionals. It is not clear, for example, that there is any important semantic difference between one saying "If it were raining they would not be playing" and "If it's raining, then they're not playing." Nor is it clear that there is any important semantic difference between one saying "If she goes to the party, he will not go" and "If she were to go, he would not go," or between one saying "If salt is mixed with water it dissolves (will dissolve)" and "If salt were to be mixed with water it would dissolve." The idea that there is an important difference here is perhaps an artifact of the empiricist outlook dominant in analytic philosophy in the last century, which endorsed the "regularity theory of causation" and the associated idea that laws of nature could be adequately expressed by the "material conditional" of standard first-order logic.

However that may be, the difference between indicative and subjunctive conditionals seems clearer in the case of past-tense conditionals. Consider

If Georges Agniel and his friends did not discover the Lascaux caves, then someone else did

and

If Georges Agniel and his friends had not discovered the Lascaux caves, then someone else would have

The difference of meaning is immediately apparent and is sufficiently shown by the fact that although one takes the first to be true, one has no reason to believe the second.

The commonly used labels ("indicative," "subjunctive," and "counterfactual") do not, however, perspicuously mark out the set of conditionals that concern philosophers when they discuss counterfactuals. The indicative/subjunctive distinction is purely syntactical and simply fails to pick out the right set of conditionals. On the one hand, "If the Palestinians declared statehood now, the Israelis would retaliate" is a counterfactual that is not grammatically subjunctive. On the other hand, one can utter a subjunctive conditional of the form "If X had happened, then Y would have happened" without having any intention to assert or imply the falsity of the antecedent. Suppose I am a detective who suspects that a criminal did A although none of my colleagues believe me. I note that the criminal did something peculiar, that is, B, and remark truly that if she had done A, she would have had to have done B in support of my case, without in any way implying that the state of affairs specified in the antecedent is not the case (alternatively, I may say this before dispatching someone to find out whether she did B). Again, I may set you a puzzle, asking you to work out what I have done, and give you clues, pointing out that if I had done X then this would have happened, that if I had done Y then this other thing would have happened, without ever asserting or implying that I did not do X or Y. Again, I may truthfully assert both "If I had come to the party I would have got drunk" and "If I had not come to the party I would have got drunk" without for a moment thinking or implying, inconsistently, that both these antecedents are false.

The purely syntactical criterion is no good, then, and blanket use of the term "counterfactual" to cover all the subjunctive conditionals that concern philosophers is no better. It remains true, nevertheless, that when one asserts a subjunctive conditional one almost invariably suggests that the state of affairs specified in the antecedent is not in fact the case. This entry will therefore use the traditional term "counterfactual" in this discussion, and contrast counterfactuals generally with indicatives in spite of the difficulties just noted.

THEORIES OF CONDITIONALS

Any theory of counterfactuals will be part of a general theory of conditionals, and the question arises as to what form a general theory of conditionals should take. Many favor a truth-conditional approach, that is, one that analyzes conditionals by offering an account of the conditions under which statements of the form "If A then C" are true or false (possible-worlds and metalinguistic accounts of conditionals are examples of truth-conditional approaches). Others seek to analyze conditionals by reference to the conditions under which they can be justifiably asserted or accepted as true (e.g., see Edgington 1986). An attractive alternative is John L. Mackie's (1973) condensed argument/supposition account, according to which conditionals are condensed arguments or suppositions and so not strictly true or false at all.

A central issue for any theory of conditionals is whether indicatives and counterfactuals should receive a uniform treatment, that is, one that uses the same theoretical apparatus across the board. David K. Lewis (1973, 1976) and Frank Jackson (1977, 1979) both reject this idea, offering nonuniform theories that fix the truth-conditions of indicatives and counterfactuals in different ways. Mackie (1973), by contrast, offers a uniform account of all conditionals in terms of the single basic notion of suppositions, and Robert C. Stalnaker (1968), having given an account of all conditionals in terms of possible worlds, accounts for the intuitive difference between indicatives and counterfactuals by appeal to pragmatic considerations.

Central to this debate is the question whether one bases one's account of indicative conditionals on the material conditional of standard first-order logic, often symbolized as "$A \supset C$," which is true just in case its antecedent is false or its consequent is true (the truth-value of the whole is determined in a purely truth-functional way by the truth-values of the parts). Lewis and Jackson are among those who think that the material-conditional approach can give an adequate account of all indicative conditionals (others think that it can only provide a necessary and not a sufficient condition), but a unified material-conditional account of both indicatives and counterfactuals seems a nonstarter. The material-conditional account, for example, classifies

If the moon had been made of cheese, I would be immortal

as just as surely true as

If this apple had been made of copper, it would have conducted electricity

simply on the ground that the antecedent is false. But one is much more discriminating about the truth-values of counterfactual conditionals than this account allows. That is why Lewis and Jackson, having accepted the material-conditional theory for indicatives, adopt a nonuniform general theory of conditionals, Lewis (1973) offering a possible-worlds account of counterfactuals and Jackson (1977) a causal account.

A further issue concerns whether one can give a uniform account of the logic of indicatives and counterfactuals. The following inference patterns

(I1) If A then C, therefore, if not-C then not-A (contraposition)

(I2) If A then B, if B then C, therefore, if A then C (hypothetical syllogism)

(I3) If A then B, therefore, if A and C then B (strengthening the antecedent)

are valid for the material conditional, but are widely agreed not to hold for counterfactual conditionals (e.g., consider the failure of (I3), in the move from the true claim "If he had walked on the ice, it would have broken" to the false claim "If he had walked on the ice and had been holding a large bunch of helium balloons, the ice would have broken"). While a nonuniform account can allow that these inference patterns hold for indicatives but fail for counterfactuals (see Lewis [1973] and Jackson [1979], who attempts to explain away apparently invalid indicative cases like "if he has made a mistake, then it is not a big mistake, therefore, if he has made a big mistake, he has not made a mistake" in terms of failure of assertibility), a uniform account must hold that if they fail for counterfactuals then they also fail for indicatives (see Stalnaker 1968).

THEORIES OF COUNTERFACTUALS

Turning now to counterfactuals, one finds three main approaches. The metalinguistic account initiated by Nelson Goodman in 1947 (see also Chisholm 1955, Mackie 1973, Tichy 1984) analyses counterfactuals in terms of an entailment relationship between the antecedent plus an additional set of statements or propositions, and the consequent. The causal approach offered by Jackson in 1977 (see also Kvart 1986) is closely related but deserves a separate category because it appeals essentially to causal concepts in its analysis of counterfactuals, thereby ruling out the popular strategy of using counterfactuals in an analysis of causation (one of the first to do this was Hume 1748/1975, p. 76; see also Lewis 1986b). Finally, there is the possible-worlds approach initiated by William Todd (1964), Stalnaker (1968), and Lewis (1973), which analyses counterfactuals in terms of similarity relations between worlds. This entry will consider them in turn, after hereby putting aside, as unimportant to the present concerns, all counterfactuals that are true (or false) as a matter of logic or *a priori* necessity, such as

If Q had been P it would have entailed P (Q)

If this number had been 2 it would have been even (odd)

If this circle had been square it would have had fewer than (more than) seven sides

THE METALINGUISTIC APPROACH. According to Goodman's (1947) metalinguistic approach a counterfactual asserts a certain connection or consequential relation between the antecedent and the consequent. Since in the case of the counterfactuals that concern this discussion the antecedent does not entail the consequent as a matter of logic or *a priori* necessity, certain other statements, including statements of laws and existing particular conditions, must be combined with the antecedent to entail the consequent. These counterfactuals, then, are true, if true at all, only if (and if) the antecedent combined with a set of statements S that meets a certain condition ϕ entails the consequent as a matter of law. The theory is metalinguistic because counterfactuals are treated as equivalent to metalinguistic statements of the relevant entailments.

A notorious difficulty for this theory has been to give an adequate specification of condition ϕ. Consider [A□→C]. Given that the assumption, in the case of a counterfactual, is that A is false, one may reasonably assert ~A. However, if ~A were admissible into S, then with A one would get the contradiction [A&~A], and since it is generally accepted that anything can be inferred from a contradiction, anything could be inferred from the conjunction of A and S, including C. All counterfactuals would therefore turn out to be true (*a priori* false counterfactuals have been excluded). To prevent this trivialization, the statements that constitute S must be (logically) compatible with A. This excludes ~A. A further requirement noted by Goodman is that the statements that constitute S must be compatible with ~C; for if they were not, C would follow from S itself, and A and the laws would play no role in the inference to C.

With this in hand Goodman offers the following analysis: "A counterfactual is true if and only if (iff) there is some set S of true sentences such that S is compatible with C and with ~C, and such that [A&S] is self-compatible and leads by law to C; while there is no set S' compatible with C and with ~C and such that [A&S] is self-compatible and leads by law to ~C" (Goodman 1947, p. 120; for a discussion of this last condition, see Bennett 2003; Parry 1957). Restricting S with the notion of compatibility does not seem to be enough, however, for counterfactuals that clearly seem false still threaten to turn out true. Consider

(1) If match m had been struck, it would have flared

and

(2) If match m had been struck, it would not have been dry

Despite the restrictions on S, one gets the unacceptable result that (1) and (2) both turn out true. To see this, assume that it is a law that (L) when oxygen is present, dry matches flare when struck. Start with the situation of the dry match (D), the presence of oxygen (O), and suppose that the match has not been struck (~S) and has not flared (~F). O, D, and L are compatible both with S and with ~F, and with S, they imply F. Thus, (1) is true. Now, however, suppose ~F: that in fact the match has not flared. ~F, O, and L are compatible both with S and with D, but with S they imply ~D. Thus, (2) is true.

To eliminate this unwanted consequence, Goodman (1947) suggests that the relevant conditions in S must be cotenable with the antecedent. A is cotenable with B if it is not the case that B would have been false if A were true. ~F is thus compatible with S but not cotenable with it, because if the match had been struck (S), it would have flared (F). So (1) is true and (2) is false. However, this solution results in a circular definition or a regress, for counterfactuals are defined in terms of cotenability and cotenability is defined in terms of counterfactuals. Goodman proposed no solution to this problem (for a short discussion, see Bennett 2003, pp. 310–312).

THE CONDENSED ARGUMENT-SUPPOSITIONAL APPROACH. Closely related to the metalinguistic account is Mackie's (1973) condensed argument or suppositional account according to which all conditionals, including all counterfactuals, are condensed or abbreviated arguments that leave certain auxiliary premises unstated. Generally, to assert [A□→C] is to assert C within the scope of the supposition A (Mackie replaced the notion of a condensed argument by that of a supposition in an attempt to cover certain atypical conditionals that do not readily expand into arguments, e.g., "If that's a Picasso I'm a Martian").

There are two central ways in which Mackie's (1973, 1974) account differs from Goodman's (1947). First, Mackie abandons any metalinguistic element. In fact, according to Mackie, this feature of Goodman's account is the reason to reject it. Mackie argues that it simply "does not ring true" that when one asserts counterfactuals one is performing a higher-level linguistic act whose subject is a lower-level linguistic act. If-sentences are about the world, not about what is said about the world.

Second, Mackie relaxes the cotenability requirement on A and S. One does not need to provide an exact criterion of cotenability. All that one needs is the idea that the speaker assumes the cotenability of A and S and a notion of cotenability that can, he claims, be elucidated simply in terms of it being reasonable to combine a belief that S with A.

This suggestion is closely in line with what are sometimes called third-parameter views of counterfactuals (see Tichy 1984, who attributes this view to Chisholm 1955; Mill 1868; Ramsey 1931). According to this view, when a speaker asserts a counterfactual, he or she implicitly assumes a set of propositions. The counterfactual is true just in case the antecedent of the counterfactual and the assumed propositions entail the consequent and the implicitly assumed propositions are true. Since the implicitly assumed propositions depend on the attitudes of the speaker, no analysis of these propositions can be given and so the cotenability problem does not arise.

One point strongly in favor of such views is their ability to deal with ambiguous counterfactuals. Consider

> If Caesar had been in command in Korea, he would have used the atom bomb

> If Caesar had been in command in Korea, he would have used catapults

Although both counterfactuals can plausibly be asserted, they make different predictions about what would have happened. By introducing a third parameter this ambiguity can be located in the set of implicitly assumed propositions. The first counterfactual is asserted by someone who is assuming that Caesar was alive during the actual Korean War, and the second counterfactual is asserted by someone who is assuming that Caesar was involved in a war in Korea during Caesar's actual lifetime.

Jonathon Bennett (2003, pp. 305–308) objects to Chisholm's (1955) version of this solution to the cotenability problem, arguing that it implausibly requires that the asserter of [A□→C] have the assumed propositions in mind, although one can, for example, be sure that the lights would have gone off if one had turned the oven on again without knowing about the faulty electrical wiring in one's kitchen. He further argues that there are no limits to what a speaker could assume in asserting [A□→C], and that this lets in unwanted counterlogical conditionals like "if that piece of cast iron were gold some things would be malleable and not malleable."

THE CAUSAL APPROACH. Another theory closely related to the metalinguistic approach is Jackson's (1977) causal theory of counterfactuals, so-called because of the central role that causality plays in it. To determine the truth-value of a counterfactual one takes the causal laws at the actual world at a time. These determine the state of the world at later times. One then takes the state of the world at the antecedent time, changes it as little as possible to make the antecedent true, and determines whether the causal laws predict subsequent states that make the consequent true.

More formally, [A□→C] is true at all the A-worlds satisfying the following:

(i) Their causal laws are identical with ours at the time of the antecedent and after

(ii) Their antecedent time-slices are the most similar to ours in particular facts

(iii) They are identical in particular fact to our world prior to the time of the antecedent

Sequential counterfactuals assert that if something had happened at one time, something else would have happened at a later time, and one difficulty for the theory is presented by asequential counterfactuals like:

If I had had a coin in my pocket, it would have been a Euro.

If Flintoff had not taken the winning wicket, Harmison would have (where this is understood as meaning that sooner or later one of them would have taken the winning wicket)

Jackson (1977) proposes to analyze asequential counterfactuals in terms of sequential counterfactuals. For example, one asserts the counterfactual about Flintoff and Harmison when one thinks that if Flintoff had failed to take the final wicket, events would have ensured Harmison's taking it (they were the only bowlers left and Australia was batting so poorly).

Jackson's account appeals to similarities between worlds. Does that mean that he is really giving a possible-worlds account of counterfactuals? Although he no longer objects to being classified as a possible-worlds theorist, in 1977 he drew a sharp division between his causal account and the possible-worlds account. He argued that a causal theorist about counterfactuals could avoid ontological commitment to possible worlds because the relevant similarities were things like the mass of an object or the magnitude of a force, similarities that could be characterized by reference to features of the actual world without any appeal to possible worlds.

THE POSSIBLE WORLDS APPROACH. In asserting a counterfactual one is of course standardly considering possibilities, how things would or might have been if certain other things had not been as they were, how things would or might be if things were not as they are, and the most influential treatment of counterfactuals has been the possible-worlds approach, which proposes to analyze counterfactuals by giving a rigorous account of their truth conditions and logical behavior using possible-worlds semantics. Stalnaker (1968) and Lewis (1973) are the most influential proponents of this view, and the basic idea is that the counterfactual [A□→C] is true just in case the closest possible A-worlds (worlds where A is true) are C-worlds (worlds where C is true), and the central notions are those of a possible world and the closeness relation. Both Stalnaker and Lewis introduce the idea of a "logical space," which is, roughly, a space of possible worlds. They locate the actual world in a "similarity structure" in such a logical space and make use of this similarity structure to determine the truth-values of counterfactuals.

More formally, for Stalnaker (1968)

[A□→C] is true iff A is impossible or C is true at $f(A, w^*)$

where f is a "selecting" function that takes the antecedent A and the actual world w^* as arguments and delivers a unique possible world as a value. The counterfactual is true if C is true at the possible world that f delivers as the value.

How exactly does the selection function select? The informal answer is that the selection is based on an ordering of possible worlds with respect to their similarity or resemblance to the actual world. More formally, for Lewis (1973)

[A□→C] is true iff either there is no A-world or some [A&C] world is more similar to the actual world than any [A&~C] world

It is convenient to represent Lewis's truth conditions in this way, with direct reference to similarity, although in his original presentation the ordering relation is explicated in terms of a system of spheres of worlds (for any possible world, all other possible worlds can be placed on spheres centered on that world, the sizes of the spheres representing how close those worlds are to that world. All worlds on a given sphere are equally close to the centered world, and inner spheres are closer to the centered world than outer spheres).

Lewis (1973) and Stalnaker (1968) agree that if the antecedent of a counterfactual is impossible than the counterfactual is trivially true. For Lewis, this is because there is no such A-world; for Stalnaker, function f selects the impossible world in which every statement is true. (It is not however clear that all impossible counterfactuals are alike in respect of truth. There is, intuitively, a difference between "If Picasso had been a sonnet, he would have had fourteen lines" and "If Picasso had been sonnet, he would have had compound eyes," and Daniel Nolan [1997] and others argue that impossible worlds, like possible worlds, can be ranked with respect to comparative similarity to the actual world.) Lewis and Stalnaker also agree that inference patterns like contraposition, hypothetical syllogism, and strengthening the antecedent ((I1) to (I3) earlier) are invalid for counterfactuals. However, they disagree about the conditional excluded middle: [[A□→C] ∨ [A□→~C]] for all A and C. Stalnaker accepts it because according to his account there will always be one closest possible world, whereas Lewis accepts ties among closest possible worlds and so the principle is not universally true.

Stalnaker and Lewis also agree in analyzing the "closeness" relation in terms of similarity between worlds. However, what makes one world more similar to the actual world than another world? Kit Fine (1975) and Bennett (1974) object that Lewis's (1973) theory does not provide the correct truth conditions if closeness of worlds is understood in terms of our everyday intuitive notion of similarity. Intuitively, the counterfactual

If Nixon had pushed the button, there would have been a nuclear holocaust

seems true, and yet it is false by the lights of one commonsense notion of similarity, according to which a world in which a nuclear holocaust does not occur although Nixon presses the button is much more similar to our unholocausted world than a world where a nuclear holocaust does occur.

Lewis responds to this objection in "Counterfactual Dependence and Time's Arrow" (1979), claiming that a possible-worlds theory of counterfactuals does not need to appeal to any everyday notion of overall similarity. It is rather up to the theorist to work out a way of weighing factors relevant to overall similarity that will deliver the right truth-values for counterfactuals. Lewis offers the follows systems of weights:

> [i] It is of the first importance to avoid big, widespread, diverse violations of law
>
> [ii] It is of the second importance to maximize the spatiotemporal region throughout which perfect match of particular fact prevails
>
> [iii] It is of the third importance to avoid even small, localized, simple violations of law
>
> [iv] It is of little or no importance to secure approximate similarity of particular fact, even in matters that concern us greatly (Lewis 1979, p. 473)

According to this system of weights, the Nixon counterfactual turns out true. Consider a world in which Nixon pushes the button and there is no nuclear holocaust; rather, events proceed in such a way as to match those in our world with perfect similarity. The trouble with claiming that this is the most similar world is that Nixon's pressing the button would have numerous effects (including the button's warming slightly, the subsequent state of Nixon's memory, and so on), and only a large miracle could wipe out all these changes. The worlds closest to ours are the ones that agree with our actual world until Nixon presses the button and then continue on in accordance with the laws of the actual world. (However, for a reformulation of the Nixon objection in the light of this reply, see Tooley 2003).

Many philosophers shy away from the apparent metaphysical commitments of the possible-worlds approach. For what is a possible world? Lewis's (1986c) answer that possible worlds are concrete entities, each as real as the actual world, seems to most hopelessly implausible, but there are many other views. Stalnaker's (1968) and Bennett's (2003) possible worlds, for example, are maximally consistent sets of propositions; Saul Kripke's are stipulations; and others hold that possible worlds are combinatorial constructions out of elements of the actual world.

Whatever one's view, and whether or not one wishes to appeal to possible worlds, counterfactual conditionals are the vehicles of two of the most fundamental forms of thought: "What if?" and "If only." They are central to imagination and invention, essential to curiosity and regret, essential, along with conditionals in general, to the fundamental capacities for debating, supposing, speculating, and hypothesizing that constitute the heart of one's intelligence.

See also Bennett, Jonathan; Chisholm, Roderick; Conditionals; Goodman, Nelson; Hume, David; Kripke, Saul; Lewis, David; Mackie, John Leslie; Modality, Philosophy and Metaphysics of; Response-Dependence Theories; Semantics.

Bibliography

Adams, Ernest W. "Subjunctive and Indicative Conditionals." *Foundations of Language* 6 (1) (1970): 89–94.

Bennett, Jonathan. "Counterfactuals and Possible Worlds." *Canadian Journal of Philosophy* 4 (1974): 381–402.

Bennett, Jonathan. *A Philosophical Guide to Conditionals.* New York: Oxford University Press, 2003.

Chisholm, Roderick M. "Law Statements and Counterfactual Inference." *Analysis* 15 (1955): 97–105.

Dudman, Vic H. "Three Twentieth-Century Commonplaces about 'If.'" *History and Philosophy of Logic* 22 (2001): 119–127.

Edgington, Dorothy. "Do Conditionals Have Truth-Conditions?" *Critica* 28 (52) (1986): 3–30.

Fine, Kit. "Review of Lewis's Counterfactuals." *Mind* 84 (335) (1975): 451–458.

Goodman, Nelson. "The Problem of Counterfactual Conditionals." *Journal of Philosophy* 44 (1947): 113–128.

Grice, Herbert Paul. "Logic and Conversation." In *Conditionals*, edited by Frank Jackson, 155–176. New York: Oxford University Press, 1991.

Hume, David. *Enquiries concerning Human Understanding and concerning the Principles of Morals* (1748), edited by L. A. Selby-Bigge. Oxford, U.K.: Clarendon Press, 1975.

Jackson, Frank. "A Causal Theory of Counterfactuals." *Australasian Journal of Philosophy* 55 (1977): 3–21.

Jackson, Frank, ed. *Conditionals*. New York: Oxford University Press, 1991.

Jackson, Frank. "On Assertion and Indicative Conditionals." *Philosophical Review* 88 (1979): 565–589.

Kvart, Igal. *A Theory of Counterfactuals*. Indianapolis, IN: Hackett, 1986.

Lewis, David K. "Causation." In *Philosophical Papers*. Vol. 2. New York: Oxford University Press, 1986a. This was originally published in the *Journal of Philosophy* 70 (1973).

Lewis, David K. "Counterfactual Dependence and Time's Arrow." In *Philosophical Papers*. Vol. 2. New York: Oxford University Press, 1986b. This was originally published in *Noûs* 13 (1979)

Lewis, David K. *Counterfactuals*. Cambridge, MA: Harvard University Press, 1973.

Lewis, David K. *On the Plurality of Worlds*. Oxford, U.K.: Blackwell, 1986c.

Lewis, David. K. *Philosophical Papers*. Vol. 2. New York: Oxford University Press, 1986d.

Lewis, David K. "Postscripts to 'Counterfactual Dependence and Time's Arrow.'" In *Philosophical Papers*. Vol. 2. New York: Oxford University Press, 1986e.

Lewis, David. K. "Probabilities of Conditionals and Conditional Probabilities." *Philosophical Review* 85 (1976): 297–315.

Mackie, John L. *The Cement of the Universe*. Oxford, U.K.: Clarendon, 1974.

Mackie, John L. *Truth, Probability, and Paradox*. Oxford, U.K.: Clarendon, 1973.

Mill, John S. *System of Logic*. London: Longmans, 1868.

Nolan, Daniel. "Impossible Worlds: A Modest Approach." *Notre Dame Journal of Formal Logic* 38 (4) (1997): 535–572.

Parry, William T. "Reexamination of the Problem of Counterfactual Conditionals." *Journal of Philosophy* 54 (1957): 85–94.

Pollock, John L. *Subjunctive Reasoning*. Dordrecht, Netherlands: D Reidel, 1976.

Ramsey, Frank P. "General Propositions and Causality." In *The Foundations of Mathematics*. New York: Humanities, 1931.

Sanford, David. *If P, then Q: Conditionals and the Foundations of Reasoning*. New York: Routledge, 1989.

Stalnaker, Robert C. "A Theory of Conditionals." *Studies in Logical Theory, American Philosophical Quarterly* 2 (1968): 98–112.

Tichy, Pavel. "Subjunctive Conditionals: Two Parameters vs. Three." *Philosophical Studies* 45 (1984): 147–179.

Todd, William. "Counterfactual Conditionals and the Presuppositions of Induction." *Philosophy of Science* 31 (1964): 101–110.

Tooley, Michael. "The Stalnaker-Lewis Approach to Counterfactuals." *Journal of Philosophy* 100 (7) (2003): 321–327.

Michelle Montague (2005)

EUDAIMONIA

Strictly speaking, the term "eudaimonia" is a transliteration of the Greek word for prosperity, good fortune, wealth, or happiness. In philosophical contexts the Greek word "eudaimonia" has traditionally been translated simply as "happiness," but a number of contemporary scholars and translators have tried to avoid this rendering on the grounds that it can suggest unhelpful connotations in the mind of the uncritical reader. (For example, it does not refer to an affective state, nor is it coextensive with the classical utilitarian conception of happiness, though both of these notions may, in some thinkers, count as aspects of *eudaimonia*.) Since the word is a compound of the prefix "eu-" (well) and the noun "daimōn" (spirit), phrases such as "living well" or "flourishing" have been proposed as possible alternatives. But the consensus appears to be that "happiness" is adequate if the term is properly understood within the philosophical context of antiquity.

Aristotle wrote that all agree that *eudaimonia* is the chief good for humans, but that there is considerable difference of opinion as to what *eudaimonia* consists in (*Nicomachean Ethics* I.2, 1095a15–30). The portrait of Socrates presented in Plato's early, Socratic dialogues has Socrates endorsing the view that *eudaimonia* consists in living a just life, which requires knowledge in the form of a kind of foresight (see especially *Gorgias*). In his later works (for example, the *Republic*), Plato continued to argue that virtue is sufficient for happiness, and that nonmoral goods do not add to *eudaimonia* (the so-called sufficiency thesis).

As is well known, Aristotle agreed that virtue is a necessary condition for *eudaimonia* but held that it is not sufficient (the so-called necessity thesis). On his account, "eudaimonia" is most properly applied not to any particular moment of a person's life, but to an entire life that has been well lived. While virtue is necessary for such a life, Aristotle argued that certain nonmoral goods can contribute to *eudaimonia* or detract from it by their absence. There is some controversy among scholars as to how Aristotle finally characterized the happy life, the life marked by *eudaimonia*. Throughout the first nine books of the *Nicomachean Ethics*, he appears to think that a happy life is a life that centrally involves civic activity. The virtues that mark the happy person are themselves defined as states of the soul that arise out of certain interactions taking place in social relations. But in book X, Aristotle's argument appears to be that a life of contemplating the theoretical (*theoria*) is the happiest sort of life, and that civic involvement can actually detract from this sort of activity (though the private life of contemplation appears to presuppose the public life, since without the public life to produce goods and services, the philosopher is incapable of living in isolation).

Where Socrates, Plato, and Aristotle agreed was in the objective nature of *eudaimonia*, which set them sharply apart from the popular morality of their day. In a famous passage from the *Gorgias* (468e–476a), Socrates shocks Polus by arguing that a wrongdoer is actually worse off than the person whom he wrongs, and that any wrongdoer is bound to be unhappy until he is punished. The person who has been wronged, by contrast, may be happy in spite of whatever physical suffering he may undergo at the hands of the wrongdoer. The *Gorgias* concludes with a myth about the fate of the human soul after death that makes it clear that only the state of the soul, not the physical state of the body, determines whether one is happy or unhappy.

Although Aristotle did not agree that happiness cannot be diminished at all by physical suffering, it is not because he thought that feelings are decisive for happiness. On the contrary, he argued for an objective standard of human happiness grounded in his metaphysical realism. In *Nicomachean Ethics* (I.7), he argued that human excellence ought to be construed in terms of what ordinarily characterizes human life (the so-called function or *ergon* argument). This argument is clearly grounded in his doctrine of causation, according to which any member of a natural kind is characterized by four causes: a formal cause, a material cause, an efficient cause, and a final cause. The final cause is inextricable from the formal cause: To be a certain kind of thing is just to function in a certain way, and to have a certain sort of function is just to be a certain kind of thing. The human function (*ergon*) is to be found in the activity of our rational faculties, particularly practical wisdom (*phronēsis*) and learning (*sophia*). Since the activity of both of these faculties is ordered not by subjective considerations but by the formal constraints of reason itself, human excellence is objectively determined: To live well is to live a life characterized by the excellent use of one's rational faculties, and this excellence is marked by successfully applying general rules for virtuous living to particular situations calling for moral deliberation.

Aristotle rejected alternative accounts of happiness as falling short of his ideal in some way (*Nicomachean Ethics* I.5, 1095b14–1096a10). The life of political honor, for example, reduces happiness to the degree to which one is esteemed by others, thus disconnecting happiness from the operation of one's own proper function. A more popularly held view equated happiness with pleasure, a view that Aristotle quickly dismissed as failing to distinguish humans as a natural kind from other animals that also feel pleasure and that rely on it as a motivating force in their daily quest for survival. For Aristotle, as for Plato before him, the hedonistic view overlooks the essential function of human rationality: to order and control human appetites and desires, channeling them into activities that, in the long run, best ensure human flourishing. Indeed, it is this very order and control that distinguishes human society from all other forms of life, so that there is an intimate connection between human excellence and the political life. This connection is subject to a certain tension, however, since both Plato, in the *Republic*, and Aristotle, in his life of theoretical contemplation, make social order a necessary condition for human excellence while simultaneously arguing that personal happiness in some sense involves disconnecting oneself from the community at large.

The Stoics agreed that happiness is our ultimate end, for which all else is done, and they defined this as consistently living in accordance with nature. By this they meant not only human nature but the nature of the entire universe, of which we are a part, and the rational order that both exhibit. Practical reason thus requires an understanding of the world and our place in it, along with our resolute acceptance of that role. Following nature in this way is a life of virtue and results in a "good flow of life," with peace and tranquility.

The Epicureans also took *eudaimonia* to be the end for humans, but they defined "eudaimonia" in terms of pleasure. Yet many of the things we take pleasure in have unpleasurable consequences, which on balance disrupt our lives, and so do not provide us with the freedom from concerns (*ataraxia*) and the absence of physical pain (*aponia*) that characterize true happiness. These traits, they believed, must be secured through the exercise of moderation, prudence, and the other virtues, yet they are not valued for their own sakes but as instrumental means to a life of pleasure and happiness.

This form of hedonistic eudaemonism is to be contrasted with the hedonism of the Cyrenaics, the main exception to Aristotle's statement that all agree that the highest good is *eudaimonia.* Sketchy accounts of the elder Aristippus suggest that his hedonism involved giving free reign to sensual desires (Xenophon, *Memorabilia* 11.1.1–34), so as always to be capable of enjoying the moment, making use of what was available (Diogenes Laertius 11.66). Later Cyrenaics refined this position as seeking to enjoy sensual pleasure to the full without sacrificing autonomy or rationality. Their conception of pleasure emphasized bodily pleasures, understood as either a kind of movement (*kinēsis*) or the supervening state of the soul (*pathos*). Because they regarded such transient states as the highest good, the Cyrenaics rejected the view that *eudaimonia,* a comprehensive and long-term type of fulfillment, is the end that should govern all our choices.

See also Aristotle; Cyrenaics; Epicurus; Phronêsis; Plato; Socrates; Sophia; Stoicism.

Bibliography

Ackrill, J. L. "Aristotle on *Eudaimonia.*" *Proceedings of the British Academy* 60 (1974): 339–359.

Aristotle. *Nicomachean Ethics.* Translated by Christopher Rowe. Oxford, U.K.: Oxford University Press, 2002.

Annas, Julia. *The Morality of Happiness.* New York: Oxford University Press, 1993.

Broadie, Sarah. *Ethics with Aristotle.* New York: Oxford University Press, 1991. See especially chapter 1, "Happiness, the Supreme End," and chapter 7, "Aristotle's Values."

Cooper, John M. "Contemplation and Happiness: A Reconsideration." In his *Reason and Emotion: Essays on Ancient Moral Psychology and Ethical Theory,* 212–236. Princeton, NJ: Princeton University Press, 1999.

Cooper, John M. "Intellectualism in the Nicomachean Ethics." In his *Reason and Human Good in Aristotle,* 144–182. Cambridge, MA: Harvard University Press, 1975.

Diogenes Laertius. *Lives of Eminent Philosophers.* Translated by R. D. Hicks. Cambridge, MA: Harvard University Press, 1972.

Gosling, J. C. B., and C. C. W. Taylor. "Epicurus." In their *The Greeks on Pleasure,* 345–364. Oxford, U.K.: Clarendon, 1982.

Irwin, Terence. "Socrates: From Happiness to Virtue." In his *Plato's Ethics,* 52–64. New York: Oxford University Press, 1995.

Plato. *The Collected Dialogues of Plato.* Princeton, NJ: Princeton University Press, 1963.

Vlastos, Gregory. "Happiness and Virtue in Socrates' Moral Theory." In his *Socrates, Ironist and Moral Philosopher,* 200–232. Ithaca, NY: Cornell University Press, 1991.

Xenophon. *Memorabilia.* Translated by Amy L. Bonnette. Ithaca, NY: Cornell University Press, 1994.

Scott Carson (2005)

EXPERIMENTATION AND INSTRUMENTATION

Experiment, William Herschel wrote, is a matter of "putting in action causes and agents over which we have control, and purposely varying their combinations, and noticing what effects take place" (Herschel 1966, p. 76). In this sense, the earliest recorded scientific experiments appeared in biological and medical contexts. In the second century CE, the physician Galen performed detailed animal experiments to find out about the functions of various organs. In the sixteenth century, Andreas Vesalius, pioneer in dissection, carried out elaborate experiments; and William Harvey, notwithstanding his Aristotelian orientation, supported his discovery of the circulation of the blood with painstaking experimental arguments. It is highly plausible that the practice of alchemy also served as an early source of experimentation. From the thirteenth century on, alchemists used laboratory equipment in order to create new agents and were arguing against the overly narrow interpretation of the art-nature divide in Aristotelian philosophy.

A third area where experimentation took place before the scientific revolution was supplied by Ptolemy's optics. Ptolemy, active in the second century CE, formulated an experimental, quantitative law of the refraction of light at the boundary of air and water and performed experiments to investigate binocular vision. In continuing this tradition in the early eleventh century CE, the Arab Ibn al-Haytham (Alhazen) wrote an impressive experimental treatise on optics in which he related in a mathematically demanding way the physics and geometry of light to the anatomy of the eye. Al-Haytham's work was translated into Latin in the thirteenth century and decisively influenced later optical research for a long time. Because of this and similar developments, Crombie saw experimental science of the modern world created by thirteenth-century philosophers of the West transforming Greek geometrical method and uniting it with the experimental habit of the practical arts.

All these different attempts of probing nature through experimental trials certainly contributed to the final emergence of experimentation in the seventeenth century as a self-conscious, methodically controlled and systematically used form of scientific experience. Galileo's new conception of motion, which was based on experiment and measurement from about 1604 on, played an instrumental and decisive role in this (Schmitt 1969). In the second half of the century, scientific academies devoted themselves to the new science and became the primary centers of experimental activity.

From the seventeenth century on, experimentation increasingly meant the implementation of new or improved scientific instruments. Following a suggestion of Thomas S. Kuhn, we can group these instruments mainly into two categories according to their origin in the classical or the Baconian tradition of physical science (Kuhn 1976). The classical sciences comprise those mathematical disciplines like astronomy, geometrical optics, statics, harmonics, and geometry itself, which were first constituted in classical antiquity and experienced their major developments already then. With the exception of harmonics, the close connections of these fields with each other lasted way up into the nineteenth century. The instruments belonging to this tradition were often called "mathematical instruments" and are of a restricted variety: ruler and compass, balance, clock, and geometrical-astronomical devices. They served as aids to "mixed mathematics," which allowed for certain physical attributes in addition to the abstract mathematical ones. To experiment with them mostly meant to confirm a belief that was established beforehand by rational considerations, or to detail a fully established theory in a special respect. Many experiments performed in this tradition proved to be in reality only thought experiments—mental constructions of possible experimental situations whose results were thought to be predictable already from everyday experience. Even Galileo participated sometimes in this attitude.

The second tradition to which we can attribute many of the new instruments of the period is the Baconian one whose disciplines owe their status as sciences mainly to the experimental movement of the seventeenth century and to the practice of "natural histories," including those of the different practical arts that experienced a tremendous re-evaluation at the time. The barrier between the craft and scholarly traditions, which had so far separated the mechanical from the liberal arts, began to break down. To the Baconian sciences belong the studies of heat, electricity, magnetism, chemistry, metallurgy, glass making, and the like. The instruments of these fields were used to investigate nature under previously unobserved or non-existent conditions and were often called "philosophical instruments." During the next decades, the Baconian movement brought forth the telescope, the microscope, the thermometer and the barometer, the air pump, electric charge detectors, the Leyden jar, and many other contrivances. It is interesting to see that these instruments were primarily used in a qualitative way and that a strictly quantitative application came only very late, mainly at the end of the eighteenth or during the early nineteenth century when the two traditions, the classical and the Baconian, started to merge with each other. From about the middle of the seventeenth century on, the Baconian movement had adopted some form of the atomic or corpuscular philosophy and became the official "experimental philosophy" of the Royal Society.

PHILOSOPHICAL ASSESSMENTS OF EXPERIMENTATION AND INSTRUMENTATION

In the second book of his *Physics*, Aristotle had developed a contrast between "physis" and "techne," that is, between natural entities that have an innate principle of change—like plants, animals and humans, but also stones and clouds—and those that are artificially constructed, like bedsteads and clothes. Until the scientific revolution, Aristotelians used this nature-artifact divide as an argument against the epistemological relevance of experimentation. In order to understand nature, they claimed, one must not intervene with her order. Intervention would either invalidate nature's innate principles or play her a trick with mechanical contrivances, but would not lead to any genuine knowledge of natural reality. Instead, one must let nature pursue her own course and purposes and gain knowledge of her principles by closely observing them. The fact that techne or art is declared by Aristotle to be able to complete nature's unfinished processes or to imitate her does not change this state of affairs. To complete nature in regard to the behavior of a natural entity meant to remove all obstacles that might have come in its way; and to imitate nature denoted the general maxim to bring form and matter of an entity in an intricate union as nature does it with her beings.

It seems that the major author in providing a *philosophical* bridge over the art-nature divide was Francis Bacon (1561–1626). This justifies Kuhn's choice of using Bacon's name for a whole new tradition of experimentation. Bacon argued that art was only a special way of arranging a state of affairs in which nature herself will then produce an intended result. He redefined Aristotle's concept of form and took it as the key to the operational features of a natural being, leaving out the teleological dimension. The discovery of operational rules of an entity can now be identified with the true form or real essence of relations among its simple natures. Consequently, Bacon rejected Aristotle's three other causes besides the formal one and took forms as "nothing more than those laws and determinations of absolute actuality which govern and constitute any simple nature, as heat, light, weight, in every kind of matter and subject that is susceptible of them" (*Nov. Org.* ii, XVII).

As a result, knowledge of our world cannot, according to Bacon, be read off from its surface, so to say. We can work our way through to the "viscera naturae," or nature's intestines, only by methodical and experimental procedures of induction. Perhaps Bacon's major insight was that simple enumerative induction, as taught by Aristotle, that is, induction without experiment and without the method of exclusion, is not enough to tell essential correlations from accidental ones.

Bacon's procedure of induction was taken as a valuable method of creating new empirical theories and laws way up into the twentieth century. The Baconian tradition culminated during the nineteenth century in John Stuart Mill's elaboration and refinement of Bacon's and Herschel's inductive rules. There is, however, a tendency visible in Mill to take experiment not quite with the same force as Bacon had taken it. For Bacon, experiment is inevitable if one wants to snatch secrets from nature—they never show up by themselves. Yet for Mill, situations are conceivable where observation can serve the same purpose as experiment: "For the purpose of varying the circumstances [in order to find out the real laws] we may have recourse … either to observation or to experiment; we may either *find* an instance in nature suited to our purposes, or, by an artificial arrangement of circumstances, *make* one. The value of the instance depends on what it is in itself, not on the mode in which it is obtained: its employment for the purposes of induction depends on the same principles in the one case and in the other, as the uses of money are the same whether it is inherited or acquired. There is, in short, no difference in kind, no real logical distinction, between the two processes of investigation" (*System of Logic*, III, vii, 2).

The belief that there is no "logical distinction" between observation and experiment became a matter of course for almost all the schools of philosophy of science of the entire twentieth century until the 1980s. It is interesting to see how an excellent nineteenth-century experimentalist, Hermann von Helmholtz, resisted this tendency, although he followed Mill in many other and important respects. His reasons, however, were different from Bacon's: If *I* can vary the conditions of an event in different respects, he argued, I can be sure that *my intervention* is the cause of observed change because I know of my will's impulse. If, however, I can only passively *observe* correlations without any help from me, I can never be sure whether these make up genuine causal relations or only accidental covariation (Helmholtz 1903). Whereas for Bacon it is the coyness of nature that compels humans to experiment, for Helmholtz it is the epistemological limitation of the passive mind that forces them to intervene in nature's course.

One of the strongest and most influential anti-inductive texts ever written is a chapter in Pierre Duhem's *Aim and Structure of Physical Theory* of 1906, titled "Physical Theory and Experiment." In order to show the general inadequacy of inductivism, Duhem picked the "Newtonian method" to pieces, as it appeared both in the hands of Newton himself as well as with Ampère's electrodynamics. He brilliantly showed that there is no question in Newton's celestial mechanics of any extraction of hypothesis by induction from experimenting, as Newton himself required in the *General Scholium*, nor in Ampère's mathematical theory of electrodynamic phenomena of any deduction "only from experiment," as stated already in the title of Ampère's treatise of 1827.

As a logical consequence, Duhem concluded that "in the course of its development, *a physical theory is free to choose any path it pleases provided that it avoids any logical contradiction; in particular, it is free not to take account of experimental facts*." It has to take account of them only "when the theory has reached its complete development" (Duhem 1974, p. 206; Duhem's emphasis). In order that experiment can unfold its true function—the testing of theories— it must be preceded by theory. Duhem intensified the priority of theory when he demanded that "this test by facts should bear exclusively on the conclusions of a theory, for only the latter are offered as an image of reality; the postulates serving as points of departure for the theory and the intermediary steps by which we go from the postulates to the conclusions do not have to be subject to this test."

Duhem's criticism was later taken up and continued by Karl Popper. In exactly the same spirit as Duhem, Popper decreed that "the theoretician puts certain definite questions to the experimenter, and the latter by his experiments tries to elicit a decisive answer to these questions and to no others" (Popper 1959, p. 107). For Popper therefore, it is only the theoretician who shows the experimenter the way, and never the other way around. The only function left for experiment is to liberate us from sterile and false theories. With Popper, experiment has altogether become the handmaiden of theory.

Duhem had even gone one step further than Popper in questioning the capability of experiment to fulfill this critical task of refuting theories as well. Even if a theory is mature enough to be tested, experiment cannot mechanically decide between it and its rival. "An experiment in physics can never condemn an isolated hypothesis but only a whole theoretical group" (p. 183). And it is hardly ever possible to decide trenchantly which of the many assumptions of a theoretical system is doubtful and responsible for the experimental contradiction. "The physicist concerned with remedying a limping theory resembles the doctor and not the watchmaker" (p. 188). A watchmaker, Duhem maintained, can take the broken watch apart and examine each component separately until he finds the defective one. The doctor, however, cannot dissect the patient to find out the problem, but has to guess its seat by inspecting disorders affecting the whole body. And even if all the assumptions of a theoretical group were known to be true except one, the rival group would not have been established as superior. This would be shown only if every possible alternative were conclusively eliminated. But we never know of course what alternatives remain to be discovered.

All these considerations led Duhem to explicitly condemn Bacon's idea of a "crucial experiment." Bacon had suggested that there do exist experiments that conclusively decide between competing theories. They do this in the way of *instantiae cruces* or "fingerposts" that are set up at crossroads to indicate the several directions. In 1951, W. V. O. Quine joined Duhem in rejecting crucial experiments. He generalized Duhem's argument to *all* of our empirical tenets. An unexpected unsuitable empirical observation does not only contradict a theoretical system, as Duhem had told us, Quine argued, but *all* our beliefs and theories: "Our statements about the external world face the tribunal of sense experience not individually but only as a corporate body. … The unit of empirical significance is the whole of science" (Quine 1961, p. 41f.). Quine used this claim for a searching critique of logical empiricism. One consequence of this is that any assumption apparently refuted by observation can be retained as true, so long as we are willing to make appropriate changes elsewhere in the system of our beliefs. This holistic argument for the underdetermination of theories by experience has become known as the "Duhem-Quine thesis."

The series of philosophical arguments to denigrate the role of experiments continued further into the 20th century. The logical empiricist Hans Reichenbach coined the influential distinction between "context of discovery" and "context of justification" which had been developed earlier by the philosophers Alois Riehl, Gottlob Frege and others under different names (Reichenbach 1951). According to this dichotomy, all the actual historical and social circumstances of the creation of a scientific theory, including its experimental generation, if there was one, cannot be used as reasons to justify it. Experiment can be good as a heuristic guide to hit upon a useful theory, but it is neither necessary nor sufficient for the validity of its results. As a result of Reichenbach's division all attention focused on the epistemology of theory and none on discovery and the possibilities of experiment.

Although Thomas S. Kuhn is routinely regarded as major critique of both logical empiricism with its forerunner Duhem and of Popper's critical rationalism, he was surprisingly enough in large agreement with his predecessors as far as the subordinate role of experiment is concerned—at least in his central work *The Structure of Scientific Revolutions* of 1962/1970. Unlike Reichenbach, however, Kuhn wanted to overcome the separation of discovery and justification, but the admissible discovery part of his logic considered the founding of theories again in overarching paradigms, but not in experiments. In this he followed his teacher Alexandre Koyré and others, who saw the success of modern science in the superiority of mathematically oriented Platonism over Aristotelianism with its "brute, common-sense experience" and over all other experimentally and technologically oriented historical endeavors. For Koyré as for Kuhn a scientific revolution is foremost an "intellectual mutation" (Koyré 1943, p. 400), i.e. a revolution of thought and not of momentous experimental innovation. Paradigms have priority over theories "in their conceptual, observational, and instrumental applications" (Kuhn 1970, p. 43). True experimental research is only possible, if questions to nature are posed in a suitable mathematical language. According to such a view, a history of experimentation could not only be a contingent epiphenomenon of the development of paradigms and would not have much explanatory value. (The contrary view is defended by deSolla Price 1984.) Only when in his later work he began to appreciate the Baconian sciences as an autonomous movement did Kuhn start to appreciate the possibility of a meaningful history of scientific experimentation (Kuhn 1976).

In retrospect, the discussion of experiment in philosophy of science from the late nineteenth century until the 1980s appears as a series of increasingly negative results: We know more and more what experiments don't accomplish and we understand better and better where earlier epistemic pretensions of experimentation find their limits. As a result, we can diagnose an "invisibility of experiment." In the same way as scientific revolutions of a field are, according to Kuhn, normally invisible to the scientific profession of the present, so experiments and their development remain largely invisible to philosophy of science because their exclusive role of testing theories seems ingrained in the ideology of its practitioners.

THE NEW EXPERIMENTALISM

Since the early 1980s, however, a change has taken place in the attitude of the study of science toward experiment. One can detect a growing awareness of the rich history of experimentation and of the vast variety of its (non-demonstrative) functions. This swing of appreciation is primarily due to detailed work of historians and sociologists of science. It is true that historiography never ceased to deal with experiment, but it had rarely put it into the center of its interest. Socio-historical analysis has now come to concentrate much more on the microstructure of experiment than before and has started to consider all kinds of other sources besides official reports, like diaries and laboratory notebooks. Especially rich sources are Faraday's laboratory notebooks and letters, Ampère's "dossier" in the archive of the Académie des Sciences and Hans Krebs' laboratory diaries and interview protocols (Gooding 1990, Steinle 2005, Holmes 1993, Graßhoff 2000). Historians even went so far as to replicate historical experiments with rebuilt apparatus and to hereby bring to light neglected or otherwise hidden dimensions of experimentation (Heering 2000). Sociologists tried to show that the formulation of experimental results requires special structures of communication in the scientific community and that there is a good deal of negotiation involved until an experimental result is considered as achieved (Shapin and Shaffer 1985, Licoppe 1996; for a discussion see Holmes 1992). The variety of fields from where these case studies come from raise hopes that the traditional concentration on physics in relation to experiment will soon be done with once and for all.

It was Ian Hacking's *Representing and Intervening* that set the ball rolling in philosophy of science. There are two phrases from Hacking's book that became the slogans of "new experimentalism": "If you can spray them, then they are real" and "Experimentation has a life of its own" (Hacking 1983, pp. 23, 150). The first catchphrase stands for a novel argument in favor of scientific realism. The philosopher's favorite theoretical entity is the electron—never given directly to our senses, but central to modern particle physics. There is an endless debate between scientific realists and their opponents whether explanatory success of a theory is ground for belief in the reality of its theoretically postulated entities. Hacking does not think very highly of this "inference to the best explanation," on which the ordinary scientific realist bases her belief in the reality of the electron. He rather sets high hopes in the fact that if you spray, say, a niobium ball with electrons, it makes a difference in the world: it decreases the charge of the niobium ball. "From that day forth," Hacking confesses, "I've been a scientific realist." In a way, Hacking's argument is a version, adapted to scientific antirealism, of Dr. Johnson's refutation of Bishop Berkeley's metaphysical antirealism concerning matter by kicking a stone. "It is not thinking about the world but changing it that in the end must make us scientific realists."

With the second catchphrase Hacking opposes the alleged theory-domination of experimentation: There actually exists experimental practice, he argues, that is *not* subordinate to theory and this practice actually proves to be very important. This claim is backed up with many intriguing examples. But liberating experiment from permanent condemnation to the role of theory's handmaiden does not automatically show what other roles it can take on and what the principles of their variations are. About this, Hacking does not say very much. The only other role he addresses in detail is, as he says, the experiment's "chief role": the "creation of phenomena." Some aspects of this role have been brought to light in Steinle's concept of "exploratory" experiments or in Heidelberger's notion of "productive" instruments (Steinle 2005; Heidelberger 1998, 2003).

All in all, Hacking seems to be largely content with a "Baconian fluster of examples of many different relationships between experiment and theory" (Hacking 1983, p. 66). This has surely proven to have been enough to initiate a "Back-to-Bacon movement, in which we attend more seriously to experimental science" (p. 150) as it had been Hacking's intention. But, if neo-Baconianism is sound, it is not enough as an explanation of what happens or should happen with other theoretical commitments of general philosophy of science, like, for example, the theory-ladenness of observation. This doctrine—dear to many philosophers of science for other reasons—comes, at least *prima facie*, into conflict with Hacking's faith in the priority of experiment.

In the wake of renewed interest in experiment, several substantial studies and edited volumes have appeared. Many of them are divided over the philosophical issue whether experiment can decide between competing theories and thus have an objective meaning or whether social and political factors are in the end responsible for scientific development. There is, for example, Pickering's sociological history of particle physics or Collins's study of gravity wave detection maintaining the social construction of scientific evidence whereas Franklin and Mayo argue for the existence of strategies that secure reliable experimental outcomes and thus of rational belief. It would be wrong, however, to perpetuate the polarization between history, sociology, and philosophy of science. One of the results of taking experiment more seriously is precisely the insight that these dichotomies have to be transcended. An attempt into this direction has been made by Rheinberger who takes "experimental systems" as functional research units, especially of the life sciences (see Hagner and Rheinberger 1998 for a programmatic overview.) They are made up of research objects, theories, experimental arrangements, instruments, as well as disciplinary, social, cultural and institutional constellations that for some time crystallize in a certain stable configuration.

EXPERIMENTATION AND THEORY-LADENNESS

The idea of theory-ladenness of experience enabled a powerful and effective criticism of logical empiricism. This is the view already encountered with Popper that there are no theory-neutral data and that the meaning of observational terms fundamentally depends upon the theoretical context in which they occur. This view can easily be strengthened to serve as the cornerstone of a constructivist and anti-empiricist account of science: The categories in terms of which we carve up our experience are not read off from the external world but follow from prior theoretical or other commitments of its observers, either individually or socially.

The implications of theory-ladenness for a view of scientific experimentation are straightforward: If observations are theory-laden and if experimentation involves observation of results, then experimentation has to be theory-laden too. Since experiments, according to this view, make sense only in relation to some theoretical background, they cannot play a role that is independent from theory.

Now, the question arises: If new experimentalism is right, do we have to give up the idea of theory-ladenness? It is difficult to imagine a straightforward "yes" as an answer, because the general spirit in which the idea of theory-ladenness has been formulated is largely the same as that of the idea that experimentation has a life of its own. It is the spirit addressed by Hacking at the beginning of his book in which philosophers finally realized that they "long made a mummy of science"—the same spirit which, in the face of history and the reality of the laboratory, denies the "Popper/Carnap common ground." To deny theory-ladenness would to some extent feel like a return to logical empiricism and thereby of mummification, even if the autonomy of experiment is the reward.

Before some kind of dénouement of this question is formulated, let us have a closer look at theory-ladenness as it appeared in the work of its most important originators. One of the first propagators of this outlook was Pierre Duhem who wrote: "An experiment in physics is the precise observation of phenomena accompanied by an *interpretation* of these phenomena; this interpretation substitutes for the concrete data really gathered by observation abstract and symbolic representations which correspond to them by virtue of the theories admitted by the observer. … The result of an experiment in physics is an abstract and symbolic judgment" (Duhem 1974, p. 147). It would not be enough for an experimental report to state, as a layman would express it, that a piece of iron carrying a mirror oscillates. Instead it should read that the electrical resistance of a coil is measured. This shows that the physicist draws conclusions from experiment only in abstract and symbolic terms "to which you can attach no meaning if you do not know the physical theories admitted by the author." In sciences less advanced than physics like physiology or certain branches of chemistry "where mathematical theory has not yet introduced its symbolic representations" and where causal explanation reigns instead of a causally neutral description, the experimenter can reason "directly on the facts by a method which is only common sense brought to greater attentiveness" (p. 180).

This kind of theory-ladenness by theoretical interpretation, as we can call it, is very often confounded with another sort which was provided by Norwood Russell Hanson in 1958 and which can be called "theory-ladenness by prior belief or knowledge." "Seeing an object *x*," Hanson wrote, "is to see that it may behave in the ways we know *x*'s do behave" (Hanson 1958, p. 22). As a result of this, Tycho and Kepler watching the sun at dawn would literally see different things: Tycho who believes in the geocentric theory sees the sun beginning its diurnal circuit, whereas Kepler as defender of heliocentrism sees the earth spinning back into the light of the sun. "Analogously," Hanson wrote, "the physicist sees an X-ray tube, not by first soaking up reflected light and then clamping on interpretations, but just as you see this page before you."

In addition, theory-ladenness in science means "causality-ladenness" for Hanson, being loaded with causal meaning. He does not exclude theory-neutral talk after all, but it only happens in the oculist's office or like circumstances but not in scientific observation or experimentation. This shows that Hanson rejects all of Duhem's points: (1) Seeing an experimental result is not interpreting it; (2) both the layman and the physicist have prior beliefs and therefore both their seeing is theory-laden; and (3) physical theory (as well as common beliefs about the world) is causal theory and not just causally neutral description. Whereas for Hanson any injection of causality into the mere registering of facts is bound to render them theoretical, for Duhem, theory begins with the representation of (causal) relations in an abstract, causally neutral structure.

In Thomas Kuhn's work we find several different conceptions of theory-ladenness that are not always separated clearly. The most frequently used is similar to Hanson's, except that it is not prior knowledge that shapes perception, but paradigm and that it stresses and utilizes the psychology of perception even more than in Hanson: "Something like a paradigm is prerequisite to perception itself. What a man sees depends both upon what he looks at and also upon what his previous visual-conceptual experience has taught him to see" (Kuhn 1970, p. 113).

In order to exhibit his other uses of theory-ladenness, let us have a look at Kuhn's treatment of scientific discovery. Kuhn admits the possibility of "fundamental novelties of fact," that go *against* a well-established paradigm. Without this possibility, as he himself realizes, science could only develop in a theoretical manner and never by adjustment to facts. "Discovery commences with the awareness of anomaly, i.e., with the recognition that nature has somehow violated the paradigm-induced expectations that govern normal science" (Kuhn 1970, pp. 52–53).

Where, according to Kuhn, does a violation of the paradigm-induced expectations come from? Does it come from a causal process that violates the received view or from a new theoretical interpretation that makes old facts appear in a new light? It seems that in Kuhn, it is almost always the *theoretical interpretation*, the assimilation to theory, that is decisive for discovery and hardly ever any causal experience. "Assimilating a new sort of fact demands a more than additive adjustment of theory, and until that adjustment is completed—until the scientist has learned to see nature in a different way—the new fact is not quite a new fact at all." That sounds more as if new facts and causal processes were created by new paradigms than the other way around. Lavoisier, we are told, for example, was enabled through his new paradigm "to see in experiments like Priestley's a gas that Priestley had been unable to see there himself" and was "to the end of his life" unable to see p. 56).

The only case where Kuhn explicitly admits that discovery has been effected by a genuinely novel causal experience appears to be the case of the X-rays. "Its story opens on the day that the physicist Roentgen interrupted a normal investigation of cathode rays because he had noticed that a barium platino-cyanide screen at some distance from his shielded apparatus glowed when the discharge was in process" (p. 57). Although Kuhn seems to consider this observation theory-laden, I maintain that, in Duhem's sense, it is not. If it were, Roentgen, by definition of theory-ladenness, would have been able to interpret it in light of the theories of physics he had at his disposal. But here it is exactly the point that his theories deserted him and he could *not* find a place for this new experience in his customary theoretical structure. For this reason he interrupted his investigation and asked himself why the screen had come to glow. Yet the novel observation is certainly theory-laden in the sense of Hanson, because Roentgen immediately looked for a causal relationship between his apparatus and the glowing of the screen, although this went completely against all his expectations!

Kuhn seems to say that Roentgen would never have paid attention to the glowing screen if he had not disposed of deeply entrenched theories of physics that *prohibited* such a phenomenon. If this is true then we have here a third sense of the notion of theory-ladenness before us. It frames a psychological hypothesis about the ease with which a phenomenon is detected or paid attention to in the light of a *contradicting* paradigm: An observation is theory-laden in this sense if it were improbable that an observer would have made it (that an observer would have noticed it or would have attributed any importance to it) without her holding a theory beforehand that created expectations *to the contrary*. It would be better to drop the term "theory-ladenness" for this case altogether and instead call it "theory-guidance" because the experimental result made sense to Roentgen as an observation in its simple causal structure already *without* the theoretical background of the theory that guided it or any other one. "Theory-guidance" refers to a psychological disposition how well one is prepared to notice a particular phenomenon in certain situations.

After Roentgen had noticed the anomaly, he conducted various experiments in order to explore the *cause* of the incident: "Further investigations—they required seven hectic weeks during which Roentgen rarely left the laboratory—indicated that the cause of the glow came in straight lines from the cathode ray tube, that the radiation cast shadows, could not be deflected by a magnet, and much else besides. Before announcing his discovery, Roentgen had convinced himself that his effect was not due to cathode rays but to an agent with at least some similarity to light" (Kuhn 1970, p. 57). This is perhaps the only place in his book where Kuhn uses the term "cause" (or an equivalent) in relation to an experimental investigation. The quotation shows vividly that Roentgen did not conduct his experiments in order to test a theory but to expand our knowledge of causal connections in relation to the scientific instruments and devices involved.

What does our discussion suggest therefore as the most adequate description of Roentgen's early experiments? They were certainly theory-guided in the sense of Kuhn and they were, or immediately became, causality-laden in the sense of Hanson, but not (or not yet) theory-laden in the sense of Duhem (which Kuhn also shares). Kuhn is right when he suggests that only after the phenomena had received an abstract and symbolic representation can we speak of a "discovery" of X-rays. Yet before this interpretation has taken place, we can say that an anomaly has occurred and that it can be replicated in certain ways; not more, but also not less.

If the case of the X-rays is in this way correctly understood, then Kuhn can give in to Hacking without loosing anything essential and admit that experimentation can be, and very often is, autonomous and free from theory. The lesson to learn is to distinguish between two kinds of experiments: those that are causal, but not (yet) embedded in a theoretical structure and those that presuppose the knowledge of such a framework. This emphasis of an autonomous "lower level" in experimentation is not a relapse into positivist observation statements and protocol sentences allegedly giving meaning to theory. The claim rather is that two types of experimentation should conceptually be kept apart: experimentation at the causal level, where the manipulation of instruments and objects under scrutiny takes place, and experimentation taking place at the theoretical level, where the results at the causal level are represented in a theoretical superstructure.

See also Ampère, André Marie; Aristotelianism; Aristotle; Bacon, Francis; Berkeley, George; Carnap, Rudolf; Duhem, Pierre Maurice Marie; Faraday, Michael; Frege, Gottlob; Galen; Galileo Galilei; Harvey, William; Helmholtz, Hermann Ludwig von; Herschel, John; Johnson, Samuel; Kepler, Johannes; Kuhn, Thomas; Lavoisier, Antoine; Logical Positivism; Mill, John Stuart; Newton, Isaac; Philosophy of Science, History of; Platonism and the Platonic Tradition; Popper, Karl Raimund; Priestley, Joseph; Quine, Willard Van Orman; Realism; Reichenbach, Hans; Riehl, Alois; Scientific Method; Thought Experiments in Science; Underdetermination Thesis, Duhem-Quine Thesis.

Bibliography

Bacon, Francis. *Novum Organum*. London: 1620.

Batens, Dederik, and Jean P. van Bendegem, eds. *Theory and Experiment: Recent Insights and New Perspectives on Their Relation*. Dordrecht: Reidel, 1988.

Buchwald, Jed Z. *Scientific Practice: Theories and Stories of Doing Physics*. Chicago: University of Chicago Press, 1995.

Collins, Harry M. *Changing Order: Replication and Induction in Scientific Practice*. Beverly Hills, CA, and London: Sage, 1985.

Crombie, Alistair C. *Robert Grosseteste and the Origins of Experimental Science, 1100–1700*. Oxford: Clarendon, 1953.

deSolla Price, Derek J. "Of Sealing Wax and String." *Natural History* 93 (1) (1984): 48–57.

Duhem, Pierre. *The Aim and Structure of Physical Theory*. New York: Atheneum, 1974. Translated by Philip P. Wiener from the 2nd ed. Paris: Chevalier & Rivière, 1914.

Franklin, Allan. *Experiment, Right or Wrong*. Cambridge, U.K.: Cambridge University Press, 1990.

Franklin, Allan. *The Neglect of Experiment*. Cambridge, U.K.: Cambridge University Press, 1986.

Galavotti, Maria Carla, ed. *Observation and Experiment in the Natural and Social Sciences*. Dordrecht: Kluwer, 2003.

Galison, Peter. *How Experiments End*. Chicago: University of Chicago Press, 1987.

Gooding, David. *Experiment and the Making of Meaning: Human Agency in Scientific Observation*. Dordrecht: Kluwer, 1990.

Gooding, David, Trevor Pinch, and Simon Schaffer, eds. *The Uses of Experiment: Studies in the Natural Sciences*. Cambridge, U.K.: Cambridge University Press, 1989.

Graßhoff, Gerd, R. Casties, and Kärin Nickelsen. *Zur Theorie des Experimentes. Untersuchungen am Beispiel der Entdeckung des Harnstoffzyklus*. Bern: Bern Studies, 2000.

Hacking, Ian. *Representing and Intervening: Introductory Topics in the Philosophy of Natural Science*. Cambridge, U.K.: Cambridge University Press, 1983.

Hacking, Ian. "The Self-Vindication of the Laboratory Sciences." In *Science as Practice and Culture*, edited by Andrew Pickering, 29–64. Chicago: University of Chicago Press, 1992.

Hagner, Michael, and Hans-Jörg Rheinberger. "Experimental Systems, Objects of Investigation, and Spaces of Representation." In *Experimental Essay—Versuche zum Experiment*, edited by Michael Heidelberger and Friedrich Steinle, 355–373. Baden-Baden: Nomos, 1998.

Hanson, Norwood Russell. *Patterns of Discovery*. Cambridge, U.K.: Cambridge University Press, 1958.

Heering, P., Falk Rieß, and C. Sichau, eds. *Im Labor der Physikgeschichte. Zur Untersuchung historischer Experimentalpraxis.* Oldenburg: BIS-Verlag, 2000.

Heidelberger, Michael. "Die Erweiterung der Wirklichkeit im Experiment." In *Experimental Essays—Versuche zum Experiment,* edited by Michael Heidelberger and Friedrich Steinle, 71–92. Baden-Baden: Nomos, 1998.

Heidelberger, Michael. "Theory-Ladenness and Scientific Instruments in Experimentation." In *The Philosophy of Scientific Experimentation,* edited by Hans Radder, 138–151. Pittsburgh: University of Pittsburgh Press, 2003.

Heidelberger, Michael, and Friedrich Steinle, eds. *Experimental Essays—Versuche zum Experiment.* Baden-Baden: Nomos, 1998.

Helmholtz, Hermann von. "Die Tatsachen in der Wahrnehmung [1878]." In *Vorträge und Reden,* 213–247. Braunschweig: Vieweg, 1903.

Herschel, John F. W. *Preliminary Discourse on the Study of Natural Philosophy* (1830). New York: Johnson Reprint Corporation, 1966.

Holmes, Frederic L. "Do We Understand Historically How Experimental Knowledge Is Acquired?" *History of Science* 30 (1992): 119–136.

Holmes, Frederic L. *Hans Krebs: Architect of Intermediary Metabolism 1933–1937.* Oxford: Oxford University Press, 1993.

Holmes, Frederic L. "The Logic of Discovery in the Experimental Life Sciences." In *Biology and Epistemology,* edited by Jane Maienschein, 167–190. Cambridge, U.K.: Cambridge University Press, 2000.

Holmes, Frederic L., Jürgen Renn, and Hans-Jörg Rheinberger, eds. *Reworking the Bench: Research Notebooks in the History of Science, New Studies in the History and Philosophy of Science and Technology.* Dordrecht: Kluwer, 2003.

Holmes, Frederic L., and Trevor H. Levere, eds. *Instruments and Experimentation in the History of Chemistry.* Cambridge, MA: MIT Press, 2000.

Koyré, Alexandre. "Galileo and Plato." *Journal of the History of Ideas* 4 (4) (1943): 400–428.

Kuhn, Thomas S. "Mathematical vs. Experimental Traditions in the Development of Physical Science." *Journal of Interdisciplinary History* 7 (1) (1976): 1–31. Reprinted in *The Essential Tension: Selected Studies in Scientific Thought and Change,* 31–65. Chicago: University of Chicago Press, 1977.

Kuhn, Thomas S. *The Structure of Scientific Revolutions.* 2nd ed. Chicago: University of Chicago Press, 1970.

Latour, Bruno, and Steve Woolgar. *Laboratory Life: The Social Construction of Scientific Facts.* 2nd ed. Princeton, NJ: Princeton University Press, 1986.

Le Grand, Homer E., ed. *Experimental Inquiries: Historical, Philosophical and Social Studies of Experimentation in Science.* Dordrecht: Kluwer, 1990.

Licoppe, Christian. *La formation de la pratique scientifique: le discours de l'expérience en France et en Angleterre* (1630–1820). Paris: Editions La Decouverte, 1996.

Mayo, Deborah G. *Error and the Growth of Experimental Knowledge, Science and Its Conceptual Foundations.* Chicago: University of Chicago Press, 1996.

Mill, John Stuart. *A System of Logic, Ratiocinative and Inductive.* London: Parker, 1843.

Pickering, Andrew. *Constructing Quarks: A Sociological History of Particle Physics.* Chicago: University of Chicago Press, 1984.

Pickering, Andrew. *The Mangle of Practice: Time, Agency, and Science.* Chicago: University of Chicago Press, 1995.

Pickering, Andrew, ed. *Science as Practice and Culture.* Chicago: University of Chicago Press, 1992.

Popper, Karl. *The Logic of Scientific Discovery.* London: Hutchinson, 1959.

Quine, Willard Van Orman. *From a Logical Point of View.* New York: Harper & Row, 1963.

Radder, Hans, ed. *The Philosophy of Scientific Experimentation.* Pittsburgh, PA: University of Pittsburgh Press, 2003.

Reichenbach, Hans. *The Rise of Scientific Philosophy.* Berkeley: University of California Press, 1951.

Schmitt, Charles B. "Experience and Experiment: Comparison of Zabarella's View with Galileo's in *De Motu.*" *Studies in the Renaissance* 16 (1969): 80–138.

Shapin, Steven, and Simon Schaffer. *Leviathan and the Air-Pump: Hobbes, Boyle, and the Experimental Life.* Princeton, NJ: Princeton University Press, 1985.

Steinle, Friedrich. *Explorative Experimente. Ampère, Faraday und die Ursprünge der Elektrodynamik.* Stuttgart: Franz Steiner, 2005.

Michael Heidelberger (2005)

MODALITY AND LANGUAGE

Modality is a category of linguistic meaning having to do with the expression of possibility and necessity. A modalized sentence locates an underlying or prejacent proposition in the space of possibilities (the term *prejacent* was introduced by medieval logicians). *Sandy might be home* says that there is a possibility that Sandy is home. *Sandy must be home* says that in all possibilities Sandy is home. The counterpart of modality in the temporal domain should be called temporality, but it is more common to talk of tense and aspect, the prototypical verbal expressions of temporality. Together, modality and temporality are at the heart of the property of displacement (one of Charles F. Hockett's design features of human language) that enables natural language to talk about affairs beyond the actual here and now.

There are numerous kinds of expression that have modal meanings, the following is just a subset of the variety one finds in English:

(1) Modal auxiliaries
  Sandy must/should/might/may/could be home.

(2) Semimodal verbs
  Sandy has to/ought to/needs to be home.

(3) Adverbs
Perhaps, Sandy is home.

(4) Nouns
There is a slight possibility that Sandy is home.

(5) Adjectives
It is far from necessary that Sandy is home.

(6) Conditionals
If the light is on, Sandy is home.

It is traditional to use English modal auxiliaries or semimodal verbs as the primary source of illustrative examples. This is in spite of the fact that these elements have a rather curious set of grammatical properties. Indeed, it appears that modal meanings are part of a natural logical vocabulary and thus elements with modal meanings easily become part of the inventory of grammatical or functional morphemes, which are typically associated with idiosyncratic, nonproductive grammatical characteristics (for a cross-linguistic survey of this process, compare Bybee, Perkins, Pagliuca 1994).

KINDS OF MODAL MEANING

One can distinguish different kinds of modal meaning. Alethic modality (Greek: *aletheia*, meaning "truth"), sometimes logical or metaphysical modality, concerns what is possible or necessary in the widest sense. It is in fact hard to find convincing examples of alethic modality in natural language, and its inclusion in this list is primarily for reason of historical completeness. The following categories, however, are of primary importance in the study of natural language. Epistemic modality (Greek: *episteme*, meaning "knowledge") concerns what is possible or necessary given what is known and what the available evidence is. Deontic modality (Greek: *deon*, meaning "duty") concerns what is possible, necessary, permissible, or obligatory, given a body of law or a set of moral principles or the like. Bouletic modality, sometimes boulomaic modality, concerns what is possible or necessary, given a person's desires. Circumstantial modality, sometimes dynamic modality, concerns what is possible or necessary, given a particular set of circumstances. Teleological modality (Greek: *telos*, meaning "goal") concerns what means are possible or necessary for achieving a particular goal. In the descriptive literature on modality, there is taxonomic exuberance far beyond these basic distinctions.

FLEXIBILITY OF MEANING

Many modal expressions can be used to express many or all these kinds of modal meaning. Witness the English semimodal *have to* in the following set of examples:

(7) It has to be raining. [after observing people coming inside with wet umbrellas; epistemic modality]

(8) You have to go to bed in ten minutes. [stern father; bouletic]

(9) Visitors have to leave by six p.m. [hospital regulations; deontic]

(10) I have to sneeze. [given the current state of one's nose; circumstantial]

(11) To get home in time, you have to take a taxi. [teleological]

Some modal expressions are more specialized in what kind of meanings they can carry. The English auxiliary *might* is most comfortable expressing epistemic modality.

(12) It might be raining.

Some modals only occur in specialized environments. The modal *need* with a bare infinitive complement can only occur in negative environments:

(13) a. You need not worry.
b. *You need worry.

(14) Nobody need worry.

Such negative polarity modals occur in other languages as well (compare the Dutch *hoeven* and the German *brauchen*).

POSSIBLE WORLDS SEMANTICS

In technical work on natural language semantics, modality is analyzed with the machinery of possible worlds semantics, developed by logicians for the artificial language of modal logic. The most influential incarnation of this idea is found in the work of the semanticist Angelika Kratzer (1981, 1991).

The starting tenet is that modal expressions express quantification over possible worlds—regardless of what those might be (most practitioners have few ontological scruples). Possibility modals correspond to existential quantification, while necessity modals correspond to universal quantification. Different kinds of modal meaning correspond to different choices of sets of possible worlds as the domain of quantification. These sets of possible worlds are assigned to the world in which the complex sentence is evaluated (the evaluation world) by an accessibility relation.

The accessibility relation underlying epistemic modality delivers as the domain of quantification for the modal those worlds that are compatible with what is known, with the available evidence in the evaluation world. Similarly, deontic modality quantifies over worlds that satisfy the relevant body of law or principles. Bouletic modality quantifies over worlds that conform to what the relevant person desires.

Actually, Kratzer (1981, 1991) argues that modal meaning does not just rely on an accessibility relation but also on an ordering of the accessible worlds. The clearest argument for this complication of the semantics comes from deontic cases. Imagine a city whose traffic bylaws outlaw the practice of double parking at any time for any reason. The bylaws further specify that anyone who is found guilty of double parking must pay a considerable fine. Robin has been found guilty of double parking, so the following sentence seems to be true:

(15) Robin must pay a fine.

Notice, however, that in all the worlds that conform to the traffic bylaws there never occurs any double parking, since that is against the law. Therefore, in none of those worlds does Robin pay a fine for double parking. Thus, the simple possible worlds analysis incorrectly predicts the sentence to be false.

Kratzer's (1981, 1991) analysis makes modal expressions doubly relative: they need to be interpreted relative to (1) a set of accessible worlds (modal base), and (2) an ordering of those worlds. For the case in hand, the accessible worlds would be those where Robin's actions hitherto are what they are (double parking occurs) and that from then on develop in many conceivable ways. The ordering would be that induced by the traffic bylaws, which would favor among the accessible worlds those where Robin pays a fine. The truth-conditions of this example are then that in all the favored worlds among the accessible worlds Robin pays a fine. The sentence could be made false either if Robin did not in fact double park or if the traffic bylaws do not in fact require a fine.

The surface variety of modal meanings is thus a product of the interplay of three factors: (1) the quantificational strength (possibility, necessity, and shadings in between, e.g. slight possibility), (2) the modal base, and (3) the ordering source.

Epistemic modality has an epistemic modal base and either no ordering or an ordering based on plausibility or stereotypicality. Deontic modality has a circumstantial modal base (because one may have to abstract away from one's knowledge that the right thing will not be done) and an ordering source based on a body of law or principles. Bouletic modality again has a circumstantial modal base and an ordering source based on a relevant person's desires.

There is much detailed research remaining to be done on the fine distinctions between different modal expressions. Consider, for example, the fact that *ought to* and *have to* somehow differ in strength in their deontic use:

(16) You ought to call your mother, but of course you don't have to.

Or, consider the fact (explored by Ninan 2005) that deontic *should* and deontic *must* differ whether one can admit that the right thing will not happen:

(17) I should go to confession, but I'm not going to.

(18) #I must go to confession, but I'm not going to.

There is also an interesting literature on fine details of epistemic meaning. Work by Ian Hacking (1967), Paul Teller (1972), and Keith DeRose (1991) shows that there is much additional complexity and context-dependency behind the phrases *what is known* or *the available evidence*, which are typically used to characterize epistemic accessibility. In particular, the context may specify whose knowledge or evidence base is relevant to the claim made with an epistemically modalized sentence.

CONTEXT-DEPENDENCY AND LEXICAL SPECIALIZATION

Kratzer (1981, 1991) argues that rather than treating the multitude of modal meanings as a case of (accidental) polysemy, it should be seen as the outcome of context-dependency. In other words, modal expressions have in of themselves a rather skeletal meaning and it is only in combination with the background context that they take on a particular shade of meaning (such as epistemic or deontic). She points to ways of making explicit what the intended conversational background is:

(19) According to the hospital regulations, visitors have to leave by six p.m.

(20) Considering the evidence before us, it has to be raining.

In the absence of such explicit markers, natural language users need to rely on contextual clues and reasoning about each other's intentions to determine what kind of modal meaning a particular sentence is intended to express in its context of use.

As seen earlier, some modals are not entirely subject to the whims of context but impose their own preferences as to what kind of modal meaning they would like to express. English *might* likes to be epistemic (with some interesting exceptions, such as the use in *You might try to put the key into this slot*, which has the force of a suggestion). This kind of behavior is not uncommon for expressions that are context-dependent: pronouns refer to contextually furnished individuals but may include restrictions on what the context can furnish, for example, the gender marking on *she* requires that the context furnish a female individual.

It has been shown that there is a recurring historical development where a modal expression that initially has a nonepistemic meaning only (something that for opaque reasons is often called a root modal) develops over time into an expression that also has epistemic meanings (e.g., Nordlinger and Traugott [1997] document this development for the case of English *ought to*).

THE ARGUMENT STRUCTURE OF MODALS

So far, this entry has been presupposing that modality concerns the possibility or necessity of a prejacent proposition. There is, however, an ancient and persistent doctrine that another kind of modality concerns the possible or necessary existence of a relation between a subject or agent and a predicate. For example, one finds the claim that deontic modality can at least sometimes concern what an agent is permitted or obliged to do.

(21) Sandy ought to call his mother.

The propositional analysis has it that the sentence expresses the necessity of the prejacent proposition that Sandy calls (will call) his mother, relative to the current circumstances and a body of ethics, for example. The predicate-level analysis has it that the sentence expresses that the agent Sandy and the property of calling his mother stand in a certain modal relation. Some authors call this the *ought to be* versus *ought to do* distinction. Certain sentences are clearly cases of propositional-level *ought to be* modality:

(22) There ought to be a law against double parking.

For sentences with an agentive subject, it is an open question, debated in the technical literature, whether a predicate-level or propositional-level analysis is correct. Whatever one's position in this debate is, one has to admit that some sentences with human subjects still do not express an obligation imposed on that subject:

(22) Jimmy ought to go in his crib now. [said of a six-month-old baby]

FURTHER AND RELATED CATEGORIES

At the outset, this entry listed a set of expressions that have modal meanings. The list was far from complete. Here, some other types of expressions that may fall under the general category of modality or at least belong to adjacent categories will be added.

A closely related category, perhaps subsumable under modality, is evidentiality. Various languages regularly add markers, inflectional or otherwise, to sentences that indicate the nature of the evidence that the speaker has for the prejacent proposition. A typical evidential system might centrally distinguish between direct and indirect evidence. The latter concept might be further subdivided into indirect reasoning from direct evidence or conclusions based on hearsay or the like. The standard European languages do not have elaborate evidential systems but find other ways of expressing evidentiality when needed. The English adverb *apparently* seems to prefer indirect evidence:

(24) Kim has apparently been offered a new job.

The German modal *sollen* has a hearsay interpretation:

(25) Kim soll einen neuen Job angeboten bekommen haben.
Kim soll a new job offered get have
"Kim has supposedly been offered a new job."

Another important category is mood, an inflectional marking on the main verb of a sentence, which expresses some kind of modal meaning. English has only a rudimentary mood system, if that. However, Romance languages, for example, productively use mood. In Italian, the complement clause of a verb like *say* occurs in the indicative mood, while the complement of *believe* appears in the subjunctive mood. There are attempts at analyzing the mood selection in such cases as depending on technical properties of the possible worlds semantics of the embedding verb. The research topic remains active and thriving.

Propositional attitude constructions are also related to modality. Consider the near equivalence of the following two sentences:

(26) Robin suspects that the butler is guilty.

(27) Given Robin's evidence, the butler might be guilty.

Jaako Hintikka (1969) proposed to analyze propositional attitudes with the same possible worlds machinery that was originally applied to modals, thus making the relation between the two categories explicit in their semantics.

Expressions of illocutionary force are also within or close to the field of modality. Consider in particular attenuating speech act markers, as explored in pioneering work by J. O. Urmson (1952):

(28) The butler is, I suspect, guilty.

The difference between attenuated assertion of a proposition and categorical assertion of a modalized proposition is small, one suspects.

One particular kind of expression deserves attention: the modal particles that are rampant in some languages, such as German:

(29) Kim hat ja einen neuen Job.
Kim has JA a new job
"Kim has a new job, as you may know already"

The gloss here is only approximate, the meaning of the modal particles is elusive and under active investigation.

Modality is a pervasive feature of natural language and sometimes it clearly appears in the semantics of an expression without a clear syntactic or morphological exponent. Such hidden modality can be detected, for example, in infinitival relatives in English (for extensive discussion, see Bhatt 2005):

(30) When you have computer trouble, Sandy is the person to talk to. [≈ Sandy is the person one ought to talk to]

Sometimes the source for the modality can be identified but its etymology and nature remains opaque:

(31) What Arlo is cooking has garlic in it.

(32) Whatever Arlo is cooking has garlic in it. [epistemic modality triggered by *-ever*: speaker does not know what precisely Arlo is cooking]

The range of modal expressions is a rich domain for language-internal and cross-linguistic investigations.

MODALITY WITHOUT CONTENT?

So far, this entry has assumed that modalized sentences express complex propositions with a possible worlds-based quantificational meaning built on top of a prejacent unmodalized proposition. While this is indeed the standard analysis in formal natural language semantics, it is not the standard assumption in descriptive and typological linguistics.

The most common analysis in descriptive work treats modality as an expression of the speaker's attitude toward the prejacent proposition, rather than giving rise to a complex proposition with its own distinct content. The prevalence of this conception can perhaps be traced back to the influence of Immanuel Kant, who wrote in his *Critique of Pure Reason* that "the modality of judgments is a very special function thereof, which has the distinguishing feature that it does not contribute to the content of the judgment" (1781, p. 74). This idea seems to have influenced both practicing linguists and a subset of logicians, including Gottlob Frege, who wrote in his *Begriffsschrift* that "[b]y saying that a proposition is necessary, I give a hint about the grounds for my judgment. But, since this does not affect the conceptual content of the judgment, the form of the apodictic judgment has no significance for us" (1879, p. 5).

It may be that scholars have typically adopted one of the two conceptions without much reflection. Within the descriptive literature, there is rarely any argumentation for the speaker's comment analysis. And the formal semantic literature rarely addresses the issue either, basically ignoring the preponderance of the speaker's comment analysis in the descriptive literature.

One rather straightforward prediction of the speaker's comment analysis is that modalized sentences should not be easily embeddable. This prediction seems to be false for at least some standard modal expressions:

(33) It might be that visitors have to leave by six p.m. [epistemic modality embedding a deontic modality]

Such iterated modality is unexpected from the point of view of the speaker's comment analysis. Better cases for a comment analysis come from speech act markers:

(34) #If yesterday, I suspect, was the worst day of the year, the market is in good shape.

The suspicion arises that some modal expressions have a comment-type meaning, while others contribute to the propositional content of the complex sentence. There is here, it seems, the opportunity for empirical and theoretical debate on this issue. It should be noted that the question here is related but not identical to the issue of whether a modal element expresses subjective or objective modality (these terms are discussed by Lyons 1977).

Independently of these ideas from descriptive linguistics, there are proposals that would give modals a meaning that goes beyond truth-conditions. In dynamic semantics, epistemic modals are treated as particular operations on an information state, see, for example, Veltman (1996). Finally, at least for deontic modals, it has been suggested that they can be used with performative force, whether or not they also have propositional content. Kamp (1973, 1978) and Lewis (1979) explore the idea that deontic 'may' is used to grant permission, while Ninan (2005) explores the idea that deontic 'must' is used to issue commands.

COMPOSITIONAL INTERACTIONS

As the examples of iterated modality in the previous section showed, at least some, if not most, modal expressions can compositionally interact with other expressions. Interactions with negation, quantifiers, and tense are particularly interesting.

The combination of modals with negation is a fountain of idiosyncratic facts. Consider that English *may* scopes under negation when read deontically, but scopes above negation when read epistemically:

(35) He may not have any cake. [deontic, "not allowed"]

(36) He may not be home. [epistemic, "possible that not"]

Or, consider that English *must* scopes above negation (in either reading) while German *müssen* scopes under negation:

(37) a. He must not have any cake. ["obligatory that not"]
b. He must not be home. ["evident that not"]

(38) Er muss nicht zuhause bleiben.
He must not at-home remain
"He doesn't have to stay home."

Lastly, note that while *can* does not easily allow an epistemic reading, negated *cannot* does have an epistemic reading:

(39) a. Sandy can be home. [?]
b. Sandy cannot be home. [epistemic]

Most of these facts have resisted systematic explanation and remain mysterious.

Sentences containing both modals and quantificational noun phrases are often ambiguous:

(40) Most of our students must get outside funding …
a. for the department budget to work out.
b. the others have already been given university fellowships.

In some of the literature, this ambiguity is assimilated to the distinction between *de dicto* and *de re* interpretations, probably inappropriately. In any case, it has been observed that not all sentences show this ambiguity. For example, epistemic modals seem to resist having quantifiers scope over them (for an exploration, see von Fintel and Iatridou 2003):

(41) Most of our students must be home by now.
a. must ≻ most of our students
b. *most of our students ≻ must

Again, this kind of fact remains mysterious, it may be an idiosyncratic syntactic fact without any grounding in semantics.

The interaction of modality and temporality is intricate and ill understood. One should first note that the aspectual nature of the prejacent sentence has a strong influence on what kind of meaning a modal sentence can carry. A nonstative prejacent typically gives rise to deontic readings, while a stative prejacent is compatible with both epistemic and deontic readings:

(42) He has to be in his office. [epistemic/deontic]

(43) He has to see his doctor this afternoon. [nonepistemic]

While modal auxiliaries do not inflect for tense (the fact that *might* may be a past-tense inflected form of *may* has reasons in the mist of history), other expressions do allow such inflection.

(44) He had to be in his office.

It is not always obvious whether what is happening here is that the modal sentence is located in the past or whether the modal has scope over a past-tense prejacent. The preceding sentence, when read epistemically, is plausibly ambiguous, reporting a past deduction about a simultaneous state of affairs or a present deduction about a past state of affairs. Finally, some modals in embedded positions seem not to express any modal meaning of their own but occur in "agreement" or "harmony" with a higher modal or mood. One relevant case is "I am convinced that it must be raining." See Portner (1997) for discussion.

CONDITIONALS

An interaction of modals with other expressions that is of paramount importance is their appearance in conditional constructions. It has been noticed again and again that for sentences of the form *if p, modal q* it is hard to find a compositional interpretation that treats the *if*-construction as expressing some kind of conditional meaning, while the modal in the consequent expresses its usual modal meaning.

Consider, for example, the following conditional:

(45) If Robin double parked her car, she must pay a fine.

A tempting idea is that the conditional construction introduces universal quantification over epistemically accessible worlds and says that the consequent is true in all epistemically accessible worlds where Robin double parked her car. The consequent in turn is true in an evaluation world if in all worlds circumstantially accessible from that world and favored by the deontic ordering source Robin pays a fine. However, now assume that one knows that Robin is invariably law abiding. She would never do anything that contravenes any law. So, among the epistemically accessible worlds there are none where she double parks against the law, so if she double parked, that must be consistent with the law. Hence, the above sentence would come out false. However, this seems wrong. The sentence does not make a claim about what the law must be like if Robin double parked her car. What it claims is that the actual law is such that double parking necessitates a fine.

The conclusion drawn from this and many parallel examples with other modal operators is that it is a mistake to analyze such structures as involving two-layered operators: a conditional construction embedding or embedded in a modal construction. Rather, the idea has been to say that in such sentences, the *if*-clause does not supply its own operator meaning but serves as a restriction on the modal base of the modal operator. The proper analysis of the previous sentence is that it says that among those circumstantially accessible worlds where Robin double parked her car, the ones favored by the law as it is in the actual world are all worlds where Robin pays a fine.

After surveying a number of such cases, Kratzer summarizes the thesis as follows, "[T]he history of the conditional is the story of a syntactic mistake. There is no two-place *if ... then* connective in the logical forms of natural languages. *If*-clauses are devices for restricting the domains of various operators" (1986).

What about bare conditionals such as *If Sandy's light is on* she is home? Here, there is no modal operator for the *if*-clause to restrict. Should one revert to treating *if* as an operator on its own? Kratzer (1986) proposes that one should not and that such cases involve covert modal operators—in this case, possibly a covert epistemic modal. This entry has nothing to say about that here.

This entry has shown that the topic of modality is characterized by rich empirical detail, considerable cross-linguistic variation, and intriguing theoretical issues. The following bibliography can serve as a start for further reading and exploration.

See also Artificial and Natural Languages; Conditionals; Hintikka, Jaakko; Kant, Immanuel; Modality, Philosophy and Metaphysics of; Philosophy of Language; Possibility; Propositional Attitudes: Issues in Semantics; Semantics.

Bibliography

van der Auwera, Johan. "On the Typology of Negative Modals." In *Perspectives on Negation and Polarity Items*, edited by Jack Hoeksema et al., 23–48. Amsterdam, Netherlands: Benjamins, 2001.

van der Auwera, Johan, and Vladimir A. Plungian. "Modality's Semantic Map." *Linguistic Typology* 2 (1998): 79–124.

Bhatt, Rajesh. *Covert Modality in Non-finite Contexts*. de Gruyter, 2005.

Bybee, Joan L., Revere Perkins, and William Pagliuca. *The Evolution of Grammar: Tense, Aspect, and Modality in the Languages of the World*. Chicago: Chicago University Press, 1994.

Condoravdi, Cleo. "Temporal Interpretation of Modals: Modals for the Present and for the Past." In *The Construction of Meaning*, edited by David I. Beaver et al. Stanford, CA: CSLI Publications, 2002.

DeRose, Keith. "Epistemic Possibilities." *Philosophical Review* 100 (4) (1991): 581–605.

Farkas, Donka. "On the Semantics of Subjunctive Complements." In *Romance Languages and Modern Linguistic Theory*, edited by Paul Hirschbühler and Konrad Koerner, 69–104. Amsterdam, Netherlands: Benjamins, 1992.

von Fintel, Kai, and Sabine Iatridou. "Epistemic Containment." *Linguistic Inquiry* 34 (2) (2003): 173–198.

Frege, Gottlob. *Begriffsschrift, eine der arithmetischen nachgebildete Formelsprache des reinen Denkens*. Halle: L. Nebert, 1879.

Hacking, Ian. "Possibility." *Philosophical Review* 76 (2) (1967): 143–168.

Hintikka, Jaako. "Semantics for Propositional Attitudes." In *Philosophical Logic*, edited by J. W. Davis, D. J. Hockney, and W. K. Wilson, 21–45. Dordrecht, Netherlands: D. Reidel, 1969.

Hockett, Charles F., and Stuart A. Altmann. "A Note on Design Features." In *Animal Communication: Techniques of Study and Results of Research*, edited by Thomas A. Sebeok, 61–72. Bloomington: Indiana University Press, 1968.

Kamp, Hans. "Free Choice Permission." *Proceedings of the Aristotelian Society, New Series*, 74: 57–74, 1973.

Kamp, Hans. "Semantics versus Pragmatics". In *Formal Semantics and Pragmatics for Natural Languages*, edited by Franz Guenthner and S. J. Schmidt, pp. 255–288. Dordrecht: Reidel, 1978.

Kant, Immanuel. *Critik der reinen Vernunft*. Riga: Johann Friedrich Hartknoch, 1781.

Karagjosova, Elena. *Modal Particles and the Common Ground: Meaning and Functions of German ja, doch, eben/halt, and auch*. Amsterdam, Netherlands: Benjamins, 2003.

Kiefer, Ferenc. "Modality." In *The Encyclopedia of Language and Linguistics*, edited by Ronald E. Asher, 2515–2520. Oxford, U.K.: Pergamon, 1994.

Kiefer, Ferenc. "On Defining Modality." *Folia Linguistica* 21 (1) (1987): 67–94.

Kratzer, Angelika. "Conditionals." *Chicago Linguistics Society* 22 (2) (1986): 1–15.

Kratzer, Angelika. "Modality." In *Semantics: An International Handbook of Contemporary Research*, edited by Arnim von Stechow and Dieter Wunderlich, 639–650. Berlin: de Gruyter, 1991.

Kratzer, Angelika. "The Notional Category of Modality." In *Words, Worlds, and Contexts: New Approaches in Word Semantics*, edited by H. J. Eikmeyer and H. Rieser, 38–74. Berlin: de Gruyter, 1981.

Lewis, David. "A Problem about Permission". In *Essays in Honour of Jaako Hintikka: On the Occasion of His Fiftieth Birthday on January 12, 1979*, edited by Esa Saarinen, Risto Hilpinen, Ilkka Niiniluoto, and Merril Provence Hintikka, pp. 163–175. Reidel, 1979.

Lyons, John. *Semantics*. New York: Cambridge University Press (1977).

Ninan, Dilip. "Two Puzzles about Deontic Necessity." In *New Work on Modality*, edited by Valentine Hacquard et al. MIT Working Papers in Linguistics, no. 52. Department of Linguistics and Philosophy, MIT, Cambridge, MA, 2005.

Nordlinger, Rachel, and Elizabeth Traugott. "Scope and the Development of Epistemic Modality: Evidence from *ought to*." *English Language and Linguistics* 1 (1997): 295–317.

Palmer, Frank Robert. *Mood and Modality*. 2nd ed. New York: Cambridge University Press, 2001.

Plungian, Vladimir A. "The Place of Evidentiality within the Universal Grammatical Space." *Journal of Pragmatics* 33 (2001): 349–357.

Portner, Paul. "The Semantics of Mood, Complementation, and Conversational Force." *Natural Language Semantics* 5 (2) (1997): 167–212.

Stowell, Tim. "Tense and Modals." In *The Syntax of Time*, edited by Jacqueline Guéron and Jacqueline Lecarme, 621–636. Cambridge, MA: MIT Press, 2004.

Teller, Paul. "Epistemic Possibility." *Philosophia* 2 (1972): 302–320.

Urmson, J. O. "Parenthetical Verbs." *Mind* 61 (1952): 192–212.

Veltman, Frank. "Defaults in Update Semantics". *Journal of Philosophical Logic* 25(3) (1996): 221–261.

Willett, Thomas. "A Cross-linguistic Survey of the Grammaticalization of Evidentiality." *Studies in Language* 12 (1) (1988): 51–97.

von Wright, Georg Henrik. *An Essay in Modal Logic*. Amsterdam, Netherlands: North-Holland, 1951.

Kai von Fintel (2005)

PHRONÊSIS

Often translated as "practical wisdom," the Greek word *phronêsis* derives from the verb *phronein*, meaning "to have understanding," or "to be wise or prudent." In its earliest uses the word is normative only in the sense that it signifies a correct cognitive grasp of some kind; only gradually does it come to be used in ethical contexts for a correct grasp of what ought to be done. For Plato and the other Socratics, *phronêsis* represents that aspect of our rational faculty that derives genuine knowledge about values and norms, that is, about the virtues (see especially *Protagoras, Gorgias*). The famous debate between the Socratics and their critics, such as the orator Isocrates, turned on the possibility of demonstrative knowledge in the sphere of virtue. Plato had attacked oratory on the grounds that its aim is not to discover what is morally right, but merely to persuade, and he offered in its place the Socratic method of dialectic, a cooperative search for the truth by means of hypothesis formation, critical examination and refutation, and hypothesis modification. Isocrates had characterized Socratic dialectic as mere eristic (*Against the Sophists* 1; *Antidosis* 261) or argument for argument's sake—probably for this reason, Plato is especially careful to distinguish the Socratic method from mere eristic in his *Euthydemus*—and referred to the Socratics as "disputers." But Plato devotes much argument to showing how the careful examination of various conceptions of the virtues can lead inexorably to a recovery of their essential nature, which resides in the soul of every person from birth.

Aristotle's treatment of *phronêsis* (*Nicomachean Ethics* VI.5 1140a24–b30; cf. 1141b8–1143a5) is similar in many respects to Plato's, but in his account the knowledge that we obtain of virtue is not the equivalent of scientific (demonstrative) knowledge (*episteme*): unlike *episteme*, which is concerned with necessary truths, *phronêsis* is always concerned with contingent truths. Aristotle defines *phronêsis* by reference to something more concrete and familiar, namely, the practically wise person, *ho phronimos*, someone who has *phronêsis*. It is the mark of the practically wise person, he says, to be able to deliberate well about what is good and advantageous for himself not merely in one area, such as health or strength, but as a means to human flourishing in general. The operation of *phronêsis* in Aristotle's account of the rational faculties appears to hinge on the application of general rules for right conduct (the *orthos logos*) to the particular circumstances of a given situation so as to result in action that will generally tend toward human flourishing. The *phronimos* is the person whose life is characterized by such applications of *phronêsis* and who, as a result, tends to flourish throughout his life. Such a person is said to be *eudaimôn* or "happy."

In contrast, the Stoics characterize *phronêsis* as a kind of scientific knowledge (*episteme*), namely, of what should be done or not. Although they differ amongst themselves about the precise relationship, the Stoics regard the other virtues as this sort of knowledge in more specific domains: justice concerns what should be done or not with regard to deserts, courage with regard to what should be endured, and moderation with regard to what should be chosen or avoided. But given the Stoics' conception of a good life as one lived in agreement with nature, knowledge of what should be done will depend on knowledge of both human nature and nature as a whole, and above all our role within the latter. *Phronêsis*, therefore, has a considerably larger scope for the Stoics than for Aristotle, and is possessed only by the Stoic ideal of the wise person.

For Epicurus, *phronêsis* has more to do with prudential reasoning. It is what enables us to assess the consequences of every choice and so calculate its overall value. It is thus crucial for leading a happy life—in fact, Epicurus regards it as even more precious than philosophy itself. In particular, he believes, it reveals that virtue and pleasure are inseparable: It is impossible to live pleasantly without living virtuously or, for that matter, to live virtuously without living pleasantly.

See also Aristotle; Dialectic; Epicureanism and the Epicurean School; Eudaimonia; Gorgias of Leontini; Plato; Protagoras of Abdera; Socrates; Stoics; Virtue and Vice; Wisdom.

Bibliography

Broadie, S. "Practical Wisdom." In *Ethics with Aristotle*. New York: Oxford University Press, 1991.

Gigon, O. "Phronesis und Sophia in der *Nicomach. Ethik des Aristoteles*." In *Mélanges de C. de Vogel*, Assen, 91–104. 1975.

Hardie, W. "Practical Wisdom." In *Aristotle's Ethical Theory*. 2nd ed. New York: Oxford University Press, 1980.

Hueffmeier, F. "Phronesis in den Schriften des Corpus Hippocraticum." *Hermes* 89 (1961): 51–84.

Kraut, R. "Function, Virtue, and Mean." In *Aristotle on the Human Good*. Princeton, NJ: Princeton University Press, 1989.

Menn, S. "Physics as a Virtue." *Proceedings of the Boston Area Colloquium in Ancient Philosophy* 11 (1995): 1–34.

Scott Carson (2005)

QUANTIFIERS IN NATURAL LANGUAGE

Quantifiers in natural language correspond to words such as *every, some, most, few*, and many others.

THE SEMANTICS OF DETERMINERS

What is the semantics of expressions like *every* and *most*? An answer to this question emerged in the early 1980s, in work of Jon Barwise and Robin Cooper (1981), James Higginbotham and Robert May (1981), Edward L. Keenan and Jonathan Stavi (1986), Johan van Benthem (1986), Dag Westerståhl (1985), and many others.

The basic idea of how to interpret quantified expressions comes from Gottlob Frege (1879). Frege observed that the familiar quantifiers ∀ (*everything*) and ∃ (*something*) can be thought of, in Frege's terms, as second-level concepts. Let us call whatever gives the interpretation of an expression its semantic value. Assuming an extensional and set-theoretic framework, we my assign predicates sets of individuals as their semantic values. Frege's idea can then be recast as saying that the semantic values of ∀ and ∃ are sets of sets. $\exists xFx$ (*something is F*) is true if the semantic value of *F* is in the interpretation of ∃, which happens just in case the semantic value of *F* is nonempty. More generally, quantifiers have as semantic values sets of the values of predicates which result in true sentences when the quantifiers are applied.

In logic, this idea was later investigated by Andrzej Mostowski (1957) and then Per Lindström (1966). But it does not apply to natural language without an important modification. Consider:

(1) Most students attended the party.

In this, *most* does not tell us something about a single predicate. Rather, it compares the students with the people attending the party. In particular, it compares the size of the set of students with the size of the set of people attending the party.

This binary or relational character of quantification in natural language is extremely widespread (as is demonstrated by the extensive list of examples in Keenan and Stavi 1986). It is also no accident. Rather, it reflects a fundamental feature of the syntax of natural languages. Simplifying somewhat, sentences break down into combinations of noun phrases (NPs) and verb phrases (VPs). Noun phrases also break down, into combinations of determiners (DETs) and common nouns (CNs) (or more complex construction with adjectival modifiers like *small brown dog*). Quantifier expressions occupy the determiner positions in noun phrases, as in:

(2) $[_S [_{NP} [_{DET}$ most $]$ $[_{CN}$ students $]$ $]$ $[_{VP}$ attended the party$]$ $]$

(See any current syntax text for a more thorough presentation of this material, or the handbook discussions of

Bernstein [2001] and Longobardi [2001]. For some interesting cross-linguistic work, see Matthewson [2001] and the papers in Bach et al. [1995].)

Quantifier expressions, such as *every* and *most*, are determiners. Their semantic values must be relations between sets of individuals, representing the semantic values of CNs and VPs in simple syntactic configurations like (2). Using some set theory, we may give examples of the semantic values of determiners explicitly. For instance, for a universe of discourse M and sets of individuals $X, Y \subseteq M$:

(3) a. $\mathbf{every}_M\ (X,Y) \longleftrightarrow \Xi \subseteq Y$

b. $\mathbf{most}_M(X,Y) \longleftrightarrow |X \cap Y| > |X \setminus Y|$

(Here the boldface $\mathbf{every}_M$ is the semantic value of the expression *every*.) This characterization of the semantic values of determiners as relations between sets is often called the relational theory of determiner denotations.

As the semantic values of determiners are relations between sets, the semantic values of noun phrases built out of determiners (or most determiners) are interpreted as sets of sets, along Fregean lines. For instance, the semantic value of *most boys* is $\boldsymbol{most}_M$ **boys** = $\{Y \subseteq M$: $|\mathbf{boys} \cap Y| > |\mathbf{boys} \setminus Y|\}$. We may use the term 'quantifier' for either sort of semantic value. The latter are often called unary or simple quantifiers. Quantifiers taking more than two arguments are well documented in natural language, and have been investigated by a number of authors, including Filippo Beghelli (1994) and Edward L. Keenan and Lawrence S. Moss (1984). Quantifiers taking as inputs relations rather than sets, called polyadic quantifiers, have also been investigated, by authors including Higginbotham and May (1981), May (1989) and van Benthem (1909), though their place in natural language remains controversial. The survey by Keenan and Westerståhl (1997) is a good place to look for an introduction to these issues.

PROPERTIES OF QUANTIFIERS

The relational theory of determiner denotations has been applied to a number of issues in logic, philosophy of language, and linguistics. Many of these are discussed in the surveys by Keenan (2002), Keenan and Westerståhl (1997), and Westerståhl (1989). These applications rely on some important properties of quantifiers, of which two examples are given here.

RESTRICTED QUANTIFIERS. Quantifiers in natural language appear to be restricted quantifiers. Whereas ∀ and ∃ range over the entire universe, a quantifier like $\mathbf{most}_M$ ranges over its first input, corresponding to the CN position in an NP. *Most boys are happy* expresses $\mathbf{Most}_M$(**boys**, **happy**). Whether this holds or not depends on the properties of the **boys**, and not anything about the rest of the universe.

The mere presence of the CN argument is not enough to show that it functions as the domain of quantification. But the CN does play an important role, which is brought out by the following pattern:

(4) a. i. Every student attended the party.

ii. Every student is a student who attended the party.

b. i. Most students attended the party.

ii. Most students are students who attended the party.

In each of these, (i) and (ii) are equivalent.

The pattern we see in (4) is called conservativity:

(5) (CONS) $\mathbf{Q}_M(X,Y)$ is conservative if and only if for all $X,Y \subseteq M$, $\mathbf{Q}_M(X,Y) \longleftrightarrow \mathbf{Q}_M(X,X \cap Y)$.

Conservativity expresses the idea that the interpretation of a sentence with a quantified noun phrase only looks as far as the CN, so the CN restricts the domain of quantification.

One of the striking facts about natural languages, observed in Barwise and Cooper (1981) and Keenan and Stavi (1986), is that the semantic values of all natural language determiners satisfy CONS. This is a proposed linguistic universals: a non-trivial empirical restrictions on natural languages.

Conservativity has proved an extremely important property. The space of conservative quantifiers is much more orderly than the full range of relations between sets. This is brought out most vividly by the conservativity theorem due initially to Keenan and Stavi (1986), further investigated by van Benthem (1983, 1986) and Keenan (1993). The key insight is that the class of conservative quantifiers can be build up inductively, from a base stock of quantifiers and some closure conditions. Let M be a fixed finite universe and let $CONS_M$ be the collection of conservative quantifiers on M. We will build up a class of quantifiers $D\text{-}GEN_M$ on M as follows. $D\text{-}GEN_M$ contains $\mathbf{every}_M$ and $\mathbf{some}_M$. We also assume that each set of members of M is definable by a predicate, and that $D\text{-}GEN_M$ is closed under Boolean combination and predicate restrictions. The latter assumes that if $\mathbf{Q}_M(X,Y)$ is in $D\text{-}GEN_M$, so is $\mathbf{Q}_M(X \cap C,Y)$ for $C \subseteq M$. This amounts to closure under (intersective) adjectival restriction in an NP.

The conservativity theorem says that for each M:

(6) $CONS_M = D\text{-}GEN_M$

This tells us that the domain of natural language determiners is far more orderly than it might have appeared. Some logical properties extending CONS have been studied, by van Benthem (1983, 1986) and Westerståhl (1985, 1989). These appear to strengthen the proposed universal as well.

LOGICALITY. Quantified NPs are often described as expressions of generality. One way to articulate the relevant notion of generality is that it requires the truth of a sentence to be independent of exactly which individuals are involved in interpreting a given quantifier. This can be captured formally by the constraint of permutation invariance. A permutation π of M is a 1-1 onto mapping of M to itself, which can be thought of as a rearranging of the elements of M. The constraint of permutation invariance then says:

(7) (PERM) Let π be a permutation of M. Then $\mathbf{Q}_M(X,Y) \longleftrightarrow \mathbf{Q}_M(\pi[X],\pi[Y])$.

(Here $\pi[X] = \{\pi(x): x \in X\}$.) PERM, or some strengthening of it, is commonly assumed in the mathematical literature, and is built into the definitions of quantifier in Lindström (1966) and Mostowski (1957). The semantic values of most natural language determiners satisfy PERM. (At least, the values of most syntactically simple determiners do.) There remain some hard cases, such as possessive constructions (as well as proper names, which can be interpreted as unary quantifiers not satisfying PERM). As these may not be examples of genuine determiners, the hypothesis that all natural language quantifiers satisfy both CONS and PERM is commonplace.

SEMANTIC COMPOSITION

The relational theory of determiner denotations does not explain how quantifiers interact with the rest of syntax and semantics. The way the values of determiners combine with other semantic values provides an example of such interaction.

According to the relational theory, the semantic values of quantified NPs are sets of sets, while the values of VPs are sets. How do these combine? When we have a quantified NP in subject position, the semantics of composition is given by set membership. For a quantified NP value α:

(8) $[_S\, [_{NP}\, \alpha\,]\, [_{VP}\, \beta\,]\,]$ is true if and only if $\beta \in \alpha$.

This simple story does not always work. Transitive verbs with quantified NPs in object position provide one sort of problem. A transitive verb will be interpreted as a relation between individuals. Now, consider an example like:

(9) a. John offended every student.

b. $[_S\, [_{NP}$ John $]\, [_{VP}\, [_V$ offended $]\, [_{NP}$ every student$]\,]\,]$

The value of *offended* is a relation between individuals, while the value of *every student* is a set of sets. We have no way to combine these to give us a set of individuals, which the value of the VP must be.

The theory of determiner denotations does not help solve this problem. Instead, some more apparatus is needed, either in the semantics or in the syntax. One approach is to posit underlying logical forms for sentences which are in some ways closer to the ones used in the standard formalisms of logic.

The goal is to replace the quantified NP *every student* with a variable that can occupy the argument position of a VP, that is, a variable over individuals. This variable is then bound by the quantifier. We thus want a structure that looks something like:

(10) $[\,[_{NP}$ every student$_x\,]\,[_S$ John offended $x\,]\,]$

In fact, many theories (following May 1977, 1985) argue that a structure like (10) is the underlying logical form of a quantified sentence. This is a substantial empirical claim about natural language, which holds that syntactic structures like (10) provide the input to semantic interpretation. Typically, such theories also hold that a syntactic process of movement produces a syntactic structure with initial quantifiers, and variables in the argument positions those quantifiers originally occupied. (For a survey of ideas about logical form in syntactic theory, see Huang 1995.)

Providing a structure like (10) does not by itself explain the semantics of binding: It does not explain semantically how the quantified NP binds the variable in the VP. The theory of the semantic values of determiners does not explain this either. Some separate account is needed.

The semantic operation that corresponds to binding is one of forming the right set to be the input of the semantic value of the determiner. Hence, even though we think of the syntactic structure *John offended x* as sentence-like (with the variable functioning like a pronoun), its interpretation needs to wind up being $\{x$: John offended $x\}$. Once we have this, we can say the sentence is true if this set is in the semantic value of the quantified

NP *every student*. Hence, binding is carried out by the appropriate form of set abstraction (as in Barwise and Cooper 1981). Many current presentations are embedded in the framework of the typed lambda-calculus, which treat sets as functions from individuals to truth values. In such a framework (Büring 2005, Heim and Kratzer 1989), set abstraction is replaced by lambda-abstraction. Other approaches use similar syntactic structures to (10), but offer a more Tarskian account of binding (Higginbotham 1985; Larson and Segal 1995). Finally, there are approaches that avoid positing syntactic structures like we see in (10), including early work of Cooper (1983), and type shifting approaches (Hendriks 1993, Jacobson 1999, Steedman 2000, van Benthem 1991). There is also an approach that seeks to explain semantic composition via a generalized account of the semantic values of determiners (Keenan 1992).

See also Artificial and Natural Languages; Frege, Gottlob; Semantics.

Bibliography

Bach, Emmon, Eloise Jelinek, Angelika Kratzer, and Barbara H. Partee, eds. *Quantification in Natural Languages*. Dordrecht: Kluwer, 1995.

Barwise, Jon, and Robin Cooper. "Generalized Quantifiers and Natural Language." *Linguistics and Philosophy* 4 (1981): 159–219.

Beghelli, Filippo. "Structured Quantifiers." In *Dynamics, Polarity, and Quantification*, edited by Makoto Kanazawa and Christopher J. Piñón. Stanford, CA: CSLI Publications, 1994.

Bernstein, Judy B. "The DP Hypothesis: Identifying Clausal Properties in the Nominal Domain." In *Handbook of Contemporary Syntactic Theory*, edited by Mark Baltin and Chris Collins. Oxford: Blackwell, 2001.

Büring, Daniel. *Binding Theory*. Cambridge, U.K.: Cambridge University Press, 2005.

Cooper, Robin. *Quantification and Syntactic Theory*. Dordrecht: Reidel, 1983.

Frege, Gottlob. *Begriffsschrift, eine der arithmetischen nachgebildete Formelsprache des reinen Denkens*. Halle: Nebert, 1979. Translated by Stefan Bauer-Mengelberg as *Begriffsschrift, a Formal Language, Modeled Upon That of Arithmetic, for Pure Thought* in *From Frege to Gödel: A Source Book in Mathematical Logic, 1879–1931*, edited by Jean van Heijenoort. Cambridge, MA: Harvard University Press, 1967.

Heim, Irene, and Angelika Kratzer. *Semantics in Generative Grammar*. Oxford: Blackwell, 1989.

Hendriks, Herman. *Studied Flexibility*. Amsterdam: ILLC Publications, 1993.

Higginbotham, James. "On Semantics." *Linguistic Inquiry* 16 (1985): 547–593.

Higginbotham, James, and Robert May. "Questions, Quantifiers and Crossing." *Linguistics Review* 1 (1981): 41–79.

Huang, C.-T. James. "Logical Form." In *Government and Binding Theory and the Minimalist Program*, edited by Gert Webelhuth. Oxford: Blackwell, 1995.

Jacobson, Pauline. "Towards a Variable-Free Semantics." *Linguistics and Philosophy* 22 (1999): 117–184.

Keenan, Edward L. "Beyond the Frege Boundary." *Linguistics and Philosophy* 15 (1992): 199–221.

Keenan, Edward L. "Natural Language, Sortal Reducibility and Generalized Quantifiers." *Journal of Symbolic Logic* 58 (1993): 314–325.

Keenan, Edward L. "Some Properties of Natural Language Quantifiers: Generalized Quantifier Theory." *Linguistics and Philosophy* 25 (2002): 627–654.

Keenan, Edward L., and Lawrence S. Moss. "Generalized Quantifiers and the Expressive Power of Natural Language." In *Generalized Quantifiers in Natural Language*, edited by Johan van Benthem and Alice ter Meulen. Dordrecht: Foris, 1984.

Keenan, Edward L., and Jonathan Stavi. "A Semantic Characterization of Natural Language Determiners." *Linguistics and Philosophy* 9 (1986): 253–326. Versions of this paper were circulated in the early 1980s.

Keenan, Edward L., and Dag Westerståhl. "Generalized Quantifiers in Linguistics and Logic." In *Handbook of Logic and Language*, edited by Johan van Benthem and Alice ter Meulen. Cambridge, MA: MIT Press, 1997.

Larson, Richard, and Gabriel Segal. *Knowledge of Meaning*. Cambridge, MA: MIT Press, 1995.

Lindström, Per. "First Order Predicate Logic with Generalized Quantifiers." *Theoria* 2 (1966): 186–195.

Longobardi, Giuseppe. "The Structure of DPs: Some Principles, Parameters, and Problems." In *Handbook of Contemporary Syntactic Theory*, edited by Mark Baltin and Chris Collins. Oxford: Blackwell, 2001.

Matthewson, Lisa. "Quantification and the Nature of Crosslinguistic Variation." *Natural Language Semantics* 9 (2001): 145–189.

May, Robert. "The Grammar of Quantification." PhD diss. Massachusetts Institute of Technology, 1977.

May, Robert. "Interpreting Logical Form." *Linguistics and Philosophy* 12 (1989): 387–435.

May, Robert. *Logical Form: Its Structure and Derivation*. Cambridge, MA: MIT Press, 1985.

Mostowski, Andrzej. "On a Generalization of Quantifiers." *Fundamenta Mathematicae* 44 (1957): 12–36.

Steedman, Mark. *The Syntactic Process*. Cambridge, MA: MIT Press, 2000.

van Benthem, Johan. "Determiners and Logic." *Linguistics and Philosophy* 6 (1983): 447–478.

van Benthem, Johan. Essays in *Logical Semantics*. Dordrecht: Reidel, 1986. Includes revised versions of van Benthem (1983, 1984).

van Benthem, Johan. *Language in Action*. Amsterdam: North-Holland, 1991.

van Benthem, Johan. "Polyadic Quantifiers." *Linguistics and Philosophy* 12 (1989): 437–464.

van Benthem, Johan. "Questions about Quantifiers." *Journal of Symbolic Logic* 49 (1984): 443–466.

van Heijenoort, Jean, ed. *From Frege to Gödel: A Source Book in Mathematical Logic, 1879–1931*. Cambridge, MA: Harvard University Press, 1967.

Westerståhl, Dag. "Logical Constants in Quantifier Languages." *Linguistics and Philosophy* 8 (1985): 387–413.

Westerståhl, Dag. "Quantifiers in Formal and Natural Languages." In *Handbook of Philosophical Logic*. Vol. 4, edited by Dov M. Gabbay and Franz Guenthner. Dordrecht: Kluwer, 1989.

Michael Glanzberg (2005)

QUESTIONS

All too often when philosophers talk and write about sentences, they have in mind only indicative sentences, that is, sentences that are true or false and that are normally used in the performance of assertions. When interrogative sentences are mentioned at all, it is usually either in the form of a gesture toward some extension of the account of indicatives or an acknowledgment of the limitations of such an account. For example, in the final two sentences of his influential paper "Truth and Meaning" (1967), Donald Davidson remarks, "And finally, there are all the sentences that seem not to have truth values at all: the imperatives, optatives, interrogatives, and a host more. A comprehensive theory of meaning for a natural language must cope successfully with each of these problems." Nonindicatives are an embarrassment to Davidson's program of identifying meaning with truth conditions. They are equally an embarrassment for the old identification of meanings with verification conditions, as well as the newer identification of meanings with inferential roles. Nonindicatives in general, and interrogatives in particular, have neither truth conditions nor verification conditions, nor do they function naturally or principally as the premises or conclusions of inferences. Yet they are no less meaningful than indicatives. And they are certainly no less important. As Nuel Belnap has observed, following David Harrah, "[We] will not assert anything ever, nor profit from the assertions of others, without at least the traces of such interests as can be expressed by interrogatives" (1990, p. 16).

Why have philosophers felt comfortable in virtually ignoring interrogatives and the other nonindicatives? Probably because of the persistent yet rather inchoate idea that indicatives and assertion are somehow fundamental to language and meaning, and that the other forms of sentences and speech acts are secondary or derivative, perhaps even unnecessary. J. L. Austin railed against this idea in *How to Do Things with Words* (1962). Austin's pioneering work gave birth to the field of speech-act theory, which found its fullest development in the work of his student John Searle. Speech-act theory is one of the few areas in philosophy that pays due attention to uses of language other than assertion. But even here one finds a residue of the tendency to subordinate the nonassertive to the assertive. We will return to this issue a bit later on.

Outside of speech-act theory, the idea that interrogatives and the other nonindicatives are secondary survives in a number of forms. The aforementioned identification of meaning with truth conditions is a primary example. One sometimes hears philosophers defend this idea by observing that everything that can be done with language can be done with just assertions. One can ask what time it is by asserting, "I wish to know what time it is"; one can command another to lower a weapon by asserting, "You will lower your weapon"; and so on. In the opposite direction, any assertion can be performed by way of a question or an order. For any *p*, one can assert that *p* by asking "Did you know that *p*?" or by commanding "Be aware that *p*." Just as questions and orders can be performed indirectly by way of assertions, assertions can be performed indirectly by way of questions and orders.

There is also the widespread view that the shared contents of all sentences and speech acts are propositions, which are nonlinguistic representations that are true or false and are the objects of belief and assertion. For example, it is thought that, in addition to its interrogative mood, the interrogative sentence "Did Martha shoot Henry?" expresses the proposition that Martha shot Henry, the same proposition expressed by the indicative sentence "Martha shot Henry." Similarly, in asking whether Martha shot Henry, a speaker expresses the very same proposition as when asserting that Martha shot Henry. The difference between these speech acts is located in what is called their illocutionary forces, not in their shared propositional content. The study of questions thus becomes a branch of the theory of force and not part of semantics proper, which is concerned with propositions and truth conditions. This provides some excuse for the philosophical focus on the truth-conditional areas of language at the expense of the vast non-truth-conditional areas.

FREGE AND WITTGENSTEIN ON QUESTIONS

The distinction between the propositional content of a sentence or speech act and its mood or force is associated with Gottlob Frege, for whom this distinction was a recurring theme. It is not often noticed, however, that Frege changed his mind about this distinction with regard to interrogatives. In his important paper "On Sense and Reference" (1970), Frege's view was that interrogative sentences do *not* express propositions (Frege's word for propositions was "thoughts"). Rather, interrogatives express what Frege called questions, where a question is not a proposition but something that "stands on the same level" as a proposition. In his later paper "Thoughts" (1984), he reversed himself, arguing, "An interrogative sentence and an assertoric one contain the same thought; but the assertoric sentence contains something else as well, namely assertion. The interrogative sentence contains something more too, namely a request" (p. 355). In other words, the sentences "Martha shot Henry" and "Did Martha shoot Henry?" express the same truth-conditional proposition. The difference is that the indicative sentence includes the force of assertion in the form of the indicative mood and the interrogative sentence contains the force of request in the form of the interrogative mood. (On imperatives, in contrast, Frege, in "Thoughts," did not reverse his earlier position. He held throughout that these sentences express commands, that is, contents that are like thoughts yet lack truth-values. Also, it must be noted that in "On Sense and Reference" Frege was discussing embedded questions, e.g., the "whether" clause in "Nancy knows whether Martha shot Henry," whereas in "Thoughts" he was concerned with stand-alone questions, e.g., "Did Martha shoot Henry?" If Frege held that the indirect reference of an embedded question should differ from the sense of its stand-alone counterpart, which seems unlikely, then we need not read him as having changed his mind.)

Ludwig Wittgenstein clearly rejected Frege's later account in *Philosophical Investigations*:

> Frege's idea that every assertion contains an assumption, which is the thing that is asserted, really rests on the possibility found in our language of writing every statement in the form: "It is asserted that such-and-such is the case." … We might very well also write every statement in the form of a question followed by a "Yes"; for instance: "Is it raining? Yes!" Would this show that every statement contained a question? (Sec. 22)

One of the ideas in this passage is a criticism of Frege's arbitrary identification of the contents of interrogatives with propositions. One could hold instead that the shared content of "Martha shot Henry" and "Did Martha shoot Henry?" is an interrogative content, something akin to a proposition except that it has interrogative-satisfaction conditions, that is, conditions of being properly answered, instead of truth conditions. Then one could say that the indicative contains this interrogative content along with an element of affirmation ("Yes!"). Wittgenstein's point is not that this alternative is preferable to Frege's, but rather that both accounts are arbitrary and should be rejected. In other words, indicatives and interrogatives have distinct kinds of contents. Of course, this was the view that Frege held in his earlier work "On Sense and Reference."

QUESTIONS IN SPEECH-ACT THEORY

Despite Wittgenstein's objections, many philosophers now accept Frege's later view that propositions are the shared contents of indicatives and interrogatives. This idea is the foundation of Searle's theory of speech acts. With a few exceptions (e.g., greetings), Searle analyzes speech acts on the basis of his schema *F*(*p*), where "F" stands for force and "*p*" for propositional content. A consequence of this is that, aside from greetings and a few other speech acts, most speech acts have propositions as their contents (a circumstance that is a residue of subordinating the nonassertive to the assertive). The distinctive feature of questions is their interrogative force, which Searle takes to be a species of request. For Searle, asking a question is a request for an answer. Questions thus fall into Searle's more general category of directives, the paradigms of which are orders and commands. The defining feature of directives is that they are attempts by speakers to get hearers to do something. So on Searle's account, a question is essentially an attempt by a speaker to get the hearer to provide an answer.

Another important feature of directives is that they have what Searle calls "world-to-words" direction of fit (1979, p. 14). This means that for a directive speech act to be satisfied, the world must come to match the proposition expressed in the performance of the speech act. When I order Martha to shoot Henry, I express the proposition that Martha will shoot Henry with the force of an order. My order is satisfied just in case Martha acts to make this proposition true. This is the sense in which the order is satisfied if the world comes to fit the words used in the order. This position, however, leads to a problem when applied to questions. When I ask whether Martha shot Henry, my question is satisfied, that is, answered, just in case the hearer provides an answer. Yet the propositional content of my question is just that Martha shot Henry; it is not that the hearer will provide an answer to the question of whether Martha shot Henry. There is no sense in which my question is satisfied when Martha shoots Henry. Another way to bring out this problem is to note that speech acts with world-to-words direction of fit require that their propositional contents describe future events or states of affairs. There is obviously no such restriction on the propositional contents of questions. The upshot of this is that questions do not fit neatly into Searle's category of directives. The fact that natural languages have a separate syntactic category of interrogative sentences, distinct from that of imperatives, further suggests that questions are not simply a variety of directives but rather constitute their own distinct category of speech acts.

THE HAMBLIN POSTULATES

The growing interdisciplinary cooperation between philosophers of language and linguists provides reason for hope that the philosophical neglect of interrogatives is coming to an end. Interrogative expressions have always occupied a central place in linguistics. For example, the behavior of so-called "wh-" words, for example, "who" and "what," provided an important source of data for early work on Chomsky's theory of transformational grammar, and the phenomenon of "wh-" movement continues to be a rich topic for linguists working on the syntax of natural language.

Interrogatives have also received a great deal of attention from linguists working in semantics. Much of this work has been guided by a set of postulates about questions and answers first laid down by the philosopher and logician C. L. Hamblin in his paper "Questions" (1958):

1. To know the meaning of a question is to know what counts as an answer to that question.

2. An answer to a question is a complete sentence or proposition.

3. The possible answers to a question form an exhaustive set of mutually exclusive possibilities.

(Hamblin's ordering and wording of these postulates is slightly different.) The first postulate is the analog for interrogatives of the idea that to know the meaning of an indicative is to know what the world would be like if it were true, that is, that to know the meaning of an indicative is to know its truth conditions. This idea is the intuitive ground for the identification of the meaning of an indicative with its truth conditions. The first Hamblin postulate plays a similar role for interrogatives. It is the intuitive motivation for the identification of the meaning of an interrogative with its answers. This first postulate is thus fundamental to semantic approaches to interrogatives.

Like the corresponding principle for indicatives, the first Hamblin postulate for interrogatives has been challenged. It seems possible to understand an interrogative without having any idea of what would count as an answer to it. The linguist Jonathan Ginzburg provides the example "What is the word for 'relaxation' in Chukotian?" (1996, p. 400). Working in the semantic framework known as situation theory, Ginzburg has developed a semantic account in which the contents of interrogatives are fine-grained structures that determine answers but are not identical with answers. This approach bears affinities to semantic accounts in which the contents of indicatives are structured propositions. Another range of counterexamples to Hamblin's first postulate derives from the work of the philosopher of science Sylvain Bromberger, who has argued that the search for answers to "why" questions for which we cannot formulate any answers is essential to the enterprise of science.

The first Hamblin postulate is also implicitly rejected by paraphrase theories of interrogatives, which analyze interrogatives by paraphrasing them into noninterrogative forms. In the theories of David Lewis and Max Cresswell, interrogatives are paraphrased as performatives. For example, "Did Martha shoot Henry?" is paraphrased as "I hereby ask you whether Martha shot Henry." A basic problem for these theories is that the interrogative reappears in the analysis in embedded form, in the example, "whether Martha shot Henry," which renders the analysis circular. In the epistemic-imperative approach of Lennart Åqvist and Jaakko Hintikka, "Did Martha shoot Henry?" is analyzed as the imperative "Bring it about that I know whether Martha shot Henry." The remaining embedded "whether" clause is then eliminated in terms of "that" clauses. "I know whether *p*," for example, is analyzed as a conjunction of conditionals: "If *p*, then I know that *p*, and if not *p*, then I know that not *p*." This account has some plausibility in this case, but as Lauri Karttunen has pointed out, it falls apart when applied to other uses of "whether" clauses. "I wonder whether *p*" is clearly not synonymous with the possibly ungrammatical "If *p*, then I wonder that *p*, and if not *p*, then I wonder that not *p*." And it is not clear even how to apply this account to a sentence like "Martha's mental health depends on whether she takes her prescriptions."

The second and third Hamblin postulates concern the nature of answers. These two postulates combine to form a conception of answers that differs from what can count as an answer in ordinary discourse. For example, the second postulate is in apparent conflict with the fact that one can often answer a question with something less than a complete sentence. For example, the proper name "Alexander Hamilton" seems like a perfectly good answer to the question "Who was the first U.S. Secretary of the Treasury?" The point of the second postulate is that, despite appearances, answers are always complete sentences or propositions, in this case, the sentence "Alexander Hamilton was the first U.S. Secretary of the Treasury" or the proposition expressed by this sentence. This postulate is motivated by the idea that a correct answer must be true, and being true is a property of sentences or propositions. Furthermore, answers always convey information, and information comes in sentences or propositions.

Despite these considerations, the second Hamblin postulate has not been universally accepted. So-called categorial theories, such as that of Roland Hausser, take seriously the surface grammatical forms of answers. On these approaches, answers can be of various categories, for example, names, common nouns, sentences, set designations, and predicates, which denote respectively individuals, objects, propositions, sets, and properties.

The third Hamblin postulate requires first that the set of answers to an interrogative be exhaustive. This is related to the fact that many interrogatives carry presuppositions. To use Hamblin's example, consider the question "In which continent is Honolulu?" (1958, p. 163). This question falsely presupposes that Honolulu is in a continent. According to one position, for the set of answers to this question to be exhaustive, it must include an answer that denies the presupposition, that is, "Honolulu is in no continent." Alternatively, one might hold that the presuppositions of a question restrict the range of possibilities to just those in which the presuppositions hold. A set of answers would then be exhaustive if it exhausts this restricted range of possibilities. On this alternative, the denial of the presupposition of a question is not an answer but rather a rejection of the question.

The third Hamblin postulate also requires that answers are mutually exclusive. This is intended to capture the idea that genuine answers are complete, in the following sense. Consider the question "Who ran the marathon?" where the candidate runners are Martha, Henry, George, and Nancy. A complete answer will indicate both who ran and who did not. For example, the proposition that only Martha and Henry ran and no one else ran is complete, whereas the proposition that Martha and Henry ran is not complete, since it leaves unspecified whether George or Nancy ran. A consequence of this is that the proposition that Martha and Henry ran is at best a *partial* answer. The fact that answers can be merely partial is what motivates the requirement that answers be mutually exclusive. Allowing partial answers requires a contrasting criterion of completeness, which is provided by the notion that answers be mutually exclusive. (Incidentally, the above example illustrates how "wh-" words are context-sensitive, as are quantifier expressions. Intuitively, a speaker who asks "Who ran the marathon?" is not asking about everyone who has ever lived but rather about some contextually determined set of candidate runners. Parallel remarks apply to someone who asserts "Everyone ran the marathon." In each case, a range of values for "who" and "everyone" is determined by features of the context of utterance. This is one of many similarities between "wh-" words and quantifiers.)

If answers are mutually exclusive, then there cannot be more than one complete and true answer to a question. This runs into problems with so-called mention-some questions. Suppose that Martha, who is new in town, asks Henry "Where can I buy an Italian newspaper?" (This example is due to Jeroen Groenendijk and Martin Stokhof.) On the most natural reading, Martha is only asking Henry to mention some place where she can buy an Italian newspaper. If so, Henry has available any number of complete and true answers, for example, "At the train station," or "At the bookstore downtown." Another sort of problem case, raised by Belnap, consists in choice questions, for example, "What are two cities that host marathons?" Intuitively, a complete answer mentions two cities that host marathons, and the choice of which two to mention is left up to the hearer. Thus, many complete and true answers are available, such as "Boston and New York host marathons," "Chicago and Los Angeles host marathons," and so on.

THREE SEMANTIC APPROACHES TO INTERROGATIVES

This section sketches three prominent approaches to the semantics of interrogatives, all of which are set in the framework of Montague semantics, also variously known as intensional semantics, model-theoretic semantics, or possible-worlds semantics. In this framework, expressions are assigned both intensions and extensions. Intensions are functions from possible worlds to entities of various kinds. The extension of an expression at a possible world is the value of its intension with respect to that world. For example, the intension of a complete indicative sentence is a function from possible worlds to truth-values. The intensions of indicatives essentially divide the set of possible worlds into two subsets: those possible worlds in which the indicative is true and those in which it is false. The proposition expressed by an indicative is normally identified either with its intension or, more simply, with the set of worlds in which the intension has the value true. This identification of propositions with sentence intensions or with sets of possible worlds is a notoriously problematic feature of the possible-worlds framework. It has the consequence that all necessarily true sentences express the same proposition. As we will see later on, a related problem arises for interrogatives.

On C. L. Hamblin's approach in his "Questions in Montague English" (1973), the intension of an interrogative is a function from possible worlds to sets of answers, where answers are propositions. The extension of an interrogative at a possible world is thus a set of propositions. This set is determined compositionally from the parts of the interrogative. For Hamblin, the extension of "who" at a possible world is a set of individuals. For example, suppose that the extension of "who" in a possible world *w* is the set {Martha, Henry, George, Nancy}. The extension of "Who runs?" in *w* is then the set of propositions {⟨Martha runs⟩, ⟨Henry runs⟩, ⟨George runs⟩, ⟨Nancy runs⟩}. (Remember that each of these propositions is itself an indicative sentence intension or a set of possible worlds.) Hamblin is aware that this approach is a departure from his own third postulate, since there is no requirement here that sets of answers be exhaustive nor that answers themselves be mutually exclusive. The extension of the yes/no interrogative "Is it the case that *p*?" in a world *w* is the set consisting of the proposition that *p* and its negation. For example, the extension of "Does Martha run?" in *w* is {⟨Martha runs⟩, ⟨Martha does not run⟩}.

Perhaps the best-known approach to interrogatives is due to Lauri Karttunen. Karttunen's account is similar to Hamblin's except that Karttunen requires that each member of the extension of an interrogative be true. In other words, on Karttunen's approach, the intension of an interrogative is a function from possible worlds to sets of true answers. Suppose that in *w* only Martha and Henry run. For Karttunen, the extension of "Who runs?" in *w* is the set {⟨Martha runs⟩, ⟨Henry runs⟩}. Similarly, the extension of "Does Martha run?" is the singleton set {⟨Martha runs⟩}. Karttunen argues that the advantage of his approach over Hamblin's is that' his approach provides a simpler account of the semantics of question-embedding verbs like "knows," as in sentences such as "Nancy knows who runs." It is widely assumed that the content of the embedded interrogative "who runs" is identical with the content of its stand-alone counterpart "Who runs?" Very roughly, Karttunen's idea is that "Nancy knows who runs" is true in *w* just in case in *w* Nancy knows each of the propositions in the extension of "who runs." The advantage of Karttunen's approach is that this extension includes only true propositions, which accords with the fact that one cannot know something false.

A third prominent approach to interrogatives is due to Jeroen Groenendijk and Martin Stokhof (1997). Unlike Hamblin and Karttunen, Groenendijk and Stokhof accept the third Hamblin postulate. On their account, the sets of answers to interrogatives are exhaustive, and each answer is mutually exclusive. A consequence of this position is that, on their view, the intension of an interrogative is a function from possible worlds to single propositions, that is, the unique, complete answers in each world. Suppose that in *w* only Martha and Henry run. Then the extension of "Who runs?" in *w* is the single proposition that Martha runs and Henry runs and no one else runs. Groenendijk and Stokhof's approach is sometimes called a partition theory. This is because on their view the intension of an interrogative partitions the set of possible worlds into jointly exhaustive, nonoverlapping subsets, one for each possible complete answer. One advantage of this model is that it captures the apparent fact that if Nancy knows who runs, she knows both who runs and who does not run. For example, if George does not run, and Nancy does not know it, then it seems that Nancy does not know who runs, even if she knows that Martha and Henry run. For Groenendijk and Stokhof, this is captured by the fact that "Nancy knows who runs" is true just in case Nancy knows the complete answer to the question "Who runs?" For Karttunen, all that is required for the truth of "Nancy knows who runs" is that Nancy knows all the true propositions of the form ⟨X runs⟩. She need not know any of the true propositions of the form ⟨X does not run⟩.

A feature shared by all three approaches is that they assign contents to interrogatives that are distinct from those for indicatives. The content of an expression is its intension. This means that for Hamblin, Karttunen, and Groenendijk and Stokhof, the contents of interrogatives are *not* propositions. Rather, they are functions from possible worlds to sets of propositions (Hamblin, Karttunen) or single propositions (Groenendijk and Stokhof). These functions can be thought of as *properties* of propositions. Thus, for Hamblin, the content of an interrogative is the property of being an answer to that interrogative (where answers can be incomplete), for Karttunen it is the property of being a true (possibly incomplete) answer, and for Groenendijk and Stokhof it is the property of being a complete and true answer.

As noted earlier, the framework of Montague semantics faces difficulties arising from its identification of propositions with sets of possible worlds. Because they are set within this framework, all three of these accounts of interrogatives face similar problems. For example, the contents of "Does 5 + 7 = 12?" and "Is first-order logic undecidable?" turn out to be identical on all three accounts. Philosophers have responded to the problems for possible-worlds accounts of propositions by searching for more fine-grained entities, such as structured propositions, to serve as the contents of indicatives. Whether or not similarly fine-grained interrogative contents can be found is a question that is currently being explored.

See also Aristotle; Carnap, Rudolf; Explanation; Mackie, John Leslie; Non-Truth-Conditional Meaning; Presupposition; Prior, Arthur Norman; Propositions; Schlick, Moritz; Strawson, Peter Frederick; Why.

Bibliography

Åqvist, Lennart. *A New Approach to the Logical Theory of Interrogatives.* Uppsala, Sweden: Filosofiska Föreningen, 1965.

Austin, J. L. *How to Do Things with Words.* Cambridge, MA: Harvard University Press, 1962.

Belnap, Nuel. "Declaratives Are Not Enough." *Philosophical Studies* 59 (1990): 1–30.

Belnap, Nuel. "Questions and Answers in Montague Grammar." In *Processes, Beliefs, and Questions*, edited by Stanley Peters and Esa Saarinen, 165–198. Dordrecht, Netherlands: D. Reidel, 1982.

Bromberger, Sylvain. *On What We Know We Don't Know.* Chicago: University of Chicago Press, 1992.

Cresswell, Max. *Logics and Languages.* London: Methuen, 1973.

Davidson, Donald. "Truth and Meaning." *Synthese* 17 (1967): 304–323.

Ginzburg, Jonathan. "Interrogatives: Questions, Facts, and Dialogue." In *The Handbook of Contemporary Semantic Theory*, edited by Shalom Lappin, 385–422. Oxford, U.K.: Blackwell, 1996.

Groenendijk, Jeroen, and Martin Stokhof. "Questions." In *Handbook of Logic and Language*, edited by Johan van Benthem and Alice ter Meulen, 1055–1124. Cambridge, MA: MIT Press, 1997.

Hamblin, Charles L. "Questions." *Australasian Journal of Philosophy* 36 (1958): 159–168.

Hamblin, Charles L. "Questions in Montague English." *Foundations of Language* 10 (1973): 41–53.

Harrah, David. *Communication: A Logical Model.* Cambridge, MA: MIT Press, 1963.

Hausser, Roland. "The Syntax and Semantics of English Mood." In *Questions and Answers*, edited by Ferenc Kiefer, 97–158. Dordrecht, Netherlands: D. Reidel, 1983.

Hintikka, Jaakko. "The Semantics of Questions and the Questions of Semantics." *Acta Philosophica Fennica* 28 (4) (1976): 1–200.

Frege, Gottlob. "On Sense and Reference." In *Translations from the Philosophical Writings of Gottlob Frege*, edited by Peter Geach and Max Black, 56–78. Oxford, U.K.: Blackwell, 1970.

Frege, Gottlob. "Thoughts." In his *Collected Papers on Mathematics, Logic, and Philosophy*, edited by Brian McGuinness, 351–372. Oxford, U.K.: Blackwell, 1984.

Karttunen, Lauri. "Syntax and Semantics of Questions." *Linguistics and Philosophy* 1 (1977): 3–44.

Lewis, David. "General Semantics." *Synthese* 22 (1970): 18–67.

Searle, John. *Speech Acts.* Cambridge, U.K.: Cambridge University Press, 1969.

Searle, John. *Expression and Meaning.* Cambridge, U.K.: Cambridge University Press, 1979.

Wittgenstein, Ludwig. *Philosophical Investigations.* New York: Macmillan, 1953.

Peter W. Hanks (2005)

REDUCTIONISM IN THE PHILOSOPHY OF MIND

Reduction can be understood in a loose or in a strict sense. In the loose sense, entities (or expressions) of a given type are reduced if they refer to "nothing over and above" other entities (expressions) that we consider well established. This is consistent with the conclusion that the reduced entities are among the posits of a mistaken world view and thus have no place in our ontology, and it is also consistent with the conclusion that the reduced entities are conserved among other accepted, better established or understood entities. In the first case we have *elimination*, and proposing this for entities of a given kind makes us eliminativists about those entities. In the second case we have *reduction in the strict sense*, and proposing this for a given kind makes us reductionists (sometimes called "conservative" or "retentive" reductionists). Reductionist projects can also be semantic or theoretical. A semantic reduction attempts to show that items belonging to a certain class of expressions are semantically equivalent to—that is, definable in terms of—another class of expressions. A theoretical reduction aims at showing that a given scientific theory can be fully subsumed under (that is, derivable from) another more basic theory.

TYPES OF MIND-BODY REDUCTIONISM

In the philosophy of mind, reductionist projects come in all formats. A reductionist effort will typically be directed against the claim that the mental has some real, independent status. But this claim has a range of versions that go from the mind being a nonphysical/biological object, to mental properties constituting a level of *sui generis* properties of organisms that is in some sense autonomous vis-à-vis the physical/biological properties, to mental expressions possessing meanings that cannot be accounted for in purely behavioral/physical terminology.

The substance dualist assertion influential until the twentieth century—that the (human) mind is an immaterial object or substance—has faced widespread philosophical criticism of an eliminativist type: "Immaterial mind" or "soul," like "élan vital," "elf," or "chupacabras," are ghostly expressions that come from mistaken frameworks or conceptions and do not refer to anything. An influential formulation of this view is Gilbert Ryle's claim that the immaterial entity posited by substance dualism is the result of a category mistake in which we reify our mental activities by placing a ghost in charge of our body. Another major reason for the eliminativist consensus about nonmaterial substances is the inability of a nonphysical substance to causally interact with the physical world, because of conservation of energy considerations and because of the difficulty of making sense of bridging mechanisms between the two ontologically diverse realms. Absent causal interaction, the argument goes, postulating souls seems pointless if not absurd.

Eliminating mental substances, however, does not directly lead to a reductive view of the mental. In the twentieth century substance materialism or physicalism has been the orthodoxy in tune with modern science, but "the reducibility of mind" has remained as a philosophical issue of first importance. It is only that the focus of the debate has now shifted to the ontological or semantic autonomy of mental *properties* or *predicates*. The first systematic attempt to fully reduce the mental to the physical comes from logical behaviorism, a position championed by Rudolf Carnap, Carl Hempel, and Gilbert Ryle in the 1930s and 1940s. The view has doctrinal connections to methodological behaviorism, the dominant methodology of psychology in the first half of the twentieth century.

Based on the logical positivist's verification criterion according to which the content of an expression is just the expressions' verification conditions and on the assumption that these conditions have to be publicly observable, logical behaviorism argues that in order for sentences including mental expressions to be meaningful they have to be translatable without loss of content into sentences including just behavioral and other physical expressions. This implies that mental expressions should be defined in terms of behavioral and other physical expressions. Following the model of definitions of dispositional properties in the natural sciences, these definitions standardly include conditional sentences showing dispositions to behave under given environmental circumstances including stimuli. So logical behaviorism is a form of semantic reduction of the mental.

Logical behaviorism has been largely abandoned for several reasons, one of them being its inability to meet the positivist standards in its own reductionist strategy. Most mental terms cannot be associated with a single behavioral disposition; there is no single behavioral manifestation of, say, "believing in God" or "loving one's country." If mental terms denote behavioral dispositions, these dispositions must be "multitracked," and this would make behavioral definitions of mental terms enormously complex. This makes the behaviorist project of defining mental terms a highly dubious project.

Moreover, it has been convincingly argued that even in simple cases a purely behavioral definition just is not possible—unless one uses some mentalistic term in the definition, which of course undermines the behaviorist enterprise. The fall of behaviorism as the accepted reductive view led to a different reductionist approach. In the 1950s U. T. Place, J. C. C. Smart, and Herbert Feigl proposed the mind-body identity theory, a simple and appealing view in line with the surge of neural research. According to the view, while there is no meaning equivalence between mental and neural terminology (thus no semantic reduction) mental states are just states of the brain or the nervous system. The claim is one of numerical identity between types of states or properties and as such it involves ontological reduction in the strict sense.

A main line of argument for the identity theory is based on ontological simplicity, a standard strategy for ontological reduction. Once we have observed a pervasive set of systematic correlations between mental occurrences and neural events, the argument goes, we should conclude that the mental and the neural are identical. For while mind-brain correlations are compatible with a range of views about the mind, simplicity dictates that we should not multiply entities that are not going to enhance our explanatory power. The view is also supported by considerations of theoretical reduction. The history of science offers countless cases of predicates of everyday frameworks being reduced to predicates of explanatorily richer scientific frameworks (a standard example is the reduction of temperature [of gases] to molecular kinetic energy). Given the advances in the neurosciences we have good reason to think a neural reduction of mentality is going to be one more item in a chain of successful theoretical reductions. This theoretical reduction would proceed by establishing "bridge laws" between mental and neural predicates and then reducing all generalizations involving the mental to the more encompassing laws of neuroscience.

Of the many attacks raised against the identity theory, two have aimed at the core of its reductive stance. Donald Davidson has argued against type-identification by claiming that there cannot be laws connecting the mental and the physical (this is called anomalism of the mental, an essential part of Davidson's nonreductive view discussed below). Mental states, in particular intentional states such as beliefs and desires, are governed by principles of rationality without which attribution of mentality would be impossible. Laws connecting the physical and the mental would constrain the mental by the principles of physical theory and thereby undermine its own peculiar rationality constraints.

Another highly influential argument against the identity theory is the "multiple realization" argument initially developed by Hilary Putnam. The identity theory requires a single physical property be the reduction base for each mental state. But surely the same mental state can occur in organisms with diverse neurophysiological structures. Nonhuman animals can be in pain and we can conceive of noncarbon based species and perhaps even artificial creatures being in pain. Mental states, Putnam argues, can be implemented or "realized" in widely diverse physical/chemical structures and so there is no unifying reduction base or structure for them. (This multiple realization objection is also at the core of the nonreductive functionalist approach discussed below.)

An alternative, eliminativist stance was defended in the 1960s by Richard Rorty and Paul Feyerabend and has as more recent versions the views of Patricia Churchland, Paul Churchland, and Stephen Stich. Learning from the failure of the identity theory to establish type-type identities between mental and neuro-chemical properties, eliminativism claims that the mental expressions used in our everyday psychological talk have no more reality or significance than "phlogiston" and "caloric fluids," terms of superseded and discarded scientific theories. It is highly unlikely that these concepts of vernacular psychology could be sharpened into concepts that will be useful to the sciences and do not correspond to the concepts of the sciences (neuroscience or cognitive science) that have the task of explaining human behavior. This radical view proposes to eliminate mental terminology for the purposes of scientific theorizing and can go as far as predicting that a full replacement is possible even for everyday purposes. The analogy with concepts in the history of science that were found to be fully misguided and therefore replaced plays an important role in the argumentation in favor of eliminativism. This view has been found by most philosophers to be unacceptably extreme since it means that an essential component of our conceptual framework has to be given up. Also, some have argued that the view is incoherent since the view cannot be expressed without the very (mental) concepts it rejects (since in the very act of affirming their view, the eliminativist is expressing a *belief*, something that, according to their view, does not exist).

TYPES OF MIND-BODY ANTI-REDUCTIONISMS AND THE REDUCTIVISTS' REACTIONS

Starting in the late 1960s, the problems plaguing reductive views let to the establishment of nonreductive physicalism as a reigning orthodoxy in the philosophy of mind. Its two most salient versions are anomalous monism and functionalism. Functionalism in fact has been the predominant view into the twenty-first century.

Davidson's anomalous monism is a physicalist view that eschews reduction. From the principles that every singular causal relation needs to be backed by strict laws (nomological character of causation) and that there are no "strict" laws about mental properties (mental anomalism), together with the assumption that at least some mental events causally interact with physical events, Davidson concludes that mental events must be identical with physical events. According to Davidson, this provides causal efficacy to mental events, even though there are no strict psychological laws governing them, and it also leads to a nonreductive view of the mental because there are no laws connecting mental properties with physical properties.

Many critics have argued that Davidson's view leaves the mental with no causal role to play. Davidson is entitled to affirm that a mental event causes a physical event (by being identical to a physical—probably neural—event). Now, an event instantiates a law—required for causation—in virtue of some of its properties, or, in other words, in virtue of falling under some event-type. Since anomalism entails that there are no laws involving mental properties or event-types, it is the physical (neural) properties of the cause event that are efficacious in the production of the effect. The fact that the cause event falls under a mental type, or the fact that the event has mental properties, is completely irrelevant for the event's causing the effect. Thus, critics conclude, Davidson's anomalous monism renders the mental epiphenomenal, making it an easy target for elimination.

The functionalist view of the mental defended by Putnam and Jerry Fodor, among others, starts with the anti-reductivist stance included in the multiple realization argument. Its positive view includes the claim that mental properties are functional properties, rather than physical/neural properties as claimed by the identity theory. On the functionalist view, for something to have a mental property M is for it to instantiate some physical property P that has the right causal connections with inputs, behavioral outputs and other mental states. Thus, a mental property is a second-order property of having a (first-order) property that fulfills a certain specified causal specification. A first-order property meeting the causal specification is called a "realizer" or "realizing property" of the second-order functional property. For any given mental property there will likely be indefinitely many realizing properties satisfying its causal specification.

The reductionist can challenge the functionalist by suggesting that the mental property be identified with the disjunction of realizers. Settling this challenge would require a metaphysical discussion on the nature of disjunctive properties. A more powerful challenge raised by Kim is the claim that since having the functional mental property implies having one of its realizing properties and since the casual powers of the instance of a functional property must be considered to be inherited from the causal powers of the realizing property, mental properties have no autonomous causal powers and so are epiphenomenal. To the reply that it is the mental kind and not the instance that has its own causal powers Kim answers that the sheer heterogeneity and diversity of the realizers of a functionally conceived mental property deprives the property of the kind of causal-nomological unity required for nomological and causally efficacious properties.

All versions of nonreductive physicalism (including anomalous monism and traditional functionalism) are targets of the exclusion argument initially put forth by Norman Malcolm and developed by Jaegwon Kim. Physicalists, even those in the nonreductive camp, accept the primacy of the physical not only in terms of substance monism but also in terms of physical properties being primary vis-à-vis mental properties. This commitment includes, according to Kim, accepting the causal closure of the physical and accepting a strong sense of dependence of the mental upon the physical. Thus, every physical event, including human behavior, has to have a complete physical cause. The mental event that is supposed to be the cause of behavior is preempted of its causal role by the physical state upon which it depends and which is the required physical cause of behavior. The upshot is that we cannot attribute a causal role to the mental unless it is identified with the physical, transforming nonreducible mental properties into epiphenomena. And epiphenomena, Kim thinks, should be cut from our ontology because they serve no purpose.

A common theme across several discussions so far has revolved around whether the mental, on one view or another, has autonomous causal powers. It is not obvious whether causal reduction or elimination implies full ontological reduction or elimination, that is, whether putative entities that are causally inefficacious or epiphenomenal can still be *bona fide* entities. To achieve full reduction we need the extra assumption that independent causal powers are necessary for the very reality of an entity. This view has been explicitly defended by Kim and Sidney Shoemaker, among others, and is largely the orthodox view. A negative answer (supported for instance by Elliott Sober and Marcelo Sabatés) makes room for epiphenomenalism as a nonreductive option about the mind.

In the first decade of the twenty-first century reductionism has gained some momentum. Kim has developed an influential functionalist view of reduction with ties to the version of functionalism defended by David Lewis in the 1970s. Kim's position, in agreement with his criticism of traditional functionalism á la Putnam, claims that "functionalizing" a property provides a form of theoretical reduction that does not require bridge laws and fully explains its reductive relationship on the base property. The view implies that on account of its multiple diverse realizability, no mental property has sufficient causal/nomological homogeneity to count as a genuine, projectible property useful in science. Instead, it proposes that we eschew talk of mental *properties* in favor of mental *predicates or concepts* that at most we get a pragmatically useful mental *predicate.* In making this move, functional reductionism appears to turn itself into a form of eliminativism with regard to mental properties.

See also Alexander, Samuel; Anomalous Monism; Broad, Charlie Dunbar; Davidson, Donald; Eliminative Materialism, Eliminativism; Emergence; Frege, Gottlob; Knowledge Argument; Logic, History of; Metaphysics, History of; Mind-Body Problem; Moral Realism; Morgan, C. Lloyd; Multiple Realizability; Phenomenalism; Philosophy of Mind; Philosophy of Science, History of; Philosophy of Science, Problems of; Physicalism; Properties; Qualia; Reduction; Russell, Bertrand Arthur William; Set Theory; Supervenience.

Bibliography

Block, Ned. "Antireductionism Slaps Back." *Philosophical Perspectives* 11 (1997): 107–132.

Carnap, Rudolf. "Psychology in Physical Language" (1931). Translated in *Logical Positivism*, edited by A. J. Ayer. Glencoe, IL: Free Press, 1959.

Churchland, Patricia. *Neurophilosophy*. Cambridge, MA: MIT Press, 1986.

Churchland, Paul. "Eliminative Materialism and the Propositional Attitudes." *Journal of Philosophy* 78 (1981).

Davidson, Donald. "Mental Events." In *Essays on Actions and Events*. Oxford: Oxford University Press, 1980.

Fodor, Jerry. "Special Sciences, or the Disunity of Science as a Working Hypothesis." *Synthese* 28 (1974): 97–115.

Fodor, Jerry. "Special Sciences: Still Autonomous after All These Years." *Philosophical Perspectives* 11 (1997): 149–163.

Hempel, Carl G. "The Logical Analysis of Psychology" (1935). In *Readings in Philosophy of Psychology*, vol. 1, edited by Ned Block, 14–23. Cambridge, MA: Harvard University Press, 1980.

Jackson, F. "Epiphenomenal Qualia." *Philosophical Quarterly* 32 (1982).

Kim, Jaegwon. *Mind in a Physical World*. Cambridge, MA: MIT Press, 1998.

Kim, Jaegwon. *Supervenience and Mind*. Cambridge, U.K. and New York: Cambridge University Press, 1993.

Lewis, David. "Psychophysical and Theoretical Identifications." *Australasian Journal of Philosophy* 50 (1972): 249–258.

Place, U. T. "Is Consciousness a Brain Process?" *British Journal of Psychology* 47 (1956): 44–50.

Putnam, Hilary. "The Nature of Mental States." In *Mind, Language and Reality*. Cambridge, U.K.: Cambridge University Press, 1978.

Rorty, Richard. "Mind-Body Identity, Privacy and Categories." *Review of Metaphysics* 19 (1965).

Ryle, Gilbert. *The Concept of Mind*. New York: Harper and Row, 1949.

Sabatés, Marcelo. "Being without Doing." *Topoi* 22 (2003).

Shoemaker, Sidney. "Causality and Properties." In *Identity, Cause and Mind*, edited by S. Shoemaker. Cambridge, U.K.: Cambridge University Press, 1984.

Smart, J.C.C. "Sensations and Brain Processes." *Philosophical Review* 68 (1959): 141–156.

Sober, Elliot. "A Plea for Pseudo-Processes." *Pacific Philosophical Quarterly* 66 (1985).

Sosa, Ernest. "Mind-Body Interaction and Supervenient Causation." *Midwest Studies in Philosophy* 9 (1984).

Stich, Stephen. *From Folk Psychology to Cognitive Science*. Cambridge, MA: MIT Press, 1983.

Marcelo H. Sabatés (2005)

SOPHIA

The Greek word *sophia* properly refers to cleverness or skill in handicraft and the productive arts, such as carpentry, music, singing, poetry, chariot driving, medicine, and even divination. In short it tends to pick out the sort of excellence in a particular domain that derives from experience and expertise. In early applications of the term to "wise men," for example the Seven Sages, the term referred primarily to the sorts of skills that would make for expertise in matters of common life and so was virtually synonymous with practical wisdom or prudence (*phronêsis*). By the late fifth century BCE, however, the term was coming to have a more specialized meaning having to do with technical skill and the expertise derived from expert training and experience; that is, it encompassed both a knowledge base and an intimate familiarity with the applications of that knowledge base. The Sophists in particular claimed to have this sort of knowledgeable expertise in many different areas, from medicine to mathematics, oratory, and political science. Indeed, the name "sophistēs" simply means someone who makes a profession of the practice and teaching of such sorts of knowledge.

In Plato, "sophia" clearly has more philosophical connotations. Already in the early, Socratic dialogues we find an attempt to draw a distinction between the kinds of "expertise" that Sophists had and the sort of genuine reflective wisdom modeled by Socrates. For Plato, the former is clearly mere logical chicanery used to generate linguistic puzzles for the purpose of winning debates (see, for example, Socrates' line of reasoning in the *Gorgias* 464b–465e). By the time Plato wrote the *Theaetetus*, he had clearly settled on an antisophistic conception of knowledge and expertise that takes the life and methodology of Socrates as its model, though even in that arguably late dialogue there is no clear line of demarcation drawn between *sophia* and *epistēmē* (knowledge). Since, for Plato, all knowledge, whether of mathematical objects or normative concepts such as the virtues, involves cognitive grasp of purely formal entities, there is less demand in his epistemology for a clear and concise differentiation between the two types of mental states and their proper objects.

Aristotle, by contrast, drew rather sharp distinctions not only between *epistēmē* and *sophia*, but also among those rational faculties and *phronêsis* (practical wisdom), *technē* (art, skill), and *nous* (intelligence, understanding). Yet the relation of *sophia* to the other rational faculties is somewhat specialized. In the *Nicomachean Ethics* (VI.7,

1141a9–b3), Aristotle began by noting the traditional use of the word "sophia" to denote those who have mastered their craft (*technē*) in a most exacting way, but added that it was also used to denote those who are "wise in general and not in one department," and he gave this as his reason for thinking that *sophia* is the "most perfect of the modes of knowledge." Thus *sophia* is associated with both *technē* and *epistēmē*, but it marks off a superlative kind of knowledge in which the knower not only fully understands the consequences of the principles of his craft but also fully understands the natures of the principles themselves. There is thus a sense in which *sophia* encompasses both the necessary truths that follow from demonstrations (the domain of *epistēmē*) and the necessary truths that are the first principles of the demonstrative sciences (the domain of *nous*). In the *Metaphysics* (981b28), this controlling wisdom is said to have the causes and first principles of all the other intellectual faculties as its proper objects, and so it is the highest form of wisdom.

The Stoics likewise took *sophia* as the perfection of human understanding (Seneca, *Epistulae* 89.4), and as consisting in a fully comprehensive and systematic grasp of the rational order in the universe. They characterized *sophia* as "knowledge of the divine and the human," with some adding "and their causes" (von Arnim, 2.35; Seneca, *Epistulae* 89.5). They also regarded this understanding as the crucial underpinning for the goal of leading a moral life and hence considered it a virtue.

In later antiquity, *sophia* held an even more elevated place. In the early Christian theologies of Philo Judaeus and Origen, it is associated with *logos* (word) and thus with the daughter or son of God, respectively. A central feature of the various Gnostic movements was the personification of *sophia* as a salvation figure. In some systems there were two sorts of *sophia*, Wisdom from above and Wisdom from below, representing the female, or noumenal, world and the male, or material, world, respectively. This dualism of *sophia* came in varying degrees. In Marcionism, a heretical doctrine of the second through fifth centuries and the most dualistic system of all, salvation consisted of accepting the wisdom that comes from the Good God and rejecting whatever comes from the Demiurge.

See also Aristotle; Gnosticism; Origen; Philo Judaeus; Phronêsis; Plato; Sophists; Stoicism.

Bibliography

Aristotle. *The Complete Works of Aristotle*, edited by Jonathan Barnes. Princeton, NJ: Princeton University Press, 1984.

Gigon, Olof. "Phronesis und Sophia in der *Nikomachischen Ethik* des Aristoteles." In *Kephalaion: Studies in Greek Philosophy and Its Continuation Offered to Professor C. J. de Vogel*, edited by J. Mansfeld and L. M. de Rijk, 91–104. Assen, Netherlands: Van Gorcum, 1975.

Gladigow, Burkhard. *Sophia und Kosmos: Untersuchungen zur Frühgeschichte von Sophos und Sophia*. Hildesheim, Germany: Olms, 1964.

Hankinson, R. J. "Natural Criteria and the Transparency of Judgment: Philo, Antiochus, and Galen on Epistemological Justification." In *Assent and Argument: Studies in Cicero's Academic Books*, edited by Brad Inwood and Jaap Mansfeld, 161–216. Leiden, Netherlands: Brill, 1997.

Menn, Stephen. "Physics as a Virtue." *Proceedings of the Boston Area Colloquium in Ancient Philosophy* 11 (1997): 1–34.

Motte, André. "Cicerón et Aristote: A propos de la distinction entre la sophia et la phronèsis." In *Aristotelica: Mélanges offerts à Marcel de Corte*, edited by André Motte and Christian Rutten, 263–303. Brussels: Éditions Ousia, 1985.

Plato. *The Collected Dialogues of Plato*. Princeton, NJ: Princeton University Press, 1963.

Seneca. *Letters from a Stoic. Epistulae morales ad Lucilium [by] Seneca*. Selected and translated by Robin Campbell. Harmondsworth: Penguin, 1969.

Von Arnim, Hans. *Stoicorum veterum fragmenta*. Leipzig, Germany: B. G. Teubneri, 1903–1924.

Woodruff, Paul. "Plato's Early Theory of Knowledge." In *Epistemology*, edited by Stephen Everson, 60–84. Cambridge, U.K.: Cambridge University Press, 1990.

Scott Carson (2005)

SÔPHROSUNÊ

Sôphrosunê is the Greek virtue of self-control, or temperance, a virtue that Aristotle says lies between self-indulgence (*akolasia*) on the one hand and insensibility (*anaisthêsia*) on the other. In its earliest uses (Homer) the word means "soundness of mind," "prudence," "discretion," and is related to the verb *sôphronein*, combining *sôs*, safe, and *phronein*, to think, a verb related to *phrên*, an archaism for mind (literally, "midriff," "heart," "the seat of thought," according to the Greeks).

Although Plato dedicated an entire dialogue (*Charmides*) to a discussion of the meaning of *sôphrosunê*, the notion of self-mastery is central to his ethical theory and he invokes it in many contexts, ranging from the *Gorgias* to the *Republic* to the *Laws*. Plato's central claim is that self-mastery is more than the mere abstention from certain forms of physical pleasure—that was the popular and sophistic characterization of the virtue—he "exalts" it (*semnunôn*, *Laws* 710a5) by equating it with *phronêsis*, practical wisdom. Already in the so-called "early" or "Socratic" dialogues (among which the *Charmides* may be counted) Plato had spoken not only of self-control but of all the virtues as reducible, in some way, to knowledge of one kind or another. Like the other "early" dialogues, the *Charmides* ends in *aporia*, puzzlement, about what *sôphrosunê* "really" is, but the suggestion is quite clear that it has to do with knowledge of what is the objectively best way for one to live. When, at *Gorgias* 491e, Callicles scorns self-control as a mere convention valued only by stupid, foolish people (*êlithious*), Socrates mounts an argument to show that those who cannot master their own desires and inclinations cannot master anything, a theme he takes up again in the *Republic*.

Aristotle regards temperance as moderation regarding pleasures and pains, and he loosely associates this virtue with courage as the two virtues of the non-rational (*alogon*) part of the soul (*Nicomachean* Ethics II.7, 1107b5–8; cf. III.10–12 1117b23–1119b10). Aristotle notes that temperance applies more to physical pleasures and pains than mental, and rather more to pleasure than to pain. On Aristotle's account, the temperate person does not crave pleasures more than is right, nor does he crave the wrong sorts of pleasures. The self-indulgent, by contrast, will crave either greater quantities of physical satisfaction than is right, for example, more food than he needs for healthy sustenance, or else he will crave the wrong sorts of physical satisfaction. Aristotle maintains that the other vice opposed to temperance, insensibility, is not merely rare but quite unnatural in humans as well as other animals. The point of both temperance and self-indulgence is the satisfaction of desire, in the one case correctly achieved in the pursuit of human flourishing, in the other a disordered pursuit of pleasure for its own sake rather than for one's natural end. Insensibility, by contrast, is an outright denial of one's basic physical needs and, by extension, a contravention of one's natural end.

Post-Aristotelian philosophy is quite heterogeneous in its treatment of ethical issues. The central conception of the virtue of self-control still has to do with controlling one's desires, though in certain cases (see, for example, *SVF* 1.200–201) it is connected more directly to the foregoing of pleasures. For the Stoics, *sôphrosunê* was counted among the cardinal virtues along with courage, prudence, and justice. Since their highest good was a life lived in accordance with nature (*kata phusin*) the wise person is one whose understanding of nature and his place in it leads him to a kind of unity with nature, and they defined *sophrosynê* very generally as practical wisdom concerned with choice and avoidance (Plut. *Stoic. rep.* 1034ce). The Epicureans, according to Cicero (*De finibus* 1.14.47–8), associated self-control with peace of mind and harmony, by freeing us from the disruptions and consequences of an unbridled pursuit of pleasure. This has value, according to them, not in itself, but because it secures greater pleasure over the long run.

See also Aristotle; Hellenistic Thought; Homer; Pain; Plato; Pleasure; Virtue and Vice.

Bibliography

Macintyre, Alisdair. "*Sôphrosunê*: How a Virtue Can Become Socially Disruptive." *Midwest Studies in Philosophy* 13 (1988): 1–11.

North, Helen. *Sophrosyne and Self-Restraint in Greek Literature.* Ithaca, NY: Cornell University Press, 1966.

Rademaker, Adriaan. *Sophrosyne and the Rhetoric of Self-Restraint: Polysemy and Persuasive Use of an Ancient Greek Value Term.* Leiden: Brill, 2005.

Santas, Gerasimos. "Socrates at Work on Virtue and Knowledge in Plato's *Charmides*." *Exegesis and Argument: Studies in Greek Philosophy Presented to Gregory Vlastos. Phronesis* suppl. vol. 1 (1973): 105–132.

Young, C. "Aristotle on Temperance." *Philosophical Review* 97 (1988): 521–542.

Scott Carson (2005)

TENSE

Tense is a grammatical category by means of which some natural languages express the temporal location of the event described by the sentence in which the grammatical tense occurs. (This definition assumes a distinction between grammatical and lexical categories. For the technically inclined, lexical categories are part of the lexicon of a language and are open classes [classes that allow new vocabulary through compounding, derivation, coining, and borrowing]. They become inflected, and do not contract, affix, or cliticize. Examples of lexical categories are nouns, adjectives, adverbs, verbs. Grammatical categories are part of the grammatical system of a language and are closed classes [classes that do not allow additions]. They may contract, affix, or cliticize. Examples include inflectional and derivational morphemes and function words, such as prepositions, determiners, conjunctions, and pronouns.) An instance of a tensed language is English. In the English unembedded sentence "Bill called," the grammatical tense "-ed" conveys the information that Bill's call happened before the time of speech. Similarly, in the English sentence "Bill will call," the grammatical tense "will" contributes the information that Bill's call occurs after the time of speech. When a language does not have grammatical tenses, as in the case of Chinese, the temporal information may be conveyed by lexical categories, such as adverbs.

The mapping between the grammatical tenses of a natural language and the expression of temporal location is very complex, and one of the goals of linguistic semantics is to investigate the relation between grammatical tenses and the expression of time. To achieve this goal, scholars in both linguistics and philosophy have proposed different theories of tense.

One type of theory, beginning with the work of the logician Arthur Prior, analyzes tenses as temporal operators. Prior (1957, 1967) treated the past and future tenses as sentential operators meaning "it was the case that" and "it will be the case that," respectively. The sentence "Bill called" is translated into $P(\wedge p)$ and is true in a world w at a time t if and only if "Bill calls" is true in w at a time t' t ($\wedge p$ is the intension of p, and "⟨" means "earlier than"). In his intensional system, Montague (1974) adopted Prior's tense logic by introducing tense operators for the past and future tenses, with the time parameter of the intensional expression embedded in the tense operator.

A different approach to the analysis of tense is that proposed by Reichenbach (1947). According to Reichenbach, tense is not a temporal operator but a complex structure built from a small set of primitives: the event time (E), the speech time (S), the reference time (R), and two relations that can hold between these times, simultaneity (symbolized with a comma) and anteriority (symbolized with an underscore). One of these relations holds between S and R, and one relation holds between R and E. The relation between S and E is not represented but is inferred from the first two. With this small set of primitives, Reichenbach was able to define the set of possible English tenses. For example, the simple past, future, and present tenses have the structures [E, R_S], [S_R, E], [S, R, E], respectively. The contribution of R becomes crucial in the analysis of complex tenses, such as the future and past perfect (which Reichenbach called "anterior future" and "anterior past"), where R overlaps neither E nor S. For example, the past perfect in "At 3:00 p.m., John had (already) called" has the structure [E_R_S], where the calling time E precedes the reference time R (3:00 p.m.), which in turn is before S.

The case of the future perfect is a little more complex. Take the sentence "By 3:00 p.m., John will have called." Our intuition is that, while 3:00 p.m. must follow the speech time, the time of John's calling must be before 3:00 p.m. but does not have to follow the speech time. The availability of the reference time R allows Reichenbach to account for this intuition easily: R must be future relative to S, and E must be past relative to R, but the relation between S and E is left unspecified, leaving open the following three possibilities: [S_E_R] or [S, E_R] or [E_S_R].

A third family of theories views tenses as temporal predicates expressing relations between times (or events). Zagona (1995), Stowell (1996), and Higginbotham (2002) are the main proponents of this view. According to these authors, tenses express temporal relations, such as anteriority, posteriority, and simultaneity, between two events (or times). However, unlike Reichenbach's theory, events (or times) are not introduced by the tenses but by verbs and adjectives instead. This view is also different from the operator analysis of tense since tenses are not operators shifting evaluation parameters

The operator theory of tense has been very influential and has inspired semantic analyses where tense is an existential quantifier binding the time argument in the predicate. Versions of the quantificational theory of tense have been proposed by David Dowty (1979), Arnim von Stechow (1995), Toshi Ogihara (1996), and Dorit Abusch (1997), among others (see Kuhn and Portner 2002 for an overview on tense logics for natural languages). Barbara Partee (1973, 1984) has observed that existential-quantifier theories are problematic when we consider some occurrences of tense in natural language. Her famous example is

(1) I didn't turn off the stove

uttered as the speaker is driving down the freeway. According to the existential analysis of tense, the sentence can be interpreted either as "There is no past time at which I turned off the stove" or as "There is a past time at which I did not turn off the stove," depending on the scope of negation with respect to the temporal quantifier. However, neither interpretation correctly captures the meaning of the sentence in the context we are considering. Clearly, the speaker did not mean to negate the existence of *any* time at which she turned off the stove, nor did she mean to assert the existence of *some* time at which she did not turn off the stove. She merely meant to assert that she did not turn off the stove at a *contextually salient past time.*

To solve this problem, Partee proposed a *referential* analysis of tense, in which tenses are linguistic devises by which we refer to times salient in the previous discourse. This analysis treats English tenses analogously to how Hans Kamp (1981) and Irene Heim (1988) treated pronouns and nominal anaphora. Variants of this idea have also been proposed by Enç (1986), Heim (1994), and

Kratzer (1998). However, there are occurrences of tenses that are not about particular times, as in the sentence

(2) Einstein visited Princeton

where a quantificational analysis of tense seems more apt. Both quantificational and referential theories of tense need to account for the occurrences of tense in (1) and (2). One possibility is to analyze the past tense as a restricted quantifier, just like ordinary nominal quantifiers. In this analysis, (1) would assert that there is no time within a contextually salient past interval at which the individual turned off the stove. The indeterminate reading of (2) would arise when the restriction of the quantifier is Einstein's entire life span.

The discussion so far has been about the meanings of the English tenses, and we have been silently assuming that there is a one-to-one correspondence between grammatical tenses and these meanings. While this is generally true in simple clauses, there are exceptions. For example, (3) illustrates a use of the grammatical present tense with the so-called *futurate* meaning.

(3) The 4:00 o'clock train leaves in five minutes.

Example (4) from Enç 1996 illustrates a mismatch between the future tense morpheme will and the semantics of the future, since Pat's sleeping is understood to be overlapping the speech time. Similarly, example (5) illustrates a mismatch between the past tense morpheme on was and the semantics of the past, since the past tense is allowed to occur with the future adverb tomorrow.

(4) Pat will be sleeping now.

(5) Pat was leaving tomorrow.

The idea of a one-to-one correspondence between tense morphology and tense meanings turns out to be even more problematic when we consider subordinate clauses and the phenomenon of sequence of tense. Consider the following sentence, where the matrix verb and the embedded verb both occur in the past tense.

(6) Bill thought that Sue was pregnant.

There are two possible readings of (6). According to the first reading, the content of Bill's thought was that Sue was pregnant at some time before the time at which Bill was having the thought. This is the so-called *shifted* reading. According to the second reading, the content of Bill's thought is that Sue was pregnant at the time when Bill was having the thought. This is the so-called *simultaneous* reading. The possible simultaneous reading, where the embedded past morpheme is not interpreted as a past tense, seems problematic for a theory in which the morpheme "-ed" is always interpreted as a semantic past. The simultaneity relation, generally expressed in English by the absence of either past or future morphemes, is expressed in sequence of tense with the past morpheme. Furthermore, notice that when we actually embed a grammatical present tense under a grammatical past tense, as in (7), we obtain not a simultaneous reading but yet a third reading, the so-called *double-access* reading. As pointed out by Enç (1987), in (7) Bill's thought is that Sue's pregnancy extends over a period of time including both the time at which Bill had the thought and the time at which (7) was uttered.

(7) Bill thought that Sue is pregnant.

Let us go back to (6). Operator theories of tense try to reconcile the occurrence of an embedded past-tense morpheme with the simultaneous reading by proposing accounts where, at the level of semantic interpretation, the embedded past tense is deleted (Ogihara 1989, 1995; von Stechow 1995) or is semantically bound by the matrix past tense (Abusch 1997) and its temporal features are deleted (von Stechow 2003).

Within the referential theories of tense, Enç (1987) proposed that the simultaneous reading of (6) is obtained when the embedded past tense is coindexed with the matrix past tense, and thus bound by it. Therefore, in her account, the embedded past tense refers to the past time referred to by the matrix past tense. Abusch (1988) points out that already in Kamp and Rohrer (1984) we can find some evidence against the claim that the morphological past tense in an embedded clause is interpreted as a semantic past tense. Abusch provides (8) as an example illustrating the fact that, the most embedded past tense, that associated with "were," cannot refer to any past time since, in the intended reading, the event of having their last meal together is understood as overlapping John's saying event.

(8) John decided a week ago that in ten days at breakfast he would say to his mother that they were having their last meal together.

Among referential theories of tense, a slightly different approach has been taken by Kratzer (1998). Kratzer's proposal, while inheriting several elements from Abusch's (1997) analysis of sequence of tense, is based on Irene Heim's observation that in some occurrences, pronouns have features that are not interpreted. For example, the second occurrence of "I" in Heim's example (9) is interpreted not as an indexical but as a bound variable in the so-called strict reading.

(9) Only I got a question that I understood.

According to Kratzer, the simultaneous reading of (6) arises when the embedded past tense is interpreted as a bound variable, just as the second occurrence of the first-person pronoun in (9) is interpreted as a bound variable, rather than as an indexical. The features on both the embedded "I" in (9) and the embedded past tense in (6) are not "interpretable" (in the sense of Chomsky 1995), that is, they do not contribute to the LF (logical form) representations of these sentences. They are zero pronouns, or zero tenses, whose morphological and phonological features probably derive from agreement with their antecedents and do not carry any semantic information. Kratzer's parallel between zero pronouns and sequence-of-tense tenses expands Partee's original insight about an analogy between pronouns and tenses. The parallel between pronouns and tenses is also at the center of recent work by Schlenker (2003) and von Stechow (2003).

The discussion of sequence-of-tense phenomena above has been concerned with sequences of tenses where th e matrix tense is a past. Hornstein (1990) claims that the availability of the simultaneous reading in sequence of tense is not restricted to the past tense but applies to all tenses. Enç (1996) challenges this claim on the basis of examples like (10), where, according to her judgment, only the shifted interpretation is possible:

(10) Mary will say that she will be tired.

Furthermore, Enç points out that the double-access reading is not forced by embedding the present tense under the future—a fact that thus sets the future tense apart from the past tense. In (11) the only reading is that Mary is upset at the time of John's assertion.

(11) John will say that Mary is upset.

On the basis of these asymmetries between the future and the past and on the basis of the observation that future-oriented modals behave like "will" with respect to sequence of tense, as in (12), Enç suggests that the future morpheme "will" is not a tense but a modal.

(12) John must claim that he is sick.

This last point raises the question of the relation between tense and two other grammatical categories: aspect and mood. Tense, aspect, and mood are intimately related, since they all contribute some information about the event that a given sentence is about: Tense, as mentioned, conveys information about the time of the event; aspect conveys information about the beginning, duration, completion, or repetition of the event; finally, mood conveys information about whether the sentence is about a possible or actual event. It is common to assume, however, that these categories are distinct, even though their boundaries are not always clear. (An example is the debate over the semantics of the present perfect in English and other languages. For a general overview of the topic, see Alexiadou, Rathert, and von Stechow 2003 and the references cited there.) Further comparative studies across Indo-European and non-Indo-European languages will, it is hoped, shed light on these intricate issues.

See also Artificial and Natural Languages; Chomsky, Noam; Intensional Transitive Verbs; Language; Montague, Richard; Prior, Arthur Norman; Quantifiers in Natural Language; Reichenbach, Hans; Semantics.

Bibliography

Abusch, Dorit. "Sequence of Tense and Temporal De Re." *Linguistics and Philosophy* 20 (1997): 1–50.

Abusch, Dorit. "Sequence of Tense, Intensionality, and Scope." In *Proceedings of the Seventh West Coast Conference on Formal Linguistics*, edited by Hagit Borer, 1–14. Stanford, CA: CSLI, 1988.

Alexiadou, Artemis, Monika Rathert, and Arnim von Stechow, eds. *Perfect Explorations*. Berlin: Mouton de Gruyter, 2003.

Chomsky, Noam. *The Minimalist Program*. Cambridge, MA: MIT Press, 1995.

Dowty, David. *Word Meaning and Montague Grammar: The Semantics of Verbs and Times in Generative Grammar and Montague PTQ*. Dordrecht, Netherlands: D. Reidel, 1979.

Enç, Mürvet. "Anchoring Conditions for Tense." *Linguistic Inquiry* 18 (1987): 633–657.

Enç, Mürvet. "Tense and Modality." In *The Handbook of Contemporary Semantic Theory*, edited by Shalom Lappin, 345–358. Oxford, U.K.: Blackwell, 1996.

Enç, Mürvet. "Towards a Referential Analysis of Temporal Expressions." *Linguistics and Philosophy* 9 (1986): 405–426.

Heim, Irene. "Comments on Abusch's Theory of Tense." In *Ellipsis, Tense, and Questions*, edited by Hans Kamp, 143–170. Amsterdam: University of Amsterdam, 1994.

Heim, Irene. "The Semantics of Definite and Indefinite Noun Phrases." PhD diss. University of Massachusetts, Amherst, 1982. Published by Garland, New York, 1988.

Higginbotham, James. "Why Is Sequence of Tense Obligatory." In *Logical Form and Language*, edited by G. Preyer and G. Peter. New York: Oxford University Press, 2002.

Hornstein, Norbert. *As Time Goes By: Tense and Universal Grammar*. Cambridge, MA: MIT Press, 1990.

Kamp, Hans. "A Theory of Truth and Semantic Representation." In *Formal Methods in the Study of Language, Part I*, edited by J. Groenendijk, T. Janssen, and M. Stokhof, 277–322. Amsterdam: Mathematisch Centrum, 1981.

Kamp, Hans, and Christian Rohrer. "Indirect Discourse." Manuscript. University of Texas, Austin, and University of Stuttgart, 1984.

Kratzer, Angelika. "More Structural Analogies between Pronouns and Tenses." In *Proceeding of Semantics and*

Linguistic Theory, VIII, edited by Devon Strolovitch and Aaron Lawson. Ithaca, NY: CLC Publications, 1998.

Kuhn, S., and P. Portner. "Tense and Time." In *The Handbook of Philosophical Logic*. 2nd ed., edited by D. Gabbay and F. Guenthner, 6: 277–346. Dordrecht, Netherlands: D. Reidel, 2002.

Montague, Richard. *Formal Philosophy: Selected Papers of Richard Montague*, edited by Richmond H. Thomason. New Haven, CT: Yale University Press, 1974.

Ogihara, Toshiyuki. "Double-Access Sentences and References to States." *Natural Language Semantics* 3 (1995): 177–210.

Ogihara, Toshiyuki. "Temporal Reference in English and Japanese." PhD diss. University of Texas at Austin, 1989.

Ogihara, Toshiyuki. *Tense, Attitudes, and Scope*. Dordrecht, Netherlands: Kluwer Academic Publishers, 1996.

Partee, Barbara. "Nominal and Temporal Anaphora." *Linguistics and Philosophy* 7 (1984): 243–286.

Partee, Barbara. "Some Structural Analogies between Tenses and Pronouns in English." *Journal of Philosophy* 18 (1973): 601–609.

Prior, Arthur N. *Past, Present, and Future*. Oxford, U.K.: Oxford University Press, 1967.

Prior, Arthur N. *Time and Modality*. Oxford, U.K.: Oxford University Press, 1957.

Reichenbach, Hans. *Elements of Symbolic Logic*. New York: Macmillan, 1947.

Schlenker, Philippe. "A Plea for Monsters." *Linguistics and Philosophy* 26 (2003): 29–120.

Stowell, Tim. "The Phrase Structure of Tense." In *Phrase Structure and the Lexicon*, edited by Johan Rooryck and Laurie Zaring, 277–291. Dordrecht, Netherlands: Kluwer, 1996.

Von Stechow, Arnim. "Feature Deletion under Semantic Binding: Tense, Person, and Mood under Verbal Quantifiers." In *Proceedings of the North East Linguistic Society 33*, edited by Makoto Kadowaki and Shigeto Kawahara. Amherst: GLSA, University of Massachusetts, 2003.

Von Stechow, Arnim. "On the Proper Treatment of Tense." In *Proceeding of Semantics and Linguistic Theory, V*, edited by Mandy Simons and Teresa Galloway. Ithaca, NY: CLC Publications, 1995.

Zagona, Karen. "Temporal Argument Structure: Configurational Elements of Construal." In *Temporal Reference, Aspect, and Actionality*. Vol. 1: *Semantic and Syntactic Perspectives*, edited by Pier Marco Bertinetto, Valentina Bianchi, James Higginbotham, and Mario Squartini. Turin, Italy: Rosenberg e Sellier, 1995.

Michela Ippolito (2005)

XENOPHON [ADDENDUM]

The central concern regarding Xenophon since the mid-1960s has been his place in the so-called Socratic problem, the question of to what extent our knowledge of the historical Socrates is accurate and on the basis of what sources we may have any confidence in the portrait of him that has come down to us. Although Xenophon's Socratic writings have been criticized on the grounds that their philosophical acumen does not compare with that of Plato, scholarship since antiquity has tended to regard them as important sources of information about the life and character of the historical Socrates. But Xenophon's portrait of Socrates has received mixed reviews. Scholars continue to debate whether the Socrates that we encounter in the early, Socratic dialogues of Plato is the historical man himself, a Platonic fiction, or something in between, and the portrait of Socrates that we find in Aristophanes is clearly something of a caricature, in which Socrates appears to serve virtually as a stock character for the ridicule of philosophers generally.

This has prompted some to claim that Xenophon is our best hope for piecing together the real life of the man. Others, however, argue that Xenophon shows no real sophistication in his writings and hence cannot be relied upon to produce an accurate portrait of such a central figure in the history of philosophy, and that if we compare Xenophon's portrait of Socrates with those of other writers of *Sōkratikoi logoi* (stories about Socrates), a genre that grew up among the followers of Socrates shortly after his death in 399 BCE, we find that we have no compelling reason to prefer his portrait to any other, including Plato's. Plato himself mentions the views of Xenophon only once (*Laws* 694c), and only to criticize an element of the political education of Cyrus as portrayed in the *Cyropaedeia*. Plato has nothing to say about Xenophon's portrait of Socrates. The other writers of *Sōkratikoi logoi* (Antisthenes, Phaedo, Eucleides, Aristippus, Aeschines, and Plato), were actively writing memoirs of Socrates as early as the 390s and 380s, but Xenophon did not begin to write his *Sōkratikoi logoi* until the 360s, and some scholars see in him a repository of recycled information, with at least one scholar suggesting that Xenophon's own youthful memories of Socrates were "filtered through the Socratic literature that had been published in the meantime" (Kahn 1996, p. 30).

Another area of scholarly attention since the mid-1960s has focused on Xenophon as comparative biographer. Even if we accept the view that his portrait of Socrates is as accurate than that of any other Socratic, some scholars maintain that we may nevertheless see in his accounts of Socrates and Cyrus an attempt at comparative biography that has value in its own right. This judgment must be weighed against the view of other scholars who argue that Xenophon's imagination is not on a par with those of the other Socratics, nor is his philosophical acumen up to the task of drawing and comparing such lives with anything like the skill that one finds in, for example, the writings of Plutarch.

See also Antisthenes; Aristippus of Cyrene; Plato; Plutarch of Chaeronea; Socrates.

Bibliography

WORKS BY XENOPHON

Xenophontis opera omnia, edited by E. C. Merchant. Oxford, U.K.: Clarendon, 1950–1954.

Mémorables, edited by Michele Bandini. Translated by Louis-André Dorion. Paris: Belles lettres, 2000–.

WORKS ON XENOPHON

Anderson, J. K. *Xenophon*. Bristol, U.K.: Bristol Classical, 2001.

Cooper, John M. "Notes on Xenophon's Socrates." In his *Reason and Emotion: Essays on Ancient Moral Psychology and Ethical Theory*, 3–28. Princeton, NJ: Princeton University Press, 1999.

Dorion, Louis-André, and Michele Bandini. "Introduction générale." In *Mémorables*, by Xenophon. Vol. 1. Paris: Belles lettres, 2000.

"Les écrits socratiques de Xénophon." Special issue, *Études philosophiques* 2 (2004).

Gray, Vivienne J. *The Framing of Socrates: The Literary Interpretation of Xenophon's "Memorabilia."* Stuttgart, Germany: F. Steiner, 1998.

Gray, Vivienne J. "Xenophon's Image of Socrates in the *Memorabilia*." *Prudentia* 27 (1995): 50–73.

Kahn, Charles H. "*Sokratikoi logoi*: The Literary and Intellectual Background of Plato's Work." In his *Plato and the Socratic Dialogue: The Philosophical Use of a Literary Form*, 29–35. Cambridge, U.K.: Cambridge University Press, 1996.

Morrison, Donald R. *Bibliography of Editions, Translations, and Commentary on Xenophon's Socratic Writings, 1600–Present.* Pittsburgh, PA: Mathesis Publications, 1988.

Morrison, Donald R. "On Professor Vlastos' Xenophon." *Ancient Philosophy* 7 (1987) 9–22.

Morrison, Donald R. "Xenophon's Socrates on the Just and the Lawful." *Ancient Philosophy* 15 (1995): 329–347.

Vander Waerdt, Paul A. *The Socratic Movement*. Ithaca, NY: Cornell University Press, 1994.

Vlastos, Gregory. "The Evidence of Aristotle and Xenophon." In his *Socrates: Ironist and Moral Philosopher*, 81–106. Ithaca, NY: Cornell University Press, 1991.

Scott Carson (2005)

thematic outline of contents

The Thematic Outline of Contents has been constructed to assist readers who wish to explore a number of entries in a specific time period or in a distinct subfield of philosophy. Entries have, accordingly, been grouped under two general headings: "Historical Periods" and "Subfields of Philosophy."

The personal entries and a few of the subject entries in the *Encyclopedia* can be placed in one of the following five historical time periods.

(1) Ancient Philosophy—from Homer in the 8th century BCE to Augustine in the 4th–5th century CE

(2) Medieval Philosophy—from Augustine to Thomas Aquinas in the 13th century CE

(3) Modern Philosophy—from Thomas Aquinas to Georg W. F. Hegel in the 18th–19th century CE

(4) Nineteenth Century

(5) Twentieth Century

To group philosophers in this fashion may give the false impression that ancient philosophy began in the time of Homer and ended with Augustine and that medieval philosophy began in the time of Augustine and ended with Aquinas after whom we get modern philosophy. The developing story of philosophy does not lend itself to such rigidly defined temporal boundaries. Indeed, Augustine was importantly influenced by ancient Platonic thought even as Aquinas was significantly indebted to ancient Aristotelian thought. Moreover, the philosophical traditions springing from Augustine and Aquinas—Augustinianism and Thomism—are very much alive in our world today. If we respect the insight that philosophical thinking develops throughout the centuries by virtue of philosophers engaging in dialogues not only with their contemporaries but also with their predecessors, then we will avoid such false notions as ancient philosophy ending at such and such a time, and we will be safe in talking about certain temporal periods of philosophy—which we are doing in this Thematic Outline of Contents.

Personal entries in the Nineteenth Century section have been divided into two groups: "major" to signify large entries containing more than 2,500 words and "minor" to indicate smaller entries. It must be noted, however, that a personal entry in the category of "minor" may discuss an enormously influential philosopher. The size of a personal entry is not always an indication of the importance of that person in a philosophical tradition. Indeed, in preparing personal entries for very influential philosophers from the current scene, our standard word allocation was between 1,000 and 1,500 words.

Personal entries in the Twentieth Century section are also divided into two groups: "early" referring to scholars whose major work was done in the first half of the twentieth century, and "recent" referring to scholars whose major work takes place in the last half of the twentieth century continuing frequently into the twenty-first century.

Some of the subject entries can be placed within Ancient Philosophy (such as Aretē and Demiurge), Medieval Philosophy (such as Liber de Causis and Scotism) and Modern Philosophy (such as Atheismusstreit and Jansenism). Most subject entries, however, defy allocation to one time frame because they relate to questions that have engaged philosophers for many centuries. Accordingly, most of the subject entries have been grouped within the following twenty-one philosophical subfields that appear in the following order: Epistemology; Philosophy of Mind and Cognitive Science; Metaphysics; Philosophy of Science; Logic, Philosophy of Logic, and Philosophy of Mathematics; Philosophy of Language; Continental Philosophy; Feminist Philosophy; Ethics; Applied Ethics; Social and Political Philosophy; Philosophy of Law; Aesthetics and Philosophy of Art; Philosophy of Religion; Buddhist Philosophy; Chinese Philosophy; Indian Philosophy; Islamic Philosophy; Japanese Philosophy; Jewish Philosophy; and Russian Philosophy. Two additional categories—Philosophical Perspectives and Movements; and Special Topics—complete the Thematic Outline of Contents.

The list of philosophical subfields into which entries have been placed is not exhaustive. Indeed, there are many additional subfields that frequently bear the title "Philosophy of . . . " such as Philosophy of Education, Philosophy of Medicine, Philosophy of Sex, Philosophy of Technology, etc. Many of these subfields have entries dedicated to them in the *Encyclopedia* and they are listed in the Thematic Outline of Contents under Special Topics.

Because most personal entries describe scholars who make contributions in more than one subfield of philosophy (such as Plato, Aristotle, Augustine, Aquinas, Descartes, Hume, Kant, Hegel, Bertrand Russell, and Hilary Putnam to mention only a few), it would be overly cumbersome to list each of them in all the subfields in which they worked. Some persons, however, can be reasonably associated with one particular subfield, such as Monroe Beardsley with "Aesthetics and Philosophy of Art," Georg Cantor with "Logic, Philosophy of Logic, and Philosophy of Mathematics," Confucius and Mencius with "Chinese Philosophy," and Mohammed Arkoun and Seyyed Hossein Nasr with "Islamic Philosophy." Such scholars are listed not only in one of the five historical periods but also within their distinctive subfields.

Clearly, the Historical Periods and the Philosophical Subfields of this Thematic Outline of Contents reflect the influence of the Western philosophical tradition originating with the ancient Greeks. Equally evident is the fact that the *Encyclopedia* contains articles devoted to non-Western philosophical traditions such as the African, Buddhist, Chinese, Indian, Japanese, and Korean. These traditions together represent a host of entries in the *Encyclopedia.* Inserting these entries into the Thematic Outline of Contents might suggest at first glance that the integrity of these traditions is being violated because they are being forced into a Procrustean Western mold. Yet it is important to remember that contemplative people from diverse cultural traditions have pondered some of the same perennial human questions for centuries. Philosophy begins with wonder, and the West has no monopoly on wonder. Human beings from diverse cultures have wondered about such things as truth, knowledge, logic, morality, and the nature of the human and also the transcendent. While the way questions are posed and answers are given may vary significantly from culture to culture, the topics of philosophy are truly multicultural. Admittedly, three of the Historical Periods used in this Thematic Outline of Contents—Ancient, Medieval, and Modern—have employed Western thinkers—Homer, Augustine, Aquinas, and Hegel—as temporal markers. Non-Western traditions would no doubt use other markers. Dividing human development into distinct periods has an element of unavoidable arbitrariness. The point to be emphasized by utilizing such divisions, however, is that philosophical thinking is a growing concern and that stages of growth are usually recognizable. The entries covering diverse philosophical traditions will, it is hoped, display that growth and also the commonality of human wonder.

HISTORICAL PERIODS IN PHILOSOPHY

Ancient Philosophy

Aenesidemus
Agent Intellect
Agrippa
Aitia
Alcinous
Alcmaeon of Croton
Alexander of Aphrodisias
Alexander of Hales
Anaxagoras of Clazomenae
Anaximander
Anaximenes
Ancient Aesthetics
Ancient Skepticism
Antiochus of Ascalon
Antiphon
Antisthenes
Apeiron/Peras
Apologists
Arcesilaus
Archē
Archytas of Tarentum
Aretē/Agathon/Kakon
Aristippus of Cyrene
Aristo of Chios
Aristotelianism
Aristotle
Arius and Arianism
Atomism
Carneades
Celsus
Chrysippus
Cicero, Marcus Tullius
Cleanthes
Clement of Alexandria
Confucius
Cosmos
Cratylus
Cynics
Cyrenaics
Demiurge
Dikē
Diodorus Cronus
Diogenes Laertius
Diogenes of Apollonia
Diogenes of Sinope
Dogma
Dong Zhongshu
Empedocles
Epictetus
Epicureanism and the Epicurean School
Epicurus
Eternity
Eudaimonia
Eusebius
Galen
Gongsun Long
Gorgias of Leontini
Greek Academy
Greek Drama
Gregory of Nazianzus
Gregory of Nyssa
Guo Xiang
Han Fei
Hen/Polla
Heraclitus of Ephesus
Hippias of Elis
Hippocrates and the Hippocratic Corpus
Homer
Hui Shi
Hypatia
Iamblichus
Impetus
Inner Senses
Kalon
Katharsis
Laozi
Leucippus and Democritus
Logos
Longinus (Pseudo)
Lucian of Samosata
Lucretius
Mani and Manichaeism
Marcion
Marcus Aurelius Antoninus
Megarians
Melissus of Samos
Mencius
Mimesis
Moira/Tychē/Anankē
Mozi
Musonius Rufus
Nāgārjuna
Nemesius of Emesa
Neoplatonism
Nomos and Phusis
Nous
Numenius of Apamea
Origen
Orphism
Ousia
Panaetius of Rhodes
Parmenides of Elea
Pelagius and Pelagianism
Peripatetics
Phantasia
Philodemus
Philo Judaeus
Philolaus of Croton
Philo of Larissa
Philo of Megara
Phronêsis
Plato
Plotinus
Plutarch of Chaeronea
Pneuma
Porphyry
Posidonius
Pre-Socratic Philosophy
Proclus
Prodicus of Ceos
Protagoras of Abdera
Psychē
Pyrrho
Pythagoras and Pythagoreanism
Seneca, Lucius Annaeus
Sextus Empiricus
Simon Magus
Socrates
Sophia
Sophists
Sôphrosunê
Stoicism
Strato and Stratonism
Tertullian, Quintus Septimius Florens
Thales of Miletus
Themistius
Theophrastus
Thucydides
Timon of Phlius
Valentinus and Valentinianism
Vasubandhu
Wang Bi
Wang Chong
Xenophanes of Colophon
Xenophon
Xunzi
Yang Xiong
Yang Zhu
Zeno of Citium
Zeno of Elea
Zhuangzi

Medieval Philosophy

Abelard, Peter
Ailly, Pierre d'
Albert of Saxony
Albert the Great
Albo, Joseph
al-Fārābī
al-Ghazālī, Ahmad
al-Ghazālī, Muhammad
al-Kindī, Abū-Yūsuf Yaʿqūb ibn Isḥāq
Anselm, St.
Augustine, St.
Augustinianism
Averroes

Avicenna
Baḥyā, ben Joseph ibn Paqūda
Bacon, Roger
Bernard of Chartres
Bernard of Clairvaux, St.
Bernard of Tours
Biel, Gabriel
Boethius, Anicius Manlius Severinus
Boetius of Dacia
Bonaventure, St.
Bradwardine, Thomas
Buridan, John
Burley, Walter
Capreolus, John
Chatton, Walter
Cheng Hao
Cheng Yi
Crescas, Hasdai
Damascius
Dante Alighieri
David of Dinant
Duns Scotus, John
Durandus of Saint-Pourçain
Eckhart, Meister
Erigena, John Scotus
Gaunilo
Gerbert of Aurillac
Gerson, Jean de
Gersonides
Gilbert of Poitiers
Giles of Rome
Godfrey of Fontaines
Gregory of Rimini
Grosseteste, Robert
Halevi, Yehuda
Han Yu
Henry of Ghent
Henry of Harclay
Hervaeus Natalis
Heytesbury, William
Hildegard of Bingen
Holkot, Robert
Hus, John
Ibn al-ʿArabī
Ibn Bājja
Ibn Gabirol, Solomon Ben Judah
Ibn Khaldūn
Ibn Ṭufayl
Ibn Zaddik, Joseph ben Jacob
Isaac of Stella
Israeli, Isaac ben Solomon
Jinul
Joachim of Fiore
John of Damascus
John of Jandun
John of La Rochelle
John of Mirecourt
John of Paris
John of Salisbury
Kilvington, Richard
Kilwardby, Robert
Li Ao
Liber de Causis
Lull, Ramón
Lu Xiangshan
Maimonides
Marsilius of Inghen
Marsilius of Padua
Marston, Roger
Matthew of Acquasparta
Medieval Philosophy
Muqammiṣ, David ben Merwan al-
Naṣīr al-Dīn al-Ṭūsī
Nicolas of Autrecourt
Olivi, Peter John
Paul of Venice
Peckham, John
Peter Aureol
Peter Damian
Peter Lombard
Peter of Spain
Petrarch
Philoponus, John
Pletho, Giorgius Gemistus
Pseudo-Dionysius
Pseudo-Grosseteste
Richard of Mediavilla
Roscelin
Rufus, Richard
Ruysbroeck, Jan van
Saadya
Saint Victor, School of
Scot, Michael
Scotism
Shao Yong
Shinran
Siger of Brabant
Simplicius
Suhrawardī, Shihāb al-Dīn Yaḥyā
Suso, Heinrich
Swineshead, Richard
Tauler, Johannes
Theodoric of Chartres
Thomas à Kempis
Thomas Aquinas, St.
Thomas of York
Ulrich (Engelbert) of Strasbourg
William of Auvergne
William of Champeaux
William of Conches
William of Moerbeke
William of Ockham
William of Sherwood
Wodeham, Adam
Wyclyf, John
Zhang Zai
Zhou Dunyi
Zhu Xi (Chu His)

Modern Philosophy

Addison, Joseph
Agrippa von Nettesheim, Henricus Cornelius
Alembert, Jean Le Rond d'
Alison, Archibald
Althusius, Johannes
Andō Shōeki
Annet, Peter
Arminius and Arminianism
Arnauld, Antoine
Astell, Mary
Atheismusstreit
Baader, Franz Xavier von
Bacon, Francis
Bahrdt, Carl Friedrich
Balguy, John
Báñez, Dominic
Basedow, Johann Bernhard
Batteux, Abbé Charles
Baumgarten, Alexander Gottlieb
Bayes, Bayes' Theorem, Bayesian Approach to Philosophy of Science
Bayle, Pierre
Beattie, James
Beccaria, Cesare Bonesana
Beck, Jakob Sigismund
Bellarmine, St. Robert
Bentham, Jeremy
Berkeley, George
Bilfinger, Georg Bernhard
Blake, William
Blount, Charles
Bodin, Jean
Boehme, Jakob
Boileau, Nicolas
Bolingbroke, Henry St. John
Bolzano, Bernard
Bonald, Louis Gabriel Ambroise, Vicomte de
Bonnet, Charles
Boscovich, Roger Joseph
Bossuet, Jacques Bénigne
Boulainvilliers, Henri, Comte de
Boyle, Robert
Brown, Thomas
Bruno, Giordano
Budde, Johann Franz
Buffon, Georges-Louis Leclerc, Comte de
Burke, Edmund
Burthogge, Richard
Butler, Joseph
Cabanis, Pierre-Jean Georges

Cajetan, Cardinal
Calvin, John
Campanella, Tommaso
Cavendish, Margaret
Charron, Pierre
Chateaubriand, François René de
Chubb, Thomas
Clarke, Samuel
Clauberg, Johannes
Cockburn, Catherine Trotter
Colet, John
Collier, Arthur
Collins, Anthony
Comenius, John Amos
Condillac, Étienne Bonnot de
Condorcet, Marquis de
Conway, Anne
Copernicus, Nicolas
Cordemoy, Géraud De
Cordovero, Moses ben Jacob
Costa, Uriel da
Crusius, Christian August
Cudworth, Ralph
Culverwel, Nathanael
Cumberland, Richard
Cyrano de Bergerac, Savinien de
Dai Zhen
Darwin, Erasmus
Descartes, René
Desgabets, Robert
Diderot, Denis
DuBos, Abbe Jean Baptiste
Eberhard, Johann August
Edwards, Jonathan
Elisabeth, Princess of Bohemia
Erasmus, Desiderius
Fénelon, François de Salignad de la Mothe
Ferguson, Adam
Fichte, Johann Gottlieb
Ficino, Marsilio
Filmer, Robert
Fludd, Robert
Fonseca, Peter
Fontenelle, Bernard Le Bovier de
Foucher, Simon
Fourier, François Marie Charles
Franck, Sebastian
Franklin, Benjamin
Galileo Galilei
Galluppi, Pasquale
Garve, Christian
Gassendi, Pierre
Gay, John
Genovesi, Antonio
Gerard, Alexander
Geulincx, Arnold
Gibbon, Edward
Glanvill, Joseph
Godwin, William
Goethe, Johann Wolfgang Von
Gottsched, Johann Christoph
Gournay, Marie le Jars de
Gracián y Morales, Baltasar
Grotius, Hugo
Hamann, Johann Georg
Harrington, James
Hartley, David
Harvey, William
Hayashi Razan
Hazlitt, William
Hegel, Georg Wilhelm Friedrich
Helvétius, Claude-Adrien
Hemsterhuis, Frans
Herbart, Johann Friedrich
Herbert of Cherbury
Herder, Johann Gottfried
Hobbes, Thomas
Holbach, Paul-Henri Thiry, Baron d'
Home, Henry
Hooker, Richard
Huang Zongxi
Huet, Pierre-Daniel
Humboldt, Wilhelm von
Hume, David
Hutcheson, Francis
Itō Jinsai
Jacobi, Friedrich Heinrich
Jansenism
Jefferson, Thomas
John of St. Thomas
John of the Cross, St.
Johnson, Samuel
Johnson, Samuel
Jungius, Joachim
Kaibara Ekken
Kant, Immanuel
Kepler, Johannes
Kleist, Heinrich von
Knutzen, Martin
Kumazawa Banzan
La Bruyère, Jean de
Lamarck, Chevalier de
Lambert, Johann Heinrich
La Mettrie, Julien Offray de
La Mothe Le Vayer, François de
La Peyrère, Isaac
Laplace, Pierre Simon de
La Rochefoucauld, Duc François de
Laromiguière, Pierre
Lavater, Johann Kaspar
Lavoisier, Antoine
Law, William
Le Clerc, Jean
Leibniz, Gottfried Wilhelm
Leonardo da Vinci
Lessing, Gotthold Ephraim
Lichtenberg, Georg Christoph
Lipsius, Justus
Locke, John
Luther, Martin
Machiavelli, Niccolò
Maillet, Benoît De
Maimon, Salomon
Maine de Biran
Maistre, Comte Joseph de
Major, John
Malebranche, Nicolas
Mandeville, Bernard
Mariana, Juan de
Marulić, Marko
Mather, Cotton
Maupertuis, Pierre-Louis Moreau de
Maxwell, James Clerk
Meier, Georg Friedrich
Melanchthon, Philipp
Menasseh (Manasseh) ben Israel
Mendelssohn, Moses
Mersenne, Marin
Meslier, Jean
Middleton, Conyers
Mill, James
Milton, John
Minagawa Kien
Miura Baien
Molina, Luis de
Montaigne, Michel Eyquem De
Montesquieu, Baron de
More, Henry
More, Thomas
Morgan, Thomas
Moritz, Karl Philipp
Mullā Ṣadrā
Muro Kyūsō
Naigeon, Jacques-André
Nakae Tōju
Newton, Isaac
Nicholas of Cusa
Nicolai, Christian Friedrich
Nicole, Pierre
Norris, John
Novalis
Ogyū Sorai
Oresme, Nicholas
Orobio de Castro, Isaac
Paine, Thomas
Paley, William
Palmer, Elihu
Paracelsus
Pascal, Blaise
Patrizi, Francesco
Pestalozzi, Johann Heinrich
Pico della Mirandola, Count Giovanni

Pico della Mirandola, Gianfrancesco
Ploucquet, Gottfried
Pomponazzi, Pietro
Pope, Alexander
Price, Richard
Priestley, Joseph
Pufendorf, Samuel von
Radishchev, Aleksandr Nikolaevich
Ramus, Peter
Régis, Pierre-Sylvain
Regius, Henricus (Henry de Roy)
Reid, Thomas
Reimarus, Hermann Samuel
Reinhold, Karl Leonhard
Robinet, Jean-Baptiste-René
Rohault, Jacques
Romagnosi, Gian Domenico
Rousseau, Jean-Jacques
Royer-Collard, Pierre Paul
Rüdiger, Andreas
Saint-Hyacinthe, Thémiseul de
Saint-Simon, Claude-Henri de Rouvroy, Comte de
Sanches, Francisco
Schiller, Friedrich
Schlegel, Friedrich von
Schulze, Gottlob Ernst
Scientia Media and Molinism
Servetus, Michael
Shaftesbury, Third Earl of (Anthony Ashley Cooper)
Shepherd, Mary
Simon, Richard
Skovoroda, Hryhorii Savych (Grigorii Savvich)
Smith, Adam
Smith, John
Socinianism
Solger, Karl Wilhelm Ferdinand
Soto, Dominic de
Spinoza, Benedict (Baruch) de
Staël-Holstein, Anne Louise Germanie Necker, Baronne de
Stahl, Georg Ernst
Stewart, Dugald
Stillingfleet, Edward
Suárez, Francisco
Sulzer, Johann Georg
Swedenborg, Emanuel
Swift, Jonathan
Sylvester of Ferrara, Francis
Telesio, Bernardino
Teresa of Avila, St.
Tetens, Johann Nicolaus
Thomasius, Christian
Thümmig, Ludwig Philipp
Tindal, Matthew
Toland, John
Toletus, Francis
Treschow, Niels
Tschirnhaus, Ehrenfried Walter von
Turgot, Anne Robert Jacques, Baron de L'Aulne
Valla, Lorenzo
Vanini, Giulio Cesare
Vasquez, Gabriel
Vauvenargues, Luc de Clapiers, Marquis de
Vico, Giambattista
Vitoria, Francisco de
Vives, Juan Luis
Volney, Constantin-François de Chasseboeuf, Comte de
Voltaire, François-Marie Arouet de
Wang Fuzhi
Wang Yang-ming
Whichcote, Benjamin
Winckelmann, Johann Joachim
Wolff, Christian
Wollaston, William
Wollstonecraft, Mary
Woolston, Thomas
Yamaga Sokō
Yamazaki Ansai
Zabarella, Jacopo

Nineteenth Century: Major Personal Entries

Avenarius, Richard
Boltzmann, Ludwig
Bosanquet, Bernard
Brentano, Franz
Buckle, Henry Thomas
Carlyle, Thomas
Clifford, William Kingdon
Cohen, Hermann
Coleridge, Samuel Taylor
Comte, Auguste
Dilthey, Wilhelm
Durkheim, Émile
Emerson, Ralph Waldo
Fechner, Gustav Theodor
Feuerbach, Ludwig Andreas
Fries, Jakob Friedrich
Green, Thomas Hill
Haeckel, Ernst Heinrich
Helmholtz, Hermann Ludwig von
Hertz, Heinrich Rudolf
Huxley, Thomas Henry
James, William
Johnson, Alexander Bryan
Kierkegaard, Søren Aabye
Lotze, Rudolf Hermann
Mach, Ernst
Mill, John Stuart
Newman, John Henry
Nietzsche, Friedrich
Peirce, Charles Sanders
Renouvier, Charles Bernard
Rosmini-Serbati, Antonio
Royce, Josiah
Schelling, Friedrich Wilhelm Joseph von
Schleiermacher, Friedrich Daniel Ernst
Schopenhauer, Arthur
Sidgwick, Henry
Simmel, Georg
Solov'ëv (Solovyov), Vladimir Sergeevich
Tolstoy, Lev (Leo) Nikolaevich

Nineteenth Century: Minor Personal Entries

Adler, Alfred
Ardigò, Roberto
Arnold, Matthew
Austin, John
Bachofen, Johann Jakob
Bain, Alexander
Bakunin, Mikhail Aleksandrovich
Bauer, Bruno
Belinskii, Vissarion Grigor'evich
Beneke, Friedrich Eduard
Bernard, Claude
Binet, Alfred
Bonatelli, Francesco
Boole, George
Boström, Christopher Jacob
Bowne, Borden Parker
Brownson, Orestes Augustus
Burckhardt, Jakob
Butler, Samuel
Caird, Edward
Calderoni, Mario
Carroll, Lewis
Carus, Carl Gustav
Carus, Paul
Caso, Antonio
Cattaneo, Carlo
Chaadaev, Pëtr Iakovlevich
Chamberlain, Houston Stewart
Channing, William Ellery
Chernyshevskii, Nikolai Gavrilovich
Chicherin, Boris Nikolaevich
Cournot, Antoine Augustin
Cousin, Victor
Darwin, Charles Robert
De Morgan, Augustus
De Sanctis, Francesco
Destutt de Tracy, Antoine Louis Claude, Comte

Deussen, Paul
Dühring, Eugen Karl
Eliot, George
Engels, Friedrich
Eucken, Rudolf Christoph
Faraday, Michael
Farias Brito, Raimundo de
Fëdorov, Nikolai Fëdorovich
Ferri, Luigi
Ferrier, James Frederick
Fischer, Kuno
Fiske, John
Fouillée, Alfred
Froebel, Friedrich
Gibbs, Josiah
Gioberti, Vincenzo
Gobineau, Comte Joseph Arthur de
Gray, Asa
Grote, John
Hamelin, Octave
Hamilton, William
Harris, William Torrey
Hartmann, Eduard von
Hebbel, Christian Friedrich
Herschel, John
Herzen, Aleksandr Ivanovich
Hess, Moses
Hickok, Laurens Perseus
Hobhouse, Leonard Trelawney
Hodgson, Shadworth Holloway
Høffding, Harald
Hölderlin, Johann Christian Friedrich
Howison, George Holmes
Hügel, Baron Friedrich von
James, Henry
Jevons, William Stanley
Jodl, Friedrich
Jouffroy, Théodore Simon
Kavelin, Konstantin Dmitrievich
Khomiakov, Aleksei Stepanovich
Kireevskii, Ivan Vasil'evich
Kozlov, Aleksei Aleksandrovich
Krause, Karl Christian Friedrich
Külpe, Oswald
Laas, Ernst
Labriola, Antonio
Lachelier, Jules
Lamennais, Hugues Félicité Robert de
Lange, Friedrich Albert
Lassalle, Ferdinand
Lavrov, Pëtr Lavrovich
Leont'ev, Konstantin Nikolaevich
Leopardi, Count Giacomo
Lequier, (Joseph Louis) Jules
Liebmann, Otto
Lipps, Theodor
Littré, Émile
Lopatin, Lev Mikhailovich
Malthus, Thomas Robert
Mansel, Henry Longueville
Marković, Svetozar
Martineau, James
Marty, Anton
Marx, Karl
McCosh, James
Mikhailovskii, Nikolai Konstantinovich
Moleschott, Jacob
Montgomery, Edmund Duncan
Morgan, Lewis Henry
Nishi Amane
Oken, Lorenz
Parker, Theodore
Pater, Walter Horatio
Paulsen, Friedrich
Petrović-Njegoš, Petar
Pisarev, Dmitri Ivanovich
Porter, Noah
Proudhon, Pierre-Joseph
Ravaisson-Mollien, Jean Gaspard Félix
Renan, Joseph Ernest
Ritschl, Albrecht Benjamin
Rosenkranz, Johann Karl Friedrich
Rozanov, Vasilii Vasil'evich
Ruskin, John
Sabatier, Auguste
Savigny, Friedrich Karl von
Schuppe, Ernst Julius Wilhelm
Shelley, Percy Bysshe
Sigwart, Christoph
Spaventa, Bertrando
Spir, Afrikan Alexandrovich
Steffens, Henrich
Stephen, Leslie
Stirner, Max
Strauss, David Friedrich
Sumner, William Graham
Taine, Hippolyte-Adolphe
Thoreau, Henry David
Trubetskoi, Sergei Nikolaevich
Vailati, Giovanni
Wallace, Alfred Russel
Wayland, Francis
Whately, Richard
Whewell, William
Wilde, Oscar Fingal O'Flahertie Wills
Wright, Chauncey

Early Twentieth Century: Personal Entries

Alexander, Samuel
Balfour, Arthur James
Banfi, Antonio
Benjamin, Walter
Benn, Gottfried
Berdyaev, Nikolai Aleksandrovich
Bergson, Henri
Blondel, Maurice
Bonhoeffer, Dietrich
Bradley, Francis Herbert
Brightman, Edgar Sheffield
Brunschvicg, Léon
Bulgakov, Sergei Nikolaevich
Bullough, Edward
Campbell, Norman Robert
Cantor, Georg
Cassirer, Ernst
Chwistek, Leon
Cohen, Morris Raphael
Collingwood, Robin George
Couturat, Louis
Creighton, James Edwin
Croce, Benedetto
Deustua, Alejandro O.
Dewey, John
Dingler, Hugo
Driesch, Hans Adolf Eduard
Duhem, Pierre Maurice Marie
Eddington, Arthur Stanley
Ehrenfels, Christian Freiherr Von
Einstein, Albert
Florenskii, Pavel Aleksandrovich
Frank, Erich
Frank, Semën Liudvigovich
Frege, Gottlob
Freud, Sigmund
Gentile, Giovanni
Geyser, Joseph
Gramsci, Antonio
Hägerström, Axel
Harnack, Carl Gustav Adolf von
Hartmann, Nicolai
Hatano Seiichi
Heim, Karl
Hilbert, David
Holt, Edwin Bissell
Hönigswald, Richard
Husserl, Edmund
Il'in, Ivan Aleksandrovich
Inge, William Ralph
Ingenieros, José
Ionescu, Nae
Iqbal, Muhammad
Ivanov, Viacheslav Ivanovich
Jeans, James Hopwood
Kafka, Franz
Kareev, Nikolai Ivanovich
Karsavin, Lev Platonovich
Kautsky, Karl
Keynes, John Maynard

Keyserling, Hermann Alexander, Graf von
Klages, Ludwig
Koffka, Kurt
Korn, Alejandro
Kropotkin, Pëtr Alekseevich
Krueger, Felix
Laberthonnière, Lucien
Lapshin, Ivan Ivanovich
Lavelle, Louis
Lenin, Vladimir Il'ich
Le Roy, Édouard
Le Senne, René
Leśniewski, Stanisław
Lévy-Bruhl, Lucien
Liebert, Arthur
Loisy, Alfred
Lunacharskii, Anatolii Vasil'evich
Maréchal, Joseph
Masaryk, Tomáš Garrigue
McDougall, William
McTaggart, John McTaggart Ellis
Mead, George Herbert
Meinecke, Friedrich
Meinong, Alexius
Mercier, Désiré Joseph
Meyerson, Émile
Miki Kiyoshi
Milhaud, Gaston
Montague, William Pepperell
Morgan, C. Lloyd
Mosca, Gaetano
Mounier, Emmanuel
Natorp, Paul
Nelson, Leonard
Neurath, Otto
Nishida, Kitarō
Oman, John Wood
Ortega y Gasset, José
Ostwald, Wilhelm
Otto, Rudolf
Palágyi, Menyhert
Papini, Giovanni
Pareto, Vilfredo
Pastore, Valentino Annibale
Pauler, Akos
Pavlov, Ivan Petrovich
Peano, Giuseppe
Pearson, Karl
Perry, Ralph Barton
Petronievic, Branislav
Petzoldt, Joseph
Pfänder, Alexander
Planck, Max
Plekhanov, Georgii Valentinovich
Poincaré, Jules Henri
Popper-Lynkeus, Josef
Pringle-Pattison, Andrew Seth
Proust, Marcel
Radbruch, Gustav
Rădulescu-Motru, Constantin
Ramsey, Frank Plumpton
Rashdall, Hastings
Rehmke, Johannes
Reich, Wilhelm
Reichenbach, Hans
Rensi, Giuseppe
Ribot, Théodule Armand
Rickert, Heinrich
Riehl, Alois
Rignano, Eugenio
Rilke, Rainer Maria (René)
Roretz, Karl
Rosenzweig, Franz
Santayana, George
Scheler, Max
Schiller, Ferdinand Canning Scott
Schlick, Moritz
Scholz, Heinrich
Schultz, Julius
Shestov, Lev Isaakovich
Shpet, Gustav Gustavovich
Smuts, Jan Christiaan
Sombart, Werner
Sorel, Georges
Spengler, Oswald
Stammler, Rudolf
Stebbing, Lizzie Susan
Stefanini, Luigi
Stein, Edith
Steiner, Rudolf
Stern, Louis William
Stöhr, Adolf
Stout, George Frederick
Stumpf, Karl
Sturzo, Luigi
Tagore, Rabindranath
Taylor, Alfred Edward
Teilhard de Chardin, Pierre
Tennant, Frederick Robert
Troeltsch, Ernst
Trubetskoi, Evgenii Nikolaevich
Trubetskoi, Nikolai Sergeevich
Turing, Alan M.
Twardowski, Kazimierz
Unamuno y Jugo, Miguel de
Vaihinger, Hans
Valéry, Paul
Varisco, Bernardino
Varona y Pera, Enrique José
Vasconcelos, José
Vaz Ferreira, Carlos
Veblen, Thorstein Bunde
Venn, John
Volski, Stanislav
Vysheslavtsev, Boris Petrovich
Wahle, Richard
Weber, Alfred
Weber, Max
Weil, Simone
Westermarck, Edward Alexander
Weyl, (Claus Hugo) Hermann
Whitehead, Alfred North
Windelband, Wilhelm
Wittgenstein, Ludwig Josef Johann
Woodbridge, Frederick James Eugene
Wundt, Wilhelm
Ziehen, Theodor

Recent Twentieth Century: Personal Entries

Abbagnano, Nicola
Adorno, Theodore Wiesengrund
Aliotta, Antonio
Al-Jabiri, ʿAbd
Alston, William P.
Anderson, John
Anscombe, Gertrude Elizabeth Margaret
Apel, Karl-Otto
Arendt, Hannah
Arkoun, Mohammed
Armstrong, David M.
Austin, John Langshaw
Ayer, Alfred Jules
Bachelard, Gaston
Baier, Annette
Baier, Kurt
Baker, Lynne Rudder
Bakhtin, Mikhail Mikhailovich
Barth, Karl
Barthes, Roland
Bataille, Georges
Baudrillard, Jean
Beardsley, Monroe
Beauvoir, Simone de
Bell, John, and Bell's Theorem
Bennett, Jonathan
Bergmann, Gustav
Berlin, Isaiah
Bertalanffy, Ludwig von
Binswanger, Ludwig
Black, Max
Blanchot, Maurice
Blanshard, Brand
Bloch, Ernst
Bohm, David
Bohr, Niels
Braithwaite, Richard Bevan
Brandt, R. B.
Bridgman, Percy William
Broad, Charlie Dunbar
Brouwer, Luitzen Egbertus Jan

Brunner, Emil
Buber, Martin
Bultmann, Rudolf
Cairns, Dorion
Camus, Albert
Card, Claudia
Carnap, Rudolf
Cartwright, Nancy
Cavell, Stanley
Chisholm, Roderick
Chomsky, Noam
Church, Alonzo
Cixous, Hélène
Code, Lorraine
Corbin, Henry
Danto, Arthur
Davidson, Donald
de Finetti, Bruno
Deleuze, Gilles
Del Vecchio, Giorgio
Dennett, Daniel Clement
Derrida, Jacques
Dretske, Fred
Ducasse, Curt John
Dummett, Michael Anthony Eardley
Dworkin, Ronald
Earman, John
Eliot, Thomas Stearns
Evans, Gareth
Feinberg, Joel
Ferguson, Ann
Field, Hartry
Fink, Eugen
Fisher, R. A.
Florovskii, Georgii Vasil'evich
Fodor, Jerry A.
Foot, Philippa
Foucault, Michel
Frankfurt, Harry
Frye, Marilyn
Gadamer, Hans-Georg
Garrigou-Lagrange, Réginald Marie
Gehlen, Arnold
Gewirth, Alan
Gilson, Étienne Henry
Gödel, Kurt
Gogarten, Friedrich
Goldman, Alvin
Goodman, Nelson
Grice, Herbert Paul
Gurwitsch, Aron
Habermas, Jürgen
Hampshire, Stuart Newton
Ḥanafī, Ḥassan
Harding, Sandra
Hare, Richard M.
Harman, Gilbert
Hart, Herbert Lionel Adolphus
Heidegger, Martin
Heisenberg, Werner
Held, Virginia
Hempel, Carl Gustav
Hintikka, Jaakko
Hocking, William Ernest
Horkheimer, Max
Hu Shi
Hyppolite, Jean
Ingarden, Roman
Irigaray, Luce
Jankélévitch, Vladimir
Jaspers, Karl
Jung, Carl Gustav
Jünger, Ernst
Kaplan, David
Kaufmann, Walter Arnold
Kelsen, Hans
Kim, Jaegwon
King, Martin Luther
Kitcher, Patricia
Köhler, Wolfgang
Kotarbiński, Tadeusz
Kripke, Saul
Kristeva, Julia
Kuhn, Thomas
Lacan, Jacques
Lakatos, Imre
Landgrebe, Ludwig
Langer, Susanne K.
Laroui, Abdullah
Lehrer, Keith
Levinas, Emmanuel
Lewis, C. S. (Clive Staples)
Lewis, Clarence Irving
Lewis, David
Lloyd, Genevieve
Losev, Aleksei Fëdorovich
Losskii, Nikolai Onufrievich
Lotman, Iurii Mikhailovich
Lovejoy, Arthur Oncken
Lukács, Georg
Łukasiewicz, Jan
Lyotard, Jean-François
MacIntyre, Alasdair
Mackie, John Leslie
Malcolm, Norman
Malraux, Georges-André
Mamardashvili, Merab Konstantinovich
Mannheim, Karl
Marcel, Gabriel
Marcus, Ruth Barcan
Marías, Julián
Maritain, Jacques
Martinetti, Piero
McDowell, John
McGilvary, Evander Bradley
Merleau-Ponty, Maurice
Miller, Dickinson S.
Millikan, Ruth
Molina Garmendia, Enrique
Montague, Richard
Moore, George Edward
Murdoch, Iris
Murphy, Arthur Edward
Nagel, Ernest
Nagel, Thomas
Nasr, Seyyed Hossein
Neumann, John von
Niebuhr, Reinhold
Nozick, Robert
Nussbaum, Martha
Oakeshott, Michael
Owen, G. E. L.
Pannenberg, Wolfhart
Parfit, Derek
Pauling, Linus
Piaget, Jean
Plantinga, Alvin
Plessner, Helmut
Popper, Karl Raimund
Posner, Richard
Prior, Arthur Norman
Putnam, Hilary
Quine, Willard Van Orman
Rahner, Karl
Rawls, John
Reale, Miguel
Rescher, Nicholas
Ricoeur, Paul
Rintelen, Fritz-Joachim von
Romero, Francisco
Rorty, Richard
Ross, William David
Rougier, Louis
Russell, Bertrand Arthur William
Ryle, Gilbert
Salmon, Wesley
Sartre, Jean-Paul
Savage, Leonard
Schrödinger, Erwin
Schutz, Alfred
Sciacca, Michele Federico
Searle, John
Sellars, Roy Wood
Sellars, Wilfrid
Sen, Amartya K.
Shariati, Ali
Shoemaker, Sydney
Sibley, Frank
Singer, Peter
Skinner, B. F.
Smart, John Jamieson Carswell
Sosa, Ernest
Spirito, Ugo

Spranger, (Franz Ernst) Eduard
Stace, Walter Terence
Stevenson, Charles L.
Strawson, Peter Frederick
Suppes, Patrick
Tarski, Alfred
Thomson, Judith Jarvis
Tillich, Paul
Toynbee, Arnold Joseph
Van Fraassen, Bas
Vlastos, Gregory
Watsuji Tetsurō
Wiggins, David
Williams, Bernard
Wilson, Edward O.
Wisdom, (Arthur) John Terence Dibben
Wollheim, Richard
Woodger, Joseph Henry
Wright, Georg Henrik von
Zen'kovskii, Vasilii Vasil'evich
Zubiri, Xavier

SUBFIELDS OF PHILOSOPHY

Epistemology

Ancient Skepticism
Apperception
A Priori and A Posteriori
Bachelard, Gaston
Basic Statements
Belief
Belief Attributions
Causal or Conditional or Explanatory-Relation Accounts
Chinese Philosophy: Metaphysics and Epistemology
Classical Foundationalism
Coherence Theory of Truth
Coherentism
Common Sense
Contextualism
Correspondence Theory of Truth
Criteriology
Critical Realism
Doubt
Epistemology
Epistemology, Circularity in
Epistemology, History of
Epistemology, Religious
Epistemology and Ethics, Parallel Between
Error
Evidentialism
Experience
Feminist Epistemology
Idealism
Ideas
Illusions
Imagination
Induction
Inference to the Best Explanation
Innate Ideas
Internalism versus Externalism
Introspection
Intuition
Irrationalism
Knowledge, A Priori
Knowledge, The Priority of
Knowledge and Belief
Knowledge and Modality
Knowledge and Truth, The Value of
Knowledge and Vagueness
Knowledge in Indian Philosophy
Moral Epistemology
Naturalized Epistemology
Other Minds
Paradigm-Case Argument
Perception
Perception, Contemporary Views
Performative Theory of Truth
Phenomenalism
Pragmatist Epistemology
Precognition
Presupposing
Primary and Secondary Qualities
Propositional Knowledge, Definition of
Pyrrhonian Problematic, The
Rationalism
Rationality
Realism
Reason
Relevant Alternatives
Reliabilism
Self-Knowledge
Self-Prediction
Sensationalism
Skepticism, Contemporary
Social Epistemology
Sociology of Knowledge
Sound
Subjectivist Epistemology
Testimony
Thinking
Time, Consciousness of
Touch
Verifiability Principle
Virtue Epistemology

Philosophy of Mind, Cognitive Science

Action
Agent Causation
Animal Mind
Anomalous Monism
Artificial Intelligence
Behaviorism
Belief
Causal Closure of the Physical Domain
Chinese Room Argument
Cognitive Science
Computationalism
Concepts
Connectionism
Consciousness
Content, Mental
Dreams
Dualism in the Philosophy of Mind
Eliminative Materialism, Eliminativism
Emotion
Existential Psychoanalysis
Folk Psychology
Frame Problem
Functionalism
Gestalt Theory
Imagery, Mental
Images
Innate Ideas
Innate Ideas, Nativism
Intention
Intentionality
Knowledge Argument
Language of Thought
Machine Intelligence
Memory
Mental Causation
Mental-Physical Distinction
Mental Representation
Mind and Mental States in Buddhist Philosophy
Mind-Body Problem
Multiple Realizability
Neuroscience
Nonreductive Physicalism
Pain
Parapsychology
Philosophy of Mind
Physicalism
Propositional Attitudes: Issues in the Philosophy of Mind and Psychology
Psychoanalysis
Psychology
Qualia
Reductionism in the Philosophy of Mind
Self
Self-Deception
Self in Indian Philosophy
Simulation Theory

Subjectivity
Supervenience
Thinking
Volition
Weakness of the Will

Metaphysics

Absolute, The
Appearance and Reality
Being
Can
Categories
Causal Approaches to the Direction of Time
Causation: Metaphysical Issues
Chance
Chinese Philosophy: Metaphysics and Epistemology
Colors
Constructivism and Conventionalism
Cosmology
Counterfactuals
Determinables and Determinates
Determinism, A Historical Survey
Determinism and Freedom
Determinism in History
Dialectic
Dialectical Materialism
Emanationism
Energy
Essence and Existence
Eternal Return
Event Theory
Existence
Extrinsic and Intrinsic Properties
Feminist Metaphysics
Fictionalism
Force
Idealism
Identity
Induction
Laws, Scientific
Laws of Nature
Macrocosm and Microcosm
Materialism
Mereology
Metaphysics
Metaphysics, History of
Metaphysics, Nature of
Modality, Philosophy and Metaphysics of
Monad and Monadology
Monism and Pluralism
Naturalism
Nature, Philosophical Ideas of
Nonexistent Object, Nonbeing
Nothing
Number
Ontology
Ontology, History of
Panpsychism
Pantheism
Persistence
Personal Identity
Personalism
Persons
Pessimism and Optimism
Possibility
Progress, The Idea of
Properties
Realism
Relations, Internal and External
Solipsism
Substance and Attribute
Teleology
Time
Time, Being, and Becoming
Unconscious
Universals, A Historical Survey
Vitalism
Voluntarism
Why

Philosophy of Science

Alembert, Jean Le Rond d'
Ampère, André Marie
Anthropic Principle, The
Bachelard, Gaston
Bacon, Francis
Bacon, Roger
Bayes, Bayes' Theorem, Bayesian Approach to Philosophy of Science
Bell, John, and Bell's Theorem
Bertalanffy, Ludwig von
Black Holes
Bohm, David
Bohmian Mechanics
Bohr, Niels
Boltzmann, Ludwig
Boscovich, Roger Joseph
Boyle, Robert
Bridgman, Percy William
Campbell, Norman Robert
Causation: Philosophy of Science
Chaos Theory
Chemistry, Philosophy of
Classical Mechanics, Philosophy of
Common Cause Principle
Confirmation Theory
Conservation Principle
Conventionalism
Copenhagen Interpretation
Copernicus, Nicolas
Counterfactuals in Science
Darwin, Charles Robert
Darwin, Erasmus
Decision Theory
de Finetti, Bruno
Determinism and Indeterminism
Dingler, Hugo
Duhem, Pierre Maurice Marie
Eddington, Arthur Stanley
Einstein, Albert
Emergence
Energy
Evolutionary Theory
Experimentation and Instrumentation
Explanation
Faraday, Michael
Feminist Philosophy of Science
Feminist Philosophy of Science: Contemporary Perspectives
Fields and Particles
Fisher, R. A.
Functionalism in Sociology
Galileo Galilei
Game Theory
Gauge Theory
Geometry
Gibbs, Josiah
Gray, Asa
Harvey, William
Heisenberg, Werner
Helmholtz, Hermann Ludwig von
Herschel, John
Hertz, Heinrich Rudolf
Hole Argument
Holism and Individualism in History and Social Science
Human Genome Project
Information Theory
Jeans, James Hopwood
Kepler, Johannes
Kuhn, Thomas
Lakatos, Imre
Lamarck, Chevalier de
Laplace, Pierre Simon de
Lavoisier, Antoine
Laws, Scientific
Life, Origin of
Logical Positivism
Mach, Ernst
Many Worlds/Many Minds Interpretation of Quantum Mechanics
Mass
Matter
Maxwell, James Clerk
Measurement and Measurement Theory
Modal Interpretation of Quantum Mechanics

Morgan, C. Lloyd
Motion
Motion, A Historical Survey
Naturalized Philosophy of Science
Natural Kinds
Neumann, John von
Newton, Isaac
Non-locality
Operationalism
Organismic Biology
Pauling, Linus
Pearson, Karl
Philosophy of Biology
Philosophy of Economics
Philosophy of Physics
Philosophy of Science, History of
Philosophy of Social Sciences
Philosophy of Statistical Mechanics
Physics and the Direction of Time
Planck, Max
Poincaré, Jules Henri
Popper, Karl Raimund
Priestley, Joseph
Probability and Chance
Psychoanalytic Theories, Logical Status of
Quantum Computing and Teleportation
Quantum Logic and Probability
Quantum Mechanics
Reduction
Reichenbach, Hans
Relativity Theory
Religion, Psychological Explanations of
Religion and the Biological Sciences
Religion and the Physical Sciences
Schrödinger, Erwin
Science, Research Ethics of
Science and Pseudoscience
Science Policy
Science Studies
Scientific Method
Scientific Realism
Scientific Revolutions
Space
Space in Physical Theories
Special Sciences
Statistics, Foundations of
String Theory
Theories and Theoretical Terms
Thought Experiments in Science
Time in Physics
Truthlikeness
Underdetermination Thesis, Duhem-Quine Thesis
Unity and Disunity of Science
Wallace, Alfred Russel
Weyl, (Claus Hugo) Hermann
Whewell, William
Wilson, Edward O.
Woodger, Joseph Henry

Logic, Philosophy of Logic, Philosophy of Mathematics

Analysis, Philosophical
Bolzano, Bernard
Boole, George
Brouwer, Luitzen Egbertus Jan
Cantor, Georg
Carroll, Lewis
Chinese Philosophy: Language and Logic
Church, Alonzo
Combinatory Logic
Computability Theory
Computing Machines
Conditionals
Continuity
Couturat, Louis
Craig's Theorem
De Morgan, Augustus
Entailment, Presupposition, and Implicature
Fallacies
First-Order Logic
Frege, Gottlob
Fuzzy Logic
Geometry
Gödel, Kurt
Gödel's Incompleteness Theorems
Hilbert, David
Induction
Infinitesimals
Infinity in Mathematics and Logic
Intuitionism and Intuitionistic Logic
Jevons, William Stanley
Kotarbiński, Tadeusz
Leśniewski, Stanisław
Liar Paradox, The
Logic, History of [overview]
Logic, History of: Ancient Logic
Logic, History of: Logic and Inference in Indian Philosophy
Logic, History of: Chinese Logic
Logic, History of: Logic in the Islamic World
Logic, History of: Logic in the Islamic World [addendum]
Logic, History of: Medieval (European) Logic
Logic, History of: The Interregnum (between Medieval and Modern)
Logic, History of: Precursors of Modern Logic [overview]
Logic, History of: Precursors of Modern Logic: Leibniz
Logic, History of: Precursors of Modern Logic: Euler
Logic, History of: Precursors of Modern Logic: Lambert and Ploucquet
Logic, History of: Precursors of Modern Logic: Bolzano
Logic, History of: Modern Logic: The Boolean Period [overview]
Logic, History of: Modern Logic: The Boolean Period: Hamilton
Logic, History of: Modern Logic: The Boolean Period: De Morgan
Logic, History of: Modern Logic: The Boolean Period: Boole
Logic, History of: Modern Logic: The Boolean Period: Jevons
Logic, History of: Modern Logic: The Boolean Period: Venn
Logic, History of: Modern Logic: The Boolean Period: Carroll
Logic, History of: Modern Logic: The Boolean Period: Peirce
Logic, History of: Modern Logic: The Boolean Period: The Heritage of Kant and Mill
Logic, History of: Modern Logic: The Boolean Period: Keynes
Logic, History of: Modern Logic: The Boolean Period: Johnson
Logic, History of: Modern Logic: From Frege to Gödel [overview]
Logic, History of: Modern Logic: From Frege to Gödel: Nineteenth-Century Mathematics
Logic, History of: Modern Logic: From Frege to Gödel: Frege
Logic, History of: Modern Logic: From Frege to Gödel: Peano
Logic, History of: Modern Logic: From Frege to Gödel: Whitehead and Russell
Logic, History of: Modern Logic: From Frege to Gödel: Post
Logic, History of: Modern Logic: From Frege to Gödel: Ramsey
Logic, History of: Modern Logic: From Frege to Gödel: Brouwer and Intuitionism
Logic, History of: Modern Logic: From Frege to Gödel: Hilbert and Formalism
Logic, History of: Modern Logic: From Frege to Gödel: Löwenheim
Logic, History of: Modern Logic: From Frege to Gödel: Skolem

Logic, History of: Modern Logic: From Frege to Gödel: Herbrand
Logic, History of: Modern Logic: From Frege to Gödel: Gödel
Logic, History of: Modern Logic: Since Gödel [overview]
Logic, History of: Modern Logic: Since Gödel: Gentzen
Logic, History of: Modern Logic: Since Gödel: Church
Logic, History of: Modern Logic: Since Gödel: Turing and Computability Theory
Logic, History of: Modern Logic: Since Gödel: Decidable and Undecidable Theories
Logic, History of: Modern Logic: Since Gödel: Model Theory: Tarski
Logic, History of: Modern Logic: Since Gödel: Model Theory: Robinson
Logic, History of: Modern Logic: Since Gödel: The Proliferation of Nonclassical Logics
Logic, History of: Modern Logic: Since Gödel: Friedman and Reverse Mathematics
Logic, Non-Classical
Logic, Traditional
Logical Knowledge
Logical Paradoxes
Logical Terms
Logical Terms, Glossary of
Logic Diagrams
Logic Machines
Łukasiewicz, Jan
Many-Valued Logics
Mathematics, Foundations of
Mill's Methods of Induction
Modality and Quantification
Modal Logic
Model Theory
Negation
Neumann, John von
Nominalism, Modern
Non-Monotonic Logic
Number
Paraconsistent Logics
Peano, Giuseppe
Probability and Chance
Proof Theory
Provability Logic
Quantifiers in Formal Logic
Ramsey, Frank Plumpton
Realism and Naturalism, Mathematical
Relevance (Relevant) Logics
Reverse Mathematics
Second-Order Logic
Set Theory
Structuralism, Mathematical
Tarski, Alfred
Type Theory
Venn, John
Whately, Richard

Philosophy of Language

Analysis, Philosophical
Analytic and Synthetic Statements
Analyticity
Anaphora
Artificial and Natural Languages
Chinese Philosophy: Language and Logic
Compositionality
Conversational Implicature
Definition
Demonstratives
Events in Semantic Theory
Generics
Indexicals
Intensional Transitive Verbs
Language
Language and Thought
Liar Paradox, The
Logical Form
Meaning
Metaphor
Modality and Language
Non-Truth-Conditional Meaning
Nouns, Mass and Count
Performative Theory of Truth
Performative Utterances
Philosophy of Language
Philosophy of Language in Continental Philosophy
Philosophy of Language in India
Phonology
Plurals
Pragmatics
Presupposition
Private Language Problem
Proper Names and Descriptions
Propositional Attitudes: Issues in Semantics
Propositions
Quantifiers in Natural Language
Questions
Reference
Religious Language
Rule Following
Semantics
Semantics, History of
Sense
Subject and Predicate
Synonymity
Syntactical and Semantical Categories
Syntax
Tense
Truth
Vagueness

Continental Philosophy

Abbagnano, Nicola
Alienation
Alterity
Apel, Karl-Otto
Bad Faith
Barthes, Roland
Bataille, Georges
Baudrillard, Jean
Beauvoir, Simone de
Binswanger, Ludwig
Blanchot, Maurice
Brunschvicg, Léon
Cairns, Dorion
Camus, Albert
Cassirer, Ernst
Cixous, Hélène
Consciousness in Phenomenology
Continental Philosophy
Critical Theory
Deconstruction
Deleuze, Gilles
Discourse Ethics
Existentialism
Existential Psychoanalysis
Feminism and Continental Philosophy
Fink, Eugen
Gadamer, Hans-Georg
Gurwitsch, Aron
Habermas, Jürgen
Heidegger, Martin
Hermeneutics
Horkheimer, Max
Husserl, Edmund
Hyppolite, Jean
Ingarden, Roman
Jaspers, Karl
Kierkegaard, Søren Aabye
Lacan, Jacques
Landgrebe, Ludwig
Lavelle, Louis
Levinas, Emmanuel
Lyotard, Jean François
Marcel, Gabriel
Merleau-Ponty, Maurice
Modernism and Postmodernism
Pfänder, Alexander
Phenomenological Psychology
Phenomenology

Philosophical Anthropology
Philosophy of Language in Continental Philosophy
Postmodernism
Sartre, Jean-Paul
Scheler, Max
Schutz, Alfred
Stein, Edith
Structuralism and Post-structuralism
Time in Continental Philosophy

Feminist Philosophy

Analytic Feminism
Astell, Mary
Beauvoir, Simone de
Card, Claudia
Code, Lorraine
Feminism and Continental Philosophy
Feminism and Pragmatism
Feminism and the History of Philosophy
Feminist Aesthetics and Criticism
Feminist Epistemology
Feminist Ethics
Feminist Legal Theory
Feminist Metaphysics
Feminist Philosophy
Feminist Philosophy of Science
Feminist Philosophy of Science: Contemporary Perspectives
Feminist Social and Political Philosophy
Ferguson, Ann
Frye, Marilyn
Irigaray, Luce
Kristeva, Julia
Lloyd, Genevieve
Sexism
Wollstonecraft, Mary
Women in the History of Philosophy

Ethics

Altruism
Asceticism
Categorical Imperative
Chinese Philosophy: Ethics
Conscience
Consequentialism
Constructivism, Moral
Contractualism
Deontological Ethics
Discourse Ethics
Divine Command Theories of Ethics
Duty
Egoism and Altruism
Emotive Theory of Ethics
Environmental Ethics
Epistemology and Ethics, Parallel Between
Equality, Moral and Social
Error Theory of Ethics
Ethical Egoism
Ethical Naturalism
Ethical Relativism
Ethical Subjectivism
Ethics
Ethics, History of
Ethics, History of: Other Developments in Twentieth-Century Ethics
Ethics and Economics
Ethics and Morality
Evil
Evolutionary Ethics
Feminist Ethics
Forgiveness
Friendship
Golden Rule
Good, The
Guilt
Happiness
Hedonism
Human Nature
Ideal Observer Theories of Ethics
Internalism and Externalism in Ethics
Intrinsic Value
Intuitionism, Ethical
Justice
Kantian Ethics
Love
Loyalty
Lying
Metaethics
Moral Dilemmas
Moral Epistemology
Moral Principles: Their Justification
Moral Psychology
Moral Realism
Moral Rules and Principles
Moral Sense
Moral Sentiments
Moral Skepticism
Noncognitivism
Objectivity in Ethics
Pain, Ethical Significance of
Pleasure
Practical Reason
Projectivism
Promises
Punishment
Racism
Rationalism in Ethics (Practical-Reason Approaches)
Religion and Morality
Respect
Response-Dependence Theories
Responsibility, Moral and Legal
Rights
Science, Research Ethics of
Self-Interest
Shame
Suicide
Sympathy and Empathy
Teleological Ethics
Toleration
Utilitarianism
Value and Valuation
Violence
Virtue and Vice
Virtue Ethics
Wisdom

Applied Ethics

Abortion
Animal Rights and Welfare
Applied Ethics
Bioethics
Business Ethics
Computer Ethics
Engineering Ethics
Euthanasia
Genetics and Reproductive Technologies
Impartiality
Informed Consent
Informed Consent in the Practice of Law
Medical Ethics
Paternalism
Patriotism

Social and Political Philosophy

Affirmative Action
Analytic Jurisprudence
Anarchism
Authority
Censorship
Chinese Philosophy: Social and Political Thought
Civil Disobedience
Communism
Communitarianism
Conservatism
Cosmopolitanism
Critical Theory
Democracy
Dialectical Materialism
Distant Peoples and Future Generations
Fascism

Feminist Social and Political Philosophy
Freedom
General Will, The
Heterosexism
Historical Materialism
Ideology
Just War Theory
Justice
Lenin, Vladimir Il'ich
Liberalism
Libertarianism
Liberty
Marxist Philosophy
Nationalism
Natural Law
Pacifism
Patriotism
Peace, War, and Philosophy
Pluralism
Political Philosophy, History of
Postcolonialism
Power
Property
Punishment
Racism
Reflective Equilibrium
Religion and Politics
Republicanism
Rights
Social and Political Philosophy
Social Contract
Socialism
Society
Sovereignty
State
Terrorism
Toleration
Traditionalism
Utopias and Utopianism
Violence

Philosophy of Law

Feminist Legal Theory
Historical School of Jurisprudence
Informed Consent in the Practice of Law
Legal Positivism
Legal Positivism: Anglo-American Legal Positiivism Since H.L.A. Hart
Legal Realism
Philosophy of Law, History of
Philosophy of Law, Problems of
Responsibility, Moral and Legal

Aesthetics and Philosophy of Art

Addison, Joseph
Adorno, Theodore Wiesengrund
Aesthetic Experience
Aesthetic Judgment
Aesthetic Qualities
Aesthetics, History of
Aesthetics, Problems of
Alison, Archibald
Ancient Aesthetics
Arnold, Matthew
Art, Authenticity in
Art, Definitions of
Art, Expression in
Art, Formalism in
Art, Interpretation of
Art, Ontology of
Art, Performance in
Art, Representation in
Art, Style and Genre in
Art, Truth in
Art, Value in
Batteux, Abbé Charles
Baumgarten, Alexander Gottlieb
Beardsley, Monroe C.
Beauty
Benjamin, Walter
Benn, Gottfried
Blake, William
Boileau, Nicolas
Bullough, Edward
Butler, Samuel
Carlyle, Thomas
Coleridge, Samuel Taylor
Creativity
Cyrano de Bergerac, Savinien de
Dante Alighieri
Danto, Arthur
Deconstruction
Eliot, George
Eliot, Thomas Stearns
Environmental Aesthetics
Feminist Aesthetics and Criticism
Gerard, Alexander
Goethe, Johann Wolfgang von
Gottsched, Johann Christoph
Hazlitt, William
Hebbel, Christian Friedrich
Hölderlin, Johann Christian Friedrich
Humor
Imagination
Jünger, Ernst
Kafka, Franz
Kleist, Heinrich von
Literature, Philosophy of
Longinus (Pseudo)
Malraux, Georges-André
Milton, John
Moritz, Karl Philipp
Music, Philosophy of
Philosophy of Film
Pope, Alexander
Proust, Marcel
Rilke, Rainer Maria (René)
Ruskin, John
Shelley, Percy Bysshe
Sibley, Frank
Structuralism and Post-structuralism
Sublime, The
Tragedy
Ugliness
Valéry, Paul
Visual Arts, Theory of the
Wilde, Oscar Fingal O'Flahertie Wills

Philosophy of Religion

Agnosticism
Analogy in Theology
Atheism
Bahrdt, Carl Friedrich
Barth, Karl
Bauer, Bruno
Berdyaev, Nikolai Aleksandrovich
Blondel, Maurice
Boehme, Jakob
Bonhoeffer, Dietrich
Brunner, Emil
Buber, Martin
Bultmann, Rudolf
Calvin, John
Chinese Philosophy: Religion
Christianity
Common Consent Arguments for the Existence of God
Cosmological Argument for the Existence of God
Costa, Uriel da
Creation and Conservation, Religious Doctrine of
Death
Degrees of Perfection, Argument for the Existence of God
Deism
Determinism, Theological
Divine Command Theories of Ethics
Edwards, Jonathan
Epistemology, Religious
Eschatology
Eternity
Evil, The Problem of
Faith
Fideism
Foreknowledge and Freedom, Theological Problem of
Franck, Sebastian
God, Concepts of

Gogarten, Friedrich
Harnack, Carl Gustav Adolf von
Heaven and Hell, Doctrines of
Heim, Karl
Hiddenness of God
Hocking, William Ernest
Hügel, Baron Friedrich von
Hus, John
Illumination
Immortality
Infinity in Theology and Metaphysics
Kierkegaard, Søren Aabye
Liberation Theology
Life, Meaning and Value of
Loisy, Alfred
Luther, Martin
Melanchthon, Philipp
Miracles
Modernism
Moral Arguments for the Existence of God
Mysticism, History of
Mysticism, Nature and Assessment of
Myth
Newman, John Henry
Niebuhr, Reinhold
Nihilism
Oman, John Wood
Ontological Argument for the Existence of God
Otto, Rudolf
Pannenberg, Wolfhart
Perfection
Philosophy of Religion
Philosophy of Religion, History of
Philosophy of Religion, Problems of
Physicotheology
Popular Arguments for the Existence of God
Providence
Reincarnation
Religion
Religion, Naturalistic Reconstructions of
Religion, Psychological Explanations of
Religion and Morality
Religion and Politics
Religion and the Biological Sciences
Religion and the Physical Sciences
Religious Experience
Religious Experience, Argument for the Existence of God
Religious Language
Religious Pluralism
Revelation
Sabatier, Auguste
Schleiermacher, Friedrich Daniel Ernst
Teleological Argument for the Existence of God
Theism, Arguments For and Against
Zoroastrianism

Buddhist Philosophy

Buddhism
Buddhism—Schools: Chan and Zen
Buddhism—Schools: Dge-lugs
Buddhism—Schools: Hua yan
Buddhism—Schools: Madhyamaka
Buddhism—Schools: Yogacārā
Buddhist Epistemology
Chinese Philosophy: Buddhism
Dōgen
Jinul
Mind and Mental States in Buddhist Philosophy
Nāgārjuna
Nirvāṇa
Shinran
Vasubandhu

Chinese Philosophy

Andō Shōeki
Cheng Hao
Cheng Yi
Chinese Philosophy [overview]
Chinese Philosophy: Buddhism
Chinese Philosophy: Confucianism
Chinese Philosophy: Contemporary
Chinese Philosophy: Daoism
Chinese Philosophy: Ethics
Chinese Philosophy: Language and Logic
Chinese Philosophy: Metaphysics and Epistemology
Chinese Philosophy: Religion
Chinese Philosophy: Social and Political Thought
Confucius
Dai Zhen
Dong Zhongshu
Gongsun Long
Guo Xiang
Han Fei
Han Yu
Hayashi Razan
Huang Zongxi
Hui Shi
Hu Shi
Itō Jinsai
Kaibara Ekken
Kumazawa Banzan
Laozi
Li Ao
Lu Xiangshan
Mencius
Minagawa Kien
Miura Baien
Mozi
Muro Kyūsō
Nakae Tōju
Ogyū Sorai
Shao Yong
Wang Bi
Wang Chong
Wang Fuzhi
Wang Yang-ming
Xunzi
Yamaga Sokō
Yamazaki Ansai
Yang Xiong
Yang Zhu
Zhang Zai
Zhou Dunyi
Zhuangzi
Zhu Xi (Chu Hsi)

Indian Philosophy

Atomic Theory in Indian Philosophy
Brahman
Causation in Indian Philosophy
God/Isvara in Indian Philosophy
Indian Philosophy
Karma
Knowledge in Indian Philosophy
Liberation in Indian Philosophy
Meditation in Indian Philosophy
Negation in Indian Philosophy
Philosophy of Language in India
Reincarnation
Self in Indian Philosophy
Truth and Falsity in Indian Philosophy
Universal Properties in Indian Philosophical Traditions

Islamic Philosophy

al-Farābī
al-Ghazālī, Ahmad
al-Ghazālī, Muhammad
al-Jabiri, ʿAbd
al-Kindī, Abū-Yūsuf Yaʿqūb ibn Isḥāq
Arkoun, Mohammed
Averroes
Avicenna
Causation in Islamic Philosophy
Corbin, Henry
Dialectic in Islamic and Jewish Philosophy

Enlightenment, Islamic
Ḥanafī, Ḥassan
Ibn al-ʿArabī
Ibn Bājja
Ibn Khaldūn
Ibn Ṭufayl
Ikhwān al-Ṣafāʾ
Illuminationism
Iqbal, Muhammad
Islamic Philosophy
Mullā Ṣadrā
Naṣīr al-Dīn al-Ṭūsī
Nasr, Seyyed Hossein
School of Qom, The
Shariati, Ali
Sufism
Suhrawardī, Shihāb al-Dīn Yaḥyā

Japanese Philosophy

Hayashi Razan
Itō Jinsai
Japanese Philosophy
Kaibara Ekken
Kumazawa Banzan
Miki Kiyoshi
Minagawa Kien
Miura Baien
Muro Kyūsō
Nakae Tōju
Nishi Amane
Nishida, Kitarō
Ogyū Sorai
Yamaga Sokō
Yamazaki Ansai

Jewish Philosophy

Albo, Joseph
Baḥyā, ben Joseph ibn Paqūda
Cordovero, Moses ben Jacob
Costa, Uriel da
Crescas, Hasdai
Dialectic in Islamic and Jewish Philosophy
Enlightenment, Jewish
Gersonides
Halevi, Yehuda
Holocaust
Ibn Gabirol, Solomon ben Judah
Ibn Zaddik, Joseph ben Jacob
Israeli, Isaac ben Solomon
Jewish Averroism
Jewish Philosophy
Kabbalah
Maimonides
Menasseh (Manasseh) ben Israel
Mendelssohn, Moses
Muqammiṣ, David ben Merwan al-
Philo Judaeus
Rosenzweig, Franz
Saadya

Russian Philosophy

Bakhtin, Mikhail Mikhailovich
Bakhtin Circle, The
Bakunin, Mikhail Aleksandrovich
Belinskii, Vissarion Grigor'evich
Berdyaev, Nikolai Aleksandrovich
Bulgakov, Sergei Nikolaevich
Chaadaev, Pëtr Iakovlevich
Chernyshevskii, Nikolai Gavrilovich
Chicherin, Boris Nikolaevich
Dostoevsky, Fyodor Mikhailovich
Eurasianism
Fëdorov, Nikolai Fëdorovich
Florenskii, Pavel Aleksandrovich
Florovskii, Georgii Vasil'evich
Frank, Semën Liudvigovich
Herzen, Aleksandr Ivanovich
Il'in, Ivan Aleksandrovich
Ivanov, Viacheslav Ivanovich
Kareev, Nikolai Ivanovich
Karsavin, Lev Platonovich
Kavelin, Konstantin Dmitrievich
Khomiakov, Aleksei Stepanovich
Kireevskii, Ivan Vasil'evich
Kozlov, Aleksei Aleksandrovich
Kropotkin, Pëtr Alekseevich
Lapshin, Ivan Ivanovich
Lavrov, Pëtr Lavrovich
Lenin, Vladimir Il'ich
Leont'ev, Konstantin Nikolaevich
Lopatin, Lev Mikhailovich
Losev, Aleksei Fëdorovich
Losskii, Nikolai Onufrievich
Lotman, Iurii Mikhailovich
Lunacharskii, Anatolii Vasil'evich
Mamardashvili, Merab Konstantinovich
Mikhailovskii, Nikolai Konstantinovich
Pavlov, Ivan Petrovich
Pisarev, Dmitri Ivanovich
Plekhanov, Georgii Valentinovich
Radishchev, Aleksandr Nikolaevich
Rozanov, Vasilii Vasil'evich
Russian Philosophy
Shestov, Lev Isaakovich
Shpet, Gustav Gustavovich
Skovoroda, Hryhorii Savych (Grigorii Savvich)
Solov'ëv (Solovyov), Vladimir Sergeevich
Spir, Afrikan Alexandrovich
Tolstoy, Lev (Leo) Nikolaevich
Trubetskoi, Evgenii Nikolaevich
Trubetskoi, Nikolai Sergeevich
Trubetskoi, Sergei Nikolaevich
Volski, Stanislav
Vysheslavtsev, Boris Petrovich
Zen'kovskii, Vasilii Vasil'evich

Philosophical Perspectives and Movements

Augustinianism
Averroism
Averroism in Modern Islamic Philosophy
Buddhism—Schools: Chan and Zen
Buddhism—Schools: Dge-lugs
Buddhism—Schools: Hua yan
Buddhism—Schools: Madhyamaka
Buddhism—Schools: Yogacārā
Byzantine Philosophy
Cambridge Platonists
Carolingian Renaissance
Cartesianism
Chartres, School of
Clandestine Philosophical Literature in France
Cynics
Cyrenaics
Darwinism
Empiricism
Encyclopédie
Enlightenment
Enlightenment, Islamic
Enlightenment, Jewish
Epicureanism and the Epicurean School
Florentine Academy
Geisteswissenschaften
Gnosticism
Greek Academy
Hegelianism
Hellenistic Thought
Hermeticism
Historical School of Jurisprudence
Historicism
Humanism
Jansenism
Logical Positivism
Mani and Manichaeism
Modernism
Modernism and Postmodernism
Multiculturalism
Mysticism, History of
Neo-Kantianism
Neoplatonism
New England Transcendentalism
New Realism
Nihilism

Ockhamism
Orphism
Panpsychism
Pantheism
Pantheismusstreit
Patristic Philosophy
Pelagius and Pelagianism
Peripatetics
Personalism
Pessimism and Optimism
Phenomenalism
Phenomenology
Physicotheology
Pietism
Platonism and the Platonic Tradition
Positivism
Postcolonialism
Postmodernism
Pragmatism
Psychologism
Pythagoras and Pythagoreanism
Rationalism
Realism
Reformation
Renaissance
Romanticism
Saint Victor, School of
School of Qom, The
Scotism
Sensationalism
Skepticism, History of
Socinianism
Sophists
Spinozism
Stoicism
Strato and Stratonism
Structuralism and Post-structuralism
Sufism
Thomism
Valentinus and Valentinianism

Special Topics

African Philosophy
Evolutionary Psychology
History and Historiography of Philosophy
Korean Philosophy
Latin American Philosophy
Philosophy
Philosophy of Education, Epistemological Issues In
Philosophy of Education, Ethical and Political Issues In
Philosophy of Education, History of
Philosophy of History
Philosophy of Medicine
Philosophy of Sex
Philosophy of Technology
Social Constructionism
Speciesism

bibliographies

The First Edition of the Encyclopedia of Philosophy *included bibliographical essays dealing with philosophy dictionaries and encyclopedias, philosophy journals, and philosophy bibliographies. To preserve and enhance these essays, they have been reproduced in this Second Edition along with detailed updates. The updates to the bibliographies cover material published between 1965 and mid-2005. All of the references appear in OCLC's WorldCat bibliographic database and are thus available either in mid- to large-size academic libraries, or through interlibrary loan. While the bibliographies are extensive, they are not exhaustive. This is especially true in the case of the journal bibliography, where less readily available non-English-language journals have been excluded, as have journals published for short periods of time. Accessibility was deemed to be more important than exhaustive coverage. The subject coverage includes both general philosophical works and works from the major sub-domains of philosophy. The bibliographic lists show that philosophy is a vital, worldwide discipline. A perusal of the journal bibliography will show that new journals are appearing every year, and the dictionary and encyclopedia bibliography identifies publications in fifty different languages. The constant stream of new journals and the accumulation of philosophical resources in so many languages are indicators of a truly vibrant discipline.*

PHILOSOPHY BIBLIOGRAPHIES

Lists of philosophers and the titles of their works were for the most part provided only *en passant* by ancient and medieval writers and scholars, as in the brief citations scattered through the first book of Aristotle's *Metaphysics* and throughout Aquinas' *Summa Theologica.* It is true that Diogenes Laërtius' listing was somewhat more systematic, but philosophical bibliographies fully worthy of the name date from more recent times.

Modern philosophy has been well supplied with bibliographies in the general sense of the term, as will be noted in the present survey, but it has been weak in a special variety of bibliographical literature, namely, journals of abstracts. The two main journals containing abstracts of current work in philosophy—the *Bibliographie de la philosophie* and the *Bulletin signalétique: Philosophie, sciences humaines*—have done and are doing a good job as far as they go, but the scope of each is limited: the first covers books only, and the two-line précis in the second are enough only to whet a desire for more.

Modern bibliographies of philosophy are of four kinds: general bibliographies; those covering a specific region or country; those covering a particular period, movement, or philosopher; and those covering a specific philosophical discipline.

GENERAL BIBLIOGRAPHIES

BIBLIOGRAPHICAL BOOKS AND PAMPHLETS. One of the earliest of the general bibliographies of philosophy is the *Bibliotheca Philosophorum Classicorum Authorum Chronologica; in qua Veterum Philosophorum Origo, Successio, Aetas, & Doctrina Compendiosa, ab Origine Mundi, Usq. ad Nostram Aetatem, Proponitur; Quibus Accessit Patrum, Ecclesiae Christi Doctorum a Temporibus Apos-*

tolorum, Usque ad Tempora Scholasticorum ad An. Usq. Do. 1140, Secundum Eandem Temporis Seriem, Enumeratio, by Johann Jacob Fries (Zürich, 1592, 110 pages), with about 2,500 entries. Three of its significant successors in the next three hundred years are the *Bibliotheca Realis Philosophica*, by Martin Lipen (2 vols., Frankfurt, 1679), with about 40,000 entries, some on subjects no longer regarded as philosophical in a strict sense; the *Bibliotheca Philosophica*, by B. G. Struve (Jena, 1704; 5th ed., 2 vols., 1740), containing about 4,000 entries; and the *Systematisch-alphabetischer Hauptkatalog der Königlichen Universitätsbibliothek zu Tübingen; Erstes Heft; A. Philosophie* (Tübingen, 1854, 63 pages), with about 3,000 entries and with annual supplements to 1880.

Of the four pre-twentieth-century bibliographies mentioned, all are available at the Library of Congress in Washington and at the British Museum in London. The last-named item is also available at the New York Public Library and at the Library of the University of Illinois.

In the twentieth century four main general philosophical bibliographies have been compiled. The first is the *Bibliography of Philosophy, Psychology, and Cognate Subjects*, by Benjamin Rand (2 vols., New York, 1905), which has about 70,000 entries and is a major work of scholarship. It was published as the two-part Volume III of the *Dictionary of Philosophy and Psychology*, edited by James M. Baldwin (3 vols., New York, 1901–1905). Part I of the two-part *Bibliography* covers histories of philosophy and works by and about philosophers from Abel to Zwingli, and Part II is systematic.

Second among the main general bibliographies of the present century is the *Bibliographische Einführung in das Studium der Philosophie*, edited by I. M. Bocheński, which consists of 20 fascicles (24 to 85 pages each) published at Bern from 1948 to 1950 and which covers philosophy in certain periods (ancient and medieval philosophy), countries (modern Italian, French existentialist, and American philosophy), religious and ethnic groups (Buddhist, patristic, Jewish, and Arabic philosophy), systems and disciplines (philosophy as a whole, symbolic logic, and logical positivism), and individuals (Plato, Aristotle, Augustine, Aquinas, and Kierkegaard).

The third principal source of this kind is Gilbert Varet's *Manuel de bibliographie philosophique* (2 vols., Paris, 1956), which contains about 25,000 entries, Volume I being historical and Volume II systematic.

Finally, there is Wilhelm Totok's *Handbuch der Geschichte der Philosophie* (Frankfurt, 1964–), of which the first volume, *Altertum* (400 pages), covers works on Indian, Chinese, Greek, and Roman philosophy, with an introduction listing works on the methodology of research in philosophy and on the general history of philosophy, dictionaries of philosophy, introductions to philosophy, and works on the philosophical disciplines. Articles from over 400 periodicals are cited.

BIBLIOGRAPHICAL SERIALS. Apparently the earliest general serial covering works in philosophy was the *Allgemeines Repertorium der Literatur; . . . philosophische Literatur*, by J. S. Ersch (Jena and Weimar, one volume each for 1785–1790, 1791–1795, and 1796–1800). Partly overlapping it in time was the *Lehrbuch der Geschichte der Philosophie und einer kritischen Literatur derselben*, by J. G. Buhle (Göttingen, one volume for each year from 1796 to 1804). After a gap of 87 years, the *Critical Review of Theological and Philosophical Literature*, edited by S. D. F. Salmond, was published at Edinburgh, covering the years 1891 to 1904. It was succeeded by the *Review of Theology and Philosophy*, edited by Allan Menzies, also at Edinburgh, which covered 1905/1906 to 1914/1915.

Meanwhile, in 1895 at Louvain a periodical was begun which was entitled the *Sommaire idéologique des ouvrages et des revues de philosophic*. After a number of changes (and with no volumes published from 1915 to 1933 and from 1941 to 1945), this periodical is now entitled the *Répertoire bibliographique de la philosophic*. It is issued four times a year and is one of the three general bibliographical serials now being published in the field of philosophy; it covers both books and periodical articles. (It is reproduced *in toto*, with Dutch headings replacing the French headings, in the *Tijdschrift voor Filosofie*, published quarterly at Louvain.) A second of the three leaders in this category is the *Bibliographie de la philosophie*, begun in 1937 as a semiannual by the International Institute of Philosophy, continued (with the omission of the years 1939 to 1945) until 1953, and issued since 1954 four times a year by the International Federation of Philosophical Societies; it covers books only, with a summary of each.

The third is the *Bulletin signalétique: Philosophie, sciences humaines* (entitled the *Bulletin analytique: Philosophie* from 1947 to 1955), published quarterly at Paris by the Centre de Documentation du Centre Nationale de la Recherche Scientifique; it is the only world-wide source of its kind which not only covers both books and periodicals but also contains a succinct abstract of each entry.

Remaining to be mentioned, as regards serial bibliographies of philosophy, are a number of sources which are either limited in scope in one way or another or are no longer issued.

A general world-wide serial no longer issued but useful for works published in the period in which it appeared is *Philosophic Abstracts*, published for the most part quarterly at New York from 1939 to 1954, with an index covering 1939 to 1950. It contains abstracts of books and lists of periodical articles.

There are two important serials, of a quasi-bibliographical character, devoted exclusively to critical reviews of philosophical books: The *Philosophischer Literaturanzeiger*, published eight times a year at Meisenheim am Glan (begun in 1949 at Schlesdorf am Kochelsee), which contains about 15 reviews in each issue; and *Philosophical Books*, issued quarterly since 1960 at Leicester, England, which contains about a dozen reviews in each issue, written largely from the viewpoint of analytical philosophy. Also deserving of mention, as regards coverage of books only, is *Scripta Recenter Edita*, issued ten times a year since 1959 at Nijmegen, the Netherlands, which is a list of books on philosophy and theology (each issue containing about 400 entries with emphasis on theology), designed especially for use by acquisitions officers of libraries.

Periodicals. It may be added, as regards serial bibliographies, that selective lists or reviews (and, in a few cases, abstracts) of current philosophical books, plus lists of periodical articles in some cases, are published either in each issue or annually or from time to time in many philosophical periodicals, and the coverage is in some cases fairly comprehensive. (For the names of periodicals in this field, see *Philosophical Periodicals, An Annotated World List*, by David Baumgardt, Washington, 1952, 89 pages, 489 entries; the list, with 157 entries, which appears under the heading "Philosophy" in *Ulrich's Periodicals Directory*, 10th ed., New York, 1963, 667 pages; and the article "Philosophy Journals" in this volume.) Especially strong in book reviews and abstracts are the German philosophical periodicals.

Of the currently published annual bibliographies in philosophical periodicals, mention may be made of the one which appears in the *Deutsche Zeitschrift für Philosophic*, published in East Berlin. Although generally global in coverage, it emphasizes works on dialectical materialism written in Eastern Europe.

Finally, topical, regional, or other summaries and evaluations of current philosophical literature (as distinguished from lists, reviews, or abstracts) appear regularly or occasionally in *The Hibbert Journal* (world-wide), *Cross Currents* (world-wide), *Philosophy* (selected countries), the *Revue philosophique de la France et de l'étranger* (selected countries), and the *Revue des sciences philosophiques et théologiques* (world-wide).

BIBLIOGRAPHICAL SECTIONS OF BOOKS. Many of the standard histories of philosophy contain bibliographical sections. The most important source of this kind is the voluminous bibliographical material in the *Grundriss der Geschichte der Philosophie*, by Friedrich Ueberweg and others (12th ed., 5 vols., Berlin, 1923–1938). The handiest is the series of lists of philosophers preceding each main part of the *History of Philosophy*, by Wilhelm Windelband, translated by James H. Tufts (2 vols., New York, 1958, paperback reprint of the rev. ed. of 1901). Also useful for the history of philosophy are the bibliographical lists (usually divided into "Fonti" and "Studi") at the ends of the chapters of the *Guida storico-bibliografica allo studio della filosofia*, by Carmelo Ferro (Milan, 1949?).

In addition, many introductory works on philosophy contain bibliographical guides. An outstanding example is the discussion of philosophical books, periodicals and dictionaries in Louis de Raeymacker's *Introduction to Philosophy*, translated by Harry McNeill (New York, 1948, 297 pages), on pp. 196–258.

NATIONAL OR REGIONAL BIBLIOGRAPHIES

BIBLIOGRAPHICAL BOOKS AND PAMPHLETS. A convenient list of the bibliographies of philosophy which are national in scope, covering some twenty countries or groups of countries, will be found in *A World Bibliography of Bibliographies*, by Theodore Besterman (4th ed., 4 vols., Lausanne, 1965–1966), Volume III, Columns 4809–4827. Outstanding among these country guides are the *Manuel de la recherche documentaire en France; . . . Philosophie*, by Raymond Bayer (Paris, 1950, 410 pages), with about 6,000 entries; the *Repertorium der Nederlandse Wijsbegeerte*, by J. J. Poortman (Amsterdam, 1948, 404 pages), with about 20,000 entries and a 168-page supplement published in 1958; the *Bibliografia filosofica italiana del 1900 al 1950* (4 vols., Rome, 1950–1957), with about 50,000 entries; the *Bibliografía filosófica española e hispanoamericana* (1940–1958), by Luis Martínez Gómez (Barcelona, 1961, 524 pages), 10,166 entries; and the anonymous *Philosophie und Grenzgebiete, 1945–1964* (Stuttgart, 1964, 434 pages), covering philosophical works in the German language, with a list of periodicals. Also deserving of mention, as regards French philosophy, are the fascicles entitled "Logique et philosophie des sciences," by Robert Blanché (1959, 54 pages), and "Morale et philosophie politique," by Georges Bastide (1961, 92 pages), in the *Bibliographie française établie à l'intention des lecteurs étrangers* (Paris).

Two volumes of a *Bibliografia Filozofii Polskiej*, covering 1750–1830 and 1831–1864, were published at Warsaw by the Polska Akademia Nauk in 1955 and 1960 (1,241 and 3,771 entries, respectively). The first volume of a *Bibliographie der sowjetischen Philosophie* (listing the articles which appeared in the Soviet periodical *Voprosy Filosofii* from 1947 to 1956; 906 entries) was compiled under the direction of I. M. Bocheński and published in 1959 by the Ost-Europa Institut at the University of Fribourg, Switzerland; four subsequent volumes, published from 1959 to 1964, covered books of 1947 to 1960 and articles of 1957 to 1960.

BIBLIOGRAPHICAL SERIALS. Serials (mostly annuals) devoted to philosophical works issued in particular countries include the following:

Abstracts of Bulgarian Scientific Literature; Philosophy and Pedagogics (Sofia; one volume for each year since 1958).

Bibliografia filosofica italiana (Milan; one volume for each year since 1949).

Bibliography of Current Philosophical Works Published in North America, issued as a supplement to certain issues of *The Modern Schoolman* (St. Louis, Mo.) and covering mainly the United States.

Die deutschen Universitätsschriften zur Philosophie und ihre Grenzgebieten, edited by Kurt Gassen (published annually at Erfurt from 1924 to 1930).

Literarische Berichte aus dem Gebiete der Philosophie, edited by Arthur Hoffman (published semi-annually at Erfurt from 1923 to 1932), which covered current German periodical publications, with special retrospective bibliographies on Hegel, Nietzsche, and others.

"Thèses de doctorat concernant les sciences philosophiques et théologiques soutenues en France," published each year since 1954 in a spring or summer issue of the *Revue des sciences philosophiques et théologiques* and covering the preceding year.

The annual *Handbook of Latin American Studies* (published since 1935, originally and now again at Gainesville, Fla.) regularly contains a chapter on philosophical studies. A "Scandinavian Bibliography," covering philosophical works published in Denmark, Finland, Norway, and Sweden, appears once a year in *Theoria* (Lund, Sweden). The *Heythrop Journal* (Oxford, quarterly) regularly contains a "select list of British books on philosophy and theology."

BIBLIOGRAPHICAL SECTIONS OF BOOKS. Many of the standard historical, critical, or documentary treatments of philosophy in particular countries or regions (American, British, French, German, Indian, etc.; and Latin American, Anglo-American, European, Scandinavian, Western, Oriental, etc.) include extensive bibliographical sections, either at the end of the book or at the end of each chapter. Examples are the bibliographies in the introductions to the several parts of the anthology *The Development of American Philosophy*, edited by W. G. Muelder and others (2d ed., Cambridge, Mass., 1960), with about 500 entries, and the bibliography at the end of Chandradhar Sharma's *Indian Philosophy* (New York, 1962, paperback reprint of the Benares edition of 1952), with about 300 entries.

PERIOD OR MOVEMENT BIBLIOGRAPHIES

BIBLIOGRAPHICAL BOOKS AND PAMPHLETS. Noteworthy among the philosophical bibliographies which cover a particular period are one on antiquity, one on the Renaissance, one on an 11-year period of the twentieth century, and one on the twentieth century as a whole:

Guía Bibliografía de la Filosofía Antigua, by Rodolfo Mondolfo (Buenos Aires, 1959, 102 pages), which is a worthy extension of the author's many substantive contributions to philosophical scholarship.

A Catalogue of Renaissance Philosophers (1350–1650), by John O. Riedl and others (Milwaukee, 1940, 179 pages), dealing with about 2,000 philosophers, with lists of writings in some cases.

Bibliographia Philosophica, 1934–1945, by G. A. de Brie (2 vols., Brussels and Antwerp, 1950–1954), Volume I historical and Volume II systematic; 48,178 entries.

Bibliografia filosofica del siglo XX.; Catalogo de la Exposición Bibliografica Internacional de la Filosofia del Siglo XX. (Buenos Aires, 1952, 465 pages), with 4,011 entries.

A period bibliography which is specialized in two senses (limited with respect to the period when the items were published and to the period with which the items deal) is the *Thomistic Bibliography, 1920–1940*, by Vernon J. Bourke (St. Louis, Mo., 1945; supplement to Vol. 21 of

The Modern Schoolman), with about 5,700 entries. It lists a number of earlier bibliographies of scholastic philosophy.

Illustrative of bibliographies covering philosophical movements is the "Bibliographic der Geschichte der idealistischen Philosophic," in *Idealismus; Jahrbuch für die idealistische Philosophie* (Zurich), Vol. I (1934), pp. 217–256 (about 350 entries). Bibliographies covering philosophical movements in particular countries include V. E. Harlow's *Bibliographical and Genetic Study of American Realism* (Oklahoma City, Okla., 1931, 132 pages), with some 700 entries, and Vito A. Belleza's "Bibliografia italiana sull'esistentialismo," in *Archivio di filosofia*, Vol. 15 (1946), 171–217, with over 700 entries. Works dealing with problems of philosophy and the history of philosophy from the standpoint of Marxism are listed in *O Marxistickej Filozofii a Vedeckom Komunizme*, compiled at the University of Bratislava (Bratislava, 1962, 146 pages), with over 400 entries.

Bibliographies covering individual philosophers are very numerous. They are listed in the appropriate sections of the general bibliographies mentioned earlier. For contemporary philosophers, the comprehensive bibliographies in the volumes of the Library of Living Philosophers, edited by Paul A. Schilpp (now published in La Salle, Ill.), are especially worthy of mention; the series covers C. D. Broad, Rudolf Carnap, Ernst Cassirer, John Dewey, Albert Einstein, Karl Jaspers, G. E. Moore, Sarvepalli Radhakrishnan, Bertrand Russell, George Santayana, and A. N. Whitehead, and volumes on others are in preparation.

BIBLIOGRAPHICAL SERIALS. The main bibliographical serial covering a specific period or movement in philosophy is the annual *Bibliographia Patristica; Internationale patristische Bibliographie*, by Wilhelm Schneemelcher (Berlin, begun with a volume for 1956 published in 1959), with about 1,000 entries in each volume.

BIBLIOGRAPHICAL SECTIONS OF BOOKS. Many of the standard works on the philosophy of a particular period or movement include extensive bibliographical sections either at the end of the volume or at the end of each chapter. As regards books on particular periods, mention may be made, for example, of Maurice de Wulf's *History of Mediaeval Philosophy*, 3d English ed., based on the 6th French ed., translated by E. C. Messenger (2 vols., London, 1935–1938; reprinted 1952); it contains (1) in Volume I an introductory chapter entitled "General Bibliography," with sections on research methods, auxiliary sciences, dictionaries and encyclopedias, collections, monographs on problems, etc. (totaling over 500 entries), and (2) at the end of each major section in each chapter a bibliographical discussion (for example, about 25 entries on John Scotus Erigena).

As regards books on particular movements, mention may similarly be made, for purposes of illustration, of *Logical Positivism* (Glencoe, Ill., 1959), edited by A. J. Ayer, which contains on pp. 381–446 a section entitled "Bibliography of Logical Positivism" (over 2,000 entries), covering not only logical positivism strictly interpreted but also "all types of analytical philosophy." Ayer's book is part of the series entitled Library of Philosophical Movements; the other books in the series (on existentialism, Scholasticism, "realism and the background of phenomenology," etc.) also contain extensive bibliographies.

BIBLIOGRAPHIES OF SPECIFIC DISCIPLINES

Among the bibliographies covering specific philosophic disciplines are the following:

I. M. Bocheński's bibliography of the history of formal logic in his *Formale Logik* (Fribourg, 1956), pp. 531–605 (over 2,000 entries), which was reproduced photographically in the English translation by Ivo Thomas, *A History of Formal Logic* (Notre Dame, Ind., 1961), on pp. 460–534, with English section headings substituted for the German headings and 34 additions to the bibliography given on p. 567.

Alonzo Church's "A Bibliography of Symbolic Logic," in *Journal of Symbolic Logic*, Vol. 1 (1936), 121–218 (about 1,800 entries), which is supplemented by abstracts of books and periodical articles on symbolic logic in each issue of the *Journal of Symbolic Logic.* Vol. 3 (1938), 178–212, contained the section "Additions and Corrections," applicable to the basic bibliography.

William A. Hammond's *A Bibliography of Aesthetics and of the Philosophy of the Fine Arts from 1900 to 1932* (rev. ed., New York, 1934, 205 pages, 2,191 entries), which also has a continuing supplement in the "Selective Current Bibliography for Aesthetics and Related Fields," now published annually in June in the *Journal of Aesthetics and Art Criticism* and originally published quarterly, under the title "Quarterly Bibliography of Aesthetic Theory, Criticism, and Psychology of Art," from the beginning of the issuance of the periodical in 1941.

Ethel M. Albert and Clyde Kluckhohn's *A Selected Bibliography on Values, Ethics, and Esthetics in the Behavioral Sciences and Philosophy, 1920–1958* (Glencoe, Ill., 1959, 342 pages), which contains 600 items in Chapter 6, "Philosophy."

John C. Rule's *Bibliography of Works in the Philosophy of History, 1945–1957* (The Hague, 1961, 87 pages, 1,307 entries), which excludes Marxist interpretations of history in the expectation of covering them separately later.

Amedeo G. Conte's "Bibliografia di logica giuridica (1936–1960)," in *Rivista internazionale di filosofia del diritto*, Vol. 38 (1961), 120–144 (about 250 entries). Addenda appeared in Vol. 39 (1962), 45–46.

For a discussion of some of the bibliographies mentioned in this article, from a librarian's standpoint, see Wilhelm Totok, "Die bibliographische Situation auf dem Gebiet der Philosophie," in *Zeitschrift für Bibliothekswesen und Bibliographie*, Vol. 5 (Frankfurt, 1958), 29–43; and his *Bibliographischer Wegweiser der philosophischen Literatur* (Frankfurt, 1959, 36 pages). See also the section on bibliographies of philosophy in Jean Hoffmans, *La Philosophie et les philosophes; ouvrages généraux* (Brussels, 1920, 395 pages).

William Gerber (1967)

PHILOSOPHY BIBLIOGRAPHIES [ADDENDUM]

The English- and non-English-language citations in this update are combined and are organized chronologically by year of publication. The citations appear within the individual year listings alphabetically by author's last name.

1965

Chan, Wing-tsit. *An Outline and an Annotated Bibliography of Chinese Philosophy.* Supp. New Haven, CT: Far Eastern Publications, 1965.

Higgins, Charles L. *The Bibliography of Philosophy; A Descriptive Account.* Ann Arbor, MI: Campus Publishers, 1965.

1966

Bibliography of Philosophy. Paris: Cultural Center of the French Embassy, 1966.

Jessop, T. E. *A Bibliography of David Hume and of Scottish Philosophy from Francis Hutcheson to Lord Balfour.* New York: Russell & Russell, 1966.

1967

Alston, R. C. *Logic, Philosophy, Epistemology, Universal Language.* Bradford, U.K.: E. Cummins, 1967.

Chan, Wing-tsit. *Chinese Philosophy, 1949–1963; An Annotated Bibliography of Mainland China Publications.* Honolulu: East-West Center Press, 1967.

Draper, John William. *Eighteenth Century English Aesthetics: A Bibliography.* New York: Octagon Books, 1967.

Hammond, William A. *A Bibliography of Aesthetics and of the Philosophy of the Fine Arts from 1900–1932.* Rev. and enl. ed. New York: Russell & Russell, 1967.

McLean, George F. *An Annotated Bibliography of Philosophy in Catholic Thought, 1900–1964.* New York: F. Ungar, 1967.

McLean, George F. *A Bibliography of Christian Philosophy and Contemporary Issues.* New York: F. Ungar, 1967.

1968

Baxandall, Lee. *Marxism and Aesthetics: A Selective Annotation Bibliography; Books and Articles in the English Language.* New York: Humanities Press, 1968.

Hessop, T. E. *A Bibliography of George Berkeley.* New York: B. Franklin, 1968.

Hoffmans, Jean. *La Philosophie et les Philosophes; Ouvrages Généraux.* New York: Burt Franklin, 1968.

Leroux, Emmanuel. *Bibliographie Méthodique du Pragmatisme Américain, Anglais et Italien.* New York: Burt Franklin, 1968.

Robert, Jean Dominique. *Philosophie et Science, Éléments de Bibliographie.* Paris: Beauchesne, 1968.

1969

Bibliography of Philosophy. New York: Cultural Center of the French Embassy, 1969.

Chan, Wing-tsit. *An Outline and an Annotated Bibliography of Chinese Philosophy.* Rev. ed. New Haven, CT: Far Eastern Publications, 1969.

1970

Adickes, Erich. *German Kantian Bibliography.* New York: B. Franklin, 1970 (reprint of the 1893–96 ed.).

Jones, Joe R., and Terry Louis White, eds. *Analytic Philosophy and Religious Language: A Bibliography.* Dallas, TX: Perkins School of Theology, Southern Methodist University, 1970.

Kraav, Marju. *Guide to Research in Philosophy.* Hamilton, ON: McMaster University Library Press, 1970–1979.

Martin, Mary Anne. *The Bibliography of Philosophy; A Guide to Basic Sources,* 1970.

Matczak, Sebastian A. *Philosophy; A Select, Classified Bibliography of Ethics, Economics, Law, Politics, Sociology.* Leuven, Belgium: Editions Nauwelaerts, 1970.

Smith, Marilynn K. *A Bibliography of Philosophy: A Partial List of Holdings in the USMA Library.* West Point, NY: U.S. Military Academy, 1970.

1971

De George, Richard T. *A Guide to Philosophical Bibliography and Research.* New York: Appleton-Century-Crofts, 1971.

1972

Barr, Mary-Margaret H. *A Century of Voltaire Study; A Bibliography of Writings on Voltaire, 1825–1925.* New York: B. Franklin, 1972 (reprint of the 1929 ed.).

Bochenski, Joseph M. *Guide to Marxist Philosophy; An Introductory Bibliography.* Chicago: Swallow Press, 1972.

Redmond, Walter Bernard. *Bibliography of the Philosophy in the Iberian Colonies of America.* The Hague: Nijhoff, 1972.

1973

Jasenas, Michael. *A History of the Bibliography of Philosophy.* Hildesheim: G. Olms, 1973.

Mitcham, Carl, and Robert Mackey, eds. *Bibliography of the Philosophy of Technology.* Chicago: University of Chicago Press, 1973.

1974

Galama, I. J. K., and A. F. Sanders. *Logic, Epistemology, and Analysis of Religious Language: A Select Bibliography.* Groningen, Netherlands: Theologisch Instituut van de Rijksuniversiteit te Groningen, 1974.

Shields, Allan. *A Bibliography of Bibliographies in Aesthetics.* San Diego: San Diego State University Press, 1974.

1975

Bochenski, Joseph M., and Kazunori Kunishima. *Marx Syugi Tetugaku: Kenkyu no hoho to Bunken.* Tokyo: Koronsha, 1975.

Inter-University Board of India. *Philosophy, Religion: A Bibliography of Doctoral Dissertations Accepted by Indian Universities, 1857–1970.* New Delhi: The Board, 1975.

Moss, Michael. *A Bibliography of Logic Books.* Oxford: Sub-Faculty of Philosophy, University of Oxford, 1975.

Negley, Glenn Robert. *Utopian Literature: A Bibliography with a Supplementary Listing of Works Significant in Utopian Philosophy.* Durham, NC: Friends of the Library, Duke University, 1975.

Peacocke, Christopher A. B., Dana S. Scott, and Martin K. Davies, eds. *A Selective Bibliography of Philosophical Logic.* 2nd ed. Oxford: Sub-Faculty of Philosophy, University of Oxford, 1975.

Seuren, Pieter A. M. *A Selective Bibliography of Philosophy of Language.* Oxford: Sub-Faculty of Philosophy, University of Oxford, 1975.

Zylstra, Bernard. *Bibliography of the Philosophy of the Cosmonomic Idea and Related Materials: English, French, and German Titles.* Toronto: Institute for Christian Studies, 1975.

1976

Lomax, Harvey. *A Contemporary Bibliography in Political Philosophy and in Other Areas.* Dallas: Lomax, 1976.

1977

Baker, John Arthur. *A Select Bibliography of Moral Philosophy.* Oxford: Sub-Faculty of Philosophy, University of Oxford, 1977.

Cortright, S. A. *A Classified Bibliography in the Philosophy of Religion.* South Bend, IN: University of Notre Dame, Center for the Study of the Philosophy of Religion, 1977.

Harre, Rom, and John Hawthorn. *A Selective Bibliography of Philosophy of Science.* 2nd ed. Oxford: Sub-Faculty of Philosophy, University of Oxford, 1977.

Lawford, Paul. *Marxist Aesthetics: A Short Bibliography of Works in English, with a Supplement on Russian Formalism, Structuralism, Semiotics.* Keele, Staffordshire, U.K.: Dept. of Sociology and Social Anthropology, University of Keele, 1977.

Lindley, Richard Charles, and J. M. Shorter. *The Philosophy of Mind: A Bibliography.* Part 1, *The Self.* Oxford: Sub-Faculty of Philosophy, University of Oxford, 1977.

1978

The Classical World Bibliography of Philosophy, Religion, and Rhetoric. New York: Garland, 1978.

Wainwright, William J. *Philosophy of Religion: An Annotated Bibliography of Twentieth-Century Writings in English.* New York: Garland, 1978.

Weber, Nancy. *Women in Philosophy, Twentieth Century: A Selectively Annotated Bibliography.* Rohnert Park, CA: Sonoma State College, 1978.

1980

McClendon, John H. *Afro-American Philosophers and Philosophy: A Selected Bibliography.* Urbana: University of Illinois, 1980–1985.

Steinhauer, Kurt, and Gitta Hausen. *Hegel Bibliography: Background Material on the International Reception of Hegel within the Context of the History of Philosophy.* Munich: Saur, 1980.

1981

Geldsetzer, Lutz. *Bibliography of the International Congresses of Philosophy: Proceedings, 1900–1978.* Munich: Saur, 1981.

1982

Gabel, Gernot U. *Canadian Theses on German Philosophy, 1925–1975: A Bibliography.* Cologne: Edition Germini, 1982.

1983

Blackwell, Richard J. *A Bibliography of the Philosophy of Science, 1945–1981.* Westport, CT: Greenwood Press, 1983.

Hernandez, Justin. *A Bibliography for the History of Medieval Philosophy.* Conception, MO: Conception Abbey, Seminary College, 1983.

Vance, Mary A. *Architecture-Philosophy: A Bibliography.* Monticello, IL: Vance Bibliographies, 1983.

1984

Nawabi, Mahyar. *Religion, Philosophy & Science.* Tehran: Mu'assasa-i mutala at wa-tahqiqat-i farhangi, 1984.

Vance, Mary A. *Aesthetics: Monographs.* Monticello, IL: Vance Bibliographies, 1984.

1986

Gombocz, Wolfgang L., Norbert Henrichs, and Rudolf Haller. *International Bibliography of Austrian Philosophy, 1974–1975.* Amsterdam: Rodopi, 1986.

1987

Chappell, V. C., and Willis Doney. *Twenty-Five Years of Descartes Scholarship, 1960–1984.* New York: Garland, 1987.

Hurley, S. L., and Jeff McMahan. *A Select Bibliography of Moral and Political Philosophy.* Oxford: Sub-Faculty of Philosophy, University of Oxford, 1987.

Swinburne, Richard. *A Selective Bibliography of the Philosophy of Mind.* New ed. Oxford: Sub-Faculty of Philosophy, University of Oxford, 1987.

Warren, Karen J. *Philosophy and Feminism, A Selected Annotated Bibliography.* 1987.

1989

Mathien, Thomas. *Bibliography of Philosophy in Canada: A Research Guide.* Kingston, ON: R. P. Frye, 1989.

1990

Brown, David. *A Selective Bibliography of the Philosophy of Religion.* Oxford: Sub-Faculty of Philosophy, University of Oxford, 1990.

1991

Bell, Albert A., and James B. Allis. *Resources in Ancient Philosophy: An Annotated Bibliography of Scholarship in English, 1965–1989.* Metuchen, NJ: Scarecrow Press, 1991.

1992

Kaylor, Noel Harold. *The Medieval Consolation of Philosophy: An Annotated Bibliography.* New York: Garland, 1992.

1993

Burr, John Roy. *World Philosophy: A Contemporary Bibliography.* Westport, CT: Greenwood Press, 1993.

Chakraborty Ganguly, Krishna. *A Bibliography of Nyaya Philosophy.* Calcutta: National Library, 1993.

1995

Navia, Luis E. *The Philosophy of Cynicism: An Annotated Bibliography.* Westport, CT: Greenwood Press, 1995.

1996

Cogswell, Robert Elzy. *Process Philosophy and Process Theology: An Annotated Bibliography of Introductory Texts.* Austin, TX: Library, Episcopal Theological Seminary of the Southwest, 1996.

Kellerwessel, Wulf. *A Bibliography on Reference and Some Related Topics in Analytical Philosophy.* New York: P. Lang, 1996.

1997

Hutchings, Noel, and William D. Rumsey. *The Collaborative Bibliography of Women in Philosophy.* Bowling Green, OH: Philosophy Documentation Center, Bowling Green State University, 1997.

Radice, Roberto. *Artistotle's Metaphysics: Annotated Bibliography of the Twentieth-Century Literature.* New York: Brill, 1997.

1998

Jones, Ward E., W. Newton-Smith, and Samir Okasha. *A Selective Bibliography of the Philosophy of Science.* New ed. Oxford: Sub-Faculty of Philosophy, University of Oxford, 1998.

Wolf, Robert G. *Analytic Philosophy of Religion: A Bibliography, 1940–1996.* Bowling Green, OH: Philosophy Documentation Center, Bowling Green State University, 1998.

1999

Daiber, Hans. *Bibliography of Islamic Philosophy.* Leiden, The Netherlands: Brill, 1999.

2000

Fieser, James. *A Bibliography of Scottish Common Sense Philosophy.* Bristol, U.K.: Thoemmes Press, 2000.

2001

Bretzke, James T. *Bibliography on East Asian Religion and Philosophy.* Lewiston, NY: E. Mellen Press, 2001.

Meissner, Werner. *Western Philosophy in China, 1993–1997: A Bibliography.* New York: P. Lang, 2001.

Stagaman, David J., James Kraft, and Kristin Sutton. *International Bibliography of Austrian Philosophy, Wittgenstein and Religion: A Bibliography of Articles, Books, and Theses in the Twentieth Century that Relate the Philosophy of Ludwig Wittgenstein to the Study of Religion and Theology.* Quezon City, Philippines: Ateneo de Manila University, 2001.

2003

Internationale Bibliographie zur österreichischen Philosophie 1993/1994. Amsterdam: Rodopi, 2003.

2004

Henrici, Peter. *A Practical Guide to Study; with a Bibliography of Tools of Work for Philosophy and Theology.* Rome: Editrice Pontificia Universita Gregoriana, 2004.

Slater, John G. *Bibliography of Modern British Philosophy.* Bristol, U.K.: Thoemmes Continuum, 2004.

Michael J. Farmer (2005)

PHILOSOPHY DICTIONARIES AND ENCYCLOPEDIAS

Aristotle compiled the first dictionary of philosophy. Other outstanding philosophers who either wrote such works or made slight beginnings in that direction include Avicenna, Leibniz, Voltaire, and Dewey. Kant lectured on *philosophische Enzyklopädie,* but his topic was really the encyclopedic scope of philosophy; Hegel wrote an "encyclopedia" of philosophy which was not an encyclopedia in the ordinary sense. Indeed, what constitutes a dictionary or encyclopedia of philosophy deserves discussion. First, it will be helpful to inspect early examples of such works as well as what might be called embedded dictionaries—the philosophical articles, alphabetically arranged but separated by nonphilosophical material, in general encyclopedias.

In Book V of Aristotle's *Metaphysics* each section consists of a definition and discussion of a philosophical concept. The various sections begin, for example, "Beginning means . . .," "Cause means . . .," "Element means . . .." He thus covered 29 topics in this first dictionary or quasi dictionary of philosophy: beginning, cause, element, nature, necessity, one, being, substance, sameness and difference, limit, that in virtue of which (or reason why), disposition, priority and posterity, potency, quantum, quality, relation, completeness (or perfection), state, being affected, privation, possession, derivation, part, whole, mutilation, genus, falsity, and accident. The rationale for the order of topics can only be conjectured.

After Aristotle dictionary-type or encyclopedic compendiums were produced by Alexandrian, Roman, and Byzantine lexicographers and doxographers, covering, for the most part, philosophy among other domains of knowledge, not philosophy exclusively. Many of these compendiums were arranged in an order other than alphabetical. Thus, in his *Bibliotheca*, or *Myriobiblion*, Photius (c. 850) summarized, in no special order, some 280 philosophical and nonphilosophical books, including works by Philo Judaeus, Justin Martyr, Origen, and Gregory of Nyssa but none by Plato or Aristotle, although he mentions having read books by Timaeus, Boëthus, and Dorotheus on Plato's use of words.

By contrast Suidas' *Lexicon* (c. 950) is arranged alphabetically. It contains articles on Aristotle (about 150 words), Zeno of Elea (about 75 words), and numerous other philosophers, as well as many topical entries, such as those on *physis, physikos*, and related terms (about nine hundred words in this group). After Suidas, however, through the rest of the medieval period and the Renaissance, most of the summaries of knowledge reverted to the nonalphabetical arrangement.

In modern times the alphabetical arrangement has been dominant in general compendiums of knowledge, and useful philosophical articles have frequently been included in them. It will be instructive, before examining the separately published dictionaries of philosophy, to survey the embedded dictionaries of philosophy.

PHILOSOPHICAL ARTICLES IN GENERAL ENCYCLOPEDIAS

From the standpoint of embedded philosophical material four French, six English, and seven other encyclopedias are especially worthy of comment. In addition, readers may note (*a*) the interest of various prominent philosophers in general encyclopedias, as illustrated by Leibniz' proposal to Louis XIV around 1675 that a group of learned persons "extract the quintessence of the best books, add the unwritten observations of experts, and thus build systems of knowledge based upon experience and demonstrations"; (*b*) the role of the *philosophes* in the work on the *Encyclopédie*; and (c) Giovanni Gentile's role in the Italian encyclopedia of 1929–1939.

FRENCH GENERAL ENCYCLOPEDIAS. Moreri, Bayle, Diderot, and Larousse are the key figures in the history of French encyclopedias. Of these four Louis Moreri and Pierre Bayle each produced an entire encyclopedia single-handedly.

Moreri. Moreri's *Le Grand Dictionnaire historique* (1st ed., Lyon, 1674, 1,346 pages; 20th ed., 10 vols., 1759) was translated twice into English and at least once into German, Italian, and Spanish. Reprintings and supplements continued to be published until 1845. By contrast with many dictionaries of philosophy which cover only topics, not individual philosophers, Moreri, in his articles on philosophy, covered many of its practitioners but offered no separate treatments of philosophical domains, problems, schools, or technical terms. Moreover, his articles on the philosophers are so thoroughly oriented toward biography that little attention is paid to doctrines.

Bayle. Bayle's *Dictionnaire historique et critique* (1st ed., 2 vols., Rotterdam, 1697; 5th ed., 5 vols., 1734; annotated ed., 16 vols., Paris, 1820–1824), two editions of which were translated or paraphrased into English, contains some basic facts plus philosophical or critical (usually impish and skeptical) comments for each entry. The comments on both the philosophical and the nonphilosophical topics support atheism, hedonism, and skepticism. As professor of philosophy at Sedan, France, and at Rotterdam, Bayle possessed the necessary technical equipment with which to support his trenchant skepticism. Acknowledging the roar of disapproval which greeted the first edition, Bayle made some revisions in the articles, but the second edition was no less outspoken than the first.

New English translations of selected articles from the *Dictionnaire* were published at Princeton in 1952, edited by E. A. Beller and M. du P. Lee, Jr., and at Indianapolis in 1965, edited by Richard H. Popkin.

"Encyclopédie." The third French general encyclopedia with significant philosophical articles was the one called simply, by common consent, the *Encyclopédie*. Its full title was *Encyclopédie, ou Dictionnaire raisonné des sciences, des arts et des métiers, par une société de gens de lettres*, edited by Denis Diderot and Jean d'Alembert.

The *Encyclopédie* had a stormy history. It was originally conceived by André F. Le Breton as merely a translation of Ephraim Chambers' *Cyclopaedia* of 1728 (described below), but the character of the project changed, especially after Diderot was put in charge. A corps of contributors was rapidly enlisted which included men of the caliber of Rousseau and Voltaire.

Among the vicissitudes which followed were the periodic banning of the work as irreligious or politically dangerous after the publication of the early volumes and the discouraged resignation of d'Alembert from the project. In 1764, while the manuscript for the final volumes was being edited, Diderot learned to his consternation that Le Breton was toning down the language in order to obviate further prosecution; some of Le Breton's most extensive changes were made in Diderot's own article "Pyrrhonienne ou sceptique philosophie," containing Diderot's most cherished ideas. The original proofs, showing Le Breton's changes and deletions, were discovered in 1933.

The *Encyclopédie* contains no articles on philosophers as such. Among its main articles dealing with philosophical schools or otherwise of philosophical interest are those on Socratic philosophy, Aristotelianism, Epicureanism, and skepticism. The spirit of the philosophical and ethical articles in the *Encyclopédie,* many of which were written by Diderot himself, was antidogmatic, but it was not atheistic or consistently skeptical. Voltaire's 40-odd articles, written in this vein, included 3 in the *E*'s ("Élégance," "Éloquence," and "Esprit"), 21 in the *F*'s ("Félicité," "Finesse," "Fornication," and so on), 11 in the *G*'s ("Goût," "Grandeur," and so on), 5 in the *H*'s ("Heureusement," "Histoire," and so on), "Idolatrie" in the *I*'s, and "Messie" (Messiah) in the *M*'s.

Rousseau wrote the articles on economics (in which he laid the groundwork for his *Contrat social*) and music. Baron de Montesquieu declined the invitation to write on democracy and despotism but promised an article on taste; the portion of it which he had finished before his death in 1755 at the age of 66 was published in Volume VII immediately after Voltaire's article on the same subject.

Eight articles from the *Encyclopédie* on ethical subjects (calumny, unhappiness, and the like) were translated by Ivan Vanslov into Russian and published in 1771 at St. Petersburg by the Imperial Academy of Science as a 21-page dictionary of ethics.

(For a full discussion of the purpose, influence, and philosophic content of the *Encyclopédie,* see the entry **Encyclopédie.**)

Larousse. The excitement aroused by Diderot's original *Encyclopédie* and by the revised editions which followed it eventually subsided, and a calm period in this field ensued. The fourth main French encyclopedia, Larousse's, had its birth in the second half of the nineteenth century. Several encyclopedias bear the name Larousse, beginning with the 15-volume *Grand Dictionnaire universel du XIXe siècle* sponsored by Pierre Larousse (Paris, 1865–1876; 2-vol. supp., 1878–1890) and extending through *Larousse de XXe siècle*, compiled by Paul Augé and published in Paris by the Librairie Larousse (6 vols., 1928–1933; supp., 1953), and the *Grand Larousse encyclopédique*, also published by the Librairie Larousse (10 vols., 1960–1964).

In the *Grand Dictionnaire* the article on philosophy, which covers only the history of philosophy, is curiously followed (perhaps to compensate for the lack of topical discussion) by 51 extensive articles on books with *philosophie* as the first or principal word of the title, such as "Philosophie (Principes de)," by Descartes; "Philosophie morale (Principes de)," by Shaftesbury; "Philosophie premiere, ou Ontologie," by Wolff; "Philosophie de la vie," by Schlegel; and "Philosophie de l'art," by Taine. This is hardly the best way to cover philosophy in an encyclopedia.

The current *Grand Larousse encyclopédique* contains numerous philosophical articles, both topical and biographical, which, although pithy, are excessively brief; for example, Bergson is covered in eight hundred words and logic in nine hundred. The space devoted to the separate articles "Logique (Grande), ouvrage de Friedrich Hegel," "Logique déductive et inductive (Système de), par John Stuart Mill," and "Logique de Port-Royal ou Art de penser" (after the fashion of the nineteenth-century edition) could have been far better used in the article on logic.

ENGLISH GENERAL ENCYCLOPEDIAS. Of the numerous English-language encyclopedias mention may be made of Harris' and the two Chambers', which are mainly of historical interest, and the *Britannica, the Americana*, and *Collier's*, which are influential today.

Harris. The *Lexicon Technicum, or an Universal English Dictionary of Arts and Sciences*, by the clergyman John Harris (1st ed., London, 1704; 5th ed., 2 vols., 1736; supp. vol., 1744), is called by the *Encyclopedia Britannica* the first alphabetical encyclopedia in English, although there seem to be other claimants to this honor. Harris wrote in the Preface, "In Logick, Metaphysicks, Ethicks, Grammar, Rhetorick, &c. I have been designedly short; giving usually the bare meaning only of the Words and Terms of

Art, with one or two instances to explain them, and illustrate them."

The book contains no articles on individual philosophers, and the articles on philosophical topics show a popular rather than a technical understanding (or misunderstanding) of the subject. For example, the article "Logick" (32 lines, mainly laudatory and, curiously, ascribing to logic our ability to explain why we dislike a painting) refers the reader, for details, to the articles "Apprehension" (7 lines), "Discourse" (5 lines defining the term as if it were a synonym of "inference"), "Judgment" (12 lines), and "Method, or Disposition" (40 lines, outlining Descartes's four methodological precepts, with condescending comment) but does not refer the reader to the articles "Conditional Propositions" (8 lines) or "Definition" (19 lines). There is no article on fallacy or syllogism.

Chambers' "Cyclopaedia." A quarter of a century after the appearance of the Harris volume Ephraim Chambers published the *Cyclopaedia, or an Universal Dictionary of Arts and Sciences* (1st ed., 2 vols., London, 1728; 5 other eds., 2 vols., London, 1739–1751/1752, and another 2-vol. ed., Dublin, 1742); supplements were published at various times from 1738 to 1753. Later editions were reportedly used in an unpublished French translation by the writers of the French *Encyclopédie*. Chambers was a freethinker, but many of his articles repeat superstitions and preposterous medical marvels as fact. The *Cyclopaedia* contains succinct articles on essence, ethics, God, knowledge, logic, metaphysics, philosophy, Sophists, truth, and will, as well as on Academic, Cartesian, Epicurean, Platonic, Pyrrhonian, Socratic, and Stoic philosophy, among others. It does not cover individual philosophers.

"Chambers's Encyclopaedia." The so-called *Chambers's Encyclopaedia, a Dictionary of Universal Knowledge for the People* (10 vols., London and Edinburgh, W. & R. Chambers, 1860–1868; rev. eds. issued periodically to 1935) was not a new edition of Ephraim Chambers' *Cyclopaedia* but a new work, written by over one hundred contributors and influenced greatly by the 15-volume tenth edition of the *Conversations-Lexikon* published from 1851 to 1855 by F. A. Brockhaus at Leipzig. The philosophical articles in *Chambers's Encyclopaedia* are uneven. Anaximander is allotted ten times as much space as Anaximenes. The article on the Gnostics is scholarly (although the author wrongly says that they "feigned a naive surprise" at not being accepted as Christians), whereas other articles are more popular in style. The article on Pascal is wholly biographical, but the one on Plotinus covers both his life and his teaching.

The current *Chambers's Encyclopaedia* (15 vols., London, George Newnes, 1950; rev. ed., 1959) is a successor of the 1860–1868 work, not of Ephraim Chambers'. Its advisers on philosophy were John Laird and A. C. Ewing. The articles on Greek philosophy incorporate recent scholarship; the one on Antisthenes, for example, avoids the error, embodied in many earlier treatments, of calling him the first Cynic. It seems odd, however, to find the intellectual work of Mohandas Gandhi and Sarvepalli Radhakrishnan discussed in A. B. Keith's article on Hinduism, which is concerned mainly with the Hindu religion, rather than in S. N. Dasgupta's article on Indian philosophy. The index volume contains a useful classified list of the philosophical articles: 29 on philosophy, metaphysics, and epistemology; 32 on logic; 8 on ethics; 41 on systems and schools; and over 200 on individual thinkers.

"Encyclopaedia Britannica." The last edition of Ephraim Chambers' *Cyclopaedia* was published in the 1750s, and the French *Encyclopédie* had appeared in the 1750s and 1760s. In the middle or late 1760s William Smellie, a printer, historian, and naturalist, wrote most of the articles for a new compendium, the *Encyclopaedia Britannica, or Dictionary of Arts and Sciences* (1st ed., 3 vols., Edinburgh, A. Bell and C. Macfarquhar, 1768–1771). It was issued in installments beginning in December 1768, and subsequent editions, some with supplements, were issued by various publishers. The numbering of the editions was discontinued after the fourteenth edition, which appeared in 1929. The *Britannica* is now published, with continuous revisions, in Chicago by William Benton.

The most famous (and on some topics the most scholarly and comprehensive) edition of the *Britannica* is the eleventh (29 vols., London and New York, 1910–1911). It was sharply attacked by Willard H. Wright (better known by his pseudonym S. S. Van Dine, under which he wrote best-selling murder mysteries) in *Misinforming a Nation* (New York, B. W. Huebsch, 1917), which made several points in Chapter XI, "Philosophy." The Britannica is provincial, he claimed, as in its description of Locke as "typically English in his reverence for facts"; dogmatic, as in the statements that Berkeley "once for all lifted the problem of metaphysics to a higher level" and that Hume "determined the form into which later metaphysical questions have been thrown"; and patronizing, as in the statement that Condillac's thought "was by no means suited to English ways of thinking." Wright also pointed out that the eleventh edition contained no articles on Bergson, Bradley, Dewey, Royce, or Santayana, and only 1 column on Nietzsche, as compared to 3 on Samuel Clarke, 5 on Spencer, 7 on Fichte, 11 on Cousin, 14 on Hume, 15 on Hegel, 15 on Locke, and 19 on Newton.

Edmund Husserl's article on phenomenology, first published in the 14th edition (1929), was included in the various printings through 1955. It was also reproduced in *Realism and the Background of Phenomenology* (Roderick M. Chisholm, ed., Glencoe, Ill., Free Press, 1961). In subsequent printings of the *Britannica* the article on phenomenology was written, at first, by J. N. Findlay and, currently, by Herbert Spiegelberg.

Many of the philosophical articles in the *Britannica* were rewritten around 1957. Some of the topical articles reflect the current Oxford philosophy. Of the current revision (1966), which for the most part reproduces the recently rewritten articles, the editors and advisers for articles on philosophy are Alonzo Church of Princeton, W. C. Kneale and W. H. Walsh of Oxford, and Sarvepalli Radhakrishnan, president of India. Contributors near the beginning of the alphabet include A. J. Ayer, Max Black, and Brand Blanshard and near the end I. A. Richards, Gilbert Ryle, A. E. Taylor, Wilbur M. Urban, and Abraham Wolf.

In a later revision Thomas E. Jessop is lively as well as scholarly on Hume. The article on Plato, by A. E. Taylor and Philip Merlan, is a comprehensive monograph of the highest value; the bibliography of over 125 items covers manuscripts, editions, commentaries, translations, and analyses. The article on aesthetics, by Thomas Munro, and "Aesthetics, History of," by Helmut Kuhn, which refer to each other, overlap somewhat; for historical data one should consult both. In his article on metaphysics Gilbert Ryle presents a penetrating survey of the status of metaphysics from the origin of the term through the twentieth-century attacks on the discipline; he predicts that the term may "come back into ordinary or pedagogic use" when the motives which generate synoptic world views swing once more into prominence.

"Encyclopedia Americana." Another major English-language encyclopedia, the *Encyclopedia Americana*, edited by Francis Lieber and Edward Wigglesworth (13 vols., Philadelphia, Carey, Lea and Carey, 1829–1833), was originally in large part a translation of the seventh edition (1827–1829) of the *Conversations-Lexikon* published by Brockhaus. Subsequent unnumbered editions, some with supplements, have been issued by various publishers.

The 1996 edition of the *Americana* has Morton G. White of Harvard University as the philosophy member of its editorial advisory board. Among the principal contributors are Brand Blanshard on idea and idealism, Richard B. Brandt on duty and ethics, Herbert Feigl on the Vienna circle, Carl G. Hempel on meaning, Walter Kaufmann on Nietzsche, C. I. Lewis on philosophy, Kingsley Price on fine arts, and Donald C. Williams on conceptualism, free will, innate ideas, mechanism, and pluralism. The article on logic, by Ernest Nagel; "Logic, Symbolic," by W. V. Quine; and the "Logic Glossary," by Arthur Danto, excel in covering a broad range of technical data briefly but comprehensibly. Some of the articles need updating; for example, the death of G. E. Moore, which is mentioned in Volume XIX, has not yet occurred in the article on common sense in Volume VII. The unsigned article on Santayana is philosophically weak.

"Collier's Encyclopedia." *Collier's Encyclopedia* (20 vols., New York, P. F. Collier & Son, 1950–1951; rev. ed., 24 vols., 1962), is published by Crowell Collier and Macmillan. It has T. V. Smith as its adviser on philosophy. Among its American contributors in the field of philosophy are Max Black, Brand Blanshard, George Boas, Roderick M. Chisholm, Raphael Demos, C. J. Ducasse, Marvin Farber, Carl Hempel, Sidney Hook, C. I. Lewis, Ernest Nagel, and Herbert W. Schneider. There are also philosophical articles by such eminent foreigners as T. M. P. Mahadevan and John Passmore. *Collier's* is stronger on the philosophical disciplines than on the schools. It contains first-class articles on aesthetics, by Van Meter Ames; epistemology, by Roderick M. Chisholm; history of ethics, by R. A. Tsanoff; logic, by I. M. Copi; metaphysics, by Blanshard; and philosophy, by a group including Blanshard, Demos, and C. W. Hendel. However, there is no article on realism, the one on naturalism has 1 paragraph, the one on monism 2 paragraphs, and the one on pragmatism 3 paragraphs. Existentialism, however, has 12 paragraphs. The bibliography of philosophy in the final volume lists over four hundred books.

OTHER GENERAL ENCYCLOPEDIAS. Of the numerous other modern encyclopedias, mention may be made of seven—three in German, one each in Italian and Spanish, and two in Russian—which are perhaps the most prominent.

German. The *Grosses vollständiges universal Lexicon*, edited by Johann Heinrich Zedler and Carl G. Ludovici (64 vols., Halle and Leipzig, 1732–1750; reprinted, 1959), was the first encyclopedia compiled on a cooperative basis. The number of its collaborators, nine, was meant to correspond to the number of the Muses. The articles display an orthodox and partly medieval point of view, acknowledging the existence of the devil and of miracles, accepting astrology ("the influence of the planets must be conceded"), and stressing the scientific contributions of Roger Bacon and Albert the Great.

Der grosse Brockhaus (16th ed., 12 vols., Wiesbaden, F. A. Brockhaus, 1952–1957; supp. vol., 1958) is the current progeny of the Brockhaus-sponsored *Conversations-Lexikon.* It is especially strong on bibliography. The bibliographical sections of some of the philosophical articles, especially those on individual philosophers, constitute one-third or more of the entire text. The bibliographical section of the article on philosophy contains seven subsections, including one on dictionaries, which lists 12 items (9 German, 2 English, and 1 French).

Of the series of encyclopedias begun by Joseph Meyer as *Das grosse Conversations-Lexicon für die gebildeten Stände* ("The Great Encyclopedia for the Educated Classes," 38 vols. in 46, Philadelphia and Hildburghausen, Germany, Bibliographisches Institut, 1840–1853; 6-vol. supp., 1853–1855) the various editions, most of which were published at Leipzig and Vienna, included, for the most part, very creditable articles on philosophers and philosophical topics. The eighth edition, called *Meyers Lexikon* (Leipzig, Bibliographisches Institut, begun 1936; Vol. XII, an atlas, published 1936), was abandoned in 1942 with the ninth volume, covering *R* and *S*. This edition showed decided Nazi influence, using, for example, the exclamation point of sarcasm in noting, in a discussion of Jewish thought, Spinoza's doctrine that God and nature (and substance also, according to the author of the article) are "identisch(!)" and in referring, in the article on Salomon Maimon, "Philosoph, Ostjude," to the baleful influence of his "Ghetto-Intellekt" on Neo-Kantianism.

Italian. Giovanni Gentile was a director and later a vice-president of the organization which produced the *Enciclopedia italiana di scienze, lettere ed arti* (36 vols., Milan and Rome, Istituto Giovanni Trecanni, later the Istituto della Enciclopedia Italiana, 1929–1939; supp. vol., 1938; 2-vol. supp., 1938–1948). The philosophical articles often include special features. For example, the one on Socrates offers a detailed analysis and appraisal of the sources, the one on Aristotle contains a section on medieval legends about Aristotle and Alexander, the one on Bruno discusses *la libertà filosofica*, and the one on *filosofia* (almost 100,000 words) quotes from a large number of writers on the nature of philosophy. Mussolini was the author of the article on fascism.

Spanish. In the Spanish *Enciclopedia universal illustrada europeo-americana* (70 vols., in 72, Bilbao, Spain, Espasa–Calpe, 1905–1930; 10-vol. appendix, 1930–1933; supp., usually biennially) many of the articles on philosophical schools or positions—materialism, utilitarianism, and so on—are usefully divided into two sections, exposition and criticism. In the article on pragmatism, for example, the sections on Anglo-American pragmatism and French pragmatism are each so divided.

Russian. The outstanding encyclopedia of prerevolutionary Russia was the *Entsiklopedichesky Slovar'* ("Encyclopedic Dictionary"), edited by Ivan E. Andreyevsky and others (43 vols. in 86, St. Petersburg and Leipzig, F. A. Brockhaus–I. A. Ephron, 1890–1907). Its philosophy articles were edited by Vladimir S. Solovyov, one of Russia's greatest philosophers, until his death in 1900 and then by Ernest L. Radlov, author of a philosophical dictionary published in 1911 (mentioned below). Solovyov himself wrote the articles on actuality, Campanella, cause, Comte, Duns Scotus, eternity, freedom of the will, Gorgias, Hartmann, Hegel (22 columns), Indian philosophy, Kant, Lully, Maine de Biran, Malebranche, metaphysics, nature, optimism, pessimism, Plato (28 columns), Plotinus, space, time, Vedānta, world process, and others.

The first edition of the *Bol'shaya Sovetskaya Entsiklopediya* ("Great Soviet Encyclopedia") was published in Moscow from 1926 to 1947 in 66 volumes. The second edition, whose chief editor was S. I. Vavilov, was published in Moscow by the Soviet Encyclopedia Publishing House from 1950 to 1958 in 53 volumes. Stalin's death during the course of publication of the second edition led to a change in the tone in the later volumes, where, for example, the cult of personality is rejected. In 1964 *Pravda* announced plans for a third edition.

The philosophical articles in both editions of the "Great Soviet Encyclopedia" are characteristically Marxist in viewpoint. Thus, Rudolf Carnap's philosophy is branded as "a typical example . . . of subjective idealism under the new labels adopted by the ideologists of the imperialist bourgeoisie in the struggle against the scientific materialist world view." In the allocation of space Hegel gets 5 pages, Kant 4, Spinoza 2, Plato 1, and G. E. Moore none; dialectical materialism gets 19 pages, philosophy 17 pages, and pragmatism half a page.

Some of the philosophical articles of the "Great Soviet Encyclopedia" were translated into German and issued in separate brochures (one each on Aristotle, Hegel, Voltaire, and idealism; one covering Bacon, Berkeley, and Bruno; and one covering Helvétius, Heraclitus,

Hobbes, and Holbach) in a series entitled *Grosse Sowjet-Enzyklopädie: Reihe Geschichte und Philosophie* (Berlin, Aufbau-Verlag, 1953–1955).

ENCYCLOPEDIC DICTIONARY. Well deserving of mention is the fact that Charles S. Peirce wrote the definitions of terms in metaphysics, logic, mathematics, and other subjects and Lyman Abbott was responsible for those in theology in *The Century Dictionary; An Encyclopedic Lexicon of the English Language*, edited by William D. Whitney (8 vols., New York, Century, 1891; issued, together with *The Century Encyclopedia of Names* and an atlas, as a 10-vol. work entitled *The Century Dictionary and Encyclopedia* in various years, with revisions, to 1911; issued in condensed form as *The New Century Dictionary*, 2 vols., D. Appleton–Century, 1943 and later years). According to the Preface, "Though it has not been possible to state all the conflicting definitions of different philosophers and schools," nevertheless, ". . . the philosophical wealth of the English language has, it is believed, never been so fully presented in any dictionary." Peirce's fine hand is evident not only in the choice of illustrative quotations but also in the breakdown of terms into subcategories; for example, the article on being includes definitions of actual being, accidental being, being in itself, connotative being, and so on.

SEMIGENERAL ENCYCLOPEDIAS. The following constitute bridges between the dictionaries of philosophy embedded in general encyclopedias and the separate dictionaries of philosophy.

"Cyclopedia of Education." Articles on 114 philosophers or groups of philosophers "whose systems have educational significance" and on 29 "philosophic views bearing on the nature of education" (atomism, determinism, dualism, empiricism, and so forth) appear in *A Cyclopedia of Education*, edited by Paul Monroe (5 vols., New York, Macmillan, 1919). John Dewey was the departmental editor for philosophy of education, and he wrote the articles on determinism, positivism, and many others. Other contributors include John Burnet, Paul Carus, Morris R. Cohen, Arthur O. Lovejoy, I. Woodbridge Riley, Frank Thilly, and Frederick J. E. Woodbridge. Cohen's article on philosophy is one of the best sources for the history of the teaching of philosophy; its bibliography contains 45 painstakingly assembled entries on philosophy in American, British, and Continental colleges, on philosophy in the secondary school, and so on.

"Encyclopaedia of the Social Sciences." The *Encyclopaedia of the Social Sciences*, edited by Edwin R. A. Seligman and Alvin Johnson (15 vols., New York, Macmillan, 1930–1935; reissued in part or in whole in various years), of which John Dewey was the advisory editor for philosophy, had over a dozen philosophers among its editorial consultants, including Morris R. Cohen, Benedetto Croce, Arthur O. Lovejoy, Ralph Barton Perry, Herbert W. Schneider, and T. V. Smith. This encyclopedia contains some extraordinarily illuminating articles on philosophical subjects.

Among the contributors of philosophical articles were George Boas on Berkeley; Léon Brunschvicg on Pascal and on Plato and Platonism; Ernst Cassirer on Kant; Cohen on atheism, belief, Bradley, Descartes, fictions, Hegel, and scientific method; Dewey on human nature, logic, and philosophy; Sidney Hook on Engels, Feuerbach, materialism, and violence; Hu Shih on Confucianism; Horace M. Kallen on behaviorism, James, modernism, morals, pragmatism, and radicalism; Lovejoy on academic freedom; Richard McKeon on Albert the Great, Anselm, Averroës, and Peter Lombard; C. R. Morris on Locke; M. C. Otto on hedonism; J. H. Randall, Jr., on Copernicus and on deism; F. C. S. Schiller on humanism; Herbert Schneider on Christian socialism, ethical culture, and transcendentalism; T. V. Smith on common sense, duty, ethics, and honor.

Dewey's article on human nature (ten columns) sets forth with clarity and force the principal meanings of the term *human nature*, the basic questions which may be asked about human nature, and the history of the understanding of human nature; his 21-item bibliography begins appropriately with his own *Human Nature and Conduct* (1922). Cassirer's article on Kant (eight columns) highlights Kant's significance for social thought and succinctly traces his impact through Fichte, the Hegelians, and the socialists; the 39-item bibliography begins with Cassirer's ten-volume edition of Kant's *Werke.* McKeon's article on Anselm brings out Anselm's little-known contribution to the problem of church–state relations.

"International Encyclopedia of the Social Sciences." The *International Encyclopedia of the Social Sciences*, a completely new encyclopedia, edited by David L. Sills, is a lineal descendant of the *Encyclopaedia of the Social Sciences.* This encyclopedia is devoted primarily to the fields of anthropology, economics, political science, psychology, sociology, and statistics. However, many of its articles are of direct relevance to philosophy; others describe the relevance of philosophical concepts to the social sciences. There are also many biographical articles on philosophers

who have made significant contributions to the social sciences.

EARLY DICTIONARIES OF PHILOSOPHY

What is to count as a dictionary of philosophy and the difference between a dictionary of philosophy and an encyclopedia of philosophy are largely matters of definition. Two definitions seem most useful for the present purpose. First, a dictionary of philosophy is an expository work setting forth information about philosophical ideas in an arrangement which either is alphabetical (as in the embedded dictionaries of philosophy already mentioned and in most of those described below) or is based on key words or concepts (as in Aristotle's "dictionary" mentioned above and the first few of those mentioned below) rather than on a systematic division of philosophy into its disciplines or parts. Second, an encyclopedia of philosophy is a comprehensive dictionary of philosophy in which various articles are monographic in scope.

Dictionaries of philosophy range from those which are purely factual through those which are partly interpretive or evaluative to those, such as Voltaire's, which present rhapsodic or satirical reflections on key general topics. Divergences from this broad range of varieties also occur—for example, a "dictionary" which merely lists philosophical terms in one language with equivalents in other languages, a "dictionary" which presents for each important philosophical term a suggested usage rather than a statement of actual usage, and an anthology of philosophical quotations arranged alphabetically by topic. Over one hundred dictionaries of philosophy of one sort or another have been published. Most have been soon forgotten, but some have gone through multiple editions over many decades.

MIDDLE AGES. Of the medieval works which may be counted as dictionaries of philosophy perhaps those of Isaac Israeli and Avicenna are most worthy of note. Israeli (c. 855–c. 955), the first Jewish Neoplatonist, wrote, in Arabic, *Kitāb al-Hudūd wal Rusum* ("Book on Definitions and Descriptions"), later translated into Latin and Hebrew. This work contains definitions, with comments thereon, of topics grouped roughly as intellect, soul, vital spirit, and so on; reason, knowledge, opinion, memory, deliberation, and so on; division, syllogism, demonstration, truth, falsehood, necessary, impossible, and so on; imagination, estimation, and sense perception; love, passion, and desire; innovation, creation, coming to be, passing away, and so on; time, eternity, and perpetuity; and other topics. The influence of al-Kindī in some 20 of the 56 sections has been noted by the latest editors of Israeli's work, A. Altmann and S. M. Stern.

Avicenna's *Kitāb al-Hudūd* ("Epistle on Definitions") contains, after an introduction on the pitfalls of the process of defining, definitions—extracted in part from Avicenna's other works—of accident, body, cause, continuous, creation, definition, form, individuality, intelligence, limit, motion, nonbeing, place, prime matter, priority, rest, soul, substance, time, universe, and other subjects. Terms having obvious mutual relations are grouped. The definitions are close to Aristotelianism in tenor.

An anonymous *Compendium Philosophiae*, based mainly on Aristotle and Albert the Great, written (probably in France) about 1327 and as yet only partly edited and published (Paris, 1936), was one of the last medieval dictionaries of philosophy. In topical groups it contains, in Books I to V, brief discussions of God, the physical features of the world, plants, animals, and man and, in Books VI to VIII, scholastic-type discussions of accident, actuality, art, becoming, being and nonbeing, cause, fate, free will, identity, language, law, motion, names, necessity, perfection, philosophy, place, potentiality, quality, quantity, relation, science, substance, time, truth and falsity, virtue and vice, and wisdom, as well as other subjects.

SIXTEENTH CENTURY. After the revival of learning and the invention of printing there appeared a number of compendiums of philosophical information. Apparently, the first formal dictionary of modern times devoted exclusively to philosophy was Giovanni Baptista Bernardo's *Seminarium Totius Philosophiae* (3 vols., Venice, Damian Zenarius, 1582–1585; 2nd ed., 3 vols. in 2, Geneva, Jacob Stoer and Franc. Faber, 1599–1605), later referred to as the *Lexicon Triplex.* In separate alphabetical dictionaries the three volumes cover, respectively, Aristotelian, Platonic, and Stoic philosophy in the writings not only of Aristotle, Plato, and the early Stoics but also of other philosophers, Greek, Roman, Christian, and Arabic. Thus, the first volume contains articles on Aristotelian philosophy from "Abstractio," "Accidens," "Actus," and other topics in the A's to "Zeleucus," "Zephirus," "Zodiacus," and other topics in the Z's.

The article "Definitio" in Volume I contains 333 paragraphs summarizing or quoting specific passages on the subject in Aristotle, Ammonius, Alexander of Aphrodisias, Themistius, Simplicius, Boethius, Averroës, Alexander of Hales, Albert the Great, Thomas Aquinas, and others. A similar approach—abstracting specific passages—is used throughout the three volumes. Accordingly, the work is essentially useful as a thorough guide to the sources but not as a synthesis.

SEVENTEENTH CENTURY. The seventeenth century provided nine principal dictionaries of philosophy, all in Latin.

1610—Nicolaus Burchardi. Buchardi's *Repertorium Philosophicum, Quo Omnes in Universa Philosophia Subinde Occurrunt Termini Perspicue Traduntur* (Leipzig, 573 pages) appeared in 1610. It was also issued at Grimma in 1613 and at Gera in 1614, 1615, and 1616. Only two copies of this work are known to exist, having been located, after many fruitless searches elsewhere, in the Universitätsbibliothek in Marburg, West Germany (the 1614 printing), and in the Sächsische Landesbibliothek in Dresden, East Germany (the 1616 printing). A microfilm copy of the 1616 printing was procured and is filed in the Public Library of the District of Columbia.

The main part of the book is not arranged alphabetically. It treats exactly one hundred topics, from philosophy, logic, metaphysics, art, nature, and word, near the beginning, to infinite soul, theology, and God, at the end. The articles are superficial in their analysis but reflect wide reading in the classic sources. An alphabetical index of topics (*abstractum, ars,* and so on) appears at the beginning, and the book ends with an alphabetically arranged index of themes discussed in the articles—for example, *abstracta saepe ponuntur pro concretis* ("the abstract is often substituted for the concrete") and *amicitia honesta cur rara* ("why true friendship is rare").

1612—Henri Louis Chasteigner. Chasteigner's *Celebriorum Distinctionum turn Philosophicarum tum Theologicarum Synopsis* (Poitiers, A. Mesner, 1612, 71 pages; subsequent eds. or reprints, various places, 1616, 1617, 1619, 1623, 1635, 1645, 1651, 1653, 1657, 1658, 1659, and 1667) made a beginning in the provision of syntheses that Bernardo's work lacked. Thus, absolute is explained as in one sense opposite to relative; in another, to dependent; and in still another, to restricted. Abstraction is broken down into real (when the thing abstracted can exist separately) and rational; rational abstraction, into negative (or divisive) and precise (or simple); and precise abstraction, finally, into physical, mathematical, and so on. A prefatory alphabetical list names 48 authors—Alexander of Hales, Aristotle, Bonaventure, Buridan, Duns Scotus, Suárez, Thomas Aquinas, William of Ockham, and so on—whose writings were chiefly used in compiling the work.

1613—Rudolf Goclenius the elder. The *Lexicon Philosophicum* (Frankfurt, Matthias Becker, 1613, 1,143 pages; additional printings or eds., Marburg, 1613, 1615 and Frankfurt, 1633, 1634; Frankfurt 1613 ed. reissued in facsimile, Hildesheim, 1964) opens with four tributes to Goclenius (Rudolf Goeckel) in Latin verse. There follow articles on terms beginning with the vowels—*absolutum, existentia, idea, obligatio, unitas,* and the like—and then articles on terms beginning with the consonants—*beatitudo, causa,* and so on. The articles are informative, presenting standard scholastic breakdowns and definitions. As has been noted by José Ferrater Mora, Goclenius, although he was the first to use the term *ontologia* (in Greek letters), did not make significant use of the term. Goclenius is cited for support on a particular point in a work as late as Eisler's *Wörterbuch der Philosophie* (1899).

1626—Johann H. Alsted. Alsted's *Compendium Lexici Philosophici* (Herborn, Germany, Georg Corvin and J. G. Muderspach, 1626, 720 pages) is a group of dictionaries on about thirty separate disciplines—anatomy, arithmetic, astronomy, and so on in nonalphabetical order—including ten on philosophy covering ethics, logic, metaphysics, philosophical "archelogy" (basic terms), philosophical didactics (teaching of philosophy), philosophical "hexilogy" (mental faculties involved in philosophy), philosophical method, pneumatics (study of spiritual beings), poetics, and politics. Some parts of the dictionaries are alphabetical; others are not. Of the ten philosophical dictionaries, the one on logic, which is 26 pages long, is perhaps the best, but most of the material in it is not arranged alphabetically and is therefore difficult to follow.

1629—George Reeb, S.J. Reeb's *Distinctiones Philosophicae* (Ingolstadt, Germany, Gregory Haenlin, 1629, 167 pages; 2nd ed., Cologne, 1630) was reprinted in 1653, 1657, and 1658 in the same volume as Chasteigner's *Synopsis.* With Reeb's *Axiomata Philosophica* it was reissued under the editorship of J. M. Cornoldi, S.J. (Bressanone, Italy, 1871 and Paris, 1873, 1875, 1891), under the title *Thesaurus Philosophorum, seu Distinctiones et Axiomata Philosophica.* Reeb's work, written from a scholastic viewpoint, discusses, as philosophical topics, such adverbial opposites as absolutely and dependently, in act and in potency, artificially and naturally, collectively and distributively, concretely and abstractly, and so on.

1653—Johann Micraelius. The *Lexicon Philosophicum Terminorum Philosophis Usitatorum* of Johann Micraelius (Jena, Jeremiah Mamphras, 1653, 667 pages; 2nd printing, 1662) contains explanations of the terms used in philosophy, broadly understood; a 51-page appended outline, by discipline, of the topics covered; a 30-page index of Greek terms; and 17 pages of illustrations, mostly geometric figures. Many articles begin with what Aristotle said on the subject and continue with the scholastic elaborations of what Aristotle said. The article "Deus," however, begins by saying flatly that Aristotle was right in calling God the prime mover but was wrong in denying God's creation of the world, God's omniscience, and so on.

1658—Johann Adam Scherzer (Schertzer) and others. Scherzer and others' *Vade Mecum, Sive Manuale Philosophicum Quadripartitum* (Leipzig, Christian Kirchner, 1658) has four parts separately paged but bound as one volume. Part I, by Scherzer, entitled *Definitiones Philosophicae*, is a scholastic-type alphabetical dictionary, with definitions, for example, under *necessarium*, of absolute, hypothetical, physical, moral, and logical kinds of necessary thing. Part II consists of Chasteigner's *Synopsis* and Reeb's *Distinctiones Philosophicae.* Part III, by Scherzer, entitled *Axiomata Resoluta*, presents a system of rules of thought (a thing cannot be and not be, a proposition must be true or false, and so on). Part IV, by Scherzer, entitled *Aurifodina Distinctionum* ("Gold Mine of Distinctions"), discusses selected distinctions in an alphabetical arrangement (for example, intrinsic and extrinsic accidents among the A's and remote and proximate cause among the C's). Scherzer's project was ambitious, but the resulting complex was too cumbersome for convenience.

1675—Heinrich Volckmar. The *Dictionarium Philosophicum, Hoc Est Enodatio Terminorum ac Distinctionum* of Heinrich Volckmar (Frankfurt, Jacob Gottfried Seyler, 1675, 798 pages; 2nd printing, 1676) is in Latin, but the author sprinkles a little German here and there. Thus, in citing the tenet "Credo quod Deus creavit me" under "Creatio," he translated it (as if it were difficult Latin) "Ich gläube dass mich Gott geschaffen hat." In an epilogue he asked the reader to ascribe any omissions not to negligence but to the enormity of the field to be covered, and he named as predecessors Chasteigner, Goclenius, Reeb, Micraelius, and Scherzer but not Alsted.

1692—Étienne Chauvin. In Chauvin's *Lexicon Rationale, Sive Thesaurus Philosophicus Ordine Alphabetico Digestus* (Rotterdam, P. van der Slaast, 1692, 756 pages; 2nd ed., entitled *Lexicon Philosophicum*, Leeuwarden, Netherlands, Franciscus Halma, 1713, 719 pages) philosophy includes natural science. Thus, there are articles, in their Latin equivalents, on acceleration, fire, meteors, and the stomach, as well as on Aristotle, Descartes (a particularly laudatory article), other philosophers, and *cognitio, simplicitas, subsistentia*, and other philosophical concepts. Cartesian influence is apparent in many of the articles.

"Nondictionaries." Mention may also be made of an unalphabetical "lexicon" of this period by Pierre Godart. The second edition of his *Totius Philosophiae Summa* (Paris, L. Billaine, 1666, 245 pages) was entitled *Lexicon Philosophicum* (2 vols. in 1, Paris, J. and R. I. B. de La Caille, 1675) although it was not really a dictionary. After an introduction on philosophy and its divisions, the philosophical schools, and some principles of philosophy the book discusses being, causes, properties, and species; physics, including matter, motion, soul, sensation, and so on, with an attack on Cartesian philosophy; economics and politics; and logic. The alphabetical index in the second edition is 47 pages long.

Wolter Schopen's *Alphabetum Philosophicum* (Nissa, John Joseph Krembsl', 1696, 105 pages), although sometimes referred to as a dictionary of philosophy, is, like Godart's *Lexicon*, not a dictionary. It is a straight exposition of twenty-odd philosophical topics, such as what a definition is, what conversion and opposition of propositions are, and how many kinds of syllogism there are, each topic being designated by a letter of the alphabet (*A, B, C*, and so on).

LEIBNIZ AND AFTER. Among the fragments of Leibniz edited in 1903 by Louis Couturat and assigned to the period 1670–1704 are two which show an interest in the Alsted work mentioned above and several which consist of lists of definitions of terms, as if Leibniz were thinking of compiling a dictionary of philosophy apart from the general encyclopedia which he had discussed with Louis XIV. One of these lists of definitions, for example, is headed "Introductio ad Encyclopaediam Arcanam." It contains definitions of *conceptus clarus, conceptus distinctus, conceptus adaequatus, conceptus primitivus*, and the like. Another, untitled, contains definitions of *amor* (love), *sapientia* (wisdom), *laetitia* (joy), *perfectio* (perfection), and so on. Illustrative are his definitions of love, the emotion by which it happens that the good or evil of another is considered part of our own, and of wisdom, the science of happiness. If Leibniz had completed a dictionary of philosophy along these lines, it would probably have constituted a vade mecum to his own philosophy rather than an exposition of historical viewpoints in philosophy.

In 1716, the year of Leibniz' death, there appeared the last Latin dictionary of philosophy before the first modern-language dictionaries. It was the *Lexicon Philo-*

sophicum; Sive Index Latinorum Verborum Descriptionumque ad Philosophos & Dialecticos Maxime Pertinentium (The Hague, Henri du Sauzet, 322 pages), of which the author is listed on the title page as Plexiacus ("Auctore Plexiaco"). Plexiacus has been identified as Charles Du-Plessis d'Argentre or Michèle Toussaint Chrétien Dupplessis (or du Plessis), but the best scholars attribute the work to one Michel Brochard. Following an extended systematic treatment of argumentation, definition, words and things, distinctions, and so on, the author presents, in an alphabetical arrangement, numerous philosophical terms and their definitions. The systematic treatment in the first part of the book, which leans heavily on the writings of Cicero, is more interesting than the somewhat routine definitions in the lexicon proper.

A Latin quasi dictionary of philosophy that may deserve mention here is the book *Philosophia Definitiva, Hoc Est Definitiones Philosophicae*, by Frederick Christian Baumeister (Wittenberg, Germany, J. J. Ahlfeld, 1738, 252 pages; 7th ed., 1746; enlarged ed., 1767), which contains definitions, grouped according to subject, of 329 logical terms, 233 terms in ontology, 95 terms in cosmology, 264 in psychology, 53 in natural theology, 182 in ethics, 69 in political philosophy, and 35 in physics, with a consolidated alphabetical index. The definitions, based in large part on the philosophy of Christian Wolff, are useful but not profound.

FIRST MODERN-LANGUAGE DICTIONARIES

In 1715 there appeared a work by J. H. (Johann Hübner) entitled *Compendieuses Lexicon Philosophicum* (Frankfurt and Leipzig, B. P. C. Monath, 208 pages; 2nd ed., 1717). The title of the second edition, varying slightly from that of the first, was *Compendieuses Lexicon Metaphysicum, zum besondern Nutzen aller Studierenden, vornemlich abet der politischen Wissenschaften befliessenen zusammen getragen* ("Compendious Metaphysical Lexicon, for Special Uses by All Students, but Chiefly Those Specializing in Political Sciences Taken as a Whole"). Although the work is in German, it discusses only Latin philosophical terms in nonalphabetical order. It begins with *ens* (a being) and among other things points out, with German examples, the distinctions among *ens, res* (a thing), and *reale* (a real thing). Other terms discussed include *verum* and *bonum* (true and real), *ubi* and *quando* (where and when), and the four causes. An alphabetical index at the end contains over four hundred entries, including about fifty under *causa—efficiens, in sensu juridico, necessaria, proxima*, and so on. The treatment is elementary, the analyses are not sharp, and the work has only historical interest today.

The first alphabetically arranged dictionary of philosophy in a modern European language appears to be Hubert Gautier's *La Bibliothèque des philosophes, et des sçavans, tant anciens que modernes* (2 vols., Paris, André Cailleau, 1723). Chauvin had treated philosophy as including the natural sciences; Gautier treated it as including the natural sciences and the humanities. Thus, his book contains articles on Alexander the Great, Copernicus, and La Fontaine, as well as on Avicenna, Descartes, Porphyry, and many others, plus a smaller number of topical articles, such as those on the Académie Royale des Sciences, *homme* (man), and *terre* (earth). Each volume has a topical index. Today, the work has interest mainly as a curiosity rather than for the information it provides.

Strictly speaking, the first dictionary of philosophy in a modern language appears to be the *Philosophisches Lexikon*, by Johann Georg Walch (Leipzig, 1726, 3,048 cols.; 2nd ed., 1733; 3rd ed., 1740; 4th ed., 2 vols., 1775), which set a new standard of comprehensiveness and scholarship for works of this kind. It reflects in part the ideas of Leibniz and Wolff, quoting or citing them in various articles as authorities. Among the more intriguing articles in this *Lexikon* are those on atheism (16 cols.), discussing arguments derived from the existence of evil, the eternity of the world, the sufficiency of nature as an explanation of events, the anthropomorphic character of our idea of God, and so on; self-knowledge, knowledge of others, knowledge of nature, and knowledge of God; fate, with summaries of the views of Parmenides, Democritus, Plato, Aristotle, the Stoics, the Epicureans, the Chaldeans and other Oriental peoples, Sextus Empiricus, Leibniz, and others; and freedom of thought (25 cols.), discussing the ipse dixit principle, freedom of interpretation, freedom of belief, the role of reason, the fate of Spinoza, the right to know the truth, and other aspects of the topic.

An appendix covers philosophers from Abelard, Albinus, and others at the beginning to the two Zenos and Zoroaster at the end. These biographical sketches are of decidedly less interest than the vivid expositions in the topical articles. Many of the biographical sketches begin, repetitiously, ". . . one of the most famous philosophers of" such-and-such a country.

In 1963 the Stuttgart firm of Friedrich Frommann Verlag was planning to issue a facsimile reprint of the fourth edition of Walch's *Philosophisches Lexikon.*

Walch's work was followed by one which originated the exact title used shortly thereafter by Voltaire. This was the *Dictionnaire philosophique portatif, ou Introduction à la connoissance de l'homme*, by Didier Pierre Chicaneau de Neuville (London, J. M. Bruyset, 1751, 381 pages; 2nd ed., Lyon, J. M. Bruyset, 1756; Italian translation of 2nd ed., Venice, 1756; 3rd ed., Paris, 1764). In de Neuville's pioneering French philosophical lexicon many of the articles are, or begin with, dictionary-type definitions, but the further explanatory material (including quotations from Boileau, Pope, Rousseau, and the early writings of Voltaire) is sometimes piquant.

VOLTAIRE AND AFTER

On September 28, 1752, Voltaire and other intellectual companions of Frederick the Great were dining with the king at Potsdam. Someone, perhaps Frederick himself, mentioned the idea of producing a philosophical dictionary on which men of letters, including Frederick, would collaborate. Voltaire began work on the project the next day and soon showed the article "Abraham" to Frederick, who considered it good and asked Voltaire to set up a list of proposed articles for the work. Voltaire instead quickly produced articles on *âme* (soul), *athéisme, baptême*, and so on, and Frederick commented that the whole book would soon be finished. Voltaire, however, interrupted the project some months later, when he left Potsdam following his break with Frederick, and he presently became involved in preparing articles for Diderot's *Encyclopédie.*

Early in 1760 Voltaire resumed work on his own dictionary. He wrote to the marquise du Deffant on February 18, "I am absorbed in rendering an alphabetical account to myself of everything that I think about this world and the other, entirely for my own use, but (perhaps after my death) for that of honest people."

In the summer of 1764 the *Dictionnaire philosophique portatif*, which was 344 pages long and contained 73 articles, was printed anonymously at Geneva with London given as the place of publication. There was a second printing later in the year. The book was banned by the Parlement of Paris on March 19, 1765, and was placed on the Index of prohibited books by the pope on July 8, 1765. Voltaire denied authorship of the book in 68 letters between July 1764 and February 1768.

A second edition was published at London in 1765 in four printings (varying from 308 to 364 pages), with eight additional articles. Three of these four printings were subsequently counted as the second, third, and fourth editions. A printing which was counted as the fifth edition was issued at Amsterdam in 1765 in two volumes with 15 additional articles. An edition specifically labeled "Sixième Édition," with 34 additional articles, was published at London in 1767 in two fascicles bound as one volume. Another edition, also called the "Sixième Édition," was printed at Geneva in 1769 under the title *La Raison par alphabet*, with further additions, in two volumes.

Subsequent editions continued to appear both during and after Voltaire's lifetime under various titles, sometimes including the articles prepared by Voltaire for the *Encyclopédie*; Voltaire's *Questions sur l'Encyclopédie*, an alphabetically arranged set of comments; *L'Opinion par alphabet*, a manuscript found after Voltaire's death; or a combination of the foregoing. One of the most useful editions was edited by Julien Benda (2 vols., Paris, Garnier Frères, 1936). Of the English versions, complete or abridged, the first appeared in 1765; a noteworthy successor appeared in 1824 (6 vols., London, J. and H. L. Hunt), comprising about three-fourths of the original, the remainder being, according to the anonymous translator, repetitive. In 1901 an "unabridged and unexpurgated" edition was translated by William F. Fleming (10 vols., London, E. R. DuMont): the latest edition, translated by Peter Gay with a preface by André Maurois, was published in 1962 (2 vols., New York, Basic Books).

Voltaire's dictionary covers primarily topics, almost totally excluding individual philosophers; among the few philosophers accorded separate treatment are Arius and "Julien le Philosophe." The topical articles are largely in the nature of discursive essays, occasionally in dialogue form, rather than directly informative expositions, but they nevertheless reflect extensive research and critical analysis. In the article on miracles Voltaire made such points as the following: if a miracle is an event to be marveled at, then everything is a miracle; if a miracle is a violation of an eternal (inviolable) law, then it is a contradiction in terms; it is a strange God who is so incapable of achieving his purposes through his own laws of nature that he must resort to changing his own "eternal" ways.

The topics covered are, for the most part, in the field of popular philosophy or religious controversy, such as Adam, apocalypse, *tout est bien* (all is good), confession, *enfer* (hell), inquisition, and so on. A few touch on technical philosophy; examples are those on *âme* (soul), *beauté* (beauty), *chain des êtres créés* ("great chain of being"), *destin* (fate), and *nécessaire* (necessary). Of the articles in his own dictionary Voltaire submitted only the one on idolatry intact to Diderot for inclusion in the *Encyclopédie*. It was reprinted there without change.

Various literary scholars have studied the sources of Voltaire's dictionary. Although Voltaire acknowledged his indebtedness to Bayle's *Dictionnaire historique et critique* and the title of his dictionary is identical with that of the one de Neuville published in 1751, it appears that he owed more to the English deists and the early French deists. As André Maurois has observed, the ideas in Voltaire's dictionary "were clichés in its epoch. Gassendi, Fontenelle, Bayle, had said all that." But the form in which the ideas are clothed in Voltaire's dictionary is inimitably adroit, vivid, chatty, anecdotal, and essentially consistent in its rough humaneness and urbanity though inconsistent in details.

REACTION TO VOLTAIRE. Reacting with indignation to the religious skepticism of the *Dictionnaire philosophique portatif* and without knowing that Voltaire was the author of the work, Louis M. Chaudon published—also anonymously—the *Dictionnaire anti-philosophique, pour servir de commentaire & de correctif au Dictionnaire philosophique & aux autres livres qui ont paru de nos jours contre le christianisme* (Avignon, 1767, 451 pages; 4th ed., 2 vols. in 1, Avignon, La Veuve Girard, 1775). Among the approximately 150 articles in the first edition are those on soul, atheism, Bayle, *Encyclopédie*, faith, hell, miracles, natural law, and reason; new articles in subsequent editions include those on deists, Spinoza, suicide, theater; and tyrannicide. Some of the articles are in two sections, presenting the orthodox view of the subject and replying to the skeptics' objections. After the alphabetical part of the work is a summary headed "Résultat des réflexions répandues dans ce *Dictionnaire*." Chaudon's defense of religion in general and of Christianity in particular was spirited and literate.

OTHER EIGHTEENTH-CENTURY DICTIONARIES. Between Voltaire and Chaudon and the end of the eighteenth century six dictionaries of philosophy appeared—three in French, two in German, and one in English—plus a number of works which have promising titles but are not dictionaries of philosophy.

French. In 1772, eight years after the first appearance of Voltaire's dictionary, a work comparable in outline, *La Petite Encyclopédie, ou Dictionnaire des philosophes*, by Abraham J. de Chaumeix, a Frenchman, was published anonymously and posthumously (Antwerp, Jean Gasbeck, 136 pages). It contains only topical articles, none on philosophers, and the articles are popular rather than strictly philosophical in tenor. The motto at the end of the book is a misquotation from Virgil, "Heu! Ubi prisca fides?" ("Alas! Where now is your former faith?").

The other two of the three French dictionaries were parts of a 166-volume rearrangement, by disciplines, of the material in the Diderot *Encyclopédie*. The rearrangement, entitled *Encyclopédie méthodique* (Paris, C. J. Panckoucke and others, 1782–1832), consisted of about fifty separate dictionaries. One of these was *Logique, métaphysique et morale*, edited by Pierre L. Lacratelle (4 vols., 1786–1791). The Lacratelle work started out to cover only logic and metaphysics, and a complete alphabetical arrangement of topics in those two disciplines was presented, from absolute (in logic, 2 cols.) and abstraction (19 cols.) at the beginning of Volume I to sensation (230 cols.) and systems (41 cols.) near the end of Volume II; however, the scope was then changed to include ethics, and the remainder of Volume II and Volumes III and IV contain an alphabetical series of articles on ethics. Volume III was the first volume to include ethics on the title page.

Immediately adjacent to the Lacratelle work in the *Encyclopédie méthodique* is *Philosophie, ancienne et moderne*, edited by Jacques A. Naigeon, an atheist who considered himself Diderot's successor (3 vols., 1791–1793). The topics range from Academics (352 cols.) and Academy (2 cols.) in Volume I to Zend-Avesta (10 cols., Diderot's article on the subject transplanted intact from the *Encyclopédie*) in Volume III. The third volume also contains, on pages 767–945, articles omitted from the first two volumes.

German. Various giants in the history of philosophy—Aristotle, Leibniz, and Voltaire—have thus far entered this record as contributors to the development of dictionaries of philosophy. Another giant—Kant—enters the record by a quirk of terminology. Kant lectured on the subject *philosophische Enzyklopädie* ten times from 1767/1768 to 1781/1782 and advertised lectures on this subject for 1785/1786 and 1787, although these did not materialize. A set of his lecture notes on *philosophische Enzyklopädie*, probably dating from the winter semester of 1781/1782, was edited by the Deutsche Akademie der Wissenschaften zu Berlin and published for the first time in 1961 in East Berlin. But the work actually deals with what might suitably be called philosophy as an encyclopedic discipline rather than philosophy expounded in encyclopedic form. It presents a structured (not alphabetical) outline of philosophy in its broadest ramifications, based on J. H. Feder's *Grundrisz der philosophischen Wissenschaften* ("Foundation of the Philosophical Sciences," Coburg, Germany, J. C. Findeisen, 1767; 2nd ed., 1769).

Thus, Kant did not write a dictionary of philosophy. However, his admirer Salomon Maimon did. Maimon was the author of *Philosophisches Wörterbuch, oder Beleuchtung der wichtigsten Gegenstände der Philosophie, in alphabetischer Ordnung* ("Philosophical Dictionary, or Illumination of the Most Important Themes of Philosophy, in Alphabetical Order," Berlin, Johann F. Unger, 1791, 222 pages). This work is an impressionistic presentation of various philosophical topics, in substance less iconoclastic than Voltaire's dictionary but just as unconventional stylistically. One of the articles, for example, includes separate vehement apostrophes, each beginning "Meine Herren!," to "die Dogmatiker oder Antikantianer" ("dogmatic philosophers or anti-Kantians") and "die kritischen Skeptiker oder Kantianer" ("critical skeptics or Kantians").

Another German dictionary of philosophy in this period, also impressionistic, was Carl Ludwig Friedrich Rabe's *Gedanken und Urtheile über philosophische, moralische und politische Gegenstände, aus guten Schriften gezogen, alphabetisch geordnet* ("Thoughts and Judgments on Philosophical, Ethical and Political Themes, Deduced From Reliable Publications, Alphabetically Arranged," Stendal, Germany, D. C. Franzen and J. C. Grosse, 1789–1790, 2 vols.). This work is even rarer than the Burchardi book of 1610. The Royal Library at Copenhagen possesses what may be the sole extant copy of it, located after the trail had run dry in many other directions. A microfilm of the Copenhagen copy is now available at the Public Library of the District of Columbia.

Volume I of Rabe's *Gedanken* contains reflections on topics with initial letters from A to Z, and Volume II likewise begins at the beginning of the alphabet and goes through to Z. Among the topics discussed are antiquity, art, business, culture, death, despotism, freedom of the press, God, guilt, happiness, language, man, religion, republic, *Schmerz*, science, soul, and time. Articles range from one or two lines to three or four pages in length. The one on freedom of the press reads, in translation, "Without freedom of the press, the soul is crippled. Freedom to think, without freedom to say, is no better than being in a straitjacket." The article on *Held* (hero) reads, "Ein Held wird nicht geformt, er wird geboren" ("A hero is born, not made").

Toward the end of the eighteenth century, there appeared two other documents like Kant's with titles that sound relevant to the story of dictionaries of philosophy but which turn out to have no relevance to the subject. The first of these was Johann Georg Büsch's *Encyclopädie der historischen, philosophischen und mathematischen Wissenschaften* (2 vols. in 1, Hamburg, Heroldsche Buchhandlung, 1775), which presents its material not in an alphabetical but in a systematic arrangement, Volume I covering history and philosophy and Volume II mathematics. The section on philosophy stresses the contributions of Descartes and Wolff and discusses philosophy in general, logic, theology, philosophical psychology, ethics, politics, economics, and related topics.

The second was the *Encyclopädische Einleitung in das Studium der Philosophie*, by Karl Heinrich Heydenricks (Leipzig, Weygandsche Buchhandlung, 1793, 249 pages), which is a systematic, nonalphabetical exposition of the nature of philosophy, systems of philosophy, the bearing of philosophy on other disciplines and on life, and the way to study philosophy.

English. In 1786, *The Philosophical Dictionary, or The Opinions of Modern Philosophers on Metaphysical, Moral, and Political Subjects*, by François Xavier Swediaur, was published (4 vols., London, G. G. J. and J. Robinson, 1786) with "F. S******r, M.D." at the end of the Preface as the only indication of the author or compiler. Many of the articles bear at the end the name of an author (Gibbon, Helvétius, Hume, Locke, Rousseau, Voltaire, and others) from whose writings the article was adapted. Swediaur did not show much understanding of or sympathy for technical philosophy. His article "Ancient Greek Philosophy" mentions Hesiod and Theognis but not Socrates, Plato, or Aristotle.

NINETEENTH CENTURY

Dictionaries of philosophy, or works purporting to be such, appeared in German, English, French, Italian, Latin, and Russian in the nineteenth century.

GERMAN. Initiating the contributions of the century to the library of dictionaries of philosophy, J. C. Lossius published *Neues philosophisches allgemeines Real-Lexikon* (4 vols., Erfurt, Germany, J. E. G. Rudolph, 1803–1805). It contains no articles on individual philosophers. Many of the articles are written from a Kantian point of view. The topics treated include not only such philosophical concepts as *angebohrne Begriffe* (innate ideas) and *cogito ergo sum* but also concepts in anthropology, mathematics, and other disciplines.

Lossius' four-volume work was followed soon after by two other works, both of which were left incomplete.

The first of these, Georg S. A. Mellin's *Allgemeines Wörterbuch der Philosophie, zur Gebrauch für gebildete Leser* ("General Dictionary of Philosophy, for Use by

Educated Readers," 2 vols., Magdeburg, Germany, Ferdinand Matthias, 1806–1807), covers the letters *A* and *B*; no more volumes were published. The work is thoroughly Kantian, as is evidenced particularly in such articles as those on apperception, on the various aspects of *Begriff* (concept), and on the various kinds of concepts.

The other, Gottfried Immanuel Wenzel's *Neues vollständiges philosophisches Real-Lexikon* ("New Complete Philosophical Encyclopedia," 2 vols., Linz, Austria, Akademische Buchhandlung, 1807–1808), was planned in four volumes, but the author died before the work was completed, and only two volumes (covering *A* to *H*) appeared. The quaint subtitle gives an adequate, if overstated, description of the work. Literally translated, the subtitle reads: "In Which the Materials and Technical Terms Appearing in All Parts of Recent and Most Recent Philosophy Are Explained, Being Developed From History Where Necessary; Disagreements of Philosophers Are Expounded and Analyzed, Many Propositions Thereof Being Corrected, Made Precise, or Expanded; Obscurities Are Lifted; New Contributions to the Stock of Philosophical Knowledge Are Presented; and Higher Pedagogy and the Science of Intellectual Excellence [*Klugheitslehre*] Are Similarly Treated."

Original works of encyclopedic scope. Each of three German works published in the subsequent years of the nineteenth century, although denominated an encyclopedia of philosophy, presented its material nonalphabetically. The works are Gottlob E. Schulze's *Enzyklopädie der philosophischen Wissenschaften, zum Gebrauche für seine Vorlesungen* ("Encyclopedia of the Philosophical Sciences, for Use With the Author's Lectures," Göttingen, Vandenhoeck und Ruprecht, 1814, 150 pages; 2rd ed., 1818; 3rd ed., 1823, 1824); Georg Friedrich Hegel's *Encyklopädie der philosophischen Wissenschaften zum Grundrisse* ("Encyclopedia of the Philosophical Sciences in Outline," Heidelberg, A. Oswald, 1817, 288 pages; 2nd and 3rd eds., 1827, 1830; 4th ed., 3 vols., Berlin, issued by Hegel's students with their lecture notes and other materials, 1840–1845); and Johann F. Herbart's *Kurze Encyklopädie der Philosophie aus praktischen Gesichtspuncten entworfen* ("Short Encyclopedia of Philosophy Designed From the Practical Standpoint," Halle, Germany, C. A. Schwetschke und Sohn, 1831, 405 pages; 2nd ed., 1841), which is reprinted in the various editions of Herbart's collected works.

Other dictionaries. German dictionaries of philosophy, more properly so designated, were written after the earliest years of the century by Krug, Furtmair, Hartsen, No-ack, and Kirchner (as well as by Eisler, who wrote a landmark work described in a section below). Of the works referred to the first four are of mainly historical interest.

The first is Wilhelm T. Krug's *Allgemeines Handwörterbuch der philosophischen Wissenschaften, nebst ihrer Literatur und Geschichte, nach dem heutigen Standpuncte der Wissenschaft* ("General Concise Dictionary of the Philosophical Sciences, Including Their Literature and History, From the Present Standpoint of Science," 4 vols., Leipzig, F. A. Brockhaus, 1827–1829, plus supp., 1829; 2nd ed., 4 vols., 1832–1833, plus supp., 1838). Krug succeeded Kant in the chair of philosophy at Königsberg. Among the more interesting and unusual articles of Krug's book, all competently written, are "Aegyptische Weisheit" (Egyptian wisdom), "Baccalaureus der Philosophie" (Ph.B. degree), "Freund und Freundschaft" (friend and friendship), "Immoralität" (immorality), "Ontologischer Beweis für's Dasein Gottes" (Ontological Proof of God's existence), Schöne Kunst" (fine art), and "Supernaturalismus" (supernaturalism). The collaborators who produced the Adolphe Franck dictionary of 1844–1852 mentioned below and Pierre Larousse of the French encyclopedia firm criticized Krug more sharply than seems warranted for working, as far as they could see, without plan or method, for giving more emphasis to the history of philosophy than to philosophy itself, and for showing, in their opinion, insufficient gravity in his style.

Another dictionary was Max Furtmair's *Philosophisches Real-Lexikon* (4 fascicles in 1 vol., Augsburg, Karl Koll-manschen Buchhandlung, 1853–1855). The third and fourth fascicles were prepared with the collaboration of Johann N. Uschold. The author, inviting attention to his title, said that his aim was to clarify not words but things. What he presented, however, is indistinguishable from the contents of lexicons with more modest pretensions. His heavy indebtedness to Krug, which he acknowledged, is evidenced by, among other things, his inclusion of the articles "Aegyptische Weisheit," "Baccalaureus der Philosophie," "Freundschaft," and others on topics suggested by Krug's work.

In 1877 appeared Frederik A. Hartsen's *Ein philosophisches Wörterbuch* (Heidelberg, Carl Winter, 45 pages). The terms defined in this work are generally philosophical expressions rather than single terms. An example is *Betrachten etwas* (*A*) *als etwas* (*B*) ("considering something [*A*] as something [*B*]"). In some cases the definitions are of the dictionary type, with little philosophical depth.

There is also Ludwig Noack's *Philosophiegeschichtliches Lexikon* (Leipzig, Erich Koschny, 1879, 936 pages). This work emphasizes individual philosophers and is especially useful for little-known Renaissance and early modern thinkers. Although some topics—the Academy, eclectics, French philosophy, Cabala—are covered, there are no articles on the philosophical disciplines—ethics, logic, metaphysics, and so on. In 1963 the Stuttgart firm of Friedrich Frommann Verlag was planning to issue a facsimile reprint of this work.

Friedrich Kirchner, author of philosophical monographs and textbooks, including a history of philosophy which went into several editions and was translated into English, wrote a *Wörterbuch der philosophischen Grundbegriffe* (Heidelberg, G. Weiss, 1886, 459 pages), which also appeared in second and third editions (1890 and 1897), by Kirchner, and in fourth, fifth, and sixth editions (1903, 1907, 1911), revised by Carl Michaëlis. The first fascicle, 96 pages, of a projected Russian translation was published at St. Petersburg by Brockhaus–Ephron in 1913. Kirchner's work contains no articles on individual philosophers. The articles are scholarly but not penetrating; the one on logic, for example, is mainly historical and biographical.

ENGLISH. The four English dictionaries of philosophy published in the nineteenth century are now outmoded.

The first one, Isaac Taylor's *Elements of Thought, or First Lessons in the Knowledge of the Mind* (London, B. J. Holdsworth, 208 pages), appeared in 1822. With some changes in the subtitle this work went through 11 British editions (11th ed., 1866) and two American editions (2nd American ed., New York, 1851). Part II contains an exposition, in alphabetical order, of about ninety topics—analysis, argument, art, axiom, being, belief, cause, and so on—bearing upon "the nature and operation of the intellectual powers."

In 1857 William Fleming's *The Vocabulary of Philosophy, Mental, Moral, and Metaphysical, With Quotations and References, for the Use of Students* (London and Glasgow, Richard Griffin, 560 pages) was published. Subsequent editions included the second (1858), an American edition, edited by Charles P. Krauth (Philadelphia, 1860; reissued 6 times, 1866–1873); a third, edited by Henry Calderwood (1876); another American edition edited and entitled *A Vocabulary of the Philosophical Sciences* by Krauth (1878; reissued, 1879); another American edition edited by Calderwood (New York, 1887, 1890); and a work by Calderwood entitled *Vocabulary of Philosophy and Student's Book of Reference, on the Basis of Fleming's Vocabulary* (1894). The illustrative quotations in the various articles are taken mainly from English writers such as Berkeley, Hume, Jeremy Taylor, Sir William Hamilton, and J. S. Mill, but there are quotations from Kant (in English) in the article "A Priori," from Cicero (in Latin) in "Faculty," and from other foreign thinkers in other articles.

In *A Dictionary of English Philosophical Terms* (London, Rivington, 1878, 161 pages) Francis Garden undertook to present a more general and less technical account of philosophical topics than had appeared in Fleming's work. Like Fleming, however, he leaned heavily on Hamilton for arguments, illustrations, and even topics, including, for example, the article "Worse Relations" (that is, more distant relations) in logic, which is written chiefly according to Hamilton's views.

Edwin S. Metcalf's *Olio of Isms, Ologies and Kindred Matter, Defined and Classified* (Chicago, L'Ora Queta P. and J. Co., 1899, 158 pages) is an elementary and popular manual. In the section "Doctrinal and Sectarian Isms" it has articles on agnosticism, antinomianism, Arminianism, and the like; the section "Civic Isms" has articles on topics like anarchism and collectivism; "Ologies" deals with such topics as aetiology and cosmology. A section headed "Miscellany" treats altruism, analogy, art, and so forth, and "Divination" has articles on aruspicy (art or practice of divination), bibliomancy, and similar topics.

The work entitled *A Dictionary of Philosophy in the Words of Philosophers,* compiled by John R. Thomson (London, R. D. Dickinson, 1887, 479 pages; 2nd ed., 1892), is not a dictionary. Its material is arranged according to a strange outline the logic of which leaves much to be desired. In some cases it is not clear whether the material presented is in Thomson's words or in those of the philosopher who is under discussion.

FRENCH, ITALIAN, AND LATIN DICTIONARIES. Adolphe Franck, a disciple of Victor Cousin, and more than fifty collaborators, including A. A. Cournot, Paul Janet, and Ernest Renan, produced the *Dictionnaire des sciences philosophiques* (6 vols., Paris, Librairie Hachette, 1844–1852; 2nd ed., 1 vol., 1875; 3rd ed., 1 vol., 1885); the second and third editions had an analytical guide to the alphabetical articles. In matters touching on religion the authors of the articles, as pointed out by Pierre Larousse in 1865, showed restraint and circumspection; indeed, in the Preface they acknowledged reverence as one of their key principles. The work is still useful today for its extensive articles on less well-known philosophers. It contains, for example, individual articles on 12 Sophists, 11 Cyrenaics, 6 Pyrrhonists, 13 Greek Stoics, 15 Roman Stoics, and 21 members of the school of Leibniz and Wolff.

Of the other French-language dictionaries of philosophy published in the nineteenth century, one was a Belgian product, and three were Parisian.

The Belgian work, (Louis J. A.) de Potter's *Dictionnaire rationnel des mots les plus usités en sciences, en philosophie, en politique, en morale et en religion* (Brussels and Leipzig, August Sehnée, 1859, 348 pages), began as a glossary at the end of the author's *La Réalité déterminée par le raisonnement* (Brussels, 1848). The glossary was reprinted under the title *A, B, C de la science sociale* (Brussels, 1848) and was then extensively elaborated into the *Dictionnaire rationnel.* The author defended middle-class conservatism in religion, politics, morals, and economics. He decried the intellectual elite and the democratic masses, the philosophical skeptics and the radical innovators.

In 1877 Bernard Pérez wrote the 16-page *Petit dictionnaire philosophique* (Paris, A. Morant). This work, intended for baccalaureate candidates, contains mostly two-line to four-line definitions or explanations of technical terms (plus identifications of a few philosophers), from *acatalepsie, actuel, and animisme* to *vitalisme,* Xenocrate, and *zététique* (persistent skepticism). Pérez also produced a similar work, *Dictionnaire abrégé de philosophie* (Paris, Félix Alcan, 1893, 90 pages).

Pages 483–521 of Henri Marion's *Leçons de psychologie appliquées à l'éducation* (Paris, Armand Colin, 1882, 538 pages; 13th ed., 1908) contained a "Vocabulaire des noms propres et des expressions philosophiques." This vocabulary covers topics in philosophy and other fields, including art, religion, and science.

Alexis Bertrand's *Lexique de philosophie* (Paris, P. Delaplane, 1892, 220 pages) has had at least four printings. This work covers topics only, on an elementary level, but the explanations are not always clear.

There were one Italian and two Latin works of this kind published in the nineteenth century.

The first Latin work was J. A. Albrand's *Lexicon Philosophicum, Quo Verba Scholastica Explicantur,* a work 68 pages long printed on pages 557–624 of Volume IV of Albrand's edition of the *Theologia Dogmatica,* by Thomas ex Charmes (4 vols., Paris, Louis Vivès, 1856–1857). The articles, explicating *absolutum, beatitudo, esse,* and so on, provide, in prosy Latin, the standard scholastic definitions of the regular scholastic philosophical terms. The *Lexicon* was intended for the use of theological students, especially those trying to understand the system of the eighteenth-century theologian Thomas ex Charmes (also called Thomas a Charmes). Of the several reprints of Albrand's edition of Thomas' *Theologia* (6, 7, or 8 vols.) some do and some do not include Albrand's *Lexicon Philosophicum.*

The Italian work was Luigi Stefanoni's *Dizionario filosofico* (2 vols, in 1, Milan, Natale Battezzati, 1873–1875). Some of the articles—for example, those on immaculate conception, matrimony, molecule, pope, and Shakers—are a bit unusual in dictionaries of philosophy, but the articles on technical philosophical subjects are useful and contain a significant amount of detail. A pro-Catholic bias is evident in the articles on theological subjects.

The second Latin work, Niceto A. Perujo's *Lexicon Philosophico-theologicum* (Valencia, Spain, Friedrich Domenech, 1883, 352 pages), had a scholastic orientation. It contains 1,364 articles, including explanations not only of terms but also of such common philosophical propositions as "Dato uno absurdo, sequitur aliud" ("If one absurdity is granted, another follows"). Some of the explanations are supported by extensive quotations from Aquinas, Bonaventure, and others.

RUSSIAN. A number of notable dictionaries of philosophy were written in Russia in the nineteenth century.

In 1819 appeared Alexander I. Galich's *Opyt Filosofskogo Slovaria* ("Toward a Philosophical Dictionary," St. Petersburg), the second fascicle of a larger work on the history of philosophical systems. This dictionary contains 217 articles, from "Absolute" to "Theurgy." The topic headings are given in the Latin alphabet—for instance, "Absolutum"—and the explanations in Russian. Special attention is paid to new philosophical terms.

Alexander I. Galich's *Leksikon Filosofskikh Predmetov* (Vol. I, No. 1, St. Petersburg, Tip. Imp. Akad. Nauk, 1845, 298 pages) is the first fascicle of a proposed set of nine (three volumes with three numbers in each). It covers about 170 terms beginning with *A* or *B* in aesthetics, ethics, logic, and metaphysics. The project was discontinued when the author's notes were destroyed in a fire.

S. S. Gogotsky's monumental work *Filosofsky Leksikon* (4 vols., Kiev, University of Kiev and other publishers, 1857–1873; 2nd ed., 1 vol., St. Petersburg, I. I. Glazunov, 1859) contains about twelve hundred articles. The articles on philosophical method, such as those on analogy, classification, dialectic, dogmatism, and method in general, are especially noteworthy. In 1876 Gogotsky produced *Filosofsky Slovar'* (Kiev, Tip. Red. "Kievsk Telegrafa," 146 pages), a one-volume condensation of his lexicon, containing approximately the same number of articles.

EISLER. Rudolf Eisler produced his *Wörterbuch der philosophischen Begriffe und Ausdrücke* ("Dictionary of Philosophical Concepts and Expressions," Berlin, E. S. Mittler und Sohn, 1899, 956 pages), which, following the setup of the *Wörterbuch* by Friedrich Kirchner, has no articles on individual philosophers. Of the three volumes of the fourth edition, whose title was shortened to *Wörterbuch der philosophischen Begriffe* (Berlin, E. S. Mittler und Sohn, published with the cooperation of the Kant-gesellschaft, 1927), the second and third were edited with the assistance of Karl Roretz, Eisler having died after the work on the first volume was completed.

This is perhaps the best technical dictionary of philosophy produced up to its time. Even now, it is probably one of the ten best available dictionaries of philosophy, ranking along with the better works of the twentieth century. Its articles contain terse definitions and are rich not only in relevant quotations in the original languages, including English, but also in bibliographical citations. On Oriental subjects the articles were weak in the first edition (Sāmkhya being dismissed with the statement that it is the system of the Indian thinker Kapila) but were strengthened somewhat in subsequent editions. The later editions, although expanded in coverage, contain fewer quotations in languages other than German.

In 1964 the Basel firm of Benno Schwabe had in preparation a new edition of the *Wörterbuch* under the editorship of Joachim Ritter.

For use by students Eisler summarized the main articles of his large dictionary in the *Handwörterbuch der Philosophie* (Berlin, E. S. Mittler und Sohn, 1913, 801 pages), of which a second edition, supervised by Richard Müller-Freienfels, was issued not only as a regular book in 1922 but also as a "microbook" (Düsseldorf, Microbuch- und Film Gesellschaft, 1922, 785 pages on 88 sides).

Eisler also produced the *Philosophen-Lexikon: Leben, Werke und Lehren der Denker* ("Dictionary of Philosophers: Lives, Works and Doctrines of the Thinkers," Berlin, E. S. Mittler und Sohn, 1912, 889 pages) to make up for the lack of treatment of individuals as such in his *Wörterbuch.* The *Philosophen-Lexikon* was the first modern biographical dictionary of philosophers. Although its articles are shorter, more numerous, and alphabetically arranged, it recalls the useful work of Diogenes Laërtius. From Anathon Aall of Norway to Ulrich Zwingli, the Reformation figure, some four thousand philosophers are identified and, when appropriate, discussed, with their main writings and writings about them listed. Eisler could perhaps be excused for according some emphasis to German philosophers, and it is not strictly fair to criticize comparative comprehensiveness on the basis of lines of print, especially since most of Eisler's allocations of space seem right; nevertheless, one may perhaps with some warrant complain that Kant gets 33 pages, Wundt 16, Spinoza 11, Plato (as well as Hegel and Leibniz) 10, and Aristotle 9 and that Hermann Cohen gets more space than Augustine, Fichte more than Descartes, Herbart more than Hume, Lotze more than Locke, Maimon more than Maimonides, and Meinong more than Bentham.

EARLY TWENTIETH CENTURY

In 1901 an important dictionary was published, and an important dictionary was begun. The early twentieth century also saw the publication of dictionary-type or supposedly encyclopedic treatments of philosophical topics by Lalande, Windelband, and less well-known writers.

GOBLOT. Edmond Goblot issued *Le Vocabulaire philosophique* (Paris, Librairie Armand Colin, 1901, 513 pages; 6th ed., 1924), in which he tried not only to record the actual meanings of terms but in part to correct confused usages by suggesting, for example, separate meanings for *général* and *universel*; for *particulier, individuel,* and *singulier;* and for *mémoire* and *souvenir.* But philosophers being the individualists that they are in the use of words, their degree of acceptance (if any) of his commendable suggestions is not perceptible. Spanish translations of this work were published at Barcelona in 1933 and at Buenos Aires in 1942 and 1945.

BALDWIN. The other important work of 1901 was Baldwin's. James M. Baldwin, a psychologist, edited, with the collaboration of an international board of advisers and contributors that included Bosanquet, Dewey, William James, Janet, Lloyd Morgan, Moore, Münsterberg, Peirce, Pringle-Pattison, Royce, Sidgwick, Stout, and Urban, the *Dictionary of Philosophy and Psychology* (3 vols. in 4, New York, Macmillan, 1901–1905; reprinted with corrections several times, in part or in entirety, by the same firm, in some cases with the designation "New Edition"; also reprinted by Peter Smith twice, partly at New York and partly at Gloucester, Mass., 1940s, 1950s). Volume III, in two parts, is a bibliography of philosophy and psychology, by Benjamin Rand, to which there were annual supplements in the *Psychological Index* from 1901 to 1908.

In the Preface the editor stated that a dictionary of terms used in Greek and scholastic philosophy "is much needed: but we have not attempted it." The dictionary does, however, include articles on Greek terminology (8 pages, by Royce) and Latin and scholastic terminology (11 pages, by Royce), as well as on analogy, nous (mind), and other special terms. Moreover, the editor aimed "to present science—physical, natural, moral—with a fullness and authority not before undertaken in a work of this character." Thus, there are articles on anthropology, brain, case law, hybrid, money, peace, pupa, and others. Like Goblot, Baldwin futilely suggested that his readers follow the recommendations made in some of the articles for preferred philosophical usage. For many entries German, French, and Italian equivalents are recommended. In addition, at the end of Volume II there is an index of Greek, Latin, German, French, and Italian terms, including those covered by separate articles on the terms as such and those merely mentioned as recommended equivalents.

Philosophically, the articles in the Baldwin dictionary are of uneven value. Some, especially the biographical articles, are too short, and there are no articles at all on Maine de Biran, Renan, and Saint-Simon. Others are broken down too minutely into terms rarely encountered, including Peirce's articles on particulate, *parva logicalia,* philosopheme, predesignate, and prosyllogism. In others there is cavalier treatment of the philosophical aspects of a subject, as in the psychologically oriented article on the self. Some articles, however, are excellent, especially the longer ones by Dewey—for example, those on nature, pluralism, and skepticism; those by Moore on cause and effect, change, nativism, quality, real, reason, relation, relativity of knowledge, spirit, substance, teleology, and truth; and the longer ones of the approximately 180 written by Peirce, including his 23 columns on syllogism, 10 columns on uniformity, and 10 on matter and form. Peirce's articles (the preparation of which, from 1901 to 1905, constituted his last steady employment) were mainly fragments of a book on logic which he never finished; only about half of these articles were reprinted in the Harvard *Collected Papers* of Peirce. Moore's 12 articles, which he later, with undue modesty, called crude, have not been reprinted.

LALANDE. With the collaboration of others André Lalande, a professor at the Sorbonne, issued the *Vocabulaire technique et critique de la philosophie* (21 fascicles, Paris, Félix Alcan, 1909–1922; revision of fascicle covering *A* in *Bulletin* of Société Française de Philosophie, 1923; 2nd ed., 2 vols., 1926; 3rd ed., 2 vols., 1928; 4th ed., 3 vols., 1931, reissued in 1932, Vols. I and II reissued, 1938; 5th–9th eds., 1 vol., 1947, 1950, 1956, 1960, 1962; 5th ed. translated into Spanish, Buenos Aires, 1953, with 2nd ed., Buenos Aires, 1964, 1,502 pages). Lalande was 95 years old when the ninth edition of the *Vocabulaire* was published. At the bottom of most of the pages appear the comments of members of the Société Française de Philosophic, including Peano and Russell among the foreign members, on the articles. The emphasis of the articles is on clarifying the meanings of terms and the usage of expressions rather than on the imparting of historical or technical information.

ORIGINAL WORKS OF ENCYCLOPEDIC SCOPE. Just as, early in the nineteenth century, the works of Schulze, Hegel, and Herbart were published as encyclopedias of the philosophical sciences, so early in the twentieth century three works of this kind were published or begun. The first "nonencyclopedia" was a series of works, edited by H. Renner and published at Charlottenburg, Germany, by O. Günther beginning in 1907, under the general title *Encyklopädie der Philosophie.* It included, for example, an introduction to philosophy and volumes on the philosophy of Rudolf Stammler and Rudolf Eucken.

Second of the three nonencyclopedias was August J. Dorner's *Encyklopädie der Philosophie* (Leipzig, Verlag der Durr'schen Buchhandlung, 1910, 334 pages); in Kantian fashion it dealt with phenomenological investigations, the construction of empirical science, and similar topics.

The third was a proposed *Encyklopädie der philosophischen Wissenschaften,* of which the first volume, *Logik,* was published in 1912, edited by Wilhelm Windelband and Arnold Ruge (Tübingen, Germany, J. C. B. Mohr, 275 pages), containing expositions of the principles of logic by Windelband, Josiah Royce (translated from English), and Louis Couturat (translated from French); of the task of logic by Benedetto Croce (translated from Italian); of the problems of logic by Federigo Enriques (translated from Italian); and of the bearing of the concepts of consciousness on logic by Nicholas Lossky (translated by Lossky himself from the original Russian).

An English edition of the Windelband–Ruge encyclopedia was projected under the editorship of Sir Henry Jones, and the first volume, *Logic,* was published in 1913 (London, Macmillan, 269 pages). For the English edition Royce's English version was available, Couturat's article was done into English from the original French rather than from the published German version, and the German of Lossky's article was his own; therefore, as the translator, B. Ethel Meyer, pointed out, only Croce's and Enriques' articles "suffered a double process of translation."

The onset of war in 1914 and the death of Windelband in 1915 resulted in the abandonment of the project. Windelband's contribution to the first volume, issued separately in German in 1913, was republished in English years later as *Theories in Logic* (New York, Philosophical Library, 1961, 81 pages). Royce's contribution was also published separately, as *The Principles of Logic* (New York, Philosophical Library, 1961, 77 pages).

OTHER WORKS. The works of the early twentieth century by less well-known writers in Italian, French, German, English, Russian, and Japanese were numerous.

In Italian there was Cesare Ranzoli's *Dizionario di scienze filosofiche* (Milan, Ulrico Hoepli, 1905, 683 pages; 2nd ed., 1916, 1,252 pages; 3rd ed., 1926, 1,207 pages; 4th ed., Maria P. Ranzoli, ed., 1943, 1,360 pages; 5th ed., Maria Ranzoli, ed., 1952, 1,313 pages). Covering only topics, not individual philosophers, the book contains articles on Pyrrhonism and Pythagoreanism (and later editions cover existentialism), but there is none on Platonism. The articles are of high quality.

In 1906 appeared Élie Blanc's *Dictionnaire de philosophie ancienne, moderne et contemporaine* (Paris, P. Lethielleux, 1,248 cols.; supp., for 1906–1907 and 1906–1908; consolidated ed., 1909). Blanc also published a vocabulary of scholastic and contemporary philosophy, presented at the beginning of his *Traité de philosophie scolastique* (3 vols., Lyon, Emmanuel Vitte, 1889; 3rd ed., Paris, 1909), and the *Dictionnaire universel de la pensée, alphabetique, logique et encyclopédique* (2 vols., Lyon, Emmanuel Vitte, 1899), which was a thesaurus-type classification of words, ideas, and things. In the *Dictionnaire de philosophie* his Catholic viewpoint is evident in many places; indeed, his starting point, he said, is moderate dogmatism.

In Germany Rudolf Odebrecht produced the *Kleines philosophisches Wörterbuch; Erklärung der Grundbegriffe der Philosophie* (Berlin, Buchverlag der "Hilfe," 1908, 83 pages; 6th ed., Leipzig, Felix Meiner, 1929). The choice of topics in this highly condensed wordbook was in some cases injudicious. There are entries on *heliozentrisch* (heliocentric) and *Hypnose* (hypnosis) but none on the Academy, Epicureanism, or Taoism.

A pocket volume, about 2½ inches by 4 inches, one of a series of about fifty covering literary terms, commercial terms, art terms, and so on was edited by Arthur Butler, *A Dictionary of Philosophical Terms* (London, G. Routledge and Sons, and New York, E. P. Dutton, 1909, 114 pages). The *Dictionary of Philosophical Terms* depends heavily on Kant, who is cited in ten of the first fifty articles. Among the topics treated are a number of German terms, such as *Anschauung* (outlook), *Begriff* (concept), and *Ding an sich* (thing-in-itself).

In 1909 also appeared Arturo Mateucci's *Vocabolarietto di termini filosofici* (Milan, Casa Editrice Sonzogno, 63 pages; 2nd ed., 1925). Intentionally elementary in its treatment, in many cases this work contains little more than dictionary definitions of the concepts covered. Some 75 percent of the articles consist of only one, two, or three lines.

Fritz Mauthner edited the *Wörterbuch der Philosophie* (2 vols., Munich, G. Muller, 1910–1911; 2nd ed., 3 vols., Leipzig, Felix Meiner, 1923). Mauthner was a literary critic and nonacademic philosopher who contributed pioneering insights on the question of what, if anything, ordinary language reveals about the world, whether the distinction between analytic and synthetic propositions is tenable, and so on. His *Wörterbuch*, after a rambling introduction of 96 pages, presents a mixture of very odd items and very useful, though informal, ones. The odd items include the articles "Babel," "Bacon's Ges'pensterlehre" (Bacon's study of ghosts), "Form" (40 cols., with only a passing reference to Aristotle), and "Graphologie." The more useful ones include "Geschichte" (history, 68 cols.), "Natur" (nature, 29 cols.), "Nichts" (nothing, 14 cols.), and "Spinoza's 'Deus'" (Spinoza's "God," 19 cols.); even these, however, should be used with caution, for they contain some questionable material.

Ernest L'vovich Radlov's *Filosofsky Slovar'* (St. Petersburg, Brockhaus–Ephron, 1911, 284 pages; 2nd ed., Moscow, G. A. Leman, 1913) covers aesthetics, ethics, logic, psychology, and the history of philosophy. It is of only limited usefulness.

Tetsujiro Inouye, Yujiro Motora, and Rikizo Nakashima edited the *Dictionary of English, German, and French Philosophical Terms, With Japanese Equivalents* (Tokyo, Maruzen Kabushiki–Kaisha, 1912, 205 pages), written in English. This is the definitive edition of the *Dictionary of Philosophical Terms* first brought out by Inouye and others in 1881 and issued in a second edition in 1884. For topical entries, including some in Arabic, Greek, and Latin besides the languages listed in the title, only the Japanese equivalents are given; the personal entries also provide identifying information.

Julius Reiner's *Philosophisches Wörterbuch* (Leipzig, Otto Tobies, 1912, 295 pages) is an elementary work in which, for example, the article on *Ambiguität* (ambiguity) consists of one word, *Zweideutigkeit* (having two meanings), and the article on *Intellekt* (intellect) consists of two words, *Geist, Verstand* (spirit or mind, understanding). Other articles, however, such as those on *Darwinismus* and *Ethik* (Darwinism and ethics), go more deeply into the subject.

Another German work was Heinrich Schmidt's *Philosophisches Wörterbuch* (Leipzig, Alfred Kröner, 1912, 106 pages; 8th ed., 1930). This was republished in the United States in 1945 by authority of the alien property custodian and went through several editions; the tenth edition (1943) was reprinted in the United States without the authority of the alien property custodian; the sixteenth edition appeared in 1961. The editions which appeared after the death of the author in 1935 were supervised by various editors. The numerous editions of this work had a vast circulation in all German-language areas. Indeed, it is perhaps the most widely used philosophical dictionary in any language at any time, the Eisler work being its main rival for this distinction. In the ninth edition (1934), while Schmidt was still alive, some pro-Nazi and anti-Jewish comments were included, and in the tenth edition (1943) the desecration of scholarship was compounded with obsequious compliments to insignificant Nazis and truly monstrous articles on Bergson, Freud, Husserl, and others. Recent editions bend over backward to rectify these aberrations.

Paul Thormeyer's *Philosophisches Wörterbuch* (Leipzig, B. G. Teubner, 1916, 96 pages; 4th ed., 1930) is an uncommonly useful short reference work. It is well organized and was up-to-date at the time it was issued.

THE NINETEEN-TWENTIES

ANGLO-SAXON SILENCE. In the 1920s 12 dictionaries of philosophy appeared or were begun—4 in German and 1 each in Hungarian, Swedish, Dutch, French, Spanish, Hebrew, Japanese, and Chinese. Not one was published in the United States or Great Britain. Indeed, the only English-language work deserving of mention here published between Butler's *Dictionary* of 1909 and Runes's *Dictionary* of 1942 was a quasi encyclopedia, the *International Encyclopedia of Unified Science*, begun in 1939. The Anglo-Saxon silence can only be recorded here. The explanation of it requires more data than are readily at hand.

GERMAN. Of the German works published in the 1920s three were published in 1923. The *Systematisches Wörterbuch der Philosophie*, by Karl W. Clauberg and Walter Dubislav (Leipzig, Felix Meiner, 1923, 565 pages), is systematic to a fault, many of the articles being broken down into standard subdivisions—for example, definition, statement, addition, and example—in a somewhat rigid fashion. Dubislav, who was a professor of philosophy at the University of Berlin, had a continuing interest in the clarification of concepts. He was close to logical empiricism and wrote the comprehensive *Die Definition* (Leipzig, Felix Meiner, 1931, 160 pages); he also made notable contributions to the philosophy of method, mathematics, and science.

In Rudolf Wagner's *Philosophisches Wörterbuch* (Munich, Rösl, 1923, 148 pages) articles range in length from one-word or two-word definitions or identifications to the six-page article on the history of philosophy, which consists mainly of a five-page outline taken from Wilhelm Wundt's *Einleitung in die Philosophie* (1914); individual philosophers are not accorded separate treatment.

In most dictionaries of philosophy that cover both topics and persons, the articles on topics are far more numerous than those on people; in Alfred Sternbeck's *Führer durch die Philosophie; Philosophenlexikon und philosophisches Sachwörterbuch* (Berlin, Globus Verlag, 1923, 306 pages), however, those on people almost equal the topical articles in number. Moreover, whereas some of the topical articles are elementary, containing little more than dictionary definitions, the biographical articles are more substantial.

Two years later, there was published the last of the German works of the 1920s, *Klare Begriffe! Lexikon der gebräuchlicheren Fachausdrücke aus Philosophie und Theologie*, by Theodor Mönnichs, S.J. ("Clear Concepts! Dictionary of the Most Common Technical Terms of Philosophy and Theology," Berlin, Ferdinand Dümmlers Verlag, 1925, 170 pages; 2nd ed., 1929). This work was written, according to the author, from the standpoint of *philosophia perennis* and Catholic theology. The longest article is the sixty-line one on religion. The pervasive scholastic emphasis in the book is indicated by the fact that many articles begin with the Latin equivalent of the term being covered, and the second edition contains, as an appendix, a 20-page alphabetical list of Latin philosophical terms with their German equivalents.

HUNGARIAN. The Hungarian work of the 1920s was *Philosophiai Szótár*, by Enyvvári Jenö (family name Enyvvári), published at Budapest by Franklin-Társulat (1923, 187 pages). The articles in this work show a creditable familiarity with West European scholarship. The titles of many of the articles are in languages other than Hungarian—for example, "Élan vital," and "Moral Insanity." Appended are a list of philosophers and a competent discussion of philosophical bibliographies.

SWEDISH. Sweden contributed the *Filosofiskt Lexikon*, edited by Alf Ahlberg (Stockholm, Bokförlaget Natur och Kultur, 1925, 207 pages; 3rd ed., 1951). In this work Swedish philosophers were given fuller treatment than others—C. J. Boström, 15 cols.; E. G. Geijer, 10 cols.; Aristotle and Plato, 6 cols. each.

DUTCH. The Dutch work of the period was C. J. Wijnaendts Francken's *Koort Woordenboek van Wijsgeerige Kunsttermen* ("Short Dictionary of Philosophical Terms," Haarlem, D. H. Tjeenk Willink & Zonen, 1925, 157 pages). It covers topics only, in a fairly popular style, and the choice of topics is liberal, making room for such terms as *kosmopolitisme, opportunisme*, and *sarcasme*, along with more technical philosophical terms.

FRENCH. In France appeared Armand Cuvillier's *Petit Vocabulaire de la langue philosophique* (Paris, Librairie Armand Colin, 1925, 109 pages; 13th ed., 1953). It was subsequently translated into Turkish (Ankara, 1944) and Portuguese (São Paulo, Brazil, 1961). This work was intended by its author to be at once *élémentaire* and *précis*. In large measure it succeeded in achieving both objectives.

SPANISH. Begun in Spain was the *Diccionario manual de filosofía* by Marcelino Arnáiz and B. Alcalde (Madrid, Talleres Voluntad, 1927–). Volume I, "Vocabulario Ideario" (659 pages), is rich in bibliography, and many of the articles contain sound historical data in addition to the conceptual explanations which the volume was essentially intended to provide. A projected second volume, covering the history of doctrines, biographies, and bibliography, was not published.

EASTERN LANGUAGES. In the 1920s dictionaries of philosophy appeared in three Eastern languages, apparently for the first time (aside from translations).

Hebrew. The Hebrew dictionary of philosophy begun in the 1920s was the *Otsar ha-Munahim ha-Filosofiyim ve-Antologiyah Filosofit* ("Thesaurus of Philosophical Terms and Philosophical Anthology"), by Jacob Klatzkin (4 vols., Leipzig, August Pries, 1928–1933); an introductory volume, published in Berlin by "Eschkol" Verlag in 1926, contains an anthology of Hebrew philosophy. Each of the four regular volumes has, as an added Latin title, *Thesaurus Philosophicus Linguae Hebraicae et Veteris et Recentioris*; Volumes III and IV had M. Zobel as coeditor. The dictionary articles are on topics only, not philosophers or schools of philosophy. Many of the articles contain the German or Latin equivalent of the title of the article; indeed, the purpose usually seems to be to explain the use of terms rather than to convey historical information on the topic as a topic, although the usage of historical writers on the subject is often indicated.

Japanese. A 1,026-page work entitled *Tetsugaku dai-Jisho* ("Dictionary of Philosophy") was published at Tokyo in 1924 by Dai Nippon Hyakka Jisho (Japanese Encyclopedia). The eighth edition (1928) consists of three volumes of text, an index volume, and a supplement. In the text volumes and in the supplement each article begins with the title in Japanese, followed usually by English, German, and French equivalents of the title. Thus, the first article in the first volume is headed, after the Japanese title, "Love. Liebe. Amour." The next several articles deal with patriotism, agape (listed alone after the Japanese title), affection, love and hate (with the Greek equivalents, φιλότηζ and νεικοζ), Aitareya Upanishad, idealism, vaguedualism, pity, and Augustine. Some of the articles, including the one on religion, are extensive, and many include references to European works.

The index volume of this Japanese dictionary has a title page in German ("Encyclopaedia Japonica, *Enzyklopädische Wörterbuch der Philosophie . . . Register . . .* Tokyo: Dobunkwan"). In addition to a Japanese index, it contains English, French, German, Latin, Pali, Sanskrit, and Chinese indexes and a *Namenregister* (index of names). In the English index approximately 35 of the first 100 entries are strictly philosophical—absolute, abstract, Academy, accident, actual, and so on; most of the others pertain to psychology. In the *Namenregister*, too, about 35 of the first 100 entries are standard names in philosophy—Abelard, Aenesidemus, Albert the Great, al-Fārābī, and so on.

Chinese. In *Chê Hsüeh Tz'ŭ Tien* ("Dictionary of Philosophy"), by Fan Ping-ch'ing (Shanghai, Commercial Press, 1926, 1,110 pages; 2nd ed., 1935; 3rd ed., 1961), the title of each article is given in Chinese, English, French, and German. The dictionary begins with an article on monism and continues with articles on monotheism, Monophysites, the seven liberal arts, the seven wise men, dualism, dilemma, antinomy, ethnology, subconscious, Albert the Great, major term, minor term, asymmetry, *credo quia absurdum*, medieval philosophy, Pascal, Parmenides, and so forth. The content is scholarly, but there are numerous errors in the Western languages. The work closes with an alphabetical index of names (in which Abelard has 8 references, Aristotle 45, Kant 28, and Marx 5) and an alphabetical index of topics from abiogenesis (1 reference) to *Zwecksystem* (1 reference).

THE NINETEEN-THIRTIES

In the 1930s there appeared four Italian and two Russian works. During this period a number of works in other languages were also published.

GERMAN. Germany began the decade with Max Apel's *Philosophisches Wörterbuch* (Berlin and Leipzig, W. de Gruyter, 1930, 155 pages). The fifth edition, which was revised by Peter Ludz, appeared in 1958, and a Spanish translation was published at Mexico City in 1961. Editions of Apel's work published since World War II are pro-Soviet.

DUTCH. In the Netherlands appeared the *Encyclopaedisch Handboek van het Moderne Denken*, edited by Willem Banning and 41 collaborators (2 vols., Arnhem, Van Loghum Slaterus, 1930–1931; 2nd ed., 1 vol., 1942; 3rd ed., 1 vol., 1950). Although the third edition emphasizes such modern ideas as anarchism, Gestalt theory, phenomenology of worship, quantification of the predicate, and the United Nations, the work does not neglect such standard philosophical ideas as category, natural law, and thing.

ENGLISH. A United States contribution, a quasi encyclopedia, in the 1930s was the inauguration of the *International Encyclopedia of Unified Science*, by Otto Neurath, Rudolf Carnap, and Charles Morris in 1936/1937 at the University of Chicago. This work, carried on after Neurath's death in 1945 by the Institute for the Unity of Science in Boston under the joint editorship of Carnap and Morris, consists thus far of 15 fascicles, of which Volume I, Number 1 (1938), contained articles by Niels Bohr on analysis and synthesis in science, by Carnap on logical foundations of the unity of science, by John Dewey on unity of science as a social problem, by Morris on scientific empiricism, by Neurath on unified science as encyclopedic integration, and by Bertrand Russell on the importance of logical form. The other 14 are monographs by individual authors. To each of these a volume and a number are assigned. The latest numerically is Volume II, Number 9 (1951), a study by Jørgen Jørgensen on the development of logical empiricism. The latest chronologically, Volume II, Number 2 (1962), is a monograph by Thomas S. Kuhn on the structure of scientific revolutions.

Thus, this "encyclopedia," like Hegel's, Herbart's, Contri's (see below), Windelband–Ruge's and the *Nouvelle Encyclopédie philosophique*, is a compendium but it is not alphabetical. The announced topics of the volumes are foundations of the unity of science, Volumes I and II; theories, induction, probability, and so on, Volume III; logic and mathematics, Volume IV; physics, Volume V; biology and psychology, Volume VI; social and humanistic science, Volume VII; and history of the scientific attitude, Volume VIII. This project, inspired by logical positivism and designed by Neurath to show that all the sciences speak the same language—essentially, physicalism—was overambitious.

FRENCH. France's contribution in the 1930s was Jean B. Domecq's *Vocabulaire de philosophie* (Tours, Alfred Cattier, 1931, 208 pages), which has separate alphabetical arrangements of topics for logic, ethics, and metaphysics and a consolidated index at the end. The author was an abbot, and the work has a Catholic orientation.

Mention may also be made of a series of monographs inaugurated in Paris in 1934 by the Presses Universitaires de France, *Nouvelle Encyclopédie philosophique*, which do not constitute an encyclopedia in the strict sense. Among the monographs published thus far are, for example, Louis Lavelle's *Introduction à l'ontologie* (No. 41, 1947) and Robert Blanché's *Les Attitudes idéalistes* (No. 45, 1949).

ITALIAN. Four Italian dictionaries of philosophy appeared or were begun in this period. The first was Giovanni Semprini's *Piccolo dizionario di coltura filosofica e scientifica* (Milan, Edizioni Athena, 1931, 502 pages). This was revised as *Nuovo dizionario di coltura filosofica e scientifica* (Turin, Società Editrice Internazionale, 1952, 470 pages). The work covers topics and individuals in philosophy, science, and education.

In 1933, Antonio Bettioli's *Il pensiero filosofico attraverso i secoli* (Urbino, Editoriale Urbinate, 234 pages) was published. The articles are grouped into schools and systems of philosophy—for example, the Academy, eclectics, idealism—and individual philosophers—113 names, including Dante, Feuerbach, Goethe, Leonardo, Swedenborg, and Tolstoy but not Bergson, Dewey, Husserl, Origen, Philo, or Proclus. The book is of limited value.

An elementary work with little penetration, Francesco Varvello's *Dizionario etimologico filosofico e teologico* (Turin, Società Editrice Internazionale, 406 pages), appeared in 1937, with a second edition in 1938. Fascism is lauded as the opposite of various false forms of government. According to the author, Marx (described as a Jew) rejected the idea that man does not live by bread alone. The articles on religion are pro-Catholic.

There was also Emilio Morselli's *Piccolo dizionario filosofico* (Milan, Carlo Signorelli, 1938, 104 pages). In this book the author aimed to help young readers who encounter in the classics of thought special philosophical expressions, expressions whose meanings differ not only from what they are in ordinary discourse but also from period to period.

An Italian work of the 1930s which called itself an encyclopedia of philosophy but which was not arranged alphabetically was Siro Contri's *Piccola enciclopedia filosofica* (Bologna, Costantino Galleri, 1931), of which only the first volume, on logic and the philosophy of science, was published.

PORTUGUESE. In Brazil appeared Renato Kehl's *Bioperspectivas; dicionário filosófico* (Rio de Janeiro, Livraria Francisco Alves, 1938, 187 pages), which is a series of Voltairian musings on art, the categorical imperative, civilization, death, education, free will, God, history, intelligence, original sin, personality, philosophy, politics, progress, work, and other subjects.

RUSSIAN. The first of the two Soviet contributions of the 1930s was Timofei S. Ishchenko's *Kratky Filosofsky Slovar'* (Moscow, Moskofsky Rabochy, 1931, 200 pages), which gave more space to Stalin (four cols.) than to Plato, Aristotle, Kant, Hegel, or Marx. Other Marxist topics, such as dictatorship of the proletariat, were accorded correspondingly disproportionate treatment with the usual positive bias. The three items in the bibliography on Aristotle are by Marx, Engels, and Stalin, respectively.

The second was a work by Mark M. Rozental' and Pavel F. Yudin, likewise entitled *Kratky Filosofsky Slovar'* (Moscow, 1939; 2nd–4th eds., 1940, 1951, 1954, each of which was reprinted the following year). A new edition appeared in 1963 with the title modified by the omission of the first word, which means "short," although the 1963 edition of 544 pages is actually shorter than the previous edition, which had 567 pages. The encyclopedia was translated into Spanish in 1945, Bulgarian in 1947, English in 1949, Ukrainian in 1952, Hebrew in 1954, and Chinese, French, Polish, and Rumanian in 1955. Reportedly, 2 million copies of the Russian original were sold in the first ten years after publication, and the press run of one of the printings in the 1950s was 500,000. The English version, adapted and translated by Howard Selsam (New York, International Publishers, 1949, 128 pages), stated in the Preface that the volume reflects Marxist partisanship (for materialism and for socialism) as contrasted with the lack of a "common approach" and the "alphabetic disorder" of other dictionaries of philosophy.

Illustrative of the topical entries in the English version are those in the *E*'s: "Eclecticism," "Economic Bases of Society," "Economic Determinism," "Economics and Politics," "Empiricism," "Empirio-criticism," "Energism (metaphysical)," "Epistemology," "Equality," and "Equilibrium, Theory of." The men treated in the *S*'s are Saint-Simon, Schelling, Spencer, Spinoza, and Stalin, and the article on Stalin is the longest of these.

The article on Kant in the English version dutifully quotes from Lenin, and those on Campanella and dualism, among others, drag in quotations from Stalin. Many of the articles on individual philosophers vapidly make a point of recounting what Marx, Engels, Lenin, or Stalin thought of the philosopher or even reverently disinter a colorless quotation from Stalin summarizing what Marx or Lenin thought of the philosopher. The article "Partisanship of Philosophy" states that the class struggle is always behind the scenes in the open struggle of philosophical opinions.

According to Alexander Philipov, a former professor of philosophy at the University of Kharkov who later emigrated in the United States, for the English version Selsam watered down two features of the original—its invective and its extravagant praise of Lenin and Stalin—in order to make the edition less offensive to Western readers.

A significant feature of the original is the fact that the article on Stalin in the fourth edition (1954) ended with a sentence which may be translated "The immortal name of Joseph Stalin will live forever in the minds and hearts of the Russian people"; that sentence vanished without a trace in the 1955 printing of the same edition. In the 1963 edition, of which 400,000 copies were printed and which had about 160 collaborators (including most of the important figures in current Soviet philosophy), there is no article on Stalin, and the Preface acknowledges the "enormous harm" resulting from the cult of Stalin. The 1963 edition is stronger than its predecessors in coverage of linguistic philosophy, logical positivism, and logic.

LITHUANIAN. Lithuania's contribution to the history of philosophical dictionaries is a 97-page article entitled "Bendroji Filosofijos Terminija" ("General Terminology of Philosophy"), by Stasys Šalkauskis; it constituted an entire issue of the periodical *Logos; Filosofijos Žurnalas* (Kaunas), 1937. The article listed some fifteen hundred Lithuanian terms useful in philosophical discussions, with their equivalents in French, German, and Russian. The list was supplemented by a discussion of synonyms of various philosophical terms in Lithuanian. In a 1938 issue of the same periodical Šalkauskis presented a list of over fifteen hundred German philosophical terms with their Lithuanian equivalents.

HEBREW. In Palestine, Zvi Hirsch Rudy produced the *Leksikon le-Filosofiyah* (Tel Aviv, Dvir, 1939, 816 cols.), with an added title page in Latin, *Philosophiae et Scientiarum Propinquarum Lexicon Hebraicum*. This work is generous with Latin terms, as the titles of articles—for example, "Actus purus," in Hebrew transliteration; as the Latin equivalents of the Hebrew titles of topical articles—for example, "Natura Naturans" as the equivalent of "Teva Tovei"; and as the titles of works cited—for example, works by Abelard and Augustine cited in the articles on those thinkers. Contemporary writers, such as Dewey and Meyerson, and topics of current interest, such as absurd and *élan vital*, are also included. The articles lack penetration. The Bibliography at the end is erratic in including, along with students' handbooks, a poorly balanced small selection of specialized monographs.

CHINESE. In 1934 appeared a new Chinese dictionary, not so strictly confined to philosophy as was the 1926 Chinese work. This was the *Ssu Hsiang Chia Ta Tz'ŭ Tien* ("Dictionary of Great Thinkers"), by P'an Nien-chih (Shanghai, Shih Chieh, 1,062 pages), which contains over five hundred articles on philosophers, writers, artists, musicians, and others. Mo Tzu quite properly is accorded 12 columns, but in the modern period Kant and Mill get only 5 columns each while Mussolini rates 6. Many names are misspelled.

THE NINETEEN-FORTIES

The 1940s saw six philosophical dictionaries in Spanish, five in English, five in German, two in Italian, two in French, and one each in Hungarian and Turkish.

FERRATER MORA. José Ferrater Mora began the decade by producing the *Diccionario de filosofía* (Mexico City, Editorial Atlante, 1941, 598 pages; 2nd ed., 1944; 3rd–4th eds., Buenos Aires, Editorial Sudamericana, 1951, 1958; 5th ed. in preparation). It is one of the most useful dictionaries published in the twentieth century. From the technical standpoint it may be mentioned that the author used a sensible system of cross references which eliminates the need for an index; he chose as topics for articles units which are neither too large nor too small. The bibliographical citations provided at the ends of some articles are judiciously selected.

The writing shows a philosophical understanding decidedly above the average for writers of philosophical dictionaries. Ferrater Mora was equally strong in his knowledge of modern logic and positivism and in the more traditional philosophical trends and developments associated with Continental metaphysics. The comprehensiveness of his scholarship and the soundness of his judgment have combined to create a monumental one-man contribution to the library of dictionaries of philosophy.

OTHER LATIN AMERICAN WORKS. In the same year, 1941, two other dictionaries were published in Latin America. One was Martín T. Ruiz Moreno's *Vocabulario filosófico* (Buenos Aires, Editorial Guillermo Kraft, 1941, 156 pages; 2nd ed., 1946, 302 pages). Among the articles of special interest in it are "Angustia" (anguish), which sets forth the viewpoints of Kierkegaard and Heidegger, and "Cosa" (thing), which distinguishes the philosophical, the (Argentine) juridical, and the economic uses of the term.

The other dictionary was César A. Guardia Mayorga's *Léxico filosófico* (Arequipa, Peru, 1941, 138 pages). A second edition was published in Arequipa in 1949 under the title *Terminología filosófica*. This work allots more space to Oriental subjects than does Ruiz Moreno's.

A work of the 1940s described as a dictionary of Argentine thought—Florencio J. Amaya's *Diccionario político, sociológico y filosófico argentino* (Mendoza, Argentina, Editorial Cuyo, 1946, 520 pages)—is more general than its title indicates. The philosophical articles are mainly subjective reflections (in the manner of Voltaire but more conservative) with occasional references to historic positions. The author's declared intention to produce sequels 6 and 12 years later (described on the title page of this book as Volumes II and III) was not carried out.

In 1947 appeared the anonymous *Pequeño diccionario de filosofía* (Buenos Aires, 156 pages), issued by Ediciones Centurión for use in conjunction with Emilio Gouiran's *Historia de la filosofía* (Buenos Aires, 1947), published by the same house. The *Pequeño diccionario* consists of two parts, one on philosophers from Peter Abelard to Xavier Zubiri, with indications of their dates and their principal works, and the other on philosophical terms, from Academia (the Academy) to *univoco* (univocal), with explanations ranging from 1 to 29 lines.

SPANISH—SPAIN. In José M. Rubert Candau's *Diccionario manual de filosofía* (Madrid, Editorial Bibliográfica Española, 1946, 658 pages) the main topics of philosophy are dealt with in extensive articles or groups of articles, and the less important topics are given merely as entries with references to the main articles where they are treated. Thus, there are articles on being (5 cols.), supreme modes of being (21 cols.), and transcendental properties of being (27 cols.); the entry "Categorías supremas" refers the reader to the articles on supreme modes of being and on predicables and predicaments. This work deserves to be better known for its clear and systematic exposition of complex subject matter, especially on topics where its Catholic orientation is not a factor.

ITALIAN. Alfredo Galluccio's *Dizionarietto dei principali vocaboli filosofici* (Cava de' Tirreni, Italy, Editore Coda, 1942, 23 pages; 3rd ed., Naples, 1952) covers only topics. Most of the eight hundred articles in the third edition are only a few lines long and are intended to identify unfamiliar terms which students may encounter in their philosophical reading.

Another miniature dictionary is Paolo Rotta's *Dizionarietto filosofico* (Milan, Carlo Marzorati, 1944, 125 pages; 5th ed., 1953), which likewise covers only topics, including concepts, problems, and movements. Many of the almost five hundred articles in the fifth edition present Kant's ideas on the subject at hand.

FRENCH. Régis Jolivet, dean of the faculty of philosophy of the Catholic University of Lyon, produced the French contribution of the 1940s, *Vocabulaire de la philosophie* (Lyon, Emmanuel Vitte, 1942, 207 pages; 2nd–4th eds., 1946, 1951, 1957; Spanish translation, Buenos Aires, 1953). The articles are brief (4 lines for "Thomisme" but 53 for "Liberté" and 52 for "Nature"). A 17-page appendix presents a "tableau historique des écoles de philosophie," showing, in conventional groupings, the dates and (in 1–11 lines) the "écoles et doctrines" of about 250 philosophers from Zoroaster to Wittgenstein.

A book described in its foreword as a "dictionnaire abrégé" is Georges Barbarin's *L'Ami des heures difficiles; un consolateur et un guide* (Paris, Éditions Niclaus, 1946, 173 pages). The author presents conventional advice, constituting a popular philosophy or a popular psychology, on more than 130 problems of life—adversity, anxiety, despair, humiliation, injustice, pain, remorse, scandal, and seduction, among others. A seduced and betrayed woman is advised to look inward and find the Divine Friend in her own soul. The friend (*Ami*) mentioned in the title is not the book but God.

ENGLISH. The *Dictionary of Philosophy* (343 pages), edited by Dagobert Runes, was published at New York by the Philosophical Library in 1942. The list of 72 contributors included some outstanding American philosophers plus a few noted Europeans. When the work was published, 13 of the contributors—C. A. Baylis, A. C. Benjamin, E. S. Brightman, Rudolf Carnap, Alonzo Church, G. W. Cunningham, C. J. Ducasse, Irwin Edman, Hunter Guthrie, Julius Kraft, Glenn R. Morrow, Joseph Ratner, and J. R. Weinberg—declared their disapproval of it. Their statement, published in various periodicals including the *Philosophical Review* and *Mind*, read in part: "We objected to the publication of the work in its present form, and some of us made vigorous efforts to persuade Mr. Runes to delay publication until it had been very materially revised. These efforts were to no avail." They added that their own articles had been altered without their consent and that although they were listed as associate or contributing editors, they "feel obliged to make a public disavowal of any editorial responsibility for it."

Despite the important defects of this work, chiefly imbalance, there are many pithy, useful identifications, descriptions, and discussions in it, especially those by Church on topics in logic. Indeed, the collection of Church's contributions to the dictionary and their issuance in a separate volume on issues and methods in logic would be a worth-while project.

A new edition of the Runes dictionary has been issued every few years (16th ed., 1960); these are, however, essentially reprints, containing only minor variations from the first edition. At least one edition, or reprint, was issued overseas (Bombay, Jaico Publishing House, 1957).

Runes also edited *Who's Who in Philosophy*, Vol. I, *Anglo-American Philosophers* (New York, Philosophical Library, 1942, 193 pages), a biographical dictionary of over five hundred living thinkers, covering not only Americans and Britons but also Indians, Europeans who came to the United States or England during Hitler's regime, and others. A contemplated second volume, for other parts of the world, was not issued. An unusual feature of the work is the listing of numerous periodical articles, as well as the major books, written by the philosophers included. Thus, the entry on Dewey runs to over 650 lines, listing over 50 books and over 250 articles.

In 1946, Father William D. Bruckmann published the third of the four American dictionaries of philosophy of this period, a volume entitled *Keystones & Theories of Philosophy* (New York, Benziger Brothers, 230 pages). This work includes comprehensive explanations—from the standpoint of Catholic philosophy—of concepts from *abstractio* (abstraction), to *voluntas* (will), of theories from absolutism to voluntarism, and of technical terms from *ab intrinseco–ab extrinseco* (from the intrinsic–from the extrinsic) to *ut sic* (as such). It also lists chronologically 121 philosophers with very brief indications of their view-points. The bulk of the work is devoted to concepts, only 19 pages being given to the individual philosophers.

Finally, John Dewey and Arthur F. Bentley, in an article in the *Journal of Philosophy* (Vol. 44, 1947, 421–434), "Concerning a Vocabulary for Inquiry Into Knowledge," presented what may, by a broad interpretation, be counted as a dictionary of philosophy. It is an array of ninety terms in alphabetical order, from *accurate, action, activity, actor, application,* and *aspect* near the beginning to *thing, trans* (as a prefix), *transaction, true, truth,* and *word* near the end. Although the entry for *mental* begins "This word is not used by us" and continues that the word usually "indicates a hypostatization arising from a primitively imperfect view of behavior," the remainder of the entry sanctions the use of the word for "emphasizing an aspect of existence." The entry for *real* reads: "Its use is to be completely avoided when not a recognized synonym for genuine as opposed to sham or counterfeit." The other entries show a similar striving for clarity and rigor.

A British dictionary of philosophy published in the 1940s is *A Rationalist Encyclopaedia: A Book of Reference on Religion, Philosophy, Ethics, and Science* (London, Watts, 1948, 633 pages; 2nd ed., 1950), by Joseph McCabe, a former priest. McCabe debunks Aquinas as bracketing "serfs and animals," Aristotle as having had almost no influence for several centuries and then a deleterious influence on science, Augustine as writing poor Latin, Avicenna as sensual and dissipated, Bacon as hypocritical, Bergson as using largely inaccurate scientific material, Buddha as unoriginal, and so on. He generally lauds philosophers who were agnostics or deists. Some of the topical articles, while equally tendentious, contain useful criticism.

GERMAN. The Kirchner work of 1886 as revised by Michaëlis in 1903 was the basis of the *Wörterbuch der philosophischen Begriffe*, by Johannes Hoffmeister (Leipzig, Felix Meiner, 1944, 776 pages; 2nd ed., 1955, 687 pages). The 1944 edition shows the influence of Adolf Hitler's regime. For example, the article "Volk" (folk) in the 1944 edition includes a lyrical exposition of the meaning of membership in a tight ethnic group and cites Hitler's *Mein Kampf* and Alfred Rosenberg's *Der Mythus des 20. Jahrhunderts*, but in the 1955 edition that exposition and those citations have vanished. The 1944 article "Rassenbiologie" (racial biology) does not appear in the later edition. The 1944 article "Demokratie" (democracy) says that pure democracy is impossible to achieve because it falsely assumes the equality of individuals; that statement is omitted in the 1955 edition. The article "Relativitätstheorie" in the 1944 edition refers to "der jüd. Gelehrte Einstein," but in the 1955 edition it says simply "Einstein"; the articles "Marxismus," "Spinozismus," and others show the same difference in the two editions.

In 1945 the Zurich firm of Rudolf Schaltegger published the first of the new German-language dictionaries of the decade, the *Ruscha Fachwörterbuch der Philosophie* ("Ruscha Dictionary of Technical Terms in Philosophy," 147 pages), in which the entries are, for the most part, a few lines long. The book would be of use to only the most elementary students.

Three years later Erwin Metzke published *Handlexikon der Philosophie* (Heidelberg, F. H. Kerle Verlag, 1948, 457 pages; 2nd ed., 1949). The wealth of topics it covers may be noted, for example, in the *L*'s, where one finds the articles "Leben" (life), with four meanings distinguished, three of them broken down into submeanings; "Lebensanschauung" (outlook on life), two meanings; "Lebensform" (form of life), two meanings; "Lebensgefühl" (feeling toward life), three meanings; "Lebenskraft" (vigor), two meanings, with cross references to "Vitalismus" (vitalism) and "Vitalität" (vitality); and "Lebensphilosophie" (philosophy of life), six meanings. A 138-page appendix consists of 1-line to 34-line identifications or brief accounts of almost two thousand philosophers, many of them living, with Americans well represented.

Walter Brugger, S.J., is the principal author of the *Philosophisches Wörterbuch,* prepared with the collaboration mainly of his colleagues at the Berchmans-Kolleg near Munich (Vienna, Herder Verlag, 1948, 532 pages). This work went into 11 editions published in various years to 1964; it was also translated into Italian (Turin, 1959) and Spanish (4th ed., Barcelona, 1964). Many of the more than two thousand articles contain bibliographical references, mostly to German works. The Catholic viewpoint from which the book was prepared is not conspicuous, and the topics are treated factually, with a minimum of controversial interpretation. An appendix of over one hundred pages (including an index of about two thousand names) presents an outline history of philosophy.

Six fascicles, covering *A* to *J*, of the *Philosophen-Lexikon* were issued in 1936–1937 by various publishers in Berlin, having been prepared under the editorship of Eugen Hauer, Werner Ziegenfuss, and Gertrud Jung. The completed work was issued in 1949–1950 by Ziegenfuss, with the collaboration of Gertrud Jung, under the title *Philosophen-Lexikon: Handwörterbuch der Philosophie nach Personen* (2 vols., Berlin, Walter de Gruyter). Most of the articles contain biographical data about the individual covered, an indication of his contribution to philosophical thought, the titles (and years of publication) of his principal works or the principal collections of his works, and the titles of selected writings about him. Some articles, such as those on von Hartmann, Friedrich Schiller, and Unamuno, present significant quotations from their writings. For Karl Barth there are, atypically, only 3 lines of text, followed by a 24-line bibliography of his writings and a 12-line list of writings about him.

The two volumes of the Ziegenfuss work are remarkably comprehensive. They are also accurate and relatively cosmopolitan. Germans, it is true, get more space than others—for example, 5 pages for Benno Erdmann, who was Gertrud Jung's teacher, and 6 pages for Fechner, compared with 1 for Democritus and 3 for Socrates. A few Marxists also get disproportionate coverage—4 pages for Lenin and 5 for Marx—and contemporaries likewise are given some preference—for example, 6 pages for Berdyaev, compared with 1 for Bentham. One is surprised to see 5 pages devoted to the racist Houston Stewart Chamberlain. But Americans are given fairly good coverage—1 page for Peirce, 3 for Emerson, 3 for James, 2 for Dewey, and 1 for Royce.

A few of the articles in the Ziegenfuss work (for example, those on Nicolai Hartmann, 17 pages; P. A. Sorokin, 3 pages; and Erich Rothacker, 7 pages) were written by the subjects themselves.

HUNGARIAN. Volume I ("Aall" to "Avicebrón") of Pal Sandor's *Filozofiai Lexikon* (Budapest, Faust Kiadás, 64 pages) appeared in 1941. No further volumes seem to have been published. This is a biographical dictionary of philosophers with some emphasis on nineteenth-century and twentieth-century thinkers—Erich Adickes, four men named Adler, Samuel Alexander, and so on—and with considerable space devoted to selected great figures of the past—Anselm, Antisthenes, Aquinas, Aristotle (32 cols.), and others.

TURKISH. The *Felsefe ve Gramer Terimleri* ("Dictionary of Philosophy and Grammar," Istanbul, Cumhuriyet Basimevi, 1942, 318 pages), prepared by the Türk Dil Kurumu (Turkish Language Society), contains a series of alphabetical three-language lists of equivalent terms (Turkish, Osmanli, French; Osmanli, French, Turkish; and French, Osmanli, Turkish) and three corresponding lists of grammatical terms. (Osmanli is a Turkish dialect.) The philosophical lists usefully include over one thousand terms in cosmology and metaphysics—*causality, demiurge,* and so on; ethics—*altruism, deontology,* and so on; logic—*amphibology, contraposition,* and so on; and other domains of philosophy, plus terms in psychology—*abulia, claustrophobia,* and so on.

THE NINETEEN-FIFTIES

The flowering begun in the 1940s continued in the 1950s. Where the previous decade saw 22 new dictionaries of philosophy that have come to the writer's attention, 24 were published in the 1950s. Nine languages were represented: English, Gaelic, German, Dutch, French, Italian, Spanish, Portuguese, and Turkish. The great landmark of the 1950s is the monumental four-volume Italian encyclopedia of philosophy written by scholars at Gallarate.

ENGLISH. A philosophical dictionary vastly different from most is *The Great Ideas: A Syntopicon of Great Books of the Western World,* compiled under the direction of Mortimer J. Adler (Chicago, Encyclopaedia Britannica, 1952), comprising Volumes II and III of the publisher's 54-volume "Great Books of the Western World." It covers 102 "great ideas," including art, being, cause, chance, change, democracy, eternity, form, God, good and evil, idea, knowledge, logic, love, matter, metaphysics, mind, nature, necessity and contingency, one and many, reasoning, sense, sign and symbol, soul, space, time, truth, will, wisdom, and world.

For each idea the work presents an analytical and expository introduction, followed by a list of elements of the idea with a series of references to pertinent passages in the great books for each element. There is also a list of related great ideas and finally a list of additional readings on the subject in classics which are not included in the "Great Books" collection. At the end of the second volume of the *Syntopicon* there are a bibliography consolidating the lists of additional readings, a discussion of "syntopical construction" (which lists, among the ideas originally considered for inclusion but rejected, becoming, belief, deduction, doubt, essence, probability, purpose, reality, self, spirit, substance, value, and many others), and an "inventory" (index) of eighteen hundred terms.

A more self-conscious book could scarcely be imagined. Virtually every portion of the book is preceded by an explanation of why that portion was formed in the way in which it was formed and not otherwise. Critics are answered before they have a chance to formulate criticisms. The reader is everywhere shown the scaffolding, and his attention is invited to a close inspection of its features.

Nevertheless, the book is highly useful. For the elements of the idea of form, for example, the reader is referred to specific passages in Plato, Aristotle, Lucretius, Augustine, Aquinas, Bacon, Descartes, Locke, Berkeley, Kant, Hegel, William James, and others. The analytical and expository introductions are for the most part general rather than technical, but they go as deeply into a subject as a thoughtful, educated reader may desire. All in all, this unique work was decidedly worth undertaking and was competently executed.

The only other English dictionary of philosophy published in the 1950s was Michael H. Briggs's *Handbook of Philosophy* (New York, Philosophical Library, 1959, 214 pages). It is difficult to see the usefulness of the article "Future," which reads, in its entirety, "Those events that will happen in time to come," or of the opening definition of the article "Change"—namely, "A constant alteration of states of the universe so that specific combinations of events do not persist." Several other articles in this handbook are equally unenlightening.

GAELIC. The *Focloir Fealsaimh* ("Vocabulary of Philosophy"), by Colmán O Huallacháin, O.F.M. (Dublin, An Clóchomhar, 1958, 169 pages), begins with a preface in French by Monsignor Louis de Raeymaeker of the University of Louvain. The book presents brief Gaelic descriptions or explanations of about two thousand Gaelic terms in philosophy and related humanistic disciplines, with the equivalent terms in German, English, French, and Latin. At the end of the book are four reciprocal word lists—German, English, French, and Latin—with the Gaelic equivalent of each word. The English word list includes not only such specifically philosophical terms as *Absolute, actual, aesthetics, agnostic,* and *aseity* but also such terms as *abnormal, acoustics, agoraphobia, anthropology*, and *atavism*.

GERMAN. In Germany and Switzerland five works were produced or begun, not counting a nonalphabetical so-called encyclopedia published in 1959. First, Carl Decurtins produced the *Kleines Philosophen-Lexikon* (Affoltern am Albis, Switzerland, Aehren Verlag, 1952, 312 pages), containing biographical sketches of three hundred individuals, among whom are not only the main figures in the history of philosophy strictly conceived but also Helena P. Blavatsky, Karl von Clausewitz, Lenin, Mussolini, the racists Chamberlain, Gobineau, and Alfred Rosenberg, as well as Jesus Christ, Dostoyevsky, Emerson, and Omar Khayyám. Chamberlain gets more space than Jesus Christ.

In 1954, Franz Austeda wrote the *Kleines Wörterbuch der Philosophie* (Frankfurt, Humboldt-Verlag, 188 pages; 2nd ed., entitled *Wörterbuch der Philosophie*, Berlin and Munich, Verlag Lebendiges Wissen, 1962, 270 pages). This work contains over eighteen hundred articles, including eight hundred which are biographical. It is a highly sensible and sound short reference work, with a reasonable proportion of space allotted to each of the standard topics in philosophy and the principal philosophers of the past and the present, as well as topics in less standard fields, such as Oriental philosophy, disciplines close to philosophy, and even old saws like Terence's "Homo sum; humani nihil a me alienum puto" ("A man am I; nothing human do I consider alien to me").

On behalf of the Kommission für Philosophie der Akademie der Wissenschaften und der Literatur zu Mainz, Erich Rothacker undertook a series of volumes under the general title *Archiv für Begriffsgeschichte; Bausteine zu einem historischen Wörterbuch der Philosophie* ("Archive for History of Concepts; Building Stones for a Historical Dictionary of Philosophy," Bonn, H. Bouvier, 1955–). Among the volumes which have appeared are Volume II (Part 2), *Kosmos* (1958, 168 pages), by Walther Kranz; Volume III, *Gewohnheit* ("Custom," 1958, 606 pages), by Gerhard Funke; Volume IV (1959, 239 pages), containing discussions by eight writers regarding various concepts or suggested texts of articles for the *Wörterbuch*; Volume V (1960, 718 pages), containing, under the headings "Absolut," "Abstrakt, Abstraktion," and "Aktivität, aktiv-passiv," the *Bibliographie deutscher Hochschulschriften von 1900–1955*, by Hans Flasche and Utta Wawrzinek; Volume VII (1962, 325 pages), containing discussions by a number of writers on such concepts as the Kantian *Analytik* and *Dialektik*; and Volume VIII (1963, 398 pages), by Karl Otto Apel, on the idea of language in the humanistic tradition from Dante to Vico. This is an ambitious and useful undertaking. Although it may not eventuate in an actual dictionary of philosophy, future writers of such dictionaries should feel obliged to utilize its findings.

In 1958, Max Müller and Alois Halder produced the paperback *Herders kleines philosophisches Wörterbuch* (Freiburg, Verlag Herder, 204 pages; 7th ed., 1965), with a bibliographical appendix citing various histories of philosophy and journals of philosophy and nine earlier dictionaries of philosophy. Portraits of Aristotle, Plato,

Augustine, Aquinas, Descartes, Leibniz, Kant, Hegel, Husserl, Bergson, Heidegger, and Jaspers appear on the back cover. The articles on medieval, modern, and contemporary thinkers are especially useful; Nicholas of Cusa is given 76 lines, Unamuno 34 lines, and Buber 28 lines.

The last of the German-language contributions of the decade is Volume II of *Das Fischer Lexikon, Enzyklopädie des Wissens*, a compilation entitled *Philosophie*, edited by Alwin Diemar and Ivo Frenzel (Frankfurt, Fischer Bucherei, 1958, 376 pages). This paperback book was reprinted in 1959 and 1960, and an English version translated by Salvatore Attanasio and prepared under the direction of James Gutmann was published as *Philosophy—A to Z* (New York, Grosset and Dunlap, 1963) in hardback and paperback editions. The collaborators consisted of 15 German authorities plus Paul K. Feyerabend of the United States. The work presents a small number of comprehensive articles—26—on such broad topics as anthropology, aesthetics, and Chinese and Japanese philosophy rather than a multitude of short ones. Historical information is given where necessary, but the emphasis is on concepts and problems. The articles show originality and penetration.

A nonalphabetical so-called encyclopedia was *Die Philosophie im XX. Jahrhundert: Eine Enzyklopädische Darstellung ihrer Geschichte, Disziplinen und Aufgaben*, edited by Frederick H. Heinemann ("Philosophy in the Twentieth Century; An Encyclopedic Presentation of Its History, Disciplines and Formulations," Stuttgart, Ernst Klett Verlag, 1959, 600 pages; 2nd edition, 1963). Heinemann begins with a discussion of the term *encyclopedia* which de-emphasizes the alphabetical order of topics, and he continues with chapters, written by himself or others, on Oriental, ancient, medieval, and modern philosophy; on movements in twentieth-century philosophy; and on epistemology, logic, philosophy of mathematics, metaphysics, philosophy of nature, and other philosophical disciplines. The treatment of the topics is mainly interpretive and constructive, rather than purely expository, especially in the chapters on the philosophical disciplines.

DUTCH. The Dutch work of this decade was edited by Johan Grooten and G. Jo Steenbergen. It is *Filosofisch Lexicon* (Antwerp, Standaard-Boekhandel, 1958, 331 pages), written by 32 collaborators, of whom the best known are perhaps E. W. Beth and Louis de Raeymaeker. The book begins with an explanation of how the topics are broken down, what type of spelling is used, how to find medieval names, and how the cross references are shown. The articles themselves are scholarly and well balanced.

FRENCH. Armand Cuvillier's *Nouveau Vocabulaire philosophique* (Paris, Librairie Armand Colin, 1956, 203 pages; 3rd ed., 1958) is a worthy successor to his *Petit Vocabulaire*, which went through 13 editions from 1925 to 1953. The new work includes a number of terms borrowed from other languages, such as *Erlehnis* (experience), *Dasein* (existence), and *pattern*. A number of articles, à la Goblot and Baldwin, set forth more than one meaning and then discourage the use of the term in one of the senses. For example, under "Empirique" (Empirical), the third meaning is "fondé sur l'expérience en général . . ." ("founded on experience in general"), but the author comments, "impropre au sens 3; dire expérienciel" ("improper in sense 3; say experiential"). A Spanish translation, entitled *Diccionario de filosofía*, was published at Buenos Aires in 1961.

J. Claude Piguet's *Le Vocabulaire intellectuel* (Paris, Centre de Documentation Universitaire et S.E.D.E.S. Réunis, 1957, 112 pages; reprinted, 1960, backstrip title, *Vocabulaire de philosophie*) disclaims being a dictionary in the sense of a list of pat definitions. It aims, instead, to stimulate students' thinking, partly by provocative opposition. For many terms an antonym is given, or two or more "opposites" are cited; for example, the article on absolute contrasts absolute with relative, and the article on duty contrasts duty not only with moral indifference but also with right. The book is probably of use mainly to students specializing in subjects other than philosophy.

ITALIAN. Of the seven Italian works of the period, three were published in 1951. Eustachio P. Lamanna and Francesco Adorno produced the *Dizionario di termini filosofici* (Florence, Felice le Monnier, 1951, 104 pages; 9th ed., 1960), in which the articles are brief, ranging from 1 line for "Verbo, (il)," ending with a cross reference to "Logos," to 47 lines for "Intelleto."

Giovanni Semprini compiled the *Nuovo dizionario di coltura filosofica e scientifica* (Turin, Società Editrice Internazionalc, 1951, 470 pages), which chiefly has articles on philosophical subjects, with errors in various articles on British and American philosophy, but also covers topics in the empirical sciences; for example, there are articles on anesthesia, clan, geology, and Mesmer.

Mario A. Boccalaro's *Dizionario filosofico* (Bologna, Licinio Cappelli, 1951, 91 pages) covers topics only. Its articles, generally a few lines long, are carefully and accurately phrased.

In 1952, Vincenzo Miano and 12 Italian collaborators produced the *Dizionario filosofico* (Turin, Società Editrice Internazionale, 1952, 693 pages), written with a Thomistic approach. Only topics are treated, but the appended "Schema della storia della filosofia" shows the name of the article in which each important philosopher is discussed; over 150 thinkers are included in the list.

Umberto Cantoro's *Vocabulario filosofico* (Bologna, Casa Editrice N. U. Gallo, 1955, 283 pages) began with an introduction on the philosophical disciplines and continued with an alphabetically arranged vocabulary which purportedly emphasized terms in common usage that have a special meaning in philosophy—for example, *absolute, concrete, and criticism*—but actually devoted most of its pages to the usual philosophical terms—*agnosticism, ambiguity, anguish, free will*, and the like. Psychology was taken by the author to be a philosophical discipline.

The *Dizionario di filosofia*, edited by Andrea Biraghi with contributions by 29 Italian collaborators (Milan, Edizioni di Comunità, 1957, 787 pages), is not strictly a dictionary since the materials in its two parts (on the history and problems of philosophy, respectively) are arranged in a nonalphabetical order, but it contains, as appendixes, three features which put it in the broad stream of dictionaries of philosophy: a dictionary of Greek terms, a dictionary of German terms, and a comprehensive alphabetical index.

The Gallarate landmark. In 1957 a group of Italian scholars in the Centro di Studi Filosofici di Gallarate, together with a few foreign collaborators, produced the *Enciclopedia filosofica* (4 vols., Venice and Rome, Istituto per la Collaborazione Culturale for the Ministry of Public Education and the Giorgio Cini and the Enrico Lossa foundations), which for the first time in half a century outshone the Baldwin work in comprehensiveness and up-to-date scholarship. The directing committee aimed to produce not "un mero *dizionario* filosofico" but a true encyclopedia of philosophy which would go beyond the dry explanation of the usages of terms and would present deeper analyses of the elements and implications both of individual problems and ideas and of more general points of view.

Each volume contains a number of full-page illustrations (mostly portraits of philosophers), and many of the articles contain bibliographical references at the end. This colossal work, totaling some 6 million words, is a basic landmark in the field of philosophical reference works, far outstripping its nearest competitors in magnitude. Physically, also, it is outstanding; the print and the 233 illustrations are not only tasteful but in some ways sumptuous. The work contains about twelve thousand articles, of which seven thousand are historical (on individual philosophers, movements, and the like) and five thousand are analytical (on concepts, problems, and the like). There are, for example, over 130 articles on past and present Russian philosophy, 82 on individual philosophical journals, over 80 on twentieth-century American philosophy, 74 on Indian philosophy, and 55 on subtopics of deduction and induction.

The contributors are mainly professors in Italian universities. Their contributions are factual, reliable, and broad in scope. The article on Aristotle (27 cols., with a full-page glossy reproduction of Raphael's head of Aristotle in the "School of Athens") is followed by articles on Pseudo-Aristotle (1 col.), Aristotle in Latin (2 cols.), and Aristotelianism (6 cols.), all of them rich in content and based on vast learning. There are worthwhile articles on neoclassicism, neocriticism, neo-empiricism, Neo-Guelphism, Neo-Hegelianism, Neo-Lutheranism, Neo-Malthusianism, Neo-Pythagoreanism, Neoplatonism, neopositivism (16 cols.), neorealism, Neo-Scholasticism, and neo-humanism.

There is some bias toward religious and idealistic positions in philosophy. Moreover, more Italian twentieth-century philosophers are treated in separate articles than either French or British. G. E. Moore gets only a column, which is less than the space assigned to Bernardo Varisco or Michele F. Sciacca, and a number of eminent American philosophers—Brand Blanshard, C. I. Lewis, Arthur O. Lovejoy, and R. W. Sellars—get less than a column.

The encyclopedia also goes far afield in including material on economics, pedagogy (with articles on *scoutismo*—the boy scouts—and on coeducation), and literary art (with articles on Joseph Addison, Sir Philip Sidney, and Jonathan Swift). Moreover, there are many minute articles which could profitably have been combined into more meaningful longer articles. However, weighing the encyclopedia's many merits against its few shortcomings, one must conclude that the work represents a highly laudable achievement, destined to be useful over a prolonged period.

SPANISH. Of the two Spanish-language dictionaries of philosophy produced in the 1950s, the first was published in Argentina and the second in Spain. Julio Rey Pastor and Ismael Quiles directed five editors and ten collaborators in the production of the *Diccionario filosófico* (Buenos Aires, Espasa–Calpe Argentina, 1952, 1,114 pages), in which the material is arranged according to a systematic outline of topics in 18 chapters instead of in alphabetical order. The 18 chapters are headed "Introducción á la historia de la filosofía"; "Lógica"; "Teoría del conocimiento"; "Epistemología y teoría de la ciencia"; "Logística, Lógica Simbólica o Lógica Matemática"; "Ontología," with 19 subheads, including "Ser," "Ente," "Existencia," and "Esencia"; "Metafisica general" (nature and structure of being and individuality); "Metafísica especial" (matter, life, mind, and spirit); "Filosofía de los valores"; "Filosofía de la religión"; "Ética"; "Estética"; "Filosofía del arte y poética"; "Psicología"; "Antropología filosófica"; "Concepción del mundo"; "Sociología"; and "Filosofía del derecho." At the end are the 45-page "Vocabulario filosófico," alphabetically arranged, and the 17-page "Equivalencias idiomáticas" (German–Spanish, English–Spanish, French–Spanish, and Italian–Spanish).

Juan Zaragüeta Bengoechea, director of the Luis Vives Institute of Philosophy in Madrid, is the author of the *Vocabulario filosófico* (Madrid, Espasa–Calpe, 1955, 571 pages), in which almost every article begins with the German, French, English, and Italian equivalents of the term being discussed. The terms are defined and explained from a scholastic point of view, generally without historical references. The articles are weak on contemporary philosophy, the one on *logística*, for example, merely setting forth in 20 lines what symbolic logic is about.

PORTUGUESE. Three Portuguese-language dictionaries of philosophy were published or were begun and dropped in the decade of the 1950s. Volume I (*A–D*) of the *Dicionário de filosofia*, by Orris Soares, was published at Rio de Janeiro in 1952 by the Instituto Nacional do Livro of the Ministério da Educação e Saúde. No other volumes have appeared. At the beginning of many of the articles are the equivalents of the term being covered in one or more of the following languages—Greek, Latin, French, Italian, English, and German. The article on Aristotle runs to more than 25 columns, with subtopics arranged alphabetically (for instance, "Aristóteles e a alma" and "Aristóteles e a astronomia"). To take the *D*'s for an example, there are useful articles on Dalton, Dante, Darwin, Descartes (15 cols.), Diogenes (four persons so named), Driesch, Duhem, Dühring, Duns Scotus, Durkheim, and others but none on Dewey.

Published at São Paulo were the first fascicle, covering the letter A, of the *Dicionario de filosofia*, by Luís Washington Vita, reprinted from the *Revista do Arquivo Municipal* (1950, 48 pages), and the *Vocabulário filosófico*, by Carlos Lopes de Mattos (Ediçôes Leia, 1957, 387 pages). Both cover only topics but include among the topics the philosophy of some individuals, in the articles on Aristotelianism, Averroism, and so forth. Vita modestly ascribes any errors which may appear in his work (of which no more has been published) to the fact that his is the first dictionary of philosophy in the Portuguese language; thus, he does not count the Voltairian 1938 work of Renato Kehl as a true dictionary of philosophy. Vita includes and Mattos excludes fields akin to philosophy. For many of his terms Mattos gives the equivalents in Esperanto, French, German, Greek, Italian, Latin, and Spanish and enumerates in the Bibliography 17 earlier dictionaries of philosophy.

TURKISH. Of Cemil Sena's *Büyük Filozoflar Ansiklopedisi* (Istanbul, Negioğlu Yayinevi, 1957–), only one volume, covering *A* to *D*, appeared. This work is a dictionary of philosophers which ranges from technical philosophers like Anaxagoras (12 cols.) to popular philosophers like Angelus Silesius and Will Durant, natural scientists like Ampère, and sociologists like Durkheim. The articles—some of them illustrated—are well balanced between biography and doctrine. Appended to Volume I are a glossary of Turkish philosophical terms with their French equivalents and an index of persons mentioned, showing, for example, 130 pages of the 642 pages in Volume I as containing references to Plato.

URMSON, ABBAGNANO, AND AFTER

ENGLISH. *The Concise Encyclopedia of Western Philosophy and Philosophers* (New York, Hawthorn Books, 1960, 431 pages), edited by James O. Urmson, contains over 150 articles on individual philosophers and about 65 articles on philosophical topics and schools. It also includes over one hundred full-page illustrations, mostly portraits of philosophers, of which eight are in color. It closes with an 11-page bibliography. Many outstanding contemporary British and American philosophers are among the 48 contributors. In the Preface the editor set forth his principles. Where it was difficult to summarize the views of a philosopher briefly, he was to be given enough space to make his position intelligible (six thousand words for Kant). More generally, it was deemed better to have fewer and longer articles than many short ones of doubtful utility. Philosophy was interpreted narrowly, excluding such popular topics as the philosophy of life. Eastern thinkers were excluded because, according to Urmson, they are philosophers in the popular, and not in the technical, sense. In recapitulation, however, he gives as the reason for their omission the fact that "their achievement is not closely related to that of western philosophers." Exception could be taken to the former of these justifications for the omission of Oriental philosophy, but the addition of the latter makes it hard to object.

Although the articles in the Urmson work are not signed, the authorship of some has become known—for instance, the article on epistemology is by Gilbert Ryle, on ethics by R. M. Hare, on Heidegger by Walter Kaufmann, and on logic by D. J. O'Connor. The articles on epistemology and ethics display a freshness seldom found in encyclopedias; they are readable, free of academicism, informative, and challenging. Many other articles are also both brilliant and original. However, the article on Heidegger not only, with some justification, makes much of his welcome of Hitlerism but also, with less warrant, dismisses the fabric of his thought as comparable to the nonexistent clothes of Hans Christian Andersen's fairy-tale emperor.

Urmson's choice of topics is questionable. Although topics outside technical philosophy were to be excluded, Karl Marx is covered in an article of fifty-three hundred words, of which the first sentence is "Marx was not primarily a philosopher." Many of the contributors are themselves the subjects of articles, but one does not find any article on Gödel, Tarski, or, among thinkers of the past, Bayle or Voltaire. Among the topical articles one does not find any on belief, causation, error, existence, identity, necessity, philosophy of history, negation, self, or vitalism.

Another English work of the 1960s was Henry Thomas' *Biographical Encyclopedia* (New York, Doubleday, 1965, 286 pages). This is a work for the general reader, not for the specialist in philosophy. For example, the more than four hundred thinkers covered include a generous selection of poets (Horace, Omar, Byron, Shakespeare), social commentators (Benjamin Franklin, Oliver Wendell Holmes, Jr.), and theosophists (Annie Besant, Helena P. Blavatsky) but not Ayer, Carnap, Jaspers, Lovejoy, Meinong, Moore, Reichenbach, Ryle, or Schlick. The expositions and evaluations are likewise on a popular level.

Another popular biographical work is Thomas Kiernan's *Who's Who in the History of Philosophy* (New York, Philosophical Library, 1965, 185 pages). The expositions of the doctrines of some of the philosophers covered are naive. For example, Aquinas is said to have redirected Aristotelianism "towards truth and away from doubt," and Mill's inductive methods are said to be based on his "advocacy of the law of the uniformity of nature."

RUSSIAN. The year 1960 saw the first volume (A to "Diderot") of a new Russian dictionary of philosophy, the *Filosofskaya Entsiklopediya*, edited by F. V. Konstantinov and others (Moscow, "Soviet Encyclopedia" Publishing House). The second volume (covering "Disjunction" to "The Comic") of the four projected volumes was published in 1962. Volume I includes four articles—"Democracy," by L. Denisova; "Dialectics," by P. Kopnin; "Humanism," by L. Denisova; and "Dialectical Materialism," by A. G. Spirkin—which are available in English, the first three having been translated by William Mandel in the quarterly *Soviet Studies in Philosophy* (Vol. I, Spring 1963) and the fourth having been translated for *Russian Philosophy: A Book of Readings*, edited by James M. Edie and others (3 vols., Chicago, Quadrangle Books, 1965).

The article on democracy attempts to show that bourgeois democracy is dictatorship of the capitalist class, with illusory freedoms, whereas socialist democracy is dictatorship of the proletarian class, with genuine freedom of speech, the press, assembly, and demonstration. The truth is also labeled elsewhere in the encyclopedia, as in the article on absolute idealism, which is described as based on "the false assumption of the existence of an absolute idea." On the positive side may be mentioned the numerous good articles on logic, the broad coverage of both topics and persons (except that Bukharin and some other heretic Marxists are omitted), and the many halftone cuts. Such sociological topics as marriage are included.

Karl G. Ballestrem's *Russian Philosophical Terminology* (Dordrecht, D. Reidel, 1964, 116 pages) contains a glossary of about one thousand philosophical terms in Russian, with English, French, and German equivalents. Emphasis is placed on terms having a special use in Soviet philosophy.

ITALIAN. Nicola Abbagnano published the *Dizionario di Filosofia* (Turin, Unione Tipografico, 1961, 905 pages; Spanish translation, Mexico City and Buenos Aires, 1963) with the collaboration of Giulio Preti on topics in the field of logic. Abbagnano is a distinguished figure in contemporary philosophy and philosophical scholarship. His dictionary, covering only topics, shows vast erudition and commendable acumen in appraising tendencies and movements in philosophy. It gives, for example, a fair and thoroughly knowledgeable treatment to contemporary Anglo-American and positivistic philosophy. In the admiring words of Urmson, who noted a few inaccuracies in the Abbagnano work in a review in *Mind* (Vol. 71,

1962, 425), Abbagnano "refers as readily to the latest numbers of American journals as to the works of Plato."

Topics for which the standard name is in a language other than Italian—for example, *Erlebnis* (living experience), *Gegenstandtheorie* (object theory), and *Weltanschauung* (world outlook)—are treated by Abbagnano or cross-referenced in their regular alphabetical order. For many of the Italian words he also gives equivalents in Greek, Latin, English, French, and German. This work is one of the outstanding dictionaries of philosophy of our time. An English translation is scheduled to be published by the University of Chicago Press.

DUTCH. K. Kuypers is the editor of a Dutch work, *Elseviers Kleine Filosofische en Psychologische Encyclopedie* (Amsterdam, Elsevier, 272 pages), that appeared in 1960. Short but useful articles are presented on obscure as well as prominent thinkers and topics. Some topics—for instance, the Gifford lectures—are not often found in dictionaries of philosophy. Appended are a 15-page historical outline showing the schools or other groupings of over five hundred philosophers; a bibliography; and a selected list of philosophical journals and organizations.

DANISH. A work of this period is Henrik Thomsen's *Hvem Taenkte Hvad; Filosofiens Hvem-Hvad-Hvor* (Copenhagen, Politikens Forlag, 1961, 390 pages), with an introductory note by Justus Hartnack. The book contains a thumbnail history of philosophy from the pre-Socratics to Husserl, Wittgenstein, and Russell; numerous illustrations and two maps; a who's who of philosophy with illustrations of Augustine reading and Heidegger hiking; a dictionary of technical terms; and a bibliography.

GERMAN. Joseph Münzhuber wrote the *Kleines Wörterbuch der Philosophie, zum Gebrauch an Schulen* (Düsseldorf, Pädagogischer Verlag Schwann, 1962, 45 pages). This work contains about 135 articles ranging from the 2-line "Transintelligibel" to the 48-line "Existenzphilosophie." Among the more unusual articles are "In-der-Welt-Sein" (being-in-the-world) and "Unschärferelation" (Heisenberg's uncertainty relation).

Anton Neuhäusler wrote *Grundbegriffe der philosophischen Sprache: Begriffe viersprachig* (Munich, Ehrenwirth Verlag, 1963, 276 pages). The length of the article on any topic covered by Neuhäusler is based not on the topic's importance but on its "Klärungs-bedurfigkeit und schwierigkeit" ("need and difficulty of explanation"). Each entry includes the English, French, and Italian equivalent of the term; an indication of the origin of the term (if this is relevant); a sophisticated but clear discussion of the use of the term; and a brief bibliography. An appendix presents a decimal classification of philosophical concepts—for example, 1 for philosophy itself; 11 for metaphysics; 11.1 for ontology; 111.11 for existence, *Dasein*, and reality; 19 for history of philosophy; 2 for theology.

In 1964 there appeared another *Philosophisches Wörterbuch* (Leipzig, VEB Bibliographisches Institut, 650 pages; reprinted 1965), edited by Georg Klaus and Manfred Buhr. It was a joint project of the Institute for Philosophy of the German Academy of Sciences in Berlin and the professorial chair for philosophy of the Institute for Economics of the Central Committee of the German Socialist Unity party. The Marxist–Leninist slant is sometimes blatant, as in the article "Demokratie," where bourgeois democracy is characterized as a form of government in which everything is subordinated to profit. Among the examples presented to illustrate the use of "is" in the article "Kopula" are (in translation): "Marx is the author of *Capital*" and "Marx is one of the greatest thinkers of mankind."

FRENCH. In 1962, Paul Foulquié, with the collaboration of Raymond Saint-Jean, produced the *Dictionnaire de la langue philosophique* (Paris, Presses Universitaires de France, 1962, 776 pages), which, as the Preface states, is heavily indebted to Lalande's work. Since Foulquié's is a dictionary of concepts, there are no articles on schools or viewpoints, such as Aristotelianism and Eleaticism. Although the basic arrangement is alphabetical, related concepts are in some cases grouped around a generic term—for example, *étant, entité, essence, exister*, and *existentialisme* around *être*. Many of the articles quote texts to support the definitions presented.

The anonymous *Dictionnaire des philosophes* (Paris, Collection Seghers, 1962, 383 pages; binder's title, *Dictionnaire illustré des philosophes*) contains biographical statements regarding approximately six hundred standard Western philosophers and philosophic thinkers, such as Ruth Benedict, Karen Horney, and Kurt Lewin, in allied fields. There follow references to about thirty Oriental thinkers and a vocabulary of some five hundred terms, most of them defined in a few lines. Scattered in the book are 64 portraits.

According to Didier Julia, the purpose of his *Dictionnaire de la philosophie* (Paris, Librairie Larousse, 1964, 320 pages) is the disclosure of eternal truths as being applicable to daily life. In keeping with that purpose, the illustrations are popular: an abstract painting, a scene in Paris after the explosion of a plastic bomb, a child peering through curtains (illustrating "Attention"), a Buddhist immolating himself at Saigon, and others. Marx gets more space than anyone else, and Trotsky gets more than Aristotle. Maimonides and Peirce are among the omissions. It is doubtful that the announced purpose of the work was achieved.

SPANISH. Paul Henri Boyer's *Diccionario breve de filosofía* (Buenos Aires, Club de Lectores, 1962, 187 pages) has some material of questionable validity. There is only one article on Oriental philosophy, on nirvana, which is wrongly defined as negation of the will to live. The spelling of non-Spanish names in the work is not reliable.

ORIENTAL LANGUAGES. Three Asian countries—nationalist China, Japan, and, most notably, Korea—have made significant contributions in the 1960s.

Chinese. The Chinese dictionary is *Chê Hsüeh Ta Tz'ŭ Tien* ("Comprehensive Dictionary of Philosophy," Taipei, Ch'i Ming Shu Chû, 1960, 464 pages), containing about one thousand five hundred articles, each printed with the equivalent of the term in at least one Western language. The first entry is on monism, and the last is on "ideal-realism." The rest cover the standard philosophical and psychological topics and personalities plus such unusual topics as dilemmatic proposition and "summists" (authors of works entitled *Summa*). Two indexes in Western languages (and roman type) list topics and personal names.

Japanese. Naomichi Takama's *Tetsugaku Yogo No Kiso Chishiki* ("Philosophical Terminology," Tokyo, Seisun Shuppan Sha, 242 pages), a Japanese work, was published in 1961. The title of each article is given with English and German equivalents. There are articles on patriotism, happiness, justice, human nature, freedom of the will, suicide, space, time, dialectical materialism, scholastic philosophy, and many other popular and technical topics. Some of the articles show an undue influence of Marxism.

Another Japanese work was edited by Yasumasa Oshima—*Shin Rinri Jiten* ("Dictionary of Ethics," Tokyo, Sobun Sha, 1961, 472 pages). The scope of this work is broader than its title indicates. Some of the articles are on ethical subjects, including agape, evil, ataraxia, will, Epicureanism, and human rights, but others transcend the domain of ethics, including those on atman, Aristotle, either–or, a priori, causality, Eleatics, entelechy, and *Dasein*. In general, this is the more scholarly of the Japanese works.

Korean. One hundred and four Korean scholars worked on the *Dictionary of Philosophy: Ch'ŏrhak Taesajŏn* (Seoul, Hagwŏnsa, 1963, 1,376 pages). A monumental job of scholarship and printing, this work contains, for many entries, the Korean expression followed by equivalents in other pertinent languages, the article in Korean with romanized transliterations where needed, and a bibliography. The field covered includes philosophy, psychology, and sociology, and the articles are of exceptionally high quality. Among the added features are about four hundred pictures of philosophers; other illustrations, including Wittgenstein's duck-rabbit and four full-page maps; a uniquely rich year-by-year chronology of philosophy, showing, for example, 1905 as the year of the inauguration or publication of specific works by 22 philosophers; and an index of about five thousand terms in Western languages.

A "NONENCYCLOPEDIA." From time to time we have paused to poke a curious finger into works which are called dictionaries or encyclopedias of philosophy but which are not arranged alphabetically. The latest of these is Ramón Conde Obregón's *Enciclopedia de la filosofía* (Barcelona, De Gassó Hernanos, 1961, 363 pages). The first four parts of the book are on philosophy in general, prephilosophy, Western philosophy, and Oriental philosophy; the fifth is headed "Conclusion." Conde's work will probably not be the last, in the march of philosophical exposition, to exploit the perennial intellectual magnetism of the term *dictionary or encyclopedia.*

DICTIONARIES OF SPECIAL PHILOSOPHICAL TOPICS

There are dictionaries which cover one or more philosophical disciplines, periods, and schools, as well as individual philosophers. The listings presented here are merely illustrative; complete coverage is not attempted.

DISCIPLINES. Some dictionaries cover a single discipline, such as aesthetics, ethics, logic, or theology; others cover a combination, such as ethics and theology or logic and philosophy of science.

Aesthetics. Among the dictionaries of aesthetics is Ignaz Jeitteles' *Aesthetisches Lexikon: Ein alphabetisches Handbuch zur Theorie der Philosophie des Schönen und der Schönen Künste* ("Dictionary of Aesthetics: An Alphabetical Handbook of the Theory of the Philosophy of Beauty and the Fine Arts," 2 vols., Vienna, Carl Gerold, 1835–1837). This is a capably written reference work, covering numerous topics in architecture, the dance, drama, drawing, music, painting, poetry, rhetoric, sculpture, and other arts, as well as topics applicable to natural beauty or to more than one of the arts. An 84-page appendix reviews the classic literature on aesthetics.

In 1946 Roger Caillois produced the *Vocabulaire esthétique* (Paris, Éditions de la Revue Fontaine, 141 pages). In addition to whole chapters on nature and art, this work contains articles on art for art's sake, authority, image, order, originality, sincerity, and other topics in nonalphabetical order. Each article is a discursive essay rather than a systematic treatment.

A curiosity among dictionaries of aesthetics is Paolo Mantegazza's *Dizionario delle cose belle* (Milan, Fratelli Treves, 1891, 346 pages; German translation, 2 vols., Jena, 1891–1892). After an introduction on elements of beauty (color, symmetry, and so on) constituting about a third of the book, the author presents over one hundred articles in alphabetical order on "beautiful things"—alabaster, eagle, gazelle, jasmine, lark, lion, moon, snow, stars—with rhapsodic comments on each.

Ethics. Among the dictionaries of ethics, mention may be made of two in particular. The first is *Dictionnaire des passions, des vertus, et des vices* (2 vols., Paris, Chez Vincent, 1769), published anonymously by Antonio F. Sticotti and Antoine Sabbatier. Discussing such topics as abasement, abominable, admiration, and adultery near the beginning of the alphabet and urbanity, utility, vivacity, and volition near the end of the alphabet, the authors epitomized the comments of famous writers—Aristotle, Bacon, Confucius, Diderot, Locke, Pascal, Voltaire, and others—on these topics.

In 1956 Vergilius Ferm's *Encyclopedia of Morals* (New York, Philosophical Library, 682 pages) appeared. The contributors to this scholarly and well-balanced volume include Lewis White Beck on Nicolai Hartmann; William K. Frankena on Ross, Sidgwick, and moral philosophy in America; Lucius Garvin on major ethical viewpoints; Walter Kaufmann on Freud, Goethe, Hammurabi, and Nietzsche; George L. Kline on current Soviet morality; Clyde Kluckhohn on Navaho morals; Swami Nikhilananda on Hindu ethics, and Frederick Sontag on Socrates, Plato, and Aristotle. Most of the articles are of substantial length and rich in content; some are a bit pedestrian.

Logic. In logic there is a Spanish *Vocabulario de Lógica*, by Baldomero Diez y Lozano (Murcia, Spain, Imp. Lourdes, 1925, 198 pages; 2nd ed., 1928), which contains about five hundred articles covering not only topics in traditional logic, such as absurd, affirmation, a fortiori, but also topics in related philosophical fields, such as change, causality, phenomena, tree of Porphyry. Given the brevity of the articles, the treatment is necessarily superficial, but the identifications of the more obscure terms are useful.

Theology. Dictionaries of theology are fairly numerous. Among them, some warrant special mention.

From 1908 to 1914 was published a work edited by Samuel M. Jackson and others, *The New Schaff–Herzog Encyclopedia of Religious Knowledge* (13 vols., New York and London, Funk and Wagnalls; reprinted, Grand Rapids, Mich., Baker Book House, 1949–1950). This work was based on the nineteenth-century works in this field edited by Philip Schaff and Johann J. Herzog. The Preface lists numerous preceding Catholic, Protestant, Anglican, Jewish, Muslim, and other theological dictionaries. More of the articles are on individuals—prophets, religious leaders, and theologians—than on topics. Most articles of philosophical interest, such as those on dualism, duty, ethics, freedom of the will, gnosticism, philosophy of religion, positivism, probabilism, Stoicism, utilitarianism, and others, as well as on individual philosophers, were written by specialists in religion; a few, however, such as those by Troeltsch on British moralists, deism, the Enlightenment, idealism, and so on, are philosophically penetrating. The 13-volume work was condensed and brought up to date in the *Twentieth Century Encyclopedia of Religious Knowledge*, edited by Lefferts A. Loetcher (2 vols., Grand Rapids, Mich., Baker Book House, 1955).

Joseph Bricout edited the *Dictionnaire pratique des connaissances réligieuses* (7 vols., Paris, Letouzey et Ané, 1925–1933). In this Catholic-sponsored work the articles of philosophic interest—prepared mostly by professors at the Séminaire des Missions located at Vals in southern France—include those on aesthetic sense, agnosticism, atheism, belief, categories, criteria of truth, deism, doubt, efficient cause, empiricism, and others, plus about 230 articles on philosophers, theologians, and schools of thought. The articles on non-Catholic viewpoints are factual and fair.

Joseph Höfer and Karl Rahner edited the *Lexikon für Theologie und Kirche* (10 vols., Freiburg, Verlag Herder, 1957–1965), a revision of the work of the same title, edited by Michael Buchberger (10 vols., 1930–1938), which was itself referred to as the second edition of Buchberger's two-volume *Kirchliches Handlexikon* (Munich, Allgemeines Verlags-Gesellschaft, 1907–1912).

The work on the philosophical articles was coordinated by Bernhard Welte of Freiburg. The Catholic viewpoint is supported throughout, but the presentation of other viewpoints is informative.

The dictionary edited by Everett F. Harrison, *Baker's Dictionary of Theology* (Grand Rapids, Mich., Baker Book House, 1960, 566 pages), includes articles on movements of theological thought—for example, Calvinism, Lutheranism, and Thomism—but none on individual thinkers as such. Only those philosophical topics which are theological in a strict sense are dealt with. The orientation is that of sophisticated fundamentalism.

In 1962 was begun *A Catholic Dictionary of Theology* (Edinburgh, Thomas Nelson and Sons), edited by Monsignor H. Francis Davis and others. One volume of the four projected volumes has been issued thus far. Very Reverend Ivo Thomas is among the editors, and Father F. C. Copleston is among the better-known contributors. Instead of the usual prosaic and often uninspired articles on individual thinkers, Volume I contains articles on special features, such as Augustine and his influence, Berkeley and Catholicism, and the system of Boscovich. The writing is lively, and the authors do not hesitate to propound new theories.

Dictionaries or encyclopedias of specific religions and denominations are also available and contain articles on theological and even general philosophical topics. Several of these sectarian dictionaries of philosophy are outstanding.

The Jewish Encyclopedia, edited by Cyrus Adler and others (12 vols., New York and London, Funk and Wagnalls, 1901–1906; reprinted in various years), contains rewarding articles on Aristotle in Jewish literature, the influence of Arabic philosophy on Judaism, Maimonides (21 cols.), Spinoza (17 cols.), ethics, theology, and numerous other topics of philosophical relevance.

The Universal Jewish Encyclopedia, edited by Isaac Landman (10 vols., New York, Universal Jewish Encyclopedia, 1939–1943), had significant contributions by Isaac Husik, perhaps the greatest historian of medieval Jewish philosophy. This encyclopedia is a worthy successor to *The Jewish Encyclopedia.*

The Catholic Encyclopedia, edited by Charles G. Herbermann and others (16 vols., New York, Robert Appleton, 1907–1912; reprinted, 1913; supp., 1917, 1922, 1954), contains over five hundred articles on cosmology, theology, metaphysics, epistemology, logic, ethics, and individual philosophers. The articles expound these topics with clarity and vigor. Noteworthy contributors include Émile Bréhier, Pierre Duhem, and Maurice de Wulf. Comparable works exist in French, German, and Italian.

Of projected works the *New Catholic Encyclopedia* being edited at the Catholic University of America, Washington, D.C., will devote about 1 million of the total of 14 million words to subjects pertinent to philosophy. *Je sais, je crois: Encyclopédie du catholique au XXeme siècle*, edited by Henri Daniel-Rops (Paris, Librairie A. Fayard, 1956–), is scheduled to comprise 150 volumes (more than 130 have been published as of 1965); it is being translated into English as *The Twentieth Century Encyclopedia of Catholicism* (New York, Hawthorn Books). It is arranged by topic rather than alphabetically. Among the volumes of philosophical interest are Claude Tresmontant's *Les Origines de la philosophic chrétienne*, Vol. XI (1962), Philippe Delhaye's *La Philosophie chrétienne au moyen âge*, Vol. XII (1959), and Régis Jolivet's *L'Homme métaphysique*, Vol. XXXV (1958).

Theology and ethics. Of the dictionaries that cover two philosophical disciplines, chief among those covering theology and ethics is the *Encyclopedia of Religion and Ethics*, edited by James Hastings and others (13 vols., Edinburgh and New York, T. and T. Clark and Charles Scribner's Sons, 1908–1926; reprinted in whole or in part in various years). This is one of the great encyclopedias of all time. In conception it is original and imaginative; in execution, apt. The choice of topics is sagacious; the research has weathered the test of time; the analyses are thorough and penetrating. Among the philosophical contributors are John Burnet on the Academy, skeptics, and Socrates; C. D. Broad on reality and time; A. F. R. Hoernlé on solipsism; the Reverend William R. Inge on logos and Neoplatonism; Rufus M. Jones on mysticism; John Laird on will; J. M. E. McTaggart on personality; John H. Muirhead on ethics and rights; Josiah Royce on axiom, error and truth, mind, monotheism, negation, and order; F. C. S. Schiller on humanism, pragmatism, spiritualism, and values; A. E. Taylor on identity and theism; Erust Troeltsch on idealism and Kant; Frederick J. E. Woodbridge on Hobbes, Hume, and pluralism; and Maurice de Wulf on aesthetics and beauty. The orientation in the articles on religion is generally that of liberal Protestantism, but opposing points of view are presented fairly. The bibliographies are compact and useful.

Also deserving of mention as covering both theology and ethics is *A Dictionary of Religion and Ethics*, edited by Shailer Mathews and Gerald B. Smith (New York, Macmillan, 1921, 513 pages), which had as contributors Franz Boas, Edgar J. Goodspeed, Rufus Jones, Eugene Lyman, George Herbert Mead, Roscoe Pound, James B. Pratt, James H. Tufts, and others. For less important topics the articles present dictionary-type definitions or identifications and little more. Imbalance in some of the articles may be illustrated by the fact that the 800-word article on Aristotle presents only one sentence on his ethics. There is a bibliography at the end, containing almost two thousand items.

Logic and philosophy of science. Major topics of another pair of philosophical disciplines—logic and the philosophy of science—are covered, though inadequately, in the *Harper Encyclopedia of Science*, edited by James R. Newman (4 vols., New York, Harper and Row, 1963), which had Ernest Nagel as its consultant on the philosophy and history of science. Among the contributors to the Newman work besides Nagel were Max Black, Irving M. Copi, Arthur C. Danto, and Milton K. Munitz. However, the philosophical articles are for the most part excessively brief. Exceptions include those on logic (four thousand words) and logical empiricism (almost five hundred words).

PERIODS. There are dictionaries covering the philosophy of specific periods, including, for example, the *Lexicon Philosophicum Graecum*, by Rudolf Goclenius the elder (Marburg, Rudolf Hutwelcker, 1615, 390 pages; 2nd ed., Frankfurt and Paris, S. Celerius, 1634), in which the terms defined are in Greek and the definitions and explanations are in Latin. Sources used by the author include the Greek philosophical classics, the New Testament, and the writings of the Greek Fathers of the Church.

The *Index zu philosophischen Problemen in der klassischen griechischen Literatur*, by Georg T. Schwarz (Bern, Francke Verlag, 1956, 109 pages), is a list of about 280 topics, such as being, definition, democracy, good, idea, life, love, philosophy, and reason, with an indication of where and how each one is discussed in pre-Aristotelian Greek literature and philosophy. Its limited objective is well carried out.

The Dictionnaire de philosophie et de théologie scolastique, ou Études sur l'enseignement philosophique et théologique au moyen âge, by Frédéric Morin, is included in the *Encyclopédie théologique*, edited by J. P. Migne (168 vols. in 170 in 3 series, Paris, 1844–1866), as Volumes XXI and XXII (1856–1857) of the third series. This dictionary covers adequately the medieval Scholastics, the main Arabic thinkers (but no Jewish philosophers), and the more important topics, problems, and movements of medieval philosophy. (The Migne encyclopedia is an unsystematic collection of dictionaries of aspects of religion—the Bible, church history, liturgy, saints, and so on.)

SCHOOLS. Movements or schools in philosophy are covered by various works. Among these is *A Biographical Dictionary of Modern Rationalists*, by Joseph McCabe (London, Watts, 1920, 934 pages). Rationalists are defined here as those who "uphold the right of reason against the authority of Church or tradition." Included are biographies of philosophers—for example, Bergson, Bradley, Lovejoy, and Moore; statesmen—for example, John Adams and Clemenceau; writers—for example, Balzac and Keats; musicians, artists, scientists, inventors, historians, sociologists, and so on.

Another school is covered in the *Dictionary of Scholastic Philosophy*, by Bernard Wuellner (Milwaukee, Wis., Bruce Publishing Co., 1956, 138 pages). Many of the articles are merely definitions. For example, the article on belief consists simply of the synonym *faith* and the article on faith gives only dictionary-type definitions of *faith* and *divine faith*, with references to two works of Aquinas. However, the book contains 33 interesting diagrams and charts, which show the subdivisions of act and potency, the categories of being, the kinds of evil, and the like.

A Concise Dictionary of Existentialism, edited by Ralph B. Winn (New York, Philosophical Library, 1960, 122 pages), contains quotations from six thinkers—Kierkegaard, Heidegger, Jaspers, Marcel, Sartre, and de Beauvoir—on anguish, being, boredom, choice, encounter, and other topics. Some of the quotations are epigrammatic; others are more extensive.

PHILOSOPHERS. Dictionaries devoted to the thought of individual philosophers are numerous. Aquinas, Aristotle, Bonaventure, Kant, Hegel, Maimonides, Plato, Russell, Schopenhauer, Spinoza, Teilhard de Chardin, and Wolff are among the main figures having special dictionaries devoted to their work. Aristotle, for example, is covered by four works.

First was Hermann Bonitz' *Index Aristotelicus* (Berlin, G. Reimer, 1870, 878 pages), which was reprinted from Volume V of the Academia Regia Borussica edition of Aristotle (5 vols., Berlin, G. Reimer, 1831–1870), with Greek texts edited by Immanuel Bekker. The index was reprinted in 1955 by the Akademie-Verlag in East Berlin. It is a complete concordance, indispensable to Aristotle scholars working with the original Greek.

Matthias Kappes' *Aristoteles-Lexikon* (Paderborn, Germany, Ferdinand Schöningh, 1894, 70 pages) contains a discussion in German of about four hundred Greek words used by Aristotle, with references to the main passages where those words play a part in his philosophy. On the basis of the 11-volume Oxford translation of Aristotle, Troy W. Organ's *An Index to Aristotle in English Translation* (Princeton, N.J., Princeton University Press, 1949, 181 pages) covers about four thousand English words, from Abdera, abdomen, and abortions to Zeno, Zeus, and zodiac, with references to the passages where they significantly occur.

In 1962 there appeared the *Aristotle Dictionary*, edited by Thomas P. Kiernan (New York, Philosophical Library, 524 pages), which has passages from Aristotle's writings, translated by H. E. Wedeck and others. It begins with a 161-page summary of the individual writings of Aristotle and continues with quotations under alphabetically arranged topic headings. The quotations chosen are not always apt; for example, the five sentences quoted under "Form" do not represent Aristotle's philosophy of form.

Plato, Aquinas, and Kant are similarly covered by three or more dictionaries each; one of the Kant dictionaries is in Russian.

CONCLUSION

In the past it was possible for a scholar to encompass in a lifetime of learning the whole of a broad domain of human interest, such as philosophy. It was possible for one person to read all the important sources, major interpretations, and critiques of the sources. One could then write a thorough, well-balanced, and accurate dictionary of philosophy for his less knowledgeable colleagues.

However, with the democratization of education and the spread of intellectual activity the philosophical sources and the critical works have become too voluminous for a single individual to master. The truly comprehensive study of what philosophers have thought and said has therefore necessarily become a cooperative venture. Although some commendable dictionaries of philosophy have been produced by great scholars singlehandedly in the twentieth century, the scholarship of a single individual is, after all, limited.

Periodically, therefore, the need arises for expert summaries and appraisals of the philosophical books and articles that rush from the presses. Thus, cooperative summings up have appeared with some regularity. This *Encyclopedia of Philosophy* is intended to provide a new, more inclusive treatment of a wide variety of philosophical topics and to be a repository of up-to-date, detailed scholarship for the use of researchers and creative philosophers alike.

Bibliography

ON GENERAL ENCYCLOPEDIAS

Especially useful are the articles on encyclopedias which appear in the *Encyclopaedia Britannica*, 11th ed., 29 vols. (Cambridge and New York, 1910–1911); in the *Encyclopedia Americana*, 30 vols. (New York, 1966); and in *Chambers's Encyclopaedia*, 15 vols. (London, 1959).

OLDER LISTS

Some 20 dictionaries of philosophy, of ethics, or of individual philosophers are listed in Johann A. Fabricius, *Abriss einer allgemeinen Historie der Gelehrsamkeit*, 3 vols. (Leipzig, 1752–1754), Vol. I, p. 422. Shorter, evaluative lists of dictionaries of philosophy appear in the Preface to the first edition of Franck's *Dictionnaire des sciences philosophiques*, 6 vols. (Paris, 1844–1852), and in the Preface to Larousse's *Grand Dictionnaire universel du XIXe siècle*, 15 vols. (Paris, 1865–1876), Vol. I, pp. xli–xlii.

TWENTIETH-CENTURY LISTS

The section "Dictionnaires de philosophic" in Jean Hoffmans, *La Philosophie et les philosophes: Ouvrages généraux* (Brussels, 1920), pp. 1–4, lists, along with 11 general dictionaries of philosophy, about 80 specialized dictionaries, on topics like ethics and aesthetics. See also the lists of philosophical dictionaries in the Alcalde *Diccionario* (Madrid, 1927), Vol. I, pp. 12–15; the section on dictionaries in the *Allgemeine philosophische Bibliographie*, by I. M. Bocheński and Florenzo Monteleone (Bern, 1948), pp. 32–33; the section on dictionaries in Carmelo Ferro's *Guida storico-bibliografica allo studio della filosofia* (Milan, 1949), pp. 187 ff.; and the section "Philosophie" in the *Index Lexicorum*, by Gert A. Zischka (Vienna, 1959), pp. 40–43.

DISCUSSIONS

André Lalande, in "Les Récents Dictionnaires de philosophie," *Revue philosophique de la France et de l'étranger*, Vol. 56 (1903), 628–648, and Frederick H. Heinemann, in "Die Aufgabe einer Enzyklopädie des XX. Jahrhunderts," pp. 1–22 of his compilation *Die Philosophie im XX. Jahrhundert*, 2nd ed. (Stuttgart, 1963), provide thoughtful comments. Also provocative is Benedetto Croce's "Un Vocabolario della lingua filosofica italiana," *La Voce*, Vol. 1 (1909), 42; in it he urged the need for historical and analytical work on philosophical terminology which would not be a mere "dizionario filosofico," with its dismembered alphabetical order; he suggested, rather, a work like "una enciclopedia filosofica," having some of the attributes of Hegel's *Encyklopädie*. The editors of the Gallarate encyclopedia, in offering more than "un mero *dizionario filosofico*" may have had Croce specifically in mind.

William Gerber (1967)

PHILOSOPHY DICTIONARIES AND ENCYCLOPEDIAS [ADDENDUM]

The English-language citations in this update are organized alphabetically by book title. The non-English language citations are grouped initially as either Asian or European, and are listed within those two categories by specific language; the citations appear alphabetically by book title within each specific language's listing.

ENGLISH LANGUAGE

Adler's Philosophical Dictionary. Adler, Mortimer Jerome. Norwalk, CT: Easton Press, 1995.

American Philosophers Before 1950. Dematteis, Philip Breed, and Leemon B. McHenry. Detroit: Gale Group, 2003.

American Philosophers, 1950–2000. Dematteis, Philip Breed, and Leemon B. McHenry. Detroit: Gale Group, 2003.

Biographical Dictionary of Twentieth Century Philosophers. Brown, Stuart C., Diané Collinson, and Robert Wilkinson. London; New York: Routledge, 1996.

Biographical Encyclopedia of Philosophy. Thomas, Henry. Garden City, NY: Doubleday, 1965.

The Blackwell Dictionary of Western Philosophy. Bunnin, Nicholas, and Jiyuan Yu. Malden, MA: Blackwell Pub., 2004.

British Philosophers, 1500–1799. Dematteis, Philip Breed, and Peter S. Fosl. Detroit: Gale Group, 2002.

British Philosophers, 1800–2000. Dematteis, Philip Breed, Peter S. Fosl, and Leemon B. McHenry. Detroit: Gale Group, 2002.

The Cambridge Dictionary of Philosophy. Audi, Robert. Cambridge, U.K.: Cambridge University Press, 1995.

The Cambridge Dictionary of Philosophy. 2nd ed. Audi, Robert. Cambridge, U.K.: Cambridge University Press, 1999.

Christian Philosophy A–Z. Hill, Daniel J. Edinburgh: Edinburgh University Press, 2005.

Companion Encyclopedia of Asian Philosophy. Carr, Brian, and Indira Mahalingam. London: Routledge, 1997.

Companion Encyclopedia of the History and Philosophy of the Mathematical Sciences. Grattan-Guinness, I. ed. London: Routledge, 1994.

A Companion to Aesthetics. Cooper, David Edward, Joseph Margolis, and Crispin Sartwell. Oxford: Blackwell Reference, 1995.

A Companion to Metaphysics. Kim, Jaegwon, and Ernest Sosa, eds. Oxford: Blackwell Reference, 1995.

A Concise Dictionary of Indian Philosophy: Sanskrit-English. Grimes, John A. Dr. S. Radhakrishnan Institute for Advanced Study in Philosophy. Madras: University of Madras, 1988.

A Concise Dictionary of Indian Philosophy: Sanskrit Terms Defined in English. Grimes, John A. New and rev. ed. Albany, NY: State University of New York Press, 1996.

A Concise Encyclopedia of Early Buddhist Philosophy: Based on the Study of the Abhidhammatthasangahasarupa. Varma, Chandra B. Delhi: Eastern Book Linkers, 1992.

The Concise Encyclopedia of Western Philosophy. 3rd ed. Rée, Jonathan., and J. O. Urmson. London: Routledge, 2005.

The Concise Encyclopedia of Western Philosophy and Philosophers. Urmson, J. O., and J. L. Ackrill, eds. New York: Hawthorn Books, 1965.

The Concise Encyclopedia of Western Philosophy and Philosophers. 2nd ed. Rev. Urmson, J. O., ed. London: Hutchinson, 1975.

The Concise Encyclopedia of Western Philosophy and Philosophers. Urmson, J. O., and Jonathan Rée. Rev. ed. London: Unwin Hyman, 1989.

The Concise Encyclopedia of Western Philosophy and Philosophers. 3rd ed. Urmson, J. O., and Jonathan Rée. London: Routledge, 2004.

Dictionary of American Philosophy. Nauman, St. Elmo, Jr. New York: Philosophical Library, 1972.

Dictionary of Asian Philosophies. Nauman, St. Elmo, Jr. New York: Philosophical Library, 1978.

Dictionary of Cognitive Science: Neuroscience, Psychology, Artificial Intelligence, Linguistics, and Philosophy. Houdé, Olivier. New York: Psychology Press, 2004.

A Dictionary of Common Philosophical Terms. Pence, Gregory E. Boston: McGraw-Hill, 2000.

The Dictionary of Eighteenth-Century German Philosophers. Kuehn, Manfred, and Heiner Klemme. Bristol, U.K.: Thoemmes, 2004.

The Dictionary of Important Ideas and Thinkers. Rohmann, Chris. London: Arrow, 2002.

Dictionary of Indian Philosophical Concepts. Singh, B. N. Varanasi: Asha Prakashan, 1988.

Dictionary of Irish Philosophers, A–Z. Duddy, Thomas, David Berman, and M. A. Stewart. Bristol, U.K.: Thoemmes Continuum, 2004.

A Dictionary of Muslim Philosophy. 2nd ed. Sheikh, M. Saeed. Lahore: Institute of Islamic Culture, 1981.

The Dictionary of Nineteenth-Century British Philosophers. Mander, W. J., and Alan P. F. Sell. Bristol, U.K.: Thoemmes, 2002.

Dictionary of Oriental Philosophy. Reyna, Ruth. New Delhi: Munshiram Manoharlal, 1984.

A Dictionary of Philosophical Concepts. Peterson, Russell Arthur. Lake Mills, LA: Graphic Pub. Co., 1977.

Dictionary of Philosophy. Angeles, Peter Adam. New York: Barnes & Noble Books, 1981.

Dictionary of Philosophy. Angeles, Peter Adam. HarperPerennial ed. New York: HarperPerennial, 1991.

A Dictionary of Philosophy. Flew, Antony. New York: St. Martin's Press, 1979.

A Dictionary of Philosophy. 2nd ed. Flew, Antony. London: Macmillan, 1984.

A Dictionary of Philosophy. 2nd ed., rev. Flew, Antony. New York: Gramercy Books, 1999.

A Dictionary of Philosophy. 3rd ed. Flew, Antony, and Stephen Priest. London: Pan, 2002.

A Dictionary of Philosophy. Lacey, A. R. New York: Scribner, 1976.

A Dictionary of Philosophy. 2nd ed. Lacey, A. R. London: Routledge & Kegan Paul, 1986.

A Dictionary of Philosophy. 3rd ed. Lacey, A. R. London: Routledge, 1996.

A Dictionary of Philosophy. Mautner, Thomas. Oxford; Cambridge, MA: Blackwell Publishers, 1996.

A Dictionary of Philosophy. Rozental, M. M., and Pavel Fedorovich Iudin. Moscow: Progress Publishers, 1967.

Dictionary of Philosophy. 15th ed., rev. Runes, Dagobert D., ed. Totowa, NJ: Littlefield, Adams, 1965.

Dictionary of Philosophy. Rev. ed. Runes, Dagobert D., ed. New York: Philosophical Library, 1983.

Dictionary of Philosophy. Saifulin, Murad, and Richard R. Dixon. New York: International Publishers, 1984.

A Dictionary of Philosophy. Srinivas, K. New Delhi: Ashish Pub. House, 1993.

Dictionary of Philosophy and Religion: Eastern and Western Thought. Reese, William L. Atlantic Highlands, NJ: Humanities Press, 1980.

Dictionary of Philosophy and Religion: Eastern and Western Thought. New and enl. ed. Reese, William L. Atlantic Highlands, NJ: Humanities Press, 1996.

Dictionary of Religion and Philosophy. MacGregor, Geddes. New York: Paragon House,1989.

A Dictionary of Scholastic Philosophy. 2nd ed. Wuellner, Bernard J. Milwaukee, WI: Bruce Pub. Co., 1966.

The Dictionary of Seventeenth-Century British Philosophers. Pyle, Andrew. Bristol, U.K.: Thoemmes, 2000.

The Dictionary of Seventeenth-Century French Philosophers. Foisneau, Luc. Bristol, U.K.: Thoemmes, 2005.

The Dictionary of Seventeenth and Eighteenth-Century Dutch Philosophers. Bunge, Wiep van. Bristol, U.K.: Thoemmes, 2003.

Dictionary of Technical Terms in Philosophy: English-Kannada-Hindi. Mahadevappa, N. G. Dharwad: Extension Service and Publications, Karnataka University, 1979.

Dictionary of Theories. Bothamley, Jennifer. New York: Barnes & Noble, 2004.

Dictionary of Twentieth-Century British Philosophers. Brown, Stuart C. Bristol, U.K.: Thoemmes Continuum, 2005.

Dictionary of World Philosophy. Iannone, A. Pablo. London: Routledge, 2001.

Encyclopaedia of Language and Linguistics. Vol. 9: Philosophy of Linguistics. Riley, Brian T. New Delhi: Cosmo Publications, 1999.

Encyclopaedia of Upanisads and Its Philosophy: An Exposition of the Fundamental Concepts, History, Philosophy, Teachings, Doctrines, and the System of Upanisads. Kapoor, Subodh. New Delhi: Cosmo Publications, 2002.

Encyclopedia of Asian Philosophy. Leaman, Oliver. London: Routledge, 2001.

Encyclopedia of Chinese Philosophy. Cua, A. S. New York: Routledge, 2003.

The Encyclopedia of Eastern Philosophy and Religion: Buddhism, Hinduism, Taoism, Zen. Fischer-Schreiber, Ingrid, and Stephan Schuhmacher. Boston: Shambhala, 1989.

The Encyclopedia of Indian Philosophies. Bhattacharya, Sibajiban, Karl H. Potter, Karl H. Larson, and Gerald James. Delhi: Motilal Banarsidass, 1970.

Encyclopedia of Indian Philosophies. Bhattacharya, Ram Shankar, and Karl H. Potter. Princeton, NJ: Princeton University Press, 1977.

The Encyclopedia of Indian Philosophies. Potter, Karl H. Princeton, NJ: Princeton University Press, 1970.

Encyclopedia of Indian Philosophies. Rev. ed. Potter, Karl H. Delhi: M. Banarsidass, 1983.

Encyclopedia of Indian Philosophies. 3rd rev. ed. Potter, Karl H. Delhi: Motilal Banarsidass Publishers, 1995.

The Encyclopedia of Indian Philosophies: Advaita Vedanta up to Samkara and His Pupils. Potter, Karl H. Delhi: Motilal Banarsidass, 1981.

Encyclopedia of Indian Philosophies, Bibliography. Potter, Karl H. Seattle: University of Washington, Center for Advanced Research Technology in the Arts and Humanities, 1999.

The Encyclopedia of Indian Philosophies: The Philosophy of the Grammarians. Coward, Harold G., and Raja K. Kunjunni. Delhi: Motilal Banarsidass, 1990.

Encyclopedia of Nineteenth Century Thought. Claeys, Gregory. London: Routledge, 2003.

Encyclopedia of the Philosophical Sciences in Outline, and Critical Writings. Hegel, Georg Wilhelm Friedrich, Ernst Behler, Arnold V. Miller, et al. New York: Continuum, 1990.

Encyclopedia of Philosophy. 2nd ed. Borchert, Donald M., ed. Detroit: Macmillan Reference USA, 2005.

Encyclopedia of Philosophy. Edwards, Paul, ed. New York: Macmillan, 1967.

Encyclopedia of Philosophy: Supplement. Borchert, Donald M., ed. New York: Macmillan Reference USA, Simon & Schuster Macmillan, 1996.

An English-Chinese Dictionary of Chinese Traditional Philosophy. Dankowski, John. Taipei: Chinese News & World Report, 1977.

English-Slovak, Slovak-English Dictionary of Philosophy. Stekauer, Pavol and L. Stekauerová. Presov: ManaCon, 1997.

Great Thinkers A–Z. Baggini, Julian, and Jeremy Stangroom. New York: Continuum, 2004.

The Greek Philosophical Vocabulary. Urmson, J. O. London: Duckworth, 1990.

The HarperCollins Dictionary of Philosophy. 2nd ed. Angeles, Peter Adam. New York: HarperPerennial, 1992.

Historical Dictionary of Descartes and Cartesian Philosophy. Ariew, Roger. Lanham, MD: Scarecrow Press, 2003.

Historical Dictionary of Hegelian Philosophy. Burbidge, John W. Lanham, MD: Scarecrow Press, 2001.

Historical Dictionary of Kierkegaard's Philosophy. Watkin, Julia. Lanham, MD: Scarecrow Press, 2001.

Historical Dictionary of Schopenhauer's Philosophy. Cartwright, David E. Lanham, MD: Scarecrow Press, 2005.

Historical Dictionary of Wittgenstein's Philosophy. Richter, Duncan. Lanham, MD: Scarecrow Press, 2004.

Indian Metaphysics and Epistemology: The Tradition of Nyaya-Vaisesika up to Gangesa. Potter, Karl H. Princeton, NJ: Princeton University Press, 1977.

Indian Philosophy A–Z. Bartley, C. J. Edinburgh: Edinburgh University Press, 2005.

Jewish Philosophy A–Z. Hughes, Aaron W. Edinburgh: Edinburgh University Press, 2005.

Key Concepts in Eastern Philosophy. Leaman, Oliver. London: Routledge, 1999.

Logic from A to Z. Detlefsen, Miael, John Bacon, and David Charles McCarty. London: Routledge, 1999

New Encyclopedia of Philosophy. Grooten, Johan, and G. J. Steenbergen, eds. New York: Philosophical Library, 1972.

Nineties Knowledge. Crystal, David. Edinburgh; Chambers, 1992.

The Oxford Companion to Philosophy. Honderich, Ted. Oxford: Oxford University Press, 2003.

The Oxford Companion to the Mind. 2nd ed. Gregory, R. L. Oxford: Oxford University Press, 2004.

The Oxford Dictionary of Philosophy. Blackburn, Simon. Oxford: Oxford University Press, 1994.

The Penguin Dictionary of Philosophy. Rev. ed. Mautner, Thomas. London: Penguin Books, 1997.

The Penguin Dictionary of Philosophy. Rev. ed. Mautner, Thomas. London: Penguin Books, 2000.

The Penguin Dictionary of Philosophy. 2nd ed. Mautner, Thomas. London: Penguin, 2005

The Philosopher's Dictionary. Martin, Robert M. Peterborough, ON: Broadview Press, 1991.

The Philosopher's Dictionary. 2nd ed. Martin, Robert M. Peterborough, ON: Broadview Press, 1994.

The Philosopher's Dictionary. 3rd ed. Martin, Robert M. Peterborough, ON: Broadview Press, 2002.

Philosophical Dictionary. Brugger, Walter, and Kenneth Baker, S. J. eds. Spokane, WA: Gonzaga University Press, 1972.

Philosophical Dictionary. Enl. ed. Bunge, Mario Augusto. Amherst, NY: Prometheus Books, 2003.

Philosophy and Connectionist Theory. Ramsey, William, and Stephen P. Stich. Hillsdale, NJ: L. Erlbaum Associates, 1991.

The Philosophy of the Grammarians. Coward, Harold G., and K. Kunjunni Raja. Princeton, NJ: Princeton University Press, 1990.

Philosophy of Religion A–Z. Quinn, Patrick. Edinburgh: Edinburgh University Press, 2005.

Quiddities: An Intermittently Philosophical Dictionary. Quine, W. V. Cambridge, MA: Belknap Press of Harvard University Press, 1987.

The Rider Encyclopedia of Eastern Philosophy and Religion: Buddhism, Hinduism, Taoism, Zen. Fischer-Schreiber, Ingrid, Stephan Schuhmacher, and Gert Woerner. London: Rider, 1989.

Sacramentum Mundi: An Encyclopedia of Theology. Rahner, Karl, Cornelius Ernst, and Kevin Smyth. London: Search Press, 1968.

Spinozistic Glossary and Index Dedicated to Spinoza's Insights. Spinoza, Benedictus de; Joseph B. Yesselman, ed. Fairfax, VA: Joseph B. Yesselman, 1999.

Stanford Encyclopedia of Philosophy. Zalta, Edward N., ed. http://plato.stanford.edu. Stanford, CA: Stanford University, Metaphysics Research Lab.

The Thinker's Dictionary: A Handbook for Philosophy and Similar Intellectual Endeavors. 2nd ed. Van de Mortel, J. A. New York, NY: McGraw-Hill, 1995.

A World of Ideas: A Dictionary of Important Theories, Concepts, Beliefs, and Thinkers. Rohmann, Chris. New York: Ballantine Books, 1999.

ASIAN LANGUAGES

ARABIC

Istilah Usuluddin dan falsafah Islam, bahasa Arab-bahasa Malaysia. Kuala Lumpur: Dewan Bahasa dan Pustaka, Kementerian Pendidikan, 1991.

Mafahim wa-al-alfaz fi al-falsafah al-hadithah. 2nd ed. Siddiq, Yusuf. Libya and Tunis: al-Dar al-ʿArabiyah lil-Kitab, 1980.

Al-Mawsuʿah al-falsafiyah al-ʿArabiyah. Ziyadah, Maʾan. Beirut: Maʿhad al-Inmaʾ al-ʿArabi, 1986–1997.

Al-Mawsuʿah al-Muyassarah fi al-Fikr al-Falsafi wa-al-Ijtimaʿi: ʿArabi-Injilizi. Hajj, Kamil. Beirut: Maktabat Lubnan Nashirun, 2000.

Al-Mawsuʿah al-naqdiyah lil-falsafah al-Yahudiyah. Hifni, ʿAbd al-Munʿim. Cairo: Maktabat Madbuli, 1980.

Mawsuʿat al-falasafah. ʿAbbas, Faysal. Beirut: Dar al-Fikr al-ʿArabi, 1996.

Mawsuʿat al-falsafah. Badawi, ʿAbd al-Rahman. Beirut: al-Muʾassasah al-ʿArabiyah lil-Dirasat wa-al-Nashr, 1984.

Mawsuʿat mustalahat al-falsafah ʿinda al-ʿArab. Jihami, Jirar. Beirut: Maktabat Lubnan Nashirun, 1998.

Mawsuʿat mustalahat al-fikr al-ʿArabi wa-al-Islami al-Hadith wa-al-Muʿasir. Dughaym, Samih, Rafiq ʿAjam, and Jirar Jihami. Beirut: Maktabat Lubnan Nashirun, 2002.

Mawsuʿat mustalahat al-Imam al-Ghazzali. ʿAjam, Rafiq. Beirut: Maktabat Lubnan Nashirun, 2000.

Mawsuʿat mustalahat al-Imam Fakhr al-Din al-Razi. Dughaym, Samih. Beirut: Maktabat Lubnan Nashirun, 2001.

Mawsuʿat mustalahat Ibn Khaldun wa-al-Sharif ʿAli Muhammad al-Jurjani. ʿAjam, Rafiq. Beirut: Maktabat Lubnan Nashirun, 2004.

Mawsuʿat mustalahat Ibn Rushd al-Faylasuf. Jihami, Jirar. Beirut: Maktabat Lubnan Nashirun, 2000.

Mawsuʿat mustalahat Ibn Sina: al-shaykh al-raʾis. Jihami, Jirar. Beirut: Maktabat Lubnan Nashirun, 2004.

Mawsuʿat mustalahat Sadr al-Din al-Shirazi. Dughaym, Samih. Beirut: Maktabat Lubnan Nashirun, 2004.

Muʿjam al-falasifah. Tarabishi, Jurj. Beirut: Dar al-Taliʿah, 1987.

Muʿjam al-falasifah al-muyassar. Aubral, François, and Jurj Saʿd. Beirut: Dar al-Hadathah lil-Tibaʿah wa-al-Nashr wa-al-Tawziʿ, 1993.

Muʿjam al-falsafah. Yaʿqubi, Mahmud. Algiers: Maktabat al-Sharikah al-Jazaʾiriyah, 1979.

Al-Muʿjam al-falsafi. Karam, Yusuf, Murad Wahbah, and Yusuf Shallalah. Cairo: Maktab Yulyu, 1966.

Al-Muʿjam al-falsafi. 2nd ed. Wahbah, Murad, Yusuf Karam, and Yusuf Shallalah. Cairo: Dar al-Thaqafah al-Jadidah, 1971.

Al-Muʿjam al-falsafi. 3rd ed. Wahbah, Murad. Cairo: Dar al-Thaqafah al-Jadidah, 1979.

Al-Muʿjam al-falsafi. Majmaʿ al-Lughah al-ʿArabiyah. Cairo: Jumhuriyat Misr al-ʿArabiyah, 1979.

Al-Muʿjam al-falsafi: ʿArabi-Injilizi-Faransi-Almani-Latini. Hifni, ʿAbd al-Munʿim. Cairo: al-Dar al-Sharqiyah, 1990.

Al-Muʿjam al-falsafi bi-al-alfaz al-ʿArabiyah wa-al-Faransiyah wa-al-Inkliziyah wa-al-Latiniyah. Saliba, Jamil. Beirut: Dar al-Kitab al-Lubnani, 1971, 1973.

Muʿjam alfaz al-qiyam al-akhlaqiyah wa-tatawwuruha al-dalali bayna lughat al-shiʿr al-Jahili wa-lughat al-Qurʾan al-karim. Zarzur, Nawal Karim. Beirut: Maktabat Lubnan Nashirun, 2001.

Muʿjam al-mustalahat al-falsafiyah: ʿArabi-Faransi-Inklizi. Khalil, Khalil Ahmad. Beirut: Dar al-Fikr al-Lubnani, 1995.

Muʿjam al-mustalahat al-falsafiyah: Faransi-ʿArabi. Hulw, ʿAbduh. Beirut: al-Markaz al-Tarbawi lil-Buhuth wa-al-Inmaʾ, 1994.

Mulhaq Mawsuʿat al-falsafah. Badawi, ʿAbd al-Rahman. Beirut: al-Muʾassasah al-ʿArabiyah lil-Dirasat wa-al-Nashr, 1996.

Mustalahat al-falsafah fi al-taʿlim al-ʿamm (Injilizi-Faransi-ʿArabi). Maktab al-Daʿim li-Tansiq al-Taʿrib fi al-ʿAlam al-ʿArabi. Casablanca: Dar al-Kitab, 1977.

Mustalahat al-Faylasuf al-Kindi: bahth tahlili. Sayf, Antuwan. Beirut: al-Jamiʿah al-Lubnaniyah, 2003.

Nahwa muʿjam lil-falsafah al-ʿArabiyah: mustalahat wa-shakhsiyat. ʿIraqi, Muhammad ʿAtif. Alexandria, Egypt: Dar al-Wafaʾ li-Dunya al-Tibaʿah wa-al-Nashr, 2001.

Sharh al-mustalahat al-falsafiyah. Bunyad-i Pizhuhishha-yi Islami; Guruh-i Kalam va Falsafah. Mashhad, Iran: al-Majmaʿ, 1993.

Sharh mustalahat al-falsafiyah. Bunyad-i Pizhuhishha-yi Islami; Guruh-i Kalam va Falsafah. Mashhad, Iran: al-Majmaʿ, 1995.

ARMENIAN

P'ilisop'ayakan bararan. Rozental', Mark Moiseevich. Yerevan, 1975.

AZERBAIJANI

Falsafa: ensiklopedik lughati. Rustamov, I. A., and Ismaiyl Omaroghlu. Baku: Azarbaijan Ensiklopediiasy, 1997.

BENGALI

Bharatiya darsana kosha. Bhattacarya, Srimohana, and Dinesh Chandra Bhattacharya. Kalikata: Samskrta Kaleja, 1978–.

Darsana o manobidya paribhashakosha. Abdul Hai, Saiyed. Dhaka: Bamla Ekademi, 1978–.

CHINESE

Beijing da xue fa xue bai ke quan shu: Zhongguo fa lü si xiang shi, Zhongguo fa zhi shi, wai guo fa lü si xiang shi, wai guo fa zhi shi [Peking University Encyclopedia]. Rao

Xinxian, Pu Jian, Wang Zhe, and You Rong. Beijing: Beijing da xue chu ban she, 2000.

Chang yong zhe xue ming ci ci dian. Huang Ming. Nanning: Guangxi ren min chu ban she; Guangxi xin hua shu dian fa xing, 1985.

Che hsüeh hsiao tz'u tien: wai kuo che hsüeh shih pu fen. Shang-hai "che hsüeh hsiao tz'u tien" pien hsieh tsu. [Beijing?], 1976.

Che hsüeh tz'u tien. Liu Yanbo. [Ch'ang-ch'un]: Chi-lin jen min ch'u pan she; Chi-lin sheng hsin hua shu tien fa hsing, 1983.

Ci hai. Shanghai: Shanghai ci shu chu ban she; Xin hua shu dian Shanghai fa xing suo fa xing, 1980.

Ci hai. 2nd ed. Shanghai: Shanghai ci shu chu ban she, 1986.

Da ci hai. Zhe xue juan. Da ci hai bian ji wei yuan hui. Shanghai: Shanghai ci shu chu ban she, 2003.

Dang dai xi fang si chao ci dian [A Dictionary of Contemporary West Trends of Thought]. Wang Miaoyang, and Zhang Huajin. Shanghai: Hua dong shi fan da xue chu ban she, 1995.

Dang dai xi fang zhe xue xin ci dian. Cheng Zhimin, and Jiang Yi. Changchun: Jilin ren min chu ban she, 2003.

Deng Xiaoping li lun ci dian. Yu Yuanpei. Shanghai: Shanghai ci shu chu ban she, 2004.

Dong xi fang zhe xue da ci dian [A Dictionary of Eastern-Western Philosophy]. Jiang Yongfu, Wu Ke, and Yue Changling. Nanchang: Jiangxi ren min chu ban she, 2000.

Han Ying zhe xue chang yong ci hui [Chinese-English Useful Terminology in Philosophy]. Zhang Junfu. [Beijing]: Beijing shi fan da xue chu ban she; Xin hua shu dian zong dian ke ji fa xing suo fa xing, 1989.

Han Ying Zhongguo zhe xue ci dian [A Dictionary of Chinese Philosophy with English Annotations]. Guo Shangxing, and Wang Chaoming.Kaifeng: Henan da xue chu ban she, 2002.

Jian ming xian dai xi fang zhe xue ci dian. Tao Yinbiao, Wu Bin, and Lü Chao. Chengdu: Sichuan ren min chu ban she; Sichuan sheng xin hua shu dian fa xing, 1988.

Jian ming xi fang zhe xue ci dian. Tao Yinbiao. Shenyang: Liaoning ren min chu ban she; Liaoning sheng xin hua shu dian fa xing, 1985.

Jian ming ying yong zhe xue ci dian. Wang Lianfa, and Huang Changjun. Beijing: Zhongguo guang bo dian shi chu ban she; Xin hua shu dian zong dian Beijing fa xing suo jing xiao, 1991.

Jian ming zhe xue bai ke ci dian. "Jian ming zhe xue bai ke ci dian" bian xie zu. Beijing: Xian dai chu ban she; Xin hua shu dian zong dian Beijing fa xing suo fa xing, 1990.

Jian ming zhe xue ci dian. Meng Xianhong. [Wuhan]: Hubei ci shu chu ban she; Xin hua shu dian Hubei fa xing suo jing xiao, 1987.

Jian ming zhe xue ci dian. Rozental', Mark Moiseevich, and Pavel Iudin. Beijing: Sheng huo, du shu, xin zhi san lian shu dian: Xin hua shu dian fa xing, 1973.

Jian ming zhe xue xiao ci dian. Zhou Lin, Li Shijia, and Yuan Youwen. Chengdu: Sichuan ren min chu ban she; Sichuan sheng xin hua shu dian fa xing, 1986.

Jianqiao zhe xue ci dian. [The Cambridge Dictionary of Philosophy]. Audi, Robert, and Lin Zhenghong. Taipei: Mao tou ying chu ban, 2002.

Kong xue zhi shi ci dian. Dong Naiqiang. Beijing: Zhongguo guo ji guang bo chu ban she; Xin hua shu dian jing xiao, 1990.

Lun heng ji jie. Wang Chong, Liu Pansui, Liang Yuandi, XieZhangting, Xiao Yi, and Jinlouzi. Taipei: Shi jie shu ju, 1966.

Makesi zhu yi ji ben yuan li jian ming jiao xue ci dian. Jun dui di fang shi yi suo yuan xiao "Makesi zhu yi ji ben yuan li jian ming jiao xue ci dian" bian xie zu. Shenyang: Liaoning jiao yu chu ban she; Liaoning sheng xin hua shu dian jing xiao, 1988.

Makesi zhu yi zhe xue ci dian. Li Shikun. [Beijing]: Zhongguo guang bo dian shi chu ban she; Xin hua shu dian zong dian Beijing fa xing suo jing xiao, 1990.

Makesi zhu yi zhe xue da ci dian. Jin Binghua. Shanghai: Shanghai ci shu chu ban she, 2003.

Makesi zhu yi zhe xue da ci dian. Wang Guoyan, Wei Xiaozhou, and Li Guozhen. Beijing: Zhongguo guang bo dian shi chu ban she, 1993.

Makesi zhu yi zhe xue quan shu. Li Huaichun. Beijing: Zhongguo ren min da xue chu ban she; Jing xiao Xin hua shu dian, 1996.

Makesi zhu yi zhe xue shi ci dian. Zhuang Fuling, and Xu Lin. Beijing: Beijing chu ban she; Xin hua shu dian Beijing fa xing suo jing xiao, 1992.

Ouzhou zhe xue shi ci dian. Ma Xiaoyan. Kaifeng: Henan da xue chu ban she; Henan sheng xin hua shu dian fa xing, 1986.

Qi meng yun dong bai ke quan shu. Reill, Peter Hanns, Ellen Judy Wilson, Liu Beicheng, and Wang Wanqiang. Shanghai: Shanghai ren min chu ban she, 2004.

Ren lei si xiang de zhu yao guan dian: xing cheng shi jie de guan nian [Guide to Human Thought]. McLeish, Kenneth. Beijing: Xin hua chu ban she, 2004.

Ru jia wen hua ci dian. Xu Xinghai, and Liu Jianli. Zhengzhou: Zhongzhou gu ji chu ban she; Xin hua shu dian jing xiao, 2000.

Si shu wu jing ming ju jian shang ci dian. Tian Ren. Huhehaote: Neimenggu ren min chu ban she, 1999.

Wai guo zhe xue da ci dian. Feng Qi and Xu Xiaotong. Shanghai: Shanghai ci shu chu ban she, 2000.

Xian dai xi fang zhe xue ci dian. Ge Li. Beijing: Qiu shi chu ban she, 1990.

Xian dai xi fang zhe xue ci dian. Xia Jisong, and Zhang Jiwu. [Hefei]: Anhui ren min chu ban she; Anhui sheng xin hua shu dian fa xing, 1987.

Xian xue ci dian. Dai Yuanchang. Taipei: Chen shan mei, 1978.

Xi fang zhe xue ci dian. Tan Xintian. Jinan: Shandong ren min chu ban she, 1992.

Xi fang zhe xue Ying Han dui zhao ci dian [Dictionary of Western Philosophy: English-Chinese]. Bunnin, Nicholas, and Yu Jiyuan. Beijing: Ren min chu ban she, 2001.

Xin bian jian ming zhe xue ci dian. Blauberg, Igor' Viktorovich, and Igor' Konstantinovich Pantin. Changchun: Jilin ren min chu ban she, 1983.

Xin bian Lun heng. Wang Chong and Xiao Dengfu. Taipei: Taiwan gu ji chu ban gong si, 2000.

Xin bian zhe xue ci dian. Wang Wenqing, Yu Dunhua, and Luo Chi. [Wuhan]: Hubei jiao yu chu ban she; Xin hua shu dian Hubei fa xing suo jing xiao, 1989.

Xin bian zhe xue da ci dian. Huang Nansen and Yang Shoukan. Taiyuan: Shanxi jiao yu chu ban she: Shanxi sheng xin hua shu dian fa xing, 1993.

Xin bian zhe xue da ci dian. Sun Yun and Sun Meiyao. [Harbin, China]: Ha'erbin chu ban she; [Beijing]: Xin hua shu dian shou du fa xing suo fa xing, 1991.

Xin Ying Han zhe xue ci dian [A New English-Chinese Dictionary of Philosophy]. Xu Changming. Chengdu: Sichuan da xue chu ban she; Sichuan sheng xin hua shu dian jing xiao, 1991.

Xi yang zhe xue ci dian. Brugger, Walter. Taipei: Guo li bian yi guan, 1976.

Ying Han zhe xue ci hui. Fu dan da xue, Xian dai zhe xue yan jiu suo, "Ying Han zhe xue ci hui" bian xie zu. Nanchang: Jiangxin ren min chu ban she; Jiangxi sheng Xin hua shu dian fa xing, 1987.

Ying Han zhe xue shu yu ci dian. Zhongguo she hui ke xue yuan; "Zhe xue yi cong" bian ji bu. Beijing: Zhong gong zhong yang dang xiao chu ban she; Xin hua shu dian jing xiao, 1991.

Zhe xue bai ke xiao ci dian. Liu Wenying, Qi Fenzhong, Zeng Xiangli, and Yang Keli. Lanzhou: Gansu ren min chu ban she; Gansu sheng xin hua shu dian fa xing, 1987.

Zhe xue ci dian. Angeles, Peter Adam. Taipei: Mao tou ying chu ban she gu fen you xian gong si, 2000.

Zhe xue ci dian. 4th ed. Fan Bingqing. Taipei: Taiwan shang wu yin shu guan, 1976.

Zhe xue ci dian. Frolov, Ivan Timofeevich, and Lin Shubo. [Canton]: Guangdong ren min chu ban she; Guangdong sheng xin hua shu dian jing xiao, 1989.

Zhe xue ci dian. Liu Yanbo. [Changchun]: Jilin ren min chu ban she; Jilin sheng xin hua shu dian fa xing, 1983.

Zhe xue da ci dian. Feng Qi. Shanghai: Shanghai ci shu chu ban she: Shanghai ci shu chu ban she fa xing suo fa xing, 2001.

Zhe xue da ci dian. Makesi zhu yi zhe xue juan. "Zhe xue da ci dian Zhongguo zhe xue shi juan" bian ji wei yuan hui. Shanghai: Shanghai ci shu chu ban she; Shanghai ci shu chu ban she fa xing suo fa xing, 1990.

Zhe xue da ci shu. Luo Guang and Li Zhen. Taipei Xian Xinzhuang: Fu ren da xue chu ban she, 1993–.

Zhe xue da ci shu. Zhe xue da ci shu bian shen wei yuan hui. Taipei Xian Xinzhuang: Fu ren da xue chu ban she, 1993–.

Zhe xue gai nian bian xi ci dian. Huang Nansen, Li Zongyang, and Tu Yinsen. Beijing: Zhong gong zhong yang dang xiao chu ban she; Jing xiao Xin hua shu dian, 1993.

Zhe xue jian ming ci. [Nanjing]: Jiangsu ren min chu ban she; Jiangsu sheng xin hua shu dian fa xing, 1985.

Zhe xue xiao bai ke. Xing Fensi and Zhao Fengqi. [Beijing]: Zhongguo qing nian chu ban she; Xin hua shu dian Beijing fa xing suo fa xing, 1986.

Zhe xue xiao ci dian. Chao yang chu ban she. Xianggang: Chao yang chu ban she, 1974.

Zhe xue xiao ci dian. Liu Yanbo. [Changchun]: Jilin ren min chu ban she; Jilin sheng xin hua shu dian fa xing, 1983.

Zhe xue xiao ci dian. Ma Quanmin and Su Houzhong. [Beijing]: Ren min chu ban she; Xin hua shu dian jing xiao, 1990.

Zhe xue xiao ci dian. Wan Zhonghang. Shanghai: Shanghai ci shu chu ban she, 2003.

Zhe xue xiao ci dian: Bian zheng wei wu zhu yi he li shi wei wu zhu yi bu fen. Shanghai Zhe xue xiao ci dian bian xie zu. Shanghai: Ren min chu ban she; Xin hua shu dian Shanghai fa xing suo fa xing, 1975.

Zhe xue xiao ci dian: Ru fa dou zheng shi bu fen. Shanghai Zhe xue xiao ci dian bian xie zu. Shanghai: Ren min chu ban she; Xin hua shu dian Shanghai fa xing suo fa xing, 1974.

Zhe xue xiao ci dian xu bian. Wai guo zhe xue shi bu fen. Chao yang chu ban she; Bian ji bu. Xianggang: Chao yang chu ban she, 1976.

Zhe xue xin gai nian ci dian. Shi Lei, Cui Xiaotian, and Wang Zhong. Ha'erbin: Heilongjiang ren min chu ban she; Heilongjiang sheng xin hua shu dian fa xing, 1988.

Zhe xue zhi shi quan shu. Han Shuying and Zhang Yongqian. Lanzhou: Gansu ren min chu ban she; Gansu sheng Xin ha shu dian fa xing, 1989.

Zhe xue zi dian. Luo Guang. Taipei: Fu ren da xue chu ban she, 1990.

Zhe xue zi dian. Zhe xue da ci shu bian shen wei yuan hui. Zhonghua min guo Taiwan Sheng Taibei Xian Xinzhuang: Fu ren da xue chu ban she, 1990.

Zhongguo da bai ke quan shu: zhe xue. Zhongguo da bai ke quan shu zong bian ji wei yuan hui, Li xue bian ji wei yuan hui. Beijing: Zhongguo da bai ke quan shu chu ban she; Shanghai: Xin hua shu dian Shanghai fa xing suo fa xing, 1987.

Zhongguo da bai ke quan shu: zhe xue. Zhongguo da bai ke quan shu zong bian ji wei yuan hui, Zhe xue bian ji wei yuan hui. Beijing: Zhongguo da bai ke quan shu chu ban she, 1992.

Zhongguo li shi da ci dian. Si xiang shi. Zhongguo li shi da ci dian si xiang shi juan bian zuan wei yuan hui. Shanghai: Shanghai ci shu chu ban she; Shanghai ci shu chu ban she fa xing suo fa xing, 1989.

Zhongguo ru xue ci dian. Zhao Jihui and Guo Hou'an. Shenyang: Liaoning ren min chu ban she; Liaoning sheng xin hua shu dian fa xing, 1988.

Zhongguo shen mi wen hua bai ke zhi shi. Jin Liangnian. Shanghai: Shanghai wen hua chu ban she, 1994.

Zhongguo zhe xue ci dian. Wei Zhengtong. Taipei: Da lin chu ban she, 1977.

Zhongguo zhe xue ci dian. Wei Zhengtong. Taipei: Da lin chu ban she, 1980.

Zhongguo zhe xue ci dian. Wei Zhengtong. Taipei: Da lin chu ban she, 1981.

Zhongguo zhe xue ci dian. Wei Zhengtong. Taipei: Shui niu tu shu chu ban shi ye you xian gong si, 1986.

Zhongguo zhe xue ci dian. Wei Zhengtong. Beijing: Shi jie tu shu chu ban gong si Beijing gong si chong yin; Xin hua shu dian Beijing fa xing suo fa xing, 1993.

Zhongguo zhe xue ci dian da quan. Wei Zhengtong. Taipei: Shui niu chu ban she, 1983.

Zhongguo zhe xue ci dian da quan. Wei Zhengtong. Taipei: Shui niu chu ban she, 1988.

Zhongguo zhe xue da ci dian. Fang Keli. Beijing: Zhongguo she hui ke xue chu ban she, 1994.

Zhongguo zhe xue shi xiao ci dian. Zhao Shulian. [Zhengzhou]: Henan ren min chu ban she; Henan sheng xin hua shu dian fa xing, 1986.

Zhongguo zhe xue xiao bai ke quan shu. Zheng Wan'geng, Wang Deyou, and Li Shen. Beijing: Zhongguo da bai ke quan shu chu ban she, 2001.

Zhonghua ru xue tong dian. Wu Feng, Song Yifu, Huo Baozhen, and Song Yanzong. Haikou: Nanhai chu ban gong si; Jilin sheng xin hua shu dian fa xing, 1992.

Zhu zi bai jia da ci dian. Feng Kezheng and Fu Qingsheng. Shenyang: Liaoning ren min chu ban she, 1996.

Zhu zi bai jia da ci dian. Huang Kaiguo. Chengdu: Sichuan ren min chu ban she, 1999.

Zhu zi bai jia da ci dian. Liu Guancai. Beijing: Hua ling chu ban she, 1994.

Zhu zi bai jia da ci dian. Liu Guancai. Taipei: Jian hong chu ban she, 2000.

Zhu zi bai jia ming ju jian shang ci dian. Tianren. Huhehaote: Nei Menggu ren min chu ban she, 1999.

Zhu zi bai jia ming pian jian shang ci dian. Ma Zhenduo, Mao Huijun, Tang Qinfu, Zhang Liangyi, and Liao Jianhua. Shanghai: Shanghai ci shu chu ban she, 2003.

GEORGIAN

K'art'vel p'ilosop'ost'a lek'sikoni: personalia. Buachidze, Tamaz. Tbilisi: Gamomc'emloba "Oazisi," 2000.

GUJARATI

Paribhashika kosa-tattvajñana. Ravala, S. V. Amadavada, India: Yunivarsiti Grantha Nirmana Borda, Gujarata Rajaya, 2001.

HINDI

Bharatiya-darsana-brhatkosa. 2nd ed. Jñana, Bacculala Avasthi. Dilli: Sarada Pablising Hausa, 2004.

Bharatiya darsana kosha. Misra, Lakshmi Kanta. Dilli: Indiyana Yunivarsiti Presa ke lie Himalaya, 1973.

Bharatiya darsana paribhasha kosa. Sukla, Dinanatha. Dilli: Pratibha Prakasana, 1993.

Jaina samskrti kosa [Encyclopaedia of Jainism]. Jain, Bhagchandra. Nagapura: Sanmati Pracya Sodha Samsthana; Varanasi: Kala evam Dharma Sodha Samsthana, 2002.

INDONESIAN

Ensiklopedi agama dan filsafat. Effendy, Mochtar. [Palembang]: Penerbit Universitas Sriwijaya, 2000–2001.

Kamus populer filsafat. Hartoko, Dick. Jakarta: Rajawali, 1986.

JAPANESE

Furansu tetsugaku shiso jiten. Kobayashi, Michio. Tokyo: Taishukan Shoten, 1999.

Gendai shiso ki wado jiten. Washida, Koyata. Tokyo: San'ichi Shobo, 1993.

Gendai tetsugaku jiten. Yamazaki, Masakazu, and Hiroshi Ichikawa. Tokyo: Kodansha, 1970.

Hikaku shiso jiten. Nakamura, Hajime, and Hideo Mineshima. Tokyo: Tokyo Shoseki, 2000.

Iwanami shojiten tetsugaku. Awata, Kenzo, and Yoshishige Kozai. Tokyo: Iwanami Shoten, 1968.

Iwanami tetsugaku, shiso jiten. Hiromatsu, Wataru. Tokyo: Iwanami Shoten, 1998.

Iwanami tetsugaku shojiten. Awata, Kenzo, and Yoshishige Kozai. Tokyo: Iwanami Shoten, 1979.

Jiten tetsugaku no ki. Nagai, Hitoshi. Tokyo: Kodansha, 2002.

Kan'i tozai tetsugaku shiso jiten. Hara, Tomio, and Shinpen sekai tetsugaku shojiten. Tokyo: Sanshin Tosho, 1983.

Rarusu tetsugaku jiten. Julia, D., Hisaaki Katayama, Yorihiro Yamagata, and Kiyokazu Washida. Tokyo: Taishukan Shoten, 1998.

Seiyo shisoshi jiten. Matsunami, Shinzaburo. Tokyo: Tokyodo Shuppan, 1973.

Sekai shiso kyoyo jiten. Kashiyama, Kinshiro. Tokyo: Tokyodo Shuppan, 1965.

Sekai shiso kyoyo jiten. Kashiyama, Kinshiro. [Tokyo]: Tokyodo Shuppan, 1978.

Sekai shiso kyoyo jiten. Nihon, Toyo hen. Nakamura, Hajime, and Sumeru Yamada. Tokyo: Tokyodo Shuppan, 1965.

Shinpan tetsugaku, ronri yogo jiten. Shiso no Kagaku Kenkyukai. Tokyo: San'ichi Shobo, 1995.

Shoshi hyakka no jiten. Ezure, Takashi. Tokyo: Taishukan Shoten, 2000.

Tetsugaku chujiten. Oda, Seiji, Ichiro Kobayashi, and Isao Kondo. Sendai-shi: Shogakusha, 1983.

Tetsugaku jii: tsuketari Shinkoku onpu. Inoue, Tetsujiro. Tokyo: Meicho Fukyukai, 1980.

Tetsugaku jii yakugo sosakuin. Hida, Yoshifumi. Tokyo: Kasama Shoin, 1979.

Tetsugaku jiten. Tokyo: Heibonsha, 1966.

Tetsugaku jiten. Tokyo: Heibonsha, 1969.

Tetsugaku jiten. Tokyo: Heibonsha, 1971.

Tetsugaku jiten. Mori, Koichi. Tokyo: Aoki Shoten, 1973.

Tetsugaku jiten. 4th ed. Mori, Koichi. Tokyo: Aoki Shoten, 1985.

Tetsugaku jiten. Mori, Koichi. Tokyo: Aoki Shoten, 1995.

Tetsugaku jiten. Mori, Koichi, and Yoshishige Kozai. Tokyo: Aoki Shoten, 1971.

Tetsugaku jiten. 2nd ed. Mori, Koichi, and Yoshishige Kozai. Tokyo: Aoki Shoten, 1972.

Tetsugaku jiten. Quine, Willard Van Orman. Tokyo: Hakuyosha, 1994.

Tetsugaku jiten. Shitanaka, Kunihiko, ed. Tokyo: Heibonsha, 1967.

Tetsugaku kihon jiten: tetsugaku nyumon. 2nd ed. Satomi, Gunshi, and Shuichi Hida. Tokyo: Fuji Shoten, 1993.

Tetsugaku, ronri yogo jiten. Ofuchi, Kazuo. Tokyo: San'ichi Shobo, 1975.

Tetsugaku shiso kopasu jiten. Alchive Co. Tokyo: Nihon Jitsugyo Shuppansha, 1987.

Tetsugaku shojiten. Komatsu, Setsuro. Kyoto: Horitsu Bunkasha, 1970.

Tetsugaku shojiten. Miwatari, Yukio. Tokyo: Kyodo Shuppan, 1974.

Tetsugaku yogo jiten. Muraji, Yoshinari. Tokyo: Tokyodo Shuppan, 1974.

Toyo tetsugaku kiwado jiten [Key Concepts in Eastern Philosophy]. Leaman, Oliver, and Hiromi Ogino. Tokyo: Seidosha, 2000.

KAZAKH

Filosofiialyq sozdik. Nurghaliev, Rymghali. Almaty: "Qazaq entsiklopediiasy" Bas redaktsiiasy, 1996.

KOREAN

Ch'oesin ch'orhak sajon. Ch'orhak Sajon P'yonch'anhoe (Korea). Seoul: Ilsinsa, 1986.

Ch'orhak sajon. Choson Minjujuui Inmin Konghwaguk Sahoe Kwahagwon; Ch'orhak Yon'guso. Tokyo: Hagu Sobang, 1971.

Ch'orhak sajon. Im, Sok-chin. Seoul: Isak, 1983.

Ch'orhak sajon. Im, Sok-chin. Seoul: Toso Ch'ulp'an Ch'ongsa, 1998.

Ch'orhak sajon. Im, Sok-chin, and Se-yon Hwang. Seoul: Chungwon Munhwa, 1987.

Ch'orhak sajon. Sahoe Kwahagwon (North Korea); Ch'orhak Yonguso; Sahoe Kwahak Ch'ulp'ansa. [P'yŏngyang]: Sahoe Kwahak Ch'ulp'ansa, 1970.

Ch'orhak sajon. Sahoe Kwahagwon (North Korea); Ch'orhak Yonguso; Sahoe Kwahak Ch'ulp'ansa; Ch'orhak Sajon P'yonjipcho. [P'yŏngyang]: Sahoe Kwahak Ch'ulp'ansa, 1985.

Ch'orhak sajon. Sahoe Kwahagwon (North Korea); Ch'orhak Yonguso. Seoul: Toso Ch'ulp'an Him, 1988.

Ch'orhak sosajon. Chongno Sojok Chusik Hoesa; P'yonjippu. Seoul: Chongno Sojok, 1989.

Ch'orhak sosajon. Han'guk Ch'orhak Sasang Yon'guhoe. Seoul: Tongnyok, 1990.

Ch'orhak sosajon. Rozental', Mark Moiseevich, and Chin Yu. Pukkyong: Minjok Ch'ulp'ansa; Sinhwa Sojom parhaeng, 1981.

Ch'orhak taesajon. Han'guk Ch'orhak Sasang Yon'guhoe. Seoul: Tongnyok, 1989.

Ch'orhak taesajon [Encyclopedia of Philosophy]. Yi, Kwang-mo. Seoul: Sin T'aeyangsa, 1991.

Segye ch'orhak taesajon [The World Dictionary of Philosophy]. Seoul: Kyoyuk Ch'ulp'an Kongsa; chon'guk ch'ongp'an Taeyong Sorim, 1985.

Segye ch'orhak taesajon [The World Dictionary of Philosophy]. Kang, Yong-son. Seoul: Songgyun Sogwan, 1977.

Segye ch'orhak taesajon. Kang, Yong-son. Seoul: Kyoyuk Ch'ulp'an Kongsa, 1980.

Segye sasang sajon. Segye Sasang P'yonjiphoe. Seoul: Yangudang, 1986.

Togyo sasang sajon. Kim, Sung-dong. Pusan: Pusan Taehakkyo Ch'ulp'anbu, 2004.

Tongyang sasang sajon. Yu, Chong-gi. Taejŏn: Umundang Ch'ulp'ansa, 1965.

Yang-su eui sae-kae. Sae-kae sa-sang kyo-yang sa-jun. Ahn, Choon-keun, comp. [Seoul]: Eul-yoo moon-wha Sa, 1969.

Yugyo taesajon. Yugyo Sajon P'yonch'an Wiwonhoe. Seoul: Pagyongsa, 1990.

MARATHI

Marathi tattvajñana-mahakosa. Vadekara, Devidasa Dattatreya. Pune: Marathi Tattvajñana-mahakosa Mandala, 1974.

MONGOLIAN

Filosofiin ukhaany Oros Mongol ner tom'ëo. Luvsantseren, G., B. Sambuu, S. Norovsambuu, and C. Dogsuren. Ulaanbaatar: BNMAU-yn Shinzhlekh Ukhaany Akademi, 1985.

PAHLAVI

A Philosophical Lexicon in Persian and Arabic. Afnan, Soheil Muhsin. Beirut: Dar el-Mashreq, 1969.

PERSIAN

Alifba-yi falsafah-i jadid: (da'irat al-ma'arif-i falsafi) Inglisi bi-Farsi. Javadi, Zabih Allah. Tehran: Intisharat-i Ibn Sina, 1969.

Dictionary of Philosophy and Social Sciences, English-Persian. Pizhuhishgah-i 'Ulum-i Insani (Iran). [Tehran]: Center, 1976.

Farhang-i falsafah va a'lam-i vabastah. Ardabili, 'Ali 'Ilmi. Mashhad: Intisharat-i imamat, 1981.

Farhang-i falsafi. Saliba, Jamil. [Tehran]: Hikmat, 1987.

Farhang-i 'ilmi va intiqadi-i falsafah. Lalande, André. Tehran: Mu'assasah-i Intisharati-i Firdawsi-i Iran, 1998.

Farhang-i istilahat-i falsafah: Inglisi-Farsi. Babayi, Parviz. Tehran: Mu'assasah-i Intisharat-i Nigah, 1995.

Farhang-i istilahat-i falsafah va 'ulum-i ijtima'i: Ingilisi-Farsi. Birijaniyan, Mari. Tehran: Mu'assasah-'i Mutala'at va Tahqiqat-i Farhangi, 1992.

Farhang-i istilahat-i falsafi-i Mulla Sadra. Sajjadi, Ja'far. Tehran: Sazman-i Chap va Intisharat-i Vizarat-i Farhang va Irshad-i Islami, 2000.

Farhang-i 'ulum-i 'aqli: shamil-i istilahat-i falsafi, kalami, mintaqi. Sajjadi, Ja'far. Tehran: Anjuman-i Islami-i Hikmat va Falsafah-'i Iran, 1982.

Istilahat-i falsafi va tafavut-i anha bayakdigar. Karaji, 'Ali. Qom: Daftar-i Tablighat-i Islami-i Hawzah-i 'Ilmiyah-i Qum, Markaz-i Intisharat, 1996.

Istilah'namah-'i falsafah-'i Islami. Ya'qub'nizhad, Muhammad Hadi. Qom: Mu'avinat-i Mutali'ati va Ittila'-i Rasani, Markaz-i Mutali'at va Tahqiqat-i Islami "Pazhuhishgah," 1997.

Sih sunnat-i falsafi: guzarishi az falsafah-i Hindi, Chini va Yahudi. Smart, Ninian, Shlomo Pines, Wing-tsit Chan, and Paul Edwards. Qom: Markaz-i Intisharat-i Daftar-i Tablighat-I Islami, Hawzah-i 'Ilmiyah-i Qum, 1999.

Vazhah'namah-'i falsafah va 'ulum-i ijtima'i: Farsi, 'Arabi, Faransah, Ingilisi, Almani, Latin. Saliba, Jamil. [Tehran]: Shirkat-i Sihami-i Intishar, 1991.

Vazhah'namah-'i falsafi: Farsi-'Arabi. Afnan, Soheil Muhsin. Beirut: Dar al-Mashriq, 1969.

Vazhah'namah-'i falsafi: Farsi-'Arabi-Inglisi-Faransah-Pahlavi-Yunani-Latin. 2nd ed. Afnan, Soheil Muhsin. [Tehran]: Nashr-i Nuqrah, 1984.

Vazhah'namah-'i tarikh-i falsafah dar Islam. Bakhtar, Zhalah-i'. Tehran: Markaz-i Nashr-i Danishgahi, 1994.

PUNJABI

Angrezi-Pañjabi takaniki shabadawali, falasafa. 2nd ed. Punjab State University Text-Book Board. Chandigarh: Pañjaba Sateta Yuniwarasiti, Taikasata-buka Borada, 1970s.

SANSKRIT

Nyayakosah: sakalasastropakarakanyayadisastriyapadarthaprakasakah. Abhyankara, Vasudevasastri. 4th ed. Punyapattana: Bhandarakarapracyavidyasamsodhanamandiradhikrtaih [1978?].

Nyayakosa, or, Dictionary of Technical Terms in Indian Philosophy. Jhalakikar, Bhimacarya, and Vasudevasastri

Abhyankara. 4th ed. Pune: Bhandarkar Oriental Research Institute, 1996.

TAMIL

Caiva camayak kalaik kalañciyam. Tiruccirrampalam, Civa. Chennai: Rajesvari Puttaka Nilaiyam, 2002.

Camayac collakarati. Cacivalli. Chennai: Ulakat Tamilaraycci Niruvanam, 1987.

TELUGU

Tattvasastranighantuvu. Rajagopalaravu, Em. Hyderabad: Telugu Akadami, 1978.

THAI

'Athibai sap pratchaya kanmu'ang læ sangkhom [Dictionary of Political and Social Philosophy]. 2nd ed. Witthayakon Chiangkun. Bangkok: Samnakphim Saithan, 2004.

Photchananukrom pratya: 'Angkrit-Thai. Chetsada Thongrungrot. Bangkok: Bo Dæng, 2004.

Sapthanukrom pratya waduai chittaniyom-watthuniyom. Methi 'Iamcharœn. Bangkok: Somchai Kanphim, 1976.

TURKISH

Ansiklopedik felsefe sözlügü. Tokatli, Attilâ. Istanbul: Bilgi Yayinevi, 1973.

Bir felsefe dili kurmak: modern felsefe ve bilim terimlerinin Türkiye'ye girisi. Kara, Ismail. Istanbul: Dergâh Yayinlari, 2001.

Ezoterik sözlük. Werner, Helmut, Bülent Atatanir, and Özgü Çelik. Istanbul: Omega Yayinlari, 2005.

Felsefe ansiklopedisi: kavramlar ve akimlar. Hançerlioglu, Orhan. Istanbul: Remzi Kitabevi, 1976–1980.

Felsefe ansiklopedisi: kavramlar ve akimlar. Hançerlioglu, Orhan. Istanbul: Remzi Kitabevi, 2000.

Felsefe okullari sistemleri: ülke, konulariyla ünlü kisiler. Göktepe, Salahattin. Izmir: Yeniyol Matbaasi, 1976.

Felsefe sözlügü. 3rd ed. Hançerlioglu, Orhan. Istanbul: Remzi Kitabevi, 1975.

Felsefe sözlügü. 6th ed. Hançerlioglu, Orhan. Istanbul: Remzi Kitabevi, 1982.

Felsefe sözlügü. Ulas, Sarp Erk, and A. Bâki Güçlü. Ankara: Bilim ve Sanat, 2002.

Felsefî doktrinler sözlügü. 2nd ed. Bolay, Süleyman Hayri. Istanbul: Ötüken, 1981.

Felsefî doktrinler ve terimler sözlügü. Bolay, S. Hayri. [Ankara]: Akçag, 1997.

Felsefî doktrinler ve terimler sözlügü. Bolay, S. Hayri. [Ankara]: Akçag, 1999.

Islâm felsefesi sözlügü. Vural, Mrhmet. Ankara: Elis, 2003.

UIGHUR

Chat'al pailasopliri qisqicha lughiti. Ahmidi, Ibrahim. Ürümqi, China: Shinjang Khalq Nashriyati, 1989.

URDU

Kashshaf-i istilahat-i falsafah: Urdu-Angrezi. Kadir, Kazi A. [Karachi]: Shu'bah-yi Tasnif o Talif o Tarjumah, Karaci Yunivarsiti, bah ishtirak-i mali, Muqtadirah-yi Qaumi Zaban, 1994.

UZBEK

Filosofiiadan qisqacha lughat. Azarov, Nikolai Ivanovich, and M. M. Khairullaev. Tashkent: "Uzbekiston" Nashriëti, 1973.

Filosofiia lughati. Abdurahmonov, Rustam. Tashkent: "Uzbekiston" Nashriëti, 1976.

VIETNAMESE

Tu' dien triet hoc. Cung, Kim Tien. Hanoi: Nhà xuat ban Van hóa-thông tin, 2002.

Tu' dien triet hoc. Rozental', Mark Moiseevich. Mát-xco'-va: Tien bo, 1986.

Tu' diên triêt hoc. Rozental', Mark Moiseevich, and Pavel Fedorovich Iudin. Hanoi: Su' Thât, 1976.

Tu' dien triet hoc gian yeu: có doi chieu tu' Nga, Anh, Đu'c, Pháp. Hu'u Ngoc, Phú Hiep Du'o'ng, and Hu'u Tang Lê. Hanoi: Đai hoc và Trung hoc chuyên nghiep, 1987.

Tu'-dien và danh-tu' triêt-hoc. Trân-van Hiên-Minh. Saigon: Tu-Sách Ra-koi, 1966.

EUROPEAN LANGUAGES

ALBANIAN

Fjalor i filozofisë. Shkolla e Partisë "V. I. Lenin." Tiranë: Shtëpia Botuese "8 Nëntori," 1981.

BULGARIAN

Anglo-bulgarski ucheben rechnik-minimum za studenti po filosofiia. Dodova, L., and R. Mukharska. Sofia: Sofiiski universitet "Kliment Okhridski," 1984.

Filosofite: kratuk rechnik. Radev, Radi, Ivan Stefanov, and Aleksandur Lichev. Sofia: Izd-vo "Khristo Botev," 1992.

Filosofski rechnik. Buchvarov, Mikhail Dimitrov, Mincho Draganov, Stoiu G. Stoev, and Mark Moiseevich Rozental'. Sofia: Partizdat, 1977.

Filosofski rechnik. 2nd ed. Buchvarov, Mikhail Dimitrov, Mincho Draganov, and Stoiu G. Stoev. Sofia: Partizdat, 1985.

Filosofski rechnik suvremenni filosofi XIX–XX vek shkoli, napravleniia. Filatov, Vladimir Petrovich, and V. S. Malakhov. Sofia: Izd-vo GAL-IKO, 1993.

CROATIAN

Covjek, odgoj, svijet: mala filozofijskoodgojna razlozba. Polic, Milan. Zagreb: Kruzak, 1997.

Filozofija. 2nd ed. Grlic, Danko. Zagreb: Panorama, 1965.

Filozofija: uvod u filozofsko mišljenje i rjecnik. Bošnjak, Branko. Zagreb: Naprijed, 1973.

Filozofija: uvod u filozofsko mišljenje i rjecnik. 2nd ed. Bošnjak, Branko. Zagreb: Naprijed, 1977.

Filozofija: uvod u filozofsko mišljenje i rjecnik. 3rd ed. Bošnjak, Branko. Zagreb: Naprijed, 1982.

Filozofijski rjecnik. Filipovic, Vladimir, and Branko Bošnjak. Zagreb: Matica hrvatska, 1965.

Filozofijski rjecnik. 2nd ed. Filipovic, Vladimir, and Branko Bošnjak. Zagreb: Nakladni zavod Matice hrvatske, 1984.

Filozofijski rjecnik. 3rd ed. Filipovic, Vladimir, and Branko Bošnjak. Zagreb: Nakladni zavod Matice hrvatske, 1989.

Filozofski recnik. Maric, Svetislav. Belgrade: Dereta, [1991?].

Leksikon filozofa. Grlic, Danko. Zagreb: Naprijed, 1968.

Rjecnik filozofskih pojmova. Misic, Anto. Split: Verbum, 2000.

CZECH

Filosofický slovník. 2nd ed. Blecha, Ivan. Olomouc: Nakl. Olomouc, 1998.

Filozofický slovník. Iudin, Pavel, and Mark Moiseevich Rozental', eds. [Bratislava]: Vydavatel'stvo politickej literatury, 1965.

Filozofický slovník. Javurek, Zdenek, E. Marešová, and M. Landová. Prague: Svoboda, 1976.

Filozofický slovník. Klaus, Georg, and Manfred Buhr. Prague: Svoboda, 1985.

Filozofický slovník pro samouky: neboli Antigorgias. 2nd ed. Neff, Vladimír. Prague: Mladá fronta, 1993.

Filozovický slovník. 4th ed. Frolov, Ivan Timofeevich. Bratislava: Pravda, 1989.

Slovník ceských filozofu. Gabriel, Jirí. Brno: Masarykova univerzita v Brne, 1998.

Slovník filosofických pojmu soucasnosti. Olsovský, Jirí. Prague: Erika, 1999.

Strucný prehled významných filosofu a filosofických pojmu. Hrubes, Jaromír. Ostrava: Ostravská univerzita, Pedagogická fakulta, 2002.

Strucny filosofický slovník. [Prague]: Svoboda, 1966.

DANISH

Filosofisk ordbog. Ord og udtryk fra oldtidens til dagens tankeverden. Hanneborg, Bente, Knut Hanneborg, and Carl Henrik Koch. Copenhagen: Høst, 1971.

DUTCH

Elseviers filosofische en psychologische encyclopedie. Kuypers, K. Amsterdam: Elsevier, 1970.

Encyclopedie van de filosofie. Kuypers, K. Amsterdam: Elsevier, 1977.

Encyclopedie van de filosofie. Waldram, Joop, and T. van Kooten. Baarn: Tirion, 1991.

Klein wijsgerig woordenboek. Schilfgaarde, Paul van. Wassenaar: Servire, 1968.

Kritisch denkerslexicon. Achterhuis, Hans. Alphen: Samsom, 1986–.

Prisma van de filosofie. Groen, Nico, and Robbert Veen. Utrecht: Het Spectrum, 1990.

Woordeboek filosofie. Willemsen, Harry. Assen: Van Gorcum, 1992.

ESTONIAN

Filosoofia leksikon. 4th ed. Frolov, Ivan Timofeevich. Tallinn: Eesti Raamat, 1985.

Lühike filosoofia leksikon. Lumi, M. Tallinn: Eesti Raamat, 1975.

FRENCH

Abécédaire de l'engagement. Benasayag, Miguel, and Béatrice Bouniol. Paris: Bayard, 2004.

L'altérité. Groux, Dominique, and Louis Porcher. Paris: Harmattan, 2003.

Bibliographie de la philosophie: glossaire [Bibliography of Philosophy: Glossary]. Unesco, Centre national de la recherche scientifique (France), and International Institute of Philosophy. Paris: J. Vrin, 1995.

Les 50 mots-clés de la philosophie contemporaine. Mantoy, Jacques. [Toulouse]: privately printed, 1971.

Dico de philosophie. Vergely, Bertrand. Toulouse: Milan, 1998.

Dictionnaire abrégé des philosophes médiévaux. Patar, Benoît. [Longueuil, Québec]: Presses philosophiques, 2000.

Dictionnaire critique à l'usage des incrédules. Memmi, Albert. Paris: Félin, 2002.

Dictionnaire de la langue philosophique. 2nd ed. Foulquié, Paul. Paris: Presses Universitaires de France, 1969.

Dictionnaire de la langue philosophique. 3rd ed. Foulquié, Paul. Paris: Presses Universitaires de France, 1978.

Dictionnaire de la philosophie. Comte-Sponville, André. Paris: Encyclopaedia Universalis, A. Michel, 2000.

Dictionnaire de la philosophie. Rev. ed. Julia, Didier. Paris: Larousse, 1970.

Dictionnaire de la philosophie. Rev. ed. Julia, Didier. Paris: Larousse, 1984.

Dictionnaire de la philosophie. Rev. ed. Julia, Didier. Paris: Larousse, 1991.

Dictionnaire de la philosophie. Rev. ed. Julia, Didier. Paris: Larousse, 1995.

Dictionnaire de la philosophie. Rev. ed. Julia, Didier. Paris: Larousse, 1998.

Dictionnaire de philosophie. Baraquin, Noëlla. Paris: A. Colin, 1995.

Dictionnaire de philosophie. 2nd ed. Baraquin, Noëlla. Paris: A. Colin, 2000.

Dictionnaire de philosophie. Durozoi, Gérard, and André Roussel. Paris: Nathan, 1987.

Dictionnaire de philosophie. Durozoi, Gérard, and André Roussel. Paris: Nathan, 1990.

Dictionnaire de philosophie. Durozoi, Gérard, and André Roussel. Paris: Nathan, 1997.

Dictionnaire de philosophie. Godin, Christian. Paris: Fayard, 2004.

Dictionnaire de philosophie. Legrand, Gérard. Paris: Bordas, 1973.

Dictionnaire de philosophie. Legrand, Gérard. Paris: Bordas, 1983.

Dictionnaire de philosophie. Russ, Jacqueline, and Clotilde Badal-Leguil. Paris: Bordas, 2004.

Dictionnaire de philosophie: les concepts, les philosophes, 1850 citations. Russ, Jacqueline. Paris: Bordas, 1991.

Dictionnaire de philosophie politique. Raynaud, Philippe, and Stéphane Rials. Paris: Presses Universitaires de France, 2003.

Dictionnaire des auteurs et des thèmes de la philosophie. Auroux, Sylvain, and Yvonne Weil. Paris: Hachette, 1975.

Dictionnaire des auteurs et des thèmes de la philosophie. Auroux, Sylvain, and Yvonne Weil. Paris: Hachette, 1984.

Dictionnaire des grandes philosophies. Jerphagnon, Lucien. Toulouse: privately printed, 1973.

Dictionnaire des idées contemporaines. Mourre, Michel, ed. Paris: Éditions Universitaires, 1966.

Dictionnaire des philosophes. 2nd ed. Baraquin, Noëlla, and Jacqueline Laffitte. Paris: A. Colin, 2000.

Dictionnaire des philosophes. Comte-Sponville, André. Paris: Encyclopaedia Universalis, A. Michel, 1998.

Dictionnaire des philosophes. Huisman, Denis, and Jean-François Braunstein. Paris: Presses Universitaires de France, 1984.

Dictionnaire des philosophes. 2nd ed. Huisman, Denis, and Marie-Agnès Malfray. Paris: Presses Universitaires de France, 1993.

Dictionnaire des philosophes antiques. Goulet, Richard. Paris: Editions du Centre national de la recherche scientifique, 1989–.

Dictionnaire des philosophes antiques. Goulet, Richard. Paris: Editions du Centre national de la recherche scientifique, 1994–.

Dictionnaire du Moyen âge: littérature et philosophie. Favier, Jean. Paris: Encyclopaedia Universalis, A. Michel, 1999.

Dictionnaire philosophique de citations. Rev. ed. Grateloup, Léon-Louis. Paris: Hachette, 1990.

Dictionnaire philosophique en langue arabe: avec index des termes français, anglais et latins. Saliba, Djemil. Beirut: Dar al-Kitab al-Lubnani, 1978–1979.

Dictionnaire Sartre. Noudelmann, François, and Gilles Philippe. Paris: Champion, 2004.

Dictionnaire Wittgenstein. Glock, Hans-Johann. [Paris]: Gallimard, 2003.

Encyclopédie philosophique universelle. Jacob, André. Paris: Presses Universitaires de France, 1989–1998.

Grand dictionnaire de la philosophie. Blay, Michel. Paris: Larousse, 2003.

Les grandes notions de la philosophie. Warin, François. Paris: Ellipses, 2001.

Histoire et mémoire. Le Goff, Jacques. [Paris]: Gallimard, 1988.

Lexique de philosophie. Stirn, François, and Hervé Vautrelle. Paris: A. Colin, 1998.

Lexique philosophique: français-arabe. Gaïd, Tahar. Algiers: Office des Publications Universitaires, 1990.

Les Notions philosophiques: dictionnaire. Auroux, Sylvain, and André Jacob. Paris: Presses Universitaires de France, 1990.

Nouveau vocabulaire des études philosophiques. Auroux, Sylvain, and Yvonne Weil. Paris: Hachette, 1975.

Nouveau vocabulaire philosohique. 13th ed. Cuvillier, Armand. Paris: A. Colin, 1967.

Petit dictionaire de la philosophie. Huisman, Denis, and André Vergez. Paris: F. Nathan, 1971.

Petit dictionnaire philosophique. Rozental', Mark Moiseevich, and Pavel Iudin, eds. Paris: E. Varlin, 1977.

Petit lexique philosophique de l'anarchisme: de Proudhon à Deleuze. Colson, Daniel. Paris: Livre de poche, 2001.

Le Petit Retz des nouvelles idées en philosophie. Huisman, Denis, and Serge Le Strat. Paris: Retz, 1987.

Philosopher au cégep: guide d'apprentissage, de vocabulaire et d'histoire. Clavet, Jean-Claude, and G.-Magella Hotton. Sainte-Foy, Quebec: Éditions Le Griffon d'argile, 1993.

Philosophes de l'humanité (Grèce, Rome, Inde, Chine, Perse, Islam, Europe médiévale et moderne). Koribaa, Nabhani. Paris: Publisud, 1995.

La Philosophie. Verviers, Belgium: Gérard, 1972.

La Philosophie. Paris: Le Livre de poche, 1977.

La Philosophie. Akoun, André. Paris: Centre d'étude et de promotion de la lecture, 1977.

La Philosophie. Noiray, André, ed. Paris: Centre d'étude et de promotion de la lecture, 1969.

La Philosophie: encyclopédie du monde actuel. Favrod, Charles-Henri. Paris: C. H. Favrod, 1977.

Philosophie, religions. Paris: Bordas. Brussels: ASEDI. Lausanne: Spes. Montréal: CEC, 1968.

Philosophie, religions. Rev. ed. Caratini, Roger, and Françoise Caratini. Paris: Bordas, 1976.

Philosophie, religions. Pascal, Georges. Paris: Bordas, 1974.

Pierre Bayle, pour une histoire critique de la philosophie: choix d'articles philosophiques du Dictionnaire historique et critique. Bayle, Pierre, Jean-Michel Gros, and Jacques Chomarat. Paris: Champion, 2001.

Pour une encyclopédia des auteurs classiques. Colli, Giorgio, Jean Christophe Bailly, Jean-Paul Manganaro, Danielle Dubroca, and Giuliana Lanata. N.p.: Christian Bourgois Editeur, 1990.

Le taureau de Phalaris: dictionnaire philosophique. Matzneff, Gabriel. Paris: Table Ronde, 1987.

Le taureau de Phalaris: dictionnaire philosophique. Matzneff, Gabriel. Paris: Table Ronde, 1994.

Vocabulaire Bordas de la philosophie. Legrand, Gérard. Paris: Bordas, 1986.

Vocabulaire Bordas de la philosophie. Legrand, Gérard. Paris: Bordas, 1987.

Vocabulaire Bordas de la philosophie. Legrand, Gérard. Paris: Bordas, 1993.

Vocabulaire de la philosophie et des sciences humaines. Morfaux, Louis Marie. Paris: A. Colin, 1980.

Vocabulaire de la philosophie; suivi d'un Tableau Historique des Écoles de Philosophie. 6th ed. Jolivet, Régis. Lyon: Emmanuel Vitte, 1966.

Vocabulaire des études philosophiques. Rev. ed. Auroux, Sylvain, Yvonne Weil, and Yvon Belaval. Paris: Hachette, 1993.

Le vocabulaire des philosophes. Zarader, Jean-Pierre. Paris: Ellipses, 2002.

Vocabulaire européen des philosophies: dictionnaire des intraduisibles. Cassin, Barbara. Paris: Le Robert, Seuil, 2004.

Le vocabulaire grec de la philosophie. Gobry, Ivan. Paris: Ellipses, 2000.

Vocabulaire philosophique arabe (avec tables françaises et anglaises). Karam, Yusuf, Murad Wahbah, and Youssef Chellalah. Cairo: Tsoumas 1966.

Le vocabulaire philosophique: français-arabe. Hulw, ʿAbduh. Beirut: Centre de recherche et de développement pédagogique, Librairie du Liban, 1994.

Vocabulaire technique et critique de la philosophie. 10th ed. Lalande, André. Paris: Presses Universitaires de France, 1968.

Vocabulaire technique et critique de la philosophie. 11th ed. Lalande, André. Paris: Presses Universitaires de France, 1972.

Vocabulaire technique et critique de la philosophie. 16th ed. Lalande, André. Paris: Presses Universitaires de France, 1988.

Vocabulaire technique et critique de la philosophie. Lalande, André. Paris: Presses Universitaires de France, 1992.

GERMAN

Chinesisch-Deutsches Lexikon der Chinesischen Philosophie. Geldsetzer, Lutz, and Han-Ding Hong. Aalen: Scientia, 1986.

Chinesisch-Deutsches Lexikon der Chinesischen Philosophie. Geldsetzer, Lutz, and Han-Ding Hong. Aalen: Scientia, 1995.

Chinesisch-Deutsches Lexikon der Klassiker und Schulen der Chinesischen Philosophie. Geldsetzer, Lutz, and Han-Ding Hong. Aalen: Scientia, 1991.

Enzyklopädie der Philosophie: von der Antike bis zur Gegenwart; Denker und Philosophen, Begriffe und Probleme, Theorien und Schulen. Augsburg: Gruppo, 1992.

Enzyklopädie Philosophie und Wissenschaftstheorie. Stuttgart: Metzler, 1995–1996.

Enzyklopädie Philosophie und Wissenschaftstheorie. Blasche, Siegfried, Gereon Wolters, and Jürgen Mittelstrass. Mannheim: Bibliographisches Institut, 1980–1996.

Enzyklopädie Philosophie und Wissenschaftstheorie. Blasche, Siegfried, Martin Carrier, Gereon Wolters, and Jürgen Mittelstrass. Stuttgart: Metzler, 1995–.

Europäische Enzyklopädie zu Philosophie und Wissenschaften. Sandkühler, Hans-Jörg, and Arnim Regenbogen. Hamburg: F. Meiner, 1990.

Grundbegriffe der altchinesischen Philosophie: ein Wörterbuch für die Klassische Periode. Unger, Ulrich. Darmstadt: Wissenschftliche Buchgesellschaft, 2000.

Grundbegriffe der analytischen Philosophie. Prechtl, Peter, and Ansgar Beckermann. Stuttgart: Metzler, 2004.

Grundbegriffe der antiken Philosophie: ein Lexikon. Bächli, Andreas, and Andreas Graeser. Stuttgart: P. Reclam, 2000.

Grundbegriffe der philosophischen Sprache. 2nd ed. Neuhäusler, Anton. Munich: Ehrenwirth, 1967.

Handbuch philosophischer Grundbegriffe. Krings, Hermann, Hans Michael Baumgartner, and Christoph Wild, eds. Munich: Kösel-Verlag, 1973.

Handlexikon zur Wissenschaftstheorie. Seiffert, Helmut, and Gerard Radnitzky. Munich: Ehrenwirth, 1989.

Handwörterbuch Philosophie. Rehfus, Wulff D. Göttingen: Vandenhoeck & Ruprecht; [Stuttgart]: UTB, 2003.

Herders kleines philosophisches Wörterbuch. 8th ed. Müller, Max, and Alois Halder. [Basel]: Herder-Bücherei, 1966.

Historisches Wörterbuch der Philosophie. Ritter, Joachim, and Rudolf Eisler. Wörterbuch der philosophischen Begriffe. Darmstadt: Wissenschaftliche Buchgesellschaft, 1971–.

Historisches Wörterbuch der Philosophie. Ritter, Joachim, Karlfried Gründer, Gottfried Gabriel, and Rudolf Eisler, eds. Wörterbuch der philosophischen Begriffe. Basel: Schwabe, 1971–.

Historisches Wörterbuch der Philosophie. Ritter, Joachim, Karlfried Gründer, and Rudolf Eisler, eds. Wörterbuch der philosophischen Begriffe. Basel: Schwabe, 1992.

Jugendlexikon Philosophie: Geschichte, Begriffe und Probleme der Philosophie. Delf, Hanna. Hamburg: Rowohlt, 1988.

Kleines philosophisches Wörterbuch. Müller, Max, and Alois Halder, eds. Freiburg, Basel, and Vienna: Herder, 1971.

Kleines philosophisches Wörterbuch. 7th ed. Müller, Max, and Alois Halder, eds. Freiburg, Basel, and Vienna: Herder, 1979.

Kleines Wörterbuch der angewandten Philosophie. Mosch, Annemarie. Zürich: Haffman, 1996.

Kleines Wörterbuch der marxistischen Philosophie. Buhr, Manfred, and Alfred Kosing. Berlin: Das Europäische Buch (Dietz), 1967.

Kleines Wörterbuch der marxistisch-leninisten Philosophie. 3rd ed. Buhr, Manfred, and Alfred Kosing. Berlin: Dietz, 1975.

Kleines Wörterbuch der marxistisch-leninisten Philosophie. 4th ed. Buhr, Manfred, and Alfred Kosing. Berlin: Dietz, 1979.

Kleines Wörterbuch der marxistisch-leninistischen Philosophie. Buhr, Manfred. Berlin: Dietz, 1966.

Kleines Wörterbuch der marxistisch-leninistischen Philosophie. 2nd ed. Buhr, Manfred, and Alfred Kosing. Berlin: Dietz, 1974.

Kleines Wörterbuch der marxistisch-leninistischen Philosophie. 5th ed. Buhr, Manfred, and Alfred Kosing. [Berlin]: Das Europäische Buch, 1981.

Kleines Wörterbuch der marxistisch-leninistischen Philosophie. 7th ed. Buhr, Manfred, and Alfred Kosing. Berlin: Dietz, 1984.

Kleines Wörterbuch der Wissenschaftstheorie. Schwarz, Gerhard, and Walter Adolf Jöhr. Saint Gall, Switzerland: Hochschule St. Gallen, 1974.

Kleines Wörterbuch zum Verständnis asiatischer Weltanschauung. Erklärungen von Worten und Begriffen. Mangoldt, Ursula von. Weilheim and Oberbayern: Barth, 1966.

Die Kunst, selber zu denken: ein philosophischer Dictionnaire. Sommer, Andreas Urs. Frankfurt am Main: Eichborn, 2002.

Lexikon der Erkenntnistheorie und Metaphysik. Ricken, Friedo. Munich: C. H. Beck, 1984.

Lexikon der Esoterik. Iwersen, Julia. Düsseldorf: Artemis & Winkler, 2001.

Lexikon der Philosophie. 5th ed. Austeda, Franz. Vienna: Hollinek, 1979.

Lexikon der Philosophie. 6th ed. Austeda, Franz. Vienna: Hollinek, 1989.

Lexikon der Philosophischen Begriffe. Ulfig, Alexander. Wiesbaden: Fourier, 1997.

Lexikon der Philosophischen Begriffe. 2nd ed. Ulfig, Alexander. Wiesbaden: Fourier, 1999.

Lexikon des Kritischen Rationalismus. Niemann, Hans-Joachim. Tübingen: Mohr Siebeck, 2004.

Marxistisch-Leninistisches Wörterbuch der Philosophie. Klaus, Georg, and Manfred Buhr, eds. Reinbek: Rowohlt, 1972.

Marxistisch-Leninistisches Wörterbuch der Philosophie. Rev. ed. Klaus, Georg, Manfred Buhr, and Karlheinz Barck, eds. Reinbek: Rowohlt, 1975.

Metzler Lexikon jüdischer Philosophen: Philosophisches Denken des Judentums von der Antike bis zur Gegenwart. Kilcher, Andreas B., Otfried Fraisse, and Yossef Schwartz. Stuttgart: Metzler, 2003.

Metzler Philosophie Lexikon: Begriffe und Definitionen. Prechtl, Peter, and Franz-Peter Burkard. Stuttgart: Metzler, 1996.

Metzler Philosophie Lexikon: Begriffe und Definitionen. 2nd ed. Prechtl, Peter, and Franz-Peter Burkard. Stuttgart: Metzler, 1999.

Onomasticon philosophicum: Latinoteutonicum et Teutonicolatinum. Aso, Ken. Tokyo: Tetsugaku-Shobo, 1989.

Philosophenlexikon. Lange, Erhard, and Dietrich Alexander. Berlin: Das Europäische Buch, 1982.

Philosophenlexikon. Lange, Erhard, and Dietrich Alexander. Berlin: Dietz, 1984.

Philosophie. Diemer, Alwin, and Ivo Frenzel. [Frankfurt am Main]: Fischer Bücherei, 1967.

Philosophie. 11th ed. Diemer, Alwin, and Ivo Frenzel. [Frankfurt am Main and Hamburg]: Fischer Bücherei, 1969.

Philosophie. 4th ed. Fiedler, Frank, and Günter Gurst. Leipzig: Bibliographisches Institut, 1986.

Philosophie. 6th ed. Fiedler, Frank, and Günter Gurst. Leipzig: Bibliographisches Institut, 1988.

Philosophie in der Geschichte ihres Begriffs: Historisches Wörterbuch der Philosophie, Sonderdruck. Gründer, Karlfried. Basel: Schwabe, 1990.

Der Philosophische Flohmarkt: Kleines Lexikon der Philosophie. Moser, Friedhelm. Frankfurt am Main: Eichborn, 1995.

Philosophisches Wörterbuch. 6th ed. Apel, Max, and Peter Christian Ludz. Berlin and New York: de Gruyter, 1976.

Philosophisches Wörterbuch. 14th ed. Brugger, Walter, ed. Freiburg, Basel, and Vienna: Herder, 1976.

Philosophisches Wörterbuch. 15th ed. Brugger, Walter, ed. Freiburg, Basel, and Vienna: Herder, 1978.

Philosophisches Wörterbuch. Halder, Alois, and Max Müller. Freiburg: Herder, 1988.

Philosophisches Wörterbuch. Rev. ed. Halder, Alois, and Max Müller. Freiburg: Herder, 1993.

Philosophisches Wörterbuch. Rev. ed. Halder, Alois, and Max Müller. Freiburg: Herder, 2000.

Philosophisches Wörterbuch. 2nd ed. Klaus, Georg, and Manfred Buhr, eds. Leipzig: Bibliographisches Institut, 1965.

Philosophisches Wörterbuch. 6th ed. Klaus, Georg, and Manfred Buhr, eds. Leipzig: VEB Bibliographisches Institut; Berlin: Das Europäische Buch, 1969.

Philosophisches Wörterbuch. 7th ed. Klaus, Georg, and Manfred Buhr, eds. Berlin: Das Europäische Buch; Leipzig: VEB Bibliographisches Institut, 1970.

Philosophisches Wörterbuch. 8th ed. Klaus, Georg, and Manfred Buhr, eds. Leipzig: VEB Verlag Enzyklopädie; Berlin: Das Europäische Buch, 1972.

Philosophisches Wörterbuch. 10th ed. Klaus, Georg, and Manfred Buhr, eds. Leipzig: Bibliographisches Institut, 1974.

Philosophisches Wörterbuch. 12th ed. Klaus, Georg, and Manfred Buhr, eds. Berlin: Das Europäische Buch; Leipzig: VEB Bibliographisches Institut, 1976.

Philosophisches Wörterbuch. 13th ed. Klaus, Georg, and Manfred Buhr, eds. Berlin: Das Europäische Buch, 1985.

Philosophisches Wörterbuch. 14th ed. Klaus, Georg, and Manfred Buhr, eds. Berlin: Das Europäische Buch, 1987.

Philosophisches Wörterbuch. 9th ed. Schmidt, Heinrich, ed. Stuttgart: A. Kröner, 1974.

Philosophisches Wörterbuch. 17th ed. Schmidt, Heinrich, and Georgi Schischkoff, eds. Stuttgart: A. Kröner, 1965.

Philosophishces Wörterbuch. 18th ed. Schmidt, Heinrich, and Georgi Schischkoff, eds. Stuttgart: A. Kröner, 1969.

Philosophisches Wörterbuch. 19th ed. Schmidt, Heinrich, and Georgi Schischkoff, eds. Stuttgart, A. Kröner, 1974.

Philosophisches Wörterbuch. 20th ed. Schmidt, Heinrich, and Georgi Schischkoff, eds. Stuttgart: Kröner, 1978.

Philosophisches Wörterbuch. 22nd ed. Schmidt, Heinrich, and Georgi Schischkoff, eds. Stuttgart: A. Kröner, 1991.

Philosophisches Wörterbuch. Stockhammer, Morris. [Cologne]: Kölner Universitäts-Verlag 1967.

Philosophisches Wörterbuch. Stockhammer, Morris. Essen: Magnus, 1980.

Philosophisches Wörterbuch. Unter Mitwirkung der Professoren des Berchmanskollegs in Pullach bei München und anderer. 12th ed. Brugger, Walter, ed. Freiburg: Herder, 1965.

Philosophisches Wörterbuch. Unter Mitwirkung der Professoren des Berchmanskollegs. 13th ed. Brugger, Walter, ed. Freiburg, Basel, and Vienna: Herder, 1967.

Schülerduden, die Philosophie. Kwiatkowski, Gerhard. Mannheim, Vienna, and Zürich: Dudenverlag, 1985.

Die sowjetische "Philosophische Enzyklopädie"; Dokument eines Politischen Umbruchs. Marko, Kurt. Cologne: Bundesinstitut für Ostwissenschaftliche und Internationale Studien, 1973.

Terminologie der frühen Philosophischen Scholastik in Indien: ein Begriffswörterbuch zur altindischen Dialektik, Erkenntnislehre und Methodologie. Oberhammer, Gerhard, Ernst Prets, and Joachim Prandstetter. Vienna: Österreichischen Akademie der Wissenschaften, 1991–.

Wissenschaftstheoretisches Lexikon. Braun, Edmund, and Hans Radermacher. Graz, Vienna, and Cologne: Styria, 1978.

Wörterbuch der antiken Philosophie. Horn, Christoph, and Christof Rapp. Munich: C. H. Beck, 2002.

Wörterbuch der Marxistisch-Leninistischen Philosophie. Kosing, Alfred. Berlin: Dietz, 1985.

Wörterbuch der Philosophie. Hegenbart, Rainer. Munich: Humboldt-Taschenbuchverlag, 1984.

Wörterbuch der Philosophie. Kosing, Alfred. Berlin: Das Europäische Buch, 1985.

Wörterbuch der Philiosophie. Pachnicke, Erich, and Richard Hönigswald. Göttingen: K. Pachnicke, 1985.

Wörterbuch der philosophischen Begriffe. Regenbogen, Arnim, and Uwe Meyer. Hamburg: F. Meiner, 1998.

GREEK

Hermeneutiko lexiko tes Indikes philosophias kai tou Gionka. Pantouvas, Theodoros. Athens: Ekdoseis Kardamitsa, 1989.

Lexikon tes prosokratikes philosophias [Lexicon of Presocratic Philosophy]. Despototpoulos, Konstantinos I. Athens: Akademia Athenon and Kentron Ereunes tes Hellenikes Philosophias, 1988.

Lexikon tes prosokratikes philosophias. Theodoracopoulos, Ioannes. Athens: Akademia Athenon, 1998.

Lexikon vasikon ennoion. Sarales, I. A. Athens, 1974.

Lexiko philosophikon horon. Dokas, Agesilaos S. Athens: Ekdot, Oikos "Aster," 1981.

Lexiko vasikon ennoion tou hylikou-technikou, pneumatikou kai ethikou politismou: themeliodeis gnoseis ennoion gia tis ektheseis. Diamantopoulos, D. P. Athens: Patake, 1984.

Neo philosophiko lexiko. Gkikas, Sokrates. Athens: Ekdoseis Savvalas, 2002.

Philosophiko lexiko. 3rd ed. Gkikas, Sokrates. Athens: Ekdoseis Pheleke, 1982.

HUNGARIAN

Filozófiai kislexikon. Szigeti, Györgyné. Budapest: Kossuth Könyvkiadó, 1970.

Filozófiai kislexikon. 2nd ed. Szigeti, Györgyné, and Györgyné Vári, eds. Budapest: Kossuth Könyvkiadó, 1972.

Filozófiai kislexikon. 3rd ed. Szigeti, Györgyné, Györgyné Vári, and Árpád Volczer. [Budapest]: Kossuth Könyvkiadó, 1973.

Filozófiai kislexikon. 4th ed. Tomori, Lajos. [Budapest]: Kossuth Könyvkiadó, 1976.

Idegen szavak a filozófiában: az arkhétól a zoón politikonig. Rathmann, János. [Budapest]: Kossuth, 1988.

ITALIAN

Antidizionario filosofico. Dizionario critico di filosofia. Testa, Aldo. Urbino: AGE, 1974.

Breve dizionario filosofico. Del Re, Raffaello. Rome: Edizioni dell'Ateneo & Bizzarri, 1979.

Concetti e problemi di filosofia. Garulli, Enrico. [Lanciano]: Editrice Itinerari, 1983.

Concetti fondamentali della filosofia. Krings, Hermann, Hans Michael Baumgartner, and Christoph Wild. Brescia: Queriniana, 1981–1982.

Dizionario critico di filosofia: rivisto dai membri e dai corrispondenti della Società francese di filosofia e pubblicato con le loro correzioni e osservazioni. 3rd ed. Lalande, André, and Mario Dal Pra. Milan: ISEDI: Mondadori, 1980.

Dizionario dei filosofi. Centro di studi filosofici di Gallarate. Florence: G. C. Sansoni, 1976.

Dizionario dei filosofi del Novecento. Centro di studi filosofici di Gallarate. [Florence]: L. S. Olschki, 1985.

Dizionario delle idee. Centro di studi filosofici di Gallarate. Florence: G. C. Sansoni, 1977.

Dizionario di filosofia. Abbagnano, Nicola. [Turin]: Unione tipografico-editrice torinese, 1968.

Dizionario di filosofia. 2nd ed. Abbagnano, Nicola. Turin: Unione tipografico-editrice torinese, 1971.

Dizionario di filosofia. 3rd ed. Abbagnano, Nicola, and Giovanni Fornero. Turin: UTET libreria, 2001.

Dizionario di filosofia. Rossi, Paolo. Florence: La nuova Italia, 1996.

Dizionario di filosofia. Runes, Dagobert David, ed. Milan: Arnoldo Mondadori, 1972.

Dizionario di filosofia: con un prospetto storico delle scuole di filosofia. Jolivet, Régis, and Luigi Castiglione. Brescia: Morcelliana, 1966.

Dizionario di filosofia: 2500 voci, 700 bibliografie, tavole cronologiche. Milan: Rizzoli, 1976.

Dizionario di filosofia: 2500 voci, 700 bibliografie, tavole cronologiche. 3rd ed. Milan: Rizzoli, 1977.

Dizionario di termini filosofici. 16th ed. Lamanna, Eustachio Paolo, and Francesco Adorno. Florence: F. Le Monnier, 1968.

Dizionario di termini filosofici. 17th ed. Lamanna, Eustachio Paolo, and Francesco Adorno. Florence: F. Le Monnier, 1969.

Dizionario filosofico. Piebe, Armando. Padua: R.A.D.A.R., 1969.

Dizionario filosofico. Zamboni, Giuseppe, and Ferdinando L. Marcolungo. Milan: Vita e pensiero, 1978.

Un dizionario filosofico ebraico del XIII secolo: l'introduzione al "Sefer De'ot ha-filosofim" di Shem Tob ibn Falaquera. Zonta, Mauro, and Shem Tov ben Joseph Falaquera. Turin: S. Zamorani, 1992.

Dizionario interdisciplinare di scienza e fede: cultura scientifica, filosofia e teologia. Tanzella-Nitti, G. and Alberto Strumia. Vatican City: Urbaniana University Press; Rome: Città Nuova, 2002.

Enciclopedia della filosofia contemporanea. Papi, Fulvio. Milan: Teti, 1979.

Enciclopedia filosofica. Rev. ed. Centro di studi filosofici di Gallarate.Florence: G. C. Sansoni, 1967.

Enciclopedia filosofica. Rev. ed. Centro di studi filosofici di Gallarate. Rome: Edipem, 1979.

Enciclopedia filosofica. Rev. ed. Centro di studi filosofici di Gallarate. [Rome?]: Lucarini, 1982.

Filosofia. Apel, Karl-Otto, and Carlo Sini. Milan: Jaca, 1992.

Il linguaggio dei filosofi: Kant, Fichte, Schelling, Hegel. Campagna, Nunzio. Naples: La città del sole: Istituto italiano per gli studi filosofici, 1998.

Parole che contano: da amicizia a volontà, piccolo dizionario politico-filosofico. Bencivenga, Ermanno. Milan: Mondadori, 2004.

Il pensiero quotidiano: piccolo sillabario filosofico per tutti. Guarini, Ruggero. Milan: BUR, 1993.

Significato, metafora e interpretazione. Welby, Lady Victoria, and Susan Petrilli. Bari: Adriatica, 1986.

Termini della filosofia contemporanea. Plebe, Armando. Rome: A. Armando, 1966.

La trama e l'ordito: storia della filosofia occidentale. Maranini, Letizia, and Ester Dolce. Milan: Hoepli, 1990.

Voci di scienze umane: dal Dizionario critico di filosofia. Testa, Aldo. Rome: Biblioteca del dialogo, 1974.

LATVIAN

Filozofijas vardniica A–Z. Rozental', Mark Moiseevich. Riga: Izdevnieciba "Liesma," 1974.

LITHUANIAN

Filosofijos zodynas. Rozental', Mark Moiseevich, and Romanas Pleckaitis, eds. Vilnius: Mintis, 1975.

MOLDAVIAN

Diktsionar de filozofie. Frolov, Ivan Timofeevich. Kishinev: Red. princlipale a Enchiklopedìei Sovietiche Moldovenesht', 1985.

NORWEGIAN

Filosofisk ordbok: [en oppslagsbok fra Tanum]. Hanneborg, Bente, and Knut Hanneborg. Oslo: Tanum, 1975.

POLISH

Filozofia a nauka: zarys encyklopedyczny. Cackowski, Zdzislaw, and Maria Izewska. Wrocław: Zaklad Narodowy im. Ossolinskich, 1987.

Filozofowie wspólczesni: leksykon. Szmyd, Jan. Kraków: Wydawn. Krakowskie, 2003.

Idee w Rosji: leksykon rosyjsko-polsko-angielski [Ideas in Russia]. Lazari, Andzhei. Warsaw: Semper, 1999–.

Leksykon filozoficzny dla mlodziezy. Delf, Hanna. Warsaw: Wiedza Powszechna, 1996.

Leksykon filozofii klasycznej. Herbut, Józef. Lublin: Tow. Nauk. Katolickiego Uniwersytetu Lubelskiego, 1997.

Leksykon filozofii: postaci i pojecia. Andrzejewski, Boleslaw. Poznań: Oficyna Wydawnicza De Facto, 2000.

Leksykon filozofów wspólczesnych. Jasinski, Boguslaw. Warszaw: Wydawn. Ethos, 1999.

Logika dla prawników: slownik encyklopedyczny. Lewandowski, Slawomir, Andrzej Malinowski, and Jacek Petzel. Warsaw: Wydawn. Prawnicze LexisNexis, 2004.

Maly slownik terminów i pojec filozoficznych, dla studiujacych filozofie chrzescijanska. Podsiad, Antoni, and Zbigniew Wieckowski. Warsaw: Instytut Wydawniczy Pax, 1983.

Podstawowe kategorie i pojecia filozofii. 2nd ed. Hull, Zbigniew, Józef Staranczak, and Witold Tulibacki. Olsztyn: [AR-T], 1976.

Slownik filozoficzny. Lacey, Alan Robert, and Roman Matuszewski. Poznań: Zysk i S-ka Wydawn, 1999.

Slownik filozofii marksistowskiej. Jaroszewski, Tadeusz M. Warsaw: Wydawn. Wiedza Powszechna, 1982.

Slownik filozofów: filozofia powszechna. Andrzejewski, Boleslaw. Poznań: Dom Wydawniczy Rebis, 1995.

Slownik filozofów polskich. Andrzejewski, Boleslaw, and Roman Kozlowski. Poznań: Wydawn, 1999.

Slownik pojec filozoficznych. Krajewski, Wladyslaw, and Ryszard Banajski. Warsaw: Wydawn, 1996.

Slownik terminów i pojec filozoficznych. Podsiad, Antoni. Warsaw: Instytut Wydawniczy Pax, 2000.

Szkolny slownik filozoficzny. Syjud, Jerzy, and Krzysztof Hermann. Katowice: Videograf II, 2000.

PORTUGUESE

Dicionário básico de filosofia. Japiassu, Hilton, and Danilo Marcondes de Souza Filho. Rio de Janeiro: J. Zahar, 1990.

Dicionário de filosofia. Abbagnano, Nicola; translated and revised by Alfredo Bosi. São Paolo: Editôra Mestre Jou, [1970?].

Dicionário de filosofia. Ferrater Mora, José. Lisbon: Publicações Dom Quixote, 1977.

Dicionário de filosofia. Legrand, Gérard. Lisbon: Edições 70, 1991.

Dicionário de filosofia. Lobo, António. Lisbon: Paralelo Editora Limitada, 1982.

Dicionario de filosofia e ciências culturais. 4th ed. Santos, Mário Dias Ferreira dos. São Paulo: Editôra Matese, 1966.

Dicionário de filosofia portuguesa. Gomes, Jesué Pinharanda. Lisbon: Publicações Dom Quixote, 1987.

Dicionário do pensamento contemporâneo. Carrilho, Manuel Maria, João Sàágua, and Diogo Pires Aurélio. Lisbon: Publicações Dom Quixote, 1991.

Dicionário universal das idéas. Castanho, César Arruda. São Paulo: Editora Meca, [1978–1986?].

Enciclopédia filosófica. Corbisier, Roland. Petrópolis, Brazil: Editora Vozes, 1974.

Logos: enciclopédia luso-brasileira de filosofia. Lisbon: Verbo, 1989–1992.

Pequeno dicionário filosófico. Pugliesi, Márcio, and Edson Bini. [São Paulo]: Hemus, 1977.

ROMANIAN

Dictionar de filosofie Indiana. Filip, Adrian. Iaşi: Glasul Bucovinei, 1996.

Dictionar de filozofie. Apostol, Pavel. Bucharest: Editura Politica, 1978.

Dictionar de termeni filosofici ai lui Lucian Blaga: introducere prin concepte. Diaconu, Florica, and Marin Diaconu. Bucharest: Univers Enciclopedic, 2000.

Dictionar filosofic: termeni, conceptii, orientari. Bujdoiu, Nicolae. Braşov: Romprint, 2002.

Dictionarul operelor filozofice românesti. Ianosi, Ion, and Vasile N. Morar. Bucharest: Humanitas, 1997.

Mic dictionar filozofic. 2nd ed. Apostol, Pavel. Bucharest: Editura Politica, 1973.

O enciclopedie a filosofiei grecesti. Vladutescu, Gheorghe. Bucharest: Paideia, 2001.

O enciclopedie a filosofiei grecesti: filosofi, filosofii, concepte fundamentale. Vladutescu, Gheorghe. Bucharest: Paideia, 1994–.

Tratat de enciclopedia dreptului. Vallimarescu, Alexandru. Bucharest: Lumina Lex, 1999.

RUSSIAN

Bukvar': Nauka, Filosofiia, Religiia. Moscow, 2001.

Chastotnyi Anglo-Russkii Slovar'. Pod'iazyk Filosofii. Razdel "Etika i estetika." Elizarova, E. F., L. K. Chernetsovskaia, N. B. Karachan, and Leonid Pavlovich Stupin. Saint Petersburg: Izd-vo Leningradskogo universiteta, 1985.

Chelovek: Entsiklopedicheskii Slovar'. Volkov, Iurii Grigor'evich, and Vitalii Semenovich Polikarpov. Moscow: Gardariki, 1999.

Entsiklopediia vysokogo uma. Taranov, Pavel Sergeevich. Moscow: Izd-vo AST, 1997.

Filosofiin tol'. Balkhaazhav, T. Ulaanbaatar: Ulsyn Khevleliin Gazar, 1990.

Filosofskaia mysl' Vostochnykh Slavian: Biobibliograficheskii Slovar'. Ogorodnik, Ivan Vasil'evich, and Leonid Vasil'evich Guberskii. Kiev: Parlamentskoe izdatel'stvo, 1999.

Filosofskii entsiklopedicheskii slovar'. 2nd ed. Averintsev, Sergei Sergeevich. Moscow: Sov. Entsiklopediia, 1989.

Filosofskii entsiklopedicheskii slovar'. Gubskii, E. F., G. V. Korableva, and V. A. Lutchenko. Moscow: INFRA-M, 1997.

Filosofskii entsiklopedicheskii slovar'. Gubskii, E. F., G. V. Korableva, and V. A. Lutchenko. Moscow: INFRA-M, 1998.

Filosofskii entsiklopedicheskii slovar'. Il'ichev, L. F. Moscow: Sov. Entsiklopediia, 1983.

Filosofskii slovar'. 4th ed. Ado, Anatolii Vasil'evich, and Ivan Timofeevich Frolov. Moscow: Izd-vo polit. lit-ry, 1980.

Filosofskii slovar'. 5th ed. Frolov, Ivan Timofeevich, and Anatolii Vasil'evich Ado. Moscow: Izd-vo polit. lit-ry, 1986.

Filosofskii slovar'. 6th ed. Frolov, Ivan Timofeevich, and Anatolii Vasil'evich Ado. Moscow: Izd-vo polit. lit-ry, 1991.

Filosofskii slovar'. 7th ed. Frolov, Ivan Timofeevich. Moscow: Izd-vo Respublika, 2001.

Filosofskii slovar'. 2nd ed. Rozental', Mark Moiseevich, and Pavel Fedorovich Iudin. Moscow: Politizdat, 1968.

Filosofskii slovar'. 3rd ed. Rozental', Mark Moiseevich, and Pavel Fedorovich Iudin. Moscow: Politizdat, 1972.

Filosofskii slovar'. 3rd ed. Rozental', Mark Moiseevich. Moscow: Izd-vo polit. lit-ry, 1975.

Filosofskii slovar' Vladimira Solov'eva. Solov'ëv, Vladimir Sergeevich. Rostov-na-Donu: Feniks, 1997.

Filosofy Rossii XIX–XX stoletii: biografii, idei, trudy. 4th ed. Alekseev, Petr Vasil'evich. Moscow: Akademicheskii proekt, 2002.

Gita: al'ternativa vybora: entsiklopedicheskii sbornik: filosofiia, religiia, istoriia, poeziia. Kulaichev, A. P. Moscow: Trivola, 1999.

Glavnyi trud Kanta: k 200-letiiu vykhoda v svet "Kritiki chistogo razuma." Abramian, Lev Arutiunovich. Yerevan, Armenia: Izd-vo Aiastan, 1981.

Kitaiskaia filosofiia: entsiklopedicheskii slovar'. Titarenko, Mikhail Leont'evich, and Nikolai Viacheslavovich Abaev. Moscow: Mysl', 1994.

Kratkaia filosofskaia entsiklopediia. Gubskii, E. F., G. V. Korableva, and V. A. Lutchenko. Moscow: Progress, 1994.

Kratkii Anglo-Russkii filosofskii slovar. Tsarev, P. V. Moscow: Izd. Mosk. un-ta, 1969.

Kratkii filosofskii slovar'. Alekseev, Aleksandr Petrovich. Moscow: Prospekt, 1998.

Kratkii Russko-Tuvinskii filosofskii slovar'. Gavrilova, Marina Mongushevna, and Maksim Shyyrapovich Artaev. Kyzyl: Tuvinskoe knizhnoe izd-vo, 1996.

Kratkii slovar' po filosofii. Blauberg, Igor' Viktorovich, Pavel Vasil'evich Kopnin, and Igor' Konstantinovich Pantin, eds. Moscow: Izd.-vo polit. lit-ry, 1966.

Kratkii slovar' po filosofii. 2nd ed. Blauberg, Igor' Viktorovich, Pavel Vasil'evich Kopnin, and Igor' Konstantinovich Pantin, eds. Moscow: Politizdat, 1970.

Kratkii slovar' po filosofii. 3rd ed. Blauberg, Igor' Viktorovich, and Igor' Konstantinovich Pantin, eds. Moscow: Politizdat, 1979.

Kratkii slovar' po filosofii. 4th ed. Blauberg, Igor' Viktorovich, Igor' Konstantinovich Pantin, and Nikolai Ivanovich Azarov, eds. Moscow: Izd-vo polit. lit-ry, 1982.

Nemetsko-russkii i Russko-Nemetskii filosofskii slovar'. Zaitseva, Zoia Nikolaevna. Moscow: Izd-vo Moskovskogo universiteta, 1998.

Novaia filosofskaia entsiklopediia: v chetyrekh tomakh. Stepin, Viacheslav Semenovich. Moscow: Mysl', 2000–2001.

Noveishii filosofskii slovar'. 2nd ed. Gritsanov, Aleksandr Alekseevich. Minsk: Interpresservis, 2001.

Proektivnyi filosofskii slovar': novye terminy i poniatiia. Tul'chinskii, Grigorii L'vovich, and Mark Naumovich Epshtein. Saint Petersburg: Aleteiia, 2003.

Russkaia filosofiia: malyi entsiklopedicheskii slovar'. Abramov, A. I. Moscow: Nauka, 1995.

Russkaia filosofiia: slovar'. Maslin, Mikhail Aleksandrovich. Moscow: Izd-vo Respublika, 1995.

Russkaia filosofiia: slovar'. Maslin, Mikhail Aleksandrovich. Moscow: Terra, 1999.

Russkie filosofy: spravochnik. Kornilov, Sergei Vladimirovich. Saint Petersburg: Lan', 2001.

Russkie mysliteli vtoroi poloviny XIX-nachala XX veka: opyt kratkogo biobibliograficheskogo Slovaria. Emel'ianov, Boris Vladimirovich, and Viacheslav Vladimirovich Kulikov. Yekaterinburg: Izd-vo Ural'skogo universiteta, 1996.

Russko-Kirgizskii slovar' geograficheskikh terminov. Amaniliev, Batyrbek. Bishkek, Kyrgyzstan: Ilim, 1967.

Slovar'. Kruglov, Aleksandr. Moscow: Gnosis, 1994–.

Slovar'-spravochnik "Chelovek i obshchestvo": Filosofiia: dlia uchashchikhsia vsekh form srednei stupeni obrazovaniia. Korotets, I. D., L. A. Shtompel', and O. M. Shtompel'. Rostov-na-Donu: Feniks, 1996.

Sovremennaia filosofiia: slovar' i khrestomatiia. Zharov, L. V. Rostov-na-Donu: Feniks, 1995.

Sovremennaia zapadnaia filosofiia: slovar'. Lektorskii, V. A., V. S. Malakhov, and Vladimir Petrovich Filatov. Moscow: Izd-vo polit. lit-ry, 1991.

Sovremennaia zapadnaia filosofiia: slovar'. 2nd ed. Malakhov, V. S., and Vladimir Petrovich Filatov. Moscow: TON, 2000.

Sovremennyi filosofskii slovar'. Kemerov, Viacheslav Evgen'evich. Moscow: Izd-vo Odissei, 1996.

Sovremennyi filosofskii slovar'. 2nd ed. Kemerov, Viacheslav Evgen'evich, and S. N. Dergachev. London: Izd-vo Panprint, 1998.

Sovremennyi filosofskii slovar'. 3rd ed. Kemerov, Viacheslav Evgen'evich. Moscow: Akademicheskii proekt, 2004.

Sto Russkikh filosofov: biograficheskii slovar'. Sukhov, Andrei Dmitrievich. Moscow: Mirta, 1995.

Sto sueverii: kratkii filosofskii slovar' predrassudkov. Bochenski, Joseph M. Moscow: Progress, 1993.

Velikie filosofy: slovar'-spravochnik. 2nd ed. Blinnikov, Leontii Vasil'evich. Moscow: Logos, 1997.

SPANISH

Breve diccionario de filosofía. Müller, Max, and Alois Halder. Barcelona: Editorial Herder, 1976.

Breve diccionario de filosofía. Müller, Max, and Alois Halder. Barcelona: Editorial Herder, 1986.

Breve diccionario filosófico. 2nd ed. Quintanilla, Miguel A. Navarra, Spain: EVD, 1996.

Breve vocabulario filosófico. Salazar Bondy, Augusto. Lima: [Editoral Universo], 1967.

Breve vocabulario filosófico. 3rd ed. Salazar Bondy, Augusto. Lima: Editoral Arica, 1974.

Conceptos fundamentales de filosofía. Krings, Hermann, Hans Michael Baumgartner, and Christoph Wild. Barcelona: Editorial Herder, 1977–1979.

Diccionario básico de filosofía. Lorenzo Lizalde, Carlos, and Andrés Plumed Allueva. Zaragoza: Mira Editores, 1992.

Diccionario bio-bibliográfico de filósofos. Menchaca, José A. Bilbao: El Mensajero del Corazón de Jesús, 1966–.

Diccionario de escuelas de pensamiento o ismos. Arroyo Fernández, Miguel. Madrid: Alderabán, 1997.

Diccionario de filosofía. Moscow: Editorial Progreso, 1984.

Diccionario de filosofia. 2nd ed. Abbagnano, Nicola. Mexico: Fondo de Cultura Económica, 1966.

Diccionario de filosofía. 2nd ed., rev. Abbagnano, Nicola. Mexico: Fondo de Cultura Económica, 1974.

Diccionario de filosofía. 2nd Spanish ed. Abbagnano, Nicola. Mexico: Fondo de Cultura Económica, 1980.

Diccionario de filosofía. Albornoz, Hernán. Valencia, Venezuela: Vadell Hermanos Editores, 1990.

Diccionario de filosofía. Blauberg, Igor' Viktorovich. Mexico, D.F.: Quinto Sol, 1986.

Diccionario de filosofía. 2nd ed. Brugger, Walter, ed. Barcelona: Editorial Herder, 1969.

Diccionario de filosofía. 10th ed. Brugger, Walter, ed. Barcelona: Editorial Herder, 1983.

Diccionario de filosofía. Durozoi, Gérard, and André Roussel. Barcelona: Editorial Teide, 1994.

Diccionario de filosofía. 5th ed. Ferrater Mora, José. Buenos Aires: Editorial Sudamericana, 1965.

Diccionario de filosofía. 6th ed. Ferrater Mora, José. Madrid: Alianza, 1979.

Diccionario de filosofía. Rev. ed. Ferrater Mora, José, and Josep-Maria Terricabras. Barcelona: Editorial Ariel, 1994.

Diccionario de filosofía. González García, Juan Carlos. [Madrid]: Edaf, 2000.

Diccionario de filosofía. 2nd ed. Herrera, Hermogenes. Quito: Santo Domingo, 1968.

Diccionario de filosofía. Julia, Didier. Mexico: Diana, 1983.

Diccionario de filosofía. Rozental', Mark Moiseevich, and Pavel Iudin. Madrid: Akal, 1975.

Diccionario de filosofia. Runes, Dagobert David. Barcelona: Ediciones Grijalbo, 1969.

Diccionario de filosofía. 7th ed. Runes, Dagobert David. Mexico: Editorial Grijalbo, 1981.

Diccionario de filosofía, abreviado. Ferrater Mora, José. Buenos Aires: Sudamericana, 1970.

Diccionario de filosofía abreviado. 2nd ed. Ferrater Mora, José. Buenos Aires: Editorial Sudamericana, 1972.

Diccionario de filosofía abreviado. Ferrater Mora, José, Eduardo García Belsunce, and Ezequiel de Olaso. Barcelona: EDHASA-Sudamericana, 1976.

Diccionario de filosofía abreviado. 3rd ed. Ferrater Mora, José, Eduardo García Belsunce, and Ezequiel de Olaso. Barcelona: EDHASA-Sudamericana, 1978.

Diccionario de filosofía abreviado. 5th ed. Ferrater Mora, José, Eduardo García Belsunce, and Ezequiel de Olaso. Barcelona: EDHASA; Buenos Aires: Sudamericana, 1980.

Diccionario de filosofía abreviado. 19th ed. Ferrater Mora, José, Eduardo García Belsunce, and Ezequiel de Olaso. Buenos Aires: Editorial Sudamericana, 1991.

Diccionario de filosofía abreviado. 24th ed. Ferrater Mora, José, Eduardo García Belsunce, and Ezequiel de Olaso. Buenos Aires: Editorial Sudamericana, 2002.

Diccionario de filosofía abreviado. 25th ed. Ferrater Mora, José, Eduardo García Belsunce, and Ezequiel de Olaso. Buenos Aires: Editorial Sudamericana, 2004.

Diccionario de filosofía: con autores y temas latinoamericanos. Bogotá: Editorial El Buho, 1986.

Diccionario de filosofía: con autores y temas latinoamericanos. 2nd ed. Bogotá: Editorial El Buho, 1994.

Diccionario de filosofía contemporánea. Quintanilla, Miguel A. Salamanca: Sígueme, 1976.

Diccionario de filosofía contemporánea. 2nd ed. Quintanilla, Miguel A. Salamanca: Sígueme, 1979.

Diccionario de filosofía de bolsillo. Ferrater Mora, José, and Priscilla Cohn. Madrid: Alianza, 1983.

Diccionario de filosofia de bolsillo. Ferrater Mora, Jose, and Priscilla Cohn. Madrid: Alianza, 2001.

Diccionario de filosofía: ilustrado: autores contemporáneos, lógica, filosofía del lenguaje. 3rd ed. Martínez Echeverri, Leonor, and Hugo Martínez Echeverri. Santa Fe de Bogotá, Colombia: Panamericana Editorial, 1998.

Diccionario de filosofía: ilustrado: autores contemporáneos, lógica, filosofía del lenguaje. 4th ed. Martínez Echeverri, Leonor, and Hugo Martínez Echeverri. Bogotá: Panamericana Editorial, 2000.

Diccionario de filosofía: ilustrado: autores contemporáneos, lógica, filosofía del lenguaje. 6th ed. Martínez Echeverri, Leonor, and Hugo Martínez Echeverri. Bogotá: Panamericana Editorial, 2000.

Diccionario de filosofía latinoamericana. Cerutti Guldberg, Horacio, Mario Magallón Anaya, Isaías Palacios Contreras, María del Rayo Ramírez Fierro, and Sandra Escutia Díaz. Toluca, Mexico: Universidad Autónoma del Estado de México, 2000.

Diccionario de filosofía oriental. Wolpin, Samuel. Buenos Aires: Kier, 1993.

Diccionario de filosofía: seguido de un cuadro histórico de las escuelas de filosofía. Jolivet, Régis. Buenos Aires: Club de lectores, 1978.

Diccionario de filosofía y sociología marxista. Iudin, Pavel, ed. Buenos Aires: Editorial Seneca, 1965.

Diccionario de filósofos. Centro de Estudios Filosóficos de Gallarte. Madrid: Ediciones Rioduero, 1986.

Diccionario de grandes filósofos, 2: (K–Z). Ferrater Mora, José. Madrid: Alianza, 2002.

Diccionario de las mil obras clave del pensamiento. Huisman, Denis. Madrid: Tecnos, 1997.

Diccionario del lenguaje filosófico. Foulquié, Paul. Barcelona: Editorial Labor, 1967.

Diccionario del lenguaje filosófico, dirigido. Foulquié, Paul. Barcelona: Editorial Labor, 1967.

Diccionario de pensamiento contemporáneo. Moreno Villa, Mariano. Madrid: San Pablo, 1997.

Diccionario de términos filosóficos. Robert, François, and José Manuel Revuelta. Madrid: Acento, 1994.

Diccionario filosófico. Ezcurdia Hijar, Agustín, and Pedro Chávez Calderón. Mexico: Limusa: Noriega Editores, 1994.

Diccionario filosófico. Hernández, Pablo María. [Dominican Republic: Universidad Autónoma de Santo Domingo], 1982.

Diccionario filosófico. 2nd ed. Hernández, Pablo María. [Dominican Republic: Universidad Autónoma de Santo Domingo], 1984.

Diccionario filosófico. Rozental', Mark Moiseevich, and Pavel Fedorovich Iudin, eds. Montevideo: Ediciones Pueblos Unidos, 1965.

Diccionario filosófico. Rozental', Mark Moiseevich, and Pavel Fedorovich Iudin, eds. [Argentina]: Ediciones Universo, 1973.

Diccionario filosófico. Rozental', Mark Moiseevich. [Havana]: Edición Revolucionaria, 1984.

Diccionario filosófico. Savater, Fernando. Barcelona: Planeta, 1995.

Diccionario filosófico. 2nd ed. Savater, Fernando. Barcelona: Planeta, 1999.

Diccionario filosófico abreviado. Rev. ed. Rozental', Mark Moiseevich, and Pavel Fedorovich Iudin. Mexico: Ediciones Quinto Sol, [1970–1979?].

Diccionario filosófico: manual de materialismo filosófico: una introducción analítica. García Sierra, Pelayo, and Gustavo Bueno. Oviedo: Fundación Gustavo Bueno, 2000.

Diccionario marxista de filosofía. Blauberg, Igor' Viktorovich, ed. Mexico: Ediciones de Cultura Popular, 1979.

Enciclopedia concisa de filosofía y filósofos. Urmson, J. O. Madrid: Cátedra, 1979.

Enciclopedia concisa de filosofía y filósofos. 2nd ed. Urmson, J. O. Madrid: Cátedra, 1982.

Enciclopedia concisa de filosofía y filósofos. 3rd ed. Urmson, J. O. Madrid: Cátedra, 1994.

Enciclopedia de la filosofía. Barcelona: Ediciones B, 1992.

La filosofía: las ideas, las obras, los hombres. Noiray, André, ed. Bilbao: Ediciones Mensajero, 1974.

Filosofía y religión. Madrid, 1991.

Los filósofos. Aubral, François. Madrid: Acento Editorial, 1994.

Grandes profecías. Madrid: Nueva Lente, 1986.

Invitación a la fenomenología. Husserl, Edmund. Barcelona: Paidós, 1992.

Léxico filosófico. Millán-Puelles, Antonio. Madrid: Rialp, 1984.

Nueva enciclopedia temática Planeta: arte y filosofá. Gutiérrez Ducóns, Juan Luis, and Javier Sánchez Almazán. Barcelona: Planeta, 1993.

Pequeña filosofía para no filósofos. Jacquard, Albert, and Huguette Planès. Mexico, D.F.: Debolsillo/Random House Mondadori, 2004.

Vocabulario técnico y crítico de la filosofía. 2nd ed. Lalande, André. Buenos Aires: El Ateneo, 1967.

UKRAINIAN

Anhlo-ukraïns'kyi filosofs'kyi slovnyk. Polishchuk, Nina Pavlovna, and Vasyl Semenovych Lisovy. Kiev: Lybid', 1996.

Filosofs'ka dumka v Ukraïni: biobibliohrafichnyi slovnyk. Tkachuk, Maryna, and Vilen Serhiiovych Hors'kyi. Kiev: Pul'sary, 2002.

Filosofs'kyi entsyklopedychnyi slovnyk. Shinkaruk, Vladimir Illarionovich. Kiev: Abrys, 2002.

Filosofs'kyi slovnyk. Shinkaruk, Vladimir Illarionovich. Kiev: Gol. Red. Ukraïns'koï Rad. Entsyklopediï, 1973.

Filosofs'kyi slovnyk. 2nd ed. Shinkaruk, Vladimir Illarionovich. Kiev: Gol. Red. Ukraïns'koï Rad. Entsyklopediï, 1986.

Michael J. Farmer (2005)

PHILOSOPHY JOURNALS

The learned journal was one of the major cultural innovations of the seventeenth century. Of the pioneering scholarly journals inaugurated during that century, the earliest one that regularly presented philosophical material is, remarkably, still being published, but, unhappily for our story, it now deals mainly with philology and related fields. This patriarch of professional periodicals, 300 years old and still lively, is the *Journal des savants* (Paris, 1665–), issued quarterly, with variations. The title was *Journal des sçavans* from 1665 to 1792. Publication was suspended from 1797 to 1816. The journal was devoted originally to book reviews, bibliographies, and news notes on philosophy, science, and literature.

In the same century similar learned journals, commenting on new books in philosophy and other fields, were issued for various periods in a number of cultural centers besides Paris. Indeed, on October 22, 1668, Leibniz wrote to Emperor Leopold I, taking note of the fact that the rival French nation had inaugurated the *Journal des sçavans* and declaring that Germany needed a similar medium of intellectual communication; Leibniz asked for a license to issue such a periodical, and the issuance of *Acta Eruditorum* beginning some 14 years later (see below) may have been the result. Prominent among the early learned journals issued outside of France which covered philosophy among other subjects were:

1668–1690. *Giornale de'letterati* (Parma), monthly. Suspended 1679–1686. Periodicals with the same title were also published in other Italian cities, including Rome, for various periods.

1681–1683. *Weekly Memorials for the Ingenious* (London), weekly.

1684–1718. *Nouvelles de la république des lettres* (Amsterdam), originally issued monthly, later issued six times a year. Founded by Pierre Bayle during his exile from France and edited by him from 1684 to 1687. Suspended 1689–1698 and 1711–1715.

1688–1690. *Freymüthige lustige und ernsthaffte Monats-Gespräche* (Halle), monthly.

In Latin, philosophical and other material appeared in *Acta Eruditorum* (Leipzig, 1682–1776), issued monthly. The title was *Nova Acta Eruditorum* from 1732 to 1776. This periodical, founded by Otto Mencke, Leibniz' friend, contained many contributions by and about Leibniz, and some authorities even say it was founded by Leibniz; he probably at least had a hand in Mencke's establishment of it. In this vehicle Leibniz first gave the world his notions respecting the differential calculus, and in it raged the controversy, beginning in 1699, over whether Leibniz or Newton first discovered the principles of the calculus.

Beginning in the eighteenth century a number of learned journals were devoted exclusively or largely to philosophy. These were the earliest instances of philosophical journals in a strict sense.

DEFINITION OF A PHILOSOPHICAL JOURNAL. A philosophical journal, for the purposes of this article, is a publication that fulfills the following criteria:

(1) It is devoted to the whole field of philosophy (and nothing else) or, more narrowly, to a part of the field of philosophy (for example, symbolic logic or Thomism) or, more broadly, to the whole field of philosophy plus one or two other fields of interest (philosophy and psychology, philosophy and theology, and so forth). The specification "part of the field of philosophy" is taken strictly, thereby excluding philosophy of education and pure theosophy, but it includes political and social philosophy. Magazines of popular philosophy or popular morals—such as Addison and Steele's *Spectator* (founded 1710), *Der Leipziger Diogenes* (founded 1723), and *Der Dresdnische Philosoph* (founded 1737)—are excluded. Student journals, such as the *Graduate Review of Philosophy* (Minneapolis), are also excluded. One theosophical journal, however, *The Aryan Path*, which contains many strictly philosophical articles, is included here.

(2) It is issued at stipulated intervals of less than a year. Thus, the intent reader will notice that this account

does not mention bibliographical yearbooks, annual collections of studies, annual proceedings of philosophical societies, or irregular collections of articles (such as the quasi journal *Polemic*, of which eight issues were published at London at irregular intervals, from 1945 to 1947). In a few cases, however, a publication which, although it had no stipulated frequency, was actually issued (say) four times a year for a period of years, is counted as a regular journal.

(3) It has survived longer than a year. This requirement leads to the exclusion of, for example, *Symposion; Philosophische Zeitschrift für Forschung und Aussprache* (Erlangen), edited by Ernst Cassirer, Hans Driesch, and others, since only four issues were published, in 1926. In the case of periodicals inaugurated just prior to the completion of this article, however, the requirement of more than a year's duration is relaxed.

Strict adherence to the second criterion listed above has led to the exclusion of at least one vitally important medium of philosophical discussion—*Proceedings of the Aristotelian Society* (London), issued annually (referred to in this Encyclopedia as *PAS*). Since its founding in 1891 this periodical has presented numerous important articles, including papers by Bertrand Russell, Gilbert Ryle, J. L. Austin, Ludwig Wittgenstein, G. E. Moore, and many others.

In our account of significant journals devoted to the whole of philosophy, we have attempted to be comprehensive. It is probable, however, that a considerable number of obscure, though worthy, journals have slipped through the net and that on these strict criteria a few borderline semiprofessional journals are omitted which may have merited inclusion. Therefore, the statistics offered from time to time in this article (for example, that so many journals originated in a certain period) are based on its author's particular standards and should be taken as approximate. For fairly complete details about philosophical journals devoted to the whole of philosophy which are still being issued, the reader is referred to the *International Directory of Philosophy and Philosophers*, edited by Gilbert Varet and Paul Kurtz (New York, 1966).

For journals devoted to a part of philosophy or to philosophy and other disciplines, the present list is definitely incomplete. For example, there have been over a hundred theological journals, past and present, but only some fifty are mentioned as outstanding examples.

Regarding each journal mentioned in this article, four facts are ordinarily presented: the year it began publication (and, if it is no longer issued, its last year of publication), its title, its place of publication, and the frequency of its issuance. Other facts, such as historic figures who were editors, periods of suspension, and changes of title, are sometimes noted, but these additions are illustrative rather than complete.

In the case of journals that have changed their titles, the latest title is usually given as the main entry, and earlier titles are noted. Where one journal has succeeded another with some definite contact or relationship between them, they are considered as a single journal with a changed title. Thus, *Ratio* is considered as continuous with its earlier incarnation and appears below as one of the two oldest living philosophical journals.

In several instances some outstanding articles that the periodicals have published or striking facts about their influence in the philosophical world are set forth. Other periodicals, such as *Philosophy* (1926–), *Voprosy Filosofii* (1947–), and some German and Italian periodicals, could also have been appropriately singled out for such an exposition, had space permitted.

STATISTICAL CONSPECTUS. From the eighteenth century to the present, approximately 70 philosophical journals have been born with more or less fanfare, have survived for a period, and have given up the ghost. About 180 others, however, are still alive, some flourishing, some bravely keeping their heads above water, some pitifully gasping for breath.

Of the philosophical journals published today, two are more than a century old, and four others are over 90 years old; their average life span, however, is about 28 years. Of those which no longer exist, the longest-lived at the time of its death was 81 years old: the *Zeitschrift für Philosophie und philosophische Kritik*, founded by the younger Fichte in 1837 and discontinued in 1918.

More births of philosophical journals occurred in the 1950s (55) and the 1940s (49) than in any other decades, but likewise more deaths of philosophical journals occurred in the 1950s (19) and the 1940s (17) than in any other decades. During World War I about 12 per cent of the philosophical journals in existence in 1914 ended their lives; during World War II about 15 per cent of those in existence in 1939 were terminated.

EARLY JOURNALS

EARLY QUASI JOURNALS. Publications devoted to philosophy that were intended to be issued from time to time (more than once a year) but not at uniform intervals may be denominated "quasi journals of philosophy" since they do not conform to the requirement of a set frequency of issuance. A number of these quasi journals came into being from about 1715 on, especially in Germany, and lasted for varying periods. The following may serve as examples:

1715–1726. *Acta Philosophorum* (Halle). In German. Covered books on the history of philosophy. Probably the earliest quasi journal of philosophy.

1741–1744. *Philosophische Büchersaal* (Leipzig). Eight issues were published.

1789–1790. *Neues philosophisches Magazin; Erläuterungen und Anwendungen des Kantischen Systems bestimmt* (Leipzig). Two volumes, each with four issues, appeared.

1790–1850. Of seven genuine philosophical journals that saw the light before 1850, two—the *Theologische Quartalschrift* and *Ratio*—still survive, but the continuity of *Ratio* with its origin is tenuous. Chronologically, the seven pre-1850 journals fall into two groups. Those in the first group are:

1794–1807. *Revue philosophique, littéraire et politique* (Paris), issued three times a month, with variations. Title was *Décade philosophique, littéraire et politique* from 1794 to 1804 and became *Revue, ou Décade philosophique* late in 1804. Merged in 1808 with the *Mercure de France* (Paris, 1672–1820) and at that point may be considered to have lost its standing as a philosophical journal.

1795–1800. *Philosophisches Journal einer Gesellschaft teutscher Gelehrten* (Neustrelitz, 1795–1796; Jena and Leipzig, 1797–1800), monthly. J. G. Fichte was coeditor from 1797 to 1800. An article that Fichte published in the *Journal* in 1798 regarding the grounds of our belief in a divine government of the universe (defining God as the moral order of the universe) caused a cry of atheism to be raised and led to the suppression of the *Journal* in all the German states except Prussia, as well as to Fichte's resignation in 1799 from his teaching position at the University of Jena (see Atheismusstreit).

1802–1803. *Kritisches Journal der Philosophie* (Tübingen), issued five times in 1802 and once in 1803. Editors, F. W. J. von Schelling and G. W. F. Hegel. Included a number of articles by Hegel.

1819–. *Theologische Quartalschrift* (Tübingen; later Ravensburg; now Stuttgart), quarterly. Suspended 1945.

The following journals belong to the second pre-1850 group:

1832–1852. *Zeitschrift für Philosophie und katholische Theologie* (Cologne, 1832–1836; Coblenz, 1836–1839; Cologne, 1840–1841; Bonn, 1842–1852), quarterly, with variations.

1837–1918. *Zeitschrift für Philosophie und philosophische Kritik; Vormals Fichte-Ulricische Zeitschrift* (Bonn, 1837–1842; Tübingen, 1843–1846; Halle, 1847–1890; Leipzig, 1891–1918), quarterly, with variations. Title was *Zeitschrift für Philosophie und spekulative Theologie*, from 1837 to 1846; subtitle varied. Founded by I. H. von Fichte (son of J. G. Fichte); later edited by him and Hermann Ulrici. Supported Christian and Hegelian views.

1847–. *Ratio* (Oxford and Frankfurt; formerly Göttingen), semiannual, with variations. Title was *Abhandlungen der Fries'schen Schule* from 1847 to 1936. Suspended 1850–1903, 1915–1917, 1919–1928, and 1937–1956. Now issued in English and German editions.

1850–1900. Of the decades from 1850 to 1899, the first produced 1 new journal of philosophy, the second and third a total of 11, and the fourth and fifth a total of 19. The lone philosophical journal born in the 1850s was *La Revue philosophique et religieuse* (Paris, 1850–1858), issued monthly.

The 1860s. In the 1860s seven philosophical journals were begun—three in Germany and one each in Belgium, France, Switzerland, and the United States. The first four journals to appear in this decade, including the first English-language journal of philosophy, are now defunct.

1861–1914. *Zeitschrift für Philosophie und Pädagogik* (Leipzig; later Langensalza), monthly, with variations. Title was *Zeitschrift für exakte Philosophie im Sinne des neuern philosophischen Realismus* (and the journal was, for the most part, a quarterly) from 1861 to 1896; suspended 1876–1882. Merged in 1896 with the *Zeitschrift für Philosophie und Pädagogik*, which had been issued since 1894; the combined publication took the title of the latter *Zeitschrift*.

1862–1864. *Athenäum; Philosophische Zeitschrift* (Munich), quarterly.

1867–1913. *L'Année philosophique* (Paris), issued annually and therefore not a "periodical" in the required sense, from 1867 to 1869 and again from 1890 to 1913, but it was a weekly (with variations) from 1872 to 1885 and a monthly from 1885 to 1889. Title was *La Critique philosophique* when the publication was issued weekly or monthly, from 1872 to 1889. C. B. Renouvier was a coeditor from 1890 to 1900.

1867–1893. *Journal of Speculative Philosophy* (St. Louis, Mo., 1867–1880; New York, 1880–1893), quarterly, with variations. Apparently the first philosophical journal in the English language. Founded by William T. Harris. Organ of the St. Louis Philosophical Society. Served as the vehicle for the first published writings of James, Royce, and Dewey. Its motto was "Philosophy can bake no bread, but she can procure for us God, freedom, and immortality."

The three philosophical journals of this period which have survived are German, Swiss, and Belgian, respectively:

1868–. *Archiv für Geschichte der Philosophie* (Berlin; previously Leipzig and Heidelberg), quarterly, with variations. Title was *Philosophische Monatshefte* from 1868 to 1887, *Archiv für Geschichte der Philosophie* from 1888 to 1894, *Archiv für Philosophie* from 1895 to 1926 (in this period the periodical was issued in two parts, *Archiv für Geschichte der Philosophie* and *Archiv für systematische Philosophie*), title was *Archiv für Philosophie und Soziologie* from 1927 to 1930 (again issued in two parts, *Archiv für Geschichte der Philosophie und Soziologie* and *Archiv für systematische Philosophie und Soziologie*), title reverted to *Archiv für Geschichte der Philosophie* in 1931; suspended 1933–1959. Original editor was Ludwig Stein, with the collaboration of Hermann Diels, Wilhelm Dilthey, Benno Erdmann, and Eduard Zeller. Paul Natorp became coeditor of the combined publication in 1895 and editor of the systematic part. Has contained articles in English, French, German, and Italian since 1895.

1868–. *Revue de théologie et de philosophie* (Lausanne), issued six times a year from 1868 to 1920, quarterly since 1921. Title has varied.

1869–. *Nouvelle Revue théologique* (Louvain, Belgium), monthly. A Jesuit organ.

THE 1870S. The 1870s are remembered as the decade which produced the *Revue philosophique de la France et de l'étranger and Mind.* However, two other journals were inaugurated during the decade:

1870–. *Rivista di filosofia* (Turin; previously Bologna-Modena, Florence, Forli, Genoa, Pavia, Rome, and Milan), quarterly, with variations. Title was *La filosofia delle scuole italiane* (Florence; then Rome), 1870–1885; title was *Rivista italiana di filosofia* (Rome) from 1886 to 1898; became two separate periodicals, *Rivista di filosofia e scienze affini* (Bologna), 1899–1908, and *Rivista filosofica* (Pavia), 1899–1908; combined under the title *Rivista di filosofia* in 1909. Suspended 1922. In 1963 it absorbed *Il pensiero critico,* a quarterly published at Milan since 1950.

1877–1916. *Vierteljahrsschrift für wissenschaftliche Philosophie und Soziologie* (Leipzig), quarterly. Title was *Vierteljahrsschrift für wissenschaftliche Philosophie* from 1877 to 1901. Coeditors at various times included Richard Avenarius, Ernst Mach, and Wilhelm Wundt.

"Revue Philosophique." The *Revue philosophique de la France et de l'étranger* (Paris, 1876–) was originally issued monthly and later issued six times a year; it is now issued quarterly. The *Revue*'s first editor, Théodule Ribot, served for 40 years, until his death in 1916. Under his direction the *Revue* gave primary emphasis to articles on psychology. Philosophy began to gain predominance under Ribot's successor, Lucien Lévy-Bruhl, who was also a long-lived editor, conducting the periodical for 23 years until his death in 1939. The editors in succeeding years, when philosophy was fully established as the main arena of discussion in the *Revue,* were Émile Bréhier and Paul Masson-Oursel (1940–1952), Masson-Oursel and Pierre-Maxime Schuhl (1952–1956), and Schuhl alone (since 1956).

Even now the *Revue*'s strongest contribution is represented not so much by publication of original hypotheses as by careful analysis and criticism of old and new viewpoints. Useful articles, for example, have been published on Leibniz, Hume, and English linguistic philosophy. An entire issue was devoted to Lévy-Bruhl in 1957 on the one hundredth anniversary of his birth. The coverage of philosophy "de l'étranger" has consisted in large part of some translations from English and German, extensive critical reviews of books, and summaries of periodical articles.

Among the more original contributions in the *Revue* have been C. S. Peirce's "La Logique de la science" (1878–1879), Étienne Gilson's "Essai sur la vie intérieure" (1920), Raymond Ruyer's "Ce qui est vivant et ce qui est mort dans la matérialisme" (1933), and Georges Gurvich's "Le Problème de la sociologie de la connaissance" (1957–1958). Famous contributors have included Rudolf

Hermann Lotze, Herbert Spencer, J. S. Mill, Wilhelm Wundt, Henri Bergson, and Georges Sorel.

"Mind." *Mind; A Quarterly Review of Psychology and Philosophy* (originally London, later Edinburgh, now Oxford, 1876–), is issued quarterly.

In 1874 Alexander Bain broached the idea of establishing the first British philosophical journal to his pupil George C. Robertson, who suggested the title *Mind.* Bain appointed Robertson editor and supported the journal financially, sinking almost £3,000 into it in 15 years, until Robertson resigned in 1891.

Robertson, on laying down his mantle as editor, lamented that the journal had attracted more attention from "the lay student" than from those "whose regular business is with Philosophy." G. F. Stout, when he succeeded Robertson in 1892, wrote that "what is of prime importance is that our pages shall be filled with genuine work to the exclusion of merely dilettante productions." The implication here is curious when one considers that among the contributors to *Mind* during Robertson's stewardship were philosophers of the caliber of Samuel Alexander, A. W. Benn, Bernard Bosanquet, F. H. Bradley, T. H. Green, William James, C. Lloyd Morgan, Hastings Rashdall, Josiah Royce, Henry Sidgwick, and John Venn.

Sidgwick, who succeeded Bain as the financial "angel" of *Mind*, died in 1900. It was then that, pursuant to a suggestion made by Sidgwick in 1899, the Mind Association was formed (with Edward Caird as the first president) to support the journal. Meanwhile, G. E. Moore and Bertrand Russell had published their earliest contributions in *Mind* in the 1890s, and the periodical was well on its way to becoming what it is now, one of the dozen most influential journals of philosophy in the world. Stout relinquished the editorship in 1920; his successors were Moore, 1921–1947, and Gilbert Ryle since 1948.

Over the decades *Mind* has published many highly influential articles, such as Moore's "The Refutation of Idealism" (1903), Russell's "On Denoting" (1905), and H. A. Prichard's "Does Moral Philosophy Rest on a Mistake?" (1912). During Moore's editorship the journal set a particularly high standard, publishing such papers as W. T. Stace's "The Refutation of Realism" (1934), A. J. Ayer's "Demonstration of the Impossibility of Metaphysics" (1934), C. L. Stevenson's "Persuasive Definitions" (1938), Norman Malcolm's "Are Necessary Propositions Really Verbal?" (1940), John Wisdom's eight articles entitled "Other Minds" (1940–1943), and Frederick Will's "Will the Future Be Like the Past?" (1947). More recently (under Ryle's editorship), *Mind* has presented such important articles as J. N. Findlay's "Can God's Existence Be Disproved?" (1948), R. M. Hare's "Imperative Sentences" (1949), Paul Edwards' "Bertrand Russell's Doubts About Induction" (1949), P. F. Strawson's "On Referring" (1950), A. J. Ayer's "Individuals" (1952), G. E. M. Anscombe's "Aristotle and the Sea Battle" (1956), Nelson Goodman's "About" (1961), and many papers—written by Wittgenstein's disciples—that helped to establish Wittgenstein's reputation before the posthumous publication of his books.

A public controversy occurred when *Mind* declined to publish a review of Ernest Gellner's *Words and Things* (London, 1959), which was critical of the ordinary-language school. Bertrand Russell, in a letter to the London *Times*, on November 5, 1959, protested against *Mind*'s decision.

Ryle's policy as editor has been to give some preference to philosophers who have not previously appeared in print. This policy, while testifying to the kindness of the editor and his concern for providing needed encouragement to tomorrow's leading spirits, has made it difficult to maintain the Olympian level of quality to which readers became accustomed during Moore's period as editor.

THE 1880S. Of the nine journals of philosophy generated in the 1880s, five are still functioning, *The Monist* being perhaps the best known. One of the nine, among the oldest Italian philosophical journals, is *Divus Thomas*; another, a Swiss product, has had *Divus Thomas* as its subtitle or (for a time) as its main title. Japan and Russia gave birth to journals of philosophy in this decade, and the Japanese entry is still in the field.

American and British. Paul Carus was associated with two of the three English-language journals begun in this decade.

1886–1915. *Review of Theology and Philosophy* (Edinburgh), quarterly. Title was *Theological Review and Free Church College Quarterly* from 1886 to 1890 and *Critical Review of Theological and Philosophical Literature* from 1890 to 1904.

1887–1936. *The Open Court* (Chicago), issued every other week from 1887 to 1888; weekly from 1888 to 1896; monthly from 1897 to 1933; quarterly from 1934 to 1936. Successor to *The Index* (published weekly at Toledo, Ohio, and later at Boston, 1870–1886), organ of the Free Religious Association. *The Open Court* was founded by Paul Carus. Devoted to the establishment of ethics and religion on a scientific basis, it was more clearly a philosophical journal than was *The Index.*

1888–. *The Monist; An International Journal of General Philosophical Inquiry* (La Salle, Ill.; previously Chicago), quarterly. Suspended 1937–1963. International editorial board. Each issue now devoted to a specific topic. Edited by Paul Carus from 1888 to his death in 1919. Contributors have included Peirce, Dewey, Bosanquet, and Russell.

European. Two of the journals first issued in the 1880s are products of Italy and two are German-language publications.

1880–. *Divus Thomas; Commentarium de Philosophia et Theologia* (Piacenza), issued six times a year. Articles in English, French, Italian, and Latin. Suspended 1906–1923.

1881–1900. *Rivista speciale di opere di filosofia scientifica* (Milan), monthly. Title was *Rivista di filosofia scientifica* from 1881 to 1891.

1886–. *Freiburger Zeitschrift für Philosophie und Theologie* (Fribourg, Switzerland), quarterly, with variations. Title was *Jahrbuch für Philosophie und spekulative Theologie* (Paderborn; later Vienna) from 1886 to 1922, with the subtitle *Divus Thomas* from 1914 to 1922; title was *Divus Thomas* from 1923 to 1953.

1888–. *Philosophisches Jahrbuch* (Munich; previously Fulda), semiannual, with variations. Title has varied. Catholic-oriented.

Japanese and Russian. The Japanese journal begun in the 1880s is still being issued. The Russian journal, *Voprosy Filosofii i Psikhologii,* died in 1917, but a new *Voprosy Filosofii,* as will be noted later, arose from its ashes 30 years later, in 1947.

1887–. *Tetsugaku Zasshi; Journal of Philosophy* (Tokyo), quarterly, with variations. Journal of the Philosophical Society of Tokyo University. Titles of articles in English.

1889–1917. *Voprosy Filosofii i Psikhologii* (Moscow), issued six times a year by the Moskovskoe Psikhologicheskoe Obshchestvo.

THE 1890S. The 1890s constituted the fertile decade of *Ethics* and *The Philosophical Review,* of the *Revue de métaphysique et de morale,* of the *Revue philosophique de Louvain,* and of *Kant-Studien,* all of which are on the scene today, plus the oldest Indian and Polish philosophical journals, which also continue to appear.

Louvain was the parent of a pair of French-language journals, both flourishing today:

1894–. *Revue philosophique de Louvain* (Louvain), quarterly. Founded by Cardinal Mercier. Published by the Société Philosophique de Louvain. Neo-Scholastic. Suspended 1915–1918 and 1941–1944. Title was *Revue néo-scolastique* from 1894 to 1910, *Revue néo-scolastique de philosophie* from 1910 to 1933, and *Revue néoscolastique de philosophie* from 1934 to 1945. A *Répertoire bibliographique* has been published as an adjunct of the *Revue* since 1895; since 1938 it has been published separately, and since 1949 it has been administratively separate. Some articles in English; others in French with English summaries.

1895–. *Répertoire bibliographique de la philosophie* (Louvain), quarterly. Title was *Sommaire idéologique des ouvrages et des revues de philosophie* (with variations) from 1895 to 1914. Suspended 1915–1933 and 1941–1945. Reproduced *in toto,* with Dutch headings, in the *Tijdschrift voor Filosofie* (Louvain, 1939–).

Two of the journals that started publication in the 1890s have ethics as their subject matter, ethics alone in one case and ethics plus metaphysics in the other:

1890–. *Ethics; An International Journal of Social, Political and Legal Philosophy* (Chicago), quarterly. Established, under the title *The International Journal of Ethics,* as an outgrowth of *The Ethical Record,* organ of the Ethical Societies; responsibility assumed by the University of Chicago in 1923; name changed to *Ethics* in 1938.

"Revue de métaphysique et de morale." The *Revue de métaphysique et de morale* (Paris, 1893–) has been issued quarterly since 1920 (previously issued six times a year). This *Revue,* now the principal French philosophical journal, was established by Xavier Léon, with the collaboration of Élie Halévy. The title of the publication reflected not only a reaction against positivism but also, affirmatively, a belief that the conclusions of speculative philosophy could have a practical value. Léon (who also founded the Société Française de Philosophie in 1901 and organized various international congresses of philosophy) served as editor of the *Revue* until his death in 1935, when he was succeeded by Dominique Parodi. Parodi died in 1955, and Jean Wahl (who had assisted Parodi on the *Revue*) took over.

Until World War II special numbers of the *Revue* were occasionally devoted to a single topic. For example, issues were devoted to Kant (1904, the centennial of his death), Rousseau (1912, the bicentennial of his birth), American philosophy (1922, with articles by John Dewey, W. E. Hocking, C. I. Lewis, R. B. Perry, and others), Pascal (1923, the tercentenary of his birth), Hegel (1931, the centennial of his death), and Descartes (1937, the tercentenary of the *Discourse on Method*).

The journal's contributors have included all French philosophers of note as well as many eminent foreigners, such as Bertrand Russell, A. N. Whitehead, and Bernard Bosanquet; Benedetto Croce and Giovanni Gentile; Miguel de Unamuno; and Edmund Husserl. Among the articles of more than ordinary interest which have appeared in the journal are Henri Poincaré's "La Logique de l'infini" (1909), Henri Bergson's "L'Intuition philosophique" (1911), Étienne Gilson's "Art et métaphysique" (1916), Gabriel Marcel's "Existence et objectivité" (1925), Léon Brunschvicg's "Religion et philosophie" (1935), José Ferrater Mora's "Philosophie et architecture" (1955), and Wahl's "Physique atomique et connaissance humaine" (1962).

"The Philosophical Review." Two of the major philosophical journals now on the scene had their origin in the *fin de siècle* decade. One of these was American, *The Philosophical Review* (Ithaca, N.Y., 1892–), which is now issued quarterly. It was previously issued six times a year. It is published by the Sage School of Philosophy at Cornell University.

The Philosophical Review was relatively undistinguished until the late 1940s. Among the few important articles that preceded the late flowering of the journal were C. I. Lewis' "Experience and Meaning" (1934) and Moritz Schlick's reply, "Meaning and Verification" (1936), which is commonly regarded as Schlick's most telling contribution to contemporary philosophy.

The *Review*'s recent burgeoning took place under the guidance of Max Black and his colleagues on the philosophy staff at Cornell. Significant contributions in this period include W. V. Quine's "Two Dogmas of Empiricism" (1951), Black's "Definition, Presupposition, and Assertion" (1952), Gilbert Ryle's "Ordinary Language" (1953), H. P. Grice and P. F. Strawson's "In Defense of a Dogma" (1956), Stuart Hampshire's "On Referring and Intending" (1956), various articles by John Rawls on justice (1958–1963), J. J. C. Smart's "Sensations and Brain Processes" (1959), Norman Malcolm's "Anselm's Ontological Arguments" (1960), and Richard Taylor's "Fatalism" (1962).

Other prominent philosophers whose work has appeared in *The Philosophical Review* include George Boas, R. M. Chisholm, P. T. Geach, Nelson Goodman, Arthur E. Murphy, Ernest Nagel, and J. A. Passmore.

"Kant-Studien." The other famous journal founded in the last decade of the nineteenth century was German: *Kant-Studien; philosophische Zeitschrift* (Hamburg and Leipzig; later Berlin; now Cologne, 1896– —), issued quarterly, with variations. The title was originally spelled *Kantstudien*. This journal has been the organ of the Kant-Gesellschaft since 1904. It was suspended twice, from 1937 to 1942 and from 1945 through 1953.

Hans Vaihinger founded *Kant-Studien* and was its editor, alone or with one or two coeditors, until 1922; Max Scheler was coeditor in 1902/1903. The periodical has published articles in English, French, German, and Italian by outstanding scholars and philosophers, including Erich Adickes, Émile Boutroux, Edward Caird, Ernst Cassirer, Rudolf Eucken, and Norman Kemp Smith. Although the periodical is specifically oriented toward Kant, it includes in its purview current thought on questions raised by Kant, pre-Kantian philosophy as part of the background of Kantianism, and other liberal extensions of the frame of reference.

For many years *Kant-Studien* published abstracts of new books in philosophy on a unique basis: the abstracts were written by the authors themselves. As another special feature, 86 separate monographs have been issued under the auspices of the journal.

During the short-lived revival of *Kant-Studien* in 1942–1944, the journal was not uninfluenced by Nazism. In 1954, however, on the 150th anniversary of Kant's death, the periodical was reborn in a new setting (Cologne), and since then it has regained its international reputation.

Other journals. Additional journals which arose in the 1890s were the following:

1893–. *Revue thomiste; Revue doctrinale de théologie et de philosophie* (originally Brussels; now Toulouse), quarterly. Founded by the Dominican order.

1895–. *The Vedanta Kesari* (Madras), monthly, with variations. Title was *The Brahmavadin; A Fortnightly Religious and Philosophical Journal* from 1895 to 1914. Organ of the world-wide Ramakrishna order.

1896–1915. *Neue metaphysische Rundschau* (Berlin), monthly. Title was *Metaphysische Rundschau* from 1896 to 1897.

1897–1949. *Przegląd Filozoficzny* (Warsaw), quarterly. English summaries of articles in some issues; table of contents also printed in French. Suspended 1940–1946. Issuance stopped by the government at the beginning of the period of militant Marxist domination of Polish philosophy (first half of the 1950s). Replaced (not succeeded) by the periodical now called *Studia Filozoficzne; Kwartalnik* (1951– —).

PREWAR PERIOD

The vital statistics for the period from 1900 to 1914 show 19 journals born, 12 of which have survived. This is the period of *The Hibbert Journal, The Journal of Philosophy, The Harvard Theological Review*, and the first of various journals called *Logos*. Czechoslovakia, Ireland, the Netherlands, and Spain are represented for the first time in this period.

THEOLOGY. The prewar period was exceptionally rich in journals which emphasized theology or the philosophy of religion:

1900–1939. *Revue de philosophie* (Paris), issued six times a year. Thomist-oriented.

1902–. *The Hibbert Journal; A Quarterly Review of Religion, Theology and Philosophy* (London), quarterly; originally issued monthly. Treats religious and humanistic questions from a philosophical or cultural point of view. Contributors have included Henri Bergson, Sarvepalli Radhakrishnan, Bertrand Russell, Rabindranath Tagore, and Leo Tolstoy.

1905–1910. *Rivista storico critica delle scienze teologiche* (Rome), monthly.

1907–. *Revue des sciences philosophiques et théologiques* (Étiolles, Soisy-sur-Seine), quarterly, with variations. Founded by the French Dominicans of the Facultés de Philosophie et de Théologie du Saulchoir. Suspended 1915–1919 and 1943–1946.

1908–. *The Harvard Theological Review* (Cambridge, Mass.), quarterly.

1909–. *Rivista di filosofia neo-scolastica* (Milan), issued six times a year, with variations. Organ of the Istituto de Filosofia, Università Cattolica del Sacro Cuore.

1910–. *La ciencia tomista* (originally Madrid; now Salamanca), issued six times a year from 1910 to 1949, quarterly since 1950. Edited by the Spanish Dominicans.

SOCIAL PHILOSOPHY AND AESTHETICS. Journals of ethics, social philosophy, philosophy of culture, and aesthetics were fostered in the prewar period in Germany and Italy:

1906–1926. *Zeitschrift für Ästhetik und allgemeine Kunstwissenschaft* (Stuttgart), quarterly. Max Dessoir, editor.

1907–. *Archiv für Rechts- und Sozialphilosophie* (Neuwied; previously Munich), quarterly. Title has varied. Contains articles mainly in German and English.

1906–. *Rivista rosminiana di filosofia e di cultura* (Milan; formerly published at Pallanza and other Italian cities), quarterly, with variations. Edited by Giuseppe Morando from 1906 to his death in 1914; edited by his son Dante since 1937. Combats positivism and subjectivism.

1910–1941. *Zeitschrift für deutsche Kulturphilosophie; Neue Folge des Logos* (Tübingen), issued three times a year. Title was *Logos; Internationale Zeitschrift für Philosophie der Kultur* from 1910 to 1933. In 1934, when the journal was completely Nazified, Richard Kroner was replaced as editor in chief (a post which he had held since 1910) and Ernst Cassirer, Edmund Husserl, Friedrich Meinecke, and Rudolf Otto were summarily removed from the roll of collaborating editors.

GENERAL PHILOSOPHY. Several of the prewar journals were general in their philosophical coverage. Two were Italian:

1903–1951. *Quaderni della critica* (Naples), issued six times a year, with variations. Founded by Benedetto Croce. Title was *La critica; Rivista di letteratura, storia e filosofia* from 1903 to 1944. Contained many articles by Croce and by Gentile.

1908–1925. *Bollettino filosofico; Organo della Biblioteca Filosofica di Firenze* (Florence), monthly, with variations. Suspended 1910, 1913–1915, and 1917–1923.

France and the Netherlands gave rise to two others:

1900–. *Bulletin de la Société Française de Philosophie* (Paris), quarterly. Contributors have included Bergson, Louis de Broglie, Brunschvicg, Croce, Einstein, and Russell.

1907–. *Algemeen Nederlands Tijdschrift voor Wijsbegeerte en Psychologie* (Assen; formerly Amsterdam), issued five times a year. Organ of the

Algemene Nederlandse Vereniging voor Wijsbegeerte. Title was *Tijdschrift voor Wijsbegeerte* from 1907 to 1934. From 1934 to 1938 this periodical included, as a separate section, *Annalen der Critische Philosophie* (Assen, 1931–1938), which was also published separately and was succeeded by *Annalen van het Genootschap voor Wetenschappelijke Philosophie* (Assen, 1939–1959), which was likewise published separately in addition to being included in this periodical. Suspended 1944–1946.

One periodical begun in this period originated in what is now Czechoslovakia, and one in what is now Poland:

1902–1937. *Česká Mysl; Casopis Filosofický* (Prague), quarterly, with variations.

1911–. *Ruch Filozoficzny* (Torun; previously Lvov), originally monthly; now quarterly. Was a supplement to *Przegląd Filozoficzny* (Warsaw, 1897–1949) from 1911 to 1914. Suspended 1915–1919, 1939–1947, and 1951–1957 (the third period being one of militant Marxist domination of Polish philosophy). Organ of the Polskie Towarzystwo Filozoficzne.

Two of the general prewar products were English-language journals. One was an Irish intellectual quarterly:

1912–. *Studies; An Irish Quarterly Review of Letters, Philosophy & Science* (Dublin), quarterly. Title on individual issues is now *Studies; An Irish Quarterly Review*, but the annual title page for bound volumes continues to use the full title.

The other English-language philosophical periodical of a general character has been associated from the start with Columbia University.

"The Journal of Philosophy." *The Journal of Philosophy* (New York, 1904–), issued fortnightly, was founded by Frederick J. E. Woodbridge and Wendell T. Bush. The title was *Journal of Philosophy, Psychology, and Scientific Methods* from 1904 to 1920. Provocative articles by William James, Arthur O. Lovejoy's "The Thirteen Pragmatisms" (1908), the "First Platform and Program of the New Realists" (1910), and numerous other notable articles have appeared in its pages. Dewey was a frequent contributor, and his philosophy has been analyzed and appraised in the *Journal* from many angles.

A few of the other important articles, on a variety of subjects, that have appeared in the *Journal* are C. I. Lewis' "A Pragmatic Conception of the A Priori" (1923), Herbert Feigl and Albert Blumberg's "Logical Positivism, A New Movement in European Philosophy" (1931), which introduced the term "logical positivism," Ernest Nagel's "Impressions and Appraisals of Analytic Philosophy in Europe" (1936), W. V. Quine's "Designation and Existence" (1939), C. G. Hempel's "The Function of General Laws in History" (1942), Nelson Goodman's "The Problem of Counterfactual Conditionals" (1947), and Norman Malcolm's "Knowledge of Other Minds" (1958). Also noteworthy are Nagel's penetrating reviews, which were frequently featured in the *Journal* in the 1930s and 1940s.

From 1933 to 1936 the *Journal* published annual world-wide bibliographies of philosophy. In more recent years it has carried texts of papers presented at the annual meetings of the Eastern Division of the American Philosophical Association. In 1963/1964 the *Journal* was involved in a minor *cause célèbre* when, after publishing an article by one of its editors on the discussion between non-Soviet and Soviet philosophers at the Thirteenth International Congress of Philosophy (Mexico City, 1963), it declined to provide equal space, although it offered some space, for an article giving a contrary view of the same discussion.

WORLD WAR I TO 1928

During World War I two new philosophical journals were begun in Europe and one each in Argentina and Japan. Only the Japanese journal is still being published. One of the European journals was a new *Logos*.

1914–1943. *Logos; Rivista trimestrale di filosofia e di storia della filosofia* (Perugia; later Naples and Florence; then Rome), quarterly. International board of editors. Suspended 1916–1919. Title was *Logos*, without the subtitle, from 1914 to 1938.

1915–1929. *Revista de filosofia, cultura, ciencias, educación* (Buenos Aires), issued six times a year, with variations.

1916–. *Tetsugaku Kenkyu; Journal of Philosophical Studies* (Kyoto), monthly. Organ of the Philosophical Society of Kyoto University. Contributors have included Heidegger and Jaspers.

1918–1943. *Blätter für deutschen Philosophie; Zeitschrift der Deutschen Philosophischen Gesellschaft* (Erfurt; later Berlin), quarterly. Title was *Beiträge zur Philosophie des deutschen Idealismus* from 1918 to 1927.

The years from 1919 to 1928 saw 32 new journals of philosophy roll off the presses, the largest quota in any ten-year period up to that time. Included were *The Per-*

sonalist, the first Chinese philosophical journals, another *Logos, The Australasian Journal of Philosophy, Philosophy*, and *The New Scholasticism*. Of the total of 32, 7 were Italian (5 survive), 5 German (2 survive), 5 French (all survive), and 4 American (all survive); the rest were scattered among China (3, none surviving), Czechoslovakia (2, none surviving), and Australia, Great Britain, India, Lithuania, the Netherlands, and Poland.

ITALIAN. Three of the Italian journals of the postwar decade have Latin names and concern theological matters chiefly:

1920–. *Gregorianum* (Rome), quarterly. Published by the Università Gregoriana di Roma. Articles in English, French, German, Italian, Latin, and Spanish.

1924–. *Angelicum* (Rome), quarterly. Journal of the Faculty of Theology, Canon Law, and Philosophy, Pontificium Athenaeum Angelicum. Articles in French, German, Italian, and Latin.

1926–. *Antonianum; Periodicum Philosophico-theologicum Trimestre* (Rome), quarterly. Published by the Athenaeum Antonianum de Urbe. Articles mainly in Latin; those in other languages are summarized in Latin

The other Italian philosophical journals of the period cover various fields:

1920–1923. *Rivista trimestrale di studi filosofici e religiosi* (Perugia), quarterly.

1920–. *Giornale critico della filosofia italiana* (Florence; previously Messina, Milan, Rome, and elsewhere), quarterly, with variations. Founded by Giovanni Gentile and edited by him until his assassination in 1944.

1921–. *Rivista internazionale di filosofia del diritto* (Milan), issued six times a year, with variations.

1924–1945. *L'idealismo realistico; Rivista di filosofia mazziniana* (Rome), monthly.

GERMAN. *Erkenntnis* (see below) was the most important journal of the postwar decade, but four other German journals also merit attention.

1919–1924. *Grundwissenschaft; Philosophische Zeitschrift der Johannes-Rehmke-Gesellschaft* (Leipzig), quarterly. Subtitle varied.

1923–1932. *Literarische Berichte aus dem Gebiete der Philosophie* (Erfurt), semiannual, with variations. Title was *Literarische Berichte der Deutschen Philosophischen Gesellschaft* from 1923 to 1924.

The two German journals begun in this period that are still on earth are concerned with heavenly matters:

1923–. *Neue Zeitschrift für systematische Theologie und Religionsphilosophie* (Berlin; originally Gütersloh), issued three times a year; formerly quarterly (irregular 1956–1959). Title was *Zeitschrift für systematische Theologie* from 1923 to 1958, and *Neue Zeitschrift für systematische Theologie* from 1959 to 1962. Suspended 1944–1949.

1926–. *Scholastik; Vierteljahresschrift für Theologie und Philosophie* (Frankfurt; previously Freiburg im Breisgau), quarterly. Published by the Jesuits of the faculties of philosophy and theology, Hochschule St. Georg, Frankfurt, and Berchmanskolleg, Pullach-am-Main. Suspended 1941–1943; combined with the *Theologische Quartalschrift* (1819–) for one year, 1944; suspended 1945–1948.

"*Erkenntnis.*" *The Journal of Unified Science (Erkenntnis)* (Leipzig; later The Hague and Chicago, 1919–1940) was issued six times a year, with variations. Its title was *Annalen der Philosophie, mit besonderer Rücksicht auf die Probleme der als ob Betrachtung* from 1919 to 1923, *Annalen der Philosophie und philosophischen Kritik* from 1924 to 1930, and *Erkenntnis, zugleich Annalen der Philosophie* from 1930 to 1939. Hans Vaihinger was coeditor from 1919 to 1930. From 1930 to 1940 the editors were Rudolf Carnap and Hans Reichenbach (but Carnap alone in 1937/1938).

In the 1930s *Erkenntnis* was perhaps the most influential philosophical periodical ever published. The Vienna circle of logical positivists took over the journal, then entitled *Annalen*, in 1930 (Vaihinger, its coeditor, was then 78 years old), renamed it *Erkenntnis*, and transformed it into a medium—which struck sparks of fire in the philosophical world—for the discussion and propagation of the circle's theses. The first issue of *Erkenntnis* contained Moritz Schlick's "Die Wende der Philosophie" ("The Turning Point in Philosophy") as the opening article and also Carnap's "Die alte und die neue Logik" ("The Old and the New Logic"). In quick succession, in the early 1930s, the periodical published Carnap's "Überwindung der Metaphysik durch logische Analyse der Sprache" ("Elimination of Metaphysics Through Logical Analysis of Language"), probably his most famous paper; Schlick's "Positivismus und Realismus" ("Positivism and Realism") and "Über das Fundament der Erkenntnis" ("On the Foundation of Knowledge"); Otto Neurath's "Protokollsätze" ("Protocol Sentences"); and Ernest Nagel's "Measurement."

Other notable articles which appeared in *Erkenntnis* are Hans Reichenbach's "Wahrscheinlichkeitslogik" ("Logic of Probability," 1935) and others by him on probability theory, Max Black's "Relations Between Logical Positivism and the Cambridge School of Analysis" (1939), and articles by Niels Bohr and other famous scientists and mathematicians, not all of whom were logical positivists. Various issues of *Erkenntnis* contained the proceedings of the Tagung für Erkenntnislehre der Exakten Wissenschaften (1929–1930), and of the International Congress for the Unity of Science (1934–1938).

Many of the articles published in *Erkenntnis* were translated into English and other languages and published in collections of the foundation papers of the logical positivist movement. Indeed, the journal had its greatest impact on philosophers in England and the United States rather than on those in continental Europe, many of whom had fallen under the spell of Martin Heidegger's *Dasein*.

FRENCH. Two of the French periodicals of the first postwar decade are religiously oriented.

1921–. *Revue d'histoire et de philosophie religieuse* (Strasbourg), quarterly. Published by the Facultéde Théologie Protestante de I'Université de Strasbourg.

1924–. *Bulletin thomiste* (Étiolles, Soisy-sur-Seine), quarterly, with variations. Organ of the Société Thomiste.

The other three are secular and humanistic.

1923–. *Archives de philosophie* (Paris), quarterly, with variations. Suspended 1953–1954.

1926–. *Les Études philosophiques* (Paris), quarterly, with variations. Founded by Gaston Berger.

1927–. *Revue des sciences humaines* (Lille and elsewhere), quarterly, with variations. Title was *Revue d'histoire de la philosophie* from 1927 to 1931 and *Revue d'histoire de la philosophie et d'histoire générale de la civilisation* from 1933 to 1946. Suspended 1932, 1940–1941, and 1945.

EASTERN EUROPEAN. During the 1920s Prague was the birthplace of two philosophical journals and Kaunas and Cracow of one each (including another *Logos*):

1920–1939. *Ruch Filosoficzký* (Prague), issued six times a year, with variations.

1921–1938. *Logos; Filosofijos Laikraštis* (Kaunas), semiannual.

1922–1950. *Kwartalnik Filozoficzny* (Cracow), quarterly. Published by the Polskiej Nakladem Akademii Umieję̨tności. Suspended 1934 and 1940–1945. Editor in the last years of the periodical was Roman Ingarden. Emphasis on phenomenology and conceptual analysis.

1927–1929. *Filosofie* (Prague), issued ten times a year. Published under the auspices of the Ministerstvo Školstvi a Národni Osvěty of Czechoslovakia.

AMERICAN. In the United States a personalistic magazine and three religious journals were founded and are still being issued:

1920–. *The Personalist* (Los Angeles), quarterly. Issued by the University of Southern California.

1923–. *The Modern Schoolman* (St. Louis, Mo.), quarterly.

1926–. *Thought; A Review of Culture and Idea* (New York), quarterly. Founded by the Jesuit periodical *America*; directed since 1940 by Fordham University. Subtitle was *A Quarterly of the Sciences and Letters* from 1926 to 1939.

1927–. *The New Scholasticism* (Washington), quarterly. Organ of the American Catholic Philosophical Association. This periodical is one of the two best sources of philosophical news (teaching appointments, publication projects, congresses, etc.), the other being the *Revue philosophique de Louvain* (1894–).

ASIAN AND AUSTRALASIAN. The three Chinese journals of philosophy that were introduced in the 1920s are:

1921–1927. *Chê Hsüeh* ["Philosophy"] (Peking), issued six times a year, with variations. Generally referred to as *Chê Hsüeh Tsa Chih* ("Philosophical Journal").

1926–1930. *Chê Hsüeh Yüeh K'an* ["Philosophical Monthly"] (Peking), monthly, with variations.

1927–1944. *Chê Hsüeh P'ing Lun* ["Philosophical Review"] (Peking), issued six times a year, with variations.

A journal published in India continues to be active:

1925–. *Philosophical Quarterly* (Calcutta; later Amalner), quarterly. Organ of the Indian Institute of Philosophy and the Indian Philosophical Congress.

"The Australasian Journal." One journal published in Australia merits a pause for special comment: *The Australasian Journal of Philosophy* (Glebe, New South Wales, Australia, 1923–), issued quarterly from 1923 to 1937 and three times a year since 1938. It is the organ of the Australasian Association of Psychology and Philosophy. The title was *The Australasian Journal of Psychology and Philosophy* from 1923 to 1946.

The *Journal* announced in its first issue that some of its articles would be technical and addressed to a few experts, whereas others would treat of "topics of universal interest, ranging from the high metaphysical quest of the secret of the Absolute, to concrete problems of social and political ethics." It undertook not to "scorn the old fogey in Philosophy, or disdain the new faddist." Bertrand Russell helped the *Journal* get off to a flourishing start by publishing in its first volume (second issue) a little-known but important article of his, "Vagueness."

In 1935 John Anderson, a controversial philosopher of Scottish origin, became the editor of the *Journal*. He thereafter exerted a strong influence not only on the *Journal* but also on the thinking of philosophers in his part of the world. The legislators of New South Wales, shocked by Anderson's militant atheism, unsuccessfully demanded his removal from his teaching post at the University of Sydney.

The current editor of *The Australasian Journal of Philosophy* is A. K. Stout, son of G. F. Stout, former editor of *Mind*. This is the third notable case in which a son followed his father's trade as editor of a philosophical journal, the other such families being the Fichtes, who respectively edited the *Philosophisches Journal*, 1795 ff., and the *Zeitschrift für Philosophie*, 1837 ff.; and the Morandos, who were editors at different times of the *Rivista rosminiana*, 1906 ff.

Among the challenging and widely discussed papers that Anderson on his pluralistic, positivistic realism; the last pieces by the elder Stout; some of the most celebrated articles by J. N. Findlay and others in the early 1940s on the philosophy of Wittgenstein; J. A. Passmore's three articles entitled "Logical Positivism" (1943, 1944, and 1948) and his "Christianity and Positivism" (1957); J. J. C. Smart's "The Reality of Theoretical Entities" (1956); A. N. Prior's "The Autonomy of Ethics" (1960); and Keith Lehrer's "Doing the Impossible" (1964). The *Journal's* influence reached a particularly high level in the period beginning about 1955.

BRITISH AND DUTCH. The remaining examples of journals begun in the first postwar decade have had London and Hilversum as their headquarters:

1926–. *Philosophy* (London), quarterly. Orgán of the British Institute of Philosophy. Title was *Journal of Philosophical Studies* from 1926 to 1931. Contributors have included Samuel Alexander, George Dawes Hicks, and Bertrand Russell.

1926–1944. *Denken en Leven; Wijsgeerig Tijdschrift* (Hilversum), issued six times a year.

1929–1938

From 1929 to 1938, 25 new journals of philosophy sought subscribers. Of these, 8 have fallen by the wayside, 6 being casualties of World War II. Among the new journals of this period were a Yugoslav quarterly, the first journals covering the philosophy of science and symbolic logic, and *Analysis*. Italy produced the most new philosophical journals (10); Germany produced none.

IDEALISTIC, RELIGIOUS, AND MYSTIC. Two publications on nonworldly philosophy were established in India:

1930–1935. *Review of Philosophy and Religion* (Poona), semiannual. Organ of the Academy of Philosophy and Religion.

1930–. *The Aryan Path* (Bombay), monthly. Popular ethics and mysticism, with emphasis on Indian philosophy.

The remaining examples of this kind of journal had their homes in Belgium, Italy, the Netherlands, and the United States, respectively:

1929–. *Recherches de théologie ancienne et médiévale* (Louvain), quarterly.

1934–. *Doctor Communis; Acta et Commentationes Pontificiae Accademiae Sanctae Thomae Aquinatis* (Rome; previously Turin), issued three times a year. Title was *Acta Pontificiae Accademiae Sanctae Thomae Aquinatis* from 1934 to 1947. Articles mainly in Latin; those in other languages are summarized in Latin.

1938–. *Bijdragen van de Philosophische en Theologische Faculteiten der Nederlandsche Jezuieten* (Maastricht), issued three times a year, with variations. Title has varied.

1938–. *Vedanta and the West* (Hollywood, Calif.), issued six times a year. Emphasis on mysticism.

Sponsored by the Vedanta Society of Southern California.

LOGIC AND RELATED DISCIPLINES. Balancing the inaugurations of religious periodicals were those of periodicals on logic, philosophy of science, and language analysis. The two most influential were *Analysis* and the *Journal of Symbolic Logic.*

"Analysis." *Analysis* (Oxford, 1933–) is issued six times a year, with variations. The journal was suspended from 1940 to 1947. This periodical was founded by a number of younger philosophers under the influence of G. E. Moore, Bertrand Russell, and Ludwig Wittgenstein. It was intended mainly as a medium for short analyses and discussions. A group of supporters pledged to pay £5 each if the venture should so require, but the journal paid its way. In 1936 an Analysis Society was formed, also aimed at guaranteeing the financial stability of the journal, but it went out of existence a few years later; some of the papers read at its meetings were published in *Analysis.*

Max Black, in America, was closely associated with the journal from its foundation, and Rudolf Carnap, Carl Hempel, and Moritz Schlick, of the Vienna circle, contributed articles to early issues. Among the memorable articles that *Analysis* has published are A. J. Ayer's "The Genesis of Metaphysics" (1934), Schlick's "Facts and Propositions" (1935), Margaret Macdonald's "Necessary Propositions" (1940), Black's "The Semantic Definition of Truth" (1948), Friedrich Waismann's six articles entitled "Analytic–Synthetic" (1949–1953), P. T. Geach's "Russell's Theory of Descriptions" (1950), Alonzo Church's "On Carnap's Analysis of Statements of Assertion and Belief" (1950), Gilbert Ryle's "Heterologicality" (1951), Karl R. Popper's "A Note on the Body–Mind Problem" (1955), Yehoshuah Bar-Hillel's "New Light on the Liar" (1957), Peter Achinstein's "The Circularity of a Self-supporting Inductive Argument" (1962), and Keith Gunderson's "Interview With a Robot" (1963).

Many highlights from the journal were reprinted in *Philosophy and Analysis* (New York, 1954), edited by Margaret Macdonald, who was editor of *Analysis* from 1948 to her death in January 1956. For a time in the 1950s, Analysis conducted "competitions" and published the best short answers to such questions as "Does it make sense to say that death is survived?"

Especially in the early years of *Analysis,* its pages crackled with iconoclasm, terseness, and wit. Currently, some of the articles are longer than the average of the early years, and a supplement containing extended articles is now issued annually.

"Journal of Symbolic Logic." The *Journal of Symbolic Logic* (Providence, R.I.; previously Menasha, Wis., and Baltimore, Md., 1936–), issued quarterly, publishes articles in English, French, and German. It is the organ of the Association for Symbolic Logic.

This journal was the first one to be devoted exclusively to its field. In April 1934, Paul Weiss called attention to the fact that papers on logic were scattered in heterogeneous periodicals, and (without specifically proposing a new periodical) he suggested the formation of a logic association. Later in the year, C. J. Ducasse and C. A. Baylis explicitly urged the establishment of a journal of symbolic logic, to be supported by an association for symbolic logic. The response was encouraging, and the venture was undertaken.

Financing the *Journal* was a problem in the early years, and it was uncertain, after the publication of the third issue, whether the publication could continue. Happily, subventions were obtained from a number of universities, and dues payments accumulated sufficiently to enable the *Journal* to meet its bills.

Aside from the high quality of many of the articles, the *Journal* is noted for an exceptionally useful section devoted to reviews and abstracts of current literature. These reviews and abstracts purport to cover all pertinent books and articles which have come to the attention of the editors; the frame of reference of publications pertinent to symbolic logic is interpreted broadly. The reviews and abstracts constitute a continuation of Alonzo Church's nonpareil bibliography of symbolic logic from 1666 to 1935 which appeared in the issue of December 1936, with a supplement in the issue of December 1938.

The well-deserved international reputation of the *Journal* derives in large part from the vast knowledge and logical acumen of Church, who is the principal editor. Among the many articles of enduring worth which have appeared in the *Journal* are Church's "A Note on the *Entscheidungs-problem*" (1936), Barkley Rosser's "Extensions of Some Theorems of Gödel" (1936), W. V. Quine's "On the Theory of Types" (1938) and his "On Universals" (1947), Carl G. Hempel's "A Purely Syntactical Definition of Confirmation" (1943), Rudolf Carnap's "Modalities and Quantification" (1946), Wilhelm Ackermann's "Begründung einer strengen Implikation" (1956), Gordon Matheson's "The Semantics of Singular Terms" (1962), and Frederic B. Fitch's "A Logical Analysis of Some Value Concepts" (1964).

Other journals. Other journals on logic, analysis, and so forth, were published in Poland, the United States, and the Netherlands:

1934–. *Studia Logica* (Warsaw), semiannual, with variations; formerly an annual. Suspended 1937–1952. Sponsored since 1953 by the Komitet Filozoficzny, Polska Akademia Nauk. Articles in English, French, German, Polish, and Russian, each with summaries in two other languages. In 1953 it absorbed the irregularly published *Studia Philosophica* (Warsaw, 1935–1951, four volumes).

1934–. *Philosophy of Science* (East Lansing, Mich.), quarterly. Organ of the Philosophy of Science Association.

1936–. *Synthese; An International Quarterly for the Logical and the Psychological Study of the Foundations of Science* (Dordrecht; previously Utrecht), quarterly, with variations. Subtitle has varied. Suspended 1940–1945 and 1964–1965. Articles in English, French, and German (originally, mainly in Dutch). Various issues have included a section (sometimes separately paged) entitled "Communications of the Institute for the Unity of Science" or "Unity of Science Forum."

SOCIAL AND MORAL PHILOSOPHY. Italy produced three, and the United States one, of the social and moral periodicals that started in this prewar period:

1932–1943. *Archivio della cultura italiana* (Rome), quarterly. Title was *Archivio di storia della filosofia italiana* from 1932 to 1938.

1935–1941. *Rassegna di morale e di diritto* (Rome), quarterly.

1935–1942. *Journal of Social Philosophy & Jurisprudence; A Quarterly Devoted to a Philosophic Synthesis of the Social Sciences* (New York), quarterly. Title was *Journal of Social Philosophy* (with the same subtitle as later) from 1935 to 1941.

1935–. *Rivista internazionale di filosofia politica e sociale* (Genoa; formerly Padua), quarterly. Suspended 1944–1963.

PHILOSOPHY, HISTORY, AND LETTERS. Italy fathered three journals linking history and literature with philosophy:

1929–1943. *Civiltà moderna; Rassegna bimestrale di critica storica, letteraria, filosofica* (Florence), issued six times a year.

1929–. *Convivium; Rivista di lettere, filosofia e storia* (Turin), issued six times a year. Suspended 1944–1946. Subtitle has varied.

1931–. *Ricerche filosofiche; Rivista di filosofia, storia e letteratura* (Messina), semiannual, with variations. Since 1948 it has been the organ of the Società Filosofica Calabrese, founded in that year.

GENERAL. Seven regular academic or professional periodicals devoted to philosophy in general were begun in this period:

1931–1959. *Annalen van het Genootschap voor Wetenschappelijke Philosophie* (Assen), issued five times a year. Title was *Annalen der critische Philosophie* from 1931 to 1938. In 1959 absorbed into *Algemeen Nederlands Tijdschrift voor Wijsbegeerte en Psychologie* (Amsterdam and later Assen, 1907–), after having been published both separately and as a section of that periodical from 1934 to 1959.

1931–. *Archivio di filosofia* (Rome), issued three times a year, with variations. Originally the organ of the Società Filosofica Italiana; more recently the organ of the Istituto di Studi Filosofici and the Associazione Filosofica Italiana. Suspended 1943–1945.

1933–. *Sophia; Rassegna critica di filosofia e storia della filosofia* (Rome; formerly Palermo, Naples, and Padua), quarterly. Became international in 1935. Subtitle has varied. Contains articles in English, French, German, Italian, and Spanish, with subtitles in these languages.

1935–1940. *Bollettino filosofico* (Rome), quarterly.

1935–. *Theoria* (Lund, Goteborg, and Copenhagen; previously Goteborg), issued three times a year. Contains articles in English, French, and German (before 1937, in Danish, Norwegian, and Swedish).

1936–1940. *Philosophia; Philosophorum Nostri Temporis Vox Universa* (Belgrade), quarterly, with variations. Contained articles in English, French, and German.

1938–. *Revue internationale de philosophie* (Brussels), quarterly, with variations. Suspended 1939–1948. Each issue is devoted to a movement, problem, or philosopher, with a comprehensive bibliography.

WORLD WAR II

In the seven years from 1939 to 1945, 21 journals of philosophy came into being. Fully 16 of these have survived, and they include a number of today's outstanding philosophical journals.

NORTH AMERICAN. Canada, the United States, and Mexico produced a total of eight philosophical journals during World War II. Canada provided a new medium for discussions of theology and philosophy, *Laval théologique et philosophique* (Quebec, 1945–), issued semiannually. This journal is published by the Facultés de Théologie et Philosophie de l'Université Laval de Québec.

In Mexico, for 17 years, a university review of philosophy and letters was published: *Filosofía y letras* (Mexico City, 1941–1957), issued quarterly, with variations. It was the organ of the Facultad de Filosofía y Letras, Universidad Nacional Autónoma.

In the United States six periodicals, varying widely in their character and in their topical focus, began in the period from 1939 to 1945. Five of these were:

1939–1954. *Philosophic Abstracts* (New York), quarterly, with variations.

1939–. *The Thomist; A Speculative Quarterly Review* (Washington; formerly New York), quarterly. Edited by the Dominican Fathers of the Province of St. Joseph.

1940–. *Journal of the History of Ideas* (New York), quarterly.

1941–. *Journal of Aesthetics and Art Criticism* (Baltimore Md.), quarterly. Organ, since 1945, of the American Society for Aesthetics. Contributors have included Croce, Dewey, and Santayana.

1943–. *Etc.: A Review of General Semantics* (San Francisco; formerly Bloomington, Ill.), quarterly. Organ of the International Society for General Semantics. Anthology volumes, consisting of selections from *Etc.*, were published in 1954 and 1959.

"Philosophy and Phenomenological Research." The most influential journal begun during World War II was *Philosophy and Phenomenological Research* (Buffalo; then Philadelphia; now Buffalo again, 1940–), which is issued quarterly. This journal is an outgrowth of the *Jahrbuch für Philosophie und phänomenologische Forschung* (Halle, 1913–1930), which was founded by Edmund Husserl.

Husserl died in 1938. In the following year the International Phenomenological Society was formed in New York City to further the understanding, development, and application of phenomenological inquiry as inaugurated by Husserl. The Society's journal, *Philosophy and Phenomenological Research*, although taking Husserl's philosophy as "the point of departure," announced at the outset that it would represent "no special school or sect." Its editor for a quarter of a century, Marvin Farber, has kept the journal's pages open to diverse points of view.

Philosophy and Phenomenological Research published the proceedings of the First Inter-American Conference of Philosophy (held at Yale University in 1943) and several stimulating symposia. The symposia dealt with meaning and truth, with articles by C. A. Baylis, C. J. Ducasse, Felix Kaufmann, C. I. Lewis, Ernest Nagel, R. W. Sellars, Alfred Tarski, W. M. Urban, A. Ushenko, and John Wild (1943–1945); probability, with articles by Gustav Bergmann, Rudolf Carnap, Kaufmann, Richard von Mises, Nagel, Hans Reichenbach, and Donald Williams (1945–1946); Russian philosophy and psychology, educational philosophy, "philosophy of freedom," and the philosophy of Arthur O. Lovejoy (various years in the 1940s and 1963); and "logical subjects and physical objects," with articles by Wilfrid Sellars and P. F. Strawson (1957).

Among the memorable individual articles in the journal were three little-known papers by Husserl entitled "Notizien zur Raumkonstitution" (Nos. 1 and 2, 1940), "Phänomenologie und Anthropologie" (1941), and "Persönliche Aufzeichnungen" (1956). Others include Paul Weiss's "The Meaning of Existence" (1940), Ernst Cassirer's "The Concept of Group and the Theory of Perception" (1944), Arthur Pap's "Logical Nonsense" (1948), Richard Mc-Keon's "Dialogue and Controversy in Philosophy" (1956), Lewis S. Feuer's "The Bearing of Psychoanalysis Upon Philosophy" (1959), Nagel's "Determinism in History" (1960), and Nicholas Rescher's "On the Logic of Presupposition" (1961). The journal publishes Spanish abstracts of its articles.

SOUTH AMERICAN. In 1944 two philosophical periodicals were established in Argentina:

1944–. *Stromata: Ciencia y fé* (Buenos Aires), issued quarterly by the Facultades de Filosofía y Teología, Colegio Máximo de San José, San Miguel. Title was *Ciencia y fé* from 1944 to 1964. Considered to be the successor to *Fascículos de biblioteca* (1937–1943) and *Stromata* (1938–1943).

1944–. *Philosophia* (Mendoza, Argentina), semiannual. Issued by the Instituto de Filosofía y Disciplinas Auxiliares, Universidad Nacional de Cuyo.

WESTERN EUROPEAN. Despite the atmosphere of war or preparations for war, new journals for philosophical discussion were begun in Belgium and France and in Spain and Portugal:

1939–. *Tijdschrift voor Filosofie* (Louvain), quarterly. Articles in English, Dutch, French, and German, with English, French, or German summaries of the articles in Dutch. Editors are chosen from Netherlands universities and Dutch-language universities of Belgium.

1942–. *Revista de filosofía* (Madrid), issued three times in 1942, quarterly since 1943. Organ of the Instituto de Filosofía Luis Vives. Scholastic. Some foreign contributors.

1945–. *Pensamiento; Revista de investigación e información filosófica* (Madrid), quarterly. Organ of the Facultades de Filosofía, Compañía de Jesús en España. Strong on the bibliography of Spanish and Latin American philosophy.

1945–. *Revista portuguesa de filosofia* (Braga; formerly Lisbon), quarterly. Organ of the Faculdade Pontifícia de Filosofia of Braga, a branch of the Society of Jesus.

1945–1955. *Dieu vivant; Perspectives religieuses et philosophiques* (Paris), quarterly, with variations.

CENTRAL AND SOUTHERN EUROPEAN. Contributions of Italy and neutral Switzerland were:

1940–1943. *Bollettino dell'Istituto di Filosofia del Diritto dell'Università di Roma* (Rome), issued six times a year.

1940–1949. *Studi filosofici; Problemi di vita contemporanea* (Milan), quarterly. Pro-Marxist from 1946 to 1949. Subtitle varied.

1945–. *Methodos; Linguaggio e cibernetica* (Milan; previously Rome), quarterly, with variations. Title was *Analisi; Rassegna di critica della scienza* from 1945 to 1947 and *Sigma; Conoscenza unitaria* from 1947 to 1948. Subtitle has varied. Contains articles in various languages. International editorial board. Organ, since 1959, of the Centro di Cibernetica e di Attività Linguistiche, Università di Milano, and of the Consiglio Nazionale delle Ricerche.

1945–. *Theologische Zeitschrift* (Basel), issued six times a year.

BULGARIAN AND ISRAELI. In Bulgaria and Israel the following journals came into being:

1945–. *Filosofska Mis'l* (Sofia), issued six times a year. Table of contents also in English, French, German, and Russian; summaries in English and Russian. Issued since 1952 by the Institut po Filosofia, Bulgarska Akademiia na Naukite.

1945–. *Iyyun* (Jerusalem), quarterly. Irregular 1945–1948; suspended 1949–1950. Contains English summaries.

POSTWAR PERIOD

In the early postwar years philosophical journals were founded at an unprecedented pace. They numbered 11 in 1946 (of which 9 have survived); 8 in 1947 (6 still alive); 5 in 1948 (4 still alive); and 7 in 1949 (3 still alive). Among them was another *Logos*.

1946. Three products of the first postwar year had humanistic titles:

1946–. *Teoresi; Rivista di cultura filosofica* (Catania; formerly Messina), quarterly, with variations. Emphasizes the synthesis of idealism and realism.

1946–. *Sapientia* (Buenos Aires), quarterly. Organ of the Facultad de Filosofía, Universidad Católica Argentina. Thomist. International contributors.

1946–. *Humanitas* (Brescia, Italy), monthly. In four parts, of which the part on philosophy is edited by Michele Federico Sciacca.

Four journals, including two from Japan, had standard, traditional titles:

1946–1949. *Tetsugaku Hyôron; Philosophical Review* (Tokyo), monthly.

1946–1949. *Tetsugaku Kikan* ["Quarterly Review of Philosophy"] (Kyoto), quarterly.

1946–. *Giornale di metafisica* (Turin), issued six times a year. Founded and edited by M. F. Sciacca. From 1946 to 1948 published by the University of Pavia; since then, by the University of Genoa. Has been described as following the Plato–Augustine–Rosmini tradition. Contributors include Maurice Blondel, Gabriel Marcel, and Jacques Maritain.

1946–. *Zeitschrift für philosophische Forschung* (Meisenheim am Glan, Germany; formerly Wurzach), quarterly.

The others cover a variety of fields:

1946–. *Otázky Marxistickej Filozofie* (Bratislava, Czechoslovakia; formerly Prague), issued six times a year, with variations. Title was *Philosophica Slovaca* from 1946 to 1949 (issued annually); *Filozofický Sborník* from 1950 to 1952 (issued annually); *Filo-*

zofický Časopis from 1953 to 1955 (quarterly); and *Slovenský Filozofický Časopis* from 1956 to 1960 (quarterly). Issued by the Slovenská Akadémie Vied. Table of contents also in English, German, and Russian. Emphasis on historical materialism.

1946–. *Rassegna di scienze filosofiche* (Naples; previously Bari and Rome), quarterly. Title was *Noesis; Rassegna internazionale di scienze filosofiche e morali* in 1946. Suspended 1947. Neo-Scholastic.

1946–. *Rivista critica di storia della filosofia* (Milan), quarterly. Title was *Rivista di storia della filosofia* from 1946 to 1949.

1946–. *Nederlands Theologisch Tijdschrift* (Wageningen), issued six times a year.

1947. Two of the 1947 products expired within 3 to 11 years:

1947–1949. *Tetsugaku* ["Philosophy"] (Tokyo), quarterly.

1947–1958. *Wiener Zeitschrift für Philosophie, Psychologie, Pädagogik* (Vienna), semiannual.

The ones that are still alive include two that are general in their scope:

1947–. *Archiv für Philosophie* (Stuttgart), quarterly. Not to be confused with the *Archiv für Geschichte der Philosophie* (Berlin, 1868–), which was entitled *Archiv für Philosophie* from 1895 to 1926. Some issues of the Stuttgart periodical, beginning in the late 1940s, incorporated issues of the irregularly published *Archiv für mathematische Logik und Grundlagenforschung*.

1947–. *Voprosy Filosofii* (Moscow), monthly, with variations. Issued by the Institut Filosofii, Akademiia Nauk SSR. Contains summaries in English and titles in English, French, German, and Spanish.

"Review of Metaphysics." The *Review of Metaphysics* (New Haven, 1947–), published quarterly, is one of the major media of discussion of the perennial problems of metaphysics. In addition, it publishes annual lists of doctoral dissertations accepted by philosophy departments in the United States and Canada, of professors who have become emeritus in philosophy, and of visiting philosophy professors from abroad. Beginning with December 1964, each issue contains abstracts of articles in certain philosophical periodicals, written (as in the case of the book abstracts formerly published in *Kant-Studien*) by the authors of the articles themselves. In earlier years the *Review* conducted competitions, comparable to those in *Analysis* (1933–), for the best short answers to piquant questions, such as why there has never been a great woman philosopher.

Outstanding among the many important articles that have appeared in the *Review* are Paul Weiss's "Being, Essence and Existence" (1947), W. V. Quine's "On What There Is" (1948), Charles Hartshorne's "The Immortality of the Past" (1953), Nathan Rotenstreich's "The Genesis of Mind" (1962), and Wilfrid Sellars' "Abstract Entities" (1963). The discussion section of the *Review* has also provided a large number of valuable contributions to current thought.

Two of the 1947 periodicals concern the philosophy of science or the unity of the sciences, and one is bibliographical:

1947–. *Dialectica; International Review of Philosophy of Knowledge* (Neuchâtel, Switzerland; and Paris), quarterly. Emphasis on philosophy of science.

1947–. *Studium Generale; Zeìtschrift für die Einheit der Wissenschaften im Zusammenhang íhrer Begriffsbildungen und Forschungsmethoden* (Berlin), monthly. Articles in English, French, and German.

1947–. *Bulletin signalétique: Philosophie, sciences humaines* (Paris), quarterly. Title was *Bulletin analytique: Philosophie* from 1947 to 1955. Contains abstracts of books and articles on philosophical subjects. Published by the Centre de Documentation du Centre Nationale de la Recherche Scientifique.

1948. Three journals begun in 1948 were founded on the European continent:

1948–. *Revue d'esthétique* (Paris), quarterly.

1948–. *Sapienza; Rivista di filosofia e di teologia dei Domenicani d'Italia* (Naples), issued six times a year. Since 1956 the organ of the Centro Italiano di Studi Scientifici, Filosofici e Teologici. Subtitle has varied.

1948–. *Roczniki Filozoficzne* (Lublin), quarterly.

The others were issued in South America:

1948–1950. *Revista colombiana de filosofía* (Bogotá), issued six times a year. Emphasis on Thomism and phenomenology.

1948–. *Filosofía, letras y ciencias de la educación* (Quito), semiannual. Published by the Facultad de Filosofía, Letras y Ciencias de la Educación, Universidad Central, Quito. Title has varied.

1949. Another *Logos* appeared in 1949, along with two periodicals called "philosophical studies" (in German and in English), and four other journals:

1949–1951. *Logos* (Mexico City), quarterly. Published by the Mesa Redonda de Filosofía, Facultad de Filosofía y Letras, Universidad Nacional Autónoma de Mexico.

1949–1952. *Philosophische Studien* (Berlin), quarterly, with variations.

1949–. *Philosophical Studies* (Minneapolis), issued six times a year. Brief articles. Many distinguished contributors.

1949–1953. *Revista de filosofía* (Santiago, Chile), quarterly. Organ of the Sociedad Chilena de Filosofía and the Universidad de Chile.

1949–1954. *Notas y estudios de filosofía* (Tucumán, Argentina), quarterly.

1949–. *Philosophischer Literaturanzeiger* (Stuttgart; formerly Schlesdorf am Kochelsee, then Stuttgart, then Meisenheim am Glan), issued eight times a year.

1949–. *Analele romåno-sovietice; Filozofie* (Bucharest), quarterly, with variations. Table of contents also in Russian. From 1949 to 1951 it was a part of *Analele romåno-sovietice; Seria istorie-filozofie* (quarterly; issued six times in 1951; title also in Russian), which itself had been a part, from 1946 to 1949, of *Analele romåno-sovietice* (issued irregularly; title also in Russian).

THE NINETEEN-FIFTIES

The decade of the 1950s saw 11 new English-language journals, 13 Spanish-language journals, 11 Italian, 4 Portuguese, 4 French, 3 German, 2 Dutch, and 1 each in Hungarian, Rumanian, Polish, Serbo-Croat, Russian, Chinese, and Japanese. As in two earlier periods, Italy was the leading or a leading producer of new philosophical journals.

ENGLISH. In continental United States and Hawaii the following journals were introduced:

1951–. *Philosophy East and West* (Honolulu), quarterly. Emphasizes Oriental and comparative thought. Suspended from 1964 to 1966.

1957–. *Philosophy Today* (Celina, Ohio), quarterly. Mainly contains reprints or translations of articles appearing elsewhere. Religious emphasis.

In Scotland are published a journal for the philosophy of science and a quarterly which has the same title as a living Indian journal begun in 1925:

1950–. *British Journal for the Philosophy of Science* (Edinburgh), quarterly.

1950–. *The Philosophical Quarterly* (St. Andrews, Scotland), quarterly. Published for the Scots Philosophical Club.

The Commonwealth countries of Canada, India, and Pakistan produced the following periodicals:

1953–. *Diogenes; An International Journal for Philosophy and Humanistic Studies* (Montreal; formerly New York), quarterly. Published under the auspices of the International Council for Philosophy and Humanistic Studies with the assistance of UNESCO.

1953–. *Journal of the Philosophical Association* (Amraoti, India; later Nagpur), quarterly. Organ of the Indian Philosophical Association. Contributors outside India have included P. T. Geach, Elizabeth Anscombe, and A. N. Prior.

1956–. *Indian Philosophy and Culture* (Vrindaban, India), quarterly. Issued by the Vaishnava Research Institute.

1957–. *Pakistan Philosophical Journal* (Lahore), quarterly.

1959–. *The Indian Journal of Philosophy* (Bombay), quarterly; formerly issued three times a year. Published for the Association for Philosophical Research.

From the Netherlands and Norway come the following:

1956–. *Phronesis; A Journal for Ancient Philosophy* (Assen), semiannual.

1958–. *Inquiry; An Interdisciplinary Journal of Philosophy and the Social Sciences* (Oslo), quarterly. Emphasis on analytic philosophy.

SPANISH. In South America five periodicals sprang to life, including one which repeated the title (*Humanitas*) of an Italian journal begun in 1946:

1950–1954. *Revista de filosofía* (La Plata, Argentina), quarterly. Issued by the Instituto de Filosofía, Universidad Nacional de La Plata.

1951–1954. *Ideas y valores* (Bogotá), quarterly. Issued by the Facultad de Filosofía y Letras de la Universidad Nacional. Title varied slightly.

1952–. *Arkhé Revista americana de filosofía sistemática y de historia de la filosofía* (Córdoba, Argentina), semiannual (formerly issued three times a year). Suspended 1955 to mid-1964. Title was originally *Arqué* subtitle varied.

1953–. *Filosofía; Revista semestral* (Quito), semiannual. Organ of the Sección de Ciencias Filosóficas y de la Educación de la Casa de la Cultura Ecuatoriana.

1953–. *Humanitas; Revista de la Facultad de Filosofía y Letras, Universidad Nacional de Tucumán* (San Miguel de Tucumán), issued three times a year, with variations.

In Central America and the Caribbean, two university *Revistas* appeared:

1956–1958. *Revista dominicana de filosofía* (Ciudad Trujillo, now called Santo Domingo), semiannual, with variations. Organ of the Facultad de Filosofía of the Universidad de Santo Domingo.

1957–. *Revista de filosofía de la Universidad de Costa Rica* (San José), semiannual.

In Spain itself six periodicals arose, including one which repeated the title (*Convivium*) of a journal begun at Turin in 1929:

1951–. *Estudios filosóficos; Revista de investigación y crítica* (Las Caldas de Besaya, Spain), issued three times a year. Organ of the Spanish Dominicans.

1951–. *Archivum; Revista de la Facultad de Filosofía y Letras, Universidad de Oviedo* (Oviedo), semiannual, with variations.

1952–. *Espíritu; Cuadernos del Instituto Filosófico de "Balmesiana"* (Barcelona), semiannual, with variations.

1954–. *Crisis; Revista española de filosofía* (Madrid), quarterly. Emphasizes Christian existentialism.

1956–1957. *Convivium; Estudios filosóficos* (Barcelona), semiannual. Issued by the Facultad de Filosofía y Letras, Universidad de Barcelona.

1956–. *Augustinus* (Madrid), quarterly. Many foreign contributors.

ITALIAN. Three of the births of Italian philosophical journals took place at Milan: one each in 1950, 1951, and 1952.

1950–1962. *Il pensiero critico* (Milan), quarterly. In 1963 absorbed into the *Rivista di filosofia* (Milan, 1870–).

1951–. *Aut Aut; Rivista di filosofia e di cultura* (Milan), issued six times a year. Title is based on the Kierkegaardian *Either/Or*

1952–. *Bollettino della Società Filosofica Italiana* (Milan), quarterly.

Three births also occurred at Rome, including that of a journal with a Latin title which contains articles in Italian and other languages:

1952–. *Rassegna di filosofia* (Rome), quarterly. Organ of the Istituto di Filosofia, Universitá di Roma.

1955–. *La nuova critica; Studi e rivista di filosofia delle scienze* (Rome; formerly Florence), semiannual. Articles mostly in Italian, but with some in English and French. International board of editors. The title may reflect a desire for association with Croce's Naples journal *La critica* (1903 ff.), which, under a slightly different title, had died in 1951.

1958–. *Aquinas; Ephemerides Thomisticae* (Rome), issued three times a year, with variations. Subtitle has varied. Now issued by the Faculty of Philosophy, and the Patristic–Medieval Institute "Joannes XXIII," of the Pontificia Universitas Lateranensis. Articles in English, French, Italian, Latin, and Spanish.

The locale of two births was Turin; of two others, Padua; and of one, Bologna:

1950–. *Filosofia* (Turin), quarterly.

1951–. *Il saggiatore; Rivista di cultura filosofica e pedagogica* (Turin), quarterly.

1954–. *Studia patavina; Rivista di filosofia e teologia* (Padua), issued three times a year; formerly a quarterly.

1956–. *Rivista di estetica* (Turin; formerly Padua), issued three times a year.

1957–. *Il dialogo* (Bologna), quarterly, with variations.

PORTUGUESE. The Portuguese-language journals which were brought into being in the 1950s were:

1951–1959. *Revista filosófica* (Coimbra, Portugal), issued three times a year, with variations.

1951–. *Revista brasileira de filosofia* (Sâo Paulo), quarterly. Organ of the Instituto Brasileiro de Filosofia. Chiefly in Portuguese, with some articles in English, French, Italian, Spanish, and other languages.

1954–. *Filosofia; Revista do Gabinete de Estudos Filosóficos* (Lisbon), quarterly. Subtitle has varied.

1959–. *Organon; Revista da Faculdade de Filosofia da Universidade do Rio Grande do Sul* (Pôrto Alegre), quarterly, with variations.

FRENCH. Four new journals of philosophy in the French language appeared in the 1950s, including two published in Belgium (one with articles in English, French, and German) and one published in the Saar (with articles in French and German), which are included here among the French journals, since the titles of two are in French, and the title of the third is in Latin and French:

1951–. *Morale et enseignement* (Brussels), quarterly, with variations. Published by the Institut de Philosophic, Université de Bruxelles.

1951–. *Revue de l'enseignement philosophique* (Paris), issued six times a year, with variations. Organ of the Association des Professeurs de Philosophie de l'Enseignement Public.

1952–. *Annales Universitatis Saraviensis; Philosophie–lettres* (Saarbrücken), quarterly, with variations. Published since 1957 by the Philosophische Fakultät, Universität des Saarlandes. Articles in English, French, and German.

1954–. *Logique et analyse* (Louvain), quarterly, with variations. Articles in English, French, and German. Organ of the Centre National (Beige) de Recherches de Logique; issued only to members from 1954 to 1957 under the title *Bulletin intérieure.*

GERMAN AND DUTCH. Three new journals of philosophy in the German language appeared during the 1950s:

1950–. *Philosophia Naturalis; Archiv für Naturphilosophie und die philosophischen Grenzgebiete der exakten Wissenschaften und Wissenschaftsgeschichte* (Meisenheim am Glan), quarterly, with variations.

1953–. *Philosophische Rundschau* (Heidelberg), quarterly, with variations. Reviews of current books. Concerned largely, in its early years, with surveys of new philosophical literature, this became a general philosophical journal. Contains occasional articles in English.

1953–. *Deutsche Zeitschrift für Philosophie* (East Berlin), monthly, with variations (quarterly, 1953–1954; issued six times a year, 1955–1959). Table of contents also in English, French, Russian, and Spanish.

The Dutch-language journals of the 1950s include one with a Dutch title and one with a Latin title:

1959–. *Dialoog; Tijdschrift voor Wijsbegeerte* (Antwerp), quarterly.

1959–. *Scripta Recenter Edita* (Nijmegen), issued ten times a year. Contains a list of books on philosophy and theology, with emphasis on theology.

RUMANIAN, HUNGARIAN, AND SLAVIC. The period produced one Rumanian and one Hungarian organ, each issued for the most part four times a year:

1954–. *Cercetári filozofice* (Bucharest), quarterly, with variations. Table of contents also in French and Russian; summaries in French or German and in Russian.

1957–. *Magyar Filozófiai Szemle* (Budapest), quarterly, with variations. Table of contents, and summaries, in English, German, and Russian. Organ of the Magyar Tudományos Akadémia Filozófiai Intézetének Folyóirata.

Of the Slavic languages, Polish, Serbo-Croatian, and Russian are represented once each in the new philosophical journals of the 1950s.

1951–. *Studia Filozoficzne; Kwartalnik* (Warsaw), quarterly, with variations. Title was *Myśl Filozoficzna* from 1951 to 1955 (issued six times a year). Sponsored from 1952 to 1955 by the Komitet Filozoficzny, Polska Akademia Nauk. Suspended 1956. Published by the Instytut Filozofii i Socjologii, Polska Akademia Nauk. Table of contents and summaries of articles in English and Russian. This periodical replaced *Przegląd Filozoficzny* (1897–1949) at the beginning of the period of militant Marxist domination. According to an article in a 1963 issue of *Studia Filozoficzne*, it was Lenin who first solved Zeno's antinomy of the arrow in flight.

1953–1958. *Filozofski Pregled* (Belgrade), issued three times a year, with variations.

1958–. *Nauchnye Doklady Vysshei Shkoly; Filosofskie Nauki* (Moscow), issued six times a year; originally issued quarterly. Often cited as *Filosofskie Nauki*, without the series title ("Scientific Reports of the Higher School") represented by the first four words.

JAPANESE AND CHINESE. Also begun in the 1950s were *Bigaku; Aesthetics* (Tokyo, 1950–), issued quarterly, and *Chê Hsüeh Yen Chiu* ["Philosophical Research"] (Peking, 1955–), issued six times a year; formerly quarterly.

THE NINETEEN-SIXTIES

The early years of the 1960s were fruitful in the production of new journals of philosophy, but not as fruitful as the record year of 1946 (11 journals). The year 1960 brought forward 9; 1961, 4; 1962, 6; 1963, 5; 1964, 3; 1965, 6; and 1966, 1 (as of the time of the completion of this article).

1960. Three philosophical journals which were started in 1960 had their origin in England:

1960–. *The Heythrop Journal; A Quarterly Review of Philosophy and Theology* (Oxford), quarterly. Issued by the Jesuit Faculties of Philosophy and Theology, Heythrop College, Oxford.

1960–. *The British Journal of Aesthetics* (London), quarterly. Published for the British Society of Aesthetics.

1960–. *Philosophical Books* (Leicester, England), originally a quarterly; now issued three times a year.

Three had their origin in the United States:

1960–. *Notre Dame Journal of Formal Logic* (Notre Dame, Ind.), quarterly.

1960–. *Studies in Philosophy and Education* (Toledo, Ohio; previously New Brunswick, N.J.), quarterly, with variations.

1960–. *Journal of Existentialism* (New York), quarterly. Title was *Journal of Existential Psychiatry* from 1960 to 1964.

Amsterdam, Madrid, and Rome fathered one philosophical journal each in 1960:

1960–. *Wijsgerig Perspectief op Maatschappij en Wetenschap* (Amsterdam), issued six times a year. Each issue devoted to a specific topic.

1960–. *Noesis; Revista de filosofía y arte* (Madrid), quarterly. Suspended 1962–1963. *Noesis* had previously been the title of a philosophical journal in Italy in 1946.

1960–. *Filosofia e vita; Quaderni trimestrali de orientamento formativo* (Turin; previously Rome), quarterly.

1961. Two journals of philosophy were inaugurated in the United States, and one each in India and the Netherlands, in 1961:

1961–. *Journal for the Scientific Study of Religion* (New Haven), semiannual.

1961–. *International Philosophical Quarterly* (New York and Heverlee–Louvain), quarterly. Edited by the department of philosophy of Fordham University and the professors of philosophy, Berchmans Philosophicum, Heverlee, Belgium.

1961–. *Darshana* (Moradabad, India), quarterly. International board of consultants.

1961–. *Studies in Soviet Thought* (Dordrecht), quarterly. Published by the Institute of East-European Studies, University of Fribourg, Switzerland. Articles in English, French, and German.

1962. Two more journals were inaugurated in the United States, and one each in Argentina, Canada, Italy, and Australia, in 1962:

1962–. *Pacific Philosophical Forum* (Stockton, Calif.), quarterly. Each issue devoted to a specific subject, with a set format (thesis and countertheses).

1962–. *Soviet Studies in Philosophy* (New York), quarterly. Contains translations from Soviet publications, mainly Soviet periodicals.

1962–. *Cuestiones de filosofía* (Buenos Aires), quarterly.

1962–. *Dialogue; Canadian Philosophical Review; Revue canadienne de philosophie* (Montreal), quarterly. Articles in English and French. Sponsored by the Canadian Philosophical Association.

1962–. *De Homine* (Rome), quarterly. Issued by the Centro di Ricerca per le Scienze Morali e Sociali, Istituto di Filosofia, Università di Roma.

1962–. *Sophia; A Journal for Discussion in Philosophical Theology* (Melbourne), issued three times a year. An Italian *Sophia* began publication in 1933.

1963. As in 1961 and 1962, two journals of philosophy were inaugurated in the United States in 1963; in addition, two were inaugurated in India and one in the Netherlands:

1963–. *Southern Journal of Philosophy* (Memphis, Tenn.), quarterly.

1963–. *Journal of the History of Philosophy* (Berkeley), semiannual.

1963–. *Indian Journal of Philosophic Studies* (Hyderabad), semiannual. Published for the Andhra Pradesh Philosophical Society by the department of philosophy of Osmanian University, Hyderabad.

1963–. *Research Journal of Philosophy and Social Sciences* (Meerut, Uttar Pradesh, India), semiannual, with variations. International editorial board. Each issue contains about 200 pages on a particular subject.

1963–. *Vivarium; A Journal for Mediaeval Philosophy and the Intellectual Life of the Middle Ages* (Assen), semiannual.

1964. Three new contributions appeared in the year 1964:

1964–. *American Philosophical Quarterly* (Pittsburgh, Pa.), quarterly. International board of consultants. Articles only; no book reviews.

1964–. *The Philosophical Journal* (Edinburgh), semiannual. Issued by the Royal Philosophical Society of Glasgow. Although mainly concerned with scientific matters, the *Journal* also contains some valuable philosophical articles.

1964–. *Documentación crítica iberoamericana de filosofía y ciencias afines* (Seville), quarterly.

1965. The following journals began publication in 1965:

1965–. *Concilium; An International Review of Theology* (London), issued ten times a year.

1965–. *Foundations of Language; International Journal of Language and Philosophy* (Dordrecht, Netherlands), issued quarterly.

1965–. *Information aus dem philosophischen Leben der Deutschen Demokratischen Republik* (East Berlin), issued quarterly.

1965–. *Religious Studies* (London), semiannual. Articles on philosophy of religion and history of religion.

1965–. *Transactions of the Charles S. Peirce Society* (Amherst, Mass.), semiannual.

1965–. *Revue universitaire de science morale* (Geneva), issued three times a year.

1966. One philosophical journal began publication in 1966 before the present article was completed:

1966–. *The Bulletin of Philosophy* (Washington), issued eight times a year. Contains news of interest to philosophers.

The expansion in the twentieth century of the number of currently published journals of philosophy has roughly paralleled the growing interest in philosophy as an academic discipline.

Bibliography

Four authors have studied philosophical journals in general. In chronological order, their reports on this field are Friedrich Medebach, "Die philosophische Fachzeitschrift," in *Zeitungswissenschaft*, Vol. II (Berlin, 1936), 210–214; David Baumgart, *Philosophical Periodicals; An Annotated World List* (Washington, 1952); Augusto da Silva, *Revistas de filosofia* (Braga, Portugal, 1955); and Tóth Ilona Kovácsné, "A Magyar Közkönyvtarakban Megtalálható Kurrens Filozófia Periodikák" ("Current Philosophical Periodicals Available in Public Libraries in Hungary"), in *Magyar Filózofiai Szemle*, Vol. 8 (Budapest, 1964), 574–601.

Three sources cover philosophical journals in particular countries: Paul Feldskeller, "Das philosophische Journal in Deutschland," in *Reichls philosophischer Almanach* (Darmstadt, 1924), pp. 302–458; Enrico Zampetti, *Bibliografia ragionata delle riviste filosofiche italiana del 1900* (Rome, 1956), and the highly knowledgeable passages on periodicals in Max Rieser, "Polish Philosophy Today," in *Journal of the History of Ideas*, Vol. 24 (1963), 423–432.

Short articles on 83 periodicals appear in the *Enciclopedia filosofica*, 4 vols. (Venice and Rome, 1957). Other pertinent sources are the list, published annually in the *Répertoire bibliographique de la philosophie*, of periodicals covered by the *Répertoire*, and the list headed "Philosophy" in *Ulrich's Periodicals Directory* (New York, 1932; 10th ed., 1963).

The titles appearing in the philosophy category in the monthly *New Serial Titles; Classed Subject Arrangement* (Washington, 1955–) are useful, as is also the record of births and deaths of periodicals (as well as of libraries which possess complete or partial sets of the periodicals) in the *Union List of Serials in Libraries of the United States and Canada*, edited by Edna Brown Titus, 3rd ed., 5 vols. (New York, 1965), continued as *New Serial Titles*, which was begun by the Library of Congress in 1953 and is published monthly.

William Gerber (1967)

PHILOSOPHY JOURNALS [ADDENDUM]

The English-language journal citations in this update are organized chronologically by year of first publication, and appear within the individual year listings alphabetically by journal title. The non-English-language journal citations directly follow the English-language list; they too are organized chronologically by year of first publication, and appear within individual year listings alphabetically by journal title.

ENGLISH LANGUAGE

1965

Foundations of Language. Dordrecht, The Netherlands; Boston: D. Reidel. 1965–1976 bimonthly (formerly quarterly).

International Directory of Philosophy and Philosophers. Bowling Green, OH: Bowling Green State University, Philosophy Documentation Center. 1965–.

Transactions of the Charles S. Peirce Society. Amherst, MA: University of Massachusetts Press. 1965– quarterly.

1966

Apeiron. University of Alberta, Dept. of Classics and Monash University, Dept. of Classical Studies. Edmonton: Academic Print. & Pub. 1966–.

The Teilhard Review. Pierre Teilhard de Chardin Association of Great Britain and Ireland (London). Teilhard Centre for the Future of Man. 1966–1981.

1967

Conceptus. Innsbruck: J. Zelger. 1967–.

Noûs. Wayne State University, Dept. of Philosophy. Detroit: Wayne State University Press. 1967– quarterly.

The Philosopher's Index. Bowling Green, OH: Bowling Green State University, Philosophy Documentation Center. 1967– quarterly.

Royal Institute of Philosophy Lectures. Royal Institute of Philosophy. London: Macmillan. New York: St. Martin's. 1967–1990; semiannual, 1987–1990.

1968

American Philosophical Quarterly. Monograph Series. University of Pittsburgh, Dept. of Philosophy. Oxford: Basil Blackwell. 1968–1978 irregular.

Kinesis. Carbondale, IL: Southern Illinois University, Dept. of Philosophy. 1968– semiannual.

Man and World. State College, PA: I.P.R. Associates.1968–1997 quarterly.

The Philosopher's Index. Richard H. Lineback. Bowling Green, OH: Philosopher's Information Center. 1968– cumulative ed.

Philosophy and History. Tubingen, Germany: Institut fur wissenschaftliche Zusammenarbeit. 1968–1991 semiannual.

Philosophy and Rhetoric. University Park, PA: Pennsylvania State University Press. 1968– quarterly.

The Philosophy Forum. DeKalb, IL: Northern Illinois University. 1968–1980 quarterly.

1969

Chinese Studies in Philosophy. White Plains, NY: International Arts and Sciences Press, M. E. Sharpe, Inc. 1969–1997.

The Journal of Critical Analysis. Bemidiji, MN: National Council of Teachers for Critical Analysis. 1969– quarterly.

The Owl of Minerva: Quarterly Journal of the Hegel Society of America. Villanova, PA: Hegel Society of America. Villanova University, Philosophy Dept., and Florida State University. 1969– semiannual.

Studies in Philosophical Linguistics. William L. Todd. Evanston, IL: Great Expectations. 1969.

The Undergraduate Journal of Philosophy. Oberlin, OH: Oberlin College, Philosophy Dept. 1969–1977.

1970

Auslegung. Lawrence, KS: Dept. of Philosophy, University of Kansas. 1970s– semiannual.

International Journal for Philosophy of Religion. Dordrecht, The Netherlands; Boston: Martinus Nijhoff. 1970– four issues per year; 1983– six issues per year.

The Journal of Philosophical Linguistics. William Todd. Evanston, IL: Great Expectations. 1970–1971.

Metaphilosophy. Oxford: Basil Blackwell for the Metaphilosophy Foundation. 1970–1999; 2000– five issues per year.

Philosophic Exchange. Brockport, NY: State University of New York College at Brockport, Center for Philosophic Exchange, College of Arts and Science. 1970–.

PSA; Proceedings of the Biennial Meeting of the Philosophy of Science Association. East Lansing, MI: Philosophy of Science Association. 1970–1994 biennial.

The Southwestern Journal of Philosophy. Norman, OK: Southwestern Philosophical Society. 1970–1980.

Studies in History and Philosophy of Science. Oxford; New York: Pergamon Press. 1970– quarterly since 1995.

Theory and Decision. Dordrecht, The Netherlands: D. Reidel. 1970– eight issues per year.

1971

Canadian Journal of Philosophy. Edmonton: Canadian Association for Publishing in Philosophy. 1971–.

Graduate Faculty Philosophy Journal. New York: New School for Social Research, Philosophy Dept. 1971– semiannual.

Idealistic Studies. Worcester, MA: Clark University Press. 1971– three issues per year.

1972

Aitia. Farmingdale, NY: State University of New York at Farmingdale. 1972– 1992 three issues per year.

Journal of Philosophical Logic. Association for Symbolic Logic. Dordrecht, The Netherlands; Boston: Kluwer Academic. 1972– bimonthly.

Paideia. Buffalo, NY: State University College at Buffalo; University of New York College at Brockport. 1972.

Philosophical Linguistics. William Todd. Evanston, IL: Great Expectations. 1972–1973.

Philosophical Papers. Dept. of Philosophy, Rhodes University, and University of the Witwatersrand. 1972– three issues per year.

Philosophy in Context. Cleveland, OH: Cleveland State University, Dept. of Philosophy. 1972–1990 annual.

Radical Philosophy. Radical Philosophy Group (Great Britain). Canterbury: Radical Philosophy Group. 1972– bimonthly.

Second Order. Ile-Ife, Nigeria: University of Ife Press. 1972— semiannual.

Thêta-pi. Leiden, The Netherlands: E. J. Brill. 1972–1974 semiannual.

1973

CIRPHO. Montreal: International Society for Computer Research in Philosophy. 1973–1976.

Gnosis. Montreal: Sir George Williams University, Dept. of Philosophy. 1973–.

Indian Philosophical Quarterly. Pratap Centre of Philosophy. Amalner, India: University of Poona, Dept. of Philosophy. 1973– quarterly.

Radical Philosophers' Newsjournal. Somerville, MA: Radical Philosophers' Newsjournal. 1973–1990s.

Revolutionary World. Amsterdam: B. R. Grüner Pub. Co. 1973–1982 five issues per year.

1974

Indian Journal of Philosophic Studies. Osmania University, Dept. of Philosophy. Hyderabad: Osmania University 1974–.

International Studies in Philosophy. State University of New York at Binghamton. Torino, Italy: Filosofia. 1974–1979 annual, 1980–1981 semiannual, 1982– three issues per year.

Journal of the Philosophy of Sport. Philosophic Society for the Study of Sport, and the International Association for the Philosophy of Sport. Champaign, IL: Human Kinetics Publishers. 1974–2000 annual, 2001– semiannual.

Lias. Amsterdam: Holland University Press. 1974– two issues per year.

1975

Canadian Journal of Philosophy. Supp. vol. Guelph, ON: Canadian Association for Pub. in Philosophy. 1975–.

Journal of the Department of Philosophy. University of Calcutta, Dept. of Philosophy. Calcutta: University of Calcutta. 1975–.

Philosophy and Medicine. Spicker, Stuart F., and H. Tristram Engelhardt. Dordrecht, The Netherlands; Boston: Reidel. 1975–.

Philosophy Research Archives. American Philosophical Association, and Canadian Philosophical Association. Bowling Green, OH: Bowling Green State University, Philosophy Documentation Center. 1975–1981 annual.

Poznan Studies in the Philosophy of the Sciences and the Humanities. Amsterdam: Rodopi. 1975– quarterly.

Teaching Philosophy. Cincinnati, OH: [s.n.]. 1975– quarterly, formerly semiannual.

1976

Midwest Studies in Philosophy. Morris, MN: University of Minnesota, Morris. 1976– annual.

Philosophical Studies in Education. Ohio Valley Philosophy of Education Society. Terre Haute, IN: School of Education, Indiana State University. 1976– annual.

Philosophy and Literature. University of Michigan, Dearborn; Whitman College. Baltimore, MD: Johns Hopkins University Press. 1976–.

Southwest Philosophical Studies. Lubbock, TX: Texas Tech Press. 1976 annual, 1982 Spring, 1988 three issues per year, 1988– annual.

1977

Aletheia. Irving, TX: International Academy of Philosophy Press. 1977– irregular.

A Directory of Women in Philosophy. Bowling Green, OH: Bowling Green State University, Philosophy Documentation Center. 1977–1982.

The Independent Journal of Philosophy. Vienna: G. E. Tucker. 1977–.

Linguistics and Philosophy. Dordrecht, The Netherlands: Kluwer Academic. 1977– bimonthly.

Reports on Philosophy. Uniwersytet Jagiellonski. Warsaw: Polish Scientific Publishers. 1977–.

Review Journal of Philosophy & Social Science. Meerut, India: Anu Prakashan. 1977–.

Towards. Northridge, CA: C. Monks. 1977– semiannual.

1978

Bulletin of the Evangelical Philosophical Society. San Bernadino, CA: Evangelical Philosophical Society. 1978–.

Eidos. Waterloo, Ontario: University of Waterloo, Philosophy Graduate Student Association. 1978–.

Human Studies. Society for Phenomenology and the Human Sciences. Dordrecht, The Netherlands: Martinus Nijhoff. 1978– quarterly.

Lonergan Workshop: Collected Essays. Fred Lawrence. Missoula, MT: Scholars Press for Longergan Workshop. 1978–.

Milltown Studies. Dublin: Milltown Institute of Theology and Philosophy. 1978– semiannual.

The Philosopher's Annual. Center for the Study of Language and Information (U.S.). Totowa, NJ: Rowman and Littlefield. 1978– annual.

Philosophical Inquiry. Aristoteleio Panepistemio Thessalonikes. Athens: [s.n.]. 1978– quarterly.

Philosophical Investigations. Oxford: Basil Blackwell. 1978– quarterly.

Philosophy & Social Criticism. Chestnut Hill, MA: [s.n.]. 1978–1994 quarterly, 1995–2003 bimonthly, 2004– seven issues per year.

Research in Philosophy & Technology. Society for Philosophy & Technology (U.S.). Greenwich, CT: JAI Press. 1978–.

1979

The Etienne Gilson Series. Pontifical Institute of Mediaeval Studies. Toronto: Pontifical Institute of Mediaeval Studies. 1979–.

Nature and System. Tucson, AZ: Nature and System. 1979–.

1980

American Journal of Theology and Philosophy. American Society for Social Philosophy and Philosophical Theology. West Lafayette, IN: American Journal of Theology and Philosophy. 1980–.

Analytic Teaching. Texas Wesleyan College and Viterbo College. Fort Worth: Texas Wesleyan College. 1980s–.

Concordia. Valencia: Concordia. 1980s– two issues per year.

The Journal of Mind and Behavior. Institute of Mind and Behavior. New York: The Journal. 1980– quarterly.

Logos: Philosophic Issues in Christian Perspective. Santa Clara, CA: University of Santa Clara, Dept. of Philosophy. 1980– annual.

The Objective Forum. New York: TOF Publications. 1980–1987 bimonthly.

Pacific Philosophical Quarterly. Los Angeles: School of Philosophy, University of Southern California. 1980– quarterly.

Southwest Philosophy Review: Papers Presented at the Annual Meeting of the Southwestern Philosophical Society. Southwestern Philosophical Society. Conway, AR: The Society. 1980s– two issues per year.

1981

Philosophical Topics. Southwestern Philosophical Society, and University of Arkansas, Fayetteville, Dept. of Philosophy. Denver, CO: Philosophical Topics. 1981– two issues per year, 1986– three issues per year plus two supplements.

World Futures. New York: Gordon and Breach. 1981– semiannual.

1982

Contemporary German Philosophy. University Park: Pennyslvania State University Press. 1982–1984 annual.

Law and Philosophy. Dordrecht, The Netherlands; Boston: D. Reidel. 1982– six issues per year.

Monograph Series. Bundoora, Victoria: Australasian Association of Philosophy. 1982– semiannual.

Philosophy Research Archives: PRA. American Philosophical Association and Canadian Philosophical Association. Bowling Green, OH: Bowling Green State University, Philosophy Documentation Center. 1982–1989 annual.

South African Journal of Philosophy. Foundation for Education, Science, and Technology, South Africa. Pretoria: Bureau for Scientific Publications of the Foundation for Education, Science, and Technology. 1982–.

Spindel Conference: Proceedings. Memphis: Dept. of Philosophy, Memphis State University. 1982– annual.

The Teilhard Review and Journal of Creative Evolution. Teilhard Centre for the Future of Man. London: Teilhard Centre. 1982–1988 three issues per year.

The Thoreau Quarterly. Minneapolis: The Thoreau Quarterly. 1982–1985 quarterly.

Topoi. Dordrecht, The Netherlands; Boston: D. Reidel. 1982– semiannual.

1983

Afro American Journal of Philosophy: AAJP. New York: Afro American Philosophy Association. 1983– quarterly.

Cognito: An International Journal for Philosophy, Society, and Politics. Quezon City, Philippines: Cogito. 1983– quarterly.

Hypatia: A Journal of Feminist Philosophy. Oxford; New York: Pergamon. 1983–.

Krisis. International Circle for Research in Philosophy. Houston: International Circle for Research in Philosophy. 1983– two issues per year.

Method. Loyola Marymount University, Boston College, Lonergan Institute, and Institute for Integrative Studies in Los Angeles. Los Angeles: Method. 1983– semiannual.

Philosophy in Science. Specola Vaticana, Center for Interdisciplinary Studies, Papieska Akademia Teologiczna (Krakow, Poland), and Pachart Foundation. Tucson: Pachart Pub. House. 1983– irregular.

Social Philosophy and Policy. Bowling Green State University, Social Philosophy and Policy Center. Oxford: Basil Blackwell, 1983– semiannual.

Theoretical Medicine. Dordrecht, The Netherlands; Boston: D. Reidel. 1983–1997 four issues per year.

1984

Explorations in Knowledge. Eastleigh, U.K.: Sombourne Press. 1984–1997 semiannual.

Faith and Philosophy: Journal of the Society of Christian Philosophers. Society of Christian Philosophers. Wilmore, KY: The Society, 1984– quarterly.

Grantees' Reports. American Philosophical Society. Philadelphia: The Society. 1984–1986 annual.

History of Philosophy Quarterly: HPQ. Bowling Green, OH: Bowling Green State University, Philosophy Documentation Center. 1984– quarterly.

Irish Philosophical Journal. Belfast: Queen's University of Belfast, Dept. of Scholastic Philosophy. 1984– semiannual.

Journal of Applied Philosophy. Society for Applied Philosophy. Abingdon, Oxfordshire, U.K.: Carfax Pub. Co. 1984– three issues per year.

Rabindra Bharati Journal of Philosophy. Rabindra Bharati University. Calcutta: Rabindra Bharati University. 1984–.

Research in Philosophy and Technology. Suppl. Society for Philosophy and Technology. Greenwich, CT: JAI Press. 1984–.

1985

CC AI. Communication and Cognition (Firm). Ghent: Communication and Cognition. 1985– quarterly.

Economics and Philosophy. Cambridge, U.K.: Cambridge University Press. 1985– semiannual.

1986

Biology and Philosophy. Dordrecht, The Netherlands; Boston: D. Reidel. 1986– five issues per year.

Current Philosophy. Randolph, MA: Honor Publications. 1986– bimonthly.

Philosophy, Theology. Milwaukee: Marquette University Press. 1986– semiannual. Formerly *International Studies in the Philosophy of ISPS.* London: Routledge and Kegan Paul.

1987

African Philosophical Inquiry. African Society for Philosophical Research. University of Ibadan, Dept. of Philosophy. Ibadan: Ibadan University Press. 1987– annual, with each issue containing two numbers.

Cognito. Cognito Society; University of Bristol. Bristol, U.K.: The Society. 1987–1999 three issues per year.

Discussions in Contemporary Culture. Dia Art Foundation and Dia Center for the Arts. New York: Bay Press. 1987–1995 irregular.

Journal of Scientific Exploration: A Publication of the Society for Scientific Exploration. New York: Pergamon. 1987– quarterly.

Medical Humanities Review. University of Texas Medical Branch at Galveston; Institute for the Medical Humanities. Galveston, TX: The Institute. 1987– semiannual.

Philosophical Perspectives. James E. Tomberlin. Atascadero, CA: Ridgeview. 1987– annual.

Quest. University of Zambia, Dept. of Philosophy, Rijkuniversiteit te Groningen, Centre for Development Studies, and University of the North (South Africa). Lusaka, Zambia: Quest. 1987– semiannual.

Science in Context. Cambridge, U.K.: Cambridge University Press. 1987– quarterly.

1988

International Journal for the Semiotics of Law. Eric Landowski. International Association for the Semiotics of Law. Merseyside, U.K.: D. Charles Publications, and Holmes Beach, FL: Wm. W. Gaunt. 1988– four issues per year.

International Journal on the Unity of the Sciences. International Cultural Foundation and International Conference on the Unity of the Sciences. New York: The Conference. 1988–1992 quarterly.

Oxford Studies in Ancient Philosophy. Supp. vol. Oberlin Colloquium in Philosophy. Oxford: Clarendon Press, and New York: Oxford University Press. 1988–.

Philosophical Psychology. Abingdon, Oxfordshire, U.K.: Carfax Pub. Co. 1988– quarterly.

1989

Bridges. Columbia, MD: [s.n.]. 1989– semiannual.

Journal of Philosophy and the Visual Arts. London: Academy Editions, and New York: St. Martin's Press. 1989–.

The Teilhard Review. Teilhard Centre for the Future of Man. London: The Centre. 1989–1994 three issues per year.

The Westminster Tanner-McMurrin Lectures on History and Philosophy of Religion at Westminster. Salt Lake City: Westminster College of Salt Lake City. 1989–1992.

1990

American Catholic Philosophical Quarterly: Journal of the American Catholic Philosophical Association. Washington, DC: The Association. 1990– quarterly.

Behavior and Philosophy. Cambridge Center for Behavioral Studies. Cambridge, MA: The Center. 1990– semiannual.

Guide to Graduate Programs in Philosophy. American Philosophical Association. Newark, DE: The Association. 1990s– biennial.

Imodoye: A Journal of African Philosophy. Lagos, Nigeria: University of Lagos, Dept. of Philosophy, Faculty of Arts. 1990–.

Journal for General Philosophy of Science. Dordrecht, The Netherlands: Kluwer Academic. 1990– two issues per year.

Journal of Philosophical Research: JPR. Bowling Green State University, Philosophy Documentation Center; American Philosophical Association; Canadian Philosophical Association; University of Nebraska; and University of Iowa. Bowling Green, OH: Bowling Green State University, Philosophy Documentation Center. 1990– annual.

Pli, Warwick Journal of Philosophy. Coventry, U.K.: University of Warwick, Dept. of Philosophy. 1990– semiannual.

1991

Dialogue and Humanism: The Universalist Quarterly. Polska Akademia Nauk; International Society for Universalism. Warsaw: Warsaw University, World Order and Universalism Research Program. 1991–1993 quarterly, 1994 bimonthly.

The Harvard Review of Philosophy. Cambridge, MA: The Harvard Review of Philosophy (Organization). 1991– annual.

Philosophical Issues. Sociedad Filosofica Ibero Americana. Atascadero, CA: Ridgeview Pub. Co. 1991– annual.

Royal Institute of Philosophy. Suppl. Royal Institute of Philosophy. Cambridge, U.K.: Cambridge University Press. 1991– semiannual.

1992

Russian Studies in Philosophy. Armonk, NY: M. E. Sharpe. 1992– quarterly.

Skeptic. Skeptics Society. Altadena, CA: The Society. 1992– quarterly.

1993

The American Philosophical Association's Guide to Graduate Programs in Philosophy. Newark, DE: American Philosophical Association. 1993– annual.

Angelaki: A New Journal in Philosophy, Literature, and the Social Sciences. Oxford: Angelaki. 1993– three issues per year.

British Journal for the History of Philosophy (BJHP): The Journal of the British Society for the History of Philosophy. Bristol, U.K.: Thoemmes Press. 1993–2001 two or three issues per year; 2002– quarterly.

Epoche. Provo, UT: Brigham Young University, Dept. of Philosophy. 1993–1998 two issues per year.

European Journal of Philosophy. Oxford: Blackwell. 1993– three issues per year.

Humanities Aitia. State University of New York College of Technology at Farmingdale. Farmingdale, NY: SUNY. 1993– three issues per year.

IJPS. London: Routledge. 1993– semiannual.

The Journal of Political Philosophy. Cambridge, MA: Blackwell. 1993–.

Perspectives on Science: Historical, Philosophical, Social. Chicago: University of Chicago Press. 1993– quarterly.

Philosophia Mathematica. Philosophy of Mathematics, Its Learning, and Its Application. Canadian Society for the History and Philosophy of Mathematics. Toronto: University of Toronto Press. 1993– semiannual.

Routledge History of Philosophy. G. H. R. Parkinson and Stuart Shanker. London: Routledge. 1993–1999 irregular.

Studies in East European Thought. Dordrecht, The Netherlands: Kluwer Academic. 1993– quarterly.

Tekhnema: Journal of Philosophy and Technology. American University of Paris. Paris: The University. 1993– annual.

1994

European Review of Philosophy. Stanford: CSLI Publications, Center for the Study of Language and Information. 1994–.

Film and Philosophy. Society for the Philosophic Study of the Contemporary Visual Arts. Portsmouth, OH: The Society. 1994– annual.

Philosophia Christi: Journal of the Evangelical Philosophical Society. Orlando: The Society. 1994– annual.

Philosophy in the Contemporary World: An International Journal Sponsored by the Society for Philosophy in the Contemporary World. Morehead, KY: The Society. 1994– quarterly.

Philosophy, Psychiatry and Psychology: PPP. Baltimore: Johns Hopkins University Press. 1994– quarterly.

1995

Dialogue and Universalism. Warsaw: Warsaw University, Centre of Universalism. 1995– monthly.

Journal of Philosophy and Development. Ago-Iwoye, Nigeria: Ogun State University, Dept. of Philosophy. 1995–.

Making the Rounds in Health, Faith, and Ethics. Chicago: Park Ridge Center. 1995–1996 semimonthly, except July and August.

Philosophy of Education. Urbana, IL: Philosophy of Education Society. 1995– annual.

Res Publica: A Journal of Legal and Social Philosophy. Association for Legal and Social Philosophy (Great Britain). Liverpool: D. Charles Publications. 1995– semiannual.

Studies in History and Philosophy of Science. Studies in History and Philosophy of Modern Physics. Oxford: Pergamon. 1995– three issues per year (April, August, December).

1996

Archimedes: New Studies in the History and Philosophy of Science and Technology. Dordrecht, The Netherlands: Kluwer Academic. 1996– annual.

Ethics and the Environment. Greenwich, CT: JAI Press. 1996– semiannual.

Philosophical Writings. Durham, U.K.: University of Durham, Dept. of Philosophy. 1996– three issues per year.

Studies in History and Philosophy of Modern Physics. Oxford: Pergamon. 1996– quarterly.

1997

Contemporary Chinese Thought: Translations and Studies. M. E. Sharpe, Inc. Armonk, NY: Sharpe. 1997– quarterly.

Crossings. Binghamton, NY: State University of New York at Binghamton. 1997– semiannual.

The Philosophers' Magazine. London: [s.n.]. 1997– quarterly.

Philosophy and Geography. Society for Philosophy and Geography. Lanham, MD: Rowman and Littlefield. 1997–.

Philosophy in Review. Edmonton: Academic Print and Pub. 1997– six issues per year.

1998

APA Newsletters. Newark, DE: American Philosophical Association. 1998– semiannual.

Biomedical Sciences. Oxford: Pergamon. 1998– four issues per year.

Continental Philosophy Review. Dordrecht, The Netherlands; Boston: Kluwer Academic. 1998– quarterly.

Critical Review of International Social and Political Philosophy. London: Frank Cass. 1998–.

Theoretical Medicine and Bioethics. Dordrecht, The Netherlands: Kluwer Academic. 1998– six issues per year.

1999

Aristoi: An Interdisciplinary Journal of Philosophy. Broome Community College, Division of Liberal Arts. Binghamton, NY: The Division. 1999–.

Foundations of Chemistry. Dordrecht, The Netherlands: Kluwer Academic. 1999– eight issues per year.

2002

Epoche. Villanova, PA: Villanova University, Philosophy Dept. 2002– two issues per year.

Politics, Philosophy, and Economics: PPE. Gerald F. Gaus and Jonathan Riley. Murphy Institute of Political Economy. London: Sage. 2002– three issues per year.

Think: A Periodical of the Royal Institute of Philosophy. London: The Royal Institute of Philosophy. 2002– three issues per year.

2004

Journal of Moral Philosophy. London: Continuum. 2004– three issues per year.

Oxford Studies in Metaphysics. Oxford: Clarendon Press. 2004– irregular.

NON-ENGLISH LANGUAGE

1965

Cuyo. Mendoza, Argentina: Universidad Nacional de Cuyo, Instituto de Filosofía, Sección de Historia del Pensamiento Argentino. 1965–1983 annual.

Al-Fikr al-muʿasir. Cairo: al-Dar al-Misriyah al-ʿAmmah lil-Taʾlif wa-al-Nashr. 1965–[?] monthly.

Praxis. Zagreb, Croatia: Hrvatsko filosofsko drustvo. 1965–1974 quarterly.

Stromata. Colegio Máximo de San José, Facultad de Filosofía, Facultad de Teología; Universidad del Salvador, Facultad de Filosofía, Facultad de Teología. San Miguel, Argentina: Universidad del Salvador, Filosofía y Teología. 1965–.

Studia metodologiczne. Uniwersytet Poznanski. Poznań, Poland: Uniwersytet im. Adama Mickiewicza. 1965–.

Studia philosophiae christianae. Warsaw: Akademia Teologii Katolickiej. 1965– semiannual.

Voprosy filosofii i psikhologii. Leningradskii gosudarstvennyi universitet, Filosofskii fakul'tet, Fakul'tet psikhologii. [Leningrad]: Izd-vo Leningradskogo universiteta. 1965–[?].

1966

A Magyar Tudományos Akadémia Filozófiai és Történettudományi Osztályának közleményei. Magyar Tudományos Akadémia, Filozófiai és Történettudományok Osztálya. Budapest: Akadémiai Kiadó. 1966–1973.

Anales del Seminario de Metafísica. Universidad Complutense de Madrid, Seminario de Metafísica. Madrid: El Seminario. 1966–1997 annual.

Annales Universitatis Scientiarum Budapestinensis de Rolando Eötvös Nominatae. Sectio philosophica et sociologica. Eötvös Loránd Tudományegyetem. Budapest: Universita. 1966–1992 irregular (formerly annual).

Azarbaijan SSR Elmlar Akademiiasynyn khabarlari. Izvestiia Akademii nauk Azerbaidzhanskoi SSR. Seriia istorii, filosofii i prava. Tarikh, falsafa va hugug seriiasy. Baku, Azerbaijan: Azarbaijan SSR Elmlar Akademiiasy Nashriiiaty. 1966–1990 quarterly.

Cahiers pour l'analyse. Paris: Le Cercle d'épistémologie de l'école normale supérieure. 1966–1969 irregular.

Dijalektika. Belgrade: Univerzitet u Beogradu. 1966–.

Filozofia. Slovenská akadémia vied, Filozofický ústav, ústav filozofie a sociológie. Bratislava, Slovakia: Vydavatelstvo Slovenskej akadémie vied. 1966–1991 six issues per year, 1992– ten issues per year.

Problemy filosofiï: mizhvidomchyi naukovyi zbirnyk. Kyïvs'kyi derzhavnyi universytet im. T. H. Shevchenka. Kiev, Ukraine: Vyd-vo Kyivs'kogo universytetu. 1966– three issues per year.

Raison présente. Paris: Editions Rationalistes. 1966–.

Rassegna bibliografica di storia della filosofia. Università di Parma, Istituto di filosofia. Padua: Liviana editrice. 1966–[?] annual.

Studia Universitatis Babes-Bolyai. Series Philosophia. Cluj-Napoca, Romania: [Universitatea Babes-Bolyai]. 1966–1974.

Theologie und Philosophie. Freiburg im Breisgau, Germany: Herder. 1966–[?] four issues per year.

Vestnik Moskovskogo universiteta. Seriia VIII: Filosofiia. Moskovskii gosudarstvennyi universitet im. M. V. Lomonosova. [Moscow]: Izd-vo Moskovskogo universiteta. 1966–1976 bimonthly.

1967

Bibliographie Philosophie. Berlin: Akademie für Gesellschaftswissenschaften beim ZK der SED, Institut für Marxistisch-leninistische Philosophie, Zentralstelle für philosophische Information und Dokumentation. 1967–1987 quarterly.

Bibliographie Philosophie. Beiheft. Berlin: Institut für Gesellschaftswissenschaften, Zentralstelle für philosophische Information und Documentation. 1967–.

Crítica: revista hispanoamericana de filosofía. Mexico: Instituto de Investigaciones Filosóficas, Universidad Nacional Autónoma de México. 1967–.

Études philosophiques et littéraires. Jamʿiyat al-Falsafah bi-al-Maghrib. Casablanca: Dar el Kitab. 1967–1981 irregular (formerly two issues per year).

Filosofija. Jugoslovensko udruzenje za filozofiju, Filozofsko drustvo Srbije. [Belgrade]. 1967–1900s quarterly.

1968

L'age de la science. Paris: Dunod. 1968–1970 quarterly.

Anuario filosófico. Universidad de Navarra, Facultad de Filosofía y Letras. Pamplona, Spain: Universidad de Navarra. 1968–.

Bibliografía filosófica mexicana. [Mexico, D.F.]: Universidad Nacional Autónoma de México, Instituto de Investigaciones Bibliográficas and Instituto de Investigaciones Filosóficas. 1968– annual.

Estudio agustiniano. Valladolid, Spain: Estudio teológico agustiniano. 1968– three issues per year.

Gnozis [Gnosis]. New York. 1968–.

Problemos. Lithuania, Aukstojo ir specialiojo vidurinio mokslo ministerija. Vilnius, Lithuania: Mintis. 1968–[?] two issues per year.

Science et esprit. Jesuits, Province du Canada français, Faculté de philosophie, Faculté de théologie. Montreal: Les Éditions Bellarmin. 1968–.

Wiener Jahrbuch für Philosophie. Vienna: W. Braumüller. 1968– annual.

1969

Analele Universitatii Bucuresti. Filozofie. Bucharest: Universitatea din Bucuresti. 1969–1973 semiannual.

Annales de l'Institut de Philosophie. Université libre de Bruxelles, Institut de Philosophie, Institut de Sociologie. [Brussels]: Editions de l'Institut de Sociologie. 1969–1978 annual.

Anthropos. Drustvo psihologov Slovenije, Slovensko filozofsko drustvo. Ljubljana, Slovenia. 1969–.

Contributi dell'Istituto di filosofia. Università cattolica del Sacro Cuore, Istituto di filosofia. Milan: Società Editrice Vita e Pensiero. 1969–[?] irregular.

Eidos; revista de filosofía. Universidad Nacional de Córdoba, Instituto de Filosofía. Córdoba, Argentina: Instituto de Filosofía. 1969–.

Filosofskie voprosy logicheskogo analiza nauchnogo znaniia. P'ilisop'ayut'yan ev Iravunk'i Institut (Haykakan SSH Gitut'yunneri Akademia), Akademiia nauk Armianskoi SSR, Baku, Institut Filosofii i Prava. Yerevan, Armenia: IZD-vo AN Armianskoi SSR. 1969–.

Philosophische Perspektiven. Frankfurt am Main: V. Klostermann. 1969–1973 annual.

Studi internazionali di filosofia. Turin: Filosofia. 1969–1973 annual.

Voprosy filosofii i sotsiologii. Leningradskii gosudarstvennyi universitet imeni A. A. Zhdanova, Filosofskii fakul'tet. Saint Petersburg: Izd-vo Leningradskogo universiteta. 1969– annual.

1970

Actualidad bibliográfica de filosofía y teología. Barcelona: Facultades de Filosofía y Teología San Francisco de Borja. 1970– semiannual.

Algemeen Nederlands tijdschrift voor wijsbegeerte. [Assen, Netherlands]: Van Gorcum. 1970– quarterly.

Auslegung. Lawrence: University of Kansas, Department of Philosophy. 1970s– semiannual (formerly three issues per year).

Discurso. Universidade de São Paulo, Departamento de Filosofia. São Paulo, Brazil: Faculdade de Filosofia, Letras e Ciências Humanas da Universidade de São Paulo. 1970– irregular.

Zeitschrift für allgemeine Wissenschaftstheorie [Journal for General Philosophy of Science]. Wiesbaden, Germany: F. Steiner. 1970–1989.

1971

Bollettino del Centro di Studi Vichiani. [Naples: Centro di studi vichianii]. 1971–.

Filosofskie nauki. Qazaqtyng S.M. Kirov atyndaghy memlekettik universiteti. Almaty, Kazakhstan: Kazakhskii gos. universitet. 1971–.

Neue Hefte für Philosophie. Göttingen, Germany: Vandenhoeck & Ruprecht. 1971–1995 irregular.

Philosophia. Athens: Kentron Ereunes tes Hellenikes Philosophias. 1971– annual.

Philosophia. Universitat Bar-Ilan, Mahlakah le-filosofyah. Ramat-Gan, Israel: Bar-Ilan University. 1971– quarterly.

Philosophica Gandensia. Meppel, Netherlands: Boom Pers. 1971–1973.

Quellen und Studien zur Philosophie. Berlin and New York: de Gruyter. 1971– irregular.

Teorema. [Valencia, Spain]: Universidad de Valencia, Departamento de Lógica y Filosofía de la Ciencia, Departamento de Historia de la Filosofía. 1971–.

Zhe xue lun ping. Taipei: Guo li Taiwan da xue zhe xue xi. 1971–[?], 2004– semiannual.

1972

Aitia. Farmingdale: State University of New York at Farmingdale. 1972–1992 three issues per year.

Godishnik na Sofiiskiia universitet, Filosofski fakultet. Sofiiski universitet, Filosofski fakultet. Sofia, Bulgaria. 1972–1979 irregular.

Philosophie. Toulouse: Université de Toulouse-Le Mirail. 1972–1989 annual.

Prace filozoficzne. Uniwersytet Jagiellonski. Kraków: Panstwowe Wydawn. Nauk. 1972–1976 irregular.

Verifiche. [Trent, Italy]. 1972– four issues per year.

Zhe xue lun ji. Fu ren da xue (Hsin-chuang shih, Taiwan), zhe xue yan jiu suo. Taipei: Fu ren chu ban she. 1972–[?] semiannual.

1973

Beijing da xue xue bao: Zhe xue she hui ke xue ban. Beijing da xue, Qing hua da xue (Beijing, China). Beijing: Beijing ren min chu ban she. 1973– bimonthly.

Diotima. Hellenike Hetaireia Philosophikon Meleton. [Athens]: Ekdosis Hellenikes Hetaireias Philosophikon Meleton. 1973–.

Obshchestvennye nauki v SSSR. Seriia 3: Filosofskie nauki. Institut nauchnoi informatsii i fundamental'naia biblioteka po obshchestvennym naukam, Institut nauchnoi informatsii po obshchestvennym naukam (Akademiia nauk SSSR). Moscow: Akademiia nauk SSSR, In-t nauch. informatsii po obshchestvennym naukam. 1973–1976 quarterly, 1977–1991 six issues per year.

Protokoly ... Vsemirnogo Kongressa po Filosofii [Proceedings of the ... World Congress of Philosophy]. World Congress of Philosophy. Sofia, Bulgaria. 1973–[?] quinquennial.

Realitas. [Madrid]: Sociedad de Estudios y Publicaciones. 1973–.

Revista venezolana de filosofía. Universidad Simón Bolívar, Departamento de Filosofía, Sociedad Venezolana de Filosofía. [Caracas]: Universidad Simón Bolívar, Sociedad Venezolana de Filosofia. 1973– semiannual.

Sprawozdania-Poznanskie Towarzystwo Przyjaciól Nauk, Wydzial Filologiczno-Filozoficzny. Poznanskie Towarzystwo Przyjaciól Nauk, Wydzial Filologiczno-Filozoficzny. Poznań, Poland: Poznanskie Towarzystwo Przyjaciól Nauk. 1973–1993 annual.

1974

Analele Universitatii Bucuresti. Filosofie, istorie, drept. Universitatea din Bucuresti. [Bucharest: Tipografia Universitatii Bucuresti]. 1974–1976.

Análisis. Bogotá, Colombia: Universidad de Santo Tomás. 1974–[?] semiannual.

Argument-Sonderbände. Berlin: Argument-Verlag. 1974–.

Cuadernos salmantinos de filosofía. [Salamanca, Spain: Universidad Pontificia de Salamanca]. 1974–.

Filosofiia i nauchnyi kommunizm. Belaruski dziarzhauny universitet imia Ul. I. Lenina. Minsk: Izd-vo BGU. 1974–1989.

Philosophica. Rijksuniversiteit te Gent. [Ghent: Rijksuniversiteit]. 1974– two issues per year.

Philosophiques. [Montreal]: Bellarmin. 1974–.

Revista de filosofía. Universidad del Zulia, Centro de Estudios Filosóficos, Revista. Maracaibo, Venezuela: Universidad del Zulia, Facultad de Humanidades y Educación. 1974– three issues per year.

Transformação. Universidade Estadual Paulista, Faculdade de Filosofia, Ciências e Letras de Assis, Departamento de Filosofia. São Paulo, Brazil: Universidade Estadual Paulista. 1974–2002 annual, 2003– semiannual.

Zhe xue yu wen hua. Taipei: Zhe xue yu wen hua yue kan bian ji wei yuan hui. 1974– monthly.

1975

Erkenntnis. Dordrecht, Netherlands: Reidel. 1975– bimonthly (formerly three issues per year).

Grazer philosophische Studien. Universität Graz, Institut für Philosophie, Forschungsstelle für Österreichische Philosophie. Amsterdam: Rodopi. 1975–1976 annual, 1977–2002 at least two issues per year, 2003– annual.

Javidan-i khirad: nashriyah-i Anjuman-i Shahanshahi-i Falsafah-i Iran. Anjuman-i Shahanshahi-i Falsafah-'i Iran. Tehran: Anjuman. 1975–[?] semiannual.

Perspektiven der Philosophie. Amsterdam: Rodopi. 1975–.

Revista de filosofía latinoamericana. [San Antonio de Padua, Argentina: Ediciones Castañeda]. 1975–1979.

Revista latinoamericana de filosofía. [Buenos Aires, Argentina: Centro de Investigaciones Filosóficas]. 1975–.

Studia Universitatis Babes-Bolyai. Philosophia. Cluj-Napoca, Romania: [Universitatea Babes-Bolyai]. 1975–1976 annual, 1977–1982 two issues per year, 1983–1985 annual, 1986– two issues per year.

1976

Allgemeine Zeitschrift für Philosophie. Allgemeine Gesellschaft für Philosophie in Deutschland. [Stuttgart]: Frommann-Holzboog. 1976–.

Annales Universitatis Mariae Curie-Sklodowska. Sectio I, Philosophia-sociologia. Lublin, Poland: Nakl. Uniwersytetu Marii Curie-Sklodowskiej. 1976– annual.

Dialéctica. Puebla, Mexico: Universidad Autónoma de Puebla, Escuela de Filosofía y Letras. 1976– three issues per year.

Theoria: casopis Filozofskog drustva Srbije. Filozofsko drustvo Srbije. Belgrade: Drustvo. 1976– four issues per year.

1977

Analele Universitatii Bucuresti. Filosofie. Bucharest: Universitatea din Bucuresti. 1977– annual.

Kennis en methode. Amsterdam: Boom Meppel. 1977–1996.

Lituanistika v SSSR: Filosofiia i psikhologiia. Lietuvos TSR Mokslu akademija, Visuomenes mokslu informacijos sektorius, Visuomenes mokslu informacijos centras (Lietuvos TSR Mokslu akademija). Vilnius, Lithuania: Akademiia nauk Litovskoi SSR, In-t filosofii, sotsiologii i prava, Sektor nauch. informatsii po obshchestvennym naukam. 1977–[?].

Manuscrito. [Campinas, Brazil]: Universidade Estadual de Campinas, Centro de Lógica, Epistemologia e História da Ciência. 1977– semiannual.

Unabhängige Zeitschrift für Philosophie [The Independent Journal of Philosophy]. Vienna: [G. E. Tucker]. 1977–.

Vestnik Moskovskogo universiteta. Seriia VII: Filosofiia. Moskovskii gosudarstvennyi universitet im. M.V. Lomonosova. [Moscow]: Izd-vo Moskovskogo universiteta. 1977– bimonthly.

Zborník Filozofickej fakulty. Philosophica. Univerzita Komenského v Bratislave, Filozofická fakulta. Bratislava: Slovenské pedagogické nakl. 1977–, 1982– annual.

1978

Epistemologia. Genoa, Italy: Tilgher-Genova. 1978.

Escritos de filosofía. Academia Nacional de Ciencias de Buenos Aires, Centro de Estudios Filosóficos. Buenos Aires, Argentina: El Centro. 1978– semiannual.

Filosofia oggi. Bologna: Tip. editrice compositori. 1978– quarterly.

Humanitas. Instytut Filozofii i Socjologii (Polska Akademia Nauk). Wrocław, Poland: Zaklad Narodowy im. Ossolinskich. 1978–1989.

Studi filosofici. Naples: Istituto universitario orientale. 1978–.

Zhe xue yan jiu. Zhexue yanjiu. [Beijing: Ren min chu ban she]. 1978–1989 monthly, 1990 bimonthly, 1991– monthly.

1979

Annales de l'Institut de philosophie et de sciences morales. Université libre de Bruxelles, Institut de philosophie et de sciences morales. [Brussels]: Editions de l'Université de Bruxelles. 1979– annual.

Annali dell'Istituto di filosofia. Università di Firenze, Istituto di filosofia. Florence: L. Olschki. 1979–1984 annual.

1980

Actas. Fundación para el Estudio del Pensamiento Argentino e Iberoamericano; Jornadas del Pensamiento Filosófico Argentino. Buenos Aires, Argentina: Ediciones FEPAI. 1980s–[?].

Anhui da xue xue bao. Zhe xue she hui ke xue ban. Anhui da xue. [Hefei, China]: Anhui da xue xue bao bian ji wei yuan hui. 1980–1994 quarterly, 1995– bimonthly.

Annales de philosophie. Beirut: Université Saint-Joseph, Faculté des lettres et des sciences humaines. 1980–2001 annual.

Cahiers du Séminaire d'histoire des mathématiques. Paris: Université Pierre et Marie Curie, Laboratoire de mathématiques fondamentales, École pratique des hautes études, 1ère section, sciences mathématiques. 1980– annual.

Concordia. Valencia, Spain: Concordia. 1980s– two issues per year.

De philosophia. Ottawa, ON: University of Ottawa, Department of Philosophy, Student Association. 1980– annual.

Dialektik: Beiträge zu Philosophie und Wissenschaften. Universität Leipzig, Zentrum für Höhere Studien, Istituto italiano per gli studi filosofici. Cologne: Pahl-Rugenstein. 1980–1989 annual, 1991–1999 three issues per year, 2000– semiannual.

Ehu. Taipei: Ehu yue kan za zhi she. 1980s– monthly.

Godishnik na Sofiiskiia universitet "Kliment Okhridski," Filosofski fakultet. Sofia, Bulgaria: Universitetska pechatnitsa. 1980–1985 annual.

Slagmark. Århus, Denmark: Slagmark. 1980s–[?].

Vestnik. Institut za marksisticne studije (Slovenska akademija znanosti in umetnosti). Ljubljana, Slovenia: SAZU. 1980–1988 two issues per year.

1981

Acta Universitatis Lodziensis. Folia philosophica. Łódź, Poland: Uniwersytet Łódźki. 1981– irregular.

Agora. Universidad de Santiago de Compostela, Sección de Filosofía, Departamento de Filosofía e Antropoloxía Social, Departamento de Lóxica e Filosofía da Ciencia-Filosofía do Dereito, Moral e Política. Santiago de Compostela, Spain: Universidad de Santiago, Sección de Filosofía. 1981–1991 annual, 1992–[?] semiannual.

Análisis filosófico. Buenos Aires, Argentina: SADAF. 1981– semiannual.

Epistemens: revista del Institute de Filosofía. Universidad Central de Venezuela, Instituto de Filosofía, Facultad de Humanidades y Educación. [Caracas]: Ediciones de la Facultad de Humanidades y Educación. 1981–.

Recherches sur la philosophie et le langage: cahier du Groupe de recherches sur la philosophie et le langage. Université des sciences sociales de Grenoble, Groupe de recherches sur la philosophie et le langage. Grenoble: Institut de philosophie et sociologie. 1981–.

Revista de la Sociedad Argentina de Filosofía. Córdoba, Argentina: La Sociedad Argentina de Filosofía. 1981–.

Tetsugaku shiso ronshu. Ibaraki, Japan: Tsukuba Daigaku Tetsugaku Shiso Gakukei. 1981–.

Uchenye zapiski kafedr obshchestvennykh nauk vuzov Leningrada. Filosofskie i sotsiologicheskie issledovaniia. Russian S.F.S.R.; Ministerstvo vysshego i srednego spetsial'nogo obrazovaniia. Saint Petersburg: Izd-vo Leningradskogo universiteta. 1981–.

Xi bei da xue xue bao [Journal of Northwest University]. Xian Shi, China: Xi bei da xue xue bao bian ji bu. 1981– quarterly.

Zhe xue nian kan [Bulletin of the Association of Philosophy of Republic of China]. Zhongguo zhe xue hui. Taipei: Gai hui. 1981–[?] annual.

1982

Anuario de filosofía. San Miguel de Tucumán, Argentina: Universidad Nacional de Tucumán, Facultad de Filosofía y Letras, Departamento de Filosofía. 1982– annual.

Chuan xi lu. Dong wu da xue, Zhe xue xi. Taipei: Dong wu da xue. 1982–1988 annual.

Revista Universidad Pontificia Bolivariana. Medellín, Colombia: La Universidad Pontificia Bolivariana. 1982–1990.

Revue sénégalaise de philosophie. [Dakar, Senegal]: Nouvelles éditions africaines. 1982– semiannual.

Studi urbinati. B2, Filosofia, pedagogia, psicologia. Università di Urbino. Urbino: Università degli studi. 1982–1987.

Suid-Afrikaanse tydskrif vir wysbegeerte [South African Journal of Philosophy]. Foundation for Education, Science, and Technology, Bureau for Scientific Publications, Philosophical Society of Southern Africa. Pretoria: Foundation for Education, Science, and Technology, Bureau for Scientific Publications. 1982–.

Topoi. Dordrecht, The Netherlands: Reidel. 1982– semiannual.

Zhongguo zhe xue nian jian. Zhongguo she hui ke xue yuan, Zhe xue yan jiu suo. Shanghai: Zhongguo da bai ke quan shu chu ban she. 1982– annual.

1983

Bao kan zi liao suo yin. Di 1 fen ce, Zhe xue, she hui xue. [Beijing]: Zhongguo ren min da xue shu bao zi liao she. 1983– annual.

Beseda. Saint Petersburg. 1983–1993.

Cahiers du séminaire de philosophie. Université des sciences humaines de Strasbourg, Centre de documentation en histoire de la philosophie. [Strasbourg, France]: Centre de documentation en histoire de la philosophie. 1983–1996.

Ch'orhak sasang ui che munje. Kyŏnggi-do Songnam-si, Korea: Han'guk Chongsin Munhwa Yon'guwon. 1983–1986 annual.

Dilthey-Jahrbuch für Philosophie und Geschichte der Geisteswissenschaften. Göttingen, Germany: Vandenhoeck & Ruprecht. 1983–2000 annual.

Filosofiia i sotsiologiia nauki i tekhniki. Nauchnyi sovet po filosofskim i sotsial'nym problemam nauki i tekhniki (Akademiia nauk SSSR). Moscow: Nauka. 1983– annual.

Revue philosophique de Kinshasa. Kinshasa, Democratic Republic of the Congo: Faculté de théologie catholique de Kinshasa, Département de philosophie et religions africaines. 1983–[?] semiannual.

Yunnan min zu xue yuan xue bao [Journal of Yunnan University of the Nationalities]. Yunnan Sheng min zu shi wu wei yuan hui, Yunnan min zu xue yuan. Kunming, China: Yunnan min zu xue yuan xue bao (she zhe ban) bian ji bu. 1983– bimonthly.

1984

Acta Universitatis Wratislaviensis. Prace filozoficzne. Historia filozofii. Uniwersytet Wrocławski im. Boleslawa Bieruta. Wrocław, Poland: Wydawn. Uniwersytetu Wrocławskiego. 1984–1992 irregular.

Análise. Lisbon: GEC Publicacões. 1984– semiannual (formerly three issues per year).

Cuyo: anuario de filosofía argentina y americana. [Mendoza, Argentina]: Universidad Nacional de Cuyo, Facultad de Filosofía y Letras, Instituto de Filosofía Argentina y Americana. 1984–.

Darshan-manjari: The Burdwan University Journal of Philosophy. Barddhaman, India: University of Burdwan. 1984– annual.

Ezhegodnik Filosofskogo obshchestva SSSR. Filosofskoe obshchestvo SSSR. Moscow: Nauka. 1984–1990 annual.

Folia philosophica. Uniwersytet Slaski w Katowicach. Katowice, Poland: Uniwersytet Slaski. 1984– annual.

Karunungan [Sophia]. Philippine Academy of Philosophical Research. Manila: De La Salle University Press. 1984– annual.

Philosophie. Paris: Les Editions de Minuit. 1984– quarterly.

Prometeo: revista latinoamericana de filosofía. Guadalajara: Universidad de Guadalajara, Facultad de Filosofía y Letras. 1984–[?] three issues per year.

Rabindra Bharati Journal of Philosophy. Calcutta: Rabindra Bharati University. 1984–.

Rivista di storia della filosofia. Milan: Franco Angeli. 1984– quarterly.

Supplemente zu den Sitzungsberichten der Heidelberger Akademie der Wissenschaften, Philosophisch-Historische Klasse. Heidelberger Akademie der Wissenschaften, Philosophisch-Historische Klasse. Heidelberg, Germany: C. Winter. 1984–1996 irregular.

1985

Annali del Dipartimento di filosofia. Università di Firenze, Dipartimento di filosofia. Florence: L. Olschki. 1985– annual.

Annuario filosofico. Milan: Mursia. 1985– annual.

Archiwum historii i filozofii medycyny. Polskie Towarzystwo Historii Medycyny i Farmacji. Wrocław, Poland: Zaklad Narodowy im. Ossolinskich. 1985– quarterly.

Boletín mexicano de historia y filosofía de la medicina. [Mexico, D.F.: Sociedad Mexicana de Historia y Filosofía de la Medicina]. 1985– irregular.

Le cahier. Collège international de philosophie. Paris: Editions Osiris. 1985–1990 annual.

Ethernité. Paris: Editions de la Différence. 1985–.

Études maritainiennes [Maritain Studies]. Ottawa, Ontario: Association canadienne Jacques Maritain [Canadian Jacques Maritain Association]. 1985– annual.

Investigación humanística. Universidad Autónoma Metropolitana, Unidad Iztapalapa, Departamento de Filosofía, Unidad Azcapotzalco, Departamento de Humanidades, Unidad Xochimilco, Departamento de Política y Cultura. Mexico, D.F.: Universidad Autónoma Metropolitana. 1985– three issues per year.

Istoriia KPSS, nauchnyi kommunizm, filosofiia, pravo. Leningradskii gosudarstvennyi universitet imeni A. A. Zhdanova. Saint Petersburg: Izd-vo Leningradskogo universiteta. 1985– quarterly.

Lexicon philosophicum. Centro per il Lessico intellettuale europeo. Rome: Edizioni dell'Ateneo. 1985– annual.

Mathesis: filosofía e historia de las matemáticas. Universidad Nacional Autónoma de México, Departamento de Matemáticas, Grupo de Filosofía e Historia de las Matemáticas. [Mexico]: Universidad Nacional Autónoma de México, Departamento de Matemáticas, Facultad de Ciencias. 1985– quarterly.

Radovi. Razdio filozofije, psihologije, sociologije i pedagogije. Sveuciliste u Splitu, Filozofski fakultet Zadar. Zadar, Croatia: Fakultet. 1985– annual.

Studies in Logic and Theory of Knowledge. Lublin, Poland: [Katolickiego Uniwersytetu Lubelskiego, Towarzystwo Naukowe]. 1985–.

1986

Filosofia. Rome: Laterza. 1986–1995 annual.

Istoriko-filosofskii ezhegodnik. Institut filosofii (Akademiia nauk SSSR). Moscow: Nauka. 1986– annual.

Pensamiento hondureño. Tegucigalpa, Honduras: Imprenta Calderón. 1986–1987 semiannual.

Revista de filosofía latinoamericana y ciencias sociales. Buenos Aires, Argentina: Asociación de Filosofía Latinoamericana y Ciencias Sociales. 1986–2000.

Sédiments. LaSalle, Quebec: Hurtubise HMH. 1986– triennial.

Synthesis philosophica. Hrvatsko filozofsko drustvo, Savez filozofskih drustava Jugoslavije. Zagreb, Croatia: Croatian Philosophical Society. 1986– semiannual.

Vestnik Leningradskogo universiteta. Seriia 6, Istoriia KPSS, nauchnyi kommunizm, filosofiia, pravo. Leningradskii gosudarstvennyi universitet imeni A. A. Zhdanova. Saint Petersburg: Izd-vo Leningradskogo universiteta. 1986–1990 four issues per year.

1987

Analogía. Dominicans, Provincia de Santiago de México, Centro de Estudios. Xochimilco, Mexico: Centro de Estudios de la Provincia de Santiago de México de la Orden de Predicadores. 1987–.

La Balsa de la medusa. Madrid: Ediciones Antonio Machado. 1987– quarterly.

Filosofia politica. Bologna: Il Mulino. 1987– semiannual.

Filosofskie nauki. Soviet Union, Ministerstvo vysshego i srednego spetsial'nogo obrazovaniia. [Moscow: Izd-vo Vysshaia shkola]. 1987– twelve issues per year.

Filosofskie osnovaniia teorii mezhdunarodnykh otnoshenii. Moscow: Institut nauchnoi informatsii po obshchestvennym naukam (Akademiia nauk SSSR). 1987– irregular.

Signos. Universidad Autónoma Metropolitana, Unidad Iztapalapa, Departamento de Filosofía. Iztapalapa, Mexico: Universidad Autónoma Metropolitana. 1987–1996 annual.

Zborník Filozofickej fakulty Univerzity Komenského. Logica et methodologica. Bratislava: Univerzita Komenského v Bratislave, Filozofická fakulta. 1987–.

Zhe xue dong tai. Zhongguo she hui ke xue yuan, Zhe xue yan jiu suo. Beijing: Zhe xue yan jiu za zhi she. 1987– monthly.

1988

Analele stiintifice ale Universitatii "Al. I. Cuza" din Iaşi. Filosofie. Iaşi, Romania: Universitatea "Al. I. Cuza" din Iaşi. 1988–[?] annual.

Athenäums monografien. Philosophie. Frankfurt am Main: Athenäum. 1988–1993 irregular.

Metalogicon: rivista internazionale di logica pura e applicata di linguistica e di filosofia. Naples: L.E.R. 1988– semiannual.

Philosophia perennis: annales française de philosophie stylistique. Association française de philosophie stylistique. Lausanne, Switzerland: Editions l'Age d'homme. 1988.

Ratio juris. Università di Bologna. Oxford, and New York: Basil Blackwell for the University of Bologna. 1988–1995 three issues per year, 1996– quarterly.

1989

Bulletin de la Société américaine de philosophie de langue française. Northern Illinois University, Société américaine de philosophie de langue française. DeKalb, IL: Société américaine de philosophie de langue française. 1989–2000 quarterly.

Daimon: revista de filosofía. Murcia, Spain: Universidad de Murcia, Departamento de Filosofía y Lógica. 1989– semiannual.

Filosofs'kaia i sotsiologicheskaia mysl'. Instytut filosofiï (Akademiia nauk Ukraïns'koï RSR). Kiev, Ukraine: Naukova dumka. 1989– monthly.

Filosofs'ka i sotsiolohichna dumka. Instytut filosofiï (Akademiia nauk Ukraïns'koï RSR). Kiev, Ukraine: Naukova dumka. 1989–1990s monthly.

Filozofski vestnik. Filozofski institut (Slovenska akademija znanosti in umetnosti). Ljubljana, Slovenia: Akademija. 1989– three issues per year.

1990

Filosofija, sociologija. Lietuvos Mokslu akademija. Vilnius, Lithuania: Mokslas. 1990– three issues per year.

I castelli di Yale. Florence: Vallecchi editore. 1990s– annual.

Ìmodòye: A Journal of African Philosophy. [Lagos, Nigeria: University of Lagos, Faculty of Arts, Department of Philosophy]. 1990–.

Isegoría: revista de filosofía moral y política. Instituto de Filosofía (Consejo Superior de Investigaciones Científicas). Madrid: Instituto de Filosofía. 1990– semiannual.

Kairos. Université de Toulouse-Le Mirail, Faculté de philosophie. Toulouse: Presses Universitaires du Mirail. 1990– irregular.

Novoe v zhizni, nauke, tekhnike. Filosofiia i zhizn'. Moscow: Izd-vo Znanie. 1990–1991 monthly.

Die Philosophin. Tübingen, Germany: Edition Diskord. 1990– semiannual.

Revista de filozofie si drept. Institutul de Filozofie, Sociologie si Drept (Akademiia nauk Respubliki Moldova). Chişinău, Moldova: Izd-vo Shtiintsa. 1990s– three issues per year.

Revue roumaine de philosophie et logique. Academia Romāna. Bucharest: Editura Academiei. 1990– quarterly.

Zeitschrift für allgemeine Wissenschaftstheorie [Journal for General Philosophy of Science]. Dordrecht, Netherlands, and Boston: Kluwer Academic. 1990– two issues per year.

1991

Filosofskii ezhegodnik. Yekaterinburg, Russia: Izd-vo Ural'skogo un-ta. 1991– annual.

Jahrbuch des Forschungsinstituts für Philosophie Hannover. Forschungsinstitut für Philosophie Hannover. Hildesheim, Germany: Bernward. 1991–1993 annual.

Nachala: organ Filosofskogo obshchestva SSSR. Filosofskoe obshchestvo SSSR, Filosofskoe obshchestvo, Assotsiatsiia prepodavatelei gumanitarnykh nauk, Vserossiiskii blagotvoritel'nyi fond kul'tury, nauki i iskusstva "Ros'." Moscow: Obshchestvo. 1991–1998 four issues per year.

Novye idei v filosofii: ezhegodnik Filosofskogo obshchestva SSSR. Filosofskoe obshchestvo SSSR. Moscow: Nauka. 1991– annual.

Philosophical Issues. Sociedad Filosófica Ibero Americana. Atascadero, CA: Ridgeview. 1991– annual.

Répertoire bibliographique de la philosophie [International Philosophical Bibliography]. Louvain-la-Neuve, Belgium: Université catholique de Louvain, Editions de l'Institut supérieur de philosophie. 1991– quarterly.

Silentium: neperiodicheskoe izdanie Filosofsko-kul'turologicheskogo issledovatel'skogo tsentra "Eidos." Saint Petersburg: Izd-vo Filosofsko-kul'turologicheskii issledovatel'skii tsentr "Eidos." 1991–[?] irregular.

Stupeni. Sovetskii fond kul'tury, Leningradskii filial "Grifon," Tvorcheskoe ob'edinenie "Stupeni." Saint Petersburg: Stupeni. 1991–1998 three issues per year.

Teoria. Pisa: ETS. 1991– semiannual.

Vestnik Leningradskogo universiteta. Seriia 6, Filosofiia, politologiia, teoriia i istoriia sotsializma, sotsiologiia, psikhologiia, pravo. Leningradskii gosudarstvennyi universitet. Saint Petersburg: Izd-vo Leningradskogo universiteta. 1991– quarterly.

1992

Dong wu zhe xue chuan xi lu. Dong wu da xue, Zhe xue xi. Taipei: Dong wu da xue. 1992–1995 annual.

Filosofski alternativi. Institut za filosofski nauki (Bulgarska akademiia na naukite). Sofia, Bulgaria: Institut po filosofski nauki pri BAN. 1992– bimonthly.

Obshchestvennye nauki v Rossii. Seriia 3, Filosofiia. Moscow: Institut nauchnoi informatsii po obshchestvennym naukam (Rossiiskaia akademiia nauk). 1992– six issues per year.

Put'. Moscow: Progress. 1992–.

Spisy Masarykovy univerzity v Brne, Filozofická fakulta. Brno, Czech Republic: Masarykova univerzita. 1992– irregular.

Vestnik Sankt-Peterburgskogo universiteta. Seriia 6, Filosofiia, politologiia, sotsiologiia, psikhologiia, pravo. Sankt-Peterburgskii gosudarstvennyi universitet. Saint Petersburg: Izd-vo Sankt-Peterburgskogo universiteta. 1992– quarterly.

Zhe xue za zhi. Taipei: Ye qiang chu ban she. 1992– quarterly.

1993

Axiomathes: quaderni del Centro studi per la filosofia mitteleuropea. Centro studi per la filosofia mitteleuropea. Trent, Italy: Il Poligrafo. 1993– three issues per year.

Comenius-Jahrbuch. Deutsche Comenius-Gesellschaft. Sankt Augustin, Germany: Academia Verlag. 1993– annual.

Cuadernos del sur. Filosofía. Bahía Blanca, Argentina: Universidad Nacional del Sur, Departamento de Humanidades. 1993–.

Filosofiia kul'tury. Samarskii gosudarstvennyi universitet, Kafedra filosofii gumanitarnykh fakul'tetov. [Samara, Russia]: Samarskii universitet. 1993–.

Ludus vitalis. Mexico, D.F.: Centro de Estudios Filosóficos, Políticos y Sociales Vicente Lombardo Toledano. 1993– semiannual.

Nemetsko-russkii filosofskii dialog. Institut nauchnoi informatsii po obshchestvennym naukam (Rossiiskaia akademiia nauk), Institut filosofskikh issledovanii. Gannovera. Moscow: INION RAN. 1993–.

Peterburgskie chteniia po teorii, istorii i filosofii kul'tury. Komitet po kul'ture i turizmu Merii Sankt-Peterburga, Filosofsko-kul'turologicheskii issledovatel'skii tsentr "Eidos." Saint Petersburg: Izd-vo Filosofsko-kul'turologicheskii issledovatel'skii tsentr "Eidos." 1993– annual.

Sotsial'nye i gumanitarnye nauki. Seriia 3, Filosofskie nauki Otechestvennaia i zarubezhnaia literatura. Institut nauchnoi informatsii po obshchestvennym naukam (Rossiiskaia akademiia nauk). Moscow: INION RAN. 1993–1994 four issues per year.

Studia philosophica. Tartu Ulikool, Filosoofia Osakond. Tartu, Estonia: Ulikool. 1993–.

Tekhnema: Journal of Philosophy and Technology. Paris: American University of Paris. 1993– annual.

1994

Eon: al'manakh staroi i novoi kul'tury. Institut nauchnoi informatsii po obshchestvennym naukam (Rossiiskaia akademiia nauk), Laboratoriia teorii i istorii kul'tury, TSentr gumanitarnykh nauchno-informatsionnykh issledovanii, Otdel kul'turologii. Moscow: INION RAN. 1994–.

Sfinks. Tvorcheskoe ob'edinenie "Stupeni." Saint Petersburg: Alga-Fond. 1994– irregular.

Sotsial'nye i gumanitarnye nauki. Seriia 3, Filosofiia. Otechestvennaia i zarubezhnaia literatura. Institut nauchnoi informatsii po obshchestvennym naukam (Rossiiskaia akademiia nauk). Moscow: INION RAN. 1994– four issues per year.

1995

Dialogue and Universalism. Uniwersytet Warszawski, Centrum Uniwersalismu, Polska Akademia Nauk, International Society for Universalism. Warsaw: Warsaw University, Centre of Universalism. 1995– monthly.

Edith Stein Jahrbuch. Stein, Edith, and Teresianum. Würzburg, Germany: Echter. 1995– annual.

Fa zhi bo lan [Legality Vision]. Gong qing tuan, Shanxi Sheng wei, Shanxi sheng Qing shao nian fan zui yan jiu hui. Taiyuan, China: Fa zhi bo lan bian ji bu. 1995– monthly.

Filosofiia nauki. Moscow: Institut filosofii (Rossiiskaia akademiia nauk). 1995– annual.

Hyle. Universität Karlsruhe, Institut für Philosophie. Karlsruhe, Germany: Hyle. 1995– annual.

Rubezhi. Demokraticheskaia al'ternativa. Moscow: Agentstvo "Vremia." 1995–1998 monthly.

1996

Dong Wu zhe xue xue bao [Soochow Journal of Philosophical Studies]. Taipei: Dong Wu da xue chu ban she. 1996–2002 annual, 2003– biennial.

Forum philosophicum: studia a Facultate Philosophica Societatis Jesu Cracoviae edita. Towarzystwo Jezusowe w Krakowie, Wydzial Filozoficzny. Kraków: WAM Press. 1996– annual.

Naukovi zapysky. Natsional'nyi universytet. Kiev, Ukraine: Kyievo-Mohylians'ka Academia. 1996–.

Pleroma. Ivano-Frankivs'k, Ukraine: Proekt "Delos'kyi nyrets'." 1996–.

Postizhenie kul'tury. Moscow: Rossiiskii institut kul'turologii. 1996– annual.

Variaciones Borges: revista del Centro de Estudios y Documentación "Jorge Luis Borges." Århus, Denmark: Århus universitet, Jorge Luis Borges Center for Studies and Documentation, Romansk institut. 1996– semiannual.

1997

Dukh i litera. Natsional'nyi universytet "Kyievo-Mohylians'ka akademiia." Kiev, Ukraine: FAKT. 1997–.

Istoriia filosofii. Moscow: Institut filosofii (Rossiiskaia akademiia nauk). 1997– irregular.

Metafizicheskie issledovaniia. Sankt-Peterburgskii gosudarstvennyi universitet, Laboratoriia metafizicheskikh issledovanii. Saint Petersburg: Aleteiia. 1997– four issues per year.

Mysl': ezhegodnik Peterburgskoi assotsiatsii filosofov. Peterburgskaia assotsiatsiia filosofov, Sankt-Peterburgskii gosudarstvennyi universitet. Saint Petersburg: Izd-vo Universiteta. 1997– annual.

Recherches de théologie et philosophie médiévales. Universität zu Köln, Thomas-Institut, Centre de Wulf-Mansion. Leuven, Belgium: Peeters. 1997– semiannual.

Vestnik Rossiiskogo filosofskogo obshchestva. Moscow: Rossiiskaia akademiia nauk, Rossiiskoe filosofskoe obshchestvo. 1997– quarterly.

1998

Alpha omega: rivista di filosofia e teologia dell'Ateneo Pontificio Regina Apostolorum. Ateneo pontificio Regina Apostolorum. Rome: L'Ateneo. 1998– three issues per year.

Bibliographie de la philosophie [Bibliography of Philosophy]. International Institute of Philosophy, Unesco, Centre national de la recherche scientifique (France). Paris: J. Vrin. 1998– annual.

Denkwege. Tübinger Gesellschaft für Phänomenologische Philosophie. Tübingen, Germany: Attempto. 1998–.

Pensamiento de los confines. Universidad de Buenos Aires, Programa de Estudios de Cultura y Pensamiento Contemporáneo, Centro de Estudios de Profesores Universitarios. Buenos Aires, Argentina: Universidad de Buenos Aires, Argentina, Diótima. 1998– semiannual.

Philosophiegeschichte und logische Analyse [Logical Analysis and History of Philosophy]. Paderborn, Germany: F. Schöningh. 1998– annual.

2000

Cités. Vendôme, France: Presses Universitaires de France. 2000– quarterly.

2002

Antropologiia kul'tury. Moskovskii gosudarstvennyi universitet im. M. V. Lomonosova, Institut mirovoi kul'tury. Moscow: OGI. 2002–.

2003

Studia antyczne i mediewistyczne. Warsaw: Wydawn. Instytut Filozofii i Socjologii (Polska Akademia Nauk). 2003– annual.

Michael J. Farmer (2005)

Terms are alphabetized on a word-by-word basis. Page references to entire articles are in ***boldface.***

A

A dicto secundum quid fallacy, 3:550
A finalidade do mundo (Farias Brito), 3:552
A fortiori
 definition of, 5:533
 reason, 7:735
A posteriori, **1:240–246**
 analytic propositions as, 1:242
 applied to concepts, 1:241–242
 Aristotle on, 1:240
 experience and, 1:240–242
 identity theory as, 7:470
 Kant on, 1:240–241
 in simulation theory, 9:38
 synthetic propositions as, 1:242–243
A posteriori argument, Hume on, 4:510
A posteriori evidence, 6:116–117
A posteriori judgments, *vs. a priori,* 1:159
A posteriori knowledge
 vs. a priori knowledge, 5:79
 as foundational, 2:276
 Kant on, 3:306
 logical positivists on, 9:665–666
 in materialism, 6:11
A posteriori metaphysics, 4:777, 8:831
A posteriori ontology, naturalism as, 6:492
A posteriori physicalism, 5:114–115
A posteriori propositions, 1:242–246
A posteriori relations, in realism, 2:101
A priori, **1:240–246**
 as absolute, 1:245–246
 Aristotle on, 1:240
 empiricism on, 1:241–242
 experience and, 1:240–242
 in human nature, 4:482
 Kant on, 1:240–241
 linguistic theory of, 5:662
 in Maréchal, 5:709–710
 mathematics as, 5:645
 McTaggart on, 6:78
 metaphysics and, 6:78, 6:204
 philosophy as, 7:331
 possibility, 7:723
 relative, 1:245–246
 in simulation theory, 9:38
A priori act, Beck on, 1:519
A priori argument
 Bayesian machines and, 1:497–498
 Hobbes's, Boyle's critique of, 1:673
 Hume on, 4:510
 for internalism, 4:715
A priori concepts, 1:241–242
 Broad on, 1:697–698
 experience and, 3:214–215
 presupposition in thought, 1:706
 in scientific theories, 2:68
 time as, critique of, 2:85
A priori conditions, for common consent arguments for God's existence, 2:346
A priori cosmology, in history of metaphysics, 6:193–194
A priori evidence, 6:116–117
A priori explanation, Bonhoeffer on, 1:656
A priori fallacies, 3:547
A priori intuition, 3:307, 5:14–15
A priori judgment(s)
 vs. a posteriori judgments, 1:159
 characteristics of, 6:117
 Kant on, 5:13–14. *See also Critique of Judgment* (Kant)
 Maimon on, 5:646
 synthetic, as principles, 5:13–14
 and understanding, 8:660
A priori justification, 5:80
A priori knowledge, **5:79–86**
 and *a posteriori* knowledge, in concept of tone, 9:280–281
 Alembert on, 1:105
 analyticity and, 1:166
 of axioms, 6:628
 Campanula on, 2:15
 in classical Indian philosophy, 9:545
 Cohen (Hermann) on, 2:302–303
 constructivism and, 9:77
 Erigena on, 3:341–342
 ethical knowledge as, 3:367

A priori knowledge, ***continued***
as evidence of incorporeality of souls, 4:606
existence of, 5:81–82, 5:85
Fechner on, 7:86
as foundational, 2:276
of good and evil, Saadya on, 4:813
as independent of experience, 5:79
Kant on, 1:160, 3:306–307, 3:410, 5:79–80, 5:101
Lewis (C. I.) on, 5:309–310
linguistic conception of, 1:150, 4:724
logical empiricism and, 8:694
logical positivists on, 9:665–666
metaphysical, Fries and, 3:752
moral realism on, 8:251–252
in naturalized philosophy of science, 6:501
necessity and, 5:151
of numbers, 6:674
Plato on, 3:358, 7:588
radical empiricism on, 5:82
Schiller (Ferdinand) on, 8:625
Schopenhauer on, 8:649–650, 8:656
Schulze on, 8:660–661
in Schuppe's epistemology, 8:663
in Shao Yong's "before Heaven" learning, 9:6
in Swedenborg's psychology, 9:337
in syntactic view of theories, 9:413–414
in theory of innate ideas, 4:686
thought experiments as, 9:455
traditional conception of, 5:80–81
of universals, 9:592
Wright (Chauncey) on, 9:847
See also Innate ideas; Rationalism
A priori metaphysics
James on, 4:777
methods of, 6:169–170
Schopenhauer on, 8:649
A priori necessary truths, knowledge and, 5:96
A priori probability, finite, 5:56
A priori propositions, 1:242–246, 8:639
analyticity of, 1:244–245
mathematical propositions as, 5:81
necessity of, 1:243–244
A priori rationalism, 8:506
A priori reasoning
in Boethius's syllogistic, 1:627–628
in Bohmain mechanics, 1:541–542
in Bohr, 1:637
coherence theory of truth and, 2:309
vs. empirical, in metaphysics, 6:202
as mathematical necessity *vs.* experience, 1:575
in observation and property set preexistence, 1:638
vs. pure *a priori,* 1:242
role of hypotheses in science, 1:643
A priori relations, in realism, 2:101
A priori statements
Ayer on, 1:437
coherence theory of truth and, 2:311–312
necessity of, 7:296
phenomenological, 7:279, 7:294–297
synonyms and, 1:167
synthetic, 1:245
A priori truth
in causality and direct realism, 2:98
in Cheng's neo-Confucian rationalism, 2:156
conventionalize and, 2:474
Aaron, R. I., on Locke, 5:378
Abbagnano, Nicola, **1:1–3**
Abbott, T. K., on Berkeley, 1:576
Abbreviatio Avicenne de Animalibus (Scot), 8:703
Abduction
and Bonaventure's reduction, 1:653
definition of, 5:533
in moral arguments for existence of God, 6:358
in scientific inference, 4:644
ʿAbduh, Muḥammad, Islamic Enlightenment and, 3:248–249
Abel, responsibility and, 4:831
Abelard, Peter, **1:3–7**
Aristotelianism of, 1:279, 5:424–425
Augustinianism of, 1:402
on being, 1:528
Bernard of Clairvaux and, 1:592
on conditionals, 5:426–429
on contradictories, 5:425
on dialectic, 1:3, 3:54, 5:424–426
ethics of, 1:3–6, 3:403
Gilbert of Poitiers and, 4:89
on inference, 1:628, 5:425–426
and logic, 1:628, 5:424–429, 5:433
in medieval philosophy, 6:99
nominalism of, 1:4–5, 9:599
philosophy of sex and, 7:522
on possibility, 7:720
on redemption, 2:249
Roscelin and, 8:495–496
on scholastic method, 7:260
School of St. Victor and, 8:592
on semantics, 8:763–764
and sermocinalism, 8:766
sermonism of, 8:764
on syncategoremata, 8:769
Theodoric of Chartres and, 9:410
on universals, 1:4–5, 3:290, 8:763–764, 9:599
William of Champeaux and, 8:592, 9:767
Abendblatter (Kleist), 5:78
Abendstunde eines Einsiedlers, Die (Pestalozzi), 7:254
Abhandlung über die Euidenz in den metaphysischen Wissenschaften (Essay on Evidence in Metaphysical Science) (Mendelssohn), 6:130
Abhandlung über die Fähigkeit der Empfindung des Schönen in der kunst und dem Uterricht in derselben (Treatise on the power of feeling beauty and on teaching it) (Winckelmann), 9:790
Abhandlungen der Fries'schen Schule (Nelson), 3:753
Abharī, al-, Arab logic and, 5:419–420
Abhidharma Buddhism, 1:740, 4:632
Abhidharmakośabháṣya (Commentary on the treasury of knowledge) (Vasubandhu), 9:650–651
Ability
Anselm on, 1:217
meaning of, 2:23–26
in mind, 6:259–260
opportunity and, 1:217, 2:25–26
possibility and, 2:25–26, 7:724–725
statements of, Austin (J. L.) on, 3:20
Ability approach, to defusing knowledge argument, 5:114
Abnormal (Foucault), 3:701
Abnormal Psychology (McDougall), 6:72
Abolitionism
Parker (T.) on, 7:122
peace and, 7:151, 7:154–157
of Wayland (Francis), 9:728
Abortion, **1:8–10**
applied ethics and, 1:236
ethical relativism and, 3:373–374
ethical treatment of future persons and, 3:393
medical ethics of, 6:93
medico-jurisprudence on, 6:95
personhood and, 1:9, 3:393, 7:242
Thomson (Judith) on, 1:9, 9:448

Abortion and Infanticide (Tooley), 7:242
"About" (Goodman), 4:159
"About the Grounds of the Mechanical Hypothesis" (Boyle), 1:673
Abrabanel, Judah. *See* Ebreo, Leone
Abraham (Biblical figure), concurring in suspension of ethical, 5:64
Abraham, Max, on electromagnetic theory of matter, 3:235–236
Abraham ben Samuel Abulafia, 5:3
Abraham ibn Daud, 5:333
Abraham ibn Ezra, 5:4
Abravanel, Isaac
  on Maimonides, 5:653
  in Renaissance Jewish philosophy, 4:824
Abravanel, Judah. *See* Ebreo, Leone
Absence
  of coercion or constraint, freedom as, 3:721
  of contradiction, principle of, 3:557
  in Indian philosophy, 6:530–532
  in knowledge of nirvāṇa, 6:622
  as means of knowledge, 5:117, 5:122
  of self-being, ontology as, 1:738–739
  as universal, 9:584
"Absent Qualia Are Impossible" (Shoemaker), 9:16
"Absoliutnaia mifologiia = absoliutnaia dialektika" (Absolute myth = absolute dialectics) (Losev), 5:575
Absolom, Absolom! (Faulkner), 4:806
Absolute, The, **1:10–13**
  aesthetic experience as revelation of, 1:679
  alienation and, 1:121–122
  as all-unity, 9:124
  being as, 1:12
  Beneke on, 8:140
  Bosanquet on, 1:662–663
  Bradley on, 1:678–679, 7:95
  Bulgakov on, 1:760
  Chicherin on, 2:147
  conceptions of, social origins of, 9:102
  in education, 7:373
  experience and, 8:12–13
  Fichte on, 1:11, 3:616
  Froebel on, 7:373
  in Gnosticism, 4:99
  God as, 1:623, 2:246, 4:111–112
  Hebbel on, 4:253–254
  Hegel on, 1:11, 1:120–121, 1:530, 4:108, 4:111, 4:264, 4:669, 5:62, 7:98, 9:289
  as identity of knower and known, 1:12
  in Indian philosophy, 4:135
  in Iqbal's theistic pluralism, 4:744
  logical positivism on, 5:526
  manifestation of, 3:616
  Pringle-Pattison on, 8:12–13
  relationship with, psychological conditions allowing, 3:607
  Schelling on, 1:11–12, 4:669, 4:749, 8:620–621
  self as allusion to, 9:237
  Spencer on, 7:714
  in Spir's principle of identity, 9:197
  Trubetskoi (Evgenii) on, 9:529–530
  Universe as, 2:563–564
  Vysheslavtsev on, 9:717–718
Absolute [term]
  Coleridge's use of, 1:10
  Hegel's use of, 1:10
  Schelling's use of, 1:10
Absolute beauty, Cousin on, 2:580
Absolute beginning, *kalām* argument on God's existence and, 2:555
Absolute being, 1:12
  God as, 1:529
  Hegel on, 1:530
  Lavelle on, 5:215
Absolute chance, as self-contradictory, 1:692
Absolute confirmation, 2:433–434
Absolute dependence, 8:634–637
Absolute essence, elevating reason to status of, 3:610
Absolute I, 3:615
Absolute idea, Hegel on, 5:62, 7:98
Absolute idealism
  as aesthetic and moral experience, 1:538
  Anderson (John) in, 1:197–198
  Beneke and, 1:543
  Bradley on, 1:12
  coherence truth theory and, 2:539
  development of, 4:557–558
  Fichte and, 4:557
  Grote and, 4:189
  Hegel on, 4:557–558, 6:193
  Kant and, 4:556
  Korn on, 5:143
  Moore on, 1:145
  personalism and, 7:234
  on reality, 8:624
  Rensi and, 8:433
  Royce on, 8:518–519
  Schelling on, 1:11–12, 4:557
  Schiller's (Ferdinand) opposition to, 8:623
  standard of rationality in, 4:784
  time in, 1:145
  world in, 1:13
Absolute identity, as intuitive, 1:704
Absolute impossibility, 7:262–263
Absolute indiscernibles, 4:569
Absolute infinite, Aristotle's denial of, 4:656
Absolute knowledge
  Bergson on, 1:567
  Hegel on, 4:264, 5:62
Absolute mind, 4:269
Absolute motion, 1:581–582, 6:592, 9:155
Absolute origin, *kalām* argument on God's existence and, 2:555
Absolute power, of God, 5:69, 6:105
Absolute reality, Brahman as, 1:684
Absolute religion, Parker (T.) on, 7:122
Absolute simples, Wittgenstein on, 9:811
Absolute simultaneity, in classical physics, 9:495
Absolute space, 1:581–582, 2:272, 9:147–148, 9:465–466
  vs. relative, 6:592
  spatial relations without, Boscovich on, 1:665
Absolute terms, Ockham on, 9:777
Absolute Thou, 5:702
Absolute truth, 3:565, 8:744
Absolute uncertainty, in Bohmian mechanics, 1:634
Absolute worth
  as categorical imperative, 2:70
  Oman on, 7:14
  supernatural and, 7:14
Absolutism, 2:466, 7:422, 8:158
Abstinence, sexual, 7:526
Abstract algebra, 5:459, 9:369
Abstract axiomatics, 4:358–359
Abstract entities
  and causality, 1:318, 5:84
  creation of, 1:318–319
  Frege on, 2:417
  ontological status of, 1:529
  in Platonism, 6:628
  rejection of, 6:627
  theories of, 6:636–637
Abstract ideas
  Berkeley on, 1:586, 4:593, 8:781–782
  in Cartesianism, 4:565–566
  Condillac on, 8:785
  as false, 1:579
  Hume on, 4:491–492

Abstract ideas, ***continued***
importance of language to, 8:785
Locke on, 4:593
as meaningless, 1:579
mental images of, 8:81–82
Abstract images, 4:590–592, 8:81–82
Abstract names, in Bentham, 1:552
Abstract natures, 1:449
Abstract nouns, 6:660
Abstract objects
vs. concrete, Brentano on, 1:691
epistemology of, 6:673–674
God's existence and, Leibniz on, 2:553
introduction of, 3:646
in ontology, 3:647, 7:26
properties of, 6:636
in science, necessity of, 6:628
Abstract terms
definition of, 5:533
elimination of, 8:553–554
Ockham on, 9:777
Abstract thought, 3:559
Abstract universals
Croce's historical knowledge and, 2:602
qualities as, 1:662
Abstract world, of eternal Forms, 5:95
Abstracta, concepts and, 2:415
Abstraction
acquisition of, 7:568
Aquinas on, 9:429
in art, 1:69, 8:620
axiom of (axiom of comprehension), 5:533
Berkeley on, 1:581–582
Campanella on, 2:15
Carnap on, 2:38
vs. concrete ideas, 4:565–566
definition of, 5:533
Diderot on, 3:72
existence of, 3:498–499
extensive, 9:748
Frege on, 6:627
Gilbert of Poitiers on, 4:88
Hugh of St. Victor on, 8:592
in inner sense theory, 4:696
in Isaac of Stella's doctrine of illumination, 4:753
Locke on, 3:300
Marcel on, 5:700
materialism and, 6:5
of meaning, 1:153
Mercier's use of, 6:144
in Neoplatonism, 8:101–102
in nominalism, 6:628
phenomenalism and, 7:273, 7:284–286
Piaget on, 7:568
principles, consistency and, 3:732
process of, 5:160
Reid on, 8:327
Russell on, 2:38
Schelling on, 8:620
in "simple act" theory of intuitive knowledge, 4:728
Toletus on, 9:511
of transcendental ego, 5:680
universals as, 1:581–582, 1:627, 9:595
Whitehead on, 9:748
Abstractionism, problems with, 9:420–421
Abstractive cognition
derivation of, 9:774–775
Duns Scotus on, 3:139–140
vs. intuitive, 3:139–140
in John of Mirecourt's epistemology, 4:841
Ockham on, 9:773–776
universality of, 9:775
Absurdity
Aristotle on, 2:74
Camus on, 2:20–21, 4:748
existentialist doctrine of, 4:748
in Peirce's logic, 5:454–455
Ryle on, 2:77–78
Sartre on, 4:748
in subject-predicate relations, 2:162
symbol for, 3:654
See also Reductio ad absurdum
Abubacer. *See* Ibn Ṭufayl
Abu'l-Barakāt al-Bahdādī
in Islamic philosophy, 4:758
in medieval Jewish philosophy, 4:817
Abu'l-Salt, Arab logic and, 5:419
Abuse of Beauty (Danto), 1:67
Abuse of Casuistry: A History of Moral Reasoning, The (Johnson and Toulmin), 1:601
ACA subsystem, 8:456
Academic freedom
Lovejoy on, 5:592
Stewart on, 9:246
Wolff on, 9:823
"Academic Freedom" (Lovejoy), 5:592
Academic laws, of Foucher, 3:702
Academic philosophy, Foucher and, 3:702
Academic principles, Leibniz on, 3:704
Academic skepticism, 1:193–195, 3:703, 4:501, 7:311–312, 8:175–176
Academica (Cicero), 2:258, 9:48
Académie Française, 3:123
Academy. *See* Florentine Academy; Greek Academy
Accelerating observer, 3:635
Acceleration
force and, 3:689, 6:2
in mass measurement, 6:2
space and, 2:522
Accentus, 5:542
Acceptance sampling, 3:665
Acceptance theory, 1:501, 3:583
Accept-West Party, 5:139
Access, to consciousness, 2:450
Access problem, 6:628
Accident(s)
in Aristotle's categories, 2:73
Boetius of Dacia on, 1:627–628
Burley on, 1:773
as change *vs.* alteration, 2:75
existence as, 5:649
Hobbes on, 4:411
vs. laws, 5:221–222, 5:225, 5:229
liability and, 7:462
in natural science, 9:867
as terms in traditional logic, 5:494
tort law and, 7:461
Zabarella on, 9:867
Accidental forms
Aquinas on, 3:115
Burley on, 1:773
vs. essential predication, 2:74
Accidental generalizations, *vs.* laws of nature, 3:709
Accidental necessity, 3:693–695
Accion consciente, theory of, 5:143
Accommodation, ethical relativism and, 3:373–374
Account of Philaretus during His Minority, An (Boyle), 1:672
Account of Reason and Faith in Relation to the Mysteries of Christianity (Norris), 6:656
"Account of the Book Entitled *Commercium Epistolicum*" (Newton), 6:591
Account of the Courts of Prussia and Hanover (Toland), 9:504
Accumulation theory, of qualities in elements, 5:118
Ach, Narziss, 4:721
Achamoth, 9:632
Achilles, on death, 5:349
Achilles argument against motion, 9:875
Achinstein, Peter, 2:435
Ackerman, James S., 1:331
Ackermann, Wilhelm, 3:639
and computing machines, 2:401
in finitary proof theory, 8:55

Ackermann functions, 2:401
Acosmism, 4:103
Acosta, Gabriel. *See* Costa, Uriel da
Acoustic (verbal) symbols, 3:670
Acquaintance
knowledge by, 1:485, 5:97, 5:114, 8:545–546
in non-inferential justification, 2:276
principle of
in Bergmann, 1:562
Russell's, 5:97
truth and, 2:277
Acquired representational states, 3:109
Acquisition of things, in Indian meditation practices, 6:108
Act
a priori, Beck on, 1:519
of abstraction theories, 4:728–729
Aquinas on, 2:679–680
Aristotle on, 2:679
of being, 1:476
belief as preparation for, 1:462
of believing, in Moore's theory of truth, 2:542
desire and, 4:714–715
ethical judgments and, 7:6
of existence, 2:551
of faith, 3:715
form as, 6:101
of God, having proximate natural or human causes, 3:534
good will and, 2:70
illocutionary, in fictional narratives, 3:627
of knowing, in Buddhism, 1:753
as knowledge, 1:103
of meaning *(das Meinen),* 5:161
meaning-endowing, in expression, 8:803
in medical ethics, 3:457–458
in medieval philosophy, 6:101
vs. omission, 3:457–458
vs. potency, 2:679–680
pure
Croce on, 2:603
Gentile on, 4:50–51, 9:197
Spirito on, 9:197
of recognition, 3:617
reflexive, intuitive cognition of, 9:774
Ross (William David) on, 8:505
temporal organization of, in computers, 6:81
unjust, 4:873–874
of will
assent as, 6:583
obligation as, 9:284
in Tennant's philosophy, 3:533
in Thomism, 3:533
Act Itself, The (Bennett), 1:549
"Act of Oblivion, The" (Culverwell), 2:613
Act utilitarianism, 3:384–385, 9:603–604
benevolence in, 9:606–607
counterintuitiveness of, 9:612–613
as descriptive ethics, 9:605–606
hedonistic, 9:607
vs. ideal rule forms, 1:687
of Mill (John Stuart), 6:227
as normative ethics, 9:606–608
praise and blame in, 9:612
probability in, 9:608–609
reflective equilibrium and, 9:611–613
rules in, 9:608, 9:612–613
and sacrifice, 9:612–613
strict, 3:749
Acta Eruditorum (journal), 5:252–254, 9:823
Action, **1:14–22**
Aecesilaus on, 1:248
agent causation and, 1:88–89
akratic, 9:728–732
Anselm on, 1:217–218
approval and disapproval of, 8:2
Arendt on, 1:253
Aristotle on, 1:15
assent and, 1:194, 1:248
Augustine on, 1:395–397
beauty of, 8:3
in behaviorism, 1:524–525
Bergson on, 1:567
capacity for, personhood and, 7:241–242
Carneades on, 1:194–195
communication and, 6:80
Condillac on, 2:423
conditions for, 6:159
consequences of, 3:708, 3:763
contemporary debate on, 3:19–20
Davidson's causal theory of, 1:17, 2:645–648
decision points leading to, 8:706
in defining truth, 4:36
in deontic logic, 9:848
at a distance
in classical mechanics, 2:281–282
criticism of, 3:688–689
in EPR theory, 8:215
by forces, 6:61
legitimacy of, 3:688
in mechanical philosophy, 6:60, 9:578
microcosm and, 5:642
in quantum mechanics, 1:539–542
divine, Malebranche on, 5:664
elucidation of, 5:673–674
evolutionary utility of, 1:565
existentialists on, 3:503
as expression, 9:833
future results of, 9:651
Gehlen on, 4:36
Geulincx on, 4:77
goals and, 7:736
goodness of, 6:159, 9:609
Hobbes on, 8:127–128
Holbach on, 6:10
in Homer, 4:460
immoral, 9:833–834
in impetus theory, 4:622
imputed to groups, 7:393–394
individuation of, 1:14–15
intent and, 1:14–15, 1:18–20, 4:700, 7:447
intrinsically good, 6:156
judgment internalism on motivation to, 4:714
justifying, might of ego in, 9:251
karma as response to, 4:625
Kierkegaard on, 3:501–503
and knowledge, 1:103, 4:77, 4:629, 9:726
Landgrebe on, 5:184
vs. legal transaction, 7:446
logic of, 9:848
luck and, 1:21
meaning attached to, revelation of, 8:664
mechanical theory of, 8:127–128
mental states and, 9:813–814
Mill (James) on, 6:219
in minimalism, 7:736
moral categories of, 6:117–118
as moral good, 1:552
as motivating force, 1:618
Nagel on, 1:17
natural meaning of, 9:833
nature of, 8:3
in neo-Confucianism, 4:795
as optimific, 1:460
palingenesis as supreme norm of, 4:95
political, 1:253
power and, 7:732
praise and blame for, 9:609, 9:612
purpose of, 9:756
as quest for truth, 1:618
reason in, 7:735–736
reasons for, 1:18–20
reductionist view of, 1:20–21

Action, *continued*
reflection on, 9:794–795
rightness of, 6:219, 9:612
Ross (William David) on, 8:505
Sartre on, 3:503
sentences as performance of, 1:154
side effects of, 1:20
as signs, 8:665
Smart on, 9:612
social, 9:93
social, science of, 6:224–225
in Stoicism, 1:194
temporal organization of, 6:80
vs. thought, in self-constitution, 4:51
thought leading to, 3:705
truth and falsity in, 9:833
ugliness of, 8:3
unfree, 9:729–731
unity of, 9:726
in utilitarianism, 9:603–609
Valla on, 9:636
virtuous, motivation to, 4:529
volitionist theory of, 1:88–89
voluntary, Augustine on, 1:395–397
von Wright's theory of, 9:847–848
Whichcote on, 9:745
will and, 1:217–218
in wisdom, 9:794–795
Wittgenstein on, 9:807, 9:813–814
Wollaston on, 9:833
wrongness of, 9:612
Action, L' (Blondel), 1:617
Action explanation, Davidson on, 2:645–648
Action theory
on agency, 3:445
ruling out causal deviance in, 5:90
of von Wright, 9:847–848
"Actions, Reasons, and Causes" (Davidson), 1:15, 1:534, 2:645–646
Activation states, 2:443
Active conditioning event, of sense object, 9:749
Active intellect
Abunaser on, 4:581
Alexander of Aphrodisias on, 1:112–113
al-Fārābī, Abū al Naṣr on, 4:756, 4:811
Averroes on, 1:424
Avicenna on, 1:433–434
in Ibn al-ʿArabī, 4:543
in Islamic Neoplatonism, 4:550, 6:557–558
itinerarium in union with, 4:544
Maimonides on, 5:651
in Maréchal on, 5:708
Themistius on, 9:409
Activism
Arnold on, 1:294
Matthew of Aquasparta on, 6:65
Activity
Berkeley on, 1:574
as character of consciousness, 5:143
as God, in Bergson, 1:570
human, Spir on, 9:196
Laromiguière on, 5:201
Leibniz on, 5:260, 5:267–268
making sense of, speech in, 9:77
philosophy as, 5:526
in Sāṃkhya cosmology, 6:107
specific forms of, 3:723
Act-object distinction, 4:560
Actor-Network Theory (ANT), 8:678–679
Actual, in ontology, 7:23
Actual being, 4:313
Actual entities, 4:627, 9:751
Actual idealism, 4:50
Gentile and, 4:49–53
Gioberti and, 4:95
Spirito on, 9:197
Actual infinite, 4:655–657, 5:533, 9:874
Actual occasions
nature and, 9:749
societies of, 9:750
Actual processes, God and, 9:752
Actual rule utilitarianism, 9:603
Actualism, Arnauld and, 1:292
Actualistic-critical metaphysics, Liebert on, 5:343–344
Actualities *(Wirklichkeiten)*, of consciousness, 5:160
Actuality
name and, in Chinese philosophy, 2:202–204
soul as, 1:274
temporally indexed, 9:481
Woodbridge on, 9:842–843
Actualization(s)
of forms, 6:101
in medieval philosophy, 6:101
Aczel, J., on rational degrees of belief, 8:685
Ad Nationes (Tertullian), 1:228, 9:399
Ad sacram (papal bull), 4:789
Adacemia, Vives on, 9:700
Adagia (Erasmus), 3:338
Adam Bede (Eliot), 3:184
Adam of Little Bridge, 5:429, 5:433
Adams, Ernest W., on conditionals, 2:424–426
Adams, Frederick, on volition, 9:705
Adams, Marilyn
on evil, 3:477–478
on free will, 4:252
on hell, 3:477–478, 4:252
Adams, Robert
on divine command theories, 3:94, 6:164
on dualism, 3:114, 3:117
moral argument and, 3:321
on omniscience, 7:479
presentism and, 9:479
Adamson, Robert, on Forberg, 1:378
Adaptation
in Darwinism, 7:342–343
evolutionary, diet and, 3:482
Gould on, 3:489–490
vs. heuristics, 8:154–155
intelligibility of world as, 9:379
Lewontin on, 3:489
in teleological argument for existence of God, 9:379–380
Tennant on, 9:392
to world, reason as, 1:559
"Adaptation of the Method of the Logical Spectrum to Boole's Problem" (Macfarlane), 5:561
Adaptationism
debate on, 3:489–490
in evolutionary psychology, 3:481–484
Adapted Mind, The (Barkow, Cosmides, and Tooby, eds.), 3:481
Adapting Minds (Buller), 3:486
Addams, Jane, 3:44
and Hull House settlement, 3:566–567
as philosopher, 3:569
Addiction, determinism and, 3:26
Addison, Joseph, 1:22
on aesthetics, 1:51, 1:513
Enlightenment and, 3:244
and Sulzer, 9:325
Additional variables theory, 8:212–213
Address on the Death of Princess Charlotte (Shelley), 9:8
Addresses to the German Nation (Fichte), 3:414, 3:614, 3:618
Adduction, 4:635
Adelard of Bath, 7:612
Adenosine triphosphate (ATP), 6:568
Adequacy
conditions of, 6:84–85
evidence in attributor contextualism and, 2:486
Adiaphoristic controversy, 6:119
Adickes, Erich
on Kant, 6:541

on Liebmann, 5:344
panpsychism and, 7:83
Adjective(s)
as descriptive uncombined expressions, 2:73
true as, 2:547–548
Adjudication
impartial, moral decision making and, 3:579
Leiter on, 1:169
logic in, 7:448–449
Adler, Alfred, **1:23–25**
Freud and, 1:23–24, 8:106, 8:146
individual psychology of, 8:146
and Jung, 4:857
in Kaufmann's volumes, 5:46
on unconscious, 9:573
Administrative law, 7:718
Admissibility, probability and, 8:38–39
Adonai (Cresca), 5:653
Adoration of the Shepherds, The (El Greco), 1:310
Adorno, Theodor Wiesengrund, **1:25–30,** 1:69–70
on Enlightenment, 3:244–245
on false consciousness, 4:574
Adrsta (invisible), karma as, 5:41–42
Adultery, 7:525
Advaita Vedānta, 4:629
on atomism, 1:383
on Brahman, 1:682–683
on knowledge, 5:117
on liberation, 5:329–330
on life, meaning and value of, 5:359
post-Śamkara, 4:629
and Schrödinger's identity theory, 8:658
Advance directives, 3:456–458
Advancement of Learning (Bacon), 1:450, 8:772
Adventures of Ideas (Whitehead), 9:746
Adventures of the Dialectic (Merleau-Ponty), 6:149, 9:491
Adverbials
Davidson on, 8:808
modification, in semantic theory, 3:462–463, 8:808
sense perception and, 8:813, 8:821
Adversus Hermogenes (Tertullian), 9:399–400
Adversus Mathematicos (Sextus Empiricus), 4:164, 9:49
on lekton, 8:757–758
on semantics, 8:757
on ultimate referents, 8:759
Adversus Pseudodialecticos (Against the pseudo dialecticians) (Vives), 7:147, 9:700
"Advice to Christian Philosophers" (Plantinga), 7:581
"Advice to French Refugees" (Bayle), 1:502
Advis et Les presens de la Demoiselle de Gournay, Les (The Advice and Presents of Mademoiselle de Gournay) (Gournay), 4:167
Aecesilaus, 1:248
Aegidius Colonna Romanus. *See* Giles of Rome
Aemilianus, P. Cornelius Scipio, 7:79
Aeneas, Dante on, 2:624
Aenesidemus, **1:30–32**
epistemology of, 3:288
Pyrrhonism and, 1:193, 9:49
ten modes of, 8:851
Aenesidemus (Schulze), 8:660
Aeons, in Valentinus, 3:189
Aeschines (Euclides of Megara), 6:110
Aeschines of Sphettus, 9:107
Aeschylus, 4:176–177
Dikē on, 3:79
Hegel on, 9:524
Nietzsche on, 9:524
Aesculapius, temple of, diagnostic technique at, 3:105
Aesthetic (Croce), 2:600
"Aesthetic Concepts" (Sibley), 9:21
Aesthetic delight, as disinterested, 5:26–27
Aesthetic Dimension, The (Marcuse), 1:70
Aesthetic education, 5:67
Aesthetic empathy, in Caso, 2:65
Aesthetic experience, **1:32–35**
Alison on, 1:303
as art, 1:298, 1:509
vs. artistic experience, 1:34–36
attitude in, 1:33, 1:36, 1:75
beauty as, 1:74, 1:511–514
Croce on, 1:57, 2:600–602
in destructive violence, 1:488–489
as distance and objectification, 1:761
imagination in, 1:50, 4:598
instrumental value of, 1:508–509
laws of appreciation and, 1:514
leading to eternal Idea, 1:538
as revelation of Absolute, 1:679
supremacy of, 1:33
viewing conditions and, 1:34
Aesthetic formalism, doctrine of, 3:572
Aesthetic judgment, **1:35–37,** 1:73–74
beauty as subjective idea in, 1:514
Boileau on, 1:640
DuBos on, 3:123
Gottsched on, 4:165–166
in *Iliad* (Homer), 1:41
Kant on, 1:35–37, 5:26, 8:630
vs. moral judgment, 5:26
Santayana on, 8:598
Schopenhauer on, 8:653
vs. scientific judgments, 5:26
Sibley on, 9:21
Aesthetic objects, identification of, 1:508–509
Aesthetic order, in teleological argument for existence of God, 9:376
Aesthetic permanence, theory of, 7:268
Aesthetic point of view, Kierkegaard on, 5:63–64
Aesthetic qualities, **1:37–41,** 1:75
Burke on, 1:51–52
Dewey on, 3:46–47
ordinary language for, 9:21
Aesthetic rationalism, in Gottsched, 4:165
Aesthetic reinforcement, 3:557
Aesthetic semblance, 8:628
Aesthetic theory
Adorno on, 1:27–29, 1:69–70
Deústua on, 5:207
of Ivanov's *theurgy,* 4:767
Aesthetic Theory (Adorno), 1:27–29, 1:69–70
Aesthetic threshold, Fechner's principle of, 3:557
Aesthetic value, 1:514, 9:641, 9:764
Aesthetica (Baumgarten), 1:50, 4:165, 9:824
Aestheticism
art in, 1:339–340, 9:764
Beardsley on, 1:508–509
Pater and, 7:136
Wilde as embodiment of, 9:764
Aesthetics, 1:73
active judgment in, 4:65
of Adorno, 1:27–28
Alexander on, 1:110–111
analytic, 1:35
ancient, **1:187–190,** 5:573–574
Anderson (John) on, 1:199
Anglo-American, 1:63–68
anti-intentionalism in, 1:509
Aquinas on, 9:435–436
Aristotle on, 1:43–45, 1:188–189
art and, 1:34–36, 1:298, 1:509, 1:548, 2:580, 4:160–161, 9:764
Augustine on, 1:46–47
authenticity and, **1:295–296**
as author-hero phenomenology, 1:469

Aesthetics, ***continued***
Bakhtin on, 1:466
Batteux on, 1:50, 1:489–490
Baumgarten on, 1:49–50
Beardsley on, 1:33, 1:64, 1:72–73, 1:508–509
beauty as concept in, 1:511–515
Benjamin on, 1:69, 1:545–547
of Blake, 1:610
Boileau on, 1:640
Bullough on, 1:36, 1:64, 1:761–762
Burke on, 1:771
as carnival, 1:466–467, 1:470
Cassirer on, 2:68
Chaadaev on, 2:121–122
Chernyshevskii on, 2:146
in Christianity, 1:46–48
of Chwistek, 2:255
in classical period, 1:41–48, 1:511–512
cognitivism in, 1:340–341
Cohen (Hermann) on, 1:65, 2:304–305
Coleridge's categories of, 2:318
Collingwood on, 2:327–328
in Confucian ethics, 2:195
contemporary developments in, 1:57–60
continental, 1:68–72
Cousin on, 2:579–580
creative process and, 2:590
in *Critique of Judgment,* 5:26–27
in *Critique of Pure Reason,* 5:15
Croce on, 1:57, 2:600–602
of deconstructionism, 1:71–72
defining, 9:562–563
Deleuze on, 2:695
Deustua on, 3:42–43
Dewey on, 1:33, 1:57, 1:75, 3:46–47
dialectic in, 1:28
dialectic materialist, 1:59
Diderot on, 3:76–77
disinterest in, 2:65
as distance and civility, 1:761–762, 2:234
Dostoevsky on, 3:100
DuBos on, 3:123
Ducasse on, 3:125
Dufrenne on, 1:59
Eagleton on, 1:70
empiricism and, 1:50–52, 1:60, 1:494, 3:556
Encyclopédie on, 3:76, 3:225
as epistemology, 4:159–161
vs. ethics, 1:37
etymology of, 1:35
existentialism and, 1:59–60
in *Faygyan,* 9:861
Fechner on, 1:514, 3:556
vs. formalism, 1:298
Foucault on, 1:71
Frazer on, 1:58
Gadamer on, 1:71
Garve on, 4:24
Gerard on, 4:65
in Gestalt psychology, 1:60
Goodman on, 1:33, 1:38, 4:160–161
Gracián on, 4:168
Hegel on, 1:54, 4:274–276, 8:629–630
Herder on, 4:331
history of, **1:41–72,** 5:575, 9:293–294
Hutcheson on, 1:35, 1:37, 4:529
imagination and, 1:50, 4:598
as imitation of nature, 1:489–490
in Ingarden's theory of art as intentional object, 4:682–683
in I-other relationships as literary transformation, 1:465
Islamic, 1:436
in Japanese philosophy, 4:793
Jouffroy on, 4:855
Jung on, 1:58
Kant on, 1:32–37, 8:598, 8:630
knowledge and, in art, 1:334–335
Külpe on, 5:161
in Latin American philosophy, 5:207
laws of nature in, 9:828–829
in Leninism, 1:59
Leont'ev on, 5:283
Lessing on, 1:50, 5:294
Lipps on, 5:363
Losev on, 5:573–574
Lukács on, 5:603
Lyotard on, 1:72
Marković on, 5:719
Marxist, 1:59, 1:68–70, 5:603, 5:737
Meier on, 6:112
Mendelssohn on, 6:131
Merleau-Ponty on, 6:150–151
metaphysics of, 1:57
in middle ages, 1:46–48
mimesis in, 6:252
morality and, 1:51, 1:67–68, 8:598, 9:563
Moritz on, 6:405–406
Munro on, 1:60
music and, 1:27–28, 9:325
in narrative time-space, 1:467
and naturalism, 1:57–58, 6:492
of nature, 1:33–34, 6:522, 9:379
in neo-classicism, 1:512
Nicolai on, 6:598–599
Nietzsche on, 1:56
19th-century, 1:514–515
of Oakeshott, 7:2
paradoxes of imagination in, 4:600–601
phenomenology and, 1:59–60, 1:70–71
philosophical
Boileau on, 1:640
developments in, 3:573
philosophy of, 7:328
philosophy *vs.,* 7:332–333
Platonic, 1:41–43, 1:187–188, 7:594–595, 9:590
Plekhanov on, 1:59, 7:628
Plotinus on, 1:45–46, 1:190
as polyphony of novelistic voices, 1:466–467
poststructuralism and, 1:71–72, 9:278
problems of, **1:72–81**
psychological, 1:514, 3:557
reader-response, 1:314
of realism, 1:39, 1:56
in Renaissance, 1:48–49
of Roretz, 8:493
Santayana on, 1:57, 1:63, 8:598
Sartre on, 1:71, 8:605–606
Schelling on, 8:620
Schiller (Ferdinand) on, 1:54, 9:325
Schiller (Friedrich) on, 8:627–628
Schlegel on, 8:627–630
in semiotics, 1:58
sensible representation in, 9:325
Shaftesbury on, 1:51, 9:3
Sibley on, 1:33–36, 1:66, 9:21
Smith (Adam) on, 9:69
and social change, 1:720
Solov'ëv on, 9:125
in Stoicism, 1:45, 1:189
Stout on, 9:261
sublime in, 9:293
Sulzer on, 9:325
symbols in, 4:161
as thinking in images, 2:100
Tolstoy on, 9:514
20th-century, 1:63–72, 1:514–515
ugliness in, 9:561–564
in unconscious, development of, 9:573
unity in, 1:33, 1:46
of Valéry, 9:634
in valuation of literature and fiction, 5:370–371
value statements in, 1:437

of Vasconcelos, 9:648–649
vital excess in, 2:65
Winckelmann on, 9:790
Wittgenstein on, 1:66, 9:819–820
Wolff on, 9:828–829
Wollheim on, 1:36, 3:257, 9:835–836
Xunzi on, 2:234
See also Environmental aesthetics
"Aesthetics and Nonaesthetics" (Sibley), 9:21
"Aesthetics and the Looks of Things" (Sibley), 9:21
Aesthetics (Estética)(Deústua), 5:207
Aesthetics of the Natural Environment (Brady), 3:256
Aesthetics: Problems in the Philosophy of Criticism (Beardsley), 1:64, 1:508
Aesthetik des reinen Gefühls (Cohen), 6:543
Äesthetische Theorie (Adorno), 1:27–29, 1:69–70
Aeterni Patris, Mercier and, 6:143, 6:144
Aether
Aristotle on, 1:271–272
in Maxwell's field theory, 6:69
Newton on, 5:642
Affection(s)
as attitude and conduct, 7:248
benevolent, bestowal by God, 1:474–476
Hartley's scale of, in theology, 2:316
human, for justice, Duns Scotus on, 3:142–143
religious, Edwards on, 3:167–168
Affectivity, Deleuze's theory of, 2:695–696
Affirmation
assumption and, 6:116
of consequent, 5:542
Affirmative, universal
in Ockham's nominalism, 9:778
simple conversion of, 3:538
Affirmative action, **1:81–82,** 6:425, 9:75
Affirmative copula, 9:777
Afflictions, in Buddhism, 1:724
Afghānī, Sayyid Jamāl ad-Dīn al-, Islamic Enlightenment and, 3:248–249
Afghanistan, U.S. war in, 7:158
Afiny i Ierusalem (Shestov), 9:11
Africa, nationalism in, 6:484
African philosophy, **1:82–88,** 9:71–72
African Religions and Philosophy (Mbitit), 1:83–84
Africans and African Americans, racist views of, 8:228
Afrocentrism, African philosophy and, 1:86
After Strange Gods (Eliot), 3:185, 3:186
After Virtue (MacIntyre), 5:636, 5:637, 9:74
Afterimages, Fechner's experiments on, 3:555
Afterlife
Adams (M.) on, 3:477–478
al-Fārābī on, 3:23
Averroes on, 3:23
Avicenna on, 3:23
belief in, Ducasse on, 3:126
belief in God and, 2:352
Buber on, 4:618
in Buddhism, 6:256–257
in Christianity. *See* Heaven and hell, doctrines of
Cicero on, 2:258
deism on, 2:682
Democritus on, 5:301
Dostoevsky on, 3:99
Ducasse on, 3:126
Dühring on, 3:131
Duns Scotus on, 3:140
Eberhard on, 3:161
and evil, problem of, 3:475
and life, meaning and value of, 5:345–346, 5:350
Losskii on, 5:577
many worlds theory and, 8:377
Marx on, 3:56
in naturalistic religion, 8:377
Old Testament (Bible) on, 3:347
in Orphism, 7:42–43
Paine on, 7:74
Rosenzweig on, 4:618
views on, 2:654
Afterthoughts (Kaplan), 5:39
Against Aristotle, on the Eternity of the World (Philoponus), 9:35
Against Christians (Porphyry), 1:228, 3:455, 6:550
Against Julian (Cyril of Alexandria), 7:143
Against Proclus (Philoponus), 6:555
Against the Academics (Augustine), 6:546
Against the Galileans (Julian), 1:228
Against the Geometers (Sextus Empiricus), 9:501
Against the Gnostics (Plotinus), 6:551
Against the Physicists (Timon of Phlius), 9:501
Against the Professors (Sextus Empiricus), 1:45
Against the Sophists (Diogenes of Apollonia), 3:89
Agape
in Christian thought, 5:586
divine command theories of ethics and, 3:93
Niebuhr on, 6:606
See also Love
Agar, W. E., 7:83–85
Agassiz, Louis, James and, 4:775
Agathias, 9:35
Agathon, **1:256**
Age
as determinable, 3:1
of Earth, and evolution, 2:636–640
in wisdom, 9:795
Age of gods, 9:675
Age of heroes, 9:675
Age of humans, 9:676
Age of Reason
end of, 2:686–687
Paine on, 2:690, 7:73
as term, 3:243
Wolff in, 9:829–830
Age of Reason, The (Paine), 2:690, 7:73
Age of Spiritual Machines (Kurzweil), 4:617
Agency
ability in, 1:217
in action, 1:15–18
action theory on, 3:445
agent-relative *vs.* agent-neutral reasons and, 3:445–446
divine, in miracles, 6:265
Hume on, 3:445
Kant on, 3:445
Lopatin on, 5:572
Nagel on, 3:445
Parfit on, 3:445
personhood and, 7:241–242
and self-determination, 3:17–18
situated epistemic, 3:576
spiritual, in human evolution, 9:721
20th-century debate on, 3:444–446
vanishing, causalism and, 1:17
in vitalism, 9:697
voluntary, and Ockham's rule of induction, 9:778
See also Free agency; Moral agency
Agent(s), patriarchal norms and, 3:588
Agent causation, **1:88–90**
determinism and, 3:26
nonmaterial, 6:60
volition and, 9:705
Agent intellect, **1:90–92,** 9:28, 9:766
Agent intelligence, William of Auvergne and, 9:766
Agent meaning, 7:405

Agent-neutral principles, 3:387–388, 3:445–446
Agent-relative principles, 3:387–388, 3:445–446
Aggregate(s)
- definition of, 5:533
- infinite, 4:186–187
- of stars, kinetic theories of, 4:804
- Vasubandhu on, 9:650–651

Aggregate features, *vs.* emergent features, 3:193
Aggregation, 7:534–535
Aggression
- definition of, 4:870
- Freud on, 9:572
- Lacan on, 5:168
- substantial, 4:870

Aging, feminist ethicists' attention to, 3:581
Agnesi, Maria, 9:839
Agnostic positivism, on "why," 9:755
Agnostic product-realism, 9:719
Agnosticism, **1:92–95,** 3:628
- *vs.* atheism, 1:359, 1:367–368
- and Christianity, 1:92–93
- Darrow on, 1:358, 1:371, 2:351
- Darwin (Charles) on, 7:561
- in defining art, 1:301
- definition of, 1:360
- Flint on, 1:94
- Galen and, 4:6
- Hélvetius and, 4:307
- Huxley (Thomas Henry) on, 1:92–93, 1:358, 4:532–533
- implied, in Darwinism, 4:171
- Kant on, 1:92, 5:709
- La Mettrie on, 5:179–180
- legal rights and, 1:358
- in logical positivism, 1:94
- Marcel on, 3:504
- mystical experience and, 6:457
- nihilism and, 6:617–618
- *philosophes* and, 2:688–691
- Sartre on, 3:427–428
- in sophism, 9:129
- Spencer on, 1:93, 7:714
- Stephen on, 1:358, 9:243
- Tyndall on, 1:371
- Vaihinger on, 9:628

Agnosticism (Flint), 1:94
"Agnosticism and Christianity" (Huxley), 1:93
Agony, in Unanumo's philosophy, 9:568
Agreement(s)
- in moral constructivism, 2:472
- in morality, 7:718
- negative method of, 6:240–242
- perception–perceived object, truth in, 1:668
- positive method of, 6:239–242
- probability of, 3:664
- reflective, between personal and social will, 7:205

Agreement methods of induction. *See* Induction, agreement methods of
Agricultural nations, 5:59
Agrippa, **1:96–97**
- epistemology of, 3:288
- Pyrrhonian skepticism and, 8:176
- *See also* Agrippan modes

Agrippa von Nettesheim, Henricus Cornelius, **1:97–98**
- and Bruno, 1:708
- Franck translation of, 3:713
- as hermetic philosopher, 1:710
- microcosm in, 5:642

Agrippan modes, 1:196, 8:176
Agrippa's trilemma, 8:176–177
Ahnung, 3:531
Ahrens, Heinrich, Krause and, 5:148
Ahura Mazdah, 3:471, 9:885–887
AI. *See* Artificial intelligence
Aids to Reflection (Coleridge), Emerson and, 3:195
Aiken, Henry, good-reasons approach and, 3:430
Ailly, Pierre d', **1:98–99,** 4:67
- on impositions and intentions, 8:765
- Luther and, 5:615–617

Aim and Structure of Physical Theory, The (La théorie physique: son objet, sa structure) (Duhem), 3:126
Air
- Anaximenes on, 1:186
- as classification of matter, Greek Academy on, 6:59
- elasticity of, 1:673

Aitia, **1:99–100**
Ajdukiewicz, Casimir
- Leśniewski and, 5:293
- on syntactical connexity, 9:353–354
- on Zeno's paradoxes, 3:60

Akaike Information Criterion, 8:685
Akhmatova, Anna, 3:454
Akratic action, 9:728–732
- *See also* Strict akratic action

Ākṛti (shape)
- in Indian semantics, 9:581
- Patañjali on, 9:581–582

Akṣapāda, on logic, 5:412
Akshobhya, 6:622
Aksimony religioznogo opyta (Axioms of religious experience) (Il'in), 4:578
Akt und Sein (Bonhoeffer), 1:655
Akutobhayā, 6:471
al-Afghānī and, 3:248
al-ʿArabī. *See* Ibn al-ʿArabī
Albalag, Isaac, 4:809, 4:820
al-Balkhī, Hayuye, 4:811–821
Albanus, Joannes, 5:439
al-Basri, Hasan, and Sufism, 9:301
Albee, Edward, on God, 9:757
Alberdi, Juan Bautista
- on identity, 5:211
- positivism and, 5:207

Alberic of Paris, on Abelard's logic, 5:428–429
Albert, David, 5:698, 8:213–214
Albert of Saxony, **1:100–102**
- on impositions and intentions, 8:765
- Nicolas of Autrecourt and, 6:601

Albert the Great, **10:1–4**
- agent intellect and, 1:91
- Aquinas and, 1:653, 9:444
- Aristotle and, 3:403
- and Bonaventure, 1:653
- David of Dinant and, 2:644
- on inner senses, 4:697
- *Liber de Causis* and, 5:334
- philosophy of logic and, 8:766
- and Siger of Barbant, 9:27

Alberti, G. W., deism and, 2:688
Albertucius. *See* Albert of Saxony
Albertus Magnus, 7:522. *See also* Albert the Great
Albinus. *See* Alcinous
Albo, Joseph, **1:102–103,** 4:823–824
Albright, W. F., 5:594
Alchemical philosophy, 1:449
- and Bacon (Roger), 1:449
- on matter, 6:59–60
- as natural philosophy, 1:444
- *See also* Esoteric philosophy

Alchemy
- Mersenne on, 6:152
- Newton in, 6:591
- Paracelsus and, 7:103–104
- Scot on, 8:703

Alcher of Clairvaux, 4:753
Alcibiades (Aeschines of Sphettus), 9:107
Alcibiades (Euclides of Megara), 6:110
Alcibiades (Plato)
- Iamblichus on, 4:540
- in Neoplatonism, 8:40
- Proclus on, 7:609
- soul as person in, 4:605

Alcidamas, logic and, 5:397
Alcinous, **1:103–104,** 5:408

Alciphron, or the Minute Philosopher (Berkeley), 1:359, 2:686
on doctrine of signs, 8:782
meaning of words in, 9:597–598
Alcmaeon of Croton, **1:104–105,** 3:395
Alcock, James E., parapsychology and, 7:116
Alcoff, Linda, 3:565, 3:586
Alcott, Amos Bronson, 6:572, 7:233
al-Dīn al Rāzī, 5:419
al-Dīn al-Tūsī, Naṣīr, 5:419–420
al-Dīn ibn Yūnus, kamāl, 5:419–420
Aldrich, Henry, 5:439–440
Aleatoric art, 1:298
Alembert, Jean Le Rond d', **1:105–107**
atheism and, 2:688
and calculus, 6:593
Cassirer and, 3:243
and Condorcet, 2:430
on Cudworth, 2:610
Encyclopédie and, 3:71, 3:221–224
Enlightenment and, 3:244
on force measurement, 3:228
Laplace and, 5:197
Newton and, 3:246
Petersburg paradox and, 5:339
Alephs, definition of, 5:533
Aletheia (truth), 4:293
Alethic modal interpretation, 6:296–297
Alexander (Lucian of Samosata), 5:597
Alexander II (czar of Russia), personal attendant to, 5:153
Alexander III (czar of Russia), Lenin and, 5:279
Alexander, Franz, Adler and, 1:24
Alexander, Samuel, **1:107–111**
Anderson (John) and, 1:197–198
on being, 7:22
on conation, 9:260
on God, concepts of, 4:109
on nature, 6:520
panpsychism and, 7:83
physicotheology and, 7:562
realism and, 3:313
Alexander of Aphrodisias, **1:112–113**
on agent intellect, 1:91
Aristotelianism and, 1:259, 5:408
atomism and, 1:384–385
Eusebius and, 3:455
on Galen, 4:6
on hylic intellect of soul, 4:68
on intellect, 4:608, 9:28
Maimonides and, 5:653
on mental modifications of words, 8:761
Simplicius on, 9:35
on syllogisms, 5:403
Themistius and, 9:409
on universals, 3:147
Alexander of Hales, **1:113–115**
apriorism of, 7:161–162
Augustinianism of, 1:402
Averroism and, 1:428
on ideas, 1:653
on illumination, 1:403
John of La Rochelle and, 4:840
on transcendentals, 3:137
Alexander the Great
Aristotle and, 1:263
Stoics and, 3:155
Alexandria
Aristotelianism in, 1:260
Neoplatonism in, 6:553–555
Platonism in, 7:142–143
Alexandrian Academy, *vs.* Greek Academy, 6:553–554
Alexandristi, Alexander of Aphrodisias and, 1:112
Alexinus of Elis, 6:111
al-Fārābī, Abū-Naṣr Muhammad, **1:115–117**
on afterlife, 3:23
on analogy, 1:139
Arab logic and, 5:418–421
on Aristotle, 1:651
Avicenna and, 1:432, 1:435
on creation, 3:360
on doctrine of intellect, 4:755
emanationism in, 3:189
on first intelligence, 4:756
on God, 5:650
and Ikhwān al-Ṣafā', 4:576
on immortality, 4:619
in Islamic philosophy, 4:755–756
Liber de Causis and, 5:333
Maimonides and, 5:649, 5:654
in medieval philosophy, 6:99
in Neoplatonism, 6:557–558
on predestination, 3:23
use of Arabic translations by, 4:754
on virtuous city, 9:315
on wisdom, 1:651
Alfonso X of Castile, 5:51
al-Futûhât al-makkiyya (Ibn al-ʿArabī), 4:541
Algazel. *See* al-Ghazālī, Muḥammad
Algebra
abstract, 5:459, 9:369
analogy in, 8:785
arithmetical, 5:460
Boolean
definition of, 5:535
diagrams in, 5:561–563
Jevons's machine and, 5:565
lattice diagram for, 5:563
logical diagrams of, 5:563
Venn diagrams and, 5:561
Cantor on, 5:463
Cauchy on, 5:459–460
cylindric, Tarski on, 9:370–372
De Morgan on, 5:461
Dedekind on, 2:500, 8:836
deductive reasoning in, 6:223
Descartes on, 4:56
equations in, logic of, 1:660
Gergonne on, 5:461
Grassmann on, 5:461
Heyting, 4:740
for intuitionistic logic, 4:740
Kant on, 5:15
language in, 8:785
laws of, 5:450
of logic
and computing machines, 2:400
definition of, 5:533
Leibniz and, 5:443
Schröder on, 5:462
logic and, 5:449–450, 5:459
Mill (John Stuart) on, 6:223
Peacock on, 5:459–460
propositional, in illative combinatory logic, 2:339
Schröder on, 5:462, 5:535
of signs, Condillac on, 2:423
symbolic, 5:460
of syntax, in formal expressions in compositionality, 2:371
Tarski on, 5:480, 9:367, 9:370–372
von Neumann, 2:343
Whitehead on, 5:461–462, 9:747
See also Mathematics
Algeria, Sufism in, 9:310
al-Ghazālī, Aḥmad, **1:117–118**
al-Ghazālī, Muḥammad, **1:118–120**
and antirationalism, 4:581
attack on philosophy, 4:758, 9:304–305
Averroes and, 1:422, 2:114
on causality, 1:118–119, 1:426, 6:558
comparison to Crescas, 2:593
on creation, 3:361
on God's omniscience, 3:23, 3:320
in Islamic philosophy, 4:758
on Neoplatonism, 6:558
on skepticism, 9:50
on Sufism, 9:304
Algorithm(s)
in combinatory logic, 2:336
in computability theory, 2:372–375, 2:388–389

Algorithm(s), ***continued***
 definition of, 5:533
 Deutsch-Jozsa, 8:200–201
 genetic, 1:348
 Grover's, 2:408
 Markov, 2:504–505
 quantum, 2:408
Algorithmic construction, of continua, 2:502–504
Algorithmic definition, of deduction, 2:254
Algorithmic quantification, of language, 5:509
al-Hallaj, Mansur, 9:303
al-Harizi, Maimonides and, 5:653
Alhazen, and Bacon (Roger), 1:453
Al-Hidaja ila Faraid al-Qulub Baḥya (Guide to the duties of the heart) (Bahya), 1:457
Alice in Wonderland (Carroll), 2:51
Alien (film), 7:385
Alienation, **1:120–127**
 Adorno and, 1:26
 alterity and, 1:133
 art and, 8:629
 contemporary interpretations of, 1:121–122
 of creator and created, 1:560
 critique and, 5:731
 definitions of, 1:122
 elimination of, 1:125
 existential angst and, 1:763
 forms of, 1:122–123
 from God, 1:762
 of God from himself, 8:621
 Hegel on, 1:120–121, 4:263
 history of, 1:120–121
 of Kafka's life, 5:5
 of labor, 2:363, 5:731, 7:544
 Mamardashvili on, 5:679
 Marx on, 2:363, 5:731, 7:544
 overcoming, 5:731, 8:629
 property and, 8:70
 Sartre on, 8:609
 self, 1:123–125
 of serial individuals and collectives, 8:609
 social wealth and, 2:362
Aliotta, Antonio, 1:1, **1:127–128**
al-Ishārāt wa al-Tanbīhāt ("The Directives and Remarks") (Avicenna), 1:432
Alison, Archibald, **1:128–129**
 on aesthetic experience, 1:303
 on taste, 1:52, 4:65
al-Jabiri, ʿAbd, **1:129–130**
al-Khūnajī, 5:419
al-Kindī, Abū-Yūsuf Yaqūb ibn Isḥāq, **1:130–131**, 3:687
 on analogy, 1:139
 and Bacon (Roger), 1:453
 on immortality, 4:618, 4:619
 on intellection, 4:755
 in Islamic philosophy, 4:755
 on logic, 5:418
 on predestination, 3:23
 Pythagoreanism and, 8:188
al-Kwarizmi, Muhammed ibn Musa, 2:399
Allais, Maurice, on decision theory, 2:659–660
Allegorical method
 Bernard of Tours on, 1:592
 Blount on, 1:619
 Boehme on, 1:623
Allegory
 Benjamin on, 1:545–546
 in Bible, 1:47, 9:844–845
 nature as, 1:48
 Philo's use of, 7:309
 on prejudice, 9:8–9
 of Prometheus, 9:9
 vs. symbol, 1:55
Allen, Colin, in ethnology, 1:202
Allen, Ethan, 2:690
"Allgemeine Deduktion des dynamischen Prozesses" (Schelling), 8:619
Allgemeine Erkenntnislehre (Schlick), 8:638
Allgemeine Gottesgelehrtheit aller gläubigen Christen und Rechtschaffenen Theologen, Die (Spener), 7:576
Allgemeine Naturgeschichte für alle Stände (Oken), 7:11
Allgemeine Pädagogik aus dem Zweck der Erziehung Abgeleitet (Herbart), 1:234
Allgemeine Psychiatrie (Jaspers), 3:507
Allgemeine Psychologie nack kritischer Methode (General psychology according to a critical method) (Natorp), 6:490, 6:543
Allgemeine Theorie der Schönen künste (General theory of the fine arts) (Sulzer), 9:324
Allgemeine Theorie des Denkens und Empfindens (General theory of thinking and feeling) (Eberhard), 3:161
Allgemeiner Deutscher Arbeiterverein, 5:203
Allocation, medical ethics and, 6:96–97
Allographic *vs.* autographic art, 1:317
Allport, Gordon, 9:260
All-Unity metaphysics, 3:669, 5:43
Almagest (Ptolemy), 2:534
al-Ma'mūn, 4:754
Almeder, Robert, 7:116
al-Miṣrī, Dhūʿl-Nūn, 9:302
al-Muhasibi, al-Harith, 9:302
Al-Muqaddimah (The prolegomena) (Ibn Khaldūn), 4:547
al-Nahawandi, Benjamin, 5:4
Alpern, Kenneth, on engineering ethics, 3:240
Alpetragius, 8:703
al-Qaeda, 9:397–398
al-Qanūn fi al-Tibb (The Canon of Medicine) (Avicenna), 1:432
al-Qazwīnī al-kātībī, 5:419–420
Alquié, Ferdinand, students of, 2:693
al-Sadiq, Abu Ja'far, 9:301
Alsted, Johann Heinrich, 5:252
Alston, William, **1:132–133**
 on belief, 3:322, 7:482
 on conditions of knowledge, 3:272
 on emotions, 3:198
 on epistemic circularity, 3:279–280
 experientialism and, 3:322–323
 on God not having beliefs, 3:696
 on mysticism, 6:462
 on perception, 7:193
 on religious experience, 7:482, 8:402
 on religious language, 8:417–418
 on Rowe's argument against existence of God, 9:408
al-Suhrawardī, Shihāb al-Dīn Yahyā. *See* Shihāb al-Dīn, Suhrawardī
al-Sulami, ʿAbd Allah al-Rahman, 9:304
al-Taḥtānī, 5:420
Altenstein, Minister von, opposition to Beneke, 1:543
Alteration
 definition of, 5:541
 persistence and, 7:208–210
Alterity, **1:133–134**
"Alternate Possibilities and Moral Responsibility" (Frankfurt), 3:718
Alternative denial. *See* Sheffer stroke function
Alternative (disjunctive) propositions, definition of, 5:553
Alternatives
 asserting, 3:538
 understanding, 3:722
"Älteste Systemprogramm des deutschen Idealismus, Das" (Rosenzweig), 8:498

Althusius, Johannes, **1:134–136**
German liberalism and, 5:321
on social contract, 9:81
Althusser, Louis
and Foucault, 3:698
in French structuralism, 9:273
on ideology, 4:574
Mamardashvili and, 5:679
Marxism of, 5:740
on structural causality, 8:610
Altmann, Alexander, on revelation, 8:587
Altra meta, La (The other half) (Papini), 7:102
Altruism, **1:136–137**
in animals, 1:204
Aquinas on, 3:170
Ardigò on, 1:252
Aristotle on, 3:170
Baier on, 1:461
Bain on, 3:174
and benevolence, 1:136–137
Bentham on, 3:173
Broad on, 9:382
Butler (Joseph) on, 3:171–172
in Christianity, 1:136
in civic affairs, 1:725
Comte on, 1:136
definition of, complexity of, 3:174–175
development of, 9:739
economics and, 7:352
empathy and, 9:345
expansion of, 9:740
in feminism, 1:137
Freud on, 3:173–174
and God, 3:172
in Greek philosophy, 3:170
Grote on, 3:173
Grotius on, 7:423
Haeckel on, 4:204
Hartley on, 3:173–174
Hobbes on, 3:170–171
Hume on, 1:136–137, 3:172–173
Hutcheson on, 1:136, 3:171
Kant on, 1:137
and love, 1:136
Mill (James) on, 6:219
Mill (John Stuart) on, 3:173–174
Nagel (Thomas) on, 1:137, 3:445, 6:475
Paley on, 3:172
Plato on, 3:170
as sacrifice, 1:136
self-referential, 9:382
Shaftesbury on, 3:171
Sidgwick on, 3:173
Tucker on, 3:172
in utilitarianism, 1:136, 3:172–173
Williams (Bernard) on, 1:136–137
See also Egoism and altruism
al-Tustarī, 5:420
al-Urmawī, Arab logic and, 5:419
Always, in Achilles paradox, 9:875
Ambiguity(ies)
as aesthetically displeasing, 3:557
Aristotle on, 8:756
Beauvoir on, 1:515
definition of, 5:534, 5:558
detection of, 3:640
in epistemology, 1:676–677
in existential ethics, 1:515
of facts, in scientific method, 8:625
fallacy and, 3:541–542, 8:767
in grammar, 6:659–660
harmfulness of, 4:5
in language, 3:549
in law, 7:455
with mass and count nouns, 6:659–660
of names, 8:756
in sensation, 8:827
state-content, 6:176
tolerance for, in fuzzy logic, 3:766
of truth, 2:310
typical. *See* Systematic ambiguity
in words and phrases, 3:542–543
See also Systematic ambiguity
Ambiguous middle fallacy, 3:542
Ame materielle, 6:9–10
Amelius, Eusebius and, 3:455
Amendola, Giovanni, Papini and, 7:102
America. *See* United States
American Association for the Advancement of Science, parapsychology and, 7:113
American Bar Association, on informed consent, 4:680
American Black theology, 5:331–333
American liberalism, 5:321–322
American Medical Association, on euthanasia, 3:456–457
American Mind, The (Commager), 5:322
American Philosophical Society, Enlightenment and, 3:244
American philosophy
vs. Continental philosophy, 2:488–489
Sumner in, 9:326–327
Suppes in, 9:333–335
American pragmatism
Apel on, 1:226
practical realism of, 1:463
American Psychiatric Association (APA)
on sexual dysfunction, 7:528
on sexual perversion, 7:527–528
American Psychological Association, symposium on death, 2:650
American Revolution
Enlightenment and, 3:247
equality as concept in, 3:330
Ferguson on, 3:604
Paine and, 7:73
American Society for Psychical Research, 7:113
Ames, Roger T., on Confucian ethics, 2:196
Amesha-Spentas ("Immortal Holy Ones"), in Zoroastrianism, 9:886
Amitābha, 6:622
devotion to, 1:723
Pure Land Buddhism's faith in, 2:168–169
Ammonius Hermeiou
Aristotelianism of, 1:260
on Aristotle's logic, 5:408
Damascius on, 6:554
and Neoplatonism, 6:553
Philoponus and, 7:313
and Simplicius, 9:34
Ammonius Saccas
and Neoplatonism, 6:553
on Plato and Aristotle, 7:571
and Plotinus, 7:631
Amor y pedagogia (Love and pedagogy) (Unamuno), 9:566
Amour de nous-mêmes, Vauvenargues on, 9:653–654
Amour propre, Vauvenargues on, 9:653–654
Ampère, André Marie, **1:137–138,** 5:656
Amphiboly, definition of, 5:534, 5:542
Amphiteatrum Aeternae Providentiae (Vanini), 7:247, 9:646
Amphiteatrum Naturae (Bodin), 1:622
Amphitryon (Kleist), 5:78
Ampliation
definition of, 5:534
doctrine of, 3:494–496
in medieval logic, 5:431–432
Ampliative induction, 6:244
Amyntor: Or, a Defence of Milton's Life (Toland), 9:504–505
An den Quellen unseres Denkens (Roretz), 8:493
Anabaptists, 8:296
Anabasis (Xenophon), 9:854

Analects (Confucius), 2:171–176
argumentation in, 2:213
ethics in, 2:194, 2:200–203
religion in, 2:228
science in, 2:218
society in, 7:486
Análisis Filosófico (periodical), 5:210
Analogical argument, as figure 2-type syllogism, 5:501
Analogical method
Chinese, 2:213, 2:217–218, 2:222
of Fourier, 3:707
in panpsychism, 7:88–89
Analogical predication, 4:108, 7:479
Analogical reason, in confirmation theory, 2:439
Analogy(ies)
argument from, 3:544, 7:51–53
of attribution *vs.* proportionality, 9:283
Bergson on, 1:570
in bioethics, 1:601
Broad on, 1:698
Bultmann on, 1:764
Butler on, 1:783
Cajetan on, 2:7
Campbell on, 2:18
definition of, 5:534
in evocative argument, 2:213–214
of experience, in *Critique of Pure Reason,* 5:19–20
fallacious, arguments from, 3:544
impairment of, by other languages, 8:784–785
in intrinsic theory of consciousness, 2:453
in macrocosm and microcosm, 5:639
metaphor and, 6:167
metaphysical, 9:344
in nature, ideas of, 6:520
origin of, 1:139
in Sufism, 9:301
in theology, **1:138–144**
first analogate in, 9:344
for ontological relation of God and creature, 4:670
theory of thought and, 9:422
Analogy *(upamana),* 5:117, 5:121
Analogy of Religion, The (Butler), 1:780–782, 2:683–686, 4:612, 7:559, 9:502
Analysis
arithmetization of, 2:495–496, 5:534–535
in axiomatic method/axiomatics, 6:22
Carnap on, 2:38
character, 8:306–307
conceptual
in analytic jurisprudence, 1:168–170
analytic/synthetic distinction and, 1:170
Moore on, 2:673, 4:150
naturalism on, 1:169
of perceiving, 7:178–179
philosophy as, 2:419
Condillac on, 8:784
in consciousness, 9:884
eidetic, 4:683
Einstein-Podolsky-Rosen. *See* Einstein-Podolsky-Rosen analysis
in ethics, 1:145
existential, 7:322–323. *See also* Existential psychoanalysis
first-pattern, in persuasion, 9:245
functional
as explanation, 3:763
of mental concepts, 3:756
in organismic biology, 7:39
uses of, 3:762
Galluppi and, 4:14
geometrical, 3:538
historical, 9:457
in informal axiomatics, 6:22
intentional, 7:294
of legal concepts, 7:447–454
linguistic
Carnap's, 2:44
by native speakers, in attributor contextualism, 2:487
logic of, 6:560
logical, of knowledge, 8:641
Mackie on, 5:638
mathematical, 6:20
definition of, 5:534–535
infinitesimal number systems and, 2:507
as means to knowledge, 8:784
Mercier's use of, 6:144
metalinguistic
of dao, 2:187
of truth, 7:196–197
metaphysical
of language, 1:769
of persistence, 7:206–211
of personalism, 7:235
of personhood, 7:238–240
metaphysics as, 6:207
Moore on, 1:144–145
of nature, 9:748–749
Neurath on, 6:560
phenomenalistic, impurity in, 7:274
philosophical, **1:144–157**
Galluppi and, 4:13–14
government reaction against, 8:638
Sellars (Wilfrid) on, 8:733
Wisdom (John) on, 9:797–798
problem of, 3:754
psychoanalytic. *See* Psychoanalysis
rigorousness of, 6:20
Russell on, 1:145–147. *See also* *Analysis of Matter, The* (Russell); *Analysis of Mind, The* (Russell)
vs. synthesis
Kant on, 1:159–161, 5:14
Quine on, 1:150
statements of, **1:159–165**
Thucydides on, 9:457
topic-neutral, of qualitative character, 8:192
Wittgenstein on, 1:147–149
Ziehen (Theodor) on, 9:884
Analysis der Wirklichkeit (Analysis of reality) (Liebmann), 3:110, 5:344
Analysis Linguarum (Leibniz), 5:441
Analysis of Matter, The (Russell), 5:131, 5:593
Analysis of Mind, The (Russell), 1:485, 8:821
on acts of perception, 4:560
Lovejoy on, 5:593
on universals, 9:601
Analysis of Sensations, The (Mach), 5:623–625
Analysis of the Phenomena of the Human Mind (Mill, James), 6:219
"Analysis of Thinking, The" (Johnson), 5:458
Analysis Terminable and Interminable (Freud), 8:105
Analyst, The (Berkeley), 1:582, 2:495, 2:686
Analytic
definition of, 7:281
of finitude, knowledge in human sciences as, 3:700
transcendental, Croce's aesthetics as, 2:602
Analytic *a posteriori* knowledge, Kant on, 3:306
Analytic *a priori* knowledge, Kant on, 3:306
Analytic aesthetics, 1:35
Analytic and synthetic statements, **1:159–165**
in analytic jurisprudence, 1:170
Grice on, 4:184

Kant on, 1:159–161, 5:14
Quine on, 1:162, 3:318, 5:84, 8:216–218, 9:345–346
Schlick on, 8:641–642
Schulze on, 8:661
synonymy and, 4:160, 9:345–346
vagueness and, 9:624
White on, 7:749
Analytic behavioralism, on materialism, 6:12
Analytic derivation, in metaphysics, 6:211
Analytic feminism, **1:157–158,** 3:586
Analytic geometry, Descartes and, 2:722–723
Analytic judgments. *See* Judgment(s), analytical
Analytic jurisprudence. *See* Jurisprudence, analytic
Analytic knowledge, Kant on, 3:306
Analytic naturalism, 3:366–367
Analytic philosophy, **1:144–155**
Austin (John Langshaw) in, 1:407–411
Black on, 1:605
Blanshard on, 1:613–614
Britain-based import of, 5:45
Carnap in, 2:35
vs. continental philosophy, 2:488–489, 5:210
death in, 2:650
on determinism, 3:6–7
education and, 7:355–356
on epistemology of technology, 7:549
existence of God in, 7:480
feminism in, **1:157–159**
Grote in, 4:190
in history of metaphysics, 6:195
Ingarden on, 4:682
Islamic antagonism to, 4:760
language and, 1:407–410
in Latin American philosophy, 5:210–211
logical positivism in, 1:149–150
logical syntax in, 9:360
Moore in, 1:144–145
political, 7:673
Quine in, 1:150–151
religion in, 7:478–479
Russell in, 1:145–147
Schlick in, 8:637–644
secular discussion of forgiveness within, 3:697
supervenience in, 9:327
Wittgenstein on, 1:147–153
Analytic pragmatism, of Rescher, 8:439
Analytic proposition(s), 1:242–244
as *a posteriori,* 1:242
Bozano on, 5:446
definition of, 5:534
Findlay on, 1:243
Frege on, 1:244
Kant on, 5:79
vs. synthetic, **1:159–165**
Analytic Psychology (Stout), 5:458
Analytic statements, **1:159–165**
coherence theory of truth and, 2:311–312
importance of, 1:163
See also Analytic and synthetic statements
Analytic tradition, on technology, 7:546
Analytic truth, *a priori* knowledge and, 5:84
Analytical engine, computing machines and, 2:400
Analytical feminism, **1:157–158,** 3:586
Analytical hierarchy, in computability theory, 2:389–390
Analytical hypotheses, in radical translation, 8:217
Analytical jurisprudence
legal positivism as, 5:237–238
Raz on, 1:169
Simchen on, 1:170
Analytical mechanics
and classical mechanics, 2:282–283
Lagrange on, 2:409
Analytical Mechanics (Lagrange), 2:409
Analytical Philosophy of History (Danto), 7:394
Analytical psychology
Dilthey on, 9:18
Jung on, 8:146–147
Analyticity, **1:165–168**
of *a priori* propositions, 1:244–245
Carnap on, 2:42–43
epistemic, 1:166–168
Frege on, 1:161, 1:166–167, 3:729
as function of logic, 1:161
as function of word meaning, 1:160
Harman on, 1:164–165
in metaphysics, 1:165–166
Quine on, 9:346
Waismann on, 1:160, 1:161
Analytic-philosophical inquiry, Kaufmann and, 5:46
Analytic-reconstructive approach, to deduction of categories, 5:34
Analytics
Aristotle on, 1:269–271, 3:53
Deleuze on, 2:696
Eudemus of Rhodes on, 5:401
Analytics (Aristotle)
on dialectic, 3:53
syllogisms in, 1:270
Analytics (Eudemus of Rhodes), 5:401
Analytic-synthetic distinction. *See* Analytic and synthetic statements
Analytische Theorie der organischen Entwicklung (Analytic theory of organic development) (Driesch), 3:110
Anan ben David, 8:585
Anankē. *See* Moira/Tychē/Anankē
Anaphora, **1:171–176**
"Anarchical Fallacies" (Bentham), 1:553
Anarchism, **1:176–180**
Arnold on, 1:294
and authoritarianism, 1:176
Bakunin on, 1:178, 1:472–473
civil disobedience and, 2:260
collectivism in, 1:178–179
cooperation in, 1:176–177
Daodejing (Lao Zi) and, 1:177
Diderot and, 1:177
and freedom, 1:176–177, 1:180
Godwin on, 1:177–178, 4:136, 8:93–94, 9:8
individualist, 1:178
and internationalism, 1:176
Kropotkin on, 1:473
Laozi and, 1:177
and Marxism, 1:178–180
mystical, Ivanov on, 4:767
and natural law, 1:176
and neo-Hegelianism, 1:178
nihilism and, 1:176, 6:617
Nozick on, 9:211
pacifist, 1:179–180
as political philosophy, 1:472–473, 7:670–671
and property, 1:176–178
Proudhon on, 8:93–95
and rebellion *vs.* revolution, 9:251
and revolutionary disciplinarianism, 3:554
scientific foundation for, 5:154
Shelley on, 9:8
socialism and, 1:178–180
on state authority, 9:210–211
Thoreau on, 9:450–451
of Tolstoy, 1:178–180
and utopianism, 1:176, 9:89
Wolff on, 2:260
Anarchist-communism, 5:153–154
Anarchosyndicalism, 1:179, 9:132
Anarchy
Arnold on, 1:293
Bentham on, 1:553–554
French Revolution and, 1:176
Nozick on, 1:603, 6:668
Proudhon on, 1:176–178

Anarchy, State, and Utopia (Nozick), 1:603, 6:668
Anatomy of Melancholy (Burton), 2:681, 7:247
"Anatomy of Some Scientific Ideas, The" (Whitehead), 9:748
Anaxagoras of Clazomenae, **1:181–183**
 atomism and, 1:384, 5:299
 on continuum, 2:490
 cosmology of, 1:271, 6:184
 Diogenes of Apollonia and, 3:89
 dynamistic teachings of, 3:686
 Leucippus and, 5:298
 Lucretius and, 5:599
 on mind, 3:211
 on nous, 6:666
 Parmenides of Elea and, 7:122
 Plato on, 2:698
 pluralism of, 1:249, 7:763
 in pre-Socratic philosophy, 7:763
 on religious discourse, 1:138
 on sensations, 8:823
 Simplicius on, 9:35
Anaxarchus, Pyrrho and, 8:173
Anaximander, **1:184–185**
 on *apeiron,* 1:225
 on coming to be as hubris, 9:12
 Empedocles and, 3:209
 on eternal return doctrine, 3:352–353
 on evolution, 3:486
 on infinity, 4:668
 monism of, 1:249
 on nature, 6:518
 Parmenides of Elea and, 7:126
 in pre-Socratic philosophy, 7:760
Anaximenes, **1:185–187**
 Diogenes of Apollonia and, 3:89
 monism of, 1:249
 panpsychism and, 7:83
 pantheism and, 7:94
 Parmenides of Elea and, 7:126
 in pre-Socratic philosophy, 7:760–761
Ancestral relation, definition of, 5:534
Ancient aesthetics, **1:187–191**
Ancient atomism, 7:764
Ancient education, 7:365
 See also Education
Ancient ethics, friendship in, 3:748
Ancient Greece
 advances in, 9:405
 awareness of death in, 2:651
 democracy in, 2:699–700
 education in, 7:364–367
 equality concept in, 3:331
 Jewish law and, 9:793
 legislative authority in, 9:139
 literature in, 4:175–176
 natural law in, 6:506
 number in, 6:670
 philosophy of, Christianity and, 9:533
 philosophy of religion in, 7:487–490
 ratio in, 6:670–671
 reality in, 7:487–488
 skepticism in, 1:191–194
 in Toynbee's historical thought, 9:517–518
 wisdom literature of, 9:794
"Ancient learning" school, Kaibara critical of, 5:7
Ancient logic, 3:54, **5:397–410**
 Aristotle and. *See* Logic, Aristotelian
 beginnings of, 5:397–398
 Diodorus Cronus and, 5:403–404
 in later antiquity, 5:407–409
 Łukasiewicz on, 5:607–608
 peripatetics and, 5:401–403
 Philo of Megara and, 5:403–404
 Plato and, 5:398
 Stoics and, 5:404–408, 5:607
 transmission to Arabs, 5:417–418, 5:421
Ancient philosophy. *See* Philosophy, ancient
Ancient skepticism, **1:191–197**
 development of, 9:48
 in Sextus Empiricus, 8:850–852
 slogans of, 8:852
Ancient Society (Morgan), 6:403–404
Ancona, Alessandro d', 4:49
Anderson, Alan
 paraconsistent logic and, 7:105
 relevant logic and, 5:491
Anderson, Elizabeth, on science, 1:158
Anderson, John, **1:197–200**
 Mackie and, 5:637
 on meaning, 3:496
 on term distribution in syllogisms, 5:499
Anderson, P. W., on emergence, 3:192
Andō Shōeki, **1:200**
André, Yves M., on Malebranche, 5:663
André le Chapelain, on love, 5:587–588
Andrea, Johann Valentin, tracts written by, 3:674
Andreas, Antonius, Duns Scotus and, 8:704
Andrew of Neufchateau, St., 3:93
Androcentrism
 pervasiveness of, 3:591
 in research, screening out, 3:594
 in Western philosophy, 3:590
Andronicus of Rhodes
 and Aristotelianism, 1:259, 1:265–266
 Peripatetics and, 7:203
Anfangsgründe aller schönen künste und Wissenschaften (Principles of All Beautiful Arts and Sciences) (Meier), 6:112
Angelic world, in Corbin, 2:537
Angell, Norman, 7:155
Angelology
 Bodin on, 1:622
 Bonaventure on, 1:653
 Swedenborg on, 9:338
Angels
 Aquinas on, 9:429–430
 composition of, Matthew of Aquasparta on, 6:65
 Malebranche on, 5:666
Anger, Philodemus on, 7:302–303
Anglia Libera (Toland), 9:504
Anglican Church
 on dogma, 3:97
 Reformation and, 8:296–297
Anglo-American tradition
 and revolution in philosophy, 7:108
 and technology, 7:546, 7:549
Anglo-Saxon philosophy, as epistemological, 5:91
Angra Mainyu, 3:471, 9:886–887
Angst
 as alienation from God, 1:762–763
 in Heidegger, 6:658
Anguish, in freedom, in Jaspers's ethics, 4:801
Anima, 4:857. *See also De Anima*
Anima, L' (periodical), 7:102
Anima motrix, transition to *vis motrix,* 5:52
Anima mundi, compared to gravity, 5:54
Animadversiones Aristotelicae (Ramus), 5:438
Animadversiones in Decimum Libri Diogenis Laertii, qui est de Vita, Moribus Placitisque Epicuri (Gassendi), 4:25
Animal(s)
 Alcmaeon of Croton on, 1:105
 altruism in, 1:204
 Aristotle on, 1:273–275
 as automata, 1:201, 1:208, 5:631
 behavior of, Rohault on, 8:483
 in behaviorism, 1:521–522
 in bioethics, 1:602
 cognition in, 1:202–203
 communication in, 1:204–205

consciousness in
vs. human consciousness, 5:78
instantiation of, 7:278
deception in, 1:206
emotion in, 1:201, 3:198–199
ethical responsibility to, 3:392–393
Haeckel on, 4:204
and human beings, comparison of, 1:105, 2:176, 7:526–527
intention in, 1:206
knowledge possessed by, 6:499
language in, 1:204–205
law of effect in, study of, 1:521
memory in, 1:206
Mencius on, 2:233
mental states of, 2:456, 2:481
morality in, 3:479, 5:155
nature of, *vs.* human nature, 5:139
pain in, and problem of evil, 3:476
persons as, Wiggins on, 9:763
problem solving in, 1:206
purposive behavior in, 1:206
rights of. *See* Animal rights
schemata of relationships among, 4:201
self-recognition in, 1:205
sexuality of, *vs.* human sexuality, 7:526–527
in sign language training experiments, 4:692
soul of, Descartes on, 2:737
speciesism and, 9:164–165
Swedenborg on, 9:336
time and, 1:203
tool making by, 1:206
unself-consciousness of, 8:725
Animal faith, Santayana on, 9:199
Animal knowledge, in virtue perspectivism, 9:136
Animal Liberation (Singer), 3:561, 9:41
Animal life, possessed of both body (Leib) and soul (Seele), 5:77
Animal magnetism, 5:642
Animal mind, **1:200–208**
Animal psychology, Reimarus in, 8:331
Animal rights, **1:208–210**, 8:667–668
human obligation to, 9:76
personhood and, 7:242–243
Singer on, 3:561, 9:41
speciesism and, 9:164–165
Animalism, personal identity and, 7:229–231
Animaux plus que machines, Les (La Mettrie), 5:180
Animism
Bruno on, 1:710
in hermetic religious philosophy, 1:711
McDougall on, 6:72
vs. microcosm, 5:639
vs. panpsychism, 7:85
Stahl on, 9:202
Stout on, 9:261
Thomasius on, 9:442
See also Macrocosm and microcosm; Panpsychism
Animistic materialism, 6:331–332
Animus, Jungian, 4:857
Anlage zur Architektonik, oder Theorie des Einfachen und Ersten in der philosophischen und mathematischen Erkentniss (Foundation of architectonic, or theory of the simple and primary elements in philosophical and mathematical knowledge) (Lambert), 5:176
Anleitung, über natürliche Begebenheiten ordentlich und vorsichtig nachzudenken (Crusius), 2:607
Anmerkungen über die Baukunst der Alten (Remarks on the architecture of the ancients) (Winckelmann), 9:790
Annalen der Philosophie (journal), 5:525
Annales school, 3:699, 7:392
Année sociologique, L' (periodical), 3:150
Annet, Peter, **1:210–211**, 2:683–685
Anniceris, Cyrenaic teaching of, 2:620
Annihilation
Kvanvig on, 4:251
pessimism and, 7:251
Russell on, 1:374
Annotata Praecurrentia, Annotata Majora (Geulincx), 4:77
Annotationes in Libros Posteriorum (Sylvester of Ferrara), 9:344
Anomalies
causal, 8:320
in rival paradigms, 8:697
scientists' response to, 5:158
Anomalism
Davidson on, 5:71
of mental, 1:211
Anomalous monism, **1:211–212**, 7:555
Davidson (Donald) on, 1:211, 2:646–648, 6:133
on determinism, 3:24
Kim on, 2:648
mental causation and, 6:133
in philosophy of mind, 7:470–471
Anomie, Durkheim on, 3:151
Anonymus Iamblichi
justice in, 6:632
sophistic ideas in, 9:129
Anorexia, 6:150
Ansai school, Yamazaki Ansai in, 9:860
Anschauung, 7:255, 7:279, 7:284
Anscombe, Gertrude Elizabeth Margaret, **1:212–213**
on causality, 2:97
on consequentialism, 2:460
on ethics, 9:687
on intention, 8:674
Lewis (C. S.) and, 5:311–312
Anselm, St., **1:214–219**
atonement theory of, 3:473
on denominatives, 8:762–763
on divine perfection, 7:194
Duns Scotus and, 3:142
on ethics, 1:216–218
on faith and reason, 1:214, 3:403
Gaunilo on, 4:33–34
on God, existence of, 3:493–494, 9:781
Henry of Ghent and, 3:136
on intentionality, 4:705
and language, 1:218–219, 6:102
on lost island *reductio*, 4:34
in medieval philosophy, 6:99
metaphysics of, 1:215–216
method of, 1:214–215
on quality and possession, 8:763
on redemption, 2:249
in religious philosophy, 7:491
on semantics, 8:762–763
See also Ontological argument for existence of God
Anselm of Laon, 7:260
"Anselmische Gottesbewies, Der" (Scholz), 8:645
Antecedent(s)
in counterfactual conditional possible world, 2:428
definition of, 5:534
denial of, 3:537, 5:543
empiricist, 3:629
in hypothetical syllogisms, 5:502
in Mill's methods of induction, 6:239
strengthening of, Lewis (D.) on, 5:314
Antecedent-consequent relationship, 3:537
anaphora and, 1:171
in thought experimentation, 9:454–455
Anthology (John of Stobi), 4:540
Anthropic principle, **1:219–222**, 3:321
Anthropocentric environmentalism, 3:258–259
Anthropocentric ideas, counterfactuals in science and, 2:575

Anthropocentrism
in metaphysics, 8:376
objective, 6:215–216
in progress, 6:215–216
Anthropological judgments, 7:244
Anthropological pessimism, of Voltaire, 9:712
Anthropologie (Steffens), 9:238
Anthropologism, Lavrov on, 5:218
Anthropology
biology and, 7:320–321
branches of, 7:320–323
common consent arguments for God's existence and, 2:349–350
cultural philosophical, 7:321–322
Gregory of Nyssa and, 4:182
knowledge and, 7:318
Landgrebe on, 5:183–184
methodology in, 7:318–319
Morgan (Lewis) and, 6:403–404
myth in, 6:465–466
natural law and, 5:714–715
philosophical, **7:315–324**
of Aquinas, 6:104
Bachofen and, 1:441
Bakhtin Circle and, 1:469
cultural, 7:321–322
in Gehlen, 4:35–36
genetic technology and, 4:48
Molina Garmendia and, 6:323–324
natural and human science demarcation, 1:470
vs. physiological, 7:317
Plessner and, 7:629
psychological, 7:322–323
Sombart on, 9:128
theological, 7:323
utopias of, 9:618
physiological *vs.* philosophical, 7:317
psychic, 3:752
psychology and, 7:322–323
of religious experience, Pannenberg on, 7:80–81
Rothacker on, 7:322
science and, 7:317–318
significance tests in, 9:214
Stein on, 9:239
theological philosophical, 7:323
Anthropology in Theological Perspective (Pannenberg), 7:80
Anthropomorphism
avoidance of, by Saadya, 8:585
of deities, Xenophanes of Colophon on, 9:853
of God, 1:359, 1:364–365, 1:370–371
in religious analogy, 1:138
Spinoza on, 9:179
Anthroposophicalism, 9:241
Anthroposophy, 9:242
Anti-Aristotelianism, of Crescas, 2:593–594
Antiatomism, of Whitehead, 6:146–147
Anti-Cartesianism
of Rorty, 8:493–494
of Vico, 9:671–672
Antichnyi kosmos i sovremennaia nauka (Losev), 5:574
Antichrist, The (Nietzsche), 6:611
Anticipations, 5:19, 9:701
Anticlericalism, deism and, 2:681
Anticonsequentialism, of Thomson (Judith), 9:449
Antidescriptivist value theory, 9:640
Anti-essentialist arguments, feminists and, 3:587
Antigone (Sophocles), 4:177
Hegel on, 9:523–524
love in, 5:583
Antihedonistic value theory, 9:639
Anti-intellectualism, in Stirner's egoism, 9:250–251
Anti-intentionalism, 1:311–312
Antike Wirtschaftsgeschichte (Neurath), 6:560
Antilanguage, use of Daoism, 2:188
Antiliteralism, 6:636
Antilogism, definition of, 5:534
Antimetaphysical movement, 4:8, 5:199
Antimetaphysics, contemporary, 6:206–207
Antinihilism, 6:618–619
Antinomianism
of Milton, 6:250
Toynbee on, 9:518
Antinomy(ies), 5:22
and dialectic, 5:9
Kantian, 2:75, 5:11
first, on time, 9:467
second, Maréchal and, 5:708
postcolonial, 7:728
"Antinomy of Pure Reason," 5:22
Antiochus Epiphanes (king of Syria), Philonides and, 3:263
Antiochus of Ascalon, **1:222–223**
Aenesidemus and, 1:30
on Aristotle, 7:571
dogmaticism of, 4:174
eclecticism of, 9:48
in Greek Academy, 4:171
Panaetius of Rhodes and, 7:79
and Platonism, 7:571, 7:607
reasonable doubt of, 3:702
Anti-Oedipus (Deleuze and Guattari), 2:694–696
Antipater of Tarsus
on logic, 5:404
Panaetius of Rhodes and, 7:78–79
Antipaternalism, hard and soft, 7:138
Antiphenomenalism
in Krueger's philosophical psychology, 5:156
of Neurath, 6:562
Antiphon, **1:223**
continua in, 2:491
on justice, 6:631–632
on nomos and phusis, 6:631
on rectilinear figures, 2:493
on sophism, 9:129–130
Anti-Platonism, 4:464–465
Anti-polemus, or the Plea of Reason, Religion and Humanity against War (Erasmus), 7:154
Antiquae Lectiones (Lipsius), 5:364
Antirationalism
on deism, 2:686
Schopenhauer on, 8:653
Antirealism
assertoric, 6:172
in British metaphysics, 6:198
ethics in, 5:704
on gender, 3:588–589
immortality in, 4:617
on meaningfulness of sentences, 9:43
in medieval philosophy, 6:101
metaphysics of, 6:171–172
in ontology, 8:275–276
sense of existence in, 8:689
on universals, 6:101
verificationist, 8:689
See also Realism
Antireductionism, properties in, 8:65–66
Anti-representationalism
of Davidson (Donald), 2:648–649
of Rorty, 8:494
Anti-Semitism
in Chamberlain, 2:123
Cohen (Hermann) on, 2:304
German, Einstein and, 3:178
in Gnosticism, 4:101
Russian, Lotman and, 5:578
Simon on, 9:33
Antisthenes, **1:224**
Diogenes Laertius on, 3:88
Diogenes of Sinope and, 3:90
logic and, 5:397
on semantics, 8:755
Socrates and, 3:399

Antisubjectivist product-objectivism, 9:719
Anti-Theistic Theories (Flint), 1:357, 1:372
Antitheoretical approaches, in bioethics, 1:601–602
Antitheses (Marcion), 5:703
Antitheses, in Bafi, 1:476
Anti-Trinitarianism, deism and, 2:681
Antitrust law, 7:718
Antiutopianism, 9:621
Antonescu, Ion, ideologies of, 3:553
Anton's syndrome, 6:566
Antony, Louise, on Quine, 1:158
Antropologicheskii printsip v filosofii (The anthropological principle in philosophy) (Chernyshevskii), 2:146
Ants, The (Wilson, E.), 9:788
Anupaladhi, 5:117
Anweisung, vernünftig zu leben (Guide to living rationally) (Crusius), 2:69, 2:607
Anxiety
  as cause of sin, 6:605
  Niebuhr on, 6:605
  precognition and, 7:755
  in psychoanalytic theory, 8:109–110
  Tillich on, 9:458–459
Apartheid, liberation theology and, 5:331
Apathy, as sign of political health, 2:703
Apeiron/Peras, **1:225**
  See also Boundless, the
Apel, Karl-Otto, **1:225–227**
Apelles, Marcion and, 5:704
Apelt, E. F., 3:753
Aperspectivity, as male strategy, 3:574–575
Aphasia, Freud on, 3:737
Aphonia, 6:150
Aphorism(s)
  of Johnson (Alexander Bryan), 4:850
  of Mīmāmsā school, 4:628
  of Nietzsche, 6:610–611
  Novalis on, 6:667
Aphrodite (love)
  in classical mythology, 5:583–584, 5:589
  Empedocles on, 3:209–213
Apocrypha
  patristic philosophy on, 7:141
  as wisdom literature, 9:793
Apodictic (apodeictic) proposition, 5:549
  See also Modality
Apodictic judgment, 1:689–690
Apodicticity, of reason, 1:429
Apoha (exclusion), as universals, 9:585–586
Apollodorus, on Democritus, 5:298
Apollonius Cronus, 3:87, 6:111
Apologetic
  Barth on, 1:478
  Butler (Joseph) on, 1:781
  Christian, Hume on, 6:266–267
  linguistic, 7:495
  negative, Plantinga on, 7:581
  religious pluralism and, 8:420
Apologetica Disceptatio pro Astrologia (Servetus), 8:831
Apologeticum (Tertullian), 1:228, 9:399
Apologetika (Zen'kovskii), 9:868–869
Apologia (King James I), 9:282
Apologia (Pico della Mirandola), 7:570–571
Apologia Compendiaria Fraternitatem de Rosea Cruce (Fludd), 3:674
Apologia Pro Vita Sua (Newman), 6:576–577, 6:583
Apologie de la religion chrétienne (Pascal), 7:131
"Apologie de Raymond Sebond" (Montaigne), 4:166, 9:52
"Apologie d'un fou, L'" ("The apology of a madman") (Chaadaev), 2:121
Apologie oder Schutzschrift für die vernunftigen Verehrer Gottes (Apology for rational worshipers of God) (Reimarus), 5:295
Apologists, **1:227–229**, 5:648
  See also Theodicy
Apology (Aristides), 1:227, 7:141
Apology (Plato), 2:260
  on Aristophanes' *The Clouds,* 9:106
  on poetry, 4:175
  on sophists, 9:109
  on wisdom of Socrates, 9:108
Apology for Mr. Toland (Toland), 9:504
Apology for Raymond Sebond (Montaigne), 2:728, 2:746, 6:333–334
Apology of Socrates (Xenophon), 9:855
Apophatic method
  in Charron, 2:134–135
  in commentaries on Brahman, 1:682–683
  in Dge-lugs Mādhyamika, 1:732
  in Huayan Buddhism, 1:738–739
  in Mādhyamika doctrine, 1:740–744
  in meditation, 1:738
  in Sanlun Buddhism, 2:162
  Svātantrika-Prāsaṅgika distinction, 1:744
Aporias, in Derrida, 2:716
Apostolic poverty, Ockham on, 9:770
Apparatus, in experiment
  indicator states of, 8:208
  in quantum theory, 8:204–208
  ready state of, 8:208
Apparatus Syllogistici Synopsis (Albanus), 5:439
Apparent being, Aureol on, 7:257
Apparent contradiction *(anupapatti),* between two means of knowledge, 5:122
Apparent reality, *vs.* true reality, 6:184
Apparitions (Tyrell), 4:603
Appeal to the Slavs (Bakunin), 1:471–472, 2:361
Appearance(s)
  Augustine on, 1:229
  Austin on, 8:819
  Berkeley on, 1:231
  Bradley on, 1:232
  grammar of, 1:229–231
  in illusory experience, 4:586
  Kant on, 1:232, 5:12
  Lambert on, 5:175–176
  Leibniz on, 1:232
  linguistics of, 1:229–231
  Protagoras on, 1:230–231
  qualities as, 1:232
  reality and, **1:229–232,** 6:79, 7:22, 7:187–188, 9:684. *See also Appearance and Reality* (Bradley)
    and evil, problem of, 3:470
    in illusory experience, 4:586
    Kant on, 5:12
    in Skovoroda's mysticism, 9:63
  substance and, 6:600
  things-in-themselves and, 5:34
  thoroughgoing affinity of, 5:17
  uniformity of, Chwistek on, 2:255
  world of, 5:22
Appearance and Reality (Bradley), 1:12, 1:232, 1:677, 4:112
  on The Absolute, 4:112
  epistemology in, 3:310–311
  on reality, 3:312
  skeptical arguments in, 9:58
  and Stebbing, 9:236
Appearance talk, constant and perspectival modes of, 7:188–190
Appearing, theories of, 8:263–264
Appellatio (property of term), 9:786
Appellation, definition of, 5:534
Appendix Scientiam Spatii Absolute Veram Exhibens (Bolyai), 5:461
Apperception, **1:233–235,** 9:850

internalized, 7:255
Kant on, 1:233–234, 3:308, 4:51, 5:17
in monadology, 3:298
unity of, 5:21
synthetic, McGilvary on, 6:75
transcendental, Kant on, 3:308
Appetites, Plato on, 9:794
Appiah, Anthony, 3:587
Appiah, Kwame, 1:86
Appleton, Jay, 3:255
Applicability, legal, 7:451
Applications of Information Theory to Psychology (Attneave), 4:72
Applied ethics, **1:235–240**, 1:599
casuistry in, 1:237–238
computer ethics as, 2:396
deduction and, 1:237
definition of, 1:236
history of, 1:236–237
informed consent in, 4:679–680
reflective equilibrium in, 1:238
relative equilibrium in, 1:238
specificity in, 1:239
vs. traditional ethical theory, 1:238–239
types of, 1:236
virtue ethics and, 9:680
Applied functional calculus, 5:536
Applied geometry, 5:15
Applied philosophy, Kant's contributions to, 5:28–30
Applied Psychology (Dewey), 3:44
Applied research, *vs.* pure research, Wolff and, 9:827
Appolonius's Problem, 3:187
Apposites (Suhrawardī), 4:582
Appraisal, legal, 7:450–452
Appraisal respect, 8:441
Appreciations (Pater), 7:136
Apprehension
abstractive. *See* Abstractive cognition
of beauty, 1:512
in Buddhist epistemology, 1:755
in Huayan Buddhism, 2:164
immediate, intuition as, 4:722
intuitive. *See* Intuitive cognition
vs. judgment, Ockham on, 9:773–774
of reasons for actions, 1:18
vs. sensing, Ehrenfels on, 3:176
in Stoicism, 1:30
Approval
faculty of, in perception of Beauty, 6:131
and moral concepts, 9:739–740
Approximation, in probability, 4:808
Apriorism, 5:84
of McCosh, 6:71
of Peckham, 7:161–162
prominent proponents of, 5:85
vs. radical empiricism, 5:85
Apriority, concept of, 5:84
A-proposition
definition of, 5:534
negating of terms in, 3:539
simple conversion of, 3:538–539
Apuleius
on logic, 5:408
in preservation of Plato's doctrine, 7:606
Aqudeza y arte de ingenio, La (Gracián), 4:168
Aquinas (Stump), 9:447
Aquinas, St. Thomas, **9:424–437**
on act *vs.* potency, 2:679–680
on aesthetics, 9:435–436
on agent intellect, 1:91
on altruism, 3:170
on analogical predication, 4:108
on analogy, 1:140–142, 1:477
on analogy of proportionality, 4:108
Aristotle and, 2:721, 3:214–216, 3:287
on atheism, 1:357
authority of, 9:436–437
on authority of prince, 9:139
Averroism and, 1:91, 1:429–430, 4:758
Avicenna and, 1:435
on Báñez, 1:476
on beauty, 1:47, 9:435–436
on being as essence, 1:528–530
Bellarmine and, 1:542
on body, 4:603–604, 8:122–123
Bonaventure and, 1:653–654
Bruno on, 1:711
in Byzantine thought, 1:789
Cajetan on, 2:7
Capreolus and, 2:30–31
censure of, 9:444
on civil state, 6:104
on cognition, 1:47, 9:426–428
on common sense, 4:697
on conscience, 3:404, 9:434–435
contrasts in, 9:444
correspondence theory of truth and, 9:534
on cosmology, 3:226–227
on creation, 1:360, 3:494, 4:109
Dante and, 2:624–626
David of Dinant and, 2:644
on determinism, 3:5, 3:9
and divine command theories of ethics, 3:93
on divine illumination, 4:580
on divine perfection, 7:194
on divine transcendence, 4:107
Dōgen and, 3:95
Dominicans and, 3:148
on dualism, 3:115
Duns Scotus and, 3:141
Durandus of Saint-Pourçain on, 3:148
empiricism and, 3:214–216, 3:221, 3:289–290
Engels on, 3:58
epistemology and, 3:289–290
on equality, 3:329
Erasmus and, 3:340
on essence and existence, 3:350, 9:283
on eternal return doctrine, 3:354
on eternity, 3:358
on ethics, 3:403–404, 9:433–435
on evil, 3:473, 9:433
on faith, 3:529–530, 3:535, 9:425–426
on family, 9:435
on forms, 1:626, 3:115, 3:289, 9:427
on free will, 3:404, 9:429, 9:433–434
Garrigou-Lagrange and, 4:23
on God
attributes of, 1:141, 2:681, 2:728
existence of, 2:551, 2:677–680, 7:557, 9:431–432
goodness of, 4:111
immanence of, 4:108
infinity of, 4:110
love of, 3:142
simplicity of, 4:116
as starting point in theology, 2:8
in theology, 2:8
Godfrey of Fontaines and, 4:131
on human nature, 9:428–430
on ideas, 4:564
on immaculate conception, 8:704
on immortal abstract intellect, 4:608–609
influences on, 9:425
on intellect, 3:289
on intentionality, 4:706
John of Paris and, 4:842
on knowledge, 3:289, 9:426–427
and Latin American philosophy, 5:205

on law, 7:421–422, 9:434
Liber de Causis and, 5:334
on light, 1:47
Luther on, 5:615
on lying, 5:619
Maritain and, 5:712–714
Marston and, 5:725–726
in medieval metaphysics, 6:189
in medieval philosophy, 6:100
on metaphysics, 3:135, 9:430–431
moderate realism of, Ockham on, 9:773
moderation of, 9:425
monophychism in, 9:28
on monotheism, 4:110
on moral obligations of merchants, 1:776–777
on natural law, 6:507–508, 7:421–422
on natural philosophy, 9:427–428, 9:772
on natural theology, 1:477
on nature, 6:519
on necessary beings, 7:26
on necessity of consequent, 3:694
on necessity of past, 3:693
occasionalism and, 5:668
on omnipotence, 4:115
on perception, 8:825
on perfection, 2:679
on person, 7:237
Philoponus and, 7:314
philosophical anthropology of, 6:104
philosophy of, 3:97, 9:425
physicotheology of, 7:557
Pico della Mirandola and, 7:571
Plato and, 3:358–359
political philosophy of, 7:659–660
on possibility, 7:720–721
on providence, 9:433
on reason, 3:404
in religious philosophy, 7:491–492
on resurrection, 3:348
Scholasticism and, 3:137
on science, 9:428
on sense perception, 3:289
on sexuality, 7:522, 7:526–528
on Siger of Brabant, 9:27
Soto and, 9:137
on soul, 3:115, 4:609–610
Stein's translations of, 9:240
and Suárez, 9:282
on substance, 1:626
on suicide, 9:319
on thought and reality, 2:539
Toletus on, 9:511
on unconscious, 9:570
on universals, 3:289, 6:189, 9:425, 9:593
on war and peace, 7:152
on will, 9:429
writings of, 9:425, 9:437–438
See also Thomism
Arab culture
Laroui on, 5:202
on state, role of, 5:202
Arabic logic. *See* Logic, in Islamic world
Arabic philosophy. *See* Islamic philosophy
Arahat, in Buddhism, 5:328
Arama, Isaac, in Renaissance Jewish philosophy, 4:824
Aratus
astrology of, 4:301–302
Cicero and, 5:598
Eudoxus and, 5:600
"Arbeiten zur Entwicklungspsychologie" (Krueger), 5:156
Arbeiter, Der (Jünger), 4:859
Arbeiterfrage, Die (Lange), 5:186
Arbeiter-Programm (Lassalle), 5:203
Arbor Scientiae (Arbre de ciència) (Lull), 5:610
Arcana Coelestia quae in Genesi et Exodo Sunt Detecta (Swedenborg), 9:338
Arcesilaus, **1:247–248**
in Greek Academy, 4:171–173, 4:301
on knowledge, 3:288
in Platonic tradition, 7:607
Pyrrho and, 1:193
and skepticism, 3:399, 9:48
Archaeology
classical, Winckelmann in, 9:790
Collingwood and, 2:325
Foucault and, 3:699–700, 7:396
Archaeology of Knowledge (Foucault), 7:396
Archaic conscious wishes, in Freud's psychology of religion, 3:745
Archē, **1:248–249,** 1:272–273, 1:276–277
Archeologie du savior, L' (The Archaeology of Knowledge) (Foucault), 3:700
Archetypes
Berkeley on, 1:581
Duns Scotus on, 3:141–142
Jungian, 1:58, 4:857
Malebranche on, 2:57
in pre-Darwinian biological theory, 2:640
Scholasticism on, 3:141
Archidoxis (Paracelsus), 7:103
Archimedean axiom, in Euclid, 2:493
Archimedean ordered fields, elementary continuum and, 2:508–509
Archimedean property, definition of, 5:534
Archimedes
on energy and work, 3:227
on equilibrium, 4:56
on flotation of bodies, 4:56
and infinitesimal calculus, 2:494
on magnitudes and ratios, 2:492–493
on method of exhaustion, 4:55
Architectonic, of Kant, 5:9
Architectonic theory of philosophy, Peirce and, 7:163–169
Architecture
aesthetic judgments and, 1:36–37
in Bentham's panopticon, 1:555
Hegel on, 4:274
Plato on, 1:41–42
theory of, 9:693–694
Wittgenstein on, 9:802
Wolff on, 9:829
Archytas of Tarentum, **1:250–251**
on eternal return doctrine, 3:353
Philolaus of Croton and, 7:310
Plato and, 8:186
Ardigò, Roberto, **1:251–252,** 7:102
"Are There *a priori* Concepts?" (Austin), 1:407
Area law, necessity and, 5:222–224
Arendt, Hannah, **1:252–256**
on evil, 3:470
extraordinary character of, 5:152
on Heidegger, 1:253
on ideology, 4:574
on violence, 9:677–678
Areopagitica (Milton), 6:250
Aretē, **1:256**
Arete of Cyrene, Cyrenaics and, 2:619
Arethas, 1:788
Argentinean philosophy
contemporary period of, 5:207–210
independentist period of, 5:205
liberation philosophy in, 5:211
positivism in, 5:206–207
Argument, 3:639
ambiguities in, detection of, 3:640
from analogy, 7:51–53
conclusion of, 7:51–53
definition of, 5:534
Strawson on, 7:57
in art, 1:334
to best explanation, 9:66

Argument, ***continued***
- in classic foundationalism, 2:276–278
- from common sense, 2:355, 7:700–701
- from design
  - Hume on, 4:511–512
  - Mendelssohn on, 6:131
  - Mill (John Stuart) on, 6:230–231
- from error, 8:519
- from essence of man, 4:383–384
- from evil, hiddenness of God and, 4:350
- fallacies in, 3:538
- forms of, 3:644
  - invalid, 3:537
- of function, definition of, 5:534
- from illusion, 3:284
- logical form and, 5:507–508
- in metaphysics, 6:204–205
- modal
  - for dualism, 3:118–119
  - in supervenience, 9:327
- from morals, 7:701–702
- narrative as, 1:336
- philosophical, *vs.* mathematical, 5:10
- from productivity, in compositionality, 2:371
- from religious experience, 3:321–322
- in Stoic logic, 5:405–406, 9:255
- validity of, 5:513
  - in classic foundationalism, 2:276–278
- veiled, 6:110

Argument against Abolishing Christianity, An (Swift), 9:341

Argumenta, in medieval logic, 5:422–423

Argumentation
- by Academy, against Stoa, 2:47
- in Chinese ethics, 2:200–201
- Chrysippus on, 2:251
- Cicero on, 2:258
- *elenchus* in, 7:593
- logical *vs.* evocative, 2:213–214

Argumentum ad baculum, definition of, 5:542

Argumentum ad hominem, 3:547–548, 3:561, 5:542

Argumentum ad ignorantiam, definition of, 5:542

Argumentum ad ignorantiam or *ad auditores,* 3:548

Argumentum ad misericordiam, definition of, 5:542

Argumentum ad personam, 3:548

Argumentum ad populum, 3:548, 5:542

Argumentum ad verecundiam, 3:548, 5:542–543

Argyropoulos, John (Johannes), 1:789, 5:437

Arhant, 6:621

Arianism
- Arius and, **1:282–284**
- in Christological debates, 2:247
- Clarke on, 2:269
- Collier on, 2:324

Ariosto, Ludovico
- and Croce, 2:601
- and Galileo, 4:9
- sentimental poetry of, 8:629

Ariosto, Orazio, Patrizi and, 7:144

Aristarchus of Samos, 4:301, 5:50, 9:405

Aristée (Hemsterhuis), 7:100

Aristides, as apologist, 1:227

Aristippus of Cyrene, **1:257**
- as founder of Cyrenaics, 2:619
- Socrates and, 3:399
- utilitarianism and, 9:605

Aristo of Ceos, *vs.* Aristo of Chios, 1:258

Aristo of Chios, **1:257–258,** 9:254

Aristocles
- Aenesidemus and, 1:31
- Eusebius and, 3:455
- on Pyrrho, 8:173

Aristocratic logic, of Ortega y Gasset, 7:47–48

Ariston of Alexandria, on logic, 5:407

Aristophanes
- Prodicus and, 8:45
- on Socrates, 3:395, 9:106
- on war and peace, 7:152

Aristotelian logic, 1:269, 5:398–401, 5:568–569, 5:607–608
- commentators on, 5:408
- and computing machines, 2:400
- creation of, 3:52–53
- Ramus on, 5:438
- Valla on, 9:635

"Aristotelian Pleasures" (Owen), 7:65

Aristotelian Society, 9:236

Aristotelian stories, 5:556–557

Aristotelian virtue ethics, 9:679

Aristotelianism, **1:258–262**
- Abelard and, 1:279
- Alexander of Aphrodisias and, 1:259
- Ammonius and, 1:260
- Andronicus and, 1:259
- Aquinas and, 3:289, 9:425, 9:432
- in Arabic world, 1:260–261
- Augustinianism and, 1:402
- Bacon (Francis) on, 1:442–443
- Buridan on, 1:430
- categories in, 2:72–74
- on causality and explanation, 1:449
- at Chartres school, 2:137
- and Christianity, 1:425, 1:428, 2:644
- commentaries in, 1:259
- cosmos in, motions of celestial bodies in, 5:54
- Crescas and, 4:822
- Culverwell on, 2:612
- David of Dinant and, 2:644
- definition of, 1:258
- Descartes and, 2:60, 2:720–721
- *vs.* divine illumination, 4:580
- empiricism of, 3:214–215
  - in medieval philosophy, 6:100–105
- ethics in, 1:256, 1:267–269, 3:397–398
  - friendship in, 3:749
- Galen on, 4:5
- Galileo on, 4:9
- Gilbert of Pointiers on, 4:88
- God in, *vs.* religious God, 4:816
- Grotius and, 4:191
- Hobbes on, 3:349
- Iamblichus and, 1:260
- Ibn Zaddik on, 4:551
- imperial age of, 1:259
- in Islamic philosophy, 1:279
- Italian, 1:430
- Kilwardby and, 5:69
- knowledge in, Sanches on, 8:595
- La Mettrie and, 5:179
- late ancient synthesis of, 1:259–260
- Latin, 1:261
- Leibniz and, 5:255, 5:265–269
- Locke on, 3:349
- MacIntyre on, 5:636–637
- Maimonides on, 5:648–651
- on matter, 6:60
- in medieval Paris, 1:452
- modern age of, 1:261–262
- moral theory of, and communitarianism, 9:74
- in natural philosophy, Ockham and, 9:778
- Nussbaum and, 6:680
- Panaetius of Rhodes and, 7:79
- Patrizi on, 7:144
- Peckham and, 7:161
- Peripatetics and, 7:202–203
- phenomenology in, Geyser on, 4:83

physics in, 1:271–273, 7:474, 9:154
Platonism and, 1:279
Plotinus and, 1:259
Pomponazzi and, 1:279, 1:430
Porphyry and, 1:259
realism in, 9:588
Aquinas and, 9:593
criticism of, 9:593–594
universals in, 9:591–593
in Reformation, 1:261
in Renaissance, 1:279–280, 8:425
Ross (William David) and, 8:504–505
vs. Saadya, 4:812
Sanches on, 8:595, 9:52
Telesio on, 9:390, 9:391
Themistius and, 1:259
Theophrastus and, 1:258
thought and thinking in, 9:419–420
Zabarella and, 1:430, 9:865–866
Aristotelicae Animadversiones (Remarks on Aristotle) (Ramus), 8:236
Aristotle, **1:263–282,** 5:422
on *a priori* and *a posteriori,* 1:240
Abelard and, 5:424–425
on absurdity, 2:74
on accidents, 1:627
on act *vs.* potency, 2:679
on aesthetics, 1:43–45, 1:188–189
on aether, 1:271–272
on *agathon,* 1:256
on agent intellect, 1:90–91
on *aitia,* 1:100
Albert the Great and, 3:403, 10:1–3
on Alcmaeon of Croton, 1:104
Alexander of Aphrodisias and, 1:112–113
Alexander the Great and, 1:263
al-Fārābī, Abū al Naṣr and, 1:116
on altruism, 3:170
on ambiguity, 8:756
on analogy, 1:139
on analytics, 1:269–271, 3:53
Anaxagoras and, 1:181–182
Anaximenes and, 1:186
Anscombe and, 1:212
on Antisthenes, 1:224
on *apeiron/peras,* 1:225
Aquinas and, 2:721, 3:214–216, 3:287, 3:403–404
and Arabic thought, 1:116, 5:417–421
archē, 1:248–249, 1:272–273
on Archytas of Tarentum, 1:250
Aristotle on, 3:538, 8:767
art in, 1:296
on astronomy, 4:301
on atomism, 1:384–385, 5:298–302
Augustine and, 1:391–392
Averroes on, 1:422–424, 1:428, 1:652, 3:134–135, 3:352, 3:403, 4:838–839
Avicenna and, 1:435, 3:134–135, 3:403
axioms and, 4:123
Bacon (Roger) on, 1:452
bans on, 1:261
on beauty and ugliness, 9:561
on being, 1:276, 1:527–528, 7:571–572
on belief and facts, correspondence of, 2:540
Boethius and, 1:625–626, 5:429
and Boileau, 1:640
Bonaventure on, 1:651–653
Boole and, 1:659
Brentano and, 3:421
Bruno on, 1:712
on categories, 1:773–774, 2:78–79, 5:536, 8:765
on causality, 1:273, 2:95
on causes, 1:100
first, 3:136
types of, 2:666–667
on change, 1:272–273, 4:621
and Christian Scholasticism, 9:772
on citizenship, 9:206
on classical identity, 4:570
and Clement of Alexandria, 2:290
on coincidence, 1:100
common sense and, 2:357
on concepts, 2:417
on consciousness, 2:453
on continuous conditions, 2:490–491
cosmological argument for God's existence and, 2:551
cosmology of, 1:271–273, 2:571, 5:640–641
on Cratylus, 2:584
critical vitalism of, 9:695
and Dante, 2:624–626
on definition, 2:665–667, 2:672–674
on Demiurge, 2:699, 5:640–641
democracy and, 1:268
on denominatives, 8:762
Descartes on, 2:738
on determinism, 3:5–6, 3:13, 3:17
Dewey on, 3:46
on dialectic, 1:269–271, 2:749, 3:52–54
in dialectic syllabus, 4:66
Dilthey and, 3:83
Diogenes Laertius and, 3:88, 3:89
Dōgen and, 3:95
on drama, 1:340
on dreams, 3:105–106
Duns Scotus and, 3:134, 3:139
on duty, 3:155
on education, 1:263, 7:367
on emanationism, 3:189
on emotions, 3:198
on energy and force, 3:225–227
Engels and, 3:61
on *episteme,* 1:270
epistemology and, 3:285–286
on equality, 3:329–331
on essence and existence, 3:349–350
essentialism in, 1:308
on eternal return doctrine, 3:353
on existence of fictitious objects, 3:493
on experience, 3:214
on fallacy, 3:538, 3:542, 8:767
on figure, 5:543
Fludd on, 3:674
Foot and, 3:684
on form, 1:273, 1:277, 1:308, 1:385, 7:65, 9:591–953
formalism in, 1:308
four elements doctrine and, 3:209
on friendship, 3:748, 7:521, 7:582–583
on future, 9:471–472
"future truth" argument for logical fatalism, 3:695
Galen on, 5:408
Galileo on, 4:9
Garve on, 4:24
on generation, 1:272–274
genetic essentialism and, 4:48
on God
mental properties of, 4:111
nature of, 5:585, 7:556
on Golden Mean, 4:152
golden rule and, 4:146
on good, 4:151, 5:8
on good man, 2:230, 5:7
Gorgias and, 8:752
and Gottsched, 4:164
on government, 1:268–269, 7:419
and Greek Academy, 1:263, 4:172
and Grice, 4:184
on habit, 5:615
on happiness, 1:267–268, 3:398
on heart, 4:6
and Heidegger, 4:290
Henry of Ghent and, 3:136
Hobbes and, 8:123, 8:774
on Homer, 1:188

Aristotle, ***continued***
on human motivation, 3:142
and Ikhwān al-Ṣafā', 4:576
on imagination, 3:286–287
on imitation, 1:43–44, 1:188, 4:599
on immortal intellect, 4:602
on immortality, 1:274, 4:608–609
on incontinence, 3:5
on incorrigibility, 8:824
on indeterminate dyad, 7:633
on inferential knowledge, 4:724
on infinite, potentially/actually distinction, 4:655
on infinite divisibility, 4:654
influence of, 1:278–280
on innate ideas, 4:691
on insensible, 6:201
on intellect, 1:275, 3:286–287
intellectual elitism of, 4:609
on intellectual virtues, 1:268, 9:682–683
on intentional action, 1:15
and Islamic philosophy, 4:754
John of Salisbury on, 4:843
on judgment, 3:286–287
on jurisprudence, 7:419
on justice, 1:267, 3:329
on katharsis, 5:44, 9:522
Kierkegaard and, 3:504, 5:62
on knowledge, 3:286–287
Laas on, 5:163
on language, 5:568
Latin American philosophy and, 5:205
on law, 7:418–419
on legislation, 7:419, 9:139
on Leucippus, 5:297–298
Liber de Causis and, 5:333
on light, 7:314
Locke and, 5:382
on logos, 5:568–569
on love, 5:585
Łukasiewicz on, 5:605–608, 5:691–692
Luther on, 5:615–617
Lyceum of, 4:172
Machiavelli and, 5:629–630
Maimonides and, 3:403, 5:648–650
Major and, 5:661
many-valued logics in, 5:688
on material world, 7:127
on matter, 1:385, 3:141, 6:58–59
in medieval education, 3:134
medieval logic and, 5:421–422, 5:429–430, 8:766
in medieval metaphysics, 6:189
in medieval philosophy, 3:403, 6:99–100
on memory, 3:286–287
on mental images, 4:592
metaphysics of, 1:275–278, 6:185–187, 6:203, 9:635–636
Scholz on, 8:645
on Millet Seed paradox, 9:877
on mimesis, 4:599, 6:252
on mind, 7:489
minima theory of, 1:385
on modality, 5:608
on moral responsibility, 3:398
on morality, 3:451
on motion, 1:273, 4:621, 6:411–412
on motion, paradoxes of
Achilles, 9:875
Dichotomy, 9:874
Flying Arrow, 9:875–876
Moving Rows, 9:876–877
natural kinds and, 6:504
natural law in, 6:506
on natural science, 4:55
on nature, 1:273, 6:519, 7:489–490
on necessary beings, 7:26
on necessity of past, 3:693
Nicolas of Autrecourt on, 6:600–601
non causa pro causa, 3:538
non causa pro causa fallacy noted by, 3:538
on nous, 1:278, 6:666
on numbers, 7:310–311
on objects, status of, 1:529
on oligarchy, 1:268
on optics, 4:301
on optimism/pessimism, 7:247
and Oresme, 7:34
organismic biology and, 7:36
Ortega y Gasset on, 7:48
Owen on, 7:64–65
Panaetius and, 4:174
on pantheism, 7:98
on paraconsistent logic, 7:105
Parmenides of Elea and, 7:122, 7:126
on parts, 6:146
Pauler on, 7:145
Paulsen and, 7:148
on perception, 8:824
on perfection, 2:677
Petrarch on, 7:264
in phantasia, 7:270
Philoponus on, 7:314
on philosophy, 1:263
philosophy of, interpreter of, 3:681
on *phronêsis,* 1:268
physicotheology in, 7:556
Pico della Mirandola and, 7:570–573
on Place of Place paradox, 9:878
Plato and, 1:267, 3:283, 3:686, 4:172, 6:548, 7:582–583, 7:634
on Platonic Forms, 1:270, 2:74, 3:350, 5:95, 9:591–593
Platonists and, 1:259–260
on pleasant, 5:8
on plenum, 3:635
on plot, 1:308
and Plotinus, 7:633
on poetry, 1:43, 1:333, 4:175–176, 7:594
vs. philosophy, 4:175–176
on polis, 9:206
on *politeia,* 1:268–269
political philosophy of, 1:267–269, 3:398, 7:656–657
on possibility, 7:719
on postsensory faculties, 4:696–697
on predicables, 5:552, 6:504
on prime mover, 4:108–110
on properties, 6:504
on Protagoras, 8:91
Psellus and, 1:279
on psyche, 1:273–275, 8:103
on Pythagoreanism, 8:185–186
and Qur'an, 1:651
on reason, locality of, 4:609
on reasoning, 1:270–271
on recognition, 1:44
in religious philosophy, 7:489
in Renaissance poetics, 1:48
on rhetoric, 1:264
Ross (William David) and, 8:504
Rufus (Richard) on, 1:454
Scholasticism and, 3:137
on scientific knowledge, 2:749
Scot's translation of, 8:703
on self-interest, 8:720
on semantics, 8:755–757
on sensationalism, 8:824
on sense perception, 3:286
on sentences, 8:756
Shestov on, 9:11
and Sidgwick, 9:25
on signification, 8:755–756
simple-body theory of, and Ibn Gabirol, 4:545
Simplicius and, 1:279, 6:555, 9:34
on social class, 7:592
on society, 5:630
on Socrates, 9:108
on sophisms, 1:270
on Sophocles, 1:188
Soto on, 9:137

on soul, 1:274–275, 3:115, 3:286, 4:607–608, 4:696–697
Gersonides on, 4:68
on sound, 9:138
on space, 9:147, 9:154
on statements, 8:756–757
Stoicism and, 4:300
on subject and predicate, 9:287–288
on subjects, 2:78–79
on substance(s), 1:4, 1:277
and attribute, 9:294–296
and essences, 9:295, 9:299
first and second, 9:288
on suicide, 9:319
and Swedenborg, 9:337
on syllogism, 1:269
Sylvester of Ferrara on, 9:344
on synonymy, 1:269–270
Syrianus on, 6:551
teleological ethics and, 9:383
Themistius on, 9:409
Theophrastus and, 1:258, 9:411–412
and theoretical-practical distinction in sciences, 3:46
on thought/thinking, 9:418
kinds of, 1:43
laws of, 5:232
nature of, 3:53
on time, 3:357–359
Toletus on, 9:511
on touch, 9:515
traditional logic and, 5:493
on tragedy, 1:43–44, 1:188, 1:297, 1:303, 1:308, 4:176, 5:44, 9:522
on true science, 4:55
on truth, 2:540–541, 5:399
definition of, 9:534
of future contingents, 3:692
on tyranny, 1:268
understanding of, 5:157
on universals, 2:15, 3:147, 3:286, 6:185, 9:586–587, 9:591–593
on universe, finitude of, 1:225
on vagueness, 9:624
Valla on, 9:635–636
on virtue, 1:267, 3:388, 7:307
on weather, 1:272
William of Moerbeke's translations of, 9:769–770
on wisdom, 1:264–265, 1:276
on women, 5:205
writings of, 1:263–267
on Xenophanes, 7:94
on Zeno's paradox, 4:655–656, 5:514
on zoology, 1:273–275
See also Aristotelianism
Aristotle: De Anima (Hicks), 4:608
Aristotle of Portugal. *See* Fonseca, Peter
Aristotle's Function Argument, 8:721
Aristotle's Syllogistic (Łukasiewicz), 5:608
Aristoxenus, 1:278, 5:44
Arithmetic
in axiomatization, 6:22
Berkeley on, 1:582
Clifford on, 2:292
in combinatory logic, 2:337
computability theory and, 2:383–387, 2:390
consistency of, 5:473
deductive reasoning in, Mill (John Stuart) on, 6:223
epistemic status of, 3:729
finite computing machines and, 2:403
first-order induction schema for, 3:650
Frege on, 1:244, 3:730–732, 5:463, 5:507, 5:516–517, 8:799
Gödel on, 5:193
happiness and, Maupertuis's application of, 6:67
Herbrand on, 5:473
and incompleteness proof, 2:41
infinite exponentiation and, 5:515
in informal axiomatics, 6:22
intuitive truth in, 4:117, 4:741, 9:593
Kant on, 1:244
language of, 1:582, 3:650, 4:120–121
logical nature of, 3:731
nonstandard number systems and, 2:506–510
Peano on, 1:146–147, 4:125, 5:463–465
Pestalozzi on, 7:371–372
provability in, 4:127–128
reduction of, to logic, 1:146, 6:674
relative interpretation of, 4:128–129
rigorousness of, 6:20
Robinson's, 4:123–124
second-order, 8:455–456
Tait on, 8:55–56
Theodoric of Chartres on, 9:410
time in, 1:244
See also Mathematics; Number
Arithmetic continuum
absolute unified framework for, 2:509
Bishop on, 2:504–505
Brouwer on, 2:502–504
geometric continuum and, 2:493–494
real number system and, 2:489
surreal number system and, 2:508
*Arithmetica Universalis (*Newton), 2:494
Arithmetical Books (De Morgan), 2:709
Arithmetical predicate, definition of, 5:534
Arithmetices Principia Nova Methodo Exposita (Peano), 5:463
Arithmétique, L' (Stevin), 2:493
Arithmetization
of analysis, 2:495–496, 5:534–535
of geometry, 5:514
of syntax, 5:535
Arity, of each relation and function symbol, 3:647
Arius, **1:282–284**
Arius Didymus, Eusebius and, 3:455
Arkoun, Mohammed, **1:284–285**
Arminianism, **1:285–286**
Chub on, 2:252
deism and, 2:681
Edwards (Jonathan) on, 3:167–169
on free will, 3:10
socinianism in, 9:99
Arminius, Jacobus, **1:285–286,** 3:167
Armstrong, David M., **1:286–287**
on body-object relation, 9:516
on colors, 2:332
on conditions of knowledge, 3:270–271
on determinables and determinates, 3:3
on Duns Scotus, 3:147
functionalist analysis of mental concepts, 3:756
on natural laws, 5:226–228
on perception, 7:191
on two-level account of introspection, 4:721
on universals, 1:287, 6:179–180, 9:585
on visual perception, 4:712
Arnauld, Antoine, **1:287–293,** 5:252, 5:439–440
and Chomsky, 2:423
Descartes and, 2:738, 2:748, 4:790–791, 5:665
Desgabets and, 2:757
epistemology of, 2:57–58
Jansenism of, 4:789–790
on La Mothe Le Vayer, 5:182
La Rochefoucauld and, 5:200
Leibniz and, 5:253, 5:257, 5:261, 5:272–276

Arnauld, Antoine, *continued*
Malebranche and, 2:61, 5:664–665, 5:670
Nicole and, 6:603
Pascal and, 7:130–131
on perception, 5:665
on providence, 5:670
on semantics, 8:775–776
Arnobius, as apologist, 1:228
Arnold, Gottfried, Franck and, 3:714
Arnold, Matthew, **1:293–295**
on Bible, 2:641
on Bolingbroke, 1:641
on Emerson, 3:197
on freedom, 5:319
on Smith's *Discourses,* 9:70
Arnold, Thomas, in legal realism, 7:428
Aron, Raymond
Dilthey and, 3:84
on ideology, 4:574
Arouet, François-Marie. *See* Voltaire, François-Marie Arouet de
Arousal theory of expression, 1:303
Arp, Hans, 8:620
Arrangement of the Philosophers (Philodemus), 7:302
Arriaga, Rodrigo, and Bayle, 1:504
Arrian, Epictetus and, 3:261
Arrow, of time, 9:498–499
Arrow, Kenneth J., general impossibility theorem of, 8:810
Ars combinatoria
definition of, 5:535
Leibniz on, 5:610
Ars disserendi (Adam of Little Bridge), 5:433
Ars Generalis Ultima (Lull), 5:610
Ars Logica (John of St. Thomas), 4:844–845, 8:772
Ars Magna (Lull), 5:442, 5:610
Art
abstraction in, 1:69
Adorno on, 1:69–70
in aestheticism, 1:339–340
and aesthetics, 1:34–36, 1:298, 1:509, 1:548, 2:580, 4:160–161, 9:764
African, 1:87
aleatoric, 1:298
Alison on, 1:129
allographic *vs.* autographic, 1:317
Anderson (John) on, 1:199
Apollonian *vs.* Dionysian, 6:609
Aquinas on, 9:435–436
argument in, 1:334
Aristotle on, 1:296
arousal theory of, 1:303
for art's sake, 1:56, 1:339–340
Lessing on, 5:294
Pater on, 7:136
authenticity in, **1:295–296**
autographic *vs.* allographic, 1:317
banality of truth in, 1:334
beauty as value of, 1:339–340
beauty of, definition of, 8:598
Belinskii on, 1:538
Bell (Clive) on, 1:59, 1:64
Benjamin on, 1:546
Bergson on, 1:57
Boileau on, 1:640
Bourdieu on, 1:300
bourgeois ideology and, 1:297
Bullough on, 1:761
Burke on, 1:771
Carroll on, 1:67–68
Caso on, 2:65
Cassirer on, 2:68
categories of, 1:316
Cavell on, 1:68
character and, 1:43
Chernyshevskii on, 2:146
Cicero on, 1:189
classical, 4:274
in cognition, 4:160–161
cognitive value of, 1:79, 1:335–337
in cognitivism, 1:340–341
Coleridge on, 2:318
Collingwood on, 1:57, 1:65, 1:304, 2:325–328
as communication, 1:57, 1:304, 1:312–313
Comte on, 1:56
contemplation and, 1:48
as conveyer of correct ideas, 7:628
Cousin on, 2:580
vs. craft, 3:572
creation of, 1:318–319
creativity and, 1:538, 2:590
Croce on, 2:601
as cultural object, 1:79, 1:514
Danto on, 1:34, 1:66–67, 1:299, 2:627–628
Daoist critique of, 2:236
De Sanctis on, 2:719
definitions of, **1:296–302**
essential, 9:820
history in, 1:300
depiction theory of, 1:328–329
Derrida on, 1:72
Deustua on, 3:42–43
Dewey on, 1:57–58, 1:64, 1:304, 3:46–47
as dialectical creation, 1:610
Dickie on, 1:67, 1:77–78
Dilthey on, 3:81, 3:83
as divine creation, 5:716
embodiment theory of, 1:305–306
emotion in, 1:54–55, 1:64–65, 1:76–80, 1:298
emotionalist theories of, 2:601, 3:125
end of, 1:341
epistemology and, 1:333–334
ethical criticism of, 1:68
ethics in, Winckelmann on, 9:790
experimentation in, 1:299
expression in, 1:64–65, **1:302–307**, 1:340
paradox of tragedy in, 4:601
as sociological statement, 7:628
film as, 7:381
formalist theory of, 1:298, **1:307–310**
found, 1:300
Fourier on, 1:56
Fry on, 1:59
functionalism on, 1:57
Gadamer on, 4:2
Gant on, 1:301
Gautier on, 1:56
in German romanticism, 8:617
in Gestalt psychology, 1:59
Gilson on, 4:93
Goodman on, 1:77–79, 1:305
Hanslick on, 1:59
Hegel on, 1:28, 1:303, 1:341, 4:269, 4:274
Heidegger on, 1:70–71
Hemsterhuis on, 4:311
Herder on, 1:55
historical context and, 1:314, 1:319–320
history as form of, 1:766
history of, 9:325
style and beauty in, 1:513
Winckelmann in, 9:790
Holocaust and, 4:452–453
Husserl on, 1:59, 1:70
and identity formation, 1:300
illusion and, 1:325–326
imagination and, 1:50, 4:596–597
as imitation, 1:75–76, 1:297, 1:489–490, 6:112
importance of, **1:337–341**
individuation of, 1:319–320
institutional theory of, 1:77–78, 1:299–300, 2:627
as instrumental value, 1:508–509
intellect and, 5:716
intent in, 1:300, 4:682–683
as interpretation, 1:314–315
interpretation of, 1:78, **1:310–315**
of invention, Wolff on, 9:826–827
Johnson (Samuel) on, 1:49

judgment and, 1:335
Kant on, 1:28
Kivy on, 1:66–67
knowledge in, 1:42, 1:79, **1:333–337**
Langer on, 1:58, 1:65–66
language and, 1:65–67
Leonardo da Vinci on, 5:281–282
Lessing on, 5:294
Levinson on, 1:67, 1:300
of living, in wisdom, 9:793
Lotze on, 5:581
Lukács on, 1:69
Lull on, 5:609–610
Malraux on, 5:674
Mandelbaum on, 1:66
Marcuse on, 1:70
Maritain on, 5:714–716
mass, *vs.* high, 1:67
meaning in, 1:78
Mill (John Stuart) on, 7:546–547
modern, philosophy of, 2:627–628
modernism in, 6:317
Molière on, 1:49
and morality, 1:42–43, 8:627, 9:514
Morris on, 1:56–58
multiplicity of, 1:76
narration theory of, 1:301–302
and nature, 1:34, 1:70, 1:641, 3:256–257, 6:522
in neo-Wittgensteinianism, 1:299
Nietzsche on, 1:56, 1:303, 9:524–525
obsolescence in, 1:335
ontology of, 1:78–79, **1:315–320,** 9:835–836
as organic whole, 1:55
orientation and, 1:335–336
original, *vs.* forged, 1:295
ownership and, 1:300
paradigmatism and, 9:237
paradox of tragedy and, 4:601
and perception, 1:336
perceptual foundations of, 6:151
performance in, **1:321–324**
personality types in, 1:335–336
philosophy of
 definition of, 7:328
 Solov'ëv on, 9:125
Plato on, 1:41–43, 1:303
play theory of, 3:100
pleasure and, 1:338–339
Plotinus on, 1:46, 1:190
postmodernism in, 7:729
products of, 4:274–275
progress in, 9:551
Proudhon on, 1:56
as pursuit of truth, 4:598
as rational reality, 1:538
reader-response theory of, 1:314–315
religion and, 9:514
as reminder of knowledge, 1:335
in Renaissance, 1:48–49
representation in, 1:297, **1:324–330**
 in painting *vs.* sculpture, 9:69
 sensitive, 1:494
 Smith (Adam) on, 9:69
in revolution, 1:69
Reynolds on, 1:49
in Romanticism, 1:297–298, 1:303–304, 8:487–488
Ruskin on, 1:56, 8:534–535
Saint-Simon on, 1:56–57
Santayana on, 1:57, 8:598–599
Sartre on, 1:71
Schelling on, 1:54, 8:620
Schiller (Ferdinand) on, 1:28, 1:54
Schopenhauer on, 1:55–56, 8:653–654, 9:524
self-conscious intelligence in, 8:620
as self-expression, 1:303–304
self-knowledge and, 1:79
self-will in, Gentile on, 4:52
semantics in, 1:67
semiotic functions of, 1:305
Seneca on, 1:189
Shpet on, 9:17
Sircello on, 1:304
site-specific works of, 3:256
in skepticism, 1:335–337
as skill, 1:296
as social capital, 1:300
social context and, 1:314
as social responsibility, 1:56–57
society and, 1:56–59, 1:69–70
spatial sense in, 9:166
style in, **1:330–333**
suffering and, 8:627
Sulzer on, 9:325
symbol systems in, 4:161
symbolisation in, 1:55, 4:594
as thinking in images, 1:538
as thought experiment, 1:336
Tolstoy on, 1:57, 1:304, 9:514
Tormey on, 1:303–306
traditional understandings of, 3:572
tragedy as synthesis of, 4:767
in transformation of future human action, 4:768
as transformed pain, 1:640
Trotsky on, 1:69
truth in, 1:28, **1:333–337,** 4:2
type theory and, 1:316
as universal imitation, 1:44
value of, 1:57, 1:80, **1:337–342**
Vasconcelos on, 9:649
virtue in, 1:67–68
Weitz on, 1:66, 1:299
Wilde on, 1:56
Wittgenstein on, 9:820
Wollheim on, 9:835–836
women and, 3:572
Wundt on, 9:850
Xunzi on, 2:234
Art (Bell), 1:64
Art and Illusion (Gombrich), 4:594
Art and Its Objects (Wollheim), 1:328
Art and Social Life (Plekhanov), 1:59
Art as Experience (Dewey), 1:57
Art Circle: A Theory of Art, The (Dickie), 1:67, 1:300
Art criticism
 in Beardsley, 1:508–509
 as detecting malperformace, 2:328
 Pater and, 7:136–137
 theories of, 2:628
"Art of Elocution or Tradition" (Bacon), 8:772
Art of Governing by Parties (Toland), 9:504
Art of Restoring (Toland), 9:504
Art of Thought, The (Wallas), 2:590
Art of War (Machiavelli), 5:626
Art Poétique (Boileau), 1:49, 1:639–640
Art, the Critics, and You (Ducasse), 3:125
"Art World, The" (Danto), 2:627
Arte Alchemie, De (Scot), 8:703
Arte of Logicke, The (Blundevile), 5:438
Arte of Reason rightly termed Witcraft, The (Lever), 5:438
Arthapatti, as means of knowledge, 5:122
"Articles of Belief and Acts of Religion" (Franklin), 2:689
Articuli Adversus Mathematicos (Bruno), 1:709
Artifact(s), 3:757
 Aquinas on, 9:435
 functions in, 9:387–389
 Plato on, 1:41–42
 in teleological argument for existence of God, 9:377–378
 women's, as decorative arts or crafts, 3:572
Artificial and natural language, **1:342–345**
 analogy in, 8:785
 autonomous idiolects in, 8:753
 Cartesian *vs.* Leibnizian, 8:779

Artificial and natural language, *continued*
Chomsky on, 9:352
Degérando on, 8:788
Frege on, 8:829
generics and, 4:43
Hamann on, 8:786–787
Humboldt on, 8:793
idéologues on, 8:788
Lambert on, 8:786
Leibniz's universal characteristics in, 8:779, 8:784
Mill (John Stuart) on, 8:797
realness in, 8:779–780
semantics for, 8:739–741
signification in, Aristotle on, 8:755–756
well-formedness of, 9:352
Artificial intelligence, **1:345–350**
autonomy of, 1:347–348
Chinese room argument and, 2:239–242
in cognitive science, 2:298–299
in computationalism, 2:394
connectionist, 1:347
conversational implicature in, 4:184
Dennett on, 2:711
emotion and, 1:349
frame problem within, 3:708
and fuzzy logic, 3:766
vs. human beings, materialism and, 6:17
vs. intelligence, 1:349
intention in, 1:349–350
learning in, 1:347
as misleading label, 1:349
non-classical logic and, 5:483
nonmonotonic reasoning in, 4:42
scope of, 1:345–456
symbolic, 1:346–347
Turing on, 2:376, 9:553
See also Machine intelligence
Artificial language(s). *See* Artificial and natural language; Language, artificial
Artificial life
artificial intelligence and, 1:345–349
cognitive science and, 2:300
Artificial virtues, 3:384, 4:508–509
Artificialization of language
in medieval philosophy, 6:101–102
reaction against, 6:103–104
Artin, Emil, 2:506
Artis Logicae Compendium (Aldrich), 5:439, 9:742
Artist(s)
authenticity of, 1:296
expertise of, 1:334–335
personalization of, 8:609
will-less perception of, 8:653
women as, 3:572
Artistic autonomy, and feminism, 3:573
Artistic form, Philodemus on, 7:302
Artistic value, 3:572
"Artists, The" (Schiller, Friedrich), 8:626
Āryadeva
on correct reasoning, 1:731
on Mādhyamaka dialectic as nihilistic, 1:742
Aryan superiority, historical determinism and, 3:37
"As if" philosophy, 9:625–628
Asaṅga
on emptiness, 1:750–751
on logic, 5:412
Vasubandhu and, 5:412
in Yogācāra Buddhism, 1:746–747
Ascent of Mount Carmel, The (John of the Cross), 4:846
Ascent Way of Life, The (Goudge), 7:337
Asceticism, **1:350–355**
arguments against, 1:352–353
arguments for, 1:351–352
in Buddhism, 1:352, 1:723–725
Cynic teaching on, 2:616
extremism of, 1:350–351
French clandestine literature and, 2:264
in Hinduism, 7:486
history of, 1:351
Jainism and, 1:351, 2:111
Nietzsche on, 1:353, 6:612
Peter Damien on, 7:258–259
Pythagoreanism and, 1:351
will and, 6:612
Asclepius, on love of God, 5:585
Ascriptivism, performative theory of truth and, 7:197
A-series, McTaggart on, 6:78
Ashtekar, Abhay, 9:269
Asia
communist mode of production and, 2:363–364
nationalism in, 6:484
Asian philosophy, on life, meaning and value of, 5:359
Askol'dov, Sergei A., Kozlov and, 5:146
Aspect, Alain, on chance and determinism in quantum theory, 2:126
Aspect theory, of self, 3:606
Aspects of the Theory of Syntax (Chomsky), 8:807
Asquith, Herbert Henry, English liberalism and, 5:320
Assassins (Persian group), 9:395
Assayer, The (Galileo), 4:9, 4:12
Assent
as act of will, 6:583
action and, 1:194, 1:248
Arcesilaus on, 1:248
to cognitive impressions, 1:194
Descartes on, 5:99
to God, 6:581
John of Mirecourt on, 4:841
Newman (John Henry) on, 6:577–581
notional, 6:580–581
probability and, 6:579–580
to proposition, 6:580
propositional attitudes and, 8:78
real, 6:580–581
in Stoicism, 1:30, 1:248
volitional and emotional parts of, 5:98
Assertibles
Clinomachus and, 6:110
in Stoic logic, 5:404–405
Assertion
Austin on, 6:650
of categorical unification, propositions as, 8:663
context and, 7:408
in definite descriptions, 9:264
vs. denial, 6:654
of ego, crime as, 9:251
of existence, Bain on, 3:496
existential, in use of "to be," 1:527–531
Marty on, 5:728–729
in neo-Russellianism, 8:89
in philosophy of language, 7:408
probable, religious truths contrary to, 3:631
in promises, 6:653
religious, 7:478
rule of, 5:88
semantics of, 8:75
in speech, 6:650
subjunctive, in definition, 9:414
of teleological functions, criteria for, 9:386
Assertion sign, definition of, 5:535
Assertoric antirealism, 6:172
Assertoric proposition, 5:549
See also Modality
Assignments, in structures, 3:651
Association
aesthetic, principle of, 3:557
vs. community, 9:96

in consciousness, Ziehen (Theodor) on, 9:884
as fallacy of mind as mechanism, 1:563–564
of ideas, 1:50, 1:138
of meaning and sensation, Berkeley on, 1:575
mind's capability of, Mill (John Stuart) on, 6:226
national state as, 9:205–206
of qualities, 1:576–578
in science of human nature, 4:491
and sensation, 1:575, 8:815

Association for Symbolic Logic, 3:124

Associationism
Bain on, 1:462–463
Bradley on, 1:677
in Britain, 19th century, 3:312
connectionism and, 2:444
Herbart in, 8:138
intelligence and, 1:596
Köhler on, 5:130–131
Martineau and, 5:726
Mead on, 6:80
Mill (John Stuart) and, 8:136
and psychology, 8:135
phenomenologists and, 3:502
sensationalism and, 8:823
in thinking counterfactuals, 1:596
Ward on, 8:137
See also Psychology

Associativity
definition of, 5:535
for extensive properties, 6:90

Assoun, Paul-Laurent, Freud and, 3:737

Assumptions
affirmation and, 6:116
in agreement methods of induction, 6:238–239
in atomism, and reductionism, 9:580
and coherence theory of truth, 2:311
and counter examples in science, 1:541–542
denial and, 6:116
in description, 4:777
in difference methods of induction, 6:238–239
in empirically equivalent theories, 9:576–577
in evocative argument, 2:213–214
in meaning, 6:83
metaphysics and, 6:199–200
in Mill's methods of induction, 6:247
phenomenology and, 7:282–283
theory of, 6:116

Aṣṭadhyāyī (Pāṇini), 5:410

Astell, Mary, **1:355–356,** 3:569, 9:838

Astrology
Gersonides on, 4:68–69
Hellenistic, 4:301–302
in natural system of mutual influences, 3:621
Pico della Mirandola (Gianfrancesco) on, 7:574
Pico della Mirandola (Giovanni) on, 7:570–573
Scot on, 8:703
Servetus on, 8:831

Astronomia Nova (Kepler), 3:687, 5:51–53

Astronomy
Alexander of Aphrodisias on, 1:113
Anaxagoras and, 1:183
Anaximander and, 1:184
Anaximenes on, 1:186
Aquinas on, 9:428
Copernican, 2:533–535
Bruno on, 1:709
cosmological models and, 2:557–560
Democritus on, 5:300
Descartes on, 2:751–752, 2:755
geocentric, 6:521
Gerbert of Aurillac and, 4:66
Greek, 2:571, 4:172, 4:301
Grosseteste on, 4:187
Hegel and, 4:266
Hellenistic, 4:301
in hermetic philosophy, 1:711
Leucippus on, 5:300
modern, founder of, 5:50
Philolaus on, 7:310–311
and physics, synthesis, 5:54
Ptolemaic theory of, 2:534
in Pythagoreanism, 8:183–184
religion and, 8:399–400
scientific method in, 8:683
Thales of Melitus on, 9:405
Zabarella on, 9:866

Astronomy (Gersonides), 4:69

Astronomy and General Physics considered with Reference to Natural Theology (Whewell), 7:561

Astrophysics, in cosmology research, 2:565

Astro-Theology (Derham), 2:686, 7:559

Asymmetric dependency theory, as atomistic account of mental content, 2:479

Asymmetric relation, definition of, 5:555

Asymmetrical reversibility, 6:149

Asymmetry
in causal relations, 2:104–106, 9:498
Cavell on, 2:116
counterfactuals in science and, 2:575–576
in direct realism, 2:98
as information in physical states, 2:105–106
of part and whole, 6:146
in possible world counterfactual conditionals, 2:429
in problem of other minds, 7:468
of properties in chemistry, 2:142–143
temporal, 7:475, 9:467–470, 9:498
in thermodynamics, 2:104–105

Asymptotic efficiency, 3:663

Asymptotic emergence, 3:193

Atala (Chateaubriand), 2:138

Atemporal being, God as, 3:693

Atemporal instantiation, persistence and, 7:208–211

"Ateneo de la Juventud" (Atheneum of youth), 5:208

Athanasia order Gründe für die Unsterblichkeit (Bolzano), 1:646

Athanasius, on Christology, 2:247

Atharvaveda, 5:116

Atheism, **1:356–377**
vs. agnosticism, 1:359, 1:367–368
arguments for, 1:360–364, 7:481
Berkeley on, 4:556
Besant and, 1:358
Bradlaugh on, 1:360
in Buddhism, 6:493
Camus on, 3:504
Chalmers on, 1:372
Charron on, 2:135
Collins on, 2:331
common consent arguments for God's existence and, 2:350
cosmic brain and, 1:368–371
Cousin on, 2:579
Cudworth on, 1:357, 2:610
Cyrenaic teaching on, 2:620
Darrow on, 1:371
in Darwinism, implied, 4:171
definition of, 1:358–360
Enlightenment and, 3:246
evil and, 1:361–364, 7:481
in existential ethics, 1:515
Fichte and, 1:358, 1:377–380, 3:614
on fideism, 1:364
Flint on, 1:357, 1:372
Forberg on, 1:378–379
Foster on, 1:372

Atheism, ***continued***
in French clandestine writings, 2:264
in Greek drama, 4:177
Holbach and, 1:358, 2:688, 3:246
hostility to, 1:357–358
hylozoism of Strato as, 9:261–262
Jodl on, 1:358
justification and, 1:373–374
Kring on, 1:372
under law, 1:358
Leopardi and, 5:286
life in, 1:373–374
Locke on, 1:357, 9:509
logical priority of, 3:745
Mackie and, 5:638
Malinowski on, 1:373
Marković and, 5:719
Marx and, 1:258
McTaggart and, 1:374
Meslier and, 6:154
in moral society, 1:357, 1:505
mystery of universe and, 1:371–372
natural *vs.* moral goodness in defense of, 9:2–3
negative impact of, 1:373–374
Nietzsche and, 1:258
objections to, 1:371–373
omniscience and, 1:372–373
Pannenberg on, 7:80–81
Pascal on, 1:373
persecution of, 1:357–358
Philosophisches Journal and, 1:377–380
Plato on, 1:357
practical, 9:628
as religion, 8:433
Rensi on, 8:433
Romanes on, 1:373
Schopenhauer and, 1:258
semantics and, 1:370
Shelley on, 1:358, 9:8
Smart on, 9:66
Smith (John) on, 9:70
of Spinoza, alleged, 9:193
theoretical, 9:628
Tillich on, 1:358
toleration for, 9:509
Tyndall on, 1:371
universe in, 1:371–372
Vaihinger and, 9:628
Atheism Doesn't Make Sense (Walsh), 2:347
Atheismus and seine Geschichte im Abendlande, Der (Mauthner), 2:349
Atheismusstreit, **1:377–380**
Atheistic materialism, 4:432
Atheistic personalism, 7:233
Athenaeum (periodical), 2:709, 8:631
Athenagoras
as apologist, 1:228
on God, nature of, 7:142
Atherton, Margaret, on dualism, 5:373
Ātman
in Advaita Vedānta, 5:359
in Buddhism, 5:328
in Jainism, 5:327
Ātmavādapratiṣedha (Refutation of the theory of a self) (Vasubandhu), 9:650
Atom(s)
as abstract natures, 1:449
in classical materialism, 6:7–8
in combinatory logic, 2:334
Cordemoy on, 2:538
Cyrano de Bergerac on, 2:618
Epicureans on, 6:59
as fiction, 9:627
Gassendi on, 4:27–28
Greek Academy on, 6:59
Heisenberg on, 4:298
in illative combinatory logic, 2:338
internal motion of, 4:298
light and, 7:476–477
in mechanical philosophy, 6:60
and nonuniform objects, 9:749
Ostwald on, 7:49
in Sanskrit, 1:380
and senses, 5:118
Whitehead on, 6:146–147
Atomenlehre (Fechner), 3:556
Atomic energy, Einstein and, 3:178–179
Atomic formula, 3:648
Atomic modal interpretation, 6:278–279
Atomic proposition, definition of, 5:553
Atomic sentences, 7:416
Atomic terms, 3:647
Atomic theory
vs. atomism, 1:385
in Bruno, 1:712
foundations of, 1:387
in Indian philosophy, **1:380–383**
condition of ātman in, 8:719
God in, 4:627
in Nyaya-Vaisesika, 4:133
soul in, 8:718
molecular behavior and, 1:643
properties *vs.* qualities in, 1:577
See also Atomism
Atomism/atomists, **1:383–389,** 3:635
Alexander of Aphrodisias and, 1:384–385
Anaxagoras and, 1:181, 1:384, 5:299
ancient, 2:491, 7:764
in Advaita Vedānta, 1:383
Aristotle and, 1:384–385
vs. atomic theory, 1:385
Avogadro and, 1:387
Bacon (Francis) on, 1:448
Bergson on, 1:563–564
Berzelius and, 1:387
Bohr and, 1:388
Boltzmann and, 1:387
Boscovich and, 1:665
Bradley on, 1:677
change in, 6:601
continua in, 2:491
cosmogony in, 5:299–300
Dalton and, 1:387
de Broglie and, 1:388
definition of, 1:384
Democritus and, 1:384, 5:297–301, 6:632, 8:182
Descartes and, 1:386
Diderot on, 3:73
Diodorus Chronus and, 3:87
Diogenes Laertius on, 3:88
in early education, 7:365
electrodynamics and, 1:388
emergence theories and, 3:191
Empedocles and, 5:299
Engels on, 3:59
Epicureans as, 3:10–11, 4:300
Epicurus and, 3:215, 3:268–270, 3:287–288, 8:759
on eternal return doctrine, 3:352–353
Galileo and, 4:8
Gassendi on, 1:386, 4:25–28
Gestalt psychology and, 8:143–144
of group phenomena, 6:481
Heisenberg and, 1:388
Hobbes on, 3:405
Hugh of St. Victor on, 8:592
in Indian philosophy, 1:381–382
informational, 2:419
in Jainism, 1:381
Jungius and, 4:861
Karaite and, 4:813–814
Köhler on, 5:130–131
Lavoisier and, 1:387
Leucippus and, 1:384, 5:297–301, 7:763
logical
Russell on, 9:535
Wittgenstein on, 9:535
See also Russell, Bertrand Arthur William; Wittgenstein, Ludwig Josef Johann
Lucretius on, 5:599–600
Maxwell and, 1:387
mental activity and, 6:60
and modern physics, 1:385

in monadology, 6:325
Mu'tazilite and, 4:813–814
nature and, 1:385
Nicolas of Autrecourt and, 6:601
Nifo and, 1:385, 3:270
nominalistic, 5:687
Parmenides of Elea and, 7:122
Philoponus and, 1:384–385
philosophical period of, 1:384–386
physicotheology and, 7:557
Planck and, 1:388
Plato and, 1:385
in pre-Socratic philosophy, 6:184, 7:763–764
Prodicus and, 8:45
psychological, 5:130, 7:282, 8:143–144
qualitative *vs.* quantitative, 1:385
quantum mechanics and, 1:388
rational necessity of, 1:383
in Renaissance philosophy, 6:60
Rutherford and, 1:388
Santayana on, 8:602
Scaliger and, 1:385–386
Schrödinger and, 1:388
scientific, 1:386–389, 8:182
and semantics, 8:759
Sennert and, 1:386
in 17th century, 1:386
Smith (John) on, 9:70
social, 5:595–596
in social sciences, 7:534
soul in, 7:764
on space, 9:147
Stoic, 8:121
string theory and, 9:268
on substance, 9:296
in theory of sensation, 8:814
Toletus and, 1:386
Udayana on, 1:383
unity and, 1:385, 9:578–580
Vasubandhu and, 1:383
in Yogācāra Buddhism, 1:383
See also Atomic theory; Chemistry; Matter
Atoms for Peace movement, 8:667
Atonement, in Christianity, 2:249
ATP (adenosine triphosphate), 6:568
ATR subsystem, 8:456
Atrocity Paradigm: A Theory of Evil, The (Card), 2:31
Attachment factors, and infant as person, 7:242
Attainment of Happiness (al-Fārābī), 7:610
'Aṭṭār, Farīd al-Dīn, 9:306
Attempt at a Critique of All Revelation (Fichte), 3:613–614
Atten, Mark van, on continuum theories, 2:505
Attention
Berkeley on, 1:587
Fichte on, 7:376
Herbart on, 7:376
in inner sense theory of consciousness, 2:453
Mansel on, 5:687
Murdoch on, 6:433–434
perception and, 7:183–184
as theoretical conation, 9:260
as will, 5:687
Attenuation of faith, 7:495
Atticus, Eusebius and, 3:455
Attig, J. C., 5:394
Attitude
in aesthetic experience, 1:33, 1:36, 1:75
belief as, 5:704–705
in computationalism, 2:391–392
doxastic, 8:175
dualism and, 8:83–84
in ethical disagreements, 9:245
ethical language and, 9:245
facts and, 8:82
mental representations and, 6:141–142
in moral constructivism, 2:472
moral judgment as expression of, 6:157
personhood and, 7:240
postcolonialism on, 7:728
presupposing and, 7:767
propositional, 8:74–80
toward objects, 6:116
Attorney for the Dammed (Darrow), 2:351
Attraction, in Yoga, 6:108
Attribute(s)
definition of, 5:535
Descartes on, 9:296–297
vs. essence, in Platonic dialogues, 7:587
existence of, in Neoplatonism, 6:188–189
as first element of nature, 9:174
of God, 4:110–111
Aquinas on, 1:141
Crescas on, 4:822
Duns Scotus on, 3:135
Gersonides on, 4:68
Israeli on, 4:814
Maimonides on, 5:649–650
Martineau on, 5:727
vs. mode, 9:173
in philosophy of religion, 7:479
Spinoza on, 6:190, 9:173
Attribution
God and, 1:141
in thinking, 9:419
Attributive monism, 6:326–327
Aubrey, John, on Hobbes, 3:171
Auctoritate Sacrae Scripturae, De (Socinus), 9:99
Audi, Robert, on existence of God, 3:535
Auditory perception, 7:180–182
Auf dem Kampffeld der Logik (On the Battlefield of Logic) (Geyser), 4:82
Auf den Marmorklippen (Jünger), 4:860
Aufbau der menschlichen Person, Der (Stein), 9:240
Aufklärung, as mission of poetry, Gottsched on, 4:164–165
Augsburg Confession, 6:119
Auguste Comte et la philosophie positive (Littré), 5:372
Augustine, St., **1:389–402**
on action, 1:395–397
on aesthetics, 1:46–47
as apologist, 1:228
on appearances, 1:229
Aquinas and, 3:403–404
on archetypes, 3:141
Arendt and, 1:253
Aristotle and, 1:391–392
autonomy of, 7:322–323
on beauty, 1:46–47, 1:74, 1:402
on belief, 1:391–392
and Boethius, 1:626
Bonaventure on, 1:651–653
books on, 1:401
in Carolingian thought, 2:49
in Cartesianism, 2:60–61
on causality, 1:398
Christianity and, 1:390–392, 2:60–61
Cicero and, 1:390, 7:421
on corporeality of God, 4:110
on creation, 1:397–398, 3:475
on curriculum, 7:368
and Dante, 2:625–626
on death, 2:652
on deception, 1:47
on design, 1:402
on destiny, 1:395
on determinism, 3:7, 3:8–9
and divine command theories of ethics, 3:93
on divine illumination, 4:580, 8:760
on doctrine of election, 3:329
on dreams, 1:393
on dualism, 1:392
Duns Scotus and, 3:139

Augustine, St., *continued*
Durandus of Saint-Pourçain and, 3:148
on duration, 9:485
Eckhart (Meister) and, 3:163
on education, 7:367–368
education of, 1:389–390
epistemology and, 3:289
on eternal return doctrine, 3:353
on eternity, 3:357–358
on ethics, 3:401–403
on evil, problem of, 3:472–474
faith and, 3:533, 5:586
on Fall, 3:473–474, 7:367–368
on fatalism, 3:692–693
on fiction, 1:47
on free will, 3:402
on freedom, 7:388
on God, 1:397–398
immanence of, 4:108
nature of, 3:357
ontological argument for existence of, 4:112
on good, 1:395
and Gregory of Rimini, 4:183
on happiness, 1:395, 3:401
on Heaven, Hell, and judgment, 2:249
Heidegger and, 3:504
Henry of Ghent and, 3:136
on history, 3:348, 7:387–388
on human nature, 7:367–368
on human sexuality, 7:521–522, 7:528
on ideas as thoughts of God, 4:564
on illumination, 1:393–395, 4:108
on imagination, 1:392–393
on innate ideas, 4:688
on intelligence, 1:393–395
Isaac of Stella on, 4:753
Kilwardby on, 5:69
on knowledge, 1:392–395
on language, 7:368, 8:759–761
Latin American philosophy and, 5:205
on law, 1:395–397
on logos, 5:569–570
on love, 1:395–397, 5:586
on lying, 1:47, 5:619
Marston and, 5:725
in medieval philosophy, 5:422, 6:99, 7:611
on memory, 1:394
on mind, 1:392–395
on mind-body problem, 6:258
on miracles, 6:267–268
on moral responsibility, 3:402
on morality, 1:395–397
on nature, 3:402, 6:519
Neoplatonism and, 1:390, 3:289, 3:401–402, 6:555
on number, 1:46
on optimism/pessimism, 7:247–248
on order, 1:397
on Origen, 3:348
on original sin, 1:399
Papini on, 7:103
on Pelagianism, 7:175
on perception, 8:824
Petrarch on, 7:264–265
Platonism and, 1:392–395, 3:357, 6:546, 7:609
Plotinus and, 3:401, 6:546
political philosophy of, 1:399–400, 7:658–659
Porphyry and, 7:143
on predestination, 3:10, 3:402, 3:473
on reason, 1:393–395
in religious philosophy, 7:491
Roman Empire and, 1:399
on Rome, 7:421
on salvation, 7:387
and Schleiermacher, 8:634
Sciacca on, 8:666
on semantics, 8:759–761
on sense perception, 1:392–393, 3:289
on sin, 3:402, 3:472
on skepticism, 9:49, 9:50
on society, 1:398–400
on soul, 3:289
on state, 7:421
Stefanini on, 9:237
and Stein, 9:239
in Sturzo's dialectic of the concrete, 9:281
on suicide, 9:319
on testimony, 9:401
theodicy and, 7:387–388
on time, 1:397–398, 3:402–403, 7:387, 9:461
on ugliness, 9:562
on understanding, 1:391–392
on unity, 1:46
on universals, 3:289, 9:593
on utility, 1:396–397
on value, 1:396–397
on virtue, 1:395–397
on vision, 1:392–393
on will, 1:395–397
Augustine: Ancient Thought Baptized (Rist), 1:401
Augustine: Confessions (O'Donnell), 1:401
Augustine of Hippo: A Biography (Brown), 1:401
Augustinian solution, 3:696
Augustinian tradition, 3:631, 7:265
Augustinianism, **1:402–404**
Averroism and, 1:429
centrality of faith to human experience in, 8:632
on civil state, 6:104
definition of, 1:402
Descartes and, 2:61
grace in, 6:99
Grosseteste and, 4:186
gulf between God and man in, 4:183
Hugh of St. Victor and, 8:592
law theory of, 6:105
Malebranche and, 5:666
Matthew of Aquasparta and, 6:64–65
and metaphysics, 6:188
Pauler and, 7:145
Peckham and, 7:161
Vives and, 9:700
voluntarism in, 6:99
See also Jansenism
Augustinus (Jansen), 1:288, 4:788–789
Aumann, Robert J., 4:19
Aurelius, Marcus, on natural law and cosmopolitanism, 2:567
Aureol, Peter. *See* Peter Aureol
Aurobindo, Sri
on Brahman, 1:684
on liberation, 5:330
Aurora, oder di Morgenro im Aufgang (Boehme), 1:624
Auschwitz (prison camp), 3:470
Ausführung des Plans und Zweckes Jesu (Bahrdt), 1:457
Ausonius, Decimus Magnus, 2:723
Aussersein doctrine, 6:115
Aussonderungsaxiom, definition of, 5:535
Austerities, karmic matter annihilated by, 5:41
Austin, John, **1:404–406**
Hart on, 5:239
on implicatures, 3:253
Kelsen and, 7:427
on law, 5:239, 7:425
legal positivism and, 5:237–238
on natural law, 6:512–513
Olivecrona on, 7:428
Paley and, 7:425
on skepticism, 9:59
Austin, John Langshaw, **1:406–412**
analytic philosophy of, 1:154
on appearances, 8:819

on argument from illusion, 4:588
on assertion in speech, 6:650
on empirical belief, 5:96
language of, 1:407–408
on locutionary and illocutionary acts in fiction, 1:509
ordinary-language philosophy and, 3:318
on performatives, 5:98, 7:199–201, 9:264
on phonetic acts, 7:551
on sense data, 8:820–821
on sovereignty, 9:141–142
on statements of human ability, 3:20
technique of, 1:407–408
Australia, first female professor of philosophy in, 5:373
Australian Feminist Studies (Lloyd), 5:373
Australian Journal of Psychology and Philosophy, 9:260
Austrian Federal Constitution of October 1920, drafting of, 5:49
Authentic, Unamuno on, 9:567
Authenticity
alienation and, 1:124
in art, **1:295–296**
Bultmann on, 1:762–763
context and, 1:295
Jaspers on, 4:800
of life, 1:762–763
as normative quality, 1:26
in performance, 1:322–323
Sartre's ethic of, 8:607, 8:610
Author
in films, 7:384
and hero, relationship of, 1:465–466, 1:469
significance of, 1:481
"Author and the Hero in Aesthetic Activity, The" (Bakhtin), 1:465–466
Authorial intention, 5:369
Authoritarianism
Adorno on, 1:26
anarchism and, 1:176
Carlyle on, 2:34
conservative view of, 2:468
de Staël on, 9:202
Godwin on, 4:136
Grotius on, 4:191
propaganda and, 1:26
Santayana on, 8:600
of Soviet Union, 9:91
Authoritative discursive practices, 3:700
Authoritative testimony, faith resting on, 5:99
"Authorité politique" (Diderot), 3:77
Authority, **1:412–418**
abandonment of, by Galileo, 4:10
Aquinas on, 9:436–437
Arendt on, 1:254
argument from, in Chinese philosophy, 2:213–214
as barrier to truth, 1:453
in case law, 1:443
in case-based reasoning, 1:237
in Christianity, 4:261
in classical world, 9:139
in Confucianism, 2:194
educational, 7:361–362
in French Revolution, 9:520
Galston on, 7:361
of group folkways, 9:326
of international law, Grotius on, 4:190–192
in knowledge of God, 1:114
of law, 7:418, 7:458
legal, 1:405–406
in medieval Europe, 9:139
of national state, 9:210–211
Pascal on, 8:46
political, Marsilius of Padua on, 5:723
of precedent, 7:449
vs. private rights, 9:204
of reason, 7:730
received, 8:46
spiritual *vs.* temporal, Giles of Rome on, 4:91
and state, 9:698
of truth, in James's pragmatism, 4:782
Weber (Max) on, 9:735
Authorship, Kierkegaard's mode of, 5:63
Autobiographical memory, 6:122, 6:125
"Autobiographical Reflections" (Sellars, Wilfrid), 8:733
Autobiography (Collingwood), 2:325
Autobiography (Darwin), 2:628–630, 7:561
Autobiography (Franklin), 3:720
Autobiography, Dilthey on, 3:84
Autographic *vs.* allographic art, 1:317
Automata
animals as, 1:201, 5:631
as model for living things, 1:593
Automatic Computing Engine, 2:399
Automatic control machinery, 6:81
Automatic sweetheart puzzle, 6:235
Automaton, parity-detecting, 3:757
Autonomism, 1:68, 9:319, 9:322
Autonomous complexes, McDougall on, 6:72
Autonomous idiolects, 8:753
Autonomy
of artificial intelligence, 1:347–348
of Augustine, 7:322–323
civil disobedience and, 2:260
conservative view of, 2:468
as crucial, 5:37
Driesch on, 3:110
education and, 7:360–361
hard, 7:331
as I-it *vs.* I-thou relationships, 1:715–716
in informed consent decision-making, 4:679–681
Marx on, 5:731
in medical ethics, 6:92–93
negative, 1:28
of philosophy, 7:331–332
of politics, 5:628
precognition and, 7:754–755
relational, 1:158
and embedded subject, 3:588
in relational terms, 3:599
soft, 7:331
of will, 5:24–25
Yang Zhu on, 9:862
See also Freedom
Autonomy-of-ethics thesis, 6:352
Autotrophism, 3:559
Autour d'un petit livre (Loisy), 5:571
Autre monde, ou les éstats et empires de la lune et du soleil, L' (Cyrano de Bergerac), 2:618
Autrement qu'être ou audelà de l'essence (Levinas), 5:304–305
Avataṃsaka (Buddhist text), 1:736
Avempace. *See* Ibn Bājja
Avenarius, Richard, **1:418–421,** 7:268
and empiriocriticism, 3:64, 7:715
Liebmann and, 5:344
Lunacharskii and, 5:611
Marxism and, 5:280
on phenomenology, 7:279, 7:282
positivistic attempts of, 5:160
Avendeath, 5:333
Avenir de la science, L' (Renan), 8:429
Averill, James, on emotions, 3:202
Averroes, **1:421–427**
on afterlife, 3:23
Alexander of Aphrodisias and, 1:112
on al-Ghazālī (Muḥammad), 6:558
and Arab logic, 5:419–421
Aristotle and, 1:260–261, 1:422–424, 1:428, 1:652, 3:134–135, 3:403, 4:838–839
and Averroism, 1:427–428
and Dante, 2:625–626
emanationism in, 3:189

Averroes, *continued*
- on essence and existence, 3:352, 4:758
- on first mover, 3:226
- Galen and, 4:5, 4:7
- and Gersonides, 4:68–69
- on God, 3:135
- Godfrey of Fontaines on, 4:131
- and Ibn al-ʿArabī, 4:541
- on immortality, 4:619, 4:744
- on inner senses, 4:697
- on intellect
  - immortal abstract, 4:608–609
  - universality of, 4:758
- in Islamic philosophy, 4:758
- on logic, 5:439
- Maimonides and, 4:820
- in medieval philosophy, 6:99
- minima theory in, 1:385
- Nicolas of Autrecourt and, 6:600
- pantheism of, 7:96
- Pico della Mirandola and, 7:571
- on Platonism, 7:611
- on predestination, 3:23
- Scot's translations of, 8:703
- writings of, 1:422–423

Averroism, **1:427–431**
- agent intellect in, 1:91
- Aquinas and, 1:91, 1:429–430
- Boethius of Dacia on, 1:628–629
- Bonaventure and, 1:650
- Burley on, 1:774
- *vs.* Christianity, 1:425, 1:430
- double truth doctrine in, 1:424–425, 1:429, 2:721
- in Islamic philosophy, modern, **1:431**
- Italian, 1:430
- Jewish. *See* Jewish Averroism
- John of Jandun and, 4:838–839
- Latin, 1:428–429
- Marsilius of Padua and, 5:722–723
- Renan and, 1:431
- Siger of Brabant on, 9:27
- Thomism and, 9:444

Aversion, Mill (James) on, 6:219

Avesta, in Zoroastrianism, 9:885

Avicebron. *See* Ibn Gabirol, Solomon ben Judah

Avicenna, **1:432–436**
- on afterlife, 3:23
- on agent intellect, 1:91
- on analogy, 1:139–140
- and Arab logic, 5:418–421
- Aristotle and, 1:260, 1:435, 1:651, 3:134–135, 3:403
- Augustinianism and, 1:402
- Averroes and, 1:422
- causal hierarchy in, 2:114
- on creation, 3:135, 3:360–361, 9:765
- Duns Scotus and, 3:134–135
- emanationism in, 3:189
- on essence and existence, 3:351, 4:757
- Galen and, 4:5–7
- Gilbert of Poitiers and, 4:89
- on God, 3:135
- on God's knowledge of things, 3:320
- and Grosseteste, 4:186
- and Ibn Da'ud, 4:817
- and Ibn Ṭufayl, 4:550
- and Ikhwān al-Ṣafāʾ, 4:576
- on immortality, 4:619
- on impetus theory, 4:622
- on inner sense, 4:697
- in Islamic philosophy, 4:757–758
- on logic, 8:766
- Maimonides and, 5:649, 5:654
- medieval European logic and, 5:422
- in medieval philosophy, 6:99
- on metaphysics, 3:135
- and Naṣīr al-Dīn al-Ṭūsī, 6:478
- on necessary being, 4:757
- and Neoplatonism, 1:426, 1:432–433, 6:557–558
- oriental philosophy of, 4:550
- Paracelsus and, 7:103
- Pico della Mirandola and, 7:571
- in Platonic tradition, 7:611
- on predestination, 3:23
- in reconciliation of emanationism and creationism, 4:755
- Scot's translations of, 8:703
- on semantic intentions, 8:765
- on universals, 1:432–433, 3:147
- and William of Auvergne, 9:766–767
- on wisdom, 1:651

Avicennism, 7:612, 8:766

Avignon papacy, Ockham and, 9:770–771

Avogadro, Amadeo, 1:387

Avtor i geroi v esteticheskoi deiatel' nosti (Bakhtin), 1:469

Awakeness, consciousness and, 2:449

Awakening
- in Buddhism, 1:722, 5:328
- in Vasubandhu, 1:751–752
- in Yogācāra practice, 1:751–752
- in Zen, 1:728–730

Awareness
- configurational, 1:328
- conscious, 4:712
- of designation, as result of comparison, 5:122
- false, asserting, 5:118
- in Gestalt theory, 8:814
- in higher-order consciousness, 2:455
- in intrinsic theory of consciousness, 2:453
- Külpe on, 5:160
- Landgrebe on, 5:184–186
- materialism and, 6:15
- *vs.* perception, 8:814–815
- as perceptual mode, 2:457
- recognitional, 1:328
- of sense datum, 8:813–814
- and successful activity, 5:119
- touch and, 9:516

Axes of subordination, 3:585

Axiology, 5:132, 9:637
- as discipline of ordinary intuition, 5:143
- epistemology as, 6:544
- *See also* Value

Axiom(s) and axiomatic method/axiomatics
- *a priori* knowledge of, 6:628
- analysis in, 6:22
- arithmetic in, 6:22
- beliefs as, 5:109
- of choice, 4:663, 8:834–836
  - Gödel on, 5:474
  - Ramsey on, 5:468
  - Skolem on, 5:471
  - surreal and hyperreal number systems and, 2:509
- combinatory, in combinatory logic, 2:337
- in computability theory, 2:382–383
- of continuity, Russell on, 2:499
- contrasted with innate ideas, 1:595
- definition of, 5:535
- of determinacy, 8:846–847
- of empty set, 4:662, 8:835
- in Euclid, 4:119
- of extensionality, 4:662, 8:835
  - Chwistek on, 2:256
  - Frege on, 5:516
- in first-order theory of identity, 4:568
- of Foucher, 3:702
- of foundation, 4:663, 8:839–840
- Frege and, 3:726, 5:464
- in game theory, 4:19
- Gödel on, 4:118
- Hilbert on, 4:358–359, 5:469
- independence of, 5:462, 6:23
- inductive, 4:125–126

of infinity, 4:662, 5:546, 8:836
of intuition, principle of, 5:19
of logic and mathematics, 5:93
logical truth and, 1:660
in many-valued logic, 5:690
Martin's, 8:844
in mathematical foundations, 6:21–25
in mathematical structuralism, 9:270
for measurement *vs.* definition, 1:633
in metamathematical foundations, 2:41
of minxent/maxent, 4:674
models in, 6:22–23
naive comprehension principle in, 4:663
in natural language, 7:404
19th century logic and, 5:459
of pairs, 4:662, 8:835
of parallels, 9:150
philosophy and, 6:20
of power set, 4:663, 8:836
of probability, 1:496, 8:24–25
process used in, 6:21–22
Proper Forcing, 8:844
Putnam on, 6:628
Quine's, 4:123
of reducibility, 8:554–555
Chwistek on, 2:256
justification of, 5:519
Russell on, 5:519
Whitehead on, 5:519
of regularity, 5:544
of replacement, 4:663, 8:837–839
in reverse mathematics, 8:455
Schiller (Ferdinand) on, 8:623–625
Scholz on, 8:644–645
for second-order arithmetic, 8:455
of separation, 4:663, 8:836
in set theory, 5:520, 8:831
in Spinoza's *Ethics*, 9:184
of strong inaccessible cardinal, 4:665
in system foundations, 2:41
Tarski on, 9:366–367
for the theory of the creating subject, 4:741–742
Toynbee on, historical, 9:519
of union, 4:663, 8:835
in unique finite systems, 1:647
Woodger on, 9:843–844
of Zermelo, 8:835–836
in Zermelo-Fraenkel set theory, 4:662–664
Axiom der fundierung, 5:544
Axiom schema, definition of, 5:535
Axiomatic Method in Biology, The (Woodger), 9:843–844
Axiomaticizability, of formal language calculability, 2:380
Axiomatics. *See* Axiom(s) and axiomatic method/axiomatics
"Axiomatik der Alten, Die" (Scholz), 8:645
Axiomatization
arithmetic in, 6:22
consequences of, 6:22–23
Craig's Theorem on, 2:583
deduction and definition in, 6:22
of logic, 5:471
in mathematical foundations, 6:21–22
of set theory and comprehension, 5:521
"Axioms as Postulates" (Schiller, Ferdinand), 8:625
Axioms of Religious Experience (Il'in), 4:578
Ayer, Alfred Jules, **1:436–438**
on adverbial analysis, 8:821
on aesthetic discourse, 1:65
on analogies for God, 1:141
on analytic statements, 1:160
on Austin, 1:154
on basic statements, 1:485
on being, 1:531
on determinism, 3:12
on doubt, 3:103
and emotivism, 1:65, 3:425–426, 3:627, 6:157
on ethical language, 9:245
on expressive meaning, 6:652
on implicatures, 3:253
on laws of thought, 5:233
and logical empiricism, 5:82
logical positivist view of, 5:526
on Malcolm (Norman), 3:106–107
on meaning, 1:149
and noncognitivism, 6:632–634
on phenomenalism, 7:273–275
and rationalist theory, 5:96
on religion, 7:478
on Sartre, 3:508
on skepticism, 9:59
on Strawson, 7:57
on verification of statements, 1:524
on verification theory of meaning, 3:317
Vienna Circle and, 5:525
Ayutasiddha, inherence and, 9:583
Az Etikai Megismerés (Pauler), 7:145
Azariel, Isaac the Blind and, 5:3
Aztec philosophy, 5:204

B

Ba gua (trigrams), in Daoist cosmology, 4:794
Baader, Franz Xavier von, **1:439–440**
Baars, Bernard J., on qualitative consciousness, 2:450
Babbage, Charles, 8:667
and early computing, 2:399–400
and machine intelligence, 5:634
physicotheology and, 7:561
Babbitt, Susan, 3:588
Babeuf, François-Noël
on equality, 3:330
and socialism, 9:87
Babylonian Captivity (Luther), 5:612
Bacchae (Euripides), 4:177
Bacciagaluppi, Guido, 6:278
Bach, Kent, on performative utterances, 7:201
Bachelard, Gaston, **1:440–441,** 9:275
Bachofen, Johann Jakob, **1:441–442**
Back-and-forth system, in model theory, 6:306–308
"Backward Look at Quine's Animadversions on Modalities" (Marcus), 6:290
Bacon, Francis, **1:442–452**
on blessings of science, 8:672
Boyle and, 1:673
Comenius and, 2:341
De Morgan on, 2:710
on definition, 2:669
Descartes and, 2:737
Diderot and, 3:72
on doctrine of idols, 1:444–446, 9:101
on eliminative induction, 1:446–450
Encyclopédie and, 3:222
on external ends, 8:675
Gassendi on, 4:27
Genovesi on, 4:49
Glanvill and, 4:97
on grammar, 8:771
on heat, 1:448, 3:229
on imagination, 1:50
Jefferson and, 4:805
on law and rhetoric, 1:443–444
legacy of, 1:451
life of, 1:443
Lipsius and, 5:364
Lloyd (G.) on, 5:373
on Lucian of Samosata, 5:597
Mill (John Stuart) and, 8:685–686
panpsychism and, 7:83
on physicotheology, 7:557

Bacon, Francis, ***continued***
on progress, 8:46
on reason, 8:772
Scholasticism and, 3:405
on science and religion, 2:685
semantics of, 8:772–773
and skepticism, 9:53
and technology, 7:546
on Telesio, 9:391
on truth, 1:450–451
Vico and, 9:672
Bacon, Roger, **1:452–455**
on Alexander of Hales, 1:114
Augustinianism of, 1:402
on divine illumination, 1:403
on forces as species, 3:687
Liber de Causis and, 5:334
on logic and mathematics, 5:442
study of optics, 1:453
on William of Sherwood, 9:786
Bad, the, Hume on, 4:502–503
Bad biases, 3:576
Bad conscience
Jankélévitch on, 4:787
in moral shame, 9:5
Bad faith, **1:455–456,** 8:608–610, 8:714
Badness
of actions, in utilitarianism, 9:609
fundamental nature of, 6:155–156
of pleasure, 4:257
Xunzi on, 9:856
Baekje, 5:134
Bagolinus, on Aristotle, 5:439
Bahir (Book of Enlightenment), 5:4
Bahnsen, Julius, on pessimism, 7:251
Bahrdt, Carl Friedrich, **1:456–457,** 2:688
Baḥyā ben Joseph ibn Paqūda, **1:457–458,** 4:816
Baier, Annette, **1:458–460**
on Hume, 3:570
on persons as essentially "second persons," 3:579
Baier, Kurt, **1:460–461**
and good-reasons approach, 3:430–431
on life, meaning and value of, 5:351–352
Baillet, Adrien, 2:721–723
Bain, Alexander, **1:461–463**
on altruism and self-interest, 3:174
on assertions of existence, 3:496
on belief, 5:91, 5:98
Condillac and, 8:826
on determinism, 3:18–19
and psychology, 8:136
Baker, Lynne Rudder, **1:463–464,** 7:239
Baker, Robert, 7:521
Baker, Theodore, 2:389
Bakhtin, Mikhail Mikhailovich, **1:464–468**
Belinskii and, 1:538
Ivanov and, 4:768
Lotman and, 5:579
Marr and, 1:469–470
Bakhtin Circle, The, **1:469–470**
Bakunin, Michael. *See* Bakunin, Mikhail Aleksandrovich
Bakunin, Mikhail Aleksandrovich, **1:471–473**
on anarchism, 1:178, 1:472–473
and collectivism, 1:178–179, 5:154
Kropotkin and, 5:154
on Soviet Union, 9:91
Balance, sense of, perception and, 7:180–182
Bald Man paradox, as semantic paradox, 5:518, 5:522
Baldhead argument, 6:110–111
Balfour, Arthur James, **1:473–474,** 4:559
Balguy, John, **1:474–476**
Ballanche, Pierre Simon, 9:520
Ballou, Adin, on pacifism, 7:67
Balzac, Honoré de, Diderot and, 3:77
Banach, Stefan, 9:366
Banach-Tarski Paradox, 8:837
Banality, of truth in artwork, 1:334
Báñez, Dominic, **1:476,** 9:445
Báñez commentary, 1:476
Banfi, Antonio, **1:476–477**
Bangs, Crunches, Whimpers, and Shrieks: Singularities and Acausalities in Relativistic Spacetimes (Earman), 3:160
Bansan, Kumazawa, **5:161–162**
Bantu Philosophy (Tempels), 1:83
Baopuzi, 2:186
Baqli, Ruzbihan, 9:306
Bar Hiyya, Abraham, 4:816
Barbapiccola, Giuseppa, 9:839
Barbaro, Ermolao
Peirce on, 7:164
Pico della Mirandola and, 7:570
Barber's paradox, of empty sets, 5:517
Barclay, Robert, 3:187
Bardi, Simone de, 2:623
Bare particulars, internal relations and, 8:342
Bare theory, 8:213
Barendregt, Henk, 4:742
Bar-Hillel, Yehoshua, 9:355–356
Barker, Ernest, 9:209
Barlaam of Calabria
and Byzantine philosophy, 1:786
on logic, 1:788–789
Barlow, Joel, 2:689
Barnes, Annette, 8:713
Barnes, Barry, 9:84
Baron, Marcia, on Kant's moral theory, 5:36
Baroque, Wolff and, 9:825
Barreda, Gabino, 5:206
Barrès, Maurice, 9:364
Barrow, Isaac, 6:590
Barruel, Augustin, 3:243
Barth, Karl, **1:477–480**
on Brunner, 1:707
on divine transcendence, 4:107
on existence of God, 7:17
Gogarten and, 4:144
Pannenberg and, 7:80, 7:81
on religious analogy, 1:142–143
theology of, 3:505
Barthes, Roland, **1:480–482**
and French structuralism, 9:273
Kristeva and, 5:151
Bartlett, Frederick, 9:77
Bartley, William Warren, 2:53
Bartolus of Sassoferrato, on natural law, 7:422
Barwise, Jon, 8:809
semantics of, 8:75–76
on truth, 5:317
Base clause, of inductive definition, 3:647
Basedow, Johann Bernhard, **1:482–483,** 5:176
Basho (logic of place), 4:798
Basic beliefs, justification of knowledge and, 3:271–272
Basic conjunction, 3:654
Basic contingent statements, 5:92–93
Basic disjunction, 3:654
Basic Facts of Mental Life (Lipps), 5:362
Basic Problems of Phenomenology, The (Heidegger), 9:490
"Basic Propositions" (Ayer), 1:485
Basic propositions, and doubt, 3:103
Basic statements, **1:483–488**
Ayer on, 1:485–486
Chisholm on, 2:242
empirical statements in, 1:484
facts in, 1:483
Hemple on, 1:485
and incorrigible, 5:93
konstatierungen characteristics of, 1:484
Neurath on, 1:484–485
Popper on, 1:486–487
Russell on, 1:485
Schlick on, 1:484
Sellars on, 8:733–734, 9:119

subjects and predicates in, 1:561–562
Wittgenstein on, 1:483–484
Basic System of Inductive Logic (Carnap), 2:437
Basil the Great, 1:786
Basilides, on God, 7:141–142
Bas-relief, 9:692–693
Bassi, Laura, 9:839
Bataille, Georges, **1:488–489,** 5:167
Batens, Diderik, paraconsistent logics and, 7:105–106
Bates, H. W., and Wallace (Alfred Russel), 9:720
Bateson, William, 2:638
Bathers, The (painting), Merleau-Ponty on, 6:151
Batterman, Robert, on emergence, 3:193
Batteux, Abbé Charles, **1:489–490**
on aesthetics, 1:50, 1:489–490
on art, 1:297
Battle of the Books, The (Swift), 9:339
Bauch, Bruno, on Liebmann, 5:344
Baudelaire, Charles
Deleuze and, 2:693
Diderot and, 3:77
Sartre on, 3:507
Swedenborg and, 9:338
Baudrillard, Jean, **1:490–492**
Bauer, Bruno, **1:492–493,** 4:573
Baumgarten, Alexander Gottlieb, **1:493–495**
on aesthetics, 1:49–50
on the beautiful, 5:26
Kant and, 5:9
in Leibnizian-Wolffian School Philosophy, 9:824
Meier and, 6:112
Mendelssohn and, 6:131
Sulzer and, 9:325
Baur, Ferdinand Christian, Parker (T.) and, 7:121
Bautain, Louis Eugene Marie, on traditionalism, 9:521
Baxandall, Michael
on painting, 1:330
on vision and pictorial idiom, 1:329
Bayes, Thomas, **1:495–502**
in arguments for existence of God, 9:407
and Bayes' rule, 1:496
and Bayesian machine, 1:60, 1:497
conditional learning model in, 8:685
and conditionalization, 1:496–497, 8:29
confirmation in, 1:499–500, 3:160–161
Earman on, 3:160–161
epistemic probability of belief in, 8:685
on evidence, 3:321
on inductive reasoning, 1:498–499, 3:666, 9:220
minimal belief change in, 4:671–672
optimality theorem and, 9:221–222
probability in
prior, 9:576
revising, 9:212
subjective, 1:495–496
and problem of old evidence, 1:500–501
in recovery of Newton's method, 8:685
Savage on, 8:612
significance tests and, 9:214
"washing out" theorem in, 8:614
Bayes or Bust?: A Critical Examination of Bayesian Confirmation Theory (Earman), 3:160
Bayes' theorem, **1:495–502**
Bayle, Pierre, **1:502–508**
on Bodin, 1:623
on common consent arguments for God's existence, 2:344
on Cudworth, 2:610
deism and, 2:682
Dictionary of
history and composition of, 1:503–504
philosophical aspects of, 1:504–505
Encyclopédie and, 3:222
Enlightenment and, 3:244
on evil, 3:469
on faith, 1:505
Foucher and, 3:704
in French clandestine literature, 2:265
on general will, 4:39
irrational fideism of, 4:96
La Mothe Le Vayer and, 5:182
on La Peyrère, 5:196
Le Clerc and, 5:236
Leibniz and, 5:254, 5:264
on metaphysics, 1:505
on optimism/pessimism, 7:248
and *philosophes,* 9:56
on reason, 3:245
on religion and morality, 1:505
on religious position, 1:506–507
on religious truths, 3:631
on revelation, 1:505–506
Shaftesbury and, 9:1
and skepticism, 1:505, 9:55
on Spinoza, 5:296, 7:99, 9:185, 9:193
on toleration, 1:503
on Viret, 2:681
Bazin, André, in film theory, 7:382
H.M.S. *Beagle,* 2:628–633, 3:487
Bealer, George, 3:273–274, 5:85
Beardsley, Monroe, **1:508–510**
on aesthetics, 1:33, 1:64, 1:72–73, 1:508–509
and anti-intentionalism, 1:311
on creative process, 2:590
Beatification, of Newman (John Henry), 6:583
Béatotide des Chrétiens ou le fléau de la foy, La (Vallée), 2:263
Beatrice (Dante's beloved), 2:623–624
Beattie, James, **1:510–511**
Gerard and, 4:64
universal grammar and, 8:791
Beatty, John, on Darwin, 7:340
Beauchamp, T. L., 7:138–139
Beaufret, Jean, and Foucault, 3:698
Beauty, **1:511–515,** 9:407–408
absolute, Cousin on, 2:580
in achievement of freedom, 8:627
of actions, 8:3
Addison on, 1:22
in aesthetics, 1:74, 1:511–514
Alexander on, 1:111
Alison on, 1:52, 1:128–129
Anderson (John) on, 1:199
Aquinas on, 1:47, 9:435–436
and art, 1:339–340, 8:620
artistic *vs.* natural, 1:70
Augustine on, 1:46–47, 1:74, 1:402
Baumgarten on, 1:494
as cause experience, 1:514
Chaadaev on, 2:121–122
Chateaubriand on, 2:138
cognition of, 1:47
Collingwood on, 2:325
Cousin on, 2:580
Croce on, 1:65, 2:602
design and, 1:402
Deustua on, 3:42–43
Diderot on, 1:52, 3:76
Dostoevsky on, 3:100
Duchamp on, 1:67
Eberhard on, 3:161
in 18th century, 1:513–514
in empiricism, 1:74
Epicurean view of, 1:45, 1:189
female use of, 9:837
Gadamer on, 4:3

Beauty, ***continued***
Gerard on, 1:52
Gottsched on, 4:165
in Greek art, as ideal, 9:791
Haeckel on, 4:204
Hegel on, 1:54, 4:275–276
Hume on, 1:35–38, 1:51, 1:74
Hutcheson on, 1:51
ideal, Cousin on, 2:580
indefinability of, 9:790
internal unity of, 1:511
as intrinsic and pure, 1:512
Jouffroy on, 4:855
judgment of, 1:74
"Kallias-Letters" on, 8:627
kalon as, 1:256
Kant on, 1:32–33, 1:38, 1:52–53, 1:308
logic of, 1:513
Mendelssohn on, 6:131
Mothersill on, 1:67
natural, 1:129, 1:339–340
Nehamas on, 1:67
in neo-classicism, 1:512
in neo-Kantianism, 1:54
in 19th and 20th centuries, 1:513–514
normativity of, 1:37, 1:46–47
number and, 1:46
objectivity in, 1:38, 1:47
in perceiving subject, 9:325
vs. perfection, 6:131
Plato on, 1:42, 1:74, 1:511–512, 7:589
Platonic Form of, 7:596, 9:590
pleasure of, 1:22, 1:44, 1:128
Plotinus on, 1:45–46, 1:190
as promise of happiness, 1:67
as property, 1:512
as resolution, 1:67
Ruskin on, 8:534
Santayana on, 1:63, 8:598
Savile on, 1:67
Schelling on, 1:54
Schlegel on, 8:630
semantics of, 1:36
Sibley on, 1:36–38
in soul's ascent to suprasensible world, 7:641–642
as spiritual force, 1:512
in Stoicism, 1:45, 1:189
as subjective idea, 1:513–514
sublime in, 8:629
vs. sublimity, 1:513
symmetry and, 1:45–46, 9:742
as term of approbation, 1:514
as truth, 8:534
ugliness and, 9:561–564
Weyl on, 9:742
Wilde on, 9:764
Winckelmann on, 9:790
Beauty and Love (Dede), 9:309
Beauval, Basnage de, 5:253
Beauvoir, Simone de, **1:515–517**
on choice, 3:504
Lloyd and, 5:373
on perception of others, 3:502
and philosophy of sex, 1:515, 7:523
on relation between the sexes, 4:745
and Sartre, 1:515–516, 8:603
on woman as the Other, 3:586
Beaux-arts réduits à un même principe, Les (Batteux), 1:489
Beauzée, Nicolas, 8:790
Beccaria, Cesare Bonesana, **1:517–519**
and Bentham, comparison of, 1:551
on law, 7:424
Voltaire and, 9:713
Becher, Erich, 4:82, 7:83
Beck, Jakob Sigismund, **1:519–520**
Beck, Ulrich, on fair distribution of goods, 7:544
Becker, Carl L., on Enlightenment, 3:243, 3:244
Becker, Oscar, in phenomenology, 7:279
Beckner, Morton
on biology, 7:337
on purposive activity, 9:385
Becoming
Anaxagoras on, 1:181
vs. being, 7:22
Hegel on, 5:62
life as process of, 9:30–31
Matthew of Aquasparta on, 6:65
physics and, 9:498
Plato on, 7:602, 7:606
Simmel on, 9:30
time and, **9:475–482**
Bedau, Mark, emergence and, 3:193
Bedersi, Yeda'ya Hapnini, 4:820
Bedeutung, 8:60–61
Bedford, Errol, on emotivism, 3:426
Beebee, Helen, on natural laws, 5:229
Beecher, Henry Knowles, 8:667
Beeckman, Isaac, Descartes and, 2:722–723
Bees, dancing by, 1:204
Beesly, E. S., Comte and, 2:413
Beethoven, Ludwig van, classical conventions and, 3:82
Begging the question (circular reasoning), definition of, 5:543
Begriff der Religion im System der Philosophie, Der (Cohen), 2:304
Begriff des absolut Wertvollen als Grundbegriff der Moralphilosophie, Der (Krueger), 5:156
Begriff des subjektiven Rechts, Der (Schuppe), 8:664
Begriffsschrift (Frege), 3:725, 4:122, 5:462–463, 8:58, 8:735, 8:799
"Begründung der Mengenlehre unabhängig vom logischen Satz vom ausgeschlossenen Dritten" (Brouwer), 1:701
Beham, Barthel, and Albrecht Durer, 3:712
Behavior
as aesthetic quality, 1:38
Armstrong on, 1:287
belief and, 1:534
Calderoni on, 2:7
causation of, 6:224–225
Chinese room argument and, 2:240–241
Chomsky on, 2:244
in cognitive science, 2:297
common sense and, 2:356
Comte on, 2:410
conative, 8:147
as conceptual connection, 7:54
conditioning and, 1:203
in Confucianism, 2:174, 2:194–195
in creativity, 2:589
desire and, 1:534
economics and, 1:777, 7:353
environment and, 8:142–143
ethics and, 1:777
goal-directed, 7:735, 8:147
inalterability of, Schopenhauer on, 8:655
inner causes and, 2:391
intentionality and, 1:549, 2:452, 4:702
in Judaism, 4:831
law of effect and, 1:521
learning as, 1:521–522
machine intelligence and, 5:634
materialist explanation for, 6:12–14
means-end rationality in, 8:715
mental states and, 7:54, 7:447
moral rules and, 1:460
nature *vs.* nurture in, 8:153–154
neuroscience and, 6:565–566
operant conditioning and, 9:61
philosophy of mind and, 7:327
predictability of, 8:164, 8:728
probability and, 8:29–30
progress and, 8:49

propositional attitudes and, 8:80
in psychoanalytic session, 8:113
psychological explanations for, 6:141
in psychological irrationalism, 4:751
purposive action and, 9:385
qualitative consciousness and, 2:450
rationalization of, 8:80
reflex theory of
Marxism and, 7:150
Pavlov and, 7:149–150
responsibility and, 8:164
and risk, in personal relationships, 1:715
sensory stimuli and, 2:456
social, probability and, Condorcet on, 2:431
societal context of, 9:93–94
in speech, 7:407
Spinoza on, 8:125
Strawson on, 7:56
teleology of, 9:388–389
in utilitarianism, 1:687
and value systems, 8:642–643
Behavior (Watson), 8:142
Behavioral environment, things *vs.* "not-things" in, 5:125
Behavioral norms, conscience and, 2:445
Behavioral scientists, physicians as, 6:95
Behavioral technology, 9:61
Behaviorism, **1:520–526**
action and intention in, 1:524–525
analytic, 1:523–525
on materialism, 6:12
objectivity in, 1:524
animal intelligence and, 1:201
Bergmann and, 1:561
Blanshard on, 4:559
Chomsky on, 2:244, 5:190, 8:151
cognition and, 1:523
cognitive psychology and, 3:675, 8:150
vs. computationalism, 2:391
conscience and, 2:445
consciousness in, 6:588
vs. dualism, 8:142
emotion in, 8:143
and Gestalt theory, 4:73
of Hélvetius, 4:306
and introspection, 4:721, 6:80
on intuition, 4:725
Köhler on, 5:129–130
on language, 5:189–191
Lashley and, 8:143
in law, 7:428
linguistic, 7:401
Locke and, 1:201
logical
and conceptual functionalism, 3:758
and mental states, 1:534
in philosophy of mind, 7:469
Ryle on, 7:469
materialism and, 6:11–13
of Mead, 6:80–81
and mental states, 1:534, 3:756
methodological, 1:525–526
other minds and, 7:53–54
personal identity and, 7:227
philosophical, 8:84
physical substances in, 3:758
and psychology, 6:141, 8:142–143
Quine and, 7:749
radical, 9:61–62
as rejection of nativism, 4:693
and response theory of intentionality, 4:706
Savage and, 8:613
as scientific hypotheses, 1:520
self-knowledge in, 8:723
Skinner on, 9:61
social, 6:80–81, 6:561
on thought and thinking, 5:191, 9:421
translation in, 1:525
types of, 8:143
Behaviorism (journal), 9:62
Behavioristic psychology, 6:80
Behemoth (Hobbes), 9:181
Beḥinat Hadat (The testing of religion) (Del Medigo), 4:824
Behn, Aphra, 9:838
Beiden Grundprobleme der Ethik, Die (Schopenhauer), 8:648
Being, **1:527–532**
Abelard on, 1:528
absolute, 1:12, 1:529–530, 5:215
of abstract entities, 1:529
act of, 1:476
actual, 4:313
analogical *vs.* univocal meaning of, 9:430
apparent, Aureol on, 7:257
Aquinas on, 1:528, 2:551, 9:430–431
in arguments for existence of God, 9:431
Aristotle on, 1:276–278, 1:527–528, 6:186–187, 7:571–572
Averroes on, 1:423–424
Ayer on, 1:531
Bakhtin on, 1:465
vs. becoming, 7:22
Blanchot on, 1:611–612
Boethius on, 1:626
Bonaventure on, 1:652
Bradley on, 1:678
in Buddhism, 1:722, 1:741
categories of, 7:23–26
causes of, 1:277, 5:714
Christ as ultimate example of, 9:460
Clauberg on, 2:285
Cohen (Hermann) on, 6:542
consciousness and, Molina Garmendia on, 6:323–324
as creating existences, 1:706
Descartes on, 1:528
Dewey on, 1:531
in distinction of substance, 1:628
Duns Scotus on, 3:135, 6:189
Edwards (Jonathan) on, 3:167
Empedocles on, 3:208
and emptiness, 1:738
Eric of Auxerre on, 1:528
vs. essence, 9:430
as eternal, 3:715
existence and, 1:476, 1:528–529, 6:188–189, 7:17
existentialism and, 3:502–503, 4:683
existents in, 4:94
experience and, 5:702
finite, 1:115
freedom as, Jaspers on, 4:801
Frege on, 1:528
Garrigou-Lagrange on, 4:23
Gioberti on, 4:93–94
Greek Academy and debate concerning, 4:173
Guo Xiang on, 4:196
Hartmann on, 1:530
Hegel on, 1:530, 4:265, 5:62
Heidegger on, 1:530–531, 3:502, 3:508, 4:290–291
Henry of Ghent on, 4:313
Ibn al-ʿArabī on, 9:308
ideal, Croce's intuition as, 2:600
independent of knowing, in new realism, 6:586
Ingarden on, 4:683
integralism and, 8:666
intuition of, 4:94, 5:713
Islamic conception of, 4:541
I-thou *vs.* I-it relationships and, 1:715–716
Kierkegaard on, 1:530
kinds of, 1:628
Leibniz on, 1:529
Levinas on, 5:305

Being, ***continued***
Locke on, 6:504
in Mādhyamika doctrine, 1:741
man as analogy for, 9:459
Marcel on, 5:702
Maréchal on, 5:709
Maritain on, 1:529, 5:713–714
Marty on, 5:728–729
meaning of, 1:527–531, 4:292
Meinong on, 6:115
as metaphysically necessary, 2:553
in *Metaphysics* (Aristotle), 1:277, 1:278
mobile, 5:713
mode of, 7:257–258, 7:297
Moore (G. E.) on, 1:528, 2:543
Mullā Ṣadrā on, 6:418
as name, 1:527
Natorp on, 6:491
vs. nonbeing, 4:196
of objects, 6:115
Odo of Tournai on, 1:528
origin of, 4:196
ousia as, 7:63
palingenesis of, in Gioberti, 4:94–95
Parmenides on, 1:527
in phenomenal world, 1:678
Pico della Mirandola on, 7:571–572
Plato on, 1:527–528, 6:185, 7:596, 7:602, 7:606
Plotinus on, 6:187, 6:547
as potentiality, 1:278
power as, 7:22
principality of, 6:418–420
Proclus on, 8:42
Quine on, 1:528
Rosmini-Serbati on, 8:501–503
Royce on, 8:519–521
salvation and, 5:702
Santayana on, 8:601
Sartre on, 8:606–608. *See also* *Being and Nothingness* (Sartre)
Scholastics on, 1:527–528, 3:137
in Sellar's critical realism, 8:732–733
Simon Magnus on, 9:34
Solov'ëv on, 9:123–124
Stein on, 9:240
Suárez on analogicity of, 9:283
subsistence *vs.* accidents in, 1:628
substantive content for, 7:22
Tauler on, 9:373
Tillich on, 3:505, 9:459–460
time and, **9:475–481**. *See also* *Being and Time* (Heidegger)
Toletus on, 9:511
transphenomenal character of, 8:606–608
Trubetskoi (Sergei) on, 9:532
unity in, 3:681, 6:187
in William of Auvergne's metaphysics, 9:765
and world as not-yet-Being, 1:468
See also Ontology
"Being and Circumstance" (Irwin), 3:256
Being and Nothingness (Sartre), 1:133, 1:515, 2:459, 6:618, 7:297, 7:522–523
ethics in, 3:427–428
on existential psychoanalysis, 3:514
as ontology, 8:606–608
Being and Time (Heidegger), 1:133, 1:657, 4:291–293, 9:490
Gadamer on, 4:2
language in, 7:411
Sartre on, 8:603
and why not "nothing," 8:622
Being-as-such, 1:529–531
Hägerström on, 4:205
in Jaspers's metaphysics, 4:802
object status and, 1:529
Being-for-itself, Sartre on, 8:606
Being-for-others, Sartre on, 8:606
Being-in-itself
Gioberti on, 4:94
Sartre on, 8:606–607
Being-in-the-world
existential psychoanalysis and, 3:512–513
Heidegger on, 3:512
Lalande and, 5:173
Beings, types of, Leibniz on, 2:552–553
Beiträge zu einer kritik der Sprache (Mauthner), 8:801
Beiträge zur Analyse der Empfindungen (Mach), 3:176
"Beiträge zur Begründung der transfiniten Mengenlehre" (Contributions to the founding of the theory of transfinite numbers) (Cantor), 2:28, 8:833
Beiträge zur Einleitung in das Alte Testament (Dewette), 7:122
Beiträge zur innern Naturgeschichte der Erde (Steffens), 9:238
Beiträge zur Optik (Goethe), 4:141
Beitz, Charles, on moral cosmopolitanism, 2:568
Bekenntnis in der Judenfrage, Eine (Cohen), 2:304
Bekenstein, Jacob, on black hole thermodynamics, 9:269
Bekhterev, V. M., 7:150–151
Bekker, Immanuel, Aristotle and, 1:266
Belief(s), **1:532–536**
and actions, 1:533–534
active *vs.* passive, 5:91
in Agrippa's trilemma, 8:177
Alston on, 3:322, 7:482
analytical behaviorism on, 1:525
apt, in Sosa's virtue perspectivism, 9:136
Armstrong on, 1:287
ascription of, 8:78
as attitude, 5:704–705
in attributor contextualism, 2:485
Augustine on, 1:391–392
authority of, 1:474
as axioms, 5:109
Bain on, 5:91, 5:98
Balfour on, 1:474
basic, justification of knowledge and, 3:271–272
and behavior, 1:534
Braithwaite on, 5:98–99
Brentano on, 5:98
Buber on, 1:716
in Buddhism, 1:754, 2:349–350
Burge on, 8:83
in Calvinism, 2:12
Carnap on, Church on, 8:739
causality and, 1:704, 2:93–94, 4:147, 8:725
chance and, 2:128–129
in Chinese religion, 2:228
in Chisholm's epistemological foundationism, 2:243
of Christianity, 2:245–249
claims of, 2:352
Clifford on, 2:292
cognitive content of, 1:142
cognitive science research on, 2:300
coherence truth theory and, 2:310, 9:536
commitment to, 7:358
in common claims *vs.* religious claims, 2:228
and common consent arguments for God's existence, 2:344–345
common sense and, 1:510, 2:355–356
community and, 1:142
computationalism and, 2:394
concepts and, 1:533
conclusive grounds for, 5:92
confirmation theory and, 2:435–436
constraints in, action and, 1:20
content of, in information semantics, Dretske on, 2:479

context and, 1:142
cosmological, of Fourier, 3:707
Daoist truth criteria and, 2:207
decisions in absence of, 1:535
definition of, mentalist, 5:98
Descartes on, 2:276, 5:91
vs. desire, 1:532
vs. disbelief, 6:526
doubt and, 1:535, 5:97, 7:166–172
education and, 7:357–358
eliminative materialism on, 3:182–183
empirical, 5:96
emunah vs. pistis, 1:716
epistemic status of, 2:278–279, 2:314, 4:716–717, 8:685
errors in, 2:276
in ethical disagreements, 9:245
ethics of, 2:292, 5:99
evaluation of, 3:325
evil demon victims of, 9:136
existence and, Quine on, 7:28
experience and, 1:533–534, 8:177–178
experimental acquisition of, 1:462
explanatory role of, 1:463, 1:533, 1:536–537
in external objects, Boscovich on, 9:248
and facts, 2:93–94, 2:540
faith in God as equivalent to, Aquinas on, 3:535
fallibility of, 4:780–781
false, 2:542–543, 5:93, 9:39
    in Moore's theory of truth, 2:542–543
    in passions, 9:190
    in Russell's theory of truth, 2:543
foundationalism and, 2:275–279, 8:177–179
in God
    Buddhism and, 2:349–350
    Darwin on, 2:349
    different senses of, 1:359
    faith and, 1:535, 3:535
    meaning of, 2:350–352
    Pascal on, 7:133, 8:713
    Plantinga on, 7:481–482
Hume on, 3:631–632, 5:16, 5:91, 5:99
ideology and, 4:575
incorrigible, doubting, 5:97
inductive inferences and, 1:698–699
infallibility of
    in attributor contextualism, 2:485
    in noninferential foundationalism, 2:277
inference and, 2:275, 9:684
information as source of, 3:108
in information semantics, 2:479
innate, 2:345–346
innate, common consent arguments for God's existence and, 2:345–346
intellectual virtue and, 9:683–684
intention and, 1:19, 4:701, 7:447
vs. intuition, 4:732
as involuntary response, 2:352
James on, 4:780–781, 7:745
justification of, 2:275, 2:314, 5:87, 7:357, 8:177
justified
    coherentism and, 2:313
    foundationalism on, 8:177–179
    inference and, 2:275–276
    knowledge and, 5:92, 9:683–684
    modal, regress of, 5:80
    reliabilist theories of, 8:362–363
    religious pluralism and, 8:420
    true, knowledge as, 5:91–93
and knowledge, 2:596, 3:270–271, 5:86–87, **5:91–100,** 5:104–107, 5:656, 9:854
as linguistic attitude, 5:704–705
in logical *vs.* evocative arguments, 2:213
Maimonides on, 5:652
Maine de Biran on, 5:656
Marcus on, 5:704–705
and meaning, 8:808
as mental content, 2:476–477
meta-incoherence and, 9:136
Mill (John Stuart) on, 2:346, 5:98
minimal change in, Bayes on, 4:671–672
in miracles, 6:273–274
monotheistic, development of, 2:350
Moore (G. E.) on, 2:542–543, 3:314
nature of, 5:98–99
necessity of, 5:652
neutral logic of, epistemological assumption about, 4:783
numerical probability and, 5:99
open-mindedness and, 7:358
pain and, 2:277, 3:758
Pascal on, 1:535, 3:531
Peirce on, 2:357, 5:91, 7:166–173, 9:537
perceptual
    in coherentism, 2:314
    formation of, 9:684–685
personal, Baker on, 1:463–464
Plantinga on, 2:12, 3:322, 7:481–482
Plato on, 2:540, 3:283–285, 5:95
political institutions and, Godwin on, 4:139
in possible worlds, skepticism and, 2:93–94
pragmatism and, 1:463, 7:745
in progress, 8:47
as proposition, 4:712, 8:81, 9:44
in Pyrrhonism, 8:174–175
rational degrees of, 8:685
realism and, 1:463
realizable desire and, 1:704
reason and, 7:581, 7:735
and reasoning, 1:510
recognition as, 1:199
as relation, 3:759
reliabilist theories of, 8:362–363
reliability of, 2:278
religious
    evidence and, 1:762
    Freud on, 3:745
    harmfulness of, 8:560
    higher power in, 4:781
    Hume on, 4:512–513
    optimism/pessimism and, 7:244, 7:245
    as self-deception, 2:12
    Shaftesbury on, 1:505
    voluntarist route to, 3:531
    Wittgenstein on, 2:228
Rescher on, 8:439–440
Russell on, 2:543
Saadya on, 8:586
and science, 1:643, 4:780
second-order, in game theory, 4:18
self-deception in, 1:535, 2:12, 8:711–713
sensation and, 1:532–533
skepticism and, 1:474, 2:12
in social epistemology, 9:84–85
Socrates on, 3:284–285
sophists on, 7:365
Spinoza on, 5:94, 9:174, 9:190
in subject contextualism, 2:482–483
suspension of, in phenomenology, 7:285–289
Swinburne on, 3:322
systems of, and coherence, 2:278–279, 2:313
theory of, apart from metaphysics, 4:783
and thoughts, 2:480

Belief(s), *continued*
- truth and, 1:532, 2:93–94, 2:277, 5:87
  - reality and, 3:709
  - Xenophanes of Colophon on, 9:854
- Unamuno on, 9:568–569
- uncertainty and, 1:535
- unconscious, 5:705
- underdetermined, evidence and, 1:535
- understanding and, 1:391–392, 5:87
- universal, 2:345–346, 2:349–350
- unjustified, as not constituting knowledge, 5:87
- in untruths, 8:81
- vague partial, 5:110
- voluntarism and, 1:534–535
- as voluntary, 9:686
- warrants of, and evidence, in Calvinism, 2:12
- as will, 1:617, 1:704
- Wodeham on, 9:822

"Belief and Unbelief: Humbly recommended to the serious consideration of creed makers" (Freneau), 2:690

Belief attributions, **1:536–538**

Belief/desire psychology, 3:675

Belinskii, Vissarion Grigor'evich, **1:538–539,** 5:48

Bell, Charles, physicotheology and, 7:561

Bell, Clive
- on aesthetic experience, 1:33
- on art, 1:59, 1:64
- formalism of, 1:295, 1:308
- Moore and, 1:64

Bell, Daniel, 6:317
- on ideology, 4:574
- on phenomenology, 7:299

Bell, John, **1:539–542**
- on Bohmian mechanics and Lorentz invariant, 1:635
- on chance and determinism, 2:126
- on entropy and information in physical states, 2:105
- on locality, 6:641–642
- on quantum mechanics, 2:126, 7:477, 8:199
- on synthetic differential geometry, 2:509–510

Bellarmine, St. Robert, **1:542–543**
- Galileo and, 2:732
- theology of, congruism in, 8:681

Bellers, John, 7:154

Bello, Andrés, positivism and, 5:207

Bell's inequality, 6:641–642

Bell's theorem, **1:539–542**
- on axioms of measurement, 8:207
- common cause principle and, 2:343
- definition of, 1:539–540
- and EPR theory, 8:215
- locality and, 6:641–642
- on quantum nonlocality, 1:630

Belnap, Nuel
- on logical terms, 5:532
- paraconsistent logic and, 7:105
- relevant logic and, 5:491
- on semantic paradoxes, 5:521

Beloff, John, 7:115–116

Bely, Andrey, and Florenskii, 3:668–669

"Bemerkungen über die kräfte der unbelebten Natur" (Mayer), on energy conservation, 3:230

Bemmei (Definitions of terms) (Ogyū), 7:10

Ben Gershon, Levi. *See* Gersonides

Benacerraf, Paul, 5:84
- and nominalism, 6:628
- on numbers as objects, 9:272

Benbow, William, deism and, 2:691

Bendardete, José A., cosmology of, 2:567

Bendō (Defining the way) (Ogyū), 7:10

Benedict, Ruth, on normative relativism, 6:159

Benedictines, Cartesianism and, 2:757

Beneficence
- Cicero on, 7:79
- Hierocles on, 7:79
- in medical ethics, 6:92–93
- Panaetius of Rhodes on, 7:79

Benefit-harm evaluation, in Mohist ethics, 2:197

Beneke, Friedrich Eduard, **1:543–544**
- and absolute idealism, 1:543
- and psychologism, 3:753
- and psychology, 8:140
- Schulze and, 8:662

Benevolence
- altruism and, 1:136–137
- Butler (Joseph) on, 1:782
- in common-sense morality, 9:23
- Confucian notion of, 2:194, 5:137
- Cumberland on, 2:615
- definition of, complexity of, 3:174–175
- *vs.* desire, 6:655
- generalized
  - in act utilitarianism, 9:606–607
  - in deontological ethics, 9:606–607
  - in rule utilitarianism, 9:607, 9:614
- in human nature, 1:781
- in moral principles, 6:374
- Price on, 8:3
- by reason alone, 1:642

Benford, Frank, law of first digits, 9:228

Benhabib, Seyla, 3:565

Benivieni, Girolamo, 3:671, 7:570

Benjamin, Walter, **1:545–547**
- Adorno and, 1:26–27
- aesthetics of, 1:69, 1:545–547

Benkert, Károly Mária, 7:523–524

Benn, Gottfried, **1:547–549,** 4:3

Bennett, Jonathan, **1:549–550**
- on event theory, 3:466–467
- on Spinoza's monism, 9:185

Bennington, Geoffrey, 5:621

Bentham, Jeremy, **1:550–558**
- on altruism and self-interest, 3:173
- and animal rights, 1:208
- on art, 1:339
- auto-icon of, 1:557
- as consequentialist, 2:460
- deontology and, 2:713
- on duty, 3:155, 7:445
- Epicurus and, 3:265
- on ethics, 3:412–413
- on fictions, 8:793, 9:796
- on government, 2:702–703
- and hedonism, 4:152, 4:719, 8:616, 8:720, 9:604
- on impartiality, 4:620
- on intentionality, 4:704
- on jurisprudence, 7:424–425
- Laas on, 5:164
- on language, 1:551–552, 8:792–793
- on law
  - codification of, 1:554–555
  - imperative theory of, 9:141
  - obligation to obey, 5:239
- legal positivism and, 5:237, 5:238
- MacIntyre on, 5:636
- on maximally desired outcomes, 3:748
- Mill (James) and, 6:218
- Mill (John Stuart) and, 6:221
- Paley and, 7:76
- panopticon of, 1:555
- on paraphrase, 3:629
- on pleasure and pain, 7:617
- political philosophy of, 7:666–667
- positivism of, 7:712
- on property, 8:69
- on religion, 1:556–557
- Sidgwick and, 9:25
- on state, conflicting interests in, 9:207

and utilitarianism, 3:382–383, 7:459, 9:604–605
on utility, 1:552–553
on war and peace, 7:155
on well-being, 8:722
Bentham, Samuel, panopticon building design by, 1:555
Bentley, A. E., 9:207
Bentley, Richard
Boyle Lectures and, 7:559
on deism, 2:686
Newton and, 5:54, 7:558
Beobachtung uber das Gefuhl des Schonen und Erhabenen (Kant), 5:26
Berdyaev, Nikolai Aleksandrovich, **1:558–561**
Dostoevsky and, 3:99
Florovskii and, 3:673
Ivanov and, 4:768
on Kant, 1:560, 9:529
Karsavin and, 5:42–43
Kireevskii and, 5:75
Losev and, 5:573
and Marxism, 5:738
Zen'kovskii and, 9:868–869
Berg, Alban, Adorno and, 1:25
Bergbohm, K. M., on obligation to obey law, 5:238–239
Berger, Gaston, 3:638
Berger, John R., 6:233
Berger, Peter
on neo-Confucianism's influence in Asia, 2:181
on self, 9:77
Bergerac, Cyrano de. *See* Cyrano de Bergerac, Savinien de
Bergmann, Gustav, **1:561–563**
Bergson, Abraham, 8:810
Bergson, Henri, **1:563–572**
on art and intuition, 1:57
on body and mind, 1:564
Brunschvicg and, 1:714
on consciousness, 9:488–489
Deleuze and, 2:694–695, 7:382, 9:275, 9:492
on determinism and freedom, 1:563–564
Deustua and, 3:42
on duration, 2:695, 4:745, 9:464, 9:488–489
Emerson and, 3:197
epistemology, 3:312–313
on evolution, 1:568–569, 2:637, 9:72
on film, 7:381
on God and nature, 2:641
on intellect
vs. intuition, 1:567, 4:749
and things, 1:566–567
on intuition, 1:567, 4:723, 4:749
James (William) and, 3:313, 4:782
Keyserling and, 5:58
Korn and, 5:142
Lachelier and, 5:169
and Latin American philosophy, 5:208
on laughter and skepticism, 1:469
Lavelle and, 5:214
Le Roy and, 5:288
Maritain and, 5:712
on memory, 1:564–565, 2:695, 3:313, 9:489
Merleau-Ponty on, 9:491
on metaphysics, 1:567–568, 9:488
on natural sciences, 1:567–568
on open and closed societies, 1:571
Papini and, 7:102
and parapsychology, 7:114, 7:116
on perception, 1:565–566
personal experience and, 8:588
on reality, 6:195
Romero on, 8:492
Sartre and, 8:606
Schutz and, 8:664
Sorel and, 9:134
on spatial concept of time, 9:487
Teilhard and, 9:374
on time, 1:563
Bergsonism (Deleuze), 2:694–695, 9:492
Bergsonism, in Taylor (Alfred), 9:373
Berheim, B. Douglas, 4:20
Berkeley (Hicks), 4:561
Berkeley (Warnock), on sound, 9:138
Berkeley, George, **1:573–588**
on abstract ideas, 1:586, 4:593, 8:781–782
on abstract images, 4:590
a-causal persistence and, 2:587
and aetheism, 6:494
on appearance, 1:231
Ayer and, 1:436
on being-as-such, 1:529
Blake and, 1:610
on Browne, 1:359
on calculus, 2:495
Coleridge and, 2:316
on common sense, 2:354–355
conceptualism of, 9:596–598
Condillac and, 2:421–422
De Morgan and, 2:709
deism and, 2:686, 5:220
Edwards (Jonathan) and, 3:168
as empiricist, 3:217–218, 3:302
Encyclopédie and, 3:223
and epistemology, 3:298–306
on essence, 6:191–192
example fallacy, 3:540
on external world problem, 1:462–463
on force as convenient auxiliary fiction, 3:689
Foucher and, 3:704
Genovesi and, 4:49
on God, 1:359, 3:217, 4:556
Hegel on, 4:557
on idea, concept of, 4:553
idealism of, 4:555, 5:230
on immaterialism, 1:576–579, 4:554–555
on immediate experience, 3:516
on infinitesimal methods, 4:652
Johnson (Samuel) and, 4:851
Laas on, 5:163
Le Clerc and, 5:236
on Locke, 4:593
Mach and, 8:827
major themes of, 1:574–575
Malebranche and, 5:671–672
Mandeville and, 5:680
mathematical philosophy of, 1:582
Maupertuis and, 8:783
on measurement, 8:11
and metaphysics, 1:579–581, 6:191–192
Mill (John Stuart) on, 3:312
natural philosophy of, 1:581–582
on nature, 6:519
on omniobserver, 6:173
on perception, 5:672
on personalism, 7:234
on phenomenalism, 7:271–273
and *philosophes,* 9:56
in Platonic tradition, 7:615
on private words, 8:782
on qualities, 8:9–11
on resemblance theory, 9:600
on scientific knowledge, 3:64
on sensa, 8:814
on sensation, 8:825
on sense experience, 4:554–555
Shelley and, 9:9
Shepherd on, 9:10
and skepticism, 7:108, 9:55
on solitary man, 8:782
on sound, 9:138
on substance, 6:191–192, 8:131, 9:298
and theology, 1:579–581
on thought and thinking, 9:420
on touch, 9:515
on universals, 1:595–598, 3:302
on words, 8:781–782

Berkeley-Hume criticism, of force, 3:689
Berleant, Arnold
 on environmental aesthetics, 3:255, 3:256
 on property, 8:70
Berlin, Isaiah, **1:588–589**
 on historical inevitability, 3:36, 3:40
 on Tolstoy, 9:512
Berlin Enlightenment, *Pantheismusstreit* and, 7:99
Berlin Society of Sciences, Leibniz and, 5:254
Berlinische Monatsschrift, 7:99
Berman, Zeke, 9:690
Bernard, Claude, **1:589–590**
Bernard of Arezzo, Nicolas of Autrecourt and, 6:601–602
Bernard of Bessa, on Alexander of Hales, 1:113
Bernard of Chartres, **1:590–591**
 in *Historia Pontificalis* (John of Salisbury), 4:844
 William of Conches and, 9:768
Bernard of Tours, **1:592–593,** 5:641
Bernardus Silvestris. *See* Bernard of Tours
Bernays, Paul, on combinatory arithmetic, 2:337–338
Bernhard, Isaak, Mendelssohn and, 6:130
Bernhardi, Friedrich vonsic, 7:154
Bernier of Nevilles, Averroism of, 1:428
Bernoulli, Daniel
 on decision theory, 2:655
 Petersburg paradox and, 5:339
 on potential energy, 3:228
 Wolff and, 9:826
Bernoulli, great-numbers theorem, 5:57
Bernoulli, Johann
 on energy conservation, 3:228
 on force measurement, 3:228
 Leibniz and, 5:253–254
Bernoulli pattern, 8:32
Bernstein, Eduard, 5:47, 5:166
Berry, Ralph Barton, 4:776
Berry's paradox, 5:518, 5:551
Bertalanffy, Ludwig von, **1:593–594**
Bertius, Pieter, Jr., Arminius and, 1:285
Bertrand, Joseph, 8:31, 9:227
"Bertrand Russell's Doubts about Induction" (Edwards), 7:108
Bérulle, Pierre de, 2:727, 5:663
Berzelius, Jöns Jakob, atomism and, 1:387
Besant, Annie, atheism of, 1:358
Beschreibung einer Reise durch Deutschland un die Schweiz im Jahre 1781 (Description of a journey through Germany and Switzerland in 1781) (Nicolai), 6:598
Best, Paul, 9:100
Best society, 6:400
Beth, E. W., 9:368
Better, Mara, 3:182
Betting odds, and probability, 2:663
Between-ness
 particulars and, 6:174
 in temporal order, 9:494
Bevezetés a Filozofiaba (Introduction to philosophy) (Pauler), 7:145
"Beweis, dass jede volle Funktion gleichmässig stetig ist" (Brouwer), 1:701
Bewusstein (consciousness), Natorp on, 6:543
Bewusstheit (known-ness), Natorp on, 6:543
Beyond Dignity and Freedom (Skinner), 9:62
Beyond Good and Evil (Nietzsche), 6:612
 on absence of moral order, 4:750
 and Shestov, 9:11
Beyond "Justification": Dimensions of Epistemic Evaluation (Alston), 1:133
Beyond Therapy: Biotechnology and the Pursuit of Happiness (Kass et al.), 7:550
Beza, Theodorus, Arminius and, 1:285
Bhabha, Homi K., on postcolonialism, 7:726
Bhagavad Gītā
 on God, personality of, 4:111–112
 on karma, 5:41
 on liberation, 5:359
 on meditation, 6:107
 as wisdom literature, 9:793
Bhakti yoga, 5:359
Bhartṛhari, 4:631, 9:581
Bhasyas, 4:132
Bhatta, Jayarasi, 5:120
Bhaṭṭa, Kumārila, 5:414
Bhāṭṭa Mīmāṃsakas, 4:628
 on absence *(abhava),* 5:122
 on certification, 9:545
 on means of knowledge, 5:117, 5:122
 on *samavāya* (inherence), 9:583
Bhāvaviveka
 in Buddhist thought, 1:731
 in Sautrānikita doctrine, 1:745
 Svātantrika-Prāsaṅgika distinction, 1:744
Bi (blindness), Xunzi on, 9:857
Bias, selection, Leslie on, 1:220
Bias paradox, 3:574–575
Biathanatos (Donne), on suicide, 9:319
Bible, 9:32
 allegory in, 1:47, 9:844–845
 anthropology of, 1:478
 apologism in, 1:227
 Arnold on, 1:294
 asceticism in, 1:351
 Barth on, 1:477
 Berdyaev on, 1:559
 Bernard of Chartres on, 1:591
 Boyle on, 1:673
 Bruno on, 7:96
 Bultmann on, 1:762
 Christological categories and, 2:247
 Collier on, 2:324
 Collins on, 2:330
 Copernicism and, 2:536
 cosmology of, 1:478
 critical evaluation of, 9:33
 Crusius on, 2:608
 Damarsais on, 2:266
 Darwinism and, 2:641
 deism and, 2:683–685, 2:690–691
 Deussen on, 3:41
 and divine command theories of ethics, 3:93
 as divine-human dialogue, 1:716
 in doctrine of Trinity, 1:456
 Encyclopédie on, 3:224
 eschatology in, 3:347–348
 eternity in, 3:357
 Herder on, 6:574
 and higher criticism, 2:691
 human beings in, 7:323
 illumination in, 4:580
 interpretation of
  Barth on, 1:477
  Blake on, 1:610
  Channing on, 2:130
 Jaspers on, 4:803
 La Peyrère on, 5:196
 Lavater on, 5:214
 Locke on, 5:395
 Loisy on, 5:570–571
 love of God in, 5:585
 Marcion on, 5:703–704
 Mirabaud on, 2:266
 on moral perfection, 7:194–195
 Nemesius of Emesa and, 6:538
 Newton (Isaac) on, 2:685
 Nietzsche's parody of, 6:611–612
 Origen on, 1:47
 Palmer (E.) on, 7:78
 Parker (T.) on, 7:121

Pascal on, 7:133
pessimism in, 7:246
Philo's use of, 7:303–304, 7:307
Plantinga on, 3:324
as record, 8:453
revelation and, 8:452–453
Rousseau on, 2:688
Simon Magnus in, 9:33
and skepticism, 9:51–52
Skovoroda on, 9:64
Sorel on, 9:132
Spinoza on, 7:97
on suicide, 9:319
Testaments of
inner concords between, 4:834
Old *vs.* New, 5:703–704
as unconscious invention of myth, 9:262
universalist message of, 4:831–832
Biblical criticism
Blount and, 1:619
Collins on, 2:331
Costa and, 2:572
in French clandestine writings, 2:265, 2:267
Bibliographies of philosophy, 10:67–75
Bibliotheca Antitrinitariorum (Sand), 9:100
Bibliotheca Fratrum Polonorum (Wiszowaty), 9:100
Bibliotheke (Photios), 1:788
Bibliothèque ancienne et moderne (LeClerc), 5:235
Bibliothèque choisie (LeClerc), 5:235–236
Bibliothèque universelle (periodical), 5:375
Bibliothèque universelle et historique (LeClerc), 5:235–236
Bickenbach, J. E., 5:512
Bickerstaff Papers (Swift), 9:340
Biconditional, definition of, 5:535
Biddle, John, 9:100
Biel, Gabriel, **1:594–595,** 5:617, 7:9
Big bang theory, 4:63
cosmological research on, 2:565
and entropy, 7:540–541, 7:565
Friedman and, 9:478
God's existence and, 2:555, 2:588
and inflationary universe theory, 2:566
Bigelow, John, 9:461
Bijoux indiscrets, Les (The indiscreet toys) (Diderot), 3:72
Bilfinger, Georg Bernhard, **1:595**
on force measurement, 3:228
on Leibnizian-Wolffian School Philosophy, 9:824
Billy Budd (Melville), 1:254
Bin Laden, Osama, 9:397
Binary, as 2-ary, 3:647
Binary connectives, in conditional sentences, 2:424
Binary relation symbol, 3:650
Binary relations, in computability theory, 2:374
Binary thought, deconstruction and, 2:661
Binding problem, 6:566–567
Binet, Alfred, **1:596–597**
Bingham, Joseph W., 7:428
Bingham, June, 6:606
Binswanger, Ludwig, **1:597–598**
and anthropology, 7:318
and existential psychiatry, 3:507, 3:510–511, 7:322–323
on Freud, 7:322
on transcendental category, 3:513
Binswanger, Otto, 6:608
Bioanthropology, 7:320
Bioengineering, 7:550
Bioethics, **1:598–605,** 7:333
as applied normative ethics, 1:598
Bentham and, 1:557
Cabanis on, 2:2
Confucianism and, 2:176
definition of, 1:598
development of, 1:599–600
as discipline, 1:598–599
distributive justice and, 1:603
general normative theories and, 1:600–601
and genetics, 4:43–48
history of, 1:599–600
informed consent in, 4:679–680
life as non-limiting condition of, 1:590
methods in, 1:600–602
morals in, 1:601–603
norms in, 1:601
philosophical assessment of, 8:675
in philosophical ethics, 1:599
and reproductive technologies, 4:43–48
social context of, 1:599–600
on suicide, 9:321
therapist's role in, 1:716
Bioethics: A Return to Fundamentals (Gert, Culver, and Clouser), 1:602
Biogenes, 8:659
Biogenetic law, 4:201
Biogeography, Wilson (Edward O.) and, 9:788
Biographia Literaria (Coleridge)
on fancy *vs.* imagination, 4:597
on Spinoza, 9:195
Biography
Carlyle on, 2:33–34
Dilthey on, 3:84
Diogenes Laertius and, 3:88
Biological functions, teleology of mental states in, 2:479
Biological need, Santayana on, 2:596
Biological philosophical anthropology, 7:320–321
Biological potentiality, 3:491
Biological Principles (Woodger), 7:37, 9:843
Biological science
and physical science
unified, 9:750
Whitehead and, 9:753
religion and, **8:393–397**
Biological theory
chance in, 2:127
of consciousness, 8:705–706
physical, 6:63
pre-Darwinian, 2:640
Biological variability, 7:465
Biological Way of Thought, The (Beckner), 7:337
Biologie als selbständige Grundwissenschaft, Die (Biology as an independent basic science) (Driesch), 3:110
Biologisches Zentralblatt (periodical), 3:110
Biology
artificial life and, 1:348–349
Beckner on, 7:337
Bergson on, 1:569
bioethics and, 1:600
Bonnet on, 1:657–658
Buffon on, 1:759
Butler (Samuel) on, 1:784
Buytendijk on, 7:320–321
Cabanis on, 2:2
Clifford on, 2:291
cognitive science and, 2:300
complementarity principle in, 1:639
Comte on, 2:411
concepts in, 3:757
definition of, 7:337
Democritus on, 5:300
development, physical, in, 7:345–347
Diderot on, 3:74–75
Diogenes of Apollonia on, 3:90
etiology in, 9:389
functional, 7:321
Goudge on, 7:337
history of, 7:337–338
inferiorities and, 3:594

Biology, *continued*
La Mettrie on, 5:178–181
language of, 7:36
machine model in, 1:593
Maritain on, 5:713
Maupertuis and, 6:66–67
Mendel and, 7:338
method in, 1:593–594
morphology and, 7:347
nonphysical forces *vs.* closed physical causality in, 2:91
as open system, 1:594
organicismic model of, 1:593
vs. other sciences, 7:337
philosophy of, **7:337–347**
Portmann on, 7:321
psychology and, 8:148–149
racism and, 8:228
reaction-theoretical model of, 1:593
scope of, 7:337–338
statistical method in, Bernard's critique of, 1:590
teleology in, 2:479–480, 7:342–343
theoretical models in, 1:593
vitalism and, 9:203, 9:696
Woodger in, 9:843–844
Biology and Gender Study Group, 3:594
Biology and Language (Woodger), 9:843–844
Biometrika (periodical), 7:159
Biometry, Pearson and, 7:159
Bion of Borysthenes, 2:617
Biophilia, 9:789
Bios of Pythagorikos (Iamblichus), 4:540
Biotechnology, philosophy of technology and, 7:550
Biran, Maine de. *See* Maine de Biran
Birch, Thomas, on Cockburn, 2:294
Birds (Aristophanes), 8:45
Birkhoff, George, 5:491, 7:539
Birnbaum, Alan, 9:217
Birth of Tragedy, The (Nietzsche), 1:56, 6:608, 8:629, 9:524–525
Bishop, Errett, on continuum, 2:501, 2:504–505
Bishop, John, on Brand, 1:16
Bishop, Michael, 3:680
Bisiach, Edoardo, on contralateral neglect, 6:566
Bismark, Otto von, 5:321
Bistami, Abu Yazid (Bayazid), 9:302
Bivalence, in theories of truth, 9:540
Bizarre skeptic, 8:531–533
Black, Joseph, on heat energy, 3:229
Black, Max, **1:605–606**
on circularity in induction, 4:640
and Frye, 3:755
and identity theory, 8:191
on scientific models and metaphors, 6:166
Black feminism, 3:575, 3:601
Black holes, **1:606–609,** 4:63
determinism and, 3:33
in string theory, 9:269
"Black International," 5:154
Black theology, American, 5:331–333
Blackburn, Simon
on emotivism, 3:206–207
and noncognitivism, 6:633–634
on nonfactualist (expressivist) suggestions, 3:627
on projectivism, 8:51–52
realism of, 8:52
on sentence meaning, 6:653
Blackett, P. M. S., on mass and energy, 3:233
Blackmore, Susan, 7:116
Blackness, of black holes, 1:609
Blackstone, Sir William
Bentham on, 1:553
on suicide, 9:319
Blackwood's Magazine (periodical), 3:184, 3:608
Bladerunner (film), 6:122
Blair, Hugh, 3:604
Blake, William, **1:609–611**
Blakeslee, Susan, 6:566
Blame, utilitarianism and, 9:609, 9:612–613
Blanchot, Maurice, **1:611–613**
Blanquerna (Lull), 5:610
Blanqui, Augusts, 9:89
Blanqui, Louis A., on eternal return doctrine, 3:354
Blanshard, Brand, **1:613–614**
and coherence theory of truth, 9:536
on evil, existence of God and, 1:362
and idealist theory, 4:559
Nagel (Ernest) on, 6:473
on perceptual consciousness, 8:817
on truth, 2:311
Blasphemy, Bataille on, 1:488
Blemmydes, Nikephoros, 1:788
Blick in die Ferne: Ein Buch der Einsichten und Hoffnungen (A look in the distance: A book of reflections and hopes) (Il'in), 4:578
Blijenbergh, Willem van, 9:176
Blind spots, perception and, 7:184
Blindness denial, 6:566
Blindsight, 6:566
Bloch, Ernst, **1:614–617**
Block, Ned, 4:591
on conscious qualitative states, 2:451
on "damn/darn" problem, 3:760
on perception, 7:192
on qualitative consciousness, 2:450
on Turing test, 5:634
Blond, Jean-Marie Le, 1:357
Blondel, Maurice, **1:617–619**
Laberthonnière and, 5:164
Lavelle and, 5:214
Sciacca and, 8:666
and Sturzo's dialectic of concrete, 9:281
Blood, in vitalism, 9:695–696
Bloor, David, 8:533, 9:78, 9:84
Blount, Charles, **1:619–620,** 2:681–682
Blue Book (Wittgenstein), 2:359, 7:109, 9:809
Blue Cliff Record (Biyan lu) (Yuanwu), 1:729
Blum, Manuel, 2:387
Blumberg, A. E., on logical positivism, 5:524
Blundevile, Thomas, 5:438
Boas, George, Lovejoy and, 5:594
Bobrow, Daniel, on logic machines, 5:566
Bodde, Derk, on Tolstoy, 9:513
Boden, Margaret A., on creativity, 2:589–590
Bodhidharma, 2:154, 2:166
Bodhisattva, 4:625, 5:41, 6:622
Bodily criterion for personal identity, 7:214–216, 7:221–222, 7:228
vs. memory criterion, 7:222–228
priority of, 7:224–225
satisfaction of, denial of, 7:226
Bodily death, personal identity and, 7:214–215
Bodily drives, in language, 5:152
Bodily transfer, personal identity and, 7:214, 7:222–228
Bodin, Jean, **1:620–623**
on determinism, 3:37
on law, 3:637, 7:422
on sovereign authority, 9:140
Bodmer, Johann Jakob, Lavater and, 5:213
Body(ies)
Alcmaeon of Croton on, 1:104
Aquinas on, 8:122–123
asceticism and, 1:353
Avicenna on, 1:433–434
Baker on, 1:463–464
Berkeley on, 1:585
Carnap on, 6:496
Carus (Carl) on, 2:63

Chisholm's metaphysics and, 2:243
in Christianity, 8:122–123
in classical mechanics, 2:280
in composition of soul, Galen on, 4:5
Condillac on of, 9:515
as corporeal form of soul, 1:622
existence and, 5:667–668, 5:701
experience of, 5:657–658
Fechner on, 8:139
Hegel on, 4:267
hierarchical classification of, 3:587
Hume on, 5:657–658, 8:133
imperfect identity of, 4:498–499
Leibniz on, 8:130
as machine, 4:609–610
Malebranche on, 5:667–668
in Manichaeism, 5:683
Marcel on, 5:701
Marcus Aurelius on, 5:707
medical knowledge of, 3:699
Merleau-Ponty on, 6:148
Milton on, 6:249
mind and, 5:22
movement of, liberty and, 5:658
as object, 6:148
and object relation, 9:516
organic, existence of, accounting for, 5:27
as perceptually spatial images, 1:564
personhood and, 7:238–240
as physical organism, *vs.* percept, 5:131
Portmann on, 7:321
reconstitution of, after death, 4:603
Regius on, 8:301
reincarnation and, 6:620–621
as self, in Cārvāka school, 8:717
self-control of, Plato on, 4:606
semantics of, and mental states, 1:370
as sensed, 6:148
as sensor, 6:148
simplicity of, 4:499
and soul, 1:433–434, 5:640, 7:319
  separability of, 1:622
  Swedenborg on, 9:336
Spinoza on, 3:294, 8:125–126
as subject, 6:148
Thomas of York on, 9:443
of universe, 5:640
Vasquez on, 9:649–650
Voltaire on, 9:710
will and, 5:656–658
Yang Zhu on, 9:862
  See also Mind-body problem; Mind-body relationship
"Body and Mind" (Clifford), 1:369
Body and Mind (McDougall), 6:72
"Body and Mind" (Stout), 9:260
Body-memory, McDougall on, 6:72
Body-mind
  dependence, 4:615
  Dōgen on, 3:95–96
Boedder, Bernard, 2:344
Boehme, Jakob, **1:624–625**
  on "dark nature" of God, 9:124
  Deussen on, 3:42
  Emerson and, 3:195
  Law (W.) and, 5:220
  on pantheism, 7:96–98
  and Schelling, 8:621
Boerhaave, Hermann
  La Mettrie and, 5:178
  and Stahlianism, 9:203
Boethian solution, 3:695
Boethius, Anicius Manlius Severinus, **1:625–628**
  Abelard and, 5:424–425
  Anselm and, 1:216
  Aristotle and, 5:408–409, 5:421–422, 7:571
  and category theory, 2:80
  on conditionals, 5:425
  Dante and, 2:624
  definition of person, 7:233
  on determinism, 3:9
  on entailments, 5:426
  on eternity, 4:110
  Gilbert of Poitier on, 4:88–89
  on God and eternity, 3:358, 3:695
  on impositions, 8:762
  "in" used by, 6:101
  on logic, 1:4, 1:627–628, 5:421–427, 5:433, 5:439
  in medieval philosophy, 6:99, 7:612
  in Neoplatonism, 6:187, 6:555
  on Plato, 7:571
  on semantics, 8:761–762
  on simple necessity, 3:694
  Theodoric of Chartres and, 9:410
  on universals, 1:626, 3:289, 8:762
  Valla on, 7:147
  William of Auvergne and, 9:765
Boethius of Sidon
  on logic, 5:407–408
  Peripatetics and, 7:203
Boetius of Dacia, **1:628–629**
  Averroism of, 1:428
  modism and, 5:432
Bogdanov, Alexander, Lenin and, 5:280
Boghossian, Paul
  on analyticity, 1:167
  on conventionalism, 1:167
  on rule following, 8:532–533
  on stipulation, 1:165
Bohm, David, **1:629–630**
  on chance, 2:126–127
  on determinism, 2:126–127, 3:33
  kalām argument for God's existence and, 2:554
  "pilot wave" theory of, 8:203
  on quantum theory, 1:541–542, 2:126–127, 3:690
Böhme, Jakob. *See* Boehme, Jakob
Bohmian mechanics, **1:630–636**
  in collapse theory, 8:212
  and Copenhagen interpretation, 1:630, 9:576–577
  eigenvalue interpretation in, 2:531
  as modal interpretation, 6:279
Bohr, Niels, **1:636–639**
  atomism and, 1:388
  Heisenberg and, 4:298
  on phenomena
    and experimentation, 2:531
    and observation, 2:530
  on quantum theory, 2:126, 2:529–530, 3:178–180
  on wave function completeness, 8:210
Boileau, Nicolas, 1:49, **1:639–641,** 5:572, 6:598
Boineburg, Johann Christian von, Leibniz and, 5:250–251, 5:266
Bois-Reymond, Paul du, 2:501
Bölcseleti Folyoirat (periodical), 7:145
Bolingbroke, Henry St. John, **1:641–642,** 2:684–685
  deism and, 2:683–684, 2:691
  friends and colleagues of, 2:687
Bolívar, Simón, 5:205
Bollack, Jean, on Empedocles, 3:209, 3:213
Bollnow, O. F., on Scheler-Hartmann school, 3:422
Bölsche, Wilhelm, 7:83
Bolsheviks
  Karsavin and, 5:42
  Lenin and, 5:279
Boltzmann, Ludwig, **1:643–645,** 4:86, 4:672
  atomism and, 1:387
  on entropy, 1:221
  on equilibrium theory, 7:538
  on Maxwell-Boltzmann energy distribution, 4:677
  on physics of gases, 7:537–538
  Planck and, 7:577–578

Boltzmann, Ludwig, ***continued***
rational "pictures" of, in Schrödinger's physics, 8:657–658
on temporal symmetry, 7:475
on time, 7:537, 7:540–542, 7:565–566, 9:470
Bolyai, János, 5:461, 9:150
Bolzano, Bernard, **1:646–648**
on continuous functions, 2:496
and history of logic, 5:445–446
and infinite set, 4:658
on logical validity, 5:234
Marty and, 5:729
Scholz and, 8:644
Bon sens du curé Meslier, Le (d'Holbach), 2:266–267, 6:154
Bonald, Louis Gabriel Ambroise, Vicomte de, **1:648–649,** 2:412
de Maistre and, 5:660
French Revolution and, 9:520
Lamennais and, 5:177
Bonatelli, Francesco, **1:649**
Bonaventure, St. *See* St. Bonaventure
Bondage, in Indian philosophy, 5:326
Bondi, Hermann, and cosmology, 2:558, 2:562, 2:565
Bonet, Nicholas, 3:354, 8:704
Bonhoeffer, Dietrich, **1:655–657**
Boniface VIII, Pope, 3:133
Bonino, José Miguez, 5:331
BonJour, Laurence
a priori justification and, 5:80
on conditions of knowledge, 3:272–273
philosophical supporting evidence, 5:85
Bonnet, Charles, **1:657–658**
Lessing and, 7:100
Maine de Biran and, 5:656
Tetens and, 9:403
Bonnety, Augustine, 9:521
"Boo-hurrah" theory of ethics, 3:204
Book of Beliefs and Opinions (Saadya), 8:586
Book of Calculations (Swineshead), 9:342
Book of Creation (Sefer ha-Yeṣīra) (Philo), 4:811
"Book of Elements" (Israeli), 4:764, 4:814
"Book of Five Substances" (Isreali), 4:814
Book of Healing (Avicenna), 7:611, 7:612
"Book of Proof and Demonstration in Aid of the Despised Religion, The" (Halevi), 4:815
Book of Roots, The (Albo), 1:102
Book of Salvation (Avicenna), 7:611
Book of Sentences (Lombard), 7:259–261
Alexander of Hales and, 1:113
in medieval philosophy, 6:99
Ockham on, 9:770–771
Olivi on, 7:12
Wodeham on, 9:821
Book of Splendor, The, 5:3
"Book of Substances" (Israeli), 4:764
Book of Supreme World-ordering Principles (Shao Yong), 9:6
Book of the Pious, 5:3
"Book on Spirit and Soul" (Israeli), 4:764
Book trade, Enlightenment and, 3:245
Boole, George, **1:658–661**
and Boolean algebra, 5:535. *See also* Boolean algebras
friends and colleagues of, 2:709
and Jevons, 4:807–808
and logic, 5:440, 5:449–450, 5:460–461, 7:163
precursors of, 2:709
and Venn, 9:657
Boolean algebras
definition of, 5:535
diagrams in, 5:561–563
Jevons's machine and, 5:565
lattice diagram for, 5:563
logical diagrams of, 5:563
Venn diagrams and, 5:561
Boolean functions, definition of, 5:535
Boole's calculus, Jevons on, 5:450
"Boole's Calculus of Logic" (Peirce), 1:659
Boolos, George
Frege and, 3:732
and logic, 5:491, 5:532, 8:708
on paradoxes in Frege, 5:517
on plural quantifiers, 8:197
on sets, 4:664
Bopp, Franz, 8:794
Borderline cases, 5:111
absolute and relative, 5:109
inquiry into, futility of, 5:111
truth-value of, 9:624
in vagueness, 9:623
Boredom, as enemy of aesthetic standpoint, 5:63
Borel, Émile, 2:501, 9:148
Borel-Kolmogorov paradox, 9:226
Borges, Jorge Luis
on autographic/allographic distinction, 1:317
Latin American philosophy and, 5:204
Borgia, Cesare, Machiavelli and, 5:627
Borgmann, Albert, on ethics and technology, 7:548
Boring, E. G., on Wundt, 9:850
Borne, Étienne, on cosmic brain argument, 1:369–370
Borozdy i mezhi (Furrows and Boundaries) (Ivanov), 4:767
Bosanquet, Bernard, **1:661–664**
Bradley and, 1:675–680, 4:559
Creighton and, 2:592
on ethics, 3:416
on matter-mind dualism, 2:595
political philosophy of, 7:668–669
Prichard on, 5:94
on punishment, 8:166
on social facts, 9:95
on state as individual, 4:560
on ugliness, 9:563
Wilson on, 5:94
Bosanquet, Philippa Ruth. *See* Foot, Philippa
Boscovich, Giussepe, on belief in external objects, 9:248
Boscovich, Roger Joseph, **1:664–666,** 3:551, 8:699
Bose-Einstein condensation, 3:178
Bosons, 3:636
Boss, Medard
on existential psychoanalysis, 3:510–511
on phenomenology, 7:301
Bosses, Bartholomew des, Leibniz and, 5:254
Bossuet, Jacques Bénigne, **1:667–668**
Augustinianism and, 1:404
Fénelon and, 3:603
on history, 7:388
La Bruyère and, 5:166–167
on providence, 3:35
Simon and, 9:33
Boström, Christopher Jacob, **1:668–669**
Boswell, James, and Johnson (Dr. Samuel), 4:853
Botanic Garden, The (Darwin), 2:631
Botanisten och filosofen (Hägerström), 4:205
Both/neither logics, 5:689–690
Botkin, S. P., 7:149
Böttger, J. F., Tschirnhaus and, 9:549
Bottom. *See* Absurdity
Boucher, François, Diderot and, 3:76
Boucher, Jonathon, on Filmer, 3:637
Bougainville, Louis-Antoine de, on human nature, 3:246
Bouillier, Francisque, on Jansenism and Cartesianism, 4:790
Boulainvilliers, Henri, Comte de, **1:669–671,** 9:193

Boulton, Matthew, and Lunar Society of Birmingham, 3:247
Bound, of set, definition of, 5:535
Bound occurrence, 3:648, 3:651, 5:535
Bound variable, definition of, 5:535
Boundless, the, 1:185. *See also* *Apeiron/Peras*
Bound-variable anaphora, 1:171–172
Bourbaki, 9:271
Bourdieu, Pierre, on art, 1:300
Bourdin, Pierre, Descartes and, 2:737–738, 2:749–750
Bourgeois drama, Diderot and, 3:76
Bourgeois ideology
 art and, 1:297
 Engels on, 3:64
 Marx on, 3:64
Bourgeois liberalism, Strauss on, 9:263
Bourgeois right, economic value equalization and, 2:362
Bourget, Paul, Taine and, 9:364
Bourguet, Louis, Leibniz and, 5:274
Boutroux, Émile
 Bergson and, 1:563
 Lachelier and, 5:169
 Latin American philosophy and, 5:208
Boutroux, Étienne, 5:164
Bowden, Peta, 3:580
Bowman, Peter, 2:524
Bowne, Borden Parker, **1:671–672**
 Lotze and, 5:583
 matter-mind dualism in, 2:595
 on personalism, 7:233–235
Bowood Circle, Bentham in, 1:551
Boyd, Richard
 Field and, 3:633
 on inference to best explanation, 8:691
 and nonreductive physicalism, 6:643
Boyle, Robert, **1:672–675**
 atomism of, 1:386–387
 on color, 2:332
 Epicurus and, 3:265
 on God, nature of, 7:557–558
 Leibniz and, 5:251
 Locke and, 5:374
 physicotheology and, 7:557–558
 on qualities, primary and secondary, 5:380, 8:8
 on science and religion, 2:685–686
 Spinoza and, 9:175
Boyle Lectures, 2:685–686
 Clarke (S.), 7:559
 Derham (W.), 7:559
 physicotheology in, 7:559
Boyle's law, 5:222–223, 6:677–678
Bracketed existence, in phenomenology, 7:285–289
Bracton, Henry de, 9:139
Bradford Books, 2:711
Bradlaugh, Charles
 on atheism, 1:360
 on existence of God, 1:362
 on rights of atheists, 1:358
Bradley, Francis Herbert, **1:675–680**
 on absolute idealism, 1:12
 on appearance, 1:232
 Bosanquet and, 1:675–680, 4:559
 on common-sense view of world, 4:558
 on duty, 3:153
 Eliot (T. S.) and, 3:185
 and epistemology, 3:310–311, 5:91
 on ethics, 3:416
 on God, personality of, 4:111–112
 on the Good, 4:153
 Hegelianism of, 6:193
 Hume's "Of Miracles" and, 6:270
 identity theory of truth and, 9:537
 on immediate experience, 3:515–516
 James's correspondence with, 4:786
 on Jevons's machine, 5:565
 Marcel and, 3:504
 on matter-mind dualism, 2:595
 on metaphysics, 6:206
 Mill (John Stuart) and, 3:312
 Moore (G. E.) and, 3:314
 pantheism and, 7:95
 on perception, 8:815
 on pragmatism, 8:799
 Prichard on, 5:94
 Royce on, 4:559
 Schiller (Ferdinand) and, 8:623
 Stebbing and, 9:236
 Taylor (Aflred) and, 9:373
 on time, 6:206
 Wilson on, 5:94
Bradwardine, Thomas, **1:680–681,** 5:69
 Albert of Saxony and, 1:101
 on Aristotelian law of motion, 3:687
 on Duns Scotus, 8:704
 Kilvington and, 5:68
 on liar paradox, 5:434
 Ockhamism and, 7:8
 Swineshead and, 9:342
Brady, Emily, on environmental aesthetics, 3:255–256
Brahe, Tycho, 5:50–51, 8:683
Brahman, **1:681–685,** 4:135
 in Advaita system, 4:629
 concept of, emergence of, 7:94–95
 in Dvaita philosophy, 4:630
 knowledge of, 7:95
 as one reality, 1:684, 4:629
 and self, 4:135, 8:719
 Tagore on, 9:363–364
 as truth, 9:542–543
Brahmanism
 vs. Buddhism, 6:255
 pessimism in, 7:246
 primary scriptures of, 5:116
Brain
 activity in, as criteria for life and death, 1:8
 Alcmaeon of Croton on, 1:104
 Bergson on, 1:564
 binding problem in, 6:566–567
 central state materialism of, 9:65
 in Chinese room argument, 2:240
 Clarke on, 2:273
 in cognitive science, 2:297
 computers and, 5:566
 conscious qualitative states and, 2:451
 cosmic, 1:368–371
 evolutionary significance of, 9:721
 function of, and consciousness, 2:456
 hemispheres in, 6:565–566
 identity theory and, 8:155
 and immortality, 4:617
 in mental states, 9:720
 and mind, 1:286–287, 6:260
 mind-body problem and, 7:468. *See also* Mind-body problem; Mind-body relationship
 in nutrient bath, existence as, 8:172
 physical causality and conservation of motion, 2:90
 physiological processes in, 5:128
 processes in, topological relations between, 5:128
 Putnam on, 8:172
 qualitative consciousness and, 2:450
 as seat of thought, 1:104
 transplantation of, personal identity and, 7:231–232
Brain death, medico-jurisprudence on, 6:95
Brain scan, religion and, 8:381
Brainchild (Dennett), 2:710–712
Brain-in-a-vat arguments, on fallibilism, 3:274–275
"Brains and Behavior" (Putnam), 1:534, 8:84
Brain-states, 5:128

Brainstorms (Dennett), on introspection, 4:721
Braithwaite, John, 9:5
Braithwaite, Richard Bevan, **1:685–687**
on belief, 5:98–99
on circularity in induction, 4:640
on purposive activity, 9:384
Brakel, Jaap van, on quantum mechanics and chemistry, 2:143
Bramhall, John, on determinism, 3:26
Branch systems, 9:469–470
Branching quantifiers, 8:197–198
Brand, Myles
on event theory, 3:467
on primary deviance, 1:16–17
Brandenburg, elector of, Locke and, 5:374
Brandenburger, Adam, 4:20
Brandom, Robert B., pragmatic theory of truth and, 9:537
Brandt, R. B., **1:687–688,** 9:82
on emotivism, 3:207, 3:426
expressivism of, 8:52
Brann, William, deism and, 2:691
Brann's Iconoclast (Brann), 2:691
Bratman, Michael, on intentions, 1:20, 4:702–703, 8:674
Braude, Stephen E., 7:116
Braudel, Fernand, on history, 7:392–393
Braun, David
on demonstratives, 2:708
on semantics, 8:77
Brave New World (Huxley), 9:621
Brazil, liberation theology in, 5:211
Brazilian philosophy
contemporary period, 5:207, 5:210
positivism in, 5:206–207
Breaks, in coherence of knowledge about man, 3:700
Brecht, Bertolt, Adorno and, 1:26
Brecht, Martin, 5:617
Breitinger, Johann Jakob, Lavater and, 5:213
Brentano, Franz, **1:688–693**
analysis of good by, 4:150
on belief, behavioral effects of, 5:98
as Cartesian dualist, 5:144
on consciousness, 2:453–455
Ehrenfels and, 3:176
on epistemology, 3:311
on essence and existence, 3:351
on ethics, 3:418, 3:421
on existence, 3:495–496
existentialism and, 3:502
Freud and, 3:737
on higher-order consciousness and, 2:454
on intentionality, 3:502, 4:704–705, 7:290–291, 8:802
on introspection, 4:720
Külpe and, 5:160–161
Marty and, 5:728
metaethics of, 6:156–157
neo-Kantianism and, 3:311
on objects of mental phenomena, 1:689–690
on phenomenology, 7:282, 7:290–291
and realism, 3:311, 6:584
on self-observation, 5:363
Stout and, 9:260
Stumpf and, 9:280
and theory of assumptions, 6:116
on thinking, 9:418
on time, 9:488–489
Twardowski and, 9:554
on unity of consciousness, 3:120
Brethren of the Common Life, 9:423
Breton, Andre-François, 3:222–223
Breuer, Josef
Freud and, 3:737
hypnosis used by, 3:737
Breuil, abbey at, prior of, 2:757
Breviary of Aesthetics (Croce), 2:601
Breviloquium (Bonaventure), 1:651–654
"Brevis Demonstratio Erroris Memorabilis Cartesii" ("A Short Demonstration of a Remarkable Error of Descartes") (Leibniz), 3:228, 5:269
Brewer, Bill, on perception, 7:192
Bride of Messina, The (Schiller, Friedrich), 8:627
Bridge identities, 3:606
Bridge principles, 4:310, 6:644, 8:285
Bridges, Douglas, on arithmetic continuum, 2:504
Bridgewater Treatises, 2:641, 7:560–561
Bridgman, Laura, on common consent for God's existence, 2:346
Bridgman, Percy William, **1:693–694**
Mach and, 5:625
operationalism and, 3:85, 7:29
Brief Disquisition of the Law of Nature, A (Cumberland, abridged by Tyrrell), 2:614
Brief Lives (Aubrey), 3:171
Brief Outline on the Study of Theology (Schleiermacher), 8:633
Briefe betreffend den allerneusten Zustand der Religion und der Wissenschaften in Gross-Brittannien (Alberti), 2:688
Briefe, den jetzigen Zustand der Schönen Wissenschaften betreffend (Letters on the state of the arts) (Nicolai), 6:598
Briefe über die ästhetische Erzieung des Menschen ("Letters on the Aesthetic Education of Man") (Schiller, Friedrich), 1:54, 8:490, 8:627
Briefe über *die Bibel im Volkston* (Bahrdt), 1:457
Brier, Robert, 7:116
Brightman, Edgar Sheffield, **1:694–695**
on evil, 3:471
on personalism, 1:362, 7:233–236
Brillo Box (Warhol), 1:299, 2:627
Bringsjord, Selmer, on induction, 3:711
Brink, David, 4:150
Brinon, Marie de, 5:253
Britain
deism in, 2:682–687, 2:691
science and religion in, 2:685–686
sovereignty issues in, 9:140–141
British empiricism, 3:216–219
antilogicism of, 5:447, 5:456
on concepts, 2:417
Dewey and, 3:45
and epistemology, 3:298–306
Helmholtz and, 4:303–304
James on, 4:784
Kant and, 3:306
Laas on, 5:163
logical positivism and, 5:524
skepticism in, 3:218–219
British idealism
and ethics, 3:416–418
Hegelianism in, 4:286
British intuitionism, 4:735
British Journal of Psychology, 9:65
British Liberal Party, 5:320
British metaphysics, 6:198
British moral philosophy, 6:433
British Museum, Westermarck at, 9:738–739
British philosophy, *vs.* continental philosophy, 2:488–489
British theology, on Fall, 3:474
Broad, Charlie Dunbar, **1:695–700**
on agent causation, 1:90
on altruism, 9:382
on Augustine, 9:485
on change, 9:498–499
on common sense, 2:357
on compromise theory of time, 9:470
on emergence, 3:192, 7:469
ethics of, 1:699
on free will, 3:14–15
on future, 9:498
on Good, 3:419

on inductive conclusions, 4:641
as intuitionist, 4:735
on knowledge, 1:696–698
on materialism, 6:15
on mind-body problem, 6:261
on moral necessity, 2:713
on parapsychology, 7:113–116
on precognition, 7:754
property dualism of, 6:133
on sensa, 8:816
on sense datum, 8:813
on Sidgwick, 3:416–418, 9:22
on specious present, 9:483
on time, 9:470, 9:475, 9:498–499
virtue ethics and, 9:687
Brochard, Victor
Lachelier and, 5:169
Łukasiewicz on, 5:607
Brockelmann, Carl, on Arab logic, 5:417
Brod, Max, 5:5
Brodbeck, May, Lehrer and, 5:248
Broglie, Louis de
on determinism, 3:33
"pilot wave" theory of, 8:203
and Schrödinger's wave mechanics, 8:657
Broken world theory, 3:254–255
Brooks, Harvey, 8:674
Brooks, Rodney
on connectionism, 2:444–445
on robotics, 1:348, 5:635
Brothers Karamazov, The (Dostoevsky), 3:99–101, 6:618
Brouwer, Luitzen Egbertus Jan, **1:700–703**
on continuum, 2:491, 2:501–504
and dimensional invariance proof, 2:27
and intuitionism, 2:491, 4:737, 5:468, 5:491, 5:546, 6:21, 6:676
on law of excluded middle, 6:527
synthetic differential geometry and, 2:510
vs. Tarski, 9:366
on transfinite induction, 4:741
on ur-intuition, 4:738
Wittgenstein and, 9:802
Brown, James Robert, on thought experiments, 9:455
Brown, John, and Parker (T.), 7:122
Brown, Lancelot 'Capability,' 3:257
Brown, Norman O., 7:523
Brown, P., on Augustine, 1:401
Brown, Thomas, **1:703–705**
and crisis of skepticism, 9:56
critique of, 3:608
Hamilton on, 8:135–136
Martineau and, 5:726
Mill (John Stuart) on, 8:136
and psychology, 18th-century British, 8:135
on relative suggestion, 9:260
Shepherd on, 9:10
on syllogism, 5:501
Brown Book (Wittgenstein), 9:809–810
Brown-Brownson case (Shoemaker), 7:231
Browne, Peter, 1:359
Brownian motion, Einstein and, 3:178, 3:181–182
Brownson, Orestes Augustus, **1:705–706,** 6:572
Brücke, Ernst von, 3:232
Brucker, Johann Jacob
Cousin and, 2:580
Encyclopédie and, 3:223
Brudzewski, Wojeich, and Copernicus, 2:533
Brueghel, Pieter, 1:304
Bruijn, Nicolaas Govert de, 4:742
Bruner, Jerome, theories of perception, 3:676
Brunner, Emil, 1:479, **1:706–708,** 3:533
Bruno, Giordano, **1:708–713**
Copernicanism of, 1:710–711
cosmology of, 1:711
death of, 1:709–710, 2:750
Ficino and, 3:624
hermetic philosophy and, 1:710
on infinity of God, 4:668–669
Jacboi and, 1:11
on material universe, 3:354
on memory, 1:711–712
and panpsychism, 7:83
and pantheism, 7:96, 8:621
on plenitude principle, 5:593
Sanches and, 8:595
Schelling and, 8:621
Sigwart on, 9:29
Spaventa and, 9:159
Toland and, 2:683
trail of, 1:709–710
on universe, 2:750–751
on world soul, 7:614
Bruno, oder über das göttliche und natüraliche Prinzip der Dinge (Schelling), 8:619
Brunschvicg, Léon, **1:713–714,** 7:567
Brunswick, Johann Friedrich, duke of
Leibniz and, 5:251
Lessing and, 5:295
Brush, Stephen G., 9:218
Brute force theories of metaphor, 6:168
Bryan, William Jennings, on evolution, 2:641
Bryce, James, 9:142
B-series, McTaggart on, 6:78
Bub, Jeffrey, 6:278–279
Buber, Martin, **1:714–717**
on afterlife, 4:618
on belief, 1:716
and existential psychoanalysis, 3:510
on faith, 1:716, 3:536
on Hasidic view of life, 5:3
and I-It relationship, 1:715, 2:167, 4:112
Kaufmann and, 5:46
Marcel and, 5:700
Mead and, comparison of, 6:82
in modern Jewish philosophy, 1:715, 4:829
Nishida and, comparison of, 6:625
Scheler and, 8:616
Shestov and, 9:13
Bucciarelli, Louis, 7:550, 9:78
Bucer, Martin, 8:830
Buch von dem Diener (The Life of the Servant) (Suso), 9:335
Buchanan, Allen, 3:562
Buchanan, George, 9:52
Buchanan, James, 7:351
Buchanan, Richard, 7:550
Buchenau, Artur, 6:543
Büchlein der ewigen Weisheit, Das (The Little Book of Eternal Wisdom) (Suso), 9:335
Büchlein der Wahrheit, Das (The Little Book of Truths) (Suso), 9:335
Büchner, Ludwig
atheism of, 3:58
on common consent for God's existence, 2:346
Engels and, 3:58–59
materialism of, 6:11
as mechanist, 3:612
nihilism and, 6:617
Buck, Brian, 4:672
Buckland, William, 7:560
Buckle, Henry Thomas, **1:717–720**
on determinism, 3:37
Gobineau on, 4:106
materialism of, 9:516
Toynbee and, 9:516
Budd, Malcolm, on environmental aesthetics, 3:256
Budde, Johann Franz, **1:721**
Buddha
being in the state of, 5:135
gurus of, 6:109
in Indian meditation practices, 6:108
life of, 1:722–724

Buddha, *continued*
soteriology of, causality in, 2:111
teaching of, deliberation and reasoning on, 5:117
trustworthiness of, 5:121
understanding of karma, 5:42
veneration of, 1:723
Buddha nature
Chan on, 2:168
li and, 4:794
realization of, 1:723
text tradition on, 1:737
Buddhabhadra, Chinese Buddhist translations of, 1:736
Buddhadatta, 4:632
Buddhaghosa, 4:632
Buddhapālita
on correct reasoning, 1:731–732
Nāgārjuna and, 5:411
Buddhism, **1:721–726,** 2:153–155, **2:160–170,** 2:220, 5:316
Abhidharma, 1:740, 4:632
act of knowing in, 1:753
afflictions in, 1:724
afterlife in, 6:256–257
analogy in, 5:122
arahat in, 5:328
asceticism in, 1:352
atheistic, 6:493
ātman in, 5:328
awakening in, 1:722, 5:328
being in, 1:722, 1:741
belief in, 1:754, 2:349–350
Buddhism, Pudgalavāda school of, 5:328
causality in, 1:734, 1:739, 1:754–757, 2:111, 2:221
Chan and Zen, 1:726–753
and Cheng Hao, 2:145
and Cheng Yi, 2:145
in Chinese culture, 2:169–170
Chinese philosophy and, 2:153–155, 2:160–170
Chinese texts in, 1:736–737
Chung on, 5:137
community in, 1:723–726
conceit in, 6:621
concentration in, 1:722, 1:729–730, 6:254
conceptual structures in, 5:119, 6:255–257
Confucianism and, 2:155, 2:163, 2:169–170, 4:794, 5:316
consciousness in, 1:724, 2:166
continuity in, 6:256
courage in, 1:722
Daoism and, 2:186, 2:191
definition of, 1:721
denial of permanent self in, 8:718
desire in, 1:352
Dge-lugs, **1:731–736**
dharma in, 1:724, 2:154
Dignaga and, 5:117
dogma and, 3:97
doubt in, 6:621
emotion in, 5:328
empiricism in, 2:164, 6:256
emptiness in, 1:731–732, 1:738–744, 2:154, 2:161–164, 2:167, 2:221, 5:328–329
enlightenment in, 2:162, 2:166–168, 2:219, 5:328, 6:621
epistemology in, 1:748, 1:753–757
eternal life in, 6:256–257
ethics in, 1:748, 2:198–199, 6:108
experience in, 6:256
faith in, 1:722, 2:168, 6:255
family in, 1:723
fictions in, 1:742–743
Four Dharmadhāus as fundamental to, 1:738–739
four noble truths of, 5:328
four-cornered negation in, 6:471, 9:543
good works in, 1:723
gurus in, 6:109
Hinayana, 5:328
history of, 7:486–487
Hua yan. *See* Huayan Buddhism
inference in, 5:122
Japanese, 4:793
karma in, as intentional activity, 1:748
knowledge in, 5:116
in Korea, 4:833, 5:134–136
liberation in, 5:328–329
literature of, 4:632–633
logic and, 5:411–413, 5:416, 9:585–586
Mādhyamaka, **1:740–746**
Mahayana. *See* Mahayana Buddhism
meditation in, 1:726–727, 6:108–109
Middle Doctrine and dharma character, summary of, 2:154
mind and mental states in, **6:253–258**
on moral perfection, 7:195
on motives, 5:41
mysticism of, 6:443–445
name of Amida Buddha in, 9:14–15
and Neo-Confucian idealistic philosophy, 2:157
neo-Daoist influence on, 2:191
nirvāṇa in, **6:620–622**
nominalism in, 9:544, 9:582–587
nonbeing in, 9:723
Pali Canon in, 7:486–487
perception in, 9:544
pessimism in, 7:246
in popular neo-Confucianism, 2:181
Prāsaṅgika-Madhyamikas vs. Svātantrika-Madhyamaka on, 1:733–734
as psychosomatic discipline, 1:730
Pure Land (Shin), 2:168–169, 9:13–14
and realism, 1:745
reality in, 4:793
rebirth in, 8:331–333
regulation of emotion in, 3:200–201
reincarnation and, 8:331
sangha in, 1:724–725
Sanlun, 2:161–163
schools of, **1:726–753**
Schopenhauer and, 8:655
self in, 2:199
senses in, 1:745, 5:118
skepticism in, 9:544
Stace and, 9:200
substance in, 5:120
Svātantrika-Prāsaṅgika distinction, 1:744
ten mysteries of, 1:737
tenet-system text analysis in, 1:733–734
Tiantai, 1:727, 2:154, 2:163–166, 2:220
ultimate reality in, 2:220–221
universal belief in God and, 2:349–350
universals in, 1:754–757, 5:119, 9:582–587
Vasubandhu on, 1:751–752
Vijñānavāda, 5:329
virtue in, 1:722
and Western philosophy, 2:159
wisdom in, 1:722–724
wisdom literature of, 9:793
Xiong Shili on, 2:159
Yogācāra, 1:745, **1:746–753**
and atomism, 1:383
and awareness, 5:120
Buddhist epistemology, **1:753–758,** 9:14
Buddhist Logic (Stcherbatsky), 4:633
Buddhist Teaching of Totality (Chang), 1:739
Budget of Paradoxes (De Morgan), 2:709

Buffier, Claude, on common sense, 2:355
Buffon, Georges-Louis Leclerc, Comte de, **1:758–759**
Diderot and, 3:72–73
on race, 3:247
Bühler, Karl, 1:469, 4:721
Building principle, in compositionality, 2:370
Bukyō shōgaku (Yamaga Sokō), 9:859
Bulgakov, Sergei Nikolaevich, **1:759–761,** 9:529
Florovskii and, 3:673
Ivanov and, 4:768
Karsavin and, 5:43
Kireevskii and, 5:75
Solov'ëv and, 9:126
Buller, David, on evolutionary psychology, 3:486
Bullough, Edward, 1:36, 1:64, **1:761–762**
Bultmann, Rudolf, **1:762–765**
on biblical eschatology, 3:348
Gogarten and, 4:144
Pannenberg and, 7:80, 7:81
theology of, 3:505–506
Bundle theory
particulars in, 6:180, 7:24
properties in, 6:199, 7:24
relations and, 7:25
Bunge, Mario
analytic philosophy and, 5:210
on philosophy of technology, 7:543
and political instability, 5:211
Burack, Benjamin, 5:566
Burali-Forti paradox, 5:551
of ordinal number, 5:517
Ramsey on, 5:468
in set theory, 5:520
Burana, on Aristotle, 5:439
Burbury, S., on physics of gases, 7:537
Burckhardt, Jakob, **1:765–766,** 8:649
Burge, Tyler, 9:351
on belief, 8:83
on externalism, 7:472
on meaning, 5:190
on mental content, 2:477–478
on semantic paradoxes, 5:522
on truth, 5:317, 5:522
Burial, as universal principle, Vico on, 9:674–675
Buridan, John, **1:766–770**
on ampliation, 5:431–432
Aristotelianism of, 1:430
on consequences, 5:434
correspondence theory of truth and, 9:534
on force, 3:687
on impetus theory, 4:621
on liar paradox, 2:541–542
Marsilius of Inghen and, 5:721
Nicolas of Autrecourt and, 6:601
Ockhamism of, 7:8
on states of affairs, 9:822
on syllogistics, 5:435
on true as adjective, 2:547
on truth, 2:541–542
Burke, Edmund, **1:770–772**
on aesthetics, 1:51–52, 1:771
Bachofen and, 1:442
on beauty and sublimity, 1:513
on Bolingbroke, 1:641
on deism, 2:691
Emerson and, 3:195
Garve on, 4:24
on law, 7:424
Mendelssohn and, 6:131
on nature, 3:254
Paine on, 7:73
political philosophy of, 4:751, 7:665–666
Savigny and, 8:614
on sublime, 9:293
on tragedy, 9:522
Burkhart, William, 5:566
Burley, Walter, **1:772–775**
Diogenes Laertius and, 3:89
on syllogism, 5:427
Burman, Frans
Clauberg and, 2:284
Descartes on, 2:739, 2:754
on Spinoza's *Theological-Political Treatise,* 9:182
Burnet, Gilbert, Norris and, 6:655
Burnet, John, 5:93, 9:107
Burnet, Thomas
and broken world theory, 3:254–255
Swedenborg and, 9:336
Burns, Robert, on Stewart, 9:246
Burrell, David, on Aquinas, 9:447
Burthogge, Richard, **1:775–776,** 8:777
Burton, David, 1:742
Burton, Robert
on deism, 2:681
pessimism of, 7:247
Bury, J. B., on chance in history, 3:38
Bush, George H. W., and Persian Gulf War, 7:157
Bush, George W., 9:42
Bushidō, ethics of, codified, 9:859
Business, 7:333
Business ethics, **1:776–780**
computer ethics and, 2:397–398
in medical ethics, 6:93
Buss, David, and evolutionary psychology, 3:481–483, 3:486
Butler, Bishop
on forgiveness, 3:697
on personal identity, 7:230
Butler, Joseph, **1:780–784**
on altruism and self-interest, 3:171–172
on benevolence, 3:408
on conscience, 2:445, 3:408
on deism, 2:683–686, 5:220
on egoism, 3:361
ethics of, 1:780–782
Green on, 4:179
on human nature, 3:171–172
Newman (Joseph Henry) and, 6:579
on personal identity, 4:612, 7:216–217
physicotheology in, 7:559
Shaftesbury and, 9:2
Sidgwick and, 9:25
on soul, 3:119–120
theology of, 1:782–783
Butler, Judith
and antirealist view of gender, 3:588–589
on identifying "woman," 3:565
on sex/gender essentialism, 3:588
Butler, Samuel, **1:784–785**
Butzer, Martin, on Franck, 3:713
Buytendijk, F. J. J., 7:320–321
Buzhen kong lun (On the emptiness of the unreal) (Sengzho), 2:221
Byrnes, James, 9:397
Bythos, 9:632
Byzantine mysticism, Gregory of Nyssa and, 4:182
Byzantine philosophy, **1:786–790**
in humanist tradition, 7:613
Pletho in, 7:630–631
Psellus and, 7:610

C

Cabala. *See* Kabbalah
Cabala del cavallo pegaseo (Cabal of the horse Pegasus) (Bruno), 1:709
Cabalistic writings, and Fludd, 3:674
Cabanis, Pierre-Jean Georges, **2:1–3**
Destutt de Tracy and, 2:760
La Mettrie and, 5:181
on language as analytic method, 8:788
Maine de Biran and, 5:655
Rapports du physique et du moral de l'homme, 6:10

Cabot, J. E., 6:572
Cady, Duane L., 7:157
Caelestius, on nature and sin, 7:175
Caelo et Mundo, De (Aristotle), 8:703
Caesoninus, Piso, 3:263
Cage, John, 1:26, 1:300, 1:321
Cahiers (Weil), 9:737
Cahiers pour une morale (Notebooks for an ethics) (Sartre), 8:607, 8:610
Cain, responsibility and, 4:831
Caird, Edward, **2:3–4**, 4:108
Cairns, Dorion, **2:4–6**
Caitanya, 4:630
Cajetan, Cardinal, **2:6–7**
 Sylvester of Ferrara and, 9:344
 Thomism and, 9:445
Cakras, in meditation, 6:109
Calabresi, Guido, 7:461
Calas, Jean, Voltaire and, 3:245, 9:712–713
Calcidius, Neoplatonism and, 6:555, 7:143, 7:611
Calcolo geometrico (Peano), 5:461
Calculability
 Church on, 5:476
 computability and, 2:380
 computing machines and, 2:402
 as conversational implicature test, 2:527–528
 decidability as, 2:378
 effective functions of, 2:374–376
 of functions, 2:401
 Kronecker on, 2:400
Calculability functions
 Dedekind on, 2:400
 Kronecker on, 2:400
Calculating machine, human consciousness as, 5:74
Calculation
 computing machines and, 2:400–402
 of partial functions in computability theory, 2:373–374
 Ryle on, 9:422
 Turing machines for, 2:375–376
"Calculations by Man and Machine: Conceptual Analysis" (Sieg), 2:407
Calculus
 actual infinities in, 4:656
 applied functional, 5:536
 Berkeley on, 2:495
 of binary relations, 9:370
 Cohen (Hermann) on, 6:542
 conceptual, 1:343
 of correlation, introduced by Krueger, 5:156
 definition of, 5:535–536
 Frege and, 1:343
 functional. *See* Functional calculus
 geometric approach to, 6:591
 infinite and continuum in, 2:494–495
 infinitesimal methods in, 2:507, 4:652
 Leibniz and, 5:442–443, 6:590
 motion and, 6:408
 Newton and, 6:590
 number and, 6:671
 of probability, 1:495–502, 8:27–28
 propositional, 3:537, 9:370
 psychology and, 8:129
 of relations, 7:168, 8:786
 scientific theory as, 1:685
 Tarski on, 9:366–367, 9:370
 time in, 9:462
"Calculus of Individuals and Its Uses" (Goodman), 4:158
Calculus Universalis (Universal calculus) (Leibniz), 5:252, 5:273
Calderoni, Mario, **2:7–8**
 de Finetti and, 2:663
 Vailati and, 9:629
Calibration, in Bohmian mechanics, 1:633–634
Calkins, Mary Whiton, on personalism, 7:233
Callahan, Daniel, 6:96
Callicott, J. Baird, on environmental ethics, 3:259
Callimachus, Diodorus Cronus and, 3:87
Calvelli-Adorno, Maria, 1:25
Calvez, Jean-Yves, on alienation, 1:122
Calvin, John, **2:8–12**, 3:530–531
 Channing on, 2:130
 colleagues of, 2:681
 and divine command theories of ethics, 3:93
 on Fall, 3:473
 on heaven, hell, and judgment, 2:249
 influence of, 2:11
 on knowledge of God and self, 2:8–10
 medieval church and, 3:405
 on predestination, 3:10
 on redemption, 2:249
 and Reformation, 8:296–298
 Schleiermacher and, 8:634
 Servetus and, 8:831
 social and political teachings of, 2:10–11
Calvinism
 Bayle on, 1:502–503
 on creation, 3:475
 Cudworth and, 2:610–611
 Culverwell and, 2:613
 Edwards (Jonathan) and, 3:166–169
 on equality, 3:329–330
 on evil, 3:474
 Johnson (Samuel) and, 4:851
 Milton and, 6:249
 as new dogmatism, 9:51
 Norris on, 6:655
 Palmer (E.) on, 7:78
 in Reformation, 8:296
 religious toleration and, 1:502
 social contract theory and, 9:81
 voluntaristic morality in, 2:13
 Whichcote on, 9:746
Calvinists, as compatibilists, 3:695
Cambridge Companion to Mill, The, 6:232
Cambridge Philosophical Transactions (periodical), contributors to, 2:709
Cambridge platonists, **2:12–14**, 7:615
 Cudworth and, 2:609
 Culverwell and, 2:612
 Cumberland and, 2:614
 deism and, 2:682, 2:685
 Edwards (Jonathan) and, 3:167
 Locke and, 3:407, 5:376–378
 More (Henry), 6:395–397
 on natural law, 3:406
 Norris as, 6:655–656
 Shaftesbury and, 9:1
 Smith (John) as, 9:69
 socinianism and, 9:100
Cambridge University, Balfour as chancellor of, 1:473
cAMP (cyclic adenosine monophosphate), 6:568
cAMP response element binding proteins (CREB), 6:568
Campanella, Tommaso, **2:14–16**
 Augustinianism and, 1:404
 panpsychism and, 7:83, 7:87
 Spaventa and, 9:159
 Telesio and, 9:391
Campbell, C. A., on determinism, 3:15–18
Campbell, George, on syllogistic reasoning, 5:501
Campbell, Norman Robert, **2:16–19**
Campbell, Sue, on memory, 6:126
Camus, Albert, **2:19–23**
 on absurdity, 2:20–21, 4:748
 on death, 2:650
 Dostoevsky and, 3:99
 ethics, 3:427
 Shestov and, 9:13
 themes in, 3:504
Camus, Jean-Pierre, 9:52

Can, **2:23–26**
"Can Quantum Mechanical Description of Reality Be Considered Complete?" (Einstein, Podolsky, and Rosen), 2:105
"Can the Will Be Caused?" (Ginet), 8:730
Can We Still Be Christians (Eucken), 3:452
Canaye, Philippes, 5:438–439
Cancelability, as conversational implicature test, 2:527–528
Candid Examination of Theism (Romanes), 1:373
Candide (Voltaire), 2:687, 9:709–711
  on evil, 3:469, 3:473
  Gracián and, 4:169
  Leibniz and, 5:254, 5:265
  Lucian of Samosata and, 5:597
  targets of, 3:409–410
Candidness, *vs.* truthfulness, 5:619
Candidus, on God's existence, 2:49
Candrakīrti, 6:470–471
  on correct reasoning, 1:731–732
  on Svātantrika-Prāsaṅgika distinction, 1:744
Candramati, 6:531
Candrānanda, 6:530
Canguilheim, Georges
  Foucault and, 9:275
  students of, 2:693
Canonical artworks, representing women and men, 3:571–572
Canonical ethical theories, women's invisibility in, 3:578
Canonists, 7:421
Canonization
  of Newman (John Henry), 6:583
  of philosophers, 3:569
  postcolonialism and, 7:727
Canons of evidence, 6:273
Canterbury v. Spence, 6:95
Canti (Leopardi), 5:284
Cantor, Georg, **2:26–30**
  on alephs, 5:533
  on algebraic numbers, 5:463
  arithmetization of mathematics and, 5:534–535
  on cardinal numbers, 4:659
  Cauchy rational number sequences in, 2:495
  on continuum, 2:498–499, 4:662, 5:538
  diagonal argument of, 8:833
  diagonal proof of, 5:541
  on Euclidean lines and real numbers, 2:500
  on infinite, 4:657, 5:515, 8:832–835, 9:148, 9:466
  kalām argument on God's existence and, 2:554
  on order types, 8:834
  Peirce and, 7:170
  Russell and, 5:466
  Schröder-Bernstein theorem and, 5:556
  on set theory, 2:500
  on transfinite numbers, 6:671, 8:832–833
  Whitehead and, 5:466
Cantor-Dedekind axiom, 2:490
Cantor-Dedekind continuum, 2:497–499
Cantor-Dedekind theory
  of continuum, 2:490
  as reductionist, 2:501
Cantor's paradox, 5:518, 5:551
Cantor's theorem
  definition of, 5:536
  Skolem on, 5:471
Capacity(ies)
  for action, personhood and, 7:241–242
  in Cartwright, 2:62
  Megarians on, 6:111–112
  mind as, 6:132, 6:259–260
Capillary phenomena, as subject to actions at a distance, 3:688
Capital (Marx), 2:642, 5:731
  on dialectic, 3:67
  Engels and, 3:238
  film version of, 7:384
  Hegel and, 3:57
  on labor, 3:68
Capital punishment
  Camus on, 2:22
  Solov'ëv on, 9:122
Capitalism
  Arendt on, 1:253
  breakdown of, 4:380
  in Chinese thought, 2:180–181
  and communism, 2:362, 2:363
  development of, Weber (Max) on, 9:735
  evolution of, 5:740
  exploitation in, 5:733–734
  feudalism and, 5:732
  global, 2:361, 5:741
  as historical individual, 9:127
  in historical materialism, 4:385
  history of, 4:385
  inevitable destruction of, 5:47
  liberation theology on, 5:331
  Marx on, 2:362, 3:68–69, 5:732–733, 9:90
  moral outlook appropriate to furtherance of, 3:765
  political philosophy and, 7:676–678
  production in, 5:732–733
  sexism and, 3:600
  social contract and, 9:80
  socialism and, 5:740–741
  Sombart on, 9:127
  Sorel on, 9:133
  statist, in Soviet Union, 9:91
  subservience in, 5:732–733
  Veblen on, 9:656
Capitalism and Schizophrenia (Deleuze and Guattari), 2:694–696
Capito, Wolfgang, 8:830
Capreolus, John, **2:30–31,** 9:445
Caractères (La Bruyère), 5:166–167
Caracteristica universalis, Leibniz on, 5:610
Caraka-saṃhitā, on logic, 5:411–413
Card, Claudia, **2:31–32**
  peeling back veils of ignorance, 3:580
Cardano, Girolamo
  Galileo on, 4:9
  panpsychism and, 7:83
  Sanches on, 8:595
  Vanini and, 9:646
Cardinal number
  Cantor on, 5:515–516, 8:833
  definition of, 5:536
  Frege on, 3:730
  Hausdorff on, 8:837
  of infinite collections, 4:659
  inner model theory of, 8:844–847
  large, 4:665, 8:839
  measurable, 8:839–840
  Peirce on, 7:170
  regular, 4:664
  representative of, definition of, 5:555
  in set theory, 8:833–834
  singular cardinals problem in, 8:845
  strongly inaccessible, 4:664–665
  supremum of, 4:664
  transfinite, definition of, 5:558
  ultrafilters in, 8:842
  Woodin on, 8:846
Cardinality(ies), set-theoretic apparatus for talking about, 3:646
Cardinality (power), definition of, 5:536
Cardinality quantifiers, 8:196–197
Cardio-pulmonary resuscitation (CPR), withholding, 6:94

Care
ethics of, 1:158, 2:31
Held on, 4:299
women and girls and, 3:579
Care-based ethics, 3:580
Careful and Strict Enquiry into the Modern Prevailing Notions of the Freedom of Will, A (Chubb), 2:253, 2:684
Carey, Helling v., 6:95
Caring, as motivation, 3:719
Carlile, Richard, deism and, 2:691
Carlson, Allen
on aesthetic experience, 1:33–34
on environmental aesthetics, 3:255–257
Carlson, Greg, 7:645
Carlyle, Alexander, and Ferguson, 3:604
Carlyle, Thomas, **2:32–35**
Emerson and, 3:195
Fichte and, 4:558
"great man" theory of, 3:37
and New England transcendentalism, 6:572
Carmelite order
reforming of, by John of the Cross, 4:845–846
Stein's profession to, 9:239
Carmen de Cometa (Sanches), 8:595
Carmichael, Stokely, Martin Luther King and, 5:73
Carnaldulensian Disputations (Laudino), 3:624
Carnap, Rudolf, **2:35–46**, 5:38
on basic statements, 1:484
on bodies, 6:496
on concepts, 2:417
on conventional truth, 2:474
on definition, 2:665, 2:670–672
early writings and projects of, 2:37–38
emotive theory and, 3:425
in epistemic materialism, 6:12
on epistemological solipsism, 9:118
on explication of inductive probability, 2:437
Frege and, 3:732
on Husserl's transcendental logic, 2:82
on inductive logic, 4:642–643, 8:28–29
on inductive probability explicatum, 2:439
on intentional isomorphism, 2:254, 9:347–348
on intentionality, 4:706
on isomorphic formulas, 8:76
on isomorphism, 2:254, 8:76, 9:347–348
Keynes's fundamental thesis and, 5:56
on L concepts, 8:738
on language, 5:527
and logical positivism, 5:526
on mathematical entities, 2:254
on meaningfulness, 9:669
on metaphysical theology, 1:360
on metaphysics, 9:808
Montague and, 6:329
Morris and, 8:797
on object languages, 8:737
on performative theory of truth, 7:196
physicalism and, 6:561–562
on positivist account of meaning, 8:737
on principle of tolerance, 3:317
on probability and confirmation theory, 2:436
on property logical independence, 2:439
Putnam and, 8:170
on quantification, 6:290
Quine on, 6:496
Salmon and, 8:594
Schlick and, 8:638–640
Sellars (Wilfrid) and, 8:733
semantics of, 5:529
on sentence testability *vs.* confirmation, 9:662
skepticism of, 9:58
on subject-predicate dualism, 9:289
on synonymy, 9:345
on syntactic view of theories, 9:415
on syntactical categories, 2:82, 9:354
on syntax, 2:42–43, 9:360
on theory of types, 9:354–355
on total evidence, 3:662
on truth, 1:166
on verifiability principle, 5:528
Vienna Circle and, 2:35, 2:38–43, 5:524
on Wittgenstein, 2:41–42
"Carnap and Logical Truth" (Quine), 1:167
Carneades, **2:46–48**
on causality, 3:17–18
Clitomachus on, 1:195
on determinism, 3:8, 3:17–18
on freedom, 3:17–18
and Greek Academy, 4:171
on knowledge, 3:288
on opinion, 1:194–195
and Platonic tradition, 7:607
and probability, 7:312, 7:607
and skepticism, 1:194–195, 3:399, 4:174, 9:48
Carnegie, Andrew, and social Darwinism, 2:642
Carnes, Patrick, on sexual addiction, 7:528
Carnot, Lazare, on energy and force, 3:229
Carnot, Sadi
heat studies of, 7:537
Helmholtz and, 3:231
Caro, Elme Marie, on Leopardi, 5:284
Carolina colony, constitution of, 5:375
Caroline (queen of England), 2:684
Carolingian renaissance, **2:49–51**
Carpenter, W. B., on unconscious, 9:571–572
Carrel, Armand, 5:372
Carrit, Edgar, Lewis (C. S.) and, 5:311
Carritt, E. F., on Good, 3:419
Carroll, Lewis, **2:51–53**, 5:452, 5:561
Carroll, Noel
on aesthetic experience, 1:33
on art, 1:67–68
on environmental aesthetics, 3:255–256
in film theory, 7:383
on prescriptivism, 7:383
Carruthers, Peter, 2:455
Carson, Rachel Louise, 8:667
Carston, Robyn, 2:527
Carta de Jamaica (Jamaica letter) (Bolívar), 5:205
Cartan, Èlie, 4:61
Carter, Brandon, 1:219
Cartesian circle, 2:743, 3:278
Cartesian dualism, 2:59, 7:468–469
as composite dualism, 3:115
and definition, 2:667–668
existential psychoanalysis and, 3:511
feminist view of, 5:373
Geulincx and, 4:80
immortality in, 4:611–612, 9:187
La Mettrie on, 5:178
Lloyd (G.) on, 5:373
Mercier and, 6:145
psychology and, 8:124–125
Santayana on, 8:597
Sartre and, 8:610–611, 8:649–650
and special mental substance, 3:756
vs. spectrum of dualisms, 3:116
See also Mind-body problem, Descartes on

Cartesian intuition, and mental content, 2:477
Cartesian Linguistics (Chomsky), 2:244
Cartesian Meditations (Husserl), 1:133
Cartesian product, definition of, 5:536
Cartesian purity, 5:34
Cartesian subject, 3:564
Cartesianism, **2:53–61**
on absolute space, 2:272, 9:147
abstract ideas in, 4:565–566
Arnauld and, 1:288–292
artificial language in, 8:779
Boulainvilliers and, 1:670
Clauberg and, 2:284–288
cognitive science and, 2:300
and consciousness, 2:459
Cordemoy and, 2:537
and crisis of skepticism, 9:54
Cudworth on, 2:610
on definition, 2:669–670
Desgabets and, 2:757–759
in Dutch Republic, 9:170
and epistemology, 3:291–294, 3:704
Eucharist in, 1:290
on faculty theory of intuitive knowledge, 4:724
Fénelon and, 3:603
Fontenelle and, 3:683
on force measurement, 3:228
Foucher and, 3:702–704
in French clandestine literature, 2:264–265
Fréret on, 2:265–266
Gassendi and, 4:26
Glanvill on, 4:97
on immortality, 4:611–612, 9:187
on intuitive knowledge, 4:726
Jansenism and, 4:790–791
Jurieu on, 6:603–604
on knowledge, 2:56–58, 2:670
Le Senne and, 5:289
Leibniz and, 1:292–293
Lichtenberg on, 5:339
Locke and, 5:378
Malebranche and, 5:663–664, 5:667–668
Mercier and, 6:145
Meslier and, 6:154
metaphysics of, 2:58–59
on moral certainty, 9:249
More (Henry) and, 6:395–396
Nicole on, 6:603
Norris and, 6:656
and ontological likeness or resemblance, 3:703
on personal identity, 9:15
and personalism, 7:233
and physics, 2:54–56, 9:154–155
on pleasure, 7:622
and rationalism, 8:243–244
of Régis and, 8:299–300
Regius and, 8:301
Rohault and, 8:483
Saint-Hyacinthe and, 8:589
Sartre and, 3:509, 8:610–611, 8:649–650
on sense perception, 4:724–725
skeptical argument of, 9:42–43
Spinoza and, 3:294, 9:175
Swedenborg and, 9:336
Tschirnhaus and, 9:549
Cartography, Anaximander in, 1:184
Cartwright, Helen, on individuation, 6:663–664
Cartwright, Nancy, **2:62–63**
on causality, 2:103
on entity realism, 8:692
on force, 3:235, 3:691
on natural laws, 5:227
on syntactic view of theories, 9:416
Carus, Carl Gustav, **2:63–64,** 9:571
Carus, E. G., and Klages, 5:77
Carus, Paul, **2:64–65**
Carus lectures, of Ducasse (Curt John), 3:124
Cārvāka school
liberation in, 4:625
self in, 8:717–718
Case law system, legal positivism on, 5:238
Case of Reason, Or Natural Religion Fairly and Fully Stated, The (Law), 2:686, 5:220
Case of Wagner, The (Nietzsche), 6:612
Case-based reasoning, 1:237–238
Casey, Edward, on phenomenology, 7:301
Caso, Antonio, **2:65–66,** 5:207–208
Cassian, John, 1:47
Cassirer, Ernst, **2:66–69**
on Alembert, 1:106
Bakhtin and, 1:467–469
on Cohen (Hermann), 6:542
and cultural anthropology, 7:322
on culture, 1:58
on Enlightenment, 3:243
Langer and, 1:58
on Machiavelli, 5:629
Natorp and, 6:491
and neo-Kantianism, 6:543
Schelling and, 8:621
on symbols, 1:65, 3:670
Urban and, 1:58
Cast sculpture, 9:692
Castañeda, Hector-Neri
on phenomenology, 7:300
political instability and, 5:211
Castells, Manuel, on globalization, 5:741
Castelvetro, Lodovico, on poetry, 1:48
Castillio, Sebastian, 3:714, 9:54
Castle, The (Kafka), 5:6
"Castle of Skepticism, The" (Beattie), 1:510
Castro, Isaac Orobio de. *See* Orobio de Castro, Isaac
Castro Leiva, Luis, 5:204
Casual sex, 7:525
Casuistry, in applied ethics, 1:237–238
Casullo, Albert
a priori justification and, 5:80
and counterfactual conditionals, 5:101
on philosophical evidence *vs.* evidence based on empirical investigations, 5:85
and Putnam-Kitcher argument, 5:100
Catastrophe
Bonnet on, 1:658
Dong Zhongshu on, 3:98
Catastrophic processes, as principle of change, 1:658
Catéchisme positiviste (Comte), 2:410
Categorematic, definition of, 5:536
Categorematic signs, in medieval logic, 9:776
Categorematic words, 5:430
Categorical concepts, set of, 3:615
Categorical grammars, 9:357–359
Categorical imperative, **2:69–72,** 5:34
conscience and, 2:447
and discourse ethics, 3:91
first and second formulation of, 5:36, 5:37
Kant on, 2:366–367, 3:154, 3:385–386, 3:411, 3:618, 5:37
Kierkegaard and, 5:63
moral cosmopolitanism and, 2:568
Williams (Bernard) on, 9:787
Categorical properties, *vs.* dispositional properties, 7:25
Categorical proposition(s)
definition of, 5:553
in traditional logic, 5:494–495
Categorical reasons, in contractualism, 2:518
Categorical system, Skolem on, 5:472

Categories (Aristotle), 1:4, 1:269, 2:490, 4:66, 5:398–399, 5:408, 9:534
- Arab logic and, 5:417
- on denominatives, 8:762
- Duns Scotus on, 3:134
- Iamblichus on, 4:540
- medieval logic and, 5:421–422
- and medieval philosophy, 6:105
- *ousia* in, 7:63
- on signification, 8:755–756
- Simplicius on, 9:34
- on substance, 9:295

Categories (Eudemus of Rhodes), 5:401

Categorization, concepts and, 2:415, 2:418

Category(ies), **2:72–83**
- Adorno on, 1:27
- Alexander on, 1:108–109
- animal understanding of, 1:203
- Aristotelian theory of, 2:72–74, 7:65, 9:635–636
- of art, 1:316
- Brahman as, 1:683–684
- Brentano on, 1:691
- Burley on, 1:773–774
- Carnap on, 2:39
- in Chatton *vs.* Ockham dispute, 2:139
- concepts and, 2:417–418
- as criteria of classification, in worldmaking, 4:161–162
- in *Critique of Pure Reason,* 5:17
- Croce's logic and, 2:602
- definition of, 3:2, 5:536
- Descartes on, 2:54
- experience and, 7:746
- of femininity, in Cixous, 2:263
- as formation of judgments, 2:75
- Gehlen on, 4:36
- historical notes on, 2:80–82
- Husserl on, 2:81–82
- in illative combinatory logic, 2:339
- Kant on, 2:74–75
  - Cohen (Hermann) on, 2:303
  - deduction of, 5:34
  - groups of, 5:19
- Lewis (C. I.) on, 7:746
- in logic of relatives, 2:81
- metaphysical implications of, 9:289
- Minagawa on, 6:253
- modal, 1:2
- of motion, 9:342
- Natorp on, 6:491
- in natural language, 2:77
- Ockham on, 1:773–774
- Otto on, 7:59–60
- Peirce on, 7:164–165, 7:168–171
- Plotinus on, 7:637
- in post-Kantian theories, 2:75–77
- restricted to phenomena, 5:18
- Russell and, 2:76–77
- Ryle on, 1:153–154, 8:581–582
- Simmel on, 6:545
- in Stammler's legal philosophy, 9:203
- subject matter exclusion from, 2:78
- of substance *vs.* dynamics in Christology, 2:247
- syntactical and semantical. *See* Syntactical and semantical categories
- as syntactical functions, 2:77
- as terms *vs.* judgments, 2:74
- theory of, 2:77–80
- toposes, 4:742
- in traditional logic, 5:494
- in transcendental logic, 2:79
- Valla on, 9:635–636
- Wittgenstein on, 2:82

Category error, in critical realism, 2:596

Category theory, synthetic differential geometry and, 2:510

Category-mistakes, 3:549, 8:581–582
- and absurdity, 2:77–78
- Aristotle on, 2:73–74
- Kant on, 2:75
- Russell's theory of types and, 2:76

Category-theoretic structuralism, 9:271–272

Caterus, Johannes. *See* Kater, Johan van

Catharsis. *See* Katharsis

Cathartic method
- of Breuer, 3:737
- and removing separately distinct symptoms, 3:740

Cathéchisme du curé Meslier, Le (Meslier), 2:267

Catherine the Great
- Diderot and, 3:71, 3:77
- Voltaire and, 9:839

Catholic Church
- censorship by, 2:732, 2:736–737, 3:342, 5:164, 5:176–177, 5:196, 5:571, 7:570
- and central fideistic thesis, 3:632
- on dogma, 3:97
- Erasmus and, 3:339
- on evolution, 2:641
- French liberalism and, 5:320
- and Galileo, 4:8–9
- Haeckel on, 4:204
- in Korea, 5:139–140
- on liberation theology, 5:331–332
- Luther and, 5:612, 5:617
- Meslier on, 6:154–155
- modernist movement in, 5:164
- natural law and, 6:513
- and papal infallibility, 3:97
- proposed union with Eastern church, 7:630–631
- reformers in, 8:296
- rule of faith in, 9:51
- sexual ethics in, 7:522–523, 7:528
- on war and peace, 7:152, 7:157
- Wyclyf and, 9:851, 9:852
- *See also* Catholicism

Catholic Demonstrations (Demonstrationes Catholicae) (Leibniz), 5:251–252, 5:266–267

Catholicism
- Anscombe and, 1:212
- Aquinas and, 9:436
- Baader on, 1:439
- de Maistre and, 5:659
- doctrine of faith in, 3:530
- double effect principle and, 1:213
- force in, 9:509
- French Revolution and, 9:520
- Ivanov's conversion to, 4:768
- Maritain and, 5:717–718
- modernism in, 6:316
- mysticism of, 6:448–450
- philosophy and
  - Mercier in, 6:144
  - Zubiri (Xavier) on, 9:888
- reality in, *vs.* science, 9:888
- on rule of faith, 9:249
- Sabatier and, 8:587
- Santayana and, 8:597
- Schlegel's conversion to, 8:632
- Servetus and, 8:831
- Stein's conversion to, 9:239
- Taine and, 9:364
- Thomism and, 9:443
- Unamuno on, 9:567
- Winckelmann and, 9:789–790
- *See also* Christianity; Roman Catholicism

Catholic-Protestant West, as profoundly rationalistic, 5:74

Cato, Dante on, 2:624–626

Cattaneo, Carol, **2:83–85**

Cattell, J. McKeen, 8:141

Cattle, in Zoroastrianism, 9:886

Cauchy, Augustine Louis
- on algebra, 5:459–460
- on calculus, 2:495, 2:496
- on infinite, 9:148
- on number, 6:671
- on statistical distribution, 9:233

Cauchy sequences
in Bishop's arithmetic continuum construction, 2:504
Brouwer on, 2:502
in Cantor's system, 2:495
Cauchy-Bolzano definition, on continuous functions, 2:496–497
Causa Dei, De (Bradwardine), 8:704
Causal anomalies, 8:320
Causal approach
to direction of time, **2:85–88**
to explanation, 3:524–525
Causal chains, deviant, 5:90
"Causal Character of Modern Physical Theory, The" (Nagel), 6:474
Causal closure of physical domain, **2:89–93**
Causal connection, inferred from positive correlation, 3:545
Causal depth, of folk psychology, 3:679
Causal determination, *vs.* causation, in NRP theory, 6:134
Causal determinism
Adler on, 1:23
and moral responsibility, 3:718
psychological development in, 1:23
Stoicism on, 9:256–257
Causal deviance, 1:15–16
Causal explanations
vs. causation, 6:134
objectivity in ethics and, 7:6
in sociology, Weber (Max) on, 9:735
Causal graph, 8:687
Causal inference, 2:107–108, 8:685–687
Causal interaction
of mind and matter, 3:703
principle of, in anomalous monism, 1:211
Causal laws
Cartwright on, 2:107
culture and, 9:733
Ziehen (Theodor) on, 9:884
"Causal Laws and Effective Strategies" (Cartwright), 2:107
Causal or conditional or explanatory-relation accounts, **2:93–95**
Causal propositions, miracles and, 6:271–272
Causal relations
events as *relata* of, 5:71
and mental states, 3:675, 8:192–193
in science, 6:247–248
Causal statements, 1:88, 7:160
Causal theory
of action, Davidson on, 2:645–648
of knowing, 4:147
of knowledge, 6:628
of metaphor, 6:167
of names, 3:459
of reference, 8:289, 9:417
Evans on, 3:459
Putnam on, 8:172
"Causal Theory of Knowing, A" (Goldman), 4:147
"Causal Theory of Names, The" (Evans), 3:459
Causal/explanatory exclusion argument, of Kim, 5:72
Causalidad (Causality) (Bunge), 5:210
Causalism, 1:15–18, 9:102
Causality
a priori principle of, 6:540
abstract entities and, 1:318, 5:84
in action, 1:15–18
Aenesidemus on, 1:31–32
in African philosophy, 1:83
agent, **1:88–90,** 3:26
al-Ghazālī (Muḥammad) on, 1:118–119, 1:426, 2:113–115, 6:558, 9:304
alternatives to, 7:715–716
analysis of, 2:99, 9:602
anomalies in, 2:106
in anomalous monism, 1:211
Anscombe on, 1:213
and antecedent necessity and divine will, 1:681
anti-fundamentalism and, 2:104
Aristotle on, 1:100, 1:273, 1:739, 2:74, 2:540–541
asymmetry of, 2:98, 2:104–106, 9:498
"at-at" theory of, 8:593
Augustine on, 1:398
and autonomy, 1:738
Avicenna on, 1:433
backward, 2:86
Bacon (Francis) on, 1:448
of behaviors, in materialism, 6:13–14
and belief, 1:704, 2:93–94, 4:147, 8:725
Berkeley on, 1:582, 1:585
in bioethics, 1:601
Boethius on, 1:626
Bohr on, 2:531
Boyle on, 1:674–675
as Brahman, 1:681–682
of brain processes, 2:92
Buckle on, 1:719
in Buddhism, 1:734, 1:739, 1:754–757, 2:111, 2:221
Buffon on, 1:759
Calderoni on, 2:7–8
Carneades on, 3:17–18
Carroll on, 2:51
in Cartesianism metaphysics, 2:58–59
vs. causal determination, 6:134
chance and, 2:125–130
Chisholm on, 2:243
Chrysuippus on, 2:252
Clarke on, 2:270
in classical mechanics, 2:281
closed physical domains and, 2:89–93
in common cause principle, 2:342–343
in conceptual role semantics, 2:479
conclusions on, 2:108
in conditional and explanatory relations, 2:93–95
in Confucianism, 2:175
Conway on, 2:529
counterfactuals and, 2:99, 2:105, 2:574–576, 3:525
Cournot on, 2:577
creative, and Universe, 2:588
in *Critique of Pure Reason,* 5:20
Crusius on, 2:606
Descartes on, 2:742–744, 2:752–753
determinables and determinates and, 3:3–4
determinism and, 3:24–26, 3:31–32, 3:36–37, 3:40–41
in Dge-lugs school of Buddhism, 1:734
Dilthey on, 3:83
and direct realism, 2:97–98
directionality of, 2:87, 2:102
DNA and, 7:345
in dogmatism, 1:32
downward, 6:648
Dretske on, 3:108–109
Driesch on, 3:111–112
Ducasse on, 3:124
Edwards (Jonathan) on, 3:168
Einstein on, 3:180–182
in eliminative induction, 1:447
emergence and, 3:192
in emergentism, 6:648
in empirical tests, 2:107
in empiriocriticism, 7:715–716
energy in, 7:49
in Epicureanism, 1:32
in event and fact statements, 1:549
in event theory, 3:467
in evolution, 1:569–570
existentialists on, 3:503

Causality, ***continued***
experience and, 2:95, 6:224
in experimentation, 2:107
in explanation, 1:449
in field theory, 2:106
as folk science, Norton on, 2:106
of Forms, 9:590
Franciscans on, 7:162
and free will, 4:109, 9:433
in functionalism, 6:645–646
in general theory of relativity, 9:157
Geulincx on, 4:77, 4:80
Geyser on, 4:83
Glanvill on, 4:96
God and, 1:139–140, 2:550
and God's existence
Aquinas on, 2:551, 9:432
in cosmological argument, 2:586
Henry of Ghent on, 3:135–136
Richard of St. Victor on, 8:592
in heredity, 7:339
in history, 9:512
Hobbes on, 4:410–411
of human behavior, 6:224–225
Hume on, 2:98–100, 3:14, 3:218, 3:304, 4:636–637, 5:20
in Ibn Khaldūn's history, 4:548
identity in, 1:741
in Indian philosophy, **2:109–113**
and indirect realism, 2:97
in individuals, 2:62
in infallibility claims, 2:277
inference in, 2:106–107, 8:685–687
informational, 3:108–109
internal relations and, 8:338–340
in Islamic philosophy, **2:113–115**
in Jainism, 2:110–111
in Kalām theology, 2:113
Kant on, 5:10, 5:20
karma and, 2:110
and knowing, Goldman on, 4:147
Köhler on, 5:131–132
Lange on, 6:540
and laws of science, 2:104
Leibniz on, 2:552–553, 6:191
Lewis (David) on, 2:105, 5:314
Locke on, 5:384
Mach on, 7:715
Mackie on, 5:638
Maimonides on, 5:650
Maine de Biran on, 5:657–658
Markov conditions and, 2:108
Maupertuis on, 6:66
Mendel on, 7:339
mental content features of, 2:477
and mental states, 6:646–647, 9:37
merely mechanical, 3:112
metaphysics of, **2:95–97**
Mill (John Stuart) on, 2:106
in mind, 7:468
and mind-body problem, 6:258–260
models of, 2:108
Mullā Ṣadrā and, 2:114
multiplication of powers and, 1:741
mutual, Zhuangzi on, 9:881
in natural philosophy, 1:449
in neo-Kantianism, 6:540
Nicolas of Autrecourt on, 6:599–600
nomological character of, 1:211
non-causal states and, 2:102
in non-Humean reductionism, 2:96, 2:100–101
of nonreal objects, 5:729
as not objectively real, 1:740–741
in NRP theory, 6:134
Nursi on, 2:114–115
Nyāya on, 2:112–113, 4:133
as objective content, 8:663
as objective reality, 3:705
observability in, 2:106–107
occasionalist theory of, 4:77
Ockham on, 7:8, 9:779–780
One and, 8:42
as ongoing concern, 2:104
overdetermination of, 2:99
parapsychology and, 7:113–114
Pastore on, 7:135
Peckham on, 7:162
in perception, 7:180–183, 7:272, 7:275–276, 7:296, 8:10–11
persistence of universe and, 2:587
Petzoldt on, 7:716
in phenomenal effects and scientific claims, 2:104
Philo on, 7:304
in physics, 6:209
Plato on, 7:601
precognition and, 7:756–757
preemption in, 2:99
primitive cultures' view of, 5:306
principle of, 1:243, 8:641–642
probabilistic, 9:334
properties and, 9:16
and psyche, 9:240
psychic, Zen'kovskii on, 9:868
in psychoanalytic theory, 8:112
in psychology, 6:646–647, 9:849
purposive activity and, 9:386
Putnam on, 8:171
in quantum theory, 1:539–542, 1:631, 1:638–639
in rationalism, 8:245–247
in realism, 2:95–102
reason and, 7:735
in reductionism, 2:101–102
in reference of theoretical terms, 9:417
Régis on, 8:299–300
Reid on, 3:18, 8:329
responsibility and, 8:164
Royer-Collard on, 8:524
Russell on, 2:103–104
Salmon on, 8:593
in Samkhya-Yaga schools, 4:134
Sankara on, 2:112
Sankhya on, 2:111–112
Schopenhauer on, 3:311
Schultz on, 8:659
and science, 2:103–104
scientific method and, 6:247–248, 9:658
second-order properties and, 3:761
self-prediction and, 8:729
of sense data, 8:819
Shepherd on, 9:10
on simultaneity and conventionalism, 2:524–525
in singularism, 2:101–102
in skepticism, 1:100
Smart on, 9:65
social, Durkheim on, 3:151
Spengler on, 9:168
in Stoicism, 1:100
structural, in Sartre, 8:610
as substantial change *vs.* alteration, 2:75
as sufficient immediate cause, 2:91–92
Taine on, 9:365
teleological order and, 9:376
as temporal directionality, 2:85–88
in Tiantai Buddhism, 2:163–164
and time, 2:87, 2:588, 9:471
ultimate end in, 4:185
universal, principle of, 1:243
and universals, 9:582–583
unobservability of, 2:106–107
of values, 9:643
vanishing agents and, 1:17
Vasubandhu on, 1:751–752
in Vedas and Upanishads, 2:109–110
as vital impetus, 1:569–570
voluntarism on, 9:715
von Wright on, 9:848
whole-making, 3:112
will and, 5:657–658
Wolff on, 9:828

Wundt on, 9:849
in Yogācāra doctrine, 1:749
"Causality and Determination" (Anscombe), 1:213
"Causality and Properties" (Shoemaker), 9:16
Causality: Models, Reasoning, and Inference (Pearl), 2:108
Causal-perceptual models, of limited utility, 5:86
Causal/theoretical strategy, 6:13–14
Causation
Philosophy of Science, **2:103–109**
See also Causality
"Causation" (Lewis), 2:105
Causation and the Types of Necessity (Ducasse), 3:124
"Causation as Folk Science" (Norton), 2:106
Cause(s)
accidental, Duns Scotus on, 3:136
of action, *vs.* reason for action, 3:20
Aristotle on, 1:100, 1:276–277, 2:666–667
and effect
in "at-at" theory of causation, 8:593
in atomism, 4:814
creative activity as escape from, 1:560
final, Ockham on, 9:780
Hume on, 4:494, 4:636–637
in introspective belief, 8:725
Karma and, 4:627
in New Nyāya, 9:583
in Ockham's metaphysics, 9:779
precognition and, 7:756
principle of proportionate reality in, 4:691
Shepherd on, 9:9–10
essential, Duns Scotus on, 3:136
higher-level events as, 6:134–135
Hobbes on, 8:127–128
in induction
agreement methods of, 6:237–238
concomitant variation method of, 6:244
difference methods of, 6:237–238
Kant on, 6:202
in metaphysics, 1:276–277, 6:202
in physics, 4:305
schema of, 5:18
of sensation, 4:304
structuring, 3:108–109
triggering, 3:108–109
unconscious, 8:113
Vasubandhu on, 9:651
Vico on, 9:674
Cause event, 5:71
Causeries du Lundi (Chateaubriand), 2:137
Causes concerning Animals (Democritus), 5:298
Causes concerning Seeds (Democritus), 5:298
Causes of Celestial Phenomena (Democritus), 5:298
Causes of the Corruption of Taste, The (Dacier), 9:839
Cavalieri, Bonaventura, on indivisibles, 5:251
Cavell, Stanley, **2:115–117**
on art, 1:68
in film theory, 7:382–384
on tragedy, 9:525
Cavendish, Margaret, **2:117–118,** 9:838
Cayley, Arthur, 4:60
Celan, Paul, 4:3
Celestial Hierarchy, On the (Pseudo-Dionysius), 7:609
Celibacy
analysis of, in philosophy of sex, 7:526
in early Christianity, Gibbon on, 4:85
Tolstoy on, 9:513
Cellular automata, computing machine development and, 2:406
Cellular cognition, 6:567–569
Cellular intervention techniques, 6:570–571
Celsus, **2:118–119,** 7:40
Cement of the Universe, The (Mackie), 5:638
Cena de le ceneri, La (The Ash Wednesday supper) (Bruno), 1:709
Censorship, **2:119–120**
of Aquinas, 9:444
by Catholic Church, 2:732, 2:736–737, 3:342, 5:164, 5:176–177, 5:196, 5:571, 7:570
in Dutch Republic, 9:182
in England, 2:682–685
in France, 2:687–688, 2:725, 3:71, 3:222–223, 5:179
French clandestine writings and, 2:264, 2:268
in Russia, 3:71, 3:77
in Soviet Union, 5:573, 5:603
Censura Philosophae Cartesiana (Huet), 9:53
Center of Logic, Epistemology and Philosophy of Science, 5:210
Centiloquium Theologicum (Ockham), 9:771
Central processing units, neural networks and, 2:444
Central Question of Philosophy, The (Ayer), 1:437–438
Central system, as Quinian and isotropic, 3:676
Centrality and Commonality (Zhongyong) (Confucian text), 2:171–173
Centralization, Taine and, 9:364–365
Central-state physicalism, 6:12
Centrifugal forces, matter and, 6:3
Century (monastic literary genre), of John of Damascus, 4:836–837
Cercidas of Megalopolis, Cynic teaching of, 2:617
Cerdo, Marcion and, 5:704
Cerebral palsy, 3:737
Cerebral transplantation, personal identity and, 7:231–232
Ceremonial rites, Xunzi and, 2:234
Ceremony, Chinese religion, 2:226
Certain Physiological Essays and Other Tracts (Boyle), 1:673
Certainty, 5:96–97
absence of, science and, 1:474
attainment of, Kant on, 4:770
vs. certitude, 6:578
Condillac on, 2:421
Condorcet on, 2:431
Descartes on, 5:95–96
empirical, 5:662
evidence for, 6:116–117
faith in, 4:771–772
Glanvill on, 4:96
illative sense and, 6:578–579
as intuitively given, 1:704
irrational, in Gehlen's social theory, 4:36
in Jaspers's epistemology, 4:800
in Kierkegaard's leap into faith, 9:58
knowledge and, 3:283
legal, myth of, 7:428
limited, as response to excessive skepticism, 9:54
Malcolm on, 5:662
Neurath on, 6:561
vs. probability, in argument from illusion, 4:587
psychological, 5:97
Sanches on, 8:595
in sense-datum theory, 8:819
skepticism and, 9:59

Certainty, ***continued***
Socrates and, 9:702
Wittgenstein on, 9:817
Certamen Philosophicum Propugnatum Veritatis Divinae ac Naturalis (Orobio), 7:41
Certification, in classical Indian philosophy, 9:545
Certitude
vs. certainty, 6:578
Duns Scotus on, 3:140–141
of faith, 6:580
Mercier's theory of, 6:145
Nicolas of Autrecourt on, 6:600
of physical science, Oresme on, 7:34
in pure mathematics, 6:217
Cerutti Guldberg, Horacio, liberation philosophy and, 5:211
Cesaire, Aime, on African philosophy, 1:84
Ceteris paribus, 3:675, 5:222–223
Cetina, Karin Knorr, 8:677
on knowledge production, 9:78
social epistemology and, 9:84
Cézanne, Paul, 6:151
Chaadaev, Pëtr Lakovlevic, **2:120–122**
Chabbi, Jacqueline, 9:302
Chaikovskii, Nikolai, 5:154
Chain of being
Bonaventure on, 1:652
Boulainvilliers on, 1:670
evolutionary view of, 1:658
La Mettrie and, 5:180
See also Lovejoy, Arthur Oncken
Chaldean Oracles, 4:540, 6:549–552, 8:43
Chaldean theology, 2:623
Challenge of Peace: God's Promise and Our Responsibility, The, 7:157
Challenger disaster, engineering ethics and, 3:240
Chalmers, David, 4:600
on dualism, 3:114, 3:117
functional reductive explanation and, 6:570
paper co-written with Jackson, 5:115
on qualitative consciousness, 2:450
on semantics, 8:77
Chalmers, Thomas
on atheism, 1:372
on nature, 2:641
on property dualism, 3:114
Chalmers, W. R., on Parmenides of Elea, 7:125
Chamberlain, Houston Steward, **2:122–124**
on historical determinism, 3:37
and Keyserling, 5:57
Chamfort, Nicolas de, Nietzsche and, 6:611
Chan, Joseph, on Confucian ethics, 2:196–197
Chan yuan zhu quanji duxu (Preface to the collected writings on the source of Chan) (Guifeng), 1:727
Chan (Zen) Buddhism, **1:726–730, 2:166–168**
and Chinese philosophy, 2:154–155
Daoism and, 2:186
Dōgen and, 3:95
summary of, 2:154–155
on ultimate reality, 2:220
on wisdom realization in daily life, 2:219
See also Zen
Chance, **2:125–130**
absolute, as self-contradictory, 1:692
in artistic composition, 1:298
asymmetry of counterfactuals and, 2:575
Buckle on, 1:718
conclusions on, 2:129
Cournot on, 2:577
in evolution, 7:339–340
exchangeability and, 2:129
history and, 3:38
mathematics of, 2:126
nature and, 6:536
in non-Humean reductionism, 2:100–101
as part of the world, 3:566
philosophical accounts of, 2:127–128
and probability, **8:24–29**
probability of truth and, 1:495
in science, 2:126–127
skepticism concerning, 2:129
statistical syllogism in, 4:641
subjectivism and, 2:129
theories of, brief history of, 2:125–126
See also Probability
Chandoux, 2:727–728
Chang Chunmai, on Chinese writing as philosophy, 4:792
Change
as alteration, 7:207
Anaximenes on, 1:186
Aquinas on, 9:427–428
Aristotle on, 1:272–273, 4:621
in atomism, 6:601
Buckle on, 1:719–720
Burley on, 1:773–775
capture of, 7:208
in Cartesianism, 2:58
as catastrophic process, 1:658
changing ideas of, 8:45–46
in classical mechanics, 2:283
conservation laws of nature and, 2:586–587
conservation principle and, 2:461
in Daoism, 2:198
Dühring on, 3:130–131
forfeiting of, 7:207–208
vs. growth, 1:186
Heraclitus on, 4:318–319
historical, 8:45–46, 9:527
in history, Vailati's work on, 9:630
Hobbes on, 6:9
linguistic stability and, 2:208–209
Melissus of Samos on, 6:120
in metaphysics, 1:568
persistence and, 7:206–211
personal identity and, 7:218–220
Plotinus on, 6:187
qualitative
addition theory of, 9:343
vs. quantitative, 1:384
quantitative, *vs.* qualitative change, 1:384
Rehmke on, 8:303
in Sanlun Buddhism, 2:161
in science, 1:568
social
in Chinese philosophy, 2:231
in French clandestine writings, 2:264
Veblen and, 9:655
societal, Godwin on, 4:137–138
in Spinoza's metaphysics, 9:172, 9:186
substance *vs.* accidents in, 2:75
Timon of Phlius on, 9:502
Turgot on, 9:551
Woodbridge on, 9:842–843
Channing, William Ellery, **2:130–131,** 6:572, 7:121
Chanut, Pierre-Hector, 2:754
Chaos
Anaxagoras on, 1:181
archē as primeval, 1:249
Carnap on, 2:38
in cosmology, 2:566
distinctions in, 2:39
as scientific starting point, 2:39
as unlimited opportunity, 9:12
Chaos theory, **2:131–134,** 3:33

Chapman, John, and Eliot (George), 3:184
"Chapter on the Elements" (Israeli), 4:764
Character
- art and, 1:43
- assessment of, 3:451
- Camus on, 2:20
- in Confucian ethics, 2:177–178
- education and, 7:370
- in ethics, 2:178
- in evocative argument, 2:213–214
- excellence in, 2:230
- failure of, 9:679
- in ideal rule utilitarianism, 1:687
- inalterability of, 8:655
- of linguistic expression, 2:707
- in psychological anthropology, 7:322–323
- qualitative, topic-neutral analysis of, 8:192
- virtue and vice as traits of, 9:678–679
- in virtue ethics, 9:679–680
- *See also* Personality

Character analysis, 8:306–307
Character and Opinion in the United States (Santayana), 8:602
Character and the Conduct of Life (McDougall), 6:72
"Character armor," 8:306–307
Character structure, Reich on, 8:310–313
Characteristic function, polynominal-time computability and, 2:388
Characteristicks of Men, Manners, Opinions, Times (Shaftesbury), 9:2
"Characteristics" (Carlyle), 2:33
Characteristics of the Present Age (Fichte), 3:618
Characterizations and Criticisms (Schlegel), 8:631
Characterology, 5:77–78
Characters, fictional
- as concepts, 1:336
- ontological status of, 5:366–367

Characters and Events (Dewey), 3:44
Chardin, Pierre Teilhard de. *See* Teilhard de Chardin, Pierre
Charge of Schism Continued, The (Norris), 6:655
Charisma, in Confucian ethics, 2:195
Charismatic authority, Weber (Max) on, 9:735
Charity
- Cousin on, 2:579
- ethics of, 1:404
- Isaac of Stella on, 4:754
- libertarian view of, 9:73
- mental content and, 2:478
- principle of, 2:646, 2:648, 6:85

Charland, Louis, on emotions, 3:201
Charles I (king of England), 5:374
Charles II (king of England)
- death of, 5:375
- Locke and, 5:388

Charles VIII (king of France), 7:570
Charles of Valois, 2:623
Charles the Bald (Holy Roman emperor), 3:340
Charlet, Étienne, 2:749–750
Charmides (Plato)
- author's family in, 7:582
- on courage, 3:396
- on historic Socrates, 9:107

Charron, Pierre, **2:134–136**
- as Christian skeptic, 3:631
- Lipsius and, 5:364
- Montaigne's skepticism and, 9:52
- Pascal and, 7:133

Chart of Biography, A (Priestley), 8:5
Chartres, School of, **2:136–137**
Chastity, 7:526
Chateaubriand, François René de, **2:137–139**
Châtelet, Émilie du, 3:246
Châtelet, Gabrielle de, Wolff and, 9:824
Châtelet, Mme. du, clandestine writings of, 2:267
Chatton, Walter, **2:139–140,** 9:821
Chauvinism/liberalism problem, 3:761
Che cosa e il fascismo (Gentile), 3:553
Chef-d'oeuvre d'un inconnu, Le (Saint-Hyacinthe), 8:588
Chellas, Brian, modal logic and, 5:491
Chelovek (Ivanov), 4:767
Chelwood, Lord Cecil of, on war and peace, 7:155
Chemical communication, Wilson (Edward O.) on, 9:788
Chemical revolution, Lavoisier and, 5:216–217
Chemistry
- atomism and, 1:386–389
- Boyle and, 1:386–387, 1:672–674
- classification and reaction method issues in, 2:141–142
- Dalton in, 1:387
- ethical implications of, 2:144
- in history and philosophy of science, 2:143–144
- language of, 8:785
- Leibniz on, 5:252
- materialism and, 6:11
- matter in, 6:61
- methodological pragmatism in, 2:141–142
- of molecular and cellular cognition, 6:568
- natural kinds in, 2:141
- in naturalism, 6:492
- natural–synthetic distinction in, 2:141
- nonphysical forces *vs.* closed physical causality in, 2:91
- ontological status and operational definitions in, 2:141
- phenomena-to-be-explained in, 8:697
- philosophy of, **2:140–144**
- phlogiston theory, 8:695, 9:202
- Priestley and, 8:6
- quantum theory and, 2:143, 9:580
- reducibility to physics, 2:142–143
- in vitalism, 9:696–697
- *See also* Atomism

Chemistry (Lavoisier), 5:157
Chen Chung Chang, many-valued logic and, 5:694
Cheng (sincerity), Zhou Dunyi on, 9:880
Cheng, Chung-ying, on Daoist ethics, 2:198
Cheng Hao, **2:144–145**
- in neo-Confucianism, 2:156, 4:794
- and Zhu Xi, 9:882

Cheng I. *See* Cheng Yi
Ch'eng Ming-Tao. *See* Cheng Hao
Cheng Yi, **2:145–146**
- Lu Xiangshan and, 5:618
- in neo-Confucianism, 2:155, 4:794
- and Zhu Xi, 9:882

Ch'eng Yi-Ch-uan. *See* Cheng Yi
Cheng Zhongying, 2:182
Chengguan, as Huayan patriarch, 1:737
Chernyshevski, Nikolai Gavrilovich. *See* Chernyshevskii, Nikolai Gavrilovich
Chernyshevskii, Nikolai Gavrilovich, **2:146–147**
- Dostoevsky on, 3:99
- Lavrov and, 5:218
- Marković and, 5:719
- nihilism of, 6:617
- Russian Populism and, 5:219

Chesselden, William, on perception, 2:421
Cheyney, E. P., on historical inevitability, 3:36
Chiasm, 6:148
Chicago laboratory school, 3:44
Chicherin, Boris Nikolaevich, **2:147–149**

Chichi keimō (Logic, an introduction) (Nishi), 6:623
Chierchia, Gennaro, on anaphora, 1:175
Child, Irvin, parapsychology and, 7:116
Child, James W., on noncombatant immunity, 4:873
Child and Curriculum, The (Dewey), 3:44, 3:48
Child development, education and, 7:254
Child labor, 2:362–363
Childhood, 1:597–598
    Freud on, 8:104–105
    Portmann on, 7:321
Children
    cognitive development of, 9:77
    cognitive research on, 2:299–300
    conscience and, 2:445
    intelligence in, 1:596
    intention in, 1:19
    irreligious education for, 3:746
    language acquisition by, Chomsky on, 2:244
    language use by, Collingwood on, 2:328
    and life, meaning and value of, 5:354–356
    pain in, reality of, 7:71–72
    personal remembering by, 6:123–124
    power over, 7:733–734
    Spranger on development of, 9:199
    as students, 7:357
    testimony and, 7:357
Childress, J. F., 7:138–139
"Child's Relations with Others, The" (Merleau-Ponty), 6:150
Chilean philosophy, 5:206–207
Chillingworth, William, 9:54, 9:100
Chimpanzees, morality in, 3:479
China
    communist, on nuclear war, 7:154
    communist mode of production and, 2:363–364
    Leibniz and, 5:253–254, 5:262–263
    Marxism in, 3:56
    mysticism of, 6:445–446
    Sufism in, 9:306
    wisdom literature of, 9:793
    Wolff on, 9:824–825
Chinese classics
    and Shao Yong, 9:6
    use of, Dai Zhen on, 2:621–622
Chinese language, structure and thinking of, 2:210–212
Chinese logic, history of, **5:414–417**
Chinese philosophy, **2:149–239**
    ancient, 2:149–152
    Buddhism in, 2:153–155, 2:159, **2:160–170,** 2:198–220, 5:316
    Chan (Zen) Buddhism in, 2:166–168
    classification as, 4:791–792
    Confucianism and, 2:149–151, **2:170–180,** 2:194, 2:220, 4:793–794
    contemporary, 2:158–160, **2:180–184**
    Daoism and, 2:151, **2:184–194,** 2:197–198, 2:205–206, 2:220–221, 2:236–237, 5:316
    development of, 2:231
    Dong Zhongshu and, 2:235
    ethics in, **2:194–202**
    Feng in, 2:159
    Guo Xiang in, 4:196
    and hermeneutics, 2:622
    history of. *See* History, of Chinese philosophy
    Huayan Buddhism in, 2:164–166
    on human nature, 5:359
    idealism in, 5:618
    inborn knowledge and, 2:221–222
    in Japan, 4:765, 4:792, 4:793
    vs. Japanese philosophy, 4:792–793
    knowledge in, 2:215–216
    language and logic in, **2:202–215**
    Laozi and, **5:194–196**
    legalism and, 2:152, 2:199–200, 2:237–238
    Leninism and, 2:180–181
    logicians school of, 2:152
    Lu Xiangshan and, **5:618**
    Malebranche on, 5:665
    Maoism and, 2:180–181
    Marxism and, 2:180–181
    Mencius and, 2:232–233
    metaphorical metaphysics of, 2:222
    metaphysical *vs.* physical in, 5:194
    metaphysics and epistemology in, **2:215–223**
    methodological issues in, 2:200–201
    middle period of, 2:152–155
    Mohist school in, 2:151, 2:197
    Mou in, 2:222
    Mozi and, 2:235–236
    neo-Confucianism in, 2:155–158, 2:181–184, 2:199
    overview of, **2:149–160**
    particularism *vs.* normative theory in, 2:200
    Pure Land Buddhism in, 2:168–169
    reality in, 2:202–208, 2:228–230, 4:793
    religion in, **2:223–231**
    ritual and, 2:226–227
    science in, 2:216–219
    self in, 2:199
    Shao Yong and, 9:6–7
    social and political thought in, **2:231–239**
    thought in, 2:208–212
    Tiantai Buddhism in, 2:163–166
    Tolstoy and, 9:513
    truth in, 2:205–208
    of ultimate reality, 2:220–221
    virtues in, 2:227–228
    Western influence on, 2:158–159, 2:180–181
    Western interest in, 2:195–196
    vs. Western philosophy, 2:205, 2:222–224, 2:230
    wisdom in, 2:219
    Xiong in, 2:159
    Xunzi in, 2:233
    Yin Yang school, 2:152
    Zhang in, 2:159–160
Chinese religion, 2:225–227
    dispassion and conventionalism in, 2:225–226
    humor as excellence in, 2:226
    New Land Buddhism and, 2:169
    skillfulness as excellence in, 2:225
    wandering as form of excellence in, 2:225
Chinese room argument, **2:239–242,** 5:634
    computationalism and, 2:395
    Searle on, 8:705
Chinul. *See* Jinul
Chiropracty, 7:466
Chisholm, Roderick, **2:242–244**
    on conditions of knowledge, 3:270–272, 3:278
    on dualism, 3:115–116, 3:121
    on epistemic use of "appears," 9:119
    on epistemology and ethics, 3:326
    on fallibilism, 3:274
    on Kant's argument on *a priori* knowledge, 5:81
    Lehrer and, 5:248
    on mereological essentialism, 6:147
    on naturalism, 6:498
    on noncognitivism, 3:327
    and pain behavior, 3:758
    on personal identity, 7:229–230

on properties, 6:199
on thinking, 9:418–419
Chmielewski, Janusz, 4:148
Cho Kwangjo, 5:137
Choi Chung, 5:136
Choi Hangi, 5:140
Choice
and action, means and conditions of, unequal control over, 3:724
and awareness of death, 2:651
axiom of (multiplicative axiom), 5:536. *See also* Set theory
Beauvoir on, 3:504
Bergson on, 1:563–564
communitarianism and, 2:369
as core of human existence, 5:62
Dewey on, 3:49
existentialism on, 3:503
freedom and, 1:563, 2:368, 2:445, 3:724–725
individual *vs.* collective in Condorcet, 2:432
Kierkegaard on, 3:501, 5:63
Sartre on, 3:504, 8:608
selection and subjectivity in, 1:565
Sen's economic theories of, 8:810
Shariati on, 9:7
subjective expected utility and, 8:613
Choice function, definition of, 5:536
Choice of Pearls (Ibn Gabirol), 4:545
Choice sequence, in Brouwer, 2:502–503
Chomskian modules, 3:485
Chomsky, Noam, **2:244–245**
on Arnauld, 2:423
on behaviorism, 1:523, 5:190, 8:151
cognitive psychology and, 8:151
in cognitive revolution, 1:522
Condillac and, 2:423
on grammatical transformations, 9:360
on innate ideas, 4:694
on language, 5:189–190
on language acquisition, 4:693
linguistics of, 8:151
in mental-physical distinction, 6:139
on phonological and logical form, 5:510
on "poverty-of-the-stimulus" arguments, 4:690
on semantics, 8:807
on Skinner's radical behaviorism, 9:62
socialism of, 9:91
on Soviet Union, 9:91
on syntactical categories, 9:355–356
on syntax, 1:344, 9:360
on universal grammar, 2:244, 2:423, 3:483
on well-formedness of natural languages, 9:352
Chong Yakyong, 5:139–140
Choses passées (Loisy), 5:571
Chosun dynasty, 5:137
Choumunos, Nikephoros, 1:788
Chreia (moral epigram), 3:90
Christ Jesus. *See* Jesus Christ
Christenheit oder Europa, Die (Novalis), 6:667
Christensen, Ferrel, presentism and, 9:479
"Christentum der Vernunft, Das" (The Christianity of reason) (Lessing), 5:296
Christian and Metaphysical Meditations (Malebranche), 5:664
Christian anthropology, Fëdorov and, 3:558–559
Christian Conversations (Malebranche), 5:664
Christian existentialism, of Zubiri (Xavier), 9:888
Christian Faith, The (Schleiermacher), 8:633
Christian Hope of Immortality (Taylor), 9:374
Christian humanism, of Milton, 6:249, 6:250
Christian liberty, Milton on, 6:250
Christian Message in a Non-Christian World (Kraemer), 1:479
Christian Neoplatonism, 3:670, 7:141
Christian philosophy
Aquinas and, 4:92
Brownson on, 1:706
Dostoevsky and, 3:99–102
and ethics, 3:401–404
Gilson on, 4:92–93
on God's existence, 2:551
Greek philosophy in, 7:387
influences on, 3:401
and Platonism, 3:669
and political philosophy, 7:657–658
rise of, 3:401
Schlegel and, 8:632
Christian Religion, as profess'd by a daughter of the Church of England (Astell), 1:355
Christian scholasticism
and Jewish philosophy, 4:820–824
problem of, 9:772
Christian Science, on evil, problem of, 3:471
Christian spiritualism, 4:53, 4:95
Christian theology
Aquinas and, 2:8
Averroism and, 1:650
Boethius on, 1:625–626
Bonald's ultramontanism and, 1:648
Bonaventure and, 1:651
Bonhoeffer on, 1:656
Boulainvilliers on, 1:670
Bulgakov and, 1:760
Bultmann on, 1:762–764
Calvin and, 2:8
Carolingian thought and, 2:50
Cartesianism and, 2:60
Channing on, 2:130–131
concept of person in, 7:237
Desgabets and, 2:61
faith in
compared to Jewish faith, 3:536
as *emunah vs. pistis,* 1:716
limits of rationalism in, 1:629
on moral perfection, 7:194–195
philosophy and, 1:650–651
reason and authority in, 1:626
revelation as dialectical discourse in, 1:707
of Solov'ëv and, 9:124
Christian Thought, Its History and Application (Troeltsch), 9:528
Christian writers, Petrarch's reading of, 7:264–265
Christianity, **2:245–251**
aesthetics in, 1:46–48
agent intellect and, 1:91
agnosticism and, 1:92–93
Albo and, 1:102–103
al-Ghazālī (Muḥammad) on, 1:119
altruism in, 1:136
analogy in, 1:140
animal cruelty and, 4:204
apologists in, **1:227–229,** 6:266–267
Aristotelianism and, 1:425, 1:428
asceticism in, 1:351
Augustine and, 1:390–392
Averroism and, 1:425, 1:430
Barth on, 1:477–480, 3:505
Bayle and, 1:506–507, 5:236
Berdyaev on, 1:561
body in, 8:122–123
Bolzano on, 1:646
Bonhoeffer on, 1:655
Bulgakov on, 1:760–761
Bultmann on, 1:762–764
Burke on, 1:771

Christianity, ***continued***
in Byzantine tradition, 1:787
Celsus on, 2:119
Chaadaev on, 2:120–121
Chateaubriand on, 2:138
and choosing to accept or to reject God's Word, 5:62
Chubb's "Christian deism" and, 2:252–253
Clement of Alexandria on, 2:289–290
Collingwood on, 2:326
Comenius on, 2:341
on creation, 3:475, 7:490
Damarsais on, 2:266
Dante on, 2:624–626
Darwin and, 2:629–630, 2:640–641
on death, 2:651, 2:652
defense of, Tillich on, 9:460
and determinism, 3:7–10
discipleship in, 1:764
doctrines in, development of, 6:581–582
dogma in, 3:97, 4:143, 7:259, 8:587–588
Eastern, in Tolstoy, 9:512
education in, 7:367–368
and Egyptian magic religion, 1:709
Eliot (George) on, 3:184
Eliot (T. S.) on, 3:186
emanationism in, 3:189
Emerson on, 6:574
Enlightenment and, 3:245–246
eschatology in, 3:347–348
on eternal return doctrine, 3:353
on eternity, 3:357–359
ethical utility of, Saint-Simon on, 8:591
evidence for, Paley on, 7:76–77
on evil, problem of, 1:363, 3:469–474, 3:477–478
in evolution of pantheism, 9:262–263
evolutionary naturalism and, 1:474
existentialism and historicity in, 1:762–764
experiential expressivism in, 8:636
freedom and, 4:274
Galen and, 4:6
Gibbon on, 4:84–86
Gnosticism as aberration of, 4:97
Goethe on, 4:143, 7:97
golden rule and, 4:144
Greek philosophy and, 9:533
Greek physicotheology and, 7:557
Haeckel on, 4:204
happiness in, 2:652
Hatano on, 4:247
heaven in, 4:249–252
Hegel on, 4:260–264, 4:276–277
Heim on, 4:297
hell in, 4:249–252
heresy in, 9:508
history and, 1:763, 2:245–246, 7:387, 8:635
Rosenzweig on, 4:829
Solov'ëv on, 9:125
Holocaust from perspective of, 4:453–454
Hume on, 6:266–267
Huxley (Thomas) on, 1:93
illumination in, 4:580
immoral society and, 1:505
and immortality, 4:618, 9:374
incarnation of Christ in, Gilbert of Poitiers on, 4:88
inclusiveness understanding of, 2:13
Judaism and, 4:826–828
in Kang's neo-Confucian political reform, 2:158
Kempis on, 9:424
Kierkegaard and, 5:64–65
La Mothe Le Vayer and, 5:182
Laberthonnière on, 5:165
Le Clerc on, 5:236
Le Roy on, 5:288
legalism in, 9:70
Lessing on, 5:295–296
Lewis (C. S.) on, 5:311–312
and life, meaning and value of, 5:345
and living before God by faith alone, 5:65
Locke on, 3:246, 5:392
logos in, 5:569–570
Losev on, 5:575
Lotze on, 5:581, 5:582
love in, 3:623, 5:585–587
Dostoevsky on, 3:99–100
Hutcheson on, 1:136
pacifism and, 7:67
Malthus on, 5:676
Manichaeism and, **5:682–685**
Martineau on, 5:726
on martyrdom, 9:320
medieval challenges to, 2:644
Meslier on, 2:266, 6:154
miracles in, 1:783
Miura on, 6:276
modern role of, Eucken on, 3:452
moral influence of
Nietzsche on, 6:611–612
Westermarck on, 9:738
mysticism of, 6:447–450
as myth, 9:262
Naigeon on, 6:476
natural law in, 7:454
and Nature, 6:519, 7:14
negative theology and, 3:401
Neoplatonism and, 1:390, 2:322, 3:403, 6:549, 6:555–556
in New England transcendentalism, 6:573
Newton on, 6:591–592
Nietzsche on, 6:612, 7:153, 9:102
Paine on, 7:73–74
Palmer (E.) on, 7:78
Pannenberg and, 7:80
Parker (T.) on, 7:121–122
Pascal on, 7:133–134
patristic philosophy and, **7:141–144**
persecution of, 9:508
personal nature of God in, 4:112
pessimism in, 7:246
philosophy and, 1:390–391, 2:246
philosophy of law and, 7:420–422
Plantinga on, 3:324, 7:580–581
and Platonism, 7:609–610
Plotinus and, 3:401
Porphyry on, 6:550
on power, 7:732
psychology and, 8:121–123
rational fideism in proof of, 4:96
rational inferiority of, 4:809
rationalization of, 1:6–7
realism in, 6:606
reason and stability in, 1:622–623
in religious philosophy, 7:490–492
on resurrection, 3:348
revelation in, 8:331, 8:451–452
Ritschl on, 8:480–481
in Roman Empire, 1:399–401, 3:401, 7:387
Rosenzweig on, 4:829
Rozanov on, 8:525
Sabatier on, 8:587–588
Schleiermacher on, 8:635
science and, 3:452, 4:297
Shelley on, 9:8
and skepticism, 9:51
Smith (John) on, 9:70
Socrates and, 9:113
Spinoza on, 9:178
Stace on, 9:200
Stoics and, 3:400
Strauss on, 6:610
on suicide, 9:319–321
Swift on, 9:341
Teilhard on, 9:375
Tillich on, 9:458–459
and toleration, 1:502, 9:507–509

transcendence in, 4:107
on unity of God, 4:110
universal salvation in, 4:251–252
and violence, 9:133
Voltaire on, 9:711–712
on war and peace, 7:152–154
Winstanley in, 1:177
Woolston and, 9:844–845
world view conflicts in, 1:762
See also Catholicism
Christianity and Morals (Westermarck), 9:738
Christianity and Positivism (McCosh), 6:71
Christianity as Old as the Creation: Or, The Gospel A Republication of the Religion of Nature (Tindal), 2:274, 2:683, 2:686, 5:220, 6:214, 9:502–503
Christianity Not Founded on Argument (Dodwell), 2:686
Christianity not Mysterious; Or a treatise Shewing That there is nothing in the Gospel Contrary to Reason, Nor above it: And that no Christian Doctrine can be properly call'd a Mystery (Toland), 2:683, 3:245–246, 6:656, 9:249, 9:504–505
Christina (queen of Sweden), 2:754–755
Descartes and, 3:188
La Peyrère and, 5:196
Christine de Pizan, on dualism, 5:373
Christliche Glaubenslehre, Die (Strauss), 9:262
Christlicher Lieder (Lavater), 5:213
Christoffel, Elwin Bruno, 4:61
Christology
in Christian Trinitarian theology, 2:248
incarnation in, 2:247
John of Damascus and, 4:837
School of St. Victor and, 8:592
Christus Unus Omnium Magister (Bonaventure), 1:651
Chronica und beschreibung der Turkey mit ihrem begriff, 3:712
Chronica, Zeytbuch und geschycht bibel (Franck), 3:712–713
Chronicle (St. Jerome), 5:598
Chronicle of the Twenty-four Generals (1370), 1:453
Chronicles of Narnia (Lewis), 5:312
Chronology, Newton in, 6:591–592
Chronomereology, 6:147
Chrosroes (king of Persia), 2:622
Chrysippus, **2:251–252**
on citizenship of world, 2:567
on combination theory, 5:441
on determinism, 3:5–6
dialectic and, 3:54
Diogenes Laertius on, 3:88
Epictetus and, 3:261
epistemology of, 3:288
and ethics, 3:400
Galen on, 5:408
Liar paradox and, 5:407
on logic, 5:404–405, 5:408
Philo of Megara and, 7:312
on semantics, 8:757
Seneca on, 8:812
Sorites paradox and, 5:407
and Stoicism, 4:301, 9:254
Chrysoloras, Manuel, 7:613
Chto delat'? (Chernyshevskii), 2:147
Chto takoe progress? (What is progress?) (Mikhailovskii), 6:215
Chu Hsi. *See* Zhu Xi
Chuang Tzu. *See* Zhuangzi
Chubb, Thomas, **2:252–253,** 2:684
deism and, 2:683, 2:691
Morgan and, 2:684
Chulhak, in Korea, 5:141
Chung Dojeon, 5:137
Chunqiu Fanlu (Copious dew in spring and autumn) (Dong Zhongshu), 3:98
Church
authority of, and state, 4:842, 9:783–784
Bultmann on, 1:763
in Christianity, 2:249–250
de Maistre on, 5:659
dogmatics and, 1:478
education and, 7:368
Kant on, 5:30
of liberal arts, in Coleridge, 2:320
Luther on, 5:612
Maritain on, 5:715–716
Marsilius of Padua on, 5:722–723
Milton on, 6:250
Naigeon on, 6:476
national, in relation to state, 9:204
nature of, Law on, 5:220
Ockham on, 9:783–784
and state
Calvin on, 2:10–11
Haeckel on, 4:203–204
source of temporal and spiritual sovereignty, 1:542
in Stillingfleets' latitudinarianism, 9:249
unity of, 1:648
Church, Alonzo, **2:253–255,** 5:536
on calculable functions, 2:401
on Carnap, 8:739, 9:348
on combinatory arithmetic, 2:337
and combinatory logic, 2:340
on computability theory, 2:375
computing machines and, 2:402–403
on effectively computable functions, 5:474
on first-order logic, 3:658
Frege and, 3:732, 5:39
on intentionality, 4:706
and lambda conversion in combinatory logic, 2:335
liar paradox and, 5:317
on mathematical logic, 5:475–476
Montague and, 6:329
on quantification, 6:290
on semantics, 8:76
on syntax, 1:344
Turing and, 5:477, 9:552
on type theory, 9:558–559
Church Dogmatics (Barth), 1:478
Church Fathers. *See* Patristic philosophy
Churchill, Winston, 5:351, 9:397
Churchland, Patricia
on connectionist models, 2:444
in early philosophical neuroscience, 6:563–564
eliminative materialism and, 3:183
Churchland, Paul
on connectionist models, 2:444
eliminative materialism and, 3:183
on knowledge by acquaintance, 5:114
Church-Rosser theorem
in illative combinatory logic, 2:339
as lambda conversion principle, 2:336
Church's theorem, 5:477, 5:536, 8:708
Church's thesis
Bishop's theory of continuum and, 2:504–505
calculability and, 2:375, 5:476
on calculable functions, 2:401
on computability, 2:379–380, 5:478
computing machines and, 2:402
definition of, 5:536
empirical evidence and, 2:380
Turing machines and, 2:376
See also Computability theory
"Church's Thesis and Principles for Mechanisms" (Gandy), 2:406
Church-Turing thesis, 5:478, 9:552
Chūshingura, 9:859
Chwistek, Leon, **2:255–257,** 5:290
Cicero, Marcus Tullius, **2:257–259**
Abelard and, 1:6
on art, 1:189
Augustine and, 1:390, 7:421

Cicero, Marcus Tullius, ***continued***
Boethius and, 1:625–626, 5:421–422
Collins on, 2:331
Dante and, 2:624–626
on decorum, 7:79
on Democritus, 5:298
on determinism, 3:17
and dialectic, 3:54, 4:66
on duty, 3:153
on Epicurus, 3:265
Garve on, 4:24
on glory, 7:79
Jerome on, 5:598
law in, 7:419–420
on logic, 5:408, 5:437
Luther on, 5:615
Machiavelli and, 5:629–630
Marsilius of Padua and, 5:724
medieval logic and, 5:422
Panaetius of Rhodes and, 7:79
panpsychism and, 7:84
Petrarch and, 7:264
Philodemus of Gadara on, 3:264
on Plato and Aristotle, 7:571
on Pyrrho, 8:173
on supernatural, 6:268
translations of, 9:50
Ciel ouvert à tous les hommes, Le (attrib: Cuppé), 2:267
Cigarette smoking, and cancer, 9:755
Cinders (Derrida), 2:717
Cinema (Deleuze), 2:695, 7:382, 9:492
Ciphers, 4:802. *See also* Symbols
Circle, arguing in, 3:546–547
Circular arguments, logical knowledge and, 5:511–512
Circular reasoning (begging the question), definition of, 5:543
Circumscription, in logic, 6:643
Circumstances
in chaos theory, 2:131
in Confucian ethics, 2:195
human freedom and, 1:763
in meaning of sentences, 9:812
in meaning of words, 9:814–815
in Mill's methods of induction, 6:239
responsibility and, 8:164
in verifiability, 9:663
Cities of Words: Pedagogical Letters on a Register of the Moral Life (Cavell), 2:116
Citizens
Bellarmine on, 1:542–543
power of, Spinoza on, 9:181–182
sovereignty and, 9:142–143
in state, 9:205–206
Stewart on, 9:247
Citizens' militias, importance of, 3:605
Citizenship
Aristotle on, 9:206
cosmopolitanism and, 2:567
in development of states, 9:204
Dong Zhongshu on, 2:235
education and, Confucius on, 2:231
French Revolution and, 8:627
vs. groupism, 9:208
vs. nationality, 6:481
Rousseau on, 9:206
Cittadini, Antonio, Pico della Mirandola and, 7:572
City of God (Augustine), 1:228, 6:519, 7:521–522
influences on, 3:401
on life, 3:402
nature *vs.* miracle in, 1:398
Roman Empire and, 1:399
"City of God" concept, origin of, 3:400
Cive, De (Hobbes), 9:177
Civic Oration (Oración cívica) (Barreda), 5:206
Civil disobedience, **2:259–262**
and criteria for selective action, 2:261
in czarist Russia, 9:89
in socialist revolution, 9:89
"Civil Disobedience" (Thoreau), 2:259
Civil liberties
Einstein and, 3:179
individualism and, 2:364
in Kant's civil contract, 9:73–74
Civil philosophy, of Romagnosi, 8:484–485
Civil rights, Einstein and, 3:179
Civil society, 9:96–98
communitarianism and, 2:369
Ferguson on, 9:247
Hegel on, 4:268, 9:206
latitudinarianism and, 9:249
Locke on, 9:207
Spinoza on, 9:181
Civil War in France, The (Marx), 5:731
Civil world, knowledge of, 9:674
Civilistische Abhandlungen (Thibaut), 8:615
Civility
in civil disobedience, 2:260
Xunzi on, 2:234
Civilization
Buckle on, 1:719
as community transformation, Collingwood on, 2:329
Comte on, 2:412
crisis of, Masaryk on, 6:2
vs. cultivation, Coleridge on, 2:320
Daoist critique of, 2:236
Dostoevsky on, 3:101
in Europe, 1:719
Gobineau's theory of, 4:106
Gracián on, 4:168
in historical process, 9:732–733
Ibn Khaldūn on, 4:548
identity of, determining, 9:518
Maritain on, 5:715
medieval *vs.* modern, 5:715
Mencius on, 2:234
Morgan (Lewis) on, 6:403–404
origin of, Diodorus on, 5:302
philosophy of, Deustua on, 3:42
Rousseau on, 3:470
Sombart on, 9:128
in Spengler's cultural morphology, 9:167
Taine on, 9:365
Toynbee on, 9:517–518
unconscious and, 9:572–573
in utopianism, 9:617–618
Xunzi on, 2:234
Civitas Solis (The city of the sun) (Campanella), 2:16
Cixous, Hélène, **2:262–263,** 3:565, 9:274
Claim of Reason, The (Cavell), 1:68, 2:115
Clairaut, Alexis-Claude, in calculus, 6:593
Clairvoyance, 7:113–114, 7:226, 7:752. *See also* Parapsychology
Clan, Durkheim on, 3:150
Clandestine philosophical literature in France, **2:263–268**
Clapeyron, Benôit, Helmholtz and, 3:231
Clapham Sect, 9:243
Clapp, Elise Ripley, 3:567
Clarity and distinctness
in metaphysics, 6:190–191
Rehmke on, 8:302
Clark, Austin, 8:193
Clark, C. H. D., 5:345, 5:350
Clark, Charles E., 5:247
Clark, Edward, 5:390
Clark, Lorene, 3:600
Clarke, James Freeman, 6:572
Clarke, John, 9:834
Clarke, Samuel, **2:268–275**
Balguy and, 1:474
conscience and, 2:445
Cumberland and, 2:615
on deism, 2:682, 2:686
on determinism, 3:15–18
on duty, 3:155

on ethics, 2:273–274
on existence of God, 9:407
on force measurement, 3:228
on free will, 2:271
on God, 2:270
Johnson (Dr. Samuel) and, 4:853–854
Leibniz and, 3:228, 3:297, 5:254, 9:155
Locke and, 5:375
on matter and laws of nature, 2:271–272
on miracles, 6:267
on naturalism and natural religion, 2:269–270
physicotheology in, 7:559
religion in, 2:273–274
Sidgwick and, 9:25
on soul, 2:273, 3:116–120
on space and time, 2:272
Wollaston and, 9:833
Clarke, W. Norris, on Aquinas, 9:448
Class
in Aristotle's metaphysics, 6:186
Boole on, 5:449–450
in bundle theory, 6:180
definition of, 5:536
of elements, in first-order model theory, 6:304–305
existential import of, Venn on, 5:451
Frege on, 5:464
indefinable, Ramsey on, 5:468
Jevons on, 5:450
membership in, and syllogistic inference, 5:502
of modal interpretations, 6:278–279
proper, definition of, 5:552
reduction of universals to, 6:176–178
requiring a translation into, 3:640
Russell on, 5:467, 8:552
of structures, in first-order model theory, 6:303–304
Venn on, 5:451
Class (mathematical and logical)
Leśniewski on, 5:290–291
predicative hierarchy and species of, 1:701
properties and, 8:64
Class (socioeconomic)
Arnold on, 1:294
education and, 7:362
exploitation and, 5:733–734
law and, 7:419
Marx on, 5:732–733, 7:390, 7:427
Mosca on, 6:407
Proudhon on, 8:94
See also Social class
Class inequality, 3:599
Class logic, Boole on, 5:450
Class names, in De Morgan's logic, 5:448
Class nominalism, 6:176–178
Class quantification, 8:197
Class struggle
Meslier on, 2:267
in Shariati's Islam, 9:7
Class theory, part and whole in, 6:146
Classical computers, *vs.* quantum computers, 8:200–201
Classical foundationalism, **2:275–279**
Classical heritage, Russia lacking, 5:75
Classical identity, 4:570–571
Classical mechanics, philosophy of, **2:279–284**
analytical mechanics in, 2:282–283
basic ontology of, 2:280
determinism and, 7:474
force in, 2:280
fundamental laws of, 2:280–281
mass in, 2:280
matter in, 2:280
mechanism in, 2:281–282
motion in, 2:280
space in, 7:474–475
teleology in, 2:283
time in, 7:474–475
time-reversal invariance, 2:281
Classical philosophy
beauty in, 1:511–512
in Byzantine tradition, 1:787
Carneades and, 2:46–48
medieval revival of, 6:189–190
metaphysics in, 6:183–188
Classicism
Boileau on, 1:639–640
Burke on, 1:771
in Cousin's aesthetics, 2:580
Croce and, 2:601
Classification
in chemistry, 2:141–142
Dge-lugs doctrinal categorization as, 1:733
of disease, 7:465–466
ethical, Carneades and, 2:48
faults in, and fallacies, 3:545
in Hua yan Buddhism, 1:736
of human cultural practices, 5:116
by hypothesis, 6:560
of knowledge, Peirce on, 7:169
of law, 7:443–444
Locke on, 9:596
of mass/count distinction, 6:659–660
process of, 5:537
by style, **1:330–333**
See also Definition
Clauberg, Johannes, 2:55, **2:284–288**
Clausewitz, Karl von, 7:154
Clausius, Rudolf
on entropy, 7:578
heat studies of, 7:537
Clavis Hieroglyphia (A hieroglyphic key) (Swedenborg), 9:337
Clavis Universalis (Collier), 2:323, 4:554
Clavius, Christopher, 2:721, 5:50, 8:595
Clay, E. R., on time, 9:483
Clay Mathematics Institute, 2:389
Clayton, Nicola, 1:203
Cleansing, 5:44
Cleanthes, **2:288–289**
and ethics, 3:400
on logic, 5:404
on love of God, 5:585
Clear cases, in law, 7:451
Clement IV, Pope, 1:452
Clement V, Pope, 3:148
Clement VIII, Pope, 7:144
Clement IX, Pope, 1:288, 6:604
Clement of Alexandria, **2:288–290**
as apologist, 1:228
Christian ethics and, 3:401
and eschatology, 3:348
on ideas as thought of God, 4:564
patristic philosophy and, 7:141–143
on purgatory, 3:348
Clerselier, Claude
Descartes and, 2:753
Desgabets and, 2:757–758
Cleve, James van, on emergence, 3:191
Clifford, William Kingdon, **2:291–294**
cosmic brain argument and, 1:369
maxim of, 5:99
panpsychism and, 7:83
Climacus writings, 5:67
Climate, A (Fūdo) (Watsuji), 9:727
Climate, historical determinism and, 3:36–37
Climbing the Mountain (Parfit), 7:120
Clinging, in Buddhism, 5:328
Clinical interpretation, in psychoanalytic theory, 8:112–114
Clinical investigation, free association and, 3:741
Clinical language, and language of rationality, 3:699
Clinical medicine, free and informed consent in, 6:97
Clinical psychology, 8:153

Clinomachus of Thurii, 6:110
Clinton, Bill, on engineering profession, 3:239
Clitomachus
- on Carneades, 1:195
- Diogenes Laertius on, 3:88
- Philo of Larissa and, 7:311
- on probable impressions, 2:48
- and skepticism, 1:195, 2:48

Cloning, 4:47, 6:96
Closed diagram, 3:656
Closed schema. *See* Closed sentence
Closed sentence (closed schema), definition of, 5:537
Closed systems
- Hamiltonian theory on energy conservation and, 2:464
- physical domain as, 2:89–93
- prediction for, 3:710
- probability and, 3:709–710

Closed term, 3:648
Closed with respect to (closed under) a relation, definition of, 5:537
Closedness
- in biology *vs.* thermodynamics, 1:594
- in society, 1:571
- of Universe as system, 1:634

Closure
- of formula, definition of, 5:537
- as gestalten factor, 5:127
- of physical, 6:134
- universal, definition of, 5:537

Cloudesley (Godwin), 4:136
Clouds, The (Aristophanes), 4:177, 9:106
"Club, The" (Johnson, Dr. Samuel), 4:852–853
Cluster theory, concepts as prototypes in, 2:418
Coady, C. A. J., on testimony, 9:400–403
Coal Question, The (Jevons), 4:807
Coase, Ronald, 7:461
Cobbett, William, 5:676, 9:88
Cobbler-prince episode, as puzzle for personal identity issue, 7:214, 7:224–227
Cobden, Richard, 7:155
Cobham, Alan, 2:388
Cocial Construction of What? (Hacking), 9:78
Cockburn, Catherine Trotter, **2:294–295,** 9:838
Code, instructional, normal form theorem and, 2:380–381
Code, Lorraine, **2:295–296,** 9:685
- and Gadamer, 3:565
- and subjectivity, 3:576

Coercion
- direct forms of, 3:722
- by God, 7:484
- indirect forms of, 3:722
- law and, 1:406, 7:444
- liberty and, 5:337–338
- meaning of, 3:722–723
- power and, 7:733

Coextension problem
- of extensionalism, 6:177
- trope theory and, 6:181

Coffa, J. Alberto, on explanation, 3:521
Coffeehouses, Enlightenment and, 3:244–245
Cogan, E. J., 2:340
Cogito ergo sum argument, 2:735–736, 2:740, 2:743, 2:758, 3:291, 5:95–96
- Kant on, 5:22
- Lichtenberg on, 5:339
- Mamardashvili on, 5:679–680
- Mansel and, 5:687
- Marcel on, 5:701
- Régis and, 8:299
- Vico on, 9:671

Cognate, in Cleanthes, 6:146–147
Cognition
- abstractive
  - derivation of, 9:774
  - *vs.* intuitive, 3:139–140
  - in John of Mirecourt's epistemology, 4:841
  - Ockham on, 9:773–776
  - universality of, 9:775
- Aquinas on, 1:47, 9:426–428
- art and, 1:335–337, 4:160–161
- Bacon (Francis) and, 1:453
- of beauty, 1:47
- in Buddhism, 1:748, 1:753
- Carneades on, 2:47
- cellular, 6:567–569
- in Chinese room argument, 2:239, 2:240
- in cognitive science, 2:297
- as communion of knower and known, 3:669
- computational models of, 6:142
- conative theory of, 9:260
- connectionism and, 2:445, 4:694
- in conventional truth and ignorance, 1:734
- cosmic correspondence to, in Xenocrates, 4:173
- Croce on, 2:600–602
- Democritus on, 5:300
- Descartes on, 4:611
- Diogenes of Apollonia on, 3:89–90
- Duns Scotus on, 3:139–140
- in ethical naturalism, 1:688
- Evans on, 2:480
- experience in, 6:74
- faith in, 4:771–772
- as general logic of relation, Natorp on, 6:490
- Geulincx on, 4:79
- gnostic reflection and memory and, 1:712
- God and, 4:818, 5:649, 6:322
- Goldman on, 4:147
- improvement of, 8:660
- in Indian philosophy, 9:542–543
- intentionality in, 1:748, 9:543
- intuitive *vs.* abstractive, 3:139–140
- in Jainism, 9:543
- judgments of responsibility and, 9:686
- in Kantian philosophy, Jacobi (Friedrich Heinrich) on, 4:770–771
- Kitcher and, 5:76
- in lower animals, 1:202
- Mannheim on, 5:685
- materialist, Voltaire and, 9:710–711
- mathematical objects in, 6:674
- in mental moments, 1:753
- metaphor in, 6:166
- molecular, 6:567–569
- Nelson (Leonard) on, 6:535
- Nietzsche on, 4:749
- nonrational, 4:749
- Nyāya, 9:543
- Peirce on, 7:165–166, 7:169–171
- perception and, 6:150
- Peter Aureol on, 7:257
- pictorialism in, 4:590
- Plato on, 7:586
- potencies in, Gerson on, 4:67
- poverty-of-stimulus paradigm and, 4:694
- Prābhākara Mīmāṃsakas on, 9:543
- pragmatic theory of, in classical Indian philosophy, 9:543–544
- psychological approach to, 1:523
- reaction time in, Pylyshyn on, 4:590
- Reinhold on, 8:334
- religion and, 1:142
- Rozanov on, 8:525
- schema correction in, 9:77
- Searle on, 8:705–706
- self-deception as pathology of, 8:711
- self-knowledge and, 8:709–710
- sensory imagination and, 4:600
- in simulation theory, 9:38

social, 8:153
social activity and, 9:77
Spinoza on, 9:174, 9:191
in subject contextualism, 2:482–483
synonymy and, 1:162
theory of value and, 7:204–205
things-in-themselves and, 4:771–772, 8:661
in thought experiments, 9:455
Trubetskoi (Evgenii) on, 9:529
Vātsyāyana on, 9:544
verbalization of, 9:543–544
William of Ockham on, 8:825
Xunzi on, 2:216
in Yogācāra doctrine, 1:747–752
See also Thinking
Cognitive access, alternative models of, 5:86
Cognitive anthropology, in study of memory, 6:126–127
Cognitive attitudes
in attributor contextualism, 2:483
in subject contextualism, 2:482
Cognitive awareness, and mimesis, 5:44
Cognitive capacity, 2:393, 2:450
Cognitive freedom, of man, 3:533
Cognitive idolatry, 7:484–485
Cognitive impression(s), 1:247, 7:271
Cognitive maps, in animals, 1:203
Cognitive processes
individuation of, 8:364
investigation of, 5:86
Cognitive psychology
computationalism and, 2:391, 2:394
epistemology and, 3:275
experimentation in, 8:152–153
Huayan Buddhism and, 1:739
linguistics and, 5:189
memory in, 6:123
mental representation in, 6:140
mental states and, 2:477
and radical behaviorism, 1:522–523
revolution of, 8:150–151
topics in, 8:151–152
Cognitive revolution, Fodor and, 3:675
Cognitive science, **2:296–301**, 7:331
Chinese room argument and, 2:241
computational models and, 2:392
computationalism and, 2:393
connectionism and, 2:443–445
on creative processes, 2:591
fiction in, 1:68
memory research in, 6:125–126
moral norms and, 3:446
pragmatics *vs.* semantics in, 7:739
Cognitive significance, Hempel on, 4:308
Cognitive states, phenomenological description of, 5:85
Cognitive transitions, in connectionist models, 2:444
Cognitive value, of expression, 5:39
Cognitively impenetrable module, visual perception occurring in, 3:676
Cognitivism
art in, 1:340–341
on emotions, 3:198–200
of Hegel, 1:341
of Moore, 6:156
moral judgments and, 6:159, 6:393
on moral truth, 6:160
in morals as constructive content, 2:471
Cognitivist value theory, 9:639–640
Cohen, Felix, 7:428
Cohen, G. A., Marxism of, 5:740
Cohen, Hermann, **2:301–306**
on aesthetics, 1:65, 2:304–305
Husserl and, 6:543
Lange and, 5:187
Meinong and, 6:543
in modern Jewish philosophy, 4:828
Natorp and, 6:490
in neo-Kantianism, 6:540–543
Cohen, Jonathan, 3:763–764, 9:352
Cohen, Morris Raphael, **2:306–308**
on Bingham, 7:428
Nagel (Ernest) and, 6:472
Cohen, Paul, 8:707
on continuum hypothesis, 2:28, 4:662
forcing method of, 8:843–844
Cohen, Stewart, on skepticism, 3:275
Coherence
in classical foundationalism, 2:278–279
criteria of, 7:292–294
of intentional acts, 7:292–295
Coherence of Theism, The (Swinburne), 1:142
Coherence theory
in applied ethics, 1:238
of knowledge, 5:93, 5:248
of truth, **2:308–313**, 3:295, 9:536–537
assumptions of, 2:309–312
Fichte and, 3:309
meaning in, 2:308–309
Neurath on, 3:317
and reflective equilibrium, 9:611
Schuppe on, 8:663
Coherentism, **2:313–315**
experience in, 8:180
in justification of knowledge, 3:271–272, 8:179–180
subject contextualism and, 2:483
Coidentification, 6:236–237
Coincidence
Aristotle on, 1:100
in no-miracles argument, 8:691
precognition as, 7:757
Coincident, in Cleanthes, 6:146
Coke, Edward, 7:423
Cold War
Pauling and, 7:146
postcolonialism and, 7:726
Colden, Cadwallader, 4:851
Colding, A., on energy conservation, 3:230
Coldness and Cruelty (Deleuze), 2:696
Colecchi, Ottavio, 9:159
Coleman, Jules
on analytic jurisprudence, 1:170
Dworkin and, 3:156
on legal positivism, 5:241–243
student of Feinberg, 3:562
Coleridge, Samuel Taylor, **2:315–321**
absolute [term] used by, 1:10
on Bible, 2:641
on Darwin (Erasmus), 2:631
Emerson and, 3:195–196
on faith, 2:316–317
Ficino and, 3:624–625
Hazlitt and, 4:248
on imagination, 1:55, 2:318–319, 4:597
Lessing and, 5:296–297
Mill (John Stuart) and, 6:221
on Milton, 1:304
on mind, 2:318
on morals, 2:319–320
on nature, 2:318
and New England transcendentalism, 6:572
Pater on, 7:136
philosophical development of, 2:315–316
on philosophy, 2:316–317
on politics, 2:319–320
on reason, 2:317
Schelling and, 1:13, 4:558, 8:618
Shelley and, 9:9
Spinoza and, 9:194–195
on understanding, 2:317

Colet, John, **2:321–322**
- Agrippa von Nettesheim and, 1:97
- Erasmus and, 3:337

Colette, 5:152
Collapse dynamics, 5:696–697
- additional variables theories and, 8:212–213
- observation and, 8:209–210
- spontaneous, 8:211–212
- of wave functions, 8:209–212

Collapse postulate, 2:126–127
Collationes (Comparisons) (Abelard), 1:3
Collationes (Duns Scotus), 3:134
Collected Essays and Reviews (James), 8:798
Collected Papers (Peirce), 4:644
Collected Works of John Stuart Mill (Robson, ed.), 6:232
Collection, as method, in Plato, 3:53
Collection of Miscellanies, A (Norris), 6:655
Collective [term], definition of, 5:537
Collective actors, as judicanda of justice, 4:863–865
Collective behavior, social sciences' analysis of, 7:534–535
Collective Choice and Social Welfare (Arrow), 8:810
Collective name, in logic, definition of, 5:549
Collective purpose, 9:281–282
Collective representations
- Durkheim on, 3:150
- Lévy-Bruhl and, 5:306–307

Collective unconscious
- existence of, 4:858
- Jung on, 4:856–858, 9:573

Collective will, and democracy, 2:701–702
Collectivism, 1:472, 4:873–874
- in anarchism, 1:178–179
- *vs.* anarchist communism, 1:179
- Bosanquet and, 1:663
- Bradley and, 1:676
- Chernyshevskii and, 2:146
- Chicherin on, 2:148

Collectivity, *vs. sobornost,* 5:60
Collectivization, 1:472
College(s)
- Dge-lugs scholastic training and, 1:734–735
- universal, Comenius on, 2:341

Collège International de Philosophie, 5:619
Collegia pietatis, 7:575
Collegial model of medical ethics, 6:93
Collegiants, 9:170, 9:175
Collier, Arthur, **2:322–324**
- on immaterialism, 4:554–555
- Norris and, 6:656

Collingwood, Robin George, **2:324–329**
- on art, 1:57, 1:65, 1:304, 1:340–341, 4:598
- Bultmann and, 1:764
- cognitivism of, 1:340–341
- on determinism, 3:40
- Gentile and, 4:53
- on historical knowledge, 7:392
- Hume's "Of Miracles" and, 6:270
- on metaphysical principles, 3:753
- on methodology, 9:36

Collins, Anthony, **2:330–332**
- colleagues of, 2:684
- deism and, 2:683, 2:691
- Priestley and, 8:4
- Swift and, 9:341
- Woolston and, 9:845

Collins, Harry, 8:677–679, 9:84
Collins, John, Leibniz and, 5:252
Collins, Patricia Hill, 3:575, 3:601
Collision(s)
- Huygens on, 2:462
- in physical processes, 6:60

Colloquies (Erasmus), 3:338
Colocated tropes, particulars as, 6:181
Colonialism
- Eurasianist view of, 3:453
- and Islamic philosophy, 4:762
- Latin American philosophy and, 5:204–205, 5:209–211
- postcolonialism and, 7:726
- Stace on, 9:201

Color(s), **2:332–334**
- Boyle on, 1:674
- Condillac and, 2:422
- as determinables, 3:1–2
- Locke on, 1:37
- Newton on, 6:590
- perception of, 1:37
- reality of, 1:39
- Schopenhauer on, 8:648
- as secondary quality, 8:8
- synthetic *a priori* truths and, 1:245

Color vision, perception and, 7:182
Color-blind society, King's vision of, 5:73
Colotes of Lampsacus, Epicurus and, 3:263
Combatants, in just war theory, 4:872–874
Combination(s)
- Chrysippus on, 5:441
- in combinatory logic, 2:334
- Kilwardby on, 5:441
- Leibniz on, 5:441

Combinatory logic, **2:334–340,** 4:671, 5:537
Combinatory Logic (Curry and Feys), 2:337
Combustion, Lavoisier on, 5:217
Comedy
- in Greek drama, 4:177
- sophism in, 9:129
- *See also* Humor

Comenius, John Amos, 2:284, **2:340–342,** 3:755, 7:254, 7:369
Coming to be, *aitia* and, 1:100
Commager, Henry Steele, on American liberalism, 5:322
Commandments (Jewish)
- Maimonides on, 4:819
- rational, 4:813

"Commandments of the Heart" (Bahya), 4:816
Commands, in computability theory, 2:378–379
Commena, Anna, Aristotelianism and, 1:260
Commentaire philosophique sur ces paroles de Jésus-Christ "Constrains les d'entrer" (Bayle), 1:503
Commentaria ac Disputationes in Primam Pattern S. Thomae (Vasquez), 9:649
Commentaria in Aristotelem Graeca (Simplicius), 9:34
Commentaria Oxoniensia. See Ordinatio (Duns Scotus)
Commentaries, in Aristotelianism, 1:259
Commentaries on the Laws of England (Blackstone), 1:553
Commentarium de Religione Christiana Libri Quatuor (Ramus), 8:236
Commentarium in Librum II Sententiarum (Bonaventure), 1:654
Commentary on Aristotle's De Anima (Aquinas), on soul as substance, 4:609
Commentary on Aristotle's Metaphysics (Aquinas), 1:528
Commentary on Boethius's On the Trinity (Thierry of Chartes), 7:612
Commentary on "Fundamental Wisdom of the Middle Way" (Buddhapālita), 1:732
Commentary on Genesis (Origen), 6:538
Commentary on Hegel's Logic (McTaggart), 6:77
Commentary on Parmenides (Proclus), 6:189
Commentary on Plato's Timaeus, A (Taylor), 9:373

"Commentary on *Summa Contra Gentiles*" (Sylvester of Ferrara), 9:343–344
Commentary on the Intimations (Ibn Kammunam), 4:584
Commentary on the Paradoxes of the Sufis (Baqli), 9:306
Commentary on the Parmenides (Proclus), 7:609
Commentary on the Philosophy of Illumination (Shahrazurī), 4:584
"Commentary on the Physics" (Averroes), on first mover, 3:226
Commentary on the Republic (Proclus), 1:190
Commentary on the Sentences (Durandus of Saint-Pourçain), 3:148
Commentary on the Sentences (Gregory of Rimini), 4:183
Commentary on the Sentences (Ockham), 9:773–774
Commentary on the Song of Songs (Gregory of Nyssa), 4:182
Commentatio Philosophica de commercio Mentis et Corporis (Wolff), 5:123
"Commentator, The" *(vrttikara),* 5:118
Commerce
  as fundamental civilizing force, 3:605
  Thoreau on, 9:451
Commerce Defended (Mill, James), 6:218
Commercial society, *vs.* military, 3:605
Commercialism, Emerson on, 3:196–197
Commiseration, as predisposition of heart/mind, 6:129
Commissurotomy, 6:565–566
Commitment
  assumption and, 6:116
  to beliefs, 7:358
  Mounier on, 6:416
  Unamuno on, 9:567
Commitments, Ontic, 8:218
Commodities, in Marx, 5:733–734
Commodities and Capabilities (Sen), 8:810
Common cause principle, **2:342–344**
  causal graphs and, 8:687
  Mill's methodology and, 8:686
  Reichenbach on, 8:686–687
  Salmon on, 8:594
Common consent arguments for the existence of God, **2:344–354**
Common destiny, as gestalten factor, 5:127
Common Faith, A (Dewey), 3:51
Common good
  communitarian ideal of, 9:74–75
  individual profit-seeking and, 1:777
  justice and, 3:684
  sovereignty and, 9:142
Common knowledge, Lewis, 4:16
Common natures
  and generality of concepts, 9:775
  in individual existents, 9:773
Common notions, of deism, 2:682–684, 6:405
Common personal language, in other minds, 7:56
Common properties
  necessity of, 9:594
  in Nyāya-Vaiśeika realism, 9:582
  perception of, 9:585
  vs. universals, 9:584
Common sense, **2:354–361**
  Aliotta on, 1:127
  Aquinas on, 4:697
  in beliefs, 1:510, 2:355–356
  Berkeley on, 1:579–580, 1:583, 3:301–302
  Black on, 1:605
  Bolzano on, 1:646
  Bradley on, 4:558
  in computationalism, 2:391–392
  Cousin on, 2:579
  double truth and contextual meaning as, 2:209
  eliminative materialism on, 3:182–183
  existence of God argued from, 7:700–701
  and external senses, 4:697
  Galluppi and, 4:14
  in Gestalt theory, 4:72–75
  Johnson and, 8:794
  Jouffroy on, 4:855
  language and, 5:662
  manifest image in, 8:734
  Moore (G. E.) and, 1:145, 3:314, 6:345–346, 7:108–109
  moral constructivism and, 2:472–473
  in moral principles, 9:23
  Peirce on, 7:171
  Priestley on, 8:6
  vs. reflection, 9:795
  Rescher on, 8:440
  Royer-Collard on, 8:524
  scientific knowledge and, 1:566
  Sellars on, 8:734
  in Sibley's method of ethics, 9:22–23
  and skepticism, 9:56
  Stewart on, 9:246–247
  Strawson on, 2:79
  theoretical science and, 8:734
  in utilitarianism, 6:227
Common Sense (Paine), 7:73
Common Sense and Nuclear Warfare (Russell), 7:155
Common Sense of the Exact Sciences (Clifford), 2:291
Common supposition, 5:557
Commonality problem, 3:586
Common-sense framework, of mentalistic understanding, 3:677
Common-sense hypothesis, 3:746
Common-sense intuitionism, 3:409, 9:22
Common-sense law, Duhem on, 3:128
Common-sense realism, 8:264–265
  McCosh on, 6:70
  perception and, 7:178–179
Commonwealth, Hobbes on, 4:418–420
Commonwealth of Oceana (Harrington), 9:504
Communal ownership
  of land, 5:75
  Plato on, 2:364
Commune(s)
  anarchist-communist view of, 5:154
  utopianism of, 9:618
Communia Mathematica (Bacon, Roger), 1:452, 5:442
Communia Naturalium (Bacon, Roger), 1:452
Communication
  action in, 6:80–81
  in animals, 1:204–205
  Apel on, 1:226
  art as, 1:57, 1:304, 1:312–313, 2:580
  chemical, Wilson (Edward O.) on, 9:788
  Chinese room argument and, 2:240
  computer ethics and, 2:396
  conversational implicature and, 2:525–526
  Cordemoy on, 2:537
  Croce's nonconceptual language of, 2:601
  as evidence of consciousness, 1:205
  explicit *vs.* implicit, 7:766
  Habermas on, 4:200
  immediate signification in, 8:792
  in introspection, 6:80–81
  Ivanov's cathartic philosophy of, 4:767–768

Communication, ***continued***
in Jaspers's psychology. *See Existenzursprung*
language and, 7:400
Mead on, 6:80–81
personhood and, 7:240
philosophy and, 7:333
pragmatism and, 7:743
presupposing and, 7:765–766
progress as, in Turgot, 9:551
of Scholastics, artificialization of language and, 6:102
Schutz on, 8:665
Shannon's mathematical theory of, 9:234
in Tolstoy, 1:57
Communicative action theory, Habermas on, 3:91
Communicative rationality, Habermas on, 4:200
Communism, **2:361–368**
American liberalism and, 5:322
anarchist, 1:179
Anderson (John) and, 1:197
Asiatic, 2:363–364
vs. collectivism, 1:179
definition of, 2:362
on distribution of social goods, 9:73
economics and, 7:353–354
emergence of, Marx on, 3:68–69
existentialism and, 3:506
and freedom, 2:362, 5:734
Gramsci on, 4:169–170
in historical materialism, 4:380
history of, 2:363–368
Marx and, 2:361, 5:734. *See also Communist Manifesto* (Marx)
Merleau-Ponty and, 6:149–150
Mutahhari and, 8:647
nihilistic *vs.* dialectical forms of, 2:361
Proudhon on, 8:94
revolution and, 9:89
Russell on, 7:156
in Russia, rise of, 3:454
Sartre and, 8:604
toleration of, 9:510
on war, 7:154
Communist Manifesto (Marx), 2:361–365, 5:730, 7:427, 9:451
Engels and, 3:238
on equality, 9:73
on ethics, 3:415
history in, 7:390
internationalism in, 9:89
law in, 7:427
philosophy of sex and, 7:522
"*Communistes ont peur de la revolution, Les*" (Sartre), 8:604
Communitarianism, **2:368–369**
in applied ethics, 1:239
on coercive institutions, 9:74–75
MacIntyre and, 5:637
nationalism in, 6:485–486
political philosophy and, 7:678–679
on Rawls's social contract theory, 9:82
Socinus and, 9:99–100
Community(ies)
Anderson (John) on, 1:199
vs. association, 9:96
Augustine on, 3:401
Bosanquet on, 1:663
Bradley (F. H.) on, 1:676, 3:416
in Buddhism, 1:723–726
business and, 1:779
Carnap on, 2:37
church and, 2:249
and civil disobedience, 2:260
Collingwood on, 2:329
of color, women *vs.* men in, 3:585
communism and, 2:365
communitarianism and, 2:368
Condorcet on, 2:433
in contractualism, 2:518
cosmopolitanism and, 2:567, 2:570
creation of, 3:611
Descartes on, 2:365
Dewey on, 3:48–49
individual in
Milton on, 6:250
Oakeshott on, 7:2
of inquiry, democratic, 3:577
Kant on, 2:367
Marx on, 2:365
in Marxist socialism *vs.* communal living, 1:716–717
in moral cosmopolitanism, 2:568
Neurath on, 6:561
nihilistic view of, 1:612
and ownership, 8:73–74
politics of, 5:637
Pufendorf on, 8:158
as reflective, 1:459
and rights *vs.* ethical responsibility for others, 2:196–197
Ritschl on, 8:481
Rousseau on, 2:366
state as, 9:204
Stein on, 9:240
Community of Rights, The (Gewirth), 4:81
Commutative justice, 4:865
Commutative law, in Boole, 5:460
Commutativity
definition of, 5:537
for extensive properties, 6:90
Comnena, Anna, and Byzantine culture, 1:788
Compactness theorem, 6:308–309
Robinson on, 5:481
Tarski on, 5:480
Companion to the Almanac (periodical), contributors to, 2:709
Comparability
equality as, 3:334
law of (law of trichotomy), definition of, 5:537
Comparative(s), superlative implied in, 2:677–679
Comparative method, in Comte, 2:411
Comparative philosophy, Corbin and, 2:537
Comparative probability axiom, in subjective expected utility, 2:658
Comparative question, of knowledge *vs.* true opinion, 5:102
Comparative relation, 6:88
Comparative religion, 2:691, 3:682
Comparison
Comte on, 2:411
in consciousness, Ziehen (Theodor) on, 9:884
in measurement of time, 9:461
Comparison theory of metaphor, 6:168
Compassion
Buddhist notion of, 5:137
Confucius on, 2:231
Eliot (George) on, 3:185
forgiveness not secured by, 3:698
in Hinduism, 7:486
in Pure Land Buddhism, 2:168–169
sympathy and, 9:345
in Tang's neo-Confucianism, 2:183
Compatibilism, 3:718
Compendium Logicae (Javellus), 5:440
Compendium Musicae (Descartes), 1:49
Compendium of Hebrew Grammar (Spinoza), 9:183–184
Compendium of the Lives and Opinions of Philosophers (Diogenes Laertius). *See Lives and Opinions of Eminent Philosophers*
Compendium Sensus Litteralis Totius Scripturae (Peter Aureol), 7:256–257
Compendium Studii Philosophiae (Bacon, Roger), 1:452
Compensation, Emerson on, 3:195–196
Competence
philosophical, 7:335–336
social, 9:198

Competition
 business moral obligations and, 1:780
 in Daoist social and political thought, 2:237
 Hegel on, 4:270
 in philosophy, 6:669
 Ruskin on, 8:534
Complement of a set, 5:537
Complementarity
 Bohr on, 2:531–532
 in quantum theory, 1:637–639, 2:531–532
Complete Neuroscientific Works of Sigmund Freud, The (Solms), 3:737
Complete proof calculus, 3:657
Complete set, definition of, 5:537
Complete states, 3:709
Complete theory, 3:650–651
Completeness
 in combinatory logic, 2:335
 computability theory axiomatization and, 2:383
 in degrees of truth, 2:309–311
 Hilbert on, 4:361–364
 of logical system, definition of, 5:537
 Łukasiewicz on, 5:607
 of physics, 7:474
 Post's definitions of, 5:467
 of quantum mechanics, 2:529
 of sense data, in Broad, 1:696
Completeness (mathematical)
 semantics and, 9:368
 Tarski on, 9:366–368
Completeness theorems, of Kripke, 5:149
Complex(es)
 in ontology, 7:25
 theory of, 6:116
Complex equipotential system, 9:697
Complex fact, functional analysis as description of, 3:763
Complex numbers, 6:671–672
Complexity
 chief use of, 3:648
 of evolution, in Teilhard, 9:374
 induction and, 3:648
 of organisms, 7:469
 of universe, atheism and, 1:371–372
 Wittgenstein on, 9:811
Complicated formations, genealogy and, 3:700
Component *vs.* resultant forces, 3:691
Composite dualism, 3:115
Composite dynamical state, 6:278
Composite objects, agnosticism about, 3:628
Composition fallacy, 3:541–543
Composition of functions, 5:554
Composition operator, 6:89–90
Compositional dualism, 3:115–116
Compositional meaning, 6:83, 7:402–405
Compositionality, **2:370–372**
 as empirically empty, 2:370
 Frege on, 8:61
 in philosophy of language, 7:403–404
 semantic, 8:61
Compositive order, Zabarella on, 9:867
Compotista, Garlandus, 5:424
Compound(s), elements in, Zabarella on, 9:866
Compound formula, 3:648
Compound terms, 3:647
Comprehension
 axiom of, 5:533
 Keynes on, 5:457
 Lewis (C. I.) on, 5:308
Comprehension scheme, for second-order arithmetic, 8:455–456
Comprehensive doctrine, Rawls on, 5:325
Compression, of sentences, 2:371
Compromise
 democracy and, 2:704
 vs. forgiveness, 3:698
 unconscious and, 3:739
Compulsion
 responsibility and, 8:163–164
 from understanding, 9:813
Computability
 calculability and, 2:380
 and partial functions, 2:380
 Turing machines and, 5:477
"Computability and λ-Definability" (Turing), 5:477
Computability theory, **2:372–390**
 analytical hierarchy in, 2:389–390
 axiomatizable theories in, 2:382–383
 basic results of, 2:380–382
 definability in arithmetic and, 2:386–387
 degrees of unsolvability in, 2:384–386
 feasibility of, 2:387–389
 formalization of, 2:375–380
 and Gödel incompleteness theorem, 2:383–384
 informal concept of, 2:372–375
 as recursive function theory, 2:378
 Turing and, 5:478, 9:552–553
Computable enumerability, 2:381
 in computability theory, 2:385
 incompleteness and, 2:383–384
Computable functions
 total
  analytical hierarchy in computability theory and, 2:389–390
  effective reducibility of, 2:385
  Kleene's theorem and, 2:382
  parameter theorem and, 2:382
 Turing on, 5:477
Computable partial functions, 2:378, 2:380
Computable relations, in arithmetic, 2:386
Computable set, 3:658
Computably enumerable sets, characterization of, 2:382
Computation
 algebraic logic and, 2:400
 Church and, 2:253–254
 in cognitive science, 2:297–298
 connectionist computation and, 2:445
 vs. embodiment, 8:155
 by entanglement, 8:200–201
 as formalism *vs.* description in science, 1:630–631
 Hobbes on, 8:773
 intelligence and, 5:632
 intentionality and, 1:350
 and metaphor, 6:167
 rules for, 2:401
 Turing on, 5:632
Computation and Cognition (Pylyshyn), 4:590
Computational model of mind. *See* Computationalism
Computationalism, **2:390–396,** 6:142
 basic idea of, 2:390–392
 Chinese room argument and, 2:239–242
 in evolutionary psychology, 3:481–484
 functionalism and, 8:155
 general issues in, 2:392–393
 in mental imagery, 4:591
 objections to, 2:395
 pragmatics and, 7:739
 vision in, 1:329, 6:142
Computational/representational theory of thought processes. *See* CRTT
Computer(s)
 and causal inference, 8:687
 classical *vs.* quantum, 8:200–201
 cognitive psychology and, 8:150–151

Computer(s), ***continued***
- digital, 5:566
- in film, 7:383–384
- formal languages and, 1:344
- functionalism and, 7:471
- human beings and, 2:395
- intelligence of, **1:345–350, 5:631–636,** 6:559–560, 9:552
- Jevons and, 5:450
- learning by, 5:635
- as logic machines, 5:565
- memory and, 6:125
- Neumann and, 6:559–560
- neural networks and, 2:444
- programs for, ownership and rights in, 2:397
- temporal organization of act in, 6:81

Computer ethics, **2:396–398**
Computer modeling, in cognitive science, 2:298
Computer science, 7:336
- computationalism and, 2:390
- effective calculability and, 2:375
- non-classical logic and, 5:483

Computer theorem, Tarski on, 5:480
Computerized system, representation of conditionals, 3:711
Computing Machinery and Intelligence (Turing), 5:633, 9:552
Computing machines, **2:398–409**
- and conceptual analysis, 2:402–404
- human calculator as paradigm of, 2:398
- idealized, 2:375
- mathematical computations and, 2:399
- physical realization of, 2:404–408
- Turing machines as, 2:375–376
- *See also* Computer(s)

Comstock, Anthony, 5:351
Comte, Auguste, **2:409–414**
- Abbagnano on, 1:3
- on altruism, 1:136
- on art, 1:56
- Buckle and, 1:718
- Carnap and, 2:36
- Dühring and, 3:130
- Hegel and, 3:63
- on humanity, 7:712
- on knowledge, 7:392
- Lange and, 5:187
- Latin American philosophy and, 5:206–207
- Lavrov and, 5:218
- law of three stages, 6:225
- Lévy-Bruhl and, 5:306
- Littré and, 5:372
- Marx and, 3:57, 3:63
- on naturalistic religion, 8:373–374
- Nishi and, 6:623
- positivism and, 2:410–413, 5:237, 7:710–712
- on progress, 7:712
- on religion, 7:712
- Saint-Simon and, 8:589
- on science, 7:711–712
- Solov'ëv and, 9:122

Comte de Saint-Simon, Engels and, 3:63
Comulgatorio, El (Gracián), 4:168
Con el eslabón (Varona), 9:648
Conant, James B., and Kuhn, 5:157
Conation, 8:126, 8:147–148, 9:260. *See also* Goals
Conative behavior, 8:147
Conative psychology, 8:147–148
Conatus, in Hobbes's materialism, 6:9
Concealment lie, 5:619
Conceit, in Buddhism, 6:621
Conceivability, 8:191–193, 9:805
Concentration, in Buddhism, 1:722, 1:729–730, 6:254
Concept(s), **2:414–420**
- *a priori* and *a posteriori* applied to, 1:241–242
- analysis, Moore on, 2:673, 4:150
- as analytically basic, 2:97
- application of, 8:171
- and belief, 1:533
- in Chatton *vs.* Aureol, 2:139
- classical theory of, 2:416–417
- Collingwood on, 2:328
- construction of
  - Kant on, 4:58
  - Rosenzweig on, 8:498
- content of, determining, 5:88
- controversy about, 2:415–416
- Croce on, 2:602
- Deleuze on, 2:696
- empiricism of, 2:417–418
- *vs.* evidence, in metaphysics, 6:184
- and experience, 1:533, 9:596
- *vs.* expression, 1:25
- extensions of, 3:731
- fictional characters as, 1:336
- formal *vs.* objective, Vasquez on, 9:649
- formation of
  - Buddhist logic on, 9:585–586
  - Hume on, 9:598
- Frege on, 3:727–728, 5:516, 9:555–556
- functional, 3:757
- generality of, 9:775
- Hegel on, 4:265–266, 4:286–287
- individuated, 5:89
- informational atomism and, 2:419
- intuitive acquaintance with, 4:728
- *vs.* judgments, 1:394–395
- language and, 2:416, 9:821
- in Mādhyamika doctrine, 1:740
- Meier's typology of, 6:112
- in metaphysics, 6:203–204
- mind-dependent, 6:176
- as natural signs, 9:775–776
- normative
  - in expressivism, 6:160
  - in metaethics, 6:158
- *vs.* object, 3:728, 9:555–556
- Ockham on, 9:775–776
- open-endedness of, Locke on, 9:596
- philosophy as analysis of, 2:419
- properties of, 3:730
- prototype theory of, 2:418
- pure
  - intellectual, experience and, 5:15
  - of understanding, 5:15–21
- Putnam on, 8:171
- Rehmke on, 8:302
- response-dependent, 8:443–444
- in Sanlun Buddhism, 2:162
- scientific
  - in metaphysics, 6:208
  - Wright (Chauncey) on, 9:846
- sensation in, 1:533
- state-content ambiguity of, 6:176
- theory and holism of, 2:418–419
- universal as, in medieval philosophy, 6:102
- use of, 2:415
- Wodeham on, 9:821
- *See also* Idea(s)

"Concept and Object" (Frege), 8:735
Concept of a Person, The (Ayer), 1:437
"Concept of Criticism in German Romanticism, The" (Benjamin), 1:545
Concept of Dread, The (Kierkegaard), 1:530, 5:64
Concept of Law, The (Hart), 3:156, 5:239
- on legal principle, 7:459
- on rules, 7:429
- on sovereignty, 9:140

Concept of Mind, The (Ryle), 2:77, 2:674, 8:581–582, 9:354, 9:421
- on imagination, 4:593, 4:597
- and logical behaviorism, 7:469
- on psychological language, 1:153
- on soul, 4:605
- on volition, 3:19

Concept of Morals, The (Stace), 9:200
Concept of Nature, The (Whitehead), 9:748
"Concept of Power, The" (Dahl), 7:733
"Concept of Truth in Formalized Languages" (Tarski), 9:354
Conception
- concepts and, 2:416
- in critical realism, 2:596
- Pearson on, 7:160
- Reid on, 8:327

Conception of Education, The (Gentile), 4:50
Conception of Reality, The (Moore, G. E.), 1:678–679, 4:559
"Concepts as Involving Laws and Inconceivable without Them" (Sellars, Wilfrid), 8:733
Conceptual analysis
- in analytic jurisprudence, 1:168–170
- analytic/synthetic distinction and, 1:170
- Moore on, 2:673, 4:150
- naturalism and, 1:169
- of perceiving, 7:178–179
- philosophy as, 2:419

Conceptual constructions, as faulty, 5:119
Conceptual determinacy, 4:286–287
Conceptual distinction, 3:138
Conceptual emergence, 3:190–193
Conceptual politics, and Carnap, 2:39–40, 2:44
Conceptual prehension, in realization, 9:752
Conceptual scheme, Conant on, 5:157
Conceptual space, psychological creativity and, 2:589–590
Conceptual systems, and external world, 3:704
Conceptualism, 7:191–192
- Aureol on, 7:256, 7:257
- Berkeley and, 9:596–598
- empiricism on, 7:722
- Hume and, 9:598–599
- Locke and, 9:594–596
- *vs.* nominalism, 9:594
- particulars in, 6:174
- universals in, 3:289–290, 6:174–176, 7:24, 9:588, 9:594–599

Conceptualization, 3:716
"Concerning the Foundation of Our Belief in Divine Government of the World" (Fichte), 1:378
Concerning the Phenomenonology of Internal Time Consciousness (Husserl), 9:489
"Concerning the Sublime" (Schiller, Friedrich), 8:629
Concienza e il meccanismo interiore, La (Bonatelli), 1:649
Conciliador, El (Menasseh ben Israel), 6:128
Conciliatory methodology
- of Leibniz, 5:255–256, 5:266–267
- Pico della Mirandola on, 5:255

Concise History of Logic (Scholz), 8:645
Concluding Unscientific Postscript (Kierkegaard), 5:64, 5:297
Conclusion
- of argument, 3:639
- definition of, 5:537
- of sequent, 3:641

Conclusiones (Pico della Mirandola), 7:614
Concomitant variation method of induction, 6:224, 6:244–247
Concord (Antiphon), 1:223
Concordia (journal), 8:632
Concordia (Molina), 8:680
Concrescence of prehensions, 9:749–750
Concrete, sensible things, unknowability and unreality of, 5:95
Concrete [term], definition of, 5:537
Concrete existent particulars, *vs.* possible particulars, 6:180
Concrete individuals, Ockham on, 9:777
Concrete metaphysics, 3:670
Concrete objects, names of, in semantic reism, 5:144
Concrete particularism, 6:174
Concrete philosophy, 5:701–702
Concrete reasoning, 6:577–578
Concrete world, of changing particulars, 5:95
Concreteness
- *vs.* abstraction, 4:565–566
- in British empiricism, 4:784
- in nominalism, 6:627

Concretism
- Kotarbiński and, 5:144
- Masaryk and, 6:1–2
- *vs.* theory of assumptions, 6:116
- theory of objects and, 6:115

Condemnation of 1277, 1:628–629, 1:650
Condensation, and fallacy, 3:549
Condestinate facts, 3:6
Condillac, Étienne Bonnot de, **2:420–424**
- on abstract ideas, 8:785
- on analogy, 8:784–785
- on analysis, 8:784
- atheism and, 2:688
- Cabanis on, 2:3
- Cousin and, 2:579
- Destutt de Tracy and, 2:760
- on equality, 3:330
- on experience, 3:517
- on human nature, 3:330
- and idéologues, 8:787–788
- Laromiguière and, 5:201
- Lavoisier and, 8:785
- on Locke's theory of knowledge, 8:784
- Maine de Biran and, 5:656
- on Maupertuis, 8:783
- Saint-Simon and, 8:589
- sensationalism and, 3:72, 8:137, 8:826
- on sensations, 8:823
- on signification, 8:783
- on terms, 5:656
- on touch, 9:515
- on universal grammar, 8:790–791

Condition(s)
- of adequacy, in semantic theories, 6:84–85
- definition of, 5:538
- INUS, 5:638
- social
  - changes to, 1:493
  - communitarianism and, 2:368
  - conservatism and, 2:465

Conditional(s), **2:424–430,** 8:358–359
- Abelard on, 5:426–429
- Boethius on, 5:425–427
- in causality and belief, 2:93–94
- in classical and non-classical logic, 5:487
- computer system representing, 3:711
- converting, 3:537
- counterfactuals and, 2:426–429, 2:573–576
- definition of, 5:545
- Diodorus Cronus on, 3:87, 5:403, 7:312
- in first-order logic, 3:646
- Grice on, 4:184
- in Humphrey's paradox, 2:128
- as indicative, 2:424–426
- Keynes on, 5:503
- material, 4:309, 8:358
- modals, appearance in, 10:25–26
- Philo of Megara on, 5:403, 7:312

Conditional(s), ***continued***
possibility and, 2:25–26
in pragmatism, 7:743
in reductionism, 2:99–100
separability *vs.* inseparability in, 1:627–628
subjunctive, 7:725
traditional logic and, 5:504
Conditional logic, 5:487, 6:299
Conditional probability, 8:25
Bayesian, 1:496–497
in common cause principle, 2:342
Conditional proof, definition of, 5:538
Conditional propositions, 5:553
and accidents *vs.* nature, 1:628
Boethius on, 5:423–424
semantics of, 1:549–550
Conditionalization
Bayesian calculus of, 1:496–497, 8:29
and evidentiary probability, 1:497–498
Conditionally, in Bloch, 1:615
Conditioned reflex(es), Pavlov on, 7:149–150
Conditioned Reflexes and Psychiatry (Pavlov), 7:150
Conditioning
classical, 1:202–203
operant, 1:203
social, meaning and, 1:152
Conditioning events, of sense object, 9:749
Conditions Handsome and Unhandsome: The Constitution of Emersonian perfectionism (Cavell), 2:116
Condorcet, Marquis de, **2:430–433**
Alembert and, 1:107
atheism and, 2:688
Comte and, 2:409–412
on death, 2:652
Destutt de Tracy and, 2:760
Enlightenment and, 3:246, 3:247
Franklin and, 3:720
on national identity, 6:481
on *philosophe,* 3:244
on progress, 8:46
Saint-Simon and, 8:589
skepticism of, 9:56
Stewart and, 9:247
Conduct
in absence of moral order, 4:750
in contractualism, 2:518
epistemology of, 1:68
as judicanda of justice, 4:863
moral action justifiability and, 2:519
psychophysical dispositions and, 9:260
social expectations of, 9:94
Socrates on, 9:108
sympathetic feelings in judgment of, 9:67
Conduct of Life (Emerson), 3:195
Conduct of the Allies, The (Swift), 9:340
Conduct of the Understanding (Locke), 1:50, 8:778
Cone, James H., on American Black theology, 5:332–333
Conee, Earl
on conditions of knowledge, 3:272–273
on skepticism, 3:275
Confabulation, 8:723
Conference of the Birds, The (ʿAṭṭār), 9:306
Confessio Philosophi (Philosopher's Confession) (Leibniz), 5:251, 5:261–263
Confession (Bakunin), 1:471–472
Confession, false, memory in, 6:126
Confessions (Augustine), 1:46, 9:461
Cicero in, 1:390
on eternity, 3:357–358
influences on, 3:401
on language, 8:760
on love, 5:586
Neoplatonism in, 1:390
on Platonism, 7:609
time in, 1:397
turn to God in, 1:395
Confessions (Rousseau), 2:687, 3:72, 7:522
Confidence
in attributor contextualism, 2:484–485
of belief and outcome, 1:533–534
probability interval as, 1:495
Confidentiality
in engineering ethics, 3:241
in form of consent, 6:95
in medical ethics, 6:94–95
Configurational force, 6:261
Confinement, in hospitals and asylums, 3:699
Confirmability, 9:661–663
meaning and, 5:528
vs. testability, 9:662
Confirmation
of diagnosis, 7:466–467
fallacies and, 3:543
in science
analytical behavior theory and, 1:524
Bayesian, 1:497–500
evidentiary relevance and, 1:501–502
probability *vs.* subjectivity and, 1:495
in theory and evidence, 1:500–501
"Confirmation and Law-likeness" (Lange), 5:230
Confirmation theory, **2:433– 442**
and absolute, 2:433–434
degrees of confirmation in, 2:438
Goodman on, 4:155–156
and incremental, 2:433–434, 2:437
induction and, 3:276
and inductive probability, 2:437
inductive underdetermination and, 9:575–576
and knowledge, 2:437
Nicod's condition and, 2:439–440
in ordinary language, 2:434–435
probability and, 2:435–437
projectability of, 2:440
and raven's paradox, 2:440–441
reasoning by analogy and, 2:439
verified consequences in, 2:439
Conflict
communism and, 5:734
Freud on, 8:145–146
in institutionalization of collective purposes, 9:281–282
of interest
engineering ethics and, 3:241
historicization of divine as solution to, 9:282
in informed consent decision-making, 4:680
in state, 9:206–208
laws of, 5:59
as morality, 1:676
national identity and, 6:482
power and, 7:731–732
psychic, 8:109–110, 8:145–146
state suppression of, 9:207
Conflict or apparent contradiction *(anupapatti),* between two means of knowledge, 5:122
Confucian classics
Chong Yakyong and, 5:139
positivistic interpretation of, 5:139
Confucianism, **2:170–180**
of Andō Shōeki, 1:200
and Buddhism, 2:155, 2:163, 2:169–170, 4:794
Chan Buddhism and, 2:168
in Chinese thought, 2:226, 2:238
and contemporary neo-Confucianism, 2:181–184
Daoism and, 2:185–186, 2:236

development of, 2:149–151, 9:856
Dong Zhongshu and, 3:98
and eclecticism in cosmology and philosophy, 2:190
ethical ideal in, 2:174–177
ethics in, 2:170–171, 2:194–197
examination system of, 3:98
golden rule and, 4:145
and harmony of individual and society, 2:150–151
Hayashi and, 4:247–248
history of, 7:486
human nature in, 2:149–150
innate good *vs.* destructive tendency in, 2:196
Itō and, 4:765
in Japan, 4:793–794, 6:477
in Korea, 5:135–136
Koryo and, 5:135–136
Li Ao and, 5:316
on life, meaning and value of, 5:359
mandate of heaven, 4:792–793
Mencius in, 6:129–130
Minagawa in, 6:253
Miura Baien and, 6:276
Mohist critique of, 2:197
morality of, in everyday life, 5:7
Mozi on, 2:235–236, 6:417
name rectification in, 2:188–189, 2:203–204
Ogyū and, 7:10
in Qing dynasty, 4:796
ren and li in, 2:194–195
rujia as ritualist bases for, 2:170–171
self in, 2:171–174
self-cultivation in, 2:177–179
social roles in, 2:188–189
society in, 2:150–151, 7:486
syncretism in, 2:153
in Tang dynasty, 5:316
and Tiantai Buddhism, 2:163
in Togukawa period, 4:794–795
ultimate reality in, 2:220
varieties of, 2:232
Wang Chong and, 9:723–724
on wisdom, 2:219
Xunzi and, 2:233, 9:856
Zhou and, 2:155
Zhu Xi, 6:477
Hayashi and, 4:247–248
Wang Yang-ming and, 6:477
Yamaga Sokō on, 9:859
Yamazaki Ansai in, 9:860
See also Chinese philosophy
Confucius, **2:442–443**
Dao in, 2:201
Emerson and, 3:195
ideal of superior man, 2:149
Itō and, 4:765
Laozi and, 5:194
Lu Xiangshan and, 5:618
Mozi on, 2:235
political and social philosophy of, 2:231–232
on ultimate reality, 2:220
on wisdom, 2:219, 9:793
Confused supposition, in medieval logic, 5:431
Confusion, in attributor contextualism, 2:486–487
Conglomeratio et exglomeratio centri, 5:43
Congregatio de Auxiliis (Congregation on grace), 4:789
Congress of Vienna, 7:155
Congruence, Helmholtz on, 4:304–305
Congruism, 8:681, 9:282
Conjecture, knowledge as, 6:595
Conjectures and Refutations (Popper), 9:94
Conjunction, 3:642
basic, 3:654
definition of, 5:538
negation of, rules for, 5:449
Conjunctive normal form, 3:654
Conjunctive propositions, definition of, 5:553
Conjuncts, 3:540, 3:642
Connectedness, in measurement, 6:88
Connectibility, in special relativity, 9:471
Connecticut, Griswold v., 6:95
Connection
creating and preserving, 3:579
vs. rules, 8:154
Connectionism, **2:443–445,** 3:679
and artificial intelligence, 1:345–347
cognitive processing and, 2:444
computationalism and, 2:392
concepts as prototypes and, 2:418
on innate ideas, 4:694
linguistic understanding and architecture in, 2:393
Connective(s)
definition of, 5:538
logical terms and, 5:531
Connective relation, definition of, 5:555
Connective words
Grice on, 7:739
Locke on, 5:385
Connectivity, as Archimedean axiom, 2:497
Connell, Desmond, on Malebranche, 5:666
Connotation
vs. denotation, 8:58
in Kant, 2:74
in Keynes, 5:457
Mill (John Stuart) on, 5:548, 8:58
of nouns in traditional logic, 5:493
Connotative terms, 9:777
Conocimiento y acción (Knowledge and action) (Vaz Ferreira), 5:208
Conquering nations, 5:59
"Conquest of Scientific Materialism, The" *(Die Überwindung des wissenschaftlichen Materialismus)* (Ostwald), 3:233
Conquete du pain, La (Kropotkin), 5:154
Conrad, Joseph, Schopenhauer and, 8:656
Conrad-Martius, Hedwig, 7:279
Conscience, **2:445–448**
Aquinas on, 3:404, 9:434–435
Ardigò on, 1:252
bad, 4:787
Butler (Joseph) on, 1:781–782, 2:686, 3:408
Calvin on, 2:9
and civil disobedience, 2:259–260
Comte on, 2:412
Dostoevsky on, 3:100
Forberg on, 1:378
freedom of
Cambridge platonists on, 2:13
Catholic Church on, 5:177
Spinoza on, 9:180
God and, 2:9, 6:581
Holbach on, 3:408
in human nature, 1:781
Mandeville on, 3:408
Marx on, 3:408
moral order and, 1:378
and moral views, 2:447
Newman (John Henry) on, 6:581
Nietzsche on, 3:408
and obedience as piety, 1:519
Paulsen on, 7:148
Price (Richard) on, 3:409
Reid (Thomas) on, 3:409
Rousseau on, 3:155
as "two parties," 9:3
Conscious, unity of, soul and, 9:429
Conscious awareness, 4:712
Conscious processes, in perception, 7:188, 7:192

Consciousness, **2:449–458**
- act and psychic content of, 1:649
- of all matter, Teilhard on, 9:374–375
- in animals, **1:200–208**
- in argument for existence of God, 9:407
- Bachofen on, 1:441
- in bad conscience, 4:787
- Bakhtin and, 1:465
- behaviorist theory of, 4:456–457, 6:588
- being and, Molina Garmendia on, 6:323–324
- Bergson on, 3:313, 9:488–489
- Binswanger on, 1:597–598, 3:507
- body as subordinate to, 3:559
- Brahman as sole, 1:684
- as brain process, 9:65
- in Buddhism, 1:724, 2:166
- Bullough on, 1:761–762
- Cassirer on, 2:66–67
- Chisholm on, 2:243
- Clarke on, 2:273
- cognito-thoughts in, 8:724
- in collapse dynamics, 8:210
- collective, Durkheim on, 3:149–150
- Collingwood on, 2:328
- colonial, 7:727
- computationalism and, 2:300, 2:394
- and concept of force, 3:689
- Condillac on, 2:421
- in Confucianism, 2:173
- connection principle of, 8:705–706
- consular nature of, 9:533
- in creative process, 2:590
- Crescas on, 2:593
- and death, medical criterion for, 2:653
- Del Vecchio on, 2:697
- Dennett on, 2:710–712
- Descartes on, 8:149
- Destutt de Tracy on, 2:760
- Dilthey on, 3:80
- as discriminative, 1:462–463
- domain of, 5:143
- Dühring on, 3:131
- eliminative materialism on, 3:182–183
- emotive and cognitive roles in, 1:462
- ethical responsibility toward, 3:392
- Evans on, 2:480
- evidence for, 1:205–206
- in evolution, 1:205
- existential psychoanalysis on, 3:512
- facts of, 5:688
- false, 4:574
- free will and, 8:125
- freedom as property of, 7:2
- Freud on, 2:449, 8:145
- Gadamer on, 4:2
- Galluppi on, 4:14
- Gentile on, 4:50–52
- in Gestalt theory, 4:74
- Gurwitsch on, 4:197
- Haeckel on, 4:203
- heart as seat of, 4:542
- Hegel on, 3:310, 3:610
- Herbart on, 7:375, 8:139, 8:145
- historical, 4:2
- history as progress of, 1:713
- history of, 3:615
- Hobbes on, 8:128
- Husserl on, 2:459, 4:290, 7:291, 9:489–490
- identity revealed by, 1:783
- image as, 8:605
- immanence of, 8:662
- impalpable *(unanschaulich)* or imageless contents of, 5:160
- in Indian philosophy, 4:626, 5:326, 9:542
- instantiation of, 7:278
- intentionality and, 1:689, 2:452, 5:701–702, 7:290–291, 8:605
- introspective operation of, 3:552
- irreducibility of, 1:649
- in Jainism, 6:254
- James (William) on, 3:313
- Kant on, 2:453, 2:758
- kinds of, 2:449
- Laas on, 5:164
- Lavrov on, 5:218
- Lequier on, 5:287
- Locke on, 5:395
- love in, in Unanumo's philosophy, 9:568
- Mamardashvili on, 5:677–679
- Marcel on, 5:701–702
- Maritain on, 5:713
- Martineau on, 5:727
- in Marxism, 5:678–679, 5:732–733
- material life and, 3:575
- in materialism, 3:182–183, 6:13
- McGilvary on, 6:75–76
- as memory images and perception, 1:565
- mental states and, 1:704
- Montgomery on, 6:340
- Moore on, 6:584
- nature and, Schelling on, 8:618–619
- in new realism, 6:587–588
- nonegological conception of, 4:197, 8:604
- objective connections and, 5:17
- ontological status of, 1:753
- origin of, dualists on, 3:116
- Ostwald on, 7:50
- particulars of, as self-consciousness, 1:668
- pastness of, 6:76
- perceptual, 7:178
  - analysis of, 7:178
  - causal argument for, 7:182–183, 7:272, 7:275–276
  - philosophical significance of, 7:185–186
  - selective nature of, 7:183–184
  - in sensing, 8:817
  - without external object, 7:182
- personhood and, 7:238–240
- Petronievič on, 7:266
- Petzoldt on, 7:268
- phenomenal, 2:450, 6:263, 7:468, 7:472–473
- phenomenological psychology and, 7:277–278, 7:282
- in phenomenology, **2:459–460,** 4:197–198
- philosophy of, 3:608
- pleasure and, 7:619
- primitive, knowledge based on, 5:146
- pure, personhood and, 7:238–239
- as pure memory, 1:564
- qualitative, 2:449–450
- raising, 3:575
- Rehmke on, 8:302–303
- Reinhold on, 8:334–335
- Renaissance view of, 5:641
- Sabatier on, 8:588
- Santayana on, 8:599
- Sartre on, 2:459, 8:604–607
- Schleiermacher on, 8:634
- and self, 2:456–457
- self-awareness in, Gentile on, 4:51
- sensing *vs.* sensa in, 2:5
- simultaneity in, Bergson on, 9:489
- as spiritual energy, Teilhard on, 9:374
- states of, in utilitarianism, 9:604
- in structuralism, 9:274
- subjectivity and, 9:290
- theories of, 2:452–456
- thought and, 1:649, 8:663
- three natures of, 9:652
- of time, **9:482–488**

Trubetskoi (Evgenii) on, 9:529
Trubetskoi (Sergei) on, 9:533
unhappy, 4:263
unity of, dualism and, 3:118–120, 4:618
and unity of ego *vs.* psychic events, 1:649
universal, in I-other relationships, 1:465
of Universe, 5:639
Varisco on, 9:647
Vasubandhu on, 1:751–752, 9:651–652
Whitehead on, 9:751
women's, uniqueness of, 3:563
Woodbridge on, 9:842
Wright (Chauncey) on, 9:847
in Yoga school, 8:718
in Yogācāra Buddhism, 1:746–752
Ziehen (Theodor) on, 9:884
See also Panpsychism

Consciousness Explained (Dennett), 2:711, 4:721
Consciousness Lost and Found (Weiskrantz), 6:566
Consciousness Only school, 2:154, 5:135
Consensus
conservatism and, 2:466
self-perfecting, 9:829
Consensus Gentium. *See* Common consent arguments for the existence of God
Consent
informed, 3:456
Malebranche on, 5:670
power and, 7:733
in social contract, 9:80
Consequence(s)
assessment of, Paley on, 7:76
definition of, 5:538
in hedonism, 4:255
individual profit-seeking and, 1:777
intended *vs.* foreseen, in just war theory, 4:871
interregnum philosophers on, 5:440
logical, 3:650
Quine on, 1:150
Tarski on, 9:368, 9:369
in thought experiments, 9:454
in medieval logic, 5:434–435
observational, deductive underdetermination and, 9:575
punishment as, 8:159
in utilitarianism, 9:603–609
determining, 9:607–608
egoistic, 9:604
hedonistic, 9:604
ideal, 9:604
probabilities assigned to, 9:608
remote, 9:607–608
universalistic, 9:604
Consequence argument, 3:33–34
Consequent
asserting, 3:537
definition of, 5:538
negating with an antecedent, 3:537
See also Antecedent-consequent relationship
Consequentia, definition of, 5:538
Consequentialism, **2:460–461**
Anscombe and, 1:213
Baier on, 1:461
common-sense morals and, 2:519
contractualism as alternative to, 2:517
critique of, 3:388
vs. deontological ethics, 3:384
in Dge-lugs Mādhyamika, 1:732–733
on ethical treatment of animals, 3:392–393
and ethics, 2:197, 3:383, 5:37
on evaluation of political and social institutions, 3:392
Finnis on, 6:513
goal-right system in, 8:810
ideal, Moore and, 6:352–353
on impartiality, 4:620
intuitionism and, 4:736
in Mohist ethics, 2:197
on principle monism, 3:441–442
principles in contractualism *vs.*, 2:518
right action in, 9:681
rule consequentialism, 9:615
in Smart's utilitarianism, 9:65–66
on suicide, 9:319
vs. teleology, 9:382
Thomson (Judith) on, 9:449
in utilitarianism, Sen on, 8:810
on virtue, 9:678
Conservation
as divine causation, 2:587
of energy
Descartes on, 8:124
discovery of, 3:226, 3:229–232, 3:236
in energetism, 7:49–50
mass and, 6:4, 6:62
materialism and, 6:11
mental causation and, 6:260
particle localization and, 8:211–212
in special relativity, 3:237
as term, 3:232
of mass, energy and, 6:4, 6:62
of matter, Moleschott on, 6:320
of motion, in physical causality, 2:90
religious doctrine of, 2:587
Conservation principle, **2:461–464,** 9:846
Conservatism, **2:464–471**
and belief, 1:535
in Bonldand, 1:648
in Chinese thought, 2:238
communitarianism and, 2:369
Confucius and, 2:231
in Greek drama, 4:177
in history, 2:465–466
individual and, 2:468–469
and laws, 1:553–554
matriarchy and, 1:441
overview of, 2:470–471
romantic historicism, 1:442
society and, 2:468–469
of utilitarian politicians, 9:23
values and, 2:466–468
Conserving causes, and existence of God, Ockham on, 9:781
Consideratio theologica (Revius), 2:284
"Considerations about Some Methods for Removing a Certain Difficulty in the Calculation of Probability in Gambling (Lichtenberg), 5:339–340
Considérations philosophiques de la gradation naturelle des formes de l'être, ou les Essais de la nature qui apprend à faire l'homme (Robinet), 8:481
Considérations sur les causes de las grandeur et de la décadence des Romains (Montesquieu), 4:86
Considérations sur les corps organisés (Bonnet), 1:657
Considérations sur l'état présent de la controverse (Desgabets), 2:757
Considered judgments, 1:238
Consilience (Wilson, E.), 9:789
Consilience of inductions, 9:789
Consistency
Aristo of Chios on, 1:257
capture of, 7:208
coherence truth theory and, 2:310
in coherentism, 2:313
counterfactual conditionals and, 2:427
definition of, 5:538
as descriptive requirement, 1:631
forfeiting of, 7:206
Gödel on, 5:473–474
Hilbert on, 4:361–364

Consistency, ***continued***
in illative combinatory logic, 2:340
internal, 1:257
in laws of probability, 9:221
Łukasiewicz on, 5:607
mathematics and, 5:470
in metamathematics, 2:41
in moral judgments, 6:158
persistence and, 7:206–211
Post's definitions of, 5:467
proof theory and, 8:54–55
in reality *vs.* dream, 3:105
relative, 5:474
and sense data *vs.* sensing, 1:696
Tarski on, 9:366–368
in theology, 1:707
unprovability of, 5:474
Consistent theory, 3:650
Consolation of Philosophy, On the (Boethius), 1:625–626, 2:136
on determinism, 3:9
Neoplatonism of, 6:555
William of Conches on, 9:768
Consolatione Philosophiae, Die (Boethius). *See Consolation of Philosophy, On the* (Boethius)
Consonance and dissonance, Krueger's theory of, 5:156
Consonants, Sanskrit, 7:413
Conspicuous consumption, 9:655
Conspiracy of the Equals, 3:330
Constancy
personal identity and, 7:219–220
in subjective probabilities, 8:37
Constant(s), 3:647, 5:538
Constant, Benjamin, French liberalism and, 5:320
Constant function, definition of, 5:554
Constant mode, of appearance talk, 7:188
Constant symbols, applying to the language, 3:655
Constantine (emperor of Rome), 3:455
Constatives, 7:200–201
Constellation, in consciousness, Ziehen (Theodor) on, 9:884
Constellation state, Wahle (Richard) on, 9:720
Constellations (Aratus), 5:600
Constituted dispositional states, role-functionalism in, 6:135
Constitution
Bentham and, 1:555–556
definition of, 7:239
vs. identity, Wiggins on, 9:762
vs. law, 7:419
as law of recognition, 9:140
and personhood, 7:239–240
Constitution, U.S., rights in, 2:701
Constitution of Liberty (Hayek), 9:72
Constitutional Code (Bentham), 1:551, 1:554–556
Constitutional government, in Cicero, 2:258
Constitutional Government and Democracy (Friedrich), 7:733
Constitutional review, centralized, 5:49
Constitutionalism, Whig, 7:663–664
Constitutive rule, 7:199
Constitutive values, 3:591–593
Constraint(s)
in computability theory, 2:387
concepts as prototypes and, 2:418
in Confucianism, 2:175
Elster's theory of creativity and, 2:590
freedom as lack of, 8:446
Construct(s)
social, 8:677
aesthetic experience and, 1:34
radically reconceived, 3:599
in science studies, 8:678–679
Construction
method of, definition of, 5:548
of models in cosmology, 2:559–563
Constructionalism
Goodman on, 4:157–158
worldmaking in, 4:161–162
Constructionism
in Chwistek's mathematical foundations, 2:255–256
reality as accessible by, 2:38
social, **9:76–79**
on animal *vs.* human sexuality, 7:526–527
on gender, 3:586, 3:589
lessons of contingency from, 3:588
"strong program" and, 8:677–678, 9:85
Constructive dilemma, definition of, 5:541
Constructive empiricism, 8:692–693, 9:645
Constructive existence proof, definition of, 5:538
Constructive interpretation, Dworkin on, 3:156, 5:243
Constructive investigations, of feminists, 3:594
Constructive skepticism, Mersenne on, 6:153
Constructivism, 5:37–38
of Brouwer's intuitionism, 4:737
and conventionalism, **2:474–476**
on infinite totalities, 4:659
Kant and, 9:76
moral, **2:471–473**, 8:644
as paradigm, 2:475
Rawls and, 8:258
Russell and, 5:467
theories of continuum and, 2:502
Constructivist logic, Bishop's theory of continuum and, 2:504–505
Consubstantiality, Losskii on, 5:577
Consumerism
Adorno on, 1:26
in Sorel's social theory, 9:133
Contact
of knowledge and world, 5:89–90
perception and, 5:118
Contact experience, notion of object from, 6:81
"Contact with the Nomic: A Challenge for Deniers of Humean Supervenience about Laws of Nature (Part II)" (Earman and Roberts), 5:230
Contemplation
Alexander on, 1:109
Ficino on, 1:48
in Huayan Buddhism, 2:164
inner ascent of, 3:622
knowledge as, 1:109
Locke on, 5:380–381
passive, rejection of, 3:559
Ruysbroeck on, 8:579–580
Contemplation de la nature (Bonnet), 1:658
Contemplation *(otium),* and practical activity *(negotium),* 1:444
Contemplative life, Ficino on, 3:621–622
"Contemporary Aesthetics and the Neglect of Natural Beauty" (Hepburn), 3:255
Contemporary New Confucianism, research program in China, 2:181–184
Contemporary Schools of Psychology (Woodworth), 8:148
"Contemporary Status of Atheism" (Le Blond), 1:357
Content
common, Schuppe's theory of, 8:663
conceptual role of, 5:88–89
of declarative sentence, 2:707
of education, 7:363
in indexicals, 4:622–623
and individualism, 8:82–83
and internalism, 8:82, 8:83

of linguistic expression, 2:707
vs. linguistic meaning, 2:705
mental, **2:476–481**
in informational semantics, 4:711
in intentions, 4:702–703
pragmatic inference and, 7:740
shaping, experience and, 9:31
theory of
adequacy condition for, 5:89
controversies in, 8:82
Content and Consciousness (Dennett), 2:710, 4:721
Content externalism, 8:82–83
Harman and, 5:88
in philosophy of mind, 3:276, 7:472
solipsism and, 9:117
Content-based objections, to folk psychology, 3:678
Context
anaphora and, 1:175–176
in animal communication, 1:204
assertion and, 7:408
authenticity and, 1:295
belief and, 1:142
Buddhist flexibility of, 1:739
in Chinese ethics, 2:200
conversational implicature and, 2:526
of demonstratives, 2:708
and "exist" as predicate, 1:662
Frege on, 3:728
and hermeneutics, 8:631
historical, art and, 1:314, 1:319–320
in indexicals, 2:707, 4:622–623
in Mohist discourse, 2:212–213
in ontology of art, 1:316–318
in personal memory, 6:123–124
in possible world counterfactual conditionals, 2:429
in pragmatics, 7:741
Putnam on, 8:171
and quantum measurement, 1:633–634
referents and, 8:62
in science studies, 8:676
sense of self and, 3:606
of sentences, Wittgenstein on, 9:812
Contextual approach to truth, 5:317
Contextual definitions, 5:540
"Contextual Implication" (Hungerland), 7:766–767
Contextual values, 3:591–592
Contextualism, **2:482–488**
on aesthetic experience, 1:33
as antiskeptical strategy, 9:46
attributor, 2:483–487
epistemic, skepticism and, 3:275
relevant alternatives and, 8:360–361
and skepticism, 9:136–137
subject, 2:482–483
Continental feminist theory, 3:586
Continental operationalism, 3:85
Continental philosophy, **2:488–489,** 5:45
aesthetics in, 1:68–72
vs. analytic philosophy, 5:210
feminism and, 3:562–566, 4:745–746
philosophy of language in, 7:410–412
time in, **9:488–493**
Contingency(ies)
of *a posteriori* propositions, 1:242–243
Cohen (Morris) on, 2:307
of commandments, 4:819
extensionalism and, 6:177
of humans, Unamuno on, 9:568
in Islamic philosophy, 4:754
Milhaud on, 6:217
Philoponus on, 7:314
Thomist argument for God's existence and, 2:553
Contingent(s)
and causality, 2:105
of conscience *vs.* utilitarian consequences, 1:782
definition of, 5:538
explanation and, 2:551
future, 1:680
God's existence and, 2:551
and time directionality, 2:105
Contingent being, Henry of Ghent on, 4:313–314
Contingent empirical propositions, as uncertain, Ayer on, 5:96
Contingent entities, in science, 6:209
Contingent existence
Aquinas on, 6:189
in ontology, 7:26
Contingent relations, qualities as, 1:575–576
Contingent statements, basic, 5:92–93
Contingent states of affairs, noninferential knowledge of, 6:210
Continua
Chatton on, 2:139
Peirce on, 7:170
Continuity, **2:489–517**
ancient geometrical conceptions of, 2:491–493
Anderson (John) on, 1:198
Aristotelian conception of, 2:490–491
arithmetic and, 2:510
arithmetization of analysis and, 2:495–496
Brouwer on, 2:499
in Buddhism, 6:256
calculus and, 2:494–495
as Cantor-Dedekind continuum, 2:497–499
choice sequence in intuitionist mathematics, 1:702
concluding remarks on, 2:510–511
constructivist theories of, 2:502–505
continuous functions and, 1:701, 2:496–497
definition of, 5:538
Deleuze on, 9:492
experience of, 1:198
in geometry, 2:499–500, 2:510, 4:361
historical
Turgot on, 9:551
Vailati on, 9:630
Infinitesimalist approaches to, 2:506–510
infinity and, 5:515
intuitionism and, 1:701, 2:503
and mathematical properties of discreteness and continuity, 1:702, 2:510
of medical test results, 7:466
nonstandard conceptions of, 2:491, 2:501–502
number theory and, 1:700
predicative theories of, 2:505–506
of processes, 6:81–82, 6:260
and real numbers, 2:493–497
Savigny on, 8:614
in scientific progress, 8:48
from sensa to public object, 4:586–587
in set-theory, 2:500–501
of time, 9:466–467
as type of religion, 2:224–225
Zeno's paradox and, 9:467
Continuum, 4:659, 4:662
definition of, 5:538
geometry and, 2:510
intuitionistic, unsplittability of, 2:503–504
in mathematics, 2:27, 2:494
nonstandard and standard analysis and, 2:510–511
number concept and, 9:741

Continuum, ***continued***
ordered fields and, 2:508–509
Poincaré on, 2:498
and set theory, 2:500
Continuum of Inductive Methods, The (Carnap), 2:439
Continuum problem. *See* Set theory
Contra Academicos (Augustine), 1:229, 9:49
Contra Celsum (Origen), 2:119, 7:40
Contra Eutychen (Boethius), 1:628
Contraception, Catholic doctrine and, 7:523
Contract(s)
in business, 1:779–780
psychology of, 7:446
in theory of states, 9:205
Contractarianism, moral cosmopolitanism and, 2:568
Contractio, notion of, 5:43
Contractual theory
in applied ethics, 1:239
Epicurus on, 3:268
Contractualism, **2:517–520**
common-sense morals and, 2:519
on evaluation of political and social institutions, 3:392
in Kant, 3:385–386
modern, 3:386
Parfit on, 7:120
self-interest and, 3:389
Contractualism and Utilitarianism (Scanlon), 2:517
Contradiction(s)
in Albo, 4:823
and analytical judgments, 5:13
and category-mistakes, 2:78
definition of, 5:538
in Dge-lugs philosophy, 1:732–733
in dialectic, 1:707, 4:260, 4:269–271
Engels on, 3:60–61
in *Guide of the Perplexed* (Maimonides), 4:818
Hegel on, 3:60–61, 4:260, 4:269–271
in law, 7:454–455
law of, 5:547, 6:527
interpretations of, 5:231–235
Lapshin on, 5:199–200
Pauler on, 7:145
vs. theory of objects, 6:115–116
traditional formulation of, 5:232–233
Lukasiewicz on, 2:547
Mao Zedong on, 3:65–66
as negations, 6:523
Nicolas of Autrecourt on, 6:600
norm of avoiding, 6:499
ordinary language and, 5:662
Ortega y Gasset on, 7:48
principle of
as *a priori* truth, 1:245
in Protagoras, 8:91
Russell on, 2:76
Saint-Hyacinthe on, 8:588
Schultze on, 8:660
sentence of propositional logic as, 3:644
theory of Forms and, 9:590
Vauvenargues and, 9:653
Wittgenstein on, 9:807
Wolff on, 9:827
Contradictory(ies)
Abelard on, 5:425
definition of, 5:538–539
in traditional logic, 5:495
Contralateral neglect, 6:566
Contraposition
definition of, 5:539
law of, 6:527
of propositions, 5:496
Contrariety, 6:523
Contrary(ies)
definition of, 5:539
in traditional logic, 5:495
Contrary-to-fact (counterfactual) conditional, definition of, 5:539
Contrast, illusions of, 3:546
Contribution to the Critique of Political Economy (Marx), 1:59, 5:731
Contributions to Philosophy (Heidegger), 4:295
Contributory value, 9:637
Controlled experiment, 6:247
"Controversy and Existence of the World" (Ingarden), 4:682
Convention(s)
in combinatory logic, 2:334
in Gricean program, 6:84
in interpretation, 1:312
Keynes on, 5:457
obligations dependent on, *vs.* obligations independent of, 4:872
in science, 7:651–652
in Tarski's truth theory, 2:548, 2:549
Convention (Lewis), 5:315
Convention T, 2:647, 6:85
Conventional implicature, 6:651–652
Conventional law, Albo on, 4:824
Conventional logics, 3:766
Conventional meaning, 6:83, 7:402
Conventional morality. *See* Morality, conventional
Conventionalism, **2:520–525**
analyticity and, 1:167
autonomous idiolects in, 8:753
in Buddhism, 1:745, 1:748, 1:757
in Daoism, 2:187–190
in Dge-lugs Mādhyamika, 1:733–734
just means challenged by, 4:872
in Mādhyamika doctrine, 1:733–734
number in, 6:675
in Plato's *Cratylus,* 8:752–754
property in, 8:69
Quine and, 6:675–677
in Sanlun Buddhism, 2:162
semantic theory of, 8:752
truth in, 2:474–475
in Yogācāra Buddhism, 1:748
Convergence, legal, 7:459
Conversation
in attributor contextualism, 2:485
common ground in, 7:406
implicature in, 2:525–528
Conversational dynamics, pragmatic presupposition and, 3:252–253
Conversational implicature, **2:525–528,** 4:184, 7:739
Conversational scorekeeping, conception of, 3:711
Conversations of Emilie, The (Epinay), 9:839
Converse domain of a relation, definition of, 5:539
Converse fallacy of the accident, 3:539–540
Converse of a relation, definition of, 5:539
Conversion
definition of, 5:539
to immanently oriented primacy of mind, 1:713–714
miracles of, in Buddhism, 6:255
of propositions, in traditional logic, 5:495–496
religious, in common consent for God's existence, 2:351
Valla on, 5:437
Convivio (Banquet) (Dante), 2:623–626
Convocation Sermon (Colet), 2:321
Convulsionnaires, Jansenism and, 4:790
Conway, Anne, **2:528–529**
and Glanvill, 4:97
Leibniz on, 9:838
on plenitude, 5:257
Conway, J. H., on surreal number system, 2:502, 2:508
Cook, James, on human nature, 3:246
Cook, Joseph, Lotze and, 5:583

Cook, Stephen, 2:387–388
Cook, Walter Wheeler, 5:245
Cook-Karp thesis, 2:388
Cook-Levin theorem, 2:389
Coomaraswamy, Ananda, 9:311
Cooper, John M., 3:748
Cooper, John W., 4:618
Cooperation
in anarchism, 1:176–177
in economics, 7:353
in ethics of preference maximization, 1:778
social, Xunzi on, 2:233
Co-operative Magazine, 9:87
Cooperative movement, 9:87
Cooperative principle, of conversation, 2:525–526
Coordinating principle, in unconscious theory, 9:573
Coordination, probability, 8:37–39
Coordinative definitions, 8:319
Coornhert, Dirck
Arminius and, 1:285
Franck and, 3:714
Cope, E. D., 2:637
Copenhagen interpretation, **2:529–532,** 6:277–279
Bell theorem and, 1:539–542
and Bohmian mechanics, 1:630, 9:576–577
and Einstein's realism, 2:530
as instrumentalist, 2:531–532
kalām argument for God's existence and, 2:554
measurement and interference in, 2:531
Copernican principle, anthropic principle and, 1:220
Copernican revolution, 2:534–535, 5:50, 7:317
Copernican Revolution: Planetary Astronomy in the Development of Western Thought, The (Kuhn), 5:157
Copernican theory, 4:8, 4:12
Bruno and, 1:709
celestial mechanics and, 2:535
Cyrano de Bergerac and, 2:618
implications of, 2:536
as mathematical supposition, 1:543
Philolaus and, 7:310–311
popularization of, 3:682
as positional astronomy, 2:534–535
and Ptolemaic astronomy, 2:535–536
simplicity and, 2:535
Copernicus, Nicolas, **2:532–536,** 5:50–51
and Cartesian physics and sciences, 2:54
censorship of, 2:732
deductive-nomological model and, 8:694
Hume and, 7:560
Leonardo da Vinci and, 5:282
as mathematician, 1:711
methodology of, 8:683
Philolaus and, 8:183
on universe, 2:750
Copula
De Morgan's generalization, 5:449
definition of, 5:539
Peirce on, 7:164–165
Copulatio (property of term), 9:786
Copy principle, in science of human nature, 4:490
Copyright, as property, 2:397
Cor Adens (Ivanov), 4:766
Corbin, Arthur, legal realism and, 5:247
Corbin, Henry, **2:536–537,** 4:541
Corbinelli, Jean, 2:757
Cordano, Girolamo, 8:426–427
Cordemoy, Géraurd de, **2:537–538**
critiques of, 2:758
on mind-body relationship, 2:59
occasionalism of, 4:77
Cordovero, Moses ben Jacob, **2:538–539**
Coriolis, Gaspard de, on energy, 3:233
Corneille, Pierre
on drama, 1:49
Fontenelle and, 3:682
Lessing on, 5:294
Cornelius, Hans
Krueger and, 5:155
in neo-Kantianism, 6:541
Cornell, Drucilla, 3:588–589
Corner, Christopher, 5:439
Cornford, Francis Macdonald, on Empedocles, 3:211
Cornhill Magazine (periodical), 9:243
Corollary, definition of, 5:539
Corpis Juris Civilis (Justinian), 7:420
Corporation(s)
Althusius on, 1:135
computers and, 2:397
in global economic logic, 2:361
as moral agents, 1:778–779
moral obligations of, 1:779–780
Corporation for the Spread of the Gospel to New England, Boyle and, 1:673
Corporeal entity, personhood and, 7:238–240
Corporeal intentionality, *vs.* dualism, 6:148
Corporeal matter
in Descartes, 2:54
in immortality of the soul, 4:605
Olivi on, 7:13
Corporeality, Conway on, 2:529
Corpus callosum, cutting of, 6:565–566
Corpus Hermeticum, Paracelsus and, 7:103
Corpuscular theory
Boyle and, 1:386–387, 1:673–674
Descartes and, 1:386
Locke and, 5:395
matter in, 6:60
Sennert and, 1:386
Corpuscularian hypothesis, 2:722
"Correct Use of Names" (Xunzi), 5:416
Corrective justice, 4:865
Correctness
dispositionalism and, 7:5
of ethical judgments
denial of, 7:5–6
opinion-independent, 9:642–643
of identification, in argument from analogy, 7:52
mind-dependence of, 7:4–5
objectivity as, 7:3, 7:4
of value judgments, 9:642
Correctorium "Circa" (John of Paris), 4:842
Correlation
in common cause principle, 2:342
in experimental predictions, 1:540–541
meaning causal connection, 3:545
Correlative principles, doctrine of, Lull on, 5:610
Correlative terms, definition by, 2:676
Correspondant, Le (periodical), 5:570
Correspondence
Cantor on, 5:463
in coherence theory of truth, 2:311
and Daoist thought, 2:207
doctrine of, 9:337–338
in Tarski's truth theory, 2:549
Correspondence (Leibniz), 9:155
Correspondence from Two Corners, The (Ivanov), 4:768
Correspondence Littéraire (Grimm), 3:71
Correspondence theory of truth, **2:539–550,** 3:317, 3:634, 9:534–538
ancient and scholastic versions of, 2:539–542
in Indian philosophy, 9:543
Locke on, 3:3

Correspondence theory of truth, *continued*
Moore on, 2:542–543
in Plato, 3:343
in Plekhanov, 7:627
presupposed by Indian philosophers, 5:119
Ramsey and, 2:545
Russell's, 2:543–545
Strawson on, 9:264
Tarski's semantic theory, 2:547–549
Wittgenstein and, 2:545
Corroboration, 7:689
Corsair, The (Kierkegaard), 5:61
Cortés, Juan Donoso, on social origin of worldviews, 9:102
Cortical correlates. *See* Brain-states
Cosmas Indicopleustes, 7:314
Cosmic blackbody radiation, cosmological observation and, 2:565
Cosmic brain, in atheistic argument, 1:368–371
Cosmic cycle, Empedocles on, 3:209, 3:213
Cosmic egg, in Orphic theogony, 7:42
Cosmic impulse, in Bloch, 1:615
Cosmic judgments, 7:244
Cosmic law, divine reason and, 2:567
Cosmic naturalism, materialism and, 6:6
Cosmic order, in Comenius, 2:341
Cosmic pantheism, 7:14
Cosmic powers, in common consent arguments for God's existence, 2:348
Cosmic Race, The (La Raza cósmica) (Vasconcelos), 5:208
Cosmic substance, Losskii on, 5:577
Cosmic sympathy, 7:638–639
Cosmic theism, of Fiske, 3:667
Cosmides, Leda, and evolutionary psychology, 3:481–486
Cosmogony
in atomism, 5:299–300
Book of Changes and Dong Zhongshu, 2:153
Fludd and, 3:674
Parmenides of Elea on, 7:125
Philolaus on, 7:310
Pythagorean, 8:183–184
sophists on, 9:131
in Stoicism, 9:256
Cosmologia Generalis (Wolff), on energy conservation, 3:228
Cosmological argument for existence of God, 2:321, **2:550–556,** 2:586–587, 3:292, 9:407
Aquinas on, 4:112
big bang theory and, 2:588
and causality, 2:586
Hume on, 4:510
kalām, 2:553–556
Cosmological constant, in cosmology research, 2:565
Cosmology, **2:556–567**
absolute in, 2:555
air in, 1:186
Alcamaeon of Croton on, 1:104–105
of al-Fārābī, 4:755
analogies in, 6:520
of Anaxagoras, 1:181, 1:271
of Anaximenes, 1:186
anthropic principle in, 1:220
Aquinas on, 3:226–227
of Archytas of Tarentum, 1:250–251
of Aristotle, 1:271–273, 5:640–641, 9:147
of Avicenna, 1:433
Bernard of Tours and, 1:592–593
in Bhagavad Gītā, 2:110
in Bible, 1:478
big bang, 9:478
Bonaventure and, 1:653
Bruno and, 1:709
of Bulgakov, 1:760
of catastrophic process and ontogenesis, 1:658
of causally closed universe, 2:89–93
at Chartres school, 2:137
in Chinese ontology of belief, 2:228
in Chinese philosophy, 2:149
Cicero and, 2:258
in Confucian eclecticism, 2:190
in Copernicus, 2:54
Crusius on, 2:607
daimones and, 4:173
in Daoist expansion by Wang Bi, 2:186
Dau Zhen on, 2:622
in Descartes, 2:53–54
description or explanation in, 2:557–558
in Dge-lugs scholasticism, 1:734–735
of Diogenes of Apollonia, 3:89–90
divine illumination in, 4:580
Earth's special place in, 1:220
energy in, 3:226–227
evolutionary
and chain of beings, 1:658
Peirce on, 7:171–174
in Sellar's critical realism, 8:732–733
of Ficino, 3:621
Fourier and, 3:707
of Galileo, 4:10
in Gnosticism, 4:99–102
in Gödel, 4:117
God's existence and, 2:550–556, 2:587–588
of Heraclitus, 4:320
in hermetic philosophy, 1:711
in hylomorphic composition of creatures, 1:653
in Ibn al-ʿArabī, 4:541
Ibn Sinā's causal hierarchy, 2:114
in illuminationism, 4:584
in Islamic philosophy, 1:433, 4:754
in Jainism, 2:111
Jeans and, 4:804
Lambert (J. H.) and, 5:175
Laplace on, 5:197
least action in, 6:66
Leibniz and, 2:551–553, 3:502, 5:256
Locke and, 5:387
Mach's principle and, 9:149
of Maimonides, 5:650–651
of Marcus Aurelius, 5:706
McTaggart on, 6:77
of Mead, 6:81–82
and metaphysics, 6:193–194
microcosm in, 5:640–641
models in
cognitive worth of models, 2:563–564
construction of, 2:559–563
multiple worlds and infinite space in, 1:711
of Naṣīr al-Dīn al-Ṭūsị, 6:478
Newton on, 5:197
of Nicholas of Cusa, 6:596–597
numbers in, 8:182–183
observation and theory in, 2:558–559
of Ockham, 9:780
Peter Aureol on, 7:256
of Philolaus, 8:183
as philosophical theology, 2:585–587
Plato and, 2:698–699, 7:601
Plutarch of Chaeronea and, 7:648
pre-Socratic, 1:271
principle of least action in, 6:66
Pythagorean, 4:173, 7:764, 8:182–185
as reason for life on Earth, 1:570
Reformation and, 8:298
relativistic, 4:117, 9:152

religion and, 8:399–400
religious, 7:310–311
Renaissance, 3:624
in Sankhya, 2:111–112
scientific
Darwinism and, 2:639–640
research in, 2:565
Shao's neo-Confucian rationalism, 2:157
space-time geometries and, 9:466
Stoic, 5:706, 8:812, 9:256
of Suhrawardī's *mundus imaginalis*, 9:316–317
of Swedenborg, 9:336
of Theophrastus, 9:412
and thermodynamic equilibrium, 1:645
Thomist, 2:551
in time directionality, 2:85–88
and Universe as existential contingent, 2:587
and Universe in future, 2:587
Valentinian, 9:632
in Vedic literature and Upanishads, 2:109–110
Whitehead on, 9:750–751
Wright (Chauncey) and, 9:846
Yin Yang school and, 2:152
Zeno on, 9:253
Zhang Zai and, 9:879
Zhu Xi on, 2:216–217
Zoroastrian, 9:887
See also Universe
Cosmopolitanism, **2:567–570**
egalitarianism in, 6:488
justice in, 6:488
of Kristeva, 1:134
vs. liberal nationalism, 6:488
nationalism in, 6:485–486
vs. patriotism, 7:140
philosophy of history in, 7:388
Rawls and, 9:98
Cosmos, **2:570–572**
in Gnosticism, 4:101–102
in Ibn al-ʿArabī, 4:541
in illuminationism, 4:584
Philolaus' explanation of, 7:310
specific model of, 3:670
in theory of divine illumination, 4:580
Costa, Newton da, paraconsistent logic and, 5:492, 7:105
Costa, Uriel da, **2:572–573,** 4:824–825
Cost-benefit analysis, and environmental ethics, 3:258
Cotes, Roger, Newton and, 6:590
Coulson, Margaret, debate in *New Left Review,* 3:600
Council and Reunion, The (Küng), 3:97
Council of Valence (855), 7:95
Council of Vienne, 5:609
Counsels, Kant on, 3:411
Count nouns, *vs.* mass nouns, **6:659–666**
Counter-examples, method of, 7:286
"Counterfactual Dependence and Time's Arrow" (Lewis), 2:575
Counterfactual intervener, Frankfurt on, 3:718
Counterfactual Test, for foreseen *vs.* intended consequences, 4:871
Counterfactuals, **10:4–10**
of asymmetry in causality, 2:105
in "at-at" theory of causation, 8:593
in Bacon (Francis), 1:448
in Berkeley, 1:583
in causal accounts of time, 2:88
and causation, 3:525
in conditional causality and reductionism, 2:99–101
conditionals and, 2:426–429, 5:101, 5:539
as events, 2:88
exclusion of forms from, 1:448
experimental predictions and, 1:540–541
as experimental questions, 1:447
Goodman on, 4:155–156
Lewis (D.) on, 5:314
Molinism on, 4:114–115
natural law and, 5:225
off-line simulation, 4:600
and omnipotence, concept of, 4:115
Peirce on, 7:167–168
realization satisfying, 3:758
representing situations, 3:710
in science, **2:573–576**
scientific law and, 5:221–224
in theory confirmation, 1:500–501
true *vs.* false, 7:518
Counterfactuals (Lewis), 5:314, 7:725
Countermovements, Wright (Chauncey) on, 9:846
Counterpart theory, 5:313. *See also* Modality
Counterstories, as narrative repair, 3:581
Counter-wish dreams, 3:744
Counting
Frege on, 6:664
vs. measuring, 6:664
Country, 2:567, 9:208
Courage
in Buddhism, 1:722
Plato on, 3:396
Courage to Be, The (Tillich), 9:458–459
Courage to Change (Bingham), 6:606
Cournot, Antoine Augustin, **2:576–578**
Cours d'analyse (Cauchy), 2:495, 5:459
Cours de l'historie de la philosophie (Cousin), 2:580
Cours de linguistique générale (Saussure), 9:273
Cours de philosophie (Gioberti), 4:93
Cours de philosophie positive (Comte), 5:372
Cours d'économie politique (Pareto), 7:117
Cours d'esthétique (Jouffroy), 4:855
Course of Lectures on Natural Philosophy (Young), on energy and work, 3:229
Course-of-values induction, definition of, 5:539
Courtly love, 5:587
Cousin, Victor, **2:578–581**
Brownson and, 1:706
Desgabets and, 2:758
Galluppi and, 4:14
Laromiguière and, 5:201
Mansel and, 5:687
and New England transcendentalism, 6:572
Pascal and, 7:132
on Spinoza, 9:195
spiritualistic school of, 3:705
Couturat, Louis, **2:581–583,** 8:645
Covenant model, of medical ethics, 6:93–95
Cowardice, 9:680
Cox, Richard T.
on basic rules of probability, 4:675
on rational degrees of belief, 8:685
on requirement of consistency, 9:221
Cradle argument, 1:222
Craft, creative process and, 2:590
Craig, Edward, epistemology of, 6:499
Craig, William
on God and time, 3:359–360
kalām cosmological argument and, 3:321
on scientific theory, 7:519
tensed theory of time and, 9:475
on token-reflexive theory, 9:476
Craig's Theorem, 2:383, **2:583–584,** 8:690
Crakanthorp, Richard, 5:439
Cramer-Rao inequality, 3:663

Cranch, Christopher Pearce, 6:572
Crane, Timothy, on perception, 7:192
Crantor of Soli, 4:173, 7:607
Crates of Thebes, Cynic teaching of, 2:617
Cratylus, **2:584–585,** 9:48
Cratylus (Plato), 2:584
  Bacon on, 8:773
  on dialectic, 3:53
  on language, 8:752–754
  mimesis in, 6:252
  Orphic influence in, 7:43
  Proclus commentary on, 7:609
  on sense perception, 3:284
  theory of Forms in, 7:595
Craving, removal of, 5:41
Crawford, Donald, 3:255–256
Creary, Lewis, 3:691
Creation
  of abstract entities, 1:318
  Alexander of Hales and, 1:115
  al-Kindī on, 1:130–131
  Anaxagoras and, 1:181
  anthropic principle and, **1:219–222**
  Aquinas on, 1:360, 3:494, 4:109
  of art, 1:318–319, 5:716
  atomists on, 5:299–300
  Augustine on, 1:397–398, 3:475
  Avicenna on, 3:135
  Basilides on, 7:141–142
  Bernard of Tours on, 1:592
  Blake on, 1:610
  Bonaventure and, 1:651
  Boyle on, 7:557
  Brahman and, 1:683
  Calvinism on, 3:475
  as causal activity, 2:586
  in Christianity, 2:246, 3:475, 7:490
  and conservation, **2:585–589**
  continuous, 1:361, 5:668–669
  Conway on, 2:529
  creativity and, 2:589
  Crescas on, 2:593–594
  Descartes on, 2:730–733, 2:751
  determinism and, 3:7–8, 3:15
  divine cooperation in, 1:760
  Duns Scotus on, 3:135
  Eckhart (Meister) on, 3:162–163
  Edwards (Jonathan) on, 3:167–168
  Ehrenfels on, 3:177
  Empedocles on, 3:209, 3:213
  Erigena on, 3:341
  of eternal truths, Descartes on, 2:728, 2:747, 2:759
  ex nihilo, 1:692, 2:49, 2:246, 2:551, 2:585, 3:494, 4:109
  Fichte on, 7:98
  Fredegisus of Tours on, 2:49
  Galen on, 4:6
  Geach on, 3:498
  vs. generation, 9:377
  Gersonides on, 4:69, 4:821–822
  Geulincx on, 4:80
  in Gnosticism, 4:99–100
  God and, 1:651
  in Greek thought, 2:698–699
  Hume on, 3:475
  Ibn Zaddik on, 4:551, 4:552
  in Indian philosophy, 4:625, 5:327
  indirect *vs.* direct, 1:651
  Irenaeus on, 3:475
  Islamic philosophy on, 1:651, 3:360–361
  Israeli on, 4:765
  in Judaism, 3:360–361, 7:490
  kalam cosmological argument, 2:551
  La Peyrère on, 5:196
  Leibniz on, 3:297, 3:494, 5:257, 5:263–265
  of literature, 1:318
  Losskii on, 5:577
  Maimonides on, 4:818, 5:650–651
  in Manichaeism, 5:683
  Milton on, 6:249
  of music, 1:318
  origin in Bernard of Tours, 1:592
  out of eternity, 9:28
  out of nothing in *kalam* argument on God's existence, 2:553–554
  Peter Lombard on, 7:260–261
  Philo on, 7:303–304
  Philoponus on, 7:314
  Plato on, 2:698–699, 6:519, 7:603
  Predelli on artistic, 1:318
  and principle of plenitude, 3:473
  as quantum event and *kalam* argument on God's existence, 2:555
  Ray on, 7:558
  Rosenzweig on, 4:829
  Ruskin on, 8:534
  Saadya on, 8:586
  semantics of, 1:370
  separability substance *vs.* God identity with that which is, 1:626
  temporality of, 1:360
  Theophilus of Antioch on, 7:142
  in *Timaeus* (Plato), William of Conches on, 9:768
  of universe ex nihilo, 2:585
  Ussher on, 5:196
  in utopianism, 9:619
  Voltaire on, 9:710
  William of Auvergne on, 9:765
Creation of substance doctrines, personal identity and, 7:219–220
Creationism, 8:670–671
  in al-Kindī, 4:755
  Longino and, 3:577
  Philoponus and, 7:314
Creative action, 1:560, 1:569–570
Creative Evolution (Bergson), 1:569, 7:382, 9:489
Creative evolution, in modernism, 6:317
Creative force, in Carus (Carl), 2:63
Creative Intuition in Art and Poetry (Maritain), 5:716
Creative Mind, The (Bergson), 1:566, 1:570, 4:782
Creative process, nature of, 2:590–591
Creative Unity (Tagore), 9:363
Creativity, **2:589–591**
  Bergson on, 1:570
  Boden on, 2:589–590
  in cognitive psychology, 8:151
  as human purpose, 1:559–560
  innovation and, 2:589
  inspiration *vs.* rationalism in, 2:589
  loss of, in societies, 9:517
  Maritain on, 5:716
  and necessity, 1:560
  in science and mathematics, 1:714
  in symbolic *vs.* empiricist thought, 1:610
  and truth, 9:57
Creator
  in Brown, 1:671
  human beings as, 7:319–320
Creature(s)
  of consciousness, 2:449
  dependence on God, 3:141
Credence, 8:27
Credibility gap, 5:110–111
Credo quia impossibile, principle of, 5:23
Credulity, 3:682, 8:402
Creighton, James Edwin, **2:591–592**
Crell, Johann, 9:100
Cremonini, Cesare, Averroism of, 1:425
Crenshaw, Kimberle, 3:586, 3:601, 8:850
Crepuscolo dei filosofi, Il (The twilight of the philosophers) (Papini), 7:102
Crescas, Hasdai, **2:592–594,** 4:822–823
  Albo and, 1:102
  Maimonides and, 5:653
  Pico della Mirandola (Gianfrancesco) and, 7:575
  on plenitude principle, 5:593

Crichton, Michael, 1:336
Crick, Francis, 2:456, 7:146
Crime
as assertion of ego, 9:251
Bosanquet on, 1:663–664
as challenge to state sovereignty, 9:146
Eliot (George) on, 3:185
Hobbes on, 6:511
Mandeville on, 5:681–682
personal identity and, 7:216, 7:217
personhood and, 7:242
punishment of, 1:517–518, 8:160–163
reform and, 8:165–167
severity of, 8:163
trivial, 8:163
Crime and Punishment (Dostoevsky), 3:100
Criminal insanity, 8:449–450
Criminal law
Beccaria on, 7:424
Posner on, 7:718
Rawls on, 4:868
utilitarian approach to, 4:868
Crimmins, Mark, on belief attribution, 1:536
Crise de la conscience europeén, La (Hazard), 3:243
Crisis (Husserl), 7:300
Crisis (Paine), 7:73
Crisis of Western Philosophy: Against Positivism (Solov'ëv), 9:122
Criteriololgy, **2:594–595**
Criterion of truth
in anonymous Mīmāmsā commentary, 5:118
skeptical response to, 5:120
Criterionless choice, 5:63–66
Critias (Plato), dating of, 9:107
Crítica (periodical), 5:210
Critical Account of the Philosophy of Kant (Caird), 4:558
Critical common sense, Peirce on, 7:171
Critical constructivism phase, of Kelsen, 5:49
Critical ethics, 6:535–537
Critical Examination of the Belief in a Life after Death, A (Ducasse), 3:126
Critical History of Greek Philosophy, A (Stace), 9:199
Critical inquiry, philosophy as, 5:91
Critical judgment, *vs.* theoretical judgment, Windelband on, 9:792
Critical legal studies, 7:463–464
Critical moral thinking, Hare on, 3:441
Critical personalism, 9:244
Critical philosophy
Kantian, Jacobi (Friedrich Heinrich) on, 4:771
Keyserling and, 5:58
Schulze and, 8:661
See also Kant, Immanuel; Neo-Kantianism
Critical positivism, 7:715–716
Critical present-aim theory, Parfit on, 7:120
Critical realism, **2:595–598,** 8:266–268
Cournot and, 2:576
dualism of, 6:75
Jodl (Friedrich) and, 4:835
Külpe and, 5:160
Lukács on, 5:603
perception and, 7:178–179
Critical Realism (Sellars), 2:595, 8:732
Critical symbolism, 8:587
Critical theory, 1:545, **2:598–599,** 3:565
Critical thinking, 7:333, 7:356–359
Critical Thinking (Black), 1:605
Critical vitalism, 9:695–697
Critical-race feminist legal theorists, 3:584
Criticism
aesthetic, 1:40, 1:508–509
Alison on, 1:128–129
of art
ethical, 1:68
moral and political role of, 1:538
Benjamin on, 1:545–547
biblical, 1:492
Carlyle and, 2:32
civic, in Russia, 1:538
in civilization, 8:460
common sense and, 2:357
conservatism and, 2:467
as Cynic virtue, 2:616
Diderot and, 3:77
and historical development, 1:493
by Jacobi (Friedrich Heinrich), 4:769–770
of law, 7:452–453
of laws of logic, 5:512
literary, 5:368–370
Eliot (T. S.), 3:185–186
in Hellenistic and Roman periods, 1:189–190
metacriticism in Beardsley, 1:508–509
Mill (John Stuart) and, 6:222
and neoclassical rules of beauty, 1:512
Philoponus and, 7:314
postcolonial, 7:727
Sibley on, 9:21
social, in Russia, 1:538
unbiased opinion and, 9:764
Vico on, 9:671
in Wolffian rationalism, Gottsched on, 4:165
"Criticism of Alexander's Theory of Mind and Knowledge" (Stout), 9:260
Criticón, El (Gracián), 4:168
Critique de la critique de la recherche del al verité (Desgabets), 2:757
Critique de la raison dialectique (Sartre), 3:427–428, 3:507
Critique de la recherche de la verité (Foucher), 2:757
Critique of Abstract Principles (Solov'ëv), 9:122
"Critique of Aesthetic Judgment," in *Critique of Judgment,* 5:26
Critique of Capitalist Democracy, The (Moore), 1:122
Critique of Dialectical Reason (Sartre), 3:510, 8:604, 9:98
Critique of Judgment (Kant), 1:74, 1:514, 2:68, 2:367, 5:8, 5:23–28
absolute in, 1:11
beauty in, 9:790
deism and, 2:689
Goethe and, 4:142
Lyotard on, 9:278
on nature, 3:254
pedantic form of, 5:9
on sublime, 9:293
on teleological judgment, 4:596–597
Critique of Practical Reason (Kant), 2:70, 2:303, 5:8
absolute in, 1:11
concept of "good" as well as "duty," 5:24
Deleuze and, 2:696
on duty, 3:153, 5:24
ethics in, 3:410
moral concepts and assumptions in, 5:23
on natural religion, 2:689
pedantic form of, 5:9
practical reason defined in, 4:613
Critique of Pure Reason (Kant), 1:519, 2:74, 2:103, 5:79
absolute in, 1:11
agnosticism in, 1:92
analytic *vs.* synthetic in, 1:159
appearance in, 1:232
apperception in, 1:233–234, 5:17
on Argument from Design, 7:560
on categories of understanding, 3:307–308

Critique of Pure Reason (Kant), ***continued***
conceptual framework in, 5:79
on dialectic, 3:54
Enlightenment and, 3:244
epistemology in, 3:306
first antinomy in, 9:467
on God, 2:689
"Idea" in, 7:389
interpreting, 5:34
on intuition as nonpropositional knowledge, 4:729
Jacobi (Friedrich Heinrich) on, 4:770–771
Kitcher (Patricia) on, 5:76
knowledge in, Goethe on, 4:142
on knowledge of inner states, 9:44
on laws of science, 3:410
Maimon on, 5:645
on metaphysics, 3:308–309
nature in, 6:520
Nelson (Leonard) on, 6:534
neo-Kantian focus on, 6:540–541
objective phenomena in, 1:245
ontology in, 7:28
pantheism and, 7:101
possibility in, 7:722–723
pragmatism and, 7:744
on productive imagination, 4:596
progressive order of, 5:9
Schopenhauer on, 8:648
second edition of, 5:23
on space and time, 2:689, 4:57, 9:148
Spaventa and, 9:159
Spir and, 9:196
on substance, 9:298
theme and preliminaries of, 5:12–14
on transcendental idealism, 4:553
Vaihinger and, 6:539
Critique of Religion and Philosophy (Kaufmann), 5:46
"Critique of Teleological Judgment," in the *Critique of Judgment*, 5:27
Critique of the Arab Mind, The (al-Jabiri), 1:129–130
Critique of the Gotha Program (Marx), 2:362, 9:73
"Critique of Utilitarianism" (Williams), 3:443
Critische Abhandlung von dem Wunderbaren in der Poesie (Bodmer), 4:166
Critische Dichtkunst (Breitinger), 4:166
Crito (Euclides of Megara), 6:110
Crito (Plato)
on duty in civil disobedience, 2:260
on historic Socrates, 9:107
on human good, 9:111
on trial of Socrates, 7:584
Critolaus, peripatetics and, 1:259
Croce, Benedetto, **2:599–605,** 9:363
on aesthetics, 1:57, 2:600–602
on beauty, 1:65
Collingwood and, 2:325–327
on economics and law, 2:603
on ethics and politics, 2:603–604
expressionism of, 1:340
Gentile and, 3:553, 4:49–51
Gramsci on, 4:169
on historical knowledge, 7:392
in historicism, 4:392
on intuition, 1:304
Labriola and, 5:165–166
Latin American philosophy and, 5:208
on logic of history and sciences, 2:602–603
Papini and, 7:102
Sorel and, 9:132
"Croce's Philosophy of History" (Collingwood), 2:325
Croll, James, 3:232
Cromwell, Oliver, Menasseh ben Israel and, 6:128
Cronus, Diodorus, "Master Argument" of, 3:692
Cross, John W., Eliot (George) and, 3:184
Cross-correspondences, parapsychology and, 7:115–116
Crowd, Kierkegaard on, 5:67
CRTT (computational/representational theory of thought processes), 3:675
Crucé, Emeric, 7:154
Crusius, C. F., Lambert and, 5:175
Crusius, Christian August, **2:605–609**
Kant and, 2:605, 2:608, 5:10, 5:124
Leibnizian-Wolffian School and, 9:825
Cruzan v. Director, Mo. Health Department, 6:95
Cryptology, Carroll and, 2:53
Crystallology, Longino on, 3:577
C-series, McTaggart on, 6:79
Cuban philosophy
contemporary period, 5:207–208
on identity, 5:211
independentist period, 5:205
positivism in, 5:206–207
Varona y Pera in, 9:647–648
Cube, duplication of, Archytas of Tarentum and, 1:250
Cudworth, Damaris, 6:655, 6:656
Cudworth, Ralph, **2:609–612**
on atheism, 1:357
Cambridge Platonism of, 2:14
Cumberland and, 2:614
deism and, 2:685
on duty, 3:155
and ethics, 3:94, 3:406
Locke and, 5:375, 5:376
More (Henry) and, 6:395
physicotheology and, 7:557, 7:558
Smith (John) and, 9:69
on Strato's "hylozoism," 9:261–262
on unconscious, 9:570–571
Cues, perceptual skill and, 7:184
Cult, Pythagoreanism as, 8:185
Cultivating Humanity (Nussbaum), 6:681
Cultivation, Confucian theory of, 5:140
Cultu et Amore Dei, De (Swedenborg), 9:336
Cultura italiana, La (Papini and Prezzolini), 7:102
Cultural influence, as criterion of validity, 3:738
Cultural objectivism, 7:316–317
Cultural philosophical anthropology, 7:321–322
Cultural relativism, 3:390–391
definition of, 3:368
as ethical subjectivism, 3:377–379
modern moral theory and, 3:374
Montesquieu and, 3:410
moral values and, 3:444
origins of, 3:405
Rorty and, 8:495
use of term, 3:369
Culturalism, 8:260
Cultural-sociology
competing terms in, 4:38
of Weber (Alfred), 9:732–733
Culture
in amplification of drives, 8:628
Arendt on, 1:254
Arnold on, 1:293–294
art and, 1:79
Bachofen on, 1:441
Bakhtin on, 1:465–468
Benjamin on, 1:546
Buddhism and, 2:169–170
in business ethical decisions, 1:778–779
Carolingian renaissance and, 2:49–51
Cassirer on, 1:58
Chamberlain on, 2:123
Chateaubriand on, 2:138
chemistry and, 2:143–144

Chernyshevskii on, 2:146
Chinese religion and, 2:226–227
classical
Eliot (T. S.) on, 3:186
Spengler on, 9:166
cognitive science and, 2:300–301
Cohen (Hermann) on, 2:304
Coleridge on, 2:320
collective representations in, 9:96
in communitarian view of nationalism, 6:486
communitarianism and, 2:368–369
Confucius on, 2:231, 2:442
contents in, 9:31
cosmopolitanism and, 2:570
crisis in, 1:254
Daoist critique of, 2:236
death instinct and, 8:310–311
as definition of nation, 6:481–482, 6:486
Dilthey on, 3:82
economics of, 7:354
education and, 7:360, 7:364
Eliot (T. S.) on, 3:186
Emerson on, 3:196
and emotion, 3:202
Fëdorov on, 3:559
Gehlen on, 4:36
geography of, 1:621–622
hero and, Carlyle on, 2:34
as historical form of *palingenesis,* 4:95
in historical materialism, 4:379
in history, 8:459, 9:733
identification with, 6:482
intelligence in, 1:596
knowledge of, 9:103
language structure and, 1:83
law and, 7:427
as machine, 8:659
Malraux on, 5:674
Mao on, 2:180
in Marxism, 1:615
as mastery of nature and law of mind, 1:719
and meaning, 1:481
in moral constructivism, 2:472
morality and, 3:685, 8:310–311
normative authority of, 1:254
objects of, 9:31
origins of
Krueger on, 5:156
Vico and, 9:674–675
Ortega y Gasset on, 7:47
philistinism in, 6:610
philosophy and, 3:404–405, 7:334–336
pluralism in, 7:642–643
in postmodernism, 7:729
as pratico-inert, 8:610
progressivist evolutionary thesis of, 9:733
Pure Land Buddhism and, 2:169
Reich on, 8:310–315
relativity of, 5:673
and religion, 2:224–225, 5:59
Rothacker on, 7:322
Schleiermacher on, 8:633–634
and secularization, 1:656
Simmel on, 6:545, 9:30–31
as social ideal, 1:293–294
in Sombart's economic system, 9:127–128
Spengler on, 3:672, 9:165–167
Spranger on, 9:199
and suicide, 9:318, 9:320
symbols in, 1:58
in Tang's neo-Confucianism, 2:183
technology and, 1:708, 7:545
transmission of, 7:364
unamism and, 1:85
universal values in, 8:459
vs. universality, 8:154
vision across, 7:334
Wundt on, 9:850
Xunzi on, 2:234
Culture and Anarchy (Arnold), 1:293
Culture and Value (Wittgenstein), 9:820
Culver, C. M., 7:138–139
Culverwell, E., on physics of gases, 7:537
Culverwell, Nathanael, **2:612–614**
Cum occasione (papal bull), 4:789
Cumberland, Richard, **2:614–615**
on duty, 3:155
ethics, 3:406
Cummins, Robert, on functions, 9:389
Cummiskey, David, grounding a consequentialist approach, 5:37
"Cunning of Reason" (Hegel), 5:653
Cunynghame, Henry, logic grid of, 5:565
Cuppé, Pierre, clandestine writings of, 2:267
Cur Deus homo (Anselm), 1:214
Curchod, Suzanne, 4:84
Curiosa Mathematica. Part 1. A New Theory of Parallels (Carroll), 2:52
Curiosity, Hobbes on, 8:128
Curriculum
in Augustine, 7:368
Comenius on, 7:369
Dewey on, 7:378
epistemology and, 7:359
Mill (John Stuart) on, 7:377
in Plato, 7:366–367
See also Education
Currie, Gregory, 7:382, 9:39
Curry, Haskel B., 2:337, 2:340, 9:354
Curry-Howard isomorphism, 4:742
Cursory Strictures on the charge delivered by Lord Chief Justice Eyre to the Grand Jury (Godwin), 4:136
Cursus Conimbricensis, 3:681
Cursus Mathematicus (Hérigone), 5:440
Cursus Philosophicus (John of St. Thomas), 4:844–845
Curves
in mathematical, 2:494
Peano and, 5:465
Cusanus. *See* Nicholas of Cusa
Custom(s)
in Chinese religion, 2:226
in Confucian ethics, 2:195
as law, 7:427
private language problem and, 8:16–17
in psychology, 9:849
Rousseau on, 3:410
social
Confucius on, 2:231
conscience and, 2:445
Daoist thought on, 2:237
sophistry on, 7:365
See also Tradition
Cut rule, 3:653, 3:657, 5:475
Cuvântul (periodical), 4:743
Cybernetics, 4:617, 6:11–12
Cybersex, 7:525
Cyclic adenosine monophosphate (cAMP), 6:568
Cyclopaedia (Chambers), 3:221
Cynicism, **2:616–617**
Antisthenes and, 1:224
asceticism of, 1:351
Diogenes Laertius on, 3:88
Diogenes of Sinope and, 3:90–91
Epictetus on, 3:262
Gregory of Nazianzus and, 4:181
language theory of, 2:669
Lucian of Samosata on, 5:597
Socrates and, 3:399, 9:113
Stoicism and, 3:399, 9:253
Zeno of Citium and, 9:869
Cynicus (Lucian of Samosata), 5:597
Cyrano de Bergerac, Savinien de, **2:618,** 5:181–182
Cyrenaics, **2:619–620,** 3:264, 3:399
Cyril of Alexandria, patristic philosophy and, 7:143
Cyropaedia (Education of Cyrus) (Xenophon), 9:856

D

Da Costa, Uriel. *See* Costa, Uriel da
Da Vinci, Leonardo. *See* Leonardo da Vinci
Dacier, Anne, 9:839
Dadaism, 1:298
Dahl, Robert, 7:733, 9:207
Dai Zhen, **2:621–622**
on neo-Confucian philosophy, 2:158
on self-cultivation, 2:177
Daigaku wakumon (Kumazawa), 5:162
Daimōn, Empedocles on, 3:210, 3:212–213
Dalgarno, George, 1:342
Dalit theology, 5:331, 5:332
Dall'uomo a Dio (Varisco), 9:647
Dalton, John, 1:387, 6:61, 8:697
Daly, Martin, evolutionary psychology and, 3:481
Damaris, Lady Masham, 2:609
Damascene, John, 4:697
Damascius, **2:622–623**
on Ammonius, 6:554
in Neoplatonism, 6:552–553
Simplicius and, 9:34
Damasio, Antonio, 3:201
Damnation, in Christianity, 2:249
Dance, representational theory of art and, 1:297
Dangun, 5:134
Daniel, Gabriel, 4:790
Daniel Säuberlich (Nicolai), 6:598
Dante Alighieri, **2:623–627**
Augustinianism and, 1:404
and Croce, 2:601
Galileo on, 4:9
on love, 5:586–587
political philosophy of, 7:660
on Scot, 8:703
on Siger of Brabant, 9:27
on war and peace, 7:152
Danto, Arthur, **2:627–628**
on action, 3:19
allographic/autographic distinction in, 1:317
on art, 1:34, 1:66–67, 1:299
and Beardsley, 1:509
on history, 7:394
on Kuhn, 7:394
on Nietzsche, 6:614
on style, 1:331
Dao
in Confucianism, 2:151
in Confucian-Mohist philosophy, 2:185
in Confucius, 2:201, 2:443
Dai Zhen on, 2:622
language engagement and, 2:205–206
Laozi on, 2:151, 2:187, 5:194, 5:195
meaning of, 2:191–193
as mysticism, 2:201
as nameless One and nonbeing, 2:151
in neo-Confucianism, 2:183
as normative practical concept, 2:184–185
Ogyū on, 7:10
as proper subject for discourse, 9:857
vs. ren, 9:726
unity with *qi* (concrete things), 9:724
Wang Bi on, 9:722
Wang Yang-ming on, 9:726
Xunzi on, 9:857
Daochuo, on chanting of Amituofo, 2:169
Daodejing (Lao Zi), 2:161, 2:185–188, 2:197–198, **5:194–196**
anarchism and, 1:177
language philosophy in, 2:205–206
mystical concept of dao, 2:151
Wang Bi on, 9:722
Zhuangzi compared with, 9:881
Daoism
ancient development and views of, 2:151
and Buddhism, 2:186, 2:191
characteristics of, 2:184
Chinese legalist social and political thought, 2:238
in Chinese philosophy, 2:184–194
on Confucian social ethics, 2:232
and Confucianism, 2:190, 4:794, 5:316
cosmic law in, 2:221
engagement with ultimate concern, 2:205–206
ethical skepticism in, 2:197–198
ethics of, *ziran* (naturally so) in, 9:722
fate under imperial rule, 2:190–191
in Guo Xiang, 4:196
historical outline of, 2:185–186, 7:486
history of, 2:187–188
Japanese interest in, 4:792
key concepts, 2:191–193
language in, 2:161
on law, 2:220–221
on life, meaning and value of, 5:359
linguistic truth and, 2:205–208
logic and, 5:416
Mencius's social and political thought and, 2:232
metaphysics of, 2:190–191
moral idealism in, 2:198
mysticism of, 6:445
on nothingness, 5:134, 5:138
ontological views of, 2:191
philosophical, 2:184–185
politics of, *ziran* (naturally so) in, 9:722
in popular neo-Confucianism, 2:181
as preparation to know external things, 2:216
reality in, 7:486
as religion, *vs.* philosophical forms of, 2:186
religious form of, 2:185
on silence, 2:220–221
social and political philosophy of, 2:236–237
syncretism in, 2:153
on ultimate reality, 2:220–221
Wei-Jin metaphysical school, 2:153
on wisdom as enlightened knowledge, 2:219
Xuan Xuanxue metaphysical school, 2:153
Dappled World (Cartwright), 2:62
Dark Ages, philosophy in, 6:99
Dark energy, in cosmology research, 2:565
Dark matter, 2:565, 8:31
Dark Night of the Soul, The (John of the Cross), 4:846
Darnton, Robert, on Enlightenment, 3:243
Darrow, Clarence
agnosticism of, 1:358, 1:371, 2:351
on atheism, 1:371
on death, 5:346, 5:349
on determinism, 3:16
on life, meaning and value of, 5:346, 5:349, 5:354
Darstellung meines Systems der Philosophie (Schelling), 1:11
Darwall, Stephen, 9:3
Darwin, Charles Robert, **2:628–630**
on animal mind, 1:201, 1:208
Beatty on, 7:340
Bergson and, 1:563, 1:568–569
on Buckle, 1:718
Butler (Samuel) on, 1:784
challenges to, 7:341–342

and Chamberlain, 2:123
and Christianity, 2:629–630, 2:685
cosmology of, 2:639–640
criticisms of, 2:636–639
Diderot and, 3:73
on emotions, 3:198
Engels on, 3:238
evolutionary psychology and, 3:481, 8:136–137
evolutionary theory of, 2:628–630, 2:632–635, 3:487–488
and feminists, 3:567
on goal-directedness of evolution, 5:159
Gobineau on, 4:106
on God, 2:349
on Goethe, 4:142
grandfather of, 2:630–631
in history of biology, 7:338
Ibn Khaldūn and, 4:549
inference regarding natural selection, 4:651
influences on, 3:487
Lamarck and, 5:174, 5:175
Malthus and, 5:675
Mendel and, 7:339
on origin of life, 5:360
Paley and, 7:75
physicotheology and, 7:561
on population, 7:338
positivism and, 7:713
Schopenhauer and, 7:522
and Steiner, 9:241
and Stephen, 9:243
taxonomy in, 7:343
variation in, 7:338
and Veblen, 9:655–656
Wallace and, 2:629, 2:632, 3:488, 8:137, 9:720–721
See also Darwinism

Darwin, Erasmus, **2:630–632**
Butler (Samuel) on evolutionary theory, 1:784
on evolution, 2:631, 3:486
and Lunar Society of Birmingham, 3:247

Darwiniana (Gray), 4:170

Darwinism, **2:632–644,** 7:341–342
adaptation in, 7:342–343
biological, 2:628–630, 2:632–635, 2:643
criticisms of, 2:636–639
Gray on, 4:170–171
directional law of evolution, 3:36
Dühring on, 3:131
on human nature, 3:480, 6:80
panpsychism and, 7:87
philosophical, 2:632, 2:639–643
vs. population theory, 5:676–677
progress and, 8:47
and scientific cosmology, 2:639–640
Smuts on, 9:72
social, 2:642–643
teleology in, 7:342–343
theology and, 2:640–641
of Wilson (Edward O.), 9:789
See also Evolution

Darwinism (Wallace), 9:721

Darwin's Dangerous Idea (Dennett), 2:711–712

"Das Christentum der Vernunft" (The Christianity of reason) (Lessing), 5:296

Das Erdbeben in Chile (Kleist), 5:78

Das Gesetz der Ursache (The law of cause) (Geyser), 4:83

Das Heilige (The idea of the Holy) (Otto), 3:753, 4:107, 6:544

Das Kathchen von Heilbronn (Kleist), 5:79

Das Kontinuum (Weyl), on continuum, 2:505

Das Krieg buchlein des Friedens (Franck), 3:713

Das menschliche Denken (Schuppe), 8:662

Das Mutterrecht. Eine Untersuchung über die Gynaikokratie der alten Welt nach ihrer religiösen und rechtlichen Natur (Bachofen), 1:441

Das Prinzip Hoffnung (Bloch), 1:614

Das Prinzip vom zureicheden Grunde (The principle of sufficient reason) (Geyser), 4:83

Das Recht des Besitzes (The right of possession) (Savigny), 8:614

"Das theologische Element im Beruf des logistischen Logikers" (Scholz), 8:645

Das Unaufhörliche (Hindemith), 1:547

Das Unbehagen in der Kultur (Freud), 7:252

Das verbüschierte mit sieben Siegeln verschlossene Buch (Franck), 3:712

Das Verhaltnis zwischen Willen und Verstand im Menschen (Fischer), 3:660

Das verloschollene Herz: Ein Buch stiller Betrachtungen (The singing heart: A book of quiet contemplations), 4:578

Das Wesen der Religion (Feuerbach), 3:609

Das Wesen des Christentums (Feuerbach), 3:609, 3:611

Daśabhūmika, 1:736

Dasan. *See* Chong Yakyong

Daśapadārthaśtra, 6:531

Dasein (temporal dimension of man), 1:70, 4:291–292, 4:800

Daseinsanalyse, 3:507

Daseinsanalytik, 7:301

Dasheng Qixin Lun (Mahayana awaking of faith), 1:737

Data
allowing to speak for themselves, 3:661
on complementarity of quantum theory and empirical phenomena, 1:637–639
in cosmological models, 2:560
cosmological science and, 2:564–565
in critical realism, 2:595
maximum information-preserving reduction of, 3:662
metaphysical, 6:170

Data structures, in computationalism, 2:391

Date theory, of time, 9:476–477

Daubenton, Louis, 3:72

Daubert, Johannes, 5:362

David of Dinant, **2:644–645**

David Strauss, the Confessor and Writer (Nietzsche), 6:610

David the Jew, *Liber de Causis* and, 5:333

Davidson, Donald, **2:645–650,** 5:71
on action, 1:15, 1:18
on anomalous monism, 1:211, 2:646–648, 6:133
on axiomatized theory of meaning, 8:743
on belief, 1:534, 1:537, 9:45
on color, 2:333
on dualism, 3:114
Evans and, 3:459
on events, 3:462–464, 3:466, 8:808
Frege and, 3:732
on intentions, 8:674
on interpretation of human behavior, 7:534
on language and thought, 5:190–5:192
on language of time, 9:463
on meaning, 1:154–155, 2:647–648
on mental content and interpretation, 2:478
on mental content and language, 2:480
on metaphor, meaning in, 6:166
on natural language, 8:807–808
Peirce and, 3:646
on primary deviance, 1:16
on rule following, 8:533

Davidson, Donald, ***continued***
on self-deception, 8:713
semantics of, 8:77–78
on supervenience, 9:331
on truth theories in natural language, 5:510
on truth-conditional format, 6:84–85
Davies, Martin, 9:38
Davies, Stephen, 1:305
Davis, Kingsley, 3:764
Davis, Larry, 9:705
Davis, Michael, 3:240
Davis, Stephen T., 4:618
Davy, Sir Humphry
Faraday and, 3:550
on heat energy, 3:229
translators of, 5:287
Dawkins, Richard, 3:490–491
Daybreak: Thoughts on the Prejudices of Morality (Nietzsche), 6:611
Daylight view, of Fechner, 3:556
De Admirandis Naturae Reginae Deaeque Mortialium Arcanis (Vanini), 9:646
De Aeternitae Mundi (Aquinas), 9:426
De Amore (André le Chapelain), 5:587
De Amore (Ficino), 1:48
De Anima (Aristotle), 2:74, 6:548
agent intellect in, 1:90–91
Aquinas and, 9:428
in Averroism, 1:430
epistemology in, 3:286
on immortal intellect, 4:602
on nature of the soul, 4:608
on non-localized nature of reason, 4:609
on postsensory faculties, 4:696–697
psyche in, 8:103
on sense perception, 3:286
Simplicius on, 9:34
soul in, 1:274
on sound, 9:138
Theophrastus on, 9:412
Toletus on, 9:511
as transition in history of psychology, 8:134–135
vitalism in, 9:695
De Anima (Averroes), 1:652
De Anima (Isaac of Stella), 4:753
De Anima (Tertullian), 4:603, 9:400
De Anima (The Soul) (William of Auvergne), 9:766
De Anima et Vita Libri Tres (Vives), 7:248
De animae (Burley), 1:774
De Arte Graphica (Du Fresnoy), 1:49
De audiendis poetis (Plutarch), 1:189
De Augmentis Scientiarum (Bacon), 8:772
De Broglie, Louis, 1:388, 1:630
De Broglie-Bohm theory. *See* Bohmian mechanics
De Bury, Richard, 5:68
De Caelo (Aristotle), 1:271
Averroes and, 1:422
on energy and force, 3:227
more mechanical conception of force, 3:686
on motion, 5:640–641
Simplicius on, 6:555, 9:34
De Carne Christi (Tertullian), 9:399
De casu Diaboli (Anselm), 1:214, 1:217
De causa Dei contra Pelagium (Bradwardine), 1:680
De causa gravitatis, et defensio sententiae auctoris de veris naturae legibus contra cartesianos (On the cause of gravity) (Leibniz), 5:253
De causis plantarum (Causes of plants) (Theophrastus), 9:411
De Christiana Religione (Ficino), 3:620
De Civitate Dei (Augustine), Plato and, 3:357
De Coelestia Hierarchia (Pseudo-Dionysius), 4:580
De Cognitione Dei et Nostri (Clauberg), 2:55
De Conceptione B.M.V. (Peter Aureol), 7:255, 7:257
De conceptu virginali (Anselm), 1:214
De Concordantia Catholica (Nicholas of Cusa), 6:595
De concordia (Anselm), 1:214
De Consideratione Dialectica Libri Sex (Titelmans), 5:439
De Consolatione Philosophiae (Boethius), 3:358, 4:110
De Constantia (Lipsius), 5:364
De Corpore (Hobbes), 5:442
De decem categoriae (Augustine), 5:422
De dialectica (Augustine), medieval logic and, 5:422
De Dieu qui vient á l'idée (Levinas), 5:305
De diffinitionibus (Victorinus), 5:422
De Diligendo Deo (On the love of God) (Bernard of Clairvaux), 1:592
De Discretione Animae, Spiritus et Mentis (Gilbert of Poitiers), 4:88
De Diversis Quaestionbus (Augustine), 4:564
De Divina Omnipotentia (Peter Damien), 7:259
De Divinus Nominibus (Pseudo-Dionysius), 4:580
De divisione (Boethius), 5:421
De Divisione Naturae (Erigena), 2:644, 7:95–96
De Doctrina Christiana (Augustine), 1:391
De Doctrina Christiana (Milton), 6:250
De Ecclesiastica Hierarchia (Pseudo-Dionysius), 4:580
De Ente et Essentia (Aquinas), 9:430
De Ente et Essentia (Cajetan), 2:6
De Ente et Uno (On being and unity) (Pico della Mirandola), 7:570, 7:571, 7:573
De Fato (Cicero), 2:258
de Finetti, Bruno, **2:662–664**
De Finibus Bonorum et Malorum (Cicero), 2:258
De formis (Burley), 1:773
De futuris contingentibus (Bradwardine), 1:680
De Generatione et corruptione (Toletus), 1:386
De Genesi ad Litteram (Augustine), 1:393, 1:395
De gli eroici furori (on heroic enthusiasms) (Bruno), 1:709
De Gournay, Mademoiselle, La Mothe Le Vayer and, 5:181
De Grammatico (Anselm), 1:214, 1:215, 1:218, 8:762–763
De Gratia et Libero Arbitro (On grade and free will) (Bernard of Clairvaux), 1:592
De Groot, Morris, gambler's ruin, 9:217
De haeresibus (John of Damascus), 4:836–837
De hypotheticis syllogismis (Boethius), 1:627–628, 5:421–423, 5:427, 5:433
De Immenso (Trismegistus), 1:711
De Immortalite Animae (Pomponazzi), on nature of the soul, 4:609
De Imperatorum et Pontificum Potestate (On the power of emperors and popes) (Ockham), 9:783–784
De incarnatione Verbi (Anselm), 1:214, 1:216
De Incertitudine et Vanitate de Scientiarum et Artium (Agrippa von Nettesheim), 1:97–98
De Insolubilibus (William of Sherwood), 9:786
De intensione et remissione formarum (Burley), 1:773
De Interpretatione (Apuleius), 5:408

De Interpretatione (Aristotle), 1:269, 3:692, 4:66, 5:398, 5:399, 5:401, 5:404, 9:471
  Abelard and, 5:425
  Arab logic and, 5:417
  Boethius' translation of, 8:761
  imposition in, 8:765
  medieval logic and, 5:421
  on semantics, 8:755
  on statements, 8:756
De interpretatione (Boethius), 5:423
De Interpretatione (Duns Scotus), 3:134
De Ipsa Natura (on nature itself) (Leibniz), 5:254
De Iside (Plutarch), 1:189
De Jure Belli ac Pacis (Grotius), 2:614, 4:190
  internationalization of natural law, 7:423, 9:81
  on war and peace, 7:152
De la causa, principio et uno (Bruno), 1:11, 1:709, 1:711
de la Cruz, Juana Inés, 3:569, 5:205, 9:838
De la fréquente communion (Arnauld), 1:288, 4:789
De la littérature considérée dans ses rapports avec les institutions sociales (de Staël), 9:201
De la monarchie selon la charte (Chateaubriand), 2:137
De la philosophie positive (Littré), 5:372
De la Sagesse (Charron), 2:135, 9:52
De la tradition de l'église sur l'institution des évêques (Lamennais), 5:177
De la Vertu des payens (La Mothe Le Vayer), 5:182
De l'Allemagne (Staël), 6:572
  censorship of, 9:201
De l'amour (Destutt de Tracy), 5:588
De Laplace, Pierre Simon, Keynes's fundamental thesis and, 5:56
De l'art de persuader (Pascal), 7:131
De legibus (Suárez), 6:509
De Legibus Naturae (Cumberland), 2:614
De l'esprit des lois (Montesquieu), 6:337
De l'esprit géométrique (Pascal), 2:670, 7:131
"De l'évasion" (Levinas), 5:304
De l'existence à l'existant (From existence to existents; From beings to beings) (Levinas), 5:304
De l'explication dans les sciences (Meyerson), 6:212
De Libero Arbitrio (On free will) (Erasmus), 3:338
De Libero Arbitrio (Valla), 9:635
De libertate arbitrii (Anselm), 1:214, 1:215, 1:217
De L'infinito, universo e mondi (Bruno), 1:709
De l'intelligence (Taine), 9:365
De l'origine des fables (Fontenelle), 3:682
De Luce (Light) (Grosseteste), 4:186
De Magistro (Augustine), on semantics, 8:760
De Magnete (Gilbert), 3:687
De Man, Paul, colleagues of, 2:715
De Methodis (On methods) (Zabarella), 9:867
De monarchia (Dante), 2:623–625, 7:152
De Morgan, Augustus, **2:709–710**, 5:439
  challenge to develop first-order logic, 3:641
  in history of logic, 5:440
  and Jevons, 4:807–808
  on logic, 5:439, 5:440, 7:163
  logic of, 5:448–449
  on mathematics, 5:461
  on relational propositions, 5:555
  rules of syllogism, 5:449
De Morgan's laws, 2:710, 3:538–540, 3:653, 5:540
De Motu (Berkeley), 3:689
De Motu (Galileo), impetus theory in, 4:622
De Motu (Newton), 6:590
De Motu Corporali et Luce (Corporal Motion and Light) (Grosseteste), 4:186
De multiplicatione specierum (Bacon, Roger), 1:455
De Mundi Universitate (Bernard of Tours), 1:592
De mundo (On the World) (anon.), 2:721
De Mysterio Trinitatis (Bonaventure), 1:652
De Natura Deorum (Cicero), 1:228, 2:258
De Natura Hominis (Nemesius of Emesa), 6:538
De Natura Rerum (Isidore of Seville), Lull and, 5:610
De naturis rerum (Neckham), 5:429
De Nominum Analogia (Cajetan), 2:7
De nostri temporis studiorum ratione (On the study methods of our time) (Vico), 9:671
De Occulta Philosophia (Agrippa von Nettesheim), 1:97, 1:708, 1:711
De Officiis (On Duties) (Cicero), 2:258, 5:724, 7:79
De Officio Hominis et Civis (Pufendorf), 8:157
De omnifaria doctrina (Psellos, Michael), 1:788
De Opifocio Mundi (Philo), 4:564
De Oratore (Cicero), 2:258
De orthodoxa fide (John of Damascus), 4:836–837
De ortu scientiarum (Kilwardby), 5:70
De Otio Religioso (On the leisure of the monks) (Petrarch), 7:264
De Philosophia Perenni (Stauchus), 3:624
De Platonis et Aristotelis philosophiae differentia (Plethon), 1:789
De Potentia (Aquinas), on intentionality, 4:706
De Potentia Dei (Aquinas), 9:431
De potentiis animae (Burley), 1:774
De Potestate Ecclesiastica (Giles of Rome), 4:91
De Potestate Regia et Papali (On royal and papal power) (John of Paris), 4:842
De principiis (On the first principles) (Damascius), 2:622, 6:551–552
De Principiis (Origen), 7:39–40
De processione Spiritus Sancti (Anselm), 1:214
De Pulchro et Apto (On the beautiful and fitting) (Augustine), 1:46
De puritate artis logicae (Burley), 1:773
  on syllogism, 5:427
De Re Publica (Cicero), 2:258
De re reading of modal claim, 5:425
De Recuperatione Terre Sancte (Dubois), 7:154
De re–de dicto distinction, 1:537
De Reductione Artium (Bonaventure), 1:652
De Regimine Principium (Giles of Rome), 4:90
De Religione Gentilium (Herbert), 2:682
De Remediis Utriusque Fortunae (Petrarch), 7:264
De Rerum Natura (Lucretius), 1:711, 5:598–601
  Croce on, 2:601–602
  Epicurus and, 3:265
  materialism in, 6:8
  on matter endowed with thought, 4:611
  on mortality, 4:606
  on origin of language, 8:759
  on *simulacra,* 4:593
  on substance and attribute, 9:296

De Rerum Natura Iuxta Propria Principia (On the Nature of Things According to Their Principles) (Telesio), 2:15, 9:390
De Rerum Principio (Vital du Four), 3:141
de Retz, Cardinal, La Rochefoucauld and, 5:200
De Revolutionibus (Copernicus), 2:534–535, 5:50
De Revolutionibus (Kepler), 6:521
De Sacramento Altaris (Ockham), 5:442
De Sanctis, Francesco, 2:600, **2:719–720**
De Sensibus (Theophrastus), 9:413
De Servo Arbitrio (The bondage of will) (Luther), 3:338
De Somniis (Aristotle), on dreams, 3:105
De Sophismatum Praestigiis Cavendis (Thomas Oliver of Bury), 5:438
De Sophisticis Elenchis (Aristotle), 5:443
  Arab logic and, 5:417
  on dialectic, 3:52
De Sophisticis Elenchis (Duns Scotus), 3:134
De Sousa, Ronald, on emotions, 3:199–201
De Sphaera (On the Sphere) (Grosseteste), 4:187
de Staël-Holstein, Mme. *See* Staël-Holstein, Anne Louise Germaine Necker, Baron de
De Stoicorum Repugnantiis (Plutarch), 7:247
De Substantia Orbis (Averroes), 1:422
De Summa Rerum (On the Greatest of Things) (Leibniz), 5:251
  on emanation, 5:259
  on mind, 5:258, 5:260, 5:261
  on plenitude, 5:257
  on substance, 5:268
  on truth, 5:272
De Summo Bono (Ulrich of Strasbourg), 9:565
De Summo Pontifice (Bellarmine), 1:543
De suppositionibus (Ockham), 1:773
De syllogismo categorico (Boethius), 5:421
De Tactu (Weber), 8:139
De Tempore, Spatio, Causalitate Atque de Analysis Infinitesimalis Logica (Dühring), 3:130
De Tomis, Hoc Est de Divisionibus (David of Dinant), 2:644
De Topica (Cicero), 2:258
De Topicis Differentiis (Boethius), 5:421–424, 5:426
De Translatione Imperii (Marsilius of Padua), 5:724
De Tribus Impostoribus Liber (Kortholt), 7:99
De Trinitate (Augustine), 1:391
  semantic theory in, 8:761
De Trinitate (Boethius), on God and eternity, 3:358
De Umbris Idearum (Shadows of Ideas) (Ficino), 1:708
De Unitate Intellectus Contra Averroistes (Aquinas)
  attack on Siger in, 9:27
  on immortal abstract intellect, 4:609
"De vera methodo philosophiae et theologiae ac de natura corporis" ("On the true method in philosophy and theology and on the nature of body") (Leibniz), 5:251
"De Vera Notione Virium Vivarum" (Bernoulli), 3:228
De veris principiis, et vera ratione philosophandi contra pseuophilosophos (On true principles, and the true method of philosophizing against the false philosophers) (Leibniz), 5:251
De Veritate (Anselm), 1:214, 1:218–219
De Veritate, Prout Distinguitur a Revelatione, a Verisimilli, a Possibili, et a Falso (Herbert), 2:682, 2:683, 4:26
De Veritate Religionis Christianae (Grotius), 4:190
De Vita (Ficino), 3:623
"De Vita Beata" (On the good life) (Seneca), 2:753
De Vita Coelitus Comparanda (Ficino), 1:710
De Vita et Moribus Epicuri (Gassendi), 4:25
De vita et moribus philosophorum (attrib: Burley), 1:774
De Vita Libri Tres (Ficino), 3:620
"De Vita Sua" (Gregory of Nazianzus), 4:181
De Voluptate (Valla), 9:634
De vulgari eloquentia (Dante), 2:623
Dealienation, 1:125
  See also Alienation
Death, **2:650–654**
  Avicenna on, 1:433–434
  awareness of, 2:650–651
  Blanchot on, 1:611–612
  Bultmann on, 1:764
  in Chinese religious thought, 2:227
  Darrow (C.) on, 5:346, 5:349
  definition of, 1:8
  as disease to be cured, 4:617
  Empedocles on, 3:208, 3:212
  Epicurus on, 2:651–652, 2:654, 3:266
  experiences after, 4:602
  fear of, 2:651–653
  Freud on, 2:651, 2:653, 8:146
  Heidegger on, 2:651, 2:653, 3:503, 9:490
  as impenetrable boundary, in Jaspers's psychology, 4:801
  Johnson (Dr. Samuel) on, 4:853
  of languages, 1:342
  Leopardi on, 5:285
  Levinas on, 9:491
  and life, incompatibility of, 4:607–608
  life after, semantics of, 1:370–371
  Marcus Aurelius on, 2:652, 5:706
  Marías on, 5:711
  materialism and, 6:14
  medical criterion for, 2:653
  naturalness of, 2:651
  normal reaction to, 5:349, 5:354
  personal identity and, 7:214–215
  pessimist's view of, 5:347–349
  as return to universal matter, 1:670
  Rosenzweig on, 4:829
  Russell on, 1:374
  Schopenhauer on, 5:346
  soul and, 1:433–434, 2:654, 4:823–825, 6:14, 9:766
  by suicide, 9:217–322
  Tillich on, 9:458–459
  Tolstoy on, 5:346–349, 9:512
  as transcendent, 4:743
  Wittgenstein on, 4:615
  See also Mortality
Death instinct, 8:310–311
Death of man theory, Foucault and, 3:564
Death penalty, personhood and, 7:242
Death Sentence (Blanchot), 1:612
Debs, Eugene V., 5:354
Decadence, in human nature, 7:319
Decalogue, as spiritualization of natural law, 1:622
Decembrio, Uberto, 7:613
Decennial Publications of the University of Chicago, 3:44
Deception
  in animals, 1:206
  Augustine on, 1:47
  vs. lying, 5:618–619
  See also Self-deception
"Deception and Division" (Donaldson), 8:713

"Deception by Subjects in Psi Research" (Hansen), 7:115
Decidability, 3:657–659
  as calculability, 2:378
  Church on, 5:475–476
  in computability theory, 2:372–373, 2:383
  Kronecker on, 2:400
  Turing on, 9:552
"Decidable and Undecidable Theories" (Monk), 5:479
Decidable theory, 3:658
Decision making
  in absence of belief, 1:535
  Arrow's general impossibility theorem and, 8:810
  Buridan's ass problem, 1:769–770
  business ethical responsibilities in, 1:779
  causality and self-prediction in, 8:731–732
  in cognitive psychology, 8:152
  competence requirement in, 4:679–680
  computer ethics and, 2:398
  conscience and, 2:445
  Dennett on, 2:711
  endowment effect and, 9:39
  and fast nondeterministic polynomial time algorithms, 2:388–389
  in genetics, 4:44
  and informed consent. *See* Informed consent
  irrational, in medical ethics, 3:456
  moral, impartially adjudication and, 3:579
  outcome confidence and, 1:533–534
  public policy and bioethics in, 1:600
  Savage on, 8:613
  in simulation theory, 9:37
  statistics and, 9:212
  in suicidal acts, 9:318–319
  underdetermined choice and, 1:535
Decision problems
  computing machines and, 2:404
  definition of, 5:539
  formulation of, 2:655
Decision procedure, 3:658
  analytical hierarchy in computability theory and, 2:390
  Church on, 5:476
  in computability theory, 2:372
  computationalism and, 2:394
  definition of, 5:479
  Löwenheim on, 5:471
  polynomial-time computability and, 2:388–239
Decision rule, compared to a significance test, 3:664
Decision theory, **2:654–661**
  formulation of decision problems, 2:655
  in game theory, 4:19–20
  in Nozick, 6:669
  prisoner's dilemma, 1:778, 3:449, 4:15, 7:353
  probability and, 8:30
  on rationality, 8:255
  Savage on, 8:613
  sure-thing principle in, 8:613
  in Tarski, 9:369–370
Decisive commitment (decision), 3:719
Declaratio Jesu Christi Filii Dei (Servetus), 8:831
Declaration of Independence, Locke and, 4:805
Declaration of the Rights of Man and Citizen, 1:518, 1:553, 3:246
Declaration of the Rights of Woman (Gouge), 9:839
Declarative, theology as, 7:258
Declarative memory, 6:123
Declarative sentences, 7:199
"Decline and Fall of the Analytical Philosophy of History" (Danto), 7:394
Decline and Fall of the Roman Empire (Gibbon), 2:690–691, 4:85–86
Decline of the West, The (Spengler), 3:36, 7:391, 9:165, 9:517
Decolonization, 7:726
Decomposition, in modal interpretations, 6:278
Decomposition of meaning, in compositionality, 2:371–372
Deconstruction, **2:661–662**
  aesthetics of, 1:71–72
  Bataille and, 1:489
  criticism on, 2:718
  Derrida and, 2:661–662, 3:565
  impact of, 2:715, 2:718
  Lloyd (G.) and, 5:373
  poststructuralism and, 9:274
  Rousseau and, 8:516
  styles of, 2:716
  supplement in, 2:716–718
  trace in, 2:661–662, 2:717–718
Decorum
  Cicero on, 7:79
  Panaetius of Rhodes on, 7:79
  Wolff on, 9:826–829
Dede, Ghalib, 9:309
Dedekind, J. W. Richard
  on arithmetic, 5:463
  arithmetization of mathematics and, 5:534–535
  axioms of, 9:270
  Cantor-Dedekind continuum, 2:497–499
  cut construction of real numbers, 2:27, 2:495–496
  on Euclidean ordered field, 2:500
  on the infinite, 4:657, 9:148
  on numbers, 6:672
  on proof in algebraic abstraction, 8:836
  on real numbers, 5:515
  on set existence, 8:834
  on sets, finite and infinite, 4:658, 5:543
  uniform calculability and, 2:400
Dedekind finite set, 5:543
Dedekind infinite set, 4:658, 5:543
Deducible, definition of, 5:539
Deduction
  in axiomatization, 6:22
  Bosanquet on, 1:662
  of categories, by Kant, 5:34
  in coherence theory of truth, 2:311
  definition of, 2:254, 5:540
  vs. evocative argumentative, 2:213–214
  illuminationist attack on, 4:760–761
  vs. induction, 4:638
  inference in, 6:222–223
  justification in, 4:638–639
  knowledge from, 5:513
  and logic, 5:532, 5:691
  Mill (John Stuart) on, 6:222–223
  in Mohist discourse, 2:212–213
  in ontology, 7:27
  of physical reality, Carnap on, 2:38
  as proof, 3:752–753
  proportional, 4:635
  and statistical syllogism, 4:635
  of substance from appearance, 6:600
  transcendental, 5:18
    and Chinese Buddhism, 2:166
    Kant on, 3:307–308
    Maréchal on, 5:709
    Nelson on, 6:544
  validity of, in classic foundationalism, 2:276–278
  Zeno of Elea and, 9:878
Déduction relativiste, La (Meyerson), 6:213

Deduction theorem, 3:653, 5:427
  definition of, 5:540
  Herbrand on, 5:472
  in Tarski, 9:367
Deductive argument, in metaphysics, 6:204–205
Deductive closure, 3:651
Deductive consequences, 4:308
Deductive logic, definition of, 5:547
Deductive method, cosmological models and, 2:562
Deductive reasoning
  common sense and, 2:356
  in law, 7:448
  Mill (John Stuart) on, 6:223
Deductive reconstruction, 4:641–643
Deductive theory, Tarski on, 5:480
Deductive underdetermination, 9:575
Deductively closed theory, 3:651
Deductive-nomological account of explanation, 3:518–520, 4:309
Deductivism
  applied ethics and, 1:237
  foundationalist, 8:178
  vs. reflective equilibrium, 1:238
Deep Democracy (Green), 3:568
Deep ecology, 3:259–260, 8:376
Default interference rule, 6:643
Default logic, 6:643
Defeasibility theory, 5:106–107, 5:248
Defeaters
  absence of, 5:106
  distinguishing feature of, 5:107
Defective object, 6:116
"Defence of Common Sense, A" (Moore), 1:144, 2:358, 6:206
Defence of Mr. Locke's Essay of Understanding (Cockburn), 2:294, 9:838
Defence of Poetry (Shelley), 9:8
Defence of the Rights of the Christian Church (Tindal), 9:502
Defending Science—Within Reason: Between Scientism and Cynicism (Haack), 8:680
Defense of an Essay of Dramatic Poesy (Dryden), 1:49
Defense of Helen (Gorgias), on sophism, 9:130
Defense of his Reply to King James I of England (Bellarmine), 1:542
Defense of Mr. Locke's Essay, A (Cockburn), 2:294, 9:838
Defense of Palamedes (Gorgias of Leontini), 4:163
Defense of Poesie (Sidney), 1:49
Defensio cartesiana (Clauberg), 2:284
Defensiones Theologiae D Thomae (Capreolus), 2:30–31
Defensor Fidei (Suárez), 9:282
Defensor Minor (Marsilius of Padua), 5:724
Defensor Pacis (Marsilius of Padua), 4:81, 4:838, 5:721–722, 5:724
Deficient cause doctrine, 3:472
Definability
  in model theory, 6:310–313
  in Tarski, 9:368–369
Definiendum, definition of, 5:540
Definiens, definition of, 5:540
Definite and infinite, argument of both, 9:873–874
Definite descriptions, 9:264
  analysis of, 3:645
  theory of, definition of, 5:540
Definition, **2:664–677**
  by abstraction, 5:540
  as analytic statement, 1:163
  Archytas of Tarentum on, 1:250
  Aristotelian theory of. *See* Predicables
  in axiomatization, 6:22
  Berkeley on, 9:597
  counterfactuals in science and, 2:573, 2:574
  crucial role of, 2:664
  definition of, 5:540
  dialectic and, 1:270–271
  essentialist, 2:664–668, 2:673–674
  experience in, 1:241
  fallacies in, 3:548
  as forms, 1:448
  Goodman on, 4:157–158
  Hempel on, 4:309
  Hobbes on, 3:349, 3:350
  of identity, 4:569–570
  illuminationist attack on, 4:760–761
  implicit, 1:167, 5:545
  impredicative, definition of, 5:545
  by likeness and difference, Speusippus on, 4:173
  linguistic, 2:664–665, 2:672–674
  Locke on, 2:667–668, 3:349, 5:384–385
  for measurement *vs.* axioms, 1:633
  in medieval philosophy, 6:101
  in metaphysics, 6:211
  ostensive, 1:241, 5:540, 7:110–111
  in Platonic dialogues, 7:586–588, 7:595
  pragmatic-contextual approach to, 2:673–676
  prescriptive, 2:664–665, 2:668–669, 2:673–674
  rules for, 2:674–675
  Sanches on, 8:595
  skeptical account of, 9:52
  Socrates on, 9:110–111
  subjunctive assertion in, 9:414
  of superlative terms, 2:678–679
  of terms in traditional logic, 5:493–494
  20th-century empiricists on, 3:219
  types of, 5:540
  of theoretical terms, 9:414–415
  in thought experiments, 9:452
  union of content in, 8:663
  in use, in linguistic phenomenalism, 7:272
  Valla on, 9:636
  Wittgenstein on, 1:241
  See also Essence
Definition (Robinson), 2:672
Definition of Good, The (Ewing), 3:420, 6:156–157
Definition per genus et differentiam, 5:540
Définitions de nom, 2:670
Deflationism, 3:634, 8:714
Degérando, Marie-Joseph, 8:788–789
  and Bentham, 8:792
Degli errori filosofici di Antonio Rosmini (Gioberti), 4:93
Degree of association, rejecting independent assortment, 3:665
Degrees of perfection, argument for the existence of God, **2:677–680**
Degrees of truth, 5:109
Déification d'Aristarchus Masso (Saint-Hyacinthe), 8:588
Deism, **2:680–693**
  of Blount, 1:619
  Bolingbroke place in, 1:642
  Boyle on science and religion and, 1:675
  in Britain, 2:682–687, 2:691, 9:194–195
  Butler (Joseph) on, 1:782
  Chub on, 2:252
  in Clarke, 2:271
  Common Notions of, 2:682, 2:684
  constructive, 2:690
  critical, 2:690
  critics of, 2:686–687
  definition of, 2:680–681
  Diderot on, 3:72
  in France, 2:687–688, 2:691
  in French clandestine writings, 2:265, 2:267
  in Germany, 2:688–689, 2:691
  and Gibbon, 4:86
  Herbert of Cherbury and, 4:328

historical, 2:690
history of, 2:681
humanistic, 2:690
Judaism identical with, Mendelssohn on, 6:132
Lamarck and, 5:173, 5:174
Law (W.) on, 5:220
legacy of, 2:690–692
of Morgan (Thomas), 6:405
and neoclassicism, 2:690
optimism/pessimism and, 7:249
Paine on, 7:73–74
Palmer (E.) and, 7:78
physicotheology and, 7:559
revelation and, 9:249
scientific, 2:690
Shelley on, 9:8
Spinoza and, 9:194–195
Swift's attacks on, 9:340–341
in United States, 2:689–691
of Vauvenargues, 9:653

Deist, The (periodical), 2:691

Deistical Society of New York, 2:690, 7:78

Deists, Franklin as, 3:720

Deist's Bible, 2:683

Deities, anthropomorphism of, Xenophanes of Colophon on, 9:853

Deity
in Bolingbroke, 1:642
of Fiske, 3:667–668
in Freudian explanation of religion, 8:378
Muro kyūsō on, 6:435
ultimate concept of, 7:16

Déjà vu, 8:332

Dejection: An Ode (Coleridge), 2:316

Del Medigo, Elijah, in Renaissance Jewish philosophy, 4:824

Del primato morale e civile degli Italiani (Gioberti), 4:93

Del Rio, Julian Sanz, 5:148

Del Vecchio, Giorgio, **2:697**

Deleuze, Gilles, **2:693–697**
Bergson and, 7:382
on difference, 9:277
on film, 7:384
in film theory, 7:382
Nietzsche and, 6:614, 9:277
poststructuralism of, 9:274
on time, 9:492

Deliberation
Aquinas on, 9:429
Dewey on, 3:49
in ethics, 7:736–737
freedom in, 1:563–564
Hobbes on, 3:11–12
Reid on, 3:18
Ryle on, 9:422

"Deliberation and Foreknowledge" (Taylor), 8:731

Deliverance (Avicenna), 4:581

Deliverances, for interpretation, 6:85

Della lezioni di commercio ossia di economia civile (Genovesi), 4:49

Della Poetica (Patrizi), 7:144

Deloraine (Godwin), 4:136

Delphy, Christine, materialist feminism introduced by, 3:601

Delrio, Martin, Lipsius and, 5:364

Delusion, in Buddhism, 1:724

DeMan, Paul, 2:661

Demandingness of moral requirement, 3:443–444

Dement, W., on dreams, 3:106

Demetrius, Cynic teaching of, 2:617

Demetrius of Laconia, Epicurean School and, 3:263

Demiurge, **2:697–699**, 5:1–2
in Aristotle, 5:640–641
in Gnosticism, 3:189, 4:99–100
in Numenius of Apamea, 6:679
and Plato, 7:489, 7:602
Simplicius adoration for, 9:35
in *Timaeus* (Plato), 5:640, 6:547–548
use of Forms by, 4:564
in Valentinianism, 9:632

Democracy, **2:699–706**
absence of famines in, 8:811
anarchism on, 1:176
in ancient Greece, 2:699–700
appraisal of, 2:704–705
in Aristotle, 1:268
Bentham on, 1:556
Christian, 9:446
as coercive, restrictive, or intolerant, 3:724
conditions for, 2:700–701, 2:704
in Condorcet, 2:433
connection with liberty, 3:724
critics of, 2:702
definition of, 2:699
Democritus on, 5:302
Dewey on, 3:48–49
education and, 5:686
Emerson on, 3:196–197
Goethe's indifference to, 4:141
Habermas and, 4:199
as haven for mediocrity, 4:686
impact of, on Thucydides, 9:457
Jeffersonian philosophy of, and Wayland (Francis), 9:728
justification of, 2:702–703, 2:705
Leont'ev on, 5:283–284
in Manheim, 5:686
Mao on, 2:180
Mariana on, 5:710–711
Maritain on, 5:715
Marsilius of Padua on, 5:722
in Mencius's social and political thought, 2:233
Mill (John Stuart) on, 6:228
in modern state, 2:700–702
Paine on, 7:73
political cosmopolitanism and, 2:569
and popular sovereignty, 2:701–702
presuppositions of, 2:704
in Protagoras, 8:92–93
as redemptive society, 4:774
in Renaissance scholasticism, 9:137
representation in, 2:700–701, 2:704
Rorty on, 8:495
Saint-Simon on, 8:591
Santayana on, 8:600
Schiller's (Ferdinand) opposition to, 8:625
Skinner's opposition to, 9:62
in socialist thought, 9:88
in socialist workplace, 9:73
sovereignty in, 9:142
Spinoza on, 9:181, 9:184
technology's impact on, 7:545
vs. theocracy, 7:307, 7:308
in Thucydides, 9:457
as utilitarian means, 1:556
in Yin Haiguang, 2:181

Democracy and Education (Dewey), 3:48

Democratization, Habermas on, 4:200

Democritus, **5:297–303**
Anaxagoras and, 1:183
atomism of, 1:384, 6:632, 8:182
continua in, 2:491
cosmogony, 5:299–300
Dilthey on, 3:84
Epicurus and, 3:264, 3:399
epistemology and, 3:282
Galileo on, 4:9
Lucian of Samosata on, 5:597
Lucretius and, 5:599
materialism of, 6:7
Metrodorus of Lampsacus on, 3:263
on physical world, 3:10
psychotherapeutics of, 3:395
on qualities, 3:209, 8:9
semantic theory of, 8:752

Democritus, **continued**
on sense experience, 4:27
on space, 9:146
Demonax of Cyprus, Cynic teaching of, 2:617
Demonology
in Boldin, 1:622
Plotinus on, 7:636
Demons (Dostoevsky), 3:100, 3:101
Demonstration
Averroes on, 1:426
Avicenna on, 1:434–435
Locke on, 5:386
as a proof, 3:752–753
Demonstration (derivation), definition of, 5:540
Demonstration of the Being and Attributes of God (Clarke), 2:268, 2:270, 2:686, 7:559
Demonstrationes Catholicae (Catholic demonstrations) (Leibniz), 5:251–252, 5:266–267
Demonstrative induction, Johnson (W. E.) on, 5:458
Demonstrative inference, theorems of, 5:56
Demonstrative knowledge, 5:96, 3:300
Demonstratives, **2:706–709**
definition of, 2:705
as devices of direct reference, 8:746
linguistic meaning *vs.* content of, 2:705
pure, 2:707
reference-fixing for, 2:707
semantics for, 2:708
"Demonstratives" (Kaplan), 3:252–253, 5:38–39
Demos, Raphael
on negation, 6:525–526
on Russell's theory of truth, 2:545
Demythologization, in Barthes, 1:481
Demythologizing, in Bultmann, 1:763
Denck, Hans, Franck's contacts with, 3:712
Deng Ziaoping, on capitalism and the socialist revolution, 2:180–181
Denial
in asceticism, 1:353
vs. assertion, 6:654
assumption and, 6:116
linguistics of, 6:654
Denial of antecedent fallacy, definition of, 5:543
Deniers, of the value of truth, 5:103
Denis, Jean-Baptiste, 2:757
Denis, St., 8:100–101
Denken und Wirklichkeit (Thought and reality) (Spir), 9:196
Dennett, Daniel Clement, **2:710–712**
cannot truly know all physical facts, 5:113
on consciousness, 2:455
consciousness theory of, 2:456
eliminative materialism and, 3:183
in ethnology, 1:202
folk psychology as an intentional system, 3:679
on imaging, 4:591
on intentionality, 4:710
on methodological behaviorism, 1:525–526
on personhood, 7:240
on qualitative consciousness, 2:450
on radical behaviorism, 1:522
on simulation theory, 9:37
on soul, 3:115–116
on Turing, 9:553
on two-level account of introspection, 4:721
on visual perception, 4:712
Denominate numbers, in quantity scales, 6:86
Denominatives, 8:762–763
Denotation
in Aristotle's categories, 2:72
vs. connotation, 8:58
in Keynes, 5:457
Lewis (C. I.) on, 5:308
Mill (John Stuart) on, 5:548, 8:58
of nouns in traditional logic, 5:493
of plural noun phrases, 7:646
Denoting
Church's view of sense and, 2:254
in semantic paradoxes, 5:518
Dense, definition of, 5:540
Density
as derived measurement, 6:90
in Newtonian mass, 6:3
Density operator *W*, 6:278
Denumerable set, definition of, 5:540
D'Enville, La Rochefoucauld, Franklin lionized by, 3:720
Deontic logic. *See* Modal logic
"Deontic Logic" (von Wright), 9:848
Deontic modal interpretation, 6:298–299
Deontic operator, reversing the order of, 3:540
Deontological ethics, **2:712–715**, 3:386–387
act utilitarians and, 9:608
as agent-relative, 3:387
arguments against, 9:606–607
conventional morality and, 3:388
definition of, 9:687
on duty of beneficence, 8:722
in education, 7:360
of intuitionism, 4:736
palingenesis as, 4:95
right action in, 9:681
on role of the Good, 4:153
vs. teleological ethics, 9:383
vs. utilitarian ethics, 3:384
Deontological methods, in bioethics, 1:600–601
Deontological nonnaturalists, 3:419–420
criticisms of, 3:420
Deontological rationality, 8:253
Deontology
definition of, 2:712–713
paradoxes of, 2:714
See also Moral deontology
Deontology (Bentham), 3:173
Dependence
absolute, 8:634–637
of body and mind in refutation of immortality, 4:615
in new realism, 6:586
relevant to *a priori* justification, 5:80
Dependency critique, 3:583
Dependency workers, 3:580
Dependent Rational Animals (MacIntyre), 5:637
Depiction theory of art, 1:328–329
Deplessis-Mornay, Philippe, critique by Charron, 2:134
Depression, and pain, 7:70
"Der Anselmische Gottesbewies" (Scholz), 8:645
Der Atheismus and seine Geschichte im Abendlande (Mauthner), 2:349
Der Begriff der Religion im System der Philosophie (Cohen), 2:304
Der Begriff des absolut Wertvollen als Grundbegriff der Moralphilosophie (Krueger), 5:156
Der einzig möglicher Beweisgrund zu einer Demonstration des Daseins Gottes (The only possible ground for a demonstration of God's existence) (Kant), 4:770
"Der Gedanke: Eine logische Untersuchung" (Frege), 3:726
Der Historismus und seine Probleme (Historicism and its problems) (Troeltsch), 9:528
Der Historismus und seine Überwindung (Troeltsch), 9:528
Der junge Hegel (Lukács), 3:84

Der logische Aufbau der Welt (The logical construction of the world) (Carnap), 2:40
on theory of types, 9:354
Der Operationskreis des Logikkalkuls (Schröder), 5:462
Der Prinz von Homburg (Kleist), 5:79
Der Raum (Carnap), space geometry theory in Carnap, 2:38
Der Römerbrief (Barth), 1:477
"Der sinnhafte Aufbau der sozialen Welt" (Schutz), 8:664
Der zerbrochene Krug (Kleist), 5:78
Derby at Epsom (painting), Merleau-Ponty on, 6:151
Derham, William
on deism, 2:686
physicotheology and, 7:559
Derivability of class terms, Bolzano on, 5:446
Derivation (deduction), of the subject, 3:615
Derivation (demonstration), definition of, 5:540
Derivations, in conduct, Pareto on, 7:118–119
Derivative knowledge
defining, 5:92
knowledge of truths, 5:97
Derived measurement, general theory of, 6:90–91
Derived rule of inference, definition of, 5:541
Derrida, Jacques, **2:715–719**
on alterity, 1:134
on art, 1:72
Bataille and, 1:489
critical legal studies and, 7:463
criticism on, 2:718
and deconstruction, 2:661–662, 3:565
Dōgen and, 3:95
on Husserl, 9:489
Lloyd (G.) and, 5:373
Nietzsche and, 6:614
on phenomenology, 7:300
in philosophy of language, 7:412
and postmodernism, 6:317, 9:59
poststructuralism of, 9:274
temporal traces in, 9:491–492
on time, phenomenology of, 9:491
on writing, 7:412
Descartes, René, **2:720–756**, 7:129
in aesthetics, 1:49
on algebra of lengths, 4:56
on animals, 1:201
on apperception, 1:233
Arnauld and, 1:288–290, 5:665
on assent as a matter of will, 5:99
and atomism, 1:386, 3:635
on automaton *vs.* man, 4:610–611
on belief, 2:276, 5:91
Berkeley and, 5:230
Boyle on, 1:674
Cambridge platonists on, 2:13–14
and Cartesian circles, 3:278
Clarke on, 2:269
Clauberg on, 2:284–288
"clear and distinct ideas," Pascal on, 4:747
on color, 2:333
common sense and, 2:355
and communism, 2:365
Comte and, contrast of, 2:411
on concepts, 9:775
Condorcet and, 2:431
on consciousness, 2:449, 2:453, 2:711, 3:511, 8:149
conservation laws of, 2:462
on correct law of inertia, 9:154
correspondence theory of truth and, 9:534
and creation of technology, 7:546
in crisis of skepticism, 9:53
Croce on, 2:602
Cudworth on, 2:611
on current conscious states, 8:723
and Cyrano de Bergerac, 2:618
deductive *a priori* arguments of, Kant's refutation of, 8:649
on definition, 2:667–668, 2:670
Desgabets on, 5:663
on determinism, 3:5, 3:12–13
Diderot and, 3:73
Discourse on the Method of Conducting One's Reason Well and Searching for Truth in the Sciences, 2:286, 2:720–725, 2:731, 2:733–737, 2:755, 3:291, 4:611, 4:692, 9:570
distance perception theory of, 1:575
on domain-specificity of language, 4:691–692
on doubt, Glanvill's objection to, 4:96
Driesch and, 3:110
and dualism, arguments for, 3:118–119
egalitarian communism of, 2:364–365
Elisabeth, princess of Bohemia, and, 3:187–188, 3:569–570
on emotions, 3:198
Encyclopédie and, 3:223
Engels on, 3:58
and epistemology, 3:291–293, 5:91, 8:243
on error, 2:276, 3:345
on eternal return doctrine, 3:354
on evil demon, 5:102, 7:385
existentialism and, 3:502, 3:509
on external ends, 8:675
on faith, 8:123
Fontenelle and, 3:683
on force measurement, 3:228
Frank (S.) on, 3:716
on free will, 2:751, 3:12–13, 6:258, 9:188
on freedom, 2:744–745, 2:751, 2:753, 2:755
in French clandestine literature, 2:264–265
on Galileo, 4:10
and Galluppi, 4:14
and Gassendi on, 4:26, 9:53
Geulincx and, 4:77, 4:78
Gewirth on, 4:81
and Glanvill, 4:96, 4:97
on God, 3:292, 8:123–124
Griesinger and, 7:151
on higher-order consciousness and, 2:454
in history of metaphysics, 6:190
in history of philosophy, 3:405
and Hobbes, 8:825
on *idea,* 4:553, 4:564–565
on idea of force acting at a distance, 5:54
idealism of, Kant on, 4:555
on ideas, 8:124
on imitation, 1:324–325
on immortality, 4:611–612, 9:187
on innate ideas, 4:687
on intentionality, 4:705
on knowledge, 3:215, 4:81, 4:561
La Mettrie on, 5:178
Laas on, 5:163
Lacan and, 5:167
on laws of physics, 9:172
Le Clerc and, 5:236
Leibniz and, 5:266, 5:269
Levinas and, 5:304
life of, 2:720–722, 2:725–728, 2:732–733, 2:736–738, 2:750, 2:754
Locke and, 3:407, 5:374, 5:376, 5:378, 5:381, 5:392
on machine intelligence, 5:631–632
Malebranche and, 1:291, 5:663–668
Mamardashvili on, 5:677, 5:679–680

Descartes, René, ***continued***
- materialism and, 2:365, 6:9
- on matter, 2:758, 6:60
- on matter-mind dualism, 2:595
- *Meditations on First Philosophy. See Meditations on First Philosophy* (Descartes)
- on mental causation, 6:132
- on mental states and consciousness, 2:457
- Mersenne and, 6:153
- on metaphysics, 6:201
- on mind, 1:201, 3:293, 8:123–124
- on mind-body problem, 2:537, 2:595, 2:720, 2:731, 2:737–738, 2:748–753, 3:12, 3:293, 6:138, 6:258, 8:124–125
- on morality, 4:78
- More (Henry) and, 6:395–396
- on motion, 9:154
- on nature, 6:519
- on necessary beings, 7:26
- on ontological argument for the existence of God, 4:112, 7:16
- on optimism/pessimism, 7:248
- Ortega y Gasset on, 7:48
- partial monism and, 6:327
- Pascal and, 7:130
- on passions, 1:233, 2:752–755, 3:188, 3:198
- *Passions of the Soul, The,* 2:752–755, 3:188, 3:198, 3:569, 3:570, 4:604
- on personalism, 7:233
- philosophy of sex and, 7:522
- on physical causality and conservation of motion, 2:90
- physicotheology and, 7:557
- on physiology, 8:124–125
- on pineal gland, 8:124–125
- and Ploucquet, 7:642
- on possibility, 7:721
- precursors of, 6:190
- on predication of existence, 1:528
- on primary certainty, 5:96
- *Principles of Philosophy, The. See Principles of Philosophy, The* (Descartes)
- privacy and, 8:125
- on progress, 8:46
- on psychology, 8:123–125
- on qualities, primary and secondary, 3:292–293, 5:380
- and rationalism, 4:746, 5:95, 9:715
- Regius and, 8:301
- in religious philosophy, 7:492
- in revival of nativism, 4:691
- *Rules for the Direction of the Mind,* 2:723–727, 2:731–732, 2:735, 4:553
- Sanches and, 8:596
- on science, 2:722, 2:724–726, 2:728–738, 2:750–754
- on scientific explanation, 8:124
- on sensation/sense perception, 3:291–293, 8:124
- and Sidgwick, 9:25
- and Smith (John), 9:70
- solipsisms in, 9:115–116
- on soul, 3:116, 3:293, 4:604, 4:610–612
- on space, 9:147
- Spinoza and, 7:101
- Suárez and, 9:282
- on the subject, 9:276
- subjectivism of, 1:491, 4:611–612
- on substance, 4:78
- on substance and attribution, 9:296–297
- and Swedenborg, 9:336
- on testimony, 9:401
- on thought and thinking, 4:611, 9:420
- and Toland, 2:683
- on unconscious, 9:570
- understanding of folk psychology, 3:677
- universal doubt, method of, 4:50
- Vasquez and, 9:649
- Vico on, 9:671–672
- voluntary error in, 1:535
- Williams (Bernard) on, 9:787
- and Wolff, 3:350, 9:826
- and women, 5:373
- *World, The,* 2:729–733, 2:736–737
- *See also* Cartesianism; *Cogito ergo sum* argument

"'Descartes' Myth' and Professor Ryle's Fallacy" (Miller), 6:235

Descartes savant (Milhaud), 6:217

Descending intuition, definition of, 5:541

Descending order, of history, 5:148

Descent of Man, The (Darwin), 2:349, 2:634–636
- cultural impact of, 2:629
- reception of, 2:629

Description(s)
- of appearance, 1:229–230
- of consciousness, 4:784
- in correspondence and theoretic progress, 1:637
- cosmology as, 2:557–558
- definite, Russell's theory of, 8:57, 9:264
- *vs.* formalism in science, 1:630–631
- in Frege, 5:516
- identity in, 4:567
- James on, 4:777
- in language engagement, 2:205
- logical forms and, 5:508–509
- measurement and object independence in, 1:638
- of mental states, in James's psychology, 4:777–778
- in metaphysics, James on, 4:782
- of nonexistent objects, 6:635
- in philosophy of language, 7:403
- *vs.* pronouns, 1:173
- of reality, 6:634
- of religious experience, 8:401–402
- Russell on, 3:315, 3:496–498, 6:635, 8:551–552
  - names and, 5:508
  - theory of, 8:59–60
- Strawson on, 7:768
- of substances, 6:78
- as typicality in theories, 1:633
- Wittgenstein on, 9:811

Description logic, 6:300

Description theory, entity reduction and, 6:172

Descriptionalism, 4:590, 6:140–141

Descriptions of Motions (Swineshead), 9:342

Descriptive anaphora, 1:173

Descriptive choice theory, 2:654–655. *See also* Decision theory

Descriptive ethics, utilitarianism as, 9:605–606

Descriptive names, Evans on, 3:460

Descriptive psychology
- Brentano on, 3:421
- of Meinong, 6:115

Descriptive relativism, 3:368, 3:370

Descriptive theories of law, 7:449–450

Descriptive theory of reference, Evans on, 3:459

Descriptive utilitarianism, 9:604

Descriptive value theory, 9:639–640

Descriptivism
- of Kripke, 8:77
- Marcus and, 5:704
- noncognitivism and, 6:633
- objections to, 8:288
- semantics in, 8:77

Desegregation, of public transportation, 5:73

Desert, principle of, with act utilitarianism, 9:613

Desert theories, 8:168

Desgabets, Robert, **2:757–760**
Cartesian eucharistic theology, 2:61
on Descartes, 5:663
dispute with Malebranche, 2:61
on Eucharist, 1:290
on Foucher, 5:663
Nicole and, 6:604
Design
aesthetic judgments and, 1:36
Augustine on, 1:402
beauty and, 1:402
philosophy of technology and, 7:549–550
in teleological argument for existence of god, 9:376–377
See also Technology, philosophy of
Design argument for the existence of God, 3:321, 4:617, 8:400–401
evolution and, 1:368
Hume on, 4:511–512
Mendelssohn on, 6:131
Mill on, 1:368
See also Physicotheology; Teleological argument for existence of God
Design of Part of the Book of Ecclesiastes, The (Wollaston), 9:832
Design stance, explanation from, 2:711
Desirability
determining, 9:643–644
in hedonism, 4:255
Desire(s)
in action, 1:19–20
in altruism and self-interest, 3:174
as argument for immortality, 4:614
asceticism and, 1:351, 1:352
Augustine on, 3:402
in Beauty *vs.* perfection, 6:131
and behaviorism, 1:534
vs. belief, 1:532
vs. benevolence, 6:655
biological teleology of mental states in, 2:479–480
in Bloch, 1:615
in Buddhism, 1:352
conscious states and rational control of, 2:457
Destutt de Tracy on, 2:760
dreams and, 8:111
eliminative materialism on, 3:182–183
Epictetus on, 3:262
Epicurus on, 3:267–268
as evil, 1:352
first-order, 7:240
in Freudian psychology, 1:352
hierarchy of, 1:351–352
Hobbes on, 3:406
influences on strength of, 9:732
intentionality in consciousness and, 2:452
intentions and, 4:701
in intrinsic theory of consciousness, 2:453
Jaegwon on, 9:388
Lacan on, 5:168
Lamarck on, 5:174
Locke on, 5:382–383
lower, 1:351–352
Marx on, 3:57
as mental content, 2:476–477
Mill (James) on, 6:219
nonaction and, in Daoism, 9:722
opposition to, 8:111
and pain behavior, 3:758
in Platonic dialogues, 7:589
in poststructuralism, 9:275
power and, 7:733
as propositional attitude, 1:532
propositional attitudes of, 4:712
realizable
and belief, 1:704
as reason to act, 4:714–715
repressed, 8:109–111
Scanlon on, 1:18–19
Schopenhauer on, 3:415
second-order, 7:240
in self-cultivation, 2:177
Spinoza on, 3:407
in strict akratic action, 9:731–732
as suffering and material attachment in Buddhist ethics, 2:199
suppression of, 1:352
vs. volition, 9:704
Desire for life, in Yoga, 6:108
Desire theory, 8:721
Desore, 2:362
Despair
rescuing a man from, 5:61
search for novelty leading to, 5:63
state of, 5:64
in Unanumo's philosophy, 9:568
Despertar y proyecto del filosofar latinoamericano (The awakening and project of Latin American philosophy) (Miró Quesada), 5:210
Dessauer, Friedrich, on philosophy of technology, 7:543
Destiny
Augustine on, 1:395
in Guo Xiang, 4:196
Jouffroy on, 4:855
Leopardi on, 5:285
Petrović-Njegoš on, 7:267
"Destiny of Man, The" (Fiske), 3:668
Destiny of Western Man, The (Stace), 9:201
Destructio Philosophorum (al-Ghazālī), 4:758
Destruction, in Nietzschian view of tragedy, 6:609–610
Destructive dilemma, definition of, 5:541
Destutt de Tracy, Antoine Louis Claude, Comte, **2:760–761**
collaboration with Cabanis, 2:2
on experience, 5:656
as idéologue, 8:787
ideology and, 4:573
on language, 8:787–788
on love, 5:588
Maine de Biran and, 5:655
on universal grammar, 8:791
Detachment, in aesthetic judgment, 1:36
Determinability
law of, 5:645
in Maimon, 5:645–646
Determinables, **3:1–4,** 8:68
Determinacy, in language, 1:72
Determinant, in historical materialism, 4:381–382
Determinate value, in quantum mechanics, 2:531
Determinately operator, introducing into language, 3:634
Determinates, **3:1–4**
Johnson (W. E.) on, 5:458
Determination, to self-determination, 3:617
Determination by the mental, 6:173
Determinationism, 6:172–173
Determining correspondence, 6:78
Determinism, **3:4–23**
as absence of spontaneity, 1:564
and absolute *vs.* conditional in divine foreknowledge, 1:628
of Anderson (John), 1:198
antecedent necessity in divine will, 1:681
Ardigò on, 1:252
Arminius on, 1:285
atomist on, 5:300
bad faith and, 8:608
in Bohmian mechanics, 8:212
Burckhardt on, 1:766
"can," meaning of, 2:23–26

Determinism, *continued*
causal
Adler on, 1:23
psychological development in, 1:23
causality and statistical relevance, 2:100
chance and credence, 2:128–129
chance and determinism in quantum theory, 2:126–127
chance in, 2:125
chaos theory simplification of probabilistic theories and, 2:133
choice misconceptualized as spatial, 1:563–564
Clarke on, 2:271
in classical mechanics, 2:281–282
classical mechanics and, 7:474
contemporary debate on, 3:19–21
in Cordemoy, 2:538
in cosmic catastrophic processes and ontogenesis, 1:658
in Crescas, 2:593
definition of, 3:4
difference, 3:31
Earman on, 3:159–160
economic, 1:125
Einstein and, 3:180–182
eliminative methods and, 6:245
Eliot (George) on, 3:184–185
Epicurus on, 3:268–269
ethical, 3:4–5
fatalism and, in Goldman, 4:148
fate and, 3:5, 3:35
and freedom, **3:24–29**
Arminians on, 3:10
Bain on, 3:18–19
Broad on, 3:14–15
Carneades on, 3:17–18
Descartes on, 3:12–13
Epicureans on, 3:10–11
in ethical determinism, 3:4–5
history and, 3:39–40
Hume, David on, 3:14
Hume on, 3:14, 3:18
Kant on, 3:15
Locke on, 3:13–14
psychiatry on, 3:16–17
Reid (Thomas) on, 3:18
in Sigwart's "I will," 9:29
Spinoza on, 3:12–13, 9:188–189
in French clandestine writings, 2:267
genetic, 4:47
in Godwin, 4:136
hard, 3:15–16
moral responsibility and, 8:448
in history, **3:35–41**
Spengler on, 9:167
Hobbes on, 3:11–12, 4:416–417
human, 3:24–29
in human character, 8:655
as hylopathic atheism in Cudworth, 2:610
Ibn Da'ud on, 4:817
and indeterminism, **3:29–35**
in Ingenieros's ethics, 4:686
in Islamic philosophy, 3:23
Laplace on, 5:197–198
Leonardo da Vinci on, 5:282
Lessing on, 5:296
liberty and, 5:658
in local theories, 6:641
logical, 3:5–7
as man-made creation, 9:132–133
materialism and, 6:6
of McTaggart, 6:77, 6:78
as metalinguistic term, 6:478
mind in associationism, 1:563–564
modern theories of, 3:12
of Moleschott, 6:320
moral judgments and, 8:7
Nagel (Ernest) on, 6:473–474
Naṣīr al-Dīn al-Ṭūsī on, 6:478
naturalism and, 6:494
as necessary in science, 1:590
nonexistence ultimate good and, 1:589
optimism/pessimism and, 7:247, 7:249
Pelagianism on, 7:175
philosophical anthropology and, 7:320
physical, 3:10–12
in physics, 6:593
Popper on, 7:690–691
possibility and, 7:724–725
in possible world counterfactual conditionals, 2:429
vs. predictability, 3:38–39
of Priestley, 8:7
psychiatry on, 3:16–17
psychological, 1:23, 3:12–19, 3:34
in Taine, 9:365
psychological development in, 1:23
punishment in, 4:193, 8:164
quantum mechanics and, 3:25, 3:29, 3:33, 3:38, 3:164, 5:697
in quantum theory, 1:539–542
relationships as I-it *vs.* I-thou and, 1:715–716
and responsibility, 3:14–15, 3:23, 3:26–28, 3:33–34, 3:40
responsibility in, 8:164
in Schultz, 8:659
scientific, 3:36–37
self-prediction and, 8:729–730
Sidgwick on, 9:24
in Siger of Brabant's morality, 9:28
singularity failure in, 1:608
sociobiology debate and, 3:491, 3:492
soft, 3:15–16
in Sorel, 9:132–133
soul as ethereal machine and, 1:658
Spinoza on, 3:407
symmetry and conservation principle of, 2:462–463
theodicy of, 6:478
theological, 3:7–10, **3:23–24**. *See also* Predestination
theological, Aquinas on, 9:433
time and, 9:471
in Toynbee, 9:519
in Turing machines, 2:376
universal, 3:24
of Varona, 9:648
in Vishnu's organization of society, 2:110
Whitehead on, 9:752
"Determinism in History" (Nagel), 3:39
Deterministic chaos, 3:33
Deterministic transitions, in wave functions, 8:210
Deterrence, in utilitarianism, 8:163
Deussen, Paul, **3:41–42**, 6:612
Deustch, David, in quantum computation, 2:408, 8:200
Deutsch, Eliot, on *Bhagavad Gita,* 5:359
Deustua, Alejandro O., **3:42–43**
Deústua, Alejandro K., as founder, 5:207
Deutsche Ideologie, Die (The German Ideology) (Marx), 4:573
Deutsch-Franzosische Jahrbucher, 3:609
Deutsch-Jozsa algorithm, 8:200–201
Deuxième sexe (The Second Sex) (Beauvoir), 1:515, 3:563, 3:586, 5:373, 7:523
Devas, Brahman as power of, 1:681–682
Development
historical, Newman on, 6:581–582
of intelligence, 1:596
of personality as genetic, 1:657
physical, 7:345–347
psychological, genius and, 1:23
social
education and, 7:372–373
Froebel on, 7:372–373
Hegel on, 3:57

Marx on, 3:57
Newman (John Henry) on, 6:581–582
in Sumner's "folkways," 9:326
Development from Kant to Hegel (Pringle-Pattison), 8:12
Development of Metaphysics in Persia, The (Iqbal), 4:743
Development of the Monist View of History (Plekhanov), on negation of negation, 3:62–63
Developmental psychology, 6:150, 8:153
Developmental systems theory, 7:345–346
Deviance
causal, 1:15–16
psychological, determinism and, 3:16–17
Deviant causal chains, 5:90
Deviant logicians, 5:109, 5:111
Device paradigm, Borgmann on, 7:548
Devices, computing machines and, 2:404
Devil, Graham on, 1:367
Devlin, Lorn, on morality, enforcement of, 5:338
Devlin, Patrick, on paternalism, 7:137
Devoir, Le (Duty) (Le Senne), 5:289
Devotees' Highroad (Razi), 9:306
Devotio moderna, and Biel, 1:594
Devotion
and development of God's role, in Indian philosophy, 4:627
to the Good, Yang Xiong on, 9:861
as means towards liberation, in Indian philosophy, 4:135
Yamazaki Ansai on, 9:860
Dewette, Wilhelm Martin, Parker (T.) and, 7:121
Dewey, John, **3:43–51**
Addams and, 3:567
on aesthetics, 1:33, 1:57, 1:75, 3:46–47
antinihilism of, 6:618
on art, 1:57–58, 1:64, 1:304, 3:46–47
and Beardsley, 1:508–510
on being, 1:531
on community, 3:48, 3:49
on concept of ideas, 4:566
critical interpretations of, 3:50–51
criticisms of, 3:425
on democracy, 3:48–49
on education, 3:44, 3:47, 7:378–379
on Emerson, 6:575
Emerson and, 3:197
on emotion, 1:64, 3:198
epistemology, 3:313
ethics, 3:418, 3:424–425, 7:378
on ethics, 3:49
evolutionary psychology and, 3:481
on experience, 3:45–47, 3:49–50
on expression, 1:304
Hegel and, 8:623
Hegelian period, 3:43–44
and Hu Shih, 2:181
on human nature, 7:378
on inquiry, 3:46, 3:47–48, 7:746
instrumentalism of, 7:745–7446
on knowledge, 7:378–379
limited impact on Korean philosophy, 5:141
on logic, 3:47–48
metaphysics of, 7:378–379
Murphy on, 6:435
Nagel (Ernest) and, 6:472
on naturalistic religion, 8:374–375
naturalization, philosophical, and, 6:501
on nature, 3:45–46
on optimism/pessimism, 7:252
Peirce and, 6:194
pragmatic theory of meaning in, 8:799
in pragmatism, 7:741, 7:745–7446
pragmatism of, 3:415–416
on role of philosophy, 3:50
Santayana and, 1:63
on social constructivism, 9:78
social epistemology and, 9:83
on social philosophy, 3:49
on society, 7:378
on transaction, 3:46, 3:49
on truth, 7:746
on valuation, 9:638
on value, 9:637–638
on war and peace, 7:155
women associated with, 3:566
Wright (Chauncey) and, 9:846
Dewey School, 3:44
DeWolf, L. Harold, on personalism, 7:236
Dexing zhi zhi (knowledge of virtue), Zhang Zai on, 9:879–880
Dge-lugs
curriculum and scholastic methods, 1:734–735
Madhyamaka and, 1:731–734
Svātantrika-Prāsaṅgika distinction, 1:732–734, 1:744
Dhammapada, as wisdom literature, 9:793
Dharma, 5:135
Buddhism in Chinese philosophy, 2:154
in Chan Buddhism, 2:167
definition of, 1:722
in Indian philosophy, 5:326
in Sanlun Buddhism, 2:162
in Tiantai Buddhism, 2:163
Vasubandhu on, 9:650
Dharmakīrti
in Buddhist epistemology, 1:753–757
criterion of truth used by, 5:119
on inference, 5:413–414
on negation, 6:530–533
proof of the reliability of a person, 5:121
science of the means of knowledge expounded by, 5:116
on universals, 9:585
in Yogācāra Buddhism, 1:745
Dharmottara, on inference, 5:414
Diacceto, Francesco da
in the circle of the Florentine Academy, 3:671
student of Ficino, 3:624
Diadocha (Diogenes Laertius), 3:88
Diagnosis, logic of, 7:466–467
Diagnostic and Statistical Manual of Mental Disorders (DSM), on sexual perversion, 7:527, 7:528
Diagonal arguments, polynomial-time *vs.* nondeterministic polynomial-time computability and, 2:389
Diagonal functions
primitive recursive functions and, 2:377
recursive function generalization and, 2:378
Diagonal proof
Cantor on, 5:463
definition of, 5:541
Diagonalization, Church on, 5:476
Diagoras of Melos, Cyrenaic teaching of, 2:620
Diagrams, method of Robinson, 5:481
Dial (periodical), 3:195
Dialectic, **3:52–56**
Abelard on, 1:3, 3:54, 5:424–426
Adorno on, 1:27–28
in aesthetics, 1:28
al-Ghazālī and, 1:118–119
Aristotle on, 1:269–271, 2:749, 5:399
Bachelard and, 1:440
Baudrillard and, 1:491
Bloch and, 1:615–616
in Chinese philosophy, 5:415

Dialectic, ***continued***
- classical syllabus of, 4:66
- Croce and, 2:602
- definition in, 1:270–271
- definition of, 3:52
- Deleuze on, 2:695
- Descartes and, 2:286
- *elenchus* in, 7:593
- Engels and, 3:238, 5:737
- of freedom as tragic, 1:559
- Genovesi on, 4:49
- Gerbert of Aurillac and, 4:66
- of grace and religion, 1:477
- in Greek Academy, 4:172, 4:301
- Hegel on, 3:309, 4:260, 8:138
- of historical materialism, 4:385–386
- in Indian philosophy, 4:627
- inquiry in, 1:192–193
- in Islamic philosophy, **3:69–70**
- in Jewish philosophy, **3:69–70**
- Kierkegaard and, 5:67
- kinds in, 7:600
- in Laozi, 5:195
- Lenin on, 5:280
- Liebert on, 5:343
- logic and, 3:53–54
    - in Daoism, 2:187–190
    - Hegel and, 2:80–81
- Losev and, 5:574–575
- Lukács and, 5:603–604
- Marx and, 3:57, 5:734
- in Marxism, 1:615–616, 7:627
- McTaggart on, 6:77
- as method, 1:476, 4:269–272
    - Bernard of Clairvaux and, 1:592
    - Kierkegaard and, 5:67
    - Solov'ëv and, 9:123
- negative, 1:27–28
- oscillation between semiotic and symbolic, 5:152
- Pannenberg and, 7:81–82
- Peter Damien on, 7:259
- Petrarch on, 7:264
- Plato and, 1:264, 4:3, 5:398, 7:592–594, 7:602
- in political conservatism, 2:465
- in psychology, 8:138
- Ramus on, 8:236–237
- in *Republic* (Plato), 1:263–264
- *vs.* rhetoric, 1:264, 1:269
- Richard of St. Victor and, 8:592
- Sartre and, 8:604
- Schleiermacher on, 8:633–634
- Solger and, 9:115
- Stoicism and, 8:757, 9:253–255
- Sturzo on, 9:281
- transcendental, 3:54
- in Western Marxism, 5:737–738
- Zeno on, 9:253

Dialectic (Valla), 9:635
Dialectic of Bruno and Spinoza, The (Lovejoy), 5:593
Dialectic of Enlightenment, Philosophical Fragments (Adorno & Horkheimer), 1:26, 1:67
Dialectica (Abelard), 1:3, 3:54, 5:424–426
- on modal logic, 5:425
- on syncategoremata, 8:769

Dialectica (Compotista), 5:424
Dialectica (Garland the Computist), 8:765
Dialectica (John of Damascus), 1:786, 4:836–837
Dialectica (Ramus), 8:236–237
Dialectica (Valla), 7:147
Dialectica ad Petrum de Medicis (Argyropulos), 5:437
Dialectica est ars artium, ad omnium methodorum principia viam habens (Buridan), 1:767–768
Dialecticae Libri Duo (Ramus), 5:438
Dialecticae Partitiones (Structure of dialectic) (Ramus), 8:236–237
Dialectical development, and modern evolutionism, 3:660
Dialectical materialism, **3:56–69,** 8:138
- aesthetics of, 1:59
- Bloch and, 1:615–616
- Engels and, 3:57–63
- historical materialism and, 4:382–383
- *vs.* idealism, 7:626
- as knowledge without mythical moment, 1:477
- Lenin and, 3:63–65, 5:279–280
- Lukács and, 1:59
- Mao Zedong and, 2:180, 3:65–66
- Marx and, 2:365, 3:56–57, 3:67–69
- and psychology, 8:138
- reflex theory of behavior and, 7:150
- Spinoza and, 9:195

Dialectical poems, metaphysical systems as, 5:143
Dialectical praxis, 8:604, 8:608
Dialectical reasoning
- Carnap on, 2:45
- Carneades on, 2:47

Dialectical theology, Gogarten on, 4:144
Dialecticam Aristotelis (Soto), 9:137
Dialecticarum Libri Tres (Valla), 5:437
Dialecticians, Diodorus Chronus and, 3:87
Dialectics of Nature (Engels), 3:58–63, 3:238
Dialektik (Schleiermacher), 8:637
Dialektika mifa (The dialectics of myth) (Losev), 5:573
Dialeth(e)ism, 7:106, 9:540–541
Diallage (Althamer), 3:712
Dialoghi d'amore (Ebreo), 4:824, 5:587–588
Dialogo della musica antica e della moderna (Galilei), 1:48
Dialogue
- Gadamer on, 7:411–412
- internal, Husserl on, 9:491
- thought as, 9:420

Dialogue (Galileo), 8:683
Dialogue (Leibniz), 8:780
Dialogue between a philosopher and a student of the common laws of England (Hobbes), 7:423
Dialogue concerning Natural Religion (Hume), 7:77–78
Dialogue concerning the Two Chief World Systems (Galileo), 2:732, 4:9–12
Dialogue entre Poliandre and Théophile (Leibniz), 5:252
Dialogue of the Two Chief World Systems (Galileo), 1:543
"Dialogue on Poetry" (Schlegel), 8:631
Dialogue on Tyndale (More), 2:322
Dialogues between Hylas and Philonous (Berkeley), 3:303
Dialogues concerning Natural Religion (Hume), 2:686–687, 9:377–380, 9:505
- on evil, 3:469
- on existence of God, 4:615
- on physicotheology, 7:559–560
- Schopenhauer on, 8:648

Dialogues des morts (Dialogues of the Dead) (Fontenelle), 3:682
Dialogues d'Oratius Tubero (La Mothe Le Vayer), 5:182
Dialogues on Death (Malebranche), 5:664
Dialogues on Metaphysics and on Religion (Malebranche), 5:664
Dialogus (William of Ockham), 7:422
"Diary of a Seducer" (Kierkegaard), 7:522
Díaz, Porfirio, 5:206
Dicaearchus, Aristotle and, 1:278
Dicaiologicae Libri Tres Totum et Universum Ius, Quo Utimur, Methodice Complectentes (Digest of jurisprudence) (Althusius), 1:135

Diceosina o sia filosofia del giusto e dell'onesto (Genovesi), 4:49
Dicey, A. V., 9:142
Dichotomies, rejection of sharp, 3:566
Dichotomy, 1:135, 5:537
Dichotomy (Stadium) argument against motion, 9:874
Dichtung (poetic fancy), in Lange, 6:540
Dichtung und Wahrheit (Poetry and truth) (Goethe), 4:141, 9:194
Dickie, George, 2:627
  on aesthetic judgment, 1:36
  on art, 1:67, 1:77–78, 1:299–300
  Bullough on, 1:762
  Levinson on, 1:300
Dickson, Michael, 6:278
Dicta Candidi de Imagine Dei (attrib: Candidus of Fluda), 2:49
Dictionaire de la langue française (Littré), 5:372
Dictionaries, philosophical, 10:75–139
Dictionary of National Biography, 9:243
Dictionary of the English Language (Johnson, Dr. Samuel), 2:681, 4:852
Dictionary definition, 5:540
Dictionnaire (Bayle), in French clandestine writings, 2:265
Dictionnaire de l'Académie Française, on French liberalism, 5:320
Dictionnaire de médecine, de chirurgie, de pharmacie, de l'art vétérinaire et des sciences qui s'y rapportent (Littré), 5:372
Dictionnaire historique et critique (Bayle), 1:503–507, 2:681
  "Rorarius" in, 9:55
  on Spinoza, 5:296
Dictionnaire philosophique (Voltaire), 2:651, 2:687
Dictionnaire portatif des beaux-arts (Lacombe), 9:324–325
Dictum de omni et nullo, definition of, 5:541
Didascalicon (Hugh of St. Victor), 8:592
Didaskalikos (Albinus of Smyrna), 4:174
Didaskalikos tôn Platonos dogmatôn (Alcinous), 1:103–104, 7:607
Diderot, Denis, **3:71–78**
  on aesthetics, 3:76–77
  Alembert and, 1:106
  anarchism and, 1:177
  atheism and, 2:688
  on beauty, 1:52
  on biology, 3:74–75
  clandestine writings influence on, 2:268
  criticism by, 3:77
  on Cudworth, 2:610
  on dreams, 3:75
  on empiricism, 3:72–73
  Encyclopédie and, 3:221–223
  Enlightenment and, 3:244
  on ethics, 3:75–76, 3:410
  French Revolution and, 3:243
  on General Will, 4:39
  on genius, 3:75
  Hélvetius and, 4:307
  on heredity, 3:74–75
  on idealism, 4:553
  on imagination, 3:73
  La Mettrie and, 5:181
  materialism and, 3:72–74, 6:10
  on matter, 3:75
  Maupertuis and, 6:67, 8:783
  on memory, 3:75
  Naigeon and, 6:476
  on national identity, 6:481
  on *philosophe,* 3:244
  philosophical attitudes, general, 3:72–73
  on politics, 3:77
  scientific background of, 3:73
  social critiques by, 3:247
  on Spinoza, 9:193
  on thought, 3:75
Dīdhiti (Raghunātha Śiromaṇi), 4:628
Didichlet, P. G. Lejune, nowhere continuous function of, 2:496–497
Die Abendstunde eines Einsiedlers (Pestalozzi), 7:254
"Die Axiomatik der Alten" (Scholz), 8:645
Die beiden Grundprobleme der Ethik (Schopenhauer), 8:648
Die christliche Glaubenslehre (Strauss), 9:262
Die Deutsche Ideologie (The German Ideology) (Marx), 4:573
Die Familie Schroffenstein (Kleist), 5:78
Die Flucht ins Vergessen: Die Anfange der Psychoanalyse Freuds bei Schopenhaeur (Zentner), 3:736
Die Freien, 9:250
Die Geschichte der Philosophie (Fries), 3:752
Die Grundgesetze der Arithmetik (Frege), 5:464
Die Grundlagen der Arithmetik (Frege), 3:725, 5:463
Die Grundlagen des 19. Jahrhunderts (Foundations of the 19th century) (Chamberlain), 2:123
Die guldin Arch (Franck), 3:712
Die Hören (journal), 8:627
"Die kausalität in der gegenwärtigen Physiks" (Schlick), 8:641
Die Lehre von dem Ganzen (Krueger), 5:156
Die Leiden des jungen Werthers (The sorrows of young Werther) (Goethe). *See Sorrows of Young Werther, The* (Goethe)
Die Logik der reinen Erkenntnis (Cohen), 2:303
"Die mathematische Logik und die metaphysik" (Scholz), 8:645
Die mathematische Naturphilosophie (Fries), 3:752
Die mitmenschlichen Begegungen in der Milieuwelt (Gurwitsch), 4:197
Die Mystik und das Wort (Brunner), 1:707
Die neue Zeit, Kautsky the editor of, 5:47
Die Philosophie der Griechen II (Zeller), 4:172
Die Philosophie des Unbewussten (von Hartmann), 7:251
Die physischen Gestalten in Ruhe und im stationaren Zustand (Köhler), 5:126
Die Posaune des jüngsten Gerichts über Hegel (Bauer), 1:492
Die Religion aus den Quellen des Judentums (Cohen), 2:304
Die Resultate der Jacobi'schen und Mendelssohn'schen Philosophie (Wizenman), 7:101
Die systematischen Begriffe in Kants vorkritischen Schriften (Cohen), 2:302
Die Überwindung des wissenschaftlichen Materialismus ("The conquest of scientific materialism") (Ostwald), 3:233
Die Verlobung in St. Domingo (Kleist), 5:78
Die vier Kronbuchlein (Franck), 3:712–713
Die vier Phasen der Philosophie (Brentano), 1:692
"Die Völlstandigkeit der Axiome des logischen Funktionkalküls" (Gödel), 5:473
Die Wahlverwandtschaften (elective affinities) (Goethe), 4:141
Die Welt als Wille und Vorstellung (The world as will and representation) (Schopenhauer), reception of, 8:648
Die Wissenschaftslehre Bolzanos (scholz), 8:645
Die Zukunft einer Illusion (Freud), 7:252
Dieks, Dennis, 6:277

Diels, Hermann
- on Democritus, 5:301
- on Empedocles, 3:210

Diet
- evolutionary adaptation and, 3:482
- in Pythagoreanism, 8:185

Diet of Worms (1521), Luther and, 5:613, 5:614

Diffeomorphism invariance
- in hole argument, 9:157
- as origin of constraint equations, 9:269

"Différance" (Derrida), 2:716, 9:277

Difference
- David of Dinant on, 2:645
- Deleuze (Gilles) on, 2:695
- erasure of, in liberation, 4:629
- Gauge Theory on, 4:31–33
- grammatical *vs.* logical, 8:580–581
- between male and female subjects, 9:276, 9:277
- in postmodernism, 6:318
- in Saussure's linguistics, 9:276
- in structuralism, 9:276–277

Différence, in Derrida, 2:661–662, 6:317, 9:277

Difference aesthetics, 3:573

Difference and Repetition (Deleuze), 2:694, 2:695, 9:274, 9:492

"Difference between Plato and Aristotle, On the" (Pletho), 7:630

Difference determinism, 3:31

Différence et répétition (Deleuze), 9:274

Difference feminism, 3:583–584, 3:600–601

Difference methods of induction, 6:224, 6:238–243
- concomitant variation analogue of, 6:245
- with conjunction of possible causes, 6:241
- with disjunction of possible causes, 6:242
- effects discovered by, 6:246
- illustration of, 6:238
- with negation of possible causes, 6:242
- use of, 6:246
- variations of, 6:239–241

Difference of sets, definition of, 5:541

Difference principle, Rawls on, 5:324

Differences, as a consuming issue, 3:599

Différend, Le (Lyotard), 9:277

Différend: Phrases in Dispute, The (Lyotard), 5:620, 5:621, 9:277

Differentia
- Johnson (W. E.) on, 3:1
- of terms in traditional logic, 5:494

Differential calculus, Fontenelle's interest in, 3:683

Differential survival, 7:338

Differenz des Fichtischen und Schellingschen Systems der Philosophie (Hegel), 1:11

Digby, Kenelm, 8:777

Digital computing machines, 2:405

Digital information, computer ethics and, 2:397

Digital media, 7:383–384

Dignāga, 6:530
- in Buddhist epistemology, 1:753
- on inference, 5:413–414

Dignities, Lull on, 5:609–610

Digression sur les Anciens et les Modernes (Fontenelle), 3:682

Dikē, **3:78–79**

Dilemma(s)
- definition of, 5:541
- horns of, 5:503
- of hypothetical and disjunctive syllogisms, 5:503
- ideas of extended things in Cartesian epistemology, 2:57
- in Marcus, 5:704
- moral, 5:704
- in Ryle, 1:153, 8:581
- use of game theory models in business ethics, 1:778

"Dilemma of Determinism" (James), 9:29

Dilemmas (Ryle), 1:153, 8:581

Dilemmatic reasoning, as categorical conclusion, 5:503

Dillingahm, William, Culverwell and, 2:612

Dilthey, Wilhelm, **3:79–85**
- Adler and, 1:24
- in anthropology, 7:318
- on descriptive psychology, 9:18
- on epistemology, 6:544
- and Gadamer, 4:2
- on *Geisteswissenschaften,* 4:37–38
- Habermas on, 4:200
- Hegelianism of, 4:287
- and Heidegger, 9:488
- on hermeneutics, 3:81–82, 3:84
- on historical reason, 3:79–80
- on history, 7:397–398
- influence of, 3:84
- influence of context on, 8:631
- Keyserling following, 5:58
- Krueger compared to, 5:156
- Liebert and, 5:343
- Lipps and, 5:363
- on methodology, 9:36
- in neo-Kantianism, 6:545
- on psychology, 3:80–81
- and Scheler, 8:615
- and Shpet, 9:17
- and Spranger, 9:198

Dilucidationes Philosophicae de Deo, Anima Humana, Mundo et Generabilis Rerum Affectionibus (Bilfinger), 1:595

Dimensionality
- in classical physics, 9:495
- of time, 9:466, 9:484

Dinet, Jacques, Descartes and, 2:749–750

Dingler, Hugo, **3:85–86**

Dio Chrysostom, Cynic teaching of, 2:617

Diodorean implication, 5:545

Diodorus Cronus, **3:87**
- on conditionals, 7:312
- Democritus and, 5:302
- on determinism, 3:5, 3:6
- on logic, 5:403–404
- Master Argument of, 3:87, 5:404
- Philo of Megara and, 7:312
- on possibility, 7:313, 7:719–720
- on propositions, 7:312
- Zeno of Citium and, 3:87, 5:404

Diogenes Laertius, **3:88–89**
- on Aenesidemus, 1:30
- Agrippa and, 1:96
- on Clinomachus of Thurii, 6:110
- correspondence truth theory in, 2:541
- on Democritus, 5:298
- on Empedocles, 3:212
- Epicurus and, 3:265
- on Leucippus, 5:299
- on pagan theology as forerunner of Christian revelation, 7:613–614
- on Parmenides of Elea, 7:125
- on Protagoras, 8:92
- on Pyrrho, 8:173
- on semantics, 8:757
- on Sextus Empiricus, 8:850
- on skepticism, 1:193, 9:49
- on Socrates, 9:106
- on ultimate referents, 8:759

Diogenes of Apollonia, **3:89–90**
- *archē* in, 1:249
- Diogenes Laertius on, 3:88
- Leucippus and, 5:298
- mind in, 7:764
- in pre-Socratic philosophy, 7:764–765
- Simplicius on, 9:35

Diogenes of Babylon
on logic, 5:404
Panaetius of Rhodes and, 7:78–79
Diogenes of Oenoanda, Epicurean School and, 3:264
Diogenes of Sinope, **3:90–91**
cosmopolitanism of, 2:567
Epictetus and, 3:261
Lucian of Samosata on, 5:597
on pleasure, 3:399
Diogenes the Cynic. *See* Diogenes of Sinope
Diogenianus, Eusebius and, 3:455
Dionis i pradionisiistvo (Dionysus and pre-Dionysianism) (Ivanov), 4:767
Dionysian man, doctrine of, pessimism and, 7:251
Dionysius the Areopagite. *See* Pseudo-Dionysius
Diop, Cheik Anta, in afrocentrism, 1:86
Dioptric (Descartes), on mind-body problem, 3:293
Dioptrics (Descartes), 1:575
Dioptrics (Molyneaux), 1:575
Dioptrics (Regius), 2:55
Diotima: Die Idee des Schonen (Fischer), 3:660
Dippel, Johann Konrad, on Spinoza, 7:99
Dirac, Paul A. M.
on big bang cosmology, 9:478
on chemistry reduction to quantum mechanics, 2:142
Dirac equation
linear operators and, 8:208–209
in quantum mathematical apparatus, 8:206
Direct awareness, 7:279
Direct evidence, 6:116–117
Direct forms, of coercion, 3:722
Direct passions, 4:505
Direct probabilities, 3:660
Direct realism, 8:262–265
perception and, 7:180, 7:182–183, 7:186
phenomenalism and, 7:273
See also Realism
Direct reduction, definition of, 5:555
Direct reference, 5:704, 8:61–62, 8:289
Direction of Time (Richenbach), 2:105
Directive correlation, in purposive activity, 9:385
Directive genetic counseling, 6:95–96
Directiveness, of organisms, 7:38
Directives and Remarks (Avicenna), 4:581
Director, Mo. Health Department, Cruzan v., 6:95
Diritto Universale (Universal Right) (Vico), 9:673–674
Disagreement
ethical, 7:6
fundamental, 3:368
Stevenson on, 9:245
ethical relativism and, 3:373–374
interminable, 5:636
Disapproval, moral concepts and, 9:739–740
Disarmonie economiche e disarmonie morali (Calderoni), 2:8
Disbelief
in common consent arguments for God's existence, 2:350–353
in God, 2:350–353, 6:618. *See also* Atheism
negation and, 6:526
Discernment
in Buddhism, 1:729–730
in Xunzi, 2:216
Discipline
bioethics legitimacy as, 1:600
in education, 7:363
Discipline and Punishment (Foucault), 1:555
Disconfirming instances, Ayers premise and, 5:82
Discontinuity
in Chinese philosophy of religion, 2:224–225
and continuous functions, 2:497
Discorrendo di socialismo e di filosofia (Labriola), 5:165
Discorsi (Galileo), 4:622
Discorso (Patrizi), 7:144
Discorso sopra il vero fine delle lettere e delle scienze (Genovesi), 4:49
Discours chrétien de l'immortalité de l'âme (La Mothe Le Vayer), 5:182
Discours de la méthode (Discourse on method) (Descartes), 2:53
Discours de métaphysique (Discourse on metaphysics) (Leibniz), 5:252, 5:255, 5:272
on emanation, 5:257, 5:259
on identity of discernibles, 5:258
on preestablished harmony, 5:271
on soul, 5:261
on substance, 5:275, 5:276
on truth, 5:273, 5:274
on universal harmony, 5:257
Discours, figure (Lyotard), 5:620, 5:621
Discours pour montrer que les doutes de la philosophie sceptique sont de grande usage dans les sciences (La Mothe Le Vayer), 5:182
Discours préliminaire (Alembert), 1:106
Discours sur la théologie naturelle des Chinois (Discourse on the natural theology of the Chinese) (Leibniz), 5:254
Discours sur le bonheur (La Mettrie), 5:178, 5:180
Discourse
colonial, 7:728
fallacies in, 3:537, 3:546–548
in myths and analogy in Bultmann, 1:764
Stoics on, 5:569
universe of, definition of, 5:559
"Discourse at the Society of Theophilanthropists, A" (Paine), 7:74
Discourse concerning a Guide in Controversies, A (Cockburn), 2:294
Discourse concerning Reason, With Regard to Religion and Divine Revelation, A (Chubb), 2:684
Discourse concerning Ridicule and Irony in Writing, A (Collins), 2:331, 2:683
Discourse concerning the Love of God (Masham), 9:838
Discourse concerning the Love of God (Norris), 6:656
Discourse concerning the Measures of Divine Love (Norris), 6:655
Discourse concerning the Unalterable Obligations of Natural Religion and the Truth and Certainty of the Christian Revelation (Clarke), 2:268, 2:686, 2:273
Discourse ethics, **3:91–92**
Discourse in Vindication of the Doctrine of the Trinity, A (Stillingfleet), 9:249
Discourse of Free-Thinking (Collins), 2:330, 2:683, 9:341
Discourse of Miracles (Locke), 6:267–268
Discourse of the Grounds and Reasons of the Christian Religion (Collins), 2:331, 2:683
Discourse on Happiness (Du Châtelet), 9:839
Discourse on Inequity (Rousseau), on evil, 3:470
Discourse on Love (Euclides of Megara), 6:110
Discourse on Matters Pertaining to Religion (Parker), 7:122
Discourse on Metaphysics (Discours de métaphysique) (Leibniz), 1:292, 5:252, 5:255, 5:272
on emanation, 5:257, 5:259
on identity of discernibles, 5:258
on preestablished harmony, 5:271
on soul, 5:261

Discourse on Metaphysics (Discours de métaphysique) (Leibniz), ***continued***
on substance, 5:275, 5:276
on truth, 5:273, 5:274
on universal harmony, 5:257
Discourse on Miracles, Considered as evidence to prove the Divine Original of a Revelation, A (Chubb), 2:684
Discourse on Style (Buffon), 1:758
Discourse on the Grounds of Reasons of the Christian Religion (Collins), 2:330
Discourse on the Method of Conducting One's Reason Well and Searching for Truth in the Sciences (Descartes), 2:286, 2:733–737, 4:611
biographical information in, 2:723
on Jesuit education, 2:721
on language use, 4:692
overview of, 2:720
publication of, 2:725
reception of, 2:755
on scientific method, 3:291
unconscious in, 9:570
on *The World,* 2:731, 2:736
Discourse on the Miracles of our Saviour In View of the Present Controversy Between Infidels and Apostates (Woolston), 2:684, 9:845
Discourse on the Origin of Inequality (Rousseau), 3:247
Discourse on Universal History (Bossuet), 3:35
Discourse physique de la parole (Cordemoy), 2:537
Discourse representation theory (DRT), 8:748–749
Discourse Representation Theory (Kamp), 8:808
Discourses (Epictetus), 3:261
Discourses (Machiavelli), 5:626, 9:101
Discourses (Smith), 9:70
Discourses in America (Arnold), on Emerson, 3:197
Discourses on Bodies of Water (Galileo), 4:8
Discourses on Livy (Machiavelli), 5:629, 5:630
Discovering the Mind (Kaufmann), 5:46
Discovery
of categories in natural language, 2:77
of causal relations in Mill, 2:106
of comparative degree in induction, 1:448
legal, 7:450–452
as legal procedure, 1:443
in scientific induction, 9:744
use of legal procedures in natural philosophy, 1:444
Discovery of the Unconscious, The (Ellenberger), 3:738
Discrete supposition, 5:557
Discreteness
definition of, 5:541
mathematical properties of, 1:702
Discretion, judicial, 7:458
Discretion thesis, of Hart, 5:240–241
Discreto, El (Gracián), 4:168
Discrimination
affirmative action and, 1:81–82
forbidding against women, 3:582
in French Second Empire, Taine and, 9:364
"Discrimination and Perceptual Knowledge" (Goldman), 4:147
Discursive thinking, real required for, 4:769
Discurus Praeliminaris de Philosophia in Genere (Discourse on philosophy in general) (Wolff), 2:556
Discussion
in Anderson (John), 1:199
types of irrelevance in, 3:547
Discussiones Peripateticae (Patrizi), 7:144
Discussive logic, as paraconsistent, 5:489
Diseases
defined as male diseases, 3:594
definition of, 7:465
genetics and, 7:466
in philosophy of medicine, 7:465–466
Disembodied existence, 7:113
Disempowerment
as sources of the problem, 3:584
of women, 3:584
Disgrace, *yi* and, 6:129
Disguised argument, 6:110, 6:111
Disinterest
in Huayan Buddhism, 2:164
medical ethics and, 6:92
vital excess and disinterest in art, 2:65
Disinterestedness, 1:53
in aesthetic experience, 1:33, 1:51
critique of, 3:573
Disjoint sets, definition of, 5:541
Disjunction(s), 3:642
assigning vague partial belief to, 5:110
basic, 3:654
in distribution-free logic, 5:489
exclusive (alteration), definition of, 5:541
Herbrand on, 5:473
inclusive, definition of, 5:541
Leibniz on, 5:444
Disjunctive expressions, 3:541
Disjunctive normal form, 3:654
Disjunctive properties, 6:644–645
Disjunctive propositions, definition of, 5:553
Disjunctive syllogism
definition of, 5:557
distortion of, 3:538
in medieval logic, 7:105
paraconsistent logic and, 7:105
reduction to categorical, 5:503
in traditional logic, 5:503
Disjunctive transcendentals, Duns Scotus on, 3:135
Disjunctivism, 7:192, 7:193
Disjuncts, 3:540, 3:642
Diskurs und Verantwortung (Apel), 1:226–227
Disorder
disciplining subjects show signs, 3:700
probability and, 8:32, 9:469
Disordine e de' rimedie delle monete nello Stato di Milano (Beccaria), 1:517
Dispositifs, studied by Foucault, 3:700
Disposition
compensatory changes in, 1:23
Hempel on, 4:309
in meaning of sentences, 6:652
psychophysical, 9:260
in rule following, 8:531–532, 8:533
in syntactic view of theories, 9:415
theories of consciousness, 2:455
Dispositional properties, *vs.* categorical properties, 7:25
Dispositional Theories. *See* Response-Dependence Theories
Dispositionalism, 7:5
Dispositions
mental, materialism and, 6:11–13
in universals, 9:598
Disputatio de casibus perplexis in jure (Disputation on difficult cases in law) (Leibniz), 5:250
Disputatio metaphysica de principio individui (Metaphysical disputation on the principle of individuation), 5:250
Disputation (Luther), 5:616
Disputationes Adversus Astrologiam Divinatricem (Disputations against astrology) (Pico della Mirandola), 7:570, 7:573
Disputationes Metaphysicae (Suárez), 9:282

Disputationes Metaphysicae (Vasquez), 9:649
Disputations on Controversial Matters (Bellarmine), 1:542
Disputed Questions (Alexander of Hales), 1:113, 1:114
Disquisitio Metaphysica (Gassendi), 4:25, 4:26
Disquisition about Final Causes of Natural Things (Boyle), 1:674–675
Disquisitions Relating Matter and Spirit (Priestley), 8:6–7
Disquotationalism, truth theories and, 9:538–539
Dissemination (Derrida), 2:715
Dissent
  engineering ethics and, 3:240
  Stephen on, 9:510
Dissertatio de arte combinatoria (Dissertation on the combinatorial arts) (Leibniz), 5:250, 5:441
Dissertatio Inauguralis Metaphysica de Universali Naturae Systemate (Maupertuis), 6:66–67
Dissertation. *See* Inaugural dissertation
"Dissertation Concerning the Fundamental Principle of Virtue or Morality" (Gay), 4:34
Dissertation on Liberty and Necessity (Collins), 2:683
Dissertation on Liberty and Necessity, Pleasure and Pain (Franklin), 2:689
Dissertation on the Combinatorial Art (Leibniz), 5:250, 5:262, 5:441
"Dissertation on Virtue" (Butler, Joseph), 1:782
Dissociated activities, McDougall on, 6:72
Dissociation of sensibility, Eliot (T. S.) on, 3:186
Dissoi Logoi, 5:397, 9:129
Distance
  in aesthetic experience and consciousness, 1:761–762
  in argument against motion, 9:874
  infinite divisibility of, 4:654–655
  invisibility of, 4:847–848
  in perception, *vs.* as judgment, 1:575–576
  temporal, 9:494
Distance components, of objectivity, 3:574
Distant peoples
  and genetic and reproductive technologies, 4:43
  moral obligation to, **3:92–93**
Distinction(s)
  Anderson (John) on, 1:198
  as category mistakes in Aristotle, 2:74
  of essence and existence, 9:283
  in Scholasticism, 6:103
  vs. separation, 3:543
"Distinction of Independent and Dependent Meanings and the Idea of Pure Grammar" (Husserl), 8:803
Distinctness, in beauty, Winckelmann on, 9:790–791. *See also* Clarity and distinctness
Distress, mental, repression of, 3:739
Distributed representation, of memory, 6:125
Distributed term
  adding conjunct to, 3:540
  definition of, 5:541
Distribution-free logic, as relevant logic, 5:489
Distributive justice, 4:865
  Dworkin on, 3:156–157
  in moral cosmopolitanism, 2:568–569
"Distributive Justice" (Rawls), 9:80
Distributive law, in Boole, 5:460
Distributivity, definition of, 5:541
Disvalue, aesthetic, in ugliness, 9:563
Divan-i Shams-i Tabriz (Rumi), 9:307
Diversification, passion for, 3:706
Diversity
  in education, 7:362
  Locke on, 5:384
  values in conservatism, 2:466
Divination, Hellenistic, 4:301
Divine
  direct revelation of, 9:123–124
  human hunger for, Unamuno on, 9:568
  location of, 8:370
  materialism and, 6:14–15
  nature of, Xenophanes of Colophon on, 9:853–854
  response to, 8:370–371
  in Wolff's ontology, 9:827
Divine action, Malebranche on, 5:664
Divine agency, in miracles, 6:265
Divine attributes
  Clarke on, 2:270
  compatibility of, 3:692
  as *kalām*-like in Crescas, 2:593
  ultramundane cause and, 2:556
Divine causality
  vs. occasionalism, 2:587
  as synchronic event, 2:588
Divine Comedy (Dante), 2:623–626, 5:587
Divine creation, optimism/pessimism and, 7:249
Divine creator, James and, 3:532
Divine essence, Ibn Gabirol on, 4:815
Divine foreknowledge
  absolute *vs.* conditional in, 1:628
  Crescas on, 2:593
  and free will, 1:626, 3:683
  in Hinduism, 2:110
  Molina on, 6:321
  Peter Aureol on, 7:256–257
  philosophical problems raised by, 3:692
Divine freedom, Henry of Ghent on, 4:313
Divine governance
  creation *ex nihilo* and, 2:585
  Philo on, 7:304
Divine ideas
  Henry of Harclay on, 4:315
  Wyclyf on, 9:852
Divine illumination
  Matthew of Aquasparta on, 6:65
  Richard of Mediavilla on, 8:458
  universals in, 9:593
Divine infallibility, correct analysis of, 3:694
Divine justice, 7:176, 7:387
Divine knowledge
  in Molina's *scientia media,* 8:681
  Philo's concept of, 7:305–306
  restriction of, to universals, 4:68
Divine law
  Albo on, 4:824
  Augustine on, 1:396
  Crusius on, 2:608
  prophets as transmitters of, Saadya on, 8:586
  Spinoza on, 9:173–174
  Suárez on, 9:284
  in volitions and bodily movements, 4:77
Divine Lawmaker: Lectures on Induction, Laws of Nature, and the Existence of God, The (Foster), 5:229
Divine love, 3:623
Divine Names (Pseudo-Dionysius), 1:140, 7:609
Divine nature, Peter Lombard on, 7:260
Divine Nature and Human Language (Alston), 1:132, 8:418
Divine omnipotence, logically impossible excluded from, 3:695
Divine order, in words, Yang Xiong on, 9:861
Divine organic life, basic laws of, 5:148
Divine perception, 7:194
Divine Person, personalism and, 7:235–236
Divine Pimander (Trismegistus), 1:711

Divine power, Brahman as, 1:681–684
Divine providence, Crescas on, 2:593
Divine reason, as cosmic law, 2:567
Divine Rectitude (Balguy), 1:475
Divine revelation
  Philo on, 7:305
  of political law, 7:307
Divine right of kings
  critique of James I by Bellarmine, 1:542
  Locke on, 5:388
Divine will
  antecedent necessity in, 1:681
  in Brightman, 1:695
  as causality as creation at every instant, 2:113
  in contiguous existence and divine causality in al-Ghazālī, 2:114
  Crusius on, 2:608
  in Descartes's physics, 9:172
  Duns Scotus on, 8:704
  in events past, present, future, 1:680
  Ibn Gabirol on, 4:545, 4:815
  justice *vs.* intellectual understanding of, 1:542
  law as, 7:454
  sin as resistance to, 2:9–10
  in theological voluntarism, 9:716
  in time, 1:704
Divine wisdom
  as eternal femininity, 1:760
  Socrates on, 9:108–109
  Sophia as personification of, 9:124
Divine-command theory, 7:479–480
  of ethics, **3:93–94,** 4:562–563
Divinity
  incarnation in Christianity, 2:247
  sense of, Plantinga on, 3:324
"Divinity School Address" (Emerson), 6:574
Divinum Humanum (Swedenborg), 9:338
Divisibility
  in Anaxagoras, 1:181, 2:490
  in Aristotle, 2:491
  Zeno of Elea on, 9:872–873
Division
  fallacy of, 3:541–543
  in Lambert, 5:445
  as method, in Plato, 3:53
Division non faciat saltum rule, 5:537
Division of labor, historical materialism and, 4:378
Division of Labor in Society (Durkheim), 3:151
Dix, Dorothea, meaningfulness of life of, 5:351
Dizionario di filosofia (Abbagnano), 1:3
DNA
  causality in, 7:345
  information theory and, 7:344–345
  and origin of life, 5:360
  structure of, discovered, 7:146
  synthesis of, 5:361–362
  See also Genetics
DNP account of explanation, 3:526
Do Not Resuscitate (DNR) guidelines, 6:94
Dobrolyubov, Nikolai
  Dostoevsky on, 3:100
  Marković and, 5:719
Dobzhansky, Theodosius, evolutionary theory and, 3:488
Docetism, Christology debates and, 2:247
Doctor Eximus, 9:282
Doctor Faustus (Mann), 1:25
Doctor-patient relationship, 6:93
Doctrinal theology, Oman in, 7:14–15
Doctrine, in religion, 8:371–372
Doctrine of choice, Kierkegaard's, 5:66
Doctrine of restraint, 8:389–391
Doctrine of the Infelicities, 7:200
Doctrine of the Logos in Its History, The (Trubetskoi), 9:533
Doctrine of the Mean (Tzu-su), 2:150, 2:219
Doctrine of the principles, Damascius on, 2:622–623
Doctrine of the Trinity and Transubstantiation Compared, The (Stillingfleet), 9:249
"Doctrine of Uniformity in Geology Briefly Refuted, The" (Kelvin), 2:637–638
Doctrine of words, 8:496
Dodd, Anthony, 8:845
Dodd, Julian, identity theory of truth and, 9:537
Dodgson, Charles Lutwidge. *See* Carroll, Lewis
Dodwell, Henry, Clarke on, 2:273
Dodwell, Henry (the younger), 2:686, 6:656
"Does Consciousness Exist?" (James, William), 4:784
Does God Exist? (Taylor), 9:374
"Does Moral Philosophy Rest on a Mistake?" (Prichard), 3:155, 3:420
"Does Tense Logic Rest upon a Mistake?" (Evans), 3:461
"Does the Inertia of a Body Depend upon Its Energy Content?" ("Ist die Trägheit eines körpers von seinem Energieinhalt abhängig?" (Einstein), 3:233–234
Doeuff, Michele Le, philosophical imaginary, 3:570
Dōgen, **3:95–96**
Dogma, **3:96–98**
  Encyclopédie on, 3:224
  as essential, McTaggart on, 6:78
  in Judaism, 1:102, 4:827
  Le Roy on, 5:288
  Meslier on, 6:154
  Saint-Simon on, 8:590
  of Stoicism, reaction against, 4:173–174
  as symbolization, 8:587
  synthesis of, at Greek Academy, 4:174
  Timon of Phlius on, 9:501
Dogmatics
  Barth on, 1:478
  ontological requirements of, 1:478
Dogmatism
  Aenesidemus and, 1:30–32
  Agrippa's trilemma and, 8:176–177
  of Antiochus of Ascalon, 1:222
  Calvinism as, 9:51
  causality in, 1:32
  in civilization, 8:460
  in critical history, 6:272
  Gassendi, 4:25–26
  in Greek Academy, 4:301, 7:607
  immense suffering caused by, 5:103
  of Maimon, 5:645
  in Plato, 6:547
  political conservatism and, 2:465
  vs. Pyrrhonism, 8:176
  rational, 5:645
  skepticism and, 1:191–192, 6:192–193
  skeptics opposition to, 8:851, 9:47, 9:48
  Vico on, 9:671–672
Dogme et critique (Le Roy), 5:288
Döhmann, Karl, on Venn diagrams, 5:562
Doing Philosophy: A Guide to the Writing of Philosophy Papers (Feinberg), 3:562
Döll, E., 3:130
Dolz, John, 5:438
Domain of a relation, definition of, 5:541

Domain of individuals, definition of, 5:541
Domain of quantification, 3:640
Domains
 Löwenheim on, 5:471
 Skolem on, 5:471
Domestic life, transformations of, 3:567
Domestic Slavery Considered as a Scriptural Institution (Fuller and Wayland), 9:728
Dominance
 in Marx, 5:732–733
 power and, 7:731–732
Dominance feminism, 3:584
Dominations and Powers (Santayana), 8:600
Dominicans
 Aquinas and, 3:148, 9:435, 9:444, 9:446
 Durandus of Saint-Pourçain and, 3:148
 Eckhart, Meister, **3:162–164**
 education of, 3:134
 on forms in things, 7:162
 vs. Franciscans, 9:445
 in medieval philosophy, 6:100
Dominion, Wyclyf on, 9:852
Dominion and grace, doctrine of, 4:91
Domitian (emperor of Rome), Epictetus and, 3:261
Domninus of Larissa, 6:552
Don Carlos (Schiller, Friedrich), 8:626
Don John of Austria, 5:364
Donagan, Alan
 deontological ethics and, 2:714
 Kant as an exemplar of moral theory, 5:37
 Lehrer and, 5:248
 on Oakeshott, 7:2
Donati, Gemma, 2:623
Donation of Constantine, 9:634, 9:635
Donatus, 8:770
Dong Zhongshu, **3:98**
 approach to Confucianism in, 2:153
 social and political thought of, 2:235
Dongyuan. *See* Dai Zhen
Donkey anaphora, 1:173–175
Donne, John
 Filmer an associate of, 3:636
 on suicide, 9:319
Donnellan, Keith, 5:102
 on direct reference theory, 8:62
 on propositional mismatches, 5:508
 work on proper names, 5:150
Donner, Wendy, 6:233
Doppelleben (Benn), 1:548
Dostoevsky, Fyodor Mikhailovich, **3:99–102**
 Bakhtin on, 1:466
 Barth and, 3:505
 existentialism and, 3:501
 and Ivanov, 4:767
 Leont'ev and, 5:283
 Masaryk and, 6:2
 nihilism in, 6:618
 on reason, 3:501
 and Shestov, 9:11
 tragic dialectic of freedom, 1:559
 on universe, nature of, 3:501
Dostojewkskij: Tragödie-Myth-Mystik (Ivanov), 4:767
Double effect principle, 1:213, 2:653
Double Negative (Heizer), 3:256
Double-truth doctrine, 1:424–425, 1:429, 2:721
 Luther on, 5:616
 Scholastics on, 5:616
 See also Averroism
Doubt, **3:102–104**
 Agrippa on, 1:96
 belief and, 1:535, 5:97, 7:166–172
 in Buddhism, 6:621
 Cartesian method of, 4:50, 8:639–640
 and conditions of indubitability, 3:102–103
 Diderot on, 3:72
 as fideistic foundation, 1:505
 immediate experience and, 3:103
 impossibility of in self-evident knowledge, 4:761
 indubitability regress, 3:104
 Lequier on, 5:287
 logical necessity and, 3:103
 in metaphysics, 6:201
 in naturalism, 6:502
 Peirce on, 7:166–167, 7:172, 7:173
 possibility and limits of, in Geulincx, 4:77
 and rational inquiry, conditions of, 3:104
 reasonable, 3:102, 4:96
 Saadya on, 8:586
 transcendence discovered through, in Jaspers's theology, 4:803
 in Unanumo's philosophy, 9:568
 universal method
  of Descartes, 4:50
  Mercier on, 6:145
Doubt-belief theory of inquiry, 7:166–172
Doubtes (attrib: Damarsais), 2:266
Doubting, in intrinsic theory of consciousness, 2:454
Doubts concerning Galen (Rhasis), 4:7
Douglas, Mary, borderline cases and, 5:111
Douglas, William O., on Darrow, 2:351
Douglass, Frederick, Martin Luther King compared to, 5:73
Doutes sur la religion proposées à Mss. les Docteurs de Sorbonne, (Fourcroy), 2:264
Dowe, Phil, on causality definition, 2:103
Downame, George, 5:438
Downward causation, 6:135
Doxastic attitudes, 8:175
Doxastic logic
 as intensional logic, 5:486
 as term, 9:848
Doxastic practice, 6:462, 8:402
"'Doxastic Practice' Approach to Epistemology, A" (Alston), 3:279–280
Doxastic responsibility, 9:685–686
Doxoscopiae Physicae Minores (Jungius), 4:861
Dragmaticon Philosophiae (William of Conches), 9:768
Drama
 Aristotle on, 1:340
 Corneille on, 1:49
 formal rules of, beauty from, 9:562
 Greek, **4:175–178**
 katharsis in, 1:340
 Kerman on, 1:308
 Plato on, 1:187
 See also Greek drama; Tragedy
Drapier's Letters to the People of Ireland, The (Swift), 9:340
Dread, 5:64
 existentialists on, 3:503, 3:508
 as experience of nothing, 1:530
 religious, Otto on, 7:60
 Sartre on, 3:503–504
Dreaming (Malcolm), 3:106–107
Dreaming, psychoanalytic theory of, 3:743–744
Dream(s), **3:105–108**
 Augustine on, 1:393
 in Carroll, 2:51
 in Cicero, 2:258
 desire and, 8:111
 Diderot on, 3:75
 finding the purported unconscious causes of, 3:743
 Freud on, 3:105–106
 vs. hallucinations, 3:105–106
 Hobbes on, 4:413
 representation in, 7:405

Dream(s), ***continued***
unconscious in, 9:572
world as, in Indian philosophy, 9:542
Dreams of a Spirit-Seer (Kant), 5:11
Drebeb, Burton, in proof theory, 8:56
Drei Nationaloekonomien, Die (Sombart), 9:128
Dreier, Jamie, on deontological ethics, 2:714
Dretske, Fred, **3:108–109**
on conditions of knowledge, 3:270–271
on consciousness, 2:455
on content of belief in information semantics, 2:479
on emotions, 3:201
on intentionality, 4:711
on natural law, 5:226–227
on perception, 7:191
on transitive conscious states, 2:457
Dreyfus, Hubert
on artificial intelligence, 1:348
on connectionism, 2:445
on phenomenology, 7:300
Dreyfus, Stuart, on connectionism, 2:445
Driesch, Hans Adolf Eduard, **3:109–113**
critical vitalism of, 9:695–697
on epistemological solipsism, 9:118
Drug-induced mysticism, 6:460
Drūj ("The Lie"), in Zoroastrianism, 9:886
Drummond, Henry, physicotheology and, 7:562
Druzhina (organized "commune"), 5:60
Dryden, John
on deism, 2:681
on drama, 1:49
Dthat (Kaplan), 5:39
dthat operator, 8:77
Du Bois, W. E. B., 3:567
Du Bois-Raymond, Emil
cosmic brain argument and, 1:369
on physiological bases of mental function, 6:11
Du Châtelet, émilie, 9:839
Du pape (de Maistre), 5:659–660, 9:520
Du Sishu Daquan Shuo (Discourse on reading the great collection of commentaries on the four books) (Wang Fuzhi), 9:724
Du Tongjian Lun (A treatise on reading Tongjian) (Wang Fuzhi), 9:724
Du vrai, du beau et du bien (Cousin), 2:579
Du Weiming, neo-Confucianism of, 2:183
Dual aspect, of every force, 3:688
Dual wish fulfillment in dreams, 3:744
Dual-aspect theory, 6:259
property dualism and, 3:113
Dualism, 6:327
agent causation and, 1:89
in Anaxagoras, 1:182
of *apeiron/peras,* 1:225
attitude, 8:83–84
of attributes, Stout's defense of, 9:260
in Augustine, 1:392
behaviorism *vs.*, 8:142
in Bergson, 1:564
Brahman as creative power, 1:683
in Brunschvicg, 1:714
in Bultmann, 1:763
Cambridge platonists on, 2:13–14
Cartesian. *See* Cartesian dualism
Christian, 3:99, 4:618
in Condillac, 2:421
of conventional-ultimate distinction in Dge-lugs, 1:733–734
vs. corporeal intentionality, 6:148
in Cudworth, 2:610
Davidson (Donald) on, 2:646–649
in doctrine of personal immortality, 4:610
Dostoevsky on, 3:99
Ducasse on, 3:125
Eddington on, 3:165–166
epiphenomenalism and, 7:469
on evaluation of political and social institutions, 3:391–392
facticity and freedom in, 1:763
feminists on, 5:373
Gehlen rejection of, 4:35
Geulincx, 4:80
in Gnosticism, 4:98–99, 4:103–104
of Hebbel, 4:253
of Hemsterhuis, 4:311
in Indian philosophy, 4:135
Lovejoy on, 5:592–593
in Mādhyamika doctrine, 1:744
in Malebranche, 5:667–668
in Manichaeism, 3:472
many minds formulation and, 5:699
of Marcus Aurelius, 5:707
materialism and, 6:9, 8:6–7
of matter and spirit, in Tolstoy, 9:512
of McDougall, 6:72
mental and physical substances, 3:758
Merleau-Ponty and, 6:148
metaphysical, James on, 4:783–784
in mind-body distinction and eucharistic theology, 2:60
mind-body problem in, 7:468
Nagel (Thomas) on, 6:475
in neo-Confucian critique of western philosophy, 2:182
in neutral monism, 6:587
in new realism, 6:585, 6:588
optimism/pessimism and, 7:245
pain and, 7:68
parapsychology and, 7:113, 7:114
personal identity and, 7:214
Petrović-Njegoš on, 7:267
of physical and mental states, 4:778
in Plato, 3:115, 3:471, 7:636
in Plotinus's indeterminate dyad, 7:635–636
psychology and, 3:182
in Sartre, 8:611
Schopenhauer on, 8:651
of souls, 6:679
in Stahl's animism, 9:202
Stumpf on, 9:280
substance, 1:89
of symbol and symbolized in Cassirer, 2:67
time and, 9:498
of Titchener, 8:142
Treschow on, 9:526
of truth between reason *vs.* revelation, 1:629
in Yin Yang school, 2:152
in Zoroastrianism, 3:471, 9:886
See also Cartesian Dualism; Mind-body problem, Descartes on
Dualism in the philosophy of mind, **3:113–122,** 7:468–469
composite dualism, 3:115
compositional dualism, 3:115–116
embodied self in, 9:259–260
modal arguments, 3:118–119
objections to, 3:116–118
Ockham's razor and, 3:118
property dualism, 3:113–115
objections to, 3:117
pure dualism, 3:115
spectrum of dualisms, 3:115–116
substance dualism, 3:113, 3:115–118
Dualist conceptions of human nature, death and, 2:654
Dualist realism, 8:265–268

Dualistic ontology, of Plato, 5:91
Dualistic realism, of critical realists, 6:75
Duality
  of Christ, 7:313
  definition of, 5:541
  in probability, 8:26
Dual-unity, of Godmanhood, 3:717
Dubois, Pierre, 7:154
DuBos, Jean Baptiste, **3:123–124**, 6:598
  Nicolai and, 6:598
Ducasse, Curt John, **3:124–126**
  on adverbial analysis, 8:821
  on immortality, 4:613
  parapsychology and, 7:116
Duchamp, Marcel
  on beauty, 1:67
  work of, 1:299, 1:310
Dudleian Lectures, 2:689
Dudman, Vic H., on conditionals, 2:424
Due care standard, in engineering ethics, 3:240
Due cheminement de la pensée (Meyerson), 6:212
Dufrenne, Mikel, on aesthetics, 1:59
Dufrennes, Michel, Ingarden and, 4:682
Dugin, Aleksandr, 3:454
Duguit, Léon, 9:143
Duhem, Pierre Maurice Marie, **3:126–129**
  on conventionalism, 2:520
  Einstein and, 3:181
  on eternal return doctrine, 3:353
  on explanation, 3:518
  on impetus theory, 4:621
  on Leonardo da Vinci, 5:281
  on observation, 8:690
  on theories, 8:677
  on thermodynamic laws, 7:537
Duhem-Quine conventionalism
  Euclidean space and, 2:521
  holism in scientific theory testing and, 2:520
Duhem-Quine thesis, 6:496, 6:497
Dühring, Eugen Karl, **3:130–132**
  Engels and, 3:57–58, 3:60–61
  on eternal return doctrine, 3:354
Dühring-Bund, 3:130
Dumarsais, César Chesneau
  Boulainvilliers's coterie in French clandestine writings, 2:266
  on grammarians, 8:790
  on *philosophe,* 3:244
Dumartheray, François, 5:154
Dumbleton, John, 9:343
Dumée, Jeanne, 9:838
Dummett, Michael Anthony Eardley, **3:132–133**
  on deductive implication, 5:513
  Evans and, 3:459
  Frege and, 3:732
  intuitionist logic and, 5:491
  on language and thought, 5:191
  on logical terms, 5:531
  on meaning, 6:676–677
  meaning theory of, 4:739
  on philosophical explanation of language, 7:551
  on Wittgenstein, 9:818
Dumon, Étienne, French translations of Bentham by, 1:551
Dumont, P.-E., 5:594
Dunn, J. Michael, relevant logic and, 5:491
Dunne, J. W., on precognition, 7:753
Dunning, Stephen N., 5:67
Dunren (feld-away-persons), 9:862
Duns Scotus, John, **3:133–148**
  on Aquinas, 9:427
  Avicenna and, 3:134–135
  and Bedersi, 4:820
  and Burley, 1:772–775
  on creation, 3:135
  and divine command theories of ethics, 3:93
  Erasmus and, 3:340
  on eternal return doctrine, 3:354
  ethical philosophy, 3:143–145
  on existence of God, 3:135–137, 3:146, 9:781
  Fonseca *vs.,* 3:682
  on forms, 1:403, 3:141–142
  on free will, 3:136–137, 3:142–143, 3:146, 3:404
  on God, 3:135–137
  on individuation, 6:102–103, 9:283
  on intuition, 3:290
  on knowledge, 3:137–140
  on knowledge of singulars, 9:283
  Liber de Causis and, 5:334
  on logic, 5:432–434
  on love of God, 3:142–144
  on matter, 3:141
  in medieval metaphysics, 6:189
  in medieval philosophy, 6:100
  on metaphysics, 3:134–137
  and Mill, 8:686
  modal theory and, 3:145–146
  moderate realism of, Ockham on, 9:773
  on necessary beings, 7:26
  and Ockham, 9:770
  Pannenberg and, 7:80
  Peirce and, 7:164
  Peter Aureol's attack on, 7:256–258
  Pico della Mirandola and, 7:571
  political philosophy, 3:143–145
  principle of individuation in, 2:139–140
  on soul, 3:141–142
  on thought and thinking, 9:420
  on transcendentals, 3:135, 3:137–138
  on universals, 3:147, 9:593
  on will and necessity, 1:680
  Wolff and, 3:350
Dupanloup, Bishop, 5:372
Dupin, Louise-Marie, 9:839
Duplex quantitas, 6:3
Duplicity, of the I's, 3:616
Durability, phenomenalism and, 7:275
Duran, Simeon ben Tzemach, 1:103
Durand, William, 3:149
Durandus of Saint-Pourçain, **3:148–149**
Durandus Petit, 3:149
Duration
  Augustine on, 9:485
  Bergson on, 2:695, 9:464, 9:488–489
  in cosmological argument for God's existence, 2:586
  Locke on, 5:382, 9:464
  metrication of, 9:494
  pure time in, 1:563
  Russell on, 9:464
  of sensa, 9:486–487
  See also Bergson, Henri; Time
Duration and Simultaneity (Bergson), 9:489
Dürer, Albrecht
  on painting, 1:48
  pessimism of, 7:247
Durkheim, Émile, **3:149–152**
  and Bergson, 1:571
  on cultural knowledge, 9:103
  functional notions used by, 3:762
  Lévy-Bruhl and, 5:306
  Pareto and, 7:118
  on rationality of social ritual, 1:488
  on social facts, 9:94
  on society as source of truth, 9:103
  on suicide, 9:320
Dürr, Karl, 4:79
Dusha cheloveka: Opyt vvedeniia v filosofskuyu psikhologiyu (Frank, S.), 3:716
Dushun, and Huayan Buddhism, 1:737, 2:164

Dussel, Enrique, liberation philosophy and, 5:211
Dutch book argument
conditional bets in, 1:497
probability calculus, 1:496
Dutch book theorem, 8:30
Dutch Republic
Cartesianism in, 9:170
organized religions in, 9:177
political tensions in, 9:176–177
Spinoza on freedom in, 9:177
"year of disaster" in, 9:182–183
Dutens, L., 5:255
Duty, **3:152–155**
Bentham on, 7:445
as branch of morality in Clarke, 2:273–274
in Cahn Yi-Zhu philosophy and neo-Confucian rationalism, 2:156
in categorical imperative, 2:71
in Cicero, 5:724
civil disobedience and, 2:260–261
to coercive institutions, 9:72
Confucian name rectification and, 2:204
Cousin on, 2:579
as creation of *volksgeist,* 8:615
in Croce, 2:603
Crusius on, 2:608
demandingness of, 3:443–444
of distributive justice in moral cosmopolitanism, 2:569
as ethical ideal of ren in Confucianism, 2:176
Fichte on, 3:414
happiness and, 2:367
of heart and limbs in Baḥyā ben Joseph ibn Paqūda, 1:457–458
Hume on, 3:384
Kant on, 3:153–155, 3:411
Kantian ethics on, 3:440
legal sense of, 7:445
in Locke, 7:370
Lunacharskii on, 5:611
in Marsilius of Padua, 5:724
Moore (G. E.) on, 3:439
in moral cosmopolitanism, 2:568
natural, 5:724
normativity of, 7:445
ordinary, 3:153–154
Paley on, 7:76
punishment for neglect of, 3:153
Ross (William David) on, 3:420, 3:440, 8:505
in Rousseau, 7:371
rule-utilitarian view of, 3:384
Stoics on, 3:154–155
utilitarianism on, 3:440–441
vs. virtue, in Kant, 8:627
in Vishnu's organization of society, 2:110
Williams (Bernard) on, 3:347
Zeno of Citium on, 9:870
See also Deontological ethics
Dvaita philosophy, 4:630
Dvaita Vedānta, on liberation, 5:330
Dwight, Timothy, deism and, 2:690
Dworkin, Andrea, work on pornography, 3:601
Dworkin, Ronald, **3:156–157**
on analytic jurisprudence, 1:169
on distribution of welfare, 8:722
on Hart, 7:459
on legal positivism, 5:240–244
on legal reasoning, 7:458–459
on natural law, 6:513
philosophy of sex and, 7:523
Dyad
as first principle, 7:606
Plato's indeterminate, 7:633, 7:636
Dyadic relation, definition of, 5:541
Dyke, Heather
tenseless theory of time and, 9:475
on token-reflexive theory, 9:476
Dynamic evolution, symmetry and conservation principle of, 2:462
Dynamic logic, 6:299
anaphora and, 1:175
as multi-modal logics, 5:487
Dynamic ontology, paradigm of, 5:43
Dynamic Predicate Logic (Groenendijk & Stokhof), 8:808
Dynamic unconscious, of Freud, 3:737–738
Dynamic unity, of the universe, 3:621
Dynamica de potentia et legibus naturae corporeae (Dynamics: Concerning the force and laws of natural bodies) (Leibniz), 5:253
Dynamical equations
in Bohmian mechanics, 8:212
operators and, 8:208–209
in quantum mathematical apparatus, 8:206
"Dynamical Model of the Electromagnetic Field, A" (Maxwell), 6:69
Dynamical principles, of Kant, 5:19
Dynamical state, modal interpretations of, 6:278
Dynamically self-regulating systems, 5:127, 5:132
Dynamics
in Cassirer's elaboration of Kant, 2:66
in chaos theory, 2:131–134
collapse, 5:696–697
Hamiltonian theory symmetries and conservation principle in, 2:463–464
language stability and dynamic expression, 2:208–209
linear, 5:696–697
sociology in Comte and, 2:412
symmetry and conservation principle of, 2:462
Dynamics in Psychology (Köhler), 5:126
Dynamis, signifying transitive activity, 3:686
Dynamism, term used by Ferri, 3:607
Dyne, metric unit of force, 3:686
Dystopia, 9:617, 9:621

E

E (badness), Xunzi on, 9:856
Eagleton, Terry, on aesthetics, 1:70
Earlier-later, McTaggart on, 6:78
Earman, John, **3:159–161**
on miracles, 6:275
on natural laws, 5:228, 5:230
on unique evolution, 3:32
Earth
age of, and evolution, 2:636–640
as classification of matter, Greek Academy on, 6:59
Luther's doctrine of two realms, 5:613–615
physical theories of, 9:154
rotation and motion in Copernicus, 2:534
rotation sun, metaphysical reasons for, 5:52
spatial references of, 9:148–149
See also World soul
Earthly existence, prolongation of, 3:745
Earthy matter, of Aristotelian doctrine, 5:53
East India Company, Mill (John Stuart) and, 6:221
Eastern Christianity, undistorted by the classical heritage, 5:75
Eastern Orthodox Church, mysticism of, 6:448
Ebbinghaus, Herman
in psychology, 8:140–141
Krueger successor to, 5:155
Ebbs, Gary, 8:533
Eberhard, Johann August, 2:688, **3:161–162**

Ebreo, Leone
on love, 5:587–588
Pico della Mirandola (Gianfrancesco) and, 7:575
in Renaissance Jewish philosophy, 4:824
Ecce Homo (Nietzsche), 6:611
Eccentrics, banished by Kepler, 5:51
Eccentrism, in progress, 6:215–216
Ecclesia spiritualis, as Franck's true church, 3:713
Ecclesianised *(votserkovlenny)* Hellenism, 3:673
Ecclesiastical society, Hooker on, 4:463–464
Ecclesiology, in Barth, 1:478, 1:479
Eckers, David, on creative process, 2:590
Eckert, J. Presper, 2:405
Eckhart, Meister, **3:162–164**
Liber de Causis and, 5:334
pantheism and, 7:96
and Suso, 9:335
Tarski and, 9:372
Thomism of, 9:444
Éclaircissement. See Enlightenment, French
Eclecticism
of Cousin, 2:579
in Greek Academy, 4:171
of Thomasius, 9:441
of Thoreau, 9:450
Eclipse of Reason, The (Horkheimer), 1:26
Ecofeminism, 3:260–261, 8:849
"École de Vienne et la philosophie traditionelle, L'" (Schlick), 8:638
École des Beaux Arts, Taine at, 9:364
Ecole freudienne, 5:167–168
École Normale, Ideology doctrine and, 2:760
Ecological Thinking (Code), 2:296
Ecology, Marxism and, 5:741
Ecomiendas, Las Casas on, 5:205
Econmion, ein Lob des Thorechten Gottlichen Worts (Franck), 3:713
Econometrics, 8:687
Economic Analysis of Law, The (Posner), 7:461
Economic and Philosophic Manuscripts of 1844 (Marx), 1:121, 1:122, 1:124, 2:363, 3:57, 3:67, 5:730
Lukács and, 5:603
Economic determinism, 1:125
Economic efficiency, of communism and western social changes, 2:361
Economic freedom, 5:143
Economic materialism, 7:627
Economic relations, Kant's kingdom of ends and, 2:366–367
Economic theory, of Mill (John Stuart), 6:228
Economic utility, Croce on, 2:603
Economics
agrarian, 9:550
alienation in, 1:121–122, 1:125
in allocation issues, 6:96–97
altruism and, 7:352
Arendt on, 1:253
of Beccaria, 1:518
and behavior, 1:777, 7:353
Berkeley on, 1:571
beyond, 7:354
boycott, Swift's advocacy of, 9:340
business ethics and, 1:777
Cartwright's machine model of, 2:63
central planning, 7:351
in Chinese philosophy, 2:200
in collectivization of means of production, 1:472
and communism, 7:353–354
cooperation in, 7:353
corporative, 9:197
criminal law and, 7:718
Croce on, 2:603
of culture, 7:354
Dühring on, 3:131
education and, 7:362
efficiency in, law and, 7:461–462
environmental, 7:353
environmental ethics and, 3:258
and ethics, **3:447–450**
and ethics of profit-seeking and self-interest, 1:777
experimental, 7:352–353
free, advantages of, 7:351
free-markets and, 1:778
in French liberal movement, 9:247
Friedman (Milton) on, 7:351–352
Genovesi on, 4:49
globalization and, 5:741, 7:351
in historical materialism, 4:379
of labor-basis of consumer rights, 1:472
law and, 2:603, 7:461–462, 7:717–718
Mandeville on, 5:681–682
Manheim on, 5:686
of market socialism, 9:92
Marx on, 5:733–734
Miura on, 6:276
moral obligations in business and, 1:779
as moral philosophy, 7:350–351
natural selection and, 7:351
Neurath on, 6:560
neuroeconomics, 7:354
Nussbaum on, 6:680
Pareto on, 7:117–118
philosophy of, **7:349–355**
and Nash equilibria, in game theory, 4:16–17
Sen on, 8:810–811
in Smith's *Wealth of Nations,* 9:68–69
Sombart on, 9:127–128
of Tagore, 9:364
in Plato's *Republic,* 7:350, 7:591
Posner on, 7:717–718
prisoner's dilemma and, 7:353
of property, 8:70–71
Robbins on, 7:351
Saint-Simon on, 8:590–591
as science, 7:351–354
self-interest in, 7:352
Sen and, 8:810
Sidgwick and, 9:26
in Smith's *Wealth of Nations,* 7:350–351, 9:68
social activity in, Weber (Max) on, 9:735
in social change, 9:656
socialist, 5:740–741, 9:88–:91
Sombart on, 9:127–128
of Soviet Union, 7:353–354
state sovereignty and, 9:146
statistical study of, 8:687
tools of, and ethics, 3:449
tort law and, 7:461
Turgot on, 9:550
value and valuation in, 9:636
welfare, Sen on, 8:810
See also Finance
Economics (Wolff), 9:825
Economistic model of causation in social sciences, 7:536
Economy, law and, 7:427
Ecosophy, 3:259
Écrit sur la signature du formulaire (Pascal), 7:131
Écrits sur la grâce (Pascal), 7:131
Ecstasy, mystic
Gregory of Nyssa on, 4:182
Philo on, 4:810
Solov'ëv on, 9:123
Ecumenical Movement, Florovskii's participation in, 3:673
Eddington, Arthur Stanley, **3:164–166**
on scientific terminology, 7:516–517
on space-time curve, 9:152
Stebbing on, 9:237
Edelmann, Johann, deism and, 2:688

Edge, Hoyt L., parapsychology and, 7:116
Edgeworth, Francis Ysidro, precision of an estimation, 3:662–663
Edgington, Dorothy, consequences of first-order logic, 3:646
Edict of Nantes, revocation of, 3:245
Edinburgh University, Balfour, chancellor, 1:473
Edith Stein Gesamtausgabe (Herder), 9:240
Edith Steins Werke (Herder), 9:240
Edmunds, Jack, on polynominal-time computability constraints, 2:388
Education
  Absolute in, 7:373
  in aesthetics, Schiller (Friedrich) on, 8:627
  affirmative action in, 1:81–82
  aim of, 7:362–363
  ancient, 7:365
  Aristotle and, 1:263, 7:367
  atomism in early, 7:365
  in Augustine, 7:367–368
  autonomy and, 7:360, 7:361
  Bacon (Roger) program of, 1:453
  beliefs and, 7:357–358
  Bentham contributions to, 1:551
  of Carneades in the Academy, 2:47
  in Carolingian renaissance, 2:49
  character and, 7:370
  in Christianity, 7:367–368
  church and, 7:368
  Cicero's on, 2:258
  in Comenius, 2:341
  communist demand for free, 2:363
  as condition of democracy, 2:704
  Confucius on, 2:231, 2:442
  content of, 7:363
  as a continuation of unceasing evolution, 3:754
  cosmopolitan and citizenship aims of, 1:483
  critical thinking in, 7:356
  criticism in, Vico on, 9:671
  cultural development and, 6:582, 7:364
  in Daoist social and political thought, 2:237
  de Staël on, 9:202
  definition of, 7:360
  deontological ethics and, 7:361
  Dewey on, 3:44, 3:47
  Dge-lugs curriculum and scholastic methods, 1:734–735
  discipline in, 7:363
  diversity in, 7:362
  in Dong Zhongshu's social and political thought, 2:235
  emotional growth and, 7:363
  in Epicurus, 7:367
  epistemic aims of, 7:356–357
  experience in, 7:371
  in fascist Italy, 4:50
  feminism and, 7:359
  free, Jodl (Friedrich) and, 4:836
  freedom and, 7:375
  Gentile on, 4:50
  gnostic, 4:98
  as governance, 7:360
  in Greece, ancient, 7:364–367
  in Greek Academy, 4:171–175
  harmony as aim of, 7:372
  Hélvetius on, 4:306
  Herbart on, 4:325
  history of, 1:599–600, 1:767, **7:364–389**
    in ancient Greece, 7:364–367
    Comenius in, 7:369
    Dewey in, 7:378–379
    Fichte in, 7:374
    Froebel in, 7:372–373
    Herbart in, 7:374–377
    Kant in, 7:373–374
    Locke in, 7:369–370
    Mill (John Stuart) and, 7:377
    Pestalozzi in, 7:371–372
    Plato in, 7:365–366
    Rousseau in, 7:370–371
    Socrates in, 7:365
    sophists in, 7:365
    Spencer in, 7:377
  human nature and, 7:367–368
  individuality and, 7:373
  indoctrination in, 7:357–358
  in Japan, Buddhism in, 4:793
  justice and, 7:366
  justification in, 7:360
  knowledge in, 7:356
  liberal, 8:5
  Locke on, 5:390–391
  Loyola and, 7:369
  Manheim on, 5:686
  metaphysics of, 7:366
  methodological opposition of Benjamin to, 1:545
  in Middle Ages, 3:134, 7:367–369
  Milton on, 6:251
  in modern period, 7:369–379
  moral, 7:363
  morality as aim of, 7:376
  multiculturalism and, 7:359
  Murphy on, 6:436
  Nelson (Leonard) on, 6:536, 6:537
  Newman (John Henry) on, 6:582
  nominalism in, 9:700
  normativity in, 7:361
  Nussbaum on, 6:681
  open-mindedness and, 7:358
  Paulsen and, 7:148
  peace as goal of, 7:373
  Pestalozzi on, 7:254–255
  philosophy in, 6:436, 7:333–334
  philosophy of
    analytic philosophy in, 7:355–356
    definition of, 7:366–367
    education as recovery of original mind, 2:168
    epistemological issues in, **7:355–360**
    ethics in, **7:360–364**
    Gentile on, 4:50–52
    Gerbert of Aurillac on, 4:66
    Hirst in, 7:355
    history of, **7:364–389**
    Peters in, 7:355
    Plato on, 7:366
    politics in, **7:360–364**
    Scheffler in, 7:355
    Spranger on, 9:199
  Plato on, 1:43, 7:365–367, 7:587–588, 7:594–595
  Platonic Forms and, 7:366
  pleasure as aim of, 7:377
  postmodernism and, 7:359
  precondition of the existence of freedom, 3:722
  Priestley on, 8:5
  privatization in, 7:362
  progress and, 8:49
  proportional, 4:635
  public, Fichte on, 3:618
  Quintilian on, 7:367
  as reform, 7:366
  in Reformation, 7:369
  reformist theory in, 7:378–379
  in Renaissance, 7:368–369
  in representative government, 6:229
  responsibility in, 7:362
  as right, 7:362
  role of learning in 16th century, 1:444
  Rosmini-Serbati on, 8:503
  Rousseau on, 7:370–371, 8:510–511
  Russell on, 8:538–539
  in self-cultivation in Confucianism, 2:177–179
  in 17th-century method of inquiry, 1:443

social competence *vs.* personal culture in, 9:198
social concerns and, 1:236
social development and, 7:372–373
as social values education, 2:231
society as product of, 7:370
sophistry in, 7:365
soul and, 7:366
Spranger on, 9:199
Stein on, 9:240
in Stoicism, 7:367
in supernaturalism, 7:379
testimony and, 7:357
testing in, 7:362
Thomasius on, 9:441
trust in, 7:357
truth in, 7:356
understanding in, 7:356–357
unity as goal of, 7:374
in utilitarianism, 7:377
values and, 7:360
veritism in, 7:358
visual, 6:562
Vives on, 9:700
Wayland's (Francis) reforms in, 9:728
of women, 9:838
Zhu Xi on, 9:883
Education of Man, The (Froebel), 3:754, 3:755
Education of the Human Race, The (Lessing), 2:688, 3:246
Education reform
in Bentham, 1:551
Croce work on, 2:599
Educational authority, 7:361–362
Educational method, in Comenius, 2:341
Educational principles, of Froebel, 3:754–755
Educational reform, at all levels, 3:618
Educational theory, in Comte, 2:413
Educational theory and practice, of Froebel, 3:754
Eductions, definition of, 5:545
Edwards, Jonathan, **3:166–170**
on Chubb, 2:253
deism and, 2:684, 2:689
on determinism, 3:9
on heaven and hell, 4:250
Locke and, 5:392
Edwards, Paul
on common consent for God's existence, 2:348
on emotivism, 3:426
on life, meaning and value of, 5:358
paradigm-case argument and, 7:108
parapsychology and, 7:116
Edwards, Ward, 8:614, 9:222
Edwards v. Aquillard, 8:671
Edwardsian solution, 3:696
Eells, Ellery, on causality definition, 2:103
Effect
definition of, 3:24
determinism and, 3:24
differences method of induction in discovering, 6:246
Effect event, 5:71
Effective calculability
Church on, 5:475
Church's thesis and Turing machines, 2:376
computing machines and, 2:402
and feasibility constraints, 2:387
as program in computability theory, 2:374–376
Effective calculable functions
in computability theory, 2:374–376
loop and while programs in computability theory, 2:378–379
Effective history, Gadamer, 4:2
Effective procedure, in computability theory, 2:372
Effectively calculable functions, first-order logic definability and, 2:380
Effectiveness
definition of, 5:541
epistemology of technology and, 7:549
Efficacious idea, 5:666–667
Efficiency
asymptotic, 3:663
definition of, 7:461
in economic theory, 3:448
epistemology of technology and, 7:549
equating information with, 3:662
Kaldor-Hicks, 7:461–462
law and, 7:461–462
liability and, 7:462
Pareto, ethics and, 3:448, 3:449
political, 5:627
Efficiency of activity
based on an awareness, 5:120
Nyaya criterion of truth, 5:119
Efficient causality
and existence of God, Ockham on, 9:781
Ockham on, 9:779–780
Effort, in strict akratic action, 9:730–731
Effort voulu, 5:655–658
Egalitarian social values
as aids in the acquisition of objective knowledge, 3:596
not compromising the objectivity of science, 3:596
Egalitarianism
in Bolzano, 1:646
cosmopolitan, Tan on, 6:488
Descartes's communism and, 2:364–365
of justice in bioethics, 1:603
luck and, 3:335–336
moral cosmopolitanism and, 2:568
Nozick on, 6:668–669
types of, 3:330–332, 3:334–335
See also Equality; Social philosophy
Egalité des hommes et des femmes (Gournay), 4:167
Egipetskii golub' (The Egyptian dove) (Leont'ev), 5:283
Egmont (Goethe), 4:140
Ego
animals' lack of, 5:77
delusions of self-power in, 9:14
embodied self and, 9:260
in Fichte, 1:11
in Freud (Sigmund), 8:146
Freud (Anna) on, 8:106
Galluppi on, 4:14
Hägerström on, 4:205
Husserl on, 7:398
as immanence of consciousness, 8:662
in Indian philosophy, 4:133
in Iqbal's theistic pluralism, 4:744
in Kant, 1:11
Krause on, 5:147
Lacan on, 5:168
Levinas on, 5:304–305
Lichtenberg on, 5:341
Lipps on, 5:363
Mach on, 5:623
in Marías, 5:711
personhood and, 7:238–239
psychology of, 8:107
as pure act, Gentile on, 4:51
reincarnation of, after death, Kozlov on, 5:146
reinstating the concept of, 5:125
resistances of a censoring force in, 3:739
Sartre on, 7:297, 8:604–605
Schelling on, 8:618–619
vs. self, Jung on, 4:857
Stein on, 9:240
Stirner on, 9:250–251

Ego, ***continued***
transcendental, abstraction of, 5:680
unconscious and, 9:572
unity *vs.* psychic events, 1:649
Wahle (Richard) on, 9:720
See also Self
Ego and His Own, The (Stirner), 9:250
Ego and the Mechanisms of Defense (Freud, A.), 8:106
"Ego-centric Predicament, The" (Perry), 7:204
Egocentric predicament, idealism and, 8:261–262
Egocentrism
in Marcel, 5:702
in new realism, 6:586–587
Egoism
as common-sense ethical method, 9:22
Dostoevsky on, 3:99–100, 3:101
of eudaimonism, 9:383
first-person, 3:362
general, 3:362
Geulincx on, 4:78
in Haeckel's ethics, 4:204
individual profit-seeking as, 1:777
Laas on, 5:164
Parfit on, 7:120
psychological
vs. ethical egoism, 3:361
Spinoza on, 9:189
rational, 3:362, 7:120
solipsism and, 9:120–121
speculative, universal idealism as, 4:770–771
in Spinoza's psychology, 9:189
in Stirner's anarchism, 9:250–251
as "union of egoists," 9:251
in Yoga, 6:108
Egoism and altruism, **3:170–175,** 9:23
Egoistic hedonism, Sidgwick on, 3:416–417
Egoistic rationality, 8:253–254
Egoistic utilitarianism, 9:604, 9:605
Egypt
interpretation of hieroglyphs from, 9:338
Sufism in, 9:309
Egyptian magic religion, in Bruno, 1:709–710
Egyptians
in afrocentrism, 1:86
Iamblichus on religion of, 6:551
in Spengler's cultural morphology, 9:166
Ehrenfels, Christian Freiherr von, **3:176–178,** 4:70, 5:156, 8:144
Ehrenfest, Paul, on electrical logic machines, 5:566
Ehrenfest, Tatiana, 4:677
on kinetic equation interpretation, 1:645
on statistical mechanics, 7:538
Ehrlich, Eugen, on law in society, 7:427
Ehrlich, Philip, on hyperreal and surreal number systems, 2:508
Eichler, Margrit, sex- and gender-related guidelines, 3:594
Eichmann, Adolph, evil of, 1:254
Eichmann in Jerusalem: A Report on the Banality of Evil (Arendt), 3:470
Eidetic analysis, 4:683
Eidetic reduction, 8:604, 8:606
Eidologie oder Philosophie als Formerkenntnis (Eidology, or philosophy as knowledge of form) (Geyser), 4:82
Eidolology, 4:323
Eigenfunctions, matter and, 6:62
Eigenstates, 8:206–207
Eigenvalues, 8:206–207
in quantum mechanics, 2:531
18th Brumaire of Louis Bonaparte, The (Marx), 5:731
18th century
materialism in, 6:9–11
women philosophers of, 9:839
18th-century philosophy
Bayle's *Dictionary* and, 1:503–504
beauty in, 1:513–514
Eihei Kōroku (Recorded sayings at Eiheiji Temple) (Dōgen), 3:95
Eihei Shingi (Monastic rules at Eiheiji Temple) (Dōgen), 3:95
Eiheiji temple, 3:96
Eimer, Theodore, Bergson on, 1:569
Eine Bekenntnis in der Judenfrage (Cohen), 2:304
Eine Untersuchung über den Staat (Stein), 9:240
Einführung in die Philosophie (Stein), 9:239–240
Einführung in die Philosophie der reinen Erfahrung (Petzoldt), 7:269
Einfülhlung, 3:750
Einheitswissenschaft (monograph series), 5:525
Einige Bermerkungen zu Jakobis Prüfung der Mendelssohnschen Morgenstunden (Kant), 7:101
Einleitung in die Geisteswissenschaften (Dilthey), 4:37
Einleitung in die Mythologie (Schelling), 8:621
Einleitung in die Philosophie (Paulsen), 7:148
Einleitung in die Psychologie (Natorp), 6:543
Einleitung zu dem Entwulf eines Systems der Naturphilosophie oder über den Begriff der spekulativen Physik (Schelling), 3:230, 8:619
Einstein, Albert, **3:178–182**
on atomic bomb, 8:667
on causality in quantum theory, 2:105
classical physics and, 6:62
Copenhagen interpretation and, 2:530
deductive-nomological model in evaluating, 8:694
on evolution of physical systems and chance, 2:126–127
on film, 7:384
in Gödel, 4:118
gravitation in, 7:476
hole argument of, 3:160, 3:180, 3:181
on Mach, 5:623
on matter as system of interrelated events, 4:745
methodology of, 8:684
Nazis and, 7:578
on neighborhood-locality, 6:639
philosophy of physics, 3:179–181
philosophy of science, 3:181–182
and philosophy of space-time, 3:159
on physics, 4:62–63
Planck and, 5:524
on quantum mechanics, 6:640, 6:641
quantum theory and, 2:643–644, 3:178, 3:180–181
realism and, 3:181–182, 7:579
Tagore and, 9:363
thought experiments, use of by, 9:452, 9:453–454
on time, 7:476
on wave function completeness, 8:209–210
Einstein equation, Friedman's solution to, 9:478
Einstein field equations, in cosmology research, 2:565
Einstein-Bose statistics, 3:178
Einstein-Podolsky-Rosen analysis
Bohm on, 1:630
Bohr on, 1:636
of chance and determinism in quantum theory, 2:126

common cause principle and, 2:343
of entropy and information in physical states, 2:105
experiment, description of, 1:540–541
impossibility proof assumptions in, 1:542
prediction *vs.* results in, 1:541–542
and quantum theory, 1:638–639, 2:126
quantum theory completeness and causality in, 1:638–639
Einstein-Podolsky-Rosen argument, 8:198–199, 8:215
Einstein's equivalence principle, conventionalism and, 2:523
Einstein's general field equations, as sources of theoretical ideas in cosmology, 2:561
Einzig möglicher Beweisgrund zu einer Demonstration des Daseins Gottes, Der (The only possible ground for a demonstration of God's existence) (Kant), 4:770
Einzige und sein Eigentum, Der (Stirner), 9:250
Eisenstein, Sergei
on film, 7:381
on *Laokoon,* 7:381–382
Eisler, Hans, Adorno and, 1:26
Eisler, Rudolf
on arguments for God's existence, 2:344
on panpsychism, 7:85
Either/Or: A Fragment of Life (Kierkegaard), 5:63–64, 7:522
Ekigaku kaibutsu (The learning of the book of changes on the discovery of things) (Minagawa), 6:253
Ekman, Paul, on emotions, 3:201
Ekpyrosis, Justin Martyr on, 7:142
El Comulgatorio (Gracián), 4:168
El criticón (Gracián), 4:168
El discreto (Gracián), 4:168
El Greco, 1:310
El héroe (Gracián), 4:168
El Oráculo manual (Gracián), 4:168
El político (Gracián), 4:168
Elaborated induction, 4:635
Élan vital, 2:695, 3:233
Elanchus, 3:52
E-languages, Chomsky on, 5:190
Elbow Room: The Varieties of Free Will Worth Wanting (Dennett), 2:711
Eleatic principle, 6:180, 7:22
"Eleatic Questions" (Owen), 7:65
Eleatics
atomism and, 5:299
Diogenes Laertius on, 3:88
Melissus of Samos, 6:120–121
one/many and, 4:312
pantheism and, 7:94
Parmenides of Elea and, 7:122
Plato and, 3:283
in pre-Socratic philosophy, 7:761–762
skepticism of, 9:48
Eleazar of Worms, 5:3
Election (religious doctrine), in Arminianism, 1:285
Elections, act utilitarians and, 9:608
Elective Affinities (Goethe), 5:588
Electra argument, 6:110, 6:111
Electra complex, 8:146
Electrical field, in unified field theory, 9:741
Electricity, Franklin's laws on, 3:720
Electrodynamics
Ampère in, 1:137–138
atomism and, 1:388
temporal direction and, 9:470
Electrolytic decomposition, Faraday's laws of, 3:550
Electromagnetic concept of mass, 6:4–5
Electromagnetic field theory
mass in, 6:5
of Maxwell, 3:551
Electromagnetic fields
energy theory and, 3:232–233, 3:235–236
Maxwell's concept of, 6:68–69
Electromagnetic force, 9:267
Electromagnetic induction
discovered by Faraday, 3:550
law of, 3:551
Electromagnetic theory of matter, 3:235–236, 6:61–62
Electronic Computer Project, memory in computing machines and, 2:406
Electronic digital machines, computing machine realization and, 2:405
Electronic Discrete Variable Calculator, 2:405
Electronic materialism, 6:6
Electrons
in chemistry and physics, 2:142
interference effects for, 5:695–696, 8:202–205
mass of, 6:4–5
Elegance, as aesthetic quality, 1:40
Elegant and Learned Discourse of the Light of Nature, An (Culverwell), 2:612
Elegantiae Linguae Latinae (Elegancies of the Latin language) (Valla), 9:636
Élémens d'idéologie (Destutt de Tracy), 8:791
Element(s)
definition of, 5:541
material, and sense, 5:118
Elementa Artis Logico-criticae (Genovesi), 4:48
Elementa juris naturalis (Elements of natural law) (Leibniz), 5:251
on evil, 5:263
on knowledge, 5:261
on mind, 5:258
on substance, 5:267
Elementa Metaphysicae Mathematicum in Modum Adornata (Genovesi), 4:48
Elementa Philosophiae Sectio Prima: De Corpore (Hobbes), 8:773
Elementa Philosophica (Johnson, Samuel), 4:851
Elementa Physicae (Mussenbroek), 4:48
Elementae Philosophiae Practica (Budde), 1:721
Elementarism, 9:244
Elementary embeddings, in model theory, 6:309–310
Elementary Lessons in Formal Logic (Jevons), 5:439
Elementary Lessons in Logic (Jevons), 4:807
Elementary Logic (Mates), 5:511
Elementary number theory, definition of, 5:541
Elementary particle theory, 4:298–299
Elementary particles
mass of, 6:4–5
in unified field theory, 9:741
Elementary propositions
definition of, 5:553
truth-functions of, 9:806–807
Wittgenstein on, 9:806
See also Basic statements
Elementary Structures of Kinship (Levi-Strauss), Lacan and, 5:168
Elemente der Psychophysik (Fechner), 3:555
Elementi di calcolo geometrico (Peano), 7:158
Elementi di economia pubblica (Beccaria), 1:518
Elementi di filosofia (Galluppi), 4:14
Elementi di scienza politica (Mosca), 6:406–407

Elements
in Aristotelian cosmology, 9:147
classes of, in first-order model theory, 6:304–305
in compounds, Zabarella on, 9:866
in Empedocles, 7:762
ontological status of chemical, 2:141
stylistic, 1:332
Elements (Euclid), 2:491–492, 2:499, 4:54, 4:55
axioms, 4:123
on compounding ratios, 9:342
number in, 6:670
Proclus and, 7:609, 8:41
Éléments de la philosophie de Newton (Voltaire), 9:708, 9:710
Éléments de physiologie (Diderot), 3:75
Elements of Law (Hobbes), 7:423
Elements of Logic (Whately), 9:742
Elements of matter, Boyle's corpuscular theory advocacy, 1:674
Elements of Metaphysics (Taylor), 2:556, 9:373
Elements of Moral Science, The (Wayland), 9:728
Elements of Natural Law (Elementa juris naturalis) (Leibniz), 5:251
on evil, 5:263
on knowledge, 5:261
on mind, 5:258
on substance, 5:267
Elements of Philosophy (Hobbes), 7:721
Elements of Physiology (Haller), 3:74
Elements of Physiophilosophy (Lehrbuch der Naturphilosophie) (Oken), 7:11
Elements of Political Economy (Mill), 6:218
Elements of Politics, The (Sidgwick), 9:26
Elements of the Philosophy of the Human Mind (Stewart), 9:247
Elements of Theology (Proclus), 1:788, 5:333–334, 6:547, 6:5527:609, 8:41–43
Elements of Rhetoric (Whately), 9:743
Elementy logiki matematycznej (Elements of mathematical logic) (Łukasiewicz), 5:608
Elenchus, 9:702, 9:855
Eleusinian mysteries, 7:488
Eleusis, Orphism and, 7:43
Eliade, Mircea, on eternal return doctrine, 3:355
Elias, in Neoplatonism, 6:555
Eliminative induction, as method in Bacon (Francis), 1:446–450
Eliminative materialism, **3:182–184**
in behaviorism, 1:520
on emotions, 3:201
Epicurus and, 3:269
on intentionality, 4:711
physicalism and, 7:553
Eliminative methods
determinism and, 6:245
induction and, 6:245
recursive axiomatization and, 2:583
Eliminative process, in cosmological models, 2:560
Eliminativism, 8:195
antirealism of, 6:172
as approach to subjectivity, 9:293
colors and, 2:333
on mind-body problem, 6:262
nature laws and, 5:227, 5:228, 5:229
properties in, 8:66
on psychological explanations of behavior, 6:141
as self-refuting or pragmatically incoherent, 3:679
Eliminativist particularism, predicate nominalism as, 6:174–175
Eliminativists, challenge of, 3:678–679
Eliminativist-vindicationist debate, 3:678
Eliot, Charles W., 4:775
Eliot, George, **3:184–185**
Eliot, Thomas Stearns, **3:185–187**, 9:507
Elisabeth, Princess of Bohemia, **3:187–188**
Conway and, 9:838
Descartes and, 2:752, 5:373
feminist attention to the philosophy of, 3:569
on mental causation, 6:132
Elisabeth of the Palatine, 3:569
Elites, in Condorcet, 2:431
Elizaeus, 7:630
Ellenberger, Henri, 3:738
Ellinskaia religiia stradaiushchego boga (The Hellenic religion of the suffering God) (Ivanov), 4:766
Ellipticality, of statements, 6:636
Ellis, Brian, 6:90
Elliston, Frederick, 7:521
Ellsberg, Daniel, on decision theory, 2:659–660
Ellul, Jacques, 9:78
on philosophy of technology, 7:544
on technology, 7:547–548
Elminativist logic, applied to reject a hypothesis, 3:666
Eloges (Fontenelle), 3:682–683
Elster, Jon
on causality in social sciences, 7:535
on creativity and rule constraints, 2:590
on emotions, 3:202
Elucidation, meaning and metalanguage in Carnap as, 2:43
Emanation, doctrine of
in al-Kindī, 4:755
in Avicenna's theory of essence and existence, 4:757
Hegel on, 4:108
of Ibn Da'ud, 4:817
in Islamic philosophy, 4:756
in Israeli, 4:765
Leibniz on, 5:256–257, 5:259, 5:262, 5:267, 5:271
in Neoplatonism, 2:644
Plotinus on, 4:108
Spinoza on, 4:108
Emanationism, **3:188–190**
in al-Kindī, 4:755
in Avicenna's theory of essence and existence, 4:757
Hegel on, 4:108
of Ibn Da'ud, 4:817
in Islamic philosophy, 4:756
in Israeli, 4:765
Leibniz on, 5:256–259, 5:262, 5:267, 5:271
in Neoplatonism, 2:644
Plotinus on, 4:108
in realm of intelligibles, 7:634–635
Spinoza on, 4:108
in Swedenborg's series and degrees, 9:337
Emanations
concept of, 5:2
doctrine of the ten, 5:3
Emancipation, in Condorcet, 2:432
Emancipatory critique, 4:573
Embeddings, elementary, in model theory, 6:309–310
Embodied appraisal theory of emotions, 3:199
Embodied eye, 9:692
Embodied self, Stout on, 9:259–260
Embodiment theory of expression, 1:305–306
Embodiment *vs.* computation, 8:155
Embryogenetic theory, Driesch on, 3:110–111, 3:112
Embryology, in developmental growth as biological system, 1:594

Emergence, **3:190–194**
asymptotic, 3:193
conceptual, 3:190–191, 3:193
Epicurus and, 3:269
epistemological, 3:190–193
Morgan (C. Lloyd) and, 6:403
ontological, 3:190–193
sociality in, 6:82
weak, 3:193
Wright (Chauncey) and, 9:846
"Emergence" (Pepper), 3:192
Emergence theories, supervenience and, 6:173
Emergent evolution, in Morgan (C. Lloyd), 6:402–403
Emergent materialism, 6:261
Emergentism, 6:648–649, 7:469
See also Emergence
Emergentists, new fundamental force/interaction, 3:691
Emergents
in Alexander, 1:108
Morgan (C. Lloyd) on, 6:402
Emerson, Ralph Waldo, **3:194–197**
on Christianity, 6:574
Dewey on, 6:575
ethics of, 3:415, 6:574
as leader of New England transcendentalism, 6:572
Nietzsche and, 6:575
Parker (T.) and, 7:121, 7:122
Sufism and, 9:311
Thoreau and, 9:450
on transcendentalism, 6:573
Émile (Rousseau), 2:366, 7:522, 9:839
Émile, ou de l'éducation, 2:687–688
education in, 7:370
Enlightenment and, 3:244
on evil, 3:470
Maine de Biran and, 5:656
Eminence, and existence of God, Henry of Ghent on, 3:135–136
Emoter, Charland (Louis) on, 3:201
Emotion(s), **3:197–203**
in aesthetic experience, 1:32–33
in African philosophy, 1:84
in animals, 1:201
apperception and, 1:234
Aquinas on, 9:429
Aristotle on, 1:188, 3:198
art as expression of, 1:54–55, 1:64–65, 1:76–77, 1:79–80, 1:298, 1:340
and assent, 5:98
Bachelard on, 1:440
beauty and, 1:513
in behaviorism, 8:143
Brentano on, 3:421
in Buddhism, 5:328
in Chinese religion, 2:224
in cognitive science, 2:297
cognitivism on, 3:198–200
in Confucianism, 2:172
correct and incorrect, 6:117
Croce on, 2:601
Dewey on, 1:64
of dread as experience of nothing, 1:530
empathy and, 9:344–345
energy and, equality of, 9:752
in ethical thought. *See* Emotivism
ethics and
deontology *vs.* utilitarianism and, 9:607
Westermarck on, 9:739–740
and facial expression, 9:39–40
in faith, 1:506
as false judgments recently formed, 2:252
fiction and, 1:68
fictional, paradox of, 4:601, 5:367–368
film and, 7:384
Hélvetius on, 4:306
Holbach on, 6:10
imaginary occurrence of, 1:306
instrumentality of, 5:716
vs. intelligence, 1:349
interactive, 3:202
in Islamic aesthetics, 1:436
katharsis of, in tragedy, 1:44
Krueger on, 5:156
Li Ao on, 5:316
Marty on, 5:729
in materialism, 6:12, 6:15–16
vs. mood, 3:199, 7:468
moral, 5:138, 9:125
moral concepts and, 9:739–740
music and, 1:303, 6:436–437
neurochemistry of, 6:12
Nussbaum on, 6:680
painful
pleasure from, 1:44
in psychoanalysis, 8:109–110
phenomenological justification of, 2:5
Philodemus on, 7:302–303
Plato on, 9:794
predication of, without body, 1:370–371
propositional nature of, 3:199–200, 5:89
rational decision-making and, 3:200–201
regulation of, 3:200–202
Scheler on, 3:422
scientific views on, 3:198–201
in Shintō, 4:796–797
in speech, 2:209
Spinoza on, 8:126–127
sublimity and, 9:294
taste and, 1:128
tragedy and, 9:521–525
valence of, 3:200
Windelband on, 9:791
Wollheim on, 9:836
Xunzi on, 2:234
See also Feeling
Emotion [term], history of, 3:197–198
Emotional distress, euthanasia and, 6:94
Emotional labor, attention to, 3:579
Emotional presentation, 6:117
Emotional reality, Johnson (Alexander Bryan) on, 4:847–848
Emotionalist theories of art, 3:125
Emotionism, Krueger on, 5:156
Emotions and the Will, The (Bain), 1:462, 5:98
Emotive theory of ethics, **3:203–208,** 3:425–426
Emotivism, **3:203–208**
Ayer on, 1:65
case for, 3:205
ethical language in, 9:245
Foot on, 6:159
Geach on, 6:652–653
history and development of, 3:204–205
in metaethics, 6:157
vs. nihilism, 6:618–619
objections to, 3:205–207
open question argument and, 6:156
vs. subjectivism, 3:204
Empathy, 3:750
aesthetic, Caso on, 2:65
friendship and, 3:749–750
Lipps on, 5:363
in simulation theory, 9:36
Stein on, 9:239
See also Sympathy, and empathy
Empedocles, **3:208–213**
atomism and, 5:299
on cosmos, 2:571
Diogenes Laertius on, 3:88
on eternal return doctrine, 3:352–353
on Four elements doctrine, 3:208–210
Freud and, 5:642
Hermarchus of Mytilene on, 3:263
on love, 5:584
Lucretius and, 5:598–599

Empedocles, ***continued***
on material world, 7:126
materialism of, 6:7–8
on mechanical process of perception, 8:823–824
Orphic influence on, 7:43
panpsychism and, 7:83, 7:89
Parmenides of Elea and, 7:122
philosophy of love *(philia)* and strife *(neikos)*, 3:686
pluralism of, 1:249
poetry of, 7:762–763
in pre-Socratic philosophy, 7:762–763
psychotherapeutics of, 3:395
Simplicius on, 9:35
Strasburg papyrus of, 3:211–212
writing style of, 4:176
Emperor's New Mind (Penrose), 2:395
Empirical awarenesses, having wholes *(avayavin)* and universals *(jati)*, 5:119
Empirical axioms, 6:89
Empirical belief, fallibilism about, 5:96
Empirical differences, in evaluative predicate application, 4:862
Empirical epistemology, of Choi Hangi, 5:140
Empirical equivalence, 9:576–578
Empirical evidence, building aesthetic theory on a foundation of, 3:556
Empirical generalizations, about intentional acts, 7:295
Empirical inquiries, use of ideas to order, 5:26
Empirical intuition, 3:752
Empirical intuitionalism, of Reid, 3:689
Empirical justification, fallible character of, 5:80
Empirical knowledge, Lewis (C. I.) on, 5:308–309
Empirical laws
vs. logical rules, 7:280–281
in science, 6:224
Empirical Logic (Venn), 9:658
Empirical metaphysics, 1:108–110
Empirical method
in Comenius, 2:341
use by Butler (Joseph), 1:781
Empirical objects, finite independent properties of, 5:56
Empirical phenomena
vs. a priori, in metaphysics, 6:202
as first principles, 1:447
as validation of inductive method, 1:447
Empirical phenomena statements, 7:295–296
Empirical predicates, 4:862, 9:660
Empirical propositions, and doubt, 3:103
Empirical psychological research, combined with philosophical, 3:675
Empirical psychological theory, 3:758
Empirical psychology, 8:133–134
Empirical Psychology (Wolff), 9:824
Empirical psychovitalism, 9:281
Empirical rationality, 4:495–496
Empirical realism, Kant's commitment to, 5:22
Empirical reasoning, nonrational basis of, 4:495–496
Empirical rules, operation of, 5:17
Empirical stance, 9:645
Empirical statements
basic statements as, 1:484
coherence truth theory and, 2:310
definition of, 7:294–295
Malcolm on, 2:359
phenomenology and, 7:279–285, 7:294
truth in, 7:295–296
Empirical supporting evidence, providing for the *a priori*, 5:85
Empirical thinking, rules of, 5:16
Empirical thought, postulates of, 5:20
Empirical values, in cosmological models, 2:560
Empirical world. *See* Sensory world
Empirically adequate theory, 5:102
Empiricism, **3:213–221**
on *a priori* concepts, 1:241–242
in accounts of sublime, 9:293
in aesthetics, 1:50–52, 1:60
American rejection of, 7:122
Anderson (John) and, 1:198
Aquinas and, 3:214–216, 3:221, 3:289–290, 9:427
Aristotelian, in medieval philosophy, 6:100–105
Ayer and, 1:436
Bachelard and, 1:440
Bacon on, Jefferson influenced by, 4:805
beauty in, 1:74
Berkeley and, 3:302
Blanshard on, 4:559
Bradley on, 1:676–677
British, James on, 4:784
Broad on, 1:697
in Buddhism, 2:164, 6:256
as Christian pessimism in politics, 1:771
concepts and, 2:417–418
and conceptualism, 7:722
consciousness of time and, 9:485–487
constructive, 8:692–693
Cousin on, 2:579
critique of, 3:220–221
Dewey and, 3:45
Diderot on, 3:72–73
discrediting of, 4:559
Edwards (Jonathan) and, 3:167
Encyclopédie and, 3:222
epistemology and, 3:275, 3:283
experience in, 9:414
externalized, 8:220
Galen and, 4:5
Garrigou-Lagrange on, 4:23
Gödel on, 4:117
Goldman on, 4:147
in Greek philosophy, 3:215–216
Green on, 4:178
Hellenistic, 4:302
Helmholtz and, 4:303–304
on human nature, 4:483
of Hume, 7:493
on immediate experience, 3:516
inductive, 5:82
on innate ideas, 8:242–243
intentionality and, 7:291–292
introspection in, 8:786
in James's psychology, 4:779, 9:483
Kant on, 8:134
in knowledge, Haeckel on, 4:202–203
Landgrebe on, 5:184
in late 19th-century science, 1:643
of legal philosophy, 7:443
Locke and, 5:376, 6:191, 7:492–493
logical, naturalism of science and, 6:501, 6:503
on loyalty, 5:595
of Mach, 5:624–625
of Maimon, 5:645
of Marsilius of Inghen, 5:721
of mathematics, 6:677
matter as the sole reality, 3:610
meaning in, 1:149
in measurement and object independence, 1:638
medical, 4:302
metaphysics and, 6:204
of Mill (James), 6:219
of Mill (John Stuart), 6:222–226
on moral judgments, 4:749
of Nagel (Ernest), 6:473
natural law and, 7:454
number and conventionalism in, 6:675
of Ockham, 9:772
optimism/pessimism and, 7:245
Ortega y Gasset on, 7:47
panpsychism and, 7:92

paradigm-case argument and, 7:107
Peripatetics and, 7:202
personalism and, 7:235
in phenomena and first principles, 1:447
phenomenalism and, 7:282, 7:285, 7:288–289, 7:294–295
philosophers' view of, 3:515
physical probability and, 8:32
Popper on, 5:625
on poverty-of-stimulus argument, 4:694
pragmatism as extension of, 4:783
prominence of, 7:494–495
of psychoanalysis, 8:110
quantum physics and, 6:502
of Quine, 8:220, 8:221
radical behaviorism and, 1:520
rational experimentation and, 1:590
vs. rationalism, 8:240
vs. realism, 6:502, 8:692–693
reductive, 8:689
in Regius's Cartesianism, 2:55
Reichenbach on, 8:170
reincarnation and, 8:332–333
religion and, 7:478
religious experience and, 8:420
in religious philosophy, 7:492–493
religious response to, 7:495–496
Russell on, 3:316
Salmon on, 8:593
and scientific theory, 7:519
scientific thought of, Mach and, 8:827
in Sellars (Wilfrid), 8:733
sensationalism and, 8:823, 8:825
sensationism and, 8:137
on sensory experience, 4:686–687
Sidgwick rejection of, 9:23
and skepticism, 3:215, 5:645
in Smart, 9:65
on sociology of knowledge, 9:101
in Spaventa's "circulation of Italian philosophy," 9:160
of Stace, 9:199–201
in Stout, 9:259
and Swedenborg, 9:336
in symbolic poetry, 1:610
in syntactic view of theories, 9:413
synthetic *a priori* truth in, 1:245
in temporal concepts, 9:483
of Tennant, 9:392
in 20th century, 3:219–221
theoretical method and, 7:331
theory of ideas in, 4:566
of thought experiments, 9:452, 9:455
threat of, to human dignity, 8:630
transcendental, of Deleuze, 2:694
in understanding disease, Galen on, 4:5
of unobservable phenomena, 8:110
of Varisco, 9:647
verifiability principle and, 9:659
view of science, 3:128
of Yin Haiguang, 2:181
See also British empiricism
Empiricism and Subjectivity (Deleuze), 2:693, 2:694
"Empiricism and the Philosophy of Mind" (Sellars, Wilfrid), 8:733
Empiricism, Semantics, and Ontology (Carnap), 2:44
Empiricist, Kepler as, 5:51
Empiricist epistemology, of Mill (John Stuart), 6:222
Empiricist language, sentences translatable to, 9:662–663
Empiricist theory, feminist reconceptualization of the agents of inquiry as communities, 3:593
Empirico-transcendental doublet, 3:700
Empiriocriticism, 3:64, 7:715–716
Employment, Mandeville on, 5:681
Employment contracts, engineering ethics and, 3:241
Empowering norms, of Kelsen, 5:49
Empowerment
in sacred-human interactions, 2:225
tradition in conservatism and, 2:469
of women, 3:584
Emptiness
as absence of self-being, 1:738
Asaṅga, 1:750–751
as being and nonbeing in subject predicate relations, 2:162
in Buddhism, 1:731–732, 1:738–744, 2:154, 2:161–164, 2:167, 2:221, 5:328–329
in Chan Buddhism, 2:167
conventional *vs.* ultimate truth and, 1:742–743
in Dge-lugs Mādhyamika, 1:732
doctrine of, 5:134–135
in Hegel, 1:530
in Huayan Buddhism, 1:738–739
in Japanese philosophy, 4:797
as knowledge, 2:162
in Mādhyamika doctrine, 1:731, 1:740–744
meditative approach to, 1:738–739
as mystical silence, 1:743
Nāgārjuna, 6:469–471
of phenomenal and nonlinguistic entities, 1:750–751
in Sanlun Buddhism, 2:161–163
in Taintai Buddhism, 2:164
in Xunzi, 2:216
in Yogācāra Buddhism, 1:746, 1:749–752
Empty set, definition of, 5:550
Empty theory, consequence of, 3:658
Emunah, 3:536
En découvrant l'existence avec Husserl et Heidegger (Levinas), 5:304
En torno a Galileo (Ortega y Gasset), 7:46
Enarratio in Summam Theologiae Divi Thomae (Toletus), 9:511
Enchiridion (Augustine), influences on, 3:401
Enchiridion (Epictetus), 9:34, 9:254
Enchiridion Militis Christiani (Handbook of a Christian soldier) (Erasmus), 3:337
Encoding
Gödel, 9:552
in Turing, 9:552
in Zalta, 6:636
Encomium Moriae (Erasmus), Lucian of Samosata and, 5:597
Encomium of Helen (Gorgias of Leontini), 1:187, 4:163
Encompassing *(das Umgreifende),* in Jaspers, 4:802
Encounter, in Heidegger, 4:296
Encounter of Man and Nature: The Spiritual Crisis of Modern Man, The (Nasr), 6:480
Encounters and Reflections: Art in the Historical Present (Danto), 2:628
Encyclopaedia Britannica, 1:503–504, 6:218
Encyclopaedia Metropolitana, contributors to, 2:710
Encyclopaedia of the Social Sciences, Lovejoy and, 5:592
Encyclopedia (Alsted), 5:252
Encyclopedia (Hegel), 4:264–265
on absolute idealism, 4:557
Engels and, 3:57–61
Marx and, 3:57
on natural science, 3:58
Encyclopedia (Leibniz), 5:442
Encyclopedia of Philosophy (Technoligia sive Technometria) (Johnson, Samuel), 4:851

Encyclopedias. *See Encyclopédie*
Encyclopedias, philosophical, 10:75–139
Encyclopedic movement, French clandestine literature and, 2:263
Encyclopédie, 2:420, 2:610, **3:221–225**
on aesthetics, 3:76, 3:225
Alembert and, 1:106
Enlightenment and, 3:244
on grammarian philosophy, 8:790
importance of, 3:71
on *philosophe,* 3:244
on politics, 3:77
and socialism, 9:87
Voltaire and, 9:709
Encyclopédie méthodique (Panckoucke), 6:476
Encyclopedism, Neurath and, 6:562
Encyclopedists, Condorcet as, 2:430
End, in postmodernism, 6:318
End of History (Fukuyama), 2:181, 7:391
End of Ideology: On the Exhaustion of Political Ideas in the Fifties (Bell), 4:574
Enden, Francis van den, 9:170
Enderton-Walkoe theorem, 8:197–198
Endliches und ewiges Sein (Stein), 9:240
Endowment effect, 9:39
Endurantism, persistence and, 7:210, 7:212
Enduring objects, 7:210–211, 9:750
Energetic personalism, 8:231
Energetics, Heom on, 3:233
Energetism, 7:49–50. *See also* Ostwald, Wilhelm
Energy(ies), **3:225–237**
accidental, 3:226
atomic stability and excitability as, 1:637
causal, 3:226
in classical mechanics, 2:282
in classical physics, 3:236–237, 6:61
connection with forces, 3:691
conservation of
as analytic statement, 8:641–642
in Descartes, 8:124
discovery of, 3:226, 3:229, 3:230–232, 3:236
in special relativity, 3:237
as term, 3:232
conversion processes, 3:229
definition of, 3:225–226
emotion and, equality of, 9:752
fields of, 3:232–233, 3:235–236
and force, 3:226–227
formal, 3:226
Hamiltonian theory on energy conservation and, 2:464
heat, 3:229
kinetic, 3:236
Aristotle on, 3:227
conservation of, 3:228
definition of, 3:226
as term, 3:231–232
mass and, 6:4
vs. matter, 6:62–63
and mechanical work, 3:227–228
in modern physics, 3:237
modern view of, 3:232–234
in natural philosophy, 6:61
in nonphysical forces *vs.* closed physical causality, 2:90–91
philosophical view of, 3:226
Planck on, 1:388
potential, 3:236
debate on, 3:232
definition of, 3:226
transformation of, 3:228–229
qualities in nature, 1:623
relational, 3:226
in relativity theory, 3:237
substantial, 3:226
types of, 3:226
universal, unity of, 3:607
Vasconcelos on, 9:648
Energy [concept], history of, 3:226–234
Energy and radiation, equipartition of, 4:804
Energy conservation, law of, in classical mechanics, 2:281
Energy-based formulations, in physics, 3:690
Energy-based theories, concepts and operative principles of, 3:690
Enforcement of Morals, The (Devlin), 7:137
Enforcers, conscience and, 2:445
Engagement, in Heidegger, 4:296
Engelmann, Paul, 9:802
Engels, Friedrich, **3:237–239**
aesthetics in, 1:59
on determinism, 3:37
dialectical materialism and, 3:57–63
Diderot and, 3:77
Dühring and, 3:131
on equality, 9:73
Feuerbach criticized by, 3:612
Fourier's criticism appreciated by, 3:707
Hegel and, 3:57–63
historical materialism and, 3:56
Kautsky and, 5:47
Labriola and, 5:165
Lavrov and, 5:218
on laws of thought, 5:232–233
Lenin and, 3:64, 3:65, 5:279–280
Lukács and, 5:603
Marx and, 3:57
Marxism and, 5:737
Marxist materialism and, 3:58–60
on negation of the negation, 3:62–63
philosophical legacy of, 3:63
philosophy of nature, 3:57–61
philosophy of sex and, 7:522
Plekhanov on, 7:626
on progress, 3:62
on revolution, 3:61–62
on state suppression of conflict, 9:207
on utopian and nihilistic communism, 2:361
Enghaus, Christine, 4:253
Engineering
history of, 3:239
social, law and, 7:428
Engineering ethics, **3:239–242**, 7:546
Engineering model of medical ethics, 6:93
Engineering philosophy of technology, 7:543
Engineering work, on using fuzzy logic, 3:766
England
absolute idealism in, 4:558
civil war in, 1:176, 1:177
concept of ideas in, 4:566
historicism in, 4:392
Jews readmitted to, 6:128
jurisprudence in, 4:389
measurement system in, 6:91
Protestantism in, 9:248–249
Schelling's influence in, 8:622
skepticism in, 9:54
social contract in, 9:81
socinianism in, 9:99
Spinoza's influence in, 9:194–195
study of philosophy in, 4:559
suppression of heterodoxy in, 2:682–685, 2:690
Taine's sympathy for, 9:364
universal grammar in, 8:791
war with Dutch Republic, 9:183
Englemeier, Peter, on philosophy of technology, 7:543
English
necessary truth in, 3:644
translating between first-order logic and, 3:644–647
English Academy, The (Newton), 5:438

English argument(s), changing to be valid, 3:641, 3:644
English liberalism, 5:319–320
English (Penny) Cyclopedia, contributors to, 2:709
English radicalism, in historiography, 1:718
English sentences, translating into first-order sentences, 3:646–647
English Traits (Emerson), 3:195, 3:197
Enlightened despotism, Voltaire on, 9:712
Enlightenment, **3:242–248**
- Adorno on, 1:69
- Aristotelianism in, 5:637
- artificial languages in, 8:779
- in Buddhism, 5:328, 6:621
- in Chan Buddhism, 2:166–168
- in Confucianism, 2:168
- in crisis of skepticism, 9:55
- on death, 2:652
- definition of, 3:242, 3:244–245
- Diderot and, 3:71
- Dōgen on, 3:95–96
- DuBos and, 3:123
- *Encyclopédie* and, 3:221–222
- epistemology of, 8:772
- Erasmus and, 3:340
- French
  - aesthetics in, 1:49–50
  - on determinism, 3:16
  - Godwin and, 1:177
  - in Germany, 2:687, 2:688–689, 6:481
- history of concept, 3:242–243
- on human nature, Schopenhauer's objections to, 8:653
- Islamic, **3:248–249**, 4:541
- Jewish, 3:246, **3:249–250**
- Russian, 8:566–567
- Lessing and, 5:294
- Locke and, 5:395, 8:777
- logic of, 8:772
- in Mahayana Buddhism, 2:219
- Meslier and, 6:155
- nirvāṇa as, 6:621
- Novalis on, 6:667
- optimism/pessimism during, 7:248–249
- Pannenberg and, 7:80
- peace proposals and, 7:155
- philosophy of history in, 7:389
- philosophy's role in, 3:243–245
- political philosophy in, 7:664–666
- political views in, 3:247
- positivism and, 7:711
- projects and agendas of, 3:245–246
- rationalism in, 4:746–747, 8:239–240
- Reinhold on, 8:334
- Romanticism and, 8:486–487
- Saint-Simon on, 8:589
- in Sanlun Buddhism, 2:162
- semantics of, 8:772, 8:775, 8:777
- sin, representation of, Green on, 4:179
- Socrates and, 9:113
- Spinoza and, 5:296
- on Strato's naturalistic atheism, 9:262
- on suicide, 9:319
- universal grammar in, 8:790–791
- wisdom in Sengzhao, 2:219
- Wolff in, 9:825, 9:829–830
- in Xunzi, 2:216
- in Yogācāra Buddhism, 1:748

Enlightenment: An Interpretation, The (Gay), 3:243
Enlightenment philosophy, Bayle in, 1:502–507
Enneads (Plotinus), 1:45–46, 1:190, 1:512, 3:400, 4:564, 5:641, 6:550, 7:271, 7:608
Ennius, Lucretius and, 5:600
Enquiry (Hume), on existence of God, 4:615
Enquiry concerning Human Understanding, An (Hume), 2:356, 4:488–489
- on altruism and self-interest, 3:173
- on knowledge, 3:218
- on miracles, 6:266–267
- on necessary connection, 4:637
- on outward impressions, 5:657
- on responsibility, 8:164

Enquiry concerning Political Justice (Godwin), 1:177, 4:136
Enquiry concerning the Principles of Morals, An (Hume), 4:488–489
- ethics in, 3:408
- outward impressions in, 5:657

Enquiry concerning the Principles of Natural Knowledge, An (Whitehead), 9:748
Enquiry into Goodness (Sparshott), 3:430
Enquiry into Plants (Theophrastus), 9:411
Enquiry Into the Ground and Foundation of Religion, Wherein is shewn, that Religion is founded in Nature, An (Chubb), 2:684
Enquiry Respecting the Relation to Cause and Effect (Shepherd), 9:10
Ens Astrale, Paracelsus on, 7:104
Ens Naturale, Paracelsus on, 7:104
Ens Seminis, Paracelsus on, 7:104
Ens Spirituale, Paracelsus on, 7:104
Ens Veneni, Paracelsus on, 7:104
Enseignement biblique, L' (periodical), 5:570
Entailment(s), **3:250–254**
- Abelard on, 5:425–426
- between belief and truth, 2:277
- in Bolzano, 1:647
- definition of, 5:541
- of facts, 1:501
- imperfect, 5:426
- in Mohist discourse, 2:212–213
- Philo of Megara on, 7:312
- *vs.* presupposition, 7:770
- supervenience in, 9:328–329

Entanglement
- computation via, 8:200–201
- Einstein on, 3:181
- of quantum states, 8:198–199
- of wave functions, 8:214–215

Entelechy
- Driesch on, 3:111, 3:112, 9:696
- in Leibniz, 8:130

Entheticus de Dogmate Philosophorum (John of Salisbury), 4:843
Enthusiasm, More (Henry) on, 6:396–397
Enthymeme, definition of, 5:542
Enthymemes
- in traditional logic, 5:500
- truncated inference, 5:500

Entity(ies)
- as absence of self-being, 1:738
- abstract. *See* Abstract entities
- actual, 4:627, 9:751
- as adventitious ideas in Cartesian epistemology, 2:56
- in animate-inanimate distinction in Cairns, 2:5
- artistic, nature of, 1:317–318
- in Bilfinger, 1:595
- character of, Whitehead on, 9:751–752
- in constructive empiricism, 8:693
- dispensability of special sciences and, 9:161
- fictitious entities in Bentham, 1:552, 1:553
- hierarchy of, Frege on, 9:555
- in Huayan Buddhism, 1:738–739
- I in relationship to, 1:715
- intrinsic value of, 4:719
- in Mādhyamika doctrine, 1:741–742
- material, Kozlov on, 5:146
- in mathematical theory, 5:465

Entity(ies), ***continued***
in metaphysical realism, 8:688–689
natural, 3:589
in neutral monism, 6:587
ontological status, 2:141, 3:727
as perceived or perceptible, 1:578
as perceptual judgment in Buddhist epistemology, 1:755
as phenomenal and nonlinguistic, 1:750–751
propositions as, 1:146
as real not constructed, 1:740
reduction of
mereological nominalism as, 6:175–176
in metaphysics, 6:172
Russell's theory of, 9:557
Stace on, 9:200
subjects and predicates as existential, 1:561–562
Swineshead on quantitative measure of, 9:342
verification and, 5:527
in Yogācāra Buddhism, 1:749
Entity commitment, Quine on, 6:198
Entity realism, 8:692
Entre nous (Levinas), 5:305
Entretien avec M. de Saci (Pascal), 7:130
Entretiens de Maxime de Thémiste (Bayle), 1:503–507
Entretiens entre d'Alembert et Diderot (Diderot), Spinozism elements in, 9:193
Entretiens sur la philosophie (Rohault), 8:483
Entretiens sur la pluralité des mondes (Fontenelle), 2:56, 3:682
Entrèves, A. Passerin, 2:626
Entropy
in black holes, 9:269
Boltzmann on, 1:221
in energetism, 7:49–50
in equilibrium model of Boltzmann, 1:644
ethics based on, 7:50
as information in physical states, 2:105
introduction of concept, 7:537
kalām argument on God's existence and, 2:555
maximizing (MAXENT), 4:672
minimizing (MINXENT), 4:672
Planck on, 7:578–579
probability and, 1:221
in Shannon's information theory, 4:672, 9:234
temporal, 9:469–470
and time, direction of, 7:537–538, 7:540–543
trace formation and, 9:469
types of, defined, 7:541
use for time directionality, 2:86
See also Statistical mechanics
Entstehung des Historismus, Die (Meinecke), 6:114
Entwurf der nothwendigen Vernunftwahrheiten (Sketch of necessary rational truths) (Crusius), 2:606
Enuma Elish, 7:759
Enumerable set, definition of, 5:542
Environing events, 9:750
Environment
behavior and, 8:142–143
in Condorcet, 2:432
as context in quantum theory, 1:634
geographical *vs.* behavioral, in Gestalt theory, 4:74
historical determinism and, 3:36–37
and history, 1:718–719
holism and property set preexistence as, 1:638
knowledge of, Oman on, 7:14
morality as response to, 9:379
observation and property set preexistence as, 1:638
quantum mechanics and, 5:698
Singer on, 9:42
state sovereignty and, 9:146
Environment of evolutionary adaptedness (EEA), 3:481–482
Environmental aesthetics, **3:254–258**
art in nature, 3:256–257
contemporary debates in, 3:255–256
gardens, 3:257
history of, 3:254–255
Environmental behaviorism, 4:306
Environmental economics, 7:353
Environmental ethics, **3:258–261**
anthropocentric environmentalism, 3:258–259
and death, 2:654
ecofeminism, 3:260–261
engineering ethics and, 3:241
holistic environmentalism, 3:259–260
moral extensionism, 3:259
moral status in, 1:603
Environmental justice, 3:258
Environmental philosophy, 3:259
Environmental racism, 3:258–259
Environmentalism
anthropocentric, 3:258–259
Carson and, 8:667
Hélvetius on, 4:306
holistic, 3:259–260
Marxism and, 5:741
Environmentalists, on technology, 7:544
Epagoge, 3:52, 5:542
Epic state of mind, 3:554
Epicheirema, definition of, 5:542
Epictetus, **3:261–263**
on death, 2:652
ethics, 3:400
on logic, 5:408
Marcus Aurelius and, 5:706–507
patristic philosophy and, 7:142
Socrates and, 9:113
in stoic tradition, 9:254
Epicureanism and the Epicurean School, **3:263–264**
application of science to morals by Beneke, 1:543
astronomy and, 4:301
beauty in, 1:45, 1:189
in Byzantine thought, 1:787
causality in, 1:32
Cyrenaicism and, 3:399
on death, 2:651–652
on determinism, 3:6, 3:10–12, 3:17
ethics, 3:399–400
on friendship, 3:268
of Gassendi, 6:8
in Hellenistic thought, 4:300–301
in hermetic religious philosophy, 1:711
on language, 4:302
on life, 3:399
on matter, 6:59, 4:611
and Meslier, 6:154
music in, 1:45
Philodemus on, 7:301–302
on physical world, 3:10–11
Plutarch of Chaeronea and, 7:649
prolepsis, 8:759
psychology in, 8:120–121
in Renaissance, 8:425
on semantics, 8:758–759
Seneca on, 8:812
on *simulacra,* 4:593
Socrates and, 3:399
Tolstoy on, 5:348
in *Utopia,* 6:399–400
Valla on, 9:635
Epicureans
atomism and, 5:302
Cicero on, 2:258

comparison to Cyrenaics, 2:619, 2:620
concept of human will, 7:305
optimism/pessimism and, 7:247
on phantasia, 7:271
Epicurus, **3:264–270**
atomism and, 3:215, 3:268–270, 5:299, 5:301
on death, 2:651–652, 2:654, 3:266
Democritus and, 3:399
Diogenes Laertius on, 3:88
education in, 7:367
empiricism and, 3:215–216
epistemology of, 3:287–288
ethics, 3:399
on free will, 3:268–269, 3:399
hedonism and, 3:267
in Hellenistic thought, 4:300–301
on knowledge, 3:269–270
Laas on, 5:164
Leibniz on, 4:552–553
on Leucippus, 5:297–298
life of, 3:264–265
Lucian of Samosata on, 5:597
Lucretius and, 5:598–601
on marriage, 5:601
materialism of, 3:265–266, 6:8
on perception, 8:824
on pleasure, 3:399, 4:255
on politics, 5:601
psychology of, 8:121
Seneca on, 8:812
on sensations, 8:823
on sense perception, 3:287–288
on sex, 5:601
on truth, 3:288
utilitarianism and, 9:605
Epicycles
banished by Kepler, 5:51
Copernicus on, 2:534
in Ptolemaic astronomy, 2:534
Epigenesis
Buffon on, 1:759
in cognitive science, 2:298
Diderot on, 3:74
Maupertuis and, 6:66
Epigenesists, 2:631
Epigrams (Callimachus), 3:87
Epilepsy, corpus callosum cutting as treatment for, 6:565–566
Epimenides
on Cretans, 5:316–317
on liars paradox, 5:514
semantic paradoxes and, 5:518
Epimenides' paradox, 5:551
Epinay, Louise d', 9:839
Epiphenomena, 5:72
"Epiphenomenal Qualia" (Jackson), 5:112–115
Epiphenomenalism
advocated by Köhler, 5:126
Broad on, 6:133
determinism and, 3:24–25
of Huxley, 4:533
mental causation and, 6:133, 6:136, 6:260
mind-body problem in, 7:469
of Ribot, 8:457
Stout on, 9:260
Epiphonomenalism, in mind-brain duality and causal closure, 2:92
Epiphyllides in Dialecticis (Maiolo), 5:439
Episodic memory, 6:122
Episteme (journal), 9:84
Episteme, in Aristotle, 1:270
Epistemes
classical, 3:700
as used by Foucault, 3:700
Epistemic attitudes, in Bayesianism, 1:501
Epistemic attributors, in attributor contextualism, 2:483
Epistemic circularity, **3:277–281**
Alston on, 3:279–280
Chisholm on, 3:278
Descartes on, 3:278
recent discussions on, 3:279
Sosa on, 3:280–281
Epistemic contextualism, skepticism and, 3:275
Epistemic distinction, between *a priori* and *a posteriori* knowledge, 5:100
Epistemic force, of prior probabilities, in inductive underdetermination, 9:576
Epistemic goals, confirmation theory and, 2:436
Epistemic hedge, adding to a statement, 5:110
Epistemic justification, 4:717, 5:85
Epistemic Justification (Alston), 1:133
Epistemic logic
as intensional logic, 5:486
as term, 9:848
vagueness and, 5:112
See also Modal logic
Epistemic materialism, 6:12
Epistemic modal interpretation, 6:298
Epistemic naturalism, 5:84
Epistemic normativity, 4:716
Epistemic norms, ideological role of, 3:574–575
Epistemic optimism, 8:690–692
Epistemic properties, in attributor contextualism, 2:485, 2:486
Epistemic rationality, 8:253
Epistemic regularity theories of natural law, 5:226
Epistemic responsibility, 9:685
Epistemic Responsibility (Code), 2:295
Epistemic status, in subject contextualism, 2:482
Epistemic-closure principle, in skepticism, 3:275
Epistemicism, 9:624–625
Epistemicists, solving the stories paradox, 5:109
Epistemological atomism, Köhler's arguments against, 5:130–131
Epistemological behaviorism, Rorty on, 8:494
Epistemological circle, in phenomenology, 7:286–287, 7:288
Epistemological criticisms, fatal to the Cartesian way of ideas originated by Foucher, 3:704
Epistemological dualism
concretism and, 5:145
of Köhler, 5:128, 5:131–132
Epistemological emergence, 3:190–193
Epistemological pacifists, 7:67
Epistemological statements
definition of, 3:325
as ethical statements, 3:326
meaning and verification theories, 3:326–328
Epistemological terms, 3:328
Epistemology, **3:270–277,** 3:311–316, 5:91
a priori and *a posteriori* in, 1:240–241
of abstract objects, 6:673–674
and abstraction by compresence, 9:344
and act of knowing, 1:753
aesthetics in, 4:159
Alston in, 1:132–133
alterity in, 1:133
ambiguity in, 1:676–677
analyticity in, 1:166–168
Aristotle and, 3:285–286
of arithmetic, 3:729
Arnauld and, 2:57–58
art and, 1:296, 1:333–334
in attributor contextualism, 2:486
Augustinian, 1:403
autonomy in, *vs.* testimony, 9:401–402
Avicenna and, 1:434–435
as axiology, 6:544
Bachelard and, 1:440

Epistemology, *continued*
Bacon (Francis) and, 1:445–446, 1:450
Barth and, 1:478
basic statements and, 1:486–487
Baumgarten and, 1:494
Bayesian, 1:495–502
of beliefs, 2:93–94, 2:98
Beneke and, 1:544
Berkeley and, 1:580, 1:586
Biel and, 1:594
Bohmian mechanics and, 1:631, 1:634
Bolzano and, 1:647
Bonaventure and, 1:403, 1:653
Bonhoeffer and, 1:655
Boole and, 1:660
Bosanquet and, 1:661
of Brahman knowability, 1:682–683
Brentano and, 1:689
Brightman and, 1:695
Broad on, 1:6971:258
Budde and, 1:721
Buddhist, 1:742–743, 1:748, 1:753–757, 2:111
Bulgakov and, 1:760
Buridan and, 1:768
Burthogge and, 1:776
Caird on, 2:4
Cairns and, 2:4, 2:5
Calvinist, 2:8–10, 2:12
of Cambridge platonists, 2:13
Campanella and, 2:14–15
Carnap and, 2:37–44
Carneades and, 2:47–48
Cartesian, 2:53–61, 2:94, 3:291–293, 3:704, 8:243
Cassirer and, 2:66–69
of causality and experience, 2:95
of causality and scientific method, 2:107
Cavell and, 2:115–116
of chance, 2:125–130
of chaos and constructed reality, 2:38–39
chemistry and, 2:141–143
Chernyshevskii and, 2:146
in Chinese philosophy, 2:215–223
Chisholm and, 2:242–243
Chrysippus on, 2:251
as circularity or infinitely regress, 1:743
clarity and distinctness in, 2:47, 2:55
in classical mechanics, 2:279
Clifford on, 2:291
Code on, 2:295–296
and cognitive processes, 5:86
coherentist, 1:695, 2:313, 8:179–180
Coleridge and, 2:317
concepts and, 1:578, 2:415
conditions for knowledge, traditional, 3:270–271
Condorcet and, 2:431
of conduct, 1:68
of constructivism, 9:78
in contemporary philosophy, 3:317–319
contextualism in, 2:482–488
and contradiction, 6:499
conventionalism and, 2:474, 2:523
Cousin's, 2:579–580
Craig (Edward) and, 6:499
Creighton and, 2:592
criteriololgy in, 2:594
and critical realism, 2:595–598
Croce's lyrical intuition and, 2:601
Cudworth and, 2:611
Culverwell on, 2:613
curriculum and, 7:359
in Daoism, 2:185, 2:188, 2:206
definition of, 3:270, 7:325
in Dge-lugs Mādhyamika, 1:732–735
of direct realism and causality, 2:97
dualism and, 3:118
in education, philosophy of, **7:355–360**
empirical inductive approach and, 1:676–677
Encyclopédie, 3:223
of Epicureanism, 4:300–301
ethics and, **3:325–329**, 5:25–26
exclusion theory in, 9:544
and experience, 1:477
externalism in, 4:716
feminism and. *See* Feminism, and epistemology
fictions and, 2:38
Florenskii and, 3:669
Foucher's, 2:57
Fréret on, 2:265–266
of game theory, 4:19–20
genetic aspect to, 6:490
Goldman (Alan) and, 4:147, 6:498
Goodman on, 4:154
Grote and, 4:189
group, 7:359
Hegel and, 2:81
Heraclitus and, 4:317–318
in hermetic philosophy, 1:712
in historical narrative, 7:395
history of, **3:281–320,** 9:83
in Huayan Buddhism, 1:738–739
Hume and, 2:80, 2:95–96
Husserl and, 2:81–82
Huxley and, 4:532–533
hypothetical-deductive approach to, 8:275
in illuminationism, 4:585
in Indian philosophy, 7:413, 9:544–545
induction justification, 1:686
infinitivist, 8:179
and informative truth, 1:450
Ingarden and, 4:682
of innate conceptions, 4:687
innate ideas *vs.* axioms in, 1:595
intellectual virtues as focus of. *See* Virtue epistemology
internalism in, 4:716
introspection and, 1:462
intuition and, 1:567, 1:578–580
and irrationalism, 4:748
Jaspers and, 4:800
John of La Rochelle and, 1:403
John of Mirecourt and, 4:841
justification in, 1:132–133
and knowledge, 7:325
by acquaintance, 1:485
vs. faith, 1:629
from interactions with world, 1:671–672
operational point of view in, 1:694
as pragmatic result, 1:566
by presence, 9:305–306, 9:316
Köhler on, 5:131–132
Leibniz and, 3:296–298
Lichtenberg on, 5:340–341
and limit of divine knowledge, 1:584
Locke and, 2:80
and logic, 1:677
and logical positivism, 3:316–317, 5:526
Lopatin on, 5:573
Losskii on, 5:576
in Mādhyamika doctrine, 1:740–744
of Maimon, 5:645–646
Malebranche's, 2:57
Manheim on, 5:685
of Maréchal, 5:707–708
Martineau and, 5:727
Marxism and, 5:736–737
mathematical judgment and, 1:714
Matthew of Aquaparta and, 1:403
Maupertuis and, 6:67
meaning and verification theories in, 3:326–328

mental content and, 2:478
mentality *vs.* sensibility and, 1:649
Mercier and, 6:145
method of, 7:329
on methodological individualism, 4:446
Meyerson and, 6:212
Mill (John Stuart) and, 6:222, 6:225–226
Miller (Dickinson) and, 6:235
Millikan and, 6:236
Minagawa and, 6:253
modal, 4:600
Moleschott and, 6:320
Montague (William) and, 6:331
Moore and, 6:347–348
moral, **6:362–369**
  Baader and, 1:439
  virtue-based, 9:135–136
moral rationalism and, 8:251–252
Mou and, 2:183
mysteries as limit of, 1:622
mysticism and, 1:711, 6:458–459, 6:462
myth and symbols and, 1:559
Natorp on, 6:490
naturalism and, 4:783, 5:72
naturalized, **6:496–500**
nature and, 1:672
nature of, 3:282–283
of neo-Wittgensteinianism, 1:299
new realism and, 6:586–588
and nonphysical realities, 2:89
nontraditional, 3:275–276, 9:685–686
normative, 7:360, 9:544, 9:683
number in, 6:673–674
and objective world, 1:631
of objectivization, 5:709
ontological, 9:529
ordinary-language philosophy, 3:317–319
other minds problem and, 1:586, 7:468
Palágyi on, 7:74–75
paranormal phenomena and, 1:698
Peirce on, 7:173
perceptions and, 2:481, 4:173
pessimism in, 9:546
phenomenology and, 7:284–285
Philo of Larissa in, 7:311
Philolaus on, 7:310–311
in philosophy, 7:325
philosophy of mind as, 8:130–131
Piaget on, 7:567
Plantinga and, 7:580–581
Plato and, 3:283–286, 7:366
Popper and, 7:690
positist, 8:180
positivistic, 9:884
postcolonial, 7:728
post-Kantian idealists and, 3:309–311
poststructuralist, 7:395
pragmatist, **7:750–752**
presupposition of objects, 1:706
primitive vagueness, 1:678
of primitivism, 8:179
principles of, 1:697
probability and, 1:782–783, 8:24–31, 9:547
Protagoras and, 8:91–92
vs. psychology, 6:497, 8:133–134
in Pyrrhonism, 8:173–176
questions on sensing and intellect, 1:698
Quine and, 6:496–497, 7:750–751, 8:220
reformed, 7:481–482
Rehmke and, 8:302–303
related disciplines, 3:276
religion and morality and, 8:386–387
religious, 1:479, **3:320–325**
Rescher and, 8:439–440
rhetoric and, 1:445
Romangnosi and, 8:484
Roretz and, 8:493
Rorty on, 7:751
Rougier and, 8:506
Russell and, 8:540–546
Sartre and, 2:459
in Sautrānikita doctrine, 1:745
Schlick and, 8:637–638
Schuppe and, 8:663
science and, 2:475, 2:557, 6:490, 7:331
selection bias and, 1:220
in Sellar's critical realism, 8:732
sensation and, 1:485
of sensationalism, 8:823
sense-datum and, 1:485–486
sense-intellect dualism in, 1:519
signification of general terms, 1:586
skepticism and, 1:30, 2:47–48, 3:274–275, 3:278, 3:282–283, 7:325, 9:48
social, 1:459, 3:276, **9:83–87,** 9:686
  feminist contribution to, 3:577
  Goldman on, 4:147
sociology of knowledge and, 5:685, 9:103
and solipsism, 9:118–119
special sciences in, 9:161
Spinoza and, 3:294–296
Stoic, 1:30, 1:247, 4:300–301, 9:255
subject and predicate in, 9:286–287
Svātantrika-Prāsaṅgika distinction, 1:744
Tarski and, 9:366
technology and, 7:548–549
of temperament, 6:574
of testimony, 9:402–403
of Theophrastus, 9:412
Thomistic, 5:708
of thought experiments, 9:455
thought-language identity, 1:648
time and, 9:462, 9:498
of Tolstoy, 9:512–513
traditional, 3:270–275
of tragedy, 9:523
truth and, 1:613
of Unamuno, 9:568–569
unperceived sensible objects and, 1:578
and utopianism, 5:74–75
Vasubandhu and, 1:751–752
virtue, 1:475, 3:276, 9:135–136
in *Warrant* trilogy, 7:580–581
Wayland (Francis) and, 9:728
Whewell and, 9:744
William of Auvergne and, 9:766
Wilson (Edward O.) and, 9:789
Windelband on, 6:544
Wittgenstein and, 2:82
Wolff and, 9:828
Wright (Chauncey) and, 9:846–847
Xenophanes of Colophon and, 9:854
Xunzi and, 2:216
and Yogācāra Buddhism, 1:745–749
Zen and, 1:730
Zen'kovskii and, 9:868
Zeno of Citium and, 9:870
Zhang and, 2:159–160
Zhu Xi and, 2:217
See also Knowledge
Epistemology and Cognition (Goldman), 4:147, 6:498
"Epistemology and the New Way of Words" (Sellars, Wilfrid), 8:733
"Epistemology Naturalized" (Quine), 5:84, 6:496–497, 6:501, 9:83
"Epistle to Yemen" (Maimonides), 5:652
Epistola de Tolerantia (First letter concerning toleration) (Locke), 5:375, 9:509
Epistolae (Augustine), 6:519

Epistolario (Leopardi), 5:284
Epistolary Discourse proving that the Soul is naturally Mortal (Dodwell), 6:656
Epistoloa de Nihilo et Tenebris (Fredegisus of Tours), 2:49
Epistulae Morales (Seneca), 2:345
Epitome Astronomiae Copernicanae (Kepler), 6:3
Épître à Uranie (Voltaire), 9:708
Epoch method, Husserl on, 3:312
Epochê, 1:31
Epochs, in historical materialism, 4:379–380
Epochs of Nature (Buffon), 1:758
EPR (Einstein, Podolsky, Rosen) paper, 3:181, 6:641
E-Proposition, definition of, 5:542
Epsilon, definition of, 5:542
Equal acceptance, of differences, 3:583
Equal consideration, as universal equality, 3:331
Equal reaction, to every action, 3:688
Equal treatment, blanket insistence on, 3:582–583
Equality
- arguments against, 3:336
- characteristics of, 3:335
- in combinatory logic, 2:336
- of consideration, 3:332
- egalitarianism and, 3:330–335
- equivalent rights as alternative to, 4:746
- and fairness, 3:335–336
- history of concept, 3:329–330
- in illative combinatory logic, 2:338
- before the law, 3:332
- law and, 7:456
- libertarianism on, 5:336
- *vs.* liberty, Dworkin on, 3:157
- in logic, definition of, 5:542
- modified or quasi-liberal theory of, 3:583
- moral, **3:329–337,** 4:38–40
- moral argument for, 7:456
- of opportunity, 3:331–332, 5:324
- property and, 8:94
- Rawls on, 8:258–259
- of rights, 3:331
- in Rousseau, 7:370–371
- social, **3:329–337,** 4:38–40
  - Dworkin on, 3:156–157
  - *vs.* freedom, 1:253
  - Mencius on, 2:233
- in socialist theory, 9:73
- of sovereign states, 9:143
- substitutivity of. *See* Leibniz's law
- universal, as ideal, 3:330–334
- in utopianism, 9:621
- Vauvenargues on, 9:654

Equality of Men and Women (Gournay), 9:838
Equanimity, in Buddhism, 1:722
Equations
- Boole on, 5:450
- formal calculus of, 2:379
- and logical propositions, 1:660
- Wittgenstein on, 9:807

Equilibrium
- average value calculation method, 1:644
- calculating values of, 4:86
- in classical mechanics, 2:281
- classicism's demand for, 1:641
- cosmic equilibrium and bidirectionality, 1:645
- cosmological research on, 2:565
- distribution probabilities, 1:644
- in game theory, 4:17
- Gibbs on, 4:87
- microscopic and macroscopic values calculation, 1:644
- oscillatory change in Boscovich, 1:666
- Pareto Optimality and market ethics, 1:778
- physical [concept], history of, 7:537–538
- reflective, 1:238, **8:290–295**
  - act utilitarianism and, 9:611–613
  - in applied ethics, 1:238
  - *vs.* deductivism, 1:238
  - Rawls on, 5:323, 8:259
  - rule utilitarianism and, 9:613–615
- statistical theory of, 7:538–539
- velocity distribution of gas in, 1:644

Equilibrium hypotheses, in quantum theory, 1:632–633
Equipollence, 2:746, 5:495
Equipollent, definition of, 5:542
Equivalence
- in Frege, 3:730, 5:464
- in indicative conditionals, 2:425
- lack of, phenomenalism and, 7:273–274
- nomic, 6:645

Equivalence classes
- construction of reality, 2:38–39
- as unsolvability degrees in computability theory, 2:385

Equivalence relation, 4:568, 5:542
Equivalent, in logic, definition of, 5:542
Equivalent translation, of material-object language, 7:276
Equivocal expression, definition of, 5:534
Equivocal relations, analogies in Cajetan, 2:7
Equivocation
- category mistakes, 2:73–75
- instances of, 3:542

Equivocation fallacy, definition of, 5:543
Erasistratus, 4:302
Erasmus, Desiderius, **3:337–340**
- on free will, 9:51
- and Grotius, 4:191
- influence of, 3:339–340
- Lucian of Samosata and, 5:597
- Luther and, 5:613
- medieval church and, 3:405
- on pacifism, 7:67
- Paracelsus and, 7:103, 7:104
- on predestination, 3:10
- Reformation and, 8:296
- skeptical basis for Catholicism, 9:50–51
- on war and peace, 7:154

Erasmus, Franck translation of, 3:713
Erasmus of Rotterdam, as a Roman heretic, 3:712
Erastianism, deism and, 2:681
Eratosthenes of Cyrene, on Aristo of Chios, 1:257–258
Ercole, Pasquale d', 7:135
Erdbeben in Chile, Das (Kleist), 5:78
Erdmann, Johann, as a secondary source for Kierkegaard, 5:67
Erewhon (Butler, Samuel), 1:785
Erewhon Revisited (Butler, Samuel), 1:785
Erfahrungsseelenlehre als Grundlage alles Wissen (Beneke), 1:543
Erfurter Programm, 5:47
Ergodic Hypothesis, 7:539
Ergodic theory, 7:539
Ergreifung des Wirklichen, Die (The grasping of reality) (Dingler), 3:85
Eric of Auxerre, being as collective, 1:528
Erickson, Gary J., 9:221
Erigena, John Scotus, **3:340–342**
- and Bernard of Chartres, 1:591
- in Carolingian period, 2:49
- and David of Dinant, 2:644
- on good, 3:403
- on life, 3:403
- in medieval philosophy, 6:99
- on nature, 1:48
- Neoplatonism and, 2:644

pantheism and, 7:95–96
predestination and salvation in Carolingian thought, 2:49
Erinnerungen (Mendelssohn), 7:100
Erinnerungen an Friedrich Nietzsche (Deussen), 3:42
Eristic, definition of, 5:542
Eristic argument, 3:52, 3:53
Erkenntnis (Journal), 5:525
Erkenntnis und Interesse (Habermas), 4:200
Erkenntnislehre nach dem Bewusstsein der reinen Vernuft (Beneke), 1:543
Erkenntnistheoretische Logik (Schuppe), 8:662
Erlangen Program, 4:60
Ernst August, Duke of Hanover, 5:252–253
Ernst Mach Society
activity of, 5:524
Vienna Circle and, 5:525
Eros. *See* Love
Eros, kalon the object of, 5:7
Eros and Civilization (Marcuse), 7:523
Eroticism, as expenditure of human limits, 1:489
Eroticized subordination, of women, 3:575
Erroneous awareness, rectifying, 5:119
Error, **3:342–346**
argument from, 8:519
Bacon on, 9:101
of belief, 2:276
Carneades probable impressions theory, 2:48
category mistakes, 2:73–75
cause as unkownable contingents, 1:678
in coherentism, 2:315
colors and, 2:333
in common consent arguments for God's existence, 2:349
in critical realism, 2:596
Croce on, 2:602
Herbert of Cherbury on, 4:327
Locke on, 5:387
as misinterpretation of fact, 9:259
Montague (William) on, 6:331
in moral constructivism, 2:472–473
objectivity of, 6:588
as original sin, 1:721
Plato's theory of, 3:343–344
in probability, Jevons, 4:808
reliability in noninferential justification, 2:278
of religious belief as self-deception, 2:12
in Sanlun Buddhism, 2:162
Spaulding on, 6:588
unreality of, in Gentile, 4:52
in velocity distribution of equilibrium of gas, 1:644
and volition, 3:345–346
in Yogācāra Buddhism, 1:746–747
Error theory, 3:628
antirealism of, 6:172
Laplace on, 5:198
in projectivism, 8:51
as response to judgment internalism, 4:714
Error theory of ethics, **3:346–347,** 6:160, 7:4
Errors, computer ethics and, 2:397–398
Erster Entwuf eines Systems der Naturphilosophie (Schelling), 8:619, 9:238
Erudition, in Comenius, 7:369
Erya, Fangyan and, 9:860
Eryxias (Prodicus), 8:45
Erziehung des Menschengeschlechts, Die (The education of the human race) (Lessing), 5:295, 5:297, 7:100
Eschatology, **3:347**
in Berdyaev, 1:560
in Bultmann, 1:764
eternal return doctrine, 3:352–354
and evil, problem of, 3:475
in Gnosticism, 4:102
of Ikhwān al-Ṣafā', 4:576
Jewish, Zoroastrianism and, 9:886
kalām argument on God's existence and, 2:555
in Neoplatonism, 6:556
of resurrection, 4:618
in Solov'ëv, 9:125–126
verifiability in, 7:478
Eschenbach, J. C.
on immaterialism, 4:555
on skepticism, 9:56
Tetens and, 9:403
Escuela de Madrid, La (Marías), 5:711
Esentialism, 2:419
Esoteric morality, in act utilitarianism, 9:613
Esoteric philosophy
and Bacon (Roger), 1:452–453
as unified science, 1:452
See also Alchemical philosophy
ESP (extrasensory perception), 7:752–757
Esperanto
Carnap use of, 2:36
Couturat work on, 2:582
Esperienza e metafisica (Spaventa), 9:160
Espinas, Alfred, Durkheim and, 3:149
"Espoir maintenant, L'" (Sartre), 8:604
Esprit, Jacques, 5:200
Esprit des lois, L' (Montesquieu), 5:238
Esprit géométrique, L' (Pascal), 7:129
Esquisse de la phénoménologie constitutive (Gurwitsch), 4:197
Esquisse d'une philosophie (Lamennais), 5:177
Esquisse d'une théorie des émotions (Sketch for a phenomenological theory of the emotions) (Sartre), 8:605
Essai de cosmologie (Maupertuis), 6:66
"Essai de dialectique rationelle" (Gergonne), 5:461
Essai de dynamique (Leibniz), on energy conservation, 3:228
Essai de philosophie morale (Maupertuis), 6:67, 7:249
Essai d'une philosophie premiÈre (Le Roy), 5:288–289
Essai historique, politique et moral su les révolutions (Chateaubriand), 2:137
Essai philosophique sur les probabilités (A philosophical essay on probabilities) (Laplace), 5:197
Essai sur le libéralisme allemand (Grandvilliers), on French liberalism, 5:320
Essai sur l'étude de la littérature (Gibbon), 4:84–86
Essai sur les conditions et les limites de la certitude logique (Milhaud), 6:217
Essai sur les fondements de nos connaissances et sur les caractères de la critique philosophique (Cournot), 2:577
Essai sur les machines en général (Carnot), on energy and force, 3:229
Essai sur les moeurs (Voltaire), 9:709, 9:713
Essai sur les règnes de Claude et Néron (Essay on the reigns of Claudius and Nero) (Diderot), 3:72
Essai sur l'inégalité des races humaines (Gobineau), 4:106
Essai sur l'origine des connaissances humaines (Essay on the origin of human knowledge) (Condillac), 2:421, 8:783
Essais (Montaigne), 4:166
Essais de critique générales (Renouvier), James and, 4:775
Essais de morale (Nicole), 6:603, 6:604
Essais de philosophie religieuse (Laberthonnière), 5:165

Essais sur la conception matérialiste de l'histoire (Labriola), 5:165
Essay concerning Human Understanding (Locke), 1:577, 1:674, 2:345, 2:356, 2:421, 2:474, 4:30, 5:376–387, 5:447, 7:215
  abstraction in, 9:595
  amendment of, 9:250
  conceptualism of, 9:594
  criticisms of, 5:376
  education in, 7:369
  Edwards (Jonathan) and, 3:166
  Enlightenment and, 3:244
  Essays on the Law of Nature and, 5:387
  ethics in, 3:407
  on faith, 3:530
  idea in, 4:553
  on imagination, 1:50
  on induction from experience, 4:638
  influence of, 5:376, 5:387
  on innate ideas, 3:216, 3:298–299, 4:688
  on knowledge of God, 4:112
  on language, 8:777
  purpose of, 5:376–377
  on substance, 9:298
  writing and publication of, 5:375, 5:376, 5:394
Essay concerning the Use of Reason, An (Collins), 2:683
Essay in Aid of a Grammar of Assent (Newman), 6:577–581
Essay in Modal Logic, An (von Wright), 9:847–848
Essay of Obedience to the Supreme Powers (Tindal), 9:502
Essay of Orthodox Theodicy, An (Florenskii), 3:669
Essay of the Application of Mathematical Analysis (Green), on potential energy, 3:228
Essay on a Course of Liberal Education (Priestley), 8:5
Essay on Christianity (Shelley), 9:8
"Essay on Cosmology, An" (Whitehead), 9:750
Essay on Criticism (Pope), 1:49
Essay on Heat, Light, and the Combinations of Light (Davy), 3:229
Essay on Man (Cassirer), 1:58, 1:65
Essay on Man (Pope), 2:685, 9:307
Essay on Metaphysics (Collingwood), on determinism, 3:40
"Essay on Nature" (Mill), 6:520
Essay on Philosophical Method (Collingwood), 2:327
Essay on Population (Malthus), 2:629
Essay on Sepulchres (Godwin), 4:136
"Essay on Species" (Darwin), 7:561
Essay on Taste (Gerard), 1:52, 4:64
"Essay on the Concept of Republicanism" (Schlegel), 8:630
Essay on the Development of Christian Doctrine (Newman), 6:581
"Essay on the Foundations of Psychology" (Maine de Biran), 5:657
Essay on the History of Civil Society (Ferguson), 3:604
Essay on the Nature and Immutability of Truth, An (Beattie), 1:510
Essay on the Nature and principles of Taste (Alison), 4:65
Essay on the Origin of Evil (King), 4:34
Essay on the Pleasures of the Imagination (Addison), 1:22
Essay on the Power of the Magistrate and the Rights of Mankind in Matters of Religion (Tindal), 9:502
Essay on the Principle of Population, An (Malthus), 3:487
Essay on the Principles of Human Action (Hazlitt), 4:248
Essay on the Resurrection (Maimonides), 4:618
Essay pour les coniques (Pascal), 7:129
Essay sceptique (Camus), 9:52
Essay sur l'indifférence en matière de religion (Lamennais), 5:177
Essay to Revive the Ancient Education of Gentlewomen, An (Makin), 9:838
Essay toward a New Theory of Vision, An (Berkeley), 1:571, 1:575–576, 9:515
"Essay Toward Solving a Problem in the Doctrine of Chances" (Bayes), 1:495
Essay toward the Present and Future Peace of Europe (Penn), 7:154
Essay towards a Real Character and a Philosophical Language (Wilkins), 8:773
Essay towards the Recovery of the Jewish Measures and Weights (Cumberland), 2:614
Essay towards the Theory of the Ideal and Sensible World (Norris), 6:656
Essay upon the Relation of Cause and Effect (Shepherd), 9:9
Essays (Emerson), 3:195
Essays Critical and Clinical (Deleuze), 2:695
Essays in Critical Realism (Santayana), 2:596
Essays in Experimental Logic (Dewey), 3:47
Essays in Radical Empiricism (James), 2:597, 4:779
  on acts of perception, 4:560
  epistemology in, 3:313
Essays in the History of Ideas (Lovejoy), 5:593
Essays Never before Published (Godwin), 4:136
"Essays on Nature and the Principles of Taste" (Alison), 1:128
Essays on Philosophical Subjects (Smith), 9:69
Essays on the Active Powers of Man (Reid), on determinism, 3:17
Essays on the Law of Nature (Locke), 5:387, 5:388
Essays on the Perception of an External Universe and other Subjects Connected with the Doctrine of Causation (Shepherd), 9:10
Essence
  absolute, elevating reason to status of, 3:610
  d'Ailly on, 1:99
  alienation from, 1:123–124
  Aquinas on, 1:528, 9:430, 9:593
  Aristotle on, 9:299
  Augustine on, 9:593
  vs. being, 9:430
  Berkeley on, 6:191–192
  in Capreolus, 2:30–31
  as concepts, 2:418
  conventional truth and ignorance, 1:734
  in critical realism, 2:595
  entities as real not constructed, 1:740
  vs. existence, 1:432–433, 9:443
  in Gilbert of Poitiers, 4:89
  in Godfrey of Fontaines, 4:131
  Hegel on, 4:265
  Heidegger on, 4:293–294
  in Huayan Buddhism, 2:164
  in Ibn Gabirol, 4:546
  in Indian grammar, 9:581
  intuition of, in phenomenology, 7:283–285
  Locke on, 6:191
  of love, 8:96–7
  in Mādhyamika doctrine, 1:740–741
  of man in community, 3:611
  in Mill's logic, 5:494
  More (Henry) on, 6:396
  multiplication of, 9:344
  ownership of, 1:124
  phenomena as lacking, 6:469, 6:471

Philo's knowledge of, 4:810
Plato on, 9:589
in Platonic dialogues, 7:587, 7:595
as primary mode of being, in Santayana, 8:601–602
real *vs.* nominal, 6:504
in self-existent God, 4:109
Socrates on, 9:589
Soto on, 9:137
as substances, 9:295
of terms in traditional logic, 5:494
Thomas of York on, 9:443
Thomist argument for God's existence and, 2:553
Toletus on, 9:511
treating as an ultimate intrinsic mode, 3:681
of truth, 4:292–294
in William of Auvergne's metaphysics, 9:765
See also Definition
Essence and existence, **3:349–352**
Aquinas on, 3:350, 6:189, 9:283
in Aristotle, 3:349–350
Averroes on, 4:758
Avicenna on, 4:757
distinction between, 9:283
Duns Scotus on, 6:189
existential psychoanalysis on, 3:512–513
Giles of Rome on, 4:89–90
in medieval metaphysics, 6:188
in medieval philosophy, 6:103
modern views on, 3:350–351
Mullā Ṣadrā on, 4:761
in ontological argument for the existence of God, 7:16–17
in ontology, 7:22–23
in Pantheism, 4:669
Rozanov on, 8:525
scholastics on, 4:669
Suhrawardī on, 6:419–420
Vasquez on, 9:649
Essence of man, as will, 3:660
Essence of objects, phenomenology and, 7:286, 7:287
Essence of Truth: On Plato's Cave Allegory and Theaetetus (Heidegger), 7:616
Essentia, Aristotle on, 3:350
Essential property, notion of, 5:70
Essentialism
Aristotelian, 5:704
in Aristotle, 1:308
charging standpoint theory with, 3:575
in definition, 2:664–668, 2:673–674
feminist discussion of, 3:586
in human genetics, 4:48
on limit to state action, 9:209
mereological, 6:147
in modal logic, 5:704
quantification and, 6:290–291
"Essentialism and Quantified Modal Logic" (Parsons), 6:290–291
Essentialist metaphysics, of Aristotle, 5:70
EST human potential movement, Kaufmann's involvement with, 5:46
Estética (Aesthetics)(Deústua), 5:207
Estetica come scienza dell'espressione e linguistica generale (Aesthetic as science of expression and general linguistic) (Croce), 1:57, 2:599
Esteticheskie fragmenty (Aesthetic fragments) (Shpet), 9:17
Esteticheskie otnosheniia iskusstva k deistvitel'nostri (The aesthetic relation of art to reality) (Chernyshevski), 2:146
Esthetics. *See* Aesthetics
Estienne, Henri, 9:50
Est-il bon? Est-il méchant? (Diderot), 3:76
Estimation
distinguished from explanation, 5:27–28
small sample theory of, 3:663
theory of, 3:661–664
Estimation errors, becoming negligible, 3:661
Estimators, achieving the minimum variance bound, 3:663
Étaples, Lefèvre d', 5:439
Etchemendy, John, on truth, 5:317
Eternal, *vs.* temporal, in Jaspers's psychology, 4:800
Eternal creation, 4:758
Eternal law, 1:396
Eternal life
in Buddhism, 6:256–257
obligation of God to bestow, Ockham on, 9:783
Eternal life force, characterized by spontaneous creativity, 5:77
Eternal mind, Cudworth on, 2:611
Eternal objects, 9:748
Eternal Peace (Kant), 7:155
Eternal recurrence, 6:611
Eternal republic, of Howison, 7:235
Eternal return, **3:352–356**
Eternal Sunshine of the Spotless Mind (film), memory in, 6:122
Eternalism, persistence and, 7:211
Eternity, **3:356–361**
as attribute of God, 4:110–111, 4:670
Averroes on, 4:758
in Christianity, 3:357–359
creation out of, 9:28
definition of, 3:356
of existents, 6:120
of God, 2:270, 7:479
in Greek philosophy, 3:357
in Islamic philosophy, 3:360–361
in Jewish philosophy, 3:360–361
Maimonides on, 5:651
of matter, as atheistic argument, 1:360–361
as mode of God, 9:173
and nature in Bernard of Tours, 1:593
in Nicolas of Autrecourt, 6:601
omniscience and, 7:479
in ontological argument for the existence of God, 7:16
in personal immortality, 4:609
Philoponus on, 7:314
in philosophy of religion, 7:479
Spinoza on, 9:190
Thomas of York on, 9:443
Ether
in Aristotle, 1:271–272
in Maxwell's field theory, 6:69
Newton on, 5:642
Ethic of Freethought, The (Pearson), 7:160
"Ethica" (Johnson, Samuel), 4:851
Ethica ordine geometrico demonstrata (Spinoza), 4:57
Ethical, definition of, 3:361
Ethical concepts, thin *vs.* thick, 3:444
Ethical Cultural movement, Jodl (Friedrich) and, 4:836
Ethical determinism, 3:4–5
Ethical egoism, **3:361–363,** 9:22, 9:25
Ethical freedom, 5:143
Ethical hedonism, 3:417, 4:254–258
Ethical individualism, 5:40
Ethical irrationalism, 4:749–750
Ethical judgments
correctness of, 7:3
denial of, 7:5–6
opinion-independent, 9:642–643
motivation to act and, 7:6
Ethical naturalism, **3:363–368,** 3:417
emotive theory and, 3:425
entity education in, 6:172
of Ingenieros, 4:686
Kant on, 3:411

Ethical naturalism, ***continued***
  Moore (G. E.) on, 3:364, 3:366–367, 3:418–419, 3:445
  20th-century debate on, 3:446–447
  in United States, 3:423–425
Ethical noncognitivism
  emotivism and, 3:203–204, 3:205–207
  in projectivism, 8:51–52
Ethical nonfactualism, 3:627
Ethical objectivism, Westermarck on, 9:739
Ethical permanence, theory of, 7:268
Ethical personalism, 7:234
Ethical point of view, Kierkegaard on, 5:63–64
Ethical properties, 7:4, 7:5
Ethical reality, 7:4
Ethical reasoning, metaethical relativism and, 3:369
Ethical relativism, **3:368–374**, 3:390–391
  descriptive, 3:368
  difficulties in, 3:370–371
  and disagreement, 3:373–374
  metaethical, 3:368–369, 3:373
  modern moral theory and, 3:374
  normative, 3:369–370, 3:372–373
  tolerance and, 3:372
  use of term, 3:369
  See also Cultural relativism
Ethical Relativity (Westermarck), 9:739–740
Ethical responsibility, as moored in the person, 5:156
Ethical skepticism. *See* Ethical relativism
Ethical statements
  definition of, 3:325
  emotivists on, 3:425–426
  good-reasons approach on, 3:430–431
  Hare (R. M.) on, 3:429–430
  meaning and verification theories in, 3:326–328
Ethical Studies (Bradley), 1:675–676, 3:416, 4:559
Ethical subjectivism, **3:375–379**
  community feeling as ethical base, 3:377–378
  definition of, 3:375
  group feeling as ethical base, 3:377–379
  ideal observer theories, 4:562–563
  language in, 9:245–246
  Ross on, 8:505
  speakers' feelings as ethical base, 3:375–377
  speakers' thoughts as ethical base, 3:377
  in Westermarck, 9:738–739
Ethical terms, need for clarification in, 3:328
Ethical theory. *See* Metaethics
Ethical Theory (Brandt), 1:687, 6:163
Ethical value, 9:641
Ethical voluntarism, 9:715–716
Ethicotheology, merits of, 5:27
Ethics, **3:379–394**
  of Abelard, 1:3, 1:5–6, 3:403
  vs. aesthetics, 1:37
  ancient, friendship in, 3:748
  of Anderson (John), 1:199
  Anselm on, 1:216–218
  anti-naturalist position on, Green on, 4:180
  in apodictic judgment, 1:689–690
  applied. *See* Applied ethics
  of Aquinas, 9:433–435
  of Aristippus of Cyrene, 1:257
  of Aristotle, 1:256, 1:267–269
  artistic imitation and, 1:490
  in beauty, Winckelmann on, 9:790
  of Beauvoir, 1:515
  of belief, 2:292, 5:99
  in Bhagavad Gītā, 2:110
  and bioethics, 1:598–599
  Boethius on, 1:628
  Bradley on, 1:675–676
  Braithwaite on, 1:686
  branches of, 3:379
  of Brandt, 1:688
  Broad on, 1:699
  Brown on, 1:705
  in Buddhism, 1:748, 2:198–199, 6:108
  of business, 1:776–780
  Caird on, 2:4
  Cairns on, 2:5
  Campanella on, 2:16
  Camus on, 2:21
  "can" and ought in, 2:25–26
  Card on, 2:31
  of care, 1:158, 7:360
  Carneades on, 2:48
  and categorical imperative, 2:69–72
  central questions of, 3:394
  of charity, 1:404
  chemistry and, 2:144
  Chen Yi-Zhu and, 2:156
  in Chinese philosophy, **2:194–202**, 2:226–227
  in Christianity, 3:401–404, 8:591
  Cicero on, 2:258
  civil disobedience and, 2:259–261
  Clarke on, 2:273–274
  of Cleanthes, 2:288
  Code on, 2:295
  Cohen (Hermann) on, 4:828
  Cohen (Morris) on, 2:307
  Collingwood on, 2:329
  computer, 2:396–398
  Comte on, 2:413
  and conflicting theoretical results, 1:601
  in Confucianism, 2:170–171, 2:174–179, 2:195, 2:442
  consequentialism and, 2:460, 5:37, 6:513. *See also* Consequentialism
  constructivism and, 2:471
  contractualism and
    Kantian, 3:385–386
    modern, 3:386
    self-interest and, 3:389
  counterutilitarian, 3:383–384
  Cousin on, 2:579
  of criminal punishment, 1:517
  critical, 6:535–537
  Crusius on, 2:607–608
  of Cudworth, 2:611–612
  Cyrenaics on, 2:619
  Dante on, 2:624–626
  in Daoism, 2:189–190, 2:197–198, 2:232, 9:722
  and deferring death, 4:617
  definition of, 3:379–380, 3:394, 7:3, 7:325–326
  Deleuze on, 2:695–696
  deliberation in, 7:736–737
  Democritus on, 5:301–302
  deontological. *See* Deontological ethics
  descriptive, utilitarianism as, 9:605–606
  of desire and predisposition in self-cultivation, 2:177
  Dewey on, 3:49, 7:378
  Dge-lugs on, 1:734–735
  Diderot on, 3:75–76
  disagreements in. *See* Disagreement, ethical
  of discipline, 7:363
  disposition-dependent, 7:5
  divine command theories of, **3:93–94**
  in divine foreknowledge, 1:628
  Dostoevsky on, 3:99–100
  Dühring on, 3:131
  Duns Scotus on, 3:143–145
  duty and, 3:153–155
  early modern period of, 3:404–412
  and economics, **3:447–450**

in Smith's *Wealth of Nations*, 9:68
in socialist thought, 9:88
Sombart on, 9:128
in education, **7:360–364**
Edwards (Jonathan) on, 3:168–169
Ehrenfels on, 3:177
of Emerson, 6:574
emotional basis of, Westermarck on, 9:739–740
emotive theory of, **3:203–208,** 5:729
Encyclopédie on, 3:224
Epicurus on, 3:265
error theory of, **3:346–347**
and evaluation of political and social institutions, 3:391–392
and evil, problem of, 3:469
evolutionary, 6:515–516
feminist, 3:578–582. *See also* Feminism, and ethics
Fichte on, 3:617
in film, 7:384
free will in, Ockham on, 9:782
friendship and, 3:748
as function of state, 1:663–664
Galluppi and, 4:13–14
of Gassendi, 4:29–30
Gay on, 4:34
general normative theories of, 1:600
and genetics and reproductive technologies, 4:43–48
in German romanticism, 8:490–491
Geulincx on, 4:78
Gewirth on, 4:81
God and, 7:479–480
golden rule and, 4:144–147
in Greece, ancient, 3:394–399
Grote and, 4:189
of Haeckel, 4:204–205
Hegel and, 4:281
Hellenistic, 3:399–401
Hélvetius on, 4:306–307
of Herbart, 4:324–325, 7:376–377
history of, **3:394–447**
contemporary, 3:418–428
in Greece, ancient, 3:394–399
Hellenistic and Roman, 3:399–401
medieval period of, 3:401–404
modern, 3:404–412
19th century, 3:412–418
recent views of, 3:428–432
20th century, 3:418–432, 3:439–447
in U.S., 3:423–425
of Hobbes, 4:414–417
of Holbach, 4:432
of Husserl, 4:525–526
of Huxley, 4:533–534
Ibn Gabirol on, 4:545
of ideal moral code utilitarianism, 1:687
impersonal, 3:388–389, 9:787
impossibility of good and, 1:721
inborn knowledge and moral metaphysics in Chinese philosophy, 2:221–222
in Indian meditation practices, 6:108
insufficiency of science in addressing, Gadamer on, 4:3
internationalization of norms, 3:382, 3:385
of irrationalism, 4:749–750
of I-thou *vs.* I-it relations, 1:715
in Jainism, 2:111, 6:254
Jaspers on, 4:801–802
Jodl (Friedrich) and, 4:835
John of La Rochelle and, 4:840
in judgment independence and moral fact, 1:549
Kantian, 2:70, 5:23–26, 5:36–38, 7:373–374
Kareev and, 5:40
Kavelin's attempt to provide a scientific foundation for, 5:48
kindness and honor in ethical character in Confucian, 2:178
Laas on, 5:164
laws of nature in, 9:828–829
Lévy-Bruhl on, 5:306
legal consciousness, 4:577–578
Leonard on, 6:535–537
Leont'ev on, 5:283
lesbian identity and ethics, 2:31
Levinas on, 4:830–832, 5:304–305
Lipps on, 5:363
in Liu's neo-Confucianism, 2:184
of logical positivism, 5:526
logo astratto in, Gentile on, 4:52
Lotze on, 5:581, 5:582
of loving and hating in Brentano, 1:690
Luther on, 5:615
of Machiavelli, 5:628
MacIntyre on, 5:636–637
of Mackie, 5:638
Manichaean, 5:684
of Marcus Aurelius, 5:706
of Martineau, 5:727
Marulić on, 5:729
in Marxism, 5:737
of Maupertuis, 6:67
of McDowell, 6:74
meaning and verification theories in, 3:326–328
medical, personhood and, 7:242
in medicine, 7:333
medieval period, 3:401–404
in medieval philosophy, 6:104–105
metaethics and, 1:599
metaphysics in, 1:599, 6:170, 9:880
of Mill (John Stuart), 6:226–228
of Milton, 6:250
of Miura, 6:276
in Mohism, 2:197
of Moleschott, 6:320–321
in monism, of Haeckel, 4:204
of Montgomery, 6:340
Moore in, 1:145, 6:349–350
moral argument for existence of God and, 6:359
moral autonomy and self-knowledge in, 1:713
moral emotions in, 9:125
moral labor and, 1:459
moral law and human understanding in, 1:542
of moral luck in Card, 2:31
moral probation in Butler (Joseph), 1:783
moral psychology in Confucian, 2:196
moral theories in, 1:599
in moral value of action and responsibility in Calderoni, 2:8
vs. morality, **3:450–451**
moral-sense questions of, 1:699
of More (Henry), 6:396–397
motivation in. *See* Motivation, ethical
Mou's moral metaphysics and metaphysics of morals, 2:222
of Murphy, 6:436
in music, 1:188
of name rectification in Chinese philosophy, 2:203–204
Naṣīr al-Dīn al-Ṭūsī's cosmogony, 6:478
natural basis for, 1:707, 3:363–364
natural law *vs.* other, 6:514
natural supremacy conscience of in Butler (Joseph), 1:781–782
naturalism in Boulainvilliers, 1:670
naturalism in U.S., 3:423–425
in neo-Confucianism, 2:199
nihilism and fraternity in Camus, 2:21
19th century, 3:412–418
of Nishi, 6:623

Ethics, ***continued***
noncognitivism in, 3:425–428, 6:632–633, 8:52, 9:611
non-human creatures and, 3:392–393
nonnaturalism, contemporary, 3:418–423
normative. *See* Normative ethics
objectivity of, 3:380–383
and obligation to future generations, **3:92–93,** 3:392–393
Ockham and, 9:782–784
ontological entities in, 1:699
Ostwald and, 7:50
ought implies can in business, 1:780
pain and pleasure as right and wrong, 1:552
parallels with science, 3:328
Parfit on, 7:120
Pauler on, 7:145
Paulsen on, 7:148–149
personalism in art, 1:538
Peter Lombard on, 7:261
Petzoldt on, 7:269
Philodemus on, 7:302
of philosophers, 7:336
philosophical analysis in, 1:145
philosophical consolation, 1:626
in philosophy, 7:325–326
vs. philosophy of right, 6:536
philosophy of technology and, 7:548
Pisarev on, 7:577
of Plotinus, purification in, 7:638
of Plutarch of Chaeronea, 7:648–649
political power and transformative character, 2:179
in popular philosophy, Green on, 4:179
of possibility, 1:2
power and speech, 2:119–120
as practical, 1:599
presented by Kropotkin as a science, 5:155
preventive, engineering and, 3:240
projectivism in, 8:51
propositions of, Wittgenstein on, 9:807
questions of, ability to settle, 7:6
of Rashdall, 8:238–239
realism in, 7:330
recent views of, 3:428–432
reflective equilibrium in, 9:611
of Régis, 8:300
of Rehmke, 8:303–304
and religion, 3:391, 5:148, 7:332
of Renouvier, 8:432
of Rescher, 8:439
of research, 8:668
and revelation in Bonhoeffer, 1:656
of Ricoeur, 8:464–465
right and wrong as objective fact, 1:552–553
ritual and propriety in Confucian, 2:195
Roman, 3:399–401
of Rosmini-Serbati, 8:502
of Ross (William David), 8:505
of Royce, 8:521–522
of Rüdiger, 8:527
of Ruskin, 8:534
of Russell, 8:555–559
Scheler on, 8:616
Schiller (Ferdinand) on, 8:625
Schleiermacher on, 8:633
Schlick on, 8:642–643
scholarship on Kant's, 5:34
Schopenhauer on, 9:717
science as spiritual, 1:714
scientific, Kavelin's, 5:48
as scientific interests and praxis, 2:218–219
secular as limited, 1:707–708
self in Confucianism, 2:171–174, 2:177–178
and self-interest, 3:380, 3:381–382
Seneca on, 8:812–813
in Shaftesbury's *Characteristicks,* 9:2
Sidgwick on, 9:22
Singer on, 9:41–42
social
and business ethics, 1:776–780
Ehrenfels on, 3:177
social action as aim of thought, 2:83
social competence *vs.* personal culture in, 9:198
social Darwinism and, 2:642–643
of social title in Chinese philosophy, 2:204
society and self in Confucianism, 2:176
Socrates on, 9:111–112
Solov'ëv on, 9:125
sophists on, 9:130
special sciences on, 9:161
in Spinoza's enlightened egoism, 9:189–190
states as morally responsible, 1:664
Stoic, 3:399–400, 5:706, 9:257
Stout on, 9:261
with a strong social orientation, 3:705
subfields of, 7:328
suffering and material attachment in Buddhist, 2:198–199
suicide as option, 9:317–322
systematic, Watsuji on, 9:727
of teaching, 7:363
technological power and, 7:545–546
teleological, **9:382–384**
Theodorus teaching on, 2:620
of Theophrastus, 9:412
vs. theory, faith in, 4:772
of Thoreau, 6:574–575
of Tolstoy, 9:513
traditional, duty in, 3:155
triadic structures in Caso, 2:65
trust in, 1:459
20th-century, 3:418–432, 3:439–447
unmasking explanation of, 7:6
utilitarian, 6:623. *See also* Utilitarianism
validity of, 6:536–537
value statements in, 1:437
of Varona, 9:648
of Vasconcelos, 9:649
of Vaz Ferreira, 9:655
of virtue, 1:213, 5:636–637
as virtue and political unity in Confucius, 2:231
virtue as principle in, 3:388
of virtues as Western interest in Confucian, 2:195–196
Voltaire on, 9:712
of Weber (Max), 9:734–735
well-being and, 8:721–722
of Williams (Bernard), 9:787
of Wilson (Edward O.), 9:789
Wittgenstein on, 9:807
of Wolff, 9:828–829
of Wollaston, 9:833–834
women's subordination and moral integrity in, 2:31
of Wundt, 9:849
xin in, 6:129–130
in Xunzi, 2:216
yi and, 6:129
of Zeno of Citium, 9:869–870
Zeno on, 9:253
in Zoroastrianism, 9:886
See also Metaethics; Morality; Individual rights
Ethics (Abelard), 1:3
Ethics (Aristotle)
Aquinas and, 9:434
on habit, 5:615

natural law in, 6:506
virtue in, 7:329
Ethics (Bonhoeffer), 1:656
Ethics (Geulincx), 4:76
Ethics (Hartmann), 3:422
Ethics (Moore)
contextual implication in, 7:767
Latin American philosophy and, 5:210
Ethics (Nowell-Smith), on Moore (G. E.), 3:419
Ethics (Spinoza), 2:265, 2:755
axioms in, 9:184
on determinism, 3:7–8
on emotions, 3:198
on eternal element of the mind, 4:602
on eternity, 3:359
Goethe on, 7:101
Leibniz and, 5:252
on love, 5:588
on mind-body identity, 9:187
on modes, 9:186
possibility in, 7:721–722
on sense perception, 3:294
translation of, 9:176
Ethics and Language (Stevenson), 9:245
Ethics and Moral Science (La Morale et la science des moeurs) (Lévy-Bruhl), 5:306
Ethics and the Limits of Philosophy (Williams), 3:347, 3:450–451, 9:787
Ethics Demonstrated in the Geometric Manner (Spinoza), 3:407
Ethics, Inventing Right and Wrong (Mackie), 3:346
Ethics of Ambiguity (Beauvoir), 1:515
"Ethics of Belief" (Clifford), 2:292
Ethics of expression and reversibility, 6:149–150
Ethics of Green, Spencer, and Martineau (Sidgwick), 3:416
Ethics, Persuasion and Truth (Smart), 9:66
Ethik (Fries), 3:751
"Ethik" (Paulsen), 7:148
Ethik des reinen Willens (Cohen), 6:543
Ethnic slurs, evaluations encapsulated in, 6:159
Ethnocentricity, Trubetskoi (Nikolai) on, 9:531
Ethnography
combining with psychoanalysis, 3:747
Encyclopédie on, 3:224
and psychoanalysis, combination of, 3:747
Ethnology, 1:202
Ethnophilosophy
African philosophy as, 1:83–84
criticisms of, 1:84–85
Ethology
on mental representation, 6:141
of Mill (John Stuart), 6:224–225
Etika (Kropotkin), 5:155
Etika Fikhte (Fichte's ethics) (Vysheslavtsev), 9:717
Etika preobrazhennogo erosa (The ethics of transfigured Eros) (Vysheslavtsev), 9:717–718
Etiologic inference, Breuer and Freud's unsound, 3:741
Etiquette
in Confucianism, 2:174–175, 2:231
Foot on, 2:71
as ritual, li, in Chinese religion, 2:226
Être et le néant, L' (Sartre), 4:748, 7:297
Étude expérimental de l'intelligence, L' (Binet), 1:596
Études sur Cournot (Milhaud), 6:217
Études sur la pensée scientifique chez les Grecs et chez les modernes (Milhaud), 6:217
Études sur Marx et Hegel (Hippolyte), 3:57
Eubulides of Miletus
arguments of, 6:110–111
dialecticians and, 5:403, 6:110
liar paradox and, 2:541, 5:316–317, 5:398
paradoxes and, 5:398
semantic paradoxes and, 5:518
vagueness used by, 9:623–624
Eucharist
Arnauld on, 1:289
Desgabets on, 1:290, 2:757
Leibniz on, 5:268–269
Eucharistic controversy, John of Paris in, 4:842
Eucharistic theology
Arnauld in, 1:289
Cartesianism as threat to, 2:60
Christ's presence in Carolingian thought, 2:50
Desgabets's Cartesian eucharistic theology, 2:61
Eucken, Rudolf Christoph, **3:451–453**
Pietism and, 7:576
and Scheler, 8:615
Euclid
axiomatic system of, 4:119, 4:123, 6:22
on compounding ratios, 9:342
and Ikhwān al-Ṣafā', 4:576
on number, 2:491–492, 6:670
on optics, 4:301
Proclus and, 8:41
Euclid (Dodgson), 2:51
Euclid and His Modern Rivals (Carroll), 2:51, 2:52
Euclidean geometry, 4:55, 4:62
continuity principles, 2:499
Helmholtz on, 6:540
Hilbert on, 4:62
Kant and, 1:244
model of, 6:23
postulates in, 4:55
and space, 2:520–521, 9:150–151
in Wolff, 9:826
"Euclidean Geometry with Infinitesimals" (Cruciani), 2:509
Euclides of Megara, 3:54, 6:110
Euclid's axiom of parallels, 5:461–462
Eudaemonism, Paulsen and, 7:148
Eudaimonia, **10:10–12**
in Aristotle, 1:267
deontological ethics and, 2:713
teleological ethics and, 9:383
in value and valuation, 9:642
Eudaimonism
Schlick's value analysis and, 8:643
as teleological ethic, 9:383
vs. utilitarianism, 9:383
Eudemian Ethics (Aristotle), 2:357, 3:397–398
Eudemonological pessimism, 7:251
Eudemus of Rhodes
Aristotle and, 1:278
on eternal return doctrine, 3:353
Galen on, 5:408
logic and, 5:401–402
Eudorus of Alexandria, 7:607, 8:187
Eudoxus
Aratus and, 5:600
on concentric spheres, 4:172
on cosmos, 2:571
physical theory of, 9:154
on proportions, 2:492, 4:54–55
Eugenics
Cabanis promotion of, 2:2
in genetic counseling, 6:96
as good human breeding, 2:2
Human Genome Project and, 4:475–476
reproductive technology and, 4:44
Schiller's (Ferdinand) interest in, 8:625
Euhemerus of Tegea, Cyrenaic teaching of, 2:620
Euler, Leonard
in calculus, 6:593
on classical mechanics, 2:279
on continuous functions, 2:496

Euler, Leonard, ***continued***
on discontinuity points, 2:497
in history of logic, 5:444
on logical diagrams, 5:560
Newtonian physics and, 6:61
on validity of syllogistic inferences, 5:499
Euler cycle, for decision procedures and polynominal-time computability, 2:388
"Eulerian Syllogistic" (Thomas), 5:444
Euler's diagrams
definition of, 5:542
of syllogistic inferences, 5:499
Eumenides (Aeschylus), Hegel on, 9:524
Eunomia, Solon on, 3:79
Euphantus of Olinthus, 6:111
Eurasian movement, Karsavin's active part in, 5:43
"Eurasian Temptation, The" (Florovskii), 3:672
Eurasianism, **3:453–454**
Florovskii a founder of, 3:672
main idea of, 9:531
Trubetskoi (Nikolai) as founder of, 9:530
Euripides, 4:176–177
love in, 5:583–584
Nietzsche on, 6:610, 9:524
on suicide, 9:322
on war and peace, 7:152
Europa (journal), 8:631
Europa i chelovechestvo (Europe and mankind) (Trubetskoi), 3:453
Europa—Mutter der Revolutionen (Heer), 2:122
Europe
environment and food supply as social growth agents, 1:719
Renaissance in, humanism in, 4:480–481
in Spengler's cultural morphology, 9:166
state sovereignty in, 9:145
Stein as copatroness of, 9:239
Sufism in, 9:309–311
unification efforts of 17th century, 7:154–155
European culture, as defined by Kireevskii, 5:75
European Journal of Parapsychology, 7:116
European philosophy, as continental philosophy, 2:488–489
European tradition
on epistemology of technology, 7:549
on technology, 7:546
Eusebius, **3:454–455**
as apologist, 1:228
patristic philosophy and, 7:143
on Simonians, 9:33
on suicide, 9:319
Eustachius of St. Paul, 2:749
Eustratios of Nica, 7:610, 1:788
Euthanasia, **3:455–459**
allocation issues and, 6:96
in debate on speciesism, 9:164
legal moralism and, 5:338
medical ethics of, 6:94
in right to die issues, 9:321–322
Euthydemus (Plato)
Colotes of Lampsacus on, 3:263
on dialectic, 3:52
on human good, 9:112
on sophists, 3:343, 9:130
Euthyphro (Plato), 2:611
on definition, 2:665, 2:666, 9:110
definition of virtue in, 7:586
on divine command theories of ethics, 3:94, 6:359
on essence, 7:595, 7:587
on historic Socrates, 9:107
Metrodorus of Lampsacus on, 3:263
ousia in, 7:62
on religion and ethics, 3:391
Socrates in, 7:584
Evaluation
in attributor contextualism, 2:483
criteria of legal, 7:453
of law, 7:452–453
in moral concepts, 6:159
Evaluative predicates, 4:862
of aesthetic qualities, 1:40
differences in application of, 4:862
Evangelische Glaubenslehre (Spener), 7:576
Evangile et l'église (Loisy), 5:570–571
Evans, C. Stephen, 5:67
Evans, Gareth, **3:459–462,** 5:102
on anaphora, 1:172–173, 1:175
on concepts, 2:415
on conceptual and nonconceptual mental content, 2:480
Evans, Marian (Mary Ann). *See* Eliot, George
Evaporation, Aristotle on, 1:272
Event, necessary connection between, 4:637
Event horizons, determinism and, 3:33
Event memory, 6:122
Event ontology, 7:24
Event theory, **3:466–468**
Events
causal account of time and, 2:87
in Davidson's adverbial modification, 8:808
as fact and event in causation statements, 1:549
as judicanda of justice, 4:863
nature analyzed in terms of, 9:748
observability of, 1:486–487
in ontology, 7:25
probability frequency of, 1:644, 9:658
property exemplication accounts of, 5:71
revelation and, 8:453
in semantic theory, **3:462–466**
Events and Their Names (Bennett), 1:549
Everett, Hugh, III
in quantum mechanics, 5:695
relative state formulation of quantum mechanics, 5:696–698
on von Neumann-Dirac collapse, 5:696–697
Everlastingness *(aevum),* in medieval philosophy, 3:358
Evidence
in Bayesian confirmation, 1:499–500
Bayes's theorem and, 3:321
of behavior and mental phenomena, 1:520
as behavior in psychology, 1:525–526
and belief, in Calvinism, 2:12
Bentham contributions to law on, 1:551
in Buckle's historiography, 1:718–719
in Cartesianism, 2:54–55
Collingwood on, 2:327
for common consent arguments for God's existence, 2:346
of complementarity of quantum theory and empirical phenomena, 1:637–639
vs. concept, in metaphysics, 6:184
for concepts in Quine, 2:417
in confirmation of hypotheses, 1:497–498
confirmation theory, 2:433– 442
conscience and, 2:447
for consciousness, 1:205–206
as convergence of opinion, 1:500
in cosmological models, 2:560
in deductive reasoning, Mill (John Stuart) on, 6:223
and doubt, 3:102–103
estimating value of, 6:275–276
historical, 6:270–273

imagery in thinking as, 1:596
incremental confirmation explication and, 2:437–438
inference from empirical generalization, 1:637
kalām argument on God's existence and, 2:555
as knowledge, 5:88
of knowledge in art, 1:334
in law, 1:444
logic of, 6:272–273
in mathematical foundations, 6:20
mathematical models of black holes and, 1:607–608
for mental qualities, 2:452
of mental sentences, Wodeham on, 9:822
of miracles, 6:269–271, 6:273–274
new theory entailment from old, 1:501
Nicod's condition and background, 2:440
observation and observers as, 1:633
Ockham on, 9:778
or probability in paradoxes of indifference, 2:436
past as, 7:452
of probability of hypothesis, 1:496–497
projectability in confirmation theory and, 2:441
Raven's paradox in confirmation relations, 2:440
relevance of, 1:501–502
reliability in Buddhist epistemology and, 1:753–754
and religious belief, 1:762
rhetoric in law, 1:443
in rhetorical method, 1:444
rules of, 7:452
scientific theory confirmation of, 1:500–501
of subjective probability, 1:497
syllogistic inference and, 5:502
in teacher-student dynamic, 7:357
in theology, 9:780
theory of, 6:116–117
in underdetermination theory, 9:575–578
and underdetermined belief, 1:535
unexamined, determining import of, 3:103
use of, 1:443
in verificationism, 8:689–690
for warrants in attributor contextualism, 2:486

Evidence for certainty, 6:116–117
Evidence for presumption, 6:116–117
"Evidences of Revealed Religion, The" (Channing), 2:130
Evident assent, in John of Mirecourt's epistemology, 4:841
Evident presumption, 6:117
Evidentialism, **3:468–469**
in justification of knowledge, 3:272
religious epistemology and, 3:321
Evil, **3:469–471**
Abelard on, 1:5
Aquinas on, 9:433
Arendt on, 1:254
Aristotle on, 3:398
of asceticism, 1:353
atheism and, 7:481
as atheistic argument, 1:361–364
in Bolingbroke, 1:642
Brentano on, 3:421
in Cambridge platonists, 2:13
as caused by unkownable contingents, 1:678
in Chen Yi-Zhu philosophy and neo-Confucian rationalism, 2:156
Christianity on, 1:363, 3:469–474, 3:477–478
Collins on freethinking and, 2:331
in common consent arguments for God's existence, 2:348
conservatism and, 2:469–470
definition and criteria for, 7:245, 7:247, 7:249
desire, lower as, 1:352
devil and, 1:367
Emerson on, 3:196
faith and, 1:363–364
free will and, 1:559, 9:408
as germ in Xunzi, 2:234
Gersonides on, 4:69
God, existence of, and, 1:361–364, 7:481, 9:380, 9:408–409
as God's "dark nature," 9:124
God's toleration of, Duns Scotus on, 3:144
Graham on, 1:367
Green (T. H.) on, 3:416
Hick on, 7:481
hiddenness of God and, 4:350–355
as human nature in Xunzi, 2:233
human propensity for, in conservatism, 2:469–470
Itō on, 4:766
justification of, 9:711
kakon as, **1:256**
Leibniz on, 5:251, 5:254, 5:263–265
as limitation of God, 1:695
in literature, 1:43
in Machiavelli, 5:627–628
in Malebranche, 5:669–670
in Manichaeism, 5:683–684, 9:380
Mansel on, 5:688
McTaggart on, 6:79
nature and, 6:520
as necessary stage toward good, 8:621
necessity of, 9:408
from nonbeing as substratum, 1:760
as obsessive superiority, 2:23
Ockham on, 9:783
origin in free choice, 1:559
Pannenberg on, 7:82
Paulsen on, 7:148
Plato on, 3:397–398
Plato's indeterminate dyad as, 7:633, 7:636
Plotinus on, 3:401
problem of, 1:623, **3:471–478**
Descartes on, 2:744–745
in divine omnipotence, 4:111
in emanation, 4:108
God's goodness and, 3:7–8
incompatibility of with God's infinity, 4:671
Lewis (C. S.) on, 5:312
Maimonides on, 3:23
moral evil, 3:469–474
Plantinga on, 7:579, 7:581
Plato on, 7:594
Plotinus on, 7:639
in Schelling, 8:621
Solov'ëv on, 9:122–123
Spinoza on, 9:176
in Stephen's agnosticism, 9:243
Proclus on, 8:41
punishment as, 8:160
Rashdall on, 8:239
reality of, 1:362–363
reason used for, 6:606
relative amounts of, 7:253
relativity to historical change, 7:247–248
resisting by force, Il'in on, 4:578
Robinet on, 8:482
Rowe on, 7:481
Socrates on, 3:397
Spinoza on, 9:174
Tennant on, 9:393
Theophrastus on, 9:412
Thomasius on, 9:441
totalitarianism and, 1:254

Evil, *continued*
types of, 3:470, 3:472
Voltaire on, 9:711
Weil (Simone) on, 9:737
Wolff on, 9:829
Wollaston on, 9:833
wrong distinguished from, 2:31
Zen'kovskii on, 9:869
in Zoroastrianism, 9:887
See also Theodicy
Evil demon scenario, as not a relevant alternative, 5:106
Evil spirits, 4:97
Evolution
action selection and subjectivity in, 1:565
in anthroposophy, 9:242
artificial intelligence and, 1:348
behavioral basis for, 1:521
Bergson on, 1:568–570
Buffon on, 1:759
in Cassirer, 2:67–68
chance in, 7:339–340
closed societies as impediment to, 1:571
cognitive science and, 2:300–301
communist society as process of, 2:362
consciousness in, 1:205
creationism and, 8:670–671
as creative holism, 9:71
as creative love in Bergson, 1:570
Descartes on, 4:611
design argument for existence of God and, 1:368
Diderot on, 3:74
duration and novelty as, 1:569
emotions and, 3:201
ethics in, 6:515–516
falsifiability and, 8:670
God as final stage of, 4:109–110
Goethe on, 4:142
Haeckel and, 4:201–202
historical laws and development in Buckle, 1:719
humanity as purpose of, 1:570
of humans
Haeckel on, 4:202
Wallace (Alfred Russel) on, 9:721
Huxley on, 4:531–532
Kimura on, 7:340
of languages, 1:342
Lewes on, 1:361
materialism and, 6:11
McCosh on, 6:71
McDougall on, 6:72
Montgomery on, 6:340
moral development as cause of final release from, 2:110
morality in, 1:204, 9:789
in Morgan (C. Lloyd), 6:402–403
Nagel on, 7:343–344
ontogenesis and, 1:658
of perception in Bergson, 1:565
Portmann on, 7:321
in pragmatic view of science, 6:502
as principle of historical reconciliation, 2:4
progress and, 8:47
in Purvamimamsa-Uttaramimamsa schools, 4:134
randomness *vs.* mechanism of appearance in, 1:632
reason degraded by, 1:474
reincarnation and, 8:333
in Samkhya-Yoga schools, 4:134
in Sankhya, 2:112
Santayana on, 8:597
Schiller's (Ferdinand) reality thesis in support of, 8:624
significance tests in, 9:214
Skelton on, 7:341
social, Habermas on, 4:200
sociocultural, Habermas on, 4:200
Spencer on, 7:714
Spencer's law of, 3:667
of state vectors in quantum mechanics, 1:635
survival of the fittest, in game theory, 4:20–22
Teilhard on, 9:374–375
teleological argument for existence of God and, 9:377–378
teleology in, 7:342–343
theories of animal consciousness and, 1:201
thought as origin of, 1:566
unique, 3:30–34
Williams on, 7:341–342
Wilson (Edward O.) on, 9:789
Wright (Chauncey) on, 9:846
Zhou's evolutionary cosmogony through yin and yang, 2:155
See also Darwinism; Natural selection
"Evolution and Ethics" (Huxley), 3:668
"Evolution by Natural Selection" (Wright), 9:846
Évolution créatrice, L' (Bergson), 1:57
Evolution de la matière, L' (Le Bon), 3:233
"Evolution of the Nature of Religion, The" (Forberg), 1:377–378
Evolution of theology in the Greek Philosophers, The (Caird), 2:4
Evolution: The Modern Synthesis (Huxley), 7:339
Evolutionary account, of human social development, 3:567
Evolutionary anthropology, on universal religious belief, 2:349
Evolutionary cosmology, Peirce on, 7:171–172, 7:174
Evolutionary creativity, pessimism and, 7:250
Evolutionary ethics, **3:478–480**, 4:686
Evolutionary homologues, 3:201
Evolutionary naturalism, Petzoldt on, 7:268–269
Evolutionary pantheism, of Hegel, 6:193
Evolutionary philosophy, brought to the defense of social conservatism, 3:668
Evolutionary positivism, 7:713–715
Evolutionary processes, permanence and, 7:268
Evolutionary programming, 1:348
Evolutionary psychology, **3:480–486,** 8:136–137
adaptationism in, 3:481–482, 3:484
computationalism in, 3:481, 3:483–484
empirical case for, 3:486
modularity in, 3:482–483, 3:484–485
problems with, 3:483–485
sociobiology debate and, 3:490–491
universality in, 3:482–483, 3:485
Evolutionary Psychology (Buss), 3:486
"Evolutionary Psychology and the Massive Modularity Hypothesis" (Samuels), 3:485
Evolutionary stable strategy (ESS), 3:480, 4:21
Evolutionary theory, **3:486–493**
adaptationism debate, 3:489–490
Bergson on, 1:569
in Cabanis, 2:2–3
causality in, 1:784
and Chamberlain, 2:123
chance in evolutionary biology, 2:127
Christian theology and, 7:557
criticisms of, 2:636–639
cultural impact of, 2:628–643, 2:711–712, 3:478
of Darwin (Charles), 2:628–630, 2:632–635, 3:487–488

of Darwin (Erasmus), 2:631, 3:486
Dennett on, 2:711–712
ethical impact of, 3:415
in James's philosophy of religion, 4:779–780
La Mettrie on, 5:180
Lamarck on, 2:635, 3:486–487, 5:174
as mechanistic, 1:568–569
modern, 2:643, 3:488–489
and moral norms, 3:446
on origin of life, 5:360
physicotheology and, 7:561–562
reproductive technologies and, 4:43
sociobiology debate, 3:490–491
and war, Bernhardi on, 7:154
Evolutionism
vs. emanationism, 3:189
of Jodl (Friedrich), 4:835
Maupertuis and, 6:67
social, Krueger on, 5:156
Evolutionist, Kropotkin as, 5:154
Evraziistvo (Eurasianism), 3:454
Evropeets (Kireevskii), 5:74
Ewing, A. C., 4:150
ethics, 3:420
as intuitionist, 4:735
metaethics of, 6:156–157
on Moore (G. E.), 3:419
Ex falso quodlibet sequitur. See Explosion
Ex impossibli quodlibet, 5:429
Exact Fitness of the Time in Which Christ Was Manifested in the Flesh, Demonstrated by Reason, Against the Objections of the Old Gentiles, and of Modern Unbelievers, The (Woolston), 9:844
Exactness, Wittgenstein on, 9:811
Examen critique des apologistes de la religion chrétienne (attrib: Fréret), 2:266
Examen critique du Nouveau Testament (attrib: Mirabaud), 2:266
Examen de la religion (attrib: Damarsais), 2:266
Examen du Nouveau Testament (attrib: Mme. du Châtelet), 2:267
Examen Vanitatis (Gianfrancesco Pico), skepticism in, 9:50
Examen vanitatis doctrinae gentium et veritatis Christianae disciplinae (Examination of the vain doctrine of the gentiles and the true Christian teaching) (Pico della Mirandola), 7:574–575
Examination dos tradiçoens Phariseas conferias con a ley escrita (Costa), 2:572
Examination of Malebranche (Locke), 5:380, 6:656
Examination of McTaggart's Philosophy (Broad), 9:485
Examination of Mr. J. S. Mill's Philosophy (McCosh), 6:71
Examination of Sir William Hamilton's Philosophy (Mill, John Stuart), 2:357, 3:629, 6:225
Examination of the Place of Reason in Ethics, An (Toulmin), 3:431
Examination of the Scotch Philosophers (Priestley), 8:6
Example, precedent as, 7:449
Excellence, ren in Confucian ethics, 2:194
Excellence and Grounds of the Mechanical Philosophy, The (Boyle), 7:557
Excellence of Technology, or the Pre-eminence of the Study of Divinity above That of Natural Philosophy (Boyle), 1:675
Exceptions to rules, miracles as, 6:265, 6:266
Exceptive clauses, Aquinas's use of, 6:104
Exchangeability, in probability theory, 2:663, 8:37
Excluded middle
law of, 5:547, 6:527, 6:676
in Brouwer, 2:502–503, 6:527
interpretations of, 5:231–235
in intuitionistic and classical logic, 2:504
proper names and, 8:59
traditional formulation of, 5:232–233
validity of, 1:701
Exclusion, in Buddhist nominalism, 9:585–586, 9:587
Exclusion principle, fermions satisfying, 3:636
Exclusion problem, 3:586
Exclusion theory, in epistemology, 9:544
Exclusive legal positivism, 5:241–242
Excusable actions, 6:118
Excusationes (Durandus of Saint-Pourçain), 3:148
Excusing, *vs.* forgiving, 3:697
Exdurantism, persistence and, 7:209–210
Exemplar Humanae Vitae (An example of human life) (Costa), 2:572, 4:825
Exemplarism, in Bonaventure, 1:651
Exemplification, in Keynes, 5:457
Exercitationes (Scalinger), 1:385
Exercitationes Paradoxica Adversus Aristotleos (Gassendi), 4:25, 9:53
Exertion, in volition, 9:703–705
Exhaustion method, on magnitude ratios, 2:493
Exhortation to Philosophy (Iamblichus), 4:540
Exigit Ordo Executionis (Nicolas of Autrecourt), 6:599–602
Exile, Adorno and, 1:26
Exist
as predicate interpreted by context, 1:662
Russell on, 7:17
use of, 7:22
Existence, **3:493–500**
with absolute worth as categorical imperative, 2:70
of abstracts, 1:529, 3:498–499
as accident, 5:649
Alexander on, 1:109
anthropology and, 7:316
Aquinas on, 2:551
Aristotle on, 2:540–541
of atoms, in Indian philosophy, 1:381–382
Avicenna on, 1:433
being as, 6:188–189, 7:17
as being in phenomenal world, 1:678
belief and, Quine on, 7:28
Bernard of Tours on, 1:592
body and, 5:701
Bohr on, 1:637
bracketing, in phenomenology, 7:285–287
Bultmann on, 1:762–763
Capreolus on, 2:30–31
in Chinese religion, 2:224
in Clarke, 2:270
common cause principle and, 2:342
common sense and, Moore on, 2:359
in content internalism, 8:82
as contingent, 2:587
continued and distinct, 4:498–499
creative activity as, 1:610
in Dge-lugs Mādhyamika, 1:732–734
in domain, 7:22
Duns Scotus on, 3:135
Einstein on, 6:639
vs. essence, 1:432–433, 9:443
essence and, 1:476

Existence, *continued*
of fictional characters, 6:635–636
of fictitious objects, 3:493–498
of fields and singularity in general relativity, 1:608
formation of concepts of, 1:578–579
Gassendi on, 2:747
of God, 2:550–556
abstract objects and, 2:553
d'Ailly on, 1:99
Alembert on, 1:106–107
Anselm on, 1:214–216, 4:112
Aquinas on, 2:677–680, 7:557, 9:431–432
Averroes on, 3:135
Avicenna on, 1:433, 3:135
beauty and, 9:407–408
being in arguments for, 9:431
belief in, self-deception in, 8:711–713
Berkeley on, 4:556
biological design and, 2:347
Blanshard on, 1:362
Bradlaugh on, 1:362
causality in argument for, 9:432
Clarke's argument for, 9:407
Collier on, 2:323
common consent arguments on, 2:344–354
consciousness and, 9:407
cosmological argument for, 9:407
degrees of perfection argument for, 2:677–680
Descartes on, 2:720, 2:728, 2:736, 2:741–748, 2:755, 3:292, 4:14, 8:123–124
design argument for, 1:368
Duns Scotus on, 3:135–137, 3:146
ethics and, 7:479–480
evil and, 1:361–364, 9:380, 9:408–409
Fackenheim on, 1:363
faith and, 1:363
Galluppi on, 4:14
Gaunilo on, 4:33–34
Geyser on, 4:83
in Gregory of Rimini, 4:183
hallmarks of successful proof of, 9:407
Hume on, 4:510
in Jaspers, 4:802
Jodl (Friedrich) on, 4:835
Johnson (Samuel) on, 4:851
Kant on, 4:556
La Bruyère on, 5:167
lack of evidence for as proof against, 1:361–362
laws of nature and, 9:407
Leibniz on, 2:553, 5:256
Lewis (C. S.) on, 5:312
Locke on, 3:300, 5:387
as logical impossibility, 7:18
as logical necessity, 1:216, 7:18
Lunn on, 1:363
in Maritain, 5:714
materialism and, 6:14
Matthew of Aquasparta on, 6:65
and meaning of life, 5:345–346, 5:352, 5:359
moral arguments for, **6:353–360**
morality and, 1:397, 9:407
motion in argument for, 9:432
in movement of atoms, 4:28
Narboni on, 4:821
Ockham on, 9:781
Paine (T.) on, 7:74
Paley on, 7:77
Pascal on, 7:133
in philosophy of religion, 7:480–481
physics and, 1:361
Plantinga on, 3:324
popular arguments for, **7:700–705**
practical reason in argument for, 4:613
probability and, 9:407
as proof of nativism, 4:687
Ray on, 7:558
relevance of, 1:363
Richard of St. Victor on, 8:592
Rowe's argument against, 9:408
Sabatier on, 8:588
Scholz on, 8:645
Spinoza on, 9:173–175, 9:185
in Stillingfleet's moral certainty, 9:249
Suárez's metaphysical proof of, 9:283–284
suffering and, 1:362
as superultimate "why," 9:758
Swinburne on, 3:321
teleological argument for, **9:376–382,** 9:407
Toletus on, 9:511
Udayana on, 4:627
Vasquez on, 9:650
Voltaire on, 9:709
Xenophanes of Colophon on, 9:854
See also Design argument for the existence of God; Ontological argument for existence of God
God as explanation of, 2:586
God as source of, scientific arguments and, 6:209
Heidegger on time and, 9:490
in Huayan Buddhism, 1:738–739, 2:164
human
moral dimension of, 3:616
tragic character of, 1:560
Hume on, 6:192
illuminationism on, 4:583
impermanence of, 6:621
of inductive probabilities, 2:437
inference of, 6:600
infinite regression of, 1:741
intentionality and, 1:689
in Jaspers. *See Existenz*
in *kalām* argument on God's existence, 2:553–554
Kant on, 7:22, 7:28
Kierkegaard on, 3:501
knowledge of, 8:131
in Leibniz on God's existence, 2:551
love in, Unamuno on, 9:568
in Mādhyamika doctrine, 1:731, 1:740–742
Maimonides on, 5:649
in Marcel, 5:701–702
Marty on, 5:729
measurement in quantum mechanics and, 1:540
in medieval metaphysics, 6:188
in metaphysics, 6:199
of mind independent as impossible, 1:578
modes of being in Ingarden, 4:683
in Moore's theory of truth, 2:542–543, 2:543
of moral facts in constructivism, 2:471
Mullā Ṣadrā on, 6:419–420
as mystery, Unamuno on, 9:568
in natural law and natural rights as fictions, 1:552
nonbeing and, God as solution to, 9:459
from nothing and causality in quantum mechanics, 2:554
of others, 5:687–688
ousia as, 7:63
pain of, 6:620
Parmenides of Elea on, 7:124–126, 7:128

as particle locality and hidden variables, 1:540
pathos of, in Schelling, 8:622
perception as necessary for, 1:574
perfection and, 7:22
permanence of, 6:601
Plato on, 6:185
in Plato's correspondence truth theory, 2:540
as possibility, 1:2
precritical writings of Kant and, 5:10
as predicate, 1:528–529, 7:17
primacy of, 6:420
private language problem and, 8:15–16
of properties, 5:667–668
reality of, Descartes on, 2:735–736, 2:740–744, 2:747–748
requirements for, 6:78
in Russell's theory of truth, 2:543
in Santayana, 2:596
Sartre on, 3:351, 3:503
of sensible qualities, 6:601
social dimension of, 7:397–398
Solov'ëv on, 9:123–124
special evidence of, 4:841
struggle for, 7:338
subjectivity of, 7:316–317
tensed *vs.* tenseless, 9:478–481
Tetens on, 9:404
Thomas of York on, 9:443
Thomist argument for God's existence and, 2:553
Toletus on, 9:511
Unamuno on, 9:567–568
unprovability of, Gorgias of Leontini on, 4:163–164
value statements of, 1:436–437
Vasubandhu on, 9:651
of work of art, 4:598
in Yogācāra Buddhism, 1:749
See also Essence and existence; Proof, of God's existence

Existence and Essence. *See* Essence and Existence

"Existence and Objectivity" (Marcel), 5:700

Existence entailing, of part and whole, 6:146

Existence proofs, as an elaborate intellectual facade, 3:746

Existent(s)
in Avicenna, 1:432–433
eternity of, 6:120
incorporeality of, 6:120
infinity of, 6:120
vs. intelligible, in Scholasticism, 9:772–773
in new realism, 6:586
in sense-datum theory, 8:819–820
vs. subsistent, 7:22
unity of, 6:120

Existential action, imaginative activity as human, 1:610

Existential analysis, 7:322–323

Existential assertions, in use of "to be," 1:527–531

Existential commitment, avoiding unwanted, 3:627

Existential feminists, 3:563

Existential function, in Frege, 5:507

Existential generalization, rule of, definition of, 5:542

Existential import
definition of, 5:542
in Venn, 5:451

Existential instantiation, rule of, definition of, 5:542

Existential moments, 4:683–684

Existential perspective, on heaven, hell, and judgment in Christianity, 2:249

Existential phenomenalism, 1:59–60

Existential phenomenology, subject/object dualism of, 3:563

Existential philosophy
introduction of, 5:45
Kaufmann and, 5:46

Existential presuppositions, 3:251

Existential propositions, 6:331
in Leibniz, 5:443
in medieval logic, 5:443

Existential psychiatry, 3:507

Existential psychoanalysis, 3:507, **3:510–514**
being-in-the-world and, 3:512–513
intentionality in, 3:512
Sartre on, 3:510–514, 8:608
subject-object split and, 3:511–512

Existential quantification
descriptions and, 5:508
in effective calculable function definability, 2:380

Existential quantifier, 3:648, 5:542

Existentialism, **3:500–510**
Abbagnano on, 1:1–2
and absurdity, 4:748
aesthetics and, 1:59–60
alienation in, 1:124
anthropology and, 7:315
anticipated, in Schelling, 8:618
of Aquinas, 9:430
authors, 3:504–505
and Barth, 1:480
Camus's relationship to, 2:20
on choice, 3:503
Christian, of Zubiri (Xavier), 9:888
in crisis of skepticism, 9:58
critique of, 3:507–509
on death, 2:652–653
on Divine personality, 4:112
Dostoevsky on, 3:99
Duns Scotus and, 3:145
epistemology and, 3:317
ethics, 3:426–428
in ethics of Beauvoir, 1:515
feminist thought and, 3:563
fideism and, 3:321
foundations of German, 3:715
free agent decisions in, 9:7
on freedom, 1:515, 3:503
German, 1:1
Gilson, 4:92–93
in Gogarten, 4:144
happiness in, 2:652
Hegelianism and, 4:285–286
in history of metaphysics, 6:195
on intentionality, 3:502
Italian, 1:1, 1:2
Jaspers in, 4:799–803
Kafka's exploration of, 5:5
of Lavelle, 5:214–215
linguistic philosophy and, 3:428–429
Lukács and, 5:604
as a major player in Korean philosophy, 5:141
Mamardashvili on, 5:679
Marcel and, 5:700
Murdoch on, 6:433
in Nietzsche, 6:612
optimism/pessimism and, 7:252–253
origins of, 3:508
of Ortega y Gasset, 7:46
Pascal and, 7:134
Pastore on, 7:135–136
personalism and, 7:236
in phenomenology, 7:285
and politics, 3:506
possibility in, 1:1–2
in postmodernism, 6:318
and psychiatry in Binswanger, 1:597–598
psychoanalysis and, 3:507
rationalism and, 3:501, 3:507–508
religious, 7:495
of Rosenzweig, 8:498
in Sabatier, 8:588
Sartre and, 1:455–456, 5:46, 6:195, 8:603, 8:610

Existentialism, ***continued***
in Schelling, 8:621–622
self-defeating aspect of, 1:1–2
in Shestov's religious philosophy, 9:11, 9:13
Stefanini on, 9:237
structuralism as reaction to, 9:273
stylistic characteristics, 3:503–504
subjective direction of, 3:715
theistic, 5:700
themes in, 3:500–504
theologians, 3:505–506
in theology of Bultmann, 1:762–764
of Unamuno, 9:566
value in, 1:2
Existentialism from Dostoevsky to Sartre (Kaufmann), 5:46
Existentialism, Religion, and Death (Kaufmann), 5:46
Existentialisme est un humanisme, L' (Sartre), 8:603
Existential-phenomenology, 8:461–462
Existentials, negative, 1:145–146
Existenz, 4:800–801
Existenzerhellung (illumination of existence), 4:800
Existenzursprung (authentic communication), in Jaspers's psychology, 4:801
Ex-Marxist intellectuals, symposium volumes published by, 3:716
"Exodus to the East," 3:672
Expectation(s)
analytical behaviorism on, 1:525
under codified law, 1:554
and mental states, 1:525
mind's capability of, Mill (John Stuart) on, 6:226
Experience(s), **3:515–518**
in *a priori* and *a posteriori,* 1:240–242
absolute and, 8:12–13
acquired after death, 4:602
as aesthetic and as ordinary, 1:508–509
as aesthetic value, 1:508–509
in analogical arguments on God in Butler and Hume, 1:783
analogies of, 5:19–20
artistic independence from, 1:508–509
of atomic properties *vs.* experiential qualities, 1:577
in behavior and psychology, 1:525–526
being and, 5:702
and belief, 1:533, 8:177–178
Benjamin on, 1:546
body in, 6:148
in Bowne, 1:671
Brightman's notion of referent as immediate, 1:695
on Brouwer's logic and, 5:468
in Buddhism, 6:256
Bultmann on, 1:763
Cassirer's concept of manifold experience, 2:66
categories and, 7:746
as causal evidence, Ockham on, 9:780
in causality and direct realism, 2:97–98
causality as unobservable in, 2:106–107
causation and, 6:224
as cause of idea of beauty, 1:514
in Chan Buddhism, 1:729, 2:167
in Chinese ethics, 2:201
Clifford on, 2:291–292
in cognition, 6:74
Cohen (Hermann) on, 2:302
in coherence theory of truth, 2:310–312
in coherentism, 8:180
colors and, 2:333
concept-immediate experience relationship in Hume, 2:95
concepts and, 1:533, 2:416, 9:596
Condillac on, 2:422
conditional, 1:598
Condorcet's probability calculus and, 2:431
consummatory, 1:64
content of, 5:528
of continuity, 1:198
Creighton on, 2:592
in Croce, 2:602
Crusius on knowledge and, 2:606
definition and, 1:241
definition of, 3:214
deriving mathematical knowledge from, 5:83
description as chaos and equivalence classes, 2:38
Destutt de Tracy on, 5:656
in development of scientific method, 1:590
Dewey on, 3:45–46, 3:49–50
dialectical resolution of antithetical experience, 1:476
as dialogue of reason and experience, 1:440
of distance perception, 1:575
dread as experience of nothing, 1:530
in education, 7:371
empiricist view of, 9:414
in empiriocriticism, 7:715
as equivalence classes, 2:38–39
evidence by, 9:778
as existential necessity, 1:579
existentialists on, 3:503
facets of, 3:552
faith as method of organization for, 9:459
fallibilism in conservatism, 2:465–466
of fiction, 1:68
in Forberg, 1:378
forms of, Collingwood on, 2:325–326
foundationalism on, 8:177–178
Four Dharmadhāus, 1:738–739
freedom as precondition of, 7:2
freedom as spontaneous, 1:564
genealogy as an attempt to remember, 3:700
generality recognized in, 9:588
in Geyser's causality, 4:83
of God, impossibility of, 8:403
habituation and, 5:656–657
Hartley on, 8:135
Held on, 4:299
Helmholtz on, 6:540
history and, 7:396–397
human, Nishida on, 6:625
illumination by God as cognitive, 1:652–653
immediate, 6:625
criteria for defining, 3:516–517
and doubt, 3:103
theories on, 3:515–516
impoverished by reduction to object, 1:545
in inclusion in moral community, 9:164
incorrigibility of basic propositions and, 1:484–487
induction from, Locke on, 4:638
inner, 1:544, 3:622, 5:655–656
instructiveness of, in Turgot, 9:551
intentionalists on, 7:191
interior, of man, 3:607
Islamic philosophy on, 4:7
in James's
metaphysics, 4:783–784
philosophy of religion, 4:779
pragmatism, 4:783, 7:744–745
psychology, 4:776, 4:779
in Jaspers's epistemology, 4:800
in Kant, 8:134
knowledge and, in Trubetskoi (Sergei), 9:532

knowledge as, 4:835. *See also* Empiricism
knowledge of, displaced-perception model of, 8:725
Lange on, 6:540
law of organization of experience, 1:476
as learning God's will, 1:574
in legal theory, 7:448
in Lewis (C. S.), 7:746
Liebmann on, 5:344–345
Locke on, 5:379, 8:149
vs. logic, in law, 7:448
in logical positivism, 4:308
Maimon on, 5:646
in Maine de Biran, 5:655–657
materialism and, 6:15–16
Maupertuis on, 6:67
medical authors on, 4:7
in metaphysics, Kant on, 6:202
Miki on, 6:216
Mill (John Stuart) on, 7:712–713
mimesis in, 4:94
in moral community, 7:2
moral order and, 1:378
in moral theory, 4:299
mystical. *See* Mystical experience
natural language in, 6:74
neural networks and, 2:444
nonveridical, 6:588
objective *vs.* subjective, 5:130
operationalism and, 7:32
in opposition to inferential knowledge, 1:453
orders of perspective on, 1:738–739
ordinary, immediate experience and, 3:517
organization by science and philosophy, 1:476
palingenesis in, 4:94–95
as part of logical space of reasons, 5:89
passive, 5:656
past as conditioned present in neurosis, 1:598
Peirce on, 6:194
perception in evaluation of, 1:533
perceptual
  transparency of, 7:191–192
  true-false evaluation in, 1:533
perceptual consciousness in, 8:817
of persons *vs.* of kerygma, 1:763
philosophers' view of, 3:515
philosophical value of ordinary everyday, 3:566
in physics and psychology, 5:528
physiology of, 8:135
plurality and relatedness as features of, 1:678
pragmatism and, 7:744–745, 7:746, 7:747
preceded by self, Nishida on, 4:798
as primitive vagueness, 1:678
principles of, in metaphysics, 6:203
as private, 5:528
private language problem and, 8:16
proof of, 8:19
in psychology
  Natorp on, 6:490
  Wundt on, 9:849
pure, 4:784
  new realism and, 6:587
  in Nishida, 4:797–798, 6:625
in pure time, 1:563
qualitative properties of, 5:72
reality of, Nagel (Thomas) on, 6:475
realm of contents in, 9:31
vs. reason, in music, 1:49
reason as law of organization, 1:476
reason as self-ordering experience, 1:477
religion and, 7:713
religious, Alston on, 7:482
as revealing morality in Cumberland, 2:615
Rickert on Kantian conception of, 6:545
Romero on, 8:492
Rosenzweig on, 8:498
in Rousseau, 7:371
Sabatier on, 8:587
sensation as, 1:576
sensation's significance in, 1:584
sensibility in, 6:74
sources of complex illusion sources in, 1:704
Spaventa's phenomenalist account of, 9:160
of spontaneity as freedom, 1:564
status of inner experience as immaterial entity, 1:544
as stories in Chinese ethics, 2:200
structure of, 5:528
thinking and, 5:687
in Tiantai Buddhism, 2:163
of time, 9:464
transcended by faith, 4:772
translation of experience in Carnap, 2:41
transparency of, 7:191–192
in truth, Unamuno on, 9:568
truth conditions and, 9:665–666
truth constituted by, 4:783
in Tschirnhaus, 9:549
Turgot on, 9:248
types of in Bacon (Roger), 1:453
understanding and, 6:74, 9:455
unity of, 5:16–17, 7:1
universals and, 9:587–588, 9:601
value of, 9:641
in verifiability, 9:663
visual, 1:325–326
of volition, 9:703–705
in wisdom, 9:795
without volition, 9:703–704
"Experience" (Emerson), 6:574
Experience and Its Modes (Oakeshott), 4:559, 7:1
Experience and Judgment (Husserl), Landgrebe and, 5:183
Experience and Nature (Dewey), 1:57, 1:64, 3:45, 3:51, 8:799
Expérience humaine et la causalité physique, L' (Brunshcvicg), 1:714
Experience Machine, 8:721
Experience of Mallarmé (Blanchot), 1:611
Experiences nouvelles touchant le vide (Pascal), 7:129
Experiencing as, 3:533
Experiential apologetics, religious pluralism and, 8:420
Experiential expressivism, 8:636
Experiential intuition, of Korn, 5:142
Experiential learning, perceptual skill and, 7:184
Experiential memory, 6:122
Experiential *vs.* metaphysical, in Rickert, 6:544–545
Experientialism
  incompatible experiences and, 3:323
  religious epistemology and, 3:322–323
  representation and, 1:327–329
Experiment(s)
  of Boyle, 1:672–673
  in Cartesianism, 2:55
  Chinese room argument as, 2:238–242
  confirmation theory and, 2:435
  controlled, difference method of induction used in, 6:247
  crucial, Duhem on, 3:128–129
  dubiousness of instrument and senses, 2:118
  Einstein-Podolsky-Rosen experiment, 1:540–541
  findings of introspective, 5:160

Experiment(s), ***continued***
frequency and propensity in chance, 2:127–128
Helmholtz on, 4:305
initial conditions in chaos theory, 2:132
measurement as empirical data, 1:637–639
medical experiments and bioethics, 1:599
in metaphysics, 6:210–211
operational point of view as theoretic basis for, 1:693–694
in psychology, Wundt on, 9:849
Experimental aesthetics, Külpe furthering the development of, 5:161
Experimental apparatus, quantum logic and, 8:204–205
Experimental design, Fisher's theory of, 3:663–664
Experimental History of Colours (Boyle), 1:674
Experimental medicine, free and informed consent in, 6:97
Experimental method, 3:218, 3:219, 3:557
Experimental philosophy, *vs.* mechanical, 6:593
Experimental Researches in Electricity (Faraday), 3:550
Experimentalism, of Maupertuis, 6:66
Experimentation
Alembert on, 1:105
in animal consciousness, 1:201–202
on animals, **1:208–209**
in art, 1:299
Bacon, Roger as proponent, 1:455
in Bohr, 2:531
causal inference and, 8:685–687
causality and scientific method, 2:107
in cognitive psychology, 8:152–153
in Comte, 2:411
economics as science of, 7:352–353
in European *vs.* Chinese science, 2:218
on extrasensory perception, 7:752–753
induction from results, 1:443
inductive method, 1:443
and instrumentation, **10:12–20**
limitations of, 1:440
mathematics and, Bachelard, 1:440
Newton on, 6:591
non-locality and, 6:640–641
operational rules as theory dictionary, 2:17–18
in parapsychology, 7:757
in philosophy, 1:451
progress and, 8:47
purpose of, 1:447
reduction in, 6:570–571
in thought *vs.* actual, 9:452
Experimentelle Studien über das Sehen von Bewegung, 4:72
Experiments and Observations on Electricity (Franklin), 3:720
"Experiments in Plant Hybridization" (Mendel), 7:338
Expertise
of artists, 1:334–335
in cognitive psychology, 8:151–152
Explaining Attitudes (Baker), 1:463
Explaining Behavior (Dretske), 3:108–109
Explanation, **3:518–527**
asymmetric contingent circumstances and, 2:576
atomic properties *vs.* experiential qualities, 1:577
in attributor contextualism, 2:486
and belief, 1:463, 1:533
of big conjunctive contingent fact in Leibniz, 2:551–552
Bonhoeffer on religious *a priori* in culture, 1:656
causal approach to, 3:524–525
causality, and, 1:449, 2:575
of cause in origin of universe, 2:554
in confirmation theory, 2:435
connectionist models in computationalism and, 2:393
cosmology as, 2:557–558
covering law account of, 3:519, 4:309–310
of creative behavior, 2:589
deductive-nomological account of, 3:518–520
distinguishing from estimation, 5:27–28
DNP account of, 3:526
Duhem on, 3:126
of error in moral constructivism, 2:473
of existence by creator God, 2:586
experimental science and religion in Boyle, 1:674–675
failure of Darwin theory, 1:569
fallacies in, 3:548
functional analysis as, 3:763
as functional in computationalism, 2:391
functional reductive, 6:570
Hempel on, 4:309–310, 8:593
in history, 2:327, 7:393–394
in Huayan Buddhism, 1:739
inductive-probabilistic, Hempel on, 4:309–310
inductive-statistical account of, 3:520–521
in Leibniz on God's existence, 2:552
in logical behaviorism, 1:534
mathematical intuitionism and, 5:469
medical, 7:466–467
mental representations in, 6:141
Meyerson on, 6:212–213
mystical experience in Bernard of Clairvaux, 1:592
Nishida on, 6:625–626
ontology and explanation in science, 1:635
of principle of sufficient reason in Leibniz, 2:551–552
Ptolemaic astronomy and, 2:534
qualitative consciousness and, 2:450, 2:451
relevancy criteria, 1:446
as result of eliminative induction, 1:446
Salmon on, 8:593
scientific
Descartes on, 8:124
Mill (John Stuart) on, 6:223–224
Wright (Chauncey) on, 9:846
scientific law and, 7:519
self-evidencing, in inference to the best explanation, 4:651
Socrates on, 7:759
Spinoza on, 7:96
statistical-relevance account of, 3:521–522
teleology in classical mechanics, 2:283
as theoretical deductions, 1:643–644
as truth criteria and Dao, 2:207
unification account of, 3:523–524
Explanation and Understanding (von Wright), 9:848
Explanatory gap, 5:114, 8:192–193
Explanatory power
of empirically equivalent theories, 9:577
scientific law and, 5:221
Explanatory realism and pluralism, combined by Kim, 5:72

Explanatory simplicity principle, as articulated by Mill (John Stuart), 5:83
Explanatory value theory, 9:639
Explanatory-relation accounts, and belief attributions, 1:536–537
Explication
- Carnap on, 5:527
- clarification of concepts in Carnap, 2:44–45
- Hempel on, 4:309
- incremental confirmation and, 2:437
- of inductive probabilities, 2:437
- reasoning by analogy in confirmation theory and, 2:439

Explicit definability, 6:312–313
Explicit *vs.* implicit, in communication, 7:766
Exploitation
- economic, Meslier on, 6:154
- in Marx, 5:733–734

Exploratio Philosophica (Grote), 4:189
Explosion *(ex falso quodlibet sequitur)*, in paraconsistent logics, 7:105
Exponential class, 3:663
Exponible proposition, 5:553, 8:770
Expositio (Porphyry), on imposition, 8:762
Expositio Aurea Super Artem Veterem (Golden exposition of the ancient art) (Ockham), 9:771
Expositio fidei (John of Damascus), 4:836–837
Expositio in Apocalypsim (Joachim of Fiore), 4:834
Exposition de la théorie des chances et des probabilités (Cournot), 2:577
Exposition du système du monde (The system of the world) (Laplace), 5:197
Exposition of Romans (Colet), 2:322
Expression(s)
- arousal theory of, 1:303
- in art, **1:302–307**
- art as, of emotion, 1:54–55, 1:64–65, 1:76–77, 1:79–80, 1:298
- in beauty, 9:563, 9:790
- catergorematic expressions and predication in Aristotle, 2:73
- character of, 5:39
- Collingwood art as, 2:328
- in compositionality, 2:370–372
- *vs.* concept, 1:25
- conditional, as indeterminate, 3:541
- content of relative to a context, 5:38–39
- Dewey on, 1:304
- embodiment theory of, 1:305–306
- in film, 7:384
- Frege on meaning of, 8:735
- in idealism, 1:303
- imagination and, 1:306
- indeterminacy of, 3:541–542
- in legal transactions, 7:445–446
- logical analysis of, 8:641
- meaning in compositionality and, 2:371
- meaning of, 7:400
- meaning-endowing act in, 8:803
- Meinong on, 8:804
- and music as analogy for, 1:25, 1:305
- pairing of, 5:39
- paronyms and names in Kant, 2:74–75
- Plato on, 8:754–755
- Santayana on, 1:305
- theory of art, 1:64–65, 1:303–306
- uncombined categorization of, 2:72–73
- Winckelmann on, 9:790
- Wollheim on, 1:306

"Expression and Meaning" (Husserl), 8:802
Expression and reversibility, ethics of, 6:149–150
Expression of Emotions in Man and Animals (Darwin), 1:201, 3:198
Expressionism
- Tolstoy on, 9:514
- on value of art, 1:340

Expression-type, definition of, 5:558
Expressive judgments, distinguished by Lewis, 5:96
Expressive meaning, 6:652, 9:835
Expressive presupposition, 3:252
Expressive-collaborative model, of morality, 3:580
Expressivism
- in metaethics, 6:160
- as projectivism, 8:51–52
- sentence meaning in, 6:653
- Thomson (Judith) on, 9:449
- *See also* Ethical noncognitivism; Nonfactualism

Extended propositional calculus, 5:536
Extension
- Condillac on, 2:422
- of continuum in Bois-Reymond, 2:501
- definition of, 5:542
- in Descartes's correct law of inertia, 9:154
- in Frege, 3:730, 5:464
- God's idea of, 5:667–668
- ideas of extended things in Cartesian epistemology, 2:57
- intelligible, 5:666–667
- in language, 5:704
- More (Henry) on, 6:396
- of nouns in traditional logic, 5:493
- as primary quality, 8:8
- *vs.* sensation, 5:667
- in Shepherd's causal realism, 9:10
- Spinoza on, 9:175
- of things in Crusius, 2:607
- in thinking, 9:419
- in Whitehead and Russell, 5:466
- *See also* Matter; Quality(ies), primary and secondary; Space

Extensional, definition of, 5:542
Extensional Cleanthes, 6:146–147
Extensional logic, Quine on, 7:28
Extensional substitution, in nonextensional contexts, 3:541
Extensionalism
- coextension problem of, 6:177
- universals in, 6:176–178

Extensionality
- axiom of, 5:542
- in Frege, 5:516, 8:61
- in linguistic descriptions of intentional phenomena, 4:710
- Russell on, 8:553

Extensions of concepts, in Frege, 3:731
Extensive abstraction, Whitehead's method of, 9:748
Extensive properties, modeling, 6:89–90
Extenuation, punishment and, 8:165
External account, of folk psychology, 3:678
External context of science, features of, 3:592
External negation, 6:523–524
External Relations. *See* Relation(s), internal and external
External universe, meaning of, 4:848
External world
- associationism, 1:462–463
- Collier on, 2:323
- conditional facts, beliefs, and explanations, 2:94
- Hume on, 3:218
- knowledge of
  - Berkeley on, 3:301–302
  - Hume on, 3:304–305
  - Locke on, 3:300–301
- Mill (John Stuart) on, 3:219, 6:226
- Moore (G. E.) on, 3:314
- Shepherd on, 9:10

Externalism, 3:760
- Burge on, 7:472
- content, 7:472, 8:82–83
- foundationalist, 8:178–179
- in justification of knowledge, 3:272–273
- mental content and, 2:477–478
- natural kinds and, 6:505
- in philosophy of mind, 3:276
- on primitivism, 8:179
- of rationality, 8:254–255
- in reliabilism, 8:365
- solipsism and, 9:120
- supervenience in distinguishing, 9:330–331

Externalized empiricism, of Quine, 8:220
Extractive proof theory, 8:55
Extrait des sentiments de Jean Meslier (Voltaire), 6:154
Extraordinary science, Kuhn on, 5:158
Extraverted psychological type, 4:856, 4:858
Extreme fideism, 3:631
Extrinsic properties, **3:527–528**
Extrinsic value, 9:637
Extroverted mysticism, 8:401
Ezorsky, Gertrude, on Dewey, 3:425
Ezra, 5:3, 9:179

F

Fabian socialism
- deism and, 2:691
- on society, 9:88

Fabians, Labriola and, 5:166
Fable, as utopian inspiration, 9:617
Fable of the Bees (Mandeville), 3:171, 3:408, 5:220, 5:680–682
Fabricius, David, Kepler's letters to, 3:687
Faces of Existence, The (Post), materialism of, 6:18
Fackenheim, Emil
- on existence of God, 1:363
- on life, meaning and value of, 5:345–346, 5:352

Fact(s)
- *a priori* necessary truths and, 2:474
- ambiguity of, in scientific method, 8:625
- in Ardigò, 1:251
- attitude and, 8:82
- basic statements, 1:483–487
- belief and, 2:93–94, 2:540
- big conjunctive contingent, in Leibniz, 2:551–552
- bioethical findings on, 1:600
- brute, Leibniz on, 2:551
- in causation statements, 1:549
- Christianity and, 2:246
- in coherence theory of truth, 2:309, 2:311
- common consent arguments for God's existence and, 2:345–346
- common sense and, 2:355
- condestinate, 3:6
- in Confucianism, 2:171–172
- in correspondence theories of truth, 2:544, 2:545
- cosmological, 2:558, 2:575
- counterfactuals. *See* Counterfactuals
- Croce's historical knowledge and, 2:602
- entailment by scientific theories, 1:501
- in fiction, 1:336
- historical and conditions in historiography, 1:718
- in Huayan Buddhism, 2:164
- ideas in, 9:744
- illusion of, 9:536
- language games and, 9:818
- logical and Bayesian conditionalization, 1:501
- Malcolm on, 5:662
- metaphysics and, 4:784, 6:203, 6:205
- in Moore's theory of truth, 2:542–543
- moral, 6:162
- moral constructivism and, 2:471–472
- in moral decisions, 1:603
- negative, 2:545, 6:525–526
- newfound respect for, 5:51
- in noninferential justification, 2:276
- objective, 1:541–542, 1:552–553, 5:132
- opinions as, Vailati on, 9:630
- in Peirce, 5:454
- in philosophy, Windelband on, 9:792
- physical *vs.* nonphysical, 2:89–93
- picture as, Wittgenstein on, 9:804
- practical *vs.* theoretical, Duhem on, 3:128
- presence of forms in, 1:448
- probability *vs.* subjectivity, 1:495
- in Ramsey's theory of truth, 2:546
- reductionism and causal relations, 2:95–96
- in relational sentences, 1:562
- and representations, 5:114
- in Russell's theory of truth, 2:543
- science concerned with, *vs.* philosophy, 9:792
- as scientific questions, 1:447
- in sentences, Wisdom (John) on, 9:797
- social, 9:94–95
- and systems, 1:661
- *vs.* theories, 8:671
- truth and, 9:534
- truth value and, 2:278
- types of, 5:220
- *vs.* value, 5:132, 9:643
  - emotivists on, 3:425
  - linguistic philosophers on, 3:429
  - Sartre on, 3:428
  - Sidgwick on, 3:417
  - Weber (Max) on, 9:734
- Wittgenstein on, 2:547, 5:150, 5:526, 9:804

Fact, Fiction and Forecast (Goodman), 4:154–155
Facticity
- hermeneutics of, 4:289–290
- in Sartre's phenomenology, 8:606
- volitization of, by bad faith, 8:608

Factive propositional attitudes, 5:89
Factory acts, communism and, 2:362
Facts of Causation, The (Mellor), 2:100
Factual knowledge, conscious qualitative states and, 2:451
Factual memory, 6:122
Factual necessity, ontological argument and, 7:18
Factual phenomenalism, 7:272
Factualism, and paradox of fiction, 5:367
Factuality, objective, 3:717
Faculties
- in Cartesian epistemology, 2:56
- Herbert of Cherbury on, 4:326–327

Facundo, o civilización y barbarie (Facundo, or civilization and barbarism) (Sarmiento), 5:206
Faguet, Émile, on French liberalism, 5:320
Fahrenheit, Daniel G., 6:87
"Failure of Impersonalism" (Bowne), 7:235
Failure; Un Uomo Finito (Papini), 7:102
"Faintest Passion, The" (Frankfurt), 3:719

Fair equality of opportunity, 8:258–259
Fairness
in computer access and social power, 2:397
and equality, 3:335–336
justice as, 8:257–258
punishment and, 8:169
vs. utilitarian ethics, 3:384
Faith, **3:529–537**
Abelard on, 1:7
and actions to achieve good purposes, 3:535
analogous to "seeing as," 3:533
Anselm on, 1:214, 3:403
Aquinas on, 3:529–530, 3:535, 9:425–426
Arnauld on, 1:289
attenuation of, 7:495
Augustinianism on, 1:402
Averroism on, 1:429
Bayle and, 1:505
being and, 5:702
Buber on, 1:716, 3:536
in Buddhism, 1:722, 2:168, 6:255
Calvin on, 2:10
Cambridge platonists on, 2:13
certitude of, 6:580
Clement on, 2:290
and cognitive freedom, 3:533
as commitment, 3:535
as communal matter, 3:536
conative element in, 3:533
Descartes on, 8:123
as direct awareness of God, 3:533
as *emunah vs. pistis,* 1:716
evil and, 1:363–364
existence of God and, 1:363, 3:535
external assessment of, 1:142
Fackenheim on, 1:363
as form of religious experience, 3:533
freedom and, 1:289, 3:533, 3:715
Gogarten on, 4:144
Haeckel on, 4:203–204
independence of God from, 8:645
as individual matter, 3:536
as interpretation, 3:533–534
Jacobi (Friedrich Heinrich) on, 4:771–772
James and, 3:531
as Jewish response to God's commitment, 3:536
justification by, in Christianity, 2:249, 8:588
Kant on, 5:23, 7:493, 7:543
Khomiakov on, 5:59–60
Kierkegaard's leap into, 9:58
knowledge and, 1:782–783, 3:529, 4:772, 9:425–426
Aquinas on, 9:426
as knowledge of God, 3:535
scientific knowledge, 3:532
Tennant on, 9:392
Leibniz on, 5:263–264
Lewis (C. S.) on, 5:312
Locke on, 5:99, 5:387, 5:392, 9:249–250
Luther on, 3:530, 5:614–617
Marcel on, 5:700
and material world, 3:532
meanings of, 3:529
Meslier on, 6:154
and miracles as probability, 1:783
modern theories of, 3:531–533
and natural philosophy, 1:451
object of, 3:529
political conservatism and, 2:465
pragmatic, 3:535
as pragmatic assumption, 3:535
precursive, 3:531
as propositional, 3:532
in Pure Land Buddhism, 2:168
pure practical, propositions in, 5:21
rationalist definition of, 3:531
reason and, 1:505, 3:530
in Averroism, 1:429
Bayle on, 1:505
Collingwood on, 2:326
John of Jandun on, 4:838–839
Newman on, 6:583
Unamuno on, 9:567
Whichcote on, 9:745
in Reformation, 8:297
Régis on, 8:300
revelation and, 8:452–453
rewarding, with verified knowledge, 3:532
risk of, measure of, 5:99
Sartre on, 1:455–456
Schleiermacher on, 8:632
Scholastics on, 5:615–616
and scientific knowledge, 3:532
as surrender, in Tillich, 9:459
Theophilus on, 1:229
Thomist analysis of, 3:531
Tillich on, 8:635, 9:459
transition to, 5:67
Trubetskoi (Sergei) on, 9:532–533
truth and, 3:530, 3:630
understanding and, 1:402, 1:479
and voluntary belief, 1:535
Faith [term], different senses of, 3:535
Faith and History (Niebuhr), 3:35
Faith and Reason (Collingwood), 2:326
Faith of a Heretic, The (Kaufmann), 5:46
Faith of a Moralist (Taylor), 9:373
Faithful model assumption, 3:30
Faktizität und Geltung (Habermas), 4:199
Falāsifa, 3:69–70
Fales, Evan
on causality in direct realism, 2:97
on properties, 5:227
Falk, W. D., 3:426
Fall, The
Augustine on, 3:473–474, 7:367–368
British theology on, 3:474
Calvin on, 3:473
in Christianity, 2:248–249
Erigena on, 3:342
and evil, problem of, 3:475–476
Losskii on, 5:577
modern theology on, 3:474
sexuality and, 7:522
Fallacie Parvipontane (anon.), 8:769
Fallacy(ies), **3:537–550**
a dicto secundum quid ad dictum simpliciter, 3:539–543, 3:550
a priori, 3:547
of accident, 3:539–540
and ambiguities, 3:541–542, 8:767
ambiguous middle, 3:542
avoidance and detection of, 3:549–550
in Carroll, 2:52
classification of, 3:537
of composition, 3:541–542
concerned with classification, 3:545
of confusion, 3:545, 3:547
of consequent and antecedent, 5:502, 5:543
of crude hypothetico-deductive (H-D) pseudo-confirmation, 3:741
definition of, 5:542–543
of denial of antecedent, 5:543
in discourse, 3:537, 3:546–548
of division, 3:541–543
of equivocation, 5:543
in evocative argumentation, 2:213–214
in explanation and definition, 3:548
formal, 3:537–541
gambler's, 3:545–546, 9:217
genetic, Freud's commission of, 3:746
ignoratio elenchi, 3:547–548, 5:543
illicit major, 3:539

Fallacy(ies), ***continued***
- illicit minor, 3:539
- illicit process, 5:543
- Indian philosophy on, 9:544–545
- inductive, 3:544
- of inductive causal inference, 3:741
- informal, 3:537, 3:541–543
- of interrogation, 3:548
- of many questions, 3:548, 5:543
- medieval logic and, 5:429–430
- of mind as mechanism, 1:563–564
- naturalistic, 3:366, 3:418–419, 3:445, 3:479, 3:548, 6:228, 8:2
- *non causa pro causa,* 3:538, 5:543
- *non sequitur,* 5:543
- in nondeductive reasoning, 3:537, 3:543–546
- in observation, 3:537, 3:543–546
- pathetic, 3:546
- *petitio principii. See* Begging the question (circular reasoning)
- philosophical, 3:548–549
- *post hoc ergo propter hoc,* 3:543–544
- of prejudice, 3:547
- *quaternio terminorum,* 5:543
- of rearranging operators, 3:540
- in reasoning about probability, 3:545–546
- of saving hypotheses, 3:544
- *secundum quid,* 5:543
- *vs.* sophistry, 3:537
- statistical, 3:545
- strict sense of, 3:537–543
- thematic affinity, 3:743
- truthlikeness of, 9:546–547
- of undistributed middle, 3:539, 5:543

Fallibilism
- about empirical belief, 5:96
- about justification, 5:104
- conservatism and, 2:465–466
- in epistemology, 3:274, 7:750–751
- Quine and, 7:750–751

Fallibility
- of belief, 4:780–781
- of introspection, 4:778
- in precognition, 7:755

Falsafat Ibn Rushd (Antūn), 1:431

False, in many-valued logic, 5:483

False awareness, asserting, 5:118

False belief(s), 2:542–543, 5:93, 9:39

False confession, memory in, 6:126

False consciousness, 4:574

Falsehood
- in Cartesian epistemology, 2:56–57
- *vs.* negation, 6:523–525
- objective, 6:525
- social factors in, 9:78
- in Wittgenstein's theory of truth, 2:547
- *See also* Lying

Falsifiability, 7:688–689, 9:661, 9:669

Falsificationist theory testing, 9:577

Falsity
- in immorality, Wollaston on, 9:833–834
- metalinguistic analysis of, 7:196–197

Fame, Johnson (Dr. Samuel) on, 4:854

Familie Schroffenstein, Die (Kleist), 5:78

Family
- Aquinas on, 9:435
- in Buddhism, 1:723
- in Confucianism, 2:174–175, 2:196
- genetic manipulation and, 4:44
- Haeckel on, 4:204
- Hegel on, 4:268
- in neo-Confucianism, 2:181
- in Plato's *Republic,* 7:591

Family Idiot, The (Sartre), 3:510, 3:514, 8:609

Family resemblances, 6:234, 9:601–602, 9:810, 9:820

Famine, Affluence, and Morality (Singer), 3:443, 9:41

Fancy
- Coleridge on, 2:318–319
- *vs.* imagination, 1:55, 2:318–319, 4:597
- Kant on, 4:596

Fang Dongmei, Buddhism and, 2:169–170

Fang Ke-li, 2:182

Fangyan (Dialect Words) (Yang Xiong), 9:860–861

Fanon, Franz, 7:728, 9:7

Farabi, al. *See* al-Fārābī, Abū-Naṣr Muhammad

Faraday, Michael, **3:550–552**
- and electromagnetic field theory, 2:282, 3:235, 3:635, 6:68
- on energy conservation, 3:232
- Engels on, 3:58
- on fields in classical mechanics, 2:282

Fardella, Michel Angelo, Leibniz and, 5:253

Farias Brito, Raimundo de, **3:552–353,** 5:207

Fascination, religious, Otto on, 7:60

Fascism, **3:553–555**
- Adorno on, 1:26
- Croce on, 2:600
- Del Vecchio and, 2:697
- Gentile and, 4:50, 4:53
- as irrationalist ideology, 4:752
- Marxism and, 5:740
- militarist tradition and, 7:154
- neoromantic universalism and, 9:158
- Pareto and, 7:117
- political philosophy and, 7:672
- propaganda and, 1:26
- Scheler on, 8:616
- Spengler and, 9:165
- Sturzo on, 9:281
- totalitarian scope of, 3:553

Faṣl al Maqāl (Averroes), 4:758

Fatal Strategies (Baudrillard), 1:491

Fatalism
- Arnauld and, 1:292
- *vs.* determinism, 3:17
- Epicurus and, 8:121
- Guo Xiang and, 4:196
- Leibniz and, 1:292
- memory and, 7:755–756
- precognition and, 7:754

Fatalistic predestinationism, Buddha and, 5:42

Fate
- Chrysippus on, 2:252
- in Confucianism, 2:175
- determinism and, 3:5, 3:35
- in Gnosticism, 4:101
- in Greek philosophy, 3:35
- Moira, 6:319
- in *Taixuan jing,* 9:861
- Wang Chong on, 9:723–724

Father, in Freudian explanation of religion, 8:378

Fathers and Sons (Turgenev), 6:617

Fathers of the Church. *See* Patristic philosophy

Faurisson, Robert, 5:620

Faust (Goethe), 4:140, 5:588

Fausto-Sterling, Anne, 3:586, 8:679

Fax Historica (Lipsius), 5:364

Fay, J., 7:97

Fayan (Model Sayings) (Yang Xiong), 9:860–861

Fazang, 1:737–739, 2:154, 2:164

Fear
- of death, 2:651–653
- freedom from, 3:723
- of nothing, 5:64
- in psychoanalytic theory, 8:111–112

Fear and Trembling (Kierkegaard), 5:64

Fearn, John, 9:10

Features, Leibniz on, 5:272

Fechner, Gustav Theodor, **3:555–558**
- on *a priori* knowledge, 7:86

on aesthetics, 1:514, 3:556
on beauty, 1:514
Carnap and, 2:35
James (W.) on, 7:84
Külpe and, 5:161
Lotze and, 5:580
panpsychism and, 7:82–89
Paulsen and, 7:149
and psychology, 8:139
on unconscious, 9:571
on Weber, 8:139
Federalism, anarchism and, 1:176
Federalism, Socialism, and Anti-Theologism (Bakunin), 1:472
Federalist, The, 7:665–666
Fëdorov, Nikolai Fëdorovich, **3:558–560**
Feeling(s)
in aesthetic experience, 1:32–33
in Buddhism, 5:328
Collingwood on, 2:328
in common consent arguments for God's existence, 2:347
Croce on, 2:601
Cyrenaics on, 2:619
Destutt de Tracy on, 2:760
Eliot (George) on, 3:184–185
gratitude as, 1:475
as judicanda of justice, 4:863
Kierkegaard on, 5:63
Langer on, 5:188
Lavater on, 5:214
Lotze on, 5:582
Mill (James) on, 6:219
Mill (John Stuart) on, 6:226
Peirce on, 7:171
personality and, 4:856
philosophy of
criticisms of, 4:772
Jacobi (Friedrich Heinrich) in, 4:769
pleasure as, 7:619–620
primacy of, in apprehension of values, 8:616
religion as determination of, 8:634
religious, Otto on, 7:59–61
in religious language, 8:414
Schleiermacher on, 8:634
sympathy-empathy distinction in, 9:344
Whitehead on, 9:751
See also Emotion(s)
Feeling and Form (Langer), 1:58, 5:187
"Feeling of Effort, The" (James), 3:689
Feenberg, Andrew, 7:544
Feferman, Solomon
on computability, 2:385, 5:478
on predicative theory and continuum, 2:501, 2:506
and proof theory, 8:55
on semantic paradoxes, 5:521
Feigl, Herbert, 4:643
on identity theory, 7:470
on justification of laws of logic, 5:512
Lehrer and, 5:248
on logical positivism, 5:524
Feinberg, Joel, **3:560–562,** 7:137
on harm, 5:337
on Wollaston, 9:834
Feldman, Fred
on hedonism, 4:152
on utilitarianism, 9:613
Feldman, Richard
on conditions of knowledge, 3:272–273
on skepticism, 3:275
Felicity, Spinoza on, 7:96
Felix (Lull), 5:610
Female Biography (Hays), 9:839
Female embodiment, experience of, 3:575
Female Genius trilogy (Kristeva), 5:152
Female heterosexism, 3:756
Female lives, alternative or resistant, 3:580
Femininity
Cixous on, 2:263
eternal, Sophia as, 1:760
role of, identifying and refiguring, 3:570
as term of deficiency, 4:745
Feminism, 3:590–591, 3:594–596
and aesthetics, **3:571–574**
in African philosophy, 1:86–87
altruism in, 1:137
analytic, **1:157–159,** 3:586
as anti-essentialist about sex and gender, 3:586
Astell and, **1:355–356**
Beauvoir and, 1:515
as bias, 1:158
on Cartesian dualism, 5:373
and challenge to category of woman, 3:575
on coercive institutions, 9:75
common theoretical basis for, 3:598–599
continental philosophy and, **3:562–566,** 9:276
education and, 7:359
and empiricism, 3:595
and epistemology, **3:574–578,** 3:590
Anderson on, 1:158
Code on, 2:295–296
core themes in, 3:574–577
domains of investigation in, 9:84
Harding and, 8:677
Hume (David) on, 1:459
pragmatist feminist development in, 3:567
and essentialism and nature of the self, 3:586
and ethics, **3:578–582**
issues addressed by, 3:580
on moral labor, 1:459
and practices of morality, 3:581
theory of, 3:748
existential freedom and, 1:515
free speech in, 7:462–463
and history of philosophy, **3:569–3:571,** 5:373
identity in, 1:158
and jurisprudence, 7:462–463
just war theory challenged by, 4:874
Latin American philosophy and, 5:208
in law, 7:462–463
Leibnizian-Wolffian School and, 9:824
liberal
beliefs of, 3:599–600
humanist, 7:462
legal theory of, inadequacies of, 3:583
scholars of, 3:582
Lloyd (Genevieve) and, **5:372–374**
MacKinnon on, 7:523
and Marxism, 3:563
and moral philosophy, 3:578
and naturalism, 3:596
networks and communities in, 3:580
Nietzsche and, 6:614
Nussbaum on, 6:681
philosophy of, **3:590–591**
Card and, 2:31
Cixous and, 2:262–263
Frye and, 3:755
Gournay and, 4:166–167
Irigaray and, 4:745–746
males in, 9:75
Stein and, 9:239
Thomson (Judith) and, 9:448
and philosophy of sex, 7:521
postmodern, 1:158, 3:564–565, 3:575, 3:585
pragmatism and, **3:566–568**
privacy in, 7:462–463
on question of subject, 9:276
radical, 7:463
Rousseau and, 8:516

Feminism, *continued*
and science, 3:596, 8:679
on sex and gender, 3:586
and social and political philosophy, **3:598–603**
socialist, 3:601, 3:606
theoretical basis for, 3:598–599
on war and peace, 7:157
Feminism and History of Philosophy (Lloyd), 5:373
Feminism Unmodified: Discourses on Life and Law (MacKinnon), 7:523
"Feminist Epistemology: An Interpretation and a Defense" (Anderson), 1:158
Feminist legal theory, **3:582–585,** 8:849–850
Feminist metaphysics, **3:585–590**
Feminist Morality (Held), 3:580
Feminist phenomenologists, 3:563
Feminist philosophy, 3:591–598
of science, **3:590–591,** 8:679
Feminist standpoint theory, 3:564, 3:575, 3:592, 3:595
Fènelon, François de Salignac de la Mothe, **3:603–604**
Feng Youlan, 2:169–170, 2:182
Ferdinand II (Holy Roman emperor), 2:723
Ferguson, Adam, **3:604–606**
Garve on, 4:24
Stewart and, 9:247
on virtue and vice, 9:247
Ferguson, Ann, 3:601, **3:606–607**
Fermat, Pierre, 2:282
Fermenta Cognitionis (Baader), 1:439
Fermentario (Fermentary) (Vaz Ferreira), 5:208
Fermions, 3:636
Fernández de Lizardi, José Joaquin, 5:205
Ferrandi, Durandus, 3:149
Ferrara, Francis Sylvester of. *See* Sylvester of Ferrara, Francis
Ferrater Mora, José, 5:209
Ferreira, M. Jamie, 5:67–68
Ferreira da Silva, Vicente, 5:210
Ferri, Luigi, **3:607–609**
Ferrier, James Frederick, 1:12, **3:607–609**
Ferrier, Jean, 2:757
Fetishism of commodity, Marx on, 3:69
Fetus
life-status of, 1:8
moral status of, 6:93
as person, 7:238–242
Feudalism
Confucius and, 2:231
as mode of production, 5:732
Feuer, Lewis, on alienation, 1:122
Feuer und Blut (Jünger), 4:859
Feuerbach, Ludwig Andreas, **3:609–613**
alienation in, 1:120–122
anthropology and, 7:316
Dühring and, 3:130
Freud and, 3:746
Hebbel and, 4:254
Hegelianism and, 3:609–610, 3:612, 4:284, 9:263
influence of, 3:612
Kozlov and, 5:146
Lange on, 5:187
Lassalle and, 5:203
Lavrov and, 5:218
Marx and, 3:56, 3:67, 3:612, 4:573
Pannenberg and, 7:80–81
translators of, 3:184
Feyerabend, Paul
eliminative materialism and, 3:182
in post-positivist debate, 8:694
on theory of relativity, 3:179
Feynman, Richard, 8:200–204
Feys, Robert, 2:337
Fichte, G. W.
on determinism, 3:15, 3:17
and pantheism, 7:97–98
on unconscious, 9:571
Fichte, Johann Gottlieb, **3:613–620,** 5:146
on absolute, 1:11, 3:616
absolute idealism and, 4:557
on apperception, 1:234
on atheism, 1:358, 1:377–380
Atheismusstreit and, 1:377–380
on authoritarianism, 3:410
Bakunin and, 1:471
and Belinskii, 1:538
coherence theory of truth and, 9:536
Deleuze on, 2:695
dialectic and, 3:54
on duty, 3:414
on education, 7:374
and epistemology, 3:309
and ethics, 3:414
on experience, 4:749
on formalism, 5:30
freedom in, 7:375
on French Revolution, 1:377
Fries and, 3:751
God in, 1:378–379
Goethe and, 1:380
on I and non-I in comparison to Mou, 2:222
influence of, 3:618–619
on intuition, 4:723
Kant and, 1:377, 3:613, 5:708, 6:539
Kierkegaard and, 5:67
Krause and, 5:147
Liebmann on, 5:344
on love, 5:588
Maréchal and, 5:708
moral ideas of, 7:374–375
on nationalism, 6:484
in neo-Kantianism, 6:541
Nicolai on, 6:598
Novalis and, 6:667
on optimism/pessimism, 7:250
on properties, 7:375
Savigny and, 7:426
Schelling and, 8:617
Schiller (Friedrich) and, 8:628
Schlegel and, 8:630
Schmid and, 1:377
Schopenhauer on, 8:648
and science of knowledge, 3:614–617, 4:50
society in, 7:375
Spinoza and, 9:194
on unity, 7:374
Vysheslavtsev and, 9:717–718
Ficino, Marsilio, **3:620–626**
and Bruno, 1:708–709
as Christian magi, 1:710
Colet and, 2:321
on human beings, nature of, 7:572
influence of, 3:624–625
on innate ideas, 4:688
Leonardo da Vinci and, 5:281, 5:282
on love, 5:587
Patrizi and, 7:144
Pico della Mirandola and, 3:624, 7:570–572
in Platonic tradition, 1:48, 7:613–614
on Pletho, 7:631
Proclus and, 8:44
scholars and, 3:671
on soul, 5:259
Fiction(s)
assessment of, 1:335
Augustine on, 1:47
in Buddhism, 1:742–743
Carnap on, 2:40
in Carroll, 2:52
characteristics of, 9:626
characters in
as concepts, 1:336
ontological status of, 5:366–367

conventional *vs.* ultimate truth, 1:742–743
definition of, 5:365–366
emotional impact of, 1:68
and entities as nonsense, 1:552
as epistemic theories, 2:38
examples of, 9:627
facts in, 1:336
in film, 7:384
horror, 1:336
as idols of mind, Bacon (Francis) on, 1:446
in knowing chaos, 2:39
vs. literature, 5:364
locutionary and illocutionary act in, 1:509
logical, definition of, 5:547
vs. logical construction, 9:796
make-believe view of, 5:365–368
of Marcel, 5:700
and moral agents, 1:779
in natural law, 1:553
in natural rights, 1:553
nonexistent objects in, 6:635
paradigm cases of, 3:626
paradox of, 5:367–368
pretense theories and, 6:637
in theories, 1:446
theses about, 3:626
utility of, 9:626–627
Vaihinger on, 9:626–627
value of, 5:370–371
See also Literature; Novel(s)

Fictionalism, **3:626–630,** 9:626–627
antirealism of, 6:172
vs. eliminativism, 3:626
fictions and, 3:626
and interpretation, 3:626–629
mathematical. *See* Nominalism
modal, Rosen-style, 3:627–629
modalism and, 6:286–287
moral, of Richard Joyce, 3:628
nominalism and, 6:630–631
noneist, challenges of, 3:629
vs. realism, 3:626
vs. reductionism, 3:626

Fictitious objects, existence of, 3:493–498

Fide Orthodoxa, De (John Damascene), 4:697

Fideism, **3:630–633**
atheism on, 1:364
Bayle on, 1:505–506, 4:96
Charron on, 2:135
Fackenheim and, 1:363
Gourney on, 4:166
Hamann and, 9:57
Hume and, 9:56
Jacobi and, 2:691
Jurieu on, 4:96
Kierkegaard and, 9:57
La Mothe Le Vayer and, 5:182
Mercier on, 6:145
moderate, 3:631–632
Montaigne on, 9:52
Nicolaus of Cusa and, 9:50
rational-skeptical, Glanvill on, 4:96–97
religious epistemology and, 3:320–321
Russell on, 8:560
Swift and, 9:341
voluntarism and, 9:716

Fidelity
vs. loyalty, 5:596
promises and, 8:54

Fides, 3:529. *See also* Faith

Fiducia, 3:529–530. *See also* Faith

Fiducial probabilities, 3:666

Field(s)
and agreement methods of induction, 6:245
in classical mechanics, 2:280–282
particles and, **3:634–636**
of a relation, definition of, 5:543
symmetry and conservation principle of, 2:462–463

Field, Hartry H., **3:633–634,** 5:85
on Craigian reaxiomatization, 2:584
on existential sentences mathematical theories, 3:628
on internal language, 8:808
on Leibniz, 2:552
in nominalism, 6:628–629
on number, 6:675
on productivity of propositional attitude states, 3:759
on semantic paradoxes, 5:521

Field equations, in cosmology, 2:561

Field of Consciousness, The (Gurwitsch), 4:197

Field operators, in elementary particle theory, 4:298–299

Field theory
beginning of, 3:551
Bohmian mechanics and, 1:635
mass in, 6:5
Maxwell and, 6:68–69
Newtonian physics and, 6:61

Fields, Factories, and Workshops (Kropotkin), 1:179

Fiery matter, of Aristotelian doctrine, 5:53

Fiesco (Schiller, Friedrich), 8:626

Fifteen Sermons Preached at the Rolls Chapel (Butler, Joseph), 1:781

Fifth Ennead (Plotinus), on eternal return doctrine, 3:353

Fifth Set of Objections (Gassendi), 4:26

Figgis, J. N., 9:143

Figurative language, definition by, 2:675–676

Figure(s)
definition of, 5:543
imperfect, definition of, 5:545

Figure-ground
irreducibility of, 6:150
perception and, 7:184

File Change Semantics (FCS), 8:748–749

Filial piety
Mencius on, 2:233
Mozi on, 2:235–236

Filler-functionalism, 6:135–136

Film, **7:381–386**

Filmer, Robert, **3:636–637,** 5:388, 9:81

Filoque, Trinity in Christianity, 2:248

Filosofia dell'arte (Gentile), 4:50

Filosofia di Gioberti, La (Spaventa), 9:160

Filosofia di Marx, La (Gentile), 4:49

Filosofia do espirito (Farias Brito), 3:552

Filosofia oggi, La (Sciacca), 8:666

Filosofiia Gegelai kak uchenie o konkretnosti Boga i cheloveka (The philosophy of Hegel as a doctrine of the concreteness of God and man) (Il'in), 4:577

Filosofiia imeni (Philosophy of the name) (Bulgakov), 1:760

Filosofiia imeni (Philosophy of the name) (Losev), 5:574

Filosofiia khoziaistva (Philosophy of the economy) (Bulgakov), 1:760

Filosofskii trekhmesiachnik (Kozlov), 5:146

Filosophfii prava (Philosophy of law) (Chicherin), 2:148

Filosophia di Giambattista Vico, La (Croce), 2:600

Filosoviia obshchego dela (Fëdorov), 3:558

Fils naturel, Le (The natural son) (Diderot), 3:71

Filum Ariadnes, 5:442

Final causes, Ockham on, 9:780, 9:781

Final state, in quantum theory, 8:209

Finalidade do mundo, A (Farias Brito), 3:552

Finality
in Aquinas, 9:431
guaranteeing a purposeful development, 3:660
Finance
power and, 7:732
Price in, 8:1
Priestley on, 8:7
See also Economics
Findlay, J. N.
on analytic propositions, 1:243
noncognitivism in, 3:327
Prior and, 8:13
Fine, Kit, 2:428, 6:290
Fine art, beauty in, 1:511
Fine Arts Reduced to the Same Principle, The (Batteux), 1:297
Finetti, Bruno de, 8:613
on convergence of opinion, 8:685
on proper scoring rule, 9:221
on subjective probability, 8:36
Fine-tuning, 8:400–401
Fingarette, Herbert, 2:195, 8:714
Finitary method, 5:543, 8:55
Finite combinatorial methods, Hilbert on, 5:470
Finite machines, computing machines and, 2:403
Finite monads, 6:325
Finite procedure, in computability theory, 2:373
Finite set, definition of, 5:543
Finitism, 4:659, 9:366
Fink, Eugen, **3:637–639**
Finkelstein, David, 8:533
Finnis, John
Dworkin and, 3:157
on natural law, 6:513
philosophy of sex and, 7:523
on Thomism, 9:383, 9:447
Finnish school, on Luther, 5:617
Fire
Heraclitus on, 4:318–319
in Pythagoreanism, 8:183
in Stoicism, 8:121
as type of matter, 6:59
Fire sacrifice, in Zoroastrianism, 9:886
First causes
Aquinas on, 2:679–680
Damascius on, 2:622–623
Darwin (Charles) on, 2:630, 7:561
Darwin (Erasmus) on, 2:631
Duns Scotus on, 3:146
God as, 4:109
Kant on, 5:23
patristic philosophy on, 7:141
Peckham on, 7:162
First Degree Entailment, 5:689–690
First Dialogue (Berkeley), on sound, 9:138
First Jansenism, 4:790
First Letter concerning Toleration (Epistola de Tolerantia) (Locke), 5:375, 9:509
First mover, Averroes on, 3:226
First Notions of Logic and Difficulties of Mathematics (De Morgan), 5:461
"First Person, The" (Anscombe), 1:213
First philosophy, 3:614
First Philosophy or Ontology (Wolff), 9:824
First (primary) intention, 5:546, 9:776
First principle(s)
Alembert on, 1:106
Arabic departures on, 7:610
certitude and, 3:140
corporeality of, 7:607
Damascius on, 2:623, 6:551–553
of materialism, 6:203
in metaphysics, 6:204
monad and dyad in, 4:312, 7:606, 7:607
Mullā Ṣadrā on, 4:759
in neo-Confucianism, 9:6
Pascal on, 7:132
Pico della Mirandola on, 7:614
Platonic-Christian synthesis of, 7:609
Reid on, 8:327–329
validation in inductive method, 1:447
First Principle of Theoretical Philosophy (Solov'ëv), 9:122
First Principles (Spencer), 3:232, 3:354
First system of freedom, 3:614
First Truths (Primae Veritates) (Leibniz), 5:253–255, 5:258, 5:272–274
First Vatican Council (1870), on faith, 3:530
Firstness, Peirce on, 7:164, 7:168, 7:171
First-order desire, personhood and, 7:240
First-order formulas, useful conventions for writing, 3:649
First-order functional calculus, 5:476, 5:536
First-order induction schema, for arithmetic, 3:650
First-order justice, 4:864
First-order languages, 3:639
changing sentences from true to false, 3:640
common core, 3:641
compared to natural, 3:640
interpretations of, 3:649–650
Robinson on, 5:481
First-order logic, **3:639–659**
compactness theorem, 8:840
completeness theorem of, 8:840
computing machines and, 2:404
definition of, 5:543
extensions of, 6:313–314
L of "constructible" sets in, 8:841
Mal'tsev on, 5:480
metatheorems and, 3:653
paradox in, 8:842
Robinson on, 5:480
on state authority, 9:211
translating between English and, 3:644–647
Zermelo's axioms in, 8:840
First-order model theory, 6:302–305
First-order Peano arithmetic, 3:650
First-order syntax, 3:647–649
First-pattern analysis, in persuasion, 9:245
First-person egoism, 3:362
First-person methods, religion and, 8:381
First-person perspective, personhood and, 7:239–240
First-Person Perspective and Other Essays, The (Shoemaker), 9:15
First-person statements, incorrigible, 7:55
First-wave feminism, 3:599
Firth, Roderick, on ideal observer, 4:562, 6:163
Fischer, Kuno, **3:659–660**
on contradiction, 4:270
controversy with Trendelenburg, 2:302
in neo-Kantianism, 6:540
Fischer, Marilyn, 3:567
Fishburn, Peter C., 2:657
Fisher, The (Lucian of Samosata), 5:597
Fisher, Ronald Aylmer, 3:488, **3:660–667,** 8:613
evolutionary theory and, 3:488
on Mill's causal inference, 8:686
on postsampling distribution, 9:230
in probability, 8:26–27
on significance testing, 9:213–215
Fisherian significance tests, 9:213–215
Fiske, John, **3:667–668**
Fitness, 7:341. *See also* Evolution; Philosophy, of biology
Fittingness, moral properties and, 6:156–157
Fitzhugh, George, 3:637

Five elements, in Daoist cosmology, 4:794
Five senses. *See* Senses
Five Types of Ethical Theories (Broad), 1:699
Five Ways (Aquinas), 2:677
Fixed-point approach to truth, 5:318
Flames, Bacon's analysis of, 1:447
Flanagan, Owen
  on Buddhism, 2:199
  on moral naturalism, 8:156
Flaubert, Gustave
  realism of, 1:56
  Sartre on, 1:455–456, 3:507, 3:510, 3:514, 8:604, 8:609
Fleck, Ludwik, 9:78
Fleetwood (Godwin), 4:136
Flesh, Merleau-Ponty on, 6:148, 6:149
Fletcher of Saltoun, 6:219–220
Flew, Antony
  on evil, 3:474
  parapsychology and, 7:116
  on personal identity, 7:215, 7:216
  on religion, 7:478
Flewelling, Ralph Tyler, on personalism, 7:235
Flexibility, in Buddhism, 1:722
Flint, Robert
  on agnosticism, 1:94
  on atheism, 1:357, 1:372
  on common consent arguments for God's existence, 2:344
  on Hamilton, 1:94
Flirting, 7:525
Florence, Italy, Dante in, 2:623
Florenskii, Pavel Aleksandrovich, **3:668–671**, 3:673, 9:529
  Bulgakov and, 1:760
  Ivanov and, 4:768
  Losev and, 5:574
  Lotman and, 5:579
  Solov'ëv and, 9:126
Florentine Academy, **3:671–672**
Florentine platonism, 2:322
Floresta, Nisia, 5:207
Florovskii, Georgii Vasil'evich, 3:453, **3:672–674**
Flower Garden of All Kinds of Loveliness (Koerbagh), 9:177
Flower Garland School (the Avatamsaka School), holistic doctrine of, 5:135
Flucht ins Vergessen: Die Anfange der Psychoanalyse Freuds bei Schopenhaeur, Die (Zentner), 3:736
Fluctibus, Robertus de. *See* Fludd, Robert
Fludd, Robert, **3:674–675,** 8:187
Fluidum theory of heat energy, 3:229
Flux
  Cratylus on, 2:584
  Diderot on, 3:73
  of energy, Whitehead on, 9:747
  Platonic Forms and, 9:590
Fluxions, in Newton's calculus, 2:495
Flying Arrow argument against motion, 6:409–410, 9:875
Focus, phenomenalism and, 7:275
Fōdo (Climate and Culture) (Watsuji), 4:797
Fodor, Jerry A., **3:675–677**
  on action explanation, 2:648
  on Chomsky, 4:695
  on color, 2:333
  on computationalism, 2:391, 4:695
  on concepts, 2:416, 2:419, 2:478
  on connectionism, 2:392, 2:444
  "damn/darn" problem, 3:760
  on emergence, 3:193
  on folk psychology, 3:678
  on innate ideas, 4:690
  on intentionality, 4:710
  on language, 5:189–191
  on mental content, 2:477
  on mental modularity, 4:695
  on mental states, 3:756
  on mentalese, 2:478–479
  on methodological solipsism, 9:117
  multiple realization argument of, 9:162
  and nonreductive physicalism, 6:643
  on phenomenology, 7:299
  on propositional attitudes, 3:759, 8:80
  on psychological modules, 3:482–485
  on reductionism, 6:644
  on systematicity of mental representations, 2:480
  on teleology of behavior, 9:388
Folie et deraison (Madness and Civilization) (Foucault), 3:699
Folk culture, in Russia, 5:60
Folk psychology, **3:677–681**
  Baker on, 1:463–464
  laws, 3:678
  mental state concepts in, 9:36
  nature of, 3:679
  theory, 3:758
  theory-theory and, 9:37
  understanding, 3:677–678
Folk theory(ies), of concepts, 2:418–419
Folkways (Sumner), 9:102, 9:326
Føllesdal, Dagfinn, 7:299
Folly of Atheism and what is now called Deism, The (Bentley), 2:686
Fons Vitae (Ibn Gabirol). *See* "Source of Life, The"
Fonseca, Peter, **3:681–682**
Fontcuberta, Joan, 9:690
Fontenelle, Bernard Le Bovier de, **3:682–683**
  Leibniz and, 5:254
  on progress, 8:46
Food of Hearts, The (al-Makki), 9:304
Food supply, and social growth, 1:719
Foot, Philippa, **3:683–685**
  on attributive good, 4:151
  on ethical naturalism, 3:364
  on ethics, 2:713, 3:432
  on killing *vs.* letting die, 9:448
  on moral concepts, 6:158–159
  on morals and etiquette, 2:71
Forberg, Carl, Vaihinger on, 9:628
Forberg, Friedrich C.
  Adamson on, 1:378
  Atheismusstreit and, **1:377–380**
  Vaihinger on, 1:378
Force(s), **3:686–692**
  acceleration and, 3:689, 6:2
  action-at-a-distance by, 6:61
  in ancient philosophy, 3:686–687
  Boscovich on, 1:665
  in Cartesian science, 2:55
  in Cheng Yi, 2:145
  in Clarke-Leibniz correspondence, 2:269
  in classical mechanics, 2:280
  in classical physics, 2:280, 3:234–235
  as common ground of nature and ego, 8:618–619
  concept, origin of, 3:689, 5:52–53
  conservation of, 3:228
  creative, Carus (Carl) on, 2:63
  Crusius on, 2:607
  differential, 3:235
  energy and, 3:226–227
  equilibrium distribution and force transfers in gas, 1:644
  fields of, 3:235–236
  in figurative sense, 3:686
  as focus of science, 8:619
  four fundamental, in string theory, 9:267
  Gauge Theory, 4:31–33
  Helmholtz on, 4:305
  Kepler on, 4:56
  mass and, 3:689, 6:2
  mathematical definition, 3:687
  measurement of, 3:228

Force(s), *continued*
- in medieval philosophy, 3:687
- mental properties and, 6:261
- and middle term in traditional syllogism, 3:689
- in modern physics, 3:235
- Moleschott on, 6:320
- and nature, 3:660
- in neo-Confucianism, 2:155–158
- Newton on, 2:520, 3:687–688
- as nonphysical *vs.* closed physical causality, 2:90–91
- in particle theory, 4:33
- Pearson on, 7:160
- philosophical difficulties inherent in, 5:53
- and physical reality, 3:686
- of production, 5:732
- qualitative definition of, 3:688
- in religious worship, Locke on, 9:509
- scientific legitimacy of, 3:688
- of sentences, 6:650
- social, 5:740
- space as conventional and, 2:522
- spiritual, beauty as, 1:512
- syllogism and, 3:689
- as tendency to action, 3:705
- Tolstoy on, 9:513
- universal, 3:235
- unnatural motions as result of, 4:621
- *vs.* violence, 9:134
- vital impetus and evolution, 1:569–570
- in Wolff's ontology, 9:828
- and worship, Locke on, 9:509
- *See also* Violence

"Force and Matter" (Tyndall), 1:371

Force of attraction, of celestial bodies, 3:687

Force-based mechanics, 3:691

Ford, Kenneth, on Turing test, 5:635

Foreknowledge and freedom, theological problem of, 1:626, **3:692–697**, 4:113–116
- God and, 4:113–116, 6:321
- Gregory of Rimini on, 4:183
- in Molinism, 8:681–682
- Ockham on, 9:782–783
- *scientia media* in solving, 9:284
- *See also* Omniscience, divine

Forensics, 7:216–217, 7:238, 7:242

Foreseen *vs.* intended consequences, in just war theory, 4:871

Forgery
- in art, 1:295
- Goodman on, 1:295

"Forget the Medium!" (Carroll), 7:383

Forgetting Foucault (Baudrillard), 1:491

Forgiveness, **3:697–698**
- personal memory and, 6:124
- and redemption, in Christianity, 2:248–249

Form(s)
- accidental, 1:773, 2:74, 3:115
- aesthetic. *See* Aesthetics
- Alexander of Aphrodisias on, 1:112
- Aquinas on, 1:626, 3:115, 3:289, 9:427
- Aristotle on, 1:273, 1:277, 1:308, 1:385, 7:65, 9:591–593
- in Augustinianism, 1:403
- Bacon on, 1:448
- beauty and, 9:562
- Burley on, 1:773
- creation of, in Israeli, 4:814
- as determinate aspects of factuality, 3:716
- Duns Scotus on, 1:403, 3:141–142
- existence of, 9:591
- as extramental object, 1:627
- good and evil and, 2:13
- grammatical form *vs.* logical form, 1:677
- Ibn Gabirol on, 4:815
- in Indian linguistics, 9:581–582
- *vs.* Indian universals, 9:586
- in individuation, 6:102
- inseparability from matter, 1:662
- Kant on, 1:308
- logical, definition of, 5:547
- matter and, 1:385
- in medieval philosophy, 6:100, 6:101, 6:102–103
- *vs.* names, 6:103
- in Ockham's metaphysics, 9:779
- ontological status of, 1:562
- particulars and, 9:591
- Plato on, 6:185, 9:589–591
- plurality of, 1:403, 8:458, 9:782
- presence of, in things, 1:447
- of pure concepts, Croce on, 2:602
- in shaping realm of content, 9:31
- similarity of, 5:127
- soul as
  - Olivi on, 7:13
  - Zabarella on, 9:866
- species as abstract and, 1:627
- Stilpo on, 6:111
- substantial
  - Aquinas on, 3:115
  - Boyle on, 1:674
  - Locke on, 1:674
- Thomistic, 5:725–726
- as true definitions, 1:448
- as universal
  - Aristotelian, 9:591–593
  - Platonic, 9:589–591
- Vlastos on, 9:702
- *See also* Form(s), Platonic

Form(s), Platonic, 2:665–666, 3:283, 3:358, 6:185, 7:588, 7:595–600
- as accidental *vs.* essential predication, 2:74
- and aesthetics, 9:590
- Aristotle on, 1:270, 2:74, 3:350, 5:95, 9:591–593
- art and, 1:333
- beauty in, 1:512, 7:596
- Bonaventure on, 1:651, 1:652
- Bulgakov on, 1:760
- challenge to, 7:597–598
- Chinese philosophy and, 2:210–211
- in *Cratylus*, 7:595
- in dialogues, 2:665, 3:283, 3:358, 6:185, 7:588, 7:595–600
- and education, 7:366
- epistemology and, 3:283–284
- and flux, 9:590
- Gilbert of Poitiers on, 4:88
- Heidegger on, 7:616
- in history of metaphysics, 6:185
- imitation and, 1:42
- immortality and, 4:608
- as living beings, 1:622
- in macrocosm and microcosm, 7:608
- and mathematics, 9:590–591
- non-identity principle and, 7:598
- in objects *vs.* mind of God, 1:591
- Plato's ethical theory and, 3:396
- in Pletho, 9:314
- Plotinus on, 3:401
- predicates in, 9:288
- in Proclus, 8:42–43
- quality-word relationships and, 1:591
- revised theory of, 7:603
- Santayana on, 2:595
- Third Man argument and, 7:598
- time and, 3:358
- and universals, 7:596, 9:590–591

Form of representation, in picture theory, 9:804

Formal calculi, 4:310

Formal concept, Vasquez on, 9:649

Formal consequentia, definition of, 5:538

Formal distinction, Duns Scotus and, 3:138–139

Formal equality, promise of, 3:582

Formal fallacies, 3:537–541
Formal implication, 8:550–551
Formal justice, 4:864–865
Formal language(s)
 decidability of, 5:479
 definability in computability theory, 2:379–380
 vs. natural, 1:344
Formal logic
 Abelard on, 1:4
 Anderson (John) and, 1:199
 Boole on, 5:449–450
 Cohen (Hermann) and, 6:542
 Hamilton on, 5:447–448
 Hegel on, 4:265–266
 John of St. Thomas on, 4:844–845
 quantifiers in, **8:196–198**
 relation to ordinary language, 9:264
 subject and predicate in, 9:287–288
Formal Logic (De Morgan), 2:709, 5:439, 5:440, 5:448, 5:461
Formal Logic (Keynes), 5:233
Formal Logic (Prior), 8:13
Formal Logic (Schiller, Ferdinand), 8:625
Formal Philosophy: Selected Papers of Richard Montague (Montague), 6:329, 8:807
Formal proof, of a sequent, 3:656
Formal properties, 1:309
Formal reasoning, Newman (John Henry) on, 6:577
Formal supposition, 5:557
Formal system(s)
 of fuzzy logic, 3:766
 logistic, 5:548
 mathematical, Tarski on, 9:366–367
Formalism
 on aesthetic experience, 1:33
 vs. aesthetics, 1:298
 antirealism of, 6:172
 of Aristotle, 1:308
 in art, 1:298, **1:307–310**
 background of, 1:308
 of Bell, 1:295, 1:308
 of Bergmann, 1:562
 definition of, 1:307–308, 5:543
 in ethics, 9:688
 of Frege, 7:405
 of Fry, 1:295, 1:308
 Gergonne on, 5:461
 of Greenberg, 1:308
 of Hilbert, 9:366
 of Kant, 1:74–75, 1:308, 9:527
 literature in, 1:309
 in mathematical foundations, 6:21
 of Montague, 7:405
 in music, 1:309, 6:437
 Newman (John Henry) and, 6:577
 number in, 6:675–676
 painting in, 1:308–309
 Philodemus on, 1:45
 in philosophy of language, 7:405
 in physics
  outdatedness of, 4:804
  quantum mechanics and, 1:630–631, 6:640–642
 vs. Platonism, 6:675–676
 problems for, 1:309
 Russian, 9:17
 Scholz and, 8:644
 Stebbing on, 9:236
 of Troeltsch, 9:527
 of Turing, 9:552
Formalism in Ethics and Non-Formal Ethics of Values (Scheler), 8:616
Formalism in Ethics and the Ethics of Intrinsic Value (Scheler), 3:421
Formalist prescriptivism, on definition, 2:668–672
Formalist school of mathematics, 5:470
Formalitatibus, De, 8:704
Formalization
 in axiomatization, 6:23–25
 definition of, 5:543
 logic in, Montague (Richard) on, 6:329–330
Formalized language, definition of, 5:544
Formally imply, definition of, 5:544
Formal'ni method v literaturovendenii (Bakhtin), 1:465
Forman, Robert, 8:402
Formas lógicas, realidad y significado (Logical forms, reality and meaning) (Moro Simpson), 5:210
Formation of the Historical World in the Human Sciences, The (Dilthey), 3:82
Formation rules, definition of, 5:544
Formey, Johann (Jean) Henri Samuel, 9:56, 9:830
Formiguera, Pere, 9:690
Forms and Limits of Utilitarianism (Lyons), 3:441
Forms of Knowledge and Society (Scheler), 3:421
Formstecher, Solomon, 4:827
Formula(s)
 closure of, definition of, 5:537
 computability decisions and, 2:388–389
 defining by induction, 3:648
 definition of, 5:544
 satisfaction and, 3:651–652
 universal, 3:658
 valid, definition of, 5:559
 well-formed, definition of, 5:559
Formula of Concord, 6:120
Formulaire de mathématiques (Peano), 5:462, 7:159
"Formulario completo" (Peano), 7:159
Forster, Malcolm, 8:685
Fortescue, John, 7:422
Fortune, 6:319
Foscarini, Paolo, 2:732
Foster, Cheryl, 3:256
Foster, John
 on atheism, 1:372
 on dualism, 3:117
 on laws of nature, 5:229
Foster, Kenelm, 2:626
Foucault, Michel, **3:698–702**
 on aesthetics, 1:71
 antihumanism of, 9:276
 on Bentham's panopticon, 1:555
 and contemporary feminism, 3:564
 critical legal studies and, 7:463
 on historical knowledge, 7:396
 on knowledge, 7:396
 Nietzsche and, 6:614
 philosophy of sex and, 7:523
 on place, 9:492
 and postmodernism, 6:317, 7:729, 9:59
 poststructuralism of, 9:274, 9:275
 Socrates and, 9:113
 on subject, 9:275
Foucher, Simon, **3:702–705**
 on Descartes' skepticism, 9:53
 Desgabets on, 5:663
 epistemology of, 2:57
 Leibniz and, 3:704, 5:253
 Malebranche and, 2:757, 5:663–664
Fouillée, Alfred, **3:705–706**
 and Bergson, 1:563
 on eternal return doctrine, 3:354
 panpsychism and, 7:83
Foumal'nyi metod v literaturovedenii (Medvedev), 1:469
Foundation, axiom of, definition of, 5:544
Foundation of the Metaphysics of Morals (Kant), 3:153, 3:411
Foundationalism
 in Chisholm, 2:242–243
 classical, **2:275–279**
  coherence theory of justification in, 2:278–279
  criticisms of, 2:276–278

Foundationalism, ***continued***
inferential justification in, 2:275
noninferential justification in, 2:276
coherentism and, 2:313
deductivist, 8:178
Descartes and, 2:735
on experience, 8:177–178
externalist, 8:178–179
infinitism and, 8:179
internalist, 8:178–179
in justification of knowledge, 3:271–272
on justified beliefs, 8:177–179
moderate, 8:178
modest, 3:272
mysticism and, 6:462
nondeductivist, 8:178
primitavist, 8:178–179
in solipsism, 9:116, 9:118
subject contextualism's critique of, 2:483
traditional, 8:178
Foundations of All Exact Sciences (Wolff), 9:823, 9:827
Foundations of Arithmetic (Frege), 7:616
Foundations of Belief (Balfour), 1:474
Foundations of Constructive Analysis (Bishop), 2:504
Foundations of Empirical Knowledge, The (Ayer), 1:437
Foundations of Geometry (Hilbert), 4:62
Foundations of Historical Knowledge (White), 7:393
Foundations of Intensional Logic (Kaplan), 5:39
Foundations of Mathematics (Ramsey), 6:521
Foundations of Measurement (Kranz), 6:89
Foundations of Medieval Spirituality in the Twelfth and Thirteenth Centuries, Mainly in Italy (Karsavin), 5:42
Foundations of Moral Goodness, The (Balguy), 1:474–1:475
Foundations of Natural Law (Fichte), 3:617
Foundations of Set Theory (Fraenkel, Bar-Hillel, Levy), 2:510
Foundations of Statistics (Savage), 2:655, 8:613
Foundations of the Theory of Probability (Kolmogorov), 2:663
Foundations of the Theory of Signs (Morris), 8:797
"Founders, The," in Latin American philosophy, 5:207
Fountain Head of Knowledge, The (John of Damascus), 4:836–837
Fountain of Life, The (Ibn Gabirol). *See* "Source of Life, The" (Ibn Gabirol)
Four Dharmadhāus, 1:738–739
Four Dissertations (Hume), 1:210
Four Dissertations (Price), 8:1–2
Four elements
doctrine of, in Empedocles, 3:208–210
in materialism, 6:7–8
William of Conches on, 9:768
Four Free-Gifts to the Clergy (Woolston), 9:845
Four Intellectual Journeys (Mullā Ṣadrā), 4:584
Four noble truths, 5:328, 6:254
Four syllogistic figures, Peirce on, 7:164
Fourberies de Scapin, Les (Cyrano de Bergerac), 2:618
Fourcroy, de Bonaventure de, 2:263–264
Four-dimensionalism, 9:762
Fourier, François Marie Charles, **3:706–708,** 7:711
on art, 1:56
James (Henry) and, 4:773–774
Kozlov and, 5:146
Lavrov and, 5:218
Phalansterian communities, 5:154
Ripley and, 6:572
socialism of, 9:88
Thoreau and, 9:451
Fourier, Jean B. J., 3:229
Fourier, Joseph, 2:497
Fourth syllogism, 4:5
Foxoles, John, 8:704
Fraassen, Bas van
on constructive empiricism, 8:692–693
on Craigian reaxiomatization, 2:584
on explanation, 3:526
on indicative conditional sentences, 2:426
on laws of nature, 5:227
on natural law, 5:226–227
on presupposition, 7:771
on probability, 8:34
on rational degrees of belief, 8:685
on semantic view of theories, 9:416–417
treatment of truth-value gaps, 5:149
Fractal structure, chaotic systems analysis, 2:132
Fraenkel, Abraham A., 2:500, 5:520, 8:838
Fraenkel, Adolf, 4:652
Frage nach der Technik, Die (Heidegger), 7:547
Fragen der Ethik (The problems of ethics) (Schlick), 8:638, 8:643
Fragility of Goodness, The (Nussbaum), 6:680
Fragment of language, Montague grammar for, 6:329–330
Fragment on Government, A (Bentham), 1:553
Fragment on Mackintosh (Mill, James), 6:219
Fragmentariness, problem of, 7:272–273
"Fragments" (Schlegel), 8:631
Fragments de philosophie positive et de sociologie contemporaine (Littré), 5:372
Fragments of an Anonymous Work Found at Wolfenbüttel (Reimarus), 2:688
Fragments of Science (Tyndall), 1:371
Fragments or Minutes of Essays (Bolingbroke), 1:642, 2:685
Fragments philosophiques (Cousin), 4:14
Frame, 3:708
Frame invariance, in subjective expected utility, 2:656
Frame problem, 2:394, **3:708–712**
France
atheism in, pre-revolution, 1:357
censorship in, 2:687–688, 2:725, 3:71, 3:222–223, 5:179
clandestine philosophical literature in, 2:263–268
as continuous state, 9:205
deism in, 2:687–688, 2:691
discrimination in Second Empire of, Taine and, 9:364
Enlightenment in. *See* French Enlightenment
invasion of Dutch Republic by, 9:183
Jansenism in, 4:789–790
Jewish philosophers of, 13th century, 4:820
liberal reform movement in, 9:247
politics of, Merleau-Ponty in, 6:149
social contract theory in, 9:81
Spinoza's influence in, 9:195
structuralism in, 9:273
student revolts in, 8:604
syndicalism in, 9:132
Taine on, 9:364, 9:365
See also French Revolution

France, Anatole, 2:366
Francis Bacon: The Logic of Sensation (Deleuze), 2:695
Francis of Assisi, St., 5:3
Francis of Marchia, 8:704
Franciscans
 apriorism of, 7:161–162
 Bacon (Roger), 1:452
 on causation, 7:162
 Dominicans *vs.*, 9:445
 Duns Scotus and, 8:704–705
 education of, 3:134
 in medieval philosophy, 6:100
 poverty of, 7:12, 9:770
Franck, Sebastian, **3:712–714**
Francke, August Hermann, 7:576
Franco, Francisco, 3:553, 5:209
Francovich, Guillermo, 5:211
Frank, Erich, **3:715–716**
Frank, Jerome, 5:245, 7:428
Frank, Philipp
 logical positivism and, 5:524
 on Mach, 5:625
Frank, Semen Liudvigovich, **3:716–717**, 5:43, 9:126
Frankena, William, 4:714
Frankfurt, Harry, **3:718–719**
 on eliminating agent alternatives, 3:696
 on love, 5:591
 on personhood, 7:240
Frankfurt Institute for Social Research, 2:598
Frankfurt School
 Habermas in, 4:199
 Peirce and, 7:173
 utopianism of, 9:619
Frankfurt-style counterexamples to PAP, 3:718
Frankl, Victor, 5:351
Franklin, Benjamin, **3:720–721**
 deism and, 2:684, 2:686, 2:689
 Enlightenment and, 3:244, 3:246
 Mandeville and, 5:680–681
 Paine (T.) and, 7:73
 Priestley and, 8:5
Franklin, Christine Ladd, 5:456
Fraser, Bruce, 7:200
Fraser, Nancy, 3:565
Fraser's Magazine (journal), 9:10
Fraternity
 as abstract in Burke, 1:771–772
 in Camus, 2:21
"Fraternity of the Rosy Cross," 3:674
Fraunce, Abraham, 5:438
Frauwallner, Erich, 9:650–651
Frayssinous, Comte Denis de, 5:177
Frazer, James G., 1:58
Frecht, Martin, 3:713
Fredegisus of Tours, 2:49
Frederick II ("The Great"; king of Prussia), 2:687–688
 Diderot and, 3:71
 Dühring and, 3:131
 Eberhard and, 3:161
 Enlightenment and, 3:247
 German literature and, 5:294
 La Mettrie and, 5:178
 Lambert (J. H.) and, 5:175
 Voltaire and, 9:709
 on war, 7:154
 Wolff and, 9:825, 9:830
Frederick V (king of Bohemia), 2:752, 3:187
Frederick William I (king of Prussia), 7:576
Frederick William II (king of Prussia), 5:30
Frederick William III (king of Prussia), 5:321
Fredkin, Edward, 2:406
Free Academy of Spiritual Culture, 5:573
Free agency
 moral responsibility and, 3:364
 mutual recognition of, 3:617
Free and informed consent, in medical ethics, 6:97
Free association
 as both investigative and therapeutic, 3:741
 Jung on, 4:857
 nontherapeutic argument for, 3:743
 pathogenic repressions in, 3:742–743
 psychoanalyst's promptings and, 3:743
 and repressions, 3:738–739
 rule of, 3:741
 techniques of, 3:738
 therapeutic success of, 3:742
 unconscious in, 9:572
Free choice, 1:700–701
Free Discussion of the Doctrines of Materialism and Philosophical Necessity (Price & Priestly), 8:4
Free economy, 7:351
Free Enquirer, The (Annet), 2:685
Free Enquiry into the Miraculous Powers, which are supposed to have subsisted in the Christian Church from the Earliest Ages, through several successive Centuries (Middleton), 2:686, 6:214
Free fall, matter and, 6:3
Free imaginative variation, in phenomenology, 7:285–287
Free Inquiry into the Nature and Origin of Evil (Jenyn), 4:853
Free law, 7:426–427
Free logic, 8:196, 9:645
"Free Man's Worship, A" (Russell), 5:348, 6:619, 7:252
Free markets, ethics of, 1:778
Free occurrence of a variable, 3:648, 5:544
Free organic unity, gathering diversity into, 5:59
Free rider genetic traits, 3:489–490
Free speech
 censorship and, 2:119–120
 computer ethics and, 2:397–398
 in feminism, 7:462–463
 Theodorus on, 2:620
Free thought, French philosophical literature and, 2:263–268
Free trade, Pareto on, 7:117
Free variable, 5:544
Free will
 agent causation and, 1:88–89
 Alexander of Hales on, 1:114
 al-Fārābī on, 3:23
 Anselm on, 1:216–217
 Aquinas on, 3:404, 9:429, 9:433–434
 Arminius on, 1:285
 Augustine on, 3:402
 Avicenna on, 3:23
 behavioral predictability and, 8:728
 Calderoni and, 2:7–8
 Cambridge platonists on, 2:13
 as "can" as metaphysical liberty, 2:24
 in Carolingian thought, 2:49
 in chance and determinism, 2:126
 Chubb on, 2:253
 in Clarke-Leibniz correspondence, 2:269
 concept of, 7:305
 consciousness and, 8:125
 as creative *vs.* deterministic causality, 1:652
 Crescas on, 2:593, 4:823
 Cudworth on, 2:611–612
 Dennett on, 2:711
 Descartes on, 2:751, 3:12–13, 6:258, 9:188
 determinism and, 1:563–564
 and divine causality, 4:109
 divine will and, 1:680–681
 doctrine of Hell and, 4:251–252
 Dostoevsky on, 3:99

Free will, ***continued***
- drive and, 3:618
- Duns Scotus on, 3:136–137, 3:142–143, 3:146, 3:404
- Edwards (Jonathan) on, 3:168–169
- Epicureans on, 3:10–11
- Epicurus on, 3:268–269, 3:399
- Erasmus on, 9:51
- and evil, 1:559, 9:408
- Gersonides on, 4:822
- of God, 1:5, 3:23
- Godfrey of Fontaine on, 4:131
- and God's foreknowledge. *See* Foreknowledge and freedom, theological problem of
- *vs.* God's grace, Melanchthon on, 6:119
- and guilt, 4:193–194
- Hegel on, 4:267
- hiddenness of God and, 7:484
- Hobbes on, 4:416–417
- Holbach on, 6:10
- human responsibility and, 1:692
- Hume on, 3:14, 3:409, 4:503–504
- Ibn Da'ud on, 4:817
- Ibn Zaddik on, 4:551
- in Islam, 2:113–115, 4:754
- James (William) on, 4:775
- Jeans on, 4:804
- John of Damascus on, 4:837
- Johnson (Samuel) on, 4:851–852
- Kant on, 3:15, 3:27, 3:412, 4:556, 8:134
- karma and, 5:42
- La Mettrie on, 5:180
- Lehrer on, 5:248
- Leibniz on, 5:252
- Lessing on, 5:296, 7:100
- Liebmann on, 5:344
- Locke on, 3:13–14, 3:407–408, 5:383
- Lopatin on, 5:573
- Luther on, 5:613
- Melanchthon on, 6:119
- as metalinguistic term, 6:478
- metaphysical liberty and, 2:24
- Mill (John Stuart) on, 6:227–228
- Miller (Dickinson) on, 6:235
- Milton on, 6:249
- Molina on, 6:322
- Molinism and, 8:681–682
- and moral causality, 2:110
- in morality, Ockham on, 9:782
- morality and, 3:364, 9:782
- Mou on, 2:183
- mutual recognition of, 3:617
- Naṣīr al-Dīn al-Ṭūsī on, 6:478
- as necessary for personhood, 1:671
- Nemesius of Emesa on, 6:538
- Nicolas of Autrecourt on, 3:404
- Ockham on, 3:404, 9:782
- omnipotence of God and, 4:115–116
- omniscience and, 4:111, 7:479
- and orderly Universe, 1:672
- paradigm-case argument and, 7:107–108, 7:111
- Pelagianism and predestination, 7:175
- personhood and, 7:240
- Petronievć on, 7:267
- Pfänder on, 7:269–270
- Philo on, 7:304–307
- Pico della Mirandola on, 7:572
- Plotinus on, 7:636
- Price on, 8:3
- Priestley on, 8:7
- psychiatry on, 3:16–17
- punishment and, 3:384
- Saadya on, 4:812–813
- salvation and, 1:288
- Schopenhauer on, 8:648
- sociobiology and, 3:491–492
- special sciences on, 9:161
- Spinoza on, 8:125
- sufficient grace on congruent action of, 9:284
- time and, 9:471–472
- Tolstoy on, 6:478, 9:512
- as tragic, 1:559
- as universal indeterminism, 4:784–785
- Valla on, 9:635
- William of Auvergne on, 9:766
- in workings of grace, in Jansenism, 4:788–789
- *See also* Will

"Free Will as Involving Determination and Inconceivable without It" (Miller), 6:235

Free-distribution warehouse, 5:154

Freedom, **3:721–725**
- academic
  - Lovejoy on, 5:592
  - Stewart on, 9:246
  - Wolff on, 9:823
- as active transcendence, 1:515
- actualization of, 3:614
- American liberalism on, 5:322
- anarchism and, 1:176–177, 1:180
- Anselm on, 1:217
- Aquinas on, 9:433
- in Arendt, 1:253
- Aristippus of Cyrene on, 1:257
- Arnauld on, 1:289
- Arnold on, 1:294
- in Augustine, 7:388
- as beginning and end of philosophy, 8:618
- body movement and, 5:658
- Boileau on, 1:640
- Bosanquet on, 1:663
- Carneades on, 3:17–18
- categorical, Kant on, 3:15
- choice and, 1:563, 2:368, 2:445, 3:724–725
- circumscribed, Merleau-Ponty on, 6:149
- communism and, 2:362, 5:734
- in Condillac, 2:423
- of conscience, 2:445
  - Cambridge platonists on, 2:13
  - Catholic Church on, 5:177
  - Spinoza on, 9:180
- in coordination of human drives, 8:628
- Cousin on, 2:579
- Croce on, 2:604
- Cynics on, 2:616
- Descartes on, 2:744–745, 2:751, 2:753, 2:755
- as direct experience, 1:564
- divine, Henry of Ghent on, 4:313
- divine cooperation in human self-creation and, 1:760
- doctrine of hell and, 4:251–252
- Dostoevsky on, 3:99–100
- Duhem on, 3:127
- Dworkin on, 3:157
- education and, 7:375
- as end goal of society, 8:810
- Eucken on, 3:452
- existentialism on, 1:515, 3:503
- facticity and limits of, 1:763
- faith and, 1:289, 3:533
- Fichte and, 3:614
- French liberalism on, 5:320
- general will and, 4:38–40
- German liberalism and, 5:321
- Gewirth on, 4:81
- of God, 7:721
  - Henry of Ghent on, 4:313
  - Ockham on, 9:781, 9:783
  - Voltaire on, 9:710
- and guilt, in Jaspers, 4:801
- Hegel on, 4:272–274, 7:390
- Henry of Ghent on, 4:313
- in Herbart, 7:375
- Hirsch (Samuel) on, 4:827
- in history, 4:273–274, 9:519
- Hume on, 3:18, 4:503–504
- in ibn al-ʿArabī, 4:542
- illusions of, 4:503–504
- imagination and, 4:597

of indifference, Leibniz on, 5:264
Jacobi on, 4:769
Jaspers on, 4:801
Kant on, 3:15, 5:321
kinds of, 3:723
Korn on, 5:208
Lachelier on, 5:170
as lack of constraint, 8:446
Lavelle on, 5:215
Leibniz on, 5:254, 5:264
Lequier on, 5:287
liberty and, 1:589
Liebert on, 5:343–344
limits to, imposed by impartiality, 4:620–621
Locke on, 5:382–383, 9:509
Malebranche on, 5:669–670
Marx on, 5:731
Merleau-Ponty on, 6:149
of mind, 4:259–260, 4:263
Naṣīr al-Dīn al-Ṭūsī on, 6:478
natural law and, 6:537
necessary conditions for, 3:721
necessity and, 1:559, 6:537, 8:620
negative, 1:589, 4:272–273
Niebuhr on, 6:605–606
Oakeshott on, 7:1–2
Ockham on, 9:782
Olivi on, 7:12–13
Oman on, 7:14
ontological status of, 1:559
Origen on, 7:39, 7:40
Paulsen on, 7:148
Pelagianism on, 7:175
Petrović-Njegoš on, 7:267
possibility and, 7:724–725
poverty as constraint of, 1:589
power and, 3:722–724
of press, political utility of, 1:556
primacy of, Jacobi on, 4:769
Reid on, 3:18, 8:329
in relationships as I-it *vs.* I-thou, 1:715–716
Rousseau on, 4:39
Sartre on, 2:459, 8:608
as self-determination, 8:447
as self-mastery, 1:663, 8:627
Sen on, 8:810–811
social decay caused by, 1:667
vs. social equality, 1:253
social harmony and, 1:180
species of, 3:723
of speech
  censorship and, 2:119–120
  computer ethics and, 2:397–398
  as condition of democracy, 2:704
  in feminism, 7:462–463
  Theodorus on, 2:620
Spinoza on, 9:180–181
state support of, 4:558–560
supposition of, 5:25
Tagore on, 9:364
Thoreau on, 9:451
of thought, Mill (John Stuart) on, 6:228
vs. toleration, 9:507
Tolstoy on, 9:512
ultimate ends in, 4:185
as universal indeterminism, 4:784–785
Varona on, 9:648
Voltaire on, 9:710–711
from want, 3:723–724
Whitehead on, 9:752
of will
  Cambridge platonists on, 2:13
  personhood and, 7:240
Wolff on, 9:827–828
Zen'kovskii on, 9:868–869
See also Determinism; Free will; Liberty
Freedom and Creation in Three Traditions (Burrell), 9:447
Freedom and Reason (Hare), 3:429–430, 6:158
Freedom and the Tragic Life (Ivanov), 4:767
Freedom and the Will (Pears), 8:730
Freedom Assumption, 3:693, 3:695
Freedom Evolves (Dennett), 2:711, 2:712
Freedom of the Will (Edwards), 3:167
"Freedom of the Will and the Concept of a Person" (Frankfurt), 3:718, 3:719
Freedom response, to divine hiddenness, 7:484
Freedom version, of Principle of Alternate Possibilities, 3:694
Freely, in Freedom Assumption, 3:693
Freemasonry
  Bahrdt and, 1:457
  Lessing and, 5:295
  Nicolai on, 6:598
Freethinkers/freethinking
  Berkeley and, 1:571
  Collins and, 2:330–331
  Cyrano de Bergerac and, 2:618
  Swift and, 9:341
Frege, Gottlob, **3:725–736**, 5:15
  on abstraction, 6:627
  on analytic propositions, 1:244
  on analyticity, 1:161, 1:166–167, 5:83
  on arithmetic, 1:244, 3:730–732, 5:463, 5:507, 5:516–517, 8:799
  assertion sign and, 5:535
  and axioms, 4:118
  on belief attributions, 1:536
  calculus of, 1:343
  Carnap and, 2:36, 5:524
  and Church, 2:254
  on cognitive access to numbers, 6:674
  and computing machines, 2:400
  on concepts, 2:417, 9:556
  on counting, 6:664
  on declarative sentences, 9:346
  Dummett on, 3:132
  on entities, hierarchy of, 9:555
  on existence as predicate, 1:528
  on explosion, 7:105
  formalism of, 7:405
  on functions, 3:727, 5:507, 5:519
  Geach on, 6:652–653
  on generality, expressions of, 8:735
  Gödel on, 4:117–118
  on illative combinatory logic, 2:340
  influence of, 3:732
  on informative identity statements, 4:567
  on Kantian view of arithmetic, 1:244
  on language, 3:727–729, 8:799–801
  Leśniewski and, 5:292–293
  liar paradox and, 5:317
  on logic, 2:36, 3:726–731, 5:463–464, 5:482, 5:511, 7:163, 9:556
  logical Platonism of, 7:616
  logicism and, 5:547
  Łukasiewicz on, 5:607
  and mathematics, 3:729–731
  on Mill (John Stuart), 5:82–83
  on names, 3:460
  on natural numbers, 6:672, 9:270
  on negation, 6:527
  and nominalism, 6:627
  on number, 6:670–672
  on objects *vs.* concepts, 9:556
  Peirce and, comparison of, 5:453
  on phenomenology, 7:299
  on proper names, 2:708, 8:58
  on psychologism, 7:280
  on questions, 10:32–33
  on reference, 8:60–61
  Russell and, 3:316
  Scholz and, 8:644
  Seale on, 8:706
  on second-order quantification, 3:726–727, 5:492

Frege, Gottlob, ***continued***
on semantics, 3:251–252, 8:60–61, 8:737, 8:799–801
on sense, 2:371, 8:736, 8:800, 8:829, 9:289
on set theory and theory of types, 2:82, 9:556
on statements of identity, 9:287
on subject-predicate dualism, 9:289
symbolic language of, 1:343
and theory of meaning, 5:548
on thought attributes, 8:829
and Vienna Circle, 2:41, 3:732
Frege argument, 6:85
Fregeanism, Kaplan and, 5:39
Frege-Geach problem, 3:206
Frege's theorem, neo-Fregeanism and, 3:731
Freidenker-Bibliothek (Thorschmid), 2:688
Freidizm: Kriticheskii ocherk (Bakhtin), 1:465
Freien, Die, 9:250
Freier deutscher Kulturbund in Grossbrittanien, 5:343
Freire, Paulo, on truth, 5:332
French, Robert, 5:634
French Encyclopedia, The. See Encyclopédie
French Encyclopedists
and ethics, 3:410
Locke and, 5:392
Sidgwick on, 3:417
French Enlightenment, 2:687–688
aesthetics in, 1:49–50
on determinism, 3:16
ethics in, 3:409
Fontenelle and, 3:683
Godwin and, 1:177
history in, 7:388
French language, defense of, 4:166
French liberalism, 5:320
French Marxism, 5:679
French Philosophical Literature. *See* Clandestine philosophical literature in France; *Encyclopédie*
French philosophy
Condillac and, 8:784
idéologues and, 8:787
signification and, 8:783
universal grammar and, 8:790
See also Clandestine philosophical literature in France
French Revolution
anarchy and, 1:176
atheism and, 1:357
Comte on, 2:412
Condorcet in, 2:430–431
equality as concept in, 3:330
failure to transform citizenry in, 8:627
Fichte on, 1:377
French liberalism and, 5:320
Godwin on, 4:136
human irrationalism and, 4:752
idéologues in, 4:573
Lavoisier and, 5:217
nation idea of, 6:481
Paine (T.) and, 7:73–74
Prince on, 8:1
Reinhold and, 8:334
Rousseau and, 4:39–40
Saint-Simon support of, 8:589
Schelling support of, 8:617
socialism and, 9:87
Taine on, 9:364, 9:365
terrorism in, 9:395
traditionalism in, 9:520–521
transcendentalism and, 6:573–574
and war, attitude toward, 7:153
Wollstonecraft and, 9:836, 9:837
Freneau, Philip, 2:690
Frequentist theory of physical probability, 8:32–33, 8:34
Fresnoy, Charles Du, 1:49
Freud, Anna, 8:106
Freud, La Philosophie, et Les Philosophes (Assoun), 3:737
Freud, Sigmund, **3:736–748,** 5:579
Adler and, 1:23–24, 8:106, 8:146
on aggression, 9:572
on altruism and self-interest, 3:173–174
on analysis, 8:105
approach to religious experience of, 3:611
Binswanger on, 3:507, 7:322
childhood in, 8:104–105
on conflict, 8:145–146
conflict in, 8:145–146
on consciousness, 2:449, 8:145
and critical theory, 2:598
on death, 2:651, 2:653, 8:146
Derrida on, 2:716, 2:717
determinism and, 3:24
on dreams, 3:105, 3:106
ego in, 8:146
Ehrenfels and, 3:177
Empedocles and, 5:642
on ethics, 5:589
evolutionary psychology and, 3:481
existential psychoanalysis and, 3:510–512
Ferguson and, 3:606
as first cognitive scientist, 5:76
Habermas on, 4:200
Herbart and, 8:145
"how" *vs.* "why" and, 9:754
influence of, 9:570
on intentionality in consciousness, 2:452
Irigaray on, 9:278
Jung and, 4:856–857, 8:106, 8:147
in Kaufmann's volumes, 5:46
on libido, 9:572
on love, 5:589
Lyotard and, 5:620
microcosm in, 5:642
on natural law, 9:572
Pareto and, 7:118
on personality, 8:146
on pessimism, 7:252
on philosophy, 3:737
philosophy of sex and, 7:522–523
and poststructuralism, 9:274
on preconscious, 8:145
precursors of, 3:736
and psychoanalysis, 5:152, 8:105–110, 8:145–146
on religion, 3:611, 3:745–747, 8:378–380
on resistance, 8:105
Sartre on, 1:455, 3:514
Schopenhauer and, 7:522, 8:652–653
self-preservation in, 8:146
on sex, 8:104–105, 8:110, 8:145–146
on suicide, 9:320
on unconscious, 3:105, 8:145–146, 8:722, 9:571–573
Freud and the Problem of God (Kung), 3:747
Freudenthal, Jacob, on Alcinous, 1:103
Freudian psychology
desire in, 1:352
evidence for, 8:107–108
meaning in, 3:511
in modern psychoanalysis, 8:107–108
Freudian slips, 3:738, 8:107
Freud's Dream (Kitcher), 5:76
Freunden des jungen Werthers, Die (Nicolai), 6:598
Freydenker-Lexicon (Trinius), 2:688
Freyer, Hans, 4:35
Friedberg, Richard, 2:385
Friedman, Alexander, 9:478
Friedman, Harvey, 5:484, 8:455
Friedman, Michael, 3:159, 3:523
Friedman, Milton, 5:335, 7:351–352, 8:613

Friedrich, C. J., 7:733
Friedrich, James, 8:715
Friedrich, Johann, Leibniz and, 5:268
Friedrich Carl Forbergs Apologie seines angeblichen Atheismus (Forberg), 1:378
Friedrich Wilhelm III (king of Prussia). *See* Frederick William III
Friend, The (Coleridge), 1:10, 1:13
Friends of God, Eckhart (Meister) and, 3:163
Friendship, **3:748–751**
- Aristippus of Cyrene on, 1:257
- Aristotle on, 3:748, 7:521, 7:582–583
- Epicurus on, 3:268
- in Godwin, 4:137
- grounded in virtue or good character, 3:749
- ideal, intensity of, 3:749
- La Rochefoucauld on, 5:201
- love of God and, 1:355–356
- modern moral theory and, 3:749
- in philosophy of sex, 7:521
- in Platonic dialogues, 7:589
- Seneca on, 8:812

Fries, Jakob Friedrich, **3:751–754**
- on faith, 3:531
- Liebmann on, 5:344
- Nelson (Leonard) on, 6:534–535
- in neo-Kantianism, 6:541
- psychological interpretation of Kant by, 6:543–544

Froben, Johann
- Erasmus and, 3:338
- Paracelsus and, 7:103

Frobenius, Leo, 7:319
Froebel, Friedrich, **3:754–755**
- on education, 7:372–373
- Kant and, 7:373
- Pestalozzi and, 7:372
- in Spranger's philosophy of education, 9:199

Frogs, The (Aristophanes), 4:177
Fröhliche Wissenschaft (Nietzsche), on eternal return doctrine, 3:354
From Being to Beings (De l'existence à l'existant) (Levinas), 5:304
From Existence to Existents (De l'existence à l'existant) (Levinas), 5:304
From Shakespeare to Existentialism (Kaufmann), 5:46
"From the Chaos to Reality" (Carnap), 2:40
From the Lectures of Zeno (Philodemus), 7:302
From Warism to Pacifism (Cady), 7:157
Fromm, Erich
- on alienation, 1:122, 1:124
- philosophy of sex and, 7:523

Fronde, The, 5:200
Frondizi, Risieri, 5:210
Fronto, 5:706
Frothingham, O. B., 6:572–573
Froude, William, 6:579
Fry, Roger
- on art, 1:59
- formalism of, 1:295, 1:308

Frye, Marilyn, **3:755–756**
- on definition of sexism, 8:848
- on individual subjectivity and choice, 3:588
- on vital concepts, 3:580

Fua de Malves, Abbé, 3:221
Fūdo (A Climate) (Watsuji), 9:727
Fuentes, Carlos, 5:204
Fujiwara Seika, 4:247–248, 6:477
Fukanzazengi (Universal recommendation for Zazen practice) (Dōgen), 3:95
Fukuyama, Francis
- on communism and liberal democracy, 2:361
- on history, 2:181, 7:391

Fulgentisu of Ruspe, 2:49
Full contraposition, definition of, 5:539
Fuller, Lon
- on law, 6:513
- legal realism of, 7:428

Fuller, Margaret, 6:572, 6:575
Fumerton, Richard, on Plantinga, 3:324
Function(s)
- and arguments, logical form and, 5:507–508
- in biological systems, 3:762
- in Bishop's theory of analysis, 2:505
- choice, definition of, 5:536
- composition of, 5:554
- in computability theory, 2:380, 2:389–390
- constant, definition of, 5:554
- as continuous, 2:496–497
- for continuum construction, 2:505
- courses-of-values of, 3:731
- definition of, 5:544
- Durkheim on, 3:151
- in early computing, 2:401
- as effectively calculable, 2:374–376
- Frege on, 3:727, 5:507, 5:519
- fundamental, 5:554
- global property of, 8:201
- identity, definition of, 5:554
- in intuitionistic logic, 2:503–504
- Kant on, 2:74
- Leibniz on, 2:494–495
- logical form and, 5:507–508
- mathematical
  - in Bishop's theory of analysis, 2:505
  - as continuous, 2:496–497
  - for continuum construction, 2:505
  - in early computing, 2:401
  - in intuitionistic logic, 2:503–504
  - notation for, 3:649
- Newton on, 2:494–495
- notation for, 3:649
- partial, in computability theory, 2:373–374
- polynomial computable feasibility of, 2:387
- predicative, 8:235
- primitive recursive
  - and computing machines, 2:401
  - numerical, 5:554
  - as polynominal-time computability constraints, 2:388
- propositional, 8:59–60, 8:550–553, 9:557
  - in *Principia Mathematica,* 5:518
  - Ramsey on, 5:468
  - with self on argument, 5:519
  - in traditional logic, 5:504
  - in Whitehead and Russell, 5:519
- recursive, definition of, 5:554
- Russell on, 5:466, 8:552–553
- successor, definition of, 5:554
- teleological
  - in artifacts *vs.* living things, 9:387, 9:389
  - criteria for assertion of, 9:386
  - explanatory role of, 9:389
  - nature of systems exhibiting, 9:386–387
  - *vs.* purposive activity, 9:388
- universals as, 9:585
- value of, definition of, 5:559

"Function and Concept" (Frege), 8:735
Function symbols, 3:645–647
Functional analysis
- as explanation, 3:763
- of mental concepts, 3:756
- in organismic biology, 7:39
- uses of, 3:762

Functional approach, in sociology, 3:765

Functional calculus, 5:535–536
applied, 5:536
first-order, 5:476, 5:536
second-order, 5:536
Skolem on, 5:470
Functional concepts, 3:757
Functional roles, 3:761, 5:88
Functional statements, about self-maintaining or self-regulating systems, 3:764
Functional states, 3:757, 6:135
Functionalism, **3:756–761**
on art, 1:57
causality in, 6:645–646
computationalism and, 8:155
computers and, 7:471
conceptual, 3:758
CRTT and, 3:675–676
development of, 6:14
historical, 1:300–301
identity theory and, 7:471
on intentionality in consciousness, 2:452
on introspection, 4:721
Kim on, 5:71–72
on mental states, 6:645–646, 9:37
motivation for, 7:471
in nonreductive materialism, 6:645–646
in philosophy of mind, 7:471, 8:85, 8:155–156
and physicalism, 3:758–759
Portmann and, 7:321
process concept in, 6:80
propositional attitudes and, 3:759, 8:84–85
psychology and, 7:471
Putnam and, 7:471, 8:172
and qualia, 8:192–193, 9:16
vs. quality space theory, 8:194
religious language and, 8:418–419
sensation in, 6:15
Shoemaker on, 9:16
in sociology, **3:762–765**
and theory of mind, 2:391
"Functionalism and Qualia" (Shoemaker), 9:16
Functionality
of cognition, in Buddhism, 1:754
in illative combinatory logic, 2:339
Functionalization, of property, 5:72
Functorial calculus, Łukasiewics on, 5:607
Fundamenta physices (Regius), 2:55, 8:301
Fundamental force or interaction, 3:691
Fundamental philosophy, of Reinhold, 8:334
Fundamental principles
in science, Whewell on, 9:744
Theophrastus on, 9:412
Fundamental Rule, of clinical investigation, 3:741
Fundamental Theory (Eddington), 3:164
Fundamental Wisdom of the Middle Way (Mūlamadhyamakakārika) (Nāgarjuna), 1:731
Fundamentalism
Islamic, 1:129–130
and Korean philosophy, 5:134
Fundamentals of Concept Formation in Empirical Science (Hempel), 4:309
Fundamentals of Marxism-Leninism: Manual, The, 3:60–61
Funk, Nanette, 3:599
Funktion und Begriff (Frege), 3:726–728, 8:801
Furlong, E. F., 4:597–598
Fushun, and Huayan Buddhism, 2:164
Fusus al-hikam (Ibn al-ʿArabī), 9:307
Futility, of CPR administration, 6:94
Future
alienation in, 1:124–125
Aristotle on, 9:471–472
Bradwardine on, 1:680
Broad on, 9:498
contemporary debate on, 3:20–21
and determinism, 3:7
Dewey on, 3:49
Dühring on, 3:130–131
events in, 1:680
Hatano on, 4:247
historical determinism and, 3:38–39
intuitive cognition of, prophecy as, 9:774
James (William) on, 9:483
kalām argument on God's existence and, 2:555
knowledge of
probabilistic nature of, 4:820
and prophecy, 9:774
Wittgenstein on, 9:807
and life, meaning and value of, 5:350–351
McTaggart on, 6:78
Mead on, 6:81–82
memory and, 6:124
necessity of, 9:472
and past, linkage of, 3:708
as present, 7:753–754
splitting worlds theory and, 5:698
statements about, 5:691–692
and time-reversal invariance of laws in physics, 2:104
traces of, 9:468–469
truth or falsity of, 9:471
Unamuno on, 9:568
Universe and, 2:587
Woodbridge on, 9:842–843
See also Determinism
Future contingents, and necessity, 1:680
Future generations
and genetic and reproductive technologies, 4:43
moral obligation to, **3:92–93**, 3:392–393
rights of, **3:92–93**, 3:258
Future of an Illusion, The (Freud), 3:745
Future tense, 2:86
Future-truth argument, for logical fatalism, 3:694
Fuxing shu (Writings on returning to one's true nature) (Li Ao), 5:316
Fuzzy controller, 3:766–767
Fuzzy logic, **3:766–767**
classical theorems rejected in, 5:109
vs. conventional logic, 3:766
foundations of, 3:766
fundamental principles of, 3:766
representation of vagueness, 5:111
as semantic multi-valued logic, 5:486
See also Many-valued logic
Fuzzy set theory, axioms of, 3:766

G

Gadamer, Hans-Georg, **4:1–4**
on art, 4:2
on dialogue, 7:411–412
hermeneutics of, 3:565
on phenomenology, 7:300
and philosophy of language, 7:411–412
Scheler and, 8:616
Gaia hypothesis, 3:259
Galápagos Archipelago, 2:629, 2:633
Galaxies, 2:560–561, 2:565
Gale, Richard
on experientialism, 3:323
on religious experience, 8:403
tensed theory of time and, 9:475
Galen, **4:4–8**
Averroes and, 1:422
Avicenna and, 5:419
on inner sense, 4:697
on logic, 4:5, 5:408
Maimonides on, 5:648
Nemesius of Emesa and, 6:538
on optimism/pessimism, 7:247

Paracelsus and, 7:103
and physicotheology, 7:557
on polysyllogism, 5:500
on Stoicism, 9:254
Galenian figure, definition of, 5:544
Galenism, 4:7
Galilean relativity, symmetry principle in, 2:462
Galilei, Vincenzo, on music, 1:48, 1:49
Galileo Galilei, **4:8–13**
on authority, 4:10
Bellarmine's admonition to, 1:543
censorship of, 2:732–733, 2:736–737
on color, 2:333
and creation of technology, 7:546
deductive-nomological model in evaluating, 8:694
Descartes and, 4:610
on energy and work, 3:227
on external ends, 8:675
on free fall of bodies, 2:721–722
Genovesi on, 4:49
on gravity as occult fancy, 5:54
Hobbes and, 3:405, 8:825
Hume and, 7:560
on impetus theory, 4:622
on infinite collections, 4:658
Leibniz and, 5:266
Leonardo da Vinci and, 5:282
on matter, 6:60
medieval philosophy and, 3:134
methodology of, 8:683
on motion of projectiles, 5:50
natural law doctrine and, 3:405
on physical causality, 5:54
Plato and, 7:602
on primary and secondary qualities, 4:11, 5:380
on scientific terminology, 7:516–517
on sensations, 8:825
temperature measurement by, 6:87
thought experiment of, 9:453
Galileo's paradox, 5:515
Gallarate movement, 8:666, 9:237
Gallese, Vittorio, 9:40
Gallicanism, Lamennais on, 5:177
Gallie, W. B.
on ethical concepts, 3:417
on history, 7:394
Galluppi, Pasquale, **4:13–14,** 9:160
Gallus, Thomas, 8:593
Galston, William, on educational authority, 7:361
Galton, Sir Francis, 4:593
in evolutionary psychology, 8:137
Pearson and, 7:159
Gambler's fallacy, 3:545–546, 9:217
Gambling, 8:26
Game of Logic, The (Carroll), 2:51–53, 5:452, 5:561
Game of truth, 3:700
Game quantifiers, 8:197
Game theory, **4:14–22**
and Bayesian machines, 1:497–498
and Buridan's ass problem, 1:769–770
and decision theory, 2:655
epistemic foundations of, 4:19–20
as ethical analysis tool, 3:449
evolutionary, 4:20–21, 4:21–22
evolutionary ethics and, 3:479–480
incomplete information in, 4:18–19
on justification of state, 9:210
Nash equilibrium in, 4:15
Neumann (John von) and, 6:559
practical reason in, 7:737
and prisoner's dilemma, 4:15
and probability, 1:495–496
and rational agent utility maximization, 1:778
Savage and, 8:612
trembling-hand metaphor in, 4:17
utilitarianism and, 9:608–609
and voting, 2:53
Gandayvūha (Buddhist text), 1:736
Gandhi, Mohandas
on civil disobedience, 2:259–261
and pacifism, 7:67
Thoreau and, 6:575, 9:451
Tolstoy and, 9:513
Gandillac, Maurice de, students of, 2:693
Gandy, Robin, 2:400, 2:406
Ganesh, in meditation, 6:108
Gant, Berys, on defining art, 1:301
Ganzheitspsychologie
of Krueger, 5:156
Wundt and, 9:849–850
Gao Zi, on evocative argumentation, 2:213–214
Gaos, José
influence of, 5:209
as *transterrados,* 5:209
Garasse, François, 9:53
Garat, Dominique Joseph, Destutt de Tracy and, 2:760
Garcia, John, 1:202
García Bacca, Juan D.
on philosophy of technology, 7:543
as *transterrados,* 5:209
Garden, The, Epicurus and, 3:264–265
Garden of Myrtles, In the (Andrea), 9:301
Garden of Pomegranates, A (Cordovero), 5:3
Garden-path sentences, meaning of, 6:140
Gardens, environmental aesthetics and, 3:257
Gardner, Catherine Villanueva, 3:570
Gardner, John, 5:241
Gardner, Martin
logical diagram method of, 5:562
and parapsychology, 7:116
Garfield, Jay L., 1:742
Garibaldi, Giuseppe, 3:554
Garland the Computist, 6:101–102, 8:765
Garrick, David
Diderot and, 3:75
Lichtenberg on, 5:338
Garrigou-Lagrange, Réginald Marie, **4:23–24,** 9:447
Garrison, William Lloyd, 7:122
Garve, Christian, 3:605, **4:24**
Garver, Newton, on violence, 9:678
Gas(es)
kinetic theory of, 4:804
Priestley's work on, 8:6
Gasking, Douglas, 2:103
Gassendi, Pierre, **4:25–31**
atomism and, 1:386
Cartesianism in early modern science, 2:60
constructive skepticism of, 9:53
corpuscular theory in Boyle, 1:673
on correct law of inertia, 9:154
criticized Fludd, 3:675
and Cyrano de Bergerac, 2:618
Descartes and, 2:738, 2:746–747
on Descartes' skepticism, 9:53
Epicurus and, 3:265
on existence, 3:495
in French clandestine literature, 2:264
and Hobbes, 8:825
on image theory of thinking, 4:565
La Mothe Le Vayer and, 5:181
La Peyrère and, 5:196
Leibniz and, 5:266
Locke and, 5:376
and materialism, 4:29–30, 6:8–9
Mersenne and, 6:153
on mind, 2:758
"objections of objections" of, 4:26, 9:53

Gassendi, Pierre, ***continued***
Pico della Mirandola (Gianfrancesco) and, 7:575
Sanches and, 8:596
on unbelief in God's existence, 2:350
Gast, Peter, Nietzsche and, 6:610, 6:612
Gastraea, 4:201–202
Gastrosophy (the science of cuisine), stressed by Fourier, 3:707
Gate of Silence, The (Stace), 9:200
Gatens, Moira, defining a bodily notion of subjectivity, 3:588
Gateway Arch (Saarinen), 3:256
Gāthās, in Zoroastrianism, 9:885
Gauge theory, **4:31–33**
Gauld, Alan, parapsychology and, 7:116
Gaunilo, **4:33–34**
Anselm and, 1:216, 3:494, 7:16
Gauss, Carl Friedrich
evidential use of likelihood function (LF), 3:661
finite sets policy of, 9:226
on geometry of surfaces, 4:61
Gauss, Cristian, Lichtenberg and, 5:338
Gauss, Karl
capillary phenomena, 3:688
on potential energy, 3:228
Gaut, Berys, on creative processes, 2:591
Gautama, Siddartha, 1:721–725
Gauthier, David, 3:381–382, 8:251
Gautier, Théophile, on art, 1:56
Gay, John, **4:34–35,** 9:340
Gay, Peter, on Enlightenment, 3:243
Gay Science, The (Nietzsche), 5:45, 6:575, 6:611
"Gaze of Orpheus" (Blanchot), 1:612
Geach, Peter
on abstractionism, 9:421
on change, 3:527
on creation, 3:498
on emotivism, 3:206, 6:652–653
on force and content, 5:424
Frege and, 3:732
on identity statements, 4:567, 4:572
on meaning, 1:154
on moral discourse, 3:364
on pain behavior and beliefs and desires, 3:758
on performative theory of truth, 7:197
on Russell's theory of truth, 2:543, 2:544
on subject-predicate dualism, 9:289
Thomism of, 9:447
on unity of the Good, 4:151
on Wittgenstein, 3:107
"Gedanke: Eine logische Untersuchung, Der" (Frege), 3:726
"Gedanken über Aufklärung" (Reinhold), 8:334
Gedanken über die Nachahmung der griechischen Werke in der Malerei und Bildhauerkunst (Thoughts on the imitation of Greek works in painting and sculpture) (Winckelmann), 9:789
Gedanken uber Tod und Unsterblichkeit (Feuerbach), 3:609
Gedanken und Tatsachen (Liebmann), 5:344, 6:541
Gedanken von der wahren Schatzung der lebendigen Krafte (Kant), 5:8, 5:124
Geertz, Clifford, on religion as a cultural idea, 2:223–224
Gegenstand der Erkenntnis, Der (Rickert), 8:458–459
Gegenstandtheorie (Meinong), 6:115
Gegoras, Nikephoros, logic use in theology and hesychasm, 1:788–789
Gehlen, Arnold, **4:35–37**
in anthropology, 7:317, 7:320
cultural anthropology and, 7:321–322
psychology of, 7:322
Geiger, Moritz, in phenomenology, 7:279
Geist, in Hegel, 7:389–390
Geist und Welt der Dialektik (Liebert), 5:343
Geisteswissenschaften, **4:37–38,** 7:317
Gehlen on, 4:35–36
Spranger and, 9:198
Geisteswissenschaften (Wundt), 9:850
Geistliche Priesterthum, Das (Spener), 7:575
"Geldzins im Altertum" (Commercial interest in antiquity) (Neurath), 6:560
Gellner, Ernest, 9:95
Gender
affirmative action and, 1:82
in analytical feminism, 1:157
as constituted and defined, 3:588
Eichler on, 3:594
Erigena on, 3:342
existential freedom of, 1:515
in feminist justice, 9:75
in history of philosophy, 3:569
as indeterminate and variable, 3:588
lesbian identity and ethics, 2:31
Lloyd on, 5:373–374
reality of, 3:588
social constructionist account of, 3:586
Turing test and, 5:633
Gender bias
in theories of art, 3:572
in the Western artistic tradition, 3:571
Gender categorization, dependent upon how bodies are perceived, 3:587
Gender differences, 3:586
Gender equality, feminists commitment to, 3:593
Gender essentialism
argument against, 3:586
remaining contested, 3:587
Gender norms, as socially constituted, 3:589
Gender politics, Code on, 2:295–296
Gender relations
maintained by aperspectivity, 3:574
reinforcing oppressive, 3:574
Gender Trouble (Butler), 3:565
Gendered metaphors, biasing theory selection, 3:574
Gendered terms, science conceptualized in, 3:591
Gene linkage, 3:489
Genealogy, and Nietzsche, 3:700, 6:610, 6:612
Genera
categories in Aristotle, 2:73
in medieval metaphysics, 6:188
in Porphyry, 6:187–188
General causal maxim, 4:494
General Considerations on the State of the Sciences and Letters (Germain), 9:839
General Cosmology (Wolff), 9:824
General covariance, Einstein and, 3:180
General History of Nature and Theory of the Heavens (Kant), 5:8
General History of the Air (Boyle), 1:674
General Introduction to Psychoanalysis (Freud), 8:110
General logic, Pastore on, 7:135
General modal status, of a proposition, 5:100
General name, in logic, definition of, 5:549
General proposition, definition of, 5:553
General recursive function, on calculable functions, 2:402
General recursive numerical function, 5:554
General relativity, 7:476, 8:353–357
determinism and, 3:33

Einstein and, 3:178
force in, 3:690–691
Gödel on, 9:499
gravity in, 3:235, 3:691, 9:267, 9:496
Mach's principle and, 9:149
mass in, 6:4
matter in, 6:62
in Newtonian empiricism, 6:593
quantum mechanics and, 3:691, 7:477
space-time curve in, 9:152
time in, 9:496–497
vs. universal gravitation, 8:684
variational principle of least action in, 9:741
General Scholium (Newton), physicotheology, 7:558
"General Semantics" (Lewis), 5:315
General System of Cartesian Philosophy (Régis), 2:287
General Systems Theory, of Bertalanffy, 1:593–594
General term, definition of, 5:544
General Theory of Employment, Interest and Money, The (Keynes), 5:55
General theory of relativity
concept of force disappearing in, 3:690–691
denial of gravitational forces, 3:691
Einstein and, 3:178
gravitational force in, 9:267
incompatibility with quantum theories, 3:691
space-time curve in, 9:152
vs. universal gravitation, 8:684
General Theory of the Fine Arts (Sulzer), 9:324
General Theory of Value (Perry), 3:423, 7:204
General *vs.* particular, in Indian grammar, 9:581
General will, **4:38–40**
as goal of moral action, Green on, 4:180
political philosophy and, 7:665
in socialism, 9:87
sovereignty and, 9:142
Generality, in illative combinatory logic, 2:340
Generality problem, 8:364
Generalizability of Critical Thinking, The (Norris), 7:358
Generalization(s)
accidental, *vs.* laws of nature, 3:709
in confirmation theory, 2:434
in cosmology, 2:557
empirical, in cosmology, 2:557
rule of, 5:544
universal
Nicod on, 2:439–440
rule of, definition of, 5:559
unwarranted, 3:543
Generalization principle, 5:36
Generalized benevolence, in act utilitarianism, 9:606
Generalized continuum hypothesis
definition of, 5:538
Gödel on, 5:474
Generalized expected utility analysis, 2:660
Generalized other, 6:81
General-sum principle, 6:146
Generation
Aristotle on, 1:272–273, 1:274
vs. creation, 9:377
Generation of Animals (Aristotle), 1:275
Generation of forgers, 5:209
Generation of 98, 5:208
Generations of Sufis, The (al-Sulami), 9:304
Generic consistency, principle of, 5:36–37
"Generic rights," 5:37
Generics, **4:40–43**
Generosity, expression through destructive violence, 1:488–489
Genes, 7:343–344
in disease transmission, 4:43
Hox, 7:346
manipulation of, techniques for, 6:571
in Mendel, 7:339
in natural selection, 7:341–342
reductionism and, 7:343–344
as units of meaning, 7:345
Genesi e struttura della società (Gentile), 4:50
Genesis
Peter Lombard on, 7:260–261
reinterpretation of the literal account of, 5:1
"Genesis of Species, The" (Wright), 9:846
Genet, Jean, 3:507, 7:253, 8:610
Genetic algorithms, 1:348
Genetic arguments for panpsychism, 7:87–88
Genetic counseling, 6:95–96
Genetic drift, 3:489, 7:340
Genetic engineering, 6:96
Genetic epistemology, 7:567, 9:686
Genetic fallacy, Freud's commission of, 3:746
Genetic psychology, of wholeness and structure, 5:155
Genetics, 4:43–48
disease and, 7:466
in ethics, Varona on, 9:648
information theory and, 7:344–345
language of, 7:345, 9:844
Love on, 7:346
medical ethics and, 6:95–96
modern evolutionary theory and, 2:634, 2:638–639, 2:643, 3:488–489
molecular *vs.* transmission, 7:344
Morgan in, 7:339
population, 7:341
in reductionism, 9:579
Scott on, 7:344
Skelton on, 7:341
teleology in, 7:342–343
See also DNA
Genetics and Evolution (Bateson), 2:638
Genetics and Reproductive Technologies, **4:43–48**
Genghis Khan
and Eurasian unity, 3:453, 3:454
moral obligation and, 6:161–162
Gengo (Abstruse words) (Miura), 6:276
Genic selectionism, 7:344
Génie du Christianisme (Chateaubriand), 2:138
Genius
Addison on, 1:23
as artistic, 1:490
Beauty produced by, 6:131
Diderot on, 3:75
DuBos on, 3:123
gendered male, 3:572
Hélvetius on, 4:306
in Kant, 1:28, 1:77
Lavater on, 5:214
as overcompensation, 1:23
Genius of Christianity Unveiled, The (Godwin), 4:136
Genlis, Madame de, 9:839
Gennadios, George Scholarios, Classical philosophy in Byzantine thought, 1:787
Genomics, 7:346
Genossenschaftsrecht (Gierke), 9:527
Genovesi, Antonio, **4:48–49**
Genre, in art, **1:330–333**
Gentile, Giovanni, **4:49–53**
converted to fascism, 3:553
Croce and, 2:600
in Gramsci, 4:169
Papini and, 7:102
on pure act, 4:50–51, 9:197

Gentile, Giovanni, ***continued***
  and Sciacca, 8:666
  Spaventa and, 9:160
Gentiles, in Levinas's ethics, 4:832
Gentner, Dedre, 6:167
Gentzen, Gerhard
  on limits in mathematics, 5:470
  on logical terms, 5:532
  on mathematical logic, 5:475
  natural deduction calculus, 3:657
  in proof theory, 8:55
  system of natural deduction of, 4:739
  in type theory, 9:558
Gentzen system, definition of, 5:544
Gentzen's consistency proof, 5:544
Genuine identity, universals and, 6:179–180
Genuine names, referents of, 5:144
Genus, Johnson (W. E.) on, 3:1
Geographical Distribution of Animals, The (Wallace), 9:720–721
Geographical environment, 5:125
Geography, and history, 1:621–622, 1:718
"Geological Climates and the Origin of Species" (Wallace), 2:637
Geological time, Buffon introduction of, 1:759
Geology, Maillet in, 5:644
Geometric continuum
  arithmetic continuum and, 2:489, 2:493–494
  Lawvere's infinitesimal approach to, 2:509
  synthetic differential geometry and, 2:509–510
Geometric model theory, 6:314–315
Geometric presentation, 9:175
Geometric structure, Hamiltonian theory on energy conservation and, 2:464
Geometrical analysis, 3:538
Geometrical objects, in ontology, 7:26
Geometrische Untersuchungen zur Theorie der Parallellinien (Lobachevski), 5:461
Geometry, 4:53–64
  and algebra of lengths, 4:56
  analytic, Descartes and, 2:722–723
  applied, 5:15
  Archimedean postulate, 4:58–59
  Archytas of Tarentum in, 1:250
  arithmetic subsumed under, 6:670
  arithmetization of, 5:514
  in Cartesian science, 2:55
  as chaos trace and trajectory and fractal structure, 2:132–133
  Clifford on, 2:291–293
  complex points, 4:60
  conventionalism in, 2:523
  coordinates, 4:56
  in cosmological model, 2:559
  in Couturat, 2:581
  deductive reasoning in, Mill (John Stuart) on, 6:223
  Descartes, 4:56
  dimensionality in, 1:576
  discrete number *vs.* continuous magnitude in ancient, 2:491–492
  as distance perception, 1:575
  Erlangen Program, 4:60
  Euclidean, 4:55, 4:62
    continuity principles, 2:499
    Helmholtz on, 6:540
    Hilbert on, 4:62
    Kant and, 1:244
    model of, 6:23
    postulates in, 4:55
    and space, 2:520–521, 9:150–151
    in Wolff, 9:826
  Eudoxus, 4:54–55
  of finite extension in Berkeley, 1:582
  foundations of, 4:358–362
  Galileo, 4:56
  Hellenistic, 4:302
  in Helmholtz, 4:304–305, 6:540
  Hilbert's axiomatization of, 8:836
  hyperbolic, 9:150
  intellect operations in terms of, 1:566
  irrationals, 4:54
  isomorphism, 4:62
  Kant on, 1:244, 4:57–58
  Kepler, 4:56
  land surveying, 4:54
  Lobachevskian, 4:59
  mathematical foundations and, 6:21
  method of exhaustion, 4:55
  model of, 6:23
  in Naṣīr al-Dīn al-Ṭūsī's refutation of matter, 6:478
  in naturalism, 6:494
  necessary truths of, Johnson (Alexander Bryan) on, 4:850
  of Newton, 4:56, 6:591
  non-Euclidean, 4:58–59
    axioms, 4:119
    interpretations in, 4:129
    Kant and, 1:244
    models of, 6:23
    in 19th century, 5:461
    Tarski on, 9:371
  planetary motion, 4:56
  Platonic Forms of, 9:590–591
  Plotinus on, 5:641
  projective
    numerical coordinates in, 4:60
    Poncelet on, 4:59–60
  propositions of, 5:95
  in Protagoras, 8:93
  pure, 5:15
  Pythagorean, 8:182–183
  of real discrete space, 7:267
  relativity of, 8:319–320
  Riemannian manifolds, 4:61–62
  segments, 4:56
  of sight and touch in Berkeley, 1:576
  solid, Archytas of Tarentum in, 1:250
  and space, 1:244, 5:11–12
  of space-time, 7:476
  spatial positions in, 9:148
  stellar parallax, 9:151
  subjectivity of sense perception and, 6:540
  of surfaces, 4:61
  synthetic, 6:591
  Thales and, 9:405
  three-dimensional space in, 9:149
  topology, 9:150
Geometry (Descartes), 2:723, 2:733
Geopolitical theory, in "Exodus to the East," 3:672
Georg Ludwig, Duke of Hanover, 5:253–254
George, Robert, Dworkin and, 3:157
George, Stefan, 4:3, 5:77
George of Poděbrad (king of Bohemia), 7:154
George of Trebizond, 7:613, 7:630
Georgetown mantra, 6:92–93
Gerard, Alexander, **4:64–66**
  Alison and, 1:129
  on beauty, 1:52
  Garve on, 4:24
Gerard of Cremona, *Liber de Causis* and, 5:333
Gerbert of Aurillac, 4:66–67
Gerdil, Giacinto Sigismondo, Malebranche and, 5:671
Gergonne, J. D.
  on algebraic calculation, 5:461
  on implicit definition, 5:545
  on validity of syllogistic inferences, 5:499
Gerhardt, C. I., 2:582 5:255
Géricault, Theodore, Merleau-Ponty on, 6:151
Germain, Christopher St., 7:422

Germain, Sophie, 9:839
German
mass/count nouns in, 6:660
real characters in, 8:779
German Enlightenment, 9:56–57
ethics, 3:410–412
Spinoza's influence on, 9:193
Sulzer's *summa* on art and aesthetics, 9:325
German existentialism, 1:1
German Hasidism, 5:3
German idealism
in aesthetics, 1:52–54
collapse of, 5:363
and critical theory, 2:598
and ethics, 3:414–415
expression in, 1:303
Florovskii on, 3:673
Geisteswissenschaften in, 4:37
German romanticism and, 8:491
Marx and, 5:730
and New England transcendentalism, 6:572
political philosophy in, 7:667–668
Rosenzweig on, 8:498
Schiller (Friedrich) and, 8:629–630
Solov'ëv and, 9:123
Sufism and, 9:311
German Ideology, The (Marx), 5:730
on repression, 3:56–57
German liberalism, 5:321
German literature, Lessing and, 5:294
German Metaphysics (Rational Thoughts on God, World, Human Soul, and All Things in General) (Wolff), 9:823–824
German pantheism, 7:97–98
German period, of Jewish philosophy, 4:826
German philosophy
Adorno and, 1:25
Apel in, **1:225–227**
Basedow in, 1:482–483
and Coleridge, 2:316
dominance in Korea, 5:141
ethics in, 3:422–423
Geisteswissenschaften in, 4:37
"I" and "Other" relation in Russian thought, 1:465
Nietzsche on, 6:611
Rosenkranz on, 8:497
in Russia, 1:471
Russian philosophy and, 1:467, 1:538
Schelling, 8:617
Scholz in, 8:644–646
Schopenhauer in, 8:647–657
Schultz in, 8:659–660
Schuppe in, 8:662–664
Sigwart in, 9:29
Simmel in, 9:30
unconscious in, 9:571
universal grammar and, 8:791
German pietist movement, 5:2–3
German positivism
development of, 6:540–541
Jhering in, 7:426
Jodl (Friedrich) in, 4:835
German psychology, 8:138–141
German romanticism, 4:254, 5:294, 8:490
German Social Democratic Party, struggle against Eduard Bernstein, 5:47
German war guilt, Weber (Max) and, 9:734
German Youth Movement, and Carnap, 2:36
Germaniae Chronicon (Franck), 3:713
Germany
cultural nationalism in, 6:481–482
deism in, 2:688–689, 2:691
Enlightenment in, 2:687, 2:688–689, 6:481
invasion of Dutch Republic by, 9:183
Jewish integration and Cohen (Hermann), 2:304–306
jurisprudence in, 4:388–389
Meinecke's patriotism for, 6:113
militarism of, 7:153–154
social positivism in, 7:713
in Spengler's cultural morphology, 9:167
Spinoza's influence in, 9:193–194
Strauss as symbol of liberalism in, 9:263
Germany and the Next War (Bernhardi), 7:154
Germenevtika i eë problemy (Hermeneutics and its problems) (Shpet), 9:17, 9:19
Gersen, John, authorship of *Imitation of Christ* and, 9:424
Gershenzon, Mikhail, 4:768
Gershon, Levi Ben. *See* Gersonides
Gerson, Jean de, **4:67–68**
authorship of *Imitation of Christ* and, 9:424
on Scotism, 8:704
Gersonides, **4:68–70**
in late medieval Jewish philosophy, 4:821–822
Maimonides and, 5:653
Gert, B., 7:138, 7:139
Gertler, Brie, recognizing an experience, 5:114
Gesammelte Schriften (Humboldt), 8:793
Gesamtausgabe (Heidegger), 7:299
Geschichte der arabischen Litteratur (Brockelmann), 5:417
Geschichte der Logik im Abendlande (Prantl), 8:765
Geschichte der neuren Philosophie (Fischer), 3:659
Geschichte der Philosophie (Deussen), 3:42
Geschichte der Philosophie, Die (Fries), 3:752
Geschichte der Reaktion, Die (Stirner), 9:251
Geschichte des gelehrten Unterrichts auf den deutschen Schulen und Universitäten (Paulsen), 7:148
Geschichte des Materialismus (Lange), 6:540, 6:608
Geschichte des römischen Rechts in Mittelalter (Savigny), 8:614
Geschichte eines dicken Mannes (The story of a fat man) (Nicolai), 6:598
Geschichte und klassenbewusstsein (History and class consciousness) (Lukács), 5:602, 5:603–604
"Geschichte und Naturwissenschaften" (Windelband), 9:792
Geschichtlichkeit, 7:397
Geschichtsphilosophie, 1:27
Gesellschaftswissenschaften, 4:38
Gesetz der Ursache, Das (The law of cause) (Geyser), 4:83
Gesetzespositivismus (statutory positivism), 5:49
Gesinnungen, 7:270
Gestalt
"actual genesis" of, 5:156
in Chamberlain, 2:122–123
chaos as scientific starting point, 2:39
as primary intuitive concept, 2:122–123
Gestalt movement, Koffka a founder of, 5:124
Gestalt principle, and origin of world, 3:177
Gestalt psychology
aesthetics in, 1:60
alternatives to, 8:144–145
art in, 1:59
Ehrenfels and, 3:176
in history of psychology, 8:143–144
perception and, 7:184, 7:568

Gestalt Psychology (Katz), 4:71
Gestalt switch
as an operative element in scientific change, 5:159
marking the transition of paradigms, 5:157
Gestalt Theory, **4:70–76**
awareness of wholes in, 8:814
in Gurwitsch, 4:197
Schelling anticipation of, 8:620
"seeing" in, 4:74–75
phenomenological psychology and, 7:277
Gestalten, 5:127
Gestell (enframing), Heidegger on, 7:547
Gesture, in action, 6:80
Gesuita moderno, Il (Gioberti), 4:93
Gettier, Edmund
belief is not sufficient for knowledge, 5:89
causality and true belief, 2:93
on conditions of knowledge, 3:270–271
seminal paper of 1963, 5:104
Gettier problem, Lehrer on, 5:248
Geulincx, Arnold, **4:76–81**
on logic, 5:440
on mind-body problem, 2:59, 3:293, 4:77, 4:80
Gewirth, Alan, **4:82,** 5:36
Gewohnheitrecht, Das (Schuppe), 8:664
Geymonat, Ludovico, 7:135
Geyser, Joseph, **4:82–84**
Ghazali, Abu Hamid Muhammad. *See* al-Ghazālī, Muhammad
Ghazali, Ahmad. *See* al-Ghazālī, Aḥmad
Ghirardi, Gian Carlo, collapse theory of, 8:211
Ghost in the machine, 8:582
Gibbard, Allan
on decision theory, 2:659
expressivism of, 6:160
on indicative conditionals sentences, 2:426
in noncognitivism, 6:633
on non-descriptivism, 4:151, 6:634
on sentence meaning, 6:653
Gibbens, Alice Howe, marriage of, 4:775
Gibbon, Edward, **4:84–86**
on atheism, 2:688
on Christianity, 2:690
Gibbon, Edward (Grandfather of the historian), Law (W.) and, 5:220
Gibbs, Josiah, **4:86–87**
on energy, 3:233
on maxent distribution, 4:677
on physics of gases, 7:537
Gibson, J. J., on intelligibility of images, 1:326
Gide, André, and Deleuze, 2:693
Giere, Ron
on semantic view of theories, 9:416–417
social epistemology and, 9:84
Gierke, Otto von
in historical school of law, 7:426
on sovereignty, 9:143
Troeltsch and, 9:527
Gifford Lectures (Driesch, Hans A. E.), 3:111
Gifford Lectures (James, William), 4:775
Gift, Derrida on, 2:718
Gigerenzer, G., on decision theory, 2:660
Gignomenal principle, 9:884
Gilbert, Scott, on genetics, 7:344
Gilbert, William, planetary force analogy with magnetism, 3:687
Gilbert of Poitiers, **4:88–89**
on conditionals, 5:428
in *Historia Pontificalis* (John of Salisbury), 4:844
School of St. Victor and, 8:592
Giles of Rome, **4:89–91,** 5:438
Aquinas and, 9:444
in Godfrey of Fontaines, 4:131
on matter, 6:3
Giles of Viterbo, Pico della Mirandola and, 7:571
Gill, John, on oracles in polynomial-time computability, 2:389
Gilligan, Carol
friendship and attachment relations, 3:749
interviewing about moral dilemmas, 3:579
Gillman, Neil, 4:618
Gilman, Charlotte Perkins, evolutionary theory of Charles Darwin, 3:567
Gilman, Daniel, 3:43
Gilmore, Grant, on legal realism, 5:246–247
Gilson, Étienne Henry, **4:91–93,** 9:754–757
on Abelard, 3:403
on Dante, 2:624–625
on Suárez's metaphysics, 9:283
Ginés de Sepúlveda, Juan
on natural law, 6:509
on rights of indigenous peoples, 5:205
Ginet, Carl, on self-prediction, 8:730
Gioberti, Vincenzo, **4:93–95**
and Brownson, 1:706
Spaventa on, 9:160
Giordani, Pietro, Leopardi and, 5:284
Giordano, Paolo, on synthetic differential geometry, 2:510
Giornale di metafisica (journal), 8:666
Gipson, Edmund, on Tindal, 9:502
Girard, Jean-Yves, linear logic and, 5:491
Gischick, Abraham, 8:613
Gitanjali (Song offerings, Tagore), 9:363
Giustizia, La (Del Vecchio), 2:697
Givant, Steven R., Tarski and, 9:371
Given, The. *See* Basic Statements
Given Time (Derrida), 2:715, 2:718
Gladstone, W. E., 2:629
Glanvill, Joseph, **4:95–97**
Cambridge platonists on, 2:14
comparison with Cudworth, 2:610
constructive skepticism of, 9:53
on limited certitude, 9:54
Glas (Derrida), 2:715
Gläserne Bienen (Jünger), 4:860
Glasner, Ruth, 4:69
Glassen, Peter, 8:721
Glaubensbekenntnis, veranlasst durch ein Kaiserliches Reichshofratconclusum (Bahrdt), 1:457
Gleitman, Lila, 4:694
Global Practice Philosophy (Wolff), 9:824
Global situations, 3:708
Global supervenience, 9:331–332
Globalization
capitalist economic logical and, 2:363
Castells on, 5:741
civil society in, 9:98
economics of, 5:741, 7:351
engineering ethics and, 3:241
and Islamic philosophy, 4:762
in Kant, 7:389
Marxism and, 5:741
postcolonialism and, 7:727
Singer on, 9:42
state sovereignty and, 9:145–146
Glory
Cicero on, 7:79
Panaetius of Rhodes on, 7:79
Glossa (Alexander of Hales), 1:113
Glossulae (Abelard), 5:422–224
Glymour, Clark, 3:743, 8:687
Gnoseology, in Maritain, 5:714–715
Gnoseo-urgy, 3:559

Gnosticism, **4:97–105**
acosmism in, 4:103
al-Jabiri and, 1:130
anti-Semitism of, 4:101
in Christology debates, 2:247
Clement on, 2:289
Demiurge and, 2:699, 4:99–100
and divine transcendence, 4:107
dualism in, 4:98–99, 4:103–104
emanationism and, 3:189
Ibn al-ʿArabī on, 9:307
Manichaean, 5:684
of Marcion, 5:703, 5:704
mysticism of, 6:447
Paracelsus and, 7:103
patristic philosophy and, 7:141
Plotinus rejection of, 7:637
role of myth in, 4:99
in Shao Yong's reflexive observation, 9:6
of Simon Magnus, 9:33–34
Simonian theory of, 9:33–34
Tertullian on, 9:400
Valentinianism, 9:631–633
Goal(s)
action and, 7:736
eschatology and, 3:347
grounds for evaluation of, 3:325
of humans, in Finnis, 6:513
judgment of, in wisdom, 9:795
in minimalism, 7:736
national identity and, 6:483
of organism behavior, 7:38
as pleasure, 4:256
in purposive activity, 9:384–385
in rationality, 8:253
reason and, 7:735, 7:736
See also Conation
Göand, Albert, in neo-kantianism, 6:543
Gobineau, Comte Joseph Arthur de, 3:37, **4:106–107**
Goclenian stories, 5:557
God
as absolute being, 1:529, 1:623
absolute dependence on, 8:634–635
absolute power of, 5:69, 6:105
as absolute sovereign, 1:706
as Absolute Thou, 5:702
acquiring conceptual knowledge of, 5:146
agnosticism and, **1:92–95**
Alexander on, 1:109
in al-Fārābī, 5:650
al-Ghazālī on, 1:119–120
all-unity of, 9:124
altruism and, 3:172
analogies for, 1:140–143
Aquinas on, 1:140–141
Ayer on, 1:141
Barth on, 1:142–143
in mathematics, 6:596
Swinburne on, 1:142
truth conditions in, 1:143
Anselm on, 1:215–216
anthropomorphic, 1:359, 1:364–365, 1:370–371
as anticipation of Hegelian Absolute, 5:62
Aristotelian idea of, 4:816
Arnauld on, 1:290–292, 2:58
assent to, 6:581
attributes of, 4:110–111
in Abu'l-Barakāt, 4:758
Aquinas on, 1:141
Crescas on, 4:822
Duns Scotus on, 3:135
Gersonides on, 4:68
Israeli on, 4:814
Maimonides on, 5:649–650
Martineau on, 5:727
in philosophy of religion, 7:479
Augustine on, 1:397–398
in Averroes, 1:424
in Avicenna, 1:433
belief in
and apprehension of wisdom, 1:457
Buddhism and, 2:349–350
Darwin on, 2:349
different senses of, 1:359
faith and, 1:535, 3:535
meaning of, 2:350–352
Pascal on, 7:133, 8:713
Plantinga on, 7:481–482
self-deception in, 8:711–713
benevolent affection bestowal by, 1:474–476
Berkeley on, 1:359, 1:580–581, 1:584–585, 3:217
Bernard of Chartres on, 1:591
Blake on, 1:610
Boethius on, 1:626
Bonaventure on, 1:653
Browne on, 1:359
Bruno on, 1:710
Budde on, 1:721
Bulgakov on, 1:760
Bultmann on, 1:762–763
Buridan on, 1:769
Burthogge on, 1:776
Butler (Samuel) on, 1:785
Calvin on, 2:8–10
in Cambridge Platonism, 2:13
Campanella on, 2:15
in Cartesianism, 2:58–59
causality of, 5:669
Celsus on, 2:119
certainty of reality of, faith in, 4:772
characteristics of
in Indian philosophy, 5:326
Leibniz on, 5:256–259, 5:263, 5:270–273
Lequier on, 5:287
Levinas on, 5:305
Lull on, 5:609–610
Luther on, 5:612–613
Newton on, 7:558–559
Paley on, 7:77
Pico della Mirandola on, 7:572
in Chartres' school philosophy, 2:137
in Chubb's "Christian deism," 2:252–253
church-state unity and, 1:648
Clarke on, 2:272, 2:274
Clement on, 2:289
Cockburn on, 2:295
coercion by, 7:484
cognition of, 5:649
Cohen (Hermann) on, 2:304, 4:828
coincidence of opposites in, 6:595–596
Coleridge on, 2:317
Collier on, 2:323–324
Comenius on, 2:341, 7:369
conception of, **4:107–117**
Anselm on, 7:16
as final cause, 4:108
foreknowledge of, in Gregory of Rimini, 4:183
in Ibn Gabirol, 4:546
immanence in, 4:107–108
Maimonides on, 4:818–819
transcendence in, 4:107–108
conscience and, 2:445, 6:581
as contingency, 2:552
Conway on, 2:529
Cordemoy on, 2:538
Cordovero on, 2:539
Cournot on, 2:577–578
creating and preserving man, 3:533
creation as sacramental mirror of, 1:652
and creation *ex nihilo*, 2:246, 2:585
creation of atoms by, in Gassendi, 4:27–28
as creative and explanatory in Boyle, 1:674–675

God, *continued*
as Creator, 1:672, 2:730–733, 2:751, 5:703
Crescas on, 2:593
cruelty of, 1:362
Crusius on, 2:607–608
Cudworth on, 2:610–611
Culverwell on, 2:613
Cumberland on, 2:615
Damarsais on, 2:266
Dante on, 2:625
Darwin (Charles) on, 2:630, 2:637
Darwin (Erasmus) on, 2:631
David of Dinant on, 2:645
death of, 1:488, 6:611–612
dependence of creatures on, 3:141
deprivation of will by, 1:217
Descartes on, 2:462
description of, 8:418–419
desire for, 6:655
and determinism, 3:6–9, 3:23, 3:35
Diderot on, 3:72, 3:73
direct relationship with man, 4:816
disbelief in, 2:350–353, 6:618
divine illumination and, 4:580
in doctrine of Hell, 4:251
Ducasse on, 3:125
education and, 7:369
emanation of wisdom from, 1:651
as emergent quality, 1:109
Emerson on, 3:195–196
as eternal contrariety, 8:621
eternal truths as constraint on, 1:291
eternity of, 7:479
ethics and, 5:148, 7:5, 7:479–480
evil as "dark nature" of, 9:124
existence of, 5:22–23
abstract objects and, 2:553
d'Ailly on, 1:99
Alembert on, 1:106–107
in analytic philosophy, 7:480
Anselm on, 1:214–216, 4:112
Aquinas on, 2:677–680, 7:557, 9:431–432
arguments for, 2:344–354
Averroes on, 3:135
Avicenna on, 1:433, 3:135
beauty and, 9:407–408
being in arguments for, 9:431
Berkeley on, 4:556
biological design and, 2:347
Blanshard on, 1:362
Bradlaugh on, 1:362
Candidus on, 2:49
causality in argument for, 9:432
Clarke's argument for, 9:407
consciousness and, 9:407
cosmological argument for, 2:550–556, 9:407
degrees of perfection argument for, 2:677–680
Descartes on, 2:720, 2:728, 2:736, 2:741–748, 2:755, 3:292, 4:14, 8:123–124
design argument for, 1:368
Duns Scotus on, 3:135–137, 3:146
ethics and, 7:479–480
evil and, 1:361–364, 7:481, 9:380, 9:408–409
Fackenheim on, 1:363
faith and, 1:363
first proof of, 5:95
Galluppi on, 4:14
Gaunilo on, 4:33–34
Geyser on, 4:83
Gregory of Rimini on, 4:183
human innate propensity to believe in, 2:346–347
Hume on, 4:510
Jaspers on, 4:802
Jodl (Friedrich) on, 4:835
Johnson (Samuel) on, 4:851
Kant on, 4:556
La Bruyère on, 5:167
lack of evidence for as proof against, 1:361–362
laws of nature and, 9:407
Leibniz on, 2:553, 5:256
Lewis (C. S.) on, 5:312
Locke on, 3:300, 5:387
as logical impossibility, 7:18
as logical necessity, 1:216, 7:18
Lunn on, 1:363
Maritain on, 5:714
materialism and, 6:14
Matthew of Aquasparta on, 6:65
and meaning of life, 5:345–346, 5:352, 5:359
moral arguments for, **6:353–360**
morality and, 1:397, 9:407
motion in argument for, 9:432
in movement of atoms, 4:28
Narboni on, 4:821
Ockham on, 9:781
ontological argument for. *See* Ontological argument for existence of God
Paine (T.) on, 7:74
Paley on, 7:77
Pascal on, 7:133
in philosophy of religion, 7:480–481
physics and, 1:361
Plantinga on, 3:324, 7:481–482
popular arguments for, **7:700–705**
practical reason in argument for, 4:613
probability and, 9:407
proof of, 5:10
as proof of nativism, 4:687
Ray on, 7:558
relevance of, 1:363
Richard of St. Victor on, 8:592
Rohault on, 8:483
Rowe's argument against, 9:408
Sabatier on, 8:588
Scholz on, 8:645
Spinoza on, 9:173–175, 9:185
Stillingfleet on, 9:249
Suárez's metaphysical proof of, 9:283–284
successful proof of, 9:407
suffering and, 1:362
as superultimate "why," 9:758
Swinburne on, 3:321
teleological argument for, **9:376–382,** 9:407
Toletus on, 9:511
Udayana on, 4:627
Vasquez on, 9:650
Voltaire on, 9:709
Xenophanes of Colophon on, 9:854
and existence of evil, Descartes on, 3:345
experience as evidence of, Tennant on, 9:392
experience of, 4:247
impossibility of, 8:403
Pannenberg on, 7:80–82
as explanation of existence, 2:586
explanation of origin of universe and, 2:554
as expressed in nature, 1:623
extension and, 5:667–668
fecundity of, 6:521
Feuerbach on, 1:121
Fichte on, 1:378–379
as final cause *vs.* creator, 1:652
finite, 1:362
foreknowledge of, 1:626, 6:321
as form of world, 4:821
in Foucher's epistemology, 2:57
as free agent, 7:308
free will of, 1:5, 1:626, 3:23

freedom of, 7:721
Henry of Ghent on, 4:313
Ockham on, 9:781, 9:783
Voltaire on, 9:710
in French clandestine writings, 2:264, 2:267
future contingents and, 1:680
general will of, 1:291, 4:39
glory of, as universal end, 9:378
in Gnosticism, 4:99–100
goodness of
Descartes on, 2:728–730, 2:739, 2:745–749, 2:753–755
Leibniz on, 5:254, 5:256
Mill (John Stuart) on, 6:229
and moral determinism, 3:7–8
as ground of being, in Schelling, 8:621
Hatano on, 4:247
Hazlitt on, 4:249
Hegel on, 4:269, 4:276
Heim on, 4:297
Hemsterhuis on, 4:311
hiddenness of, **4:352–356**, 7:483–484
in Hindu philosophy, 5:329
Hobbes on, 4:421, 6:9
human beings as, 1:372–373
and human freedom, Descartes on, 2:751–755
and human hunger for immortality, Unamuno on, 9:568
human knowledge of, Eckhart (Meister) on, 3:162
human nature and, 7:368
human perception and, 1:584
human preconceptions of, 1:477
in human self-creation, 1:760
as human symbol, 1:519
in human-divine dialogue in Bible, 1:716
humans loved by, 4:828
Hume on, 4:509–510
Huxley on, 4:533
Idea and, in Philo, 4:810
ideas as thoughts of, 4:564
ideas caused by, 1:580
identity with that which is, 1:626
illumination and, 1:453, 1:652–653, 8:760
in illuminationism, 4:761
imitation of, 5:652, 5:653
immanence of, 9:526
immutability of, 1:680
as individual, 1:216
inference of, 6:580–581
infinity of
John of Damascus on, 4:837
Nicholas of Cusa on, 6:595–596
in Tolstoy, 9:512
instinctive approach to, 5:714
as intellect, 4:818, 5:650–651
intellect of, 5:649–650
in Iqbal's theistic pluralism, 4:745
in Islamic Neoplatonism, 6:557
isolation from, 1:477
James (William) on, 3:531, 4:781
justness of, Saadya on, 4:813
Kant on, 1:232, 2:689
karma theory and, 5:42
as knowable through grace, 1:479
knowledge of, 3:622, 7:305–306
Alexander of Hales on, 1:114
Aquinas on, 9:432
Calvin on, 2:9
as cause, 1:139–140
Charron on, 2:134–135
Halevi on, 4:816
Isaac of Stella on, 4:753–754
Leibniz on, 5:261–264
Maimonides on, 4:818, 5:652
Naṣīr al-Dīn al-Ṭūsī on, 6:478
Philo Judaeus on, 8:122
postvolitional, 6:321–322
prevolitional, 6:321–322
in Pseudo-Dionysius, 8:101–102
Rosenzweig on, 4:829
Scholastics on, 3:137–138
self-revelation in nature, 1:580
Ulrich of Strasbourg on, 9:565
Vives on, 9:701
knowledge possessed by, 3:320, 7:479
Laberthonnière on, 5:165
Lavater on, 5:214
Leibniz on, 5:261–264, 5:671
Leont'ev on, 5:283
as limited maintainer of world, 1:695
linguistics of, 1:94–95
love of
Aquinas on, 3:142
Astell on, 1:355–356
in Christianity, 5:585–586, 5:589
Duns Scotus on, 3:142–144
by humans, 4:828
Spinoza on, 5:588
as supreme goal, 4:823
in Tauler, 9:372
Maimonides on, 5:649–650
Malebranche on, 2:57, 5:664–669
as man in the world, 9:263
in Manichaeism, 5:683
Mansel on, 1:359, 1:362
Marcel on, 5:702
Marston on, 5:726
Marx on, 3:56
as maximum, 6:596
McTaggart on, 6:78
meaningfulness of life and, 6:619
mediation of, 3:533
mental properties of, 4:111
as metaphor, 1:142, 9:8
metaphysical, 1:359, 1:362
Mill (John Stuart) on, 1:93, 1:359
mind of, Wyclyf on, 9:851
in mind-body problem, 6:258–259
in mind-nature relationship, 1:672
misery of man without, Pascal on, 7:133–134
modalities and, 3:145–146
modes of discourse about, 1:764
in Moore's theory of truth, 2:542
and morality, 1:380, 1:475, 1:542, 1:556, 2:274
multiplicity of, 1:433, 1:681–682
Muqammiṣ on, 6:432
mutuality of revelation of, 1:559
Naṣīr al-Dīn al-Ṭūsī on, 6:478
Nasr on, 6:479–480
natural law and, 6:507–509, 6:512–515
and nature, 1:398, 9:646
nature as objectification of, 1:672
nature of. *See also* Pantheism; Physicotheology
Adams (M.) on, 3:477–478
Aquinas on, 2:681, 2:728, 9:432–433
Aristotle on, 5:585, 7:556
Augustine on, 3:357, 3:402–403
Barth on, 7:81
Boyle on, 7:557–558
Clarke on, 7:559
Driesch on, 3:112
Dühring on, 3:130
Eckhart (Meister) on, 3:162–163
Edwards (Jonathan) on, 3:167
Erigena on, 3:341, 7:95
and evil, problem of, 3:469–478
Goethe on, 4:143
in Jewish philosophy, 3:401
Kant on, 3:410–411
Lamarck on, 5:173
Leibniz on, 7:559
Lombard on, 7:260
Lotman on, 5:579
Lotze on, 5:581–582
naturalist theories of, 3:367
Ockham on, 9:781

God, *continued*
Pannenberg on, 7:80–81
patristic philosophy on, 7:141–143
Pauler on, 7:145
Paulsen on, 7:149
Philo on, 7:306
Pico della Mirandola on, 7:573
Plato on, 3:96–97
Stoics on, 5:569
Tillich on, 3:505
time and, 3:8–9, 3:357–360
Whitehead on, 9:752
Xenophanes of Colophon on, 9:854
nature's return to, 1:652
as necessary independent being, 1:706
Nietzsche on, 1:362
Norris on, 6:655–656
as nothing, 9:335
as nous, 6:666
in Nursi, 2:114–115
as object of faith, 3:529
in Old *vs.* New Testament, 5:703
omnipotence of
Abelard on, 1:5
d'Ailly on, 1:99
goodness and, 1:362
logical contradictions and, 6:599
Mansel on, 5:688
Ockham on, 9:781
and predestination, 3:9–10, 3:23
Russel on, 1:361
omniscience of
atheism and, 1:372–373
and determinism, 3:6–9, 3:23
Gersonides on, 4:822
Lequier on, 5:287
or Essence, Krause on, 5:147
Peirce on, 7:164
perception of, 1:132
perfection of, 7:16, 7:194
as perpetually active creator, 4:765
persistence and existence of universe and, 2:587
personalism and, 1:362, 7:235–236
personality of, 4:111–112
personhood of, 7:237
Peter Aureol on, 7:256
Philo's concept of, 7:303–308
in philosophy of religion, 7:479
Plato on, 2:698, 3:94, 7:303–304
as positive nothingness, 9:123
possibility and, 7:721
presence of, contingencies of, 4:831
prime matter in thought of, 4:821
principle of limit upheld in, 4:668
Pseudo-Dionysius on, 8:101–102
in psychology, of Tauler, 9:372–373
as radiant freedom, 1:559
as redeemer in Christianity, 2:248–249
Régis on, 5:666–667
rejection of, 4:251
relation to persons, 1:672
revelation as encounter with, 1:707, 8:453
Rosenzweig on, 4:829, 8:498
Rosmini-Serbati on, 8:503
Rousseau on, 2:687–688
Russell no, 8:559
Sartre on, 3:351
science and, 5:727
secularization and, historical implications of, 1:656
self-alienation of, 1:121
self-contraction of, 5:2
self-knowledge of, 1:433
as self-revealing, 2:247
self-sufficiency of, 4:109
semantics of, 7:483
Shakyamuni Buddha as, 1:723
simplicity of, 1:114, 1:140, 4:110, 4:116
sin by, Ockham on, 9:783
as solution to problem of nonbeing, 9:459
as source of wisdom, 1:651
Spinoza on, 1:11, 7:96–97, 8:125, 9:173–174, 9:191
stoic conception of, 9:254
Stout on, 9:261
as substance, in Thomism, 7:24
supercomprehension of, 6:322
as supreme agent, 3:692
Tagore on, 9:363–364
as teacher of men, 5:65
Teilhard on, 9:375
Telesio on, 9:391
as term, 7:483
in theological anthropology, 7:323
in theological "why," 9:757
Theophilus on, 1:228
in thought and thinking, 9:420
Tillich on, 9:459
Tindal on, 2:683, 9:503
Tolstoy on, 9:512
transcendence of, 1:477, 4:99, 5:1, 9:526
Treschow on, 9:526
in Trinity, 1:652
as Trinity in Christianity, 2:247–248
true love and friendship derived from, 3:623
Tschirnhaus on, physics and, 9:549
ugliness and, 9:562
Unamo y Jugo on, 1:359
Unamuno on, 9:567–568
unity of, Saadya on, 4:812–813, 8:586
as universal, Carus (Carl) on, 2:63
unknowability of, 7:306
in Valentinianism, 9:632
Vanini on, 9:646
Varisco on, 9:647
verum-factum principle and, 9:672
vision in, 5:666–667
volitional conformity with, 1:595
Voltaire on, 9:710
as voluntary creator in Islam, 2:113
Wallace (A. R.) on, 2:637
Weil (Simone) on, 9:737
will and heart of, 1:623
will of
as criterion of virtue, Gay on, 4:34–35
Gay on, 4:34–35
learned through experience, 1:574
Maimonides on, 4:818
moral objectivism and, 6:164–165
Paley on, 7:76
in time, 1:704
truth and, 5:666
William of Auvergne on, 9:765
Wolff on, 9:827–828
in Wollaston's ethics, 9:834
world soul as alternative to, 9:8
zero as, 7:11
in Zoroastrianism, 9:886
God and Other Minds (Plantinga), 7:581
God and Philosophy (Gilson), 4:92
God Assumption, 3:693, 3:695
God, Freedom and Evil (Plantinga), 7:581
"God Glorified in Man's Dependence" (Edwards), 3:167
God in Indian philosophy, **4:132–135**
Brahman as one reality, 1:681–684
Udayana on existence of, 4:627
God the Known and God the Unknown (Butler, Samuel), 1:785

Gödel, Kurt, 2:402, **4:117–119**
analyticity criteria, 2:42–43
arithmetic formal incompleteness, 2:41
axioms, 4:118
on calculable functions, 2:402–403
on completeness, 4:364
on continuum hypothesis, 2:28, 4:662, 8:707
dialectica interpretation of arithmetic, 4:741
field equation closed causal curves, 2:106
on finitary consistency, 5:470
on formal calculus of equations, 2:379
on general relativity, 9:499
on impredicative definitions and vicious circles, 2:256
incompleteness and general recursive functions, 2:401
incompleteness theorem of, 8:840
on intuitionistic logic, 4:739
metalanguage necessary incompleteness, 2:42
on primitive recursive functions in computability theory, 2:378
in proof theory, 8:56
on Ramified Theory, 9:557
self-reference lemma, 4:124–125
on set theory, 2:500, 5:520
space-time of, 9:497
transitive collapse in, 8:842
on Turing formalization, 2:376
in Vienna Circle, 8:638
work with *L* of "constructible" sets, 8:841
Gödel numeration, in combinatory arithmetic, 2:338, 5:544
Gödel set theory, in illative combinatory logic, 2:340
Gödel-Hebrand computability, 2:379
Gödel's completeness theorem, 5:544, 7:106
Gödel's incompeteness theorems, **4:119–131**, 5:544, 8:840
computability theory, 2:383–384
in computability theory, 2:382
on consistency, 5:473
first-order logic and computability theory axiomatization, 2:383
Friedman on incompleteness and, 5:484
Hilbert and, 6:676
machine intelligence and, 5:634
recursive inseparability theorem, 4:125
and strong and weak systems, 5:478
Tarski and, 9:368, 9:369
Turing and, 9:552
Gödel's Proof (Nagel), 6:473
Gödel-von Neumann-Bernays set theory, 5:544
Godfrey of Fontaines, **4:131–132**
Godhead
Eckhart (Meister) on, 3:162, 3:163
in Suso's trinitarian theology, 9:335
Godlovitch, Stan, on performance integrity, 1:322
Godmanhood, Frank generalized the notion of, 3:717
Gods
age of, 9:675
in classical mythology, 5:585
Democritus on, 5:301
and determinism, 3:5–6, 3:8
Empedocles on, 3:211
Epictetus on, 3:262
establishing the reliability of, 5:121
in Homer, 4:459–460
morality of, 4:111
Plato on, 7:594
in Shintō, 4:796–797
Socrates on, 9:109–110
Xenophanes of Colophon on, 3:211
"Gods of Greece, The" (Schiller, Friedrich), 8:626
Godwin, William, **4:135–140**
on anarchism, 1:177–178, 4:136, 8:93–94, 9:8
and Coleridge, 2:316
and cooperative movement, 9:87
in evolutionary psychology, 8:137–138
on government, 7:73
Hazlitt and, 4:248
on natural law, 9:251
on oppressiveness of social institutions, 9:9
on property, 8:69
and Shelley, 9:7
utilitarianism and, 9:605
Goethe, Johann Wolfgang von, **4:140–144**
anthropology, 7:316
Carlyle on, 2:32–33
and Carnap, 2:35
Chamberlain on, 2:124
and Croce, 2:601
Diderot and, 3:77
Dühring on, 3:131
ein offenes Geheimnis, 3:717
Emerson and, 3:195
Fichte and, 1:380
Gadamer on, 4:3
in Kaufmann's volumes, 5:46
and Klages, 5:77
Lavater and, 5:213
Lessing and, 5:296
on love, 5:588
as naive poet, 8:629
and New England transcendentalism, 6:572
on Newton, 3:57–58
Nicolai on, 6:598
Novalis and, 6:667
on optimism/pessimism, 7:250
in pantheism dispute, 9:194
pantheism of, 7:97
Pantheismusstreit and, 7:99, 7:101
Renaissance demythification, 1:470
Rintelen and, 8:479–480
and Schelling's pantheism, 8:621
and Schiller (Friedrich), 8:627
and Schopenhauer, 8:648
Spinoza and, 7:101, 9:194
in Spranger's philosophy of education, 9:199
and Steiner, 9:241
Sufism's influence on, 9:311
Sulzer and, 9:325
on tragedy, 9:523
on unconscious, 9:571
Goethe dessen seine Bedeutung für unsere und die kommende Zeit (Carus, Carl), 2:63
Goetheanum, 9:242
Goette, A., Driesch and, 3:110
Goeze, Johann Melchior, Lessing and, 5:295
Gogarten, Friedrich, **4:144**
Gogol, Nikolai Vasil'evich, 2:122
Gold, Thomas
on branch systems, 9:469–470
on cosmological theorizing, 2:562
Goldbach's Conjecture, 2:383, 5:101
Golden Age
in Chinese social and political thought, 2:238
Empedocles on, 3:210
of Russian philosophy, 8:567–571
Golden Bough, The (Frazer), 1:58
Golden Rule, **4:144–147**
Confucius and, 2:213
reversibility of, 1:460
Golden section, special aesthetic status of, 3:557
Golden Verses (Pythagoras), 6:553
Golden Words (Pythagoras), 4:6

Golding, Joshua, on faith, 3:535
Goldman, Alan
naturalism of, 8:156
philosophy of sex and, 7:523
Goldman, Alvin, **4:147–148,** 4:600
barn case imagined by, 5:89
on communication control, 9:84
on conditions of knowledge, 3:270–271
epistemology of, 6:498, 9:84
on innate ideas, 4:694
nominalism and, 6:628
on primary deviance, 1:17
psychological capacities mediated, 3:680
on reliabilism, 9:120
on simulation theory, 9:37
on social epistemology, 3:276
on volition, 9:705
Goldmann, Lucien
Dilthey and, 3:84
Kristeva's graduate work with, 5:151
Goldstein, Bernard R., 4:69
Goldstein, Kurt, as a founder of Psychologische Forschung, 5:126
Goldsworthy, Andy, 3:256
Golgotha und Scheblimini (Hamann), 7:99
Gombrich, E. H., 4:594
on illusion, 1:325–326
on images, 1:325–326
Plato and, 1:325–326
on vision, 1:329
Wollheim and, 1:306
Gondi, Jean-François-Paul de (Cardinal de Retz), 2:757
Gongan meditation, in Jinul's Buddhism, 4:833
Gongsun Long, 2:204–205, **4:148–149**
Gongsun Longzi (Gongsun Long), 4:148
Good, The, 4:150–153, **4:150–153**
Anselm on, 1:215
in antihedonistic value theory, 9:639
Aquinas on, 9:434, 9:435
Aristotle on, 1:267, 1:276, 3:398
attributive and predicative uses of, 4:151
Augustine on, 1:395
beauty and, 9:435
Brentano on, 3:421, 6:157
Broad (C. D.) on, 3:419
Carritt (E. F.) on, 3:419
in Coleridge, 2:319
as contemplation and virtue, 1:629
correctness of loving in Brentano, 1:690
in Cudworth, 2:611
Culverwell on, 2:613
Cumberland on, 2:615
definition and criteria for, 7:245, 7:249
Descartes on, 3:188
as deterministically ultimate, nonexistence, 1:589
Diderot on, 3:75
Duns Scotus on, 3:135, 3:142, 3:143
Epicureans on, 3:10–11
Erigena on, 3:403
Euclides on, 6:110
evil in progress toward, 8:621
Ewing on, 6:156–157
Green on, 4:180
Hare on, 3:429–430, 6:633
as highest ideal in communism, 2:367
Hobbes on, 3:406
Hume on, 3:408, 4:502–503
individual profit-seeking as, 1:777
intuitive knowledge of *(liangzhi),* 9:726–727
Jouffroy on, 4:855
Locke on, 3:407
McTaggart on, 6:79
in *Metaphysics* (Aristotle), 1:276
Mill (John Stuart) on, 6:227
Moore (G. E.) on, 3:418–419, 3:439, 6:352
vs. moral, in teleological ethics, 9:382–383
as moral property, 6:352
moral values as forms, 2:13
morality and, in Taylor (Alfred), 9:373–374
in Nicolas of Autrecourt, 6:601
in normative value theory, 9:639
One as, 8:41–42
in Plato, 3:398, 4:172, 6:548, 7:488, 7:601
in Platonic dialogues, 7:585
pleasure as, 4:257
in Plotinus, 6:547–548
pluralism in conservatism and, 2:467
presupposition of, in moral arguments for existence of God, 6:355–357
Prichard (H. A.) on, 3:419
in Proclus, 8:41–42
Rashdall on, 8:238–239
Rawls on, 9:83
relative amounts of, 7:253
relativity to historical change, 7:247, 7:248
Robinet on, 8:482
Ross (William David) on, 3:419, 8:505
in rule utilitarianism, 9:615
Scholastics on, 3:137
social, 2:364, 2:464–465
Socrates on, 9:111–112
Spinoza on, 9:172
stoics on man's pursuit of, 9:257
temporal *vs.* eternal, in Taylor (Alfred), 9:373–374
truth as, in James's pragmatism, 4:782
unity and, 8:41–42
utilitarian theory of, 4:189
value as, 9:637
as volitional conformity to God, 1:595
in wisdom, 9:795
Wolff on, 9:829
Yang Xiong on, 9:861
Good, Irving John, 4:672
on Nicod's condition and background evidence, 2:440
positive statistical relevance in causality, 2:100
on rational degrees of belief, 8:685
Good biases, distinguishing from bad, 3:576
Good gestalt, as a gestalten factor, 5:127
Good life, The
Aristotle on, 3:398
cultural cosmopolitanism and, 2:569–570
Habermas on, 3:91
Good lives, conservatism and, 2:466
"Good Samaritan" laws, 4:867
Good will
act as duty, 2:70
Kant on, 3:154
manifesting, 5:26
Good works
in Buddhism, 1:723
Ruysbroeck on, 8:579–580
Goodman, Nelson, **4:154–162**
on aesthetics, 1:33, 1:38, 4:160–161
on art, 1:77, 1:78–79, 1:305
art referential value, 1:509
on conditions of knowledge, 3:272
on confirmation theory, 2:441
on constructivism, 2:475
on counterfactuals, 2:427, 2:573–574, 4:156–157
criterion for classes, 6:176–177
on definition, 2:665, 2:670–671
in early nominalism, 6:627
on forgery, 1:295
on image semiotics, 1:327

incremental confirmation theory and, 2:434–435
on induction, 4:638, 5:229–230
mereology and, 6:146
in possible world counterfactual conditionals, 2:429
in post-positivist debates, 8:694
on style, 1:332
on Synonymy, 9:348
theories of perception, 3:676
on vagueness, 9:624
Goodman's grue puzzle, in Bayesian approach, 1:499
Goodness
of actions
conditions for, 6:159
in utilitarianism, 9:609
Whichcote on, 9:745
agathon as, **1:256**
in Anselm, 1:215
as attribute of God, 1:215, 4:111
Clement on, 2:289
definability of, 6:155–156
Epictetus on, 3:261–262
fundamental nature of, 6:155–156
as germ in Xunzi, 2:234
intuitive knowledge of, 6:156
in Machiavelli, 5:627
in metanormative value theory, 9:639
Moore on, 6:156
moral sense of, 1:474–475
natural *vs.* moral, 9:2–3
in naturalism, 6:495
of nature, 6:520
omnipotence and, 1:362
ontological character of, 1:628
Plotinus on, 6:187
reasonableness of, 1:475
as satisfaction and fulfillment, 1:614
Thomson (Judith) on, 9:449
Wollaston on, 9:833
Xunzi on, 9:856
Goodness-of-fit tests, 9:219–220
Good-reasons approach, 3:430–431
Gorbachev, Mikhail, Lenin and, 5:281
Gordon, Robert, 4:600
on emotions, 3:199
propositional emotions, 5:89
psychological capacities mediated, 3:680
on simulation theory, 9:37
Gorgias
in ancient aesthetics, 1:187
Antisthenes and, 1:224
in early education, 7:365
epistemology and, 3:282
ethics of, 3:395
logos in, 5:568
semantic naturalism in, 8:752
semantics in, 8:751
skeptical-nihilist thesis of, 9:48
on sophism, 9:130
as sophist, 9:129
Gorgias (Plato), 2:571, 5:8
author's family in, 7:582
elenchus in, 7:593
on human expertise, 9:109
on human good, 9:111
on judgment, 7:584
justice in, 6:632
Metrodorus of Lampsacus on, 3:263
natural law in, 6:506
Orphic influence in, 7:43
on rhetoric, 7:592
rhetoric in, 1:187–188
on social context of technology, 7:546
on sophists, 9:130
on tragedy, 4:175
on virtue, 7:589–590
Gorgias of Leontini, **4:162–164**
Gorski Vijenac (Njegoš), 7:267–268
Gosala, Makkhali, 5:42
Gospel(s)
Bultmann on, 1:764
literary criticism of, 1:492
and moral society, 2:367
as unconscious invention of myth, 9:262
Gospel of John, logos in, 5:569
Gosse, Philip, creationist theory of, 5:172
Gossett, William Seely, on postsampling distribution, 9:230
exact distribution of the statistic, 3:662
on rejecting a hypothesis or a model, 3:666
Gosudarstvennyi element v budushchem obshchestve (The state element in future society) (Lavrov), 5:219
Gott (Herder), 7:101
Gottfried Wilhelm Leibniz: Sämtliche Schriften und Briefe (Akademie der Wissenschaften, eds.), 5:250
Göttingen neo-kantianism, 6:543–544
Göttinger Taschen-Calender (periodical), 5:338
Göttingisches Magazin der Wissenschaften und Litteratur (periodical), 5:338
Gottsched, Johann Christoph, **4:164–166,** 9:824
Götz von Berlichingen (Goethe), 4:140
Goudge, Thomas, 7:337
Gouge, Olympe de, 9:839
Gould, Carol, 9:73
Gould, Steven Jay
on adaptation, 3:489–490
Dennett and, 2:712
on evolutionary psychology, 3:484
on selection, 7:342
Gournay, Marie le Jars de, **4:166–167,** 9:838
Gouvea, André de, 9:52
Governance, education as, 7:360
Government
al-Fārābī, Abū al Naṣr on, 1:117, 4:756, 4:811
Aristotle on, 1:268–269, 7:419
Buddhist civic participation, 1:725
in Chinese thought, 2:231
civil disobedience and, 2:260
corrupting influence of, Godwin on, 4:136–137
corruption and sinister interests, 1:555
Croce on, 2:604
Daoist, 2:236–237, 9:722
de Maistre on, 5:659
as distributor of pain and pleasure, 1:556
Dong Zhongshu on, 2:235, 3:98
Gautama on taxation and education, 1:725
Godwin on, 7:73
in Islamic state, 4:763
Japanese, philosophy under, 4:792
liberal view of, 5:319–322
libertarianism on, 5:335, 5:336
limit of actions by, 9:209
as limited in conservatism and, 2:469
Locke on, 2:699, 5:388–390, 7:153
Machiavelli on, 5:627, 5:629
Maimonides on, 5:652
mandate of heaven of, 4:792–793
Mariana on, 5:710–711
Marsilius of Padua on, 5:722, 5:724
in Mencius's political thought, 2:233
Mill (James) on, 6:219
Mill (John Stuart) on, 3:414
and nationalism, rise of, 7:152–153
as negative historical change agent, 1:720
Ogyū on, 7:10
Ortega y Gasset on, 7:47
Paine on, 7:73

Government, *continued*
Philo on, 7:306–307
power and, 7:369–370, 7:732–733
Priestley on, 8:5
of primitive humans, 9:675
promotion of bioethics, 1:599–600
Protagoras on, 8:92–93
in protecting freedom, Gewirth on, 4:81
protection of individual rights, 1:552
public scrutiny, 1:555
relation to society, 9:96
ren in, Mencius on, 6:130
Risorgimento, Gioberti on, 4:93
role of, Rawls on, 5:324
Rousseau on, 7:73
self-cultivation *vs.* economic status in Chinese philosophy, 2:200
in Shelley's anarchism, 9:8
in social contract, 9:80
Thoreau on resistance to, 6:575
Vitoria on, 9:698
Wang Fuzhi on, 9:724–725
Xunzi on, 2:233, 9:856
See also Politics; State
Grabasso, A., 7:135
Grace
Arnauld on, 1:288
attitude and attainment of, in Tauler, 9:372, 9:373
in Augustinianism, 6:99
authentic life availability of, 1:763
in Barth, 1:477
in beauty, Winckelmann on, 9:790
in Calvin, 2:10
divine immanence and, 1:618
in dominion, Wyclyf on, 9:852
effect on individual's congruent action, 9:284
emanationism and, 3:190
as the foundation of sobornost, 5:59
vs. free will, Melanchthon on, 6:119
free will in workings of, in Jansenism, 4:788–789
future contingents and necessity and, 1:680
God's obligation to bestow, Ockham on, 9:783
of grace and religion, 1:477
human action and, 1:618
Kempis on, 9:424
as knowable through grace, 1:479
Luther on, 5:613, 5:614
Malebranche on, 5:664, 5:670
Milton on, 6:250
in Molinism, 8:681–682
Nicole on, 6:604
Pascal on, 7:133–134
Pelagians as enemies of, 7:175
rationality as act of, 1:479
rationality of revelation and, 1:479
religion and, 1:477
role divine grace and human action, 1:618
salvation and, 1:288
sufficient *vs.* efficacious, 8:681
in Taylor (Alfred), 9:374
in Thomism, 8:681
in wisdom and virtue, 6:99
Grace and Personality (Oman), 7:14
Gracia, Jorge, political instability and, 5:211
Gracián y Morales, Baltasar, **4:168–169**
Graef, Hilda, on Newman (John Henry), 6:583
Graf, Arturo, 7:135
Graham, Angus C., 4:149
on Chinese epistemology, 2:206
on language engagement imperfection, 2:205
Graham, Billy
on Bible as revelation, 8:452
on devil, 1:367
Graham, Daniel, on Empedocles, 3:213
Gram force, 3:686
Grammaire (Condillac), 8:791
Grammaire générale (Beauzée), 8:790
Grammaire générale et raisonnée, ou La grammaire de Port-Royal, 2:423
Grammar
ambiguity in, 6:659–660
anaphora in, **1:171–175**
Anselm on, 1:218–219
of appearance, 1:229–231
behaviorists on, 5:189–190
in Bernard of Chartres, 1:591
categorical, 9:356–359
Chomsky linguistic competence in, 2:244
cognitive limits and categories in Husserl, 2:81–82
Condillac on, 8:790–791
context-free phrase structured, 9:356
criterion of sentencehood in, 8:804
existential reference *vs.* grammatical subject, 1:677
Hellenistic, 4:302
history of, Bacon (Roger) on, 1:455
identity in, 4:567
in Indian philosophy, universals in, 9:580–582
Leibniz on logic and, 5:442
logical form and, 5:508
mass/count distinction in, **6:659–666**
mentalists on, 5:189–190
of naming conventions and mass nouns in Chinese, 2:211–212
in natural *vs.* artificial language, 1:344
negation in, 6:524–525
nondescriptivism and, 6:634
of Pāṇini, 5:410, 7:413–415
philosophy and, 8:770
phrase-structured, 9:355
Platonists on, 5:189
Port-Royal Grammar, 8:775
Priestley in, 8:5
propositional types and, 5:507
quality-word relationships, 1:591
in Sanskrit, 7:413
Schleiermacher on, 8:636–637
as sermocinal science, 8:766
in sophism, 8:751–752
speculative, 1:591, 8:770–771
Bernard of Chartres on, 1:590
in medieval logic, 5:432–433
Stoicism's influence on, 9:255
subject and predicate in, 9:285–286
transformational, 9:355–356
universal. *See* Universal grammar
William of Champeaux, 9:767
Grammar of Science, The (Pearson), 7:160
Grammarian philosophy, 4:626, 4:631
Bacon and, 8:770, 8:773
of Bentham, 8:792
Condillac on, 8:790–791
imposition and, 8:762
in Middle Ages, 8:770–771
origin of, 8:790
of sophists, 8:751
Grammatical consequences, Leibniz on, 5:442
Grammatical forms
performative utterances and, 7:199–200
truth and, 7:196
Grammatical relation, coindexing of, 5:509
Grammatical structure
and logical form, 5:506
phonological form mismatches and, 5:509
transformational grammars and, 5:509

Grammatici Latini (Kiel), 8:769
Grammatologie L'écriture et la différence, De la (Derrida), 9:274
Grammatology, 7:412
Gramsci, Antonio, **4:169–170**
  on ideology, 4:574
  Labriola and, 5:165
Grand Cyrus, Le (Scudéry), 5:588
"Grand Design, The," 7:154
Grand Mystery Laid Open, The (Toland), 9:504
Grand theory, feminists retreat from, 3:601–602
Grande, Can, 2:626
Grande Encyclopedie, La, 1:504
Grandjouan, Fanny (Denise Paul), 2:694
Grandvilliers, Jean de, on French liberalism, 5:320
Grant, R. M., on miracles, 6:266
Graphic representation
  in Peirce's logic, 5:454–455
  in Venn's logic, 5:451–452
Graphology, 5:77
Grassmann, Hermann
  on algebra, 5:461
  and Carus, 2:64
  and Peano, 5:461
  and Whitehead, 2:64
Gratitude, reason, conformity with, 1:475
Grave, Christian, on Mendelssohn, 7:99
Gravesande, Willem Jakob, on force measurement, 3:228
Gravitation
  determinism and, 3:32
  in Einstein, 7:476
  vs. general theory of relativity, 8:684
  as sources of theoretical ideas in cosmology, 2:561
  universal, 5:54, 8:683–684
Gravitational attraction, Newtonian theory of, 5:123
Gravitational equations, in cosmology research, 2:565
Gravitational field
  of Newton, 3:635
  in unified field theory, 9:741
Gravitational force
  Kepler's conception of, 3:687
  not maintained for GTR, 3:691
Gravitational mass, 4:804, 6:4
Gravitatione (Newton), 9:155
Gravitons, 6:62
Gravity
  absolute-relative debate in, 9:157
  action-at-a-distance in, 9:578
  attempts underway to quantize, 3:691
  compared to *anima mundi* of the ancients, 5:54
  cosmic equilibrium bidirectionality and, 1:645
  dropped as an answer by Kepler, 5:54
  Einstein on, 3:178
  Galileo on, 8:683
  in general relativity, 3:235, 9:496
  loop quantum, 9:269–270
  mass in, 6:3
  in Newton, 6:593
  pre-Newtonian formulations in the *Astronomia Nova,* 5:53–54
  quantum, 9:267, 9:497
  space as conventional and, 2:522
  in string theory, 9:267–268
Gray, Asa, 3:488, **4:170–171**
Gray, John Chipman
  on legal realism, 5:246
  on philosophy of law, 7:425
Gray, Robert, philosophy of sex and, 7:523
Graz, University of, Meinong at, 6:114
"Great Affirmation" (Simon Magnus), 9:34
Great Awakening
  deism and, 2:689
  Edwards (Jonathan) and, 3:167
Great Britain. *See* Britain
Great chain of being
  Lamarck and, 5:174
  Lovejoy on, 5:593
Great Chain of Being, The (Lovejoy), 5:592–5:593
Great Change, principle of, 5:138
"Great Diakosmos," 6:7
Great Didactic, The (Comenius), 2:341, 7:369
Great Dispute and Christian Politics, The (Solov'ëv), 9:122
Great Harmony, Zhang's neo-Confucian rationalism, 2:157
Great Illusion, The (Angell), 7:155
"Great Instaurration" (Francis Bacon), 1:445
Great Is Diana of the Ephesians, or the Original Idolatry. (Blount), 1:619
Great Learning (Zengzi), 2:150, 2:171, 4:795
  on heart/mind watchfulness, 2:173
  virtue in Confucianism, 2:174
Great man model, of history, 3:569
"Great man" theories, 3:37
Great Ultimate
  in neo-Confucian rationalism, 2:155–157
  Zhou Dunyi on, 9:880
  Zhu Xi on, 9:883
Great Vacuity, Zhang's neo-Confucian rationalism, 2:157
Great World-System (Leucippus), 5:298
Great Year, in eternal return doctrine, 3:353
Greater Hippias (Plato), 1:41, 1:42
"Greatest good for the greatest number," 3:383, 3:412
Greatness, as quality, 1:22
Greece, ancient
  advances in, 9:405
  awareness of death in, 2:651
  democracy in, 2:699–700
  education in, 7:364–367
  equality concept in, 3:331
  Jewish law and, 9:793
  legislative authority in, 9:139
  literature in, 4:175–176
  natural law in, 6:506
  number in, 6:670
  philosophy of, Christianity and, 9:533
  philosophy of religion in, 7:487–490
  ratio in, 6:670–671
  reality in, 7:487–488
  religion, philosophy of, in, 7:487–490
  skepticism in, 1:191–194
  in Toynbee's historical thought, 9:517–518
  wisdom literature of, 9:794
Greed, Buddhism on, 1:724
Greek Academy, **4:171–175**
  Aenesidemus in, 1:30
  vs. Alexandrian Academy, 6:553–554
  Aristotle in, 1:263
  Damascius and, 2:622, 6:552, 6:553
  dialectic and, 3:53, 3:54
  Diogenes Laertius on, 3:88
  in Hellenistic thought, 4:300
  on matter, 6:58–59
  in Platonic tradition, 7:606–609
  Plutarch of Athens and, 6:551
  skepticism in, 1:247, 9:48–49, 9:253
Greek art, ideal of beauty in, 9:791
Greek drama, **4:177–178**
Greek fathers, teachings of, 3:672

Greek philosophy
access to, in early Middle Ages, 8:586
altruism in, 3:170
applied to Jewish doctrine, 4:810–811
Arabic translations of, 7:610–611
in Christian philosophy, 7:387
on cosmos, 2:571
on creation, 2:698–699
and David of Dinant, 2:644
Dikē in, **3:78–79**
empiricism in, 3:215–216
epistemology in, 3:283–289
eschatology in, 3:347, 3:348
as eternal source for philosophical thought, 3:673
eternity in, 3:357
ethics, 3:394–399
on existence of fictitious objects, 3:493
fate in, 3:35
on infinity, 4:668
on inner senses, 4:696
Islamic philosophy and, 1:423
Islamic translations of, 4:754
Laberthonnière on, 5:165
love in, 5:584–585
matter in, 6:58–59
microcosm in, 5:639
myth in, 6:463–464
Parmenides of Elea, **7:122–129**
Philo's revival of, 7:303–305, 7:308
physicotheology in, 7:556–557
political philsoophy, 7:655–657
Santayana affinity for, 8:597
and Schiller (Friedrich), 8:627
semantics in, 8:751–759
on sensationalism, 8:823–824
Servetus on, 8:831
Simplicius in preserving, 9:35
sophists and, 9:129
Stoicism in, 9:253
substance and attribute in, 9:294
and Sufism, 9:301
on war and peace, 7:152, 7:154
wisdom literature of, 9:794
See also Atomism
Greeley, Horace, Liberal Republican Party and, 5:321
Green, Edmund Fisk. *See* Fiske, John
Green, George, on potential energy, 3:228
Green, Judith, radical critical pragmatism, 3:568
Green, Leon, legal realism and, 5:247, 7:428
Green, Thomas Hill, **4:178–181**
English liberalism and, 5:320
epistemological studies of, 5:91
ethics, 3:416
on freedom, 5:319
idealism of, 4:558
on limit to state action, 9:209
political philosophy of, 7:668–669
and Sidgwick, 9:25
state as manifestation of common purpose, 4:560
Green Revolution, environmental ethics and, 3:260
Greenberg, Clement
formalism of, 1:308
on painting, 1:331
Gregory of Nazianzus, **4:181**
patristic philosophy and, 7:143
on Sextus Empiricus, 8:850
Gregory of Nyssa, **4:181–183**
and Byzantine view of philosophy, 1:786
Erigena and, 3:341
eschatology, 3:348
patristic philosophy and, 7:143
Gregory of Rimini, **4:183–184**
Giles of Rome and, 4:89
on natural law, 6:509
Ockhamism of, 7:8
Gregory of St. Vincent, on Eudoxus method of ratio, 2:492
Grelling, Kurt, on set theoretic paradoxes, 5:518
Grelling-Nelson paradox of heterologicality, 5:551
Grennadios, George Scholarios, Latin scholasticism in Byzantine thought, 1:789
Grenzsituationen (impenetrable boundaries), in Jaspers's psychology, 4:801
Gresham's law, necessity and, 5:222, 5:223
Greuze, Jean-Baptiste, Diderot and, 3:76
Grew, Nehemiah, physicotheology and, 7:557
Grews, Ivan, 5:42
Grice, Herbert Paul, **4:184–185**
on connective words, 7:739
on conversational implicature, 2:525
on implication, 6:651
on implicatures, 3:253
on indicative conditional sentences, 2:425
on language and thought, 5:191
on natural and nonnatural meaning, 4:711
on pragmatics, 7:738, 8:747–748
on truth of sentences, 6:651
"what is said" and "what is implicated," 3:646
Grice, Paul. *See* Grice, Herbert Paul
Gricean analytical program, 6:83–84
Grief Observed, A (Lewis), 5:311–312
Griesinger, Wilhelm, 7:151
Griffin, David Ray, parapsychology and, 7:116
Griffin, Donald
on animal communication, 1:204, 1:205
on animal consciousness, 1:201–202
Griffin, James, 8:721, 9:643, 9:681
Griffin, Miriam, 8:811
Griffiths, Paul, on emotions, 3:201
Grimaldi, Claudio, Leibniz and, 5:253
Grimes, John, on conscious qualitative states, 2:451
Grimm, Friedrich, 2:688, 3:71, 3:683
Grisez, Germain
on natural law, 6:513
philosophy of sex and, 7:523
Griswold v. Connecticut, 6:95
Groenendijk, Jeroen, 1:175, 8:808
Groos, Karl, play theory of art, 3:100
Gross, Paul, 8:677, 8:679
Grosseteste, Pseudo-. *See* Pseudo-Grosseteste
Grosseteste, Robert, **4:185–189**
Averroism and, 1:428
Bacon (Roger) and, 1:453
Bonaventure and, 1:653–654
Thomas of York and, 9:443
Grote, John, **4:189–190**
on altruism and self-interest, 3:173
and Sidgwick, 9:21, 9:25
Grotius, Hugo, **4:190–193**
cosmopolitanism and, 2:567
Culverwell use of, 2:613
and Cumberland, 2:614
in international law, 7:422
on justice, 9:673
La Peyrère and, 5:196
on natural law, 6:510
on property, 8:69
Pufendorf and, 8:157
on social contract, 9:81
Socinus and, 9:100
Suárez and, 9:284
Vico and, 9:672–673
on war and peace, 7:152
and Wolff, 9:826
Grouchy, Sophie de, Marquise de Condorcet, 9:839

Groundedness, explicating an intuitive notion of, 5:149
Grounds of Natural Philosophy (Cavendish), 2:117
Groundwork of the Metaphysics of Morals (Kant), 2:70, 2:366, 3:749, 4:557, 5:23, 6:512
Group, individual in, 6:81
Group identity, as politically necessary, 3:587
Group Mind, The (McDougall), 6:72
Group selection, 7:342
Groupism, 9:208
Groups
 size of, and impartiality, 4:620–621
 theory of in 19th century mathematics, 5:462
Grover's algorithm, quantum computing and, 2:408
Growing block view, persistence and, 7:211
Growth
 vs. change, 1:186
 developmental, as biological system, 1:594
 emotional, education and, 7:363
 McDougall on, 6:72
 physical, 7:345–347
Growth of the Mind, The (Koffka), 5:124
Grudenlagen (Cantor), 8:832
Grudriss der Psychologie (Wundt), 1:234
Gruhle, Hans, as a founder of Psychologische Forschung, 5:126
Grumbling Hive (Mandeville). *See Fable of the Bees* (Mandeville)
Grünbaum, Adolf
 on direction of time, 9:470
 on non-epistemological conventionalism, 2:523
 on psychoanalysis, 8:108
 on tensed theory of time, 9:477–478
 tenseless theory of time and, 9:475
Grundgesetze der Arithmetik (Frege), 2:400, 3:726, 5:464, 5:466, 5:517, 8:799
Grundlage der gesamten Wissenschaftslehre (Fichte), 1:11, 3:54
Grundlagen (Frege), 5:464
Grundlagen der Arithmetik, Die (Frege), 3:725, 5:463, 8:799
Grundlagen der Geometrie, Die (Dingler), 3:86
Grundlagen der Geometrie (Hilbert), 8:836
Grundlagen der Mathematik (Hilbert and Bernays), 2:401
Grundlagen des 19. Jahrhunderts, Die (Foundations of the 19th century) (Chamberlain), 2:123
Grundlagen einer allgemeinen Mannigfaltigkreislehre (Foundations of a General Theory of Sets) (Cantor), 2:27–28
Grundlagenforshung (Research on the foundations of the exact sciences) (periodical), 3:85
Grundlegung der allgemeinen Grammatik und Sprachphilosophie (Marty), 8:803
Grundlegung der Dialektik (Liebert), 5:343
Grundlegung der Logik und Erkenntnistheorie (Foundations of logic and epistemology) (Geyser), 4:82
Grundlegung und Aufbau der Ethik (Brentano), 1:690, 3:421
Grundlegung zur Physik der Sitten (Beneke), 1:543
Grundlinien einer Kritik der bisherigen Sittenlehre (Outline of a critique of previous ethical theory) (Schleiermacher), 8:633
Grundlinien einer Kritik und exakten Theorie der Wissenschaften, insbesondere der mathematischen (Essentials of a critique and rigorous theory of the sciences, especially of the mathematical ones) (Dingler), 3:85
Grundlinien einer Philosophie der Technik (Kapp), 7:543
Grundprobleme der Ethik (Troeltsch), 9:527
Grundriss der Erkenntnistheorie und Logik (Schuppe), 8:662
Grundriss der Geschichte der Philosophie seit Beginn des neunzehnten Jahrhunderts (Wundt), 1:234
Grundrisse (Marx), 5:731
Grundsatze der Philosophie der Zukunft (Feuerbach), 3:609
Grundzüge der Ethik und Rechtsphilosopie (Schuppe), 8:664
Grundzüge der mathematischen Logik (Scholz), 8:645
Grundzüge der Mengenlehre (Hausdorff), 8:837
Grundzuge der Theoretischen Logik (Hilbert, Ackermann), 2:404, 3:639
Gruppentheorie und Quantenmechanik (Theory of Groups and Quantum Mechanics) (Weyl), 9:741
Grutter v. Bollinger (2003), 1:82
GRW collapse, 8:211–212
Gryphius, Wolff and, 9:825–826
GTR. *See* General theory of relativity
Guardini, Romano, on philosophy of technology, 7:545
Guattari, Felix, 2:694, 2:696
Guénon, René, 9:311
Guernica (Picasso), 1:328
Guessing, aiming at the truth, 5:87
Guettard, Jean-Étienne, Lavoisier and, 5:216
Guide of the Perplexed (Maimonides), 1:505, 4:818–819, 5:648
 analogy in, 1:140
 creation in, 5:650
 influence of, 5:653
 microcosm in, 5:641
 Narboni commentary on, 4:821
 Scot on, 8:703
 special providence in, 4:68
Guido da Montefeltro, Dante on, 2:625
Guidobaldo del Monte, on energy and work, 3:227
Guillaumin, Colette, materialist feminism introduced by, 3:601
Guilt, **4:193–195**
 collective, 4:194–195
 extenuation and, 8:165
 German war, 9:734
 as impenetrable boundary, in Jaspers's psychology, 4:801
 internalization of moral norms and, 3:382
 Nietzsche on, 6:612
 vs. shame, 9:4–5
 Tillich on, 9:458–459
 in Wollheim's psychology, 9:836
Guitton, Jean, on optimism/pessimism, 7:249
Guizot, François, French liberalism and, 5:320
Guldin Arch, Die (Franck), 3:712
Gulliver's Travels (Swift), 9:340
 on scientific method, 4:688
 utopianism of, 9:619
Gumilev, Lev, neo-eurasianism and, 3:454
Gumilev, Nikolai, 3:454
Guṇa (particular qualities), *vs.* Western particulars, 9:587
Gundlegung der Soziologie des Rechts (Ehrlich), 7:427
Guo Xiang, **4:196–197**
 contributions to Daoism, 2:153
 ontological view of, 2:191
 on transformation in Daoist ontology, 2:153

Gupta, Anil, on semantic paradoxes, 5:521
Gupta dynasty, Hindu systems of philosophy and, 5:329
Gurevich, Aron, 5:42
Guru, 4:626, 6:109
Gurwitsch, Aron, **4:197–198**, 7:299, 7:301
Gustafson, Richard F., on Tolstoy, 9:512
Gustatory sense, 5:118
Guth, Alan, on inflationary universe theory, 2:566
Gutiérrez, Gustavo, liberation theology and, 5:331–333
Gutting, Gary, argument from religious experience and, 3:321
Guyau, Jean Marie, on eternal return doctrine, 3:354
Guyton de Morveau, Louis-Bernard, 5:216–217
Gyandry, advocacy of, 3:606
Gyeke, Kwame, on African philosophy, 1:85
Gymnosophism, 8:173

H

Haack, Susan, 3:272, 8:680
Haag-Hall-Whiteman theorem, 3:635
Haak, Theodore, Elisabeth, princess of Bohemia and, 3:187
Habermas, Jürgen, 2:599, **4:199–201**
  Adorno and, 1:26
  on Arendt, 1:255
  on civil society, 9:98
  in concert with Ricoeur, 3:744
  critical legal studies and, 7:463
  on discourse ethics, 3:91
  on emancipatory critique, 4:574
  on Hegel, 4:280
  influencing feminists, 3:565
  Marxism of, 5:739–740
  socialism of, 9:91
Habilitation (Apel), 1:225
Habit
  in act utilitarianism, 9:608
  in animals, 1:202
  Dewey on, 3:48
  experience and, 5:656–657
  Luther on, 5:615
  Maine de Biran on, 5:656–657
  Peirce on, 7:167, 7:171–172, 7:174
  society as, 7:378
  of thought in Berkeley, 1:587
Habit memory, 6:123
Hacking, Ian, 8:594
  on emotion, 3:202
  on entity realism, 8:692
  on logical terms, 5:532
  on probability, 8:37–38
  on social constructionism, 9:78
"Haddocks' Eyes" (Carroll), 2:52
Hades, in Orphism, 7:43
Hadras, Lull's Dignities and, 5:610
Haeberlin, Paul, 7:83
Haecceitism. *See* Modality, Philosophy and Metaphysics of
Haecceity
  Duns Scotus on, 3:138–139, 3:145, 3:147
  Peirce on, 7:168–170
Haeckel, Ernst Heinrich, **4:201–205**
  Driesch and, 3:109, 3:110
  on evolution, 2:635
  monism of, 7:714
  panpsychism and, 7:83
  and Steiner, 9:241
Hägerström, Axel, **4:205–208**
  emotive theory and, 3:425, 3:426
  on Kelsen, 7:428
  in legal philosophy, 7:428
  logical positivism and, 5:525
Hahn, Hans
  on continuity and number system, 2:501
  logical positivism and, 5:524
Haight, Mary, on self-deception, 8:712, 8:714
Halachah, Maimonides on, 5:647
Halakhah (Jewish law)
  Levinas's defense of, 4:832
  as wisdom literature, 9:793
Halbwachs, Maurice, on collective memory, 6:126
Haldane, J. J., 9:66
Hale, Bob, on Leibniz's argument for God's existence, 2:552
Hale, Lord Chief Justice, 2:682
Halevi, Yehuda, **4:208–210,** 4:815–816
Hall, David L, on individual rights *vs.* ethical responsibility for others in Confucian ethics, 2:196
Hall, E. W., on Moore (G. E.), 3:419
Hall, G. S., students of, 3:43
Hall, Joseph, Lipsius and, 5:364
Hall, Roland, 5:394
Hall, Stanley, 8:141
Haller, Albrecht von, 3:74
  and Cabanis, 2:2
  La Mettrie and, 5:179
Halley, Edmund
  Berkeley on, 2:686
  Enlightenment and, 3:246
  Newton and, 6:590
Hallische Jahrbucher für deutsche Wissenschaft und Kunst (Ruge), 3:609
Hallucinations, 7:177–178, 7:182, 7:184, 7:187–189
  in argument from significance of continuity, 4:587–588
  astral bodies as, 4:603
  causes of, 4:586–587
  in critique of shadow-man doctrine, 4:603
  disjunctivism and, 7:193
  displace-perception model and, 8:725
  vs. dreams, 3:105–106
  phenomenalism and, 7:274
  in sense-datum theory, 8:820
Halting problem
  computing machines and, 2:404
  Turing on, 5:477
  unsolvability in computability theory, 2:382
Halwachs, Maurice, 2:693
Halwachs, Pierre, 2:693
Halyburton, Thomas, on deism, 2:682
Hamann, Johann Georg, **4:210–213**
  in crisis of skepticism, 9:57
  as an extreme fideist, 3:631
  geist as term in, 4:37
  Jacobi (Friedrich Heinrich) and, 4:769
  on Kant's use of language, 8:787
  on language, 8:785–787
  and Mauthner, 8:801
  Pantheismusstreit and, 7:99, 7:101
  on unconscious, 9:571
  on verbalism, 8:786
Hamblin postulates, 10:34–35
"Hamburg Logic" (Jugius), 4:861
Hamelin, Octave, **4:213–214**
  Lavelle and, 5:214
  Le Senne and, 5:289
Hamilton, James, Locke and, 5:392
Hamilton, William, **4:214–216**
  on agnosticism, 1:92
  on Brown (T.), 8:135–136
  on classical mechanics, 2:279
  on complex numbers, 5:514
  De Morgan and, 2:709
  on Flint, 1:94
  friends and colleagues of, 2:709
  intellectual circle of, 3:608
  inverse variation of feeling and knowledge, 3:608
  on logic, 5:439, 5:447
  Mansel and, 5:687
  McCosh and, 6:71
  on phenomenology, 7:278

quantification of predicate and, 5:553
sensation inverse relationship with perception, 1:462–463
on unconscious, 9:572
Hamiltonian cycles, for decision procedures and polynominal-time computability, 2:388
Hamiltonian mechanics, conservation principle in, 2:463
Hamiltonian theory, symmetries and conservation principle in, 2:463–464
Hamlyn, D. W., 8:824
Hammond, Peter, on decision theory, 2:655
Hampshire, Stuart Newton, **4:216–218**, 8:730
Han dynasty, Confucianism in, 3:98
Han Fei, 2:237, 2:238, **4:219–220**
self-cultivation *vs.* economic status in Chinese philosophy, 2:200
on Yang Zhu, 9:862
Han Fei Tzu. *See* Han Fei
Han Yu, **4:220–221**, 9:861
Hanafī, Hasan, **4:218–219**, 4:762
Hanay, Alastair, on method in Chinese ethics, 2:200
Hand, Its Mechanism and Vital Endowments as Evincing Design, The (Bell), 7:561
Hand, Learned, Dworkin and, 3:156
Handbook of Platonism (Alcinous), 5:408
Handbuch der psychischen Anthropologie (Fries), 3:752
Hanfeizi. *See* Han Fei
Hankel, Hermann, continuous magnitude and irrational numbers, 2:501
Hannay, Alastair, 5:68
Hansel, Charles E. M., parapsychology and, 7:116
Hansen, Chad, 4:149
on Chinese ethics, 2:201
on mass nouns in Chinese, 2:210–212
on Mohist ethics, 2:197
Hansen, George P., 7:115
Hanslick, Eduard
on arousal theory of expression, 1:303
on art, 1:59
on music, 1:56, 1:303
Hanson, Norwood, in post-positivist debates, 8:694
Hanzawa, Masao, on electrical logic machines, 5:566
Happenings, mental, brain physiology in, 9:720
Happiness, **4:221–224**
Anselm on, 1:218
Antiochus of Ascalon on, 1:222–223
Aristotle on, 1:267, 1:268, 3:398
Augustine on, 1:395, 3:401
beauty as promise of, 1:67
in Christianity, 2:652
as creative labor in Marx, 2:367
deontological ethics and, 2:713
Descartes on, 2:753
Diogenes of Sinope on, 3:90
Dühring on, 3:131
duty and, 2:367
as ethical criteria in Bentham, 1:552–553
in existentialism, 2:652
and future, irrelevance of, 5:350–351
harmonious, 7:205
Hélvetius on, 4:307
Hemsterhuis on, 4:311
as hypothetical imperative, 2:70
Ikkhwān al-ṣafā, pursuit of, 4:576
in indirect utilitarianism, 7:460
La Mettrie on, 5:180
law and, 7:456
McTaggart on, 6:78
Mill (John Stuart) on, 7:377–378
Moore's open question on, 4:736
morality and, 1:218
Paley on, 7:76
Panaetius of Rhodes on, 7:79
Pascal on, 7:132
Paul (St.) on, 3:401
as philosophical aim, 1:390
Plotinus on, 7:639–640
as principle of utility in Bentham, 1:551
promotion of, and justice, 4:867
reason in, Wollaston on, 9:833–834
research on, 9:642
Schlick on, 8:643
Schopenhauer on, 5:345–346
Skovoroda on, 9:64
stoics on, 9:254
Tabataba'i on, 8:646–647
through congenial tasks, 9:64
in utilitarian societies, 9:66
Vauvenargues on, 9:654
virtue and, 1:222–223, 1:267, 1:268
Wollaston on, 2:684, 9:833–834
Zeno of Citium on, 9:870
Haraway, Sandra
objectivity meaning situated knowledges, 3:577
reflections on hybrid constructions of nature, 3:592
Hard facts, necessity of the past applicable to, 3:694
Hardenberg, Friedrich Leopold von. *See* Novalis
Hardie, Keir, 9:89
Hardin, C. L., on color, 2:333
Harding, Sandra, **4:224–225**
on African struggles, 1:87
arguing for multiple standpoints and views, 3:576
drawing on earlier proposals of feminists, 3:592
feminist standpoint epistemology and, 8:677
postmodern epistemic stance, 3:592
on strong objectivity in science, 8:679
working within standpoint theory, 3:576–577
Hardware-independence, in Chinese room argument, 2:239
Hare, Richard M., **4:225–226, 5:37**
on act and rule utilitarianism, 9:603–604
on continental philosophy, 2:488
criticism of, 3:430
ethics, 3:429–430
on meaning, 1:154
on Moore (G. E.), 3:418, 3:419
on moral principles, 2:447
on moral reason, 6:158
on moral thinking, 3:441
prescriptions in ethical language, 4:150
prescriptivism of, 3:684
on principle monism, 3:441
on Rawls's social contract theory, 9:82
Sidgwick and, 9:25
and Singer, 9:42
on use of "good," 6:633
on valuation, 9:638
Hare Krishna movement, 4:630
Harlay de Champvallon, François de, 2:757
Harley, Robert, Toland and, 9:504
Harm, definition of
in medical ethics, 3:456
in social and political philosophy, 5:337
Harm principle, of Feinberg, 3:561
Harm to Others (Feinberg), 3:561

Harm to Self (Feinberg), 3:561
Harman, Gilbert, **4:226–228**
- on analyticity, 1:164–165
- basic mental notions, 5:88
- on consciousness, 2:455
- on intentional action, 4:703
- on language acquisition, 4:694
- on moral facts, 6:162
- on moral relativism, 3:372–373, 9:449
- on moral skepticism, 6:394
- on perception, 7:190–191
- on side effects of action, 1:20
- theory of meaning further developed by, 3:756

Harmless Wrongdoing (Feinberg), 3:561
Harmonice Mundi (Kepler), 3:675, 5:51
Harmonics (Archytas of Tarentum), 1:250
Harmonics (Ptolemy), 1:189
Harmonie universelle (Mersenne), 6:152
Harmonious equipotential system, 9:697
Harmonious happiness, 7:205
Harmoniousness
- in Coleridge, 2:320
- in criteria of experience, 1:678
- as criteria of real, 1:678

Harmony
- in antiutopianism, 9:621
- and barbarians, 3:707
- as Confucian ideal, 2:150–151
- in Confucianism-Mohism and Daoism, 2:185
- in Croce, 2:603
- in Daoism, 2:198
- as educational aim, 7:372
- in Froebel, 7:372
- Laozi on, 5:194–195
- Leibniz's republic of monadic spirits and, 2:365–366
- in monadology, 6:324–325
- passion for, 3:706
- Perry's concept of, 7:205
- Philolaus on, 7:310–311
- preestablished
  - Leibniz on, 5:254, 5:270–276
  - Wolff on, 5:123
- replacing Civilization, 3:706
- symmetry and, Weyl on, 9:742
- in Tiantai Buddhism, 2:163
- universal, Leibniz on, 5:257, 5:260–263, 5:271
- in utopianism, 9:617–618

Harmony between Plato and Aristotle (al-Fārābī), 1:423
Harms, suffered by women, 3:584
Harnack, Carl Gustav Adolf von, **4:228–229**
- Barth on, 1:477
- Loisy and, 5:570
- on Marcel, 5:703
- Trubetskoi (Sergei) and, 9:533

Harnish, Robert, on performative utterances, 7:201
Harper, William, on decision theory, 2:659
Harre, R. M., on categorical imperative, 2:71
Harrel, David, modal logic and, 5:491
Harrington, James, 2:681, 2:682, **4:229–230**
Harris, James, on universal grammar, 8:790
Harris, William Torrey, **4:230–232**
- Dewey and, 3:43
- Emerson and, 3:196

Harris, Zellig, 9:355, 9:360
Harrison, Andrew, on image symbols, 1:327
Harrison, Jane Ellen, on myth, 1:58
Harrison, John, nautical chronometer of, 6:91
Harrod, R. F., on induction, 4:641
Harsanyi, John C., 3:449, 4:18
Hart, Herbert Lionel Adolphus, **4:232–234**
- Dworkin on, 3:156, 7:459
- on law, 1:168–169
- legal philosophy of, 7:429
- legal positivism of, 5:239–241
- on legal principles, 7:459
- on legal rules, 5:247
- on morality, enforcement of, 5:338, 7:137
- on sovereignty, 9:140

Hart, W. D., on soul, 3:116, 3:117
Hartle, James, *kalām* argument on God's existence and, 2:555
Hartley, David, **4:234–236**
- on altruism and self-interest, 3:173–174
- on association of ideas, 1:50
- and Coleridge, 2:315–316
- ether theory of, 8:699
- Gay and, 4:34
- on human nature, 3:173
- Lichtenberg and, 5:341
- moral-sense theory in, 3:408
- neurophysiology of, 8:135
- on pleasure and pain, 7:621
- Priestley and, 8:4, 8:6
- in psychology, 18th-century British, 8:135
- sensationalism in, 8:826
- on sensations, 8:135, 8:823
- Tetens and, 9:403

Hartlib, Samuel, and Boyle, 1:672
Hartman, David, on Maimonides, 5:654
Hartman, Geoffrey, 2:661
Hartman, Heidi, as a socialist feminist, 3:601
Hartmann, Eduard von, **4:236–238**
- and Kozlov, 5:146
- on life, meaning and value of, 5:356
- Nietzsche and, 6:610
- panpsychism and, 7:83
- Paulsen and, 7:149
- on pessimism, 7:245, 7:250–251
- on phenomenology, 7:278
- on philosophical method, 7:86
- and Solov'ëv, 9:123
- on unconscious, 9:571

Hartmann, Heinz, 8:106
Hartmann, Klaus, on Hegel, 4:280
Hartmann, Nicolai, **4:239–245**
- being, 1:530
- ethics, 3:422
- and Gadamer, 4:1
- German reaction to, 3:422
- Geyser and, 4:83
- Ingarden and, 4:682
- Latin American philosophy and, 5:209
- Scheler and, 8:616
- on value, 9:638

Hartshorne, Charles, 9:752
- on determinism, 3:7, 3:9
- ontological argument and, 3:321, 7:18
- panpsychism and, 7:83, 7:85
- process philosophy of, 7:478

Hartsock, Nancy
- grounds for the feminist standpoint, 3:575
- influence of, 3:592
- Marx's theory of the standpoint, 3:563–564

Hartsoeker, Niklaas, 3:73
Harvard University, James at, 4:775
Harvey, William, **4:245–246**, 4:610
"Has Austin Refuted the Sense Datum Theory" (Ayer), 1:154
Hasard, 4:306
Hasidism, mysticism of, 6:447
Haskalah. See Enlightenment, Jewish
Hasker, William, 3:116, 3:117, 3:119–120, 4:618
Haslanger, Sally
- materialist approach to gender essentialism, 3:587
- on persistence, 7:206

unmasking of natural categories or properties as social, 3:586
Hatano Seiichi, **4:247**
Hate, Empedocles on, 6:8
Hatred, Buddhism on, 1:724
Hatzfeldt, Countess von, Lassalle and, 5:203
Haugeland, John
on intentionality, 4:710
on symbolic artificial intelligence, 1:346
Hauriou, Maurice, 4:35
Hausdorff, Felix, 8:837
Hausdorff's Paradox, 8:837
Haven, Joseph, Nishi translates, 6:623
Haverfield, F. J., and Collingwood, 2:324
Having, in inherence, 9:583
Hawking, Stephen
on black hole thermodynamics, 9:269
kalām argument on God's existence and, 2:555
Hawthorne, John, on skepticism, 3:275
Hawthorne, Nathaniel, 6:572–573
Hayashi Razan, **4:247–248**
enemy of Kumazawa, 5:161
Yamaga Sokō and, 9:859
Haydn, Joseph, classical conventions and, 3:82
Hayek, Frederich A. von
on equality, 5:336
on libertarianism, 5:336
on liberty, 5:334, 9:72
on limit to state action, 9:209
moral obligations in business, 1:779
Hayes, Patrick J.
conception advanced by, 3:709
objections about inferences supported by conditions, 3:711
situational calculus as a solution for the frame problem, 3:708
on Turing test, 5:635
Haykuichi shinron (A new theory on many doctrines) (Nishi), 6:623
Hays, Mary, 9:839
Ḥayy ibn Yaqẓān (Ibn Ṭufayl), 4:550, 4:551
Hazard, Paul, on Enlightenment, 3:243–244
Hazlitt, William, **4:248–249,** 5:676
H-D pseudo-confirmation, spurious causal inferences, 3:741
He Lin, in Contemporary New Confucianism research program, 2:182
Heal, Jane, 4:600
psychological capacities mediated, 3:680
on simulation theory, 9:37
Healey, Richard, 6:278–279
Healing (Avicenna), 4:581
Health, 7:333
genetics and, 7:466
in philsoophy of medicine, 7:465–466
Health care
allocation of, 6:96
effects on women's, 3:594
Health studies, religion and, 8:381–382
Heaper argument, 6:110–111, 9:623–624
Heard, Gerald, 7:155
Hearing
perception and, 7:180–182
sense of, 5:117
Hearsay, 7:452
Heart
desire and predisposition in self-cultivation, 2:177
heart/mind in Confucianism, 2:172–173
in religious consciousness, 1:506
Heart disease, in women, 3:594
Heat
Bacon's (Francis) analysis of, 1:447–448
death, 9:469
definition of, 6:87
Hegel on, 4:266–267
natural, heart as source of, in Galen, 4:5
in Telesio, 9:390
Heaven
in Buddhism, 6:257
in Christianity, 2:249
in Confucianism, 2:176, 2:220, 5:139
as cosmos, 2:571
doctrine of. *See* Heaven and hell, doctrines of
as life-giving force, 2:176
Luther's doctrine of two realms, 5:613, 5:614, 5:615
Mozi on, 6:417
as Supreme Reality in Confucianism, 2:151
Wang Chong on, 9:723
Heaven *(Tian),* Dong Zhongshu on, 3:98
Heaven and hell, doctrines of, **4:249–253**
contemporary accounts of, 4:250–251
contemporary challenges to, 4:251–252
in Gnosticism, 4:101–102
historical development of, 4:250
Heavenly City of the 18th Century Philosophers, The (Becker), 3:243
Heaviside, Oliver, electromagnetic field theory, 3:235
Hebart, Johann Friedrich, activities of mind in Beneke, 1:544
Hebbel, Christian Friedrich, **4:253–254**
Hebrew
dictionary of, 8:585
Gersonides' reliance on, 4:69
Jewish philosophy written in, 4:819–820
Simon on, 9:33
Spinoza's compendium of, 9:183, 9:184
Hedenius, Ingmar, emotive theory and, 3:425
Hedge, Frederic Henry, 6:572
Hedged performatives, 7:200
Hedgehog and the Fox, The (Berlin), 9:512
Hedonic calculus
Bentham on, 3:413
of Maupertuis, 6:67
Hedonic treadmill, 9:642
Hedonism, **4:254–258,** 7:245
art as, 1:338–339
in Barthes, 1:481
as consequentialism, 2:460
criticism of, 4:257–258
of Cyrenaics, 2:619
Epicurus on, 3:267
in Greek Academy, 4:172
on intrinsic goodness, 4:719
Marulić on, 5:729
Moleschott on, 6:320–321
of moral sense theories, Green on, 4:180
pleasure in, 7:617
preference, 8:721
property and, 8:70
the prudentially good and, 4:151–152
psychological, 4:256–257, 8:132
of Mill (James), 6:219
Sidgwick on, 3:417
Sidgwick on, 3:417
as theory of well-being, 8:720–721
utilitarianistic, 9:382
in *Utopia,* 6:399
See also Ethical hedonism
Hedonist paradox, Epicurus and, 3:268
Hedonistic act utilitarianism, 9:607

Hedonistic ethics, in Epicureanism, 4:300
Hedonistic school, 4:300
Hedonistic utilitarianism, 4:254–255, 9:604
of Mill (John Stuart), 6:233
Hedonistic value theory, 9:639
Heelan, Patrick, on phenomenology, 7:300
Heereboord, Adriaan, 2:753
Hegel, Georg Wilhelm Friedrich, **4:258–283,** 5:59
on Absolute, 1:10–11, 1:120–121, 1:530, 4:108, 4:111, 4:264, 4:557–558, 4:669, 5:62, 6:193, 7:98, 9:289
on aesthetics, 1:54, 4:274–276, 8:629–630
on alienation, 1:120–122
anthropology and, 7:316
on apprehension of God, 4:111
on art, 1:28, 1:303, 1:341
Bachofen and, 1:442
Bakunin and, 1:471
and Bataille and post-historical negativity, 1:488–489
on beauty, 1:54, 4:275–276
being-as-being as emptiness, 1:530
and Belinskii, 1:538
Beneke opposition to, 1:543–544
on Berkeley's immaterialism, 4:557–558
in Bradley's ethics, 1:676
Caird and, 2:4
Chicherin and, 2:147
on Christ, 3:97
on Christianity, 4:260–264, 4:276–277
on civil society, 9:96, 9:206
cognitivism of, 1:341
Cohen (Hermann) and, 2:303
coherence theory of truth and, 9:536
communism and, 2:367
and critical theory, 2:598
Croce and, 2:602
Danto on, 2:627
on definition of tragedy, 4:177
Deleuze and, 2:694–695
Dewey and, 3:43, 8:623
dialectic and, 2:80–81, 3:54–55, 4:260, 8:138
dialetheism of, 7:106
Dilthey and, 3:79, 3:84
Driesch on, 3:112
early writings of, 4:261–262
on emanation, 4:108
Emerson and, 3:196
Engels and, 3:57–63, 3:238
Enlightenment and, 3:243, 7:390
epistemology and, 3:309–310, 5:91
Erigena and, 3:342
on essence and existence, 3:350
and ethics, 3:414–415
and existentialism, development of, 3:508
Ferrier and, 3:608
Feuerbach and, 3:609
Fischer and, 3:660
Frank (S.) and, 3:716
on freedom, 4:272–274, 7:390
Fries and, 3:751
Gadamer and, 4:2
on *geist,* 4:37
on general will, 4:38
on God, 2:641, 4:110, 4:668–669, 7:17
Green on, 4:179
Hirsch (Samuel) and, 4:827
on historical development, 2:410–411
and history, 1:442, 3:36, 4:260, 4:268–269, 4:273–274, 7:386–390, 9:166
Ibn Khaldūn and, 4:549
on idea, 3:67–68
Il'in on, 4:577
on infinity, 1:12, 4:668–669
on Judaism, 3:249
Kant and, 2:71, 6:539
in Kaufmann's volumes, 5:46
Kierkegaard and, 3:504, 5:62
Kireevskii and, 5:74
Kleist and, 5:78–79
Labriola and, 5:165–:5:166
Lacan and, 5:168
Lange on, 5:187
Lassalle and, 5:203
Lavrov and, 5:218
on law, 7:425–426
Lenin and, 3:65, 5:280
Lessing and, 3:246
Liebmann on, 5:344
life of, 4:258–259
on logic, 4:265–266
Losev and, 5:573
Lotman and, 5:579
Maimonides and, 5:653
Marx and, 3:57, 3:67–69, 3:348, 5:603, 5:731, 5:740, 7:390, 8:70
on master and slave, 4:262–263
McTaggart on, 6:77
and metaphysics, 6:193
on mind, 4:259–260, 4:267–269, 4:280
monism of, 6:326
on morality, 4:261–263, 4:267–268
on motion, 6:408
on myth, 9:262
Natorp and, 6:543
on nature, 4:266–267, 6:520
in neo-Kantianism, 6:541
on Newton, 3:57–58
Pannenberg and, 7:81–82
pantheism of, 7:97, 7:98
Pantheismusstreit and, 7:101–102
Paulsen and, 7:148
on personalism, 7:234
on phenomena, 8:138
on phenomenology, 7:278
phenomenology of mind, 4:262–264
philosophical system of, 5:62
philosophy of sex and, 7:522
political philosophy of, 7:668
in postmodernism, 7:730
Pringle-Pattison and, 8:12
on Proclean triad, 7:616
progress in, 8:46–47
on property, 8:70
Proudhon and, 8:94–95
on providence, 3:35, 7:389
on psychology, 8:138
on punishment, 8:161
rationalism of, 5:74, 8:138
Rawls and, 3:470
on reason, 4:263, 5:232
rehabilitation of, 5:45–46
on religion, 4:264, 4:276–277
Renan and, 8:428–429
Rosenkranz and, 8:496–497
Rosenzweig and, 8:498
Santayana and, 8:599
Schelling and, 1:12, 8:617–619
Schiller (Ferdinand) and, 8:623, 8:629
Schopenhauer and, 3:311
on self-alienation, 1:123, 5:67
Shestov on, 9:11
on skepticism, 9:58
on social development, 3:57
Socrates and, 9:113
and Solov'ëv, 9:123
Spaventa and, 9:160
Spinoza and, 9:194
spirit in, 7:389–390
on state, 3:415, 7:153, 9:143
Stirner and, 9:250
Taine and, 9:365
on thought, laws of, 5:232–233
on thought and language, 7:534–535
on totalitarianism, 9:96
on tragedy, 9:523–524

on unconscious, 9:262, 9:571
on unhappy consciousness, 4:263
on war and peace, 7:153
on will, 4:272
on women, 3:570
See also Hegelian idealism
Hegel: A Reinterpretation (Kaufmann), 5:46
Hegel und der Staat (Rosenzweig), 8:498
Hegelian idealism, 4:280, 4:286, 6:193, 7:390
Gentile and, 4:49–53
McTaggart and, 6:77
Schelling and, 8:618
and socialism, Gramsci on, 4:169
sovereignty and, 9:143
Spaventa and, 9:160
Strauss and, 9:262
Hegelianism, 4:264–269, **4:283–288**
Bakhtin Circle and, 1:469–470
Beneke and, 1:543
contradictions in, 3:609
Dewey and, 3:43–44, 3:45
Die Freien and, 9:250
as esoteric psychology, 3:610
Feuerbach and, 3:609–612, 4:284, 9:263
on the Good, 4:153
Khomiakov and, 5:59
Kierkegaard and, 3:501, 5:64–67, 9:57
left *vs.* right, 4:285
Left-wing, Bauer on, 1:492
logical monism in, 6:184
of McGilvary, 6:75
metaphysics of, 6:203
on moral and religious development, 5:62
and ontological argument for the existence of God, 7:17
on organic nature of state, 9:205
Pastore and, 7:135
in philosophy of law, 7:425–426
property in, 8:70
and rationalism, 3:610
on revelation, 4:112
revolutionary views and, 1:471
Rickert on, 8:459
Rosenkranz and, 8:496–497
Russell and, 8:536
Schopenhauer and, 8:648
on social facts, 9:95
See also Neo-Hegelianism
Hegelianism and Personality (Pringle-Pattison), 4:558
Hegel's Dialectic (Gadamer), 4:2
Hegel's Political Philosophy (Kaufmann), 5:46
Hegesias, Cyrenaic teaching of, 2:619
Heiberg, Johan Ludvig, as a secondary source for Kierkegaard, 5:67
Heidegger, Martin, **4:288–296**
Abbagnano and, 1:1
application by Binswanger, 1:597–598
Arendt and, 1:252–253
on art, 1:70–71
on being, 3:502, 3:508, 3:512
being and nothing, 1:530–531
and *Being and Nothingness,* 8:606
Binswanger and, 3:510
and Bonhoeffer, 1:656–657
Bultmann use of, 1:762–763
compared to S. Frank, 3:717
on consciousness, 3:507
on death, 2:651, 2:653, 3:503, 9:490
and Derrida, 2:716, 2:661, 9:275
Dilthey and, 1:70, 3:79, 3:84
discussions with Fink, 3:639
Dōgen and, 3:95
on dread, 3:503
early thought, 4:289–290
ethics, 3:422
existential psychiatry and, 3:507
existential psychoanalysis and, 3:510
existential temporality, 4:2
existentialism and, 6:195
Fink and, 3:637
Frank on, 3:715
and Gadamer, 4:1
Gehlen and, 4:35
on history, 7:397–398
in history of ontology, 7:28
on human beings, nature of, 3:512
on Husserl, 9:490
influences on, 3:504, 4:288, 9:488
on intentionality, 3:512
Japanese philosophy and, 4:797
in Kaufmann's volumes, 5:46
Kierkegaard and, 3:502
Klages work similar to, 5:77
Lacan and, 5:167
Levinas and, 5:303–304
on measurement of time, 9:490
on metaphor as structure, 2:222
on modern society, 3:506
Natorp and, 6:491
Nazism of, 1:253
on negativity, 8:606
in neo-Kantianism, 6:542
Nietzsche and, 6:607, 6:613–614
on nothing, 6:658
ontology of, 3:502–503
on optimism/pessimism, 7:253
phenomenological approach of, 3:563
phenomenology and, 6:195, 7:297–300, 7:397–398
on philosophy, 7:399
in philosophy of language in, 7:410–411
on philosophy of technology, 7:544
on Platonic Forms, 7:616
Platonism in, 7:616
politics of, 3:506
and postmodernism, 9:59
and poststructuralism, 9:275
on present, 9:490
on pre-Socratic philosophy, 1:530–531
Sartre and, 3:504, 8:603, 8:606
Scheler and, 8:616
and School of Qom, 8:647
on science, 1:252–253
silence in, 7:411
on something rather than nothing, 9:754
on speech, 7:411
on superultimate "why," 9:759, 9:760
on technology, 7:547
themes in, 3:504
on understanding, 4:2
on why not "nothing," 8:622
and Zubiri (Xavier), 9:888
Heidelberg Institute of Social Sciences, Weber (Alfred) at, 9:732
Heidelberg neo-Kantianism, 6:544–545. *See also* Neo-Kantianism
Heidelberg School. *See* Neo-Kantianism
Heidenhain, Rudolf, 7:149
Heilige, Das (The idea of the Holy) (Otto), 3:753, 4:107, 6:544
Heilsgeschichtlich conception of revelation, 8:452
Heim, Irene
on dynamic semantics, 8:808
File Change Semantics (FCS) of, 8:748
on presupposition, 7:771
Heim, Karl, **4:296–297**
Heimsoeth, Heinz, in neo-Kantianism, 6:542
Heineg, approach to truth of, 2:166
Heinrich von Ofterdingen (Novalis), 6:667

Heisenberg, Werner, **4:297–299**
atomism and, 1:388
chance and determinism in quantum theory, 2:126
complementarity of quantum theory and empirical phenomena, 1:638
on Copenhagen interpretation, 2:530
Mach and, 5:624
Plato and, 7:602
on reality of particles, 8:641
uncertainty relations, 8:658
Heisenberg's uncertainty principle
as absolute in quantum theory, 1:634
in Copenhagen interpretation, 2:530
correspondence of theory and data, 1:638
and Lorenz invariance, 1:539
matter in, 6:63
in quantum mechanics, 2:531
wave function and, 7:477
Heitler, Walter, 7:146
Held, David, on political cosmopolitanism, 2:569
Held, Klaus, Landgrebe and, 5:183
Held, Virginia, 3:580, **4:299–300**
Heldke, Lisa, corresponsible model of objectivity, 3:568
Heliocentric astronomy
concept of, 5:52
in late medieval period, 2:533
Ptolemaic astronomy reform using, 2:534
Pythagorean idea of, 5:50
Heliopolis (Jünger), 4:860
Hell
Adams on, 3:477–478
in Christianity, 2:249
doctrine of, 4:250–251
Hellenism, ecclesianised, 3:673
Hellenistic Judaism, patristic philosophy and, 7:141, 7:142
Hellenistic philosophy, phantasia in, 7:270–271
Hellenistic thought, **4:300–303**
anger-management in, 8:812
didactic poetry in, 5:598
epistemology and, 3:287–289
ethics in, 3:399–400
Galen and, 4:7
and Gregory of Nyssa, 4:182
Iamblichus in, 4:539
Jewish philosophy in, 4:810–811
logos in, 5:569
on mimesis, 6:252
optimism/pessimism in, 7:246–247
Peripatetics and, 7:202
Roman references to, 7:264
theory of illumination in, 4:580
Helling v. Carey, 6:95
Hellman, Geoffrey
on hermeneutic nominalism, 6:630
modal structuralism, 3:627
on modal structuralism, 9:271
Helm, George
on energy, 3:233
Planck and, 7:577
Helm, Karl, on existentialism, 3:505
Helm, Paul, faith involving trust, 3:535
Helmholtz, Hermann Ludwig von, **4:303–305**
conservation of energy, 3:551
on energy conservation, 3:231
in neo-Kantianism, 6:540
Planck and, 7:577
Plekhanov and, 3:64
in psychology, 8:140
and Schlick, 8:638–639
on scientific method, 3:230–231
on senses, 6:540
Helmont, J. B. van, occultist biology of, 9:202
Helvétius, Claude-Adrien, **4:305–307**
atheism and, 2:688
Diderot and, 3:74
empiricism of, 8:137–138
Enlightenment and, 3:244
on equality, 3:330
ethics, 3:410
in evolutionary psychology, 8:37–38
and Garve, 4:24
and Godwin, 4:135
on human nature, 3:330
Laas on, 5:164
Tetens and, 9:403
utilitarianism and, 9:605
Helvétius, Madame, Destutt de Tracy and, 2:760
Hemineglect, 6:566
Hemmings, Sally, 4:806
Hemodynamic response, 6:564
Hemoglobin, in MRI, 6:564–565
Hempel, Carl Gustav, **4:308–311**
Basic statements, 1:485
causality definition, 2:103
covering law model of, Salmon's alternative to, 8:593
deductive-nomological model of, 8:694
on definition, 2:665, 2:670–672
Earman and, 3:159
on explanation, 3:518–520, 3:523–524
failure of verifiability principle and, 9:669
on history, 7:393
on incremental and absolute confirmation, 2:433–434
logical empiricism and, 5:82
on meaning, 1:149
on Nicod's condition and background evidence, 2:440
on physical domain causal closure and current science, 2:91
on scientific law, 7:519
on scientific terminology, 7:517
on scientific theory, 7:520
on sentence meaning, translatable, 9:662–663
on syntactic view of theories, 9:415
theoretician's dilemma in semantics, 8:690
Hempel's dilemma, 6:139
Hemsterhuis, Frans, **4:311–312,** 7:100
Henderson, David, on subject contextual cognitive competence, 2:483
Henkin, Leon, 8:197
Henkin quantifiers, 8:197–198
Henkin semantic consequence, 8:707
Henkin's completeness theorem, 5:544, 8:707
Henological Argument, 2:677–680
Hen/Polla, **4:312**
Henri Bergson (Jankélévitch), 4:787
Henriade (Voltaire), 9:708
Henry, Frederick, Arminianism and, 1:286
Henry IV (king of France)
education and, 2:720
on European unity, 7:154–155
Henry VII of Luxembourg, 2:625, 2:626
Henry of Ghent, **4:312–315**
on certitude, 3:140
Duns Scotus and, 3:135–136, 3:137–138, 3:140
on God, 3:135–136
in Godfrey of Fontaine, 4:131
on properties, 3:138
on transcendentals, 3:137–138
Henry of Harclay, **4:315–316**
Henslow, J. T., 2:628
Hepatitis, Willowbrook experiment on, 6:97
Hepburn, Ronald, on environmental aesthetics, 3:255, 3:256

Heptaplomeres Sive Colloquium de Abditu Rerum Subliminum Arcanus (Bodin), 1:622
Heptaplus (Pico della Mirandola), 2:322, 7:570, 7:571, 7:573
Heptateuch (Theodoric of Chartres), 2:136, 9:410
Heraclides of Pontus, in Greek Academy, 4:173
Heraclitus of Ephesus, **4:316–321**
Bernhardi and, 7:154
on cosmos, 2:571
and Cratylus, 2:584
dialectic and, 3:55
Diderot and, 3:73
Dikē in, 3:79
Dilthey on, 3:84
Diogenes Laertius on, 3:88
Diogenes of Apollonia and, 3:89
doctrine of opposing tensions, 3:686
epistemology and, 3:281
on eternal return doctrine, 3:353
on Homer, 1:41
on identity, 5:232
influence of, 4:320
Justin Martyr on, 5:569, 7:142
on language, 8:751
Lassalle and, 5:203
Lucretius and, 5:599
monism of, 1:249
Parmenides of Elea on, 7:124
on persistence, 7:207
Plato and, 3:283, 3:284–285, 7:606
in pre-Socratic philosophy, 7:761
on Pythagoras, 8:185
in religious philosophy, 7:487–488
and Stoicism, 9:253
on temporary identity, 4:570
universal flux doctrine, 3:357
on war, 7:152
writing style of, 4:176
and Zeno of Citium, 9:870–871
Herbart, Johann Friedrich, **4:321–325**
on apperception, 1:234
in associationism, 8:138
on consciousness, 8:139, 8:145
on education, 7:374–375, 7:374–377
ethics of, 7:376–377
Freud and, 8:145
on ideas, 7:375–376, 8:139
Labriola and, 5:165
Lange and, 5:186
Liebmann on, 5:344
Lotze and, 5:580
metaphysics of, 7:376
in neo-Kantianism, 6:541
in psychology, 8:138–139
psychology of, 7:376
on soul, 1:234
soul in, 7:376
Herbert, George
Filmer an associate of, 3:636
influence of, 2:683
Herbert of Cherbury, **4:325–329**
on crisis of skepticism, 9:53
deism and, 2:682, 2:684
Ficino a forerunner of, 3:623
Gassendi's objections on, 4:26
on innate ideas, 4:688
Kortholt on, 7:99
on optimism/pessimism, 7:249
and unbelief in God's existence, 2:350
Herbrand, Jacques
finitary method and, 5:543, 8:55
on finite calculability, 2:401
logic of, 5:472
Herbrand's theorem, on quantification theory, 5:473
Herculean jurisprudence, 7:458–459
Herder, Johann Gottfried, **4:329–334**
anthropology and, 7:316
on art and nature, 1:55
Atheismusstreit and, 1:377
on biblical account of creation, 9:101
and Buckle, 1:718
Carlyle use of, 2:33
Emerson and, 3:195
geist as term in, 4:37
on history, 7:389
on language, 8:785, 8:787
Lavater and, 5:213
on Mendelssohn, 7:99
in pantheism dispute, 9:194
Pantheismusstreit and, 7:99, 7:101
romanticism, 1:442
and Schelling's pantheism, 8:621
Spinoza and, 9:194
on thought and language, 7:534–535
in transcendentalist departure from Unitarianism, 6:574
on unconscious, 9:571
Heredity
Diderot on, 3:74–75
Hélvetius on, 4:306
Maupertuis's study of, 6:66–67
McDougall on, 6:72
Heredity and the Aetiology of the Neuroses (Freud), 3:737
Herepath, W., on physics of gases, 7:537
Heresy
charges of, against Montaigne, 4:166
Christian view of, 9:508
in Islamic mysticism, 6:451–452
of Jansenism, 4:789
rational speculation as path to, 8:586
of Servetus, 8:831
of Siger of Brabant, 9:27, 9:28
Hérigone, Pierre, 5:440
Hering, Jean, 4:682
Heritage, as definition of national identity, 6:482
Herman, Barbara, 2:71, 2:715, 3:570, 5:36
Hermarchus of Mytilene, Epicurean School and, 3:263
Hermeneutic circle, 1:311
Hermeneutic methods
Dge-lugs doctrinal categorization, 1:733
in Huayan Buddhism, 1:736
Hermeneutic reconstruction, of psychoanalysis, 3:744–745
Hermeneutics, **4:334–336**
Apel on, 1:226
of cooperation, pragmatic, 3:567
of Dai Zhen, 2:621–622
in development of pluralism, 7:642
Dilthey on, 3:81–82, 3:84
in *Faygyan*, 9:861
feminism and, 3:565
Gadamer on, 4:1–2
interpretation and, 1:311
of Ivanov, 4:768
on methodology for science, 9:36–37
naturalism on, 6:493
of Philo, 4:810
of Ricoeur, 8:462–463
in Schleiermacher, 8:636–637
in Shpet's phenomenology, 9:17
on social sciences metaideology, 7:533–534
spiritual, in Corbin, 2:537
tension between phenomenology and, 7:299–300
Vedic, universals in, 9:581
Wang Bi on, 9:722
Hermeneutics and Criticism (Schleiermacher), 8:637
Hermeneutics of facticity, 4:289–290
Hermes, or a Philosophical Inquiry concerning Language and Universal Grammar (Harris), 8:790

Hermes Trismegistus
- heliocentrism in hermetic philosophy, 1:711
- Patrizi and, 7:144
- Pico della Mirandola and, 7:570, 7:571
- in Renaissance, 1:710

Hermetic philosophy
- art of memory in, 1:712
- in Bernard of Tours, 1:592
- Bruno and, 1:708–712
- mathesis works by Bruno, 1:709
- in Renaissance, 1:710

Hermetica, on love of God, 5:585

Hermeticism, **4:337–339**
- history of, 4:337
- in Pletho, 9:314

Hermias, 6:552

Hermitian operator, 8:206–207

Hermogenes, Tertullian on, 9:399–400

Hermotimus (Lucian of Samosata), 5:597

Hero of Alexandria, on energy and work, 3:227

Herodotus
- on land surveying, 4:54
- on Thales of Miletus, 9:405

Héroe, El (Gracián), 4:168

Heroes, 2:33–34, 9:675

Heroism, in Milton's poetry, 6:251

Herophilus, 3:87, 4:302

Herr Bastiat-Schulze von Delitzsch, der ökonomische Julian, oder Kapital und Arbeit (Lassalle), 5:203

Herr Eugen Dühring's Revolution in Science (Engels), 3:57–58, 3:60–61, 3:62, 3:65, 3:238

Herring, Ewald, 6:133, 6:260

Herschel, John, **4:339–340**
- and Darwin, 2:628
- on energy, 3:231–232
- friends and colleagues of, 2:709
- physicotheology and, 7:562

Hertz, Heinrich Rudolf, **4:340–343**
- contribution to classical mechanics, 2:280
- electromagnetic field theory, 3:235
- on Maxwell's theory, 9:578

Hervaeus Natalis, **4:343–344**

Hervetius, Gentian
- Pico della Mirandola (Gianfrancesco) and, 7:575
- skepticism of, 9:51
- translations of Sextus Empiricus, 9:50

Herz, Marcus
- Jewish Enlightenment and, 3:249
- Kant's letter to, 5:15

Herzberger, Hans, on semantic paradoxes, 5:521

Herzen, Aleksandr Ivanovich, **4:344–345**
- ideas restated by Kavelin, 5:48
- and Kareev, 5:40
- Lavrov and, 5:218
- Russian Populism and, 5:219
- studied by Florovskii, 3:672
- writings of, 5:153

Heschel, Abraham Joshua, kinship with Hasidic social ethics, 5:3

Hesiod
- Dikē in, 3:79
- on love, 5:583
- Parmenides of Elea and, 7:128
- truth in poetry and, 1:41
- Xenophanes on, 7:94

Hess, Moses, **4:345–346**

Hesse, Mary
- on metaphor in science, 6:167
- in post-positivist debate, 8:694
- on property logical independence, 2:439
- rejecting Jammer's instrumentalism, 3:690
- on semantic view of theories, 9:416

Hessen-Rheinfels, Ernst von, 5:252

Hesychasm
- controversy over, 1:789
- mysticism of, 6:448

Heterodoxy, suppression of, in England, 2:682–683, 2:684, 2:685, 2:690

Heteropathic laws, Mill (John Stuart) on, 3:191

Heterosexism, 3:756, **4:346–350**

Heterosexual sex, dangers and coercion of, 3:601

Heterosexuality
- as not threatened by homosexuality, 3:602
- taken to be normative, 3:756

Hetubindu, 6:533

Hetu-cakra (wheel of reasons), 5:413

Heuristics, *vs.* adaptation, 8:154–155

Hexaëmeron (Basil the Great), 4:577

Hexameron (Grosseteste), 4:186

Hexaméron rustique (La Mothe Le Vayer), 5:182

Heyd, Thomas, on environmental aesthetics, 3:256

Heytesbury, William, 1:101, **4:350–351**

Heyting, Arend
- Heyting algebras, 4:740
- on intuition of propositional calculus, 5:473
- intuitionist logic and, 4:738, 5:491
- intuitionistic account of mathematics and, 6:676
- logic of, 6:527
- on proof interpretation of truth, 4:738

Hibben, John Grier, on Enlightenment, 3:243

Hibbert Lectures, 4:775, 9:364

Hicesias, 3:90

Hick, John, 4:617
- on evil, 3:477, 7:481
- faith and, 3:535
- on religion, 7:478, 7:482

Hickok, Laurens Perseus, **4:351–352**

Hicks, R. D., 4:608

Hidden variable theories of wave functions, 8:209–214

Hiddenness of God, **4:352–357**, 7:483–484

Hiding from Humanity (Nussbaum), 6:680

Hierarchical structure, doctrine of, 5:49

Hierarchies
- in arithmetic relations under computability theory, 2:386
- in Bonaventure, 1:652
- in Bradley, 1:678
- in computability theory, 2:389–390
- Descartes and, 2:364–365
- of entities, Frege on, 9:555
- Ibn Sīnā's causal hierarchy, 2:114
- Kant's kingdom of ends and, 2:366–367
- ordered field structure and simplicity, 2:509
- orders of infinite series and transfinite numbers, 2:27–28
- in Plato's communism, 2:364
- of propositions, in Russell, 5:519, 9:557
- in Pythagoreanism, 8:187
- Russell's theory of types, 2:76
- in set theory, 9:368
- in Spann's neoromantic universalism, 9:158

Hierarchy, Ficino's concept of a great, 3:621

Hierocles
- on beneficence, 7:79
- in Neoplatonism, 6:553

Hieroglyphic Key, A (Swedenborg), 9:337

Higginbotham, James, on referents, 8:89

Higher criticism
of Bible, 2:691
La Peyrère and, 5:196
Higher Learning in America, A Memorandum on the Conduct of Universities by Businessmen, The (Veblen), 9:655
Higher morality, 3:618
Higher order vagueness, 5:111
Higher power, in James's religious belief, 4:781
Higher Superstitions: The Academic Left and Its Quarrels with Science (Gross), 8:679
Higher understanding, Dilthey on, 3:83
Higher-level events, as causes, 6:134–135
Higher-order events, mental causation and, 6:135
Hilary of Poitiers, 1:47
Hilbert, David, 3:639, **4:357–368**
on axioms, 9:270–271
and Carnap, 2:42
computing machines and, 2:399
on continuum problem, 8:834
cosmology and actual infinity, 2:567
Dingler and, 3:85
on Euclidean geometry, 4:62
finitary method and, 5:543
on first-order logic, 8:840
formalism and, 5:54, 6:213
Gödel on, 4:117
in mathematics, 6:676
synthetic *a priori* propositions and, 8:639
on geometry, 4:358–362, 5:462
on ideal mathematics, 5:544
logic of, 5:469
Łukasiewicz on, 5:607
on metamathematical effectiveness of theories, 2:400
positive propositional calculus, 5:536
on proof interpretation, 4:738
proof theory and, 8:54–55
on real mathematics, 5:554
and Schlick, 8:640
set-theoretic paradoxes, 4:121
vs. Tarski, 9:366
Hilbert program, reverse mathematics and, 8:456
Hilbert school, computability theory origins in, 2:400
Hilbert space
subspaces of, propositions associated with, 8:205
mathematics, quantum mechanical, 6:277–278
Hilbert-style calculi, 3:657
Hildegard of Bingen, **4:368–370,** 5:641
Hill, T. P., on base invariance, 9:228
Hill, Thomas, interpreting the metaphysical elements of Kant's theory, 5:37
Hinayana Buddhism, 5:328
Hinchcliff, Mark, on time, 9:478
Hindemith, Paul, collaboration with Benn, 1:547
Hindu theology, causality in Vishnu's organization of society, 2:110
Hinduism
asceticism in, 7:486
dogma and, 3:97
on evil, problem of, 3:471
God, concept of, in schools of philosophy, 4:132–135
history of, 7:485–486
liberation in, 5:329–330
meditation in, 6:108
mysticism of, 6:444–445
pessimism in, 7:246
primary scriptures of, 5:116
reality in, 7:486
reincarnation in, 8:332
Santayana affinity for, 8:597
on suicide, 9:320
Tagore's concept of God in, 9:363–364
wisdom literature of, 9:793
Hintikka, Jaakko, **4:370–372**
on Carnap's construction, 4:642
game-theoretical semantics of, 8:808
on logical terms, 5:531
modal logic and, 5:491
nonbranching notation of, 8:197–198
on phenomenology, 7:299
on quantifiers, 5:492
suggestions of, 3:654
Hintikka set, 3:654–656
Hinton, C. Howard, syllogism diagram method of, 5:562
Hinton, Geoffrey, 4:591
Hipparchia of Crete, Cyrenaic teaching of, 2:620
Hipparchus, 4:301
Hippasus of Metapontum, 8:185
Hippias Major (attrib: Plato), 1:511
on definition, 9:110
on sophists, 9:130
unsuccessful attempt to define the *kalon,* 5:7
Hippias of Elis, **4:372–373**
Hippocrates and the Hippocratic Corpus, **4:373–376**
on curvilinear area, 2:493
Diogenes of Apollonia and, 3:89
and Galen, 4:6
Leibniz and, 5:257
Hippocratic oath, 6:92
Hippolyte, Jean
on Marx, 3:57
students of, 2:693
Hippolytus
on Marcion, 5:703
on Simon Magnus, 9:33
traditional theology and, 7:142–143
Hippolytus (Euripides), 4:177, 5:583–584
Hiroshima, bombing of, 4:871–872, 9:396
Hirsch, Samuel, in modern Jewish philosophy, 4:827–828
Hirst, Paul, in education, philosophy of, 7:355
His, W., Driesch and, 3:110
Hispanidad (Hispanicity)
transterrados and, 5:209
Unamuno on, 5:208
Hispanization of Europe, Unamuno on, 5:208
Histoire de Charles XII (Voltaire), 9:713
Histoire de la langue universelle (Lé and Couturat), 2:582
Histoire de la littérature anglaise (Taine), 9:364–365
Histoire de la sexualite (History of sexuality) (Foucault), 3:701, 7:523
Histoire de l'Academie royale des sciences (Fontenelle), 3:683
Histoire des Oracles (Fontenelle), 3:682
Histoire du prince Titi (Saint-Hyacinthe), 8:589
Histoire naturelle de l'âme (La Mettrie), 5:178–179
Histoire naturelle des animaux sans vertèbres (Lamarck), 5:173, 5:174
Historia Animalium (Aristotle), 8:703
Historia Critica Philosophiae (Brucker), 3:223
Historia de la filosofía (Marías), 5:711
Historia Ecclesiastica (Eusebius), 3:455
Historia Inquisitionis (Limborch), 7:41
Historia Pontificalis (John of Salisbury), 4:844
Historia Reformationis Polonicae (Lubieniecki), 9:100
Historia Theologiae Dogmaticae et Moralis (Budde), 1:721
Historiae (Agathias), 9:35

Historiae de Rebus Hispaniae (Mariana), 5:710
Historian, Franck as a, 3:713
Historic Doubts Relative to Napoleon Bonaparte (Whately), 9:743
Historic force, externalizing the spiritual, 3:713
Historical and Critical Dictionary (Bayle), 3:244
Historical and Moral View of the Origin and Progress of the French Revolution (Wollstonecraft), 9:837
Historical conditions, for knowledge in the human sciences, 3:699
Historical development, social principles and, 6:581–582
Historical epochs, in historical materialism, 4:379–380
Historical evidence, 3:224, 6:270–273
Historical functionalism, 1:300–301
Historical inevitability, 3:35–38
Historical Inevitability (Berlin), 3:36, 3:40
Historical judgments, in Croce, 2:602
Historical knowledge, combining with philosophical thought, 3:715
Historical materialism, 3:56, **4:376–388,** 5:731–733, 5:738
  human nature in, 4:383–384
  in Marxism, 1:615–616, 9:92
  Miki and, 6:216
  origin of, 4:376–377
  Sartre and, 8:609
  validity of, 4:382–385
Historical meaning, in painting, 9:835
Historical method
  as Baconian in Collingwood, 2:327
  Pater on, 7:136–137
Historical narrative, art as, 1:301–302
Historical phenomenalist strand, of empiricist antecedents, 3:629
Historical philosophy, of Voltaire, 9:713
Historical process
  Saint-Simon on, 8:590
  Weber (Alfred) on, 9:732–733
Historical reason, Dilthey on, 3:79–80
Historical record, utopian works as, 9:620
Historical school of jurisprudence, **4:388–390,** 8:614–615
Historical school of law, 7:426
Historical sciences
  vs. natural sciences, Windelband on, 9:792
  representation of the past, 3:594
Historical skepticism, as a form of psychotherapy, 5:150
Historical stages, theory of, 3:605
Historical theory, in study of memory, 6:126–127
Historicism, **4:390–396**
  in Collingwood's metaphysics, 2:328
  critical ontogenological, 8:260
  cultural anthropology and, 7:321
  definition of, 4:392–393
  in Ibn Khaldūn, 4:548
  Lotman and, 5:578
  Meinecke and, 6:114
  nonidealistic views of Cattaneo, 2:83–84
  of Popper, 7:398
  Pufendorf and, 8:158–159
  Reale and, 8:260
  of Romangnosi, 8:484
  social development, 1:442
  Stefanini on, 9:237
  in Troeltsch, 9:527
Historicistic judgments, 7:244
Historicity
  existentialism and Christianity in Bultmann, 1:762–764
  Levi-Strauss on, 7:398
  in philosophy of history, 7:397–399
Historie critique du vieux testament (Simon), 9:33
Historie des variations des eglises rotestants (History of the variations of the Protestant churches) (anon.), 1:667
Historie naturelle (Natural history) (Buffon), 1:758
Histories (Polybius), 7:308
Histories (Thucydides), 4:563
Historiography
  of Bennett, 1:550
  Bible as, 1:716
  Buckle in, 1:720
  Burckhardt on, 1:765–766
  and Chan (Zen) Buddhism, 1:726
  Cousin on, 2:580, 6:572
  critical intellect *vs.* poetic imagination in Carnap, 2:40
  in demonstration of spiritual unification, 1:714
  in Dge-lugs philosophy, 1:731
  difficulty of Bruno's works, 1:710
  as empirical inductivist approach, 1:718
  geography in, 1:621–622
  Lovejoy on, 5:593
  in Marx, 1:720
  race in Chamberlain, 2:123
  sociological data use in Buckle, 1:718–719
  text interdependence in Buddhist development, 1:729
  Zhuangzi on Daoist development, 2:187
"Historiography of Ideas" (Lovejoy), 5:593
Historismus und seine Probleme, Der (Historicism and its problems) (Troeltsch), 9:528
Historismus und seine Überwindung, Der (Troeltsch), 9:528
History
  of aesthetics, **1:41–72,** 5:575
    sublimity in, 9:293–294
  of alienation, 1:120–121
  analysis of, 9:457
  of applied ethics, 1:236–237
  Arab, Laroui on, 5:202
  Arkoun on, 1:284
  of art, 9:325
    Blake on, 1:610
    style and beauty in, 1:513
    Winckelmann in, 9:790
  ascending order of, 5:148
  of asceticism, 1:351
  Augustine on, 3:348, 7:387–388
  Benjamin on, 1:545–546
  Berdyaev on, 1:560–561
  of bioethics, 1:599–600
  of biology, 7:337–338
  Bloch on, 1:615–616
  Bolingbroke on, 1:641
  Bonhoeffer on, 1:655
  Bossuet on, 7:388
  botanized view of, 3:672
  Braudel on, 7:392–393
  Buckle and, 1:718
  Burckhardt on, 1:766
  of capitalism, 4:385
  Carlyle on, 2:33–34
  causality in, 4:548, 9:512
  change in, 8:45–46
  Chateaubriand on, 2:138
  of Chinese philosophy
    Buddhism in, 2:153–155, 2:169–170
    and Chan (Zen) Buddhism, 2:166
    Cheng Hao in, 2:144–145
    Cheng Yi in, 2:145
    Confucianism in, 2:149–153, 2:170–171
    contemporary era of, 2:180–184
    Daoism in, 2:151–153, 2:184–191
    Huayan Buddhism in, 2:163
    Legalist school in, 2:152

logic, **5:414–417**
Logicians school in, 2:152
Maoism and, 2:180–181
Mohist school in, 2:151
neo-Daoism in, 2:152
overview of, 2:149
Pure Land Buddhism in, 2:168–169
Sanlun Buddhism in, 2:161
Tiantai Buddhism in, 2:163
Yin Yang school in, 2:152
Christianity and, 1:763, 2:245–247, 4:289, 8:635
Gibbon on, 4:84–86
Rosenzweig on, 4:829
as class struggle, 7:390
Coleridge on, 2:319
Collingwood on, 2:324–327, 2:325, 2:326, 6:270
Comenius on, 7:369
communism and, 2:361–362, 2:367
as comparative morphology, 9:165–167
Comte on, 2:409–411, 2:414
of Confucianism, 7:486
conservatism in, 2:465–466
continuity in, Vailati's work on, 9:630
critical periods of, 6:221
Croce on, 2:325, 2:600–604
and cultural types in I-other relationships, 1:465
culture in, 8:459
cyclical nature of, 7:387
of Cynics, 2:617
Danto on, 7:394
of Daoism, 2:187–188
in defining art, 1:300
descending order of, 5:148
determinism in, **3:35–41,** 6:473–474
development through criticism, 1:492–493
Dilthey on, 3:83–84, 7:397–398
direction of, 6:582
discussion of, *vs.* philosophy of, 7:398
divine will disclosed in, 2:9
of education. *See* Education, history of
Emerson on, 3:196
end of, Fukuyama on, 2:181, 7:391
of engineering, 3:239
environment and, 1:718–719
of environmental aesthetics, 3:254–255
of epistemology. *See* Epistemology, history of
of ethics. *See* Ethics, history of
existential possibility disclosed in, 1:763
experience and, 7:396–397
explanation in, 2:327, 7:393–394
Foucault on, 7:396
free will and, 3:40
freedom in, 4:273–274, 9:519
in French Enlightenment, 7:388
Fukuyama on, 2:181, 7:391
Gadamer on, 4:2
geography and, 1:621–622, 1:718
God in, 2:10, 3:713
Spinoza on, 4:108
Gödel on, 9:497
Gogarten on, 4:144
"great man" theories of, 3:37
Hegel on, 1:120–121, 1:442, 3:36, 4:260, 4:268–269, 4:273–274, 4:285, 5:62, 9:166
Heidegger on, 7:397–398
Hempel on, 7:393
Herder on, 4:332, 7:389
of hermeticism, 4:337
heroes in, Carlyle on, 2:33–34
hidden plan of nature in, 5:29
of Hinduism, 7:485–486
Hobbes in, 4:425
holism and individualism in, **4:442–450**
Huizinga on, 3:40, 7:395
human nature and, 7:398
humans as subject of, 1:766
Humboldt on, 4:485
Husserl on, 4:525–526, 7:397–398
of ideas
Bergson and, 1:571
Berlin and, 1:589
and bioethics, 1:599–600
Boethius and, 1:626
Boulainvilliers in, 1:669
Bruno and, 1:708–712
Buddhism in, 1:736–737
Buffon and, 1:758–759
Carlyle and, 2:33
chance in, 2:125–126
Channing and, 2:130–131
Chinese science and, 2:216–219
Chinese social and political thought and, 2:231–239
Copernicus and, 2:536
Cousin on, 2:580
Creighton on, 2:592
French clandestine literature and, 2:263–268
Ptolemy and, 2:536
individualizing thought in, 8:459
induction and, 9:744
intellectual, 7:334
intelligibility of, 9:518
interpretation of, 1:762, 9:456–457
irrationality in, 9:626
of Islamic philosophy, causality in, 2:113–115
Jewish
Cumberland on, 2:614
La Peyrère on, 5:196
and Judaism, 4:809–810, 4:829, 7:387
Kant on, 6:514, 7:374, 7:388–389
Karsavin on, 5:42
Landgrebe on, 5:185
Lavrov on, 5:218–219
and law, 8:620, 9:519
Leont'ev on, 5:283
Lessing on, 5:295
as literature, 7:394
of literature
Blake in, 1:610
Boileau on, 1:640
Ivanov on, 4:768
Loewith on, 7:391
of logic, 2:80–82
Boethius and, 1:625–626
Boole and, 1:658–660
category theory in, 2:72–83
Cleanthes and, 2:288
Euler in, 5:444
in Indian philosophy, 4:627, 4:631–632
in Jainism, 4:631–632
Lambert in, 5:444–445
Leibniz in, 5:444
Ploucquet in, 5:445
logic of, 1:492–493
Lukács on, 5:603–604, 7:391
Manheim on, 5:685–686
Marcuse on, 7:391
of marriage, 9:739
Marx on, 1:615–616, 3:415, 9:677
of materialism, 5:186, 6:7–8, 6:540, 7:148, 9:625–626
of mathematics
Boethius on, 1:625
Boole and, 1:658–660
Cantor and, 2:26–29
computing machines and, 2:399–400
infinity in, 2:26–29
meaning of
in Augustinianism, 1:404
Hoyle on, 5:351
of metaphysics. *See* Metaphysics, history of

History, ***continued***
metaphysics and, 1:713–714, 1:785, 6:205
methodology in, on miracles, 6:272–273
of militarism, 7:153–154
of modal logic, 6:291
moral decadence caused by freedom and individual liberty, 1:667
moral judgment in, 1:765–766
of mystical Messianism, 5:2
of mysticism, **6:441–453**
mythical language and, 1:762
myths and, 1:442
Nagel (Ernest) on, 6:473–474
and narrative, 7:394–398
natural. *See* Natural history
of natural theology, 7:494
nature and, 1:718, 2:410
nature of inquiry in, 7:398
in neo-Kantianism, 7:392
Nietzsche on, 6:610
of number, 6:670
Ogyū on, 7:10
of ontology, **7:27–29**
operationalism of, 4:2
of optimism, 7:246–253
order in, 9:518
organic periods of, 6:221
Pannenberg on, 7:81–82
of pantheism, 2:683
Pareto on, 7:119
patterns in, 9:518
perfection as aim of, 7:390
of Peripatetics, 3:399
of pessimism, 7:246–253
phases of, Hegel on, 5:62
phenomenology of, 7:301
philosophical
as alternative to everyday history, 5:29
Vico on, 9:672–674
of philosophy, **4:396–402**
Anscombe in, 1:212
approaches to, 4:401
Bacon (Francis) and, 1:443, 1:451
Bayle's *Dictionary* and, 1:503–504
Bennett and, 1:550
Bentham (Jeremy) and, 1:551
Berkeley and, 1:576–577, 1:583
and bioethics, 1:599–600
Black and, 1:606
Boethius and, 1:625–627
Boulainvilliers in, 1:670
Brentano and, 1:692
Bruno and, 1:708–712
Byzantine, 1:786–790
Capreolus on, 2:30–31
Carnap and, 2:38–41
Carneades and, 2:46–48
Carolingian renaissance and, 2:49–51
Cartesianism and, 2:53–61
categories in, 2:72–83
Cavendish in, 2:117–118
Chaadaev and, 2:120–122
Charron and, 2:135
Chartres school in, 2:136–137
chemistry and, 2:143–144
claims of, 4:397–398
Confucianism and, 2:170–180
Cousin on, 2:580, 6:572
Croce on, 2:602
Daoism and, 2:184–194
definition of, 7:326–327
Deussen on, 3:41
Encyclopédie and, 3:223
in England, 1:444
feminism and, 1:515, 3:569–571, 4:745–746
genres in, 4:401
Geyser on, 4:82
Gilson on, 4:92–93
gnostic sources and, 4:98
Hegel and, 4:287
in India, 2:109–113
Laas on, 5:163
of law, **7:418–430**
Levinas on, 5:304
logic and, 5:456–457
Marías in, 5:711
mediaeval, St. Bonaventure and, 1:649–650
of philosophy, 3:65, 3:243, 4:557
vs. philosophy, 4:398–399
of religion, **7:485–498**
in Renaissance, 1:710
as revealing activity of mind, 1:713
Romanticism in, 8:490
Spaventa and, 9:159–160
Stefanini's paradigmatism and, 9:237
texts of, 4:400–401
Theophrastus on, 9:413
value of, 4:399
Vienna Circle and, 2:38–41
women in, 9:837–839
philosophy and, 2:325–327, 9:676
philosophy of, **7:386–399**
Berdyaev on, 1:560–561
Bloch and, 1:615–616
Bosanquet on, 1:663
Buckle and, 1:720
Burckhardt on, 1:765–766
Carlyle on, 2:33–34
Carnap on, 2:44
Cattaneo on, 2:83
Chamberlain on, 2:123
Chicherin on, 2:147–148
Christian philosophy and, 7:387, 7:613–614
Collingwood and, 2:325–327
critical, 7:392–395
Croce on, 2:602
vs. discussion of history, 7:398
Dostoevsky on, 3:101
empirical inductivist approach to, 1:718
Encyclopédie on, 3:224
in Enlightenment, 7:389
Fichte and, 3:618
Geyser on, 4:82
Hegel and, 4:263, 4:268–269, 7:386–390
historians and, 7:396
historicity in, 7:397–399
Ibn Khaldūn on, 4:547
Joachim of Fiore and, 4:834
Kant and, 5:29, 7:388–389
Khomiakov and, 5:59
Krause and, 5:148
on language misuse, 1:545
Marx and, 1:615–616, 1:720, 7:390–391
Miki and, 6:216
moral certainty in, 9:249
Morgan (Lewis) and, 6:403–404
Mosca and, 6:406–407
neo-Confucianism and, 2:158
non-rational forces and, 1:441
pagan theology and, 7:613–614
Philo and, 7:308
Plekhanov on, 7:627
in postmodernism, 7:395–397
primitive communities and, 1:442
and progress, 1:718
rational and irrational elements in, 1:442
revelation and, 1:655–656, 7:613–614
Saint-Simonian–Comtian, Mill (John Stuart) and, 6:221
scope of, 7:386
as secular Messianic redemption, 1:545
secularization and, 1:656
Solov'ëv's world spirit in, 9:123

Spengler on, 9:165–167
substantive, 7:386–392
Turgot on, 9:512, 9:516–519, 9:526, 9:551
utopias of, 9:618
Voltaire in, 7:386–388
of Wang Fuzhi, 9:724–725
of philosophy of sex, 7:521–524
of political philosophy, **7:654–680**
in Greek Academy, 4:172
Popper on, 7:391, 7:691
in positivism, 7:392–393
of possibility, 7:719–723
post-historical negativity, 1:488–489
of presentism, 9:479
of probability theory, 7:537–538
and progress, 1:718, 7:388–389
purpose of, 3:347
as reality, 1:695, 7:396–397
of reason, critical theory and, 2:599
reason in, Voltaire on, 9:713
and reconciliation of non-rational forces, 1:441
reconstruction of, 2:327
of religion, 1:727–728, 2:247, 9:262
as revelation, Pannenberg on, 7:81–82
Ricoeur on, 7:395–396
Rilke on, 8:478
Ritschl on, 8:480–481
in Romanticism, 8:488
Rorty on, 7:399
Russian, Trubetskoi on, 9:531
of Russian philosophy
Chernyshevskii in, 2:146–147
Chicherin in, 2:147–149
Sartre on, 3:510
Schiller (Friedrich) on, 8:626
Schlegel on, 8:632
and science, 1:718–719, 7:393, 8:428–429
of science. *See* Science(s), history of
as science of values, 8:459
secularization and, 1:656
self-alienation and, 1:124–125
as self-annihilating, 1:611
of semantics, 1:455, **8:750–810**
of semiotics, 1:455
of sexuality, Foucault on, 3:701
Shpet on, 9:17
of skepticism, **9:47–61**
and social change, 9:656
socialism and, 1:561
of Stoicism, 3:400
in structuralism, 7:395
successful outcome of, 3:559
of technology, computing machine physical realization in, 2:404–408
of terrorism, 9:395
theological philosophies of, 3:35
theological stage of, Comte on, 2:410
three-stage pattern of, 5:148
Tolstoy on, 9:512
Toynbee on, 3:36, 7:391, 9:165, 9:517–519
Turgot on, 9:551
universal, 3:35, 5:59, 7:389, 8:459–460
Vaihinger on, 9:626
Vailati on, 9:630–631
value of, 6:610
Vico on, 2:431, 7:388
violence in, 9:677
Voltaire on, 9:713
White (H.) on, 7:395
White (M.) on, 7:393
Whitehead's education in, 9:746
Zoroastrian theory of, 9:887
"History" (Emerson), 6:574
History and Eschatology (Bultmann), 1:764
History and the Future of Theocracy, The (Solov'ëv), 9:122
History of Ancient and Modern Literature (Schlegel), 8:632
History of British India (Mill), 6:218
History of Civilization (Buckle), 1:718
History of Early Opinions concerning Jesus Christ (Priestley), 8:6
History of England (Hume), 2:681
History of Florence (Machiavelli), 5:626
History of Frederick the Great (Carlyle), 2:34
History of Greater Britain, A (Major), 5:661
History of Human Marriage, The (Westermarck), 9:739
History of Man (Buffon), 1:758
History of Materialism (Lange), 5:186, 6:540, 7:148, 9:625–626
History of Philosophical Systems, A (Ferm), 7:234
History of Philosophy (Stanley), 9:50
History of Scientific Ideas (Whewell), 9:743
History of the Decline and Fall of the Roman Empire (Gibbon), 4:84–86
History of the Inductive Sciences, from the Earliest to the Present Time (Whewell), 9:743
History of the Man after God's own Heart (anon.), 1:210, 2:685
History of the Poetry of the Greeks and Romans (Schlegel), 8:630
History of the Progress and Termination of the Roman Republic (Ferguson), 3:604
History of the Revolt of the Netherlands (Schiller, Friedrich), 8:626
History of the Royal Society (Sprat), 1:50
History of the Two Indies (Raynal), 3:244
History of the Work of Redemption, The (Edwards), 3:167
History of Unitarianism commonly called Socinianism (Nye), 9:100
History of Western Philosophy (Russell), 1:438, 9:464
History of Women Philosophers, A (Waithe), 9:838
Hitler, Adolf
Driesch and, 3:111
moral depravity of, 6:163
national socialism of, 3:553
Planck and, 7:578
racism of, 8:225–226
Hjelmslev, Johannes, on non-zero infinitesimal geometry, 2:509
Hoadly, Benjamin, Law and, 5:220
Hobart, R. E. *See* Miller, Dickinson S.
Hobbes, Thomas, **4:403–426**
on action, 8:127–128
on altruism and self-interest, 3:170–171
on Aristotelianism, 3:349
Aristotle and, 8:123
Boyle on, 1:673
Butler (Joseph) on, 1:781
Cambridge platonists on, 2:13
causes in, 8:127–128
on civil disobedience and duty, 2:260
Clarke on, 2:271
as classical politics in Collingwood, 2:329
communism metaphysical basis and, 2:365
comparison to Xunzi's social and political philosophy, 2:233
concept of ideas in, 4:564
consciousness in, 8:128
contemporary of Filmer, 3:636
on corporate state, 9:205
in crisis of skepticism, 9:54
Cudworth's ethics and, 2:611
Cumberland on, 2:614
on curiosity, 8:128
on definition, 2:665, 2:669, 3:349, 3:350
deism and, 2:682

Hobbes, Thomas, *continued*
on deliberation, 3:11–12
Descartes and, 2:738, 2:742
on determinism, 3:5, 3:11–12, 3:13, 3:15–16, 3:26
Dilthey on, 3:84
and Dutch Republic, 9:177–178
on emotions, 3:198
in enlightenment rationalism, 4:746
Epicurus and, 3:265
on equality, 3:330
on essence and existence, 3:349
ethics, 3:405–406, 3:407, 4:414–417
on evaluation of political and social institutions, 3:392
on government, role of, 7:153
on historicity of Bible, 9:179
in history of philosophy, 3:405
on human nature, 3:170–171
as hylopathic atheist in Cudworth, 2:610
on imagination, 1:50, 4:593
on knowledge, 2:669
Kortholt on, 7:99
on law, 7:423
Leibniz and, 4:552, 4:553, 5:251, 5:266
on liberty, 3:169, 5:319
life of, 4:403–406, 4:423
Locke and, 5:376, 7:424
on logic and mathematics, 5:442
logic of, 4:406–410
on machine intelligence, 5:631
on man as machine, 4:610
materialism of, 2:365, 6:9, 8:825
on meaning, 7:401
mechanism of, 8:127–128
methodology of, 4:406–410, 4:424
and Mill (John Stuart), 8:795
on mind, 6:259
on mind-body problem, 8:127
and modern ethical theory, 3:406
on morality and self-interest, 3:381–382
on motivation in ethics, 3:389
natural law in, 6:510–511
nominalism of, 9:599
origin of rights in, 4:180
Pascal and, 7:129
on passions, 8:128
philosophy of nature of, 4:410–411
philosophy of sex and, 7:522
political philosophy of, 4:417–420, 7:662–663
possibility in, 7:721
on power of citizens, 9:181–182
on propositions, 8:796
on prudence, 8:128
psychology of, 4:411–414, 8:127–128
Pufendorf and, 8:157
on religion, 4:420–422, 4:424
reversibility of moral rules, 1:460
Rousseau on, 2:366
Scholastics and, 3:294
on self-interest and origins of communism, 2:364
on self-preservation, 9:715
semantics in, 8:773–775
on sensationalism, 8:825
Shaftesbury's opposition to, 9:1
Sidgwick on, 3:417
on social contract, 9:81
on social wholes, 9:94
on soul, 3:11
on sovereignty, 9:140–141
and Spinoza, 3:294, 9:177
on the state, 4:51
on state of nature, 3:405, 4:415–416, 7:153, 9:79
and Stout, 9:259
Telesio and, 9:391
on thought and language, 7:534, 9:420
on toleration, 9:507
on universals, 4:407, 9:599
voluntarism of, 9:714
on war and peace, 7:153
on will, 3:406, 8:128
Hobhouse, Leonard Trelawney, **4:426–427**
Hoboth Ha-Lebaboth (Duties of the heart) (Baḥya), 1:457
Hocking, William Ernest, **4:427–428**
Hodge, Charles
on common consent for God's existence, 2:345, 2:348
on unbelief in God's existence, 2:350
Hodgson, Shadworth Holloway, 3:609, **4:428–429**
Høffding, Harald, **4:429–430**, 7:83
Hoffmann, A. F.
and Crusius, 2:605, 2:607
Lambert and, 5:175
Hoffmann, Freidrich, and Stahlianism, 9:203
Hofstadter, Douglas
on mind, 2:711
on Turing, 9:553
Hogarth, William, Lichtenberg on, 5:338
Hohenheim, Philippus Aureolus Theophrastus Bombastus von. *See* Paracelsus
Hoist, Amelia, 9:839
Hoitenga, Dewey, 3:535
Holbach, Paul-Henri Thiry, Baron d', **4:430–433**, 6:10
atheism and, 1:358, 2:688, 3:246
on conscience, 3:408
controversy generated by, 3:71
on determinism, 3:16
Encyclopédie and, 3:223
Enlightenment and, 3:244
Epicurus and, 3:265, 3:269
ethics, 3:410
influence of, 4:433
La Mettrie and, 5:181
Naigeon and, 6:476
Holbein, Hans, controversy over two paintings of, 3:556
Hölderlin, Johann Christian Friedrich, **4:433–436**, 8:617
Gadamer on, 4:3
on Schiller's *Letters,* 8:629
Hole argument, **4:436–441**
diffeomorphism invariance in, 9:157
of Einstein, 3:160, 3:180, 3:181
1987 hole argument, 4:437–438
responses to, 4:438–440
Hole diffeomorphism, Earman on, 3:160
Holiness, in Collingwood, 2:325–326
Holism, **4:441–450**
in Brouwer on continuum and rational numbers, 2:502
Buddhism and, 2:163–164
coherence theory of truth and, 9:536
of concepts, 2:418–419
Duhem-Quine conventionalism and, 2:520
Einstein and, 3:181–182
emergence and, 3:193
epistemic justification of belief and, 2:314
evolutionary, in Smute, 9:71–72
of functionalism, 3:760
harmony of whole by mutual penetration, 2:165
in illuminationism, 4:584
in intepretationsit theories of mental content, 2:478
in Krueger's philosophical psychology, 5:156
meaning, eliminative materialism on, 3:183
in medicine, 7:467

methodological, 4:443
in naming conventions and mass nouns in Chinese and, 2:210–211
of Oakeshott, 7:1, 7:2
observation and property set preexistence, 1:638
round teaching of Tainti Buddhism, 2:163–164
in Smuts' political theory, 9:71
social *vs.* mechanical wholes, 9:95
in Spann's neoromantic universalism, 9:158–159
in statement of social facts, 9:94–95
Holism and Evolution (Smuts), 9:71
Holistic empiricism, mathematical knowledge as a version of, 5:83
Holistic environmentalism, 3:259–260
Holistic medicine, 7:467
Holistic tradition, in European philosophical thought, 3:766
Holkot, Robert, **4:450–451**
double truth doctrine and, 5:616
Ockhamism of, 7:8
Thomism and, 9:445
Holland, as center of Jewish thought, 4:824
Holldöbler, Bert, 9:788
Holmes, John Haynes, on common consent for God's existence, 2:348–349
Holmes, Oliver Wendell, legal realism and, 5:246–248
Holmes, United States v., 6:97
Holmstrom, Nancy, socialist feminism used more broadly, 3:601
Holobolos, Manuel, in Byzantine thought, 1:789
Holocaust, **4:451–454**
Faurisson on, 5:620
indescribability thesis of, 4:454
Lyotard on, 5:620
uniqueness of, 4:451–453
Holophrastic meaning, Lewis (C. I.) on, 5:308–309
Holt, Edwin Bissell, **4:454–457**
neutral monism of, 6:587
in new realism, 6:585
realism and, 3:313
Holy, Otto on, 7:61
Holy Family, The (Marx) 1:493, 3:56–57
Holy Spirit
as an active agent driving the planets, 5:52
Luther on, 5:613
Plantinga on, 3:324
Pletho on procession of, 7:630
Holy will, 5:25
Hombre mediocre, El (Ingenieros), 4:686
Home, Henry, 3:720, **4:457–458**
Homeless objects, 6:115
Homemakers, extending social security to career, 3:583
Homeomorphic models of religious language, 8:418
Homeostasis, in Spinoza, 8:126
Homer, **4:458–460**
Aristotle on, 1:188
Demiurge in, 2:698
Dikē in, 3:79
Heraclitus on, 1:41
integrative writing of, 4:176
nous in, 6:666
Parmenides of Elea and, 7:128
pessimism of, 7:246
Philodemus of Gadara on, 3:263
psyche in, 8:103
truthfulness of poetry and, 1:41
Xenophanes on, 1:41, 7:94
Homeric Problems (Zeno), 9:253
"Homer's Contest" (Nietzsche), 6:610
Homicide, in Antiphon, 1:223
Homme machine, L' (La Mettrie), 5:178–180, 6:10
Homme planté, L' (La Mettrie), 5:178–180
Homo Viator (Marcel), 7:253
Homogeneity, cosmological models and, 2:560
Homoia (Resemblance) (Speusippus), 4:173
Homoiomereity, in Anaxagoras, 1:181–182
Homophobia, heterosexism and, 4:349
Homosexuality
invention of term for, 7:524
legal moralism and, 5:338
repression of, 8:112
views on, 7:523–524, 7:528
Honduran philosophy, independentist period, 5:205
Hone, William, deism and, 2:691
Honest to God (Robinson), 1:364, 1:656
Honesty, as thick moral concept, 6:164
Hong Daeyong, leading figure in the Study-North Scholars, 5:140
Hönigswald, Richard, in neo-kantianism, **4:460–461**, 6:541
Honor, in Confucianism, 2:175, 2:178–179
Honoré, A. M., on property, 8:71
Honorius III, Pope, on Erigena, 7:95
Hooded Man paradox, as semantic paradox, 5:518
Hook, Sidney, on Dewey, 3:425
Hooke, Robert, 7:558
Cavendish on, 2:118
Leibniz and, 5:251
Newton and, 6:590
physicotheology and, 7:558
Hooker, Sir Joseph, 2:628, 2:629
Hooker, Richard, **4:461–465**
on common consent for God's existence, 2:344
Locke and, 5:376
on social contract, 9:79
Hooker, Thomas, 7:422
Hooks, bell, articulating commonality and exclusion problems, 3:586
Hope
in Bloch, 1:615
mobilization of the patient's by the therapist, 3:742
Hope of Israel (Menasseh ben Israel), 6:128
Hopi Ethics (Brandt), 1:687
Hopkins, Gerard Manley, Duns Scotus and, 3:144
Horace, and Boileau, 1:640
Ho-Rak debate, in Korea, 5:139
Horde, Durkheim on, 3:150
Hören, Die (journal), 8:627
Horgan, Terence
on connectionism, 2:445
on Davidson, 3:466
Horizon, of intentional acts, 7:293–294
Horizons, for Gadamer, 3:565
Horizontal universal, 9:582
Horkheimer, Max, **4:465–466**
Adorno and, 1:26
critical theory and, 2:598
on Enlightenment, 3:244–245
on history, 7:391
Hormic psychology, 6:72, 8:147–148
Horn, Laurence, on generalized conversational implicature, 2:527
Horned argument, 6:110, 6:111
Horney, Karen, Adler and, 1:24
Hornsby, Jennifer
on action, 1:15
identity theory of truth and, 9:537
Horologium Sapientiae (Suso), 9:335
Horowitz, Alexandra, work in animal cognition, 1:206
Hors sujet (Levinas), 5:305
Hortensius (Cicero), 1:390
Horton, Joseph, 6:91
Horwich, Paul, 2:648, 8:533, 9:539
Hoshina Masayuki, Yamazaki Ansai and, 9:860

Hospers, John
on creative process, 2:590
on determinism, 3:16, 3:17
Lehrer and, 5:248
on libertarianism, 5:334, 5:336
on liberty, 9:72
Hospinianus, John, 5:439
Hostility, to atheism, 1:357–358
Hostos, Eugenio María, 5:204
Hotelling, Harold, 8:613
Houghton, Samuel, physicotheology and, 7:561
Hountoundji, Paulin, on unamism, 1:85
House of Wisdom, 4:754
"How"
causal *vs.* state or condition, 9:756
and "why"
as different questions, 9:755–756
as same question, 9:755
How the Laws of Physics Lie (Cartwright), 2:62, 5:227
How to Do Things with Words (Austin), 1:154, 1:407–408, 7:199
"How to Make Our Ideas Clear" (Peirce), 4:781, 7:742–743, 8:799
How We Think (Dewey), 3:47
Howard, William, in proof theory, 8:56
Howison, George Holmes, **4:467**
matter-mind dualism in, 2:595
and McGilvary, 6:75
on personalism, 7:235
Howson, Colin, 8:34
Hox genes, 7:346
Hoyle, Fred
on cosmological theorizing, 2:562
on meaning of history, 5:351
Hsiao-ch'ü, 5:415–416
Hsun Tzu. *See* Xunzi
Hu Shi, **4:520–421**
on Dai Zhen, 2:621
on social reform, 2:181
Hua Yen metaphysics, *li* in, 4:794
Hua yua
central texts, 1:736–737
Four Dharmadhāus, 1:738–739
patriarchal lineage in, 1:737–738
Huainanzi, 2:186, 9:862
Huairang, and Chan (Zen) Buddhism, 2:167
Huang Zongxi, **4:467–468**
Huangbo, use of metaphor and rhetoric by, 1:729
Huanglao, on method preparation to know external things, 2:216
Huart, Claude, 9:50
Huayan Buddhism, **1:736–740**, 2:154, 2:164–166
in Chinese philosophy, 2:154
on Huangbo metaphor, 1:729
and Zen, comparison of, 1:737–738
Huayan Fajie Guanmen (Meditative approaches to the Huayan Dharmadhātu) (Dashun), 1:737
Huayan jing (Avatamsaka sutra, Flower-wreath sutra), 1:736, 2:164
Hubble, Edwin, 4:63
Huber, Marie, 9:839
Huemer, Michael, on conditions of knowledge, 3:272
Huet, Pierre-Daniel, **4:468–471**, 9:53
Hügel, Baron Friedrich von, 4:111, **4:471–472**
Hugh of Saint Victor, 1:402–403, 8:592
See also Saint Victor, School of
Hugo, Victor, Diderot and, 3:77
Huguenots, Louis XIV's campaign against, 3:245
Hui Neng, and Buddhism, 2:155, 2:168
Hui Shi, **4:472–473**
on logic, 5:415
on names as relative indexicals, 2:189
Huiwen, in Taintai Buddhism, 2:163
Huizinga, Johan
on death, 2:651
on free will, 3:40
on history, 7:395
Hull, Clark
behaviorism of, 8:143
Pavlov and, 7:151
radical behaviorism, 1:520
Hull House, 3:44, 3:566–567
Hulst, Monsignor d', 5:570
Human, All Too Human (Nietzsche), 6:611
Human action, in Homer, 4:460
Human activity, on Brouwer's logic and, 5:468
Human beings
ability to respond to God, 1:707
as abstract idea, 1:586
age of, 9:676
alienation in, 1:121, 1:123–124, 3:611
as *animal metaphysicum*, 8:649
animals *vs.*, 1:105, 1:602
anthropic principle and, **1:219–222**
in anthropology, philosophical, 7:319
aspirations of, utopias as record of, 9:620
avoidance of sin by, 7:175
as bees in Mandeville, 5:681–682
Biblical conception of, 7:323
bioethical definition, 1:602
biological propensity to believe in God's existence, 2:346–347
in Christianity, 2:248–249, 9:768
cognition and computationalism, 2:395
cognition and connectionist models, 2:444
cognitively free in relation to God, 3:533
composite nature of, in doctrine of immortality, 4:602
in Confucianism, 2:171, 2:443
connectionism and, 2:445
contingency of, Unamuno on, 9:568
contrasted with nature, 6:518
de Maistre on, 5:660
as defined by labor in Marx, 2:363
definition of, 2:699
dignity of, 7:572–573
equality of, Vauvenargues on, 9:654
essence of, Reale on, 8:260
evolution and, 2:635–636, 2:637, 2:640–641, 2:642–643
evolution of
Haeckel on, 4:202
Wallace (Alfred Russel) on, 9:721
existential authenticity and, 1:762–763
finite computing machines and, 2:403–404
finitude of, 6:667
in flesh of the world, 6:148–149
as free creative activity, 8:621
God and world and, Rosenzweig on, 4:829
happiness *(eudaimonia)* for, 3:749
as higher organism than state in Chicherin, 2:147
history of, in Gnosticism, 4:101
in Homer, 4:460
improvement of, 5:675–676
as individual *vs.* person, 5:715
in James's philosophy, 4:776
Kant on, 2:367 2:714
Leibniz's republic of monadic spirits, 2:365–366
love for God, 4:828
loved by God, 4:828
Maritain on, 5:715
Marx on, 3:67–69
materialism and, 6:11, 6:17

as means, 6:656
as measure of things, 8:91–93
Mencius on government service to, 2:233
microcosm and, 5:639
Mill (John Stuart) on, 6:224–225, 7:377
Morgan (Lewis) on, 6:404
nature of
  Dostoevsky on, 3:99
  Edwards (Jonathan) on, 3:169
  Encyclopédie on, 3:224, 3:225
  Heidegger on, 3:512
  Hobbes on, 3:405
  La Mettrie on, 5:179–181
  Lamarck on, 5:174–175
  Landgrebe on, 5:183
  Parmenides of Elea on, 7:124–125
  Plantinga on, 3:324
  Rousseau on, 3:410
  Sartre on, 3:428
needs of, 4:483
in Nietzsche, 7:320
Oken on, 7:11
omniscience of, 1:372–373
ontological status of, 2:654
Origen on, 7:39
as paradigm for computing machines and, 2:398–399
as part of nature, 6:518
vs. "person," 1:463–464, 7:215–216
in Plato's hierarchical communism, 2:364
plurality of forms in, Ockham on, 9:782
proprium in identity of, 8:634
protean nature of, 5:58
pure, Zhuangzi on, 9:881
purpose of, 9:756
reduction to physics and physiology, 2:2
Régis on, 8:300
rights of, 4:483
Rousseau on, 2:688
Sartre on reality of, 8:607
in Schultz's typology, 8:659
self-government by. *See* Democracy
self-image of, 7:319–320
sexuality, *vs.* animals, 7:526–527
social nature of, 9:648, 9:673
as soul and body construct, 4:605
sovereignty of, 9:142
specifying the essence of, 3:611
tai qi of, Zhu Xi on, 4:794
unworthiness of Culverwell, 2:613
and vagueness of material objects, 3:121–122
Vaihinger in, 9:625
in Valentinianism, 9:632
Vico on, 9:673
as volitional not rational, 1:595
Weil's (Simone) concept of, 9:737
Wollaston on, 2:684
Zabarella on, 9:867
Zen'kovskii on, 9:868
Zubiri (Xavier) on, 9:888
Human body, as a collection of less conscious spiritual substances, 5:146
Human capacity
  to characterize others, 3:677
  to describe and to understand the mental, 3:677
  reasons and justification in contractualism, 2:518
Human condition
  in Bultmann, 1:762–763
  Camus on revolting against, 2:21–22
  fraternal solidarity in Camus, 2:21
  in Heidegger, 1:762–763
  moral cosmopolitanism and, 2:568, 2:569
  moral responsibility in Camus, 2:22–23
  Pascal on, 7:132–133
Human consciousness
  vs. animal consciousness, 5:78
  privacy of, 3:610–611
Human culture
  Coleridge on, 2:316–317
  cosmopolitanism and, 2:567, 2:569–570
Human determinism, 3:24–29
Human experience, Nishida on, 6:625
Human experience plateau (Dewey), 3:46
Human fare, transformation into human thought, 3:612
Human freedom, 3:616. *See also* Freedom
Human Freedom, Of (Schelling), 8:621
Human Genome Project, 4:43, 4:46, **4:473–476,** 6:96, 7:346
Human ideal, 2:149, 3:578
Human intellect, Yang Zhu on, 9:862
Human knowledge
  Dostoevsky on, 3:99
  limitations of, 3:616
Human Knowledge: Its Scopes and Limits (Russell), 3:234, 8:819
Human learning, ontological explanation of the process of, 3:755
Human life
  conscience and, 2:445
  as value in contractualism, 2:518
Human love, Ficino's doctrine of, 3:623–624
Human mind, physical possibility determined by, 5:30
Human misery, Cynic teaching on, 2:616
Human nature, **4:481–484**
  a priori, 4:482
  in anarchism, 1:177–178
  vs. animal nature, 5:139
  in antiutopianism, 9:621
  Aquinas on, 9:428–430
  Asian philosophies on, 5:359
  in Augustine, 7:367–368
  in Bacon (Francis), 1:445
  in Bible, 1:478
  in Blake, 1:610
  in Bodin, 1:620
  Butler (Joseph) on, 3:171–172
  in Calvin, 2:10
  Cambridge platonists on, 2:13
  as capacity to pursue ends and categorical imperative, 2:70
  in Cassirer, 2:67
  in Cheng, 2:156
  in Cheng Hao, 2:144
  in Chernyshevskii, 2:146
  cloning effect on, 4:47
  Coleridge on, 2:317
  complexity of, 3:174–175
  components of, 1:781
  Condillac on, 3:330
  in Condorcet, 2:433
  in Confucian ethics, 2:196
  conservatism and, 2:469–470
  culture and geography and, 1:621–622
  Cumberland on, 2:615
  Darwinists on, 3:480
  decadence in, 7:319
  in Dewey, 7:378
  divine rationality of, in Stoicism, 9:254
  Dong Zhongshu on innate good and evil as normative in, 2:235
  dualist conceptions of, 2:654
  in early Confucian thought, 2:149–150
  education and, 7:367–368
  empiricism on, 4:483
  Enlightenment on, 3:246–247
  Erigena on, 3:341–342
  as evil in Xunzi, 2:233
  evolution of, in morality, 9:789
  existentialism on, 3:503, 3:508

Human nature, *continued*
as fundamentally irrational, 4:751
in Gnosticism, 4:101–102
God and, 7:368
as God-seeker, 2:352–353
Godwin on, 1:177–178
Hartley (David) on, 3:173
Helvétius on, 3:330
Hemsterhuis on, 4:311
Herbart on, 7:376
historical criticism and, 1:622
in historical materialism, 4:383–384
history and, 1:718–719, 7:398, 7:629
in history and human behavior, 1:718–719
Hobbes on, 3:170–171, 3:405, 4:424–425
human response to God, 1:707
Hume on, 4:488–493, 8:132
ideal moral code utilitarianism and, 1:687
Indian philosophy on, 5:359
Isaac of Stella on, 4:753
in I-thou *vs.* I-it relationships, 1:715–716
in Itō's *kogigaku,* 4:766
La Bruyère on, 5:167
La Rochefoucauld on, 5:200–201
Latin American philosophy on, 5:205
Li Ao on, 5:316
love and, 4:483–484
in Lu's neo-Confucian idealistic philosophy, 2:157
Maistre on, 9:520
in medieval philosophy, 6:99
in Mencius, 2:150, 2:231, 2:233–234
Mill (John Stuart) on, 6:230, 6:521
Morgan (Thomas) on, 6:405
natural law and, 6:515
vs. nature in Xunzi, 2:233–234
needs and, 4:483
Nietzsche on, 6:609–610
in normative ethics, 1:687
as not God-given, 1:515
nurture and, 2:233–234, 4:483
Ogyū on, 7:10
Paley (William) on, 3:172
Pelagianism and predestination, 7:175
Plato on, 7:591
pluralism in conservatism and, 2:467
potentialities of, in Schiller (Friedrich), 8:627–628
rationality in, 4:482
rationality of social ritual and, 1:488
recovery through education, 2:168
as religious, 2:345–346
Renaissance view of, 5:641–642
rights and, 4:483
Rousseau on, 7:370–371, 8:508–510
Schopenhauer on, 7:153, 8:651–652, 8:653
science of, 4:488–493
sensuous and formal drives in, 8:628
Shaftesbury on, 3:171
Soto on, 9:137
in Stoicism, 9:794
Thomasius on, 9:441
in Thucydides, 9:457
Tucker (Abraham) on, 3:172
as unchanging in Confucius, 2:236
understood through Darwinism, 6:80
in utopianism, 9:620–621
voluntarism on, 9:715
Wilson's (Edward O.) on, 9:788–789
Xunzi on, 2:233–234, 9:856–857
Yamaga Sokō on, 9:859
Zhang Zai on, 9:879
Zhu Xi on, 9:883
Human Nature (Hobbes), 7:522
on language, 8:773
on speech, 8:775
Human Nature and Conduct (Dewey), 3:48, 3:51
Human rights, 2:568, 8:474–475
Human Rights and Global Justice (Gewirth), 4:81
Human sciences
categories of, 3:82–83
Dilthey on, 3:79–85
methodology for, 9:36–37
structuralism and, 9:273
Human Sexuality (Primoratz), 7:521
Human society(s)
divided, 3:604
Duns Scotus on, 3:144–145
Human Society in Ethics and Politics (Russell), 1:374
Human subjectivity
in deduction of categories, 5:34
strictly moral core of, 3:616
Human vulnerability and interdependence, 3:580
Human World in the Physical Universe (Maxwell), materialism of, 6:18
Human worth, in moral cosmopolitanism, 2:568
Humanae Vitae (Pope Paul VI), 6:513
Human-animal distinction, bioethical issues, 1:602–603
Humaneness, on Confucius, 2:443
Humanism, **4:477–481**
in Bacon (Francis), 1:450
in Berdyaev, 1:560
at Chartres school, 2:136–137
in Cicero, 2:257–258
Comenius on, 2:341
of communism, 2:363
Eliot (George) and, 3:184–185
Encyclopédie and, 3:225
in feminism, 7:462
Foucault's resistance to, 3:698
of Godfrey of St. Victor, 8:592
of Grotius, 4:191
Heidegger on, 4:295
historical knowledge in, 7:392
on horror fiction, 1:336
Hugh of St. Victor and, 8:592
in Latin American philosophy, 5:204–205
Lucian of Samosata and, 5:597
of Masaryk, 6:2
in neo-Confucianism, Japanese acceptance of, 4:795, 4:796
Peter Damien on, 7:258
Petrarch as representative of, 7:263, 7:265
in Platonic tradition, 7:613
Pletho and, 7:630
Reformation and, 8:296
in Renaissance, 8:424–426, 9:441
Sartrean, 8:607
of Schiller (Ferdinand), 8:623–624
Spranger and, 9:198
in Tagore's philosophy, 9:364
of Valla, 9:635
Humanism and Terror (Merleau-Ponty), 6:149
Humanisme de l'autre homme (Levinas), 5:305
Humanismen som livhsållning (Humanism as a way of life) (von Wright), 9:847
Humanist Manifesto of 1933, 8:733
Humanitarianism
of Channing, 2:130–131
human irrationality in contravening, 4:751–752
Humanitas (journal), 8:666
Humanities
competing terminology for study of, 4:37–38
Geisteswissenschaften, 4:37–38

memory studied in, 6:122
use in logical *vs.* evocative argument, 2:213
Humanity
as alienated in sale of labor, 2:363
in Brunschvicg, 1:714
Coleridge on, 2:320
Comte on, 7:712
in Confucianism, 2:150
cosmopolitanism and, 2:570
Croce's cosmic intuition and, 2:601
as distinct from animals, 2:226
divided into a series of social organisms, 5:148
Krause on, 5:147
maximum stability of, 7:268
in neo-Confucian rationalism, 2:155–156
as new religion in Comte, 2:412–413
of nonwhites, 4:806
obsessive's superiority as evil in Camus, 2:23
perfectibility of, in Turgot, 9:551
principle of, 6:85
as reason for life on earth in Bergson, 1:570
right of, 5:148
of sages, 9:723
social differentiation as characteristic of, 2:176
as subject of history, Burckhardt on, 1:766
as unitary organism in Chernyshevskii, 2:146
universal religion of, Comte on, 2:410
as value of in Chinese philosophy, 2:168
Wang on, 2:152
Humanness, in Confucianism view of ultimate reality, 2:220
Humans, Turing machines and, 2:408
Humboldt, Alexander von, Lichtenberg and, 5:338, 5:339
Humboldt, Wilhelm von, **4:484–486**
and Croce, 2:601
and Darwin, 2:628
German liberalism and, 5:321
on inner form of natural language, 8:794
on language, 8:793–794
and Mauthner, 8:801
and Schiller (Friedrich), 8:627
and Shpet, 9:17
in Spranger's philosophy of education, 9:199
Hume, David, **4:486–514**
on *a priori* knowledge, 4:611
on *a priori* metaphysics, 6:170
on aesthetic experience, 1:33
on aesthetic judgment, 1:35–37
on agency, 3:445
on altruism and self-interest, 1:136–137, 3:172–173
as an epistemologist, 5:91
analysis of causation, 4:636–637
Anscombe on, 1:213
anthropology and, 7:316
on apprehension, 3:176
arguing from premises containing only descriptive terms, 3:548–549
on artificial virtues, 3:384
on association of ideas, 1:50
on atheism, 2:688
awakening of Kant, 5:10
Ayer and, 1:436
on Beattie, 1:510
on beauty, 1:35–36, 1:37–38, 1:51, 1:74, 1:513
on belief, 3:631–632, 5:16, 5:91, 5:99
on Berkeley's view of general ideas, 9:596
on body, 5:657–658, 8:133
on Bolingbroke, 1:641–642, 2:684–685
Cartwright on, 2:62
on categories and knowability, 2:80
on causality, 2:95, 2:103, 2:106–107, 2:114, 5:10, 5:20
causality in, Shepherd on, 9:10
on causation, 3:124
on cause and effect, 4:637
censorship of, 1:210
central doctrines of the analytic as an answer to, 5:16
on clarity and distinctness, 6:192
on Clarke, 2:274
close friend of Ferguson, 3:604
committee of minor deities of, 9:407
common sense and, 2:356
on concepts, 2:417
on conceptual intuitions, 4:732
conceptualism of, 9:598–599
on creation, 3:475
in crisis of skepticism, 9:55–56
critique of metaphysics and, 5:526
on dangers of imagination, 4:596
de Finetti and, 2:663
on definition, 2:667–668
deism and, 2:681, 2:686–687, 2:691
Deleuze on, 2:693, 2:694, 2:695
denial of the unity of the self, 5:76
on determinism, 3:8, 3:13, 3:14, 3:15–16, 3:27
division of propositions, 5:13
Driesch and, 3:110
on duty, 3:155
Earman on, 3:161
Einstein and, 3:179
emotivism and, 3:204
empiricism of, 3:218–219, 7:493
Encyclopédie and, 3:223
Enlightenment and, 3:244, 3:246
in enlightenment rationalism, 4:746
epistemology, 3:298, 3:303–305, 3:711
on epistemology of testimony, 9:402
ethical subjectivism in, 3:375
ethics, 3:408–409
on evil, 1:362, 3:469–470
on existence, 3:495
on existence of God, 1:362, 4:615
expectations about the future as habits of the mind, 3:708
on experience and Cohen (Hermann) on Kant, 2:302
on experience in analogical arguments on God, 1:783
on faith, 4:771
feelings, reality of, Green on, 4:179
feminist epistemology, 1:459
force as merely a construct, 3:689
Foucher's arguments used by, 3:704
Franklin a friend of, 3:720
on free will, 3:14, 3:409, 4:503–504
Frege on, 3:730
on future, 4:641, 5:16
and Gibbon, 2:690–691, 4:84, 4:86
Glanvill and, 4:96
and Godwin, 4:138
Green on, 4:179–180
in history of metaphysics, 6:191–192
on human nature, 4:488–493, 8:132
on ideas, 1:50, 3:218, 3:303–304, 8:131
on images, 8:131
imagination in, 8:131–132
on impressions, 3:218, 3:303, 8:131
on individuals, 4:497–499
induction, problem of, 4:154
on inferential justification, 2:275
on innateness of principle of induction, 4:693

Hume, David, *continued*
on intuition, 4:724
on judgments, 3:495
on justice, 3:409
on justification, 6:498–499
and Kant, 2:689, 3:306
Keynes's fundamental thesis and, 5:56
Köhler on, 5:131
Kripke comparing to Wittgenstein, 5:150
literary fame of, 5:364
logic subordination to psychology, 1:677
on loyalty, 5:595
Lucian of Samosata and, 5:597
and Mach, 8:827
MacIntyre on, 5:636
Maine de Biran and, 5:657–658
Malebranche and, 5:671–672
on manifest image, 8:734
on mathematics, 6:202
and Mauthner, 8:801
on mental images, 4:592–593
on mental states, 2:457
methodism of, 3:278
Middleton and, 6:214
mind in, 8:132, 8:133
on mind-body problem, 8:133
on miracles, 4:109, 6:266–267, 6:269–270, 6:274–275, 7:76
Moore on, 7:109
on moral distinctions, 7:424
on moral responsibility, 3:409
on morality, 4:506–509
on motivation in ethics, 3:389, 4:715
on natural law, 5:225, 6:512, 6:515
on nature, 7:559–560, 8:133
on necessary connection, 4:637
Newton and, 8:133
Nicolas of Autrecourt and, 6:600
in noncognitivism, 1:141
nonfactionalist strand of empiricist thought discerned in, 3:629
on outward impressions, 5:657–658
Paley and, 7:77–78
on passions, 4:504–505, 8:132
on perception, 8:815
on personal identity, 4:612, 7:213, 7:218–221
on phenomenalism, 7:272, 7:275, 7:276, 7:282
phenomenalism of, 6:192
and philosophy of religion, 2:691
philosophy of sex and, 7:522
physicotheology and, 7:559–560
on pleasure, 8:132
on pleasure and pain, 7:621
possibility in, 7:722
practical effectiveness of reason, 5:24
predecessors of, 8:131
Price and, 8:1–2
projectivism of, 8:51
on properties, 3:527
on property, 8:69
psychology in, 8:130–133
Ramsey (Michael) and, 5:672
on reasoning, 7:735, 8:132
recognizing the virtue of small, egalitarian societies, 3:605
regularity theory of, 5:132
Reid on, 3:305–306, 9:248
on religion, 4:509–513
in religious philosophy, 7:493
on resemblance, 9:599–600
on responsibility, 8:164
Rousseau and, 3:410
rules for judging causes and effects, 5:99
Schopenhauer on, 8:648
Schultze on skepticism of, 8:660
on self, 2:199, 8:132–133
on sensa, 8:814
on sensation, 8:131, 8:826
Shaftesbury and, 9:2
skepticism of, 3:218, 4:500–501, 9:47
Smart and, 9:65
on Spinoza, 9:193, 9:297
Stace and, 9:200
on subjectivity of moral judgments, 3:381
on substance, 7:24, 9:298
on suicide, 9:319
on sympathy, 1:136–137, 3:750, 8:132, 9:345
on taste, 4:65
on teleological argument for existence of God, 9:377–380
on testimony, 7:357
theory of origins, 4:490
on thought and thinking, 9:420
on tragedy, 9:523
on understanding, 4:493–497, 4:596. *See also Enquiry concerning Human Understanding, An* (Hume)
on universals, 3:303–304, 9:598–599
utilitarianism and, 3:382–383, 3:384, 9:605
Veblen and, 9:655–656
on virtue and vice, 9:247
voluntarism of, 9:714–715
on "why," 9:755
on will, 4:501–504
on Wollaston, 9:834
Humean best-system theory
causal reduction and realism in, 2:96–100
chance and credence, 2:128–129
Humean (regularity) view of laws of nature, 5:225–231
Humean supervenience, 3:191
Hume's Abject Failure: The Argument against Miracles (Earman), 3:161
Hume's principle, 6:672
Frege and, 3:730, 5:517
neo-Fregeanism and, 3:731
Humor, **4:514–519**
as Chinese religious excellence, 2:226
incongruity theories of, 4:516–517
melancholy, 7:247–248
in Schiller's *Mind!,* 8:625
Seneca's *Pumpkinification of Claudius,* 8:813
in Stace's "Refutation of Realism," 9:200
in Swift's social satire, 9:339–341
theories of, 4:515–517, 4:517–518
types of, 4:514–515, 4:517–518
See also Comedy
Humphreys, Paul, on explanation, 3:525–526
Humphrey's paradox, conditional probability and propensity, 2:128
Humpty Dumpty, as nominalist, 9:599
Hunger, 20th-century debate on, 3:443
Hungerland, Isabel C., on presupposing, 7:766–767
Hunt, William H., 4:774
Hunter, W. S., 8:143
"Hunting of the Snark, The" (Carroll), 2:52
Huntington, Edward V., infinity characterization in set theory, 2:498
Huntington, Ellsworth, 3:37
Huntington's disease, 7:466
Hurka, Tom, on virtue and vice, 9:678–679
Hursthouse, Rosalind, 9:681
Hus, John, **4:519–520**
Husserl, Edmund, **4:521–527**
Abbagnano and, 1:1
on alterity, 1:133
in anthropology, 7:318
on art, 1:59, 1:70
and Banfi, 1:476–477
Brentano and, 1:690

on Buddhism, 2:165–166
categories and cognitive limits in, 2:81–82
Cohen (Hermann) and, 6:543
on consciousness, 2:459
on consciousness of time, 4:290, 9:489
on definition, 2:665, 2:667–668
Derrida on, 2:715–717, 9:489
development of phenomenology and, 7:299
Dilthey and, 3:84
Dingler and, 3:85, 3:86
doctrine of intentionality, 7:290–291, 7:293–294, 7:299
on ego, 7:398
elaboration of Cairns, 2:5–6
on empathy, 9:345
epistemology, 3:312
on essence and existence, 3:351
existential psychoanalysis and, 3:510
existentialism and, 3:317, 3:502
Fink and, 3:637–639
and Frege, 3:728, 3:732
Gadamer, 4:3
in Gödel, 4:118
and Gurwitsch, 4:197
Hartmann and, 3:422
and Heidegger, 3:504, 4:290–291, 9:490
on history, 7:397–398
influences on, concept of time, 9:488
and Ingarden, 4:682
on intentionality, 3:502, 4:704
intentionality and, 3:512
on internal dialogue, 9:491
on intentionality, 8:605
and Jaspers, 4:799
Köhler's debt to the phenomenology of, 5:126
Külpe's indebtedness to, 5:160
Landgrebe and, 5:183
on language, 8:802–803
Leśniewski and, 5:292–293
Levinas and, 5:303–304
Lipps and, 5:363
Losev and, 5:573
Mamardashvili on, 5:677
Mead and, 6:82
on meaning categories, 9:352
Merleau-Ponty on, 9:491
on Mill's connotation-denotation distinction, 8:803
Natorp and, 6:490
noema, 4:198
opposition to psychologism, 7:280–281
on parts, 6:146
Pfänder and, 7:269
on phenomenology, 3:563, 3:753, 4:82, 4:522–523, 7:277, 7:279, 7:282, 7:283, 7:285, 7:288–290, 7:397–398
and Plessner, 7:629
on psychologism, 4:522–523, 8:115–116
on psychology, 4:522–523
and Santayana, 8:598
Sartre and, 3:317, 8:603
Scheler and, 3:421, 8:616
and Schutz, 8:664
Shestov on, 9:11
and Shpet, 9:17
Simmel and, 9:30
Stein and, 9:239–240
Stumpf and, 9:280
Twardowski and, 9:554
use by Binswanger, 1:597–598

Husserl Circle, 4:198
Husserlian semantics, in compositionality, 2:371
Husserliana, 7:299
Hussites, social egalitarianism and, 3:329
Hutcheson, Francis, **4:527–530**
on aesthetics, 1:35–37, 4:529
on altruism and self-interest, 1:136, 3:171
in arousal theory of art, 1:303
and Balguy, 1:474
on beauty, 1:51, 1:513–514
conscience and, 2:445
Cumberland and, 2:615
Edwards (Jonathan) and, 3:167
ethics, 3:408
Kant on, 5:26
on morality, civic and social character of, 3:605
on perception of virtue and vice, 1:474–475, 8:2
Price on, 8:2
on reflexive sense, 4:65
Shaftesbury and, 9:2
and Smith (Adam), 9:66
on virtue and vice, 9:247
on Wollaston, 9:834

Hutchinson, Keith, on unique evolution, 3:32
Hutten, Ulrich von, 9:263
Hutton, James, 2:640, 7:561
Huxley, Aldous, 7:155, 9:311
antiutopianism of, 9:621
on intentional properties, 6:263

Huxley, Julian
evolutionary ethics and, 3:479
evolutionary theory and, 3:488
on naturalistic religion, 8:375–376
on superultimate "why," 9:758
on synthesis, 7:339

Huxley, Thomas Henry, **4:530–534**
agnosticism of, 1:92–93, 1:358, 4:532–533
on Christianity, 1:93
Darwin and, 2:628, 2:629
Dewey and, 3:43
on energy conservation, 3:232
epistemology of, 4:532–533
ethics of, 4:533–534
on evolution, 2:641, 4:531–532
on evolutionary ethics, 3:479
evolutionary theory and, 2:635
on mental causation, 6:133, 6:260
metaphysics of, 4:532–533
Romanes lecture, 3:668

Huygens, Christiaan
Cartesian contributions, 2:56
clock built by, 6:91
on elastic collisions and conservation laws, 2:462
on force and momentum, 3:228
on hypothetico-deductive method, 8:684–685
Leibniz and, 5:251, 5:269
Newton and, 6:590

Huygens, Constantijn, Elisabeth, princess of Bohemia and, 3:187
Hyakugaku renkon (Nishi), 6:623
Hyaptia, lynching of, 6:553
Hybrid logic, 6:300
Hybridization, in Mendel, 7:338–339
Hydrodynamica, sive de Viribus et Motibus Fluidorum Commentarri (Bernoulli), on potential energy, 3:228
Hydrostatic paradox, Descartes and, 2:721–722
Hygrometry, science of, 3:702
Hylomorphism, 1:403, 8:458
Hylozoism, 7:84, 7:91
Hyman, Ray, parapsychology and, 7:116
Hymn to Zeus (Cleanthes), 5:585, 9:35
Hymnen an die Nacht (Novalis), 6:667
Hypatia, **4:534–535**
Hyperaspistes (Erasmus), 3:338–339
Hyperbolic geometry, 9:150
Hyperproof, 3:656
Hyperreal number systems
of Robinson, 2:506–507
of Skolem, 2:507

Hypertime, 9:462, 9:471
Hypnosis, 5:642
Hypocrisy, 6:435, 9:680

Hypomnemata Mathematica (Stevin), on energy and work, 3:227
Hypostasis
in al-Fārābī's metaphysics, 7:610
concept of infinity in, 4:668
as hierarchy of reality, 7:609
in medieval Platonic thought, 7:611, 7:612
in Plotinus's theory of the One, 7:633–634
as reflection of Christian trinity, 7:615
soul in, 7:614
Hypothesis/hypotheses
alternative, neglect of, 3:545
analytical, in radical translation, 8:217
Bayesianism and, 1:497–502
behaviorism as, 1:520
Campbell on, 2:17–18
of causal relationships, 2:107
classification by, 6:560
in confirmation theory, 2:434–435
continuum (CH), 8:832–833
in cosmological argument for God's existence, 2:586
creation of, 3:532
of design, probability of agreement on, 3:664
ether theories of, 8:699
in experimental economics, 7:353
fallacy of saving, 3:544
falsifiability of, Popper on, 8:683
fictions *vs.*, 9:626
as fictitious construction, 1:575
Fisher on, 9:218
as images constructed from observation, 1:643–644
as imagination not beliefs, 1:643
in inference to best explanation, 4:651
logical consequences verification of, 2:438
plausibility of, 1:500
Poincaré on, 7:652
probability of, 1:496–498
as scientific theory, 1:685
Socratic
Wolff on, 9:827
in Xenophon, 9:855
synthetic statements as, 5:529
testing
Neyman-Pearson theory of, 9:215–218
selection for, 3:664
for self-deception, 8:715–716
universal, probability of, 5:56
Hypothesis physica nova (New physical hypothesis) (Leibniz), 5:251, 5:260, 5:269
Hypothetic methods of science, limits to, 1:590
Hypothetical and disjunctive reasoning, systematizing, 3:537–538
Hypothetical imperatives, in Kant, 2:70
Hypothetical intentionalism, 1:313–314
Hypothetical propositions, 5:553
Hypothetical syllogism
Abelard on, 5:427
Boethius on, 5:427
definition of, 5:557
impossibilities and, 1:627–628
in traditional logic, 5:502
Hypotheticals, as statement form in Keynes, 5:503
Hypothetico-deductivism, 4:639, 8:684–685, 8:699, 9:575
Hypotyposes (Clement of Alexandria), 7:142
Hypotyposes (Outlines of Pyrrhonism) (Sextus Empiricus), 9:49–50
Hyppolite, Jean, **4:535–537**
on history, 7:391
Lacan and, 5:168
Hyslop, James, parapsychology and, 7:116
Hysterical symptoms, disappearance of, 3:740
Hythlodaeus, Raphael (character), 6:400

I

I
The, 3:615
absolute, 3:615
in introspection, 6:81
and Other, 1:465
practical, 3:615
that acts, and the I that knows, 8:620
I and Thou (Nishida), 6:625
I Ching. See Yijing
"I See the Promised Land" (King), 5:73
"I Have a Dream" (King), 5:73
I massimi problemi (Varisco), 9:647
"I principî della filosofia practica di Giordano Bruno" (Spaventa), 9:159
"I think"
rational psychology developed around, 5:21–22
"therefore I exist," 5:95
Iakubinskii, Lev, and Bakhtin Circle, 1:469–470
Iamblichus, **4:539–541**
Aristotelianism of, 1:260
Chaldaean Oracles and, 6:549
and Ikhwān al-Ṣafāʾ, 4:576
and Neoplatonism, 6:550–551
on *phantasia,* 7:271
and Platonic tradition, 7:608–609
vs. Porphyry, 6:550
Pythagoreanism of, 6:550, 8:188
on religious rites, 6:551
on sophists, 9:129
Iamblichus: De Anima (Iamblichus), 4:539
Iatromechanism, 5:178
Iavlenie i smysl (Appearance and sense) (Shpet), 9:17
Ibn Abdūn, Muḥammad, 5:419
Ibn Adī, Yaḥyā, 5:418
Ibn al-ʿArabī, **4:541–544**
on Islamic gnosis, 9:307
Lull and, 5:610
mysticism of, 4:760
pantheism, 4:743
on theophany, 9:307
Ibn al-Kindī, Abū-Yūsuf Yaʿqūb, 4:814
Ibn Bājja, **4:544–545**
Arab logic and, 5:419
Maimonides and, 5:654
Ibn Caspi, Joseph, 4:809, 4:820–821
Ibn Da'ud, Abraham, 4:817
Ibn Ezra, Abraham
on biblical history, 9:179
and Ibn Gabirol, 4:815
in medieval Jewish philosophy, 4:816
Ibn Gabirol, Solomon ben Judah, **4:545–547**
on divine will, 9:765
Grosseteste and, 4:186
on hylomorphic composition of creatures, 1:653
on matter and form, 3:141
in medieval philosophy, 4:814–815, 6:100
in Platonic tradition, 7:611
Ibn Haylān, Yuhannā, 1:115
Ibn Kammunā, 4:817
Ibn Khaldūn, **4:547–550**
on al-Fārābī, Abū al Naṣr, 1:115
Arab logic and, 5:420
Ibn Kurrah, Thabit, 3:227
Ibn Paqūda, Baḥyā ben Joseph. *See* Bahyā ben Joseph ibn Paqūda
Ibn Rushd. *See* Averroes
Ibn Sina. *See* Avicenna
Ibn Tibbon, Samuel, 4:820, 5:648, 5:653
Ibn Ṭufayl, **4:550–551**
Ibn Wāqār, Joseph, 4:821

Ibn Yūnus, Abū Bishr Mattā, 5:418
Ibn Zaddik, Joseph ben Jacob, **4:551–552**
  and Ibn Gabirol, 4:815
  on microcosm, 5:641
Ich schaue in Leben: Ein Buch der Besinnung (I am peering into life: A book of thoughts) (Il'in), 4:578
Icon(s), as names, Peirce on, 5:453
Id, 8:146
  pessimism and, 7:252
  unconscious and, 9:572
Idea(s), **4:563–567**
  absolute, Hegel on, 5:62, 7:98
  abstract. *See* Abstract ideas
  as abstract ideal content, 1:677
  accessory, 8:776
  Alexander of Hales and, 1:653
  Ampère on, 1:138
  Arnauld on, 1:291, 2:57–58
  association of, 1:50, 1:138
  Augustine on, 9:593
  of beauty, 1:513–514
  Berkeley on, 1:574–576, 1:579, 1:586–587, 3:217, 3:302, 8:825, 9:596–597
  Bolzano on, 1:647
  Bonaventure on, 1:653
  Boulainvilliers on, 1:670
  in Buddhist epistemology, 1:754–755
  Campanella on, 2:15
  Campbell on, 2:17
  in Cartesian epistemology, 2:55–57
  Coleridge on, 2:317
  Collier on, 2:323
  common sense and, 2:356
  complex
    Locke on, 5:379–385
    and simple, in content externalism, 9:117
  concept of, 4:553
  concepts and, 2:417
  Condillac on, 8:826
  as conventional *vs.* ultimate truth, 1:742–743
  cosmological model theoretical, 2:561
  Deleuze on, 2:695
  Descartes on, 2:54, 8:124
    vs. judgments, 2:744, 3:291–292
    reality content of, 2:742–743
  Destutt de Tracy on, 2:760–761
  in Dewey's instrumentalism, as law of action, 4:566
  efficacious, 5:666–667
  empiricists on, 3:219
  expressibility of, 2:208–210
  in facts, 9:744
  Foucher on, 2:57, 3:703
  Fouillee on, 3:705
  Gilbert of Poitiers on, 4:88
  and God, 1:580, 4:810
  Hartley on, 8:826
  Hazlitt on, 4:249
  Hegel on, 3:67, 3:68
  Henry of Harclay on, 4:315
  Herbart on, 7:375–376, 8:139
  history of. *See* History, of ideas
  Hume and, 1:50, 2:95, 3:218, 3:303–304, 8:131, 9:598
  idéologues on, 8:788
  as images
    Berkeley on, 9:596–597
    in Locke, 9:594–596
  as indirect perception objects, 1:577
  innate. *See* Innate ideas
  intentionality and existence of, 1:689
  James (William) on, 3:313, 4:782–783
  language stability and dynamic expression and, 2:208–209
  Laromiguière on, 5:201
  Leibniz on, 3:298
  Locke on, 1:200–201, 3:216–217, 3:299, 3:301, 5:377–379, 5:385–387, 5:395, 9:594–596
  in Mādhyamika doctrine, 1:740
  Malebranche on, 2:57, 5:665–666
  Marx on, 3:67, 3:68
  materialist science of, 4:574
  Mead on, 6:80
  as mental phenomena, 1:689
  Mill (James) on, 6:219
  Moore (G. E.) on, 3:314
  object of, 6:116
  Otto on, 7:59–60
  Price on, 8:2
  as private events, 1:586
  proportionate reality in causes of, 4:691
  of reason, 3:752, 5:21
  Reed (T.) on, 3:494–495
  Régis on, 8:300
  Reid on, 8:323–324
  Rosmini-Serbati on, 8:501
  in Russell's theory of truth, 2:543
  Schopenhauer on, 3:311, 8:650, 8:654
  serial, of society, 8:609
  simple
    Locke on, 5:379–380, 5:385
    Price on, 8:2
  social origin of, 9:101–102
  Spinoza on, 3:294–295
  as theological issue, 1:291
  unification in antitheses of, 1:476
  universals and, 1:591, 9:586
  Weber's elective affinity of, 9:102
  Whewell on, 9:744
  See also Concept(s); Thought
Idea de principio en Leibniz y la evolución de la teoría deductiva, La (The Idea of Principle in Leibniz and the Evolution of Deductive Theory) (Ortega y Gasset), 7:47
Idea for a Universal History from a Cosmopolitan Point of View (Kant), 6:514, 7:388–389
Idea of a Christian Society, The (Eliot), 3:185–186
Idea of a Patriot King (Bolingbroke), 1:641
Idea of a University, The (Newman), 6:576, 6:582, 9:240
Idea of History, The (Collingwood), 2:326, 6:270
"Idea of History" (Huizinga), on free will, 3:40
Idea of Nature, The (Collingwood), 2:327
Idea of Principle in Leibniz and the Evolution of Deductive Theory, The (La Idea de principio en Leibniz y la evolución de la teoría deductiva) (Ortega y Gasset), 7:47
Idea of the Holy (Otto), 6:544, 7:59, 8:634–635
Ideal(s)
  of beauty, Winckelmann on, 9:790
  of good, in communism, 2:367
  Herbart on, 7:375
  in human symbolic consciousness, 2:68
  as presupposition in thought, 1:706
Ideal beauty, Cousin on, 2:580
Ideal being, Croce's intuition as, 2:600
Ideal consequentialism, Moore and, 6:352–353
Ideal human, Confucius on, 2:149
Ideal judgments, Mercier on, 6:145
Ideal language(s), 1:561
  Frege on, 5:507
  Russell on, 8:543–545
Ideal limit theories of truth, mind-dependence in, 6:173
Ideal mathematics, 5:544
Ideal name, 8:754
Ideal numbers, 7:637
Ideal observer theory, **4:562–563,** 6:163

"Ideal of Pure Reason, The," 5:22
Ideal type, 9:735
Ideal utilitarianism, 3:439, 9:604
 as normative ethics, 9:607
 Ross on, 8:505
Ideal World, The (Norris), 6:656
Idealism, **4:552–562**
 about universals, conceptualism as, 6:176
 absolute. *See* Absolute idealism
 and act-object distinction, 4:560
 actual, 4:50
  Gentile and, 4:49–53
  Gioberti and, 4:95
  Spirito on, 9:197
 Aliotta and, 1:127
 Anderson (John) and, 1:197–198
 apperception in, 1:234
 Arendt on, 1:254
 Bergson on, 1:565
 Berkeley and, 1:574, 6:192
 Bosanquet and, 1:663
 Boström and, 1:668
 Bradley and, 3:310
 British, 4:286, 9:373
 Brown and, 1:671
 Brunschvicg on, 1:713
 Burthogge on, 1:776
 in Chinese philosophy, 2:238, 5:618
 Christian
  of Stefanini, 9:237
  of Tolstoy, 9:512
 Cohen (Morris) on, 2:306
 coherence theory of truth and, 9:536
 Coleridge and, 2:315
 Collingwood on, 2:325–328
 concrete universal in, 9:289
 constructivism and, 2:475
 continental philosophy and, 2:488
 cosmology of, 6:193–194
 and crisis of skepticism, 9:57–58
 criterion of truth in, 5:120
 critical
  Jacobi (Friedrich Heinrich) and, 4:771
  Kant on, 4:553, 5:10
 critical realism and, 2:595
 Croce on, 2:600
 in Daoism, 2:198
 Dewey and, 3:43–45
 Dummett and, 3:132
 Eddington and, 3:165–166
 Edwards (Jonathan) and, 3:168
 egocentrism in, 6:586
 Eliot (T. S.) on, 3:185
 Engels on, 3:58
 and ethics, 3:414–415
 expression theory of art and, 1:303–304
 failure of, 9:791
 Fouillee and, 3:705
 of freedom, Dilthey on, 3:84
 Genovesi and, 4:49
 German
  German romanticism and, 8:491
  Marx and, 5:730
  and New England transcendentalism, 6:572
 and God, 3:610
 Gödel on, 4:117
 Gogarten and, 4:144
 Green on, 4:178
 Haeckel on, 4:202
 Hegel and. *See* Hegelian idealism
 humanist ethical, 2:697
 Husserl and, 3:312
 immaterialism and, 4:554
 Jacobi (Friedrich Heinrich) and, 4:771
 Kant and, 7:493–494
 Külpe and, 5:160
 Laas on, 5:163–164
 Lenin on, 3:63–64
 logical positivism on, 5:526
 Lotze on, 5:581
 on loyalty, 5:595–596
 Mach and, 5:625
 Malthus and, 5:676
 Marx and, 7:390
 metaphysical, 4:554, 6:170, 6:494
 vs. metaphysical realism, 8:688–689
 mind-body problem in, 7:468
 mind-dependence as, 6:173
 on mind-independence, 9:43
 monistic, 1:713
 Moore (G. E.) and, 3:314, 8:149
 Mou and, 2:222
 Nagel (Ernest) on, 6:473
 Natorp and, 6:490
 vs. naturalism, 6:499
 nature and, 1:672
 in neo-Confucianism, 2:157–158, 2:221–222
 in neo-Kantianism, 2:697
 new realism *vs.*, 6:584
 objective
  Dilthey on, 3:84
  on thought and thinking, 9:420
 optimism/pessimism and, 7:249–250
 parapsychology and, 7:113–114
 Pearson and, 7:160
 Peirce (C. S.) and, 7:164
 on perception, 8:815
 Perry and, 7:203–204
 personalism and, 7:234–235
 pragmatic, 7:748, 8:440
 Rashdall and, 8:238
 realism as polemic against, 8:261–262
 Renan on, 8:428–429
 Royce and, 4:286
 Russell and, 3:315
 Santayana and, 8:599
 Schelling on, 8:617
 Schiller (Ferdinand) and, 8:623
 Schleiermacher on, 8:632
 Schlick on, 8:640–641
 and scientific naturalism, 3:705
 Shelley and, 9:9
 social theory of, 4:559–560
 Spaventa and, 9:160
 speculative
  Creighton on, 2:592
  Gramsci on, 4:169–170
 Stalin on, 3:63
 Stout on, 9:259
 subjective
  Kantian philosophy as, 4:770
  Protagoras and, 8:91
  Schelling on, 8:618
 Taylor (Alfred) and, 9:373
 theory of art in, 4:597
 thought and, 4:561
 transcendental, 4:555–556, 6:573
 Trubetskoi (Sergei) and, 9:532–533
 universal, as speculative egoism, 4:770–771
 in utopianism, 9:616–617
 Vasquez and, 9:649
 voluntaristic, 3:705, 8:520–521
 Wittgenstein on, 9:818
 Wundt and, 9:850
 in Yogācāra Buddhism, 1:745
Idealismus und Positivismus (Laas), 5:163
Idealist school. *See Xin Xue* school
Idealistic positivism, of Vaihinger, 9:625
Ideality, materiality and, intertwining of, 6:150
Idealization
 of properties in cosmological models, 2:560
 scientific theory utility, 1:644
 suspicion of, 3:581
"Ideas" (Schlegel), 8:631
Ideas for a Descriptive and Analytic Psychology (Dilthey), 3:80–81, 3:84, 9:18

Ideas Pertaining to a Pure Phenomenology (Husserl), 9:18
Ideas Which Plato Mentions, On the (Psellus), 7:610
Ideas y creencias ("Ideas and Beliefs") (Ortega y Gasset), 7:47, 8:180
Idee der Staaträson in der neueren Geschichte, Die (Meinecke), 6:113
Idée directrice de la dissolution opposée de l'évolution, L' (Lalande), 5:172
"Idee zu einer allgemeinen Geschichte in Weltburgerlicher Absicht" (Kant), 5:29
Ideen zu einem Versuch, die Grenzen der Wirksamkeit des Staates zu bestimmen (Ideas toward an investigation to determine the proper limits of the activity of the state) (Humboldt), 5:321
Ideen zu einer Philosophie der Natur (Schelling), 1:11, 8:618
Ideen zur Philosophie der Geschichte der Menscheit (Herder), 7:389
Idees-forces, 3:705
Idempotency, definition of, 5:544
Identically false, definition of, 5:544
Identically true, definition of, 5:545
Identicals, indiscernibility of, 4:568
Identification
- correctness of, argument from analogy and, 7:52, 7:53
- cultural, 6:482
- explanation as, 6:212–213
- in film, 7:384
- forming second-order volition, 3:719
- in mental representations, 6:236
- operating within the body, 5:152

"Identification and Wholeheartedness" (Frankfurt), 3:719
Identité et réalité (Meyerson), 6:212
Identity(ies), **4:567–572**
- absolute, as intuitive, 1:704
- absolute dependence in, 8:634–635
- as agent-relative role, 8:710–711
- Aristotle on, 5:232
- art and, 1:300
- Bradley on, 1:679
- Brahman and, 1:683, 8:719
- in Buddhism, 1:757, 6:256
- in Chinese philosophy, 2:204
- in Chisholm's metaphysics, 2:243
- Church's axiomatic treatment of, 2:254
- of classical and quantum particles, 3:636
- cloning and, 4:47
- Crusius on, 2:606
- death and, 2:654
- definition of, 5:545
- denoting, 3:730
- in Dge-lugs, 1:733–734
- of discernibles, Leibniz on, 5:258
- in feminism, 1:158
- Frege on, 3:726, 3:728, 8:800
- Heraclitus on, 5:232
- ideology and, 4:573
- image recognition of, 4:594–595
- in Indian philosophy, 8:719
- of indiscernibles, 5:545
  - in bundle theory of particulars, 6:180
  - McTaggart on, 6:78
- intersectional nodes of, 3:575
- Jevons on, 5:450
- in Latin American philosophy, 5:211–212
- law of, definition of, 5:547
- in Leibniz's calculus, 5:443
- Lewis (D.) on, 5:314
- in linguistic reference, 2:205
- Locke on, 5:379, 5:384
- in Mādhyamika doctrine, 1:741–742
- mindreading and, 9:38
- in Mohist discourse, 2:212–213
- in multiple realizability, 6:429–431
- as narratively constructed, 3:581
- of national state, 9:204–205
- as non-innate idea, 4:693
- numerical
  - persistence and, 7:210
  - personal identity and, 7:220
- as objective content, 8:663
- in ontology of mental moment and act of knowing, 1:753
- over time, persistence and, 7:209–210
- of parents and offspring, 1:785
- of people, 5:38
- perfect, 4:497–498
- personal. *See* Personal identity
- and personhood, 1:463–464
- philosophy of, 7:11
- in postmodernism, 7:730
- proprium and, 8:634
- Ramsey on, 5:468
- reality and, 6:213
- reconstituting politically, 3:606
- reincarnation and, 8:333
- Romero on, 8:492
- Russell's definition of, 5:468
- in Sankhya, 2:112
- Schelling on, 8:620–621
- Scholz on, 8:645
- Schulze on, 8:660
- socially constructed, 3:589
- of societies, 9:96
- Spir on, 9:196–197
- statements of, 4:567, 9:162, 9:287
- and theory of truth, 9:537
- understanding in, 6:112
- Wiggins on, 9:762
- *See also* Law, of identity

"Identity and Predication" (Evans), 3:461
Identity and Spatio-temporal Continuity (Wiggins), 9:762
Identity function, definition of, 5:554
Identity theory
- of the mind, 7:470, 8:155
  - anomalous monism and, 7:470
  - entity education in, 6:172
  - functionalism and, 7:471
  - monism and, 6:326
  - propositional attitudes and, 8:84
  - qualia and, 8:191–192
  - types of, 7:553
- of Schrödinger, 8:658

Ideocracy, principle of, 3:672
Ideologie und Utopie (Manheim), 5:685
Idéologues
- and Bentham, 8:792
- Cabanis and, 2:1
- and Comte, 2:409
- on language, 8:787–790
- Laromiguière and, 5:201
- Maine de Biran and, 5:655–656
- Napoleon and, 2:760–761
- origin of, 2:760
- on signs, 8:788
- on universal grammar, 8:791

Ideology, **4:573–575**
- Destutt de Tracy and, 2:760–761
- Engels on, 3:64
- Manheim on, 5:685–686
- Marx on, 3:64

Ideology and Utopia (Mannheim), 4:574
Ideology of the Aesthetic, The (Eagleton), 1:70
Idiolects, autonomous, 8:753
Idiom(s)
- looking, 1:230
- seeming, 1:230

Idioscopy, branches of, Peirce on, 7:169
Idiot, The (Dostoevsky), 3:100
Idiot de la famille: Gustave Flaubert de 1821 à 1857, L' (Sartre), 8:604
Idle argument, the, 3:6
Idler, The (Johnson, Dr. Samuel), 4:853
Ido, Couturat work on, 2:582
Idolatry, cognitive, 7:484–485

Idols of mind, Bacon (Francis) on, 1:445–446
"Idols of the Market Place" (Bacon), 8:772
Idziak, Janine M., 3:93
If, definition of, 5:545
If and only if symbol, in propositional logic, 3:642
If...then..., 8:358–359
"Ifs and Cans" (Austin), 1:408
in statements of human ability, 3:20
Ignatius of Antioch, on Christ, 7:141
Ignorance
Buddhism and, 1:748, 1:753
conventional truth and, 1:734
explanation of, 5:111
as goal for philosophy, 9:719
learned, knowledge as, 6:595
of native speakers, in attributor contextualism, 2:486–487
prior probabilities and, 9:222
rhetorical teaching and, 1:729
vagueness as, 9:624–625
veil of, Rawls on, 5:323, 8:258
in Yoga, 6:108
in Yogācāra Buddhism, 1:746–747
Ignoratio elenchi fallacy, 3:547–548, 5:543
Ihara, Craig, 2:196
Ihde, Don, 7:544–545
Ihering, Rudolf von, 4:35
Iḥya (al-Ghazālī), 1:119
I-intentionality, 7:299
I-it relationship, and Chan (Zen) Buddhism, 2:167
Ikeda Mitsumasa, and Kumazawa, 5:161
Ikhwān al-Ṣafā', **4:575–577,** 4:756–757
Il gesuita moderno (Gioberti), 4:93
Il XX secolo (Sciacca), 8:666
I-languages, Chomsky on, 5:190
Iliad (Homer)
aesthetic judgment in, 1:41
on death, 5:349
Dikē in, 3:79
Il'in, Ivan Aleksandrovich, **4:577–579**
Il'in: Sobranie sochinenii v desiati tomakh (Il'in, I. A., Collected Works), 4:579
Illative sense, 6:578–579
Illative theory, in combinatory logic, 2:335, 2:338–340
Illicit major fallacy, 3:539
Illicit minor fallacy, 3:539
Illicit process fallacy, definition of, 5:543
Illocution
in Austin (John Langshaw), 1:408–410
in Gricean pragmatics, 7:739
Illocutionary act(s), 7:199
vs. locutionary acts, 7:201
in fictional narratives, 3:627
Illocutionary Acts and Sentence Meaning (Alston), 1:132
Illumination, **4:579–581**
Alexander of Hales on, 1:403
Augustine on, 1:393–395, 8:760
Bacon (Roger) on, 1:403
by God, John of the Cross on, 4:846
Isaac of Stella on, 4:753
Marston on, 5:725
theory of, universals and, 9:593
William of Auvergne on, 1:403
Illumination of Sufism (al-Tusi), 9:303
Illuminationism, **4:581–585,** 6:418
Ikhwān al-Ṣafa' and, 4:576
in Islamic philosophy, 4:760–761
in Sufism, 9:305–306
of Suhrawardī, 9:315
theory of light in, 4:761
Illusion(s), **4:585–590,** 7:177–178, 7:183, 7:187–188
alternating, 7:184
argument from, 1:231–232, 7:189–190, 8:816, 8:820
art and, 1:325–326
in Buddhist epistemology, 1:755
Chrysippus on, 2:251
disjunctivism and, 7:193
film as, 7:384
Gombrich on, 1:325–326
optimistic, 7:250
personal identity and, 7:223
phenomenalism and, 7:274
sensations and, 7:181
truth criteria and Dao, 2:207
Illusionistic school, criterion of truth in, 5:120
"Illustrations of the Dynamical Theory of Gases" (Maxwell), 6:70
Illyricus, Matthias Flacius, 5:439
Image(s), **4:592–596**
abstract, 4:590–592, 8:81–82
as actual picture, 4:594–595
Bergson on, 1:565–566
of body, 1:567
body as, 1:564
in Buddhist epistemology, 1:754–755
Bultmann on, 1:764
Chwistek on, 2:255
concepts and, 2:416
in critical realism, 2:596
Croce on, 2:601
definition of, 5:545
Descartes on, 2:54, 2:744
Gibson on, 1:326
Hume on, 8:131
ideas as
Berkeley on, 9:596–597
in Descartes, 2:54
in Locke, 9:594–596
intelligibility of, 1:326–327
Jungian, 4:857
in literature, 4:596–597
in memory, 1:564
mental, 4:590–592
concepts and, 2:416
propositional attitudes and, 8:81–82
naturalistic, 1:325, 1:326
ontological identity in mental moment, 1:753
outlines in, 1:327
production of, in Plato, 1:41–42
vs. proposition, 8:154
and reality, 1:538
representational nature of, 7:405
Sartre on, 4:594–595, 8:604–605
Schier on, 1:326–327
scientific hypothesized theories as, 1:643–644
semiotics and, 1:327
vs. sensation, 8:131
in thinking, 1:596
of Trinity, 1:652
in Vasubandhu, 1:751–752
Image and Brain (Kosslyn), 4:591, 6:565
Image and Mind (Currie), 7:382
Image and Mind (Kosslyn), 4:590
"Image in Psychological Life: Role and Nature, The" (Sartre), 8:604
Imageless thought, capacity for, 5:161
Image-making powers, phantasia and, 7:271
Imagery
enrichment of perception by, 7:184
mental, **4:590–592**
during hallucination, 4:587–588
in mindreading, 9:38–39
other than visual, 4:595
personal identity and, 7:223–224, 7:227
Imagery Debate (Tye), 4:591
Images of Mind (Posner & Raichle), 6:565
Images or Shadows of Divine Things (Edwards), 3:168

Imaginaire, L' (Sartre), 4:594, 4:598, 8:604
Imaginaire; psychologie (The psychology of imagination) (Sartre), 1:71
Imaginary, The (Sartre), 2:459
Imaginary numbers, 6:671
Imaginary Portraits (Pater), 7:136
Imagination, **4:596–602**
Addison on, 1:22
aesthetics and, 1:50, 4:598
Alison on, 1:128
Aristotle on, 3:286–287
art and, 1:50, 1:341
artistic, 1:306, 4:596–597
Augustine on, 1:392–393
Bachelard on emotions and, 1:440
Bacon on, 1:50
Blake on, 1:610
Brady (Emily) on, 3:255
Burke on, 1:771
Carnap on, 2:40
cognitivism and, 1:341
Coleridge on, 1:55, 2:318, 4:597
Collingwood on, 2:327–328
compound, 1:50
conation in, 9:260
Condillac on, 2:422
Deustua on, 3:42–43
Diderot on, 3:73
dreams and, 3:106
enactive, 9:38–39
vs. fancy, 1:55, 2:318–319, 4:597
as function of the soul, 4:596
Gassendi on, 4:28–29
Goethe on, 4:142
Gottsched on, 4:165
Hazlitt on, 4:248
Hobbes on, 1:50, 4:412–413, 4:592–593
Hume on, 4:496–497, 8:131–132
hypotheses formation, 1:643
in Ibn al-ʿArabī, 4:541
as instrument of knowledge, Descartes on, 2:727, 2:741
vs. intellect, 5:651–652
Kant and, 5:18
language games of, 9:810
Locke on, 1:50
Maimonides on, 4:819, 5:651–652
in mental pretense, 9:38
Mullā Ṣadrā on, 6:419
vs. perception, 1:393
in perception of time, 9:491–492
pleasures of, 1:22
of prophets
Maimonides on, 4:819
Spinoza on, 4:825
qualities in, 1:22
reality and, 1:341
recreative, 4:600
in revealing truth, 4:597–598
in romanticism, 1:55
Ryle on, 4:597
Santayana on, 8:597–598
Sartre on, 1:71, 8:604–606
vs. sense, 8:131
sensory, 4:600
as sole cognitive power, 1:711
Spinoza on, 4:825, 9:174
suppositional, 9:38–39
and taste, 4:65
in thought experiments, 9:452–455
in utopianism, 9:619
Walton on, 1:328–329
will and, 8:619–620
world in, 4:496–497
Imagination (Furlong), 4:598
"Imagination of the Poet: Elements for a Poetics, The" (Dilthey), 3:81
Imaginative engagement, value of, 5:370
Imaginative variation, in phenomenology, 7:285–287
Imagism, on thought and thinking, 9:421
Iman, and belief in God's existence, 3:536
Imitation
Aristotle on, 1:43–44, 1:188, 4:599
art as, 1:75–76, 1:297, 1:490
Descartes on, 1:324–325
of God, 5:652–653
in *Iliad,* 1:41
imagination and, 4:599
Moritz on, 6:406
of nature, 1:490
in pictorial representation, 9:69
Plato on, 1:41–42, 1:187, 1:303, 1:324–325
synonyms for, 1:42
Turing test and, 5:633
of universals, 1:44
Imitation of Christ (unknown), 9:423–424
Imitationism, 5:145
Immaculate conception, 8:704
Immanence
in conception of God, 4:107–108
of consciousness, 8:662
Deleuze on, 2:694
Gentile on, 4:50
of properties, 8:67
Rilke on, 8:477–478
Romero on, 8:492
Sartre on, 8:606
Tillich on, 4:108
Immanentism, of Lessing, 5:296–297
Immaterialism, 4:554
Berkeley and, 1:574, 1:583, 8:781
in Germany, 4:555
Immediacy
Dewey on, 3:46
Nishida on, 6:625
in sense-datum theory, 8:819
Immediate inference
by conversion of propositions, 5:496
definition of, 5:545
Immediate knowledge
of truths, 5:97
types of, 3:752
Immediate metaphysical cognition, 3:752
Immerman, Karl Leberecht, Gadamer on, 4:3
Immorality, 9:833–834. *See also* Evil; Morality
Immortalitate Animae, De (Pomponazzi), 7:681–684
Immortality, **4:602–619**
agent intellect and, 1:91
al-Fārābī, Abū al Naṣr on, 4:619
al-Kindī, Abu-Yusuf Yaqūb ibn Isḥāq on, 4:618–619
in antirealism, 4:617
arguments against, 4:615
Aristotle on, 1:274, 4:602, 4:608–609
Averroes on, 1:424, 4:619, 4:744
Avicenna on, 4:619
Cartesianism on, 4:611–612, 9:187
Christianity and, 4:618, 9:374
desire as argument for, 4:614
Ducasse on, 4:613
Duns Scotus on, 3:141
of ego, in Iqbal's theistic pluralism, 4:744
Empedocles on, 3:210–213
eternity in, 4:609
and existence of God, 4:613–614
Fechner on, 3:556
Ficino on, 3:622–623
Gibbon on, 4:85
human existence and, 3:622
in Indian philosophy, 5:327
interior objectivity and, 8:666
in Islam, 4:619, 6:558
Judaism on, 4:618
Kant on, 4:612–614, 4:669
Maimonides on, 4:618
Malthus on, 5:676

Immortality, ***continued***
materialism and, 8:7
McTaggart on, 4:613, 6:77–78
Mendelssohn (Moses) on, 4:618, 6:131
Mill (John Stuart) on, 6:230–231
moral arguments for, 4:613–614
as moral duty, 4:745
and morality, 4:613–614, 8:13
Nietzsche on, 4:744
parapsychology and, 4:612, 7:115–116
personal, eternity in, 4:609
personal identity and, 7:214–215
Plato on, 7:634
Pomponazzi on, 1:91
Pringle-Pattison on, 8:13
and punishment, 4:603, 4:612–613
question of, brain in, 4:617
in Qur'an, 6:558
Radishchev on, 8:230–231
reincarnation and, 4:617
religious view of, 4:618–619
Russell (Bertrand) on, 4:615, 8:559–560
śatapatha Brāhmaṇa on, 5:327
shadow-man doctrine of, 4:603
Sidgwick on, 4:614
Smith (John) on, 9:70
in socinianism, 9:99
Socrates on, 4:602
of soul, 1:105, 1:274, 2:654, 4:602, 9:429
Aristotle on, 1:274
Dostoevsky on, 3:99
Meier on, 6:112
Mendelssohn on, 6:131
Mill (John Stuart) on, 6:230–231
More (Henry) on, 6:396
Norris on, 6:656
Plato on, 4:602, 4:608, 6:258
Smith (John) on, 9:70
Spinoza on, 9:174
Taylor (Alfred) on, 9:374
Tolstoy on, 9:512
Unamuno on, 9:567–568
"unnatural" desire for, 5:78
See also Soul, immortality of
"Immortality" (Hume), 4:614
Immunity, from error, 5:106
Impact phenomena, matter and, 6:3
Impanation, 4:842
Impartiality, **4:619–621**
Cheng Hao on, 2:144
Daoism on, 2:187
equality as, 3:334
in ideal observer theories, 4:562–563
legal, 7:455
in Mohist ethics, 2:197
in moral principles, 6:374
Impenetrability, Ostwald on, 7:49
Impenetrable boundaries *(Grenzsituationen),* Jaspers on, 4:801
Imperative(s)
"can" and ought and, 2:25–26
categorical, 2:69–72
Kant on, 3:154, 5:24–25
Imperative theory of law, legal positivism and, 5:237
Imperfect figures, definition of, 5:545
Imperfection, of world, 1:361
Imperialism
African philosophy and, 1:85–86
moral, ethical relativism and, 3:372
Sidgwick on, 9:26
Imperialism, the Highest Stage of Capitalism (Lenin), 5:280
Impermanence
of existence, 6:621
in ontology of nirvāṇa, 6:622
Vasubandhu on, 9:651
Impersonal, in ethics, Williams (Bernard) on, 9:787
Impersonal "itness," Heidegger on, 3:717
Impersonality, objectivity as, 7:4
Impetus, **4:621–622,** 6:9
Impiété des déistes, athées et libertins de ce temps, L' (The Impiety of the Deists, Atheists, and Libertines of Our Time) (Mersenne), 2:725, 6:152
Implication
contextual, 7:765–769
definition of, 5:545
different degrees of, 5:56
explicit *vs.* implicit, 7:766
formal, 8:550–551
law of, 6:528
material, 3:642, 5:545, 8:548–549
Peirce on, 5:454
Implicature, 3:253
conventional, 6:651–652
conversational, 2:525–528
in pragmatics, 7:739
Implicit definition, 1:167, 5:545, 6:312–313
"Importance of What We Care About, The" (Frankfurt), 3:719
Impossibilia, 6:172
Impossibility
absolute, 7:262–263
appearance and, 1:232
in existentialism, 1:1–2
in nature *vs.* mathematics, 1:541–542
as non-innate idea, 4:693
in ontology, 7:23
Parmenides on, 1:232
in possible world counterfactual conditionals, 2:428
in private language problem, 8:14–15
and separability *vs.* inseparability, 1:627–628
in syllogisms, 1:627–628
"Impossibility of a Paretian Liberal, The" (Sen), 8:810
Impossible objects, 6:115
Impossible state of affairs, 7:262–263
Impossible worlds, in relevant logic, 5:488
Impredicative definition, 5:534, 5:545
Impredicative methods, necessity of, 8:456
Impredicative systems, 8:56
Impressions
Carneades on, 2:47–48
Hume on, 3:218, 3:303, 8:131
in intrinsic theory of consciousness, 2:453
Maine de Biran on, 5:655–657
Mill (James) on, 6:219
in Stoicism, 1:194, 1:247
Improvement, Enlightenment and, 3:247
Improvement of the Moral Qualities, The (Ibn Gabirol), 4:545
Improvisation, in animals, 1:522
Impulse, 3:688
"In," Boethius' use of, 6:101
In Advance of a Broken Arm (Duchamp), 1:299, 1:310
In Boethium de Hebdomadibus (Aquinas), on God's goodness, 4:111
In Defense of Reason (Paton), 9:483
In Harm's Way: Essays in Honor of Joel Feinberg, 3:562
In Job's Balances (Shestov), 9:12
In Metaphysica (Simplicius), 9:35
In My Father's House (Appiah), 1:86
In rebus realism, about universals, 6:179
In Stahlgewittern (Jünger), 4:859
In Topica Ciceronis (Boethius), 5:422
In vitro fertilization, 7:525
Inaccuracy, in conscious qualitative states, 2:451
Inalienable rights, Ockham on, 9:783–784

"Inaugural Address of the Working Men's International Association, September 28, 1864" (Marx), 2:362
Inaugural dissertation, of Kant, 5:11–12
Incan philosophy, 5:204
Incarnation
  Celsus on, 2:119
  of Christ, 4:88
  Christian beliefs on, 2:246–247
  as contrary to rational evidence, 3:631
  Kierkegaard on, 3:533
  Marcel on, 5:701
  patristic philosophy and, 7:142
  Plotinus on, 7:635
  theory of substance and, 9:296
"Incipit Vita Nova" (Korn), 5:142
Inclusion
  appearance and reality and, 6:79
  definition of, 5:545
Inclusion *(sambhava),* as means of knowledge, 5:117
Inclusive legal positivism, 5:241–243
Incoherence, of intentional acts, 7:292–293
Incoherence of Incoherence, The (Averroes), 1:422
Incoherence of the Philosophers, The (al-Ghazālī), 1:422, 3:23, 4:758, 9:304
Income distribution, bourgeois right principle and, 2:362
Incommensurability
  criticism of, 8:696–697
  in Greek geometry, 2:492
  Kuhn on, 8:695–697
  mathematics and, 7:35
  vs. moral disagreement, 6:161–162
  as shifts-in-standards, 8:697–698
Incommensurable world, accompanying paradigm shift, 5:159
Incompatibility, in negation, 6:525–526
Incompatible manuals of translation, 8:217–218
Incompetent patients, and euthanasia, 3:456–458
Incomplete object, 6:115
Incompleteness
  in computability theory, 2:382–384
  Friedman on, 5:484
  metalanguages and, 2:42
  in quantum theory, 1:630
Incompleteness theorems, 4:116, 8:456
Incongruity theories of humor, 4:516–517
Inconsistency
  confirmation theory and, 2:434
  in discourse, 3:546
  Frege on, 3:731
  in illative combinatory logic, 2:339
  vs. impartiality, 4:619
  Kierkegaard on, 5:64
  Vaihinger on, 9:625
Inconsistent, definition of, 5:545
Incontinence, ethical determinism and, 3:5
Incorporationalism. *See* Inclusive legal positivism
Incorporeal things, reality of, 3:622
Incorporeality, of existents, 6:120
Incorrigibility
  Aristotle on, 8:824
  certainty and, 5:97
  conditions implying, 3:103
  Epicurus on, 8:824
Incorrigible belief, doubting, 5:97
Incorrigible statements, 5:93
Indecidability, of first-order predicate logic, 2:254
Indefinability, of knowledge, 5:94
Indefinite dyad, in Aristotle, 3:189
Indefinite propositions, definition of, 5:553
Indemonstrables
  definition of, 5:545
  in Stoic logic, 5:406–407
Independence
  of axioms, 5:461–462
  definition of, 5:545
  feminism and, 3:599
  of immanent, 7:204
  logical, of properties under inductive probability, 2:439
  Łukasiewicz on, 5:607
  mathematical, Tarski on, 9:366–368
  of objects, Berkeley on, 1:585
  in probability, 8:25–26
  Proudhon on, 8:94
  realist theory of, 6:331
  Schröder on, 5:462
  of substance, in ontology of substance, 7:24
Independence axiom, in subjective expected utility, 2:658–660
Independence-friendly logic, 8:198
Indeterminacy
  in Buddhist epistemology, 1:755
  in causal relations, 2:106
  of chance and credence, 2:128–129
  in Chinese room argument, 2:241
  Chisholm on, 2:243
  of colors, 2:332–333
  in Daoism, 2:198
  of expressions, 3:541–542
  human ambivalence and, 5:110
  in law, 7:464
  in legal theory, 7:450
  in Mādhyamika doctrine, 1:740–743
  Nash equilibrium and, 4:16–17
  Pyrrho on, 8:174
  in quantum theory, 1:539–542, 2:106
  of translation, 8:217
Indeterminism
  implications of, 3:33–34
  of local theories, 6:641
  as metalinguistic term, 6:478
  moral responsibility and, 8:447–448
  Naṣīr al-Dīn al-Ṭūsị on, 6:478
  in quantum theory, 6:474
  Renouvier on, 8:431
  time and, 9:471
  universal, human freedom as, 4:784–785
  See also Chance; Determinism
Indeterministic transitions, in wave functions, 8:210
Index, 5:453
Index librorum prohibitorum. See Index of prohibited books
Index of prohibited books
  Dante on, 2:625
  Laberthonnière on, 5:164
  Loisy on, 5:571
Index scolastico-cartésien (Gilson), 4:91
Indexicals, **4:622–623**
  agent-relative knowledge as, 8:710
  directly referential, 5:39, 8:746
  linguistic meaning *vs.* content of, 2:705
  perspectival character of, 9:292
  pure, 2:705
  self-knowledge as, 8:709
  semantic paradoxes and, 5:518
  semantics for, 2:707
  of time, 9:462–463
  variable contents *vs.* stable characters of, 5:39
  See also Demonstratives
India
  Dalit theology in, 5:331–332
  mysticism of, 6:442–445
  nirvāṇa concept in, 6:620
  religious pessimism in, 7:246
  Sufism in, 9:310–311
  suicide in, 9:320
  terrorism in, 9:395
  wisdom literature of, 9:793

Indian philosophy, **4:623–634**
absence in, 6:530–532
actual entities in, 4:627
atomic theory in, **1:380–383**
atomism and, 1:381–382
beginninglessness in, 4:625
bhakti period in, 4:624
and Boström, 1:668
Brahman and, 1:681–684
Cairns and, 2:5
causality in, 2:109–113
certification in, 9:545
consciousness in, 9:542
debate in, 4:627
Deussen on, 3:41
Dvaita, 4:630
emptiness in, 6:471
epistemology in, 9:544–545
eschatology in, 3:347
eternity in, 3:359
on fallacies, 9:544–545
God/Isvara in, 4:132–135
Hare Krishna movement in, 4:630
heterodox schools of, 6:254
on human nature, 5:359
inference in, 5:412–414, 6:532
knowledge in, 5:115–123, 7:413
knowledge *vs.* action in, 4:629
literature in, 4:623–624
logic in. *See* Logic, in Indian philosophy
and medieval Jewish philosophy, 4:812
mereology in, 1:381
modern period in, 4:624
negation in, **6:530–533**
nonexistence in, 6:531
Pantheism in, 7:94–95
perception in, 6:254, 6:532–533, 7:413, 9:543
philosophy of language in, 7:412–417
realism in, 9:543
referentialism in, 9:544
reincarnation in, 8:331–332
religion in, 4:624
Śaiva, 4:631
Schlegel on, 8:631–632
Schopenhauer and, 8:655
soul in, 6:254
Steiner and, 9:241
sutras of, 4:624
testimony in, 9:544–545
truth in, **9:542–546**
universe in, 9:380
Indian Question, Las Casas on, 5:205
Indicative sentences
conditionals in, 2:424–426
in first-order logic, 3:646
Indicator states, of experimental apparatus, 8:208
Indifference
objective plausibility and, 1:500
probability and, 8:28, 8:31–32
vs. toleration, 9:507
Indifference principle, probability theory paradoxes of, 2:436
Indigenous peoples
rights of, Las Casas on, 5:205
societies of, ecofeminism on, 3:260
Indirect evidence, 6:116–117
Indirect passions, 4:505–506
Indirect proof. *See Reductio ad absurdum*
Indirect realism, 6:124, 8:265–268. *See also* Realism
Indirect reduction, definition of, 5:555
Indirect speech acts, 7:405–406
Indirect utilitarianism, 7:459–460
Indiscernibility equivalence relation, in measurement, 6:88
Indiscernibility of identicals, 6:173–174
Indiscernible(s)
absolute, 4:569
identity of, 4:568–569, 5:545. *See also* Identity
Indispensability, of mathematics, 6:677–678
Individual(s)
Aristotle on, 6:186–187
Bradley on, 1:676
categorical imperative and, 2:71
in clinical psychology, 1:597–598
Cohen (Hermann) on, 4:828
communism and, 2:362
in community
in Milton's ethics, 6:250
Oakeshott on, 7:2
as concrete, 1:662, 9:777
in Confucianism, 2:150–151, 2:442
conservatism and, 2:468–469
corporations as, 1:778–779
existentialism and, 1:597–598, 3:501–502
Garve on, 4:24
in German romanticism, 8:617
God as, 1:216
in group, 6:81
Hazlitt on, 4:248
Hebbel on, 4:253–254
Hemsterhuis on, 4:311
as heroes, and hero worship, 2:34
Hume on, 4:497–499
idealist view of, 4:560
as judicanda of justice, 4:863
Kierkegaard on, 3:501, 5:67
Mill (John Stuart) on, 6:229
in moral cosmopolitanism, 2:568
Ockham on, 9:777
vs. person, 5:715
power of, computer access and, 2:397
rational economic behavior and, 1:777
and reproductive cloning, 4:47–48
Ritschl on, 8:481
social action and, 9:95
in social contract, 9:79
social functions and, 1:662
in state, 6:481
style and, 1:331
Unamuno on, 9:566
vs. universals, in moderate realism, 9:773
Williams (Bernard) on, 9:787
Zhuangzi on, 9:881–882
"Individual and Collective Representations" (Durkheim), 3:150
Individual and Society (Eucken), 3:452
Individual autonomy
Kareev on, 5:40
sphere of, 3:582
Individual constant symbols. *See* Constant(s)
Individual decision theory, 2:655
Individual (particular), definition of, 5:545
Individual psychology, 1:24, 8:146
Individual rights
communitarianism and, 2:369
contractualist view of, 3:386
as counterutilitarian norm, 3:383–384
Hume on, 3:384
in Kantian contractualism, 3:385–386
in libertarianism, 9:72–73
Locke on, 4:190
rule-utilitarian view of, 3:384
and state sovereignty, 9:146
Individualism
Adorno on, 1:26
and anarchism, 1:178
anthroposophy and, 9:242
in Chomsky's linguistics, 2:245
and communism, 2:364
communitarianism and, 2:369
in Confucian ethics, 2:196–197
content, 8:82–83
in Cynic teaching, 2:616
discrediting of, 4:559–660
in French Revolution, 9:520

group phenomena in, 6:481
illusion of, 1:26
Lunacharskii on, 5:611
methodological, 4:442–443
Mill (John Stuart) on, 9:510
moral cosmopolitanism and, 2:568
vs. neoromantic universalism, 9:158
refinements of, 4:443–444
in Reformation, 8:297
rise of, 7:323–324
Ruskin on, 8:534
Santayana on, 8:600
social, critics of, 4:558
social contract and, 9:80
social science methodology and, 7:535–536
Stirner on, 9:250–251
Tagore on, 9:364
Thoreau on, 9:451
Treschow and, 9:526
See also Holism
"Individualism and the Mental" (Burge), 8:83
Individuality, 3:723
education and, 7:373
of ethical personalism, 1:538
and evil, 9:124
Heidegger on, 2:653
introspection in, 6:81
Kant on, 7:373
of man, 7:321
matter in, 6:189
Matthew of Aquasparta on, 6:65
Meinecke on, 6:114
Mill (John Stuart) on, 6:227–228
Schuppe on, 8:663
social subordination and, 1:538
of substance, in ontology, 7:23–24
Individuals (Strawson), 2:79, 9:138, 9:265
Individuals: An Essay in Descriptive Metaphysics (Strawson), 6:197–198
Individuated concepts, 5:89
Individuation
action and, 1:14–15
of art, 1:319–320
Cartwright on, 6:663–664
Duns Scotus on, 3:139, 6:102–103, 8:704
intuition and, 1:320
Jung on, 9:573
Peter Aureol on, 7:257
positive difference and, 3:681–682
of propositions, 8:89
vs. reidentification, 7:213–214
Suárez on, 9:283
Thomas of York on, 9:443
as universal, 9:584
Individuum und Gemeinschaft (Stein), 9:240
Indivisibility, of substance, in ontology, 7:23–24
Indoctrination
common consent arguments for God's existence and, 2:348
in education, 7:357–358
Indologìa (Indology) (Vasconcellos), 5:208
Indra, in Indian theology, 7:94
Indubitability, 3:102–104
Induction, **4:635–650**, 9:744
agreement methods of, 6:224, 6:238–243
concomitant variation analogue of, 6:244–245
field concept for, 6:245
illustration of, 6:237–238
negative, 6:240–242
positive, 6:239–242
use of, 6:246–247
ampliative, 6:244
arguments in, types of, 4:635
backward, in game theory, 4:18
Bacon (Francis) on, 1:445–451
bar, 4:741
Barbara on, 5:501
in Bayesian confirmation, 1:498–499
Bonaventure on, 1:653
Bosanquet and, 1:662
Bradley on, 1:676
in Buddhist epistemology, 1:757
Carnap on, 4:642–643, 8:28–29, 8:594
circularity in, 4:640
in cosmological argument for God's existence, 2:585–586
cosmological models and, 2:562
as criterion for demarcation, 8:670
vs. deduction, 4:638
definition by, 3:648
definition of, 5:545–546
eliminative methods and, 1:445–450, 6:245
epistemology and, 3:276
evident presumption in, 6:117
fallacies in, 3:543
as formal, 5:501
frame problem solution and, 3:711
Goodman on, 4:154–155
Hamilton on, 2:357
history of, 4:635
Hume on, 3:711, 4:637
hypothetico-deduction method and, 4:639
innateness of ideas and, 4:693
in intuitionistic logic, 2:503
intuitive, 1:243, 9:592–593
and true knowledge, 5:95
of universals, 9:592–593
Jevons on, 4:808
justification and, 1:447, 1:686, 4:636
Keynes on, 5:56–57
Lachelier on, 5:169–170
laws of nature and, 5:229–230
in legal theory, 7:448–449
linguistic approach to, 4:645–646
Locke on, 4:638
mathematical, 4:635, 5:546, 9:270
in metaphysics, 6:204–205, 6:210–211
method of elimination, 1:446
Mill (James) on, 6:219
Mill (John Stuart) on, 2:106, 6:222–224
Ockham on, 9:778
paradigm-case argument and, 7:107–108
Peirce on, 1:653, 4:644
pessimistic, 8:692
Popper on, 4:640
problem of, special case of, 3:708
proportional, 4:635
regularity (Humean) theorists on, 5:225
Royer-Collard on, 8:524
Russell on, 3:316
Salmon on, 8:593, 8:594
in science, 6:209, 8:682–688
scientific *vs.* logical, 9:744
straight rule of, 8:594
Strawson on, 9:265
syllogistic major and, 5:501–502
in traditional logic, 5:500
transfinite, 4:741, 5:558
of universals, 9:592–593
untrustworthiness of, 5:96
Whately on, 9:743
Whewell on, 9:743, 9:744
"Induction and Probability" (Broad), 1:698–699
Induction axiom, 3:650, 8:455
Inductive clause, of inductive definition, 3:647
Inductive consequences, Hempel on, 4:308
Inductive fallacies, 3:544
Inductive logic
definition of, 5:547
Hempel on, 4:308

Inductive probability, confirmation theory and, 2:435
Inductive (recursive) definition, 3:647, 5:540
Inductive set, definition of, 5:543
Inductive underdetermination, 9:575–576
Industrial capitalism, Ruskin on, 8:534–535
Industrial revolution, Pascal and, 7:129
Industrialization
  free law and, 7:426
  Gehlen on, 4:36
  Leont'ev on, 5:283
  nihilism and, 6:618–619
  Saint-Simon on, 8:590–591
  and socialism, 9:87
Industrie, L' (journal), 8:589
Inequality(ies)
  affirmative action and, 1:82
  Bell's, 6:641–642
  Hayek on, 9:72
  Spann on, 9:159
  for women in the sciences, 3:591
Inequality of Human Races, The (Gobineau), 4:106
Inertia
  Descartes on, 9:154
  God and, 9:172
  Kant on, 6:3
  mass in, 6:2
  in Newtonian dynamics, 9:148, 9:155
  principle of, as conservation principle, 2:462
  See also Mass
Inertial frames, and laws of classical mechanics, 2:280–281
Inertial mass, 6:4
Inevident assent, John of Mirecourt on, 4:841
Inevitability
  historical, 3:35–38
  and moral responsibility, 3:719
Inexcusable actions, 6:118
Inexpressibility
  Brahman meaning of, 1:682
  philosophers and, 4:730–731
Infallibility
  of belief
    in attributor contextualism, 2:485
    in noninferential foundationalism, 2:277
  causal sufficiency and, 2:277
  divine, analysis of, 3:694
  See also Papal infallibility
Infancy, prolonged, 3:667
Infant(s)
  emotion in, 3:199
  as persons, 7:238–242
Infantile episodes, 3:743
Inference
  a priori facts and, 1:677
  Abelard on, 1:628, 5:425–426
  Akaike Information Criterion for, 8:685
  in axiomatization, 6:23
  Bayesian theory of, 8:30
  and belief, 9:684
  to the best explanation, **4:651–652**
    as antiskeptical strategy, 9:44
    no-miracles argument of, 8:691
  Boethius on, 5:422–423
  Bosanquet on, 1:661
  in Buddhism, 1:753, 1:756, 4:633
  Carroll on, 5:452
  causal, 2:107, 8:685–687
  in cognitive psychology, 8:152
  in coherentism, 2:315
  in computability theory, 2:383
  concepts and, 2:415
  in conceptual role semantics, 2:479
  conclusions of, testing, 7:53
  by conversion of propositions, 5:496
  De Morgan on, 5:449
  definition of, 5:546
  demonstrative and nondemonstrative, 5:56
  in Dge-lugs Mādhyamika, 1:732
  empiricism and, 9:23
  of existence, Nicolas of Autrecourt on, 6:600
  Frege on, 2:400, 3:726, 5:507
  and fuzzy connectives, 3:767
  of God, 6:580–581
  Goodman on, 4:154–155
  Hamilton on, 5:448
  in hypotheses, 4:639
  illative sense and, 6:578–579
  immediate, definition of, 5:545
  in Indian philosophy, 5:412–414, 6:532
  indicative conditionals and, 2:423, 2:426
  inductive, 4:635, 4:646, 5:501, 8:682. *See also* Inference, to the best explanation
    Bayesian, 9:220
    justification of, 1:698–699
    straight rule of, 8:594
  informal omission of, 5:500
  intentionality and, 7:291
  in intuitionist logic, 5:488
  Jevons on, 4:807–808, 5:451
  justified belief and, 2:275–276
  logical construction substituted for, 2:39
  in many-valued logic, 5:690
  materialism and, 6:16
  McCosh on, 6:70–71
  McTaggart on, 6:78
  as means of knowledge, 5:117
  mediate, definition of, 5:548
  in medieval logic, 5:422–423
  in methodological behaviorism, 9:61
  Mill (John Stuart) on, 6:222, 6:225
  in Mohist discourse, 2:212–213
  myth of the given and, 8:733–734
  Newman (John Henry) on, 6:577, 6:580
  Newton on, 6:592–593
  of nirvāṇa, 6:622
  no-miracle argument of, 8:691
  as non-monotonic, 5:490
  optimality theorem, 9:221–222
  in other minds problem, 7:468
  paraconsistent logics and, 5:483
  Peirce on, 5:453, 5:454–455, 7:164
  from phenomena, 8:684
  in possible world counterfactual conditionals, 2:428
  pragmatic, 7:740
  rules of, 3:726, 5:93, 5:109, 5:448, 5:507, 5:511, 6:222
  Salmon on, 8:593–594
  in scientific method, 8:682–688, 8:700
  "seeing" and, in Gestalt theory, 4:74–75
  sense in, 8:830
  as source of knowledge, 4:812
  in Stoic logic, 9:255
  by subalteration elimination, 5:504
  syllogism and, 5:502
  syllogistic, 5:499
  unconscious, 4:726–727
  universals and, 1:676–677
  valid, definition of, 5:559
Inference *(anumana),* 5:117
Inferiority, in Adler, 8:106
Inferno (Dante), 2:626
Infertility, 7:466
Infimae species, 5:537
Infini mathématique L' (Coutuart), 2:581
Infinitary proof theory, 8:55–56
Infinite
  absolute, Aristotle's denial of, 4:656

actual, 4:655–657
definition of, 5:533
vs. potential, 4:655–656, 9:874
as aesthetic principle, Cousin on, 2:580
Collier on, 2:323
Crescas on, 2:594, 4:822–823
and definite, argument of both, 9:873–874
Hegel on, 4:265
traversing, *kalām* argument on God's existence and, 2:554
See also Infinity
Infinite aggregates, 4:186–187
Infinite classes, Ramsey on, 5:468
Infinite degrees of freedom, 3:635
Infinite divisibility, 1:181, 4:493. *See also* Infinity, in mathematics and logic
Infinite propositions, 5:553
Infinite regress, 1:757, 3:271–272, 5:109, 5:122
kalām argument on God's existence and, 2:554
Infinite sets
Cantor on, 5:463
and real numbers, 5:515
Skolem on, 5:471
Infinite totality, Intuitionist logic and, 5:469
Infinitesimal deferential geometry, Lawver's theory of, 2:509
Infinitesimal magnitudes, in Euclid, 2:492
Infinitesimals, 2:494, **4:652–653**
Cantor-Dedekind theory and, 2:490
Lawvere's differential geometry of, 2:509
in mathematics, 2:495
as numerical entities, 6:671
Peirce on, 2:501
in potentially/actually infinite distinction, 4:656
Robinson on, 5:481–482
in synthetic differential geometry, 2:509–510
Weierstrass on, 6:671
Infinitism, 8:179
Infinity
apeiron/peras and, 1:225
Aristotle and, 2:491
in art, 1:771
Avicenna on, 1:433
axiom of, 5:546–547, 9:557
Couturat on, 2:581
in dichotomy paradox, 9:874
of existents, 6:120
God and, 4:110, 4:822
John of Damascus on, 4:837
Nicholas of Cusa on, 6:595–596
Grosseteste on, 4:186–187
Hegel on, 1:12
Hilbert on, 5:470
Kant on, in first antinomy, 9:467
Levinas on, 5:304
Locke on, 5:382
in mathematics and logic, **4:654–667**
potentially/actually infinite distinction, 4:655–656
set theory and, 4:657, 9:366
supertask, 4:666
in Zeno's paradoxes on motion, 4:654–655
in metamathematics, 4:121
Naṣīr al-Dīn al-Ṭūsị on, 6:478–479
nature and, 6:521
Nicholas of Cusa on, 6:595
number theory and, 1:700
probability and, 8:33–34
Ramified Theory and, 9:557
Solger on, 9:114
in theology and metaphysics, **4:668–671**
time and, 9:466–467
Tolstoy on, 9:512
types of, 9:466–467
Zeno's paradox on, 5:514
See also Infinite
Inflation, Jung on, 4:857
Influence
power and, 7:733–734
in Schutz's mundane phenomenology, 8:664
Influence of Habit of the Faculty of Thinking, The (Maine de Biran), 5:656
Influx, Wolff on, 9:826
Informal fallacies, 3:537, 3:541–543
Informal reasoning, Newman (John Henry) on, 6:577
Information
in computationalism, 2:393
computer ethics and, 2:396
computing machine development and, 2:407
concepts and, 2:416, 2:419
Evans on, 3:461
identity in, 4:567
in indicative conditionals sentences, 2:426
in language, 9:597
mental content and, 2:480
in paraconsistent logic, 5:489
in physical states, 2:105
quantum computing and, 2:407
in social welfare judgment, 8:810
as source of knowledge, 3:108, 4:812
Information loss paradox, black holes and, 1:609
Information processing, by neural networks, 2:443–444
Information technology, non-classical logic and, 5:483
Information theory, **4:671–679**
entropy and, 9:469–470
genetics and, 7:344–345
Information Theory and Statistics (Kullback), 4:672
Informational causation, 3:108–109
Informational semantics, 4:711
Information-friendly logic, 8:198
Informed consent, 3:456, **4:679–680**
engineering ethics and, 3:241
in genetic and reproductive issues, 4:43
in medical ethics, 6:97
medico-jurisprudence on, 6:95
in practice of law, **4:680–682**
technology and, 7:545–546
Ingarden, Roman, **4:682–685**
on literature, 1:59
Scheler and, 8:616
Inge, William Ralph, **4:685–686**
Ingenieros, José, **4:686,** 5:207
Ingersoll, Robert, deism and, 2:691
Ingredient, in Cleanthes, 6:146
Inherence
of properties, 7:25
of universals
in Nyāya-Vaiśeka realism, 9:583–584
Western realism and, 9:587
Inherent value, 9:637
Inheritance, 6:72–73, 7:338
Inheritance (Saadya), 8:585
Inheritance networks, 6:642–643
Inhibitions, Symptoms, and Anxieties (Freud), 8:105
Initial conditions, in chaos theory, 2:131
Initial ordinal, definition of, 5:546
Initiation, in Orphism, 7:43
Initiative, spiritual, 6:217
Injury, power and, 7:732
Injustice
morality and, 4:866
potential costs of, 3:684
victimless, 4:864
Innate disposition to goodness, Mencius on, 2:233

Innate ideas, **4:686–689**
vs. axioms, 1:595
common consent arguments for God's existence and, 2:345
in Confucianism, 2:196
Culverwell on, 2:613
Descartes on, 2:54, 2:56
of geometry in vision, 1:575
of God, in Calvin, 2:9
Leibniz on, 3:298, 4:565, 5:260–262
Locke (John) on, 3:216, 3:298–299, 3:407, 5:377–378
nativism and, **4:690–696**
Plato on, 5:261
in rationalism, 8:240–243
Innate knowledge, in Chinese philosophy, 2:221–222
Innate principles, 8:241–242
Innateness, of concepts, 2:416–417
Inner psychophysics, 3:555
"Inner Sense" (Shoemaker), 9:15
Inner senses, **4:696–697**
consciousness and, 2:453
Croce on, 2:600
higher-order consciousness and, 2:454
Inner voice, conscience as, 2:447
Inner Word, 3:712, 3:713
Innocent VIII, Pope, Pico della Mirandola and, 7:570
Innocents
vs. noncombatants, in just war theory, 4:872
punishment of, 8:161–162
act utilitarianism on, 9:612
rule utilitarian on, 9:606, 9:613
Innovation, creative process and, 2:590
Inputs, characterizing, 3:761
Inquiries into Human Faculty and Its Development (Galton), 4:593
Inquiry
Dewey on, 3:46–48, 7:746
dialectic, 1:192–193
as experiential and experimental, 3:566
goodness of, improving, 3:566
historical, nature of, 7:398
knowledge as, 1:192
limits to, in Schopenhauer, 8:650
Peirce on, 3:48, 7:166–173
pragmatism and, 7:744–746
in skepticism, 1:191–192
in social epistemology, 9:84
in Socratic dialogues, 9:108
values in, 3:576
Inquiry concerning Beauty, Order, Harmony, and Design (Hutcheson), 1:51
Inquiry concerning Political Justice (Godwin), 2:316
Inquiry concerning the Distinctness of the Principles of Natural Theology and Morality (Kant), 2:69
Inquiry concerning Virtue and Merit (Shaftesbury), 3:71, 9:2
Inquiry into Goodness (Yuan shan) (Dai Zhen), 2:621
Inquiry into Meaning and Truth, An (Russell), 1:485, 9:600–601
Inquiry into the Good, An (Zen no kenkyo) (Nishida kitarō), 4:791, 6:623
Inquiry into the Human Mind on the Principles of Common Sense (Reid), 2:356
Inquiry into the Nature and Causes of the Wealth of Nations (Smith), 3:247, 9:67
Inquisition
Galileo and, 2:732
Spinoza and, 9:169
Insanity
criminal, 8:449–450
responsibility and, 8:163–164
Insect Societies, The (Wilson, E.), 9:788
Inseparability
Abelard on, 5:427–428
Ockham on, 5:434
Insight
heroes', into culture, 2:34
as knowledge, 8:126
Köhler on, 5:132
Manheim on, 5:686
materialism and, 6:16
rational, 8:126
Spinoza on, 8:126
Insolubilia (Bradwardine), 5:434
Insolubilia, definition of, 5:546
Insolubilia Monacensis, 5:434
Insolubles, in medieval logic, 5:433–434
Inspiration
creativity and, 2:589–590
in *Odyssey,* 1:41
Plato on, 1:187
Installation art, 9:692–693
Instantiation
atemporal, persistence and, 7:208–211
universal, rule of, definition of, 5:559
Instinct
in common consent arguments for God's existence, 2:344–346
God and, 5:714
intuition and, 1:567
Locke on, 7:369
Maritain on, 5:715
McDougall on, 6:72, 8:147
reincarnation and, 8:332–333
teleological order and, 9:376
Instinct and Experience (Morgan), 6:402
Instinct of Workmanship, The (Veblen), 9:656
Instinctual meaning, in Freudian psychology, 3:511
Institut für mathematische Logik und Grundlagenforschung, 8:645
Institut National, Ideology doctrine and, 2:760
Institute for the Unity of Science, 6:562
Institute of Philosophy, University of Louvain, 6:143, 6:144
Institutes of Metaphysics (Ferrier), 1:12, 3:608–609
Institutes of Moral Philosophy (Ferguson), 3:604
Institutes of the Christian Religion (Calvin), 2:8
Institutio Logicae (Wallis), 5:439
Institutio Oratoria (Quintilian), 7:367
Institutional structure
Dilthey on, 3:82
legitimacy of, in Gehlen, 4:36
Institutional theory of art, 1:77–78, 1:299–300, 2:627
Institutionalized suicide, 9:320
Institutiones Dialecticae (Training in dialectic) (Ramus), 8:236
Institutiones grammaticae (Priscian), 5:422
Institutiones Philosophiae Eclecticae (Bude), 1:721
Institutioni Armoniche (Zarloni), 1:48
Institutionum Dialecticarum (Fonseca), 3:681
Instituto de Filosofia del Diritto, 2:697
Instituto de Investigacioines Filosóficas, 5:210
Instruction, miracles of, in Buddhism, 6:255
Instruction chrétienne, 2:681
Instruction code, normal form theorem and, 2:380–381
Instructions, in computability theory, 2:373–374
Instrumental reason, 7:735–736
Instrumental value, 3:176, 9:637, 9:641–642
Instrumentalism
antirealism of, 6:172
Baier on, 1:461

in Copenhagen interpretation, 2:531–532
Dewey on, 4:566, 7:745–7446
on intentionality, 4:711
interpretive, on intentionality, 4:711
Kuhn and, 8:701
pragmatism and, 7:745–7446
in quantum mechanics, 7:477
recursive axiomatization and, 2:583
on scientific law, 7:518
in scientific realism, 8:690
Wright (Chauncey) and, 9:846
See also Dewey, John; Nonfactualism; Pragmatism
Instrumentation and experimentation, **10:12–20**
Integral thinking, 5:74
Integralism, 8:666
Integration studies, religion and, 8:381
Integrationalism, Gehlen affinity with, 4:35
Integrationism
Buddhism and, 5:135–136
in Korean philosophy, 5:134
Integrity
Confucius on, 2:443
La Rochefoucauld on, 5:201
law and, 7:458–459
performance and, 1:322–323
Unamuno on, 9:567
Intellect, 4:608–609
acquired, Gersonides on, 4:68
active. *See* Active intellect
agent, **1:90–92,** 1:453 9:28, 9:766
Aquinas on, 3:289
Aristotle on, 1:275, 3:286–287, 4:602, 4:608–609
art and, 5:716
in ascent of soul, 3:622
Averroes on, 4:758
Bergson on, 1:566
Carnap on, 2:40
in common consent arguments for God's existence, 2:348
divine, 5:649–650
evolutionary origin of, 1:566
external world in, 1:566–567
and free will, Descartes on, 3:12
God as, 4:818, 5:650–651
Godfrey of Fontaine on, 4:131
Grosseteste on, 4:186
Iamblichus on, 4:540
vs. imagination, 5:651–652
vs. intuition, 4:749
Israeli on, 2:539–540
Jaspers on. *See Verstand*
and knowledge, 4:812
and liberation, 4:628
and logic, 1:566
Maréchal on, 5:709
Maritain on, 5:716
and mathematics, 1:566
matter and form in, 4:814–815
monopsychism and, 9:28
in Neoplatonism, 6:547
Ockham on, 3:290, 9:782
passive, Averroes on, 1:424
pleasure in, 1:338
potential, 1:91
Proclus on, 8:42–43
in religion, 1:782–783
and science, 1:567–568
and sensory material, 8:650
in soul, 1:112
spatial analysis by, 1:566
and theology, 1:707
Tschirnhaus on, 9:549
as understanding, 1:594
virtue-based epistemology of, 9:135–136
and will, 8:652
Winckelmann on, 9:790
Zabarella on, 9:866
See also Reason
Intellectual history, Lovejoy on, 5:593–594
Intellectual intuition
recording the results of, 5:93
through faith, 4:772
Intellectual Intuition and Chinese Philosophy (Mou), 2:183
Intellectual meaning, Johnson (Alexander Bryan) on, 4:849–850
Intellectual property
computer ethics and, 2:397
in engineering ethics, 3:241
Intellectual reality, Johnson (Alexander Bryan) on, 4:847–848
Intellectual virtues, 5:105
vs. moral, 1:268
in virtue epistemology, 9:682–686
Intellectualism, Croce on, 2:601
Intellectus archetypus, 5:16, 5:21
Intellectus ectypus, 5:15–16
Intelligence
agent, 9:766
in animals, **1:200–208**
artificial. *See* Artificial intelligence
Augustine on, 1:393–395
in children, 1:596
computation and, 5:632
computing machines and, 2:408
Dewey on, 3:49
vs. emotion, 1:349
evolutionary significance of, 9:721
Garrigou-Lagrange on, 4:23
Gassendi on, 4:29
Gehlen on, 4:35–36
human
vs. animal, 1:549
vs. machine, 5:634–635
machine, **5:631–636**
Neumann (John von) on, 6:559–560
Turing on, 9:552
natural law and, Grotius on, 6:510
Piaget's theory of, 9:77
Plato on, 7:633–634
Plotinus on, 3:189, 6:187
as skills and cultural factors, 1:596
Turing on, 9:552–553
Turing test and, 5:633–635, 9:553
types of, 5:15–16
Zeno of Citium on, 9:870
Intelligence quotient, 5:129, 9:244
Intelligent design, 8:396–397
arguments for, 3:321
as pseudoscience, 8:671
See also Teleology
Intelligent Woman's Guide to Socialism and Capitalism (Shaw), 9:87
Intelligenzprufungen an Anthropoiden (Köhler), 5:126
Intelligibility
of anthropomorphic theology, 1:369
Gibson on, 1:326
of history, 9:518
of intentional acts, 7:292–293
of representation, 1:326–327
of world, as adaptation, 9:379
Intelligible, *vs.* existent, in Scholasticism, 9:772–773
Intelligible essence, *vs.* primary substance, Ockham and, 9:778
Intelligible extension, 5:666–667
Intelligible world, 5:25
Intension
content of expressions and, 5:39
definition of, 5:546
Hamilton on, 5:448
Lewis (C. I.) on, 5:308
of nouns in traditional logic, 5:493
in properties, 8:65
Intensional, definition of, 5:546
Intensional account of universals, 6:177
Intensional logic
of Montague, 6:329–330
Quine on, 7:28
world-semantics and, 5:486
Intensional operators, types of, 5:487

Intensional semantics, 1:345, 4:622, 9:347–348
Intensional transitive verbs, **4:697–700**
Intensionality, in logical formalization, 6:329
Intention, **4:700–704**
  action and, 1:18–20, 1:524–525, 5:90, 7:447
  in animals, 1:206
  Anscombe on, 1:213
  in art, 1:300, 1:316–318
  in artificial intelligence, 1:349–350
  author *vs.* reader and, 1:314
  in behaviorism, 1:524–525
  belief and, 1:19, 4:701, 7:447
  Bratman on, 1:20
  "can" as, 2:24
  computation and, 1:350
  in Confucianism, 2:172
  consciousness and, 5:48
  contemporary debate on, 3:19–20
  in film, 7:384
  first (primary), definition of, 5:546
  functions attributed to, 1:19–20
  Harman on, 1:20
  interpretation and, 1:312–313
  Kavka's "toxin puzzle" of, 4:702–703
  knowledge and, 7:447
  law and, 7:446–447
  luck and, 1:21
  McCann on, 1:20
  moral judgments and, 5:24
  normativity in, 1:20
  physicalists on, 7:553
  policy as, 8:674
  power and, 7:733–734
  propositional attitudes of, 4:712
  proximal, 1:16–17
  reductionist view of, 1:20–21
  of saying a thing, 9:814–815
  second (secondary), definition of, 5:546
  in semantics, 7:402
  in sexism, 8:848
  side effects of, 1:20
  in strict akratic action, 9:729–730
  supremacy of, 7:447
  vs. volition, 9:704
  Wilson (George) on, 1:16
Intention (Anscombe), 1:213
Intention perseverance, 4:703
Intentional acts, 7:290–295
Intentional analysis, 7:294
Intentional being, Peter Aureol on, 7:257
Intentional calculus, 3:710
Intentional characterization, scheme of, 3:677
Intentional content, 2:449–451, 7:192
Intentional level, of cognitive psychology, 3:676
Intentional mental states, folk psychology and, 3:678
Intentional properties
  of mental representations, in explanatory role, 6:141
  naturalization of, 6:263–264
  in physical universe, 3:678
Intentional realism, Fodor on, 3:675
Intentional stance
  antirealism of, 6:172
  explanation from, 2:711
Intentional Stance, The (Dennett), 2:711
Intentional states, 7:191
  Chisholm on, 2:242
  mental causation and, 6:136
  perception as, 7:192
Intentionalism, 1:312–314
Intentionalist theories, of perception, 7:191–193
Intentionality, **4:704–714,** 8:802
  in actions and events, 1:15–16, 1:18–20, 1:549
  in aesthetic experience, 1:509
  Ayer on, 1:437
  Beardsley on, 1:509
  Brentano on, 1:689–690
  in Buddhism, 1:748, 1:754
  Cairns on, 2:5
  in Chinese religion, 2:225
  Chisholm on, 2:243
  in cognitive science, 2:299–300
  consciousness and, 2:452, 2:459
  Davidson (Donald) on, 2:646
  definition of, 7:290
  in deontological ethics, 3:387
  derived *vs.* underived, 4:710
  Desgabets on, 2:759
  in existential psychoanalysis, 3:512
  existentialism on, 3:502
  Galen on, 4:6
  Heidegger on, 3:512
  of language, 3:744
  in linguistic reference, 2:205
  materialism and, 6:17
  in Meinong's theory of objects, 8:803
  mental, 1:689, 7:468, 9:290–291
  Millikan on, 6:236
  in mind-body problem, 6:262–264
  noninference criterion for, 7:290–292
  original, in conscious subject, 9:291
  phenomenology and, 7:282, 7:289–292, 7:299
  in philosophy of mind, 7:471–472
  propositional attitudes and, 8:81
  Sartre on, 3:502, 8:605
  Searle on, 8:705
  in self-knowledge, 8:726
  in social context, 9:77
  subjectivity and, 9:290–291
Intentionality (Searle), 3:744
"Intentionality of Sensation: A Grammatical Feature, The" (Anscombe), 1:213
"Intentions and Interpretations: A Fallacy Revived" (Beardsley), 1:509
"Intentions of the Philosophers" (al-Ghazālī), Albalag commentary on, 4:820
"Interaction between Heaven and Man," theory of, Wang Chong on, 9:723
Interaction theory of metaphor, 6:166–167
Interactionism
  of Descartes, 6:259
  of McDougall, 6:72, 8:147–148
Interdisciplinary perspective, 7:334
Interdisciplinary theory construction, psychoanalysis as, 5:76
Interests
  exercise and satisfaction of, 3:723
  shared by women, 3:600
Interference, in quantum mechanics, 2:531
Interference bands, 8:202–203
Interference effects, for electrons, 5:695–696, 8:202–205
Interference rule, default, 6:643
Interior Castle, The (Teresa of Ávila), 9:394
Interiorità oggettiva (Sciacca), 8:666
Interiority, 1:403, 8:666
Interminable disagreement, 5:636
Internal and External Reasons (Williams), 4:714
Internal causality, in Aristotle, 2:666–667
Internal Constitution of the Stars, The (Eddington), 3:164
Internal folk psychology, 3:678
Internal Form of the Word (Shpet), 9:18
Internal negation, 6:523–524
Internal principles, 4:310
Internal properties, relativity of, 8:342–344
Internal realism, mind-dependence in, 6:173

Internal relations, 2:308–309
Internal representation
in cognitive science, 2:299
in computationalism, 2:391–392
connectionism in, 2:444–445
Internal states
certitude and, 3:140
in computationalism, 2:392
in methodological solipsism, 9:117
Internalism
Chisholm on, 2:243
content, 8:82–83
on ethical naturalism, 3:367
in ethics, **4:714–716**
vs. externalism, **4:716–719**
foundationalist, 8:178–179
and knowledge, 3:272–273
on primitivism, 8:179
of rationality, 8:254–255
reasoning in, 7:737
in reliabilism, 8:365
supervenience and, 9:327, 9:330–331
Internality, of memory, 7:223, 7:227
Internalization of moral norms
ethical relativism and, 3:390–391
and self-interest, 3:382
utilitarianism and, 3:385
Internalized apperception, 7:255
International Association for the Study of Pain (IASP), 7:68
International Atomic Energy Commission, 8:667
International Brotherhood, Bakunin foundation of, 1:472
International Encyclopedia of Unified Science (Carnap, Morris, & Neurath, editors), 6:562
International Journal of Parapsychology, 7:116
International justice, 4:865
International language, in Comenius, 2:341
International law, 4:191–192, 7:422–423
auto-limitation of, 9:143
computer ethics and, 2:397
in consolidation of national states, 9:204
cosmopolitanism and, 2:567
Grotius on, 4:191–192
legal positivism in, 5:237–238
in philosophy of law, 7:422–423
Soto on, 9:137
sovereignty and, 1:621, 9:143–144
Suárez in, 7:423
Vitoria and, 7:422, 9:699
International Law (Wolff), 9:825
International relations
Bentham and, 1:551
sovereignty in, 9:143–144
International society, 5:29, 9:698–699
International Workingmen's Association
Bakunin and, 1:472
British trade unions and, 9:89
Marx's address to, 2:362
Internationalism
anarchism and, 1:176
Rawls on, 9:83
in socialist thought, 9:89–90
and war, ending of, 7:154–156
Internet
ethics and, 2:397
illegality of digital copy and, 2:397
property rights and, 2:397
Interpenetration of opposites, law of, Engels on, 3:238
Interpersonal relations, 3:615
Interpersonal transactions, between psychoanalyst and patient, 3:742
Interpolation, in model theory, 6:310–313
Interpretants, 8:798
Interpretation
anti-intentionalism and, 1:311–312
art and, 1:78, **1:310–315**
Camus on, 2:20
candidates for, 1:310
Carnap on, 2:43
categorical *vs.* hypothetical judgments and, 1:661
clinical, 8:112–114
in combinatory logic, 2:335
vs. computationalism, 2:395
constraints on, 6:85
convention in, 1:312
Dao and, 2:192, 2:205
definition of, 1:310, 5:546
Duhem on, 3:128
exegetical, 1:47
"exist" as predicate in, 1:662
faith as, 3:533–534
fictionalist strategies of, 3:626–629
of first-order language, 3:641
of functional analyses, 3:763
functions, in computationalism, 2:390–391
hermeneutics and, 1:311
of historical materialism, 4:380–382
and history, 1:762
holistic nature of, 1:310–311
in impartiality, 4:619–620
intent and, 1:312–313
intentionalism and, 1:312–313
irony and, 1:311–312
linguistic meaning and, 1:311
literal, 1:310
of literary works, 5:368–370
meaning and, 1:311, 2:192
of metaphor, 1:311
morality in, 1:313
nonfactualist strategy of, 3:627
vs. observation, 3:128, 3:546
of performance, 1:321–322
principal, definition of, 5:546
purpose of, 1:310
reader-response theory of, 1:314–315
of religious experience, 8:401–402
secondary, definition of, 5:546
in semantic theory, 6:85
of theory, 1:685
Bell and, 1:539–542
Bohmian mechanics and, 1:630–636
kinetic equation and, 1:645
unity and, 1:311
Interpretation and Analysis (Wisdom), 9:796
Interpretation of Quantum Mechanics (Schrödinger), 8:658
Interpretation of Visual Motion, The (Ullman), 2:394
Interpretation of Whitehead's Metaphysics, An (Christian), 9:751
Interpretatione, De (Aristotle), on determinism, 3:6
Interpretationist theories, of mental content, 2:478
Interpretations of Poetry and Religion (Santayana), 8:602
Interpretivism, as normative jurisprudence, 1:169–170
Interregnum, history of logic in, **5:437–440**
Interrogation, fallacies of, 3:548
Intersection of sets, definition of, 5:546
Intersectionality
concept of, 3:601
doctrine of, 3:586–587
Intersubjectivity, in basic statements, 1:484–487
Intertextuality, in Derrida, 2:716
Intertheoretic reduction, 6:569
Intertwining, 6:148
Interval quantity scales, 6:88
Intimations (Suhrawardī), 4:582
Intransitive relation, definition of, 5:555
Intrigue and Love (Schiller, Friedrich), 8:626

Intrinsic properties, **3:527–528,** 7:25
Intrinsic value, 3:176, **4:719–720,** 9:637, 9:641–642
Introception, 9:245
Introducción a la filosofía (Marías), 5:711
Introductio ad Philosophiam Ebraeorum (Budde), 1:721
Introductio ad Philosophium Aulicam (Thomasius), 9:441
Introductio ad syllogismos categoricos (Boethius), 5:421
Introduction à la connaissance de l'esprit humain (Vauvenargues), 9:653
Introduction à l'analyse des sciences, ou de la génération, des fondements, et des instruments de nos connaissances (Lancelin), 8:788
Introduction à l'etude de las medicine experimental (Bernard), 1:590
Introduction à l'histoire de la philosophie (Cousin), 6:572
"Introduction to a General Theory of Elementary Propositions" (Post), 5:467
Introduction to Arithmetic (Nicomachus of Gerasa), 4:540
Introduction to History: The Theory of History (Karsavin), 5:42
Introduction to Logic (Galen), 5:408
Introduction to Logic (Joseph), 5:231
Introduction to Logic and Scientific Method, An (Nagel & Cohen), 6:472
Introduction to Logical Theory (Strawson), 3:252, 9:264
Introduction to Mathematical Logic (Church), 4:706
Introduction to Mathematical Logic (Frege), 1:343
Introduction to Metaphysics (Bergson), 1:567–568
Introduction to Philosophy (Paulsen), 7:83–7:88, 7:149
Introduction to Political Science (Seeley), 9:26
Introduction to Social Psychology (McDougall), 8:147
Introduction to the Creed of the Sufis (al-Kalabadhi), 9:303–304
Introduction to the Critique of Political Economy (Marx), 9:101
Introduction to the Human Sciences (Dilthey), 3:80–82
Introduction to the Middle Way (Madhyamakāvatāra) (Candrakīrti), 1:732
Introduction to the Principles of Morals and Legislation (Bentham), 1:551, 3:412–413, 7:76, 8:720
Introduction to Wittgenstein's "Tractatus" (Anscombe), 1:212
Introductiones in Logicam (William of Sherwood), 5:430, 9:786
Introductory Discourse (Middleton), 6:214
Introduzione allo studio della filosofia (Gioberti), 4:93
Introspection, **4:720–722**
  in analysis of sense contents, 8:821
  behaviorism and, 6:80
  Buckle on, 1:718
  in classification of mental states, 9:38
  Comte on, 2:413
  in Confucianism, 2:173
  consciousness and, 2:449, 2:457
  epistemological role of, 1:462
  in James's psychology, 4:778
  Lipps on, 5:363
  materialism and, 6:17
  of mental, 6:138–139
  Mill (James) on, 6:219
  qualitative consciousness and, 2:451
  religion and, 8:381
  in self-knowledge, 8:724, 8:726
  in social behaviorism, 6:80
  Titchener on, 8:149
  two-level account of, 4:721
  untrustworthiness of, 5:96
  Wundt on, 9:849
Introspectionism, 5:130, 8:149, 8:724
Introverted mysticism, 8:401
Introverted psychological type, 4:856–858
Intuition, **4:722–735**
  absolute identity as, 1:704
  and action, 1:567
  aesthetic, 2:600–601
  in analyticity, 1:148
  appeals to, role of, 7:409
  artistic, 1:54, 1:57
  axioms of, 5:19
  of being, 4:94, 5:713
  Bergson on, 1:57, 1:568–570
  Brouwer on, 1:700, 5:468, 9:366
  Campanella on, 2:15
  and causality, 1:704
  conceptual, linguistic theory of, 4:728–729
  Croce on, 1:304, 2:600–601
  in Daoist thought, 2:185
  Descartes on, 2:724–726, 2:734–736, 2:740
  disciplines of, 5:143
  as disinterested instinct, 1:567
  Duns Scotus on, 3:290
  Emerson on, 6:573
  of essences, in phenomenology, 7:283–285
  in ethical intuitionism, 4:736
  Gioberti on, 4:94
  in historians, 1:766
  indefinitely progressive, 1:567
  individuation and, 1:320
  vs. intellect, 4:749
  intellectual, through faith, 4:772
  Kant on, 3:306–307
  and knowledge, 1:567, 2:724–726, 2:734–736, 2:740
  Korn on, 5:142–143
  in legal appraisal, 7:450
  Locke on, 5:386
  lyrical, 2:601
  Maritain on, 5:713
  Martineau on, 5:727
  mathematical, 1:700, 4:118, 9:366
  metaphysics and, 5:713, 6:211
  Mill (John Stuart) on, 6:225–226
  moral, Habermas on, 3:91
  mystery and, 5:701
  mystical experience as, 1:570
  Nishida on, 1:728
  as non-perceptual, 1:697
  in nonrational cognition, 4:749
  of noumenal, 5:708
  Ockham on, 3:290
  Ortega y Gasset on, 7:47
  perception and, 7:177, 7:182, 7:185
  personal identity and, 7:231–232
  personality and, 4:856
  poetic, 5:716
  primordial, 5:468
  pure, 3:752
  and qualia, 8:195
  rational, 4:733
  Santayana on, 8:602
  in Shepherd's causality, 9:10
  "simple act" theory of, 4:728
  Spinoza on, 3:295
  spiritual, 5:147
  in Suhrawardī's knowledge by presence, 9:305
  and temporal perception, 1:700
  in theistic pluralism of Iqbal, 4:744
  and value judgments, 9:643
  in wisdom, 9:795
  See also Intuitionistic logic
"Intuition und Intellekt bei Henri Bergson" (Ingarden), 4:682

Intuitionalist mathematics, Brouwer on, 1:700–702
Intuitionism, 3:386–387, **4:737–743**
 and association of proof with truth, 5:109
 Brouwer on, 5:468
 commonsense, 3:409, 9:22
 in Daoism, 2:185
 definition of, 5:546
 as descriptivism, 6:633
 early development of, 3:406
 emotive theory and, 3:425
 ethical, **4:735–737**
 fan theorem, 4:741
 and Gentzen's rules of natural deduction, 4:739
 Grote on, 4:189
 in Latin American philosophy, 5:208
 and mathematics, 5:468, 5:469, 6:21
 Mill (John Stuart) and, 6:222, 6:227
 on moral knowledge, 3:445
 on nonexistence of infinite totalities, 4:659
 number in, 6:676–677
 phenomenology as, 7:284
 Piaget and, 7:567
 quantificational language used by, 8:196
 Rashdall on, 8:238–239
 Sidgwick on, 3:416–417
 vs. utilitarianism, 9:22
 and value theory, 9:640
Intuitionisme en Formalisme (Brouwer), 1:701
Intuitionist logic, **4:737–743**, 5:487, 6:528, 9:559
 Bishop on, 2:504–505
 continuum and real numbers in, 2:502–504
 as critique of logical Platonism, 5:487
 fan theorem, 4:741
 Gentzen and, 4:739
 Grote on, 4:189
 modal logic and, 5:483
 negation in, 6:528
 and principle of excluded middle, 4:738
 quantificational language used by, 8:196
 synthetic differential geometry and, 2:510
Intuitionist rationality, 8:254
Intuitionistic propositional calculus, 5:536
Intuitions of the Mind, Inductively Investigated, The (McCosh), 6:71
Intuitive appreciation, Keyserling on, 5:58
Intuitive cognition
 of causality, 9:779–780
 of God, 9:780–781
 John of Mirecourt on, 4:841
 of mental states, 9:774
 of nonexistents, 9:774
 Ockham on, 9:773–776
Intuitive contingent truths, 5:93
Intuitive knowledge, 5:92
 of goodness, 6:156
 Locke on, 3:300, 5:96
 Spinoza on, 7:97
Intuitive moral thinking, Hare on, 3:441
Intuitive set theory, intuitionism and, 5:546
Intuitivism
 Kozlov and, 5:146
 Losskii on, 5:576
INUS conditions, 5:638
Invalid arguments, 3:538, 3:639
Invalidity, *vs.* inconsistency, 3:546
Invariance, Cohen (Morris) on, 2:307
Invariances (Nozick), 6:669
"Invariant Variational Problems" ("Invariante Variationsprobleme") (Noether), 3:234
Invention, art of, Wolff's study of, 9:826
Inverse compositionality, 2:372
Inverse of a relation, definition of, 5:539
Inverse probability
 Bayesian, 3:660
 Jevons on, 4:808
Inversion
 definition of, 5:546
 of great-numbers theorem of Bernoulli, 5:57
"Inverted Spectrum, The" (Shoemaker), 9:16
Inverted spectrum hypothesis, 8:193
Investigation of the Laws of Thought, An (Boole), 5:460
Investigations in Currency and Finance (Jevons), 4:807
Investors, moral obligations of, 1:779–780
Invisible College, and Boyle, 1:672–673
Invisible hand
 and social Darwinism, 2:642
 and social moral good, 1:777
Involuntary active euthanasia, 3:456
Involuntary passive euthanasia, 3:456
Involution, Lalande on, 5:172–173
Inwagen, Peter van, 4:618
 on event theory, 3:467
 on possibility, 7:725
Inwood, Brad, on Empedocles, 3:212
Ion (Plato)
 aesthetics in, 1:41
 on knowledge claims of poets, 7:585–586
 on poetry, 4:175, 7:595
Ionescu, Nae, **4:743**
Ionian physicists, Diogenes Laertius on, 3:88
Ionian School. *See* Pre-Socratic philosophy
IOT. *See* Ideal observer theory
Iota operator, definition of, 5:546
Iphigenie auf Tauris (Goethe), 4:140
I-proposition, definition of, 5:547
Iqbal, Muhammad, **4:743–745**
Iran
 Iḥya in, 1:119
 modern philosophy in, 4:762
 Sufism in, 9:310
Iranism, 5:59
Iraq
 as center of Jewry, 4:810
 U.S. war in, 7:158
Ireland, Swift's defense of, 9:340
Irenaeus, 3:533
 on creation, 3:475
 on God, 7:142
 on Simon Magnus, 9:33
 theodicy of, 3:474, 9:393
 on Valentinus, 9:631
Irène (Voltaire), 9:709
Irenicum (Stillingfleet), 9:249
Irigaray, Luce, **4:745–746**
 on deconstructing dualisms, 3:565
 and essentialist theory of sexual difference, 3:570, 3:573, 3:586
 on moments of instability in philosophical texts, 3:570
 poststructuralism of, 9:274
 on speaking subjects, 9:276
 on women, 3:570, 3:573
Irma Dream, 3:743
Irony
 Baudrillard and, 1:491
 interpretation and, 1:311–312
 in Solger's philosophy of art, 9:114
 in Stace's "Refutation of Realism," 9:200
 in Swift's religious commentary, 9:340
"Irrational," conduct-guiding function of, 4:862–863
Irrational decision, in medical ethics, 3:456

Irrational fideism, 3:632, 4:96
Irrational numbers, 6:670–671
 continuous magnitude and, 2:501
 as incommensurable magnitudes, 2:492
Irrationalism, **4:746–753**
 dominance of, 8:645
 moral judgments and, 4:749
 Pastore and, 7:135
 psychological, 4:751
Irrationality
 in history, 9:626
 in nature, 9:626
 in racism, 8:225–226
 Spinoza on, 8:126–127
 Vysheslavtsev on, 9:717–718
Irreducibility, 1:741, 6:644–645
Irreferentialism, analytical behaviorism and, 1:523–524
Irreflexive relation, definition of, 5:555
Irrelevance, in discussion, common and important types of, 3:547
Irreversible phenomena, 2:575
Irreversible processes
 in causality, 2:99
 and directional causality for time, 2:87
 entropy and, 7:537–541
Irrgang, Bernhard, 7:549
Irwin, Harvey J., 7:116
Irwin, Robert, on site-specific art, 3:256
Is
 of constitution, 4:570
 in identity, 4:567
Is America Safe for Democracy? (McDougall), 6:72
"Is Consciousness a Brain Process?" (Place), 9:65
"Is Consciousness a Type of Behavior?" (Miller), 6:235
Isaac of Stella, **4:753–754**
Isaac the Blind, 5:3
Isagoge (Porphyry), 2:80, 4:66, 5:408, 5:421, 6:188
 Abelard and, 5:427
 Arab logic and, 5:417
 Duns Scotus on, 3:134
 Kilwardby's commentary on Porphyry's, 5:70
 predication in, 6:187
Ischod k vostoku, Predchuvstviia i sversheniia, Utverzhdenie Evraziitsev (Exodus to the East: Forebodings and events: An affirmation of the Eurasians), 3:453
Isendoorn, Gisbertus, 5:438
Ishiguro, Hidé, 9:817
Ishrāq (Surawardī), 9:314
Ishrāqī, Islamic Neoplatonism and, 6:558
Isidore of Seville, 2:622
 on law, 7:421
 Lull and, 5:610
Islam
 accepting, 3:536
 and aesthetics, 1:436
 al-Fārābī, Abū al Naṣr and, 1:116
 Avicenna on, 1:426
 Christian missionaries to, 5:609–610
 dogma in, 3:97
 emanationism in, 3:189–190, 4:576
 eschatology in, 3:347
 European unification and, 7:154
 and faith as religious duty or virtue, 3:536
 fundamentalism in, 1:129–130
 illuminationism in, 4:576
 immortality in, 4:619, 6:558
 in medieval Jewish philosophy, 4:811
 monotheism in, 4:110
 mysticism of, 4:549, 6:450–452
 natural in, 7:14
 Neoplatonism in, 3:190
 People of the Book and, 8:647
 political theory and, 7:679
 reproductive technologies and, 4:46
 on resurrection, 4:619
 Shariati on, 9:7
 Shi'ite, 1:116
 in Spengler's cultural morphology, 9:166
 and state, role of, 5:202
 on suicide and martyrdom, 9:320
 tolerance in, 8:647
 truth in, 8:647
 Zoroastrianism and, 9:887
Islamic Enlightenment, **3:248–249**, 4:541
Islamic Neoplatonic Aristotelians, 2:114
Islamic philosophy, **4:754–764**
 Abu'l-Barakāt al-Baghđađi and, 4:817
 active intellect in, 4:550
 aesthetics in, 1:436
 Alexander of Aphrodisias in, 1:112–113
 al-Fārābī, Abū al Naṣr, in, 1:116, 4:811
 al-Ghazālī, Muhammad, in, 1:118, 2:114, 9:304–305
 al-Kindī in, 1:131
 analogy in, 1:139–140
 antirational skepticism in, 9:50
 Aristotelianism and, 1:116, 1:260–261, 1:279
 Arkoun in, **1:284–285**
 Averroism in, 1:431
 causality in, 2:113–115
 at Chartres school, 2:137
 classical period, end of, 3:70
 Corbin on, 2:537
 cosmology in, 1:433
 on creation, 3:360–361
 determinism in, 3:23
 dialectic in, **3:69–70**
 East *vs.* West in, 1:130
 enlightenment in, 4:762
 epistemology in, 3:319–320
 essence and existence in, **3:351–352**
 eternity in, 3:360–361
 on experience, 4:7
 Galen and, 4:6–7
 Gerbert of Aurillac and, 4:66
 and God's existence, 2:551
 on God's knowledge of things, 3:320
 Greek thought in, 1:423
 Grosseteste and, 4:186
 haqq concept in, 4:542
 Ibn al-ʿArabī and, 4:541
 Ibn Bājja and, 4:544–545
 Ibn Khaldūn and, 4:547–550
 Ibn Ṭufayl and, 4:550
 Ikhwān al-Ṣafā' (Brethren of Purity) in, 4:575–577, 4:756–757
 illuminationism in, 4:580–585
 indirect *vs.* direct creation in, 1:651
 on inner senses, 4:697
 Jewish participation in, 4:811
 kalām in, 2:551, 3:69–70, 4:762
 in medieval philosophy, 6:99–100
 modern, 1:431
 Mullā Ṣadrā in, 2:114, 6:418–419
 Muqammiṣ and, 6:432
 Muʿtazilite school of, 8:586
 mysticism in, 4:759
 Neoplatonism and, 1:426, 3:403, 6:557–558, 9:301–303
 and *Organon*, 4:582–583
 peripatetic, 4:581
 Persians in, 4:761
 and Platonism, 1:116, 7:610–612
 Plotinus and, 1:423, 3:401
 prophetic, of Shi'ism, 4:550
 Pythagoreanism in, 8:188
 reason in, 1:130
 reproductive technologies and, 4:46
 on resurrection, 4:619

School of Baghdad, 9:301
School of Qom, 8:646
science and, 3:248–249
scope of, 4:759
on self-evident knowledge, 4:761
sharīʿa subordinated to, 4:755
Shariati in, 9:7
Socrates and, 9:113
Suhrawardī in, 4:581, 9:305, 9:314–317
syncretism in, 1:423
theology and, 4:759
theory of intellection in, 4:755
vocabulary in, 1:131
worldview of, 1:652, 4:756
Islamic Renaissance
Averroes and, 1:427
Islamic Enlightenment and, 3:248–249
in modern Islamic debate, 4:762
Islamic Republic, 8:646
Islamic revolution, 4:763, 9:7
Isma'ili
Brethrens of Purity and, 4:756–757
Islamic Neoplatonism and, 1:432, 6:558
Isocrates
Cicero on, 2:257
rhetoric and, 1:264
Isolation
as androcentric bias, 1:158
perfection and, 1:294
private language and, 8:15
Isomorphic predicates, 8:65
Isomorphic relationships, 5:131
Isomorphism, 5:127–129
Carnap on, 8:76, 8:738–739, 9:347–348
Curry-Howard, 4:742
extensional, 4:157–158
geometric models, 4:62
Gestalt theory and, 4:70–73, 8:144
intentional, 9:347–348
and phenomenal world and brain-states, 5:128
Scotism and, 8:704
Israë vengé (Orobio), 2:267
Israel
Holocaust and, 4:454
occupation of Palestine by, 9:396–398
Israeli, Isaac ben Solomon, **4:764–765**
in medieval Jewish philosophy, 4:814
on truth as correspondence, 2:539–540
Issuant conception of hell, 4:251
"Ist die Trägheit eines körpers von seinem Energieinhalt abhängig?" ("Does the Inertia of a Body Depend upon Its Energy Content?") (Einstein), 3:233–234
Istoria e dimostrazioni intorno alle macchie solari (Letters on sunspots) (Galileo), 4:8
Istoricheskie pis'ma (Historical letters) (Lavrov), 5:218–219
Istoriia antichnoi estetiki (History of ancient aesthetics) (Losev), 5:575
Istoriia kak problema logiki (History as a problem of logic) (Shpet), 9:17
Istoriia russkoi filosofii (Zen'kovskii), 9:868
Istorija Svete Udovice Judit (History of the Widow Judith) (Marulić), 5:729
Īśvara, 6:108
Italia (newspaper), 2:719
Italian philosophy, Spaventa's "circulation" of, 9:159
Italienische Reise (Goethe), 4:141
Italy
Aristotelianism in, 1:430
Averroism in, 1:430
existentialism in, 1:1–2
fascist regime in, 4:50
federalism in unity of, Gioberti on, 4:93
Jewish scholars of, 13th-c., 4:820
Marxism in, 5:165
neo-Hegelianism in, 1:1
Renaissance in, humanism in, 4:479–480
social positivism in, 7:713
Sturzo in, 9:281
Italy and Fascism (Sturzo), 9:281
I-thou and I-it relationship, 1:715, 2:167, 4:112
Itō Jinsai, **4:765–766,** 5:7
Śunyatāsaptati (Seventy Verses on Emptiness), 6:470
Iurkevich, P. D., 9:123
Ivanhoe, Philip J., 2:196
Ivanov, Viacheslav Ivanovich, **4:766–768,** 5:574
Iz glubiny, 3:716

J

Jackiw, Roman W., 1:539
Jackson, Frank, 8:192
on Churchland, 5:114
conscious qualitative states and, 2:451
"Epiphenomenal Qualia," 5:112–115
on indicative conditionals, 2:425
on qualia, 5:112–115, 9:292
Jackson, Lydia, 3:195
Jacobi, Friedrich Heinrich, 3:531, **4:769–773**
on absolute, 1:11
Baader and, 1:439
Dilthey and, 8:631
fideism of, 2:691
Fries and, 3:751
Goethe and, 4:141
Kant and, 5:20
Lessing and, 5:296
Mendelssohn and, 6:131
in pantheism dispute, 9:194
Pantheismusstreit and, 7:99–101
Steinheim and, 4:828
Jacquard, Joseph Marie, 2:400
Jacques le Fataliste (Jacques the Fatalist) (Diderot), 3:71–73, 3:410
Jaeger, Werner
Aristotelianism of, 1:262
on *Metaphysics* (Aristotle), 1:276
Jäger, Gerhard, 8:56
Jaggar, Alison, 3:581, 3:599
Jahn, Otto, Nietzsche and, 6:608
Jahrbuch für Philosophie und phänomenologische Forschung (Husserl), 7:279
Jainism
on actions, 5:41
and asceticism, 1:351
and atomism, 1:381
and causality, 2:110–111
cognition in, 9:543
ethics of, 6:108
liberation in, 5:327–328
literature of, 4:631–632
logic in, 9:543
matter in, 1:381, 5:41
meditation in, 6:108
on memory and knowledge, 5:122
mind and mental states in, 6:254
mysticism of, 6:442–443
self in, 8:718
on suicide, 9:320
on universals, 9:586
Jaja, Donato, 4:49, 9:160
Jakobson, Roman, 9:273
Jamaica Letter (Carta de Jamaica) (Bolívar), 5:205
James, Henry, **4:773–774,** 4:779–781
James, Robert, 3:71, 3:73
James, Susan, 3:570

James, William, 3:531–532, **4:774–787,** 7:203–204
- Aliotta and, 1:127
- Anderson (John) and, 1:197
- artistic aspirations of, 4:774–775
- on belief, 1:535, 3:632, 7:745
- Bergson and, 3:313
- on commitment, 3:632
- on determinism, 3:5, 3:15–16, 3:31
- on dreams, 3:105
- education of, 4:774–775
- Emerson and, 3:197
- on emotions, 3:198–199
- empiricism of, 9:483
- and epistemology, 3:313
- health of, 4:775
- on human motivation, 5:104
- on ideas, 4:566
- on immediate experience, 3:515–516
- influences on, 4:775
- on intention of saying a thing, 9:814–815
- on introspection, 4:721
- Judeo-Christian religious hypothesis and, 3:531
- Lequier and, 5:287
- Mach and, 5:623
- on matter-mind dualism, 2:595–597
- McDougall and, 6:71
- McGilvary and, 6:75
- on mental causation, 6:133, 6:260
- metaphysics of, 4:783–785
- Miller (Dickinson) and, 6:234–235
- on naturalism, 1:373
- and new realism, 6:584–585
- Niebuhr and, 6:606
- nominalism of, 7:744
- on optimism and pessimism, 7:245, 7:252
- on pacifism, 7:67
- on panpsychism, 7:84
- Papini and, 7:102
- parapsychology and, 7:116
- personal experience and, 8:588
- philosophy of, 4:775–776
- pluralism of, 6:328
- Pound and, 7:427
- and pragmatism, 3:415–416, 4:781–783, 7:102, 7:427, 7:741–745, 8:798, 9:537
- precursive faith and, 3:532
- on present, 9:484
- on psychology, 4:776–779
- on reality, 3:689
- and religion, 3:531, 3:611, 4:781
- Santayana on, 8:602
- Schiller (Ferdinand) and, 8:623
- on self-preservation, 9:715
- Sigwart and, 9:29
- on *Studies in Logical Theory,* 3:44
- on thought, 7:744
- on time, 9:482–483, 9:487
- on truth, 9:537
- on value, 7:744–745
- on world, why it exists, 9:759

James I (king of England), 9:282

James II (king of England), 3:245, 5:375, 9:81

James II (king of Majorca), 5:609

James of Lausanne, 3:148

James of Metz, 3:148

James of Venice, 5:422

James-Lange theory of emotions, 3:198–199

Janet, Paul, Cudworth and, 2:610

Janet, Pierre
- Adler and, 1:24
- on Spinoza, 9:195
- Taine and, 9:364

Jankélévitch, Vladimir, **4:787–788**

Jansen, Cornelius, 4:788
- Arnauld and, 1:288
- Geulincx and, 4:76
- Nicole and, 6:603

Jansenism, **4:788–791**
- Arnauld and, 1:288
- Descartes and, 2:60–61
- Desgabets and, 2:757
- Fénelon and, 3:603
- Jesuits and, 4:168
- Pascal and, 7:130–131
- Pope Clement IX and, 6:604

Janssen, T. M. V., on compositionality, 2:370

Japan
- annexation of Korea, 5:140
- Buddhism in, 4:793
- Confucianism in, 4:765
- government of, philosophy under, 4:792
- mysticism in, 6:445–446
- suicide in, 9:320
- Western philosophy in, 6:623
- in World War II
  - bombing of, 9:397
  - defeat of, 6:624

Japanese language, mass/count nouns in, 6:660

Japanese philosophy, **4:791–799**
- Andō Shōeki in, 1:200
- *vs.* Chinese philosophy, 4:792–793
- Shin Buddhism in, 9:13–14
- texts of, 4:793
- as transplanted tradition, 4:792

Jaśkowski, Stanislaw, 5:492, 5:608, 7:105

Jaspers, Karl, **4:799–804**
- Abbagnano and, 1:1
- on dread, 3:503
- on existentialism, 3:501–502
- Frank and, 3:715
- influences on, 3:504
- on modern society, 3:506
- Nietzsche and, 6:607
- politics of, 3:506
- positivism and, 3:501–502
- on psychology, 3:507
- Ricoeur and, 3:744
- themes in, 3:504
- on the transcendent, 3:508

Jāti (class)
- in Indian grammar, 9:581
- *vs.* Western universals, 9:587

Javellus, Chrysostom, 5:440

Jayanta, on awareness, 5:119

Jayarasi, on possibility of knowledge, 5:117

Jaynes, Edwin T.
- Fisher and, 3:661
- on Gibb's maxent method, 4:677
- and probability theory, 4:672, 8:31, 9:223
- on sampling distributions, 3:663
- and thick coin example, 9:219

Jealousy, 7:525

Jean of Labadie, 7:575

Jeanne Grey (de Staél), 9:201

Jeans, James Hopwood, **4:804–805**
- Fisher and, 3:661
- Stebbing on, 9:237

Jefferson, Thomas, **4:805–807**
- deism and, 2:689
- on democracy, and Wayland (Francis), 9:728
- Enlightenment and, 3:246
- on equality, 3:329
- Locke and, 5:392
- Priestley and, 8:8

Jefferson Bible, being The Life and Morals of Jesus Christ of Nazareth, The (Jefferson), 2:689

Jeffrey, Richard, on decision theory, 2:657–659

Jeffreys, Harold, 3:661, 9:222

Jekyll, Gertrude, 3:257

Jellema, Harry, 7:580

Jellinek, Georg, 9:143

Jen "humaneness," Confucian virtue of, 5:7

Jenkin, Fleemingsic, 2:638

Jennings, Raymond, paraconsistent logic and, 5:492

Jensen, Ronald, 8:845

Jerome, St. *See* St. Jerome
Jerusalem, Karl Wilhelm, Lessing and, 5:296
Jerusalem oder über religiöse Macht und Judentum (Jerusalem, or on Religious Power and Judaism) (Mendelssohn), 3:245, 6:132, 7:99
Jessell, Thomas, on neuroscience, 6:567–568
Jesu Christu Servatore, De (Socinus), 9:99
Jesuits
  Arnauld and, 1:288
  defense of, by Gournay, 4:167
  Descartes and, 2:720–721, 2:737, 2:749–753
  Encyclopédie and, 3:222
  Gioberti on, 4:93
  Gracián as, 4:168
  Jansenism and, 4:168
  Pascal on, 1:288, 7:130–131
  scientia media and, 8:680
  Suárez as, 9:282
Jesus Christ
  as allusion to Absolute, 9:237
  Arius on, 1:283
  Arnauld on, 1:290
  asceticism of, 1:351
  Bahrdt on, 1:457
  Barth on, 1:478
  Bonaventure on, 1:652
  Bonhoeffer on, 1:655–657
  Bultmann on, 1:763–764
  in Carolingian thought, 2:50
  in Christianity, 2:246–247
  Collier on, 2:324
  Conway on, 2:529
  deists on, 2:681, 2:685
  and divine command theories of ethics, 3:93
  duality of, 7:313
  Eckhart (Meister) on, 3:162
  as genuinely human, 3:534
  Hegel on, 4:261, 4:276
  historicity of, 1:492
  as incarnation of God, 2:247
  Kushitism and, 5:59
  life of, historicity of, 9:262–263
  Manichaeism and, 5:683–684
  Marcion on, 5:703–704
  Mirabaud on, 2:266
  on moral perfection, 7:194–195
  patristic philosophy on, 7:141–143
  Philoponus on, 7:313
  Priestley on, 8:5–6
  revelation and, 7:490–491
  in self-consciousness of Christians, 8:635
  Servetus on, 8:831
  Shelley on, 9:8
  in socinianism, 9:99
  Spinoza on, 4:825–826
  Suso on, 9:335
  Swedenborg on, 9:338
  in Trinity, 2:248
  Valentinianism and, 9:632
  Woolston on, 9:844–845
Jesus Messias (Lavater), 5:213
Jeune parque, La (The young fate) (Valéry), 9:634
Jevons, William Stanley, **4:807–809**
  De Morgan and, 2:710
  and logic, 5:439, 5:450–451
  logical piano of, 5:565
Jevons's machine, as logic machine, 5:565
Jewish Averroism, **4:809**. *See also* Albalag, Isaac; Del Medigo, Elijah; Ibn Caspi, Joseph; Narboni, Moses
Jewish Enlightenment, 3:246, **3:249–250**, 9:42
Jewish Gnosticism, 5:2
Jewish history
  Cumberland on, 2:614
  La Peyrère on, 5:196
Jewish mysticism, 1:709, 5:1
Jewish orthodoxy, rebellion against, 4:824
Jewish philosophy, **4:809–833**
  continuity in, 4:819
  on creation, 3:360–361
  Crescas and, 2:592–593
  dialectic in, **3:69–70**
  Elisaeus in, 7:630
  emanationism in, 3:189–190
  eternity in, 3:360–361
  German period of, 4:826
  Gersonides in, 4:69
  on God, nature of, 3:401
  Guide of the Perplexed (Maimonides) and, 5:648–653
  Hellenistic period of, 4:810–811
  Ibn Gabirol and, 4:545–547
  Ibn Zaddik and, 4:551–552
  illumination in, 4:580
  on immortality, 4:618
  Israeli in, 4:764–765
  kalām in, 3:69–70
  Maimonides in, **5:647–654**
  medieval, 4:811–824
  Menasseh ben Israel in, 6:128
  modern and contemporary, 4:824–829
  Muqammiṣ in, 6:432
  Neoplatonism and, 1:457–458, 3:403
  Nussbaum and, 6:680
  Orobio in, 7:41
  philosophers classified in, 4:825
  in Platonic tradition, 7:611
  Plotinus and, 3:401
  and political philosophy, 7:657–658, 7:679–680
  Pythagoreanism in, 8:188
  Rosenzweig in, 8:499
  Saadya in, 8:585–587
  Shestov in, 9:13
  Spinoza in, 9:169–192
  Sufism and, 1:458
  13th-century, 4:819–821
  time in, 7:387
  See also Judaism
Jewish terrorism, 9:395
Jewish theology
  Buber and, 1:715, 4:829
  Celsus on, 2:119
  Cohen (Hermann) on, 2:304
  faith in, 1:716, 3:536
  See also Judaism
Jews
  Ashkenazic, *Haskalah,* 3:246
  characteristics of, Pareto on, 7:118
  Cohen (Hermann) on, 2:304–306
  Dostoevsky on, 3:101
  Dühring on, 3:131
  in England, readmission of, 6:128
  in Germany, 2:304–306
  Mirabaud on, 2:266
  Pascal on, 7:133
  racism and, 8:228
  and Scriptures, 5:2
Jhana, 6:254–255
Jhering, Rudolf von, on law, 7:426
Ji Kan, on speech, 2:208
Ji Zang
  and Buddhism, 2:154
  on double truth and contextual meaning, 2:209
  on truth as conventional *vs.* absolute, 2:162
  on wisdom, 2:219
Jianwen zhi zhi (Knowledge of seeing and hearing), Zhang Zai on, 9:879–880
Jina, 1:722
Jing (emperor of China), 3:98
Jingde Chuandeng Lu (Chan text), 2:167
Jinsei, 5:162
"*Jinsei sampǫ-setsu*" ("The three treasures of theory of man's life"), 6:623
Jinul, **4:833–834,** 5:136
Jīva, in Jainism, 5:327, 6:254
Jixia Academy, 2:216

Jnana, 5:116
Joachim, Harold H., 9:536
Joachim of Fiore, **4:834–835**
Joachim of Floris, 1:452
Joachimsen, Paul, 2:123
Job, Book of, 9:793
Jodl, Friedrich, **4:835–836**
  on atheism, 1:358
  Laas and, 5:164
Johann Friedrich, Duke of Hanover, Leibniz and, 5:252
John XXII, Pope
  Eckhart (Meister) and, 3:162
  Ockham and, 9:770–771
  Philip VI and, 3:148
John Duns Scotus. *See* Duns Scotus, John
John Italos, 1:786–788
John Locke Lectures, 2:711
John of Damascus, 1:786, **4:836–837**
John of Fidanza. *See* St. Bonaventure
John of Jandun, **4:838–840**
  Averroism of, 1:428
  Siger of Brabant and, 9:27
John of La Rochelle, **4:840–841**
  Alexander of Hales and, 1:114–115
  Augustinianism of, 1:402
  epistemology of, 1:403
John of Mirecourt, **4:841–842**
  d'Ailly and, 1:99
  on Nicolas of Autrecourt, 6:599
  Ockhamism of, 7:8
John of Paris, **4:842,** 9:444
John of St. Thomas, **4:843–844,** 8:765
John of Salisbury, **4:844–845**
  on Bernard of Chartres, 1:590
  on *ex impossibli quodlibet,* 5:429
  Gilbert of Poitiers and, 4:88
  on grammar, 8:770
  on syncategoremata, 8:769
  William of Conches and, 9:768
John of the Cross, St. *See* St. John of the Cross
John Paul II, Pope
  on liberation theology, 5:332
  on Newman (John Henry), 6:583
  Scheler and, 8:616
  on sex outside of marriage, 7:529
John Scotus Erigena. *See* Erigena, John Scotus
John Stuart Mill (Skorupski), 6:232
John's Gospel, on incarnation in Christianity, 2:247
Johnson, Alexander Bryan, **4:847–851,** 8:794–795
Johnson, Rodney W., 4:675
Johnson, Samuel (American philosopher), **4:851–852**
  on Berkeley, 1:581
  on common sense, 2:354
  Edwards (Jonathan) and, 3:166
Johnson, Samuel (English litterateur), **4:852–854**
  on art, 1:49
  on Bolingbroke, 1:641–642, 2:684
  on deism, 2:681
Johnson, William Ernest
  on determinables and determinates, 3:1
  Keynes and, 5:457
  logic of, 5:458
  Stebbing and, 9:236
Johnston, Mark, 8:443, 8:714
Johnstone, Peter T., 4:740
Joint denial, definition of, 5:547
Joint methods of agreement and difference of induction, 6:224, 6:240–242
Jokes, as absurdity *vs.* nonsense, 2:77
Joly, Eugene, 3:530
Jonas, Hans, 7:548–549, 9:78
Jones, Sir Henry, 4:108
Jones, W. T., on Plotinus, 3:401
Jordanus Brunus Redivivus, 2:267
Jordanus Nemorarius, on energy and work, 3:227
Jørgensen, Jørgen, 5:525
Joris, David, Franck and, 3:714
Josef K, in *The Trial,* 5:5
Joseph, H. W. B., on laws of thought, 5:231
Joseph II (king of Austria), Enlightenment and, 3:247
Joseph ben Abraham Gikatilia, 5:3
Joseph ben Jacob al-Kirkisani, 5:2
Joseph von Arimathia (Lavater), 5:213
Josephson, Eric, on alienation, 1:122
Josephson, Mary, on alienation, 1:122
Josephus
  as apologist, 1:227
  on suicide, 9:319
Jouffroy, Théodore Simon, **4:855–856**
  Laromiguière and, 5:201
  on Spinoza's pantheism, 9:195
Joule, James Prescott
  on energy conservation, 3:230, 3:551
  physicotheology and, 7:560
Journal (Emerson), 3:194–196
Journal des Savants (periodical), 5:253, 5:275
Journal des Sçavans (periodical), 5:253
Journal intime (Maine de Biran), 5:655
Journal of a Tour to the Hebrides with Samuel Johnson, The (Boswell), 4:853
Journal of Applied Behavior Analysis, 9:61
Journal of Consciousness Studies, 7:116
Journal of Parapsychology, 7:116
Journal of Philosophy, 3:44
Journal of Psychic Research, 7:116
Journal of Scientific Exploration, 7:116
Journal of Speculative Philosophy, 3:43, 3:196, 4:286, 4:558, 7:165–166
Journal of the American Society of Psychical Research, 7:116
Journal of the Experimental Analysis of Behavior, 9:61
Journal of the History of Ideas, 5:593
Journal of Unified Science, 5:525
Journalism
  philosophy and, 7:333
  social role of, 1:556
Journals, philosophical, 10:139–177
Journey from St. Petersburg to Moscow (Puteschestvie iz Peterburga v Moskvu), (Radishchev), 8:230
Jouvenel, Bertrand de, 3:722
Joyce, G. H., on common consent arguments for God's existence, 2:344, 2:347–349
Joyce, James, and Cixous, 2:262
Joyce, James M., on decision theory, 2:655
Joyce, Richard, moral fictionalism of, 3:628
Juárez, Benito, Barreda and, 5:206
Judah ha-Levi, 9:50
Judah the Faithful, 9:182
Judah the Hasid, 5:2, 5:3
Judaism
  Albo on, 1:102
  Christianity and, 3:536, 4:826–827
  Costa and, 2:572
  as covenantal relationship, 3:536
  creation in, 7:490
  and deism, Mendelssohn on, 6:132
  and divine transcendence, 4:107
  dogma in, 1:102, 3:97, 4:827
  eschatology in, 3:347
  on eternal return doctrine, 3:353
  excommunication in, 9:169
  and Gnosticism, 4:101
  on God's righteousness, 4:111
  Heaven and Hell in, 4:250
  Hegel on, 4:261–262
  Hellenistic, patristic philosophy and, 7:141–142
  history and, 4:809–810, 4:829, 7:387
  on immortality, 4:618

intolerance of, Gibbon on, 4:85
love of God in, 5:585–586
and martyrdom, 9:182, 9:320
Messiah in, 1:102–103
and monotheism, 4:110
mysticism of, 6:446–447
natural in, 7:14
purpose of, Spinoza on, 4:827
rational superiority of, 4:809
reproductive technologies and, 4:46
Saadya on, 8:586
Simon on, 9:33
Spinoza on, 4:826–827
on suicide, 9:319–320
universalization of, 4:827
wisdom literature of, 9:793
Zoroastrianism and, 9:886
See also Jewish philosophy; Jewish theology; Rabbinical Judaism

Judeo-Christian tradition, pessimism in, 7:246

Judging for Ourselves: Or Free-Thinking, the Great Duty of Religion. Display'd in Two Lectures, deliver'd at Plaisterers-Hall (Annet), 1:210

Judgment(s)
a priori
vs. a posteriori, 1:159
characteristics of, 6:117
Kant on, 5:13–14. *See also Critique of Judgment* (Kant)
Maimon on, 5:646
and synthetic, 5:13–14
and understanding, 8:660
abstractive cognition and, 9:774–775
and act expressed as synsemantic term, 1:690
aesthetic. *See* Aesthetic judgment
analytical
Bolzano on, 5:446
contradiction and, 5:13
Kant on, 1:242, 5:13–14. *See also Critique of Judgment* (Kant)
vs. synthetic, 1:159–161
anthropological, 7:244
as appetite, 8:51
vs. apprehension, Ockham on, 9:773–774
Arendt on, 1:254–255
Aristotle on, 3:286–287
art and, 1:335
ascribing maxims to, 5:26
Bonaventure on, 1:653
Bosanquet on, 1:661–662
Bradley on, 3:310
Brentano on, 1:689–690
in Buddhist epistemology, 1:755
in Cartesian epistemology, 2:56–57
in Chinese philosophy, 2:188–190
in Christianity, 2:249
circumstantial discretion in, 2:200
Clarke on, 2:271
Clauberg on, 2:286
in coherence theory of truth, 2:309–312
colors and, 2:332
vs. concepts, 1:394–395
as conclusion of inference, 5:94
considered, 1:238
contents required for, 8:663
counterfactuals and, 2:428, 2:574
Creighton on, 2:592
criteriololgy in, 2:594
Croce on, 2:602
in Daoism, 2:197–198
De Morgan on, 5:461
definition of, 5:547
Descartes on, 2:744, 3:291–292
Destutt de Tracy on, 2:760
divine, 1:394–395
emotion and, 2:252
ethical, correctness of, 7:3
evident *vs.* blind, 1:690–691
existential, 5:708
false yet evident, 6:117
formal properties of, 5:17–18
Frege on, 3:726
Hegel on, 4:265–266
Hume on, 3:495
ideal, Mercier on, 6:145
incremental confirmation explication and, 2:437–438
Kant on, 1:242, 2:74–75, 3:306–309, 5:13–16, 5:456, 6:193. *See also Critique of Judgment* (Kant)
Locke on, 5:386
as logic of propositions, 5:494
Malebranche on, 3:293–294
Mansel on, 5:687
mathematical, 1:714
McTaggart on, 6:78
mental content and, 2:478
metalinguistic analysis and, 2:187
moral. *See* Moral judgment(s)
in moral constructivism, 2:473
normative, Lewis (C. I.) on, 5:310–311
object of, 6:116
objective, Westermarck and, 9:739
in paradoxes of indifference, 2:436
perception as, 3:675, 7:179
of personal responsibility, 8:444–445
of pleasure, 1:339
political, Niebuhr on, 6:606
predicative, and existence, 3:495–496
propositional attitudes of, 4:712
psychological, 7:244
in Pyrrhonism, 1:195–196
qualities of, 1:575
Rawls on, 5:323
and reality of objects, 8:660–661
reasoning and, 3:675
reflection by community and, 1:459
relational, 1:676
of responsibility, cognition and, 9:686
of revelation, 8:454
Rickert on, 6:544
Russell on, 2:544
Scanlon on, 2:517
of self as of others, 9:67
Sigwart on, 9:29
Spinoza on, 3:295
suspension of, 1:31, 1:247–248, 8:175–176
taste and, 1:35
tranquility and, 1:195–196
types of, 1:662, 5:13, 7:244
universal, 7:244
value. *See* Value judgment(s)
Windelband on, 9:792
in wisdom, 9:795

Judgment internalism, 4:714

Judicanda, 4:863

Judicial activism
legal positivism on, 5:238
legal realism on, 5:245–246

Judicial discretion
legal positivism on, 5:238–241
legal realism on, 5:245–246

Judith (Hebbel), 4:253

Jugendgeschichte Hegels (Dilthey), 3:84

Jugendschriften (Hegel), 5:30

Julian (bishop of Eclanum), 7:522

Julian (emperor of Rome), as apologist, 1:228

Julian the Chaldaean, 6:549

Jung, Carl Gustav, **4:856–859**
on aesthetics, 1:58
analytical psychology of, 8:146–147
on common consent argument for God's existence, 2:345
Freud and, 4:856–857, 8:106, 8:147
Kaufmann and, 5:46
on microcosm, 5:642

Jung, Carl Gustav, ***continued***
and modern psychoanalysis, 8:107
on mythology, 8:146–147
on patients' purposelessness, 5:352
on personality, 8:146–147
on religion, 8:146–147, 8:379
on sex, 8:146
on synchronicity, 7:757
on unconscious, 9:573
Junge Hegel, Der (Lukács), 3:84
Jünger, Ernst, **4:859–861**
Klages and, 5:77
on philosophy of technology, 7:545
Jungius, Joachim, **4:861–862,** 5:440
Juridico-philosophical work, of Kelsen, 5:49
Jurieu, Pierre, 6:603–604
Bayle and, 1:503
irrational fideism of, 4:96
Jurisprudence
analytic, **1:168–171**
legal positivism as, 5:237–238
Raz on, 1:169
Simchen on, 1:170
Aristotle on, 7:419
Austin (John) on, 1:405–406, 7:425
Bentham on, 7:424–425
Cohen (Hermann) on, 2:303–304
Cohen (Morris) on, 2:307
feminist, 7:462–463
Herculean, 7:458–459
as intellectually derived from Divine will, 1:542
Kant and, 7:424
medico-legal, 6:95
normative, 1:169–170
ownership and, 8:72
vs. philosophy of law, 7:443
pragmatism in, 7:718
Priestley on, 8:5
procedural justice in, 4:864
province of, 1:405–406
Pufendorf on, 8:158
science in, Haeckel on, 4:204
substantive, 1:168
See also Law; Legal positivism
Juristic theories, 8:469–470
Just, The (Camus), 2:22
Just and Unjust Wars (Walzer), 7:157
Just cause
definition of, 4:870–871
feminist challenge to, 4:874
Just defense, 4:871
Just means
collectivism and, 4:873–874
conventionalism and, 4:872
definition of, 4:870–871
feminism and, 4:874
Just War: Force and Political Responsibility, The (Ramsey), 7:157
Just war theory, **4:870–874,** 7:157–158
feminism and, 4:874
Grotius on, 4:191–192, 7:423
intended *vs.* foreseen consequences in, 4:871
Suárez on, 9:285
terrorism in, 9:396–397
Justianus (emperor of Rome), 2:622, 6:553
Justice, **4:862–870**
Anaximander on, 1:184–185
in *Anonymus Iamblichi,* 6:632
Antiphon on, 6:631–632
Aquinas on, 9:434
Aristotle on, 1:267, 3:329
cause and effect and, 4:814
in Chinese thought, 2:238
civil disobedience and, 2:259–261
in coercive institutions, 9:74
Cohen (Hermann) on, 2:303–304
conduct-guiding function of, 4:862–863
conservatism on, 2:470
cosmic, 1:184–185
cosmopolitanist, 6:488
Cousin on, 2:579
in criminal punishment, 1:517
Dante on, 2:626
Del Vecchio on, 2:697
demands of, fulfillment of, 3:745
distribution of, and bioethics, 1:600–603
divine, 1:542, 7:387
Dworkin on, 3:156–157
education and, 7:366
egalitarian, 6:488
enforceability of, 4:866
environmental, 3:258
Epicurus on, 3:268
as fairness, 8:257–258
and family, 3:599
feminist ideal of, 9:75
first-order, 4:864
formal, 4:864–865
general will in, 4:38–40
Gewirth on, 4:81
golden rule and, 4:146
Habermas on, 3:91
human affection for, Duns Scotus on, 3:142–143
as human awareness, 1:542
and human happiness, 3:684
Hume on, 3:409
judicanda of, 4:863
Latin American philosophy on, 5:205
law and, 7:455–456, 8:230
liberal, 6:488–489
libertarianism on, 5:336–337
vs. liberty, 5:336
Luther on, 5:612
material, 4:865–866
in medical ethics, 6:92–93
moral cosmopolitanism and, 2:568–569
in moral voices of males, 3:579
Niebuhr on, 6:606
normative function of, 4:862–863
Nozick on, 6:668
optimism/pessimism and, 7:248
vs. other moral qualities, 4:866
Pelagianism on, 7:175
in Platonic dialogues, 7:584–585
principles of, 5:38, 8:258–259
procedural, 4:864
punishment and, 8:160–162
Rawls on, 3:470, 4:867–868, 5:323–324, 6:488, 8:258–259, 9:80
recipient-oriented, 4:867–868
Rüdiger on, 8:527
Saadya on, 4:812–813
and sanction of the will, 8:620
shaming punishment as, 9:5
social
communism and, 2:361
liberation theology on, 5:331
Pestalozzi on, 7:255
Rawls on, 5:323–324
technology and, 7:544
social positivism and, 7:711
in socialist thought, 9:88–89
Socrates on, 9:855
sophists on, 9:130
as sovereign authority, 1:621
Stammler on, 9:203
unified concept of, 4:863–869
utilitarianism and, 8:162, 9:66
utility and, 7:455–456
Vico on, 9:673–674
as virtue, 3:684, 7:307
Voltaire on, 9:712–713
in wage value, 2:363
as will of God, 1:542, 7:387
Justice as Fairness (Rawls), 3:470, 9:80
Justice, Gender and the Family (Okin), 9:75
Justification
a priori, 5:80
of aesthetic ascriptions, 1:40
in Agrippa's trilemma, 8:177
Alston on, 1:132–133

atheism and, 1:373–374
of belief, 2:275, 2:314, 5:87, 7:357, 8:177
Bickenbach on, 5:512
of cognitive attitudes, 2:483
in coherentism, 8:179–180
of conduct, 2:519
in conservatism, 2:467
considered judgments and, 1:238
in contractualism, 2:518–519
deductive, 4:638–639, 5:511
in education, 7:360
in epistemology, 1:132–133, 9:135–136
ethical, of civil disobedience, 2:260–261
evidentialism and, 3:468
of evil, 9:711
by faith, Sabatier on, 2:249, 8:588
in foundationalism, 2:277–279, 8:177–179
good-reasons approach on, 3:430
of heterosexism, 4:347–348
Hume on, 3:304
in induction, 4:636, 9:265, 9:575
inferential, 2:275–276
infinite regress of, 5:109
in infinitism, 8:179
of intuitions, 4:734–735
knowledge and. *See* Knowledge, justification of
Lehrer on, 5:248–249
moral, in Christianity, 2:248–249
of moral principles, **6:369–376**, 8:50
of morality, 5:715, 6:619, 9:449
Nozick on, 6:669
objectivity as, 7:3, 7:4
Plantinga on, 7:580
in positivism, 8:180
of property, 8:69–70
of punishment, 8:160–162
in Pyrrhonism, 8:174–175
Rawls on, 5:323
retributivism and, 8:162
social epistemology and, 9:83
standard conception of, 5:104
and swamping problem, 5:105
of validity, 5:511
of values, 2:467
"vindication," 4:644
of violence, 9:677
and virtues, 9:135–136, 9:688
Justification of Paternalism, The (Gert and Culver), 6:92
Justification of the Good, The (Solov'ëv), 9:122, 9:125
Justified belief. *See* Belief(s), justified
Justin Martyr
as apologist, 1:227–228
on logos, 5:569
patristic philosophy and, 7:142
on Socrates, 9:113
Justinian, 7:420
Justitia et Jure, De (Soto), 9:137

K

K (land surveyor), in *The Castle,* 5:6
K filolsofii postupka (Bakhtin), 1:469
Kabbalah, **5:1–5**
Agrippa von Nettesheim and, 1:97–98
emanationism in, 3:190
God as positive nothingness in, 9:123
in Jewish philosophy, 4:821
microcosm in, 5:642
mysticism of, 6:446–447
Pico della Mirandola and, 7:571–573
in universal philosophical system, 7:614
Kabbalism
Conway and, 2:529
Cordovero and, 2:539
Leibniz and, 5:256
Paracelsus and, 7:103–104
Kafka, Franz, **5:5–6**
Lukács and, 5:603
Mamardashvili on, 5:680
nihilism in, 6:618
Kagan, Matvei, 1:468
Kagan, Shelly, 8:721, 9:613
Kagen (The origin of price) (Miura), 6:276
Kahan, Dan, 9:5
Kahn, Herman, 7:157
Kaibara Ekken (Ekiken), **5:7**
Kaila, Eino, 5:525, 9:847
Kairos Document, Challenge to the Church, The, 5:331–332
Kakon, **1:256**
Kala, and idea of knowledge, 5:117
Kalām
cosmological argument, 2:113, 2:551–554, 2:593, 3:321
on "creative word" of God, 5:4
dialectic and, 3:69–70
La Peyrère on, 5:196
Leibniz on, 3:297, 3:494, 5:257, 5:263–265
of literature, 1:318
Losskii on, 5:577
Maimonides on, 4:818, 5:650–651
in Manichaeism, 5:683
meanings of, 1:360
Milton on, 6:249
of music, 1:318
Muʿtazilite, 4:811
out of eternity, 9:28
Peter Lombard on, 7:260–261
Philo on, 7:303–304
Philoponus on, 7:314
Plato on, 2:698–699, 6:519, 7:603
Predelli on artistic, 1:318
and principle of plenitude, 3:473
as quantum event and *kalām* argument on God's existence, 2:555
Qur'anic understanding in, 2:113
Ray on, 7:558
Rosenzweig on, 4:829
Ruskin on, 8:534
Saadya on, 8:586
semantics of, 1:370
separability substance *vs.* God identity with that which is, 1:626
temporal, Saadya on, 4:812
temporality of, 1:360
Theophilus of Antioch on, 7:142
in *Timaeus* (Plato), William of Conches on, 9:768
Ussher on, 5:196
in utopianism, 9:619
Voltaire on, 9:710
William of Auvergne on, 9:765
See also Emanationism
Kalbfleisch, J. G., 3:665
Kaldor-Hicks efficiency, 7:461–462
Kāli, in meditation, 6:108
Kalima, in Islamic thought, 3:97
Kalin, Theodore A., 5:566
Kalin-Burkhart, as electrical logic machine, 5:566
Kalkreuth, Graf Adolf, Maimon and, 5:645
"Kallias-Letters" (Schiller, Friedrich), 8:627
Kalon, 1:256, **5:7–8**
Kames, Lord. *See* Home, Henry
Kami, in Japanese philosophy, 4:796
Kamlah, Wilhelm, Bultmann and, 3:506
Kamm, Frances, on human dignity, 2:714
Kamp, Hans, 4:623
on anaphora, 1:174
discourse representation theory (DRT) of, 8:748–749
on dynamic semantics, 8:808
on temporal coordinates, 8:745
Kampf als innerres Erlebnis, Der (Jünger), 4:859

Kaṇāda, on logic, 5:412
Kanazawa, Makoto, on anaphora, 1:175
Kandel, Eric, 6:567–568
Kango (Presumptuous words) (Miura), 6:276
Kant, Immanuel, **5:8–35**
- on *a posteriori* knowledge, 3:306
- on *a priori* and *a posteriori,* 1:240–242
- on *a priori* and necessary, 5:100
- on *a priori* knowledge, 1:160, 3:306–307, 3:410, 5:79–80, 5:101
- *a priori* metaphysics of, 6:170
- on *a priori vs.* empirical, 6:202
- Abbagnano on, 1:2
- on absolute, 1:11
- and absolute idealism, 4:556
- Adickes on, 6:541
- on aesthetic experience, 1:32–34
- on aesthetic judgment, 1:35–37, 5:26, 8:630
- on aesthetic pleasure, 8:598
- on agency, 3:445
- on agnosticism, 1:92, 5:709
- on altruism, 1:137
- on analytic propositions, 5:79
- on analytic *vs.* synthetic distinction, 1:159–161, 5:14
- on animal rights, 1:208
- anthropology and, 7:316
- on antinomies, 9:47
- Apel on, 1:226
- on appearance, 1:232, 5:12
- on apperception, 1:233–234, 3:308, 4:51, 5:17
- Arendt on, 1:255
- on argument from design, 7:560
- on arithmetic, 1:244
- on art, 1:28, 1:34
- Baader on, 1:439
- Bakhtin and, 1:467
- Baron on, 5:36
- Baumgarten and, 1:493
- on beauty, 1:32–33, 1:38–39, 1:52–53, 1:308
- Berdyaev on, 1:560, 9:529
- on Berkeley, 4:555
- British empricism and, 3:306
- Caird and, 2:4
- Cassirer and, 2:66
- categorical imperative of, 2:69–72, 3:385–386
  - and conscience, 2:447
  - golden rule as basis of, 4:146
- on categories, 2:74–75, 5:536
- on causality, 2:103, 6:202
- on certainty, 4:770
- Chamberlain and, 2:122
- Chicherin on, 2:147
- Chisholm on, 5:81
- on civil contract, 9:73–74
- civil liberties in, 9:73–74
- Clifford on, 2:291
- Cohen (Hermann) on, 2:301–306
- coherence theory of truth and, 9:536
- Coleridge and, 2:315
- common sense and, 2:357
- on community, 2:367
- on concepts, 2:415–417, 4:58
- connotation in, 2:74
- on consciousness, 2:453, 2:758
- constructivism and, 2:475, 9:76
- contractualism of, 3:385–386
- on cosmology, 2:556
- cosmopolitanism and, 2:567
- on councils, 3:411
- Cournot and, 2:576
- Couturat on, 2:581–582
- on critical idealism, 4:553, 5:10
- and critical theory, 2:598
- critique of metaphysics and, 5:526
- Croce and, 2:600–602
- Crusius and, 2:605, 2:608, 5:124
- on definition, 2:665–668
- deism and, 2:689–691
- Deleuze and, 2:694–696
- deontological ethics and, 2:714
- on Descartes, 8:649
- on determinism, 3:15, 3:27
- Deussen and, 3:41
- Dewey and, 3:44
- dialectic and, 3:54
- Dilthey and, 3:79, 3:84
- Dingler and, 3:85
- Driesch and, 3:110
- dualism of, 8:627
- Dühring and, 3:130
- Duns Scotus and, 3:136
- on duty, 3:153–155, 3:411, 8:627
- Eberhard and, 3:161–162
- Eddington and, 3:165
- on education, 7:373–374
- Einstein and, 3:179
- on empathy, 9:37
- on empiricism, 3:215, 8:134
- Enlightenment and, 3:242–245
- epistemology of, 3:306–309, 5:91
- on equality, 3:330
- on evil, 3:469–470
- on existence, 3:495, 7:22
- on experience, 3:517, 8:134
- faith in, 5:23, 7:493, 7:543
- on feeling, 7:620
- Fichte and, 1:377, 3:613, 5:708, 6:539
- first large German monograph on, 3:659–660
- Fischer-Trendelenburg controversy on, 2:302
- formalism and, 1:74–75, 1:308
- on free will, 3:15, 3:27, 3:412, 4:556, 8:134
- on freedom, 3:15, 5:321
- Frege on, 3:729
- Freud on, 3:746
- Fries and, 3:752
- Froebel and, 7:373
- Garve on, 4:24
- on general will, 4:38
- on genius, 1:28, 1:77
- Gentile and, 4:50
- on geometry, 1:244, 4:57–58, 4:305
- Gestalt psychology and, 8:144
- on globalization, 7:389
- on God, 1:232, 2:689, 7:17
- Gödel on, 4:117
- Goethe and, 4:141–142
- on good will, 2:715
- Grice and, 4:184
- Habermas and, 3:91
- Hägerström and, 4:205
- Hegel and, 3:309–310
- Helmholtz and, 4:303
- on history, 7:374, 7:389
- on Hume's skepticism, 9:57
- idealists and, 7:493–494
- on ideas, 4:565
- on I-in-itself, 1:519
- on immortality, 4:612–614, 4:669
- on impartiality, 4:620
- on individuality, 7:373
- on inertia, 6:3
- on infinity, 9:467
- on innate ideas, 4:693
- on inner sense, 4:697
- on intellectual intuition, 4:772
- on internalism, 4:714
- on intrinsic value, 4:719
- on intuition, 4:723, 4:729, 4:772
- and Iqbals' theistic pluralism, 4:744
- Jacobi (Friedrich Heinrich) on, 4:770–771
- Jaspers and, 4:799
- journals on, 6:539
- on Judaism, 3:249
- on judgment. *See also Critique of Judgment* (Kant)
  - aesthetic, 1:35–37, 5:26, 8:630
  - analytic, 1:242, 5:13–14
  - felt effects of, 9:294
  - synthetic, 5:13–14

teleological, 4:596–597
transcendental, 3:308
on jurisprudence, 7:424
Kaufmann on, 5:46
Kierkegaard and, 3:504, 5:62
on kingdom of ends and categorical imperative, 2:366–367
Kleist on, 5:78
on knowledge of God, 4:112
on knowledge of inner states, 9:44
on knowledge *vs.* faith, 7:543
Knutzen and, 5:124
Köhler and, 5:131
Korn and, 5:142
Kozlov and, 5:146
Krueger on, 5:156
Laas on, 5:163
Lacan and, 5:167
Lambert and, 5:176
Landgrebe on, 5:183–184
Lange on, 5:186–187
language used by, abstruseness of, 8:787
Latin American philosophy and, 5:208
Lavelle on, 5:214
Lavrov and, 5:218
on law, 7:424, 9:203
on laws of thought, 5:234
Lichtenberg and, 5:339–341
Liebert and, 5:343
Liebmann on, 6:545
on life, meaning and value of, 5:355
on limits of rational inquiry, 4:748
logic of, 5:456
Lotman and, 5:579
on lying, 5:619
Lyotard and, 5:620–621
Mach and, 5:623
MacIntyre on, 5:636
Maimon and, 5:645–646
Maine de Biran and, 5:656
Mamardashvili on, 5:677, 5:680
Maréchal and, 5:708–710
on mass, 6:3
on *mathesis universalis,* 8:645
mature philosophy of, formula for, 5:9
Mendelssohn and, 6:131, 7:99
on mental states and consciousness, 2:457
Mercier on, 6:145
and metaphysics, 3:308–309, 6:192–193, 7:374, 8:645
on mind, 5:709, 8:133–134
in modernism, 6:316–317
on monadology, 6:325
on moral agency, 3:364
on moral community, 2:518
on moral compliance, 6:394
on moral goodness, 4:152
on moral law, 3:154
on moral necessity, 2:713
on moral perfection, 7:195
on moral reasoning, 7:737
on moral responsibility, influence on Schopenhauer, 8:655
on moral theology, Schulze on, 8:661
on moral truths, 6:163
on moral universe, 8:619
Moritz and, 6:406
on motivation in ethics, 3:389–390
in Mou's neo-Confucianism, 2:183
on nationalism, 6:484
on natural law, 6:512–514
on nature, 1:36, 3:254, 6:519–520
nebular hypothesis on, 3:354
Nelson (Leonard) on, 6:534–535
on Newtonian mechanics, validity of, 8:639
Nicolai on, 6:598
Nietzsche on, 6:611–613
Nussbaum and, 6:680
on objective phenomena, 1:245
and ontology, 6:188, 7:16–17, 7:28, 9:287
on optimism/pessimism, 7:249
on pacifism, 7:67
Paley and, 7:76
on pantheism, 7:101
Pantheismusstreit and, 7:99–101
Parfit and, 7:120
Parker (T.) and, 7:121
Paulsen and, 7:148
Peirce and, 5:453, 7:163–167
on personal values, 3:442
on personalism, 7:234
on phenomena *vs.* noumena, 5:131
on phenomenology, 7:278–279
philosophical work of, 5:9–10
and philosophy of history, 7:388–389
philosophy of sex and, 7:522
plant theory of, 9:336
in Platonic tradition, 7:615
on political cosmopolitanism, 2:569
political philosophy of, 7:667–668
on possibility, 7:722–723
post-Hegelian ethical theory and, 3:415
postmodernism and, 7:729
on practical reason, 4:613
precritical writings of, 5:10–11
Pringle-Pattison and, 8:12
private life of, 5:9
on productive imagination, 4:596
on promises, 7:373–374
on property, 8:69
and psychology, 8:133–134
on punishment, 8:160–162
quid facti vs. quid juris in, 5:646
Rawls on, 9:82
on real predicates, 9:287
reason in, 7:729
Reinhold and, 8:334
in religious philosophy, 7:493
on respect, 8:441–442
retributivism of, 8:160
Riehl and, 8:467
Rousseau and, 2:366, 7:424
Scheler and, 3:421
Schelling and, 8:617
Schiller (Friedrich) and, 8:626–627
Schlegel on, 8:630
Schleiermacher and, 8:633, 8:637
Schopenhauer and, 3:311, 8:648–649
Schultz and, 8:659
Schuppe and, 8:663
on science, 7:317–318
on self, 8:134
on self-deception, 8:713
Shelley and, 9:9
Shestov on, 9:11
Sidgwick and, 9:25
Simmel and, 9:31
skepticism of, 9:47
sociology of knowledge and, 9:101
Solov'ëv and, 9:123
on soul, 3:118
on space, 4:58, 9:147–148
Spir and, 9:196
Stoics and, 3:400
Stumpf on, 9:280
on sublime, 1:53–54, 8:627, 9:293–294
on substance, 9:298
on suicide, 9:319
Sulzer and, 9:325
on syllogism, reduction of, 5:498
on synthetic *a priori* truths, 1:244
on taste, 1:36, 1:52–53
Teten and, 9:404
on thought and thinking, 4:561, 9:420–421
on time, 9:467
on transcendental idealism, 4:555–556
on transcendental logic, 2:79

Kant, Immanuel, ***continued***
on understanding, 3:80
on universal causality, 1:244
on universal history, 6:514, 7:388–389
Vaihinger and, 9:625
on virtue, 8:627
on war and peace, 7:155
Windelband on, 6:545, 9:791
wisdom and, 9:794
Wolff and, 5:124, 9:825, 9:830
and women philosophers, 9:839
and Zhang's neo-Confucianism, 2:159–160
Kant als Metaphysiker (Wundt), 6:542
Kant and the Problem of Metaphysics (Heidegger), 6:542, 9:490
Kant, Ontologie und Wissenschaftslehre (Martin), 6:542
Kant und die Epigonen (Liebmann), 5:344, 6:539, 6:541
Kantian constructivism, in moral constructivism, 2:472
Kantian critical philosophy, Mercier on, 6:145
Kantian ethics, 3:410–412, **5:36–38,** 5:76, 7:325–326, 7:373–374
applied, 1:239
deontological theory and, 4:153
on duty, 3:440
Gewirth on, 4:81
on moral principles, 3:445
Scheler on, 8:616
utilitarian strain in, 9:603
on value, 3:443
Westermarck on, 9:739–740
Kantian idealism
failure of, 9:791
Rensi on, 8:433
Kantian morality, 2:69, 4:613, 5:24–25
Hegel on, 4:261–262
Mou on, 2:183
practical reason as source of, 4:613
Kantianism
altruism in, 1:137
Bonhoeffer on, 1:655
Cohen (Hermann) and, 4:828
as consequentialism, 2:460
and crisis of skepticism, 9:57
and friendship, 3:749
Galluppi and, 4:13
Helmholtz and, 4:303–304
Lipps and, 5:363
on love, 5:591
on moral goodness, 4:152
Nussbaum and, 6:680
in philosophy of law, 7:424
Piaget and, 7:567
Schlick on, 8:639
Schulze on, 8:660
on sense perception, 4:729
on sexual objectification, 7:529
as subject idealism, 4:770
on virtue, 9:678
See also Neo-Kantianism
Kants Analogien der Erfahrung (Laas), 5:163
Kants Begründung der Ästhetik (Cohen), 2:305, 6:453
Kants Begründung der Ethik (Cohen), 2:303
Kants Erkenntnistheorie (Volkelt), 6:541–542
Kants Leben und die Grundlagen seine Lehre (Fischer), 3:660, 6:540
Kants Lehre von der doppelten Affektion unseres Ich (Adickes), 6:541
Kant's Metaphysics and Theory of Science (Martin), 6:542
Kants Theorie der Erfahrung (Cohen), 2:302
Kants Theorie der Ethik (Cohen), 6:543
Kants Theorie des Verstehens (Gurwitsch), 4:198
Kant's Thinker (Kitcher), 5:76
Kant's Transcendental Psychology (Kitcher), 5:76
Kantstudien (periodical), 5:343
Kaplan, David, **5:38–40**
and direct reference theory, 8:61, 8:289
Frege and, 3:732
on indexicals, 2:706–708, 4:622–623
on presupposition, 3:252–253
on propositions, 8:88–89
on semantic paradoxes, 5:522
Kaplan, Mark, on decision theory, 2:657
Kapp, Ernst, 7:543
Karaites, 4:813–814, 8:585
Karamzin, N. M., Lotman and, 5:578
Kareev, Nikolai Ivanovich, **5:40–41**
Kareyev, Nicholas Ivanovich. *See* Kareev, Nikolai Ivanovich
Karl, Gregory, on music, 1:306
Karma, **5:41–42**
in Buddhism, 1:748, 5:328, 6:256
causality and, 2:110
Chung on, 5:137
doctrine of, pessimism in, 7:246
Dōgen and, 3:96
God and, 4:133
in Indian philosophy, 2:110, 5:326
in Jainism, 8:718
law of, 5:121
meditation and, 6:108
as moral law, 2:110
prakṛti in, 4:626
process of, 4:624
in Purvamimamsa-Uttaramimamsa schools, 4:134
in reincarnation, 8:332
theory of, in liberation, 4:625
in *Yoga Sūtra,* 6:109
in Yogācāra Buddhism, 1:749–750
Karmic action-at-a-distance, 5:42
Karnaugh, Maurice, 5:563
Karnaugh map, for complex logical propositions, 5:563
Karplus, Margarethe "Gretel," 1:25
Karsavin, Lev Platonovich, 3:453, **5:42–44,** 9:529
Karsavina, Tamara, 5:42
Karttunen, Lauri, on implicatures, 3:253
Kāshmir Śaivism, 1:684, 4:631
Kaspi, Joseph. *See* Ibn Caspi, Joseph
Kass, Leon R., 4:617, 7:550
Kata Christianon (Against the Christians) (Porphyry), 3:455
Katalēptikē phantasia, 7:271
Katastemmatic pleasure, Epicurus on, 3:267
Kater, Johan van, 2:738
Katharsis, **5:44–45**
in aesthetic experience, 1:33
in Aristotle's *Poetics,* 1:188, 1:308, 9:522
in drama, 1:340
psychological, 5:44
in tragedy, 1:44–45
Kathā-vatthu (Points of Controversy) (Tissa), 5:411
Kathchen von Heilbronn, Das (Kleist), 5:79
Kathêkon (duty), Zeno of Citium on, 9:870
Kattunen, L., on anaphora, 1:173
Katz, David, 4:71, 9:516
Katz, Jerrold, 9:351
on language, 5:189
on utterative performances, 7:200
Katz, Steven, 6:461, 8:402
Kaufmann, Walter Arnold, **5:45–47,** 6:613
"Kausalität in der gegenwärtigen Physiks, Die" (Schlick), 8:641
Kautsky, Karl, **5:47–48,** 5:280
Kavelin, Konstantin Dmitrievich, **5:48–49**
Kavka, Gregory
on noncombatant immunity, 4:873
on nuclear deterrence, 7:157

"toxin puzzle" of intentions, 4:702–703
Kavod ("glory"), 5:4
Keinai gigai (Devotion within, righteousness without), 9:860
Keisler, H. Jerome, on hyperreal number systems, 2:506–507
Keller, Evelyn Fox, on masculine orientation of science, 3:592
Kellert, Stephen, 2:133
Kelsen, Hans, **5:49–50**
on basic law, 9:142
Hart on, 5:239
on just war theory, 7:423
legal positivism and, 5:237
pure legal theory of, 7:427
on sovereignty, 9:139
Kelvin, William Thomson, Lord, 2:637–638
on energy conservation, 3:231
Maxwell and, 6:68
Kemeny, John G., 2:439, 4:642
Kennedy, Gail, on Dewey, 3:425
Kenny, Anthony, 3:535
on continuity in Wittgenstein, 9:817
on emotions, 3:199
on omniscience, 7:479
Kephalaia (Mani), 5:683
Kepler, Johannes, **5:50–55**
astrology and, 7:573
and celestial mechanics, 2:535
and Copernican astronomy, 2:535
deductive-nomological model and, 8:694
ellipse and area rules of, 8:683
Fludd and, 3:675
Galileo and, 4:13
on mass, 6:3
on matter, 6:60
methodology of, 8:683
on nature, 6:519
personality of, 5:51
on physical causality, 5:54
Pico della Mirandola and, 7:573
Plato and, 7:602
Pythagoreanism and, 8:187
and quantitative determination of dynamic activity, 3:687
syntax of scientific laws and, 7:518
Kepler's laws, in cosmology, 2:558
Kerman, Joseph, on opera, 1:308
Kerygma and Myth (Bultmann), 1:764
Kessler, K. F., Kropotkin and, 5:155
Kett, Henry, 5:440
Keynes, John Maynard, **5:55–57**
on inductive conclusions, 4:641
on inductive probability and confirmation theory, 2:436
on Malthus, 5:676
on probability, 3:327, 8:27–28
Keynes, John Neville
on disjunctive syllogism, 5:503
on laws of thought, 5:233
logic of, 5:457–458
on predicative forms, 3:496
Keyserling, Hermann Alexander, Graf von, **5:57–58**
Khan, Genghis, 6:477
Khan, Helagu, 6:477–478
Khan, Inayat, 9:311
Kharakter Chelovecheskovo Znaniya (The character of human knowledge) (Chernyshevskii), 2:147
Khazars, conversion of, in Halevi, 4:815–816
Khinchin, Aleksandr, 4:677
Khomeini, Rohallah, 4:763, 8:647
Khomiakov, Aleksei Stepanovich, **5:58–61**
Khrushchev, Nikita, Lenin and, 5:281
Ki. See Qi
Kidd, John, physicotheology and, 7:560
Kierkegaard, Mikael Pederson, 5:61
Kierkegaard, Søren Aabye, **5:61–68**
Abbagnano and, 1:1
on actions, 3:501–503
and anthropology, 7:316
Barth and, 1:480, 3:505
on being, 1:530
and crisis of skepticism, 9:57
criticisms of, 3:508–509, 5:65–66
and divine command theories of ethics, 3:93
on divine incognito, 3:533
on divine transcendence, 4:107
on divine will, 9:716
on dread, 3:503, 3:508
and ethics, 3:415
on existence, 3:501
existentialism and, 4:285
as fideist, 3:631–632
Frank and, 3:715
Hegel and, 3:55
Heidegger and, 3:502
on individual, 3:501
influences on, 3:504
Jaspers and, 3:504, 4:799
on leap into faith, 9:58
Lequier and, 5:287
Lessing and, 5:297
literary style of, 3:504
on man's will, 5:91
on objective uncertainty, 3:531
on philosophers' view of reality, 3:502
on philosophical systems, 3:501
philosophy of sex and, 7:522
politics of, 3:506
on radical freedom, 8:608
on rationalism, 4:748
on religious truths contrary to probable assertions, 3:631
Shestov and, 9:11
Socrates and, 9:113
Stein and, 9:239
themes in, 3:504
Kierkegaard: Construction of the Aesthetic (Adorno), 1:27
Kiesow, Friedrich, 7:135
Killing, Wilhelm, 4:61
Killiyat (Averroes), 1:422
Kilogram, 6:2, 6:91
Kilvington, Richard, **5:68–69**
on *positio,* 5:433
Swineshead and, 9:343
Kilwardby, Robert, **5:69–71**
on Aristotle, 5:439
on invention *vs.* judgment, 5:438
on modality, 5:435
on plurality of forms, 1:403
on speculative grammar, 8:771
Thomism and, 9:444
Kim, Jaegwon, **5:71–72**
on causality of mental states, 6:646–647
on desire, 9:388
on dualism, 3:114
on emergence, 3:191–192
on event theory, 3:466–467
on functionalism, 6:645
on functionalizing reductionism, 6:570, 9:163
on multiple realizability, 6:644–645
on nonreductive materialism, 6:648
Sosa and, 9:135
Kimura, Motoo, on evolution, 7:340
Kind(s)
Aristotle on, 6:504
bridge principles and, 6:644
Kripke on, 6:504
linguistics of, 6:504–505
natural, **6:503–505**
of number, 6:670–671
ontology of art and, 1:315–316
Kindergarten movement, 3:754
Kindi, Abu-Yusuf Yaqub ibn Isaq al-. *See* al-Kindī, Abū-Yūsuf Yaʿqūb ibn Ishāq

Kind-nature, 3:147
Kindness
in Buddhism, 6:255
in Confucianism, 2:175–179
and ren in Confucian ethics, 2:175–176, 2:194
Kinds of Minds (Dennett), 2:711
Kinematic effects, Aristotelian notion of, 3:686
Kinematics, 2:559, 2:562, 6:412–413
Kinesthetic sense, perception and, 7:181
Kinetic pleasure, Epicurus on, 3:267
Kinetic theory, 1:644–645, 6:69–70
King, Jeffrey C.
on anaphora, 1:175–176
on demonstratives, 2:708
King, Martin Luther, Jr., **5:73–74**
on civil disobedience, 2:259–261
Marxism of, 5:741
pacifism and, 7:67
Thoreau and, 6:575
Kingdom of ends, Kant on, 3:154
Kingdom of God, Vaihinger on, 9:628
Kingly Crown, The (Ibn Gabirol), 4:545, 7:611
Kingsley, Charles, 2:641
Kinoshita Junan, 5:7
Kinsey, Alfred, 7:523
Kinship, universal, attainment of, 3:559
Kirchhoff, Gustav
Planck and, 7:577
on presence of iron in the sun, 3:664
Kireevskii, Ivan Vasil'evich, **5:74–76**
Kirmmse, Bruce, 5:68
Kirsteva, Julia, 3:565
Kitāb al-Amānāt wa'l'i tiqādāt ("The Book of Beliefs and Creeds") (Saadya), 4:812
Kitāb al-ʿIbar (Ibn Khaldūm), 4:547
Kitāb al-Muʿtabar (Abu'l-Barakāt al-Baghdādī), 4:817
Kitāb al-shifāʾ (Avicenna), 5:418
Kitcher, Patricia, **5:76–77**
Kitcher, Philip, 5:77
a priori justification and, 5:80
on *a priori* knowledge, 3:273
on dispensability of special sciences, 9:162
on explanation, 3:523–524
on linearity policy, 8:675
on propositions, general modal status of, 5:101
Putnam and, 5:84, 5:100
social epistemology and, 9:84
on theory-change, 8:692
Kittay, Eva, on Rawls, 1:158
Kivy, Peter
on art, 1:66–67
on music, 1:305
KK thesis, 5:108
Klaesges, Ulrich, Landgrebe and, 5:183
Klagen über das verdorbene Christenthum (Spener), 7:576
Klages, Ludwig, **5:77–78,** 7:319
Klee, Paul, and Benjamin, 1:546
Kleene, Stephen Cole
computing machines and, 2:402
on formal languages in computability theory and, 2:379
many-valued logic and, 5:491
on provability of equational calculus, 2:401
on truth-value gaps, 5:149
Kleene T-predicates, in computability theory, 2:389
Kleene's theorem, in computability theory, 2:382, 2:386, 2:401
Klein, Felix
Dingler and, 3:85
Erlangen Program, 4:60
Klein, Melanie, 5:152, 8:106
Klein, Peter, on conditions of knowledge, 3:270–271
Klein-Braslavy, Sara, 4:69
Kleist, Heinrich von, **5:78–79**
Kleitman, N., on dreams, 3:106
Klemperer, O., on mass and energy, 3:233
Kleptomania, determinism and, 3:16–17
Klimovsky, Gregorio, 5:210
Klopstock, Friedrich Gottlieb, Lavater and, 5:213
Knight, Richard Payne, on picturesque, 3:254
"Know Thyself," 8:722
Knowability, mental content features of, 2:477
Knowers, deauthorizing women as, 3:574
Knowing
Daoism as preparation for, 2:216
in phenomenology, 7:287
Russell on, 2:543
Knowing how, 5:94, 5:98, 8:582–584
Knowing subject, in *Critique of Pure Reason*, 5:21
Knowing that, 5:94, 5:98, 8:582–584
Knowledge, 9:547
a priori. See A priori knowledge; Rationalism
a priori geometry in vision and, 1:575
absence as means of, 5:117, 5:122
absolute
Bergson on, 1:567
Hegel on, 4:264, 5:62
abstraction in, 8:619
by acquaintance, 1:485, 5:97, 5:114, 8:545–546
act as, 1:103
and action, unity of, 9:726
Aeschylus on, 4:177
agent-relative, 8:710
Alexander on, 1:109
ambiguity as precondition for, 1:676–677
analytic
a posteriori, Kant on, 3:306
a priori, Kant on, 3:306
Anaxagoras on, 1:182–183
in animals, 6:499, 9:136
anthropology and, 7:318
apprehension in, 1:30
Aquinas on, 3:289, 9:426–427
Arcesilaus on, 3:288
Ardigò on, 1:251
Aristotle on, 3:286–287, 9:592–593
Armstrong on, 1:287
art and, 1:42, 1:79, 1:333–337, 8:653–654
asceticism and, 1:352
in attributor contextualism, 2:484–486
Augustine on, 1:392–395
Bacon (Francis) on, 1:445
and beauty, 1:511
in beauty *vs.* perfection, 6:131
belief and, 2:596, 3:270–271, 5:86–87, **5:91–100,** 5:656, 9:854
as belief attribution, 1:536–537
Bergson on, 1:566–567
Berkeley on, 3:217, 3:302–303, 8:783
Bernard of Clairvaux on, 1:592
Bodin on, 1:620
in Bohmian mechanics, 1:634
Bonaventure on, 1:653
Brahman and, 1:682–684
Broad on, 1:696
Bruno on, 1:711
Brunschvicg on, 1:713
in Buddhist epistemology, 1:753–754
in Byzantine view of philosophy, 1:786
Calvin on, 2:8–9
Campanella on, 2:15
Carnap on, 2:45
Carneades on, 3:288
Cartesians on, 2:670
causal theory of, 4:147, 6:628

certainty and, 2:431, 3:283
in Chan (Zen) Buddhism, 2:166
in Chinese philosophy, 2:215–216
Chisholm on, 2:243, 3:278
Chrysippus on, 2:252
Cicero on, 2:258
classification of, Peirce on, 7:169
Clifford on, 2:291
Code on, 2:296
Cohen (Morris) on, 2:307
in coherence theory of truth, 2:311
Collingwood on, 2:327
colors and, 2:333
Comenius on, 2:341
common, 4:16, 4:19–20
common consent arguments for God's existence and, 2:346
common sense and
  Hamilton on, 2:357
  Moore on, 2:358–359
as completely *sui generis,* 5:94
in computationalism, 2:394–395
Comte on, 2:410, 2:413, 7:392
Condillac on, 2:421–422, 8:784, 8:826
conditions for, traditional, 3:270–271
as conjecture, 6:595
conscience and, 2:445
of conscience *vs.* utilitarian consequences, 1:782
conscious qualitative states and, 2:451
as contemplation, 1:109
counterfactual conditionals and, 2:427
Cournot on, 2:576
Craig (Edward) on, 6:499
in critical realism, 2:596
Croce on, 2:602
Crusius on, 2:606
Cudworth on, 2:611
Cyrenaics on, 2:619
declarative *vs.* practical, 4:690
deductive reasoning and, 5:513
definability of, 5:94
definition of, 5:91–98, 7:586–587
Democritus on, 5:300
Descartes on, 2:365, 2:726–727
Dewey on, 3:45–48, 7:378–379
with direct object, 5:94
in direct realism and causality, 2:97
divine, 1:592, 6:65, 7:479
Dühring on, 3:130
Duns Scotus on, 3:137–140
Eddington on, 3:165
in education, 7:356
eidetic reduction and, 8:606
by eliminative induction, 1:446
emotion in, Windelband on, 9:791
as emptiness, 2:162
Encyclopédie on, 3:223–224
Engels on, 3:58–59
Epicurus on, 3:269–270
in epistemology, 7:325
of existence, 8:131
experience and, 1:453, 8:725. *See also* Empiricism
of external world
  Berkeley on, 3:301
  Hume on, 3:304–305
of facts, 1:251
factual, conscious qualitative states and, 2:451
faith and, 1:782–783, 3:529, 4:772, 9:425–426
  Aquinas on, 9:426
  as knowledge of God, 3:535
  scientific knowledge, 3:532
  Tennant on, 9:392
Foucault on, 7:396
foundationalism and, 2:275–279
fourth condition for, 5:106–107
Fries on, 3:752
Galluppi on, 4:14
in game theory, 4:19–20
of God, 3:622, 6:478, 7:305–306
  Alexander of Hales on, 1:114
  Aquinas on, 9:432
  as cause, 1:139–140
  Charron on, 2:134–135
  in Gnosticism, 4:102
  Halevi on, 4:816
  as innate, Calvin on, 2:9
  Isaac of Stella on, 4:753–754
  Leibniz on, 5:261–264
  Maimonides on, 4:818, 5:652
  Philo Judaeus on, 8:122
  Pseudo-Dionysius on, 8:101–102
  Rosenzweig on, 4:829
  Scholastics on, 3:137–138
  self-revelation of, in nature, 1:580
  Ulrich of Strasbourg on, 9:565
  Vives on, 9:701
Godwin on, 4:138
Goethe on, 4:142
Goldman on, 4:147
grades of, 8:126
Grosseteste on, 4:186
Habermas on, 4:200
Haeckel on, 4:202–203
Hegel on, 3:309–310
Helmholtz on, 4:304
Hempel on, 4:308
historical, 2:602, 7:388–395
in history, 1:719–720, 2:325
Hobbes on, 2:669, 4:424
Hume on, 3:218–219
and identity of knower and known, 1:12
in I-it *vs.* I-thou relations, 1:716
as illumination, 1:652, 4:579, 6:65
imagination and, 9:454–455
independent of being, in new realism, 6:586
in Indian philosophy
in Indian philosophy, 4:135, 4:627–468, **5:115–123,** 5:327, 7:95, 7:413
in indicative conditionals sentences, 2:425
indoctrination and, 7:358
of inductive probability, 2:437
inferential, 1:453, 3:108, 4:723–724
information as source of, 3:108
insight as, 8:126
integrity and universality of, 3:559
intellectual, in Tschirnhaus, 9:549
intention and, 7:447
intuitive, 1:567, 4:723–726
and intuitive participation *vs.* intellectual analysis, 1:567
Islamic view of, 3:319–320
in Jainism, 8:718
James (William) on, 3:313
justification of, 3:270–274, 5:88, 5:92–93, 5:104–106, 5:511
  a priori vs. a posteriori, 3:273–274
  Chisholm on, 2:242
  coherentism in, 3:271–272, 8:179–180
  ethical, 3:273
  evidentialism in, 3:272
  foundationalism and, 2:242, 3:271–272
  internalist *vs.* externalist, 3:272–273
  noninferential, 2:276
  positism on, 8:180
  proper functionalist theory in, 3:273
  reliabilism in, 3:272–273
justified belief and, 2:93, 9:683–684
Kant on, 3:306–309, 5:708, 7:543, 9:791
kinds of, 5:96
  Locke on, 3:300
  Spinoza on, 3:295–296

Knowledge, *continued*
as knower-known *vs.* wisdom as capacity, 2:215–216
Kuhn on, 2:475
language as condition of, 8:785
of laws of logic, 5:511
Le Clerc on, 5:236
Le Roy on, 5:288
as learned ignorance, 6:595
Lehrer on, 5:248–249
Leibniz on, 5:259–262
Lenin on, 3:64–65
Leonardo da Vinci on, 5:282
Lewis (C. I.) on, 5:307–308
light as metaphor for, 3:242
linguistic expression of, 8:640
linguistic theory of, 4:724
locations of, 5:116
Locke on, 2:597, 3:216–217, 3:300, 5:96, 5:376–379, 5:385–387, 7:370
logical analysis of, 8:641
Lotze on, 5:581
Lukács on, 5:604
Maimon on, 9:57
Maimonides on, 5:651–652
Maréchal on, 5:708–709
Maritain on, 5:712–713
Martineau on, 5:727
in Marxism, 5:737–738
mathematical
Mill (John Stuart) on, 5:82
objects of, 5:95
Quine on, 5:83–84
mathematical model of, 3:396
Matthew of Aquasparta on, 6:64–65
mental image representation in, 4:590
metaphysical, Fries and, 3:752
Mill (John Stuart) on, 7:392
and modality, **5:100–102**
in modernism, 6:316–317
moral
in Chinese philosophy, 2:221–222
prospective, 9:726
prospective *vs.* retrospective, 9:726
retrospective, 9:726
Wang Yang-ming on, 9:726
of moral action conformity to reason, 1:475
mystical, 1:423
Nāgārjuna on, 6:470
natural, Nicolas of Autrecourt on, 6:599–600
of natural law, 5:714–715
in naturalism, 6:499–500
of necessity for return to God, 1:652–653
in neo-Confucianism, 2:157–158, 4:795
in new realism, 6:584
Nicholas of Cusa on, 6:595
Nicolas of Autrecourt on, 6:601
nonexistence as instrument of, 6:531
noninferential, 4:726–727, 9:23
nonpropositional, 4:729–730
nonpropositional, intuition as, 4:729–730
as object of inquiry, 1:192
Ockham on, 9:780
vs. opinion, 1:42
Oresme on, 7:34
Ortega y Gasset on, 5:208–209, 7:46
of other minds, Wisdom (John) on, 9:798–799
overvaluation of, 9:547
Parmenides of Elea on, 7:122–128
partiality and authority of, 3:592
Pascal on, 7:132–134
Pearson on, 7:160
Peckham on, 7:161–162
Peirce on, 7:163–165, 7:171–173
perception and, 4:585, 7:178
personal and sub-personal, 4:690
Pestalozzi on, 7:371–372
in phenomenology, 7:287
Philo of Larissa on, 7:305, 7:312
in philosophy of language, 7:400
Plantinga on, 3:323–324, 7:580
Plato's theory of, 2:665, 3:283–286, 3:396, 3:736, 5:93, 5:259–260, 5:568, 7:586–590, 7:602
poetic, 5:716, 7:585
Popper on, 7:691
in positive social change, 2:83
in postmodernism, 6:317–318
practicality and, 1:450, 9:855
as pragmatic result, 1:566
prevolitional, 6:321–322
priority of, **5:86–90**
probability and, 8:26–31
process of, *vs.* object of, 6:585
proper function theory of, 6:498
prophetic, 7:305
propositional, 1:335, 5:92, **8:86–88**
in Pyrrhonism, 8:174–175
rational *vs.* sensible, 9:404
in rationalism, 5:95–96, 8:243–244
as rationality, 1:559
of rationality, in game theory, 4:18
of reality, 5:712–713
as relative, 3:667
in reliabilism, 6:498
religious, 7:61
Otto on, 7:59
Sabatier's critical symbolism as, 8:587
representation problem, in computationalism, 2:394
Rothacker on, 7:318
Rousseau on, 7:371
Rufus on, 8:528–529
Russell on, 3:315, 8:545–546
Saadya on, 4:812, 8:586
Sanskrit terms for, 5:115–116
Santayana on, 8:597
Scheler on, 7:318
Schelling on, 1:12, 8:619
Schiller (Ferdinand) on, 8:623
Schlick on, 8:640
Schopenhauer on, 8:653–654
Schuppe on, 8:662
science and, 4:424, 5:528
scientific, 2:602
Aristotle on, 2:667, 2:749
Averroes on, 1:423–424
Berkeley on, 3:64
Mach on, 3:64
Ockham on, 9:778
self-consciousness and, 2:15
as self-control, 9:855
self-knowledge and, in Ibn Zaddik, 4:551
Sellar on, 8:732
sensationalism and, 8:823
in Shao Yong's "before Heaven" learning, 9:6
in simulation theory, 9:37
skepticism and, 1:191, 3:318, 4:173, 9:42, 9:47
social constructionism and, 9:78
social epistemology and, 9:83
sociology of, *vs.* epistemology, 5:685
Socrates on, 9:794, 9:855
soul and, 9:70
sound and, 9:138
special sources of. *See* Introspection; Intuition; Memory; Perception; Testimony
Spinoza on, 8:126
in Stoicism, 1:247, 7:312
subjective, 1:495, 8:623
Suhrawardī on, 4:583
syllogism as means to, 1:450
systemization and reconstruction of, 2:37
taste and, 1:490
Tennant on, 9:392

testimony and, 9:401–403
Tetens on, 9:404
theological mysteries and, 1:622
theoretical
Avicenna on, 1:434
faith as, 4:772
theory of, 4:10, 9:122
Avicenna and, 4:757–758
crisis in, 7:318
myth of the given in, 8:733–734
reliabilist, 9:44
Sigwart on, 9:29
Soto on, 9:137
Spinoza and, 9:171
thing known and, 6:586
in thought experiments, nature of, 9:454–455
Toletus on, 9:511
transformative purpose of, 1:444
and true belief, 2:277, 2:596, 3:284–285, 5:93–95, 5:104–107
and truth, 2:166, 5:91–92, **5:102–108**
20th-century empiricists on, 3:219–220
twofold nature of, 9:791–792
types of, 3:752, 7:287
as unconscious memory, 1:784, 3:736
unified system of, 2:36
uninferred, 5:92
universal, 2:341
of universals, Aristotle on, 9:592–593
vagueness and, **5:108–112**
Vaihinger on, 9:627
in Valentinianism, 9:632
of validity of rule of inference, 5:511
value of, 5:104–107
virtue and, 9:135–136, 9:683–685, 9:794
vision-illumination and, 4:584
Voltaire on, 9:709
Wahle (Richard) on, 9:719
Wang Yangming on, 2:219, 9:726
Whewell on, 9:789
will and, 1:12, 8:620, 9:791
Windelband on, 9:791–792
in wisdom, 9:795
Wodeham on, 9:822
Xenophanes of Colophon on, 9:854
Zeno of Citium on, 9:870
Zhang Zai on, 9:879–880
Zhu Xi's scientific work and, 2:217
See also Epistemology
Knowledge and Action (Conocimiento y acción) (Vaz Ferreira), 5:208
Knowledge and Certainty (Malcolm), 5:662
Knowledge and Experience in the Philosophy of F. H. Bradley (Eliot), 3:185
Knowledge and Reality (Bosanquet), 1:661, 1:663, 4:559
Knowledge and the Flow of Information (Dretske), 3:108
Knowledge and the Sacred (Nasr), 6:479
Knowledge argument, **5:112–115,** 8:192
Knowledge in a Social World (Goldman), 4:147
Knowledge-by-presence
in illuminationism, 4:583–585
in modern Islamic philosophy, 4:762
Mullā Ṣadrā on, 3:320
in Sufism, 4:761, 9:305–306
of Suhrawardī, 9:316
Knudson, Albert C., on personalism, 7:233–235
Knutzen, Martin, 5:8–10, **5:123–124**
Koch, Christoph, on neural activity and consciousness, 2:456
Kochen, Simon, 6:277
Kochen-Dieks interpretation, 6:277–279
Kochen-Specker theorem. *See* Quantum mechanics
Kock, Anders, on synthetic differential geometry, 2:509
Kockelmans, J., on phenomenology, 7:300
Kock-Lawvere axiom, of non-zero infinitesimals, 2:509
Koder, Rudolf, 9:801
Koelling, R. A., 1:202
Koen, Billy Vaughn, 7:543
Koerbagh, Adriaan, 9:177
Koffka, Kurt, **5:124–125**
and Gestalt theory, 4:70
Köhler and, 5:124–126
and Psychologische Forschung, 5:126
Koguryo, and Buddhism, 5:134
Köhler, Josef, Pound and, 7:427
Köhler, Wolfgang, **5:126–134**
and behaviorism, 4:73
on consciousness, 4:74
and Gestalt theory, 4:70
Koffka and, 5:124–126
Kohut, Heinz, 8:107
Kojève, Alexandre, 4:285–286, 5:167, 7:391
Kojiki, in Japanese philosophy, 4:796
Kolmogorov, Andrei Nikolajevich
on intuitionist logic, 4:738, 5:491
on probability, 2:663
and problem interpretation, 4:738
theory of chance, 2:126
Kommunismus (Lukács), 5:602
Komplexqualitaten, 5:156
Kongzi. *See* Confucius
König, Samuel, on force measurement, 3:228
König's paradox, 5:518
Kontinuum, Das (Weyl), 2:505, 9:741
Kook, Abraham Isaac, 5:3
Koopman-Darmois form, 9:225–226
Koran. *See* Qur'an
Korea
Buddhism in, 4:833, 5:134–136
Confucianism in, *qi* and *li* in, 4:795
Minjung theology in, 5:331–333
Western culture in, 5:140
Korean philosophy, 4:792, **5:134–142,** 5:140–142
Kormchie Zvezdy (Pilot Stars) (Ivanov), 4:766
Korn, Alejandro, **5:142–143,** 5:207–208
Kornblith, Hilary, 3:275, 6:499
Korsch, Karl, 2:598
Korsgaard, Christine, 5:38, 8:251
Kortholt, Christian K., on Spinoza, 7:99
Koryo dynasty, and Confucianism, 5:135–136
Köselitz, Heinrich, Nietzsche and, 6:610
Koslow, A., on logical terms, 5:532
Kosmogonie (Ehrenfels), 3:177
Kosmologische Briefe über die Einrichtung des Weltbaues (Cosmological letters on the structure of the universe) (Lambert), 5:175
Kōsōryoku no ronri (The logic of the power of imagination) (Miki), 6:216
Kosslyn, Stephen, 4:590, 6:565
Kotarbiński, Tadeusz, **5:143–146,** 6:627
Tarski and, 9:370
Twardowski and, 9:554
Kovalinski, M. I., 9:63
Kozhevnikov, V. A., 3:558
Kozlov, Aleksei Aleksandrovich, **5:146–147,** 5:572
Krabbe, Hugo, on sovereignty, 9:143
Kracauer, Siegfried, Adorno and, 1:26–27
Kraemer, Hendrick, 1:479
Kraft, Julius, and *Ratio,* 3:753
Kraft und Stoff (Buchner), 3:58, 6:11
Kranz, Walther, on Democritus, 5:301
Kraus, Christian, German liberalism and, 5:321

Krause, Karl Christian Friedrich, 3:42, **5:147–149**
Krausism, in Spain, 5:148
Kraut, Robert, 8:533
Kreisel, Georg, 4:741, 8:55
Kreislauf des Lebens, Der (Moleschott), 6:319
Kretzmann, Norman
on Aquinas, 9:447
on God and time, 3:359–360
Kreutzer Sonata, The (Tolstoy), 9:513
Krieg buchlein des Friedens, Das (Franck), 3:713
Kring, W. D., on atheism, 1:372
Kripke, Saul, **5:149–151**
a priori justification and, 5:80
on *a priori* knowledge, 3:274
on belief attribution, 1:536
on color error, 2:333
on contingent truths known *a priori,* 5:101–102
and descriptivism, 8:77, 8:706, 8:746–747
on direct reference, 8:61
on identities as *a posteriori,* 5:114
on intuitionistic logic, 4:740
on Kant, 5:100
on language, 1:155
on materialism, 7:409
on meaning and belief, 8:808
modal logic and, 3:766, 5:483, 8:739–740
on names, 1:155, 7:407–409, 8:706, 8:746–747
on natural kinds, 6:504
on natural law, 5:227
on necessary truths as *a posteriori,* 2:474, 5:101
on necessity, 7:724
on open question argument, 6:156
on philosophical logic, 5:474
on possibility, 7:723–724
on possible worlds, 3:766, 5:491, 7:724
on private language problem, 8:23
on propositions, 8:88–89
on quantification, 6:290
on reference, 7:409
on rule following, 8:531–533
on semantic paradoxes, 5:521
on semantics, 3:766, 8:77, 8:739–740
on truth, 5:318, 9:540
Twin Earth analogy in, 7:406–408
on Wittgenstein, 8:23, 8:531–532, 9:818
Kripke-Putnam picture, 8:288–289
Krishna, in meditation, 6:108
Kristeva, Julia, **5:151–153**
on alterity, 1:134
on distinctive methods of women, 3:573
and postmodernism, 6:318
and poststructuralism, 9:274
on speaking subject, 9:276
Kritische Theorie der Formbildung (Modern Theories of Development) (Bertalanffy), 1:593
Kritisches Journal der Philosophie, 8:617
Kritizismus (Criticism) (Riehl), 3:110
Krochmal, Nachman, 3:249, 4:828
Kroes, Peter, 7:549
Kronecker, Leopold
on arithmetization and continua, 2:501
on decidability and calculability of functions, 2:400
on existence and constructibility, 5:469
Kronig, A., on physics of gases, 7:537
Kropotkin, Pëtr, **5:153–155**
and anarchist communism, 1:179
Bakunin and, 1:473
evolutionary ethics and, 3:479
on natural law, 9:251
Krueger, Felix, **5:155–157,** 9:850
Krugman, Saul, 6:97
Krylov, N., 7:540
Kuhn, Thomas, **5:157–160**
constructionism and, 2:475, 9:78
Danto on, 7:394
on incommensurability, 8:695–696
on Lavoisier, 5:217
and naturalism, 6:501, 9:84
on perception, 3:676
on phenomenology, 7:300
on philosophy of science, 5:171–172
on reference of theoretical terms, 9:417
on relativity, 3:179
and science, 6:501, 8:677
on scientific revolutions, 8:683–688, 8:694–703, 9:235
on shifts-in-standards, 8:697–698
Kuleshov, Lev, in film theory, 7:381
Kullback, Solomon, 9:219
Külpe, Oswald, 4:82, 5:124, **5:160–161,** 8:140–141
Kulturgeschichte als Kultursoziologie (Weber, A.), 9:732
Kulturphilosophie (Simmel), 9:31
Kulturwissenschaft(en), 4:38, 8:459
Kumārila, Mīmāmsaka
on absence, 6:530–532
on Buddhist nominalism, 9:586
Kumazawa Banzan, **5:161–162,** 6:477
Kun, Béla, 5:602
Kundalini, 6:109
Kunen, Kenneth, 8:845
Küng, Hans, 3:97, 3:747
Kung-sun Lung, 5:415, 5:416
Kuong Tang Hôi, 1:728
Kupperman, Joel J., on Daoist ethics, 2:197
Kuratowski, Kazimierz
on ordered pair, 8:837
Tarski and, 9:368
Kuriai Doxai (Epicurus), 3:265
Kurtz, Paul, 7:115–116
Kurzweil, Ray, 4:617
Kushitism, 5:59
Kvanvig, Jonathan, 9:686
on hell, 4:251
on presentism, 9:479
and swamping problem, 5:105
Kvitko, David, on Tolstoy, 9:512–513
Kwame Ture. *See* Carmichael, Stokely
Kyburg, Henry, on explanation, 3:519
Kydones, Demetrios, 1:789
Kydones, Prochoros, 1:789
Kyōto School, 3:95, 4:797–798

L

La Béatotide des Chrétiens ou le fléau de la foy (Vallée), 2:263
La Bruyère, Jean de, **5:166–167**
La Cena de le ceneri (The Ash Wednesday supper) (Bruno), 1:709
La Concienza e il meccanismo interiore (Bonatelli), 1:649
La Conquete du pain (Kropotkin), 5:154
La Crise de la conscience europeén (Hazard), 3:243
La Cultura italiana (Papini and Prezzolini), 7:102
La Déduction relativiste (Meyerson), 6:213
La Filosofia di Gioberti (Spaventa), 9:160
La Filosofia di Marx (Gentile), 4:49
La Filosofia oggi (Sciacca), 8:666
La Filosophia di Giambattista Vico (Croce), 2:600
La Forge, Louis de, on mind-body relationship, 2:58–59
La Giustizia (Del Vecchio), 2:697
La Grande Encyclopedie, 1:504

La Idea de principio en Leibniz y la evolución de la teoría deductiva (The Idea of Principle in Leibniz and the Evolution of Deductive Theory) (Ortega y Gasset), 7:47
La Jeune parque (The young fate) (Valéry), 9:634
La Langue des calculs (Condillac), 8:785
La Libertad creadora (Korn), 5:142
La Liberté chez Descartes et la theologie (Gilson), 4:91
La Mauvaise conscience (Jankélévitch), 4:787
La Mettrie, Julien Offray de, **5:178–181**, 6:10
atheism and, 2:688
Cabanis and, 2:2
Diderot and, 3:75
Epicurus and, 3:269
in French clandestine literature, 2:265
on machine intelligence, 5:631
La Modalité de jugement (Brunschvicg), 1:714
La Morale et la science des moeurs (Ethics and Moral Science) (Lévy-Bruhl), 5:306
La Mort d'agrippine (Cyrano de Bergerac), 2:618
La Mothe Le Vayer, François, **5:181–183**
La Peyrère and, 5:196
Pascal and, 7:133
La Nausée (Sartre), 4:748, 8:603, 8:606
La Nouvelle Héloïse (Rousseau), 5:588
La Passion de Husayn Ibn Mansur Hallaj: martyr mystique de l'Islam (Massignon), 9:303
La Pensée (Blondel), 1:618
La Perception de la causalité (Michotte), 4:72
La Perpétuité de la foy (Arnauld & Nicole), 6:604
La Peyrère, Isaac, **5:196–197**
La Philosophie de Charles Renouvier (Milhaud), 6:217
"La Philosophie des mathématiques de Kant" (Couturat), 2:582
La Philosophie positive (periodical), 5:372
La Poesia (Croce), 2:601
La Politique du clergé de France (Jurieu), 6:603–604
La Porée, Gilbert de, 1:592
La Prose chagrine (La Mothe Le Vayer), 5:182
La Psicologia come scienza positiva (Ardigò), 1:252
La Psychologie allemande contemporaine (Ribot), 8:457
La Psychologie anglaise contemporaine (Ribot), 8:457
La Psychologie de l'attention (Ribot), 8:457
La Psychologie des sentiments (Ribot), 8:457
La Raison et les normes (Lalande), 5:173
La Raza cósmica (The Cosmic Race) (Vasconcelos), 5:208
La Reazione idealistica contro la scienza (Aliotta), 1:127
La Rebelión de las masas (The Revolt of the Masses) (Ortega y Gasset), 7:47, 7:547
La Recherche d'une première vérité (Lequier), 5:287
La Religieuse (The nun) (Diderot), 3:71, 3:76
La Rochefoucauld, Duc François de, **5:200–201**
on death, 2:652
Garve and, 4:24
Gracián and, 4:168
La Bruyère and, 5:166
Nietzsche and, 6:611
La Roi naturelle, ou Catéchisme du citoyen français (Volney), 9:707
La Storia del regno di Napoli (History of the Kingdom of Naples) (Croce), 2:604
"La Storia ridotto sotto il concetto generale dell'arte" (Croce), 2:599
La Struttura dell'esistenza (Abbagnano), 1:1
La Technique (The Technological Society) (Ellul), 7:547–548
La Tentation de l'occident (Malraux), 5:673
La Théorie de l'intuition dans la phénoménologie de Husserl (Levinas), 5:303–304
La Théorie physique: son objet, sa structure (The Aim and Structure of Physical Theory) (Duhem), 3:126
La Venue à l'écrotire (Derrida), 2:263
La Vérité des sciences contre les septiques ou Pyrrhoniens (Mersenne), 2:725, 6:152
La Vita come ricerca (Spirito), 9:197
La Vita delle forme letterarie (The life of literary forms) (Pastore), 7:135
La Voix et le phénomène (Derrida), 9:274
Laas, Ernst, **5:163–164**
Laberthonnière, Lucien, **5:164–165**
Labor, 1:472
as defining human being, 2:363
division of, historical materialism and, 4:378
Hegel on, 4:270–271
as life's prime want, 2:362
Marx on, 3:68–69, 5:732–733
Ruskin on, 8:534
Smith on, 7:350, 9:68
socialist ideal of, 9:73
women and, 3:579
Labor protection legislation, 2:361–362
Labriola, Antonio, **5:165–166**
Croce and, 2:599
Sorel and, 9:132
Labyrinthus Medicorum (Paracelsus), 7:103
Lacan, Jacques, **5:167–169**
Cixous on, 2:263
in French structuralism, 9:273
Lyotard and, 5:620
Merleau-Ponty and, 6:150
philosophy of sex and, 7:522
Lacerba (periodical), 7:102
Lacey, Hugh, 9:62
Lachelier, Jules, **5:169–170**
Laches (Plato)
on battle of Delium, 9:106
on courage, 3:396
definition of virtue in, 7:586, 9:110
on Socrates, 7:584, 9:107
Lackey, Douglas P.
on Counterfactual Test, 4:871
on nuclear weapons and war, 7:157
Laclos, Choderlos de, 5:588
Lacombe, Jacques, 9:324–325
Lactantius, as apologist, 1:228
Ladd, G. T., Lotze and, 5:583
Ladd, John, Lehrer and, 5:248
Ladd-Franklin, Christine, 5:534
"Lady Mary Shepherd's Metaphysics" (Shepherd), 9:10
Lae, Radbruch on, 7:427
Lafargue, Michael, 2:198
Lafayette, Marquis de, Paine and, 7:73
Lafayette, Mme. de, La Rochefoucauld and, 5:200
Lafuma, Louis, Pascal and, 7:132
Lagardelle, Hubert, 3:553
Lagneau, Jules, Lachelier and, 5:169
Lagrange, Joseph Louis
on action at a distance, 3:688
on classical mechanics, 2:279
Comte and, 2:409
on energy and work, 3:227
on energy conservation, 3:229
on force measurement, 3:228
on potential energy, 3:228

Lagrangian dynamics, and Newtonian dynamics, 3:691
Laing, R. D., Sartre and, 3:507
Laissez-faire doctrine, liberalism and, 5:319, 5:322
Lakatos, Imre, **5:171–172**, 8:677
Lakatos Prize, 3:159
Lakoff, George, 8:807
Lalande, André, **5:172–173**, 7:567
L'Altra meta (The other half) (Papini), 7:102
Lamarck, Chevalier de, **5:173–175**
  Bergson on, 1:569
  Butler (Samuel) on, 1:784
  Darwin (Charles) and, 3:488
  Darwin (Erasmus) and, 2:631
  on evolution, 2:635, 3:486–487, 5:174
Lamarckism, 3:486–487
  Darwin and, 2:635–639, 2:643
  McDougall and, 6:72
Lambda-Calculus
  and computability theory, 2:375, 2:379
  computing machines and, 2:402
Lambda-Conversion theory, in combinatory logic, 2:335–336
Lambda-Definability, of Church, 5:476
Lambert, Johann Heinrich, **5:175–176**
  on axiom of parallels, 9:150
  on calculus of relations, 8:786
  Eberhard and, 3:161
  on language, 8:785–787
  on Lobachevskian geometry, 4:59
  on logical diagrams, 5:560
  on phenomenology, 7:278
  universal grammar and, 8:791
Lambert of Auxerre, 5:430–431, 8:767
Lambert's diagrams, definition of, 5:547
Lamennais, Hugues Félicité Robert de, 3:631, **5:176–178**, 9:57
Lamentabili (papal decree, 1907), 3:97, 5:571
Lamprias (Euclides of Megara), 6:110
Lamy, François, 5:665, 5:671
Lancaster, Duke of (John of Gaunt), 9:851
Lancelin, P. F., 8:788
Lancelot, Claude
  Arnauld and, 1:288
  Chomsky and, 2:423
  Port-Royal Grammar and, 8:775
  universal grammar and, 8:790
Lancelot, Dante on, 2:625
Land
  communal ownership of, 5:75
  national identity and, 6:482
  as property, 8:69
Landau, Barbara, 4:694
Landgrebe, Ludwig, **5:183–186**
  Fink and, 3:638
  on Kant, 5:183–184
Landino, Cristoforo, 3:624, 3:671
Landsberg, Paul-Louis, on death, 2:651
Lanford, O., 7:540
Lang, Andrew, myth in, 6:464
Lange, Albert, Lavrov and, 5:218
Lange, Friedrich Albert, **5:186–187**
  in neo-Kantianism, 6:540
  Paulsen and, 7:148
  Vaihinger and, 9:625–626
Lange, Joachim
  Thomasius and, 9:442
  Wolff and, 9:826
Lange, Konrad, 3:100
Lange, Marc, 5:230
Lange-Eichbaum, Wilhelm, 6:609
Langer, Susanne K., **5:187–188**
  on art, 1:58, 1:65–66
  Cassirer and, 1:58, 1:65
  on music, 1:305
  on virtual objects, 9:691
Langmuir, Irving, 7:146
Langsam, Harold, on perception, 7:193
Langton, Rae, Dworkin and, 3:157
Language(s), 1:760, **5:188–190**
  absurdity *vs.* nonsense in, 2:77
  acquisition of, Chomsky on, 2:244
  aesthetic, Wittgenstein on, 9:820
  ambiguous use of, 3:549
  analogy in, 1:141–142, 8:784–785
  analysis of. *See also* Linguistic analysis
    Frege's, 8:829
    metaphysical, Buridan on, 1:769
  as analytic method, 8:784
  analytic philosophy and, 1:407–410
  analytic/synthetic distinction in. *See also* Analytic and synthetic statements
    Goodman on, 4:160
    Wittgenstein on, 1:163
  in animals, 1:204–205
  Anselm on, 1:218–219
  antimetaphysics and, 6:206–207
  of arithmetic, 3:650
  art and, 1:65–67
  artificial, **1:342–345**
    Carnap on, 2:42–43
    logical categories and, 2:79
    and natural. *See* Artificial and natural language
    syntactical functions in, 2:77
  artificialization of
    in medieval philosophy, 6:101–102
    reaction against, 6:103–104
  Augustine on, 7:368, 8:759
  aural and visual recognition of, 9:334
  Austin (John Langshaw) on, 1:407–410
  Averroes on, 1:426
  Bacon and, 8:772
  Bakhtin on, 1:466
  Barth on, 1:480
  "being" as lexical unit in, 1:527
  belief attribution and, 1:536–537
  Bentham on, 1:551–552, 8:792–793
  Berkeley on, 1:587, 3:302, 9:597
  in biology, use of, 7:36, 9:843–844
  Boethius on, 8:761–762
  Bolzano on, 1:647
  Brouwer on, 5:468
  in Buddhist epistemology, 1:755
  Buridan on, 1:769
  Cabanis on, 2:2, 8:788
  Carnap on, 2:42–43, 5:527
  Cassirer on, 2:68
  causal concepts in, 2:95
  causation statements and, 1:549
  Cavell and, 2:115–116
  Chinese, pronouns in, 2:172
  in Chinese thought, 2:187–190, 2:201–215, 2:229–230
  in Chisholm's metaphysics, 2:243
  Chomsky on, 2:245
  in Cixous écriture feminine project, 2:262
  in cognitive psychology, 8:151
  Collingwood on, 2:327–328
  common, in other minds, 7:56
  complex illusion sources in, 1:704
  in complex reasoning, 9:77
  compositionality in, 2:370, 7:403–404
  computers and, 1:344
  concepts and, 2:415–416
  in conceptualization of suicide, 9:318
  concrete/physical distinction in, 1:691
  Condillac on, 2:422–423, 8:784–785
  connectionist models and, 2:444
  connotation-denotation distinction and, 8:796
  as continuous process, 8:793
  on conventional truth, 2:474

conversational implicature in, 4:184
Cordemoy on, 2:537
Croce on, 2:601
culture and, 1:83
as custom, 8:16–17
Daoism and, 2:161–162, 2:187–190, 2:205–208, 2:220–221
Davidson (Donald) on, 2:647–648
death of, 1:342
deficiencies of, 1:446
as definition of nation, 6:481–482
Derrida on, 7:412
Descartes on, 4:691–692
descriptions and, 5:508
determinacy of, 1:72
in Dge-lugs Mādhyamika, 1:732–733
divine, sensible object as, 1:574
as divine gift, 1:648
Dummett on, 3:132–133
Eliot (T. S.) on, 3:186
as epitome of human connectedness, 2:363
ethical, in shaping attitudes, 9:245
Evans on, 3:459–462
exactness of, 9:811
and expressive range of speech, 2:209
as flesh, 6:149
Florenskii on, 3:670
formal, 9:540
  vs. natural, 1:344
  and nonlogical symbol meaning, 1:660
formalization
  in Carnap, 2:42–43
  in logic, 1:660
formalized, definition of, 5:544
fragment of, Montague grammar for, 6:329–330
Frege on, 2:82, 5:507, 8:736
French, defense of, 4:166
French interest in, 8:783
Frye on, 3:755
functions of, 9:19–20
Gadamer on, 7:411–412
generics in, 4:40
of genetics, 7:345
Gioberti on, 4:94
God and, 1:94–95, 1:707, 4:767–768, 6:432
Goodman on, 4:157
Gorgias of Leontini on, 4:164
Habermas on, 4:200
Heidegger on, 4:295, 7:410–411
in Hellenistic thought, 4:302
Herder on, 4:329–330, 8:787
Hobbes on, 6:9
and "horizon of meaning," 3:565
Hui Shi on, 2:189
human, *vs.* animal intelligence, 1:549
Humboldt on, 4:485–486, 8:793–794, 9:17–18
Husserl on, 8:802–803
idéologues on, 8:787–790
ideal, 1:342–343, 1:561–562
  Frege on, 5:507
  Russell on, 8:543–545
identity statements in, 4:568
of Illumination, 4:582
imposition, first and second, 8:762
incommensurability in, of rival paradigms, 8:696–697
indexicals and, 4:622–623
innate, 8:784
and intellect, 1:566
intensional transitive verbs in, 4:697
intersubjectivity of sentences in, 1:484–487
in Islamic aesthetics, 1:436
isomorphism and, 5:129
Johnson (Alexander Bryan) on, 4:847–848, 8:794–795
Kripke on, 1:155, 7:406–408, 8:746–747
Lacan on, 5:168
law and, 7:464
learning, Ryle on, 8:582–583
legal, 7:444–446
Leibniz on, 1:342–343, 5:441, 8:779
Lewis (D.) on, 5:315
Lichtenberg on, 5:342
linguistic fictions in, 8:793
linguistic signs in, 9:273–274
Locke on, 3:300, 5:384–385, 8:777
logic and, 1:147, 2:41, 2:525, 6:495, 9:776
logical positivism and, 5:527, 6:194
Losev on, 5:574
Lucretius on, 8:759
Malcolm (Norman) on, 3:106–107, 5:662
Marty on, 5:728–729
Marx on, 3:68
mass/count nouns in, **6:659–666**
materialism and, 6:9, 6:12
mathematical, 3:639, 8:785
of mathematics, 8:785
Maupertuis on, 8:783–784
Mauthner on, 8:801–802
and meaning, 1:154, 1:545, 7:400–402, 8:808
as meaning-delivery-within-speech-capacity, 2:208–209
in medieval philosophy, 6:101–102
Meinong on, 8:803–804
memory and, 7:414
mental content and, 2:480
Merleau-Ponty on, 7:411
and metaphysics, 6:194–195, 7:409–410
Mill (John Stuart) on, 6:234, 8:795–797
and modality, **10:20–27**
Montague on, 6:329–330
Moore on, 2:358
mystical and, 6:456–457, 6:461, 9:808
natural quantifiers in, **10:28–32**
nature of, 4:847–848, **5:188–190**
non-descriptivist, 4:150
nouns in, 6:660
Ockham on, 9:776
and ontology, 1:83
ordinary. *See* Ordinary language
in organismic biology, 7:36–37
origin of, 8:787
pain description and, 7:70–71
Peirce on, 8:797–799
perception and, 6:149
personal identity and, 7:215, 7:219, 7:227
personalism and, 7:236
phallocentric view of, Cixous on, 2:263
philosophy and, 1:152–153, 9:629–630, 9:798
philosophy of, **7:400–410**
  in anti-intentional aesthetics, 1:509
  appeals to intuition in, 7:409
  assertion in, 7:408
  basic statements and, 1:483–488
  Chinese, 2:202–215
  communication in, 7:400
  in continental philosophy, 7:410–412
  definition of, 7:328
  of Epicureans, 8:758–759
  formalism in, 7:405
  in Germany, 8:785
  idéologues and, 8:788
  implications of, 7:409–410
  importance of, 7:400
  incommensurability in, 8:696–697

Language(s), ***continued***
indeterminacy of translation, 1:525
indexicals, 4:622–623
in India, 4:631, **7:412–417**
intensional semantics, 9:347–350
knowledge in, 7:400
methodology in, 7:408–409
name rectification as, 2:203–204
naturalism *vs.* conventionalism, 8:752
pragmatics in, 7:402
questions in, 7:400
reference in, 7:408
semantic externalism, 9:45
semantics in, 7:402
sentences as proper names in, 8:801
social epistemology and, 9:84
subject and predicate in, 9:287
synonymy in, 9:345–352
syntactical and semantical categories, 9:352–359
syntax, 9:359–361
translation in, 7:404–405
Twin Earth analogy in, 7:406–408
universal grammar and, 8:790–791
phonological and logical form in, 5:509–510
phrase-structured, 9:355
Plato on, 5:398, 5:568
in Plato's *Cratylus*, 8:752–754
plurals and plurality in, 7:644–647
polynominal-time computability and, 2:388
possibility of revolution in, 5:152
possible-world semantics and, 1:155
in poststructuralism, 9:275
pragmatism and, 7:742–744
private. *See* Private language/private language problem
processing programs, 1:346
productivity in, 7:403–404
programming, 1:344
proof in, 1:343
in propositions, 9:809–810
Putnam on, 7:406–408
radical behaviorism and, 1:522–523
and radical negation of things, 1:611–612
and reality, 4:543, 7:262–263
Cassirer on, 2:67
Wittgenstein on, 9:806
reference in, 8:288–290
regimentation of, 8:218–219
rules and, 8:16–19
verifiability principle and, 9:665–666
Wittgenstein on, 7:109, 9:815
in Sanlun Buddhism, 2:161–162
Saussure on, 7:411
Schleiermacher on, 8:636–637
of science, 7:516–517, 8:785, 8:789
science and, 5:529
Searle on, 8:706
in self-constitution, 4:51
as semantically compositional, 5:510
sense-datum terminology and translation in, 1:486
Shpet on, 9:17–20
sign systems in, 8:784–788
silence and, 7:411
as social phenomena and tradition, 1:648
and social reality, 8:665
sophists on, 9:131
of space, 9:465
in speech and meaning-delivery-beyond-speech-capacity, 2:208
Sprat on, 1:50
stability, and dynamic expression, 2:208–209
Stöhr on, 9:252
Stoics and, 8:757, 9:255
Strawson on, 2:79
structuralism and, 9:273
as structured response, 1:522–523
subject-predicate in, 9:286
Tarski and, 2:549
term *policy* in, 8:673–674
Theophrastus on, 9:411
and thought, 1:648, 4:693–694, **5:191–192**
analytic priority of, 5:191–192
analytical behaviorism on, 1:523–524
epistemological priority of, 5:191–192
intentional attitudes in, 4:706
ontological priority of, 5:191–192
priority of, 5:191–192
relative priority of, 5:190–191
of thought, **5:192–194**, 6:141
concepts as prototypes and, 2:418
in content, 2:478
Fodor on, 2:393, 8:80
postulating, 3:759
of time, 9:462–464, 9:470, 9:478
translation of, transition accompanying, 5:159
Turgot on, 8:784
and ultimate concern, 2:205–206
Unamuno on, 9:568
as unifying justification for monarchy, 1:648
universal, 1:342, 9:810
Couturat on, 2:582
Leibniz on, 5:262, 5:441, 5:535, 8:779, 8:786
of science, Condorcet on, 2:432
universal grammar and, 8:790–791
universals and, 9:601
unthinkable shown by, 9:805
vs. use of language, 7:402
Vailati on, 9:629–630
verbalism in, 8:786
verifiability principle and, 9:669
Wittgenstein on, 1:66, 1:480, 2:82, 2:359, 3:317–318, 9:805, 9:809–810
Wodeham on, 9:821
as world-view, 2:229, 8:801
See also Semantics
Language and Time (Smith), 9:478, 9:479
Language game
absolute simples defined by, 9:811
antimetaphysics and, 6:206–207
facts and, 9:818
Lyotard on, 5:620
in propositions, 9:809–810
use in, 9:812
Language of Morals, The (Hare), 3:419, 3:429–430
Language of New Media, The (Manovich), 7:384
Language of Thought, The (Fodor), 2:393, 8:80
Language theory
of cynics, 2:669
metaphor in, 6:166
of scholastics, 2:669, 3:493–494
of sophists, 2:669
Language, Truth, and Logic (Ayer), 1:65–66, 1:149, 1:436–437, 5:233
Languages and Language (Lewis), 5:315, 8:808
Languages of Art, The (Goodman), 1:305, 4:159–161
Langue des calculs, La (Condillac), 8:785
L'Anima (periodical), 7:102
L'Année sociologique (periodical), 3:150

Lao Tzu. *See* Laozi
Laokoon (Lessing), 1:50, 2:688, 5:294, 7:381
Laozi, 2:186, 5:194, **5:194–196**
  anarchism and, 1:177
  use of anti-language interpretation, 2:188
  Wang Bi on, 9:722
  Zhuangzi compared with, 9:881
Laplace, Pierre Simon de, **5:197–199**
  in astronomy, 6:593
  on black holes, 1:607
  on cosmic brain argument, 1:369
  and De Morgan, 2:710
  on determinism, 2:282, 3:30–31
  Earman on, 3:160
  evidential use of likelihood function (LF), 3:661
  Fisher and, 3:665
  on forces acting at a distance, 3:688
  nebular hypothesis on, 3:354
  plant theory of, 9:336
  on potential energy, 3:228
  on probability, 3:664, 8:26
  on statistical inference, 5:57
"L'Apologie d'un fou" ("The apology of a madman") (Chaadaev), 2:121
Lapshin, Ivan Ivanovich, **5:199–200**
L'Aqudeza y arte de ingenio (Gracián), 4:168
L'Archeologie du savior (The Archaeology of Knowledge) (Foucault), 3:700
Large and small, 9:872
Large numbers, law of, 8:25, 8:35
Large sample theory, 3:662
L'Arithmétique (Stevin), 2:493
Laromiguière, Pierre, 2:760, **5:201–202**
Laroui, Abdullah, **5:202**
Larson, Richard, on propositional attitudes, 8:78
Las Casas, Bartolomé de
  on Indian Question, 5:205
  on natural law, 6:509
Lashley, Karl, 1:522–523, 8:143
Laski, H. J., 9:143
Laslett, Peter, 5:388, 5:395
Lasnik, H., 9:360
Lassalle, Ferdinand, **5:202–204**
Lasswell, Harold, 8:675, 9:207
Last Saying, or Dying Legacy of Mr. Thomas Hobbs (Blount), 1:619
Last Word, The (Nagel), 6:475
Latent force. *See* Energy, potential
Latent functions, 3:763–765
Latent-dream-thoughts, examining, 3:743
Later Roman Empire (Bury), 3:38
Latin American philosophy, **5:204–213**
  characteristics of, 5:204
  colonial period, 5:204–205
  contemporary period, 5:207–212
  independentist period, 5:205
  Ingenieros in, 4:686
  liberation philosophy in, 5:211, **5:331–333**
  positivism in, 5:206–208, 5:210
  Romero in, 8:491–492
  two trends in, 5:204–205
Latin Aristotelianism, 1:261
Latin Averroism, 1:428–429
Latin Christendom, 9:410
Latin language, artificialization of, in medieval philosophy, 6:102
Latitudinarianism
  in Cambridge platonists, 2:13
  Cudworth on, 2:609
  deism and, 2:682, 2:685
  Law on, 5:220
  on science and religion, 2:685
  Stillingfleet on, 9:249
Latour, Bruno, 8:677
  on knowledge production, 9:78
  social epistemology and, 9:84
Latterday Pamphlets (Carlyle), 2:34
Laudan, Larry, 8:692, 9:84
"Laugh of the Medusa" (Cixous), 2:263
Laughter, 1:469, 1:470, 7:629
L'Autre monde, ou les éstats et empires de la lune et du soleil (Cyrano de Bergerac), 2:618
Lavater, Johann Kaspar, **5:213–214**
  Goethe and, 4:143
  Lichtenberg and, 5:338
  Pantheismusstreit and, 7:99
Lavelle, Louis, **5:214–216**
  Abbagnano on, 1:1
  Le Senne and, 5:289
L'Avenir de la science (Renan), 8:429
Lavoce (periodical), 7:102
Lavoisier, Antoine, **5:216–218**
  atomism and, 1:387
  Bentham and, 8:792
  Condillac and, 8:785
  Newtonian physics and, 6:61
  paradigm-defining work of, 5:157
  on phenomena-to-be-explained, 8:697
Lavrov, Pëtr Lavrovich, 5:40, **5:218–219,** 6:215
Law(s)
  academic, of Foucher, 3:702
  administrative, 7:718
  alienation in, 1:120
  ambiguity in, 7:455
  Ambrose on, 7:420
  analysis of, 7:447–454
  analytic jurisprudence and, **1:168–170**
  in ancient Greece, 9:457
  animal rights in, 1:209
  applied ethics and, 1:235
  Aquinas on, 7:421–422, 9:434
  Aristotle on, 7:418–419
  "as it is" *vs.* "as it ought" and, 1:553
  atheists and, 1:358
  Augustine on, 1:395–397, 6:105
  Austin (John) on, 1:405–406, 7:425
  authority of, 7:418, 7:458
  Avicenna on, 1:434
  Bacon (Francis) on, 1:443
  Bartolus on, 7:422
  basic, in validifying legal order, 9:142
  behaviorism in, 7:428
  Bentham on, 1:551–554
  bioethical issues in, 1:600
  Bodin on, 1:621, 7:422, 9:140
  branches of, 7:443
  Buckle on, 1:719
  Burke on, 7:424
  and business, 1:778
  of calculus, Leibniz on, 5:443
  Calvin on, 2:11
  causal, 2:96
  of causality, 2:87, 2:106
  character of, 7:454–455
  Chicherin and, 2:147–148
  Chinese, 2:152, 2:200
  in Christianity, 4:261–262
  Cicero on, 7:419–420
  civil disobedience and, 2:11, 2:259–261
  class and, 7:419
  of classification, Pauler on, 7:145
  classification of, 7:443–444
  clear cases in, 7:451
  codification of, 1:554–555
  coercion and, 1:406, 7:444
  Cohen (Hermann) on, 2:303–304
  Cohen (Morris) on, 2:307
  command theory of, 6:512–513
  common, as arbitrary, 1:554
  common-sense, Duhem on, 3:128
  and communism, 2:364, 7:427
  computer ethics and, 2:397
  conscience and, 2:445
  of conservation, and change over time, 2:586
  vs. constitution, 7:419
  of continuity, Leibniz on, 2:494
  of contradiction, 5:547

Law(s), *continued*
interpretations of, 5:231–235
Lapshin on, 5:199–200
Pauler on, 7:145
traditional formulation of, 5:232–233
contradiction in, 7:455
of conversion, of syllogism, 5:499
of correlativity, Pauler on, 7:145
as court directive, 7:428
Cousin on, 2:579
criminal
Posner on, 7:718
utilitarian approach to, 4:868
criticism of, 7:452–453
Croce on, 2:603
as cultural phenomenon, 7:427
custom as, 7:427
Daoist opposition to, 2:237
deductive reasoning and, 7:448
as defense of liberty, 1:518
definition of, 7:443–444
of distribution, in model theory, 6:311–312
divine, 1:396, 4:824, 7:454
Albo on, 4:824
Augustine on, 1:396
in volitions and bodily movements, 4:77
Duhem on, 3:127–129
Dworkin on, 3:156
economics and, 2:364, 2:603, 7:427, 7:461–462, 7:717–718
of effect, in radical behaviorism, 1:520–522
efficiency and, 7:461–462
of efficient causes, Lachelier on, 5:169–170
equality and, 7:456
eternal, 1:396, 9:284
ethical evaluation of, 3:391–392
evaluation of, 7:452–453
and evidence, 7:452
of excluded middle, 3:692, 3:766, 5:547
in Brouwer, 2:502–503, 6:527
interpretations of, 5:231–235
in intuitionistic and classical logic, 2:504
proper names and, 8:59
traditional formulation of, 5:232–233
experience and, 7:448
feminism in, 7:462–463
Fichte on, 3:617
of final causes, Lachelier on, 5:169–170
free, 7:426–427
Fréret on, 2:265–266
Fuller on, 6:513
general will and, 4:38–39
God and, 1:706, 2:10
of gravity, 2:463
Gray on, 7:425
grounds of grounds ofsic, legal positivism on, 5:242–244
and guilt, moral *vs.* legal, 4:193–194
happiness and, 7:456
and harm and privacy in speech, 2:119–120
Hart on, 5:239–240
Hegel on, 4:261–262, 4:267, 7:425–426
historical school of, 7:426
history and, 1:718–719, 8:620
Hobbes on, 4:420, 7:423
of identity
definition of, 5:547
interpretations of, 5:231–235
Pauler on, 7:145
traditional formulation of, 5:232–233
as ideological superstructure, 7:427
Il'in on, 4:577
impartiality of, 7:455
imperative theory of, 9:141
indeterminacy in, 7:450, 7:464
and informed consent doctrine, 4:680–681
integrity and, 7:458–459
of intensity, of Fechner, 3:556
intention and, 7:446–447
international. *See* International law
Isidore on, 7:421
Jhering on, 7:426
justice and, 7:455–456
justness of, 8:230
Kant and, 5:29–30, 7:424
of large numbers, 8:25, 8:35
lexical definition of, 7:443–444
liability and, 7:462
of logic
conceptions of, 5:511
definition of, 5:547
identification of, 5:512
justification of, 5:511–512
Peirce on, 5:454
logical consistency of, legal realism on, 5:245–246
love and, 9:533
Luther on, 5:612–613
Maine on, 7:425
Mariana on, 5:711
Marsilius of Padua on, 5:722
in Marxism, 7:427
of mathematics, Peano on, 5:465
and "maxims of participation," 9:203
mental states in, 7:446–447
of mind, Fechner and, 3:557
Montesquieu on, 6:337–338, 7:424
moral. *See* Moral law
morality and, 3:617, 5:237–243, 7:137, 7:444
of nations, cosmopolitanism and, 2:567
natural. *See* Natural law
of nature, 3:709, **5:225–231**
vs. accidents, 5:225, 5:229
in arguments for existence of God, 9:407
in Aristotle, 7:489–490
black holes and, 1:609
Bruno and, 1:712
Cambridge Platonists on, 3:406
Cartwright on, 2:62
categorical imperative and, 2:70
as causes and nomological conditions, 2:98–99
in chance and credence, 2:128–129
Clarke on, 2:269–272
in classical mechanics, 2:280–281, 2:282–283
Condorcet on, 2:433
constructive empiricism and, 9:645
and Copernican astronomy, 2:535
in cosmology, 2:221, 2:557, 2:562
vs. creativity, 1:610
Crusius on, 2:607
Daoism and, 2:219–221
as descriptive, 1:582
Driesch on, 9:697
eliminativist view of, 5:227–229
Hobbes on, 3:405, 4:415–416
induction and, 5:229–230
Kant on, 3:411
Kepler and, 5:50
Lewis (D.) on, 5:314
in logical positivism, 5:528
as mathematical hypotheses, 1:582
in Milton's ethics, 6:250
necessity of, internal, 1:580
nomic necessity and, 5:225
Philo on, 7:304–306

in possible world counterfactual conditionals, 2:429
primary and secondary, 6:250
in reductionism and causal relations, 2:96
regularity (Humean) view of, 5:225–231
science and, 2:573–574
strong law theories and, 5:226–231
supervenience and, 5:228–229
symmetry and causal directionality in, 2:98–99
temporal asymmetry and, 9:468–469
Theophrastus on, 9:412
time-reversal invariance in, 2:104
truth by convention and, 2:520
verifiability principle and, 5:528
Wolff on, 9:828–829
of negation, 6:527
in neo-Confucian rationalism, 2:155
nominalism in, 7:428
obedience and, 1:405–406, 2:10, 5:238–239, 7:456–457
Ockham on, 7:422
of opposition, of syllogism, 5:499
oral (Jewish). *See also* Mishnah; Talmud
Karaite and, 4:813–814
Philo and, 4:810
origin of, in *volksgeist,* 8:615
ownership and, 8:72
patriarchy in, 7:463
Peirce on, 5:454
Penna on, 7:422
penumbra of, Hart on, 5:240
of peoples, 8:259
Pericles on, 7:418
philosophers and, 1:235
vs. philosophy, 7:332
philosophy of, 1:443, 3:617
absolutism and, 7:422
Chinese, 2:237–238
Christianity and, 7:420–422
empiricism of, 7:443
history of, **7:418–433**
Italian, 2:697
vs. jurisprudence, 7:443
and "law as it is" *vs.* "law as it ought," 1:553
legal policy and, 7:426
in Middle Ages, 7:420–422
modernism in, 7:460–461
and monarchy, 1:621
positivism in, 7:424–425
postmodernism in, 7:460–461
problems of, **7:443–464**
pure and practical reason in, 9:203
in Renaissance, 7:422–423
in Roman Empire, 7:419–420
Scandinavian, 7:428–429
and social contract, 9:79–81
Stoics in, 7:419
in Suárez, 9:284
in 20th c., 7:426
utilitarianism in, 7:424–425
of physics, 2:90
of planetary motion, necessity and, 5:222
Plato on, 7:418
politics and, 7:444
positive, 7:424
in positivism, 7:424–425
Posner on, 7:717–718
practicality in, 7:428
in pragmatism, 7:444
Priestley on, 8:5
principles and, 7:458–459
and "principles of respect," 9:203
of probability, 2:438
procedural, 7:454–455
as protection, 7:454
Pufendorf on, 8:157–158
and punishment, 1:517–518, 8:160–161, 8:169
Reale and, 8:260
reason and, 6:73, 7:418
and records, 1:443
reform of, 1:552–553
relativism in, 7:427
and rhetorical method, 1:443–444
Roman, 1:135, 7:420
Ross on, 7:428
Rousseau on, 3:410
rule of, in conservatism, 2:470
as rules, 7:429
Savigny on, 8:615
Schuppe on, 8:664
scientific, **5:220–225**
as a-causal principles, 2:104
vs. accidents, 5:221–222
Cartwright on, 2:62
Clifford on, 2:293
cosmology and, 2:558
Duhem on, 3:128
in empiriocriticism, 7:715
in inexact sciences, 5:222–224
nomic necessity and, 5:221–224
Pearson on, 7:715–716
problems of, 7:517–518
Wittgenstein on, 2:41
of the sea, 4:190–191
and security, 1:554
Seneca on, 7:419–420
skepticism in, 7:451
Smith on, 2:364
and social change, 1:720
social engineering approach to, 7:428
social life and, 7:444
of social phenomenon, in Comte and, 2:411–412
and social practice, 7:458
and social purpose, 7:453–454
in society, 7:426–427
sociological theory of, 7:426–427
Socrates on, 7:418, 9:106
Sophists on, 7:418–419
Soto on, 9:137
sources of, 7:448, 7:458
sovereignty and, 1:621, 7:423
Stammler on, 7:424, 9:203
Stone on, 7:428
subjectivity and, 1:554
substantive, 7:453–454
of sufficient reason
as law of thought, 5:231
Pauler on, 7:145
of supply and demand, 2:367
and testimony, 1:443
Thomasius on, 9:440
of thought, **5:231–235**
Boole on, 1:659, 5:450, 5:561
definition of, 5:547
descriptive interpretations of, 5:232–233
formal interpretations of, 5:233–234
Lapshin on, 5:199
modern logic on, 5:234–235
prescriptive interpretations of, 5:233
Thucydides on, 9:457
Tolstoy on, 9:513
tort, 7:461
types of, Hart on, 5:239–240
Ulpian on, 7:420
and understanding, 9:137
of uniform motion, 6:9
of uniqueness, Petzoldt on, 7:268
universal, 1:622, 2:70
unlawful, 8:230
unwritten, 9:510
in utilitarianism, 7:424–425, 7:455–456
utility of, 1:554, 7:455–456
validity of, 7:458

Law(s), ***continued***
and values, 7:455
Vico on, 9:673
vocabulary of, 7:444
Volney on, 9:707
Voltaire on, 9:713
wealth as goal of, 7:717–718
will theory of, 5:49, 7:446
and women, 3:584
See also Jurisprudence
Law, William, **5:220**
Johnson (Dr. Samuel) and, 4:853–854
on reason, 2:686
Law and the Modern Mind (Frank), 7:428
Law, Liberty, and Morality (Hart), 7:137
Law of Determinate Number, 3:130
Law of Peoples, The (Rawls), 9:74
closed society in, 9:98
internationalism of, 9:83
"Law of the Preponderance of the Means of the End" (Vaihinger), 9:627–628
Law of Violence and the Law of Love, The (Tolstoy), 9:513
Lawiers Logike, The (Fraunce), 5:438
Lawlikeness, Hegel on, 3:310
Lawrence, D. H., 2:694, 3:720
Lawrence, William, 9:10
Laws (Plato), 1:512
aesthetics in, 1:41
on arts in education, 7:595
atheism in, 1:357
dating of, 9:107
on dogma, 3:97
editing of, 4:172
on leadership, 7:591–592
soul in, 4:607–608, 6:185
on suicide, 9:319
Laws (Pletho), 7:630
Laws and Symmetry (van Fraassen), 5:227, 9:645
Law's Empire (Dworkin), 3:156, 5:243, 7:459
Laws of the Communication of Motions (Malebranche), 5:664
Laws of Thought (Boole), 1:659, 5:561
Lawvere, W., 2:509
Lazar, Ariela, 8:715
Lazarsfield, Paul, Adorno and, 1:26
Le Blond, Jean-Marie, atheism of, 1:357
Le Bon, Gustave
on eternal return doctrine, 3:354–355
on matter and energy, 3:233
Le Bon sens du curé Meslier (d'Holbach), 2:266–267, 6:154
Le Cathéchisme du curé Meslier (Meslier), 2:267
Le Chef-d'oeuvre d'un inconnu (Saint-Hyacinthe), 8:588
Le Ciel ouvert à tous les hommes (attrib: Cuppé), 2:267
Le Clerc, Jean, **5:235–237**
Le Correspondant (periodical), 5:570
Le Devoir (Duty) (Le Senne), 5:289
Le Différend (Lyotard), 9:277
Le Doeuff, Michèle, Lloyd and, 5:373
Le Fils naturel (The natural son) (Diderot), 3:71
Le Grand Cyrus (Scudéry), 5:588
Le Maistre de Saci, Isaac, Pascal and, 7:130
Le Mariage forcé (Molière), 5:181–182
Le Mémorial (Pascal), 7:130
Le Militaire philosophe, or Difficultés sur la religion proposées au P. Malebranche (Naigeon), 2:267, 6:476
Le Mythe de Sisyphe (Camus). *See Myth of Sisyphus, The* (Camus
Le National (periodical), 5:372
Le Neveu de Rameau (Rameau's nephew) (Diderot), 3:71–77, 3:410
Le Notre, Andre, 3:257
Le Pédamt joué (Cyrano de Bergerac), 2:618
Le Père de famille (The father of the family) (Diderot), 3:71, 3:76
Le Personnalisme (Renouvier), 7:233
Le Philosophe (attrib: Damarsais), 2:266
Le Philosophe ignorant (Voltaire), 9:193
Le Progrès de la conscience dans la philosphie occidentale (Brunschvicg), 1:714
Le Réalisme chrétien et l'idéalisme grec (Laberthonnière), 5:165
Le Revolte Kropotkin and, 5:154
Le Rire (Bergson), 1:57
Le Roy, Édouard, **5:288–289**
Garrigou-Lagrange and, 4:23
and *sens commun,* 4:23
Teilhard and, 9:374
Le Senne, René, 1:1, **5:289–290**
Le Sens commun, la philosophie de l'être et les formules dogmatiques (Garrigou-Lagrange), 4:23
Le Sorgenti irrazionali del pensiero (Abbagnano), 1:1
Le Souici de soi (Care of the Self) (Foucault), 3:701
Le Système du monde (Duhem), 3:126
Le Temps et l'autre (Time and the Other) (Levinas), 5:304
Leaders, unjust acts by, dissociation from, 4:873
Leadership
al-Fārābī on, 4:756
in Daoism, 2:198
Plato on, 7:591–592
power and, 7:731–732
League for Peace and Freedom, Bakunin and, 1:472
League of Humanity, of Krause, 5:147
League of Nations, 7:152, 7:155
League of Nations: A Practical Suggestion, The (Smuts), 9:71
Leap into faith, Kierkegaard on, 3:631
Learned Ignorance, On (Nicholas of Cusa), 7:613
Learning
in animals, 1:521–522
by artificial intelligence, 1:347
in Buddhism, 1:724
in cognitive science, 2:298
Comenius on, 2:341
in computationalism, 2:392
by computers, 5:635
in Confucianism, 2:173, 2:177–179
conscience and, 2:445
culture as, 1:293
Daoist concepts of, 2:192–193
Destutt de Tracy on, 5:656
Dretske on, 3:109
in Elizabethan England, 1:444
God and, 1:652–653
habituation and, 5:656–657
language of thought thesis and, 5:192
Maine de Biran on, 5:656–657
McDougall on, 6:72
in neo-Confucianism, 2:156, 2:183, 4:795
by neural networks, 2:444
perceptual skill and, 7:184
recognizing as, 1:44
Shao Yong on, 9:6
stochastic models of, 9:334
Tolman's studies on, 1:201
Yang Zhu's philosophy of, 9:862
Zhou Dunyi on, 9:880–881
Learning from Six Philosophers (Bennett), 1:550
Learning of the Mysterious, 4:196
Learning of the Way movement, 9:6
Least action, principle of, 6:66
Least-number operator, 5:554
Leben Jesu, Das (Strauss), 3:184, 9:262–263
Lebensformen, Die (Spranger), 9:198
Lebensgestaltung und Klassenkampf (Neurath), 6:561
Lebenslehere (Chamberlain), 2:123

Lebensphilosophie
anthropology and, 7:316–317
Pietism and, 7:576
Lebensphilosophie und Phänomenologie: eine Auseinandersetzung der Diltheyschen Richtung mit Heidegger und Husserl (Misch), 3:638
Lebenswelt, 7:297
Lecky, William E. H., on miracles, 6:266
Leclerc, Jean, Locke and, 5:375
"L'École de Vienne et la philosophie traditionelle" (Schlick), 8:638
Leçon de philosophie (Laromiguière), 5:201–202
Leçons sur les hypothèses cosmogoniques (Poincaré), on eternal return doctrine, 3:355
Leçons sur les origines de la science grecque (Milhaud), 6:217
Lectura (Chatton), 2:139
Lectura super librum de Anima (Paul of Venice), 7:147
Lectura super librum Posteriorum Analyticorum (Paul of Venice), 7:147
Lectures and Remains (Ferrier), 3:608
Lectures on Godmanhood (Solov'ëv), 9:122, 9:124
Lectures on Greek Philosophy (Ferrier), 3:609
Lectures on Logic (Hamilton), 5:439, 5:447
Lectures on Mechanics (Kirchhoff), 3:689
Lectures on Metaphysics (Hamilton), 7:278
Lectures on Modern Idealism (Royce), 4:286
"Lectures on Natural Philosophy" *(Vorlesungen über Naturphilosophie)* (Ostwald), 3:233
Lectures on the Experimental Psychology of Thought (Titchener), 8:142
Lectures on the History of Philosophy. See Lectures on the Philosophy of History (Hegel)
Lectures on the Philosophy of History (Hegel), 7:386
on Berkeley's immaterialism, 4:557
on Enlightenment, 3:243
Lenin and, 3:65
Platonism in, 7:616
Lectures on the Philosophy of Kant (Sidgwick), 2:358
Lee, Steven P., 7:157
Leeuwenhoek, Antoni van, Leibniz and, 5:252
Left Hegelianism, 4:284
Leftow, Brian, 3:115
Legacy of Genghis Khan: A Perspective on Russian History Not from the West but from the East (Trubetskoi), 9:531
Legacy to Gaius (Philo), 7:303
Legal applicability, 7:451
Legal appraisal, 7:450–452
Legal consciousness, 4:577
Legal context, memory in, 6:124
Legal convergence, 7:459
Legal discovery, 7:450–452
Legal language, 7:444–445
Legal obligations
definition of, 7:445
moral obligations and, 5:29
Legal paradox, 7:452
Legal persons, definition of, 7:237–238, 7:242
Legal philosophy
of Radbruch, 8:229–230
of Stammler, 9:203
Legal positivism, **5:237–239,** 7:425
Anglo-American, **5:239–245**
definition of, 5:237
exclusive, 5:241–242
as form of legal study, 5:237–238
on grounds of grounds of lawsic, 5:242–244
Hart on, 5:239–241
imperative theory of law and, 5:237
inclusive, 5:241–243
vs. natural law, 5:237–238
Nazism and, 7:427
on obligation to obey law, 5:238–239
Legal protection, for women, 3:584
Legal realism, **5:245–247**
Legal rules, and women, 3:583
Legal science, 7:427
Legal studies, critical, 7:463–464
Legal systems, 7:443
Legal theory, feminist, **3:54–57,** 3:582–585, 8:849–850
Legal transactions, 7:445–446
Legalism, Chinese, 2:232–234, 2:237–238
Legality
objective, 3:618
optimism/pessimism and, 7:249
Legatio (Athenagoras), 7:142
Legibus ac Deo Legislatore, De (Suárez), 9:282
Legibus et Consuetudinibus Angliae, De (Bracton), 9:139
Legislation
Aristotle on, 7:419
Carlyle on, 2:33
folkways and, 9:326
in legal pragmatism, 7:718
precedent and, 7:448–449
as will of supreme authority, 9:140
Legislators
Buchanan on, 7:351
and real issues *vs.* ideals, Burke on, 1:771–772
Smith on, 7:351
Legitimacy, Arendt on, 1:253–254
Lehmann, Erich, 9:218
Lehrbuch der allgemeinen Chemie (Ostwald), 3:233
Lehrbuch der allgemeinen Psychologie (Geyser), 4:82
Lehrbuch der Allgemeinen Psychologie (Rehmke), 8:303
Lehrbuch der exakten Naturwissenschaften (Dingler), 3:86
Lehrbuch der Logik (Stöhr), 9:252
Lehrbuch der Naturphilosophie (Elements of Physiophilosophy) (Oken), 7:11
Lehre von dem Ganzen, Die (Krueger), 5:156
Lehre von der Energie, Die (Helm), 3:233
Lehrer, Keith, 3:272, **5:248–249**
Lehringe zu Sais, Die (Novalis), 6:667
Leib und Seele (Body and soul) (Driesch), 3:111
Leibniz, Friedrich, 5:250
on universal harmony, 5:257, 5:260–263, 5:271
Leibniz, Gottfried Wilhelm, **5:249–279**
on *a priori* and *a posteriori,* 1:159, 1:240
on action at a distance, 3:688
on analogy of concurrent clocks, 4:77–78
on appearance, 1:232
on apperception, 1:233
and Aristotelianism, 5:265–269
Arnauld and, 1:288–293
ars combinatoria and, 5:535
on attributes, 5:494
Augustinianism and, 1:404
Baumgarten on, 5:9
on being-as-such, 1:529
on best possible world, 5:254, 5:263–265
on body, 8:130
Bruno and, 1:712
calculus and, 6:590
and Cartesianism, 2:56–59
on causality, 2:90
Chisholm and, 2:243
Chomsky and, 2:244

Leibniz, Gottfried Wilhelm, *continued*
on clarity and distinctness, 6:190–191
Clarke and, 2:269, 7:559
conciliatory focus of, 5:251–256, 5:266–267
concomitance in, 1:292–293
on continuum, 2:494–495
Conway and, 2:528–529
on Cordemoy's atoms, 2:538
Couturat on, 2:581–582
on creation, 3:297, 3:494, 5:257, 5:263–265
and crisis of skepticism, 9:55
Crusius and, 2:606
Deleuze on, 2:695
Descartes and, 2:748, 5:274–275
on determinism, 3:5, 3:8, 3:30
Diderot and, 3:73
Dilthey on, 3:84
Eberhard on, 3:161
Elisabeth, princess of Bohemia, and, 3:187
on emanation, 5:256–259, 5:262, 5:267, 5:271
Emerson and, 3:195
Encyclopédie and, 3:223
on energy conservation, 3:228
Enlightenment and, 3:243
entelechy in, 8:130
and epistemology, 3:296–298
on essence and existence, 3:351
on Eucharist, 5:268–269
on Euclid, 2:499
on evil, 3:469, 3:473, 5:263–265
on faith, 5:263–264
fatalism of, 1:292
on features, 5:272
on force measurement, 3:228
Foucher and, 3:704
on freedom, 5:254, 5:264
Genovesi and, 4:49
Geyser and, 4:82
on God, 5:256–264, 5:270–273, 5:671
existence of, 2:551–553
nature of, 7:559
Gödel and, 4:117
Goethe and, 4:141
Gottsched and, 4:165
and history of logic, 5:441–444
and history of philosophy, 3:405
on Hobbes' super-nominalism, 8:780
ideal language of, 1:342–343
on ideas, 3:298
on identity and possibility, 8:645
on identity of discernibles, 5:258
on identity of indiscernibles, 5:545
on infinite, 2:494–495, 4:659
and infinitesimal methods, 4:652
on innate ideas, 4:565, 4:692, 5:260–262
on knowledge, 5:259–262
Knutzen and, 5:123
La Mettrie on, 5:178
Laas on, 5:163
Lambert and, 8:785–786
on language, 8:779–781
on laws of thought, 5:233–234
Le Clerc and, 5:236
Lessing and, 5:295–296, 7:100
on life, purpose of, 5:261
life of, 5:250–254
Locke and, 1:233, 3:298, 5:378, 8:129–130
on logic, 5:272–274, 5:440
on logical diagrams, 5:560
Lotman and, 5:579
Lotze and, 5:582
Lull and, 5:610
Malebranche and, 5:671
on mass, 6:3
on mechanism, 5:265–269, 8:129
and metaphysics, 6:169, 6:190–191, 6:199, 8:645
methodology of, 5:255–256
microcosm in, 5:639
on mind, 5:258–262, 5:267–268, 6:259, 8:128–130
on mind-body union, 5:275–276
on mind-brain duality, 2:92
and monadology, 3:296–298, 4:141, 4:554, 5:260, 5:276–277, 6:324–325, 9:288–289
on monism, 6:326–327
on motion, 5:251–253, 5:269–270
and mystical idealism, 4:552–554
on nature, 7:559, 8:129
Newton and, 7:475
ontology of, 3:502
on optimism/pessimism, 7:244–245, 7:248–249
panpsychism and, 7:83, 7:86
Pantheismusstreit and, 7:99–101
on perception, 3:298, 5:11, 5:270, 8:129–130
phenomenalism of, 5:270–272
on philosophical corpus, 5:254–255
physicotheology and, 7:559
Pico della Mirandola (Gianfrancesco) and, 7:575
and Platonism, 5:255–260, 7:615
on plenitude, 5:257–258, 5:260, 5:593
and pluralism, 5:146, 6:328
on possibility, 7:722
on possible worlds, 7:23
on preestablished harmony, 5:254, 5:270–276, 9:336
preformationism of, 8:129
and principle of sufficient reason, 3:297, 5:270, 5:274
on probability coordination, 8:37
on properties, 3:528
and psychology, 8:128–130
on Pufendorf, 8:158
on qualities, 1:232
and rationalism, 4:746
and relationism, 9:147, 9:155–156
on republic of monadic spirits, 2:365–366
on resurrection, 5:268
Russian philosophy and, 5:572
Sanches and, 8:596
Schleiermacher and, 8:637
Scholz and, 8:644–645
on second-order logic, 8:707
on self-sufficiency of matter, 5:266–268, 5:274–275
on sense experience, 3:298, 4:554
on soul, 1:292, 3:117, 3:298, 5:251, 5:260, 5:267, 8:130
on space, 9:147
Spinoza and, 3:296
on Stahl's animism, 9:202
on study of arguments, 3:639
Sturzo and, 9:281
Suárez and, 9:282
on subject, 5:272–274
on subjects and predicates, 9:288–289
on substance, 5:256, 5:265–277, 8:128–129, 9:297–298
on subthreshold sensory perceptions, 3:736
Sulzer and, 9:325
Swedenborg and, 9:336
on Swineshead, 9:342
on sympathy, 5:257
on synonymy, 9:346
Tetens and, 9:403
and theodicy, 5:671
on thought and thinking, 9:420
on time, 9:467
Toland and, 2:683, 9:504
on truth, 3:296–297, 5:262–263, 5:272–274
on unconscious, 9:571
on universal characteristic, 8:779, 8:786
on universal language, 5:262, 5:441, 5:535

Wolff and, 3:350, 5:9, 5:123, 7:27, 9:824–826, 9:830
Wundt and, 9:849
Leibniz: Philosophie des Panlogismus (Gurwitsch), 4:198
Leibnizian rationalism, Kant and, 5:21
Leibnizian thinking, 5:10
Leibnizian-Wolffian School, 9:824–825, 9:830
Leibniz's law, 4:568
and Frege's sense and reference, 8:801
and proper names, 8:58
and relative identity, 9:762
and semantics, 8:781
Leiden des jungen Werthers, Die (The Sorrows of Young Werther) (Goethe). *See Sorrows of Young Werther, The* (Goethe)
Leiter, Brian, on law, 1:169
"Leitgedanken meiner naturwissenschaftlichen Erkenntnislehre, Die" (The primary ideas of my scientific epistemology) (Mach), 5:339
Lekton, 5:547, 8:757–758
Lektsii po struktural'noi poetike (Lectures on structural poetics) (Lotman), 5:578
Lemos, Miguel, 5:207
Lenard, Phillip, Einstein and, 7:578
Length measurement, 6:89–90, 7:29–30
Lenin, Vladimir Ilich, **5:279–281**, 5:351
on authoritarianism, 3:410
dialectical materialism and, 3:63–65
Engels and, 3:64–65
Hegel and, 3:65
and history, 3:37
on ideology, 4:574
influence of, 5:280–281
Kautsky and, 5:48
Lukács and, 5:603
on Marxism, 5:737
Pastore on, 7:136
Plekhanov and, 7:626–628
on revolutionary legality, 7:427
Leninism
aesthetics in, 1:59
Gramsci and, 4:170
Lenk, Hans, 7:549
L'Enseignement biblique (periodical), 5:570
Lensing, Elise, 4:253
Lenz, John, Lehrer and, 5:248
Leo XII, Pope, Lamennais and, 5:177
Leo XIII, Pope
Aquinas and, 9:436, 9:446
Erasmus and, 3:338
Loisy and, 5:570
Leo Tolstoy, Resident and Stranger (Gustafson), 9:512
Leonard, H. S., 6:146
Leonardo (periodical), 7:102
Leonardo da Vinci, **5:281–282**
on art, 1:48
on death, 2:652
Leonhardi, Hermann von, Krause and, 5:148
Leont'ev, Konstantin Nikolaevich, **5:283–284**
Leontius (Plato), 7:590
Leopardi, Count Giacomo, **5:284–286**
Leopold, Aldo, on environmental ethics, 3:259
Leopold, Nathan, Darrow (C.) and, 5:346
Leplin, Jarrett, 8:690
Lequier, (Joseph Louis) Jules, **5:287–288**
Les Advis et Les presens de la Demoiselle de Gournay (The Advice and Presents of Mademoiselle de Gournay) (Gournay), 4:167
Les Animaux plus que machines (La Mettrie), 5:180
Les Beaux-arts réduits à un même principe (Batteux), 1:489
Les Bijoux indiscrets (The indiscreet toys) (Diderot), 3:72
"*Les Communistes ont peur de la revolution*" (Sartre), 8:604
Les Fourberies de Scapin (Cyrano de Bergerac), 2:618
Les Lettres Persanes (Montesquieu), 6:336–337
Les Liaisons dangereuses (Laclos), 5:588
Les Maximes des saints (Fénelon), 3:603
Les Mots (Sartre), 8:604
Les Mots et les choses: Une archéologie des sciences humaines (Foucault), 3:698, 9:274
Les Origines de la France contemporaine, 9:365
Les Origines de la statique (Duhem), 3:126
Les Philosophes géomètres de la Grèce (Milhaud), 6:217
Les Ruines, ou Méditations sur les révolutions des empires (Ruins of Empires) (Volney), 9:707
Les Systèmes socialistes (Pareto), 7:117
Les Temps modernes (journal), 6:148
Lesage, George Louis, 3:688, 8:699
Lesbian Choices (Card), 2:31
Lesbian identity and ethics, 2:31
L'Escuela de Madrid (Marías), 5:711
Leslie, Alan, 9:39
Leslie, Charles, on deism, 2:691
Leslie, John
design argument and, 3:321
on selection bias, 1:220
Leśniewski, Jan, and Tarski, 5:480
Leśniewski, Stanisław, **5:290–293**
Cleanthes and, 6:147
nominalism and, 6:627
and ontology, 5:144
on part and whole, 6:146
protothetic and, 5:553, 5:607
Tarski and, 9:371
on theory of types, 9:353
Twardowski and, 9:554
"*L'Espoir maintenant*" (Sartre), 8:604
L'Esprit des lois (Montesquieu), 5:238
L'Esprit géométrique (Pascal), 7:129
Lessing, Gottfried, Ferguson and, 3:605
Lessing, Gotthold Ephraim, **5:293–297**
on aesthetics, 1:50, 5:294
Christianity and, 3:246
deism and, 2:688–689
Eisenstein and, 7:381
Enlightenment and, 3:243
Mendelssohn and, 6:130–131
and pantheism, 7:97, 9:193–194
Pantheismusstreit and, 7:99–100
Reimarus and, 2:688
on Spinoza, 4:770
on tragedy, 9:523
Lessing, Karl, 5:296
Lessings Leben (Lessing, Karl), 5:296
L'Être et le néant (Sartre), 4:748, 7:297
Letter concerning Toleration (Locke), 3:245, 5:390–391
"Letter from a Birmingham Jail" (King), 2:261, 5:73
Letter from Rome, showing an exact conformity between Popery and Paganism, A (Middleton), 6:214
"Letter on Humanism" (Heidegger), 4:295–296
Letter to a Deist (Stillingfleet), 2:682
Letter to a Deist concerning Beauty and Excellency or Moral Virtue (Balguy), 1:474
"Letter to a German Friend" (Camus), 2:21, 3:427
Letter to a Young Gentleman (Swift), 9:340
"Letter to Anebo" (Porphyry), 3:455, 6:551
Letter to Christina (Galileo), 4:11
"Letter to Gogol" (Belinskii), 1:538
Letter to Herodotus (Epicurus), 5:600
"Letter to His Father" (Kafka), 5:5

Letter to Lord Ellenborough (Shelley), 9:8
Letter to Menoeceus (Epicurus), on death, 2:652
Letter to Queen Charlotte of Prussia (Leibniz), 4:554
Letter to the abbé Raynal, on the Affairs of North America (Paine), 7:73
Letter to Waterland (Middleton), 6:214
Lettere a Engels (Labriola), 5:165
Lettere filosofiche sulle vicende della filosofia relativamente ai principî delle conoscenze umane da Cartesio sino a Kant inclusivamente (Galluppi), 4:14
Letters and Journal (Jevons), 4:807
Letters and Social Aims (Emerson), 3:195
Letters concerning the English Nation (Lettres philosophiques) (Voltaire), 2:687, 9:708
Letters concerning the Love of God (Astell), 1:355–356, 6:655, 9:838
Letters from the Anglican Period (Newman), Stein's translation of, 9:240
Letters Giving an Account of Several Conversations upon Important and Entertaining Subjects (Saint-Hyacinthe), 8:589
Letters on Aesthetic Education (Schiller), 1:54, 8:490, 8:627
Letters on Education (Macaulay), 9:839
Letters on Sunspots (Galileo), 4:8
Letters on the Religion Essential to Man (Huber), 9:839
Letters on the Study and Use of History (Bolingbroke), 1:641
Letters on Theron and Aspasio (Sandeman), 4:773
Letters to Malcolm (Lewis), 5:312
Letters to Serena (Toland), 9:504–506
Letters to the Inhabitants of Northumberland (Priestley), 8:8
Letters Written during a Short Residence in Sweden, Norway, and Denmark (Wollstonecraft), 9:837
Lettre à M. Hemsterhuis (Jacobi), 7:100
Lettre à Sorbière (Denis), 2:757
"Lettre à un ami, touchant le progrès du déisme en Angleterre" (Saint-Hyacinthe), 8:589
Lettre contre les sorciers (Cyrano de Bergerac), 2:618
Lettre de Thrasibule à Leucippe (Fréret), 2:265
Lettre écrite à un scavant religieux (Cordemoy), 2:537
Lettre sur la sculpture (Hemsterhuis), 4:311
Lettre sur les aveugles (Letter on the blind) (Diderot), 2:421, 3:71–73, 4:553
Lettre sur les désirs (Hemsterhuis), 4:311
Lettre sur les sourds et muets (Letter on the deaf and dumb) (Diderot), 3:71, 3:76
Lettre sur l'homme (Hemsterhuis), 4:311
Lettres à Mme. Dacier (Saint-Hyacinthe), 8:589
Lettres à un grand vicaire sur la tolérance (Letters to a grand vicar on toleration) (Turgot), 9:550
Lettres à une princesse d'Allemagne (Euler), 5:444
Lettres écrites de la campagne (Saint-Hyacinthe), 8:588
Lettres Persanes, Les (Montesquieu), 6:336–337
Lettres philosophiques (Chaadaev), 2:120–122
Lettres philosophiques (Letters concerning the English Nation) (Voltaire), 2:687, 9:708
Lettres provinciales (Pascal), 1:288, 4:789, 7:130–131
Lettres sur divers sujets de metaphysique et de religion (Fénelon), 3:603
L'Étude expérimental de l'intelligence (Binet), 1:596
Leucippus, **5:297–303**
  atomism and, 1:384, 7:763
  Diogenes of Apollonia and, 3:89
  materialism of, 6:7
  Parmenides of Elea and, 7:122
  on physical world, 3:10
Level of significance, 3:665
Level (order), definition of, 5:547
Levelers, on equality, 3:329–330
Leven, Kunst, en Mystiek (Brouwer), 1:700
Lever, Ralphe, 5:438
Leverkühn, Adrian, Adorno and, 1:25
Levi, Isaac, on decision theory, 2:657, 2:658
Leviathan (Hobbes), 2:260, 2:364
  on corporate state, 9:205
  on definition, 2:669
  on emotions, 3:198
  ethics in, 3:405
  in French clandestine writings, 2:265
  on imagination, 1:50, 4:593
  influence in Dutch Republic, 9:177–178
  on language, 8:773
  law in, 7:423
  on social contract, 9:81
  on social wholes, 9:94
  suppression of, 9:182
  on universals, 9:599
Levin, Leonid, 2:389
Levin, Murray, on alienation, 1:122
Levinas, Emmanuel, **5:303–306**
  on alterity, 1:134
  on death, 9:491
  Derrida on, 2:716–718
  in modern Jewish philosophy, 4:830–832
  on time, 9:491
Levine, Andrew, on socialism, 9:91
Levine, Joseph
  and explanatory gap, 5:114
  and functional reductive explanation, 6:570
  on qualitative consciousness, 2:450
Levinson, Jerrold
  on art, 1:67, 1:300, 1:318
  on Dickie, 1:300
  on music, 1:303, 1:306
Levinson, Stephen, on generalized conversational implicature, 2:527
Lèvi-Strauss, Claude, 2:715
  and French structuralism, 9:273
  on historicity, 7:398
  Lacan and, 5:168
  structural analysis of myths, 9:274
Levitt, Norman, 8:677–679
L'Évolution créatrice (Bergson), 1:57
L'Evolution de la matière (Le Bon), 3:233
Lévy, Benny, 8:604
Lévy-Bruhl, Lucien, **5:306–307**
  in ethnophilosophy, 1:83
  Gilson and, 4:92
Lewes, George Henry
  Eliot (George) and, 3:184
  on evolution, 1:361
  Pavlov and, 7:149
Lewin, Kurt, 5:563, 8:144
Lewis, C. S. (Clive Staples), 4:607, **5:311–313**
  on categories, 7:746
  on experience, 7:746
  on hell, 4:251
  pragmatism of, 7:746
Lewis, Clarence Irving, **5:307–311**
  on definition, 2:668
  on doubt, 3:103
  Malcolm and, 5:662

and modal logic, 5:483, 5:491
and rationalist theory, 5:96
on valuation, 9:638
on value, 9:637
Lewis, David, **5:313–315**
on admissibility, 8:38–39
on Bayesian conditionalized learning model, 8:685
on causality, 2:99, 2:103, 2:281
on chance and credence, 2:128
conditional logic and, 5:491
on common knowledge, 4:15
and conversational scorekeeping, 3:711
on counterfactuals in science, 2:574
and eliminative materialism, 3:182
on epistemological skepticism, 7:409
on event theory, 3:466–467
on explanation, 3:525
frequentism of, 8:34
functionalist analysis of mental concepts, 3:756
on indicative conditionals, 2:425–426
and knowledge argument, 5:114
on language, 5:189
metaphysics of, 6:170
and minimal-change semantics, 3:710
on natural laws, 5:226–229
on persistence, 7:207
on personal identity, 7:229–231
on plurality of worlds, 3:627
on possibility, 7:724
on possible world counterfactual conditionals, 2:247–249
on presupposition, 3:252
on probability, 8:34, 8:37
on propositional attitudes, 8:808
Ramsey and, 8:34
on skepticism, 3:275
on subjunctive conditionals, 2:99, 7:725
on supervenience, 3:191, 9:331
Lewis, G. N., 3:354–355, 7:146
Lewis Carroll's Symbolic Logic (Bartley), 5:452
Lewontin, Richard
on adaptation, 3:489
on evolutionary psychology, 3:484
Lex aeterna, 4:463
Lexical constituents, in compositionality, 2:372
Lexical definition, 5:540, 7:444
Lexical modulation, 7:740
Lexical units, as concepts, 2:419
Lexicon Philosophicum (Goclenius), 4:564
L'Existentialisme est un humanisme (Sartre), 8:603
L'Expérience humaine et la causalité physique (Brunschvicg), 1:714
Leyden, W. von, 5:387
Lezioni di filosofia del diritto (Del Vecchio), 2:697
L'Homme machine (La Mettrie), 5:178–180, 6:10
L'Homme planté (La Mettrie), 5:178–180
Li, 2:226–227
as abstract being, 5:137
in Confucianism, 2:220
in Daoist cosmology, 4:794
Japanese rejection of, 4:795
Mencius on, 6:129
and movement of *qi*, 5:138
in neo-Confucianism, 4:795
as unity in being, 1:738
Wang Fuzhi on, 9:724
Xunzi on, 2:234, 9:856–857
Zhang Zai on, 9:879
Zhu Xi on, 9:883
Li Ao, **5:316**
Li Ji, decorum in, 9:826
Li Tong, and Zhu Xi, 9:882
Li Xue school, 4:794
Li Zhicai, 9:6
Liability
computer ethics and, 2:397–398
in law, 7:462
Liaisons dangereuses, Les (Laclos), 5:588
Liang Shuming
on Chinese writing as philosophy, 4:792
and New Confucianism, 2:182
Liangzhi (intuitive knowledge of the good), Wang Yang-ming on, 9:726–727
Liar paradox, 5:149, **5:316–319**, 5:398, 6:110, 9:540
and correspondence truth theory, 2:541
dialetheism and, 7:106
in medieval logic, 5:433–434
presupposition and, 7:771
resolution of, 7:196–197
Russell on, 2:544
semantic paradox and, 5:521–522
and set theory, 5:518
Stoic logic and, 5:407
in Tarski's truth theory, 2:547
See also Epimenides' paradox
Liar sentence, as semantic paradox, 5:521
Liber Aristotelis de Expositione Bonitatis Purae. See Liber de Causis
Liber Astronomiae (On the spheres) (Alpetragius), 8:703
Liber Concordiae (Joachim of Fiore), 4:834
Liber Contra Gradus et Pluralitatem Formarum (Giles of Rome), 4:89
Liber de anima sextus de naturalibus (Avicenna), 4:697
Liber de Causis, 4:90, **5:333–334**, 8:41, 9:770
Liber Figurarum (Joachim of Fiore), 4:834
Liber Introductorius (Scot), 8:703
Liber Karastonis (Ibn Kurrah), on energy and work, 3:227
Liber Particularis (Scot), 8:703
Liber Sententiarum (Aureoli), on force and energy, 3:227
Liber Sex Principiorum (Gilbert of Poitiers), 4:88
Liberal arts
painting in, 1:48
Theodoric of Chartres on, 9:410
Liberal culture, Meinecke and, 6:113
Liberal democracy, 2:361, 8:389–390
Liberal education, Cicero on, 2:258
Liberal feminism
beliefs of, 3:599–600
humanist, 7:462
legal theory of, inadequacies of, 3:583
scholars of, 3:582
Liberal Imagination, The (Trilling), 5:322
Liberal ironism, 8:495
"Liberal Legislation and Freedom of Contract" (Green), 4:179
Liberal Republican Party, 5:321
Liberal thought, Condorcet on, 2:431
Liberalism, **5:319–326**
American, 5:321–322
Arab, 1:130
Arnold and, 1:294
Chicherin on, 2:148
communitarianism and, 2:368
vs. conservatism, 2:467–470
critiques and revisions of, 3:599–600
Darwinism and, 2:711–712
Dworkin on, 3:156
English, 5:319–320
Feinberg and, 3:560
French, 2:263, 5:320
German, 5:321

Liberalism, ***continued***
Gogarten and, 4:144
laissez-faire, Green on, 4:179
MacIntyre on, 9:75
Manheim on, 5:686
Marcuse on, 3:156
Maritain and, 5:717–718
and nationalism, 6:485–488
paternalism and, 7:137–138
Rawls and, 3:156, 5:323–325, 6:487–488
and rights, 1:589
Santayana on, 8:600
social-welfare, 3:599
Liberalism and Social Action (Dewey), 3:51
Liberation
in Asian philosophy, 3:95–96
Dōgen on, 3:95–96
in Indian philosophy, 4:133, **5:326–331**
in Cārvāka school, 4:625
empirical self and, 8:717
Hare Krishna movement and, 4:630
intellect and, 4:627
karma theory of, 4:625
and life, meaning of, 5:359
in literary tradition, 4:623
meditation and, 6:107–108
in Nyaya-Vaisesika schools, 4:133
in Purvamimamsa-Uttaramimamsa schools, 4:135
in Samkhya-Yoga schools, 4:134
Liberation philosophy, 5:211
Liberation theology, 5:211, **5:331–333,** 9:73
Liberi Arbitrii cum Gratiae Donis, Divina Praescientia, Providentia, Praedestinatione et Reprobatione Concordia (Molina), 8:680
Libero Arbitrio, De (Erasmus), 9:51
Libertad creadora, La (Korn), 5:142
Libertarianism, **5:334–337**
agent causation and, 1:90
on coercive institutions, 9:72–73
computer ethics and, 2:397
Epicurus and, 3:269
on evaluation of political and social institutions, 3:391–392
on historical causation, 3:40
and justice in bioethics, 1:603
political philosophy and, 7:676–678
Proudhon and, 8:94–95
Rawls and, 9:82
Toynbee and, 9:519
Winstanley and, 1:177
Liberté chez Descartes et la theologie, La (Gilson), 4:91
Libertins érudits, La Mothe Le Vayer and, 5:181
Liberty(ies)
Burke on, 1:771–772
Carlyle and, 2:34
and censorship, 2:119–120
Chicherin on, 2:148
Christian, Milton on, 6:250
in common consent arguments for God's existence, 2:347–348
Croce on, 2:604
in de Staël's Protestantism, 9:202
and democracy, 3:724
determinism and, 5:658
Deustua on, 3:42–43
vs. equality, Dworkin on, 3:157
freedom and, 3:723
as "freedom from," 1:589
general will and, 4:38–40
Hobbes on, 3:169, 5:319
of indifference, Descartes on, 2:744–745
indivisibility of, 1:472
vs. justice, libertarianism on, 5:336
law and, 1:518
libertarians on, 5:334–337
Maine de Biran on, 5:657–658
Mill (John Stuart) on, 6:233, 9:510
and monarchy *vs.* democracy, 1:621
and moral improvement, 9:3
in moral principles, 6:374–375
negative, 3:724, 5:334–335
positive, 3:724, 5:334–335
presumption in favor of (individual), 3:561
Priestley on, 8:5
in Russian society, 2:148
and social decay, 1:667
socialists on, 5:334–335
speech and, 2:119–120
Spinoza on, 9:181
of spontaneity, Descartes on, 2:744–745
state power and, **5:337–338**
vs. toleration, 9:507
welfare liberals on, 5:334–335
See also Freedom
Liberty, Equality, Fraternity (Stephen), 9:510
Liberty of the Press, The (Tindal), 9:502
Liberty-limiting principles, 3:561
Libidinal Economy (Lyotard), 5:620–621
Libido
Bloch on, 1:615
Freud on, 9:572
Library(ies), 3:559
Libri Quatuor Sententiarum (Book of Sentences) (Peter Lombard), 7:259–261
Libros Physicorum (Soto), 9:137
Lichtenberg, Georg Christoph, **5:338–343**
and epistemology of exact sciences, 5:340
Lavater and, 5:214
and philosophy of language, 5:342
and philosophy of mathematics, 5:339–340
and thought experiments, 9:452
L'Idée directrice de la dissolution opposée de l'évolution (Lalande), 5:172
L'Idiot de la famille: Gustave Flaubert de 1821 à 1857 (Sartre), 8:604
Lie of omission, 5:619
Liebert, Arthur, **5:343–344**
Liebig, Justus von, on mechanical energy of animals, 3:229
Liebknecht, Karl, Kautsky and, 5:47
Liebmann, Otto, **5:344–345**
Driesch on, 3:110
on Kant, 6:545
and neo-Kantianism, 6:539–541
Liezi, 2:186, 9:862
Life, 1:654
after death, semantics of, 1:370–371
artificial, 1:345–349
atheism and, 1:373
Augustine on, 3:402
as autopoetic system, 2:300
biological capacities and, 1:602
Butler (Samuel) on, 1:785
Carus (Carl) on, 2:63
Cheng Hao on, 2:144
in Chinese philosophy, 2:224–227
Cicero on, 2:258
Cournot's vital principle and, 2:577
definition of, 1:8
desirability of, 9:642–644
desire for, in Yoga, 6:108
Erigena on, 3:403
Eucken on, 3:451–452
Freud on, 8:146
"historylessness" of, 9:165
human
Bergson on, 1:570
Bultmann on, 1:764
existential authenticity and, 1:762–763

as impersonal, 1:548
incompatibility with death, 4:607–608
leading, meaning of, 9:836
Leopardi on, 5:285–286
love in, atheism and, 1:373–374
material, and consciousness, 3:575
meaning and value of, **5:345–359**
in cosmic sense, 5:351–352
Darrow (C.) on, 5:346, 5:349, 5:354
Emerson on, 3:195
in existential sense, 5:354–357
future, irrelevance of, 5:350–351
God's existence and, 5:345–346, 5:352, 5:359
normal view of, 5:354
objective sense of, 5:353
pessimistic view of, 5:345–356
Sabatier on, 8:588
Schopenhauer on, 5:345–346, 5:350, 5:354
sources of, 5:351–357
speciesism and, 9:164
subjective sense of, 5:353
in terrestrial sense, 5:351–353
Tolstoy on, 5:346–349, 5:356, 9:512
meaninglessness of, 6:619
origin of, 5:174, **5:359–362**
Ortega y Gasset on, 7:45, 7:46
physics of conditions for, 2:567
as process of becoming, 9:30–31
purpose of
Leibniz on, 5:261
in wisdom, 9:795
Zen'kovskii on, 9:868
as quality in space-time, 1:109
RNA world and, 5:361–362
sanctity of, 7:694–697
solitary, Levinas and, 4:831
soul as principle of, 4:607
as substance, 9:695
Unamuno on, 9:566–569
unity of learning as, 9:862
unsupportability of, in universal equilibrium, 1:645
as utopia, 9:621
Woodbridge on, 9:842
zeal in, atheism and, 1:373–374
Life (Teresa of Ávila), 9:394
Life after Life (Moody), 4:618
Life at the Limits (Kaufmann), 5:46
Life in a Jewish Family (Stein), 9:239
Life of Antonio Carafa, The (Vico), 9:672
Life of Chaucer (Godwin), 4:136
Life of Cicero (Middleton), 6:214
Life of Demonax (Lucian of Samosata), 5:597
Life of Don Quixote and Sancho (Vida de Don Quijote y Sancho) (Unamuno), 9:566
"Life of Gregory Skovoroda, The" (Kovalinski), 9:63
Life of Isidore (Damascius), 2:622, 6:552
"Life of Jesus" (Hegel), 4:261
Life of John Milton (Toland), 9:504–505
Life of John Stuart Mill, The (Packe), 6:233
Life of Moses (Gregory of Nyssa), 4:182
Life of Plotinus (Porphyry), 6:549–550, 7:608
Life of Reason, The (Santayana), 8:597–599
Life of Samuel Johnson, The (Boswell), 4:853
Life of the Mind, The (Arendt), 1:255
Life of the Servant, The (Suso), 9:335
Life sciences
and bioethical issues, 1:603–604
and overtly gendered subject matter, 3:591
Life world, Landgrebe on, 5:185–186
Lifeboat model of allocation, 6:96–97
Life-drawing classes, women and, 3:572
"Life-knowledge," and scientific knowledge, 5:60
Lifestyles, communitarianism and, 2:369
Lifeworld, 3:564, 4:200
Light
Aquinas on, 1:47
Aristotle on, 7:314
atoms and, 7:476–477
Bacon (Francis) on, 1:448
Bonaventure on, 1:653–654
in classical mechanics, 2:282, 7:474
Comenius on, 2:341
corpuscular theory of, 6:591
as creative substantial radiation, 1:654
Crescas on, 2:593
in divine illumination, 4:579–580
Grosseteste on, 1:453, 1:653–654
in illuminationism, 4:761
Kepler on, 5:53
and knowledge, 3:242
in language of illumination, 4:582
in Manichaeism, 5:683
matter and, 6:62
Michelson-Morley experiment and, 9:149
Newton on, 6:590–591
Philoponus on, 7:314
in special theory of relativity, 9:149
velocity of, 2:523–524, 2:559, 7:476, 9:149
wave hypothesis for, 6:69, 6:591
Light cones, in local theories, 6:641
Light of Nature Pursued, The (Tucker), 3:172, 4:34
Lightning, as electrical discharge, 3:720
Lightning rod, Franklin and, 3:720
Like and unlike, 9:872
Likelihood equation, 3:661–663
Likelihood principle, 9:212–213
Fisher and, 3:662
in Neyman-Pearson statistical theory, 9:217
Likelihood ratio test, logic of, 3:664
"Likeness to God" (Channing), 2:130–131
L'Imaginaire (Sartre), 4:594, 4:598, 8:604
Limborch, Philip van, 5:391
Orobio and, 7:41
on Spinoza's *Theological-Political Treatise*, 9:182
Limit(s)
definition of, 5:547
Hilbert on, 5:470
infinity and, 5:470, 5:515
in Leibniz's calculus, 2:495
in Pythagoreanism, 8:183
Limit number, definition of, 5:547
Limit ordinal. *See* Limit number
Limitative propositions, 5:553
Limited and unlimited, 4:312, 9:873–874
Limited Inc. (Derrida), 2:718
Limited independent variety, principle of, 5:56
Limiters, 7:310–311
Limits of Jurisprudence Defined (Bentham), 7:425
"Limits of Natural Selection, The" (Wright), 9:846
Limits of Religious Thought, The (Mansel), 1:92–93, 1:362
"Limits of Self Awareness, The" (Martin), 7:193
L'Impiété des déistes, athées et libertins de ce temps (The impiety of the deists, atheists, and libertines of our time) (Mersenne), 2:725, 6:152
Linde, Andrei, on chaotic inflationary cosmology, 2:566
Lindemann, Hans A., 5:210
Lindley, Dennis V., 9:222
Lindman, Harold, 8:614, 9:222
Lindström, P., on logical terms, 5:531

L'Industrie (journal), 8:589
Line, Whitehead's definition of, 9:748
Linear dynamics, 5:696–697
Linear operator
  on Hilbert space, 6:277–278
  on vector space, 8:208
Linear ordering, 3:646
Lines of force
  concept of, 3:551
  Maxwell and, 6:68
"Lines of identity," Peirce on, 5:455
Linguistic analysis, by native speakers in attributor contextualism, 2:487
Linguistic apologetic, 7:495
Linguistic Behavior (Bennett), 1:549
Linguistic behaviorism, 7:401
Linguistic capacity, Condillac on, 2:423
Linguistic competence, 2:650
  Chomsky on, 9:360
  Davidson (Donald) on, 2:647–648
Linguistic conventions, 5:501, 7:199–200
Linguistic differences
  in conceptualization of suicide, 9:318
  in evaluative predicate application, 4:862
  in Swedenborg's doctrine of correspondence, 9:337
Linguistic fictions, 8:793
Linguistic meaning
  compositional, 6:83, 8:735
  vs. content, 2:705
  conventional, 6:83
  defining, 6:82–83
  vs. sense, 8:830
Linguistic necessity, 1:148
Linguistic phenomenalism, 7:271–273
Linguistic philosophy, 3:428–430, 8:494
Linguistic processing, modularity theory of, 3:675
Linguistic rules, types of, 2:674
Linguistic sign, 9:273–274
Linguistic theory(ies), 5:188–189
  Encyclopédie on, 3:224
  on grammatical transformations, 9:360
  Köhler and, 5:129
Linguistics
  a priori knowledge in, 1:150, 5:662
  of appearance, 1:229–231
  Bakhtin on, 1:466
  belief as attitude in, 5:704–705
  Carnap on, 2:42–44
  Cassirer on, 2:67
  Chinese, 2:191
  Chomsky and, 2:245, 8:151
  in cognitive science, 2:297
  compositionality in, 2:370
  computational models and, 2:392
  concreteness in, 6:627
  conversational implicature in, 4:184
  in expression of knowledge, 8:640
  in foundation of mathematics, 8:640
  Frege on, 9:555–556
  of God, 1:94–95
  guise in, 7:403
  Humboldt and, 8:793
  in Indian philosophy, 4:631
  in induction, 4:641, 4:645–646
  of kinds, 6:504–505
  and logical form, 5:510
  machine intelligence and, 5:634
  metalinguistic-linguistic distinction, 1:702
  on methodological individualism, 4:446
  in morality, 6:632–634
  natural language and, 2:77, 8:794
  necessity in, 1:148, 1:166
  of nothing, 1:218
  philosophical use of, 1:605–606
  philosophy as, 8:149–150
  and phonology, 5:510, 7:551–553
  in physicalism, 6:562
  of present, 9:498
  of promises, 8:53
  propositional attitudes and, 8:78, 8:808
  Quine and, 8:216–221
  religion and, 7:495
  Ryle on, 2:77
  Saint-Hyacinthe and, 8:588
  of Sanskrit, 7:414–417
  semantic view of, 9:416–417
  speaking body and, 5:151
  speech and, 1:469–470
  Strawson and, 2:79
  testimony in, 9:401
  of theoretical definitions, 9:414–415
  time in, 9:463–464, 9:470, 9:478
  Trubetskoi (Nikolai) on, 9:531
  in understanding, Heidegger on, 4:2
  utterance and, 1:469
  vernacular tongue and, 2:623
Linkage parameters, 3:664
Linnaean Society, 2:629–634, 2:639
Linnaeus, Carl, 3:247, 9:411
Linné, Carl von. *See* Linnaeus, Carl
Linsky, Leonard, 9:347
Linton, Ralph, on universal values, 3:420
Liouville's Theorem, 4:87
Lippmann, Walter, on government, 2:702
Lippo Lippi, Merleau-Ponty on, 6:151
Lipps, Theodor, **5:362–363**
  Ebbinghaus and, 8:141
  on empathy, 5:161, 9:239
  Klages and, 5:77
  Krueger and, 5:155
Lipset, Seymour, on ideology, 4:574
Lipsius, Justus, 3:262, **5:363–364**
Lisbon earthquake, Voltaire and, 9:711
Lishi wuai, 1:738
LISP, "cond" function in, 3:711
Listening
  Adorno on, 1:26–27
  borrowed-meaning knowledge and, 9:138
  in I-it *vs.* I-thou relations, 1:716
  to music, 6:439
Literacy
  and freedom, 3:722
  and suffrage, 1:556
Literal, 3:654, 4:809
Literalism
  nonbeing and, 6:635–636
  pretense theories and, 6:637
Literary criticism
  Benjamin on, 1:546
  Derrida and, 9:278
  Eliot (T. S.) and, 3:185–186
  in Hellenistic and Roman periods, 1:189–190
  vs. metaphysics, 6:205
  in postcolonialism, 7:727
  Solov'ëv and, 9:125
Literary devices, used by Kierkegaard, 5:68
Literary genres, of Cynics, 2:617
Literary Notebooks (Schlegel), 8:630–631
Literary Remains of the Late Henry James, The (James, William), 4:779
Literary studies, as academic discipline, 5:369
Literary theory
  and deconstruction, 2:661–662
  Milton and, 6:251
  Romanticism and, 8:631
Literature
  as allographic, 1:317
  anti-intentionalism and, 1:311–312
  Arnold on, 1:294
  and authorial intention, 5:369
  Bakhtin on, 1:465–468
  Beauvoir and, 1:516
  Benn on, 1:548

Blake and, 1:611
Blanchot and, 1:611–612
Boileau on, 1:640
characters in, ontological status of, 5:366–367
Chernyshevskii on, 2:146
in Chinese ethics, 2:200
in Cixous écriture feminine project, 2:262
in Confucian ethics, 2:196
creation of, 1:318
criticism and interpretation of, 2:33, 5:368–370
Croce's aesthetic theory of, 2:601–602
definition of, 5:368
evil in, 1:43
vs. fiction, 5:364
in formalism, 1:309
genre in, **1:330–332,** 1:469
history as, 7:394
Ingarden on, 1:59
intentionality in, 1:469
irony in, 1:311
locutionary and illocutionary acts in, 1:509
Lukács on, 1:69, 5:603
Marković on, 5:719
modernism in, 6:317
morality and, 1:67
novel as, 8:631
as persuasive world-view representation, 2:229
philosophical *vs.* other, 7:332–333
philosophy of, **5:364–372**
in ancient Greek drama, 4:175–177
and artistic imagination, 4:596–597
in Buddhism, 4:632–633
De Sanctis on, 2:719–720
in Hinduism, 4:623–624
Plato on, 1:41–42
reader-response theory of, 1:314–315
realism in, 1:337
in Roman period, 1:45
Romanticism and, 8:487–488
structuralism and, 9:273
Sulzer on, 9:325
value of, 5:370–371
See also Fiction
Literature and Dogma (Arnold), 1:294
Literature and the Right to Death (Blanchot), 1:611
Little Book of Eternal Wisdom (Suso), 9:335
Little Book of Truths, The (Suso), 9:335
Little World-System (Democritus), 5:298
Littré, Émile, **5:372**
Liu Shuxian, 2:182–184
Liubov-mirazh? (Is Love a Mirage?) (Ivanov), 4:767
Liuzu tanjing (Platform sutra of the sixth patriarch) (Huineng), 2:198–199
Live option, as psychological category, 3:532
Lived body, 6:148
Lives and Opinions of Eminent Philosophers (Diogenes Laertius), 1:96, 1:193, 3:88, 8:850, 9:106
Living
art of, in wisdom, 9:793
vs. nonliving, 9:694–695
Living Flame of Love, The (John of the Cross), 4:846
Living force. *See* Energy, kinetic
"Living On" (Derrida), 2:718
Living things
Boyle on, 1:674
Cyrano de Bergerac and, 2:618
functions in, 9:387
as illustration of teleological order, 9:376
as organisms, 1:593–594
Tennant on, 9:393
unity of learning as, 9:862
Livingston, Paisley, 7:385
Llewellyn, Karl N.
on behavior analysis, 7:428
Ehrlich and, 7:427
legal realism and, 5:245–247
Lloyd, Genevieve, **5:372–374**
presentism and, 9:479
study of the "maleness" of reason, 3:570
Loa Zi, 2:205
Loar, Brian, 5:114
Lobachevski, Nikolai Ivanovich, 4:59, 5:461, 9:150
Lobachevskian geometry, 2:521, 4:59
Local situations, 3:708
Localist memory scheme, 6:125
Locality
and causal account of time, 2:87
and non-locality, **6:638–642**
in quantum mechanics, 2:530
of reason, 4:608
superpositioning and, 5:695–696
Location(s), 7:23
"Location of Sound, The" (O'Shaughnessy), 9:138
Loci, in medieval logic, 5:422–423
Loci Communes Rerum Theologicarum (Melanchthon), 6:119
Locke, Alain, 3:567
Locke, John, 3:530, 3:636, **5:374–396**
on abstraction, 3:300, 4:565, 4:593
Alembert and, 1:106
as antilogical, 5:447
on Aristotelianism, 3:349
Arminianism and, 1:286
on atheism, 1:357, 9:509
behaviorism and, 1:201
Beneke and, 1:544
Bentham and, 8:792
Berkeley and, 1:586, 3:301, 8:782
bibliographic resources on, 5:394–395
Bilfinger and, 1:595
Boulainvilliers and, 1:670
Budde and, 1:721
Burthogge and, 1:776
Cartesian epistemology and, 2:58
on causation, 5:384
character of, 5:375–376
on Christianity, 3:246, 5:392
on church and state roles, 3:245
on civil disobedience, 2:261
on civil society, 9:207
Cockburn on, 2:294
Coleridge and, 2:316
Collingwood on, 2:329
Collins and, 2:330
on color, 1:37, 2:332
on common consent for God's existence, 2:345
on common sense, 2:356
on concepts, 2:417
conceptualism of, 9:594–596
Condillac and, 2:420–423, 8:826
on consciousness, 2:449, 2:453, 5:395
on contemplation, 5:380–381
Cousin and, 2:580
and crisis of skepticism, 9:54
and critical realism, 2:597
Culverwell and, 2:613
Declaration of Independence influenced by, 4:805
on definition, 2:667–668, 3:349
deism and, 2:682–683, 2:690
Descartes and, 3:407
on desire, 5:382–383
Destutt de Tracy and, 2:760
on determinism, 3:5, 3:13–14
Diderot and, 3:72–75
on diversity, 5:384
and divine command theories of ethics, 3:93
Driesch and, 3:110
DuBos and, 3:123
Duns Scotus and, 3:144

Locke, John, ***continued***
on duration, 5:382, 9:464
on duty, 7:370
Eberhard and, 3:161
on education, 5:390–391, 7:369–370
Edwards (Jonathan) and, 3:166–167
on elementary notions, 5:175–176
empiricism of, 3:214–217, 3:221, 7:492–493
Encyclopédie and, 3:222–224
Enlightenment and, 3:244–245, 4:746
and epistemology, 3:298–301, 5:91
on equality, 3:330
on error, 5:387
on essence and existence, 3:349
and ethics, 3:407–408
on experience, 3:517, 5:379, 8:149
on faith, 5:99, 5:387, 5:392, 9:249–250
and feminism, 3:600
on Filmer, 9:81
on free will, 3:13–14, 3:407–408, 5:383
on freedom, 5:382–383, 9:509
Galluppi and, 4:14
on geometry, 4:57
Gibbon and, 4:86
on God, 2:346, 4:112, 5:387
Goodman on, 4:159
on government, 2:699, 5:388–390, 7:153
Green on, 4:179
Hartley and, 8:826
on higher-order consciousness, 2:454
on Hobbes, 7:424
Hoffman and, 2:607
on ideas, 1:200–201, 3:298–300, 5:395
complex, 5:379–385
definition of, 5:377, 5:385
as images, in Descartes, 2:54
innate, 3:216, 3:298–299, 3:407, 5:377–378
and knowledge of reality, 5:387
as representation, 1:577
simple, 5:379–380, 5:385
source of, 5:379
on identity, 5:379, 5:384
on imagination, 1:50
on induction from experience, 4:638
on infinity, 5:382
influence of, 5:376, 5:387, 5:391–394
influences on, 5:376
on innate ideas, 4:688, 4:692
on inner sense, 4:697
on instinct, 7:369
Johnson and, 8:794
on knowledge, 3:216–217, 3:300, 5:96, 5:376–379, 5:385–387, 7:370
Lambert and, 5:176
on language, 3:300, 5:384–385, 8:777–779
Le Clerc and, 5:235
Leibniz and, 1:233, 3:298, 5:254–256, 5:261, 8:129–130, 8:779
liberalism and, 5:319–322
libertarianism and, 5:334–335
on liberty, 3:169
on limited certitude, 9:54
Maine de Biran and, 5:656
Malebranche and, 5:671, 6:656
on material world, 3:301, 5:377–379, 5:395
matter-mind dualism in, 2:595
Mauthner and, 8:801
on memory, 5:380–381
and metaphysics, 6:191
methodism of, 3:278
Mill (John Stuart) and, 8:795
on mind, 5:378, 8:129–130
on mind-body problem, 3:13
on miracles, 6:267–268
on mixed modes, 5:383
on modes, 5:381–383
on morality, 5:378, 5:386
on national identity, 6:481
on natural law, 6:511–512
Norris and, 6:655–656
on number, 5:382
on optimism/pessimism, 7:248
on perceiving and mental qualities, 2:452
on perception, 1:233, 5:395
on personal identity, 4:604, 4:612, 5:379, 5:395, 7:214–227, 7:232, 7:238, 9:762–763
on personhood, 7:238
and *philosophes,* 9:56
and philosophy, 3:405
physicotheology in, 7:559
Piaget on, 7:568
on pleasure, 3:267, 4:257, 7:621
political philosophy of, 5:387–390, 5:395, 7:663–664
on power, 5:382–383, 5:395
on primary and secondary qualities, 3:2, 3:217, 3:299–302, 5:379–380, 6:670, 8:8
on probability, 5:387, 6:579–580
on properties, 3:528
on property, 5:389, 5:395, 8:69
and psychology, 8:135
on public interest, 9:207
on qualitative consciousness, 2:450
and rationalism, 4:746
Rawls on, 9:82
on real *vs.* nominal essences, 6:504
on reason, 5:379, 5:387, 5:392
on reflection, 5:380–381, 5:385
on relations, 5:381, 5:384
on religion and ethics, 3:391, 5:391–392, 5:395
on resemblance, 9:599–600
on rights of individuals, 4:190
on sensa, 8:814
on sensations, 8:823–825
on sense perception, 3:299–300, 5:379, 5:385
Shaftesbury and, 9:1
on social contract, 9:80
on society, 7:369–370
socinianism and, 9:100
on soul, 3:118
on sovereignty, 1:542–543
on space, 5:381–382
on the state, 9:205
on state of nature, 5:388, 7:153
on substance, 1:674, 5:381–384, 7:23, 7:369, 9:298
Swedenborg and, 9:336
on testimony, 9:401
Tetens and, 9:403
Thomasius and, 2:606
on thought and thinking, 5:382, 9:420
on time, 5:382
Tindal and, 2:683, 9:502–503
Toland and, 2:683, 9:249
on toleration, 5:391–395, 9:507–509
on touch, 9:515
on truth, 5:377–378, 8:588
on understanding, 1:50, 5:377, 8:778
on universals, 9:594–596
unknown substance and category theory, 2:80
Voltaire and, 2:687, 9:709
on war and peace, 7:153
Wiggins and, 9:762–763
on will, 5:382–383
Wittgenstein on, 1:203
and Wolff, 9:826
Locke Newsletter, The (periodical), 5:394
Locus, Abelard on, 5:425–426

Locutionary acts, *vs.* illocutionary acts, 7:201
Lodestone, used by Fludd, 3:674
Loeb, Louis, on Hume, 6:498–499
Loeb, Richard, Darrow (C.) and, 5:346
Loewer, Barry, 8:214
  on many minds formulation, 5:698
  on natural laws, 5:228
  on semantic notions of mental content, 2:479
Logic, 6:490, 8:592
  Abelard on, 1:4, 5:424–428
  of action, 9:848
  in adjudication, 7:448–449
  Albert of Saxony on, 1:101
  algebra of
    and computing machines, 2:400
    Leibniz and, 5:443
    Schröder on, 5:462
  of algebraic equation, 1:660
  of analogies, in Cajetan, 2:7
  of analysis, in Neurath, 6:560
  analyticity as function of, 1:161
  ancient. *See* Ancient logic
  Anderson (John) on, 1:199
  arguments and, 1:773, 3:639–642
  Ariston of Alexandria on, 5:407
  Aristotelian, 1:269, 2:72–74, 3:52–53, 5:398–401, 5:568–569, 9:635
  artificial languages and, 1:342–343
  Avicenna and, 1:434–435
  axiomatizable *vs.* tool for axiomatics, 1:660
  and axiomatization
    Boole and, 5:450
    for deduction and definition, 6:22
  axioms of, 5:93
  Bacon (Francis) on, 1:445
  Bayle on, 5:236
  of "bear on" *vs.* "influence" in Chinese, 2:210
  Biel on, 1:594
  in biology, 9:844
  Boethius on, 1:626
  Bolzano and, 1:647, 5:445–446
  Boole and, 1:658–660, **5:447–458**, 5:449–450
  Bosanquet on, 1:661
  both/neither and, 5:689–690
  Boyle on, 7:163
  Bradley and, 1:676–679
  Brentano on, 1:689–692
  Brouwer and, 5:468–469
  in Buddhism, 1:733, 1:756, 4:633
  Buridan on, 1:768
  Burley on, 1:773
  Burthogge on, 1:776
  in Byzantine thought, 1:788–789
  Carnap on, 2:43
  Carroll (Lewis) and, 2:51–53, 5:452
  in Cartesianism, 2:285–286
  categories and, 2:77–80
  category theory, 2:72–83
  causal powers and, 1:741
  Chinese, 2:152, 2:210–214
  Chrysippus on, 2:251
  Church (Alonzo) and, 2:253–254, 5:475–476
  Chwistek on, 2:255–256
  circumscription in, 6:643
  classical
    eliminating terms in, 8:196
    and interference effects for electrons, 8:203–204
    and quantum logic, 8:205
    weakening, 5:109
  classification of, Peirce on, 7:169
  Cohen (Hermann) on, 6:542
  Cohen (Morris) on, 2:306–307
  coherence and, 1:695
  combinatory. *See* Combinatory Logic
  computability theory and, 2:400
  in computationalism, 2:391
  Comte on, 2:411
  conditional, 5:487
  contradiction in, 4:270
  conversational implicature in, 4:184
  Croce and, 2:602
  Crusius and, 2:606
  De Morgan and, 2:709–710, 5:448–449, 7:163
  default, 6:643
  definition of, 5:547, 7:326
  Dewey on, 3:47–48
  in Dge-lugs Mādhyamika, 1:732–733
  dialectic and, 1:626, 3:53–54
  Diodorus Chronus and, 3:87
  of directional causality for time, 2:87
  distribution-free, 5:489
  Dodgson and, 2:51–53
  Driesch on, 3:111
  dynamic, anaphora and, 1:175
  empiriocriticism and, 7:716
  Engels on, 3:63
  Epicurus on, 3:269, 4:300
  and epistemology, 1:445
  as ethics of thought, 9:29
  Euler and, 5:444
  of evocative argument, 2:213–214
  and excluded middle validity, 1:701
  vs. experience, in law, 7:448
  fatal abstractions of, 8:625
  First Degree Entailment in, 5:689–690
  first-order, 2:254, 2:380–384, **3:639–659**
  and five indemonstrables, 9:255–256
  formal
    Abelard on, 1:4
    Anderson (John) and, 1:199
    Boole on, 5:449–450
    Cohen (Hermann) and, 6:542
    Hamilton on, 5:447–448
    Hegel on, 4:265–266
    John of St. Thomas on, 4:844–845
    and ordinary language, 9:264
    quantifiers in, **8:196–198**
    subject and predicate in, 9:287–288
  free, 8:196
  and free will, 9:29
  Frege on, 2:36, 3:726–731, 5:463–464, 5:482, 5:551, 7:163, 9:556
  Friedman and, 5:484
  function spaces and, 4:742
  Galen on, 4:5
  in game theory, 4:19
  generics in, 4:42
  Gentile on, 4:49
  Gentzen and, 4:739, 5:475
  Gödel and, 4:119–131, 5:473–474
  as grammar of rationality, 1:768
  grammatical form *vs.*, 1:677
  Hamilton and, 5:447–448
  Hegel and, 2:81, 4:265–266, 4:270, 4:286–287
  Herbrand and, 5:472–473
  Hilbert and, 5:469–470
  history of. *See* History, of logic
  Hobbes and, 4:406–410, 6:9
  Husserl on, 2:81–82
  of identity, 1:679, 4:568
  independence-friendly, 8:198
  of indexicals, 4:623
  in Indian philosophy, **5:410–414**
  infinitesimals, 4:652–653
  in informal axiomatics, 6:22
  intensional, 5:486–487
  intuitionist. *See* Intuitionism; Intuitionist logic

Logic, *continued*
in Islamic world, history of, **5:417–421**
Avicenna and, 5:418–419
eastern and western schools of, 5:419–420
Greek logic and, 5:417–418, 5:421
logicians of Andalusia and, 5:419
School of Baghdad and, 5:418
in Jainism, 9:543
Jevons on, 4:807–808, 5:450–451
John of St. Thomas on, 4:845
Johnson on, 5:458
Jungius and, 4:861
Kant and, 2:74–75, 5:17–18, 5:456–457
Keynes and, 5:457–458
Kotarbiński on, 5:144
Lambert on, 5:175–176
and language, 1:147, 2:647–648
law of, definition of, 5:547
on laws of thought, 5:234–235
Le Clerc on, 5:236
in legal appraisal, 7:450
Leibniz on, 5:262, 5:272–274, 5:441
Leśniewski on, 5:290–293
and logical *vs.* non-logical constants, 5:234
Löwenheim and, 5:470–471
Łukasiewicz on, 5:605–608
Mackie and, 5:638
in Mādhyamika doctrine, 1:740–743, 4:633
many-valued. *See* Many-valued logic
Marsilius of Inghen and, 5:721
masculinism of, 1:157
mathematical, 1:147, 5:459–463, 8:541, 8:546–548, 8:834, 9:747
Boole and, 1:659–660, 5:460
combinatory, 2:334–340
computable partial functions as class in, 2:380
effective calculability in computability theory and, 2:375
in mathematical foundations, 6:20–21
modern, origin of, 5:482
Montague in, 6:329
Royce and, 8:521
of medical diagnosis, 7:466–467
medieval, 3:54, 8:765–770, 8:767
Megarian tradition, 3:54
Mill (John Stuart) and, 1:676, 5:456–457, 8:795
miracles and, 6:266–270
Miura on, 6:276
modal. *See* Modal logic
vs. models, 8:154
modern, **5:447–484,** 8:840
Bolzano on, 5:445–446
Boolean period of, **5:447–458**
computing machines and, 2:399
decidable and undecidable theories and, 5:478–479
disjunctive reasoning and, 5:503
from Frege to Gödel, **5:458–474**
hypothetical reasoning and, 5:503–504
and traditional logic, 5:504
monotonicity in, 6:642
Mozi and, 6:417
Nagel (Ernest) on, 6:473
natural language and, 2:77
necessary beings and, 7:26
negation in, 6:523–529
non-classical, **5:485–493**
and extensions *vs.* rivals, 5:485
proliferation of, 5:482–484
quantifiers and, 5:490
non-monotonic, 5:490–491, **6:642–643**
normative aim of, 9:29
notation of
Boole and, 5:450
Frege on, 3:726
Marcus and, 5:704
negation in, 6:527–528
Peano on, 5:465
Venn on, 5:451–452
objects of, in naturalism, 6:494
Ockham and, 2:80, 9:776–778
omniscience principle and, 4:738
one/many in, 4:312
in ontology, 2:41, 7:26
ordinary language approach to, 5:438
Ortega y Gasset and, 7:47–48
paraconsistent, 5:489, **7:105–106**
paradoxes and, 5:317
Pastore on, 7:135
Paul of Venice on, 7:147
Pauler on, 7:145
Peirce on, 5:453–456, 7:163–165, 7:168, 7:174
Pfänder on, 7:270
phenomenology and, 7:279–280
in philosophy, 7:326
Piaget on, 7:568–569
of place, Nishida on, 4:798
Poincaré on, 7:653
of possibility, 1:2
Post and, 5:467, 5:538, 5:606
in post-Kantian thought, 2:75–77
post-Renaissance status of, 9:742
precursors of, **5:440–446**
predicate
Frege on, 3:726, 3:731
mereology in, 6:146
predicate modal
semantics of, 6:294–296
syntax of, 6:292
Prior in, 8:13
private language problem and, 8:19–21
probability and, 8:27–29, 9:220–222
probative *vs.* proairetic reasoning and, 2:213–214
proof theory and, **8:54–57**
propositional, 1:660, 3:642–644
Abelard on, 1:4
Boethius on, 1:4
Burley on, 1:773
Diodorus Cronus and, 3:87
Frege and, 9:556
Geulincx on, 4:79
Łukasiewicz on, 5:605–607
many-valued logic and, 5:688–689
in medieval logic, 5:424–425
Russell (Bertrand) and, 9:557
Ryle on, 2:78
in Stoicism, 1:4, 5:405
Tarski on, 9:367
type theory and, 9:555
propositional modal
semantics of, 6:293–294
syntax of, 6:292
of propositions, 5:494–496
provability, 4:127–128, 5:486, **8:97–99**
and psychology, 1:677, 7:279–280
quantificational, type theory and, 9:555
quantum. *See* Quantum logic
Ramsey and, 5:467–468
Ramus on, 8:236–237
reduction of arithmetic to, 1:146, 6:674
Régis and, 8:300
regulative principle in, 6:577
Rehmke and, 8:303
of relations, Peirce and, 7:166
of relatives, 2:81
relevant, 5:488

rhetorical tradition in, 5:437–438
Robinson and, 5:481
Rüdiger on, 8:527
Russell on, 2:76–77, 5:466–467, 8:541, 8:546–551
Ryle on, 2:77, 8:580–581
in Sanlun Buddhism, 2:161–162
Schiller (Ferdinand) on, 8:625
Schuppe on, 8:663
as scientific research method, 2:40
second-order, 5:556, **8:707–708,** 9:368–369
semantic understanding and, 8:807
Seneca on, 8:812
and separability *vs.* inseparability in conditionals, 1:627–628
of significance tests, 9:213
since Gödel, **5:474–484**
Skolem and, 5:471–472
as specialized thinking, 1:661
statement forms and, 5:234
Stebbing and, 9:236–237
in Stoicism, 4:300, 9:255
strength of, truthlikeness and, 9:547
in style, 1:331
subject and predicate in, 9:287–288
and subject-accident distinction, 2:73
of syllogisms, 5:496–503
dilemmas in, 5:503
distribution of terms in, 5:498–499
Euler's diagrams and, 5:499–500
figures and moods and, 5:496–497
hypothetical and disjunctive syllogisms and, 5:502–503
and polysyllogisms, enthymemes, and induction, 5:500–501
and reduction, 5:497–498
skeptical criticisms of, 5:501–502
symbolic. *See* Symbolic logic
synsemantic terms and, 1:690
tense, 8:13
termist, 5:430–432
of terms, 5:493–494
tertium non datut dictum and, 3:5
Thomasius on, 9:441
topic-neutrality of, 8:708
traditional, **5:493–506**
transcendental. *See also* Kant, Immanuel
vs. Chinese Buddhism, 2:166
Husserl on, 2:81–82, 4:524–525
Kant on, 2:79
Turing and, 5:476–478
Twardowski and, 9:554
Vailati and, 9:631
Varona and, 9:648
Vasubandhu on, 9:651
Venn and, 5:451–452, 9:657–658
Whately on, 9:742–743
Whitehead and, 5:466–467, 9:753
William of Champeaux and, 9:767
William of Sherwood and, 9:786
Wittgenstein on, 2:82, 9:800
Wolff on, 9:827
Wundt and, 9:849
Xunzi on, 2:216
Zabarella and, 9:866–867
Logic (Arnauld), Wolff on, 9:827
"Logic" (De Morgan), 5:448
Logic (Dewey), 7:746
Logic (Hegel), 3:57
Engels and, 3:59–60
on natural science, 3:58
Logic (Johnson), 3:1, 5:458
Logic (Mill, John Stuart), 4:37, 7:546–547
"Logic and Conversation" (Grice), 2:525
Logic and Knowledge (Russell), 2:544, 2:544–545
"Logic and Metaphysics in Some Earlier Works of Aristotle" (Owen), 7:65
Logic and the Basis of Ethics (Prior), 8:13
"Logic as the Science of Knowledge" (Bosanquet), 1:662
"Logic at the Crossroads" *(Logik aud dem Scheidewege, Die)* (Palgyi), 7:75
Logic diagram(s), 5:547, **5:560–564**
Logic for Use (Schiller, Ferdinand), on truth, 8:625
Logic machines, 5:562, **5:565–567**
Logic Machines and Diagrams (Gardner), 5:562, 5:566
Logic Made Easy (Kett), 5:440
Logic of Hegel (Marx), 3:68
Logic of Modern Physics (Bridgman), 7:30
Logic of Perfection, The (Hartshorne), 9:752
Logic of Scientific Discovery (Popper), 1:486, 8:670
Logic of Sense (Deleuze), 2:694, 9:492
Logic of the Morphology of Knowledge (Bosanquet), 1:661–662
"Logic without Ontology" (Nagel), 6:473
Logica (Abelard), 5:424–425
Logica contracta (Clauberg), 2:286
Logica formale e dedotta dalla considerazione dei modelli meccanici (Formal logic deduced by the consideration of mechanical models) (Pastore), 7:135
Logica Fundamentis Suis a Quibus Hactenus Collapsa Fuerat Restituta (Geulincx), 4:76, 5:440, 8:772
Logica Hamburgensis (Jung), 5:440
Logica Ingredientibus (Abelard), 1:3, 3:54
Logica Magma (Paul of Venice), 7:147
Logica mexicana (Mexican Logic) (Rubio), 5:204
Logica moderna, William of Sherwood in, 9:786
Logica modernorum, development of, 5:429–432
Logica Nostrorum Petitioni Sociorum (Abelard), 1:3
Logica nova, 5:422, 5:429–430
Logica Parya (Paul of Venice), 7:147
Logica vetus, 5:421–422
Logica vetus et nova (Clauberg), 2:286
Lógica viva (Vital Logic) (Vaz Ferreira), 5:208
Logicae Artis Compendium (Sanderson), 5:440
Logicae Libri Quinque (Crakanthorp), 5:439
Logical adequacy, in Strawson, 7:57
Logical analysis, 8:237, 8:641
Logical atomism
logical pluralism in, 6:184
on purpose of philosophy, 9:796–797
Russell and, 3:315–316, 8:543–545
Ryle and, 8:581
Wittgenstein on, 3:317
See also Russell, Bertrand Arthur William; Wittgenstein, Ludwig Josef Johann
Logical behaviorism
and conceptual functionalism, 3:758
and mental states, 1:534
in philosophy of mind, 7:469
Ryle on, 7:469
Logical calculus
Johnson on, 5:458
Leibniz on, 5:441–442
"Logical Calculus, The" (Johnson), 5:458
Logical certainty, 5:97

Logical compulsion, Wittgenstein on, 9:813–814
Logical connections, materialism and, 6:17
Logical connectives
 characteristics of, 5:530–532
 Frege on, 3:726
 truth-functionality of, 5:109
Logical consequence, 2:434, 3:650
Logical constants, 5:234, 5:512
Logical construction, *vs.* fiction, Wisdom (John) on, 9:796–797
Logical constructionism, of Russell, 8:541–543
"Logical Constructions" (Wisdom), 9:797
Logical contingency, *vs.* dubitability, 3:103
Logical Demonstrativa (Saccheri), 5:440
Logical determinism, 3:5–7
Logical device, of Jevons, 5:451
Logical empiricism, 3:219, 5:82
 Carnap and, 2:35
 deductive-nomological model in, 8:694
 Einstein and, 3:180
 naturalism in science and, 6:501–503
 and scientific revolution, 8:694–695
 Sellars (Wilfrid) and, 8:733
 See also Logical positivism
Logical equivalences, involving quantifiers, 3:654
Logical expressions, as syncategorematic terms, 2:73
Logical fallacies, Black on, 1:606
Logical fatalism
 future-truth argument for, 3:694
 vs. theological fatalism, 3:692
Logical fiction, definition of, 5:547
Logical form, **5:506–510**
 definition of, 5:547
 depiction of, 9:804
 grammar and, 5:508
 and mismatches between sentential and propositional structure, 5:508
 in picture theory, 9:804
Logical Form of Action Sentences, The (Davidson), 8:808
Logical formalization, Montague (Richard) and, 6:329
Logical formulas, Peirce on, 5:454
Logical Foundations of Probability (Carnap), 2:436, 2:439
Logical grammar
 and belief attribution, 1:537
 and "to be" as name, 1:527–531
 and "to be" as verb, 1:527–531
Logical implication, definition of, 5:547
Logical impossibility, of God's existence, 7:18
Logical Investigation on Expression and Meaning (Husserl), and Shpet, 9:19
Logical Investigations (Chrysippus), 9:254
Logical Investigations (Derrida), 9:491
Logical Investigations (Husserl), 7:269–270
Logical knowledge, **5:511–514**
Logical laws, Ziehen (Theodor) on, 9:884
Logical monism, of Parmenides, 6:184
Logical necessity
 of God's existence, 7:18
 vs. indubitability, 3:103
 ontological argument and, 7:18
Logical notions
 Carroll and, 5:452
 Frege and, 5:464
 Jevons and, 5:450
 Peirce and, 5:453–454
 Post and, 5:467
Logical operators
 Boole on, 5:450
 metatheorems and, 3:653
 in non-classical logic, 5:485
"Logical Paradox, A" (Carroll), 5:452
Logical paradoxes, **5:514–524**
 Banach-Tarski and, 8:837
 Bernardete's, 4:666
 Borel-Kolmogorov and, 9:226
 chord, 9:227
 of confirmation, 9:288
 counting beyond the finite and, 5:514–516
 Hausdorff and, 8:837
 Mr. Russell's barber and, 5:516–517
 nonconglomerability, 9:226
 Principia Mathematica and, 5:518–521
 Russell's, 4:663, 8:834
 semantic paradoxes and, 5:517–522
 Skolem and, 8:840
 Thompson's lamp, 4:666
 of Zeno, on motion, 4:654–655
 Zermelo-Fraenkel set theory and, 5:520–521
Logical pluralism, 6:184
Logical positivism, **5:524–530**, 7:273
 agnosticism in, 1:94
 in analytical philosophy, 1:149–150
 and causality, 2:104
 coherence truth theory and, 2:308–310
 on conceptual intuitions, 4:732
 emergence of, 1:149
 empiricism of, 3:219–220
 epistemic materialism and, 6:12
 and epistemology, 3:316–317
 Hempel and, 4:308
 and innate ideas, 4:693
 meaning in, 1:149
 and mental states as behavior pattern, 1:534
 and metaphysics, 4:561, 6:170, 6:194, 6:202
 in modernism, 6:317
 necessary truth and, 2:474
 operationalism and, 7:31
 positivism and, 5:527–530
 and protocol sentences, 1:484–486
 Quine and, 6:198
 recursive axiomatization and, 2:583
 Rougier and, 8:506
 Russell and, 1:149
 science and, 2:104, 9:668
 on semantics, 8:737
 skepticism in, 9:58
 Tractatus and, 9:808
 and traditional philosophy, 5:525–527
 on underdetermination, 9:577
 verifiability principle and, 9:659
 verificationism in, 8:689
 Yin Haiguang and, 2:181
Logical possibility
 definition of, 5:547
 Duns Scotus on, 3:146
Logical pragmatism, 9:630
Logical probability, confirmation theory and, 2:435
"Logical" proof of determinism, 3:540
Logical reasons, science of, 5:116
Logical relations, in noninferential justification, 2:276
Logical rules, *vs.* empirical laws, 7:280–281
Logical scheme, as formulation of relationships, 9:748
Logical Structure of the World, The (Carnap), 1:149, 6:496
Logical symbols
 in first-order languages, 3:641
 of propositional logic, 3:642
Logical Syntax of Language, The (Carnap), 2:671–672, 4:706, 5:529
Logical system, completeness of, definition of, 5:537

Logical terms, **5:530–533**
glossary of, **5:533–560**
Logical truth
vs. necessity, 5:39
Quine on, 8:216
Logical types, Russell on, 2:76–77
Logical words, 8:19–21
Logically equivalent pairs, 3:653
Logicism, 8:274–275
definition of, 5:547
in mathematical foundations, 6:21
reducibility in, 6:172
Logico modernorum, 5:422
Logico-informational requirement, and performance characteristic, 3:662
Logik (Lotze), 5:580
Logik (Pfänder), 7:270
Logik (Sigwart), 9:29
Logik als Aufgabe, Die (Logic as a task) (Driesch), 3:110–111
Logik aud dem Scheidewege, Die ("Logic at the Crossroads") (Palgyi), 7:75
Logik der reinen Erkenntnis, Die (Cohen), 2:303, 6:543
"Logik, Grammatik, Metaphysik" (Scholz), 8:645
Logique (Roure), 2:285–286
Logique du sens (Deleuze), 9:274
Logique, ou l'art de penser (The Port-Royal Logic) (Arnauld and Nicole), 2:55, 4:790, 5:439–440
Logische Aufbau der Welt, Der (The logical construction of the world) (Carnap), 2:40
Logische Syntax der Sprache (Logical Syntax of Language) (Carnap), 2:42, 9:354
Logische Untersuchungen (Husserl), 4:705, 7:280, 8:115–116, 8:802
Logischen Grundlagen der exakten Wissenschaften, Die (The logical foundations of the exact sciences) (Natorp), 6:490, 6:543
Logistic (formal) system, definition of, 5:548
Logistic method, definition of, 5:548
Logistik als Versuch einer neuen Begründung der Mathematik, Die (Ionescu), 4:743
Logo astratto, Gentile on, 4:52–53
Logology (Collier), 2:324
Logos, **5:567–570,** 7:304, 7:308
in apologism, 1:227–228
Aristotle on, 5:568–569
in Christianity, 2:247, 5:569–570
of God, 4:810
in Hellenistic philosophy, 5:569
Heraclitus on, 4:316–317
Justin on, 1:228
in Kabbalah, 5:4
in Neoplatonism, 5:569–570
patristic philosophy on, 7:141, 7:142
Philo on, 4:810
Plato on, 3:285, 5:568
Pre-Socratics on, 5:567–568
in Stoicism, 6:506
Theophilus of Antioch on, 7:142
Loisy, Alfred, **5:570–571**
Lokācārya Pillai, 4:630
Lokalisation morphogenetischer Vorgänge (The localization of morphogenetic processes) (Driesch), 3:110
Lokayata school, 5:120
Lollards, social egalitarianism and, 3:329
Lombard, Lawrence Brian, on event theory, 3:466–467
Lombard, Peter. *See* Peter Lombard
L'Ombre de la Damoiselle de Gournay (The Shadow of Mademoiselle de Gournay) (Gournay), 4:167
Lombroso, Cesare, positivism of, 7:714
London, Fritz, 7:146
Long, A. A., on Parmenides of Elea, 7:126
Long-arm inputs and outputs, 3:760
Longfellow, Samuel, 6:572
Longino, Helen, 8:679
on contextual and constitutive values, 3:591
critical contextual empiricism of, 9:84
as feminist empiricist, 3:595
formulation of descriptive categories, 3:592–593
on models representing complex human potentialities, 3:576
on objectivity as property of communities, 3:577
on science, 1:158
Longinus (Pseudo), **5:571–572**
literary criticism of, 1:189–190
on sublime, 4:166
Longinus, Cassius, 5:571–572, 9:293
Long-term potentiation (LTP), 6:568
Looking idioms, 1:230
Loop quantum gravity, 9:269–270
Lopatin, Lev Mikhailovich, **5:572–573**
Lord of the Light (Or Adonai), The (Crescas), 2:592
L'Ordine nuovo (Gramsci), 4:169
Lorentz transformations, 3:179, 7:476
Lorenzen, Paul, in proof theory, 8:55
L'Organem (Canaye), 5:438–439
L'Organisateur (journal), 8:590
Lortz, Joseph, 5:617
Loschmidt, J., on physics of gases, 7:537
Losev, Aleksei Fëdorovich, 4:768, **5:573–576**
Losskii, Nikolai Onufrievich, 5:43, **5:576–578,** 9:529
Frank and, 3:716
Kozlov and, 5:146
Solov'ëv and, 9:126
Lost Island *reductio,* 4:33–34
Lotman, Iurii Mikhailovich, **5:578–580**
Lotus Sutra, 1:723
Lotze, Hermann. *See* Lotze, Rudolf Hermann
Lotze, Rudolf Hermann, **5:580–583**
on acute-angle hypothesis, 4:59
on panpsychism, 7:83
Paulsen and, 7:149
on Pennsylvania, 7:84
on personalism, 7:234
in psychology, 8:139
Santayana on, 8:597
on soul, 3:116–120
Stumpf and, 9:280
Louis VII (king of France), 4:843
Louis XIV (king of France)
Arnauld and, 1:288
Desgabets and, 2:757
Enlightenment and, 3:245
and Jansenism, 4:790
La Bruyère and, 5:167
Leibniz and, 5:251
Louis XVI (king of France), 7:73–74
Louis of Bavaria (Holy Roman Emperor), 9:770–771
Louis Philippe (king of France), 5:320
Louvain, University of, Mercier at, 6:143
Love, **5:583–591**
altruism and, 1:136
Aristotle on, 3:142
atheism and, 1:373–374
Augustine on, 1:395–397
being and, 5:702
Bernard of Clairvaux on, 1:592
Christian, 5:585–587
Dostoevsky on, 3:99–100
Hutcheson on, 1:136
in classical mythology, 5:583–584
in classical philosophy, 5:584–585
consent and, 5:670
definition of, 5:43
Edwards (Jonathan) on, 3:168
Empedocles on, 6:8. *See also* Aphrodite (love)
as essence of perfection, 7:195
Fénelon and, 3:603

Love, *continued*
of friendship, Duns Scotus on, 3:143
al-Ghazālī (Aḥmad) on, 1:117
as God, Bergson on, 1:570
of God
Astell on, 1:355–356
by humans, 4:828
as supreme goal, 4:823
Tauler on, 9:372
in human nature, 4:483–484
of humans, by God, 4:828
La Rochefoucauld on, 5:201
lack of, atheism and, 1:373–374
Levinas on, 4:831
Luther on, 5:617
Malebranche on, 5:670
as manifestation of divine reality, 9:512
McTaggart on, 6:77
in middle ages, 5:586–587
in modern period, 5:588–589
in Mohism, 2:151, 6:417
morality and, 1:46, 3:719, 5:670–671
in Mozi's social philosophy, 2:235
Niebuhr on, 6:606
Norris on, 6:655
Nussbaum on, 6:680
in philosophy of sex, 7:521
Plato on, 1:188, 3:142, 7:521, 7:589, 9:702
Plotinus on, 1:46
Proust on, 8:96–7
psychological view of, 5:590–591
in religion, 1:373–374
in Renaissance Neoplatonism, 5:587–588
Rosenzweig on, 8:498
Schopenhauer on, 8:653
self, 1:781, 5:670–671, 8:132
in *Symposium,* 1:42
20th-century views on, 5:590–591
Thomasius on, 9:441
Tolstoy on, 9:512
Trubetskoi on, 9:533
trust in, 1:68
Unanumo on, 9:568
of wishing one well, Duns Scotus on, 3:143
Love, Alan, on genetics, 7:346
Love, On (Ficino), 7:614
Love mysticism, 8:401
Love-hate relations
Brentano on, 1:690
as mental phenomena, 1:689
Love-idea-monads, connecting, 3:669
Lovejoy, Arthur Oncken, **5:591–594**
on dualism, 2:597–598
on James's pragmatism, 4:781
on new realism, 6:588
on pragmatism, 7:742
on principle of plenitude, 3:473
Lovelace, Ada, on Turing test, 5:634
Löwenheim, Leopold, logic of, 5:471
Löwenheim's theorem. *See* Skolem–Löwenheim theorem
Lowenstein, George, 9:39
Löwenthal, Elsa Einstein, 3:178
Löwenthal, Leo, Adorno and, 1:26
Löwith, Karl, 7:391
Nietzsche and, 6:607
on Vico, 9:670–671
Loyalty, **5:595–596**
in Confucianism, 2:231
engineering ethics and, 3:240
vs. fidelity, 5:596
Royce on, 8:521
to state, 9:208
Loyola, Ignatius, education and, 7:369
LTP (long-term potentiation), 6:568
Lu Chiu-Yüan. *See* Lu Xiangshan
Lu Hsiang-Shan. *See* Lu Xiangshan
Lu Jiuyuan. *See* Lu Xiangshan
Lu Xiangshan, **5:618**
on innate moral knowledge, 2:221–222
and neo-Confucianism, 2:157, 4:794
on ultimate reality, 2:220
Lubbock, John, on universal belief in God, 2:349
Lubieniecki, Stanislas, 9:100
Luca Mikrokozma (Njegoš), 7:267
Lucas, J. R., on machine intelligence, 5:634
Luce, R. Duncan, on decision theory, 2:656
Lucian of Antioch, Arius and, 1:283
Lucian of Samosata, **5:596–598**
Lucifer, Anselm on, 1:214
Lucinde (Schlegel), 5:588, 8:631
Luck
Card on, 2:31
intention and, 1:21
Luck egalitarianism, 3:335–336
Luckmann, Thomas, on self, 9:77
Lucretius, **5:598–602**
atomism of, Santayana on, 8:602
Epicureanism and, 3:399–400
Epicurus and, 3:265
on love, 5:585
on marriage, 5:601
materialism of, 6:8
on matter, 6:59
on mortality, 4:606
on origin of language, 8:759
on politics, 5:601
on sex, 5:601
on *simulacra,* 4:593
on space, 9:147
Lucy's child, identification of, 5:108
Ludlow, Peter
on propositional attitudes, 8:78
on token-reflexive theory, 9:476
Ludwig, Karl, 7:149
Ludwig Feuerbach and the Outcome of Classical German Philosophy (Engels), 3:58–59
Lugone, Maria, 3:580
Luhmann, Niklas, 9:98
Lukács, Georg, 1:69, **5:602–605**
Adorno and, 1:27
on art in society, 1:69
and Bakhtin Circle, 1:469
dialectical materialism of, 1:59
Dilthey and, 3:84
on existentialism, 3:509
on historical materialism, 5:738
on history, 7:391
on ideology, 4:574
Marxism and, 2:598, 5:735–736
Łukzasiewicz, Jan, **5:605–609**
on ancient logic, 5:607–608
on Aristotle, 5:691–692
and computing machines, 5:566
on continuum-valued logic, as paraconsistent, 5:489
on functorial calculus, 5:607
on instructions in proof, 3:646
Leśniewski and, 5:290
many-valued logic and, 5:485–486, 5:491, 5:688–689
on modal logic, 5:608
on polysyllogism, 5:500
on propositional logic, 5:605–607
on quantification in syllogism, 5:505
Scholz and, 8:645
Stoic logic and, 5:405
Tarski and, 2:547, 9:367
Twardowski and, 9:554
Lull, Ramón, **5:609–611**
Bruno on, 1:709
on logic and computing machines, 2:400
on logic and mathematics, 5:442
and reasoning, 5:565
Lumen, as radiant medium, 1:654
Luminous conditions, 5:88
Lunacharski, Anatoli Vasilyevich. *See* Lunacharskii, Anatolii Vasil'evich

Lunacharskii, Anatolii Vasil'evich, 5:280, **5:611–612**
Lunar Society of Birmingham, 3:247
Lund, Anne Sorensdatter, 5:61
Lunheng (Wang Chong), 9:723
Lunn, Arnold, on evil and existence of God, 1:363
Lunstedt, Vilhelm, in legal philosophy, 7:428
Lunyu (Collected Works) (Confucius), 2:442, 9:860
Luria, Isaac, 6:446–447
  doctrine of transmigration, 5:2
  Moses ben Jacob Cordovero and, 5:3
L'Usage des plaisirs (The Use of Pleasure) (Foucault), 3:701
Lushi Chunqiu, on Yang Zhu, 9:862
Luther, Martin, **5:612–618**
  Copernicism and, 2:536
  definition of faith, 3:530
  and divine command theories of ethics, 3:93
  on dogma, 3:97
  Erasmus and, 3:338–339, 9:50–51
  on faith, 3:530, 5:614–617
  on Franck's unorthodox thoughts, 3:713
  on God, characteristics of, 5:612–613
  Gogarten and, 4:144
  Kierkegaard and, 5:65
  medieval church and, 3:405
  Melanchthon and, 6:119
  metaphysics and, 4:144
  on philosophy, 5:613–617
  Pietism and, 7:575
  on power, 7:732
  on predestination, 3:10
  on reason, 5:613–617
  on redemption in Christianity, 2:249
  and Reformation, 8:295–298
  Stein and, 9:239
  20th-century views on, 5:617
  theological development, 5:612–613
Lutheranism, 8:296, 9:441
Lutterel, John, and Ockham, 9:770
Luxemburg, Rosa, 9:91
  Kautsky and, 5:47
  Lukács and, 5:603
Luynes, Louis Charles d'Albert, duke of, 2:753
Lycan, W. G., 3:760
Lyceum, 1:258, 1:263, 4:301
Lyco, Diogenes Laertius on, 3:88
Lyell, Charles
  Darwin and, 2:628–629, 2:640, 3:487
  on evolutionary theory, 2:635–638
  physicotheology and, 7:560–561
  positivism of, 7:713
  Wallace (Alfred Russel) and, 9:720–721
Lying, **5:618–619**
  Augustine on, 1:47
  definition of, 5:618–619
  See also Falsehood
Lyons, David
  on principle monism, 3:441
  on utilitarianism, 7:459
Lyons, Harold, 6:91
Lyotard, Jean François, **5:619–621**
  on aesthetics, 1:72
  on difference, 9:277
  and film theory, 7:382
  and postmodernism, 6:318, 9:59, 9:277
  poststructuralism of, 9:274
  on sublime, 9:294
Lysis (Plato)
  Colotes of Lampsacus on, 3:263
  friendship and love in, 7:587
Lysistrata (Aristophanes), 7:152

M

Ma Yufu, 2:182
Mably, Gabriel de, Lotman and, 5:579
MacArthur, Robert, 9:788
Macaulay, Catherine, 9:839
Macaulay, Charles P. R., logic machines of, 5:565
Macaulay, Vincent A., 4:672
Macbeth (Shakespeare), 5:351
MacCrimmon, Kenneth R., 2:660
MacDowell, John, on projectivism, 8:51
Macfarlane, Alexander, logical chart method of, 5:561
Mach, Ernst, **5:623–626**
  antimetaphysical attitude of, 3:689
  Carnap and, 5:524
  on causality, 7:715
  classical mechanics and, 2:280
  on cosmological theorizing, 2:562
  critique of metaphysics and, 5:526
  Duhem and, 3:126
  Ehrenfels and, 3:176
  Einstein and, 3:179
  empiricism of, 8:657–658
  empiriocriticism and, 3:64, 7:715
  on energy, 3:233
  exclusion from science, 2:103–104
  on history of science, 3:227
  on inertial system, 9:148
  influence of, 5:624
  Lichtenberg and, 5:339
  logical positivism and, 3:316, 5:524, 6:194
  Marxism and, 5:280
  mass defined by, 6:4
  Mauthner and, 8:801
  on mechanics of space, 9:156
  on metaphysics, 5:526
  in neo-Kantianism, 6:541
  Pearson and, 7:160
  on phenomenology, 7:279, 7:282
  Planck and, 7:577
  positivistic attempts of, 5:160
  in psychology, 1:252
  Schlick and, 8:638
  Schrödinger and, 8:657–658
  on scientific statements, 8:826–827
  on self-knowledge, 8:709
  on sensations, 8:823, 8:826–827
  and skepticism, 9:58
  on space, mechanics of, 9:156
  on space-time, 9:466
  on thermodynamic laws, 7:537
  and thought experimentation, 9:452–455
  on unified science, 5:525, 5:528
Machiavel en médecine (La Mettrie), 5:178
Machiavelli, Niccolò, **5:626–631**
  deontological ethics and, 2:714
  in history of philosophy, 3:405
  on human nature, 3:170
  Ibn Khaldūn and, 4:549
  political philosophy of, 7:660–661
  as prophet of Italian unity, 3:554
  on sociology of knowledge, 9:101
  on state, 9:204
  on war and peace, 7:152
Machina, Mark, on decision theory, 2:660
Machine(s)
  as adjuncts to organisms, 1:784
  computing machines and, 2:402–408
  humans as, materialism and, 6:17
  logical, Jevons on, 5:450
  Turing and, 2:376, 5:632–633, 9:552
Machine intelligence, **5:631–636**
  Neumann (John von) on, 6:559–560
  Turing on, 5:633, 9:552
  See also Artificial intelligence

Machine model
in biology, 1:593
Bonnet on, 1:658
consciousness in, 1:649
as ethereal machine of subtle matter, 1:658
Mach's Principle, 3:179, 5:624
MacIntyre, Alasdair, **5:636–637**
on Aquinas, 9:447
on Aristotelian moral theory, 9:74
on cultural relativism, 3:444
on human telos, 9:74
on perfectionism, 4:152
on practice of virtue, 9:74
on Rawls's social contract theory, 9:82
Mackey, Louis, 5:68
Mackie, David, causality definition of, 2:103
Mackie, John Leslie, **5:637–639**
on atheism, 3:321–322
on causality, 2:99
and error theory of ethics, 3:346–347, 3:364, 7:4
on evil, 3:474
on evolutionary ethics, 3:480
on Locke, 3:628
on miracles, 6:274–275
on moral skepticism, 6:393–394
noncognitivism and, 6:633–634
on values, moral *vs.* personal, 3:443
on Wollaston, 9:834
MacKinnon, Catharine
Dworkin and, 3:157
on objectivity, 3:574
philosophy of sex and, 7:523
as radical feminist, 3:600
Mackintosh, James, Mill (James) and, 6:219
Mackintosh, R. H., and Christology, 2:247
Maclaurin, Colin
on force measurement, 3:228
Hume and, 7:560
Macroallocation, 6:96–97
Macrobius, 7:611
Macrocosm and microcosm, **5:639–643**
Bosanquet on, 1:663
Boscovich on, 1:666
Brahman and, 1:681
Coleridge's theory of imagination and, 2:318
in cosmology, 1:645
in Gnosticism, 4:101–102
Ibn al-ʿArabī on, 4:543
Ibn Zaddik on, 4:551
Ikhwān al-Ṣafāʾ on, 4:576
Israeli on, 4:765
in medieval Platonic thought, 7:611–612
Platonic Forms in, 7:608
Schopenhauer on, 8:651
Skovoroda on, 9:64
Steffen on, 9:238
Macroscopic and microscopic, in scientific theories, 1:643
Madame Bovary (Flaubert), 8:609
Mademoiselle de Maupin (Gautier), 1:56
Madhva, 4:135, 4:630
on Brahman as creative power, 1:683
on liberation, 5:330
on resemblance theory, 9:586
Mādhyamika Buddhism, **1:740–746,** 5:134–135
causality in, 1:741
in China, as Sanlun Buddhism, 2:161
contradiction in, 1:742–743
Dge-lugs and, 1:731–734
emptiness in, 1:731–732, 1:740–744
epistemology of, 1:732–733, 1:740–744, 1:757
knowledge in, 5:117
as mysticism, 1:742–744
Nāgārjuna and, 5:329, 6:470–471
as nihilism, 1:742
ontology in, 1:306, 1:731, 1:740–742
paradox in, 1:740–743
on possibility of knowledge, 5:117
property-bearer relation in, 1:740–742
as quietism, 1:743–744
skepticism in, 1:743
and Svātatrika-Prāsṅgika distinction, 1:744
syncretism in, 1:744–745
See also Buddhism
Madison, James, 2:701–702
Madness, at margins of community, 3:699
Magazin: Monatschrift für Litteratur (periodical), 9:241
Magentios, Leo, 1:788
Magentios, Sophonias, 1:788
Magi, in Zoroastrianism, 9:886
Magic
Bruno and, 1:708–712
Simon Magnus and, 9:33
Wang Chong and, 9:723
and world-reflection within memory, 1:712
in Zoroastrianism, 9:886
Magie der Seele, Die (Spranger), 9:199
Magna Moralia (attrib: Aristotle), on love of gods, 5:585
Magnetic field
Ampère's work on, 1:137–138
in unified field theory, 9:741
Magnetic lines of force, 3:551, 6:69
Magnetic resonance imaging (MRI), 6:564–565
Magnetic stimulation, transcranial, 6:571
Magnetism, animal, 5:642
Magnitude
Aristotle on, 2:490
Couturat on, 2:581
Euclid on, 2:492
as extensive continuum, 2:490
of infinity, Buridan on, 1:769
Stevin on, 2:493
Mahāvaipulya Buddhāvataṃsaka Sūtra, 1:736
Mahavira
on bondage and liberation, 5:327
Jainism and, 2:110–111
Mahayana Buddhism, 5:41
Chan (Zen) Buddhism and, 2:167–168
double truth and contextual meaning in, 2:209
enlightenment in, 2:219
Huayan Buddhism and, 2:164–166
influence of, 1:723
liberation in, 5:328
on life, meaning and value of, 5:359
literature of, 4:633
Nāgārjuna and, 6:469–470
and Pure Land Buddhism, 2:168–169
on reality, 2:221
Sanlun Buddhism and, 2:161–163
Tiantai Buddhism and, 2:163–164
wisdom in, 2:219
See also Buddhism
Mahayānaśraddhotpāda (Buddhist text), 1:737
Maher, M., 4:614
Maher, Patrick, 2:439–440
Maia Neto, José, 7:133
Maid of Orleans, The (Schiller, Friedrich), 8:627
Maignan, Emmanuel, in French clandestine literature, 2:264
Maillet, Benoît De, **5:644**

Maimon, Salomon, **5:644–647**
- critical idealism of, 8:661
- Deleuze and, 2:694–695
- Jewish Enlightenment and, 3:249
- partial skepticism of, 9:57

Maimonides, **5:647–655**
- Albo on, 1:103
- on analogy, 1:140
- Aquinas and, 9:425
- Aristotle and, 3:403
- Averroes and, 4:820
- on creation, 3:361
- Crescas on, 2:593, 4:822–823
- on evil, 3:23
- and Gersonides, 4:69
- on immortality, 4:618
- on Isaac Israeli, 4:764
- in Jewish Averroism, 4:809
- Maimon and, 5:644
- in medieval philosophy, 4:817–819, 6:100
- microcosm in, 5:641
- on prophets, 4:825
- on Saadya, 8:587
- on soul, 3:23
- Spinoza and, 4:825–826
- on world, 5:641

Main Currents in American Thought (Parrington), 5:322

Maine, Henry, on law, 7:425

Maine de Biran, **5:655–659**
- Ampère and, 1:138
- Bergson and, 1:563
- Cousin and, 2:579
- ideology doctrine and, 2:760
- Laberthonnière and, 5:164
- Lavelle and, 5:214
- Le Senne and, 5:289
- on will, 3:689

Mainländer, Philipp, on pessimism, 7:251

Maiolo, Lorenzo, 5:439

Maistre, Comte Joseph de, **5:659–660**
- Comte and, 2:412
- conservatism and, 2:465
- fideism of, 9:57
- French Revolution and, 9:520

Maitland, F. W., on sovereignty, 9:143

Major, John, **5:661**

Major premise, definition of, 5:548

Major term, definition of, 5:548

Majority, Mosca on, 6:407

Majority rule, 3:637

Make-believe, value of, 5:365–370
- *See also* Imagination

Makin, Bathsua, on women, 9:838

Malament, David, 2:524

Malamud, Margaret, 9:302

Malantschuk, Gregor, 5:67

Malay Archipelago, The (Wallace), 9:720

Malcolm, Norman, **5:661–663**
- on common sense, 2:359
- on dreams, 3:106–107
- on empiricism, 5:96
- ontological argument and, 3:321, 7:18
- in Wittgenstinian approach to religion, 7:478

Malcolm X, 5:73

Male bias, 3:574

Male chauvinism, Frye and, 3:756

Male dominance, Ferguson on, 3:606

Male gaze, 3:571

Male psychosocial development, cognitive styles arising from, 3:574

Malebranche, Nicolas, **5:663–673**
- André on, 5:663
- Arnauld and, 1:288–292, 5:665, 5:670
- Augustinianism of, 5:666
- on bodies, 5:667–668
- and Cartesianism, 2:54–56, 2:61, 5:663–668
- on Chinese philosophy, 5:665
- Collier and, 2:323
- Connell on, 5:666
- and crisis of skepticism, 9:53–54
- Descartes and, 1:291, 5:663–668
- Desgabets and, 2:757–758
- on divine illumination, 4:580
- dualism in, 5:667–668
- Elisabeth, princess of Bohemia, and, 3:187
- *Encyclopédie* and, 3:223
- epistemology of, 2:57–58, 3:293–294
- ethics in, 3:406
- evil in, 5:669–670
- Foucher and, 2:757, 5:663–664
- on freedom, 5:669–670
- on general will, 4:39
- on God, 4:790, 5:665–669, 6:258–259
- on grace, 5:664, 5:670
- on ideas, 3:703–704, 5:665–666
- influence of, 5:671–672
- on judgment, 3:293–294
- La Mettrie on, 5:178
- on language, philosophical, 9:338
- Lavelle and, 5:214
- Le Clerc and, 5:236
- Leibniz and, 5:252, 5:671
- Locke on, 6:656
- love in, 5:670
- on mind-body problem, 2:57–59, 2:757, 3:293, 5:667–668, 6:258–259
- morality of, 5:670–671
- on motion, 5:664
- Nicole and, 6:604
- Norris and, 6:655
- and occasionalism, 4:77–80, 5:665, 5:670
- on original sin, 5:671
- on perception, 3:293–294, 5:665–667
- on pleasure, 5:671
- Ploucquet and, 7:642
- Régis and, 5:665–666
- on salvation, 1:290–291
- on sensation, 3:703–704, 5:667–668
- on sense perception, 3:293–294, 5:667
- skepticism and, 9:53–54
- on soul, 3:703–704, 5:665–666
- Spinoza and, 5:666
- Suárez and, 5:666
- theodicy of, 5:669–670

Malines, Mercier at, 6:143

Malinowski, Bronislaw
- on atheism, 1:373
- functionalism and, 3:762
- on myths, 3:764

Mallet, David, Bolingbroke and, 2:684

Malpractice, in medico-legal jurisprudence, 6:95

Malraux, Georges-André, **5:673–675**

Malthus, Thomas Robert, 2:629, 3:487–488, **5:675–677**

Mal'tsev, Anatolii, on first-order logic, 5:480

Mamardashvili, Merab Konstantinovich, **5:677–680**

Mamiani, Terenzio, 3:607

Man. *See* Human beings

Man (Tagore), 9:363

"Man against Darkness" (Stace), 9:200

Man of Reason: "Male" and "Female" in Western Philosophy, The (Lloyd), 5:373

Man Starving Himself to Death, The (Hegesias), 2:619

Man without Qualities (Musil), 6:618

Manar, al- (The Lighthouse) (periodical), 3:249

Mandaeism, *vs.* Manichaeism, 5:684

Mandarin Chinese, mass/count nouns in, 6:660

Mandate of heaven, in Japanese philosophy, 4:792–793

Mandelbaum, Maurice
on art, 1:66
on societal facts, 9:95
Mandeville (Godwin), 4:136
Mandeville, Bernard, **5:680–682**
on altruism and self-interest, 3:171
on conscience, 3:408
deism and, 2:683
philosophy of sex and, 7:522
on vice, 5:220
Mandonnet, Pierre, 2:626
Manekin, Charles, 4:69
Manhood, concept of, 7:262–265
M'ani al-Nafs (Baḥya), 1:458
Mani and Manichaeism, 4:104, **5:682–685**
al-Balkhī and, 4:811–821
Andover and, 4:811–821
Augustine and, 3:472, 7:176
Bayle on, 3:469
creation in, 5:683
dualism of, 6:327
ethics of, 5:684
in Gnosticism, 4:98, 4:104, 5:684
God and, 4:110
Jesus in, 5:683–684
vs. Mandaeism, 5:684
Robinet and, 8:482
system of, 5:683–684
on universe, 9:380
Manifest functions, 3:763–764
"Manifesto for the Reappraisal of Sinology and Reconstruction of Chinese Culture" (Tang et al), 2:182
Manifesto of the Communist Party (Marx), 4:573
Manipulation, in modern societies, 3:723–724
Man-machine-beast-machine debate, Cyrano de Bergerac and, 2:618
Man-measure principle, 8:91–93
Mann, Thomas
Adorno and, 1:25
Schopenhauer and, 8:656
Manner, in conversational implicature, 2:526
Mannermaa, Tuomo, on Luther, 5:617
Mannheim, Karl, **5:685–687**
on cultural knowledge, 9:103
and historicism, 4:391
on ideology, 4:574
Lukács and, 5:604
on society as source of truth, 9:103
Mannour, Gerrit, and Brouwer, 1:701
Manovich, Lev, on film, 7:384
Man's Hope (Malraux), 5:673
Man's Lot (Kaufmann), 5:46
Man's Mortality (Overton), 9:70
Man's Place in the Universe (Wallace), 9:721
Mansel, Henry Longueville, **5:687–688**
on agnosticism, 1:92–93
on determinism, 3:15
on metaphysical God, 1:359–362
Mantra, in Indian meditation practices, 6:108
Manual (Epictetus), 3:261–262
Manual of Modern Scholastic Philosophy (Mercier), 2:344
Manual of Psychology (Stout), 9:259
Manuductio ad Stoicam Philosophiam (Lipsius), 5:364
Manuel d'économie politique (Pareto), 7:117
Manuscrito (periodical), 5:210
Many minds theory, 8:214
Many questions fallacy, definition of, 3:548, 5:543
Many worlds theory, 7:23, 8:213–214
afterlife and, 8:377
vs. many minds theory, 8:214
Many worlds/Many minds interpretation of quantum mechanics, **5:695–699**
vs. multiple universe theories, 1:221
naturalism and, 6:492
Many-and-one, Brahman and, 1:684
Many-one correspondence, definition of, 5:548
Many-valued logic, 5:485–486, **5:688–695**
applications of
philosophical, 5:691–692
technical, 5:693–694
definition of, 5:548, 5:690
development of, 5:482–483
Łukasiewicz on, 5:605–607
in 19th-c. mathematics, 5:462
other logics and, 5:691
Peirce on, 5:453
proof procedures in, 5:690–691
propositional, 3:642
semantics in, 5:689–690
sentences in, 5:688
vagueness and, 9:624
Mao Tse-Tung. *See* Mao Zedong
Mao Zedong
as communist leader, 2:363–364
in contemporary Chinese philosophy, 2:180–181
dialectical materialism and, 3:65–66
Map(s), robots and, 3:708
Mapping, of sets, 5:548
Marbe, Karl, and Koffka, 5:124
Marburg neo-Kantianism, 1:476, 1:480, 6:542–543
Bakhtin Circle and, 1:469
Banfi and, 1:476
Barth and, 1:480
See also Neo-Kantianism
Marcel, Gabriel, 3:504, **5:699–703**
Abbagnano on, 1:1
influences on, 3:504
on modern society, 3:506
on optimism/pessimism, 7:253
Scheler and, 8:616
Marche, François de la, 3:354
Marcion, 2:289, **5:703–704,** 9:33
Marcus, Ruth Barcan, **5:704–705,** 6:290
on logical terms, 5:531
on quantifiers, 5:492
Marcus Aurelius Antoninus, **5:705–707**
on death, 2:652
Epictetus and, 3:262
ethics of, 3:400
Lucian of Samosata on, 5:597
on natural law and cosmopolitanism, 2:567
pantheism in, 7:94
Stoicism of, 9:254
on wisdom, 9:794
Marcuse, Herbert, 4:573
Adorno and, 1:25
on art, 1:70
Dilthey and, 3:84
Hegelianism of, 4:287
on history, 7:391
on liberalism, 3:156
and Marxism, 5:739
philosophy of sex and, 7:523
on social change, 2:599
on technology, 7:544
Mare Clausum (Selden), 4:191
Mare Liberum (Grotius), 4:190
Maréchal, Joseph, **5:707–710,** 9:446
Margin of error principle, 5:111
Marginal Consciousness (Gurwitsch), 4:198, 7:301
Marginalization
multiple forms of, 3:585
victims of, perspectives of, 3:568
of women, 3:574
Margolin, Victor, on design, 7:550
Marheinecke, Reinhard, Kierkegaard and, 5:67
Maria, or the Wrongs of Woman (Wollstonecraft), 9:837
Maria Stuart (Schiller, Friedrich), 8:627
Mariage forcé, Le (Molière), 5:181–182
Mariana, Juan de, **5:710–711**
Marías, Julián, **5:711–712**
Mariátegui, Carlos, 5:209–211

Maric, Mileva, 3:178
Maritain, Jacques, **5:712–718**
- on being, 1:529–530
- knowledge theory of, 5:712–713
- metaphysics of, 5:713–714
- moral philosophy of, 5:714–715
- political philosophy of, 5:715–716
- Thomism and, 9:446

Marius the Epicurean (Pater), 7:136
Market(s)
- business ethics of, 1:778
- in Marxist socialism, 9:92

Market economy
- communism and, 2:362
- libertarianism and, 5:336

Markov algorithms, 2:504–505
Markov conditions, 2:108, 8:687
Marković, Svetozar, **5:718–720**
Marksizm i filosofiia iazyka (attrib: Voloshinov), 1:465, 1:469
Marmontel, Jean-François, 3:223–225
Marquand, Allan
- logical chart method of, 5:561
- on logical machines, 5:565

Marr, David, on vision, 1:329
Marr, Nikolai, on semantic paleontology, 1:469–470
Marriage
- Aquinas on, 9:435
- Epicurus on, 5:601
- Fuller on, 6:575
- history of, 9:739
- Lucretius on, 5:601
- in Manichaeism, 5:684
- and sex, 7:529
- as universal principle, Vico on, 9:674–675

Mars, orbit of, Kepler's efforts to determine, 5:51
Marsh, Adam
- Bacon (Roger) and, 1:452
- Thomas of York and, 9:443

Marshall, Alfred, Anderson (John) and, 1:199
Marsilius of Inghen, **5:720–721**
Marsilius of Padua, **5:721–725**
- Gewirth on, 4:81
- John of Jandun and, 4:838
- political philosophy of, 7:660
- on sovereignty, 1:542–543
- on supreme authority, 9:140

Marsilius of Padua and Medieval Political Philosophy (Gewirth), 4:81
Marston, Roger, **5:725–726**
- Augustinianism of, 1:402
- Greek philosophy and, 7:161

Martensen, Hans Lassen, 5:61, 5:67
Martí, José, 5:204–205, 5:211
Martianus Capella, in Neoplatonism, 6:555
Martin, Alain, on Empedocles, 3:211
Martin, C. B., on properties, 5:227
Martin, Donald, 8:844
Martin, Gottfried, in neo-Kantianism, 6:542
Martin, Michael
- on atheism, 3:321–322
- on perception, 7:193

Martin, Robert, on truth, 5:318
Martin of Dacia, modism and, 5:432
Martineau, James, **5:726–727**
- on cosmic brain argument, 1:369
- on God's existence, 2:348–349

Martinetti, Piero, **5:727–728**
Martin-Löf, Per, 4:739
Martinus, Raymundus, 7:133
Martius, Hedwig Conrad, 4:682
Marty, Anton, **5:728–729,** 8:803
Martyrdom
- in Judaism, 9:182
- Meslier on, 6:154
- responsibility and, 8:164
- suicide as, 9:317, 9:320

Marulić, Marko, **5:729–730**
Marvin, Walter T., and new realism, 6:585
Marx, Karl, **5:730–735**
- on alienation, 1:120–125, 5:604, 5:731
- Anderson (John) and, 1:199
- anthropology and, 7:316
- atheism of, 1:258
- Bakunin and, 1:471–473
- Bloch on, 1:616
- on capitalism, 3:68–69, 5:732–733
- Chinese critique of, 2:180–181
- on civil disobedience, 2:260
- on class, 7:390
- Cohen (Hermann) on, 2:304
- and communism, 2:365, 5:734
- Comte and, 2:413
- on conscience, 3:408
- and constructivism, 9:76
- and critical theory, 2:599
- Croce and, 2:603
- Darwinism and, 2:642
- on determinism, 3:37
- dialectic materialism and, 3:56–57, 3:67–69
- on economic bases of society, 2:364
- Engels and, 3:238
- Enlightenment and, 7:390
- on equality, 9:73
- ethics in, 3:415
- on exploitation, 5:733–734
- Ferguson and, 3:605
- on fetishism of commodity, 3:69
- Feuerbach and, 3:56, 3:67, 3:612, 4:573
- on Fourier, 3:707
- on freedom, 5:731
- Gentile on, 4:49
- on happiness as creative labor, 2:367
- Hegel and, 3:57, 3:67–69, 4:285, 5:731, 5:740, 7:390, 8:70
- historiographic influence of, 1:720
- on history, 3:415, 9:677
- on human nature, 3:67–69
- Ibn Khaldūn and, 4:549
- idealism of, 7:390
- on ideology, 4:573
- Jewish political rights and, 1:493
- Kautsky on, 5:47
- on labor, 3:68–69
- Lassalle and, 5:203
- Lavrov and, 5:218
- on laws of thought, 5:232–233
- Lenin and, 3:64, 5:279–280
- literary remains of, editing and publishing of, 5:47
- Lukács on, 5:603–604
- Lyotard and, 5:620
- Manheim and, 5:685
- Marković and, 5:719
- on Marxism, 5:735
- Nussbaum and, 6:680
- Pareto and, 7:118
- Pastore on, 7:136
- and philosophy of history, 7:390–391
- and philosophy of sex, 7:522–523
- Plekhanov on, 7:626
- political philosophy of, 7:669–670
- and poststructuralism, 9:274
- on progress, 3:62
- on property, 2:260, 8:73
- on reason, 3:68
- on religion, 3:745
- on revolution of proletariat, 3:62
- Ruge and, 3:609
- Saint-Simon and, 8:591
- on self-alienation, 1:123
- on social development, 3:57
- social epistemology and, 9:83
- on social relations, 3:68–69
- on sociology of knowledge, 9:101–102
- Sombart and, 9:127
- Sorel and, 9:132

Marx, Karl, ***continued***
on state suppression of conflict, 9:207
on Strauss, 9:263
utopianism of, 9:618
Veblen and, 9:655–656
Marxe, Roberto Burle, 3:257
Marxism, **5:735–742**
Adorno and, 1:27
and aesthetics, 1:59, 1:68–70, 5:603, 5:737
anarchism and, 1:178–180
Bloch on, 1:615–616
Bulgakov on, 1:759–760
in China, 2:180–181
class in, 7:427
communitarianism and, 9:75
consciousness in, 5:678–679
critical theory and, 2:598
definition of, 5:735–736
on democracy, 2:702
Dühring and, 3:131
Engels and, 3:58–60, 3:237–238
epistemology of, 5:736–737
on equality, 9:73
eschatology in, 3:347–348
ethics in, 5:737
and existentialism, 3:509
feminism and, 3:563–564
Feng and, 2:159
French, 5:679
Gramsci on, 4:169–170
Hägerström and, 4:205
Hegel and, 4:262–263, 5:736
idealist *vs.* materialist, 5:736–738
on ideology, 4:573–574
in Korea, 5:141
Labriola and, 5:165–166
Lakatos and, 5:171
Lavrov on, 5:219
law in, 7:427
Lenin and, 5:279–281
liberation theology and, 5:331–332
Losev and, 5:573–575
Lotman and, 5:579
Lukács and, 5:602–604
Lunacharskii and, 5:611–612
Lyotard and, 5:620
MacIntyre and, 5:636
Malraux and, 5:673
Mamardashvili on, 5:678–679
Mariátegui on, 5:209
Marx on, 5:735
materialism in, 3:58–60, 3:238, 5:732–734
economic, 7:627
historical, 1:615–616
vs. idealism, 5:736–738
Merleau-Ponty and, 6:149–150
Meslier and, 6:155
metaphysics of, 5:737
Miki and, 6:216
nature in, 3:57–58
Neurath and, 6:560–561
opposition to, 1:178–179
orthodox, 5:47, 5:736–737
overview of, 3:56
philosophy and, 4:169–170
political, 7:669–670
traditional, 5:735–736
Plekhanov and, 7:626
postmodernism and, 5:740
post–World War II, 5:739–740
principles of, 4:552
property in, 8:70
pseudoscience in, 3:238
on racism, 8:228
reflex theory of behavior and, 7:150
religion and, 5:737, 8:377–379
revisionism and, 1:616, 9:132
and Social Darwinism, 3:479
social forces and, 5:740
and socialism, 1:716–717, 9:90
Sombart on, 9:127
as Soviet religion, 1:560
Spinoza and, 9:195
split in, 5:738
structuralism and, 9:273
on technology, 7:544
Viconian revision of, 9:133
Volski and, 9:707
Western, 5:737–738
and women's oppression, 3:600
See also Historical materialism
Marxism: An Interpretation (MacIntyre), 5:636
Marxism-Leninism, 3:56
See also Historical materialism; Leninism; Marxism
Marxism-Leninism-Maoism, 2:180–181
Marxist societies, Diderot and, 3:77
Mary II (queen of England), Locke and, 5:375
Masao Abe, 5:359
Masaryk, Tomáš Garrigue, 5:166, **6:1–2**
Maschinentheorie des Lebens, Die (Schultz), 8:659
"Maschinentheorie des Lebens, Die" (The machine theory of life) (Driesch), 3:110
Masculine biases, traditional theories and, 3:573
Masculinism, of logic, 1:157
Masham, Damaris Cudworth, 5:254, 9:838
Masham, Sir Francis and Lady, 5:375
Masonic movement, Enlightenment and, 3:245
Mass, **6:2–5**
in black holes, 1:606–609
in Cartesian science, 2:55
in classical mechanics, 2:280
concepts of, 6:2–3, 6:81
definition of, 6:4
electromagnetic, 6:4–5
energy and, 6:4
gravitational, 6:4
inertial, 6:4
Mach on, 5:624
Ostwald on, 7:50
as quantity of matter, 6:3
in theory of relativity, 3:179–180, 3:237
in Wolff's ontology, 9:828
See also Matter
Mass media
Adorno on, 1:26
Carroll on, 7:383
vs. high art, 1:67
Mass nouns, *vs.* count nouns, **6:659–665**
Mass persuasion, techniques of, 5:158
Mass society, Emerson on, 3:196–197
Massaro, Toni, 9:5
Mass-energy relation, 3:233, 3:237
Masses (of people), Ortega y Gasset on, 7:47
Massignon, Louis, 9:303
Master argument, of Diodorus Cronus, 3:87, 3:692, 5:404
Master concept, in Hegel, 4:262–263, 4:271
Masterpiece, as having male gender, 3:572
Masturbation
analysis of, in philosophy of sex, 7:525
Rousseau on, 7:522
Material conditional, 4:309, 8:358
Material consequentia, definition of, 5:538
Material development, in history, Comte on, 2:410
Material elements, and sense, 5:118
Material entities, Kozlov on, 5:146
Material essence realism, 9:767
Material implication, 3:642, 5:545, 8:548–549
Material justice, 4:864–865
Material life, and consciousness, 3:575
Material logic, John of St. Thomas on, 4:845

Material objects
essence of, 7:286–287
McTaggart on, 6:78
Mill (John Stuart) on, 3:312
permanence of, 7:271–272
persistence of, 7:274–275
and perspective, 1:147
phenomenalism and, 7:271
as sense datum, 8:818–819
vagueness of, dualism and, 3:120–122
Material processes, causative continuity of, 6:133, 6:260
Material substance
Leibniz on, 5:256, 5:265–277
Platonism on, 5:232
Material supposition, 5:557, 9:776
Material thing(s)
definition of, 6:5
not represented by unextended ideas, 3:703
Material unification, of Russia, 5:75
Material world, 1:577
Aristotle on, 7:127
Berkeley on, 3:301–302
Descartes on, 2:746
Desgabets on, 2:759
Empedocles on, 7:127
in Indian philosophy, 7:95
Lavelle on, 5:215
Locke on, 3:301, 5:377–379, 5:395
Origen on, 7:39
patristic philosophy on, 7:141
Materialism, 5:116, 5:132, **6:5–19**
a posteriori knowledge in, 6:11
and abstraction, 6:5
Anderson (John) and, 1:198
animistic, 6:331–332
appeal of, 6:6
atheistic, 4:432
and awareness, 6:15
and behaviorism, 6:11–13
Berkeley and, 1:574
Bosanquet and, 1:663
Broad on, 6:15
Büchner and, 6:11
Buckle and, 9:516
in Buddhist ethics, 2:199
Cabanis and, 2:1
Carlyle on, 2:34
Cavendish on, 2:117–118
and chemistry, 6:11
Chernyshevskii and, 2:146
in classical period, 6:7–8
Cleanthes and, 2:288
on cognition, 9:710–711
communism and, 2:365
Condillac on, 2:421
contemporary, 6:13–14
in controversies over time, 9:498
cosmic brain argument and, 1:369–371
Cousin on, 2:579
criticism of, 4:558
and cybernetics, 6:11–12
Cyrano de Bergerac and, 2:618
Daoism and, 2:237
David of Dinant and, 2:644–645
and death, 6:14
Democritus and, 6:7
Descartes and, 2:365, 6:9
and determinism, 6:6
dialectical. *See* Dialectical materialism
Diderot on, 3:72–74
and divine, 6:14–15
and dualism, 6:9, 8:6–7
economic, 7:627
in 18th c., 6:9–11
electronic, 6:6
eliminative. *See* Eliminative materialism
emergent, 6:261
emotion in, 6:12, 6:15–16
Empedocles and, 6:7–8
Encyclopédie on, 3:224
Engels and, 3:58–60, 3:238
Epicurus and, 3:265–266, 6:8
epistemic, 6:12
and evolution, 6:11
existentialists on, 3:503
and feminism, 3:601, 3:606
first principles of, 6:203
Fiske and, 3:668
Foucault and, 3:699
Fouillee and, 3:705
in French clandestine writings, 2:267
Gassendi and, 4:29–30, 6:8–9
Gehlen and, 4:35
and gender essentialism, 3:587
Glanvill on, 4:97
Gödel on, 4:117
Green on, 4:179–180
Haeckel on, 4:202
Hägerström and, 4:205–206
historical. *See* Historical materialism
history of, 5:186, 6:7–8, 6:540, 7:148, 9:625–626
Hobbes and, 2:365, 6:9, 8:825
Holbach and, 4:432
idealism and, 3:611, 4:552
Bosanquet and, 1:663
and Marxism, 5:736–738
immortality and, 8:7
Indian
perception in, 6:254
soul in, 6:254
intuitive resistance to, 8:195
Kripke on, 7:409
La Mettrie and, 5:178–181
Lange on, 5:186–187, 6:540
Lavrov on, 5:218
Lenin on, 3:64–65, 5:280
Lichtenberg on, 5:341
Lucretius on, 6:8
Marković and, 5:719
Martineau and, 1:369
Marxism and, 3:56–57, 4:552, 5:731–733, 5:736–738
mechanical. *See* Mechanical materialism
medical, 6:6, 6:10
Meslier and, 6:154
metaphysics of, 6:204
mind-body problem in, 7:468–469
Moleschott in, 6:320–321
Nagel (Ernest) on, 6:473
Naigeon and, 6:476
naturalism and, 6:473, 6:492–493
nature of, 6:6
neo-Confucianism and, 2:158
new, 3:56
in 19th c., 6:11
nonreductive, 6:17–18, 6:643
functionalism in, 6:645–646
Kim on, 6:648
mental states in, 6:646–647
objections to, 6:14–17
objects in, 3:120–122
Paulsen on, 7:148
physicalism and, 6:643, 7:553
Priestley and, 8:6–7
propositional attitudes and, 8:83–85
qualia and, 8:191–195
reductive, in theology, 1:370
Rensi on, 8:433
resistance to, 8:195
Santayana on, 8:599
in 17th century, 1:576–577
Smart on, 9:65
on sociology of knowledge, 9:101–102
Strauss on, 9:263
on teleology, 2:641
and vagueness of material objects, 3:120–122
Vaihinger and, 9:625–626
vitalism and, 9:695
Voltaire and, 9:710–711

Materialism, ***continued***
Wolff on, 4:553
world-as-container view in, 1:577
and Yogācāra Buddhism, 1:748
Materialism and Empirio-Criticism (Lenin), 3:64–65, 5:280
"Materialism and Revolution" (Michelson), 8:607
Matérialisme, vitalisme, rationalisme (Cournot), 2:577
Materialismo storico ed economia marxista (Croce), 2:600
Materialist Conception of History, The (Plekhanov), 7:627
Materialist school (Lokayata), 5:117
Materialist Theory of the Mind, A (Armstrong), 1:286–287, 4:721
Materialist-feminist multisystems theory, of oppression, 3:606
Materiality, ideality and, intertwining of, 6:150
Material-object language, 7:274–276, 7:296
Maternal Thinking: Toward a Politics of Peace (Ruddick), 3:579, 7:157
Mates, Benson, 7:725, 9:346, 9:350
Mathematical Analysis of Logic, The (Boole), 5:440, 5:460
Mathematical definitions, 3:652
Mathematical Foundations of Quantum Mechanics (Neumann), 8:210
"Mathematical Games" (Gardner), 5:566
Mathematical hypotheses, in science, 1:582
Mathematical knowledge. *See* Knowledge, mathematical
Mathematical logic. *See* Logic, mathematical
Mathematical model(s)
and black holes, 1:607–608
in cosmology, 2:559
interpretations of, 6:297
of knowledge, Plato on, 3:396
and maxent in probability distribution, 4:673
Mathematical Models (Cundy and Rollett), 5:566
Mathematical objects
in cognition, 6:674
Hellman on, 6:630
in nominalism, 6:626–628
Mathematical physics, and cosmology, 2:561
Mathematical principles, of Kant, 5:19
Mathematical Principles of Philosophy (Newton), 2:279
Mathematical structures
classes of, 3:651
nature and, 7:11
Mathematical theory
of evolution. *See* Population, genetics and
of irrationals, Theaetetus on, 4:172
Peano and, 5:465
semantic approach to, 9:334
Mathematical Theory of Relativity, The (Eddington), 3:164
Mathematical truth, as type of fact, 5:220
Mathematics
a priori construction of, 5:645
a priori necessity of, *vs.* experience of, 1:575
and actual infinity, 2:567
analogies in, on God, 6:596
analytic truths in, 1:244
Anderson (John) and, 1:199
application of, 1:199
applied, 5:15
argument in, 5:10–11
arithmetization of (arithmetization of analysis), definition of, 5:534–535
axioms of, 5:93
Bachelard and, 1:440
beauty in, 1:511–512
Berkeley on, 1:574–575, 1:582, 2:495, 3:217–218, 3:302
Black on, 1:605
Bohmian mechanic equations, 1:631–632
Bohr and, 1:637
Bolzano and, 1:646
Boscovich and, 1:665–666
branches of, Peirce on, 7:169
Brouwer and, 1:700–702
Bruno on, 1:709
calculus of probability and, 1:495
Campbell and, 2:18
Carroll (Lewis) and, 2:51–53
certitude in, 6:217
and chance, study of, 2:125–126
and chaos theory, 2:131–134
characterization of world, 1:577
in Chinese science, 2:218
Cohen (Morris) on, 2:306
coherence truth test in, 2:308–309
compactness theorem, 4:653
computability theory as, 2:372
computing machines and, 2:399, 2:404
Comte on, 2:411
Condorcet on, 2:431
connectionism and, 2:445
conservativeness of, 3:633
continuity and, 1:702
in cosmology, 2:560–567
Crusius and, 2:606
De Morgan and, 5:461
deductive reasoning in, 6:223
Democritus on, 5:301
Descartes and, 2:720–728, 2:735, 2:739, 3:292–293
diagonal argument in, 8:833
discreteness and, 1:702
of divisibility of line segments, 4:655
Dodgson and, 2:51–53
early computing and, 2:399
empiricism of, 6:677
epistemology of, Tarski and, 9:366
error theories about, 3:628
in European science, 2:218
Field on, 3:633
finitary, 4:118
formalist account of, 6:675–676
foundations of, **6:20–57**
and arithmetic and geometry, 2:510–511
Berkeley on, 2:495
Bolzano on, 1:646
Cantor-Dedekind theory and, 2:490
and Cauchy's foundation of calculus, 2:495
and chaos and probability theory, 2:133
choice in, 1:700–702
Chwistek's nominalist construction of, 2:255–256
combinatory logic and, 2:334–340
Frege on, 2:82, 3:729
Friedman and, 5:484
Fries on, 3:753
Galileo on, 4:10
and gambler's ruin, 9:217
and game theory, 1:778
and Gauge theory, 4:31–33
and generalized continuum hypothesis, 8:837
geometry and, 4:53
Gerbert of Aurillac on, 4:66
in Gödel, 4:119
Goethe on, 4:142
in Greek Academy, 4:172
Grosseteste on, 4:187
Hegel on, 4:271
Hellenistic, 4:302
Helmholtz and, 4:303
Hilbert and, 4:62, 5:469, 6:676

history of. *See* History, of mathematics
Hume on, 3:218
ideal, 5:544
impossibility proofs in, nature and, 1:541–542
impredicative methods in, necessity of, 8:456
incommensurability and, 7:35
indispensability of, 6:677–678
indivisibles in, 4:12
induction in, 4:125–126
infinitesimal methods in, 4:652–653
intuitionalist, 1:700–702
intuitionism and, 5:469, 6:676–677
Jeans on, 4:804
kalām argument on God's existence and, 2:554
Kant on, 3:307, 5:15, 5:19
Kolmogorov on, 2:126
Lakatos on, 5:171
Lambert (J. H.) on, 5:175
Laplace on, 5:197
Leibniz on, 5:251–252
Leonardo da Vinci on, 5:282
Leśniewski on, 5:290
Lichtenberg on, 5:339–340
linguistic foundations of, 8:640
in local motion, 4:187
as logic, 1:147, 1:659–660, 8:541, 8:546–548
logical truth test in, 2:308
Maimon on, 5:645
Maritain on, 5:713
Maupertuis on, 6:67
meaning in, 6:677
meaningfulness in, 5:469
in medieval philosophy, 6:105
vs. metamathematics, 1:702
vs. metaphysics, 6:202
Mill (John Stuart) on, 3:214, 3:219, 6:222–223
models in, Tarski on, 9:367–369
monotonicity in, 6:642
moral nature of, 1:714
of music, 8:185
natural phenomena and, 1:630
in naturalism, 6:494
Neumann (John von) on, 6:559
Newton and, 6:591
Nicholas of Cusa and, 6:596
19th-c. logic and, 5:459
nominalism and, 6:628–630
number in, **6:670–678**
ontological scope of, 2:41
Oresme on, 7:34–35
Ortega y Gasset on, 7:48
Pascal and, 7:129–131
Patrizi on, 7:144
Peano and, 7:158–159
Peirce on, 7:169
Petronievič and, 7:267
philosophy of, 1:701, 5:487
and analytic method, 1:646
consistency and set theory paradoxes in, 2:29
and intuitionalism, 1:700
in physics, 2:574
Plato/Platonism and, 1:250, 5:487, 6:673, 7:602–603, 7:614–615, 8:186, 9:590
Poincaré on, 7:652–653
presuppositions of, 6:171
of probability, 8:24–26
Protagoras and, 8:93
pure, 5:15, 5:467
in Pythagoreanism, 8:182–183, 8:186
as quantitative analytical method, 1:646
in quantum mechanics, 1:637–639
Ramsey and, 8:235
real, definition of, 5:554
religion and, 8:398–399
Robinson and, 5:482
Russell on, 3:316, 5:467, 8:541, 8:546–555
Sanches on, 8:595
Scholz on, 8:645
semantic models in, 4:740
and sensations, 5:19
set theory in, 2:82, 8:831–832
social, Condorcet on, 2:432
in subjective probability, 8:30
sublimity in, 1:54, 9:294
as superficial, 1:711
syntax in, 9:360
synthetic *a priori* truth in, 1:244
Tarski on, 9:366
timeless present in, 3:356
transfinite numbers in, 8:832
truth in, 4:130, 8:595
20th-century empiricists on, 3:219–220
type theoretic approach to, 2:82, 4:742
universal, Leibniz on, 5:535
well-ordering and, 8:832–833
Weyl on, 9:741
Whitehead on, 3:316, 9:747
Wolff and, 9:826–827
See also Metamathematics; *specific types*
"Mathematische Logik und die metaphysik, Die" (Scholz), 8:645
Mathematische Naturphilosophie, Die (Fries), 3:752
Mathematisch-mechanische Behandlung morphologischer Probleme der Biologie, Die (Mathematico-mechanical treatment of morphological problem of biology) (Driesch), 3:110
Mather, Cotton, **6:57–58**
Mathesis Universalis (Scholz), 8:645
Mathnawi-yi ma'nawi (Rumi), 9:307
Matijacevič Yuri, 2:386
Matilal, Bimal Krishna, 1:743
Matriarchy, in primitive society, 1:441
Matrices (mathematical), Tarski on, 9:367
Matrix (film), 7:385
Matrix mechanics, 4:298
Matter, **6:58–64**
Alexander on, 1:110
alternative conception of, 5:28
Ampère on, 1:138
Aquinas on, 6:189, 9:427, 9:436
Aristotle on, 1:385, 3:141
atomic theory and, 1:643
Bergson on, 1:566–567
Bernard of Tours on, 1:592
Bonaventure on, 1:653
Boscovich on, 1:665–666, 1:666
Campanella on, 2:15–16
in Cartesian science, 2:55
Chrysippus on, 2:252
Clarke on, 2:272
in Clarke-Leibniz correspondence, 2:269
in classical mechanics, 2:280
in classical physics, *vs.* energy, 6:62–63
Collier on, 2:323–234
colors as texture of, 2:332
dark, 8:31
David of Dinant on, 2:645
Descartes on, 1:386, 9:154
Desgabets on, 2:758
Diderot on, 3:73–75
Diogenes of Apollonia on, 3:89–90
Duns Scotus on, 3:141
ego's relation to, 4:745
electromagnetic theory of, 3:235–236, 6:69
in elementary particle theory, 4:298–299
Epicureans on, 6:59
eternity of, as atheistic argument, 1:360–361
form and, 1:385
Greek Academy on, 6:59
Greek philosophers on, 6:59
historical concepts of, 6:58

Matter, *continued*
Holbach on, 6:10
hylozoism and, 9:261
Ibn Gabirol on, 4:546, 4:815
in immaterialism, 4:554
in individuality, 6:189
inseparability from form, 1:662
Israeli on, 4:814
in Jainism, 1:381
in Kabbalism, 5:4
Leibniz on, 3:296
Lenin on, 3:64–65, 5:280
Lichtenberg on, 5:341
Marxism and, 1:615–616
in materialism, 6:5
Maupertuis on, 6:67
in medieval philosophy, 6:100
Mill (John Stuart) on, 6:226
Milton on, 6:249
mind and, Johnson (Samuel) on, 4:851
molecular composition of, 1:643
Moleschott on, 6:320
Naṣīr al-Dīn al-Ṭūsī on, 6:478
in Neoplatonism, 6:2–3
in Ockham's metaphysics, 9:779
Olivi on, 7:13
Ostwald on, 7:49
Paracelsus on, 7:104
Peirce on, 7:164
Plekhanov on, 7:626
Priestley on, 8:7
primary qualities and, 8:8–9
prime
in medieval philosophy, 6:101
in thought of God, 4:821
and problems of perception. *See* Illusion(s); Perception; Phenomenalism; Realism; Sensa
of proposition, definition of, 5:547
psychic properties of, 6:67
as reality, 3:610
Rehmke on, 8:303
reification of energy and, 3:233
Rohault on, 8:483
Santayana on, 8:602
secondary qualities of, 8:8–9
space-time curve near, 9:152
in Stoicism, 1:100
as system of interrelated events, 4:745
Telesio on, 9:390
Theodoric of Chartres on, 9:410
in theory of relativity, 3:179
Thomas of York on, 9:443
Voltaire on, 9:709–710
See also Atomism; Mass; Materialism
Matter and Memory (Bergson), 1:564–567, 9:489
Matter of Baby M, 6:95
Matter of Karen Quinlan, An Alleged Incompetent, 6:95
Matter-mind dualism, critical realism and, 2:595
Matthaüs, Anton, 1:135
Mattheson, Johann, on music, 1:305
Matthew (Biblical book), divine command theories of ethics and, 3:93
Matthew of Aquasparta, **6:64–65**
Augustinianism of, 1:402
epistemology of, 1:403
Greek philosophy and, 7:161
Matthias (Holy Roman emperor), Kepler and, 5:50
Matthiessen, F. O., on American liberalism, 5:321–322
Mauchly, John, 2:405
Maudsley, H., on unconscious, 9:571–572
Maupertuis, Pierre-Louis Moreau de, **6:66–67**
and Berlin circle, 5:124
Diderot and, 3:72
on force, 3:689
on optimism/pessimism, 7:249
on private language, 8:783
on signification, 8:783–784
Maurice, Frederick Denison
Lessing and, 5:296
on Mansel, 5:688
Maurice of Nassau, 2:721
Maurras, Charles, on nationalism, 6:484
Mauthner, Fritz
on language, 8:801–802
linguistic skepticism of, 9:58
on universal religious belief, 2:349
Mauvaise conscience, La (Jankélévitch), 4:787
Mavrodes, George, on just means, 4:872
Max Schelers Phänomenologie der Religion (Geyser), 4:83
Maxent, 4:672, 4:673
Maxent distributions, class of, 3:663
Maxim(s), 5:26, 5:36
of Kant, 3:618, 5:26, 5:36
Kitcher on, 5:76
of La Rochefoucauld, 4:168, 5:200–201
Maximal intrinsic fixed point, obtaining, 5:149
Maximal specificity, requirement of, 3:710
Maximal-change semantics, 3:710
Maximen und Reflexionen (Goethe), 3:195, 4:143
Maximes (La Rochefoucauld), 4:168, 5:200–201
Maximes des saints, Les (Fénelon), 3:603
Maximilian Joseph III (king of Bavaria), 2:723, 9:825
Maximos the Confessor, and John of Damascus, 4:837
Maximum entropy formalism, endorsed by Fisher, 3:663
Maximum Entropy in Action (Buck & Macaulay), 4:672
Maximum entropy method, 3:666
Maximum likelihood estimate. *See* MLE
Maxwell, Grover, 8:693
Maxwell, James Clerk, 1:643–644, 4:86, **6:68–70**
atomism and, 1:387
Boltzmann, and, 1:644–645
and classical mechanics, 2:280–282
on electromagnetism, 3:232–236, 3:551
on energy, 3:233
on equilibrium theory, 7:538
on Faraday, 3:551
on gases, 7:537
Lichtenberg and, 5:340
Pearson and, 7:159
physicotheology and, 7:562
on physics of gases, 7:537
unity and, 9:578
Maxwell, Nicholas, materialism of, 6:18
Maxwell-Boltzmann energy distribution, 4:677
Maxwell's demon, 6:70
Maxwell's equations, 7:476
Māyā (illusion), 3:471
doctrine of, pessimism in, 7:246
Indian pantheism and, 7:95
See also Indian philosophy
Mayan philosophy, 5:204
Mayer, Julius, 3:551
Mayer, Robert von, 3:230
Maynard, Patrick, 1:329
Mayo, Deborah G., 9:217
Mayr, Ernst, 3:488
Mayz Vallenilla, Ernesto, 5:211
Mazarin, Jules (Cardinal)
and Jansenism, 4:789
La Rochefoucauld and, 5:200
Mazzini, Giuseppe
on nationalism, 6:483–484
on state, 4:51
Mazzoni, Jacopo, Patrizi and, 7:144
Mbiti, John, on African philosophy, 1:83–84

McCall, Storrs
on future in theory of time, 9:478
Stoic logic and, 5:407
on time, 9:470–471, 9:478
McCann, Hugh
on intention, 1:20
on volition, 9:705
McCarthy, John
conception advanced by, 3:709
solution for the frame problem, 3:708
McCarthy, T., on logical terms, 5:532
McCarthyism, Einstein and, 3:179
McCawley, James, 8:807
McClennen, Edward, on decision theory, 2:655
McCloskey, H. J., 6:234
McCosh, James, **6:70–71**
McCulloch, Warren, on cognitive science, 2:298
McDougall, William, **6:71–73**
conative psychology of, 8:147–148
on instinct, 8:147
parapsychology and, 7:116
Stout and, 9:260
McDowell, John, **6:73–74**
Evans and, 3:459
on internalism, 4:714
as intuitionist, 4:735
on motivation in ethics, 4:715
on nonconceptual mental content, 2:480
on perception, 7:192
on space of reasons, 5:89
McGilvary, Evander Bradley, **6:75–77**
McGinn, Colin, on qualitative consciousness, 2:450
McIntyre, Ronald, on phenomenology, 7:299
McKenna, Erin, 3:568
McKeon, Richard, 2:623, 4:81
McKinsey, J. C. C.
on semantic account of theories, 9:334
Tarski and, 9:370
McLaughlin, Andrew, on Marxism, 5:741
McTaggart, John Ellis, **6:77–79,** 7:233
on absolute, 1:12–13
atheism of, 1:374
on being, 7:22
on contradiction, 4:269
Hegelianism of, 6:193
on immortality, 4:613
Iqbal and, 4:743
on metaphysics, 4:560
paradox of, 9:498
on pluralistic idealism, 4:559
terminology of, 9:497
on time, unreality of, 9:464
wisdom and, 9:794
Me, in introspection, 6:81
Mead, George Herbert, **6:79–82**
Aliotta and, 1:127
constructivism of, 9:77
Gehlen and, 4:35
and policy sciences, 8:675
Meaning, **6:82–86**
Abelard on, 1:5
abstraction and, 1:153, 1:586
in actions, truth and falsity of, 9:833
agent, 7:405
Alston on, 1:132
as ambiguous word, 3:744
of analytic judgments, 1:160
in animal communication, 1:204
Anselm on, 1:218–219
anthropology and, 7:318
anti-intentionalism and, 1:311–312
in art, 1:78, 9:835
articulated *vs.* hidden, 1:28
Augustine on, 8:759
Ayer on, 1:149
behavior of speaker and, 7:407
of being, 4:292
Benjamin on, 1:546
Berkeley on, 1:587–588
in Bible, 1:47
Black on, 1:605
of Brahman, 1:682
in Buddhist epistemology, 1:756
Bulgakov on, 1:760
Burge (T.) on, 5:190
Carnap on, 2:43, 5:529
Cassirer on, 2:67
in Chinese philosophy, 9:722
Chinese room argument symbol and, 2:241
as cognitive, 5:526
in cognitive science, 2:299–300
compositionality and, 2:370, 7:402–405
in computationalism, 2:393
concepts and, 2:414, 2:415
conditions of satisfaction in, 8:706
content externalism and, 9:117
in context-sensitivity in speech, 2:209
as convention truth, 2:474–475
conventional, 7:402
conversational implicature and, 2:525–528
as creative activity, 1:559–560, 1:560
Creighton on, 2:592
in critical realism, 2:596
in Daoism, 2:187–190
das Meinen, act of, 5:161
Davidson (Donald) on, 1:154–155, 2:647–648
death and, 1:611–612
definition of, 4:184, 7:400–401
and delivery-within-speech-capacity, 2:208–209
Dilthey on, 3:83
distinction and category mistakes in Aristotle, 2:74
Dummett on, 6:676–677
emotive, 9:245
in empiricism, 1:149–150, 9:414, 9:808
as existential reference, 1:677
of expressions, 7:400
expressive, 6:652
extrinsic nature of, 7:401–402
Frege on, 3:728, 5:548, 6:505
in Freudian psychology, 3:511
functionalism about, 3:760
Geach on, 1:154
genes as units of, 7:345
Grice on, 2:528, 4:184, 7:738
Hare on, 1:154
Hempel on, 1:149
hidden *vs.* articulated, 1:28
Hobbes on, 7:401
illocutionary acts and, 1:132
image as bearer of, 4:594
in Indian philosophy, 9:580–582
in indicative conditional sentences, 2:426
instinctual, 3:511
intellectual, 4:849–850
interpretation and, 1:311
Johnson (Alexander Bryan) on, 4:848–850
Langer on, 5:187–188
language and, 1:154, 1:545, 2:208–209, 7:401
in legal transactions, 7:446
Lewis (C. I.) on, 5:308–309
in logical positivism, 1:149
Mansel on, 5:687
Marty on, 5:728–729
in mathematics, 6:677
Meinong on, 3:312
in metaethics, 6:155–160
in metaphor, 6:166
metaphysical status of, 1:605
Millikan on, 6:236
natural
of actions, 9:833
vs. nonnatural, 4:711

Meaning, *continued*
- nihilism and, 6:617–618
- nonpropositional, 6:652–654
- non-truth-conditional, **6:649–655**, 8:532
- Novalis on, 6:667
- operational theory of, 4:849
- Peirce (C. S.) on, 3:313, 5:453, 7:167
- in philosophy of language, 7:400–402
- in Plato's dialogues, 8:755
- polarity in, 2:67–68
- in pragmatics, 7:738
- and pragmatism, 4:781–783, 7:743–744
- in private language problem, 8:15
- as private perception, 1:586
- Proclus on, 8:45
- of propositions, 4:849
- Putnam (H.) on, 5:190, 7:409
- of questions, 4:850
- Quine on, 1:149–150, 8:89
- reality of, 7:401–402
- referents as, 8:759, 8:794
- relational nature of, 7:401–402
- representational, 7:402–405
- in rule following, 8:531–533
- in rules of language, 4:622
- Russell on, 1:146, 5:97
- Ryle on, 8:582–583
- in Sanlun Buddhism, 2:161–162
- Schiller (Ferdinand) on, 8:625
- in science, 2:41
- of scientific *vs.* metaphysical statements, 5:528
- Searle on, 1:154
- of sentences, 5:510, 7:406
    - circumstances of, 9:812
    - Johnson (Alexander Bryan) on, 4:849
    - as logical picture, 2:41
    - in use, 9:811–813
    - what cannot be said, 9:804
- shared, Eliot (T. S.) on, 3:186
- social conditioning and, 1:152
- solipsism and, 9:116
- speaker's, 6:83–84, 7:405–406
- in speech and delivery-beyond-speech-capacity, 2:208
- subject-predicate relations and, 2:162
- synonymy and, 1:162–163, 9:346
- in tautologies, 1:148
- truth and, 1:166, 2:310, 9:665
- and universe of discourse, 1:660
- use and, 6:85–86, 9:624, 9:811–813
- vagueness and, 9:624
- verifiability of, 9:659–666
- verification and, 1:523, 3:316–317, 5:527, 5:687, 9:414
- and Western *vs.* Buddhist semantics of reference, 1:756
- and what cannot be said, 9:804
- Wittgenstein on, 8:531–533, 9:811–813
- Wollheim on, 9:835
- of words, 5:510
    - in Indian theories of language, 7:414–416
    - in relation to function, 3:760
    - in syllogisms, 5:501
- in writing, 1:71–72

"Meaning and Illocutionary Force" (Frye), 3:755

Meaning and Necessity (Carnap), 8:737
- on intensional structure, 9:347
- on synonymy, 9:345

Meaning equations, definition by, 2:676

Meaning of Love, The (Solov'ëv), 9:122, 9:125

Meaning of Meaning, The (Ogden & Richards), 1:58, 8:799

Meaning of Words, The (Johnson), 8:795

Meaning rationalism, Millikan on, 6:236

Meaningfulness
- falsifiability and, 9:669
- measurement models and, 6:88
- in operationalism, 7:31–32
- qualitative, 6:89

Meaninglessness
- of life, 6:619
- *vs.* meaningfulness, in expression, 8:803
- Tillich on, 9:458–459
- Unamuno on, 9:567

Meaning-skeptic, 8:531–533

Means of knowledge *(pramana),* 5:117

Mean-speed theorem, 7:35

Measurable property, fundamental, 6:90–91

Measure, in beauty, Winckelmann on, 9:790

Measurement, and measurement theory, 2:19, **6:86–92**
- in additional variables theory, 8:212
- as axioms *vs.* definitions, 1:633
- Berkeley on, 8:11
- in Bohmian mechanics, 1:633–634
- in chemistry, 2:142
- in collapse dynamics, 8:210
- common cause principle and, 2:343
- in Copenhagen interpretation, 2:531
- *vs.* counting, 6:664
- definition of, 6:86
- derived, general theory of, 6:90–91
- devices for, 6:91
- Giles of Rome on, 4:90
- Goodman on, 4:157
- Jevons on, 4:808
- Kilvington on, 5:69
- of mass, 6:2
- models in, 6:87–88
- of motion, 9:342
- of particle spin, 1:540
- perception and, 8:10
- of pleasure, 1:339
- in probability, 4:808
- of qualities, 8:9–10
- quantum, problem of, 5:695–696, 8:207
- in quantum experimental apparatus, 8:206–209
- quantum mechanics and, 1:540, 1:631, 1:637–639, 2:531, 7:477, 8:658
- Reichenbach on, 8:170
- representation theorems in, 9:334
- representational theory of, 6:89–91
- in science, 1:637
- scientific terminology and, 7:517
- of sensory experience, 8:10
- spatial, intellect as, 1:566
- splitting worlds and, 5:697–698
- in spontaneous collapse theory, 8:211
- standards in, 8:10
- of time, 9:461, 9:483
    - Anaximander and, 1:184
    - Heidegger on, 9:490

Measurement and Calculation (Campbell), 2:19

Measurement domain, 6:87

Mécanique analytique (Lagrange), 3:688
- on energy and work, 3:227
- on force measurement, 3:228

Mecanique celeste (Laplace), 3:688

Mécanique industrielle (Poncelet), 3:229

Meccan Revelations, The (Ibn al-ʿArabī), 9:307

Mechanica (Aristotle), on energy and force, 3:227

Mechanica (Guidobaldo del Monte), on energy and work, 3:227

Mechanical calculators, historical overview of, 2:399–400

Mechanical devices, and computing machine development, 2:406

Mechanical materialism
Driesch on, 3:110–111
Elisabeth, princess of Bohemia, and, 3:188
Engels on, 3:59–60
Gassendi and, 4:30
and human dignity, 8:630
Mechanical philosophy
Boyle and, 1:673–674
Conway on, 2:529
Descartes on, 2:722, 2:729–730
vs. experimental, 6:593
Leibniz and, 5:255, 5:265–269
matter in, 6:60
unity in, 9:578
Mechanical work. *See* Work, mechanical
Mechanics
analytical, 2:282–283
classical, **2:279–284**
basic ontology of, 2:280
determinism and, 7:474
force in, 2:280
fundamental laws of, 2:280–281
mass in, 2:280
matter in, 2:280
mechanism in, 2:281–282
motion in, 2:280
space in, 7:474–475
teleology in, 2:283
time in, 7:474–475
time-reversal invariance, 2:281
Hegel on, 4:266
Hertz on, 4:342–343
representations of, 4:341–342
in Stern's theory of teleomechanics, 9:244
Mechanik in ihrer Entwicklung, Die (The Science of Mechanics) (Mach), 3:227
Mechanism(s), 5:132
action in, 8:127–128
Bertalanffy on, 1:593
Cabanis on, 2:1
Cartesianism and, 2:60
Cartwright on, 2:63
Cavendish on, 2:118
in classical mechanics, 2:281–282
as closed society, 1:571
consciousness and, 1:649
Crusius on, 2:607
Cudworth on, 2:610
in French clandestine literature, 2:264–265
Helmholtz and, 4:305
Hobbes and, 8:127–128
in Indian philosophy, 2:110
Leibniz on, 8:129
Meslier on, 2:266–267
microcosm and, 5:642
mind in, 8:127
and moral causality in Vishnu's organization of society, 2:110
Ostwald on, 7:49–50
on particulate motion, 2:272
in society and morality, 2:33
Mechanistic thought, 1:563
Mechanization, and Turing machines, 2:375–376
Media, mass
Adorno on, 1:26
Carroll on, 7:383
vs. high art, 1:67
Mediate inference, definition of, 5:548
Mediate knowledge, types of, 3:752
Mediating third, 8:609
Mediationism, in Tagore, 9:364
Mediavilla, Richard of. *See* Richard of Mediavilla
Medical ethics, **6:92–98**
act *vs.* omission in, 3:457–458
and advance directives, 3:456–458
and animal research, 1:208–209
and assisted suicide, 9:321
and bioethics, 1:599
death criteria and, 2:653
euthanasia and, 3:455–459
and genetic and reproductive technologies, 4:43–48
informed consent in, 3:456, 4:679–680
paternalism and, 7:138–139
personhood and, 7:242
practical nature of, 6:92
refusal of permission *vs.* request in, 3:457–458
and withholding of treatment, 3:456–458
Medical knowledge, of body, 3:699
Medical materialism, 6:6, 6:10
Medical research
agenda of, allocation and, 6:96
Bentham and, 1:557
bioethical issues in, 1:603
Medici, Cosimo de, academy founded by, 3:671
Medici, Giulio de, Machiavelli and, 5:626
Medici, Lorenzo de, 7:570
Ficino and, 3:624
Machiavelli and, 5:626
Medici, Piero de, 7:570
Medicina Mentis (Tschirnhaus), 9:549
Medicinal Dictionary (James), 3:71–73
Medicine
Adler's work in, 1:23
Hellenistic, 4:302
Helmholtz in, 4:303
holistic, 7:467
phenomenal effects and scientific causal claims in, 2:104
philosophy and, 7:333
philosophy of, **7:465–467**
animism of animal organism, 9:202
in Galen, 4:4–6
Servetus and, 8:830
therapist in, 1:716
Medieval civilization, *vs.* modern, 5:715
Medieval cosmology, crystal spheres of, 5:51
Medieval courtly love, 3:623
Medieval logic, **5:421–437**
Abelard and, 5:424–428
Boethius and, 5:421–424
consequences in, 5:434–435
disjunctive syllogism in, 7:105
English schools of, 5:430, 5:434
explosion in, 7:105
fallacies in, 5:429–430
insolubles in, 5:433–434
on logic of sentences, 5:506
logica modernorum, development of, 5:429–432
modality in, 5:435
modism in, 5:432–433
obligations in, 5:433
Parisian schools of, 5:428–430
on predicables, 5:552
truth conditions in, 2:541
Medieval period
Carolingian renaissance in, 2:49–51
Copernicus and astronomy in, 2:533
optimism/pessimism in, 7:247
Medieval philosophy, **6:99–107**
altruism in, 3:170
Being in, 1:528
branches of, 2:624
on causation, 7:162
Dante in, 2:625
and epistemology, 3:289–291
on eternal return doctrine, 3:353–354
and ethics, 3:401–404
force as concept in, 3:687
Galileo and, 3:134
Gilson on, 4:92
Locke and, 5:376
matter in, 6:60
microcosm in, 5:641–642

Medieval philosophy, ***continued***
natural law in, 3:404, 6:507–509
nominalism in, 1:769, 9:599
Peter Lombard and, 7:261
physicotheology in, 7:557
political, 7:659–660
and science, 2:669
universals in, 3:289–291, 6:101–102, 6:188, 9:593
Medieval science, 1:769, 2:669
Medieval Studies, 4:92
Medieval theology, 7:522
"Meditación de la técnica" (Ortega), 7:547
Meditaciones del Quijote (Ortega y Gasset), 7:45
Meditation
Bernard of Clairvaux on, 1:592
Buddhism and, 2:154, 5:328–329, 6:254–256
Chan Buddhism and, 1:729, 2:155, 2:167
depictions of, 6:107
Hua yan Buddhism and, 1:738–739
in Indian philosophy, **6:107–110,** 9:542
after enlightenment, 4:629
Isvara and, 4:134
practice of, 6:108–109
jhāna and, 1:726–727
Marcus Aurelius and, 5:706
as monastic practice, 1:727–728
orders of perspective on, 1:738–739
Meditation on Emptiness (Hopkins), 1:733
Meditationes Philosophicae de Nonnullis ad Poema Pertinentibus (Baumgarten), 1:50, 1:494
Meditations (Marcus Aurelius), 5:706, 9:254
Meditations on First Philosophy (Descartes), 2:738–749, 2:758, 4:25, 4:564
Arnauld on, 1:288–290
Cartesian circles and, 3:278
composition of, 2:738
on determinism, 3:12
on doubt, 3:102
on dreams, 3:105
early versions of, 2:728
on error, 3:345
Gassendi on, 4:25
on man as thinking substance, 4:612
on matter, 2:758
on mind-body problem, 6:258
overview of, 2:720
publication of, 2:737
reception of, 2:749–757
on *semel in vita,* 2:727
on sense perception, 3:292
solipsisms in, 9:115–116
translation of, 2:753
on truth, 2:735–736
Meditative Approaches to the Huayan Dharmadhātu (Dushun), 1:738
Mediterranean and the Mediterranean World (Braudel), 7:395
Medium extrinsecum, 9:778
Medizinische Psychologie (Lotze), 8:139
Medlin, Brian, on values, moral *vs.* personal, 3:443
Medvedev, Pavel Nikolaevich, and Bakhtin Circle, 1:469
Megarians, **6:110–112**
on determinism, 3:5
and dialectic, 3:54, 3:87
and possibility, 7:719–720
Megillat ha-Megalleh (Bar Hiyya), 4:816
Meichū rokkan (Six chapters on categories) (Minagawa), 6:253
Meier, Georg Friedrich, **6:112–113**
Baumgarten and, 1:494
Kant and, 5:9
Mendelssohn and, 6:131
Sulzer and, 9:325
Meijers, Anthonie, 7:549
Meiji period, Japanese philosophy during, 4:791
Meiji Restoration, 1:728
"Meine Nachforschungen über den Gang der Natur in der Entwicklung des Menschengeschlechtes" (Pestalozzi), 7:255
Meinecke, Friedrich, 4:391, **6:113–114**
Meinong, Alexius, **6:114–119**
Cohen (Hermann) and, 6:543
Ehrenfels and, 3:176
and epistemology, 3:311–312
on existence, 3:495
on intentionality, 4:709
on linguistic meaning, 8:803–804
Marty and, 5:729
neo-Kantianism and, 3:311
in new realism, 6:584
realism and, 3:313
Russell and, 3:315
Twardowski and, 9:554
Meinongianism. *See* Noneism
Meirokusha (Japanese intellectual group), 6:623
Meizer, Michael, 3:256
Melancholia, 7:247–248
Melancholy, of Kierkegaard, 5:61
Melancholy humor, 7:247
Melanchthon, Philipp, **6:119–120**
Copernicism and, 2:536
on Franck's unorthodox thoughts, 3:713
on logic, 5:437–438
Pico della Mirandola and, 7:570
Mélanges philosophiques (Jouffroy), 4:854–855
Melden, A. I., 3:19–20, 3:430
Mele, Alfred
on static puzzle of self-deception, 8:713
on volition, 9:705
Melerebuts, Alfred, on action, 1:15
Melia, Joseph, 3:628
Melian Dialogue (Thucydides), sophism in, 9:129
Melidunenses, on conditionals, 5:429
Meliorism, 7:245
Melissus of Samos, **6:120–121**
atomism and, 5:299
metaphysical criticism of, 6:184
Parmenides of Elea and, 7:122, 7:125
in pre-Socratic philosophy, 7:762
Simplicius on, 9:35
on space, 9:146
Mellor, D. H.
on probability, 9:471
on tensed theory of time, 9:475
on token-reflexive theory, 9:476
Membership, definition of, 5:548
Memento (film), memory in, 6:122
Memoire sur la faculté pensée (Destutt de Tracy), 8:788
Mémoire sur l'habitude (Maine de Biran), 2:760
Mémoires (La Rochefoucauld), 5:200
Memoires de l'Institut National des Sciences et Arts (Cabanis), 8:788
Mémoires de Trévoux, 7:244
Mémoires d'outretombe (Chateaubriand), 2:137
Mémoires historiques et philosophiques sur la vie et les ouvrages de Diderot (Naigeon), 6:476
Memoirs Illustrating the History of Jacobinism (Barruel), 3:243
Memoirs of a Revolutionist (Kropotkin), 5:154
Memoirs of the Author of A Vindication of the Rights of Woman (Godwin), 4:136
Memorabilia (Recollections of Socrates) (Xenophon), 2:698, 3:90, 8:751, 9:855

"Memoranda concerning the Aristotelian Syllogism" (Peirce), 5:453, 7:164
Memoria et Reminiscentia, De (Aristotle), 4:696–697, 8:824
Mémorial, Le (Pascal), 7:130
Memories and Studies (James), 7:84
Memories of My Life (Westermarck), 9:738
Memory, 2:596, **6:122–128**
  a priori, in Plato's doctrine of reminiscence, 4:606
  in animals, 1:206
  Anscombe on, 1:213
  Aristotle on, 3:286–287
  asymmetry of, 9:498
  Augustine on, 1:394
  autobiographical, 6:122, 6:125
  Bergson on, 1:564, 2:695, 3:313, 9:489
  Bruno on, 1:708
  in Buddhism, 1:722
  chemistry of, 6:568
  Chisholm on, 2:242–243
  in cognitive psychology, 8:151
  collective, 6:126
  in computability theory, 2:387
  computationalism and, 2:394
  in computing machines, 2:405
  Condillac on, 2:422
  as consciousness, 1:564
  construction of, 6:126
  Destutt de Tracy on, 2:760
  Diderot on, 3:75
  evident presumption in, 6:117
  and experience, 3:214
  external influences on, 6:126
  factual, 6:122
  fallibility of, 5:96
  forms of, 6:122–123
  forward, 7:755–756
  Hobbes on, 4:412–413
  imagery and, 7:223–224
  as images, 1:564
  in imagination, 1:711–712
  in Indian theories of language, 7:414
  internality of, 7:223, 7:227
  Locke on, 5:380–381
  McDougall on, 6:72
  as modular process, 2:394
  in molecular and cellular cognition, 6:568
  in national identity, 6:482
  and personal identity, 7:214–228
  philosophy of, 6:122
  Plato on, 1:394, 5:640
  precognition and, 7:755–756
  procedural, 6:123
  public, personal identity and, 7:226–227
  pure, as consciousness, 1:564
  Reid on, 8:326–327
  reliability of, 6:124
  vs. retention, in Husserl, 9:489
  Ribot on, 8:457
  Rignano on, 8:476
  Russell on, 3:316
  Schopenhauer on, 8:652
  sensory-motor response and, 1:564
  social, 6:126–127
  theories of, 6:124–125
  time and, 9:462–463
  and unconscious knowledge, 1:784
Memory systems, 6:123
Memory trace, 6:124–126
Men
  Cabanis on, 2:2
  values and roles associated with, as normative, 3:591
  worship of, required by heterosexuality, 3:756
Menasseh (Manasseh) ben Israel, **6:128**
Mencius, **6:129–130**
  and Confucianism, 2:195–196, 2:443
  Dai Zhen on, 2:621
  on evocative argumentative, 2:213–214
  on good, capacity for, 2:173
  on human nature, 2:150, 4:766
  on humanity (ren) and righteousness (yi), 2:150
  Itō and, 4:765
  and Japanese philosophy, 4:792–793
  on life, meaning and value of, 5:359
  Lu Xiangshan and, 5:618
  on moral virtue, 2:234
  and neo-Confucianism, 2:157, 4:794
  politics in, 2:179
  on self-cultivation, 2:177
  on social differentiation, 2:176
  on speech protection, 2:196–197
  wisdom literature of, 9:793
  Xunzi and, 9:856
  Yang Zhu and, 2:186–188, 9:862
  Yin Haiguang and, 2:181
Mencius (Mengzi) (Mencius), 2:171, 2:234, 6:129
  ceremonial behavior in, 2:175
  on heart/mind guiding role, 2:173
  on political action and character in Confucianism, 2:179
  on social and political reform, 2:176
Mencke, Otto, 5:252
Mendel, Gregor
  on causality, 7:339
  Darwin and, 7:339
  evolution and, 2:634, 2:638–639, 2:643
  genetic theory of, 3:488–489, 7:339, 9:579
  in history of biology, 7:338–339
"Mendelism and Biometry" (Fisher), 3:661
Mendelssohn, Moses, **6:130–132**
  on absolute, 1:11
  on church and state, 3:245
  Eberhard and, 3:161
  on feeling, 7:620
  Hamann on, 7:99
  on immortality, 4:618, 6:131
  Jacobi (Friedrich Heinrich) and, 4:770
  in Jewish philosophy, 3:249, 4:826–827
  Lavater and, 5:213
  Lessing and, 2:688, 5:294–296
  Maimon and, 5:645
  in pantheism dispute, 9:194
  Pantheismusstreit and, 7:99–101
  Spinoza and, 1:11, 4:770
  Sulzer and, 9:325
Menexemus (Philo of Megara), 7:312
Mengzi. *See* Mencius
"Mengzi" ziyi shuzheng (Commentary on the meaning of terms in *Mengzi*) (Dai Zhen), 2:621
Meno (Plato), 4:54, 5:65, 5:102, 5:106
  on *a priori* knowledge, 4:606
  on essence, 7:595
  geometry in, 4:54
  Gorgias of Leontini in, 4:162–163
  on human good, 9:111
  hypothesis in, 7:593
  on innate ideas, 4:691
  on knowledge
    nature and value of, 5:102
    vs. true belief, 3:284–285, 5:106
  Orphic influence in, 7:43
  paradox posed by Socrates in, 5:65
  recollection in, 7:588–589
  on virtue
    definition of, 9:110
    as knowledge, 7:589–590, 9:112
    teachability of, 7:586
Mens rea, 7:446, 8:448–449
Mensch, Der (Gehlen), 4:36

Menschliche Denken, Das (Schuppe), 8:662
Mental, the
 introspection of, 6:138–139
 vs. nonmental, 7:468
 and nonmental language, 3:757
"'Mental' and the 'Physical,' The" (Friegl), 7:470
Mental causation, **6:132–137**, 7:468
 and conservation of energy, 6:260
 in mind-body problem, 6:258–260
 pain and, 7:69–70
Mental constructions, freedom from, 9:652
Mental development
 in cognitive science, 2:298
 Comte on, 2:410
Mental dispositions, Wollheim on, 9:836
Mental entities
 concepts as, 2:417
 direct acquaintance with, 6:210
Mental faculties doctrine, 6:131
Mental force, 2:90–91
Mental illness
 Fries on, 3:753
 personhood and, 7:241
 suicide as, 9:320
Mental imagery. *See* Imagery, mental
Mental life
 and active impulses from external stimuli, 1:544
 of plants, 3:555
Mental logic, *vs.* mental models, 8:154
Mental maps, 4:590
Mental modularity, 4:695
Mental operations, Condillac on, 2:422
Mental phenomena, 7:52
 behaviorism and, 1:520
 brain in, 6:260, 9:270
 Brentano on, 3:311, 3:421
 causally inert, 6:133
 computationalism and, 2:391–394
 connectionism and, 2:444–445
 content of
  Dennett on, 2:710–711
  features of, 2:477
  in sensationalism, 8:823
 eliminative materialism and, 3:182–183
 Freud on, 9:572
 Hobbes on, 6:9
 Husserl on, 3:312
 intentionality in, 4:704
 and intuitionist mathematics, 1:700
 intuitions as, 4:734
 kind of, *vs.* content of, 1:562
 and knowledge, 1:544, 5:161
 La Mettrie on, 6:10
 vs. logical content, 3:753
 in materialism, 6:9–11
 physiological events as, 6:133, 6:261
 realization of, by microphysical events, 6:135
 representational theory of mind on, 6:142
 Ryle on, 8:581–582
 in supervenience thesis, 6:263, 9:327
 as volition, 9:703–704
Mental Philosophy (Haven), 6:623
Mental predicates, 2:646
Mental properties
 color as, 2:333
 definition of, 3:113–114
 force-generating, 6:261
 in functional reductionism, 5:72
 in higher-order consciousness, 2:454
 intrinsic nature of, 3:528
 perceiving and, 2:451–452
 vs. physical properties, in property dualism, 6:132–133
 as second-order properties, 3:761
 shared, type-identity and causality in, 2:92–93
 supervenience of, on physical properties, 9:327
Mental representation(s), **6:140–143**
 concepts and, 2:416–418
 language of thought thesis on, 5:191–192
 Millikan on, 6:236
 semantics of, 6:142
Mental residue, 5:72
Mental sentences, Wodeham on, 9:821–822
Mental state(s)
 "aboutness" of, 8:81
 analytical behaviorism on, 1:524
 in animals, 2:456
 Armstrong on, 1:286–287
 vs. automaton states, 3:757
 Ayer on, 1:437
 behavior and, 7:447
  as conceptual connection, 7:54
  Strawson on, 7:56
 Berkeley on, 1:586
 in Buddhist philosophy, **6:253–257**
 causal-functional nature of, 9:16
 causality of, 6:646–647, 8:192–193
 in Chinese room argument, 2:238
 in computationalism, 2:390–391
 concept of, having, 7:56–57
 consciousness and, 1:704, 2:449–451, 2:455–456, 4:712
 contentful, 2:477–478, 8:79–81
 Dennett on, 2:456
 description of, 7:52
 in desire for pleasure, 8:721
 epistemological content of, 2:478
 in functionalism, 3:756, 6:645–646, 9:37
 as functionally discrete internal states, 3:679
 in higher-order consciousness, 2:454
 higher-order thought (HOT) theory of, 4:713
 individuating, 3:760
 inner processes and outward criteria in, 1:525
 intentionality and, 3:677, 4:700–701, 4:709, 7:468, 8:81, 9:291
 in James's psychology, 4:777–778
 in law, 7:446–447
 Lewis (D.) on, 5:314–315
 in logical behaviorism, 1:534, 9:61
 materialism and, 6:12–16, 6:646–647
 nature and, 6:262
 negative sentences and, 8:804
 Ockham on, 9:774
 ontological status of, 1:565
 of others, personal identity and, 7:221
 overdetermination of, 2:92
 ownership of, 1:437
 physical states and
  asymmetrical knowledge of, 6:16–17
  logical connections between, 6:17
 qualitative *vs.* contentful, 8:79
 quantum mechanics and, 5:698
 Searle on, 8:705–706
 simulation theory and, 9:36
 in solipsism, 9:115, 9:118
 in subjectivity models, 9:292
 "theory-theory" of, 4:148, 9:36
 Wittgenstein on, 9:813–814
 Wollheim on, 9:836
Mentalese
 Fodor on, 2:478
 predication in, 2:479
Mentalism, 2:90–93
 and characterization of minds and behavior of others, 3:677
 on language, 5:189
 and neo-Confucianism, 2:157–158

revival of, 4:693
subjectivity in, 9:290–291
Mentality
connectionism and, 2:444
Cousin on, 2:579
Mentality of Apes, The (Köhler), 4:72
Mentalizing, 9:36
Mental-physical distinction, **6:138–140**
Mention of term, definition of, 5:548
Menzer, Paul, 5:343
Mercier, Désiré Joseph, 2:344, **6:143–146,** 9:446
Méré, Antoine Gombault de, 5:166
Mere Addition Paradox, Parfit on, 7:120
Mere Cambridge properties, 3:527
Mere Christianity (Lewis), 5:311
Meredith, C. A.
on *CN*-calculus, 5:607
on functorial calculus, 5:607
Łukasiewicz and, 5:608
Mereological composition, unrestricted, 6:176
Mereology, **6:146–147**
and essentialism, 6:147
in Gongson Long's white horse thesis, 4:149
in Indian philosophy, 1:381
Leśniewski on, 5:290–291
and nominalism, as entity reduction, 6:175–176
and particularism, 6:176
tenseless theory of time and, 9:471
and universalism, 9:762
Merezhkovskii, Dmitrii, and Kireevskii, 5:75
Mérian, Johann Bernhard, 9:56
Merit
in Buddhism, 1:723
ethical properties and, 7:5
Meritorious actions, 6:118, 6:233
Merkl, Adolf Julius, 5:49
Merleau-Ponty, Maurice, 3:638, **6:147–152**
on Bergson, 9:491
Ferrier and, 3:608
in film theory, 7:382
Foucault and, 3:698
Gurwitsch and, 4:197
Husserl and, 3:317, 8:803, 9:491
and ontology, 3:510, 9:491
and phenomenology, 3:563, 7:297–298
in philosophy of language, 7:411
and poststructuralism, 9:275
Sartre and, 6:149, 8:603
Scheler and, 8:616
on sense, 9:491
on speech, 7:411
on touch, 9:516
trace in, 2:717
Merlino, Saverio, Labriola and, 5:166
Merriam, Charles E., 8:675
Mersenne, Marin, **6:152–153**
Descartes and, 2:725–733, 2:738, 2:753, 2:759, 9:53
Fludd and, 3:675
Gassendi and, 4:30
Hobbes and, 8:825
La Mothe Le Vayer and, 5:181
Pascal and, 7:129
Sanches and, 8:596
skepticism of, 4:30, 9:53
Merton, Robert, 8:677, 9:78
Merton, Thomas, 3:763
Merton Schoolmen, 3:134
Mervis, Carolyn, 2:418
Meslier, Jean, 2:266–267, **6:153–155,** 9:712
Mesmer, Franz Anton, 5:642
Mesmerism, 8:670
Messiah
coming of, date of, calculating, 5:2
of Davidic line, Kabbalist belief in, 5:2
of Ismir, 5:2
Messianic expectancy, in Bloch, 1:616
Messianism
as idea, Cohen (Hermann) on, 4:828
as utopianism, 9:620
Mestizo consciousness, Zea on, 5:209–210
Meta logou, 5:93
Metabasis, Aristotelian prohibition against, 5:69
Metabeliefs, in coherentism, 2:315
Metacriticism, DuBos and, 3:123
Metaepistemology, 3:326–328
Metaethical relativism, 3:368–373
Metaethics, **6:155–165**
Daoism and, 2:184–185
definition of, 3:379
history of. *See* Ethics, history of
and ideal observer theories, 4:562–563
intuitionism in, 4:735–736
meaning in, 6:155–160
moral objectivism in, 6:160–161
arguments against, 6:161–162
arguments for, 6:162–165
moral reality in, 6:160–161
moral truth in, 6:160–161
vs. normative ethics, 7:326
on objectivity of standards, 3:381
persuasion in, 9:246
in sanctity of life issues, 9:42
Smart on, 9:66
Metafizicheskie predposylki poznaniya (Metaphysical premises of knowledge) (Trubetskoi), 9:529
Metaideology, in social sciences, 7:533–534
Metalanguage, 1:343–344
Carnap on, 2:42–43
definition of, 5:548
and foundations of science, 2:41–42
vs. language, 1:702
Lukasiewicz on, 2:547
necessary incompleteness of, 2:42
semantic paradoxes and, 5:521–522
Tarski on, 2:547–549, 5:474
and type theory, 2:76–77
Metalinguistics
and dao, 2:187
and grammar preservation, 2:78
Naṣīr al-Dīn al-Ṭūsī on, 6:478
on synonymy, 9:351
of theories, 9:414
of time, 9:463
and truth, 7:196–197
Metalogic
Frank on, 3:716
Leśniewski on, 5:292–293
Russell and, 5:466
Whitehead and, 5:466
Metalogicon (John of Salisbury), 4:843–844, 5:429
on artificialization of language, 6:102
on syncategoremata, 8:769
Metamathematics
and Barendregt's cube, 4:742
and Curry-Howard isomorphism, 4:742
definability in, 9:369
definition of, 5:548, 9:366
by Gödel, 4:117, 4:121–123
intuitionistic logic and, 4:742
Suppes on, 9:416
system foundations and, 2:41
Tarski on, 9:366–367
See also Mathematics
"Metamorphosis of Metaphysics, The" (Wisdom), 9:799
Metanormative theories of value, 9:638–640
Metaphor, **6:166–169**
analogy and, affinity between, 6:167
Aquinas on, 1:140–141

Metaphor, ***continued***
brute force theories of, 6:168
in Buddhism, 1:729
in Chinese metaphysics, 2:222
clarity of, 1:606
as communication between intellect and intuition, 1:567
complex illusion sources in, 1:704
conceptual theories of, 6:168
elements as, 1:440
in genetics, 7:345
God and, 1:140–142
Goodman on, 4:161
interpretation of, 1:311
in painting, 9:835
in religious language, 8:417–418
Ricoeur on, 7:300, 8:463–464
Tillich on, 1:365–366
of trembling hand, 4:17
untranslatable, 1:365–366
value of, 2:666
Metaphor and Religious Language (Soskice), 8:417–418
Metaphysic of Morals (Kant), 5:8, 5:24
Metaphysica (Baumgarten), 9:824
Metaphysical analysis
of language, 1:769
of persistence, 7:206–211
of personalism, 7:235
of personhood, 7:238–240
Metaphysical Club, 7:741
Metaphysical data
Ockham's razor applied to, 6:171
presuppositions of, 6:171
scientific *vs.* common-sense, 6:170
Metaphysical Foundations of Natural Science (Kant), 5:23, 5:28–30
Metaphysical necessities, examples of, 5:151
Metaphysical Principles of the Virtues (Kant), on self-deception, 8:713
Metaphysical solipsism, 9:115–116
Metaphysical stage, in Comte, 2:412
Metaphysical status, of conventional truths, 2:475
Metaphysical theology
Mansel and, 1:362
rejection of, 1:364–365
unfalsifiability of, 1:366–367
unintelligibility of, 1:365–366
Metaphysical Tree, The (Shahrazurī), 4:584
Metaphysical truth, 6:205, 6:210–211
Metaphysical *vs.* experiential, Rickert on, 6:544–545
Metaphysician, psychological data indispensable to, 3:552
Metaphysics, 1:750–751, 2:89–93, **6:169–181**
Abelard on, 1:4–5, 1:528
abstract entities and, 1:529
of aesthetics, 1:57
Alembert on, 1:106
Alexander of Hales and, 1:115
al-Fārābī, Abū al Naṣr and, 1:116
of All-Unity, 3:669
Anselm on, 1:215–216
anthropocentric, naturalistic religion and, 8:376
approaches to, 6:170–173
Aquinas and, 1:528, 9:430–431, 9:436
Ardigò on, 1:251
Aristotle and, 1:264–265, 1:275–278, 1:527–528, 2:72–74, 6:185–186, 7:65, 9:635–636. *See also Metaphysics* (Aristotle)
asymmetry and causal relations in, 2:104–106
asymmetry of counterfactuals in, 2:575
Averroes and, 1:424–425
Avicenna and, 1:432–433, 3:135, 4:757
Ayer on, 1:531
Bacon (Francis) and, 1:449
Bayle on, 1:505
being in, 1:527–532
and being qua being, 9:283
Bergson on, 1:568, 9:488
Berkeley and, 1:529
Biel on, 1:594
Blanshard on, 1:613
Boethius on, 1:628
Bohr and, 1:637–639
Bonaventure on, 1:651
Bonhoeffer on, 1:656
Bonnet and, 1:658
Boström and, 1:668
Boyle on, 1:674–675
Bradley on, 1:676
Brentano on, 1:689–691
Brouwer on, 2:504
Brown on, 1:704
Buckle on, 1:718
Budde and, 1:721
in Buddhism, 1:737, 1:742–745, 1:755
Buridan on, 1:768
Burthogge and, 1:776
in Byzantine thought, 1:787
Caird on, 2:4
Cajetan on, 2:6–7
Calderoni on, 2:7
Camus on, 2:20–21
"can" in, 2:23–26
Capreolus and, 2:30–31
Carnap and, 2:40–44, 9:808
Carroll on, 2:51
Cartwright on, 2:62
Carus (Carl) and, 2:63–64
Carus (Paul) and, 2:64
Caso and, 2:65
Cassirer on, 2:66
categories and, 2:72–83
causality and, 1:741, 2:85–88, 2:95–97, 2:98–99, 2:101, 2:107, 2:125
chance and, 2:125–128
in chaos and probability theory foundations, 2:133
in Chinese philosophy, 2:215–223, 2:220–221
Clifford on, 2:293
Cohen (Morris) on, 2:306–307
coherence theory of truth and, 2:308–309
Collier and, 2:324
Collingwood on, 2:327–328
of common cause principle, 2:342
common sense and, 1:510, 2:358
communism and, 2:365
comprehensiveness of, 6:199
Comte on, 2:410, 6:225
concepts in, 6:203–204
conservatism and, 2:465–466
constructive empiricism and, 9:645
conventionalism and, 2:474
Corbin and, 2:537
cosmology and, 2:551, 2:556
critique of, 6:197
Crusius and, 2:606–607
Cudworth and, 2:609–610
Dante on, 2:624
in Daoism, 2:185, 2:192, 2:198, 2:205–207
as deductive, 1:697
definition of, 6:169, 7:326
Descartes and, 1:528, 2:285
descriptive *vs.* reversionary, 2:79
descriptive *vs.* revisionary, 2:79, 9:265
Dewey and, 1:531, 7:378–379
in Dge-lugs Mādhyamika, 1:732
in direct *vs.* indirect creation by God, 1:651
of disease, 7:465–466
of double truth and contextual meaning, 2:209
Duns Scotus on, 3:134–137
of education, 7:366
Ehrenfels on, 3:177

and elimination of dogmatic, 5:21–23
Eliot (George) on, 3:184
as emanation for Christ, 1:651
empirical, 1:108–110
Encyclopédie on, 3:223
of enduring things, persistence and, 7:210–211
of entropy and information in physical states, 2:105
Eric of Auxerre and, 1:528
in evolutionary theory, 1:569
features of, 6:199
feminist, **3:57–62**, 3:585–590
as form and substance, 1:626
Frege on, 1:528
fundamentality of, 6:199
future of, 6:181
Gassendi and, 6:8–9
Genovesi on, 4:49
Geulincx and, 4:79–80
Giles of Rome on, 4:89–90
Gogarten on, 4:144
Green on, 4:179–180
Hägerström on, 4:206
Hartmann and, 1:530
Hazlitt and, 4:248–249
Hegelian, 1:530, 2:81, 4:283–286
Heidegger on, 1:530–531
Helmholtz on, 4:303–304
Herbart and, 4:322–323, 7:376
and history, 1:713–714, 1:785, 6:205
history of, 1:527–531, **6:183–200,** 8:645
and human condition, 2:22
Hume on, 2:80, 2:95–96
Husserl on, 2:81–82
Huxley and, 4:532–533
Ibn al-ʿArabī and, 9:308
and idealism, 4:561, 6:170
impossibility of, verifiability principle and, 9:659
Indian, 9:542–544, 9:580–582
of inexperiential, 4:686
infinite regress and, 1:741
intuitionism and, 1:568, 5:713
James (William) and, 4:782–785
Jankélévitch on, 4:787
Jodl (Friedrich) on, 4:835
Johnson (Dr. Samuel) and, 4:853
Jünger and, 4:859
Kant on, 2:66, 2:74–75, 3:308–309, 4:57, 5:36, 7:374
Kierkegaard on, 1:530
Kim on, 5:72
Kozlov and, 5:146
language and, 7:409–410
Lavelle on, 5:214–216
in legal philosophy, 7:428
Leibniz on, 1:529, 4:165–166, 5:256
Liebert on, 5:343
of life as unified organism, 1:785
of light, Grosseteste on, 4:186
Locke on, 2:80
logical positivism and, 5:525–526
Lotze on, 5:581
in Mādhyamika doctrine, 1:740–744
Maritain on, 1:529–530, 5:713–714
Martinetti and, 5:728
Marxism and, 5:737
materialism and, 6:15
mathematics in, 9:342
Maupertuis and, 6:67
McTaggart on, 4:560, 6:78
of meaning, 1:605
meaninglessness and, 6:170
Mercier and, 6:144
method of, 4:322, 6:169–171, 6:210–211, 7:329–330
on methodological individualism, 4:444–446
Mill (John Stuart) and, 6:225–226
Millikan and, 6:236
modality and, 6:287–288, 7:580
Moore and, 1:528, 6:346–347
moral constructivism and, 2:472
moral rationalism and, 8:251
More (Henry) and, 6:395–396
Mou and, 2:183
Mullā Ṣadrā and, 6:419–420
on multiplication of pure essences, 9:344
Nasr on, 6:479–480
nature of, **6:200–212**
necessary *vs.* contingent propositions in, 5:100
and neo-Confucianism, 2:156–157
and neo-Daoism, 2:190–191
and neo-Kantianism, 6:541–542
Neurath on, 6:561
and nomological conditions, 2:98–99
Norris and, 6:656
Nozick and, 6:669
number in, 6:670
in Nyaya-Vaisesika schools, 4:133
object permanence in, 1:579–580
Ockham and, 2:80, 6:171, 7:7, 9:779–781
Odo of Tournai on, 1:528
Oken and, 7:11
Olivi and, 7:13
one/many in, 4:312
ontological, 1:613, 7:743
optimism/pessimism and, 7:245, 7:250
Ortega y Gasset and, 7:45
and pairs of contradictory doctrines, proven by Kant, 5:22
panpsychism and, 7:86
paranormal phenomena and, 1:698
Parmenides on, 1:527, 7:122
particulars in, 6:173–174
Pauler on, 7:145
Pearson on, 7:160
perception and, 1:755, 7:188
personhood and, 1:463–464
and pessimism, 7:245, 7:250
Peter Aureol on, 7:258
Petronievič's contribution to, 7:266
philosophers classified in, 6:199
philosophy and, 4:8, 7:326
Plato and, 1:187, 7:608, 9:702
Plutarch of Chaeronea and, 7:648
Popper-Lynkeus on, 7:697–699
of possibility, 7:723–724
possible worlds and, 6:284–286
in post-Kantian thought, 2:75–77
postmodern culture and, 1:491
of presence, 3:565
presupposing in, 7:768–769
principles of
    discovery of, 3:752
    Philolaus' concept of, 7:310–311
probability and, 2:127–128, 8:35–36, 9:381
"problem of the many" in, 6:663
of propositions, 8:81–85
and psychology, 8:457
and quantum mechanics, 5:697
Quine on, 1:528
of real entities, 1:740
and realism, 1:745, 2:64, 8:688–689
and reality, 1:662, 2:20–21, 5:143
and reason, 5:13
in reductionism and causal relations, 2:96
refutations of, 6:202
of Régis, 8:300
reincarnation and, 8:332
Renan and, 8:428–429
Rescher and, 8:439
responsibility in, 4:830–831
Richard of Mediavilla and, 8:458
Riehl and, 8:467
Rignano and, 8:476
Rüdiger on, 8:527
Rufus and, 8:529–530

Metaphysics, ***continued***
Russell on, 2:76–77, 2:358, 8:540–546
in Samkhya-Yoga schools, 4:134
in Sankhya, 2:111–112
in Sautrānikita doctrine, 1:745
scandal of, 5:13
Schopenhauer on, 8:647
Schrödinger's identity theory of, 8:658
and science, 1:568, 4:532, 5:728, 6:199–200, 6:208–210, 7:331
Duhem on, 3:126–127
and Gauge Theory, 4:31–33
James (William) on, 4:777, 4:782
Kant on, 6:170
scientific, 5:728
scope of, 6:183, 6:208–210
Seneca on, 8:812
Shepherd and, 9:10
social sciences and, 7:534–535
and society's presuppositions, 2:328
Sophia and, 3:669
sophists on, 9:131
and soul, 1:652
special sciences on, 9:161
as speculative suprascience, 1:697
Spencer and, 7:377
Spinoza on, 9:171–172, 9:174, 9:186–187
Spir and, 9:197
Stöhr's theorogonous, 9:252
Stoicism and, 9:256
Suárez and, 9:283–285
subject and predicate in, 9:288–289
as subject-object relationship, 1:491
of substance, 3:588, 9:762
supersensible in, 6:201–202
Svātantrika-Prāsaṅgika distinction, 1:744
Swedenborg and, 5:11
in syntax and meaning, 2:41–42
Tagore and, 9:364
task of, 6:169–171
of temporal parts, persistence and, 7:208–210
Tetens on, 9:404
theology as, 1:436–437
Theophrastus and, 9:412
of theory and categories, 2:77–80
Thomas of York and, 9:443
Thomasius and, 9:442
Thomistic, 1:476, 5:708, 9:443
Thomson (Judith) and, 9:449
Tillich and, 9:459–460
of time, 7:211
Toletus and, 9:511
Tolstoy and, 9:512–513
of *Tractatus,* 9:805
and transcendental, 5:526
in transcendental logic, 2:79
in transformation of knower into object known, 2:15
ugliness and, 9:562
Unamuno and, 9:568–569
universals in, 6:173–174
Valla on, 9:635–636
value and, 8:51–52, 9:640
Varisco and, 9:647
Vasconcelos and, 9:649
Vasquez and, 9:649
Vaz Ferreira on, 9:654–655
Vico and, 9:672
vital impetus and evolution in, 1:569–570
Voltaire and, 9:710–711
Wahle (Richard) on, 9:719
Wang Fuzhi and, 9:724
Weil (Simone) and, 9:737
Whitehead on, 2:81, 9:747–752
Wiggins and, 9:762
William of Auvergne and, 9:765
without ontology, 6:202–204
Wittgenstein on, 2:82, 9:808
Wolff and, 9:827–828
and Yogācāra Buddhism, 1:745–749
Zhou Dunyi on, 9:880
Zhu Xi and, 9:883
Metaphysics [term], meaning of, 6:183
Metaphysics (al-Kindī), 4:542
Metaphysics (Aristotle), 1:527, 2:74, 2:217, 5:398, 9:534
on Anaxagoras, 2:698
archē in, 1:248–249, 1:276–277
being in, 1:278, 7:571–572
cause in, 1:276, 1:277
David of Dinant and, 2:644
Duns Scotus on, 3:134
on essence, 3:350, 9:295
Good in, 1:276
in history of metaphysics, 6:183
Jaeger on, 1:276
Jesuit education and, 2:721
Megarians in, 6:111
ousia in, 7:63
on persistence, 7:206
on Plato's philosophy, 7:634
Simplicius on, 9:34
on Socrates, 9:108
terminology in, 1:423
Theophrastus on, 1:258
on truth in words, 8:756–757
on unity, 1:275–276, 7:571–572
William of Moerbeke's translation of, 9:769
wisdom in, 1:276
Metaphysics (Geulincx), 4:77
Metaphysics in Ancient Greece (Trubetskoi), 9:533
Metaphysics of Creation (Kretsmann), 9:447
Metaphysics of Morals (Kant), 2:71, 5:34
"Metaphysics of the Love of the Sexes" (Schopenhauer), 5:589
Metaphysics of Theism (Kretzmann), 9:447
Metaphysik (Lotze), 5:580
Metaphysik (Meier), 6:112
Metaphysik der Erkenntnis (Hartmann), 1:530
Metasemantic theories, 6:83–84
Metatheorem(s)
definition of, 5:548
of first-order logic, 3:647–654, 3:653–654
Metatheory(ies)
definition of, 5:548
Tarski on, 5:480
Metazoa, Haeckel on, 4:201–202
Metempsychosis. *See* Reincarnation
Meteorology
Anaxagoras on, 1:183
Anaximenes on, 1:186
Aristotle on, 1:271–272
Descartes on, 2:729–733
Philoponus on, 7:314
Seneca on, 8:812
Meteorology (Aristotle), 1:271–272
Meteorology (Descartes), 2:729–733
Meteorology (Diogenes of Apollonia), 3:89
Meteors (Regius), 2:55
Method(s)
bioethics and, 1:600
Burley on, 1:773
Cohen (Morris) on, 2:306
of construction, definition of, 5:548
Descartes on, 2:286, 6:190
of difference, Mill (John Stuart) on, 3:124
of doubt, in Descartes, 2:735–736, 2:753, 3:291, 3:683. *See also* Skepticism, Descartes on
Lequier on, 5:287
general normative ethics and, 1:600–601
in historiography, Burckhardt on, 1:765–766

in Huayan Buddhism, 2:164
in logic, Zabarella on, 9:866–867
of measuring common objects, 3:557
naturalism as, 6:492–493
philosophical, 7:330–331, 8:580–581, 9:554, 9:648
Bacon (Francis) on, 1:444–446
Bayle and, 1:504–505
in Buddhism, 2:163–166
Byzantine, 1:787
Cairns on, 2:6
Calvin on, 2:11–12
Carneades and, 2:47
Cavendish on, 2:118
Charron and, 2:135
in Chinese thought, 2:200–201, 2:210–212, 2:222
Collingwood on, 2:327
Comte on, 2:411
Crusius on, 2:605–606
in Huayan Buddhism, 2:164
and ideal-language formalism, 1:561
logical positivism and, 5:527
logical *vs.* evocative argument as, 2:213–214
in Mohist discourse, 2:212–213
Rescher and, 8:439–440
solipsism as, 9:199
Stace on, 9:199
in Tainti Buddhism, 2:163–164
Xunzi on, 2:216
of postulation, definition of, 5:548
of production or construction, 3:557
of selection or choice, 3:557
Stace on, 9:199
of truth tables, 9:807
Xunzi on, 2:216
Method for the Easy Comprehension of History (Methodus ad Facilem) (Bodin), 1:620–622
Method of the Divine Government, Physical and Moral, The (McCosh), 6:71
Méthod de nomenclature chimique (Lavoisier), 8:785
Methode der Physik, Der (Dingler), 3:86
Methodenbuch für Väter und Mütter der Familien und Vöker (Basedow), 1:482
Methodism
epistemology and, 3:278
Pietism and, 7:575–576
"Methodological Character of Theoretical Concepts, The" (Carnap), 7:31, 9:669
Methodological circle, phenomenological, 7:283, 7:287–288
Methodological holism, 4:443
Methodological individualism, 4:442–443
Methodological naturalism, 6:501
Methodological solipsism, 9:117–118
Methodology
Basedow and, 1:483
in bioethics, 1:601–602
in epistemology, 7:329
feminist, 3:580–581, 3:590
Green on, 4:179
of Hobbes, 4:406–410, 4:424
hypothetico-deductivism and, 8:684–685, 8:699
and language, 7:408–409
in metaphysics, 7:329–330
miracles and, 6:266–270
modern, research in, 8:682–683
Mozi on, 6:417
naturalism as, *vs.* metaphysics, 6:501
of neuropsychology, 6:568
philosophical, 7:329–331
pragmatism as, 7:748
Reimarus on, 8:330–331
religion and science and, 8:398
scientific, 3:594–595
Shoemaker on, 9:15
and social sciences, 7:535–536
vs. technique, 1:407
theoretical, 7:331
See also Scientific method
Methods of Ethics (Sidgwick), 2:358, 3:416–418, 4:614
common sense in, 9:22
on pleasure as desired mental state, 8:721
Methodus Inveniendi Argumenta (Geulincx), 4:76
Metochites, Theodore, 1:788
Metric system, 6:91
Metrical geometry, 9:150
Metrication
of space-time, in general relativity, 9:496
of time, 9:476–477, 9:494–495
Metrodorus of Chios, skepticism of, 1:192
Metrodorus of Lampsacus, Epicurus and, 3:263–264
Metropolita Ilarion, 5:59
Mexican logic (Logica mexicana) (Rubio), 5:204
Mexican philosophy
colonial period, 5:204–205
contemporary, 5:207–211
independentist period, 5:205
positivism in, 5:206–207
Vasconcelos in, 9:648–649
Mexico, in Spengler's cultural morphology, 9:167
Meyer, Gertrud, 4:800
Meyer, Lodewijk, 9:170, 9:175
Meyer, Robert, 5:491
Meyers, Diana, 3:586–588
Meyerson, Émile, **6:212–214**
Meyronnes, Francis, Duns Scotus and, 8:704
Miaphysitism, 7:313
Michael of Cesena, and apostolic poverty, 9:770
Michael Scot. *See* Scot, Michael
Michell, John
on black holes, 1:607
Priestley and, 8:7
Michels, Robert, on democracy, 2:702
Michelson-Morley experiment, 3:165, 9:149
Michotte, André, 2:107
Microallocation, 6:96–97
Microcanonical ensemble, method of, 7:538
Microcosm. *See* Macrocosm and microcosm
Microcosmus (Lotze), 7:83
Micrographia (Hooke), 7:558
Microphysical events, mental causation and, 6:134–136
Microstates, in statistical thermodynamics, 9:468–469
Middle Ages
aesthetics in, 1:46–48
challenges to Christianity in, 2:644
concept of state in, 9:204
definition in, 2:669
dialectic in, 3:54
education in, 3:134, 7:367–369
emanationism in, 3:189
and eternity, 3:358
friars in, education of, 3:134
humanism in, 4:477–478
and infinity, 4:668–671
Jewish philosophy in, 4:811–821
logic in, 3:54
love in, 5:586–587
metaphysics in, 6:188–189
natural law in, 7:421
optimism/pessimism in, 7:247
pantheism in, 7:95
philosophy of law in, 7:420–422
Platonism in, 7:609–612
Savigny on, 8:614
semantics in, 8:759–771
skepticism in, 9:50

Middle Ages, ***continued***
social egalitarianism in, 3:329
sovereign authority in, 9:139
in Spengler's cultural morphology, 9:166
and substance, 9:296
and suicide, 9:319–321
traditional logic and, 5:493
and war and peace, 7:152–154
Middle class, Marx's conception of, 2:362
Middle knowledge, 6:321
Middle Platonism, 1:227, 6:546
Celsus and, 2:118–119
Clement and, 2:289
Middle term, in syllogism, definition of, 5:548
Middlemarch (Eliot), 3:184
Middleton, Conyers, 2:686, **6:214–215**
Middleton, Richard of. *See* Richard of Mediavilla
Middle-Way school, of Buddhism, 1:731–735, 2:154
Midrash Rabbah (Menasseh ben Israel), 6:128
Midrashim, 4:811
Mie, Gustav, on electromagnetic theory, 3:235–236
Mifologiia grekov i rimlian (The mythology of the Greeks and Romans) (Losev), 5:575
Mikhailov, M. L., and Kropotkin, 5:153
Mikhailovskii, Nikolai Konstantinovich, **6:215–216**
Kareev and, 5:40
Lenin and, 5:280
on negation of negation, 3:62–63
Miki Kiyoshi, **6:216–217**, 6:624
Mikrokosmus (Lotze), 5:582, 7:234
Milesian school
Anaximenes in, 1:185
philosophers of, 7:759–761
Miletus, School of. *See* Pre-Socratic Philosophy
Milhamot Adonai (The war of the Lord) (Gersonides), 4:68, 4:821, 5:653
Milhaud, Gaston, **6:217**
Militaire philosophe, Le (clandestine tract), 2:267
Militaire philosophe, or Difficultés sur la religion proposées au P. Malebranche, Le (Naigeon), 6:476
Militarism
history of, 7:153–154
Machiavelli and, 5:626–627
sexism inextricable from, 4:874
Military science, 9:859
Military service, as legal obligation, 7:445
Military societies, as impoverished, violent, and "rude," 3:605
Militia(s), as paradigmatic egalitarian, socially activist institution, 3:605
Mill, James, **6:218–220**
Bentham and, 1:555
Condillac and, 8:826
on government, 2:702–703
Martineau and, 5:726
on perception, 3:312, 8:815
on pleasure and pain, 7:621
positivism of, 7:712
and psychology, 8:136
on sensations, 8:823, 8:826
utilitarianism and, 3:412
on war and peace, 7:155
Mill, John Stuart, 3:721, **6:220–234**
on altruism and self-interest, 3:173–174
Anderson (John) and, 1:199
and animal rights, 1:208, 3:392
on art, 7:546–547
on attributes, 5:494
Bain and, 1:462
Balfour on, 1:474
on belief
behavioral effects of, 5:98
without instinctive knowledge, 2:346
Bentham and, 8:792
on Brown (T.), 8:136
Buckle on, 1:717–721
Carlyle and, 2:33
on causal inference, 8:685–686
causality definition, 2:103
on causation, 3:124
on cause and effect, 4:636–637
on Coleridge, 2:316, 2:320
on common consent arguments for God's existence, 2:344
common sense and, 2:357
on Comte, 2:413
Condillac and, 8:826
on connotation-denotation distinction, 8:796, 8:803, 9:287
as consequentialist, 2:460
on definition, 2:665, 2:672
Demiurge and, 2:699
on design argument, 1:368
on determinism, 3:15–16
Durkheim and, 3:151
on duty, 3:155
on education, 7:377
education of, 6:218, 6:221, 8:614
as empiricist, 3:214, 3:219
Epicurus and, 3:265
epistemology and, 3:312, 5:91
on ethical treatment of animals, 3:392
and ethics, 3:413–414
on evil, 3:470, 3:471
on experience, 7:713
on externalism, 4:714
Frege on, 3:729
Geisteswissenschaften, origin of, 4:37
on God, 1:93, 1:359
on government, 2:702
on happiness, 7:378
on hedonism, 4:152, 9:382
on heteropathic laws, 3:191
on human nature, 6:521, 7:377
on ideal utilitarianism, 9:604
on induction, 4:641, 5:82, 6:224, **6:237–248**
Varona and, 9:648
Venn and, 9:658
Keynes and, 5:56
on knowledge, 7:392
on knowledge from deduction, 5:513
Laas on, 5:163
on language, 8:795–797
on laws of thought, 5:233
on liberty, 9:510
life of, 6:220–222
on limit to state action, 9:209
logic of, 5:456
MacIntyre on, 5:636
on Mansel, 5:688
Moore and, 3:419
on moral community, 2:518
on names, 5:548, 8:58, 8:62–63
on nationalism, 6:483
on natural law, 6:512
on nature, 6:520–521
Nishi and, 6:623
Nussbaum and, 6:680
on paternalism, 7:137
on perception, 3:312, 8:815
on phenomenalism, 7:272–273
philosophy of sex and, 7:522
physicotheology and, 7:561
on pleasure, 1:339
political philosophy of, 7:667
positivism of, 7:712–713
principle monism and, 3:440
on projection, 4:156
on property, 8:69–70
and psychology, 8:136
and radical empiricism, 5:82–83
on religion, 7:713
on rewards and punishments, 4:614

on science, 2:106, 7:546–547
on self-determination, 2:702
on sexual consent, 7:529
Sidgwick and, 9:25
on sight as muscular sense, 1:463
Stephen and, 9:243
on syllogisms, 5:501–502
on toleration, 9:510
and utilitarianism, 3:382–383, 6:222, 6:227, 6:232–233, 7:459–460, 9:382, 9:603–606
Venn and, 9:657–658
on virtue, 3:413–414
on war and peace, 7:155
on well-being, 8:722
Whewell and, 9:744
on women's liberation, 9:75
Mill Newsletter, The, 6:232
Mill on the Floss, The (Eliot), 3:184
Millenarianism, 3:348
Miller, Arthur, Prior and, 8:13
Miller, David
on justice, 2:568
on moral cosmopolitanism, 2:568
on probability coordination, 8:38
Miller, Dickinson S., **6:234–235**
Miller, George, 8:150
Miller, J. Hillis, and deconstruction, 2:661
Miller, Mara, on environmental aesthetics, 3:257
Miller, Stanley, on origin of life, 5:360
Millet Seed paradox, 9:877
Millian theory of names, 8:58, 8:62–63
Millianism, 8:6–7, 8:76–77
Millikan, Ruth Garrett, **6:235–237**
on biological teleology, 9:389
in ethnology, 1:202
on property naturalism, 6:498
on rule following, 8:532–533
on teleosemantics, 4:711
Milne, Edward Arthur, on cosmology, 2:558, 2:562, 2:566
Milton, John, 1:304, **6:248–251**
Mīmāṃsa, 5:122, 6:530
self in, 8:719
sentences in, 7:416
Mīmāṃsa realism, universals in, 9:582
Mīmāṃsakas
analogy accepted by, 5:121–122
on senses, 5:118
Mīmāṃsā-sūtra (Jaimini), 5:414
Mimesis, 4:599, **6:252–253,** 9:632–633
See also Imitation
Mimesis as Make-Believe (Walton), 1:68
Mimetic art forms, 5:44
Mimimalization, 2:376–378
Minagawa Kien, **6:253**
Minar, Edward, 8:533
Mind, 1:750–751
absolute, 4:269
and act of knowing, 1:753
Alexander on, 1:108
alienation of, 1:120–121
Anaxagoras on, 1:182–183, 3:211
animal, **1:200–208**
Aristotle on, 7:489
Arnauld on, 2:58
in associationism, 1:563–564
in atomism, 6:60
Augustine on, 1:392–395
Bacon (Francis) on, 1:445–446
Bain on, 1:462
Bergson on, 1:565–566
Berkeley on, 1:580, 1:584–587
Bernard of Tours on, 1:592
and body, 4:615, 5:22
Bolzano on, 1:647
Bradley on, 1:678–679
brain and, 1:286–287, 6:260
in Buddhism, 1:724, 2:166, **6:253–258**
Cabanis on, 2:2
Calvin on, 2:10
as capacities, 2:726–727, 2:741, 6:132
causality in, 7:468
central state materialism of, 9:65
in Chan (Zen) Buddhism, 2:166–167
Charron on, 2:135
in Chinese thought, 2:168
in cognitive science, 2:296–301
Coleridge on, 2:316, 2:318
Collingwood on, 2:326–328, 2:328
common sense and, 2:358
computationalism and, 2:390–394
Comte on, 2:411
concepts and, 2:414
Condillac on, 2:421
in Confucianism, 2:173
in connectionism, 2:393, 2:444
and consciousness, 1:564–565, 1:704
construction of, 8:542–543
Cousin on, 2:579
creative freedom of, 1:714
Creighton on, 2:592
in critical realism, 2:596
Cudworth on, 2:610
Davidson (Donald) on, 2:646–649
Descartes on, 1:201, 2:56, 2:57, 2:726–727, 2:741, 3:293, 6:138, 8:123–124
Diderot on, 3:72
Diongenes of Apollonia on, 7:764
Dostoevsky on, 3:99
Dretske on, 3:108–109
Ducasse on, 3:124–125
Dühring on, 3:130–131
Eddington on, 3:165
Edwards (Jonathan) on, 3:167–168
as emergent, 1:108
Emerson on, 3:196
Engels on, 3:58
Epicurus on, 3:269
existential psychoanalysis on, 3:512
expressive range of speech and, 2:209
Fechner on, 8:139
feminists on, 5:373–374
Foucher on, 2:57
freedom of, 4:259–260, 4:263
in functionalism, 6:14
Garrigou-Lagrange on, 4:23
Geulincx on, 4:77–78
God and, 1:453, 1:580–581, 2:58
Goldman on, 4:147
Grosseteste on, 4:186
Hegel on, 4:259–260, 4:264–269, 4:280, 4:283, 4:558
Hélvetius on, 4:306–307
Herder on, 4:330–331
Holbach on, 6:10–11
Hume on, 4:499, 8:132
in idealism, 4:560–561
ideas in, 1:653
identity theory of, 7:470, 7:553, 8:155
entity education in, 6:172
monism and, 6:326
propositional attitudes and, 8:84
qualia and, 8:191–192
illative sense in theory of, 6:578–579
and images, 4:592–593
imagination and, 4:600
imperfect identity of, 4:499
independent existence of, as impossible, 1:578
and intentionality, 1:689
and intuition, 1:704
in Iqbal's theistic pluralism, 4:745
as irreducible to machine, 1:649
James on, 4:778–779
Johnson (Samuel) on, 4:851
Kant on, 5:22, 5:709, 8:133–134
La Mettrie on, 5:179, 5:180
Laromiguière on, 5:201
Le Roy on, 5:288
Leibniz on, 2:553, 5:251, 5:258–262, 5:267–268, 8:128–129

Mind, *continued*
Lewis (D.) on, 5:314–315
location of, 6:259, 9:248
Locke on, 5:378, 8:129–130
Lu Xiangshan on, 5:618
in Mādhyamika doctrine, 1:740–744
Marcus Aurelius on, 5:706
Maréchal on, 5:708
Maritain on, 5:713
and matter, 2:358, 3:703, 8:657
mechanical theory of, 8:127
memory in, 6:124
and mental state attribution, "theory-theory" of, 4:148
Mill (John Stuart) on, 6:226
Morgan (C. Lloyd) on, 6:403
Mou on, 2:183
in neo-Confucianism, 2:157–160, 2:183, 4:795
neuroscience and, 6:569–570
Newman on, 6:578–579
objective, 4:267–269
and objects of vision, 1:576
Oken on, 7:11
panpsychism and, 9:188
Peckham on, 7:162
Peirce on, 7:164, 7:173
philosophy of, **7:467–473**
in Bacon (Francis), 1:445–446
behavior and, 7:317
Chinese, 2:208–210
cognitive science and, 2:300
Collingwood on, 2:328
computationalism and, 2:391
concepts and, 2:414
content externalism in, 7:472
definition of, 7:327
determinism and, 3:24–25
epistemology and, 3:276, 8:130–131
functionalism in, 7:471, 8:85, 8:155–156, 9:16
of Hegel, 4:259–260, 4:267–269
intentionality in, 7:471–472
introspection in, 4:720–722
of Kant, 5:34
Kim's work in, 5:71
materialism and, 6:11–12
mental content and, 2:478
mental-physical distinction in, 6:138
of Millikan, 6:236
mind-body problem in, 7:468. *See also* Mind-body problem; Mind-body relationship
myth of the given in, 8:733–734
on object-directedness, 4:712
of Olivi, 7:13
physical domain closed causality and, 2:89–93
propositional attitudes in, **8:79–86**
scope of, 7:467–468
in Shoemaker, 9:15
in Spinoza's panpsychism, 9:188
Stewart on, 9:248
Stout on, 9:259
supervenience in, 7:471
of Wollheim, 9:836
physical basis of
Nagel (Ernest) on, 6:473
Nagel (Thomas) on, 6:475
Turing on, 9:552–553
physiologist study of, 1:462
Plato on, 7:556
Plotinus on, 5:569, 6:187
preparation to know external things, 2:216
psychological modules in, 3:482–485
psychological processes of, 1:544
qualities in, 1:578–579
quantum mechanics and, 9:553
and radical behaviorism, 1:520
and reality, 1:671–672
reflexivity and, 6:81
representational theory of, 2:391–392, 6:124
as revealed in history, 1:713
Rohault on, 8:483
Russell on, 8:542–543
Santayana on, 8:597
Searle on, 8:705–706
in shaping sensory material, 8:650
Shelley on, 9:9
species and genera in, 1:627
in speech and ideas, 2:208–210
Spinoza on, 3:294, 4:602, 8:125–126
in Stoicism, 5:706
Stout on, 2:358
subjective, 4:267
as substance, 7:468–469
tabula rasa theory of, 8:129–130
Taine on, 9:365
temporal properties of, 6:259
Tetens on, 9:404
theory of
innate ideas in, 4:694
introspection in, 4:721
subjectivity in naturalistic framework of, 9:291–292
Vaihinger on, 9:627–628
time as, 1:109–110
Titchener on, 8:147
Turing on, 9:552
and unconscious ideas, 1:544
Vasubandhu on, 1:751–752
Wang Yang-ming on, 9:726
Woodbridge on, 9:842
Xunzi on, 2:216
in Yogācāra Buddhism, 1:746–749
See also Idealism; Mind-body problem; Nous; Other minds; Personal identity; Psychology; Reason; Thinking
"Mind, The" (Edwards), 3:166–168
Mind (journal), 9:236, 9:258
Mind! (Schiller, Ferdinand), 8:625
Mind; A Quarterly Review of Psychology and Philosophy, 1:462
"Mind and Behavior" (Shoemaker), 9:15
Mind and Its Place in Nature, The (Broad), 3:192, 6:15, 7:469
Mind and Matter (Schrödinger), 8:657
Mind and Matter (Stout), 2:358
Mind and Morals (Russell), 7:522
Mind and World (McDowell), 4:287, 6:74
"Mind, Brains, and Programs" (Searle), 2:395
Mind Doesn't Work That Way, The (Fodor), 3:485
Mind in a Physical World (Kim), 5:71
Mind independence, objectivity as, 7:4
Mind, Self, and Society (Mead), 9:77
Mind-body problem, **6:258–265,** 7:468
Augustine on, 6:258
and brain, 7:468
Broad on, 6:261
causality in, 6:258
computation and, 5:632
in contemporary philosophy, 3:12
Cordemoy on, 2:59
Descartes on, 2:537, 2:595, 2:720, 2:731, 2:737–738, 2:748–753, 3:12, 3:293, 6:138, 6:258, 8:124–125, 9:187
Desgabets on, 2:757–758
determinism and, 3:24–25
in dualism, 7:468
eliminativism on, 6:262
Elisabeth, princess of Bohemia, on, 3:188
Encyclopédie on, 3:224
in epiphenomenalism, 7:469
Fechner on, 8:139
Geulincx on, 2:59, 3:293, 4:77, 4:80
God in, 6:258–259
Hobbes on, 8:127

Hume on, 8:133
in idealism, 7:468
importance of, 7:467–468
intentionality in, 6:262–264
Leibniz on, 5:275–276
Locke on, 3:13
Malebranche on, 2:57–59, 2:757, 3:293, 5:667–668, 6:258–259
many minds formulation and, 5:699
Marx on, 3:56–57
in materialism, 7:468–469
mental causation in, 6:260
Montague (William) on, 6:331–332
Montgomery on, 6:340
nature in, 6:262
Ostwald on, 7:50
parallelism in, 6:258–259
Paulsen on, 7:149
perceptual consciousness and, 7:183, 7:186
in phenomenalism, 7:468
physics in, 6:261–262
propositional attitudes in, 6:262–263
psychophysical dispositions, 9:260
qualia in, 6:263
reason in, 6:262
Régis on, 8:299–301
Reich on, 8:309–310
Ryle on, 1:154, 8:581–582
scholasticism on, 2:750
self-consciousness in, 6:262
Sellars on, 8:733
solutions to, 3:756
Spinoza on, 8:125–126, 9:187
Strawson on, 9:265
subjectivity in, 9:292
supervenience in, 5:72, 6:263–264
Vasquez on, 9:650
See also Mind-body relationship

Mind-body relationship
Bergson on, 1:564
Berkeley on, 1:585
Blake on, 1:610
Bodin on, 1:622
Bosanquet on, 1:663
Cabanis on, 2:2
Carroll on, 2:51
Clarke on, 2:273
Clauberg's occasionalism and, 2:55
Collingwood on, 2:328
Condillac on, 2:421
in Confucianism, 2:173
and conservation of motion and energy, 2:90
Conway on, 2:529
Cordemoy on, 2:59
Descartes on, 2:54, 2:537, 8:124–125
eucharistic theology and, 2:60
La Forge on, 2:58–59
Leibniz on, 5:275–276
Malebranche on, 2:57–59, 2:757, 3:293, 5:667–668, 6:258–259
mental *vs.* brain events in, 1:697
personhood and, 1:464
physical causality and, 2:90
pineal gland and, 1:658
preestablished harmony and, 1:494
psychogenic factor in, 1:697
reincarnation and, 8:332–333
Ryle on, 1:154
sense data as private objects in, 1:697
special sciences and, 9:161
Spinoza on, 8:125–126, 9:187
time in, 1:565
See also Mind-body problem

Mind-Brain Continuum, The (Charland & Llinás), 6:567
Mind-brain duality, parapsychology and, 7:114
Mind-dependence, 6:173, 6:176, 7:4–5
Mindfulness, in Buddhism, 1:722, 6:255
Mind-independence
in constructivism, 2:475
conventionalism and, 2:474
in Moore's theory of truth, 2:547
Mind-matter dualism
Cordemoy on, 2:538
critical realism and, 2:597
Mindreading, 2:241, 9:36–39
Minds, other, **7:51–59,** 7:468
Berkeley on, 1:580, 1:586–587
Chinese room argument and, 2:241
critical realism on, 2:596
Cyrenaics teaching and, 2:619
Davidson (Donald) on, 2:646–648
existence of, 5:687–688
Lipps on, 5:363
in logical behaviorism, 7:469
problem of, 7:468
Wisdom (John) on, 9:798–799
Mind's I, The (Dennett and Hofstadter), 2:711
Mind-talk, presuppositions of, 6:171
Ming dynasty, neo-Confucianism in, 2:622
Ming-shi, on name reality, 2:202
"Ming-Shi-Lun" ("On name and actuality") (Gongsun Long), 2:204
Minima theory, Aristotelian, 1:385–387
Minimal fixed point, obtaining, 5:149
Minimal sufficient statistic, 3:662
Minimal theory of reference, 8:290
Minimal-change semantics, 3:710
Minimalism
goal-oriented behavior in, 7:735–736
Kotarbiński and, 5:143
Minimax theorem, 6:559
Minjung theology, 5:331–333
Minkowski, Herman
Dingler and, 3:85
on phenomenology, 7:301
on relativity of simultaneity, 9:150
Minkowski space-time, 2:524, 7:476, 9:464, 9:484
Minor premise, in syllogism, definition of, 5:548
Minor term, in syllogism, definition of, 5:548
Minority culture
Eliot (T. S.) on, 3:186
Mosca on, 6:407
Minority races, oppression of, 3:756
Mints, Grigori, in proof theory, 8:56
Minucius Felix, as apologism, 1:228
Minxent, 4:672
Mirabaud, Jean-Baptise de, 2:266
Miracle(s), **6:265–276**
Annet on, 1:210
in Avicenna's theory of knowledge, 4:758
belief in, 6:273–274
in Buddhism, 6:255
Bultmann on, 1:762
Clarke on, 2:271
evidence of, 6:269–270, 6:275–276
Galen on, 4:6
Gersonides on, 4:69
Gibbon on, 4:85
Hirsch (Samuel) on, 4:827
Hume on, 7:76
Huxley on, 4:533
Ibn Caspi on, 4:809
identifying, 6:268–269
Lewis (C. S.) on, 5:312
Lipsius on, 5:364
Maimonides on, 4:818
materialism and, 6:14
Meslier on, 6:154
Middleton on, 6:214–215
Mill (John Stuart) on, 6:230–231
as natural, 6:492
nature *vs.*, 1:398
Paley on, 7:76–77
Philo on, 7:304
probability of, in natural law, 1:783
proving, 6:269–270

Miracle(s), ***continued***
- as revelation, 8:453
- Spinoza on, 9:175
- Stokes (G.) on, 7:562
- as suspended secondary causes, 4:109
- use of term, 6:265
- Wolff on, 9:828
- Woolston on, 9:845

Miracle of Theism, The (Mackie), 5:638
Miracles (Lewis), 5:311
Mirandola, Count Giovanni Pico Della. *See* Pico Della Mirandola, Count Giovanni
Mirari Vos (papal encyclical), 5:177
Mirimanoff, Dimitry, 8:837
Mirimanoff's paradox, in set theory, 5:517, 5:520
Miró Quesada, Francisco
- analytic philosophy and, 5:210
- on generation of forgers, 5:209
- *mestizo* consciousness and, 5:210

Mirosozertsaine V. S. Solov'eva (V. S. Solov'ev's world view) (Trubetskoi), 9:529
Mirror stage, Lacan on, 5:168
Miscellaneous Works (Gibbon), 4:84
Misch, Georg, 3:638
Mischief of Separation, The (Stillingfleet), 9:249
Mises, Dr. *See* Fechner, Gustav Theodor
Mises, Richard von
- Lichtenberg and, 5:339
- in probability theory, 8:32

Mishnah (codified Jewish oral law)
- Maimonides and, 5:647
- popular philosophy in, 4:810–811

Misinformation, in moral constructivism, 2:472
Miskawayh, Arkoun and, 1:284
Mislocation, of observations, 3:546
Misner, Charles W., on cosmology, 2:566
Misobservation, 3:546
Misogyny, 3:594
Misperception(s), 7:184–189
- personal identity and, 7:223
- phenomenalism and, 7:274
- of reality, McTaggart on, 6:77
- sense-data theory and, 7:190

Mission, Ortega y Gasset on, 7:46
Mistake(s)
- category
  - Aristotle on, 2:73–74
  - Kant on, 2:75
- Malcolm on, 2:359
- noninferential justification and, 2:278

"Mistaken Subtlety of the Four Syllogistic Figures, The" (Peirce), 7:164
Misura in psicologia sperimentale (Aliotta), 1:127
Mitcham, Carl, on technology, 7:543, 7:549
Mitchell, Basil, on standards of validity, 3:321
Mitchell, Lucy Sprague, 3:567
Mitchell, O. H., Peirce and, 5:454, 7:168
Mitchell, O. M., 7:562
Mithraism
- eschatology in, 3:347
- Zoroastrianism and, 9:887

Mitigated skepticism, 4:26–27, 4:30
- Mersenne on, 6:153
- Sanches on, 9:52

Mitmenschlichen Begegungen in der Milieuwelt, Die (Gurwitsch), 4:197
Mitsein, Heidegger on, 3:717
Mittelstrass, J., on phenomenology, 7:300
Mitzvot (religious commandments), Ibn Ezra's emphasis on, 5:4
Miura Baien, **6:276–277**
Mixed modes, Locke on, 5:383
Mixed Opinions and Maxims (Nietzsche), 6:611
Mixed strategy, in act utilitarianism, 9:608–609
Mixed syllogisms, definition of, 5:557
Mixtum, problem of, 4:90
Mixture, universal, Anaxagoras on, 1:181–182
Mladenchestvo (Infancy) (Ivanov), 4:767
MLE (maximum likelihood estimate), 3:661
- as invariant, 3:661
- justification of, 3:662
- large-sample properties of, 3:662
- as most concentrated, 3:662
- as unequivocally superior, 3:662

Mme. de Staël, Anne Louise Germaine Necker, Baronne de. *See* Staël-Holstein, Anne Louise Germaine Necker, Baronne de
M'Naghten rules, 8:163
Mnemonic terms, 5:548–549
Mo Di, on knower-known *vs.* wisdom as capacity, 2:215–216
Mo Tzu. *See* Mozi
Mob psychology. *See* Psychology
Möbius strip, locality in, 6:639
Modal arguments
- for dualism, 3:118–119
- in supervenience, 9:327

Modal categories, Abbagnano on, 1:2
Modal Cleanthes, 6:147
"Modal Fictionalism" (Rosen), 3:627
Modal interpretation of quantum mechanics, **6:277–280**, 8:213
Modal logic, 5:486, 5:704, **6:292–301**, 8:740
- Abelard on, 5:425
- Aristotle on, 5:401
- Chrysippus and, 5:405
- definition of, 5:549
- essentialism in, 5:704
- extensions of, 6:299–300
- in game theory, 4:19–20
- history of, 6:291
- interpretations of, 6:296–299
- intuitionistic logic translated into, 4:739
- Kripke and, 5:149, 8:739
- Lewis (C. I.) and, 5:307, 5:483
- Marcus and, 5:704–705
- and modern classical logic, 5:485
- Peirce on, 5:455
- possible worlds and, 5:486, 6:283–284, 8:807
- propositions in, 8:740–741
- quantified, 6:289–291
- semantics of, 5:486, 6:292–296, 8:807
- syntax of, 6:292
- Tarski on, 9:370
- Theophrastus on, 9:411
- von Wright and, 9:847–848

Modal theory
- Duns Scotus and, 3:145–146
- Eudemus on, 5:401–402
- Theophrastus on, 5:401–402

Modalism, fictionalism and, 6:286–287
Modalité de jugement, La (Brunschvicg), 1:714
Modality(ies)
- Aristotle on, 5:608
- Chrysippus and, 5:405
- definition of, 5:549
- Diodorus on, 5:403–404
- in epistemological discussions, 5:100
- and language, 4:568, **10:20–27**
- Lewis (D.) on, 5:313–314
- Łukasiewicz on, 5:608
- Marcus on, 5:704–705
- in medieval logic, 5:435
- mereology and, 6:147
- metaphysics and, 6:199, 6:287–288
- in naturalism, 6:494–495
- Philo of Megara on, 5:403–404

philosophy and metaphysics of, **6:280–289**, 9:327
Plantinga on, 7:580
and quantification, **6:289–291**
supervenience and, 9:327–328
Van Fraassen on, 9:645
Modality *cum dito,* 5:549
Modal-reliability approach, to *a priori* knowledge, 3:273–274
Mode(s)
Agrippan, 1:196
of being, Peter Aureol on, 7:257–258
of causal efficacy, perception in, 9:750
Locke on, 5:381–383
terminology of, 3:681
of thinking, Locke on, 5:382
Model(s)
of axiomatic theory, 6:22–23
and causal modeling, 2:108
and chaos model simplicity, 2:131–134
in chemistry, 2:143
in Chinese science, 2:217–218
in Confucian ethics, 2:196
construction of, 3:654–656
definition of, 5:549
of economic behavior and ethics, 1:777
game theory, in business ethics, 1:778
in Huayan Buddhism, 1:738–739
vs. logic, 8:154
measurement as, 6:87
of molecular ontological status, 2:140–141
phenomenological foundations for, 2:62
in physics, discarded, 4:804
Ramus's use of, 8:237
of religious language, 8:418
of theory, 3:650–651
unity in science and, 9:579–580
"Model of Rules, The" (Dworkin), 5:241
Model theory, **6:301–315**
back-and-forth system in, 6:306–308
compactness theorem in, 6:308–309
definability in, 6:310–313
elementary embeddings in, 6:309–310
elimination of quantifiers in, 6:305–306
enlargements in, 4:653
first-order, 6:302–305
geometric, 6:314–315
interpolation in, 6:310–313
large cardinals and, 8:844–847
logical terms and, 5:531
for nonclassical logic, 5:474
Robinson diagram method and, 5:481
in semantic view of theories, 9:334, 9:416
set theory and, 8:840–843, 9:271
and stability, 6:314–315
substructures in, 6:309–310
Tarski and, 5:479–484, 8:841, 9:367–369
and theory of infinitesimals, 4:653
thought experiments in, 9:455
ultrafilters in, 8:842
Modeling
in cognitive science, 2:298
of human behavior, 8:612
in Toynbee's historical work, 9:517–518
Moderation
Aquinas and, 9:425
in Confucianism, 2:150–151
Moderator between an Infidel and an Apostate, The (Woolston), 9:845
Modern Atheism (Étienne), 1:369
Modern Introduction to Logic, A (Stebbing), 9:236
Modern Introduction to Metaphysics, A (Drennan), 1:530
Modern Introduction to Philosophy (Edwards and Pap), 2:348
Modern Man in Search of Soul (Jung), 2:345
Modern Materialism and Its Relation to Religion and Theology (Martineau), 1:369
"Modern Moral Philosophy" (Anscombe), 1:213, 2:460
Modern Science and Anarchism (Kropotkin), 5:154
Modern society
Eliot (T. S.) on, 3:186
Habermas on, 4:200
Modern Times (journal), 8:603
Modern way
Biel on, 1:594
Ockhamism and, 7:8–9
Moderne Kapitalismus, Der (Sombart), 9:127
Modernism, **6:316–319**
in legal philosophy, 7:460–461
Loisy and, 5:570–571
Pius X on, 5:571
Modernity
alienation in, art and, 8:629
Aristotelianism in, 1:261–262
Barth on, 1:480
Benjamin on, 1:545–546
Cavell on, 2:116
Hegel on, 4:280
Islamic debate on, 4:764
Islamic Enlightenment and, 3:249
vs. tradition, Nasr on, 6:480
Modernization, 4:280
Moderns, Fontenelle on, 3:682
Modes of Thought (Whitehead), 9:749–750
Modest Defence of Publick Stews, A (Mandeville), 7:522
Modest Proposal, A (Swift), 9:340
Modism, in medieval logic, 5:432–433
Modisti, 5:432
Modularity
in evolutionary psychology, 3:482–485
of perception and linguistic processing, 3:675
Modulation, lexical, 7:740
Modules, psychological, 3:482–483
Modus ponendo tollens, 5:549
Modus ponens, 3:653, 5:549
distortion of, 3:537
forerunners of, 5:402
Frege on, 3:726
Gentzen on, 5:475
in Indian philosophy, 5:411
Peano on, 5:463
Modus tollendo ponens, 5:549
Modus tollens, 5:549
distortion of, 3:537–538
forerunners of, 5:402
in Indian philosophy, 5:411
probabilistic form of, 3:666
Moebius, August, 4:60
Mohanty, Chandra, 3:602, 7:299
Mohism, 2:197, 2:238, 6:417
and Daoism, 2:185–187
reasoning patterns in, 2:212–213
Mohr, Friedrich, on energy, 3:229
Moine, Alphonse Le, Nicole and, 6:603
Moira/Tychē/Anankē, **6:319**
Moism, 5:414–416
"Moist Canons," 5:415
Mokṣākaras Gupta, 4:634
Molecular cognition, 6:567–569
Molecular genetics, 9:579
Molecular intervention techniques, 6:570–571
Molecular proposition, definition of, 5:553
Molecular structure, Pauling on, 7:146

Molecule(s)
- in chemistry, 2:140–141
- as nonuniform object, 9:749
- quantum mechanics and, 2:143
- in temperature, 6:87

Moleschott, Jacob, 6:11, **6:319–321**

Molière
- on art, 1:49
- Diderot and, 3:77
- Fénelon on, 3:603
- La Mothe Le Vayer and, 5:181–182

Molina, Luis de, **6:321–323**
- on divine foreknowledge, 4:114–115, 7:479, 9:284
- on free will in workings of grace, 4:788–789

Molina Garmendia, Enrique, 5:207, **6:323–324**

Molinism, 4:114–115, 8:680–682

Moller, Poul Martin, and Kierkegaard, 5:67

Molyneaux, William, 1:575, 2:421

"Molyneaux's Question" (Evans), 3:462

Momentary, everything as, 5:120

Momentum, 2:462–464, 3:228

Monad(s) and monadology, 5:146, **6:324–326**
- appearance and, 1:232
- apperception in, 3:298
- appetition in, 3:297
- Bruno and, 1:712
- cause-following, 6:72
- definition of, 6:324
- and dyad, 7:607
  - in medieval Platonic thought, 7:612
  - in Pythagoras's principle of infinity, 4:668
- Genovesi and, 4:49
- goal-seeking, 6:72
- Leibniz on, 3:296–298, 4:141, 4:554, 5:260, 5:276–277. *See also* *Monadology* (Leibniz)
- life, karma and, 5:42
- logical pluralism in, 6:184
- Lopatin on, 5:572
- Lotman and, 5:579
- mass in, 6:3
- Maupertuis and, 6:66–67
- in McDougall's personality theory, 6:72
- metaphysics and, 6:202
- perception in, 3:297
- as perspectives, 8:129–130
- in relational theory of space, 9:147
- self-consciousness in, 3:298
- as spiritual substance, 7:642
- subject-predicate in, 9:288–289
- substance and, 8:129, 9:297
- Wolff and, 9:826–828

Monadism, Lotze and, 5:582

Monadology (Leibniz), 2:551, 5:254–255, 5:270
- on body-soul union, 5:277
- on causation, 5:266
- on God, 5:256, 5:259
- on identity of discernibles, 5:258
- metaphysical methods in, 6:169
- on mind, 5:258–259, 5:262
- on plenitude, 5:258
- on soul, 5:260
- on substance, 5:276–277, 8:128–129, 9:297
- on sympathy, 5:257
- on truth, 5:274

Monadology (Nicholas of Cusa), 6:596

Monarchia Messiae (The Messiah's Monarchy) (Campanella), 2:16

Monarchism
- Bodin on, 1:620–621
- Chateaubriand on, 2:137
- papal, in Campanella, 2:16
- as social tradition, 1:648
- and sovereign autonomy, 1:621
- *See also* Monarchy

Monarchomachi, 9:81

Monarchy
- absolute, by divine choice, 1:667
- Dante on, 2:625
- Dong Zhongshu on, 3:98
- Dostoevsky on, 3:100
- as personification of public weal, 1:621
- as social tradition, 1:648
- Vitoria on, 9:698
- *See also* Monarchism

Monasticism/monastic practices
- in Buddhism, 1:723
- in Chan (Zen) Buddhism, meditation in, 1:727–728
- Dge-lugs scholastic training and, 1:734–735
- mysticism of, 6:447
- Vasubandhu on, 1:751–752
- in Yogācāra Buddhism, 1:751–752
- Zen awakening of self as, 1:728–729

Monde, ou Traité de la lumière (The World, or Treatise on Light) (Descartes). *See World, The* (Descartes)

Money
- action as, 1:14
- Jevons on, 4:807
- and power, 3:564, 7:732

Money and the Mechanism of Exchange (Jevons), 4:807

Money, Sex, and Power (Hartsock), 3:564

Monism, **6:326–329**
- Anaximander and, 1:249
- Anaximenes and, 1:249
- anomalous, **1:211–212,** 7:555
  - Davidson (Donald) on, 1:211, 2:646–648
  - on determinism, 3:24
  - Kim on, 2:648
  - mental causation and, 6:133
  - in philosophy of mind, 7:470–471
- Aristotle and, 4:610
- Carus on, 2:64
- David of Dinant and, 2:645
- Diderot and, 9:193
- Diogenes of Apollonia and, 3:89
- on evaluation of political and social institutions, 3:391–392
- Haeckel and, 4:202–204, 7:714
- Heraclitus and, 1:249
- Herder and, 9:194
- in Hinduism, 3:471
- Indian
  - in Advaita school, 4:629
  - personality of God in, 4:111–112
- *vs.* intuitionism, 4:735
- Itō and, 4:765
- James (Henry) and, 4:779
- Jodl (Friedrich) and, 4:835
- Köhler and, 5:132
- Lichtenberg and, 5:341
- Lovejoy on, 5:592
- in Mill's utilitarianism, 4:735
- Moleschott and, 6:320
- of monads, Leibniz's development of, 3:704
- of Mullā Ṣadrā, 4:759
- naturalistic, 4:835
- neutral, 6:587, 7:468, 8:149
- new realism and, 6:586–587
- Ostwald and, 7:50
- Palágyi and, 7:75
- of Parmenides, Zeno of Elea and, 9:871–872
- Paulsen and, 7:148–149
- and possibility of knowledge, 5:117
- and realism, of new realists, 6:75
- Rehmke and, 8:302
- reification of energy and, 3:233
- Russell and, 8:149
- Spinoza and, 3:294, 9:185, 9:193
- Steiner and, 9:241

substantival, 6:326–327
in Śuddhādvaita Vedānta school, 4:630
Taine and, 9:365
Thales and, 1:249
Toland and, 9:506
Treschow and, 9:526
Vasconcelos and, 9:648
Monism and Meliorism (Carus), 2:64
Monist, The, Carus (Paul) and, 2:64
Monistic value theory, 9:639
Monistic vitalism, of Conway, 9:838
Monlorius, on Aristotle, 5:439
Monmouth, Duke of, rebellion by, 5:375
Monoculus. *See* John of Paris
Monologion (Anselm), 1:214–216, 3:136
Monomachos, Constantine, 1:787
Monophychism, of Aquinas, 9:28
Monotechnics, Mumford on, 7:543–544
Monotheism
common consent arguments for God's existence and, 2:348
development of, 2:349–350
Krause on, 5:148
in Platonic tradition, 7:609–610
Stillingfleet on, 9:249
suicide and martyrdom in, 9:320
trinity and, 1:283
Xenophanes of Colophon and, 9:853–854
Monothelitism, free will in, 4:837
Monotonicity, 3:653
for extensive properties, 6:90
in logic, 5:490
in mathematical reasoning, 6:642
Montage, Eisenstein on, 7:381–382
Montague, Richard, **6:329–330**
on algorithmic quantification, 5:509
on compositionality, 2:371
formalism of, 7:405
Frege and, 3:732
on intensional logic, 8:807
on semantic paradoxes, 5:522
on semantics, 1:345, 8:740–743
Tarski and, 1:345
on verbs, 8:742–743
Montague, William Pepperell, 3:313, **6:330–332,** 6:584–585
Montague grammar, 6:329–330
Montaigne, Michel Eyquem de, **6:332–335**
Charron and, 2:134–136
as Christian skeptic, 3:631
on concept of ideas, 4:564
and crisis of skepticism, 9:51–52
De Gournay and, 5:181
deism and, 2:683
Emerson and, 3:195
Epicurus and, 3:265
on epistemology, 9:52
French clandestine writings and, 2:264
Gassendi and, 4:30
La Mothe Le Vayer and, 5:182
Lipsius and, 5:364
Meslier and, 6:154
Nietzsche and, 6:611
Pascal and, 7:133
philosophy of sex and, 7:522
and Pyrrhonian skepticism, 2:725, 2:728–729, 2:746
Montalte, Louis de, 7:131
Montani, on conditionals, 5:428
Montanism
Ballanche and, 9:521
Tertullian and, 9:399
Montesquieu, Baron de (Charles Louis de Secondat), **6:335–339**
Comte and, 2:411–412
on determinism, 3:37
Emerson and, 3:195
Encyclopédie and, 3:223
Engels and, 3:61
and ethics, 3:410
Ferguson and, 3:605
French liberalism and, 5:320
on general will, 4:39
Gibbon and, 4:86
on government, 4:136
Ibn Khaldūn and, 4:549
on law, 5:238, 7:424
Locke and, 5:392
political philosophy of, 7:664–665
social critiques by, 3:247
Montgomery, Edmund Duncan, **6:339–340**
Montmarquet, James, 9:685–686
Monument architecture, 9:693
Mood
Croce's lyrical intuition and, 2:601
definition of, 5:549
vs. emotion, 3:199, 7:468
epistemology of, in Emerson, 6:574
of sentences, 6:650
Moods of syllogisms
in disjunctive, 5:503
division of, 5:496
in hypothetical, 5:502
reduction of, 5:497
Moody, Raymond A., 4:618
Moon Unification Church, 5:46
Moore, Edward F., on logic machines, 5:566
Moore, George Edward, **6:340–353**
on act-object distinction, 4:560–561
on adverbial analysis, 8:821
on aesthetics, 1:63–64
in analytic philosophy, 1:144–145
Anderson (John) and, 1:197–199
in antimetaphysics, 6:206
on beauty, 8:722
on belief and unbelief in doing and saying, 2:352
Bell and, 1:64
Black and, 1:606
Blanshard and, 1:614
on Brentano, 3:421
on certitude, 9:59
on common sense, 2:358, 7:108–109
on consciousness, 6:584
as consequentialist, 2:460
on contextual implication, 7:767
on correspondence theory of truth, 9:535
counterparts of Fries's "self-reliance of Reason," 3:753
criticisms of, 3:419, 6:350–351
on definition, 2:665–668, 2:672–673
on egoism, 9:120
epistemology of, 3:314–316, 6:347–348
on error, 3:343–344
on ethical naturalism, 3:364–367, 3:418–419, 3:445
on ethical subjectivism, 3:375–377
on ethics, 1:145, 3:418–419, 3:439–440, 6:349–350
on existence, 1:528
and fallibilism about empirical belief, 5:96–97
on the Good, 3:418–419, 3:439, 4:150
ideal utilitarianism of, 3:439, 9:604
on idealism, 4:559, 8:149
on intrinsic goodness, 4:719
Latin American philosophy and, 5:210
life of, 6:340–341
linguistic philosophers on, 3:429
Malcolm and, 5:661
metaethics of, 6:155–156
metaphysics of, 6:346–347
method of, 6:343–346
Mill (John Stuart) and, 3:419, 6:228
monism of, 4:735
on moral knowledge, 3:445
naturalistic fallacy, 3:548

Moore, George Edward, *continued*
and new realism, 2:595, 6:584
nonnaturalism of, 3:204
and open question argument, 3:366, 3:418–419, 3:439, 3:444–445
and open question on happiness, 4:736
on organic unities, 4:719, 6:353
paradigm-case argument and, 7:108–109
paradoxical sentence of, 5:110
and paritive argument on sensa, 8:816
particularism of, 3:278
on perception, 6:348–349
on philosophy, purpose of, 9:796–797
philosophy of, 6:342–350
on pragmatism, 8:799
and Ramsey's theory of truth, 2:547
realism and, 3:313–314
on right, 3:419
on sensation, 3:125
on sense datum, 8:813
Sidgwick and, 3:417, 9:25
on skepticism, 7:108–109
Stace and, 9:200
on statements of existence, 3:497–498
Stebbing and, 9:236
Stout and, 9:259
on truth, 2:542–545
and utilitarianism, 9:605–606
on value, 3:439, 3:442–444
on value judgments, 9:643
von Wright and, 9:847
Wittgenstein and, 9:817
Moore, Henry, Norris and, 6:655
Moore, Stanley, on alienation, 1:122
Moore, Underhill, legal realism and, 5:245
"Moore and Ordinary Language" (Malcolm), 2:359
Moore's Paradox, 5:87–88
Moral action, 1:475
Croce on, 2:603
in *Groundwork of the Metaphysic of Morals,* 5:23–24
as highest action, 1:618
intention of, evaluation of, 4:700
intrinsic value and, 4:719
Moral agency
empathy and, 9:345
in ethics, 9:688
Kant on, 3:364
Murdoch on, 6:433
Moral agents
in business ethics, 1:777–779
freedom of, limiting, 4:620–621
Moral argument(s)
for equality, 7:456
for existence of God, **6:353–360**
immortality as, 4:613–614
renewed attention to, 3:321
Moral Boundaries (Tronto), 3:581
Moral certitude, as logic of probability, Crusius on, 2:606
Moral choices, Anselm on, 1:218
Moral clarity, in utopianism, 9:619
Moral code
religion and, 6:230
in utilitarian ethics, 1:687
Moral community, 3:561, 7:2
Moral compliance, 6:394
Moral concepts
in metaethics, 6:158–159
religion and, 8:385–386
thick, 6:159
thin, 6:159
Moral consciousness
Croce on, 2:603
Kant on, 2:366–367
liangzhi as seat of, 9:726–727
Moral considerations, personal identity and, 7:215–218
Moral cultivation, in neo-Confucianism, 2:156
Moral damage, of oppression, 3:579
Moral defect, 3:685
Moral deontology, and divine command theories of ethics, 3:93–94
Moral dilemmas, 1:218, **6:360–362**
Moral disagreement
emotivism and, 6:157
vs. incommensurability, 6:161–162
moral objectivism and, 6:161
normative relativism and, 6:159–160
Moral doctrine
Ficino and, 3:622
vs. natural science, 7:265
Peter Lombard and, 7:261
Moral drive, 3:618
Moral education, 3:603, 7:363
Moral endeavor, persistence in, 5:30
Moral epigram. *See Chreia*
Moral epistemology, **6:362–369**
Moral Epistles (Seneca), 8:811–812, 9:254
Moral error, Descartes on, 3:12
Moral evil, problem of, 3:469–474
Moral experience, 4:299, 5:48
Moral explanations, 6:162
Moral extensionism, in environmental ethics, 3:259
Moral faculty, conscience and, 2:445
Moral gap, 6:359
Moral goodness, Crusius on, 2:608
Moral harm, paternalism and, 7:137
Moral identity, 5:38
Moral imperatives
Kant on, 5:24–25
Lavrov on, 5:218
Moral inadequacy, Kierkegaard's intellectual opponents and, 5:63
Moral judgment(s), 5:727
vs. aesthetic judgments, 5:26
attitude and, 6:157
Burckhardt on, 1:765–766
and cognitivism, 6:159, 6:393
conscience in, 1:781
consistency in, 6:158
Croce on, 2:603
and determinism, 8:7
emotive theory of ethics on, 3:203–207
empiricism and, 4:749
epistemic evaluation of, 6:364–368
in ethical irrationalism, 4:749
in history, 1:765–766
Hume on, 3:381
intentions and, 5:24
and irrationalism, 4:749
judgment internalism as, 4:714
justification of, 6:370–371
law and, 2:603
Moore on, 6:352
and noncognitivism, 6:159–160, 6:393, 6:632–634
Nowell-Smith on, 3:429–430
overriding, 6:157–158
on public interest, 9:207–208
reflection and, 9:739
and responsibility, 8:446–447
skepticism of, 6:393–394
Smart's utilitarian theory of, 9:66
on suicide, 9:318
truth fixed by facts, 3:684
truth of, 6:160–161
universalizable, 6:157
vs. value judgments, 1:461
Moral justification
of civil disobedience, 2:260
of heterosexism, 4:347–348
Moral law
consequences of, 5:24
Costa on, 4:825
Cumberland on, 2:615
kings and, 3:604
See also Kant, Immanuel
Moral Laws (Brightman), 7:235

Moral life, passions in, 4:529
Moral Limits of the Criminal Law (Feinberg), 3:560
Moral luck, Williams (Bernard) on, 9:788
Moral metalogic, defense of, by Whately, 9:742–743
Moral methodology, of Rawls, 9:611
Moral norms
biological science and, 3:446–447
Habermas on, 3:91
See also Internalization of moral norms
Moral objectivism, 3:561
arguments against, 6:161–162
arguments for, 6:162–165
intolerance and, 6:162
in metaethics, 6:160–161
moral realism and, 6:162
normative ethics and, 6:164
rationality in, 6:163
Moral obligation
belief and unbelief in God and, 2:351–352
to distant peoples, 3:92–93
to future generations, 3:92–93, 3:392–393
incommensurability of, 6:161
lending content and specificity to, 3:618
Mill (John Stuart) on, 6:233
oddity of, 6:358–359
Prichard on, 3:420
Moral order
absence of, in ethical irrationalism, 4:750
in conservatism, 2:465
in metaphor of personal God, 9:8
Moral Order and Progress (Alexander), 1:107
Moral organ, 4:311
Moral Paradoxes of Nuclear Deterrence (Kavka), 7:157
Moral Philosopher, in a Dialogue between Philalethes, a Christian Deist, and Theophanes, a Christian Jew, The (Morgan), 2:684
Moral philosophy
absent normative implication, 1:461
Baier and, 1:461
Balguy and, 1:475
Chinese, 2:234
Chinese name rectification and, 2:203–204
Chrysippus on, 2:252
Coleridge on, 2:319
Confucian, 2:213, 2:231–239
cosmopolitanism as, 2:568–569
Culverwell's Calvinist, 2:613
economics as, 7:350–351
ethical language, 1:461
Geulincx and, 4:77, 4:80
Grote and, 4:189
Jakélévitch and, 4:787–788
Maimonides and, 5:652–653
Maritain and, 5:714–715
modern, neglect of friendship in, 3:748–749
Mozi on, 2:235
Murdoch and, 6:433–434
passions and, 3:570
Price and, 8:2–3
Reid and, 8:329
respect in, 8:441–442
rules of, 1:460
See also Morality
Moral Philosophy (Wolff), 9:825
Moral Point of View, The (Baier), 3:431
Moral principles
justification of, **6:369–376**
in Sidgwick's common-sense ethics, 9:23
transcendental arguments for, 6:373–376
20th-century debate on, 3:439–442
See also Moral rules
Moral Principles and Nuclear Weapons (Lackey), 7:157
Moral Problem, The (Smith), 6:163
Moral proof, of existence of God, 5:23
Moral properties, as nonnatural relational properties of fittingness, 6:156–157
Moral psychology, **6:376–379**
Descartes on, 3:188
Philodemus on, 7:302
Plutarch of Chaeronea and, 7:648–649
Moral questions, answering, 3:380
Moral rationalism, **8:247–251**
Moral realism, 6:161–163, **6:379–382**
Moral Relativism and Moral Objectivity (Thomson & Harman), 9:449
Moral requirement
categorical, 3:443
demandingness of, 3:443–444
dilemma between, 6:360–362
hypothetical, 3:443
Moral responsibility, 9:685
approach to, 8:450
in Carolingian thought, 2:49
Cudworth on, 2:611–612
dilemma of, 8:446–448
free will and, 3:718
freedom and, 8:445–446
and legal responsibility, **8:444–451**
meaning of, 8:445
personhood and, 7:240
Moral rules, 6:370–371, **6:382–385**
application of, 6:375–376
autonomy of, 6:372–373
as commands, in moral arguments for existence of God, 6:353
completeness of, 6:375–376
consistency among, 9:611–612
emotions and, 9:739–740
justification of, **6:369–376**
objectivity of, 6:372–373
origin and development of, 9:739
proof of, 9:606
teachability of, 1:460
ultimate, 6:371–372
Volney on, 9:707
Moral sciences, Mill (John Stuart) on, 6:224–225
Moral sense, **6:385–388**
conscience and, 2:445
Green on, 4:180
habituation of, Gay on, 4:34–35
Hutcheson on, 4:527–529
Mill (James) on, 6:219
Saint-Hyacinthe on, 8:588
sympathy in, 9:67
theories, 3:408
Moral sentiment, **6:388–393**
causation of, 4:506–507
empathy and, 9:345
in personality, 6:72
in Shaftesbury's natural goodness, 9:3
Moral shortcomings, repair of, 5:30
Moral skepticism, **6:393–394**
Moral solidarity, communitarianism and, 2:369
Moral status
in bioethics, 1:602–603
in business ethics, 1:776
in environmental ethics, 1:603
Moral subject, producing, 3:700
Moral theory
biases in, 3:578
common core, 5:37
Foot and, 3:684
Held on, 4:299
idealizing in, 3:580
Ortega y Gasset and, 7:46
Socrates and, 9:702
Wayland (Francis) and, 9:728
women's experience in, 4:299
Moral Thinking (Hare), 3:441, 6:160

Moral value
    of informed consent decision-making, 4:679–680
    objective, Machie on, 3:346–347
    Perry on, 7:205
    vs. personal value, 3:442–444
    in socialist thought, 9:88
Moral virtues
    defining, 9:688
    vs. intellectual, 1:268, 9:682
    vs. natural, 9:2
Morale et la science des moeurs, La (Ethics and Moral Science) (Lévy-Bruhl), 5:306
Moralia (Plutarch), 4:172
Moralis philosophia (Bacon, Roger), 1:455
Moralism
    Franklin and, 3:720
    legal
        Feinberg and, 3:561
        liberty and, 5:338
    and optimism, 7:252
Morality
    Abelard on, 1:5–6, 3:403
    of abortion, 1:8–10
    abuse of, in injustice, 4:866
    aesthetics and, 1:51, 1:67–68, 2:121–122, 8:598, 9:563
    aging and, 2:2
    agnostic, 9:243
    agreement in, 7:718
    animals and, 5:155
    Anscombe and, 1:212–213
    as apprehension of universalizable principles, 5:36
    Aquinas on, 9:434
    in arguments for existence of God, 9:406–409
    Aristotle on, 3:451
    art and, 1:42–43, 2:146, 8:627, 9:514
    of asceticism, 1:352
    of atheism, 1:357
    Augustine on, 1:395–397
    authority of, Williams (Bernard) on, 9:787
    Balguy on, 1:475
    Beneke on, 1:543
    and bioethics, 1:601
    Bolingbroke on, 1:642
    Bosanquet on, 1:663
    Brandt on, 8:52
    Brentano on, 1:690
    in Buddhism, 1:723–724, 6:255
    Cabanis on, 2:2
    Calvin on, 2:9
    of Cambridge Platonists, 9:1
    Camus on, 2:22–23
    Caso on, 5:208
    Cavell on, 2:116
    Chaadaev on, 2:121–122
    Cheng Hao on, 2:144
    Cheng Yi on, 2:145
    Chernyshevskii on, 2:146
    in Chinese religious thought, 2:226–227
    and civil disobedience, 2:261
    Clarke on, 2:273
    Cockburn on, 2:295
    cognitive science and, 8:156
    Cohen (Hermann) on, 2:303
    Coleridge on, 2:319
    Collingwood on, 2:329
    common sense and, 2:358
    Condorcet on, 2:432
    conflict and, 1:676
    in Confucianism, 2:150–151, 2:177–178, 2:196–197, 2:442, 4:796, 5:7
    conscience and, 1:378, 1:781, 6:581
    consequentialism and, 2:461, 2:518
    in contractualism, 2:518
    conventional
        deontological ethics and, 3:388
        and impersonal morality, resistance to, 3:389
        Nietzsche on, 9:263
        rights and obligations in, 3:383–384
        Singer on, 3:389
        as static, 1:571
    corruption of, 2:2, 6:598
    creation *ex nihilo* and, 2:585
    Cudworth on, 2:609
    Cumberland on, 2:615
    Daoist view on, 2:187–190, 2:198, 2:236
    death instinct and, 8:310–311
    of deferring death, 4:617
    definition of, 3:380
    determinism and, 8:7
    divine will and, 7:422
    and doing *vs.* letting, 1:549
    education and, 7:363, 7:376
    Eliot (George) on, 3:184–185
    emotions and, 5:138, 9:739–740
    empathy and, 9:345
    enforcement of, 5:338, 7:137
    environment and, 9:379
    esoteric, in act utilitarianism, 9:613
    ethical egoism and, 3:361–362
    vs. ethics, **3:450–451**
    etiquette and, 2:71
    in everyday life, 5:7
    in evocative argument, 2:213–214
    in evolution, 1:204, 9:789
    experience as foundation of, 1:378
    expressive-collaborative model of, 3:580
    free will in, 9:782
    Galluppi on, 4:14
    Garve on, 4:24
    Gay on, 4:34
    Gewirth on, 4:81
    goal of, 3:380
    God and, 1:380, 1:397, 7:701, 9:407
    of gods, 4:111
    golden rule and, 4:144–147
    and The Good, 9:373–374
    vs. good, in teleological ethics, 9:382–383
    and good and bad as apodictic judgment, 1:690
    and good and evil as ontologically real forms, 2:13
    Greek Academy on, 4:174
    Grotius on, 6:510
    and guilt *vs.* shame, 9:4–5
    happiness and, 1:218
    Hegel on, 4:261–263, 4:267–268
    Herbart on, 7:374–375
    higher, 3:618
    Hobbes on, 3:381–382, 4:424–425
    Holocaust and, 4:454–455
    and human nature, 1:781
    humanism and, 1:450
    Hume on, 4:506–509, 7:424
    Hutcheson on, 3:605
    ideal observer theory of, 2:190
    immortality and, 4:613–614, 8:13
    immutability of, 8:2
    impartiality and, 2:235, 4:619, 4:620
    imperatives of, Kant on, 5:24–25
    impersonal, resistance to, 3:388–389
    innate principles of, Locke on, 5:378
    as intellectually derived from Divine will, 1:542
    in interpretation, 1:313
    "is" *vs.* "ought" in, 6:515
    in Japanese philosophy, 4:796
    Jodl (Friedrich) on, 4:835
    Johnson (Dr. Samuel) on, 4:853–854
    judgments in, 6:632–634
    justification of, 5:715, 6:619, 8:50, 9:449
    Kant on, 2:69, 4:613, 5:24–25

Kantian
Hegel on, 4:261–262
Mou on, 2:183
language of, noncognitivism and, 6:632–633
Laplace on, 5:198
law and, 2:329, 3:617, 5:237–243, 7:137, 7:444
Law (W.) on, 5:220
legal enforcement of. *See* Paternalism
legal positivism on, 5:237–243
and legal reasoning, 3:156
Leibniz's republic of monadic spirits and, 2:366
and life, meaning and value of, 5:355
linguistics in, 6:632–634
literature and, 1:67
Locke on, 5:378, 5:386
Lopatin on, 5:573
and love, 1:46, 3:719, 5:670–671
and loyalty, 5:595–596
Machiavelli on, 5:627
MacIntyre on, 5:636
Maimonides on, 5:652–653
Malebranche on, 5:670–671
Mandeville on, 5:682
Marcus on, 5:704
Martineau on, 5:727
merchants and, 1:777
as method of assessment, 1:688
Mill (John Stuart) on, 6:233
Milton on, 6:250
Mozi on, 2:235
Murdoch (Iris) on, 3:451, 6:433–434
Nakae Tōju on, 6:477
nationalism and, 6:485
in natural law, 6:505–506
in natural philosophy, 1:451
naturalism and, 2:190, 3:363–366, 6:476, 6:495, 8:156
naturalistic utilitarian, 6:476
nature and, Thoreau on, 9:451
in neo-Confucian rationalism, 2:155–156
Nietzsche on, 3:389, 4:153, 6:611–612, 9:263
nihilism and, 6:617–619
noncognitivism in, 6:632–633
norms of, internationalization of, 3:382, 3:385
Nussbaum on, 6:680
objective, 6:495, 8:239
Ockham on, 9:782
optimism/pessimism and, 7:249
origin and development of, 9:739
pain and, 8:3
Paley on, 7:76
Pelagianism on, 7:175
Pestalozzi on, 7:372
Plato on, 1:43, 7:585
pleasure and, 8:3
poetry and, 1:444
and point of view, 1:460
and politics, 3:605
population theory and, 5:676–677
pornography and, 7:530
practices of, 3:581
presuppositions of, 6:171
pretense of, in injustice, 4:866
principle of, detailed derivation of, 3:617
progress and, 8:47–50
of promises, 8:53
as public system, 1:602
of punishment, 8:161–162, 8:168–169
pure religion of, 5:30
Rashdall on, 8:239
Rawls on, 3:479
reality of
Price on, 8:2
Taylor (Alfred) on, 9:373–374
reasoning in, 7:736–737
reflective *vs.* obligatory basis for, 1:459
relativism in, 7:718, 8:50
religion and, 1:505, 6:598, **8:382–389**
Baader on, 1:439
causal dependence of, 8:384–385
conceptual dependence of, 8:385–386
epistemic dependence of, 8:386–387
in James's philosophy, 4:779
metaphysical dependence of, 8:387
Nicolai on, 6:598
as rational relationship, 1:505
Saint-Simon on, 8:591
Sidgwick on, 9:22
and suicide, 9:320
Swift's satires on, 9:340–341
Taylor (Alfred) on, 9:373
threat posed to, 8:388
rewards and punishments in, 4:614
rights in, 9:448–449
Saint-Hyacinthe on, 8:589
Santayana on, 1:63, 8:600–601
as secondary quality, 8:51
and self-interest, 3:380–382, 3:389, 3:408
as self-realization, 1:676
sexual, Russell on, 8:538–539
and sexual consent, 7:529
sexual perversion and, 7:528
and sexuality, 3:450, 7:529, 8:538–539
Sidgwick on, 2:358
Singer on, 3:443, 9:41
skepticism in, 6:618–619
Smith (Adam) on, 7:350–351
social, 4:268, 7:454
and social decay caused by freedom, 1:667
social utility *vs.*, 5:48
speculation and, 1:378
stability and historical change in, 1:720
as struggle in Cynic teaching, 2:616
supreme principle of, 5:23–24
Swift on, 9:341
Taylor (Alfred) on, 9:373–374
Tennant on, 9:393
of terrorism, 9:396–398
Theophrastus on, 9:412
in theories of population, 5:676–677
Thomson (Judith) on, 9:448–449
Tindal on, 9:502–503
toleration in, 9:510
Tolstoy on, 9:513
Troeltsch on, 9:527
in unbelievers in God, 2:351
as universal, 2:273, 3:380, 9:378
utopianism and, 9:620–621
Vasubandhu and, 1:751–752
violence of, 6:680
and volitional conformity to God, 1:595
Voltaire on, 9:712
Williams (Bernard) on, 9:787
women philosophers on, 9:838
Xunzi on, 2:234
in Yogācāra Buddhism, 1:749–750
See also Ethics
Morality [term], Hegel's use of, 4:261–262
Morality, Prudence, and Nuclear Weapons (Lee), 7:157
Moralium Dogma Philosophorum, William of Conches and, 9:768
Moralization of life, 7:205
Moravec, Hans, on machine intelligence, 5:635
More, George Edward, on Bradley, 1:679

More, Henry, **6:395–398**
Cambridge platonists on, 2:14
Cudworth and, comparison of, 2:610
on Descartes's cosmology, 9:249
and ethics, 3:406
Glanvill and, 4:95–97
More, Thomas, **6:398–401**
Colet and, 2:322
Erasmus and, 3:337–338
on suicide, 9:319
Utopia, 5:154
utopia [term] coined by, 9:616
on war and peace, 7:152
"More Is Different" (Anderson), 3:192
Moreh Nebukhei ha-Zman (Guide of the perplexed for our time) (Krochmal), 4:828
Moreland, J. P., 4:618
Moreno, Mariano, 5:205
Moréri, Louis, 1:503–507
Mores, conscience and, 2:445
Morgan, Augustus de. *See* De Morgan, Augustus
Morgan, C. Lloyd, **6:401–403,** 9:72
Morgan, George A., 6:613
Morgan, Lewis Henry, 1:442, **6:403–404**
Morgan, Lloyd, Pearson and, 7:160
Morgan, Thomas, **6:405**
deism and, 2:683–684, 2:691
in genetics, 3:488, 7:339
Morgenstern, Oskar, Neumann (John von) and, 6:559
Morgenstuden oder Vorlesungen über das Daseyn Gottes (Morning Hours, or Lectures on the Existence of God) (Mendelssohn), 1:11, 6:131, 7:99
Moriae Encomium (In praise of folly) (Erasmus), 3:338
Moritz, Karl Philipp, **6:405–406**
Moro Simpson, Tomás, 5:210
Morphologists, 2:635
Morphology
biology and, 7:347
plural, mass/count distinction in, 6:660
syntax and, 9:359–361
Morphosyntax, 9:361
Morris, Charles W.
on art, 1:58
on formal semantics, 5:556
and pragmatics, 7:738
semotics and, 7:173
on signification, 8:797
Vienna Circle and, 5:525
Morris, G. S., Dewey and, 3:43, 3:44
Morris, William
on art, 1:56
and socialism, 9:88–89
utopianism of, 9:619
Morrison, Gary Saul, on Dostoevsky, 3:99
Morrison, Wayne, 6:91
Mort d'agrippine, La (Cyrano de Bergerac), 2:618
Mortal Questions (Nagel), 6:475
Mortality
Abelard on, 1:5
Lucretius on, 4:606
Overton on, 9:70
of phenomena, 4:293
of soul, Costa on, 4:824
See also Death; Immortality
Morte ed immortalità (Sciacca), 8:666
Mosaic law
Albo on, 1:102
Ambrose on, 7:420
as social contract, 4:826
Mosaic theory, Köhler on, 5:130
Mosaics, 9:691
Mosca, Gaetano, 2:702, **6:406–408**
Moscow Linguistic Circle, 9:17
Moscow Metaphysical School, 9:17
Mosersky, J. M., 9:475–477
Moses
Maimonides on, 4:826, 5:651–654
prophecy of, 4:825
Moses ben Jacob Cordovero, 5:3
Moses ben Shemtob de Leon, 5:3
Moses' Chapters (Maimonides), 5:648
Moskovitianin (The Muscovite), 5:74
Moskovsii Sbornik (Kireevskii), 5:74
Mosley, Oswald, 8:625, 9:510
Most High, The (Blanchot), 1:612
Most normal model, in non-monotonic logic, 5:491
Mostler, Fredrick, 8:613
Mostowski, Andrzej, 5:531, 8:842
Mostowski-Linström-Tarski approach, 5:531
Mothersill, Mary, on beauty, 1:67
Motion, **6:408–411**
absolute, 1:581–582, 6:592, 9:155
ancient concepts of, 6:412
Aquinas on, 2:551
in argument for existence of God, 2:551, 9:432
arguments against, 9:874–877
Aristotelian law of, 3:686–687
Aristotle on, 1:273, 2:490–491, 6:411–412
Arnauld on, 2:58
Berkeley on, 1:567–568
of body, Geulincx on, 4:77
in Bohmian mechanics, 1:631–632
Boscovich on, 1:665
Boyle on, 1:674
Burley on, 1:773–774
cinematographic analysis of, 1:566
Clarke on, 2:272
in classical mechanics, 2:280
Collier on, 2:323
complete theory of, 7:476
conservation of, 2:90, 2:462
Conway on, 2:529
Descartes on, 2:54, 2:58, 9:154
early concepts of, 6:411
entropy and, 2:106
equilibrium of, 1:644–645
Eudoxus on, 4:54–55
of falling body, 4:9
Galileo on, 4:8–11, 8:683
God as cause of, 2:58
Hamiltonian theory on, 2:463–464
of heat, Bacon (Francis) on, 1:448
historical survey of, **6:411–415**
Hobbes on, 4:410, 8:825
Huygens on, 2:462
idealized, in Galileo, 8:683
as illusory experience, 4:585
in immortality of soul, 1:105
impetus theory of, 1:769, 4:621–622
laws of
Newton's, 3:234–235
in Wolff's ontology, 9:828
Leibniz on, 5:251–253, 5:269–270
limited conception of, 1:567–568
Malebranche on, 5:664
medieval concepts of, 6:105, 6:412
in medium *vs.* in vacuum, Giles of Rome on, 4:90
Melissus of Samos on, 6:120
and mind-body relationship, Berkeley on, 1:585
natural and unnatural, 4:621
Newton on, 3:234–235, 6:592, 7:559
in Nyāya-Vaiśeika realism, 9:582
Oresme on, 7:34–35
particle nonlocality and, 1:631–632
particulate, 1:577
perception of, 7:184–185
Philoponus on, 7:314
physical causality and, in mind-body relationship, 1:585
in physics, 7:474
planetary, 4:56
Plotinus on, 6:187
as primary quality, 8:8
projectile, 4:621
by psychokinesis, 7:753
quantum computing and, 2:408

in quantum theory, 1:631, 1:635
relativity of, 4:11, 6:413–415
in Sanlun Buddhism, 2:161
of self, as property of purity, 2:117–118
substantial, principle of, 6:419
Swineshead on, 9:342
as temporal metaphor, 9:487
through space-time, 9:465
time and, 9:496
touch and, 9:516
Zeno of Elea on, 9:872–877
Zeno's paradoxes and, 1:568, 4:654–655, 9:467
See also Movement
Motivated forgetting, Freud's thesis of, 3:739
Motivation
in capitalist system, 9:69
ethical, 3:381
agent-relative *vs.* agent-neutral reasons, 3:445–446
biological science on, 3:446–447
creation of, 3:389
Hobbes on, 3:389
Hume on, 3:389
impersonal moral theories and, 3:389
Kant on, 3:389–390
relativism and, 3:390–391
rule-utilitarianism and, 3:385
Sidgwick on, 3:417
ethical judgments and, 7:6
in internalism, 7:737
judgment internalism in, 4:714
moral, 2:519
empathy as, 9:345
in internalism and externalism, 4:714–716
pleasure and, 4:256–257, 7:622–623
reason and, 7:737
Schopenhauer on, 8:652
self-love and, 1:781
in sentences, 6:653
Sidgwick on, 9:24
and soul, 9:240
and strict akratic action, 9:731
of tragic writing, 1:43–44
Motivation and Agency (Melerebuts), 1:15
Motive
determining, 3:175
determinism and, 3:18–19, 3:26
intention and, 7:447
law and, 7:446–447
Melden (A. I.) on, 3:19–20
Reid on, 3:19–20
Motoori Norinaga, 4:796–797
Mots, Les (Sartre), 8:604
Mots et les choses: Une archéologie des sciences humaines, Les (Foucault), 3:698, 9:274
Mou Zongsan
Buddhism and, 2:169–170
on moral metaphysics and metaphysics of morals, 2:222
neo-Confucianism of, 2:182–184
Moulton, Janice, 7:523
Mounier, Emmanuel, **6:415–416**
Mountain Gloom and Mountain Glory (Nicholson), 3:255
Mouton, Gabriel, 6:91
Movement
in Avicenna's theory of essence and existence, 4:757
Bergson on, 7:382
Landgrebe on, 5:184–185
See also Motion
Movies, **7:381–386**
Moving Rows argument against motion, 9:876–877
Mozart, Wolfgang Amadeus, 3:82
Mozi, **6:417–418**
on impartial concern and benefit-harm evaluation, 2:197
on logic, 5:414–415
on predispositions of heart/mind, 6:129
on religious rite, 2:151
social and political philosophy of, 2:235–236
on universal love, 2:151
M-predicates, 7:239
"Mr. —bov and the Question of Art" (Dostoevsky), 3:100
Mr. C——n's Discourse of Freethinking (Swift), 9:341
MRI scan, 6:564–565
Mučnik, A. A., 2:385
Mueller, Joel, 8:585
Muhammad
al-Fārābī, Abū-Naṣr Muhammad on, 4:756, 4:811
Emerson and, 3:195
islam (submission) and *Iman* (faith) and, 3:536
and Sufism, 9:300
Muirhead, J. H., on the Good, 4:153
Mūlamadhyamakakārikā (Fundamental Verses on the Middle Way), 6:470–471
Mulhall, Stephen, 7:385
Mullā Ṣadrā, 4:761, **6:418–421**
on essence and existence, 3:352, 4:761
on knowledge-by-presence, 3:320
on metaphysical philosophy, 4:584
philosophic mysticism of, 4:759
on primacy of existence and causality, 2:114
Müller, Adam, 5:78
on nationalism, 6:484
Spann and, 9:158
Müller, Ernst, 7:578
Müller, Georg, 5:576
Müller, Johannes, 8:140
Müller, Max
Durkheim and, 3:151
on myth, 6:464
Müller-Lyer illusion, 8:177
Multiculturalism, **6:421–427**
communitarianism and, 2:369
education and, 7:359
liberalism *vs.* naturalism in, 6:487
nationalism in, 6:485, 6:487
and pluralism, 7:643
Multifunctionalism, Nowell-Smith and, 6:633
Multi-modal logics, dynamic logic on, 5:487
Multiple Drafts Model (MDM) of consciousness, 2:711
Multiple occupancy thesis, on personal identity, 7:229
Multiple personalities, McDougall on, 6:72
Multiple realizability, **6:427–432,** 6:644–646, 8:285–286
Multiple relation theory, Russell on, 3:345
Multiplicatio Specierum (Bacon, Roger), 1:452
Multiplication, Lambert on, 5:445
Multiplicative axiom, 5:468. *See also* Choice, axiom of
Multiplicative inverse function, 3:645
Multiplicity
of art, 1:76
from first principle, 4:312
of God, in Avicenna, 1:433
in negation, 6:525
in Plato's realm of intelligibles, 7:633
in Proclus, 8:41–42
of universes, cosmology models and, 2:563–566
Multiverse hypothesis, 8:400–401
Mumford, Lewis, on philosophy of technology, 7:543–544
Muṇḍaka Upanishad, 6:107

Mundane phenomenology, 8:664
Mundle, C. W. K., 7:116
Mundus imaginalis, 9:315
Munich Circle, Lipps and, 5:362
Munitz, Milton K., on cosmology, 2:564
Munro, Thomas, on aesthetics, 1:60
Münster uprising, 8:296
Munsterberg, Hugo, 7:381, 8:141
mu-operator, in computability theory, 2:401
Muqammiṣ, David ben Merwan al-, **6:432**
Murat, Achille, Emerson and, 3:194–195
Murder
- abortion as, 1:8
- Antiphon on, 1:223

Murdoch, Iris, **6:433–434**
- on emotions, 3:202
- on morality, 3:451
- on Sartre, 8:610

Mure, G. R. G., 4:269–270
Muro kyūsō, **6:434–435**
Murphy, Arthur Edward, 3:430, **6:435–436**
Murphy, Gardner, on parapsychology, 7:115–116
Murphy, Nancy, 4:618
Murray, Gilbert
- on decline of Roman Empire, 3:400
- on war and peace, 7:155

Muscle sense, *vs.* touch, 8:139
Museum(s), activity of, 3:559
Museum of Natural History, burglary of, 9:755–756
Musgrave, Alan, on epistemic optimism, 8:690
Music
- Adorno on, 1:25–28
- and aesthetics, 1:27–28, 9:325
- African, 1:87
- Alembert on, 1:106
- as allographic, 1:317
- as analogy of expression, 1:305
- Archytas of Tarentum on, 1:250
- artificial intelligence and, 1:346
- of Cage, 1:26, 1:300, 1:321
- creation of, 1:318
- Davies on, 1:305
- Descartes on, 2:722
- emotion and, 1:303
- Epicurean view of, 1:45
- ethics in, 1:188
- as expression of imagined emotion, 1:306
- folk, 9:514
- in formalism, 1:309, 6:437
- Galilei on, 1:48–49
- Hanslick on, 1:56, 1:303
- Hegel on, 4:275
- instrumentation in, 1:322
- Karl on, 1:306
- Kivy on, 1:305
- Langer on, 1:305
- Levinson on, 1:303, 1:306
- Losev on, 5:575
- Marcel and, 5:700
- mathematics of, 8:185
- Mattheson on, 1:305
- in Neoplatonism, 1:190
- Nietzsche on, 9:525
- as nonreducible mode of thought, 1:25
- number in, 8:185
- Philodemus on, 1:45, 1:189
- philosophy of, **6:436–440**
- Phonogram Archives, 9:280
- Plato on, 1:188
- pleasure in, 1:338–339
- pseudo-individualism in, 1:26
- Ptolemy on, 1:189
- Pythagoras on, 1:41, 8:185
- reason *vs.* experience in, 1:49
- representational theory of art and, 1:297
- Ridley on, 1:303
- Robinson (Jenefer) on, 1:303, 1:306
- Schopenhauer on, 1:56, 8:654
- Tolstoy on, 9:514
- Vasconcelos on, 9:648–649
- Vermazen on, 1:306
- Wagner on, 1:56
- Walton on, 1:306
- Wittgenstein and, 9:800
- Zarlino on, 1:48, 1:49

Musical harmonies, planetary motions governed by, 5:51
Musical katharsis, in Aristotle's *Politics,* 5:44
Musical scale, Philolaus' use of, 7:310
Musil, Robert, 6:618
Muslim League, 4:744
Muslim philosophy. *See* Islamic philosophy
Musonius Rufus, **6:440–441**
- Epictetus and, 3:261, 9:254
- Justin Martyr on, 7:142
- patristic philosophy and, 7:142

Musschenbroek, Pieter van, 4:48
Mussolini, Benito, 3:553–554
- Pareto and, 7:117
- Sorel and, 9:132

Must, unconditional value of, as absolute moral duty, 2:70
"Must We Burn Sade?" (Beauvoir), 7:523
Must We Mean What We Say (Cavell), 2:115
Mutahhari, Murttaz, 8:647
Mutations, in evolution, 9:377
Muʿtazilites
- and al-Kindī, 4:755
- atomism of, 4:813–814
- on free will, 4:754
- theodices of, 8:586

Muthmasslicher Anfang der Menschengeschichte (Kant), 7:249
Mutterrecht. Eine Untersuchung, Das (Bachofen), 1:441
Mutual Aid (Kropotkin), 1:179, 5:154, 5:155
Mutual Assured Destruction (MAD), 7:157
Mutual causation, Zhuangzi on, 9:881
Mutual empathy, 3:749
Mutual recognition, in contractualism, 2:518
Mutualism, 1:178, 8:94
Muzyka kak predmet logiki (Music as the subject of logic) (Losev), 5:575
MVB estimators, replacing asymptotic efficiency, 3:663
My Confession (Tolstoy), 9:512
My Pedagogic Creed (Dewey), 3:48
"My Station and Its Duties" (Bradley), 1:676
My View of the World (Schrödinger), 8:657
Myers, Frederic, 7:116
Myerson, Émile, 3:355
Myhill, John, 2:386
Mynster, Bishop, 5:61
Myrvold, Wayne, 8:685
Mysterium Cosmographicum (Kepler), 3:687, 5:50–52
Mystery
- Marcel on, 5:701
- Pastore on, 7:135–136
- Swift on, 9:340
- and truth, 9:12

Mystic, Kepler as, 5:51
Mystic ecstasy
- Philo on, 4:810
- of whirling dervishes, 9:307

Mystical, Wittgenstein on, 9:808
Mystical anarchism, 4:767
Mystical experience
- agnosticism and, 6:457
- alternative interpretations of, 6:454–455

ascent to, as wisdom, 1:650
Bernard of Clairvaux on, 1:592
Boehme and, 1:623
Bonaventure on, 1:653
Bruno on, 1:711
in Buddhism, 1:722–724
Bulgakov on, 1:760
content and quality of, 6:458–459
Dostoevsky on, 3:99
"I" and "Other" relationship as, 1:465
intuition and, 1:570
language and, 6:456–457
as learning God's will, 1:574
objectivity and, 6:457–458
paradoxes of, 6:455–457
Reich on, 8:313–314
Solov'ëv on, 9:123
Suso and, 9:335
in Yogācāra Buddhism, 1:751–752
in Zen, 1:728–730
Mystical love, in Sufism, 9:303
Mystical Messianism, history of, 5:2
Mystical Theology (Pseudo-Dionysius), 1:140, 7:609
Mysticism
assessment of, 6:462
Averroes and, 1:426–427
Baader and, 1:439
Bergson on, 1:571
Bernard of Clairvaux on, 1:592
Bohm on, 1:630
Bonaventure and, 1:403
Brouwer on, 1:702
in Buddhism, 2:221
Chinese philosophy misunderstood as, 2:201
Christian, 6:447–450
Corbin on, 2:537
in Daoism, 2:151, 2:185
drug-induced, 6:460
Eckhart (Meister) and, 3:162–163
evolutionary future, 1:571
Fénelon and, 3:603
Gerson and, 4:67
God's love and, 1:570–571
Gregory of Nyssa and, 4:182
history of, **6:441–453**
in Ibn al-ʿArabī, 4:541
Indian, 6:442–445
in Islam, 4:549, 4:759–760
Jewish, 1:447–458, 5:1, 6:446–447
Joachim of Fiore and, 4:834
John of the Cross and, 4:846
language and, 6:461
Lavater and, 5:214
of Law (W.), 5:220
love of God in, 5:586–587
in Mādhyamika, 1:742–744
Naṣīr al-Dīn al-Ṭūsī on, 6:478–479
nature and assessment of, **6:453–462**
neural science and, 6:460
pantheism and, 7:95
reductionist, 6:493
in release from enslavement by will, 8:655
and religious attitude to life, 4:685
in religious language interpretation, 8:416–417
Saadya on, 8:585
Schelling on, 4:749, 8:621
in School of St. Victor, 8:592
Solov'ëv on, 9:124–125
Stace on, 9:200–201
Stein on, 9:240
in Sufism, 9:300
Swedenborg and, 9:338
Tarski and, 9:372–373
Tennant on, 9:392
Teresa of Ávila and, 9:394
theism and, 6:460
types of, 8:401
Weil (Simone) and, 9:736
Mysticism and Logic (Russell), 7:272, 8:819
Mysticism and Philosophy (Stace), 9:201
Mystik und das Wort, Die (Brunner), 1:707
Myth, **6:463–468**
in anthropology, 6:465–466
Bachofen on, 1:441
Barthes on, 1:480–481
Blanchot on, 1:612
Bultmann on, 1:762–764
Cassirer on, 2:67–68
in Chinese philosophy of religion, 2:224
in Gnosticism, 4:99
gospels as unconscious invention of, 9:262
in Greek philosophy, 6:463–464
Harrison on, 1:58
and history, 2:34
and knowledge, 1:559
Losev on, 5:574–575
in Manichaeism, 5:683–684
in modern thought, 6:464–466
nonexistent objects in, 6:635
in psychology, 9:849
in religious language interpretation, 8:416–417
revolutionary use of, 9:134
ritual and, 1:58
Schelling on, 1:234
Steffens on, 9:238
structural analysis of, 9:274
in Toynbee's historical work, 9:518
as utopian inspiration, 9:617
"Myth of Functional Analysis as a Special Method in Sociology and Anthropology The" (Davis, K.), 3:764
Myth of Sisyphus, The (Camus), 2:20–21, 4:748, 9:58
on death, 2:650
ethics in, 3:427
"Myth of the Aesthetic Attitude, The" (Dickie), 1:36
Mythe de Sisyphe, Le (Camus). *See Myth of Sisyphus, The* (Camus)
Mythology
a priori structure of, 8:621
ancient, 7:759–760
classical
love in, 5:583–585
Pico della Mirandola on, 7:572
collective unconscious in, 4:857–858
Greek, 7:759–760
human significance of, 3:611
Jung on, 8:146–147
modern poets' need for, 8:631
pre-Socratic philosophy and, 7:764
Proclus on, 8:43
Schelling on, 8:621
Schlegel on, 8:631
Mythos, *vs.* logos, 5:567
Mythus des 20.Jahrhunderts (Myths of the 20th century) (Rosenberg), 2:123

N

Nachlass (Nietzsche), 6:611
Nachlass (Wittgenstein), 9:817
Nachmanides, 4:618
Naess, Arne
deep ecology and, 3:260
logical positivism and, 5:525
on method in Chinese ethics, 2:200
on skepticism, 9:59
Nāgārjuna, 2:168, 4:633, 5:123, **6:469–472**
and Buddhism, 1:731, 2:154, 2:167
as dialetheist, 1:742–743
on emptiness and knowability, 1:740–743
on logic, 5:411
on possibility of knowledge, 5:117
on truth, 5:329

Nagel, Ernest, **6:472–474**
on action, 1:17
on agency, 3:445
on determinism, 3:39, 3:41
on distinguishing properties, 7:87
on emergence, 3:192
on evolution, 7:343–344
on factual content of functional statements, 3:764
on functions (teleological), 9:386
La Mettrie and, 5:181
on objectivity, 7:3–4
philosophical naturalism and, 6:501
on purposive activity, 9:385
on reduction, 6:569, 8:283–285, 9:162
on semantic view of theories, 9:416
Suppes and, 9:333
on theological "why," 9:758
Vienna Circle and, 5:525
Nagel, Thomas, **6:474–476**
on altruism, 1:137, 3:445, 6:475
on consciousness, 2:449
and deontological ethics, 2:714
echolocation experiments of, 5:113, 9:292
on ethical relativism, 3:374
on explanatory gap, 8:192
on internalism, 4:714
on life, meaning and value of, 5:358
on mental-physical distinction, 6:139
philosophy of sex and, 7:523, 7:526
on principle monism, 3:442
on qualia, 9:292
on qualitative consciousness, 2:450
on self, 8:709
"What Is It Like to Be a Bat?", 5:112
Nägeli, Karl, 2:637
Nahḍah. See Enlightenment, Islamic
Naigeon, Jacques-André, **6:476**
Naissance de la clinique (The Birth of the Clinic) (Foucault), 3:699
Naissance du christianisme (Loisy), 5:571
Naive observer, *vs.* trained observer, 5:130
Naive realism, 5:160, 7:189–190, 8:818. *See also* Realism
Naive set theory, 3:766
Naive theory of names, 8:58
Naive vitalism, 9:695
Naiyayikas
and analogy, 5:121–122
and nonperception, 5:122
and pragmatic principle of confirmation, 5:119
and senses, 5:118
Nakae Tōju, 5:161–162, **6:477**
Nakamura Yōjirō, 4:791
Nakasima, Akira, on electrical logic machines, 5:566
Naked singularities, unique evolution and, 3:33
Namarupa, 6:256
Name(s)
Abelard on, 8:764
abstract, 1:552, 1:586
Anselm on, 1:216–218
and autonomous idiolects, 8:753
"being" status as, 1:527
of belief attributions, 1:536
Bentham and, 1:552, 8:792
Biel on, 1:594
in Buddhism, 1:723
in Chinese, 2:203–204, 2:210–212, 5:415–416
in Confucianism, 2:150
and connotation-denotation distinction, 8:796
conventional *vs.* ultimate, 1:734
Cratylus on, 2:584
in *Daode Jing,* 2:187–188
in Daoism, 2:161, 2:187–190
vs. descriptions, 8:288
descriptive theory of, 8:746–747
in elementary propositions, 9:806
Epicureans on, 8:759
Evans on, 3:459–461
false, Plato on, 8:754–755
vs. forms, 6:103
Frege on, 5:548, 8:800
God as, 7:483
Hobbes on, 4:406–407, 8:773–774
Hui Shi on, 2:189
Husserl on, 8:803
idéologues on, 8:788
ideal, 8:754
identity in, 4:567
immediate referent of, 8:759
and inward locution, 8:761
Kant on, 2:74–75
Kripke on, 1:155, 5:150–151, 6:290, 7:724, 8:746–747
Leibniz on, 8:779
Locke on, 5:385
in logic, definition of, 5:549
Losev on, 5:574
as many-to-one *vs.* one-to-one mappings, 2:205
meaning of, correspondence theory and, 2:546
in medieval philosophy, 5:430, 6:101
Mill (John Stuart) on, 8:795–796
Ming-shi on, 2:202
in modism, 5:432
in Moism, 5:415–416
negative, definition of, 5:549–550
and non-existential references, 1:446
Peirce on, 5:453
Plato on, 8:752–754
privative, definition of, 5:552
proper. *See* Proper name(s)
as relative indexicals, 2:189
Roscelin on, 8:496
Russell on, 1:146, 2:545–546, 5:508
in Sanlun Buddhism, 2:161
Socrates on, 8:751–753
Sophists on, 8:751
syncategoremata and, 8:756
Tarski on, 2:547–548
types of, 8:759
Wittgenstein on, 2:547, 9:805, 9:812
words as, 9:599–602
Xunzi on, 2:216
Name rectification
in Chinese thought, 2:188–189, 2:203–204, 2:238
in Confucianism, 2:203–204
Mencius on, 2:232
Naming and Necessity (Kripke), 1:155, 5:150, 6:290, 7:724, 8:746–747
Nanak (Sikh guru), 6:108–109
Nanna oder das Seelenleben der Pflanzen (Fechner), 3:555
Napoleon III, French liberalism and, 5:320
Napoleon Bonaparte
de Staël and, 9:201
French liberalism and, 5:320
and history, 3:37
Idéologues and, 3:1
Laplace and, 5:197
Spengler on, 9:167
Taine on, 9:365
Tolstoy on, 9:512
Volney and, 9:707
Narayan, Uma, 3:581
Narboni, Moses, 4:809, 4:821
Narodnaia volia (The people's will) party, 5:219
Narratio Prima (Rheticus), 2:533
Narrative
as argument, 1:336
history and, 7:394–398

in medical ethics pedagogy, 6:93
in philosophy, 7:332–333
Ricoeur on, 8:463–464
in virtue, 9:685
Narrative repair, 3:581
Narrativism, as theory of art, 1:301–302
Narveson, Jan, on liberty, 9:72
N-ary function, 3:649
N-ary relation, 3:649
Nash equilibrium, evolutionary ethics and, 3:479–480
"Nashi novye khristiane: F. M. Dostoevskii i graf Lev Tolstoi" ("Our New Christians: F. M. Dostoevsky and Count Lev Tolstoy") (Leont'ev), 5:283
Nashi zadachi: Stat'i 1948–1954 (Our tasks: Articles 1948–1954) (Il'in), 4:578
Naṣīr al-Dīn al-Ṭūsī, **6:477–479,** 8:646
Nāṣir khosrow, 6:478, 8:646
Nasr, Seyyed Hossein, 4:764, **6:479–481**
Nathan the Wise (Nathan der Weise) (Lessing), 2:688, 5:295, 6:130
Nation(s), 6:481–483, 9:208
Chamberlain on, 2:123
Miller on, 2:568
prehistory of, 5:59
rights of, Vitoria and, 9:698–699
types of, Khomiakov on, 5:59
Nation, The, art critic for, 2:628
National, Le (periodical), 5:372
National Book Critics Circle Prize for Criticism, 2:628
National Learning philosophy, 4:796
National Question in Russia, The (Solov'ëv), 9:122
National Socialism. *See* Nazism
National spirit, Krochmal on, 4:828
National state, Croce on, 2:604
Nationalism, **6:481–489**
in Africa, 1:84–86, 6:484
in Asia, 6:484
as breakdown of racial solidarity, Gobineau on, 4:106
civic, 6:485
in communitarianism, 6:485, 6:486
cosmopolitanism and, 2:570, 6:485–486
definition of, 6:481
Dühring and, 3:131
globalization and, 9:98
Gobineau on, 4:106
Goethe and, 4:141
Hegelian view of, 9:208
Heidegger and, 4:294
in Japanese philosophy, 4:796–797
just war and, 7:157–158
law and, 8:615
liberal, 6:487–489
and liberalism, 6:486–487
and morality, 6:485
multiculturalism in, 6:485–487
vs. patriotism, 7:140
Rawls on, 6:485–488
Schopenhauer on, 8:648
scientific, 7:323
socialism and, 9:89
Spengler and, 9:165
Third-World, 7:726
and war, conceptions of, 7:152–153
Nationality
vs. citizenship, 6:481
moral cosmopolitanism and, 2:568
Nativism
behaviorism and, 4:693
Reid and, 8:325–326
on sensory experience, 4:686–687
Natorp, Paul, **6:490–491**
Gadamer and, 4:1
Hegel and, 6:543
Lange and, 5:187
in neo-Kantianism, 6:542–543
in psychology, 6:490, 6:543
Natur und Leben (Chamberlain), 2:123
Natura Deorum, De (Cicero), skepticism in, 9:48–49
Natura et Gratia, De (Soto), 9:137
Natura Hominis, De (Nemesius), 4:697
Natural and the Supernatural, The (Oman), 7:14
Natural assets, redress of, 6:96
Natural beauty, 1:129, 1:339–340, 4:275–276
Natural conditions, and freedom, 3:721
Natural deduction calculus, Gerhard Gentzen on, 3:657
Natural disaster, Mandeville on, 5:681–682
Natural drive, 3:618
Natural Goodness (Foot), 3:684–685
Natural history
Bodin on, 1:622
Buffon on, 1:759, 3:73
cosmic catastrophic process and, 1:658
evolution and, 1:785
Jungius and, 4:861
Natural History (Buffon), 3:73
Natural History of Religion (Hume), 2:686, 9:505
Natural kinds, **6:503–505**
Natural knowledge, Ockham's theory of, 9:775
Natural language(s), **1:342–345,** 5:509
artificialization of
in medieval philosophy, 6:101–102
reaction against, 6:103–104
axioms in, 7:404
in experience, 6:74
and first-order language, 3:639
vs. formal, 1:344
logic and, 6:329
in philosophy of language, 7:403
quantifiers in, **10:28–32**
Natural law, **6:505–517**
Abelard on, 1:6–7
Albo on, 4:823–824
anarchism and, 1:176
in ancient sources, 6:506–507
anthropology and, 5:714–715
Aquinas on, 3:404, 6:104, 6:507–508, 7:421–422, 9:434
Aristotle on, 6:506
Austin on, 5:239, 6:512–513
Bentham on, 1:553, 5:239
Blackstone on, 1:553
Cambridge Platonists on, 3:406
Campbell and, 2:17
in Catholicism, 6:513
in Christianity, 7:454
civilization and, 4:549
common sense in, Jouffroy on, 4:855
contemporary, 6:510–516
cosmopolitanism and, 2:567
Culverwell on, 2:613
Cumberland on, 2:614–615
Decalogue and, 1:622
definition of, 6:505–506
denial of, 7:423
Dworkin and, 3:156
empiricism and, 7:454
as fiction, 1:553
Finnis on, 6:513
freedom and, 6:537
Freud on, 9:572
Galileo and, 3:405
general will in, 4:38–40
generics in, 4:43
genetics and, 4:47
Germain on, 7:422
God and, 6:507–509, 6:512, 9:284
Grotius on, 4:191, 6:510
Hobbes on, 6:510–511
Hooker on, 4:463
Hume on, 6:512, 6:515
as invalid for positive law, 1:553
as justification of common law, 9:141
Kant on, 6:512–514

Natural law, ***continued***
legal consciousness and, 4:577
in legal evaluation, 7:453
vs. legal positivism, 5:237–238
Locke on, 5:388, 6:511–512
logical nature of, 6:271
in Maritain, 5:714–715
medieval, 3:404, 6:507–509, 7:421
Mendelssohn on, 4:827
Mill (John Stuart) on, 6:512
miracles and, 1:783
Montesquieu on, 7:424
in Nelson (Leonard), 6:537
origins of, 9:673
other ethical theories and, 6:514
Philo on, 7:304–306
political philosophy and, 7:658, 7:661–662
in political society, 9:698
problems for, 6:514–516
property in, 8:69
Pufendorf on, 8:158
relativism and, 6:514–515
religion and, 6:514–515
religious *vs.* secular, 6:510
reproductive technologies and, 4:47
in Roman jurisprudence, 9:139
Savigny on, 8:615
scientific, 8:158
Smart on, 9:65
social contract theory and, 9:80–81
social Darwinism and, 2:642–643
species of, 3:709
Spinoza and, 9:189
Stirner and, 9:251
Stoics on, 3:400
Suárez on, 7:423
teleology of, 7:454
Thomasius and, 9:440–441
Thomism and, 9:447
utilitarian criticism of, 9:81
Vico on, 9:673
Volney on, 9:707
Natural Law (Wolff), 9:825
Natural Law and Natural Rights (Finnis), 6:513, 9:447
Natural Law in the Spiritual World (Drummond), 7:562
Natural Laws in Scientific Practice (Lange), 5:230
Natural light, in d'Ailly, 1:98
Natural necessity, 5:25
Natural numbers, 6:672
addition and multiplication of, 3:650
definition of, 5:549
first-order language for, 3:649–650
intuitionism and, 4:738, 5:469
as potentially infinite, 4:656
Skolem on, 5:472
Natural order, miracles and, 6:265–266
Natural philosophy
of Anaxagoras, 1:183
of Anaximenes, 1:186
Aristotelianism in, 9:778
of Averroes, 1:424–425
Bacon (Francis) and, 1:442–445
Bonaventure and, 1:651
Budde and, 1:721
Buridan and, 1:769, 7:8
Burley on, 1:772–775
Burthogge and, 1:776
Cambridge platonists on, 2:14
Cartesianism and, 2:53–61
Cavendish and, 2:117–118
Chatton on, 2:139
and Christian theology, Aquinas on, 9:772
Chrysippus on, 2:252
Copernicus and, 2:536
Crusius and, 2:607
Descartes and, 2:53–54
double truth doctrine in, 1:424–425
Enlightenment and, 3:246
Gersonides on, 4:69
in Islam, 1:651
Leonard on, 6:535
Mach in, 5:623–625
Maillet in, 5:644
Marsilius of Inghen and, 5:721
matter and energy in, 6:61
and method, 1:444–446
moral philosophy and, 1:444, 1:450–451
and neo-Confucian rationalism, 2:157
Ockham and, 7:8–9, 9:778
Philoponus and, 7:313–314
pre-Socratic, 7:758–759
religious purpose of, 1:444
and rhetorical method, 1:444
of Rüdiger, 8:527
Rufus on, 8:528
sense data and, 5:721
Steffens on, 9:238
of Stöhr, 9:252
transformation of, to physical science, 1:451, 5:51, 6:590
unity in, 9:578
women philosophers of, 9:838
Zhu Xi and, 2:216–217
Natural properties, 8:67
Natural Questions (Seneca), 8:812, 9:254
Natural religion
Bahrdt and, 1:457
Bolingbroke on, 1:642
Budde on, 1:721
Butler (Joseph) on, 1:782
Chubb on, 2:253
Clarke on, 2:269
Costa on, 2:572
deism and, 1:782, 2:681, 2:684, 2:688
Ficino and, 3:623, 7:571
in French clandestine writings, 2:268
Hume on, 7:77–78
in United States, 2:689
Voltaire and, 2:687
Wollaston on, 9:834
Natural Religion Insufficient (Halyburton), 2:682
Natural resources
environment and, 1:719
and future generations, 3:92–93
state sovereignty over, 9:146
Natural rights
Austin on, 5:239
Bentham on, 5:239
Godwin on, 4:139
nonexistence of, 1:553
Natural science
certitude and, 3:140
classification in, Aristotle on, 9:592
Cohen (Hermann) on, 2:303
Collingwood on, 2:327
Diderot on, 3:72–73
Dilthey on, 3:80
Engels on, 3:57–61, 3:238
existential psychoanalysis and, 3:510–511
Gehlen and, 4:35
induction methods and, 4:636
Kant on, 3:411
moral doctrine and, 7:265
Oken in, 7:11
vs. psychology, Ziehen (Theodor) on, 9:884
Rescher on, 8:439
Rickert on, 8:458–459
sophists on, 9:131
Steffens on, 9:238
Weyl on, 9:741
Windelband on, 9:792
Natural selection, 7:338
biological teleology of mental states and, 2:479–480
challenges to, 7:341–342

debate on, 3:489–490
Diderot on, 3:72
economics and, 7:351
evolutionary ethics and, 3:478–479
formulation of theory, 9:720–721
genes in, 7:341–342
Gould on, 7:342
group selection, 7:342
law of effect, 1:521
necessity and, 5:222
Skelton on, 7:341
teleology and, 7:342–343
utility in, 9:721
See also Evolution
Natural significance, of events, 3:534
Natural theology
Calvin and, 2:10
history of, 7:494
Ockham on, 7:7, 9:780–781
Paley on, 2:641, 7:75–77, 7:560, 9:392
Palmer (E.) on, 7:78
Peckham on, 7:162
propositions of, 3:530
revelation and, 8:452, 8:453
standards of validity in, 3:321
Stokes on, 7:562
Wolff on, 9:824
See also Physicotheology
Natural Theology (Paley), 2:641, 7:75–77, 7:560, 9:392
Natural Theology (Stokes), 7:562
Natural Theology (Wolff), 9:824
Naturalism, **6:492–495,** 8:276–278
a priori knowledge in, 6:501
adjudication in, 1:169
and aesthetics, 1:57–58, 6:492
analytic, 3:366–367
Aristotle and, 3:397
Baier and, 1:458–460
Cartesian doubt in, 6:502
case for, 6:493
causal order and, 9:381
Clarke on, 2:269
conceptual, 1:169, 6:497–498
Cornell and, 4:150
Daoism and, 2:190, 2:236
definition of, 3:363
as descriptivism, 6:633
determinism and, 6:494
Dilthey on, 3:84
doubt and, 1:474
Eleatic argument for, 6:493
in epistemology, 3:275, 3:327, 4:147
in ethics, 3:327, 3:479. *See also* Ethical naturalism
Eucken on, 3:452
evolutionary, 7:268–269, 7:579–580
fallacy of, 8:2
Foot and, 3:684
gloom and, 1:373
on God, nature of, 3:367
of Goldman, 8:156
Green on, 4:179–180
hermeneutics and, 6:493
Hooker and, 4:464–465
vs. idealism, 4:552, 6:499
implications of, 6:493–494
James (William) on, 1:373
Jodl (Friedrich) and, 4:835
Kelsen and, 5:49
knowledge in, 6:499–500
legal, 1:169
Marx and, 3:56
materialism and, 6:6, 6:473
mental content and, 2:477
metaphysical, and epistemology, 4:783
methodological, 6:492–493, 6:498, 6:501
of miracles, 6:492
modality of, 6:494–495
monistic, 4:835, 9:506
moral, 8:156
morality and, 2:190, 3:363–366, 6:476, 6:495, 8:156
mysticism in, 6:493
Nagel (Ernest) on, 6:473–474
nonmaterialistic, 6:492–493
in normative ethics, 1:688
normativity and, 6:501–502
as ontology, 6:492–493
origins of, 3:405
philosophical, 7:331, 8:156
physicalism as, 6:492–493
in Plato's *Cratylus,* 8:752–754
pragmatism and, 6:502–503
property, 6:498
of Quine, 7:751, 8:156, 8:220–221
realist, 6:162–163, 6:494
religion and, 3:552, 6:493, 7:59
Sanches on, 8:595
Santayana and, 8:598
Schiller on, 8:629
in science, 3:596, **6:500–503,** 8:700–701
semantic theory of, 8:752
social epistemology and, 9:83
special relativity and, 9:499
strong, 3:366–367
substantive, 6:498
supervenience, 6:498
synthetic, 3:366–367
Tagore on, 9:364
Taine on, 9:365
Telesio and, 9:391
and time, 7:564–565
utilitarianism and, 4:736, 6:476
value and, 6:171
weak, 3:366–367
Woodbridge and, 9:842
Naturalism and Agnosticism (Ward), 1:94
"Naturalism and Liberalism in the Philosophy of Ralph Barton Perry" (Feinberg), 3:560
Naturalism and Religion (Otto), 7:59
Naturalist value theory, 9:640
Naturalistic constraint, in computationalism and cognitive science, 2:393
Naturalistic fallacy, 3:366, 3:418–419, 3:445, 3:479, 3:548, 6:228, 8:2
Naturalistic humanism, of Feuerbach, 3:612
Naturalistic images, 1:325–326
Naturalistic psychology, of Haeckel, 4:203
Naturalistic reconstructions of religion. *See* Religion, naturalistic reconstructions of
Naturalization projects, in mind-body problem, 6:263–264
Naturalized epistemology, 3:576–577, 3:596, **6:496–500**
Naturalized philosophy of science, **6:500–503**
Naturalizing the Mind (Dretske), 3:109
Naturalness. *See Ziran*
Naturbegriffe und Natururteile (Concepts of nature and judgments of nature) (Driesch), 3:110
Nature, **6:517–522**
Adorno on, 1:70
aesthetics and, 1:33–34, 6:522, 9:379
alienation from, 1:610
as alive, 8:129
as allegory, 1:48
analogies of, 6:520
analysis of
into actual occasions, 9:749
in terms of events and objects, 9:748–749
Andō Shōeki on, 1:200
Aquinas on, 6:519
as architecture and organism, 1:593–594
Aristotle on, 1:273, 6:519, 7:489–490
and art, 1:34, 1:70, 1:489–490, 1:641, 6:112

Nature, *continued*
atomism and, 1:385
Augustine on, 3:402, 6:519
in Barthes, 1:480–481
in Bayes, 1:498–499
beauty in, 1:129, 9:790
Berkeley on, 1:581–582, 6:519
Bernard of Tours on, 1:593
black hole as singularity in, 1:606–609
Bohm on, 1:630
Bruno on, 1:710, 1:711
Burthogge on, 1:776
Cambridge Platonists on, 2:14
Carlson on, 1:33–34
Cassirer on, 2:66–67
chance in, 6:536
Chateaubriand on, 2:138
Cheng Hao on, 2:144
in Chinese thought, 2:168
Chwistek on, 2:255
Cohen (Morris) on, 2:307
cosmic equilibrium and bidirectionality of, 1:645
of creation as sacrament, 1:652
Cudworth on, 2:610
in Daoism, 2:191–193, 2:219–221
definition of, 3:256, 6:517–518
Descartes on, 6:519
Dewey on, 3:45–46
divine workmanship in, 2:9
divinity of, 9:646
and doctrine of series and degrees, 9:337
Ducasse on, 3:124–125
education and, 7:254
Emerson on, 3:196
Erigena on, 3:341
and essence of man, 3:611
Eucken on, 3:452
evil in, 6:521
as flesh, 6:148
Formstecher on, 4:827
freaks of, Dong Zhongshu on, 3:98
and freedom, 3:614
in game theory, 4:19
Gentile on, 4:52
Glanvill on, 4:96
God and, 1:398, 1:623, 1:672, 5:669, 9:646
Goethe on, 4:141, 4:142–143
goodness of, 6:520
Guo Xiang and, 4:196
Haeckel on, 4:201
Hegel on, 4:264–267, 6:520
Herder on, 1:55
hidden variables *vs.* local causality in, 1:540–542
and history, 1:718, 2:410
Holbach on, 6:10
human. *See* Human nature
humans and, 6:518
Hume on, 7:559–560, 8:133
infinity and, 6:521
in James's psychology, 4:778
Johnson (Alexander Bryan) on, 4:847–848
Kant on, 1:36, 6:519–520
Kepler on, 6:519
knowledge of, 9:103
Krause on, 5:147
La Mothe Le Vayer and, 5:182
Lamarck on, 5:173–174
language and, 4:847–848
laws of, 3:709, 7:489–490
Leibniz on, 7:559, 8:129
Leonardo da Vinci on, 5:282
Leopardi on, 5:285
Liebmann on, 5:345
Lotze on, 5:582
Maimonides on, 5:651
Marxist theory of, 3:57–58
mathematical conception of, 7:602, 9:336
mathematical structures and, 7:11
mathematics impossibility proofs and, 1:541–542
mental states and, 6:262
Mill (John Stuart) on, 6:229–230
in mind-body problem, 6:262
vs. miracle, 1:398
model of, and reification of energy, 3:233
moral actions and, 1:781–782
Nasr on, 6:480
and natural *vs.* unnatural, 6:517–518
in neo-Confucianism, 2:156–158, 2:183
19th century view of, 2:641
normativity and, 6:520–522, 6:632
vs. nurture, 8:153–154
animal *vs.* human sexuality and, 7:527
sociobiology debate and, 3:490–491
organic, 4:201, 4:267
pantheistic view of, 6:518
Paracelsus on, 7:104
Peirce on, 2:357
periodicity of. *See* Eternal return
philosophical ideas of, **6:517–522**
philosophy of
Bonnet on, 1:658
Campanella on, 2:15–16
Engels on, 3:57–61
Hegel and, 4:266–267
Hobbes and, 4:410–411
John of St. Thomas and, 4:845
Kant and, 5:28–29
Lachelier on, 5:169–170
Miura on, 6:276
Schelling on, 8:618–619
Schlegel on, 8:631
Schultz and, 8:659
Plato on, 6:519, 7:602
Plotinus on, 1:46
pre-Socratics on, 6:518–519
qualities in, 1:623
regulation of, 3:558–559
restoration of, human role in, 1:444
Robinet on, 8:482
Rousseau on, 8:508–510
Santayana on, 8:597
Schelling on, 8:618–619
Shaftesbury on, 1:51
simplicity of, 7:652
Spinoza on, 7:96–97, 9:172
state of, 2:260, 7:369–370, 9:79
in Steffens's pantheism, 9:238
in Stoicism, 9:254, 9:794
vs. supernature, 6:518
in Swedenborg's *harmonia constabilita,* 9:336
Telesio on, 9:390–391
Tennant on, 9:393
that which is *vs.* being of, 1:628
Theophrastus on, 9:412
Thoreau on, 9:450–451
uniformity of, 2:255, 6:224, 6:245, 9:778
unity of, 7:652
and universal equality, 3:331–332
Vaihinger on, 9:626
as violent, 1:488
waste in, 1:361
William of Conches on, 9:768
Wilson (Edward O.) on, 9:789
Winckelmann on, 9:790
Wolff on, 9:827
Woodbridge on, 9:842
in Yin Yang school, 2:152
Zhu Xi and, 2:216–217, 9:883
Zhuangzi on, 9:881–882
See also Environmental aesthetics; Pantheism
Nature (Emerson), 3:195, 6:574
"Nature" (Mill, John Stuart), 6:515
Nature and Destiny of Man (Niebuhr), 6:605
Nature and Forms of Sympathy, The (Scheler), 1:469
Nature and principle school, 2:144–145

Nature and Sources of the Law (Gray), 7:425
Nature and the Greeks (Schrödinger), 8:657
Nature, Mind, and Death (Ducasse), 3:124–125, 3:125
Nature of Existence, The (McTaggart), 4:559, 6:78–79, 9:464
Nature of Life, The (Waddington), 7:87–88
Nature of Mathematics (Black), 1:605
"Nature of Mental States, The" (Putnam), 7:471
Nature of Necessity, The (Plantinga), 7:580, 7:581
Nature of Sympathy, The (Scheler), 3:421, 8:616
Nature of the Chemical Bond (Pauling), 7:146
"Nature of the Gothic, The" (Ruskin), 1:56–57
Nature of the Physical World (Eddington), 3:164–165
Nature of the Universe, The (Hoyle), 5:351
Nature of Thought, The (Blanshard), 1:613, 2:309, 4:559, 8:817
Nature of True Virtue, The (Edwards), 3:167
Nature religion, Hermetic magic as, 1:710
Nature's Capacities and Their Measurement (Cartwright), 2:62, 5:227
Natürliche Dialektik (Dühring), 3:130
Naturphilosophie, 3:230, 5:28
Naturrechts school, German liberalism and, 5:321
Naudé, Gabriel, 5:181, 9:52
Nausée, La (Sartre), 4:748, 8:603, 8:606
Nazism (National Socialism)
- Benn on, 1:548
- Bonhoeffer and, 1:655
- Buber and, 1:715
- Camus and, 2:21
- Chamberlain and, 2:123
- critical theory and, 2:598–599
- Driesch and, 3:111
- evolutionary ethics and, 3:479
- Heidegger and, 1:253, 4:294
- Jünger and, 4:860
- Köhler and, 5:126
- Lakatos and, 5:171
- legal positivism and, 7:427
- Meinecke and, 6:114
- militarist tradition and, 7:154
- moral consistency of, 6:158
- Planck and, 7:578
- political philosophy and, 7:672
- Putnam and, 8:170
- racial hygiene in, 4:44
- racism of, 8:228
- Scheler on, 8:616

Neander, Karen, 9:389
Nebular hypothesis, Wright (Chauncey) and, 9:846
Necessary, Ockham's razor and, 9:772
Necessary and sufficient condition, definition of, 5:538
Necessary being
- Avicenna on, 4:757
- Henry of Ghent on, 4:313–314
- in Islamic philosophy, 4:754
- in ontology, 7:26
- in possible worlds, 7:23
- in William of Auvergne's metaphysics, 9:765

Necessary condition(s)
- for causality, with subjunctive conditionals, 2:99
- definition of, 5:538

Necessary connection, 4:494–495
Necessary existence, Aquinas on, 6:189
Necessary extension problem, 6:177, 6:181
Necessary phenomena statements, 7:296–297
Necessary proposition(s), 5:70, 5:100
Necessary-contingent distinction, 1:561
Necessitarianism
- Clarke on, 2:271
- Collins on, 2:683
- Martineau on, 5:726

Necessity
- and *a priori,* 1:243–244, 5:79–81, 7:296
- Abbagnano on, 1:2
- Abelard on, 5:426–427
- absolute *vs.* conditional, 1:628
- accidental, 3:693–695
- of analytic statements, 1:164
- Boethius on, 5:426
- in Buddhist epistemology, 1:757
- in classical Greek thought, 2:698
- creative activity and, 1:559
- factual, ontological argument and, 7:18
- freedom and, 6:537
- future contingents and, 1:680
- kinds of, 6:280–282
- Kripke on, 5:151, 7:724
- Lessing on, 5:296
- Lewis (D.) on, 5:313
- linguistic, 1:148, 1:166
- Mill (John Stuart) on, 6:227–228
- moral
  - deontological, 2:713
  - teleological, 2:713
- nomic
  - and natural law, 5:225
  - and scientific law, 5:221–224
- ontological argument and, 7:18
- of the past, 3:693
- Pearson on, 7:160
- Peter of Spain on, 7:262
- Philo of Megara on, 7:313
- physical, 5:221–225
- Plantinga on, 7:579
- proof theory and, 5:472
- qua phenomenon, 5:25
- schema of, 5:18
- sources of, 6:282–283
- Spinoza on, 9:187
- Wittgenstein on, 9:807, 9:813–814
- world characterized by, 1:559–560

Necessity of Atheism, The (Shelley), 1:358, 9:8
Necker, Jacques, 3:247
Neckham, Alexander, 5:429
Nectar of Devotion, The (Bhaktivedanta Swami), 4:630
Neddham, Joseph, 2:216
Nedelia (Week) (periodical), 5:218
Nédellec, Hervé, 3:148
Needham, Joseph, 3:73
Negate of a set, 5:537
Negation, **6:522–530**
- Abelard on, 5:424–425, 5:428
- aesthetic expression through destructive violence, 1:488–489
- apodictic judgment as, 1:690
- Bachelard on, 1:440
- Blake and, 1:611
- Blanchot on, 1:611–612
- within the body prior to signification, 5:152
- Boethius on, 1:628
- Buridan on, 1:768
- "can" and, 2:24–25
- complex, 6:525–526
- contradiction as, 6:523
- in contraposition of terms, 5:496
- creative, 2:22–23
- definition of, 5:549, 6:522–523
- Demos on, 6:525–526
- in dialectical method, 4:271
- disbelief and, 6:526
- elimination of, 6:528–529
- external, 6:523–524
- *vs.* falsehood, 6:523, 6:525
- four-cornered, 6:471, 9:543
- in grammar, 6:524–525
- Hegel on, 4:271

Negation, *continued*
incompatibility in, 6:525–526
in Indian philosophy, **6:530–533**
internal, 6:523–524
in intuitionist logic, 5:488
laws of, 6:527
in logic, 5:495, 6:523–529
in Marxism, 5:737
multiplicity in, 6:525
and mystical transformation of self, 1:623
of negation, 3:62–63
notation of, 6:527–528, 6:532–533
otherness and, 6:523, 6:526
Peirce on, 5:454
in phenomenology, 2:165–166
of properties, 8:66
propositional, 1:4, 1:628
in relevant logic, 5:488, 8:358–359
in Sanlun Buddhism, 2:162
Stoics on, 6:523
Wittgenstein and, 2:544
and world as self-annihilating, 1:611
Negation sign, 3:642
Negation-free logic, as paraconsistent, 5:489
Negative dialectic, 1:27–29
Negative Dialectics (Adorno), 1:27–29
Negative duties, violation of, as injustice, 4:866
Negative existentials, 1:145–146
Negative experiences, Freud on, 3:739
Negative freedom, 3:721, 4:272–273
Negative instance, in induction, 6:238
Negative method of agreement, 6:240–242
Negative name, definition of, 5:549–550
Negative premises, fallacies and, 3:539
Negative propositions, definition of, 5:553
Negative terms
in De Morgan's logic, 5:448
definition by, 2:676
Negative theology, 4:818, 5:649, 5:652
Neglect, contralateral, 6:566
Nehamas, Alexander, on beauty, 1:67
Neighborhood-locality, 6:638–640
Nein! Antwort an Emil Brunner (Barth), 1:707
Neisser, Ulrich, 5:190
Nelkin, Dana, 8:715
Nelles, Walter, 7:428
Nelson, Hilde Lindemann, 3:581, 3:593
Nelson, Leonard, 3:753, **6:534–538,** 6:543–544
Nemesius of Emesa, **6:538–539**
on eternal return doctrine, 3:353
on inner sense, 4:697
Nemirow, Laurence, 5:114
Neoclassicism
Chateaubriand on, 2:138
deism and, 2:690
Neo-Confucianism
Buddhism and, 2:155–158, 2:169–170
Cheng Hao and, 2:144–145
Cheng Yi and, 2:145
Cheng-Zhu and, 2:155–156
contemporary, 2:181–184
Dai Zhen and, 2:158
development of, 2:157–158
Du Weiming and, 2:183
and ethics, 2:199
Feng and, 2:159
first principle in, 9:6
on innate moral knowledge, 2:221–222
in Japan, 4:793–795
Kaibara Ekken and, 5:7
Kang and, 2:158
in Korea, 5:136–139
Kumazawa and, 5:161
'Learning of the Way' movement in, 9:6
Liu Shuxian and, 2:183–184
logic and, 5:416
in Ming dynasty, 2:622
of Mou, 2:183–184, 2:222
of Muro kyūsō, 6:434–435
mysticism of, 6:445
in Qing dynasty, 2:621–622
in Song dynasty, 2:622
spiritual view of, 2:181–184
Tang and, 2:182–183
three generations and, 2:182–183
three traditions doctrine, 2:183–184
and Western philosophy, 2:182
Wolff and, 9:823
Xiong and, 2:159
Zhu Xi and, 4:794, 5:138–139, 9:882
Neocriticism, of Renouvier, 8:430
Neo-Daoism
on logic, 5:416
Xuanxue (Wang Bi) and, 9:722
Neo-Darwinism, 2:637–639, 2:643, 7:340, 9:721
Neo-eurasianism, 3:454
Neo-Fregeanism, 3:731–732
Neo-Hegelianism, 4:558–659
anarchism and, 1:178
in Italy, 1:1
Marx on, 4:573
Nietzsche on, 6:610
Spranger and, 9:198
Taylor (Alfred) and, 9:373
Neo-Hobbesianism, 8:249–251
Neo-intensionalism, 9:351–352
Neo-Kantianism, **6:539–546,** 8:249–250
on *a priori* knowledge, 8:252
and analytic metaphysics, 5:34
Apel on, 1:226
and Bakhtin Circle, 1:469
beauty in, 1:54
beginnings of, 6:539–541
and critical theory, 2:598
critique of metaphysics and, 5:526
Critique of Pure Reason and, 6:540–541
definition of, 6:539
empiricism and, 3:311
Geyser on, 4:82
Göttingen, 6:543–544
Hegel and, 4:280–281
Heidelberg, 6:544–545
Helmholtz in, 6:540
history in, 7:392
Lange in, 6:540
Lapshin and, 5:199–200
Lavrov and, 5:218
Lewis (C. I.) and, 5:307
Liebmann and, 5:344
Lukács and, 5:603
Marburg, 1:469, 6:542–543
metaphysical, 6:541–542
on moral commitments, 8:251
moral education in, 7:363
Natorp and, 6:490–491, 6:543
Rickert on, 8:459
Riehl in, 8:467
Sabatier and, 8:588
Sellars and, 8:734
sociological, 6:545
Stammler and, 9:203
on virtue, 9:678
Neo-Lamarckians, 2:639
Neo-Manichaeism. *See* Mani and Manichaeism
Neo-Marxism, 3:238
Neo-Nagelian reduction, 8:284
Neoneo-Kantian period, of Kelsen, 5:49
Neoorthodoxy, decline of, 3:321
Neopatristic Synthesis (Noital), 3:673
Neoplatonism, **6:546–559**
abstraction in, 8:101–102
aesthetics and, 1:45–46
in Alexandria, 6:553–555
of al-Kindī, 4:755
of Aquinas, 9:425
and Aristotle, 6:548

attacks on, 6:558
attributes in, 6:188–189
Augustine and, 1:390, 3:289, 3:401–402
Averroes and, 1:423
of Avicenna, 1:426, 1:432–433
Bacon (Roger) and, 1:452
of Baḥyā ben Joseph ibn Paqūda, 1:457–458
on being and unity, 7:572
Bernard of Clairvaux and, 1:592
Boethius and, 1:625, 6:187
of Brethrens of Purity epistles, 4:756
Cambridge Platonists and, 2:12–14
Christianity and, 1:390, 2:644, 3:401–403, 3:670, 6:549, 6:555–556, 7:141
Comenius and, 2:341
Conway and, 2:529
cosmic hierarchy in, 4:580
Damascius and, 2:622–623
Dante and, 2:626
Demiurge and, 2:699
dialectic and, 3:55
on divine transcendence, 4:107
emanationism in, 3:189–190
Emerson and, 3:195
epistemology of, 3:288–289
on eternal return doctrine, 3:353
and ethics, 3:399–401
and Giles of Rome, 4:90
God in, 9:123
Greek Academy and, 4:171
Gregory of Nyssa and, 4:182
Hegel and, 3:309
Hellenic culture and, 6:548–549
historical survey of, 6:549–555
in Ibn Gabirol, 4:546
in Ibn Zaddik, 4:551
on innate ideas, 4:688
Isaac of Stella and, 4:753
in Islam, 1:426, 3:403, 4:754, 6:557–558
of Israeli, 4:764, 4:765
Jewish philosophy and, 3:403
Latin, 6:555
logical categories of, 2:80
logical monism in, 6:184
logos in, 5:569–570
Losev and, 5:573
on love, 5:587–589
Lull and, 5:610
matter in, 6:2–3
metaphysics and, 6:187–188
microcosm in, 5:641
on mimesis, 6:252
More (Henry) and, 6:395
music in, 1:190
mysticism of, 6:447–448
Nicholas of Cusa on, 6:595
Numenius of Apamea and, 6:679
on one/many, 4:312
Origen and, 7:40
pantheism and, 7:95
Paracelsus and, 7:103
patristic philosophy and, 7:143
Pauler and, 7:145
phantasia and, 7:271
vs. Platonism, 6:546
plenitude principle in, 5:593
Pletho and, 9:314
Plotinus and, 6:546–549, 7:631–642
possibility in, 7:720
of Pseudo-Dionysius, 8:101–102
Pythagoreanism and, 8:187
rational mysticism of, 4:685
reality in, 6:548
on reason, 3:400
in religious philosophy, 7:490
Renaissance, on love, 5:587–588
Simplicius and, 9:34–35
Skovoroda and, 9:63
soul in, 6:547
Speusippus and, 7:606
spirituality of, 6:548
Stoicism and, 9:253
Sufism and, 9:301
Suso and, 9:335
syncretism in, 4:174
Tarski and, 9:372
Thomism and, 9:443
on universals, 3:147
Neopositivism, 3:179, 7:716, 8:260
Neo-Pythagoreanism, 3:189, 8:183–184
Neo-Quineanism, 9:351
Neoromantic universalism, 9:158–159
Neo-Russellianism, 8:89
Neo-Scholasticism, 1:262, 4:23–24
Neospiritualist movement, Lachelier and, 5:169
Neo-Stoicism, Lipsius and, 5:363
Neo-Thomism, 4:91–93, 9:446. *See also* Thomism
Neoverificationism, Dummett and, 3:132
Neovitalism, Driesch and, 3:109–111
Neo-Wittgensteinianism
art in, 1:299
epistemology of, 1:299
Nerlich, Graham
on date theory, 9:477
on linguistics of time, 9:478
on nature of space, 9:466
tensed theory of time and, 9:475
Nernst, Walther, Planck and, 7:578
Nerve cells, computers and, 5:566
Nervous impulses, and perceptual consciousness, 7:181–183
Nervous system
in functionalism, 6:14
in mental states, 6:12
qualia and, 6:16
Neta, Ram, 2:487
Nettesheim, H. C. Agrippa von, 9:51
Nettler, Gwynn, 1:122
Networks
computationalism and, 2:392
concepts as prototypes and, 2:418
inheritance, 6:642–643
linguistic understanding and, 2:393
Neue Apologie des Socrates (New Apology of Socrates) (Eberhard), 3:161
"*Neue Grundlegung der logik*" ("New foundation of logic") (Carnap), 2:41
Neue Hypothese uber die Evangelisten als bloss menschliche Geschichtsschreiber betrachtet (New Hypothesis concerning the Evangelists Regarded as Merely Human Historians) (Lessing), 5:295
Neue Kritik der Vernunft (New critique of reason) (Fries), 3:751
Neue oder anthropologische Kritik der Vernunft (Fries), 3:751
"Neue psychologische Studien" (Krueger), 5:156
Neue Zeit, Die (periodical), 3:58, 5:47
Neues Organon (New organon) (Lambert), 5:175–176, 7:278, 8:786
Neueste Offenbarungen Gottes (Bahrdt), 1:456–457
Neumann, John von, **6:559–560**
artificial life and, 1:348
on axiomatics, 8:837
on Bohmian mechanics and mathematical impossibility, 1:541–542
on computing machines, 2:405–406
on ergodic theory, 7:539
in finitary proof theory, 8:55
and quantum logic, 5:491
and quantum theory, 1:638
Savage and, 8:612
on set theory, 5:521, 6:673
on transfinite numbers, 8:837
on wave function, 8:210
Neural activity, and consciousness, 2:451, 2:454, 2:456

Neural networks
concepts and, 2:416
connectionism and, 2:443
human cognition and, 2:445
Neural science, mysticism and, 6:460
Neural states, color as, 2:333
Neurath, Marie Reidemeister, 6:562
Neurath, Otto, **6:560–563**
in epistemic materialism, 6:12
logical positivism and, 5:524
naturalization of philosophy of science and, 6:501
on protocol propositions, 3:317
on protocol statements, 5:529
on truth, 3:317
Neurocognitive sciences, memory studied in, 6:122
Neuroeconomics, 7:354
Neuroethics, memory studied in, 6:122
Neuroimaging, functional, 6:564–565, 7:354, 8:152
Neurology
clinical neuropsychology and, 6:565–566
and consciousness, 1:205
Hartley and, 8:135
qualities in, 8:11
of universe, 1:369
Neurophilosophy (Churchland), 6:563–564, 6:569
Neurophysiology, 6:133
Neuropsychology, 6:565–568
Neuropsychopharmacology, Freud and, 3:737
Neuroscience, **6:563–572**
basic, 3:737
binding problem in, 6:566–567
in cognitive science, 2:297, 8:152
definition of, 6:563
determinism and, 3:25
on emotion, 3:200, 3:201
experimental techniques in, 6:570–571
moral norms and, 3:446
neuroimaging in, 6:564–565
pain in, 6:564
reduction in, 6:569–571
Neuroses
Adler on, 1:23
alienation and, 1:125
Freudian unconscious in, 9:572
in Jungian psychotherapy, 4:857
past as conditioned present in, 1:598
religion and, 8:379–380
repression and, 3:739, 3:740
Neurotic Constitution, The (Adler), 1:23
Neutral monism, 6:587, 7:204, 7:468, 8:149
Neutralism, 7:340
Never, in Achilles paradox, 9:875
Neveu de Rameau, Le (Rameau's nephew) (Diderot), 3:71–77, 3:410
Neville, Robert, on Daoist ethics, 2:198
New Academy, 2:48, 2:257, 7:607
New Chart of History, A (Priestley), 8:5
New Cyneas, The (Crucé), 7:154
New England Transcendentalism, **6:572–576.** *See also* Transcendentalism
New Essays on Human Understanding (Leibniz), 3:736, 4:565, 4:692–693, 5:254–256, 5:261
New Experiments Physico-Mechanical Touching the Spring of the Air and Its Effects (Boyle), 1:673
New Foundations of Ontology (Bergmann), 1:562
New Hopes for a Changing World (Russell), 7:156
New Law of Righteousness, The (Winstanley), 1:177
New Leviathan (Collingwood), 2:328
New Look theories, of perception, 3:676
New materialism, 3:56
New Natural Lawyers, philosophy of sex and, 7:523
New Nyāya, 9:583
New Pathways in Science (Eddington), 3:164
New Philosophy, The (Ibn Kammunam), 4:584
"New Philosophy of Experience, A" (Schlick), 9:663
New Phrenology, The (Uttal), 6:565
New Physical Hypothesis (Hypothesis physica nova) (Leibniz), 5:251, 5:260, 5:269
New Presentation of the Science of Knowledge (Fichte), 3:614–615
New realism, 4:455–456, 5:592, **6:584–589,** 7:204, 8:263
on matter-mind dualism, 2:595
monism of, 6:75
New Realism, The, 4:559–561
New Realism; Cooperative Studies in Philosophy (Holt, Marvin, Montague, Perry, Pitkin, & Spaulding), 6:585
New Republic (periodical), contributors to, 3:44
"New Riddle of Induction, The" (Goodman), 5:229
New Science, The (Vico), 7:388, 9:670–676
New System of Chemical Philosophy, A (Dalton), 1:387
New Testament, 2:247–249
Bultmann on, 3:505
Collins on, 2:331
on equality, 3:329
Erasmus' edition of, 3:337–338
eschatology in, 3:347–348
and existential authenticity, 1:762–763
on heaven and hell, 4:250
inner concords with Old Testament, 4:834
Lessing on, 5:295
Loisy on, 5:571
patristic philosophy on, 7:141
on suicide, 9:319
See also Scripture
New Theory of Vision, A (Berkeley), 4:553, 9:515
epistemology in, 3:301
Le Clerc and, 5:236
Mill (John Stuart) on, 3:312
on sense experience, 8:782
New York, as art center, 2:627
New York Review of Books, Dennett-Gould debate in, 2:712
Newborns, as persons, 7:238–241
Newcomb, Simon, 9:228
Newcomb's Problem. *See* Decision Theory
"Newcomb's Problem and Two Principles of Choice" (Nozick), 6:669
Newcomb's puzzle, 3:696
Newly Born Woman, The (Cixous), 2:262
Newman, James R., 6:473
Newman, John Henry, **6:576–584,** 9:240
News from Nowhere (Morris), 9:89, 9:619
Newton, Isaac, 3:686, **6:590–594**
on absolute motion, 9:155
and action at a distance, 5:642
Alembert and, 1:106
arianism of, 1:284
Bayes and, 8:685
Bentley and, 7:559
Berkeley on, 1:581–582
calculus of, 2:494–495
on Cartesianism, 2:56
Clarke and, 2:268–269, 7:559
classical mechanics and, 2:279
and conservation of motion and energy, 2:90
on cosmological theory, 2:561
critics of, 3:57–58

deductive-nomological model and, 8:694
deism and, 2:682
determinism and, 3:32
Earman on, 3:159, 3:160
Edwards (Jonathan) and, 3:166–167
Einstein on, 3:179
Enlightenment and, 3:244, 3:246
on force, 2:520, 3:687–688
grave of, 2:628
on gravity, 3:635, 5:54, 9:578
greatness of, 5:9
Hartley and, 8:826
Hume and, 8:133
inertial system of, 9:148
Laplace and, 5:197–198
Leibniz and, 5:251–253, 5:269, 7:475
Lichtenberg and, 5:340
Locke and, 5:375, 5:395
Mach and, 5:624
on magnitude, 2:494
on mass, 6:3
matter and, 6:61
methodology of, 8:684
motion laws of, 3:234–235
on numbers, 2:494, 4:57
paradigm-defining work of, 5:157
physicotheology in, 7:558–559
religious views of, 2:685
and Saint-Simon, 8:589
socinianism and, 9:100
on space, 2:272, 5:11, 7:474–475
theory of light, Goethe on, 4:141, 4:142
on time, 3:354, 7:475, 9:465
view of space, Kant on, 5:11
Voltaire and, 2:687, 9:709
"why" addressed by, 9:754
Wolff and, 9:826, 9:829

Newton, John, 5:438

Newtonian physics, 7:474
black holes in, 1:607
as classical mechanics, 2:279–281
Cohen (Hermann) and, 2:303
and cosmological ideas, 2:561
inertial system in, 9:148–149
space in, 9:155

Neyman, Jerzy, 8:613
on Mill's causal inference, 8:686
on testing statistical hypotheses, 9:215–218

Neyman-Pearson theory, 3:664–665, 9:215–218

Nezhnaia taina (The Tender Mystery) (Ivanov), 4:767

Nhât Hahn, 1:728

Nicaea, Council of, Arius and, 1:283

Nicene Creed (Christian dogmatic text), 2:248

Nicholas III, Pope, on apostolic poverty, 9:770

Nicholas of Cusa, 3:716, 5:43, **6:594–597**
David of Dinant and, 2:644
emanationism in, 3:189
on God as synthesis of opposites, 4:669
in humanist tradition, 7:613
Leonardo da Vinci and, 5:281
on plenitude principle, 5:593

Nicholas of Methone, 1:788, 7:610

Nicholas of Oresme. *See* Oresme, Nicholas

Nichols, Shaun, 9:39

Nicholson, Marjorie Hope, on Romanticism, 3:255

Nichomachean Ethics (Aristotle), 2:201, 2:357, 3:397–398
Aquinas and, 9:434
on friendship, 3:748, 7:521
on habit, 5:615
intellectual elitism in, 4:609
on justice, 3:329
Kilwardby's commentary on, 5:70
on love, 5:585
natural law in, 6:506
pleasure in, 7:65
on self-interest, 8:720
on suicide, 9:319
virtue in, 3:388, 7:329

Nichomachus of Gerasa, Iamblichus and, 6:550

Nichtseinsfreude, 6:117

Nichtseinsleid, 6:117

Nicod, Jean, 2:439–440, 4:635

Nicol, Eduardo, 5:209

Nicolai, Christian Friedrich, **6:598–599**
Eberhard and, 3:161
Lessing and, 5:294
Pantheismusstreit and, 7:99

Nicolas of Autrecourt, **6:599–603**
Buridan and, 1:769
on free will, 3:404
Ockhamism of, 7:8

Nicole, Pierre, 5:439–440, **6:603–604,** 7:131
Arnauld and, 1:288
Cartesianism in work of, 4:790
Desgabets and, 2:757

Nicomachus of Gerasa, use by Boethius, 1:625

Niebuhr, Barthold Georg, 8:614

Niebuhr, Reinhold, 3:35, **6:604–607**

Nielsen, Kai, 9:73
on emotivism, 3:426
good-reasons approach and, 3:430

Nietzsche, Friedrich, **6:607–617**
Adler on, 1:23
on aesthetics, 1:56
on Anaximander, 1:185
anthropology and, 7:316
aphoristic style of, 6:610–611
on art, 1:56, 1:303, 9:524–525
on asceticism, 1:353
atheism of, 1:258
Bataille and, 1:488
Benn and, 1:548
biography of, 6:607–609
Burckhardt and, 1:765
Camus and, 2:21
Carlyle and, 2:34
on classical man, 9:166
on conscience, 3:408
critical legal studies and, 7:463
Danto on, 2:627
on death, 2:653
on decadence, 7:319
Deleuze and, 2:694–696, 9:275
Derrida on, 2:716–718
Deussen and, 3:41
Dōgen and, 3:95
Dostoevsky and, 3:99
Emerson and, 3:194–197, 6:575
on empathy, 9:37
epistemology and, 5:91
on eternal return doctrine, 3:354–355
on ethics, 3:415
on facial mimicry, 9:39–40
and genealogy, 3:700
on God, 1:362
Gracián and, 4:168
health of, 6:608–609
Heidegger and, 3:504, 6:607, 6:613–614
on image of man, 7:320
on immortality, 4:744
on impersonal morality, 3:389
influence of, 6:613–615
Ivanov and, 4:766–767
Jaspers and, 3:504, 4:799
Kaufmann on, 5:46
Keyserling and, 5:58
Klages and, 5:77
Latin American philosophy and, 5:208
on life, meaning and value of, 5:356
Lunacharskii and, 5:611
Lyotard and, 5:620
MacIntyre and, 5:636

Nietzsche, Friedrich, ***continued***
 on moral order, 4:750
 on morality, 3:389, 4:153, 6:611–612, 9:263
 on music, 9:525
 nihilism of, 6:618
 Papini and, 7:102
 on pessimism, 7:247, 7:251–252
 philosophy of sex and, 7:522
 posthumous appropriation of, 6:607
 and postmodernism, 3:564, 7:730
 and poststructuralism, 3:564, 9:274
 psychoanalytic doctrines of, 3:736
 on rational inquiry, 4:749
 rehabilitation of, 5:45–46
 and Sartrean existentialism, 5:45
 Schiller and, 8:629
 Schopenhauer and, 8:649
 Shestov and, 9:11
 on social origin of ideas, 9:101–102
 Socrates and, 9:113
 Steiner and, 9:241
 Stirner and, 9:251
 on Strauss's conventional morality, 9:263
 on suicide, 9:320
 textuality in, 6:614
 on tragedy, 1:56, 9:523–524
 translations of, 5:45
 on übermensch, 6:612
 on unconscious, 9:571
 on virtue, 5:628
 Wagner and, 6:608, 6:611, 9:525
 on war and peace, 7:153
 writings of, 6:609–613
Nietzsche, Karl Ludwig, 6:608
Nietzsche and Philosophy (Deleuze), 2:694–695, 9:277
Nietzsche as Philosopher (Danto), 6:614
Nietzsche: Krankheit und Wirkung (Lange-Eichbaum), 6:609
Nietzsche: Philosopher, Psychologist, Antichrist (Kaufmann), 5:45, 6:613
Nieuwenhuis, Domela, 1:180
Nieuwyntit, Barnard, 3:73
Nifo, Agostino, 1:385, 3:270, 5:439
"Night among the American Savages" (Chateaubriand), 2:138
Night view, of Fechner, 3:556
Nigidius Figulus, 8:186–187
Nigrinus (Lucian of Samosata), 5:597
Nihilism, **6:617–620**
 anarchism and, 1:176, 6:617
 and antinihilism, 6:618–619
 in Blanchot, 1:611–612
 Blondel and, 1:618
 Camus and, 2:21–22
 Chernyshevskii and, 2:146
 communism and, 2:361
 in Dge-lugs, 1:734
 in Gnosticism, 4:103
 in Mādhyamika, 1:742
 Malraux on, 5:674
 neo-Confucianism on, 2:182
 and persistence, 7:207
 pessimism and, 7:251, 7:252
 Saint-Hyacinthe and, 8:589
 science and, 1:253
 semantics and, 8:751
 Svātantrika-Prāsaṅgika distinction, 1:732–734
Nihilism (Thielicke), 6:618
Nihon kodai bunka (Ancient Japanese culture) (Watsuji), 9:727
Nihon rinri shisōshi (History of Japanese ethical thought) (Watsuji), 9:727
Nihon seishin-shi (The history of Japanese spirit) (Watsuji), 9:727
Nineteen Eighty-Four (Orwell), as dystopia, 9:617
1987 hole argument, 4:437–438
19th-century philosophy
 associationism in, 3:311
 beauty in, 1:514–515
 epistemology on, 3:311–313
 ethics in, 3:412–418
 irrationalism in, 4:746
 Islamic renaissance in, 4:762
 materialism in, 6:11
 sensationalism in, 3:312
 Thomistic revival in, 1:262
 view of nature in, 2:641
Ninety-five Theses (Luther), 5:612
Ningen (human being), 4:797
Ningengaku toshite no rinrigaku (Ethics as anthropology) (Watsuji), 9:727
Ninth Bridgewater Treatise (Babbage), 7:561
Nirvāṇa, **6:620–622**
 in Buddhism, 1:724, 5:328–329, 6:257
 concentration in, 6:254
 in Jainism, 5:327–328
Nirvāṇa Sutra, 1:729
Nishi Amane, 4:791, **6:622–623**
Nishida, Kitarō, **6:623–626**
 Dōgen and, 3:95
 in Japanese philosophy, 4:791, 4:797–798
 use of Zen, 1:728
Nishitani Keiji, 3:95, 6:624
Nivison, David S., on Confucian ethics, 2:196
Nizolio, Mario, Leibniz and, 5:255–256
Nizolius, Marius, Leibniz and, 5:251
No Exit (Sartre), 8:604
No Hair Theorem, 1:607
Nobel Prize
 for chemistry, Pauling (Linus) and, 7:146
 for literature
  Eliot (Thomas Stearns) and, 3:185
  Eucken (Rudolf Christoph) and, 3:451
 for peace, Pauling (Linus) and, 7:146
 for physics, Einstein and, 3:178
 for physiology, Pavlov and, 7:149–150
Nobility
 in Confucian ethics, 2:194
 Dante on, 2:624–625
Noble savage
 Charron on, 2:135
 Chateaubriand on, 2:138
Noble truths
 of Buddhism, 1:725
 establishing, 5:121
Nochlin, Linda, 3:572
Nodding, Nel, 3:602
Nodes, connectionism and, 2:443
Noel, Estienne, Pascal and, 7:129–130, 8:46
Noel-Baker, P. J., on war and peace, 7:155
Noema, 7:299
Noether, Emmy, 3:234
Noether's theorem, 2:464, 3:234
Noetic synthesis, 9:259
"Noetica" (Johnson, Samuel), 4:851
Noetics
 Oriel and, 6:576
 religious experience and, 8:402–403
 Shpet and, 9:18
 Siger of Brabant and, 9:28
 Thomism in, 9:443
Nolan, Daniel, 2:428
Nomadism, 6:317–318
Nomic equivalence, 6:645
Nomic necessity
 and natural law, 5:225
 and scientific law, 5:221–224
Nomic preservation, 5:221, 5:224
Nominal(s), perfect *vs.* imperfect, 3:466
Nominales
 on conditionals, 5:428

on impossible position, 5:433
on syllogism, 5:426
Nominalism, **6:626–631**
Abelard (Peter) and, 1:4–5, 9:599
Alexander of Aphrodisias and, 4:68
Anselm on, 1:216
apoha and, 9:585–586
Aristotelianism and, 1:261
being in, 1:528
Biel and, 1:594
Buddhist, 9:544
Buridan and, 1:768
Chwistek and, 2:255–256
vs. conceptualism, 9:594
and concretism, 5:144
definition of, 6:626–627
in education, 9:700
fictionalism and, 6:630–631
Garrigou-Lagrange on, 4:23
Gerson and, 4:67–68
Goodman on, 4:158–159
hermeneutic, 6:629–630
Hobbes and, 8:774
James (William) and, 7:744
language and, 6:102
in law, 7:428
Luther and, 5:615–617
Maimonides and, 4:68
Marsilius of Inghen and, 5:720–721
on measurement, 6:86
mereology and, 6:146
moderate, universals and, 9:599
motivations for, 6:627–629
number and, 6:675
Ockham and, 6:627–628, 9:599, 9:772, 9:777–778
particulars in, 6:174
vs. Platonism, 6:626–627
private language problem and, 8:20
psychological, on thought and thinking, 9:420–421
vs. realism, 2:254
resemblance and, 8:68, 9:599–600
revolutionary *vs.* hermeneutic, 6:629–630
sameness and, 8:20
Sanches on, 8:595
Sellars (Wilfrid) on, 8:734
Smart on, 9:65
Spinoza and, 3:294
Tarski on, 9:370
Thomasius and, 9:441
Thomism and, 9:443
and universals, 1:769, 3:289–291, 6:174–175, 7:24, 9:585–586, 9:599–600
Wodeham and, 9:821–822
Wyclyf on, 9:851
See also Goodman, Nelson; Hobbes, Thomas; Quine, Willard Van Orman; Roscelin
Nominalism [term], 6:174
Nominalist prescriptivism, on definition, 2:668–669
Nominalistic theory, finding, 3:633
No-miracles argument, 8:691
Nomological attitude, 9:578–579
Nomological connections, and causal relations, 1:211, 5:71
Nomological danglers, 6:261
Nomological propositions, miracles and, 6:271–272
Nomos, **6:631–632,** 9:130–131
Non causa pro causa fallacy, 3:538, 5:543
Non sequitur fallacy, definition of, 5:543
Nonabrogatory policy, in Scholasticism, 6:100–105
Nonaccidentality, and knowledge, 5:106
Nonaction *(wuwei)*
in Daoist government, 9:722
Wang Bi on, 9:722
Nonaesthetic, 9:563
Non-Archimedian geometry(ies), 4:359–360
Nonassertoric antirealism, 6:171–172
Nonatomists, in social sciences, 7:534–535
Nonbeing, **6:635–638**
in Buddhism, 9:723
Dao as, Wang Bi on, 9:722
of objects, Meinong on, 6:115
Tillich on, 9:459
Noncausal cementing relations, 5:71
Nonclosure, relevant alternatives and, 8:360
Noncognitivism, **6:632–635**
antirealism of, 6:172
contemporary, 3:425–428
definition of, 6:156
emotivism and, 3:203–207
in epistemology, 3:327–328
and ethics, 3:203–207, 3:327–328, 7:4, 9:245
Foot and, 3:684
Hume and, 1:141
and moral judgments, 6:159–160, 6:393, 6:632–634
open question argument and, 6:156
as projectivism, 8:51–52
and value theory, 9:640
See also Nonfactualism
Noncombatants
immunity from harm, 4:872–873
vs. innocents, in just war theory, 4:872
Noncomparable probabilities, 5:56
Nonconceptual content, Evans on, 3:461
Noncontradiction
in Mohist discourse, 2:212–213
Nicolas of Autrecourt on, 6:602
principles of
Leibniz on, 6:169, 6:173–174
Wolff on, 7:27
Nondeductive determinationism, 6:172
Nondeductive reasoning, fallacies in, 3:537, 3:543–546
Nondeductivism, foundationalist, 8:178
Nondescriptivism, 8:288–290. *See also* Noncognitivism
Noneism, 3:627, 3:629
Nonempirical rules, 5:17
Nonepistemic rationality, 8:253
Nonepistemic seeing, 3:108
Nonepistemic values, 3:576
Nonequilibrium theory, in statistical mechanics, 7:539–540
Non-Euclidean geometry, 4:58–59, 5:461
axioms of, 4:119
interpretations in, 4:129
Kant and, 1:244
model of, 6:23
Tarski on, 9:371
Nonexistence, **6:635–638**
in Buddhism, 2:111
in Indian philosophy, 6:531
Nonexistent entities, cognition of, 1:523
Nonexistent object(s), 6:115, **6:635–638**
cognition of, Ockham on, 9:774
in intentional inexistence, 4:704–705
Meinong on, 6:115
Russell on, 6:172
Nonexistential claims, 3:628
Nonexplanation Test, for foreseen consequences, 4:871–872
Nonextensional contexts, 3:540–541
Nonfactive operator, 3:629
Nonfactualism, 3:627
and empiricist thought, Hume on, 3:629
and ethical naturalism, 3:364
and fictionalism, 3:629
"Non-governing Conception of Laws of Nature, The" (Beebee), 5:229
Non-Identity Problem, Parfit on, 7:120

Non-indicative sentences, 3:646–647
Noninference criterion, for intentionality, 7:290–292
Noninferential knowledge, of contingent states of affairs, 6:210
Noninstrumental value, 9:641–644
Nonliving, *vs.* living, 9:694–695
Non-locality, **6:638–642**
Nonlogical conduct, Pareto on, 7:117–118
Nonlogical constants, 5:234
Nonlogical symbols, in first-order languages, 3:641
Non-malfeasance, in medical ethics, 6:92–93
Nonmental, physical as, 6:139
Nonmental entities, direct perception of, 6:210
Nonmodal syllogism, Aristotle on, 5:400–401
Non-monotonic logic, 4:42, **6:642–643**
Nonmoral emotions, as manifestations of *qi*, 5:138
Nonnaturalism
- in epistemology, 3:326–327
- and ethics, 3:326–327, 3:417–423
- *See also* Moore, George Edward

Nonnaturalist value theory, 9:640
Nonobjectivism, unqualified, 6:160–161
Nonobservation, errors of, 3:546
Nonparticipation, Proclus on, 8:42–43
Nonperception
- in Indian philosophy, 6:532–533
- and knowledge, 5:117

Nonperformance, 6:118
Nonphysical states, qualitative consciousness and, 2:450
Nonrealism
- moral, 6:161
- and universals, 6:174–178

Nonreductive physicalism, 5:71–72, 6:134–135, **6:643–649**
Nonreflexive relation, definition of, 5:555
Nonrigid designator, 3:759
Non-self-predicating particulars, 6:179
Nonsense
- Bentham and, 1:552–553
- and fictitious entities, 1:552
- Russell on, 2:76, 2:545

"Nonsense on Stilts" (Bentham), 1:553
Nonsortal concepts, *vs.* sortal concepts, Wiggins on, 9:762
Nonstandard model, definition of, 5:549
Nonsymmetric relation, definition of, 5:555
Nontransitive relation, definition of, 5:555
Non-truth-conditional meaning, **6:649–655**, 8:532
Nonuniform objects, 9:749
Nonviolence
- in Indian meditation practices, 6:108
- in Jainism, 6:254
- *See also* Violence

Nonviolent passive resistance, 5:73
Noosphere, 9:375
Norm(s)
- in bioethics, 1:601
- Boileau on, 1:640
- in business ethics, 1:778
- Confucianism and, 2:170–171
- conscience and, 2:445
- criteriololgy and, 2:594
- Daoism and, 2:187
- in moral constructivism, 2:472
- in natural ethics, 1:704
- of objectivity, and male bias, 3:574
- philosophy and, 9:792
- in societal expectations, 9:94

Norm and Action (von Wright), 9:848
Normal
- in philosophy of medicine, 7:465–466
- scientific psychology and, 3:699
- separation from pathological or criminal, 3:700–701

Normal form
- Bozano on, 5:445
- in combinatory logic, 2:336
- in computing, 2:401
- Schrdöer on, 5:462
- Skolem on, 5:471
- universal partial computable functions and, 2:381

Normal form theorem, in computability theory, 2:380–282, 2:389–390
Normal science, Kuhn on, 5:157
Normal system of domains, 5:550
Normative category, of legal science, 5:49
Normative ethics, 1:599, 7:326, 7:335
- act utilitarianism as, 9:606–608
- and business, 1:777–778
- "can" and ought in, 2:25–26
- categorical imperative and, 2:71
- content of, 3:380
- definition of, 3:379
- goal of, 3:380
- ideal moral code utilitarianism and, 1:687
- metaethical relativism and, 3:373
- moral objectivism and, 6:164
- moral rationalism and, 8:252
- and morality, definition of, 3:380
- naturalism in, 1:688
- proof of, 9:611

Normative relativism, 3:369–373
- difficulties in, 3:371
- in metaethics, 6:159–160

Normative science, branches of, Peirce on, 7:169
Normative status, mental content features of, 2:477
Normativity
- Adorno on, 1:26
- of beauty, 1:37, 1:46–47
- concept of, 5:49
- of culture, 1:254
- in education, 7:361
- in ethics, 7:335
- in intention, 1:20
- in jurisprudence, 1:169–170
- of legal duty, 7:445
- of meaning, 8:531–533
- in medical diagnosis, 7:466–467
- naturalism and, 6:501–502
- nature and, 6:520–522, 6:632
- of ownership, 8:71
- philosophy and, 7:332–334
- presupposing and, 7:767
- in projectivism, 6:633
- promises and, 8:53–54
- propaganda and, 1:26
- rationalistic, 1:211
- self-evidence and, 1:26
- in sentences, 6:653
- sources of, 5:38
- of truth, 1:218–219

Norris, John, **6:655–657**
- Astell and, 1:355
- Collier and, 2:323
- occasionalism of, 1:356

Norton, J., on space-time, 3:160
Norton, John, on thought experiments, 9:455
No-substance theories, 7:24
Not Guilty, 3:44
Not I, 3:615
Not stealing, in Indian meditation practices, 6:108
Notae in Programma (Regius), 2:55
Notae in programma quoddam (Notes on a Program; Comments on a Certain Broadsheet) (Descartes), 2:754
Notation
- Lambert and, 5:445
- of logic, Skolem on, 5:471

logical
Marcus and, 5:704
negation in, 6:527–528
"Note on Categories" (Smart), 2:78
Note sur les Réflexions (Biran), 8:784
Notebooks, 1914–1916 (Wittgenstein), 2:544
Notebooks for an Ethics (Sartre), 8:607, 8:610
Notes Directed against a Certain Program (Descartes), 4:565
Notes from Underground (Dostoevsky), 3:99–101
"Notes on Ryle's Plato" (Owen), 7:64–65
Notes on the State of Virginia (Jefferson), 4:805
Notes to Literature (Adorno), 1:29
Notes to Tübingen Theology (Wolff), 9:824
Notes towards the Definition of Culture (Eliot), 3:185–186
Nothing, **6:657–659**
Anselm on, 1:218
and being, Heidegger on, 1:530–531
Blondel on, 1:618
Carroll on, 2:51
and creation *ex nihilo,* 2:246
Damascius on, 6:552
Dge-lugs Mādhyamika on, 1:732
divine fused with, 1:760
experienced as dread, 1:530–531
God as, 9:335
Hegel on, 5:62
Leibniz on, 2:551
linguistics of, 1:218
in Mādhyamika doctrine, 1:740–742
meditative approach to, 1:738
as pseudo problem, 1:568
vs. something, 8:622, 9:754
Nothing-but philosophies, 7:281
Notions, Berkeley's doctrine of, 9:597
Noumenal love-idea-monad, 3:669
Noumenon (pl. noumena)
in Huayan Buddhism, 2:164–165
Kant and, 3:308, 5:21
Maréchal on, 5:708
in metaphysics, 6:202
in Tiantai Buddhism, 2:163
Noun(s)
abstract, 6:660
in categorical syllogism, 5:493
Chinese, 2:191–193, 2:210–211
and construals, 7:645
as descriptive uncombined expressions, 2:73
Leibniz on, 5:441
mass *vs.* count, 2:210–211, **6:659–666**
Peirce on, 5:453
Plato on, 9:286
plural, 7:644–646
quantified, 1:171–172, 3:645
Noun phrases
complex, 3:645
in first-order logic, 3:644–646
Nous, **6:666**
Anaxagoras on, 1:181
Aristotle on, 1:278
microcosm and, 5:640
Plato on, 2:698
Plotinus on, 7:633
Nous (journal), 9:135
Nouveau Christianisme (Saint-Simon), 8:590
Nouveaux Essais (Leibniz), 5:447, 9:403
on *a priori* and *a posteriori,* 1:240
Eberhard and, 3:161
on language, 8:779
See also New Essays on Human Understanding (Leibniz)
Nouveaux Mélanges philosophiques (Jouffroy), 4:855
Nouvelle Héloïse, La (Rousseau), 5:588
Nouvelle Mécanique ou statique (Varignon), on energy and work, 3:227
Nouvelles Ecclésiastiques (journal), 4:790
Nouvelles études sur l'histoire de la pensée scientifique (Milhaud), 6:217
Nouvelles Libertes de penser, 3:683
Nova de Universis Philosophia (Patrizi), 7:144
Novalis, **6:666–668**
on love, 5:588
and New England transcendentalism, 6:572
Schelling and, 8:617
Schlegel and, 6:667, 8:631
on Spinoza, 9:193
Novara, Dominico Maria da, and Copernicus, 2:533
Novel(s)
Bakhtin on, 1:465–468
of Malraux, 5:673–674
See also Fiction
Novelty
exclusion by intellect, 1:566
psychological creativity and, 2:589–590
as quality, 1:22
Noverre, Georges, 1:297
Novikov, I. D., 9:478
Novissima Sinica (Latest news from China) (Leibniz), 5:253
Novitz, David, 2:590
Novum Organon Renovatum (Whewell), 9:743
Novum Organum (Bacon), 1:447
on blessings of science, 8:672
on definition, 2:669
on doctrine of "idols," 9:101
on heat energy, 3:229
on semantics, 8:772
Now, Gersonides on, 4:821–822
Nowell-Smith, Patrick
on determinism, 3:18
ethical theory of, 3:327
on Hare, 3:430
on Moore (G. E.), 3:419
on moral judgments, 3:429–430
on noncognitivism, 6:633
on presupposing, 7:767–768
Nozick, Robert, **6:668–670**
conditional accounts and Cartesian demons, 2:94
on equality, 5:336
experience machine of, 8:721
on knowledge, 3:270–271
on libertarianism, 5:334–336, 8:810
on liberty, 9:72
on life, meaning and value of, 5:358
on personal identity, 7:229–230
on Rawls, 5:324, 9:82
on state authority, 9:211
N-tuple, as an ordered list, 3:649
Nuchelmans, Gabriël, 4:79
Nuclear deterrence, 7:157
Nuclear disarmament, Pauling and, 7:146
Nuclear weapons, and war, 7:154–157
Null hypothesis, 3:665
Null set, definition of, 5:550
Numan, Max, and Turing, 2:375
Number(s), **6:670–679**
algebraic, Cantor on, 5:463
Aristotle on, 2:490
Augustine on, 1:46
beauty and, 1:46
Berkeley on, 1:582
calculus and, 6:671
Cantor on, 5:463, 8:833
cardinal. *See* Cardinal number
in combinatory logic, 2:337
complex, 6:671–672
in computability theory, 2:372, 2:383, 2:386
continuum and, 9:741
in conventionalism, 6:675

Number(s), *continued*
in cosmology, 8:182–183
definition of, 3:730
as determinable, 3:1
effectively enumerable, 4:121
in epistemology, 6:673–674
in formalism, 6:675–676
Frege on, 3:729–730, 5:463–464
Hilbert on, 5:470
history of, 6:670
ideal, 7:637
imaginary, 6:671
infinite series of, finite sum of, 4:655
infinitesimal, 4:652
infinity and, 5:515
in intuitionism, 6:676–677
irrational. *See* Irrational numbers
kinds of, 6:670–671
large, law of, 8:25, 8:35
Leibniz on, 2:552–553
Locke on, 5:382
as magnitude ratio, 2:493–494
in mathematical Platonism, 7:614–615
in music, 8:185
natural, 2:372, 6:672
Newton on, 4:57
in ontology, 7:26
ordinal. *See* Ordinal number(s)
Philolaus' use of, 7:310
in Platonism, 6:670–676, 7:634
plurality of, 7:644–647
as primary property/quality, 6:670, 8:8
as property of property, 6:672
in Pythagoreanism, 8:182–183
rational, definition of, 5:554
real. *See* Real number(s)
realism and, 6:171
and reality, 9:6
Roman *vs.* Indian, 4:66
surreal
Conway on, 2:502, 2:508
ordered field simplicity hierarchy and, 2:509
transfinite, 6:671, 8:832–833
Cantor and, 2:27–28
religion, and, 2:29
type theory and, 6:672–673
well-ordering of, in set theory, 8:833
Number systems, nonstandard approaches to, 2:506–510
Number theory
Cantor and, 2:26–29
Church on, 5:476
in combinatory arithmetic, 2:337
as continuum of free choice series, 1:700
Couturat on, 2:581
and definition of real numbers as cuts, 2:27
elementary, definition of, 5:541
Gödel on, 5:473
Hilbert on, 5:470
model-theoretic methods in, 5:482
Newton on, 2:494
and orders of infinity, 2:27
real numbers in, 2:27, 2:493–494
religion and, 2:29
Numenius of Apamea, **6:679–680**
Eusebius and, 3:455
Pythagoreanism in, 8:187
Numerical equivalent, in Frege, 5:464
Numerical identity, 4:567, 7:210, 7:220
Numerical representation, measurement models and, 6:88
Numinous, concept of, Otto on, 7:60–61
Nunn, T. P., in new realism, 6:584–585
Nuremberg Code, 8:667
Nuremberg trials, 1:236
Nursi, Bediüzzaman Said, on causality, 2:114–115
Nurture, human nature and, 4:483
Nussbaum, Martha, **6:680–681**
on emotions, 3:202
and feminism, 3:581
on moral cosmopolitanism, 2:568
on tragedy, 9:525
Nute, Donald, 3:711
Nutrition, patient refusal of, 3:456–458
Nyāya, 4:132, 6:530
on certification, 9:545
cognition in, 9:543
on liberation, 5:329
new, 6:530
nonexistence in, 6:531
reality in, 6:531
testimony in, 9:544–545
Nyāyabhāṣa, 6:531
Nyāya-bindu (Dharmakirti), 5:414
Nyāyamañjarī (Udayana), 4:627
Nyāya-praveśa (Beginning logic) (Śankaras-vāmin), 5:413
Nyāyasūtra, 4:627
absence in, 6:531
truth in, 9:544
Nyāya-sūtra (Aphorisms on logic) (Akṣapāda), 5:412–414
Nyaya-Vaisesika, 4:133, 4:628
realism, 9:582–584
self in, 8:718
Veda and, 5:121
Nye, Stephen, 9:100

O

O cheloveke, o ego smertnosti i bessmertii (On man, his mortality and immortality) (Radishchev), 8:230–231
O ponimanii (On the understanding) (Rozanov), 8:524
O prirode chelovecheskogo soznaniia (On the nature of human consciousness) (Trubetskoi), 9:532
O soprotivlenii zlu siloiu (On resistance to evil by force) (Il'in), 4:578
O sushchnosti pravosoznaniia (On the essence of legal consciousness) (Il'in), 4:577
O zasadzie sprzeczości u Arystotelesa (On the principle of contradiction in Aristotle) (Łukasiewicz), 5:605
Oakeshott, Michael, 4:269, 4:559, 7:1–3
Oaklander, L. Nathan
on date theory, 9:477
tenseless theory of time and, 9:475
on token-reflexive theory, 9:476
Obedience
Alcibiades on, 7:418
Austin on, 1:405, 9:141
Culverwell on, 2:613
Cumberland on, 2:615
law and, 1:405–406
as necessary to knowledge of God, 2:10
Obiter Scripta (Santayana), 8:602
Object(s)
abstract
vs. concrete, Brentano on, 1:691
epistemology of, 6:673–674
God's existence and, Leibniz on, 2:553
introduction of, 3:646
in ontology, 3:647, 7:26
properties of, 6:636
in science, necessity of, 6:628
as aesthetic, 1:508–509
analytic judgments of, 1:160
Aristotle on, 9:592
as art, 9:691
artistic, 1:315–319
attitudes toward, 6:116
attributes of, perspective and, 6:76
body and, 6:148, 9:516
and Brahman, inseparability of, 1:683
in Buddhism, 6:621
Caird on, 2:4
Clifford on, 2:293

coincident of, 6:146
vs. concepts, Frege on, 9:555–556
concrete
vs. abstract, Brentano on, 1:691
vs. physical, 1:691
constancy of, in perception, 7:185
of cosmology, 2:558
defective, 6:116
desired, representations of, and strict akratic actions, 9:731–732
in Dge-lugs Mādhyamika, 1:732
as divine language, 1:574
eternal, 9:748
expressions for, Tarski on, 9:367
as families of sensation, 1:584
form of, beauty from, 9:562
found, as art, 1:300
Frege on, 3:728, 3:729–730
homeless, 6:115
and ideas, 4:782, 6:116
impossible, 6:115
incompatible properties of, persistence and, 7:207
incomplete, 6:115
independence of, 1:584
ingredient of, 6:146
in intentionality, 4:705
of judgment, 6:116
in Kantian subjective idealism, 4:770
of knowledge, 5:94
knowledge of, in understanding propositions, 9:809
Lacan on, 5:168
from manipulatory experience, 6:81
Maréchal on, 5:708–709
Marsilius of Inghen on, 5:720–721
Marty on, 5:728–729
material. *See* Material objects
Meinong on, 6:115, 8:803
naming, 3:648
in Natorp's psychology, 6:490
nature analyzed in terms of, 9:748–749
nonexistent. *See* Nonexistent object(s)
nonreal, 5:729
numbers as, 3:729–730
numerical identity between, persistence and, 7:210
in ontological reism, 5:144
organism and, relations between, 6:75–76
Peirce on, 7:167
of perception, in idealism, 8:261
permanence of, 1:584
as phenomenal, 1:519
in photography, 9:689–690
physical, 9:749
construction of, 8:541–542
geometric properties of, in operationalism, 7:29
Russell on, 8:541–542
of power, 7:731
predicates and, 8:65
presupposition of, in thought, 1:706
private, in analytical behaviorism, 1:523
public, phenomenalism and, 7:274–275
qualities of, perception as indirect representation of, 1:577
reality of, 6:621
reductionism on, *vs.* sense experience, 9:798
relationship between, identity in, 4:567
in science of human nature, 4:489–490
as sense datum, 8:817–819, 9:138
simple, Wittgenstein on, 9:805, 9:808
skepticism on, *vs.* sense experience, 9:797–798
social relation to, 6:81
and subject
Baudrillard on, 1:491
correlation, 6:491
temporal parts of, persistence and, 7:208–210
in truth theory
Ramsey and Moore's, 2:547
Russell's, 2:544–545
Twardowski on, 9:554
uniform, 9:749
as universals, 9:588
vagueness in, 4:570
virtual, 9:691
visible, as divine language, 1:574
Wittgenstein on, 9:805
Object language, definition of, 5:550
Object theory, Meinong on, 6:115–116
Object-directed thought, Evans on, 3:460
Objectification
of actual entities, 9:751
as human enslavement, 1:560
Sartre on, 8:607
of women, 3:574
Objections and Replies (Descartes), translation of, 2:753
Objections of objections, 4:26, 9:53
Objections to Descartes's Meditations (Hobbes), 8:775
Objective(s), Meinong on, 3:312, 6:117
Objective anthropocentrism, in progress, 6:215–216
Objective concept, Vasquez on, 9:649
Objective connections, for Kant, 5:17
Objective experience, *vs.* subjective, 5:130
Objective factuality, 3:717
Objective idealism
Dilthey on, 3:84
on thought and thinking, 9:420
Objective legality, 3:618
Objective list theory, 8:721
Objective mind, 4:267–269
Objective moral value, 3:346–347
Objective morality, 6:495, 8:239
Objective phenomena, Kant on, 1:245
Objective prescriptivity, existence of, 3:628
Objective reality
to be known, 3:715
causality as, 3:705
certainty of, faith in, 4:771–772
existential experience of, 3:715
Objective reference, Kant and, 5:15–16
Objective relativism
McGilvary and, 6:75
Murphy and, 6:435–436
"Objective Relativism in Dewey and Whitehead" (Murphy), 6:435
Objective spirit
Dilthey on, 3:83
Simmel on, 6:545
Spranger on, 9:199
Objective truth
in Hegelianism, 4:287
meaninglessness of, 9:568
of moral judgments, 6:160–161
Unamuno on, 9:568
Objective *vs.* subjective
Natorp on, 6:543
Nishida on, 6:625–626
Objective will, Paulsen on, 7:148–149
Objectives of the Philosophers (al-Ghazālī, Muḥammad), 9:304
Objectivism
and Bayesianism, 1:500, 3:666
cultural, 7:316–317
Geyser on, 4:83
Kavelin on, 5:48
Moleschott and, 6:320
in moral life, 9:125
qualified, 6:160–161
Stace on, 9:200
unqualified, 6:160–161

Objectivity
in aesthetic experience, 1:509, 1:761–762
of aesthetic judgments, 1:36
and analytic behaviorism, 1:524
in Bayesian confirmation, 1:499–500
and beauty, 1:38, 1:47
Berkeley on, 1:585
Bohmian mechanics as counterexample for, 1:631
in Cartesian epistemology, 2:57
Cassirer on, 2:67
of chance, in reductionism, 2:100–101
Cohen (Hermann) on, 2:302
as correctness, 7:3, 7:4
criteria for, 1:525
Davidson (Donald) on, 2:650
in Dge-lugs Mādhyamika, 1:732
Driesch on, 3:111
Einstein on, 3:180
of ethical standards, 3:380–383
in ethics, 4:562–563, **7:3–7**, 9:787–788
experience and, 5:528
in feminist metaphysics, 3:568
Fichte on, 3:309
Gadamer on, 4:2
Hegel on, 4:263, 4:287
historical, 7:396
Humboldt on, 8:793
as impersonality, 7:4
James (William) on, 4:776
as justification, 7:3–4
Kant on, 3:307–309
and law, 1:554
in mental–physical distinction, 6:139
as mind independence, 7:4
in moral constructivism, 2:472
of moral principles, 6:372–373
mystical experience and, 6:457–458
nature of, 3:576–577
in observation, 1:633
in quantum mechanics, 1:541–542
and relationship to entities, 1:715
and right and wrong, 1:552–553
Schopenhauer on, 3:311
in scientific realism, 8:689
in social constructionism, 9:77–78
in subject contextualism, 2:482
in subjective probability, 8:36
as truth, 7:3, 7:4
types of, 9:642
Williams (Bernard) on, 9:787
Object-relations theory, 8:106–107
Obligation(s)
as act of will, 9:284
in action of states, 9:205
Austin (John) on, 1:405
to church *vs.* society, 9:509
Clarke on, 2:273
in Confucianism, 2:176
convention-dependent *vs.* convention-independent, 4:872
as counterutilitarian norm, 3:384
ethical, 2:273, 3:451
Hume on, 3:384
Kant on, 8:616
and law, 7:456–457, 9:284
legal, 7:445
Liebert on, 5:343
Lunacharskii on, 5:611
in medieval logic, 5:433
moral, 3:451, 8:616, 9:3
in moral cosmopolitanism, 2:568
promises and, 8:53
in rationality, 8:253
in relational terms, 3:599
rule-utilitarian view of, 3:384
Shaftesbury on, 9:3
universal, categorical imperative as, 2:69–72
to virtue, 9:3
Williams (Bernard) on, 3:347
Obligationenrecht als heute röminschen Rechts (Savigny), 8:614
Obligationes (Swineshead), 5:433
Obligationes (William of Sherwood), 9:786
Obligationes Parisiensis, 5:433
O'Brien, Denis, on Empedocles, 3:212–213
Observable(s)
Bohr on, 2:531
causality as, 2:107
phenomenalism and, 7:282
in quantum mechanics, 2:530
theories referring to, inductive underdetermination and, 9:576
Observation, 1:638
anthropic principle and, **1:219–222**
and causality, 2:96, 2:106–107
in classical physics, 9:495
in collapse dynamics, 8:210
Comte on, 2:411
conation in, 9:260
confirmation theory and, 2:433–442
Copenhagen interpretation and, 2:530
cosmology and, 2:557–559, 2:563–566
Dai Zhen on, 2:158
in Daoism, 2:189–190
Duhem on, 3:128
eliminative materialism on, 3:182–183
environmental influence on, 1:633
in European *vs.* Chinese science, 2:218
in experimental economics, 7:353
fallacies, 3:537, 3:546
of four-dimensional motion, 9:484
Galileo on, 4:9
and gnosis, 9:6
holism and, 1:638
in Huayan Buddhism, 2:164
and induction
in agreement methods, 6:238
in difference methods, 6:238
introspective, in James's psychology, 4:778
in medieval astronomy, 2:533
mental state and, 5:698
operationalism and, 7:32
as primitive concept, 1:486–487
and psychoanalytic theory, 8:110
in Pythagoreanism, 8:182
scale-dependent, 6:87
Schrödinger on, 8:658
in science, 1:637
scientific terminology and, 7:517
scientific theory and, 1:685
selection bias and, 1:220
semantics and, 8:690
and senses, 2:118
as systematically ambiguous, 3:542
in Tiantai Buddhism, 2:163
of time, in special relativity, 9:495–496
Observation language, 4:308
Observation statements, 6:89, 9:663
Observational consequences, deductive underdetermination and, 9:575
Observations (Diderot), 3:77
Observations on Man (Hartley), 1:50, 4:34, 8:4, 8:135
Observations on the Equality of the Sexes and of Their Difference (Dupin), 9:839
Observations on the Nature of Civil Liberty (Price), 8:1
Observations upon Experimental Philosophy (Cavendish), 2:117–118
Observer(s)
accelerating, 3:635
conscience and, 2:445
and entities, 1:715
in quantum theory, 1:630–631
and sense data variation, 1:696

Obshchestvo liubomudrov (Society of the lovers of wisdom), 5:74
Obshchina (Russian commune), 5:60, 5:75
Obsolescence, in art, 1:335
Obversion, definition of, 5:550
Occasion(s)
actual
nature and, 9:749
societies of, 9:750
Vico's use of, 9:674
Occasion sensitivity, 8:171–172
Occasion sentences, in radical translation, 8:217
Occasional Thoughts (Masham), 9:838
Occasionalism
Arnauld on, 1:292
Astell on, 1:356
Clauberg on, 2:55
Cordemoy on, 2:538
Cudworth on, 2:610
Descartes and, 2:58–59, 3:293
Geulincx on, 4:77–78
Leibniz on, 3:704
Malebranche and, 1:292, 2:587, 5:665, 5:668–670, 6:258–259
Norris and, 1:356
omnipotence and, 5:668
Rohault on, 8:483
women philosophers on, 9:838
See also Cartesianism; Geulincx, Arnold; Malebranche, Nicolas
Occhialini, G. P. S., on mass and energy, 3:233
Occult, 8:426. *See also De Occulta Philosophia* (Agrippa von Nettesheim)
Occultism
and biology, Helmont and, 9:202
Steiner and, 9:241
Occurrences
brain physiology in, 9:720
nonextensional, as criterion of intentional, 4:707
philosophy of, 9:719
Ocellus Lucanus, 7:607
Ocherki antichnogo simvolizma i mifologii (Essays on ancient symbolism and mythology) (Losev), 5:575
Ockham, William of, 5:69, **9:770–785**
d'Ailly and, 1:98–99
Albert of Saxony and, 1:101
on ampliation, 5:431
artificialization of language and, 6:103–104
Biel and, 1:594
Burley and, 1:773
Chatton on, 2:139–140
on cognition, 8:825
on consequences, 5:434–435
correspondence theory of truth and, 9:534
on determinism, 3:9
and divine command theories of ethics, 3:93
on divine foreknowledge, 4:113–114
on divine will, 9:716
Duns Scotus and, 3:141, 8:704
Durandus of Saint-Pourçain and, 3:148
Erasmus and, 3:340
on eternal return doctrine, 3:354
on formal individuation, 6:102–103
on free will, 3:404
Gregory of Rimini and, 4:183
on hard and soft facts, 3:695
on intellect, 3:290
on intentionality, 4:705
Kilvington and, 5:69
on law, 7:422
on levels of signification, 8:765
on logic, 5:437, 5:440–442
Luther and, 5:615–617
on mathematics, 5:442
and metaphysics, 6:190
Mill (John Stuart) and, 8:686
on modality, 5:435
on natural signs and nominal essence, 2:80
Nicolas of Autrecourt and, 6:601
and nominalism, 6:627–628, 9:599
philosophy of, 6:100, 9:771–772
on property, 8:73
on propositional theory, 1:773
and religious philosophy, 7:9, 7:492
on sense perception, 3:290
on skepticism, 9:50
Spinoza and, 3:294
on universals, 1:773, 3:290–291, 9:283, 9:599, 9:773
Wodeham and, 9:821
writings of, 9:771
Ockhamism, 4:113–114, **7:7–10**
Albert of Saxony and, 1:101
Catholicism and, 9:436
concepts of God in, 4:113–114
Gerson on, 4:67
Marsilius of Inghen on, 5:721
on natural knowledge, 4:183
Sylvester of Ferrara on, 9:344
Ockhamist solution, 3:695–696
Ockham's razor, 9:772
appropriate application of, 3:690
dualism and, 3:118
logical constructions and, 9:796
in metaphysics, 6:171
nominalism and, 6:627–628
Peter Aureol on, 7:256
O'Connor, Sandra Day, on affirmative action, 1:82
O'Connor, Timothy, on volition, 9:705
Octavius (Minucius Felix), 1:228
"Ode to Joy" (Schiller, Friedrich), 8:626
Odes, Fangyan and, 9:860
Odin put' psikhologii i kuda on vedët (One way of psychology and where it leads) (Shpet), 9:18
Odo of Tournai, 1:528
Odoevskii, Prince Vladimir, 5:74
O'Donnell, J., on Augustine, 1:401
Odyssey (Homer), artistic inspiration in, 1:41
Oecolampadius, Paracelsus and, 7:103
Oeconomia Regni Animalis (Swedenborg), 9:336
Oeconomicus (Household management) (Xenophon), 9:855
Oedipal complex, 8:106, 8:111, 8:146
Oedipal conflict, 8:378
Oedipus at Colonus (Sophocles), 7:246, 9:524
Oedipus Tyrannus (Sophocles), 1:188, 4:177, 9:524
Oenomaus of Garda
Cynic teaching of, 2:617
Eusebius and, 3:455
Oettingen, A. J. von, on energy, 3:233
Oeuvres (Descartes), on Gassendi's "objections of objections," 4:26
Oeuvres pastorales (Mercier), 6:143
"Of a Particular Providence and of a Future State" (Hume), 2:686
"Of Being" (Edwards), 3:166–167
"Of Generation" (Darwin), 2:631
Of Grammatology (Derrida), 2:715–718, 7:412
"Of Insects" (Edwards), 3:166
Of Miracles (Hume), 2:686, 6:266–271, 8:1–2, 9:505
"Of Personal Identities" (Butler, Joseph), 1:783
Of Population (Godwin), 4:136
"Of the Nature of that Imitation which takes place in what are called the Imitative Arts" (Smith), 9:69
"Of the Power of the Imagination" (Montaigne), 7:522
Of the Soul of the Word, and of Particular Souls, (Burthogge), 1:776

Of the Vanitie and uncertaintie of artes and sciences (Agrippa von Nettesheim), 1:97–98
Offenbarung nach dem lehrbegriff der Synagoge, Die (Revelation according to the doctrine of the synagogue) (Steinheim), 4:828
Offense principle, of Feinberg, 3:561
Offense to Others (Feinberg), 3:561
Officio Missae, De (Isaac of Stella), 4:753
Ogburn, William Fielding, 7:545
Ogden, S. N., 3:506
Ogyū Sorai, 5:7, **7:10–11**
Ohcerki gogolevskogo perioda russkoi literatury (Essays on the Gogol Period of Russian Literature) (Chernyshevskii), 2:146
Oken, Lorenz, **7:11–12**
Okin, Susan Moller, 9:75
  on multiculturalism, 3:602
  on Rawls, 3:600, 9:82
Olam Katon (The Microcosm) (Ibn Zaddik), 4:551
Old Academy
  emanationism in, 3:189
  in Platonic tradition, 7:606–607
Old Apology for the Truth of the Christian Religion against the Jews and Gentiles Revived, The (Wollaston), 2:684, 9:845
Old Testament (Bible)
  Arabic translation of, 8:585
  Collins on, 2:331
  eschatology in, 3:347
  Ezra as editor of, 9:179
  Gersonides on, 4:69
  and New Testament, inner concords of, 4:834
  Spinoza on, 9:178–179
  on suicide, 9:319
  as wisdom literature, 9:793
  See also Scripture
Oldenburg, Henry, 5:251–252, 9:175
Oligarchy, in Aristotle, 1:268
Oliphant, Herman, legal realism and, 5:245, 7:428
Olivecroma, Karl
  legal philosophy of, 7:428
  on ownership, 8:71
Oliver Cromwell's Letters and Speeches, with Elucidations (Carlyle), 2:34
Olivi, Peter John, **7:12–13**
Ollman, Bertell, 9:91
Olsen, Regine, 5:61, 7:522
Olson, Eric, on dualism, 3:115
Olympiodorus, in Neoplatonism, 6:555
Oman, John Wood, **7:13–15**
Ombre de la Damoiselle de Gournay, L' (The Shadow of Mademoiselle de Gournay) (Gournay), 4:167
Omega, definition of, 5:550
Omega-complete, definition of, 5:550
Omega-consistent, definition of, 5:550
Omens, and determinism, 3:5–6
Omission, *vs.* act, in medical ethics, 3:457–458
Omnia Opera Ysaac (Israeli), 4:764
Omniobserver, 6:173
Omnipotence, divine, 4:111
  Abelard on, 1:5
  d'Ailly on, 1:99
  free will and, 4:115–116
  goodness and, 1:362
  logical contradictions and, 6:599
  Mansel on, 5:688
  occasionalism and, 5:668
  Ockham on, 9:781
  and predestination, 3:10, 3:23
  in problem of foreknowledge and free will, 4:115–116
  Russell on, 1:361
Omniscience
  divine, 4:111, 9:173
    Adams on, 7:479
    al-Fārābī on, 3:23
    atheism and, 1:372–373
    Augustine on, 3:402–403
    Avicenna on, 3:23
    and determinism, 3:6–9, 3:23
    eternity and, 7:479
    free will and, 7:479
    Gersonides on, 4:822
    in human beings, 1:372–373
    Kenny on, 7:479
    Lequier on, 5:287
    in philosophy of religion, 7:479
  of ideal observer, 6:163
Omnitemporality of truth, 3:693
"On a Generalization of Quantifiers" (Mostowski), 5:531
"On a New List of Categories" (Peirce), 7:165
"On Abstinence" (Porphyry), 3:455
On Anger (Philodemus), 7:302–303
On Anger (Seneca), 8:811–812
On Animal and Vegetable Physiology Considered in Relation to Natural Theology (Roget), 7:560
On Being Buddha: The Classical Doctrine of Buddhahood (Griffiths), 1:723
On Benefits (Seneca), 8:812, 9:254
On Categories (Aristotle), 2:72
On Certainty (Wittgenstein), 8:180, 9:59, 9:817
On Characters and Ways of Life (Philodemus), 7:302
On Choices and Avoidances (Philodemus), 7:302
On Colors (Democritus), 5:298
"On Computable Numbers, with an Application to the Entscheidungsproblem" (Turing), 5:476
On Constancy (Seneca), 8:812
"On Contradiction" (Mao Zedong), 2:180, 3:65–66
On Conversation (Philodemus), 7:302
On Crimes and Punishments (Beccaria), 1:517–519
On Death (Philodemus), 7:303
On Demonstration (Galen), 5:408
"On Denoting" (Russell), 1:145–146, 3:252
On Dreams (Synesius), 6:553
On Duties (De Officiis) (Cicero), 7:79
On Duty or Appropriate Action (Peri tou kathêknotos) (Panaetius of Rhodes), 7:79
On Education (Alexinus of Elis), 6:111
On Epicurus (Philodemus), 7:302
On Eternal Peace (Kant), 6:623
"On Faraday's Lines of Force" (Maxwell), 6:68
"On Fate" (Alexander of Aphrodisias), 3:455
On Fate (Cicero), 3:17
On Feminism (Sobre feminismo) (Vaz Ferreira), 5:208
On Frank Speech (Philodemus), 7:302
On Free Choice of the Will (Augustine), 3:692
On Freedom of the Will (Augustine), 3:401
"On Friendship" (Montaigne), 7:522
On Generation and Corruption (Aristotle), 1:271–272
On Geology and Mineralogy (Buckland), 7:560
"On Grace and Dignity" (Schiller, Friedrich), 8:627
On Gratitude (Philodemus), 7:302
"On Gravitation and the Conservation of Force" (Brücke), 3:232
On Greek Education (Zeno), 9:253
"On Hardness and Whiteness" (Gongsun Long), 4:148
On Heroes, Hero Worship, and the Heroic in History (Carlyle), 2:34
"On History" (Carlyle), 2:33
On Human Nature (Wilson, E.), 9:788–789
On Human Nature (Zeno), 9:253

On Hypothetical Syllogisms (Boethius), 5:408
On Insolubles (Swineshead), 9:342
"On Language as Such and on the Language of Mankind" (Benjamin), 1:545
On Law (Zeno), 9:253
On Law and Justice (Ross), 7:428
On Leisure (Seneca), 8:812
On Liberty (Mill, John Stuart), 1:717, 2:34, 2:119–120, 3:724, 6:228, 6:232–233, 7:522, 9:510
 on coercion and state power, 5:337
 on freedom, 3:721
On Life (Shelley), 9:9
"On Likeness of Meaning" (Goodman), 4:159, 9:348
On Listening to Poetry (Zeno), 9:253
"On Love" (Hegel), 7:522
On Love (Stendhal), 5:588
On Mathematical Concepts of the Material World (Whitehead), 9:747
On Medical Experience (Galen), 4:4
On Melissus, Xenophanes and Gorgias, 4:164, 6:120
On Memory and Recollection (Aristotle), 4:592
On Methods of Inference (Philodemus of Gadara), 3:263
On Mind (Leucippus), 5:298
On Modern History (Schlegel), 8:632
On Music (Philodemus), 1:45, 3:263, 7:302
On My Own Opinions (Galen), 4:4–6
On Naive and Sentimental Poetry (Schiller, Friedrich), 8:629–630
On Nature (Democritus), 5:298
On Nature (Diogenes of Apollonia), 3:89
On Nature (Epicurus), 3:265, 5:599
"On Nature" (Mill, John Stuart), 6:229–230
On Nature (Parmenides), 7:123–124
On Nature (Philolaus), 7:310
On Nature Itself (De Ipsa Natura) (Leibniz), 5:254
On Nature or What Exists (Melissus of Samos), 6:120
"On New Democracy" (Mao), 2:180
On Not Being (Gorgias of Leontini), 4:163–164, 9:130–131
On Obligations (Swineshead), 9:342
On Passions (Zeno), 9:253
On Photography (Sontag), 1:324
"On Physical Lines of Force" (Maxwell), 6:69
On Piety (Philodemus), 7:302
"On Pleasure" (Valla), 9:635
On Poems (Peri Poematon) (Philodemus), 1:45, 3:263, 7:302
"On Practice" (Mao Zedong), 2:180, 3:65–66
On Prayer (Origen), 7:40
"On Predicting Our Future" (Stenner), 8:731
On Problem Solving (Duncker), 4:72
On Providence (Alexander of Aphrodisias), 1:113
On Providence (Hierocles), 6:553
On Providence (Seneca), 8:812
"On Referring" (Strawson), 3:252–253, 3:628, 9:264–265
"On Referring to Things" (Gongsun Long), 4:148
On Religion: Speeches to Its Cultural Despisers (Schleiermacher), 8:632, 8:636
On Resurrection (Athenagoras), 1:228
On Rhetoric (Philodemus), 3:263, 7:302
On Saying That (Davidson), 8:808
On Scientific Discovery (Galen), 4:4
On Sensations (Timon of Phlius), 9:501
On Signs (Philodemus), 7:302
On Signs (Zeno), 9:253
"On Some Novelties of the New Realism" (Lovejoy), 5:592
"On Some Recent Criticism of Church's Thesis" (Mendelson), 5:476
On Speech (Eudemus of Rhodes), 5:401
"On Statues" (Porphyry), 3:455
On the Adaptation of External Nature to the Physical Condition of Man (Kidd), 7:560
On the Aesthetic Education of Man in a Series of Letters (Schiller, Friedrich), 1:54, 8:490, 8:627
"On the Art of Tragedy" (Schiller, Friedrich), 8:627
On the Brevity of Life (Seneca), 8:812
"On the Caloric Effects of Magneto-electricity, and on the Mechanical Value of Heat" (Joule), 3:230
On the Citizen (Hobbes), 9:177
On the Concept of Irony (Kierkegaard), 5:61
"On the Concept of Logical Consequence" (Tarski), 5:531
"On the Connection of the Animal Nature of Man with his Spiritual Nature" (Schiller, Friedrich), 8:626
"On the Conservation of Force" (Faraday), 3:232
"On the Conservation of Force" (Helmholtz), 3:230–231
On the Constitution of the Church and State (Coleridge), 2:319
On the Contradictions of the Stoics (Plutarch), 8:758
On the Divine Names (Dionysius the Areopagite), 6:552
"On the Duty of Philosophy in Our Age" *(von der Pflicht der Philosophie in unserer Zeit)* (Liebert), 5:343
"On the Electrodynamics of Moving Bodies" (Einstein), 2:523
On the Equilibrium of Planes (Archimedes), 3:227
On the Essence of Truth (Heidegger), 4:293–294
On the Eternity of the World (Aquinas), 1:360
On the Existence of Evils (Proclus), 8:41
On the First Principles (De principiis) (Damascius), 2:622, 6:551–552
"On the Form and Principles of the Sensible and Intelligible Worlds" (Kant), 5:11
On the Genealogy of Morals (Nietzsche), 6:612
"On the General Law of the Transformation of Energy" (Rankine), 3:231
On the General Science of Mathematics (Iamblichus), 4:540
On the Generation of Animals (Aristotle), 1:91, 9:695
On the Gods (Philodemus), 3:263, 7:302
On the Gods (Sallustius), 6:551
On the Good King According to Homer (Philodemus), 3:263, 7:302
On the Greatest of Things (De Summa Rerum) (Leibniz), 5:251
 on emanation, 5:259
 on mind, 5:258–261
 on plenitude, 5:257
 on substance, 5:268
 on truth, 5:272
On the Happy Life (Seneca), 8:812
On the Harmony between Religion and Philosophy (Averroes), 1:425
On the History of the Psychoanalytic Movement (Freud), 3:738, 3:743
"On the Infinite" (Hilbert), 2:400, 3:627
On the Influence of the Passions on the Happiness of Individuals and Nations (Staël), 9:839
On the Intension and Remission of Forms (Burley), 1:775
"On the Jewish Question" (Marx), 1:493, 8:73
On the Language and Wisdom of India (Schlegel), 8:631
On the Life According to Nature (Zeno), 9:253

On the Life and Manners of the Philosophers (Burley), 3:89
"On the Limits of Art" (Ivanov), 4:768
On the Literal Interpretation of Genesis (Augustine), 7:609
"On the Logical Positivist's Theory of Truth" (Neurath, Carnap, and Hempel), 1:485
"On the Management of Property" (Philodemus of Gadara), 3:263
On the Marriage of Philology and Mercury (Martianus Capella), 6:555
"On the Mathematical Foundations of Theoretical Statistics" (Fisher), 3:662
On the Mind (Helvétius), 3:74
On the Most Ancient Wisdom of the Italians (Vico), 9:671
On the Musically Beautiful (Hanslick), 1:303
On the Mysteries of the Egyptians (Iamblichus), 4:539–540, 6:551
"On the Nature of European Culture and on Its Relationship to Russian Culture" (Kireevskii), 5:74
On the Nature of Man (Democritus), 5:298
On the Nature of Man (Diogenes of Apollonia), 3:89
On the Nature of the Gods (Cicero), 7:84
On the Nature of the Universe (Ocellus Lucanus), 7:607
On the Nature of Things (Anaximander), 1:184
On the Nature of Things (De rerum natura) (Lucretius), 3:399–400, 5:598–601
On the Nature of Things (Empedocles), 3:208–213
"On the Nature of Things-in-Themselves" (Clifford), 2:293
"On the Nature of Truth" (Russell), 2:545
"On the Notion of Cause" (Russell), 2:103–106
"On the Object of Jesus and His Apostles" (Reimarus), 2:688
On the Opinions of Hippocrates and Plato (Galen), 4:6
"On the Origin of Force" (Herschel), 3:231–232
On the Passions (Philodemus), 7:302–303
"On the Pathetic" (Schiller, Friedrich), 8:627
On the Peace of Faith (Nicholas of Cusa), 6:597
On the Philosophy of Discovery (Whewell), 9:743
"On the Philosophy to Be Derived from Oracles" (Porphyry), 3:455
On the Planets (Democritus), 5:298
On the Prevention of War (Strachey), 7:155
On the Principle of Contradiction in Aristotle (Łukzasiewicz), 5:290
On the Principles of the Universe (Alexander of Aphrodisias), 1:113
On the Problem of Empathy (Stein), 9:239
On the Proportions of Velocities in Motion (Bradwardine), 9:342
"On the Reason for Taking Pleasure in Tragic Subjects" (Schiller, Friedrich), 8:627
"On the Regress" (Zabarella), 9:867
"On the Religion of Nature " (Freneau), 2:690
On the Revolutions of the Heavenly Spheres (Copernicus), censorship of, 2:732
"On the Russian Idea" (Ivanov), 4:768
On the Senses (Democritus), 5:298
On the Soul (Aristotle). *See De Anima* (Aristotle)
On the Soul (Iamblichus), 4:540
"On the Soul against Boethius" (Porphyry), 3:455
On the Soul of the Universe and On Nature (Timaeus of Locri), 7:607
On the Source of Authority (Durandus of Saint-Pourçain), 3:148
"On the Space-Theory of Matter" (Clifford), 2:293
On the Stoics (Philodemus), 7:302
"On the Story of the Resurrection" (Reimarus), 2:688
On the Study and Difficulties of Mathematics (De Morgan), 5:461
On the Study Methods of Our Time (De nostri temporis studiorum ratione) (Vico), 9:671
"On the Study of Greek Poetry" (Schlegel), 8:630
On the Sublime (Longinus), 1:189–190, 7:271, 9:293
On the Sublime and the Beautiful (Burke), 1:771
On the Syllogism (De Morgan), 2:709
"On the Tendency of Varieties to Depart Indefinitely from the Original Type" (Wallace), 2:632, 9:721
On the Tides (Galileo), 3:687
"On the Transfer of Energy in the Electromagnetic Field" (Poynting), 3:232
"On the Transformation of Gravity" (Croll), 3:232
On the Trinity (Victorinus), 7:143
"On the True Method in Philosophy and Theology and on the Nature of Body" *(De vera methodo philosophiae et theologiae ac de natura corporis)* (Leibniz), 5:251
On the True Mystical Theology (Leibniz), 5:262
On the True Principles and the True Method of Philosophy (Nizolio), 5:256
"On the Truth of Moral Propositions" (Hägerström), 3:425
On the Ultimate Origination of Things (Leibniz), on plenitude, 5:257
"On the Uniformity and Perfection of Nature" (Freneau), 2:690
On the Universe (Heraclitus), 7:207
On the Universe (Zeno), 9:253
On the Use and Disadvantage of History for Life (Nietzsche), 6:610
"On the Use of the Chorus in Tragedy" (Schiller, Friedrich), 8:629
On the Use of the Parts of the Body (Galen), 6:538
On the Usefulness of Parts (Galen), 4:6
On the Way of Life of the Gods (Philodemus), 7:302
On the Way to Language (Heidegger), 7:410–411
"On the White Horse" (Gongsun Long), 4:148
On the World (De mundo) (anon.), 2:721
On Thermonuclear war (Kahn), 7:157
On Time and Being (Heidegger), 9:490
On Topical Differentiae (Boethius), 5:408
On Tranquility (Seneca), 8:812
On True and False Ideas (Arnauld), 1:291, 2:57, 5:664
On Truth (Antiphon)
  nomos and phusis in, 6:631
  on sophism, 9:130
"On Truth and Lies in an Extra-Moral Sense" (Nietzsche), 6:610
"On Two New Properties of Mathematical Likelihood" (Fisher), 3:662
"On Unreasonable Contempt for Popular Opinion," 3:263

On Vices and the Opposite Virtues and the People in whom they occur and the Situations in which they are found (Philodemus), 7:302
On Violence (Arendt), 9:677–678
"On Wealth" (Philodemus of Gadara), 3:263
On Words (Democritus), 8:752
"On Words" (Locke), 8:777
"On Zermelo's Paper 'On the Mechanical Explanation of Irreversible Processes'" (Boltzmann), 7:565
One, the
  Aristotle on, 3:189
  Averroes and, 1:423
  beauty and, 1:45
  causality and, 8:42
  Cheng Yi on, 2:145
  good and, 8:41–42
  knowledge of, problem of, 7:636
  as Lord of itself, 7:637
  in monadology, 6:325
  Neoplatonism on, 6:547–548
  Parmenides on, 8:43
  in *Parmenides* (Plato), 8:43–44
  perfection and, 8:41–42
  Plato on, 7:632–633
  Plotinus on, 3:400–401, 4:668
  Proclus on, 5:333, 8:41–42
120 Days of Sodom (Sade), 7:522
One Step Forward, Two Steps Back (Lenin), 5:280
One World (Singer), 9:42
One-Dimensional Man (Marcuse), 4:574
O'Neill, Onora, on Kant's moral theory, 5:36
One-many correspondence, definition of, 5:550
One/many problem, 7:44
  See also Hen/Polla
Onesicarus, Cynic philosophy of, 2:617
One-sidedness, Mill (John Stuart) on, 6:221
One-to-many relations, 2:7
One-to-one correspondence
  Cantor on, 5:463
  definition of, 5:550
  Frege on, 5:464
  in Skolem logic, 5:471
"Only Possible Ground of Proof of God's Existence, The" (Kant), 5:10
Only x and y rule, 7:229–231
Onna daigaku (The great learning for women), 5:7
Onomatodoxy, Losev and, 5:574
Ontic commitments, 8:218
Ontic theories, 8:218
Ontically deterministic, draws of cards from decks as, 3:709
Ontogenesis
  Bonnet on, 1:658
  cosmic, 1:658
  La Mettrie on, 5:180
Ontogenetic psychoanalytic assumptions, 3:746
Ontological argument for existence of God, 3:292, **7:15–21**, 9:406–407, 9:781
  Anselm on, 1:214–216, 3:493–494, 4:112, 8:645
  Augustine on, 4:112
  Barth on, 7:17
  criticism of, 7:18–19
  Descartes on, 4:112, 7:16
  failure of, 7:18–19
  Gassendi on, 3:495
  Gaunilo on, 4:33–34
  Geyser on, 4:83
  Gödel on, 4:117
  Hegel on, 7:17
  Kant on, 3:495, 5:10, 5:23, 6:188, 7:28, 8:660
  Kierkegaard on, 3:501
  Leibniz on, 5:256
  Matthew of Aquasparta on, 6:65
  in medieval philosophy, 6:99, 6:188–189
  Mendelssohn on, 6:131
  modal, 7:20–21, 7:581
  More (Henry) on, 6:396
  Ockham on, 9:781
  perfection in, 7:16, 7:20–22
  in philosophy of religion, 7:480
  Plantinga and, 3:321, 7:20–21, 9:406–407
  possibility proof of, 7:21
  reconstruction of, 7:18
  Russell on, 3:498, 7:17
  Scholz's investigation of, 8:645
  Spinoza and, 3:350
  Tillich on, 7:17
  versions of, 3:321
  Wolff and, 3:350
Ontological attitude, toward fiction, 3:626
Ontological commitments, 3:629, 6:198
Ontological dynamics, stages of, 5:43
Ontological emergence, 3:190–193
Ontological irrationalism, 4:747
Ontological notions, in Karsavin's system, 5:43
Ontological reductionism, 9:162–163
Ontological reism, 5:144–145
Ontological relativity, Quine on, 8:220
Ontological similarity, between sensations and conceptual ideas, 3:703
Ontological simplification, provided by reductive functionalization, 5:72
Ontological skepticism, of Voltaire, 9:709
Ontological status
  of essence, in critical realism, 2:596
  of forces, 3:690
  of freedom, 1:559
  of infinitesimals, in Newton and Leibniz, 2:494
Ontological undertaking, philosophy as, 5:91
Ontologism
  as being-in-itself, Gioberti on, 4:94
  Brownson on, 1:706
  Italian, 3:607
Ontology, **7:21–27**
  a posteriori, 6:493
  of *a priori* truths, Bolzano on, 1:647
  as absence of self-being, 1:738–739
  and Absolute, Chicherin on, 2:147
  antirealism in, 8:275–276
  art and, 1:78–79, **1:315–320**, 9:835–836
  axiomatization in, 1:660
  and being in general as unthinkable, 1:587
  Berkeley on, 1:574, 1:577–580, 1:586–587
  Biel on, 1:594
  and bioethics, 1:600
  Blanshard on, 1:613
  Boethius on, 1:628
  in Bohmian mechanics, 1:635
  Bonaventure on, 1:652
  Bonhoeffer on, 1:656–657
  Bonnet on, 1:658
  Bosanquet on, 1:663
  Boulainvilliers on, 1:670
  Bradley on, 1:677–679
  Brahman, 1:683–684
  Brentano on, 1:689
  Brightman on, 1:695
  Brownson on, 1:706
  Buddhist, 1:722, 1:729, 1:733, 1:745–749, 1:755, 2:161–164
  Burley on, 1:773–774
  Campanella on, 2:15
  Capreolus on, 2:30–31
  Carnap on, 2:44, 2:474
  in Carolingian thought, 2:50
  Cartwright on, 2:62
  of categories, 2:75

Ontology, *continued*
of causality, 2:101
Chan (Zen) Buddhism and, 1:729
chance and, 2:125–130
Chatton on, 2:139
in chemistry, 2:140–141
Cheng Hao on, 2:144
Chernyshevskii on, 2:146
in classical mechanics, 2:280
Cohen (Morris) on, 2:306
concepts and, 1:578–579, 2:415–416
concrete/physical distinction in, 1:691
of conventional truths, 1:742–743, 2:475
cosmology models and, 2:563–564
Crusius and, 2:606
in Daoism, 2:198
in Dge-lugs Mādhyamika, 1:294, 1:733–734
Encyclopédie, 3:223
of entities, 1:561–562, 1:740
of essence, in critical realism, 2:596
Fredegisus of Tours on, 2:49
Frege on, 3:727
of good and evil, 2:13
Guo Xiang on, 2:153, 4:196
Heidegger on, 1:656–657, 9:488–490
Herbart on, 4:322–323
history of, **7:27–29**
in Huayan Buddhism, 2:164
Husserl on, 2:82
of "I and other" relations, 1:465
of Ibn al-ʿArabī, 4:541
Ibn Sīnā's causal hierarchy in, 2:114
ideal-language method and, 1:561
in illuminationist "primacy of quiddity," 4:583
Ingarden on, 4:683
of intentionality, 4:705
of irrationalism, 4:747
Kant and, 5:21
of karma, 1:748
of knowing, 1:753, 2:15
Kuhn on, 2:475
Leśniewski on, 5:290–292
Levinson on, 1:318
linguistic influence on, 1:83
logic and, 6:473, 9:827
Losskii on, 5:577
in Mādhyamika doctrine, 1:306, 1:731, 1:740–742
Marcel and, 5:702
measurement and, 1:638
Merleau-Ponty and, 6:148
and metaphysics, 6:202–204, 7:743
Millikan and, 6:237
in modern art, 2:627–628
Mou on, 2:183
Mullā Ṣadra on, 2:114
of *mundus imaginalis,* 9:315
Nagel (Ernest) on, 6:473
of name, in Chinese philosophy, 2:189
naturalism and, 6:492–493
necessary-contingent distinction in, 1:561
neo-Daoist metaphysics and, 2:190–191
in new realism, 6:587–588
of nirvāṇa, 6:622
in non-Humean reductionism, 2:100–101
Nursi on, 2:114–115
object independence in, 1:584
Ockham on, 2:139
parsimony in, 6:628
personalism in, 5:702
personhood and, 1:463–464
phenomenological, 8:606
Plato and, 1:527
of possible things, 1:595
in possible-world counterfactual conditionals, 2:428
in quantum mechanics, 2:142–143, 5:698
in quantum physics, 9:888
in quantum theory, 1:637
Quine on, 8:218–221
of real world, 1:671
realism and, 1:672
Rehmke and, 8:303
religion and, 9:459
in Sanlun Buddhism, 2:161–163
Sartre on, 1:456, 8:606–609
in Sautrānikita doctrine, 1:745
of self, in Buddhism, 1:722
of self-realization, in Śaiva systems, 4:631
Stein on, 9:240
and subject–predicate relations, 2:162
Suhrawardī on, 9:316
Svātantrika-Prāsaṅgika distinction, 1:732–734
Tillich on, 9:459
in time, philosophy of, 9:478–479
of truth judgments, 1:690
of ultimate truth, 1:742–743
Vienna Circle and, 2:41
of "what is," 1:626
Wodeham and, 9:821–822
Wolff on, 9:827–828
Wollheim and, 9:835–836
of the word, in Shpet's linguistics, 9:19
Yin Yang school and, 2:152
in Yogācāra Buddhism, 1:745–749
Zhu Xi and, 9:883
See also Being
"Ontology of the Photographic Image, The" (Bazin), 7:382
Ontosophia (Clauberg), 2:285
"Opacity" (Kaplan), 6:290
Oparin, Alexandre Ivanovich, on origin of life, 5:360
Open question argument, 3:366, 3:418–419, 3:439, 3:444–445, 6:155–156
Open schema, definition of, 5:550
Open sentence, definition of, 5:550
Open Society, Popper on, 5:171
Open systems, *vs.* closed, and frame problem, 3:710
Open Theists, 3:695
Open-mindedness, in education, 7:358
Opera, Kerman on, 1:308
Opera as Drama (Kerman), 1:308
Opera Omnia (Henry of Ghent), 4:315
Opera Philosophica et Mineralia (Swedenborg), 9:336
Operant conditioning, 1:521, 9:61
Operational theory of meaning, 4:849
Operationalism, **7:29–33**
as antimetaphysical movement, 4:8
Bridgman and, 1:693–694
Dingler and, 3:85
of history, 4:2
Mach and, 5:625
phenomenalism and, 7:273
verifiability principle and, 9:659
Operations, in combinatory logic, 2:334
Operationskreis des Logikkalkuls, Der (Schröder), 5:462
Operative words, 7:446
Operator(s)
definition of, 5:550
fallacy of rearranging, 3:542
Lambert on, 5:444–445
Leibniz on, 5:444
logical, ontological status, 1:562
multiple and nonextensional, 3:540–541
and realism in quantum theory, 1:634
on vector space, 8:208
Operator order, ambiguities about, 3:542
Opere (Ardigò), 1:251–252

Operette morali (Leopardi), 5:284–285
Opinion
- Arcesilaus on, 1:247
- Carneades on, 1:194–195
- and common consent arguments for God's existence, 2:349
- common sense and, Stout on, 2:358
- as fact, Vailati on, 9:630
- faith ranking above, 3:529
- *vs.* knowledge, 1:42
- Spinoza on, 9:174
- in Stoicism, 1:194, 1:247
- and volition, 3:345

Opinion des anciens sur le monde (attrib: Mirabaud), 2:266
Opinions of the Inhabitants of the Virtuous City (Abunaser), 4:581, 7:610
Opium, religion as, 3:745
Oppenheim, David, 9:42
Oppenheimer, Robert, 8:667
Opportunity
- Anselm on, 1:217
- and "can" as subjunctive conditional, 2:24

Opposites
- Heraclitus on, 4:316–317
- interpenetration of, Engels on, 3:62
- in Marxism, 5:737
- negation with, 6:523
- in perception, 1:182
- unity of, 4:316–317, 9:881
- Zhuangzi on, 9:881

Opposition
- in nature, *vs.* in logic, 5:10
- of propositions, 5:545
- traditional theory of, 5:495

Oppressed class, 3:563
Oppression, 3:578–579
- bases for, 3:578
- clarifying, 3:755
- and ethics, 3:578
- feminist consciousness of, 3:563
- forms of, 3:578, 3:601
- Marxism and, 3:563
- by men, uniting women, 3:601
- phenomenology of, 7:728

"Oppression" (Frye), 3:755
O-proposition
- conversion of, 3:539
- definition of, 5:550

Oproverzhenie solipizma (A refutation of solipsism) (Lapshin), 5:200
Optical diagrams, of Fludd, 3:674
Optical illusions, 1:229–230
Optical rays, force propagated by, 3:687
Opticks (Newton), 3:688, 6:590–591
- Edwards (Jonathan) and, 3:166
- Enlightenment and, 3:246
- Hartley and, 8:135
- physicotheology in, 7:558

Optics
- Bacon (Roger) and, 1:453
- Descartes on, 2:725–726, 2:729–735. *See also Optics* (Descartes)
- Hellenistic, 4:301
- Neurath and, 6:560
- Philoponus on, 7:314

Optics (Descartes), 2:725–726, 2:729–731
- composition of, 2:733
- critiques of, 2:737
- on resemblance, 1:325

Optimality theorem, 9:221–222
Optimism, **7:244–254**
- conservatism and, 2:470
- history of, 7:246–253
- moral principles and, 2:447
- moralistic, 7:252
- progress and, 8:45–46
- rationalistic, Johnson (Dr. Samuel) on, 4:853
- and religious and philosophical issues, 7:245–246
- Sturzo and, 9:282
- teleologico-evolutionary, 7:251
- transcendental, 7:267
- of Voltaire, 9:711

Optimisme, 7:244
Opus Maius (Bacon), 5:442
Opus Oxoniense. See Ordinatio (Duns Scotus)
Opus Paragranum (Paracelsus), 7:103
Opus Paramirum (Paracelsus), 7:103
Opus Postumum (Kant), 5:9, 5:30, 5:35, 5:708–710
Opus Tertium (Bacon, R.), on William of Sherwood, 9:786
Opuscula Sacra (Boethius), 2:136
Or Adonai (The light of the Lord) (Crescas), 4:822
Oración cívica (Civic Oration) (Barreda), 5:206
Oracle of computability
- hierarchy and, 2:389
- in polynomial-time *vs.* nondeterministic polynomial-time, 2:389
- Turning on, 5:478
- unsolvability degrees and, 2:384–385

Oráculo manual, El (Gracián), 4:168
Oral law (Jewish)
- Karaite and, 4:813–814
- Philo and, 4:810
- *See also* Mishnah; Talmud

Orality, in Buddhism, 6:255
Oratio de Sinarum philosophia practica (Wolff), 9:824
Oration (Pico della Mirandola), 7:570–572
Oratory, Quintilian on, 7:367
Orbs of Heaven, The (Mitchell), 7:562
Orcibal, Jean, on Jansenism, 4:788
Ordained power, of God, 5:69
Order
- aesthetic
  - Aquinas on, 9:435
  - definition of, 9:376
  - *vs.* teleological order, 9:376
- Augustine on, 1:397
- causal
  - definition of, 9:376
  - naturalism and, 9:381
  - *vs.* teleological, 9:376
- Deustua on, 3:42
- Driesch on, 3:111
- in history, 9:518
- in logic, Zabarella on, 9:866–867
- miracles and, 6:265–266
- properties of, 9:494
- social, Althusius on, 1:135
- teleological
  - *vs.* aesthetic, 9:376
  - *vs.* causal, 9:376
  - definition of, 9:376
  - in life, 9:376
- temporal
  - in arguments for existence of God, 9:407
  - in Minkowski space-time, 9:496
  - in physics, 9:494
  - in Schutz's life-world, 8:665
- of universe, 5:640
- of world as cosmos, 2:571

Order (level), definition of, 5:547
Order of Things, The (Foucault), 3:698, 3:699–700, 7:396, 9:274, 9:275
Order type, definition of, 5:550
Ordered
- partially, definition of, 5:550
- simply, definition of, 5:550
- well, definition of, 5:550

Ordered fields
- Archimedean, and surreal number system, 2:508–509
- elementary continuum and, 2:506–509
- real-closed, 2:506
- simplicity hierarchy in, 2:509

Ordered pair, definition of, 5:550

Ordering principle, in subjective expected utility, 2:657–658
Ordinal
  initial, definition of, 5:546
  transfinite, definition of, 5:558
Ordinal number(s), 8:834
  Burali-Forti paradox of, 5:517
  Cantor on, 5:516
  definition of, 5:551
  generalized continuum hypothesis of, 4:662
  Hume's principle for, 4:659
  in measurement of sets, 4:660
  in set theory, 4:660, 8:834
  Zermelo on, 5:516
Ordinal utilities, 3:447
Ordinally similar, definition of, 5:550
Ordinary language, 1:153–154, 5:662
  common sense and, 2:357–359
  confirmation theory and, 2:434–436
  inductive probability and, 2:437
  as philosophically salient in Cavell, 2:115
  school of, 1:153–154
  subjunctives in, distinguishing, 3:710
Ordinary-language philosophy, 3:317–319
  and formal logic, 9:264
  and metaphysics, 6:170, 6:194–195
  Strawson and, 2:79, 6:197–198, 9:264–266
  on synonymy, 9:348–349
  syntax in, 9:360
Ordinatio (Duns Scotus), 3:134, 8:704
Ordinatio (Ockham), 9:771
Ordine nuovo, L' (Gramsci), 4:169
Ordnungslehre (Theory of order) (Driesch), 3:110–111
Ordo Amoris (Scheler), 8:616
Oresme, Nicholas, 6:105, **7:33–36**
Oresteia (Aeschylus), 3:79, 4:176–177
Organem, L' (Canaye), 5:438–439
Organic bodies, existence of, accounting for, 5:27
Organic development
  Driesch on, 3:110–112
  in Goethe's "primal plant," 9:241
  Stahl on, 9:202
  of states, 9:205
  Sumner on, 9:326
Organic life, laws of, Darwin on, 2:631
Organic logic, of Vasconcelos, 9:648
Organic nature, 4:201, 4:267
Organic periods of history, 6:221
Organic perspective, Dewey and, 3:43–45
Organic principle, and interpretation of spiritual phenomena, 5:60
Organic progress, Fëdorov on, 3:559
Organic structures, 1:593
Organic unity
  free, gathering diversity into, 5:59
  Moore on, 4:719, 6:353
  in organismic biology, 7:37
Organisateur, L' (journal), 8:590
Organische Bewegung, Die (Mayer), on energy conservation, 3:230
Organischen Regulationen, Die (Organic regulations) (Driesch), 3:110
Organism(s)
  art in, 1:55
  in biology, 1:593
  complexity of, 7:469
  directiveness of, 7:38
  memory in, 1:564
  object and, relations between, 6:75–76
  organization of, 7:37
  and parent-offspring identity, 1:785
  in perspectives, 6:76
  philosophy of (Whitehead), 9:750
  properties of, Greek Academy on, 6:59
  purposive activity in, 1:784
  state as, 9:205
  supremacy of, 7:347
  teleological behavior of, 7:38
  unconscious memory in, 1:784
  world as, 2:65, 5:641
Organismic biology, **7:36–39**, 9:696
Organon (Aristotle), 2:136, 2:286, 4:582–583, 5:69, 5:398–401, 5:408–409, 5:417–419
Organs, fullness of, 3:559
Organum Vetus et Novum (Burthogge), 8:777
Oriel noetics, Newman (John Henry) and, 6:576
Orientalism, postcolonialism and, 7:728
Orientalism: Western Representations of the Orient (Said), 7:728
Orientation, art and, 1:335–336
Origen, **7:39–41**
  Arius and, 1:283
  biblical interpretations of, 1:47
  on Celsus, 2:118–119
  Christian ethics and, 3:401
  and eschatology, 3:348
  on eternal return doctrine, 3:353
  on Greco-Roman theory of history, 3:348
  Gregory of Nyssa and, 4:182
  and library at Caesarea, 3:455
  on logos, 5:569
  Nemesius of Emesa and, 6:538
  and patristic philosophy, 7:141–143
  on purgatory, 3:348
  on Simonians, 9:33
  Wollaston and, 2:684, 9:844, 9:845
Origin(s), Hume's theory of, 4:490
Origin and Development of the Moral Ideas, The (Westermarck), 9:739–740
Origin of a Work of Art (Heidegger), 1:71, 4:2
Origin of Forms and Qualities (Boyle), 7:557
Origin of Geometry (Husserl), Derrida on, 2:715
Origin of German Tragic Drama (Benjamin), 1:545
"Origin of Human Races and the Antiquity of Man Deduced from the Theory of Natural Selection, The" (Wallace), 2:635
Origin of Our Knowledge of Right and Wrong (Brentano), 3:421
Origin of Species, The (Darwin), 1:568
  contents of, 2:633–635
  cultural impact of, 2:629, 2:640–643, 2:685, 3:478
  evolutionary psychology and, 8:136–137
  Gray's review of, 4:170
  in history of biology, 7:338
  McCosh and, 6:71
  on origin of life, 5:360
  physicotheology and, 7:561
  positivism and, 7:713
  precursors of, 2:631
  publication of, 3:488
  reception of, 2:629, 2:636, 2:641
  theism in, 2:630
  Wallace (Alfred Russel) and, 9:721
  writing of, 2:629
  See also Darwinism
"Origin of Species, The" (Jenkin), 2:638
Original contract, explaining political authority, Kant on, 5:29
Original enlightenment (*hongaku*), Tendai church and, 3:95
Original mind, Lu Xiangshan on, 5:618
Original or immediate knowledge, 3:752
Original position, Rawls on, 5:323–324, 8:258
Original sin
  Anselm on, 1:217
  Augustine on, 1:399
  choice as, 4:801
  in collective guilt, 4:194

and doctrine of radical evil, 5:30
Eberhard on, 3:161
Edwards (Jonathan) on, 3:169
and evil, problem of, 3:469–470
ignorance resulting from, 4:96
Jaspers on, 4:801
Locke on, 5:395
Losskii on, 5:577
Malebranche on, 5:671
Maritain on, 5:714
modern theology on, 3:474
in Pelagianism, 7:175
society and, 1:399
in Stephen's agnosticism, 9:243
Originality, in introspection, 6:81
Origination
in machine intelligence, 5:634
in reliable process, 8:363–364
Origines Britannicae (Stillingfleet), 9:249
Origines de la France contemporaine, Les, 9:365
Origines de la statique, Les (Duhem), 3:126
Origines Gentium Antiquissimae; or Attempts for Discovering the Times of the First Planting of Nations (Cumberland), 2:614
Origines Sacrae (Stillingfleet), 9:249
Origini e dottrina del fascismo (Gentile), 3:553
Origins of Forms and Qualities (Boyle), 1:577
"*Origo Largitatis et Causa Essendi*" (Ibn Gabirol), 4:546
Ornstein, D. S., 4:677
Oro, Juan, on origin of life, 5:360
Orobio de Castro, Isaac, 2:267, **7:41–42**
Orogeny, Zhu Xi on, 2:216–217
Orpheus, 7:42
Patrizi and, 7:144
Pico della Mirandola and, 7:570
Orphic theology, 2:623
Orphism, **7:42–45**
Empedocles and, 3:210
Pythagoreanism and, 8:182
Ørsted, Hans Christian
Ampère, 1:137
and magnetism, 3:551
and thought experiments, 9:452
Ortega y Gasset, José, **7:45–49**
Dilthey and, 3:84
Gaos and, 5:209
Latin American philosophy and, 5:208, 5:209
Marías and, 5:711
perspectivism of, 5:208–209
on positivism, 8:180
Scheler and, 8:616
on technology, 7:544, 7:547
Zea and, 5:209
Zubiri (Xavier) and, 9:888
Orthodox Christianity, Chaadaev on, 2:121
Orthodox Church
on dogma, 3:97
Eurasian unity and, 3:454
Ivanov and, 4:768
Orthodoxy, as principle unifying all spheres of life, 5:74
Orthogenesis
Bergson on, 1:569
Darwinism and, 2:637
Oruka, Odera, on African philosophy, 1:85
Orwell, George, on public opinion, 1:180
Osborne, Catherine, on Empedocles, 3:212
O'Shaughnessy, Brian
on location of sound, 9:138
on luck, 1:21
Oshio Heihachirō, 4:795
Oslo Peace Accords, 9:397–398
Osnovy gosudarstvennogo ustroistva: Proekt Osnovnogo Zakona Rossii (The foundations of government: A proposal for the fundamental law of Russia) (Il'in), 4:578
Ostensive definition, 1:241, 5:540, 7:110–111
Ostrorodt, Christoph, 9:100
Ostwald, Wilhelm, **7:49–51**
Carnap and, 2:35–36
on energy, 3:226, 3:233
on life, meaning and value of, 5:348
Planck and, 7:577
Taine and, 9:365
Osvobozhdenie (Liberation), 3:716
Oswald, James, on common sense, 2:357
Ot Marksizma k idealizmu (From Marxism to idealism) (Bulgakov), 1:760
Other
Adorno and, 1:26
Arkoun on, 1:284
in course of action, 6:80–81
generalized, 6:81
in Hegelianism, 4:285–286
Lacan on, 5:168
Levinas on, 4:830–831, 5:304–305
negation and, 6:523, 6:526
paradigmatism and, 9:237
self and, 5:702
woman defined as, 3:586
See also Alterity
Other minds, **7:51–59,** 7:468
Berkeley on, 1:586–587
Chinese room argument and, 2:241
critical realism on, 2:596
Cyrenaics and, 2:619
Davidson (Donald) on, 2:646–648
existence of, 5:687–688
Lipps on, 5:363
in logical behaviorism, 7:469
Schelling on, 8:619
in skeptical reasoning, 9:43
solipsism and, 9:115–121
Wisdom (John) on, 9:798–799
"Other Minds" (Wisdom), 9:798–799
Other persons, Del Vecchio on, 2:697
Otherwise Than Being (Levinas), 1:134
Otto, Rudolf, **7:59–62**
on divine transcendence, 4:107
on Fries's concept of "presage," 3:753
and natural theology, 7:494
on śankara and Eckhart, 3:163
Otto of Lucca, 7:261
Ottoman Empire, Sufism in, 9:309
Ought, "can" and, 1:780, 2:25–26
Our Knowledge of the External World as a Field for Scientific Method in Philosophy (Russell), 1:147, 2:38, 8:819, 9:200
Our Place in the Universe (Smart), 9:65
Ousia, **7:62–64**
Outer psychophysics, 3:555
Outer Word, 3:712–713
Outline of a System of Utilitarian Ethics, An (Smart), 9:66
"Outline of a Theory of Truth" (Kripke), 5:149
Outline of Abnormal Psychology, An (McDougall), 6:72
Outline of Philosophy, The (Russell), 5:131
Outline of Psychology, An (McDougall), 6:72
Outlines of Cosmic Philosophy (Fiske), 3:667
Outlines of Philosophy of Art (Collingwood), 2:327
Outlines of Pyrrhonism (Sextus Empiricus), 1:31
Mersenne on, 6:152
on semantics, 8:757
on skepticism, 8:850
Outlines of the History of Ethics (Sidgewick), 9:2
Outputs, characterizing, 3:761

Outsiders, voices of, respecting and honoring, 3:585
Ouyang Jingwu, 2:159, 2:208–209
Overbeck, France, Nietzsche and, 6:612
Overdetermination, mental causation and, 6:134–135
Overman, in Nietzsche, 6:612
Oversoul
Dante on, 2:626
Emerson on, 3:196
Overton, Richard, 9:70
Ovum, as developmentally determined system, 1:594
Owen, G. E. L., **7:64–65**
Owen, Robert, 9:87–89
Owenite cooperative, 9:87
Owens, Joseph, on Aristotle, 3:350
Ownership
artistic creation and, 1:300
communal, 8:73–74
computer ethics and, 2:397
definition of, 8:71
law and, 7:445, 8:72
normativity of, 8:71
Plato on, 2:364
of property, 8:71–72
Ox Soul, in Zoroastrianism, 9:886
Oxfam, Foot and, 3:684
Oxford, University of
Bacon (Roger) and, 1:452
Ockhamism at, 7:7
Oxford Calculators, 5:68, 9:343
Oxford Dictionary, on dreams, 3:105
Oxford philosophy, in Strawson, 9:264
Oxford University Sermons (Newman), 6:583
Ōyōmei. *See* Wang Yang-ming

P

Paccekabuddhas, 5:328
Pachymeres, George, 1:279, 1:788
Pacidius Philalethi Prima de Motu Philosophia (Pacidius to Philalethes: A First Philosophy of Motion) (Leibniz), 5:252
Pacifism, **7:67–68**, 7:155–157
just war theory and, 4:874
Russell and, 8:536–539
types of, 7:67–68
Pacifist anarchism, 1:179–180
Pacius, on Aristotle, 5:439
Paderewski, Ignacy, 5:605
Padgett, Alan, on God and time, 3:360
Padoa, Alessandro, on independence, 5:462
Paedagogus (Clement of Alexandria), 2:289–290
Pagan religion, Vico on, 9:675
Pagan Tribes of Borneo, The (McDougall), 6:71
Paganism, Clement on, 2:289
Pagels, Elaine, 7:522
Pagin, Peter, 9:351
Paglia, Camille, 7:523
Paidomorphosis, 7:320
Pain, **7:68–72**
and aesthetics, 5:63
asceticism and, 1:352–353
in assimilation of sensation, 8:824
and belief, 2:277, 3:758
in calculus of utility, 7:617
in children, reality of, 7:71–72
concept of, 7:56–57
consciousness and, 2:449
Dühring on, 3:131
emotional, 5:44, 8:109–110
ethical significance of, 3:474–475, **7:72–73**
euthanasia and, **3:455–459**
and evil, as theological problem, 3:474–475
of existence, 6:620
expressions of, as learned behavior, 7:71
folkway descriptions of, 7:70–71
God's experience of, 4:110
Lewis (D.) on, 5:315
in materialism, 6:9–10, 6:15–16
medical ethics and, 6:97
morality and, 8:3
nature of, 7:68
neurophysiology of, 7:68–69
neuroscience and, 6:564
nirvāṇa as relief of, 6:620
Nishida on, 6:624
optimism/pessimism and, 7:249–253
in pathogonous metaphysics, 9:252
perception of, 7:181
Philodemus on, 7:303
philosophical views on, 7:68–73
and pleasure
balance of, 7:251–253
and behavior, 1:552
Bentham on, 1:552
Berkeley on, 1:586
Boileau on, 1:640
felicific calculus, 1:552
government and, 1:556
mind and, 1:578
as moral standard, 1:552
as private sensa, 4:588
and psychological development, 7:71–72
speciesism and, 9:164
in tragedy, pleasure from, 1:44, 9:561–562
treatment of, ethics of, 7:71–72
ugliness and, 9:561
unreality of, Gentile on, 4:52
Paine, Thomas, **7:73–74**
deism of, 2:689–691
political philosophy of, 7:665–666
Painlev, Paul, on unique evolution, 3:32
Painting
artificial intelligence and, 1:346
Baxandall on, 1:330
Carroll on, 7:383
DuBos on, 3:123
in formalism, 1:308–309
Gilson on, 4:92
Hegel on, 4:275
perspective as meaning in, 1:312
Plato on, 1:324
Renaissance, 1:330–331
theory of, 9:690–692
titles of, 9:691
Wölfflin on, 1:330–331
Wollheim on, 9:835
Painting and Reality (Gilson), 4:92
Painting as an Art (Wollheim), 9:835
Pair set, definition of, 5:551
Pairing axiom, definition of, 5:551
Pakistan
Iqbal and, 4:744
Sufism in, 9:310
Palágyi, Menyhert, **7:74–75**
Palamas, Gregory, 1:788–789
Palatine Anthology (Philodemus), 7:302
Paley, William, **7:75–78**
on altruism and self-interest, 3:172
Austin and, 7:425
Channing and, 2:130
and ethics, 3:93, 3:412
on God
characteristics of, 7:77
existence of, 7:77, 9:377
on human nature, 3:172
Hume and, 7:77–78
Malthus and, 5:676
on miracles, 6:267
on nature, 2:641
physicotheology and, 7:560
Thoreau and, 9:450
utilitarianism and, 9:605
Pali Canon, 7:486–487
Palingénésie philosophique, ou Idées sur l'état passé (Bonnet), 1:658, 7:100
Palingénésie sociale (Ballanche), 9:520

Palingenesis, 4:94–95
Palmer, Elihu, 2:690–691, **7:78**
Pampsychia (Patrizi), 7:144
Panaetius of Rhodes, **7:78–80**
  Aristotle and, 4:174
  and ethics, 3:400
Panamanian philosophy, contemporary period of, 5:211
Pan-Americanism, in Latin American philosophy, 5:210
Panarchia (Patrizi), 7:144
Panaugia (Patrizi), 7:144
Pañcaśikha, 5:412
Pañcaskandhakaprakaraṇa (A treatise on the five aggregates), 9:651
Pancosmia (Patrizi), 7:144
Panentheism
  Bulgakov on, 1:760
  emanationism as, 3:189
  Franck and, 3:713
  Krause and, 5:147
  See also Emanationism; Krause, Karl Christian Friedrich
Pangenesis theory, Democritus on, 5:300
Pāṇini, 4:631
  grammar of, 5:410, 7:413–415
  on speech, 7:413
  universals used by, 9:581
Panlogism
  Natorp and, 6:543
  Trubetskoi (Sergei) on, 9:532
Pannenberg, Wolfhart, **7:80–82**
  on anthropology of religious experience, 7:80–81
  on history as revelation, 7:81–82
Panopticon, 1:555, 2:396–397
Panpsychism, **7:82–94,** 9:390
  arguments for, 7:86–90
  and consciousness, degrees of, 7:85
  Empedocles on, 3:209–210
  Fechner on, 3:556
  hylozoism and, 7:84
  intelligibility of, 7:90–92
  Kozlov on, 5:146
  vs. materialism, 6:6
  naive *vs.* critical, 7:85–86
  parapsychology and, 7:114
  Spinoza on, 9:188
  Strato and, 9:261
  Telesio on, 9:390
  world soul and, 7:84–85
Panpsychistic idealism, personalism and, 7:234
Pan-Slavism, Bakunin and, 1:471–472
Pansomatism, 5:144
Pantagruel (Rabelais), 4:564
Pantaṇjali, yoga and, 5:329
Pantheism, **7:94–99**
  and absolute, 1:12
  in all-unity of God, 9:124
  Butler (Samuel) and, 1:785
  Caird and, 4:108
  Christianity and, 9:262–263
  Comenius on, 2:341
  controversy about. *See Pantheismusstreit*
  criticisms of, 7:98–99
  David of Dinant and, 2:644–645
  dynamic *vs.* immanentist, 7:634
  Fiske on, 3:667
  German, 7:97–98
  Goethe and, 4:141–143, 9:194
  Hegel and, 3:610
  history of, 2:683
  ibn al-ʿArabī and, 4:743
  and idealism, 3:610, 4:552
  in Indian philosophy, 7:94–95
  on infinity of God, 4:669
  in Islamic mysticism, 6:452
  Jacobi (Friedrich Heinrich) and, 4:769
  Kabbalah and, 5:2
  Nakae Tōju and, 6:477
  as naturalistic religion, 8:376
  of nature, 6:518
  Paulsen and, 7:148
  Scheler on, 8:616
  Schelling on, 4:557, 8:621
  Schlegel and, 8:632
  Servetus and, 8:830
  Skovoroda and, 9:63
  Spinoza and, 4:108, 7:95–97, 9:185, 9:193
  Steffens and, 9:238
  Teilhard and, 9:375
  as theological atheism, 3:610
  Toland and, 9:506
  Trubetskoi (Sergei) on, 9:532
  Vaihinger and, 9:628
  Viśiṣṭādvaita on, 4:630
Pantheismusstreit, 5:296, **7:99–102,** 9:193
Pantheisticon: sive Formula celebrandae Sodalitatis (Toland), 9:506
Panthoides, 6:111
PAP (Principle of Alternative Possibilities), 3:694, 3:718
Pap, Arthur, 2:348
Papacy
  Aquinas on, 6:104
  authority of, 9:783–784
  at Avignon, 9:770–771
  and nationalism, rise of, 7:152–153
  Ockham and, 9:770–771, 9:783–784
  on war and peace, 7:154
  Wyclyf on, 9:851
  See also specific pope
Papal infallibility
  Catholic Church and, 3:97
  Lamennais on, 5:177
  Luther on, 5:612
Papillone (butterfly), 3:706
Papini, Giovanni, 2:663, **7:102–103**
Papirius Fabianus, 8:811
Paracelsus, **7:103–105**
  Franck and, 3:712
  Judah the Hasid compared to, 5:3
  panpsychism and, 7:83
Paraconsistent logics, **7:105–106**
  applications of, 7:106
  inference and, 5:483
  information and, 5:489
Paradigm(s), 8:695–697
  bioethics and, 1:601
  competing, 5:158–159
  in Confucian ethics, 2:196
  constructivism and, 2:475
  creative process and, 2:590
  incommensurability of, 5:157
  Malcolm on, 2:359
  as models, 5:158
  value of, 1:606
Paradigm concept, of Kuhn, 5:157
Paradigm physical object view, 6:139
Paradigm shifts, 5:158
Paradigmata, Lichtenberg on, 5:340
Paradigmatism, 9:237
Paradigm-case argument, **7:106–113**
Paradigm-defining works, 5:157
Paradise Lost (Milton), 1:304, 4:166, 6:251
Paradise Regained (Milton), 6:251
Paradox(es)
  Borel-Kolmogorov, 9:226
  in Buddhism, 1:738
  Buridan on, 1:768–770
  of Carroll, 5:452
  category mistakes and, 2:75, 2:78
  in Chan Buddhism, 2:167
  in Chinese philosophy, 2:189, 5:415
  chord, 9:227
  in classical philosophy, 5:398
  in combinatory logic, 2:337
  of conditional probability, 2:128
  and conventional *vs.* ultimate truth, 1:742–743
  definition of, 5:551
  as dialectic result of freedom, 1:559

Paradox(es), *continued*
Einstein, Podolsky, Rosen argument and, 1:630
of fiction, 5:367–368
of finite and infinite sets, 2:28
of freedom, Niebuhr on, 6:605
Frege on, 9:556
of imagination, 4:600–601
of indifference, 2:436
information loss, in black holes, 1:609
in Laozi, 5:195
legal, 7:452
liar's. *See* Liar paradox
logic and, 5:317
logical, 5:551
Lukasiewicz truth theory and, 2:547
in Mādhyamika doctrine, 1:740–743
Malcolm on common sense, 2:359
of material implication, 3:643, 5:551
vs. mere inconsistency, 5:65
Nāgārjuna as dialetheist, 1:742–743, 1:742–743
nonconglomerability, 9:226
Petersburg, 5:339
in physics, 2:106
in presentation of religious ideas, 2:229–230
Raven's, 2:440–441
and revelation as dialectical discourse, 1:707
of round square, 8:804
Russell on, 2:76, 2:544, 5:466, 8:834
of self-deception, 8:714
semantic, 5:551
and set theory, 5:520, 5:551, 6:21, 6:672–673, 9:555
of skepticism, 8:23, 9:136–137
Skolem's, 5:556
Socratic, 9:111
in Stace's metaphysics, 9:200
Stoic logic and, 5:407
of strict implication, 5:429
of subjective truth, 9:11
in Tarski's truth theory, 2:547
with time, 9:465
truth and, 9:534, 9:540
water-and-wine, 9:226
Wittgenstein on, 2:359
Zeno on, 1:568, 2:491, 7:598
"Paradox of the Thinking Behaviorist" (Lovejoy), 5:592
"Paradox of the Time-Retarding Journey, The" (Lovejoy), 5:592
Paradoxa (Lipsius), 5:364
Paradoxa ducenta octoginta (Franck), 3:712
Paradoxe sur le comédien (The Paradox of the actor) (Diderot), 3:71
Paradoxien des Unendlichen (The Paradoxes of the Infinite) (Bolzano), 1:646
Paralipomena Dialectices (Illyricus), 5:439
Parallel distributed processing, 1:347, 2:299
Parallel laws, Ziehen (Theodor) on, 9:884
Paralleli Militari (Patrizi), 7:144
Parallelism
in mind-body problem, 6:258–259
psychophysical, 7:268
Paralogism, definition of, 5:551
Paralysis denial, 6:566
Parameter theorem, in computability theory, 2:382
Paramorphic models of religious language, 8:418
Paranormal phenomena
Broad and, 1:698
Ducasse on, 3:125–126
naturalism and, 6:492, 6:501
See also Parapsychology; Precognition
Paraphrase, 3:627–628
notion of, 3:629
Quine on, 8:219
Paraphrasis, 3:627–628
Paraphrastic fictionalists, invoking nonfactive operators, 3:629
Parapraxis, 3:738
Parapsychological Association, 7:113–115
Parapsychology, **7:113–117**
case for, 7:115–116
controversies about, 7:114–115
Driesch on, 3:112
as evidence of immortality, 4:612
experimentation in, 7:752–753, 7:757
materialism and, 6:14
McDougall on, 6:72
philosophical implications of, 7:113–114
research on, problems in, 7:114
See also Precognition
Pardes Rimmonim (A garden of pomegranates) (Cordovero), 2:539
Parerga and Paralipomena (Schopenhauer), 8:648
Pareto, Vilfredo, **7:117–119**
on decision theory, 2:655
on democracy, 2:702
on economics, 7:117–118
on senses as source of knowledge, 9:103
on social origin of ideas, 9:102
on sociology, 7:117–119
Pareto efficiency
ethics and, 3:448–449
law and, 7:461
Pareto optimality, 1:778
Pareto superiority, 7:461
"Pari de Pascal, Le" (Lachelier), 5:170
Parfit, Derek, **7:119–121**
on agency, 3:445
on Buddhism, 2:199
on Hume, 2:199
as intuitionist, 4:735
on personal identity, 7:229–231, 9:762–763
on self-effacing standards of conduct, 3:441
Sidgwick and, 9:25
on utilitarianism, 9:613
on vagueness, 9:624
Wiggins and, 9:762–763
Parhelia, Descartes on, 2:729
Paris, University of, 1:650
Bacon (Roger) and, 1:452
and lectures on Aristotle, 1:454
and Ockhamism, 7:7
Parisian schools, of medieval logic, 5:428–429
Parity-detecting automaton, 3:757
Parker, Theodore, 1:718, 6:572, **7:121–122**
Parmenides (Plato)
author's family in, 7:582
commentaries on, 2:622
dating of, 9:107
Forms in, 3:283, 6:185, 7:597–598
Hegel on, 3:54
Iamblichus on, 4:540
on ideas as paradigms, 4:563–564
metaphysics in, 6:185
Neoplatonism and, 8:40
nothing in, 6:657
nous in, 6:666
on one idea in multiple particulars, 7:638
One in, 8:43–44
Owen on, 7:64–65
Parmenides of Elea and, 7:122
Proclus on, 6:552, 7:609
on statements, 8:754–755
theology in, 8:43–44
on three first principles, 7:608
Zeno of Elea in, 9:871

Parmenides of Elea, **7:122–129**
vs. Anaxagoras, 1:181
Anscombe on, 1:213
apeiron/peras in, 1:225
atomism and, 5:299
on being and tautology, 1:527
Empedocles and, 3:208
epistemology and, 3:281
on error, 3:343, 5:146
on eternity, 3:357
on impossibility, 1:232
on logos, 5:568
on love, 5:584
Lucretius and, 5:598
and Melissus of Samos, 6:120
and metaphysics, 6:183–184
monism of, 6:7, 6:326
on one/many, 4:312
Owen on, 7:64–65
parody of, in Gorgias of Leontini, 4:164
Plato and, 7:606
in pre-Socratic philosophy, 7:762
on reality, 7:762
and religious philosophy, 7:487–488
semantic theory in monism of, 8:751
Shestov on, 9:11
Simplicius on, 9:35
on space, 9:146
Zeno of Elea's defense of, 9:871
Parody
Kant's, on analysis without synthesis, 8:734
Nietzsche on, 6:611–612
of Parmenides of Elea, in Gorgias of Leontini, 4:164
of self, in Romantic poetry, 8:631
Paroles d'un croyant (Lamennais), 5:177
Paroles d'un revolte (Kropotkin), 5:154
Parr, Samuel, 9:10
Parriana (Barker), 9:10
Parrington, Vernon Louis, on American liberalism, 5:322
Parse trees, in computational model of language, 2:392
Parsi community, 9:887
Parsimony
in nominalism, 6:627–628
Ockham's principle of, 9:772
Parsons, Charles, on truth, 5:317, 5:522
Parsons, Talcott, 9:94–96
Parsons, Terence, 6:290–291
Part(s)
in Cleanthes, 6:146–147
James (William) on, 4:784
in organismic biology, 7:37, 7:38
and whole
general theory of, 6:146
Leśniewski on, 5:290–291
Partial contraposition, definition of, 5:539
Partial functions
in computability theory, 2:373–380, 2:389
normal form theorem and, 2:380–381
and Turing machines, 2:376
Partial identity, 4:570
Partial monism, 6:327
Partial propositional calculus, 5:536
Partially ordered, definition of, 5:550
Participation
Bonaventure on, 1:652
in conservatism, 2:468–469
Copenhagen interpretation and, 2:530
direct, intuition as, 1:567
in God's love, by mystics, 1:570–571
between Kinds, 7:600
laws of, 1:83
Plato on, 7:596, 8:42
Proclus on, 8:42–43
quality-word relationships, 1:591
soul and, 8:43
Particle(s), 3:634
classical, 3:636
fields and, 3:634–636
moving in space, 3:688
non-existence of, in Schrödinger, 8:658
singlet state of, 6:640
in string theory, 9:268
symmetry and conservation principle of, 2:462–463
triplet state of, 6:640
Whitehead's definition of, 9:747
See also Particulate matter
Particle physics, 2:566, 9:152–153
Particle theories, reformulating, 3:634
Particular(s)
Abelard on, 1:4–5
abstract, 8:67
Aquinas on, 6:189
Aristotle on, 6:185, 9:592
bare, internal relations and, 8:342
in Buddhist epistemology, 1:755
concrete existent vs. possible, 6:180
Cudworth on, 2:611
essence realized in, 9:592
essential properties of, 6:180
Forms and, 9:591
God's knowledge of, 4:758
imperfection of, 9:590–591
inference from, Mill (John Stuart) on, 6:223
locations as, 7:23
in metaphysics, 6:173–174, 6:188
non-self-predicating, 6:179
Ockham on, 6:190
Plato on, 9:589–590
properties as, 7:25
realism about
nonrealism about universals and, 6:174–178
realism about universals and, 6:178–180
rejection of, 6:180–181
reductionism and, 6:180
Rehmke on, 8:302–303
in states of affairs, 7:25
Strawson on, 6:198
of substance, in ontology, 7:23–24
as trope class, 6:181
universals from, 9:595, 9:598
Particular (individual)
definition of, 5:545
knowledge of, through sensory intuition, 4:724
"Particular and General" (Owen), 7:65
Particular negative, in Ockham's nominalism, 9:778
Particular proposition, definition of, 5:553
Particularism, 3:278, 6:174–178
Particulate matter, 1:643
Boscovich on, 1:666
Clarke on, 2:272
in classical mechanics, 2:280
unobservable, 1:643
See also Particle(s)
Partiia Evraziia (Eurasian Party), 3:454
Partiinost, 3:63–64
Partnership tracks, 3:583
Parts of Animals (Aristotle), 1:273–275
Parvipontani, on conditionals, 5:429
Pascal, Blaise, **7:129–135**
anthropology and, 7:316
Arnauld and, 1:288
on atheism, 1:373
on authority, 8:46
and crisis of skepticism, 9:54
on decision theory, 2:655
on definition, 2:665, 2:670
on Descartes's "clear and distinct ideas," 4:747
Diderot and, 3:75
Emerson and, 3:195
Gassendi and, 4:27
on general will, 4:39
on God, belief in, 7:133, 8:713

Pascal, Blaise, ***continued***
- on human condition, 7:132–133
- Jansenism of, 4:789, 7:130–131
- Kierkegaard and, 5:62
- La Bruyère and, 5:166
- and mathematics, 7:129–130
- moderate fideism of, 3:632
- Nicole and, 6:603
- Noel and, 8:46
- on optimism/pessimism, 7:248
- and philosophy of science, 7:130–131
- on progress, 8:46
- on rational belief, 1:535
- on religion, 3:531, 7:130–134
- on revelation, 3:533
- scientific work of, 7:129–130, 7:134
- Shestov and, 9:11–13
- skepticism of, 4:747
- Voltaire on, 2:687

Pascal, Jacqueline, 3:569
Pascal et Leibniz (Guitton), 7:249
Pascendi Dominici Gregis (papal encyclical, 1907), 5:571
Pasch, Moritz, 4:62
Paschasius Radbertus, 2:50
Passages from the Life of a Philosopher (Babbage), 2:400
Passion(s)
- in belief, 3:531
- Clarke on, 2:274
- crimes of, 8:165
- Descartes on, 1:233, 2:754–755, 3:188. *See also Passions of the Soul, The* (Descartes)
- DuBos on, 3:123
- Edwards (Jonathan) on, 3:168
- Epictetus on, 3:262
- false beliefs in, 9:190
- Hazlitt on, 4:249
- Hobbes on, 4:413–414, 8:128
- and human nature, 1:781
- Hume on, 4:504–505, 8:132
- Hutcheson on, 4:529
- Jainism on, 5:327
- of man, 3:706
- in materialism, 6:9–10
- in moral life, 4:529
- in moral philosophy, 3:570
- reason and, 9:715
- as self-love, 8:132
- Spinoza on, 9:174
- Stoic rejection of, 9:257
- Vauvenargues on, 9:653
- women philosophers on, 9:838

Passion de Husayn Ibn Mansur Hallaj: martyr mystique de l'Islam, La (Massignon), 9:303
Passional desire, to believe, 3:531
Passionate engagement, and possibility of critical appraisal, 5:68
Passions of the Soul, The (Descartes), 2:752–755, 3:188, 3:569, 3:570, 4:604
- on emotions, 3:198
- philosophy of sex and, 7:522

Passive conditioning event, of sense object, 9:749
Passive synthesis, 4:523
Past
- Carnap on, 2:39
- and coherence theory of truth, 2:309
- in critical realism, 2:596
- as evidence, 7:452
- *kalām* argument on God's existence and, 2:554–555
- McGilvary on, 6:76
- McTaggart on, 6:78
- Mead on, 6:81–82
- in memory, access to, 6:124
- neurosis and, 1:598
- physics and, 2:104–105
- reality of, paradigm-case argument and, 7:107
- relevance to present states, 5:350–351
- Woodbridge on, 9:842–843

Past and Present (Carlyle), 2:34
Past lives, 6:109, 8:332–333
Past tense, in medieval logic, 2:541
Pasteur, Louis, 5:351, 5:360
Pastoralism, in Zoroastrianism, 9:886
Pastore, Valentino Annibale, 5:565, **7:135–136**
Patañjali, 4:626, 9:581
Pateman, Carole, 3:599
Patents, in engineering ethics, 3:241
Pater, Walter Horatio, **7:136–137**
Paternalism, **7:137–140**
- in genetic counseling, 6:95–96
- hard, 7:137–139
- legal, 3:561, 7:137–138
- and liberty, 5:337–338
- medical ethics and, 6:92–95, 7:138–139
- moral, 7:137
- physical, 7:137
- soft, 7:137–139

"Path of Law, The" (Holmes), 7:428
Pathetic fallacy, 3:546
Pathogenic repressions, 3:739–740
Pathology of the Mind, The (Maudsley), 9:571
Paths and Havens (Suhrawardī), 4:582
Patient(s)
- advance directives made by, 3:456
- consciousness and, 1:597
- and euthanasia, 3:455–459, 6:94
- incompetent, 3:456
- refusal of hydration and nutrition by, 3:456–458
- rights of, 6:93
- transference in, 3:742

Patin, Guy, 9:52
- La Mothe Le Vayer and, 5:181
- La Peyrère and, 5:196

Patocka, Jan, and Fink, 3:639
Paton, H. J.
- on sensa, 9:486
- on specious present, 9:483

Patriarcha; or the Natural Power of Kings (Filmer), 3:636–637, 5:388
Patriarchy
- and female heterosexuality, 3:756
- in feminist jurisprudence, 7:462
- law and, 3:584, 7:463
- in Marxism, 5:740
- as oppression, 3:563
- prohibition of, 3:584
- Wollstonecraft on, 9:836–837
- and women, 3:575, 3:584, 3:756

Patrimonial individual, 5:152
Patriotism, **7:140–141**
- communitarianism and, 2:369
- Meinecke and, 6:113
- Santayana on, 8:600
- types of, 7:140

Patristic philosophy, 3:558, **7:141–144**
- Gregory of Nazianzus and, 4:181
- Gregory of Nyssa and, 4:181–182
- Isaac of Stella on, 4:753
- in preservation of gnostic sources, 4:98
- and shadow-man doctrine of immortality, 4:603

Patritius. *See* Patrizi, Francesco
Patrizi, Francesco, 3:624, **7:144–145**
Pattern recognition, in medical diagnosis, 7:467
Pattison, Mark, deism and, 2:691
Pauer, Imre, 7:145
Paul, L. A., on date theory, 9:477
Paul, St. *See* St. Paul
Paul of Pergula, 8:765
Paul of Venice, **7:146–147**
- on existential proposition, 5:443
- on impositions and intentions, 8:765

Pauler, Akos, **7:145**
Pauli, Wolfgang H., 2:530–532
Pauling, Linus, **7:145–146**

Paulsen, Friedrich, **7:147–149**
Liebert and, 5:343
in neo-Kantianism, 6:541–542
on panpsychism, 7:83, 7:87–89
Spranger and, 9:198
on world soul, 7:84–85
Paulze, Marie Anne, 5:216
Pausanias, Empedocles and, 3:212
Pavlov, Ivan Petrovich, 1:201, **7:149–151**
Paz, Octavio, 5:204
Peace, **7:151–158**
abolitionism and, 7:151, 7:154–157
atomic warfare and, 8:667
conservatism and, 7:151–154
as educational goal, 7:373
experimentation with, 8:667
Grotius on, 4:191–192
Kant on, 7:373
political cosmopolitanism and, 2:569
Suárez on, 9:284–285
Peace of Westphalia, 9:145
Peace with God (Graham), 1:367
Peacock, George, on algebra, 5:459–460
Peacocke, Christopher
on concepts, 2:417, 5:89
on logical terms, 5:532
on luck, 1:21
on perception, 7:192–193
Peano, Giuseppe, **7:158–159**
axioms of, 5:465, 6:672, 9:556
Grassmann and, 5:461
on mathematical logic, 5:462–466
Pastore and, 7:135
Russell and, 5:466
Whitehead and, 5:466
Peano arithmetic, 1:146–147, 5:465
axioms in, 5:465
Frege on, 3:730
unsolvability degrees and, 2:385
Peano's postulates, 5:551, 7:158
Pearce, David G., 4:20
Pears, David
on self-deception, 8:714
on self-prediction, 8:730
Pearson, Egon S., on testing statistical hypotheses, 9:215–218
Pearson, Karl, **7:159–161**
and chi-squared measure of deviation, 4:672
Fisher and, 3:661
goodness-of-fit tests of, 9:219–220
on "how" in science, 9:755
on Mill's causal inference, 8:686
on precision, 3:662–663
on scientific law, 7:715–716
Peasant of the Garonne, The (Maritain), 5:717–718
Peasant Wedding Dance (Brueghel), 1:304
Peckham, John, **7:161–163**
on matter, 3:141
on plurality of forms, 1:403
Thomism and, 9:444
Pedagogy
instructional appeal and, 1:483
of medical ethics, 6:93
Pedagogy of the Oppressed (Freire), 5:332
Pédamt joué, Le (Cyrano de Bergerac), 2:618
Peer groups, conscience and, 2:447
Peguy, Charles, and fascism, 3:553
Peine (pain), 7:249
Peirce, Benjamin, 7:163
Peirce, Charles Sanders, 4:781, **7:163–174**
on abduction, 1:653, 5:533
on actions, 3:646
on ampliative arguments, 4:635
Apel and, 1:226
on belief, 5:91, 7:166–173, 9:537
Bonaventure and, 1:653
on Boole, 1:659
on categories, 2:75, 2:81, 7:164–171
on cognition, 7:165–171
and coherence theories of knowledge, 5:93
common sense and, 2:357
on continuum and infinitesimals, 2:501
on doubt, 3:103
Duns Scotus and, 3:139, 3:144–145
and epistemology, 3:313
on eternal return doctrine, 3:355
and "first-intentional logic of relatives," 3:639
Habermas on, 4:200
on haecceity, 7:168–170
on ideas, 4:566
on induction, 1:686, 4:644
influence of, 7:173–174
on inquiry, 3:48, 7:166–167, 7:171–173
vs. James (William), 7:742
on language, 8:797–799
logic of, 5:453–456
logical chart method of, 5:561
on logical interpretant, 8:798
and metaphysics, 6:194
Nagel (Ernest) and, 6:472
on negation, 6:528
ordinary-language philosophy of, 6:195
panpsychism and, 7:83
on phenomenology, 7:278
philosophical orientation of, 7:163–164
philosophical system of
first, 7:164
fourth, 7:168–172
second, 7:165–166
third, 7:166–168
and pragmatism, 7:741–744, 8:798, 9:537
precursors of, 2:710
on premises in syllogisms, 5:502
realism of, 7:744
on relational propositions, 5:555
Rescher on, 7:751
on Schiller (Ferdinand), 8:623
on semiosis, 8:797
on social constructivism, 9:78
social epistemology and, 9:83
students of, 3:43
and syllogistic logic, 5:504
truth in, 7:744
on vagueness, 9:624
Vailati and, 9:630
on "would be" of events, 4:645
Pejorism, 7:245
Pelagius and Pelagianism, **7:174–176**
Descartes and, 2:753–755
as historical movement *vs.* theological system, 7:175
on nature and sin, 7:175
and necessity, 1:680
Ockham and, 9:778
philosophy of sex and, 7:522
on predestination, 8:681
Pell, John, 3:187
Pellisson-Fontanier, Paul, 5:253
Pelloutier, Fernand, 1:178
Penn, William, 3:187, 7:154
Penna, Lucas de, 7:422
Pennsylvania Gazette (Franklin), 3:720
Penny Cyclopaedia (periodical). *See English (Penny) Cyclopedia*
Penrose, Roger
on computationalism, 2:395
on machine intelligence, 5:634
Pensée, La (Blondel), 1:618
Pensées (Pascal), 1:535, 3:531, 3:632, 7:130–132, 9:11
on case for skepticism, 9:54
on knowledge and faith, 7:132–134
Pensées philosophiques (Diderot), 3:71, 3:75

Pensées sur l'interprétation de la nature (Thoughts on the interpretation of nature) (Diderot), 3:71–75
Penthesilea (Kleist), 5:79
Penumbra of law, Hart on, 5:240
Penzias, Arno, 4:63
People. *See* Human beings; Persons
Pepper, Stephen, on emergence, 3:192
Per accidens, 5:70, 5:551
Per se, definition of, 5:551
Per se necessity, 5:70
Per se terms, 5:70
Peras. See Apeiron/Peras
Perceivability, of *qi,* 5:140
Perceived world, behavioral environment as, 5:125
Perceiving, 7:178
- conceptual analysis of, 7:179–180
- in conscious qualitative states, 2:452
- Dennett on, 2:456
- Russell on, 2:543
- as skill, 7:180–184
- *See also* Perception

Perceiving God (Alston), 1:132
Perception, **7:177–187,** 8:648
- of abstract and concrete ideas, 4:565–566
- achieving aspect of, 5:129
- active *vs.* passive, 1:578
- and act-object distinction, 4:560
- Aenesidemus on, 1:31
- in aesthetic appraisal and criticism, 8:654
- ambiguity of, 3:542
- analysis of, 7:177–180
- Anaxagoras on, 1:182
- anticipations of, 5:19
- *vs.* apperception, 1:233
- Aquinas on, 3:289, 8:825, 9:426–427
- Aristotle on, 3:286, 9:592–593
- Armstrong on, 1:287
- Arnauld on, 2:57–58, 5:665
- art and, 1:336, 9:835
- auditory, 7:180–182
- Augustine on, 3:289
- *vs.* awareness, 8:814–815
- Balguy on, 1:475
- of beauty *vs.* ugliness, 9:564
- and belief, 1:287, 1:533, 2:314
- Bergson on, 1:565, 3:312–313
- Berkeley on, 1:583, 1:586, 3:301–303, 5:672
- binding problem in, 6:566–567
- Blanshard on, 1:613
- Brown on, 1:704–705
- in Buddhism, 1:753, 9:544
- Carneades on, 2:47
- Carroll on, 2:51–52
- in Cartesianism, 2:58
- causal processes in, 7:180–183, 7:272, 7:275–276, 7:296
- and causality, 2:97–98, 2:103, 2:107, 8:10–11
- in children, 2:103
- in Chinese ethics, 2:200
- Clifford on, 2:292
- cognition and, relation of, 6:150
- in cognitive psychology, 8:151
- Collier on, 2:323
- Collingwood on, 2:326
- of colors, 2:333, 8:648
- common sense and, 2:355
- complexities of, 7:181–182
- and computationalism, 2:394
- conceptual analysis of, 7:179–180
- Condillac on, 2:421
- confusing relations with intrinsic qualities, 3:546
- in conscious qualitative states, 2:452
- and consciousness, 1:565, 2:453–455
- contact and, 5:118
- contemporary views on, **7:187–194**
- continuity and stability of, 1:566
- conversational implicature in, 4:184
- in critical realism, 2:595–596
- definition of, 7:177
- in definition of beauty, 8:598
- Dennett on, 2:456
- Descartes on, 3:278, 3:291–293
- as direct, 1:584–585
- divine, 7:194
- divine *vs.* human, 1:580–581
- Dretske on, 3:108
- Eddington on, 3:164–165
- Engels on, 3:58–59
- enrichment of, 7:184
- Epicurus on, 3:287–288
- in epistemology, 4:173
- errors in, 7:184–190, 7:223, 7:274
- evidence of, 7:177–180
- evident presumption in, 6:117
- evident *vs.* blind judgment, 1:691
- of experience, 8:725
- extrasensory, 7:752–757
- Fichte on, 3:309
- of film, 7:384
- force in, 8:618–619
- Gerard on, 4:65
- in Gestalt theory, 4:72, 4:75
- of God, 1:132, 2:58
- Greek philosophers on, 8:823–824
- Grice on, 4:184
- Grote on, 4:189
- Hegel on, 3:310
- Helmholtz on, 4:304
- Hemsterhuis on, 4:311
- Hobbes on, 4:412
- Hume on, 3:303–305
- in idealism, 8:261
- illusions and, 5:96
- *vs.* imagination, 1:393
- in Indian materialism, 6:254
- in Indian philosophy, 5:117, 6:532–533, 7:413, 9:543
- as indirect representation in qualities, 1:577
- initial evidence and analysis, 7:177–180
- innate ideas in, 4:565, 4:691
- intellectual virtue and, 9:685
- intentionalist theories of, 7:191–193
- in intrinsic theory of consciousness, 2:453
- Kant on, 3:306–308, 4:555, 6:193
- and knowledge, 5:93, 7:178
- language and, intertwining of, 6:149
- language of, 8:821–822
- language of thought and, 5:192
- Leibniz on, 3:298, 5:270, 8:129–130
- Liebmann on, 5:344
- Locke on, 1:233, 3:299–300, 5:395
- Mach on, 8:827
- Maine de Biran on, 5:656–657
- Malebranche on, 2:57, 3:293–294, 5:665–667
- Marx on, 3:59
- Matthew of Aquasparta on, 6:64–65
- Maupertuis on, 8:783
- measurement and, 8:10
- as mental content, 2:476–477
- Merleau-Ponty on, 6:149, 6:151
- Mill (James) on, 3:312
- Mill (John Stuart) on, 3:312
- modes of, 1:578
- modularity theory of, 2:394, 3:675
- Moore (G. E.) on, 1:145, 3:314–315, 6:348–349
- of moral agents, 8:2
- Nagel (Ernest) on, 6:474
- in new realism, 6:584
- as nonconceptual information, 2:481
- and nonepistemic seeing, 3:108
- of nonmental entities, 6:210

and non-perception, 6:532–533
nonveridical, 9:542
object permanence of, 1:579–580
objects of awareness in, 8:813
Ockham on, 3:290
opportunistic processing in, 4:592
optimism/pessimism and, 7:249
of other minds and qualities, 1:586
of outlines, 1:327
of pain, 8:824
Palágyi on, 7:75
paradigm-case argument and, 7:107–110
Pearson on, 7:160
Peirce on, 7:169–170
Perry on, 7:205
personal identity and, 7:218–220
Peter Aureol on, 7:257
phenomenal character of, 1:519
phenomenalism and, 7:271, 7:275–276
of physical objects, 6:81, 6:138–139
Piaget on, 7:568
in pictorial representation, 9:835
Plotinus on, 3:288–289
problems of, 7:177–178
and proof of God's existence, 1:585
propositional content in, 9:44
Protagoras on, 8:91–92
psychological processes in, 7:183–186
pure, 5:667
of qualities, 1:575, 1:578, 8:10
quality and accuracy of, 7:183–184
Reid on, 3:305, 8:324–325
of relations *vs.* intrinsic qualities, 3:546
relativity of, 1:31, 4:586
and religious experience, 7:482, 8:402
representative theory of, 4:564–565
Riehl on, 8:467
Rosmini-Serbati on, 8:501
Royer-Collard on, 8:524
in Russell's theory of truth, 2:543
vs. Sartre's imaging consciousness, 8:605
scholastics on, 8:824–826
Schopenhauer on, 8:650
in self-knowledge, 9:16
Sellars on, 2:597, 8:732
sensation and, 1:578, 1:704–705, 8:814, 8:823
sense
Aquinas on, 3:289
Aristotle on, 3:286
Augustine on, 3:289
Berkeley on, 3:301, 3:302–303
Democritus on, 5:300–301
Descartes on, 3:291–293
Epicurus on, 3:287–288
Hegel on, 3:310
Hume on, 3:303–305
Kant on, 3:306–307
Leibniz on, 3:298
Leucippus on, 5:300
Lewis (C. I.) on, 5:307–309
Locke on, 3:299–300, 5:379, 5:385
Mach on, 5:625
Malebranche on, 3:293–294
Ockham on, 3:290
Plotinus on, 3:288–289
Spinoza on, 3:294
universals proved by, 9:582
vs. sense, 9:484
sense-datum theory and, 1:696, 7:178, 7:183–191
of sensible ideas, 1:579
sensing and, 8:817
sensory imagination and, 4:600
in Shin Buddhism, 9:14
as skill, 7:180–184
Socratics on, 8:823–824
of sound, 9:280
speech and, 5:657
Spinoza on, 3:294, 9:174
Stern on, 9:244
in Stoicism, 9:255
sublating, 9:542–543
as tainted by illusions, hallucinations, and dreams, 5:96
taste in, 1:38
and theme, thematic field, and margin, 4:197–198
Theophrastus on, 9:412
vs. thinking, 7:192
of time, 9:482–483
truth and, 5:118
unity of, neuroscience and, 6:567
of universals, 9:582–585, 9:592–593
veil of, 7:190
veridical, 7:187–189, 7:193
visual, 4:712, 6:566–567, 7:182
volition and, 9:703
Whitehead on, 3:316, 9:750
Wittgenstein on, 9:820
Wollheim on, 1:328
in Yogācāra Buddhism, 1:747–749
Perception (Price), 1:576, 8:815
Perception and Identity (Ayer), 1:438
Perception and the Physical World (Armstrong), 7:191
Perception de la causalité, La (Michotte), 4:72
Percepts, 5:128, 5:131
Perceptual belief, forming, 9:684–685
Perceptual body, place in perceptual space, 5:131
Perceptual gestalten, physical structures analogous to, 5:127–129
Perceptual mechanisms, errors by, 3:546
Perceptual object, 9:749
Perceptual reduction, 7:184
Perceptual similitude, 4:590
Perceptual space, and physical space, 5:131
Perceptual states, mental content and, 2:478
Percipient event, 9:749–750
Percipient particles of matter, Maupertuis on, 6:67
Perdurantism, persistence and, 7:208–209
Père de famille, Le (The father of the family) (Diderot), 3:71, 3:76
Peregrinus, Lucian of Samosata on, 5:597
Peregrinus Proteus, Cynic teaching of, 2:617
Pereira Barreto, Luis, positivism and, 5:207
Perepiska iz dvukh uglov (The correspondence from two corners) (Ivanov), 4:767
Perestroika, Lenin and, 5:281
Perfect cosmological principle, 2:562
Perfect Crime, The (Baudrillard), 1:491
Perfect entailments, 5:426
Perfect figure, definition of, 5:551
Perfect identity, 4:497–498
Perfect number, in eternal return doctrine, 3:353
Perfect ("Pythagorean") solids, 5:51
Perfection, **7:194–195**
as aim of history, 7:390
Arnold on, 1:294
vs. beauty, 6:131
degrees of, as argument for existence of God, 2:677–680
existence and, 7:22
in good and evil, 9:829
of man, in socialist theory, 9:88
metaphysical, Mendelssohn on, 6:131
moral, 7:194–195
in nature, Lamarck on, 5:174–175

Perfection, ***continued***
One and, 8:41–42
in ontological argument for existence of God, 7:16, 7:20–22
optimism/pessimism and, 7:245
scale of, in Candidus's proof of God's existence, 2:49
in utopianism, 9:617
Wolff on, 9:826–829
Perfectionism, and rationality, 8:254
Perfil del hombre y la cultura en México, El (Profile of man and culture in Mexico) (Ramos), 5:209
Performance
ability and, 2:25–26
in art, **1:321–323**
artificial intelligence and, 1:346
authenticity in, 1:322–323
in Confucian ethics, 2:195
Godlovitch on, 1:322
integrity and, 1:322–323
interpretation of, 1:321–322
meritorious, 6:118
of music, 6:438–439
in studio, 1:323
Performance art, **1:321–323**
Performative theory of truth, **7:195–202,** 9:264
Performative utterances, **7:199–202**
explicit, 7:199
hedged, 7:200
linguistic conventions and, 7:199–200
self-verifying, 7:201
statements and, 7:200–201
Performative verbs, 5:98, 7:200
Performativity, phenomenon of, 7:199
Pergamum, school of. *See* Neoplatonism
Peri Hermeneias (Aristotle), 5:462
Peri hypsous (Longinus), 5:571–572
Peri Penthous (On grief) (Crantor of Soli), 4:173
Peri tou kathêknotos (*On Duty or Appropriate Action)* (Panaetius of Rhodes), 7:79
Pericles
on law, 7:418
in Thucydides, 9:457
Peripatetics, **7:202–203**
Avicenna and, 4:550
on causality, 1:32
Diogenes Laertius on, 3:88
Galileo and, 4:12
history of, 3:399
Ibn al-ʿArabī and, 4:541
illuminationists and, 4:582, 4:760–761
Islamic, 9:301
Avicenna as, 4:581
on knowledge, 3:320
Mullā Ṣadrā in, 6:418
Justin Martyr and, 7:142
logic and, 5:401–403, 5:407–408
and *Organon,* 4:582
patristic philosophy and, 7:142
and Plato's doctrines, 7:606
semantics of, 8:762
Simplicius on, 9:35
Stoicism and, 1:259, 5:407
Themistius as, 9:409
on virtue, 7:307
Peripatos, 1:258, 1:263, 7:202
Periphyseon (Erigena), 3:341, 3:342
Permanence
and change, religion and, 9:752
Petzoldt on, 7:268
phenomenalism and, 7:271–272
of substance, in *Critique of Pure Reason,* 5:19–20
Permission, refusal of, *vs.* request, in medical ethics, 3:457–458
Permissiveness, in contractualism *vs.* consequentialism, 2:518
Peron, Juan, ideologies of, 3:553
Perovitch, Anthony, 8:402
Perpetual motion, energy conservation and, 3:231
Perpetual Peace (Kant), 2:567
Perpétuité de la foy, La (Arnauld & Nicole), 6:604
Perrin, Jean-Baptiste
on atoms, 9:579
on common cause principle, 8:594
Perry, John, 8:809
on belief attribution, 1:536
on personal identity, 7:229
semantics of, 8:75–76
Perry, Ralph Barton, **7:203–206**
on egocentrism, 6:586
and ethics, 3:418, 3:423
and idealism, 7:203–204
neutral monism of, 6:587
realism and, 3:313, 6:584–585
on valuation, 9:638
on value, 7:204–205, 9:637
Perry, Stephen, on normative jurisprudence, 1:170
Persecution
of atheists, 1:357–358
of Christians, 9:508
vs. toleration, 9:507
Persia
Ibn al-ʿArabī's influence in, 9:308
and Islamic philosophy, 4:761
metaphysics in, Iqbal on, 4:743
terrorism in, 9:395
Persian Gulf War, just war theory and, 7:157
Persian Letters (Montesquieu), 3:247
Persian philosophy, Corbin on, 2:537
Persians, The (Aeschylus), 4:176
Persistence, **7:206–213**
capture of, 7:208
Chisholm on, 2:243
everyday understanding of, argument against, 7:208
forfeiting of, 7:207
initial worry and, 7:206–211
in no-substance theories, 7:24
phenomenalism and, 7:274–275
stage view of, in identity, 4:571
of substance, in ontology, 7:24
as survival, 7:207–210
Persistence nihilism, 7:207
Persistent vegetative state, medico-jurisprudence on, 6:95
Person(s), 7:233, **7:237–244**
as animals, Wiggins on, 9:763
and business ethics, 1:777
categories of, 7:237
as context of experience, 1:695
definition of, 7:237
as dependencies communities, 1:676
and God, 1:672, 1:695
Held's concept of, 4:299
Hume on, 4:499
as individual substance, 1:628
individual *vs.*, 5:715
knowledge of, 5:94
legal concept of, 7:237–238, 7:242
vs. "man," 7:215–216
metaphysical, 7:240
moral, 7:240–241
in moral action justifiability, 2:519
Mounier on, 6:416
necessity of corporeal form to, 4:603
other, Del Vecchio on, 2:697
personal identity and, 7:220–221, 7:231–232
relational conception of, 3:579
reliability of, proof of, 5:121
respect for, 5:37
Rosmini-Serbati on, 8:502
social, 7:238
in social relationships, 3:579
unable to create selves, 1:671
Vasubandhu on, 9:650–651
Person und Sache (Stern), 7:233

Persona, 7:233
- in Christian Trinitarian thought, 2:248
- Jungian, 4:856

Personal agent predicates, in religious language, 8:418

Personal idealism
- personalism and, 7:234–235
- of Rashdall, 8:238

Personal identity, **7:213–233**
- criteria for, 7:214–216, 7:221–228
- Hume on, 3:305
- incomplete concept of, 7:215
- indeterminate, 7:230–232
- Leibniz and, 4:568
- Locke on, 4:604, 5:379, 5:395, 7:214–218
- memory and, 4:606, 9:15
- objective-subjective perspectives in, 9:291–292
- Parfit on, 7:120
- personhood and, 7:239–240
- preservation of, in resurrection, 4:618
- problems of, 7:213–214
- reduplication argument for, 7:229
- self and, 8:708–711
- Shoemaker on, 9:15–16
- in social relationships, 9:77
- soul as, 4:605–606
- special sciences on, 9:161
- survival and, 7:230
- theory of substance and, 9:296–297
- thought experiments in, 9:15
- Wiggins on, 9:762–763
- Williams (Bernard) on, 9:787

"Personal Identity" (Butler), 4:612

"Personal Identity" (Parfit), 7:229

Personal Identity (Shoemaker & Swinburne), 9:15

"Personal Identity and Individuation" (Williams), 7:229–230

Personal information, computer ethics and, 2:396

Personal injury law, 6:95

Personal language, in other minds, 7:56

Personal memory, 6:122–124

Personal Narrative (Edwards), 3:166

Personal relationships, faith in, 3:531

Personalism, **7:233–237**
- atheistic, 7:233
- Berdyaev on, 1:559
- Biran and, 3:689
- Bowne and, 1:671–672
- Brightman and, 1:362
- ethical, 7:234
- God in, 1:362
- historical antecedents of, 7:233–234
- idealistic, 7:234–235
- Marcel and, 5:702
- Mounier and, 6:416
- realistic, 7:234
- Stefanini and, 9:237–238
- Stern on, 9:244
- systematic themes in, 7:235–236
- theistic, 7:233–236
- types of, 7:234–235

Personalism (Bowne), 7:235

Personalismul Energetic (Rădulescu-Motru), 8:230–231

Personalist and Emanzipator (periodical), 3:130

Personality
- Adler on, 1:23–24
- of Augustine, 7:322–323
- in Buddhism, 1:724
- compensatory changes in, 1:23
- in Confucianism, 2:172–173, 2:177, 2:195
- Emerson on, 3:196
- Freud on, 8:146
- genetic development of, 1:657
- and hero worship in history, 2:34
- identity and, 7:227
- Jungian, 4:856, 8:146–147
- Le Senne on, 5:289
- MacIntyre on, 5:637
- Malraux on, 5:673
- Mamardashvili and, 5:679
- McDougall on, 6:72, 8:147
- meaning of sentences and, 6:652
- personal identity and, 7:227
- in psychological anthropology, 7:322–323
- Rashdall on, 8:238–239
- Rintelen on, 8:479
- Schopenhauer on, 8:655
- self-cultivation of, 2:177
- Spranger's typological analysis of, 9:198
- studies on, 9:678–679
- style and, 1:331
- in syntactic view of theories, 9:415
- types, in art, 1:335–336
- virtue and, 5:637
- *See also* Character

Personality (Tagore), 9:363

Personhood
- abortion and, 1:9, 3:393, 7:242
- in bioethics, 1:602
- conditions for, 7:238–240
- in Confucianism, 2:171–174
- constitution of, 1:463–464, 7:239–240
- dehumanization of, by technology, 1:707–708
- human *vs.* divine, 1:704
- I-it and I-thou relationships and, 1:715
- induction into, 1:459
- moral aspects of, 7:240–243
- as rational individual substance, 1:628
- social title as attribute of, 2:203–204
- vagueness of, 9:624
- Zen'kovskii on, 9:868

Personnalisme, Le (Renouvier), 7:233

Persons and Bodies (Baker), 1:463–464, 7:239

"Persons and Their Pasts" (Shoemaker), 7:230, 9:15

Person-stages, Parfit on, 7:120

Person-thing distinction, 9:244

Perspectival mode, of appearance talk, 7:188–190

Perspectivalism, 6:279

Perspective
- Berkeley on, 1:583
- in consciousness, 6:75–76
- in Daoist morality, 2:189–190
- epidynamic relatedness of, 6:76
- geometry and, 1:575
- in Huayan Buddhism, 1:738–739
- linguistic reference and, 2:205
- material objects and, 1:147
- monads as, 8:129–130
- moral, of men and women, 3:579
- as nonexclusive view of unobservable, 1:643–644
- operational point of view and, 1:694
- in paintings, 1:312
- past and, 1:597–598
- in reality, 6:82
- in rhetoric and language, 2:230
- on sacred, in thinking, 2:225
- space-time and, 1:108
- subjective *vs.* objective, Nagel (Thomas) on, 6:475
- temporal, in clinical psychology, 1:597–598

Perspective realism. *See* Realism

Perspective theory, of McGilvary, 6:75

Perspectivia (Bacon, Roger), 1:455

Perspectivism
- Nietzsche on, 6:612
- Ortega y Gasset and, 5:208–209, 7:46
- and pluralistic conception of art, 3:572–573

Persuasion
in Chinese philosophical discourse, 2:200–201
ethical language and, 9:245
first-pattern analysis of, 9:245
Gorgias of Leontini on, 4:162–163
rational, 7:731–732
world-view representation on, 2:229
Persuasive definition, 3:548
Pertaining to a Pure Phenomenology and Phenomenological Philosophy (Pfänder), 7:269
Perturbation, in Newtonian mechanics, 6:593
Perturbative string theory, 9:268
Pertutilis logica (Very Useful Logic) (Albert of Saxony), 1:101
Peru, liberation theology in, 5:211
Peruvian philosophy, 5:204, 5:209–211
Pervasion, in Indian philosophy, 5:413–414
Pervasive quality, Dewey on, 3:46
Pessimism, **7:244–254**
anthropological, of Voltaire, 9:712
conservatism and, 2:470
epistemic, 9:546
eudemonological, 7:251
Gobineau and, 4:106
in Gracián, 4:168
in Hegesias, 2:619
history of, 7:246–253
industrialization and, Gehlen on, 4:36
Leopardi and, 5:285
on life, meaning and value of, 5:345–356
metaphysical, 7:250
moral principles and, 2:447
religious, 7:245–246
Schopenhauer on, 8:647, 8:653
Taine on, 9:365
Vaihinger on, 9:626
Pessimistic induction, 8:692
Pestalozzi, Johann Heinrich, **7:254–255**
on arithmetic, 7:371–372
on education, 7:371–372
Froebel and, 3:754–755, 7:372
on knowledge, 7:371–372
on morality, 7:372
Rousseau and, 7:371
in Spranger's philosophy of education, 9:199
Pestalozzianism, 7:254–255
PET scan, 6:564
Peter Aureol, **7:255–258**
Chatton on, 2:139–140
on determinism, 3:9
on Duns Scotus, 8:704
on intentionality, 4:705
Peter Bell the Third (Shelley), 9:9
Peter Damian, **7:258–259,** 9:716
Peter Lombard, 5:70, **7:259–262**
Abelard and, 1:7
Alexander of Hales and, 1:113
Duns Scotus and, 3:133–134
Durandus of Saint-Pourçain and, 3:148
Major and, 5:661
in medieval philosophy, 6:99
School of St. Victor and, 8:592
Peter of Candia, 8:704
Peter of Celle, John of Salisbury and, 4:843
Peter of Maricourt, Bacon (Roger) and, 1:453
Peter of Spain, **7:262–263**
and Byzantine thought, 1:789
on logic, 5:430–432, 5:440
Major and, 5:661
on syncategoremata, 8:769
on terms, 8:767
Peter the Great (Czar of Russia)
Eurasianists on, 3:454
Leibniz and, 5:254
Peters, Richard, 7:355
Peters, Stanley, on implicatures, 3:253
Petersburg paradox, 5:339
Petersen, Steve, in neuroscience, 6:565
Peterson, N. P., and Fëdorov, 3:558
Petit Traité sceptique sur cette façon de parler, n'avoir pas le sens commun (La Mothe Le Vayer), 5:182
Petite traité de sagesse (Charron), 2:135
Petitio principii, 3:546. *See also* Begging the question (circular reasoning)
Petitiones Contrariorum (William of Sherwood), 9:786
Petrarch, **7:263–266**
Petronievié, Branislav, **7:266–267**
Petrović-Njegoš, Petar, **7:267–268**
Pettit, Philip, 8:533
Petzäll, Åke, 5:525
Petzoldt, Joseph, **7:268–269,** 7:716
Peyrère, Isaac La, 2:265, **5:196–197,** 9:33, 9:179
Pfänder, Alexander, 5:362, **7:269–270,** 7:279, 9:239
Pfister, Oskar, 3:745
Phädon oder über die Unsterblichkeit der Seele (Phaedo, or on the Immortality of the Soul) (Mendelssohn), 6:131
Phaedo (Plato)
on body, value of, 3:397
commentaries on, 2:622
on cosmology, 2:698
definition in, 7:595
Euclides in, 6:110
Forms in, 6:185, 7:595
Form-sensible relation in, 7:596
hypothesis in, 7:593
on matter, 5:269
metaphysics in, 6:184–185
on nature as purification, 7:608
Orphic influence in, 7:43
ousia in, 7:62–63
Philo of Larissa and, 7:311
psyche in, 8:103
on recollection, 3:284, 7:588
on Socrates
death of, 9:106
piety of, 9:110
on soul, 4:602, 4:608
on suicide, 9:319
thought in, 9:420
Phaedrus (Plato)
beauty in, 1:512
Cicero and, 2:257
dating of, 9:107
on dialectic, 3:53
Ficino on, 3:623
Forms in, 7:595
Iamblichus on, 4:540
natural law in, 6:506
on poetry, 1:42, 7:595
on recollection, 7:588
on rhetoric, 1:188, 7:592
sex in, 7:521
on soul, 4:607, 6:185
Phaenomena (Aratus), 5:600
Phalansterian communities, 5:154
Phalanxes, organizing humanity into, 3:706–707
Phanes, in Orphic theogony, 7:42
Phantasia, **7:270–271**
Phantasiae, in Epicurus, 3:215–216
Phantoms of the Brain (Blakeslee & Ramachandran), 6:566
"Pharisaical Righteousness" (Smith), 9:70
Pharmacology, Boyle and, 1:672–673
Pharmakon, in deconstruction, 2:661–662
Phase sortals, 9:762
Phenomena, 5:128
of acoustics, 9:280
analysis of, 2:224, 6:219, 8:705
Bohr on, 2:531
categories of, 2:75, 5:18
Cavendish on, 2:117
chaos model simplicity, 2:131–134
Clifford on, 2:293
of colors, 2:332–334

common sense and, Moore on, 2:358–359
Comte on, 2:411
conventional *vs.* ultimate, 1:734
Copenhagen interpretation and, 2:530
Cratylus on, 2:584
definition of, 7:278, 7:281–283, 7:289, 7:292
in Dge-lugs Mādhyamika, 1:732–734
diachronic connection among, 5:71
empirical, 1:447
experience of, as learning God's will, 1:574
forms as instances of, 1:447
frequency of instances *vs.* frequency over time, 1:644
group, 6:481
Hegel on, 8:138
Heidegger on, 4:290–291
in Huayan Buddhism, 1:738–739, 2:164–165
identification of, 7:284–285, 7:288–294
inference from, 6:592–593, 8:684
in intellectual analysis, as static, 1:566
intentionality and, 1:689, 7:292
Kant on, 1:245, 2:75
lack of essence in
Nāgārjuna on, 6:469–471
and reality, 6:470
manifestation of, 1:739, 4:290–291
measurement of, 1:638
mortality of, 4:293
Newton on, 6:592–593, 8:684
nonempirical status of, 7:288–289
and nonlinguistic entities, 1:750–751
object permanence of, 1:579–580
and operations definitions, 2:141
paranormal, 6:492
perceptibility and perception of, 1:579–580
in quantum theory, 1:637
recurrence of, Lachelier on, 5:169
referents as, 8:759, 8:794
Renouvier on, 8:430–431
Riehl on, 6:541
Romero on, 8:492
Sartre on, 8:606
Schultz on, 8:659
as static in intellectual analysis, 1:566
vs. things-in-themselves, 1:232, 5:20–21
in Tiantai Buddhism, 2:163
Vasubandhu on, 9:650, 9:651
Phenomena statements
empirical, 7:295–296
necessary, 7:296–297
Phenomenal character
naturalization of, 6:263–264
of perceptual experiences, 7:188
Phenomenal concept, 8:195
Phenomenal event, with physiological correlate, 5:129
Phenomenal gestalten, and dynamically self-regulating physical systems, 5:127
Phenomenal mental properties, 6:136
Phenomenal states, and phenomenal properties, 3:760
Phenomenal world
of Kant's inaugural dissertation, 5:12
knowers and, 1:671
Phenomenalism, **7:271–277**
and analysis, impurity in, 7:274
argument from illusion and, 1:231
on basis of truth, 3:220
Berkeley and, 3:301, 6:192
difficulties in, 7:273–276
Eberhard and, 3:161
existential, 1:59–60
factual, 7:272
fragmentariness and, 7:272–273
Gehlen on, 4:36
Goodman on, 4:158–159
Hume and, 6:192
Leibniz and, 5:270–272
linguistic, 7:271–273
Mersenne and, 6:153
vs. metaphysical realism, 8:688–689
Mill (John Stuart) on, 3:312
mind-body problem in, 7:468
naturalism and, 6:494
Neurath and, 6:562
on noninferential knowledge, 4:727
opposition to, 7:282
perception and, 7:275–276
Petronievié on, 7:266
Plessner and, 7:629
Ploucquet on, 7:642
self in, 6:256
Stern and, 9:244
well-founded, 5:270
Woodger on, 9:843–844
Phenomenological embeddedness, 5:34
Phenomenological observation, 7:184
Phenomenological philosophy, cognitive science and, 2:300
"Phenomenological Philosophy of Edmund Husserl and Contemporary Criticism, The" (Fink), 3:638
Phenomenological program, Fink and, 3:639
Phenomenological psychology, **7:277–278,** 7:301
Phenomenological reduction, 4:523, 7:277, 7:281–285
Phenomenological statements
a priori, 7:279, 7:294–297
derived from examples, 7:285–287
properties of, 7:283
Phénoménologie (Phenomenology) (Lyotard), 5:620
Phenomenologie der Thematik und des reinen Ich (Gurwitsch), 4:197
Phenomenology, **7:278–301**
act-, *vs.* phenomenology of facts, 8:616
and action *vs.* realization, 1:618
aesthetics and, 1:59–60, 1:70–71
Arendt and, 1:252–253
associationist psychology and, 3:502
Bakhtin Circle and, 1:469
Bergmann on, 1:562
Binswanger on, 1:597–598
Bonhoeffer on, 1:655
bracketing existence in, 7:285–289
branches of, Peirce on, 7:169
Brentano and, 1:690, 3:421
Cairns and, 2:6
Camus and, 2:20
Carnap on, 2:38
Cartwright on, 2:62
chaos distinctions within, 2:39
in clinical psychology, 1:597–598
cognitive science and, 2:300
coherence in, criteria of, 7:292–294
Condillac on, 2:421
of consciousness, 2:459
Cassirer on, 2:67
of time, 9:484
contemporary, 3:317, 7:297–298
Corbin on, 2:537
description in, 4:777
description of, 7:279–281
development of, 7:299–300
eidetic reduction in, 8:604
epistemological circle in, 7:286–288
ethics in, 3:421–423
of experience, 5:688
feminism and, 3:563
Gadamer on, 4:3
Gehlen on, 4:36

Phenomenology, ***continued***
Geyser on, 4:83
Gurwitsch on, 4:197
Hegelianism in, 4:285–286
Heidegger and, 4:288–291
hermeneutics and, 7:299–300, 9:17
historical particularity in, 4:289
of history, 7:301
Huayan Buddhism and, 1:739, 2:165–166
Husserl on, 2:81–82, 4:522–523, 7:397–398, 8:802
Ingarden and, 4:683
intentionality and, 7:282, 7:289–292, 7:299
intuition of essences in, 7:283–285
Landgrebe and, 5:183–185
Levinas on, 5:304–305
of living discourse, 9:17–18
as logically independent, 5:125
Lyotard on, 5:620
Mansel and, 5:688
in medical ethics, 6:93
and memory, 6:122
and metaphysics, 6:195
methodological circle in, 7:283, 7:287–288
in modernism, 6:317
narrative as bioethical method, 1:601–602
neo-Kantianism and, 3:311
nondescriptivism and, 6:634
origins of, 7:279
Peirce on, 7:174
personalism and, 7:236
Pfänder in, 7:269
Philolaus on, 7:310–311
postcolonialism and, 7:727
in postmodernism, 6:318
and psychology, 7:300–301
rationality and, 5:679
Reale and, 8:260
reflection in, 7:287–289, 7:297
of religious experience, 8:401–402
Rickert on, 8:459
Santayana on, 8:598
Sartre on, 6:195, 7:297, 8:603
Scheler on, 8:616
Schlick on, 8:642
social, 7:727
in social sciences, 8:664
Spaventa on, 9:159
speaking body and, 5:151
Stefanini on, 9:237
Stein on, 9:239–240
and technology, 7:546, 7:549
Tiantai Buddhism and, 2:165–166
transcendental, 7:277–278
and truth, 2:62
of womanhood, 9:240
Phenomenology and the Theory of Science (Gurwitsch), 4:198
Phenomenology of Moral Consciousness (von Hartmann), 7:278
Phenomenology of Perception (Merleau-Ponty), 3:510, 4:197, 6:148–150, 7:297, 9:491
language in, 7:411
trace in, 2:717
"Phenomenology of Reason" (Husserl), 9:18
Phenomenology of Spirit (Hegel), 4:262–264, 5:62, 7:278, 8:599
Engels and, 3:61
on knowledge, 3:309–310
Marx and, 7:390
Russian translation of, 9:18
on Schelling's absolute, 1:12
Phenomenology of Willing (Pfänder), 7:269–270
Phenomenon of Man, The (Teilhard), 9:374–375
Pheromones, Wilson (Edward O.) on, 9:788
Phi phenomenon, 7:184
Philalethie (Basedow), 1:483, 5:176
Philebus (Plato), 1:511–512, 7:311
apeiron/peras and, 1:225
beauty in, 1:42
commentaries on, 2:622
cosmology in, 8:185
dating of, 9:107
on dialectic, 7:593–594
Gadamer on, 4:1
on infinity, 4:654
microcosm in, 5:640
persuasion in, 4:162
on pleasure, 3:397
Socrates in, 7:601
Philia. See Friendship
Philip the Fair (king of France), 3:133
Philippi, Guillaume, and Geulincx, 4:76
Philippus of Opus, 4:172
Phillips, D. Z., 1:141, 4:617
Phillips, Wendell, Parker (T.) and, 7:122
Philo
Christian writers on, 5:569
Clement and, 2:289
on divine illumination, 4:580
on divine transcendence, 4:107
on emanationism, 3:189
Eusebius and, 3:455
on ideas as thoughts of God, 4:564
patristic philosophy and, 7:141–143
on possible, 3:87
and religious philosophy, 7:490
Philo Judaeus, **7:303–309**
on God, 7:303–306
in Jewish philosophy, 4:810
on knowledge, 7:305
on love of God, 5:585
and philosophy of history, 7:308
Plotinus and, 3:401
on providence and laws of nature, 7:304
psychology of, 8:122
on soul and free will, 7:304–305
on theocratic government, 7:306–307
on virtue, 7:307–308
on world soul, 5:641
Philo of Alexandria
Aenesidemus and, 1:31
apologism and, 1:227
Bible and, 3:357
in exegetical interpretation, 1:47
logos in, 5:569
patristic philosophy and, 7:141
skepticism of, 1:191
Philo of Larissa, **7:311–312**
Aenesidemus and, 1:30
eclecticism of, 9:48
in Greek Academy, 4:171
in Platonic tradition, 7:607
reasonable doubt of, 3:702
and skepticism, 1:191, 2:48
Philo of Megara, 5:403–404, 5:607, **7:312–313**
Philo the Dialectician, 3:87
Philodemus, **7:301–303**
Epicurean School and, 3:263–264
on formalism, 1:45
Lucretius and, 5:599
on music, 1:45, 1:189
on poetry, 1:45, 1:189
surviving works of, 3:265
Philolaus of Croton, **7:310–311**
cosmology of, 8:183
on Pythagoreanism, 8:185
"Philological Lectures" (Porphyry), 3:455
Philology
Biblical, and Trinity, 1:456
Hellenistic, 4:302
Valla and, 9:635
Vico on, 9:674
Philonian implication, 5:545
Philonides, Epicurean School and, 3:263
Philoponus, John, **7:313–315**
Aristotle and, 1:279, 5:408
atomism and, 1:384–385

on continuity, 2:493
on logic, 5:408, 5:439
in Neoplatonism, 6:554–555
Pico della Mirandola (Gianfrancesco) and, 7:575
on Proclus, 6:554–555
on projectile motion, 4:621
Simplicius on, 6:555, 9:35
Philosophe, Le (attrib: Damarsais), 2:266
Philosophe ignorant, Le (Voltaire), 9:193
Philosopher(s), 7:335–336
atheism of, 1:357
in Byzantine society, 1:787
definition of, 7:335
ethics of, 7:336
on gender issues, 9:75
in imperfect societies, 4:545
in industrial societies, 4:36
medical doctors as, 4:4
Plato on, 7:591, 7:597
as poets, 4:176
pre-Socratic
in history of metaphysics, 6:184
Orphism and, 7:44
Simplicius on, 9:35
prophets as, 4:819
as rulers, 1:117
sophists as, 9:129
Unamuno on, 9:567
Valéry on, 9:634
Vico on, 9:674
"Philosophers Are Back on the Job" (Singer), 9:41
Philosopher's Brief, 3:458
Philosopher's Confession (Confessio Philosophi) (Leibniz), 5:251, 5:261–263
Philosophers in Exile (Gurwitsch), 4:197
Philosophers Speak of God (Harshorne and Reese), 9:752
Philosophes
and atheism, 2:688–691
and crisis of skepticism, 9:56
deism and, 2:687–688
Enlightenment view of, 3:244
in French Revolution, 3:243, 8:589
German, deism and, 2:688
Latin American philosophy and, 5:205
Paine as, 7:74
Volney as, 9:706–707
Philosophes géomètres de la Grèce, Les (Milhaud), 6:217
Philosophia Militans (Paulsen), 7:148
Philosophia Mundi (William of Conches), 9:768
"Philosophia Naturalis" (John of St. Thomas), 4:844–845
Philosophia Naturalis (Ockham). *See Summulae in Libros Physicorum* (Ockham)
Philosophia Naturalis (Regius), 8:301
Philosophia perennis, 7:248
Philosophia Perennis, Festgabe Joseph Geyser (Huber), 4:83
Philosophia Prima (Avicenna), 8:766
Philosophia Sagax (Paracelsus), 7:103
Philosophia Synthetica (Rüdiger), 8:527
Philosophiae Naturalis Principia Mathematica (Newton), 3:246
Philosophia: Philosophorum Nostri Temporis Vox Universa (periodical), 5:343
Philosophic emanationism, 3:189
Philosophic faith *(philosophische Glaube),* Jaspers on, 4:802–803
Philosophic Society of Louvain, 6:143
Philosophic Study of Tolstoy, A (Kvitko), 9:512–513
Philosophical aesthetics
Boileau on, 1:640
developments in, 3:573
Philosophical anthropology
Aquinas and, 6:104
Bachofen and, 1:441
Bakhtin Circle and, 1:469
in Gehlen, 4:35–36
genetic technology and, 4:48
Molina Garmendia and, 6:323–324
and natural and human science demarcation, 1:470
Plessner and, 7:629
Sombart on, 9:128
utopias of, 9:618
Philosophical Arguments (Ryle), 8:581
Philosophical bibliographies, 10:67–75
Philosophical Commentaries (Berkeley), on significance of words, 8:781
Philosophical community, Patricia Kitcher and, 5:76
"Philosophical Conceptions and Practical Results" (James, William), 4:781, 7:744
Philosophical dictionaries and encyclopedias, 10:75–139
Philosophical Dictionary (Voltaire)
Enlightenment and, 3:244
targets of, 3:409–410
Philosophical Discourse Concerning the Natural Immortality of the Soul (Norris), 6:656
Philosophical Enquiry into the Origins of Our Ideas of the Sublime and the Beautiful, A (Burke), 1:51–52, 3:254, 9:293, 9:522
Philosophical Essay on Probabilities, A (Essai philosophique sur les probabilités) (Laplace), 5:197
Philosophical Essays (Ayer), 1:437
Philosophical Essays (Stewart), 9:248
Philosophical Explanations (Nozick), 6:669, 7:230
Philosophical fallacies, 3:548–549
Philosophical Fragments (Kierkegaard), 5:65
Philosophical grammar, history of, Bacon (Roger) on, 1:455
Philosophical Guide to Conditionals (Bennett), 1:549–550
Philosophical Hermeneutics (Gadamer), 4:2
Philosophical history
as alternative to everyday history, 5:29
Vico on, 9:672–674
Philosophical imaginary, feminism and, 3:570
Philosophical inquiry, as expression of individual existence, 5:61
Philosophical Inquiry concerning Human Liberty (Collins), 2:683, 8:4
Philosophical Investigations (Wittgenstein), 9:802, 9:809–815
a priori and *a posteriori* in, 1:241
analytic philosophy in, 1:151–152
"arm going up" analogy in, 8:674
art in, 1:66
faith in, 3:533
image in, 4:594
Kripke and, 5:149
on panpsychism, 7:90
private language problem in, 8:22
on rule-following, 8:530–531
truth theory in, 2:544–546
Philosophical journals, 10:139–177
Philosophical legitimacy, of action at a distance, 3:688
Philosophical Letters (Cavendish), 2:117–118
"Philosophical Letters" (Schiller, Friedrich), 8:626
Philosophical logic
development of, 5:474
non-classical logic and, 5:483
Van Fraassen and, 9:644–645
Philosophical method. *See* Method(s); Methodology
Philosophical Notebooks (Lenin), 3:65, 5:280

Philosophical Papers (Lewis), on supervenience, 3:191
Philosophical Papers (Moore), 5:97
"Philosophical Papers" *(Philosophische Aufsätze)* (Jerusalem), 5:296
"Philosophical Perplexity" (Wisdom), 9:797–799
Philosophical Poems (More), 6:395
Philosophical Principles of Integral knowledge (Solov'ëv), 9:122
Philosophical problems
  in bioethics, 1:602
  senseless, Vaihinger on, 9:627–628
  Vailati and, 9:629
  Wisdom on, 7:57–58
Philosophical Propositions (Agnesi), 9:839
Philosophical Review, The (journal), 9:65
Philosophical schools, Cyrenaics and, 2:619
Philosophical Scrutiny of Religion, A (Ducasse), 3:125
Philosophical Society, The, 4:286
Philosophical Society at Derby, 2:630
Philosophical Studies (journal), 8:733
Philosophical Studies (Moore), 3:314
Philosophical systems
  existentialism on, 3:501–502
  irreducibility of knowledge to, 1:559
  Kierkegaard on, 3:501
Philosophical terminology, Lalande on, 5:172
Philosophical Theology (Tennant), 7:562, 9:379, 9:392
Philosophical Theory of the State (Bosanquet), 1:663, 4:560
Philosophical Understanding and Religious Truth (Frank), 3:715
Philosophical View of Reform, A (Shelley), 9:8
Philosophical Works (Descartes), on attribute, 9:297
Philosophico-science revolution, and *philosophe* movement, 3:683
Philosophie (Jaspers), 4:800
"Philosophie als strenge Wissenschaft" (Husserl), 7:282
Philosophie am Scheidewege, Die (Schultz), 8:659
Philosophie Bemerkungen (Wittgenstein), 9:809
Philosophie de Charles Renouvier, La (Milhaud), 6:217
Philosophie de l'art (Taine), 9:364–365
"Philosophie de l'esprit" (Lavelle and Le Senne, eds.), 5:289
Philosophie der Arithmetik (Husserl), 3:732, 7:280
Philosophie der Aufklärung, Die (Cassirer), 3:243
Philosophie der Erlösung (Mainländer)}, 7:251
Philosophie der Freiheit (Steiner), 9:241
Philosophie der Griechen, Die II (Zeller), 4:172
Philosophie der Logik und Arithmetik (Dingler), 3:86
Philosophie der Mathematik und Naturwissenschaft (Philosophy of Mathematics and Natural Science) (Weyl), 9:741–742
Philosophie der Mythologie (Schelling), 8:621
Philosophie der Offenbarung (Schelling), 8:621
Philosophie der symbolischen Formen (Cassirer), 1:65
Philosophie des Als-Ob, Die (Vaihinger), 9:625
"Philosophie des mathématiques de Kant, La" (Couturat), 2:582
Philosophie des Unbewussten, Die (von Hartmann), 7:251
Philosophie Herakleitos des Dunkeln von Ephesos, Die (Lassalle), 5:203
Philosophie. Ihr Problem und ihre Probleme, Die (Philosophy. Its problem and its problems) (Natorp), 6:490
Philosophie positive, La (periodical), 5:372
Philosophie première (Jankélévitch), 4:787
Philosophie sensualiste au XVIII siècle (Cousin), 2:580
Philosophie und Religion (Schelling), 1:12, 4:749
Philosophie Zoologique (Lamarck), 3:486–487, 5:173–174
Philosophiea Naturalis Theoria Redacta ad Unicam Legem Virum in (Boscovich), 1:665
Philosophies of Arts (Kivy), 1:67
Philosophische Archiv (periodical), 3:161
Philosophische Aufsätze ("Philosophical Papers") (Jerusalem), 5:296
Philosophische Briefe über Dogmatismus und kritizismus (Schelling), 4:557, 8:618
Philosophische Glaube (philosophic faith), Jaspers on, 4:802–803
Philosophische Kritizismus, Der (Riehl), 8:467
Philosophische Rundschau (journal), 4:2
Philosophische Sytematik (Philosophical systematics) (Natorp), 6:490–491
Philosophische Untersuchungen üuber das Wesen der menschlichen Freiheit (Schelling), 8:621
Philosophische Versuche uber die menschliche Natur und ihre Entwicklung (Philosophical essays on human nature and its development) (Tetens), 9:404
Philosophischen Schriften (journal), 4:552
Philosophisches Journal, 1:377–380
Philosophisches Magazin (periodical), 3:161
Philosophoe der Symbolischen Formen (Cassirer), 1:58
Philosophy, **7:325–337**
  as *a priori,* 7:331
  absolute as aim of, 1:11
  academic, Foucher and, 3:702
  as activity, 5:526
  activity of mind and, 1:713
  Adorno on, 1:25
  of aesthetics, 7:328
  vs. aesthetics, 7:332–333
  alchemical. *See* Alchemical philosophy; Esoteric philosophy
  al-Fārābī, Abū-Naṣr Muhammad on, 1:116
  analytic, **1:144–157,** 2:419
    Austin (John Langshaw) in, 1:407–411
    education and, 7:355–356
    feminism in, **1:157–159**
    language and, 1:407–410
    logical positivism in, 1:149–150
    Quine in, 1:150–151
    religion in, 7:478–479
    Wisdom (John) in, 9:797–798
    Wittgenstein on, 1:147–153
  ancient
    Losev on, 5:575
    modernism *vs.,* 6:316
    optimism/pessimism in, 7:246–247
    Owen and, 7:64–65
    Vlastos and, 9:701
    women in, 9:837–838
  Antiochus of Ascalon on, 1:222
  antithetical experience in, 1:476
  applied, Kant's contributions to, 5:28–30
  Aquinas on, 9:426
  Ardigò on, 1:251
  argument in, 5:10–11
  Aristotle on, 1:263

of art, 1:610
Bullough on, 1:761
definition of, 7:328
enthusiasm and irony in, 9:114–115
Langer on, 5:187–188
as assistive to theology, 1:650
autonomy of, 1:650, 1:767, 7:331–332
Ayer on, 1:437
being as object of, 1:527
Bentham and, 1:551
Berkeley and, 1:576–577
bibliographies, 10:67–75
bioethics and, 1:600
of biology, **7:337–349**
in evolutionary game theory, 4:20–22
and genetics and reproductive technologies, 4:46–48
teleology and, 9:389
in Bonaventure's theology, 1:650–651
Bonhoeffer on, 1:655
branches of, Peirce on, 7:169
of Buddhism, 1:725
Buridan on, 1:767
business and, 7:333
Byzantine, 1:786, 1:789–790
Carnap on, 2:44–45
Carolingian renaissance and, 2:49–51
Carus (Paul) and, 2:64
Cattaneo on, 2:83
central categories of, formation of, 3:570
chance in, 2:127–128
Chateaubriand on, 2:138
Chinese, 2:227, 5:665
Christian, 1:390–391, 1:650, 7:141
of Dostoevsky, 3:99–102
and ethics, 3:401–404
influences on, 3:401
Neoplatonism and, 3:403
philosophy of history and, 7:387
rise of, 3:401
circulation of, 4:49
of circumstance, Ortega y Gasset on, 5:208
Clement of Alexandria on, 2:290
Collingwood on, 2:325–327
common sense and, 2:356
as communal discipline, 1:451
communication and, 7:333
competence in, 7:335–336
competition in, 6:669
conceptual analysis in, 1:170
as craft for good of common people, 2:83
critical judgment in, 9:792
Croce on, 2:602
Crusius on, 2:606
cultural significance of, 7:334–336
cultural upheaval and, 3:404–405
of culture
Cassirer on, 2:67–68
Roretz and, 8:493
Dante on, 2:624
and data of reason, 1:706
definition of, 7:325, 7:336–337
Descartes on, 2:750
descriptive *vs.* reversionary metaphysical theories and, 2:79
Dge-lugs scholastic training and, 1:734–736
dictionaries and encyclopedias, 10:75–139
of economics. *See* Economics, philosophy of
in education, 7:333–334
of education. *See* Education, philosophy of
Elizabethan view of, 1:444
empiricist view of, 9:644–645
encyclopedias, 10:75–139
in England, role of learning in, 1:444
in Enlightenment, 3:243–245
epistemology in, 7:325
esoteric. *See* Alchemical philosophy; Esoteric philosophy
ethics in, 7:325–326
etymology of, 7:335
facts and, Windelband on, 9:792
feminist. *See* Feminism; Feminist philosophy of science
fields in, major, 7:325–329
of film, **7:381–386**
French. *See* French philosophy
German
Adorno and, 1:25
Apel in, **1:225–227**
Basedow and, 1:482–483
Coleridge and, 2:316
ethics in, 3:422–423
Geisteswissenschaften in, 4:37
and "I" and "Other" relation in Russian thought, 1:465
in Korea, 5:141
Nietzsche on, 6:611
Rosenkranz on, 8:497
in Russia, 1:465–467, 1:471, 1:538
Schelling, 8:617
Scholz in, 8:644–646
Schopenhauer in, 8:647–657
Schultz in, 8:659–660
Schuppe in, 8:662–664
Sigwart in, 9:29
Simmel in, 9:30
unconscious in, 9:571
universal grammar and, 8:791
Geyser on, 4:82
goal of, 1:11, 5:342, 9:719
God as standard of accuracy in, 2:8
grammar and, 8:770
happiness as aim of, 1:390
Hegel on, 4:269
Heidegger on, 7:399
Helmholtz on, 4:304
Hilbert and, 4:62
historicization of, 7:397–399
and history, 2:325–327, 9:676
of history. *See* History, philosophy of
history of. *See* History, of philosophy
Hobbes in, 4:425
of identity, 7:11
ignorance as goal of, 9:719
importance of, 7:332, 8:494
Indian, **4:623–634**
absence in, 6:530–532
atomic theory in, **1:380–383**
atomism in, 1:381–382
causality in, 2:109–113
certification in, 9:545
consciousness in, 9:542
Deussen on, 3:41
emptiness in, 6:471
epistemology in, 9:544–545
eschatology in, 3:347
eternity in, 3:359
on fallacies, 9:544–545
on human nature, 5:359
inference in, 5:412–414, 6:532
logic in. *See* Logic, in Indian philosophy
and medieval Jewish philosophy, 4:812
mereology in, 1:381
negation in, **6:530–533**
nonexistence in, 6:531
Pantheism in, 7:94–95
perception in, 6:532–533, 9:543
philosophy of language in, 7:412–417
realism in, 9:543
referentialism in, 9:544
testimony in, 9:544–545
truth in, **9:542–546**
universe in, 9:380

Philosophy, ***continued***
in intellectual history, 7:334
interdisciplinary perspective in, 7:334
Islamic, **4:754–764**
Abu'l-Barakāt al-Baghdādī and, 4:817
active intellect in, 4:550
Alexander of Aphrodisias in, 1:112–113
al-Fārābī, Abū-Naṣr in, 4:811
al-Ghazālī (Muhammad) in, 1:118
al-Kindī in, 1:131
analogy in, 1:139–140
Aristotle in, 1:116
classical period of, 3:70
cosmology in, 1:433
determinism in, 3:23
dialectic in, **3:69–70**
East *vs.* West in, 1:130
on experience, 4:7
Galen and, 4:6–7
and Grosseteste, 4:186
haqq, concept of, 4:542
Ibn al-ʿArabī and, 4:541
Ibn Bājja and, 4:544–545
Ibn Khaldūn and, 4:547–550
Ibn Ṭufayl and, 4:550
illuminationism and, 4:581–585
Jewish participation in, 4:811
kalām in, 3:69–70
Neoplatonism in, 6:557–558
peripatetic, 4:581
Plato in, 1:116
prophetic, of Shi'ism, 4:550–551
Pythagoreanism in, 8:188
reason in, 1:130
reproductive technologies and, 4:46
science and, 3:248–249
Suhrawardī in, 4:581
vocabulary in, 1:131
James on, 4:786
Jaspers on, 4:799
journalism and, 7:333
journals, 10:139–177
Kabbalists on, 4:821
of language. *See* Language, philosophy of
language and, 1:152–153
of law. *See* Law(s), philosophy of
vs. law, 7:332
of liberation. *See* Liberation philosophy
Lichtenberg on, 5:342
limits to, 1:629, 5:620
and linguistics, 7:173, 8:149–150
of logic, Frege and, 2:82
logic in, 1:768, 6:329–330, 7:326
logical positivism and, 5:526, 5:529
Luther on, 5:613–617
Lyotard on, 5:620
of mathematics. *See* Mathematics, philosophy of
of medicine. *See* Medicine, philosophy of
medicine and, 7:333
of memory, 6:122
Mercier on, 6:145
metaphysical, 4:584
metaphysics in, 7:326
method of. *See* Method(s), philosophical
of mind, 2:89–93, **7:467–473**
Bacon (Francis) and, 1:445–446
Chinese, 2:208–210
cognitive science and, 2:300
Collingwood on, 2:328
computationalism and, 2:391
concepts and, 2:414
definition of, 7:327
determinism and, 3:24–25
epistemology and, 3:276, 8:130–131
functionalism in, 8:85, 8:155–156, 9:16
Hegel and, 4:259–260, 4:267–269
introspection in, 4:720–722
Kant and, 5:34
Kim on, 5:71
materialism and, 6:11–12
mental content and, 2:478
mental-physical distinction in, 6:138
Millikan and, 6:236
on object-directedness, 4:712
Olivi and, 7:13
propositional attitudes in, 8:79–85
Shoemaker on, 9:15
Spinoza on, 9:188
Stewart on, 9:248
Stout on, 9:259
Wollheim and, 9:836
modern, development of, Feuerbach on, 3:610
Montague (Richard) on, 6:329–330
Moore on, 1:145
Mou on, 2:222
of music, Losev on, 5:575
narrative in, 7:332–333
natural. *See* Natural philosophy
natural science and, 8:458–459
naturalism in, 7:331
of nature
Bonnet and, 1:658
Campanella on, 2:15–16
Engels on, 3:57–61
Hegel and, 4:266–267
Hobbes and, 4:410–411
John of St. Thomas and, 4:845
Kant and, 5:28–29
Lachelier on, 5:169–170
Miura on, 6:276
Schelling on, 8:618–619
Schlegel on, 8:631
Schultz and, 8:659
nature of
Ducasse on, 3:124
Lichtenberg on, 5:341–342
Mercier on, 6:144
Vailati on, 9:629
Wisdom (John) on, 9:796–799
new, development of, Eucken on, 3:451–452
as nonreducible mode of thought, 1:25
normativity and, 7:332–334
Ortega y Gasset on, 7:48
vs. other disciplines, 7:332–333
parts of, 4:321–322
Pascal on, 7:133
of physics, **7:473–478**
Descartes and, 9:172
Einstein and, 3:179–181
Helmholtz and, 4:305
on inertial systems, 9:149
Schrödinger and, 8:657–658
Taine on, 9:365
Plato on, 1:263, 7:597
and poetry, 4:175–176, 5:68, 7:586, 7:594–595
political. *See* Political philosophy
Popper on, 7:691
poststructuralism and, 9:278
practical
Fichte and, 3:618
Kotarbiński and, 5:145
as practical tool, Shaftesbury on, 9:2
pre-Socratic. *See* Pre-Socratic philosophy
Pringle-Pattison on, 8:12
of probability, of Keynes, 5:55–56
as profession, multiculturalism in, 6:422–423

professionalization of, verifiability principle and, 9:668
pseudo problems in, 1:568
pseudo sentences in, 5:527
of psychiatry, memory studied in, 6:122
of psychology. *See* Psychology, philosophy of
psychology and, 1:544, 5:362–363, 8:148–150, 8:155–156
public policy and, 7:335
purpose of
Husserl on, 3:312
Laberthonnière on, 5:164–165
Windelband on, 9:791
Wisdom (John) on, 9:796–799
in Pythagoreanism, 8:181–182
and reason *vs.* revelation, 1:629
of religion, **7:478–503**
Abelard on, 1:7
Athens *vs.* Jerusalem in, 9:11
Baader (Franz Xavier von) and, 1:439
Braithwaite and, 1:686
Bruno and, 1:710
Calvin and, 2:8, 2:12
Card on, 2:4
Chaadaev and, 2:120–121
Chinese, 2:223–231
Chinese approach to, 2:226–227
Collingwood on, 2:326
in common claims *vs.* religious claims in virtue, 2:228
consolation and death in, 2:227
definition of, 7:327
Ducasse on, 3:125
Fichte and, 3:618
genre and persuasion in, 2:228–230
God in, 7:479
Hatano and, 4:247
Hegelian, 4:276–277, 4:284
historical *vs.* phenomenal analysis in, 2:224
history of, **7:485–498**
Hume's "Of Miracles" in, 6:270
Ii'in in, 4:577
Ionescu on, 4:743
I-thou *vs.* I-it relationships and, 1:716
Jacobi (Friedrich Heinrich) and, 4:772
James (William) and, 4:779–781
Kant and, 5:30
literalism and indirect discourse in, 2:230
omniscience in, 7:479
origins of, 2:691
paradox in, 2:229–230
Plantinga and, 7:581
problems of, **7:499–503**
Roman Catholicism harmony with common sense, 1:646
Royce on, 8:521–522
Shestov and, 9:13
social values in, 2:226–227
spiritual attitude–social manipulation analysis in, 2:226–227
Ziehen (Theodor) on, 9:884
vs. religion
in The Absolute, 4:111–112
Pico della Mirandola on, 7:573
religion and, in Maimonides, 5:648
and rhetoric, in Cicero, 2:257
role of
Dewey on, 3:50
Eucken on, 3:451
Lucian of Samosata on, 5:597
Paulsen on, 7:148
in Romanticism, 8:488–489
Rorty on, 7:399, 8:494
Ryle on, 8:580–581
Schelling on, 1:11
Schlick on, 8:638–641
scholastic. *See* Scholastics/Scholasticism
and science, 1:151, 7:183, 7:187, 7:282, 7:331–332, 9:197
Jungius and, 4:861
Mercier on, 6:145
Pastore on, 7:135
in phenomenology, 7:282
realism on, 7:183, 7:187
Spirito on, 9:197
Windelband on, 9:791–792
Zubiri (Xavier) on, 9:888
as science, 1:451, 7:282
of science. *See* Science(s), philosophy of
self-consciousness and, 1:713
of sex. *See* Sex, philosophy of
Sidgwick on, 9:22
social. *See* Social philosophy
of social sciences. *See* Social science(s), philosophy of
and society, 5:648
special sciences in, 9:161
speculative. *See* Speculative philosophy
of spirit, in Croce, 2:600
of statistical mechanics. *See* Statistical mechanics, philosophy of
Stoicism on, 9:257
subfields of, 7:328–329
of technics, outlines of, 3:670
of technology. *See* Technology, philosophy of
theological, *vs.* philosophy of religion, 7:478–479
and theology, 1:479, 1:767–786, 4:840, 7:332, 9:28, 9:772
Alexander of Hales on, 1:114
Aquinas on, 9:772
Arnauld on, 1:289
Barth on, 1:479
Buridan on, 1:767–768
Duns Scotus on, 3:134
John of La Rochelle on, 4:840
Siger of Brabant on, 9:28
therapeutic role of, 1:152
Thoreau on, 6:575
transcendental
psychological considerations in, 5:34
Twardowski on, 9:554
universal grammar and, 8:790
universal language of, 9:338
uses of, 7:336–337
value of, 7:336–337
Vasconcelos on, 9:648
Vico on, 9:676
Vienna Circle and, 2:38–41, 5:525
Wahle (Richard) on, 9:719
Western, neo-Confucian critique of, 2:182
wisdom and, 7:335
Wittgenstein on, 1:148, 1:152
women's exclusion from, 3:590
world views and, 7:334–335
Philosophy (Korean academic journal), 5:141
Philosophy and Historical Understanding (Gallie), 7:394
Philosophy and Phenomenological Research (journal), 9:135
Philosophy and Public Affairs (journal), 9:41
Philosophy and Scientific Realism (Smart), 9:66
Philosophy and Sex (Baker and Elliston, eds.), 7:521
Philosophy and the Mirror of Nature (Rorty), 8:494
Philosophy and the Modern Mind (Stace), 9:200
Philosophy and the Physicists (Stebbing), 9:236

"Philosophy and the Scientific Image of Man" (Sellars, Wilfrid), 8:734
Philosophy as a Science: Its Matter and Method (Ducasse), 3:124
Philosophy in a New Key (Langer), 1:58
"Philosophy in the Tragic Age of the Greeks" (Nietzsche), 6:610
Philosophy in the 20th Century (Ayer), 1:438
Philosophy, Interpreter of Holy Scripture (Meyer), 9:170, 9:182
Philosophy of Art, The (Ducasse), 3:125
Philosophy of Art, The (Schelling), 1:54, 8:622
Philosophy of "As If" (Vaihinger), 1:24, 2:38
Philosophy of Discovery (Whewell), 1:677
Philosophy of Hegel, The (Stace), 9:199
Philosophy of History (Collingwood), 2:326
Philosophy of History (Hegel), 5:59
Philosophy of History (Karsavin), 5:42
Philosophy of Illumination (Suhrawardī), 4:582
Philosophy of Language (Alston), 1:132
Philosophy of Leibniz, The (Russell), on substance, 9:298
"Philosophy of Life" (Dilthey), and Shpet, 9:19
"Philosophy of Logical Atomism, The" (Russell), 3:345
Philosophy of Mass Art, A (Carroll), 1:67
Philosophy of Mathematics (Comte), 7:712
Philosophy of Mind (Hegel), 1:12
Philosophy of Natural Science, The (Hempel), 8:694
"Philosophy of Nature" (Hegel), Engels and, 3:58, 3:60
Philosophy of New Music (Adorno), 1:26
Philosophy of occurrences, 9:719
Philosophy of organism (Whitehead), 9:750
Philosophy of Oriental Illumination (Suhrawardī), 9:305
Philosophy of Personalism, The (Knudson), 7:233
Philosophy of Physical Science (Eddington), 3:164
Philosophy of Plato (al-Fārābī), 7:610
Philosophy of Psychology and the Humanities (Stein), 9:240
"Philosophy of Pure Sciences, The" (Clifford), 2:293
Philosophy of Religion Based on Kant and Fries, The (Otto), 7:59
Philosophy of Right (Hegel), 2:320, 7:425–426, 9:96
Philosophy of Science (Bergmann), 1:561
Philosophy of Symbolic Forms, The (Cassirer), 8:621
Philosophy of the Active and Moral Powers of Man (Stewart), 2:347
Philosophy of the Common Task, The (Fëdorov), 3:560
Philosophy of the Human Mind (Brown), 1:704
Philosophy of the Inductive Sciences, Founded upon Their History (Whewell), 9:743
Philosophy of the Present, The (Mead), 6:81–82
Philosophy of the Sciences (Tennant), 9:392
"Philosophy of the Unconditioned" (William), 1:92
Philosophy of the Unconscious (Hartmann), 6:610, 9:571
Philosophy of Theism (Croll), 3:232
Philosophy of Whitehead, The (Mays), 9:751
Philostratus, on phantasia, 7:271
Phlogiston, 5:216–217
Phobias, in psychoanalytic theory, 8:111–112
Phobus (literary magazine), 5:78
Phoenix (Euclides of Megara), 6:110
Phonogram Archive, 9:280
Phonological form, and transformational grammar, 5:509
Phonology, **7:551–553,** 9:531
Photios, Patriarch of Constantinople, on universals, 1:788
Photography, 9:689–690
Photons, 6:62
    in PET scans, 6:564
    quantum computing and, 2:407
Photoplay: A Psychological Study, The (Munsterberg), 7:381
Phrase(s)
    ambiguous, 3:542–543
    meaning assigned to, Davidson on, 6:85
Phrenology, 2:413, 8:670
Phronêsis, 1:268, **10:27–28**
Phusis, **6:631–632**
Phylogenetic psychoanalytic assumptions, 3:746
Physica Vera (Geulincx), 4:77
Physical
    concept of, 2:91
    definition of, 6:139, 7:553
    as nonmental, 6:139
    operationalism and, 7:29–32
    perception of, 6:138–139
Physical body, in ontological reism, 5:144
Physical forces
    concept of, 5:52
    human intellect *vs.*, 9:862
Physical influence, Pietist doctrine of, 5:123
Physical laws, in view from nowhere, 6:73
Physical Monadology (Kant), 6:325
Physical processes
    collision and, 6:60
    electromagnetic theory and, 6:62
Physical properties
    color as, 2:333
    definition of, 3:113–114
    of material things, 6:5–6
    vs. mental properties, in property dualism, 6:132–133
    supervenience of mental properties on, 9:327
Physical science
    and biological science
        unified, 9:750
        Whitehead and, 9:753
    certitude of, Oresme on, 7:34
    determinism and, 3:10–12, 3:29–33
    religion and, **8:397–401**
    Schelling on, 8:618–619
    truth by convention in, 2:520
Physical Society, Eddington and, 3:164
Physical space
    and mathematical space, 4:848
    and perceptual space, 5:131
Physical stance, explanation from, 2:711
Physical states
    entropy and information in, 2:105
    and functional states, 3:757
    Gauge Theory and, 4:31–33
    mental states and
        asymmetrical knowledge of, 6:16–17
        in James's psychology, 4:777–778
        logical connections between, 6:17
    qualitative consciousness and, 2:450
Physical systems, and phenomenal gestalten, 5:127
Physical theory, physical defined by, 6:139
Physicalism, 2:92–93, 3:758, **7:553–556**
    anomalous monism and, 1:211

body-mind dependence in, 4:617
Carnap and, 6:561–562
colors and, 2:332
computationalism and, 2:391
development of, 6:561–562
doubt about, sources of, 5:112–113
doubts in, 5:112–113
emergence and, 3:193
and functionalism, 3:758–759
as global supervenience thesis, 9:331
and identifying mental states with brain states, 3:756
on intentionality, 4:711
on introspection, 4:721
Köhler and, 5:132
as linguistic doctrine, 6:562
logical positivism and, 5:528–529
in modern science, 6:138
Nagel (Thomas) on, 6:475
naturalism as, 6:492–493
Neurath on, 6:561–562
nonreductive, **6:643–649**
phenomena in, 3:691
physics and, 6:139
Quine and, 8:220
token, 7:555
truth and, 3:220
type, 7:553–555
Physicalism, or Something Near Enough (Kim), 5:71
Physicalistic judgments, 7:244
Physician-assisted suicide, 3:456, 3:458, 6:94, 9:321. *See also* Euthanasia
Physicochemical plateau, 3:46
Physico-formal properties, of mental representations, in explanatory role, 6:141
Physicophysical properties, Ducasse on, 3:125
Physicopsychical properties, Ducasse on, 3:125
Physicotheology, **7:556–563**
Derham and, 2:686, 7:559
Kant on, 5:23
Physico-Theology (Derham), 2:686, 7:559
Physics, 2:37–38
a priori basis of, Kant on, 5:28
Albert of Saxony and, 1:101
Anaxagoras on, 1:183
Aquinas and, 9:427–428
Aristotle and, 1:271–273, 7:474. *See also Physics* (Aristotle)
and astronomy, 5:54
atomism and, 1:385
of black holes, 1:606–609
Boltzmann and, 1:644–645
Boscovich on, 1:666
Buridan on, 1:769
Burley and, 1:773
Cartesian, 2:285
and causal account of time, 2:87
chemistry's reduction to, 2:142–143
Chwistek on, 2:255
classical
locality in, 6:638–639
matter in, 6:61
matter *vs.* energy in, 6:62–63
Taine on, 9:365
time in, 9:495
and classical mechanics, 2:279
color in, 2:333–334
completeness of, 7:474
contemporary, 3:690
cosmological models and, 2:562
counterfactuals and mathematical relations in, 2:574
Crescas and, 4:822–823
Crusius on, 2:607
Descartes and, 2:53–54
determinism and, 3:10–12, 3:29–33
and direction of time, **7:563–567**
domain of, as closed, 2:89–93
Duhem (Pierre Maurice Marie) and, 3:126
Einstein, Albert, **3:178–182**
elementary particles in, 9:267
emergence theories and, 3:191
Epicureanism and, 4:300
and epistemology, Eddington on, 3:164
equations as models in, 3:30
and existence of God, 1:361, 7:703–704
faithful model assumption in, 3:30
field theory and, 2:106
force in, 3:688
formalism in, outdatedness of, 4:804
Gauge Theory and, 4:31–33
Hegel on, 4:266–267
Heisenberg and, 4:297–299
Helmholtz and, 4:303
Hugh of St. Victor on, 8:592
hypothesized theory and, 1:644
and impetus theory of projectile motion, 1:769
Kant on, 5:30
Laplace on, 5:197
laws of, time-reversal invariance of, 2:104–105
Lenin on, 3:65
on life, conditions for, 2:567
local magnitudes in, 6:638–639
Mach in, 5:623
Maritain on, 5:713
mathematics and, Oresme on, 7:34–35
Maxwell and, 1:644–645
in medieval philosophy, 6:105
in mind-body problem, 6:261–262
models in, discarded, 4:804
motion in, 7:474
natural philosophy and, 6:590
naturalism and, primacy of, 6:492
neighborhood-locality in, 6:639–640
Newtonian, 7:474
black holes in, 1:607
as classical mechanics, 2:279
in Cohen (Hermann), 2:303
inertial system in, 9:148–149
as source for cosmological ideas, 2:561
space in, 9:155
observation and observers in, 1:633
Ockham and, 9:780
ontological assumptions in, 1:635
phenomenalism and, 2:104, 7:273
and philosophy, Earman on, 3:159–161
vs. philosophy, 4:10
philosophy of, **7:473–477**
Descartes on, 9:172
Einstein and, 3:179–181
Helmholtz and, 4:305
on inertial systems, 9:149
Schrödinger and, 8:657–658
scope of, 7:473–474
Taine on, 9:365
physical events in, causation of, 6:209
physicalism and, 6:139
psychology and, 5:129
public language of, 5:528
pure, accounting for, 5:20
in quantum mechanics, 2:143
Quine and, 6:198
Schlick on, 8:641
Seneca on, 8:812
of sky, 5:54
soul in, 1:274
and special sciences, 9:161
statistical reasoning in, 6:70
in Stoicism, 4:300, 9:254, 9:256
Strato and, 9:261
symmetry and conservation principle of, 2:462–463
terminist, Crescas and, 4:822–823

Physics, ***continued***
time in, 2:85–86, **9:493–501**
Tschirnhaus on, 9:549
virtual image in, 4:594
vitalism and, 9:696–697
Wolff on, 9:828
Zabarella and, 9:866
See also Energy; Force; Quantum mechanics
Physics (Aristotle), 1:272–273, 2:95, 2:490, 5:157
Averroes and, 1:422
causality in, 2:95, 2:666–667
David of Dinant and, 2:644
on energy and force, 3:226
on geometrical theorems, 4:55
Giles of Rome on, 4:90
Grosseteste on, 4:186
microcosm in, 5:641
motion in, 1:273, 3:686, 9:874
natural law in, 6:506
number in, 2:490
Ockham on, 9:771
as paradigm-defining work, 5:157
Philoponus on, 7:314
Simplicius on, 9:34
Physics and Philosophy (Jeans), 4:804
Physics: The Elements (Campbell), 2:17, 6:89
Physikalische Begriffsbildug (Physical concept formation) (Carnap), 2:41
Physiochemical theory, of perception, 5:127–129
Physiognomia (Scot), 8:703
Physiognomische Fragmente zur Beforderung der Menschenkenntnis und Menschenliebe (Physiognomic fragments for furthering the knowledge and love of man) (Lavater), 5:213
Physiognomy, Lavater and, 5:213–214
Physiologia Stoicorum (Lipsius), 5:364
Physiological psychology, 3:552, 9:849–850
Physiological Psychology (McDougall), 6:71, 8:147–148
Physiologische Psychologie (Wundt), 9:849
Physiology
of brain, 5:128
Buytendijk on, 7:320–321
Cabanis on, 2:2–3
Descartes and, 8:124–125
Empedocles on, 3:209–210
of experience, 8:135
Helmholtz and, 4:304
mental events and, 6:133, 6:261
in mental states, 9:720
of mind, 1:462
neural, Taine on, 9:365
of universe, 1:369
Physiology (Lewes), 7:149–150
Physiophilosophy-Lehrbuch der Naturgeschichte (Oken), 7:11
Physiotheology, shortcomings of, 5:27
Physischen Gestalten in Ruhe und im stationaren Zustand, Die (Köhler), 5:126
Phytologia or the Philosophy of Agriculture and Gardening (Darwin), 2:631
Pia Desideria (Spener), 7:575
Piaget, Jean, **7:567–569**
developmental psychology and, 8:153
Merleau-Ponty and, 6:150
on schemata, 9:77
Picasso, Pablo, 1:328
Pickering, Andrew, 8:677, 9:84
Pico della Mirandola, Count Giovanni, **7:570–574**
as Christian magi, 1:710
on conciliatory methodology, 5:255
Ficino and, 3:624, 7:570, 7:571, 7:572
on first principles, 7:614
and Florentine Academy, 3:671
on love, 5:587
on Plato and Aristotle, 7:571–573
in Platonic tradition, 7:614
Sigwart on, 9:29
syncretism of, 7:570–573
Pico della Mirandola, Gianfrancesco, **7:574–575**
Pico della Mirandola (Giovanni) and, 7:572–574
skepticism of, 9:50
Picot, Claude, 2:753
Pictorialism, 4:590
Picture of Dorian Gray, The (Wilde), 9:763–764
Picture theory, 9:803–804
elementary propositions in, 9:806
as nature of thought, 9:804–805
in *Philosophical Investigations,* 9:811–813
Picturesque, the, 3:254
Piecemeal super-naturalism, 4:781
"Pierre Menard, Author of the Quixote" (Borges), 1:317
Pietism, **7:575–576**
Budde and, 1:721
Crusius and, 2:605
Kant and, 5:124
Lambert and, 5:175–176
Major and, 5:661
natural philosophy and, 2:607
Thomasius and, 9:441–442
Wolff and, 9:823
Piety
Bonhoeffer on, 1:656
and conscience, 1:519
knowledge of, Socrates on, 9:855
Lotze on, 5:582
Santayana on, 8:599
Piggyback genetic traits, 3:489–490
Pilgrim (*saṁsāri*), in Jainism, 5:327
Pillar and Ground of the Truth, The (Florenskii), 3:669, 3:670
Pillow Problems (Carroll), 2:51
Pilot-wave theory, 3:33, 8:203. *See also* Bohmian mechanics
Pinch, Trevor, 8:677, 8:679
Pindar, on poetry, 1:41
Pineal gland
Descartes on, 8:124–125
as location of soul, 1:658
Pines, Shlomo, on Maimonides, 5:654
Pini, Ermenegildo, 4:94
Pinker, Steven, 3:481, 8:152
Pinsent, David, 9:800
Pisan, Christine Di, 3:600
Pisarev, Dmitri Ivanovich, **7:576–577**
Kareev and, 5:40
Lavrov and, 5:218
Marković and, 5:718
on nihilism, 6:617
Pistis Sophia (Faith-wisdom), emanationism in, 3:189
Pitcher, George, 5:76
Pitkin, Walter B.
on external relations, 6:587
in new realism, 6:585
Pitt, Joseph C., 7:549
Pitt, William, Price and, 8:1
Pitts, Walter, on cognitive science, 2:298
Pius IX, Pope, French liberalism and, 5:320
Pius X, Pope, on modernism, 5:571
Pius XI, Pope, Stein's letter to, 9:239
Pius XII, Pope
on evolution, 2:641
Loisy and, 5:571
PKA (protein kinase A), 6:568
Place
Foucault on, 9:492
knowledge of, 5:94
Nishida on, 6:625–626
Philoponus on, 7:314
Place (Basho) (Nishida), 6:625
Place of Place paradox, 9:877–878
Place of Value in a World of Fact, The (Köhler), 4:73, 5:126, 5:131–132

Placebo effect
likelihood of, 3:740
rival hypothesis to, 3:742
Placita philsophorum (Plutarch), 8:188
Plague, The (Camus), 2:22, 3:427
Plaisir (pleasure), 7:249
Plamenatz, John, on equality, 3:331
Plan, Cyrenaics teaching on, 2:619
Plan of Parliamentary Reform (Bentham), 1:555
Planck, Max, **7:577–579**
atomism and, 1:388
on energy, 1:388
Köhler and, 5:126
Schlick and, 8:637
scientific discoveries of, 7:578–579
Vienna Circle and, 5:524
Planck's constant, 7:577
Plane, characterization of, 4:360–361
Planetary kinematics, Copernican theory as, 2:535
Planetary motion
causes of, 3:687
Copernicus on, 2:534
external agent and, 3:686
Kepler's three laws of, 5:50–51
in late medieval astronomy, 2:533
matter and, 6:3
Plant(s)
mental life of, 3:555
Plantin, Christophe, Lipsius and, 5:364
Plantinga, Alvin, 5:85, 5:102, **7:579–581**
a priori justification and, 5:80
on belief, 2:12, 3:322, 7:481–482
on direct demonstration of soft fact, 3:696
on existence of God, 3:321, 7:20–21, 7:481–482, 9:406–407
experientialism and, 3:322
on knowledge, 3:273, 3:323–324
on proper function theory, 6:498
reformed epistemology, 7:481–482
on seeings *vs.* seemings, 5:85
on warrant, 3:323–324
Plants and Fruits (Democritus), 5:298
Plastic arts, visual symbols provided by, 3:670
Plastic nature, 2:610, 5:236
Platner, Ernst, 9:56
Plato, 4:2, **7:581–605**
on *a priori* knowledge, 3:358
on abstractions, 3:499
and aesthetic history, 1:41–43, 1:187–188
aitia in, 1:99–100
on altruism, 3:170
analogy in, 1:139
on Anaxagoras, 1:183
Anselm and, 1:215
Antisthenes and, 1:224
apeiron/peras in, 1:225
apologism and, 1:228–229
on applying predicates, 9:288
Aquinas and, 3:358–359, 9:425
and Arabic thought, 1:116
archē in, 1:249
Archytas of Tarentum and, 1:250
Arethas and, 1:788
on art, 1:41–42, 1:303, 1:333
on atheism, 1:357
and atomism, 1:385, 5:302
Augustine and, 1:392–396, 3:357, 6:546
Averroes and, 1:422
Bacon (Francis) and, 1:451
on battle of Delium, 9:106
on beauty, 1:42, 1:74, 1:511, 5:584–586
on being, 1:527, 7:596
on being-as-such, 1:529
on belief, 3:284–285, 5:95, 5:106
on bodily self-control, 4:605
on body, 3:397, 4:5
Boethius and, 1:625–626
Bonaventure on, 1:651
and Byzantine thought, 1:787
and Christianity, 2:246
Colotes of Lampsacus on, 3:263
on composite nature of man, 4:605
on concepts, 2:417
on conflicting interests, 9:206
on conventionalism, 8:753
on cosmos, 2:571
on courage, 3:396
Couturat on, 2:581
on Cratylus, 2:584
Cudworth and, 2:610
Culverwell on, 2:612
Damascius on, 2:622
Davidson (Donald) and, 2:645
on death, 2:652
on definition, 2:665–666
on demiurge, 2:698–699, 7:489, 7:602
on determinism, 3:4–5
Deussen and, 3:41
and dialectic, 1:263–264, 3:52–53, 7:592–594, 7:602
Dikē and, 3:79
Dilthey on, 3:84
Diogenes Laertius on, 3:88
Diogenes of Sinope and, 3:90
on dogma, 3:96–97
dogmatism in, 6:547
on dreams, 3:105
dualism in, 3:115, 3:471, 4:610, 6:327
on duty, 3:155
on economics, 7:350, 7:591
on education, 7:365–367
on elementary triangles, 7:603
emanationism in, 3:189
on empirical judgments, 3:284–285
epistemology in, 3:283–286, 7:366
on equality, 3:329
error theory of, 3:343–344
eschatology in, 3:347
on eternal return doctrine, 3:353
on eternity, 3:358
on ethics, 3:395–398
Euclides and, 6:110
Eusebius and, 3:455
on evil, 3:397, 3:473
family of, 7:582
Fénelon and, 3:603
finitude of universe in, 1:225
four elements doctrine and, 3:209
Gadamer and, 4:2–3
Galileo on, 4:9
geometry in, 4:54
on God, 4:108–111, 7:303–305
on gods, 7:594
Gombrich and, 1:325–326
on the Good, 4:172, 6:548, 7:488, 7:632
Gorgias and, 4:162–163, 8:752
grammarian philosophy in, 8:751
in Greek Academy, 4:171–172, 4:300
and hierarchical communism, 2:364
on human expertise, 9:109
on human motivation, 3:142
on human sexuality, 7:521, 7:528
and humanism, 7:613
on ideal numbers, 7:637
on idealism, 4:553
on ideas, 4:563–564, 5:261
and Ikhwān al-Ṣafā', 4:576
on illumination, 4:579
on imitation, 1:41–42, 1:187, 1:303, 1:324–325
on immortality, 4:602, 4:609, 6:258, 7:634
on indeterminate dyad, 7:633
on infinity, 4:654, 4:668
Inge and, 4:685
on innate ideas, 4:687, 4:691
on intellect, 9:28
and Ivanov's *theurgy*, 4:767
on justice, 3:174
Justin Martyr and, 5:569

Plato, *continued*
on *kalon,* 5:7
on katharsis, 5:44
Kierkegaard and, 3:504
on knowledge, 3:214, 5:568, 7:599, 7:602, 9:100
vs. opinion, 1:42
poets' claims of, 7:585
Laas on, 5:163–164
on language, 5:568, 8:752–754
and Latin American philosophy, 5:208
on law, 7:418
on lawgiver as linguistic authority, 8:753
on leadership, 7:591–592
Levinas and, 5:305
on light, analogy of, 4:579–580
on limit and unlimited, 7:601
on limitation, 4:668
logic and, 5:398
on logos, 5:568
on love, 1:188, 3:142, 5:584–586, 9:702
Maimonides on, 5:648
on mathematics, 1:250, 8:186
on matter, 5:269, 6:58–59
memory in, 1:394, 5:640
and metaphysics, 1:187, 6:184–185, 7:608, 9:702
Metrodorus of Lampsacus on, 3:263
on microcosm, 5:640–641
on mimesis, 6:252
on mind, 7:556
on moral responsibility, 3:398
on morality of art, 1:43
on music, 1:188
on myth, 6:463–464
on names, 8:752–754
Natorp on, 6:490
natural law in, 6:506
on naturalism, 8:753
nature in, 6:519
on nothing, 6:657
on nouns and verbs, 9:286
on nous, 2:698, 6:666
on number, 6:670
Numenius of Apamea on, 6:679
on obligation to be just, 2:398
on the One, 7:632, 7:633
on one/many, 4:312
on optimism/pessimism, 7:247
Orphism and, 7:43
Ortega y Gasset on, 7:48
on *ousia,* 7:62–63
Owen on, 7:64–65
on painting, 1:324
Parmenides of Elea and, 7:122, 7:127
on participation, 1:652, 8:42
on perception, 8:824
on phantasia, 7:270–271
on philosophy, 1:263
on philosophy *vs.* poetry, 4:175–176, 7:594–595
physicotheology and, 7:556
Pico della Mirandola and, 7:570–573
on pleasure, 3:396–397
on plenitude, 5:593
Plotinus and, 3:400, 3:401
on poetry, 1:187–188, 1:333, 7:585
political philosophy of, 3:397, 7:656
possibility in, 7:720
on pre-Socratic cosmology, 1:271
Proclus on, 1:190, 6:546, 8:40–41
on profit-seeking by individuals, 1:777
as prophet, 8:40
on Protagoras, 1:230–231
on psyche, **8:103**
and Pythagoras, 7:488–489, 8:181, 8:186
rationalism of, 9:714–715
realism of, 9:588–591
reality in, 7:488
on receptacle, 7:632
on recollection, 3:283–284, 4:691
on regulation of emotion, 3:200–201
on religion and ethics, 3:391
and religious philosophy, 7:488–489
on reminiscence, 3:358, 4:606
on rhetoric, 2:257, 5:568
Schleiermacher and, 8:633
Schopenhauer and, 8:648, 8:654
Sciacca on, 8:666
on self-control, 3:396–397
on sense experience, 3:283–286
Shaftesbury and, 9:1
Shelley and, 9:9
Shestov on, 9:11
Sidgwick and, 9:25
Simplicius on, 6:554
skepticism of, 1:192–193
on social class, 7:591, 7:592
on Socrates
life of, 9:105
piety of, 9:109
trial of, 9:106
Socratic dialogues of, 9:107–108
on sophists, 9:129–130
on soul, 4:5, 4:602, 4:605–608, 5:259, 6:258, 7:44
on space, 9:147
on statements, 8:754–755
Stoicism and, 4:300
on suicide, 9:319
Taylor (Alfred) on, 9:373
teaching practice of, 4:172
and technology, 7:546
on testimony, 9:401
on theory of kinds, 7:600
on thought, nature of, 3:53
on time, 3:357
on tragedy, 9:521–523
transcendence in, 7:488
on truth, 2:540
on understanding, 1:393–394
on universals, 2:15, 4:563–564, 9:587–591
on unseen, 6:201
Utopia and, 6:400
Vico and, 9:672
on virtue, 1:256, 7:307, 9:112
on war and peace, 7:152
on wisdom, 9:794
on world soul, 3:686
on Zeno of Elea, 9:871
Plato and His Doctrine, On (Apuleius), 7:606–607
"Plato and Parmenides on the Timeless Present" (Owen), 7:65
Plato and Platonism (Pater), 7:136
"Plato on Not-Being" (Owen), 7:64–65
Plato: The Man and His Work (Taylor), 9:373
Plato und die sogenannten Pythagoreer (Frank, E.), 3:715
Platone et eius dogmate (Apuleius), 1:104
Platonic Academy of Florence, 3:621. *See also* Florentine Academy
Platonic dialogues
akrasia in, 7:589–590
chronology of, 7:583, 9:107
definition in, 7:586–587, 9:110–111
dialectic in, 7:592–594
elenchus in, 7:593
essences in, 7:587
friendship in, 7:587
Gadamer on, 4:1
of Hemsterhuis, 4:311
on human good, 9:111–112
on love, 7:589
morality in, 7:585
participation in, 7:596, 7:601
on piety, 9:109–110
recollection in, 7:588–589

rhetoric in, 7:592–594
semantics in, 8:751–754
social and political theory in, 7:590–592
Socrates in, 7:583–584
historical, 9:108
vs. real Socrates, 8:504–505, 9:589
on statements, 8:754–755
on virtue, 7:586, 7:589–590, 9:112
Platonic dualism, Petrović-Njegoš on, 7:267
Platonic love, 3:623
Platonic realism
Augustine and, 9:593
criticism of, 9:593–594
Gongsun Long and, 4:148
theory of objects and, 6:115
universals in, 9:588–591
Platonic reason, and Christianity, 3:624
Platonic studies, Vlastos in, 9:701–702
Platonic Theology (Ficino), 5:259
Platonic Theology (Proclus), 6:546, 6:552, 7:609, 8:41
Platonic tradition, continuity of, 3:624
Platonism, **7:605–617**
abstract entities in, 6:628
on abstractions, 3:499
Alcinous on, 1:104
Anselm and, 1:215
in apologism, 1:228
and Aristotle, 1:259–260, 1:279, 6:548
Augustine and, 3:289
belief in axioms and, 6:628
Bernard of Chartres and, 1:591
Brown (James Robert) and, 9:455
Cambridge, 2:682, 2:685, 6:655–656
at Chartres school, 2:137
and Christianity, 7:609
conventionalism as alternative to, 6:675
Cudworth and, 2:611
on determinism, 3:4
on eternity, 4:110
Eusebius and, 3:455
Ficino and, 3:620, 7:614
Florenskii and, 3:669
formalism as alternative to, 6:675–676
fragmentation of influence in, 7:615
Frank and, 3:716
Frege and, 3:728
Freud and, 5:589
Galileo and, 4:9–10
on God, 4:110
Hegel and, 3:309, 4:260
Henry of Ghent and, 4:313
Iamblichus and, 4:540
Ibn Zaddik and, 4:551
idea in, 4:553
influence of, 3:624
and Islamic philosophy, 7:610–611
Johnson (Samuel) and, 4:851
Justin Martyr and, 7:142
on knowledge, 5:259–260
on language, 5:189
Leibniz and, 5:255–260
Leonardo da Vinci and, 5:282
logic and, 5:408
love in, 5:583
Lucian of Samosata on, 5:597
Maimonides and, 5:648
Marcus Aurelius and, 5:707
on material realism, nature of, 5:232
mathematical, 4:117. *See also* Realism, and naturalism, mathematical
middle, 1:227, 6:546
Milton and, 6:250
vs. Neoplatonism, 6:546
vs. nominalism, 6:626–627, 6:675
Norris and, 6:655
number in, 6:670–676
Nussbaum on, 6:680
Panaetius of Rhodes and, 7:79
Pater on, 7:136
patristic philosophy and, 7:141–142
Patrizi and, 7:144
Pauler and, 7:145
Petrarch on, 7:264
Philo on, 7:303–305
Pico della Mirandola and, 7:571
Pletho and, 7:630
Plutarch of Chaeronea and, 7:649
Proust and, 8:96–97
Puritan, Edwards (Jonathan) and, 3:167
Pythagoreanism and, 8:185
realist alternatives to, 6:674–676
Renaissance and, 1:48, 8:425
Russell and, 8:536
"Russell-revised," 8:645
Santayana and, 8:598
Scholtz and, 8:644
School of St. Victor and, 8:592
sociology of knowledge in, 9:100–101
on soul, 4:604
vs. structuralism, 6:674–675
Sufi school of Isfahan and, 9:308
Taylor (Alfred) and, 9:373
Tertullian on, 9:400
Themistius and, 9:409
thought and thinking in, 9:419–421
Trubetskoi (Sergei) and, 9:532
usefulness of, *vs.* positivism, 8:645
Valentinianism and, 9:632–633
Vives on, 9:701
See also Neoplatonism
Platonism and the Spiritual Life (Santayana), 8:602
"Platonism of Aristotle, The" (Owen), 7:65
Platons Ideenlehre (Plato's theory of ideas) (Natorp), 6:490
Plato's Earlier Dialetic (Robinson), 2:665
Plato's Psychogony, On (Psellus), 7:610
Plato's Theory of Ideas (Ross), 8:504–505
Plattner, Ernst, 3:751
Plausibility, in attributor contextualism, 2:485
Plautus, Lipsius and, 5:364
Play
in construction of personal identity, 9:77
Schiller on, 1:54, 8:628
Playfair, John, physicotheology and, 7:560
"Plea for Excuses" (Austin), 1:408
"Plea for Psychology as a 'Natural Science'" (James, William), 4:777
Plea for the Christians (Athenagoras), 1:228
Plea for the Constitution, A (Austin), 1:405
Pleasant, 4:502–503, 5:8
Pleasure, **7:617–625**
Addison on, 1:22
Aristippus of Cyrene on, 1:257
Aristotle on, 1:44, 7:65
art and, 1:338–339
in asceticism, 1:352–353
Augustine on, 3:401
badness of, 4:257
beauty and, 1:44, 1:128, 1:512, 9:561
Bentham on, 1:339, 3:413
conditioning by, 4:257
Cyrenaics on, 2:619
Democritus on, 5:301
Diderot on, 3:410
Diogenes of Apollonia on, 3:90
as educational aim, 7:377
Epicurus on, 3:267, 3:399
Gay on, 4:35
Gentile on, 4:53

Pleasure, ***continued***
- as good, 4:256, 4:257
- Gottsched on, 4:165
- in happiness, 1:267, 9:833
- hedonism and, 4:152, 4:255–256
- Hegesias on, 2:619
- Helvétius on, 3:410
- Holbach on, 3:410
- Hume on, 8:132
- imagination and, 1:22
- intellectual, 1:338
- judgment of, 1:339
- Locke on, 3:407
- Malebranche on, 5:671
- in materialism, 6:9–10
- measurement of, 1:339
- Mill (John Stuart) on, 1:339, 3:413, 6:228, 6:232–233
- morality and, 8:3
- in motivation, 4:256–257
- in music, 1:338–339
- in narrow hedonism, 8:720
- in normative value theory, 9:639
- optimism/pessimism and, 7:249–253
- from painful emotions, 1:44
- Plato on, 3:396–397, 4:1
- Plotinus on, 3:401
- research on, levels of, 9:642
- in rule utilitarianism, 9:615
- sexual nature of, 8:145–146
- Socrates on, 3:396–397
- Speusippus on, 4:173
- Theodorus on, 2:620
- in tragedy, 9:522
- *vs.* utility, 1:396–397
- in *Utopia,* 6:399–400
- from utopian works, 9:620
- Valla on, 9:635
- Wollaston on, 9:833

Pleasure principle, 8:146, 9:572

Pleasure-pain balance, 7:251, 7:253

Pleasures, combining, 3:706

Pleitropy, 3:489

Plekhanov, Georgii Valentinovich, **7:626–629**
- aesthetics of, 1:59
- on determinism, 3:37
- dialectical materialism and, 3:56
- Lenin and, 5:279–280
- on negation of negation, 3:62–63
- on sensation, 3:64–65
- on Spinoza, 9:195

Plenitude
- in Christian thought, 5:593
- Conway (A.) on, 5:257
- Leibniz on, 5:257–258, 5:260
- Lovejoy on, 5:593
- in Neoplatonism, 5:593
- Plato on, 5:593
- Spinoza on, 5:257

Plenum
- Aristotle and, 3:635
- atomists and, 3:635

Plessner, Helmut, 7:318–319, **7:629–630**

Pletho, Giorgius Gemistus, 1:787–789, 3:671, **7:630–631,** 9:314

Plotinus, **7:631–642**
- on Aenesidemus, 1:30
- on aesthetics, 1:45–46, 1:190
- Aristotelianism of, 1:259
- on art, 1:46, 1:190
- Augustine on, 6:546
- on beauty, 1:45, 1:190, 1:512
- on being, 6:547, 7:572
- Bergson and, 1:563
- on cosmic sympathy, 7:638–639
- Cousin and, 2:580
- and emanationism, 3:189, 4:108
- epistemology of, 3:288–289
- on eternal return doctrine, 3:353
- and ethics, 3:400–401
- on evil, 3:401, 3:472, 7:639
- Ficino and, 3:621
- on geometry, 5:641
- on God, 4:564, 5:585
- on happiness, 7:639–640
- and Ikhwān al-Ṣafā', 4:576
- on infinity, 4:668
- Inge and, 4:685
- on innate ideas, 4:688
- and Islamic philosophy, 1:423
- *vs.* later Neoplatonists, 6:548–549
- Leibniz and, 5:256
- on logos, 5:569
- on love, 1:46
- on material world, 3:360
- and metaphysics, 6:187–188
- on microcosm, 5:641
- on mimesis, 6:252
- on mind, 5:569
- on nature, 1:46
- on necessary beings, 7:26
- and Neoplatonism, 6:546–549
- on the One, 7:633, 7:636
- panpsychism and, 7:83
- patristic philosophy and, 7:143
- on phantasia, 7:271
- Plato and, 3:400–401, 3:401, 7:608
- on pleasure, 3:401
- on poetry, 7:595
- Porphyry on, 6:549–550
- and positive "total-unity," 3:716
- Proclus on, 6:546, 8:42
- psychology in, 8:122
- on purification, 7:638
- on reality, 6:548, 7:608
- on reincarnation, 7:634
- on sense perception, 3:288–289
- Shestov on, 9:11
- spirituality of, 6:548
- and Sufism, 9:303
- on unconscious, 9:570
- unity in, 6:547

Ploucquet, Gottfried, 5:445, **7:642**

Plücker, Julius, 4:60

Plümacher, Olga, on optimism/pessimism, 7:250

Plural morphology, mass/count distinction in, 6:660

Plural quantifiers, 8:196–197

Pluralism, **6:326–329, 7:642–644**
- Anaxagoras and, 1:249, 7:763
- Anderson (John) and, 1:198
- in coercive institutions, 9:74
- Cournot and, 2:577
- in Dvaita philosophy, 4:630
- Empedocles and, 1:249
- in ethical intuitionism, 4:735
- on government, 2:702
- moral, 7:642–643
- on moral principles, 3:439–442
- of new realism, 6:587
- physical, Zeno of Elea on, 9:873
- in pre-Socratic philosophy, 7:762–763
- Rawls on, 5:325
- religious, **8:419–420**
- Russell on, 8:545–546
- theistic, of Iqbal, 4:744
- of values, in conservatism, 2:467–468

Pluralist realism, cognitive value of explanations, 5:72

Pluralistic idealism, personalism and, 7:234–235

Pluralistic Universe, A (James, William), 4:775

Plurality
- of forms, 8:458
- plurals and, **7:644–647**
- Zeno of Elea on, 9:872–874

Plurals and plurality, **7:644–647**

Plutarch of Athens, and Neoplatonism, 6:551

Plutarch of Chaeronea, **7:647–649**
- on Colotes of Lampsacus, 3:263
- on Demiurge, 2:699
- on Empedocles, 3:212
- Eusebius and, 3:455
- influences on, 7:647–648
- on optimism/pessimism, 7:247
- on phantasia, 7:271

on poetry, 1:189
on Stoic semantics, 8:758
Pneuma, **7:649–650**
Chrysippus on, 2:252
Diogenes of Apollonia and, 3:89
Stoics on, 6:59
Po zvezdam (By the stars) (Ivanov), 4:766
Podipki (Leont'ev), 5:283
Podolsky, Boris, on quantum theory, 2:105, 2:126, 3:181, 6:641
Podro, Michael, on visual representation, 1:328
Poèla désastre de Lisbonne (Voltaire), 2:687, 9:711
Poème sur la loi naturelle (Voltaire), 2:687
Poems and Discourses (Norris), 6:655
Poesia, La (Croce), 2:601
Poetic philosophers, 5:68
Poetics (Aristotle), 1:43–45, 1:188, 1:308, 1:512, 2:571, 5:44, 5:417, 9:522
and Arab logic, 5:418
on imitation, 4:599
mimesis in, 6:252
Patrizi on, 7:144
Poetics (Scaliger), 1:48–49
Poetics, sociological approach to, 1:469
Poetry
Aristotle on, 1:43, 1:188, 1:333, 7:594. *See also Poetics* (Aristotle)
in Aufklärung, 4:165–166
Benn on, 1:548
Blake's symbolic, 1:610
Boileau on, 1:640
Carnap on, 2:40
Castelvetro on, 1:48
in Cixous écriture feminine project, 2:262
classical and romantic, 8:629–631
Coleridge and, 2:316, 2:318–319
creative imagination in, 4:166
Croce on, 2:601
Dadaist, 1:298
of Dōgen, 3:96
DuBos on, 3:123
Empedocles and, 7:762–763
film and, 7:381
Gadamer on, 4:3
Gottsched on, 4:165–166
Green on, 4:179
Gregory of Nazianzus and, 4:181
Hegel on, 4:275
Ibn Gabirol and, 4:545
Ibn Zaddik and, 4:551
Iqbal and, 4:743
Ivanov and, 4:766
katharsis in, 1:44
Maritain on, 5:714
of Marulić, 5:729
Milton and, 6:251
Orphic, 7:42
in *Phaedrus,* 1:42
Philodemus on, 1:45, 1:189, 7:302
and philosophy, 1:444, 4:175–176, 5:68, 7:594–595
Pindar on, 1:41
Plato on, 1:187–188, 1:333, 7:585–586, 7:594–595
Plutarch on, 1:189
pre-Islamic subthemes and, 9:300
Proclus on, 8:43
of Rilke, 8:477–478
in Romanticism, 8:487–488
of Rumi, 9:306–307
Scaliger on, 1:48–49
Schiller on, 8:629–630
Schlegel on, 8:630, 8:631
as sensitive discourse, 1:494
of Shao Yong, 9:6
Shelley on, 9:8
Sidney on, 1:49
of Skovoroda, 9:64
of Solov'ëv, 9:122
of Stace, 9:200
in Sufism, 9:306
symbolism in, 1:55
of Timon of Phlius, 9:501
truthfulness of, 1:41
Wordsworth on, 1:298
of Yang Xiong, 9:860–861
Zeno on, 9:253
Pohlers, Wolfram, in proof theory, 8:56
Poidevin, Robin Le
on date theory, 9:477
tenseless theory of time and, 9:475
on token-reflexive theory, 9:476
Poiesis, 1:43
"Poimandres," 4:102
Poincaré, Henri, 1:700, **7:650–654,** 8:638
Campbell and, 2:17
Carnap and, 2:37–38
on conventional truth, 2:474
on conventionalism of space, 2:521
Couturat and, 2:582
Duhem and, 3:126
Einstein and, 3:181–182
on eternal return doctrine, 3:355
on Euclidean geometry, 9:151
on force, 3:235
on Fourier series, 2:497
new positivism of, 5:524
on physics of gases, 7:537
Piaget and, 7:567
Schlick and, 8:639
on scientific theory, 3:129
on set theory, 5:520
on vicious circle principle, 5:519
Point, Whitehead's definition of, 9:747–748
Point de départ de la métaphysique (Maréchal), 5:707–708
Point masses, symmetry and conservation principle of, 2:462
Points of time, 3:646
Poisson distribution, 9:224
Pojman, Louis, 3:535
Poland, socinianism in, 9:99
Polanyi, Michael, 5:158
Polarity
Cohen (Morris) on, 2:307
Palágyi on, 7:75
Polarization, of society, 5:685–686
Pole, Cardinal Reginald, on Machiavelli, 5:628
Polemo, on life according to nature, 7:606–607
Polemon of Athens, in Greek Academy, 4:173
Polenta, Guido da, Lord of Ravenna, 2:623
Policraticus (The statesman) (John of Salisbury), 4:843–844
Policy, 8:673–674
Policy sciences, 8:675
Polish Hasidism, 5:3
Polish philosophy, 9:554–555
Ingarden in, 4:682–685
Twardowski and, 9:553
Politecnico, Cattaneo and, 2:83
Politeia, Aristotle on, 1:268–269
Politian, 9:50
Politica Methodice Digesta et Exemplis Sacris et Profanis Illustrata (Politics methodically arranged and illustrated by holy and profane examples) (Althusius), 1:135
Political action
Arendt on, 1:254–255
revolution by, 1:472–473
Political and economic arrangements, institution of, 3:723
Political arrangements, evil in conservatism, 2:470
Political authority, political cosmopolitanism and, 2:569
Political economy
highest good in communism and, 2:367
and labor protection legislation, 2:362
Political equality, Bentham on, 1:551

Political ethics
in Chinese philosophy, 2:200
and civil disobedience, 2:260–261
in Confucianism, 2:179
Political institutions
coercive, justifications for, 9:72
ethical evaluation of, 3:391–392
Political Justice (Godwin), 4:248, 8:137–138, 9:87
Political Liberalism (Rawls), 5:324–325, 8:259, 9:74, 9:83
Political liberty
Blount on, 1:619
and other liberties, 3:724
Political organization
Plato on, 3:397
in transition to states, 9:204
Political participation, and meaning of "liberty," 3:724
Political philosophy
analytic, 7:673
anarchism as, 1:472–473, 7:670–671
Anderson (John) and, 1:199
Aquinas and, 9:433–435
Augustine and, 7:658–659
authoritarianism as, in Carlyle, 2:34
Avicenna and, 1:434
Bakunin and, 1:471–473
Berlin and, 1:588–590
bioethics and, 1:600–603
Bosanquet on, 1:663
Boulainvilliers and, 1:669–671
Brownson and, 1:706
Burke on, 1:771–772
Burley on, 1:774
Calvin on, 2:11
capitalism as, 7:676–678
Carlyle on, 2:33
Carroll on, 2:52
Chateaubriand on, 2:137
Chinese, 2:152, 2:231–239
Christian, 7:657–658
on clemency, 8:812–813
communitarianism as, 2:369, 7:678–679
Comte on, 2:412–413
Condorcet on, 2:432
of Confucius, 2:231–232
conservatism and, 2:464–471
cosmopolitanism and, 2:569
Cousin and, 2:579
in Daoism, 2:186, 2:236–237
Dong Zhongshu and, 2:235
Duns Scotus on, 3:143–145
Dworkin on, 3:156–157
in Enlightenment, 3:247
feminist, 3:598–603
general will in, 4:38–40
in German idealism, 7:667–668
Gerson and, 4:67
Gersonides and, 4:822
Giles of Rome and, 4:90–91
Greek, 7:655–657
Green and, 4:178–180
Guo Xiang and, 4:196
Habermas and, 4:199–200
Hegelian, 4:284–285
history of, 4:172, **7:654–680**
Hobbes and, 4:417–420, 7:662–663
human law exemplified in, 9:284–285
Islamic, 4:549, 7:679
Judaic, 7:657–658, 7:679–680
language in, 1:648
of legal consciousness, 4:577
libertarianism as, 7:676–678
liberty in, **5:337–338**
on limits to state action, 9:208–209
Locke and, 5:387–390, 5:395, 7:663–664
Machiavelli and, 7:660–661
Maimonides and, 5:652
Mao Zedong and, 2:180–181
Maritain and, 5:715–716
in Marxist socialism, 1:716–717
medieval, 7:659–660
Mencius and, 2:232–233
methodology of, 7:673
Mill (John Stuart) and, 6:228–229
monarchism as, 1:620–621
Mozi and, 2:235–236
name rectification in, 2:231
neo-Confucianism and, 2:158
Nozick and, 6:668–669
Oakeshott and, 7:1–2
Ockham and, 9:782–784
papal monarchism as, in Campanella, 2:16
policy [term] and, absence of, 8:673–674
Rawls in, 8:257–259
in Reformation, 7:661–662
of revolution, 1:471–473
Rosmini-Serbati and, 8:503
Russian, 2:148
Saint-Simon on, 8:589–591
Sartre on, 8:607
science policy in, 8:675
sovereignty issues in, 9:139
Stoic, 7:658
transformative nature of, 2:179
Troeltsch and, 9:527–528
20th-c., 7:672–673
in utilitarianism, 7:666–667
welfare state and, 7:678
wrong in, 1:664
Xunzi and, 2:233–234
Yin Haiguang and, 2:181
Young Hegelian, 1:471
Political power
for black Americans, 5:73
in Chinese thought, 2:237
Mariana on, 5:710
Olivi on, 7:12
Political protest, as civil disobedience, 2:259–261
Political reform
of capitalism, as emergent communism, 2:363
Chinese religious dimension in, 2:225
in Confucianism, 2:176
Hu Shih and, 2:181
Stewart on, 9:247
Political relevance, of traditional personal values, 3:720
Political revolutions, and scientific revolutions, 5:158–159
Political rights
Bentham and, 1:551
communitarianism and, 2:369
in Rousseau's social contract, 2:366
as sphere of autonomy, 1:589
Political science
Bentham on, 1:555–556
Condorcet on, 2:432
legislation based on, 1:556
Political self-determination, cultural cosmopolitanism and, 2:570
Political society, Vitoria on, 9:698
Political speech, computer ethics and, 2:397–398
Political theory. *See* Politics/political theory
Political Treatise (Spinoza), 9:183–184
Political violence, Arendt on, 1:253–254
Politicians
in Confucian ethics, 2:195
professional class of, Weber (Max) on, 9:734
Político, El (Gracián), 4:168
Politicorum Libri Sex (Lipsius), 5:364
Politics/political theory, 3:595–596
action in, 1:253
of al-Fārābī, 4:755
Aristotle on, 1:267–269, 3:398. *See also Politics* (Aristotle)
Augustine on, 1:399–400
and autonomy, 5:628
Benjamin on, 1:547

Bentham on, 1:556–557
and bioethics, 1:603
of civil disobedience, 2:259–261
Cohen (Hermann) on, 2:303
Collingwood on, 2:329
of community, 5:637
conservatism and, 2:464–467
Croce on, 2:604
Daoist, *ziran* (naturally so) in, 9:722
De Sanctis on, 2:719–720
and decision making, Condorcet on, 2:431
Deleuze on, 2:696
Diderot on, 3:77
and education, philosophy of, **7:360–363**
Encyclopédie on, 3:224
Epicurus on, 3:265, 5:601
existentialism and, 3:506
and free speech, 2:119–120
of Fries, 3:751–752
in German romanticism, 8:490–491
and government, 1:552
Herder on, 4:332–333
in historical materialism, 4:379
Hobbes on, 4:424–425, 9:140–141
of Holbach, 4:432–433
of Islamic Neoplatonism, 6:558
of Ivanov, 4:767
Johnson (Dr. Samuel) on, 4:852
justice in, 4:864
Kant on, 5:29–30
of Khomeini, 8:647
of Kierkegaard, 5:68
and law, 7:444
Lucretius on, 5:601
Luther on, 5:613
in Machiavelli, 5:626–628
of Marković, 5:719–720
of Marsilius of Padua, 5:722
in medieval philosophy, 6:104–105
of Merleau-Ponty, 6:149–150
modern view of, 2:703
of Mosca, 6:406–407
in Mou's neo-Confucianism, 2:183
as negative historical change agent, 1:720
as negotiation, 1:589
Nelson (Leonard) on, 6:536–537
of Niebuhr, 6:606–607
optimism/pessimism and, 7:248
Philo on, 7:306–307
in Plato, 7:590–592
power in, 7:733–734
of Priestley, 8:7–8
public interest in, 9:207
of Ricoeur, 8:464–465
in Romanticism, 8:488
of Rosenkranz, 8:497
of Rousseau, 8:511–513
Saint-Simon's, industrialists' role in, 8:590–591
Schlegel on, 8:630
science in
Haeckel on, 4:204
Mill (John Stuart) and, 6:225
Shelley on, 9:7–8
and social change, 1:720, 9:656
social contract and, 9:79–83
sophists on, 9:130
Spinoza and, 9:178–184
in Stewart's liberal reform, 9:247
technological power and, 7:544–545
toleration in, 9:510
utilitarianism and, 9:24
utopias of, 9:618
of Weber (Max), 9:734–735
Zeno on, 9:253
See also Government
Politics (Aristotle), 1:268, 3:397–398, 5:44
forms of government in, 7:419
law in, 7:418–419
mimesis in, 6:252
natural law in, 6:506
Politics and Vision (Wolin), 9:208
Politics of Conscience. T. H. Green and His Age (Richter), 4:558
Politics of Friendship, The (Derrida), 2:715
Politics of Reality, The (Frye), 3:755
Politique du clergé de France, La (Jurieu), 6:603–604
Politische und der theologische Liberalismus, Der (Strauss), 9:263
Poliziano, Angelo, and Florentine Academy, 3:671
Polla. *See* Hen/Polla
Pollock, Frederick, on property, 8:71
Pollock, Sheldon, 5:116
Pollution, technology and, 7:545
Polyhistor, Alexander, 3:89
Polymath, 8:185
Polyphonic thinking, 5:58
Polystratus, Epicurean School and, 3:263
Polysyllogism
definition of, 5:551–552
in traditional logic, 5:500
Polytheism
Christian misunderstanding of, 2:119
vs. pantheism, 7:94
Pletho on, 7:630
Simplicius on, 6:555
toleration of, 9:508
universal belief in God and, 2:349–350
Polyxenus, 6:110
Pomponazzi, Pietro, **7:680–685**
on Aquinas, 2:721
Aristotelianism of, 1:279, 1:430
Ficino and, 3:624
on immortality, 1:91
on soul, 4:609
Vanini and, 9:646
Ponce, John, 8:705
Poncelet, Jean Victor
on energy and work, 3:229
on projective geometry, 4:59–60
Poor, the
in liberation theology, 5:331–332
Meslier and, 6:154
Rousseau on, 2:366
Poor Law Amendment Act, Bentham, 1:551
Poor Richard, aphorisms of, 3:720
Poor Richard's Almanack (Franklin), 2:689, 3:720
Pope (Holy Father of Catholic Church)
Arnauld on, 1:288
authority of, 9:139
de Maistre on, :659–660
infallibility of. *See* Papal infallibility
Marsilius of Padua on, 5:721–723
political philosophy and, 7:659–660
powers of, Suárez on, 9:285
in Solov'ëv's theocracy, 9:125
sovereignty of, 5:659
See also specific pope
Pope, Alexander, **7:686–688**
and aesthetics, 1:49
Bolingbroke and, 2:685
Swift and, 9:340
Voltaire and, 2:687
on whirling dervishes, 9:307
Popper, Joseph, on energy, 3:233
Popper, Karl Raimund, **7:688–692**
Adorno and, 1:26
antipredictive argument of, 8:730
Apel and, 1:226
asymmetrical confirmation theory of, 8:640
on basic statements, 1:486
and coherence theories of knowledge, 5:93
on demarcation, 8:670
on Duhem, 3:129
on empiricism, 5:625

Popper, Karl Raimund, *continued*
on Enlightenment, 3:244–245
faith and, 5:99
on falsifiability of scientific hypotheses, 8:683
on historical inevitability, 3:36, 3:39
on historicism, 7:398
on history, 7:391
on induction, 4:640
Kuhn on, 8:683
Lakatos and, 5:171
on Leibniz's calculus, 5:443
on probability, 8:35
on properties, 3:528
on science, 3:317, 7:352, 9:547
on scientific law, 7:518
on scientific method, 4:640
on scientific progress, 8:48
and skepticism, 9:58
on social wholes, 9:94, 9:95
on time, 9:470
on true scientific doctrines, 5:120
on truthlikeness, 9:547
and Vienna Circle, 5:524
Popper-Lynkeus, Josef, 6:560, **7:692–700**
Popple, William, 5:391
Popular arguments for the existence of God, **7:700–705**
Popular culture, Benjamin on, 1:546
Popular philosophy
corrective to, Green on, 4:179
Mendelssohn and, 6:131
in Mishnah, 4:810–811
Nicolai and, 6:598
"Popular Philosophy in Its Relation to Life" (Green), 4:179
Popular Science Monthly (periodical), 7:166
Popular sovereignty, and democracy, 2:701–702
Population
checks to, 5:675
Darwin on, 7:338
environment and, 1:719
food supply and, 1:719
genetics and, 3:660, 7:341
Malthus on, 5:675–677
theories of, morality in, 5:676–677
Population biology, in game theory, 4:20–22
Populism, Russian, Lavrov and, 5:218, 5:219
Pornography
analysis of, in philosophy of sex, 7:529–530
as attack on women's self-esteem, 3:584
computer ethics and, 2:398
legal moralism and, 5:338
Porphyry, **7:705–707**
Abelard and, 5:424
apologism and, 1:228
Aristotelianism of, 1:259, 2:80, 5:408
Boethius on, 1:626
Christian Neoplatonism and, 7:141
and Christianity, 6:549–550, 7:143
in dialectic syllabus, 4:66
Duns Scotus on, 3:134
and enneads, 7:632
Eusebius and, 3:455
vs. Iamblichus, 6:550
and Ikhwān al-Ṣafā', 4:576
logical chart method of, 5:563
medieval logic and, 5:421
on Origen, 7:40
patristic philosophy and, 7:143
Plotinus and, 3:400, 6:549–550
on predicables, 5:552
on semantics, 8:762
on substance, 6:187–188
on universals, 1:627, 3:289
Porretani, on conditionals, 5:428
Port Royal circle, La Rochefoucauld and, 5:200
Portable Nietzsche, The (Nietzsche), 5:45
Porter, Noah, **7:708**
Portmann, Adolf, in anthropology, 7:321
Port-Royal des Champs (convent)
Cartesianism at, 2:757, 4:790–791
Jansenism at, 4:789
Port-Royal Grammar (Arnauld), 8:775
Port-Royal Logic, The (Logique, ou l'art de penser) (Arnauld and Nicole), 5:439–440, 8:775
Port-Royal Logic (Descartes), 2:286–287, 4:565
Port-Royalists. *See* Arnauld, Antoine; Nicole, Pierre
Portugal, Aristotle of. *See* Fonseca, Peter
Posaune des jüngsten Gerichts über Hegel, Die (Bauer), 1:492
Posidonius, **7:708–710**
on determinism, 3:5–6
on ethics, 9:257
investigations of tides, 3:686
on logic, 5:408
Marcus Aurelius and, 5:707
Panaetius of Rhodes and, 7:79–80
Positing, 3:615
Positio, in medieval logic, 5:433–434
Positism
on justification of knowledge, 8:180
relativistic, 8:180
Positive instance, in induction, 6:238
Positive law, definition of, 5:237
Positive metaphysics, 3:705
Positive method of agreement, 6:239–242
Positive presuppositions, 6:524–525
Positive propositional calculus, 5:536
Positive strand, of feminist research, 3:574
Positivism, **7:710–717**
Abbagnano on, 1:3
agnostic, on "why," 9:755
of Alembert, 1:106
of Anderson (John), 1:198
as antimetaphysical movement, 4:8
of Austin (John), 1:406, 7:425
of Ayer, 6:633
of Bentham, 7:712
Cabanis on, 2:1
Carnap on, 2:38
in classical dialectical argumentation, 2:47
Cohen (Hermann) on, 2:302–303
Cohen (Morris) on, 2:306–307
Comte and, 1:3, 2:413, 5:237, 7:710, 7:711–712
critical, 7:715–716
criticism of, 4:558
deterministic, 7:714
Ehrlich on, 7:427
Einstein and, 3:180
Encyclopédie and, 3:223
Engels and, 3:63, 3:238
and ethics, 5:142
evolutionary, 7:713–715
German, Jodl (Friedrich) in, 4:835
Gestalt theory and, 4:73
Gobineau and, 4:106–107
Gödel on, 4:117
Habermas on, 4:200
Henri in, 7:710
history in, 7:392–393
of Ingenieros, 4:686
Jaspers and, 3:504
Korn and, 5:142
Laas on, 5:163
lack of scientific usefulness, 8:645
Langer on, 5:187
in Latin American philosophy, 5:206–208, 5:210
Lavrov on, 5:218
law in, 7:424–425
Le Senne on, 5:289

legal, Dworkin on, 3:156
Lessing on, 5:295–296
Littré and, 5:372
logical, 7:273
agnosticism in, 1:94
in analytical philosophy, 1:149–150
emergence of, 1:149
empiricism of, 3:219–220
meaning in, 1:149
on metaphysical systems, 4:561
Russell and, 1:149
Schlick on, 8:637
of Lombroso, 7:714
of Marsilius of Padua, 5:722
Martinetti on, 5:728
Marx and, 3:56
Mercier and, 6:144–145
of Mikhailovskii, 6:215
of Mill (James), 7:712
of Mill (John Stuart), 7:712–713
mind-dependence in, 6:173
modern, early proponents of, 3:689
Nazism and, 7:427
and neopositivism, 7:716
Nietzsche on, 6:610
nihilistic, avoidance of, by Sabatier, 8:588
Nishi Amane and, 6:623
number in, 6:675
Papini on, 7:102
Pauler on, 7:145
Pearson and, 7:160
Planck on, 7:578
relativistic, 7:268
and science, 3:128, 7:710, 9:36–37
social, 7:711–713
of Spencer, 7:713–714
Spengler and, 9:168
Stace on, 9:200
Stevenson (Charles) and, 6:633
Strauss and, 9:263
Taine on, 9:364
utilitarianism and, 7:711–713
Vaihinger and, 9:625
of Varisco, 9:647
of Wundt, 7:714, 9:849
Ziehen and, 9:884
See also Scientific method
"Positivism" (Stace), 9:200
Positivismo en México, El (Positivism in Mexico) (Zea), 5:209
Positivity
for extensive properties, 6:90
in religion, 4:261
Positivity of the Christian Religion, The (Hegel), 4:261
Positron emission tomography (PET) scan, 6:564
Posner, Michael, on neuroimaging, 6:565
Posner, Richard, **7:717–719**
on law and economics, 7:461
philosophy of sex and, 7:523
Possessed, The (Dostoevsky), 6:618
Possibilia, 6:172
Possibilità e libertà (Abbagnano), 1:2
Possibility, **7:719–726**
a priori, 7:723
Abelard on, 7:720
and ability, 2:25–26, 7:724–725
absolute *vs.* relative, 7:721–722
of apodictic judgments, 1:689–690
Aquinas on, 7:720–721
Aristotle on, 7:719
Bergson on, 1:568
Bloch on, 1:615
Cleanthes on, 2:288
in contemporary thought, 7:723–725
counterfactuals in science and, 2:573
Descartes on, 7:721
determinism and, 7:724–725
Diodorus Cronus on, 3:87, 7:313
of events, and causal accounts of time, 2:87–88
existence as, 1:2
existential, 1:1–2, 1:763
formal, 7:719
freedom and, 7:724–725
God and, 7:721
Herbert of Cherbury on, 4:327
history of, 7:719–723
Hobbes on, 7:721
Hume on, 7:722
hypothetical, 7:725
James on, 4:786–787
Kant on, 7:722–723
Kripke on, 7:723–724
Leibniz on, 7:722
in Mādhyamika doctrine, 1:741
in Megarianism, 7:719–720
metaphysics of, 7:723–724
natural, 6:494–495
in Neoplatonism, 7:720
Philo on, 3:87, 7:313
Plato on, 7:720
potentiality as, 7:719
primacy of, 1:595
probability and, 8:26
relative, 7:719
semantics of, 7:724
Spinoza on, 7:721–722
in Stoicism, 7:720
theses of, 4:600
truthlikeness and, 9:547–548
in utopianism, 1:615, 9:620
Wittgenstein on, 9:805
Possibility of Altruism, The (Nagel), 3:445, 6:475
Possibility proof, of ontological argument, 7:21
Possible, in ontology, 7:21–23
Possible being, in William of Auvergne's metaphysics, 9:765
Possible causes, in Mill's methods of induction, 6:239
conjunctions of, 6:241–243
disjunction of, 6:242
negations, 6:242
Possible objects theory, bundle theory and, 6:180
Possible particulars, *vs.* concrete existent particulars, 6:180
Possible rule utilitarianism, 9:603
Possible universes, cosmology models and, 2:563–566
Possible worlds, 2:102, 7:580
and beliefs, 2:93–94
counterfactuals and, 2:427–429, 2:574–575
Crescas on, 2:594
in Huayan Buddhism, 2:165
and information as mental content, 2:480–481
kalām argument on God's existence and, 2:553
Kripke on, 7:724
Leibniz on, 2:553
in metaphysics, 6:199
metaphysics and, 6:284–286
modal logic and, 5:486, 6:283–284
in ontology, 7:23
Peirce on, 5:455
in relevant logic, 5:488
teleological arguments for God's existence and, 2:588
understanding and, 5:513
Possible-world semantics, 1:155, 8:75–76, 9:330
Post, Emil
and computability theory, 2:375, 2:385
computing machines and, 2:399
on logic, 5:467, 5:538, 5:606
on mathematical logic, 5:467
Post, J. F., materialism of, 6:18
Post Card, The (Derrida), 2:715
Post hoc ergo propter hoc fallacy, 3:543–544
Postcelestial *qi,* 5:138
Postcolonialism, **7:726–729**

Posterior Analytics (Aristotle), 2:74, 5:398, 5:400
- and Arab logic, 5:417–418
- on definition, 2:667
- grammar and, 8:770
- Grosseteste on, 4:186
- on inferential knowledge, 4:724
- Scholz on, 8:645
- on sense perception, 3:286
- syllogism in, 1:269

Post-Hegelian ethical theories, 3:415–416

Post-Kantian tradition
- Deleuze and, 2:694–695
- development of, 2:694
- on dogma, 3:97
- epistemology in, 3:309–311

Postmodern Condition, The (Lyotard), 5:619–620, 6:318, 9:277, 9:294

Postmodernism, **7:729–731**
- education and, 7:359
- feminism and, 1:158, 1:158, 3:564–565, 3:575, 3:585
- in legal philosophy, 7:460–461
- Lyotard on, 5:620, 9:277
- Marxism and, 5:740
- philosophy of history in, 7:395–397
- poststructuralism and, 9:274
- and racist or heterosexist assumptions, 3:584
- skepticism in, 7:395–397, 9:59
- social organization in, 1:491
- sublimity and, 9:294
- and traditional philosophical practice, 3:699

Postpositivist philosophy, of science, 3:592

Post's theorem, on arithmetical definability in computability theory, 2:387

Postscript, 5:67

"Postscript: After Twenty Years" (Popper), 8:730

Poststructuralism, 6:318
- aesthetics and, 1:71–72, 9:278
- epistemology in, 7:395
- feminism and, 3:564
- *See also* Structuralism

Postulates
- of adequacy, 8:665
- of biogenes, 8:659
- in cosmological idea creation, 2:562
- definition of, 5:552
- of *formalitates,* 8:704
- Kant on, 5:20, 8:661
- scientific theory formal requirements, 1:685
- theoretical, 9:414

"Postulates of Empirical Thought, The," in the *Critique of Pure Reason,* 5:20

Postvolitional knowledge, 6:321–322

Potency
- *vs.* act
  - Aquinas on, 2:679–680
  - Aristotle on, 2:679, 7:22
- Bonaventure on, 1:654
- Gerson on, 4:67
- of soul, 1:274

Potential, Aquinas on, 2:551

Potential infinite, definition of, 5:552

Potentiality
- Aquinas on, 9:431
- being as, 1:278
- of matter, 1:654
- possibility as, 7:719
- power and, 7:733–734
- as property, 6:495
- Rozanov on, 8:525
- in Sankhya, 2:112
- Woodbridge on, 9:842–843
- *See also* Possibility

Potenz und Akt (Stein), 9:240

Potter, Van Rensselaer, on bioethics, 1:599

Pound, Roscoe
- on legal realism, 5:246, 7:427
- on state policy, 9:207

Poundal (British unit of force), 3:686

Poussin, Nicolas, 1:304–305

Pouvoir Ouvrier (Worker's Power), 5:619

Poverty
- contractualist view of, 3:386
- of Franciscans, subjective right of, 7:12
- and freedom, 1:589
- globalization and, 5:741
- Marxism and, 5:741
- Priestley on, 8:7
- Rousseau on, 2:366
- 20th-c. debate on, 3:443
- utilitarian view of, 3:385
- world, act utilitarianism on, 9:612–613
- *See also* Poor, the

Poverty and Famines: An Essay on Entitlement and Deprivation (Sen), 8:811

Poverty of Historicism, The (Popper), 3:36, 7:391

Poverty of Philosophy (Marx), 3:62

Poverty-of-stimulus arguments, 4:690, 4:694

Powell, Louis, on affirmative action, 1:82

Power, **7:731–735**
- absolute, of God, 5:69, 6:105
- Anselm on, 1:217
- Austin (John) on, 1:405
- as being, 7:22
- Brahman, definition of, 1:681
- in Chinese thought, 2:237
- in Cixous écriture feminine project, 2:262
- computer ethics and, 2:397
- conflict and, 7:731–732
- in Confucian ethics, 2:195
- Daoism and, 2:192–193
- and freedom, 3:722–724
- of God, 4:814
- governmental, 7:369–370
- Hegel on, 4:262
- human
  - predestination and, 3:10
  - Wittgenstein on, 9:807
- knowledge and, 1:444
- Locke on, 5:382–383, 5:395
- Marsilius of Padua on, 5:723
- meditation and, 6:109
- nihilism on, 6:619
- optimism/pessimism and, 7:248
- papal, 5:721–722
- political
  - Arendt on, 1:253–254
  - Mariana on, 5:710
- in postcolonialism, 7:728
- in poststructuralism, 9:275
- production and, 5:732
- property and, in historical materialism, 4:378–379
- and reality, 6:493
- as relation, 7:732–733
- and restriction of less powerful, 3:724
- in Simon Magnus's Gnosticism, 9:34
- social, hierarchical grid of, 3:587
- state use of, Meinecke on, 6:113
- unequal, and unequal freedom, 3:724
- vegetative, 1:274
- violence and, 9:677–678

Power to punish, emergence of, 3:700

Power vacuum, in contemporary culture, 5:152

Power-conferring rules, Hart on, 5:239–240

Powers, in ontology, 7:25

Powers and Limits of Psychoanalysis, The (Kristeva), 5:152
Powers of Horror (Kristeva), 5:152
Power-set axiom, definition of, 5:552
Poynting, John Henry, on electromagnetism, 3:232, 3:236
Poynting vector, 3:236
P-predicates, 7:239
Prābhākara, 4:628, 6:530
  on certification, 9:545
  on cognition, 9:543–545
  and five means of knowledge, 5:117
  nonperception in, 5:122
  resemblance theory of, 9:586
Prābhākara Mīmāṃsakas, on cognition, 9:543
Practical atheism, 9:628
Practical facts, Duhem on, 3:128
Practical knowledge, as Chinese approach to science, 2:217–218
Practical reason, **7:735–738**
Practical Study School, emergence of in Korea, 5:139
Practicality
  Carnap on, 2:39
  and computability theory, 2:387–389
  in law, 7:428
Practice(s)
  Croce on, 2:603
  ethical, scientific interests and, 2:218–219
  Korean philosophers and, 5:141
  of morality, 3:581
  primacy over theory, 3:615
Practico-inert field, 8:609
Prado, Juan de, 7:41
Prae-Adamitae (La Peyrère), 5:196
Praeparatio Evangelica (Preparation for the Gospel) (Eusebius), 1:228, 3:455
Pragmatic account, of truth *vs.* empirical adequacy, 5:102
Pragmatic circularity, logical knowledge and, 5:511–512
Pragmatic justification, of logical laws, 5:512
Pragmatic twist theories of metaphor, 6:168
Pragmatically circular arguments, logical knowledge and, 5:512
Pragmaticism
  concept of ideas in, 4:566
  Gehlen and, 4:35
  of James, Santayana on, 8:602
  meaning theory in, 8:798
  of Sorel, 9:132
  on underdetermination, 9:577
  See also Pragmatism
Pragmatics, 6:83, **7:738–741**
  in formal semantics, 5:556
  Grice on, 8:748
  in philosophy of language, 7:402
  post-Gricean, 7:740–741
  Sellars (Wilfrid) on, 8:733
  vs. semantics, 7:738–739
  transcendental, 1:226–227
Pragmatism, 3:567, **7:741–750**
  of Aliotta, 1:127
  American
    Apel on, 1:226
    practical realism of, 1:463
  anthropology and, 7:315
  in applied ethics, 1:239
  on asceticism, 1:352
  belief and, 1:463, 7:745
  in Chinese thought, 2:238
  in classical Indian concepts of cognition, 9:543–544
  Cohen (Morris) on, 2:307
  communication and, 7:743
  and critical realism, 2:596–597
  de Finetti and, 2:663
  on death, 2:652
  definition of, 7:742–743
  Dewey on, 7:745–7446
  ethics in, 3:415–416
  evolution and, 6:502
  experience and, 7:744–747
  feminism and, **3:38–40**, 3:566–568
  fictionalism and, 9:626
  Gricean, 7:738
  inquiry and, 7:744–746
  instrumentalism and, 7:745–7446
  interpretation of, 7:742
  James (William) and, 4:777, 4:781–783, 4:786, 7:427, 7:742
  language and, 7:742
  and law, 7:444
  legal, 7:718
  meaning theory in, 7:743–744, 8:799
  Mercier and, 6:145
  as method, 7:748
  naturalism and, 6:502–503
  origins of, 7:741–742
  Papini and, 7:102
  Peirce and, 3:313, 7:163, 7:167–168, 7:172–173, 7:741–744
  and pluralism, 7:642
  Posner on, 7:718
  of Putnam, 7:749
  Quine and, 1:162, 7:749
  of Rescher, 7:748, 7:751
  of Rorty, 8:494–495
  of Schiller (Ferdinand), 7:742, 8:623–624
  and Schutz, 8:664
  on self-preservation, 9:715
  signs in, 7:743
  speech act theory and, 1:226
  truth and, 7:744–746, 8:624–625, 9:537
  in United States, 7:741
  of Vailati, 9:630
  value in, 7:744–745
  verifiability principle and, 9:659
  Vienna Circle and, 5:525
  women and feminists and, 3:566
Pragmatism: A New Name for Some Old Ways of Thinking (James, William), 4:744, 4:775, 4:776, 4:781
Pragmatism and Feminism (Siegfried), 3:567
Pragmatismo (Papini), 7:102
Pragmatist epistemology, **7:750–752**
Praise, utilitarianism and, 9:609, 9:612–613
Prajñā, soteriology in Buddhism, 1:730
Prajñāpāramitā sūtras, 6:469
Praktische Philosophie für alle Stände (Basedow), 1:482
Pralaya (cosmic night), in Indian philosophy, 5:326
Pramanas, 5:117, 5:122–123
Pramáṇavārtikka, 6:533
Prañjā-pradīpaḥ: A Commentary on the Madhyamaka Sūtra, 1:732
Prantl, Carl, 5:607, 8:765
Prāsaṅgika, 1:732–734, 1:744–745, 5:411
Prāsaṅgika-Madhyamikas, in Dge-lugs thought, 1:732
Praśastapāda, on inference, 5:414
Praśastapádabhāṣya, 6:531
Pratt, Vaughn, modal logic and, 5:491
Pratyaksa (perception), 5:117
Prawitz, Dag, in proof theory, 8:56
Praxeology, 5:145
Prayer
  Carus (Paul) on, 2:64
  Origen on, 7:40
Preaching of Peter, on God, nature of, 7:141
Preambles to faith. *See Preambula fidei*
Preambula fidei, doctrine of, 3:530
Precedent, legal
  authority of, 7:449
  indeterminacy of, 7:450
  legal realism on, 5:246
  legislation and, 7:448–449
Precelestial *qi,* 5:138

Precognition, **7:752–758**
- Augustine on, 3:402–403
- implications of, 7:114
- research on, 7:113
- views on, 7:115
- *See also* Parapsychology

Preconscious
- Freud on, 8:145
- Maritain on, 5:713

Predania (periodical), 4:743
Predelli, Stefano, on creation, 1:318
Predestination
- Arminius on, 1:285
- Augustine on, 3:10, 3:402, 3:473
- Barth on, 1:478–479
- Bradwardine on, 1:681
- Carolingian theories on, 2:49
- in Christianity, 2:249
- and divine causality, 4:109
- God's omnipotence and, 3:9–10, 3:23
- Isaac of Stella on, 4:754
- Molinism on, 8:681–682
- Ockham on, 3:695
- Peter Aureol on, 7:257
- Wyclyf on, 9:852
- *See also* Determinism

Predestination, God's Foreknowledge and Future Contingents (Ockham), 3:695
Predicables, definition of, 5:552
Predicate(s)
- in analogy, 1:139
- in analytic judgments, 1:159
- in anaphora, 1:174
- Aristotle on, 2:73, 8:756
- being and nonbeing and, 2:162
- "believes" as, 1:537
- Boole and, 1:660
- in Buddhist epistemology, 1:757
- Church on, 5:475
- Clinomachus and, 6:110
- definition of, 5:552
- dispositional/nondispositional distinction in, 9:16
- empirical, 4:862
- entities as, 1:561–562
- in entrenchment of extensions, Goodman on, 4:156–157
- evaluative, 4:862
- "exist" as, 1:662
- existence as, 1:528–529, 7:17
- Frege on, 2:417, 3:728, 9:555
- isomorphic, 8:65
- Kant on, 9:287
- of kind, 6:644
- Leibniz on, 5:441
- in Maimon, 5:645–646
- in medieval logic, 8:765–766
- mental causation and, 6:133
- modality and, Van Fraassen on, 9:645
- moral, 4:862
- objects and, 8:65
- physical, 2:646
- quantification of, 5:553
- in Russell's theory of descriptions, 8:59
- in Spinoza's monism, 9:185
- of style, 1:331–332
- subject and, 1:561–562, 9:266, 9:286–289
- synonymy of, 9:349
- in Tarski's truth theory, 2:548
- term distribution and, 5:498
- theological, meaning of, 8:411–412
- and "to be," 1:527
- transcendent realism and, 6:179
- translating expressions into, 3:640
- truth as, 9:538–539
- use of, 9:666
- vague, 5:111, 5:693

Predicate calculus
- Gentzen on, 5:475
- Ramsey on, 5:468
- unsolvability degrees and, 2:385

Predicate nominalism, as eliminativist particularism, 6:174–175
Predication
- analogical, 4:108, 7:479
- Aristotle on, 2:73
- Chwistek on, 2:256
- De Morgan on, 5:449
- definition of, 5:552
- dialectical
  - in Suhrawardī's illuminationism, 4:583
  - Theophrastus on, 9:411
- essential, Descartes on, 2:747–748
- in *Isagoge* (Porphyry), 6:187
- in Kant's logic, 5:456
- one/many in, 4:312
- of properties, 8:65
- recursive axiomatization and, 2:583
- scientific, Neurath on, 6:561
- Stilpo on, 6:111

Predicative judgments, and existence, 3:495–496
Predicativism, set-theoretic approach to continuum in, 2:505–506
Predictability
- of behavior, 8:164
- determinism and, 3:38–39
- responsibility and, 8:164

Prediction
- Bayesian confirmation and, 1:495–502
- chance and, 2:125–130
- in chaos theory, 2:131, 2:133
- in classical foundationalism, 2:275
- for closed systems, 3:710
- in confirmation of hypotheses, 1:497
- in confirmation of theories, 1:500–501
- confirmation theory, 2:433– 442
- in cosmology, 2:566
- empiriocriticism and, 7:716
- experimental counterfactuals and, 1:540–541
- Hempel on, 4:310
- in historical materialism, 4:380
- in late medieval astronomy, 2:533
- and Markov causal conditions, 2:108
- maxent-based, 4:673
- positivism and, 7:716
- of probabilistic correlations, 2:342
- in quantum theory, 1:539–540, 1:630, 8:206
- scientific law and, 7:519
- scientific theory and, 7:519–520
- in theory comparison and primitive ontology, 1:635

Predispositions, of *xin,* 6:129–130
Predmet znaniia (The object of knowledge) (Frank, S.), 3:716
Preemptive overdetermination, 3:718
Preexistence, McTaggart on, 6:78
Preface des elements de la geometrie de l'infini (Fontenelle), 3:683
Preface to Metaphysics (Maritain), 1:529–530
Preference(s)
- as behavior in psychology, 1:525–526
- in decision making, 8:613, 8:810
- economic modeling of, 1:777
- in ethics of rational agent utility maximization, 1:778
- moral prescriptions as, 5:37
- satisfaction of, as measure of well-being, 3:448
- Scheler on, 8:616

Preference ordering, in non-monotonic logic, 5:491
Preferential treatment. *See* Affirmative action
Preferred basis problem, 8:213–214
Preformationism, 2:631
- Diderot on, 3:74

Leibniz on, 8:129
Maupertuis and, 6:66
Prehistoric Times (Lubbock), 2:349
Prejudice
in allegory of painted veil, 9:8–9
fallacy of, 3:547
government and, Godwin on, 4:137
propaganda and, 1:26
wisdom and, 9:795
Preliminary Communication (Freud), 3:737
Preliminary Discourse on Philosophy (Wolff), 9:824
Premise(s)
of argument, 3:639
common sense and, 2:357
conclusions following from, 3:538
definition of, 5:552
disjunctive, 5:503
evocative argumentative, 2:214
inconsistencies in, detecting, 3:546
major, definition of, 5:548
propositions taken as, 5:55
of sequent, 3:641
in syllogisms, 5:502
Prenatal genetic selection, 6:96
Prenex form theorem, 3:654
Prenex formula, 3:654
Prenex normal form
Peirce on, 5:454
Skolem on, 5:471
Preposition, as syntactic category, 9:357
Presbyterianism, 8:296
Prescription(s)
moral, universalizability of, 2:447
moral principles as, 5:37
Prescriptive definition, 2:664–665, 2:668–669, 2:673–674
Prescriptive theories of law, 7:449–450
Prescriptivism
Carroll on, 7:383
Foot on, 6:159
in metaethics, 6:157
on moral truth, 6:160
open question argument and, 6:156
in sanctity of life issues, 9:42
See also Metaethics; Noncognitivism
Presence, in Derrida, 2:716
Present
alienation in, 1:124
Carnap on, 2:39
definitions of, 9:486
Deleuze on, 9:492
future and, 5:350–351
future as, 7:753–754
Heidegger on, 9:490
linguistics of, 9:498
living, 9:489–490
McTaggart on, 6:78
Mead on, 6:81–82
neurosis as conditioned form of past in, 1:598
past and, 5:350–351
in physics, 9:498
punctiform, 9:484
special relativity and, 9:499
specious, 9:483–484, 9:487
word as omnipotent state of, 1:739
Present age
of complete sinfulness, 3:618
Kierkegaard on, 9:451
Present Age, The (Kierkegaard), 9:451
Present Philosophical Tendencies (Perry), 7:204
Presentation
principle of, ontological status of forms and, 1:562
in Russell's theory of truth, 2:543–545
Schopenhauer on, 3:311
Presentational immediacy, perception and, 9:750
Presentational symbolic forms, Langer on, 5:187–188
Presentationism, 8:823
Presentism
degree, 9:480
history of, 9:479
persistence and, 7:211
tensed theory and, 9:479
time and, 9:461–463
President of Good and Evil, The (Singer), 9:42
President's Council on Bioethics, 7:550
Pre-Socratic philosophy, **7:758–765**
Anaxagoras in, 7:763
Anaximander in, 7:760
Anaximenes in, 7:760–761
archē in, 1:249
atomism in, 7:763–764
cosmology in, 1:271
definition of, 7:758–759
Eleatics in, 7:761–762
Empedocles in, 7:762–763
epistemology and, 3:281–282
on eternal return doctrine, 3:352–353
Heidegger and, 1:253, 1:530–531
Heraclitus in, 7:761
logos in, 5:567–568
on matter, 6:58
Melissus in, 7:762
microcosm in, 5:639
mythology and, 7:764
nature in, 6:518–519
Nietzsche on, 6:610
pantheism in, 7:94
vs. philosophy, 7:759
pluralism in, 7:762–763
Pythagoreanism in, 7:761
sources in, 7:759
Thales in, 7:760
Theophrastus on, 9:413
Zeno of Elea in, 7:762
Press Licensing Act (Britain; 1662), 2:682
Pre-suggestion era, 3:740
Presumption
evidence for, 6:116–117
in favor of liberty, 3:561
inference and, 5:122
types of, 5:122
Presumption (*arthapatti*), as means of knowledge, 5:117
Presupposing, **7:765–769**
Presupposition, **3:250–254, 7:770–771**
asking question with, 3:548
definition of, 3:2
vs. entailment, 7:770
in Mill's methods of induction, 6:247
positive, 6:524–525
pragmatic, 3:252–253, 7:770–771
in science, 6:209
Strawson's theory of, 3:252–253
and success of inquiry, 3:576
Presuppositionism, 3:628
Presuppositionless inquiry, phenomenology and, 7:282–283
"Presuppositions of Critical History, The" (Bradley), 6:270
"Pretending" (Austin), 1:408
Pretense
mental, in simulation theory, 9:38–39
of morality, in injustice, 4:866
Pretense theories, 6:637
Prevalence of Humbug, The (Black), 1:606
Prevenciones divinas contra la vana idolatria de las gentes (Orobio), 7:41
Prévost, Pierre, 8:788
Prezzolini, Giuseppe, 7:102
Price, George R., 4:21, 8:7
Price, Henry Habberley, 4:593
on Berkeley, 1:576
and certainty argument on sensa, 8:815–816
on directly present sense data, 8:815

Price, Henry Habberley, ***continued***
and mentalist definition of belief, 5:98
parapsychology and, 7:114–116
on perceptual consciousness, 8:817
on phenomenalism, 7:272
on resemblance theory, 9:600–601
on sense datum, 8:813
on touch, 9:515
on universals, 9:600–601
Price, Huw, on temporal symmetry, 9:470
Price, Richard, **8:1–4**
common-sense intuitionism of, 3:409
conscience and, 2:445, 3:409
on duty, 3:155
Enlightenment and, 3:245
Franklin and, 3:720
Priestley and, 8:5
Price, Uvedale, on picturesque, 3:254
Prichard, H. A.
and ethics, 3:418
on Good, 3:419
as intuitionist, 4:735
on knowledge, 3:315, 5:94
Ross and, 8:505
on traditional ethics, 3:155
Pride
object of, 6:159
Vives on, 9:701
Priest, Graham
and dialetheism, 1:742, 7:106
many-valued logic and, 5:491
on motion, 6:410
Priestcraft in Perfection (Collins), 2:330–331, 2:683
Priesthood of all believers, 8:297
Priestley, Joseph, **8:4–8**
Darwin (Erasmus) and, 2:630
Enlightenment and, 3:245
Lichtenberg and, 5:341
and Lunar Society of Birmingham, 3:247
materialism of, 6:11
Price and, 8:4
and Unitarianism, 2:690
Priest-to-supplicant model of medical ethics, 6:93
Prima facie duty, Ross (W. D.) on, 3:440
Primae Veritates (First Truths) (Leibniz), 5:253–255, 5:272
on identity of discernibles, 5:258
on plenitude, 5:258
on truth, 5:273–274
Primal being, in Valentinianism, 9:632
Primary and secondary qualities. *See* Quality(ies), primary and secondary
Primary (first) intention, definition of, 5:546
Primary goods, 8:258–259
Primas, Hans, 2:143
Primavesi, Oliver, on Empedocles, 3:211
Prime factors, Leibniz on, 5:441
Prime mover
Aquinas on, 9:432
Aristotle on, 6:186
Gassendi on, 4:28
Telesio on, 9:391
Prime social determinant, in historical materialism, 4:381–382
Primer on Determinism, A (Earman), 3:159
Primitive(s), 3:641
Primitive basis, definition of, 5:552
Primitive Christianity Revived (Whiston), 2:252
Primitive people
common consent arguments for God's existence and, 2:349–350
on death, 2:651
Enlightenment and, 3:246–247
Lévy-Bruhl on, 5:306–307
and monotheistic belief, 2:350
Primitive recursiveness, formalization in computability theory, 2:376–378
Primitive tribes. *See* Primitive people
Primitivism
in Daoism, 2:185, 2:187–188, 2:236–237
Diderot on, 3:76
epistemology of, 8:179
externalism on, 8:179
foundationalism and, 8:178–179
internalism on, 8:179
Lovejoy and, 5:593–594
Primitivism and Related Ideas in Antiquity (Lovejoy and Boas), 5:594
"Primitivism in Ancient Western Asia" (Albright), 5:594
"Primitivism in Indian Literature (Dumont, P.-E.), 5:594
Primo Principio, De (Duns Scotus), 8:704
Primoratz, Igor, 7:521
Primordial unity, of real, 3:716
Prince, The (Machiavelli), 3:554, 4:168, 5:626–629
Principal interpretation, definition of, 5:546
Principal Truths of Natural Religion Defended and Illustrated, The (Reimarus), 2:688
Principality of being, 6:418–420
Principes de la nature et de la grace, fondés en raison (The Principles of nature and grace, based on reason) (Leibniz), 1:233, 5:254
Principes fondamentaux de l'équilibre et du mouvement (Carnot), on energy and force, 3:229
Principes physiques de la raison et les passions de l'homme (Maubec), 6:10
Principia Dialecticae (Augustine), on semantics, 8:760
Principia Ethica (Moore), 2:673, 3:418, 6:352–353
analytic philosophy in, 1:145
on beauty, 8:722
on duty, 3:439
evolutionary ethics and, 3:479
on the Good, 4:150
in metaethics, 6:155
Principia Mathematica (Newton), 3:687, 5:157, 6:590–593
Enlightenment and, 3:246
ether in, 5:642
force in, 3:687
Krueger and, 5:157
Leibniz and, 5:269
physicotheology in, 7:558
and physics, 2:279
on space and motion, 9:155
Principia Mathematica (Russell and Whitehead), 2:29, 2:76, 3:316, 9:746–747
combinatory logic in, 2:335
definition in, use of, 2:671
in history of modern logic, 5:462–468, 5:472
Leśniewski and, 5:290
logic machines and, 5:566
paradoxes in
logical, 5:518–521
semantic, 5:522
Pearson and, 7:159
Peirce (Charles) and, 7:163
type theory and, 9:557
Principia Philosophiae (Principles of Philosophy) (Descartes). *See Principles of Philosophy, The* (Descartes)
Principia Rerum Naturalium (Swedenborg), 9:336
Principien der Metaphysik (Petronievíć), 7:266
Principium Primorum Cognitionis Metaphysicae Nova Dilucidatio (Kant), 5:10

Principle(s)
abstract use of, Dai Zhen on, 2:621
academic, Leibniz on, 3:704
of aesthetic association, 3:557
of alternative possibilities. *See* PAP
bridge, 6:644
of charity, 2:646–648, 6:85
in Cheng Hao, 2:144
in Cheng Yi, 2:145
of clarity, 3:557
in Confucianism, 2:220
of contradiction
as *a priori* truth, 1:245
in modern logic, 5:234
in Descartes, 2:54
of excluded middle, in modern logic, 5:234
Hart on, 7:459
of humanity, 6:85
of identity, 5:234, 9:196–197
of indiscernibility, in calculus of Leibniz, 5:443
law and, 7:458–459
of least action, 6:66
of minimum effort, 3:557
in neo-Confucianism, 2:155–158
of noncontradiction, 6:173–174
Ortega y Gasset on, 7:48
of plenitude, 3:473
practical, Locke on, 3:407
speculative *vs.* practical, Locke on, 3:407
of sufficient reason, 2:551
in cosmological argument for God's existence, 2:585
Crusius and, 2:606
Leibniz on, 2:551, 3:297, 5:270, 5:274, 9:156
triadic system of, Iamblichus on, 4:540
of utility
definition of, 1:551
as greatest happiness, 1:551
source as pain and pleasure, 1:552
Wang Fuzhi on, 2:158
Principle monism, defense of, 3:440–442
Principle of Alternative Possibilities (PAP), 3:694, 3:718
Principle of Relativity, The (Whitehead), 9:749
"Principle of the All" (Alexander of Aphrodisias), 5:653
Principles (Regius), 8:301
Principles of Animal Mechanics (Houghton), 7:561
Principles of Art, The (Collingwood), 1:57, 1:65, 2:327, 4:598
Principles of Bioethics, The (Beauchamp and Childress), 6:93
Principles of Economics, The (Jevons), 4:807
Principles of Electricity, The (Campbell), 2:17
Principles of Geology (Lyell), 2:638, 2:640, 3:487, 7:713
Principles of Gestalt Psychology (Koffka), 4:70, 4:71, 5:124–125
Principles of Human Knowledge (Berkeley), 2:422, 9:515
appearance in, 1:231
on ideas, concept of, 4:553
on Locke, 4:593, 9:596
"notions" in, 9:597
on sense perception, 3:301
on words, 8:781
Principles of Individuality and Value (Bosanquet), 1:662
Principles of Logic (Bradley), 1:676, 3:310, 5:565
Principles of Mathematics, The (Ramsey), 5:467
Principles of Mathematics (Russell), 3:316, 5:463, 5:466, 6:172
Principles of Mental Physiology (Carpenter), 9:571–572
Principles of Moral and Political Philosophy (Paley), 3:412, 7:75–76
Principles of Moral and Political Science (Ferguson), 3:604
Principles of Morals and Legislation (Bentham), 8:793
Principles of Natural and International Law (Wolff), 9:825
Principles of Natural Knowledge, The (Whitehead), 9:748
Principles of Natural Theology (Joyce), 2:347
"Principles of Nature and of Grace, Based on Reason, The" (Leibniz), 2:551
Principles of Nature; or, a Development of the Moral Causes of Happiness and Misery among the Human Species (Palmer), 2:690
Principles of Neuroscience (Kandel, Jessell, & Schwartz), 6:567–568
Principles of Parliamentary Representation, The (Carroll), 2:53
Principles of Philosophy, The (Descartes), 2:53, 2:60, 2:285, 2:749–755
clarity in, 2:741
composition of, 2:729
Elisabeth, princess of Bohemia, and, 3:188
on extension, 9:154
on force measurement, 3:228
on freedom, 9:188
overview of, 2:720, 2:749
reception of, 2:755
on *semel in vita,* 2:727
Spinoza and, 9:175
on thought, 4:611
translations of, 2:753
Principles of Philosophy (Geulincx), 4:77
Principles of Physics (Du Châtelet), 9:839
Principles of Political Economy (Malthus), 5:675
Principles of Political Economy, The (Sidgwick), 9:26
"Principles of Problematic Induction" (Broad), 1:698
Principles of Psychology (James, William), 3:105, 3:313, 4:776–779, 9:482–483
Principles of Science, The (Jevons), 4:807, 5:450
Principles of the Civil Codes, Works (Bentham), 9:207
Principles of the Most Ancient and Modern Philosophy, The (Conway), 2:14, 2:528
Principles of the Theory of Probability (Nagel), 6:473
Principles of Topological Psychology (Lewin), 4:72, 5:563
Pringle-Pattison, Andrew Seth, 1:12, **8:12–13**
Prints, *vs.* paintings, 9:691
Prinz, Jesse, on emotions, 3:199, 3:201
Prinz von Homburg, Der (Kleist), 5:79
Prinzip der Wissenschaft, Das (Hägerström), 4:205
Prinzip Hoffnung, Das (Bloch), 1:614
Prinzip vom zureicheden Grunde, Das (The Principle of Sufficient Reason) (Geyser), 4:83
Prinzip von Gut und Böse, Das (Reiner), 3:422–423
Prior, Arthur Norman, **8:13–14**
on "believes" as predicate, 1:537
on determinables and determinates, 3:1–2
on logical terms, 5:532
modal logic and, 5:491
on Moore (G. E.), 3:419
on pastness, 9:480
presentism and, 3:627, 9:479
tensed theory of time and, 9:475

Prior Analytics (Aristotle), 2:136, 5:398–401, 5:455
Abelard and, 5:425–426
Arab logic and, 5:417–418
Interrregnum commentaries on, 5:439
Kilwardby on, 5:70
medieval philosophy and, 5:421–422, 5:430
on modality, 5:435
Ramus on, 5:438
"Prior Probabilities" (Jaynes), 9:223
Priority, of knowledge. *See* Knowledge, priority of
Priscian
Abelard and, 5:424
on grammar, 8:770
medieval logic and, 5:422
on syncategoremata, 8:756, 8:769
Priscianus minor, Kilwardby on, 5:70
Priscianus the Lydian, exile of, 6:553
Prison(s)
panopticon and, 1:555
and recognition of delinquency, 3:700
Prisoner for God (Bonhoeffer), 1:656
Prisoner's dilemma, 1:778, 3:449, 4:15, 7:353. *See also* Decision theory
Privacy
computer ethics and, 2:396–397
Descartes and, 8:125
feminism and, 3:599, 7:462–463
justice in, 4:864
in medical ethics, 6:94–95
medico-jurisprudence on, 6:95
Private language/private language problem, **8:14–24,** 8:783, 9:814–815
applications of, 8:15–19
arguments for, 8:16–19
in basic sentences, 1:484–486
Berkeley on, 8:782
Biran on, 8:784
impossibility and, 8:14–15
logical words and, 8:19–21
Maupertuis on, 8:783
in *Philosophical Investigations,* 9:814–815
"same" in, 8:20–21
solipsism and, 9:116–117
in Wittgenstein, 8:20–23
Private life, justice in, 4:864
Private objects, in analytical behaviorism, 1:523
Private power-conferring rules, Hart on, 5:240
Private property, 8:73–74. *See also* Property
Privation, in Cartesian epistemology, 2:56–57
Privative name, definition of, 5:552
Privative theory, 7:249
Privatization, of schools, 7:362
"Privatization of the Good" (MacIntyre), 9:75
Privilege, bases for, 3:578
Prix de la justice et de l'humanité (Voltaire), 9:713
Probabilism, *vs.* subjectivism, 8:31
"Probabilismo" (de Finetti), 2:662
Probability, **8:24–40**
a priori
finite, 5:56
vs. a posteriori, 2:101
of acts, 9:608–609
admissibility and, 8:38–39
in analogical reasoning, 2:439
assent and, 6:579–580
axioms of, 1:496, 8:24–26
Bayesian approach to, 1:495–502, 6:274–275
Boltzmann on, 1:644
Bolzano on, 5:446
Bruno on, 9:221
Butler on, 1:781, 6:579
calculus of, 8:27–28
and "can" as extensional permissive, 2:24
and "can" as inclination or intention, 2:24
card shuffling analogy for, 9:469
Carneades on, 2:47–48, 7:312, 9:48
Cartwright on, 2:62
and causal closure of physical domain, 2:92
and causality and statistical relevance, 2:100
Cavendish on, 2:118
vs. certainty, in argument from illusion, 4:587
and chance, 2:125–129
chaos modeling and, 2:133
classical, 8:26–27
closed systems and, 3:709–710
and common cause principle, 2:342–343
and computing machine development, 2:407
conditional, 8:25
Condorcet on, 2:431
confirmation principles for, 1:498
in confirmation theory, 2:435–437, 2:441
conscience and, 2:445–446
of consequences, 9:608
and convergence of opinion, 1:500
coordination, 8:37–39
Cournot's calculus of, 2:577
and credence, 2:128–129
Crusius's logic of, 2:606
Cyrano de Bergerac on, 2:618
de Finetti on, 2:662–664
De Morgan on, 2:710
definition of, 8:26
degree of, and conscience, 2:445–446
disorder and, 8:32, 9:469
duality in, 8:26
entropy and, 1:221, 1:644, 9:469
epistemology and, 8:24–31, 9:547
equilibrium theory and, 1:644, 7:538–539
exchangeability in, 8:37
of existence of God, 3:321, 9:407
fallacies involving, 3:545–546
and fallibility of reason, 1:629
finite-frequency, 1:686
Fisher on, 3:660
and formalism *vs.* description in science, 1:630–631
frequency interpretation of, 1:644, 9:212, 9:220
and gambler's ruin, 9:217
in game theory, 4:18
Herbert of Cherbury on, 4:327
history of, 7:537–538
Humphrey on, 2:128
incremental and absolute confirmation and, 2:433–434
independence and, 8:25
in indicative conditional sentences, 2:425–426
indifference and, 8:28, 8:31–32
induction and, 1:698, 4:635, 4:642
infinity and, 8:33–34
in infomatics, 4:671
initial conditions and, 8:36
and intellectual limits of knowledge, 1:782–783
interference effects for electrons and, 8:203–204
interpretations of, 7:538
Jevons on, 4:808
Keynes on, 3:327, 8:27–28
Kolmogorov on, 2:126
Laplace on, 5:197–198
and law of effect, 1:521
and law of first digits, 9:227–228
Locke on, 5:387
logic of, 8:27–29, 9:220–222
log-uniform prior of, 9:222
many minds formulation and, 5:698–699
in many worlds theory, 8:213–214

Markov on, 2:108
mathematics of, 8:24–26
maxent distribution in, 4:673
Maxwell on, 1:644
metaphysics of, 8:35–36, 9:381
and microscopic and macroscopic values calculation, 1:644
miracles and, 1:783, 6:274–275
multiple universes and, 1:221
Newman (John Henry) on, 6:579–580
Nicolas of Autrecourt on, 6:601
nonequilibrium theory and, 7:539–540
in operant conditioning, 9:61
optimality theorem, 9:221–222
paradoxes in, 9:226–227
philosophical, 4:496
physical, 8:24–27, 8:32–37
Poisson distribution in, 9:224
Popper on, 7:690
prior, 9:222–228
propensity theory of, 8:34–36
quantum computing and, 2:407
in quantum theory, 1:540–541, 1:632–633, 6:640
Ramsey on, 8:29–30, 8:235
repeat rate, 4:675
Salmon on, 8:593–594
Savage on, 8:613
scientific law and, 7:518–519
single-case, 8:34
in subject contextualism, 2:482
subjective, 2:435–437, 8:27–31
vs. physical, 8:37–38
of truth in sentences, 6:652
vs. truthlikeness, 9:547
subjectivist interpretations of, 2:663–664, 8:36–37
of success, intention and, 1:21
of theories, in inductive underdetermination, 9:576
in thermodynamics, 9:468–469
time asymmetry and, 7:537–543, 7:564–565
time directionality and, 2:105
unphilosophical, 4:496
Venn on, 9:658
Wolff and, 9:826
See also Chance
"Problem about Truth–A Reply to Mr. Warnock" (Strawson), 7:198
Problem of Conduct, The (Taylor), 9:373
Problem of Counterfactuals, The (Goodman), 4:155
"Problem of De Re Modality" (Fine), 6:290
"Problem of Hell: A Problem of Evil for Christians" (Adams), 3:477–478
Problem of Knowledge (Ayer), 1:437, 1:486
Problem of Pain, The (Lewis), 5:311–312
Problem of Symbol and Realistic Art, The (Losev), 5:574–575
"Problem of the Counterfactual Conditional, The" (Goodman), 2:427
Problem of the thinking animal, 7:232
Problem solving
in animals, 1:206
creative process as, 2:590
Machiavelli on, 5:629
reflection and, 5:700–701
Problema de la filosofia latinoamericana, El (The problem of Latin American philosophy) (Miró Quesada), 5:210
Problema della causalità (The problem of causality) (Pastore), 7:135
Problema prichinnosti u Iuma i Kanta (The problem of causality in Hume and Kant) (Shpet), 9:17
"Problema rechevykh zhanrov" (Problem of speech genres) (Bakhtin), 1:466
Problema simvola i realisticheskoe iskusstvo (The problem of symbol and realistic art) (Losev), 5:574–575
Problemata (Aristotle), on eternal return doctrine, 3:353
Problematica de Vacuo (Hobbes), 1:673
Problemizations, genealogy of, 3:701
Problems from Locke (Mackie), 5:638
Problems in Dostoevsky's Poetics (Bakhtin), 1:466
Problems in Philosophy (Russell), on knowledge, 3:315
Problems of Art (Langer), 1:58
Problems of Belief (Schiller, Ferdinand), 8:625
Problems of Philosophy, The (Russell), 1:229, 3:345, 4:729, 5:210, 9:600
Problemy idealizma, 3:716
Problemy tvorchestva Dostoevskogo (Bakhtin), 1:464–466, 1:469
Procedural justice, 4:864–865
Procedural law, 7:454–455
Procedure(s)
determining fundamental moral principles, 5:38
effective, in computability theory, 2:372
Proceedings of the Aristotelian Society (journal), 9:236
Process(es)
actual, God and, 9:752
classification and reaction methods, 2:141–142
continuity of, Mead on, 6:81–82
material, causative continuity of, 6:133, 6:260
in monadology, 6:325
in nature, and vital force *vs.* continuous process flow, 1:593
in ontology, 7:25
reality as, 1:110
Whitehead on, 9:750–752
Process and Reality (Whitehead), 2:81, 2:557, 7:25
Process philosophy, 8:376
Huayan Buddhism and, 1:739
Whitehead in, 7:478
Processing, parallel distributed, 1:347
Proclus, **8:40–44**
apeiron/peras in, 1:225
in Byzantine thought, 1:787
Christian Neoplatonism and, 7:141
on continuity, 2:493
Damascius on, 2:622
dialectic and, 3:55
emanationism in, 3:189
in Greek Academy, 4:171
Hellenism and, 2:623
Iamblichus and, 4:540
influence of, 6:552
Liber de Causis and, 5:333–334
in Neoplatonism, 6:551–552
Nicholas of Cusa and, 6:597
patristic philosophy and, 7:143
on phantasia, 7:271
Philoponus on, 6:554–555, 7:314
on Plato, 1:190, 6:546
in Platonic tradition, 7:609
on Plotinus, 6:546, 8:42
William of Moerbeke's translation of, 9:770
Prodicus of Ceos, **8:44–45**
on meaning of words, 9:131
semantic naturalism in, 8:752
as sophist, 9:129
on synonyms, 8:751
Product of sets, definition of, 5:546
Product states, 8:214–215
Production
exploitative modes of, 3:600
Marx on, 5:732–733
in neo-Confucian rationalism, 2:156
Posner on, 7:718
in reliable process, 8:363–364

Productive forces, in historical materialism, 4:384–385
Productive system, Dilthey on, 3:82
Productive Thinking (Wertheimer), 4:72
Productivity
arguments from, in compositionality, 2:371
of life *(shengsheng),* Dau Zhen on, 2:622
linguistic, 7:403–404
mental content and, 2:478
Professional ethics
computer ethics and, 2:398
and medicine, 1:603–604
virtue ethics and, 9:680
"Professor Dewey's 'Essays in Experimental Logic'" (Russell), 8:624
Profit, Marx on, 5:733–734
Profit-seeking, by individuals, 1:777
Programming, evolutionary, 1:348
Programming languages, in computability theory, 2:378–379
Programs
in computability theory, 2:373, 2:378–379
computer, as data, 2:373–374
in Turing machines, 2:376
Progress, **8:45–51**
Comte on, 2:412, 7:712
Condorcet on, 2:432
conservatism and, 2:469–470
cost of, 8:49–50
de Staël on, 9:201
Engels on, 3:62
Gobineau on, 4:106
Haeckel on, 4:204
in history, 1:713, 2:410–411, 7:388–389
idea of, history of, 8:46–47
legitimization of, by Schiller's man-made reality, 8:624
Marx on, 3:62
Mikhailovskii on, 6:215–216
in modern Islamic debate, 4:762
Paine on, 7:73
Rescher on, 8:440
Schopenhauer on, 8:653
scientific, 8:48
socialist view of, 9:88
Solov'ëv on, 9:125
Turgot on, 9:551
Progrès de la conscience dans la philosphie occidentale, Le (Brunschvicg), 1:714
Progression, dialectic, 8:138
Progressive political views, of Fries, 3:751–752
Progressivism, of Hegel, 4:260
Prohibitions, in Orphism, 7:43
Project for Settling an Everlasting Peace in Europe (Saint-Pierre), 7:154–155
Project of Perpetual Peace, A (Rousseau), 7:155
Project Zero, 4:160
Projectability, in confirmation theory, 2:441–442
Projection
and social power, 3:575
theory of, Goodman on, 4:154–157
Projective spirit, in man, 3:611
Projectivism, **8:51–53**
Goodman on, 4:156–157
Humean, 6:633
Prolegomena (Kant), absolute theory of space in, 9:147
Prolegomena to a Christian Dogmatics (Barth), 1:478
Prolegomena to Any Future Metaphysics That Will Be Able to Come Forward as Science, with Selections from the Critique of Pure Reason (Kant), 1:232, 2:417, 4:553, 5:8, 5:14, 5:623
Prolegomena to Ethics (Green), 3:416, 4:178, 4:179, 4:558
Prolegomena to the Law of War and Peace (Grotius), 6:510
Prolepsis, in Epicurus, 3:215–216
Proletarian, *vs.* capitalist, 5:733–734
Proletariat
Comte on, 2:413
Lukács on, 5:604
Marx on, 5:604
Prometei (Prometheus) (Ivanov), 4:767
Prometheanism, Losev on, 5:575
Prometheus
love and, 5:585
Pythagoras and, 8:185–186
"Prometheus" (Goethe), 7:99
Prometheus Bound (Aeschylus), 4:177
Prometheus Unbound (Shelley), 9:9
Promiscuity, sexual, 7:525
Promises, **8:53–54**
assertion in, 6:653
to dead persons, 2:654
Kant on, 7:373–374
personal memory and, 6:124
power and, 7:732
rule-utilitarianism on, 3:384
Pronoun(s)
in anaphora, **1:171–176**
vs. descriptions, 1:173
Evans on, 3:461
"Pronouns, Quantifiers, and Relative Clauses" (Evans), 3:461
Proof
Bohmian mechanics and mathematical impossibility of, 1:541–542
Brouwer on, 5:468
in computability theory, 2:373, 2:382–383
definition of, 5:552
Euclides on, 6:110
of experience, 8:19
Gentzen on, 5:475
of God's existence
Aquinas on, 1:528
Barth on, 1:478
Berkeley on, 1:580–581, 1:585
Blondel on, 1:618
Bonnet on, 1:658
Brentano on, 1:692
Candidus on, 2:49
Chatton on, 2:139
by common consent arguments, 2:344–354
Crusius on, 2:607
Descartes on, 1:528, 2:61
Kant on, Mou's critique of, 2:183
metaphysical requirements for, 1:478
Ockham on, 2:139
from hypothesis, definition of, 5:552
by induction, on complexity, 3:648
interpretation, 4:738
kinds of, 3:752–753
legal transaction and, 7:446
Leibniz on, 5:441
Peano on, 5:462
Post and, 5:467
in private language problem, 8:19
Proof calculi, 3:656–657
"Proof of an External World" (Moore), 1:145, 3:314
Proof theory, 3:752–753, 4:362–366, 6:559, **8:54–57**
Gödel and, 5:474
Herbrand and, 5:472
in 19th-century mathematics, 5:462
Proof theory (metamathematics), definition of, 5:548
Proofs and Refutations (Lakatos), 5:171
Propaganda
Adorno on, 1:26
authoritarianism and, 1:26
in Stevenson's metaethics, 9:246
Propagande par le fait (propaganda by deed), 3:554

Propensity theory
of evolution, 7:341
of probability, 8:34–36
Proper class, definition of, 5:552
Proper functionalist theory
in justification of knowledge, 3:273
Millikan and, 6:236
Proper name(s), **8:57–64**
anaphora and, 1:171
Anselm on, 1:218
Aristotle on, 2:73
descriptive theories of, 8:706
Frege on, 5:516, 8:829
Kripke on, 7:407, 7:409
Marcus on, 5:704
mass/count distinction in, 6:660
in Mill (John Stuart)'s logic, 5:494
nonreferring, 8:58–59
references in, 5:548, 8:829
sense of, 5:548
Proper subset, definition of, 5:552
Proper-motivation response, to hiddenness of God, 7:484
Properties, **8:64–68**
of abstract objects, 6:636
Anselm on, 1:218
Archimedean, definition of, 5:534
Aristotle on, 6:504
being and existence as, 1:528–529
being and unity as, 6:187
Berkeley on, 1:587
in bundle theory, 6:199
categorical view of, 5:227, 6:494–495, 7:25
causal theory of, 9:16
in causality of continuous processes, 2:100–101
chemical, 2:141
of colors, 2:332–334
conceptions of
abundant, 8:64–66
intensional, 8:65
sparse, 8:66–68
cosmological models and, 2:559–560
definite, in set theory, 8:836
disjunctive, 6:644–645
dispositional view of, 5:227, 6:494–495, 7:25
Ducasse on, 3:124–125
in eliminativism, 8:66
ethical, 7:4
existence of, 5:667–668
explanation and behavior of, 1:674
of external objects, qualia as, 8:194
extrinsic, **3:527–528**
formal, 1:309
Frege on, 5:516
Gauge Theory on, 4:31–33
of God, 4:116, 9:185–186
Gongsun Long on, 4:149
of the Good, 4:150
Herbart on, 7:375
immanent *vs.* transcendent, 8:67
in Indian philosophy, 4:133, 4:627, 4:633
instantiation, temporally mediated, persistence and, 7:210–211
intrinsic, **3:527–528,** 4:719
Leibniz on, 3:297
linguistics and, 1:218
in love, 8:96–97
in Mādhyamika doctrine, 1:741–742
medieval logic truth condition as, 2:541
mental, definition of, 3:113–114
in mental acts, 1:562
mental causation and, 6:133
in metaphysical solipsism, 9:115
Mill (James) on, 6:219
mind-dependence of, 7:4
modal, 7:580
in Moore's theory of truth, 2:543
natural, 8:67
negation of, 8:66
neighborhood-locality of, 6:638–639
number as, 6:670–672
of objectives of negative sentences, 8:804
in ontology, 7:24–25
particulars and, 6:174, 6:180, 7:25
physical, definition of, 3:113–114
Plato on, 3:284
potentiality as, 6:495
protomental, 6:263
quantification of, by Leibniz's law, 4:569
Quine on, 6:199
in realism, 8:65–66
realization of, 6:644–645
in reductionism, 2:96, 8:65–66
redundancy of, 8:66–67
resultant *vs.* emergent, 6:648–649
Scholasticism on, 3:138–139
secondary, Descartes on, 2:749
Shoemaker (Sydney) on, 3:3–4, 9:16
Socratic fallacy in, 9:110
special sciences and, 9:161
in states of affairs, 7:25
Strawson on, 6:198
structural, as aesthetic properties, 1:39
of substances, in chemistry and physics, 2:142
supervenience and, 6:134, 9:327–329
symmetry and conservation principle of, 2:462–463
as term for substance, 9:295
touch and, 9:515
as universals, 7:24–25, 9:587
of Universe, 2:557
value as, 9:639
warrant, 7:580
words for, **8:64**
"Properties of Terms" (William of Sherwood), 9:786
Property, **8:68–74**
anarchism and, 1:176–178
appropriation of, 8:68–69
computer ethics and, 2:397
Comte on, 2:413
in conventionalism, 8:69
definition of, 8:72–73
economics and, 8:70–71
equality and, 8:94
existence and, Kant on, 7:22
Filmer's doctrine of, 3:637
Godwin on, 1:177–178
in Hegelianism, 8:70
justification of, 8:69–70
land as, 8:69
in libertarianism, 9:73
Locke on, 5:389, 5:395, 8:69
Mariana on, 5:710–711
Marx on, 8:73
in Marxism, 8:70
and monarchy, 1:621
in natural law, 8:69, 9:284
power and, in historical materialism, 4:378–379
primary-kind, personhood and, 7:239
private, 8:73–74
as property (logical), 8:71
Proudhon on, 8:94
public, 8:73–74
Rand on, 8:74
in socialism, 9:73
society and, 8:70–71, 8:73–74
theories of, 8:69–71
Tolstoy on, 1:179–180, 9:513
in utilitarianism, 8:69–70
value of, 8:69
Property dualism, 3:113–117, 6:132, 8:191
Property exemplification account, of events, 5:71

Property rights, 3:384, 7:75–76, 8:71
Prophasis, 1:99
Prophecy. *See* Prophets and prophecy
Prophetic knowledge, Philo on, 7:305
Prophets and prophecy
al-Fārābī, Abū-Naṣr on, 4:811
al-Ghazālī (Muhammad) on, 9:304
al-Kindī on, 1:130–131
Avicenna on, 1:434, 4:757
Collins on, 2:331
and future contingents and free will, 1:680
Gersonides on, 4:68–69, 4:822
in Gnosticism, 4:101
Ibn Caspi on, 4:820
Ikhwān al-Ṣafā' on, 4:576
imitation of God and, 5:653
as intuitive cognition of future things, 9:774
in Islamic philosophy, 4:754
Israeli on, 4:814
in Jewish Averroism, 4:809
Maimonides on, 4:819, 4:825, 5:651–653
Meslier on, 6:154
as philosophers, 4:819
Plato as, 8:40
Saadya on, 8:586
self-fulfilling, 8:728
Spinoza on, 4:825, 9:179
utopianism of, 9:618
Proportion
of alternatives, Laplace on, 5:198
in beauty, Winckelmann on, 9:790
in Euclidean geometry, 2:492
Eudoxus on, 4:54–55
symmetry and, Weyl on, 9:742
Proportionality, Cajetan on, 2:7
Proposiciones relativas al porvenir de la filosofía (Ingenieros), 4:686
Proposition(s), **8:88–91**
a posteriori. See A posteriori propositions
a priori. See A priori propositions
alternative (disjunctive), definition of, 5:553
analysis of, 1:484, 9:806
analytic, 1:242–244
as *a posteriori,* 1:242
Bozano on, 5:446
definition of, 5:534
Findlay on, 1:243
Frege on, 1:244
Kant on, 5:79
vs. synthetic, **1:159–165**
apodictic (apodeictic), definition of, 5:549
Aristotelian, subject/predicate in, 1:660
assent to, 6:580
as assertions of categorical unification, 8:663
assertoric, 5:549
atomic, definition of, 5:553
basic
Ayer on, 1:485
and doubt, 3:103
and belief attribution, 1:536–537
Bentham on, 8:792
Berkeley on, 8:782
bivalence, 9:256–257
Bolzano on, 1:647, 5:446
Boole on, 5:449–450
boundaries between, Wittgenstein on, 4:862
Buridan on, 1:768
categorical (subject-predicate), definition of, 5:553
in categorical syllogism, 5:493
Chisholm on, 2:242
Chrysippus on, 2:251
in classification of moral methods, 9:23
compound (molecular), definition of, 5:553
conditional (hypothetical), 5:553
conditionals of accidents *vs.* nature, 1:628
conjunctive, definition of, 5:553
contents of, 6:136
conversion of, 5:495–496
in critical realism, 8:639–640
of declarative sentence, 2:707
deductive justification of, 5:511
definition of, 5:553
design of, 8:782
Diodorus Cronus on, 7:312
as distributed or as undistributed, 5:498
as element of significance, 8:792
elementary
truth-functions of, 9:806–807
Wittgenstein on, 9:806
entertaining, 5:98
as entities, 1:146
essence of, 9:809
Euler on, 5:444
existential import of
Leibniz on, 5:443
Venn on, 5:451
exponible, 5:553, 8:770
as extralinguistic, extramental schemata, 8:780
fictional, 6:637
form of, 1:677, 5:448, 5:547, 9:810
foundational knowledge as knowledge of, 2:278
Frege on, 5:453, 5:507, 9:556
Fries on, 3:754
general, definition of, 5:553
Geulincx on, 4:79
grammatical form *vs.* logical form, 1:677
Hamilton on, 5:448
with Hilbert subspaces, 8:205
Hobbes on, 8:774–775
identical, 8:785
vs. image, 8:154
indefinite, definition of, 5:553
individuation of, 8:89
infinite (limitative), 5:553
interpretants and, 8:797–798
Jevons on, 5:450
Johnson (Alexander Bryan) on, 4:849, 8:795
Keynes on, 5:55
language game in, 9:809–810
Leibniz on, 5:441, 8:780
linguistic *vs.* conceived, 1:647
Locke on, 5:385–386
logic of, 4:79, 5:494–496
Malcolm on, 5:662
mathematical
as *a priori,* 5:81
justifying empirically, 5:80
matter of, definition of, 5:547
medieval logic and, 2:541
on mental content, 2:476–477
metaphysical
Descartes on, 6:201
Kant and, 5:10–11
Vienna Circle on, 3:316
metaphysics of, 8:81–82
Mill (John Stuart) on, 8:796
in minimal theory of truth, 9:539
Moore (G. E.) on, 2:542–543, 2:547, 3:314
necessary, 5:662
negative, definition of, 5:553
nonlogical elements and, 1:660
Ockham on, 1:773, 9:777–778
as ordered sequences of terms, 1:647
particular, definition of, 5:553
as patterns of reasoning, 5:506–507
Peirce on, 5:453–454, 8:797–798
Philo of Megara on, 7:312
philosophical, Wisdom (John) on, 9:797
in physics, 8:641
in Plato's *Cratylus,* 8:752
plausibility of, 1:495

probability and, 5:55, 8:25
problematic, definition of, 5:549
Proclus on, 7:609
proper names and, 8:57
protocol, in Neurath, 3:317
in Pyrrhonism, 8:176
quality of, definition of, 5:553
quantity of, definition of, 5:553
Quine on, 6:199
ramification levels of, 9:557
relational, definition of, 5:553
Russell (Bertrand) on, 2:544, 8:736, 9:557
simple (atomic; elementary), definition of, 5:553
singular, 5:39, 5:495
  definition of, 5:553
  Kaplan on, 2:708
  vs. universal, Ockham on, 9:778
solvability as equation, 1:660
specific modal status of, 5:101
in Stoic dialectic, 9:255
structure of, 5:506, 5:509
subcontrary, 5:557
subjective probability and, 8:29
syllogistic, 1:660
synthetic, 1:242–243
theological, 4:849
truth of, 1:768
  limiting cases of, 9:807
  Malcolm on, 5:662
  Newton on, 6:593
  stipulation, 1:165
truth-functions of, 9:806–807
types of, 5:495, 5:553, 9:657
understanding, 9:806
universal
  Boole on, 5:449
  definition of, 5:553
  form of, 9:809
  Johnson (Alexander Bryan) on, 4:849
  vs. singular propositions, Ockham on, 9:778
  terms in, 5:498
universal grammar and, 8:791
utility of, 8:89
verifiability principle and, 9:659–660
verification theory of meaning and, 3:316–317
volition as, 9:705
whole of language presupposed in, 9:809–810
Wittgenstein on, 2:546–547
Wolff on, 9:827
See also Statement(s)

Propositional algebra, in illative combinatory logic, 2:339
Propositional attitudes, 5:89, 8:79–80
  ascription of, 8:75
  behavior and, 6:141, 8:80
  in behaviorism, 8:84
  as belief with mind-to-world direction, 1:532
  causal profile of, 8:84
  causal-explanatory approach to, 8:80
  content of, 8:81–83
  examples of, 8:74
  functionalism and, 3:759, 8:84–85
  materialism and, 8:83–85
  and mental representations, 6:141–142
  mental states and, 8:81
  metaphysics of, 8:83–85
  in mind-body problem, 6:262–263
  possible-world semantics and, 8:75–76
  presupposition of belief, 1:533
  in psychology, **8:79–86**
  in semantics, **8:74–79**
  and sensation, 1:532
  and thoughts, 2:480
Propositional calculus, 5:535–536
  Church on, 5:476
  diagrams in, 5:562
  Frege on, 5:463
  Gentzen on, 5:475
  Gödel on, 5:473
  in illative combinatory logic, 2:339
  Peirce on, 5:454
  Post on, 5:467
  and pure hypothetical statements, 5:504
  Stoics and, 3:54
  Venn on, 5:452
Propositional connective, definition of, 5:538
Propositional knowledge, **8:86–89**
Propositional liar sentence, as semantic paradox, 5:521
Propositional logic. *See* Logic, propositional
Propositional operators, 3:643
Propositionalism, 4:699
Proposition-factors, Ryle on, 2:78
Propriety, in Confucianism, 2:194–195, 2:443
Proprium, 5:552, 8:634
Prose chagrine, La (La Mothe Le Vayer), 5:182
Prosentences, 9:538
Proslogion (Anselm), 1:214–216, 7:15

Prospect; or, View of the Moral World (periodical), 2:690, 7:78
Prospect-refuge theory, 3:255
Prospectus (Hazlitt), 4:249
"Prospecus des travaux scientifiques nécessaires pour réorganiser la société" (Comte), 2:410
Prostitution
  analysis of, in philosophy of sex, 7:524–526, 7:529–530
  Mandeville on, 7:522
  as morally risky, 3:606
  pornography and, 7:530
Prosyllogism, definition of, 5:551–552
Protagoras (Plato)
  akratic action in, 9:729
  on courage, 3:396
  on death, 3:397
  Dikē and, 3:79
  on evil, 3:397
  on historic Socrates, 9:107
  on human good, 9:111–112
  on irrational emotion, 7:589
  natural law in, 6:506
  on pleasure, 3:396–397
  rational choice theory in, 7:586
  on rhetoric, 7:592
  on self-control, 3:396–397
  social theory in, 8:92–93
  Socrates in, 7:584
  on sophists, 9:109, 9:129–130
  on virtue
    definition of, 9:110
    as knowledge, 9:112
    teachability of, 7:586
Protagoras of Abdera, **8:91–93**
  on appearance, 1:230–231
  Aristotle and, 3:285
  on democracy, 9:457
  dialectic and, 3:52
  Diogenes Laertius on, 3:88
  in early education, 7:365
  epistemology and, 3:282
  ethics of, 3:395
  as first grammarian, 8:751
  Laas on, 5:163
  logic and, 5:397
  on man as measure of all things, 5:93
  one/many and, 4:312
  on perception, 8:824
  Plato on, 1:230–231
  Schiller (Ferdinand) on, 8:623
  on self-preservation, 9:715
  skeptical relativism of, 9:48
  as sophist, 9:129
  syllogistic dilemma of, 5:503
Protagorean relativism, 1:230–231

Protection
equal, under law, 7:456
need for, 3:745
from violence, 7:454
Protein kinase A (PKA), 6:568
"Protest against Gentile's "Manifesto of Fascist Intellectuals"" (Croce), 2:600
Protestant Church, 2:249
on dogma, 3:97
Enlightenment and, 3:245
Pietism and, 7:575–576
Protestant Ethic and the Spirit of Capitalism (Weber, M.), 9:735
Protestant Reformation, 8:296–297
in development of states, 9:204
Novalis on, 6:667
predestination debate in, 3:10
Protestant theology. *See* Protestantism
Protestantism
Christocentrism in, 8:635
Comte on, 2:412–413
essential doctrines of, 8:297
as ideology, 1:477
latitudinarianism in, 9:249
Melanchthon in, 6:119
and mysticism, 6:450, 8:621
personal liberty in, 9:202
redemption in, 2:249
revelation in, 8:452
Sabatier's critical symbolism in, 8:587–588
Schleiermacher on, 8:633
Stillingfleet on, 9:249
Protocol sentences, 1:484–485, 6:562
analyticity and utility in, 2:43
private experience and, 5:528
truth and, 5:529
See also Basic statements
Proto-genetic engineering, medical ethics and, 6:95–96
"Protokollsätze" (Neurath), 6:562
Protologia, 4:93–94
Protoscience, folk psychology as, 3:677
Protothetic
definition of, 5:553
Leśniewski on, 5:290, 5:292
Prototypes, concepts as, 2:418
Proto-writing, Derrida on, 2:716
Protozoa, Haeckel on, 4:201–202
Protrepticus (Aristotle), epistemology in, 3:285–286
Protrepticus (Iamblichus), 9:129
Proudfoot, Wayne, 8:402–403
Proudhon, Pierre Joseph, **8:93–96**
on anarchy, 1:176–178
on art, 1:56
Bakunin and, 1:471
Lavrov and, 5:218
on natural law, 9:251
on property, 9:88
social positivism and, 7:711
socialism of, 9:89
Sorel and, 9:132
writings of, 5:153
Proust, Marcel, **8:96–97**, 8:656
Provability, Turing on, 9:552
Provability logic. *See* Logic, provability
Provability modal interpretation, 6:297
Proverbs (biblical book), as wisdom literature, 9:793
Providence, **8:99–100**
Abelard on, 1:5
Aquinas on, 9:433
Arnauld on, 5:670
definition of, 9:433
deism on, 2:682
determinism and, 3:35
Hegel on, 7:389
Philo on, 7:304–308
Plotinus on, 7:639
in political conservatism, 2:465
Vico on, 9:675
Providentissimus Deus (papal encyclical, 1893), 5:570
Province and Function of Law (Stone), 7:428
Province of Jurisprudence Determined, The (Austin), 1:405
Provinciales (Pascal), 6:603
Provisos, 4:310
Proximal intention, 1:16–17
Proximity, as gestalten factor, 5:127
Proximum genus, 5:537
Proxy, *vs.* description, 1:173
Prozrachnost' (Transparency) (Ivanov), 4:766
Prudence
Hobbes on, 8:128
as hypothetical imperative, 2:70
Rüdiger on, 8:527
Prussia, Hegelianism in, 4:285
Pryor, James, on fallibilism, 3:274
Przypkowski, Samuel, 9:100
Przywara, Erich, 9:240
Psalms, as wisdom literature, 9:793
Psalterium Decem Chordarum (Joachim of Fiore), 4:834
Psarros, Nikos, 2:143
Psellos, Michael
Aristotle and, 1:279
in Platonic tradition, 7:610
Pletho and, 7:630
work of, 1:788
Pseudocertification, 9:546
Pseudo-Dionysius, **8:100–102**
analogies for God in, 1:140
apeiron/peras in, 1:225
on divine illumination, 4:580
on divine transcendence, 4:107
emanationism in, 3:189
Erigena and, 3:340–341
Isaac of Stella and, 4:753
in Platonic tradition, 7:609
Proclus and, 6:552, 7:143
School of St. Victor and, 8:593
Stein on, 9:240
on unity of pagan theology with Christian revelation, 7:614
Pseudo-Grosseteste, **8:102–103**
Pseudo-memories, inducing, 3:743
Pseudonyms, used by Kierkegaard, 5:62–63
Pseudo-Plutarch, Eusebius and, 3:455
Pseudoscience, **8:669–673**
Psi. *See* Parapsychology
Psicologia come scienza positiva, La (Ardigò), 1:252
Psillos, Stathis, on theory change, 8:692
Psyche, **8:103**
causality and, 9:240
Plotinus on, 3:189
Sartre on, 8:605
Vaihinger on, 9:627
Psyche (Carus), 9:571
Psyché (Derrida), 2:715
Psychiatric disorders
concept of personhood and, 7:241
treatment, 1:598
Psychiatry
in ancient Greece, 3:395
Binswanger on, 7:322
consent in, 6:95
on determinism, 3:16–17
existential, 3:507, 7:322–323
memory in, 6:122
Pavlov and, 7:150
Sartre on, 3:507
Psychic states, unpleasurable, 3:738
Psychical activity, Biel on, 1:594–595
"'Psychical Distance' as a Factor in Art and an Aesthetic Principle" (Bullough), 1:64, 1:761–762
Psychical research, 1:698. *See also* Parapsychology
Psychoanalysis, **8:103–109**
cornerstone of, 3:738–740
derivative schools of, 8:145–148
existential. *See* Existential psychoanalysis
existentialism and, 3:507
free association in, 3:741–743
Freudian, 5:152, 8:105–110, 8:145–146

hermeneutic reconstruction of, 3:744–745
in history of psychology, 8:145–148
Lacan and, 5:167–169
Malraux on, 5:673
Merleau-Ponty and, 6:150
Spinoza and, 8:126–127
structuralism and, 9:273
vs. traditional practice, 3:699
Western culture and, 3:738
"why" and, 9:754
Wollheim and, 9:835
Psychoanalysis [term], first published use, 3:737
Psychoanalytic Studies of the Personality (Fairbarn), 8:107
Psychoanalytic theory(ies), 3:743, **8:109–114**
Psychofunctionalism, 3:758
Psychogenetic portrait, of religious creeds, 3:746
Psychokinesis, 7:113–114, 7:753. *See also* Parapsychology
Psycholinguistics
Chomsky and, 2:244–245
computational models and, 2:392
Psychologia Empirica (Wolff), 9:338
Psychological analysis, Fouillee and, 3:705
Psychological data, in metaphysics, 3:552
Psychological development, pain and, 7:71–72
Psychological investigations, of Fries, 3:753
Psychological method, common sense and, 2:357
Psychological modules, 3:482–485
Psychological processes
in perception, 7:183–186
personal identity and, 7:231
Psychological properties, materialism on, 6:6
Psychological propositions, Johnson (Alexander Bryan) on, 4:849
Psychological statements
behaviorist accounts of, 7:54
incorrigible, 7:55
nature of, 5:145
Psychological states
in attributor contextualism, 2:486
Dennett and, 2:456
intention as, 4:702
object-directed, 4:712
as propositional attitudes, 1:532
Psychological types, Jungian, 4:856
Psychological wholeness, theory of, 5:156
Psychologie allemande contemporaine, La (Ribot), 8:457
Psychologie als Wissenschaft (Herbart), 1:234
Psychologie anglaise contemporaine, La (Ribot), 8:457
Psychologie de l'attention, La (Ribot), 8:457
Psychologie der Weltanschauungen (Jaspers), 3:715, 4:800
Psychologie des grands calculateurs et jouveurs d'eche (Binet), 1:596
Psychologie des Jugendalters (Spranger), 9:199
Psychologie des sentiments, La (Ribot), 8:457
"Psychologie et métaphysique" (Lachelier), 5:170
Psychologie vom empirischen Standpunkte (Brentano), 1:688, 4:704, 8:802
Psychologische Forschung, 5:124–126
Psychologism, 4:783, 6:498, 6:534, 7:280–282, **8:114–116**
active impulses from external stimuli, 1:544
Fries and, 3:753
Husserl on, 4:522–523
logic subordination to psychology, 1:677
opposition to, 7:280
Wundt on, 9:849
Psychology, **8:117–157**
a priori and *a posteriori* in, 1:241
Adler and, 1:23–24
alienation in, 1:120–125
altruism and self-interest in, 3:173–174
analytical, 8:146–147
Dilthey on, 9:18
Jung on, 8:146–147
animal, 1:202, 8:331
approaches in, *vs.* schools of, 8:148
Aquinas on, 9:429–430
Ardigò on, 1:252
Aristotle and, 1:273–275
artificial intelligence and, 1:349–350
atomism in, 8:143–144
in Augustinianism, 1:402–403
Bacon (Francis) and, 1:445–446
Baker on, 1:463–464
behaviorism and, 1:520–526, 8:142–143
Beneke and, 8:140
Bergson and, 1:564–565
Biel and, 1:594
Binswanger and, 7:322
Bonnet and, 1:657
Brentano and, 1:689, 3:311
British, in 18th c., 8:135
Bruno on, 1:712
Buddhism and, 1:724, 2:199
Bultmann on, 1:762–763
Butler (Joseph) and, 1:781–783
calculus and, 8:129
Calderoni and, 2:7
Campanella and, 2:15
Carus (Carl) and, 2:63–64
Cattaneo and, 2:83
causality in, 6:646–647
in children, 1:596, 2:103
Chomsky on, 2:245
Christianity and, 8:121–123
Cleanthes and, 2:288
clinical, 6:95, 8:153
cognitive, 1:523, 2:297, 3:275, 8:150–152
common consent arguments for God's existence and, 2:348
compositional theories of meaning and, 7:404–405
computationalism and, 2:392
computational-representational theory and, 1:523, 1:526
and computing machine development, 2:406
Comte and, 2:413
conative, 8:147–148
concepts and, 2:415–419
Condorcet and, 2:432
in Confucianism, 2:173, 2:196
connectionism and, 2:444
conscience and, 2:445
consent in, 6:95
constructivism in, 9:76–77
of contracts, 7:446
controversies in, 8:153–155
conversational implicature tests and, 2:528
of creative processes, 2:591
Crusius and, 2:606–608
Cudworth and, 2:611
Daseinanalyse, 1:597–598
Descartes and, 8:123–125
descriptive, 1:598, 9:18
determinism in, Taine on, 9:365
Dewey on, 3:44
dialectic in, 8:138
Dilthey on, 3:80–81
Dong Zhongshu on, 2:235
drive, 1:23
Ebbinghaus and, 8:140–141
Eckhart (Meister) on, 3:162

Psychology, *continued*
eliminative materialism and, 3:182–183, 3:201
Empedocles on, 3:209–210
empirical, 1:595, 3:173–174, 6:112, 6:496, 8:133–134
endowment effect in, 9:39
Epicureanism and, 8:120–121
and epistemology, 1:445, 3:275, 3:282, 6:497, 8:133–134
and ethics, 7:4–5
evolutionary, 8:136–137
and existential meaning, 1:597
explanation *vs.* phenomena in, 1:596
false belief in, 9:39
folk, 1:463–464, 3:182–183, 3:201
Freudian, 1:352, 3:511
desire in, 1:352
evidence for, 8:107–108
meaning in, 3:511
in modern psychoanalysis, 8:107–108
functionalism and, 7:471
Gassendi on, 4:28–29
Gehlen and, 7:322
German, 8:138–141
Gestalt. *See* Gestalt theory
Geyser and, 4:82
Haeckel and, 4:203
Hegel and, 8:138
Heidegger on, 1:762–763
Helmholtz and, 8:140
Hélvetius and, 4:306–307
Herbart and, 4:323–324, 7:376, 8:138–139
of hero worship, 2:34
and higher-order consciousness, 2:454
historiographic use of, 1:719
Hobbes and, 4:411–414, 8:127–128
Hormic, 8:147–148
Hume and, 8:130–133
Husserl on, 4:522–523
Ibn Da'ud and, 4:817
idols of mind in, 1:445–446
individual, 1:24
as inductive presupposition to philosophy, 1:544
inferiority of women to men, 3:594
in inner sense theory of consciousness, 2:453
intellectual abstraction by compresence, 9:344
and intelligence testing, 1:596
James and, 4:776–784
Jaspers on, 4:800–801
Jodl (Friedrich) and, 4:835
John of La Rochelle on, 4:840
Jouffroy and, 4:855
Kant and, 8:133–134
kinds in, 6:644
Krueger and, 5:156
laws of, Mill (John Stuart) and, 6:225
Leibniz and, 8:128–130
liberation from, metaphysics and, 8:457
Lichtenberg on, 5:341
and logic, 7:279–280, 9:827
Lotze in, 8:139
Mach in, 1:252, 5:624
materialism and, 6:11
McDougall and, 8:147–148
of meaning, in critical realism, 2:596
Meier on, 6:112
of memory, 1:564–565, 1:712, 6:125
Mendelssohn and, 6:131
mental representation and, 6:141
Mercier and, 6:145
Merleau-Ponty and, 6:150
metaphorical elements in, 1:440
Mill (John Stuart) and, 6:225, 6:233
mob, Taine on, 9:365
moral, 2:196, **6:376–379**
and moral principle, 2:447
Morgan (C. Lloyd) and, 6:402
Natorp on, 6:490, 6:543
vs. natural science, Ziehen (Theodor) on, 9:884
"normal" in, establishing limits of, 3:699
objects in, Natorp on, 6:490
operant conditioning and, 9:61
operationalism in, 1:693–694, 7:32
Palágyi on, 7:74–75
Pavlov and, 7:149–150
phenomenological, **7:277–278**, 7:300–301
philosophical
Blanshard on, 1:613
Krueger's, 5:156
philosophy and, 5:362–363, 8:148–150, 8:155–156
philosophy of
Evans on, 3:462
human as object *vs.* person in, 1:596
inner processes and outward criteria in, 1:525
physics and, 5:129
Plotinus and, 8:122
process concept in, 6:80
propositional attitudes in, **8:79–86**
in psychologism, 8:114–115
Putnam and, 8:172
reconstructive, 6:490
refutation of rational, 5:21–22
Rehmke and, 8:303–304
reinforcement in, 9:62
research in, 8:152
revolts in, 8:142–148
Ribot in, 8:457
Roretz and, 8:493
Sartre on, 1:455, 3:507
schemata in, 9:77
in Scholasticism, 8:123
schools in, era of, 8:142–148
science of, 4:855, 8:134–150
scientific theorizing in, three stages of, 7:30–31
of sensory systems, 1:202
shared memories in, 6:126
Shpet on, 9:18
Sidgwick on, 9:24
social. *See* Social psychology
Soto and, 9:137
Spinoza on, 3:407, 8:125–127, 9:189
Stern and, 9:244
in Stoicism, 8:120–121
Stout and, 8:141, 9:259
subject-object split and, 3:511
Summa de Anima (John of La Rochelle) as textbook of, 4:840
Swedenborg and, 9:337
Tauler on, 9:372
theological, 8:121–123
Theophrastus on, 9:412
therapists in, 1:716
transference in, 9:38
transition from philosophy to science, 8:134–150
Treschow and, 9:526
Twardowski on, 9:554
unconscious/conscious relationship in, 2:63–64
unified science and, 5:528
in United States, emergence of, 8:141
Varona and, 9:648
Vasquez and, 9:649–650
Vasubandhu and, 1:751–752
vocabulary of, 2:646–648
Wahle (Richard) and, 9:719–720
Ward in, 8:141
Watt in, 8:144–145
Wittgenstein on, 9:817
Wolff on, 9:827
Wollheim on, 9:835–836

Wundt in, 8:140, 9:848–850
Xunzi and, 2:234
in Yogācāra Buddhism, 1:749–750
Ziehen (Theodor) on, 9:884
See also Evolutionary psychology; Existential psychoanalysis
Psychology (Dewey), 3:44
Psychology from an Empirical Standpoint (Brentano), 3:737, 4:708
Psychology of Number and Its Applications to Methods of Teaching Arithmetic (Dewey), 3:44
Psychoneuroses, pathogenesis of, 3:740–741
Psychopathology
Ribot on, 8:457
Taine on, 9:365
Psychophysics
disciplines of, 3:555
dispositions of, 9:260
parallelism in, Petzoldt on, 7:268
plateau of, 3:46
properties in, Ducasse on, 3:125
Psychosemantics, 2:391–393
Psychosemantics (Fodor), 2:391
Psychoses, Adler on, 1:23
Psychosomatic discipline, Buddhism as, 1:730
Psychotherapy
Jungian, 4:857–858
Reich and, 8:305–310
Ptolemaic astronomy
Copernican theory and, 2:533–536
on planetary motion, 2:534
Ptolemaic Universe, 5:50
Ptolemy
Avicenna and, 1:433
on music, 1:189
physical theory of, 9:154
ultraempiricism of, 6:105
Public
definition of, in engineering ethics, 3:240
vs. private, contradictions in, 4:806
Public and Its Problems, Individualism Old and New, The (Dewey), 3:51
Public discourse, doctrine of restraint and, 8:392–393
Public good, Plato on, 2:364
Public opinion, Orwell on, 1:180
Public policy, 7:335, 7:353–354
Public power-conferring rules, Hart on, 5:240
Public safety, engineering ethics and, 3:239–241
Public spiritedness, *vs.* patriotism, 7:140
Pudgalavāda school of Buddhism, 5:328–329
Pudovkin, V. I., in film theory, 7:381
Pufendorf, Samuel von, **8:157–159**
cosmopolitanism and, 2:567
Encyclopédie and, 3:224
on natural law, 6:511
on social contract, 9:80
Pugio Fidei (Martinus), 7:133
Pulitzer Prize, for Wilson (Edward O.), 9:788
Pumpkinification of Claudius, The (Seneca), 8:813
Punctum aequans, in Ptolemaic astronomy, 2:534
Punishment, **8:159–170**
civil disobedience and, 2:260
of crime, 1:517–518, 8:160–161
de Maistre on, 5:660
desert theories of, 8:168
in determinism, 8:164
as deterrent, 1:551, 4:193, 8:163
extenuation and, 8:165
fairness and, 8:169
Hegel on, 8:161
in Hell, doctrine of, 4:250–251
of immortal abstract intellect, Aquinas on, 4:608
immortality and, 4:603, 4:612–613
of innocents, 8:161–162, 9:612
justice and, 8:161–162
justification of, 8:160–162
Kant on, 8:160–162
law and, 7:445, 8:160–161, 8:169, 8:448–450
Mill (John Stuart) on, 6:233
morality of, 4:614, 8:161–162, 8:168–169
nature of, 1:517–518
need for, 4:194
panopticon and, 1:555
power and, 7:732
preventive, 8:168–169
prison and, 1:555
proportionality of, 1:551
questions surrounding, 8:159–160
reform and, 8:165–167
and rehabilitation, 1:551
responsibility and, 8:163–165
retributivism in, 8:160–163, 8:168
and rewards
Beccaria on, 1:517–518
Chinese thought on, 2:237–238
Clarke on, 2:273–274
in Xunzi's philosophy, 2:233
severity of, 8:162–163
and shaming, 9:5
in social science, 8:168
types of, 8:159
utilitarianism and, 3:384, 8:161, 8:166–167
Punishment of Death, On the (Shelley), 9:8
Punto de partida del filosofar, El (Philosophizing's point of departure) (Frondizi), 5:210
Pure act
Croce on, 2:603
Gentile on, 4:50–51, 9:197
Spirito on, 9:197
Pure drive, 3:618
Pure functional calculus, 5:536
Pure Land (Shin) Buddhism, 2:168–169, 9:13–14
Pure Land sutras (Buddhist scripture), history of, 1:723
Pure Logic and Other Minor Works (Jevons), 4:807, 5:450
Pure man, Zhuangzi on, 9:881
Pure Pragmatics and Possible Worlds: The Early Essays of Wilfrid Sellars (Sellars), 8:733
Pure syllogisms, definition of, 5:557
Purgation, in Aristotle's concept of katharsis, 9:522
Purgatorio (Dante), 2:626
Purgatory
Clement of Alexandria on, 3:348
Origen on, 3:348
in reincarnation beliefs, 8:331–332
Purification
in Plotinus's ethics, 7:638
in Yogācāra Buddhism, 1:751–752
Purifications (Empedocles), 3:208–213
Purify Your Hearts! (Kierkegaard), 5:63
Puritanism and Puritans
decline of, 2:690
deism and, 2:689
Edwards (Jonathan) and, **3:166–170**
Milton and, 6:250
Toland on, 2:683
Purity, through meditation, 6:108
Purity and Danger (Douglas), 5:111
Purity postulate, of Kelsen, 5:49
Purpose, in human sciences, Dilthey on, 3:83
Purposive activity
in animals, 1:206
behavioral criteria in, 9:385
causality and, 9:386
criteria for, 9:384–385
vs. function, 9:388
phenomenology and, 7:292
systems exhibiting, 9:385–386

Purposive activity, ***continued***
as teleological explanation, 9:388–389
Tolman on, 1:201
Purposiveness, McDougall on, 6:71
Pursuit of Truth (Quine), 8:220
Pursuits of Happiness (Cavell), 7:384
Pūrvamimāmsā, 4:132–135, 4:628
Pushing Time Away (Singer), 9:42
Put' k ochevidnosti (The path to self-evidence) (Il'in), 4:578
Puteschestvie iz Peterburga v Moskvu (Journey from St. Petersburg to Moscow) (Radishchev), 8:230
Putnam, Hilary, 5:88, **8:170–173**
a priori justification and, 5:80
on axioms, 6:628
on belief, 8:808
on Carnap's intensional structure, 9:348
on concepts, 2:417–418
and empirical computational theory of mind, 3:756
Field and, 3:633
Fodor and, 3:675
on functionalism, 7:471
on inference to best explanation, 8:691
on James (William), 4:786
Kitcher and, 5:100
and Kripke-Putnam picture, 8:288–289
on language acquisition, 4:694
on mathematics, 6:677–678
on meaning, 5:190, 7:409, 8:808
on mental content, 2:477
on methodological solipsism, 9:117
on multiple realizability, 6:644
on natural kind terms, 5:150
on naturalism in science, 6:504
and nonreductive physicalism, 6:643
on open question argument, 6:156
on philosophical behaviorism, **8:84**
pragmatism of, 7:749
on preclusion of behavior by desire, 1:534
on present in special relativity, 9:499
Quine and, 5:84
realism of, 7:749
on reference of theoretical terms, 9:417
on referents, 8:62
on skepticism, 3:274
on truth, 2:648
Twin Earth analogy of, 7:406–408, 9:45
Putti razvitiia russkoi literatury preddekabristskogo perioda (Paths of the development of Russian literature in the pre-Decembrist period) (Lotman), 5:578
"Puzzle about Belief, A" (Kripke), 5:150, 8:77
Puzzle cases, for personal identity theory, 7:214, 7:224–228
Puzzles
of Carroll, 2:51
Kavka's "toxin puzzle" of intentions, 4:702–703
solving, normal science likened to, 5:158
Pylyshyn, Zenon, 4:590
on connectionism, 2:392, 2:444
on sensory imagination, 4:600
on visual perception, 3:676
Pyrrho, **8:173–174**
Diogenes Laertius on, 3:88
skepticism of, 1:192–193, 3:399, 8:850, 9:49
Timon of Phlius on, 9:501
Pyrrhonian Discourses (Aenesidemus), 1:30, 1:31
Pyrrhonian school, sensitivity to dogmatism, 5:103
Pyrrhonian skepticism, 2:725, 2:728–729, 2:746, 5:103
Pyrrhonism, **8:174–181**
vs. academic skepticism, 1:195–196
Aecesilaus and, 1:248
Aenesidemus and, 1:31, 1:193
Agrippa and, 8:176–177
belief in, 8:174–175
development of, 9:49
vs. dogmatism, 8:176
epistemology in, 8:174–176
German enlightenment and, 9:56–57
Gournay on, 4:167
Hervet and, 9:51
judgment in, 1:195–196
justification in, 8:174–175
knowledge in, 8:174–175
Malebranchism and, 9:53
Montaigne and, 9:51–52
Pascal on, 7:132, 7:133
propositions in, 8:176
Sextus Empiricus and, 1:31, 8:850
Shestov and, 9:13
skepticism and, 1:195–196, 2:48, 8:175–176
tranquility in, 1:195–196
tropes in, 9:49
Voltaire on, 2:687
Pythagoras and Pythagoreanism, **8:181–190**
after Plato, 8:186–187
Archytas of Tarentum and, 1:250
Aristotle on, 8:185–186
asceticism and, 1:351
astronomy in, 8:183–184
cosmogony in, 8:183–184
cosmology in, 7:764, 8:182–183, 8:183–184, 8:185
and Dante, 2:624
diet in, 8:185
Diogenes Laertius on, 3:88, 3:89
dualism of, 6:327
early, 8:185–186
Empedocles and, 3:208, 3:210
on eternal return doctrine, 3:353
and Galen, 4:6
at Greek Academy, 4:173
Heraclitus on, 8:185
Iamblichus on, 4:540, 6:550, 8:188
and Ikhwān al-Ṣafā', 4:576
on infinity, 4:668
in Islamic philosophy, 8:188
Justin Martyr and, 7:142
and katharsis, 5:44
in land surveying, 4:54
on language, 8:751
Lloyd on, 5:373
mathematics in, 8:182–183, 8:186
music in, 1:41, 8:185
nature in, 6:518–519
Neoplatonism and, 6:548
Neo-Pythagoreanism, 8:184
of Nigidius Figulus, 8:186–187
number in, 8:182–183
one/many in, 4:312
Orphic influence on, 7:43
Philolaus in, 7:310
Pico della Mirandola and, 7:570
Plato on, 7:488–489, 8:186
Platonism and, 8:185
as pre-Socratics, 7:761
Prometheus as, 8:185–186
revivals of, 8:186–187
in Roman Empire, 8:187
secrecy in, 8:181
semantic naturalism in, 8:752
skepticism over, 8:184–185
soul in, 8:186
on space, 9:146
on suicide, 9:319
sympathy in, 8:182
on time, 3:357
ultimate principles in, 8:183

on unity, 5:639
Valentinianism and, 9:632
as way of life, 8:181–182
Xenophanes on, 8:181
Pytho (Timon of Phlius), 9:501

Q

Qi (concrete things) and Dao, 9:724
Qi (force), 5:137–140
in Daoist cosmology, 4:794
elevation over *ri*, 5:7
Ogyū on, 7:10
Wang Fuzhi on, 9:724
Zhang Zai on, 9:879
Zhu Xi on, 9:883
Qing dynasty
Confucianism during, 4:796
neo-Confucianism during, 2:621–622
rise of textual criticism in, 2:621–622
Quadratus, as apologist, 1:227
Quadrivium, 4:66
Quaestiones Disputatae de Cognitione (Matthew of Aquasparta), 6:64–65
Quaestiones Disputate de Potentia Dei (Aquinas), 9:430
Quaestiones Quodlibetales (Aquinas), 4:564
Quaestiones Quodlibetales (Duns Scotus), 3:134
Quaestiones Subtilissimae in Metaphysicam (Duns Scotus), 3:134
Quaestiones Super de Generatione et Corruptione, 5:68
Quaestiones Super Libris Quattuor de Caelo et Mundo (Buridan), 3:687
Quaestiones Super Libros Ethicorum (Kilvington), 5:69
Quaestiones Super Libros Physicorum (Ockham), 9:771
Quaestiones Super Physicam (Kilvington), 5:69
Quaestionum Libri de Anima (Sylvester of Ferrara), 9:344
Quakers
on conscience, 2:445
Voltaire on, 2:687
Winstanley and, 1:177
Qualia, 6:15–16, **8:191–195**
conscious and, 2:451
direct acquaintance with, 6:210
as discriminatory computation *vs.* irreducible information, 2:300
epiphenomenal, 5:112
inverted, 9:16
Jackson (Frank) on, 5:112–115, 9:292
as mental representations, 4:713
in mind-body problem, 6:263
Nagel on, 9:292
and nervous system, 6:16
Shoemaker on, 9:16
and subjectivity, 9:292
Qualitative character, topic-neutral analysis of, 8:192
Qualitative dialectic, of Kierkegaard, 5:67
Qualitative meaningfulness, 6:89
Qualitative methods, for psychology, 5:129
Qualitative states, folk psychology and, 3:678
Quality(ies)
aesthetic, **1:37–41,** 3:46–47
in analogy, 1:139
Anaxagoras on, 1:182
as appearances, 1:232
as association, 1:578
beauty as, 1:512
Berkeley on, 8:9–11
biological capacities and moral status, 1:602
Carnap on, 2:39
Cartesianism and, 2:55–57
causal powers and infinite regress, 1:741
conditionals of accidents *vs.* nature, 1:628
and conscious, 2:451–452
in conversational implicature, 2:526
Democritus on, 3:209, 8:9
dualism of, in embodied self, 9:260
emergents and, 1:108
evaluation of, 1:446–447
existence of, 6:601
Hegel on, 4:265
Hobbes on, 4:410
in imagination, 1:22
induction, 1:447
as judgments *vs.* perceptions, 1:575
Leibniz on, 1:232
life as, 1:109
in Mādhyamika doctrine, 1:741–742
measurement of, 8:9–10
in nature, 1:623
neurology and, 8:11
in Nyāya-Vaiśeika realism, 9:582
Ockham on, 9:777, 9:779
opposite, 1:182
Oresme on, 7:34–35
perception of, 1:575, 8:10, 8:91–92
primary and secondary, 1:577–578, **8:8–12**
Bayle on, 3:469
Berkeley on, 3:217, 3:301–302
Boyle on, 1:674, 5:380
Democritus on, 3:209
Descartes on, 3:292–293, 5:380
Edwards (Jonathan) on, 3:167–168
Galileo on, 4:11, 5:380
intrinsic nature of, 3:528
location of, Johnson (Alexander Bryan) on, 4:848–849
Locke on, 3:2, 3:217, 3:299–302, 5:379–380, 6:670, 8:8
in materialism, Leucippus-Democritus on, 6:7
qualities beyond, in panpsychism, 7:86
sound as, 9:138
of proposition, definition of, 5:553
Protagoras on, 8:91–92
and quantity, 3:61–62. *See also* Categories; Dialectical materialism
and relations, 3:549
relativism of, 8:9
in science, 8:10–11
as self-contradictory, 1:678
sensing, in absence of intellectual analogue, 1:698
separable *vs.* inseparable, accidents as, 1:627
vs. stuffs, 1:182
of substance, 9:296
of substance *vs.* accidents, 1:628
substantial change *vs.* alteration and, 2:75
tertiary, 7:86
as universals, 9:587
Valla on, 9:636
visual, in neuroscience, 6:566–567
word relationships with, 1:591
Quality of Life, The (Nussbaum), 6:680
Quality space theory, 8:193–194
Quanta, 3:636
Quantifiability, of *qi*, in Choi's theory, 5:140
Quantification/Quantification theory
in axiomatization, 6:22
Chwistek on, 2:256
classical, 8:196–198
De Morgan on, 5:448

Quantification/Quantification theory, ***continued***
existential formulas in effective calculable function definability, 2:380
Frege on, 5:507
Hamilton on, 5:448
Herbrand's theorem on, 5:472–473
Lukasiewicz on, 5:505
of mass nouns, 6:662–663
measurement models and, 6:88
modality and, **6:289–291**
Peirce on, 5:455, 7:168
restricted, 1:172
Russell on, 8:551
second-order, 3:726–727, 5:489–492
Skolem on, 5:472
Smiley on, 5:505
substitutional, in non-classical logic, 5:490
suppressed, 3:541
Quantificational sentences, in natural language, 5:509
Quantified modal logic, 6:289–291
Quantifier(s)
binary, in non-classical logic, 5:490
cardinality as, 5:490
classical logic and, 5:485, 5:489
clauses for, 3:652
computability theory and, 2:386
elimination of
in model theory, 6:305–306
Tarski and, 5:480
in formal logic, 5:553, **8:196–198**
free, 5:490
Frege on, 3:726, 5:507
game, 8:197
language expression and, 5:490
logical equivalences involving, 3:654
logical terms and, 5:531
monadism and, 5:490
in natural language, **10:28–32**
in non-classical logic, 5:490
in noun phrases, 3:645
order of, changing, 3:540
Peirce on, 5:454
prefix, 3:654
in Russell's theory of descriptions, 8:59
Tarski on, 2:548, 5:480
in traditional logic/grammar, 5:506–507
universal, 3:648
definition of, 5:559
order of, 3:540
in Tarski's truth theory, 2:548
Quantifier-free formula, 3:654
Quantifying In (Kaplan), 5:39, 6:290
Quantitative atomism, 1:385
Quantitative dialectic, Kierkegaard on, 5:67
Quantitative measure, of information, 3:662
Quantity
Bolzano on, 1:646
in conversational implicature, 2:526
Maritain on, 5:713
of proposition, definition of, 5:553
See also Measurement
Quantity scale
definition of, 6:86
interval, 6:88
observation dependent on, 6:87
ratio, 6:88
Quantum algorithm, in quantum computing, 2:408
Quantum chromodynamics, 4:31–33
Quantum computers
vs. classical computers, 8:200–201
computing machine development and, 2:407
Quantum computing
computing machines and, 2:399
and teleportation, **8:198–202**
Quantum Dialogue (Beller), 3:182
Quantum field theory, 2:565–566, 3:635
Quantum indeterminacy, 3:690–691
Quantum interactions, exchanges of momentum in, 3:691
Quantum logic
Birkhoff (George) and, 5:491
distribution failure in, 5:489
Neumann (John von) and, 5:491
and probability, **8:202–205,** 8:214
Restall and, 5:492
Quantum logicians, 8:204–205
Quantum measurement, 1:633–634, 5:695–696, 7:477, 8:207
Quantum mechanics, **8:206–215**
atomism and, 1:388
Bell and, 1:539–542, 7:477
and black holes, 1:608
Bohr's complementarity interpretation of, 2:531–532
and cat paradox, 8:657
causality and, 2:92, 2:100
chemistry and, 2:142
common cause principle and, 2:343
computing machine development and, 2:407
Copenhagen interpretation of, 1:539–542, 2:529–532
determinism and, 1:539–542, 3:25, 3:29, 3:33, 3:38, 3:164, 5:697
development of, 7:476–477
Einstein on, 6:640–641
energy in, 3:237
in EPR (Einstein, Podolsky, Rosen) paper, 6:641
Everett and, 5:695
as formalism, 1:630–631, 4:678
general relativity and, 9:152
and gravitation, 1:608
Huayan Buddhism and, 1:739
incompleteness of, 8:198–199
instrumentalism in, 7:477
interference in, 2:531
kalām argument for God's existence and, 2:554
locality principle and, 1:539–540
Mach and, 5:624
many worlds interpretation of, 1:221, **5:695–699,** 6:492
matter and, 6:62–63
measurement and, 1:540, 1:631, 1:637–639, 2:531, 7:477, 8:658
mental causation and, 6:133–134
mental energy and, 6:261–262
mental states and, 5:698
mind and, 9:553
modal interpretation of, **6:277–280,** 8:213
and molecular structure, 2:143
neighborhood locality in, 6:640
objectivity *vs.* subjectivity in, 1:541–542
origin of Universe and, 2:554
and particles, 3:635
Pauling on, 7:146
probability in, 6:640
puzzles in, 7:477
realism and, 1:539, 7:477
Reichenbach on, 8:320–321
relative-formulation of, 5:696–698
Schrödinger on, 8:657
temporal symmetry of, 9:468
theories in, empirical equivalence of, 9:576–577
von Neumann-Dirac collapse formulation in, 5:696–697
Quantum Mechanics: An Empiricist View (Van Fraasen), 9:645
Quantum particles, wavefunctions for, 3:635
Quantum physics
Bohr and, 1:636–639
natural law and, 5:225
ontology and, 9:888

Quantum states
entangled, 8:198–199, 8:657
evolution of, 8:208–209
in quantum mathematical apparatus, 8:206
teleportation of, 8:199–200
Quantum theory
Bohmian
vs. Copenhagen, empirical equivalence of, 9:576–577
external objectivity in, 1:631
Bohr and, 1:637–639
and causality, 1:638–639
chance and determinism in, 2:126–127
chemistry and, 9:580
cosmology research and, 2:565–566
Einstein and, 3:178–182
Einstein, Podolsky, Rosen paradox and, 1:630
empiricism and, 6:502, 9:645
entropy and, 2:105
equilibrium hypotheses and, 1:632–633
Heisenberg and, 4:298
many worlds theory in, 7:23
Meyerson on, 6:213
Nagel (Ernest) on, 6:474
naturalism and, 6:492
Neumann (John von) and, 1:638, 6:559
and nonlocality *vs.* incompleteness, 1:630
objective world incompatibility and, 1:631
ontological implications of, 8:212–213
phenomena in, status of, 1:637
Planck on, 7:578–579
predictions in, 8:206–207
randomness *vs.* mechanism of appearance and, 1:632
and reality of events, 3:180–181
scientific law and, 7:518–519
on simultaneity and conventionalism, 2:524
space-time continuity and, 2:499
subject and object in, 9:741–742
unity of science and, 9:580
and Universe as closed and open system, 1:634
Quantum Theory (Bohm), 1:629–630
Quantum-mechanical Hilbert-space mathematics, 6:277–278
Quarks, in gauge theory, 4:31–32
Quasi-hedonistic value theory, 9:639
Quasi-theological "why," 9:757
Quaternio terminorum fallacy, 5:543
Quaternuli (David of Dinant), 2:644
Queer theorists, 3:585
Quellen zur Geschichte des christlichen Gnosis (Völker), 9:34
Querelle de femme (Woman question), 9:838
Querelle des Anciens et des Modernes, DuBos in, 3:123
Queries (Newton), physicotheology in, 7:558
Quesnay, François
Encyclopédie and, 3:223
and Stewart, 9:247
Quesnel, Pasquier, 4:790
Quest of the Ordinary: Lines of Skepticism and Romanticism (Cavell), 2:116
Qu'est-ce que la littérature (Sartre), 8:603
Qu'est-ce-que la propriété? (What is property?) (Proudhon), 1:176
Question(s), **10:32–37**
answerability of, 9:759
in ethics, ability to settle, 7:6
factual, in moral disagreements, 6:157
Johnson (Alexander Bryan) on, 4:850
meaningfulness of, 9:759–760
philosophical, Wisdom (John) on, 9:797–798
Question of a Weltanschauung, The (Freud), 3:745
Question of Animal Awareness, The (Griffin), 1:201
Question of the King of Milinda (Conze), 2:199
Questiones Celeberrimae in Genesim (Mersenne), 6:152
Questions on Aristotle's Metaphysics (Buridan), 1:768–769
Questions on Aristotle's Physics (Buridan), 1:769
Questions on Genesis (Philo Judaeus), 5:585
Questions on Physics (Ockham), 1:773
Quetelet, Adolphe, 2:411, 8:26–27
Quia arguments, 9:431
Quicunque vult ("Athanasian Creed"), 2:248
Quiddity, 4:583
Quidort, John. *See* John of Paris
Quietism
Cheng Hao on, 2:145
of Epicureanism, 4:300
Fénelon and, 3:603
Quijano, Anibal, on postcolonialism, 7:726
Quincey, Thomas De, 3:608
Quine, Willard Van Orman, **8:216–221**
on *a priori* knowledge, 1:150
in analytic philosophy, 1:150–151
on analyticity, 1:166–168
on analytic–synthetic distinction, 1:162, 3:318, 5:84, 8:216–218, 9:345–346
Antony (Louise) on, 1:158
on attitude ascriptions, 9:37
on axiom of reducibility, 5:519
and behaviorism, 7:749, 9:62
on being as value of variable, 1:528
on "believes" as semantically unstructured predicate, 1:537
on Carnap, 2:43, 6:496
and coherence theories of knowledge, 5:93
on concepts, 2:417–419
confirmation of theory, 1:524
conventionalism and, 2:520, 6:675–677
Davidson (Donald) and, 2:646
de re–de dicto distinction in Quine, 1:537
on definite descriptions theory, 5:540
on definition, 2:665, 2:670–671
disquotational theory of truth and, 9:539
eliminative materialism and, 3:182
on empathy, 9:37
on empirical meaning, 1:149–150
and epistemology, 3:275, 7:750–751
on event theory, 3:467
fallibilism of, 7:750–751
on implicit definition, 1:167–168
indeterminacy of translation, 1:525
on indiscernibility of identicals, 5:443–545
and inductive empiricism, 5:83–84
influence of, 6:198–199
on innate similarity space, 4:693
on intensional semantics, 4:706, 9:345–346, 9:350
on intentional object, 4:709–710
Kim on, 5:72
on language, 5:189
Leśniewski and, 5:290–293
Lewis (D.) and, 5:313
on logical and grammatical form, mismatches between, 5:508
on logical consequence, 1:150

Quine, Willard Van Orman, ***continued***
on logical terms, 5:531
Marcus and, 5:704
on mass/count nouns, 6:661
and metaphysics, 6:198
naturalism of, 7:751, 8:156
on naturalized epistemology, 6:496–497
and nominalism, 6:627
on number, 6:670
on ontological commitment, 9:152
and ontology, 7:28
on paraphrase, 3:629
on Platonic view of thinking, 9:420
and post-positivist debates, 8:694
and pragmatism, 1:162, 7:749
on quantification, 6:289–291
and radical behaviorism, 1:520
and radical empiricism, 5:82
on relational/notional distinction, 4:698
on Russell's paradox, 8:553
on second-order logic, 8:708
on semantic ascent, 4:710
on semantics, 5:556
on sentences, 1:151
on set theory, 5:520, 5:553–554
Smart and, 9:65
on social constructivism, 9:78
social epistemology and, 9:83
students of, 2:710
on synonymy, 1:162
on theories, 8:677
on truth, 2:649–650, 3:318
verifiability principle and, 9:669–670
and verificationism, 1:151
Vienna Circle and, 5:525
"Quine as Feminist: The Radical Import of Naturalized Epistemology" (Antony), 1:158
Quineanism, meaning in, 8:89
Quine-Duhem conventionalist thesis, 8:217
Quine-Duhem problem, 1:498, 3:160
Quineian naturalism, 8:276–277
Quinn, Philip
on divine-command theory, 7:479
on life, meaning and value of, 5:358–359
on natural law, 6:514
Quinn, Warren, on deontological ethics, 2:714
Quinque voces, 5:408
Quintessence, Aristotle on, 6:59
Quintilian
on Aristotle, 3:350
on education, 7:367
on logic, 5:437
on oratory, 7:367
Quod nihil scitur (That Nothing Is Known) (Sanches), 8:595, 9:52
Quodlibet (Durandus of Saint-Pourçain), 3:148
Quodlibeta Septem (Ockham), 9:771
Quodlibetal Questions (Chatton), 2:139
Quodlibets (Godfrey of Fontaines), 4:131
Qur'an, 3:536
al-Fārābī, Abū al Naṣr on, 4:811
al-Ghazālī (Muḥammad) on, 1:119
analogy in, 1:139–140
Aristotle and, 1:651
contemplative discipline in, 9:300
creation in, 6:557
God and, 2:113
immortality in, 6:558
liberation in, 9:7
Necessary Wujûd in, 4:543
Quus, 8:532

R

Rabbinical Judaism
Karaite rejection of, 4:813
Saadya's defense of, 8:586
Rabelais, François, 4:564
anarchism and, 1:177
Bakhtin on, 1:466
French clandestine writings and, 2:264
Lucian of Samosata and, 5:597
on rebellion, 1:470
Rabin, Michael, on feasibility in computability theory, 2:387
Rabossi, Eduardo, analytic philosophy and, 5:210
Race
African philosophy and, 1:86
biological, existence of, 6:423–424
Ehrenfels on, 3:177
Enlightenment on, 3:246–247
environmental conditioning and, Gobineau on, 4:106–107
German-Aryan superiority in Chamberlain, 2:123
Gobineau, 4:106–107
historical determinism and, 3:36–37
in human genome mapping, 4:46
Jefferson and, 4:806
nationalism and, 6:484
in "positive eugenics" issues, 4:44
as psychosocial factor for Taine, 9:365
Rachlin, Howard, 9:62
Racial hygiene, Cabanis and, 2:2
Racine, Jean
Diderot and, 3:77
Fénelon on, 3:603
Lessing on, 5:294
Racism, **8:223–229**
affirmative action and, 1:81–82, 9:75
criticism of, 8:224–225
Dühring and, 3:131
Einstein and, 3:179
environmental, 3:258–259
Frye and, 3:756
Gobineau on, 4:106–107
institutional *vs.* covert, 8:848
La Peyrère's pre-Adamite theory and, 5:196
in Marxism, 5:740
multiculturalism and, 6:424–425
Mussolini on, 3:554
sociobiology as, 3:491
theory, 8:224
Racovian Catechism, 9:99–100
Racowitza, Count von, Lassalle and, 5:203
Radbruch, Gustav, 7:427, **8:229–230**
Radcliffe-Brown, A. R., on functional methods, 3:762–763
Radford, Colin, in arousal theory of art, 1:303
Radhakrishnan, Sarvepali, on Tagore, Rabindranath, 9:363
Radiation
background, cosmological observation and, 2:565
equipartition of, 4:804
Radiative values, 9:245
Radical empiricism, 5:82, 5:85, 6:317
Radical feminism, 3:584, 3:600–601, 7:463
Radical reductionism, 1:151
Radical reformers, 8:296
Radical translation, Quine on, 8:216–218, 8:221
Radicalism
philosophical
of Mill (James), 6:218
of Mill (John Stuart), 6:221
political, of Priestley, 8:7–8
Radishchev, Aleksandr Nikolaevich, 5:578–579, **8:230–231**
Rădulescu-Motru, Constantin, **8:231**
Rae, Scott B., 4:618
Rahner, Karl, **8:231–234**

Raichle, Marcus, on neuroimaging, 6:565
Raiffa, Howard, on decision theory, 2:656
Railton, Peter, 3:441, 3:526
Raison et les normes, La (Lalande), 5:173
Raleigh, Sir Walter, 9:50
Rama, in meditation, 6:108
Ramachandran, Vilayanur, 6:566
Rāmājuna, 4:135, 4:630
  Brahman as one reality, 1:683
  on liberation, 5:330
  on life, meaning and value of, 5:359
  resemblance theory of, 9:586
Rambler, The (Johnson, Dr. Samuel), 4:852
Rameau, Jean Philippe
  in aesthetics, 1:49
  Alembert and, 1:106
Rameau's nephew (Le Neveu de Rameau) (Diderot), 3:71–77, 3:410
Ramée, Pierre de la, 5:438
Ramified theory, 5:558, 8:554–555, 9:557–558
Ramified Theory of Types (Russell), 9:557
Ramism, syllogistic moods of, 5:497
Ramos, Samuel
  Bolívar and, 5:205
  generation of forgers and, 5:209
  Zea and, 5:209
Ramsey, Frank Plumpton, **8:234–235**
  on axiom of reducibility, 5:519
  on decision theory, 2:655, 2:656
  on events, 3:462
  on existence, 3:498
  Lewis (D.) and, 8:34
  logic of, 5:467–468
  and Moor's theory of truth, 2:547
  on natural laws, 5:226
  on nature, 6:521
  on paradox, 5:551
  on performative theory of truth, 7:196, 7:198
  on physical theories, 9:417
  pragmatism of, 7:747
  on probability theory, 2:663, 8:29
  on ramification, 9:557–558
  on rational degrees of belief, 8:685
  subjective expected utility and, 8:613
  on truth, 2:546, 9:538
  on values probability and confirmation theory, 2:436
  Wittgenstein and, 9:801–802
Ramsey, Michael, Hume and, 5:672
Ramsey, Paul, on war, 7:157
Ramsey test, of indicative conditionals sentences, 2:425–426
Ramsey-sentence approach, 9:417
Ramus, Peter, **8:236–238**
  Althusius and, 1:135
  Edwards (Jonathan) and, 3:167
  Leibniz on, 5:441
  on logic, 5:437, 5:438
  logical chart method of, 5:563
Rand, Ayn, on property, 8:74
Randall, John Herman, 4:81
Randolph, John F., logical diagram method of, 5:562
Random sampling, 4:644, 8:686
Randomness
  chaos modeling and, 2:133
  as evolutionary organization agency, 1:569
  in quantum mechanics, 1:540
  in quantum theory, 1:632–633
  See also Chance; Chaos; Probability
Range
  of relation, definition of, 5:539
  of values, definition of, 5:554
Rank, Otto, on unconscious, 9:573
Ranke, Leopold von, Machiavelli and, 5:628
Rankine, William, on energy conservation, 3:231
Rape
  analysis of, in philosophy of sex, 7:525–526, 7:530
  Posner on, 7:718
  in utilitarianism, 7:718
Rape law, as instrument of terror by the white state, 3:584–585
Rape of the Sabine Women (Poussin), 1:304–305
Raphael, D. D., on equality, 3:331–332
Rapports du physique et du moral de l'homme (Cabanis), 2:2, 6:10, 8:788
Rasā'il Ikhwān al-Ṣafā' (The epistles of the brethren of purity), 4:575
Rashdall, Hastings, **8:238–239**
  on punishment, 8:161
  utilitarianism of, 9:605
Rasselas (Johnson, Dr. Samuel), 4:852, 4:853
Ratio
  Berkeley on, 2:495
  compounding, 9:342
  in Euclid, 2:492
  Eudoxian-Euclidean, and real numbers, 2:493–494
  in music, 1:41
  of numbers, 6:670–671
Ratio (journal), 3:753
Ratio Inveniendi Medium Terminum (Corner), 5:439
Ratio quantity scales, 6:88
"Rational," conduct-guiding function of, 4:862–863
Rational, faith as, 3:534–537
Rational Account of the Grounds of Protestant Religion, A (Stillingfleet), 9:249
Rational authority, Weber (Max) on, 9:735
Rational benevolence, in moral principles, 6:374
Rational choice/rational choice theory
  Davidson (Donald) on, 2:645–648
  and decision theory, 2:654
  duty and, 3:152–153
  emotion and, 3:200–201
  goal of, 2:655
  language of thought and, 5:192
  Savage on, 8:613
  See also Decision theory
Rational consensus, theory of, Lehrer and Wagner on, 5:248
Rational Dependent Animals (MacIntyre), 9:75
Rational inquiry
  conditions of, and doubt, 3:104
  revealing the need to accept some fundamental principles on faith, 3:631
Rational intuition. *See* Intuition
Rational moral discourse, emotivism and, 3:207
Rational number(s)
  Brouwer on, 2:502
  as commensurable magnitudes, 2:492
  definition of, 5:554
Rational or "intelligible" world, 5:36
Rational persuasion, 7:731–732
Rational Philosophy or Logic (Wolff), 9:824
Rational preference
  cycles, 2:657
  representation of, 2:656
Rational Psychology (Wolff), 9:824
Rational psychology, refutation of, 5:21–22
Rational standards, of knowing and doing, 3:617
Rationalism, **8:239–247**
  a priori, 8:506
  in aesthetics, 1:49–50, 2:580, 4:165
  Ardigò on, 1:252
  of Averroes, 1:650
  Bachelard and, 1:440

Rationalism, ***continued***
Bahrdt and, 1:457
Berkeley on, 1:574
in Carnap, 2:40–41
causality in, 8:245–247
Chubb on, 2:253
Collins on, 2:330–331
Cordovero and, 2:539
in Cournot, 2:576
creativity and, 2:589
critical intellect *vs.* poetic imagination in Carnap, 2:40–41
critique of Deist arguments, 1:782
Croce lyrical intuition and, 2:601
defining, 5:95
Deist arguments and, 1:782
Descartes and, 2:54, 8:240–243
empiricism and, 3:215, 8:240
in Enlightenment, 8:239–240
epistemology and, 3:283, 3:291–298
on essence and existence, 3:350
in ethics, 4:81, **8:247–252**
existentialism and, 3:501, 3:507–508
on experience, 3:517
Gehlen and, 4:35
Gibbon and, 4:86
Haeckel on, 4:202–203
Hegel and, 8:138
Heraclitus and, 4:317–318
Hume and, 6:192
Inge and, 4:685
introspection in, 8:786
Islamic, Muqammiş and, 6:432
Jacobi's (Friedrich Heinrich) rejection of, 4:770, 4:772
Johnson (Dr. Samuel) on, 4:853
Kant and, 3:306, 5:21
and knowledge, 4:202–203, 5:95–96, 8:243–244
Landgrebe on, 5:184
limits to, 1:629
Maillet and, 5:644
Maimon and, 5:645
on mathematical propositions, 9:101
moral, **8:247–251**
in Muslim theology, 4:548
in neo-Confucianism, 2:155–159, 4:795
normativity in, 1:211
Oakeshott on, 7:2
one-sidedness of, 5:74
optimism/pessimism and, 7:245, 7:248
Philoponus and, 7:313
in proofs of God, 9:407
Reformation and, 8:296
in religious philosophy, 7:492
Rougier on, 8:506
in science, 8:244–245
scientific, of Renan, 8:428–429
sensationalism and, 8:825
Shestov on, 9:11
skepticism and, 4:749
in socinianism, 9:100
in Spaventa's "circulation of Italian philosophy," 9:160
Spinoza and, 3:294
Stout on, 9:259
substance in, 8:245–247
Swedenborg and, 9:336
in theology, 8:240
theory of ideas in, 4:566
Tindal and, 9:503
Trubetskoi (Sergei) and, 9:532
on truth, 9:101
vs. voluntarism, 9:714–715
Whichcote and, 9:745–746
Rationalism in Politics (Oakeshott), 7:2
Rationalist school. *See Li Xue* school
Rationality, **8:253–255**
of action, 1:18
akratic action in, 9:729
Bulgakov and, 1:760
Carneades and, 2:47–48
and causation in social sciences, 7:536
in Chinese discursive style ethics, 2:200
classical, 5:679
Cockburn on, 2:295
Cohen (Morris) on, 2:306–307
Collingwood on, 2:326
common knowledge of, 4:18
comparative analysis of, 5:679
confirmation theory and, 2:436
conscience and, 2:445–447
in conscious qualitative states, 2:451
Cynic teaching on, 2:616
in Dge-lugs philosophy, 1:732–733
in economics, 1:777, 3:447
in education, 7:356
and emotions, 3:202
empirical, 4:495–496
escaping confines of, 3:631
in ethical naturalism, 1:688
evolution and, 1:566
in expressivism, 6:160
Florenskii and, 1:760
folk psychology and, 3:679
Habermas on, 4:200
in Hegelianism, 4:273, 4:283
in human nature, 4:482
in human response to God, 1:707
in ideal type, 9:735
in judgment, 7:5
logic as grammar of, 1:768
MacIntyre on, 5:636
Mamardashvili on, 5:679
Mencius on, 2:233
mental content and, 2:478
in metaethics, 6:163–164
Millikan on, 6:236
and morality, 1:461, 1:505
in Nishida, 1:728
occasion-sensitivity of, 8:171–172
Parfit on, 7:120
personhood and, 7:240–241
phenomenology and, 5:679
Putnam on, 8:171–172
and religion, 1:505, 8:420
respect and, 8:441–442
of revelation, 1:479
Searle on, 8:705–706
social, Lehrer and Wagner on, 5:248
in subject contextualism, 2:483
tradition-constituted, 5:636
of world, Zeno of Citium on, 9:870
Rationality axioms, 6:89
Rationalization, of behavior, 8:80
Rationes seminales, 1:403
Ratio-vitalism, 5:711, 7:45
Ratnāvalī (Jeweled Garland of Advice to the King) (Nāgārjuna), 6:469–470
Ratramnus, 2:50
Ratzenhofer, Gustav, 9:102
Rauh, Frédéric, 5:289
Raum, Der (Carnap), space geometry theory in Carnap, 2:38
Raum, Zeit, Materie (Space-Time-Matter) (Weyl), 9:741
Raum und Zeit in der gegenwärtigen Physik (Schlick), 8:639
Ravaisson-Mollien, Jean Gaspard Félix, **8:255–257**
Bergson and, 1:563
Lachelier and, 5:169
Raven's paradox, in confirmation theory, 2:440–441
Ravenscroft, Ian, 3:678, 9:39
Raw and the Cooked, The (Lèvi-Strauss), 9:274
Rawls, John, **8:257–259**
on civil disobedience, 2:260
on closed society, 9:98
on contractualism, 3:386
difference principle of, 8:810
on ethics, 7:119
on evil, 3:470–471

gender-free society and, 9:75
on general will, 4:40
on the Good, 4:150
good-reasons approach and, 3:430–432
influence of, 9:611
on justice, 2:568–569, 3:386, 3:391–392, 4:867–868, 6:488, 9:74
Kant and, 2:71, 5:37–38
King and, 5:73
Kittay on, 1:158
on liberalism, 3:156, 5:323–325
on moral constructivism, 2:472
on morality, 3:479
on nationalism, 6:485–488
neo-Kantian political philosophy of, 5:34
Nozick and, 6:668
Nussbaum and, 6:680
Okin on, 3:600
on principle monism, 3:440–441
on redress of natural assets, 6:96
on reflective equilibrium, 1:238
on Rousseau, 4:40
on self-respect, 8:442
Sidgwick and, 9:25
on social contract, 9:80–82
on utilitarianism, 7:459
on "veil of ignorance," 9:74, 9:82
Ray, John
Cudworth and, 2:610
physicotheology and, 7:557–558
Raynal, Guillaume-Thomas-François de, 3:244
Raz, Joseph
in analytical jurisprudence, 1:169
on authority, 9:211
Dworkin and, 3:156–157
on legal positivism, 5:241–242
on strong normative thesis, 5:49
Raza cósmica, La (The Cosmic Race) (Vasconcelos), 5:208
RCA (Recursive Comprehension Axiom), 8:455–456
"Reaction in German–A Fragment by a Frenchman" (Bakunin), 1:471
Reaction time, to mental imagery, 4:590–591
Reader-response theory of interpretation, 1:314–315
Reading, Sartre on, 4:598
Ready state, of experimental apparatus, 8:208
Real
abstract entity status as, 1:529
in Dge-lugs Mādhyamika, 1:732
Lacan on, 5:168
in Mādhyamika doctrine, 1:740–742
vs. potency, Aristotle on, 7:22
Rehmke on, 8:303
religions on, 8:419–420
Zen awakening of self as, 1:728–729
Real mathematics, definition of, 5:554
Real number(s)
as Archimedean fields, 2:497–498
as arithmetic continuum, 2:489
arithmetico-set-theoretic concept of, 2:495–499, 2:510–511
Bishop on, 2:504
Cantor on, 2:495, 5:463
Cantor-Dedekind theory of, 2:497–499, 2:510–511
continuum hypotheses for, 2:27, 2:489
as Dedekind cuts of rational numbers, 2:495–496
definition of, 2:27, 5:554
and Euclidean ordered fields, 2:500
as Eudoxian-Euclidean ratios, 2:494
Frege on, 5:464
infinity and, 5:514
mathematical foundations and, 2:490
of ordering, 5:516
Robinson on, 2:506–507
Stevin on, 2:493
Tarski on, 5:480
Weyl on, 2:506
Real objects, knowable by reason, 5:12
Real possibility, *vs.* logical and empirical possibility, 5:20
Real Presence, doctrine of, Luther and, 5:615
Real-closed ordered fields, elementary continua and, 2:506
Reale, Miguel, **8:260**
Realism, **8:260–273,** 8:274–276
act-object distinction and, 4:560
aesthetics of, 1:39, 1:56
alethic, 1:132
Anderson (John) and, 1:198
Anselm and, 1:216
as antiskeptical strategy, 9:45
Armstrong and, 1:287
being in, 1:528
Bergson on, 1:565
Berkeley and, 1:574
Bernard of Chartres and, 1:591
Bingham and, 7:428
Blackburn and, 8:52
in British metaphysics, 6:198
Cajetan on, 2:7
causality and, 2:97, 2:101
in Chinese philosophy, 2:188–189
in Chinese thought, 2:237–238
Chomsky and, 2:244–245
Christian, 6:606
on connotative terms, 9:777
conservatism and, 2:470
constructivism and, 2:471
conventional *vs.* ultimate, Dge-lugs on, 1:733–734
cosmology models and, 2:563–564
Cournot and, 2:576
critical
of Jodl (Friedrich), 4:835
in Schlick, 8:639–640
of Sellars (Roy), 8:732
criticism of, 9:593–594
Diderot and, 3:77
direct, 2:97, 8:262–265
discrediting of, 4:559
dualist, 8:265–268
Dummett and, 3:132
Einstein and, 3:181–182, 7:579
Einstein's, Copenhagen interpretation and, 2:530
vs. empiricism, 6:502
entity, 2:142, 8:692
epistemic optimism of, 8:690–692
epistemology, 3:313–316
in ethics, 7:330
existence in, 8:689
Flaubert and, 1:56
Geyser and, 4:82
and good and evil, 2:13
Husserl and, 3:312
vs. idealism, 4:552
on idealist metaphysics, 6:170
in illusory experiences, 4:588–589
immanent
metaphysics of, 6:171
and universals, 6:179–180
in Indian philosophy, 5:413, 9:543
indirect, 2:101, 8:265–268
internal, 7:749, 8:171–172
Kim on, 5:72
legal, **5:245–247,** 7:427–429, 7:461, 8:71
economics and, 7:461
influence of, 5:247
as legal positivism, 5:238
rise of, 5:246–247
Lewis (C. I.) on, 5:308–309
in literature, 1:337
logical positivism on, 5:526
Lukács on, 5:603
Masaryk and, 6:1–2
McCosh and, 6:71

Realism, *continued*
Meinong on, 3:312
metaphysical, 6:171, 7:749
Millikan and, 6:237
mind-independence of world in, 8:689
modal, 5:313, 7:23
moderate
of Aquinas, 9:425
Ockham on, 9:772
in Scholasticism, 9:773
Montague (William) and, 6:331
Moore and, 6:352
moral, 6:161–163, **6:379–382**
naive, 7:189–190
natural, critical realism and, 8:732
and naturalism, mathematical, **8:273–278**
in neo-Confucianism, 2:158, 5:137
neo-Kantianism and, 3:311
new, **6:584–589,** 7:204
and nominalism, in Burley and Ockham, 1:773
number in, 6:673
Nyāya-Vaiśeika. *See* Nyāya-Vaiśeika realism
ownership in, 8:71
particulars in, 6:174–181
Peirce and, 7:744
perception and, 7:178–190
perspective, 6:75, 8:263–264
pessimistic induction and, 8:692
phenomenalism and, 7:271–273
photographic, 9:690
Planck and, 7:579
Platonic, 6:674–676, 9:587–591
Pound and, 7:427
practical, and beliefs, 1:463
on properties, 8:65–66
in Purvamimamsa-Uttaramimamsa schools, 4:134
Putnam and, 7:749, 8:171–172
and quantum mechanics, 1:539, 7:477
in quantum theory, 1:634
of representational theory of mind, 6:141–142
representative, 8:8–9
on causation of sense data, 8:819
on memory, 6:124
perception and, 7:179–183, 7:186
phenomenalism and, 7:271–273
Rosmini-Serbati on, 8:501–502
Royce on, 6:584
Russell and, 3:315–316, 8:540–541
in Sautrānikita doctrine, 1:745
Scandinavian, 8:71
Schlick on, 8:640–641
scientific, **8:688–694,** 8:700–701
Rescher on, 8:440
of Vasconcelos, 9:648
on sense data, 8:818
in Shepherd's causality, 9:10
socialist, 1:59, 1:68–69
Solov'ëv on, 9:123
Stout on, 9:259
structural, 8:692
Svātantrika-Prāsaṅgika distinction, 1:732–734
truth in, 1:132
and universals, 1:287, 3:289–290, 6:174–181, 7:24–25, 9:582–594, 9:773
Vasubandhu and, 1:751–752
William of Champeaux and, 8:592
Woodbridge and, 9:842
Wyclif and, 9:851
Zola and, 1:56
"Realism and the New Way of Words" (Sellars, Wilfrid), 8:733
Realism with a Human Face (Putnam), 8:170
Réalisme chrétien et l'idéalisme grec, Le (Laberthonnière), 5:165
Realist Conception of Truth, A (Alston), 1:132
Realist theory of independence, 6:331
Realistic monism, of Riehl, 8:467
Realistic personalism, 7:234
Realistische Grundzüge (Riehl), 8:467
Reality
absolute, Brahman as, 1:684
African *vs.* European view of, 1:83
in ancient Greece, 7:487–488
apparent *vs.* true, 6:184
appearance and, **1:229–232,** 6:79, 7:22, 7:187–188, 9:684
Aquinas on, 2:539
Averroes on, 1:424
Bergson on, 9:488
Berkeley on, 1:581–582
Bloch on, 1:615
Bosanquet on, 1:662
Bradley on, 3:310–311
Brahman as, 1:684
Buddhism on, 2:221
Carnap on, 2:38–40
in Cartesian epistemology, 2:57
Cassirer on, 2:67
in Catholicism, *vs.* science, 9:888
and certainty, 4:770
chaos partitioning and, 2:39
Chernyshevskii on, 2:146
in Chinese Buddhism, 4:793
in Chinese philosophy of language, 2:202–208
in Chinese philosophy on ultimate, 2:220–221
Chwistek's plurality of, 2:255
coherence truth theory and, 2:310
Coleridge on, 2:318
of color, 1:39
common sense and, Moore on, 2:359
communism and, 2:367
Confucius on, 2:201
as consistent and harmonious, 1:678
construction of, 8:623–624, 9:76
contradictions and, 9:590, 9:807
Creighton on, 2:592
in Daoism, 2:221, 7:486
Dau Zhen on, 2:622
David of Dinant on, 2:645
Descartes on, 2:742–744
description of, 6:634
Dilthey on, 3:80
of disease, 7:465–466
Dōgen on, 3:95–96
Dostoevsky on, 3:99
vs. dreams, 3:105–108
Driesch on, 3:111–112
Dühring on, 3:130
Eddington on, 3:165
Edwards (Jonathan) on, 3:167–168
efficaciousness as mark of, 6:493
Einstein on, 3:180
emanationism and, 3:188–190
emptiness of phenomena and, 6:470
Encyclopédie on, 3:223
of error, 6:588
European *vs.* African view of, 1:83
of evil, 1:362–363
existentialism and, 3:501–502, 6:195
of film, 7:382
Fries on, 3:752
generality and, 1:581–582
Gentile on, 4:50
in Gestalt theory, 4:73–74
Gongsun Long and, 4:148
Hägerström on, 4:205
Herbart and, 7:376
hierarchy of, 1:423
in Hinduism, 7:486
historical narrative and, 7:396–397
hypostasis as hierarchy of, 7:609
and identity, 6:213
in illusory experience, 4:586
imagination and, 1:341

in Indian philosophy, 4:135, 5:326, 6:531, 9:542
intellectual inaccessibility of, 1:570
intuition and, 1:570
Jainism on, 4:631
in James's evolutionary theory, 4:780
in James's metaphysics, 4:784
Jeans on, 4:804
John of St. Thomas on, 4:845
Johnson (Alexander Bryan) on, 4:847–848
Kant on, 5:12
knowable as, 7:330
knowledge and, 4:771, 5:712–713, 9:792
Laas on, 5:164
language and, 2:201–208, 4:543, 7:262–263, 9:806
layered view of, 5:71
Leopardi on, 5:285–286
Levinas on, 5:304
Liebmann on, 5:344–345
and "living knowledge," 3:717
Locke on, 3:2–3
Losskii on, 5:577
Lotze on, 5:581, 5:582
Luther on, 5:613–615
in Mādhyamika doctrine, 1:744
Maritain on, 5:712–714
Marty on, 5:729
and mathematical models in black holes, 1:607–608
McCall on, 9:470–471
of meaning, 7:401–402
mental content and, 2:477, 4:804
in metaphysics, 6:199, 6:208–210
in mimesis, 6:252
mind-body problem in, Geulincx on, 4:80
as "monodual" coincidence of opposites, 3:716
Moore (G. E.) on, 3:314
moral
 in metaethics, 6:160–161
 Murdoch on, 6:434
of morality
 in Price, 8:2
 in Taylor (Alfred), 9:373–374
mutually constitutive transactions and, 3:566
Nagel (Thomas) on, 6:475
name identity and, 2:204
Nasr on, 6:480
in naturalism, 6:492
in Neoplatonism, 6:548
number as basis of, 9:6
objectification and, 1:560
objective. *See* Objective reality
in ontological argument for the existence of God, 7:15
optimistic doctrine of, 7:248
Otto on, 7:59–60
Parmenides on, 7:762
Peirce on, 6:194, 7:166–173
perspectives in, 6:82
in phenomenology, 2:38, 6:195
in philosophical methodology, 7:330
physical
 Davidson (Donald) on, 2:646–647, 2:648
 and evil, problem of, 3:470, 3:472
 Hinduism on, 3:471
 Johnson (Alexander Bryan) on, 4:847–848
 Zoroastrianism on, 3:471
physicalism on, 7:553
Platonic, 6:185, 7:488, 7:608
Plotinus on, 3:401
pragmatic theory of truth and, 9:537
pragmatism and, 4:781
of present, *vs.* past and future, in Augustine, 9:461
as process, 1:110
Proclus on, 8:41, 8:42
in Purvamimamsa-Uttaramimamsa schools, Samkara on, 4:135
quantum theory and, 3:180–181
rational coherence and, 6:606
representing, 5:114
Rickert on, 8:459
Riehl on, 6:541
Royce on, 8:519–520
Santayana on, 2:595
Schiller (Ferdinand) on, 8:624
in science, *vs.* Catholicism, 9:888
scientific conventions and, 2:521–522
of self, 8:132–133
sentence as model of, 9:803–804
in Shin Buddhism, 9:14
social
 language and, 3:563
 as objectification, 1:559–560
Spencer on, 7:377
spiritual, physics as external manifestation of, 3:556
of style, 1:331
subject–object and, 1:615, 5:708
Svātantrika-Prāsaṅgika distinction, 1:744
in Taintai Buddhism, 2:163–164
tautologies and, 9:807
theory of Forms and, 9:590
theurgy and, 9:125
Tillich on, 9:459
of time
 Augustine on, 9:485
 McTaggart on, 9:464
time as attribute of, 1:110
Tolstoy on, 9:512
Tooley on, 9:471
of Trinity in Christianity, 2:248
in truth, authority derived from, 4:782
ultimate. *See* Ultimate reality
Unamuno on, 9:569
unity of, 7:761–762, 9:647
Vaihinger on, 9:628
Varisco on, 9:647
Voltaire on, 9:710–711
Whitehead on, 9:750–752
Wittgenstein on, 2:546, 9:806
Wolff on, 9:827
Ziehen (Theodor) on, 9:884
"Reality of the Past, The" (Anscombe), 1:213
Reality principle, 8:146
Realizability, 6:428
 Kleene and, 4:741
 modified, 4:741
 multiple, **6:427–432**, 6:644–646, 8:285
Realization
 action *vs.*, 1:618
 in Buddhism, 1:724
 conceptual prehension in, 9:752
 counterfactuals and, 3:758
 of functional properties, 3:757
 mental causation and, 6:135–136
 of philosophy, revolution as, 5:735
Realm of Matter, The (Santayana), 2:597
Realms of Being (Santayana), 8:597
Realms of value, 9:637
Realms of Value (Perry), 3:423, 7:204
Realpolitik, 7:660–661
Reardon, Betty, 4:874
Rearranging operators, fallacy of, 3:540–542
Reason, **8:279–282**
 a fortiori, 7:735
 for action
  vs. cause of action, 3:20
  in explanation, 2:645–648
 as adaptation to world, 1:559
 in aesthetics, 9:820
 d'Ailly on, 1:98
 Anselm of Canterbury on, 3:403
 in anthropology, 7:319–320
 apodicticity of, 1:429

Reason, *continued*
Aquinas on, 3:404, 9:426, 9:434
in Arab thought, 1:130
ascribing maxims to, 5:26
Augustine on, 1:393–395, 3:402
authority of, 7:730
Averroes on, 1:422, 1:429
Balguy on, 1:475
belief and, 7:581, 7:735
Bernard of Clairvaux on, 3:403
Boileau on, 1:640
Bradley on, 3:311
Calvin on, 2:10
Cambridge Platonists on, 2:13
causality and, 7:735
and Christianity, 1:650, 3:246
classical, emergence of, 3:699
cognitive powers of, 5:12
Coleridge on, 2:317
Collins on, 2:330
common consent arguments for God's existence and, 2:348
conscience and, 2:445
conversational implicature in, 4:184
Cournot on, 2:576–577
Croce on, 2:602
Crusius on, 2:606
Dai Zhen on, 2:621–622
Damascius on, 2:623
in decision theory, 2:655
in definition of irrationalism, 4:746
Deleuze on, 2:694
and democracy, 2:704
demonstration as highest, 1:426
Descartes on, 2:723–724, 2:733–739, 2:745–746
determinism and, 3:5
in dialectical method, 4:271–272
Diderot on, 3:223
Dilthey on, 3:79–80
Dostoevsky on, 3:99–100, 3:501
Duhem on, 3:127
Duns Scotus on, 3:143–144
Enlightenment and, 3:242–246
and ethics, 3:143–144, 7:736–737, 8:633
in European *vs.* Chinese science, 2:218
in existentialism, 7:46
experience and, 1:49, 1:476, 3:214–215
faith and, 1:505, 3:530
in Averroism, 1:429
Bayle on, 1:505
Collingwood on, 2:326
John of Jandun on, 4:838–839
Newman on, 6:583
Unamuno on, 9:567
Whichcote on, 9:745
Foucault on, 7:729
Gay on, 4:34–35
Gerson on, 4:67
Gewirth on, 4:81
Glanvill on, 4:96–97
goal-oriented behavior and, 7:735, 7:736
and God, knowledge of, 1:114, 4:112–113
and good of man, 9:457
as guide, 7:735
Hegel on, 3:309–310, 3:610, 4:263, 4:266, 4:271–272, 5:232
Hobbes on, 3:405–406
Hume on, 7:735
and induction, 1:653, 1:686
instrumental, 7:735–736
as intellectual faculty, 5:21
in internalism, 4:714–716, 7:737
intuitive, 5:713
Islamic Enlightenment and, 3:249
in Jansenism, 4:790
in Jaspers's psychology. *See Vernunft*
Jewish Enlightenment and, 3:249–250
kalām on, 3:69–70
Kant on, 3:308, 3:410, 7:729
and knowledge, 4:812
Krause on, 5:147
La Mothe Le Vayer on, 5:182
La Rochefoucauld on, 5:201
Lalande on, 5:172–173
Lamennais on, 5:177
and language structure, 2:647–648
law and, 6:73, 7:418, 8:615
Law (W.) on, 5:220
Le Roy on, 5:288
Leopardi on, 5:286
Lewis (C. S.) on, 4:607
liberation theology on, 5:332
limits of, 1:707, 3:99–100, 3:699
linguistic operation in, 8:787
Lloyd on, 5:373
locality of, 4:609
Locke on, 5:379, 5:387, 5:392
Lotze on, 5:581
Lu Xiangshan on, 5:618
Luther on, 5:613–617
Maimonides on, 5:651
Maritain on, 5:713–714
Marx on, 3:68
in materialism, 6:10
Mercier on, 6:144–145
and metaphysics, 3:752, 6:201
Meyerson on, 6:213
Milton on, 6:250
in mind-body problem, 6:262
Molina Garmendia on, 6:324
and morality, 1:461, 4:81, 5:24, 5:138, 9:833
motivation and, 7:737
Mullā Ṣadrā on, 6:418
music and, 1:49
in Muʿtazilite theology, 4:811–812
Nagel (Thomas) on, 6:475
natural law and, 6:508, 6:512
Nelson (Leonard) on, 6:535
in neo-Confucianism, 2:622
Neoplatonists on, 3:400
Newman (John Henry) on, 6:577–578
Niebuhr on, 6:606
non-localized nature of, 4:609
normative, in moral rightness, 6:163–164
Oakeshott on, 7:2
objects of, 8:280–281
Ortega y Gasset on, 7:46
Otto on, 7:59–60
Paine on, 7:73
Pannenberg on, 7:82
Parmenides of Elea on, 7:123–124
Pascal on, 7:132
passion and, 9:715
Plato on, 2:698, 9:794
possessing concepts of its own, 5:12
in postmodernism, 7:729, 7:730
powers of, 8:281–282
practical, **7:735–738**. *See also* Rationalism
and contemplation *(otium) vs.* practical life *(negotium)*, 1:444
Habermas on, 3:91
highest good in communism and, 2:367
Kant on, 4:613, 5:24
and naturalistic understanding of virtue and vice, 3:685
novel conception of, 3:685
Ritschl on, 8:480–481
practical effectiveness of, 5:24
"pure," capacities of, 5:12–13
in Pythagoreanism, 8:182
questions and, 8:279–281
rationality and, 8:253
Régis on, 8:300
regulative employment of, 5:26
religious truth and, 7:59
repudiation of, 5:77

revelation and, 1:505–506, 1:707, 4:828
Hobbes on, 4:421–422
Hume on, 4:512
role of, 7:735
Romero on, 8:492
rules and, 7:736
Saadya on, 8:586
Saint-Hyacinthe on, 8:588
Santayana on, 8:598–599
Sartre on, 3:503
Schelling's law of identity in, 8:621
Schleiermacher on, 8:633
Scholastics on, 5:615–616
as self-ordering experience, 1:477
self-reliance of, principle of, 3:753
Shestov on, 9:11–12
skepticism and, 1:505, 4:500–501
and soul, 7:319–320
speculative, 5:713–714, 9:426
Spinoza on, 3:295–296
Steinheim on, 4:828
Stoics on, 3:400, 5:569
sufficient
in argument for existence of God, 9:407
Geyser on, 4:83
insufficiency of, 4:787–788
vs. superstition, 8:47
Thomasius on, 9:441
Tindal on, 5:220, 9:503
Trubetskoi (Sergei) and, 9:532
and truth, 3:631, 9:833–834
Tschirnhaus on, 9:549
Voltaire on, 9:713
and will, 9:250–251
Wollaston on, 9:833–834
women and, 9:836–837
Zen'kovskii on, 9:868
See also Intellect
Reason [term], 8:280
Reason and Analysis (Blanshard), 1:613–614
"Reason and Belief in God" (Plantinga), 7:581
Reason and Goodness (Blanshard), 1:614
Reason and Morality (Gewirth), 4:81
Reason and Nature (Cohen, Morris), 2:307
Reason and Religion (Norris), 6:655–656
Reason and Responsibility: Readings in Some Basic Problems of Philosophy (Feinberg), 3:562
Reason and Revelation in the Middle Ages (Gilson), 4:92
Reason in Art (Santayana), 1:57, 1:63, 8:598
Reason in Common Sense (Santayana), 8:599
Reason in Religion (Santayana), 8:599
"Reason Is Faith Cultivating Itself" (Collingwood), 2:326
Reason of Wolff's Classes in Mathematics and Global Philosophy (Wolff), 9:823–824
Reason the Only Oracle of Man, or a Compendious System of Natural Religion (Allen), 2:690
Reasonable, in European *vs.* Chinese science, 2:218
Reasonableness
in Balguy, 1:475
induction justification, 1:686
Reasonableness of Christianity, The (Locke), 3:246, 4:112, 5:375, 5:390–395, 9:505
Reasoning
by analogy, in confirmation theory, 2:439
Aristotle on, 1:270–271
Bayle and, 1:502–503, 1:507
beliefs and, 1:510
biological matrix of, 8:625
case-based, 1:237–238
as causal process, 6:133
concrete, 6:577–578
Crusius on, 2:607
defeasible, 6:642
dialectic *vs.* scientific, 1:270
discursive, 9:427
formal *vs.* informal, 6:577
Hobbes on, 5:631
Hume on, 8:132
from known to unknown, 9:408–409
legal, 3:156, 7:447–452, 7:458–459
mathematical
formalization of, 3:646
Frege on, 5:463
metaphor in, in Chinese metaphysics, 2:222
modeling, imprecision and, 3:766
monotonicity in, 6:642
moral
Ayer on, 6:157
Baier on, 3:431
circularity in, 3:547
Dau Zhen on, 2:622
emotion in, 3:579
Hare on, 6:158
vs. nonmoral, 7:737
Toulmin on, 3:431
truth in religion derived from, 5:30
nature and, 8:633–634
Newton on, 6:592–593
Nicholas of Cusa on, 6:595
patterns of, 5:506–507
precognition and, 7:754
probability and, 6:579–580
"reason preserving" in, 4:184
Reinhold on, 8:334
Rignano on, 8:476
semantics and, 1:343
as sensation, 4:637
society and, 8:633–634
by syllogism, 6:600
in theology, 1:93
theoretical, belief in, 1:533
by women, 1:355
See also Thinking
Reasons
for actions, 1:18
internalism of, 4:714
moral, as hypothetical, not categorical, 3:685
subject contextual epistemic structure of, 2:482–483
Reasons against Restraining the Press (Tindal), 9:502
Reasons and Persons (Parfit), 7:229
ethics and, 7:119–120
on self-effacing standards of conduct, 3:441
Reazione idealistica contro la scienza, La (Aliotta), 1:127
Rebel, The (Camus), 2:22, 3:427
Rebelión de las masas, La (The Revolt of the Masses) (Ortega y Gasset), 7:47, 7:547
Rebirth, 8:331–333. *See also* Reincarnation
Rebuttal, of syllogistic dilemma, 5:503
Recaséns Siches, Luis, as *transterrados,* 5:209
Recherche de la verité (Malebranche), 1:288, 2:57, 2:757, 5:663–666
"Recherche des loix du mouvement" (Maupertuis), 6:66
Recherche d'une première vérité, La (Lequier), 5:287
Recherches philosophiques sur la nécessité de s'assurer par soi-même de la vérité (Saint-Hyacinthe), 8:588
Recherches sur la theorie de la demonstration (Hilbert), 5:472
"Recherches sur l'attraction des spheroides homogènes" (Lagrange), on potential energy, 3:228

Rechérches sur l'organisation des corps vivans (Lamarck), 5:173
Recht des Besitzes, Das (The right of possession) (Savigny), 8:614
Recht des Besitzes, Das (Schuppe), 8:664
Recipients
of injustice, requirement of, 4:863–864
justice oriented on, 4:867–868
Reciprocity (causal interaction), in *Critique of Pure Reason* (Kant), 5:20
"Reclamation of the Freedom of Thought from the Princes of Europe" (Fichte), 1:377
Reclus, Elisee, 5:154
Recognition
act of, 3:617
in agent-relative knowledge, 8:710
as belief, 1:199
false picture of, 4:594
Hegel on, 4:262
of law, 7:458
as learning, 1:44
in phenomenology, 7:287
rule of, 7:458
in Schlick's knowledge of sameness, 8:640
of three-dimensional object, 4:594
Recognition respect, 8:441
Recollection
conation in, 9:260
theory of
in Platonic dialogues, 7:588–589
Socrates on, 3:283–284
Reconciliation of Two Sages (al-Fārābī), 7:610
Reconsiderations (Toynbee), 9:517
Reconstruction in Philosophy (Dewey), 3:44
Records of History (Sima Qian), 5:194
Rectangular charts, as logical diagrams, 5:561
Recurrence of phenomena, Lachelier on, 5:169
Recursion, transfinite, definition of, 5:558
Recursion theorem, in computability theory, 2:382. *See also* Computability theory
Recursive Comprehension Axiom (RCA), 8:455–456
Recursive enumerability, computing machines and, 2:402
Recursive function(s)
in combinatory arithmetic, 2:338
definition of, 5:554
in early computing, 2:401
Gödel on, 5:474
Skolem on, 5:472
terminology of, 2:378
Recursive (inductive) definition, 5:540
in Peano, 5:465
in Tarski's truth theory, 2:548–549
Recursive number theory, definition of, 5:554
Recursive set, definition of, 5:554
Recursively enumerable, 2:583–584, 5:554
Recursiveness
Church on, 5:476
in computability theory, 2:376–378
Redargutio Philosophiarum (Bacon, Francis), 1:451
Redelmeier, D., on decision theory, 2:657
Redemption
Benjamin on, 1:546
in Blake, 1:611
in Christianity, 2:248–249
Kabbalists on, 5:2
from selfhood, through society, 4:773–774
Reden über die Religion (Speeches on Religion) (Schleiermacher), 5:297
Redfield, Robert, on universal values, 3:420
Redi, Francesco, on spontaneous generation, 5:359–360
Rediscovery of the Mind, The (Searle), 2:395
Reducibility
axiom of, 5:554–557
in combinatory logic, 2:336
multiple realizability and, 6:644
supervenience and, 9:327
Reductio ad absurdum arguments
Anselm on, 1:216
definition of, 5:545–555
in Dge-lugs Mādhyamika, 1:732
improper, 3:538
in Indian philosophy, 5:411
Leibniz on, 5:443
Nāgārjuna on, 6:470
Svātantrika-Prāsaṅgika distinction, 1:744
Valla on, 5:437
in Zeno of Elea, 9:872
Reduction, **8:282–287**
Bolzano's method of, 5:445–446
as functional explanation, 6:570
in Husserl, 9:489
intertheoretic, 6:569
in multiple realizability, 6:429–431
Nagelian, 6:569, 8:283–285, 9:162
neo-Nagelian, 8:284
in neuroscience, 6:569–571
Pauler's method of, 7:145
perceptual, 7:184
scientific, 7:520
of second-figure, 5:498
of syllogisms, 5:497, 5:555
of universals, 6:176–178
Reductionism, 2:89–93, 7:277, 7:285
Baker (Lynne Rudder) on, 1:463–464
behaviorism and, 1:520
on belief, justification of, 7:357
Cantor-Dedekind theory and, 2:501
causality and, 2:95–96, 2:98–102
and chaos theory in science, 2:133
of Chernyshevskii, 2:146
computationalism and, 2:391
and determinationism, 6:172
Epicurus and, 3:269
Fodor on, 6:644
functional, 5:72, 6:570
genes and, 7:343–344
Humean, 2:96–100
intention in, 1:20–21
in medicine, 7:467
in non-Humean reductionism, 2:100–101
opposition to, 7:281–283
personal identity in, 7:230
in philosophy of mind, 1:520, 1:526, **10:37–40**
and physics, 2:142–143
properties in, 8:65–66
radical, 1:151
and science, 9:579–580
singularism and, 2:101–102
special sciences and, 9:161
of Titchener, 8:142
Reductive empiricism, 8:689
Reductive explanation, functional, 6:570
Reductive functionalization, 5:72
Reductive methods
in Abhidharma Buddhism, 1:740
in Buddhist epistemology, 1:756–757
in Carneades, 2:47–48
Charron's, 2:135
in Dge-lugs Mādhyamika, 1:732
of Pauler, 7:145
Svātantrika-Prāsaṅgika distinction, 1:744
Reductive psychologism, 5:34
Redundancy, of properties, 8:66–67
Redundancy argument, 3:690

Reduplication argument, for personal identity, 7:229
Rée, Paul, Nietzsche and, 6:611
Reference, **8:288–290**
accessory ideas and, 8:776
anaphora and, 1:171–174
in animal communication, 1:204
of belief attributions, 1:536
Brightman on, 1:694–695
causal theory of, 8:172, 8:289, 9:417
in Chinese philosophy, 2:188–189, 2:202–204
in Chisholm's metaphysics, 2:243
concepts and, 2:415–417
in definite descriptions, 9:264
demonstratives and, 8:746
descriptivist theory of, 9:417
in Dge-lugs Mādhyamika, 1:732
direct, 5:704, 8:61–62, 8:289
Evans on, 3:459–461
as external and sensation of touch, 1:705
Frege on, 3:727–728, 5:464, 8:60–61, 8:736, 8:800
Kripke on, 7:409
as many-to-one *vs.* one-to-one mappings, 2:205
in mental direction, 1:689
minimal theory of, 8:290
new semantic theory of, 8:747
personalism and, 7:235
in philosophy of language, 7:408
and probabilities in possible worlds, 2:94
probability and, 8:32–33
of proper name, 5:548
in purpose-perspective-sensitivity, 2:204–205
Putnam on, 2:417
in Quineanism, 8:89
in religious language, 8:419
sense and, 8:736, 8:800, 8:829
in speech, 7:407
symbol grounding as, 2:241
of theoretical terms, 9:417
in time, 9:462–463
See also Private language/private language problem
"Reference and Contingency" (Evans), 3:461
Reference Guide (Yolton and Yolton), 5:394
Referential anaphora, 1:171
Referential opacity, 5:555, 5:704
Referentialism, in classical Indian philosophy, 9:544
Referents, 8:759, 8:794
context and, 8:62
in neo-Russellianism, 8:89
Refinement, and incremental attainment of nirvāṇa, 1:724
Reflection
and action, 1:565
anti-theory of, 1:459
in Buddhism, 1:724
colors as, 2:332
as community activity, 1:459
Condillac on, 2:423
in Confucianism, 2:173, 2:177–179
in judgment, 7:5
law of, in classical mechanics, 2:282
Locke on, 5:380–381, 5:385
Marcel on, 5:700–701
and moral judgments, 9:739
mystery and, 5:701
in phenomenology, 7:287–289, 7:297
primary and secondary, 5:700–701
Reinhold on, 8:334
transcendental, 5:709
in wisdom, 9:794–795
"Reflections of a Temporalist on the New Realism" (Lovejoy), 5:592
Reflections on the Conduct of Human Life (Norris), 6:655
Reflections on the Formation and the Distribution of Riches (Turgot), 9:550
Reflections on the Revolution in France (Burke), 1:771–772, 7:73, 9:837
Reflections on Violence (Sorel), 9:677
Reflective agreement, between personal and social will, 7:205
Reflective equilibrium, **8:290–295**
act utilitarianism and, 9:611–613
in applied ethics, 1:238
vs. deductivism, 1:238
Rawls on, 5:323, 8:259
rule utilitarianism and, 9:613–615
Reflective examination, perception and, 7:177
Reflective or mediate knowledge, 3:752
Reflective thinking, in phenomenology, 7:288
Reflectiveness, consciousness and, 2:449
"Reflex Arc Concept in Psychology, The" (Dewey), 3:45
Reflex theory of behavior
Marxism and, 7:150
Pavlov and, 7:149–150
Reflexes of the Brain (Sechenov), 7:151
Réflexions critiques sur la poésie et sur la peinture (DuBos), 3:123
Reflexions critiques sur quelques passage de rhéteur Longin (Boileau), 1:640
Réflexions philosophiques sur l'origine des langues et la signification des mots (Maurertuis), 8:783
Réflexions sur la formation et la distribution des richesses (Turgot), 9:550
Réflexions sur la peine capital (Reflections on the Guillotine) (Camus), 2:23
Réflexions sur la Question Juive (Anti-Semite and Jew) (Sartre), 8:610
Reflexions sur la violence (Réflections on violence) (Sorel), 9:132
"Réflexions sur le Phlogistique" (Lavoisier), 5:217
Reflexive act, intuitive cognition of, 9:774
Reflexive relation, 4:568, 5:555
Reflexivity, mind and, 6:81
Reform
Bergson on, 1:571
education as, 7:366
irrationality and, 4:752
and "law as it ought," 1:553
and moral obligations in business, 1:779–780
neo-Confucian, 2:158
punishment and, 8:165–167
utopianism and, 9:619–620
Reformation, **8:295–298**
age of, 8:295–297
Aristotelianism in, 1:261
deists on, 2:683
education in, 7:369
Erasmus and, 3:338–339
Franck on, 3:713
Lucian of Samosata and, 5:597
Melanchthon in, 6:119
moral, 8:166–167
political philosophy and, 7:661–662
Servetus and, 8:831
skepticism in, 9:50–52
social contract theory and, 9:81
Reformed churches, 8:296
Reformed epistemology, 7:481–482
Refusal of permission, *vs.* request, in medical ethics, 3:457–458
Refutation by logical analogy, definition of, 5:534
Réfutation de l'ouvrage d'Helvétius (Refutation of Helvétius) (Diderot), 3:71
Réfutation de Spinoza (Boulainvilliers), 9:193

Refutation des erreurs de Bonoit de Spinoza (Boulainvilliers), 1:670
Refutation of Deism (Shelley), 9:8
"Refutation of Idealism" (Kant), 9:44
"Refutation of Idealism, The" (Moore), 3:125, 3:314, 4:559, 8:821, 9:200
"Refutation of Philosophy" (al-Ghazālī), 6:558
"Refutation of Realism, The" (Stace), 9:200
Refutation of the Materalists (al-Afghānī), 3:248–249
"Refutation of the Principles of Christianity" (Crescas), 2:592
Refutations (Zeno), 9:253
Regan, Tom, on environmental ethics, 3:259
Regeneration, will in, 6:119
Regents of the State of California, Tarisoff v., 6:95
Regents of the University of California v. Blake (1978), 1:82
Regicide, in Mencius, 2:232
Regimented language, 8:218–219
Régis, Pierre Sylvain, **8:299–300**
  Cartesianism of, 2:56
  Desgabets and, 2:759
  on God, 5:666–667
  Malebranche and, 2:61, 5:665–666
  Tschirnhaus and, 9:549
Regius, Henricus (Henry de Roy), **8:301**
  Descartes and, 2:55, 2:754
  empiricism of, 2:55
  on mind-body problem, 2:750
Regnum Animale (Swedenborg), 9:336
Regress
  in classical foundationalism, 2:275
  of justification, terminating, 5:92
  of justified modal beliefs, 5:80
  in resemblance theory, 9:601
  Zabarella on, 9:867
Regress-generating property, 9:584
Regularities of convention, in meaning, 6:84
Regularity (Humean) view of laws of nature, 5:225–231
Regularity theory, Köhler criticized by defenders of, 5:132
Regularity view, of causation, 7:276
Rehabilitation, 8:165–167
Rehmke, Johannes, **8:302–304**
Reich, Wilhelm, 7:523, **8:304–316**
Reichenbach, Hans, **8:318–322**
  on common cause principle, 2:342, 8:686
  on conventionalism of space, 2:521–522
  on direction of time, 7:542
  emotive theory and, 3:425
  on empirical methodology, 8:170, 8:693
  on explanation, 3:524
  on force, 3:235
  interpretations of, 8:321–322
  life of, 8:318–319
  and Markov condition, 8:687
  on measurement, 8:170
  on paradigmatic inductive situation, 4:643
  in probability theory, 8:32
  Putnam and, 8:170
  Salmon and, 8:593
  on straight rule of inductive inferences, 8:594
  on temporal entropy, 9:469
  on temporal metric, 9:494
  on time, 7:566
    entropy and, 9:469
    measurement of, 9:494
    tenseless theory of, 9:475
Reid, Thomas, **8:322–329**
  on active judgment in aesthetic process, 4:65
  Alison and, 1:128–129
  on causation, 3:18
  common-sense theory of, 2:356
    intuition in, 3:409
    Stewart on, 9:246–247
  on conscience, 3:409
  and Cousin, 2:579
  and crisis of skepticism, 9:56
  on deliberation, 3:18
  on determinism, 3:15, 3:17, 3:18, 3:19
  on epistemology of testimony, 9:402
  on ether theories, 8:700
  on fictional objects, existence of, 3:494–495
  on force and consciousness, 3:689
  Gerard and, 4:64
  on Hume, 3:305–306, 9:248
  on ideas, 3:494–495
  Lehrer and, 5:248
  Mansel and, 5:687
  Martineau and, 5:726
  on memory, 6:125
  on motive, 3:19, 3:20
  particularism of, 3:278
  on personal identity, 4:612, 7:230
  Royer-Collard and, 8:523–524
  Sciacca on, 8:666
  Shepherd on, 9:10
  Sidgwick and, 9:23
  skepticism of, 9:56
  on testimony, 7:357
  on virtue and vice, 9:247
Reidentification
  criteria for, 7:221–223, 7:226
  vs. individuation, 7:213–214
  processes of, 7:213, 7:215
Reification, in classical Indian philosophy, 6:470
Reign of Terror, 9:395
Reikon ichigenron (Monism of the soul) (Nishi), 6:623
Reimarus, Elise, *Pantheismusstreit* and, 7:100
Reimarus, Hermann Samuel, **8:330–331**
  deism and, 2:688
  Lessing and, 5:295
Reinach, Adolf
  in phenomenology, 7:279
  Stein and, 9:239
Reincarnation, **8:331–333**
  in Buddhism, 1:723, 2:111, 6:255–256
  cause of, 6:620
  Empedocles on, 3:210, 3:212
  and evil, problem of, 3:476
  and immortality, 4:617
  in Indian philosophy, 5:326–327
  Jainism on, 2:111, 5:327
  karma and, 2:110, 2:111, 5:41
  materialism and, 6:14
  McTaggart on, 6:77
  nirvāṇa and, 6:620–621
  in Orphism, 7:43
  parapsychology and, 7:113–116
  personal identity and, 7:229–230
  Plotinus on, 7:634
  See also Rebirth
Reiner, Hans
  ethics, 3:422–423
  on life, meaning and value of, 5:354–355
Reinforcement, 9:61, 9:62
Reinhard, A. F., Crusius and, 2:605
Reinhardt, K., on Parmenides of Elea, 7:126
Reinhardt, William, 8:845
Reinhold, Fichte und Schelling (Fries), 3:751
Reinhold, Karl Leonhard, **8:333–335**
  Fries and, 3:751
  Maimon and, 5:646–647
  Schulze on, 8:660
Reism, 5:144
  vs. theory of assumptions, 6:116
  theory of objects and, 6:115
  See also Concretism
Reject-West Party, 5:139

Rekishi tetsugaku (Philosophy of history) (Miki), 6:216
Relation(s), 3:642
 Carnap on, 2:40
 Cassirer on, 2:67
 Chatton on, 2:139
 consciousness as, 6:75
 in conversational implicature, 2:526
 De Morgan on, 5:448, 5:449
 definition of, 5:555
 existential, 1:689
 external, Pitkin on, 6:587
 in identity, 4:568
 inferential, in Buddhist epistemology, 1:757
 internal and external, **8:335–344**
 Locke on, 5:381, 5:384
 meaning and, 7:401–402
 in monadology, 6:324–325
 natural, 4:491
 as object of knowledge, 8:640
 to objects, 6:81
 Ockham on, 2:139
 ontology and, 1:562, 7:25
 philosophical, 4:491
 power as, 7:731–733
 psychical, 1:689
 vs. qualities, 3:549
 in reductionist causality, 2:96
 of reproduction, 3:601
 in science of human nature, 4:490–491
 as self-contradictory appearance, 1:678
 in states of affairs, 7:25
 of substances to parts, 6:78
 in Tetens, establishment of, 9:404
 vs. things, 3:549
 types of, 5:555
 universal, in logic, 9:827
Relation de Groenland (La Peyrère), 5:196
Relation de l'Islande (La Peyrère), 5:196
Relation symbol, 3:645
Relational arguments, as fallacies, 3:540
Relational autonomy, 1:158
Relational conception
 of person, 3:579
 of self-hood, in Hegel *vs.* Kierkegaard, 5:67
Relational dualism, 6:331
Relational good, of friendship, 3:749
Relational proposition, definition of, 5:553
Relational syllogisms, 5:408
Relational symbols, 3:647
Relationism, 5:686, 9:155
Relations theory, of McGilvary, 6:75–76
Relationships
 Buber on, 1:715
 causal, 2:107
 centrality of, 3:579
 in Confucianism, 2:172–173
 I-it and I-thou, 1:715
 of law, 3:617
 logical formulation of, 9:748
 looking/looked at model of, 8:607–608
 ontology and, 1:562
 Spann on, 9:158
 of things, as observer *vs.* as person, 1:715
Relative identity, 4:572, 9:762
Relative-state quantum mechanics, 5:696–698
Relativism
 aesthetic qualities in, 1:39–40
 Aliotta on, 1:127
 Anderson (John) on, 1:198
 Buddhism and, 1:745
 conservatism and, 2:466–467
 cultural, 3:368, 5:673
 Eddington on, 3:165
 Geyser on, 4:82
 of health, 7:465
 of historical knowledge, 7:398–399
 of illusions, 4:588–589
 incommensurability as, 8:696–697
 in induction, 8:28–29
 of internal properties, 8:342–344
 Kuhn and, 5:159
 in law, 7:427
 Lukács on, 5:604
 and mechanics, cosmological principle creation and, 2:562
 on miracles, 6:267–268
 Moleschott and, 6:320
 moral, 2:472, 7:718, 8:50
 of motion, in Newton, 6:592
 natural law and, 6:514–515
 of neopragmatism, 7:642
 new realism and, 6:585–586
 of normality, 7:465
 objective
  McGilvary and, 6:75
  Murphy and, 6:435–436
 of perception, 1:31
 and positivism, 7:268, 8:180
 Posner on, 7:718
 in pragmatic theory of truth, 9:537
 Prodicus and, 8:45
 progress and, 8:50
 Protagorean, 1:230–231
 of qualities, 8:9
 Radbruch and, 8:229–230
 Rorty and, 7:751
 in science, 6:502
 Shestov on, 9:12
 of shifts-in-standards, 8:698–699
 Stich and, 7:751
 Sumner and, 9:326
 of taste, 1:39–40
 Thomson (Judith) on, 9:449
 time in, 7:475
 Williams (Bernard) and, 9:787
 Wittgenstein and, 9:818
Relativism [term], 3:369
Relativismo e idealismo (Aliotta), 1:127
Relativity, **8:345–357**
 Bergson on, 9:489
 in Bohmian mechanics, 1:635
 in Buddhism, 1:745
 Carroll and, 2:51–52
 common cause principle and, 2:343
 connectibility in, 9:471
 consciousness and, 5:143
 conservation laws and, 3:234
 and cosmology, 2:559–562
 determinism and, 3:32–33
 Eddington on, 3:164–165
 Einstein and, 3:178–180
 Galilean, 2:462, 4:11
 Gauge Theory and, 4:31–33
 general. *See* General relativity
 geometries of, 4:61, 8:319–320
 of illusions, 4:588–589
 of internal properties, 8:342–344
 intuitive time in, 4:118–119
 Lovejoy on, 5:592
 Meyerson on, 6:213
 of motion, 4:11, 6:413–415
 naturalism and, 9:499
 Newton and, 6:592
 nominalism and, 6:628–629
 Palágyi on, 7:74
 of perception, 4:586
 Platonism and, 8:645
 quantum theory and, 6:639–642
 in Schlick's critique of Kantianism, 8:639
 science and, 1:694, 9:580
 in sense-datum theory, 8:816, 8:820
 of simultaneity, 9:150
 space and, 2:522–523
 space-time in, 3:159, 9:464–465, 9:496–497
 special. *See* Special relativity
 statements on physical states in, 8:639

Relativity, ***continued***
of theoretical truth, Shestov on, 9:12
thought experiment in, 9:453–454
unified field theory in, Weyl and, 9:741
verified consequences and, 2:438
Whitehead and, 9:749
Relativity Theory of Protons and Electrons (Eddington), 3:164
Relevance
Abelard on, 5:427–428
attributor contextualism and, 2:486
definition of, 5:106
determination of, 1:446
systems of, 8:665
Relevance of Beauty, The (Gadamer), 4:3
Relevance (relevant) logics, **8:358–359**
Relevant alternatives, 5:106, **8:359–362**
Relevant logic, 5:488
Relevant-information rationality, 8:254
Reliabilism, **8:362–366**
accidental *vs.* non-accidental, 9:136
as antiskeptical strategy, 9:44
in justification of knowledge, 3:272–273
naturalism of, 6:498
problems with, 8:363–365
solipsism and, 9:120
and subjectivism, 9:290
virtue perspectivism as, 9:136
Reliability, of beliefs, in noninferential foundationalism, 2:278
Reliability of Sense Perception, The (Alston), 1:132
Relief theories of humor, 4:517
"Religation," 9:888
Religieuse, La (The nun) (Diderot), 3:71, 3:76
Religiia Dionisa (The religion of Dionysus) (Ivanov), 4:766
Religio catholica, of Spinoza, 4:826
Religio Laici (Blount), 1:619
Religio Laici (Dryden), 2:681
Religio Rationalis (Wiszowaty), 9:100
Religion, **8:366–372**
absolute, Parker (T.) on, 7:122
adherents, arguments among, 3:536
agnosticism and, 1:92–95
allegorical nature of, in moral order, 9:8
in analytic philosophy, 7:478–479
in ancient Greece, 7:487–490
Anselm in, 7:491
antecedents of, James on, 4:780
Aquinas in, 7:491–492
Aristotelian God and, 4:816
Aristotle in, 7:489
art in, Tolstoy on, 9:514
Augustine in, 7:491
Averroes on, 1:426–427
Avicenna on, 1:434
Ayer on, 7:478
Bentham on, 1:556–557
Bergson on, 1:571
Berkeley on, 3:301
and biological sciences, 4:43–48, **8:393–397**
Blake on, 1:610
Boulainvilliers on, 1:670
Bultmann on, 1:762–764
characteristics of, 8:368–369
in Chinese philosophy, 2:223–231
Cicero on, 2:258
Cockburn on, 2:295
cognitive aspects of, 1:142, 7:59
collective guilt in, 4:194–195
collective unconscious in, 4:857–858
Collins on, 2:330–331
Comenius on, 2:341
Comte on, 2:410–412, 7:712
Confucius on, 2:443
conservatism and, 2:466
Costa on, 2:572
Cousin on, 2:579
critical symbolism and, 8:587
Croce on, 2:602
cultural concept of, 2:223–224
Damarsais on, 2:266
Daoist, *vs.* philosophy, 2:186
and death, 2:227
Destutt de Tracy on, 2:760–761
Diderot on, 3:77
discontinuous and ameliorative types of, 2:224–225
divine illumination in, 4:580
dogma in, 1:571, 6:78
Dühring on, 3:131
Durkheim on, 3:151–152
Edwards (Jonathan) on, 3:168–169
Eliot (George) on, 3:184
empiricism and, 7:478, 7:492–496
Encyclopédie on, 3:224
Enlightenment and, 3:243–246
eschatological verifiability in, 7:478
and ethics, 3:391, 7:261, 7:332, 8:591
experience and, 7:713
experimental science and, 1:674–675
features of, 8:368–369
Fëdorov and, 3:558
Feuerbach on, 3:611–612
Fiske on, 3:668
Flew on, 7:478
Franck on, 3:713
in French Revolution, 9:520
Fréret on, 2:265–266
Freud on, 3:611, 3:745–747, 8:378–380
fulfillment through, 2:224–225
fundamentalist, as reaction to globalization, 9:98
Gassendi on, 4:29–30
Glanvill on, 4:96–97
God in, 7:479
Goethe on, 4:143
and grace, 1:477
Haeckel on, 4:203–204
Hazlitt and, 4:249
Hegel and, 3:610, 4:264, 4:269
Heraclitus in, 7:487–488
Herbert of Cherbury on, 4:327–328
Herder on, 4:333–334
Hermetic magic as, 1:710
Hick on, 7:478, 7:482
historical recollections and, 3:747
Hobbes on, 4:420–424
of humanity, 3:668, 6:230
Hume on, 4:509–513
Huxley on, 4:533
I-it *vs.* I-thou relations in, 1:716
immortality in, 4:618–619
in Indian philosophy, 4:624
Islamic philosophy and, 4:550
James (William) on, 3:531–532
belief in, 4:780–781
evolutionary theory in, 4:779–780
experience in, 4:779
Johnson (Dr. Samuel) on, 4:853–854
Jung on, 8:146–147, 8:379
Kant and, 5:30, 7:493
Kaufmann and, 5:46
Lamennais on, 5:177
Leibniz on, 5:253
Leopardi on, 5:286
linguistics and, 7:495
Locke on, 3:391, 5:391–392, 5:395
Lotze on, 5:581–581
love in, 1:373–374
Lunacharskii on, 5:611–612
in Marxism, 5:737
of Masaryk, 6:2
materialism and, 6:7–9
McTaggart on, 6:78

Meslier on, 6:154–155
Mill (John Stuart) on, 6:229–230, 7:713
Mohist teaching on, 2:151
Montague (William) on, 6:332
Montesquieu on, 6:338–339
and morality, **8:382–388,** 9:739
atheism and, 1:505
Baader and, 1:439
causal dependence of, 8:384–385
conceptual dependence of, 8:385–386
epistemic dependence of, 8:386–387
in James's philosophy of religion, 4:779
metaphysical dependence of, 8:387
Nicolai on, 6:598
as rational relationship, 1:505
Saint-Simon on, 8:591
Shestov on, 9:11, 9:13
Sidgwick on, 9:22
on suicide, 9:320
Swift's satires on, 9:340–341
Taylor (Alfred) on, 9:373
More (Henry) and, 6:396–397
myth and, 2:68, 9:262
Napoleon and, 4:573
natural. *See* Natural religion
natural law and, 6:510, 6:514–515
natural philosophy and, 1:444
naturalism and, 6:493, 7:59
naturalistic reconstructions of, **8:373–377**
Neoplatonism in, 7:490
Niebuhr on, 6:605–606
noncognitive/nonpropositional and, 3:535
Oman on, 7:14
omniscience in, 7:479
Otto on, 7:59–61
pagan, Vico on, 9:675
Paine on, 7:73–74
Palmer (E.) on, 7:78
Parker (T.) on, 7:121
Parmenides in, 7:487–488
Pascal on, 7:131–134
Pater on, 7:136
personalism and, 7:235–236
persuasive world-view representation by, 2:229
Peter Lombard on, 7:261
philosophical
Carus (Paul) on, 2:64
Channing and, 2:130–131
and philosophy, 3:623, 4:111–112, 7:573
Green on, 4:179
Maimonides on, 5:648
Pico della Mirandola on, 7:573
as philosophy for the masses, 4:757
philosophy of, 7:327, **7:478–503**
Abelard on, 1:7
animism in, 1:710
Athens *vs.* Jerusalem in, 9:11
of Baader (Franz Xavier von), 1:439
Braithwaite and, 1:686
in Bruno's hermeticism, 1:710
in Calvin, 2:8–12
in Card, 2:4
Chaadaev and, 2:120–121
Chinese, 2:223–231
Collingwood on, 2:326
in common claims *vs.* religious claims, 2:228
consolation and death in, 2:227
definition of, 7:327
Ducasse on, 3:125
of Fichte, 3:618
genre and persuasion in, 2:228–230
of Hatano, 4:247
of Hegel, 4:276–277, 4:284
historical *vs.* phenomenal analysis in, 2:224
history of, **7:485–498**
Hume's "Of Miracles" in, 6:270
Ii'in in, 4:577
in Ionescu, 4:743
I-thou *vs.* I-it relationships, 1:716
Jacobi (Friedrich Heinrich), 4:772
literalism and indirect discourse in, 2:230
origins of, 2:691
Plantinga and, 7:581
Royce on, 8:521–522
Shestov in, 9:13
social manipulation analysis in, 2:226–227
social values in, 2:226–227
Ziehen (Theodor) on, 9:884
and physical sciences, **8:397–401,** 8:588
as pious study, 1:506
Planck on, 7:579
Plato on, 7:488–489
and politics, **8:389–393**
Popper-Lynkeus on, 7:697–699
primitive
common consent arguments for God's existence and, 2:348
supernatural in, 7:14
prophetic, natural in, 7:14
psychological explanations of, **8:377–382**
of Pythagoreans, 8:181–182
rationalism in, 7:492
Reformation and, 8:295–298, 9:50–52
Reich on, 8:313–315
and religious pluralism, 8:420
Renan on, 8:429
Rensi on, 8:433
repression and, 1:374
reproductive technologies and, 4:45
Ritschl on, 8:480–481
Rousseau on, 8:513–515
Rozanov on, 8:525
Russell on, 8:559–561
Saint-Simon on, 8:591
Santayana on, 8:599
Schiller (Ferdinand) on, 8:625
Schlegel on, 8:631
Schleiermacher on, 7:97, 8:632–635
science and, 9:393
"how" and "why" in, 9:754
interaction of, 8:395
separation of, 8:394–395
skepticism and, 9:50–52
Smith (John) on, 9:70
Socrates on, 9:109–110
sophists on, 9:130
Spinoza on, 4:826, 9:191
stability and historical change in, 1:720
Stoicism in, 7:489
Swift on, 9:340
teleological argument in, 7:481
Tennant on, 9:393
vs. theological philosophy, 7:478–479
Tillich on, 9:460
Tindal on, 9:503
toleration and, 1:502, 9:507–509
Tolstoy on, 9:512
traditions in, 1:284, 2:225
and truth, 3:630, 7:14, 7:478, 7:482
in 20th century, 7:497–498
types of, 8:369–372
Unamuno on, 9:567
in unconscious, development of, 9:573
universal, 2:410, 9:674–675
utopianism of, 9:618

Religion, ***continued***
Vaihinger on, 9:628
value of
James on, 4:780
Nasr on, 6:479, 6:480
Vaz Ferreira on, 9:654–655
Vico on, 9:674–675
virtue and, 2:227–228, 9:2–3
Voltaire and, 9:709–712
Whitehead on, 9:752
"why" questions in, 9:754
Wilson (Edward O.) on, 9:789
wish-fulfillments and, 3:747
Wittgenstinian approach to, 7:478
Woolston and, 9:844–845
Wright (Chauncey) and, 9:847
See also Belief(s), religious
Religion and Philosophy (Collingwood), 2:325
Religion and the Order of Nature (Nasr), 6:480
Religion aus den Quellen des Judentums, Die (Cohen), 2:304
Religion der Vernunft aus den Quellen de Judentums, Die (Religion of reason from sources of Judaism) (Cohen), 4:828–829
Religion des Geistes, Die (The religion of the spirit) (Formstecher), 4:827
Religion of a Scientist (Fechner), 7:82–83
Religion of Man, The (Tagore), 9:363, 9:364
Religion of Nature Delineated, The (Wollaston), 2:683–684, 9:833
Religion und Philosophie (Brentano), 1:692
Religion within the Limits of Reason Alone (Kant), 2:689, 5:8, 5:30, 8:627
Religions in Four Dimensions: Existential and Aesthetic, Historical and Comparative (Kaufmann), 5:46
Religionsphilosophie (Scholz), 8:645
Religionsphilosophie der Juden, Die (The philosophy of religion of the Jews) (Hirsch), 4:827
Religionznyi smysl filosofii (The religious meaning of philosophy) (Il'in), 4:577
Religious Aspect of Philosophy, The (Royce), 4:286
Religious assertion, 7:478
Religious beliefs. *See* Belief(s), religious
Religious believer, faith possessed by, 3:532
Religious cognition, and knowledge, 3:532
Religious conversion, Kierkegaard on, 5:67
Religious cosmology, 7:310–311
Religious education, Pestalozzi on, 7:255
Religious emanationism, 3:189
Religious existentialism, 7:495, 8:498
Religious experience, 1:711–712, **8:401–403**
and absolute dependence, 8:636–637
Alston on, 7:482
anthropology of, Pannenberg on, 7:80–81
in argument for existence of God, **8:404–410**
Bruno on, 1:711
empiricism and, 8:420
epistemological status of, 8:406–407
faith and, 3:533
in knowledge of God, 4:112
Mead on, 6:81
nature of, 8:405–406
psychological explanations for, 8:409–410
rationality of, 1:479
verifiability of, 8:407–409
See also Mystical experience
Religious humanism, in existentialism, 3:506
Religious knowledge
gaining, 3:531
Otto on, 7:59, 7:61
Religious language, 7:478, **8:411–419**
Barthes on, 1:481
nonassertive interpretations of, 8:414–417
ritualistic interpretation of, 8:415
Religious law
Maimonides on, 4:819
philosophy and, 4:811
Saadya on, 4:813
Religious life, 2:224–225
Religious metaphysics, Karsavin's system of, 5:43
Religious Musings (Coleridge), 2:316
Religious pessimism, history of, 7:246
Religious pluralism, 4:744, 8:389–390, **8:419–420**
Religious rites, Iamblichus on, 6:551
Religious significance, of events, 3:534
Religious texts
critical evaluation of, 9:33
literal sense of, *vs.* philosophical sense, 4:809
Religious truth
Oman on, 7:15
reason and, 7:59
Religious verification
vs. scientific verification, 3:532
Tennant and, 3:532
Religious warfare, 8:392
Religious-Philosophical Society, 5:573
Remarks on Colour (Wittgenstein), 9:817
"Remarks on Frazier's *Golden Bough*" (Wittgenstein), 9:818
Remarks on the Foundations of Mathematics (Wittgenstein), 9:809
Remarks upon Some Writers in the Controversy concerning the Foundation of Moral Virtue and Obligation (Cockburn), 2:294
Remarks upon the Principles of Reasonings of Dr. Rutherforth's Essay (Cockburn), 2:294
Remarques critiques (Turgot), 8:784
Remarques sur les pensées de Pascal (Voltaire), 9:708
Remembering (Bartlett), 9:77
Remembering (Martin and Deutscher), 6:124
Remembering how, *vs.* remembering that, 5:98
Reminiscence
in Condillac, 2:422
doctrine of, 4:606–607
Remond, Nicolas, Leibniz and, 5:254
Remonstrance, Great, 1:285–286
Remote "steering," teleportation as, 8:199
Remote viewing, 7:113
Ren (human-heartedness)
in Confucian ultimate reality, 2:220
vs. Dao, Wang Yang-ming on, 9:726
Mencius on, 6:129–130
in *tai qi*, Zhu Xi on, 4:794
Wang Yang-mingo and, 9:725–726
Xunzi on, 9:856–857
Zhang Zai on, 9:880
Renaissance, **8:421–427**
aesthetics in, 1:48–49
Aristotelianism in, 1:261, 1:279–280
art in, 1:48–49
awareness of death in, 2:651
chronological limits of, 8:422
democratic thinking in, 9:137
education and, 7:368–369
epistemology of, 3:291, 8:772
Erasmus and, 3:338
geographical limits of, 8:422–423
Gerson as typifying, 4:67
hermeticism in, 4:337–338

hieroglyphic interpretation in, 9:338
humanism in, 4:478–481, 8:424–426
and education in 17th century, 2:720–721
Petrarch and, 7:263–265
Islamic, 1:427, 3:248–249
Jewish philosophy in, 4:824
law in, 7:422–423
logic of, 8:772
love in, 5:587–588
microcosm in, 5:641–642
Neoplatonism in
Colet and, 2:322
in hermetic philosophy, 1:710
optimism/pessimism in, 7:247
painting, 1:330–331
philosophy
Bruno and, 1:708–712
and contemplative *vs.* practical life, 1:444
Goethe and, 1:470
humanism and, 1:450
philosophy of law in, 7:422–423
Platonism in, 1:48, 3:671, 7:612–613
republicanism in, 8:435
science in, 8:423
semantics of, 8:772
skepticism in, 4:30, 9:50
social values in, 8:423–424
in Spengler's cultural morphology, 9:166
state in, 9:204
Thomism in, 9:445
on war and peace, 7:152, 7:154
Renaissance, The (Gobineau), 4:106
Renaissance, The (Pater), 7:136–137
Renaissance episteme, 3:700
Renan, Joseph Ernest, **8:428–429**
Averroism and, 1:430–431
Loisy and, 5:570
on nationality as language, 6:482
on Spinoza, 9:191–192
Tagore and, 9:364
Reneri, Henri, 2:736
Renner, Karl, on law and economy, 7:427
Renoir, Pierre-Auguste, Merleau-Ponty on, 6:151
Renouvier, Charles Bernard, 4:775, **8:429–432**
James and, 4:775
Lequier and, 5:287
panpsychism and, 7:83
on personalism, 7:233
Rensi, Giuseppe, **8:433**
Renunciation, Mill (John Stuart) on, 3:413
Repentance, 7:307
Repercussorium (Peter Aureol), 7:255–257
Replacement, axiom of (axiom of substitution), 5:520, 5:555
Replicas
in architecture, 9:693–694
in painting, 9:691
in sculpture, 9:692
Reply (Anselm), 7:15
"Reply on Behalf of the Fool" (Gaunilo), 4:33
Reply to Boindin (Maupertuis), 8:783–784
Reply to Colotes (Plutarch), 3:263
"Reply to Leonard Linsky" (Carnap), 9:347
"Reply to My Critics" (Moore), 2:673
Reply to the Letter of Porphyry to Anebo (Iamblichus), 4:539
Réponse aux reflections de Bayle (Leibniz), 4:552
Reporario (Chatton), 2:139
Report on the EDVAC (von Neumann), 2:405
Reportatio (Ockham), 9:771
Representation
in art, 1:297, **1:324–330**
axioms of, 6:88–90
Cassirer on, 2:66–67
cognitive science and, 2:299
colors and, 2:333
in combinatory logic, 2:334
compositionality and, 2:370
concepts and, 2:416, 2:480–481
connectionist models in computationalism and, 2:392
disintegration of, 3:700
in dreams, 7:405
experientialism and, 1:327–329
form of, in picture theory, 9:804
in images, 7:405
intelligibility of, 1:326–327
limits of, 3:700
Marxist epistemology as, 5:736–737
memory as, 6:124–125
mimesis and, 6:251
in music, 6:437–438
and nonconceptual mental content, 2:480–481
in picture theory, 9:804
political, 2:700–701
in postcolonialism, 7:727–728
primacy of, 3:700
problem of, resolving, 3:710
proportional, 6:229
Régis on, 8:299–300
semiotics and, 1:327
by soul, 9:325
sublimity in, 9:293
systemic *vs.* acquired, 3:109
in Yogācāra Buddhism, 1:747–749
Representation and Invariance of Scientific Structures (Suppes), 9:334
Representation 'I,' for Kant, 5:21
Representation theorem, 9:334
Representational meaning, 7:402–405, 9:835
Representational part, of computational/representational theory of thought, 3:675
Representational theory
of measurement, 6:89–91
of mind, 6:141–142
computationalism and, 2:391–392
language of thought and, 5:191–192
memory in, 6:124
Representationalism, 8:194
consciousness in, 2:455
Jackson (Frank) on, 5:115
Marxist epistemology as, 5:736–737
propositional attitudes and, 8:78
Representative, of cardinal number, definition of, 5:555
Representative government
vs. democracy, 2:700–701, 2:704
Mill (James) on, 6:219
Mill (John Stuart) on, 6:228–229
Representative Government (Mill, John Stuart), 2:34
Representative Men (Emerson), 3:195
Representative realism, 8:8–9, 8:265–266
on causation of sense data, 8:819
on memory, 6:124
perception and, 7:179–186
phenomenalism and, 7:271–273
Repression
cathartic lifting of, 3:737
and consciousness, 3:739
in dynamic unconscious, 3:738
in Freudian unconscious, 9:572
of homosexuality, 8:112
Merleau-Ponty on, 6:150
and neurosis, 3:742
psychic mechanism of, 3:738
in psychoanalytic theory, 8:109–111
Reich on, 8:307–309
religion and, 1:374
theory of, 3:738

Repressive hypothesis, 3:701
Reproduction
differential, 7:338
ethical issues in, 4:43–48
in Manichaeism, 5:683
of performances, 1:323
Robinet on, 8:482
See also Sex
Republic (Bodin), 1:621
*Republic (*Diogenes of Sinope), 3:90
Republic (Plato), 1:512, 1:777, 2:16, 2:201, 7:247
on aesthetics, 1:41, 1:187
on altruism, 3:170
on analogy of light, 4:579–580
on art, 1:333
author's family in, 7:582
Averroes on, 1:422
beauty in, 1:512
Campanella and, 2:16
on civil disobedience, 2:260
on civilization, 9:617–618
Colotes of Lampsacus on, 3:263
on conflicting interests, 9:206
dating of, 9:107
on dialectic, 3:53, 7:593
on dogma, 3:96–97
on economics, 7:350
on education, 1:263–264, 7:365–366, 7:594
on embodiment, 7:635
ethics in, 1:777, 2:201, 3:396
on Forms, 2:665, 3:358, 7:595–596
on geometry, 4:54
on God, 3:358, 4:111
on the Good, 7:608, 9:112
on Greek Academy, 4:172
on human good, 9:112
on imitation, 1:324, 6:252
on immortality, 4:609
on justice, 3:174
on knowledge, 7:599
on love, 7:589
on metaphor, 2:699
on metaphysics, 1:187
on mimesis, 6:252
on natural law, 6:506
Orphic influence in, 7:43
ousia in, 7:63
on poetry, 4:175, 7:585–586
on political organization, 3:397
as political utopia, 9:618
Proclus on, 1:190, 7:609
on profitability of justice, 3:174
on psychic disorder, 7:590
on sense experience, 8:824
on social theory, 7:590–591
on sophists, 9:130
on soul, 4:607, 8:103
on suicide, 9:319
on tragedy, 9:521–522
on virtue, 1:256
on vision and understanding, 1:393–394
on war and peace, 7:152
and Zeno of Citium, 9:253, 9:869
Republic (Zeno of Citium), 9:253, 9:869
Republicanism, **8:434–438**
communitarianism and, 2:369
of Jefferson, 4:805
of Marsilius of Padua, 5:723
Palmer (E.) and, 7:78
Schlegel on, 8:630
Repugnant conclusion, Parfit on, 7:120
Repulsion, in Yoga, 6:108
Request, *vs.* refusal of permission, in medical ethics, 3:457–458
Required actions, 6:118
Requiredness, Köhler on, 5:132
Requirements of significance, neglect of, 3:545
Rescher, Nicholas, **8:438–440**
on Peirce, 7:751
pragmatism of, 7:748, 7:751
Research
androcentrism in, screening out, 3:594
animal, 1:208–209
applied *vs.* pure, 9:827
cognitive science, 2:299–300
Confucian, 2:182
cosmology, 2:565–566
ethics of, 8:668
feminist, 3:574
on happiness, 9:642
intelligence, 1:596
logic and, 2:40
medical
agenda of, allocation and, 6:96
auto-icon of Bentham, 1:557
bioethical issues in, 1:603
in methodology, 8:682–683
psychical, 1:698. *See also* Parapsychology
in psychology, 8:152
pure *vs.* applied, Wolff and, 9:827
questions for, values influencing choice of, 3:576
scientific, ethics of, **8:667–669**
sexism in, 3:594
sociology, imperative in, 8:675
Resemblance
appearance and, 1:230
in conceptualism, 9:599
family
concepts as prototypes in, 2:418
as concepts in Wittgenstein, 2:417
nominalism and, 8:68, 9:599–600
particulars and, 6:174
theories, 9:586, 9:600–602
in nominalism, 9:600
objections to, 9:600–601
and universals, 6:178, 9:586, 9:589–602
Wittgenstein on, 9:601–602
Resentment
forgiveness as overcoming of, 3:697
as not necessarily vengeful or malicious, 3:697
Scheler on, 8:616
Residues, Pareto on, 7:118–119
Residues method of induction, 6:224, 6:243–244
Resistance
Aquinas on, 6:104
Freud on, 8:105
imaginative, paradox of, 4:601
to power, difficulty of, 3:701
in strict akratic action, 9:730–731
Resistance, Rebellion and Death (Camus), ethics in, 3:427
"Resistance to Civil Government" (Thoreau), 6:575
Resnik, Michael, on structures as patterns, 9:271
Resolution, beauty as, 1:67
Resolution calculus, 3:657
Resolutive order, Zabarella on, 9:867
Respect, 8:391, **8:441–442**
conduct justifiability and, 2:519
in contractualism, 2:518
deontological ethic of, 7:360
for persons, 5:37
in politics, 8:391
punishment and, 8:161–162
Respiration, Lavoisier on, 5:217
"Response to Sor Filotea" (Juana Inés de la Cruz), on women, 9:838
Response-dependence theories, **8:443–444**
Responsibility
in actions of states, 9:205
in Anscombe, 1:212–213
behavior and, 8:164
belief and unbelief in God and, 2:351
in Cain and Abel story, 4:831
in Calderoni, 2:8
in Card, 2:31
causality and, 8:164

in Chinese religion, 2:225
circumstance and, 8:164
compulsion and, 8:163–164
computer ethics and, 2:397
conscience and, 2:446
in consequentialism, 2:460
in determinism, 8:164
doxastic, 9:685–686
in education, 7:362
of elected officials in democracy, 2:701
epistemic, 9:685
extenuation and, 8:165
in Greek drama, 4:176–177
of group members, 8:609
Hume on, 8:164
insanity and, 8:163–164
intention and, 7:447
judgments of, 8:444–445, 9:686
legal, 8:448–450. *See also* Punishment
Levinas on, 4:830–831
luck egalitarianism and, 3:335
moral agents in business ethics, 1:778–779
moral and legal, **8:444–450,** 9:685
Aristotle on, 3:398
Augustine on, 3:402
behavior and, 1:460
in business ethics, 1:778–780
in Christian philosophy, 3:402
determinism and, 3:14–15, 3:23, 3:26–28, 3:33–34, 3:40
Dostoevsky on, 3:100
Duns Scotus on, 3:143
free agency and, 3:364
freedom and, 8:445–446
Hobbes on, 3:12
Hume on, 3:14, 3:409
meaning of, 8:445
Plato on, 3:398
punishment and, 3:384, 8:448–450
to others, Levinas on, 4:830–831
Pelagianism on, 7:175
personal, judgments of, 8:444–445
personhood and, 7:240
precognition and, 7:755
predictability and, 8:164
punishment and, 8:163–165
and recipient-oriented justice, 4:869
social, art as, 1:56–57
in state action, 9:205
technological power and, 7:545–546
temptation and, 8:163–164
women and, 2:31
Ressentiment (Scheler), 8:616
Rest, in Sanlun Buddhism, 2:161
Restall, Greg, and quantum logic, 5:492
Restitutio Christianismi (Servetus), 8:831
Restitutive justice, 4:865
Restraint, doctrine of, 8:389–391
Restriction, in medieval logic, 5:431–432
Restrictive terms, and syntax of scientific laws, 7:518
Resultant forces, *vs.* component, 3:691
Resultants, Morgan (C. Lloyd) on, 6:403
Resultate der Jacobi'schen und Mendelssohn'schen Philosophie, Die (Wizenman), 7:101
Resurrection
Aquinas on, 3:348, 4:603
Averroes on, 4:758
Christian monists on, 4:618
Christianity on, 3:348
Islamic philosophy on, 4:619
Leibniz on, 5:251, 5:268
reconstitution doctrine of, 4:602–603
in socinianism, 9:99
Resurrection (Tolstoy), 9:513
Resurrection of Jesus Considered: In Answer To the Tryal of the Witnesses (Annet), 1:210
Retributive justice, 4:865
Retributivism
justice and, 8:162
of Kant, 8:160
legalistic, 8:169
in punishment, 8:160–163, 8:168
Retrocognition, 7:113–114
Retrocognitive clairvoyance, 7:226
Retrocognizance, 7:226–227
Retrospection, bad conscience from, 4:787
Rettungen (Vindications) (Lessing), 5:294–295
Reuchlin, Johannes
Melanchthon and, 6:119
Pico della Mirandola and, 7:571
Reuleaux, Franz, 7:543
Reunion in Philosophy (White), 2:673
Réve de d'Alembert (D'Alembert's dream) (Diderot), 3:71–76
materialism in, 6:10
themes in, 3:410
Revealed law, Hooker on, 4:463
Revealed theology, 8:452
Revelation, **8:451–454**
as act of grace, 1:479
al-Fārābī on, 4:756
al-Kindī on, 1:130–131
Altmann on, 8:587
availability of, 1:763
Bonhoeffer on, 1:655
Boyle on, 1:675
Bulgakov on, 1:760
Cambridge Platonists on, 2:13
capacity for response to, 8:454
Charron on, 2:135
in Christianity, 1:650, 7:490–491
Chubb on, 2:253
Cumberland on, 2:615
deism on, 2:682, 2:685–686
as dialectical discourse, 1:707
in French clandestine writings, 2:265
general, 8:454
in Gnosticism, 4:102
of God, in nature, 1:580
Haeckel on, 4:203–204
Heilsgeschichtlich and, 8:453
history as, 7:81–82
Hobbes on, 4:421–422
Hume on, 4:512
judgment of, 8:454
Maimonides on, 5:652
Meslier on, 6:154
in miracles, 6:267–268
Mullā Ṣadrā on, 6:418
and pagan theology, 7:613–614
Pannenberg on, 7:81–82
as personal act, 1:707
vs. philosophical truth, 6:144
and philosophy of history, 1:655–656, 7:613–614
probability and, 1:782–783
in Proclus, 8:40
propositional concept of, 8:452
vs. rational, 1:505–506
of reality of things, 4:771
vs. reason, Steinheim on, 4:828
Reimarus on, 8:331
relational conception of, 1:479
Rosenzweig on, 4:829
Saadya on, 8:586
as sacrosanct and unchangeable, 5:2
special, 8:454
Swift on, 9:340
as symbolic truth, 4:757
Taylor (Alfred) on, 9:374
Thomasius on, 9:440
Revelation as History (Pannenberg, ed.), 7:81
Reverence, as predisposition of heart/mind, 6:129
Reverse mathematics, **8:455–456**
Reversibility thesis, 6:148–151

Review of the Principal Questions in Morals, A (Price), 8:2, 8:4
"Revision of Philosophy" (Goodman), 4:158
Revisionism, of aesthetic theory, 3:573
Revista de Filosofia, 4:686
Revius, Jocobus, 2:285, 2:753
Revivification of the Sciences of Religion (al-Ghazālī), 1:117, 9:305
Revolt
against human conditions *vs.* against injustice, 2:21–22
in psychology, 8:142–148
Revolt against Dualism, The (Lovejoy), 5:592
Revolt of the Masses, The (La Rebelion de las masas) (Ortega y Gasset), 7:47
Revolte, Le Kropotkin and, 5:154
Revolution
American, Price and, 8:1
art in, 1:69
Bakunin on, 2:361
Chateaubriand on, 2:137
in collectivism, 1:179
Comte on, 2:412
Engels on, 3:61–62
folkways as unchanged by, 9:326
French
anarchy and, 1:176
atheism and, 1:357
equality as concept in, 3:330
Fichte on, 1:377
French liberalism and, 5:320
Godwin on, 4:136
idéologues in, 4:573
Lavoisier and, 5:217
nation in, idea of, 6:481
Price on, 8:1
Taine on, 9:364, 9:365
terrorism in, 9:395
traditionalism in, 9:520–521
transcendentalism and, 6:573–574
Hegel on, 3:61
Manheim on, 5:685
Marković on, 5:719
Marsilius of Padua on, 5:722
Marx and, 5:730, 5:734
in mutualism, 1:179
myth in, 9:132–134, 9:134
nihilism and, 6:617
perpetual, 1:471
in philosophy, 7:108
political, and scientific, 5:158–159
in psychology, 8:142–148
as realization of philosophy, 5:735
vs. rebellion, in Stirner's anarchism, 9:251
right of
Locke on, 5:390
in Rousseau, 3:410
scientific progress as, 8:48
social
Bakunin and, 1:472
as primary, 1:472
in socialist thought, 9:89
Thoreau on, 9:451
Trotsky on, 1:69
violence in, 9:132–134
Young Hegelian argument for, 1:471
Revolution in Poetic Language (Kristeva), 5:152
Revolutionary(ies)
utopianism of, 9:618
women's potential as, 3:606
Revolutionary disciplinarianism, anarchism and, 3:554
Revolutionary legality, 7:427
Revolutionary movements
Burke on, 1:771–772
Maoism, 2:180–181
as radical rejection of human condition, 2:22
Revolutionary paradigm shift, 5:159
Revue de mathématique (periodical), 7:158
Revue de metaphysique et morale (Le Roy), 4:23
Revue philosophique (periodical), 5:306
Revue philosophique de la France et de l'étranger (journal), 8:457
Revue philosophique de Louvain (periodical), 6:143
Reward and punishment
Cumberland on, 2:615
Cyrenaics teaching on, 2:619
Mozi social and political philosophy, 2:236
Xunzi's social and political philosophy, 2:233
Rey, Abel, on eternal return doctrine, 3:355
Rey, Georges, 2:417, 3:183
Rey Pastor, Julio, 5:210
Reynolds, Edward, 3:187
Reynolds, Joshua, on art, 1:49
Ṛgveda, 5:116
liberation in, 5:327
meditation in, 6:107
on primordial oneness, 5:326
speech in, 7:413
Rhees, Rush, 9:806
Rheinische Thalia (journal), 8:626
Rhemes, in Peirce, 5:453
Rhetoric
argumentation and persuasion in, 2:229
in Aristotle, 1:264
Bacon (Francis) on, 1:443–445
Bain and, 1:463
in Chinese thought, 2:200–201, 2:222, 2:228–230
Cicero and, 2:258, 5:630
vs. dialectic, 1:264, 1:269
Epicurean School on, 3:263
in epistemology, 1:445
Gorgias of Leontini and, 4:162–163
as investigative method, 1:444
metaphor in, 1:729, 2:222
Newman (John Henry) and, 6:583
perspective and, 2:230
persuasion by, 2:229
in *Phaedrus* (Plato), 1:188
Philodemus on, 7:302
Plato and, 1:187–188, 4:175, 5:568, 7:592–594
probative *vs.* proairetic reasoning and, 2:213
purpose of, 1:443
Ramus on, 8:237
self-cultivation and, 2:230
sophistic teaching of, 9:130
in Stoicism, 9:255
William of Champeaux, 9:767
in Zen, 1:729
Rhetoric (Aristotle), 9:522
Arab logic and, 5:417
on emotions, 1:188, 3:198
tragedy in, 9:522
Rhetorical Spaces: Essays on Gendered Locations (Code), 2:296
Rhine, Joseph Banks, 7:113
Rhizomal thinking, 6:317
Rhymes (Dante), 2:623
Ri
elevating *ki* over, 5:7
Hayashi on, 4:248
Ogyū on, 7:10
Ribot, Théodule Armand, **8:456–457,** 9:364
Rice's theorem, in computability theory, 2:382
Richard, Mark, 1:536–537
Richard of Mediavilla, 3:141, **8:457–458**
Richard of Middleton. *See* Richard of Mediavilla
Richard of Saint Victor. *See* Saint Victor, School of
Richard Wagner in Bayreuth (Nietzsche), 6:608, 6:610

Richards, I. A., emotive theory and, 3:425
Richard's paradox, 5:518, 5:551
Richardson, Samuel, on love, 5:588
Richelieu, Cardinal de
La Mothe Le Vayer and, 5:182
La Rochefoucauld and, 5:200
Richenbach, Hans, on causality, 2:100–106
Richter, J. P. F., on unconscious, 9:571
Rickert, Heinrich, **8:458–460**
on definition, 2:667–668
on experience, 6:545
Fink and, 3:637
Frank (Erich) and, 3:715
on judgment, 6:544
in neo-Kantianism, 6:544
Pauler and, 7:145
Simmel and, 9:30
use of defining terms by, 4:38
Ricoeur, Paul, **8:460–466**
Dilthey and, 3:84
on Freud, 3:744
on history, 7:395–396
Lacan and, 5:168
on phenomenology, 7:300, 7:301
on postcolonialism, 7:727
Riḍā, Rashīd, 3:249
Ridicule
in Collins, 2:331
use of, 3:549
Ridley, Aaron, on music, 1:303
Rieber, Steven, 2:486
Riegl, Alois, on style, 1:331
Riehl, Alois, **8:467–468**
Driesch and, 3:110
on eternal return doctrine, 3:354
Liebert and, 5:343
in neo-Kantianism, 6:540–541
Riemann, Bernhard, 5:461
on derivatives and integrals in calculus, 2:496
on *n*-manifold *M*, 4:61–62
Riemannian Manifolds, 4:61–62
Rietdijk, C. W., 9:499
Right(s), **8:468–475**
of animals, **1:208–210**
to believe, and wishful thinking, 3:532
Bentham on, 1:553
in bioethics, 1:603
of citizens, 9:247
to commit suicide, 9:321
computer ethics and, 2:397
conceptual analyses of, 8:470–472
Condorcet on, 2:432
as creation of *volksgeist,* 8:615
of dead persons, 2:654
democratic government and, 2:701–704
of distant peoples, **3:92–93**
Dworkin on, 3:156
education as, 7:362
equivalent, for men and women, 4:746
of future generations, **3:92–93,** 3:258
Gewirth on, 4:81
Godwin on, 4:139
Green on, 4:180
human, 8:474–475
human nature and, 4:483
inalienable, Ockham on, 9:783–784
of individuals, in Confucian ethics, 2:196–197
juristic theories of, 8:469–470
legal sense of, 7:445
in libertarianism, 9:73
to life, personhood and, 7:242
Mill (John Stuart) on, 6:233
moral, 8:473
moral origin of, 4:180
Nozick on, 6:668
of ownership, 8:71–72
of patients, 6:93
philosophy of, *vs.* ethics, 6:536
possible possessors of, 8:472–473
private *vs.* public authority and, 9:204
property, 3:384, 7:75–76, 8:71
Cousin on, 2:579
ownership and, 8:71
in ultutarianism, 3:384
in Sen's economic theory, 8:810–811
sexual, 4:746
in social contract, 9:80
of suicide, 9:321
utilitarianism and, 7:459–460
violation of, as injustice, 4:866
See also Individual rights
Right and the Good, The (Ross), 3:440, 8:505
Right Hegelianism, 4:284
Righteousness
in Confucianism, 2:231
Yamazaki Ansai on, 9:860
Rightness, of actions
in act utilitarianism, 9:612
"can" as extensional permissive, 2:24
community governed by, Krause on, 5:148
deontological nonnaturalists on, 3:419
Krause on, 5:148
Mill (James) on, 6:219
Moore (G. E.) on, 3:419
objective and subjective senses of, 3:377
Ross (William David) on, 8:505
in rule utilitarianism, 9:613
in virtue ethics, 9:681
and wrong
distinction, conscience and, 2:445
as predisposition of heart/mind, 6:129
"Rights and Agency" (Sen), 8:810
Rights of Man, The (Paine), 7:73
Rights of the Christian Church Asserted, The (Tindal), 9:502
Rights of War and Peace, The (Grotius), 6:510
"Rights, Representation, and Reform" (Bentham), 1:553
Rigid designator, of a functional property, 3:759
Rignano, Eugenio, **8:476**
Rilke, Rainer Maria (René), **8:477–478**
Gadamer on, 4:3
Simmel and, 9:30
Rimini, Alberto, collapse theory of, 8:211
Rindler particles, 3:635
Rinrigaku (Ethics) (Watsuji), 4:797
Rintelen, Fritz-Joachim von, **8:479–480**
Ripheus, Dante on, 2:626
Ripley, George, 6:572
Rire, Le (Bergson), 1:57
"Rise of Hermeneutics, The" (Dilthey), 3:81–82
Rishis, revealing the Veda, 5:121
Risk
in decision theory, 2:656, 2:659–660
in personal relationships, 1:715
Ristay, Carolyn, 1:206
Rites, religious, Iamblichus on, 6:551
Ritschl, Albrecht Benjamin, **8:480–481,** 9:527
Ritschl, Friedrich Wilhelm, Nietzsche and, 6:608
Ritschlain school, Christology in, 2:247
Ritter, Johann Wilhelm, 6:667
Ritter, W. E., 7:36
Ritual
in Chinese religion, 2:226–227
in Confucianism, 2:171–177, 2:194–195
in Ivanov's mystical anarchism, 4:767
myth and, 1:58

Ritual, ***continued***
in religious language interpretation, 8:415
Xunzi and, 2:234
Zoroastrian, 9:886–887
Riurik, descent from, 5:153
Rivista di estetica (journal), 9:237
Rivista di matematica (periodical), 7:158
Rivista internazionale di filosofia del diritto (periodical), 2:697
Rivista italiana di filosofia (journal), 3:607
RNA world, and origin of life, 5:361–362
Road to Revolution (Yarmolinsky), 6:617
Robbers, The (Schiller, Friedrich), 8:626
Robbins, Lionel
on economics, 7:351
on measures of well-being, 3:448
Robert, Jason, on physical development, 7:347
Robert de Courçon, 2:644
Robert Guiskard (Kleist), 5:78
Robert of Melun, 5:429, 8:592
Robertelli, Francesco, 7:144
Roberts, John, on natural laws, 5:230
Robertson, William, friend of Ferguson, 3:604
Robertson-Walker expression, as model in cosmology, 2:559
Robinet, Jean-Baptiste-René, **8:481–482**
Robinson, Abraham, 4:652
on first-order logic, 5:480
on infinitesimals, 2:502, 2:506
on model theory, 5:481–482
Robinson, J. A. T., on metaphysical theology, 1:364–365
Robinson, Jenefer
on music, 1:303, 1:306
on style, 1:331–332
Robinson, Richard
on definition, 2:665, 2:672
emotive theory and, 3:425
Robot(s)
in Chinese room argument, 2:240–241
directional capabilities of, 3:708
worlds of, 3:708–709
Robotics, situated, 1:347–348
Rockefeller, John D., and social Darwinism, 2:642
Rodell, Fred, legal realism and, 7:428
Roden Crater (Turrell), 3:256
Rodin, Auguste, 8:477
Rodnoe i vselenskoe (Matters Native and Universal) (Ivanov), 4:767
Rodó, José Enrique, 5:204
Roe vs. Wade (1973), 1:236
Roget, Peter, physicotheology and, 7:560
Rohault, Jacques, **8:482–484**
Cartesianism of, 2:55–56, 3:702
Tschirnhaus and, 9:549
Roi naturelle, ou Catéchisme du citoyen français, La (Volney), 9:707
Roig, Arturo Andrés
liberation philosophy and, 5:211
mestizo consciousness and, 5:210
Roland, Per, in neuroimaging, 6:565
Role of the Individual in History, The (Plekhanov), 3:37
Role-functionalism, mental causation and, 6:135
Rolland, Romain, on Tagore, Rabindranath, 9:363
Rolls Sermons (Butler), 2:686
Romagnosi, Gian Domenico, 2:83, **8:484–485**
Roman Catholicism, 2:249, 3:530
Bodin, 1:622–623
Chaadaev on, 2:120–121
Charron and, 2:134
Chateaubriand on, 2:138
Comte on, 2:412–413
faith in, 3:529–530
on miracles, 6:267
mysticism of, 6:448
redemption in, 2:249
See also Catholic Church; Catholicism
Roman Empire
Augustine and, 1:399, 7:421
authority in, 9:139
Christianity in, 1:399–401, 4:261, 7:387
City of God (Augustine) and, 1:399
Dante on, 2:625
ethics in, 3:399–400
Greek sources referenced during, 7:264
and historical inevitability, 3:37, 3:38
law in, 1:135, 7:420
canonists in, 7:421
majesty in, 1:621
social contract in, 9:81
synthesis with French monarchy, 1:621
in transition to states, 9:204
types of, 7:420
universal law as replacement for, 1:622
and literature, 1:45
Machiavelli and, 5:629–630
measurement system of, 6:91
natural law in, 6:507
optimism/pessimism in, 7:247
philosophy of law in, 7:419–420
Plotinus and, 7:631–632
Pythagoreanism in, 8:187
slavery in, 7:420
in Spengler's cultural morphology, 9:168
Stoicism in, 9:253
on war and peace, 7:152, 7:154
Roman philosophy
eschatology in, 3:348
and republicanism, 8:435
See also Cicero, Marcus Tullius; Lucretius; Marcus Aurelius Antoninus; Seneca, Lucius Annaeus; Stoicism
Romance, culture of, 3:584
Romanes, G. J., on atheism, 1:373
Romania, 4:743
Romanovs, Eurasianists on, 3:454
Romantic art, 4:274
Romanticism, **8:485–491**
aesthetics in, 1:54–56, 1:771
of Alison, 1:129
art in, 1:297–298, 1:303–304
Cavell on, 2:116
in Coleridge, 2:320
on creative genius, 7:595
in Denmark, 9:238
Eliot (T. S.) on, 3:185–186
Enlightenment and, 8:486–487
German
Hibbel and, 4:254
Lessing and, 5:294
Gracián on, 4:168
and history, 1:442
imagination in, 1:55
literary theory and, 8:631
and New England transcendentalism, 6:572
novels in, 8:631
optimism/pessimism and, 7:249–250
poetic theory in, 8:631
polarity of finite and infinite in, 9:114
vs. representational theory of art, 1:297–298
Schelling as epitome of, 8:617
Schiller (Friedrich) and, 8:629–630
of Schlegel, 8:630–631
Schleiermacher and, 8:632
of Solger, 9:114
sublimity and, 9:294
Swedenborg and, 9:338
temperament of, 8:485–486

on thought and language, 7:534–535
Rome. *See* Roman Empire
Rømer, Olaus, 9:149
Römerbrief, Der (Barth), 1:477
Romero, Francisco, 5:207–209, **8:491–492**
Rommen, Heinrich A., on property, 8:73
Röntgen, Wilhelm, Dingler and, 3:85
Rooijen, Rudolphus Snel van, Arminius and, 1:285
Roosevelt, Franklin D., atomic bomb and, 3:178
Roosevelt, Theodore, and social Darwinism, 2:642
Ropohl, Gunter, on epistemology of technology, 7:549
"Rorarius" (Leibniz), 9:55
Roretz, Karl, **8:492–493**
Rorty, Richard, **8:493–495**
eliminative materialism and, 3:183
espousing views while denying their accuracy, 5:103
on history, 7:399
on personhood, 7:238
on phenomenology, 7:300
on philosophy, 7:399
and postmodernism, 9:59
pragmatic theory of truth and, 9:537
pragmatism and, 7:173, 7:749, 7:751
Roscelin, **8:495–496**
Anselm and, 1:216
nominalism of, 3:290
on universals, 6:101–102, 8:496
Rosch, Eleanor, on concepts as prototypes, 2:418
Roscoe, Mary Anne, 4:807
Rose, Alan, 5:694
Rosemont, Henry, 2:196
Rosen, Nathan, on quantum theory, 2:105, 2:126, 3:181, 6:641
Rosenberg, Alfred, Chamberlain and, 2:123
Rosenberg, Charles, on connectionism, 2:444
Rosenberg, Gregg, on dualism, 3:117
Rosenkranz, Johann Karl Friedrich, **8:496–497**
Rosenthal, David M., 2:454, 4:712
Rosenzweig, Franz, 4:618, 4:829, **8:498–499**
Rosicrucian Fraternity, 3:674
Rosmini e Gioberti (Gentile), 4:49
Rosmini-Serbati, Antonio, 2:602, 7:83, **8:500–503**
and Sciacca, 8:666
Spaventa on, 9:160
Thomism and, 9:446
Ross, Alf
emotive theory and, 3:425
legal philosophy of, 7:428
on ownership, 8:71–72
on value, 3:443
Ross, David, on Aristotle, 5:439
Ross, William David, **8:504–505**
on Aristotle, 3:350
on deontological theory, 2:714, 4:153
on duty, 3:440
and ethics, 3:420
on Good, 3:419
on happiness, distribution of, 8:722
intuitionism of, 3:386–387, 4:735
on Moore, 3:440
on pluralism, 4:735
on right, 3:419
on value, use of, 9:637–638
Rosser, Berkeley, 5:694
Rossi, Alejandro, 5:210
Rossiia i chelovechestvo (Russia and mankind) (Trubetskoi), 9:531
Rotating gravitational masses, equilibrium of, 4:804
Rothacker, Erich, 7:318, 7:322
Rothschild, M., on risk theory, 2:660
Rouelle, Guillaume-François, Diderot and, 3:73
Rougier, Louis, 5:525, **8:506**
Round approach
in Huayan Buddhism, 2:164
and phenomenology, 2:165
in Tiantai Buddhism, 2:163–164
Round method, similarities with western phenomenology, 2:165
Roush, Sherrilyn, 2:435
Rousseau, Jean-Jacques, **8:507–516**
Bonald and, 1:648
Bosanquet and, 1:663
on citizenship, 9:206
on civilization, 3:470
on conscience, 3:155
Constant on, 5:320
Darwin (Erasmus) and, 2:630
de Staël and, 9:201
deism and, 2:687–691
Derrida on, 2:715–717
Diderot and, 3:72, 3:77
on duty, 3:155, 7:371
on education, 7:370–371
Emerson and, 3:195
Encyclopédie and, 3:223
Enlightenment and, 3:244
Epicurus and, 3:265
on equality, 3:330, 7:370–371
ethics in, 3:409–410
on evil, 3:470
experience in, 7:371
French Revolution and, 4:39–40, 9:520
Froebel and, 3:755
on general will, 4:38–40
on government, 2:701, 7:73
Green on, 4:179
on human nature, 7:370–371
Hume and, 3:410
Kant and, 5:29, 7:424
knowledge in, 7:371
Lamarck and, 5:173
on language, 8:787
literary style of, 3:410
Lotman and, 5:579
on love, 5:588
Maine de Biran and, 5:656
peace proposals of, 7:155
Pestalozzi and, 7:371
on *philosophes*, 2:688
philosophy of sex and, 7:522
political philosophy of, 7:665
on public interest, 9:207
Rawls on, 9:82
Scanlon and, 2:517
on self-determination, 2:702
sensationalism and, 3:72
on social contract, 2:366, 9:80
social critiques by, 3:247
and socialism, 9:87
on society, 7:370–371
on sovereignty, 9:142–143
in Spranger's philosophy of education, 9:199
on thought and language, 7:534–535
on unconscious, 9:571
wisdom and, 9:794
Routley, Richard, 3:627, 5:491
Roux, Wilhelm, 3:110
Rowe, William I., 3:321, 7:481, 9:408
Rowlands, Mark, 6:126
Rowse, A. L., on historical inevitability, 3:36
Roy, Henry de. *See* Regius
Royal absolution, 3:603
Royal Astronomical Society, 2:709
Royal authority, Buddhism and, 5:134
Royal Society
Desgabets and, 2:757
Leibniz and, 5:253
Locke and, 5:375
members of, 3:164, 7:159

Royalism, of de Maistre, 5:660
Royall, Richard M., 9:212
Royce, Josiah, **8:518–522**
Ducasse and, 3:124
Eliot (T. S.) and, 3:185
and ethics, 3:415
Hegelianism of, 4:286
on idealism, 4:559
Lotze and, 5:583
on loyalty, 5:595–596
Marcel and, 3:504
on panpsychism, 7:83–92
and realism, 6:584
Royer-Collard, Pierre Paul, **8:523–524**
Rozanov, Vasilii Vasil'evich, **8:524–526**
Rubins, Edgar, 4:71
Rubio, Antonio, 5:204
Ruddick, Sara
on moral reasoning of mothers, 3:579–580
on mothering connected to peace politics, 3:602
philosophy of sex and, 7:523
on war and peace, 7:157
Rüdiger, Andreas, **8:526–527**
Rudiments of English Grammar, The (Priestley), 8:5
Rudolf II, 5:50
"Rudolf Stammlers Überwindung des materialistischen Geschichtsauffassung" (Weber), 9:203
Ruegg, David Seyfort, 1:743
Rufus, Richard, 1:454, 5:70, **8:527–530**
Ruge, Arnold
Feuerbach and, 3:609
Lavrov and, 5:218
Ruggiero, Guido de, 5:321
Ruines, ou Méditations sur les révolutions des empires, Les (Ruins of Empires) (Volney), 9:707
Rule(s), **8:531–533**
in act utilitarianism, 9:608, 9:612–613
of argument, 3:644
Austin (John) on, 1:405
of compositionality, 2:370
of conditionalization, definition of, 5:538
conference of social roles by, 9:94
and connections, 5:17, 8:154
exceptions to, miracles as, 6:265, 6:266
of generalization, 5:544
Hart on, 7:429
in ideal moral utilitarianism, 1:687
indeterminate, 7:451–452
indirect utilitarianism on, 7:460
of inference, 5:555
language and, 8:16–19, 9:815
law as, 7:429
linguistic meaning of, 6:83
miracles as exceptions to, 6:265, 6:266
monastic, in Buddhism, 1:725
on operative words, 7:446
and perception of order, 3:700
from precedents, 7:449
primary, Hart on, 5:239–240
private language and, 8:16–17, 9:815
programmable, human cognition and, 2:445
reason and, 7:736
of recognition, 5:240–241, 5:244, 7:458
in rule utilitarianism, 9:613–614
for sameness, 8:20
scientific understanding and, 6:73
of skill, Kant on, 3:411
social, as judicanda of justice, 4:863–865
of succession, 5:57
in Turing, 9:552
types of, Hart on, 5:239–240
Wittgenstein on, 1:152, 9:814–815
Rule consequentialism, 9:615
Rule following, **8:531–533**
Rule models, in ethics, 9:687–688
Rule of Reason, The (Wilson), 5:438–439
Rule utilitarianism, 3:384–385, 3:748–749, 9:603–604
actual, 9:603
aim of, 9:614
defense of, 9:614
as descriptive ethics, 9:605–606
the good in, 9:615
Hare on, 3:441
inconsistency in, 9:614
of Mill (John Stuart), 6:233
as normative ethics, 9:607
praise and blame in, 9:613
reflective equilibrium and, 9:613–615
rules in, cost of internalizing, 9:613–614
weakness of, 9:607
Rule-governed practice, Novits's theory of creativity and, 2:590
Rulers, in Chinese thought, 2:237
Rules for Solving Sophisms (Heytesbury), 9:342
Rules for the Direction of the Mind (Regulae) (Descartes), 2:723–727, 2:731–735, 4:553
Rule-to-rule principle, in compositionality, 2:370
Rumford, Count, on heat energy, 3:229
Rumi, Jalal al-Din, 4:744, 9:306–307
"Runabout Inference-Ticket, The" (Prior), 8:14
Ruse, Michael, on evolutionary ethics, 3:480
Ruskin, John, **8:534–535**
on art, 1:56
on evolution, 2:641
Ruskin's Philosophy (Collingwood), 2:325
Russell, Bertrand Arthur William, 2:652, **8:535–561**
on *a priori* knowledge, 4:729
on Absolute, 9:289
on abstraction principle, 2:38
on adverbial analysis, 8:821
analysis of definite descriptions, 3:645
in analytic philosophy, 1:145–147
Anderson (John) and, 1:197
on appearance *vs.* reality, 1:229, 1:230
on assumptions of science, 3:632
on axiom of continuity, 2:499
Ayer and, 1:436
on basic statements, 1:485
on belief
attributions, 1:536
behavioral effects of, 5:98
in God, 2:352
on body-mind dependence, 4:615
Bradley (F. H.) and, 1:675–676, 3:416
and Carnap, 5:524
on causality, 2:103–104, 2:281
and Chwistek, 2:255
coherence theory of truth and, 9:536
on common cause principle, 8:594
on common sense, 2:358
on correspondence theory of truth, 2:539, 9:535
on death, 1:374, 2:652
on definite descriptions, 1:523, 5:540, 9:264
on definition, 2:665, 2:670–671
on derivative knowledge, 5:92
on descriptions, 3:315, 3:496–498, 5:508, 6:635, 8:59–60
Dewey and, 3:44
on doubt, 3:103
on duration of time, 9:464
Eliot (T. S.) and, 3:185
emotive theory and, 3:425
on empiricism, 3:219–220

epistemology and, 3:315–316, 5:91, 8:540–546
on error, 3:345
ethics of, 8:555–559
on Euler, 5:444
Evans and, 3:460
on existence, 3:495
on explosion, 7:105
and fictionalism, 3:629–630
on freedom, 3:722
Frege and, 2:82, 3:732, 5:464, 5:517, 9:289
on future and past, 3:708
Hegelianism of, 8:536
hierarchical theories of truth and, 9:540
and idealism, 4:559
on immortality, 4:615
on information contents of sentences, 8:736
on intentional object, 4:709
on intuition, 4:724
Kaplan and, 5:39
on knowledge of things *vs.* knowledge of truths, 5:97
and Köhler, comparison of, 5:131
and Korean philosophy, 5:141
on language, Wittgenstein and, 9:806
Latin American philosophy and, 5:210
on laws of logic, 5:511
on Leibniz, 5:272, 9:298
on life, meaning and value of, 5:345, 5:348
life of, 8:535–539
and logic, 5:482, 8:546–551
on logical constructions, Wisdom (John) on, 9:796
logical positivism and, 1:149
logicism and, 5:547, 6:21
Lovejoy on, 5:593
Łukasiewicz on, 5:605–607
on man-made reality, 8:624
on mass and energy, 3:234
on mathematics, 8:546–555
on meaning, 1:146
on Meinong, 8:804
metaphysics of, 8:540–546
on method of construction, 5:548
monism of, 8:149
Moore on, 7:109
on motion, 6:408–409
and multiple relation theory, 3:345
Nagel (Ernest) and, 6:472
on naive comprehension principle, 4:663
on natural numbers, 9:270
on negative existentials, 1:146
neo-Kantianism and, 3:311
new realism and, 2:595, 6:584–585
on nonbeing, 6:635
no-substance theory of, 7:24
on nothing, 6:657
on number, 6:670
on omnipotence, 1:361
on ontological argument for existence of God, 3:498, 7:17
on optimism/pessimism, 7:252
ordinary-language philosophy of, 6:194–195
pacifism of, 8:536–539
Pastore and, 7:135
Peano and, 1:146–147, 7:158–159
on phenomenalism, 7:272
philosophy of sex and, 7:522
Platonism of, 8:536
pluralism of, 6:328
precursors of, 7:163
on presupposition, 7:770
on propositional attitudes, 4:712
rationalism and, 5:96
realism and, 3:313–314
and religion, 6:619, 8:559–561
on resemblance theory, 9:600–601
on Rousseau, 4:40
and Santayana, 8:598
on Sartre, 8:610
and Schlick, 8:640
and Scholz, 8:645
and School of Qom, 8:647
on science, 3:632
search for certain knowledge, 5:97
second-order quantification and, 5:492
on semantic paradoxes, 5:518
semantics of, 3:252
on sensa, 8:815–816
sensationalism and, 8:827
on sense datum, 8:813
on "sensible" space, 8:819
on sentences, 7:768, 8:801
on set theory, 5:518, 8:834
Sidgwick and, 9:25
skepticism in, 9:58
social theories of, 8:535–539
on specious present, 9:483
Stace and, 9:200
on statements of identity, 9:287
Stout and, 9:259
Strawson on, 7:768
on subject-predicate logic, 9:287–289
on supervenience, 9:328–329
and systematic ambiguity, 5:558
Tagore and, 9:363
on tenseless theory of time, 9:475
on theory of objects, 6:115–116
theory of types and, 2:76–77, 2:256, 5:558, 8:547–548, 8:554–555, 9:353, 9:555–558
on truth, 2:543–545
Turing and, 9:552
on universals, 9:585, 9:600–601
vicious-circle principle, 5:555
and Vienna Circle, 2:41
on war and peace, 7:155–156
and Whitehead, 9:746–747
on "why," answers to, 9:757–758
Wittgenstein and, 9:800–801
Russellian singular terms, 3:460–461
Russell's paradox, 4:663, 5:551, 8:834
in combinatory logic, 2:337
dialetheism and, 7:106
Frege on, 3:731, 5:464
Leśniewski and, 5:290
Ramsey on, 5:468
Russell on, 5:466
set-theory and, 4:663, 5:517–518, 8:834
type theory and, 2:76, 8:547–548, 9:555
unrestricted transcendent realism and, 6:179
verifiability principle and, 9:668–669
"Russell's Philosophy of Science" (Nagel), 6:474
Russia
censorship in, 3:71, 3:77
civil disobedience in, 9:89
communist mode of production and, 2:363–364
constructivism in, Bishop's theory of continuum and, 2:504–505
cultural and spiritual evolution in, 3:673
Eurasianism and, 3:453–454
formalism in, 9:17
Husserl's phenomenology in, 9:17
Leont'ev on, 5:283–284
materialism in, Dostoevsky on, 3:99
nihilism, origin of word in, 6:617
populism in, 5:48, 6:215–216
religious renaissance in, 9:13
religious-philosophical tradition in, 5:575–576
in Solov'ëv's theocracy, 9:125
in Spengler's cultural morphology, 9:166–167
Spinoza and, 9:195

Russia, *continued*
symbolist literary movement in, 4:766
Symbolist movement in, 3:668
See also Soviet Union
Russia (Cobden), 7:155
Russia and the Universal Church (Solov'ëv), 9:124
Russia idea, The, Dostoevsky on, 3:101
Russian philosophy, **8:564–578**
Bakhtin in, 1:464–469
Bakunin, 1:471
Chaadaev in, 2:120–122
civic criticism, 1:538
Dostoevsky in, 3:99–102
Enlightenment, 8:566–567
German philosophy and, 1:538
Golden Age of, 8:567–571
historical evolution of, 8:565–578
Il'in and, 4:577
Ivanov in, 4:766–768
Kievan period of, 8:565
Lavrov and, 5:218–219
Lenin and, 5:279–281
Leont'ev and, 5:283–284
Lopatin and, 5:572–573
Losev and, 5:573–576
Losskii and, 5:576–578
Lotman and, 5:578–579
Mamardashvili in, 5:677–680
Muscovite period, 8:565–566
Pisarev and, 7:576–577
Plekhanov in, 7:626
post-Soviet, 8:578–579
Radishchev in, 8:230–231
realistic metaphysics in, 9:18
Rozanov in, 8:524–526
Shestov in, 9:11–13
Shpet in, 9:17–20
Silver Age of, 8:571–575, 9:126
Skovoroda in, 9:63–65
Solov'ëv in, 9:122–127
Soviet period, 8:575–577
Spir in, 9:196–197
typical features of, 8:564–565
Zen'kovskii in, 9:868
Russian Philosophy (Kline), 9:63
Russian revolution, 4:752, 4:767, 7:626
Russian school, on continuum, 2:501
Rutherford, Ernest, atomism and, 1:388
Ruysbroeck, Jan van, **8:579–580**
Brethren of the Common Life and, 9:423
Eckhart (Meister) and, 3:163
Rwanda, genocide in, just war theory and, 7:157
Ryle, Gilbert, **8:580–584**
on absurdity, 2:77–78
on category mistakes, 9:354
category theory of, 2:77–78
on continental philosophy, 2:488
on definition, 2:673–675
on determinism, 3:7
on imagination, 4:593, 4:597
on introspection, 4:721
on knowing how and knowing that, 5:92, 5:94, 5:98
on lawlike statements, 5:502
on logical behaviorism, 7:469
on mental terms, 1:523
on mind-body relationship, 1:154
on natural language, 2:77
ordinary-language philosophy and, 1:153, 3:318, 6:195
on perceiving, 7:180
on personal identity, 7:227
on pleasure and pain, 7:618–619
on prelinguistic knowledge, 4:725
on scientific law, 7:518
on self-knowledge, 8:723
on sense data, 8:820
and Sibley, 9:20
and Smart, 9:65
on soul, 4:605
on states of mind, 6:12
students of, 2:710
on thought and thinking, 9:421–422
Vienna Circle and, 5:525
on volition, 3:19
Rynin, David, on truth and falsity, 7:768
Ryōchi, 6:477

S

S. Agustino (Papini), 7:103
Saadya, **8:585–587**
Gersonides on, 4:68
and Kabbalah, 5:4
in medieval Jewish philosophy, 4:811–813
Pythagoreanism and, 8:188
Saarinen, Eero, 3:256
Śabara, on inference, 5:414
Sabatier, Auguste, **8:587–588**
Sablé, Mme. de, La Rochefoucauld and, 5:200
Saccheri, Gerolamo, 5:440, 9:150
Sacks, Gerald, on computability theory, 2:385
Sacrament(s)
creation as, 1:652
Luther on, 5:612
Melanchthon on, 6:119
Sacramentalism, 1:652
Sacred, supernatural and, Oman on, 7:14
Sacred power, Brahman, definition of, 1:681
Sacred realm, as perspective for thinking, 2:224–225
Sacred Theory of the Earth, The (Burnet), 9:336
Sacrifice
act utilitarian requirement for, 9:612–613
altruism as, 1:136
as choice, 5:43
Kempis on, 9:424
suicide as, 9:320
Sacrificio come significato del monado (Aliotta), 1:127
Sacrobosco, Johannes de, 1:101, 1:708
Sacrorum Antistitum, 6:316
Saddharmapuṇḍarīka (Lotus of the wonderful law) (Buddhist scripture), 2:163
Sade, Marquis de, 1:488, 7:522
Sadhana: The Realisation of Life (Tagore), 9:363–364
Sadock, Jerrold, on conversational implicature tests, 2:527–528
Sadra, Mulla, 9:308, 9:316
Sadyajyotis, 5:121
Safety
in contextualist solution to skepticism, 9:136
engineering ethics and, 3:239–241
relevant alternatives and, 8:361–362
Sages
Li Ao on, 5:316
and Stoicism, 9:257–258
Wang Bi on, 9:722–723
Zeno of Citium on, 9:870
Saggio filosofico sulla critica della conoscenza (Philosophical essay on the critique of knowledge), 4:14
Said, Edward, on postcolonialism, 7:728
St. Ambrose
Christian ethics and, 3:401
on law, 7:420
on moral perfection, 7:195
Porphyry and, 7:143
on suicide, 9:319
St. Andrew of Neufchateau, 3:93
St. Anselm. *See* Anselm, St.
St. Bernard, Dante on, 2:626
St. Bernard of Clairvaux, **1:591–592,** 5:586
ethics of, 3:93
Gilbert of Poitiers and, 4:88–89

on reason, 3:403
School of St. Victor and, 8:592
St. Bonaventure, **1:649–655**
vs. Alexander of Hales, 1:114
Augustinianism of, 1:402
on divine illumination, 4:580
doctrines of, 1:653–654
Duns Scotus and, 3:135
Durandus of Saint-Pourçain and, 3:148
epistemology of, 1:403
Marston and, 5:726
in medieval philosophy, 6:100
on metaphysics, 1:651–653
mysticism of, 1:403
Pearson and, 7:161
Philoponus and, 7:314–315
philosophy of, 1:650–651
Stefanini on, 9:237
on transcendentals, 3:137
Saint Genet: Comédien et martyre (Sartre), 3:507, 8:610
St. Jerome, 7:175
on Lucretius, 5:598
philosophy of sex and, 7:522
on suicide, 9:319
St. John of the Cross, **4:846–847**
Teresa of Ávila and, 9:394
three-dark-nights theory, Stein on, 9:240
St. Leon (Godwin), 4:136
Saint Louis School, The, 3:196. *See also* Harris, William Torrey
St. Maximus the Confessor, Erigena and, 3:341
St. Paul
attack upon philosophers, 3:674
and Byzantine view of philosophy, 1:786
on Cretans, 5:316–317
deists on, 2:685
epistles of, 5:391, 7:141
ethics of, 2:714
on happiness, 3:401
Locke on, 5:375, 5:391
Marcion on, 5:703–704
on moral perfection, 7:195
on philosophers, 3:674
St. Thomas Aquinas. *See* Aquinas, St. Thomas
Saint Victor, School of, 3:136, **8:591–593**
Saint-Cyran, Jean Duvergier de Hauranne, abbé de
Arnauld and, 1:288
in Jansenism, 4:789–790
Sainte-Beauve, Nicole and, 6:603
Saint-Hyacinthe, Thémiseul de, **8:588–589**
Saint-Médard cemetery, 4:790
Saint-Pierre, Abbé, 7:154–155
Saint-Simon, Claude-Henri de Rouvroy, Comte de, **8:589–591**
on art, 1:56–57
positivism and, 7:710, 7:711
scientific socialism of, 9:89
Saint-Simonian movement, 9:88
Carlyle and, 2:33
Mill (John Stuart) and, 6:221
Saisset, Émile, on Spinoza's pantheism, 9:195
Saito, Yuriko, on environmental aesthetics, 3:256
Śaiva Siddhānta, Brahman as sole existential, 1:684
Sakamoto Hyakudai, 4:791
Sakoku Nihon no higeki (National seclusion, Japan's tragedy) (Watsuji), 9:727
Śakya (reference), 9:582–583
Śakyatāvacchedaka (sense), 9:582–583
Salamanca, University of, 3:148–149
Sale of Lives, The (Lucian of Samosata), 5:597
Sallustius, in Neoplatonism, 6:551
Salmerón, Fernando, 5:210
Salmon, Nathan
on demonstratives, 2:708
on names as devices of direct reference, 8:747
on semantics, 8:77
Salmon, Wesley, **8:593–594**
on causality, 2:103
on explanation, 3:519–525
fallacy of inductive causal inference, 3:741
Lehrer and, 5:248
Reichenbach's vindication and, 4:644
Salons (Diderot), 3:71, 3:76–77
Salons, Enlightenment and, 3:244–245
Salvation
apokatastasis doctrine of, 4:182
Arnauld and, 1:288
Augustine on, 7:387
being and, 5:702
Culverwell on, 2:613
Eberhard on, 3:161
Edwards (Jonathan) on, 3:167
Erigena on, 3:341
free will and, 1:288
in Gnosticism, 4:97, 4:102
good works in, Melanchthon on, 6:119
grace and, 1:288
granting of, 4:39
Gregory of Nyssa on, 4:182
Jansenism on, 4:788–789
as liberation from existence, 9:124
Luther on, 5:612–615
Malebranche on, 1:290–291
Marcel on, 5:702
Palmer (E.) on, 7:78
Pelagianism and predestination and, 7:175
in Pure Land Buddhism, 2:169
Rosenzweig on, 4:829
of society, by worker-soldier, 4:859–860
theurgy in, Iamblichus on, 4:540
universal, 4:251–252
Samādhi, 1:730, 4:833
Samaveda, 5:116
Sambursky, Samuel, 2:491, 5:641, 6:63
Sameness
personal identity and, 7:219–220
in private language problem, 8:20–21
Śamkara, 1:682–683, 4:135, 4:629
Samkhya school, 4:132, 6:107, 8:332
absence in, 5:122
analogy in, 5:122
cognition in, 5:116
epistemology in, 5:117
Sāmkhyakārikās (Iśvarakṛṣṇa), 4:626
Samkhya-Yoga, 4:134, 4:626–627
Samples, statistical, 3:662, 3:663
Sampson Agonistes (Milton), 6:251
Samsara, 5:326
in Buddhism, 5:329
in Hindu philosophy, 5:329
in Jainism, 5:327
in Uttara Mīmāṁsā, 5:329
Samuel the Hasid, 5:2
Samuels, Richard, 3:485
Samuelson, Paul A., 8:810
Samurai class, Minagawa on, 6:253
San Giovanni, order of, founding of, 4:834
San Manuel bueno, mártir (Saint Emanuel the Good, martyr) (Unamuno), 9:566
San Marco, Convent of, 7:574
Sanatana dharma, 5:326–327
Sanches, Francisco, **8:594–596**
and crisis of skepticism, 9:51–52
Gassendi and, 4:30
Pico della Mirandola (Gianfrancesco) and, 7:575
Sanchoniatho's Phoenician History (Payne), 2:614
Sanctification, in Christianity, 2:249

Sanctis, Francesco de. *See* De Sanctis, Francesco
Sanctity of human life, 7:694–697
Sand, Christoph, 9:100
Sandel, Michael, on Rawls, 5:324, 9:82
Sandeman, Robert, and James (Henry), 4:773
Sanderson, Robert, 5:440
Sanford, David, 5:109
Sanger, Margaret, 5:351
Sangha, 1:722–726
Śankara
  Eckhart (Meister) and, 3:163
  on empirical awarenesses, 5:120
  on liberation, 5:329–330
  on life, meaning and value of, 5:359
  on power of karma depending on ignorance, 5:41
Śankaras-vāmin, on inference, 5:413
Sankhya, 2:111–112
Sankhyakarika (Isvarakrishna), 2:111
Sanlun Buddhism, 2:161–163
Sanlun xuanyi (Profound meaning of the three treatises) (Jizang), 2:162
Sanskrit, 4:133
  atom in, 1:380
  consonants in, 7:413
  Hindu literature in, 4:624
  linguistics of, 7:414–417
  rules of, Pāṇini on, 4:631
  Schlegel's study of, 8:631
  units of speech in, 7:413
  verbs in, 7:413
  vowels in, 7:413
Śāntarakṣita, in Dge-lugs philosophy, 1:732–733
Santayana, George, **8:597–603**
  on aesthetics, 1:57, 1:63, 8:598
  on animal faith, 3:632, 9:199
  on beauty, 1:63
  on biological need, 2:596
  Dewey and, 1:63
  on expression, 1:305
  on knowledge symbol mediated faith, 2:597
  metaphysical monism and, 2:598
  Miller (Dickinson) and, 6:235
  on morality, 1:63, 8:600–601
  on mortality, 4:606–607
  Nagel (Ernest) and, 6:472
  naturalistic skepticism of, 9:58
  on pessimism, 7:252
  on religion, 8:599–600
  on sense data, 2:595
Sapentiale (Thomas of York), 9:443
Sapir-Whorf thesis, 1:83
Sarewitz, Daniel, 8:675
Sarmiento, Domingo Faustino, 5:206
Sartre, Jean-Paul, **8:603–612**
  Abbagnano on, 1:1
  on absurdity, 4:748
  on action, 3:503
  on aesthetics, 1:71, 8:605–606
  on agnosticism, 3:427–428
  on alienation, 8:609
  on alterity, 1:133
  on art, 1:71
  Ayer on, 3:508
  Beauvoir and, 1:515–516, 8:603
  on being, 8:606–608
  Camus and, 2:20
  Cartesianism and, 3:509, 8:610–611
  on causal theories of behavior, 3:507
  on choice, 3:504, 8:608
  on "city of ends," 8:606–607
  communism and, 8:604
  on consciousness, 2:459, 8:604–607
  Danto on, 2:627
  on death, 2:653
  Deleuze and, 2:693
  Dilthey and, 3:84
  on dread, 3:503–504
  on eidetic reduction, 8:604–606
  on essence and existence, 3:351
  on ethics, 3:427–428
  on existence, 3:351, 3:503
  on existential psychoanalysis, 3:510–514, 8:608
  and existentialism, 1:455–456, 6:195, 8:603, 8:610
  on faith, 1:455–456
  Ferrier and, 3:608
  on Flaubert, 1:455–456, 3:507, 3:510, 3:514, 8:604, 8:609
  on freedom of imagination, 4:597
  on Freud, 1:455, 3:514
  on God, 3:351
  Heidegger and, 3:504, 8:603, 8:606
  on history, 3:510
  on human nature, 3:428
  Husserl and, 3:317, 8:603
  on images, 4:594–595, 8:604–605
  on imagination, 1:71, 8:604–606
  on individual, 3:509
  influences on, 3:504
  on intentionality, 3:502, 8:605
  literary fame of, 5:364
  Mamardashvili and, 5:679
  on man as totality, 8:608
  Marxism of, 5:739
  on mediating third, 8:609
  Merleau-Ponty and, 6:149, 8:603
  on negativity, 8:606–607
  nihilism of, 6:618
  on nothing, 6:657–658
  on nothingness, 8:605
  on optimism/pessimism, 7:253
  on original choice, 3:513
  on perception of others, 3:502
  on phenomenology, 6:195, 7:297, 8:603
  philosophy of sex and, 7:522–523
  politics of, 3:506
  on practico-inert, 8:609
  on progressive-regressive method, 8:604
  on psychology, 1:455, 3:507
  on reading, 4:598
  on reason, 3:503
  Russell on, 8:610
  Scheler and, 8:603, 8:616
  on self-deception as bad faith, 8:608–610, 8:714
  Shariati and, 9:7
  on social ontology, 3:510
  on social relations, 3:514, 8:608, 9:98
  on subjectivity, 9:491
  on "the look," 8:607
  themes in, 3:504
  on unconscious, 8:608–610
Ṣaṣṭi-tantra (Sixty doctrines), 5:412–414
SAT tests, 7:362
Śatapatha Brāhmaṇa, on immortality, 5:327
Satire
  in Burke (Edmund), 1:770–771
  in Swift, 9:339–341
  utopianism and, 9:619
  of Voltaire, 9:708
Satisfaction, 3:448
  in first-order model theory, 6:302–303
  formulas and, 3:651–652
  in identification, 3:719
  levels of, 9:642
  in Tarski's truth theory, 2:548–549
Satisfactione, De (Crell), 9:100
Satisfiability, 5:556
Satisficing, in utilitarianism, 9:383
Saturated-unsaturated dichotomy, Frege on, 3:727
Saturation axioms, in hyperreal number systems, 2:508
Satyagraha (truth force), Gandhi and, 7:67
Saudi Arabia, Sufism in, 9:309–310
Saunderson, Nicholas, 3:72

Saussure, Ferdinand de
Barthes and, 1:481
Chomsky and, 2:244
Derrida on, 2:715–716
on language, 7:411
and semiology, 1:481, 5:152
and structuralism, 9:273
Sautrāntika-Yogacara Buddhism, on universals, 9:585
Savage, J. J., on frequency theory, 9:220
Savage, Leonard, **8:612–614**
de Finetti and, 2:663
on decision theory, 2:655, 2:658
on rational degrees of belief, 8:685
on stable estimation, 9:222
Savigny, Friedrich Karl von, **8:614–615**
in historical school of law, 7:426
on social wholes, 9:95
Savile, Anthony, on beauty, 1:67
Saving Belief (Baker), 1:463
Saving hypotheses, fallacy of, 3:544
Savitskii, P. N., Eurasianism and, 3:453
Savonarola, Girolamo, 5:626, 7:570, 7:574, 9:50
Sawanih al-'ushshaq (The lovers' experiences) (al-Ghazālī, Aḥmad), 1:117
Sax, Leonard, on Nietzsche, 6:609
Sayables, in Stoic logic, 5:404
Scaliger, Julius Caesar
atomism and, 1:385–386
on poetics, 1:48–49
and Vanini, 9:646
Scaling model, of temperature measurement, 6:87
Scandinavian legal philosophy, 7:428–429
Scanlon, Thomas
on action, 1:18
contractualist theory of, 2:517, 2:714–715, 3:386
on desire, 1:18–19
as intuitionist, 4:735
on moral reasoning, 7:737
on self-interest, 3:389
on value (analysis of), 4:150
on well-being, 8:722
Scapegoat, and utilitarianism, 9:606, 9:612–613
Scarpellini, Bruno, many-valued logic and, 5:694
Scepsis Scientifica (Glanvill), 4:95
Sceptic Chymist, The (Boyle), 1:387
Scepticism. *See* Skepticism
Scepticism (Naess), 9:59
Scepticism and Animal Faith (Santayana), 2:596–597, 8:601, 9:58
Schacher, Quirinus, Leibniz and, 5:250
Schachtel, Ernest, on alienation, 1:122
Schaffer, Jonathan, 2:99
Schaffer, Simon, 9:84
Schaffner, Kenneth, 7:343–346
Schattländer, Richard, on Scheler-Hartmann school, 3:422
Scheffler, Israel
in education, philosophy of, 7:355
on intentional semantics, 4:706
on scientific law, 7:519
on vagueness, 9:624
Scheffler, Samuel
consequentialism and, 2:461
on ethics, 2:713
on utilitarianism, 9:383
Scheiermacher, Friedrich, 1:707, 7:494
Schein, Barry, 3:464–465
Scheines, Richard, 8:687
Scheler, Max, **8:615–617**
on anthropology, 7:317
Bakhtin and, 1:468
on death, 2:651
on empathy, 9:239, 9:345
on ethics, 3:418, 3:421–422
German reaction to, 3:422
on God's existence, 2:352–353
Hartmann and, 3:422
Ingarden and, 4:682
on knowledge, 7:318
Latin American philosophy and, 5:209
and phenomenology, 7:279
on resentment, 8:616
Sartre and, 8:603, 8:616
on social influence on thoughts, 9:103
social theory of, Plato's influence on, 9:101
on value, 9:638
Schellenberg, John, 4:351–352
Schelling, Friedrich Wilhelm Joseph von, **8:617–623**
on absolute, 1:10, 1:11–12, 4:669
on absolute idealism, 1:11–12, 4:557
on abstraction, 8:619
on apperception, 1:234
on art, 1:54
Baader and, 1:439
on beauty, 1:54
Coleridge and, 1:13, 2:316
Deleuze on, 2:695
dialectic and, 3:54
Emerson and, 3:196
on energy conservation, 3:230
Erigena and, 3:342
on essence and existence, 3:350
Ferrier and, 3:608
Hegel on, 1:12
on intuition, 4:749
Kant and, 6:539
Kierkegaard and, 5:67
Kireevskii and, 5:74
Krause and, 5:147
Losev and, 5:573
monism of, 6:326
on myth, 1:234
and neo-Kantianism, 6:541
on Newton, 3:57–58
Novalis and, 6:667
panpsychism and, 7:83
pantheism of, 7:97, 7:98
Pantheismusstreit and, 7:101
and romanticism, 8:618
Rosensweig on, 8:498
Schopenhauer on, 8:649
Solov'ëv and, 9:123
Spinoza and, 9:194
Steffens and, 9:238
on unconscious, 9:571
on why not "nothing," 8:622
Wundt and, 1:234
Schema
Gentzen on logic of, 5:475
open, definition of, 5:550
Schemata, 5:18, 9:77
Schematizing concepts, Otto on, 7:61
Scheme of Literal Prophecy Considered (Collins), 2:331, 2:683
Scherk, Jöel, 9:268
Scherzer, Johann Adam, Leibniz and, 5:250
Scheutz, Georg Edward, 2:400, 7:537, 7:540, 7:565
Schiebinger, Londa, 8:679
Schier, Flint, on image intelligibility, 1:326–327
Schiffer, Steven
on borderline cases, 5:110
on propositions, 8:89
Schiller, Ferdinand Canning Scott, **8:623–626**
and aesthetics, 1:54, 9:325
on art, 1:28, 1:54
Gehlen and, 4:35
Goethe and, 4:141
and panpsychism, 7:83, 7:91–92
Papini and, 7:102
on play, 1:54
pragmatism of, 4:35, 7:742, 8:623–624, 8:799
Sulzer and, 9:325
on tragedy, 9:523
on truth, 8:624–625

Schiller, Friedrich, **8:626–630**
and aesthetics, 1:54
Belinskii, influence on, 2:538
and Goethe, 4:145
and Hegel, 4:274
and Lange, 5:186
and Schlegel, 8:630
Schlegel, Friedrich von, 5:588, **8:630–632**
on aesthetics, 8:627–630
Coleridge and, 2:316
Ferguson and, 3:605
Fichte and, 8:630
Lange and, 5:186
Liebmann on, 5:344
on love, 5:588
Moritz and, 6:406
Novalis and, 6:667, 8:631
on opposed races, 5:59
on play, 8:628
and Romanticism, 8:490
Schelling and, 8:617
Schiller (Friedrich) and, 8:629
on tragedy, 9:523
Schlegel, Fritz, 5:61, 5:588
Schleiermacher, Friedrich Daniel Ernst, 4:2, **8:632–637**
Dilthey and, 3:79
on evil, 3:474
Gadamer and, 4:2
on language as national identity, 6:481
Lessing and, 5:297
pantheism of, 7:97, 7:101
Pantheismusstreit and, 7:101
Pietism and, 7:576
and Platonism, 7:612, 7:615
on proprium, 8:634
on religion, 7:97
Schlegel and, 8:631
Scholz and, 8:644
Schopenhauer on, 8:648
Sigwart on, 9:29
Tennant and, 9:393
Schlesinger, George, 9:475, 9:478
Schlick, Moritz, **8:637–644**
on basic statements, 1:484
and coherence theory of truth, 9:536
and correspondence theory of truth, 3:317
on determinism, 3:12
ethical theory of, 8:642–643
on knowledge as sameness, 8:640
logical positivist view of, 5:526
and neo-Kantianism, 6:541
philosophical methodology of, 8:637–638
on *Tractatus,* 9:808
Twardowski and, 9:554
on unified science, 5:528
on verifiability principle, 5:528
on verification theory of meaning, 3:316–317
Vienna Circle and, 5:524
Wittgenstein and, 9:802
Schmid, C. C. E., Fichte and, 1:377
Schmidt, Wilhelm, 2:350
Schmitt, Carl, 4:35
Schmitt, Frederick, 3:276
Schmuck, Catharina, 5:250
Schoenberg, Arnold, Adorno and, 1:25
Scholarius, Gennadius, 7:630
Scholarship, historians and, 1:766
Scholastic method
Buddhist
Dge-lugs and, 1:733–735
Hua yan doctrinal classification and, 1:736
and Mādhyamika dialectic on emptiness, 1:740–743
Svātantrika-Prāsaṅgika distinction, 1:732–734, 1:744
Burley and, 1:773
description of, 1:767
Peter Lombard on, 7:260
Scholastica Commentaria in Primam Partem Angelici Doctoris (Báñez), 1:476
Scholastics/Scholasticism
vs. Calvin, 2:8–11
and abstract natures, 1:449
Abubacer in, 4:550
Alexander of Hales in, 1:114
Anselm in, 6:99
and archetypes, 3:141
Aristotelianism and, 1:261
Avempace in, 4:544
Avicenna and, 4:757
on being, 1:528
Boethius and, 1:626
and Byzantine thought, 1:789
vs. Calvin, 2:8–11
Capreolus on, 2:30–31
Cartesianism and, 2:285–286
Christian
and Jewish philosophy, 4:820, 4:824
problem of, 9:772
on concepts, 2:417
Culverwell and, 2:613
Dante and, 2:624
on determinism, 3:7
dialectic and, 3:54
double truth doctrine and, 5:616
Duns Scotus and, 3:133
Durandus of Saint-Pourçain and, **3:148–149**
Erasmus and, 3:339–340
on essence and existence, 2:747, 3:350–351
and ethics, 3:404
on existence of fictitious objects, 3:493–494
on faith, 5:615–616
French clandestine literature and, 2:264
Geulincx and, 4:76
Giles of Rome and, 4:89–91
on God, 2:728, 4:669
Godfrey of Fontaine and, 4:131–132
Heidegger on, 4:290
Hobbes and, 3:294
Ibn Gabirol and, 7:611
intelligible *vs.* existent in, 9:772–773
Kilwardby and, 5:69
language in, 2:669, 6:101–102
in Latin American philosophy, 5:204–206
logical and methodological interests of, 1:626, 2:285–286
Luther and, 5:615–617
Malebranche and, 5:663
matter in, 6:3
in medieval philosophy, 6:100–105
Merton Schoolmen and, 3:134
on mind-body problem, 2:750
Molina and, 6:321–322
More (Thomas) and, 6:398
in natural philosophy, 1:444
and Ockhamism, 7:8, 9:771–772
Peirce and, 7:164
on perception, 8:824–826
Petrarch and, 7:263–265
phenomenology and, 9:240
Pico della Mirandola and, 7:570–572
on properties, 3:138–139
and psychology, 8:123
on reason, 5:615–616
in Renaissance England, 1:444
Richard of St. Victor and, 8:592
Scholz on, 8:645
School of St. Victor and, 8:592
on science, 3:134
Scot and, 8:703
Soto and, 9:137
on soul, 4:608
Spanish, 9:443
Spinoza and, 3:294
Suárez and, 9:282–283
on theology, 3:134, 5:615

Thomism and, 9:445
on transcendentals, 3:137–138
true as adjective in, 2:547
on truth as signified thing, 2:540
Wolff and, 9:825–826
See also Augustinianism; Averroism; Medieval philosophy; Ockhamism; Scotism; Thomism
Scholz, Heinrich, 5:525, **8:644–646**
Schönborn, Johann Philipp von, 5:250
Schönfinkel, Moses, 2:340
Schoock, Martin, 2:750
School(s)
Carolingian renaissance, 2:49–51
in Hellenistic philosophy, 4:300
privatization of, 7:362
See also Education
School and Society, The (Dewey), 3:44, 3:48
School of Baghdad, 5:418
"School of Giorgione, The" (Pater), 7:136–137
School of Names, 4:148
School of Precepts, endorsed by Three Kingdoms, 5:134
School of Qom, The, 4:763, **8:646–647**
School of Wisdom, of Keyserling, 5:58
Schopenhauer, Arthur, **8:647–657**
on aesthetics, 1:36, 1:55–56, 8:653
on art, 1:55–56, 9:524
on artists, 8:653
asceticism of, 1:351
atheism of, 1:258
Brouwer and, 1:700
Burckhardt and, 1:766
on death, 2:650–653, 5:346
on determinism, 3:12, 3:16
Deussen on, 3:41–42
Driesch and, 3:110
Dühring and, 3:130
on empathy, 9:37
and epistemology, 3:311, 5:91
on ethics, 3:415
on evil, 3:469
on existence governed by will, 4:747
Fischer and, 3:660
Freud and, 7:522, 8:652–653
Geyser on, 4:83
Gracián and, 4:168
Griesinger and, 7:151
on happiness, 5:345–346
on human nature, 7:153
on ideas of reflection, 8:650
Ivanov and, 4:767
Keyserling and, 5:58
Korn and, 5:142
Kozlov and, 5:146
Latin American philosophy and, 5:208
Leopardi and, 5:285
Liebmann on, 5:344
on life, meaning and value of, 5:345–346, 5:350, 5:354
on love, 5:588–589, 8:653
on moral principles, 2:447
on music, 1:56
and neo-Kantianism, 6:541
Nietzsche and, 6:608–610
panpsychism and, 7:83–86
on pessimism, 7:244–246, 7:250–251
philosophy of sex and, 7:522
on principle of sufficient reason, 4:83
and psychoanalytic doctrines, 3:736
Romero on, 8:492
Schulze and, 8:660
Solov'ëv and, 9:123
on Suárez's scholasticism, 9:282
Sufism and, 9:311
on suicide, 9:319
Tolstoy and, 9:512
on tragedy, 9:523–524
on unconscious, 9:571
Vaihinger on, 9:626
voluntarism of, 9:714–717
on war and peace, 7:153
on will, 8:655
on women, 4:168–169
on world, why it exists, 9:758
on *Zeugungsproblem,* 5:356
Schopenhauer as Educator (Nietzsche), 6:610
Schotch, Peter, paraconsistent logic and, 5:492
Schreier, Otto, 2:506
Schröder, Ernst, 5:462
and Boolean algebra, 5:535
Leśniewski and, 5:291–292
Schröder-Bernstein theorem and, 5:462, 5:556
Schröder-Bernstein theorem, 5:462, 5:556
Schrödinger, Erwin, **8:657–659**
atomism and, 1:388
Einstein and, 3:181
Schrödinger's cat paradox, 1:631
Schrödinger's equation
and evolution of physical systems, 2:126
linear operators and, 8:208–209
and particles in quantum physics, 1:631
in quantum mathematical apparatus, 8:206
Schubert, Glendon, 9:207
Schubert, Gotthilf Heinrich von, 4:254
Schultz, Julius, **8:659–660**
Schulze, Gottlob Ernst, **8:660–662,** 9:57
Schuppe, Ernst Julius Wilhelm, **8:662–664**
Schur, Friedrich, 4:61
Schurman, Maria van, 3:187, 9:838
Schuster, John, on Descartes, 2:723
Schütte, Kurt, 8:55
Schutz, Alfred, 4:197, **8:664–666**
Schutzschriften (Wolff), 9:824
Schwabl, Hans, on Parmenides of Elea, 7:125
Schwarschild solution, in cosmology, 2:561
Schwartz, Barry, 9:62
Schwartz, Benjamin Isadore, 2:194, 2:197
Schwartz, James, on neuroscience, 6:567–568
Schwartz, John, 9:268
Schwartz, Peter, on biological teleology, 9:389
Schwarz inequality, 3:663
Schwarzschild, Karl, 1:607, 9:151
Schwendendörffer, Bartholomäus, 5:250
Schwenkfeld, Kaspar, 3:713, 8:830
Sciacca, Michele Federico, **8:666–667**
Sciama, Dennis, on cosmology, 2:558, 2:562, 9:478
Science(s), 2:68
a priori argument in, Boyle on, 1:673
abstract objects in, necessity of, 6:628
a-causal principles in, 2:104
aims of, 7:578, 7:650–651, 8:827
in ancient India, 5:116
Aquinas on, 9:428
Aristotle and, Zabarella on, 9:866
of art, 1:514
autonomy of, 7:331–332
Bachelard on, 1:440
Bacon (Francis) and, 1:442–443
Balfour on, 1:473–474
Bayesianism and, 1:495–502
and belief, 1:643, 4:780
Bergson on, 1:568
Berkeley on, 1:573–574, 1:583
Bernard of Tours and, 1:592
and bioethics, 1:599–600, 1:603
biological *vs.* other, 7:337
Bohmian mechanics in, 1:629–630, 1:635–636

Science(s), *continued*
Boltzmann and, 1:644–645
Boscovich and, 1:664–666
Boyle and, 1:672–674
Bozano and, 5:445
branches of, methodological uniqueness of, 1:647
Buckle on, 1:718–719
Buridan and, 1:769
Cabanis and, 2:2
Campbell and, 2:17–19
Carnap and, 2:37–45
Cartesianism and, 2:53–61, 2:365, 2:722–738, 2:750–754
Cartwright and, 2:62
Cassirer on, 2:67
causality and, 1:449, 2:103, 2:106–108, 6:247–248
chance and, 2:127–129
chaos and, 2:39, 2:133
character of, 7:650–651
in Chinese thought, 2:216–219, 4:792
Christianity and, 3:452, 4:297
cinematographic method of analysis in, 1:566
and classical mechanics, 2:279
classical physics as model for, 9:365
classification of, by Kilwardby, 5:70
Clifford on, 2:291
cognitive, and pragmatics *vs.* semantics, 7:739
Cohen (Morris) on, 2:307
Collingwood on, 2:326
Comenius on, 2:341
common sense and, 2:358
communities in, 8:695
cognitive labor in, distribution of, 9:85–86
domination by men, 3:595
and linguistic communities, Kuhn's analogy of, 5:159
sociology of, 9:78
Comte on, 2:410–411, 6:225, 7:711–712
concepts in
as functional, 3:757
in operationalism, 7:29–32
Condorcet on, 2:431
constructivism and, 2:475, 9:76–78, 9:645
cosmology and, 2:556–557
counterfactuals in, 2:573–576
crisis of, 7:317–318
critical limits of, 1:474
Cyrano de Bergerac on, 2:618
deists on, 2:683
demonstration in, 8:595
Descartes on, 2:365, 2:722–738, 2:750–754
description in, 6:561
as descriptive, 1:574, 1:582
determinism and, 3:10
as dialectical process, 1:440
Diderot on, 3:72
disciplines in, differentiation of, 9:792
and discreteness and continuity, 1:702
dissent in, 1:500
Dostoevsky on, 3:99
drug efficacy testing as causal inference model for, 2:107
Duhem (Pierre Maurice Marie) and, 3:126–129
Dühring on, 3:131
economics as, 7:351–354
18th-c. enthusiasm for, 8:46
emotion and, 3:198–201
empirical laws of, 6:224
empiricism and, 3:128, 9:644–645
in empiriocriticism, 7:715
and end-benefit outcomes, in policy formulation, 8:675
Engels on, 3:57–63
Enlightenment and, 3:246
and entropy and information in physical states, 2:105
epistemology and, 3:275, 5:340, 7:331, 9:84
errors in, 9:631
ethical naturalism and, 3:363
and ethics, 2:218–219, 3:328, 5:142
Eucken on, 3:452
European *vs.* Chinese, 2:218
evidence in, 1:500–501, 9:778
evolutionary theory and, 1:569
existence of God argued from, 7:703–704
and experience, 1:476, 2:326, 5:528
experimental, economics as, 7:352–353
Fludd on, 3:674
formalism *vs.* description in, 1:630–631
Fries and, 3:753
Gadamer on, 4:3
Geisteswissenschaften and, 4:37
gender and, 3:593, 8:679
of genetics, 4:43
Gestalt theory and, 4:72–73
Giles of Rome on, 4:90
and God, 5:727, 7:703–704
Goodman on, 4:157
in Greek thought, 2:217
Grosseteste on, 4:187
Haeckel and, 4:201–204
Heidegger on, 1:252–253, 3:502
Heim on, 4:297
in Hellenistic thought, 4:301
Helmholtz and, 4:303–304
Hempel and, 4:308
hermeneutical phenomenology of, 7:300
hermeticism and, 1:712
history and, 1:718–719, 7:393, 8:428–429
history of, 3:227, 3:291, 6:501
chemistry and, 2:143–144
and contemporary methodology, 8:683
naturalism and, 6:501
19th-c., 1:643–644
as revealing activity of mind, 1:713
scientific revolution in, 8:695
Hobbes and, 4:408, 4:423–424
"how" questions in, 9:754–755
Human Genome Initiative and, 4:43
incompleteness of, 1:568
induction in, 6:209, 9:743
inexact, scientific laws in, 5:222–224
intellect and, 1:566–568
intuition and, 5:143
Islamic philosophy and, 3:248–249
James (William) on, 4:780
Jaspers on, 4:800
Jeans on, 4:804
Jung on, 4:858
Kim and, 5:72
and knowledge, 4:424, 9:791
of knowledge
Bosanquet and, 1:662
Fichte and, 3:614–617, 4:50
knowledge in
Aristotle on, 2:667, 2:749
Averroes on, 1:423–424
Berkeley on, 3:64
in critical realism, 2:597
Croce on, 2:602
as extension of common science, 1:566
Kuhn and, 5:159
as logical error, 2:602
Mach on, 3:64
Mersenne on, 6:152–153
nativism on, 4:687
Ockham on, 9:778
Schlick on, 8:638
as social construction, 9:78

La Mothe Le Vayer and, 5:182
Lakatos on, 5:171–172
language used in, 8:789
Laplace on, 5:198–199
Lavoisier and, 5:216–217
laws of, as a-causal principles, 2:104
Le Roy on, 5:288
legal, 7:427
Leonardo da Vinci on, 5:281–282
Lichtenberg on, 5:340
limitations of, 3:99
linearity thesis of, 8:674–675
logical positivism and, 6:194
Longino on, 1:158
Lotze on, 5:581–581
Mach on, 3:227, 8:827
Malraux on, 5:673
Maritain on, 5:713
Marković on, 5:719
Marsilius of Inghen on, 5:720–721
Marx on, 3:57
Masaryk on, 6:2
materialism and, 6:6, 6:14
mathematics in, indispensability of, 6:677–678
Maxwell and, 1:644–645
Mead on, 6:81
and medieval thought, 2:669, 6:105
memory studied in, 6:122
mental states as subject of, 1:201
mental-physical distinction in, 6:138
Mersenne in, 6:152–153
metaphor in, 6:167
and metaphysics. *See* Metaphysics, and science
Meyerson and, 6:212
Mill (John Stuart) and, 2:106, 6:247–248, 7:546–547
Milton and, 6:251
of mind, re-establishment of, 5:156
models in
  in cosmology, 2:559–564
  equilibrium, of Boltzmann, 1:644
  interpretive alternatives of, 1:685
  and kinetic probability, 1:644
  metaphor and, 6:166
  of Universe, 2:557–558
modern concept of, formation of, 1:451
in modernism, 6:316
moral nature of, 1:714
Nasr on, 6:480
nationalism in, 7:323
Natorp on, 6:490
natural and human, demarcation of, 1:470
and natural law, 3:404
naturalism and, 6:496, **6:500–503**
and nature, 1:593–594, 1:628, 4:858
nature of, 4:531–532
neo-Platonism and, 4:90
Nietzsche on, 6:610
nihilism and, 1:253
nominalism in, 6:628–629
vs. non-science, 7:352
normal, 8:699
normativity in, 6:502, 8:695
objectivity in, 2:126, 4:2, 9:787
Ockham on, 9:778–780
ontological aspects of, 1:635, 7:300
operationalism and, 1:693–694, 2:17–18, 7:31
optimism/pessimism and, 7:246
Ortega y Gasset on, 7:48
Ostwald and, 7:50
Pannenberg on, 7:82
Paracelsus and, 7:103
paradigms in, 8:695
paranormal phenomena and, 1:698
parapsychology and, 7:113–115
Pascal and, 7:129–131, 7:134
Pearson and, 7:159–161
Peirce on, 6:194, 7:173
and pervasive causal ideas *vs.* deep physical principles, 2:108
phenomenal effects and, 2:104
philosophy and. *See* Philosophy, and science
philosophy as, 1:151, 4:792
philosophy of, 4:8
  Aenesidemus on, 1:32
  Austrian suppression of, 8:639
  Bayesianism and, 1:501–502
  bioethics in, 1:600
  chemistry and, 2:141–144
  Chinese, 2:216–219
  consistency in, 1:631
  and correspondence between theories, 1:637
  definition of, 7:327–328
  demarcation problem in, 8:670, 8:673
  descriptive correlation and, 1:574
  efforts to historicize, 3:596–597
  efforts to "socialize," 3:597
  of Einstein, 3:181–182
  eliminative materialism and, 3:182–183
  European *vs.* Chinese, 2:218
  and explanations as theoretical deduction, 1:643–644
  feminist, **3:63–70**, 3:590–598, 8:679
  Fontenelle as historian of, 3:683
  Greek theoretic *vs.* Chinese pragmatic, 2:217
  history of, 1:440, **7:503–7:515**
  on hypotheses, 1:643–644, 9:218
  and idealization of theories, 1:644
  innate ideas debated in, 4:688
  and knowability of variables, 1:631
  and logical empiricism, 8:694
  and measurement as axiom *vs.* definition, 1:633
  metaphor and, 6:166
  method development, 1:590
  moral implications of, 1:603, 1:714
  naturalized, **6:500–503**
physical domain and, 2:91, 2:105
physicotheology and, 7:557–562
Planck on, 7:578
and plausible supposition, 1:495
Poincaré on, 7:650–651
Popper on, 3:317, 7:352, 7:688–691, 9:547
positivism and, 3:128, 5:206, 7:710
possibility and, 1:595
practice of, *vs.* product of, 6:501
and prescriptive probabilities, 1:495–496
presupposition in, 6:209
probability and, 1:495–496, 1:632
problems of, **7:516–521**, 8:670–673
professionalization of, verifiability principle and, 9:668
progress and, 1:637, 8:46–48
projectively gendered, 3:591
and pseudoscience, **8:669–673**
psychological origin of, 6:81
of psychology. *See* Psychology
qualities in, 8:10–11
Quine on, 1:151
Ramsey and, 8:235
rationalism in, 1:440, 1:637, 8:244–245
realism in, **8:688–694**
  vs. empiricism, 8:692–693
  no-miracles argument in, 8:691

Science(s), *continued*
objectivity in, 8:689
Rescher on, 8:440
Vasconcelos and, 9:648
reality in, *vs.* Catholicism, 9:888
of reasons, status of, 5:116
reduction/replacement model in, 7:343–344
Reformation and, 8:297–298
and relative *a priori* concepts in theories, 2:68
and religion, 1:93, 1:473–474, 2:685–686, 8:377, 8:394–395, 9:393
"how" and "why" in, 9:754
in Renaissance, 8:423
research ethics of, **8:667–669**
Russell on, 2:358
Salmon (Wesley) on, 8:593–594
Sanches on, 8:595
Santayana on, 8:601
Scholastics on, 3:134
simplicity and, 1:666, 4:157
social consequences of, 3:597
social epistemology and, 9:84
societizing, 3:597
Sorel on, 9:132–133
Spinoza on, 3:296, 7:98, 9:172
and statistical mechanics, 2:126
supernatural and, 6:268
symbols in, 4:161
as system of statements, 1:484–485
Taine on, 9:365
teleology in, 9:387
Tennant on, 9:392–393
theism and, 1:474, 4:204
theology and, 3:134, 7:82, 9:392, 9:780
theoretical judgment in, 9:792
timeless present in, 3:356–357
and truth, 2:724, 2:733–735, 4:408, 9:547
Tschirnhaus on, 9:549
typicality and, 1:633–635
unconscious and, 9:570
unified
as calculus, 1:685
Carnap on, 2:38–45
Cartesianism and, 2:53–61
Cartwright on, 2:62
and chemistry's reduction to physics, 2:142–143
logical positivism and, 5:525, 5:528
and speculative suprascience, 1:697
systems approach to, 1:594
as theoretic *vs.* praxis, 2:217
Zhu Xi and, 2:217
See also Unified science
unity in, 1:423–424
U.S. policy for, 8:674–675
Vailati on, 9:631
verification principle and, 5:527–528
as well-made language, 8:785
Whewell on, 9:743
Whitehead on, 9:747–749
Williams (Bernard) on, 9:787
Windelband on, 9:791–792
Wolff and, 9:827
Wright (Chauncey) and, 9:846
See also Law(s), scientific; Neuroscience; Physics; Quantum mechanics; Scientific revolution
Science and Civilization in China (Neddham), 2:216
Science and Humanism (Schrödinger), 8:658
Science and Philosophy of the Organism, The (Driesch), 3:110
Science and the Modern World (Whitehead), 9:746, 9:749
Science as Golem (Collins), 8:679
Science as Social Knowledge (Longino), 1:158
"Science et philosophie" (Le Roy), 5:288
Science of Ethics, The (Stephen), 9:243
Science of Logic, The (Hegel), 5:62
Engels on, 3:60–61
on idealism, 4:557
on knowledge, 3:309–310
Lenin and, 3:65, 5:280
Science of Mathematics, The (Mach), 5:624
Science of Mechanics, The (Die Mechanik in Ihrer Entwicklung, historisch-kritisch dargestellt) (Mach), 3:689, 9:156
on history of science, 3:227
mass defined in, 6:4
Science of the Cross, The (Stein), 9:240
Science, Perception, and Reality (Sellars, Wilfrid), 8:733
Science policy, **8:673–676**
Science studies, **8:676–680**
Science wars, 8:677, 9:78
Science without Numbers (Field), 3:633
Scientia Media and Molinism, 6:321–323, **8:680–682**
Scientific Aspect of the Supernatural, The (Wallace), 9:721
Scientific classification, in Condorcet, 2:432
Scientific determinism, 3:36–37
Scientific dogmatism, Milhaud on, 6:217
Scientific ethics, Kavelin's, 5:48
Scientific explanation, 3:518, 3:526
Braithwaite on, 9:385
Descartes on, 8:124
Hempel on, 4:309
mathematical hypotheses, and, 1:582
Mill (John Stuart) on, 6:223–224
Salmon on, 8:593
Wright (Chauncey) on, 9:846
Scientific Explanation (Braithwaite), 9:385
Scientific Explanation and the Causal Structure of the World (Salmon), 8:593
Scientific inquiry, 3:674, 5:508. *See also* Scientific method
Scientific instruments
for astronomical research, 2:564–565
in cosmology, 2:557–559
Scientific judgments, *vs.* aesthetic judgments, 5:26
Scientific laws, **5:220–225**
vs. accidents, 5:221–222
Cartwright on, 2:62
Duhem on, 3:128
in empiriocriticism, 7:715
in inexact sciences, 5:222–224
nomic necessity and, 5:221–224
outside of fundamental physics, 5:222
Pearson on, 7:160, 7:715–716
problems of, 7:517–518
Scientific method, **8:682–688**
Bacon (Francis) and, 1:443
Bayesianism and, 1:500–501, 9:220
behaviorism and, 1:522–525
belief in, James (William) on, 4:780
Bohr on, 1:637
Boyle on, 1:673
in Cartesianism, 2:54–55
causation and, 2:107–108, 6:247–248, 8:686–687
chance and, 2:129
in chemistry, 2:142–143
in Chinese science, 2:217–218
Chomsky and, 2:244
and conditional probability and hypothesis, 1:496–497
and *Daseinanalyse* in clinical psychology, 1:597–598
determinism and, 1:590
development of, 1:590
as dialogue of reason and experience, 1:440

and empirical phenomena and first principles, 1:447
in ethics, Dewey on, 3:424
Gersonides and, 4:69
Goethe on, 4:142
Grosseteste on, 4:187
Habermas on, 4:200
in historical study, 9:517
Hobbes on, 4:408–410
in humanities, 4:37
inductive, 1:446
Laplace on, 5:198–199
in late medieval astronomy, 2:533
Mill (John Stuart) on, 5:456
and morals, 1:686
naturalism and, 6:492, 8:700–701
Neurath on, 6:561–562
objectivation in, 8:658
and operational point of view, 1:693–694
Pascal on, 7:130
Pearson on, 7:160
Peirce on, 4:644, 7:167
philosophical methodology and, 7:330–331
in physics, 2:142–143
Popper on, 4:640
in psychoanalytic theory, 8:113
rationalism in, 8:244–245
realism and, 8:700–701
and religion, 1:686
Rescher on, 8:439
rhetoric and, 1:444–445
Schiller (Ferdinand) on, 8:625
Schlick on, 8:642
in science and pseudoscience, 8:670–671
skepticism and, 4:11–12
Suppes on, 9:333–334
Telesio and, 9:391
as term, 8:596
Theophrastus and, 9:412
traditional, reform of, 3:594
Venn on, 9:658
See also Positivism

Scientific objects, 9:749
Scientific principles, Wright (Chauncey) on, 9:846
Scientific psychology. *See* Psychology
Scientific rationalism, of Renan, 8:428–429
Scientific reduction, 7:520
Scientific revolution(s), 8:694–695, **8:694–703**
gradualist model of change in, 8:699
Kepler on, 5:53
Kuhn on, 8:683–688
Mersenne and, 6:153
and organism system theory, 1:594
and political revolution, parallels between, 5:158–159
shifts-in-standards in, 8:697–698
thought experiments before, use of, 9:452

Scientific spirit, Fontenelle and, 3:682
Scientific terminology, problems of, 7:516–517
Scientific tests, of cosmological models, 2:561
Scientific theory(ies)
a-causal principles and, 2:104
axiom *vs.* definition and, 1:633
axiomatization and, 2:37–38
Bayesianism and, 1:497–498
and bioethics, 1:600–601
Bohmian mechanics and, 1:630–636
Boltzmann and, 1:644–645
Campbell on, 2:17
Carnap and, 2:37–38
in Cartesianism, 2:54–55
Cartwright on, 2:62
chance and, 2:129
chaos modeling and, 2:133
in Chinese thought, 2:217–218
Chomsky and, 2:244
confirmation and, 1:500–501, 2:435
conservation principle in, 2:462
consistency in, 1:631
convergence of opinion and, 1:500
Copernican and Ptolemaic meaning as, 2:535–536
correspondence principle in, 1:637
in cosmology, 2:557–561
counterfactuals and, 1:501, 2:574
and current science, 2:91
Duhem-Quine conventionalism and, 2:520
electrons and, 2:142
entropy and, 2:105
in European *vs.* Chinese science, 2:218
formal requirements, 1:685
frequency of instances *vs.* frequency over time and, 1:644–645
Greek theoretic *vs.* Chinese pragmatic, 2:217
Hempel on, 4:308
hypotheses and, 1:643–644
idealization in, 1:644
inductive probabilities and, 2:437
inference from empirical generalization and, 1:637
kalām argument as, 2:555
vs. laws, 2:17
in logical positivism, 4:308
Maxwell and, 1:644–645
Milhaud on, 6:217
naturalization of mental content in, 2:480
nature *vs.* mathematical impossibility and, 1:541–542
object independence and, 1:638
observation and, 1:638, 1:643–644
ontology and, 1:635
operational rules and, 2:17–18
on planetary motion, 2:533–534
Popper on, 7:690
probability statement in, 1:686
problems in, 7:519–520
quantum theory and, 1:637–639, 2:143
relative *a priori* concepts in, 2:68
semantic approach to, 9:333–334, 9:645
skepticism and, 1:643
stages of, 7:30–31
testing of, 1:685, 3:128–129
typicality and, 1:633–635
unobservable entities in, 1:643–644

Scientific thought, 5:157
Scientific Thought (Broad), 1:698–699, 9:470, 9:485
Scientific verification, 3:532. *See also* Science(s), and truth
Scientism
of McDowell, 6:74
opposition to, 7:282

Scientist(s)
in cognitive science, 2:297
mopping-up operations of, 5:157–158

Scienza e opinioni (Varisco), 9:647
Scipionic Circle, 7:79
Scito teipsum (Know yourself) (Abelard), 1:3
Scleiermacher, Friedrich, 3:531
Scope, of quantifier, definition of, 5:556
Scopes trial, 2:641
"Scorekeeping in a Language Game" (Lewis), 5:315
Scot, Michael, **8:703**
Scotism, 3:696, **8:704–705**
Catholicism and, 9:436
Gerson and, 4:67
Henry of Harclay on, 4:315
Marsilius of Inghen on, 5:721
Soto and, 9:137
Sylvester of Ferrara on, 9:344
Thomism and, 9:445

Scott, Dana, 2:337, 8:842
Scottish Cato, 3:604
Scottish Enlightenment, 3:246
Scottish philosophy
Emerson and, 3:195
Ferrier on, 3:608
McCosh and, 6:70
and psychology, 4:855
Scottish Philosophy, the Old and the New (Ferrier), 3:608
Scottish school, on common sense, 2:356–357
Scotus, John Duns. *See* Duns Scotus, John
Scotus Erigena, John, on emanationism, 3:189
"Scotus Hiberniae restitutus" (Ponce), 8:705
Screwtape Letters, The (Lewis), 5:311
Scriabin, Aleksandr, 4:767
Scriblerus Club, 9:340
Scriptum Super I Sententiarum (Peter Aureol), 7:255
Scripture
al-Ghazālī (Muhammad) on, 1:119
al-Kindī on, 1:130–131
Annet on, 1:210
and crisis of skepticism, 9:51, 9:52
deists on, 2:683
historicity of, 9:178–179
interpretation of
Cordovero on, 2:539
philosophical, 9:170
Isaac of Stella on, 4:753
Jews and, 5:2
in Jinul's Buddhism, 4:833
Luther on, 5:612–614
Meslier on, 6:154
Milton on, 6:249
Morgan (Thomas) on, 6:405
Origen on, 7:39–40
Pico della Mirandola on, 7:571
in Protestant Reformation, 8:297
as record, 8:453
as revelation, 8:452
socinian interpretation of, 9:99
Spinoza on, 9:176
on suicide, 9:319
Tindal on, 9:503
Toland on, 9:505
Scripture of the Doctrine of Reason, The (Priestley), 8:5
Scripture Vindicated (Waterland), 6:214
Scriven, Michael
Lehrer and, 5:248
in post-positivist debates, 8:694
Scruton, Roger, 7:523, 7:526
Scudéry, George de, on drama, 1:49
Scudéry, Madeleine de, 5:588, 9:838
Sculpture, 4:274–275, 9:692–693
Search for a Method (Sartre), 8:604, 8:609
Searle, John, **8:705–707**
and Chinese room argument, 2:239–242
on consciousness, 2:449
on determinables and determinates, 3:1–2
on emotivism, 3:206
on human mind *vs.* computers, 2:395
on intentionality, 2:452, 4:710
on language, 3:744
on machine intelligence, 5:634
on meaning, 1:154
on mental states *vs.* awareness, 2:456
on performative utterances, 7:199
on phenomenology, 7:299
on volition, 9:705
Sebaldus Nothanker (Nicolai), 6:598
Sebond, Raimond, 9:52
Sechenov, I. M., 7:150–151
Secombe, Wally, 3:600
Second incompleteness theorem, 8:456
Second Jansenism, 4:790
Second law of thermodynamics
kalām argument on God's existence and, 2:555
necessity and, 5:222
See also Thermodynamics
Second Meditation (Descartes), 3:677
Second (secondary) intention
definition of, 5:546
terms of, in medieval logic, 9:776
Second Sex, The (Deuxième sexe) (Beauvoir), 1:515, 3:563, 3:586, 5:373, 7:523
Second Thoughts in Moral Philosophy (Ewing)
ethics in, 3:420
on Moore (G. E.), 3:419
Second Treatise on Civil Government (Locke), 2:261, 7:369, 7:424
Secondarily satisfiable, definition of, 5:556
Secondarily valid, definition of, 5:556
Secondary interpretation, definition of, 5:546
Secondary meaning, in painting, 9:835
Secondary modeling systems, Lotman on, 5:578
Secondary rules
Hart on, 5:239–240
Mill (John Stuart) on, 6:227
Second-figure, syllogism of, 5:498
Secondness, Peirce on, 7:164, 7:168, 7:171
Second-order arithmetic, 8:455–456
Second-order belief, in game theory, 4:18
Second-order desire, personhood and, 7:240
Second-order functional calculus, 5:536
Second-order logic, 5:556, **8:707–708**
Second-order mathematics, in axiomatization of set theory, 8:455
Second-order preferences, 3:718
Second-order quantification, 3:726–727, 5:489–492
Second-order state, 3:757
Second-order volition(s), 3:718–719, 7:240
Second-wave feminism, 3:599
Secrecy
in engineering ethics, 3:241
in Pythagoreanism, 8:181
Secret of Hegel, The (Stirling), 4:558
Secret of the Self (Iqbal), 4:744
Secrets of Secrets (pseudo-Aristotle), influence on Bacon (Roger), 1:452
Secretum (Petrarch), 7:264
Sectarianism, Thomasius on, 9:441
Section of set (segment of set), definition of, 5:556
Secular society, Hooker on, 4:463–464
Secularism
deism and, 2:681
Green and, 4:179
historical implications of, 1:656
School of Qom on, 8:647
of science, Nasr on, 6:480
in Sibley's common-sense ethics, 9:22–23
Secundum imaginationem (according to imagination), 5:69
Secundum quid fallacy, 5:543
Security, computer ethics and, 2:398
Sedgwick, Adam, 2:640
Sedley, David
on Euclides, followers of, 6:110
on Lucretius, 5:599
Seduction, sexual, 7:525
Seebohm, Frederick, on phenomenology, 7:299
Seeds, in Anaxagoras, 1:182
Seeing and Knowing (Dretske), 3:108
Seeing as, concept of, 3:533
Seeings, 5:85
"Seele" als elementarer Naturfaktor, Die (The "Soul" as elementary factor of nature) (Driesch), 3:110
Seele und die Formen, Die (The soul and the forms) (Lukács), 5:603

Seeman, Melvin, on alienation, 1:122–123
Seeming idioms, 1:230
Seemings, 5:85
Sefer ha-emunah ha-ramah (The book of sublime religion) (Ibn Da'ud), 4:817
Sefer ha-emunoth weha-deoth (The book of beliefs and opinions) (Saadya), 8:586
Sefer ha-Ikkarim (The Book of Principles) (Albo), 4:823
Sefer Yetsirah (Book of Formation), 5:4, 8:585
Sefirot (emanations from the Divine), 5:4, 5:610
Segerberg, Krister, 5:491
Segment of set (section of set), definition of, 5:556
Segundo, Juan Luis, on truth, 5:332
Sehnsucht, 5:588
Seidan (Discourses on government) (Ogyū), 7:10
Seikyō yōroku (The essence of Confucianism) (Yamaga Sokō), 9:859
Sein (being), 7:297
Sein und Zeit (Heidegger), 1:762–763, 7:297
Seinsfreude (joy), 6:117
Seinsleid (sadness), 6:117
Sejnowski, Terry, on connectionism, 2:444
Selbald, Hans, 3:712
Selden, John, 3:636
Selected Passages from a Correspondence with Friends (Gogol), 2:122
Selection
    fitness and, 7:341
    levels of, 7:341–342
    perception and, 7:183–184
Selection bias, Leslie on, 1:220
Selection set, definition of, 5:556
Selective breeding, Ehrenfels on, 3:177
Selective subjectivism, Eddington on, 3:164–165
Selective theory, 8:263
Selety, Franz, on eternal return doctrine, 3:354
Self, **8:708–711**
    Alexander on, 1:109–110
    as allusion to absolute, 9:237
    art as expression of, 1:303–304
    Beck and, 1:519
    Bergson on, 1:564
    in Buddhism, 2:199, 6:256
    capacities of, 1:459
    in Chinese, 2:172
    in Chinese name rectification, 2:203
    Confucian concept of, 2:171–176
    consciousness and, 5:143
    Deleuze on, 2:694
    Descartes on, 2:720, 2:728, 2:740–741, 2:755
    destruction of, Weil (Simone) on, 9:737
    Dilthey on, 3:80
    vs. ego, Jung on, 4:857
    embodied, 9:259–260
    empirical, 8:134
    as existence that alludes to God, 9:237
    experience preceded by, Nishida on, 4:798
    Green (T. H.) on, 3:416
    Hume on, 3:218, 4:179, 4:499, 8:132–133
    and I-in-itself, 1:519
    image of, 7:319–320
    in Indian philosophy, **8:717–720**
        atman as, 4:133
        God as another, 4:627
        identification of, with Brahman, 4:135, 4:628
        in Sāmkhya-Yoga schools, 4:626
    in Japanese philosophy, 4:797
    Kant on, 1:519, 8:134
    Kohut on, 8:107
    Le Roy on, 5:288–289
    Le Senne on, 5:289
    in Levinas's metaphysics, 4:830–831
    Lichtenberg on, 5:341
    Maine be Biran on, 5:657–658
    Maritain on, 5:714
    Martineau on, 5:727
    Marx on, 5:731
    in metaphysical solipsism, 9:115
    in metaphysics, 4:830–831, 5:728, 9:115
    Mou on, 2:222
    Nāgārjuna on, 6:471
    in Neoplatonism, 6:556
    Ortega y Gasset on, 5:208
    other and, 5:702
    personal identity and, 7:215
    personality and, 5:673
    as pronoun, in Chinese, 2:172
    psychology of, 8:107
    reality of, 8:132–133
    reformation by, 8:166
    relational theory of, 3:588
    Ribot on, 8:457
    in scientific metaphysics, 5:728
    serial theory of, 4:612
    shame and, 9:3
    Shoemaker on, 9:15
    in social constructionism, 9:77
    solitude of, 5:67
    as special case of universal, 1:755
    Taine on, 9:365
    things and, Ortega y Gasset on, 7:45
    understanding of, autonomy and, 5:731
    unified and coherent, rejection of, 3:587–588
    unity of, 1:109–110
    Vasubandhu on, 9:650
    Williams (Bernard) on, 9:787
    Yang Zhu on, 9:862
    in Yogācāra Buddhism, 1:749
    See also Ego
Self (*ātman*), in Indian philosophy, 5:327
Self and Future, The (Williams, B.), 9:787
Self Trust (Lehrer), 5:248
Self-alienation, 1:123–125
Self-awareness
    and Chinese room argument, 2:238
    of God, 1:433
    in Nishida, 6:626
    in ontology of being, Tillich on, 9:459
    Waddington on, 7:87–88
Self-certification, 9:545
Self-consciousness, 3:615
    animals' lack of, 8:725
    Carlyle on, 2:33
    Christians and, 8:635
    Coleridge's theory of imagination and, 2:318–319
    communism and, 2:365
    in computational terms, 2:300
    conditions for, 3:617
    Emerson on, 3:196
    as goal of philosophical reflection, 1:713
    Hegel on, 4:280–281
    Husserl on, 2:459
    vs. introspection, 4:720
    and knowledge, 2:15
    in mind-body problem, 6:262
    in monadology, 3:298
    particulars as, 1:668
    personhood and, 7:240–242
    religious pessimism and, 7:246
    Sartre on, 2:459
    Schopenhauer on, 8:650–651
    social interaction and, 9:77

Self-constitution, Gentile on, 4:50–51
Self-contradiction
Bradley on, 1:678
definition of, 5:556
Łukasiewicz on, 2:547
Malcolm on, 2:359
Self-control
of body, Plato on, 4:605
in Buddhism, 1:722
knowledge as, 9:855
Plato on, 3:396–397, 4:605
Socrates on, 3:396–397
as wisdom, 1:722
See also Self-discipline
Self-cultivation
Cheng Hao on, 2:145
Cheng Yi on, 2:145
Chinese legalists on, 2:200
in Confucianism, 2:173, 2:176–179, 2:442
desire and, 2:177
ethical attributes and, 2:177
in neo-Confucianism, 4:794
predisposition and, 2:177
rhetorical presentation in, 2:230
Self-deception, **8:711–717**
bad faith and, 1:455–456, 8:608
belief and, 1:535, 2:12, 8:711–713
confabulation in, 8:723
Fingarette on, 8:714
in judgment of right conduct, 9:67
religion as, 2:12
Sartre on, 8:608–610, 8:714
Self-Deception (Fingarette), 8:714
Self-destruction, materialism and, 6:16
Self-determination
Cudworth on, 2:611–612
freedom as, 8:447
in informed consent, 4:679–681
in nationalism, 6:483–484
right to die issues and, 9:321–322
theory of, 3:17–18
Self-development, Mill (John Stuart) on, 6:227–228
Self-discipline, 1:353, 2:616. *See also* Self-control
Self-effacing standards of conduct, 3:441
Self-evidence
Adorno on, 1:26, 1:29
cosmological principle and, 2:562–563
Cudworth on, 2:611
development of, 9:744
normativity and, 1:26
Ockham on, 9:778
Stumpf on, 9:280
subjectivity of, 1:29
Self-evident truth(s)
common sense and, 2:356
necessary, 5:92–93
Self-examination, in Confucianism, 2:172–173
Self-fulfillment (Gewirth), 4:81
Self-government. *See* Democracy
Selfhood, as sin, James (Henry) on, 4:773–774
Selfhood step, in ascending order, 5:148
Self-identity
internal relations and, 8:337–338
personal identity and, 7:220
Self-ignorance, in attributor contextualism, 2:486–487
Self-image, of human beings, 7:319–320
Self-imitation, 5:145
Self-interest, **8:720–722**
and altruism. *See* Egoism and altruism
and business, 1:779–780
Chinese legalists on, 2:238
Clarke on, 2:274
in communism, 2:364
constraint of, by general will, 4:39
contractualist view of, 3:386
definition of, 3:174, 3:361
in economics, 7:352
ethics and, 3:380–382
Green (T. H.) on, 3:416
Hélvetius on, 4:307
Kant on, 2:367
La Rochefoucauld on, 5:201
Laas on, 5:164
and morality, 1:461, 1:779–780, 3:380–382, 3:389, 3:408
as motive of human action, 2:1–2
and profit-seeking by individuals, 1:777
Sidgwick on, 3:417
in Smith's *Wealth of Nations,* 9:69
Socrates on, 3:395
utilitarianism and, 3:389
Vauvenargues on, 9:653–654
virtue as advantageous to, 9:3
in western thought, 2:364
Self-interpretation, Dennett's consciousness theory and, 2:456
Selfish Gene, The (Dawkins), 3:490
Selfishness
ChenYi-Zhu on, 2:156
in Christianity, 2:248–249
Comte on, 2:413
Confucianism on, 2:177–179
consequentialism and, 2:461
Self-knowledge, **8:722–728**
art and, 1:79
Dretske on, 3:109
friends and, 3:749
Hegel on, 4:262
Heidegger on, 4:290–291
as indexical, 8:709
indubitability of, 3:608
Israeli on, 4:765
Mach on, 8:709
Millikan on, 6:236
moral self-transformation in, 9:2
personal identity and, 7:214
Plotinus on, 7:640
and purity, 2:117
Schleiermacher on, 8:634
Shoemaker on, 9:15–16
Skovoroda on, 9:64
Zhu Xi and, 2:217
Self-Knowledge and Self-Identity (Shoemaker), 9:15
Selflessness, Eliot (George) on, 3:185
Self-love
act utilitarianism and, 9:606
in human nature, 1:781
Malebranche on, 5:670–671
passions as, 8:132
Self-lover, good person as, 5:7
Self-mastery
Bosanquet on, 1:663
and totalitarianism, 1:589
Self-mortification, in Tauler, 9:372
Self-observation
concept of, 3:751
Lipps on, 5:363
Self-other relationship, Cixous on, 2:262
Self-predicating universals, 6:179
Self-prediction, **8:728–732**
Self-presentation, of direct evidence, 6:117
Self-preservation
Freud on, 8:146
Hobbes on, 3:405
in object-relations theory, 8:106
Spinoza on, 3:407
Telesio on, 9:390–391
urge for, 5:78
voluntarism and, 9:715
Self-protection, Mill (John Stuart) on, 6:228
Self-realization
Cynic teaching on, 2:616
Ortega y Gasset on, 7:46
Royce on, 3:415
transcendentalists on, 3:415
Self-recognition, in animals, 1:205
Self-reference
in Confucianism, 2:442
semantic paradoxes and, 5:522

Self-referential paradoxes, type theory, 2:76
Self-regarding sentiment, in personality, 6:72
Self-regulating systems, functional statements and, 3:764
Self-reliance, Epictetus on, 3:262
Self-respect, 2:442–443, 8:442
Self-sacrifice
Mill (John Stuart) on, 3:413
suicide and, 9:318
Self-sufficiency
Diogenes of Sinope on, 3:90
of matter, Leibniz on, 5:266–268, 5:274–275
Self-transcendence, Niebuhr on, 6:605
Self-transformation, Guo Xiang on, 4:196
Self-understanding, Confucius on, 2:219
Self-validation, in phenomenological statements, 7:285
Sellars, Roy Wood, **8:732–733**
on critical realism, 2:595–598
metaphysical monism and, 2:598
on perception, 2:597
Sellars, Wilfrid, **8:733–735**
on basic statements, 8:733–734, 9:119
on consciousness, 2:455
eliminative materialism and, 3:182
Lehrer and, 5:248
on mentalistic talk of human beings, 3:677
Millikan and, 6:235
on place in space of reasons, 5:89
in post-positivist debates, 8:694
on theory of meaning, 3:756
on volition, 9:705
Selten, R., 4:17
Semanalysis, of Kristeva, 5:152
Semantic compatibility, in Indian theories of language, 7:416–417
"Semantic Considerations on Modal Logic" (Kripke), 5:149
Semantic externalism, 9:45
Semantic instrumentalism, 9:414
Semantic interpretation, in neural networks, 2:444
Semantic memory, 6:122
Semantic presupposition, 7:770–771
Semantic realism, 8:689–690
Semantic reism, 5:144
"Semantic Structure and Logical Form" (Evans), 3:461
Semantic tableaux, in Peirce, 5:455
"Semantic Theory and Tacit Knowledge?" (Evans), 3:461
Semantic thesis, 3:626
Semantic twist theories of metaphor, 6:168
Semantical role, definition of, 5:556
"Semantical Solution of the Mind-Body Problem, A" (Sellars, Wilfrid), 8:733
Semantics, 6:83, **8:735–749**
Abelard on, 1:5, 8:763–764
adverbial modification in, 3:462–463, 8:808
aims of, 6:649–650
analogy in, 8:784–785
analytic-synthetic distinction in, 9:345–346
in ancient logic, 5:397–398
and anthropomorphic theology, 1:370
Aristotle on, 5:399, 8:755–757
in art, 1:67
in artificial languages, 1:344–345
of assertion, 8:75
atheism and, 1:370
attributor context-sensitivity to, 2:487
Augustine on, 8:759–761
autonomous syntax and, 8:807
Bacon (Roger) on, 1:455
Barwise on, 8:75–76
of beauty, 1:36
behaviorism and, 1:520
belief ascriptions in, 8:739
Bentham on, 8:792–793
Berkeley on, 1:587
bivalence in, 9:540
of body, mental states and, 1:370
Boethius on, 8:761–762
Bolzano on, 5:446
in Buddhist epistemology, 1:756
Carroll on, 2:51–52
categories in, 9:352–359
in category theory, 4:742
in Chinese, 2:188–189, 2:203–204, 2:211–212
Church on, 8:76
Chwistek on, 2:256
completeness and, 9:368
compositionality and, 2:370–371, 5:510, 8:61
comprehension and extension of terms in, 8:777
computationalism and, 2:392
concepts and, 2:415, 2:419
conceptual role of, 1:164, 2:479, 3:760, 8:734
Condillac on, 8:784–785
of conditional statements, 1:549–550, 2:424
and conditions of adequacy, 6:84–85
consequence in, 9:368, 9:369
in constructivism, 2:471
conventional *vs.* ultimate, Dge-lugs on, 1:734
of creation, 1:370
criterion of meaningfulness in, 8:795
critical forces, pre-class society origin of, 1:469
and Dao, 2:205–208
in date theory of time, 9:477
Davidson on, 8:77–78
decompositional approach to, 8:807
denominatives in, 8:762–763
in descriptivism, 8:77
discourse representation theory (DRT) of, 8:748–749
in distribution-free logic, 5:489
doctrine of objectives, 8:804
dynamic, 8:749, 8:808
early theory of, 8:752
Enlightenment and, 8:772
of Epicureans, 8:758–759
events in, **3:462–466**
expressions of generality in, 8:735
extensionality in, 8:61
File Change Semantics (FCS), 8:748–749
force in, 6:650
formal, 5:556, 8:808. *See also* Semiotics
Frege and, 3:251–252, 8:60–61, 8:737, 8:799–801
for fuzzy logic, 3:766
generative, 8:807
generics in, 4:40–43
of God, 7:483
Henkin on, 8:707
history of, 1:455, **8:750–810**
Hui Shi on, 2:189
Humboldt on, 8:793–794
Husserl on, 2:371, 8:802–803
idéologues on, 8:787–790
illocutionary acts in, 8:706
imposition and intentions in, 8:764–765
index of evaluation in, 8:745
Indian, 9:580–582
of indirect discourse, theory of, 8:808
informational, 2:479
intensional, 1:345, 4:622
intentionality and, 4:706, 7:402, 8:764–765, 8:802
and intuitionism, 4:739–740, 5:488

Semantics, *continued*
inward locutions in, 8:761
Johnson on, 8:794–795
Kaplan on, 4:622, 5:38–39
and knowledge, 8:777
Lambert on, 8:786
Leibniz's Law and, 8:781
lekton, doctrine of, 8:757–758
lexical, 1:164
of life after death, 1:370–371
Locke on, 8:777
logical terms and, 5:532
in machine intelligence, 5:634
many-to-one *vs.* one-to-one mappings in, 2:205
in many-valued logic, 5:689–690
Marsilius of Inghen and, 5:721
of mass/count nouns, 6:661–662
Maupertuis on, 8:783–784
Mauthner on, 8:801–802
meaning-delivery-within-speech-capacity in, 2:208–209
Meinong on, 8:803–804
mental representations in, 2:479, 6:141
metaphor and, 6:166–169
Mill (John Stuart) on, 8:795–797
Millianistic, 8:76–77
modal logic and, 5:483, 5:486, 6:293–296
model theoretic approaches to, *vs.* absolute truth theory, 8:744
Montague on, 1:345, 6:329
mood in, 6:650
of moral sentences, 2:471
in naive theory, 8:58
in natural language, 1:344–345, 5:510
of negative sentences, 8:804
new theory of reference in, 8:747
nominalism and, 6:626, 6:629–630
ordinary language category theory of, 2:79
of paraconsistent logics, 7:105
paradoxes in, 5:551, 8:555
denoting in, 5:518
Kripke on, 5:149
in logic, 5:521–522
in parallel distributed processing, 1:347
Peirce on, 8:797–799
Perry and, 8:75–76
and philosophy, 9:367
in philosophy of language, 7:402
in Plato's *Cratylus,* 8:752–754
Plutarch on, 8:758
of possibility, 7:724
possible-world, 1:155, 8:75–76, 8:807
vs. pragmatics, 7:409, 7:738–739
procedural, 3:760
of programming languages, 1:344
prolepsis, 8:759
of proper names, 8:57–63
propositional attitudes, 8:74–78, 8:808
in Putnam's Twin Earth analogy, 9:45
quantifiers as arguments to verbs in, 4:699
reference as purpose-perspective-sensitivity in, 2:204–205
of relevant logic, 5:488, 8:358–359
Renaissance, 8:772
Russellian, 8:59–60, 8:737, 8:747
for scientific conditionals and lawlike sentences, 3:710
of scientific laws, 7:517–518
for second-order logic, 8:707
of self-knowledge, 8:723
Sellars (Wilfrid) on, 8:733–734
semiosis in, 8:797
of sentences, 1:5
sequents in, 3:650. *See also* Sequents
sermonism and, 8:764
in set theory, 9:368
and signs, doctrine of, 8:782
Soames on, 8:75–76, 8:77
sophismata, 8:770
speculative grammar and, 8:771
speech and meaning-delivery-beyond-speech-capacity in, 2:208
Stalnaker on, 8:76, 8:748
state-descriptions in, 8:738
of statements, Plato on, 8:755
Stoics and, 5:405, 8:757–758, 9:255
Strawson on, 2:79
subject and predicate in, 9:286–287
syncategoremata, 8:756
synsemantic terms and, 1:691
vs. syntactics, 9:368–369
Tarskian, 1:343, 2:547, 5:517, 8:841, 9:367–369
teleosemantics, 4:711
of tense, in *kalām* argument on God's existence, 2:553
in tensed theory of time, 9:477–478
thematic elaboration, 3:464–465
theoretician's dilemma in, 8:690
on theories, 9:416–417
theory of reference and, 8:746–747
theory of truth and, 8:744, 9:537–538
of thought attributions, in natural language, 8:829
three discourses of, 8:761–762
of truth, 7:196
truth in, 8:737, 9:264
T-schemata, 8:808
universals and, 8:762–764, 9:602
value in
in attributor contextualism, 2:484
as degrees of truth, 5:486
of verbs, 8:741–742
verifiability principle and, 9:666
See also Language
Semasiology, 5:728–729
Semblance, Langer on, 5:188
Semel in vita, Descartes on, 2:727
Semiactivism, of Matthew of Aquasparta, 6:65
Seminal reasons, as potency of matter in Bonaventure, 1:654
Semiology
Barthes on, 1:481
Ferdinand de Saussure and, 5:152
vs. semiotics, Peirce on, 7:173–174
Semiosis, 8:797
Semiosphere, Lotman on, 5:578–579
Semiotic elements, 5:152
Semiotics
aesthetics in, 1:58
art in, 1:305
Bacon (Roger) on, 1:455
Blanchot on, 1:611–612
Bulgakov on, 1:760
Cassirer on, 2:67
definition of, 5:556
development of, 8:808
Goodman on, 1:327
history of, 1:455
images and, 1:327
Lotman on, 5:578–579
Merleau-Ponty and, 6:150
Peirce and, 7:165, 7:173–174
pragmatics in, **7:738–741**
representation and, 1:327
vs. semiology, Peirce on, 7:173–174
Shpet and, 9:17–18
sign, symbol, and meaning in, 2:67
and signification of general terms, 1:586
Soviet, 9:17–18
transcendental, 1:225–226
See also Semantics
"Semiotik, oder die Lehre von der Bezeichnung der Gedanken und Dinge" (Lambert), 8:786

Semipositivist, Kareev as, 5:40
Semiramida (Khomiakov), 5:59
Semler, J. S., Lessing and, 5:295
Sempiternity, 3:693
Sempronius Gundibert (Nicolai), 6:598
Sen, Amartya K., **8:810–811**
  on measures of well-being, 3:448
  Nussbaum and, 6:680
  on profit-seeking by individuals, 1:777
Seneca, Lucius Annaeus, **8:811–813**
  on Aristotle, 3:350
  on art, 1:189
  on common consent for God's existence, 2:345
  on death, 2:652
  Descartes on, 2:753
  on dialectic, 3:54
  Diderot on, 3:72, 3:76
  Galileo on, 4:9
  on law, 7:419–420
  Lipsius and, 5:364
  Naigeon and, 6:476
  on Petrarch, 7:264
Seneca the Younger, stoic writings of, 9:254
Senghor, Leopold, on African philosophy, 1:84
Sengshao
  on emptiness of motion, 2:161
  on ultimate reality, 2:221
  on wisdom as absolute pure intuition, 2:219
Senior, Nassau, *vs.* Malthus, 5:677
Sennert, Daniel, atomism and, 1:386
Sens commun, la philosophie de l'être et les formules dogmatiques, Le (Garrigou-Lagrange), 4:23
Sensa, **8:813–823**
  adverbial analysis and, 8:821
  arguments concerning, 8:815–816, 8:819–820
  causal chains of, 7:180–181, 7:272, 7:275–276, 7:296
  duration of, 9:486–487
  in illusory experience, 4:586–587
  language of, 8:821–822
  Paton on, 9:486
  perception and, 7:178–188
  phenomenalism and, 7:271
  properties of, 8:816–817
  realism in, 8:818
  Sellar on, 8:732
  sense contents of, 8:821
  in "sensible" space, 8:819
  of time, 9:484–485
  See also Sense data; Sense-datum theory
Sensation(s)
  as act of soul, 1:403
  and afterimages, 8:814–815
  ambiguities in, 8:827
  in anomalous monism, 1:211
  vs. apprehension, 5:160
  Aquinas on, 9:428–429
  Ardigò on, 1:252
  Aristotle on, 8:824
  Armstrong on, 1:287
  association and, 8:815
  Astell on, 1:356
  awareness of, *vs.* perception, 8:814–815
  vs. belief, 1:532
  Berkeley on, 1:575, 1:585, 3:217–218
  Boulainvilliers on, 1:670
  Boyle on, 1:674
  in Brouwer's ur-intuition, 4:738
  Brown on, 1:705
  Cabanis on, 2:2
  Campanella on, 2:15
  cause of, 4:304
  Chwistek on, 2:255
  of colors, 2:332–334
  Condillac on, 2:421–422, 9:515
  Culverwell on, 2:613
  definition of, 8:813
  Descartes on, 8:124
  Destutt de Tracy on, 2:760
  Ducasse on, 3:124–125
  in empiriocriticism, 7:715
  Epicurus on, 3:269
  as experience, 1:576
  vs. extension, 5:667
  formal properties of, attention to, 5:19
  Foucher on, 3:703
  Gassendi on, 4:28–29
  Greek philosophers on, 8:823–824
  Hartley on, 8:135
  Helmholtz on, 4:304
  Hobbes on, 6:9, 8:825
  Hume on, 8:131
  idéologues on, 8:788
  ideologues on, 8:788
  vs. image, 8:131
  in inner sense theory of consciousness, 2:453
  James (William) on, 3:313
  judging, criteria for, 1:696
  Kant on, 3:306
  knowledge and, 8:126
  Leucippus-Democritus on, 6:7
  Lichtenberg on, 5:341
  Locke on, 1:201
  Mach on, 3:64
  Malebranche on, 2:57, 5:667–668
  in materialism, 6:7, 6:15
  Mill (James) on, 6:219
  Mill (John Stuart) on, 6:226
  natural expressions of, 7:54–55
  neurophysiology of, 8:135
  and ontological proof of God's existence, 1:585
  pain in assimilation of, 8:824
  vs. perception, 8:814–815, 8:823. *See also* Sense perception
  personality and, 4:856
  physicalists on, 3:220, 7:553
  pleasure-pain dimension of, 7:617–618
  Plekhanov on, 3:64–65
  primary *vs.* secondary qualities of, 1:674
  in psychology, 18th-century British, 8:135
  Reid on, 3:305, 8:324–325
  relevancy of, 1:356
  in representational theories of consciousness, 2:455
  Rohault on, 8:483
  Royer-Collard on, 8:524
  Russell on, 3:315
  as self-intimating, 5:93
  vs. sense datum, 1:485
  shared, 8:15
  significance of, in experience, 1:584
  Spinoza on, 8:126
  in Stoicism, 8:121
  in theory of self-constitution, 4:50–51
  of things *vs.* qualities, 1:578
  thought experiments and, 9:455
  Wittgenstein on, 7:54
  words referring to, 7:54
  in Yogācāra Buddhism, 1:748–749
  See also Sensa
Sensational realism, adherence to, 5:145
Sensationalism, 8:135–137, **8:823–829**
  atomistic, 8:140
  in Britain, 19th century, 3:312
  Condillac and, 2:422, 8:137
  Cousin on, 2:579
  de Staël on, 9:202
  Diderot and, 3:72
  Epicurean semantics and, 8:759
  inappropriate groupings in, 8:827
  Pearson and, 7:160
  and perception, 8:815
  Royer-Collard on, 8:523
  scientific statements and, 8:826–827
  Wundt and, 8:140

"Sensations and Brain Processes" (Smart), 7:470, 9:65

Sense(s), **8:829–830**
- acquisition of knowledge by, 1:653
- Aristotle on, 2:74
- Augustine on, 1:392–393
- Bacon (Francis) on, 1:450
- beauty felt by, 9:790
- borrowed-meaning knowledge and, 9:138
- Church on, 2:254
- in compositionality, 2:371
- correction of, by reason, 4:186
- Cudworth on, 2:611
- denotation and, 2:254
- Eddington on, 3:164–165
- Edwards (Jonathan) on, 3:167
- and empirical psychology, 1:494
- Epicureans on, 8:758
- Frege on, 3:728, 5:464, 8:735–736, 8:800
- Grosseteste on, 4:186
- Haeckel on, 4:202–203
- Helmholtz on, 6:540
- and ideas, 8:596
- in illusory experiences, 4:586
- *vs.* imagination, 8:131
- inward, 5:655–656
- knowledge from, 9:879–880. *See also* Empiricism
- La Mothe Le Vayer and, 5:182
- Lenin on, 3:64–65
- limitations of, 7:182
- *vs.* linguistic meaning, 8:830
- Locke on, 3:217
- Maine de Biran on, 5:655–656
- Malebranche on, 5:667
- Merleau-Ponty on, 9:491
- in metaphysics, 6:184
- modalities of, 2:39
- Nicolas of Autrecourt on, 6:600
- perception. *See* Sense perception
- and perceptual discreteness, 1:575
- Plato on, 3:284–285
- of proper name, 5:548
- psychological laws of, 1:202
- in rational inference, 8:830
- reference and, 8:736, 8:800
- reflexive, 4:65
- Saadya on, 4:812, 8:586–587
- Sanches on, 8:596
- of "see," 8:820
- semantic, 8:60–61
- skepticism of, 4:501
- and social roles assigned to women, 3:572
- as source of truth, 1:450, 2:727–729, 2:739–741, 2:749, 9:103
- subjectivity of, 6:540
- *vs.* taste, 1:38
- Telesio on, 9:390
- of time, *vs.* perception, 9:484
- universals proved by, 9:582
- Winckelmann on, 9:790
- Zeno of Elea on, 9:877
- Zhang Zai on, 9:879–880
- *See also* Common sense; Qualia

"Sense and Certainty" (Goodman), 4:159

Sense and Non-Sense (Merleau-Ponty), 6:149

Sense and Nonsense of Revolt, The (Kristeva), 5:152

"Sense and Reference" (Frege), 8:735

Sense and Sensibilia (Austin), 1:154, 1:407

Sense contents, phenomenalism and, 7:273

Sense data
- Ayer on, 1:437
- Broad on, 1:696
- colors as, 2:333
- in Huayan Buddhism, 2:164–165
- in logical constructions, 9:796
- McTaggart on, 6:78
- natural philosophy and, 5:721
- objectivity of, 1:519
- persistent and sense-qualified, 1:696
- and qualia, 8:191
- terminology of, 1:437
- *See also* Sensa; Sense-datum theory

Sense experience
- Ayer on, 1:437
- Berkeley on, 4:554, 8:782–783
- Democritus on, 4:27
- discovery of natural objects in, Santayana on, 8:599
- empiricism on, 4:686–687
- Galileo on, 4:12
- Gassendi on, 4:25–26
- in Gestalt theory, 4:74–75
- Godfrey of Fontaine on, 4:131
- Green on, 4:558
- Hobbes on, 8:825
- illusory, 4:585
- imagination and, 4:600
- independence from, in Hilbert, 4:62
- Leibniz on, 4:554
- measurement of, 8:10
- nativism on, 4:686–687
- Plato on, 3:283–286
- religious experience and, 8:402–403
- in skeptical argument, 9:42–43
- solipsism and, 9:115–116
- Spinoza on, 3:295–296
- Stout's noetic synthesis of, 9:259
- and taste, 4:65
- unreliability of, in Sanches, 8:596
- *See also* Sense perception

Sense impression, 8:813

Sense object, 9:749

Sense of Beauty, The (Santayana), 1:57, 1:63, 8:597–598

Sense organs
- in Buddhist epistemology, 1:754–755
- Haeckel on, 4:203
- perception and, 7:180–182
- properties not transducible by, 3:676
- in Yogācāra Buddhism, 1:749

Sense perception
- Alston on, 7:482
- Aquinas on, 3:289
- Aristotle on, 3:286
- and association, 1:575
- Augustine on, 3:289
- Berkeley on, 3:301–303
- Cartesians on, 2:56–57, 4:725
- Democritus on, 5:300–301
- Descartes on, 3:291–293
- Epicurus on, 3:287–288
- Ferrier on, 3:608
- Hazlitt on, 4:248
- Hegel on, 3:310, 4:262
- Hume on, 3:303–305
- Kant on, 3:306–307
- and knowledge of nature, 1:453
- Kozlov on, 5:146
- Leibniz on, 3:298
- Leucippus on, 5:300
- Lewis (C. I.) on, 5:307–309
- Locke on, 3:299–300, 5:379, 5:385
- Mach on, 5:625
- Maine de Biran on, 5:656–657
- Malebranche on, 3:293–294
- and materially false ideas, 2:56–57
- Ockham on, 3:290
- Plato on, 7:599
- Plotinus on, 3:288–289
- as *pratyaksa,* 5:117
- Reinhold on, 8:334
- in Sautrānikita doctrine, 1:745
- Spinoza on, 3:294
- *See also* Perception; Sense experience

Sense qualities, Zabarella on, 9:866

Sensed, body as, 6:148
Sense-datum theory, 1:154
  perception and, 7:178, 7:183–186, 7:189–192
  phenomenalism and, 7:273–274
  sensa and, 8:813–822
  Stace on, 9:200
Senseless problems, Vaihinger on, 9:627–628
Sense-reference distinction, in Frege, 3:728
Senses and the Intellect, The (Bain), 1:462
Sensibilia
  phenomenalism and, 7:272
  Russell on, 8:821
  Schulze on, 8:660–661
  See also Phenomenalism
Sensibility
  in experience, 6:74
  Hegel on, 3:610
  standpoint of, 3:618
  and things *vs.* qualities, 1:578
Sensible qualities, 1:578
  as divine language, 1:574
  in Ockham's metaphysics, 9:779
Sensible space
  sensa in, 8:819
  and verbal space, 4:848–849
Sensible things, Locke and Berkeley on, 1:574
Sensible world, 5:25
Sensing
  in absence of intellectual analogue, 1:698
  adverbials in, 8:813
  vs. apprehension, Ehrenfels on, 3:176
  perception and, 8:817
  sense-datum theory and, 8:813–814
Sensism, 4:94
Sensitive knowledge
  Locke on, 3:300, 5:96
  Sosa on, 9:136
Sensitivity(ies)
  relevant alternatives and, 8:359–360
  to stimuli of indefinite logical complexity, 3:676
Sensor, body as, 6:148
Sensory imagination, 4:600
Sensory intuition, 4:724
Sensory knowledge, *a priori* elements in, 5:14
Sensory stimuli
  and behavior, 2:456
  consciousness and, 2:449
Sensory taste, 8:8, 9:515
Sensory world, 5:36
Sensory-motor activity, 1:564–565
Sensualism, 4:306, 7:47
Sensuous impulses, of man, 5:24
Sensuousness, Cousin on, 2:580
Sentence(s)
  Abelard on, 1:4
  as abstract structures, 1:318
  as actions, 1:154
  anaphora of, **1:171–176**
  Aristotle's semantics of, 8:756
  Arnauld on, 8:776
  atomic, 7:416
  attitude-ascribing, 8:80
  Austin (John Langshaw) on, 1:408
  as belief attributions, 1:536–538
  Bentham on, 1:552
  Blackburn on, 6:653
  Bolzano on, 1:647, 5:445–446
  Carnap on, 5:527
  composite sense of, 1:4
  in computability theory, 2:387
  concepts and, 2:415
  as conditionals, 2:424
  content of, 8:746
  context and, 7:766, 8:746
  conversational implicature tests and, 2:527–528
  counterfactual, *vs.* indicative conditional, 1:550
  Davidson on, 6:85
  declarative, meaning of, 9:346
  denial in, 6:654
  dispositions of speakers and, 6:652
  entailment in, 7:770
  expressivism on, 6:653
  facts represented by, 9:797
  force of, 6:650
  formula as, 3:648
  Frege on, 3:728, 9:556
  future contingent, 5:692
  Gibbard on, 6:653
  Grice on, 6:651
  Hempel on, 4:308
  illocution in, 1:132
  in Indian theories of language, 7:416–417
  indices of truth in, 8:808–809
  inferential role of, 3:629
  intension of, 1:345
  intentional, inscriptional theory of, 4:706
  L concepts in, 8:738–739
  logic and, 3:643, 5:506, 5:688
  Mauthner on, 8:802
  meaning of, 5:510, 6:85, 7:406, 9:264
    Alston on, 1:132
    analyticity and, 1:166–167
    conventional, 6:83
    correspondence theory and, 2:546
    Johnson (Alexander Bryan) on, 4:849
    Quine on, 1:151
    use and, 9:811–813
    in verifiability principle, 9:660
    and what cannot be said, 9:804
    Wittgenstein on, 1:147–148
  meaningfulness of, 9:43, 9:669
  Meinong on, 8:804
  mental content and, 2:476–477
  mood of, 6:650
  in Moore's theory of truth, 2:542
  motivation in, 6:653
  multiplicity of, 7:404
  negation of, 6:523
  negative, 8:804
  negative existential, 1:145–146
  normative, 6:653
  object-language and, 9:353
  open, definition of, 5:550
  paraphrasis and phraseoplerosis in, 1:552
  Peirce on, 5:453
  phrase structure of, 9:360
  as picture, 9:803–804
  Plato on, 7:600
  presupposing in, 7:766, 7:770
  previously unheard, understanding, 2:371
  of probability and confirmation theory, 2:436
  proper use of, 3:627
  of propositional logic, 3:643
  protocol. *See* Protocol sentences
  as pseudo-statements, 8:737
  reference of, 8:800–801, 8:804
  referential opacity in, 4:707
  relational, ontology in, 1:562
  Russell on, 2:546, 7:768, 8:736–737
  science as system of, 1:484
  semantics of, 1:5, 6:649–650, 8:74–75
  sense of, 3:728, 8:800–801
  senseless, 9:812–813
  Stoics on, 8:757
  subject–predicate relations in, 2:162, 9:285–286
  synonymous, 7:403
  syntax and, 9:359–360
  Tarski on, 2:387, 2:547–549
  thoughts as, 9:804–805
  transitive verbs in, intensional, 4:698

Sentence(s), ***continued***
- translatable into empiricist language, 9:662–663
- understanding of, 2:371, 7:406, 9:664–665
- unused, 6:84
- verifiability principle applied to, 9:659–660
- in verificationism, 7:31, 9:43
- Wisdom (John) on, 9:797
- Wittgenstein on, 2:546, 9:803–805, 9:812–813

Sentence need, grammatical form of, 5:509
Sentences (Kilvington), 5:69
Sentences (Lombard), 5:70, 7:259–261
- Alexander of Hales and, 1:113
- Duns Scotus on, 3:133–134
- Durandus of Saint-Pourçain on, 3:148
- John of Mirecourt on, 4:841
- in medieval philosophy, 6:99
- Ockham on, 9:770–771
- Olivi on, 7:12
- Wodeham on, 9:821

Sententiae (William of Champeaux), 9:767
Sententiae Vaticanae (Epicurus), 3:265
Sentential connective, definition of, 5:538
Sentential forms, Bolzano on, 5:446
Sententialism, 8:82–83
Sentience
- abortion and, 1:8
- and inclusion in moral community, 9:164
- in Stout's noetic synthesis, 9:259
- Whitehead on, 9:751

Sentient entity, in ontological reism, 5:144
Sentiment(s)
- Boileau on, 1:640
- instinct in, 6:72
- in personality, 6:72
- Pfänder on, 7:270
- reflective, in Shaftesbury's moral sense, 9:3
- in Smith's moral theory, 9:67
- and taste, 4:65

"Sentiment of Rationality, The" (James, William), on objectivity, 4:776
Sentimentalism, Mercier on, 6:145
Sentimiento trágico de la vida, Del (The Tragic Sense of Life) (Unamuno), 9:566–567
Seo Kyeongdeok, theory of cosmology and human nature, 5:138
Seon Buddhism, Jinul in, 4:833
Seonggwangsa monastery, founding of, 4:833
Separability thesis, 5:240–241
Separation, and distinction, confusion of, 3:543
September 11, 2001, 9:395–397
Sequence, definition of, 5:556
Sequents, 3:641, 3:644, 3:650–651, 3:656
Serial idea, 8:609
Series
- converging, Newton on, 6:591
- infinite, Kant on, 9:467
- *kalām* argument on God's existence and, 2:555
- in Swedenborg's philosophy of nature, 9:337

Serious Call to a Devout and Holy Life, A (Law), 2:686, 4:854, 5:220
Serious Proposal to the Ladies, A (Astell), 1:355–356
- *Part II,* 9:838

Sermocinalism, 8:766
Sermon before the House of Commons, March 31, 1647, A (Cudworth), 2:685
"Sermon on Law and Grace," 5:59
Sermon on the Mount, Tolstoy on, 9:513
Sermons on the Canticle (Bernard of Clairvaux), 1:592
Serra, Richard, 3:256
Servetus, Michael, 3:338, 8:296, **8:830–831**
Servo Arbitrio, De (Luther), 9:51
Sessions, William Lad, 3:535–536
Sestakov, V. I., on electrical logic machines, 5:566
Set(s)
- of axioms, 3:651
- Cantor on, 5:516
- "constructible," *L* of, 8:841
- decidable, in computability theory, 2:372
- Dedekind infinite, 4:658
- definition of, 5:556
- empty, 4:657
- finite and infinite, 2:28
- Frege on, 5:516
- Hume's principle for, 4:659
- indefinitely extensible, 4:665
- intersection of, definition of, 5:546
- iterative conception of, 4:664
- order type principle for, 4:661
- product of, 5:546
- Russell on, 2:76
- size of, limitation of, 4:664
- totally ordered, 4:660
- union of, definition of, 5:559
- universal, definition of, 5:559
- well-ordered, 4:663, 5:516, 8:832–833

Set theory, 3:649, **8:831–847**
- actually infinite collections in, 4:657
- axiomatic system of, 6:559
- axiomatization of, 5:471, 8:455, 8:835–840
- Bolzano and, 1:646
- Cantor on, 6:671, 8:832–835
- Cantor-Dedekind theory of continuum and, 2:500–501
- comprehensive, 5:521
- consistency strength in, 8:841
- continuum hypothesis and, 2:500, 4:659, 4:662, 8:832–833
  - generalized, 8:837
  - predicative theories on, 2:505–506
- covering theorem for *L,* 8:845
- definability in, 9:368
- definite property in, 8:836
- dimensionality in, 9:466–467
- forcing method in, 8:843–844
- Frege and, 5:516
- Gödel's incompleteness theorem and, 8:840
- hierarchies in, 9:368
- hyperreal number systems and, 2:506–507
- in illative combinatory logic, 2:340
- infinitistic, 9:366
- and infinity, 5:515
- in informal axiomatics, 6:22
- inner model theory, 8:844–847
- instants in, 9:467
- intuitionism and, 1:701, 4:739–741, 5:546
- iterative conception in, 8:842
- *kalām* argument on God's existence and, 2:554
- many-valued logics and, 5:693, 5:694
- in mathematical foundations, 6:20–21
- mereology as alternative to, 6:147
- method of diagonalization, 4:661–662
- Montague and, 6:329
- naive comprehension principle, 4:663
- Neumann (John von) and, 6:559
- ontology and, 7:26
- and orders of infinite series, 2:27–28
- ordinal numbers in, 4:660, 8:834

paradoxes and, 5:520–521, 6:21, 6:672–673, 9:555
Peano's axioms and, 5:465
Peirce on, 7:170
reflection method in, 4:665
relativism and, 5:472
replacement and foundation in, 8:841–842
in semantic account of theories, 9:334
semantics in, 4:739–741, 9:368
set-theoretic reductionism in, 8:836
of simultaneity, in classical physics, 9:495
Skolem on, 5:471–472
Tarski and, 9:366
temporal order in, 9:494
transfinite numbers in, 2:27–28, 8:832
type theory and, 9:555
well-ordering principle in, 4:663, 8:832–833
Zermelo-Fraenkel, 4:662–664
See also Mathematics
Seth, Andrew. *See* Pringle-Pattison, Andrew Seth
Set-theoretic structuralism, 9:271
17th century
atomism in, 1:386
materialism in, 6:8–9
optimism/pessimism in, 7:247
rejection of medieval philosophy, 2:669
women philosophers of, 9:838–839
Seventh Letter (Plato), 4:579, 7:582
Severus, Eusebius and, 3:455
Sévigne, Mme. de, La Rochefoucauld and, 5:200
Sex
Epicurus on, 5:601
Freud on, 8:104–105, 8:110, 8:145–146
Jung on, 8:146
Lucretius on, 5:601
and neuroses, 3:742
in object-relations theory, 8:106
philosophy of, **7:521–532**
and animal *vs.* human sexuality, 7:526–527
Beauvoir and, 1:515, 7:523
concepts analyzed in, 7:524–726
expression of, in destructive violence, 1:488–489
history of, 7:521–524
and sex/gender distinction, 1:515
and sexual objectification, 7:529
sexual perversion and, 7:527–529
subjects of investigation in, 7:521
as pleasure, 8:145–146
See also Reproduction
Sex and Reason (Posner), 7:523
Sex and Social Justice (Nussbaum), 6:681
Sex, Art, and American Culture (Paglia), 7:523
Sex differences, distinction between, 3:586
Sex from Plato to Paglia (Soble), 7:521
Sex-affective production, 3:601, 3:606
Sex/gender distinction, 1:515
Sexism, **8:847–850**
affirmative action and, 9:75
benefits of, for capitalism, 3:600
as characterizing social structures, 3:756
as ineliminable from some political theories, 3:600
Marxism and, 5:740
militarism inextricable from, 4:874
in research, screening out, 3:594
in science, as bad science, 3:594
sociobiology as, 3:491–492
"Sexism" (Frye), 3:756
Sextus Empiricus, **8:850–852**
on Aenesidemus, 1:31–32
correspondence truth theory of, 2:541
on Democritus, 5:300
Diodorus Cronus and, 3:87
on dogmatists, 8:851–852
Gassendi and, 4:30
La Mothe Le Vayer and, 5:182
on lekton, 8:757–758
Parmenides of Elea and, 7:122–123
Pico della Mirandola (Gianfrancesco) and, 7:574
on Pyrrhonism, 1:31, 8:173
on quietude, 9:49
on semantics, 8:757
on skepticism, 1:191–192, 3:88, 3:288
on subjectivity, 8:91
on syllogistic reasoning, 5:501
on Timon of Phlius, 9:501–502
translations of, 9:50
on ultimate referents, 8:759
use of tropes by, 9:49
Sexual activity, 7:524
Sexual addiction, 7:528–529
Sexual consent, morality and, 7:529
Sexual Democracy (Ferguson), 3:606
Sexual desire, 7:523–524
Sexual Desire: A Moral Philosophy of the Erotic (Scruton), 7:523
Sexual development
Freud on, 8:104–105
in psychoanalytic theory, 8:109
Sexual difference
Irigaray on, 4:746
politics of, philosophy of sex and, 7:521
Sexual division of labor, 3:575
Sexual dysfunction, *vs.* sexual perversion, 7:528
Sexual expression, Victorian-era, 3:701
Sexual fantasy, 7:525
Sexual harassment, 3:585
Sexual inhibitions, mystical experience and, 8:313–314
Sexual minorities, oppression of, by heterosexuals, 3:756
Sexual objectification, 7:529
Sexual obsession, abandoning, in Indian meditation practices, 6:108
Sexual orientation
analysis of, in philosophy of sex, 7:524
as social construct, 3:585
Sexual personification, 7:529
Sexual perversion, 7:527–529
"Sexual Perversion" (Nagel), 7:523
Sexual repression, Diderot on, 3:76
Sexual selection, 2:633–634, 2:643
"Sexuales Ober- und Unterbewusstsein" (Ehrenfels), 3:177
Sexualethik (Ehrenfels), 3:177
Sexuality
asceticism and, 1:353
Blake on, 1:611
Card on, 2:31
Cixous and, 2:262–263
commonality of, 2:2
Ehrenfels on, 3:177
experience of, genealogy of, 3:701
expression through destructive violence, 1:488–489
Freud on, 9:572
Haeckel on, 4:204
and lesbian identity and ethics, 2:31
and moral luck, 2:31
morality and, 3:450, 7:529, 8:538–539
and neuroses, 4:857
sanctification of, 8:524–525
Schopenhauer on, 8:652–653
as social construct, 7:523

Sexuality, *continued*
Spinoza on, 9:190
Tolstoy on, 9:513
"Sexualmoral der Zukunft" (Ehrenfels), 3:177
Seymour, Charles, 4:251
Shadow, Jungian, 4:857
Shadow-man doctrine, 4:603
Shaffer, Jerome, 7:523
Shafir, E., on decision theory, 2:656–657
Shaftesbury, Third Earl of (Anthony Ashley Cooper), **9:1–4**
on aesthetics, 1:51
on altruism and self-interest, 3:171
on conscience, 2:445
Cumberland and, 2:615
deism and, 2:683
Diderot and, 3:71
Edwards (Jonathan) and, 3:169
on ethics, 3:408
and French clandestine writings, 2:268
on human nature, 3:171
Kant on, 5:26
Locke and, 5:374–375, 5:388
Mandeville and, 5:682
on religious belief, 1:505
Spalding (J. J.) and, 5:213
theory of taste and, 4:65
Shah, Idries, 9:311
Shakespeare, William
on death, 5:349
Diderot and, 3:77
and German romanticism, 8:617
Lessing on, 5:294
Lichtenberg on, 5:338
Schlegel on, 8:630
Shestov and, 9:11
Shakyamuni Buddha, as cosmic, 1:723
Shame, **9:4–6**
in Confucianism, 2:175
as predisposition of heart/mind, 6:129
Sartre on, 8:607
Wollheim on, 9:836
Shame and Necessity (Williams, B.), 9:787
Shan (goodness), Xunzi on, 9:856
Shandao, 2:169
Shangshu (Book of documents), on ultimate reality, 2:220
Shannon, Claude
in cognitive psychology, 8:150
on electrical logic machines, 5:566
information theory of, 4:672, 9:234
Shannon, Moor, on logic machines, 5:566
Shao Gu, 9:6
Shao Kangjie, 5:138
Shao Yong, 2:157, **9:6–7**
Shape
Cordemoy on, 2:538
as determinable, 3:1
outlines, 1:327
as primary quality, 8:8
Shapin, Steven, 9:84
Shapiro, Stewart, 9:271
Shapur, Mani and, 5:683
Shapurakan (Mani), 5:683
Shared memory, 6:126–127
Shariati, Ali, **9:7**
Sharon, Ariel, 9:397–398
Sharp thresholds, 5:111
Shaw, George Bernard
Darwinism and, 2:642
on socialism, 9:87–88
Shaw, Mary, Lehrer and, 5:248
Sheffer stroke function, 5:556
Shelley, Percy Bysshe, **9:7–9**
atheism of, 1:358
pantheism of, 7:98
Shema, in Judaism, 3:97
Shen Dao, on name theory in Chinese philosophy, 2:187
Shengsheng (productivity of life), Dau Zhen on, 2:622
Shepard, Roger, 4:590
Shepherd, Mary, **9:9–11**, 9:839
Sherlock, Thomas
Annet on, 1:210
on religion, 9:503
Sherrington, Charles Scott, 6:71
Shestov, Lev Isaakovich, **9:11–13**
Dostoevsky and, 3:99
rejection of rational standards, 3:631
on religious truths, 3:631
Shi, as perspective on phenomena, 1:738
Shidō (Yamaga Sokō), 9:859
Shi'ite sect
al-Fārābī, Abū-Naṣr Muhammad and, 1:116, 4:756
independent judgment in, Shariati on, 9:7
School of Qom and, 8:646
Shilla, 5:134–135
Shils, Edward, on ideology, 4:574
Shimony, Abner, on rational degrees of belief, 8:685
Shin Buddhism, 9:13–14
Shinran, **9:13–15**
Shintoism
Confucian rationalization of, 9:860
in Japanese philosophy, 4:796
Kojiki in, 4:796
Shishi wuai, in Huayan Buddhism, 1:739
Shiva, Vandana, on Green Revolution, 3:260
Shoah. *See* Holocaust
Shōbōgenzō (Treasury of the true dharma-eye) (Dōgen), 3:95–96
Shōbōgenzō Zuimonki (Miscellaneous talks) (Dōgen), 3:95
Shoemaker, Sydney, **9:15–17**
on consciousness, 2:455
on natural law, 5:227
on personal identity, 7:222–223, 7:229–232
on properties, 3:3–4
Shor, Peter, on quantum computing, 2:408
Shore, John E., 4:675
Short and Easy Method with the Deists (Leslie), 2:691
"Short Demonstration of a Remarkable Error of Descartes, A" ("Brevis Demonstratio Erroris Memorabilis Cartesii") (Leibniz), 3:228
Short Treatise on God, Man, and His Well-Being (Spinoza), 9:173
Short-arm inputs and outputs, 3:760
Shōwa Research Society, 6:216
Shpet, Gustav Gustavovich, **9:17–20**
Shrader-Frechette, Kristin S., 7:544
Shun Kwong-loi
on Chinese ethics, 2:201
on Confucian concept of ren, 2:195
Shùn Zhèng Lùn (Asanga), 5:412
Shunmin (conforming persons), 9:862
Shushu. *See* Zhu Xi
Shyness effect, in parapsychology, 7:114
Sibbern, Frederik Christian, and Kierkegaard, 5:67
Sibley, Frank, **9:20–21**
on aesthetics, 1:33–36, 1:66, 9:21
on beauty, 1:38
on nonaesthetic properties, 1:39
on taste, 1:38
Sic et Non (Abelard), 7:260
Sicarii, 9:395
Sickle-cell anemia, 7:146, 7:466
Sickness unto Death, The (Kierkegaard), 5:64
Siddartha Gautama, 2:111
Siddha (perfect one), in Jainism, 5:327–328

Sidereus Nuncius (The starry messenger) (Galileo), 4:8
Sidgwick, Henry, **9:21–27**
- on altruism and self-interest, 3:173
- on Cicero's influence, 7:79
- on common sense, 2:358
- as consequentialist, 2:460
- on esoteric morality, 9:613
- ethics and, 3:416–418
- on Green (T. H.), 3:416
- on hedonistic utilitarianism, 9:382
- on ideal observer, 4:562
- on immortality, 4:614
- on inclination *vs.* obligation, 3:414
- on intrinsic value of hedonism, 4:719
- as intuitionist, 4:735
- on preference hedonism, 8:721
- on self-effacing standards of conduct, 3:441
- on Shaftesbury's *Characteristicks*, 9:2
- on Sophists, 3:395
- and utilitarianism, 3:382–383, 9:605–606
- on well-being, 8:722

"Sidgwick's Pessimism" (Mackie), 3:443
Sidney, Algernon
- and deism, 2:681
- on poetry, 1:49

Siècle de Louis XIV (Voltaire), 9:708–709, 9:713
Siegfried, Charlene Haddock, 3:567
Sierra, Justo, 5:204, 5:206
Siete ensayos de interpretación de la realidad peruana (Seven interpretative essays on Peruvian reality) (Mariátegui), 5:209
Sieyès, Abbé, definition of nation, 6:481
Siger of Brabant, **9:27–29**
- Averroism on, 1:428
- Bonaventure on, 7:161
- Dante on, 2:626

Siger of Courtrai, on grammar, 8:771
Sight
- and distance perception, 1:575
- perception and, 7:180–185
- sense of, 5:117
- *See also* Vision

Sight and Touch (Abbott), 1:576
Sign(s)
- Cassirer on, 2:67
- Condillac on, 2:422
- miracles as, 6:267
- and polarity in symbol and significance, 2:67–68
- in pragmatism, 7:742, 7:743
- and sensible object as divine language, 1:574

Sign Systems Studies, Semiotics (Trudy po znakovym sistemam, Semiotika), 5:578
Sign theory
- Aenesidemus on, 1:31
- local, 9:515
- Maine de Biran and, 5:657
- Peirce (C. S.) on, 3:313, 7:165, 7:173–174

Signals, in Anselm, 1:218
Signature, of first-order language, 3:641
"Signature of the Age" (Schlegel), 8:632
Signes envisagés relativement à leur influence sur la formation des ideés (Prévost), 8:788
Signes et de l'art de penser, considérés dans leurs rapports mutuels (Degérando), 8:788
Significance (statistical), 3:665
Significance tests, 3:664–666
- as extensions of likelihood ratio tests, 3:665
- Fisherian, 9:213–215
- Laplacean logic of, 3:666
- purely negative, possibility of, 3:665

Significant truth, inquiry aiming for, 3:576
Significatio (property of term), 9:786
Signification
- accessory words in, 8:776
- Aristotle on, 8:755
- Arnauld on, 8:776
- Bentham on, 8:792
- Condillac on, 8:784
- French interest in, 8:783
- heterogeneous elements in, 5:152
- immediate, 8:792
- impositions and intentions in, 8:764–765
- in Indian theories of language, 7:414
- Johnson on, 8:794
- Kant on, 2:74–75
- levels of, among intentions, 8:765
- Lewis (C. I.) on, 5:308
- Locke on, 8:777–778
- in medieval truth theory, 2:541
- Mill (John Stuart) on, 8:796
- of names and paronyms, 2:74–75
- Peirce on, 8:797
- in *Port-Royal Logic*, 8:775
- Ryle on, 2:78
- semiosis as, 8:797
- semiotic element of, 5:152
- signifier and, 1:481
- in Tarski's truth theory, 2:547

Signifiers
- Lacan on, 5:168
- in signification, 1:481

Signs and portents, and determinism, 3:5–6
"Signs of the Times" (Carlyle), 2:33
Sigwart, Christoph, 4:266, 5:456, 7:279, **9:29–30**
Sikhism, meditation in, 6:108
Śīla, 1:730
Silas Marner (Eliot), 3:184
Silence
- Daoism on, 2:205, 2:220–221
- double truth and contextual meaning of, 2:209
- Heidegger on, 7:411
- linguistic truth and, 2:205
- as manifestation of wisdom, 2:162
- in Sanlun Buddhism, 2:162

Sillogismi (Dolz), 5:438
Sillogismo e proporzione (Syllogism and proportion) (Pastore), 7:135
Silloi (Timon of Phlius), 9:501
Silpas. See Kala
Silva, Alcino, 6:568
Silver, Jack, 8:845
Silvester III, Pope, 4:66
Sima Guang
- on Laozi, 5:194
- on Yang Xiong, 9:861

Simchen, Ori, on analytical jurisprudence, 1:170
Simeon Stylites, St., 1:350
Similarity(ies)
- counterfactuals in science and, 2:574
- as gestalten factor, 5:127
- grammatical *vs.* logical, 8:580–581
- in mathematics, 8:546–547
- in metaphor, 6:166
- in neo-Wittgensteinianism, 1:299

Similarity circle, 6:178
Simmel, Georg, **9:30–32**
- on culture, 6:545
- Lukács and, 5:602
- in neo-Kantianism, 6:545
- and Scheler, 8:615

Simmons, Keith, on truth, 5:317
Simocatta, Theophylactus, Copernicus on, 2:533
Simon, Richard, **9:32–33**
- higher criticism and, 5:196
- on Spinoza, 2:265

Simon Magus, 4:98, 4:100, **9:33–34**
Simondon, Gilbert, on philosophy of technology, 7:543

Simonianism, 9:34
Simons, Menno, Franck and, 3:714
Simple(s), Wittgenstein on, 9:805, 9:808, 9:811
Simple laws, of nomic form, 3:709
Simple supposition, 5:557, 9:776
Simple theory of types, definition of, 5:558
Simpliciter predication, concepts of, 5:70
Simplicity
- in beauty, Winckelmann on, 9:790
- Campbell on, 2:18
- in chaos theory analysis, 2:131–133
- Copernican theory and, 2:535
- Daoism and, 2:237
- of God, 1:114, 1:140, 4:110, 4:116
- Goodman on, 4:157
- of nature, 7:652
- Rehmke on, 8:303
- in scientific theories, 2:18
- structural, theory of, 4:157
- in utopianism, 9:617
- Wittgenstein on, 9:811

Simplicius, **9:34–36**
- Aristotle and, 1:279, 5:408, 6:555
- on concentric spheres, 4:172
- Diogenes of Apollonia and, 3:89
- on Empedocles, 3:212
- Epictetus on, 3:262
- on eternal return doctrine, 3:353
- exile of, 6:553
- on limited and unlimited argument, 9:874
- Melissus and, 6:120
- on Moving Rows paradox, 9:876
- and Neoplatonism, 6:554
- panpsychism and, 7:83
- Parmenides of Elea and, 7:122–123
- on Philoponus, 6:555
- on polytheism, 6:555

Simply ordered, definition of, 5:550
Simulating Minds: The Philosophy of Psychology and Neuroscience Mindreading (Goldman), 4:148
Simulation account, of folk psychology, 3:680
Simulation theory, **9:36–41**
Simultaneity
- absolute, in classical physics, 9:495
- Bergson on, 9:489
- causality and, 2:586–588
- conventionalism and, 2:523–525
- divine causality and, 2:588
- relative, in special relativity, 9:496
- Salmon on, 8:594
- theory of relativity and, 3:179, 9:496
- thought experiment on, 9:453–454

Simultaneously satisfiable, definition of, 5:556
Sin
- Abelard on, 1:6
- as act of will, 7:175
- Anselm on, 1:214, 1:217
- anxiety as cause of, 6:605
- Augustine on, 3:402, 3:472
- Calvin on, 2:12
- Camus on, 2:23
- in Christianity, 2:248–249
- Descartes on, 3:12
- and determinism, 3:8
- Erigena on, 3:341
- free will and, 1:217
- hiddenness and, 7:484
- as *logo astratto,* in Gentile, 4:52
- nature and, 6:521
- New Land Buddhism and, 2:169
- Niebuhr on, 6:605
- noetic effect of, 2:12
- Ockham on, 9:783
- original
  - Anselm on, 1:217
  - Augustine on, 1:399
  - choice as, 4:801
  - in collective guilt, 4:194
  - and doctrine of radical evil, 5:30
  - Eberhard on, 3:161
  - Edwards (Jonathan) on, 3:169
  - and evil, problem of, 3:469–470
  - ignorance resulting from, 4:96
  - Jaspers on, 4:801
  - Locke on, 5:395
  - Losskii on, 5:577
  - Malebranche on, 5:671
  - Maritain on, 5:714
  - modern theology on, 3:474
  - in Pelagianism, 7:175
  - society and, 1:399
  - in Stephen's agnosticism, 9:243
- Pelagianism on, 7:175
- predestination and, 3:10
- as resistance to God's will, 2:9
- Schleiermacher on, 8:634
- as source of error, 1:721
- subjectivity of, 1:6
- Taylor (Alfred) on, 9:374
- Wolff on, 9:827–828
- *See also* Morality

Sincerity, Zhou Dunyi on, 9:880
Singer, Marcus, 3:430, 5:36, 9:25
Singer, Michael, 3:256
Singer, Peter, 3:561, **9:41–42**
- on act utilitarianism, 9:612–613
- on animal rights, 1:208, 8:667–668
- consequentialism and, 2:461
- on conventional morality, 3:389
- on duty to aid others, 3:443
- on economic inequality, 3:385
- Sidgwick and, 9:25
- on utilitarian moral cosmopolitanism, 2:569

Single-party system, representation in, 2:701
Singlet state, 6:640, 8:214–215
Singular name, in logic, definition of, 5:549
Singular proposition(s)
- definition of, 5:553
- Kaplan on, 2:708
- Suárez on, 9:283
- *vs.* universal propositions, Ockham on, 9:778

Singular term, definition of, 5:556
Singularity (grammatical), semantics of, 8:57
Singularity (in physics)
- black hole as, 1:606–609
- in chance, frequency and propensity of, 2:127–128
- *kalām* argument on God's existence and, 2:555
- space-time, Earman on, 3:160
- unique evolution and, 3:33

Sinn, 7:299, 8:60–61
Sinn unseres Daseins, Der (Reiner), 5:354
"Sinnhafte Aufbau der sozialen Welt, Der" (Schutz), 8:664
Sircello, Guy, on art, 1:304
Siris (Berkeley), 7:615
Siro, Philodemus of Gadara and, 3:264
Sistema di logica come teoria del conoscere (Gentile), 4:50
Sisterhood, obstructions to, 3:606
Sisterhood Is Powerful (slogan), 3:599
Sisyphus fragment, 6:632
Situated epistemic agency, 3:576
Situated knowers, partiality of their perspectives, 3:577
Situated knowledge, 3:575–576, 3:592
Situated robotics, 1:347–348
Situation
- being-in, 8:607
- definition of, 1:456
- Dewey on, 3:49
- Sartre on, 1:456, 8:607
- of sense object, 9:749

Situation Semantics (Barwise & Perry), 8:809

Situationality, Jaspers on, 4:801
Siva, in meditation, 6:108
Six livres de la république (Bodin), 7:422, 9:140
"Sixth Cartesian Mediation: The Idea of a Transcendental Theory of Method" (Fink), 3:638
Size
  as determinable, 3:1–2
  paradox of, 9:872–873
Skandhas (aggregates), Vasubandhu on, 9:650–651
Skelton, Peter, on natural selection, 7:341
Skeptical Chemist (Boyle), 1:674
Skeptical idealism, of Oakeshott, 7:1
Skeptical Inquirer (periodical), 7:116
"Skeptical paradox," Kripke on, 5:150
"Skeptical solution," Kripke on, 5:150
Skeptical Zetetic (periodical), 7:116
Skepticism
  academic, 1:193–195, 3:703, 4:501, 7:311–312, 8:175–176
  Aenesidemus on, 1:30
  Agrippa and, 1:96
  aitia in, 1:100
  ancient, **1:191–197**
  Antiochus of Ascalon and, 1:222
  and apologism, 1:229
  Arcesilaus and, 1:247–248
  arguments for, 5:103
  art in, 1:335–337
  and astrology, 4:302
  and atomic theory, 1:643
  attributor contextualism and, 2:485–487
  in autonomous idiolects, 8:753
  Bayle on, 1:506–507
  and belief, 1:474, 2:12, 2:93–94
  Berkeley on, 3:302, 4:556
  Boyle on, 1:675
  in British empiricism, 3:218–219
  Buddhism and, 9:544
  Calvinism and, 2:12
  Carneades and, 1:194–195, 2:46, 4:174, 7:312
  and Catholic rule of faith, 9:51
  Cavell on, 2:115–116
  and chance, 2:129
  Charron on, 2:134–135
  in Chinese philosophy, 2:189, 2:200, 2:227
  in civilization, 8:460
  Clitomachus and, 1:195
  common consent arguments for God's existence and, 2:347–348
  common sense and, 1:510, 2:355–356
  contemporary, **9:42–47**
  contextualist solution to, 9:136–137
  Daoism and, 2:189–190
  on definition, 2:668
  vs. deism, 2:681
  Descartes on, 2:727–729, 2:738–741, 2:745–746, 3:291
  in dialectical method, 4:272
  Diogenes Laertius on, 3:88
  dogmatism and, 1:191–193
  empiricism and, 3:215, 3:220, 5:645
  Encyclopédie and, 3:222
  Epicurus and, 3:269
  epistemology and, 3:274–275, 3:278, 3:282–283, 3:288, 7:325, 7:409
  ethical, in Daoism, 2:197–198
  and ethics, 3:399
  evidentialism and, 3:468
  fictionalism and, 9:626
  in film, 7:384
  in French clandestine writings, 2:264
  and Galen, 4:6
  Galileo on, 4:11–12
  Glanvill on, 4:95–97
  Gödel on, 4:117
  Gournay on, 4:166
  in Greece, 1:191–194
  in Greek Academy, 1:247, 4:171, 4:174
  Hegel on, 4:272
  history of, **9:47–61**
  in history of metaphysics, 6:192–193
  Huet and, 4:469–470
  Hume and, 3:303–305, 4:500–501, 4:637
  and indirect perception, 1:577
  inferential justification and, 2:275
  inquiry in, 1:191–192
  in Islamic Spain, 9:50
  on justice, 9:673
  on knowledge, 3:318
  La Mothe Le Vayer on, 5:182
  and laughter, 1:469
  Le Clerc on, 5:236
  in legal theory, 7:451
  and limited certitude, 9:54
  and linguistic negativity as intellectualized disappointment, 2:115
  Locke (John) and, 3:216
  in logical positivism, 9:58
  Lucian of Samosata on, 5:597
  in Mādhyamika doctrine, 1:743
  Maimon and, 5:645–646
  Manheim and, 5:686
  in mental-physical distinction, 6:140
  Mersenne on, 6:152–153
  in metaphysical solipsism, 9:115–116
  in Middle Ages, 9:50
  Mill (John Stuart) on, 6:225, 6:230
  mitigated, 4:26–27, 9:52
  Moore on, 7:108–109, 9:817
  moral, **6:393–394**
  in morality, 6:618–619
  of natural law, 6:510
  of New Academy, 7:607
  Nicolas of Autrecourt on, 6:602
  optimism/pessimism and, 7:247
  paradigm-case argument against, **7:106–113**
  paradox of, 8:23
  Pascal on, 7:131–134
  patristic philosophy and, 7:141–142
  Philo of Larissa and, 7:311
  Pico della Mirandola (Gianfrancesco) on, 7:574–575
  and pious fideism, 1:506–507
  Plato and, 1:192–193
  postmodern, 7:395–397, 9:59
  precursors to, 1:192–193
  probable impressions and, 2:48
  Pyrrhonian, 1:192–193, 3:399, 8:173–176
  and Pythagoreanism, 8:184–185
  questions asked in, 9:797–798
  reason and, 1:505
  and religious pluralism, 8:419
  in Renaissance, 8:425
  Rensi and, 8:433
  Sanches on, 8:595–596, 9:52
  Santayana and, 8:601
  Schulze and, 8:660
  and science, 1:474, 4:11–12
  Sextus Empiricus on, 1:191–192
  Shakespearean tragedy and, 9:525
  Socrates and, 3:399, 4:173, 9:113
  sophists and, 9:130–131
  Stoicism and, 1:193–194, 4:173
  suicide and, 9:319
  of supernatural religion, 6:230
  as theoretical problem, 9:684–685
  Timon of Phlius on, 9:501
  on underdetermination, 9:577
  and unobservables, 1:643
  and value of knowledge and truth, 5:102–103
  Vico on, 9:671–672

Skepticism, ***continued***
virtue epistemology and, 9:684–685
Wittgenstein and, 9:817
Wolff on, 4:553
Xenophanes and, 1:192
"Skepticke, The" (Raleigh), 9:50
Skeptic's Handbook of Parapsychology, A (Kurtz), 7:115
Sketch for a Historical Picture of the Progress of the Human Mind (Condorcet), 2:409, 2:431–432, 3:244
Skill
art as, in Aristotle, 1:296
Daoist concepts of de and dao and, 2:192–193
Skillfulness, as excellence in Chinese religion, 2:225
Skinner, B. F., **9:61–63**
Chomsky on, 2:244
on introspection, 4:721
on language acquisition, 4:693
and law of effect, 1:521
on mental states, 1:201
on mentalism, 1:524–525
and radical behaviorism, 1:520
utopianism of, 9:618–619
Sklar, Larry, on space and time, 3:159
Skolem, Thoralf, 5:694, 9:369
on axiom of replacement, 8:838
on first-order sentence, 3:658–659
hyperreal number system of, 2:507
logic of, 5:471
on Peano's axioms, 5:465
recursive number theory and, 5:554
Skolem-Löwenheim theorem and, 5:556, 9:369
Skolem functions, 3:658
Skolem-Löwenheim theorem, 5:556, 9:369
Skolem's paradox, 5:471, 5:556
Skovoroda, Hryhorii Savych (Grigorii Savvich), 8:566–567, **9:63–65**
Sky god, in Zoroastrianism, 9:886
Skyrms, Brian
on convergence of opinion, 8:685
on decision theory, 2:659
evolutionary ethics and, 3:480
on natural laws, 5:226
Slater, John Clarke, 7:146
Slavery
in Brazil, 5:207
Channing and, 2:130–131
contractualist view of, 3:386
Hegel on, 3:415, 4:262–263, 4:271
Jefferson and, 4:806
Locke on, 5:389
as mode of production, 5:732
postcolonialism and, 7:728
in Rome, 7:420
Thoreau on, 6:575
Ulpian on, 7:420
utilitarian view of, 3:386
Wayland's (Francis) rejection of, 9:728
Slavic national soul, 5:75
Slavophilism
Eurasianists and, 3:453–454
founding of, 5:58
of Kireevskii, 5:74
philosophical romanticism and, 5:60
Slipher, Vesto, 4:63
Ślokavārtiika, 6:532
Slote, Michael
consequentialism and, 2:461
on utilitarianism, 9:383
on virtue ethics, 9:679
Slupecki, Jerzy, 5:694
Small and large, argument of both, 9:872
Small samples, study of, facilitating, 3:662
Smart, John Jamieson Carswell, **9:65–66**
on causal account of time, 2:87
on change and time, 9:498–499
on colors, 2:332
on cosmic coincidence, 8:691
on deontological theory, 4:153
on identity theory, 7:470, 8:191
on Ryle, 2:78
on sensations and brain processes as identical, 5:133
on soul, 3:11
tenseless theory of time and, 9:475
on topic-neutral analyses, 3:756
utilitarianism of, 9:611
Smart, Ninian, 8:401–402
Smell
perception and, 7:181–182
sense of, 5:117
Smiley, T. J., on quantification in syllogism, 5:505
Smith, Adam, **9:66–69**
anthropology and, 7:316
and communism, 2:365
on economics, 7:350–351
on empathy, 9:37, 9:67, 9:345
Enlightenment and, 3:246–247
Garve on, 4:24
German liberalism and, 5:321
on ideal observer, 4:562
on imitation in art, 9:69
Kant on, 2:367
legacy of, 7:351
on legislators, 7:351
Mandeville and, 5:681
on material prosperity *vs.* wealth, 3:605
on morality, 7:350–351
on moral-sense theory, 3:408
on profit-seeking by individuals, 1:777
on self-interest, and origins of communism, 2:364
and social Darwinism, 2:642
spectator theory of, 7:316
Stewart on, 9:246–247
on sympathy, 3:750
Smith, C. A. B., 9:217
Smith, David, on phenomenology, 7:299
Smith, Dorothy
on "lifeworld" of women, 3:564
and Marx's theory of standpoint, 3:563–564
Smith, Hilda, on dualism, 5:373
Smith, John, **9:69–71**
Smith, John Maynard, 4:20–21
Smith, Michael, 4:715, 8:251
Smith, Murray, 7:385
Smith, Peter, 2:133
Smith, Quentin
on date theory, 9:477
on language of time, 9:463
on pastness, 9:480
presentism and, 9:479
tensed theory of time and, 9:475
Smith, Ray, 9:221
Smith, W. John, 1:204
Smith, W. Robertson, 3:762
Smithson, Robert, 3:256
Smullyan, Arthur F., 6:290
Smuts, Jan Christiaan, 4:559, **9:71–72**
Smyslzhizn (The meaning of life) (Trubetskoi), 9:529
Snell, Willebrord, 2:725–726
Snell's law, 2:725–726
Soal, Samuel G., 7:115
Soames, Scott
on belief attributions, 1:536
on language, 5:189
on names as devices of direct reference, 8:747
on presupposition, 3:252–253
on semantics, 8:75–76, 8:77
Sobel, Jordan Howard
on determinism, 3:29
on miracles, 6:275
Sober, Elliott, 5:230, 8:685
Soble, Alan, 7:521

Sobociński, Boleslaw
on *CN*-calculus, 5:607
Leśniewski and, 5:290
Łukasiewicz and, 5:607–608
Sobornost
vs. collectivity, 5:60
extended beyond theology, 5:60
Khomiakov and, 5:59
material, 5:75
principle of, 3:559
Sobre a Mortalidade da Alma (On the mortality of the soul) (Costa), 4:825
Sobre feminismo (On Feminism) (Vaz Ferreira), 5:208
Sobstvennost' i gosudarstavo (Property and the state) (Chicherin), 2:148
Social abuse, Meslier on, 6:154
Social action, science of, 6:224–225
Social aggregation, 7:534–535
Social and behavioral sciences, overtly gendered subject matter in, 3:591
Social and Cultural Dynamics (Sorokin), 9:102
Social approach, 3:595
Social atomism, 5:595–596
Social behavior, probability and, Condorcet on, 2:431
Social behaviorism, of Mead, 6:80–81
Social Bliss Considered (Annet), 1:210
Social capital, art as, 1:300
Social change
in Chinese philosophy, 2:231
in French clandestine writings, 2:264
Veblen and, 9:655
Social choice theory, as ethical analysis tool, 3:449
Social class
Aristotle on, 7:592
critical theory and, 2:599
Descartes on, 2:365
Eliot (T. S.) on, 3:186
Plato on, 7:591–592
socialism and, 9:87–89
sociology of knowledge and, 9:101
See also Class (socioeconomic
Social cognition, 8:153
Social competence, 9:198
Social conditioning, meaning and, 1:152
Social conditions
changes to, 1:493
communitarianism and, 2:368
conservatism and, 2:465
Social consciousness, 2:362
Social consequences, of science, 3:597
Social construct, 8:677
aesthetic experience and, 1:34
radically reconceived, 3:599
in science studies, 8:678–679
Social Construction of Reality, The (Berger & Luckmann), 9:77
Social constructionism, **9:76–79**
on animal *vs.* human sexuality, 7:526–527
on gender, 3:586, 3:589
lessons of contingency from, 3:588
"strong program" and, 8:677–678, 9:85
Social constructivism, on underdetermination, 9:577
Social context, art and, 1:314
Social contract, **9:79–83**
Blackstone on, 1:553
and deterrence of crime, 1:518
as fiction, 9:627
Grotius on, 4:191
Hobbes on, 2:366, 3:405, 4:417–418, 6:511
justice and, 8:257–258
Locke on, 5:388–389, 6:511–512
Milton on, 6:250–251
Mosaic law as, 4:826
obligation to law and, 7:457
personhood and, 1:9
Rawls on, 5:323–324
Scanlon's contractualism and, 2:517
theoretical context of, 9:95
in welfare state, 9:829
Social Contract (Rousseau), 4:38, 5:320, 9:80
Constant on, 5:320
on general will, 4:38
on government, 3:410
on private interests, 9:206
on sovereignty, 9:142
Social Control through Law (Pound), 9:207
Social conventions, performative utterances and, 7:200
Social cooperation, Xunzi on, 2:233
Social creatures, humans as, 3:749
Social critic, Fourier's influence as, 3:707
Social customs
Confucius on, 2:231
conscience and, 2:445
Daoist thought on, 2:237
Social Darwinism, 2:642–643
evolutionary ethics and, 3:478–479
Latin American philosophy and, 5:206–207
race and, 8:227–228
Social determinant, in historical materialism, 4:381–382
Social development
Hegel on, 3:57
Marx on, 3:57
Newman (John Henry) on, 6:581–582
in Sumner's "folkways," 9:326
Social doctrine, Darwinism and, 2:642–643
Social elites, Comte on, 2:412
Social engineering, law and, 7:428
Social entities, 3:589
Social epistemology, 3:276, **9:83–87**, 9:686
feminist contribution to, 3:577
Goldman on, 4:147
Social Epistemology (journal), 9:84
Social equality
Dworkin on, 3:156–157
vs. freedom, 1:253
Mencius on, 2:233
Social ethics
and business ethics, 1:776–780
Ehrenfels on, 3:177
Social evolution, Habermas on, 4:200
Social evolutionism, Krueger on, 5:156
Social facts, 9:94–95
Social forces, 5:740
Social fragmentation, Vico on, 9:676
Social framework, memory in, 6:126
Social good, in conservatism, 2:464–465
Social harmony, in utopianism, 9:617–618
Social injustice, Latin American philosophy on, 5:205
Social institutions
coercive, justifications for, 9:72
ethical evaluation of, 3:391–392
justice as first virtue of, 4:867–868
oppressiveness of, 9:9
socialist thought on, 9:88
socialist workplace as, 9:73
in Spann's neoromantic universalism, 9:158
Social interaction, norms of
Habermas on, 3:91
in role-setting, 9:94
Social irrationalism, 4:751
Social issues, Voltaire and, 9:712
Social justice
communism and, 2:361
liberation theology on, 5:331
Pestalozzi on, 7:255
Rawls on, 5:323–324
technology and, 7:544
Social legislation
Bentham and, 1:551
communism and, 2:362

Social life
  law and, 7:444
  Lotze on, 5:582
  morality in, 7:454
  organization of, principle of, 5:75
  Pufendorf on, 8:158
Social location, as epistemic resource or liability, 3:575–576
Social mathematics, Condorcet on, 2:432
Social memory, 6:126–127
Social morality, 4:268, 7:454
Social norms
  Chinese names as prescriptive in, 2:203–204
  Confucianism and, 2:174–177
Social opportunities, Bentham and, 1:551
Social order
  Comte on, 2:412
  conservative view of, 2:468
  Plato on, 2:364
  Pufendorf on, 8:158
Social organization, Eliot (T. S.) on, 3:186
Social ownership, of means of production, 5:47
Social person, definition of, 7:238
Social phenomena
  empirical scientific investigation into, 9:734
  philosophical analysis of, 9:734
  Taine on, 9:365
Social philosophy, **9:72–76**
  and allocation issues, 6:96–97
  Ayatollah Khomeini and, 4:763
  Bellarmine and, 1:542–543
  Bolingbroke on, 1:770–771
  Bradley on, 1:676
  Bruno on, 1:709
  Buddhist, 1:725
  Burke (Edmund) on, 1:770–771
  Butler (Samuel) on, 1:785
  Carlyle on, 2:33
  Cartwright on, 2:63
  Cattaneo and, 2:83–84
  and censorship, 2:119–120
  Chaadaev and, 2:120–121
  Chernyshevskii and, 2:147
  Chicherin on, 2:147
  Chinese, 2:188–189, 2:199–200, 2:231–239
  Cicero on, 2:258
  Coleridge on, 2:319
  Confucianism and, 2:150–151, 2:170–171, 2:174, 2:178–179, 2:185, 2:199–200, 2:231–232
  Daoism and, 2:185–188, 2:198, 2:236–237
  on dehumanization by technology, 1:708
  Dewey on, 3:49
  Dong Zhongshu and, 2:235
  Dostoevsky on, 3:100–101
  Fārābī's virtuous city and, 9:315
  Feinberg and, 3:561
  feminist, **3:70–75**, 3:598–603
  Filmer and, 3:637
  and free speech, 2:119–120
  on freedom and individual liberty, 1:667
  irrationality of human nature and, 4:751–752
  Kierkegaard and, 5:68
  Korkeimer on, 2:598–599
  law in, 7:453–454
  liberty in, **5:337–338**
  Mao on, 2:180
  Maritain and, 5:715–716
  Marx and, 9:90
  Marxist, 1:716–717
  Mencius on, 2:232–233
  Mill (John Stuart) and, 6:228–229
  in Mohism, 2:185
  moral causality in, 2:110
  Morgan (Lewis) and, 6:403–404
  Mozi on, 2:235–236
  neo-Confucianism and, 2:183
  New England transcendentalists and, 6:574
  Oakeshott and, 7:1–2
  Olivi and, 7:12
  and pluralistic societies, 7:643
  pragmatism and, 3:568
  and primitivism in Daoism, 2:185–186
  resource reallocation in, 9:41
  on revolt against human conditions *vs.* revolt against injustice, 2:21–22
  Ruskin and, 8:534
  Saint-Simon on, 8:589–590
  Sartre on, 8:607
  Sen on, 8:810
  Shin Buddhism and, 9:15
  and social contract, 9:79–83
  Sombart and, 9:127–128
  Sumner's social evolutionism and, 9:326
  Tagore and, 9:364
  Tang on, 2:183
  Thoreau and, 9:451
  Xunzi on, 2:233–234
Social positivism, 7:711–713
Social power, hierarchical grid of, 3:587
Social practice, legal systems and, 7:458
Social prediction, 4:380
Social principles, historical development of, 6:581–582
Social problems
  secondary to spiritual, 1:560
  suicide as alleviating, 9:321–322
Social process, in historical process, 9:732–733
Social progress, critical theory and, 2:599
Social psychology, 8:153
  Comte on, 2:410
  on intentionality in consciousness, 2:452
  McDougall and, 8:147–148
  Mead and, 6:80–81
  moral norms and, 3:446
  in social change, 9:656
  Wundt and, 9:850
Social rationality, Lehrer and Wagner on, 5:248
Social reality
  language and, 3:563
  as objectification, 1:559–560
Social reconstruction, Comte on, 2:410
Social reform
  Carnap on, 2:37
  Chinese, religious dimension of, 2:225–227
  civil disobedience and, 2:259–260
  Cixous and, 2:262–263
  Confucianism and, 2:176
  Haeckel on, 4:204
  and "law as it ought," 1:553
  Mill (John Stuart) on, 6:221–222
Social relations
  and Confucianism, 2:175
  Marx on, 3:68–69
  Sartre on, 3:514, 8:607–608, 9:98
  Weber on, 9:93
Social restrictions, faced by men, 3:756
Social revolution, Bakunin and, 1:472
Social roles, Confucianism and, 2:231
Social rules, as judicanda of justice, 4:863–865
Social science(s)
  chance and, 2:125–126
  Chomsky and, 2:244
  competing terms for, 4:38
  Comte on, 2:411
  Condorcet on, 2:431
  determinism and, 3:36
  holism and individualism in, **4:441–450**
  Mill (John Stuart) and, 6:225
  mundane phenomenology in, 8:664

and natural and human science demarcation, 1:470
operationalism in, 7:31–32
philosophy of, **7:533–536**
Geisteswissenschaften, 4:37–38
ideology (concept of) in, 4:572–574
metaideological questions in, 7:533–534
metaphysical questions in, 7:534–535
methodological questions in, 7:535–536
and probability, 2:431
punishment in, 8:168
and religion, 8:377. *See also* Religion, psychological explanations of
Sombart on, 9:127–128
sophists and, 9:130
statistical methods and, 2:125–126
Social Security, state paternalism and, 5:338
"Social Situation of Music" (Adorno), 1:27
Social solidarity, Durkheim on, 3:150
Social states, in Comte, 2:411
Social Statics (Spencer), 7:155
Social status
art and, 1:300
bioethical issues and, 1:603
Social structure
historical materialism and, 4:378–379
Radcliffe-Brown on, 3:763
Wundt on, 9:850
Social system, Radcliffe-Brown on, 3:763
Social Teaching of the Christian Churches, The (Troeltsch), 9:527
Social teleologi i marxismen (Hägerström), 4:205
Social terms, defining man in, 3:707
Social Text (Sokal), 8:680
Social theory
class conflict in, Saint-Simon on, 8:590
of collective purpose, 9:281–282
of concepts, 2:416
Encyclopédie on, 3:224
Gehlen on, 4:36
Gobineau on, 4:106
idealist, 4:559–560
ideology in, 4:573–574
Lukács on, 5:603–604
Ortega y Gasset and, 7:46
Ostwald and, 7:50
Plato and, 7:590–592
poststructuralism and, 9:278
Protagoras and, 8:92–93
Rousseau on, 4:39
Russell and, 8:536–539
Santayana and, 8:600
Shelley on, 9:8
social constructionism in, 9:77–78
and social contract, 9:79–83
Sorel on, 9:133
Spann and, 9:158
Sumner's "folkways" and, 9:326
Social transformation, 1:471
Social types, Durkheim on, 3:150–151
Social utility
Croce on, 2:603
law and, 2:603
vs. morality, 5:48
Social values
in Confucianism, 2:231
and needs of society, 3:596
Social wealth, alienation and, 2:362
Socialism, **9:87–93**
American liberalism and, 5:322
and anarchism, 1:178–180
Bolzano on, 1:646
classless society and, 7:427
on coercive institutions, 9:73
Coleridge and, 2:316
and communal living, 1:716–717
and communism, 2:362–363
Comte on, 2:413
and conservatism, contrast of, 2:470
Dostoevsky on, 3:100–101
Engels on, 3:238
Eucken on, 3:452
Fourier and, 3:707
German, Sombart on, 9:127
Gramsci on, 4:169–170
as historical epoch, 1:561
individualism in, 1:538
King on, 5:73
Lange on, 5:186
Lassalle on, 5:203
Lavrov on, 5:218–219
on liberty, 5:334–335
Lunacharskii on, 5:611–612
Mao on, 2:180
Marković on, 5:719
Marxism and, 1:716–717, 5:740–741
and philosophy of history, 1:442
Proudhon and, 8:94
Saint-Simon on, 8:589
and Solov'ëv, 9:122
Sombart on, 9:127
in Sorel's social theory, 9:133
utopian, 1:646, 3:59, 3:238
Socialism: An Analysis (Eucken), 3:452
Socialism ou Barbarie (either socialism or barbarism), 5:619–620
Socialism: Utopian and Scientific (Engels), 3:59, 3:238
Socialist calculation debate, 7:351
Socialist feminism, 3:601, 3:606
Socialist legality, 7:427
Socialist realism, 1:59, 1:68–69
Sociality
Mead on, 6:82
transcendental conditions of, 3:617
Socialization
Habermas on, 4:200
as oppression, 1:515
Social-welfare liberalism, 3:599
Sociedad Argentina de Análisis Filosófico (SADAF), 5:210
Società Italiana di Filosofia del Diritto, 2:697
"Societal Facts" (Mandelbaum), 9:95
Societas Ereunetica, 4:861
Société française de psychanalyse, 5:167
Société Psychoanalytique de Paris, 5:167
Societized philosophy of science, 3:597
Society, **9:93–99**
al-Fārābī on, 4:756
and alienation, 1:121–122, 5:731
ancient Chinese, 2:149
Anderson (John) on, 1:199
Aristotle on, 5:630
art and, 1:56–59, 1:69–70, 1:538
atheism and, 1:505
Augustine on, 1:398–400
Bergson on, 1:571
Bosanquet on, 1:663–664
boundary maintenance in, 9:96
Bradley on, 1:676
Brandt on, 1:688
Buddhist, 1:725
Butler (Samuel) on, 1:785
Calvin on, 2:10–11
Carlyle on, 2:33
character structure and, 8:311–313
Chateaubriand on, 2:138
Chernyshevskii on, 2:146–147
Chicherin on, 2:147–148
Chinese social title and, 2:204
in Chinese thought, 2:194–202, 2:226–227, 2:231
civil, 9:96–98
classless, 7:427
Cohen (Hermann) on, 2:304
Coleridge on, 2:319–320
and collectivization of means of production, 1:472

Society, *continued*
communism and, 2:361
Comte on, 2:410, 2:414
Condorcet on, 2:432
in Confucianism, 2:150–151, 2:176–177, 2:195, 2:443, 7:486
constructivism in, 9:76
corrupting influence of, 4:136–137
Croce on, 2:604
and cultural critical forces, 1:469
decline of, 9:517
and deterrence of crime, 1:518
development in, 5:731–732
in development of states, 9:204
Dewey on, 7:378
ecclesiastical, Aquinas on, 9:435
education and, 7:370
Eliot (T. S.) on, 3:186
Emerson on, 3:196–197
entropic trends in, 9:133
Epicurus on, 4:300
ethical agents in, 8:633
ethics in, 1:778, 2:194–202
evil in, necessity of, 1:771
exclusivity in, 1:662
family as foundation of, 4:204
Gehlen on, 4:36
gender and, 1:515, 3:565
Giles of Rome on, 4:91
goal-right system in, 8:810
Godwin on, 4:136–137
good in, 2:364
groupism and, 9:208
growth in, 9:517
Habermas on, 4:199–200
as habit, 7:378
Haeckel on, 4:204
Hegel on, 4:284
Herbart on, 7:375
Ibn Khaldūn on, 4:548
ideal, 4:137
idealist view of, 4:559–660
immoral, 1:505
indictment of, utopianism and, 9:619
and individual behavior, 1:676
individual profit-seeking and, 1:777
individuality and social subordination in, 1:538
Jouffroy on, 4:855
justice in, as bioethical issue, 1:603
Kant on, 4:558
language in, 1:648
law in, 7:426–427
Leibniz on, 2:365–366
Locke on, 7:369–370
love in, 9:533
Lukács on, 1:69
Luther on, 5:613
Machiavelli on, 5:627–628
Maimonides on, 5:652
Mandeville on, 5:681–682
Manheim on, 5:685–686
Marković on, 5:719–720
Marsilius of Padua on, 5:722
Marx on, 5:732–733
matriarchal, 1:441
Meslier on, 2:267
metaphysics and, 2:328
Mill (John Stuart) on, 6:229, 7:377
modern, 3:186, 4:200
and morals, 1:461, 1:505, 1:779
music as model for, 1:27–28
nature *vs.* art in, 1:641
obligation to, *vs.* to church, 9:509
open *vs.* closed, 1:571
as order of creation, 1:707
original sin and, 1:399
philosophical anthropology on, 7:323–324
philosophy as threat to, 5:648
polarization of, 5:685–686
political
Aquinas on, 9:435
in civic paradigm, 6:485
Giles of Rome on, 4:90–91
Locke on, 7:369–370
Mosca on, 6:406–407
political changes in, 2:361
Popper on, 7:691
postmodern organization of, 1:491
progress of, 8:48–49
promises in, 8:53–54
property and, 8:70–74
as redemption, *vs.* selfhood, 4:773–774
reform of, utopianism and, 9:619–620
Reich on, 8:310–313
religion in, 8:378
and religious toleration, 1:502
and ritual, 1:488, 2:226–227
Romagnosi on, 8:484–485
Rousseau on, 7:370–371, 8:508–510
Santayana on, 8:600
Schiller (Friedrich) on, 8:627
Schopenhauer on, 8:653
scientific method and, 8:46
as secular Messianic redemption, 1:545
security in, 1:554
shaming punishment in, 9:5
in social contract, 9:79
social facts in, 9:94–95
social growth agents in, 1:719
socialist critique of, 9:88
Sorel on, 9:133
and sovereign authority, 1:621
vs. state, 1:663–664
in state of nature, 7:369–370
Stein on, 9:240
Stoics on, 4:300
structure of, 8:377
superstructure of, 5:732–733
Thoreau on, 9:450–451
Toynbee on, 9:517
tradition in, 2:469, 9:521
Trubetskoi on, 9:533
ultimate good in, as nonexistent, 1:589
utilitarianism on, 1:687
in *Utopia*, 6:400
utopianism and, 9:617–620
Vishnu's organization of, 2:110
Volski on, 9:707
wealth as evolutionary fitness in, 1:785
Weil (Simone) on, 9:737
well-ordered, Rawls on, 5:323–325
women in, 3:563
Xunzi on, 2:233–234
See also State
Society and Solitude (Emerson), 3:195
Society for Empirical Philosophy, Vienna Circle and, 5:525
Society for Phenomenology and Existential Philosophy, 4:198
Society for Propagating the Gospel in Foreign Parts, Collins on, 2:331
Society for Psychical Research, 1:473, 7:113
Society for the Philosophy of Sex and Love, 7:521
Society Must Be Defended (Foucault), 3:701
Society of the Lovers of Russian Literature, Khomiakov and, 5:58
Socinianism, **9:99–100**
deism and, 2:681
Stillingfleet on, 9:249
Socinianism Truly Stated (Toland), 2:683, 7:97
Socinus, Laelius and Faustus. *See* Socinianism
Sociobiology
debate on, 3:490–491
successful critiques of, 3:576
Wilson (Edward O.) and, 3:490, 9:788–789
Sociobiology: The New Synthesis (Wilson), 3:490, 9:788

Sociocultural evolution, Habermas on, 4:200
Socioeconomic conditions, Sartre on, 1:456
Sociological factors, 1:469
Sociological neo-Kantianism, 6:545
    See also Neo-Kantianism
Sociological theory of law, 7:426–427
Sociologism, 8:260
Sociology
    alienation in, 1:120
    Althusius on, 1:135
    causal explanations in, 9:735
    Comte on, 2:413–414
    constructivism in, 9:76–77
    Darwinism and, 2:642
    Durkheim and, 3:149–152
    educational theory and, 2:413
    empirical, 6:561
    Encyclopédie on, 3:224
    functionalism in, 3:762–765
    historicocultural approach to, 9:732–733
    of knowledge, **9:100–105**
    Masaryk on, 6:2
    Morgan (Lewis) and, 6:403–404
    Neurath and, 6:561
    paradigm-change in, 8:696
    Pareto on, 7:117–119
    phenomenological approach in, 8:664
    postmodernism in, 7:729
    research imperative in, 8:675
    of science
        naturalism and, 6:503
        "strong program" in, 8:677–678, 9:85
    Simmel and, 9:30
    Sombart on, 9:128
    Spencer in, 7:714
    understanding *(Verstehen)* in, 9:735
    utopianism and, 9:620
    Weber (Alfred) on, 9:732–733
    Weber (Max) on, 9:734–735
    Whitehead and, 9:753
Socrates, **9:105–114**
    on *akrasia,* 7:589–590
    Antisthenes and, 1:224
    Arcesilaus and, 1:247
    on belief, 3:284–285
    on body, value of, 3:397
    Chaucer on, 9:106
    on civil disobedience, 2:260
    on conventionalism, 8:753
    on correctness of names, 8:751–753
    daimon of, 6:611
    death of, 6:611
    on definition, 2:665–666
    on determinism, 3:4
    dialectic and, 3:52–53
    Diogenes Laertius on, 3:88
    on divine command theories of ethics, 3:94
    in early education, 7:365
    on empirical judgments, 3:284–285
    Epictetus and, 3:261
    on ethics, 3:395–398
    Euclides of Megara and, 6:110
    on evil, 3:397
    on explanation, 7:759
    Galileo on, 4:9
    and Hellenistic philosophers, 3:399
    on human expertise, 9:109
    on human good, 9:111–112
    Ikhwān al-Ṣafā' and, 4:576
    on immortality, 4:602
    on incorporeality of souls, 4:607
    influence of, 9:113
    Justin Martyr on, 7:142
    Kierkegaard and, 3:504
    on knowledge, 4:173
    on law, 7:418
    logic and, 5:398
    methodology of, 8:638
    on naturalism, 8:753
    Nietzsche on, 6:611–613
    on optimism/pessimism, 7:247
    paradoxes cited by, 9:111
    Parmenides of Elea and, 7:122
    parody of, in *The Clouds,* 4:177
    physicotheology and, 7:556
    piety of, 9:109–110
    Plato and, 9:589
    in Platonic dialogues, 7:583–584
    vs. Platonic "Socrates," 8:504–505, 9:589
    on pleasure, 3:396–397
    political philosophy of, 7:656
    on profitability of justice, 3:174
    on recollection theory, 3:283–284
    on reducing fine to good, pleasant, or both, 5:8
    on self-control, 3:396–397
    skepticism of, 9:48
    Skovoroda and, 9:63
    social contract and, 9:81
    sophism and, 9:129–130
    and Stoicism, 4:300, 9:869
    suicide of, 9:318
    trial of, 7:584, 9:106
    on universals, 9:589
    on virtue, 1:256, 7:585
    Vlastos on, 9:702
    on wisdom, 9:794
    Xenophon and, 9:854–856
Socrates, Ironist and Moral Philosopher (Vlastos), 9:702
"Socratic Elenchus, The" (Vlastos), 9:702
Socratic ignorance, and reasonable doubt, 3:702
Socratic love, 3:623
Socratic method, 7:329
Socratic Puzzles (Nozick), 6:669
Soderini, Gonfalonier Piero, Machiavelli and, 5:626
Sodipo, J. O., on African philosophy, 1:85
Soft facts, 3:694
Soft positivism. *See* Inclusive legal positivism
Sogolo, Godwin, on African philosophy, 1:85
Sokal, Alan, 8:680
Sokolowski, R., on phenomenology, 7:299–300
Soler, Ricaurte, 5:211
Solger, Karl Wilhelm Ferdinand, **9:114–115**
Solids, perfect, 5:51
Soliloquies (Augustine), 1:47
Soliloquies (Schleiermacher), 8:632–633
Soliloquy, as self-analysis, 9:3–4
Solipsism, **9:115–122**
    animal consciousness and, 1:206
    basic statements and, 1:484–487
    egoism as, 4:553
    in Gestalt theory, 4:74
    Stace and, 9:199–200
    in Yogācāra Buddhism, 1:748
Solitary life, Levinas and, 4:831
"Solitary Man" (Berkeley), 8:782
Solitude of the self, 5:67
Solms, Mark, 3:737
Solomon, Robert C., 3:199, 7:523
Solovay, Robert, 2:389, 8:844–845
Solov'ëv, Vladimir Sergeevich, 5:43, 5:572, **9:122–127**
    central doctrine of positive "total-unity," 3:716
    Fëdorov and, 3:558
    Kavelin and, 5:48
    Leont'ev and, 5:283
    Losev and, 5:573
    and metaphysics, 3:669, 9:18
    Trubetskoi (Evgenii) and, 9:529
    Trubetskoi (Sergei) and, 9:532
    Zen'kovskii and, 9:868
Solovine, Maurice, 3:180
Solutions (Zeno), 9:253

Somatic marker hypothesis, 3:201
Somatic wisdom, emotions and, 3:200–201
Somatism, ontological reism as, 5:144
Sombart, Werner, **9:127–129**
"Some Antecedents of the Philosophy of Bergson" (Lovejoy), 5:592
Some Dogmas of Religion (McTaggart), 6:78
Some Main Problems of Philosophy (Moore), 2:542, 3:343
"Some Major Strands of Theodicy" (Swinburne), 3:478
"Some Meanings of 'Nature'" (Lovejoy), 5:594
"Some Misinterpretations of Empiricism" (Stace), 9:200
"Some Properties of Conversion" (Church and Rosser), 2:336
"Some Questions concerning Validity" (Urmson), 7:111
Some Reasons for an European State (Bellers), 7:154
"Some Reflections on Moral-Sense Theories in Ethics" (Broad), 1:699
"Some Remarks on Logical Form" (Wittgenstein), 1:148, 9:802
Some Thoughts concerning Education (Locke), 5:375, 5:390, 7:369
"Some Varieties of Functionalism" (Shoemaker), 9:16
"Somehow view" of Jainism, 6:254
"Something about One Way of Possibly Doing One Part of Philosophy" (Austin), 1:408
Something, rather than nothing, "why," 9:754
Sommario di pedagogia come scienza filosofica (Gentile), 4:50
Sommerhoff, George, on purposive activity, 9:385
"Somnium–A Dream of the Moon" (Kepler), 5:54
Song dynasty
  Chan Buddhism in, 1:727, 3:95
  neo-Confucianism in, 2:622
Song of Solomon, and medieval views of love, 5:586–587
Sontag, Susan, 1:324
Soo-Hong Chew, 2:660
Sophia, **10:41–42**
  Losskii on, 5:577
  mythological, 3:669
  in Valentinianism, 9:632
  Zen'kovskii on, 9:868
Sophie (de Staél), 9:201
Sophie Charlotte (queen of Prussia), 5:253–254, 5:264–265
Sophie, Duchess of Brunswick, 5:252–253
Sophimata (Albert of Saxony), 1:101
Sophiology, 3:669
  Bulgakov and, 1:760
  Solov'ëv and, 9:124
  Zen'kovskii and, 9:868
Sophism
  Aristotle on, 1:270
  epistemology and, 3:282
  on language, 8:751–752
  in Platonic dialogues, 9:109
  Schopenhauer on, 8:648
  semantics in, 8:751–752
Sophismata, 8:770
Sophismata (Kilvington), 5:68–69, 5:433
Sophismata grammaticalia logicalia (Kilwardby), 5:69–70
Sophist (Plato)
  aesthetics in, 1:41
  alterity in, 1:134
  being and unity in, 6:186
  on change in realm of ideas, 7:632
  on classes of names, 9:286
  dating of, 9:107
  Deussen and, 3:41
  on dialectic, 3:53, 7:594
  elenchus in, 7:593
  existence in, 7:22
  on falsity, 3:343
  Forms in, 7:596–600
  on knowledge, 3:285
  Levinas and, 5:304
  on logic, 5:398
  metaphysics in, 6:185
  mimesis in, 6:252
  naturalism in, 6:493
  on ontology, 7:600
  Owen on, 7:64–65
  Parmenides of Elea and, 7:122
  on statements, 8:754–755
  statements in, 2:540
  on theory of kinds, 7:600
  thought in, 9:420
  truth in, 9:534
Sophistical Refutations (Aristotle), 1:4, 2:136, 5:398–399
  Abelard and, 5:425
  on fallacy, 8:767
  and medieval thought, 5:422, 5:429–430
  on signification, 8:755–756
  syllogism in, 1:269
Sophistry, *vs.* fallacy, 3:537
Sophists, **9:129–131**
  on belief, 7:365
  on convention, 7:365
  on definition, 2:668
  dialectic and, 3:52
  in early education, 7:365
  epideixis and, 4:163
  epistemology and, 3:282
  on error, 3:343
  ethics of, 3:395
  golden rule and, 4:146
  Gorgias of Leontini as, 4:162
  Green on, 4:179
  language theory of, 2:669
  law in, 7:419
  logic and, 5:397
  on logos, 5:567–568
  in philosophy of law, 7:418
  Plato and, 3:283
Sophocles, 4:176–177
  Aristotle on, 1:188
  Hegel on, 9:523–524
  on love, 5:583
  Nietzsche on, 9:524
  on optimism/pessimism, 7:246
  on rival moral goods, 9:74
Sôphrosunê, **10:42–43**
Sopra le teorie della scienza: logica, matematica, fisica (On the theories of science: logic, mathematics, physics) (Pastore), 7:135
Sorbière, Samuel, 9:50
Sorel, Georges, **9:132–135**
  anarchism of, 1:178–179
  Anderson (John) and, 1:199
  and fascism, 3:553
  Gramsci on, 4:169
  Labriola and, 5:165–166
  Lukács and, 5:603
  on violence, 9:677
Sorensen, Roy, 5:111, 9:625
Sorgenti irrazionali del pensiero, Le (Abbagnano), 1:1
Sorites, 5:556–557
  Carroll's logic system for, 5:453
  valid, rules for, 3:539
Sorites paradox, 5:108–109
  Eubulides and, 5:398
  Stoic logic and, 5:407
  vagueness in, 9:623–624
Sorokin, Pitirim, 9:102
Soroush, Abdul, 4:763
Sorrows of Young Werther, The (Goethe), 4:140, 5:588, 7:250, 8:629
Sortal concepts, *vs.* nonsortal concepts, Wiggins on, 9:762
Sosa, Ernest, **9:135–136**
  on conditions of knowledge, 3:272
  on dualism, 3:117
  on epistemic circularity, 3:280–281
  on intellectual virtues, 9:682–683

on philosophical supporting evidence, 5:85
political instability and, 5:211
on virtue epistemology, 3:276
Soskice, Janet, 8:417
Soteriology
in Buddhism, 1:754, 2:111, 2:162, 2:166–169
and Carolingian philosophy, 2:49
in Cartesianism, 2:60
Chaadaev and, 2:120–121
Charron and, 2:135
and Christianity, 2:60, 2:120–121
and ethical ideal of ren in Confucianism, 2:176
in Jainism, 2:111
and karma, 2:110–111
and moral development, 2:110
in Zen, 1:729–730
Sotion, 8:811
Soto, Dominic de, **9:137–138,** 9:511
Souici de soi, Le (Care of the Self) (Foucault), 3:701
Soul
abortion and, 1:8
accent of, 3:622
in activity of representation, 9:325
Alexander of Aphrodisias on, 4:68
al-Ghazālī, Muhammad on, 1:118
Aquinas on, 4:609–610, 9:429–430, 9:437
Aristotle on, 1:274–275, 3:286, 4:68, 4:608–609. *See also De Anima* (Aristotle)
in atomism, 4:28, 7:764
Augustine on, 1:402–403, 3:289
Averroes on, 1:423, 1:652
Avicenna on, 1:433–434
and beauty, 1:512
body and, 1:433–434, 1:494, 1:622, 4:5, 4:608, 5:640, 7:319, 9:336
Brahman relation to, 1:683–684
Brentano on, 1:692
as bundle of powers, 1:544
as center of Universe, 3:621
Clarke on, 2:273
in classical Greek thought, 2:698
Cleanthes on, 2:288
Clement on, 2:290
Comenius on, 7:369
composition of, 6:65, 9:372–373
Crusius on, 2:607
Cudworth on, 2:611
Culverwell on, 2:613
dark night of, 4:846
death and, 1:433–434, 2:654, 4:823–825, 6:14, 9:766. *See also* Soul, immortality of
Democritus on, 5:300
Descartes on, 1:201, 2:728, 2:753, 3:116, 3:293, 4:610–612
Dostoevsky on, 3:99
Driesch on, 3:112
Duns Scotus on, 3:141–142
Eckhart (Meister) on, 3:162
education and, 7:366
Emerson on, 3:195
Empedocles on, 3:210–213
Epicureans on, 3:10
Epicurus on, 3:269
Erigena on, 3:341–342
as ethereal machine of subtle matter, 1:658
Eucken on, 3:452
evidences of, 3:556
as exemplar of God, 1:652
Ficino on, 5:259
Galen on, 4:5
Gassendi on, 4:28
Gersonides on, 4:68
Gorgias of Leontini on, 4:163
Haeckel on, 4:203
Hegel on, 4:267
Henry of Harclay on, 4:315
Herbart on, 1:234, 7:376
Hobbes on, 3:11
Holbach on, 6:10
hylic intellect of, 4:68
hylomorphism of, in Ibn Gabirol, 4:546
in hypostatic system, 7:614
Iamblichus on, 4:540
as immaterial, 2:273
immortality of, 1:105, 2:654, 4:602, 9:429
Aristotle on, 1:274
Dostoevsky on, 3:99
Meier on, 6:112
Mendelssohn on, 6:131
Mill (John Stuart) on, 6:230–231
More (Henry) on, 6:396
Norris on, 6:656
Plato on, 4:602, 4:608, 6:258
Smith (John) on, 9:70
in Indian materialism, 6:254
intellect and, 1:112, 4:608–609
Isaac of Stella on, 4:753
Israeli's double account of, 4:765
in Jainism, 6:254, 8:718
John of La Rochelle on, 4:840
Kant on, 4:556
La Mettrie on, 5:178–179, 6:10
Laromiguière on, 5:201
Leibniz on, 1:292, 3:117, 3:298, 5:251, 5:260, 5:267, 8:130
Leucippus on, 5:300
Lichtenberg on, 5:340–341
light in operation of, 4:186
Lotze on, 5:581
Maimonides on, 3:23
Malebranche on, 5:665–666
Marx on, 3:56
materialism and, 6:9, 6:14
as matter, 6:59–60
Matthew of Aquasparta on, 6:65
Meier on, 6:112
Mendelssohn on, 6:131
Mill (John Stuart) on, 6:230–231
Milton on, 6:249
Mirabaud on, 2:266
in monadology, 6:325
Montague (William) on, 6:331
More (Henry) on, 6:396
motivation in inspiring, 9:240
Nemesius of Emesa on, 6:538–539
in Neoplatonism, 6:547
Norris on, 6:656
Ockham on, 9:782
Olivi on, 7:13
in Orphism, 7:42–44
participation and, 8:43
Paulsen on, 7:87
Philo on, 7:304–305
in physics, 1:274
Platonic view of, 2:364, 4:54, 4:602–604, 5:258–259, 6:185, 6:258, 6:547–548, 8:103
Plotinus on, 3:288–289, 6:187, 7:634
postsensory faculties of, 4:696–697
powers of, 1:275, 1:594
as principle of life, 4:607
Proclus on, 8:43
in Pythagoreanism, 8:182, 8:186
reason as separate from, 7:319–320
Regius on, 8:301
in reincarnation, 8:332–333
in *Republic* (Plato), 8:103
St. Victor on, 1:403, 8:592
Schulze on, 8:662
sensation as act of, 1:403
Smith (John) on, 9:70
speech and, 4:163
spiritual multitudes inhabiting, 1:622
in Stahl's animism, 9:202
in Stoicism, 8:121, 9:257
Strato on, 9:261
survival after death, 4:823–825, 9:766. *See also* Soul, immortality of
Swedenborg on, 9:336
Tauler on, 9:372–373

Soul, *continued*
Tertullian on, 4:603, 9:400
theories of, 4:605
as thinking substance, 4:610
Thomas of York on, 9:443
in *Timaeus* (Plato), 6:547–548
transmigration of, 8:182
and unity of ego *vs.* psychic events, 1:649
Vasquez on, 9:649–650
in vitalism, 9:695
Voltaire on, 9:710
of Westerners, as fragmented, 5:74
William of Auvergne on, 9:766
William of Conches on, 9:768
Wolff on, 9:827–828
Woodbridge on, 9:842
world, Burthogge on, 1:776
Zabarella on, 9:866
See also Anima; Panpsychism; Psyche
Soul, The (De Anima) (William of Auvergne), 9:766
Soul-making theodicy, 4:355
Sound(s), **9:138–139**
in film, 7:383
in Indian philosophy of language, 7:413
interpretation of logical system, definition of 5:557
Mach's work in, 5:624
perception of, psychology of, 9:280
in phonology, 9:531
as secondary quality, 8:8
Wundt's experiments on, 9:483
Sound of Two Hands Clapping (Dreyfus), 1:732–733
Sound proof calculus, 3:657
"Source of Life, The" (Ibn Gabirol), 4:545–547, 4:815, 7:611
Sources thesis, 5:241–242
South American Philosophy. *See* Latin American Philosophy
Southey, Robert, and Coleridge, 2:316
Souvenirs d'enfance et de jeunesse (Loisy), 5:570
Sovereign authority, 1:621
"Sovereign Reason" (Nagel), 6:473
Sovereignty, **9:139–146**
absolute, indissolubility of, 1:621
Bellarmine on, 1:542
Bodin on, 1:621
de Maistre on, 5:659
and divine right of kings, 1:542
just war and, 7:157–158
knowledge, purpose of, 1:444
laws and, 7:423
in legislatures, 1:554
Mariana on, 5:710–711
of pope, 5:659
popular
and democracy, 2:701–702
nationalism and, 6:483
as power of republic, 1:621
of state, 9:210
Suárez on, 9:284–285
as translation of divine power, 1:542–543
and war, 7:155
Sovereignty of Good (Murdoch), 6:433
Soviet philosophy, 8:575–577
Bakhtin and, 1:464–469
Plekhanov and, 7:628
Soviet Union
Bakhtin studies, 1:467
ban on Shestov, 9:13
censorship in, 5:573, 5:603
communism in, 2:363–364, 7:353–354
Darwinism in, 2:643
dissolution of, as practical defeat of communism, 2:361
economics of, 7:353–354
founding of, 5:279
Ivanov and, 4:767–768
Lenin and, 5:280–281
Mamardashvili and, 5:678
Marxism and, 3:56, 5:739
and nuclear arms, 7:157
public celebrations in, 4:768
Russell on, 8:538
and socialism, 9:73, 9:91
Spinoza and, 9:195
See also Russia
Soziallehren der christlichen Kirchen und Gruppen, Die (Troeltsch), 9:527
Sozialwissenschaften, 4:38
Spaccio de la bestia trionfante (The expulsion of the triumphant beast) (Bruno), 1:709
Space, 2:15, **9:146–153**
absolute, 1:581–582, 2:272, 9:147–148, 9:465–466
vs. relative, 6:592
spatial relations without, Boscovich on, 1:665
Aquinas on, 9:428
Aristotle on, 9:147, 9:154
atomism on, 9:147
Boscovich on, 1:666
Campanella on, 2:15
Carnap on, 2:40
Carroll on, 2:51
Clarke on, 2:272, 7:559
in classical mechanics, 2:281, 7:474–475
Clifford on, 2:292
Cohen (Hermann) on, 2:303
common cause principle and, 2:343
concept of, abstracted from experience, 6:81
conceptual, psychological creativity and, 2:589–590
continuum and infinity in, 2:491
conventionalism and, 2:520–525
Copernicus on, 2:54
cosmological modeling of, 2:559
Crescas on, 2:593
in *Critique of Pure Reason* (Kant), 2:689, 4:57, 9:148
Crusius on, 2:607
curvature of, constancy in cosmological models, 2:560
Democritus on, 9:146
density and pressure of, 3:178
Descartes on, 2:54, 9:154
Dühring on, 3:130
Euclidean, 2:520–521, 9:150–151
and Duhem-Quine conventionalism, 2:521
and non-Euclidean, 9:150–151
existence of, McTaggart's denial of, 6:78
as form of empirical intuition, 3:752
Friedman on, 3:159
and geometry, 1:244, 5:11–12, 9:149
Hamiltonian mechanics and conservation principle in, 2:463
Heidegger on, 3:512
Helmholtz on, 4:304–305
Hilbert on, 6:277–278, 8:205
homaloidal, Whitehead on, 9:749
homogeneity of, in cosmological models, 2:560
Hume on, 3:304, 4:492–493
inflationary universe theory and, 2:566
intellect and, 1:566
intrinsic metric of, 7:29
in Japanese philosophy, 4:797
Kant on, 2:689, 3:304–307, 4:57–58, 5:11–12, 9:147–148
Kozlov on, 5:146
language of, 9:465
Leibniz on, 4:554, 6:191, 9:147
Lenin on, 5:280
Liebmann on, 5:345
Locke on, 3:304, 5:381–382
Lucretius on, 9:147
Mach on, 5:624
mathematical, 1:700, 4:848

mathematical, physical space and, 4:848
Melissus of Samos on, 9:146
mereology and, 6:147
metrication of, *vs.* time, 9:495
Moore on, 2:358
nature of, operationalism and, 7:29
Nerlich on, 9:466
Newton on, 7:474–475, 7:559, 9:471
Parmenides on, 9:146
Pearson on, 7:160–161
perception of, 2:51, 2:292
perceptual, and physical space, 5:131
Petronievič on, 7:267
in physical theories, **9:154–158**
Plato on, 9:147
Plotinus on, 6:187
primitive cultures' view of, 5:306
Pythagoras on, 9:146
relational theory of, 9:147
Riemann on, 5:461
sense of, Piaget on, 7:568
"sensible," in sense-datum theory, 8:819
in Spengler's cultural morphology, 9:166
stellar parallax, 9:151
symmetry in, 2:462, 9:468
as term, rules for linguistic use of, 8:641
three-dimensional, in geometry, 9:149
and time, 2:87–88, 9:487, 9:495. *See also* Space-time
as *a priori* forms of perception, 4:693
in circumscribing human thought, 4:744
Earman on, 3:159
in human representation, 7:642
ideas of, examination of, 5:14–15
in Iqbal's theistic pluralism, 4:744
Kant on, 5:11–12
objective *vs.* subjective, 9:741
philosophy of, 3:159, 7:642
as universal form of sensibility, 5:12
Space, Time and Deity (Alexander), 1:197–198
Space-time
Alexander on, 1:108–109, 7:22
Augustinian confusion resolved by, 9:461
Copernican principle and, 1:220
cosmological modeling of, 2:559
curvature of, 9:465, 9:496
decomposition of, 9:497
Earman on, 3:160
Einstein on, 3:179–180
empirical features of, 1:109
four-dimensional conception of, 9:65
free will and, 9:471
in general relativity, 9:496–497
geometry of, 7:476
Gödel on, 9:496–497
infinite divisibility of, 4:655–656
kalām argument on God's existence and, 2:555
locality in, 6:638
in materialism, 6:5
mental events in, 6:261
Minkowski on, 9:464, 9:484
movement through, 9:465
overview of, 9:464–465
perspective and, 1:108
Salmon on, 8:594
as singularity, 2:565, 3:160
Smart on, 9:65
in special relativity, 9:149–150, 9:495
in string theory, 9:270
substantivalism of, 3:160
Space-Time-Matter (Raum, Zeit, Materie) (Weyl), 9:741
Spain
anarchism in, 1:178
antirational skepticism in, 9:50
Ibn Bājja, 4:544
Jewish philosophers of
Galen and, 4:6
13th century, 4:820
Thomism in, 9:137
Unamuno on, 9:567
Spalding, Johann Jakob, Lavater and, 5:213
Spandrels of San Marco and the Panglossian Paradigm, The (Gould and Lewontin), 3:484
Spanheim, Friedrich, Toland and, 9:504
Spaniard, Unamuno on, 9:567
Spanish Civil War, 5:209
Spanish Inquisition, Erasmus and, 3:339
Spanish philosophy
Latin American philosophy and, 5:204–205, 5:208–209
Ortega y Gasset in, 7:45
Spann, Othmar, **9:158–159**
Spannung (tension between eternal and temporal), 4:800
Sparshott, Francis, on creative process, 2:590, 3:430
Sparsity, of properties, 8:66–68
Spartacus, anarchism and, 1:177
Spatial co-ordinates, system of, origin of, 5:125
Spatial parts, of objects, persistence and, 7:208
Spatial relations
isomorphism principle for, 5:128
sound and, 9:138
without absolute space, Boscovich on, 1:665
Spaulding, Edward, and new realism, 6:585–587
Spaventa, Bertrando, 4:49, **9:159–161**
Speaker meaning, 6:83–84, 7:405–406
"Speaker's Reference and Semantic Reference" (Kripke), 5:150
Speaking of Art (Kivy), 1:66
Spearman, Charles, and Krueger, 5:156
Special evidence, in John of Mirecourt's epistemology, 4:841
Special relativity
absolute-relative debate in, 9:156
connectibility in, 9:471
conservation of energy in, 3:237
conventionalism and simultaneity in, 2:523–525
determinism and, 3:32–33
Einstein and, 3:179
mass in, 6:4
and naturalism, 9:499
observation of time in, 9:495–496
and present, 9:499
Putnam on, 9:499
relative simultaneity in, 9:496
Rietdijk on, 9:499
space and time in, 9:149–150, 9:495–496
and tense, 9:499
time in, 9:149–150, 9:495–496
Special sciences, **9:161–164**
metaphysics and, Aristotle on, 6:185
microphysical events in, 6:135
ontology separate from, 7:27
"Special Sciences" (Fodor), 3:193
Species, 7:343
Aristotle on, 2:73
Avicenna on, 1:433
Johnson (W. E.) on, 3:1
in medieval metaphysics, 6:188
Porphyry on, 6:187–188
of terms, in traditional logic, 5:494
theory of, 9:559
Speciesism, 9:76, **9:164–165**
Specific modal status, 5:100–101

Specific nerve energies, 4:304
Specificity, in applied ethics, 1:239
Specimen geometriae luciferae (Leibniz), 2:499
Specimen Irma Dream (Freud), 3:743
Specimen of Dynamics (Leibniz), 5:269, 9:156
Specimen of True Philosophy, in a Discourse on Genesis (Collier), 2:324
Specious Present. *See* Time, consciousness of
Spectator (Addison), 1:51
Spectator (periodical), Enlightenment and, 3:244
Spectator theory, of Adam Smith, 7:316
Spector, Clifford, 8:56
Spectral modal interpretation, 6:278–279
Speculation, moral order and, 1:378
Speculative egoism, universal idealism as, 4:770–771
Speculative grammar, 1:591, 8:770–771
 Bernard of Chartres on, 1:590
 in medieval logic, 5:432–433
Speculative idealism
 Creighton on, 2:592
 Gramsci on, 4:169–170
Speculative philosophy, 1:476
 in *Cursus Theologicus* (John of St. Thomas), 4:845
 Schopenhauer and, 8:656
 state support for, 8:638
 Twardowski on, 9:554
Speculative principles, Locke on, 3:407
Speculative proofs, of existence of God, 5:23
Speculum Mentis (Collingwood), 2:325
Speech
 assertion in, 6:650
 behavior in, 7:407
 censorship and, 2:119–120
 in Cixous écriture feminine project, 2:262
 conversational implicature in, 2:525–528
 entailment in, 7:770
 expressive ability and, 2:208–210
 free
  censorship and, 2:119–120
  computer ethics and, 2:397–398
  in feminism, 7:462–463
  Theodorus on, 2:620
 Heidegger on, 7:411
 Hobbes on, 8:773
 identification of particular objects in, 9:265
 illocutionary acts in, 8:706
 in Indian theories of language, 7:414–416
 indirect, 7:405–406
 Lambert on, 8:786
 in making sense of activity, 9:77
 meaning of, context-sensitivity of, 2:209
 meaning of Dao in, 2:191–193
 and meaning-delivery-within-speech-capacity, 2:208–209
 Merleau-Ponty on, 7:411
 Pāṇini on, 7:413
 perception and, 5:657
 Philodemus on, 7:302
 proof in, 8:19
 in psychology, 9:849
 reference in, 7:407
 stability and dynamic expression in, 2:208–209
 thought and, Vailati on, 9:629
 units, of Sanskrit, 7:413
Speech and Phenomena (Derrida), 2:715–717, 9:491
Speech Genres and Other Late Essays (Bakhtin), 1:470
Speech on the Morals of the Chinese (Wolff), 9:824
Speech-act theory, 1:226, 6:167
Speeches on Religion (Reden über die Religion) (Schleiermacher), 5:297
Speed
 computing machine realization and, 2:405
 of light, 7:476
Spekulative Dogmatik (Baader), 1:439
Spelke, Elizabeth, 4:694
Spelman, Elizabeth, 3:586
Spelman, Sir Henry, 3:636
Spence, Canterbury v., 6:95
Spencer, Herbert
 on Absolute, 7:714
 on agnosticism, 1:93, 7:714
 Balfour on, 1:474
 Bergson on, 1:569
 Condillac and, 8:826
 Darwinism and, 2:642
 Durkheim and, 3:149, 3:151
 on education, 7:377
 Eliot (George) and, 3:184
 on energy conservation, 3:232
 on eternal return doctrine, 3:354
 on evolution, 7:714
 evolutionary psychology and, 3:481
 Fiske and, 3:667–668
 Ibn Khaldūn and, 4:549
 Lalande on, 5:172
 Latin American philosophy and, 5:206–207
 libertarianism and, 5:334–335
 Liebmann and, 5:344
 metaphysics of, 7:377
 Ostwald and, comparison of, 7:50
 positivism of, 7:713–714
 on reality, 7:377
 social Darwinism and, 3:479
 "survival of the fittest" doctrine, 3:415
 Taine and, 9:365
 utopianism of, 9:618
 on war and peace, 7:155
 Wilson (Edward O.) and, 9:789
 Wright (Chauncey) on, 9:846
Spener, Philipp Jakob, 7:575–576
Spengler, Oswald, **9:165–169**
 on decadence, 7:319
 on determinism, 3:36
 Gehlen and, 4:35
 Klages and, 5:77
 Toynbee and, 9:517
Sperry, Roger, 6:565–566
Speusippus
 Aristotle and, 1:263
 on first principles, 7:606
 in Greek Academy, 4:171
Spiegelberg, Herbert, 4:682
Spin (of particle), measuring apparatus for, 8:208
Spinoza, Benedict (Baruch) de, 3:405, 7:248, 7:308, **9:169–193**
 on absolute, 1:11
 on affect imitation, 9:345
 on behavior, 8:125
 on belief, 5:94, 9:174, 9:190
 on Bible, 7:97
 on body, 3:294
 Boulainvilliers on, 1:670
 on Brahman, 1:682–683
 Cartesianism of, 2:59
 censorship of, 9:182
 on clarity and distinctness, 6:190
 coherence theory of truth and, 9:536
 on conation, 8:126
 Crescas and, 2:593
 and crisis of skepticism, 9:54
 Cumberland and, 2:615
 on death, 2:650–652
 deep ecology and, 3:260
 deism and, 2:682, 9:194–195
 Deleuze on, 2:695–696
 on Descartes, 2:745, 2:755
 on determinism, 3:5–8, 9:188–189
 Einstein and, 3:179–181
 on emanation, 4:108

on emotions, 3:198, 8:126–127
on empathy, 9:345
Encyclopédie and, 3:223
Enlightenment and, 3:246, 4:746, 5:296
and epistemology, 3:294–296
on essence and existence, 3:350
on eternity, 3:357–359
and ethics, 3:406–407
on free will, 3:12–13, 8:125
on freedom, 9:188
and French clandestine literature, 2:265
geometric presentations of, 9:175
German pantheism and, 7:97–98
Geulincx and, 4:80
on God, 4:111, 4:668–669, 8:125, 9:184
  and nature, 1:11, 2:641, 4:107
Goethe and, 4:141, 7:101
Hebrew grammar of, 9:183–184
higher criticism and, 5:196
on historicity of scripture, 9:178–179
Hobbes and, 3:294
on ideas, 3:294–295
on insight, 8:126
on intuition, 3:295, 7:97
on irrationality, 8:126–127
Jacobi (Friedrich Heinrich) on, 4:770
on judgment, 3:295
on knowledge, types of, 3:295–296, 8:126
La Peyrère and, 5:196
on laws of physics, 9:172
Le Clerc and, 5:236
Leibniz and, 3:296, 5:251–252, 5:269
Lessing and, 5:294–296
Lichtenberg and, 5:339–341
on life, meaning and value of, 5:356
Lloyd on, 5:373
Locke and, 5:392
on logical monism, 6:184
on love, 5:588
Maimonides and, 5:652, 5:653
Malebranche and, 5:666
on material universe, 3:354
Mendelssohn and, 1:11
Meslier and, 6:154
on metaphysics, 6:169, 9:172–173
on mind, 3:294, 4:602, 6:259
on mind-body identity, 8:125–126, 9:187
on miracles and natural order, 6:266
in modern Jewish philosophy, 4:825–826
on monism, 3:294, 6:326–327, 9:185
mysticism of, Schlegel on, 8:630
on *natura naturans,* 9:175, 9:185
on nature of being, 5:148
on opinion, differences of, 9:182
Orobio and, 7:41
on panpsychism, 9:188
pantheism of, 4:108, 7:96–98, 8:621, 9:185, 9:193
Pantheismusstreit and, 7:99–101
on passions, 9:190
Paulsen and, 7:149
in Platonic tradition, 7:615
on pleasure, 4:257
on plenitude, 5:257, 5:593
on political state, 9:180–181
on possibility, 7:721–722
and psychoanalysis, 8:126–127
on psychology, 8:125–127, 9:189
and rationalism, 4:746
on reason, 3:295–296
on rights, origin of, 4:180
Sanches and, 8:596
Santayana and, 8:597
Schelling and, 8:617
Schleiermacher and, 8:637
Scholasticism and, 3:294
on science, 3:296, 7:98
on sensation, 8:126
on sense experience, 3:295–296
on sense perception, 3:294
Shelley and, 9:9
Shestov on, 9:11
Sigwart on, 9:29
Simon and, 9:33
on social contract, 9:80–81
Solov'ëv and, 9:123
on state of nature, 7:153, 9:180
Steffens and, 9:238
Stout and, 9:259
on substance, 4:78, 4:770, 8:125, 9:297
on substance independence, 7:24
Taine and, 9:364–365
Toland and, 2:683
translators of, 3:184
Tschirnhaus and, 9:549
on understanding and free will, 3:12–13
on war and peace, 7:153
wisdom of, 9:794
Spinozism, **9:193–196**
  of Lessing, Mendelssohn and, 6:131
  of Malebranche, 5:666
  of Wolff, 9:828
Spinula, Stephanus, 2:755
Spir, Afrikan Alexandrovich, **9:196–197**
Spiral Jetty (Smithson), 3:256
Spirit
  alienation of, 1:120–121
  in atomism, 6:60
  autonomy of, 7:61
  Berkeley on, 1:579–580, 3:301–302
  and Christian Trinity, 2:248
  Chrysippus on, 2:252
  Croce on, 2:600
  Crusius on, 2:607
  Farias Brito's philosophy of, 3:552
  Hegel on, 7:389–390
  history as typology of, 4:743
  integrity of, 5:74
  Krochmal on, 4:828
  Leibniz on, 2:366
  Lopatin on, 5:572–573
  as manifestation of divine, Formstecher on, 4:827
  Milton on, 6:249
  Molina Garmendia on, 6:324
  Morgan (C. Lloyd) on, 6:403
  myths as collective embodiment of, 1:441
  objective. *See* Objective spirit
  opposition to unfreedom, 1:559
  Otto on, 7:61
  phenomenology of, 4:544
  philosophy of, Croce on, 2:600
  as pure act, Gentile on, 4:50
  Santayana on, 8:602
  in Spengler's cultural morphology, 9:166
  Telesio on, 9:390
  threat to, in modern tendency to objectify and systematize, 5:67
  unconscious in, 5:713
  unity as, 3:668
  Vasconcelos on, 9:648
Spirit (*Geist*), emergence of, in man, 5:77–78
Spirit forces, replaced by physical forces, 5:51
Spirit of Christianity, The (Hegel), 4:261–262
Spirit of Hebrew Poetry (Herder), 6:574
Spirit of Medieval Philosophy, The (Gilson), 4:92
"Spirit of the Age, The" (Mill, John Stuart), 2:33
Spirit of the Laws (Ferguson), 3:605
Spirit of the Laws (Montesquieu), 3:410
Spiritlessness of modernity, 5:67
Spirito, Ugo, 4:53, **9:197–198**

Spiritu et Anima, De (Alcher of Clairvaux), 4:753
Spiritual agency, in human evolution, 9:721
Spiritual Canticle, The (John of the Cross), 4:846
Spiritual force, beauty as, 1:512
Spiritual formation, Dge-lugs scholastic training and, 1:734–735
Spiritual Foundations of Life (Solov'ëv), 9:122
Spiritual initiative, 6:217
Spiritual intuition, 5:147
Spiritual life
  Dilthey on, 3:79–80
  Eucken on, 3:452
Spiritual matter
  and hylomorphic composition of creatures, 1:653
  Olivi on, 7:13
Spiritual Opticks: or a Glasse discovering the weaknessese and imperfection of a Christians knowledge in this life (Culverwell), 2:612
Spiritual phenomena, interpretation of, 5:60
Spiritual reality, physics as external manifestation of, 3:556
Spiritual realm, Dante on, 2:625
Spiritual security, Cynic teaching and, 2:616
Spiritual substance, doctrine of, and personal identity, 7:217–220
Spiritual world, relationships of, 3:607
Spiritualism, 8:296
  and communism, 2:365
  Franck and, 3:712–713
  Gödel on, 4:117
  as pseudoscience, 8:670
  shadow-man doctrine of immortality in, 4:603
  Stefanini and, 9:237
  Wallace (Alfred Russel) and, 9:721
Spiritualistic school, of Victor Cousin, 3:705
Spirituality
  of beauty, Winckelmann on, 9:790
  Bonhoeffer on, 1:656
  as characteristic of God, 4:670
  contemplative, 8:592
  Eucken on, 3:452
  of Neoplatonism, 6:548
  Rilke on, 8:477–478
  Spann on, 9:158
  work and, integration of, 9:737
Spirituality of John Henry Newman, The (Graef), 6:583
Spirtes, Peter, 8:687
Spitzel, Theophil Gottlieb, on Spinoza, 7:99
Splitting worlds formulation of quantum mechanics, 5:697–698
Spontaneity
  and creativity, 1:714, 2:590
  as direct experience of freedom, 1:564
  doctrine of, 1:462
  Kant on, 5:36
  Sartre on, 2:459
Spontaneous collapse theories, 8:211–212
Spontaneous generation, 5:359–360
Spontaneous localization theory, 8:211–212
Spór o Istnienie Świata (The controversy over the existence of the world) (Ingarden), 4:683
Spranger, (Franz Ernst) Eduard, 6:545, **9:198–199**
Sprat, Thomas, on language, 1:50
Sprichworter (Franck), republished by G. E. Lessing, 3:713
Spring and Autumn (Confucian classic), 3:98
Sprott, D. A., 3:665
Square of opposition
  definition of, 5:557
  in traditional logic, 5:495
Sriharsa, denial of possibility of knowledge, 5:117
Srīnivāsa, 4:630
Stability
  in Buddhist epistemology, 1:757
  of language, and dynamic expression, 2:208–209
  Rawls on, 8:259
Stability theory, 6:314–315
Stable subjectivities, dissolution of, 3:588
Stace, Walter Terence, 8:401, **9:199–201,** 9:563
Staddon, John, 9:62
Stadium (Dichotomy) argument against motion, 9:874
Staël-Holstein, Anne Louise Germaine Necker, Baronne de, 3:195, 6:572, **9:201–202,** 9:319, 9:839
Stafford-Clark, David
  on "how" and "why," 9:754
  on superultimate "why," 9:758
Stage theory, persistence and, 7:209–210
Stahl, Georg Ernst, **9:202–203**
Stakeholders, in business moral obligations, 1:779
Stalin, Joseph
  as communist leader, 2:363–364
  on dialectic, 5:737
  Lenin and, 5:281
  and Mussolini, comparison of, 3:554
  on revolution, 3:61
Stalnaker, Robert C.
  conditional logic and, 5:491
  on decision theory, 2:659
  on internal language, 8:808
  on possible world counterfactual conditionals, 2:427
  on possible world representations of mental content, 2:481
  on presupposition, 3:252, 8:748
  on propositions and understanding, 5:513
  on semantics, 3:710, 8:76
Stammler, Rudolf, **9:203–204**
  on law, 7:424
  and neo-Kantianism, 6:543
Stampioen, Johan, 3:187
Stance, in Blackburn, 6:634
Standard(s)
  of conduct, self-effacing, 3:441
  in contractualism, 2:518
  of practice, 1:239
  universal, conservatism and, 2:466
Standard model, definition of, 5:549
Standardism
  philosophical, 8:439
Standardism, philosophical, 8:439
Standardization, Adorno on, 1:26
Standing sentences, in radical translation, 8:217
Standpoint
  Marx's theory of, 3:563
  and patriarchal social relations, 3:575
  theorists of, and bias paradox, 3:575
  women and, 3:595
Stanhope, Charles, logic machine of, 5:565
Stanley, Jason
  on contextualism, 3:275
  on pragmatics, 7:741
Stanley, Thomas
  Encyclopédie and, 3:223
  on skepticism, 9:50
Stanton, Betty, 2:711
Stanton, Harry, 2:711
Star of Redemption, The (Der Stern der Erlösung) (Rosenzweig), 8:498
Stark, Johannes, Einstein and, 7:578
Starry Messenger, The (Galileo), 4:8

Stars
- aggregates of, kinetic theories of, 4:804
- and black holes, 1:607–608
- stellar parallax and, 9:151

State, **9:204–211**
- al-Fārābī, Abū-Naṣr Muhammad on, 1:117
- Aquinas on, 6:104
- Arab view of, 5:202
- Arnold on, 1:294
- Augustine on, 6:104, 7:421
- Bosanquet on, 1:663
- Calvin on, 2:10–11
- Chicherin on, 2:148
- civil disobedience and, 2:260
- civilizing influence of, on individuals, 1:663
- coercive, justifications for, 9:72
- as collective actor, in justice, 4:865
- of consciousness, 2:449
- contractual nature of, 9:73–74
- Croce on, 2:604
- economic bases of, 2:364
- as enemy of individual, 9:251
- Fichte on, 3:617
- and freedom, 4:558
- General Will in, Rousseau on, 4:38–40
- Gentile on, 4:51
- geography and culture of, 1:621–622
- Green on, 4:180
- Haeckel on, 4:203–204
- Hegel on, 3:415, 4:268, 7:153
- Hobbes on, 3:405
- ibn Bājja on, 4:544
- Ibn Khaldūn on, 4:548
- incapacity for wrong, 1:664
- in international law, Grotius on, 4:190–191
- Islamic, in Khomeini's political philosophy, 4:763
- Lavrov on, 5:219
- legal consciousness in, 4:577–578
- Leonard on, 6:536–537
- liberalism on, 5:319–322
- Locke on, 9:509
- Machiavelli on, 5:629
- Marsilius of Padua on, 5:722
- Marx on, 3:415
- Meinecke on, 6:113
- Milton on, 6:250–251
- and morality, enforcement of, 5:338. *See also* Paternalism
- as more real than people, 1:663
- nation defined by, 6:481
- as national community, 9:208
- as natural property, 9:284
- phenomenologically distinct, identifying, 5:85
- pluralism in, 7:642
- post-Westphalian model of, 9:145
- powers of, 3:617
  - *vs.* liberty, 5:337–338
  - Meinecke on, 6:113
- Pufendorf on, 8:158
- punishment by, 8:160
- religion and, 4:203–204
- Rousseau on, 3:410, 4:38–40
- Saint-Simon on, 8:591
- Schlegel on, 8:632
- Smith on, 2:364
- in social contract, 9:79
- social rules and, 4:865
- and society, relation of, 9:96
- sovereignty of, 9:139
- in Spengler's cultural morphology, 9:166
- Spinoza on, 9:180–181. *See also* *Religio catholica*
- Stein on, 9:240
- in Sumner's laissez-faire social theory, 9:326
- as threat to liberty, 2:148
- Tolstoy on, 9:513–514
- totalitarianism in, 9:96
- Treitschke on, 7:153
- welfare and, 7:426
- withering away of, 8:591
- *See also* Government; Society

State and Revolution (Lenin), 5:280

State in Relation to Labour, The (Jevons), 4:807

State of affairs
- in events, 7:25
- in hedonism, 4:255
- impossible, 7:262–263
- as judicanda of justice, 4:863
- in ontology, 7:25
- in processes, 7:25
- in science, 6:209
- in Wodeham's ontology, 9:821–822

State of Fear (Crichton), 1:336

State of nature
- Collingwood on, 2:329
- Cumberland on, 2:615
- Hobbes on, 3:405, 4:415–416, 7:153, 9:79
- Locke on, 5:388, 7:153
- primitivism on, 5:594
- Rawls on, 5:323–324
- society in, 7:369–370
- Spinoza on, 7:153, 9:180

State of Souls Separated from their Bodies, The (Huber), 9:839

State structures, of Kushitism, 5:59

State transformation, quantum computing machine development and, 2:407

State-content ambiguity, 6:176

Statement(s)
- analytic, **1:159–165**
- Aristotle on, 2:540–541, 8:756–757
- Ayer on, 1:436–437
- basic. *See* Basic statements
- Carroll on, 5:453
- causal, 1:88, 1:549
- conditional, semantics in, 1:549–550
- confirmability of, 9:661–663
- correctness of, 8:171
- correspondence truth theory and, 2:540–541, 9:264
- falsifiability of, 9:661
- future, 5:691–692
- in illative combinatory logic, 2:339
- intensional transitive verbs in, 4:698
- meaning of, 9:660
- metaphysical, 1:436–437
- multilateral, 5:453
- necessary-contingent distinction and, 1:561
- Plato on, 2:540, 8:754–755
- of probability, 1:686
- scientific, Mach on, 8:826–827
- in sensationalism, 8:823
- Stoics on, 2:541
- superfluous components of, 9:662
- synthetic, **1:159–165**
- truth in, 9:264
- truth-conditions of, 4:622
- universal, 7:768
- vague, as objects of knowledge, 5:111
- validity of, proving, 5:121
- verifiability principle applied to, 9:659–660
- verification and, 5:527
- *See also* Proposition(s)

Statement forms, valid, in modern logic, 5:234

Statement of the method, by Malinowski, 3:762

Statesman (Plato), 7:591–594, 9:107

Statesman, wisdom required by, 9:795

State-type mapping, in computationalism, 2:390–391

Statistical conclusions, probability measures and, 5:57

Statistical deduction, 4:644

Statistical Explanation and Statistical Relevance (Salmon), 3:741

Statistical fallacies, 3:545
Statistical frequency of events, 9:658
Statistical inference, Keynes and, 5:57
Statistical laws, as scientific law, 7:518–519
Statistical mechanics
  Boltzmann and, 1:644–645
  chance and credence in, 2:128–129
  and chaos modeling of probabilistic characterizations, 2:133
  development of, 6:70
  and information theory, 4:677–678
  Maxwell and, 1:644–645
  objective chance and, 2:126
  philosophy of, 4:86–87, **7:537–543**
    canonical ensembles, Gibbs on, 4:86–87
    causal inference in, 8:685–687
    entropy and, 7:537–543
    equilibrium theory and, 7:538–539
    Gibbs on, 4:86–87
    history of, 7:537–538
    nonequilibrium theory and, 7:539–540
    and probability, 7:538
    and time, direction of, 7:537–543
  probability in, 7:538, 9:499–500
  thermodynamics and, 7:537–538, 7:541–542, 9:579
Statistical methods
  and chance in social sciences, 2:125–126
  and directionality and asymmetry, 2:98
  Fisherian significance tests, 9:213–215
  gambler's ruin, 9:217
  goodness-of-fit tests, 9:219–220
  invariance in, 9:223
  Neyman-Pearson theory of, 9:215–218
  Poisson distribution in, 9:224
  postsampling distribution in, 9:230
  randomization in, 9:214
  for small samples, 3:662
Statistical reasoning, in physics, 6:70
Statistical relevance, 2:100, 3:521–522, 4:310
Statistical syllogism, 4:635, 4:641
Statistical theory, Pearson and, 7:159
Statistics
  Akaike Information Criterion and, 8:685
  Behrens-Fisher problem in, 9:231
  Buckle on, 1:718–719
  Cauchy distribution in, 9:231
  Comte and, 2:412
  confidence intervals in, 9:231
  confounders in, 8:686
  and decision making under uncertainty, 3:660
  degrees of association in, 8:686
  of distribution in equilibrium of gas, 1:644–645
  econometrics in, 8:687
  exact distribution of, 3:662
  foundations of, 8:613, **9:212–236**
  frequentist paradigm in, 8:613
  in infomatics, 4:671
  informed priors and, 9:233–234
  Koopman-Darmois form, 9:225–226
  likelihood principle of, 9:212–213
  optimality theorem and, 9:221–222
  overfitting data in, 8:685
  precognition as explanation for, 7:757
  principle of stable estimation in, 8:614
  probable error of, 3:663
  randomization in, 8:686
  Salmon's relevance model of, 8:593
  Savage and, 8:613–614
  subjective expected utility theory and, 8:613
  tea-tasting lady in, 9:213
  in thermodynamics, 9:468–469
  thick coin example, 9:219
Staudt, Karl Georg Christian von, 4:60
Stcherbatsky, T., 4:633
Steady state model, cosmological idea creation and, 2:562
Stebbing, Lizzie Susan, **9:236–237**
  on Le Roy, 5:288
  Vienna Circle and, 5:525
Stechus, Augustinus, 3:624
Stecker, Robert, on art, 1:300
Steele, Richard
  Addison and, 1:22
  Enlightenment and, 3:244
Stefanini, Luigi, **9:237–238**
Steffens, Henrich, **9:238–239**
Stein, Charles, 9:225
Stein, Edith, **9:239–241**
  on empathy, 9:345
  Lipps and, 5:363
Stein, Howard, on space and time, 3:159
Steiner, Rudolf, **9:241–242**
Steinheim, Solomon Ludwig, 4:828
Stella (Goethe), 4:140
Stellar evolution, Eddington on, 3:164
Stendhal, on love, 5:588
Stenius, Erik, on rhythm of *Tractatus*, 9:803
Stenner, A. J., 8:731
Steno, Nicolaus, Leibniz and, 5:252
Stephen, James Fitzjames, on toleration, 9:508–510
Stephen, Leslie, **9:243–244**
  agnosticism of, 1:358, 9:243
  deism and, 2:691
"Steps Toward a Constructive Nominalism" (Goodman & Quine), 4:158, 6:627
Sterba, James, on Rawls, 5:324
Stern, Louis William, 7:233
Stern der Erlösung, Der (The star of redemption) (Rosenzweig), 4:829, 8:498
Stern-Gerlach experiment, 1:633–634
Stevens, Michael, on probability, 8:39
Stevenson, Charles L., **9:245–246**
  on Dewey, 3:425
  on emotivism, 3:204–207, 3:425–426, 3:684, 6:157
  ethical theory of, 3:327
  on expressive meaning, 6:652
  on Moore (G. E.), 3:376–377, 3:418
  in noncognitivism, 6:632
Stevin, Simon
  Descartes and, 2:721
  on energy and work, 3:227
  inclined plane thought experiment of, 9:453
  on real numbers, 2:493
Stewart, Balfour, physicotheology and, 7:561–562
Stewart, Dugald, **9:246–248**
  on common consent for God's existence, 2:347
  on common sense, 2:358
  Johnson and, 8:794
  Mansel and, 5:687
  Mill (John Stuart) and, 8:795
  Shepherd on, 9:10
Sthavīravāda Buddhism, on logic, 5:411
Stich, Stephen
  eliminative materialism and, 3:183
  on endowment effect, 9:39
  on folk psychology, 3:678
  on pragmatism, 7:751
Stiglitz, J. E., on risk theory, 2:660
Stillingfleet, Edward, 2:682, 5:375–377, 5:386, 5:391, **9:248–250**
Stilpo of Megara, 6:111, 8:755

Stimulus, in intrinsic theory of consciousness, 2:453
Stimulus meaning, in radical translation, 8:216–217
Stimulus-response
- in biology, 1:593
- in communication, 6:80–81
- as memory, 1:564
- Weber on, 8:139

Stipulation, Boghossian on, 1:165
Stipulative definition, 3:548, 5:540
Stirling, James, on force measurement, 3:228
Stirner, Max, **9:250–251**
- anarchism of, 1:178
- ideology of, Marx on, 4:573

Stitch, Stephen, 3:680
Stockdale, James, Epictetus and, 3:262
Stocker, Michael, 3:749
Stoddard, Solomon, 3:166
Stöhr, Adolf, **9:251–253**
Stoicism/Stoics, **9:253–258**
- and the Academy, 2:46, 2:48
- action in, 1:194
- on active and passive principles, 7:607
- aesthetics in, 1:45, 1:189
- *aitia* in, 1:100
- on anger, 8:812
- Antiochus of Ascalon and, 1:222
- apprehension in, 1:30
- Aquinas and, 9:425
- Arcesilaus on, 1:247
- asceticism and, 1:351
- assent in, 1:30, 1:248
- astrology and, 4:301–302
- astronomy and, 4:301
- atomism in, 8:121
- Avicenna and, 5:419
- Bacon (Roger) on, 1:455
- beauty in, 1:45, 1:189
- Boethius on, 1:625
- and Byzantine thought, 1:787
- Carneades and, 2:48
- Christianity and, 3:401
- Cicero on, 2:258
- Cleanthes and, 2:288
- Clement on, 2:290
- Clinomachus and, 6:110
- continua in, 2:491
- and correspondence theory of truth, 2:541, 9:534
- cosmology in, 5:706
- cosmopolitanism and, 2:567
- Cudworth on, 2:610
- cynicism and, 2:617, 3:399
- on death, 2:652
- deep ecology and, 3:260
- definition of virtue by, 7:307
- on determinism, 3:5–7
- dialectic and, 3:54
- Diderot on, 3:72, 3:76
- Diogenes Laertius on, 3:88
- Diogenes of Apollonia and, 3:89
- on discourse, 5:569
- on duty, 3:154–155
- education in, 7:367
- emanationism in, 3:189
- Epictetus and, 3:261–262
- Epicurean School and, 3:263
- epistemology of, 1:30, 1:247, 3:288
- on equality, 3:329
- on eternal return doctrine, 3:353
- and ethics, 3:399–400, 5:706
- explanation and causality in, 1:449
- Ferguson and, 9:247
- fire in, 8:121
- on five indemonstrables, 9:255–256
- on force, 3:686–687
- and God, 4:110, 5:569, 7:306
- Gournay on, 4:167
- and Gregory of Nazianzus, 4:181
- Grotius on, 4:191
- on the heart, 4:6
- Hegel on, 4:263
- and Hellenistic thought, 4:300–301
- history of, 3:400
- and Ikhwān al-Ṣafāʾ, 4:576
- and illuminationism, 4:582–583
- impressions in, 1:194, 1:247
- on innate ideas, 4:688
- inspiration as breath in, 4:579
- on intermediate natural things, 4:174
- Justin Martyr and, 7:142
- knowledge in, 1:247, 7:312
- La Mettrie on, 5:180
- on language, 4:302
- law in, 7:419
- and lekton, doctrine of, 8:757–758
- on life, 3:399
- Lipsius on, 5:364
- logic and, 3:54, 5:404–408, 5:493, 5:607, 6:110
- logical categories of, 2:80
- logos in, 5:569, 6:506
- Lucian of Samosata on, 5:597
- Marcus Aurelius and, 5:706
- Marulić on, 5:729
- on matter, 1:100, 6:59
- microcosm in, 5:641–642
- mind in, 5:706
- on moral perfection, 7:194
- More (Thomas) on, 6:399
- Musonius Rufus and, 6:440–441
- natural law and, 3:400, 6:506–507
- negation in, 6:523
- opinion in, 1:194, 1:247
- optimism/pessimism and, 7:247
- *ousia* in, 7:62–63
- Panaetius of Rhodes and, 7:78–80
- panpsychism and, 7:83
- pantheism in, 7:94
- patristic philosophy and, 7:141–142
- on perception, 8:824
- periodization of, 7:79
- peripatetics and, 1:259
- on phantasia, 7:271, 8:824
- Philodemus on, 7:302
- Plutarch of Chaeronea and, 7:649
- political philosophy of, 7:658
- possibility in, 7:720
- power in, 7:732
- propositional logic in, 1:4
- psychology in, 8:120–121
- on reason, 3:400, 5:569
- religion in, 7:489
- in Renaissance, 8:425
- semantics in, 8:757–758
- Seneca and, 8:811
- sensation in, 8:121
- Shaftesbury and, 9:1
- Simplicius on, 9:35
- skepticism and, 1:193–194, 4:173
- Skovoroda on, 9:63
- social contract and, 9:81
- Socrates and, 3:399, 9:113
- soul in, 8:121
- on suicide, 9:319
- and theory of knowledge, 4:173
- on universe, 3:687
- Valla on, 9:635
- Vives and, 9:701
- on war and peace, 7:154
- on wisdom, 1:194, 9:794
- *See also* Zeno of Citium

"Stoicism and Mental Health" (Russell), 2:352
Stoics. *See* Stoicism/Stoics
Stokes, Donald E., 8:675
Stokes, George
- Pearson and, 7:159
- physicotheology and, 7:562

Stokhof, Martin, 1:175, 8:808
Stoljar, Natalie, 3:587
Stolnitz, Jerome, on aesthetics, 1:33, 1:36
Stolz, Otto, on Euclid, 2:492
Stone, Julius, in law, 7:428
Stone, Tony, 9:38
Stone Spaces (Johnstone), 4:740

Storage, memory as, 6:125
Storia del regno di Napoli, La (History of the Kingdom of Naples) (Croce), 2:604
Storia della filosofia (Abbagnano), 1:1
Storia della letteratura italiana (History of Italian literature) (De Sanctis), 2:719
"Storia ridotto sotto il concetto generale dell'arte, La" (Croce), 2:599
Stories, in Chinese ethics, 2:200
Storr, Anthony, on Freud as semanticist, 3:744
Stosszahlansatz, 7:539
Stout, George Frederick, **9:258–261**
 on common sense, 2:358
 and evolutionary psychology, 8:137
 Johnson (William Ernest) and, 5:458
 and psychology, 8:137, 8:141
Strachey, John, 7:155
Strachey, Lytton, on Queen Victoria's dying thoughts, 3:107
Strahlungen (Jünger), 4:860
Stranger, The (Camus), 2:21
Strangers to Ourselves (Kristeva), 1:134
Strasburg papyrus of Empedocles, 3:211–212
Strategy, Neumann's (John von) work on, 6:559
Stratification, definition of, 5:557
Strato and Stratonism, **9:261–262**
 in Greek Academy, 4:300
 in Lyceum, 1:258
 Peripatetics and, 7:202
Strauss, David Friedrich, **9:262–264**
 assumption of, 3:611
 on Christianity, 6:610
 Hegel and, 4:276
 Lassalle and, 5:203
 Loisy and, 5:570
 on miracles, 6:266
 Nietzsche on, 6:610
 Parker (T.) and, 7:121
 translators of, 3:184
Strauss, Leo
 on Maimonides, 5:654
 Rousseau and, 8:516
Stravinsky, Igor, Adorno on, 1:26
Strawson, Peter Frederick, **9:264–267**
 on argument from analogy, 7:52
 on descriptions, 7:768
 essay "On Referring," 3:628
 Evans and, 3:459
 Hungerland on, 7:767
 Kitcher (Patricia) and, 5:76
 and metaphysics, 5:34, 6:197–198
 ordinary language conceptual system of, 2:79
 on ordinary logic, 8:807
 on other minds, 7:56–57
 on performative theory of truth, 7:195–198
 on performative utterances, 7:200
 on presupposition, 3:252–253, 7:767–768
 on propositional mismatches, 5:508
 on Russell, 7:768
 on sound, 9:138
 theory of person, 7:238–239
Stream, of conscious qualitative states, 2:451–452
"Stream of Thought, The" (Hamlyn), 4:595
Streben, Fichte on, 5:588
Streit der Psychologisten und Formalisten in der modernen Logik, Der (Palágyi), 7:75
Streng, Frederick J., 1:743
Strengthened syllogism, definition of, 5:557
Strengthening the antecedent, Lewis (D.) on, 5:314
Strevens, Michael, on explanation, 3:525–526
Strict act utilitarian, 3:749
Strict akratic action, 9:729–732
 definition of, 9:729
 effort in, 9:730–731
 resistance in, 9:730–731
Strife (Quarrel), in Empedocles, 3:209–213, 7:762–763
Striking the Earth at Yi River (Shao Yong), 9:6
Strindberg, August, 9:338
String theory, **9:267–270**
Strings, of Post, 5:467
Stroboscopic motion, experiments on, 5:126
Stromateis (Patchwork) (Clement of Alexandria), 2:289, 4:564, 7:142
Strong, A. H., on unbelief in God's existence, 2:350
Strong, Charles Augustus, 6:235, 7:83
Strong analogies, *vs.* weak analogies, 3:544
Strong Archimedeanness, for extensive properties, 6:90
Strong force, 9:267
Strong law theories of natural law, 5:226–231
Strong objectivity
 Harding's thesis of, 3:592
 and reflexivity, 3:576
Strong Program, 8:677–678, 9:85
Strong verifiability, 9:660–661
Structural axioms, 6:89
Structural properties, as aesthetic properties, 1:39
Structural realism, 8:692
Structuralism, 8:275, **9:273–279**
 Barthes on, 1:481
 Eddington on, 3:164–165
 history in, 7:395
 "I and other" as universal ontological in, 1:465
 Lacan and, 5:168
 Lotman and, 5:578
 Lyotard on, 5:620
 mathematical, **9:270–272**
 modal, 9:271–272
 vs. Platonism, 6:674–675
 Shpet and, 9:17
 vs. traditional philosophical practice, 3:699
Structure(s)
 in first-order model theory, 6:302–304
 and function, linkage of, 3:763
 Krueger's theory of, 5:156
 personal, existence and individuality of, 5:156
Structure of Appearance, The (Goodman), 2:671
 and constructionalism, 4:158
 on theory of systems, 4:157
Structure of Behavior, The (Merleau-Ponty), 6:150
Structure of Science, The (Nagel), 3:192, 6:472–473
Structure of Scientific Revolutions, The (Kuhn), 2:475, 5:157–159, 5:217, 6:501, 7:394, 8:683, 8:694, 9:84
"Structure of the Continuum, The" (Brouwer), 1:702
Strukturwandel der Öffentlichkeit (Habermas), 4:199
Struttura dell'esistenza, La (Abbagnano), 1:1
Struve, Peter B., 3:63, 3:716
Stuart, Elizabeth, 2:752, 3:187
Studi filosofici, 1:476
"Studi sopra la filosofia di Hegel" (Spaventa), 9:159
Studia Cartesiana (periodical), 2:757
Studia Philonica Annual, The, 7:308
Studies and Exercises in Deductive Logic (Jevons), 4:807, 5:450, 5:565
Studies and Exercises in Formal Logic (Keynes), 3:496, 5:457
Studies in Hegelian Cosmology (McTaggart), 4:560

Studies in Humanism (Schiller), 7:83
Studies in Logical Theory (Dewey *et al.*), 3:44, 3:47
Studies in Phenomenology and Psychology (Gurwitsch), 4:198
"Studies in the Logic of Confirmation" (Hempel), 2:434
Studies on Hysteria (Freud), 3:737
Study in Organ Inferiority and Its Physical Compensation (Adler), 1:23
Study of History, A (Toynbee), 3:36, 7:391, 9:165, 9:517–519
Study of Natural Philosophy (Herschel), 7:562
Study-North Scholars, 5:140
Stuerman, Walter E., 5:562
Stufenbaulehre (doctrine of hierarchical structure), Kelsen's adoption of, 5:49
"Stuff"/"Thing" dichotomy, 6:663
Stump, Eleonore
- on Aquinas, 9:447
- on God and time, 3:359–360
- on Thomistic doctrine of soul, 3:115

Stumpf, Karl, **9:280–281**
- Gurwitsch and, 4:197
- Köhler and, 5:126

Stupecki, Jerzy
- on Aristotle, 5:608
- Leśniewski and, 5:290
- on logic, 5:606
- Łukasiewicz and, 5:608

Sturm, Johann Christophorus, on Spinoza, 7:99
Sturm und Drang (Goethe), 8:626
- Lavater and, 5:214
- Lichtenberg and, 5:338
- Sulzer and, 9:325

Sturzo, Luigi, **9:281–282**
Style
- in art, **1:330–333**
- Ackerman on, 1:331
- Boileau on, 1:640
- Danto on, 1:331
- development of, 1:331
- as different realities in Chwistek, 2:255
- elements of, 1:332
- as exclusive concern of art, 1:548
- Goodman on, 1:332
- in history *vs.* criticism, 1:332
- individual *vs.* general, 1:331
- logic and, 1:331
- predicates of, 1:331–332
- Riegl on, 1:331
- Robinson (Jenefer) on, 1:331–332
- as taxonomy, 1:331
- term, history of, 1:330
- Walton on, 1:332
- Wölfflin on, 1:331
- Wollheim on, 1:331, 1:332

Stylites, St. Simeon, 1:350
"Su la Scoemza nova del Vico" (Cattaneo), 2:83
Suárez, Francisco, 1:542–543, 9:137, **9:282–285**
- Aristotelianism of, 1:279
- colonialism and, 5:204
- congruism in theology of, 8:681
- Duns Scotus and, 3:144
- Erasmus and, 3:340
- on essence and existence, 3:350
- and international law, 7:422–423
- Malebranche and, 5:666
- on natural law, 3:404, 6:509
- on political sovereignty, 1:542–543
- Thomism and, 9:445
- on war and peace, 7:152

Subaltern genera, 5:537
Subaltern syllogisms, 5:407
Subalternant
- definition of, 5:557
- in traditional logic, 5:495

Subalternate, definition of, 5:557
Subalternation
- definition of, 5:557
- Valla on, 5:437

Subalterns, in traditional logic, 5:495
Subconscious. *See* Unconscious
Subcontrary(ies), 5:495, 5:557
Subformulas, 3:649
Subgroups, functional practices of, 3:763
Subject
- achieving consciousness of itself, 3:615
- in Aristotle's metaphysics, 9:288
- Baudrillard on, 1:491
- body as, 6:148
- in Buddhist epistemology, 1:757
- of categorical proposition, definition of, 5:557
- content internalism and, 8:82
- "death of," in structuralism, 9:274–275
- feminist thinkers on, 9:276
- grammatical, as existential entities, 1:561–562
- Heim on, 4:297
- identity and, 2:204
- Leibniz on, 5:272–274
- Maimon on, 5:645
- and object correlation, 6:491
- and predicate, 9:266, **9:285–290**
- as relationally constituted and historically embedded, 3:588
- in Varisco's metaphysics, 9:647

Subjection of Women, The (Mill, John Stuart), 6:232, 7:522, 9:75
Subjectivation, formations of, 3:700
Subjective aesthetics, of Mendelssohn, 6:131
Subjective anthropocentrism, in progress, 6:215–216
Subjective expected utility, 2:655
- alternatives to, 2:660
- comparative probability axiom in, 2:658
- frame invariance in, 2:656
- independence axiom in, 2:658–659
- objections to, 2:659–660
- ordering principle in, 2:657–658
- representation of rational preference in, 2:656
- Savage on, 8:613
- sure-thing principle in, 2:658–660
- value independence in, 2:656–657

Subjective experience, *vs.* objective, 5:130
Subjective idealism
- Kantian philosophy as, 4:770
- Schelling on, 8:618

Subjective mind, 4:267
Subjective perspective, Davidson (Donald) on, 2:646
Subjective probability, 2:435–437, 8:27–31
Subjective realism, Rosmini-Serbati on, 8:501–502
Subjective right, in Franciscan poverty, 7:12
Subjective theory, of justification, 5:105
Subjective truth, Unamuno on, 9:568
Subjectivism
- and chance, 2:129
- Descartes and, 4:611–612
- *vs.* emotivism, 3:204
- in empirical psychology, 6:112
- in ethics. *See* Ethical subjectivism
- and European philosophy, 9:533
- Finetti and, 8:36
- Garrigou-Lagrange on, 4:23
- Hägerström on, 4:206
- Kierkegaard and, 5:62
- Le Senne on, 5:289
- Lewis (C. I.) on, 5:308
- *vs.* logical probabilism, 8:30–31
- Maupertuis and, 6:67
- Meier on, 6:112
- on moral discourse, 3:364
- in moral life, 9:125
- new realism on, 6:585–586

Subjectivism, ***continued***
origins of, 3:405
Ploucquet on, 7:642
in probability analysis, 2:663–664, 8:27–31
reliabilism as test of, 9:290
Russell and, 8:556–559
in social constructionism, 9:77
Stace and, 9:200
Subjectivist epistemology, **9:290**
Subjectivist theory of probability, 8:36–37
Subjectivity, 1:554, **9:290–293**
of aesthetic judgments, 1:35
Bayesian, 1:499–501
and beauty as idea, 1:513–514
Bultmann on, 1:764
Calvin on, 2:9
Carnap on, 2:41
in deduction of categories, 5:34
as environment and observation, 1:633
of existence, 7:316–317
experience and, 5:130, 5:528
feminist accounts of, 3:587–588
Helmholtz on, 6:540
higher-order thought model of, 9:292
Humboldt on, 8:793
in indicative conditionals sentences, 2:425
in intuitionist mathematics, 1:700
Jaspers and, 4:800–801
Kant on, 5:34
Lacan on, 5:167
McDougall on, 6:71
of medical diagnosis, 7:467
as memory and perception convergence, 1:565
of mental images, 8:81
in mental-physical distinction, 6:139
Nagel (Thomas) on, 6:475
Natorp on, 6:543
Nishida on, 6:625–626
vs. objective, 5:130, 6:543, 6:625–626
vs. objectivity, in perspective, 6:475
vs. probability, 1:495
in quantum mechanics, 1:541–542
Sartre on, 9:491
of self-evidence, 1:29
of self-image, 7:319
of sensory qualities, 6:540
Sextus Empiricus on, 8:91
speaking subject in, 9:276
in structuralism, 9:274
truth as, 5:64
in Yogācāra Buddhism, 1:745–748
Subject–object
dualism, 3:564
existential psychoanalysis and, 3:511–512
Maréchal on, 5:708
mystery and, 5:701
Nietzche on, 3:564
reality of, 5:708
Subject–predicate proposition, definition of, 5:553
Subjects of resistance, political stance of, 3:606
Subjunctive conditionals, 3:710, 7:725
Sublating awareness *(badhaka-jnana)*, 5:118
Sublation
as criterion of truth, 5:118–120
in perception, 9:542–543
Sublime, The, **9:293–294**
Alison on, 1:128
vs. beauty, 1:513
Boileau on, 1:640
Burke on, 1:771, 3:254
concept of, 5:27
dynamical, 1:54
Kant on, 1:53–54, 3:254, 8:627
Lyotard on, 5:620–621
mathematical, 1:54
Mendelssohn on, 6:131
pain from, beauty and, 9:562
Schiller (Friedrich) on, 8:629
Subsentential expressions, meaning of, 6:84
Subservience, in Marx, 5:732–733
Subset
definition of, 5:557
proper, definition of, 5:552
Subsistential realism, of Montague (William), 6:331
Subsistents
vs. existents, 7:22
in new realism, 6:586
Substance
Anselm on, 1:216
Aquinas on, 2:551, 4:609, 9:432
Aristotle on, 1:4, 1:277, 2:73, 7:65, 9:288, 9:295–296, 9:592
and attribute, 9:288–289, **9:294–300**
Berkeley on, 6:191–192, 8:131
in Buddhism, 6:254
as category of being, 7:23–24
Cavendish on, 2:117–118
in chemistry, 2:141
in Christology, 2:247
as concrete individual thing, 9:300
Crusius on, 2:607
Descartes on, 2:54, 9:296–297
divisibility of, 6:78
in dualism, 6:327
facts about, realists on, 9:777
Geulincx on, 4:78
Gilbert of Poitiers on, 4:88
Giles of Rome on, 4:90
Haeckel on, 4:202
Hegel on, 6:193
Hobbes on, 4:411
Hume on, 4:499, 8:826
Ibn Gabirol on, 4:546
Kant on, 6:202, 7:28
Leibniz on, 5:256, 5:265–277, 6:191, 8:128–129, 9:297–298
life as, 9:695
limitless infinity as, 4:668
Locke on, 5:381–384, 6:191, 7:369
material
Leibniz on, 5:256, 5:265–277
Platonism on, 5:232
in medieval philosophy, 6:100–101
Millikan on, 6:237
mind as, 7:468–469
in monadology, 4:555, 6:325
in monism, 6:326–327
More (Henry) on, 6:396
Nicolas of Autrecourt on, 6:600
in Nyāya-Vaiśeika realism, 9:582
Ockham on, 7:8, 9:777–779
Ostwald on, 7:49
ousia as, 7:63
as owned property, 9:295
Patañjali on, 9:581–582
Pauler on, 7:145
permanence of, 5:19–20
Porphyry on, 6:187–188
primary, Ockham on, 9:778
in rationalism, 8:245–247
Régis on, 8:299–300
rejection of, 5:120
schema of, 5:18
soul as, 4:602–604, 4:609
Spinoza on, 4:770, 6:169, 6:190, 7:96, 8:125, 9:173, 9:185
Stillingfleet on, 9:249
as substratum of qualities, 9:299
in thinking, 9:418–419
in trinity, 1:283–284
as unity of qualities and relations, 9:280
Voltaire on, 9:709
Wittgenstein on, 9:805
Woodbridge on, 9:842
Wright (Chauncey) on, 9:847
Zabarella on, 9:867

Substance dualism, 3:113–116
mental causation and, 6:132
objections to, 3:117–118
See also Dualism in the philosophy of mind
Substance sortals, 9:762
Substantial aggression, definition of, 4:870
Substantial forms
Aquinas on, 3:115
Boyle on, 1:674
Locke on, 1:674
Substantial motion, principle of, 6:419
Substantival monism, 6:326–327
Substantivalism, space-time, Earman on, 3:160
Substantive law, 7:453–454
Substitution
axiom of (axiom of replacement), 5:555
rule of, 5:557
Substitution of Similars, The (Jevons), 4:807, 5:450
Substitutional quantification, 8:196
Substitutivity principle, in compositionality, 2:370
Substratum
as abstraction, 1:579
Bulgakov on, 1:760
in Indian philosophy, 5:413
Locke on, 7:23
as unthinkable, 1:587
Substructural logics, as non-classical, 5:489
Substructures, in model theory, 6:309–310
Subtraction, Lambert on, 5:445
Successions (Diogenes Laertius), 3:88
Successive operators, 3:540
Successor
definition of, 5:557
in Peano, 5:465
Successor function, definition of, 5:554
Successor relation, Frege on, 3:730–731
Suchon, Gabrielle, 9:838–839
"Sudden enlightenment followed by gradual practice," 4:833
Suessanus, Niphus. *See* Nifo, Agostino
Suffering
actual *vs.* portrayed, 9:522–523
Adams (M.) on, 3:478
of animals, 1:208–209
and art, 8:627
avoiding and ending, 3:579
Bayle on, 5:236
in Buddhism, 1:723–725, 1:748, 2:199
caused by ignorance of nonself, 1:740
in common consent arguments for God's existence, 2:348
elimination of, in Buddhism, 1:723–725
ethical significance of, and evil, as theological problem, 3:474–475
existence of God and, 1:362, 2:348, 9:408
Kempis on, 9:424
Le Clerc on, 5:236
medical ethics and, 6:97
moral value of, Dostoevsky on, 3:100
nirvāṇa and, 6:622
Nishida on, 6:624
Philodemus on, 7:303
power and, 7:732
punishment and, 8:163
Schopenhauer on, 8:655
sources of, 7:252
speciesism and, 9:164
Swinburne on, 3:478
Volney on, 9:707
Sufficiency
Carnap's total evidence and, 3:662
of maximum likelihood estimates, 3:662
new criterion of, 3:662
proof theory and, 5:472
Sufficient conditions
for causality with subjunctive conditionals, 2:99
definition of, 5:538
Sufficient estimators, 3:662
Sufficient reason
Clarke on, 2:271
Crusius on, 2:606–608
God and, 2:550
Heidegger on, 7:28
Leibniz on, 6:169, 6:191
Parmenides on, 6:183–184
Wolff on, 7:27
Sufficient statistic
distributions admitting, 3:663
recognizing at sight, 3:662
Sufism, **9:300–314**
annihilation of self in, 9:302
Baḥya and, 1:458
Bayazidian, 9:302
Brethrens of Purity and, 4:757
Central Asian school of, 9:306
doctrinal development in, 9:302
emanationism in, 3:190
Ibn al-ʿArabī and, 4:541
Ibn Khaldūn on, 4:549
illuminationist thought in, 4:760–761
in Islamic philosophy, 4:759, 9:309
and Kabbalah, comparison of, 5:4
Mevlevi order in, 9:307–309
on mystical love, 9:303
mysticism of, 6:452
Naqshbandi order in, 9:306
Qadiri order in, 9:306
school of Isfahan in, 9:308
whirling dervishes in, 9:307
Sugden, Robert, on decision theory, 2:660
Suhrawardī, Shihāb al-Dīn Yaḥyā, 2:537, **9:314–317**
Corbin, influence on, 2:537
on essence and existence, 3:352
illuminationism and, 4:581, 4:760
on knowledge, 3:320
metaphysics of, 6:419–420
in restructuring of *Organon,* 4:582–583
Sui dynasty, Buddhism under, 4:793
Suicide, **9:317–324**
Camus on, 2:20–21, 2:650
in debate on speciesism, 9:164
Dostoevsky on, 6:618
Durkheim on, 3:150–151
Hegesias on, 2:619
institutionalized, 9:320
meaningless, 2:20–21
physician-assisted, 3:456–458, 6:94, 9:321
Tolstoy on, 5:348
Suicide (Durkheim), 3:150
Suika Shintō, 9:860
Suireau, Marie des Agnes, 6:603
"Sul significato soggetiva della probabilità" (de Finetti), 2:662
Sull'analisi e sulla sintesi (On analysis and synthesis) (Galluppi), 4:13
Sullivan, Harry Stack, Adler and, 1:24
Sullivan, Shannon, 3:567–568
Sully, duke of, 7:154–155
Sulzer, Johann Georg, **9:324–326**
Lavater and, 5:213
on Pyrrhonism, 9:56
Tetens and, 9:403
Sum set, definition of, 5:557
Summa (Alexander of Hales), 7:161–162
Summa Contra Gentiles (Aquinas), 7:526, 9:426
analogy in, 1:140–141
on divine transcendence, 4:107
purpose of, 3:403
Sylvester of Ferrara on, 9:343–344

Summa de Anima (Summa on the soul) (John of La Rochelle), 4:840
Summa De Articulis Fidei (Summa on the articles of faith) (John of La Rochelle), 4:840
Summa de Ente (Wyclyf), 9:851–852
Summa de Vitiis (John of La Rochelle), 4:840
Summa Lamberti (Lambert of Auxerre), 5:430
Summa Logicae (Ockham), 1:773, 5:431–437, 5:435, 8:765, 8:769, 9:771, 9:776
Summa logicae et philosophiae naturalis (Dumbleton), 9:343
Summa Minorum (Alexander of Hales), 1:114–115
Summa Modorum Significandi (Siger of Courtrai), 8:771
Summa Naturalium (Paul of Venice), 7:147
"Summa of Alexander Hales" (John of La Rochelle), 4:840
Summa philosophiae (Eustachius of St. Paul), 2:749
Summa Sententiarum (Peter Lombard), 7:261
Summa Theologiae (Aquinas), 1:542, 3:529
  analogy in, 1:140–141, 2:677–679, 9:426, 9:511
  beauty in, 1:47
  on eternity, 3:358
  on incorruptible nature of soul, 4:609
  on intentionality, 4:706
  on monotheism, 4:110
  on natural law, 6:507–508
  on nature, 6:519
  on omnipotence, 4:115
  on omnipresence of God, 4:108
  purpose of, 3:403
  on sexuality, 7:522
  on war and peace, 7:152
Summa Theologica (Alexander of Hales), 1:653
Summa Theologica (Wyclyf), 9:852
Summa Theologicae Disciplinae (Summa of theological learning) (John of La Rochelle), 4:840
Summary Account of the Deist's Religion (Blount), 2:682
"A Summary View of the Rights of British America" (Jefferson), 4:805
Summerfield, Donna, 8:533
Summulae (Soto), 9:137
Summulae de dialectica (Buridan), on ampliation, 5:431–432
Summulae in Libros Physicorum (Ockham), 9:771
Summulae Logicales (Compendia of logics) (Peter of Spain), 1:767, 5:430
Summum genus, 5:537
Sumner, J. B., social Darwinism and, 3:479
Sumner, L. W., 8:721
Sumner, William Graham, **9:326–327**
  Darwinism and, 2:642
  on normative relativism, 6:159
  on sociology of knowledge, 9:102
Sum-set axiom, definition of, 5:557
Sun
  as analogy for nirvana in Buddhism, 1:724
  as magical, Bruno on, 1:710–711
  as nirvāṇa, analogy of, 1:724
  as source of power, 5:52
Sunlun School, 2:219
Sunspots, 4:12
Sunyata, 1:731
Supercomprehension, 6:322
Superego, 8:146, 9:572
Super-essentialism, in bundle theory, 6:180
Superficiality, of folk psychological explanations, 3:680
Superior man, Confucian ideal of, 2:149
Superiority theories of humor, 4:515
Superlative(s), 2:677–679
Superman, pessimism and, 7:251–252
Supernaturalism
  education in, 7:379
  materialism and, 6:14–15
  in miracles, 6:267–268
  vs. natural, 6:518
  naturalistic religion and, 8:376
  Oman on, 7:14
  Paulsen on, 7:148
  piecemeal, 4:781
  Renan on, 8:429
Superposition, 5:696–697, 8:204
Supersensible, in metaphysics, 6:201–202
Superstition
  bold attack on, 3:682
  as enemy of religion, 9:70
  in fiction, 1:336
  vs. reason, 8:47
  Spinoza on, 9:178
  Toland on, 9:505
Superstratum, in Indian philosophy, 5:413
Superstructure, of society, 5:732–733
Super-truth, notion of, 5:110
Superultimate "why," 9:758–761
  answerability of, 9:759
  as meaningless, 9:759–760
Supervaluationists
  borderline statements and, 5:110, 9:624
  rejection of inference rules, 5:109
  Van Fraassen and, 9:645
Supervenience, 7:191, 7:471, **9:327–333**
  and causation, 5:71
  dualism and, 3:114–115
  emergence and, 3:191
  entity reduction and, 6:172–173
  mental causation and, 6:134
  mental phenomena in, 6:263
  in mind-body problem, 5:72, 6:263–264
  natural laws and, 5:228–229
  nonreductive determinationism and, 6:172–173
  in token physicalism, 7:555
  of universals, 6:178
Supervenience and Mind (Kim), 5:71
Suppes, Patrick, **9:333–335**
  on causality, 2:100–103
  colleagues of, 2:645
  on semantic approach to theories, 9:416
"Supplément" (Desgabets), 2:758–759
Supplement, in Derrida, 2:716–717
Supplément au voyage de Bougainville (Supplement to Bougainville's voyage) (Diderot), 3:76, 3:247
Supplementativity, of part and whole, 6:146
Supplices (Euripides), 4:607, 9:322
Supposal, 4:597
Suppositio (property of term), 6:101, 9:786
Supposition, 8:767–768
  definition of, 5:557
  interregnum philosophers on, 5:440
  material, 5:557, 9:776
  in medieval philosophy, 5:430–432
  Ockham on, 9:776–777
  personal, 5:430–431, 5:557, 9:776
  simple, 9:776
  types of, 5:557
Suppressed quantification, 3:541
Suppression, of desire, 1:352
Supramoralism, of Fëdorov, 3:559
Supremacy of the Father Asserted (Chub), 2:252
Supreme being, common consent arguments for God's existence and, 2:348

Supreme Court, U.S., on euthanasia, 3:456–458
"Sur la Non-contradiction de l'arithmétique" (Herbrand), 5:473
"Sur une Courbe, qui remplit toute une aire plaine" (Peano), 5:465
Surdus. *See* John of Paris
Sure-thing principle, in subjective expected utility, 2:658–660
Surreal numbers
  Conway on, 2:502, 2:508
  ordered field simplicity hierarchy and, 2:508–509
Surrealism
  Benjamin on, 1:546
  Lacan and, 5:167
Surrender, concept of, 5:68
Surrogate motherhood, 5:338, 6:95
Surveillance, power of, 3:700
Surveiller et punir (Discipline and Punish) (Foucault), 3:700
Survival
  differential, 7:338
  persistence as, 7:207–210
  personal identity and, 7:230
Suso, Heinrich, 3:163, **9:335–336**
Suspension of belief, in phenomenology, 7:285–289
Suspicion of idealization, 3:581
Süszmilch, J. P., 8:787
Sutras, 4:132–133, 4:624
  Buddhist, 4:632–633
  definition of, 1:722
  Jain, 4:631
Suttie, Ian, Adler and, 1:24
Sutton, Oliver, 3:133
Sutton, Thomas, 9:444
Suvchinskii, P. P., Eurasianism and, 3:453
Suzuki, Taitaro, Nishida and, 6:623–624
Svātantrika, emptiness and method in, 1:732–734, 1:744–745
Svātantrika-Madhyamaka, 1:732
Svet vechernii (The fading light) (Ivanov), 4:767
Svetasvatara Upanishad, meditation in, 6:107
Svoe slovo (private journal of Kozlov), 5:146
Swammerdam, Jan, Leibniz and, 5:252
Swamping problem, 5:105
Swanton, Christine, 9:679–681
Swanwick, H. M., 7:155
Swedenborg, Emanuel, **9:336–339**
  Blake and, 1:610
  Emerson and, 3:195
  fantasies of, metaphysics compared to, 5:11
  James (Henry) and, 4:773
Swift, Jonathan, **9:339–341**
  anarchism and, 1:177
  on scientific method, 4:688
  utopianism of, 9:619
  and Voltaire, 2:687
Swinburne, Richard
  on belief, 3:322
  on Christian apologetics, 3:324
  design argument and, 3:321
  on dualism, 3:114–115, 3:119–121, 4:618
  on evil, 3:477–478
  experientialism and, 3:322
  faith and, 3:535
  on God's existence, 2:551–552, 3:321, 9:381–382, 9:407
  on miracles, 6:274
  on mysticism, 6:462
  on personal identity, 7:229–230
  on religious analogy, 1:142
  on religious experience, 8:402
  and swamping problem, 5:105
Swineshead, Richard, 5:433, **9:342–343**
Switching circuits, computers and, 5:566
Swoyer, Chris, on natural law, 5:227
Sydenham, Thomas, Locke and, 5:374
Syllabus of a Proposed System of Logic (De Morgan), 2:709, 5:448
Syllogism
  Abelard on, 5:427
  and action explanations, 1:533
  Aristotle and, 1:269, 3:53, 5:70, 5:400–401, 8:595
  Averroes on, 1:426
  Avicenna on, 1:434–435
  Barbara on, 5:499–501, 5:505
  Baroco on, 5:497–499
  Bocardo on, 5:497
  Boethius on, 5:427
  Camestres on, 5:497–499
  Carroll on, 5:452
  as categorical, 5:493
  categorical, definition of, 5:557
  Celarent on, 5:497–499
  Cesare on, 5:497
  compound, types of, 5:500
  conclusive, by force of axiom, 5:408
  and conditionals of accidents *vs.* nature, 1:628
  Darapti on, 5:497
  Datisi on, 5:497
  De Morgan on, 2:710, 5:449
  definition of, 5:557
  Descartes on, 2:724
  disjunctive categorical, reduction of, 5:503
  Eudemus on, 5:402
  Euler on, 5:444, 5:560
  Felapton on, 5:497
  Ferison on, 5:497
  Festino on, 5:497
  figures of, 5:496–497
    division of, 5:496
    first, 5:497–498, 5:504
    fourth, 5:498
    second, derivability from first figure, 5:504–505
    third, 5:498
  Galen on, 5:408
  Hamilton on, 5:448
  Hinton on, 5:562
  horned, 5:503
  hypothetical, 1:627–628, 5:402–403, 5:502
  middle term in, definition of, 5:548
  minor premise in, definition of, 5:548
  minor term in, definition of, 5:548
  and Mohist discourse, 2:212–213
  moods of, 5:496–497
  names of, 5:496
  Nicolas of Autrecourt on, 6:600
  and nontrivial knowledge, 1:450
  Peirce on, 5:504
  prosleptic, 5:402
  pure, definition of, 5:557
  reduction of, 5:555
  relational, 5:408
  rhetorical treatment of, 5:438
  Sanches on, 8:595
  Schiller (Ferdinand) on, 8:625
  in Stoic logic, 5:406–407
  subaltern, 5:407
  Theophrastus on, 5:402, 9:411
  in traditional logic, 5:493, 5:496–503
  types of, 5:557
  valid, rules for, 3:539
  validity of, 5:499
  Venn and, 5:451, 5:561
  Whately on, 9:742–743
Syllogistic logic, 1:660
  Brentano on, 1:691–692
  Kant's, Peirce on, 5:453
  Lambert on, 5:445
  laws of identity in, 5:443
  Leibniz on, 5:441
  limitations of, 1:676
  Ploucquet and, 5:445
Sylvan, Richard, dialetheism of, 7:106

Sylvester of Ferrara, Francis, **9:343–344**
Sylvie and Bruno (Carroll), 2:51
Symbolic algebra, Peacock on, 5:460
Symbolic art, 4:274
Symbolic artificial intelligence, 1:346–347
Symbolic language, of Peano, 5:465
Symbolic logic
  Boole and, 1:660
  Carroll and, 2:53, 5:452–453
  development of, 6:642
  Frege on, 5:464
  Peano and, 7:159
  Post and, 5:467
  Venn and, 5:451, 9:657
Symbolic Logic (Carroll), 2:53
  Part I, 5:452
  Part II, 5:453
Symbolic Logic (Venn), 5:451, 9:657
Symbolic reference, 9:750
Symbolism
  Florenskii and, 3:670
  Frege on, 5:464
  in religion, Collingwood on, 2:326
  Stern's radiative values in, 9:245
Symbolization, 4:594
Symbols
  in algebraic logic, 1:660
  vs. allegory, 1:55
  in art, 1:55
  Baker on, 1:463–464
  Cassirer on, 1:65, 2:66–67
  in Chinese room argument, 2:240–241
  classes of, 3:670
  computationalism and, 2:395
  as constitutive elements, 3:670
  in culture, 1:58
  in first-order languages, 3:647
  general ideas as, 1:581–582
  improper, definition of, 5:558
  Jaspers on. *See* Ciphers
  Kristeva on, 5:152
  logical, 5:454
  Losev on, 5:574
  Peirce on, 5:454
  and phenomena, 3:675
  in poetry, 1:55
  proper, definition of, 5:558
  propositional, 3:643, 3:647
  in quantum mechanics, 1:638
  religious, 8:414–415, 8:587, 9:460
  as representation of knowledge, 1:559
  Sabatier on, 8:587
  Santayana on, 2:597
  and significance, polarity in, 2:67–68
  Spengler on, 9:166
  of truth, religion as, 4:550–551
  20th-c. empiricists on, 3:219–220
  Unamuno's use of, 9:566
Symmetric relation(s)
  in computability theory, 2:386
  definition of, 5:555
Symmetry
  beauty and, 1:45–46
  causal directionality and, 2:98–99
  Cavell on, 2:116
  conservation principle and, 2:462–463
  in physical laws, time and, 2:104–105
  probability and, 8:26
  spatial, in universe, 9:468
  temporal, 7:475
Symmetry (Weyl), 9:742
Symons, Donald, 3:481
Sympathetic magic, Wang Chong on, 9:723
Sympathy
  cosmic, in Plotinus's organic universe, 7:638–639
  Eliot (George) on, 3:185
  and empathy, **9:344–345**
  Grotius on, 6:510
  Hume on, 1:136–137, 4:506, 8:132
  Leibniz on, 5:257
  in Pythagoreanism, 8:182
  Smith (Adam) on, 9:67
Sympathy [term], used by Hume and Smith, 3:750
Symphonic persons, 5:43
Symposium (Banquet) (Xenophon), 9:855
  definition in, 7:595
  theory of forms in, 7:595
Symposium (Plato), 1:512
  aesthetics in, 1:41, 1:188
  beauty in, 1:42, 1:512
  Ficino's commentary on, 3:620–623, 3:671, 7:614
  on human sexuality, 7:521
  on love, 3:623, 5:584–585, 5:589
  on pleasure, 3:396–397
  on poetry, 7:585
  on self-control, 3:396–397
Symposium Aristotelicum, 7:65
Symptoms
  in logic of diagnosis, 7:466
  sense or meaning of, 3:744
Syncategoremata, 8:769–770, 9:776
Syncategoremata (Peter of Spain), 5:440
Syncategoremata (William of Sherwood), 9:786
Syncategorematic, definition of, 5:558
Syncategorematic terms, 5:430–432
  as logical expressions, 2:73
  in traditional logic, 5:495
Synchronicity
  and binding problem, 6:567
  precognition and, 7:757
Syncretism
  in Confucianism, 2:153
  in Daoism, 2:153
  in Gnosticism, 4:97–98
  Ikhwān al-Ṣafā' and, 4:576
  in Islamic philosophy, 1:423
  in Mādhyamika doctrine, 1:744–745
  in Middle Platonism, 7:607
  in Neoplatonism, 4:174
  Pico della Mirandola and, 7:570–571
Syndicalism, 9:132
Synechiology, 4:323
Synechism, Peirce on, 7:170–171
Synergism controversy, 6:119
Synergistic environmental ethics, 3:260–261
Synesius
  Hyaptia and, 6:553
  on phantasia, 7:271
Synonymity, **9:345–352**
  a priori statements and, 1:167
  analytic statements and, 1:161–162
  and analytic/synthetic distinction, 4:160, 9:345–346
  Aristotle on, 1:269–270
  cognitive, 1:162
  definition by, 2:675
  Goodman on, 4:158
  meaning and, 1:162–163
  Prodicus on, 8:45
  Quine on, 1:162, 8:216–219
  in sentences, 7:403
Synonymous expressions, in compositionality, 2:370
Synopsis Philosophiae Naturalis (Johnson, Samuel), 4:851
Synsoplevede Figurer (Rubin), 4:72
Syntactic processes, computational, 3:676
Syntactic rules, in compositionality, 2:370
Syntactic sequent, 3:657
Syntactical and semantical categories, 9:352–359, **9:352–359**
Syntactical variable, definition of, 5:558
Syntactics
  autonomous, 8:807
  consequence in, 9:368–369
  criticism of, 9:415
  selectional restrictions and, 8:807

vs. semantics, 9:368–369
on theories, 9:413–416
See also Semantics
Syntagma Philosophiae Epicuri, cum Refutationibus Dogmatum, Quae Contra Fidem Christianum ab eo Asserta Sunt (Gassendi), 4:25–26
Syntax, **9:359–361**
in ancient logic, 5:397–398
Aristotle on, 5:399
arithmetization of, 2:42, 5:535, 8:840
Carnap on, 2:42–43
Chomsky on, 1:344
Church on, 1:344
compositionality and, 2:370–371
in computationalism, 2:391
of English, 7:400
in formal language, 1:343
in formal semantics, 5:556
Herbrand proof theory and, 5:472
metalanguage formalization and, 2:42–43
Post on, 5:467
of scientific laws, 7:517–518
in Stoic logic, 5:405
synsemantic terms and, 1:691
in Tarski, 9:368
See also Semantics
Synthesis, 5:16–18
of *a priori* truth, 1:244
vs. analysis, Quine on, 1:150
of apprehension, Kant on, 3:307–308
in consciousness, Ziehen (Theodor) on, 9:884
definition of, 5:558
in evolutionary theory, 7:339
Huxley on, 7:339
Kant on, 3:307–308
Martinetti on, 5:728
Mercier's use of, 6:144
of objective and relative, 6:75–76
Plato and, 3:53
of recognition, 3:308
of reproduction, 3:307–308
in scientific metaphysics, 5:728
Synthetic *a posteriori* knowledge, Kant on, 3:306
Synthetic *a priori* judgments, 5:13–14
Synthetic *a priori* knowledge
Kant on, 3:306–307
in Spir's principle of identity, 9:196
Synthetic *a priori* principles, demonstrations of, 5:19
Synthetic differential geometry, use of infinitesimals, 2:509–510
Synthetic judgments, Kant on, 5:13–14
Synthetic knowledge, Kant on, 3:306
Synthetic naturalism, 3:366–367
Synthetic propositions, Kant on, 5:79
Synthetic statements, **1:159–165**
Synthetic theory, 2:336–337, 2:643
Syntheticity, in Frege, 3:729
Syrianus, in Neoplatonism, 6:551
System der erworbenen Rechte, Das (Lassalle), 5:203
System der Ethik (Paulsen), 7:148
System der Logik (Ueberweg), 5:231
System der Logik und Metaphysik oder Wissenschaftslehre (Fischer), 3:660
System der Metaphysik (Fries), 3:752
System der philosophichen Rechtslehre und Politik (Leonard), 6:537
System der Werttheorie (Ehrenfels), 3:176
System der Wissenschaft (Ostwald), 2:36
System des heutigen römischen Rechts (Savigny), 8:614
System des transzendentalen Idealismus (Schelling), 1:11, 4:557, 8:620
System of Ethics, The (Fichte), 3:617
System of Logic (Mill, John Stuart), 2:672, 5:456–457, 6:222–225
Bain and, 1:461
on heteropathic laws, 3:191
influences of, 8:795
on laws of thought, 5:233
naive theory in, 8:58
on principle monism, 3:440
"System of Modal Logic, A" (Łukasiewicz), 5:608
System of Nature (Holbach), 3:246
System of Philosophy (Régis), 5:665–667
System of the Vedanta, The (Zeller), 3:41
System of the World, The (Exposition du système du monde) (Laplace), 5:197
System of Transcendental Idealism (Schelling), 1:54
Systema Theologicum ex Prae-Adamitarum Hypothesi (La Peyrère), 5:196
Systematic ambiguity, 3:534, 5:558
definition of, 5:558
and perception, 3:542
Russell and, 5:558
Whitehead and, 5:558
and words, 3:542
Systematic ethics, Watsuji on, 9:727
Systematic regularity theories of natural law, 5:226
Systematic theology, Pannenberg and, 7:80
Systematic Theology (Hodge), 2:345
Systematic Theology (Pannenberg), 7:82
Systematic Theology (Tillich), 1:364, 9:459
"Systematically Misleading Expressions" (Ryle), 8:580–581
Systematicity
compositionality and, 2:371
connectionist models in computationalism and, 2:393
in language, 7:404
mental content and, 2:478
Systematischen Begriffe in Kants vorkritischen Schriften, Die (Cohen), 2:302
Systematization, in mathematics foundations, 6:20
Systeme de la nature (Holbach), 6:10
Système de philosophia (Régis), Cartesianism of, 2:56
Système de politique positive (Comte), 2:410
Système d'Epicure (La Mettrie), 5:178, 5:180
Système des animaux sans vertèbres (Lamarck), 5:173
Système du monde, Le (Duhem), 3:126
Système International d'Unites (SI), 6:91
Système nouveau de la nature et des la communication de substances (New system of nature) (Leibniz), 5:253–255, 5:270, 5:275
Systèmes socialistes, Les (Pareto), 7:117
Systemic representational states, 3:109
Systems
of belief, and coherence, 2:278–279, 2:313
Bergson on, 1:568
in biology, 1:594
Bosanquet on, 1:662
Carnap on, 2:41
in chaos theory, 2:131–134
in Chinese room argument, 2:240
in Copernican theory, 2:535
of Creighton, 2:592
existentialism on, 3:501–502
formal
in combinatory logic, 2:334–344
Gödel's Theorem, 4:119–131
Habermas's paradigm of, 4:200
joint descriptions of, 6:279
of life, Eucken on, 3:451–452
morals as, 1:602
of philosophy, of Hobbes, 4:423
and randomness *vs.* appearance in equilibrium, 1:633
of reality, Hegel's dialectic as, 2:81
science as, 2:36–41

Systems, *continued*
of scientific laws, in *Critique of Judgment,* 5:26
truth and, 1:661
unified total, science as, 2:38–41
Universe as, 1:634
value state of, 6:278
"Systems of Logic Based on Ordinals" (Turing), 5:478
Szilard, Leo, 3:178

T

Tabaqat (al-Sulami), 9:304
Tabataba'i, Hussein, 8:646–647
Tableau du climat et du sol des états-Unis d'Amérique (Volney), 9:707
"Tableau général de la science, qui a pour objet l'application du calcul aux sciences morales et politiques" (General View of the Sciences Comprising the Mathematical Treatment of the Moral and Political Sciences) (Condorcet), 2:432
Tableau philosophique des progrès successifs de l'esprit humaine (Philosophic panorama of the progress of the human mind) (Turgot), 9:551
Ta-ch'ü, 5:415–416
Tacit knowledge, Evans on, 3:461
Tacitus
Lipsius and, 5:364
Vico and, 9:672
Tacitus (Lipsius), 5:364
Tactile space, 4:848–849
Tadbīr al-motawaḥḥid (The rule of the solitary) (Ibn Bājja), 4:544
Tagore, Rabindranath, **9:363–364**
Tahāfut al-Tahāfut (Avicenna), 1:426
Tahiti, Diderot on, 3:76
Tai qi (Supreme Ultimate)
Guo Xiang on, 4:196
Zhu Xi on, 4:794
Taigiroku (The great doubt), 5:7
Taiheisaku (A policy for great peace) (Ogyú), 7:10
Taiji tu (Diagram of the Great Ultimate), comments on, 9:880
Taiji tushuo (An Explanation of the Diagram of the Great Ultimate) (Zhou Dunyi), 9:880
Tail areas, in significance testing, 3:666
Taine, Hippolyte-Adolphe, **9:364–366**
Laromiguière and, 5:201–202
on sociology of knowledge, 9:102
Tait, Peter Guthrie
and classical mechanics, 2:280
physicotheology and, 7:561–562
Tait, William, in proof theory, 8:55–56
Taixu (Great void), Zhang Zai on, 9:879
Taixuan jing (Canon of Supreme Mystery) (Yang Xiong), 9:860–861
Takeuti, Gaisi, in proof theory, 8:56
Taking Rights Seriously (Dworkin), 3:156
Talbott, William, 4:251–252, 8:715
Tale of a Tub (Swift), 9:339
Taliaferro, Charles, on soul, 3:116
Taliban, 9:397–398
Talmud
in Hellenistic Jewish philosophy, 4:810–811
Saadya's legal commentaries on, 8:585
Talon, Omer, 8:236
Tan, Kok-Chor, on cosmopolitan egalitarianism, 6:488
Tanabe, Hajime, Nishida and, 6:624
Tang dynasty
Confucianism in, 5:316
logic in, 5:416
Tang Junyi
Buddhism's influence on, 2:169–170
and neo-Confucianism, 2:182–183
Tangled Tale, A (Carroll), 2:51
Tanke och förkunnelse (Thought and prophecy) (von Wright), 9:847
Tanluan, on Pure Land Buddhism, 2:168
Tanqīh al-abhāth bi'l-mabhath 'an al-milal al-thalāth (Ibn Kammūna), 4:817
Tantra, meditation practice of, 6:109
Tantravártikka, 6:532
Tao. *See* Dao
Taoism. *See* Daoism; Laozi
Tao-te-ching. See Laozi
Tarabhāṣā (Mokṣākara Gupta), 4:634
Taran, Leonardo, on Parmenides of Elea, 7:126
Tarasoff v. The Regents of the State of California, 6:95
Tarski, Alfred, **9:366–372**
on calculus, 5:607, 9:367
and Carnap, 2:43
convention T, 5:109
on definability, 9:368–369
definition of truth, 8:841
on formal models, 9:334
immigration of, 9:371
on language, logical structure of, 2:647
Leśniewski and, 5:290
on logic, 5:234, 5:479–480, 5:531, 5:538
logical positivism and, 5:525
Łukasiewicz and, 5:607–608
many-valued logic and, 5:491, 5:694
on mathematics, 9:366, 9:370, 9:371–372
on metamathematics, 9:366–367
on model theory, 3:766, 9:367–368
Montague and, 1:345
on natural languages, 5:510
philosophy of, 9:370
Platonism and, 8:645
on propositional logic, 9:367
on real-closed order fields, 2:506
on semantic paradoxes, 5:521–522
on semantic theory of truth, 9:537–538
on semantics, 5:517, 9:367–369
set-theoretical topological interpretation of, 4:740
on syntactical categories, 9:354
on true sentence of English, 8:737
on truth, 2:541, 2:547–549, 5:510, 8:196, 9:537–538
on T-schemata, 8:808
and Vienna Circle, 2:41
Tarski's theorem, and computability theory, 2:383, 2:386–387
"Tarski's Theory of Truth" (Field), 3:633
Tart, Charles, parapsychology and, 7:116
Tartaglia, Joannes, 2:755
Tartu-Moscow School of Semiotics, 5:578, 5:579
Task of Utopia, The (McKenna), 3:568
Tasso, Torquato
Galileo on, 4:9
Patrizi and, 7:144
Taste, 1:50–51
absolute standard of, 9:790
and aesthetics, 1:513, 4:165
Alison on, 1:52, 1:128, 4:65
Batteux on, 1:489–490
emotion and, 1:128
Gerard on, 4:64–66
Hume on, 1:35
judgment as, 8:51
judgments of, 5:26–27
Kant on, 1:36, 1:52–53
perception and, 7:181
and presupposition of knowledge, 1:490
and relativism, 1:39, 1:40
sense of, 5:117

vs. senses, 1:38
sensory, 8:8, 9:515
Sibley on, 1:38, 9:21
as transition between thinking and feeling, 9:325
Tatale Mobilmachung (Jünger), 4:859
Tathāgata, definition, 1:722
Tatian
as apologist, 1:227–228
and Byzantine view of philosophy, 1:786
philosophy and, 7:142
Tatsachen in der Wahrnehmung, Die (The facts of perception) (Helmholtz), 4:303–304
Tattler (periodical), Enlightenment and, 3:244
Tattvacintāmani (Gangeśa), 4:628
Tattvakaumudī (Vāscaspati Miśra), 4:626
Tattvārtha Sūtra, meditation in, 6:109
Tattvarthadhigama Sutra (Discourse on the Nature of Things) (Umasvati), 2:111
Tauler, Johannes, **9:372–373**
Eckhart (Meister) and, 3:163
pantheism of, 7:96
and Suso, 9:335
Tautology
in Buddhist epistemology, 1:757
in compositionality, 2:370
confirmation theory and, 2:434
definition of, 5:558
examples of, 3:644
necessity in, Wittgenstein on, 9:807
propositional logic and, 3:644
quantifier-free, 5:472
Ramsey on, 5:468
in Sanlun Buddhism, 2:161
in set theory, Tarski on, 9:367
as super-true, 5:110
Wittgenstein on, 1:148, 9:807
Tawney, R. H., on equality of consideration, 3:332
Taxation, libertarianism on, 5:336
Taxation No Tyranny (Johnson, Dr. Samuel), 4:852
Taxonomy
in Darwin, 7:343
as defeasible reasoning, 6:642
genre as, 1:330
style as, 1:331
Taylor, Alfred Edward, **9:373–374**
on cosmology, 2:556
on historic Socrates, 9:107
Taylor, Charles, on Hegel, 4:280
Taylor, E. B., 2:349
Taylor, Harriet, 3:599, 6:220
Taylor, Mark C., 5:67
Taylor, Paul, 3:259, 9:637
Taylor, Richard, 5:248, 8:731
TDCT. *See* Traditional divine command theory
Teacher, as bringing truth, 5:65
Teaching
Augustine on, 7:368
as bringing truth, 5:65
Comenius on, 7:369
ethics of, 7:363
by Ockham, 9:770
in Pestalozzi, 7:372
by Wittgenstein, 9:801–803
by Wolff, 9:823
in Zen, 1:729
Tea-tasting lady, 3:664–665
Teatrum Vitae Humanae (Zwinger), 5:442
Technē, 1:41–42
Technicism, 7:547
Technicity, development into technology, 7:546–547
Technics, philosophy of, 3:670
Technique, La (The Technological Society) (Ellul), 7:547–548
Technique of Theory Construction, The (Woodger), 9:844
Technique of variation, Bozano on, 5:446
Technological Society, The (La Technique) (Ellul), 7:547–548
Technology
and artificial intelligence, **1:345–350**
in cognitive science, 2:298–299
computer ethics and, 2:396
constructivism in, 9:76–78
dehumanization by, 1:707–708
development of technicity into, 7:546–547
engineering ethics and, 3:242
in film, 7:383
Heidegger on, 4:295–296
Jünger on, 4:859–860
and machine intelligence, **5:631–636**
Marx on, 5:732–734
need creation from, 5:732
one-sided, defects of, 3:559
philosophy of, **7:543–551**
empirical turn in, 7:549
epistemological issues, 7:548–549
ethical and political issues in, 7:544–546
ethics and, 7:548
government policy and, 7:550
historical emergence, 7:543–544
metaphysical issues, 7:546–548
quantum computing and, 2:407
social justice and, 7:544
style and, 1:331
war inseparable from, 4:859–860
Teichmuller, Gustav, influence on Kozlov, 5:146
Teilhard de Chardin, Pierre, **9:374–376**
Diderot and, 3:76–77
Duns Scotus and, 3:144
Maritain and, 5:717
panpsychism and, 7:83
Teixeira Mendes, Raimundo, positivism and, 5:207
"Tektonische Studien an Hydroidpolypen" (Tectonic studies of hydroid polyps) (Driesch), 3:109
Teleological argument for existence of God, 7:701–702, **9:376–382,** 9:407
adaptation in, 9:379–380
artifacts in, 9:377, 9:378
cosmology and, 2:588
criticisms of, 9:377
design in, 9:376–377
evil in, 9:380
evolution and, 9:377–378
in Indian philosophy, 4:133
naturalism and, 9:381
overview of, 7:701–702
in philosophy of religion, 7:481
Swinburne on, 9:381–382
teleological order and, 9:376
Tennant on, 9:379, 9:392–393
universe in, 9:378–379
Teleological ethical theories, 2:713
Teleological ethics, 4:153, **9:382–384,** 9:687
Teleologico-evolutionary optimism, 7:251
Teleology, **9:384–390**
anthropocosmic, 4:543
Aquinas and, 9:431
of art and nature, 8:620
Bakhtin and, 1:465
Bergson and, 1:570
in biology, 1:594, 7:342–343, 9:389
in Blanshard's ethics, 1:614
Bonnet and, 1:658
in Buddhist epistemology, 1:753–754, 1:755
Burckhardt on, 1:766
Butler (Samuel) and, 1:784–785
Carneades and, 2:48
in Cartesian science, 2:55

Teleology, ***continued***
- and categorical imperative, 2:69–70
- Chrysippus on, 2:252
- in classical mechanics, 2:283
- Collingwood and, 2:329
- common consent arguments for God's existence and, 2:347
- of computationalism, 2:393
- *vs.* consequentialism, 9:382
- and creativity, 1:559–560
- in *Critique of Judgment,* 5:27–28
- Darwinism and, 2:641, 7:342–343
- definition of, 9:384
- *vs.* deontology, 9:383
- Diogenes of Apollonia and, 3:89–90
- of eroticism, 1:489
- in evolution, 2:112, 7:342–343
- functional roles and, 3:761
- functions in, 9:386–389
- Galen on, 4:5
- in genetics, 7:342–343
- God and, 1:652
- in Kant, 2:366–367, 5:27–28
- language of, 9:387
- Masaryk on, 6:2
- of mental representation and computationalism, 2:393
- in mental states, 2:479
- of natural law, 7:454
- in natural selection, 7:342–343
- order in, 9:376
- in perfectionism, 4:152
- in post-historical negativity, 1:488–489
- purposive activity in, 9:384–389
- of Pyrrhonism, 1:195–196
- questions in, 9:384
- Rozanov on, 8:525
- Sabatier and, 8:588
- in Sankhya, 2:112
- in science, 9:387
- of Shakyamuni Buddha, 1:723
- Stern and, 9:244
- as subject-object reunion, 1:615
- Swedenborg and, 9:337
- Theophrastus on, 9:412
- Woodbridge on, 9:842

Teleomechanics, 9:244

Teleosemantics, 4:711, 7:345

Telepathy, 7:52, 7:113–114, 7:752
- *See also* Parapsychology

Teles, Cynic teaching of, 2:617

Telesio, Bernardino, **9:390–391**
- Campanella and, 2:15
- Galileo on, 4:9
- panpsychism and, 7:83, 7:87
- Patrizi and, 7:144

Teller, Paul, on emergence, 3:193

Telliamed (Maillet), 5:644

Telluris Theoria Sacra (The sacred theory of the earth) (Burnet), 9:336

Telos, 1:43, 9:74

Tempels, Placide, 1:83–85

Temperature
- classical measurement of, 6:86–87
- definition of, 6:86–87
- operational definition of, 7:30
- as quality, 8:10

Tempered equality, of intellectual authority, 3:595

Tempier, Étienne, 9:444

Tempier, Stephen
- on Averroism, 1:650
- propositions condemned by, 8:457

Template-directed synthesis, 5:361

Temple du goût (Voltaire), 9:708

Temple of Nature, The (Darwin), 2:631

Temporal asymmetry, 7:475, 9:467–470, 9:498

Temporal creation
- Aquinas on, 1:360
- Saadya on, 4:812

Temporal modal interpretation, 6:297–298

Temporal or tense logic. *See* Modal logic

Temporal parts, metaphysics of, persistence and, 7:208–210

Temporal sequences, Helmholtz on, 4:304

Temporal-historical occurrence, 4:289

"Temporalistic Realism, A" (Lovejoy), 5:592

Temporality, 4:523

Temporariness, in Taintai Buddhism, 2:164

Temporary identity, 4:570–571

Temps et l'autre, Le (Time and the Other) (Levinas), 5:304

Temps modernes, Les (journal), 6:148

Temptation
- in Milton's poetry, 6:251
- responsibility and, 8:163–164

Ten corporeal intellects, 4:817

Ten Hours Bill (English labor statute), communism and, 2:361–362

"Ten Modes of Aenesidemus" (Aenesidemus), 1:31

Tendency
- in Malthus, 5:677
- progress as, 8:47

Tennant, Frederick Robert, **9:392–394**
- in natural theology, 7:494
- physicotheology and, 7:562
- on teleological argument for existence of God, 9:379, 9:380
- and voluntarist apologetic for theistic faith, 3:532–533

Tennant's theory, Thomist analysis of faith in, 3:532

Tennemann, W. G., 2:580

Tense, **10:43–47**
- causal construction of, 2:85–86
- general relativity and, 9:499
- McTaggart on, 9:497–498
- medieval logic correspondence truth conditions and, 2:541
- physics and, 9:497–499
- special relativity and, 9:499
- theory of time, 9:463, 9:475, 9:478–481
- time-reversal invariance of laws in physics, 2:104–105
- truth condition and, 6:650

Tense logic, 5:486, 8:13

Tense operators, in intensional logic, 5:487

Tension
- Helmholtz on, 3:231
- in Unanumo's philosophy, 9:568
- universal, Posidonius on, 3:686

Tensors, locality and, 6:638

Tentation de l'occident, La (Malraux), 5:673

Tenure policies, applying equally, 3:583

Teoría del hombre (Theory of man) (Romero), 5:209

Teoria della probabilità (de Finetti), 2:663

Teoria generale della spirito come atto puro (Gentile), 4:50

Teorica del sovrannaturale (Gioberti), 4:93

Teresa of Ávila, St.,**9:394–395**
- Báñez on, 1:476
- John of the Cross and, 4:845
- Stein and, 9:239

Term(s)/terminology
- absolute, Ockham on, 9:777
- abstract
  - definition of, 5:533
  - elimination of, 8:553–554
  - Ockham on, 9:777
- atomic, 3:647
- Austin (John Langshaw) and, 1:407
- in Boethius, development of, 1:626
- Bolzano on, 5:446
- in categorical syllogism, 5:493
- in classical logic, eliminating, 8:196

coined by Kepler, 5:50
complexity of, 5:494
comprehension and extension of, 8:777
Condillac on, 5:656
connotative, Ockham on, 9:777
De Morgan on, 5:449
definition of, 5:558
as descriptive uncombined expressions, 2:73
as empty or non-empty, 1:647
evidence by, 9:778
general, definition of, 5:544
God as, 7:483
Lalande on, 5:172
Leśniewski on, 5:292
in logic, 5:494, 8:764–768, 9:776
logical behavior of, 5:494
major, definition of, 5:548
mention of, definition of, 5:548
observable *vs.* theoretical, 9:415–416
Peirce on, 5:453
as rhemes in Peirce, 5:453
in science, use of, 9:843–844
signification as property of, 8:767
singular, definition of, 5:556
supposition as property of, 8:767–768
in syllogism, 5:498
syncategoremata, 8:769–770
theoretical, **9:413–417**
canonical formulation of, 9:414
illustration of, by thought experiment, 9:452–455
intertheoretic reduction of, 6:569
vs. observable, 9:415–416
Ramsey-sentence approach to, 9:417
reference of, 9:417
in scientific theory, 7:519
semantic approach to, 9:416–417
syntactic view of, 9:413–416
in thought experiments, 9:452–455
types of, 3:647
ultimate referents of, 8:759
unique parsing of, 3:647–648
use of, definition of, 5:548
Terminating judgments, Lewis (C. I.) on, 5:308–309
Terminist physics, Crescas and, 4:822–823
Termist logic, 5:430–432
Territory, national identity and, 6:482
Terrorism, **9:395–399**
anarchism and, 1:176
as challenge to state sovereignty, 9:146
defining, 9:395–396
in just war theory, 9:396–397
State Department definition of, 9:395
suicide tactics in, 9:317, 9:320
and war, nature of, 7:158
Tertiary qualities, 7:86
Tertium non datur, 3:5
See also Excluded middle, law of
Tertullian, Quintus Septimius Florens, **9:399–400**
apologism of, 1:228
Christian ethics and, 3:401
credo quia absurdum of, 3:631
Kierkegaard and, 5:62
Marcion and, 5:704
on shadow-man doctrine of immortality, 4:603
traditional theology and, 7:142–143
on Valentinus, 9:631–632
Tesserae, 9:691
Test(s)
in Blanshard's epistemology, 1:613
for category difference in Ryle, 2:77
of conversational implicature, 2:527–528
in education, 7:362
for empirical causality, 2:107
medical, 7:466–467
for morality of point of view, 1:460
"Test of Simplicity, The" (Goodman), 4:157
Test of Time, The (Savile), 1:67
Testability
vs. confirmability, 9:662
meaning and, 5:528
"Testability and Meaning" (Carnap), 9:662
Testament (Meslier), 2:266, 6:154, 9:712
Testimony, **9:400–403**
aesthetic qualities and, 1:39–40
appropriateness of, 9:403
authoritative, faith resting on, 5:99
children and, 7:357
Collins on, 2:330
definition of, 9:400
education and, 7:357
vs. epistemic autonomy, 9:401–402
as epistemologic necessity, 9:86, 9:402
epistemology of, 9:402–403
faith and, 5:99
vs. hearsay, 7:452
Hume on, 6:269, 7:357
Indian philosophy on, 9:544–545
as knowledge source, 9:401–402
in law, 7:452
as linguistic entity, 9:401
on miracles, 6:269, 6:274
Reid on, 7:357
of Thucydides, 9:456–457
untrustworthiness of, 5:96
Testimony: A Philosophical Study (Coady), 9:400
Testing for Truth (Lampkin), 5:566
Testing Statistical Hypotheses (Lehmann), 9:218
Tetens, Johann Nicolaus, **9:403–404**
Eberhard and, 3:161
Lambert and, 5:176
Tetralemma, 6:471
Tetralogies (Antiphon), 1:223
Tetsugaku (science of seeking wisdom), 4:791, 6:623
Textual commentary, Chinese, 2:226
Textual criticism
in Buddhism, 1:729
Dai Zhen on, 2:621–622
Dge-lugs and, 1:733–734
Textual meaning, in painting, 9:835
Textualism, 7:173
Textuality, 6:614
Texture, as determinable, 3:1
Thagard, Paul, social epistemology and, 9:84
Thales of Miletus, **9:405–406**
Diogenes Laertius on, 3:88
geometric theorem, 4:54
materialism of, 6:7
on matter, 6:58
monism of, 1:249
panpsychism and, 7:83
pantheism and, 7:94
Parmenides of Elea and, 7:126
in pre-Socratic philosophy, 7:760
Tharp, L. H., 5:531
"That" clauses, 8:89
"That the Doctrines of the Other Philosophers Actually Make Life Impossible" (Colotes of Lampsacus), 3:263
Thatcher, Margaret, 9:98
Thätigen Christenthums Nothwendigkeit (Spener), 7:575–576
Theatetus (Clement of Alexandria), 2:289
Theaetetus (Plato), 2:540–542, 3:105, 5:91–94, 9:420
dating of, 9:107

Theaetetus (Plato), ***continued***
dreams in, 3:105
epistemology in, 8:91
Euclides in, 6:110
Forms in, 7:598–600
on knowledge, 3:284–286, 3:343, 5:91–94, 7:599
on nouns and verbs, 9:287
Parmenides of Elea and, 7:122
Protagorean relativism in, 4:164
sense experience in, 8:824
on Sophists, 3:343, 9:130
subjectivism in, 9:131
thought in, 9:420
truth in, 2:540, 2:542
Theaetetus of Athens, 4:172
"Theatre Considered as a Moral Institution" (Schiller, Friedrich), 8:626
Theft, Hobbes on, 6:511
Theiler, Willy, on Diogenes of Apollonia, 3:90
Theism, **9:406–409**
Baader and, 1:439
Brightman and, 1:694–695
and compatibilism, 3:696
Darwin and, 8:395–396
Eddington and, 9:237
evolution and, 9:378
Freud on, 3:745–747
Haeckel on, 4:204
idealistic view of, 4:552
on infinity of God, 4:669–671
Jeans and, 9:237
Masaryk and, 6:1–2
McTaggart and, 6:78
mysticism and, 6:460
of Nakae Tōju, 6:477
naturalism and, 6:474
and personalism, 7:233–236
and pluralism, 4:744
psychoanalytic ontogeny of, 3:747
psychoanalytic phylogeny of, 3:747
on religious experience, 8:403
Rensi and, 8:433
Shaftesbury and, 9:3
Tennant and, 9:392–393
Tillich on, 1:364
Toland and, 9:505
Vaihinger and, 9:628
Varisco and, 9:647
Vasconcelos and, 9:648
Voltaire and, 9:711
"Theism" (Mill, John Stuart), 2:699, 6:230
Theism and Thought (Balfour), 1:474
Themata, in Stoic logic, 5:406–407
Thematic affinity fallacy, 3:743
Thematic elaboration, in semantic theory, 3:464–465
Thematic reenactments, as pathogenically recapitulatory, 3:742–743
Theme-horizon structure, irreducibility of, 6:150
Themis: A Study of the Social Origins of Greek Religion (Harrison), 1:58
Themistius, **9:409**
Aristotelianism of, 1:259
Boethius and, 5:421, 5:422
Theobald, Archbishop of Canterbury, John of Salisbury and, 4:843
Theocracy
in Bonalnd, 1:648
in Calvin, 2:11
in Campanella, 2:16
vs. democracy, 7:307–308
Philo on, 7:306–307
Solov'ëv on, 9:122, 9:125
Théodicée (Leibniz), 3:469, 3:473, 5:254, 5:263–265, 5:274, 7:248–249
Theodicy
Adams and, 3:477–478
Augustine and, 3:472–474, 7:387–388
Berdyaev and, 1:559
Brentano and, 1:692
Butler (Joseph) and, 1:783
definition of, 3:472
Hick and, 3:477
hiddenness of God and, 4:355–356
Irenaeus and, 3:474–475
Leibniz and, 3:469, 3:473, 5:263–265, 5:671
Malebranche and, 5:669–670
Malthus and, 5:676
in Naṣīr al-Dīn al-Ṭūsị, 6:478
Nursi and, 2:114–115
Schelling and, 8:621
soul-making, 4:355
Swinburne and, 3:477–478
See also Evil; Leibniz, Gottfried Wilhelm
Theodicy (Essais de Théodicée) (Leibniz), 1:505, 5:254, 5:263–265, 5:274
Bayle and, 1:505
evil in, 3:469, 3:473
optimism/pessimism in, 7:248–249
Spinoza and, 7:99
Theodoric of Chartres, 2:136–137, 7:612, **9:410–411**
Theodorus, Cyrenaic teaching of, 2:620
Theogonie (Feuerbach), 3:609
Theogony, Orphic, 7:42
Theogony (Hesiod), on love, 5:583
Theologia Christiana (Abelard), 1:3
Theologia Platonica (Ficino), 1:48, 2:322, 3:620–625, 7:144
Theologia Scholarium (Abelard), 1:3, 7:260
Theologia Summi Boni (Abelard), 1:3, 1:6–7
Theological determinism, 3:7–10, **3:23–24**
See also Predestination
Theological fatalism
argument for, 3:693–694
denying the Freedom Assumption, 3:695
vs. logical fatalism, 3:692
as thought problem, 3:696
Theological fatalists, denying the Freedom Assumption, 3:695
Theological Notebook (Newman), 6:583
Theological Papers (Newman), 6:583
Theological philosophy
and anthropology, 7:323
of history, determinism in, 3:35
vs. philosophy of religion, 7:478–479
Theological propositions, Johnson (Alexander Bryan) on, 4:849
Theological psychology, 8:121–123
Theological statements
meaning of, 8:411–412
verifiability of, 8:412–414
Theological voluntarism, 3:93, 9:716
Theological "why," 9:756–758
"Theologische Element im Beruf des logistischen Logikers, Das" (Scholz), 8:645
Theologische Nachlass (Lessing), 5:295, 5:296
Theology
analogy in, **1:138–144**
anthropology and, 7:323
Aquinas on, 9:426, 9:772
areopagitic, Stein on, 9:240
Arnauld on, 1:289
Averroes and, 1:424–425
Baader and, 1:439
Bacon (Roger) and, 1:454
Bayle and, 1:505–506
Bernard of Clairvaux and, 1:592
Bodin and, 1:622
Boyle and, 1:675
Buridan and, 1:767
Butler (Samuel) and, 1:785
in Byzantine thought, 1:788–789
Comte and, 6:225
congruism and, 8:681

Crusius and, 2:608
Darwinism and, 2:630, 2:637, 2:640–641
as declarative, 7:258
and divine unity, 4:551–552
Duns Scotus and, 8:704
and ethics, duty in, 3:155
Eucharistic, 1:289
and evil, problem of, 3:469–470
existentialism in, 3:505–506
general will in, 4:39
Gilbert of Poitiers on, 4:88
gnostic, 4:99–100
God as transsubjective datum in, 8:645
Gödel and, 4:117
Hartley and, 2:316
Hegelian, 4:284
Heidegger and, 4:289
Heraclitus and, 4:319–320
history and, 3:35
impossibility of, 9:780–781
Islamic
  al-Fārābī, Abū al Naṣr in, 1:116
  Jewish participation in, 4:811
Jansenist, 4:788–789
Kempis and, 9:424
Khomiakov and, 5:60
King (Martin Luther) and, 5:741
Luther on, 5:615
Mackie in, 5:638
Marsilius of Inghen and, 5:721
materialism and, 6:14–15
metaphysical, 1:436–437
  Carnap on, 1:360
  Mansel and, 1:362
  rejection of, 1:364–365
  Tillich on, 1:364–365
  unintelligibility of, 1:365–366
Milton and, 6:249
Molina's *scientia media* and, 8:680–682
moral
  Crusius on, 2:608
  Kant on, 5:23, 8:661
mystical
  in Baḥyā ben Joseph ibn Paqūda, 1:457–458
  Bernard of Clairvaux on, 1:592
  Boehme and, 1:623
  Bonaventure and, 1:652
  Bulgakov and, 1:760
  of Gregory of Nyssa, 4:182
  interpenetration and non-obstruction principle in, 1:737
natural, 9:406–408
negative, 1:93, 5:649, 5:652
  vs. affirmative, 7:613
  Maimonides on, 4:818
Newton in, 6:591–592
Ockham and, 9:779–781
Oman and, 7:14–15
Peter Lombard and, 7:261
Philodemus on, 7:302
philosophical
  Butler (Joseph) and, 1:780–784
  creation *ex nihilo* and, 2:585
  Tennant on, 7:562, 9:379, 9:392
and philosophy, 1:478, 1:650, 4:840, 7:332
  Alexander of Hales on, 1:114
  Arnauld on, 1:289
  Duns Scotus on, 3:134
  13th-c. syntheses of, 9:772
vs. philosophy of religion, 7:478–479
Platonic, 8:43–44
positive
  evidence in, 9:778
  Ockham on, 9:772, 9:778, 9:781
predestination and, 8:681–682
Proclus and, 8:41–43
Protestant. *See* Protestantism
Pseudo-Dionysius and, 8:101–102
rational demonstration in, 4:92
rationalism in, 8:240
reasoning in, 1:93
reductive materialism in, 1:370
reincarnation and, 8:332–333
revelation and, 8:452–453
Ritschl and, 8:480–481
Saadya on, 4:812
Scholastics on, 5:615
School of St. Victor and, 8:592–593
vs. science
  Pannenberg on, 7:82
  Scholastics on, 3:134
of socinianism, 9:99
as solution to nonbeing, 9:459
Soto and, 9:137
as speculative independence, 1:477
Spinoza and, 9:180
statements of
  meaning of, 8:411–412
  verifiability of, 8:412–414
Swedenborg and, 9:338
theory of substance in, 9:296
Thomasius and, 9:440–441
trinitarian, Gregory of Nazianzus on, 4:181
Troeltsch on, 9:527
ugliness and, 9:562
Ulrich of Strasbourg on, 9:565
as understanding by faith, 1:479
Vives on, 9:700
Whichcote and, 9:746
Wolff and, 9:825, 9:829
Wyclyf and, 9:851
Xenophanes of Colophon and, 9:853
Zen'kovskii and, 9:868–869
See also God, existence of; Philosophy of religion; Physicotheology; Religion; Theism
Theology of Liberation: History, Politics, and Salvation, A (Gutiérrez), 5:331–332
Theomonism, 9:307
Theophania, Erigena on, 7:95
Theophilus
  as apologist, 1:228
  on faith, 1:229
  on God, 1:228, 7:142
Theophrastus, 7:202–203, 9:35, **9:411–413**
  on agent intellect, 1:91
  Anaximenes and, 1:186
  Arcesilaus and, 1:247
  Aristotle and, 1:258, 9:411–412
  on atomism, 5:298
  on Democritus, 5:298, 5:300
  Diogenes Laertius and, 3:89
  Diogenes of Apollonia and, 3:89, 5:298
  Empedocles and, 3:208
  Galen on, 5:408
  in Greek Academy, 4:300
  La Bruyère and, 5:166
  on Leucippus, 5:298
  on logic, 5:401–403
  on *Metaphysics* (Aristotle), 1:258
Theophrastus Redivivus, 2:264
Theorem(s), 3:650
  about first-order logic, 3:647
  definition of, 5:558
  elementary, in combinatory logic, 2:334
  Gödel's, 4:119–131
  well-ordered, definition of, 5:559
Theorem schema, definition of, 5:558
Theoremata (Duns Scotus), 3:134
Theoremata de Corpere (Giles of Rome), 6:3
Theoremhood, testing first-order sentences, 3:658
Theoretical atheism, 9:628
Theoretical concepts, Wright (Chauncey) on, 9:846
Theoretical differences, in evaluative predicate application, 4:862

Theoretical facts, Duhem on, 3:128
Theoretical I, 3:615
Theoretical ideas, 2:561–563
Theoretical judgment, *vs.* critical judgment, Windelband on, 9:792
Theoretical language, 4:308
Theoretical method, 7:331
Theoretical physics, cosmology and, 2:558
Theoretical terms. *See* Term(s)/terminology
Theoretical-empirical terms, in verificationism, 7:31
Theoretical-practical rationality, potential for, 3:617
Theoretische Kinematik (Reuleaux), 7:543
Theoria Medica Vera (Stahl), 9:202
Theoria motus abstracti (Theory of Abstract Motion) (Leibniz), 5:251, 5:260, 5:269
Théorie analytique de la chaleur (Fourier), 3:229
Théorie de l'intuition dans la phénoménologie de Husserl, La (Levinas), 5:303–304
Theorie des kommunikativen Handelns (Habermas), 4:200
Theorie des quatres mouvements et des destinees generales (Fourier), 3:706
Theorie des Romans, Die (The soul and the forms) (Lukács), 5:603
Theorie des tourbillons cartesiens (Fontenelle), 3:683
Théorie physique: son objet, sa structure, La (The Aim and Structure of Physical Theory) (Duhem), 3:126
Theorie und Praxis (Habermas), 4:199–200
Theories of conditionals, **10:5–6**
Theories of Societies (Parson), 9:96
Theories of Surplus Value (Marx), 5:731
Theory(ies), 3:650–651, **9:413–418**
- of assumptions, 6:116
- axiomatizing, in mathematical foundations, 6:21–22
- belief in, reasons for, 9:577
- canonical formulation of, 9:414
- of causality, in realism, 2:101
- of causation, and solution of the frame problem, 3:711
- Chomsky and, 2:244
- of complexes, 6:116
- concepts as, 2:418–419
- Croce on, 2:603
- definition of, 9:413
- of descriptions, 8:196
- descriptive set, 8:833
- Duhem on, 3:127–129
- Einstein on, 3:181–182
- eliminative materialism on, 3:182–183
- empirically adequate, 5:102
- empirically equivalent rivals of, 9:576–578
- *vs.* ethics, faith in, 4:772
- evocative argumentative and, 2:213–214
- exclusion of fictitious entities and, 1:446
- *vs.* fact, 8:671
- falsifiability of, in demarcation, 8:670
- first-order, decidability of, 5:479
- of forms
  - Aristotle on, 9:591
  - and definition, 2:665–666
  - universals in, 9:590–591
- in Ibn al-ʿArabī, 4:542
- illustration of, by thought experiment, 9:452–455
- inference to the best explanation and, 4:652
- and intertheoretic reduction, 6:569
- and intertheoretic relations, asymmetric, 9:580
- Johnson (Alexander Bryan) on, 4:849
- locality of, 6:641
- of meaning, 6:83
  - deflationist perspective, 3:634
  - Dummett on, 3:132–133
- of mind, 3:758
- of models, Tarski on, 5:480
- of objects, Meinong and, 6:115–116
- and observable *vs.* theoretical, 9:415–416
- pessimistic induction and, 8:692
- Poincaré on, 7:652–653
- probabilistic, common cause principle and, 2:342–343
- provability logic and, 8:98–99
- in psychology, 5:129
- Ramsey-sentence approach to, 9:417
- reference of, 9:417
- of repression, and psychoanalysis, 3:738
- semantic approach to, 9:334, 9:416–417
- study of changes in, 8:692
- Suppes and, 9:334
- syntactic view of, 9:413–416
- of types
  - definition of, 5:558
  - in illative combinatory logic, 2:339
- types of, 7:400–401
- in underdetermination, 9:575–578
- voluntarist, 3:531–533
- *See also* Term(s)/terminology, theoretical

Theory and Regulation of Love, The (Norris), 6:655
Theory of Abstract Motion (Theoria motus abstracti) (Leibniz), 5:251, 5:260, 5:269
Theory of Committees (Carroll), 2:51
Theory of Games and Economic Behavior (Neumann & Morgenstern), 6:559
Theory of Good and Evil, The (Rashdall), 8:238
Theory of Groups and Quantum Mechanics (Gruppentheorie und Quantenmechanik) (Weyl), 9:741
Theory of Heat (Maxwell), 6:70
Theory of Human Action (Goldman), 4:148
Theory of Justice, A (Rawls), 5:323–324, 9:611
- bioethics in, 1:603
- on coercive institutions, 9:74
- ethics in, 7:119
- on evil, 3:471
- justice in, 4:867–868
- on morality, 3:479
- nationalism in, 6:485
- on social contract, 9:82
- stability in, 8:259

Theory of Knowledge (Lehrer), 5:248
Theory of Knowledge and Existence, The (Stace), 9:199
Theory of Literature (Welleck & Warren), 4:597
Theory of Meaningfulness (Narens), 6:87
Theory of Moral Sentiments (Smith), 3:246, 7:350, 9:67
"Theory of Probabilities" (De Morgan), 2:710
Theory of Science (Wissenschaftslehre) (Fichte), on reality, 3:414
Theory of Social and Economic Organizations (Weber), 9:93
Theory of the Earth (Buffon), 1:758
Theory of the Good and the Right, A (Brandt), 1:687
Theory of the Living Organism, The (Agar), 7:83
Theory of the Moral Sentiments (Grouchy), 9:839

Theory-dependence, of method, 3:576
Theory-theory
endowment effect in, 9:39
of folk psychology, 3:677
innate ideas in, 4:694
as knowledge-rich approach, 9:37
in mental state attribution, 4:148, 9:36
reevaluation of, 3:680
Theosis, Luther and, 5:617
Theosophism, 9:241–242, 9:338. *See also* Steiner, Rudolf; Swedenborg, Emanuel
Theosophy. *See* Steiner, Rudolf; Swedenborg, Emanuel
Therapy, psychoanalytic, 8:105–106
See also Psychoanalysis
Theravāda
meditation in, 6:109
on nirvāṇa, 5:328
Therefore, in an argument, 3:639
Thermodynamics
of black holes, 9:269
Boltzmann and, 1:644
chemical potential in, Gibbs on, 4:86
of entropy, 2:105
equilibrium bidirectionality in, 1:645
and microcanonical ensembles, 4:86–87
Planck on, 7:578
reduction of, 9:579
statistical mechanics and, 2:126, 7:537–538, 7:541–542
statistical *vs.* phenomenological, 9:468–469
Taine on, 9:365
temporal asymmetry and, 2:104–105, 7:537–542, 7:564–565
temporal symmetry and, 2:104–105, 9:468
time reversal in, 9:499–500
Thermometer
Fludd and, 3:674
invention of, 6:87
"Theses on Feuerbach" (Marx), 3:59, 3:612
Theurgic aesthetics, of Fëdorov, 3:560
Theurgy, 4:767
Thibaut, A. F. J., 8:615
Thick moral concepts, 6:159, 6:164
Thielicke, Helmut, on nihilism, 6:618
Thiên, on Zen Buddhism, 1:726
Thierry, Augustin, 8:589
Thierry of Chartres. *See* Theodoric of Chartres
Thin moral concepts, 6:159
Thin particulars, 6:199
Thing-in-itself
Ampère on, 1:138
appearances and, 5:34
certainty of existence of, faith in, 4:771–772
existence of, impossibility of proving, 8:660
Fichte on, 3:309, 6:541
Fries on, 6:541
Green on, 4:179
Haeckel on, 4:202
Hegel on, 6:541
Herbart on, 6:541
as inaccessible to rational investigation, 4:748
Jacobi (Friedrich Heinrich) on, 4:770–771
Kant on, 3:306–307, 4:556, 8:650
Liebmann on, 6:541
Mach on, 5:623
Maréchal and, 5:709
Nietzsche on, 6:612
as non-spatial-temporal pure rational minds, 1:668
phenomena and, 1:232, 5:20–21
Reinhold on, 8:334–335, 8:661
Riehl on, 6:541
Schelling on, 6:541
Schlick on, 8:639
Schopenhauer on, 3:311
in sense-datum theory, 8:818
Thing-language, Carnap on, 3:317
Things
characteristics of, 5:125
examples of, 5:125
Israeli on, 2:539–540
in ontological reism, 5:144
as physical in critical realism, 2:595
in Scholastic correspondence theories of truth, 2:540
self and, Ortega y Gasset on, 7:45
Things as They Are; or, the Adventures of Caleb Williams (Godwin), 4:136
"Things without the Mind" (Evans), 3:461–462
Things-in-themselves. *See* Thing-in-itself
Thinking, **9:418–423**
analogy theory of, 9:422
attribution in, 9:419
Chinese linguistic structure and reflective thought, 2:210–212
Collingwood on, 2:328
conceptual view of, 9:420
consciousness and, 2:449
correspondence theory and, 2:546
Destutt de Tracy on, 2:760
evolutionary theory and, 2:637
experience and, 5:687
Green on, 4:179
image theory of, 4:565
images in, 4:592–595
as inner side of speaking, 8:633
interior nature of, 9:418
as intuition *vs.* rationality, 1:728
James *vs.* Schiller (Ferdinand) on, 8:623
Kant on, 4:561
Langer on, 5:187–188
language and, 8:14–23
logic and, 1:661
Marcel on, 5:700–701
Marx on, 3:57
moral, Hare on, 3:441, 6:160
overt, 9:422
vs. perception, 7:192
personal identity and, 7:232
personality and, 4:856
phenomenology and, 7:279–280, 7:288
in Platonism, 9:419–421
reflective, 7:288
Rehmke on, 8:302
Ryle on, 9:421–422
Schopenhauer on, 8:656
stability and, 7:268
supposal as, 4:597
traditional theories of, 9:419–421
types of, 9:418
Vico on, 9:672
as visual inspection *vs.* action affinity, 1:596
See also Cognition; Thought
Thinking and Experience (Price), 4:593–594, 9:600
Thinking and Meaning (Ayer), 1:437
Thinking and Representation (Price), 9:601
Thinking to Some Purpose (Stebbing), 9:237
Third man argument, 6:111
"Third Man Argument in the *Parmenides,* The" (Vlastos), 9:701–702
Third Set of Objections, The (Hobbes), 4:564
Thirdness, Peirce on, 7:164, 7:168–171
Third-World nationalism, 7:726
"Thirteen Pragmatisms, The" (Lovejoy), 4:781, 5:592
Thirty Years War
Descartes and, 2:723
Elisabeth, princess of Bohemia, and, 3:187
Leibniz and, 5:255

Thirty-Nine Articles of Religion, 8:297
Thomas, M. H., on Dewey, 3:45
Thomas, Vincent
on creative process, 2:590
Lehrer and, 5:248
Thomas à Kempis, **9:423–424**
Thomas Aquinas, St. *See* Aquinas, St. Thomas; Thomism
Thomas Becket, John of Salisbury and, 4:843
Thomas of Erfurt, modism and, 5:432
Thomas of York, **9:443**
Thomas Oliver of Bury, 5:438
Thomasius, Christian, 5:250, **9:440–442**
Budde and, 1:721
Crusius and, 2:605
on decorum, 9:826
Rüdiger and, 8:526–527
Thomasius, Jakob, Leibniz and, 5:250, 5:265
Thomism, 1:364, 3:531, **9:443–448**
analogy in, 1:364
as authentic existentialism, Gilson on, 4:92
Báñez on, 1:476
Cajetan and, 2:7
Catholicism and, 9:436
and Dante, 2:625–626
definition of, 9:443
Descartes and, 2:720–721
on divine perfection, 7:194
epistemology in, 5:708
existentialism in, 1:476
Finnis on, 9:383
Fonseca and, 3:681
Garrigou-Lagrange and, 4:23
in Geyser, 4:82–84
Giles of Rome and, 4:89–91
history of, 1:262, 9:445–447
Hooker and, 4:462–463
Maréchal and, 5:708
in medieval philosophy, 6:100
Mercier and, 6:143–145
modern revival of, 9:436
vs. Molinism, 8:680
natural law in, 6:508
and Ockhamism, 3:696
periods of, 9:443–444
in Renaissance, 9:445
renewal of, 6:143, 6:144
Soto and, 9:137
substance in, God as, 7:24
Sylvester of Ferrara and, 9:343
Taylor (Alfred) and, 9:373
Tennant on, 3:532
tension in, 9:448
Vasquez and, 9:649–650
See also Thomas Aquinas, St.
Thomson, Judith Jarvis, **9:448–450**
on abortion, 1:9, 9:448
on event theory, 3:466
Thomson, William, 2:280, 3:551
Thoreau, Henry David, **9:450–452**
on civil disobedience, 2:259
ethics of, 6:574–575
Thorndike, Edward, 1:520, 7:150
Thorschmid, U. G., on deism, 2:688
Thou, absolute, 5:702
Thought
abstract, 3:559
and action, 1:596, 4:36, 4:51
in actual idealism, 4:49
Aquinas on, 2:539
Aristotle on, 1:43
belief attribution and, 1:536–537
Bergson on, 1:566
Blake on, 1:610
Block on, 2:457
categories of, 4:265
Chisholm on, 2:243
circumscription of, by space and time, 4:744
in cognitive science, 2:299, 8:152
computationalism and, 2:393
concepts and, 2:415
Condillac on, 2:423
consciousness and, 1:649, 2:454, 2:457, 4:713, 8:663
as content of mental states, 2:478
creative process and, 2:590
Crusius on, 2:606
Davidson (Donald) on, 2:650
Democritus on, 5:301
Descartes on, 4:611
Diderot on, 3:75
Engels on, 3:59
evolutionary origin of, 1:566
and fallacies, 2:213–214
freedom of, 6:228
Frege on, 3:728, 5:507, 8:829
Gehlen on, 4:36
generalizing, 8:459
Gentile on, 4:49
glossmorphy of, 9:252
Hegel on, 4:265
Heidegger on, 4:294–295
higher-order consciousness and, 2:454, 4:713
historical particularity and, 4:289
Hobbes on, 4:413, 6:9
in idealism, 4:561
idealization of, 5:685–686
as imageless, 1:596
imaginative activity as normative, 1:610
individualizing, 8:459
intentionality in, 2:452
and intuition, 1:567
James and, 4:778–779, 4:784, 7:744
Lachelier on, 5:170
language and, 5:468, 8:793
language of, **5:191–194**
law and, 7:418
Lessing on, 7:100
logic as ethics of, 9:29
Lotze on, 5:581
Maimon on, 5:645–646
Manheim on, 5:685–686
mental images in, 2:393, 4:593
metaphysical attitude of, Engels on, 3:59–60
Millikan on, 6:236
nature of
Aristotle on, 3:53
Plato on, 3:53
Wittgenstein on, 9:804–805
nonreducible, 1:25
ontologism, 4:94
Pastore on, 7:135
Peirce on, 5:454
philosophical, presupposing an object beyond itself, 3:715
philosophy as clarification of, 2:44–45
philosophy of, 6:212
as pictures, 9:804–805
in Plato's theory of truth, 2:540
as product of being, 3:610
projective, necessity of, 3:559
psychological, optimism/pessimism in, 7:247–248
rational control of, 2:457
rhetoric in, 1:443
Rickert on, 8:459
Rosenzweig on, 8:498
Royce on, 8:519–520
Santayana on, 8:599
scientific, *vs.* thought experiments, 9:452
as secretion of mind, 2:2
in self-constitution, 4:51
silent, 9:422
solipsism and, 9:117–119
in solution of problem, 8:625
and speech, 2:209, 9:629
Stephen's history of, 9:243
Stout on, 9:259
tradition and, 1:284
traits of, 4:778
turning movement in, 4:289
universals and, 1:613, 9:601
Vaihinger on, 9:627–628
Vailati on, 9:629

Wodeham on, 9:821
See also Ideas; Laws of thought; Thinking
Thought and Action (Hampshire), 8:730
Thought contents (*Gedanken*), Külpe on, 5:160
Thought experiments, **9:452–456**
analytical behaviorism and, 1:525
art as, 1:336
in attributor contextualism, 2:485
Chinese room argument and, 2:239–242
on impossibilities in syllogisms, 1:627–628
Philoponus and, 7:314
philosophical problems as, 3:696
in problem of qualia, 9:292
Twin Earth, 7:406–408
Thought force, 3:705
Thought News (periodical), 3:44
Thought processes, 1:596, 5:160
Thought theory, paradox of fiction and, 5:367–368
Thoughts Occasioned by Dr. Parr's Spital Sermon (Godwin), 4:136
Thoughts on Man (Godwin), 4:136
Thoughts on The Late Transactions Respecting The Falkland Islands (Johnson, Dr. Samuel), 4:852
Thoughts on Various Subjects (Swift), 2:131
Thousand Plateaus, A (Deleuze), 2:696
Thrasylus, on Democritus, 5:298
Thrasymachus, ethics of, 3:395
Thread of Life (Wollheim), 6:124
Three body problem, chaos model simplicity in, 2:132
Three Conversations (Solov'ëv), 9:122, 9:125
Three Dialogues between Hylas and Philonous (Berkeley), 1:573, 1:576–579, 2:355, 4:555, 4:560
Three Essays on Religion (Mill, John Stuart), 1:93, 1:368, 2:346, 4:614, 6:229, 7:561
Three Essays on the Theory of Sexuality (Freud), 7:522
Three Letters to Lamy (Malebranche), 5:665
Three Letters to the Bishop of Bangor (Law), 5:220
"Three Meetings" (Solov'ëv), 9:122
Three Philosophical Poets (Santayana), 8:602
Three Physico-theological Discourses (Ray), 7:558
Three Rival Versions of Moral Inquiry (McIntyre), 9:447
Three Speeches in Memory of Dostoevsky (Solov'ëv), 9:122
Three Treatise School (the Mādhyamika School), 5:134–135
Three-body problem, in classical mechanics, 2:282
Threefold unity, in Taintai Buddhism, 2:164
Through Nature to God (Fiske), 3:668
Through the Looking-Glass (Carroll), 2:51
Thucydides, **9:456–458**
aitia in, 1:99
on equality, 3:329
Hobbes on, 3:170
property in, 8:73–74
sophism in, 9:129
Thugs of India, 9:395
Thulstrup, Niels, 5:67
Thümmig, Ludwig Philipp, **9:458**
Thus Spoke Zarathustra (Nietzsche), 6:611–612
Emerson and, 6:575
on eternal return doctrine, 3:354
on war and peace, 7:153
Tianli (heavenly principle)
Wang Yang-ming on, 9:726
Zhu Xi on, 9:883
Tiantai Buddhism, 2:154, 2:163–166
Chan Buddhism and, 1:727
on ultimate reality, 2:220
Tibetan Buddhism, Dge-lugs tradition in, 1:731–735
Tides, theory of, 5:54
Tieck, Ludwig
Novalis and, 6:667
Schelling and, 8:617
Schlegel and, 8:631
Tiedemann, Dietrich, 2:580
Tien Tai metaphysics, *li* in, 4:794
Tienson, John, 2:445
Tikhie dumy (Bulgakov), 1:760
Tilde, definition of, 5:558
Till Frågan om den Gällande Rättens Begrepp (Hägeström), 3:425
Till We Have Faces (Lewis), 5:312
Tillich, Paul, **9:458–461**
on atheism, 1:358, 2:350
criticism of, 1:364–367
existentialism of, 3:505
on God
immanence of, 4:108
ontological argument for existence of, 7:17
metaphor in, 1:365–366
on metaphysical theology, 1:364–365
nothing in, 6:658
on rationality of faith, 3:535
on redemption in Christianity, 2:249
on ultimate concerns, 8:635
Tillotson, John, 2:683–685
Tilted Arc (Serra), 3:256
Timaeus (Plato), 1:591–592, 2:136, 7:270, 7:303–305
atomists and, 5:302
author's family in, 7:582
Bernard of Chartres and, 1:591
Bernard of Clairvaux and, 1:592
on body, 4:5
Chartres school and, 2:136
cosmology in, 7:601
creation in, 6:519
creator god in, 9:256
dating of, 7:583, 9:107
Demiurge in, 2:698–699, 4:668, 5:640, 6:547–548
on dreams, 3:105
on elementary triangles, 7:603
on eternity, 3:358
on evil, 3:397
Forms in, 3:283, 3:358, 6:185
God in, 4:108–109
Hugh of St. Victor on, 8:592
Iamblichus on, 4:540
Justin Martyr on, 5:569
Leonardo da Vinci and, 5:282
microcosm in, 5:640
mimesis in, 6:252
in Neoplatonism, 8:40
on pleasure, 3:397
Proclus on, 7:609, 8:41
psyche in, 8:103
on realm of sensibles, 7:632
on sense perception, 3:284
on soul, 6:547–548, 7:635
on space, 9:147
Theodoric of Chartres and, 9:410
theory of ideas in, 4:564
on virtue and vice, 7:590
William of Conches's commentary on, 9:768
Zeno of Citium and, 9:870
Timaeus of Locri, 7:607
Time, **9:461–475**
in absolute idealism, 1:145
absolute theories of, 7:475, 9:465–466
in Achilles paradox, 9:875
in African philosophy, 1:83–84
alienation in, 1:124–125
animal knowledge of, 1:203
Aquinas on, 9:428
Aristotle on, 2:490, 3:357–359
in arithmetic, 1:244

Time, *continued*
arrow of, 9:498–499
asymmetry and, 2:575, 9:467–470
Augustine on, 1:397–398, 3:402–403, 7:387, 9:485
backward causation and, 2:99
in bad conscience, 4:787
and becoming, **9:475–482**
Bergson on, 1:563–564, 9:487, 9:489
Berkeley on, 1:581–582
big bang cosmology and, 9:478
Boltzmann on, 1:644–645
Bradwardine on, 1:680
Buffon on, 1:759
Carnap on, 2:39
Carroll on, 2:51–52
causal theories of, 9:471
causality of continuous processes and, 2:101–102
Clarke on, 2:272
in classical mechanics, 2:281, 2:282, 7:474–475
in classical physics, 9:495
Cohen (Hermann) on, 2:303
common sense and, Moore on, 2:358
in computability theory, 2:387
concept of, abstracted from experience, 6:81
and consciousness, 2:459, 5:143
consciousness of, 4:290, **9:482–488**
in continental philosophy, **9:488–493**
continuum and, 9:466–467
controversies about, 9:497
as conventional truth, 2:520
Conway on, 2:529
coordinate, 9:495
as cosmic, historical, and existential, 1:560
in cosmological argument for God's existence, 2:586
of creation, 1:360
Crescas on, 2:593
in *Critique of Pure Reason* (Kant), 2:689, 4:57, 9:148
Crusius on, 2:607
date theory of, 9:476–477
Deleuze on, 9:492
Derrida on, 9:491
direction of, 1:645, 7:475, **7:563–567,** 9:468–470, 9:499–500
causal approaches to, 2:85–88
entropy and, 7:537–543
naturalistic theories of, 7:564–565
open and closed contingencies in, 2:105
directional causality for, 2:87
Dühring on, 3:130
duration of, 9:464
Eckhart (Meister) on, 3:163
Einstein on, 7:476
emergent qualities in, 1:110
as empirical intuition, 3:752
empiricism and, 9:483
entropy of, 9:469
epistemology of, 9:462, 9:498
in Flying Arrow paradox, 9:876
as fourth dimension, 9:484
free will and, 9:471–472
freedom and, 1:563–564
Friedman on, 3:159
futurity as tense concept in, 2:86
in general relativity, 9:496–497
in geology, Darwinism and, 2:640
Gödel on, 4:118
God's relationship to, 1:626, 3:8–9, 3:357–360
Hatano on, 4:247
Heidegger on, 3:512, 4:290–292
historical, 7:387
Hume on, 3:304, 4:492–493
hypertime, 9:462
ideas of, examination of, 5:14–15
in I-it *vs.* I-thou relations, 1:716
in Indian philosophy, 5:326
infinity and, 9:466–467
Ingarden on, 4:683
intellect's understanding of, 1:567–568
James (William) on, 9:482–483, 9:487
in Japanese philosophy, 4:797
Jewish conception of, 7:387
in *kalām* argument on God's existence, 2:553, 2:554
Kant on, 3:304–307, 5:11, 9:467
Kozlov on, 5:146
Lalande on, 5:173
language of, 9:462–464, 9:470, 9:478–481
Leibniz on, 4:554, 6:191, 9:467
Lenin on, 5:280
Levinas on, 9:491
Liebmann on, 5:345
Locke on, 3:304, 5:382
Mach on, 5:624
mathematical intuition of, 1:700
as mathematical *vs.* continuous flow, 1:563
McTaggart on, 6:78–79
measurement of, 9:461, 9:483
Anaximander in, 1:184
devices for, 6:91
Heidegger on, 9:490
memory and, 9:462, 9:463
mereology and, 6:147
Merleau-Ponty on, 9:491
metaphysics of, 7:211
metrication of, 9:476–477, 9:494
in micro *vs.* macrophysics, 9:499
as mind, 1:109–110
in mind-body relationship, 1:565
in motion, 9:876
in Moving Rows paradox, 9:877
neurosis and, 1:598
Newton on, 7:475, 9:465
objective unity in, 9:489
as omnipotent present, 1:739
order in, 9:494
Paracelsus on, 7:104
paradoxes with, 9:465
passage of, 9:462–464, 9:496
Pearson on, 7:160–161
perception of, 9:482–483
periodicity of. *See* Eternal return
persistence and, 7:208–211
Petronievič on, 7:267
philosophy of
ontology in, 9:478–479
in physics, 2:104, **9:493–501**
Piaget on, 7:568
Plato on, 3:357, 3:358
Plotinus on, 6:187
plurality in experience in, 1:679
polynominal-time computability constraints and, 2:388–389
Popper on, 9:470
Price (Huw) on, 9:470
probability frequency of instances *vs.* frequency over, 1:644
progress and, 8:49
proper, 9:495–496
as reality attribute, 1:110
reference in, 9:462–463
in relativism, 7:475
reversal of
in classical mechanics, 2:281
in classical physics, 2:104, 9:495
in thermodynamics, 9:499–500
scientific concept as falsification of, 1:567–568
as semantical indices, 8:807
simultaneity and, 2:523–525
and space, objective *vs.* subjective, 9:741
space-time, 9:464–465
spatial metaphors for, 9:487

in special relativity, 9:149–150, 9:495–496
speed of, 9:462
splitting worlds theory and, 5:698
in spontaneous collapse theory, 8:211
as successive duration, 2:16
Taine on, 9:365
in Taintai Buddhism, 2:164
in *Taixuan jing*, 9:861
tense and, 9:463, 9:475–481
tensed *vs.* tenseless, 9:478–481
thermodynamic asymmetry and, 2:104–105
Timon of Phlius on, 9:501–502
token-relflexiveness of, 9:462–463, 9:475–476
Tooley on, 9:470–471
topology of, 9:494
touch and, 9:516
travel, 9:497
unreality of, 6:77, 6:206, 9:464
visual sensations and, 9:485–487
will of God in, 1:704
Woodbridge on, 9:842–843
See also Eternity
Time and Eternity (Stace), 9:200
Time and Free Will (Bergson), 1:563, 9:487–488
Time and Modality (Prior), 8:13
Time and Modes of Being (Ingarden), 4:683
Time and Narrative (Ricoeur), 7:395
Time and Space-Time (Nerlich), 9:478
Time and the Other (Le temps et l'autre) (Levinas), 5:304, 9:491
Time Is an Artist (Kaufmann), 5:46
Time lag, perceptual consciousness and, 7:181–182
Time, Tense, and Causation (Tooley), 9:471
Timeless deity, 3:695
Timeless present, in science, 3:356–357
Times Arrow and Archimedes' Point (Price), 9:470
"Times, Beginnings, and Causes" (Anscombe), 1:213
Timon of Phlius, **9:501–502**
Pyrrho and, 1:193, 8:173
skepticism of, 9:49
Tindal, Matthew, **9:502–504**
on Clarke, 2:274
critics of, 2:684
deism and, 2:683, 2:686, 2:691
on reason, 5:220
Swift and, 9:341
Tipler, Frank J., 4:617, 8:377
Tīrthaṅkāra, in meditation, 6:108
Tissa, Moggaliputta, 5:411
Titchener, Edward, 8:141–142
on emotions, 3:198
on feelings as bearers of ultimate qualities, 7:620
on introspection, 4:721
introspection in, 8:149
on mind, 8:147
in psychology, 8:141
Titelmans, Franciscus, 5:439
Titgemeyer, Rainer, 2:340
Titular properties, *vs.* universals, 9:584
Tocqueville, Alexis de, on government, 2:702
Todhunter, Isaac, Pearson and, 7:159
Toegye. *See* Yi Hwang
Togetherness, in consciousness, 6:75
Token, definition of, 5:558
Token identity theories, 7:553
Token physicalism, 3:759, 7:553–555
Token-token identity theory, pain and, 7:68–69
Tokugawa period
Andō Shōeki in, 1:200
Chanzong during, 1:727–728
Confucianism under, 4:794–795
Hayashi in, 4:247
Toland, John, **9:504–507**
on Christianity, 3:245, 3:246
Chubb and, 2:684
deism and, 2:683, 2:691
Diderot and, 3:73
Enlightenment and, 3:245, 3:246
Locke and, 9:249
Morgan and, 2:684
Norris and, 6:656
pantheism and, 7:97
on reason, 3:245
on rules of faith, 9:249
Swift and, 9:341
Toleration, **9:507–511**
alternatives to, 9:507–508
of atheism, 9:509
Carnap's principle of, 2:43
conservatism and, 2:469
definition of, 9:507
dissenters' call for, 9:249
Enlightenment and, 3:245–246
ethical relativism and, 3:372
in Islam, 8:647
Judeo-Christian denial of, Gibbon on, 4:85
Locke on, 5:391–395, 9:507–509
logical positivist principle of, 5:529
Mill (John Stuart) on, 9:510
of moral views, 6:162
objectivity in ethics and, 7:6
political, 9:510
principal theory of, 3:317
of religion
Bayle on, 1:502
class behavior and, 1:493
Jewish political rights and, 1:493
Turgot on, 9:550
Schiller (Friedrich) on, 8:626
Shaftesbury and, 9:3
Spinoza on, 4:826
in Sufism, 9:311
Voltaire on, 9:712–713
Toletus, Francis, 1:386, **9:511**
Tolman, Edward
on animal learning, 1:522
behaviorism of, 8:143
on purposive activity, 9:384
studies on learning, 1:201
Tolochinov, I. E., 7:150
Tolstoy, Lev (Leo) Nikolaevich, **9:512–514**
and anarchism, 1:178–180
on art, 1:57, 1:304, 9:514
on conscience, 2:445
conversion crisis of, 6:619
on death, 5:346–349, 9:512
expressionism of, 1:340
Fëdorov and, 3:558
on free will, 6:478
Kareev and, 5:40
on Kropotkin, 5:154
Leont'ev and, 5:283
on life, meaning and value of, 5:346–347, 5:356
Schopenhauer and, 8:656
Wittgenstein and, 9:801
Tolstoy and China (Bodde), 9:513
Toltec philosophy, 5:204
Tongshu (Penetrating the Book of Changes) (Zhou Dunyi), 9:880
Tönnies, Ferdinand, 9:95
Tonpsychologie (Stumpf), 9:280
Too Many Minds Objection, to personal identity theory, 7:231–232
Tooby, John, 3:481–486
Tooke, John Home, 8:791–792
Tooley, Michael
on date theory, 9:477
on motion, 6:409–410
on natural laws, 5:226–229
on personhood, 7:238–242
on present, 9:480
on Prior's syntactics of tense, 9:480
on tensed theory, 9:478–480
on time, 9:470–471
Topica (Aristotle), 2:674

Topica (Cicero), 5:422
Topic-neutral analysis of qualitative character, 8:192
Topic-neutral mental states, 6:13
Topics (Aristotle), 2:73, 2:136, 5:398–399, 5:408, 5:443
  Arab logic and, 5:417
  on dialectic, 1:264, 3:53
  logic in, 5:398–399, 5:408, 5:443
  medieval logic and, 5:422
  medieval philosophy and, 5:430
Topics (Cicero), 4:66
Topics, in Mohist discourse, 2:212–213
Topological Cleanthes, 6:147
Topological modal interpretation, 6:297
Topology
  Brouwer contributions to, 1:700
  Lacan on, 5:168–169
  properties in, 9:494
  of space, 9:150
  of space-time, 9:466
  of time, 9:494
Toposes, 9:272
Torah
  Albo on, 1:103
  on resurrection, 4:618
Tormey, Alan, 1:303–306
Torquato Tasso (Goethe), 4:140
Torrey, H. A. P., Dewey and, 3:43
Torricelli, Evangelista, 4:27, 7:129–130
Tort law, 7:461
Torture, Beccaria on, 1:518
Total evidence, Carnap's requirement of, 3:662
Total social life, functions contributing to, 3:762–763
Totalitarianism
  Arendt on, 1:254
  civil society in, 9:96, 9:97
  evil and, 1:254
  as extension of freedom to master, 1:589
  as extension of self-mastery, 1:589
  ideology and, 4:574
  Il'in on, 4:577
  Jünger's approach to, 4:860
  as revolt against human conditions *vs.* revolt against injustice, 2:21–22
  Stace on, 9:201
  state and society in, 9:96
  technological dehumanizing, 1:708
  violence and, 1:254
  See also Fascism
Totalité et infini, Essai sur l'extériorité (Levinas), 5:304
Totality and Infinity (Levinas), 1:134, 5:304, 9:491
Total-unity, of the real, 3:716
Totemism, Durkheim on, 3:151–152
Touati, Charles, 4:69
Touch, **9:515–516**
  Brown on, 1:705
  as dimensionality in geometry, 1:576
  vs. muscle sense, 8:139
  Wever on, 8:139
Toulmin, Stephen
  on atheism, 1:358
  criticism of, 3:431–432
  good-reasons approach and, 3:430–431
  noncognitivism in, 3:327
  in post-positivist debates, 8:694
  on scientific law, 7:518
  utilitarianism and, 9:603
Tourneur, Zacharie, Pascal and, 7:132
Tout en Dieu (Voltaire), 9:710
Toward a Feminist Theory of the State (MacKinnon), 7:523
Toward a Perspective Realism (McGilvary), 6:75
"Toward a Philosophy of Act" (Bakhtin), 1:465
"Toward Perpetual Peace" (Kant), 8:630
"Tower of Babel, The" (Oakeshott), 7:2
Towerson, Gabriel, Locke and, 5:387
Toynbee, Arnold Joseph, **9:516–519**
  on determinism, 3:36
  on Ibn Khaldūn, 4:547
  influence of, 9:165
Trace(s)
  in deconstruction, 2:661–662, 2:717–718
  temporal
    in Derrida, 9:491–492
    entropy and, 9:469
    future *vs.* past, 9:468
Tractatus (Peter of Spain), 5:430
Tractatus adversus Reprobationis absolutae Decretum (Norris), 6:655
Tractatus de Anima et de Virtutibus (Tract on the soul and virtues) (John of La Rochelle), 4:840
Tractatus de Corpore Christi (Ockham), 9:771
Tractatus de Paupertate (Peter Aureol), 7:257
Tractatus de Praedestinatione et de Praescientia Dei et de Futuris Contingentibus (Ockham), 9:771
Tractatus de Primo Principio (Duns Scotus), 3:134, 3:136
Tractatus de Sacramento Altaris (Ockham), 9:771
Tractatus de Sphaera Mundi (Sacrobosco), 1:708
Tractatus Emmeranus, 5:433
Tractatus Logico-Philosophicus (Wittgenstein), 1:66, 1:147, 1:483, 2:41, 2:82, 2:546, 4:559, 5:129, 5:467, 5:524–526, 6:526, 9:803–808
  aesthetics in, 1:66
  analytic philosophy in, 1:147
  analytic/synthetic distinction in, 1:163
  basic statements in, 1:483
  Carnap and, 2:41
  cognition in, 2:82
  on existence, 3:498
  facts in, 5:526
  on finality of death, 4:615
  idealism in, 4:559
  linguistic necessity in, 1:148
  logic in, 5:467
  logical atomism in, 3:315–316
  logical positivism and, 3:316, 9:808
  meaning in, 5:129
  negation in, 6:526
  Philosophical Investigations and, 9:809
  on propositions, 8:737
  publication of, 9:801
  Schopenhauer and, 8:656
  on self, 8:709
  on sentences, Wisdom (John) on, 9:797
  truth in, 2:546
  Vienna Circle and, 5:524
Tractatus Primus (Burley), 1:773
Tractatus Theologico-Politicus (Spinoza), 1:670, 2:265, 4:825
  on Dutch Republic, 9:177
  on freedom of thought, 9:180
  on history of scripture, 9:178–179
  Lessing and, 5:295
  Maimonides in, 5:653
  on miracles, 6:266
  on power of citizenry, 9:181
  on social contract, 9:81
Tracy, Destutt de. *See* Destutt de Tracy, Antoine Louis Claude, Comte
Trade, Mandeville on, 5:681
Trade secrets, in engineering ethics, 3:241
Tradition
  Arkoun on, 1:284
  Cassirer on, 2:68

communitarianism and, 2:369
in Confucianism, 2:176–177, 2:442
in conservatism, 2:468–469
cultural cosmopolitanism and, 2:570
Eliot (T. S.) on, 3:186
as means of knowledge, 5:117
in medical ethics, 6:94
religious
Chinese, 2:226–227
and common life, 2:224–225
Meslier on, 6:154
See also Custom; Kabbalah
Tradition of Fathers, all-embracing normative role of, 3:673
Traditional authority, Weber (Max) on, 9:735
Traditional divine command theory, 6:164–165
Traditional logic, figures and moods, 5:496–497
Traditionalism, **9:520–521**
de Maistre and, 5:659–660
Lamennais and, 5:177
Mercier on, 6:145
vs. modernity, 6:480
Nasr and, 6:479
in national identity, 6:482
Tragedy, **9:521–525**
Aristotle on, 1:43–44, 1:188, 1:297, 1:303, 1:308, 4:176, 5:44, 9:522
Boileau on, 1:640
classical, 9:524
in conflict between rival goods, 9:74
faith and, 1:364
in Greek drama, 4:176–177
Ivanov on, 4:767
katharsis in, 1:44–45
Mendelssohn on, 6:131
moral luck in, 9:788
motivations for, 1:43–44
Nietzsche on, 1:56, 6:609–610
paradox of, 4:601, 9:561–562
Romantic, 9:524
Schiller (Friedrich) on, 8:627
as social panacea, 4:768
sophism in, 9:129
Tragedy and Philosophy (Kaufmann), 5:46
Tragic art, Boileau on, 1:640
Tragic Sense of Life in Men and Peoples (Unamo y Jugo), 1:359
Traité de botanique (Van Tieghem), 3:62–63
Traité de dynamique (Alembert), 1:105
Traité de Homme (Treatise of Man) (Descartes), 2:53, 2:729, 2:731, 5:663
Traite de la cognissance de Diue et de soi-meme (Bossuet), 1:667
Traite de la liberte (Fontenelle), 3:683
Traité de la méchanique (Coriolis), 3:233
Traité de la nature et la grâce (Malebranche), 5:664
Traité de l'esprit de l'homme (La Forge), 2:58
Traité de l'harmonie réduite à ses principes naturels (Rameau), 1:49
"Traité de l'indéfectibilité des creatures" (Desgabets), 2:757
Traité de physique (Rohault), 2:55, 8:483
Traité des passions (Descartes), 1:233
Traité des sensations (Condillac), 2:421
Traité des vertus (Jankélévitch), 4:787
Traité du vide (Pascal), 7:130
Traité Elémentaire de Chimie (Lavoisier), 5:216, 5:217
Traité philosophique (Huet), 4:470
Traité sur la tolérance à l'occasion de la mort de Jean Calas (Voltaire), 2:687, 9:713
Traités de législation civile et pénale (The Theory of Legislation) (Bentham/Dumont), 1:551
Tranquility, in Pyrrhonism, 1:195–196
Transaction(s)
Dewey on, 3:46, 3:49
legal, 7:445–446
Transactional flourishing, truth as, 3:567
Transcendence
Aquinas on, 4:107
Barth on, 4:107
Bonhoeffer on, 1:656
in conception of God, 4:107–108
as existential freedom, 1:515
Gregory of Nyssa on, 4:182
Jaspers on, 4:800, 4:802–803
Kierkegaard on, 4:107
Levinas on, 5:305
Niebuhr on, 6:605
Otto on, 4:107
Philo on, 4:107
in Plato, 7:488
Rilke on, 8:477–478
Romero on, 8:491–492
of sparse properties, 8:66
Transcendence of the Ego, The (Sartre), 7:297, 8:604
Transcendent psychology, 3:552
Transcendent realism
about universals, 6:178–179
metaphysics of, 6:171
Transcendental(s)
Duns Scotus on, 3:135–138
Scholastics on, 3:137–138
Transcendental aesthetic, 2:302, 5:14
Transcendental analytic, 2:602, 5:16, 5:16
Transcendental apperception, 5:17
Transcendental arguments
force of, 5:34
from possibility of experience, 5:19
Transcendental deduction, 5:18
Kant on, 3:307–308
Nelson on, 6:544
Transcendental dialectic, 3:54, 5:16, 5:21
Transcendental empiricism, of Deleuze, 2:694
Transcendental historical awareness, Landgrebe on, 5:185–186
Transcendental idealism, 4:555–556
Fichte on, 3:615
Kant on, 3:615, 4:553, 5:34
Transcendental ideality, of space and time, 5:15
Transcendental judgment, Kant on, 3:308
Transcendental logic
vs. Chinese Buddhism, 2:166
in Husserl, 2:81–82, 4:524–525
Kant on, 2:79, 5:16
Transcendental method
of Cohen (Hermann), 2:303
in *Critique of Pure Reason* (Kant), 4:771
in Maréchal, 5:709
Transcendental perfection, Aquinas on, 2:679
Transcendental phenomenology, 4:523, 7:277–278
in modernism, 6:317
radical recasting of, 3:638
Transcendental pragmatics, 1:226–227
Transcendental schema, 5:18
Transcendental sciences, Peirce and, 7:164
Transcendental subject of thoughts, 5:21
Transcendental subjectivity, in Santayana, 8:597, 8:602
Transcendental terms, in medieval logic, 5:443
Transcendental unity of apperception, Kant on, 3:308
Transcendentalism
American *vs.* European, 6:573–574
Apel on, 1:225–226
cogito ergo argument and, 5:679

Transcendentalism, ***continued***
- development of, 4:558–659
- Duns Scotus on, 3:135–138
- Emerson and, 3:196, 6:573
- and ethics, 3:415
- Hazlitt and, 4:249
- Merleau-Ponty and, 6:148
- Nelson (Leonard) on, 6:534
- in neo-Kantianism, 6:541
- New England, **6:572–576**
- Parker (T.) on, 7:122
- productive imagination in, 4:596
- Puritanism and, 3:169
- Scholastics on, 3:137–138
- Sufism and, 9:311
- of Thoreau, 9:450–451
- and Unitarianism, 6:574
- Weber (Alfred) on, 9:733
- *See also* Kant, Immanuel; Neo-Kantianism; New England Transcendentalism

Transcendentally necessary judgments, 5:14

Transcranial magnetic stimulation, 6:571

Transfer principle, 3:696

Transference, 3:742, 9:38
- in Freud, 8:105
- in Kohut, 8:107
- legal, 7:445

Transfiguration of the Commonplace, The (Danto), 1:66–67, 1:317, 2:627

Transfinite cardinals, definition of, 5:558

Transfinite induction
- definition of, 5:558
- Gentzen on, 5:475

Transfinite mathematics, in Hilbert, 5:470

Transfinite numbers. *See* Number(s), transfinite

Transfinite ordinal, definition of, 5:558

Transfinite recursion, definition of, 5:558

Transfinite recursion theorem, 8:838

Transformation, all change as, 5:19

Transformation rule. *See* Rule(s), of inference

Transformational grammar, logical form and, 5:509–510

Transformism, Diderot on, 3:72

"Transient and Permanent in Christianity, The" (Parker), 6:572, 7:121–122

Transient attribute, 3:709

Transition, from ethical to religious, 5:64

"Transition from Metaphysical Foundations of Natural Science to Physics" (Kant), 5:30

Transitional feminist morality, 3:606

Transitive relation, definition of, 5:555

Transitivity
- of consciousness, 2:449
- in measurement, 6:88
- of part and whole, 6:146

Translation
- adequacy of, 6:85
- belief attribution and, 1:537
- Carnap on, 2:41
- Chomsky on, 2:245
- from first-order logic to English, 3:644
- in identity theory, 7:470
- incompatible manuals of, 8:217–218
- indeterminacy of, 1:525, 8:217
- language engagement and Dao, 2:205
- meaning of, 1:545
- personal identity and, 7:222
- in philosophy of language, 7:404–405
- and sense-datum terminology, 1:486
- Tarski on, 2:548
- truth and, 7:196, 7:222

Translations from the Philosophical Writings of Gottlob Frege (Geach & Black), 8:799

Transmigration
- Avicenna on, 1:433
- Luria's doctrine of, 5:2
- in Pythagoreanism, 8:182

Transordinal laws, 6:261

Transparency, of experience, 7:191–192

Transparency thesis, 9:690

Transposition
- definition of, 5:558
- law of, 6:527, 9:287

Transrationalism, in Cournot, 2:577–578

Transterrados (the trans-landed), 5:209

Transubstantiation
- Descartes on, 2:757
- matter in, 6:3
- Rohault on, 8:483–484
- Stillingfleet on, 9:249
- theory of substance and, 9:296
- Wyclyf on, 9:851–852

Transverse waves, velocity of propagation of, 6:69

Trattato di sociologia generale (Pareto), on social origin of ideas, 9:102

Travel Diary (Keyserling), 5:58

"Travels of Peter, Paul and Zebedee, The" (Lovejoy), 5:592

Traversarius, Ambrosius, 3:89

Treachery, as thick moral concept, 6:164

Treatise concerning Religious Affections, A (Edwards), 3:167–168

Treatise concerning the Principles of Human Knowledge, A (Berkeley), 1:573, 1:576–579, 1:586, 7:615

"Treatise of Corrections" (Xunzi), 5:416

Treatise of Eternal and Immutable Morality (Cudworth), 2:611, 2:685, 3:94

Treatise of Human Nature, A (Hume), 2:199, 2:356, 3:172, 4:488–489, 4:593, 6:498–499, 7:218
- anthropology and, 7:316
- on association of ideas, 1:50
- on cause and effect, 4:637
- Enlightenment and, 3:244–246
- ethics in, 3:408
- on imagination, 4:596
- Kant and, 5:16
- on knowledge, 3:218
- passions in, 8:132
- on personal identity, 3:305, 4:612
- philosophy of sex and, 7:522
- projectivism in, 8:51
- Ramsey (Michael) and, 5:672
- skeptical arguments in, 9:55–56
- on universals, 9:598

Treatise of Man (Traité de Homme) (Descartes), 2:53, 2:729, 2:731, 5:663

Treatise of Morals and of Politics (Suchon), 9:838–839

Treatise of the Passions and the Faculties of the Soule of Man (Reynolds), 3:187

Treatise of the Three Imposters (anon.), 3:245

Treatise on Algebra, A (Peacock), 5:460

Treatise on Electricity and Magnetism (Maxwell), 3:232

"Treatise on *Esse*, The" (Ibn Gabirol), 4:546

Treatise on Freewill (Cudworth), 2:611

Treatise on Human Nature (Hume), on personal identity, 4:612

Treatise on Language (Johnson), 8:794

Treatise on Light (Huygens), 8:684

Treatise on Money, A (Keynes), 5:55

Treatise on Painting (Leonardo da Vinci), 5:281–282

Treatise on Probability, A (Keynes), 5:55

Treatise on the Emendation of the Intellect, The (Spinoza), 9:171

Treatise on the Laws of Ecclesiastical Polity (Hooker), 2:344

Treatise on the Love of God (Malebranche), 5:665
Treatise on the power of feeling beauty and on teaching it (Winckelmann), 9:790
Treatise on the Projective Properties of Figures (Poncelet), 4:59
"Treatise on the Resurrention" (Aquinas), 4:603
Treatise on the Soul (Ibn Kammunam), 4:584
Treatise on the Sphere, The (Clavius), 5:50
Treatise on the stages of yogic practice (Asanga), 5:412
Treatise on Universal Algebra with Applications, A (Whitehead), 5:461–462, 9:747
Treatise on Virginity (Gregory of Nyssa), 4:182
"The Treatise Which Reconciles Philosophy and Religious Law" (Ibn Wāqār), 4:821
Treaty of Paris (1763), 2:689
Tredennick, Hugh, on Aristotle, 3:350
Tree graph, as logical chart, 5:563
Treisman, Anne, on visual processing independence, 2:456
Treitschke, Heinrich von
- on state, function of, 7:153
- on war and peace, 7:153–154

Trembley, Abraham, 3:73
Trembling hand metaphor, 4:17
Trendelenburg, Adolf
- on Aristotle's logic, 5:65
- Fischer and, 2:302
- Kierkegaard and, 5:67
- in neo-Kantianism, 6:540
- Paulsen and, 7:148

Trennung von Staat und Kirche, Die (Separation of state and church) (Troeltsch), 9:527
Trépanier, Simon, on Empedocles, 3:212
Treschow, Niels, **9:526**
Trevor, William, 9:5
Trial, The (Kafka), 5:5–6, 6:618
Trichotomy, law of, 5:537
Tricontinentalism, 7:726
Triggering cause, 3:108–109
Triginta Sigilli (Thirty Seals) (Bruno), 1:708
Trigonometry and Double Algebra (De Morgan), 5:461
Trilling, Lionel, on American liberalism, 5:322
Trimśikākarikāvṛtti (Thirty verse treatise) (Vasubandhu), 9:651
Trinitarian theology
- arithmetical expression of, 7:612
- Boehme on, 1:623
- Bonaventure on, 1:651
- in Bulgakov's view of Sophia, 1:760
- in Christianity, 2:247–248
- Clarke and, 2:269
- Isaac of Stella on, 4:754
- non-ontological distinction in, 9:335
- of person as rational individual substance, 1:628
- Platonic hypostasis as reflection of, 7:615
- Pletho on, 7:630
- as rational individual substance, 1:628
- socinianism and, 9:100
- in Solov'ëv's all-unity, 9:124
- Stillingfleet on, 9:249
- Swedenborg and, 9:338
- Swift on, 9:340
- *See also* Trinitarianism

Trinitarianism
- Servetus on, 8:830
- Theodoric of Chartres and, 9:410
- *See also* Trinitarian theology

Trinitate, De (Servetus), 8:830
Trinitatis Erroribus, De (Servetus), 8:830
Trinity
- Abelard on, 1:6–7
- analogies for, 1:140
- arithmetical expression of, 7:612
- Arius on, 1:283
- in Augustinianism, 1:402–403
- Boehme on, 1:623
- Bonaventure on, 1:651
- in Bulgakov's view of Sophia, 1:760
- in Christianity, 2:247–248
- Clarke and, 2:269
- doctrine of
  - Christ revelation of, 1:478
  - proof for, 1:456–457
- Duns Scotus on, 3:139, 3:144
- Erasmus on, 3:338
- God's personhood and, 7:237
- Isaac of Stella on, 4:754
- Joachim of Fiore on, 4:834
- Milton on, 6:249
- monotheism and, 1:283
- Newton on, 6:591
- non-ontological distinction in, 9:335
- of person as rational individual substance, 1:628
- Philoponus on, 7:313
- Platonic hypostasis as reflection of, 7:615
- Pletho on, 7:630
- as rational individual substance, 1:628
- Richard of St. Victor on, 8:592
- Roscelin on, 8:495–496
- Saadya on, 8:586
- Servetus on, 8:830
- socinianism and, 9:100
- Solov'ëv on, 9:124
- soul as image of, 1:402–403
- Stillingfleet on, 9:249
- substance of, 1:283–284
- Swedenborg and, 9:338
- Swift on, 9:340
- Theodoric of Chartres and, 9:410
- Tolstoy on, 9:512
- Tri-Unity modeled on, 5:43
- William of Conches on, 9:768

Trinius, J. A., 2:688
Triplet state, 6:640
Tri-rūpa-hetu, 5:412, 5:413
Trismegistus, Hermes, 3:620
Tristan und Isolde (opera), 8:654
Trisvabhābanirdeśa (Teaching on the three natures) (Vasubandhu), 9:651
Tritheism, Roscelin and, 8:496
Triumph of Fame (Petrarch), 7:264
"Triumph of Infidelity, The" (Dwight), 2:690
Tri-Unity, modeled on Holy Trinity, 5:43
Trivium, 4:66, 8:772, 8:797
Trobriand Islanders, empirical phenomena statements by, 7:295–296
Troeltsch, Ernst, **9:526–528**
- in historicism, 4:390–391
- on Scheler, 8:616

Trois discours sur la condition des grands (Pascal), 7:131
Trois verites (Charron), 2:134
Trojan Women, The (Euripides), 7:152
Trolley problem, 9:448
Tronto, Joan, 3:581
Tropes
- in Pyrrhonism, 1:196
- as sparse properties, 8:67–68
- theory of, 4:32, 6:181, 9:49
- universals as, 6:181

Trotsky, Leon
- Kautsky and, 5:48
- socialist realism of, 1:68–69
- trial of, 3:44

Trubetskoi, Evgenii Nikolaevich, 3:453, **9:528–530**

Trubetskoi, Nikolai Sergeevich, **9:530–532**
Trubetskoi, Sergei Nikolaevich, 9:529, **9:532–534**
realistic metaphysics and, 9:18
Solov'ëv and, 9:126
Trudy po znakovym sistemam, Semiotika (Sign Systems Studies, Semiotics), 5:578
True
as adjective
in medieval truth theory, 2:547
in Tarski's truth theory, 2:547–548
"blind" uses of, 7:197–198
expressive use of, 7:196–197
True awareness, produced by undisturbed causes, 5:119
True belief
knowledge and, 2:277, 2:596, 3:284–285, 5:93–5:95, 5:106
meta logou, 5:93
True faith, Khomiakov on, 5:59
True friendship, Ficino on, 3:623
True Gospel of Jesus Christ Asserted, The (Chubb), 2:253, 2:684
True Gospel of Jesus Christ Vindicated, The (Chubb), 2:253, 2:684
True Intellectual System of the Universe, The (Cudworth), 1:357, 2:609–610, 2:685, 7:557
True reality, *vs.* apparent reality, 6:184
True self, 3:719
True-false evaluations, 1:532
Truman, David, 9:207
Truman, Harry, 9:397
Trust
in attributor contextualism, 2:485
in education, 7:357
as *emunah vs. pistis,* Buber on, 1:716
epistemology of testimony and, 9:403
love and, 1:68
as moral foundation, 1:459
of patients, euthanasia and, 6:94
Truth, **9:534–542**
a priori, 3:547
Leibniz on, 1:240
necessary, knowledge and, 5:96
synthetic, 1:244–245
absolute, 3:565, 8:744
action as quest for, 1:618
as adjective
in medieval truth theory, 2:547
in Tarski's truth theory, 2:547–548
as aim of memory, 6:123
Alembert on, 1:105
Aliotta on, 1:127
ambiguities of, 2:310
analytical, 1:160, 5:446
analyticity criteria of, 2:42–43
Anselm on, 1:218–219
Aristotle on, 5:399, 8:756–757, 9:534
in art, 1:28, **1:333–337,** 4:2–3
Averroes on, 1:425, 1:426
Bacon (Francis) on, 1:450–451
Bacon (Roger) on, 1:453
in basic statements, 1:483–487
and beauty, 4:3, 8:534
belief and, 1:532, 2:93–94, 5:87
"blind" uses of, 7:197–198
Bolzano on, 5:446
Boole and, 1:660
in Buddhism, 1:745, 2:167, 5:121, 6:255
Burthogge on, 1:776
vs. candidness, 5:619
Carlyle and, 2:32
Carnap on, 1:166, 2:417, 5:527
Cartwright on, 2:62
Cassirer on, 2:67–68
in Chan Buddhism, 2:166–167
characteristics of transactions in, 3:568
in Chinese philosophy, 2:201, 2:207
Clement on, 2:290
cognition and, 3:753
coherence theory of, 1:613, 2:308–313, 3:295, 4:189, 8:663, 9:536–537
Collingwood on, 2:325
common sense and, 1:510, 2:356
conceptual
Bolzano on, 1:647
as type of fact, 5:220
as condition for knowledge, 3:270–271
Condorcet's probability calculus and, 2:431
as constructive and conventional, 2:474–476
contextual approach to, 5:317
contingent
God's knowledge of, 6:321–322
Leibniz on, 3:296–297
vs. necessary, 5:662
as type of fact, 5:220
contradictions in, Shestov on, 9:11
as convention or ignorance, 1:734
conventional, 9:14
vs. absolute, in Sanlun Buddhism, 2:162
vs. ultimate, in Buddhism, 1:733–734, 1:742–743
in conventionalism, 2:474–475
as convergence of opinion, 1:500
correspondence theory of, 2:539–550, 3:317, 9:534–538, 9:543
counterfactuals and, 2:573
Couturat on, 2:581–582
creativity and, 1:545
criterion for, 2:309, 5:120
finding, 3:703
Galileo's, 4:10
critical theory and, 2:599
criticism and, Vico on, 9:671
Crusius on, 2:606
and Dao, 2:205–208
Davidson (Donald) on, 2:647–648
as decision of meaning, 1:166
deflationary theories of, 9:538–540
degrees of, 2:309, 5:109, 5:486
dependence on systems, 1:661
Descartes on, 2:365, 2:724–730, 2:735, 2:739, 2:745–749, 2:753–755, 6:190
Deussen on, 3:41
Deustua on, 3:43
Dewey on, 7:746
in Dge-lugs Mādhyamika, 1:732–733
dialtheism and, 9:540–541
disquotational theories of, 9:538–539
double
and contextual meaning, 2:209
doctrine of, 1:424–425, 1:429, 2:721
Duhem-Quine conventionalism and, 2:520
Dummett on, 3:132–133
Eckhart (Meister) on, 3:163
in education, 7:356
vs. empirical adequacy, 5:104
in empirical statements, 7:295–296
empiricists on, 3:219–220
Epicurus on, 3:288
in epistemological inquiry, 9:84
essence of, 4:292–294
in ethical hedonism, 4:257
in evident *vs.* blind judgment, 1:690–691
in exclusion theory and conventionality, 1:757
existence and, 2:596
experience and, 1:671
expressive use of, 1:691, 7:196–197
facts and, 9:534

and falsity, in Indian philosophy, **9:542–546**
in first-order model theory, 6:302–303
fixed-point approach to, 5:318
Foucault on, 3:564
Frege on, 3:727–729
functional definitions of, 4:783
Gadamer on, 4:3
Gehlen on, 4:36
geometry as standard of, 4:54
God's will and, 5:666
Grote on, 4:189
in Hegelianism, 4:287
Heidegger on, 4:293–294
Herbert of Cherbury on, 4:326
hierarchical theories of, 9:540
of historical materialism, 4:383
Hobbes on, 4:408
Horwich on, 9:539
as human and fallible, 3:703
identity theory of, 9:537
illusion and, 1:231–232
images and, 1:545
imagination and, 4:597–598
independent of world, 1:165
in Indian philosophy, 4:133, 6:471, **9:542–546**
indicative conditionals and, 2:425–426
as intrinsically valuable, 5:104
intuitionistic, 4:737–738
in James's pragmatism, 4:782–783, 4:783
in Jewish Averroism, 4:809
Kierkegaard on, 5:65
knowledge and, 5:91–92
Kripke on, 9:540
La Mothe Le Vayer and, 5:182
Lavater on, 5:214
Le Roy on, 4:23, 5:288
Leibniz on, 3:296–297, 5:262–263, 5:272–274
liar's paradox and, 5:317
liberation theology on, 5:332
linguistic
 Bolzano on, 1:647
 and Dao, 2:205–208
Locke on, 3:3, 5:377–378
logical atomism and, 9:535
of logical entailment in scientific theories, 1:501
Lotze on, 5:581
Lukács on, 5:604
Malebranche on, 5:666
many-valued logic and, 5:483
in Marxism, 5:738
mathematical
 definition of, 4:130
 as type of fact, 5:220, 5:220
in medical ethics, 6:94–95
in mental acts, 1:562
in metalanguages, 2:42
in metaphysics, 6:205
minimal theory of, 9:539
modes of access to, 1:425
Moore (George) on, 9:535
moral
 analytic, 6:358
 in constructivism, 2:471–473
 in metaethics, 6:160–161
 moral error *vs.*, 2:473
 as object of investigation, 5:38
moral constructivism and, 2:471–473
mystery and, 9:12
nature and tests of, 1:613
necessary, 5:95
 analytic truth and, 5:84
 vs. contingent, 5:662
 de Maistre on, 5:662
 Johnson (Alexander Bryan) on, 4:850
 Leibniz on, 3:296–297
 in metaphysics, 6:208–209
Neurath on, 3:317
Nicholas of Cusa on, 6:595
in Nietzsche, 6:612
noninferential, 9:23
in noninferential justification, 2:276
normativity of, 1:218–219
objective. *See* Objective truth
objective likelihood of, 5:105
objectivity as, 7:3–4
omnitemporality of, 3:693
in ontology, 7:27
Pannenberg on, 7:82
paradoxes and, 9:534
Pascal on, 7:132
Peirce on, 5:455, 7:173
perception and, 5:118, 7:179
in perception–perceived object agreement, 1:668
vs. perspective, 6:612
and phenomena statements, 7:295–296
philosophical *vs.* revealed, 6:144
Pico della Mirandola on, 7:570–571
in Plato's dialogues, 8:755
of poetry, 1:41
Popper on, 9:547
possible, 5:65, 5:547
as practical knowledge, 1:450
pragmatism and, 4:781–786, 7:744–746, 9:537
predicate, 9:539
principle of sufficient reason and, 2:585
Proclus on, 8:40
of propositions, 5:662
 Malcolm on, 5:662
 Newton on, 6:593
 stipulation, 1:165
prosentential theory of, 9:538
Protagoras on, 8:91–92
in protocol sentences, 1:484–487
as quasi-object in Ramsey and Moore's truth theory, 2:547
realist view of, 1:132
as relational and perspectival, 3:564
in reliabilism, 6:498
religion as symbol of, 4:550–551
religious, Oman on, 7:15
Rescher on, 8:439
revelation and, 1:629, 8:40, 8:452
revision approach to, 5:318
Rorty on, 8:494–495
Ruskin on, 8:534
Russell on, 9:535
Saint-Hyacinthe on, 8:588
Santayana on, 8:602
Scholastics on, 3:137
in science, 2:475, 5:528, 9:547
of science of private, 5:528
semantic paradoxes and, 5:522
semantic theory of, 7:196, 9:537–538
sensation and, 1:532
sentential necessity *vs.* contingency in, 1:561
in Shin Buddhism, 9:14
in simultaneity and conventionalism, 2:525
skeptics on, 3:288
as social construct, 9:78, 9:85
solipsism and, 9:116
sophists on, 9:131
in Stoic logic, 5:404
subjective, Unamuno on, 9:568
subjective probability of, 1:495, 9:547
as subjectivity, 5:64
syllogisms and, 1:450
Tagore on, 9:364
Tarski on, 2:387, 2:549, 5:474, 8:196, 9:369, 9:537–538
Thomasius on, 9:442
and truthlikeness, 9:547
Tschirnhaus on, 9:549
types of, 5:220, 5:233

Truth, *continued*
Ulrich of Strasbourg on, 9:565
Unamuno on, 9:568–569
universal
Cheng Yi on, 2:145
Plato on, 9:591
value of, 5:104
in verificationist antirealism, 8:689
by virtue of form, 1:660
Williams (Bernard) on, 9:788
Wittgenstein on, 9:535
Wolf on, 7:27
Wollaston on, 9:833–834
Truth (Antiphon), 1:223
"Truth" (Strawson), 7:196, 9:264
Truth and Contradictions (Collingwood), 2:325, 2:328
Truth and Meaning (Davidson), 8:808
Truth and Meaning: Essays in Semantics (Evans and McDowell), 3:459
Truth and Method (Gadamer), 4:1–2, 7:411
"Truth and Probability" (Ramsey), 8:29
Truth and Truthfulness (Williams, B.), 9:788
"Truth by Convention" (Quine), 1:150, 1:167, 2:671
Truth conduciveness, and epistemic justification, 5:85
Truth memory, personal identity and, 7:222
Truth of Artwork, The (Gadamer), 4:3
Truth of the Sciences, The (La vérité des sciences contre les sceptiques ou pyrrhoniens) (Mersenne), 2:725
Truth, Probability, and Paradox (Mackie), 5:638
Truth theory
ideal limit, mind-dependence in, 6:173
of meaning, verifiability principle and, 9:665
Truth trees, 3:657
Truth-conditions, 6:84–85
in analytic statements, 1:164
for attributor contextualism, 2:485
Chrysippus on, 2:251
for conditional logic, 5:487
of conventional implicature, 6:651–652
in counterfactual conditionals, 2:427–429
counterfactuals and, 2:574
for disjunction, 5:489
in epistemic contextualism, 3:275
experience and, 9:665–666
in Gricean pragmatics, 7:739
in impossible worlds, 5:488
in medieval logic, 2:541
psychological roles and, 6:652
in religious analogy, 1:143
in semantics, 6:649
Truthfulness
vs. candidness, 5:619
in medical ethics, 6:94–95
Truth-functions
Boole on, 5:450
classical logic and, 5:485
definition of, 5:558
Gödel on, 5:473
many-valued logic and, 5:483–485
Peirce on, 5:454
Russell on, 5:467
theory of, 9:806–807
Whitehead on, 5:467
Truthlikeness, **9:546–549**
Truthmaker gaps, 5:111
Truthmakers
borderline cases and, 9:625
in metaphysics, 6:211
Truth-predicate, liar paradox and, 5:149
Truth-tables, 3:644, 5:559
and computability, 2:388
method of, 9:807
Post on, 5:467
Truth-theoretic semantics, Evans on, 3:459
Truth-tracking, good biases allowing, 3:576
Truth-value
in attributor contextualism, 2:484
Church on, 5:476
in conditionals, 2:424
conversational implicature and, 2:525
of counterfactuals in causality, 2:100
definition of, 5:559
facts and, 2:278
Frege on, 3:728
gaps
supervaluationists and, 5:110
treatments of, 5:149
knowledge and, 2:309
in many-valued logics, 5:692–693
Peirce on, 5:453
persistence and, 7:211
of proposition, 5:100
of propositional symbols, 3:643–644
realism in, 8:276
Russell on, 5:467
of sentences, 3:642, 3:728
in subject contextualism, 2:483
in truth-function logic, 1:660
vagueness and, 9:624
Whitehead on, 5:467
T-schemata, 8:808
Tschirnhaus, Ehrenfried Walter von, 5:251, **9:549–550** 9:826
T-sentences, 2:647
Tsong-kha-pa
in Dge-lugs philosophy, 1:732–733
in Mādhyamika doctrine, 1:744–745
Tsuda Masamichi, 6:623
Tyson, I. F., 7:149–150
Tu quoque, 3:547–548
Tu Wei-Ming, 5:359
Tucker, Abraham
on altruism and self-interest, 3:172
Gay and, 4:34
on human nature, 3:172
Tetens and, 9:403
utilitarianism and, 9:605
Tucker, Benjamin, 1:178
Tucker, Ellen Louisa, 3:195
Tuckney, Anthony, 9:745
Tullock, Gordon, 7:351
Tung Chung-Shu. *See* Dong Zhongshu
Turanic peoples, Eurasianism and, 3:453–454
Turgenev, Ivan, 6:617
Turgot, Anne Robert Jacques, Baron de L'Aulne, **9:550–551**
Encyclopédie and, 3:223–224
on experience, 9:248
on Maupertuis's solitary man, 8:784
and Stewart, 9:247
Turing, Alan M., 4:672, **9:552–553**
artificial life and, 1:348
on computability, 5:476–478
computational approach derived from, 3:675
on computing, 5:477
and computing machines, 2:375–376, 2:399, 2:403
on effective calculability, 2:375
on machine intelligence, 5:632–635
on repeat rate, 4:675
on universal programmable computer, 5:474
Turing computability, 2:376, 5:559
Church's thesis and, 2:254
lambda definability and, 2:254
Turing machine, 5:632, 9:552
calculability on, 5:477
in cognitive science, 2:299
in computability theory, 2:375–376

computing machines and, 2:399, 2:403–408
definition of, 5:559
nondeterministic polynominal-time computability and, 2:388
normal form theorem and, 2:380
problem unsolvability and, 2:385
quantum computing and, 2:407
Turing test, 2:394, 5:633–635, 9:553
See also Machine intelligence
Turing-computable, definition of, 5:559
Turning movement, in thought, 4:289
Turrell, James, 3:256
Tusculanae Disputationes (Cicero), 2:258
Tuskegee Syphilis Study, 8:667
Tversky, A., on decision theory, 2:656
Twardowski, Kazimierz, **9:553–555**
and Ingarden, 4:682
Leśniewski and, 5:290, 5:292
Łukasiewicz and, 5:605
20th century
awareness of death in, 2:651
beauty in, 1:514–515
continental philosophy and, 2:488–489
Frege and, 8:799
materialism in, 6:11–13
optimism/pessimism in, 7:252–253
20th Century Encyclopedia of Catholicism, Faith article, 3:530
Twersky, Isadore, 5:654
Twilight of the Idols (Nietzsche), 6:612
Twin Earth analogy, 3:760, 5:88, 7:406–408, 9:45
"Two Concepts of Rules" (Rawls), 3:440
"Two Dogmas of Empiricism" (Quine), 1:150, 1:167, 5:83, 9:346, 9:350, 9:669
Two New Sciences (Galileo), 4:9, 4:11, 4:12, 8:683
Two Sources of Morality and Religion, The (Bergson), 1:570, 1:573
Two Treatises (Digby), 8:777
Two Treatises of Government (Locke), 3:636, 5:388–390, 5:395
Essays on the Law of Nature and, 5:387
Filmer and, 9:81
influence of, 5:376
writing and publication of, 5:375–376
"Two wrongs" technique, 3:547–548
Two-aspect view, 5:34
Twofold truth, 9:14
Two-object view, 5:34
Two-slit experiment, 8:202–205, 8:206
Tyché. *See* Moira/Tyché/Ananké
Tychism, Peirce on, 7:172
Tydeman, Daniel, 9:176
Tye, Michael, 4:591, 7:190–191
Tylor, E. B., Durkheim and, 3:151
Tyndall, John
agnosticism of, 1:371
on atheism, 1:371
Tynianov, Jurii, Lotman and, 5:578
Type(s)
definition of, 5:559
Russell on. *See also* Type theory
Schröder on, 5:462
Type I error probability, in Neyman-Pearsonite theory, 3:665
Type physicalism, 3:759, 7:553–555
Type theory, **9:555–560**
art in, 1:316
Church (Alonzo) on, 9:558–559
Chwistek and, 2:255
constructed *vs.* discovered syntactical functions, 2:77
definition of, 5:558, 9:555
Gentzen on, 9:558
in illative combinatory logic, 2:339
in intuitionistic logic, 4:742
Leśniewski on, 9:353
number and, 6:672–673
predicate restriction by, 6:179
Ramsey on, 5:468, 9:555–558
Russell (Betrand) and, 2:76–77, 2:256, 2:544, 5:467, 8:547–548, 9:556–558
Type-identity theory, 8:84
Types of Men (Spranger), 9:198
Type-token distinction
in elimination of universals, 6:179
in nominalism, 9:600
Type-type identity theories, 7:553
Typical ambiguity. *See* Systematic ambiguity
Typicality, 1:633–635
Tyranny, in Aristotle, 1:268
Tyrell, G. N. M., 4:603
Tyrrell, James
on Cumberland, 2:614
Locke and, 5:375–376, 5:387
Tzara, Tristan, poetry of, 1:298

U

Über Annahmen ("On Assumptions") (Meinong), 6:116, 8:803
Über Bedetung und Aufgabe der Erkenntnistheorie (Zeller), 6:540
Über Begriff und Form der Philosophie (Riehl), 8:467
"Über Begriff und Gegenstand" (Frege), 3:726
"Über das Entstehen der grammtischen Formen und ihren Eisfluss auf die Ideenentwickelung" (Humboldt), 8:794
Über das Fundament der Erkenntnis" (Schlick), 1:484
Über das Sehn und die Farben (Schopenhauer), 8:648
Über das Verhältniss der bildenden künste zu der Natur (Schelling), 8:620
"Über das Verhaltniss der empirischen Psychologie zur Metaphysik" (Fries), 3:751
"Über Definitionsbereiche von Funktionen" (Brouwer), 1:701
Über den individuellen Beweis für die Freiheit des Willens (Liebmann), 5:344–345
Über den objektiven Anblick (Liebmann), 5:344
Über den Standort der Industrien (Weber, A.), 9:732
Über den wahren Begriff der Naturphilosophie; Darstellung meines Systems der Philosophie (Schelling), 8:619
Über den Willen in der Natur (Schopenhauer), 7:86, 8:648
Über die allgemeine spekulativische Philosophie (On general speculative philosophy) (Tetens), 9:404
"Über die Definition der Masse" (Mach), mass defined in, 6:4
Über die Erhaltung der kraft (Helmholtz), 4:303
"Über die Freiheit des Willens" (Schopenhauer), 8:648
"Über die Grundlage der Moral" (Schopenhauer), 8:648
"Über die Grundlagen der Geometrie" (Frege), 3:727
Über die Kawi-Sprache auf der Insel Jawa (Humboldt), 8:793
Über die Lehre des Spinoza in Briefen an den Herrn Moses Mendelssohn (Jacobi), 1:11, 5:296, 7:99
"Über die teutschen Beurtheilungen der französischen Revolution" (Reinhold), 8:334
"Über die Verschiedenheit des menschlichen Sprachbaues und ihren Einflussz auf die geistige Entwickelung des Menschengeschlechts" (Humboldt), 8:793

Über die vierfache Wurzel des Satzes vom zureichen Grunde (On the Fourfold Root of the Principle of Sufficent Reason) (Schopenhauer), 8:648
"Über die Wirklichkeit der Dinge ausser Gott" (On the Reality of Things outside God) (Lessing), 5:296
Über eine Entdeckung nach der alle neue kritik der reinen Vernunft durch eine ältere entbehrlich gemacht werden soll (Kant), 3:161–162
Über Entwicklungspsychologie, ihre historische und sachliche Notwendigkeit (Krueger), 5:156
"Über formal unentscheidbare Sätze der Principia Mathematica and verwandter Systeme I" (Gödel), 5:473
Über Gegenstandstheorie (Meinong), 8:804
"Über Gestaltqualitäten" (Ehrenfels), 3:176
"Über Möglichkeiten im Relativkalkül" (Löwenheim), 5:471
"Über Sinn und Bedeutung" (Frege), 3:726–728, 5:464, 8:799–801
Über Verfassungswesen; Die indirekte Steuer und die Lage der arbeitende klassen (Lassalle), 5:203
Überweg, Friedrich, on laws of thought, 5:231
Überwindung des wissenschaftlichen Materialismus, Die ("The conquest of scientific materialism") (Ostwald), 3:233
Udayana, 1:383, 4:627
Udayanācārya, universals and causation in, 9:582
Uddyotakara, 5:414
Ueber... *See* Über...
Uelsmann, Jerry, 9:690
Uexküll, 7:320
Ugliness, 8:3, **9:561–564**
Uisang, and Buddhist schools in Korea, 5:135
Ukrainian philosophy, 9:63
Ulam, Stanislaw
- on computing machine development, 2:406
- on measurable cardinals, 8:839–840

Ulpian, on law, 7:420
Ulrich (Engelbert) of Strasbourg, **9:565**
Ultimate concern, in Daoism, 2:205–206
Ultimate personality, in Indian philosophy, 5:326
"Ultimate Principles and Ethical Egoism" (Medlin), 3:443
Ultimate reality
- beyond consciousness, 5:143
- in Buddhism, 2:220–221
- in Confucianism, 2:220
- in Daoism, 2:220–221
- McTaggart on, 6:77

Ultimatum game, 7:354
Ultraempiricism, in medieval philosophy, 6:105
Ultramontanism
- Bonald on, 1:648
- de Maistre and, 5:659–660
- Lamennais and, 5:176–177

Ultramundane being, Leibniz on, 2:551
Ultramundane cause, in *kalām* argument on God's existence, 2:556
Ultranationalism, Miki and, 6:216
Umayyad Empire, John of Damascus and, 4:836
Umgreifende, das (encompassing), Jaspers on, 4:802
Umma (community), in Arab culture, 5:202
Umwelt (Buytendijk), 7:320
Unamism, African philosophy and, 1:85
Unamuno y Jugo, Miguel de, **9:565–569**
- on common consent for God's existence, 2:352–353
- on death, 2:652
- on eternal return doctrine, 3:355
- existentialism and, 3:505
- Generation of 98 and, 5:208
- on God, 1:359

Unanticipated consequences, of activities, 3:765
Unaufhörliche, Das (Hindemith), 1:547
Unavowable Community, The (Blanchot), 1:612
Unbeautiful, 9:563
Unbehagen in der Kultur, Das (Freud), 7:252
Unbelief. *See* Atheism; Disbelief
Unbiased estimators, 3:661
Unboundedness, in compositionality, 2:371
Uncertainty
- absolute, in Bohmian mechanics, 1:634
- and belief, 1:535
- Brouwer on, 1:701
- in decision theory, 2:656, 2:659–660
- Fisher's third measure of, 3:666
- frequentist or subjective types of, 3:766
- modeling decisions under, 8:613
- probability and, 8:29
- in quantum theory, 1:539–542, 1:634, 1:638
- and world, 3:566
- *See also* Uncertainty principle

Uncertainty principle
- and correspondence of theory and data, 1:638
- and Lorenz invariance, 1:539
- matter in, 6:63
- in quantum theory, 1:539, 1:634
- wave function and, 7:477

Unconditioned imperative, Kant on, 3:154
Unconscious, **9:570–575**
- Bergson on, 1:564–565
- concept of, future of, 9:573–574
- desire in, 8:111
- determinism and, 3:17
- floodgates of, unlocking, 3:741
- Freud on, 3:105, 8:145–146, 8:722, 9:571–573
- Herbart on, 7:375–376
- Maritain on, 5:713
- Merleau-Ponty on, 6:150
- personal, Jung on, 4:856–857
- pessimism and, 7:250
- pre-Freudian history of, 3:736
- representations of, 9:574
- Sartre on, 8:608–610
- Schopenhauer on, 8:652
- semanalysis on, 5:152

Unconscious Memory (Butler, Samuel), 1:785
Unconscious processes
- cognitive psychology on, 3:737
- in perceptual consciousness, 7:186–188, 7:192

Undecidability
- in computability theory, 2:373, 2:382, 2:404
- computationalism and, 2:395
- in Pyrrhonism, 1:196
- Tarski on, 5:480, 9:370

Undecidable, The (Turing), 2:404
Undecidable Theories (Tarski), 9:370
Undenkbare, das (unthinkable), God as, Jaspers on, 4:802
Underdetermination thesis, Duheim-Quine thesis, **9:575–578**
Understanding
- *a priori* judgments and, 8:660
- in analogy of illumination, 4:580
- Anselm on, 1:215
- Astell on, 1:356
- Augustine on, 1:391–392, 1:402
- Balguy on, 1:475
- belief and, 1:391–392, 5:87

body in, 6:148
categories of
Kant on, 3:307–308
and objectivity, 1:519
in Chinese room argument, 2:240
Coleridge on, 2:317
common sense and, 2:355
compulsion from, 9:813
in computationalism, 2:393
conversational implicature and, 2:525
created by acquaintance, 5:97
in dialectical method, 4:271–272
in education, 7:356–357
Edwards (Jonathan) on, 3:167–168
in experience, 6:74
faith and, 1:402
Gadamer on, 4:2
Gassendi on, 4:29
Hegel on, 4:266, 4:271–272
Heidegger on, 4:2
higher, Dilthey on, 3:83
history and, Heidegger on, 4:2
in humans *vs.* animals, 1:105
Hume on, 4:493–497, 4:596. *See also Enquiry concerning Human Understanding, An* (Hume)
in identity, 6:112
of I-in-itself, 1:519
illumination and, 4:579–580
imagination and, 4:596, 5:18, 8:619–620
improvement of, 1:356
intellect as, 1:594
Kant on, 3:80, 3:307–308, 5:18
Laromiguière on, 5:201
and law, 9:137
Leibniz on, 2:561, 3:736, 4:565, 4:692–693, 5:254–256
limits of, Meier on, 6:112
Locke on, 1:50, 5:377, 8:778. *See also Essay concerning Human Understanding* (Locke)
materialism and, 6:16
morality as perception of, 8:2
of music, 6:437
Plato on, 1:393–394
and possible worlds, 5:513
presupposing and, 7:765–766
principles of
in metaphysics, 6:203
proving, 5:19
pure concepts of, 5:15–21
Rozanov on, 8:524
Schutz on, 8:665
of self
autonomy and, 5:731
Confucius on, 2:219
of sentences, 2:371, 7:406, 9:664–665
Shpet on, 9:19
Spinoza on, 3:12–13
Spranger on, 9:198
of time, 1:567–568
valid argument and, 5:513
vision and, 1:393–394
of what cannot be said, 9:804
of words, 5:120, 9:664–665
See also Verstehen (understanding)
Understanding *(Verstehen). See Verstehen* (understanding)
Understanding Whitehead (Lowe), 9:751
Undetermined choice, ultimacy of, 5:62
Undistributed middle fallacy, 3:539, 5:543
Undistributed term, 3:540
Undue harm, as injustice, 4:866–867
Unfree action, and strict akratic action, 9:729–731
Unger, Peter
on dualism, 3:117
on priority of knowledge, 5:87–88
Unger, Roberto, Dworkin and, 3:157
Ungrund, Boehme on, 7:96
Unhappy consciousness, 4:263
Unification account of explanation, 3:523–524
Unified field theory
Einstein and, 3:178, 3:181
Weyl and, 9:741
Unified science
as calculus, 1:685
Carnap on, 2:38–45
Cartesianism and, 2:53–61
Cartwright on, 2:62
and chemistry's reduction to physics, 2:142–143
logical positivism and, 5:525, 5:528
and speculative suprascience, 1:697
systems approach to, 1:594
as theoretic *vs.* praxis, 2:217
Zhu Xi and, 2:217
Uniform connection within the manifold, principle, 3:557
Uniform motion, laws of, 6:9
Uniform objects, 9:749
Uniformitarianism, 2:638–640, 3:487, 3:611
Uniformity
Lalande on, 5:172–173
of nature
Mill (John Stuart) on, 6:224, 6:245
in Ockham's rule of induction, 9:778
Unigenitus (papal bull), 4:790
Unintelligibility
of intentional acts, 7:292–293
of metaphysical theology, 1:365–366
Union of sets (sum of sets), definition of, 5:559
Unique evolution, 3:30–34
Unique parsing lemma, 3:647
Unique parsing of terms, 3:647–648
Uniqueness
law of, Petzoldt on, 7:268
of representation, measurement models and, 6:88
Unit set, definition of, 5:559
"Unitarian Christianity" (Channing), 2:130
Unitarianism
Channing and, 2:130–131
deism and, 2:681, 2:690–691
Emerson and, 3:194–195
Priestley and, 8:5–6
rise of, in New England, 3:169
socinianism and, 9:99–100
transcendentalist departure from, 6:574
Unitary consciousness, in *Critique of Pure Reason,* 5:17
Unitate Intellectus, De (Aquinas), 4:758
United Nations, 7:152, 7:155
United Shilla, 5:135
United States
absolute idealism in, 4:558
aesthetics in, history of, 1:63–68
affirmative action in, 1:82
Arendt on, 1:253
concept of ideas in, 4:566
critical legal studies in, 7:463
deism in, 2:689–691
democracy of, as redemptive society, 4:774
ethical naturalism in, 3:423–425
Hegelianism in, 4:286
hermeneutics in, 4:2
historicism in, 4:392
Latin American philosophy and, 5:211–212
legal philosophy in, 7:427
pragmatism in, 7:741
Price and, 8:1
property in, 8:70
psychology in, 8:141
science policy in, 8:674–675
Sufism and, 9:311
Veblen on, 9:655–656
United States v. Holmes, 6:97

Unity(ies)
- Absolute as all-one, 9:124
- in aesthetic experience, 1:33, 1:46
- in ancient mythology, 7:759–760
- of apperception, 5:21
- Aristotle on, 6:186
- atomism and, 1:385
- Augustine on, 1:46
- in beauty, 9:790
- in being, 6:187
- of consciousness
  - Aquinas and, 9:28
  - dualism and, 3:118–120
- de Maistre on, 5:660
- and disunity, in science, **9:578–580**
- education and, 7:374
- of existents, 6:120
- Fichte on, 7:374
- Gentile on "pure act" and, 9:197
- of God, 4:110, 4:812–813
- of the Good, 4:151, 8:41–42
- of intellect, Averroes on, 4:758
- interpretation and, 1:311
- Martinetti on, 5:728
- microcosm and, 5:639
- in monadology, 6:324–325
- in monism, 6:327
- Mullā Ṣadrā on, 6:418
- Muqammiṣ on, 6:432
- of nation, 6:481
- of nature, 7:652
- objective, in time, 9:489
- of objects, in Natorp, 6:491
- of opposites
  - Heraclitus on, 4:316–317
  - Zhuangzi on, 9:881
- in organismic biology, 7:37
- of perception, neuroscience and, 6:567
- of person, personal identity and, 7:214–215, 7:218–220, 7:228
- Plato on, 6:185, 8:43
- Plotinus on, 6:187, 6:547
- Proclus on, 8:41–42
- psychological, ecclesiastical endorsement of, 9:444
- in Pythagoreanism, 5:639
- of reality, 7:761–762
- Rehmke on, 8:303
- in science, 1:423–424, 9:197
- of self, 1:109–110
- and struggle of opposites, law of, 3:62
- Tagore on, 9:364
- Theodoric of Chartres on, 9:410
- in Tiantai Buddhism, 2:163
- of Trinity, in Christianity, 2:248
- unconscious need for, 9:573
- Whitehead on, 9:749
- Winckelmann on, 9:790
- Wolff on, 9:827

Unity of Philosophical Experience (Gilson), 4:92

Unity of Science, The (Carnap), 1:484, 5:525

Universae Christianae Theologiae Elementa (Genovesi), 4:48

Universal affirmative
- in Ockham's nominalism, 9:778
- simple conversion of, 3:538

Universal belief, 2:349–350
- common consent arguments for God's existence and, 2:345–346

Universal Calculus (Calculus Iniversalis) (Leibniz), 5:252, 5:273

Universal causality, principle of, 1:243

Universal closure, definition of, 5:537

Universal college, in Comenius, 2:341

"Universal computing machine," Turing on, 5:477–478

Universal consciousness in I-other relationships, 1:465

Universal Declaration of Human Rights (UN), on equality, 3:330

Universal determinism, 3:24

Universal energy, unity of, 3:607

Universal equality, as ideal, 3:330–334

Universal formula, 3:658

Universal generalization, rule of, definition of, 5:559

Universal grammar, 8:790–791
- Chomsky on, 2:244, 2:423, 3:483
- Humboldt on, 8:794
- Husserl on, 8:803
- language-acquisition device as, 4:694
- Mauthner on, 8:802

Universal gravitation. *See* Gravitation, universal

Universal harmony, Leibniz on, 5:257, 5:260–263, 5:271

Universal history, 3:35, 5:59, 7:389, 8:459–460
- Kant on, 6:514, 7:388–389
- Schiller (Friedrich) on, 8:626

Universal History of Philosophy (Deussen), 3:41

Universal hylomorphism, 8:458

Universal hypothesis, probability of, 5:56

Universal idealism, as speculative egoism, 4:770–771

Universal indeterminism, human freedom as, 4:784–785

Universal instantiation, rule of, definition of, 5:559

Universal judgments, 7:244

Universal kinship, attainment of, 3:559

Universal knowledge, in Comenius, 2:341

Universal language, 1:342
- Couturat on, 2:582
- Leibniz on, 5:262, 5:441, 5:535
- of science, Condorcet on, 2:432

Universal law, as Roman law replacement, 1:622

Universal love, in Mohism, 6:417

Universal mathematics, Leibniz on, 5:535

Universal methodic doubt, Mercier on, 6:145

Universal Mind, Shelley on, 9:9

Universal mixture, Anaxagoras on, 1:181–182

Universal Postal Union, 7:155

Universal prescriptions, moral principles as, 5:37

Universal properties in Indian philosophy, 4:133, 4:627, 4:633, **9:580–587**

Universal proposition(s)
- Boole on, 5:449
- definition of, 5:553
- Johnson (Alexander Bryan) on, 4:849
- *vs.* singular propositions, Ockham on, 9:778
- terms in, 5:498

Universal quantifier(s), 3:648
- definition of, 5:559
- order of, 3:540
- in Tarski's truth theory, 2:548

Universal religion, Comte on, 2:410

Universal responsiveness, of Russian people, Dostoevsky on, 3:101

Universal Right (Diritto Universale) (Vico), 9:673–674

Universal set, definition of, 5:559

Universal standards, conservatism and, 2:466

Universal tension, Posidonius on, 3:686

Universal Treatise (Nicolas of Autrecourt). *See Exigit Ordo Executionis* (Nicolas of Autrecourt)

Universal truth, Plato on, 9:591

Universal values, 3:420, 8:459

Universal-blockers, 9:584

Universal-hood, 9:584

Universalism, 2:568, 3:348, 9:158–159

Universalistic utilitarianism, 9:604–605

Universality
- *vs.* culture, 8:154
- law of, 6:528

Universalizability
- conscience and, 2:447–448
- Kant on, 3:385–386, 3:411–412
- Kantian ethicists and, 5:36–37
- Williams (Bernard) on, 9:787

Universals
- *a priori* knowledge of, 9:592
- Abelard on, 1:4–5, 3:290, 8:763–764, 9:599
- abstract
  - Croce on, 2:602
  - qualities as, 1:662
- as abstractions, 1:627, 9:595
  - *vs.* generalities, Berkeley on, 1:581–582
- Alexander of Aphrodisias on, 3:147
- Anselm on, 1:216
- antirealism and, 6:101
- *Apoha* (exclusion) as, 9:585–586
- apprehension of, 9:592
- Aquinas on, 3:289, 6:189, 9:425, 9:593
- Aristotle on, 2:15, 3:147, 3:286, 6:185, 9:586–587, 9:591–593
- Armstrong on, 1:287, 6:179–180, 9:585
- art as imitation of, 1:44
- Augustine on, 3:289, 9:593
- Avicenna on, 1:432–433, 3:147
- Berkeley on, 1:595–598, 3:302
- Boethius on, 1:626, 3:289, 8:762
- Bradley on, 3:310
- in Buddhism, 1:754–757, 5:119, 9:582–587
- Buridan on, 1:769
- Burley on, 1:773
- categorical imperative and, 2:69–72, 2:447
- causality and, 9:582–583
- Chinese language and, 2:210–211
- *vs.* common properties, 9:584
- in conceptualism, 3:289–290, 6:174–176, 7:24, 9:594–599
  - *vs.* realism, 9:588
- conceptualist theories of, 3:290
- Cudworth on, 2:611
- definition of, 9:587–588
- domains of, intersecting, 9:584
- Duns Scotus on, 3:147, 9:593
- Eleatic principle for, 6:180
- existence of, 3:498–499, 9:599–600
- and experience, 9:587–588, 9:601
- in extensionalism, 6:176–178
- as extramental object, 1:627
- formation of, Hume on, 9:598
- Forms and, 6:590–591, 7:596, 9:586
- Garland the Computist on, 6:101–102
- Gauge Theory on, 4:31–33
- Giles of Rome on, 4:89
- as God, Carus (Carl) on, 2:63
- Gongsun Long on, 4:148
- Henry of Harclay on, 4:315
- historical survey of, **9:587–603**
- Hobbes on, 4:407, 9:599
- horizontal, 9:582
- Hume on, 3:303–304, 9:598–599
- idealism about, conceptualism as, 6:176
- and Ideas, 1:591, 9:586
- in Indian philosophy, **9:580–587**
- intensional account of, 6:177
- internal relations and, 8:340–341
- Islamic philosophy on, 3:320
- John of Salisbury on, 4:843
- in judgment, 1:677
- knowledge of
  - Aristotle on, 9:592–593
  - Plato on, 9:591
- Locke on, 9:594–596
- in logic, Wolff on, 9:827
- Marsilius of Inghen on, 5:720–721
- in mathematical study, Sanches on, 8:595
- in medieval philosophy, 3:289–291, 6:101–102, 6:188, 9:593
- in metaphysics, 6:173–174
- moral prescriptions as, 2:447
- naturalism and, 6:494
- nominalism and, 1:769, 3:289–291, 6:174–175, 7:24, 9:585–586, 9:599–600
- nonrealism and, 6:174–178
- number and, 6:670
- in Nyāya-Vaiśeka realism, 9:582–584
- objectivity of, 8:302
- Ockham on, 1:773, 3:290–291, 9:283, 9:599, 9:773
- Peirce on, 7:166
- perceptibility of, 9:582–585, 9:592–593
- Photios on, 1:788
- Platonic, 2:15, 4:563–564, 9:588–591
- Porphyry on, 1:627, 3:289
- prenatal knowledge of, 9:592
- properties as, 7:24–25, 9:587
- realism and, 1:287, 3:289–290, 6:174–181, 7:24–25, 9:582–584, 9:587–594, 9:773
- reduction to classes, 6:176–178
- Rehmke on, 8:302–303
- representation of, subjects and predicates in, 9:288
- resemblance and, 6:178, 9:586, 9:598–602
- restriction of God's knowledge to, in Gersonides, 4:68
- Roscelin on, 6:101–102, 8:496
- Russell on, 9:585, 9:600–601
- self as special case of, 1:755
- self-predicating, 6:179
- semantics of, 8:762–764, 9:602
- Siger of Brabant on, 9:28
- Solov'ëv on, 9:122–123
- as species and genera, 1:627
- Strawson on, 6:198
- Suárez on, 9:283
- theory of, properties and, 8:67–68
- in theory of Forms, 9:590–591
- in thought and perception, 1:613, 9:601
- *vs.* titular properties, 9:584
- Treschow on, 9:526
- as trope class, 6:181
- Venn on, 5:451
- vertical, 9:582
- William of Champeaux on, 9:767
- words and, 8:764, 9:580–583
- word-types as, 6:175
- Wyclyf on, 9:851

Universe
- as absolute, 2:563–564
- adaptiveness in, 9:380
- anthropic principle and, **1:219–222**
- in Aristotelian metaphysics, 6:186
- in Aristotelian physics, 9:154
- asymmetry of, temporal, 9:467–470
- atheism on, 1:371–374
- Bernard of Tours on, 1:592
- big-bang models of, 4:63
- body of, 5:640
- in Cartesian physics, 9:154–155
- in Christian theology, William of Conches on, 9:768
- closed physical domain of, 2:89–93
- as closed *vs.* open system, 1:634
- cognitive worth and, 2:563–564
- coherence theory of truth and, 2:308
- in Confucianism, 2:153
- consciousness of, 5:639
- conservation of, 2:585–589
- in Copenhagen interpretation, 2:530
- cosmology of, 2:557–558, 2:565–566
  - in ancient philosophy, 2:571

Universe, *continued*
creation of, 2:585–589
light in, Grosseteste on, 4:186
Creighton on, 2:592
Descartes on, 2:750–751
entropy in, 7:540
Erigena on, 7:95
external, meaning of, 4:848
finitude of, 1:225
geometry of, 4:62–63
God and, 2:587
Leibniz on, 2:551–553
Gödel on, 4:118–119
ground of, Laozi on, 5:194
in Huayan Buddhism, 2:165
inclusivity of, and superultimate "why," 9:760
inflationary theory of, 2:566
in Israeli, 4:765
in *kalām* argument on God's existence, 2:555
laws of, syntax of scientific laws and, 7:518
Leibniz on, 2:551–553
Losskii on, 5:577
loveless, 1:373–374
Lu Xiangshan on, 5:618
Manichaean view of, 9:380
men as citizens of, Krause on, 5:148
as multiplicity via black holes, 1:608
mystery of, atheism and, 1:371–372
nature of
existentialists on, 3:501
Newton on, 7:558
Peirce on, 7:171, 7:174
in neo-Confucianism, 2:157
neural physiology in, 1:369
Nicholas of Cusa on, 6:596–597
number as basis of, 9:6
in ontology of classical mechanics, 2:281
order of, 5:640
origins of, 2:565
oscillating model of, *kalām* argument on God's existence and, 2:555
as passing phase of consciousness, 4:745
as process, Mead on, 6:80
Ptolemaic, 5:50
purpose of, glory of God as, 9:378
in Pythagoreanism, 8:182
as quantum creation event, 2:555
rationality of, Jeans on, 4:804
Robinet on, 8:482
in scientific cosmology, 2:557
stability of, 1:220–221
symmetry of, spatial, 9:468
in teleological argument for existence of God, 9:378–379
temporal beginning of, 2:588
Theophrastus on, 9:412
as unity in sympathy with itself, 7:638–639
value of, McTaggart on, 6:79
Yamaga Sokō on, 9:859
See also Cosmogony; Cosmology
Universe of discourse, 3:496
Boole on, 1:660, 5:450
definition of, 5:559
Universes, multiple, 1:221–222
Universes (Leslie), 1:220
University, Newman (John Henry) on, 6:582
University of Constantinople, in Byzantine thought, 1:787
University of London, Bentham contributions to, 1:551
University of Munich, appointment of Baader, 1:439
University of Paris
Buridan at, 1:767
and *logica modernorum,* development of, 5:429
Univocal, definition of, 5:559
Univocation, Abelard on, 5:429
Univocative relations, in Cajetan theory of analogy, 2:7
Unjust acts
contributions to, 4:873–874
by leaders, dissociation from, 4:873
Unknowable. *See* Deity
Unlawful law, 8:230
Unlike and like, argument of both, 9:872
Unlimited and limited, argument of both, 9:873–874
Unlimiteds, 7:310–311
Unmoved mover, Aristotle on, 5:585–586, 6:186
Unnatural, *vs.* natural, 6:492
"Unnatural" desire, for immortality, 5:78
Unnatural Lottery: Character and Moral Luck, The (Card), 2:31
Unnatural urge, to self-preservation, 5:78
Uno Deo Patre, De (Crell), 9:100
Unobservable(s)
causality as, 2:106–107
empiricism and, 8:110
particulates as, and scientific theory, 1:643–644
perspective as nonexclusive view of, 1:643–644
theories referring to, inductive underdetermination and, 9:576
Unpleasant, Hume on, 4:502–503
Unpredictability, emergence and, 3:192
Unqualified nonobjectivism, 6:160–161
Unqualified objectivism, 6:160–161
Unreasonableness of Separation, The (Stillingfleet), 9:249
Unrestricted composition, 9:762
Unrestricted mereological composition, 6:176
Unrestricted transcendent realism, 6:179
Unsayable
existence of, 9:808
Wittgenstein on, 9:804
Unseen Universe, The (Tait and Stewart), 7:561–562
"Unseen World, The" (Fiske), 3:668
"Unsocial sociability," of human beings, 5:29
Unsolvability, in computability theory, 2:384–386
"Unsolvable Problem of Elementary Number Theory, An" (Church), 2:336, 2:375
Unsuccessful repressions, as pathogens of psychoneuroses, 3:740–741
Untersuchung über den Staat, Eine (Stein), 9:240
Untersuchung über die Deutlichkeit der Grundsätze der naturlichen Theologie und der Moral (Kant), 2:608, 5:10
"Untersuchungen über das logische Schliessen" (Gentzen), 5:472
"Untersuchungen über en Aussagenkalkül," 5:607
Untersuchungen zur Grundlegung der allgemeinen Sprachtheorie (Marty), 5:728
Unthinkable (*das Undenkbare*), God as, in Jaspers, 4:802
Untimely Meditations (Nietzsche), 6:575, 6:609–610
Unum nomen unum nominatum
Berkeley on, 9:596–597
Hume and, 9:598
Unwarranted generalization, 3:543
Unzer, Johanna Charlotte, Wolff and, 9:824, 9:830
Uomo finito, Un (Failure; Un Uomo Finito) (Papini), 7:102
Upadanakthandhas (clinging), in Buddhism, 5:328

Upaniṣads
Brahman in, 1:681–682
consciousness in, 9:542
history of, 7:485
on karma, 2:110
knowledge of reality and, 4:134
on liberation, 5:327
Tagore on, 9:364
See also Hinduism
Upheavals of Thought: The Intelligence of Emotions (Nussbaum), 6:680
Urbach, Peter, 8:34
Urban, Wilbur Marshall, Cassirer and, 1:58
Urban VIII, Pope
Augustinus condemned by, 4:789
Galileo and, 2:732
Urban of Bologna, Averroism of, 1:428
Urey, Harold, on origin of life, 5:360
Urmson, J. O., 6:233, 7:111
Ursprung sittlicher Erkenntinis (The Origin of Our Knowledge of Right and Wrong) (Brentano), 1:690
Uruguayan philosophy, 5:206–207
Usage des plaisirs, L' (The Use of Pleasure) (Foucault), 3:701
Use
of force, in justice enforcement, 4:866
of term, definition of, 5:548
Use and Abuse of History, The (Nietzsche), 1:765
Use theory of meaning, 6:85–86
vagueness and, 9:624
Wittgenstein on, 9:811–813
Ussher, James, on creation, 5:196
Utilias: A Journal of Utilitarian Studies, 6:232
Utilitarian rationality, 8:254
Utilitarianism, **9:603–616**
Abelard on, 1:6
act. *See* Act utilitarianism
altruism in, 1:136, 3:172–173
animal rights in, 1:208–209, 3:392
in applied ethics, 1:239
Bentham amd, 7:459
and bioethics, 1:603
Bolzano on, 1:646
Bradley on, 1:676
calculus of justified action, 7:624
calculus of pain in, 7:617
Chernyshevskii on, 2:146–147
Coleridge on, 2:319
as common-sense ethical method, 9:22
consequences in, 9:603–609
determining, 9:607–608
egoistic, 9:604
hedonistic, 9:604
ideal, 9:604
probabilities assigned to, 9:608
remote, 9:607–608
universalistic, 9:604
as consequentialism, 2:460
cost-benefit analysis and, 1:551
critique of, 3:383–384, 3:389
Croce and, 2:603
as descriptive ethics, 9:604–606
deterrence in, 8:163
discrediting of, by idealism, 4:559–560
on duty, 3:440–441
education in, 7:377
as egalitarian good, 1:646
egoistic, 9:604–605
Eliot (T. S.) on, 3:185
Encyclopédie on, 3:224
on ethical treatment of animals, 3:392
and ethics, 3:382–383, 3:412–414, 5:24, 7:325, 9:605–606
vs. eudaimonism, 9:383
on evaluation of political and social institutions, 3:391–392
and friendship, 3:748–749
Gay and, 4:34–35
Godwin on, 4:138
golden rule and, 4:146
on the Good, 4:153
on government, 2:702–703
Grote on, 4:189
happiness principle in, 1:551
hedonistic, 4:254–255, 6:233, 9:382, 9:604
in historiography, 1:718
history of, 9:604–605
Hume on, 3:408–409
ideal, 3:439, 9:604
as normative ethics, 9:607
Ross on, 8:505
ideal moral code in, 1:687
ignorance of consequences and, 1:782
images of man in, 7:323
inadequacy of, 7:455–456
on inclination *vs.* obligation, 3:414
indirect, 7:459–460
on intrinsic value of hedonism, 4:719
vs. intuitionism, 9:22
just distribution and, 7:456
and justice, 1:603, 4:867, 8:162
Kant and, 5:37
in Latin American philosophy, 5:205
law in, 7:424–425, 7:455–456
Locke on, 3:407
on love, 5:591
on loyalty, 5:595
Lyons on, 7:459
Marsilius of Padua and, 5:722
maximization in, 9:383
Mill (James) and, 6:218–220
Mill (John Stuart) and, 6:222, 6:227, 6:232–233, 7:459–460
mitigation in, 8:165
in Mohist ethics, 2:197
moral cosmopolitanism and, 2:568
and natural law, 9:81
naturalist and nonnaturalist, 4:736
naturalistic morality and, 6:476
neo-Hegelianism and, 4:558
Nishi and, 6:623
normative, 9:604
Parker (T.) and, 7:122
Paulsen and, 7:148
pluralist critique of, 3:439–440
political conservatism of, 9:23
political philosophy in, 7:666–667
positivism and, 7:712–713
precursors of, 9:605
promises in, 8:53
proof of, 9:606
property in, 8:69–70
punishment in, 8:161, 8:166–167
rape in, 7:718
Rawls and, 5:324, 7:459, 9:82
rights and, 7:459–460
rule. *See* Rule utilitarianism
self-interest and, 3:389
Sen on, 8:810
Sidgwick on, 3:416–417, 9:23–24
in Singer's practical ethics, 9:42
in Smart's consequentialism, 9:65
social positivism and, 7:711
Sombart on, 9:127
Stace on, 9:200
on state action, 9:207
in Stephen's morality, 9:243
universalistic, 9:604–605
on value, 3:443
on war and peace, 7:155
on well-being, 8:722
Williams (Bernard) on, 9:787
Utilitarianism (Mill, John Stuart), 6:227–228, 6:232, 6:623
on altruism and self-interest, 3:173
society in, 7:377
Utility
in act *vs.* ideal rule utilitarianism, 1:687
Bacon (Francis) on, 1:450
Bentham's principle of, 1:551
Croce on, 2:603

Utility, ***continued***
in economic theory, 3:447–448
vs. enjoyment, 1:396–397
Hélvetius on, 4:306–307
as informative truth criteria, 1:450
judging the rightness of actions by, 3:547
justice and, 7:455–456
of law, 7:455–456
as measure of ethical value, 3:383
in natural selection, 9:721
Nozick on, 6:669
of perception, in evolution, 1:565
proof of, Mill (John Stuart) on, 6:232–233
of property, 8:69
of propositions, 8:89
as secondary by-product of development, Gehlen on, 4:36
Sidgwick on, 3:417
social
Croce on, 2:603
law and, 2:603
vs. morality, 5:48
Valla on, 9:635
as value, 9:637
of vice, 5:682
"Utility of Religion, The" (Mill, John Stuart), 6:230
Utopia [term], use of, 9:616–617
Utopia (More), 2:16, 5:154, 6:398–400, 9:616
on suicide, 9:319
on war and peace, 7:152
Utopias and utopianism, **9:616–622**
anarchism and, 1:176, 9:89
Bloch on, 1:615–616
Bolzano on, 1:646
Butler (Samuel) on, 1:785
causes of, 9:619–620
Comenius on, 2:341
communism and, 2:361
definition of, 9:617
inspiration of, 9:617–618
Malthus on, 5:675
Manheim on, 5:685–686
Mao on, 2:180
in Marxist socialism *vs.* communal living, 1:716–717
neo-Confucian political reform as, 2:158
pragmatist feminist concept of, 3:568
Saint-Simon on, 8:590
in Schiller's coordination of human drives, 8:628
in Solov'ëv's theocracy, 9:125
uses of, 9:620–621
varieties of, 9:618–619
Utriusque Cosmi, Maioris Scilicet et Minoris, Metaphysica, Physica atque Technica Historia (Fludd), 3:674
Uttal, William, in neuroscience, 6:565
Uttaramiesika, 4:132–135
Uytenbogaert, Johannes, Arminius and, 1:285

V

V svoem kraiu (In my own land) (Leont'ev), 5:283
Vacuity, in neo-Confucian rationalism, 2:157
Vacuum and void
atomists on, 5:299
Crusius on, 2:607
Pascal on, 7:129–130
Strato on, 9:261
See also Quantum mechanics
Vāda-vidhi (Rules of debate) (Vasubandhu), 5:412
Vague partial belief, 5:110
Vague predicates, thresholds for, 5:111
Vague statements, as objects of knowledge, 5:111
Vagueness, **9:623–625**
as aesthetically displeasing, 3:557
epistemic logic and, 5:112
and fallacy, 3:541
higher-order, 5:111
in identity, 4:570
of knowledge, 5:108
many-valued logics and, 5:694
in self-knowledge, 8:723
views in, 9:624–625
virtue and, 9:680–681
Vaibhāṣika Buddhism, Vasubandhu in, 9:650–651
Vaidalyasūtra (Devastating Discourse), 6:470
Vaihinger, Hans, **9:625–629**
Adler and, 1:24
Carnap and, 2:38
on *Critique of Pure Reason* (Kant), 6:539
on Forberg, 1:378
Lange and, 5:187
and neo-Kantianism, 6:541
Schultz and, 8:659
Vailati, Giovanni, **9:629–631**
de Finetti and, 2:663
Peano and, 7:159
Vair, Guillaume de, Lipsius and, 5:364
Vaiśeṣika, 4:132, 5:117, 6:530
on analogy, 5:122
on liberation, 5:329
on nonperception, 5:122
on person, 9:650–651
Vaiśeṣika-sūtra (Aphorisms pertaining to individuation) (Kaṇāda), 4:627, 5:412, 6:530–531
Vākyapadīya (Bhartṛhari), 4:631
Valdés, Juan de, 9:99
Valence, of emotion, 3:200
Valentinus and Valentinianism, 4:104, **9:631–634**
emanationism in, 3:189
and Gnosticism, 4:98
Valerius Terminus (Bacon, Francis), 1:449–450
Valéry, Paul, **9:634**
Valid, secondarily, definition of, 5:556
Valid arguments, 3:639
Valid form transposition, minimizing, 3:538
Valid formula, definition of, 5:559
Valid inference, definition of, 5:559
Valid sentence, of propositional logic, 3:644
Valid sequent, 3:641, 3:650
Validity
in contractualism *vs.* consequentialism, 2:519
of laws, 3:617, 7:458
of legal transactions, 7:446
in paraconsistent logics, 7:105
of psychoanalysis, 8:110
in relevant logic, 5:488
and understanding, 5:513
Valla, Lorenzo, **9:634–636**
on Boethius, 7:147
on logic, 5:437
Valle, José Cecilio del, 5:205
Vallenilla, Ernesto Mayz, on epistemology of technology, 7:549
Valuation, Köhler on, 5:132
Value(s), **9:636–644**
Abbagnano on, 1:2
in absence of moral order, 4:750
aesthetic, 9:561–564, 9:764
Alexander on, 1:110–111
apprehension of, feelings in, 8:616
of art, 1:57, 1:80, **1:337–342**, 1:508–509
Augustine on, 1:396–397
Calderoni on, 2:8
in categorical imperative, 2:70
causal analysis of, 9:643
in Confucianism, 2:231
in consequentialism, 2:460
conservatism and, 2:466–468

in contractualism, 2:517
Cynic teaching on, 2:616
definition of, 5:559, 9:636–637
Deustua on, 3:43
Dewey on, 3:49
education and, 7:360
egoist's view of, 9:121
endowment effect and, 9:39
in evocative argumentation, 2:213–214
existence of, Wittgenstein on, 9:807
in existentialism, 1:2
facts and, 5:132, 9:643
  emotivists on, 3:425
  linguistic philosophers on, 3:429
  Sartre on, 3:428
  Sidgwick on, 3:417
  Weber (Max) on, 9:734
final causation for, Grice on, 4:185
of function, definition of, 5:559
Gentile on, 4:52–53
Hägerström on, 4:206–207
in historical materialism, 4:382
history as science of, 8:459–460
in human sciences, Dilthey on, 3:83
as innate moral knowledge, 2:221–222
in inquiry, 3:576
instrumental, 1:339
intrinsic, 1:339, 4:719
James (William) on, 7:744–745
Kantian ethics on, 3:443
of knowledge and truth, 5:103–107
Korn's theory of, 5:143
law and, 7:428, 7:455
of literature and fiction, 5:370–371
Lotze on, 5:581
metaphysics of, 8:51–52
Molina Garmendia on, 6:324
Moore on, 3:439, 3:442–444
moral, 3:442–444, 7:205
and needs of society, 3:596
negative, Gentile on, 4:52–53
non-moral, 3:442
normative theories of, 9:638–639
Novits's theory of creativity and, 2:590
as objective fact, 5:132
Perry (R. B.) on, 3:423, 7:204–205
personal *vs.* moral, 3:442–444
personalism and, 7:235–236
philosophical theories of, 9:638–640
of philosophy, 7:336–337
Popper on, 7:690–691
in pragmatism, 7:744–745
in projectivism, 8:51
of property, 8:69
range of, definition of, 5:554
realms of, 9:637
as reference of art, 1:509
Rintelen on, 8:479
Ruskin on, 8:534
Russell on, 8:556–557
Santayana on, 8:598
Scheler on, 8:616–617
subjectivity of, 8:556–557
transcendent realist theory of, 6:171
universal in, 3:420, 8:459
of Universe, McTaggart on, 6:79
uses of, 9:637
utilitarianism on, 3:443
utility as independent form of, 2:603
in visual experience, 9:691–692
Value and Destiny of the Individual, The (Bosanquet), 1:662
Value criteria, in historical understanding, 8:459
Value empiricism, personalism and, 7:235
Value feelings, 6:117
Value independence, in subjective expected utility, 2:656–657
Value judgment(s), 9:638
  correctness of, 9:642
  derivative, 9:640
  intuition and, 9:643
  Lewis (C. I.) on, 5:310–311
  in metanormative value theory, 9:639–640
  Moore (G. E.) on, 9:643
  vs. moral judgment, 1:461
  in notion of function, 3:765
  proving, 9:640
  in wisdom, 9:795
Value predicates, 9:638
Value state of system, 6:278–279
Value statements, on existence, 1:436–437
Value theory
  Cairns' phenomenology and, 2:5
  death and, 2:654
  Ehrenfels and, 3:176–177
  Lunacharskii on, 5:611
  Meinong and, 6:117–118
  Scheler and, 8:616–617
  Schlick on, 8:642–643
Value-free science, ideal of, 3:594–595
Valuing, 9:638
Van Breda, Herman Leo, 3:638
Van Fraassen, Bas C., 3:628, 3:690, 6:277, **9:644–646**
Van Helmont, Francis Mercury, 3:187, 5:253
Van Schurman, Anna Maria, 3:569
Van Tieghem, Philippe, 3:62–63
Vanderschraaf, Peter, 4:20
Vanderveken, Daniel, 8:706
Vane, Walter, Locke and, 5:374
Vanini, Giulio Cesare, 2:725, **9:646**
Vanishing-point perspective, 9:692
Vanity of Dogmatizing (Glanvill), 4:95
Vanity of Human Wishes, The (Johnson, Dr. Samuel), 4:854
Vardhaamana, in Jainism, 2:110–111
Vargas Llosa, Mario, 5:204
Varia Opuscula Theologica (Suárez), 9:282
Variability, biological, 7:465
Variable(s)
  being as value of, 1:528
  bound
    definition of, 5:535
    in Peirce, 5:455
  definition of, 5:559
  in first-order language, 3:647
  free occurrences of, in formula, 3:651
  independent limitation principle for probability analysis, 1:698
  in Leibniz's calculus, 5:443
  naming objects, 3:648
  proper names and, 8:62–63
  in quantum theory, 1:630
  syntactical, definition of, 5:558
Variable binding, 1:172
Variation, Darwin on, 7:338
Variational principle of least action, in general relativity, 9:741
Varieties of Goodness (Wright), 3:432
Varieties of Reference, The (Evans), 3:459–460, 3:462
Varieties of Religious Experience, The (James, William), 4:775, 4:780, 7:84
Variety
  Mill (John Stuart) on, 9:510
  Stephen on, 9:510
  Tagore on, 9:364
Varignon, Pierre, on energy and work, 3:227
Varisco, Bernardino, 7:83, **9:646–647**
Varona y Pera, Enrique José, 5:206–207, **9:647–648**
Varro, 9:399
Varṣaṇya, 5:412
Vasconcelos, José, 5:207–208, **9:648–649**

Vasquez, Gabriel, **9:649–650**
Vasubandhu, **9:650–653**
on atomism, 1:383
on Dignāga, 5:413
on inference, 5:412–413
on realism refutation and moral implications, 1:751–752
in Yogācāra Buddhism, 1:746–747, 1:751–752, 9:650–652
Vatican II
communism and, 5:741
Maritain and, 5:717
Vatier, Antoine, 2:733, 2:737
Vātsīputrīya Buddhism, on person, 9:650–651
Vātsyāyana
on cognition, 9:544
on inference, 5:414
on trustworthy or authoritative person, 5:121
Vaucel, Louis-Paul du, 6:603
Vauvenargues, Luc de Clapiers, Marquis de, **9:653–654**
Vaz Ferreira, Carlos, 5:207–208, **9:654–655**
Veblen, Thorstein Bunde, **9:655–656**
Vecchio, Giorgio Del. *See* Del Vecchio, Giorgio
Vector calculus, Peano and, 7:158
Vector space, 8:208
Veda(s), 5:116, 5:121
cosmological evolution in, 2:109–110
language in, 7:412–413
See also Indian philosophy
Vedānta, 4:132
Brahman on, 1:682–684
and knowledge, 5:122
on liberation, 5:329–330
self in, 8:719–720
See also Indian philosophy
Vedānta Deśika, 4:630
Vedantins, 5:120
Vedic hermeneutics, universals in, 9:581
Vedic literature, concept of karma in, 5:41
Vegetarianism, in Pythagoreanism, 8:185
Vegetative powers, 1:274
Veil of ignorance, Rawls on, 5:323, 8:258
Veil of perception, 7:190
Veiled argument, 6:110
Veitch chart, as logical diagram, 5:563
Vekhi, 3:716
Velleman, J. David
on action, 1:17–18
on love, 5:591
Velocity
in classical mechanics, 2:280
in gas distribution and equilibrium probabilities, 1:644–645
Huygens on, 2:462
of light, 2:559, 7:476, 9:149
Oresme on, 7:35
Tooley on, 6:409–410
Vendidād, in Zoroastrianism, 9:885
Vendler, Zeno, on event theory, 3:466
Venevitinov, Dmitrii, 5:74
Venezuelan philosophy, 5:205–207, 5:211
Venn, John, **9:657–658**
Carroll and, 2:53, 5:452–453
Jevons and, 5:565
logic of, 5:451–452
on predicative judgments, 3:496
See also Venn diagrams
Venn diagrams, 5:559–561
Carroll's method and, 5:452–453
definition of, 5:559
syllogisms and, 5:451–452
Venue à l'écrotire, La (Derrida), 2:263
Vénus physique (Maupertuis), 6:66–67
Vera, Augusto, 9:160
Vera Cruz, Alonso de la, 5:204
Vera Religione, De (Völkel), 9:100
Verbal Behavior (Skinner), 4:693, 9:62
Verbal communication
Indian philosophy on, 5:117, 5:120–121
personhood and, 7:240
Verbal space, and sensible space, 4:848–849
Verbalism, 8:786
Verbs
Anselm on, 1:218
Chinese, 2:191–193
intensional transitive, 4:697–699, 8:78
Leibniz on, 5:441
nonassertive speech and, 6:650
propositional attitude and, 8:75
Sanskrit, 7:413
Verbütschierte mit sieben Siegeln verschlossene Buch, Das (Franck), 3:712
Verdenius, W. J., on Parmenides of Elea, 7:125
Verdicts out of Court (Darrow), 1:371
Vergil, Dante on, 2:626
Verhaltnis zwischen Willen und Verstand im Menschen, Das (Fischer), 3:660
Veridical perception, 7:187–189, 7:193
Verifiability
Carnap on, 5:527
eschatological, 7:478
of mathematical proofs, 2:373
and problems of positivism, 5:527–528
strong, 9:660–661
weak, 9:661
Verifiability principle, **9:659–670**
in analytical behaviorism, 1:523
application of, 9:659–660
Ayer on, 1:436
of basic statements, 1:483–487
Carneades and, 9:48
criticisms of, 9:664–666
in denial of skeptical argument, 9:43
failure of, 9:669
logical behaviorism and, 1:534
in logical positivism, 5:527–528, 7:31
meaningfulness of, 9:664
Popper on, 7:688
problems raised by, 9:659–666
in Schlick's analytical procedure, 8:642
science and, 5:528
in scientific realism, 8:689
in syntactic view of theories, 9:414
theological statements and, 8:412–414
Verification
in Aristotle's theory of truth, 2:540–541
in coherence theory of truth, 2:311
in illative combinatory logic, 2:339
mathematical intuitionism and, 5:469
meaning and, 3:316–317, 5:84, 5:527, 5:687
of psychoanalytic theory, 8:111–112
of reality and convention, 2:522
Tractatus and, 9:808
Verificationism
concepts and, 2:417
Dummett and, 3:132
Mansel and, 5:687
on meaningfulness of sentences, 9:43
operationalism and, 7:31
Quine and, 1:151
Verisimilitude, Boileau on, 1:640
Véritables Principes de la Grammarie (Dumarsais), 8:790
Veritate, De (Herbert of Cherbury), 9:53

Vérité des sciences contre les septiques ou Pyrrhoniens, La (Mersenne), 2:725, 6:152
Verite evident, as a rule of truth, 3:702
Veritism, in education, 7:358
Verlobung in St. Domingo, Die (Kleist), 5:78
Verloschollene Herz: Ein Buch stiller Betrachtungen, Das (The singing heart: A book of quiet contemplations), 4:578
Vermazen, Bruce, on music, 1:306
Vermischte Schriften (Lichtenberg), 5:339
Vermischte Schriften (Savigny), 8:614
Vernadskii, G. V., 3:453, 5:578
Vernadskii, V. I., 3:559
Vernichtungswille, 7:251
Vernunft (reason), Jaspers on, 4:801
Vernünftige Gedanken von den Cometen (Knutzen), 5:123
Vernunftlehre (Meier), 6:112
Veröffentlichungen des Vereines Ernst Mach (monograph series), 5:525
Veron, François, 9:52
Veronese, Giuseppe, on continuum, 2:501
Verrti, Alessandro, and Beccaria, 1:517
Verrti, Pietro, and Beccaria, 1:517
Verstand (intellect), Jaspers on, 4:801
Verstehen (understanding), 9:93
 methodology of, 9:36
 in sociology, Weber (Max) on, 9:735
 in Spranger's analysis of personality types, 9:198
Versuch den Begriff der negativen Grossen in die Weltweisheit einzuführen (Kant), 5:10
Versuch die Metamorphose der Pflanzen zu erklaren (Goethe), 4:140
Versuch einer Critischen Dichtkunst (Gottsched), 4:164
"Versuch einer Selbstkritik" (Nietzsche), 7:251
Versuch einiger Betrachungen über den Optimismus (Kant), 7:249
Versuch über die Erkenntnis (Inquiry into the nature of knowledge) (Brentano), 1:692
Versuch über die Tranzscendentalphilosophie (An essay on Transcendental Philosophy) (Maimon), 5:645
Vertical universal, 9:582
Vertraute Briefe von Adelheid B. an ihre Freundin Julie S. (Confidential letters from Adelaide B. to her friend Julie S.) (Nicolai), 6:598
Verum-factum principle, 9:672
Very, Jones, 6:572
Vesey, G. N. A., on sound, 9:138
Vetenskapen ock förnuftet (Science and reason) (von Wright), 9:847
Viau, Théophile de, trial of, 2:725
Vice, **9:678–683**
 as component of human nature, 1:781
 Eliot (George) on, 3:185
 Mandeville on, 5:682
 range of, 9:680
 social utility of, 5:682
 stoics on, 9:257
Vicious-circle principle
 impredicative concepts and, 2:256
 mathematics and, 5:519
 natural language and, 2:77
 Russell on, 2:76, 5:466–467, 5:555
 Whitehead on, 5:519
Vico, Giambattista, **9:670–677**
 Cattaneo on, 2:83
 Condorcet and, 2:431
 Croce and, 2:600–602
 Genovesi and, 4:48
 Gioberti and, 4:94
 on history, 3:36, 7:388
 Ibn Khaldūn and, 4:549
 method of, 9:675
 on myth, 6:464
 on sociology of knowledge, 9:101
 Sorel and, 9:133
 Sturzo's dialectic of concrete and, 9:281
Victoria (queen of England), dying thoughts of, 3:107
Victorinus, Boethius on, 1:625–626
Victorinus, Marius
 medieval logic and, 5:422
 Porphyry and, 7:143
Vida de Don Quijote y Sancho (Life of Don Quixote and Sancho) (Unamuno), 9:566
Video installation, 9:693
Vidya. See Veda(s)
Vienna Circle, 5:525
 on basic statements, 1:484
 Bergmann in, 1:561
 break-up of, 8:638
 Carnap and, 2:35, 2:38–43, 5:524
 Frege and, 2:41, 3:732
 Gödel in, 8:638
 Latin American philosophy and, 5:210
 logical positivism and, 5:524, 9:58
 Schlick and, 8:637, 8:642
 Scholz on, 8:645
 and verification theory of meaning, 3:316–317
 Wittgenstein and, 2:41–42, 5:524, 9:802
 See also Logical positivism
Vienna method, of education, 6:562
Vier Kronbüchlein, Die (Franck), 3:712–714
Vier Phasen der Philosophie, Die (Brentano), 1:692
View from nowhere
 McDowell on, 6:73–74
 Nagel on, 6:474–475
View from Nowhere, The (Nagel), 6:474–475
View of the Evidences of Christianity, A (Paley), 7:75–77
Vigrahavyāvartanī (Replies to Objections) (Nāgārjuna), 6:470
Vijñānavāda Buddhism, on liberation, 5:329
Villegas, Abelardo, 5:211
Villoro, Luis, 5:210
Viṃśatikā (Twenty Verses) (Vasubandhu), 1:751–752, 9:652
Vinaya, 1:722, 1:725
Vincent of Beauvais, 8:767
Vincent of Lérins, 3:97
Vincenti, Walter G., 7:549–550
Vindication, thesis of, 3:626
Vindication of Natural Science, A (Burke), 1:770–771
Vindication of the Reasonableness of Christianity (Locke), 5:375, 5:391–392
Vindication of the Rights of Men (Wollstonecraft), 9:837
Vindication of the Rights of Woman (Wollstonecraft), 4:136, 9:836–837
Vindicationism, 3:678, 4:644
Vindiciae Contra Tyrannos, 9:81
Vio, Tommaso de. *See* Cajetan, Cardinal
Violence, **9:677–678**
 Arendt on, 1:253–254
 in civil disobedience, 2:260
 fascism and, 3:554
 in French liberal movement, 9:247
 Mariana on, 5:711
 in natural order, 1:488
 and patriarchal cultural region, 3:584
 protection from, 7:454
 refutation of, in Shelley's anarchism, 9:8
 revolutionary use of, 9:133–134
 in socialist revolution, 9:89

Violence, ***continued***
in Stirner's egoist rebellion, 9:251
symbolic use of, 9:134
Tolstoy on, 9:513
See also Force; Nonviolence
"Violence and Metaphysics" (Derrida), 2:717–718
Viret, Pierre, on deism, 2:681
Virgil
Dante on, 2:626
on Lucretius, 5:601
Philodemus of Gadara and, 3:264
Virgin birth, 9:627
Virginia Statute for Religious Freedom, 3:246, 4:805
Virginity, 7:526
Virtual distinction, 3:138
Virtual objects, 9:691
Virtue(s), **9:678–682**
Abelard on, 1:6
abstract, 8:3
altruism as, 1:136
Antiochus of Ascalon on, 1:222–223
Antisthenes on, 1:224
application of, 9:688–689
approval of, 4:528
aretē as, **1:256**
Aristo of Chios on, 1:257
Aristotle on, 1:267, 3:398, 7:329
in art, 1:67–68
artificial, 4:508–509
Hume on, 3:384
asceticism and, 1:353
Augustine on, 1:395–397, 3:401–402
Balguy on, 1:475
benevolence as, 1:782, 3:174
in Buddhism, 1:722
in Chinese religion, 2:227–228
Clarke on, 2:274
Cleanthes on, 2:288
Clement on, 2:290
as cognitive, 1:450
in Confucianism, 2:150–151, 2:174, 2:194, 2:200, 2:231
Cumberland on, 2:615
Cynic teaching on, 2:616
Dante on, 2:624–625
in Daoism, 2:185, 2:192–193
definition of, by Socrates, 9:110–111, 9:589, 9:794
demand requirements of, common *vs.* religious, 2:228
Descartes on, 3:188
as dharma, 1:724
Diogenes of Sinope on, 3:90
vs. duty, Kant on, 8:627
Edwards (Jonathan) on, 3:167–169
Eliot (George) on, 3:185
as end in itself, 7:307–308
Epicurus on, 3:268
and ethics, 3:388, 4:78, 5:636–637
evil as cause of, 3:475–476
Gay on, 4:34–35
Geulincx on, 4:78
Haeckel on, 4:204
happiness and, 1:222–223, 1:267–268
Hobbes on, 3:406
in human nature, 1:781
in Itō's Confucianism, 4:766
Jankélévitch on, 4:788
justification of, 9:688
Kant on, 3:411
as knowledge, 9:112, 9:794
knowledge of, Zhang Zai on, 9:879–880
La Rochefoucauld on, 5:201
Locke on, 3:407
love in, 1:136
Machiavelli on, 5:627
MacIntyre on, 5:636–637
Mandeville on, 5:682
in medieval philosophy, 6:99
Mencius on, 2:233
Mill (John Stuart) on, 3:413–414, 6:230
moral sense of, 1:474–476
natural *vs.* moral, 9:2
necessity of, 2:713
in *Nichomachean Ethics* (Aristotle), 7:329
Nietzsche on, 5:628
Paley on, 7:76
Panaetius of Rhodes on, 7:79
perception of, 4:528
Philo on, 7:307–308
Plato on, 1:256, 7:585, 7:589–590, 7:595
practical, 8:3
as practice, 9:74
Price on, 8:3
in Renaissance, 8:423
Ruysbroeck on, 8:579–580
self-interest and, 8:720
Smith (Adam) on, 9:68
Socrates on, 9:110–111, 9:589, 9:702
sophistic teaching of, 9:130
in Stoicism, 9:255–257
teachability of, 7:586, 7:594
teaching of, Dewey on, 3:48
Telesio on, 9:390–391
transformative action by, 2:227–228
Vauvenargues on, 9:654
and vice
comparison of, 9:680
Golden Mean, Aristotle on, 4:152
Hume on, 4:507–508
Ibn Gabirol on, 4:545
in Platonic dialogues, 7:589–590
Schopenhauer on, 8:655
Smith (Adam) on, 9:68
Stewart on, 9:247
typology of, 4:507–508
Vico on, 9:673
Western understanding of, 2:227
Zeno of Citium on, 9:870
See also Intellectual virtues; Moral virtues
Virtue accounts, 9:686
Virtue epistemology, 3:276, **9:682–687**
appealing to, 5:105
in Sosa, 9:135–136
Virtue ethics, 1:213, **9:687–689**
in bioethics, 1:601
constructive program of, 9:688–689
critical program of, 9:687–688
development of, 3:748
right action in, 9:681
vs. virtue theory, 9:679–680
Virtue perspectivism, 9:136
Virtue theory
inference in, 9:684
vs. virtue ethics, 9:679–680
Virtue-centered naturalism, of Foot, 3:684
Virtues of Authenticity (Nehamas), 1:67
Virtues of humanity *(ren)*, Dau Zhen on, 2:622
Virtuous citizenry, creating, 3:605
Virtuousness, 9:680–681
Vis motrix, transition to, 5:52
Vis viva, as measure of force, 3:228
Vishinsky, Andrei, on revolutionary legality, 7:427
Vishtaspa (Persian king), conversion to Zoroastrianism, 9:885
Visible and the Invisible, The (Merleau-Ponty), 3:510, 6:150
Visible objects, as divine language, 1:574
Vision
Augustine on, 1:392–393
Berkeley on, 1:575–576
in cognitive psychology, 8:151
in commissurotomy patients, 6:566

computationalism and, 1:329, 2:394
in conscious qualitative states, 2:451
cross-cultural, 7:334
Currie on, 7:382
defects in, perception and, 7:184
description of, 8:820
distance in, 1:575
film and, 7:382
geometry of, 8:326
in Gestalt theory, 4:70–71, 4:74–75
in God, 5:666–667
Gombrich on, 1:329
vs. hearing, 9:138
Helmholtz on, 4:304
imaging as form of, 4:591
in James's philosophy, 4:781–782
Koffka on, 4:70–71, 4:74–75
Marr on, 1:329
mechanics of, 8:326
modular computational account of, 1:329
nonconceptual mental states and, 2:480
vs. photography, 9:690
sensations of, and time, 9:485–487
spiritual *vs.* corporeal, 1:393
topographic representations in, 4:591
understanding and, 1:393–394
in Weiskrantz, 2:451
Vision-illumination, 4:584
Viśiṣṭādvaita Vedānta, 1:683–684, 4:629, 5:330
Visual arts
female nudes in, 3:571
formal rules of, beauty from, 9:562
theory of, **9:689–694**
Visual experience, 1:325–326, 8:724–725, 9:691–692
Visual field, 5:130, 6:140
Visual information, Dennett's consciousness theory and, 2:456
Visual perception, 7:180–185. *See also* Vision
Visual processes, mental representation in, 6:142
Visual qualities, in neuroscience, 6:566–567
Visual space, 4:848–849
Visual (spatial) symbols, 3:670
Visualisation, in neuroscience, 6:565
Vita come ricerca, La (Spirito), 9:197
Vita delle forme letterarie, La (The life of literary forms) (Pastore), 7:135
Vita Fausti Socini (Przypkowski), 9:100
Vita Nuova (Dante), 2:623–624, 5:587
Vital du Four, 3:141, 7:161
Vital entity, 9:695
Vital force
Cavendish on, 2:117–118
Cheng Yi on, 2:145
vs. closed physical causality, 2:90–91
in Confucianism, 2:172
in craft work, 2:200
and disinterest in art, 2:65
as fiction, 9:627
as heaven, 2:176
in science and mathematics, 1:714
See also Qi
Vital impetus, in Bergson, 1:570
Vital Logic (Lógica viva) (Vaz Ferreira), 5:208
Vital motion, Conway on, 2:529
Vital principle, Cournot on, 2:577
Vital reason, metaphysics of, 7:45
Vitalism, 5:77, 5:132, **9:694–698**
Bertalanffy on, 1:593
Driesch on, 3:110–111
evolution and, 1:569–570
Helmholtz and, 4:303
in Latin American philosophy, 5:208
Marías and, 5:711
McDougall and, 6:72
monistic, of Conway, 9:838
nonmental in, 6:139
organismic biology and, 7:36
proofs of, 9:697
Schlick on, 8:642
Stahl and, 9:203
Stumpf on, 9:281
Vitalismus als Geschichte und als Lehre, Der (The History and Theory of Vitalism) (Driesch), 3:110
Vitality, Croce on, 2:603
Vitoria, Francisco de, **9:698–699**
colonialism and, 5:204
international law and, 7:422
Thomism and, 9:445
Vivarana (Prakāśātman), 4:629
Vives, Juan Luis, 7:147, 7:248, **9:699–701**
"*Vizantizm i slavianstvo*" (Byzantinism and Slavdom), 5:283
Vlastos, Gregory, **9:701–703**
on equality, 3:331–332
on historical Socrates, 9:107
on Parmenides of Elea, 7:125
Vnutrenniaia forma slova (The internal form of the word) (Shpet), 9:17
Vocabulaire technique et critique de la philosophie (Lalande), 5:172
Vocabulary
in Islamic philosophy, 1:131
of Krause, 5:147
of law, 7:444
of psychology, 2:646–648
Vocalism, 8:496
Vocation of Man, The (Fichte), 3:414, 3:616
Voetius, Gisbert, 2:750, 2:753
Vogel, Henriette, 5:78
Vogel, Jonathan, on fallibilism, 3:274
Vogt, Karl, 6:11
"Voice of Poetry in the Conversation of Mankind, The" (Oakeshott), 7:2
Void. *See* Vacuum and void
Voigt, Woldemar, Dingler and, 3:85
Voix et le phénomène, La (Derrida), 9:274
Volckmann, W., Lotze and, 5:580
Volder, Burchard de, Leibniz and, 5:254
Volition, **9:703–706**
action and, 1:88–89
Aquinas on, 9:433–434
and assent, 5:98
and consciousness, 5:48
contemporary debate on, 3:19–21
Croce on, 2:603
vs. desire, 9:704
Epictetus on, 3:262
error and, 3:345–346
vs. intention, 9:704
McDougall on, 8:147
mental action of, 9:704
Peirce on, 7:171
Rehmke on, 8:303
Ryle on, 3:19
second-order, 3:718–719, 7:240
without experience, 9:703–704
See also Will
Volitional necessities, 3:719
Volkelt, Johannes, in neo-Kantianism, 6:540–542
Völkerpsychologie (Wundt), 9:849–850
Volland, Sophie, 3:71–72
"Völlstandigkeit der Axiome des logischen Funktionkalküls, Die" (Gödel), 5:473
Volksgeist (spirit of a people), 8:497, 8:615
Volney, Constantin-François de Chasseboeuf, Comte de, 2:760, **9:706–707**
Voloshinov, Valentin Nikolaeovich, and Bakhtin Circle, 1:469
Volski, Stanislav, **9:707–708**
"Voltaire" (Carlyle), 2:33

Voltaire, François-Marie Arouet de, 4:169, **9:708–714**
Bolingbroke and, 2:685
Boulainvilliers and, 2:265
Carlyle on, 2:33
clandestine literature and, 2:264, 2:267
on creation, biblical account of, 9:101
on death, 2:651
deism and, 2:687–691
Encyclopédie and, 3:223–225
Enlightenment and, 3:244
on ethics, 3:409
on evil, 3:469–470, 3:473
Franklin lionized by, 3:720
French liberalism and, 5:320
French Revolution and, 3:243, 9:520
Gibbon and, 4:86
Gracián and, 4:169
Holbach and, 3:71
Leibniz and, 5:254, 5:265
Locke and, 5:392
Lucian of Samosata and, 5:597
Maillet and, 5:644
Meslier and, 2:266
Mirabaud and, 2:266
Newton and, 3:246
Nietzsche and, 6:611
on *philosophes,* 2:688
in philosophy of history, 7:386–388
Rousseau and, 2:687
Saint-Hyacinthe and, 8:588
sensationalism and, 3:72
Socrates and, 9:113
on Spinoza, 9:193
Strauss on, 9:263
on toleration, 3:245
on "why" questions, meaningful and meaningless, 9:760
on world, why it exists, 9:759
Voluntarism, **9:714–717**
in Augustinianism, 6:99
and belief, 1:534–535
Bellarmine on, 1:542
Biel on, 1:594
Carnap on, 2:36, 2:44
free will in, William of Auvergne on, 9:766
Godfrey of Fontaine on, 4:131
Iqbal on, 4:744
Mercier on, 6:145
metaphysical, 9:716–717
psychological, 9:714–715
of Schiller (Ferdinand), 8:623–624
Sigwart on, 9:29
Solov'ëv and, 9:123
Voluntarist theories, 3:531–533
Voluntaristic idealism, 3:705, 8:520–521
Voluntary action
Augustine on, 1:395–397
Bergson on, 1:565
in legal theory, 7:447
and perception, 1:565
Voluntary agencies, and Ockham's rule of induction, 9:778
Voluntary euthanasia
active, 3:456–458
passive, 3:456–458
Vom Baum des Wissens Guts and Boss (Franck), 3:713
Vom Beruf unserer Zeit für Gesetzgebung und Rechtswissenschaft (Savigny), 8:615
Vom Dasein Gottes (Brentano), 1:692
Vom Erkennen und Empfinden der Menschlichen Seele (Herder), 1:55
Vom Ich als Prinzip der Philosophie (Schelling), 4:557, 8:618
Vom Menschen (Sombart), 9:128
Vom Musikalisch-Schönen (Hanslick), 1:56
Von dem grewlichen laster der trunckenheyt (Franck), 3:712
Von der Pflicht der Philosophie in unserer Zeit ("On the Duty of Philosophy in Our Age") (Liebert), 5:343
Von der Physiognomik (Lavater), 5:213
von Neumann algebra, 2:343
von Neumann-Bernays-Gödel set theory, surreal numbers system and, 2:508
von Neumann-Dirac collapse, 5:696–697
von Wright, Henrik, modal logic and, 5:491
Voprosy Filosoffii i Psikhologii (Problems of Philosophy and Psychology) (Lopatin), 5:572
Vorländer, Karl, 6:543
Vorlesungen über die Algebra der Logik (Schröder), 5:462
Vorlesungen über die Methode des academischen Studiums (Schelling), 8:620
Vorlesungen über praktische Philosophie (Lectures on practical philosophy) (Natorp), 6:490–491
Vorschule der Aesthetik (Fechner), 3:556
Vortices theory, in Cartesianism, 2:54, 3:683
Vorwärts (periodical), 3:57
Vostok, Rossiia i slavianstvo (The East, Russia, and Slavdom) (Leont'ev), 5:283
Voting, game theory and, 2:53
Vouillemin, General, Vienna Circle and, 5:525
Vowels, Sanskrit, 7:413
Voyage du Monde (Daniel), 4:790
Voyage en égypte et Syrie (Volney), 9:706
Vperyed! (Forward!) (periodical), 5:219
Vṛtra, 5:327
Vvedenskii, Aleksandr, 5:199, 5:576
Vyakti (particular), in Indian grammar, 9:581
Vygotsky, Lev Semyonovitch, 9:77
Vyrubov, G. N., 5:372
Vysheslavtsev, Boris Petrovich, **9:717–718**

W

Wadding, Luke, 8:705
Waddington, C. H., 7:83, 7:87–88
Wage, in Marx, 5:733–734
Wager passage, 3:531
Wagner, Carl, 5:248
Wagner, Richard
Chamberlain and, 2:122
Ehrenfels and, 3:176
on music, 1:56
Nietzsche and, 6:608, 6:611–612, 9:525
Schopenhauer on, 8:654
Wahl, Jean, on Lequier, 5:287
Wahle, Richard, **9:719–720**
Wahlverwandtschaften, Die (Elective affinities) (Goethe), 4:141
Wahreit und Methode (Gadamer), 1:71
"Wahrheitsbegriff in den formalisierten Sprachen, Der" (Tarski), 9:354
Wainright, William, 8:402
Waismann, Friedrich
on analyticity, 1:160–161
Lichtenberg and, 5:339
on meaning of sentences, 9:660–661
Wajsberg, Mordchaj
and logic, 5:606, 5:694
Łukasiewicz and, 5:607–608
Wald, Abraham, 8:612, 9:215
Wäldchen 125, Das (Jünger), 4:859
Walden, or Life in the Woods (Thoreau), 6:574, 9:450–451
Walden Two (Skinner), utopianism of, 9:618–619
Waldgang, Der (Jünger), 4:860

Walker, Margaret Urban, on morality, 3:580–581
Wallace, Alfred Russel, **9:720–721**
Darwin and, 2:629, 2:632, 3:488, 8:137
evolutionary theory of, 2:632, 2:635–637, 2:641
Malthus and, 5:675
on origin of life, 5:360
social Darwinism and, 2:642
"Wallace's line," 9:720
Wallas, Graham
on creative process, 2:590
on freedom, 3:724
Wallenstein (duke of), Kepler and, 5:50
Wallenstein trilogy (Schiller, Friedrich), 8:627
Wallis, John, 4:58, 5:439
Walras, Léon, Pareto and, 7:117
Walsh, Chad, 2:347
Walton, Kendall
on aesthetic experience, 1:33
on art, 1:68
on imagination, 1:328–329
on music, 1:306
on photography, 9:690
on style, 1:332
on visual representation, 1:328–329
Walzer, Michael
on justice in moral cosmopolitanism, 2:568
on Rawls's social contract theory, 9:82
on war and peace, 7:157
Walzer, Raphael, 9:239
Walzer, Richard, on British bombing of Germany, 9:397
Wanderer and His Shadow, The (Nietzsche), 6:611
Wang Bi, **9:722–723**
on cosmology and ontology, 2:190–191
harmonization of Daoism and Confucianism, 2:186
on nonbeing, 2:153, 4:196
on speech and meaning-delivery-beyond-speech-capacity, 2:208
Wang Chong, **9:723–724**
Wang Chuanshan. *See* Wang Fuzhi
Wang Fuzhi, 2:158, **9:724–725**
Wang Hao, on digital computers, 5:566
Wang Shou-Jen. *See* Wang Yang-ming
Wang Yang-ming, **9:725–727**
on Confucianism, 2:173, 2:177
doctrine of, 5:161
on moral knowledge, 2:221–222
Nakae Tōju and, 6:477
and neo-Confucianism, 2:157–158, 2:199, 4:794–795
on philosophy of mind, 4:795
ryōchi in, 6:477
on ultimate reality, 2:220
on wisdom, 2:219
Wang Yang-ming school, 5:7
Waning of the Middle Ages (Huizinga), 7:395
War/warfare
atomic, 8:667
Hegel on, 4:268
and international law, Grotius on, 4:191–192
Jünger's metaphysics and, 4:859–860
just war theory of, 4:191–192, 7:157–158
justice and, 4:865
Machiavelli on, 5:626–627
Mandeville on, 5:681–682
natural law and, 6:509
nuclear weapons and, views on, 7:154–157
optimism/pessimism and, 7:248
religious, doctrine of restraint and, 8:392
in Suárez's human law, 9:284–285
technology and, 4:859–860
in Thucydides, 9:457
Vitoria on, 9:699
War and Peace (Tolstoy), 9:512–513
War and the Christian Conscience (Ramsey), 7:157
War guilt, German, Weber (Max) and, 9:734
Ward, James, 6:260
on agnosticism, 1:94
on associationism, 8:137
in evolutionary psychology, 8:137
and Iqbal, 4:743
in psychology, 8:141, 9:259–260
on sensationalism, 8:823
and Stout, 9:259–260
Ward, Keith, 5:359
"Ward as a Psychologist" (Stout), 9:260
Warfare. *See* War/warfare
Warfield, Ted, 3:696
Warheit und Evidenz (Brentano), 1:690–691
Warhol, Andy, 1:299, 2:627
Warnock, Geoffrey
on ethical naturalism, 3:364
on principle of universal causality, 1:243
on sound, 9:138
Warrant trilogy (Plantinga), 3:323–324, 7:580
Warrants
in attributor contextualism, 2:484–486
of belief, and evidence, in Calvinism, 2:12
in criteriololgy, 2:594
induction justification and, 1:686
in subject contextualism, 2:483
Warren, Austin
on artistic imagination, 4:597
on genre, 1:330
Warsaw School of logic
Leśniewski and, 5:290, 5:293
Łukasiewicz and, 5:608
Wartenberg, Thomas, 7:385
"Was heisst: sich im Denken orientieren?" (Kant), 7:101
Was ist der Mensch? (Stein), 9:240
Was ist Philosophie? (Scholz), 8:644
"Was ist Philosophie" (Windelband), 9:792
Was ist Philosophie? Ein Gespräch zwischen Edmund Husserl und Thomas von Aquino (Stein), 9:240
Was sind und was sollen die Zahlen? (Dedekind), 2:400, 5:463, 8:836
Washington, George, deism and, 2:689
Was-sein. See Essence
Wasserstrom, Richard, on institutional sexism, 8:848
"Waste Book 1664" (Newton), 3:687
Water
as classification of matter, Greek Academy on, 6:59
in Thales of Miletus' natural philosophy, 9:405
Water-solubility, 6:135
Waterston, J., on physics of gases, 7:537
Watkins, J. W. N., on principle of universal causality, 1:243
Watson, Gary, on strict akratic action, 9:730–731
Watson, James
and behaviorism, 1:201
Pauling and, 7:146
Watson, John
and behaviorism, 1:520, 8:142–143
on introspection, 4:721
Pavlov and, 7:151
Watsuji Tetsurō, 4:797, 6:624, **9:727–727**
Watt, Henry J., in history of psychology, 8:144–145
Wave fields, of elementary particles, in unified field theory, 9:741

Wave function, 7:477, 8:202
- collapse interpretations of, 8:209–212
- completeness of, 8:209–214
- eigenstates, 8:206–207
- entangled, 8:214–215
- evolution of, 8:210
- expression of, 8:206–207
- non-locality of, 6:640–641
- in quantum mathematical apparatus, 8:206
- Schrödinger on, 8:658
- superposition of, 8:204

Wave mechanics, 8:657
Wave theory, of light, 6:591
Way, The. *See* Dao
Way of Light, The (Comenius), 2:341, 7:369
Way of Seeming, Parmenides of Elea on, 7:122, 7:125–126
"Way of the warrior," 9:859
"Way of Truth" (Parmenides), 3:357, 7:122–126
"Way the World Is, The" (Goodman), 4:159
Way towards the Blessed Life, The (Fichte), 3:618
Wayland, Francis, **9:728**
Ways of Russian Theology (Florovskii), 3:673
Ways of World-making (Goodman), 2:475, 4:161
Weak analogies, *vs.* strong, 3:544
Weak emergence, 3:193
Weak force, 9:267
Weak verifiability, 9:661
Weakened syllogism, definition of, 5:557
Weakness
- in perception of ugliness, 9:563
- of will, 8:711, **9:728–732**

Wealth
- alienation and, 2:362
- as consumable good, 9:68
- as evolutionary fitness, Butler (Samuel) on, 1:785
- food supply and, 1:719
- as goal of law, 7:717–718
- Posner on, 7:717–718
- Rousseau on, 2:366
- Ruskin on, 8:534
- Smith (Adam) on, 9:68–69
- social, alienation and, 2:362
- Spinoza on, 9:171
- Turgot on, 9:550

Wealth of Nations (Smith), 1:777, 2:364, 5:321, 7:350–351
Weather
- Anaxagoras on, 1:183
- Anaximenes on, 1:186
- Aristotle on, 1:272
- Philoponus on, 7:314

Webb, Sidney, 9:89
Weber, Alfred, **9:732–734**
- critical legal studies and, 7:463
- Manheim and, 5:685
- on metaideology in social sciences, 7:534

Weber, Ernst Heinrich
- Fechner's principle and, 3:556
- Lotze and, 5:580
- in psychology, 8:139

Weber, Jean-Paul, on Descartes, 2:723
Weber, Max, 9:732–733, **9:734–736**
- on capitalism, 3:765
- and critical theory, 2:598–599
- Dilthey and, 3:84
- on elective affinity, 9:102
- Lukács and, 5:602
- in neo-Kantianism, 6:545
- on objective possibility, 8:607
- Schutz and, 8:664
- Simmel and, 9:30
- on social action, 9:93
- on social influence on thoughts, 9:103
- on Sombart, 9:128
- on Stammler's progressive generalizations, 9:203
- Troeltsch and, 9:527

Weber, Tulio, collapse theory of, 8:211
Weber, Wilhelm, theory of forces, 3:551
Webern, Anton, Adorno and, 1:25
Weber's law, 3:556, 8:139
Wedgewood, Josiah, and Lunar Society of Birmingham, 3:247
Weg zur Gewissheit und Zuverlässigkeit der menschlichen Erkenntnis (Way to certainty and reliability of human knowledge) (Crusius), 2:606
"Wege der Gotteserkenntnis" (Stein), 9:240
Wege des Glaubens (Stöhr), 9:252
Weierstrass, Karl
- arithmetization of mathematics, 5:534–535
- Cantor and, 5:463
- on infinite, 9:148
- on number, 6:671
- on real numbers, 2:496

Weigel, Erhard
- Leibniz and, 5:250
- Pufendorf and, 8:157
- Wolff and, 9:826

Weigel, Valentin, Franck and, 3:714
Weight
- as determinable, 3:1
- as manifestation of natural motion, 3:686

Weighted utility model, 2:660
Weights, as measuring devices, 6:91
Weil, Simone, 6:433, **9:736–738**
Weimar Republic, Kautsky in, 5:48
Wein, Hermann, on nihilism, 6:618
Weiner, Norbert, on axiom of reducibility, 5:519
Weiner Kries (discussion society), 8:638
Weinreich, Uriel, 9:356
We-intentionality, 7:299
Weis, John, 6:572
Weishi School, on wisdom as transforming consciousness, 2:219
Weiskrantz, Lawrence
- on blindsight, 6:566
- on vision and consciousness, 2:451

Weismann, August, 2:639, 3:109
Weiss, Frederick A., on alienation, 1:122
Weisse, C. H., Lotze and, 5:580
Weitz, Morris, on art, 1:66, 1:299
Weizsäcker, C. F. von, on phenomenology, 7:300
Welfare
- economic measures of, 3:447–448
- as highest good, Mill (John Stuart) on, 6:227
- in Hinduism, 7:486
- in indirect utilitarianism, 7:460
- libertarian view of, 5:335, 9:72–73
- in rule utilitarianism, 9:615

Welfare liberalism
- on coercive institutions, 9:73–74
- feminist justice and, 9:75
- on liberty, 5:334–335

Welfare state
- political philosophy and, 7:678
- universal equality and, 3:331–332
- Wolff and, 9:829

Welfarism, in utilitarianism, Sen on, 8:810
Well-being
- of animals, **1:208–210**
- definition of, and justice, 4:867–868
- economic measures of, 3:448
- functional capability as measure of, 8:810–811
- Sen on, 8:810–811
- subjective, psychological research on, 9:642
- *See also* Eudaimonia; Happiness; Self-Interest

Welleck, René, 4:682
  on artistic imagination, 4:597
  on genre, 1:330
Well-formed formulas, definition of, 5:559
Well-founded phenomenalism, 5:270
Well-ordered, definition of, 5:550
Well-ordered theorem, 5:559, 8:832–833
Wells, H. G., utopian works of, 9:620
Welt als Wille und Vorstellung, Die (The World as Will and Representation) (Schopenhauer), 1:55–56, 6:608, 7:86, 8:648
Weltalter, Die (Schelling), 8:621
Weltanschauliche Gedichte (Goethe), 4:143
Weltbuch, Spiegel un bildtniss des gantzen Erdbodens (Franck), 3:713, 3:714
Weltbürgertum und Nationalstaat (Meinecke), 6:113
Welton, Donn, Landgrebe and, 5:183
Welträthsel, Die (Haeckel), 4:202
Weltschmerz, 7:250
Weltseele, von der (Schelling), 8:619
Weltstaat, Der (Jünger), 4:860
Welty, Chris, 3:711
Wenj (Collected writings) (Zhu Xi), 2:216
Wenzel, Aloys, 7:83
Werder, as secondary source for Kierkegaard, 5:67
Werkmeister, W. H., in neo-Kantianism, 6:543
Wert des Lebens (Dühring), 3:131
Wertheimer, Max
  and Gestalt theory, 4:70, 8:144
  Koffka and, 5:124
  Köhler and, 5:126
  and Psychologische Forschung, 5:126
  set of dynamic factors, 5:127
Wertmasstäbe, 7:251
"Werttheorie und Ethik" (Ehrenfels), 3:176, 3:177
Wesen der Freiheit, Das (Liebert), 5:343
Wesen der Religion, Das (Feuerbach), 3:609
Wesen des Christentums, Das (Feuerbach), 3:184, 3:609, 3:611
Wesen des Christentums (von Harnack), 5:570
Wesley, John
  on deism, 2:686–687
  forerunners of, 2:686
  on Smith (John), 9:71
  on suicide, 9:319
  Zinzendorf and, 7:576
West, Henry, 6:233
Westermarck, Edward Alexander, 3:375, **9:738–740**
Western civilizations, Kireevskii's principles of, 5:75
Western culture, memory and, 6:122
Western democracies, Eliot (T. S.) on, 3:186
Western philosophy
  Christian dogma and, 3:97
  in Korea, 5:139–141
Western religions, pessimism in, 7:246
Western society
  communism as internal evolution of, 2:361
  limitations of, Kireevskii on, 5:74
Western thought
  Nietzsche on, 3:564
  parapsychology and, 7:113–114
Westminster Abbey, burials at, 2:628
Westminster Review (periodical), 3:184
Westphal, Merold, 5:68
Westphalia, treaty of, 9:145, 9:176
Weyl, (Claus Hugo) Hermann, 4:61, **9:740–742**
  on Cantor-Dedekind set theory, 2:501
  on continuum, 2:505–506
  on mathematical foundation, 5:469
Wff, definition of, 5:559
What Can She Know? (Code), 2:295
What Does It All Mean? (Nagel), 6:475
"What Does the Phenomenology of Edmund Husserl Want to Accomplish?" (Fink), 3:638
"What Does 'Universal History' Mean and to What End Is It Studied?" (Schiller, Friedrich), 8:626
"What I Believe" (Russell), 1:374
What I Believe (Tolstoy), 9:512
"What Is an Author?" (Foucault), 9:276
"What Is an Emotion?" (James), 3:198–199
What Is Art? (Tolstoy), 1:57, 1:304, 9:514
What Is Faith? (Kenny), 3:535
"What Is Folk Psychology?" (Stich, Ravenscroft), 3:678
"What Is It Like to Be a Bat?" (Nagel), 5:112, 6:475
"What Is Justified Belief?" (Goldman), 4:147
What Is Life? (Schrödinger), 8:657
What Is Man? (Kaufmann), 5:46
What Is Philosophy (Deleuze and Guattari), 2:696
"What Is the Law?" (Bingham), 7:428
What Is to Be Done? (Lenin), 4:574, 5:280
What Nietzsche Means (Morgan), 6:613
What People Live By (Tolstoy), 9:512
"What Pragmatism Is" (Peirce), 8:798
What the "Friends of the People" Are (Lenin), 3:65, 5:280
"What the Tortoise Said to Achilles" (Carroll), 5:452
"What Violence Is" (Garver), 9:678
What We Owe to Each Other (Scanlon), 2:517
Whately, Richard, **9:742–743**
  on Leibniz, 5:447
  logic textbook of (1826), 3:641
  on long discussion veiling fallacy, 3:549
  Malthus and, 5:677
  and Oriel noetics, 6:576
  on syllogistic reasoning, 5:501
Wheeler, John Archibald
  on black holes, 1:606–609
  on Copenhagen interpretation, 2:530
Whether a Maid May Be a Scholar? (Schurman), 9:838
Whewell, William, **9:743–745**
  Bradley and, 1:677
  on consilience of inductions, 8:699
  De Morgan and, 2:710
  on deductive logic, 4:640
  friends and colleagues of, 2:709
  physicotheology and, 7:561
  Sidgwick and, 9:25
  Wilson (Edward O.) and, 9:789
Whichcote, Benjamin, **9:745–746**
  Culverwell and, 2:612
  deism and, 2:685
  Locke and, 5:376
  More (Henry) and, 6:395
  on natural goodness of man, 9:1
  Smith (John) and, 9:69
  socinianism and, 9:100
Whigs, political philosophy of, 7:663–664
Whipps, Judy D., 3:567–568
Whirling dervishes, 9:307–309
Whistle-blowing, engineering ethics and, 3:240
Whiston, William
  Arianism of, 1:284
  and Chubb, 2:252
Whitcote, Benjamin, 2:14
White, Hayden, on history, 7:395

White, Morton
  on analytic-synthetic distinction, 7:749
  Austin (John Langshaw) and, **1:406–412**
  on definition, 2:673
  on Dewey, 3:425
  on history, 7:393
White Mountain, battle of, 3:187
Whitefield, George, deism and, 2:689
Whitehead, Alfred North, **9:746–754**
  on atoms, 6:146–147
  on categories, 2:81
  on cosmology, 2:557
  on definition, 2:670–671
  epistemology of, 3:316
  on event theory, 3:466
  on God, 2:641, 4:110
  Grassmann and, 5:461
  influence of, 9:753
  Lovejoy on, 5:592–593
  on matter, 4:745
  metaphysics of, 9:749–752
  Murphy on, 6:435
  natural theology of, 9:752
  on nature, 2:641, 6:520
  on Newton, 9:754
  on optimism/pessimism, 7:252
  panpsychism and, 7:83
  on part and whole, 6:146
  Peano and, 7:159
  periods of work of, 9:747
  physicotheology and, 7:562
  Plato and, 7:602
  precursors of, 7:163
  in process philosophy, 7:478
  on processes, 7:25
  on reality, 6:195
  Scholz and, 8:645
  on set-theoretic and semantic paradoxes, 5:518
  and systematic ambiguity, 5:558
  and theory of types, 5:558, 6:672
  on universe, 6:146
Whitehead's Metaphysics (Leclerc), 9:751
Whiteness, Bacon (Francis) on, 1:447
Whitman, Walt, on personalism, 7:233
Whole
  harmony of, 2:165
  in mereology, 6:146–147
  as more than sum of its parts, 5:127
  in Ockham's metaphysics, 9:779
  in organismic biology, 7:37, 7:38
  part and, 6:146
Wholeness, Ruskin on, 8:534
Wholeness and the Implicate Order (Bohm), 1:630
Wholeness step, in ascending order, 5:148
Wholly-unified-selfhood, in ascending order, 5:148
"Who's Afraid of Absolute Space" (Earman), 3:159
"Why," **9:754–761**
  answers to, 9:757–758
  causal *vs.* purpose, 9:756
  as complaint, 9:757
  cosmic, 9:756–758
  "how" and, 9:754–756
    as different questions, 9:755–756
    as same question, 9:755
  superultimate, 9:758–761
  theological, 9:756–758
Why I Am Not a Christian (Russell), 4:615
Why Should I Be Moral? (Singer), 9:41
Wien, Wilhelm, 3:235–236
Wierenga, Edward R., 3:93–94
Wiggins, David, **9:762–763**
  on life, meaning and value of, 5:358
  on personal identity, 7:229
Wigner, Eugene P.
  on collapse dynamics, 8:210
  on Copenhagen interpretation, 2:530
Wilamowitz-Moellendorff, Ulrich von, 3:210, 4:1
Wilberforce, Bishop, 2:629, 2:641
Wilde, Oscar Fingal O'Flahertie Wills, **9:763–765**
  on art, 1:56
  Pater and, 7:136
Wildelband, Wilhelm, Fink and, 3:637
Wildman, Sir John, and deism, 2:681
Wilhelm II (king of Prussia), 7:578
Wilhelm Meister (Goethe), 6:667, 8:631
Wilhelm Tell (Schiller, Friedrich), 8:627
Wilhelm von Humboldt und die Humanitätsidee (Spranger), 9:198
Wilkins, John, 4:95
  constructive skepticism of, 9:53
  on limited certitude, 9:54
  on real characters, 8:773
  on universal language, 1:342
Will
  act of
    assent as, 6:583
    obligation as, 9:284
    in Tennant's philosophy, 3:533
    in Thomism, 3:533
  Adler on, 1:23
  to annihilation, pessimism and, 7:251
  Anselm on, 1:217
  Aquinas on, 9:429
  Aristotle on, 3:398
  in ascent of soul, 3:622
  asceticism and, 6:612
  attention as, 5:687
  Augustine on, 1:395–397
  in Augustinianism, 1:404
  in Bain's defense of determinism, 1:462
  belief as, 1:617, 1:704
  body and, 5:656–658, 8:651
  in Cairns' phenomenology, 2:5
  categorical imperative and, 2:70
  causation in, in Geyser, 4:83
  collective, and democracy, 2:701–702
  in Confucianism, 2:172
  contemporary debate on, 3:19–21
  in contracts, 7:446
  Crusius on, 2:607–608
  deprivation of, by God, 1:217
  and desire, 1:594, 1:692
  Diderot on, 3:72
  divine, 7:422, 7:454, 9:372
    al-Ghazālī on, 2:114
    antecedent necessity in, 1:681
    Brightman on, 1:695
    and creation at every instant, 2:113
    Crusius on, 2:608
    in events past, present, and future, 1:680
    Ibn Gabirol on, 4:815
    justice *vs.* intellectual understanding of, 1:542
    law as, 7:454
    sin as resistance to, 2:9–10
    in theological voluntarism, 9:716
    in time, 1:704
  Edwards (Jonathan) on, 3:168–169
  as essence of man, 3:660
  finite and Cosmic, nature as objectification of, 1:672
  as force, 6:261
  free. *See* Free will
  general, 1:291, 4:39
  of God, 4:814. *See also* Will, divine
    Maimonides on, 4:818
  good, Kant on, 2:715
  in governing thought, 9:29
  as heart/mind capacity, in Confucianism, 2:172
  Hegel on, 4:272

Hobbes on, 3:406, 8:128
Hume on, 4:501–504
identifying with one's, 3:719
imagination and, 8:619–620
intellect and, 8:652, 9:28
in intentional action, 1:14–15
justice and, 8:620
Kierkegaard on, 5:62
knowledge and, 1:12, 8:620
Windelband on, 9:791
Laromiguière on, 5:201
in law, 7:446–447
Locke on, 5:382–383
Luther on, 3:10
Maine de Biran on, 5:657–658
Naṣīr al-Dīn al-Ṭūsī on, 6:478
national, 6:484
in neo-Confucianism, 2:158
neuroses and, 1:23
Nietzsche on, 6:612
objective, Paulsen on, 7:148–149
Ockham on, 9:782
perception and, 1:233
to power
Adler on, 1:23
in neuroses, 4:857
Nietzsche on, 6:612. *See also* *Will to Power, The* (Nietzsche)
technological, 1:253
in Thucydides, 9:457
public and private, Rousseau on, 4:39
and reason, 9:250–251
in rebellion against God, 1:707–708, 2:9–10
Rehmke on, 8:304
Ribot on, 8:457
Schopenhauer on, 3:311, 3:415, 4:747, 8:647, 8:650–654, 9:716–717
Spinoza on, 9:175
superiority of, 1:404
Tauler on, 9:372–373
Telesio on, 9:390
Tetens on, 9:404
Thomasius on, 9:441
Trubetskoi (Sergei) on, 9:533
voluntarism and, 9:714–715
Wahle (Richard) on, 9:720
Wittgenstein on, 9:807
Wundt on, 1:234
See also Free Will; Volition
"Will: Its Structure and Mode of Operation, The" (Ceighton), 2:591
Will theory of law, 5:49, 7:446
"Will to Believe, The" (James, William), 1:535, 2:292, 3:531–532, 3:632, 4:780, 4:786
Will to Power, The (Nietzsche), 1:56, 5:45, 6:613–614
on eternal return doctrine, 3:354
on war and peace, 7:153
Willats, John, on vision and pictorial idiom, 1:329
Wille, Bruno, 7:83
Willful Virgin: Essays in Feminism (Frye), 3:756
"Willful Virgin, or Do You Have to Be a Lesbian to Be a Feminist" (Frye), 3:756
William III (king of England), Locke and, 5:375, 5:388
William Heytesbury. *See* Heytesbury, William
William James Lectures (Grice), 7:738
William of Alnwick, Duns Scotus and, 8:704
William of Auvergne, **9:765–767**
Augustinianism of, 1:403
Averroism and, 1:428
Duns Scotus and, 3:135
on illumination, 1:403
Liber de Causis and, 5:334
William of Champeaux, 8:591, **9:767**
William of Conches, **9:768–769**
on Platonic world soul, 7:612
School of St. Victor and, 8:592
William of Militona, Alexander of Hales and, 1:114
William of Moerbeke, 5:344, **9:769–770**
William of Ockham. *See* Ockham, William of
William of Orange. *See* William III (king of England)
William of Paris. *See* William of Auvergne
William of Saint Thierry
on love, 5:586
and William of Conches, 9:768
William of Sherwood, 5:430, **9:786**
on logic, 5:432
on syncategoremata, 8:769
on terms, 8:767
William of Soissons, 5:429
Williams, Bernard, **9:786–788**
on altruism, 1:136–137
on consequentialism, 2:460
on cultural relativism, 3:444
deniers of the value of truth, 5:103
error theory of ethics and, 3:347
on ethical relativism, 3:372
on ethics *vs.* morality, 3:450–451
on heaven, eternal joy of, 4:252
on impersonal morality, 3:388
on impossibility of believing at will, 5:87
on internal and external reasons, 4:714
on moral *vs.* prudential, 4:152–153
on oneself as causal lever of optimal outcomes, 3:748
on personal identity, 7:224
on tragedy, 9:525
on value, 3:443
Williams, D. C., on induction, 4:641
Williams, Donald, bundle theory of, 7:24
Williams, G. C.
on evolution, 7:341–342
on genic selectionism, 7:344
Williams, N. P., on the Fall, 3:474
Williams, Owen, on personal identity, 7:229–231
Williams, Patricia. *See* Kitcher, Patricia
Williamson, Timothy
on conditions of knowledge, 3:270–271
logic of clarity, 5:112
on priority of knowledge, 5:88
on unknowability of borderline statements, 5:111
on vagueness, 9:624–625
Willing, Kant's notion of pure practical reason and, 3:616
Willoughby, Francis, physicotheology and, 7:557
Willowbrook State School, 6:97
Wilson, Edward O., **9:788–789**
evolutionary ethics and, 3:479–480
sociobiology debate and, 3:490–491
Wilson, George
on action explanation, 2:648
on anaphora, 1:175–176
on intention, 1:16
on rule following, 8:533
Wilson, Harold, 9:510
Wilson, John Cook
on determinables and determinates, 3:1–2
on knowledge, 3:315, 5:94
Wilson, Margo, 3:481
Wilson, Rob, on social memory, 6:126
Wilson, Robert, 4:63
Wilson, Thomas, 5:438–439
Wilson, Woodrow, 9:71
Wilton, Thomas, 1:773
Wimsatt, William, 9:162

Winckelmann, Johann Joachim, **9:789–791**
on beauty, 1:513
Cousin and, 2:580
Lessing on, 5:294
on style, 1:330, 1:513
Sulzer and, 9:325
Windelband, Wilhelm, **9:791–793**
on epistemology as axiology, 6:544
Frank (Erich) and, 3:715
on Kant, 6:545
and Liebmann, 5:344, 5:345
Losskii and, 5:576
in neo-Kantianism, 6:540, 6:544
use of defining terms by, 4:38
Winds of Doctrine (Santayana), 8:602
Winner, Langdon, 7:544–545, 9:78
Winstanley, Gerrard, 1:177
Winston, David, on Philo, 7:309
Wipple, John F., on Thomism, 9:447–448
Wiredu, Kwasi, on African philosophy, 1:84–85
Wirklichkeit (Hegel), 3:716
Wirklichkeitslehre (Theory of reality) (Driesch), 3:111, 3:112
Wisdom, **9:793–796**
Aristotle on, 1:264–265, 1:276, 4:290
in Buddhism, 1:722–724
in Chinese epistemology, 2:215–216, 2:219
Chrysippus on, 2:252
components of, 9:794–795
definition of, 9:793
Dge-lugs scholastic training for, 1:734–735
as divine illumination, 4:580
in etymology of philosophy, 7:335
evil in society and, 1:771
as femininity, 1:760
of God, as metaphysical concept, 3:669
God as source of, 1:651
Ibn al-ʿArabī on, 4:542
Ibn Gabirol on, 4:546–547
in medieval philosophy, 6:99
in *Metaphysics* (Aristotle), 1:276
in neo-Confucianism, 2:183
Plato's view's of, Bonaventure on, 1:651
of previous generations, 8:46
in Sanlun Buddhism, 2:162
Socrates on, 9:108–109
in Stoicism, 1:194
Telesio on, 9:390–391
Zeno of Citium on, 9:870
Wisdom, (Arthur) John Terence Dibben, **9:796–799**
on experiences after death, 4:602
on other minds, 7:57–58
Wittgenstein and, 9:798–799
Wisdom, John, Vienna Circle and, 5:525
Wisdom literature, 2:200, 9:793–794
Wisdom of God Manifested in the Works of Creation (Ray), 7:558
"Wisdom of Ptah-hotep," 9:793
Wisdom of Solomon (Apocrypha), as wisdom literature, 9:793
Wiseman, Richard, 7:116
Wish-content, of dynamic unconscious, 3:738
Wish-contravening dreams, reconciling, 3:744
Wishful impulses, in latent dream-thoughts, 3:743
Wissen, Glaube und Ahndung (Fries), 3:751
Wissen und Denken (Knowing and thinking) (Driesch), 3:111
Wissen, Wollen, Glauben (Frank), 3:715
Wissenschaftliche Weltauffassung, Der Wiener Kreis (The Scientific World View: The Vienna Circle), 5:525
Wissenschaftslehre (Science of Knowledge) (Fichte), 3:414, 3:614–617, 4:50, 5:30, 6:667
Wissenschaftslehre Bolzanos, Die (Scholz), 8:645
Wiszowaty, Andreas, 9:100
Witchcraft, 4:97, 8:669–670
Without Guilt and Justice (Kaufmann), 5:46
Witnesses, 3:655
Witt, Charlotte, essentialist theories of gender, 3:587
Witt, Jan de, 9:177, 9:183
Witten, Ed, 9:268
Wittgenstein, Ludwig Josef Johann, **9:799–821**
Abbagnano on, 1:3
on action, 3:19
on actions of states, 9:205
aesthetics of, 1:66, 9:819–820
and analytic philosophy, 1:147–153
on analytic/synthetic distinction, 1:163
on animal intelligence, 1:203
Anscombe and, 1:212
in antimetaphysics, 6:206
antispeculative approach of, 4:559
Ayer and, 1:436
Barth on, 1:480
basic statements in, 1:483–484
Black and, 1:605
on boundaries between propositions, 4:862
Carnap and, 2:37, 2:41–42
on Cavell, 2:115–116
on certitude, 9:59
on cognitive limits and categorical illusion, 2:82
on concepts, 2:417
on correspondence theory of truth, 2:545
counterparts of Fries's "self-reliance of Reason," 3:753
on criteriology, 2:594
criterion of verification of, 8:642
Daoism and, 2:185, 2:205
on death, 4:615
on definition, 1:241
"duck-rabbit," 8:637
Dummett and, 3:132
Duns Scotus and, 3:137–139
education of, 9:800
employing words without reducing their meaning, 5:158
on existence, 3:498
and existential quantification, 5:508
faith as "seeing as," 3:533
fallibilism about empirical belief resisted by, 5:96
fideism and, 3:321
in film theory, 7:383
Frege and, 3:414, 3:732, 9:289
good-reasons approach and, 3:430, 3:431
on honest thinker in religious claim balancing, 2:228
idea of meaning, 3:756
on image as bearer of meaning, 4:593
on induction, 4:648
on inner processes and outward criteria, 1:525
on intentionality, 4:705–706
Kripke on, 5:149–150, 8:23, 8:531–533
on language, 1:66, 8:760
lectures of, 9:802
Lichtenberg and, 5:342
on Locke, 1:203
logical positivism and, 3:316
on logical syntax, 9:360
Lyotard and, 5:620
Malcolm (Norman) and, 3:106–107, 5:661
materialism and, 6:12
Mauthner and, 8:802

on memory, 6:125
mental terms in, 1:523–524
on mindreading, 9:38
Moore (G. E.) on, 3:314
"my arm going up" analogy, 8:674
on negation, 6:526
ordinary-language philosophy of, 1:153–154, 3:317–318, 6:195
other minds and, 7:54–56
on panpsychism, 7:90
paradigm-case argument and, 7:109–110
on personal identity, 7:221
and philosophy of religion, 7:478
picture theory of meaning, 5:129
positivism of, 8:180
postmodernism of, 7:730
on prelinguistic knowledge, 4:725
on private language problem, 5:149–150, 8:20–23, 8:531–533
on propositional mismatches, 5:508
on propositions, 8:737
on questions, 10:32–33
reception of, 9:818
on refutation, 7:400
on resemblance, 9:601–602
on rules, 1:152, 8:530–531
Russell and, 2:543–544, 3:315–316
Schlick and, 8:638–640
and School of Qom, 8:647
Schopenhauer and, 8:656
on self, 8:709
social epistemology and, 9:83
on social nature of meaning, 9:116
on social sciences metaideology, 7:533–534
on speech and meaning-delivery-beyond-speech-capacity, 2:208
on statements of identity, 9:287
Stout and, 9:259
Strawson on, 7:56
on subject-predicate dualism, 9:289
on tautologies, 1:148
as "therapist," 5:150
on thinking words, 4:612
on thought and language, 7:535
on truth, 2:546–547, 9:535
on "truth" and "facts," 2:547, 5:150, 5:526, 9:804
Turing and, 9:552
and Vienna Circle, 2:41–42, 5:524, 9:802
von Wright and, 9:847
Wisdom (John) and, 9:797, 9:799
Wollheim and, 1:306
See also Neo-Wittgensteinianism

Wittgenstein on Rules and Private Language (Kripke), 5:149, 8:23, 8:531–533
Wittig, Monique, 3:587
Witwicki, Władysław, 9:554
Wizenman, Thomas W., *Pantheismusstreit* and, 7:101
WKL subsystem, 8:456
Wodeham, Adam, **9:821–822**
on Chatton, 2:140
on individuation, 2:139–140
influence of, 9:822
Ockhamism of, 7:8
on Scotism, 8:704
Woldemar (Jacobi), Schlegel on, 8:631
Wolf, Rudolph, 4:673
Wolff, Christian, **9:822–832**
Bilfinger and, 1:595
Crusius and, 2:605
on essence and existence, 3:350–351
on evil, 3:470
on force measurement, 3:228
Galluppi and, 4:13
Gottsched and, 4:165
Hegel on, 3:59
on hieroglyphics, 9:338
and history of ontology, 7:27
influence of, 9:829–830
influences on, 9:825–826
and Kant, 5:9
on knowledge of beauty, 1:494
Knutzen and, 5:123
Lambert on, 5:175–176
Leibniz and, 3:228, 5:254
Lessing and, 5:294
monism of, 6:326
on real and logical, 5:10
Suárez and, 9:282
Thomasius and, 9:442
on "three bad sects," 4:553
Thümmig and, 9:458
Tschirnhaus and, 9:549
and universal grammar, 8:791
Wolff, G., Driesch and, 3:110
Wolff, Robert Paul
on anarchism, 2:260
on civil disobedience, 2:260
on state authority, 9:210
Wolffianism
Baumgarten and, 1:493
Crusius and, 2:605
of Kant, 5:124
of Meier, 6:112
of Reimarus, 8:330–331
Wölfflin, Heinrich, on painting, 1:330–331
Wolfson, Harry, on Philo, 7:308

Wolin, Sheldon S., 9:97, 9:208
Wollaston, William, **9:832–834**
deism and, 2:683–684
Franklin (Benjamin) on, 2:689
Wollheim, Richard, **9:835–836**
on aesthetics, 1:36, 3:257, 9:835–836
on artistic expression, 1:306
on style, 1:331–332
on visual perception, 1:328
Wollstonecraft, Mary, 4:136, **9:836–837**
as feminist, 3:599
as philosopher, 3:569
Wolterstorff, Nicholas
on Calvinism, 2:12
on Gaunilo, 4:34
on religious devotion, 3:535
Woman in the 19th Century (Fuller), 6:575
Woman question, 9:838
Womanism, 3:601
Women
art of, risk of ghettoizing, 3:573
bonding of, 3:580
Cabanis on, 2:2
in Cixous écriture feminine project, 2:262–263
Code on, 2:295
Comte on, 2:413
cultural preservation by, 1:441
differences among, 3:599
and ecofeminism, 3:260
existential freedom of, 1:515
feminist attention to, 3:569–570
in history of philosophy, 4:166–167, 4:299, 4:745–746, 9:9–11, 9:201–202, 9:236–241, 9:301, 9:836–837, **9:837–841**
labor protection of, 2:362
in Latin American philosophy, 5:205
liberation of, Mill (John Stuart) on, 9:75
lifeworld of, 3:564
and material life, 3:575
vs. men, 3:583
Musonius Rufus on, 6:440–441
needs of, 3:582
as objects of sexual desire, 3:571
opportunities for, Bentham's support of, 1:551
oppression of, 3:755–756
perspectives of, as privileged over men's, 3:595
as philosophers, 3:569–570
philosophers' perceptions of, 3:570
rational faculties of, 1:355

Women, ***continued***
sex-based caricatures of, critiques of, 4:745–746
social primacy of, 1:441
subordination and integrity of, 2:31
Women and Economics (Gilman), 3:567
Women and Human Development (Nussbaum), 6:681
Woncheuk, 5:135
Wonhyo, Buddhist theory established by, 5:135
Wood, Thomas E., 1:742
Woodbridge, Frederick James Eugene, **9:841–843**
and *Journal of Philosophy,* 3:44
Nagel (Ernest) and, 6:472
in new realism, 6:585
Woodger, Joseph Henry, 7:37, **9:843–844**
Woodin, Hugh, 8:846
Woodruff, Peter, on truth, 5:318
Woods, James Houghton, and Cairns, 2:5
Woodward, James, 2:103, 3:525
Woodworth, Robert S., 8:148
Woolgar, Steve, 9:78, 9:84
Woolley, Guy, on quantum mechanics, 2:143
Woolston, Thomas, **9:844–845**
Chubb and, 2:684
deism and, 2:683–684
Word, Franck von. *See* Franck, Sebastian
Word and Image (Gadamer), 4:3
Word and Object (Quine), 1:151, 6:197, 6:198, 9:62
Word nominalism, 6:174–175
Words
ambiguous, 3:542–543
analogy and, 8:784–785
analyticity as function of meaning in, 1:160
Aristotle's semantics of, 8:755–757
Augustine on, 8:760
Berkeley on, 1:587–588, 8:781–782, 9:597
Buddhism on, 1:756, 9:14
Bulgakov on, 1:760
in Christianity, 2:247
concepts and, 2:415
contract making and, 7:446
counterinstances of, Berkeley on, 8:781–782
Cratylus on, 2:585
definitions of, Berkeley on, 9:597
denominative, 8:762–763
doctrine of, 8:496
features as properties of, 9:357
Hobbes on, 4:407–408
Humboldt on, 8:793
impositions, first and second, 8:762
inferences from, 1:756
inner form in, 8:794
Johnson on, 8:794
in legal transactions, 7:445–446
Locke on, 8:777–778
in locutions, 8:761
logical, 8:19–21
Mauthner on, 8:802
meaning of
in Chinese philosophy, 9:722
Davidson on, 6:85
in Indian theories of language, 7:414–416
vs. things, 9:812
use and, 9:811–815
Meinong on, 8:803–804
misuse of, 4:407–408
music and, 6:438
as names, 9:599–602
nominalism and, 9:600
ontology of, in Shpet's linguistics, 9:19
operative, 7:446
particular *vs.* general, 9:598
Peirce on, 8:797–798
prolepsis and, 8:759
for properties, 8:64
reference and, 1:611–612
signification of, 8:794
Stoics on, 8:757
subject and predicate as, 9:285
syncategoremata, 8:769–770
as synsemantic terms, 1:691
as things, 9:600
ultimate referents of, 8:759
understanding, 5:120, 9:664–665
universality of, in nominalism, 9:599–600
and universals, 8:764, 9:580–583
unum nomen unum nominatum, 9:596–598
use of, 9:812
confusion about, 3:549
without meaning, 3:548
vagueness of, 1:446
veracity of, Indian philosophy and, 5:120
Wittgenstein on, 8:531–532
Words (Kaplan), 5:39
Wordsworth, William
Emerson and, 3:195
Mill (John Stuart) and, 6:221
and New England transcendentalism, 6:572
pantheism of, 7:98
on poetry, 1:298
Spinoza and, 9:195
Word-tokens, 6:175
Word-types, 6:175
Work
in anarchist communism, 1:179
as congenial to one's nature, 9:64
Hegel on, 4:262
Kropotkin on, 1:179
mechanical, energy and, 3:227–228
of relationship, 3:579
Ruskin on, 8:534
in socialist society, 9:73
and spirituality, integration of, 9:737
"Work of Art in the Age of its Technological Reproducibility, The" (Benjamin), 1:546
Work of the Digestive Glands (Pavlov), 7:149–150
Workers
alienation of, Marxism on, 7:544
Jünger on, 4:859–860
in Merleau-Ponty's politics, 6:149
Working class
communism and, 2:362
women in, 3:600
Works
of faith and truth in natural philosophy, 1:451
Ruysbroeck on, 8:579–580
Works (Bolingbroke), 2:684–685
Works (Wordsworth), 4:179
Works of Love (Kierkegaard), 3:93
Works of the Six Days, On the (Thierry of Chartes), 7:612
Works on the Records of Epicurus and Some Others (Philodemus), 7:302
World(s)
in absolute idealism, 1:13
alienation and, 1:610
angelic, Corbin on, 2:537
as anticreation, Blake on, 1:610
of appearances, 5:22
atomic basis of, Gassendi on, 4:27–28
Augustine on, 1:397–398
beginning of, William of Auvergne on, 9:765–766
Bergson on, 1:565–566
in Bohmian mechanics, 1:631
Brahman as creative power of, 1:683
Burthogge on, 1:776
causal account of time in, 2:88

Collier on, 2:323–324
concepts and, 2:414
Confucianism and, 2:150–151
contingency of, 7:314
cosmopolitanism and, 2:567–569
as cosmos, 2:571
in critical realism, 2:595
as discrete by intellect, 1:566–567
disunity of, 2:62
as eternal, William of Auvergne on, 9:765–766
existence of, 9:758
as fallen, 1:559
as flesh, 6:148
God and, Rosenzweig on, 4:829
God as form of, 4:821
as God becoming, 1:760
Homer on, 4:459
horribleness of, 8:560–561
Huayan Buddhism and, 1:738–739
imperfection of, 1:361
interpretation of, 1:566
Kant on, 5:36
as karmic construction, 4:633
language and, 2:205–206
Leibniz on, 2:366
Maimonides on, 5:641
in Manichaeism, 5:683
material. *See* Material world
materialistic conception of, 9:627
as mind-dependent, 1:579
mind-independence of, in metaphysical realism, 8:688–689
natural, 6:492
as omnipotent present, 1:739
ordering of, religion and, 9:752
as organism, 2:65, 5:640–641
origin of
  Gersonides on, 4:69
  Maimonides on, 5:650–651
perception of
  Bentham on, 1:551–552
  indirect, 1:577
possible. *See* Possible worlds
in Pythagoreanism, 8:185–186
rationality of, Zeno of Citium on, 9:870
reality of, in Indian philosophy, 9:542
as representation, 8:650
Russell on, 2:543
Schultz on, 8:659
as self-annihilating, 1:611
sensible
  as illusion, 6:121
  and intelligible, 5:25
sensory, 5:36
Shelley on, 9:8–9
spiritual, relationships of, 3:607
truth independent of, 1:165
variability *vs.* stability of, 1:579
in Yogācāra Buddhism, 1:748
See also Cosmogony; Cosmology; Many worlds/Many minds interpretation of quantum mechanics
World, The (Descartes), 2:729–733, 2:736–737
World and the Individual, The (Royce), 4:559, 7:83–85, 7:92
World as Will and Representation (Schopenhauer), 7:522
World Chaos (McDougall), 6:72
World enigmas, 4:202
World Enough and Space-Time: Absolute vs. Relational Theories of Space and Time (Earman), 3:160
World government, proposals for, 7:154–158
World of Colour, The (Katz), 4:72
"World of Individuals, A" (Goodman), 4:158
World of Life, The (Wallace), 9:721
World of States of Affairs, A (Armstrong), 1:287
World poverty, act utilitarianism on, 9:612–613
World process, Karsavin's description of, 5:43
World soul
  as alternative to metaphor of personal God, 9:8
  in Bruno's cosmology, 7:614
  Ficino and, 3:621
  panpsychism and, 7:84–85
  Plotinus on, 3:401
  Solov'ëv on, 9:123
  Stoics on, 5:569
  Swedenborg on, 9:337
  William of Conches on, 7:612
  See also Macrocosm and microcosm; Panpsychism; Pantheism
World Unmask'd, The (Huber), 9:839
World War I
  idea of progress and, 8:47
  Marcel in, 5:699
  Toynbee and, 9:517
  Vaihinger on, 9:626
  and views on war, 7:155
  Weber (Max) and, 9:734
  Wittgenstein in, 9:801
World War II
  Adorno in, 1:28–29
  Anscombe on, 1:212
  Austin (John Langshaw) in, 1:406
  emotivism and, 3:205
  Marxism post-, 5:739–740
  Nishida on, 6:624
  philosophy of history and, 7:391
  terrorism in, 9:397
  Turing in, 5:632
  and views on war, 7:155
  Wittgenstein in, 9:802–803
World-cementing objective relations, 5:72
World-semantics, logic and, 5:483, 5:486–488
World-traveling, concept of, 3:580
World-view(s)
  causal-mechanistic, in Schultz, 8:659
  Christian and scientific, incompatibility of, Stace on, 9:200
  Christianity as, 2:245
  Dilthey on, 3:84
  Fichte on, 3:618
  Franck on, 3:713
  in French clandestine writings, 2:264
  of Muslim philosophy, 4:756
  persuasive representation of, 2:229
  philosophy and, 7:334–335
  religion as, 2:224
  social origin of, 9:102
Worry, initial, 7:206–211
Worship, as necessary to knowledge of God, 2:10
Wörterbuch der philosophischen Begriffe (Eisler), 2:344, 7:85
Worth
  absolute
    as categorical imperative, 2:70
    Oman on, 7:14
    supernatural and, 7:14
  in value, 9:636
Wright, Chauncey, **9:845–847**
Wright, Crispin
  on Blackburn, 8:52
  on borderline cases, 5:110
  Frege and, 3:732
  on Leibniz's argument for God's existence, 2:552
Wright, Georg Henrik von, 2:103, 3:432, **9:847–848**
Wright, Larry, on biological teleology, 9:389
Wright, Sewall, 7:83
Writer's Diary, A (Dostoevsky), 3:100–101
Writing, Derrida on, 2:715–718, 7:412
Writing and Difference (Derrida), 2:715–718

Wrongness
in act utilitarianism, 9:612
vs. evil, 2:31
in rule utilitarianism, 9:613
sense of, in utopianism, 9:620
seriousness of, affirming, 3:697
Wu (Emperor of China), 3:98
Wu (nonbeing), Dao as, Wang Bi on, 9:722
Wu buquian lun (Things do not shift) (Sengzhao), 2:161
Wundt, Max, 6:542, 7:86
Wundt, Wilhelm, **9:848–850**
on apperception, 1:234
Durkheim and, 3:150
on emotions, 3:198
on feeling, 7:620
on introspection, 4:721
Krueger and, 5:155
Külpe and, 5:160–161
Mercier on, 6:145
panpsychism and, 7:83
positivism of, 7:714
on psychological atomism, 7:282
in psychology, 8:140
Schelling and, 1:234
sensationalism of, 8:140
sound experiments by, 9:483
on will, 1:234
Würzburg school, 4:593
Wuwei (nonaction)
Laozi on, 5:195
Wang Bi on, 9:722
Wuxing (five phases), in Diagram of Great Ultimate, 9:880
Wyclyf, John, 4:91, **9:851–852**
Wyman, Jeffries, 4:775

X

Xenocrates of Chalcedon
on first principle, 7:606
in Greek Academy, 4:173
and Stoicism, 9:253
Xenophanes of Colophon, **9:853–854**
Aristotle on, 7:94
and constructivism, 9:76
on God, 7:142
on gods, 3:211
on Homer, 1:41
and pantheism, 7:94
Parmenides of Elea and, 7:128
Plato on, 7:122
on Pythagoras, 8:181
skepticism of, 1:192, 9:48
Xenophon, **9:854–856, 10:47–48**
on cosmos, 2:571
on Demiurge, 2:698
on Socrates, 3:90, 9:109
trial of, 9:106
"Ximing" (Western inscription) (Zhang Zai), 9:879–880
Xin (heart/mind), 6:129
Xin lixue (Feng), 2:169–170
Xin xue (philosophy of the mind), Wang Yangming on, 4:795
Xin Xue school, 4:794
Xing (human nature)
Mencius on, 6:129–130
Xunzi on, 9:856–857
Yangists on, 6:129–130
Xiong Shili
Buddhism and, 2:169–170
and neo-Confucianism, 2:159, 2:182
Xirau, Joaquín, as *transterrados,* 5:209
Xu Fuguan, 2:182
Xuan (Qi king), Mencius and, 6:130
Xuanxue (Learning of the mysterious)
Wang Bi and, 9:722
Wang Chong and, 9:724
Xuedou Zhuongxian, 1:729
Xunzi, **9:856–857**
argument in, 2:201
on Confucianism, 2:173, 2:196
on correctness through law and propriety, 2:150
on heart/mind watchfulness, 2:173
on human nature as evil, 2:150
on knower-known *vs.* wisdom, 2:215–216
legalists and, 2:238
on logic, 5:416
methods of, 2:216
on rationality and animal nature, 2:234
social and political thought of, 2:233–234
Xunzi, The (Xunzi), 2:175–176, 2:234, 9:856
Xuyan (Prefatory words) (Dai Zhen), 2:621
XX secolo, Il (Sciacca), 8:666

Y

Yad Hazakah (Maimonides), 5:647
Yajurveda, 5:116
Yale School, 2:661
Yamaga Sokō, **9:859–860**
Yamazaki Ansai, 5:7, **9:860**
Yāmuna, 4:630
Yan Hui, as example of *cheng* (sincerity), 9:880
Yang Jian, Lu Xiangshan and, 5:618
Yang Xiong, **9:860–862**
Yang Zhu, **9:862–863**
in Daoism, 2:185–186
Mencius and, 2:186–188, 9:862
Yangists, on *xing,* 6:129–130
Yangming philosophy, Chinese, in Korea, 5:139
Yashts, in Zoroastrianism, 9:885
Yearnings, in common consent arguments for God's existence, 2:347
Yeats, William Butler, 9:363
Yi (change), Zhang Zai on, 9:879
Yi (propriety), 6:129
Yi (rightness), Xunzi on, 9:856–857
Yi Hwang, 5:138
Yi I, 5:138
Yi Ik, and Western thought in Korea, 5:139
Yi li (moral pattern), Zhu Xi on, 9:883
Yi Saek, and later Korean Confucians, 5:136
Yijing (Classic of Changes), 2:152, 2:155, 2:159–161, 2:186, 9:6
Dau Zhen on, 2:622
Minagawa's use of, 6:253
principle of Great Change in, 5:138
Taixuan jing and, 9:860–861
Yin and *yang*
Confucian eclecticism and, 2:190
in Daoist cosmology, 4:794
Dau Zhen on, 2:622
in Diagram of Great Ultimate, 9:880
Zhou's evolutionary cosmogony and, 2:155
Yin Haiguang, 2:181
Yin-Yang school, 2:152, 2:163
Yoga, 4:132, 4:626, 9:542
Bhakti, 5:359
and cognitive and psychological processes, 5:116
gurus in, 6:109
liberation in, 5:329
meditation in, 6:107–108
and mysticism, 6:442–443
self in, 8:718–719
Yogācāra Buddhism, **1:746–753**
atomism in, 1:383
and awareness, 5:120
eight consciousnesses in, 1:749–750
five stages of, 1:752
Vasubandhu in, 1:746–747, 1:751–752, 9:650–652
Vihñapti-mārtra and, 1:747–749

Yogācārabhūmi-śāstra (Treatise on the stages of yogic practice) (Asanga), 5:412
Yogasūtras (Patañjali), 4:626, 5:329
on law of karma, 4:625
on meditation, 6:107–108
paths in, 6:109
Yogōcōra idealism, Japanese rejection of, 4:795
Yolton, Jean S., 5:394–395
Yolton, John W., 5:385, 5:394
Yorck of Wartenburg, Count, 3:79
Young, Edwards, and Sulzer, 9:325
Young, Ella Flagg, 3:567
Young, Iris Marion, 3:563, 3:599
Young, Robert J. C., on postcolonialism, 7:726
Young, Thomas, on energy and work, 3:229
Young Hegelians, and Bakunin, 1:471
Yuan shan (Inquiry into Goodness) (Dai Zhen), 2:621
Yuanwu Keqin, Chan teaching of, 1:729
Yugoslavia, ethnic cleansing in, 7:157
YuktiΣaΣ†ika (Sixty Verses of Reasoning), 6:470
Yulgok. *See* Yi I
Yulre (Classified conversations) (Zhu Xi), 2:216
Yunmen, on Buddhism, 2:166
Yutasiddha, 9:583

Z

Zabarella, Jacopo, **9:865–867**
on agent intellect, 1:91
Aristotelianism of, 1:430
on logic, 5:439
Philoponus and, 7:314
Zack, Naomi, 3:586–587
Zadachi etiki (Tasks [or problems] of ethics), 5:48
Zadeh, Lotfi, 2:491, 3:766
Zadig (Voltaire), targets of, 3:409–410
Zadrozny, W., on compositionality, 2:370
Zaehner, R. C., 8:401
Zagzebski, Linda, 9:682
on swamping problem, 5:105
and Thomistic Ockhamism, 3:696
Základové konkretné logiky (Masaryk), 6:2
Zakony myshleniia i formy poznaniia (The laws of thought and the forms of cognition) (Lapshin), 5:199
Zalabardo, José, 8:533
Zalta, Edward, 6:636
Zarathustra, 9:885–886. *See also* Zoroastrianism
Zarlino, Gioseffe, on music, 1:48–49
Zea, Leopoldo
Bolívar and, 5:205
on identity, 5:211
influences on, 5:209
on *mestizo* consciousness, 5:209–210
Zeal, atheism and, 1:373–374
Zeigo (Superfluous words) (Miura), 6:276
Zeitschrift für geschichtlichen Rechtswissenschaft, 8:614
Zeitschrift für Sozialforschung (journal), 2:599
Zeller, Eduard
friends and colleagues of, 3:41
on Kant, 6:540
Łukasiewicz on, 5:607
on Parmenides of Elea, 7:125
Zellner, Arnold, on informed priors, 9:234
Zen
geography of, 1:726
and Huayan Buddhism, comparison of, 1:737–738
in Korea, 5:135–136
school of, 1:726–730
Sōtō, 3:95–96
vs. Western philosophy, 6:625
See also Buddhism; Chan (Zen) Buddhism
Zen no kenkyō (An Inquiry into the Good) (Nishida), 4:797–798
Zend-Avesta (Fechner), 3:347, 7:84–86
Zen'kovskii, Vasilii Vasil'evich, 5:75, **9:867–869**
Zeno of Citium, **9:869–871**
Alexinus and, 6:111
Antiochus of Ascalon and, 1:222
Aristo of Chios and, 1:257
on citizenship of world, 2:567
on dialectic and rhetoric, 9:255
Diodorus Cronus and, 3:87, 5:404
Diogenes of Sinope and, 3:90
Epictetus and, 3:261
on epistemology, 1:247, 3:288
in Hellenistic thought, 4:300
on logic, 5:404
on natural law, 6:507
panpsychism and, 7:84
Plato and, 7:606
Seneca on, 8:812
Simplicius on, 9:35
Stoicism of, 9:253
writings of, 9:253
See also Stoicism
Zeno of Cyprus, ethics of, 3:400
Zeno of Elea, **9:871–879**
dialectic and, 3:52
Diogenes Laertius on, 3:88
on impossibility, 1:232
logic and, 5:398
metaphysical criticism of, 6:184
on motion and change, 2:161
Owen on, 7:64–65
on paradoxes of motion, 4:654
Parmenides of Elea and, 7:122
on plurality, 7:598
and pre-Socratic philosophy, 7:762
on time, 3:357
See also Zeno's paradox
Zeno of Sidon, Epicurean School and, 3:263
"Zeno the Mathematician" (Owen), 7:65
Zenophanes, on time, 3:357
Zeno's paradox (Zeno of Elea), 3:52–54, 9:874–878
Ajdukiewicz on, 3:60
Aristotle and, 2:491
Hegel on, 3:60
logic of, 5:514
motion in, 1:568, 2:161, 4:654, 6:408
Parmenides's metaphysics and, 6:184
time and, 9:467
Zentner, Marcel, 3:736
Zerbrochene Krug, Der (Kleist), 5:78
Zermelo, Ernst
aussonderungsaxiom and, 5:535
on definite property, 8:836
on number
cardinal and ordinal, 5:516
definitions of, 6:674–675
on set theory, 2:29, 2:500, 5:520, 8:835–836
well-ordering theorem of, 8:834
Zermelo-Fraenkel set theory, 2:500, 4:662–664, 5:520, 5:560, 8:835–836
axioms as computable set in, 2:383
Friedman on, 5:484
Gödel's theorems and, 5:474
Skolem on, 5:472
unsolvability degrees and, 2:385
Zero
Frege on, 3:729
as God, 7:11
Newton on, 2:494
as number, 6:671
Zero situation, Dingler on, 3:86
Zetetic (Voltaire), 9:710
Zettel (Wittgenstein), 9:818
Zeugungsproblem, 5:354–356

Zeuner, Gustav, on energy, 3:233
Zeus, in Stoicism, 9:256
Zevi, Sabbatai, 5:2
Zhang Dongsun, 2:159–160
Zhang Hengqi, 5:138
Zhang Zai, **9:879–880**
on neo-Confucian rationalism, 2:156–157
on ultimate reality, 2:220
Zhao Qi, *Mengzi* edited by, 6:129
Zhdanov, Andrei, 1:59, 1:68–69
Zhe xue. See Chinese philosophy
Zheng meng (Rectifying the obscure) (Zhang Zai), 9:879
Zhi (wisdom), Mencius on, 6:129
Zhihong Xia, 3:32
Zhikai, Taintai Buddhism and, 2:163
Zhishi (ultimate in discrimination), 9:861
"Zhi-Wu-Lun" ("On referring to things") (Gongsun Long), 2:204
Zhiyan, 1:737
Zhiyi, and Buddhism, 1:727, 2:154, 2:163
Zhong Yong (Doctrine of the Mean), in neo-Confucianism, 4:795
Zhou Dunyi, **9:880–881**
on evolutionary cosmogony through yin and yang, 2:155
on ultimate reality, 2:220
and Zhang Zai, comparison of, 9:879
Zhouyi Neizhuan (Internal commentary on the book of changes) (Wang Fuzhi), 9:724
Zhouyi Waizhuan (External commentary on the book of changes) (Wang Fuzhi), 9:724
Zhozhou, 2:167
Zhu Xi (Chu Hsi), **9:882–884**
on Confucian ethics, 2:173, 2:177
in Japanese philosophy, 4:793–794
Lu Xiangshan and, 5:618
Muro kyūsō and, 6:434–435
natural philosophy of, 2:216–217
on neo-Confucianism, 2:155, 2:199
on self-cultivation, 2:177
on ultimate reality, 2:220
writings of, introduced into Korea, 5:136
on Yang Xiong, 9:861
Zhu Xi Confucianism, 6:477
Hayashi and, 4:247–248
Wang Yang-ming and, 6:477
Yamaga Sokō on, 9:859
Yamazaki Ansai in, 9:860
Zhu Xi neo-Confucianism, 4:794, 5:138–139, 9:882
Kaibara Ekken and, 5:7
Kumazawa and, 5:161
Zhuangzi, **9:881–882**
antirationalism of, 5:415
and Chinese legalist social and political thought, 2:238
on Daoism, 2:151, 2:190
on names and reference, 2:204
on purpose in linguistic reference, 2:205
Zhuangzi (Yang Zhu), 2:185–187, 2:197–198, 4:196
Zhuangzi Zhengmeng Zhu (Commentary on Zhang Zai's zhengmeng) (Wang Fuzhi), 9:724
Zhukovskii, Vasilii, 5:74
Zibaldone (Leopardi), 5:284
Ziegler, Theobald, Laas and, 5:164
Ziehen, Theodor, **9:884–885**
Zimzum, Cordovero on, 2:539
Zinzendorf, Nikolaus Ludwig von, 7:576
Zionism
and Islamic philosophy, 4:762
Jewish Enlightenment and, 3:250
Ziran (naturally so)
Laozi on, 5:194–195
Wang Bi on, 9:722
Zisi, on ultimate reality, 2:220
Zizek, Slavoy, 7:522
Zognmi, 1:737
Zohar, book of, emanationism in, 3:189
Zola, Emile, realism of, 1:56
Zombies, 6:263–264, 8:193
Zoological Philosophy (Philosophie zoologique) (Lamarck), 5:173–174
Zoology
Aristotle on, 1:273–275
Haeckel and, 4:201
Zoonomia or the Laws of Organic Life (Darwin), 2:631
Zor'kin, Valerii Dimitrievich, 2:148
Zoroaster
Emerson and, 3:195
Patrizi and, 7:144
Pico della Mirandola and, 7:570–571
Zoroastrianism, **9:885–887**
eschatology in, 3:347
on evil, problem of, 3:471
Manichaeism and, 5:684
in Pletho's theory of Platonic Forms, 9:314
Zou Yan, and Yin Yang school, 2:152
"Zu den Sachen!", 7:281–283
Zuangzuang, in Chinese philosophy, 2:154
Zubiri, Xavier, **9:888–889**
Zukunft einer Illusion, Die (Freud), 7:252
Zur Analysis der Wirklichkeit (Liebmann), 6:541
Zur Entwicklungspsychologie des Rechts (Krueger), 5:156
Zur Ethik und Politik (Paulsen), 7:148
Zur Farbenlehre (Toward the Theory of Colors) (Goethe), 4:141
Zur Kritik der hegelschen Philosophie (Feuerbach), 3:609
Zur Lehre vom Inhalt und Gegenstand der Vorstellungen (Twardowski), 9:554
Zur Logik der Sozialwissenschaften (Habermas), 4:200
Zur Morphologie (Goethe), 4:141
Zurvān (Infinite Time), 9:887
Zurvanism, 9:887
Zuse, Konrad, 2:406
Zwingliism, 8:296